THE
ALMANAC
OF
AMERICAN
POLITICS
1982

D1563573

THE ALMANAC OF AMERICAN POLITICS 1982

The President, the Senators,
the Representatives, the Governors:
Their Records and Election Results,
Their States and Districts

Michael Barone
and
Grant Ujifusa

BARONE & COMPANY
Washington, D.C.

Text design by Lee E. Fischer, Fine Print & Production, Inc., Cambridge, Mass.
Photography by Shepard Sherbell, Washington, D.C.

Library of Congress Cataloging in Publication Data

Barone, Michael
   Almanac of American politics 1982
   Includes index.
   1. Politics in the United States
2. U.S. president, vice president, congressmen, governors
3. Election results.   4. Biographies   5. Key votes   6. Group ratings
I. Ujifusa, Grant, joint author
II. Title
PE0000.X0   000.0'00   70–160417
Library of Congress Catalog Card Number: 70–160417
ISBN 0-940702-00-2 (Cloth)
ISBN 0-940702-01-0 (Paper)

FIRST EDITION

10 9 8 7 6 5 4 3 2 1

ACKNOWLEDGMENTS

For their help in the preparation of this book, we wish to thank the following: Paul Harstad, West Coghlan, Scott Gale, Steve Ramirez, Jane Beard, Edward Halpern, Michael Davis, Gary Logan, Lawrence M. Knopp, Jr., Brad Bannon, Gail Backman, and Linda Reinisch.

Special thanks should go to Shepard Sherbell, who provided the photographs; to Lee Fischer, of Fine Print & Production, Inc., who single-handedly redesigned the body of the book and supervised the composition as well; and to Guy Oliver, of Fine Print & Production, Inc., who handled the difficult and crucial details of printing.

Amy Gussack and Roberta Whalen, of O. Positive, Inc., were invaluable in trade sales as were Roger Craver and Elizabeth Corley, of Craver, Mathews & Smith, and Jeff Hills, of Specialized Marketing Services, in direct mail sales. We are especially indebted to Ethan Siegal, who helped to organize mountains of data and to keep the whole process moving. And we are grateful to Joan S. Barone and Amy Ujifusa, for their help and encouragement.

The Almanac of American Politics 1982 is dedicated to Walter H. Shorenstein, who made its publication possible, with thanks for his encouragement and counsel.

CONTENTS

THE PRESIDENCY:
THE 1980 ELECTIONS

The American presidency is the most important public office in the world, and the one whose holder is chosen by the most intricate and protracted process. No other major democratic nation reposes so much power in a single elected official, and no other nation spends so much time and energy determining who the next president is going to be. Prime ministers in other countries, leaders in such dictatorships as Russia and China — each is one in a crowd of many politicians struggling for power. But the president stands alone. The Constitution sets him apart, and his at least theoretical control over the huge executive branch gives him power far outweighing that of any member of Congress. The most important powers of the president are not necessarily formal; he is circumscribed by law and custom and can seldom achieve his major goals by command. What the president does have is the spotlight. More than any other American, or any other world leader, he has the power and the ability to frame issues, to set a national agenda, to dominate the public dialogue, and to set the terms of discussion. The president can set the tone of our public life.

And inevitably he does — for better or worse. Franklin Roosevelt, entering the presidency in 1933, had few clear ideas of how to extricate the nation from economic catastrophe. But from the time he told Americans that they had nothing to fear but fear itself, he made people believe that something would be done and that it would work. Roosevelt was one of the two Americans who have been nominated for national office by a major political party five times, and he set a tone for his generation and the one after. The other American nominated for national office five times was Richard Nixon, and it is tempting to say that he set a very different tone for our own times. Certainly the Watergate scandal helped create a negative national mood, as had the Vietnam war before it. Lyndon Johnson ran in 1964 promising not to send American boys to fight where Asian boys should fight and then did just the opposite; Richard Nixon ran in 1968 promising to uphold middle-class morality and then was forced out of office for breaking the law. Vietnam, Watergate, the new experience of persistent inflation, the various energy crises of the 1970s — these all contributed to a very negative climate of public opinion, a climate none of the presidents of the 1965–80 period could alter.

Nor did they have much luck winning reelection. Americans in the 1960s assumed that most presidents could win a second term; since then only one president has, and he was forced out of office soon after. In the 1970s we adjusted our presidential selection system; we hoped to get better results out of a better system. But the new process is so complicated and the primary season so long that it seems that only politicians who campaign full time can win; and in any case no process can guarantee good results. The nation also needs luck — the kind of luck that gave America Franklin Roosevelt in 1932. One president after another has been ousted — Johnson in 1968, Nixon in 1974, Ford in 1976, and Carter in 1980. Each time we were surprised, and never more than we were in 1980 by the size of Ronald Reagan's margin. Carter did not have a good job rating and was not personally popular, but no one expected that he would be beaten by 10% by a 69-year-old former governor; no one expected that the Democratic Party would lose control of the Senate. Indeed, as the 1980 campaign began, the focus was on the Democrats, and many thought Carter's real battle was for the nomination, not the general election.

The Democratic Nomination. Edward Kennedy entered the race a clear favorite on November 4, 1979. That was also the date the Iranians seized the hostages. From that time until the Democratic nomination was effectively decided, Jimmy Carter stayed in the White House and attended to the hostage problem — with occasional strategic phone calls to Democratic Party activists and officeholders in key caucus and primary states. Kennedy was hurt by his faltering performance in an interview in October with Roger Mudd on CBS and was hurt further in December when he condemned the Shah of Iran. By the end of the year, Carter had taken the lead over Kennedy in the polls; California Governor Jerry Brown, also a candidate, never was a significant factor.

The nomination was essentially decided in three contests: the Iowa caucuses and the New Hampshire and Illinois primaries. Kennedy campaigned actively in Iowa, but he was overwhelmed by Carter support; the president had kept close touch with the Iowa Democrats who had given him his first important victory four years before, but his triumph was more than a matter of personal contact with a few hundred key leaders; more than 100,000 Iowa Democrats participated and the anti-Kennedy trend was unmistakable. New Hampshire, for years the first primary, is next door to Kennedy's Massachusetts; but here Carter again prevailed. Finally, Illinois was the first of the nation's big industrial states to have a primary. Again Kennedy campaigned hard; here the response was unequivocal, a better than 2-to-1 victory for the president.

Kennedy did not withdraw from the election then; indeed, he stayed in the competition for five months, until the Democrats held their convention in New York. He even won some primaries, including strong wins in Massachusetts and New York, but he was unable to win outside the East Coast and California with two minor exceptions, and his showings tended to get better when voters thought he had little chance for the nomination. Kennedy impressed voters of all parties with his grace and composure during this period and managed to make a plausible case against proposed convention rules that would have made Carter's nomination mathematically certain. But the high point of Kennedy's candidacy came in New York, on the second night of the convention, when he addressed the delegates purportedly in support of a minority platform plank. This is Kennedy's metier: a stirring speech before a large and friendly crowd. He disappointed no one: he defended the Democratic vision of a compassionate government, attacked Ronald Reagan, even made a few bows to Jimmy Carter. His doomed campaign had won 40% of the delegates; the Carter managers must have reflected, as they saw the crowd's emotion at Kennedy's speech, on how easily he might have taken control of the convention if he had won just a few more delegates.

Kennedy's performance dominated Carter's convention; on the last night, when Kennedy came up on the platform, he gave Carter only the most lukewarm of handshakes, and that was the picture that made the newsmagazines. Carter failed to stir the delegates and he did not get far in making a case for himself with the voters. He surely blames Kennedy's persistence for that, and with some justice, but it is also true that there was little positive enthusiasm among either the delegates or, if we can trust the polls, from the voters who renominated the president.

The Republican Nomination. The contest for the Republican nomination was largely the process of the initial favorite, Ronald Reagan, overcoming his disadvantages and capturing a victory at last after two unsuccessful races. Reagan's disadvantages were two, his age (69) and his lack of experience in national government; his identification with ideological conservatives was an asset, not a liability, in the Republican delegate selection process. Initially, in the Iowa caucuses, his strategy seemed to be to keep a light schedule and avoid appearances with other candidates; when George Bush won the Iowa caucuses after Reagan refused to appear at a multicandidate debate, that strategy changed. Reagan campaigned hard in New Hampshire and accepted the invitation of the Nashua newspaper to debate George Bush one-on-one. When the paper backed out of paying for the hall (someone questioned whether it would be a corporate contribution), Reagan agreed to foot the bill; he then invited the other Republican candidates. Bush, caught off guard, declined to appear with the others; Reagan, when the newspaper's editor turned off the sound in his microphone, was outraged and came out with the campaign's best line: "I paid for this microphone, Mr. Breen." Reagan's support had been climbing rapidly and Bush's falling in New Hampshire before the debate; after it Reagan beat Bush by nearly a 2-to-1 margin. After big victories in southern states, including a triumph over John Connally in South Carolina where the Texan had campaigned intensively, Reagan beat Bush and John Anderson handily in Illinois.

In effect the fight was over. Other candidacies had been dispatched. Senator Bob Dole was never able to get a campaign organized. Connally, with strong support from business executives and $11 million in contributions, could not charm ordinary people and ended up with a single delegate; he gracefully bowed out and supported Reagan. Congressman Philip Crane had support from activists of the right but won few votes. John Anderson, having failed to win a single Republican primary, perceived a call for an independent candidacy. Senator Howard Baker blamed his lack of success on his failure to abandon his duties as minority leader. Bush kept on campaigning for a while and even won some primaries, but by June the Republicans were united around Reagan. The Republican National Convention was his to command, and while there were some missteps — notably the effort to persuade Gerald Ford to take the vice presidential nomination in return for promises of a "co-presidency" — on the whole the proceedings in Detroit were devoted to expounding the ideas that Reagan and other Republicans had been spreading and which had been proving so persuasive to so many voters.

The Anderson Difference. John Anderson's candidacy in 1980 had its genesis in the 1978 primary election in the 16th congressional district of Illinois. After 18 years in office, Anderson was unable to win more than 58% of the vote against a dull-witted right-wing minister; disgusted, he decided not to run for Congress again and to try for the presidency instead. He did not find it difficult to distinguish himself from the other candidates. He looked askance at the Kemp–Roth tax cut (although he had supported it as a House Republican), and in the Iowa debate he cited as his greatest mistake his vote for the Gulf of Tonkin resolution in 1964 — making him perhaps the last presidential candidate to win votes on his position on Vietnam. He also had a distinctive and original proposal for a 50¢ gas tax. Anderson's distinctiveness earned him some votes in Iowa and, more important, prominent and repeated mention in *Doonesbury,* which helped him become a kind of hero to college and postcollege voters. But not even in New England, where Republican primary voters are more liberally inclined than anywhere else, could Anderson actually win a primary; Bush edged him in Massachusetts and Reagan in Vermont. For a time Anderson led the polls in Illinois, more on the basis of his issue stands than local popularity because his congressional district is only a small part of the state; but in the end Reagan had a handsome victory there.

Anderson faced a quandary. Should he continue what must inevitably be a losing race for the Republican nomination? Or should he run as an independent or third party candidate? The latter possibility was tempting. There was an obvious constituency, voters who think of themselves as liberal on cultural issues and conservative on economic issues, a body increasing in size as the Vietnam generation of college graduates moves into the voting stream. Anderson fit their politics pretty well, although there were a few embarrassing exceptions; he had always been a backer of nuclear power, for example, and now had to search his record for votes that might be plausibly claimed as skepticism. And there were many other voters who were simply dissatisfied with the choice of Jimmy Carter and Ronald Reagan, and were looking for someone else.

There was an opening, in other words, and the potential for a candidate such as Anderson to become competitive for the electoral votes of many states. In polls through the summer he got more than 20% and, when voters were asked to assume he had a chance of winning, he was more competitive with Carter and Reagan. Yet in the end his campaign fizzled; he had only 7% of the vote, with his best showings (15%) in Massachusetts and Vermont. Why didn't he do better? First of all, there was the tactical error of spending too much time and campaign money on qualifying Anderson for the ballot in all 50 states. George Wallace, operating 12 years before in a less hospitable legal environment, had accomplished the same thing with much less fuss. Second, Anderson forces spent little money on television advertising although his campaign manager, David Garth, is one of the most skillful makers of political commercials around. Third, the candidate showed little ability to communicate ideas. He was still a man of the House, ready to speak in a loud scolding tone on any subject for two minutes; he never understood that a candidate has to speak in a conversational tone for 30 seconds on the subject he wants to emphasize. Consequently, many of the original ideas his campaign developed simply never got communicated, as he spent his time responding to questions on stray topics such as abortion or his chances to win.

Anderson nevertheless won one victory: by getting 7% of the vote, he qualified for federal matching funds and paid off his campaign debts. He also left the race with a mailing list of contributors three times larger than that of the Democratic Party. Anderson thus has the potential of reviving his candidacy in 1984 and may be an important political factor in the years in between.

The General Election. The fundamentals of the general election were fairly apparent early on. Jimmy Carter had a low job rating; voters wanted to get rid of him if they could find a good alternative. Ronald Reagan was for many voters an unknown quantity; they had their doubts about him (was he too old? was he too impulsive or warlike?) that they wanted resolved before they made a decision. The fall campaign can be divided into three periods, and only during the first of those did Ronald Reagan seem to be making the kind of mistakes that could cost him the presidency.

These were Reagan's initial bloopers, when he talked too freely and without discipline to the press, between the Democratic Convention and early September. Reagan got into avoidable trouble by questioning the theory of evolution and asserting that the creation theory should be taught in high schools as well. Gratuitously, he offered the opinion that the Vietnam war was a moral cause. While Los Angeles was suffering its worst air pollution in recent years, Reagan was saying that Mount Saint Helens and the Great Smoky Mountains cause more pollution than does man's civilization. All of these statements might be defensible; but they ran against voters' conventional wisdom and they were peripheral to the main economic and foreign policy concerns voters had. It was odd as well to see a man who preaches against federal intrusion offering, as a candidate for the presidency, opinions on high school curriculums.

By early September Reagan had evidently been convinced that greater circumspection was necessary, and afterwards he disciplined himself very well indeed. The undisciplined candidate during the second period was President Carter. This was the time when he charged that Reagan's election would divide black and white, Christian and Jew — a particularly inappropriate comment when one considers that throughout the campaign Reagan refrained from capitalizing on the one ethnic prejudice that was really flaring in America, the dislike of the sudden influx of Cuban refugees. Carter suddenly found himself under attack for his "meanness" (an attack begun by a *Washington Post* editorial) and actually had to apologize for it in an interview with Barbara Walters. Carter strategists had hoped to find Reagan by mid-October on the defensive on charges that he was too likely to risk war and was too unsympathetic to blacks and the poor. Instead Carter was on the defensive for his tactics.

Even so, Carter was inching upward in the polls. But he was doing little more than corralling some, but not all, traditional Democratic voters, and neither he nor Reagan was running consistently over 40% in published polls through mid-October, even though Anderson was sinking fast. The nation had not yet made its choice. Against this backdrop, Carter, who had resisted debates throughout the campaign, agreed to debate his challenger. The debate was held the Tuesday before the election, and many professional observers thought the crisp, factual, serious Carter had won. But voters — at first by a small plurality, then a few days later in much larger numbers — made Reagan the winner. The reason was not so much what happened in the debate as it was in the dynamics of the campaign. Voters wanted to reject Carter and were looking for reassurance that Reagan was acceptable. In the debate they got it. Reagan made no obvious mistakes; he stressed convincingly his desire for peace; he presented himself as an amiable and knowledgeable man, and one capable of inspiration.

The result was the massive Reagan victory: 51% for Reagan, 41% for Carter, 7% for Anderson, 1% for others (mostly the Libertarian ticket of Ed Clark and David Koch, which had advertised heavily on television). Hopes were raised during the last weekend that the hostages would be returned by Iran. But those hopes were dashed before election day, and for once the hostage situation did not work in Carter's political favor. He had defended himself against Kennedy's attacks on the Shah and some Republicans' desire for stronger action by citing his concern for the hostages' safety; but by November 4 — exactly one year after the hostages were seized — it was apparent that Carter's policy had failed, and he paid the price for making the hostages the central focus of American politics. Reagan's victory was not just a personal one; it was a victory of ideas. The Republicans captured 12 Democratic Senate seats and won control of the Senate for the first time since 1952, and they made substantial gains in the House as well. They were running, moreover, all on roughly the same issues and the same philosophy — in vivid contrast to the Democrats, who tend to adapt their politics to the local terrain.

The Reagan Victory. It is worth considering the dimensions of Ronald Reagan's victory. Whatever happens to his administration, the support won in 1980 gives us a good picture of the kind of nation we were that year and what we were seeking in our government. It was certainly a decisive victory, but not quite the landslide that has been claimed: of the two-party vote, Reagan got about the same share as Eisenhower in 1952 or 1956, and only about half the percentage margin of big landslide winners such as Nixon (1972), Johnson (1964), Roosevelt (1932 and 1936), and Harding (1920). Reagan had 489 electoral votes, but if Carter had gotten just 2% more and Reagan 2% less, Reagan's electoral vote total would have been 365 — 95 more than is needed to win, but not quite a unanimous victory. Still, it was a victory over an incumbent president; and if one looks at Carter's electoral votes they were all from states that are special cases: the president's and vice president's home states; D.C. with its black majority and Maryland with its many government workers; the most heavily Democratic states in the east and south (Rhode Island and West Virginia), each with a sagging economy; and Hawaii, a state that leans strongly to Democrats and to incumbent presidents.

Reagan's biggest percentage margins came in the West, where he carried every state but Hawaii; the best Carter did in other western states was 39%. But there are really two Wests, as shown by the returns. One is the Rocky Mountains (plus Alaska), where Reagan was as strong as anywhere in the country. He had 61% of the vote there, to only 29% for Carter. In his home area, on the Pacific Coast, Reagan was not quite so strong. He had only a bare majority, indeed fell below an absolute majority in Oregon and Washington as well as Hawaii. On the booming West Coast feeling on economic issues tends to be conservative, but opinion on cultural issues increasingly is liberal. This was the part of the nation that started the late 1970s tax revolt, with the passage of Proposition 13 in California in 1978; but it is also the part of the country where marijuana use is most common and where there is the strongest opposition to nuclear power. In 1980 California and the other West Coast states started out with a large bloc of voters committed to Ronald Reagan, perhaps as many as 45%, but they also started out with a large bloc of voters committed to vote against him, in California (where memories of Governor Reagan sending the police onto campuses are still fresh among some young voters) as much as 40%. The anti-Reagan vote was ultimately split between Carter and Anderson. But this may well be the part of the country where Reagan's Republicans will find it hardest to improve on his 1980 percentages.

The Midwest, the region that is often the political fulcrum of the country, was almost as strong for Reagan as the West. He had 51% of all the votes here and absolute majorities in every state except the Upper Midwest trio of Minnesota (which the Carter–Mondale ticket carried), Wisconsin, and Michigan. These three states have much the same combination of cultural liberalism and economic conservatism as the West Coast, and they will be hard for Republicans to carry if they concentrate on cultural rather than economic issues. The four states through which run the major east–west transportation routes of the nation — the Old National Road, now U.S. 40 and Interstate 70; the great railroads; airline routes requiring changes at O'Hare as railroads once required changing at Dearborn Station — Ohio, Indiana, Illinois, and Missouri, taken together usually duplicate the national voter preference; they did in 1980 as well. Reagan's best showings in the Midwest came in the belt of plains states from Kansas to North Dakota, where altogether he ran as well as he did in the Rocky Mountain states (61%-30%). These states used to react against national administrations in farm revolts. But farm prices are relatively high (although affected by the grain embargo against Russia) and the plains states, for the first time in the 20th century, are generating enough jobs that they can hold their young people rather than lose them to other states. The same kind of buoyant prosperity at home and disaffection for government in Washington that has made Reagan-style conservatism almost the politics of consensus in the mountain states seems to have had the same effect on the plains.

The East had been the Democrats' stronghold in the electoral college since 1960, but

Ronald Reagan took all but 17 electoral votes there. The one area of Carter strength was the Chesapeake Bay area: he carried Washington, D.C., with its black majority, and Maryland and nearly carried Delaware. One reason: Maryland and Delaware have higher percentages of blacks and of southern whites than other eastern states, plus significant white ethnic groups that go Democratic. John Anderson's 14% in New England—the one part of the country where he got over 10%—was largely responsible for Ronald Reagan's victories there; no one sees Massachusetts as part of an emerging Republican majority. Apparently voters in these states did not see a need, as some of their mayors did, to keep the Democrats in to maintain federal aid programs; neither did voters in the three big states of New York, New Jersey, and Pennsylvania. There is a tendency to forget that in every close election in 35 years there at least 45% of the voters in these states have supported the Republican candidate. Reagan got that vote and a little more, which was enough for him to carry all three in three-way races.

Finally, there is the South, which went almost unanimously for Jimmy Carter in 1976 but gave him only Georgia and West Virginia in 1980. For purposes of analysis, there are really three Souths. The first is the Oil South—Louisiana, Oklahoma, and Texas—which has become a political unit since energy has become a major national issue. The political heritage in these states is Democratic, but as the nation's major producers of oil and natural gas they favor removal of price controls and accordingly tend to lean Republican. These states have had rapid economic growth in the late 1970s, and the fast-growing affluent parts of their big cities are not only heavily Republican, but are capable of producing the kind of elan and financial support that build real political strength. It is no accident that Texas and Louisiana, for the first time in more than 100 years, both have Republican governors. The Oil South was narrowly for Carter in 1976, when his position on energy issues was not clear; in 1980 it produced a 55%–41% margin for Reagan.

Another segment of the South that can be identified politically may be called the Growth South—Florida and Virginia, the only southern states whose rapid population growth has come in large part from outside the South. The economy of Virginia is buoyant, and its conservative political tradition still intact from the days of Harry Byrd, Sr.'s, political machine. Florida, rapidly growing in the 1970s, found itself facing hard times in 1980, particularly because of the unexpected and unwanted influx of Cuban refugees. The refugee issue turned Miami and south Florida against Carter by September 1980, and Florida was the first large state he had clearly irretrievably lost to Reagan.

Finally, there is the heartland of the South, from West Virginia and Kentucky down through Arkansas and the belt of Deep South states from Mississippi to North Carolina. Over the past 20 years this part of the country has undergone greater social and political change than any other region. In 1960, the southern heartland was still segregated by law and segregated even more firmly by the iron hand of custom; it was by far the poorest region in the nation, a region that regularly exported most of its young people to the great industrial cities of the North. Today all that has changed. The civil rights movement and national civil rights legislation have changed the way southerners of both races behave and, against the predictions of conservatives, changed the way white southerners feel. There is no parallel in the history of advanced nations to the change in attitude among white southerners—from a determined and even violent resistance to any form of integration to a calm, sometimes casual, often pleased acceptance of contact with blacks and equal opportunity. For that the black civil rights leaders, who pressed their cause when more prudent people urged caution, deserve the greatest measure of credit; but white southerners deserve some as well. They are proud of how they have changed and entitled to that pride.

With integration has come, coincidentally or not, a vast increase in the South's prosperity. The South is still the lowest wage part of the country and attracts much industry because there are few unions here and more positive attitudes toward business. But wages are much higher, relative to the national average, than they were 20 years ago, and differences in the cost of living have enabled affluent people in the South to enjoy the same standard of living as people making double the dollars in the Northeast.

Jimmy Carter's election as president in 1976 was a kind of symbolic ratification of the changes in the South. As the first white southerner to win the presidency in more than 100 years, Carter ran as a supporter of civil rights; and who can forget the moment on the podium after his 1976 acceptance speech when Carter led Democrats such as George Wallace to listen to the benediction delivered by Martin Luther King, Sr.? In the 1968 and 1972 elections, Democratic nominees had won less than 20% of the votes of southern whites. In 1976 Carter carried enough votes among southern whites to win 57% of the votes in the southern heartland — by far his strongest region in the country. Regional pride certainly played a part in that result — not a mindless affection for a southern accent or the stars and bars, but a real sense that the people of this nation have accomplished something important, have worked successfully to build a better society where black and white can work and live together.

By 1980, of course, such factors were not as important: southerners no longer had to prove that a southerner could be elected president. Still, Carter's showing in the southern heartland was as strong as his performance in any region of the country. He actually led Reagan, 49%-48%, in this area, and if he failed to beat Reagan in more than two states, he came within 2% of the Reagan totals in every one of the others. Ironically, John Anderson's minuscule vote here — his weakest showing in the nation — may have made the difference in several states.

Looking Ahead. It is risky in the extreme to try to forecast the result or even the contours of support in an election still several years away. Who in 1977 forecast that Jimmy Carter would lose by 10% to Ronald Reagan in 1980? Looking ahead to 1984, much depends on the success — or failure — of the Reagan Administration, particularly since voters chose both a president and, for the most part, a Congress pledged to some rather specific policy goals. In his debate with Jimmy Carter, Ronald Reagan in his summation asked voters to consider several questions when they made their choice for president — questions that will be as important in determining the outcome of the 1984 election as they were in 1980.

> Are you better off than you were four years ago? Is it easier for you to go and buy things in the stores than it was four years ago? Is there more or less unemployment in the country than there was four years ago? Is America as respected throughout the world as it was? Do you feel that our security is as safe, that we're as strong as we were four years ago?

No precise predictions are possible. But it is possible to get a sense of how the future is evolving from the past, to get a sense of where we are going by looking back at where we have been. One perspective is to look back over the past four presidential elections, from 1968 to 1980. The period is suitable for analysis: it covers the years in which America experienced the shocks of Vietnam and Watergate, years in which the country for the first time experienced persistent inflation, years in which the Great Society legislation had been enacted and the United States for the first time had the functional equivalent of a welfare state, years in which civil rights had been secured for blacks in the South and elsewhere.

We have been operating in this period as if the Democratic Party had a natural majority. Yet the figures tell a different story.

Percentage of Democratic, Republican, and major third candidates' votes for president, 1968–80

	1968	1972	1976	1980	Average
Democratic	43	38	50	41	43
Republican	43	61	48	51	51
Third candidates	14	—	—	7	5

It would be going too far to say that the Republicans have become a natural majority party; their average is a bare majority and only once in four times did they exceed it. But it seems pretty clear that the Democrats no longer have a natural majority in presidential elections. Only once — after the Republicans produced the worst scandal in American history — were the Democrats able to win even a bare majority, and overall they averaged only 43% of the vote. It may be objected that each of the Democratic losses was, in some way, a special case. And of course each presidential election is unique. But continued failure over an extended period raises the presumption that something serious is wrong. The results suggest that neither major party has a natural majority in presidential elections any longer; and they suggest as well that Democratic candidates, coming from a more diverse and less united party, have more difficulty in amassing a national coalition than Republicans do.

What has happened in the 1968–80 period is that the Democratic Party has lost strength in its traditional base support groups outside the South without gaining much strength in the Republican Party's traditional base support groups. The big industrial states of the East have been voting closer to the national average than they used to. Big central cities, which have been losing population, may be producing higher Democratic percentages but they are producing smaller Democratic margins than they used to; and Democratically inclined metro areas as a whole, suburbs with central city, are not showing the kinds of Democratic margins they used to. Democratic percentages have declined sharply among blue collar and Catholic voters and have increased only a little among professional/executive and white Protestant voters. In essence, the Democratic Party has lost its base and has gained nothing in return.

Percentages of total vote won by Republican, Democratic, and major third candidates in presidential elections, 1968–80

	1968 Nixon– Humphrey– Wallace	1972 Nixon– McGovern	1976 Ford– Carter	1980 Reagan– Carter– Anderson
United States	43–43–14	61–38	48–50	51–41–7
East	43–50–7	58–41	47–51	47–42–9
Midwest	47–44–9	59–39	50–48	51–41–7
West	49–44–7	57–39	51–46	54–34–9
South	36–32–32	69–29	45–54	52–44–3

The Republican Party has made corresponding gains but has not assured itself of a natural majority position—a difficult task in any case in a time when increasing numbers of voters refuse to identify with or consistently support candidates of one party. Some of the Republicans' gains—among blue collar workers, for example—come among groups that are going to be smaller, not larger, shares of the total population in the future. There was much publicity in 1980 about the support Republicans had from the Moral Majority. But the long-range trend in cultural attitudes has been away from the traditional values these groups purport to defend and toward a greater tolerance of different life-styles and behavior. The way in which the younger, baby-boom generation of Americans are living their personal lives—with many divorces and relatively few children—tends to ratify these cultural attitudes, even as they move into their thirties, an age when traditional cultural attitudes have in the past taken hold. The Reagan Republicans will be under great pressure from many of their supporters to enact their own personal moral codes into law—to outlaw abortion, to stiffen laws against drugs, to ban circulation of schoolbooks that undermine traditional attitudes, to foster an atmosphere in which prayers are effectively required in public schools. But heavy concentration on such cultural issues will antagonize a significant portion of the potential Republican constituency. Among an increasing group of Americans, particularly in the baby-boom generation, and especially on Reagan's own West Coast, the trend is toward a politics that is liberal on cultural matters and conservative on economic issues. The long-term interest of the Republican Party is to attract these voters, not repel them. As he took office, Reagan's apparent decision to concentrate on economic issues and foreign policy seemed well calculated to achieve that goal.

Kevin Phillips, whose book *The Emerging Republican Majority* seemed less than prophetic in the middle 1970s, now argues that the emergence was only delayed. The Democrats gained temporary advantage from the shocks of Vietnam (which produced a new generation of Democratic activists) and Watergate (which won Democrats votes they would not have gotten otherwise in 1974 and 1976). But the results of 1980—not only on the presidential but also on the congressional level—show that the Democrats have squandered these advantages. They were unable to convert the negative feelings people directed toward the Republicans because of Vietnam and Watergate into positive feelings directed toward Democrats for their accomplishments.

Politics at the national level in America is always a matter of personality, because of the central importance of the presidency, but it is also a product of ideas. For 40 years the ideas that have been associated with the term liberal have prevailed. In 1930 most Americans did not believe that the federal government had a responsibility to maintain a strong economy with low unemployment and to provide sustenance for those who could not find it for themselves; in 1980 most Americans do. In 1930 most Americans did not believe that the federal government should guarantee the civil rights of blacks; in 1980 most Americans do. Liberals have, in effect, written the history books: most Americans believe that Franklin Roosevelt was a good president and Richard Nixon a bad one, and they believe that John Kennedy was the best of all. They believe that isolationism before World War II was wrong and that the Vietnam war was wrong.

These basic values underlie the surface political dialogue that seems to favor the people we call conservative and to work against the people we call liberal. Voters want government spending controlled, but they want continuation of just about every government program they can think of. They want a tougher foreign policy, but after Vietnam they are hesitant indeed to risk any American military involvement abroad. The Reagan Administration must be careful to avoid collision with the underlying liberal consensus even as it seeks to carry out its conservative mandate.

For Ronald Reagan, this may be easier than for many other Republicans. He is the first presidential nominee to mention Franklin Roosevelt with approval at a Republican National Convention, and he was once a Democrat—indeed, a very active and liberal Democrat. Reagan sees himself not as repealing what Roosevelt did, but as restoring what Roosevelt had sought; the Democrats and the liberals, in his view, are the ones who went astray. A good case can be made for that proposition. There is some point, after all, if you raise taxes and increase regulation, where you seriously impair the market capitalism which in fact provides most of the wealth of this country; and Reagan and his followers may be correct in believing that we have reached that point. The Reagan economic program seems, at this writing, designed to produce a buoyant prosperity of a sort that we have not seen since the middle 1960s—even at the risk of heating up inflation. The Reagan foreign policy seems designed to take a more aggressive posture to reduce the risk of actually having to back it up. All of these ideas have a chance of working—although at this writing it is still not clear to what extent they will be acted on.

What is clear is that in 1981, for the first time in 15 years, the basic idea of the nation's surface political dialogue and the basic ideas of the administration in office seem to be in accord rather than in counterpoint. Richard Nixon came to office in 1969 in a nation still determined to expand the role of government and generally inclined to liquidate the American commitment in Vietnam. Nixon, against all his personal inclinations, presided over a government that saw domestic spending increase and defense spending decrease, that saw the development of a youth culture, the legalization of abortion, and the effective legalization of marijuana. Ideas that were abroad in the land moved the nation much more than the administration did, and well before Watergate. Then the Carter Administration came to office, staffed by people determined to continue in the direction opinion seemed to be moving around 1970, only to see the tide of opinion change. Now people wanted less government and a more aggressive, truculent foreign policy. Now we have the Reagan Administration, which seems to be moving in the direction people say they want. We shall see whether things work out better for this administration than they have for its four predecessors.

The Reagan Government. There is an old saying among political consultants that the campaign always reflects the candidate. The personal character of the candidate, his interests and priorities, his way of doing business—all these things inevitably affect everyone up and down the chain of command and influence what the public finally sees. It is the same with forming a government. An administration will always reflect the president. It is obviously not possible now to reach final judgments on the Reagan government. But it is possible to discern the direction in which it is going. President Reagan's initial major appointments and the policies he adopted in his first months in office give us a fair idea of what the Reagan government will be like. They sugggest that it will be quite a different

government in domestic and foreign policy, and that the White House itself will operate with unusual harmony but not always efficiency.

**OMB Director
David Stockman**

The Reagan government has shown a very clear sense of where it wants to go in domestic policy and how to get there. The key move was the appointment of David Stockman as director of the Office of Management and the Budget. In many respects Stockman was the odd man out in the Reagan Cabinet: he was appointed at age 34, he had never been a successful businessman or lawyer, he had made his whole adult career in Washington. There were other differences. Stockman, more than any other Cabinet-level appointee, knew just what he wanted to do. Ronald Reagan's acquaintance with him was brief—they first met when Stockman took the part of his onetime boss, John Anderson, in a practice session for the Reagan–Anderson debate—but evidently it was enough to tell Reagan that Stockman had the intellect and the temperament to do the job Reagan wanted.

After four years as an iconoclastic congressman and several years before that as a congressional aide, Stockman knew the federal budget cold—where the big money was, where cuts could be made, which programs were intellectually indefensible or vulnerable to attack. Yet he had not been in Washington long enough and had not operated at a high enough level to make the kind of personal alliances and institutional commitments that would inhibit his budget-cutting. Stockman knew more about government than the other Reagan appointees, and he operated with fewer constraints.

If you wanted to make major cuts in the federal budget to go along with major tax cuts — if you wanted, in other words, to reduce the role government plays in our society and our economy — Stockman is exactly the kind of person you would want to appoint to a job that, given those goals, is the most important in government. There was speculation in the early months of the Reagan Administration about the possibility of fights between Stockman and Treasury Secretary Donald Regan. But Regan, an extremely innovative and successful businessman at Merrill Lynch, seemed to enter government without much of a specific agenda other

**Secretary of the Treasury
Donald Regan**

than the desire of any conservative Republican to hold down spending, lower taxes, and control inflation. Stockman had a specific program, and in the first months he and Regan worked in tandem. Regan, moreover, staffed many of the high positions in the Treasury Department with supply-siders, who are likely to be Stockman's intellectual allies on budget and tax questions to come.

**Secretary of Health
and Human Services
Richard Schweiker**

The other major domestic Cabinet appointees had less to say about their initial budgets than Stockman. But in some cases there are possibilities of battles to come. Richard Schweiker at Health and Human Services, for example, came to the job after 20 years in Congress (12 in the Senate, 8 in the House), during much of which he had high ratings from liberal and labor groups; he is likely to be committed to programs Stockman is going to want to cut. The biggest fight in his area may come over Social Security. Stockman's 1981 budget cuts avoided any change in Social Security old age and disability benefits. Yet if you are going to cut the federal budget really significantly, you must go after basic Social Security benefits — either cut the cost-of-living increase, raise the age of retirement, or make some other major change.

Other department heads are likely to become — or were from the inception — advocates of their agencies' constituencies. John Block came to the Department of Agriculture as a fervent opponent of the Russian grain embargo the administration first continued and then ended. Drew Lewis was not in long at Transportation before he proposed limits on Japanese car imports to help the auto companies; Malcolm Baldridge at Commerce joined him. Raymond Donovan at Labor was in the headlines first because of the difficulties he had winning confirmation. But the holder of his office usually ends up as the inside advocate of organized labor or (less likely, but possible) of the kind of employers — major contractors — Donovan once was.

Secretary of Agriculture
John Block

Terrell Bell at Education seemed unenthusiastic about abolishing his department, although candidate Reagan had promised to do so. Samuel Pierce at Housing and Urban Development and James Edwards at Energy had fewer ties with their agencies and their constituencies; they seem to have been appointed more for their characteristics (distinguished black, southern governor) than for their familiarity with their fields. Pierce's views are not clear, and the agency he heads has become visibly less important in the last decade. Edwards's views are clearer — he supports energy price deregulation and development of nuclear power — and if his talents are generally disparaged around Washington it is worth recalling that he left the governorship of South Carolina, an office he had won unexpectedly, with substantial respect from the state's voters.

Secretary of Transportation
Drew Lewis

Secretary of Education
Terrell Bell

U.S. Ambassador to the UN
Jeanne Kirkpatrick

One Cabinet appointee is there because of his close ties with the president: Attorney General William French Smith. Another, James Watt at Interior, is more like Stockman. He knows his stuff — he first came to Washington in 1962 and served in a high post in the Interior Department during the Ford Administration — and he has strong views. Yet he has pursued his career in such a way — heading the Mountain States Legal Foundation, financed by conservative foundations as a counterweight to environmental litigation groups — as to preserve his own independence from environmental lobbies. Watt knows what he wants and how to get it — and the president, as he made clear when Watt's nomination was criticized, understands exactly what Watt intends to do and supports it wholeheartedly.

**Attorney General
William French Smith**

Thus where the president saw the need for major change, he appointed men committed to it and competent enough to obtain it — Stockman, Watt. For other departments, whose budgets may be cut but whose essential functions are not to be impaired, more conventional appointments were made. Most of the appointees dealing directly with Capitol Hill are not personally committed to doing things all that much differently from the past. They are clearly taking their orders, however, from men who are.

In foreign policy it was not so clear from the early months of the Reagan Administration who was giving the orders. Alexander Haig, as incoming secretary of State, made a big to-do about his primacy in the foreign policy making process. But no secretary of State can impose an organization chart on a president who does not want to observe it. Haig and Reagan did not know each other; Haig might reflect that he

**Secretary of the Interior
James Watt**

was running the White House while Reagan was serving out his last term as governor in Sacramento and that he was hobnobbing with the leaders of Western Europe when Reagan was preparing radio broadcasts in Pacific Palisades. But Reagan had been elected president and Haig, after a brief media flurry, in 1979 declined to run. It seemed that Reagan was seeking top appointees with experience, such as Haig, or at least a reputation for caution, such as Defense Secretary Caspar Weinberger. He did not give the right-wing defense intellectuals the high posts some of his backers had hoped, and for all their commitment to higher defense spending neither Weinberger nor Haig endorsed every expensive new weapons system proposed.

**Secretary of State
Alexander Haig**

**Secretary of Defense
Caspar Weinberger**

The difference between foreign and domestic policy is that on foreign policy the Reagan Administration entered office with a general attitude but not with a detailed agenda. Admittedly that is more difficult in foreign policy; there is no single document like a budget that can incorporate all of an administration's policies. Neither, or so it seemed in the spring of 1981, was there a foreign policy equivalent of David Stockman, no Henry Kissinger. President Reagan himself seems to have made a decision to concentrate first on his economic policy—an entirely defensible decision, given the nature of the domestic economy. But that decision, if such it was, still left the direction and the success of his administration in foreign policy in doubt.

After a few months of the Reagan Administration, and particularly in the crisis following the March 30 assassination attempt on the president, it became clear that three men had emerged as dominant in the Reagan White House: Chief of Staff James Baker, Counselor Edwin Meese, and Deputy Chief of Staff Michael Deaver. Deaver and Meese were longtime Reagan loyalists, Meese a top aide when Reagan was in Sacramento, Deaver the public relations man who had helped to set up Reagan's successful enterprises when he retired; Baker was an outsider, one of the leaders of the nearly successful Ford campaign in 1976 and George Bush's campaign manager in 1980. Despite these diverse origins, the three seemed to work closely together and to harbor few of those jealousies that are a staple of Washington journalism. That may simply reflect President Reagan's distaste for such things and his unwillingness to tolerate serious dissension among his staff, an unwillingness that produced his decision to fire campaign manager John Sears in February 1980. No one supposes that there will be no feuds during the Reagan years. But it looks likely to be a more serene and united administration than many others.

One political institution that has prospered over the past six years is that perennial stepchild of American politics, the vice presidency. This owes much to Vice Presidents Walter Mondale and George Bush as well as to the presidents they have served under. Mondale on leaving office offered some advice for his successors. The gist was that the vice president should be loyal and should publicly support the president's decisions, even if he does not agree with them; he should give his advice forcefully but desist if it is not taken; he should shun line responsibilities, which inevitably get him into struggles with the president's appointees and staff, and he should in fact serve as a sort of special, exalted staffer instead. Implicit in this advice is that the vice president should accept his place happily.

Vice President George Bush

He may indeed be president someday, but there is not an awful lot he can do about becoming president; he does not want to succeed after a tragedy, and his fate as a candidate someday is tied to the fate of an administration he is not in charge of. If he can accept these things, and if he can hold the confidence of the president, then he can be a useful public official; and, after all, how many people have the opportunity to be that? Mondale proved to be a useful public official indeed, a valued staffer inside the White House and a respected public figure outside. George Bush, to a considerable extent, seems to be following the same course, although he may make what Mondale would regard as the mistake of accepting line responsibilities.

Both men may have been trained, inadvertently, for the office, since they owed so much of their respective careers to the support of more powerful men. Mondale owed all his offices — Minnesota attorney general, U.S. senator, vice president — to appointment, although he won impressive election victories for the former two once in office and may still be a presidential candidate in 1984. Bush owed much of his advancement to appointment as well. He did succeed in getting elected to the House in 1966 and 1968 from one of the most Republican congressional districts in the United States, but he failed twice, in 1964 and 1970, to win election to the U.S. Senate. Instead, he served with some distinction in a series of appointive positions in the Nixon and Ford Administrations — Republican national chairman, ambassador to the United Nations, ambassador to China, head of the Central Intelligence Agency. Bush, like Mondale, is a man who is loyal to his political patrons without being sycophantic. He has accepted disappointment gracefully and instinctively behaved just as he should have when Reagan was shot — assuring the nation that the government was in good hands, but not in any way trespassing on the prerogatives of the presidency. Historians may someday say that in the late 1960s and early 1970s we were unlucky in our presidents, that we elected men of considerable talents but of the wrong temperaments for the time. They might also say that we were lucky in the late 1970s and early 1980s in our vice presidents — for which, of course, we can thank the presidents they served under.

THE SENATE

The Republican Takeover. There were two stunning surprises on election night 1980. The first was the size of Ronald Reagan's margin, and the second was the Republican takeover of the Senate. The first surprise seems, in retrospect, almost inevitable: the challenger had survived scrutiny by an electorate deeply dissatisfied with the incumbent. The second was, to an extent almost forgotten, the result of luck. To understand that we need only look at the results in the 34 senatorial elections. Nine were decided by 2% of the vote or less. The Republican candidates won seven of these nine elections. Without them, they would have ended up with 46 senators out of 100. With them, they had a 53–47 majority.

1980 Senate Elections

State	Republican candidate	%	Democratic candidate	%
EAST				
Connecticut	James L. Buckley	41	Christopher J. Dodd	54
Maryland	Charles McC. Mathias	66	Edward T. Conroy	34
*New Hampshire	Warren Rudman	52	John A. Durkin	48
New York	Alfonse M. D'Amato	45	Elizabeth Holtzman	44
	Jacob K. Javits (Liberal)	11		
Pennsylvania	Arlen Specter	50	Peter F. Flaherty	48
Vermont	Stewart M. Ledbetter	49	Patrick J. Leahy	50
MIDWEST				
Illinois	David C. O'Neal	42	Alan J. Dixon	56
*Indiana	J. Danforth (Dan) Quayle	54	Birch Bayh	46
*Iowa	Charles E. Grassley	53	John Culver	46
Kansas	Robert Dole	64	John Simpson	36
Missouri	Gene McNary	48	Thomas F. Eagleton	52
North Dakota	Mark Andrews	70	Kent Johanneson	29
Ohio	James E. Betts	28	John Glenn	69
*South Dakota	James Abdnor	58	George McGovern	39
*Wisconsin	Robert Kasten	50	Gaylord Nelson	48
WEST				
*Alaska	Frank H. Murkowski	54	Clark Gruening	46
Arizona	Barry Goldwater	50	Bill Schulz	49
California	Paul Gann	37	Alan Cranston	57
Colorado	Mary Estill Buchanan	49	Gary Hart	50
Hawaii	Cooper Brown	18	Daniel K. Inouye	78
*Idaho	Steven D. Symms	50	Frank Church	49
Nevada	Paul Laxalt	59	Mary Gojack	37
Oregon	Bob Packwood	52	Ted Kulongoski	44
Utah	Jake Garn	74	Dan Berman	26
*Washington	Slade Gorton	54	Warren G. Magnuson	46
SOUTH				
*Alabama	Jeremiah Denton	50	Jim Folsom, Jr.	47
Arkansas	Bill Clark	41	Dale Bumpers	59
*Florida	Paula Hawkins	52	Bill Gunter	48
*Georgia	Mack Mattingly	51	Herman E. Talmadge	49
Kentucky	Mary Louise Foust	35	Wendell H. Ford	65
Louisiana			Russell B. Long	58
			Louis (Woody) Jenkins	39
*North Carolina	John P. East	50	Robert Morgan	49
Oklahoma	Don Nickles	53	Andy Coats	44
South Carolina	Marshall Mays	30	Ernest F. Hollings	70

Seats gained by Republicans and lost by Democrats.

But luck usually comes to those who are well prepared. And there is no question that the Republicans outcampaigned the Democrats in 1980 Senate races. They did not, as it happens, outpoll them, but that is because Democrats in the big states of California, Illinois, and Ohio had weak opponents and piled up huge margins, while Republicans won many more seats by smaller margins in smaller states. But by every other measure this was indeed a Republican victory. The Republicans gained 12 seats, the biggest turnaround since the

Democrats gained 13 seats in the 1958 elections. Moreover, the Republican victories were not concentrated in any one region of the country. They gained only one seat in the East but held hotly contested seats in New York and Pennsylvania without the benefit of incumbency. They won four seats in the Midwest, three in the West, and four in the South. They did not lose a single seat although ironically, in a conservative year and in a conservative state, Mr. Conservative, Barry Goldwater, was almost beaten in Arizona.

It would be a mistake to ascribe the Republican takeover of the Senate to presidential coattails. Some of the newly elected Republicans—Mack Mattingly in Georgia, for example—actually ran ahead of the new president. But the Republicans did undoubtedly benefit from the efforts of the party to present a united front on the issues and to organize its political efforts effectively. Credit for the latter must start with Bill Brock, the Republican national chairman during the Carter years, who pushed Republican fund-raising programs to great success (largely through direct mail solicitations of relatively small contributions) and who saw that the money went to the candidates who could use it best. That is an effort that takes years of preparation, and one that the Democrats did not come close to duplicating. But the Republicans won not only the battle of organization but the battle of ideas. The Republican Party had united itself around a series of themes: a strong defense, stricter control of government spending, a more positive cultural attitude toward America. It had managed to secure nearly unanimous public support for a program as original and intellectually daring as the Kemp–Roth tax cut. At its Detroit convention in 1980 it presented speaker after speaker with essentially the same message—a message that was not only Ronald Reagan's but that had already become the message of the large majority of Republican officeholders and candidates.

Against this the Democrats were reduced to scrambling. The Carter Administration, for whatever reasons, never succeeded in presenting the kind of reasonably coherent and unifying program and themes that the Democrats had presented when they were in power in the early 1960s and that the Republicans were presenting when they were out of power in the late 1970s. Democratic senators and Senate candidates were forced to come up with their own platforms and to emphasize their own special achievements. A senator in one state might talk of his water projects, a senator in another his concern for the union member whose job is threatened, a Senate candidate in another his support of conservative fiscal policies. But most of the Democrats found themselves on the wrong side of most of the big issues of the economy and foreign policy. The fact that most voters were more concerned about inflation and government spending than they were about unemployment and deprivation hurt most Democrats. The Iran hostage crisis may particularly have hurt those Democrats who were associated with dovish foreign policies in the past. Just two Democrats who turned out to have serious contests survived: Gary Hart in Colorado and Patrick Leahy in Vermont. Both had established, not in 1980 but as long ago as their campaigns in 1974, that they stood for something rather different from the national Democratic issue positions, something more in line with the traditions and feelings of their states.

The Sources of Power. For 20 years after their gain of 13 seats in the 1958 Senate elections, Democrats—and generally liberal Democrats—dominated the Senate. There was seldom a reliable liberal majority, but the liberals had the initiative on the issues, they had elan and enthusiasm, and they were usually sooner or later able to build majorities on all their issues, winning some allies on some issues and some on others. The Republicans may hope for similar dominance and, as we shall see below, their chances for additional gains in 1982 are good. Already they are in some ways in a stronger position than liberal Democrats were in 1959. They have a president who agrees strongly with their views on most issues. They have very few dissenters in their own ranks. Out of power in the Carter years, the Republicans have developed an impressive cohesion and solidarity. They have not lost it — at least not by the spring of 1981. That does not mean that there will not be some fissures someday; it is not hard to find major philosophic differences among Republican senators. But so far the Republicans have emphasized programs and policies on which their differences are few and neither the Democrats nor events have advanced onto center stage issues that split the Republicans apart.

The Republicans have an additional advantage today that liberal Democrats did not enjoy in 1959, and that is seasoned and effective leadership. Howard Baker was as surprised as anyone on election night when Republicans won a Senate majority — but not too surprised to act soon and make sure that he would be Senate majority leader. He quickly enlisted Ronald Reagan's close friend — and Baker's only plausible rival for the post — Paul Laxalt to nominate him for the job. And even before the inauguration he seemed to establish a good working relationship with the Reagan White House. One reason for this is that Baker himself seems unusually serene and unjealous for a senator who was, after all, just beaten and beaten fairly badly in a race for the presidency. But like George Bush, and like Laxalt (who hoped for the vice presidential nomination), Baker shows no signs of regret; rather, he seems to regard himself as a man with interesting, useful work to do and the opportunity to play a major role in what he considers to be the good fight. Of Baker's talents there can be no doubt. He is not the master of the Senate Rules that Robert Byrd, now the uncomfortable minority leader, is. But he has a style more readily adaptable to television and the temperament to deal easily with his colleagues.

In his first months as majority leader Baker seemed to stay in close touch with his colleagues and made special efforts to get to know the junior Republicans, many of them political allies of the New Right. His views are not a problem, for the most part. He is a hard-liner on foreign policy (although some on the right cannot forget his role in securing approval of the Panama Canal Treaties). He backs budget-cutting and tax cuts (but the Clinch River Breeder Reactor in Tennessee remains untouched). He has supported civil rights measures throughout his career — one of the few southern Republicans to do so — but does not back all the procedures urged by civil rights advocates. Someday Baker may have trouble keeping together the Jesse Helmses of the right and the much less numerous Lowell Weickers of the left. But the major Reagan budget cuts passed the Senate before that day arrived — and most observers would say it is still quite a way off.

Besides Baker, it is hard to say who the sources of power are in the Senate today; and Baker himself would probably emphasize that most of his power comes from hard work and communicating with his colleagues, not any capacity to command allegiance. The leading powers among the Democrats are no longer committee chairmen — Henry Jackson, Edward Kennedy, Russell Long — or no longer in the Senate at all — Warren Magnuson, Frank Church, Herman Talmadge. Gone also — although their disappearance is less noted by observers — are most of the Democratic Senate staffs that played such an important part in putting together legislation and building the big government that Republicans decry.

This liberal Democratic staff grew because senators who wanted an energetic government active in many areas could not by themselves master the details to create and monitor such a government. Staff members advise senators during sessions or at hearings, keep in touch with people in critical positions in the executive branch, and create, nurture, and perpetuate federal programs that few senators give much thought to. These "submerged horizontal bureaucracies that link the three branches of government," as Senator Daniel Moynihan calls them, are responsible for many of the programs and policies whose unpopularity or cost helped produce votes for Republicans.

The Republicans understood the power of the staff and moved quickly once they had the votes to dismantle it. The majority party is entitled to two-thirds of the staff appointments; that meant that as soon as the Republicans took control, half the Democratic staff would be gone. In addition, Republicans such as Strom Thurmond cut the total number of staff positions — thus reducing further the number of positions for the Democratic minority.

To see what the dismantling of the Democratic staff means, consider the differences between how the Senate handled the incoming Reagan Administration and the way the Senate hamstrung the Nixon Administration 12 years ago. This time Democratic senators got nowhere in their attempts to raise questions about Cabinet and sub-Cabinet appointees; in 1969, Democratic senators, well briefed by their staffs and allied lobbyists, extracted policy concessions from such appointees as Walter Hickel as the price of confirmation. Over the next three years, the Senate almost voted to end a war the administration wanted prosecuted and it defeated major administration projects such as the supersonic transport. It rejected two of the president's Supreme Court nominees.

Staff played a major role in all of these fights, assembling facts and arguments for the senators' positions and helping to frame the issues. A prime example is James Flug, then a staffer for Senator Edward Kennedy. Flug got the idea into his head that the Supreme Court nomination of Judge G. Harrold Carswell should and could be stopped and recruited a senator to lead the fight against Carswell. And it was staff who directed the research and raised the arguments that defeated him. This is not said to minimize the role Birch Bayh and other senators played in that fight. But it was a Senate majority — ably assisted and sometimes guided by staff — that gave the Nixon Administration so much trouble.

Before the 1980 election, in program after program, the Senate staffers and agency appointees or high bureaucrats kept programs going that might otherwise have disappeared and started programs that might otherwise never have existed. There was nothing illegitimate about this; it is not improper to use ingenuity and skill to achieve political ends. But now the staffers and their Rolodexes are gone; the critical phone calls to bureaucrats are not made; hearings are not set up; regulations are not pushed through. The consequences are immeasurable.

Who, besides Baker, and in the absence of the old Democratic staff and before the development of a really powerful Republican staff, are the real powers in the Senate today? Any list is a distortion. But it may be worthwhile to try to list the dozen senators who seem most likely to have major influence over what seem most likely to be major decisions in the next several years. Some are powerful because of their committee positions, some by virtue of their expertise or parliamentary skill, most by some combination of the two. The senator's primary committee positions, the year he is up for reelection, and his percentage margin over his major party opponent in his most recent election is included.

Senator	Party/ State	Committee	Year	%
Howard H. Baker, Jr.	R-Tenn.	Majority Leader	1984	56–42
Pete V. Domenici	R-N.M.	Chairman, Budget	1984	53–47
Paul Laxalt	R-Nev.		1986	59–37
Robert Dole	R-Kan.	Chairman, Finance	1986	64–36
Russell B. Long	D-La.	Ranking Minority Member, Finance	1986	58–39
John Tower	R-Tex.	Chairman, Armed Services	1984	50–49
Strom Thurmond	R-S.C.	Chairman, Judiciary	1984	56–44
Orrin G. Hatch	R-Utah	Chairman, Labor and Human Resources	1982	54–45
Charles H. Percy	R-Ill.	Chairman, Foreign Relations	1984	53–46
Robert C. Byrd	D-W.Va.	Minority Leader	1982	100–0
Jesse Helms	R-N.C.	Chairman, Agriculture	1984	55–45
Henry M. Jackson	D-Wash.	Ranking Minority Member, Energy and Natural Resources	1982	72–24

Some senators are on the list for what amount to unofficial positions: Paul Laxalt is the senator personally closest to the president (although he seems careful not to tread on Baker's prerogatives), and Jesse Helms is there primarily because he is the unofficial Senate leader of the New Right. Only one man on the list is a freshman: Orrin Hatch, assigned to what was considered a hopelessly liberal committee, suddenly finds himself chairman. Robert Byrd is low on the list but could easily rise if Democrats get more cohesive and Republicans splinter; the chairman and ranking minority member of Appropriations do not appear because subcommittee chairmen there traditionally have held great power and because their own sway is encroached upon by the Budget Committee.

Note that some of the Republicans on the list seem anything but politically secure: Domenici, Tower, Helms, and Hatch all won by narrow margins last time. But Hatch upset a Democratic incumbent in what has become the most Republican state in the Union, and he is the only Republican on this list up for reelection in 1982. Overall, the success of these Republicans — like the success of the Republican Party generally — seems tied to the success of the Reagan Administration. If the Republicans can produce, or seem to produce, an improvement in the economy, if they can provide a more assertive foreign policy but one that does not result in unpleasant entanglements abroad, then they and their party are in good shape for future elections. If not, they may find themselves where Jimmy Carter and the Democrats found themselves in November 1980.

The Prospects for 1982. Much has been made of the role of the New Right and of cultural issues such as abortion in the Republican successes of 1980. But the New Right attacks only served as one prong in a multi-prong attack on Democratic incumbents, and the Republicans won much more because of their positions on what are traditionally regarded as central issues — the economy and foreign policy — than because of their positions on issues most observers consider peripheral, such as abortion. For 1982, these issues will probably be dispositive again, and voters in effect will be called upon to render a verdict on the Republicans' performance after two years in power. It is the tradition in America for the in party to lose seats in the off-year elections. But like many hoary traditions, this one is not always observed. There is in fact one example of just the opposite: the Democrats in 1962 picked up four Senate seats two years after John F. Kennedy was elected president (they lost four House seats, but actually more liberals were elected than in 1960 because of primary victories). The Democrats, beginning with larger majorities, were rewarded for what voters considered a good performance; there is no reason to believe that voters will not reward Reagan and his Republicans if they believe that their performance is good.

Republicans have one additional advantage in the 1982 Senate races, one they also enjoyed in 1980: most of the Senate seats up are held by Democrats. Democrats currently hold a 21–12 advantage among this class of Senate seats; moreover, few of the Republicans are considered especially vulnerable. In recent years there has been a tendency, particularly in large states where almost no voters know a senator personally and few have much idea of what he is up to, for voters in Senate races to vent their frustrations with things as they are, and to throw out incumbents. If this continues, Democrats will be hurt—whatever the verdict on the Reagan Administration. Moreover, in early 1981 at least, it appeared that Republicans would enjoy a significant fund-raising edge over Democrats, at least in terms of party funding; this means that Republican candidates can concentrate on campaigning while Democratic candidates will have to spend much time on fund-raising.

The following list of senators up in 1982 is divided by party and region and shows age on election day 1982 and year first elected, with percentage margins over major party candidates in their last election and the percentages for Ronald Reagan, Jimmy Carter, and John Anderson in the 1980 general election.

This is a young class of senators by and large. Stennis is expected to retire at age 81; Hayakawa, at age 76, is expected to have difficulty winning reelection. There are relatively few senior senators here, and some of the most senior—Henry Jackson, William Proxmire—are in very strong shape. But otherwise there are not a great many sure things on the list. Still, there are far fewer obviously vulnerable incumbents among the Republicans than the Democrats. There is no way the Democrats can regain control of the Senate without making a concerted drive to win most of the Republican seats; indeed, without such a drive, Democrats will likely lose more seats and see Republicans expand on their current 53–47 advantage. That will leave the Democrats waiting for 1984, when for the first time since 1962 they will be facing a Senate class made up mostly of Republicans.

State	Senator	1982 Age	Year App'd or Elected	%	Reagan/ Carter/ Anderson %

DEMOCRATIC SENATORS

State	Senator	1982 Age	Year App'd or Elected	%	Reagan/ Carter/ Anderson %
EAST					
Maine	George J. Mitchell	49	1980	Appointed	46–42–10
Maryland	Paul S. Sarbanes	49	1976	57–39	44–47–8
Massachusetts	Edward M. Kennedy	50	1962	69–29	42–42–15
New Jersey	Harrison A. Williams, Jr.	62	1958	61–38	52–39–8
New York	Daniel Patrick Moynihan	55	1976	54–45	47–44–8
MIDWEST					
Michigan	Donald W. Riegle, Jr.	44	1976	52–48	49–42–7
Nebraska	Edward Zorinsky	53	1976	53–47	66–26–7
North Dakota	Quentin N. Burdick	74	1960	62–37	64–26–8
Ohio	Howard M. Metzenbaum	65	1976	50–47	52–41–6
Wisconsin	William Proxmire	66	1957	72–27	48–43–7
WEST					
Arizona	Dennis DeConcini	45	1976	54–43	61–28–9
Hawaii	Spark M. Matsunaga	66	1976	54–41	43–45–11
Montana	John Melcher	58	1976	64–36	57–32–8
Nevada	Howard W. Cannon	70	1958	63–31	64–27–7
Washington	Henry M. Jackson	70	1952	72–24	50–37–11
SOUTH					
Florida	Lawton Chiles	52	1970	63–37	56–39–5
Mississippi	John C. Stennis	81	1947	100–0	49–48–1
Tennessee	James R. (Jim) Sasser	46	1976	52–47	49–48–2
Texas	Lloyd Bentsen	61	1970	57–42	55–41–2
Virginia	Harry F. Byrd, Jr.	67	1965	57–38*	53–40–5
West Virginia	Robert C. Byrd	64	1958	100–0	45–50–4

REPUBLICAN SENATORS

State	Senator	1982 Age	Year App'd or Elected	%	Reagan/ Carter/ Anderson %
EAST					
Connecticut	Lowell P. Weicker, Jr.	51	1970	58–41	48–39–12
Delaware	William V. Roth, Jr.	61	1970	56–44	47–45–7
Pennsylvania	H. John Heinz III	44	1976	52–47	50–42–6
Rhode Island	John H. Chafee	60	1976	58–42	37–48–14
Vermont	Robert T. Stafford	69	1971	50–45	44–38–15
MIDWEST					
Indiana	Richard G. Lugar	50	1976	59–40	56–38–5
Minnesota	David Durenberger	48	1978	61–35	43–47–9
Missouri	John C. Danforth	46	1976	57–42	51–44–4
WEST					
California	S. I. Hayakawa	76	1976	50–47	53–36–9
New Mexico	Harrison H. Schmitt	47	1976	57–43	55–37–6
Utah	Orrin G. Hatch	48	1976	54–45	73–21–5
Wyoming	Malcolm Wallop	49	1976	55–45	63–28–7

*Harry F. Byrd, Jr., ran as an Independent against a Democrat but votes with the Democrats to organize the Senate.

THE HOUSE

The 1980 Elections. In November 1980 the Democrats won 243 House seats and the Republicans won 192. Those results seem like a pretty conclusive Democratic victory. Yet they must be considered a major advance by the Republicans. The Democrats actually lost 33 seats in the election. When we add to that the much smaller Democratic losses in 1976 and 1978, we find that the Democrats are reduced essentially from their 1974 level (291 seats, a 2–1 margin) to their 1972 level (240 seats). This is not a safe margin for the Democratic leadership. If Republicans stay united on an issue — and that was their tendency in the later Carter years and the early Reagan months — then the Democrats cannot carry the House if they lose 26 votes. There are, at this writing, 46 members of the Conservative Democratic Forum — a group of largely low-seniority southern conservatives who share few views with the majority of House Democrats. Among many of the other younger Democrats there is skepticism about many traditional Democratic programs and no sense of obligation to go along with the Democratic leadership and organized labor on important issues. When Democrats had 280–290 votes, the Democratic leadership could, for practical purposes, exert control. When they have only about 240 votes, the leadership cannot. The 1980 elections reduced the Democrats from a position of control to a position where everything is contingent. From that point of view, the elections were clearly a Republican victory.

Another way to consider the results is in terms of numbers of votes. The Democrats, as has been true in every set of House elections since 1952, outpolled the Republicans. But not by much.

1980 House Election Results by Region, with Percentages

Area	Democrats	%	Republicans	%	Carter–Reagan %
U.S.	39,166,261	50	37,228,051	48	41–51
East	9,787,839	51	9,195,421	48	42–47
Midwest	11,392,612	48	12,187,890	51	41–51
West	7,303,060	47	7,590,754	49	34–54
South*	10,682,750	56	8,293,986	43	44–52

Includes Louisiana September election.

The Democrats' percentage was, as always, higher in the South. There are many districts there where the Republicans do not field candidates or which they do not contest seriously. Nevertheless, the Democratic margin in the South is no longer overwhelming. But even more important is the Democrats' performance outside the South. In 1980, for the first time since 1968, the Democrats failed to carry a plurality of the votes cast for House candidates outside the South. Since 1958 there have been only three occasions when the Democrats have failed to win a plurality in House elections outside the South: 1966, 1968, and 1980. The dates are suggestive. Each occurred not during the triumphant period of a Republican national administration but during a period when an unpopular Democratic administration was in office. Each represented a turning away from Democrats generally. Each gave the Republicans effective control of the House, or something very close to it.

House elections are not perfectly representative of public opinion about the two parties. Increasingly in the 1960s and 1970s incumbent congressmen became more adept in using the advantages of incumbency to increase their margins and to ensure their reelections even when their party was unpopular. The result can be seen graphically in the 1972 general election. The Democratic presidential candidate that year, George McGovern, carried only 89 of the 435 congressional districts. But Democratic House candidates carried 240 districts. Literally half of the districts that elected Democratic congressmen voted Republican for presidents (and three districts that elected Republican congressmen voted for McGovern, all in Massachusetts). That kind of ticket-splitting can be explained only by the strength of House incumbents (and, in some cases, by the vigor of Democratic challengers). Each year they send out hundreds of thousands of pieces of mail, they help thousands of constituents solve their problems with government, and they tend to appear far more often on local television and radio and in local newspapers than their challengers ever could. For a while in the middle 1970s it looked as if incumbent congressmen could have indefinitely long careers, regardless of trends in public opinion. More specifically, it looked as though the large number of Democrats elected in 1974 might, in effect, prolong Democratic control of the House regardless of what happened to the presidency and the Senate.

Now the trend seems to be going, slowly, in the other direction. The advantages of incumbency are still important. But there are disadvantages as well. As Democratic congressmen begin to take lead roles on national issues, they lose the power to define their image to their constituents; they become known not only for constituency service and attention to local problems but also for what may be an unpopular stand on national issues. Thus congressmen of national stature such as Morris Udall and Thomas Foley had trouble in recent elections. Moreover, taking thorough advantage of incumbency is an exhausting business. It requires flying home to the district every weekend, working long hours during the week, never really having much personal time at one's disposal. Thus congressmen in their 30s with good prospects for reelection—for example, Richard Nolan of Minnesota and John Cavanaugh of Nebraska—simply quit in 1980. It is not insignificant that many of the Republicans elected that year are young, single, and have never held major jobs before. (They resemble, in those respects, many of the young Democrats elected in 1974 and 1976.) Such persons are far more likely than married persons with established careers to withstand the rigors of a House career.

In the 1968 election, despite turmoil and dissatisfaction among the voters, 91% of the incumbent congressmen were reelected—the highest figure in American history. In 1980 the reelection rate was 83%—still very high (it was as high as 50% only twice in the 19th century) but a definite drop: turnover was twice as high as in 1968. Most of the turnover resulted from retirements rather than defeats, but many of those retirements were not entirely voluntary: some congressmen faced sure defeat, many others faced the likelihood of a tough election with an uncertain outcome. The result is that the Democrats have not been able to preserve their 1974 gains in the face of adverse trends in public opinion. The Republicans in fact won a larger percentage of votes in House than Senate races in 1980 (they were able to convert their Senate votes into more victories, because many Democratic votes were concentrated in the big states of California, Ohio, and Illinois, where Republicans never seriously threatened the Democrats). Their current share of House seats in fact represents a more accurate picture of partisan voting patterns in congressional elections than their current share of Senate seats.

There is little evidence that Reagan coattails, as such, were decisive in more than a handful

of House elections — if that. Nationally, Reagan carried just 51% of the vote, a good performance in a three-way race, but one not likely to produce a landslide in House elections
where there are typically only two significant candidates. Republican House candidates, as
a whole, actually ran behind Reagan in the East and even with him in the Midwest; he ran
9% ahead of Republican House candidates in the South, but in many cases there were no
serious candidates running to take advantage of whatever coattails he might have had. A
closer look at those seats that the Republicans actually won away from the Democrats (see
table below) demolishes the theory that coattails were decisive. In most Republican pickups
in the East and virtually all of them in the Midwest, the Republican House candidates actually ran ahead of Reagan. In the seats Republicans picked up in the South, Reagan had no
more than 56% of the vote; Republican House candidates ran ahead of him in five out of 11
districts and no more than 3% behind him in all but one. Even in the West — Reagan's strongest region and the only one where he ran ahead of almost all Republicans in Republican
pickup districts, there is little evidence that Reagan somehow mechanically pulled voters
into the Republican column. Some of these races — the defeat of Ways and Means Chairman Al Ullman in Oregon, the defeat of Democrat James Corman in the San Fernando
Valley, the defeat of Public Works Committee Chairman Bizz Johnson in northern California — were among the best financed and best publicized in the country; voters may have
known more about them than about the presidential race.

Moreover, even defeated Democrats showed the capacity to run far ahead of Jimmy Carter. The major exceptions were Abscam defendants and poorly financed nominees in districts where an incumbent Democrat retired. Democrat Gunn McKay in Utah ran 30%
ahead of Carter; unfortunately for McKay, this was the strongest Reagan district in the
country, and the Republican won. Some results were simply odd. In New Mexico, the governor's nephew wangled the Democratic nomination after the incumbent died, and the
courts would not allow a Republican or the late congressman's widow on the ballot. They
ran as write-ins, and the Republican won.

Taken together, the House races across the nation or in a single region seem to give a pretty clear portrait of national or regional opinion. But that is because peculiar circumstances
tend to balance each other out. The partisan composition of the House can be predicted fairly well from the Gallup Polls that ask voters which party's candidate they will vote for. But
the actual composition of the House — who holds which seat, which subcommittee chairman is reelected and which defeated, all the questions that determine the actors in the legislative process and the outcome — all these in our system are still very much the product of the
particularities of local politics. Anyone who seeks to understand the Congress and the way it
works has to understand each of the 435 congressional districts. The Republicans in 1980
won not because of some mechanical coattail effect, but because they put on aggressive, intelligent campaigns in more Democratic-held seats than Democrats did in Republican-held
seats. Republican candidates had the advantage of a reasonably coherent and attractive
Republican national message and of better national organization. But if the Republicans
had not had the good local campaigns, the Democrats would still be holding a secure margin
in the House.

Coattails Effect? Districts Where Republicans Captured Democratic Seats

Seat	Winning Candidate	R–D % Congress	R–D % President	Difference in R%	Difference in D%
EAST					
Conn. 3	Lawrence DeNardis	52–46	50–39	+ 2	+ 7
N.J. 4	*Christopher Smith	57–41	47–44	+10	– 3
N.J. 7	Marge Roukema	51–47	57–32	– 5	+15
N.Y. 3	Gregory Carman	50–47	57–34	– 7	+13
N.Y. 6	John LeBoutillier	53–47	54–36	– 1	+11
N.Y. 17	*Guy Molinari	48–35	49–42	– 1	– 7
N.Y. 32	George Wortley	60–32	51–37	+ 9	– 5
Pa. 8	James Coyne	51–49	55–33	– 8	+17
Pa. 11	James Nelligan	52–48	51–43	+ 1	+ 5
R.I. 2	Claudine Schneider	55–45	38–47	+17	– 2
MIDWEST					
Ind. 3	John Hiler	55–45	54–39	+ 1	+ 6
Mich. 6	Jim Dunn	51–49	50–37	+ 1	+12
Minn. 6	Vin Weber	53–47	48–43	+ 5	+ 4
Mo. 8	Wendell Bailey	57–43	57–39	—	+ 4
Mo. 10	Bill Emerson	55–45	53–44	+ 2	+ 1
Neb. 2	Hal Daub	53–44	61–30	– 8	+14
Ohio 9	Ed Weber	56–40	44–46	+10	– 6
Wis. 3	Steven Gunderson	51–49	48–43	+ 3	+ 6
WEST					
Cal. 1	Eugene Chappie	54–40	57–32	– 3	+ 8
Cal. 21	Bobbi Fiedler	49–48	51–38	– 2	+10
Cal. 35	David Dreier	52–45	62–29	–10	+16
Cal. 42	Duncan Hunter	53–47	53–37	—	+10
N.M. 2	Joe Skeen (write-in)	38–34	60–35	–22	– 1
Oreg. 2	Denny Smith	49–47	55–34	– 6	+13
Utah 1	James Hansen	52–48	77–18	–25	+30
Wash. 4	Sid Morrison	57–43	55–36	+ 2	+ 7
SOUTH					
Fla. 12	Clay Shaw	55–45	56–36	– 1	+ 9
N.C. 6	Eugene Johnston	51–49	52–44	– 1	+ 5
N.C. 11	William Hendon	54–46	51–45	+ 3	+ 1
S.C. 1	Tom Hartnett	52–48	53–44	– 1	+ 4
S.C. 6	*John Napier	52–48	45–53	+ 7	– 5
Tex. 8	Jack Fields	52–48	45–52	+ 7	– 4
Va. 3	Thomas Bliley	52–33	55–40	– 3	– 7
Va. 8	Stanford Parris	49–48	56–33	– 7	+15
Va. 10	Frank Wolf	51–49	53–34	– 2	+15
W.Va. 2	Cleveland Benedict	56–44	47–48	+ 9	– 4
W.Va. 3	Mick Staton	53–47	47–48	+ 6	– 1

Ran against Democratic incumbent involved in the Abscam scandals.

The Sources of Power. The House is a complicated institution, and generalization is dangerous — particularly ahead of the fact. Yet it seems likely that a generalization can be made about power in the House of Representatives of 1981–82, and that is that power will be split: the Republicans have the votes and the power to prevail on most substantive issues (although many will be closely contested), while the Democrats have control of most of the major committees and the power to prevail on most procedural matters. That means that the outcome of most legislative battles is likely to hinge on skill and imagination — the legislative skill to take maximum advantage of every parliamentary device and the imagination to frame issues in terms most favorable to one's side.

How can substantive and procedural power be split? There are two answers. One is that the majority of the majority party controls committee assignments and chairmanships. Most House members are, nominally at least, Democrats, and most Democrats are most or less solidly aligned with the liberal side of their party. One of the reforms put through in the wake of the 1974 elections that has been most successful is the requirement that committee chairmen and chairmen of Appropriations subcommittees be elected by all Democrats in their caucus. Initially it resulted in the ousting of some chairmen. This has not happened recently, but the effect has been more profound. Committee chairmen know now that they are accountable, and those whose views are far out of line with those of the majority of Democrats know that there are limits to how far they can push those views. The conduct of Jamie Whitten, the most senior member of the House, is instructive. Before 1974, he had a solidly conservative voting record and ran the Agriculture Appropriations Subcommittee as a personal fiefdom. After 1974, his voting record changed enough that his labor voting record went up 40%, and he began to strongly support the food stamp program, a favorite of urban Democrats. The obvious reason: Whitten was second in line for chairman of Appropriations, and he wanted the post when Chairman George Mahon stepped down. Mahon retired in 1978, and Whitten was elected (although not without a fair number of dissenters, even though there was no organized opposition). He holds his chair on sufferance, and he is not the kind of chairman he almost certainly would have been ten years ago. Conservatively inclined Democrats know therefore that there are limits as to how far they can go in expressing their feelings and still get the kind of advancement they want. The easiest way for them to make concessions to northern liberals is on procedural matters. Therefore, it is likely that the House Democratic leadership will find it easier to win procedural than substantive votes.

The other major way the Democrats have effective control of procedure is through the House Rules Committee. There is no equivalent for this body in the Senate or indeed in most legislatures in the world. Almost every major bill that comes before the House (with only a few minor exceptions) must have a rule, that is, the Rules Committee must pass and get the House to agree to a set of terms and conditions under which it may be considered. These typically include restrictions on amendments and time limits on speeches; the latter simply keep the House acting quickly, but the former, obviously, can affect the outcome. The majority party traditionally has a 2–1 margin on Rules, and the Democrats' 11 members are all pretty solidly loyal to the leadership. Indeed, Democratic Rules members are now appointed directly by the speaker, which resolves any ambiguity about who is in charge. The five Republicans have little leverage. It is not likely that the Democrats will throttle a major Reagan initiative by refusing to allow it to be introduced in amendment form, but theoretically they could do so — and the possession of such theoretical power is a strong bargaining chip in any negotiations. The Democrats do have the capacity to see that issues are framed favorably to their cause; they can give their leaders a stronger position from which to conduct negotiations in conference committee with Republican senators.

It is going to be difficult for Democrats to summon majorities on substantive issues, however—not impossible, but difficult. Once we get into the area of substantive issues, however, we are into the most complex of inquiries—one where further generalizations are not only dangerous but are almost certain to be misleading. There is really no substitute, at this point, for considering matters issue by issue and committee by committee, in the material that makes up the bulk of this book. It is possible here, as it was in the Senate, however, to attempt to indicate who the most important players are likely to be on the most important issues of the next two years. Most of them are subcommittee chairmen—a reflection of the power that really important subcommittees have. This is not so much an unintended consequence of House reforms as it is a reflection of how the House has always worked. The House has many more members than the Senate and, much more than in the Senate, House members actually work personally on legislation. They depend much less on staff; most of their staff handles casework. Detail work on legislation, given the large size of full committees, is often done in subcommittee. And the fact that subcommittee chairmen are now elected (typically, by all the Democrats on the full committee) means that most important subcommittees have chairmen of considerable competence and the confidence of most of the committee's Democrats—not as in the past a member who simply has a few years more seniority (or who won a coin toss with his fellow freshmen some years ago) than anyone else.

In that spirit, let us present this list of powerful congressmen, with their parties and districts, their committee or subcommittee positions, the year they were first elected, their percentage margin over their major party opponent in the 1980 election, and the percentages in their districts for Reagan, Carter, and Anderson in 1980.

Congressman	Party–State	Committee/Subcommittee	Year	%	Reagan/Carter/Anderson %
Thomas P. O'Neill	D-Mass. 8	Speaker	1952	78–22	31–51–16
Dan Rostenkowski	D-Ill. 8	Chmn., Ways & Means	1958	85–15	24–70–4
Robert H. Michel	R-Ill. 18	Minority Leader	1956	62–38	60–32–6
Richard Bolling	D-Mo. 5	Chmn., Rules	1948	70–30	35–59–5
Jim Wright	D-Tex. 12	Majority Leader	1954	60–39	51–46–2
James Jones	D-Okla. 1	Chmn., Budget; Member, Ways & Means	1972	58–42	66–29–4
Delbert L. Latta	R-Ohio 5	Ranking Minor. Mem., Budget; Member, Rules	1958	70–30	59–32–8
John D. Dingell	D-Mich 16	Chmn., Energy & Commerce	1955	70–28	45–47–6
Henry A. Waxman	D-Cal. 24	Chmn., Health & Environment Subc. (Energy & Commerce)	1974	64–27	41–47–8
Carl D. Perkins	D-Ky. 7	Chmn., Education & Labor	1948	100–0	43–55–1
Jamie Whitten	D-Miss. 1	Chmn., Appropriations; Chmn., Agricult. Subc. (Appropriat.)	1941	63–37	42–55–2
Thomas S. Foley	D-Wash. 5	Majority Whip; Chmn., Wheat, Soybeans, & Feed Grains Subc. (Agriculture)	1964	52–48	56–34–8
Sam Gibbons	D-Fla. 7	Chmn., Trade Subc. (Ways & Means)	1962	72–28	52–43–5
Don Edwards	D-Cal. 10	Chmn., Civil & Constitutional Rights Subc. (Judiciary)	1962	62–28	45–41–11

Congressman	Party-State	Committee/Subcommittee	Year	%	Reagan/Carter/Anderson %
Henry J. Hyde	R-Ill. 6	Ranking Minor. Mbr., Civil & Constitutional Rights Subc. (Judiciary)	1974	63–37	52–39–8
Barber Conable	R-N.Y. 35	Ranking Minor. Mbr., Ways & Means	1964	72–28	46–44–8
Phil Gramm	D-Tex. 6	Mbr., Budget	1978	71–29	54–43–2
Leon Panetta	D-Cal. 16	Mbr., Budget	1976	71–25	50–34–11
Richard Cheney	D-Wyo. a-l	Chmn., Republican Policy Committee	1978	69–31	63–28–7
Morris K. Udall	D-Ariz. 2	Chmn., Interior & Insular Affairs	1961	58–40	56–34–8
Richard Gephardt	D-Mo. 3	Mbr., Budget; Ways & Means	1976	78–22	51–44–4
Phillip Burton	D-Cal. 6	Chmn., Labor–Mgmt. Relations Subc. (Education & Labor)	1965	69–26	33–53–11
Timothy Wirth	D-Col. 2	Chmn., Telecommunications, Consumer Protect., & Finance Subc. (Energy & Commerce)	1974	56–41	54–30–13
Lee H. Hamilton	D-Ind. 9	Chmn., Europe & Middle East Subc. (Foreign Affairs)	1964	64–46	54–41–4
Trent Lott	R-Miss. 5	Minority Whip	1972	74–26	58–40–1

There are, of course, plenty of House veterans on this list. But what is striking is how many junior members there are. Election of committee and subcommittee chairmen has made the House more of a meritocracy, and every individual on this list has shown considerable legislative and political skill as well as the endurance and luck necessary to achieve a high seniority position.

Redistricting and the 1982 Elections. By now, almost everyone must know that the House will be reapportioned in line with the results of the 1980 census. Some states, all in the East and Midwest, will lose seats; some states, all in the West and South, will gain. The table shows the changes, with the total number of seats in 1980 and 1982 for each region.

House Seats by Region

Region	1972–80	1982–90	Gain/Loss	Region	1972–80	1982–90	Gain/Loss
East	113	104	– 9	West	76	85	+ 9
Midwest	121	113	– 8	South	125	133	+ 8

For the first time in American history, the West and South as they are defined here (the census defines them differently, including Delaware, Maryland, and D.C. in the South) have more representations than the North and the East.

There has been much talk that this shift of representation to the Sun Belt will provide a major boost for Republicans in the House. That prognostication is almost certainly exaggerated. In the first place, this is not such an extraordinary regional shift; more House seats shifted around after, for example, the 1960 census than after this one. In the addition, it also makes a difference who is doing the redistricting. Three states—Florida, Texas, and California—have between them nine of the 17 House seats the Sun Belt is gaining. All three

Changes in House Representation

Region/State	1972–80	1982–90	Difference	Region/State	1972–80	1982–90	Difference
EAST	**113**	**104**	**– 9**				
Connecticut	6	6	—	New Jersey	15	14	– 1
Delaware	1	1	—	New York	39	34	– 5
Maine	2	2	—	Pennsylvania	25	23	– 2
Maryland	8	8	—	Rhode Island	2	2	—
Massachusetts	12	11	– 1	Vermont	1	1	—
New Hampshire	2	2	—				
MIDWEST	**121**	**113**	**– 8**				
Illinois	24	22	– 2	Missouri	10	9	– 1
Indiana	11	10	– 1	Nebraska	3	3	—
Iowa	6	6	—	North Dakota	1	1	—
Kansas	5	5	—	Ohio	23	21	– 2
Michigan	19	18	– 1	South Dakota	2	1	– 1
Minnesota	8	8	—	Wisconsin	9	9	—
WEST	**76**	**85**	**+ 9**				
Alaska	1	1	—	Nevada	1	2	+ 1
Arizona	4	5	+ 1	New Mexico	2	3	+ 1
California	43	45	+ 2	Oregon	4	5	+ 1
Colorado	5	6	+ 1	Utah	2	3	+ 1
Hawaii	2	2	—	Washington	7	8	+ 1
Idaho	2	2	—	Wyoming	1	1	—
Montana	2	2	—				
SOUTH	**125**	**133**	**+ 8**				
Alabama	7	7	—	North Carolina	11	11	—
Arkansas	4	4	—	Oklahoma	6	6	—
Florida	15	19	+ 4	South Carolina	6	6	—
Georgia	10	10	—	Tennessee	8	9	+ 1
Kentucky	7	7	—	Texas	24	27	+ 3
Louisiana	8	8	—	Virginia	10	10	—
Mississippi	5	5	—	West Virginia	4	4	—

states have Democratic legislatures, however; California and Florida have Democratic governors as well, and there are more than enough Democrats in Texas to override the Republican governor's veto. Consequently, the Republicans are not likely to make massive gains simply on the basis of reapportionment.

Finally, there is less leeway than is often supposed under the one-person-one-vote rule for eking out partisan advantage in redistricting. The courts have imposed a very tight equal population requirement that sharply limits what legislatures can do: thus the Democratic legislature in California will have to create a new Republican district in the San Diego area, because there are so many people there now and such a large percentage of them vote Republican. Similarly, the Republican legislature in Pennsylvania is not going to be able to eliminate most of the state's Democratic congressional districts. Republicans are spending a great deal of money and are using lots of computer time on the national level to get as favorable redistricting plans as they can. It is not clear that all the technology is necessary. The real difficulty in redistricting for partisan advantage is not in determining where the votes are going to be in 1982 but where they will be in 1986 or 1990. That involves a certain amount of intuition and guesswork. Will the Mexican–Americans break sharply to the Republicans, or will they become even more heavily Democratic? Will they move out and scatter in working-class suburbs, or will they cluster in a few Mexican–American communities? No one can know the answers for sure, yet these questions can make a great deal of difference to a partisan redistricter in California. The success of gerrymanders is actually pretty dismal. In 1962 the redistricting process in New York was completely controlled by Republicans and the process in California completely controlled by Democrats. Both controlling groups had plenty of expert help in drawing new congressional and state legislative district lines; they drew their districts carefully, block by block, and had all the necessary data at hand. Yet the Republicans never made their hoped-for gains in New York congressional districts, and the Democrats lost half a dozen districts intended to be Democratic in California before the decade was over. By 1968 the Democrats had captured control of the New York legislature and the Republicans had captured control of the California legislature.

The conclusion is inescapable that in any state where the parties are in reasonable balance one party cannot through redistricting put a legislature or a majority of a large congressional delegation out of reach of the other party over a decade's elections under the limitations imposed by the one-person-one-vote rule.

Much of the congressional redistricting that takes place for 1982 will be automatic (as in South Dakota, which loses one of its two seats) or Iowa (where the controlling Republicans are likely to allow a nonpartisan expert agency to draw the lines, as they did ten years ago). The important redistricting situations, where sizable numbers of congressional seats are at stake, and where differences in drawing the lines can make significant differences in the results, are limited to a relatively small number of states. The following table shows such situations, indicating the number of seats before and after redistricting, the present party balance of the House delegation, and the party controlling the governorship and each house of the state legislature. States with a single representative at large (and South Dakota, which will have one representative in 1982) have been omitted.

Thus for all the ballyhoo about Republican chances, they have control of redistricting in only six states with a total of 53 districts. In three the process is likely to be noncontroversial (Iowa, Nebraska, Utah), and in one (Washington) Republican control hinges on the vote of one state senator who switched parties and would presumably subordinate Republicans' desires for partisan gains to his own personal desire for a House seat. This means Republicans have control in two major states, Pennsylvania and Indiana. One might add to that Illinois, where Republicans missed control by one vote in the state Senate; they might be able to negotiate for that support.

The Democrats, in contrast, have theoretical redistricting control in 22 states with 223 seats—a majority of all 435 House seats. In some of these states, however, their control hinges on their possession of legislative majorities large enough to override a governor's veto (Arkansas, Louisiana, Missouri, Texas, and Virginia). In practice the process in these southern or southern-oriented states is not likely to be partisan (many Democratic legislators prefer the politics of Ronald Reagan to the politics of Jimmy Carter). In some other states there is hardly likely to be any controversy. Still, the Democrats can at least match the Republicans in the number of important states where they have redistricting control: California, Florida, New Jersey, and Texas.

State	House Seats Before	House Seats After	D–R	Gov.	Legislature Upper D–R	Legislature Lower D–R	Theoretical Control
Ala.	7	7	4–3	D	35–0	105–4	Democrat
Ariz.	4	5	2–2	D	14–16	17–43	Split
Ark.	4	4	2–2	D	34–1	93–7	Democrat
Cal.	43	45	22–21	D	23–17	48–32	Democrat
Colo.	5	6	3–2	D	15–20	27–38	Split
Conn.	6	6	4–2	D	22–13	83–68	Democrat
Fla.	15	19	11–4	D	27–13	81–39	Democrat
Ga.	10	10	9–1	D	51–5	157–23	Democrat
Hawaii	2	2	2–0	D	17–8	39–12	Democrat
Idaho	2	2	0–2	D	12–23	15–56	Split
Ill.	24	22	10–14	R	30–29	85–91	Split
Ind.	11	10	6–5	R	15–35	37–63	Republican
Iowa	6	6	3–3	R	21–29	42–58	Republican
Kan.	5	5	1–4	D	16–24	53–72	Split
Ky.	7	7	4–3	D	28–10	74–26	Democrat
La.	8	8	6–2	R	39–0	95–10	Democrat
Maine	2	2	0–2	D	16–17	84–67	Split
Md.	8	8	7–1	D	40–7	125–16	Democrat
Mass.	12	11	10–2	D	32–7	128–31	Democrat
Mich.	19	18	12–7	R	24–14	64–46	Split
Minn.	8	8	3–5	R	45–22	70–64	Split
Miss.	5	5	3–2	D	43–4	116–4	Democrat
Mo.	10	9	6–4	R	23–11	111–52	Democrat
Mont.	2	2	1–1	D	22–28	43–57	Split
Neb.	3	3	0–3	R	16–32	None	Republican
Nev.	1	2	1–0	R	15–5	26–14	Split
N.H.	2	2	1–1	D	10–13	160–239	Split
N.J.	15	14	8–7	D*	25–13*	44–36*	Democrat
N.M.	2	3	0–2	D	22–20	41–29	Democrat
N.Y.	39	34	22–17	D	25–35	86–64	Split
N.C.	11	11	7–4	D	40–10	96–24	Democrat
Ohio	23	21	10–13	R	15–18	56–43	Split
Okla.	6	6	5–1	D	37–11	73–28	Democrat
Oreg.	4	5	3–1	R	21–9	33–27	Split
Pa.	25	23	13–12	R	23–25	100–103	Republican
R.I.	2	2	1–1	D	43–7	72–18	Democrat
S.C.	6	6	2–4	D	41–5	107–17	Democrat
Tenn.	8	9	5–3	R	20–12	58–39	Split
Tex.	24	27	19–5	R	24–7	114–36	Democrat
Utah	2	3	0–2	D	7–22	17–58	Republican
Va.	10	10	1–9	R	31–9	74–25	Democrat
Wash.	7	8	5–2	R	24–25	42–56	Republican
W.Va.	4	4	2–2	D	27–7	77–22	Democrat
Wis.	9	9	5–4	R	19–14	58–40	Split

*State elections November 1981.

The bulk of House districts in the new Congress, however, are likely to be drawn in those 16 states where redistricting control is divided between the parties (they have 152 districts altogether) or where the process will proceed noncontroversially. Some states, particularly those without large metropolitan areas, have not had major demographic shifts within their bounds; they can redistrict by changing boundaries very slightly, and that is probably what most of them will do. In others the obvious compromise will be to protect incumbents and put any new seats up for grabs or allocate them to the party that is obviously entitled to them demographically (the Republicans in Colorado, for instance). Overall, it is our estimate that reapportionment and redistricting, taken together, will give the Republicans a net gain of between five and ten House seats—a helpful number for them, but not one that will, without further efforts, give them control of the House. To win that the Republicans will have to make the kind of effort they did in 1980—and hope that the Democrats, as in 1980, fail to mount serious challenges in most Republican districts.

THE GOVERNORS AND BIG-CITY MAYORS

Does it really matter to citizens of one state who is governor of another? Often it seems the answer is no. Citizens of Virginia, even well-informed ones, spend their whole lives knowing nothing of what the governor of North Dakota does and are none the worse for it. Yet there are reasons to give at least some attention to the governors and the state governments they head. After all, our incumbent president and his predecessor served as governors—and had never been in the federal government except as members of the military services before they were elected. Governors are executives, in charge of an administration—something senators and congressmen cannot claim about themselves. Governors even have command of military forces—a technical responsibility in most circumstances, perhaps, but a vital one when a riot breaks out in a big city or on a large campus. Our most eminent political writer, David Broder, believes strongly that a governorship, at least of a large state, provides training for the presidency at least as good as a seat in the Senate; and there is certainly nothing that is a duplicate of executive responsibility. Some of our greatest presidents served as governors, but not as members of Congress—Thomas Jefferson, Theodore Roosevelt, Woodrow Wilson, Franklin Roosevelt.

And it can matter to the rest of us what the governor of North Dakota does. North Dakota, as it happens, sits atop huge strata of low sulphur coal. Decisions that its state government makes—the amount of the coal severance tax, environmental restrictions on strip mining—can make as much difference to our energy supply as decisions made on Capitol Hill. Moreover, over the past decade, the government spending that has been rising most rapidly—and, in the opinion of some, most uncontrollably—is state government spending. Most of the government services that we enjoy—or disparage—are at some point funded or delivered by the state governments.

Finally, the states really do matter — even still. Critics are fond of pointing out that many state boundaries don't make sense. Many of our major metropolitan areas sit astride state boundaries — New York, Philadelphia, Washington, Chicago, Cincinnati, St. Louis, Kansas City, Portland. (Others are astride international boundaries — Detroit, Buffalo, San Diego, El Paso.) Nevertheless our states continue to have political and governmental personalities. With surprisingly few exceptions, most Americans feel some sort of allegiance to or bond with their state. We are not where we were in the early 19th century, when, if someone was asked what country he was from, he would say Pennsylvania or Virginia. But the states do mean something and do merit a little attention in a book covering American politics.

The 1980 Elections. Not many states hold gubernatorial elections in the presidential year anymore. There are still four states that elect their governors every two years (New Hampshire, Vermont, Rhode Island, and Arkansas) — a vestige of the old colonial mistrust of executives that, inter alia, led Massachusetts to elect its governor every year until 1920. A few other small states have gubernatorial elections in presidential years (Delaware, North Dakota, Montana, Utah, and West Virginia). Only four fairly large states do so (North Carolina, Indiana, Missouri, and Washington) and it is not surprising perhaps that none of these has generated a governor who became a serious presidential candidate since Paul McNutt of Indiana in the 1930s.

1980 Governor Elections

State	Republican Candidate	%	Democratic Candidate	%
EAST				
Delaware	Pierre S. du Pont IV	71	William J. Gordy	29
New Hampshire	Meldrim Thomson, Jr.	41	Hugh J. Gallen	59
Rhode Island	Vincent A. Cianci	26	J. Joseph Garrahy	74
Vermont	Richard A. Snelling	59	M. Jerome Diamond	37
MIDWEST				
Indiana	Robert D. Orr	58	John A. Hillenbrand II	42
Missouri	Christopher S. Bond	53	Joseph P. Teasdale	47
North Dakota	Allen I. Olson	54	Arthur A. Link	46
WEST				
Montana	Jack Ramirez	45	Ted Schwinden	55
Utah	Bob Wright	44	Scott M. Matheson	55
Washington	John Spellman	57	James A. McDermott	43
SOUTH				
Arkansas	Frank D. White	52	Bill Clinton	48
North Carolina	I. Beverly Lake, Jr.	37	James B. Hunt, Jr.	62
West Virginia	Arch A. Moore, Jr.	45	John D. Rockefeller IV	54

1979 Governor Elections

State	Republican Candidate	%	Democratic Candidate	%
SOUTH				
Kentucky	Louie B. Nunn	41	John Y. Brown, Jr.	59
Louisiana	David C. Treen	50.3	Louis Lambert	49.7
Mississippi	Gil Carmichael	39	William F. Winter	61

There are a few states still that hold gubernatorial elections in the odd-numbered years. Kentucky, Louisiana, and Mississippi had contests in 1979; Virginia and New Jersey have them in 1981.

A look at the results of the 1979 and 1980 gubernatorial elections shows how difficult it is to come up with any meaningful generalizations about them. The popularity of particular individuals was critical in most of these elections. Several—the contests in Louisiana and Kentucky particularly—were free-for-alls with many candidates and lavish spending. Some —Missouri and West Virginia—were rematches in which the loser of the earlier election prevailed this time. Republicans picked up five governorships, but there seems not to have been any single, overriding reason for that.

The 1982 Elections for Governor. In 1982 we will have a more representative sample of gubernatorial elections; some 36 states will elect governors, including all of the nine largest. The table shows the governors, their parties, their age at the time of the 1982 general election, the year they were first elected, and their margins over their major party opponents in their last election.

State	Governor	D/R	Age	Year First Elected	%	
EAST						
Connecticut	William A. O'Neill	D	52	1981	—	Succeeded to office on resignation of Ella Grasso
Maine	Joseph E. Brennan	D	48	1978	48–34	
Maryland	Harry R. Hughes	D	55	1978	71–29	
Massachusetts	Edward J. King	D	57	1978	52–47	
New Hampshire	Hugh J. Gallen	D	58	1978	59–41	
New York	Hugh L. Carey	D	63	1974	51–45	
Pennsylvania	Richard L. Thornburgh	R	50	1978	53–46	
Rhode Island	J. Joseph Garrahy	D	61	1976	74–26	
Vermont	Richard A. Snelling	R	54	1976	59–37	
MIDWEST						
Illinois	James R. Thompson	R	46	1976	59–40	
Iowa	Robert D. Ray	R	54	1968	58–41	
Kansas	John W. Carlin	D	42	1978	49–47	
Michigan	William G. Milliken	R	60	1968	57–43	Succeeded to office on resignation of Geo. Romney
Minnesota	Albert H. Quie	R	59	1978	52–45	
Nebraska	Charles Thone	R	58	1978	56–44	
Ohio	James A. Rhodes	R	73	1974	49–48	Also elected 1962, 1970; ineligible to run in 1982
South Dakota	William J. Janklow	R	43	1978	57–43	
Wisconsin	Lee S. Dreyfus	R	56	1978	54–45	

State	Governor	D/R	Age	Year First Elected	%	
WEST						
Alaska	Jay S. Hammond	R	60	1974	40–21	
Arizona	Bruce E. Babbitt	D	44	1978	52–45	Succeeded to office on death of Wesley Bolin
California	Edmund G. Brown, Jr.	D	44	1974	56–37	
Colorado	Richard D. Lamm	D	47	1974	58–39	
Hawaii	George R. Ariyoshi	D	56	1974	54–44	
Idaho	John V. Evans	D	57	1977	59–40	Succeeded to office on resignation of Cecil Andrus
Nevada	Robert F. List	R	46	1978	56–40	
New Mexico	Bruce King	D	58	1978	51–49	Also elected 1970; ineligible to run in 1982
Oregon	Victor G. Atiyeh	R	59	1978	55–45	
Wyoming	Ed Herschler	D	64	1974	51–49	
SOUTH						
Alabama	Forrest (Fob) James., Jr.	D	48	1978	73–26	
Arkansas	Frank D. White	R	49	1980	52–48	
Florida	Robert (Bob) Graham	D	45	1978	56–44	
Georgia	George Busbee	D	55	1974	81–19	Ineligible to run in 1982. Also served on resignations of govs., 1963, 1969
Oklahoma	George Nigh	D	55	1978	52–47	
South Carolina	Richard W. Riley	D	50	1978	61–38	
Tennessee	Lamar Alexander	R	42	1978	56–44	
Texas	William (Bill) Clements	R	65	1978	50–49	

Most of the eastern governors up for reelection are Democrats and most of the midwesterners are Republicans. Those party affiliations match roughly those regions' recent voting habits. The preponderance of Democrats over Republicans in the South is similarly representative. In the West, however, most of the governorships are currently held by the Democrats, even though in presidential elections this has been the most Republican region of the country. Most of these Democrats have established their own identity with regional attitudes; many of them fought the Carter Administration. But can they match the appeal of Republicans in line with the Reagan Administration?

The fiercest political battles will be waged for the big governorships: New York, Pennsylvania, Ohio, Michigan, Illinois, Texas, California. On the basis of previous results and current popularity only one governor enters any of these big state races with great strength: Thompson of Illinois, although Milliken of Michigan would have to be added to that short list if he were to seek another term. The national implications of these races do not seem too great, however. Congressional redistricting will, presumably, have been taken care of before the governors elected in 1982 take office. None of the likely contenders in these big states seems a likely presidential candidate for 1984.

State and Major Local Governments. The magnitude of state and local governments has grown far beyond expectations; at the end of the 1970s the state governments were spending about $1,000 for every person in the nation. Local governments were spending additional sums — sometimes doubling the state total in major cities. The table below shows the magnitude of the state governments, from $28 billion California to $612 million Vermont. It also shows the amount they spend per capita, which varies quite substantially. It is highest in the West, where living costs are high (this is the major reason for the high figures in Alaska and Hawaii), and in the East, where the highest per capita spending is in New York and Rhode Island, both of which lost population in the 1970s. A major portion of the expenditures of any state or local government are wages, salaries, and fringe benefits (notably including pensions). Since government workers seldom can be fired, their numbers tend not to decrease, even if population does. By the same token, they do not necessarily increase as fast as population in areas with high private sector growth and population gain. Two of the three lowest per capita state spending figures are in Texas and Florida, the two booming Sun Belt states that, between them, gained seven congressional districts in the 1970s.

It is interesting to set beside the state figures those for the cities that are as high as the lowest state. Note that none of the new Sun Belt cities is among them. Houston is the fourth largest city in the country now (counting within city limits, not whole metropolitan areas), but it does not spend as much money as the state of Vermont, which has one-third its population. The cities with the largest per capita spending are those with the longest-established large-city governments — New York and Boston — plus Washington, D.C., which fills the functions of both city and state and has part of its budget supplied by the federal government. The impact of high state and local spending can be judged by combining the per capita figures for New York state and city. They total nearly $3,000 per capita — a pretty heavy load for taxpayers to carry. The figure for a resident of Los Angeles, by contrast, is less than half that.

Expenditures of State Governments and Major City Governments — in Millions of Dollars and Per Capita, by Region

State	$million	$ Per Capita	State	$million	$ Per Capita
EAST	**60,351**	**1,108**	**MIDWEST**	**55,965**	**951**
New York	22,708	1,293	Michigan	10,507	1,135
Pennsylvania	11,575	975	Illinois	10,418	912
New Jersey	7,718	1,048	Ohio	9,762	904
Massachusetts	6,377	1,112	Wisconsin	5,381	1,144
Maryland	4,678	1,109	Minnesota	4,779	1,172
Connecticut	2,963	953	Indiana	4,089	745
Maine	1,183	1,052	Missouri	3,337	679
Rhode Island	1,171	1,236	Iowa	3,011	1,034
New Hampshire	784	852	Kansas	2,012	851
Delaware	762	1,280	Nebraska	1,250	796
Vermont	612	1,197	North Dakota	777	1,190
			South Dakota	642	930
New York City	11,963	1,692			
Washington	1,844	2,892	Chicago	1,304	434
Philadelphia	1,409	835	Detroit	989	822
Baltimore	940	1,195			
Boston	897	1,593			

State	$million	$ Per Capita	State	$million	$ Per Capita
WEST	**50,210**	**1,163**	**SOUTH**	**57,949**	**829**
California	28,319	1,196	Texas	9,665	679
Washington	4,860	1,177	Florida	6,462	663
Oregon	2,906	1,104	North Carolina	5,249	894
Colorado	2,518	872	Virginia	4,876	912
Arizona	2,288	842	Georgia	4,437	796
New Mexico	1,578	1,214	Louisiana	4,123	981
Hawaii	1,524	1,579	Kentucky	3,880	1,060
Alaska	1,466	3,661	Alabama	3,558	915
Utah	1,464	1,002	Tennessee	3,361	732
Montana	901	1,145	South Carolina	3,007	964
Idaho	891	944	Oklahoma	2,733	903
Nevada	862	1,079	West Virginia	2,424	1,243
Wyoming	633	1,344	Mississippi	2,367	939
			Arkansas	1,897	830
Los Angeles	1,093	368			
San Francisco	804	1,184			

The Big-City Mayors. Politically, the most important mayors in the country remain those who head the largest city governments. Houston may have more residents than Detroit now, but the mayor of Houston has less clout than the mayor of Detroit, whether the forum is the U.S. Conference of Mayors, the Democratic National Convention, or a committee meeting room on Capitol Hill. The mayor of Detroit (despite the budget problems that he, like other big-city mayors, must deal with) has more city employees and more public spending behind him, a bigger and more powerful city government. Much more than Houston, it performs more than housekeeping functions. The elections of mayors in these big cities are contested as hard as governorships, if not more so, and the mayors are mentioned — and not without reason — from time to time as possible candidates for president or vice president. The table lists the mayors of these big cities, their partisan affiliation, whether they are elected on a partisan or nonpartisan basis, and when they must next face the voters.

City	Mayor	Party	Type of Election	Next Election
New York City	Edward I. Koch	D	Partisan	Nov. 1981
Chicago	Jane Byrne	D	Partisan	Mar. 1983
Los Angeles	Thomas Bradley	D	Nonpartisan	April 1985
Philadelphia	William J. Green	D	Partisan	Nov. 1983
Detroit	Coleman Young	D	Nonpartisan	Nov. 1981
Baltimore	William Donald Schaefer	D	Partisan	Nov. 1983
San Francisco	Dianne Feinstein	D	Nonpartisan	Nov. 1983
Washington	Marion Barry, Jr.	D	Partisan	Nov. 1982
Boston	Kevin H. White	D	Nonpartisan	Nov. 1983

1982 ELECTION CALENDAR

What follows is a calendar of primary and runoff election dates tentatively scheduled for 1982. The reader should remember that states can change their primary dates for any reason and often do. At this writing, for example, Colorado is considering changing its primary from September 14 to August 3. Despite this freedom, states seem to be gravitating to just a few primary dates. Nine states have primaries in May and 13 states have primaries in the first eight days of June; 20 states have primaries between September 7 and September 18. This leaves just eight states as odd men out.

March 16	Tuesday	Illinois
May 1	Saturday	Texas
May 4	Tuesday	Indiana, North Carolina
May 11	Tuesday	Nebraska
May 18	Tuesday	Oregon, Pennsylvania
May 25	Tuesday	Arkansas, Idaho, Kentucky
June 1	Tuesday	Mississippi, New Mexico, South Dakota, West Virginia
June 5	Saturday	Texas runoff
June 8	Tuesday	California, Iowa, Maine, Montana, New Jersey, North Dakota, Ohio, South Carolina, Virginia, Arkansas runoff
June 22	Tuesday	Mississippi runoff, South Carolina runoff
August 3	Tuesday	Kansas, Michigan, Missouri
August 5	Thursday	Tennessee
August 10	Tuesday	Georgia
August 24	Tuesday	Alaska, Oklahoma
August 31	Tuesday	Georgia runoff
September 7	Tuesday	Alabama, Arizona, Connecticut, D.C., Florida
September 11	Saturday	Delaware
September 14	Tuesday	Colorado, Maryland, Massachusetts, Minnesota, Nevada, New Hampshire, New York, Rhode Island, Utah, Vermont, Washington, Wisconsin, Wyoming
September 18	Saturday	Hawaii, Louisiana
September 21	Tuesday	Oklahoma runoff
September 28	Tuesday	Alabama runoff
October 5	Tuesday	Florida runoff

THE PEOPLE
AND THE REGIONS

The 1980 Census. Attacked as inaccurate and too expensive, the subject of lawsuits and denunciations, the 1980 census is still the best statistical picture of the United States we can get at this time. It tells us not only about those trends we have already observed — the growth in California, for example — but it also alerts us to new trends and changes in our country that we did not expect and which, without the milepost of the census, we might not have noticed. Such information is critical: no one can understand a nation as large and complex as ours without resort to statistical evidence. Let us examine briefly some of those noticed and unnoticed trends.

The most obvious trend is the movement of population from the East and Midwest to the West and South. Every one of the southern and western states had greater than average population growth during the 1970s; every eastern and midwestern state with three small exceptions (Maine, New Hampshire, and Vermont) had less than average population growth during the 1970s. Such a total contrast is the exception, not the rule, during the post–World War II era. Put it another way: only 1% of the nation's population growth during the 1970s occurred in the East and only 10% in the Midwest. In contrast, 36% of the nation's population growth was in the West and a majority of it, 53%, in the South. What this means in personal terms is clear: there was substantial outmigration from the North and East, since their growth rates were well below the rate of natural increase, and massive migration from them (and from other places, such as Latin America) into the South and West.

State	1980 Pop.	1970 Pop.	Change	% Change
U.S.	**226,504,825**	**203,302,031**	**+23,202,794**	**+ 11**
EAST	**54,585,989**	**54,289,183**	**+ 296,806**	**+ 1**
Connecticut	3,107,576	3,032,217	+ 75,359	+ 2
Delaware	595,225	548,104	+ 47,121	+ 9
Dist. of Colum.	637,651	756,668	– 119,017	– 16
Maine	1,124,660	993,722	+ 130,938	+ 13
Maryland	4,216,446	3,923,897	+ 292,549	+ 7
Massachusetts	5,737,037	5,689,170	+ 47,867	+ 1
New Hampshire	920,610	737,681	+ 182,929	+ 25
New Jersey	7,364,158	7,171,112	+ 193,046	+ 3
New York	17,557,288	18,241,391	– 684,103	– 4
Pennsylvania	11,866,728	11,800,766	+ 65,962	+ 1
Rhode Island	947,154	949,723	– 2,569	– 0
Vermont	511,456	444,732	+ 66,724	+ 15
MIDWEST	**58,853,804**	**56,590,294**	**+ 2,263,510**	**+ 4**
Illinois	11,418,461	11,110,285	+ 308,176	+ 3
Indiana	5,490,179	5,195,391	+ 294,788	+ 6
Iowa	2,913,387	2,825,368	+ 88,019	+ 3
Kansas	2,363,208	2,249,071	+ 114,137	+ 5
Michigan	9,258,344	8,881,826	+ 376,518	+ 4

State	1980 Pop.	1970 Pop.	Change	% Change
Minnesota	4,077,148	3,806,103	+ 271,045	+ 7
Missouri	4,917,444	4,677,623	+ 239,821	+ 5
Nebraska	1,570,006	1,485,333	+ 84,673	+ 6
North Dakota	652,695	617,792	+ 34,903	+ 6
Ohio	10,797,419	10,657,423	+ 139,996	+ 1
South Dakota	690,178	666,257	+ 23,921	+ 4
Wisconsin	4,705,335	4,417,821	+ 287,514	+ 7
WEST	**43,165,199**	**34,838,243**	**+ 8,325,956**	**+ 24**
Alaska	400,481	302,583	+ 97,898	+ 32
Arizona	2,717,866	1,775,399	+ 942,467	+ 53
California	23,668,562	19,971,069	+3,697,493	+ 19
Colorado	2,888,834	2,209,596	+ 679,238	+ 31
Hawaii	965,000	769,913	+ 195,087	+ 25
Idaho	943,935	713,015	+ 230,920	+ 32
Montana	786,690	694,409	+ 92,281	+ 13
Nevada	799,184	488,738	+ 310,456	+ 64
New Mexico	1,299,968	1,017,055	+ 282,913	+ 28
Oregon	2,632,663	2,091,533	+ 541,130	+ 26
Utah	1,461,037	1,059,273	+ 401,764	+ 38
Washington	4,130,163	3,413,244	+ 716,919	+ 21
Wyoming	470,816	332,416	+ 138,400	+ 42
SOUTH	**69,899,833**	**57,584,311**	**+12,315,522**	**+ 21**
Alabama	3,890,061	3,444,354	+ 445,707	+ 13
Arkansas	2,285,513	1,923,322	+ 362,191	+ 19
Florida	9,739,992	6,791,418	+ 2,948,574	+ 43
Georgia	5,464,265	4,587,930	+ 876,334	+ 19
Kentucky	3,661,433	3,220,711	+ 440,722	+ 14
Louisiana	4,203,972	3,644,637	+ 559,335	+ 15
Mississippi	2,520,638	2,216,994	+ 303,644	+ 14
North Carolina	5,874,429	5,084,411	+ 790,018	+ 16
Oklahoma	3,025,266	2,559,463	+ 465,803	+ 18
South Carolina	3,119,208	2,590,713	+ 528,495	+ 20
Tennessee	4,590,750	3,926,018	+ 664,732	+ 17
Texas	14,228,383	11,198,655	+ 3,029,728	+ 27
Virginia	5,346,279	4,651,448	+ 694,831	+ 15
West Virginia	1,949,644	1,744,237	+ 205,407	+ 12

Some of this migration represents movement out of ailing industrial cities, the one-industry towns whose industries are in trouble. The paradigms are Youngstown, Ohio (steel), and Flint, Michigan (automobiles); although one should probably include as well factory towns that have been declining for generations: Scranton, Pennsylvania (anthracite coal), and Lawrence, Massachusetts (textiles). But there are not all that many Youngstowns and Flints. A much larger component of this migration is movement out of our largest metropolitan areas — not only out of such predominantly industrial metropolitan areas as Pittsburgh, Cleveland, and Detroit, but also out of diversified metropolitan areas such as New York, Philadelphia, Boston, and Chicago. One cannot explain the outmigration from the latter as the result of economic disaster, and perhaps it is the result of something very much like the opposite. These metropolitan areas have plenty of economic vitality and growth, but they are metropolitan in atmosphere, and most Americans—as polls have showed for years—would rather live in small towns or in the countryside. In the 1970s, after years of economic growth, more Americans were affluent enough to do just that, and some of the movement out of the metropolitan areas represents positive choices, made possible by affluence, not negative choices made necessary by economic stagnation.

That is true as well of another kind of population loss: the decline in population of most central cities and many close-in suburbs. The main reason for this (and leaving aside certain slums such as the south Bronx and inner-city Detroit, which are another story) is not that there is any decline in the number of housing units, but that people who used to double up are now living alone or in smaller groups and that people are having fewer children. Young people out of school are getting their own apartments; older people often live on their own rather than move in with relatives. In the close-in suburbs the parents of the 1950s and 1960s have seen their children grow up and move away, to a farther-out suburb, a central city neighborhood, or a smaller city somewhere else; the same house that registered five residents in the 1960 census registers two in 1980. Such population loss—the empty nest syndrome—represents not decline but aging, and it is as American as apple pie. You can follow, in successive censuses, the settlement of urban or suburban neighborhoods or even of whole states (for example, Nebraska in the 1880s) by young people, which shows up as a sudden and startling population increase; the maturing of their children, which shows up as a steady population; and their moving away, which shows up as population loss. In the process, the community is probably becoming more rather than less affluent, more rather than less comfortable.

Note that the change we have been talking about is the change in our metropolitan area populations. Much attention has been focused on the loss of population in most of our central cities and on the gains in some Sun Belt central cities. But neither of these changes necessarily means much, except for municipal finance officers; the changes just indicate whether a central city is hemmed in by incorporated areas (such as Boston or St. Louis) or whether it can annex adjacent territory in which there is population growth (such as Houston or Phoenix). Using just central city populations makes San Antonio the tenth largest city in the country, a result that, if one looks at metropolitan populations, is absurd; on that basis, the two-million-plus people of Metropolitan Boston would be represented by just the half a million who still live within the central city. Movement outward from a central base is a natural concomitant of urban growth and happens in Europe as well as here: there were more people within the corporate limits of Paris 100 years ago than there are today (but its metropolitan area has grown substantially). Downtown New York City, the area around Wall Street and City Hall, had a much larger population in 1820 than it has had since, as the city has moved outward; for that matter, Manhattan had 2.3 million people in 1910, 1.6 million in 1920, and 1.4 million today. In the 1910–20 decade, people moved out to Brooklyn and the Bronx as the new subways made those outer boroughs accessible to their jobs; in later decades, people moved out as transportation facilities improved or as the jobs themselves moved farther out.

That said, there is still an obvious difference between the metro areas of the East and Midwest, which have either been losing population or gaining slowly, and those of the West and South, which have been gaining much more rapidly. There is evidence here of the vitality of economic growth in the Sun Belt and of a lack of economic growth in the Snow Belt. Let us look at each of the major regions of the country and examine some of the factors that have or have not produced growth—and see what they mean.

Metro Area	1980 Pop.	1970 Pop.	Change	% Change
EAST	**30,916,316**	**32,110,574**	**−1,194,258**	**− 4**
New York, N.Y.–N.J.	14,695,411	15,655,663	− 960,252	− 6
Philadelphia, Pa.–N.J.	4,716,818	4,824,110	− 107,292	− 2
Washington, D.C.–Md.–Va.	3,060,240	2,910,111	+ 150,129	+ 5
Boston, Mass.	2,763,357	2,899,101	− 135,744	− 5
Pittsburgh, Pa.	2,263,894	2,401,362	− 137,468	− 6
Baltimore, Md.	2,174,023	2,071,016	+ 103,007	+ 5
Buffalo, N.Y.	1,242,573	1,349,211	− 106,638	− 8
MIDWEST	**24,851,910**	**24,668,393**	**+ 183,517**	**+ 1**
Chicago, Ill.–Ind.	7,745,109	7,608,122	+ 136,987	+ 2
Detroit, Mich.	4,352,762	4,435,051	− 82,289	− 2
St. Louis, Mo.–Ill.	2,355,275	2,401,884	− 55,609	− 2
Minneapolis–St. Paul, Minn.–Wis.	2,114,256	1,965,391	+ 148,865	+ 8
Cleveland, Ohio	1,898,720	2,063,729	− 165,009	− 8
Cincinnati, Ohio–Ky.–Ind.	1,401,403	1,387,207	+ 14,196	+ 1
Milwaukee, Wis.	1,397,143	1,403,884	− 6,741	− 0
Kansas City, Mo.–Kans.	1,327,020	1,273,926	+ 53,094	+ 4
Indianapolis, Ind.	1,166,929	1,111,352	+ 55,527	+ 5
Columbus, Ohio	1,093,293	1,017,847	+ 75,446	+ 7
WEST	**25,349,392**	**21,371,920**	**+3,977,472**	**+ 19**
Los Angeles, Calif.	11,463,206	9,980,859	+1,482,347	+ 15
San Francisco, Calif.	4,547,792	4,174,562	+ 373,230	+ 9
Seattle, Wash.	2,092,408	1,836,949	+ 255,459	+ 14
San Diego, Calif.	1,861,846	1,357,854	+ 503,992	+ 37
Denver, Colo.	1,619,921	1,239,545	+ 380,376	+ 31
Phoenix, Ariz.	1,508,030	971,228	+ 536,802	+ 55
Portland, Oreg.–Wash.	1,242,187	1,007,130	+ 235,057	+ 23
Sacramento, Calif.	1,014,002	803,793	+ 120,209	+ 26
SOUTH	**15,761,010**	**12,112,122**	**+3,648,888**	**+ 30**
Houston, Texas	3,101,290	2,169,128	+ 932,162	+ 43
Dallas–Fort Worth, Texas	2,974,878	2,377,623	+ 597,255	+ 25
Miami, Florida	2,640,002	1,887,892	+ 752,110	+ 40
Atlanta, Georgia	2,029,618	1,595,517	+ 434,101	+ 27
Tampa–St. Petersburg, Fla.	1,596,492	1,088,549	+ 507,943	+ 44
New Orleans, La.	1,186,725	1,046,470	+ 140,255	+ 13
Norfolk, Va.	1,160,051	1,058,764	+ 101,287	+ 10
San Antonio, Texas	1,071,954	888,179	+ 183,775	+ 21

Areas indicated here are Standard Metropolitan Statistical Areas or combinations thereof. Combinations include (Nassau–Suffolk, Jersey City, Newark, Paterson), Chicago (Gary), Los Angeles (Anaheim, Riverside, Oxnard), San Francisco (San Jose), Seattle (Tacoma), Houston (Galveston), Miami (Fort Lauderdale), Norfolk (Newport News).

The Troubled East. The major metro areas of the East have lost population, and the only significant population gains in the region have been in the rural hinterland, northern New England and parts of outstate Pennsylvania, and nonmetropolitan Maryland. Metro New York lost nearly a million people in the 1970s. This population loss has been disastrous for state and local governments, especially that of New York City. But it is not clear how disastrous it has been for the quality of life for those who continue to live there. Essentially, the

East has been losing low-wage jobs—the predictable consequence of its high degree of unionization, high minimum wages, and high required costs of employment (such as unemployment compensation, safety standards, etc.). The East has lost low-wage jobs and has not replaced them. It has lost low-wage workers—after a time lag—and has not replaced them either. One of the more interesting migrations in the United States is the net movement of people from New York City to Puerto Rico, as New York no longer offers opportunities to compensate for giving up the pleasures of living in one's native area. Another trend is the migration that didn't happen. In the 1950s and the 1960s whole high school graduating classes in heavily black counties in the coastal Carolinas would get on the bus and go to New York. Very few people do that anymore. But the absence of low-wage jobs doesn't mean that a good community cannot be built on a high-income wage base. Massachusetts seems to have done that already.

Unfortunately for the East, the cost of state and local government per capita rises very rapidly when there is no population growth. Governments naturally tend to grow, and government workers—especially the unionized militants in the eastern metro areas—demand wage and benefit increases that exceed inflation, even as their productivity declines. Eventually governments must resist or face bankruptcy, as New York City has since 1975. The long-range outlook for the East is favorable, just as the long-range outlook for London is favorable, whatever the problems of industrial northern England. But first the East must ease the burden it is carrying of an expensive government designed to help low-wage workers who are no longer there.

The Midwest Heartland. The census shows us three Midwests, in quite different condition. The smallest, and probably least noticed, is the north woods. Northern Michigan, Wisconsin, and Minnesota enjoyed boom times in the 1970s, based not just on tourism but also on increased population. Essentially people from the big metro areas were using their affluence to build retirement homes here or to move here, accepting lower dollar wages in return for more pleasant living conditions. As a result, the north woods are enjoying their most prosperous times since the lumber barons cleaned them bare of trees around the turn of the century.

In vivid contrast is the condition of the industrial Midwest. Such metro areas as Detroit, Cleveland, Milwaukee, and Buffalo (technically in the East, but socioeconomically almost a smaller brother of Cleveland), have lost population in the 1970s; Chicago, despite its booming white collar sector, has gained only a little. These areas have been the Democratic heartland of the Midwest since the New Deal, and the percentages there may be even more Democratic than they used to be; but the absolute number of votes is on the decline. (Note, however, that areas in very special trouble, such as Detroit, had rising turnouts in 1980, as if people here were seeking some special help from government and politicians.) The primary industries in this Great Lakes area are autos and steel, the two industries with the highest wage structures in the nation. Unfortunately, as the 1970s turned into 1980s, it was becoming clear that consumers would not buy products with the price tags required to finance these high wages. So what we have had is the late 20th-century equivalent of pay cuts: massive layoffs (one-third of auto employment), explicit wage cuts (as at Chrysler), disguised wage cuts (reduced overtime, longer vacations). Workers here are protected from many of the risks of market capitalism by generous unemployment benefits. But for many these are running out, and they—especially the younger workers—are drawing the obvious conclusion: they would be better off moving elsewhere where there are jobs. In early 1981 there were long lines at the newspaper counter in a bookstore in Dearborn, Michigan—blue collar workers waiting for copies of the *Houston Chronicle,* to read the help wanted ads.

This kind of movement is always sad, but what would be sadder is if it did not occur. The Great Lakes industrial cities cannot support all their people, and it would be very expensive for the rest of society to do so. It is sad to see the great civic institutions of such cities as Detroit and Cleveland—once among the largest, proudest cities in the nation—fall into disrepair. But someone must pay for them, and the local economy cannot. The one city here that seems sure to survive as a world center is Chicago. Its blue collar job base may be eroding, but its white collar job base is booming. Chicago's blue collar neighborhoods and suburbs lost population in the 1970s, but its affluent suburbs gained population as rapidly as most places in the Sun Belt.

The Booming West. Most Americans don't realize it, but the West is our most urban and metropolitan region, not because its metropolitan population is so large but because its non-metropolitan population is so small. There just aren't very many places in the West out of the range of a city water system where any sizable number of people can live comfortably. Therefore, the population follows the city limits—or the water lines. It is fitting then that the biggest population increase—1.5 million people, 6% of the population increase in the entire nation—comes in the Greater Los Angeles area. The Rocky Mountain states have the highest percentage rates of increase, but they start from a low base; in actual numbers, the largest increases are in the states of the Pacific Coast.

Some critics see the growth in the West as the result of low wages, low degrees of unionization, and corporate greed. But these explain very little of the growth that has occurred. The Rocky Mountain states have historically had low-wage economies but, with their recent growth, personal incomes there have risen markedly as well. Moreover, the Pacific Coast states, where most of the growth has occurred, are not low-wage states at all. They have high degrees of unionization, high wages, and, in California anyway, large numbers of blacks and Mexican-Americans. Affluent Americans seem to be moving to these regions because they love the physical environment, the climate, and the life-style, and they are generating, through their creativity and hard work, an exceedingly productive economy. It is hard to avoid the conclusion that the magic ingredient is not some economic factor but rather a spiritual one—a habit of mind, an attitude. California and the West in the early 1970s seemed unsure of themselves and for a moment paused in their growth. By the middle and late 1970s, however, California and the West were growing as rapidly and productively as ever before.

In the past California led the West in growth. In the 1970s, despite California's massive growth, percentage growth was faster in almost all the other states of the West. The West, like all other regions of the country except the South, also saw its nonmetropolitan areas grow faster than its metropolitan areas. Some of this growth occurred because of rising energy prices and mineral exploration in the West. Mineral finds, after all, tend over time to be proportionate to area, and the West has 49% of the land area of the United States. In the 1970s major oil, coal, and other mineral resources were developed in the West; Denver became a major regional center for exploration; rural counties in Wyoming and the northern reaches of Alaska experienced a modern-day version of the mining booms that were seen in California's Mother Lode country, Nevada, Colorado, Montana, and the Klondike in the 19th century. Moreover, in nonmineral areas there was substantial growth also. The paradigm here is Utah, whose population increased by 38% in the decade, largely because of in-migration by Mormons, Mormon converts, and those who yearned for the moderation, confidence, and respect for tradition they find in the life-style here. The new subdivisions of Utah's Wasatch Front and of Boise are filling up with refugees from southern California, people who found Orange County too hectic, too smoggy, and too risque for their tastes. They are raising their families now in an atmosphere that seems close to the stereotypical idea of the American small town—which is probably just what they want. Affluence, once again, is giving Americans an opportunity to have the life-style they want.

The New South. The major demographic story in the South in the 1970s is the migration that didn't happen. For 100 years, from the end of Reconstruction until the 1970s, blacks left the South. There was steady and massive outmigration in every decade until the 1980s. As a result, black percentages in the population fell—although blacks have always, on the average, had higher birth rates than whites. In the 1970s, the outmigration, for all practical purposes, stopped. What black migration there was was largely to the large- and middle-sized metropolitan areas in the South itself—one of the reasons for their population increases. As a result, blacks are almost certain to be a more important political force in the South as the century ends. Black birth rates continue to be notably higher than white (in part because blacks are, on the average, younger). In Massachusetts in 1920 most of the adults were Protestants and Republicans, and most of the children were Catholics and Democrats. Forty years later, Massachusetts had changed from one of our most Republican states to one of our most Democratic. The change in the South is not likely to be so drastic; there is no southern state today, not even Mississippi, where a majority of children are black. But the long-range trend—and southern politicians know this—is for the black percentages to rise, not fall as they have in the past. And this, more than anything else, means blacks are likely to remain an integral force in the politics and the economic life of the South in the decades to come.

   It is probably not a coincidence that black outmigration stopped in the first full decade after the success of the civil rights revolution in the South. It is probably not a coincidence either that economic and therefore population growth in the South accelerated at the same time. Segregation was a damper on economic growth in a number of ways. It deterred investment, because many nonsouthern investors found segregation distasteful or possibly disruptive; no investor wants to take undue risks. It diverted economic resources to the enforcement of segregation rules. It often barred blacks from moving ahead economically as they might otherwise do; probably one of the untold stories of the 1970s is the economic success—not wealth, but simply solid personal success—achieved by hundreds of thousands of southern blacks over the past decade. We forget now what a vast change the civil rights revolution made in the behavior and attitudes of whites—and blacks—in the South. Black gains seem secure now: no one is going to deny them the vote, bar them from working with whites, or bar access to public accommodations. Traditional southern courtesy, once extended only to whites, is often extended now to blacks as well. One reason blacks are not leaving the South as often as they used to is that there are fewer opportunities in the East and the industrial Midwest. But another reason is that life in the South for blacks is much more pleasant than it used to be.

   It is ironic that many of those who take much of the credit—and often deserve it—for the booming growth of the South were the opponents of the civil rights measures that in large part made that growth possible. It is true that one of the advantages the South still enjoys is its low wage structure; its low degree of unionization is attractive to many employers from the North and abroad who set up plants here. The South — or part of it: Texas, Oklahoma, Louisiana — benefits from the boom in energy prices and from the expertise these states have developed in getting oil out of the ground, by no means an automatic process. But the South had low wages and lots of oil long before the 1970s. Now its wages are approaching the national average (getting very close if one considers local taxes as well), and its oil is running out. Nevertheless the growth the South has generated using these advantages now seems to have developed a momentum of its own.

Minorities, Ethnics, and Immigration. The United States has been shaped — created, really — by successive tides of immigration. The first was in the 1600s, when the colonies were established. They grew through the Revolutionary period largely by natural increase; the first immigrants, like all our later ones, were young, fertile people who had the childbearing habits of the peasantry from which they came. The second major wave of immigration sprang from the Irish potato famine and upheavals in German Europe; it lasted from the 1840s to the Civil War. Then, in the 1880s, immigration began from lands formerly so undeveloped that their residents never even thought of leaving: southern Italy, eastern Germany, Poland and other parts of eastern Europe. That immigration lasted until it was shut off first by World War I and then by the immigration laws of 1921 and 1924.

We are now in the midst of what we might consider a fourth wave of immigration, primarily from Latin America and the Caribbean, the eastern Mediterranean, and eastern Asia. Before we exaggerate the problems connected with it, we should realize that it is very much smaller in magnitude than the earlier waves. In one calendar year, 1907, the United States absorbed 1,700,000 immigrants in a nation with a population of 86 million. Today we groan under the burdens of absorbing some 600,000 immigrants a year in a much more prosperous nation of 226 million. The earlier burden was more than seven times as great.

We are just waking up to the fact that our nation will be changed by this immigration as it was changed by earlier ones. Immigrants and groups with below-average incomes — notably blacks — have more children than affluent Americans; our population in the future is sure to be more Hispanic and black than it is today, just as our population today is more Italian and Polish than it was 80 years ago. American history, demographically, has been a history of taking people from lower socioeconomic groups, from within our borders and abroad, and enabling them to rise substantially in the social scale. In general, our economy has expanded, the number of affluent people has increased, and yet affluent people themselves do not produce enough offspring to fill all those places in the next generation. Past immigrants worked their way up to them, and there is no reason to believe that today's immigrants — or today's blacks, freed finally from segregation — will not do the same. Nor is there any great reason to fear that today's immigrants will not be assimilated. The only danger is if we should artificially fence them off from the mainstream culture, in schools and jobs where only their native language is used. Fortunately, the country seems to be moving rapidly away from the idea of language-segregated education and toward the kind of assimilation that eighty years of history assures us works.

Minorities Population (Rounded Off to Nearest Thousand)

State	Total Pop.	Black Pop.	%	Hispanic Pop.	%	Am. Ind. Pop.	%	Asian Pop.	%
U.S.	226,505	26,488	12	14,606	6	1,418	1	3,501	2
EAST	**54,586**	**6,351**	**12**	**2,696**	**5**	**89**	**—**	**635**	**1**
Conn.	3,108	217	7	124	4	5	—	19	1
Del.	595	96	16	10	2	1	—	4	1
D.C.	638	448	70	18	3	1	—	7	1
Maine	1,124	3	—	5	—	4	—	3	1
Md.	4,216	958	23	65	2	8	—	64	2
Mass.	5,737	221	4	141	2	8	—	50	1
N.H.	921	4	—	6	1	1	—	3	1
N.J.	7,364	925	13	492	7	8	—	104	1
N.Y.	17,557	2,402	14	1,659	9	39	—	311	2
Pa.	11,867	1,048	9	154	1	9	—	64	1
R.I.	947	28	3	20	2	3	—	5	1
Vt.	511	1	—	3	1	1	—	1	—
MIDWEST	**58,853**	**5,337**	**9**	**1,276**	**2**	**249**	**—**	**390**	**1**
Ill.	11,418	1,675	15	635	6	16	—	160	1
Ind.	5,490	415	8	87	2	8	—	20	—
Iowa	2,913	42	1	26	1	5	—	12	—
Kans.	2,363	126	5	63	3	15	1	15	1
Mich.	9,258	1,199	13	162	2	40	—	57	1
Minn.	4,077	53	1	32	1	35	1	27	1
Mo.	4,917	514	10	52	1	12	—	23	—
Neb.	1,570	48	3	28	2	9	1	7	—
N.D.	653	3	—	4	1	20	3	2	—
Ohio	10,797	1,077	10	120	1	12	—	48	—
S.D.	690	2	—	4	1	45	7	2	—
Wis.	4,705	183	4	63	1	29	1	18	—
WEST	**43,165**	**2,262**	**5**	**6,252**	**14**	**719**	**2**	**2,081**	**5**
Alaska	400	14	3	9	2	64	16	8	2
Ariz.	2,718	75	3	441	16	153	6	22	1
Cal.	23,669	1,819	8	4,544	19	201	1	1,254	5
Colo.	2,889	102	4	339	12	18	1	30	1
Hawaii	965	17	2	71	7	3	—	584	60
Idaho	944	3	—	37	4	11	1	6	1
Mont.	787	2	—	10	1	37	5	3	—
Nev.	799	51	6	54	7	13	2	14	2
N.M.	1,300	24	2	476	37	105	8	7	1
Oreg.	2,633	37	1	66	3	27	1	35	1
Utah	1,461	9	1	60	4	19	1	15	1
Wash.	4,130	106	3	120	3	61	1	103	2
Wyo.	471	3	1	24	5	7	2	2	—

State	Total Pop.	Black Pop.	%	Hispanic Pop.	%	Am. Ind. Pop.	%	Asian Pop.	%
SOUTH	**69,900**	**12,539**	**18**	**4,381**	**6**	**362**	**1**	**395**	**1**
Ala.	3,890	996	26	33	1	8	—	10	—
Ark.	2,286	373	16	18	1	9	—	7	—
Fla.	9,740	1,342	14	858	9	19	—	57	1
Ga.	5,464	1,465	27	61	1	8	—	24	—
Ky.	3,661	259	7	27	1	4	—	10	—
La.	4,204	1,237	29	99	2	12	—	24	1
Miss.	2,521	887	35	25	1	6	—	7	—
N.C.	5,874	1,316	22	57	1	65	1	21	—
Okla.	3,025	205	7	57	2	169	6	17	1
S.C.	3,119	948	30	33	1	6	—	12	—
Tenn.	4,591	726	16	34	1	5	—	14	—
Tex.	14,228	1,710	12	2,986	21	40	—	120	1
Va.	5,346	1,008	19	80	1	9	—	66	1
W.Va	1,950	65	3	13	1	2	—	5	—

No definable ethnic or racial group assimilates in quite the same way, however, and none assimilates completely; thank goodness we enjoy the cultural variety we gain from our various heritages. The 1980 census — the most comprehensive count ever of these minorities, since special pains and great expense were taken to include them — gives us clues about their futures.

It shows us, first of all, that nearly half of American blacks remain in the South — because of the 1970s migration that didn't take place. It also shows, however, that blacks are becoming an increasingly large percentage in some northern states: in Maryland (23%), where blacks are moving out from Washington, D.C., to Prince Georges County; in New York (14%), where most of the 1970s outmigration was among whites and Puerto Ricans, not blacks; in Illinois (15%), where many blacks live not only in Chicago but in many of the city's southern suburbs and, in smaller numbers, scattered around the new and affluent suburbs in a semicircle 30 miles from the Loop; in Michigan (15%), where blacks are in a majority in Detroit and are also present in many, although by no means all, of the city's suburbs. In the South, 35% of the population of Mississippi is black, a 2% drop since 1970, but the prospect is for an increase; other states more than one-quarter black include South Carolina, Louisiana, Georgia, and Alabama.

Hispanics are a varied group but, taken together, they are highly concentrated. Some 19% of California's residents are of Spanish origin, and most of them are no longer concentrated in all-Spanish neighborhoods. They are spread out with high percentages in some working-class suburbs and significant percentages just about everywhere else in the state. The evidence suggests that they do not suffer much from discrimination and that they are moving rapidly up the economic ladder in this booming state. This is all the more encouraging since some of these people come directly from the subsistence economy of rural Mexico. Mexican–Americans are also a major factor in Texas (21%), but they seem more segregated there and less prosperous in what is still, for many, a low-wage state. Mexamerica, in Joel Garreau's terminology, extends up from the Rio Grande into San Antonio and across the river into El Paso, and there the population is poor and almost entirely Mexican. New York is the other major locus of Americans of Spanish origin, and most there are Puerto Rican. But the 1970s saw a net migration back to Puerto Rico, which is more pleasant and more prosperous than the south Bronx; indeed, many of the south Bronx's problems, dwelled on by so many journalists and politicians, derive from the fact that Puerto Rico has been doing well. There has, however, been an important Latin American migration to New York, other eastern cities, and to Florida from other countries. Many of these people are illegal aliens, and some undoubtedly were missed by the Census Bureau. Far from placing a burden on American institutions, however, they pay taxes (sales tax and withheld income taxes and Social Security) and do not demand public services (because they might be identified as aliens). They come here to work, not collect welfare; they contribute to our economy; they are young, eager, hardworking, family-oriented — just the kind of people any country should want. They are no harder to assimilate than the Italian–Americans of the early 20th century were, although many of them, like many of those Italian–Americans, will probably choose someday to return to their native lands. The last major cluster of Hispanics is not a group of immigrants but the Spanish-speaking people of northern New Mexico, most of whose ancestors lived there 350 years ago.

The final group, not much noticed, are Asians. People of Asian descent are now 2% of our total population. They are the majority in Hawaii, and they include one out of 20 Californians. This is a group that is disadvantaged in the sense that many come from poor economic conditions and they suffer occasionally from racial prejudice. But they don't behave as if they were underprivileged. In early 1981 some Californians were concerned because Asian–Americans formed 20% of the student body of the University of California at Berkeley and because they were doing so well in mathematics and computer sciences. This is the kind of problem every part of the country should be so fortunate to have. Asians otherwise are scattered around the country, with concentrations in the New York area, the Chicago area, the Seattle area, and — interestingly — Texas. It seems that many Vietnamese refugees have made their way to Texas; the climate they find familiar, but the real reason they come is that they recognize the possibilities for economic advancement.

Age Groups, Life-Styles, and Fundamental Political Attitudes. A continual topic of discussion in American demographics is the baby boom — the unusually large number of babies born to Americans in the 1945–61 period. We are just beginning to realize what an unusual demographic event this was: such a high birth rate has never before or since been recorded in an affluent developed nation with no significant immigrant population. For some years afterward, however, we assumed that it was the norm; thus Social Security planners assumed that the low birth rates of the 1960s and 1970s, which historically are much more typical of advanced societies, would suddenly change and produce enough young Americans who would, in their adult years, pay for the Social Security benefits of the elderly baby boomers. But no such baby boom has occurred, and the Social Security system is now threatened with bankruptcy.

The baby boom generation has been blamed for this and for all kinds of social ills: for the rising crime rates of the 1960s and 1970s (because young people commit most crimes), for the low rises in productivity in the late 1970s (because new workers have low productivity, and large numbers of baby boomers entered the work force in this period), and for lower moral standards (because baby boomers tended to have sex earlier, to smoke marijuana as well as drink beer, to postpone earning wages for the pleasures of an affluent adolescence). Now the baby boom generation is entering the family formation years. It is in some ways, as its elders always gloatingly predicted, getting more conservative — but not in the same way its elders did. The experiences of the generations, after all, are very different. The baby boomers' parents endured the poverty of the Depression and the uncertainty of World War II and the bomb. The baby boomers have lived in a generation-long period of prosperity and (despite Vietnam) an absence of major war.

The voters of the older generation sought economic security through government action and, as they grew older, they sought from government a reaffirmation of the conservative cultural tradition in which they had been raised. The baby boom generation for some years took prosperity for granted and was busy spending American society's wealth on such worthwhile things as cutting down air and water pollution, giving more generous payments and services to the poor, and simply enjoying its own leisure time rather than working. By the late 1970s, however, it was becoming clear that the economy would not automatically grow. But the baby boomers, stunned by Vietnam, were skeptical of the government's ability to improve things. They were ready to accept the interesting intellectual arguments of Ronald Reagan and the supply-side economists. On the cultural issues — and in the political arena they include such matters as abortion, gun control, the environment, drugs — the baby boomers, reflecting the atmosphere in which they were brought up and the youth culture in which they moved to maturity, are much more liberal than their elders.

So we are heading, slowly, toward a reversal of the standard American political paradigm. It used to be that the typical American voter was liberal on economic issues and conservative on cultural issues. There are still plenty of such voters around, although they are outnumbered by those who are conservative on both sets of issues. But the growing number is of those who are conservative on economic issues and liberal on cultural issues. The diagram below assigns approximate percentages to each group — a procedure done totally unscientifically and strictly on the basis of intuition. Nonetheless, it provides at least a beginning for an understanding of the complexity of American political attitudes and illustrates the terminology that is used throughout this book.

CULTURAL ISSUES

	Liberal	Conservative
ECONOMIC ISSUES Liberal	10%	30%
Conservative	25%	35%

The balance is quite different in different states and regions. In California, for example, the lower left box would have a much larger percentage; in Texas, the lower right box would have a larger percentage; and in Massachusetts we would see a majority in one of the two top boxes. Overall, this matrix shows that, despite the Democratic advantage in party iden-tification, it is easier for a Ronald Reagan than a George McGovern to win the presidency: Reagan starts out with a lot more people in his box (although some of them in 1980 voted for their fellow white southerner Jimmy Carter). These figures should not, finally, be regard-ed as etched in stone. There were more economic liberals five years ago, before the Carter economic programs, than there are today; and the results of the Reagan economic programs may affect the numbers again, one way or the other. Changes in cultural attitudes proceed more slowly, although the initial evidence is that the generation younger than the baby boomers — few of whom are voting yet — are going to be more conservative on cultural is-sues than those who cherish memories of the 1960s.

GUIDE TO USAGE

The Almanac of American Politics is designed to be self-explanatory. The basic data for each section are derived from public sources. We have used the final results of the 1980 census for **total population,** for **racially defined ethnic groups** (blacks, American Indians, Asians) and for Hispanics (the term the Census Bureau uses now is "Spanish origin") Unfortunately, 1980 figures are not yet available for **foreign stock** and **other ethnic groups;** 1970 figures are used and are so labeled. **Median 4-person family income** is a Census Bureau estimate, provided for each state; for congressional districts, we have **1970 median family income,** and we have indicated its **percentage relationship to the national average,** to give a sense of whether a district had an above- or below-average income. The **federal tax burden** is provided by the Tax Foundation, Inc., and the **federal outlays** are provided by the Community Services Administration. HEW is listed here rather than HHS because the separate Department of Education had not yet been created at the time the data here was provided.

Voting data come from state and local election authorities. The **presidential vote by congressional district** was calculated by *The Almanac* from state and local sources. Percentages shown indicate **percentage of total vote cast,** including votes for minor candidates not shown. For president the vote for every candidate who received 5% or more nationally is shown for every district; for president and other offices, in general elections the vote for every candidate who received 5% or more of the vote in a constituency is shown. In primaries, votes for minor candidates are lumped together. **Group ratings** are provided by the groups listed, all of which have offices in Washington; several (LCV, RPN, NAB, NSI) calculate no ratings for odd-numbered years, and RPN at the time we had to go to press had not calculated its 1980 ratings. **Biographies, committee memberships,** and **key votes** are compiled from official congressional publications and other public sources.

Here is a list of the rating groups, with their basic orientation and major concerns.

ADA   **Americans for Democratic Action.** Liberal, concerned about both economic and cultural issues.

COPE   **Committee on Political Education** of the AFL–CIO. Liberal, concerned primarily about economic and labor issues.

PC   **Public Citizen.** One of the organizations associated with Ralph Nader, concerned especially about the workings of the political and governmental processes.

LCV   **League of Conservation Voters.** Environmental, concerned with environmental issues.

CFA   **Consumer Federation of America.** Concerned with consumer and economic issues, considered proconsumer.

RPN   **Ripon Society.** The liberal Republican organization.

NAB   **National Association of Businessmen.** Conservative, concerned primarily about economic and business issues.

NSI   **National Security Index** of the American Security Council. Conservative, concerned with defense and foreign policy issues.

NTU   **National Taxpayers Union.** Concerned with and generally opposed to federal government spending.

ACA   **Americans for Constitutional Action.** Conservative, concerned about both economic and cultural issues.

ACU   **American Conservative Union.** Conservative, concerned about both economic and cultural issues. Closer to the New Right than ACA.

Because of the difficulty in summing up a legislator's position on a complex issue in a single vote, we list the specific roll call votes that were used.

SENATE VOTES

1) **Draft Registn $**
   H.J.Res. 521, June 12, 1980. Passage of the bill to spend $13.3 million for registering 19- and 20-year-old males for the draft. Passed 58–34.

2) **Ban $ to Nicrgua**
   H.R.7542, June 28, 1980. Motion to table an amendment to delete $75 million in foreign aid to Nicaragua. Passed 44–33.

3) **Dlay MX Missile**
   H.R.8105, Nov. 21, 1980. Amendment to cut $120 million appropriation for the MX missile. Rejected 12–65.

4) **Nuclr Mortorium**
   S.562, July 17, 1979. Amendment to block new construction permits for nuclear power plants for six months. Rejected 35–57.

5) **Alaska Lands Bill**
   H.R.39, Aug. 18, 1980. Motion to invoke cloture (limit debate) on bill. Passed 63–25 (60 votes needed).

6) **Fair Housng Cloture**
   H.R.5200, Dec. 9, 1980. Motion to invoke cloture (limit debate) on bill. Rejected 54–43 (60 votes needed).

7) **Ban $ Rape Abortns**
   H.J.Res.610, Sept. 29, 1980. Motion to table an amendment to allow use of federal funds to pay for abortions when needed to save the life of the mother or in the event of rape or incest. Rejected 34–45.

8) **Cap on Food Stmp $**
   S.1309, July 23, 1979. Amendment to delete section eliminating ceiling (cap) on food stamp expenditures. Rejected 37–57.

9) **New US Dep Edcatn**
   S.210, April 30, 1979. Passage of bill to create a new U.S. Department of Education. Passed 72–21.

10) **Cut OSHA Inspctns**
    H.R.3904, July 29, 1980. Amendment to exempt businesses with ten or less employees and with low injury rates from routine safety inspections by the Occupational Safety and Health Administration. Passed 48–36.

11) **Cut Socl Incr Defns**
    S.Con.Res.86, May 7, 1980. Motion to kill amendment cutting $2 billion from defense outlays and $400 million from interest payments and transferring the funds to domestic programs on the budget resolution. Passed 64–30.

12) **Income Tax Indexing**
    H.R.3919, Dec. 6, 1979. Amendment to adjust individual income tax rates to inflation. Rejected 41–47.

13) **Lim Spdg 21% GNP**
S.Res.380, March 25, 1980. Motion to table an amendment and to require that outlays be reduced to 21% of the gross national product. Rejected 45–52.

14) **Incr Wndfll Prof Tax**
H.R.3919, Dec. 4, 1979, Amendment to increase tax rate on oil discovered 1973–78 from 60% to 75%. Passed 58–35.

15) **Chryslr Loan Grntee**
H.R.5860, Dec. 19, 1979. Passage of bill to authorize $1.5 billion in federal loan guarantees to the Chrysler Corp. Passed 53–44.

HOUSE VOTES

1) **Draft Registn $**
H.J.Res. 521, April 22, 1980. Passage of bill to spend $13.3 million for registering 19- and 20-year-old males for the draft. Passed 219–180.

2) **Ban $ to Nicrgua**
H.R.4473, Sept. 6, 1979. Amendment to prohibit aid to Nicaragua without prior congressional approval. Rejected 189–221.

3) **Dlay MX Missile**
H.R.6974, May 15, 1980. Amendment to reduce appropriations for MX missile by $500 million. Rejected 152–250.

4) **Nuclr Mortorium**
H.R. 2608, Nov. 29, 1979. Amendment to block new construction permits for nuclear power plants for six months. Rejected 135–254.

5) **Alaska Lands Bill**
H.R.39, May 16, 1979. Amendment to create 125 million acres of national parks, wildlife refuges, and forests in Alaska. Passed 268–157.

6) **Fair Hsg DOJ Enfrc**
H.R.5200, June 11, 1980. Amendment to provide for enforcement of fair housing law through administrative law judges in the Department of Justice. Passed 205–204.

7) **Lim PAC Contrbtns**
S.832, Oct. 17, 1979. Amendment to limit contributions by political action committees to House candidates. Passed 217–198.

8) **Cap on Food Stmp $**
H.Con.Res.107, May 2, 1979. Amendment to reduce proposed increased budget for food stamps so as to continue the ceiling (cap) on food stamp expenditures. Rejected 146–276.

9) **New US Dep Edcatn**
H.R.2444, July 11, 1979. Passage of bill to create a new U.S. Department of Education. Passed 210–206.

10) **Cut OSHA $**
Amendment to reduce by $10 million the appropriation for the Occupational Safety and Health Administration. Rejected 177–240.

11) **Cut Socl Incr Defns $**
H.Con.Res.307, May 1, 1980. Amendment to budget resolution to increase defense programs by $5.8 and to reduce other programs correspondingly. Rejected 164–264.

12) **Hosptl Cost Controls**
H.R.2626, Nov. 15, 1979. Amendment to cut administration hospital cost containment program and to establish a study commission and fund state programs instead. Passed 234–166.

13) **Gasln Ctrls & Allctns**
H.R.3000, Oct. 24, 1979. Amendment to prohibit use of federal funds to allocate or control the price of gasoline. Rejected 189–225.

14) **Lim Wndfll Prof Tax**
    H.R.3919, June 28, 1979. Amendment to provide a windfall profits tax of 60% and to discontinue the tax in 1990. Passed 236–183.
15) **Chryslr Loan Grntee**
    H.J.Res.467, Dec. 20, 1979. Passage of bill to authorize $1.5 billion in federal loan guarantees to the Chrysler Corp. Passed 252–141.

ABBREVIATIONS

ACA	Americans for Constitutional Action
ACU	American Conservative Union
ADA	Americans for Democratic Action
Asst.	Assistant
CFA	Consumer Federation of America
C	Conservative Party (New York)
CG	Coast Guard
Chmn.	Chairman
CHOB	Cannon House Office Building
Chwmn.	Chairwoman
COPE	Committee on Political Education (AFL–CIO)
D	Democrat
DFL	Democratic–Farmer–Labor Party (Minnesota)
Dir.	Director
DOC	Department of Commerce
DOD	Department of Defense
DOE	Department of Energy
DOI	Department of the Interior
DOJ	Department of Justice
DOT	Department of Transportation
Dpty.	Deputy
DSOB	Dirksen Senate Office Building
EPA	Environmental Protection Agency
ERDA	Energy Research and Development Administration
HEW	Department of Health, Education and Welfare
HHS	Department of Health and Human Services
HUD	Department of Housing and Urban Development
I, Ind.	Independent
IR	Independent–Republican Party (Minnesota)
Jt.Com.	Joint Committee

L	Liberal Party (New York)
LCV	League of Conservation Voters
LHOB	Longworth House Office Building
Lib.	Libertarian Party
NAB	National Association of Businessmen
NSI	National Security Index of the American Security Council
NTU	National Taxpayers Union
PC	Public Citizen
R	Republican
Rank.Mbr.	Ranking Member
RHOB	Rayburn House Office Building
RPN	Ripon Society
RSOB	Russell Senate Office Building
Sel.Com.	Select Committee
Sp.Com.	Special Committee
Sub.	Subcommittee
USAF	United States Air Force
USAFR	United States Air Force Reserve
USDA	United States Department of Agriculture
USMC	United States Marine Corps
USMCR	United States Marine Corps Reserve
VA	Veterans Administration

ALABAMA

Alabama is now a state without a political identity. It has clearly moved out of one era of its history—one dominated by George Wallace—but it is not clear where it is going or where it wants to go. Out of the Wallace period we did get a clear picture of the state's personality. This has always been a feisty, populist state, from the time it was settled by poor dirt farmers; the big plantations came later, and their owners never really controlled Alabama's politics. In the 20th century, Alabama was one of the southern states most hostile to its big business interests and elected politicians such as Hugo Black, later a U.S. Supreme Court justice; Lister Hill and John Sparkman, in their times effective populist senators, perhaps the most accomplished pair of senators in Washington during the 1950s and early 1960s; and Governor Kissin' Jim Folsom, one of the few southern politicians who refused in the 1950s to endorse segregation.

Wallace drew on the spirit of these men even as he worked against their aims. He felt he had been "out-segged" in the 1958 Democratic gubernatorial primary, and he vowed he would never let that happen again. In 1962 Wallace whipped Folsom, whose problems included not only his stand on racial issues but his alcoholism, and went on to rule state government for all but 1½ of the next 16 years. The governor directed the anger of Alabama's whites against civil rights leaders and pointy-headed bureaucrats; and unlike most southern segregationists he had the political acumen to appeal to the racial fears of northern whites in what were technically nonracial terms. His success in northern primaries made him a hero in Alabama; Wallace won 67% of its votes—i.e., virtually all its white votes—in the 1968 presidential election. But in the old state Capitol in Montgomery his policies were more hospitable to business than populistic, and his old platform—segregation forever—was soon discredited by history.

Physically crippled by a gunshot wound in 1972, politically crippled by his defeat by Jimmy Carter in the 1976 Florida presidential primary, Wallace was a spent force in Alabama politics by 1978. He prudently declined to run for the Senate although, as it happened, both the state's Senate seats were up that year. He retired to become suddenly a rather warmly regarded figure, even among the state's blacks.

Wallace's retirement left Alabama the choice of several directions. It could once again become a kind of populist state, electing Democrats in line with their party's national positions on economic though not cultural issues. Alabama seemed to have done that in 1978 when it elected as its two U.S. senators former state Chief Justice Howell Heflin and state Senator Donald Stewart. But Stewart was upset in the 1980 runoff (his initial election was to fill the unexpired term of the late Senator James Allen), and Heflin meanwhile turned out to be more cautious or conservative on economic issues than Sparkman or Hill had been in the 1940s and 1950s.

Another possible direction for politics here was suggested by the election of Governor Fob James, a Republican (and member of the party's state executive committee) as recently as 1976, who prevailed in a multicandidate Democratic primary field. Finally, the election of Admiral Jeremiah Denton as U.S. senator in 1980 suggests that Alabama might finally go Republican. Republicans had swept several House seats as long ago as 1964, in the Goldwater landslide and had launched serious statewide candidacies in 1966, 1972, and 1978. But before 1980 none ever succeeded.

But most of these results seemed more accidental — or idiosyncratic — than the beginning of a long-term trend. Take the gubernatorial race. The key factor, as it turned out, was money. A former Auburn football player, James, after his playing career, went into business and invented a barbell made of high-density plastic. Improbably, this invention revolutionized the weight lifting equipment industry and James became a very rich man indeed — the kind of new rich entrepreneur who does so much for the Republican Party in the Sun Belt these days. But James, prudently perhaps, decided that it would be better to run for governor as a Democrat. It was not for lack of competition. Former Governor Albert Brewer (who had succeeded in the post in 1968 when George Wallace's wife Lurleen died in office), Lieutenant Jere Beasley (a Wallace protege who had fallen out with the governor), Attorney General Bill Baxley (who had strong black support and had prosecuted those who had allegedly bombed the Birmingham black church in 1963), and state Senator Sid McDonald all had significant support. James's big spending and a "new era" theme put him on top in the first primary and Baxley's black support got him second place; in the runoff Baxley was crippled by charges that he owed gambling debts in six figures. James won the runoff and the Republicans made no serious effort in the general election.

The governor's race in 1982 should be quite a different matter. Alabama governors are now permitted a second consecutive term, and an incumbent who has done a reasonably good job will probably not attract strong primary opposition. Nor is it clear that the Republicans will be able to generate much enthusiasm to oppose a man who is so close to them. James's wife ostentatiously endorsed Ronald Reagan in 1980, and James himself declined to formally endorse Jimmy Carter; there have even been rumors that James would seek re-election as a Republican. Nonetheless, it is not clear that James has produced for Alabamians as bright a new post-Wallace day as they hoped for, and there is no shortage of men with recent experience as statewide candidates who might be looking for some office to run for — and there are no Senate seats up in 1982.

Howell Heflin is a man without a very political background, although he does have a political pedigree: his uncle, "Cotton Tom" Heflin, was a fierce segregationist who served in the Senate from 1920 to 1931. This generation's Heflin has a different temperament and attitudes. A painstaking legal craftsman, Heflin served as chief justice of Alabama's Supreme Court, his only elective office before the Senate. He was elected to the post in 1970 as a reformer and a critic of George Wallace, effected a thorough reform of the state's court system, and then retired to private life. In 1978 he expected his chief rival for the Senate to be Wallace; instead, when Wallace dropped out, it was U.S. Congressman Walter Flowers. Flowers ran as the candidate with experience in Washington; Heflin ran against "the Washington crowd." Heflin won the runoff easily, so easily that the Republican candidate, Jim Martin, switched to the other Senate race.

Heflin was a natural to serve on the Senate Judiciary Committee because of his interest in legal issues; he also serves on Agriculture and Commerce. He views national issues as most Alabamians do: he is a strong advocate of a tougher national defense, a mild populist on economic issues, a supporter of the basic civil rights laws. Heflin has not been a crusader on economic issues in one direction or the other; rather, as his background suggests, he has devoted much of his attention to technical, but potentially very important, matters such as the details of administrative law. Heflin has worked to separate the large number of administrative law judges from the agencies whose work they pass on, and he sponsored a move to take away from the FTC power to order divestiture of certain shared monopolies. Heflin's seat is up in 1984 and, while it is far too early for definitive predictions, he does not seem to have antagonized any major bloc of voters in Alabama.

The state's other Senate seat has had four occupants over the past five years: James Allen, the conservative master of the Senate's parliamentary rules, who died suddenly in 1978 after leading the unsuccessful fight against the Panama Canal Treaties; Maryon Allen, his unexpectedly spunky widow who was appointed in his place and who was defeated in the 1978 runoff for the nomination for the rest of her husband's term; Donald Stewart, an aggressive and populistic state legislator who beat Maryon Allen and Republican Jim Martin in 1978 but fell victim to Public Service Commissioner Jim Folsom, Jr., in the Democratic runoff in 1980; and Admiral Jeremiah Denton, a prisoner of war in North Vietnam for seven years, who surprised almost everyone by winning the seat in November 1980.

The bigger surprise here, however, was the defeat of Stewart, a young man (40 when he was beaten) who had compiled a liberal record on economic issues and had shown the kind of feisty fighting spirit Alabama voters have liked in the past. But Stewart's defeat was a kind of fluke. He had 49% of the votes in the first primary, coming 6,249 votes short of winning without a runoff. In that contest, the 31-year-old Folsom benefited from his father's populist reputation in the northern counties of the state and from his own more conservative politics in the southern parts. Stewart's support from blacks and in the Birmingham and Mobile areas was not enough to win for him.

Meanwhile Denton had beaten former Congressman, Pentagon official, and Ambassador to New Zealand Armistead Selden in the Republican primary—another example of Alabama's preference for candidates from home over "the Washington crowd." Denton was an authentic hero—a prisoner of war who had blinked out the word "torture" when being filmed in North Vietnam, the first POW to return, a man whose story had become a made-for-television movie. He is also a person of strong beliefs: very religious (although a Catholic, not a Moral Majority Protestant) and concerned about problems that senators do not ordinarily consider solvable. He is supposed to have told an Alabama audience that one of the world's greatest problems is sex before marriage in underdeveloped countries, and he considers "instant gratification" and "promiscuity" as among the nation's most serious problems. The new senator has been at pains to assure official Washington that he is not a nut and appears in fact to be more original and thoughtful than Washington expected.

On the Judiciary Committee Denton was assigned the chairmanship of a new subcommittee on internal security. The specter of a revival of the abuses of the old House Un-American Activities Committee was raised, although again Denton tried to be reassuring to everyone. He also chairs a subcommittee on Aging, Family, and Human Services, which gives him an opportunity to affect government actions that do in fact advance or retard family values. The course of his Senate career is, at this writing, by no means clear. He is a man whose convictions as well as his experiences seem entirely original for the Senate, and the question is whether he will leave a distinctive imprint, whether he will just blend in, or whether he will have little effect one way or the other. In the meantime, he can be counted on as a generally reliable vote for measures favored by the Reagan Administration and by Senate conservatives of the stripe of Jesse Helms of North Carolina.

For the first time in several decades, Alabama did not lose substantial population through outmigration in the 1970s. This means, among other things, that the black percentage of the population here will tend to rise rather than fall as it did for 100 years until 1970; black Alabamians tend to have more children than whites. Another effect is that Alabama does not have to redraw its congressional district lines drastically. The major changes will occur in the Birmingham area, where the Democratic legislature might try to hurt the reelection chances of freshman Republican Albert Lee Smith of the 6th district.

Census Data   Pop. (1980 final) 3,890,061, up 13% in 1970s: 1.72% of U.S. total, 22d largest. Central city, 26%; suburban, 36%. Median 4-person family income, 1978, $18,352, 95% of U.S.; 41st highest.

1979 Share of Federal Tax Burden $5,906,000,000; 1.31% of U.S. total, 24th largest.

1979 Share of Federal Outlays $7,419,140,000; 1.60% of U.S. total, 22d largest.

DOD	$1,687,078,000	19th	(1.58%)	HEW	$2,966,764,000	20th	(1.65%)
DOE	$32,784,000	30th	(0.27%)	ERDA	$8,043,000	30th	(0.29%)
HUD	$112,467,000	19th	(1.70%)	NASA	$212,296,000	6th	(4.53%)
VA	$414,541,000	17th	(1.99%)	DOT	$216,640,000	25th	(1.31%)
EPA	$54,954,000	30th	(1.03%)	DOC	$38,167,000	17th	(1.20%)
DOI	$20,816,000	43d	(0.37%)	USDA	$366,932,000	28th	(1.52%)

Economic Base   Agriculture, notably broilers, cattle, cotton lint, and eggs; primary metal industries, especially blast furnaces and basic steel products, and iron and steel foundries; finance, insurance, and real estate; apparel and other textile products, especially men's and boys' furnishings; textile mill products, especially cotton weaving mills; food and kindred products, especially meat products; lumber and wood products, especially sawmills and planing mills.

Political Lineup   Governor, Forrest (Fob) James, Jr. (D). Senators, Howell Heflin (D) and Jeremiah Denton (R). Representatives, 7 (4 D and 3 R); 7 in 1982. State Senate, 35 D; State House of Representatives, 109 (105 D and 4 R).

The Voters

Registration   2,132,139 Total. No party registration.
Employment profile 1970   White collar, 41%. Blue collar, 43%. Service, 13%. Farm, 3%.
Ethnic groups   Black 1980, 26%. Total foreign stock 1970, 2%.
Presidential Vote

1980	Reagan (R)	654,192	(49%)
	Carter (D)	636,730	(47%)
	Anderson (I)	16,481	(1%)
1976	Ford (R)	504,070	(43%)
	Carter (D)	659,170	(56%)

1980 Democratic Presidential Primary			*1980 Republican Presidential Primary*		
Carter	193,734	(82%)	Reagan	147,352	(70%)
Kennedy	30,667	(13%)	Bush	54,730	(26%)
Three others	10,678	(4%)	Six others	9,271	(4%)
Uncommitted	1,670	(1%)			

SENATORS

Sen. Howell Heflin (D) Elected 1978, seat up 1984; b. June 19, 1921, Lovina, Georgia; home, Tuscumbia; Birmingham-Southern College, B.A., U. of Ala., J.D. 1948.

Career USMC, WWII; Practicing atty., 1948–71; Pres., Ala. State Bar, 1965–68; Chief Justice, Ala. Supreme Court, 1971–77.

Offices 3107 DSOB, 202-224-4124. Also P.O. Box 3294, Montgomery 36101, 205-832-7287.

Committees *Agriculture, Nutrition, and Forestry* (8th). Subcommittees: Soil and Water Conservation; Agricultural Credit and Rural Electrification; Agricultural Research and General Legislation.

Commerce, Science, and Transportation (8th). Subcommittees: Science, Technology and Space; Surface Transportation.

Judiciary (8th). Subcommittees: Courts; Separation of Power.

Select Committee on Ethics (Vice-chairman).

Group Ratings

	ADA	COPE	PC	LCV	CFA	RPN	NAB	NSI	NTU	ACA	ACU
1980	39	63	33	20	27	—	64.	80	39	50	43
1979	26	53	20	—	19	—	—	—	37	46	44

Key Votes

1) Draft Registn $	FOR	6) Fair Housng Cloture	AGN	11) Cut Socl Incr Defns	FOR
2) Ban $ to Nicrgua	AGN	7) Ban $ Rape Abortns	FOR	12) Income Tax Indexing	FOR
3) Dlay MX Missile	AGN	8) Cap on Food Stmp $	FOR	13) Lim Spdg 21% GNP	AGN
4) Nuclr Mortorium	AGN	9) New US Dep Edcatn	FOR	14) Incr Wndfll Prof Tax	FOR
5) Alaska Lands Bill	AGN	10) Cut OSHA Inspctns	AGN	15) Chryslr Loan Grntee	FOR

Election Results

1978 general	Howell Heflin (D)	547,054	(94%)	($1,059,113)
	Jerome B. Couch (ProL)	34,951	(6%)	
1978 runoff	Howell Heflin (D)	556,685	(65%)	
	Walter Flowers (D)	300,654	(35%)	($755,259)
1978 primary	Howell Heflin (D)	369,270	(48%)	
	Walter Flowers (D)	236,894	(31%)	
	John Baker (D)	101,110	(13%)	($179,388)
	Four others (D)	56,179	(8%)	
1972 general	John Sparkman (D)	654,491	(62%)	($702,109)
	Winton M. Blount (R)	347,523	(33%)	($764,961)

Sen. Jeremiah Denton (R) Elected 1980, seat up 1986; b. July 15, 1924, Mobile; home, Mobile; Spring Hill Col., 1942–43, U.S. Naval Acad., B.A. 1946, Geo. Wash. U., M.A. 1964.

Career U.S. Naval Officer, 1946–77; Rear Admiral, 1973; Commandant, Armed Forces Staff Col., Norfolk, Va., 1974–77.

Offices 110 RSOB, 202-224-5744. Also 3280 Dauphin St., Suite B121, Mobile 36616, 205-690-3222, and Suite 1701, Daniel Bldg., 15–20th St., S., Birmingham 35233, 205-254-0806.

Committees *Armed Services* (9th). Subcommittees: Military Construction; Seapower and Force Projection; Manpower and Personnel.

Judiciary (9th). Subcommittees: Juvenile Justice; Separation of Power; Security and Terrorism (Chairman).

Labor and Human Resources (8th). Subcommittees: Education; Alcoholism and Drug Abuse; Aging Family and Human Services (Chairman).

Veterans' Affairs (5th).

Group Ratings and Key Votes: Newly Elected

Election Results

1980 general	Jeremiah Denton (R)	650,362	(50%)	($855,346)
	Jim Folsom, Jr. (D)	617,175	(47%)	($356,647)
1980 primary	Jeremiah Denton (R)	73,708	(64%)	
	Armistead Selden (R)	41,825	(36%)	($269,965)
1978 general	Donald W. Stewart (D)	401,852	(55%)	($816,456)
	James D. Martin (R)	316,170	(43%)	($552,504)
1978 runoff	Donald W. Stewart (D)	502,346	(57%)	
	Mrs. Jim Allen (D)	375,894	(43%)	($305,498)

1978 primary	Mrs. Jim Allen (D)	334,758	(46%)	
	Donald W. Stewart (D)	259,795	(35%)	
	Two others (D)	137,583	(19%)	
1974 general	Jim Allen (D)	501,541	(96%)	($37,328)

GOVERNOR

Gov. Forrest (Fob) James, Jr. (D) Elected 1978, term expires Jan. 1983; b.Sept. 15, 1934, Lanett; Auburn U., B.S. 1955.

Career Pro Football Player, Montreal Alouettes, 1956; U.S. Army Corps of Engineers, 1957, Construction Engineer, 1958–59, Supt., 1960–61; Pres. and Bd. Chmn., Diversified Products Corp., 1962–78.

Offices Executive Dept., Montgomery 36130, 205-832-3511.

Election Results

1978 gen.	Forrest (Fob) James, Jr. (D)	551,886	(73%)
	Guy Hunt (R)	196,963	(26%)
1978 runoff	Forrest (Fob) James, Jr. (D)	515,520	(55%)
	Bill Baxley (D)	418,932	(45%)
1978 prim.	Forrest (Fob) James, Jr. (D)	256,196	(28%)
	Bill Baxley (D)	210,089	(23%)
	Albert Brewer (D)........	193,479	(21%)
	Sid McDonald (D)	143,930	(16%)
	Nine others (D)..........	96,223	(11%)
1974 gen.	George C. Wallace (D).....	497,574	(83%)
	Elvin McCary (R)........	88,381	(15%)

FIRST DISTRICT

The Tombigbee and Alabama Rivers flow south from Alabama's Black Belt—named for the fertility of its black cotton-growing soil—to the port of Mobile and the Gulf of Mexico. Mobile is Alabama's second largest city and the largest port on the Gulf between Tampa and New Orleans. Dominated by industries sensitive to economic cycles—shipping, shipbuilding, paper—the Mobile area had little population growth during the 1950s and 1960s but, like many parts of the South, grew at a faster rate in the 1970s as migration to the North essentially ended.

Mobile is the most blue collar of Alabama's large cities and, although its proximity to New Orleans and vaguely French name suggest a certain Creole urbanity, it is in fact a rough-and-tumble town. Politically the Mobile area is feisty: it was the urban area in Alabama that most strongly supported George Wallace, and in recent years it veered away from the Democrats of Jimmy Carter toward the more pugnacious politics of right-wing Republicans. Locally, Mobile has been one of the last cities in the South where blacks have failed to win representation and influence in proportion to their numbers, although the industrial suburb of Prichard has had a black mayor since 1972.

Alabama's 1st congressional district extends from Mobile north to the Black Belt and includes one black-majority county (Wilcox). But most of the people live in and around Mobile,

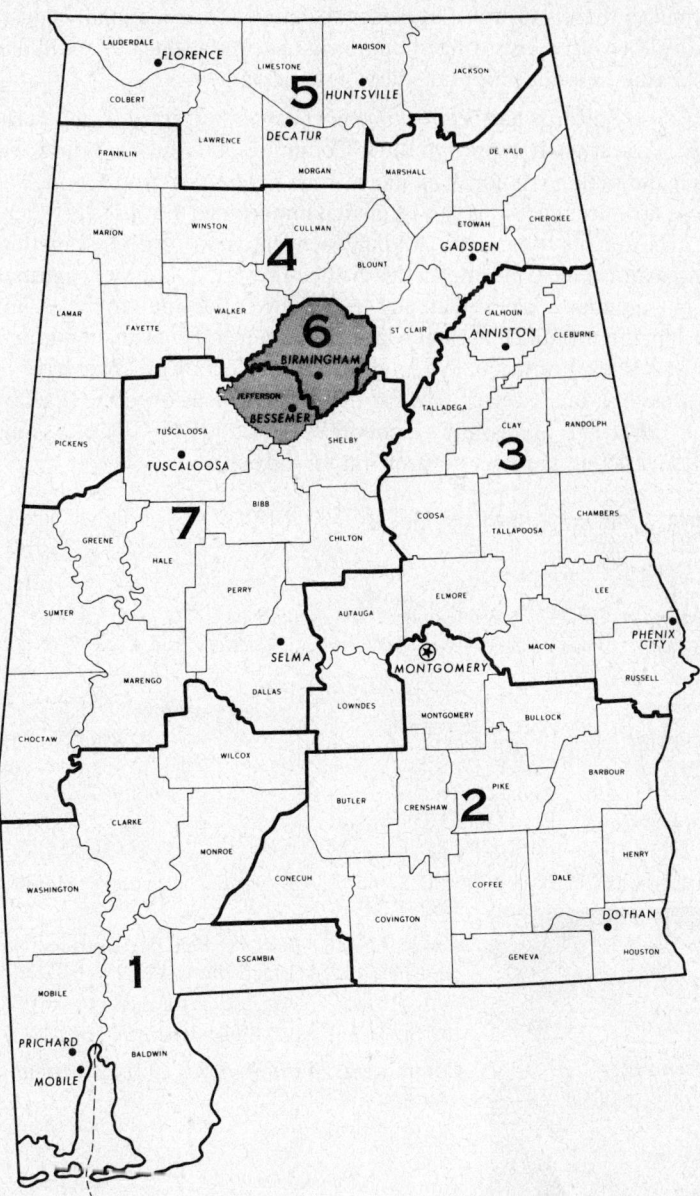

and most of its votes are cast in Mobile County and next-door Baldwin County. (Baldwin, with its retirement settlements on the Gulf, has become the most Republican county in Alabama in recent elections.) The 1st was an area that went solidly for Barry Goldwater in 1964, when most blacks here could not vote, and it still has a congressman who was initially swept in in the Goldwater landslide, Republican Jack Edwards. Edwards has survived and thrived politically since, thanks to his solid personal character and his solidly conservative voting record. In 1978 he faced his strongest opponent in years, a state senator and former University of Alabama football star, and still won handily.

In the House Edwards has become one of the most respected of southern Republicans. He early won a seat on the Appropriations Committee, on which he is now the third ranking Republican and ranking minority member of the Defense Appropriations Subcommittee, a body whose technical decisions can be of vital importance. Edwards is widely respected for his intelligence and his conservative and independent views on defense matters; there are, by the way, no major defense facilities in this district. Edwards is also vice chairman of the House Republican Conference, a post with no formal powers but one that makes him a member of the leadership; the current chairman is Jack Kemp, a member of greater originality, although perhaps, in the view of some, not so solidly reliable. Will Edwards ever have a top leadership position? Possibly, but it seems that for the moment he is overshadowed by men such as Kemp and Edwards's Mississippi neighbor, Trent Lott (who, however, might run for the Senate). Redistricting presents no problem for Edwards.

Census Data   Pop. (1980 final) 563,140, up 15% in 1970s. Median family income, 1970, $7,305, 76% of U.S.

The Voters

   Employment profile 1970   White collar, 41%. Blue collar, 42%. Service, 14%. Farm, 3%.
   Ethnic groups   Black 1980, 31%. Hispanic 1980, 1%. Amer. Ind. 1980, 1%. Total foreign stock 1970, 2%.

Presidential Vote

1980	Reagan (R)	107,659	(56%)
	Carter (D)	77,758	(41%)
	Anderson (I)	1,969	(1%)
1976	Ford (R)	83,622	(50%)
	Carter (D)	81,012	(48%)

Rep. Jack Edwards (R) Elected 1964; b. Sept. 20, 1928, Birmingham; home, Mobile; U. of Ala., B.S. 1952, LL.B. 1954.

Career   USMC, 1946–48, 1950–51; Instructor in Business Law, U. of Ala., 1954; Practicing atty., 1954–64.

Offices   2369 RHOB, 202-225-4931. Also 8011 Fed. Ofc. Bldg., 109 St. Joseph St., Mobile 36602, 205-690-2811.

Committees   *Appropriations* (3d). Subcommittees: Defense; Transportation.

Group Ratings

	ADA	COPE	PC	LCV	CFA	RPN	NAB	NSI	NTU	ACA	ACU
1980	17	11	17	22	7	—	91	83	42	83	87
1979	11	21	8	9	4	—	—	—	48	78	74
1978	20	11	13	23	14	50	100	90	24	89	70

Key Votes

1) Draft Registn $	FOR	6) Fair Hsg DOJ Enfrc	AGN	11) Cut Socl Incr Dfns $	FOR
2) Ban $ to Nicrgua	AGN	7) Lim PAC Contrbtns	AGN	12) Hosptl Cost Controls	AGN
3) Dlay MX Missile	AGN	8) Cap on Food Stmp $	FOR	13) Gasln Ctrls & Allctns	AGN
4) Nuclr Mortorium	AGN	9) New US Dep Edcatn	AGN	14) Lim Wndfll Prof Tax	FOR
5) Alaska Lands Bill	AGN	10) Cut OSHA $	FOR	15) Chryslr Loan Grntee	AGN

Election Results

1980 general	Jack Edwards (R)	111,089	(95%)	($26,731)
	Steve Smith (Libertarian)	6,130	(5%)	($0)
1980 primary	Jack Edwards (R), unopposed			
1978 general	Jack Edwards (R)	71,711	(64%)	($166,456)
	L. W. Noonan (D)	40,450	(36%)	($85,773)

SECOND DISTRICT

It was not until some years after Alabama was admitted to the Union that southern planters, their soil in Virginia and the Carolinas grown tired, discovered the Black Belt of Alabama. The fertile black soil gave the region its name and almost cried out for the crop that came to characterize the Confederacy: King Cotton. As every schoolchild knows, cotton was a crop that required cheap, abundant labor, and Alabama's Black Belt became slave territory; before the Civil War slaves outnumbered whites by as much as 10–1 in some counties. For years after the Civil War the majority of the Black Belt's citizens were the descendants of slaves. But as black migration to the North continued, the black percentage here diminished, and by the time the 1965 Voting Rights Act gave blacks the ballot, only a handful of small rural counties were left with black majorities.

On a map Alabama's congressional district lines look perfectly regular. Closer inspection, however, shows them to have been carefully crafted to divide the black majority counties among several districts, to prevent black voters from exerting a major influence in any congressional election. The 2d district, for example, contains only one black majority county (Bullock), but just outside the district lines there are three others (Macon, Lowndes, and Wilcox). So the blacks in the 2d are heavily outnumbered by the white majority in Montgomery, the state's capital, and by those in the nearly all-white "piney woods" counties to the south of the Black Belt. Yet this may change in time as well: the end of the black migration northward in the 1970s means that blacks, who have more children than whites, will inevitably increase their percentage of the population in states such as Alabama; and this is the kind of development we can expect politicians to pay attention to. It would be ironic if that trend should result someday in a black majority in Montgomery, a city with a special kind of Deep South heritage. It was the Cradle of the Confederacy, the rebels' capital before Richmond. And it was the site of the 1956 Montgomery bus boycott that gave national prominence to a young black minister named Martin Luther King, Jr.

This is one of three Alabama districts with a Republican congressman, a man who seemed to be in some political trouble back home during the late 1970s but who seems politically very well positioned for the 1980s. Bill Dickinson was first elected in 1964, when Barry Goldwater swept the state (few blacks voted in Alabama then) and Republicans won five house seats and wiped out 87 years of Democratic seniority. Redistricting after the 1970 census, which cost Alabama a seat, caused Dickinson some problems by adding rural Democratic counties to the district; his strength has always been in urban Montgomery. He attracted significant opponents and was attacked for not doing enough for the district's military installations (they include Montgomery's Maxwell Air Force Base and Dothan's Fort Rucker). In 1978 Dickinson was cut to as low as 54% of the vote.

In 1980, although he again had tough opposition, he did better, winning 61% of the vote. One reason was the tide of national issues: he had the endorsement of Jerry Falwell of the Moral Majority and the benefit of a reputation as a firm opponent of government spending. He may also have been helped by Ronald Reagan's unexpected carrying of the district—a turnaround of the 1976 result. Dickinson also benefited as the man in line to become ranking minority member of the House Armed Services Committee in the next Congress. Dickinson has been a vocal supporter, if not an articulate leader or a vocal proponent of any one of the services, in the fight for higher defense spending; and that is an issue stance very much in line with opinion in this always hawkish district in the particular circumstances of 1980. He now serves in that position, and the possibility that he might someday be chairman, in the not entirely remote contingency that the Republicans control the House, will surely be an asset for him in the next one or two elections. Redistricting will not be, as it was ten years ago, a problem. Alabama loses no seats and, if anything, the 2d will lose one or two counties to other districts but will not otherwise be changed.

Census Data   Pop. (1980 final) 549,505, up 12% in 1970s. Median family income, 1970, $6,749, 70% of U.S.

The Voters

Employment profile 1970   White collar, 42%. Blue collar, 39%. Service, 14%. Farm, 5%.
Ethnic groups   Black 1980, 31%. Hispanic 1980, 1%. Total foreign stock 1970, 2%.

Presidential Vote

1980	Reagan (R)	99,583	(52%)
	Carter (D)	83,717	(44%)
	Anderson (I)	1,991	(1%)
1976	Ford (R)	75,528	(46%)
	Carter (D)	88,208	(53%)

Rep. William L. Dickinson (R) Elected 1964; b. June 5, 1925, Opelika; home, Montgomery; U. of Ala., A.B. 1948, LL.B. 1950.

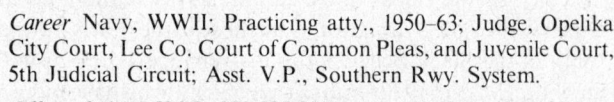

Career Navy, WWII; Practicing atty., 1950–63; Judge, Opelika City Court, Lee Co. Court of Common Pleas, and Juvenile Court, 5th Judicial Circuit; Asst. V.P., Southern Rwy. System.

Offices 2406 RHOB, 202-225-2901. Also 401 Fed. Court Bldg., Montgomery 36104, 205-832-7292.

Committees Armed Services (Ranking Member). Subcommittees: Research and Development; Military Installations and Facilities; Readiness.

House Administration (2d). Subcommittee: Services.

Group Ratings

	ADA	COPE	PC	LCV	CFA	RPN	NAB	NSI	NTU	ACA	ACU
1980	11	10	20	17	14	—	100	100	59	83	94
1979	5	6	10	3	7	—	—	—	54	88	95
1978	5	16	10	2	5	60	100	100	29	96	83

Key Votes

1) Draft Registn $	FOR	6) Fair Hsg DOJ Enfrc	AGN	11) Cut Socl Incr Dfns $	FOR
2) Ban $ to Nicrgua	FOR	7) Lim PAC Contrbtns	AGN	12) Hosptl Cost Controls	AGN
3) Dlay MX Missile	AGN	8) Cap on Food Stmp $	FOR	13) Gasln Ctrls & Allctns	AGN
4) Nuclr Mortorium	—	9) New US Dep Edcatn	AGN	14) Lim Wndfll Prof Tax	FOR
5) Alaska Lands Bill	AGN	10) Cut OSHA $	FOR	15) Chryslr Loan Grntee	AGN

Election Results

1980 general	William L. Dickinson (R)	104,796	(61%)	($116,504)
	Cecil Wyatt (D)	63,447	(37%)	($27,952)
1980 primary	William. L. Dickinson (R), unopp.			
1978 general	William L. Dickinson (R)	57,924	(54%)	($139,313)
	Wendell Mitchell (D)	49,341	(46%)	($115,372)

THIRD DISTRICT

The 3d district of Alabama extends from the cotton-growing Black Belt in the southern part of the state to the red clay hills of the north. In the south is Tuskegee, a black-majority town in a black-majority county, and the home of Booker T. Washington's Tuskegee Institute. Also in the southern portion is Phenix City, a onetime Alabama "sin city" across the Chatta-hoochee River from Georgia's huge Fort Benning. A mid-1950s cleanup of Phenix City pro-pelled a young prosecutor, John Patterson, into the governor's chair in 1958; he beat George Wallace in the Democratic primary, the one time Wallace allowed himself to be "out-segged." In the northern part of the district is the small industrial city of Anniston, home of a distin-guished small southern newspaper and of the Army's Fort McClellan.

Outside the Black Belt counties in the south, the 3d district is mostly white, and the whites living in the district's small factory towns and rugged farm country were for years the heart of George Wallace's constituency. The current congressman, Bill Nichols, was a Wallace floor leader in the Alabama Senate in the 1960s, and it was as a Wallace Democrat that in 1966 he captured the district by beating a Republican elected in the Goldwater landslide two years before. Since then Nichols has been sent back to Washington every two years without difficulty; he has not had a Republican opponent since 1972. His voting record on most is-sues is solidly conservative, more so than the populist tone (if not the substance) of Wallace's rhetoric would lead one to expect.

Nichols is now the fifth-ranking Democrat on the House Armed Services Committee. He has always been in line with the hawkish tone of the majority of the members of this body and has at least some chance of being chairman someday. He chairs a subcommittee on Mil-itary Personnel and Compensation which is responsible at least technically for determining the level of military pay and fringe benefits. There has been much criticism lately that skilled military technicians and line officers are not sufficiently well paid to keep them in the service. Nichols and his subcommittee are not necessarily to blame, however, since the amount of money to be made available for military pay is essentially a budgetary decision, and his sub-committee is just one actor in the process. He tends to favor the Army rather than the Navy or Air Force.

Census Data Pop. (1980 final) 565,749, up 15% in 1970s. Median family income, 1970, $6,817, 71% of U.S.

The Voters

Employment profile 1970   White collar, 34%. Blue collar, 50%. Service, 14%. Farm, 2%.
Ethnic groups   Black 1980, 29%. Total foreign stock 1970, 1%.

Presidential Vote

1980	Reagan (R)	81,520	(46%)
	Carter (D)	90,029	(50%)
	Anderson (I)	2,063	(1%)
1976	Ford (R)	63,819	(40%)
	Carter (D)	93,776	(58%)

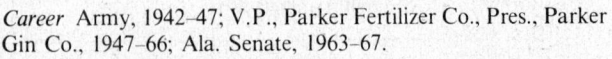

Rep. Bill Nichols (D) Elected 1966; b. Oct. 16, 1918, near Becker; home, Sylacauga; Auburn U., B.S. 1939, M.S. 1941.

Career Army, 1942–47; V.P., Parker Fertilizer Co., Pres., Parker Gin Co., 1947–66; Ala. Senate, 1963–67.

Offices 2417 RHOB, 202-225-3261. Also Fed. Bldg., P.O. Box 2042, Anniston 36201, 205-236-5655.

Committees *Armed Services* (5th). Subcommittees: Research and Development; Military Personnel and Compensation (Chairman).

Group Ratings

	ADA	COPE	PC	LCV	CFA	RPN	NAB	NSI	NTU	ACA	ACU
1980	17	25	33	17	14	—	91	100	44	59	59
1979	11	45	30	14	37	—	—	—	53	73	69
1978	5	20	25	15	9	50	100	100	22	83	78

Key Votes

1) Draft Registn $	FOR	6) Fair Hsg DOJ Enfrc	AGN	11) Cut Socl Incr Dfns $	FOR
2) Ban $ to Nicrgua	FOR	7) Lim PAC Contrbtns	FOR	12) Hosptl Cost Controls	AGN
3) Dlay MX Missile	AGN	8) Cap on Food Stmp $	FOR	13) Gasln Ctrls & Allctns	FOR
4) Nuclr Mortorium	AGN	9) New US Dep Edcatn	AGN	14) Lim Wndfll Prof Tax	AGN
5) Alaska Lands Bill	AGN	10) Cut OSHA $		FOR	15) Chryslr Loan Grntee	AGN

Election Results

1980 general	Bill Nichols (D)	107,654	(99%)	($33,572)
1980 primary	Bill Nichols (D)	49,323	(85%)	
	Charlie Baker (D)	8,608	(15%)	
1978 general	Bill Nichols (D), unopposed			($13,212)

FOURTH DISTRICT

Nowhere were the shifting tides of Alabama politics during the past 20 years more clearly evident than in the 4th congressional district. During the late 1950s and early 1960s, when everyone thought massive desegregation in the South was impossible, this part of northern Alabama, between Birmingham on the south and the Tennessee River valley on the north, was considered a populist stronghold. The local congressman, Carl Elliott, was considered reliable enough by the Kennedy Administration to have been rewarded with one of the two new seats created, after a bitter struggle, on the Rules Committee in 1961. Organized labor was strong enough here to play some part in the district's politics, and Elliott always had a good labor rating. The workingmen from the industrial towns such as Gadsden, Jasper, and Cullman, and the leatherhanded farmers of the red clay hills consistently supported economic liberals such as Senators (1938–69) Lister Hill and (1946–79) John Sparkman and Governor (1947–51, 1955–59) Kissin' Jim Folsom against more business-oriented candidates.

Then suddenly race became the major factor in politics here, and everything else changed. George Wallace was elected governor by promising to stand in the schoolhouse door to prevent desegregation — somehow. Barry Goldwater swept the state and in the process helped elect a Republican congressman, Jim Martin, for the 4th district. Martin, a successful businessman, voted a solid pro-business line in Washington and probably could have held the seat had he not unwisely run for governor in 1966. Meanwhile, the voters in the 4th — almost all white, even after the Voting Rights Act of 1965, because there never were many blacks in these hills — had stopped thinking of themselves as working people and voted instead simply as white people. The results show near unanimity: 71% for Wallace in 1968, 78% for Nixon in 1972.

The Republicans were unable to duplicate Martin's victory when he stepped aside in 1966, and Democrat Tom Bevill won the seat. Although it was not clear at the time, Bevill's election meant at least a partial return to the populist tradition of representation — and presaged the change in attitudes that was to come in northern Alabama.

For even as northern Alabama was giving Wallace large majorities in his last race for governor in 1974, race was becoming less and less important a factor in politics. Integration had proceeded so far (in public accommodations, schools, jobs) and seemed likely to proceed no further (in bars, churches, private clubs, housing). In any case, it has been more the idea of integration than the fact of it that irritated whites. And when integration finally came, it seemed, if not the best thing that ever happened to the South, as Jimmy Carter said, then at least tolerable enough. The 1976 election results showed how things had changed: the last two presidential candidates with black support had won 10% and 22% of the vote here; Carter won with 65%. Even in 1980, with his popularity far lower and his symbolic value to white southerners already achieved, Carter still carried the 4th district — one of the relatively few throughout the nation in which he got an absolute majority of the votes.

Bevill's voting record is better suited to this kind of constituency than the one he served in the late 1960s. He has generally had a voting record rated at about 50% by organized labor, with ratings much lower from liberal groups more concerned with noneconomic cultural issues. He is chairman of the Energy and Water Development Appropriations Subcommittee, formerly known as Public Works — or pork barrel. In this capacity he has reported out the rivers and harbors or water projects bills that were vetoed or cut so abruptly by President Carter. Bevill adheres to the philosophy, shared by many of Alabama's populist Democrats, that the government should spend liberally on public works projects in order to build things people need and to create jobs. That philosophy is a little out of fashion today with many liberals, who worry about the environmental effects of such projects, and with conservatives, who don't like to spend money at all; Bevill's viewpoint may ultimately be squeezed out between the Carter and the Reagan Administrations. But as late as 1980, at least, it still commanded a majority on the floor of the House.

Bevill is also an at-large Democratic whip and so technically a member of the House leadership. He is usually the leadership's most loyal follower on the Alabama delegation. Electorally, he appears to have nothing to worry about. His constituents, no longer concerned about racial issues, seem to have no complaints about his performance.

Census Data   Pop. (1980 final) 594,974, up 21% in 1970s. Median family income, 1970, $6,350, 66% of U.S.

The Voters

Employment profile 1970   White collar, 31%. Blue collar, 53%. Service, 11%. Farm, 5%.
Ethnic groups   Black 1980, 7%. Hispanic 1980, 1%.

Presidential Vote

1980	Reagan (R)	95,402	(46%)
	Carter (D)	108,327	(52%)
	Anderson (I)	1,627	(1%)
1976	Ford (R)	66,263	(34%)
	Carter (D)	124,601	(65%)

Rep. Tom Bevill (D) Elected 1966; b. Mar. 27, 1921, Townley; home, Jasper; U. of Ala., B.S. 1943, LL.B. 1948.

Career   Army, WWII; Practicing atty., 1949–67; Ala. House of Reps., 1958–66.

Offices   2302 RHOB, 202-225-4876. Also 600 Broad St., Gadsden 35901, 205-546-0201.

Committees   *Appropriations* (11th). Subcommittees: Military Construction; Energy and Water Development (Chairman).

Group Ratings

	ADA	COPE	PC	LCV	CFA	RPN	NAB	NSI	NTU	ACA	ACU
1980	22	42	37	31	36	—	91	89	35	35	58
1979	26	50	38	31	37	—	—	—	34	52	61
1978	15	40	28	38	18	42	75	90	19	67	46

Key Votes

1) Draft Registn $	FOR	6) Fair Hsg DOJ Enfrc	AGN	11) Cut Socl Incr Dfns $	FOR
2) Ban $ to Nicrgua	FOR	7) Lim PAC Contrbtns	FOR	12) Hosptl Cost Controls	AGN
3) Dlay MX Missile	AGN	8) Cap on Food Stmp $	FOR	13) Gasln Ctrls & Allctns	FOR
4) Nuclr Mortorium	AGN	9) New US Dep Edcatn	FOR	14) Lim Wndfll Prof Tax	AGN
5) Alaska Lands Bill	FOR	10) Cut OSHA $	FOR	15) Chryslr Loan Grntee	AGN

Election Results

1980 general	Tom Bevill (D)	129,365	(98%)	($16,495)
1980 primary	Tom Bevill (D), unopposed		
1978 general	Tom Bevill (D), unopposed			($8,413)

FIFTH DISTRICT

Fifty years ago the Tennessee River coursed through Alabama's northern counties and every spring flooded the farm country and small towns along its banks. Then the Tennessee Valley Authority, TVA, was created in the 1930s. The agency dammed the wild river for most of its length, controlled the flooding, and produced cheap public power. This part of Alabama has had a populistic streak since the time of Andrew Jackson, and with the coming of TVA it elected to Congress New Dealers such as John Sparkman, who served in the House from what is now the 5th district from 1937 to 1946, and Bob Jones, who succeeded Sparkman and served until his retirement in 1976.

These men helped to bring to the 5th other benefits from the federal government, and the changes in the district have been striking. In 1950 Huntsville, considered a big town in these parts, was just a sleepy hill town of 14,000. Today its population is more than ten times that, and still growing. The principal agent of change has been the Redstone Missile Arsenal, the home of hundreds of Army and NASA rocket engineers and technicians. In recent years the Pentagon and NASA have pumped into the seven counties that make up the 5th district about $400 million a year, with most of it going to Huntsville.

In 1976 there was naturally a spirited contest for the district's seat. In the Democratic primary and runoff the winner over nine other candidates was Ronnie Flippo, a former state legislator. He has seats on two committees of great importance to the district: Public Works, which has oversight of TVA, and Science, which oversees research and development on the space program (he is chairman of the subcommittee that has jurisdiction over this). He seems more interested in proceeding in the footsteps of his immediate predecessor, Jones, who retired as chairman of the Public Works Committee, than of Sparkman, who worked on broad national issues as well as local ones. Flippo has a record that is closer to that of most Democrats than anyone else in the Alabama delegation except the 4th district's Tom Bevill. Since 1976 he has had only nominal opposition, and redistricting is unlikely to have any effect on the political balance in the district.

Census Data Pop. (1980 final) 549,802, up 12% in 1970s. Median family income, 1970, $8,271, 86% of U.S.

The Voters

Employment profile 1970 White collar, 47%. Blue collar, 38%. Service, 12%. Farm, 3%.
Ethnic groups Black 1980, 14%. Hispanic 1980, 1%. Total foreign stock 1970, 2%.

Presidential Vote

1980	Reagan (R)	72,831	(41%)
	Carter (D)	96,169	(54%)
	Anderson (I)	3,746	(2%)
1976	Ford (R)	50,039	(32%)
	Carter (D)	106,191	(67%)

Rep. Ronnie G. Flippo (D) Elected 1976; b. Aug. 15, 1937, Florence; home, Florence; U. of N. Ala., B.S. 1965; U. of Ala., M.A. 1966.

Career CPA, 1966–77; Ala. House of Reps., 1971–75; Ala. Senate, 1975–77.

Offices 405 CHOB, 202-225-4801. Also 122 Hilton Ct., Florence 35630, 205-766-7692.

Committees *Public Works and Transportation* (15th). Subcommittees: Economic Development; Investigation and Oversight; Water Resources.

Science and Technology (10th). Subcommittees: Energy Research and Production; Space Science and Applications (Chairman); Transportation; Aviation and Materials.

Group Ratings

	ADA	COPE	PC	LCV	CFA	RPN	NAB	NSI	NTU	ACA	ACU
1980	28	40	30	31	36	—	92	100	35	42	53
1979	16	35	26	28	8	—	—	—	34	46	53
1978	10	42	33	27	9	50	70	88	20	74	41

Key Votes

1) Draft Registn $	FOR	6) Fair Hsg DOJ Enfrc	AGN	11) Cut Socl Incr Dfns $	FOR
2) Ban $ to Nicrgua	FOR	7) Lim PAC Contrbtns	AGN	12) Hosptl Cost Controls	AGN
3) Dlay MX Missile	AGN	8) Cap on Food Stmp $	AGN	13) Gasln Ctrls & Allctns	FOR
4) Nuclr Mortorium	AGN	9) New US Dep Edcatn	FOR	14) Lim Wndfll Prof Tax	FOR
5) Alaska Lands Bill	FOR	10) Cut OSHA $		FOR	15) Chryslr Loan Grntee	AGN

Election Results

1980 general	Ronnie G. Flippo (D)	117,626	(94%)	($77,827)
	Betty Benson (Libertarian)	7,341	(6%)	($0)
1980 primary	Ronnie G. Flippo (D), unopposed			
1978 general	Ronnie G. Flippo (D)	68,985	(97%)	($41,660)

SIXTH DISTRICT

Birmingham is one of the few major southern cities that did not exist at the time of the Civil War. It was founded a few years after the conflict and was named, in the hope of a great industrial future, for the great English manufacturing center. The hopes of the founders have been realized, although incompletely. Birmingham is where it is because it sits on a mountain — one of the southernmost in the Appalachian chain — that is made of iron-rich ore; it was recognized even in Reconstruction days as the natural site for a steel industry. Today, as it has been for years, Birmingham is the major, indeed really the only, significant steel producer in the South. But it has not been a city with an especially robust local economy. A generation ago it was about equal to Atlanta in size and importance. Since then Atlanta has boomed and Birmingham has stagnated, to the point that Atlanta is the undisputed capital of the South and Birmingham is just another regional center.

Part of the reason is economic. Birmingham is dangerously close to being a one-industry town, and in the last generation the steel industry in the United States has been anything but healthy. Moreover, in an era when business is increasingly dependent on airline travel, Atlanta has the busiest airport in the South, while Birmingham has relatively few flights, except those coming in from or going out to Atlanta. Another reason for Birmingham's lack of growth was the city's response to the civil rights revolution. As Atlanta was billing itself as the city too busy to hate, Birmingham's Police Commissioner Bull Connor set dogs and fire-hoses against civil rights demonstrators. That same year, 1963, Connor seemed unperturbed when someone set off a bomb in a black church and killed four young girls. Those events in Birmingham supplied some of the momentum that produced the Civil Rights Act of 1964; and they also damaged the city's economy. Investors, after all, shun commotion and uncertainty of any kind. During the 1960s metropolitan Atlanta grew 37% while metropolitan Birmingham grew 3%. In the 1970s the percentage difference was not so great, but by that time Atlanta was building on a much bigger base.

Despite the turmoil of 1963, Birmingham is one part of Alabama that always tended to oppose George Wallace. The city voted heavily against him in 1970, his toughest election, when he was nearly beaten by Albert Brewer. This is the only part of Alabama with a really substantial high-income vote — a group that produces solid Republican majorities any time the Republicans come close to contesting a statewide race seriously. The blacks here of course always opposed Wallace unanimously; unlike blacks in small towns, they could not be swayed by the urgings or threats of pro-Wallace neighbors. That leaves relatively few Wallace-type Democrats, and not many votes for a Democrat like Jimmy Carter either; in fact, Carter failed to carry Birmingham's Jefferson County in both 1976 and 1980.

Alabama's 6th congressional district currently includes all of Birmingham and most of its Jefferson County suburbs, excluding only that area to the west, much of it industrial, that is in the 7th district. It includes the high-income suburbs on the hillsides and the steel factories they overlook; it includes working-class whites (although many seem to be moving to counties farther out now) and blacks. On balance it has been essentially a Republican district, and its congressional politics has been played out largely in that most unusual of southern institutions, the seriously contested Republican primary.

The main reason for this unusual situation is that for some years the 6th had an unusual congressman. John Buchanan was a Republican, first elected in the Goldwater year of 1964, and in his early congressional career counted as a reliable conservative vote. He is also a Baptist minister and in Washington began attending a predominantly black church — which must have been an unusual experience for someone fresh from the Birmingham of 1963. In the 1970s, as Buchanan became closer to many black fellow church members, he shifted positions on some issues. Not only on civil rights but on some economic matters as well, Buchanan broke with the standard Republican position. In the late 1970s, as Republicans in the House were becoming more partisan and cohesive, Buchanan was moving in just the other direction, concentrating on issues such as home rule for the District of Columbia. His conversion should not be overstated; on national liberal ratings indexes he stood well below 50%. But he also got higher ratings on them than any other member of the Alabama delegation at a time when most southern Republicans were getting ratings near zero.

There are significant constituencies for this kind of representation in this country, in high-income neighborhoods such as New York's Upper East Side or in very affluent or well-educated suburbs of cities such as Boston and Chicago and Philadelphia; but there is not much of such a constituency in Birmingham. Buchanan had some trouble from liberal and conservative Democratic opponents in 1974 and 1976, but his real problems came in 1978 when Albert Lee Smith, a former member of the John Birch Society, ran against him in the primary. Alabama, like most southern states, does not have party registration, and voters are free to vote in whichever primary they want. Few are used to voting in Republican primaries — where seldom are there significant contests — and in 1978, with Democrats staging seriously contested primaries for governor and both Senate seats, only 15,000-odd voted in the 6th district Republican primary. Buchanan won, but with only 57% of the vote — a clear warning signal. In 1980 Smith ran again. This time nearly three times as many people voted in the Republican primary, and Smith won a 55%–45% victory. A few weeks later the Whig Party — remnant of the 19th-century organization — tried to put Buchanan on the ballot, but failed. The Democratic nominee, a minister himself and a member of the Birmingham Council, was prepared to run against Buchanan as too liberal; he had little rationale left when Smith became the Republican nominee. The result was close, however, as Smith trailed behind the showings here of Ronald Reagan and Admiral Jeremiah Denton, who carried the Birmingham area by similar margins.

Smith can be counted on to vote with the currently well-disciplined and enthusiastic bloc of Republicans in the House; and in this respect the district's Republican primary voters are surely represented more accurately, if less interestingly, than they were by Buchanan. But Smith's narrow margin in 1980 suggests he may be more vulnerable in a future general election than Buchanan. Moreover, the Democratic legislature may try to redraw the district lines to Smith's disadvantage. This would not be difficult. The 6th district must be somewhat enlarged, and the obvious addition would be the industrial suburbs just west of Birmingham, which are heavily Democratic.

Census Data   Pop. (1980 final) 518,032, up 5% in 1970s. Median family income, 1970, $8,683, 91% of U.S.

The Voters

Employment profile 1970   White collar, 52%. Blue collar, 34%. Service, 14%. Farm, –%.
Ethnic groups   Black 1980, 32%. Hispanic 1980, 1%. Total foreign stock 1970, 3%.

Presidential Vote

1980	Reagan (R)	104,374	(53%)
	Carter (D)	82,538	(42%)
	Anderson (I)	3,040	(2%)
1976	Ford (R)	90,928	(55%)
	Carter (D)	70,995	(43%)

Rep. Albert Lee Smith, Jr. (R) Elected 1980; b. Aug. 31, 1931, Birmingham; home, Mountain Brook; Auburn U., B.S. 1954.

Career   U.S. Navy, 1954–56; Life insurance underwriter; Delegate, Rep. Nat. Conv., 1968, 1972, 1976.

Offices   1723 LHOB, 202-225-4921. Also 105 Fed. Ct. Bldg., 1800 5th Ave, N., Birmingham 35203, 205-254-1525.

Committees   *Budget* (10th).

Veterans' Affairs (11th). Subcommittees: Compensation, Pension and Insurance; Hospitals and Health Care.

Group Ratings and Key Votes: Newly Elected

Election Results

1980 general	Albert Lee Smith, Jr. (R)	95,019	(51%)	($264,199)
	W. B. (Pete) Clifford (D)	87,536	(47%)	($41,812)
1980 primary	Albert Lee Smith, Jr. (R)	25,857	(55%)	
	John H. Buchanan, Jr. (R).......	20,855	(45%)	($186,925)
1978 general	John H. Buchanan, Jr. (R).......	65,700	(62%)	($123,808)
	Don Hawkins (D)	40,771	(38%)	($20,238)

SEVENTH DISTRICT

The 7th congressional district of Alabama contains a virtual cross-section of the state. It includes a substantial part of metropolitan Birmingham, including Bessemer, the steel mill suburb, and Fairfield, site of Miles College—both with black majorities. At the other end of the district are Black Belt counties with the highest black percentages and lowest incomes in Alabama. They are, however, far less important politically than they would have been if blacks had got the vote earlier; their population is less than half that of 50 years ago, as a result of the great migrations to the North. In the 1970s those migrations mostly stopped, but it is probably too late for these small counties to recover. A local economy of any real strength does not appear to be a possibility here, and migration will probably continue, this time to the urban areas of the South. In between Birmingham and the Black Belt is Tuscaloosa, the geographical center of the district, a reasonably properous middle-sized city, and the proud home of the University of Alabama and of Paul Bear Bryant.

The 7th district lacks a uniform political identity. It has the largest black percentage of any Alabama congressional district—38% in 1970, 36% in 1980. Yet for years the congressmen elected by this district seemed to have voting records more conservative than the state average. The politicians seemed to think of themselves as representing the well-to-do—culturally and politically conservative people whom they knew from the local country club. And of course, back in the days when blacks did not dare vote and many whites didn't keep up their poll taxes, this is exactly whom they did represent.

Certainly this seemed to be the view of the 7th district held by Congressman Walter Flowers when, as a member of the House Judiciary Committee in 1974, he voted for the impeachment of Richard Nixon. Of all the committee's members, Flowers seemed most wrenched by this decision and most fearful of its political effect back home. In fact, it hurt him scarcely at all—and not simply because Nixon resigned a short time later. The district's black people, who had opposed Flowers in 1972 and 1974 primaries, were pleased with his vote, and so were far more whites than he apparently assumed. Flowers had no trouble whatever holding onto the seat and indeed could still be in Congress had he not suddenly entered the 1978 Senate race when George Wallace declined to run. His political instincts again proved defective when he campaigned as the candidate who knew Washington; he was beaten by a wide margin by Howell Heflin who stressed that he was not part of "the Washington crowd."

Flowers's sudden Senate candidacy created an unexpected opening in the 7th district. The congressman's Tuscaloosa law partner, Richard Shelby, had been running for lieutenant governor; he switched to the congressional race and won. In the runoff he was opposed by state legislator Chris McNair, who had received a respectable percentage; it is symbolic of how far the South has come that not much, one way or the other, was made of the fact that McNair is black. Meanwhile, the Republican candidate expressly conceded the general election. Shelby compiled a voting record similar to that of Flowers—more conservative than those of Alabama's northern hill country Democrats—and had no difficulty winning re-election in 1980. Redistricting may cost him some black precincts in the Birmingham sub-urbs, but that should not hurt him politically.

Census Data Pop. (1980 final) 548,859, up 12% in 1970s. Median family income, 1970, $6,806, 71% of U.S.

The Voters

Employment profile 1970 White collar, 38%. Blue collar, 43%. Service, 15%. Farm, 4%.
Ethnic groups Black 1980, 36%. Hispanic 1980, 1%. Total foreign stock 1970, 1%.

Presidential Vote

1980	Reagan (R)	90,008	(45%)
	Carter (D)	97,158	(49%)
	Anderson (I)	2,004	(1%)
1976	Ford (R)	71,799	(42%)
	Carter (D)	93,693	(56%)

Rep. Richard C. Shelby (D) Elected 1978; b. May 6, 1934, Fairfield; home, Tuscaloosa; U. of Ala., A.B. 1957, LL.B. 1963.

Career Practicing atty., 1963– ; Ala. Senate, 1971–79.

Offices 1705 LHOB, 202-225-2511. Also P.O. Box 2627, Tusca-loosa 35401, 205-752-3578.

Committees *Energy and Commerce* (19th). Subcommittees: En-ergy Conservation and Power; Fossil and Synthetic Fuels; Health and the Environment; Oversight and Investigations.

Veterans' Affairs (11th). Subcommittees: Hospitals and Health Care; Housing and Memorial Affairs.

Group Ratings

	ADA	COPE	PC	LCV	CFA	RPN	NAB	NSI	NTU	ACA	ACU
1980	11	20	20	17	7	—	92	100	45	67	68
1979	5	40	23	24	4	—	—	—	44	68	76

Key Votes

1) Draft Registn $	FOR	6) Fair Hsg DOJ Enfrc	AGN	11) Cut Socl Incr Dfns $	FOR
2) Ban $ to Nicrgua	FOR	7) Lim PAC Contrbtns	AGN	12) Hosptl Cost Controls	AGN
3) Dlay MX Missile	AGN	8) Cap on Food Stmp $	FOR	13) Gasln Ctrls & Allctns	AGN
4) Nuclr Mortorium	AGN	9) New US Dep Edcatn	FOR	14) Lim Wndfll Prof Tax	AGN
5) Alaska Lands Bill	AGN	10) Cut OSHA $	FOR	15) Chryslr Loan Grntee	AGN

Election Results

1980 general	Richard C. Shelby (D)	122,505	(73%)	($126,936)
	James E. Bacon (R)	43,000	(26%)	($0)
1980 primary	Richard C. Shelby (D), unopposed			
1978 general	Richard C. Shelby (D), unopposed	77,742	(96%)	($181,405)

ALASKA

Alaska is the nation's largest state (586,000 square miles) and also its smallest (400,000 residents in 1980—and one-quarter of that is growth in the last 10 years). Alaskans live in the land of the midnight sun and of darkness at noon; of winter wind-chill factors that reach 100 below and of muggy, mosquito-filled summers; of the tallest mountains in North America and thousands of miles of rugged seacoast. It is a land where a penniless immigrant, Walter Hickel, can make millions in the construction business, and where some Eskimos and Aleuts still live in grinding poverty. Most important these days, Alaska is the land of the great North Slope oil strike, of sudden boom—and the nation's highest unemployment.

It is hard for someone from the "Lower 48" to grasp the size of Alaska. More than twice as large as Texas, the state spans four different time zones. But for all its expanse, Alaska has only one railroad and a few paved highways—the only way to get around is by airplane. Even the most isolated villages in the interior have an airstrip cleared in the bush or on a frozen river. Politicians especially have to fly a lot, and crashes are not uncommon; one killed Congressman Nick Begich and House Majority Leader Hale Boggs in 1972, and another seriously injured Senator Ted Stevens and killed his wife in 1978.

Most of Alaska still belongs to nature; it remains the home of the caribou and perhaps an occasional Eskimo hunter. Most of the population is clustered in a few small urban areas, with 43% of the people living in greater Anchorage. Dreams of sudden riches still bring men to Alaska (and this is one state that has many more men than women), but riches are seldom found. Life here can be hard: high wages are eaten up by high prices, and there are fewer people proportionately over 65 than in any other state. After a while, things are just too rough, and people tend to move back south.

The familiar image of Alaska is of a place with almost uncharted wilderness. Yet Alaska, like most western states, is essentially an urban place for people who live and work there. Nearly half the state's population is in Anchorage, which is not where the state's oil is found, nor even the southern terminus of the pipeline. The city owes its location initially to its good natural port, but today Anchorage is the economic center of almost all of Alaska, the one place where services and amenities are generally available and the site of the major airport that connects Alaska to the Lower 48 and the Orient. The other major center, with about one-eighth of the state's population is Fairbanks. Located in the interior, unprotected from the Arctic winds as Anchorage is by the towering Alaska Range, Fairbanks is exceedingly hot in its brief summer and terrifyingly cold in its long winter. Economically, Fairbanks is primarily a service town for the pipeline and for other mineral extraction enterprises in the interior. But Fairbanks has suffered from great unemployment here since the pipeline was completed; the men who had come up from the Lower 48 were left with little to do but grumble and make trouble after months of working for high dollar wages. A vast amount of coal lies under the land near Fairbanks, and other minerals as well, but the environment still puts up formidable obstacles to commercial exploitation of resources—obstacles with which most Americans are no longer familiar.

There is an older Alaska as well, in the fishing towns of the Panhandle and the old tiny capital of Juneau, located on an inlet of the Pacific up against a steep mountain. There is the

Alaska of the Bush, the villages where Alaska's Natives—Indians, Aleuts, Eskimos— live, often in poverty. Torn away from their traditional culture, they are uncomfortable with what has replaced it. And there are the smaller settlements in a 200-mile arc around Anchorage, the place where boomers from the Lower 48 have come up to make their fortunes: the Matanuska Valley, one of the few places in Alaska where there is any farming; Seward; the Kenai Peninsula; the little port of Valdez, the southern terminus of the oil pipeline. Yet almost all of Alaska is still physically vacant, devoid of human habitation, perhaps unseen by human eyes. What to do with the vast expanse is the continuing and enduring question of Alaska politics.

For years Alaska longed for statehood, for control of its own affairs and release from the economic thrall of Seattle and the political hegemony of Washington, D.C. Alaska has succeeded in generating a boom economy—thanks largely to the huge North Slope oil find of the late 1960s, which was finally put into production when the Trans-Alaska Pipeline System began to operate in 1977. But Alaska, probably more than any other state, has had to endure the discomfort of having the federal government make decisions that will continue to shape its future as surely as the Northwest Ordinance did Ohio's or the Homestead Act Nebraska's.

Many of these decisions were made during the 1970s and in 1980, and in no case was the decision made in the way that a clear majority of Alaska voters would have preferred. The first of these decisions concerned the very basic question of the ownership of Alaska's land. The Statehood Act of 1959 had promised Alaska the right to select 103 million acres as state lands, but that right was subject to the claims of Alaska Natives—Eskimos, Aleuts, and Indians—who had never surrendered their claims to anyone. In 1966 the federal government imposed a freeze, refusing to allow Alaska to select any more land until the Natives' claims were settled, which happened at just about the time oil was being discovered on the North Slope. Naturally Alaskans were eager for the state government, which supported rapid development of resources, to claim all the lands with mineral potential it could. But the Alaska Native Claims Act of 1971 forced them to wait until 12 regional Native corporations selected their own 44 million acres (12% of the state's land area): these corporations were also given $962 million. All this proved to be a frustrating and time-consuming process.

But it was probably not as frustrating to development-minded Alaskans as was the delay in the building of the oil pipeline. Proposed in the early 1970s, the pipeline was the only practical way to get that much oil from the North Slope to civilization. But environmentalists charged that the pipeline as originally designed would destroy the permafrost (land that remains frozen year round except for a few inches at the top), would interfere with caribou migrations, and would otherwise irreparably injure Alaska's unique and fragile environment. The environmentalists went to court and in 1973 got a ruling halting pipeline construction. Alaskans could have taken their chances on the Supreme Court, but they preferred to overturn a lower court decision by congressional action. So in 1973, by a one-vote margin in the Senate, the pipeline was exempted from submitting an environmental impact statement; in return, its builders had to agree to an expensive and time-consuming redesign, including building the pipeline on platforms above ground level. Construction was not completed and pumping not begun until almost ten years after the oil was found—and after truly grotesque cost overruns.

The third major decision made in the 1970s affecting Alaska concerned the lands that should be set aside as wilderness or otherwise protected by the federal government from various kinds of use and development. Under the Native Claims Act, the Carter Interior Department withdrew from all development some 80 million acres until December 1978, pending a congressional decision on how much should be protected. The issue was one around which environmentalists from the Lower 48 — Alaska's name for the contiguous states — had organized intensively; it seemed obvious to them that never again would the nation have such an opportunity to protect so much wilderness. They had the sympathy of the Carter Administration, the support of most congressional Democrats, and they also enlisted such conservative conservationists as ex-Senator James Buckley and Ford Administration Interior officials. The result was the Alaska Lands Law of 1980, which protected 159 million acres from various forms of development; altogether,49% of Alaska's land is so protected. This was the single major victory of liberal-oriented groups in the 96th Congress, and it may turn out to be the last major achievement of the environmental movement of the late 1960s and 1970s. Certainly Alaska will be affected for years to come. President Reagan would never have signed such a bill, but it is unlikely to be repealed or substantially altered for the foreseeable future.

None of the three major decisions made by Congress during the decade would have come out the way they did if Alaskans themselves had decided matters. Four out of five Alaskans are white, and they would never have been as generous to the Natives as Congress was; the pipeline would have been built earlier and without environmental safeguards; and nothing like the Alaska Lands Bill would ever have come out of the Alaska legislature. The major forces in Alaska politics, the *Anchorage Times* and Jesse Carr's Teamsters Union, are strongly in favor of development — as much and as fast as possible. Most of the state's politicians, such as Governor Jay Hammond, are a little more equivocal, but only a little. Every indication is that the overwhelming majority of voters are boomers (boosters of development) rather than greenies (environmentalists). Alaskans, after all, have a high-wage and high-cost economy in a forbidding physical environment (it enrages them to hear it described as fragile). The state's economy is subject to wide fluctuations, and Alaskans are determined to see it prosper. Future generations may very well thank the Congresses of the 1970s for preserving so much of Alaska, but very few Alaskans today will.

That reaction against the environmental movement has made Alaska very much a Republican state in national politics. In the tight presidential elections of 1960 and 1968, Alaska came very close to the national average in its preferences. In 1976 and 1980, however, it was one of the most Republican — or least Democratic — states. Indeed, in 1980 Jimmy Carter got only 26% of the votes here, and in some parts of the state Carter ran behind Libertarian Party candidate Ed Clark. This was the Libertarians' strongest state: they took 12% of the vote for Clark, and in 1978 and in 1980 elected members of the legislature. The success of this small, rough-and-ready party in Alaska makes a certain amount of sense. A strong desire for untrammeled development, together with an equally strong desire to be left alone characterize Alaska politics: the state hates federal regulations and has decriminalized marijuana. The Panhandle area, the oldest part of Alaska, used to be Democratic but in 1980 went solidly for Reagan; the Bush was the only part of the state Carter could carry, thanks to his support from Natives. Reagan had majorities everywhere else. In Metropolitan Fairbanks Ed Clark won 19% of the vote and in the southern region beyond Metropolitan Anchorage he had 16%.

Representation in the Senate is obviously of great importance to a state such as Alaska, when so many of its basic decisions are made in Congress. Its influence in the House is necessarily limited by the fact that it has only one congressman-at-large. Don Young, the incumbent since a 1973 special election, spoke out vociferously against the Alaska Lands Bill, for instance, but he could do nothing to prevent House passage; the other side had the votes and House rules don't allow obstructive tactics. The Senate is different. But here Alaska was hobbled in the 1970s by severe professional and, ultimately, personal differences between the men who were its senators for 12 years, Republican Ted Stevens and Democrat Mike Gravel. They came to the Senate at almost precisely the same time — Stevens by appointment after the death in 1968 of Democrat Bob Bartlett, one of the architects of statehood, and Gravel after the 1968 election, when with a TV blitz he upset incumbent Ernest Gruening in the primary.

Temperamentally they are very different. Stevens fit in well in the Senate: he is bright and knowledgeable about Washington; he can fashion a compromise or defend a hard-line position. In 1975 he became Republican campaign committee chairman and Republican whip in 1977; he is now majority whip, the number two position in the leadership. Gravel, in contrast, was always something of a maverick. Having gotten his seat by unseating one of the two dissenters from the Gulf of Tonkin resolution, Gravel tried a few years later to read into the Senate record massive excerpts from the then-banned Pentagon Papers; foiled by a timely objection, he began to cry. Then in 1972 he nominated himself for vice president at the Democratic National Convention. Gravel was always a loner in the Senate, a man who would try to use the rules to maximum advantage and who, in the opinion of some colleagues, welshed on commitments.

Stevens's instinct on Alaska issues was always to compromise. A tough negotiator, he would attempt to get the opposition to give up the gains made in the House. Stevens worked with such senators as Henry Jackson of Washington, long chairman of the Interior Committee. Gravel's inclination was just the opposite. He wanted no compromise at all; he tried to defeat the environmentalists utterly. On one occasion he succeeded. In 1973 he persuaded the Senate, by a 50–49 vote, to exempt the Alaska pipeline from the Environmental Protection Act altogether. That made the building of the pipeline possible, and it helped Gravel win reelection in 1974 against an opponent who was a member of the John Birch Society. But it also infuriated Stevens and Jackson, who were committed to a broad-gauged revision of federal pipeline statutes and thought they also had had a commitment from Gravel to support them.

In 1978 Gravel tried the same kind of manuever against the House-passed Alaska Lands Bill but this time failed. Stevens had been laboriously negotiating a compromise and had obtained one that dismayed environmentalists. Gravel then tried to filibuster the bill to death at the end of the session and succeeded. Unfortunately for him, the Carter Administration by executive action immediately created 56 million acres of national monuments, protected another 40 million, and had the president designate 6 million more for protection under the Antiquities Act. This protected more land than the House bill would have and was exactly what Stevens had feared. Stevens himself was easily reelected in 1978, but shortly thereafter he was involved in the plane crash that killed his wife. Relations between Stevens and Gravel, never warm, became as vitriolic as relations between any two Senate colleagues ever have been.

Predictably, in the next Congress the House passed an expansive Alaska Lands Bill, and Stevens again tried to compromise it down. Gravel on his own tried to filibuster it. In the summer of 1980, just weeks before Gravel faced a Democratic primary contest, the Senate voted for cloture on Gravel's filibuster by a 63 to 25 vote. Alaskans, like residents of most small states, are pretty sophisticated about the way the Senate works, and they cannot fail to have been impressed by this scathing rebuff of Gravel. It was humiliating for a senator to be able to muster so few votes against a remedy so extreme as cloture on a matter so important to his state. It was as if senators were trying to send a signal to the voters of Alaska. In any case, Gravel was defeated by a 55%–44% margin by Clark Gruening, a young lawyer and the grandson of the man Gravel had defeated 12 years before.

Gruening had great momentum from that victory; the race against Gravel had been the central focus of Alaska politics, and no one had paid much attention to Frank Murkowski, the Fairbanks banker who won the Republican nomination easily. But Murkowski ended up winning the general election. He probably broke the race open when he attacked Gruening for having supported in the legislature a measure committing Alaska to "environmental purity." The vehement — almost violent — feeling against environmentalists of most Alaskans was directed against Gruening.

Gruening claimed the amendment was innocuous; Murkowski brought in lawyers to say that weaker amendments in other states had generated numerous lawsuits and held up development. And that turned the election around. Gruening ran well for a Democrat in Anchorage, which is a Republican town in the tradition of Phoenix or Boise; but Murkowski ran as well in his hometown of Fairbanks, and managed to hold Gruening just about even in the area where Murkowski grew up, the Panhandle. Overall Murkowski won with 54% of the vote — not an overwhelming victory, but a clear one.

So Alaska, which had had one of the most divided Senate delegations, now has one of the most united. Stevens is now not only majority whip, but also the second-ranking member of the Appropriations Committee, chairman of its Defense Subcommittee, and a senior member of its Interior Subcommittee, always important to Alaska. He is also a member of the Commerce Committee and a supporter there of maritime subsidies; he had served on Energy and Interior, to work on the Alaska Lands Bill, but in 1981 switched back to Commerce.

Stevens is by no means a member of the New Right. He gets along with labor in Alaska as well as with business; he has what is considered a moderate record on most issues. Because of his leadership position and because his basic views are in line with those of the Republican majority's, he can be expected to support the Reagan Administration. But he is less likely to go along with some measures sought by the Moral Majority (e.g., banning abortion) or laws to reduce the power of unions.

Murkowski, who was a respected banker and businessman in Alaska, seems to have similar views. He serves on two committees with important implications for Alaska: Energy (the old Interior Committee) and Environment and Public Works. Congress has made many major decisions for Alaska over the last ten years, but some others still must be made; and on those the likelihood is that Stevens and Murkowski will be working closely together. In a Republican Senate, they should receive more deference to their views than Gravel did. One of those issues is the possible purchase by Alaska of the federally owned Alaska Railroad. Another is the financing of the proposed gas pipeline that would extend from the North Slope across northeastern Alaska, through Canada, and down to the Pacific Northwest. A third provides for the exploration and development of Alaska's supplies of coal, nickel, and strategic minerals such as cobalt, molybdenum, and platinum.

Congressman Young is also likely to work well with Stevens. First elected after Nick Begich was killed in a plane crash, Young is a Republican from the Bush. He serves on the Interior Committee and is ranking Republican on the Public Lands and National Parks

Subcommittee, the body that will handle any revisions of the Alaska Lands Bill; it is chaired by John Seiberling, one of the architects of the present legislation, who is likely to have a majority over Young on this issue. Young is also a new member of the Merchant Marine Subcommittee and a supporter of maritime subsidies. He has been reelected generally with large margins but had a fairly close race against state Senator Patrick Rodey of Anchorage in 1978; Rodey may run against him again in 1982. Young's main problem is, of course, the success of the Alaska Lands Bill in the House.

Alaska's governor, Jay Hammond, is known as someone who does not believe unequivocally in growth and development, but he too has strongly opposed measures such as the Alaska Lands Bill. He is just the kind of man you would cast for an Alaska version of *Mr. Smith Goes to Washington:* a bearded bush pilot (who rescued people from a downed plane in the 1978 campaign), a sometime poet (or doggerel writer), a former trapper, commercial fisherman, and air taxi operator. Hammond is open and informal, and always ready to concede the strong points of his adversaries' positions. He won two elections, and primaries as well, by exceedingly close margins; in fact he has beaten, at one time or another, every one of the state's former governors. His most difficult tasks as governor include moving the state capital from Juneau to a site near Anchorage, as ordered by voters in a referendum, and figuring out what to do with the huge surplus the state receives from its royalties on North Slope oil. Under his leadership Alaska abolished its state income tax; the legislature also passed a controversial bill returning money to residents, with those who have lived longer in the state getting more.

Hammond reportedly plans to return to Naknek after the 1982 campaign. The leading competitor for his place is his lieutenant governor, Terry Miller, a personable young man who has had considerable experience in Alaska politics. His toughest Republican competitor is likely to be Tom Fink, who ran third in the primary between Hammond and former Governor Walter Hickel in 1978; Fink is an intellectual conservative and a stronger backer of growth and development than Hammond. A leading Democrat is Bill Sheffield, owner of a chain of hotels in the state. But party labels mean less here than in the Lower 48. In primary elections Alaskans can vote for a Senate candidate of one party and a gubernatorial candidate of another; consequently, voters go where the action is, and personality plays a major role in the results. But it is not like Wyoming, where everyone expects to meet all the candidates; the distances are too vast and the population too urbanized. Alaska indeed has become a state where campaigning by television is all-important. It is also a state whose concerns seem increasingly to diverge from those of the Lower 48 and whose mentality seems to be growing more colonial the further we get beyond statehood. The question for the 1980s is whether Alaska issues will continue to be paramount in Alaskans' voting in national elections, or whether voters here will return to their earlier practice of making decisions on the same factors as other Americans.

Census Data Pop. (1980 final) 400,481, up 32% in 1970s: 0.18% of U.S. total, 50th largest. Central city, 43%; suburban, 0%. Median 4-person family income, 1978, $27,572, 135% of U.S., 1st highest.

1979 Share of Federal Tax Burden $1,533,000,000; 0.34% of U.S. total, 43d largest.

1979 Share of Federal Outlays $1,932,153,000; 0.42% of U.S. total, 41st largest.

DOD	$634,487,000	34th	(0.60%)	HEW	$201,158,000	51st	(0.11%)
DOE	$3,483,000	42d	(0.03%)	ERDA	$873,000	44th	(0.03%)

HUD	$9,127,000	50th	(0.14%)	NASA	$815,000	38th	(0.02%)
VA	$27,333,000	51st	(0.13%)	DOT	$257,121,000	22d	(1.56%)
EPA	$23,858,000	44th	(0.45%)	DOC	$38,290,000	16th	(1.20%)
DOI	$390,907,000	4th	(7.04%)	USDA	$115,778,000	43d	(0.48%)

Economic Base   Finance, insurance, and real estate; food and kindred products, especially canned and cured sea foods; agriculture and fishing, notably fish, dairy products, eggs, potatoes, and cattle; oil and gas field services, and other oil and gas extraction activity; paper pulp, and other paper and allied products.

Political Lineup   Governor, Jay S. Hammond (R). Senators, Ted Stevens (R) and Frank H. Mur-kowski (R). Representatives, 1 R at large; 1 in 1982. State Senate, 21 (11 D and 10 R); State House of Representatives, 41 (23 D, 16 R, and 2 Libertarian).

The Voters

Registration   261,536 Total. 69,224 D (26%); 43,265 R (17%); 139,911 Nonpartisan (54%); 9,136 Others (3%)
Employment profile 1970   White collar, 55%. Blue collar, 30%. Service, 15%. Farm, –%.
Ethnic groups   Black 1980, 3%. Hispanic 1980, 2%. Am. Ind. 1980, 16%. Asian 1980, 3%. Total foreign stock 1970, 11%.

Presidential Vote

1980	Reagan (R)	86,112	(55%)
	Carter (D)	41,842	(27%)
	Anderson (I)	11,155	(7%)
	Clark (Libertarian)	18,479	(10%)
1976	Ford (R)	71,555	(58%)
	Carter (D)	44,058	(36%)
	MacBride (Libertarian).....	6,785	(6%)

SENATORS

Sen. Ted Stevens (R) Appointed Dec. 23, 1968, elected 1970, seat up 1984; b. Nov. 18, 1923, Indianap-olis, Ind.; home, Anchorage; Oreg. St. U., Mont. St. U., UCLA, A.B. 1947, Harvard U., LL.B. 1950.

Career Air Force, WWII; Practicing atty., 1950–53, 1961–68; U.S. Atty., 1953–56; U.S. Dept. of Interior, Legis. Council, 1956–58, Asst. to the Secy., 1958–60, Solicitor 1960–61; Alaska House of Reps., 1964–68.

Offices 127 RSOB, 202-224-3004. Also 221 Fed. Bldg., Anchor-age 99501, 907-272-9561; and 200 Fed. Bldg., Fairbanks 99701, 907-452-5264.

Committees *Majority Whip.*

Appropriations (2d). Subcommittees: Interior; Legislative Branch; State, Justice, Commerce, and the Judiciary; Defense (Chairman); Labor, Health and Human Services, Education.

Commerce, Science and Transportation (8th). Subcommittees: Aviation; Communications; Mer-chant Marine and Tourism.

Governmental Affairs (3d). Subcommittees: Civil Service, Post Office, and General Services (Chair-man); Oversight of Government Management; Congressional Operations and Oversight.

Group Ratings

	ADA	COPE	PC	LCV	CFA	RPN	NAB	NSI	NTU	ACA	ACU
1980	39	50	17	5	7	—	50	89	39	71	50
1979	21	35	12	—	10	—	—	—	30	43	67
1978	10	33	13	15	20	78	42	70	14	61	67

Key Votes

1) Draft Registn $	FOR	6) Fair Housng Cloture	AGN	11) Cut Socl Incr Defns	FOR
2) Ban $ to Nicrgua	FOR	7) Ban $ Rape Abortns	AGN	12) Income Tax Indexing	—
3) Dlay MX Missile	—	8) Cap on Food Stmp $	FOR	13) Lim Spdg 21% GNP	FOR
4) Nuclr Mortorium	AGN	9) New US Dep Edcatn	FOR	14) Incr Wndfll Prof Tax	AGN
5) Alaska Lands Bill	AGN	10) Cut OSHA Inspctns	FOR	15) Chryslr Loan Grntee	FOR

Election Results

1978 general	Ted Stevens (R)...............	92,783	(76%)	($346,837)
	Donald W. Hobbs (D)	29,574	(24%)	($21,234)
1978 primary	Ted Stevens (R), unopposed			
1972 general	Ted Stevens (R)...............	74,216	(77%)	($195,123)
	Gene Guess (D)	21,791	(23%)	($47,131)

Sen. Frank H. Murkowski (R) Elected 1980, seat up 1986; b. Mar. 28, 1933, Seattle, Wash.; home, Fairbanks; Seattle U., B.A. 1955.

Career U.S. Coast Guard, 1955–56; Pres., Alaska Nat. Bank of the North, 1971; Alaska Commissioner of Econ. Devel., 1967–70; Pres., Alaska Chamber of Comm, 1977.

Offices 2104 RSOB, 202-224-6665. Also Fed. Bldg., 701 C St., Box 1, Anchorage 99513, 907-271-3735; 101 12th Ave., Box 7, Fairbanks 99701, 907-452-6227; and Fed. Bldg., Box 1647, Juneau 99802, 907-586-7463.

Committees *Energy and Natural Resources* (8th). Subcommittees: Energy and Mineral Resources; Water and Power (Chairman); Public Lands and Reserved Water.

Environment and Public Works (9th). Subcommittees: Water Resources; Toxic Substances and Environmental Oversight; Regional and Community Development (Chairman).

Veterans' Affairs (6th).

Group Ratings and Key Votes: Newly Elected

Election Results

1980 general	Frank H. Murkowski (R)........	84,159	(54%)	($496,854)
	Clark Gruening (D).............	72,007	(46%)	($507,445)
1980 primary	Frank H. Murkowski (R)........	16,292	(59%)	
	Art Kennedy (R)	5,527	(20%)	($97,530)
	Four others (R)	5,813	(21%)	
1974 general	Mike Gravel (D)	54,361	(58%)	($469,300)
	C. R. Lewis (R)................	38,914	(42%)	($353,701)

GOVERNOR

Gov. Jay S. Hammond (R) Elected 1974, term expires Dec. 1982; b.July 21, 1922, Troy, N.Y.; Penn. St. U., 1940–42, U. of Alaska, B.S. 1948.

Career Navy, WWII; Bush pilot, trapper, and guide, 1946–48; Pilot Agent, U.S. Fish and Wildlife Svc., 1948–56; Commercial fisherman and air taxi operator, 1956–74; Alaska House of Reps., 1959–65; Mgr., Bristol Bay Borough, 1965–67; Alaska Senate, 1967–72; Mayor, Bristol Bay Borough, 1972–74.

Offices Pouch A, State Capitol, Juneau 99811, 907-465-3500.

Election Results

1978 gen.	Jay S. Hammond (R)	49,580	(39%)
	Walter J. Hickel (write-in)	33,555	(26%)
	Chancy Croft (D)	25,656	(20%)
	Tom Kelly (I)	15,656	(12%)
1978 prim.	Jay S. Hammond (R)	31,896	(39%)
	Walter J. Hickel (R)	31,798	(39%)
	Tom Fink (R)	17,487	(22%)
1974 gen.	Jay S. Hammond (R)	45,840	(48%)
	William A. Egan (D)	45,553	(47%)

Rep. Don Young (R) Elected Mar. 6, 1973; b. June 9, 1933, Meridian, Cal.; home, Fort Yukon; Chico St. Col., B.A. 1956.

Career Construction work, 1959; Teacher, 1960–69; Riverboat capt.; Fort Yukon City Cncl., Mayor; Alaska House of Reps., 1966–70; Alaska Senate, 1970–73.

Offices 2331 RHOB, 202-225-5765. Also 115 Fed. Bldg., Anchorage 99501, 907-279-1587.

Committees *Interior and Insular Affairs* (3d). Subcommittees: Mines and Mining; Public Lands and National Parks.

Merchant Marine and Fisheries (5th). Subcommittees: Coast Guard and Navigation; Fisheries and Wildlife Conservation and the Environment.

Group Ratings

	ADA	COPE	PC	LCV	CFA	RPN	NAB	NSI	NTU	ACA	ACU
1980	22	31	13	6	14	—	89	100	55	70	67
1979	11	22	3	16	0	—	—	—	49	71	71
1978	5	53	8	8	5	25	89	100	25	73	84

Key Votes

1) Draft Registn $	AGN	6) Fair Hsg DOJ Enfrc	AGN	11) Cut Socl Incr Dfns $	FOR
2) Ban $ to Nicrgua	—	7) Lim PAC Contrbtns	AGN	12) Hosptl Cost Controls	—
3) Dlay MX Missile	AGN	8) Cap on Food Stmp $	FOR	13) Gasln Ctrls & Allctns	AGN
4) Nuclr Mortorium	AGN	9) New US Dep Edcatn	FOR	14) Lim Wndfll Prof Tax	FOR
5) Alaska Lands Bill	AGN	10) Cut OSHA $	FOR	15) Chryslr Loan Grntee	FOR

Election Results

1980 general	Don Young (R)	114,089	(74%)	($285,594)
	Pat Parnell (D)	39,922	(26%)	($51,065)
1980 primary	Don Young (R)	68,920	(100%)	
1978 general	Don Young (R)	68,811	(55%)	($270,359)
	Patrick Rodey (D)	55,176	(45%)	

ARIZONA

Arizona, the last of the 48 contiguous states to be admitted to the Union, was for years terra incognita to most Americans: a vast expanse of thinly populated desert, with almost as many Indians as whites, a place that impinged very little on the national consciousness. People had heard stories about the fierce Apaches and the sheepherding Navajo, and they knew about Arizona's tourist attractions, especially the Grand Canyon and those Saguaro cactuses behind which the sun set. In the 1930s, as farmers from the Dust Bowl of Oklahoma and Kansas sought a better life in California they found themselves coming across northern Arizona along Route 66, a road celebrated in song and which was the setting of the play *The Petrified Forest*. Americans also knew vaguely that Arizona was a place with copper mines and that it had had its share of western outlaws and lawmen (such as Wyatt Earp). Meanwhile, economically and politically, Arizona was a sleepy state, a constituency that sent to Washington conservative Democrats who concentrated on aiding the state (the most famous of whom was Carl Hayden) and wealthy mine owners (Lewis Douglas).

All this was changed by two inventions that became commercially practical in the years after World War II—the passenger airplane and the air conditioner. The airplane made it possible for tourists to visit Arizona in the winter; those visits gave people in the Midwest the idea that this state, with its warm winters and hot but dry summers, might be a good place to retire. Air service also made Arizona a practical place to do business, and today booming Phoenix is the central focus of such major corporations as Greyhound and Motorola. Air conditioning made Arizona's summer heat bearable. People here like to say that the dry heat is not so bad, but the fact is that for three or four months of the year the heat would be unbearable for most Americans. Airline service and air conditioning became commonplace in the decade after World War II, and that is when Arizona started to be transformed by vast population growth. In 1940 this state had 550,000 people, mostly scattered in small towns. In the early 1960s it passed the one million mark, and by 1980 there were 2,700,000 Arizonans.

These newcomers inhabit an almost entirely new Arizona. There are still remnants of an older Arizona: mining towns such as Bisbee, pleasant country towns such as Prescott that but for the mountains could be in the midwestern plains, and such sun-baked agricultural market centers as Yuma. But today most Arizonans live in the large metropolitan areas: 56% of the state's population is in Phoenix and surrounding Maricopa County and another 21% is in Tucson and Pima County. The new Arizonans like to think of themselves as upholding traditional values, but Phoenix has little of the stability or tradition that are found in more politically liberal places like Boston or Philadelphia. Phoenix proclaims itself, with the glare of chrome and glass, new and contemporary. The main streets proceed straight north and south or east and west, separated one mile apart on the remorseless grid transplanted from the Midwest, until a mountain prevents them from going any farther. Inside an automobile — life in Arizona is very difficult without one — with the windows up and the air conditioning on, Phoenix seems to be an exceedingly silent city, quiet and orderly as cities where you travel by foot never are.

Yet there is something vibrant and chaotic about life in Phoenix — a lack of an established order and, often, of established standards of legality and fair play. The establishment occupies a very thin layer atop local society; there are not any really old families here, and the men who have guided the destiny of the city and state are businessmen and lawyers whose names are not generally known. Underneath, there is plenty of money but few prevailing standards. The lures of Arizona have brought in big corporations, and there are plenty of jobs; contrary to popular impression, Arizona is not just a retirement haven and has about an average percentage of the elderly in its population. But Arizona has also lured many of the unscrupulous con men and fast-buck artists: drifters and grifters who would have been at home in Raymond Chandler's Los Angeles (although not in the more stratified and sophisticated Los Angeles of today). This aspect of life in Phoenix was revealed to the general public a few years ago by the Don Bolles murder case. Bolles, an investigative reporter looking into land-selling scandals, was murdered by a bomb that exploded in his car; a group of substantial businessmen and a small-time hoodlum were accused of the crime and convicted, although their conviction was overturned by the state Supreme Court.

Arizona's sudden growth literally transformed the state's politics. The change — from an old-fashioned Democratic state to a sleek and brash conservative one — is best illustrated by the contrasting careers of the men who have so far been the state's best-known politicians: Carl Hayden and Barry Goldwater. Hayden began his political career as a councilman in Tempe (formerly Hayden's Crossing) in 1902, when Phoenix was just a hot, sleepy depot on the Southern Pacific Railroad. He was a Democrat in a state much of whose small population came mainly from the South and that was both conservative and Democratic. Although Arizona occasionally went Republican in national elections (it never supported a losing presidential candidate until 1960), Hayden and most Arizona Democrats seldom were seriously challenged. Hayden's career was built around bringing federal money and Colorado River water to Arizona, and he used all his seniority — he represented Arizona in Congress from statehood in 1912 until his retirement in 1969 — to that end. His monument was the Central Arizona Project, finally approved in 1968, when he was 91 years old. Interestingly, most of this water goes not to residential Phoenix, but to the agribusiness farmers in the otherwise parched Gila River valley around the city. Jimmy Carter tried to phase out the CAP, but Arizona politicians of all stripes — liberal Democrat Morris Udall and conservative Republicans John Rhodes and Barry Goldwater — rallied to protect Hayden's legacy.

The birth of Arizona's dominant conservative Republicanism can be dated with some precision to the year 1949, when Barry Goldwater, then proprietor of his family's Phoenix department store, was elected to the Phoenix city council. The next year Goldwater helped a Republican win the governorship, and in 1952 Republicans swept the state, and Goldwater himself was elected to the Senate. (The man he beat, Ernest MacFarland, was then Senate majority leader, and his defeat set the stage for Lyndon Johnson's ascent to that post.) Goldwater won reelection by a large margin in 1958, and in a bad year for Republicans nationwide distinguished himself as the sole successful conservative Republican. His frank, often blunt and impolitic articulation of his beliefs brought him so much devotion and volunteer support from all over the country that he won the 1964 Republican presidential nomination despite his malapropisms, his modesty, and his evident distaste for running.

Goldwater's resolute conservatism — he said he wanted to repeal federal programs, not start new ones — was vastly appealing to the new Arizonans of the 1950s and 1960s. These people were mostly white collar workers, professionals, and technicians, from traditional cultural backgrounds in the Midwest and South. Their desire for stability in a patently unstable cultural environment and their affection for the system of free enterprise that enabled them to be more successful and more productive than most of them had ever dreamed: these basic impulses were given detail and thrust in Goldwater's politics. The older "pinto" Democrats were unappealing — dusty, rural, old, and more concerned about a few federal dollars when the real growth of the local economy seemed to come from private investment. These are the kind of voters who have made Metropolitan Phoenix more Republican in the last three presidential elections than Orange County, California. In fact, the years 1958 to 1972 were almost entirely Republican in Arizona — the only state that has gone Republican in every presidential election since 1948, where Republicans held the governorship for all but two years in the 1958–74 period, whose congressional delegation was, with the exception of Morris Udall, all Republican during the entire Nixon and Ford Administrations.

Yet all has not gone well for Arizona Republicans. They lost the governorship in 1974 and 1978; they lost one of the state's Senate seats in 1976 and nearly saw Barry Goldwater lose the other in 1980, despite the Republican trend. In the early and middle 1970s the Democrats here were on the offensive, although they did not win many races; in the late 1970s, the Democrats ran strong candidates who managed to win despite the Republican tide in state and nation.

The most surprising result, however, was Barry Goldwater's near defeat. Coming as it did in a heavily Republican year, it cannot be considered a repudiation of Goldwater's philosophy; Ronald Reagan at the same time was carrying Arizona by a 61%–28% margin over Jimmy Carter. Much more important was the impression that Goldwater was not only old (71, two years older than Reagan), but also tired and no longer enthusiastic. A hip injury has caused him pain for some years, and at his appearance before the 1980 Republican National Convention he looked and sounded more irritable than usual, distracted and prone to inappropriate frankness (he said,"this might be the last Republican convention"). Goldwater has always concentrated more on articulating positions on national issues than on providing services for constituents. Although he is the only Senate Republican who has served before as part of a Republican Senate majority, he does not have all that much seniority, because he gave up his seat to run for president in 1964. Back in Arizona, the senator certainly has many admirers, but he does not often evoke warm feelings from voters; he is a politician who seems more interested in principles than people, and many of his conservative constituents turned out to be more interested in principles than in him.

So in 1980 Goldwater was more vulnerable than many supposed. He had an active Democratic opponent in Bill Schulz, a businessman who claims to own more garden apartments than anyone else in Phoenix. Schulz spent liberally from his own personal fortune, beat a more liberal opponent, Jim McNulty, in the primary, and stressed his West Point background and conservative views on issues. His argument was that Goldwater would not get things done. He came very close to winning, keeping Goldwater uncertain all night even as Ronald Reagan's landslide became readily apparent.

Nevertheless, Goldwater has won more vindication for his views than most politicians. Many of the things he believed and articulated, once considered irresponsible, have now become the conventional wisdom, and the conservative tide he always predicted seems to be occurring now. But Goldwater himself has not been a central figure in the process. He holds no leadership position in the Senate and is not chairman of any regular standing committee —even though less senior Republicans are. His first love is probably the Armed Services Committee; he holds the rank of general in the Air Force, loves to fly, and of course has always been a strong backer of bigger defense (and especially Air Force) budgets (he has been ready on occasion to cut Navy spending). But John Tower of Texas has more seniority on that committee than Goldwater, and so is chairman. Similarly, on the Commerce Committee Goldwater is outranked by the much younger and slightly less senior Bob Packwood of Oregon. Goldwater is a reliable vote for Republicans and a spokesman on defense and intelligence issues; he chairs the Select Committee on Intelligence, whose Republican members are almost all resolutely conservative on these issues. Goldwater believes strongly that the intelligence agencies should not be regulated too closely by the Congress, which means that he will not be as active a chairman as some more critical senators would be.

For Arizona politics, 1982 is a kind of make-or-break year for both the state's Democrats and Republicans. The Democrats' two major officeholders are up for reelection, Senator Dennis DeConcini and Governor Bruce Babbitt; and while both won their first terms with more than narrow margins, both also won under special circumstances that may not be repeated in 1982. Both have substantial talents and proven political appeal, but both must swim against a strong Republican current.

Senator DeConcini ran in 1976 for the seat vacated by Republican Paul Fannin, and he was fortunate enough to encounter one of the most vituperative Republican primary battles in recent American politics. One candidate, Congressman John Conlan, is an evangelical Christian; many of his backers shared his strong religious beliefs. He called for the election of more Christians in politics, infuriating his opponent, Congressman Sam Steiger, who is Jewish, and causing Barry Goldwater, who is not, to charge Conlan with anti-Semitism. Steiger was no less controversial. Once in Arizona he shot two burros, in self-defense, he claimed; the autopsy, however, showed that they had been shot from behind. Steiger won the Republican primary but, seriously wounded, could do no better than split usually heavily Republican Maricopa County even in the general election. Meanwhile, DeConcini capitalized on his own assets. He is from a politically prominent family in Tucson, he had a strong record as prosecutor there, and in an anti-Washington year he could claim strong roots in Arizona.

Winning an election at age 39, DeConcini has the potential of staying in as long as Carl Hayden, but he favors limiting senators to 12 years of service and announced that he would seek no more than two terms. In the Senate he has proceeded sometimes in the Hayden, sometimes in the Goldwater tradition. He does tend toward state problems, but he has also had impact on major national issues. In the Panama Canal Treaty debate DeConcini suddenly became the center of national attention when he advanced his own understanding that the treaty did not bar the United States from using military force to keep the canal open in the future. The Carter Administration had to negotiate carefully with DeConcini, then with Panama's Torrijos, then back to DeConcini again, in order to get the treaty through. DeConcini's vote turned out to be crucial. It also caused him some problems in Arizona. Treaty opponents seemed to see him, not as a brave young senator wringing a concession out of the national administration, but as a sneaky politician who was seeking excuses for supporting the treaty. Recall petitions were circulated for a while, and DeConcini's popularity was not helped.

In the Carter years DeConcini was—as the Canal Treaty episode showed—a key swing vote in the Senate, a Democrat who by no means uniformly followed the liberal bloc but who would support Democratic leadership positions much of the time. He retains an interest in law enforcement, narcotics control, and organized crime, and has a seat on the Judiciary Committee; one of the really touchy issues he must deal with there, and one that stimulates a lot of strong feeling in Arizona, is immigration control. He also has a seat on the Appropriations Committee and its Interior Subcommittee—positions of great importance to Arizona interests. But in running for reelection he cannot claim, as Arizona Democrats such as Hayden used to, that he has overwhelming clout in Washington; he must make his case on the basis of his positions on issues and on the issues he has himself emphasized. There is no shortage of possible Republican challengers to DeConcini in 1982. The list begins with former Congressman John Conlan, who has always had backing from evangelical Christians, and concludes with an unlikely candidate, but one who would be formidable if she runs: Phoenix Mayor Margaret Hance. DeConcini has a strong base in Tucson and will almost certainly carry the smaller counties. But the Phoenix area casts more votes than both put together and media campaigns have become a must in Arizona politics.

Arizona's governor, Bruce Babbitt, came to office in an accidental, almost bizarre way and has distinguished himself as one of the nation's brightest and most thoughtful governors. Elected attorney general in 1974, Babbitt won fame for prosecuting the Bolles case and for winning refunds for consumers in suits against companies that fixed prices. The incumbent governor, Raul Castro, was a Democrat who did not achieve great popularity; in 1977 he was appointed ambassador to Argentina. His successor, Wesley Bolin, was a Democrat who had held the office of Arizona secretary of state since 1948, a man with a fine silvery mane who liked to ride horses and wear western clothes, and whose top advisors were conservative Republicans. Dino DeConcini, brother of the senator and top aide to Castro, was preparing to run against Bolin in the primary when the new governor suddenly died in March 1978. Now Babbitt, who was not running for governor, was governor. Not quite 40, he was personally attractive: he comes from an old Flagstaff family, he goes backpacking with his family in the Grand Canyon, he remains unpretentious and unflappable despite his sudden rise and despite the death threats he received in the Bolles case. Proof that Arizona has been leaning Republican is that Babbitt—a strong Democrat who was even endorsed by the conservative *Arizona Republic*—did not win a particularly impressive margin over his 1978 Republican opponent, Pontiac dealer and former state Senator Evan Meacham, a perennial candidate who had never before come close to winning statewide office.

Babbitt, although governor of a state that is far away from most Americans, has developed a somewhat national reputation. He served on the commission appointed by President Carter to investigate the Three Mile Island nuclear plant accident and drew on his own background as an engineering student to help draft a report that reached definite conclusions and was widely accepted as responsible. He began his Arizona political career with a reputation as a liberal. He has since achieved national notice as one who questions liberal shibboleths. As a governor who must administer federal programs, he has attacked them as requiring too much paperwork and giving too much control to Washington. When Ronald Reagan announced his budget cuts in early 1981, Babbitt alone among governors came forward with an alternative: the idea that some functions that the states had traditionally handled and that Washington still largely funded should be abandoned by the federal government while other functions that had long had federal involvement should not necessarily be cut. This is a position more rigorous intellectually than that of the administration or those of its chief critics and is typical of Babbitt's originality and verve. He must run for reelection in 1982, and at this writing the identity of his Republican opponent is far from clear. Given Arizona's Republican leanings, however, even a governor with as many claims to reelection as Babbitt cannot be assured of winning. He has been mentioned as a candidate for senator, but he would surely not run until at least 1986, when Goldwater's seat is up, and that is still a long way away.

A word should be said about Arizona's House delegation. What other state with such a small delegation has had two leaders, of different parties, of the brainpower, clout, and integrity of Morris Udall and John Rhodes? Udall, the chairman of the House Interior Committee, has been one of the most legislatively productive members of the House; he beat back a strong conservative challenge and was reelected with an increased margin in 1980. Rhodes stepped down as House minority leader in 1981 but retains an important role in the House. Arizona has gained one House seat in every census since 1950, and 1980 is no exception. The new district lines will be drawn by the Republican legislature, which will likely try to create a new Republican seat in the Phoenix area. The current 3d and 4th districts, both partially in the Phoenix area and partially in the outer counties, would lose substantial numbers of voters in the Phoenix area but probably would not be altered significantly in political leanings.

Census Data Pop. (1980 final) 2,717,866, up 53% in 1970s: 1.20% of U.S. total, 29th largest. Central city, 41%; suburban, 35%. Median 4-person family income, 1978, $20,863, 102% of U.S., 19th highest.

1979 Share of Federal Tax Burden $4,238,000,000; 0.94% of U.S. total, 31st largest.

1979 Share of Federal Outlays $5,538,668,000; 1.20% of U.S. total, 28th largest.

DOD	$1,519,313,000	22d	(1.43%)	HEW	$1,843,600,000	32d	(1.03%)
DOE	$2,855,000	43d	(0.02%)	ERDA	$1,026,000	43d	(0.03%)
HUD	$48,931,000	35th	(0.74%)	NASA	$18,854,000	19th	(0.40%)
VA	$309,298,000	26th	(1.49%)	DOT	$174,604,000	29th	(1.06%)
EPA	$66,892,000	25th	(1.26%)	DOC	$14,268,000	36th	(0.45%)
DOI	$473,080,000	3d	(8.52%)	USDA	$229,428,000	38th	(0.95%)

Economic Base Finance, insurance, and real estate; electrical equipment and supplies, especially electronic components and accessories; agriculture, notably cattle, cotton lint, lettuce, and dairy products; metal mining, especially copper ores; machinery, especially office and computing machines; food and kindred products; tourism.

Political Lineup Governor, Bruce E. Babbitt (D). Senators, Barry Goldwater (R) and Dennis DeConcini (D). Representatives, 4 (2 R and 2 D); 5 in 1982. State Senate, 30 (16 R and 14 D); State House of Representatives, 60 (43 R and 17 D).

The Voters

Registration 1,121,169 Total.
Employment profile 1970 White collar, 51%. Blue collar, 32%. Service, 14%. Farm, 3%.

Ethnic groups   Black 1980, 3%. Hispanic 1980, 19%. Am. Ind. 1980, 6%. Asian 1980, 1%. Total foreign stock 1970, 17%. Canada, Germany, 1% each.

Presidential Vote

1980	Reagan (R)	529,688	(61%)
	Carter (D)	246,843	(28%)
	Anderson (I)	76,952	(9%)
1976	Ford (R)	418,642	(56%)
	Carter (D)	295,602	(40%)

SENATORS

Sen. Barry Goldwater (R) Elected 1968, seat up 1986; b. Jan. 1, 1909, Phoenix; home, Phoenix; U. of Ariz., 1928.

Career Maj. Gen., USAFR, 1937–67; Phoenix City Cncl., 1949–51; U.S. Sen., 1952–64; Repub. nominee for Pres., 1964.

Offices 337 RSOB, 202-224-2235. Also 5429 Fed. Bldg., Phoenix 85025, 602-261-4086, and Suite 7-G, Fed. Bldg., Tucson 85701, 602-792-6334.

Committees *Armed Services* (3d). Subcommittees: Tactical Warfare (Chairman); Strategic and Theatre Nuclear Forces; Preparedness.

Commerce, Science and Transportation (2d). Subcommittees: Aviation; Communications; Science, Technology and Space.

Select Committee on Indian Affairs (2d).

Select Committee on Intelligence (Chairman).

Group Ratings

	ADA	COPE	PC	LCV	CFA	RPN	NAB	NSI	NTU	ACA	ACU
1980	0	18	20	12	7	—	100	86	63	100	91
1979	5	6	12	—	5	—	—	—	59	95	92
1978	10	12	23	8	15	33	100	90	57	95	89

Key Votes

1) Draft Registn $	FOR	6) Fair Housng Cloture	AGN	11) Cut Socl Incr Defns	FOR
2) Ban $ to Nicrgua	—	7) Ban $ Rape Abortns	—	12) Income Tax Indexing	—
3) Dlay MX Missile	AGN	8) Cap on Food Stmp $	FOR	13) Lim Spdg 21% GNP	FOR
4) Nuclr Mortorium	AGN	9) New US Dep Edcatn	AGN	14) Incr Wndfll Prof Tax	—
5) Alaska Lands Bill	FOR	10) Cut OSHA Inspctns	—	15) Chryslr Loan Grntee	—

Election Results

1980 general	Barry Goldwater (R)	432,371	(50%)	($949,992)
	Bill Schulz (D)	422,972	(49%)	($2,073,232)
1980 primary	Barry Goldwater (R)	140,765	(100%)	
1974 general	Barry Goldwater (R)	320,396	(58%)	($394,042)
	Jonathan Marshall (D)	229,523	(42%)	($129,260)

Sen. Dennis DeConcini (D) Elected 1976, seat up 1982; b. May 8, 1937, Tucson; home, Tucson; U. of Ariz., B.A. 1959, LL.B. 1963.

Career Army Adjutant General Corps, 1959–60; Practicing atty., 1963–65, 1968–73; Special Counsel, Admin. Asst. to Gov. Samuel P. Goddard, 1965–67; Pima Co. Atty., 1973–76.

Offices 3230 DSOB, 202-224-4521. Also Ariz. Bank Bldg., 101 N. 1st St., Suite 1634, Phoenix 85003, 602-261-6756, and 301 W. Congress, Tucson 85701, 602-792-6831.

Committees *Appropriations* (13th). Subcommittees: Foreign Operations; Interior; State, Justice, Commerce, and the Judiciary; Treasury, Postal Service, and General Government.

Judiciary (6th). Subcommittees: Constitution; Immigration and Refugee Policy.

Veterans' Affairs (4th). *Select Committee on Indian Affairs* (3d).

Group Ratings

	ADA	COPE	PC	LCV	CFA	RPN	NAB	NSI	NTU	ACA	ACU
1980	67	67	23	34	20	—	46	60	40	39	30
1979	26	42	46	—	38	—	—	—	33	64	47
1978	35	58	55	43	30	60	64	40	27	39	33

Key Votes

1) Draft Registn $	FOR	6) Fair Housng Cloture	FOR	11) Cut Socl Incr Defns	AGN
2) Ban $ to Nicrgua	FOR	7) Ban $ Rape Abortns	FOR	12) Income Tax Indexing	FOR
3) Dlay MX Missile	AGN	8) Cap on Food Stmp $	FOR	13) Lim Spdg 21% GNP	AGN
4) Nuclr Mortorium	FOR	9) New US Dep Edcatn	FOR	14) Incr Wndfll Prof Tax	FOR
5) Alaska Lands Bill	FOR	10) Cut OSHA Inspctns	FOR	15) Chryslr Loan Grntee	AGN

Election Results

1976 general	Dennis DeConcini (D)	400,334	(54%)	($597,405)
	Sam Steiger (R)	321,236	(43%)	($679,384)
1976 primary	Dennis DeConcini (D)	121,423	(53%)	
	Carolyn Warner (D)	71,612	(32%)	
	Wade Church (D)	34,266	(15%)	
1970 general	Paul Fannin (R)	228,284	(56%)	
	Sam Grossman (D)	179,512	(44%)	

GOVERNOR

Gov. Bruce E. Babbitt (D) Elected 1978, term expires Jan. 1983; b. June 27, 1938, Flagstaff; Notre Dame U., B.S., Marshall Scholar, U. of Newcastle, England, M.S. 1963, Harvard U., J.D. 1965.

Career Spec. Asst. to the Dir. of VISTA, 1965–67; Practicing atty., 1967–74; Atty. Gen. of Ariz., 1974–78.

Offices Capitol West Wing, 9th flr., Phoenix 85007, 602-255-4331.

Election Results

1978 gen.	Bruce E. Babbitt (D)	282,605	(52%)
	Evan Mecham (R)	241,093	(45%)
1978 prim.	Bruce E. Babbitt (D)	108,548	(77%)
	One other (D)	32,785	(23%)
1974 gen.	Raul H. Castro (D)	278,375	(50%)
	Russ Williams (R)	273,674	(50%)

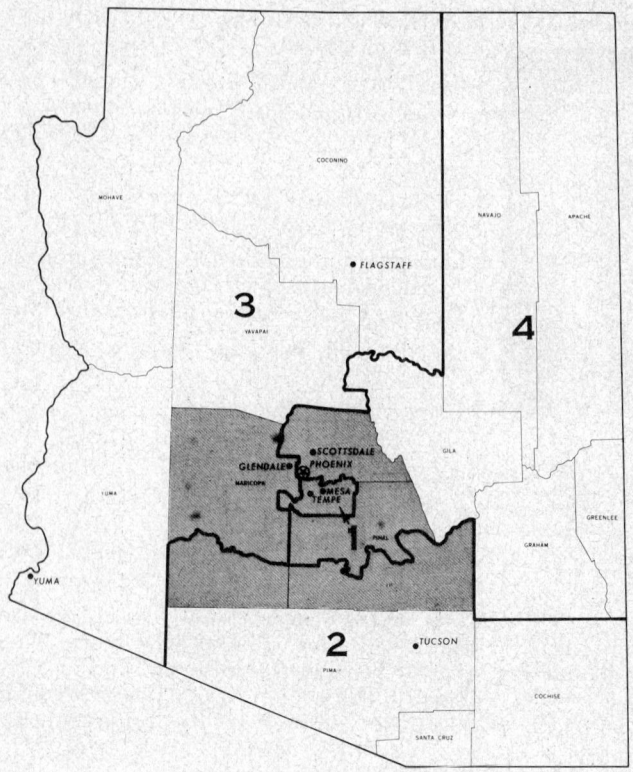

FIRST DISTRICT

Phoenix is one, perhaps the prototype, of those instant cities in what Kevin Phillips named the Sun Belt. It is almost totally the creation of the air-conditioned years after World War II. In 1940 Phoenix had 65,000 residents; in 1950, 106,000; by 1970 the metropolitan area was nearly one million and in 1980, 1½ million. Once a sleepy stop on the Southern Pacific Railroad, Phoenix is now one of the nation's major metropolitan areas, the headquarters of such national corporations as Greyhound and the home of national figures such as Barry Goldwater. There is little evidence of tradition or heritage here: almost every building is new, and the bows to Indian or Mexican styles are clearly in the idiom of the 1970s. Phoenix is considered by many people to be a retirement village, a sort of St. Petersburg West, and there are major retirement centers, e.g., Del Webb's Sun City, northwest across the desert. But statistically Phoenix is a young city, drawing fewer retirees in search of sun than young energetic people in search of jobs and sudden riches. Little heavy industry exists here, many low-paying service jobs do; the real boom is in white collar industries.

Technologically advanced, Phoenix is politically conservative. No other major metropolitan area in the country has consistently voted so heavily Republican. Part of the reason is in the conservative attitudes of retirees, at least those well enough off to afford to live here; part is in the fact that people in technical occupations seem to have an affinity for the certainties and hard edges of conservatism, just as those in what we call the humanities and social sciences tend to prefer the generosity and lack of precision that often characterize American liberalism. For whatever reasons, Phoenix's Republicanism is not in doubt. There are Democratic areas here: the black and Mexican neighborhoods south of downtown, laced with gas-station-sized factories and with often unpaved streets, crisscrossed by railroad tracks. But blacks and Mexicans do not form a major part of the Phoenix area's population, and migration seems to be heavily white; and hardly an Anglo white precinct in this city regularly goes Democratic. It is like some of the industrial cities of the Midwest in the 1920s, from whose voting returns one can find no evidence of a white working-class consciousness or of ethnic neighborhoods; if there is some variation in local elections, there is a virtually identical response to national contests.

Phoenix has always been the heartland of Goldwater conservatism in Arizona. It was Phoenix's growth that made possible Goldwater's initial victories in the 1950s and the conservative successes of the years after that. One of the original Goldwater conservatives is 1st district Congressman John Rhodes. In 1952, when Goldwater was first elected to the Senate, Rhodes became the first Republican ever elected to the House from Arizona. He is now one of only two Republican House members who can remember what it was like serving as part of a Republican majority there. Rhodes rose quietly in the House hierarchy, becoming the second-ranking minority member of Appropriations and chairman of the House Republican Policy Committee and, in 1973, when Gerald Ford became vice president, Rhodes was elected House minority leader. It was a kind of nadir for the Republican Party, about to suffer big losses in the 1974 election and seeing the initiative swing almost wholly to the Democrats. Rhodes himself faced unexpected trouble at home. The 1st district fashioned by the legislature after the 1970 census gave him all of Phoenix's black and Mexican precincts, and in 1972, 1974, and 1976 he was held to less than 60% of the vote. In 1974 he had only 51%, with 7% going to an antiabortion independent candidate.

The years since have seen a revival of the Republican Party in the House and nation, a process in which Rhodes has played some part. In the House he was less accommodating to the Democrats than Ford had sometimes been, and under Rhodes's leadership a cadre of aggressive young Republicans began challenging the Democrats more vigorously—and calling for tougher leadership than they thought they were getting under Rhodes. In the late 1970s, increasingly the Republicans, not the Democrats, were crackling with new ideas and coming up with new legislative initiatives for solutions to the nation's problems. Rhodes was not such an initiator himself, but he was astute enough to recognize such initiatives as good partisan measures when they came along, and he probably deserves some of the credit for the fact that they were endorsed by every segment of what previously had been a fractious Republican Party. During the Carter years particularly Rhodes helped to move the House away from what he had described in his early 1970s book as *The Futile System*.

Nonetheless, Rhodes decided to step down as minority leader after the 1980 election. (He said that if Republicans won a majority, he would run for speaker.) One reason was criticism he was receiving from younger members, who wanted Democrats challenged more aggressively than was in Rhodes's nature. They found him perhaps too much of a Republican of another generation, intelligent but not inclined to challenge conventional liberal wisdom as much as they would like. Another reason may simply have been the pace of the job. Rhodes quit the leadership at age 64, when many successful men seek lighter schedules. He serves now on the House Rules Committee—a good place for the Republicans to use his talents—

and he has some voice in the leadership councils if he wants it. Rhodes had no trouble winning reelection in 1978 or 1980 and could continue to serve if he wants to, but he has announced that he will retire in 1982.

The 1st district as currently constituted includes the southern half, approximately, of the city of Phoenix, including most of its slum neighborhoods, but some prosperous middle- and upper-income neighborhoods as well. To the east, across the Salt River, are the suburban communities of Tempe, the home of Arizona State University, and Mesa, site of a large Mormon temple. As suggested by their major institutions, Tempe leans a little liberal (for Arizona) in elections while Mesa is solidly conservative. Arizona's district lines will have to be changed and a new district added for 1982. The heavily Republican legislature will probably not choose to retain the current contours, since if the 1st is reduced in size and still left with all the minority precincts, it stands a chance of going Democratic sometime in the 1980s. What the legislators will probably do, instead of having one district running east–west across southern Maricopa County, is to run two districts north–south from the southern part of the Phoenix area to the northern part of the city. Both such districts would likely be heavily Republican — more Republican than the current 1st district — and would elect either Rhodes or whoever is nominated in the Republican primary.

Census Data   Pop. (1980 final) 624,551, up 41% in 1970s. Median family income, 1970, $9,126, 95% of U.S.

The Voters
  Employment profile 1970   White collar, 52%. Blue collar, 32%. Service, 14%. Farm, 2%.
  Ethnic groups   Black 1980, 5%. Hispanic 1980, 16%. Am. Ind. 1980, 2%. Asian 1980, 1%. Total foreign stock 1970, 16%. Canada, Germany, 2% each.

Presidential Vote

1980	Reagan (R)	118,001	(62%)
	Carter (D)	51,119	(27%)
	Anderson (I)	16,390	(9%)
1976	Ford (R)	99,375	(59%)
	Carter (D)	62,632	(37%)

Rep. John J. Rhodes (R) Elected 1952; b. Sept. 18, 1916, Council Grove, Kans.; home, Mesa; Kans. St. U., B.S. 1938, Harvard U., LL.B. 1941.

Career   Air Force, WWII; Practicing atty., 1949–53; V.P., Harm & Home Life Ins. Co.

Offices   2310 RHOB, 202-225-2635. Also 1930 Valley Ctr., Phoenix 85073, 602-261-3181.

Committee   *Rules* (5th). Subcommittee: Rules of the House.

Group Ratings

	ADA	COPE	PC	LCV	CFA	RPN	NAB	NSI	NTU	ACA	ACU
1980	0	8	17	—	7	—	89	90	44	86	69
1979	11	10	10	7	4	—	—	—	47	81	82
1978	15	13	13	15	18	89	100	100	21	70	90

Key Votes

1) Draft Registn $	—	6) Fair Hsg DOJ Enfrc	AGN	11) Cut Socl Incr Dfns $	FOR
2) Ban $ to Nicrgua	FOR	7) Lim PAC Contrbtns	AGN	12) Hosptl Cost Controls	—
3) Dlay MX Missile	AGN	8) Cap on Food Stmp $	FOR	13) Gasln Ctrls & Allctns	AGN
4) Nuclr Mortorium	AGN	9) New US Dep Edcatn	AGN	14) Lim Wndfll Prof Tax	FOR
5) Alaska Lands Bill	AGN	10) Cut OSHA $	FOR	15) Chryslr Loan Grntee	AGN

Election Results

1980 general	John J. Rhodes (R)	136,961	(73%)	($191,809)
	Steve Jancek (D)	40,045	(21%)	($0)
1980 primary	John J. Rhodes (R)	34,185	(100%)	
1978 general	John J. Rhodes (R)	81,108	(71%)	($201,177)
	Ken Graves (D)	33,178	(29%)	($6,306)

SECOND DISTRICT

Tucson is the second of Arizona's two cities, a place overshadowed demographically and politically by Phoenix, although in another, smaller western state Tucson would be the metropolis. The city has about one-third the population of Phoenix and a rather different economic base. Like Phoenix, it is not primarily a resort or retirement center, although it does have such communities; but Tucson is more blue collar than the capital city. It does not have so many corporate headquarters or high technology industries. A major industry in these parts is copper. Although it is not actually mined in Tucson, most of the U.S. copper supply comes from within a 100-mile radius of the city, and many of the services ancillary to the copper industry are here. Tucson also has some notable defense plants and it is the home of the University of Arizona.

Tucson has always been the more Democratic of Arizona's two cities, and it is today. In state elections it tends to be Democratic and Dennis DeConcini and Bruce Babbitt have both emerged from Tucson with big margins. But in national matters Tucson has been moving perceptibly to the right. It has been growing rapidly, and most of the new migrants tend to be prosperous, conservative folks from the Midwest; the comfortable neighborhoods of east Tucson and in the foothills of the mountains north of the city deliver Republican margins almost as high as comparable neighborhoods in Phoenix. In the close presidential election of 1976, Tucson and surrounding Pima County went for Gerald Ford; in 1980, they gave Ronald Reagan a 50%-34% margin over Jimmy Carter.

That trend has meant trouble for Morris Udall, who as congressman from the 2d district of Arizona represents Pima County and southeastern Arizona, including the border town of Nogales and the copper mining town of Bisbee (where the big Phelps Dodge mine closed down in the middle 1970s) and the ghost town of Tombstone in Cochise County. Udall is by all measures a politician of national stature. This is not simply because he was a presidential candidate, although he did turn out to be Jimmy Carter's most enduring rival for the 1976 Democratic nomination and finished second in seven primaries from New Hampshire to South Dakota; he missed finishing first by heartbreaking margins several times. Udall made himself somewhat the liberal standard-bearer in that race, although he avoided the term liberal.

But his real national standing derives more from his work in the House, where he is one of the hardest-working and most accomplished legislators the Congress has seen in some time.

As much as anyone, he fashioned our campaign finance reform laws, which despite much carping have eliminated many abuses and still have allowed candidates to raise enough to communicate their messages. For years he labored in the dull vineyards of the Post Office and Civil Service Committee, setting pay for government workers and trying to reform the Post Office; in 1978 he achieved the considerable success of putting together, with the help of the Carter Administration and fellow committee members Edward Derwinski and William Ford, the civil service reform bill that at last moves in the direction of making government employees more accountable.

Udall's most noted efforts have probably been in the environmental field. His brother Stewart was Secretary of the Interior in the Kennedy–Johnson Administration (Morris Udall ran for Stewart's seat when he resigned from Congress to take the post); and Congressman Udall, like many western members, got a seat on the Interior Committee. In 1977, he faced the delicious choice between chairmanships; he passed up the Post Office and took Interior. That body has jurisdiction over national parks, mining and mineral exploration of government land, Indian tribes, and American overseas possessions. Udall has always been counted as a friend by environmentalists, and he has strong interests in many of these areas; he has worked, for example, to maintain as federal parklands some of the mountain ranges around Tucson. During the Carter years Udall had several major accomplishments. In the 95th Congress he pushed through a comprehensive strip mining law, a measure necessarily of great complexity which has not since been assailed. In the 96th Congress he got through the House and enacted into law the Alaska Lands Bill, setting aside millions of acres of Alaska's lands and allowing others to be explored for minerals. This was the foremost achievement of the environmental movement in the Congress in the late 1970s, and Udall got it through the House not once but twice (the Senate killed it the first time).

Udall has also had his disappointments legislatively. He was unable to persuade the House, despite its then heavy Democratic majorities, to favor universal voter registration by postcard and other devices. His proposals for public financing of congressional elections have gone nowhere and are now dead. He ran into heavy opposition at home to his proposals to reform federal mining laws generally; there were charges that his bill would shut down Arizona's copper industry. Udall backed down on this issue, but it still hurt him at home; he lost normally Democratic Cochise County in 1978 and 1980.

Indeed, overall, Udall's national stature seems to have hurt rather than helped his standing in the 2d district. His opponents have regularly charged that he was a liberal after his 1976 presidential campaign, and the fact that he did best in New England and the Upper Midwest — places very different in their attitudes from Arizona — may have hurt him back home. His role on national issues may look constructive in Washington, but some Arizona voters question whether he should spend so much time on issues that primarily affect Alaska. In 1976 Udall's percentage in the general election fell, even though his Republican opponent dropped out of the race. In 1978, a Republican who admitted running misleading ads nonetheless held Udall to 54% of the vote — his lowest percentage since he first won in 1961. In 1980 Republicans targeted this seat. But by this time Udall had learned how to fight back. He worked hard at serving the district's needs, returned often, and took pains to educate new residents on what he had done for Tucson and southern Arizona and how he had killed efforts to stop the Central Arizona Project. Despite a stronger Republican campaign than in the previous two elections, Udall's margin rose to 58%–40%.

That suggests that Udall is less likely to be challenged seriously in the future. There is one problem for him; he announced during the 1980 campaign that he has Parkinson's disease, which causes his hands to shake but otherwise is not likely to have significant effects for years. The 1980 verdict suggests that 2d district voters still regard Udall as able to do his job, and he remains one of the most influential and productive members of the House. Redistricting, even though it will be done by a Republican legislature, may help him, since the easiest way to reduce the size of the 2d district is to remove Cochise County; it is not likely the Democratic Governor Bruce Babbitt will allow the legislature to split Tucson and its Democratic votes between two districts.

Census Data   Pop. (1980 final) 658,936, up 49% in 1970s. Median family income, 1970, $8,832, 92% of U.S.

The Voters

Employment profile 1970   White collar, 51%. Blue collar, 32%. Service, 15%. Farm, 2%.
Ethnic groups   Black 1980, 3%. Hispanic 1980, 24%. Am. Ind. 1980, 3%. Asian 1980, 1%. Total foreign stock 1970, 23%. Canada, Germany, 2% each.

Presidential Vote

1980	Reagan (R)	111,164	(51%)
	Carter (D)	75,694	(35%)
	Anderson (I)	27,721	(13%)
1976	Ford (R)	91,113	(50%)
	Carter (D)	85,224	(46%)

Rep. Morris K. Udall (D) Elected May 2, 1961; b. June 15, 1922, St. Johns; home, Tucson; U. of Ariz., J.D. 1949.

Career Air Force, WWII; Pro basketball player, Denver Nuggets, 1948–49; Practicing atty., 1949–61; Pima Co. Atty., 1952–54.

Offices 235 CHOB, 202-225-4065. Also 301 W. Congress, Tucson 85701, 602-792-6404.

Committees *Interior and Insular Affairs* (Chairman). Subcommittees: Energy and the Environment (Chairman); Insular Affairs; Water and Power Resources.

Post Office and Civil Service (2d). Subcommittees: Civil Service; Investigations.

Group Ratings

	ADA	COPE	PC	LCV	CFA	RPN	NAB	NSI	NTU	ACA	ACU
1980	61	67	53	59	50	—	10	25	16	14	9
1979	74	79	73	85	63	—	—	—	26	9	11
1978	70	79	73	66	73	58	0	10	9	13	13

Key Votes

1) Draft Registn $	AGN	6) Fair Hsg DOJ Enfrc	FOR	11) Cut Socl Incr Dfns $	AGN
2) Ban $ to Nicrgua	AGN	7) Lim PAC Contrbtns	FOR	12) Hosptl Cost Controls	AGN
3) Dlay MX Missile	—	8) Cap on Food Stmp $	AGN	13) Gasln Ctrls & Allctns	FOR
4) Nuclr Mortorium	FOR	9) New US Dep Edcatn	FOR	14) Lim Wndfll Prof Tax	AGN
5) Alaska Lands Bill	FOR	10) Cut OSHA $	AGN	15) Chryslr Loan Grntee	FOR

Election Results

1980 general	Morris K. Udall (D)	127,786	(58%)	($763,650)
	Richard H. Huff (R)	88,653	(40%)	($696,954)
1980 primary	Morris K. Udall (D)	43,448	(100%)	
1978 general	Morris K. Udall (D)	67,878	(53%)	($294,849)
	Tom Richey (R)	58,697	(45%)	($134,130)

THIRD DISTRICT

Arizona's 3d congressional district is a hybrid, a combination of part of the heavily Republican Phoenix area and of the sparsely populated, traditionally Democratic counties of the western half of the state. The district includes Yuma, an agricultural town on the sun-baked banks of the lower Colorado River, whose last waters irrigate the desert lands in the area (the Colorado's water is used so intensively that only a trickle actually flows into the Gulf of California). The district includes the Grand Canyon and the small city of Flagstaff nearby; it has some Indians, although most of the Navajo live primarily in the 4th district to the east. The northwestern part of the state was almost empty 20 years ago. Today it boasts such towns as Lake Havasu City, a retirement development whose owner purchased London Bridge from Britain and plopped it down in the Arizona desert. Prescott, an older town where almost everyone wears western hats, has been a Republican stronghold so long that it is the place where Barry Goldwater has begun each of his campaigns. The tradition in this part of the state (except for Prescott) is Democratic, but the recent trend, mostly because of new migrants, has been Republican.

Within the current boundaries of the 3d, nearly 60% of the votes are cast in the Phoenix metropolitan area. The 3d includes the whole west side of Phoenix and just wings the city's small black and Mexican–American neighborhoods. Phoenix is a new city; here on the west side the vacant lots between the small stucco houses and the gaudy roadside establishments grow easily back into small patches of Arizona desert. The 3d does not take in the richest parts of Phoenix; there is less grass here (water is expensive) and fewer palm trees. Communities are segregated by age as much as anything else. Younger people with families live near the Christown shopping center, one of Phoenix's largest. Farther out is Del Webb's Sun City, which allows no residents under 50, no schoolchildren, and which spreads over acres of former desert. This part of the Phoenix area really has no political tradition; almost no one lived here 30 years ago. It votes heavily Republican in national elections, almost as strongly Republican as the expensive and stylish suburb of Scottsdale across town.

Nonetheless the 3d district has a congressman who is at least nominally a Democrat. When Republican Sam Steiger left the House to run for the Senate in 1976, he left the seat wide open, and there was naturally some competition. Ordinarily the Republican nominee, a state senator, would have been expected to win. But another Republican state senator was running as an independent (he ultimately won 10% of the vote), and the victor by a narrow margin in the Democratic primary was Bob Stump, a state senator of very conservative views. Stump had represented a low-income area at the ragged western edge of Metropolitan Phoenix, the kind of place where fundamentalist religion is far more attractive than liberal political doctrine. In Congress Stump has had one of the most conservative voting records of any Democrat; his voting record is almost indistinguishable from those of most Republicans. He serves on Armed Services and Veterans' Affairs and is predictably hawkish. Indeed, there was talk that he would run in 1980 for Barry Goldwater's seat as a Republican—although nothing came of that when Goldwater decided to seek another term himself. Stump got more opposition in 1978 in the Democratic primary (he was held to 61%) than in the general election; he was reelected easily in 1980.

Stump seems to have found a successful formula; the only question is whether redistricting will hurt him. The Republican legislature might try to slice up his district so that a real Republican could win it. The easier route would be to excise much of the fast-growing Phoenix area and make it part of the new 5th district Arizona gets from the 1980 census, a district that almost certainly will go Republican. In the meantime, Stump would presumably hold the seat, but should he not seek reelection a Republican would be the favorite to win.

Census Data Pop. (1980 final) 745,635, up 68% in 1970s. Median family income, 1970, $8,964, 94% of U.S.

The Voters

Employment profile 1970 White collar, 46%. Blue collar, 36%. Service, 13%. Farm, 5%.
Ethnic groups Black 1980, 2%. Hispanic 1980, 17%. Am. Ind. 1980, 4%. Asian 1980, 1%. Total foreign stock 1970, 15%. Canada, Germany, 1% each.

Presidential Vote

1980	Reagan (R)	148,411	(65%)
	Carter (D)	60,656	(26%)
	Anderson (I)	15,468	(7%)
1976	Ford (R)	111,116	(58%)
	Carter (D)	74,467	(39%)

Rep. Bob Stump (D) Elected 1976; b. Apr. 4, 1927, Phoenix; home, Tolleson; Ariz. St. U., B.S. 1951.

Career Navy, WWII; Cotton and grain farmer; Ariz. House of Reps, 1958–66; Ariz. Senate, 1967–76, Senate Pres., 1975–76.

Offices 211 CHOB, 202-225-4576. Also Fed. Bldg., Phoenix 85025, 606-261-6923.

Committees *Armed Services* (16th). Subcommittees: Readiness; Research and Development.

Veterans' Affairs (14th). Subcommittee: Oversight and Investigations.

Select Committee on Intelligence (9th). Subcommittee: Program and Budget Authorization.

Group Ratings

	ADA	COPE	PC	LCV	CFA	RPN	NAB	NSI	NTU	ACA	ACU
1980	0	17	13	13	14		100	100	73	83	89
1979	0	10	10	3	4	—	—	—	72	96	97
1978	5	10	18	0	9	56	100	100	60	100	91

Key Votes

1) Draft Registn $	FOR	6) Fair Hsg DOJ Enfrc	AGN	11) Cut Socl Incr Dfns $	FOR
2) Ban $ to Nicrgua	FOR	7) Lim PAC Contrbtns	AGN	12) Hosptl Cost Controls	AGN
3) Dlay MX Missile	AGN	8) Cap on Food Stmp $	FOR	13) Gasln Ctrls & Allctns	AGN
4) Nuclr Mortorium	AGN	9) New US Dep Edcatn	AGN	14) Lim Wndfll Prof Tax	FOR
5) Alaska Lands Bill	AGN	10) Cut OSHA $	FOR	15) Chryslr Loan Grntee	AGN

Election Results

1980 general	Bob Stump (D)	141,448	(64%)	($88,979)
	Bob Croft (R)	65,845	(30%)	($2,799)
1980 primary	Bob Stump (D)	36,028	(100%)	
1978 general	Bob Stump (D)	111,850	(85%)	($198,085)
	Kathleen Cooke (Libertarian)	19,813	(15%)	

FOURTH DISTRICT

The 4th congressional district of Arizona is the northeast corner of the state, running from the Four Corners region and the Navajo Reservation to the posh suburb of Scottsdale nestling behind Phoenix's Camelback Mountain. The Four Corners presents the harsher side of the west: a windswept land where coal is strip-mined and giant electrical generating plants belch black smoke into the sky. This is good business for the Navajo but also the kind of degradation of a pristine environment that the Clean Air Act in its present form tries to prevent. The Navajo are Arizona's and the nation's most populous tribe, and within the bounds of their reservation (and of the Hopi Reservation it surrounds) the 1980 census counted 74,000 residents—up substantially from ten years before. South of the reservation are the gas station stops along Route 66, and below them the mountains where towns have such picturesque names as Show Low (relic of a long-ago poker game) and Snowflake. In the southeastern part of the district are some of Arizona's copper mining towns, places such as Globe and Morenci, isolated from the rest of the state. These parts of the 4th district are among the more Democratic parts of Republican Arizona. Voter turnout among the Navajo rose dramatically in the 1970s, and the beneficiaries have mostly been Democrats; the copper mining towns are staunchly Democratic, although they have little impact since their population is small and declining.

However, these two areas have only 30% of the votes in the 4th district; the rest are cast in Maricopa County, the Phoenix metropolitan area. The 4th includes most of Scottsdale and Paradise Valley, Phoenix's most expensive and prestigious suburbs, and the city of Phoenix itself north of Camelback Mountain and west of one of the city's main dividing streets. This is probably the most heavily Republican part of a Republican state, a prosperous area whose citizens are very proud of what they and the private enterprise system have achieved and who are almost totally innocent of the liberal guilt that affects so deeply the attitudes of rich people in such places as New York and Boston.

Given the population balance, the 4th could be expected to be heavily Republican, and since its creation in 1972 it has elected only Republican congressmen. Yet it has been seriously contested by Democrats twice and may be the scene of a serious contest in the 1980s, depending on redistricting. In 1972 Democrat Jack Brown and Republican John Conlan made this the most expensive House race in the nation; Conlan won narrowly and went on to run for the Senate in 1976. That year, Democrat Tony Mason ran an expensive race, carrying the outer counties but came up 719 votes short of beating Republican Eldon Rudd, who had big margins in Maricopa County.

Rudd has held the district ever since. A former FBI agent, he is considered a dull speaker and campaigner, but his record is solidly conservative by almost every measure, and he has been mentioned on occasion as a candidate for statewide office. He could, for example, run against Senator Dennis DeConcini in 1982 and would have to be conceded a reasonable chance of winning. In the 4th, Rudd has not had serious competition since 1976, but he could be hurt by redistricting. In 1980, against an underfinanced opponent, he won only 52% of the vote in the outer counties, as compared to 67% in Maricopa County. He still won a big victory; but if redistricting removes much of the Maricopa part of the district, as is necessary if a new Phoenix area district is to be created, the 4th will move much closer to the marginal category. Extrapolating from the 1980 result. Rudd's 63% would look more like 57%. In those circumstances, it is possible that the Democrats would make a greater effort and might have a chance of pulling off an upset.

Census Data   Pop. (1980 final) 688,744, up 55% in 1970s.Median family income, 1970, $9,886, 103% of U.S.

The Voters

   Employment profile 1970   White collar, 56%. Blue collar, 29%. Service, 12%. Farm, 3%.
   Ethnic groups   Black 1980, 2%. Hispanic 1980, 9%. Am. Ind. 1980, 14%. Asian 1980, 1%. Total foreign stock 1970, 13%. Canada, Germany, 1% each.

Presidential Vote

1980	Reagan (R)	151,495	(65%)
	Carter (D)	58,941	(25%)
	Anderson (I)	16,784	(7%)
1976	Ford (R)	116,475	(60%)
	Carter (D)	72,578	(37%)

Rep. Eldon Rudd (R) Elected 1976; b. July 15, 1920, Camp Verde; home, Scottsdale; Ariz. St. U., B.A. 1947, U. of Ariz., J.D. 1949.

Career USMC, WWII; Practicing atty., 1949; Spec. Investigator, FBI, 1950–70; Maricopa Co. Bd. of Supervisors, 1972–76.

Offices 1110 LHOB, 202-225-3361. Also 6009 Fed. Bldg., 230 N. 1st Ave., Phoenix 85025, 602-261-4803.

Committee *Appropriations* (14th). Subcommittees: Energy and Water Development; Treasury, Postal Service, and General Government.

Group Ratings

	ADA	COPE	PC	LCV	CFA	RPN	NAB	NSI	NTU	ACA	ACU
1980	6	11	13	17	7	—	100	100	59	95	93
1979	0	5	10	5	4	—	—	—	72	100	97
1978	0	0	13	5	5	67	100	100	56	96	95

Key Votes

1) Draft Registn $	FOR	6) Fair Hsg DOJ Enfrc	AGN	11) Cut Socl Incr Dfns $	—
2) Ban $ to Nicrgua	FOR	7) Lim PAC Contrbtns	AGN	12) Hosptl Cost Controls	—
3) Dlay MX Missile	—	8) Cap on Food Stmp $	FOR	13) Gasln Ctrls & Allctns	AGN
4) Nuclr Mortorium	AGN	9) New US Dep Edcatn	AGN	14) Lim Wndfll Prof Tax	FOR
5) Alaska Lands Bill	AGN	10) Cut OSHA $		FOR	15) Chryslr Loan Grntee	AGN

Election Results

1980 general	Eldon Rudd (R)	142,565	(63%)	($228,663)
	Les Miller (D)	85,046	(37%)	($153,345)
1980 primary	Eldon Rudd (R)	35,515	(88%)	
	One other (R)	4,718	(12%)	
1978 general	Eldon Rudd (R)	90,768	(63%)	($178,134)
	Michael McCormick (D)	48,661	(34%)	($23,548)

ARKANSAS

Fifteen years ago the outlook for Arkansas was bleak. The state had pretty well earned the Dogpatch reputation it held across the nation. Since the days of the Great Depression, its young people continued to leave by the thousands, looking for jobs elsewhere. The state's population had peaked at nearly 2 million in 1940 and had fallen 163,000 between that census and 1960. Moreover, Arkansas's reputation as a relatively tolerant border state was shattered by the machinations of Governor Orval Faubus, who blocked implementation of a federal court integration order and forced President Eisenhower to send federal troops into Little Rock's Central High. (The Little Rock episode, however, guaranteed political success for Faubus, who was able to break the state's two-term tradition and remained governor through 1966.) Meanwhile, Arkansas's income levels and educational achievement were among the lowest in the nation. By any measure Arkansas was in trouble in 1965.

Today Arkansas is in much better shape. Its income levels are still below the national average, but the gap has narrowed and increasing differentials in the cost of living have made Arkansas's relatively low wages and salaries buy much more than they could in a northeastern metropolitan area. Segregation has long since been left behind, and education and other state services have been improved. Much of the credit for these developments must go to the late Governor Winthrop Rockefeller, who served only four years (1966–70), but who turned the state around in that short time. Rockefeller, like many southern governors, worked hard at attracting jobs, particularly in small factories that could be located out near where people had grown up; he repudiated segregation and in effect liberated every politician since from the race issue. He helped to build a more positive attitude toward the state, a sense that Arkansas was more than a backwater and that it could accomplish things.

The other major reason for the change in Arkansas's fortunes is a basic change in American patterns of migration. In the 20 years after World War II, there were great internal migrations in this country from the rural areas of the South and, to some extent, of the Midwest toward the giant metropolitan areas with their expanding economies. People went where opportunity was during a time of economic expansion. But in the 1970s, a contrary trend became evident. Americans, starting off with a level of prosperity and a standard of living much higher than those of 25 years before, no longer felt as much of an urge to leave their native lands for higher incomes. Local economies in the rural South were improving, and the negative aspects of life in the big metropolitan areas had become more apparent even as the supply of new jobs in many of them seemed to dry up.

The result was a gigantic migration that did not take place: people in the rural southern and plains states stayed put rather than moving, and the population of states such as Arkansas, after plummeting for 20 years, began moving upward again. Arkansas stopped losing all its most talented young people, and during the 1970s there was net migration into, not out of, the state. In addition, there was a migration here that did occur, a migration of people from northern cities and from Arkansas's own urban areas to the more rural, mountainous counties of the northern part of the state. This is one of those resort areas that has been attracting thousands of new year-round residents in the 1970s. All in all, the 1970s saw the fastest population growth in Arkansas since the 1900–10 period.

For 30 years Arkansas had the same two senators: John McClellan, an austere conservative, and J. William Fulbright, the aloof, sometimes moody, always thoughtful chairman of the Foreign Relations Committee. Today it has two Democratic senators who seem to be almost equally secure politically and have the prospect of remaining together in the Senate for a comparable period of time. They are Dale Bumpers, the governor who succeeded Rockefeller and who defeated Fulbright in the 1974 Democratic primary, and David Pryor, who nearly beat McClellan in the 1972 Democratic primary and then won his seat in a hotly contested three-way primary in 1978 after serving as governor himself. They are much more alike—although not identical—in temperament and voting pattern than were McClellan and Fulbright. But the current senators owe at least something to a man of the other party, Winthrop Rockefeller, whom Bumpers beat in the 1970 gubernatorial election—and admitted that a supporter of civil rights such as himself could not have won without the example Rockefeller set.

Bumpers is in many ways an extraordinary political figure—a man who came out of a small southern town and almost immediately became a national political figure. He is pleasant, fluent, sincere but not cloying, able to master difficult issues easily. He was mentioned before 1974 as a potential presidential candidate, but he ran for the Senate instead of becoming, as his fellow southern governor Jimmy Carter did, a full-time candidate in 1975 and 1976. Now one wonders whether the nation is ready for another "New South moderate." Bumpers's voting record probably puts him closer to northern Democrats than to stereotypical southern conservatives. On the Energy Committee he has generally taken positions opposed by the oil companies—in contrast with the senators from the surrounding oil-producing states. He has also championed federal energy conservation programs. After McClellan's death he also won a seat on Appropriations—a sign that he has the favor of the leadership. He has also shown some suspicion of big government; he sponsored a bill to remove the presumption in federal courts that federal regulations are valid. He has not yet succeeded, however, in achieving his potential as a major leader in the Senate, and he has made some enemies, as when he was one of several senators who refused to provide the 60th vote for cloture for the labor law reform pushed by the AFL–CIO when Democrats still had the majority.

Bumpers was reelected in 1980 without serious opposition but won just 59% of the vote—far lower than had been expected. One reason was a sudden decline in Democratic support in Arkansas generally. The dropoff was evident in the presidential election, where Jimmy Carter's percentage sagged from 65% to 48% in four years and, to everyone's surprise, Carter lost the state; and in the race for governor (Arkansas is one of four states that still elects its governors every two years) where incumbent Bill Clinton was upset by Republican Frank White.

Arkansas in the late 1970s was one of the most Democratic of states. It has produced a series of outstanding young liberal Democratic candidates and seemed to have no Republican Party capable of competing. Then, to some extent in 1978 and to a very definite extent in 1980, the Republicans turned things around. One reason is that they came up with better candidates. Another is that, in Little Rock and other urban centers, they corralled the country club vote that had been the foundation of Republican strength in most southern states. A third reason is a resurgence of the traditional Republicanism of the mountains and hills of northwestern Arkansas, coupled with a strong Republican trend in Fort Smith, a natural gas producing town on the border of Oklahoma, at a time when Democrats increasingly became identified as opponents of the interests of oil. (Jimmy Carter got only 27% of the vote in Fort Smith's Sebastian County; Dale Bumpers got only 29%.) But perhaps the most important reason is that the issues and ideas — opposition to government spending, support for a stronger defense — that had been working for Republicans throughout the nation for several years all of a sudden began working for them in Arkansas and swamped the Democrats.

One local issue also played an important part in the governor's race: Cuban refugees. Fort Chaffee, near Fort Smith, was one of the major entry points for the rush of Cuban refugees in the spring and summer of 1980. There were lurid stories about crimes committed by the refugees and about homosexual refugees. Local people in this homogeneous area were surely terrified about these alien creatures in their midst and, like most Americans called on to make a sacrifice these days, angry that they had been singled out. The Carter Administration received much of the blame for the situation; but voters also turned against Governor Clinton, elected almost without opposition in 1978 at age 32. But in 1980 he was unfortunate enough to have a creditable opponent, businessman Frank White, and to have accumulated some grievances because of the refugee situation and because of an increase in license plate fees. Clinton was upset by a narrow margin — one of the biggest surprises on an election night full of surprises — but no one believes that his career in Arkansas politics is over. Clinton declined to run for Democratic national chairman, preferring to remain in Arkansas, and chances are that he will oppose White again in two years. Voters will have a chance to choose, with some perspective, which of these two governors they prefer.

Arkansas's other senator, David Pryor, had the good fortune of not having to run in 1980, although everyone believes that he, like Bumpers, would have won. Pryor is another prodigy from a small town: elected to Congress in 1966 at age 32, nearly elected to the Senate in 1972, elected governor at age 40 in 1974, and elected to the Senate in 1978. From his time in the House he has the reputation of a liberal. He voted against the seating of the regular Mississippi delegation at the 1968 national convention, he supported civil rights legislation and, when denied funds to investigate nursing homes, he set up his own volunteer committee and worked in a nursing home incognito to learn of conditions firsthand. This was quite extraordinary behavior for a congressman from the most Deep South part of the state. But it also caused Pryor some difficulty when he ran against Senator McClellan in 1972. McClellan's achievements, such as the Arkansas River navigational system, had not been enough to beat Pryor outright in the first primary, and in the runoff the old senator attacked the young congressman as a liberal and a tool of organized labor.

Such attacks would be less plausible today. As governor, Pryor antagonized labor by sending in the National Guard when firemen struck in Pine Bluff and disappointed education and other lobbies with his tight budgets. In the 1978 Senate primary he faced two tough opponents: Congressman and former Attorney General Jim Guy Tucker, who had the support of organized labor, and Congressman Ray Thornton, also a former attorney general, who had served on the House Judiciary Committee that voted to impeach Richard Nixon. It was almost a perfectly even three-way race, and in the runoff this time it was Pryor attacking his opponent Tucker for labor and liberal ties — and winning. Pryor serves on the Agriculture, Governmental Affairs, and Select Aging Committees. His voting record on most issues is somewhat more conservative than Bumpers's but more liberal than that of most southern Democratic senators. His seat is up in 1984 and, while previous speculation has centered on the outside chance that he might have serious Democratic primary opposition, it seems more likely that his problems will come from Republicans who, in Governor Frank White and 2d district Congressman Ed Bethune, have developed at least two plausible candidates — and who might, as the Democrats did in the past, come up with some unknown young lawyer from a small town who could sweep the state.

Arkansas is one state that doesn't have to worry much about redistricting. It has the same number of congressional seats as it has had for the past 20 years (four), and the populations of the current districts are not that far from average. In 1981 it shifted a few counties from the 2d and 3d to the 1st and 4th districts and met the one-person-one-vote standard without upsetting the political balance anywhere.

Census Data   Pop. (1980 final) 2,285,513, up 19% in 1970s: 1.01% of U.S. total, 33d largest. Central city, 19%; suburban, 20%. Median 4-person family income, 1978, $15,669, 77% of U.S.; 50th highest.

1979 Share of Federal Tax Burden $3,291,000,000; 0.73% of U.S. total, 32d largest.

1979 Share of Federal Outlays $3,957,784,000; 0.86% of U.S. total, 34th largest.

DOD	$514,494,000	38th	(0.48%)	HEW	$1,875,109,000	31st	(1.05%)
DOE	$2,286,000	45th	(0.02%)	ERDA	$2,081,000	40th	(0.07%)
HUD	$57,862,000	32d	(0.88%)	NASA	$88,000	47th	(0.00%)
VA	$317,736,000	25th	(1.53%)	DOT	$144,249,000	32d	(0.87%)
EPA	$23,985,000	43d	(0.45%)	DOC	$17,161,000	27th	(0.54%)
DOI	$27,040,000	41st	(0.49%)	USDA	$426,200,000	23d	(1.77%)

Economic Base   Agriculture, notably soybeans, broilers, cattle, and cotton lint; food and kindred products, especially meat products; finance, insurance, and real estate; lumber and wood products, especially sawmills and planing mills; electrical equipment and supplies, especially electrical industrial apparatus; apparel and other textile products, especially men's and boys' furnishings; furniture and fixtures, especially household furniture.

Political Lineup   Governor, Frank White (R). Senators, Dale Bumpers (D) and David Pryor (D). Representatives, 4 (2 D and 2 R); 4 in 1982. State Senate, 35 (34 D and 1 R); State House of Representatives, 100 (93 D and 7 R).

The Voters
  Registration   1,185,902 Total.
  Employment profile 1970   White collar, 39%. Blue collar, 41%. Service, 13%. Farm, 7%.
  Ethnic groups   Black 1980, 16%. Total foreign stock 1970, 2%.

Presidential Vote

1980	Reagan (R)	403,164	(48%)
	Carter (D)	398,041	(48%)
	Anderson (I)	22,468	(3%)
1976	Ford (R)	267,903	(35%)
	Carter (D)	498,604	(65%)
1980 Democratic Presidential Primary	Carter	269,290	(60%)
	Kennedy	78,503	(18%)
	One other	19,459	(4%)
	Uncommitted	80,940	(18%)

SENATORS

Sen. Dale Bumpers (D) Elected 1974, seat up 1986; b. Aug. 12, 1925, Charleston; home, Charleston; U. of Ark., Northwestern U., LL.B. 1951.

Career USMC, WWII; Practicing atty., 1951–70; Charleston City Atty.; Gov. of Ark., 1970–74.

Offices 3229 DSOB, 202-224-4843. Also 2527 Fed. Bldg., 700 W. Capitol, Little Rock 72201, 501-378-6286.

Committees *Appropriations* (14th). Subcommittees: District of Columbia; Interior; Legislative Branch; State, Justice, Commerce, and the Judiciary.

Energy and Natural Resources (3d). Subcommittees: Energy Research and Development; Energy and Mineral Resources; Public Lands and Reserved Water.

Select Committee on Small Business (3d). Subcommittee: Government Regulation and Paperwork.

Group Ratings

	ADA	COPE	PC	LCV	CFA	RPN	NAB	NSI	NTU	ACA	ACU
1980	56	53	43	58	27	—	40	33	35	35	31
1979	53	63	58	—	52	—	—	—	26	35	30
1978	45	26	53	79	35	67	82	20	16	35	30

Key Votes

1) Draft Registn $	FOR	6) Fair Housng Cloture	FOR	11) Cut Socl Incr Defns	FOR
2) Ban $ to Nicrgua	FOR	7) Ban $ Rape Abortns	AGN	12) Income Tax Indexing	AGN
3) Dlay MX Missile	AGN	8) Cap on Food Stmp $	AGN	13) Lim Spdg 21% GNP	AGN
4) Nuclr Mortorium	FOR	9) New US Dep Edcatn	FOR	14) Incr Wndfll Prof Tax	FOR
5) Alaska Lands Bill	FOR	10) Cut OSHA Inspctns	FOR	15) Chryslr Loan Grntee	AGN

Election Results

1980 general	Dale Bumpers (D)	477,905	(59%)	($220,861)
	Bill Clark (R)	330,576	(41%)	($119,196)
1980 primary	Dale Bumpers (D), unopposed			
1974 general	Dale Bumpers (D)	461,056	(85%)	($335,874)
	John Harris Jones (R)	82,026	(15%)	($18,651)

Sen. David Pryor (D) Elected 1978, seat up 1984; b. Aug. 29, 1934, Camden; home, Camden; U. of Ark., B.A. 1957, LL.B. 1964.

Career Ed. and Publisher, *Ouachita Citizen,* Camden, 1957–61; Practicing atty., 1964–66; U.S. House of Reps., 1967–72; Candidate for Dem. nomination for U.S. Senate, 1972; Gov. of Ark., 1975–78.

Offices 248 RSOB, 202-224-2353. Also Suite 3030 Fed. Bldg., Little Rock 72201, 501-387-6336.

Committees *Agriculture, Nutrition and Forestry* (5th). Subcommittees: Agriculture Research and General Legislation; Rural Development, Oversight, and Investigations; Foreign Agricultural Policy.

Governmental Affairs (7th). Subcommittees: Civil Service, Post Office, and General Services; Oversight of Government Management; Congressional Operations and Oversight.

Special Committee on Aging (4th).   *Select Committee on Ethics* (2d).

Group Ratings

	ADA	COPE	PC	LCV	CFA	RPN	NAB	NSI	NTU	ACA	ACU
1980	44	42	33	33	7	—	55	44	38	46	26
1979	42	58	46	—	43	—	—	—	32	42	27

Key Votes

1) Draft Registn $	FOR	6) Fair Housng Cloture	FOR
2) Ban $ to Nicrgua	FOR	7) Ban $ Rape Abortns	AGN
3) Dlay MX Missile	AGN	8) Cap on Food Stmp $	AGN
4) Nuclr Mortorium	—	9) New US Dep Edcatn	FOR
5) Alaska Lands Bill	FOR	10) Cut OSHA Inspctns	FOR

11) Cut Socl Incr Defns	FOR
12) Income Tax Indexing	AGN
13) Lim Spdg 21% GNP	AGN
14) Incr Wndfll Prof Tax	AGN
15) Chryslr Loan Grntee	AGN

Election Results

1978 general	David Pryor (D)	395,506	(77%)	($774,824)
	Thomas Kelly, Jr. (R)	84,308	(16%)	($16,208)
	John G. Black (I)	37,211	(7%)	($32,863)
1978 runoff	David Pryor (D)	265,525	(55%)	
	Jim Guy Tucker (D)	218,026	(45%)	($1,019,659)
1978 primary	David Pryor (D)	198,039	(34%)	
	Jim Guy Tucker (D)	187,568	(32%)	
	Ray Thornton (D)	184,095	(32%)	($1,004,515)
	One other (D)	8,166	(1%)	
1972 general	John L. McClellan (D)	386,398	(61%)	($516,573)
	Wayne H. Babbitt (R)	248,238	(39%)	

GOVERNOR

Gov. Frank White (R) Elected Nov. 1980, term expires Jan. 1985; b. June 4, 1933, Texarkana; home, Little Rock; U.S. Naval Acad., Enginnering Degree, 1956.

Career Capt., USAF, 1956–61; Exec., Merrill Lynch, 1961–73; Exec., Commercial Nat. Bank of Little Rock, 1973–75; Dir., Ark. Indust. Devel. Commission, 1975–77; Pres. & CEO, Capitol S&L, 1977–80.

Offices State Capitol, Little Rock 72201, 501-371-2345.

Election Results

1980 gen.	Frank White (R)	435,684	(52%)
	Bill Clinton (D)	403,241	(48%)
1980 prim.	Frank White (R)	5,867	(72%)
	Marshall Chrisman (R)	2,310	(28%)
1978 gen.	Bill Clinton (D)	335,101	(63%)
	A. Lynn Lowe (R)	193,746	(37%)

FIRST DISTRICT

Eastern Arkansas—the flat, fertile, cotton-growing plains that line the west bank of the Mississippi River—is economically more tied to the state of Mississippi or to Memphis, Tennessee, than to the hilly regions of central Arkansas or the Ozark Mountains. Like the Delta in Mississippi and the Bootheel in Missouri, eastern Arkansas is occupied by large farms and even plantations where, until the last 15 years or so, whites imposed a life of segregation on the large number of blacks. This part of the state has seldom favored any form of upcountry populism, although it has always retained at least a nominal Democratic allegi-

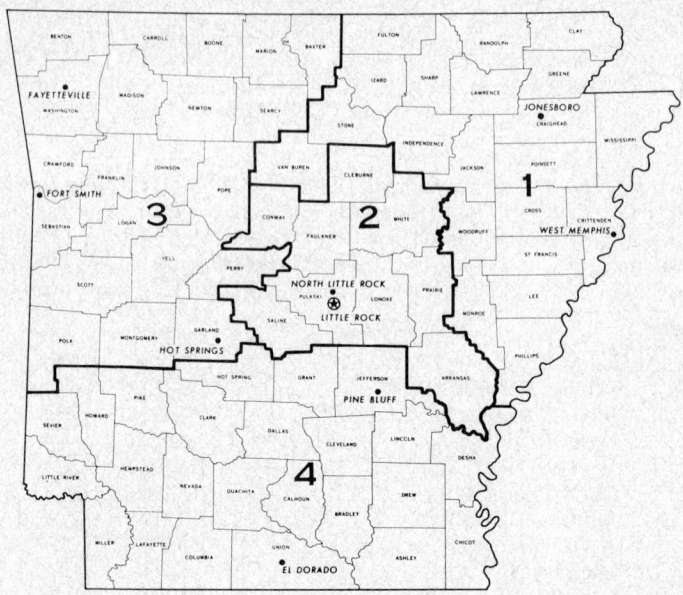

ance. In 1980, when President Jimmy Carter and Governor Bill Clinton failed to carry the state, both were still able to win these counties in eastern Arkansas.

Eastern Arkansas forms about half of Arkansas's 1st congressional district. The district also includes some hill counties to the northwest, added in redistricting after the 1970 census, and will probably add one or two flatland counties along the Arkansas River from the 2d district after the 1980 census. Nonetheless, the district basically considers itself agricultural; its largest cities are West Memphis, a tiny hamlet staring across levees and the river and barely able to make out the towers of Memphis in the distance, and Jonesboro, home of Arkansas State University, one of those small Arkansas cities that trended sharply Republican in 1980.

The district has been represented for years by southern Democrats. For 30 years its congressman was Ezekiel C. Gathings, who rose on the seniority ladder to become chairman of Agriculture's Cotton Subcommittee. Its current congressman, Bill Alexander, is a member of the Appropriations's Agriculture Subcommittee, a body that has been for 30 years a major force in the governance of the U.S. Department of Agriculture. His best chance of a chairmanship, however, is on the State, Justice, Commerce, and the Judiciary Subcommittee of Appropriations, a body of great importance but one presumably of less immediate interest to his constituents.

But Alexander's most important position is as assistant majority whip, the number four position in the Democratic leadership. He was chosen for that post after the 1980 election by Speaker O'Neill and Majority Leader Jim Wright; they evidently saw him as bright and hardworking, close enough to northern liberals to be acceptable to the majority of House Democrats and with a district and voting record not totally uncongenial to most southern conservatives. The early 1980s, however, promise to be a time when it will be hard to hold together these two groups of Democrats, particularly if the Reagan economic programs prove to be popular. Alexander may find himself stuck in a position where he must argue for policies somewhat more liberal than those he would formulate on his own and where he will be hard-pressed to win many votes among the southerners whom other Democrats suppose to be his natural constituency. Conceivably his current position could lead someday to the speaker's chair; but if he does make it he will have been sorely tested in the process.

Census Data Pop. (1980 final) 521,904, up 9% in 1970s. Median family income, 1970, $5,381, 56% of U.S.

The Voters

Employment profile 1970 White collar, 34%. Blue collar, 40%. Service, 13%. Farm, 13%.
Ethnic groups Black 1980, 19%. Hispanic 1980, 1%. Total foreign stock 1970, 1%.

Presidential Vote

1980	Reagan (R)	79,426	(44%)
	Carter (D)	93,654	(52%)
	Anderson (I)	3,588	(2%)
1976	Ford (R)	52,491	(30%)
	Carter (D)	120,799	(70%)

Rep. Bill Alexander (D) Elected 1968; b. Jan. 16, 1934, Memphis, Tenn.; home, Osceola; U. of Ark., Southwestern U. at Memphis, B.A. 1957, Vanderbilt U., LL.B. 1960.

Career Army, 1951–53; Practicing atty., 1960–69.

Offices 201 CHOB, 202-225-4076. Also Fed. Bldg., Jonesboro 72401, 501-972-1550.

Committees Appropriations (13th). Subcommittees: Agriculture, Rural Development and Related Agencies; Commerce, Justice, State and Judiciary; Military Construction.

Standards of Official Conduct (3d).

Group Ratings

	ADA	COPE	PC	LCV	CFA	RPN	NAB	NSI	NTU	ACA	ACU
1980	44	56	23	31	43	—	18	25	15	33	21
1979	37	50	20	28	12	—	—	—	17	4	20
1978	25	59	30	44	23	50	18	60	5	41	50

Key Votes

1) Draft Registn $	FOR	6) Fair Hsg DOJ Enfrc	FOR	11) Cut Socl Incr Dfns $	AGN
2) Ban $ to Nicrgua	AGN	7) Lim PAC Contribtns	AGN	12) Hosptl Cost Controls	AGN
3) Dlay MX Missile	AGN	8) Cap on Food Stmp $	AGN	13) Gasln Ctrls & Alletns	AGN
4) Nuclr Mortorium	AGN	9) New US Dep Edcatn	FOR	14) Lim Wndfll Prof Tax	FOR
5) Alaska Lands Bill	FOR	10) Cut OSHA $	AGN	15) Chryslr Loan Grntee	FOR

Election Results

1980 general	Bill Alexander (D), unopposed	($50,289)
1980 primary	Bill Alexander (D), unopposed	
1978 general	Bill Alexander (D), unopposed	($37,844)

SECOND DISTRICT

The 2d congressional district of Arkansas is the center of the state — politically as well as geographically. Somewhat more than half its population can be found in Pulaski County, including the state capital of Little Rock, with its large black and affluent white neighborhoods, and North Little Rock, a kind of industrial suburb across the Arkansas River. The district also includes a number of hill counties to the north and, in the southeast, part of the flat, cotton-growing Mississippi plain. Little Rock made an international name for itself by forcibly resisting integration of Central High School in 1957; President Eisenhower had to send in federal troops when Governor Orval Faubus refused to obey the law. But Little Rock has since lived down its bad reputation and has become one of the more politically progressive cities in the South. It supported Republican Governor Winthrop Rockefeller and his three Democratic successors, Dale Bumpers, David Pryor, and Bill Clinton; and it has elected progressive candidates at about every level. Unlike most southern cities, Little Rock is not the Republican bastion of the state; indeed, it gave Jimmy Carter a hefty plurality in the 1980 general election even as he lost the state as a whole.

In congressional politics the 2d district has been a good example of the recent changes in Arkansas's House representation — from the tradition of building up great seniority over the years to one of electing popular new officeholders frequently. Until 1976 the district was represented by Wilbur Mills, first elected in 1938 and chairman of the House Ways and Means Committee from 1958 until his downfall in 1974 following the Fanne Fox scandal. Mills's original district was in the hills and had not included Little Rock, but the capital was added to his district in redistricting in the 1960s and, until the scandal made it obvious he had lost his clout, was pleased to support him. Now the congressional seat here seems to be vying with the office of attorney general as a launching pad for ambitious young politicians. Mills was never interested in statewide office, but those who are must be aware that being congressman from Little Rock gives statewide exposure on television and in newspapers. Thus Jim Guy Tucker, who succeeded Mills and had been state attorney general, served here for just one term and then ran for the Senate in 1978.

The 2d's current congressman is Ed Bethune, who in many respects is an unusual choice. For one thing, he is from the mountains rather than from Little Rock, although he managed to win difficult races in 1978 anyway. Second, he is a Republican — the first elected to the House from these parts since 1868. He is Little Rock's kind of Republican, however: a protege of Winthrop Rockefeller who never embraced the anti–civil rights politics so prevalent among so many southern Republicans. Bethune ran a well-financed campaign in 1978 and managed to beat a Little Rock-based Democrat. In the House, he was elected chairman of the 35-member freshman class. This proved to be an unusually assertive group, pressing the Republican leadership for better committee assignments and the Democratic leadership on all kinds of procedural and substantive issues. Despite his moderate reputation, Bethune emerged as a tough partisan Republican at a time when Republicans increasingly had the initiative on issues of all kinds.

Against a weak opponent in 1980, Bethune was elected with a stunning margin. His performance so far suggests he may have the potential for statewide office and could someday be a serious competitor for one of the state's two Senate seats.

Census Data   Pop. (1980 final) 595,768, up 24% in 1970s. Median family income, 1970, $7,484, 78% of U.S.

The Voters

Employment profile 1970 White collar, 46%. Blue collar, 37%. Service, 13%. Farm, 4%.
Ethnic groups Black 1980, 17%. Hispanic 1980, 1%. Total foreign stock 1970, 3%.

Presidential Vote

1980	Reagan (R)	95,148	(46%)
	Carter (D)	103,040	(50%)
	Anderson (I)	7,317	(4%)
1976	Ford (R)	60,457	(32%)
	Carter (D)	126,790	(68%)

Rep. Ed Bethune (R) Elected 1978; b. Dec. 19, 1935, Pocahontas; home, Searcy; Little Rock Jr. Col., 1957–58, U. of Ark., B.S. 1961, J.D. 1963.

Career USMC, 1954–57; Randolph Co. Dpty. Prosecuting Atty., 1963–64; FBI Agent, 1964–68; Practicing atty., 1968–.

Offices 1535 LHOB, 202-225-2506. Also 1527 New. Fed. Ofc. Bldg., Little Rock 72201, 501-378-5941.

Committees *Banking, Finance and Urban Affairs* (9th). Subcommittees: Economic Stabilization; Financial Institutions Supervision, Regulation and Insurance; Housing and Community Development.

Budget (8th).

Group Ratings

	ADA	COPE	PC	LCV	CFA	RPN	NAB	NSI	NTU	ACA	ACU
1980	11	11	20	17	29	—	92	100	54	74	89
1979	16	25	18	33	7	—	—	—	53	84	89

Key Votes

1) Draft Registn $	FOR	6) Fair Hsg DOJ Enfrc	AGN	11) Cut Socl Incr Dfns $	FOR
2) Ban $ to Nicrgua	FOR	7) Lim PAC Contrbtns	AGN	12) Hosptl Cost Controls	AGN
3) Dlay MX Missile	AGN	8) Cap on Food Stmp $	FOR	13) Gasln Ctrls & Allctns	AGN
4) Nuclr Mortorium	—	9) New US Dep Edcatn	AGN	14) Lim Wndfll Prof Tax	FOR
5) Alaska Lands Bill	FOR	10) Cut OSHA $		FOR	15) Chryslr Loan Grntee	AGN

Election Results

1980 general	Ed Bethune (R)	159,148	(79%)	($193,207)
	James Reid (D)	42,278	(21%)	($14,919)
1980 primary	Ed Bethune (R), unopposed			
1978 general	Ed Bethune (R)	65,285	(51%)	($255,098)
	Doug Brandon (D)	62,140	(49%)	($329,590)

THIRD DISTRICT

The 3d district of Arkansas is the northwest quadrant of the state — a region of green hills rising to mountains, of historic poverty but recent prosperity. The new economic climate comes in large part from retirees and younger people attracted by the area's mild climate, its scenic mountains and reservoirs, by its jobs in small industries, by its low-keyed pace of life, and by its fidelity to traditional values. The cities of the 3d are medium-sized, the kind that most Americans say they prefer. Among them are such places as Fort Smith, on the Oklahoma border; Fayetteville, site of the University of Arkansas; and Hot Springs, the onetime gambling center that is still a popular resort and retirement center. The district also contains Arkansas's most solidly Republican areas, the mountain counties in the north that opposed the Confederacy and even in the Depression of the 1930s remained faithful to the party of the Union.

For the first three-quarters of the 20th century, this was the only Arkansas district to be the scene of two-party contests, and until 1978 it was the only one represented by a Republican congressman. In 1966 the 3d surprised practically everyone when it ousted longtime incumbent James Trimble, then 72 and a member of the House Rules Committee, and elected in his place Republican State Chairman John Paul Hammerschmidt. The new congressman carried the Republican counties in the north and profited generally from Winston Rockefeller's strong showing in the gubernatorial race that year.

As a congressman Hammerschmidt has been a reliable member of the Republican Conference and on the Public Works Committee has tended to support pork barrel projects and to oppose diverting money from highways to mass transit—what one would expect from a representative of a rural district whose lakes were largely created by federally built dams and whose barge industry depends on federal navigation projects. Hammerschmidt is ranking Republican on the House Veterans' Affairs Committee and tends to take the point of view of the traditional veterans' organizations, which—more oriented to World War II era veterans—are skeptical about increasing benefits for Vietnam era veterans and oppose cuts in or elimination of the separate system of VA hospitals. Hammerschmidt's issue positions have been a good recipe for political success. Hammerschmidt has had significant opposition only once, in 1974, when Bill Clinton, then a 28-year-old law professor at the University of Arkansas, ran a vigorous campaign here and in that Watergate year held him to 52% of the vote.

In 1980 there was a major shift of public opinion in the district, but one that did not affect Hammerschmidt adversely—the reaction to the choice of Fort Chaffee, a military base near Fort Smith, as one of the main centers for Cuban refugees. There were charges that the refugees were not properly resettled, that they were committing crimes in the area. There must have been fears that they would just remain in Arkansas, an alien presence, sopping up local tax dollars and committing all sorts of mayhem. Unrealistic and unfounded as the fears and rumors may have been, the impact of the refugees was clear in the election returns.

The Carter Administration was given the primary blame for the situation, and the president, who had carried this district comfortably in 1976, got only 37% of the vote here in 1980. Governor Bill Clinton was also blamed and, after carrying the district in 1978 and winning 48% against a popular congressman in 1974, he could take only 40% of the vote against his Republican opponent, Little Rock businessman Frank White. How lasting this surge will be to the Republican is unclear—particularly now that the Republicans are in office and in a position to be blamed if more refugees are sent to Fort Chaffee. It is entirely possible that the issue will be forgotten in 1982, like a cyclone that blows through town. But the very force of its impact shows what strong feelings lurk beneath a pleasant surface ambience.

Census Data   Pop. (1980 final) 638,607, up 33% in 1970s. Median family income, 1970, $6,057, 63% of U.S.

The Voters

Employment profile 1970 White collar, 38%. Blue collar, 42%. Service, 13%. Farm, 7%.
Ethnic groups Black 1980, 2%. Hispanic 1980, 1%. Am. Ind. 1980, 1%. Total foreign stock 1970, 3%.

Presidential Vote

1980	Reagan (R)	150,405	(58%)
	Carter (D)	96,831	(37%)
	Anderson (I)	8,365	(3%)
1976	Ford (R)	99,178	(44%)
	Carter (D)	128,322	(56%)

Rep. John Paul Hammerschmidt (R) Elected 1966; b. May 4, 1922, Harrison; home, Harrison; The Citadel, Okla. A&M Col., U. of Ark.

Career Army Air Corps, WWII; Bd. Chmn., Hammerschmidt Lumber Co., Chmn., Rep. State Central Comm., 1964-.

Offices 2207 RHOB, 202-225-4301. Also Fed. Bldg., Fayetteville 72701, 501-442-5215.

Committees *Public Works and Transportation* (3d). Subcommittees: Aviation; Economic Development; Water Resources.

Veterans' Affairs (Ranking Member). Subcommittees: Compensation, Pension and Insurance; Hospitals and Health Care; Oversight and Investigations.

Select Committee on Aging (3d). Subcommittees: Housing and Consumer Interests; Human Services.

Group Ratings

	ADA	COPE	PC	LCV	CFA	RPN	NAB	NSI	NTU	ACA	ACU
1980	6	10	13	17	14	—	91	100	49	77	89
1979	16	16	20	38	7	—	—	—	52	92	95
1978	10	11	13	10	14	45	100	100	27	88	83

Key Votes

1) Draft Registn $	—	6) Fair Hsg DOJ Enfrc	AGN	11) Cut Socl Incr Dfns $	FOR
2) Ban $ to Nicrgua	FOR	7) Lim PAC Contrbtns	AGN	12) Hosptl Cost Controls	AGN
3) Dlay MX Missile	AGN	8) Cap on Food Stmp $	FOR	13) Gasln Ctrls & Allctns	AGN
4) Nuclr Mortorium	FOR	9) New US Dep Edcatn	AGN	14) Lim Wndfll Prof Tax	FOR
5) Alaska Lands Bill	FOR	10) Cut OSHA $	FOR	15) Chryslr Loan Grntee	AGN

Election Results

1980 general	J. P. Hammerschmidt (R), unop.			($42,307)
1980 primary	J. P. Hammerschmidt (R), unop.			
1978 general	John Paul Hammerschmidt (R) .	130,086	(78%)	($47,521)
	William C Mears (D).........	35,748	(22%)	

FOURTH DISTRICT

Geographically the 4th congressional district of Arkansas takes in the southern third of the state. It stretches from the flat Delta lands along the Mississippi River, west across rolling hills to Texarkana, a city situated so squarely on the Texas–Arkansas border that the state line runs through City Hall. The principal towns in the district are quiet places: El Dorado, in an area of considerable oil production; Camden, the home of Senator David Pryor and of the late Senator John McClellan; Arkadelphia; and Pine Bluff, the childhood home of the late Martha Mitchell. By many indices the 4th district is more like neighboring Mississippi or northern Louisiana than the rest of Arkansas. This is the part of the state most like the Deep South. It has the largest black percentage of any of the state's districts, and it produced the largest vote for George Wallace when he ran in 1968.

For some years the 4th had a tradition, quite out of line with most of the Deep South at that time, of electing moderate or even liberal Democrats to the Congress. In 1966 it elected David Pryor, a 32-year-old lawyer who fought to regulate nursing homes; in 1972 it elected Ray Thornton, who voted as a member of the Judiciary Committee to impeach Richard Nixon. Both men eventually ran, unsuccessfully, for the Senate (although Pryor won on his second try, in 1978). The primary race here in 1978 produced a more conservative Democrat, Beryl Anthony. He beat Secretary of State Winston Bryant in the runoff by a 52%–48% margin — this was tantamount to the general election victory in this district, where the Republicans have not fielded a candidate since 1966. The 4th district was one part of Arkansas that supported the whole Democratic ticket even when Jimmy Carter and Governor Bill Clinton were upset in the 1980 election. But Anthony supported the national administration not all that often in the House. He has seats on the Agriculture Committee and (since 1981) on Budget. As one of the more conservative southern Democrats, he may be a pivotal vote on many issues in 1981 and 1982, since he will be the kind of Democrat the Reagan Administration will look to, to provide majorities for its programs in the House.

Census Data Pop. (1980 final) 529,234, up 10% in 1970s. Median family income, 1970, $6,191, 65% of U.S.

The Voters

Employment profile 1970 White collar, 36%. Blue collar, 44%. Service, 14%. Farm, 6%.
Ethnic groups Black 1980, 30%. Hispanic 1980, 1%. Total foreign stock 1970, 1%.

Presidential Vote

1980	Reagan (R)	78,185	(41%)
	Carter (D)	104,516	(55%)
	Anderson (I)	3,198	(2%)
1976	Ford (R)	55,777	(31%)
	Carter (D)	122,693	(69%)

Rep. Beryl F. Anthony, Jr. (D) Elected 1978; b. Feb. 21, 1931, El Dorado; home, El Dorado; U. of Ark., B.S., B.A. 1961, J.D. 1963.

Career Asst. Atty. Gen. of Ark., 1964–65; Dpty. Union Co. Prosecutor, 1966–70; Prosecuting Atty., 13th Judicial Dist., 1971–76; Legal Counsel, Anthony Forest Products Co., 1977; Practicing atty., 1977–.

Offices 213 CHOB, 202-225-3772. Also Fed. Bldg., P.O. Box 2021, El Dorado 71730, 501-863-0121.

Committees *Agriculture* (20th). Subcommittees: Conservation, Credit and Rural Development; Cotton, Rice and Sugar; Forests, Family Farms and Energy.

Budget (17th).

Group Ratings

	ADA	COPE	PC	LCV	CFA	RPN	NAB	NSI	NTU	ACA	ACU
1980	22	44	30	26	36	—	42	56	29	36	37
1979	26	37	15	24	11	—	—	—	30	21	44

Key Votes

1) Draft Registn $	—	6) Fair Hsg DOJ Enfrc AGN	11) Cut Socl Incr Dfns $ AGN
2) Ban $ to Nicrgua	AGN	7) Lim PAC Contrbtns AGN	12) Hosptl Cost Controls AGN
3) Dlay MX Missile	AGN	8) Cap on Food Stmp $ AGN	13) Gasln Ctrls & Allctns FOR
4) Nuclr Mortorium	—	9) New US Dep Edcatn FOR	14) Lim Wndfll Prof Tax FOR
5) Alaska Lands Bill	AGN	10) Cut OSHA $ AGN	15) Chryslr Loan Grntee —

Election Results

1980 general	Beryl F. Anthony, Jr. (D), unopp. .	($101,235)
1980 primary	Beryl F. Anthony, Jr. (D), unopp.	
1978 general	Beryl F. Anthony, Jr. (D), unopp. .	($372,652)

CALIFORNIA

California, in giving the nation our 40th president, also gave us a paradox: this state, the setter of political and cultural trends, the home of hot tubs and est and *The Whole Earth Catalogue,* has produced perhaps our most tradition-minded and our oldest president. Reagan, moreover, cannot be dismissed as something alien to California: he is as Californian in one way as Jerry Brown is in another. Indeed, Reagan is really the first California president; earlier presidents who claimed residence in California, Hoover and Nixon, made their public careers almost entirely in Washington and ultimately retired to New York City. Reagan lived like an ordinary citizen (or as much like an ordinary citizen as a successful second-rank movie star can) for three decades in Los Angeles, and saw that city change from a far-off regional center to the nation's second great metropolis. Most of his public service was in the still rather isolated and parochial capital city of Sacramento, and no one imagines that he would choose to retire anywhere but in California.

Yet Reagan, despite his eight years as a popular governor, was never able to achieve many of his goals. He wanted to make California like Disneyland's Main Street, but it has ended up in some respects more like Haight-Ashbury. Reagan came to office preaching against the drug culture and student rioting. He left the governorship with marijuana effectively legalized and the values of the student generation spreading to all age groups. He came to office as an opponent of civil rights legislation. Yet when he left office there was a black mayor of Los Angeles and a black superintendent of public instruction, both elected over conservative opposition. He came to office as a champion of traditional family values. Yet he signed a law effectively legalizing abortion in California—an act he now considers a mistake. This politician who has always called for limited government had in the late 1960s and early 1970s the ambitious goal of using government to encourage one life-style and discourage others. The inevitable failure led to some loss of popularity. It is not generally recalled now that Reagan's margin was cut in half in his second gubernatorial election and that he left office without overwhelming popularity—and without a like-minded successor. This experience may have been instructive for Reagan. He campaigned in 1980 and came to office in 1981 downplaying the cultural issues that were so important to so many of his strong supporters. The Ronald Reagan of the 1980s was a mellower politician than the Reagan of the 1960s; if he still described himself as a politician who believed in family values, he was careful—running in a society where so many voters are single or divorced—not to characterize himself as a scourge of those who do not. Reagan's election as president has been called a ratification of conservative cultural values. But it is more accurate to call it an acceptance by cultural conservatives of different life-styles.

California seems to have taught Reagan some lessons, but he can claim that he has taught California some as well. Much has been made of the fact that California's state budgets increased during Reagan's governorship—just as the federal budget increased rapidly during the overlapping years of the Nixon presidency. But Reagan also had considerable success in popularizing the idea that big government had become a burden rather than a boon. Reagan was not the driving force behind California's Proposition 13, the ballot measure that forced a cut in property taxes in June 1978. Indeed, a spending limit measure he did sponsor failed in 1973. But Proposition 13 hit hard at a tax on the asset that most middle- and upper-income families now rely on to build up their net worth—their homes. The surprising success of Proposition 13 crystallized a national mood and seems increasingly to mark a turning point in public attitudes and public policy, between the time when people were happy to have government grow faster than GNP and when they demanded that its growth be slowed. That basic thrust in turn found expression in Reagan's 1980 national campaign and in his 1981 proposals for budget and tax cuts.

In California it was not Reagan's cultural attitudes but his economic policies that enabled him to carry—by a very solid 53% to 36% margin—the state over Jimmy Carter in 1980. This represents a reversal of his experience in gubernatorial elections and it stands on its head the conventional wisdom of American politics. That conventional wisdom is that the electorate is essentially conservative on cultural issues and liberal on economic issues. That is still true, for example, in a Pennsylvania mill town, where the population is largely Catholic and devoted to its local church and where people have low incomes and want government assistance. But it has very little to do anymore with a state like California. There are two demographic facts about California that explain its different politics. First, it is a state of newcomers: most voters, like Reagan, came from somewhere else. Second, it is a state of great affluence: most of the rest of the voters, like Jerry Brown, grew up in a setting of affluence and comfort and take it for granted.

The affluence of California can hardly be overstated. Reagan in 1980 repeated over and again that if California were a separate nation it would have the seventh largest gross national product in the world—his way of embellishing his credential as governor. But even as he was speaking, California seemed headed up into sixth or fifth place. No one is entirely sure why. The economists of the right, the supply siders, argue that Proposition 13 and other tax-cutting measures in the late 1970s stimulated the state's economy, and there may be something to that. All the indicators seem to show extraordinary growth and considerable in-migration during this period. But from a broader perspective the supply-side explanation fails. California has been a high tax state since the 1940s, when Earl Warren deliberately kept taxes up during World War II; California is not a tax haven, not a giant New Hampshire, and never has been. On the left, some critics have argued that California has grown because of the spasmodic growth of single industries, such as entertainment (first the movies, then TV) and defense (first aircraft, then aerospace). But over the long term California has grown rapidly regardless of the health of these industries. The prime example is cited by Jane Jacobs in *The Economy of Cities*. In 18 months at the end of World War II, metropolitan Los Angeles lost 230,000 jobs in defense industries. Every sign pointed to vast depression and depopulation for the Los Angeles Basin in the postwar years. The exact opposite happened. In the 1945–55 period the Los Angeles area was the fastest-growing major metro area in the nation; it generated one out of eight new jobs in the nation during this period. Standard economic analysis tells us that growth comes where there are basic resources and access to markets. But California is thousands of miles from any other significant market, and its basic resources are limited. It has been a net importer of oil since the 1950s (although it is a significant producer as well), it is hundreds of miles from basic fuels such as coal and raw materials such as iron ore; southern California is always in danger of being short of water. California has one basic industry due to its geographic endowment: agriculture (although that depends on irrigation as well). But the conclusion is unavoidable that the only reason a major thriving economy exists in California is because people want it to. It is a creation of will.

The people who created and filled the jobs that California has continuously been creating since the end of World War II acted in large part because they wanted to stay here. No one should underestimate the attraction of California's climate and physical beauty in stimulating the growth of the economy and — in the 1970s — arousing concern about the consequences of that growth. The climate is for most Americans near perfect, and in the years after World War II almost all of California, even the large metropolitan areas, had the small-town atmosphere that most Americans consider ideal. As California has developed its own sophisticated urban centers — not only in San Francisco but in Beverly Hills and university towns as well — middle-class Californians have fanned out, using their affluence to buy homes in farther counties and what once were rural areas, 50 or 60 miles away from their jobs on the freeway. The affluence of California can support not only Rodeo Drive and Union Square, but also decorated vans and weekend skydiving and skiing and surfing and jacuzzis. What products does California produce to earn all this income? It is like asking what New York or Chicago produces. California is famous lately for Silicon Valley, the concentration of the microprocessor industry south of San Francisco, but this is only a small part of the state's economy. The fact is that California makes practically everything today, shipping out goods over thousands of miles or just making things and performing services for the affluent local market

It is against this background that California politics of the 1970s and 1980s must be understood. California has an electorate that is essentially conservative on economic issues and liberal on cultural issues — the exact reverse of the old New Deal model. Its conservatism on economic issues was most apparent in Proposition 13, but it has been clear also in the years since, when Californians have mourned very little the public services that have been cut. Even California's identifiable minorities, with the possible exception of blacks, do not seem to be voting strongly to restore services or make government more generous. That is an effect of affluence: Mexican-Americans in California in 1979 had a median family income of $15,000 — not rich, but far removed from the barrio stereotype, and especially remarkable when you consider how many impoverished Mexicans have been moving rapidly to California in recent years. Some have predicted that California will soon have a "third world" majority; already 8% of its residents are black, 19% of Spanish origin, and 5% Asian. But the evidence of the census suggests that the large majority of Mexican–Americans and Asians and a larger than supposed number of blacks are assimilating comfortably into the affluent middle-class life-style of suburban California; the evidence of election returns suggests they do not see themselves as oppressed or downtrodden masses. California's liberalism on cultural issues is obvious from the results of successive referenda, from 1972 when one-third of the state's voters favored outright legalization of marijuana to 1978 when a majority rejected a measure to prohibit homosexuals and advocates of homosexual rights from teaching in public schools. The Jimmy Carter of 1980 had the worst of both worlds in California: he was seen as an advocate of big government in comparison to Ronald Reagan (although he lost the Democratic primary to Edward Kennedy), and he was seen, despite his liberal stands on issues from foreign policy to the environment, as a southern Baptist unsympathetic to the cultural liberalism of California. Reagan, by stressing his economic conservatism and downplaying his cultural conservatism, was able to carry his native state easily—and by a larger margin than probably would have been possible a few years ago, when feelings on the old cultural issues burned hotter.

The politician who seems most clearly fitted to California's new politics is Jerry Brown. Yet it is not altogether clear that Brown has the unalloyed allegiance of most of the state's voters. Brown was undeniably popular early in his governorship. Voters (although not politicians) were enchanted by his unusual personal habits (living in an unfurnished room, working late, riding in unobtrusive cars) and by his original philosophy of government. Back in 1975 and 1976 he was questioning liberal shibboleths and big government while most Democrats were basking in the afterglow of Watergate. In the 1976 presidential primary, Brown won a huge majority—a strong testimonial from the voters who knew him the best, although its force was diluted by the fact that his chances to win the nomination were obviously nil by the time the California primary was held in June. Brown fascinated young voters and converted old voters to his vision of an era of limits and a more disciplined, intellectually rigorous approach to government.

Proposition 13 was a disaster for Brown, although it seemed to embody most of his principles and although he seemed to recover adeptly afterwards. The problem was that he opposed the measure vehemently and used against it the standard arsenal of arguments—government would go bankrupt, all worthwhile programs would have to be slashed—that turned out to be false. He allied himself uncharacteristically with the public employee unions and the advocates of bigger government. After the victory of Proposition 13, Brown made an adroit about-face—or so it seemed to most observers. Yet his very adroitness seems to have worked against him. He returned to the rhetoric of the era of limits. He worked with the legislature to repair the damage to local government (although such legislators as then Assembly Speaker Leo McCarthy did much of the hard work). He called for a federal constitutional convention to pass an amendment requiring a balanced federal budget unless Congress passed such an amendment itself—a proposal most political experts considered irresponsible (since a convention could, among other things, repeal the Bill of Rights) and a transparent attempt to focus attention on his 1980 presidential campaign.

But first Brown had to get reelected governor in 1978. In retrospect, it seems easy: he won 61% of the two-party vote over the bland Republican candidate, Evelle Younger, more than Reagan or his father had ever won. Yet it was not so automatic. Brown was on the wrong side of issues from nuclear power (to which he is strongly opposed) to capital punishment (again, opposed) to Proposition 13 (quick switch after it passed in June). He bragged about the number of jobs California had gained while he was governor, and he relied on his liberal stands on cultural issues (nuclear power again, notably) to attract the young voters and his record of appointing blacks and Mexican–Americans to attract the minorities. But Brown may have scored as many points by attacking Younger for his high government pensions and for installing a shower in his Sacramento office — in unstated contrast to Brown's well-known austerity.

Brown's performance in the 1980 presidential election was, in contrast, a clear flop. Unlike 1976, he was unable to capture voters' imaginations, and he ran a poor third to Jimmy Carter and Edward Kennedy in the primaries. He made his big effort in Wisconsin, and won only 12% of the vote and retired from competition. By the time the California primary came around, Brown was an also-ran and won only 4% of the state's votes. A more vivid contrast with 1976 cannot be imagined.

In early 1981 Brown was generally considered unlikely to run for governor again, and the betting was that he would run for senator. In many ways, his career seems to have taken the same turns as that of one of California's greatest politicians, Hiram Johnson. Like Johnson, he was elected governor at a young age, in a sharp break with the past; like Johnson, he effected some major reforms and changed the direction of state government. (He is like Johnson also in the fact that his father was successful in politics, although Johnson hated his father and said so publicly while Brown seems only disdainful of his father, who has worked hard for him in all his campaigns.) After two terms as governor, Johnson went on to the Senate, as Brown evidently wants to. The omens there are not terribly auspicious. Johnson was senator for nearly 30 years, but he was never very effective. He was a loner, unable to influence his colleagues, a bitter and unpleasant man whose nation seemed little interested in his once sparklingly new reformist ideas. Brown is not nearly so vituperative, nor does he have some of Johnson's other negative characteristics. But the question remains how well this individualist would be suited to a lifetime of service in the collegial atmosphere of the Senate.

The succession in any case is not likely to be as automatic as it was in Johnson's case. Most observers assume that the incumbent senator, S. I. Hayakawa, cannot be reelected. His victory over Democrat John Tunney in 1976 was an upset, and Hayakawa was 70 then. He amused Californians with his repartee during the campaign, but once in office he became known for his habit of sleeping in public hearings. Hayakawa vows to run for reelection, but the best he can say for his chances is that he hopes to slip through the crowd and win a minority victory in the Republican primary; he does not disclose how he hopes to win the general election. He is likely to have a large and illustrious field of competitors: Congressman Barry Goldwater, Jr., who declined to run in 1976; Congressman Pete McCloskey, who ran against Richard Nixon as an anti–Vietnam war candidate in 1972; Maureen Reagan, daughter of the president who disagrees with him on a few issues (the Equal Rights Amendment, for one); Congressman Robert Dornan, whose district may be eliminated by redistricting and who raised record sums by direct mail in 1980. Less likely to run — although nothing is certain in California politics — is San Diego Mayor Pete Wilson, a Republican with a moderate reputation who is, at the same time, not as far from the Reagan Republican consensus as some suppose.

On the Democratic side Brown may have competition from John Tunney or from former Speaker Leo McCarthy. McCarthy ran the Assembly for six of the eight Brown years and kept the wheels of government running while Brown went on in his unorthodox manner. McCarthy lost the speakership after he was challenged by the majority leader, Howard Berman of Los Angeles; but Berman in turn was beaten by Willie Brown. Another possible candidate, but only if Brown does not run, is Tom Hayden, the founder of Students for a Democratic Society, who now runs a Committee for Economic Democracy with his wife, Jane Fonda, from their Santa Monica base. Hayden ran a respectable second to John Tunney in the 1976 Senate primary, and his allies have won city elections in Santa Monica (where their big issue is rent control) and in university towns.

The field for the governorship is likely to be crowded as well—which is hardly surprising, given the prize. It is generally assumed that Brown will not run again. The chief Democratic contenders are Thomas Bradley, fresh in 1981 from a rousing reelection as mayor of Los Angeles, and Kenneth Cory, the state controller, a former Orange County assemblyman. Each would be an unusual candidate: Bradley is black, Cory is 6'7". No state has ever elected a black governor, or ever really given a black candidate serious consideration. Bradley, after nine years' service as mayor, after years as a policeman, is about as reassuring to whites as a black candidate could be; he has steadily borne great responsibilities, and he is by no stretch of the imagination a radical. But one may wonder whether voters, even in this tolerant and culturally liberal state, are ready to consider him solely on his merits. On the Republican side, the obvious candidate is Lieutenant Governor Mike Curb. A solid Reagan loyalist, he is even younger than Brown; he was a successful entrepreneur in popular music and won his current office in large part because of the problems of his predecessor, Mervyn Dymally. Some observers consider Curb a little shallow, however. He may very well be challenged by Attorney General George Deukmejian, older, more aggressive, a strong advocate of the death penalty. Dark horses include state Senator Ken Maddy, who ran a strong but ultimately losing race in the 1978 Republican gubernatorial primary, and Pete Wilson. There is, obviously, no clear favorite.

The most experienced statewide official in California today is Senator Alan Cranston, elected state controller in 1958 and 1962 and U.S. senator in 1968, 1974, and 1980. His career has had its ups and downs: he was defeated for controller in 1966, and he won the Senate seat only when the incumbent, Thomas Kuchel, was defeated in the primary by Max Rafferty, the conservative superintendent of public instruction. It is a measure of how well right-wing candidates were doing then that even after certain facts about Rafferty's past had come out —he had sat out World War II with an alleged injury and then had thrown away his crutches on V–J Day—Cranston still won with only 53%.

Cranston began his political career as a founder of the California Democratic Council, a liberal volunteer group important in the 1950s and early 1960s. He was expected to gravitate naturally to the articulate, but often powerless, liberal wing of the Senate. Instead he showed an unusual talent for maintaining good relations with conservatives and for becoming a dealmaker when he sensed that compromises could be struck. By 1974, when he sought his second term, Cranston had won the reputation in some quarters as the best liberal vote counter in the Senate. He shows the enthusiasm one expects from a young liberal idealist and the physical energy one expects from a man who holds the world 100-yard dash record for his age group.

Those were the qualities that enabled Cranston to win the position of Democratic whip— the number two spot in the leadership. Majority Leader Mike Mansfield retired in 1976, and Whip Robert Byrd ran for the leadership. He had opposition, but Cranston was unopposed for the whip post. Now that the Democrats have lost their Senate majority, Cranston is minority rather than majority whip. He is not the kind of person concerned about the loss of ceremonial place, but he will certainly regret the fact that he will have many fewer opportunities for influencing policy in the directions he wants.

Cranston, for all his capacities as an operator, has always been concerned about certain issues and has quietly concentrated on them. One is controlling the arms race. Cranston was one of the early leaders of the United World Federalists, and he was one of the chief Senate backers of the SALT Treaties, although he did not sit on the committees that held hearings on them. He is concerned about involving young people in public service. He himself was involved in politics young; as a journalist he published an unexpurgated translation of Hitler's *Mein Kampf* in the 1930s, and he is now interested in revitalizing the Peace Corps and the whole idea of public service jobs for the young. He has put in hard work on such worthy causes as encouraging adoption of children with special needs. Cranston has also worked hard, probably harder than any other member of the state's delegation, for California's economic interests. He was singlehandedly responsible for passing the $250 million loan guarantee for Lockheed a decade ago, when he talked an errant colleague into switching his vote at the last minute. More recently, he saw that the state of California, which owns major oil properties, was exempted from the windfall profits tax. He keeps an eye out for the agricultural interests of the state and for its major corporations, for its labor unions and its universities.

Cranston was rewarded for all his hard work with a resounding reelection in 1980. He was initially targeted by the New Right, but they were scared off by the high cost of television advertising in California; potentially strong Republican opponents were scared off by Cranston's leads in fund-raising and endorsements. His opponent turned out to be Paul Gann, the less articulate of the two main sponsors of Proposition 13; at 66, Cranston was blessed with an opponent who was older than he. Cranston achieved a resounding 57%–37% victory. No U.S. senator had ever won four million votes in an election before; Cranston won 4,700,000. Cranston will have difficulty pursuing some — although not all — of his causes with a new Republican majority. But he specializes in quiet persuasion and keeps in touch with those whose views might be assumed to be quite different.

California has been the nation's largest state in population for nearly 20 years; its size may be gauged from the fact that for 1982 it will have 45 congressional districts, as compared to 34 for New York and 27 for Texas, the next two largest states. In California the control of redistricting is in the hands of the Democrats, although there is an outside chance that a coalition of Republicans and minorities will be formed to create a series of heavily Democratic and heavily Republican seats. The more likely result is a districting scheme very much like the one that exists now. The House seats are now Democratic by only a 22–21 margin, and at least two of the new seats, one in the Orange County area and one around San Diego, are certain to be Republican. A third new seat will probably be created somewhere in the Central Valley and Sierras area, and that could go for either party; the Democrats will draw the lines, but Republicans made big gains throughout that area in the 1980 elections. Los Angeles County will in effect lose a seat, and the legislature will try to see that it is Republican. Otherwise, the congressional delegation, led by Phillip Burton, will probably seek what amounts to an incumbent protection plan; and the legislators, who are increasingly happy with the good life in Sacramento, and less interested than they were 10 or 20 years ago in moving to Washington, will probably go along.

Census Data   Pop. (1980 final) 23,668,562, up 19% in 1970s: 10.45% of U.S. total, 1st largest. Central city, 36%; suburban, 56%. Median 4-person family income, 1978, $22,294, 109% of U.S.; 5th highest.

1979 Share of Federal Tax Burden $51,573,000,000; 11.44% of U.S. total, 1st largest.

1979 Share of Federal Outlays $52,534,139,000; 11.35% of U.S. total, 1st largest.

DOD	$18,592,547,000	1st	(17.52%)	HEW	$17,524,914,000	2d	(9.80%)
DOE	$1,009,411,000	3d	(8.57%)	ERDA	$420,976,000	2d	(15.53%)
HUD	$522,499,000	2d	(7.93%)	NASA	$1,864,248,000	1st	(39.87%)
VA	$2,003,753,000	1st	(9.66%)	DOT	$1,009,429,000	3d	(6.12%)
EPA	$400,262,000	2d	(7.54%)	DOC	$169,118,000	6th	(5.34%)
DOI	$583,268,000	2d	(10.50%)	USDA	$1,747,930,000	2d	(7.27%)

Economic Base   Finance, insurance, and real estate; agriculture, notably cattle, dairy products, grapes, and hay; transportation equipment, especially aircraft and parts; electrical equipment and supplies, especially radio and television communication equipment; food and kindred products; machinery, especially office and computing machines; tourism; ordnance and accessories.

Political Lineup   Governor, Edmund G, Brown, Jr. (D). Senators, Alan Cranston (D) and S. I. Hayakawa (R). Representatives, 43 (22 D and 21 R); 45 in 1982. State Senate, 40 (23 D and 17 R); State House of Representatives, 80 (48 D and 32 R).

The Voters

   Registration   11,361,020 Total. 6,042,989 D (53%); 3,942,468 R (35%); 147,198 American Independent (1%); 86,193 Libertarian (1%); 44,806 Peace and Freedom (0%); 26,545 Miscellaneous (0%); 1,070,821 declined to state (9%).
   Employment profile 1970   White collar, 54%. Blue collar, 31%. Service, 13%. Farm, 2%.
   Ethnic groups   Black 1980, 8%. Hispanic 1980, 19%. Asian 1980, 5%. Total foreign stock 1970, 25%. Japanese, 1%. Canada, UK, Germany, Italy, 2% each. USSR, 1%.

Presidential Vote	1980	Reagan (R)	4,524,835	(53%)
		Carter (D)	3,083,652	(36%)
		Anderson (I)	739,832	(9%)
	1976	Ford (R)	3,882,244	(49%)
		Carter (D)	3,742,284	(48%)

1980 Democratic Presidential Primary			*1980 Republican Presidential Primary*		
Kennedy	1,507,142	(45%)	Ronald Reagan	2,057,923	(80%)
Carter	1,266,276	(38%)	Anderson	349,315	(14%)
Unpledged delegation.	382,759	(11%)	Bush	125,113	(5%)
Brown	135,962	(4%)	Two others	31,707	(1%)
One other	71,779	(2%)			

SENATORS

Sen. Alan Cranston (D) Elected 1968, seat up 1986; b. June 19, 1914, Palo Alto; home, Los Angeles; Pomona Col., 1932–33, U. of Mexico, 1935, Stanford U., B.A. 1936.

Career   Foreign Correspondent, Internatl. News Svc., 1936–38; Lobbyist, Common Cncl. for American Unity, 1939; Army, WWII; Real estate business, 1947–67; Pres., United World Federalists, 1949–52; State Comptroller of Cal., 1958–66.

Offices   229 RSOB, 202-224-3553. Also 10960 Wilshire Blvd., Los Angeles 90024, 213-824-7641, and One Hallidie Plaza, Suite 301, San Francisco 94102, 415-556-8440.

Committees   *Minority Whip.*

Banking, Housing, and Urban Affairs (3d). Subcommittees: Housing and Urban Affairs; Financial Institutions; Economic Policy.

Foreign Relations (7th). Subcommittees: Arms Control, Oceans and International Operations, and Environment; East Asian and Pacific Affairs; Near Eastern and South Asian Affairs.

Veterans' Affairs (1st).

Group Ratings

	ADA	COPE	PC	LCV	CFA	RPN	NAB	NSI	NTU	ACA	ACU
1980	83	88	57	78	67	—	20	0	25	5	7
1979	88	88	60	—	57	—	—	—	26	4	3
1978	85	89	68	85	55	60	27	20	8	8	17

Key Votes

1) Draft Registn $	AGN	6) Fair Housng Cloture	FOR	11) Cut Socl Incr Defns	AGN
2) Ban $ to Nicrgua	FOR	7) Ban $ Rape Abortns	AGN	12) Income Tax Indexing	AGN
3) Dlay MX Missile	AGN	8) Cap on Food Stmp $	AGN	13) Lim Spdg 21% GNP	AGN
4) Nuclr Mortorium	FOR	9) New US Dep Edcatn	FOR	14) Incr Wndfll Prof Tax	FOR
5) Alaska Lands Bill	FOR	10) Cut OSHA Inspctns	AGN	15) Chryslr Loan Grntee	FOR

Election Results

1980 general	Alan Cranston (D)	4,705,399	(57%)	($2,823,462)
	Paul Gann (R)	3,093,426	(37%)	($1,705,523)
1980 primary	Alan Cranston (D)	2,608,746	(80%)	
	Richard Morgan (D)	350,394	(11%)	
	Two others (D)	305,476	(9%)	
1974 general	Alan Cranston (D)	3,693,160	(61%)	($1,336,202)
	H. L. Richardson (R)	2,210,267	(36%)	($702,767)

Sen. S. I. Hayakawa (R) Elected 1976, seat up 1982; b. July 18, 1906, Vancouver, B.C., Canada; home, Mill Valley; U. of Manitoba, B.A. 1927, McGill U., M.A. 1928, U. of Wis., Ph.D. 1935.

Career Professor, U. of Wis., Illinois Inst. of Tech., U. of Chicago, San Fran. St. Col., 1955–68, Acting Pres., San Fran. St. Col., 1968, Pres., 1969–73.

Offices 6217 DSOB, 202-224-3841. Also Rm. 812, 523 W. 6th St., Los Angeles 90014, 213-688-6081.

Committees *Agriculture, Nutrition, and Forestry* (3d). Subcommittees: Soil and Water Conservation; Agricultural Research and General Legislation; Nutrition; Forestry, Water Resources, and Environment (Chairman).

Foreign Relations (4th). Subcommittees: African Affairs; East Asian and Pacific Affairs (Chairman); Western Hemisphere Affairs.

Select Committee on Small Business (4th). Subcommittees: Export Promotion and Market Development; Advocacy and the Future of Small Business (Chairman).

Group Ratings

	ADA	COPE	PC	LCV	CFA	RPN	NAB	NSI	NTU	ACA	ACU
1980	22	22	20	33	0	—	91	90	50	92	80
1979	11	11	26	—	10	—	—	—	48	65	84
1978	15	18	30	12	25	70	82	80	30	68	77

Key Votes

1) Draft Registn $	FOR	6) Fair Housng Cloture	AGN	11) Cut Socl Incr Defns	FOR
2) Ban $ to Nicrgua	AGN	7) Ban $ Rape Abortns	AGN	12) Income Tax Indexing	FOR
3) Dlay MX Missile	AGN	8) Cap on Food Stmp $	FOR	13) Lim Spdg 21% GNP	FOR
4) Nuclr Mortorium	AGN	9) New US Dep Edcatn	AGN	14) Incr Wndfll Prof Tax	AGN
5) Alaska Lands Bill	FOR	10) Cut OSHA Inspctns	FOR	15) Chryslr Loan Grntee	AGN

Election Results

1976 general	S. I. Hayakawa (R)	3,748,973	(50%)	($1,184,624)
	John Tunney (D)	3,502,862	(47%)	($1,940,988)
1976 primary	S. I. Hayakawa (R)	886,743	(38%)	
	Bob Finch (R)	614,240	(26%)	
	Alphonzo Bell (R)	532,969	(23%)	
	Seven others (R)	285,822	(12%)	
1970 general	John Tunney (D)	3,496,558	(54%)	
	George Murphy (R)	2,877,617	(44%)	

GOVERNOR

Gov. Edmund G. Brown, Jr. (D) Elected 1974, term expires Jan. 1983; b. Apr. 7, 1938, San Francisco; U. of Cal., B.A. 1961, Yale U., J.D. 1964, U. of Santa Clara.

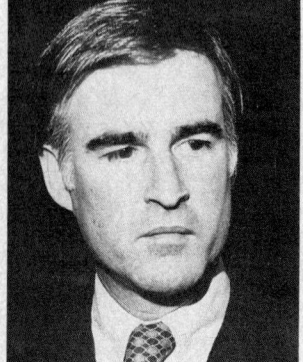

Career Research Atty., Cal. Supreme Ct.; Practicing atty.; Study for the priesthood, Sacred Heart Novitiate, Los Gatos; Secy. of State of Cal., 1971–75.

Offices State Capitol, Sacramento 95814, 916-445-2841.

Election Results

1978 gen.	Edmund G. Brown, Jr. (D) .	3,878,812	(56%)
	Evelle J. Younger (R)	2,526,534	(37%)
	Ed Clark (Libertarian)	377,960	(5%)
1978 prim.	Edmund G. Brown, Jr. (D) .	2,567,067	(78%)
	Eight others (D)	743,673	(22%)
1974 gen.	Edmund G. Brown, Jr. (D) .	3,131,648	(50%)
	Houston I. Flourney (R) . . .	2,952,954	(47%)

FIRST DISTRICT

The 1st is physically the largest of California's congressional districts: with 2% of the state's population, the district covers 22% of its terrain. And varied terrain it is: the 1st extends from the Oregon border to a point south of Lake Tahoe. It does not take in any of the state's Pacific coastline; the western border is the Coast Range. Within the 1st is a substantial part of the northern reaches of the great valley that supplies so much of the nation's food. The district also takes in much of the Sierra Nevada, including the resort area around Tahoe and most of California's ski resorts; most of the Sacramento River valley; and most of what is called the Mother Lode country. The last is the land where the Sierra slants down to the valley, the place where gold was discovered in 1849; some of the county names — Placer, El Dorado — recall those fabled days.

This part of California has been the state's boom area in the 1970s. People, especially young people, have been moving out of the great urban agglomerations of Los Angeles and San Francisco Bay — the boom areas of the 1940s, 1950s, and 1960s — to the hills of the Mother Lode country and the small towns and farms of the upper Sacramento valley. Many of the Mother Lode counties still retain the look of the 1850s, with many of the old buildings standing. There were fewer people here in 1970 than in 1850, but in the ten years after 1970 these counties almost doubled in population. Affluent California has moved into the Mother Lode country, renovating intricately carved redwood houses and building its own new condominiums and subdivisions.

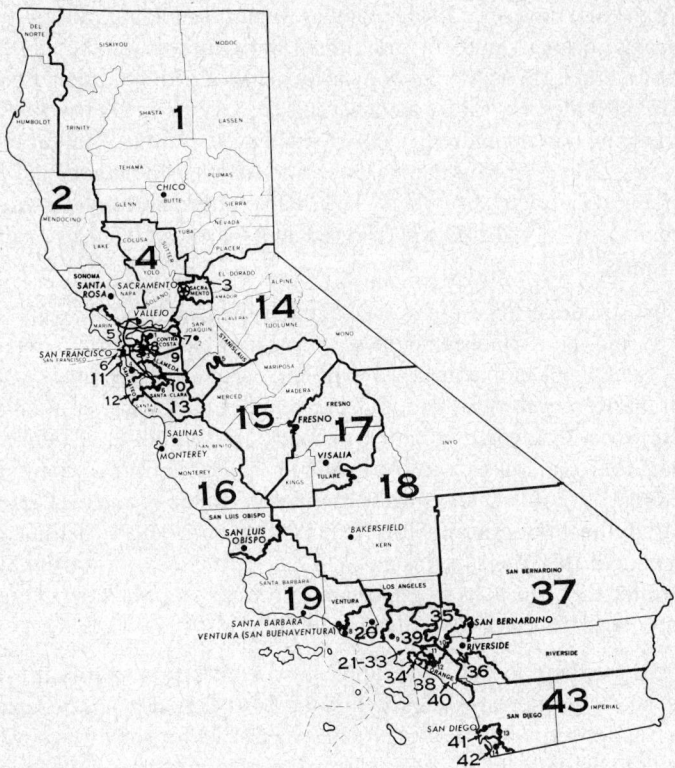

Meanwhile, the streams coming down from the Sierra, the Coast Range, and the giant (active or dormant) volcanoes such as Mount Shasta and Mount Lassen are important today not for the gold that is in them but for the water that is sometimes not. This is the part of California that provides the lion's share of the state's water. And the state's water plan, begun under the first Governor Brown but still not entirely completed, involves sending it from this part of northern California down to the southern Central Valley as well as to the Los Angeles Basin. The dependence of southern California's cities and the Central Valley's farms on aqueduct water was shown vividly by the 1976–77 drought, which seriously damaged California's economy. It is a reminder of how our affluent economy rests on a physical environment that is not particularly hospitable to our form of civilization.

The voters in the 1st district are not spread out equally over this vast and often hauntingly beautiful country. There are two significant concentrations of people. The first is to be found in the upper Sacramento valley, around such towns as Redding, Red Bluff, Chico, and Oroville. This is the northern tip of the Central Valley, the nation's richest agricultural area. About 40% of the 1st's residents live here. Another 20% live in the northeast suburbs of Sacramento, stretched out along Interstate 80 as it heads for the Sierras.

The 1st is historically a Democratic district, but the 1980 returns suggest that it is in the midst of a sharp change in political preference. Up through 1976 its traditional Republican areas (Chico, Oroville) were outnumbered and outpolled by Democratic places (Red Bluff, Redding, the Sacramento suburbs). But in 1980 the whole district went Republican for president and, for the first time since 1940, for congressman. The results cannot be chalked up to Ronald Reagan's personal popularity; no similar shifts are seen in other parts of California. Rather, what we find is the sudden unpopularity of liberal economic policies and perhaps of liberal cultural attitudes as well. A tendency exists to see migrants from the metropolitan areas as left-leaning flower children, intent on building communes. But far more numerous are young family people, who dislike the glitter and sophistication that make San Francisco and Los Angeles so attractive to others. They want communities where traditional values are respected and traditional rules are followed, and they want political candidates who respect those values.

The shift in attitudes is apparent if one contrasts the Democratic congressman who was beaten in 1980 and the Republican elected in his place. Harold "Bizz" Johnson was one of the last New Deal type Democrats in the House, 72 years old at the time of the election. He remembered the Roosevelt years and in his 22 years in Congress supported most spending programs. He especially favored programs to build dams, harbors, and public buildings; and during his last four years in Congress he chaired the Public Works Committee. He must have been bewildered by the attacks made by environmentalists and the Carter Administration on the traditional pork barrel bills. He must have been equally bewildered by the electoral preferences of the voters of this now affluent district. They show little interest in the kind of programs that had been so important to people here when they were poor and felt they needed government projects to help them get by.

The new congressman is Eugene Chappie, a wisecracking Republican who has a solid political base in the Sacramento suburbs and the Mother Lode country. Chappie knew his way around Sacramento and had been eyeing the district for some years; when Johnson's share of the vote fell suddenly in 1978, Chappie moved. Chappie campaigned vigorously; Johnson did very little. He sits on the Agriculture Committee—a useful place for a congressman from this district. Redistricting is going to make a considerable difference in the district's boundaries, since it has gained so much population; the lst will lose quite a bit of its territory, probably in the southern Mother Lode and suburban Sacramento counties. This is Chappie's home territory, but unless the Republican trend of 1980 here turns out to be a fluke, the incumbent appears to have a safe seat.

Census Data   Pop. (1980 final) 652,219, up 41% in 1970s. Median family income, 1970, $8,681, 91% of U.S.

The Voters

   Employment profile 1970   White collar, 45%. Blue collar, 33%. Service, 16%. Farm, 6%.
   Ethnic groups   Black 1980, 1%. Hispanic 1980, 5%. Am. Ind. 1980, 2%. Asian 1980, 1%. Total foreign stock 1970, 13%. Canada, 2%; UK, Germany, Italy, 1% each.

Presidential Vote

1980	Reagan (R)	158,846	(57%)
	Carter (D)	88,189	(32%)
	Anderson (I)	22,249	(8%)
1976	Ford (R)	106,842	(48%)
	Carter (D)	110,186	(49%)

Rep. Eugene A. Chappie (R) Elected 1980; b. Mar. 28, 1920, Sacramento; home, Roseville.

Career Army, WWII; El Dorado Co. Supervisor, 1950–64; Cal. Assembly, 1965–80.

Offices 1730 LHOB, 202-225-3076. Also 270 E. 4th St., Chico 95926, 916-893-8365.

Committees *Agriculture* (19th). Subcommittees: Cotton, Rice and Sugar; Domestic Marketing, Consumer Relations and Nutrition; Forests, Family Farms and Energy.

Group Ratings and Key Votes: Newly Elected

Election Results

1980 general	Eugene A. Chappie (R)..........	145,585	(54%)	($375,721)
	Harold T. Johnson (D)..........	107,993	(40%)	($378,764)
	Jim McClarin (Libertarian)	17,497	(6%)	($0)
1980 primary	Eugene A. Chappie (R)..........	69,307	(100%)	
1978 general	Harold T. Johnson (D)..........	125,122	(59%)	($26,620)
	James E. Taylor (R)	85,690	(41%)	($10,617)

SECOND DISTRICT

For 300 miles north out of San Francisco the California coast stands in massive grandeur, and cut off from the interior by the Coast Range, the region is covered with Douglas firs and redwoods. The first white settlers here were Russians, down from Alaska, but little evidence of their activities remains except for a number of place names, e.g., the Russian River and the town of Sebastopol. More enduring are the rocky, foggy coastline and the redwoods; the new Redwoods National Park, a subject of continuing controversy, attracts many tourists. This was lumbering country in the late 19th century, and the Victorian mansions in such towns as Eureka and Mendocino testify to the riches of the harvest. But today this is not an area of steady prosperity. Any decline in the demand for housing—and there have been many in recent years—depresses the local lumber industry. Meanwhile, proposals to expand the redwoods park, pushed through by San Francisco's Phillip Burton, excite protest demonstrations by lumbermen. Despite the district's natural beauty there has traditionally been outmigration here, but that trend was reversed sharply in the 1970s. Formerly young people from the coastal region left to probe the mysteries of San Francisco and Berkeley; now many young people, fed up with the smog and congestion of California's big metropolitan areas, are swelling the population of the small towns and farming areas of the coast.

The Redwood Empire, as it is sometimes called, makes up most of the 2d congressional district of California. It stretches from the Marin County line, just a few miles north of the Golden Gate, to the Oregon border. Metropolitan growth intrudes in the southern part of Sonoma County, up to Santa Rosa, where Luther Burbank had his laboratory, and the southern edge of wine-growing Napa County. Politically just about the whole area is marginal territory. It went for Carter over Ford by a small margin in 1976, for Nixon over Humphrey by a small margin in 1968. In 1980, like much of nonmetropolitan California, it swung sharply to Ronald Reagan and the Republicans.

The swing was enough to determine the outcome of the race for the House. In congressional races the 2d followed for years the pattern of most California districts: regularly reelecting its congressman, regardless of party. Republican Del Clausen first won in a 1963 special election, to replace a Democrat killed in a plane crash; Clausen is now one of California's most senior House members. Clausen has not, however, been reelected with the kind of majority most incumbents achieve. He was held under 60% by a weak Democrat in 1974 and 1976, and in 1978 and 1980 he received serious challenges from speech pathologist Norma Bork. The first time she held him to 52% of the vote; better prepared, and operating in a more favorable climate of opinion, Clausen was reelected with 55% in 1980.

Clausen is the most senior Republican on two House committees. In 1981 he had his choice of being the ranking Republican member on either one. His decision tells something about his basic attitude. He had served as ranking member on Interior, an environment-oriented committee that had handled the redwoods park issue. Clausen tended to take the side of the local lumbermen and, although he won some concessions, essentially he was beaten by Phil Burton. He chose in 1981 to become ranking member on Public Works, a committee traditionally much more hospitable to development and economic activity and less interested in preserving a pristine environment. It is not clear, however, how interested northern Californians are in dams and federal buildings, the special concerns of this committee. In 1980 the voters of the 1st district defeated Democrat Bizz Johnson, although he was chairman of Public Works.

Clausen's chances of winning reelection in 1982 might be reduced somewhat by redistricting, since the population figures suggest he might lose some of the southern part of the district, where he has received his highest percentages. Even if that happens, however, it is not clear that he will encounter as strenuous an opponent as he has in the last two elections. If Clausen retires, the most likely successor is Democratic Assemblyman Barry Keane.

Census Data   Pop. (1980 final) 622,027, up 34% in 1970s. Median family income, 1970, $9,497, 99% of U.S.

The Voters

Employment profile 1970   White collar, 47%. Blue collar, 34%. Service, 15%. Farm, 4%.
Ethnic groups   Black 1980, 9%. Hispanic 1980, 6%. Am. Ind. 1980, 2%. Asian 1980, 1%. Total foreign stock 1970, 18%. Canada, UK, Germany, Italy, 2% each.

Presidential Vote

1980	Reagan (R)	132,531	(50%)
	Carter (D)	95,971	(36%)
	Anderson (I)	27,869	(10%)
1976	Ford (R)	106,197	(47%)
	Carter (D)	111,043	(50%)

Rep. Don H. Clausen (R) Elected Jan. 22, 1963; b. Apr. 27, 1923, Humboldt Co.; home, Crescent City; San Jose St. Col., Cal. Poly., Weber Col., St. Mary's Col.

Career Navy, WWII; Banking, insurance, professional aviation; Del Norte Co. Supervisor.

Offices 2308 RHOB, 202-225-3311. Also Rm. 216 Eureka Inn, Eureka 95501, 707-442-0912.

Committees *Interior and Insular Affairs* (2d). Subcommittees: Insular Affairs; Public Lands and National Parks; Water and Power Resources.

Public Works and Transportation (Ranking Member).

Group Ratings

	ADA	COPE	PC	LCV	CFA	RPN	NAB	NSI	NTU	ACA	ACU
1980	22	28	23	39	21	—	75	100	38	64	74
1979	11	22	13	24	7	—	—	—	46	71	78
1978	10	24	5	27	14	42	100	100	22	89	90

Key Votes

1) Draft Registn $	AGN	6) Fair Hsg DOJ Enfrc	AGN	11) Cut Socl Incr Dfns $	FOR
2) Ban $ to Nicrgua	FOR	7) Lim PAC Contrbtns	AGN	12) Hosptl Cost Controls	AGN
3) Dlay MX Missile	AGN	8) Cap on Food Stmp $	FOR	13) Gasln Ctrls & Allctns	AGN
4) Nuclr Mortorium	AGN	9) New US Dep Edcatn	FOR	14) Lim Wndfll Prof Tax	FOR
5) Alaska Lands Bill	AGN	10) Cut OSHA $	AGN	15) Chryslr Loan Grntee	FOR

Election Results

1980 general	Don H. Clausen (R)	141,698	(54%)	($451,056)
	Norma K. Bork (D)	109,789	(42%)	($190,689)
1980 primary	Don H. Clausen (R)	62,970	(100%)	
1978 general	Don H. Clausen (R)	114,451	(52%)	($200,924)
	Norma Bork (D)	99,712	(45%)	($80,437)

THIRD DISTRICT

The 3d district of California contains most of the city of Sacramento and some of its suburbs. The site of Sutter's Fort, Sacramento has been an important urban center since the Gold Rush of 1849. Today it is the largest city in the Central Valley, the much irrigated and incalculably rich farmland north along the Sacramento River and south along the San Joaquin. Ever since the Gold Rush, Sacramento has been a Democratic stronghold. These days that preference can be seen as a function of the large number of public employees in this capital city, who tend to be more favorably disposed than the ordinary citizen toward the concept of big government. In fact the 3d district has a higher proportion of public employees than all but four others in the nation—three districts in the suburbs of Washington, D.C., and the state of Alaska. Nonetheless there are limits: Sacramento gave a majority of its votes to Proposition 13 in June 1978.

Sacramento is one of the few American cities with staunchly Democratic newspapers — part of the McClatchy chain that also dominates journalism in Modesto and Fresno farther south in the Valley. As a result, Sacramento's Democratic voting habits are strong enough that this middle-class, middle-income district just missed by a hair going for George McGovern in 1972. Sacramento has its problems with Democrats who run against big government: Jimmy Carter got an unimpressive margin in 1976 and actually lost this Democratic area in 1980, and Jerry Brown ran behind his statewide percentage here in 1978.

The 3d district has been solidly Democratic for years. In 1978, when 26-year incumbent John Moss retired, Republicans seriously contested the district but were not able to win it. Robert Matsui, then a Sacramento councilman, won the five-candidate Democratic primary and prevailed in the general election over County Supervisor Sandy Smoley. Matsui appears to be a solid Democratic Party loyalist in the House. He was rewarded in 1981 with a seat on the Ways and Means Committee, where he seems likely to support Democratic positions on taxes and welfare. Redistricting will probably not affect the composition of this district much.

Census Data   Pop. (1980 final) 585,264, up 26% in 1970s. Median family income, 1970, $11,019, 115% of U.S.

The Voters

Employment profile 1970   White collar, 62%. Blue collar, 25%. Service, 12%. Farm, 1%.
Ethnic groups   Black 1980, 8%. Hispanic 1980, 9%. Am. Ind. 1980, 1%. Asian 1980, 6%. Total foreign stock 1970, 20%. Canada, U.K., Germany, Italy, 2% each.

Presidential Vote

1980	Reagan (R)	118,814	(48%)
	Carter (D)	99,225	(40%)
	Anderson (I)	23,357	(9%)
1976	Ford (R)	98,706	(46%)
	Carter (D)	110,313	(52%)

Rep. Robert T. Matsui (D) Elected 1978; b. Sept. 17, 1941, Sacramento; home, Sacramento; U. of Cal., B.A. 1963, Hastings Col. of Law, J.D. 1966.

Career Practicing atty., 1967– ; Sacramento City Cncl., 1971–78.

Offices 329 CHOB, 202-225-7163. Also 8058 Fed. Bldg., Sacramento 95814, 916-440-3543.

Committees *Ways and Means* (22d). Subcommittees: Public Assistance and Unemployment Compensation; Select Subcommittee on Revenue Measures.

Select Committee on Narcotics Abuse and Control (11th).

Group Ratings

	ADA	COPE	PC	LCV	CFA	RPN	NAB	NSI	NTU	ACA	ACU
1980	94	79	67	76	71	—	0	20	11	13	11
1979	89	90	83	88	89	—	—	—	16	12	8

Key Votes

1) Draft Registn $	AGN	6) Fair Hsg DOJ Enfrc	FOR	11) Cut Socl Incr Dfns $	AGN
2) Ban $ to Nicrgua	AGN	7) Lim PAC Contrbtns	FOR	12) Hosptl Cost Controls	FOR
3) Dlay MX Missile	FOR	8) Cap on Food Stmp $	AGN	13) Gasln Ctrls & Allctns	FOR
4) Nuclr Mortorium	FOR	9) New US Dep Edcatn	FOR	14) Lim Wndfll Prof Tax	AGN
5) Alaska Lands Bill	FOR	10) Cut OSHA $	AGN	15) Chryslr Loan Grntee	FOR

Election Results

1980 general	Robert T. Matsui (D)	170,670	(71%)	($211,981)
	Joseph Murphy (R)	64,215	(26%)	($0)
1980 primary	Robert T. Matsui (D)	95,565	(89%)	
	One other (D)	11,967	(11%)	
1978 general	Robert T. Matsui (D)	105,537	(53%)	($468,028)
	Sandy Smoley (R)	91,966	(47%)	($329,408)

FOURTH DISTRICT

The low, flat delta lands where the Sacramento and San Joaquin Rivers empty into San Francisco Bay; the rich fruit-growing land of the lower Sacramento valley; and some of the fast-growing suburbs of Sacramento itself make up the 4th congressional district of California. The southern part of the district — Vallejo and surrounding Solano County — has long been industrial and Democratic. The same inclination is shared by the Sacramento suburbs in Yolo and Sacramento Counties. Only the more sparsely populated northern counties — Colusa, Sutter — regularly turn in Republican majorities, and these are, at the very least, balanced by a new center of Democratic strength, the University of California at Davis. Situated on flat delta lands, Davis seems to have the nation's best developed set of bicycle paths and highest population of bicycles.

The 4th district has never been considered especially interesting territory politically, yet it has provided a pivot for several of the most interesting political stories of the late 1970s — all stories that tended to hurt the district's dominant Democrats. The first of these is the Bakke case, which concerned admission to Davis's medical school. Bakke spotlighted the injustices and absurdities of many affirmative action programs; and although the Davis campus itself probably was persuaded that the medical school's quota system should have been upheld, relatively few ordinary citizens agreed. Then there was Proposition 13, another blow to liberalism; although the ballot measure passed the entire state, it was prompted by the failure of the governor and legislature in Sacramento, just on the edge of the 4th district, to extend property tax relief.

Finally, there is the Koreagate scandal. The 4th is one of the nation's two major rice growing areas, and many of Tongsun Park's activities were connected with rice. One of the congressmen he befriended was the 4th district's Robert Leggett. But Leggett was never criminally charged in the Koreagate case, nor did the Bakke case or Proposition 13 cause him any problems. His career, at age 52, was already over before these issues came to a head. For in 1976 it had been revealed that Leggett had not only had an affair with a secretary but had actually had two children by her and was maintaining two households. Leggett beat a weak Republican opponent that year, but with only 51% of the vote. It was clear that he could not win in 1978, and he did not run.

So despite all the potential problems for Democrats here—and adverse national trends—the Democratic hold on the district has actually been strengthened. The main reason is the strength of the new congressman, Vic Fazio, who won 57% of the vote in a four-candidate primary in 1978, and prevailed over a strong Republican challenge in the general election. He was reelected easily in 1980, although Ronald Reagan carried this once dependably Democratic district. Fazio is one of several congressmen who are veterans of the California Assembly; he is also, and this is likely a first, a former professional Assembly staffer. That is a formidable background. The Assembly is known for the competence of its operations, and Fazio was involved as well in founding that estimable publication, the *California Journal*.

He has shown his legislative abilities in the House. In his second term he won a seat on the Appropriations Committee and a subcommittee chairmanship as well. This is the Legislative Subcommittee, and while its subject matter is not earthshaking, it is very important to members of Congress: it sets the budget for Congress and all its committees and subcommittees. Fazio appears to be the kind of knowledgeable and politically adept legislator who can fill such a position comfortably.

Census Data   Pop. (1980 final) 581,198, up 25% in 1970s. Median family income, 1970, $9,556, 99% of U.S.

The Voters

Employment profile 1970   White collar, 51%. Blue collar, 30%. Service, 14%. Farm, 5%.
Ethnic groups   Black 1980, 8%. Hispanic 1980, 12%. Am. Ind. 1980, 1%. Asian 1980, 5%. Total foreign stock 1970, 18%. Canada, Germany, 2% each; UK, Italy, 1% each.

Presidential Vote

1980	Reagan (R)	103,541	(48%)
	Carter (D)	86,427	(40%)
	Anderson (I)	20,295	(9%)
1976	Ford (R)	76,230	(43%)
	Carter (D)	96,028	(55%)

Rep. Vic Fazio (D) Elected 1978; b. Oct. 11, 1942, Winchester, Mass.; home, Sacramento; Union Col., B.A. 1965.

Career Aide to U.S. Rep. Ronald Cameron; Consultant, Cal. Assembly, 1967; founder, *The California Journal*; Dir., Office of Assembly Major. Consultants and Asst. to Assembly Spkr., 1971; Cal. Assembly, 1975–78.

Offices 1421 LHOB, 202-225-5716. Also 823 Marin St., Rm. 8, Vallejo 94590, 707-552-0720.

Committees *Appropriations* (27th). Subcommittees: Energy and Water Development; Legislative (Chairman).

Group Ratings

	ADA	COPE	PC	LCV	CFA	RPN	NAB	NSI	NTU	ACA	ACU
1980	89	79	53	58	71	—	8	22	12	23	11
1979	84	79	70	76	63	—	—	—	12	8	5

Key Votes

1) Draft Registn $	FOR	6) Fair Hsg DOJ Enfrc	FOR	11) Cut Socl Incr Dfns $	AGN
2) Ban $ to Nicrgua	AGN	7) Lim PAC Contrbtns	FOR	12) Hosptl Cost Controls	FOR
3) Dlay MX Missile	AGN	8) Cap on Food Stmp $	AGN	13) Gasln Ctrls & Allctns	FOR
4) Nuclr Mortorium	FOR	9) New US Dep Edcatn	FOR	14) Lim Wndfll Prof Tax	AGN
5) Alaska Lands Bill	FOR	10) Cut OSHA $	AGN	15) Chryslr Loan Grntee	FOR

Election Results

1980 general	Vic Fazio (D)	133,853	(65%)	($185,300)
	Albert Dehr (R)	60,935	(30%)	($5,517)
	Robert J. Burnside (Libertarian)	10,267	(5%)	($0)
1980 primary	Vic Fazio (D)	71,344	(80%)	
	One other (D)	18,100	(20%)	
1978 general	Vic Fazio (D)	87,764	(55%)	($235,600)
	Rex Hime (R)	70,733	(45%)	($138,085)

FIFTH DISTRICT

The 5th congressional district of California takes in the northwest portion of San Francisco and all of Marin County, two of the more prosperous and scenic parts of the cosmopolitan San Francisco Bay area. The San Francisco portion includes the highest-income parts of the city; the expensive Pacific Heights, Marina, and Sea Cliff districts. These neighborhoods are on hilltops or near water. In valleys inland are some of San Francisco's poorer neighborhoods; the black Fillmore district, the Western Addition, and the Haight–Ashbury area, famous a decade ago as the center of hippie culture in America and now being revived by young people renovating homes.

But most of this part of San Francisco is solid middle-class country. It is not quite suburbia: the houses are older, sitting amidst the unburied telephone and electric wires, and there are not as many young families as in the suburbs. A tradition of tolerance typical of San Francisco exists here, and majorities of even middle-class voters never went over to the politics of Richard Nixon or Spiro Agnew. It is not their middle-class sensibilities, but their pocketbooks, they worry about. Even before Proposition 13, there was a backlash in San Francisco against the demands of the municipal employees' unions; and while Proposition 13 was beaten in the ghetto and trendy parts of the district, it prevailed in the more middle-class areas.

The Marin County portion of the 5th lies just across the Golden Gate Bridge. A series of suburbs nestled between rugged mountains and the Bay, this is the West Coast origin of what Tom Wolfe called "The Me Decade." Marin's life style has been captured neatly in Cyra McFadden's spiral-bound book, *The Serial*. If the traditional politics of the standard Middle American has been liberal on economic issues and conservative on social issues, the politics of Marin County has been just the reverse. This is traditionally a Republican area, one of the few parts of California that supports liberal over conservative Republicans in primaries.

Marin moved away from Richard Nixon's Republicans the more they waved the flag and attacked unusual life-styles, and back in 1972, 49% of its voters supported legalization of marijuana in a referendum. At the same time, Marin is a wealthy county, and one that does not believe that it has any particular obligation to give its money away. It voted 62% for

Proposition 13 in 1978, just about the state average, and in the same year it ousted a Democratic assemblyman. Marin was never very warm toward Jimmy Carter, who as a Georgia Baptist seems inherently unsimpatico.

These unusual attitudes have left the 5th congressional district out of kilter with national trends. In 1972 this district went for George McGovern and in 1976 for Gerald Ford. In 1980 Marin backed Reagan over Carter, but Carter got large margins in San Francisco from voters who evidently could not stomach Reagan; John Anderson also ran well here, better than in all but one of California's other districts. The result: this is the only congressional district in the nation that has supported the loser in each of the last three presidential elections.

The current congressman from the 5th district, John Burton, has had a long career in San Francisco, in California, and in national politics. He succeeded his brother Phil in the California Assembly in 1964 at a time when both Burtons were considered wild radicals because, among other things, they wanted to abolish the House Un-American Activities Committee. Less than ten years later John Burton was chairman of both the Assembly Rules Committee and the California state Democratic Party. That was also the year he ran for Congress in the last of those special elections in the spring of 1974 that did so much to show how unpopular Richard Nixon was throughout the country. John Burton remains close to his brother and would have become a power if Phil Burton had been elected majority leader in 1976 — a position he missed by just one vote in the Democratic Caucus. Instead the younger Burton has some interesting committee positions: he chaired the subcommittee investigating government regulation of the DC–10 after the Chicago crash.

In 1980 Burton attracted strong Republican opposition for the first time in his House career. Republican Dennis McQuaid had a base in northern Marin, the least trendy part of the county, and he attacked Burton as "unconventional" and "off the wall." Burton does in fact tend to harangue, and with his drooping mustache and rumpled clothes he is not anyone's idea of pin-striped propriety. But McQuaid's personal attacks evidently did not work. Burton did indeed lose Marin County, but his liberal record on economic issues — the Burtons are as interested as anyone in Congress in raising the level of transfer payments to the poor — probably cost him more than his unconventional style in a county where conventions are scarcely traditional. Burton carried the San Francisco portion of the district solidly, which was enough for a greater than expected margin of victory. More than that, the Burtons took revenge on the Republicans in another district. Reportedly they told the Republicans that if John Burton was given a hard race, they would make sure that Bill Royer, the Republican who had won a 1979 special election in the 11th district just south of San Francisco, would also get a tough race. John Burton won and Royer lost.

All that would suggest that John Burton will not have such a difficult challenge next time. Redistricting, however, may pose a problem. San Francisco has lost population, and both Burtons' districts will have to move outward. That means, in John Burton's case, to territory he lost in 1980. But in the past Phil Burton put together California's congressional redistricting and one can be reasonably sure that there will be a Democratic district, or as Democratic as possible, for John Burton to run in in 1982.

Census Data   Pop. (1980 final) 467,013, up 1% in 1970s. Median family income, 1970, $12,010, 125% of U.S.

The Voters

Employment profile 1970   White collar, 69%. Blue collar, 17%. Service, 14%. Farm, –%.

Ethnic groups   Black 1980, 9%. Hispanic 1980, 5%. Asian 1980, 12%. Total foreign stock 1970, 34%. UK, Germany, Italy, 3% each; USSR, Ireland, 2% each.

Presidential Vote

1980	Reagan (R)	80,930	(38%)
	Carter (D)	91,480	(44%)
	Anderson (I)	26,904	(13%)
1976	Ford (R)	95,721	(48%)
	Carter (D)	94,329	(48%)

Rep. John L. Burton (D) Elected June 4, 1974; b. Dec. 15, 1932; home, San Francisco; San. Fran. St. Col., B.A. 1954; U. of San. Fran., LL.B. 1960.

Career Army 1954–56; Deputy Atty. Gen. of Cal.; Cal. Assembly, 1965–74; Chmn., Cal. Dem. Party, 1973–74.

Offices 1714 LHOB, 202-225-5161. Also 450 Golden Gate Ave., Box 36024, San Francisco 94102, 415-556-1333.

Committees *Government Operations* (8th). Subcommittees: Government Activities and Transportation (Chairman); Government Information and Individual Rights.

House Administration (8th). Subcommittees: Accounts; Office Systems; Policy Group on Information and Computers.

Select Committee on Aging (5th). Subcommittee: Retirement Income and Employment (Chairman).

Group Ratings

	ADA	COPE	PC	LCV	CFA	RPN	NAB	NSI	NTU	ACA	ACU
1980	94	88	69	94	79	—	0	0	30	33	17
1979	84	100	73	88	78	—	—	—	32	14	6
1978	80	100	80	82	77	27	0	0	43	13	10

Key Votes

1) Draft Registn $	AGN	6) Fair Hsg DOJ Enfrc	FOR	11) Cut Socl Incr Dfns $	AGN
2) Ban $ to Nicrgua	AGN	7) Lim PAC Contrbtns	FOR	12) Hosptl Cost Controls	FOR
3) Dlay MX Missile	FOR	8) Cap on Food Stmp $	AGN	13) Gasln Ctrls & Allctns	FOR
4) Nuclr Mortorium	FOR	9) New US Dep Edcatn	—	14) Lim Wndfll Prof Tax	—
5) Alaska Lands Bill	FOR	10) Cut OSHA $	AGN	15) Chryslr Loan Grntee	FOR

Election Results

1980 general	John L. Burton (D).............	101,105	(51%)	($369,237)
	Dennis McQuaid (R)	89,624	(45%)	($484,140)
1980 primary	John L. Burton (D).............	59,735	(100%)	
1978 general	John L. Burton (D).............	106,046	(67%)	($88,923)
	Dolores Skore (R)..............	52,603	(33%)	

SIXTH DISTRICT

San Francisco is a special city, named over and over as the city where most Americans would like to live and as the American city most foreigners would like to visit. It has a unique climate, physical beauty, and a special atmosphere spiritually. Yet San Francisco passed through some difficult years in the late 1970s, and although its spirit seems to be recovering, it has still not regained the serene confidence it once enjoyed. For a few years, San Francisco seemed to be under siege. There was the Patricia Hearst kidnapping and the bizarre bank robbery by the Symbionese Liberation Army, Sara Jane Moore's attempt to assassinate President Ford, the Guyana massacre of the San Francisco–based People's Temple, and the murders of Mayor George Moscone and Supervisor Harvey Milk. People began to wonder whether something had gone terribly wrong with San Francisco.

San Francisco has always had the reputation of an exotic city, hospitable to political radicals and cultural deviants when most American cities wanted no part of them. The city got its start as the supply center of the gold mining camps — springing suddenly into existence in 1849 — and some of its raffish character was established during those lawless days. The city also had its own unique ethnic migrations (many Chinese, many Italians). And instead of standard machine politics it spawned its own breed of radicals, e.g., Denis Kearney, who wanted to prohibit Chinese immigration, and its own kind of political boss, such as Abe Ruef, who was finally thrown out by the progressive reformer Hiram Johnson. By the turn of the century San Francisco had developed its own sensibility in the arts and its own literary heroes: Jack London, Frank Norris, and Ambrose Bierce. It also fostered one of the strongest union movements in the nation, one whose successes were probably made possible by the fact that the city's economy had such a solid base: the city's economy is based solidly on that most prosaic of commodities, food. It is through San Francisco's port and rail facilities that most of California's incredibly rich harvest of vegetables, fruits, and other agricultural products are transported to the rest of the world. This is the mouth of the Central Valley's cornucopia.

San Francisco's political tradition was progressive Republican until the 1930s, when it became Democratic. But it was a political tradition that in many ways seemed peculiarly distant from the rest of the country. San Francisco was a place apart, and proud of it. Since that time, changes in transportation and communication have made San Francisco less distinctive; the sheer physical distances that isolated it from other American cities are no longer much of a barrier. Nevertheless, no one would deny that San Francisco has remained unique. Its early reputation as a home for writers and artists has attracted several generations of bohemians here; the climate is pleasant, people are used to unusual neighbors, and the artistic atmosphere is not as exacting or as bitchy as New York's. The economy has remained prosperous — it was not hit as hard by the Depression of the 1930s as many cities, for people still have to eat — and population has risen and spread from the city to the various lowlands between the Bay and the mountains. The city itself has become increasingly the home of the very rich and the very poor, of the single and the elderly and the homosexual, of the black and the Chinese and the Filipino.

In the early 1970s, San Francisco seemed sure of where it was going. Riding on its continuing prosperity and growth, it could afford to become the largest office center in the nation after New York and Chicago — and to conduct campaigns against high rises at the same time. This was a city where the majority was determined to tolerate all of its minorities; San Francisco voted to legalize marijuana in 1972, it favored gay rights, it opposed capital punishment. And it had a group of savvy political leaders who seemed destined for positions of greater power. Foremost among them was Congressman Phillip Burton, who as head of the Democratic Study Group in the 1970s was the major force behind critical reforms in the House. The group also included John Burton, Phil's brother, who was a leading member of the State Assembly and Democratic state chairman as well, and Willie Brown, chairman of the Assembly Ways and Means Committee and head of the 1972 California McGovern delegation. Another was George Moscone, a leading state senator who was then widely expected to be the next mayor. All personal friends, these men represented a set of ideas of what government should be. Their first priority was the poor—increasing welfare payments, providing more benefits, instituting national health insurance. They were strong supporters of labor unions. They worked to preserve the environment. They were classic California liberals—and also practical, hardheaded politicians.

By the late 1970s they had accomplished much of what they set out to do. But some of their dreams had gone sour. Phil Burton had failed, by one vote, to be elected House majority leader after the 1976 elections; his heavy-handed tactics and alliance with Wayne Hays alienated one too many of his Democratic colleagues. Willie Brown had been beaten two years before in a contest for Assembly speaker by Leo McCarthy, another San Franciscan whose personal style is closer to that of the residential neighborhoods he represents in the southern part of the city. McCarthy, by any measure, was a solid liberal Democrat, and a talented legislator as well; he held the Assembly on a straight course during the first six years of the Brown years, when the governor couldn't be bothered with legislative lobbying; and he beat Brown's effort to have the California legislature endorse the proposal for a constitutional amendment to prohibit federal deficit spending.

George Moscone, as predicted, was elected mayor in 1975 to replace Joseph Alioto, who had gotten on well with both the unions and the business community. But even as Moscone won, San Francisco seemed to be changing. Voters had rejected a salary increase for city employees and nearly elected a budget-cutter over Moscone. It was clear that the majority felt that enough was being done for the unions and the poor—and by most standards they were doing well. The great battles of the early 1970s had been won: Vietnam was over, Nixon was out, and under Moscone the city behaved about as tolerantly and nurturingly toward minorities as a city government can. Moscone and his friends who had burned to accomplish things suddenly found themselves in positions of power with most of their goals achieved.

That was the context in which the Guyana massacre and, weeks later, the Moscone and Milk murders occurred. In Guyana a man who had hovered around the edges of the liberal subculture and had been accepted by the political community turned out to be a homicidal maniac; Moscone and other Democrats who had accepted Jim Jones's support in the past were dismayed at their misjudgment. Dan White, the former supervisor who shot Moscone and Milk, had represented the part of the city least sympathetic to the Mayor's tolerant policies—a kind of Middle America at the edge of San Francisco—and his act was reminiscent of the cultural conflicts of the 1960s and early 1970s. Ironically, White was found guilty only of manslaughter—leniency that suggested that some San Franciscans considered the killings of a liberal mayor and a gay supervisor not particularly heinous crimes. The street riot by gays that followed suggested a breakdown of the apparent truce between different segments of the city. The new Mayor, Dianne Feinstein, took pains to point out that San Francisco was a city of family people with traditional values, not just kooks, even as she appointed a homosexual to Milk's supervisor seat. San Francisco and its politics remain distinctive, but the city that had seemed to reach a liberal consensus became a place of civil discord instead. Its economy, as always, remains strong, and its appeal to outsiders continues, but the political future of San Francisco is far from clear.

San Francisco now seems to be in better shape, and the fortunes of its leading politicians have improved. Dianne Feinstein was reelected mayor, over the opposition of a supervisor backed by conservative homeowners and Jerry Brown. Leo McCarthy was ousted as speaker but was replaced by none other than Willie Brown, his onetime rival but current ally; McCarthy himself may run for the U.S. Senate in 1982. Phil Burton has been a very active and productive member of the House, and John Burton was able to repel a strong Republican challenge in 1980. San Francisco's skyline gets more impressive, and the city thrives even as the suburbs grow. The media always talks about San Francisco's gay community, but even more important demographically—and an important force for stability are the city's large Oriental communities. Indeed, Asians and Pacific Islanders (the category the census uses) are now by far San Francisco's largest minority, with 22% of the city's population, almost as many as blacks and Mexican–Americans put together.

Most of the city of San Francisco is within the 6th congressional district, the seat represented by Phil Burton. It includes all of San Francisco's downtown and most of its tourist attractions—Chinatown, Telegraph Hill and North Beach, Nob Hill and Union Square. The district includes the middle-income Sunset district near the Ocean and St. Francis Wood, home of the conservative Catholic upper class. It includes also the city's docks, the foundation of its prosperity, although they look anything but prosperous themselves. The 6th also includes the Mission district, mostly Mexican but with many gingerbread houses restored by Anglos; the geographically isolated Hunters Point ghetto; the dreary sameness of the subdivisions visible from the Bayshore Freeway. This could be the most polyglot district in the nation: with large numbers of blacks, Mexican–Americans, Chinese–Americans, and Filipinos. White Anglos are a minority here as well. Not surprisingly, this is a solidly Democratic district—one of the most reliably Democratic in California.

Phillip Burton, despite his defeat in the majority leader race in 1976, remains one of the nation's most important congressmen. He is probably more responsible than any other single person for the changes that have made the House of Representatives an open, responsive place today—in stark contrast to what it was a decade ago. Burton's achievements are all the more notable because he seemed so unlikely, when first elected, ever to be a power in Washington. Back in 1964, he was part of the tiny left wing of the House: an opponent of the Vietnam war and an advocate of the abolition of the House Un-American Activities Committee. But he was not just a protestor; he also worked hard on legislation. As a member of the Education and Labor Committee, he became a generally recognized expert on welfare legislation.

Burton is also a kind of instinctive dealmaker, with a taste for unusual alliances. Thus he got labor Democrats to join southerners to oppose modest limits on farm subsidy payments in return for more money for welfare. In 1971 he assembled the whole California delegation, Republicans as well as Democrats, to support redistricting plans that would return all incumbents; he will try to do so again in 1982. When he became head of the Democratic Study Group in 1971, he made the organization a real power—perhaps the real power in the House. The DSG rounded up votes on important issues, prepared crucial amendments, and raised campaign money for candidates who Phil Burton thought could win.

Burton could not have hoped to ascend to the leadership, however, without the support of the 75 freshman Democrats elected in 1974. They helped him beat fellow Californian Bernie Sisk for the Steering Committee chair and seemed likely to elect him majority leader. But his alliance with Wayne Hays hurt after the Elizabeth Ray scandal. In December 1976

Burton led on the first ballots as Californian John McFall and then Richard Bolling, considered his toughest rival, were eliminated. But in the final race he was beaten by Jim Wright of Texas by a single vote. It was a defeat that had to be interpreted as a personal rejection of Phil Burton.

Such a setback would effectively end the congressional careers of many men, but this has not happened in Burton's case. He has no leadership role, and the DSG is no longer so responsive to him—nor is its work so important since Tip O'Neill has become speaker. Burton is not one of O'Neill's favorites, and he is a natural rival of Majority Leader Wright, Majority Whip Thomas Foley, and Rules Committee Chairman Bolling, all of whom might be his competitors for the speakership someday. And Burton is not a full committee chairman.

Burton is nevertheless one of the major legislators in the House. During the Carter years he was chairman of the Interior subcommittee with jurisdiction over American territories overseas—Insular Affairs, in the old-fashioned term. He has brought the benefits of the American welfare state—food stamps, other welfare programs—to places as distant as Puerto Rico, Guam, and American Samoa. His clout in these areas was memorialized in the comment that the sun never sets on the Burton empire. Burton also put together major parks legislation, establishing new national parks and wilderness areas from one end of the country to the other, from the controversial Redwoods park in northern California to urban parks in New York and other major cities.

Burton showed a real flair for his work on the Interior Committee, but in 1981 he gave up his subcommittee chair there for one on Labor–Management Relations. Organized labor feared Republicans' assaults on the labor laws; a move was made to repeal the Davis–Bacon Act and it was possible that the major labor laws would be changed. Burton can be counted on to provide aggressive leadership and uncompromising advocacy of positions he considers in the interest of the poor and working people. Immediately after his defeat for majority leader, Burton seemed preoccupied with regaining a chance for a leadership position. But in the years that have followed, he has been such a productive and active legislator that he had little time for such preoccupations. There is no vacancy in the leadership now, but as things now stand Burton could be doing nothing more productive than he is now.

Census Data   Pop. (1980 final) 441,257, down 5% in 1970s. Median family income, 1970, $10,606, 111% of U.S.

The Voters

Employment profile 1970   White collar, 58%. Blue collar, 26%. Service, 16%. Farm, –%.
Ethnic groups   Black 1980, 12%. Hispanic 1980, 17%. Am. Ind. 1980, 1%. Asian 1980, 22%. Total foreign stock 1970, 47%. Italy, 5%; Ireland, 3%; Canada, UK, 2% each; USSR, 1%.

Presidential Vote

1980	Reagan (R)	50,967	(33%)
	Carter (D)	81,691	(53%)
	Anderson (I)	16,502	(11%)
1976	Ford (R)	62,223	(40%)
	Carter (D)	83,668	(54%)

Rep. Phillip Burton (D) Elected Feb. 18, 1964; b. June 1, 1926, Cincinnati, Ohio; home, San Francisco; USC, A.B. 1947, Golden Gate Law School, LL.B. 1952.

Career Army, WWII and Korea; Practicing atty.; Cal. Assembly, 1956–64.

Offices 2304 RHOB, 202-225-4965. Also Rm. 11104 Fed. Ofc. Bldg., 450 Golden Gate Ave., San Francisco 94102, 415-556-4862.

Committees *Education and Labor* (4th). Subcommittees: Labor–Management Relations (Chairman); Labor Standards.

Interior and Insular Affairs (2d). Subcommittees: Insular Affairs; Public Lands and National Parks.

Group Ratings

	ADA	COPE	PC	LCV	CFA	RPN	NAB	NSI	NTU	ACA	ACU
1980	83	89	73	88	93	—	0	0	21	25	11
1979	95	89	88	95	89	—	—	—	16	0	3
1978	95	94	85	86	86	45	0	0	26	4	10

Key Votes

1) Draft Registn $	AGN	6) Fair Hsg DOJ Enfrc	FOR	11) Cut Socl Incr Dfns $	AGN
2) Ban $ to Nicrgua	AGN	7) Lim PAC Contrbtns	FOR	12) Hosptl Cost Controls	FOR
3) Dlay MX Missile	FOR	8) Cap on Food Stmp $	AGN	13) Gasln Ctrls & Allctns	FOR
4) Nuclr Mortorium	FOR	9) New US Dep Edcatn	FOR	14) Lim Wndfll Prof Tax	AGN
5) Alaska Lands Bill	FOR	10) Cut OSHA $		AGN	15) Chryslr Loan Grntee	—

Election Results

1980 general	Phillip Burton (D)	93,400	(69%)	($140,812)
	Tom Spinosa (R)	34,500	(26%)	($6,906)
	Roy Childs (Libertarian)	6,750	(5%)	($0)
1980 primary	Phillip Burton (D)	57,463	(81%)	
	Two others (D)	13,351	(19%)	
1978 general	Phillip Burton (D)	81,801	(68%)	($96,933)
	Tom Spinosa (R)	33,515	(28%)	

SEVENTH DISTRICT

The 7th congressional district of California is one of the more politically marginal parts of the San Francisco Bay area. Although of apparently regular, rectangular shape and lying wholly within Contra Costa County, the 7th is really a collection of heterogeneous industrial and suburban communities separated by high mountains. Richmond, a working-class city facing San Francisco Bay, is the anchor to the west. It supplies large Democratic margins in all elections, in part because of its large (48%) black population. Along the bay that leads to the Sacramento River Delta are the industrial towns of Martinez, Pittsburg, and Antioch — more Democratic bastions. Republican margins come from the more prosperous, faster-growing inland suburbs such as middle-income Concord (now the 7th's largest city with 103,000 people) and high-income Walnut Creek. These affluent communities have been moving the 7th toward the Republican column in statewide elections. But in congressional contests it has remained Democratic.

The 7th's congressman, George Miller, might be called a fairly typical member of the freshman class of 1974. The seat was opened up for him when incumbent Jerome Waldie, an early proimpeachment voice on the House Judiciary Committee, ran unsuccessfully for governor, and two popular local state legislators decided not to leave Sacramento. That left the field pretty clear for Miller. As the son of a former state senator, he had a well-known name in Contra Costa County, and he won the Democratic primary fairly easily. In the general election, he had a significant opponent. But the issues of 1974 favored Democrats, he had a well-financed, well-run campaign, and he won the election with a solid 56%—above Democratic levels in close statewide contests.

In the House Miller was one of the freshmen who supported the 6th district's Phillip Burton for House majority leader; he serves on the same committees as Burton, Interior and Education and Labor. While some freshmen have expressed doubts about the efficacy of government spending programs, Miller generally supports them and has high labor and liberal voting records. Like most other freshmen, he has managed to maintain a high profile in his district, using the advantages of incumbency to the maximum. He was reelected with 76% of the vote in 1976 and with lower but still comfortable percentages in 1978 and 1980. The key question for the future about the freshman of 1974 is how long people like Miller will be willing to exert all the effort that is needed to keep a district like this safe: regular trips back on weekends, frequent telephoning to key constituents, maintaining efficient constituency service.

A conflict may present itself here with Miller's increasing legislative duties. He is now chairman of the Labor Standards Subcommittee of Education and Labor, the body that considers such controversial legislation as the proposal for a subminimum wage for teenagers (shelved by Reagan's Republicans, at least for a while, in early 1981). Still in his 30s, Miller has the potential for a long House career; redistricting should pose no problem since Burton will likely have a say in drawing the lines.

Census Data   Pop. (1980 final) 555,306, up 20% in 1970s. Median family income, 1970, $11,826, 123% of U.S.

The Voters

Employment profile 1970   White collar, 52%. Blue collar, 35%. Service, 12%. Farm, 1%.

Ethnic groups   Black 1980, 10% Hispanic 1980, 9%. Am. Ind. 1980, 1%. Asian 1980, 4%. Total foreign stock 1970, 19%. Canada, UK, Germany, Italy, 2% each.

Presidential Vote

1980	Reagan (R)	113,690	(59%)
	Carter (D)	90,975	(39%)
	Anderson (I)	21,827	(9%)
1976	Ford (R)	95,241	(47%)
	Carter (D)	104,664	(51%)

Rep. George Miller (D) Elected 1974; b. May 17, 1945, Richmond; home, Martinez; Diablo Valley Col., San Fran. St. Col., B.A. 1968, U. of Cal. at Davis, J.D., 1972.

Career Legis. Aide to Cal. Senate Major. Ldr., 1969–74.

Offices 2422 RHOB, 202-225-2095. Also 367 Civic Dr., Pleasant Hill 94523, 415-687-3260.

Committees *Education and Labor* (10th). Subcommittees: Elementary, Secondary and Vocational Education; Labor Standards (Chairman); Select Education.

Interior and Insular Affairs (10th). Subcommittee: Water and Power Resources.

Group Ratings

	ADA	COPE	PC	LCV	CFA	RPN	NAB	NSI	NTU	ACA	ACU
1980	94	88	87	88	93	—	0	0	25	27	17
1979	84	94	93	93	93	—	—	—	29	8	3
1978	85	94	75	87	59	25	11	0	32	6	9

Key Votes

1) Draft Registn $	AGN	6) Fair Hsg DOJ Enfrc	FOR	11) Cut Socl Incr Dfns $	AGN
2) Ban $ to Nicrgua	—	7) Lim PAC Contrbtns	FOR	12) Hosptl Cost Controls	FOR
3) Dlay MX Missile	FOR	8) Cap on Food Stmp $	AGN	13) Gasln Ctrls & Allctns	FOR
4) Nuclr Mortorium	FOR	9) New US Dep Edcatn	FOR	14) Lim Wndfll Prof Tax	AGN
5) Alaska Lands Bill	FOR	10) Cut OSHA $	AGN	15) Chryslr Loan Grntee	FOR

Election Results

1980 general	George Miller (D)	142,044	(63%)	($132,477)
	Giles St. Clair (R)	70,479	(31%)	($38,434)
1980 primary	George Miller (D)	81,956	(85%)	
	One other (D)	14,253	(15%)	
1978 general	George Miller (D)	109,676	(63%)	($65,404)
	Paula Gordon (R)	58,332	(34%)	($57,786)

EIGHTH DISTRICT

The closest thing we have to a self-consciously radical congressional district in the United States is the 8th district of California. This is where the first great student rebellion of the 1960s broke out, the Free Speech Movement of 1964 at the University of California's Berkeley campus. The city itself has a unique sort of politics—one of a few places in the United States where an elected school board imposed a busing program for integration, to bring together black children from the flatlands along San Francisco Bay and affluent whites from the hills above the campus. In the late 1960s and early 1970s there was one crisis here after another, such as the People's Park riots when Ronald Reagan sent in state troopers because students were walking across two vacant blocks owned by the university. In 1971 a slate of self-styled radicals won control of the city government; council meetings for years afterward were dominated by quarrels between members of the original group.

Berkeley is not the only distinctive part of the 8th. The district also includes the north Oakland ghetto, the Black Panthers' birthplace. The Panthers have gone through several stages, from something like guerrilla warfare to quasimilitary breakfast programs for school-children to the 1973 candidacy of Bobby Seale for mayor of Oakland—a solid campaign that won 36% of the vote. Groups with rhetoric as grandiose as the Panthers but whose membership can be counted on the fingers of one hand spring up from time to time, like the now famous Symbionese Liberation Army, which murdered Oakland School Superinten-dent Marcus Foster and kidnapped Patricia Hearst.

Today the campus is quieter; toga parties have replaced genuine riots, and student politi-cal activism has almost vanished. The ghetto is quiet too, and there are few lurid rebel armies in evidence. But the politics of the 8th congressional district still is rooted in the turbulent period of protest and rebellion, and the district's congressman is as explicit a product of those movements as there is in Congress. He is Ronald Dellums, a former social worker and Berkeley council member, who was first elected in 1970. Dellums won that year by defeating the incumbent, Jeffrey Cohelan, in the Democratic primary. The complaint against Cohelan was not his voting record—it was solidly liberal and antiwar—as it was stylistic. Cohelan had the support of older liberals and organized labor, Dellums of students and blacks; and in the politics of 1970, that was enough for a Dellums victory.

Dellums's explicitly radical stance infuriated California Republicans, who in 1970—the midpoint of Ronald Reagan's service as governor—and 1972 poured considerable amounts of money into this highly un-Republican district. Dellums has consistently lost some votes that usually go to Democrats. But there are enough Democratic votes to spare in this district, and Dellums has always gotten at least 55% of the vote. He might have a problem with redis-tricting after the 1980 census; but most likely he, like other California Democrats, will be protected by the legislature.

In the House, Dellums now has nearly a decade of seniority and considerable clout for a member with his beliefs. He became chairman of the House District of Columbia Commit-tee when his predecessor, Charles Diggs, was barred from the position because of his convic-tion on payroll-padding charges. The D.C. Committee is not as powerful as it was before the District got home rule; but it still carries some clout, and there is a certain symbolic value to having someone like Dellums chair a House committee. Dellums has also advanced to a fairly high position (11th) on the House Armed Services Committee, a body to which he won assignment over the objections of the then chairman and on which he seldom finds himself in agreement with the majority. Such positions tend to limit Dellums's legislative output, and he is perhaps as active on welfare bills as he is on military matters. For example, he opposed with some passion a move to prescribe the kinds of food recipients of food stamps could purchase with their coupons. Neither is Dellums unafraid to take up exotic causes. He argues, for example, that Puerto Rico should be given some form of independence so that it can vote on whether it wants to be independent—although in perfectly free elections, more than 90% of the Puerto Ricans have rejected independence.

Such stands apparently do not generate controversy in the 8th district. Dellums is disliked by a large number of his constituents, including some who vote for him every November; but he has not attracted primary opposition since 1974 and cannot be beaten in the general. So while it is unlikely that even this district would pick, ab initio, this kind of congressman today, he remains in the House as a kind of reminder of the politics of protest that carried all before it in Berkeley not so long ago.

Census Data   Pop. (1980 final) 439,310, down 5% in 1970s. Median family income, 1970, $11,401, 119% of U.S.

The Voters

Employment profile 1970   White collar, 66%. Blue collar, 22%. Service, 12%. Farm, –%.
Ethnic groups   Black 1980, 24%. Hispanic 1980, 7%. Am. Ind. 1980, 1%. Asian 1980, 9%. Total foreign stock 1970, 27%. Canada, UK, Germany, Italy, 2% each.

Presidential Vote

1980	Reagan (R)	65,088	(32%)
	Carter (D)	106,500	(52%)
	Anderson (I)	22,813	(11%)
1976	Ford (R)	79,368	(39%)
	Carter (D)	115,361	(57%)

Rep. Ronald V. Dellums (D) Elected 1970; b. Nov. 24, 1935, Oakland; home, Berkeley; Oakland City Col., A.A. 1958, San Fran. St. Col., B.A. 1960, U. of Cal., M.S.W. 1962.

Career USMC, 1954–56; Psychiatric Social Worker, Cal. Dept. of Mental Hygiene, 1962–64; Program Dir., Bayview Community Ctr., 1964–65; Dir., Hunter's Pt. Bayview Youth Opp. Ctr., 1965–66; Assoc. Dir., San Fran. Econ. Opp. Council's Concentrated Empl. Program, 1967–68; Berkeley City Cncl., 1967–71.

Offices 2136 RHOB, 202-225-2661. Also 2490 Channing Way, Rm. 202, Berkeley 94704, 415-548-7767.

Committees *District of Columbia* (Chairman). Subcommittee: Fiscal Affairs and Health (Chairman).

Armed Services (11th). Subcommittee: Research and Development.

Post Office and Civil Service (13th). Subcommittees: Human Resources; Postal Operations and Services; Postal Personnel and Modernization.

Group Ratings

	ADA	COPE	PC	LCV	CFA	RPN	NAB	NSI	NTU	ACA	ACU
1980	100	89	97	92	100	—	10	0	31	23	11
1979	95	95	90	94	96	—	—	—	28	4	3
1978	95	95	95	92	96	44	0	0	42	8	5

Key Votes

1) Draft Registn $	AGN	6) Fair Hsg DOJ Enfrc	FOR	11) Cut Socl Incr Dfns $	AGN
2) Ban $ to Nicrgua	AGN	7) Lim PAC Contrbtns	FOR	12) Hosptl Cost Controls	FOR
3) Dlay MX Missile	FOR	8) Cap on Food Stmp $	AGN	13) Gasln Ctrls & Allctns	FOR
4) Nuclr Mortorium	FOR	9) New US Dep Edcatn	FOR	14) Lim Wndfll Prof Tax	AGN
5) Alaska Lands Bill	FOR	10) Cut OSHA $	AGN	15) Chryslr Loan Grntee	FOR

Election Results

1980 general	Ronald V. Dellums (D)	108,380	(56%)	($312,128)
	Charles V. Hughes (R)	76,580	(39%)	($82,500)
	Tod Mikuriya (Libertarian)	10,465	(5%)	($0)
1980 primary	Ronald V. Dellums (D)	72,325	(100%)	
1978 general	Ronald V. Dellums (D)	94,824	(57%)	($75,945)
	Charles V. Hughes (R)	70,481	(43%)	($7,933)

NINTH DISTRICT

Not all of the East Bay across from San Francisco was a hotbed of political radicalism during the 1960s. The suburbs south of Oakland—San Leandro, San Lorenzo, Castro Valley, and the old middle-class city of Alameda—often seemed like outposts of Middle America, just a few miles south of student-filled Berkeley and the Oakland ghetto, along San Francisco Bay. None of these are elite suburbs; they are working-class and middle-class communities. While the student radicals and Black Panthers were winning headlines, people here were making a different kind of history, and some unnoted progress. The image these communities have is of middle-class whites, but in fact they are more various. The resolutely middle-class neighborhoods of the southern part of Oakland are mostly black, and there are a few blacks as well in the suburbs; there are many more Mexican–Americans, living unobtrusively in neighborhoods that were once all whites, and many families of Asian descent as well.

This area has no radical tinge, despite its increasing variety of ethnic backgrounds. But this part of the San Francisco Bay area, with portions of more affluent Alameda and Contra Costa suburbs over the Diablo Range, forms California's 9th congressional district. Basically Democratic, the 9th missed going Democratic in the two Republican presidential landslides of 1972 and 1980 by just a hair each time, and it has sent Democrats to Washington for as long as anyone can remember. For 28 years the congressman was George Miller (no relation to current 7th district incumbent George Miller) who rose silently to become chairman of the House Space Committee. Miller, in the tradition of many oldtimers, got out of touch with his district. In 1972, at age 81 and against strong competition, Miller could win only a pathetic 22% of the primary vote.

The winner of that primary was Fortney (Pete) Stark, a strong opponent of the Vietnam war and local banker. Stark had combined ideology and financial interest by erecting a large peace symbol over his suburban bank in Walnut Creek; he attracted the accounts of peace activists all over the Bay area by printing checks with the peace symbol on them. Stark spent liberally on his own campaign and won the general election even though George McGovern failed, although just barely, to carry the 9th.

In his first term, Stark won assignment to the Banking Committee. He reversed the usual pattern: many members have acquired banking interests and voted for them once they got on the committee; Stark sold his bank stock and often voted against the bank lobbies. In his second term he moved to the Ways and Means Committee, where he is one of the most reliable backers of such measures as progressive tax reform and national health insurance. Stark now chairs the subcommittee on Public Assistance and Unemployment Compensation, a body charged with passing on many of the biggest of President Reagan's 1981 proposed budget cuts. Stark's tendency is to oppose cuts and to fund the programs generously, but he will have some difficulty persuading a majority on his subcommittee and on Ways and Means—much less the full House—to go along.

Redistricting could be a problem for Stark, since the Bay area has not gained much population in the 1970s, which will put some squeeze on incumbents. Most likely, however, the Democrats in charge of redistricting will give him a district not too different in character and composition from the present 9th.

Census Data Pop. (1980 final) 474,611, up 2% in 1970s. Median family income, 1970, $11,309, 118% of U.S.

The Voters

Employment profile 1970 White collar, 52%. Blue collar, 35%. Service, 12%. Farm, 1%.
Ethnic groups Black 1980, 19%. Hispanic 1980, 10%. Am. Ind. 1980, 1%. Asian 1980, 5%. Total foreign stock 1970, 22%. Canada, UK, Germany, Italy, Portugal, 2% each.

Presidential Vote

1980	Reagan (R)	77,897	(45%)
	Carter (D)	75,961	(44%)
	Anderson (I)	15,400	(9%)
1976	Ford (R)	72,063	(43%)
	Carter (D)	91,871	(55%)

Rep. Fortney H. (Pete) **Stark** (D) Elected 1972; b. Nov. 11, 1931, Milwaukee, Wis.; home, Oakland; MIT, B.S. 1953, U. of Cal., M.B.A. 1959.

Career Air Force, 1955–57; Founder, Beacon Savings and Loan Assn., 1961; Founder and Pres., Security Natl. Bank, Walnut Creek, 1963–72.

Offices 1034 LHOB, 202-225-5065. Also 7 Eastmont Mall, Oakland 94605, 415-635-1092.

Committees *District of Columbia* (4th). Subcommittee: Fiscal Affairs and Health; Government Operations and Metropolitan Affairs.

Ways and Means (6th). Subcommittees: Public Assistance and Unemployment Compensation (Chairman); Select Subcommittee on Revenue Measures.

Select Committee on Narcotics Abuse and Control (4th).

Group Ratings

	ADA	COPE	PC	LCV	CFA	RPN	NAB	NSI	NTU	ACA	ACU
1980	94	83	90	87	93	—	11	11	24	17	6
1979	84	88	85	88	93	—	—	—	29	5	3
1978	95	95	90	90	96	50	0	0	41	17	8

Key Votes

1) Draft Registn $	AGN	6) Fair Hsg DOJ Enfrc	FOR	11) Cut Socl Incr Dfns $	AGN
2) Ban $ to Nicrgua	AGN	7) Lim PAC Contrbtns	FOR	12) Hosptl Cost Controls	FOR
3) Dlay MX Missile	FOR	8) Cap on Food Stmp $	AGN	13) Gasln Ctrls & Allctns	FOR
4) Nuclr Mortorium	FOR	9) New US Dep Edcatn	FOR	14) Lim Wndfll Prof Tax	AGN
5) Alaska Lands Bill	FOR	10) Cut OSHA $	—	15) Chryslr Loan Grntee	AGN

Election Results

1980 general	Fortney H. (Pete) Stark (D)	90,504	(53%)	($62,905)
	William J. Kennedy (R)	67,265	(41%)	($28,806)
1980 primary	Fortney H. (Pete) Stark (D)	67,262	(100%)	
1978 general	Fortney H. (Pete) Stark (D)	88,179	(65%)	($24,697)
	Robert S. Allen (R).............	41,138	(30%)	($7,234)

TENTH DISTRICT

During the last two decades, population growth in the San Francisco Bay area has been concentrated near the southern end of the Bay. The growth has been centered around the old farm market town of San Jose — now mostly indistinguishable from its suburban neighbors. The growth has come from two directions: from the industrial East Bay suburbs and from the center of San Jose itself. The once fertile farmland here has provided enough space for dozens of factories, and the white working class and Mexican–American population has supplied a large work force, augmented by many migrants from other parts of the country. The east side of San Jose is thus largely blue collar, as are the East Bay suburbs to the north: Fremont, Newark, Union City.

The other stream of migration to San Jose has come from the northwest. Here, along U.S. 101 and Interstate 280, is the Silicon Valley, the heart of much of the nation's microcomputer industry. People here are highly educated, affluent, addicted to Perrier and bicycling and jogging. The heart of the Silicon Valley is a dozen or so miles up the freeways from San Jose, but the entire area has benefited from its prosperity. This has in fact been one of the nation's boom areas, and if the growth in the San Jose area tapered off somewhat in the 1970s, residents were compensated by the rapidly escalating real estate values.

California's 10th congressional district consists essentially of eastern San Jose and the East Bay suburbs to the north. Its terrain spans the southern edge of the bay from Hayward in Alameda County, not far south of Oakland, to the edge of the Lockheed Sunnyvale plant, west of San Jose. The district has the largest Mexican–American population in the Bay area, some concentrated in the old Mexican neighborhoods in San Jose. But to a substantial extent Mexican–Americans are scattered about the district much as Italian–Americans are. This is a solidly Democratic district, solid enough to have voted for George McGovern in 1972, although not enough for Jimmy Carter in 1980.

For almost 20 years now this part of California has been represented by Democratic Congressman Don Edwards. Edwards is one of those relatively senior congressmen who was a prime beneficiary of the tidal wave of Democratic freshmen of 1974. He had the seniority and experience to hold high committee positions, and at the same time he reflected the views of the freshmen well enough that he could, for the first time, be sure of a large number of votes on the floor. Edwards has an odd background for a liberal: he was once an FBI agent, and he got rich as the owner of the only title company in San Jose and Santa Clara County, which increased in size from 290,000 in 1950 to 1.1. million in 1970 (it is now 1.3 million).

Edwards is nonetheless one of the most liberal members of the House; an early opponent of the Vietnam war and onetime chairman of Americans for Democratic Action, and he and Phillip Burton were among the few members in the 1960s who voted to abolish the House Un-American Activities Committee. He is also the fourth-ranking Democrat on the House Judiciary Committee and chairman of the Civil and Constitutional Rights Subcommittee. In this capacity he was in 1980 the chief sponsor of revisions to the Fair Housing Act, one of the few liberal initiatives in the 96th Congress and one that passed the House mostly intact only to be killed in the Senate. Edwards is likely to be in a hot seat in 1981 and 1982. His subcommittee has jurisdiction not only over fair housing, but also over extension of the Voting Rights Act and is responsible as well for considering constitutional amendments. Edwards has consistently opposed reporting out any of the myriad of amendments proposed to ban abortion, impose prayer in schools, and ban school busing, and the Democratic majority on his subcommittee is likely to remain firm in that resolve. The Republicans, led by Henry Hyde, a strong opponent of abortion, will take just the opposite view. Edwards and Hyde are worthy adversaries: both idealistic men who are accomplished practical politicians and who have a history of taking up seemingly hopeless causes and then achieving goals.

Edwards has a deserved reputation for being scrupulously fair when it comes to procedure and pleasant on a personal level; but he also fights hard for what he believes in and does not make concessions easily.

Edwards is one of the few House liberals who has a district that is expanding substantially in population. As a result, redistricting is probably not a great threat to him. Democrats control the process, and there is plenty of heavily Democratic territory in eastern San Jose and the East Bay from which to fashion another district with political inclinations very much like the 10th.

Census Data   Pop. (1980 final) 586,818, up 27% in 1970s. Median family income, 1970, $11,095, 116% of U.S.

The Voters

    Employment profile 1970   White collar, 47%. Blue collar, 40%. Service, 12%. Farm, 1%.
    Ethnic groups   Black 1980, 5%. Hispanic 1980, 25%. Am. Ind. 1980, 1%. Asian 1980, 9%. Total foreign stock 1970, 26%. Italy, 3%; Canada, Portugal, 2% each; UK, Germany, 1% each.

Presidential Vote

1980	Reagan (R)	78,689	(45%)
	Carter (D)	71,937	(41%)
	Anderson (I)	18,622	(11%)
1976	Ford (R)	65,121	(40%)
	Carter (D)	92,239	(57%)

Rep. Don Edwards (D) Elected 1962; b. Jan. 6, 1915, San Jose; home, San Jose; Stanford U., Stanford U. Law School.

    Career FBI Agent, 1940–41; Navy, WWII; Pres., Valley Title Co., San Jose.

    Offices 2307 RHOB, 202-225-3072. Also 1625 The Alameda, San Jose 95126, 408-292-0143.

    Committees *Judiciary* (4th). Subcommittees: Civil and Constitutional Rights (Chairman); Criminal Justice; Monopolies and Commercial Law.

    Veterans' Affairs (2d). Subcommittees: Education, Training, and Employment; Hospitals and Health Care.

Group Ratings

	ADA	COPE	PC	LCV	CFA	RPN	NAB	NSI	NTU	ACA	ACU
1980	100	89	73	96	100	—	9	0	21	17	11
1979	95	95	83	87	81	—	—	—	26	0	3
1978	80	84	75	93	73	27	9	10	32	4	11

Key Votes

1) Draft Registn $	AGN	6) Fair Hsg DOJ Enfrc	FOR	11) Cut Socl Incr Dfns $	AGN
2) Ban $ to Nicrgua	AGN	7) Lim PAC Contrbtns	FOR	12) Hosptl Cost Controls	FOR
3) Dlay MX Missile	FOR	8) Cap on Food Stmp $	AGN	13) Gasln Ctrls & Allctns	FOR
4) Nuclr Mortorium	FOR	9) New US Dep Edcatn	FOR	14) Lim Wndfll Prof Tax	AGN
5) Alaska Lands Bill	FOR	10) Cut OSHA $	AGN	15) Chrysl Loan Grntee	—

Election Results

1980 general	Don Edwards (D)	102,231	(62%)	($29,151)
	John M. Lutton (R)	45,987	(28%)	($1,542)
	Joseph Fuhrig (Libertarian)	11,904	(7%)	($0)
1980 primary	Don Edwards (D)	64,507	(100%)	
1978 general	Don Edwards (D)	84,488	(67%)	($31,740)
	Rudy Hansen (R)	41,374	(33%)	($25,124)

ELEVENTH DISTRICT

The Peninsula is the bony finger of land south of San Francisco that connects the city to the rest of California. Almost down the middle of the Peninsula runs the San Andreas Fault, which some experts believe will shift again within the next 20 years or so and produce an earthquake like the one that devastated San Francisco in 1906. To the west of the Fault the land is mountainous enough to have discouraged development, except in the suburb of Pacifica, which clings to the foggy mountainsides above the ocean, directly south of San Francisco. Most of the Peninsula's population is packed into neat little suburbs between the Fault and the salt flats and industrial areas created by landfill dumped into San Francisco Bay.

The Peninsula suburbs, notably sunnier and warmer than the city, are occupied mainly by white collar people who commute to San Francisco or, more likely, work around San Jose or on the Peninsula itself. Politically these towns behave more like eastern upper-middle-class suburbs than like the archconservative wealthy towns around Los Angeles. These are people who trend Democratic when social issues dominate the political dialogue, as they did in the years of the Vietnam war, student rebellion, and the debate over legalization of marijuana. They trend Republican, however, when purely economic issues are at stake, as was the case in 1978 with Proposition 13 and, evidently, in the 1980 presidential race as well.

The 11th congressional district includes the northern Peninsula suburbs—Daly City, South San Francisco ("the industrial city," it says in big letters on a mountain near the Bayshore Freeway), and San Bruno, on down to Redwood City. There are really two sets of suburbs here. In the northern part of the Peninsula, just south of San Francisco, are Daly City, Pacifica, and South San Francisco; these are really extensions of the blue collar neighborhoods of the city itself with large numbers of Oriental and Mexican–American as well as white working-class residents. To the south, starting at the San Francisco Airport, are the traditionally Republican towns—San Bruno, Millbrae, Burlingame, San Mateo, Belmont, San Carlos. Some of these are now Democratic in many elections, but this part of the Peninsula elects a Republican assemblyman and in 1978 defeated an incumbent Democratic state senator. In the hills above is the town of Hillsborough, the home of many of San Francisco's wealthiest and most socially prominent families.

This is the district that elected Congressman Leo Ryan, whose death in Jonestown, Guyana, made international news in November 1978. Ryan had gone to Guyana to investigate the People's Temple cult of Jim Jones, which had been centered in San Francisco and which had attracted, among others, relatives of many of Ryan's constituents. There were allegations that members were tortured and held in Jonestown against their will—allegations that seemed fully verified when several of them attempted to leave Jonestown with Ryan. Just as a plane was being boarded, Ryan and several newsmen were shot. The world knows the rest of the story: how Jones persuaded almost all his followers to kill their children and themselves.

Since Ryan's death the district has had two different congressmen. In a special election to fill the seat in 1979, Republican Bill Royer, a member of the San Mateo County Board of Supervisors, managed to beat a former Ryan aide after the Democrats had a divisive primary. Royer benefited from a well-financed campaign and local disgust with high-spending Democrats less than a year after the passage of Proposition 13, and he was helped by the support of the 12th district's Pete McCloskey (who once represented all the territory within the 11th).

The result of the special election was reversed in 1980 by Democrat Tom Lantos. A successful professional economist with an imposing appearance, he united Democratic factions and avoided primary opposition. He spent liberally, ran an astute campaign, and at the same time managed to argue for a larger defense budget and to attack Royer's allegedly conservative voting record (it was not all that far removed from that of most House Republicans). Royer may indeed be the first victim of the solidarity of House Republicans, since conservative Republican positions have never been particularly popular in the Peninsula. Lantos was in any case one of only three Democrats to beat an incumbent Republican congressman in 1980.

Lantos's political talents are evident from his upset victory. He sits on the Foreign Affairs Committee and has a natural interest in foreign policy; he was born in Budapest and fought in the underground against the Nazis. His major political problem for 1982 will be redistricting. The northern part of the Peninsula is the most Democratic, but pressure exists to take some of that territory and add it to the population-shy districts of the Burton brothers in San Francisco. Phil Burton himself will probably work to see that Lantos ends up with a favorable district, but that will take some adroit district-drawing.

Census Data   Pop. (1980 final) 498,238, up 7% in 1970s. Median family income, 1970, $13,062, 136% of U.S.

The Voters

  Employment profile 1970   White collar, 59%. Blue collar, 29%. Service, 12%. Farm, -%.
  Ethnic groups   Black 1980, 5%. Hispanic 1980, 13%. Am. Ind. 1980, 1%. Asian 1980, 11%. Total foreign stock 1970, 32%. Italy, 4%; Canada, UK, Germany, 3% each; USSR, Ireland, 1% each.

Presidential Vote

1980	Reagan (R)	 96,108	(49%)	1976	Ford (R)	.... 94,646 (51%)
	Carter (D)	 72,391	(37%)		Carter (D)	...... 85,027 (45%)
	Anderson (I)	... 22,081	(11%)			

Rep. Tom Lantos (D) Elected 1980; b. Feb. 1, 1928, Budapest, Hungary; home, Hillsborough; U. of Wash., B.A., 1949, M.A. 1950, U. of Cal., Berkeley, Ph.D. 1953.

Career Econ.–Foreign Policy Advisor to Sens. Joseph R. Biden, Jr., Del., 1978–78; Consultant to Senate Foreign Relations and Judiciary Committees; Member, Pres. Task Force on Defense and Foreign Policy; Faculty, San Fran. St. U., 1950–; Member, Millbrae Sch. Bd.

Offices 1123 LHOB, 202-225-3531. Also 520 S. El Camino Real, Suite 800, San Mateo 94402, 415-342-0300.

Committees *Foreign Affairs* (20th). Subcommittees: Asian and Pacific Affairs; Europe and the Middle East.

Government Operations (23d). Subcommittees: Environment, Energy and Natural Resources; Government Activities and Transportation.

Select Committee on Aging (27th). Subcommittees: Retirement Income and Employment; Housing and Consumer Interests.

Group Ratings and Key Votes: Newly Elected

Election Results

1980 general	Tom Lantos (D)	85,823	(46%)	($554,718)
	Bill Royer (R)	80,100	(43%)	($781,795)
	Wilson Branch (Peace & Freedom)	13,723	(7%)	($0)
1980 primary	Tom Lantos (D)	52,722	(100%)	
1979 special	Bill Royer (R)	52,585	(58%)	
	Joe Holsinger (D)	37,685	(42%)	
1979 spec. prim.	Bill Royer (R)	19,409	(52%)	
	Les Kelting (R)	6,562	(18%)	
	Bruce Maker (R)	5,980	(16%)	
	Two others (R)	5,189	(14%)	
1978 general	Leo J. Ryan (D)	92,882	(61%)	($40,588)
	Dave Welch (R)	54,621	(36%)	($26,229)

TWELFTH DISTRICT

The 12th congressional district of California is a part of the Peninsula south of San Francisco. Its northern end lies in Redwood City, in San Mateo County about 10 miles south of the San Francisco city limit; it extends south and east to the boundaries of San Jose. The district's central communities are probably Palo Alto and Menlo Park, the former the home of Stanford University and the latter the home of such diverse California life-style publications as the *Whole Earth Catalogue* and *Sunset* magazine. The 12th includes the woodsy suburbs of Portola Valley and Woodside and the affluent suburb of Atherton on land between the hills and the Bay. South of Palo Alto, in Santa Clara County, are the more middle-class suburbs of Santa Clara, Sunnyvale, and Mountain View.

Silicon Valley is the name given to this area over the last few years. Silicon chips have revolutionized computer production, and probably the world's major center of the silicon chip industry is in the corridor between U.S. 101 and Interstate 280 from Menlo Park through Palo Alto, Los Altos, Mountain View, and Sunnyvale. There has been no population growth in this area in the 1970s, but there was great economic growth; property values, both commercial and residential, were buoyed by the success of the Silicon Valley pioneers.

Yet this is an area that prides itself less on its economic productivity than on its attitude toward the environment. This is an area with a disproportionately large number of Sierra Club members; there are bicycle paths everywhere and tennis courts are in constant use. And the feeling for the environment here is not just an academic impulse. From the hilly affluent areas or the valley below you cannot avoid seeing how fast the available land has been occupied. Nor can you help noticing, as you drive on the Bayshore Freeway that links the communities of the 12th together, how the ugly industrial fill land is gradually eating away at the expanse of San Francisco Bay.

This is the district that has elected, for more than ten years now, Congressman Pete McCloskey. His is a political career more full of pitfalls than the Perils of Pauline, but he has survived and politically seems in better shape than ever, poised to run for the Senate in 1982. At the heart of McCloskey's appeal has always been the environmental issue. When he first ran for Congress, in a 1967 special election, it was his environmental interests that made this

Menlo Park lawyer the winner over Shirley Temple Black. (Mrs. Black may also have been hurt by her movie star background. That was right after the elections of Governor Ronald Reagan and Senator George Murphy—neither of whom had great support in the Peninsula.)

It was only after his first election that McCloskey became known as an ultraliberal Republican. And that was really only because of his views on the war; on economic issues he has tended to reflect the caution of his upper-income constituents and their aversion to organized labor. Even his opposition to the Vietnam war came from an unlikely source; his feelings, as a decorated Marine veteran, that the war was perverting the corps and military generally. With a fervor that may come only from experience in battle, McCloskey argued against unnecessary war and bloodshed and made as strong a case as was made against the Vietnam adventure.

All this was during the years when Ronald Reagan conservatives dominated California's Republican Party. They opposed McCloskey in primary after primary, holding him to 53% in 1968, 60% in 1970, 44% in 1972 (against two opponents) and 50% in 1974. In 1972 McCloskey ran for president against Richard Nixon, receiving microscopically less than his goal of 20% in New Hampshire and dropping out of the race in time to run again in California. In 1973 McCloskey considered switching parties, as his friend Donald Riegle did. But McCloskey decided to stay a Republican and was encouraged to do so by the friendly support he received from President Ford, who as vice president came out and campaigned for him in the 1974 primary.

McCloskey had reason to feel much more comfortable in the Republican Party during the late 1970s. As the focus of public affairs shifted from Vietnam to economic issues, he found himself instinctively on the Republican side. He believes strongly in the free-market economic system and has no problem supporting such measures as deregulation of energy prices and the Kemp–Roth tax cut. In the Carter years he devoted much of his legislative attention to the Merchant Marine and Fisheries Committee, on which he was ranking Republican; he opposed the cozy arrangements that had granted maritime companies and maritime union members massive federal subsidies, and he led on the floor the successful fight to kill the bill requiring that 9.5% of oil imported into the U.S. be shipped in U.S. flag carriers. On most issues, McCloskey does not seem too uncomfortable in the Republican Party of Ronald Reagan, although he was not an admirer of the president when he was governor of California. The major exception certainly would be environmental issues, on which McCloskey must find himself very much at odds with the positions of Interior Secretary James Watt.

McCloskey now seems bent on running for the Senate, although the 12th district seems perfectly suited to him in this year's political climate. He has said he wants the seat of incumbent S. I. Hayakawa, who appears vulnerable in both the Republican primary and in the general election. McCloskey's problem, as it was in 1968–74, is the Republican primary. He would almost certainly lose a one-on-one contest with a conservative. His chances rest on the possibility that enough conservatives will enter the race against Hayakawa—possible entrants include Barry Goldwater, Jr., Maureen Reagan, and Robert Dornan—to allow McCloskey to win with a minority of the votes. In a general election he would certainly be a strong contender.

The 12th district's boundaries will undoubtedly be modified somewhat in redistricting. Democrats might be tempted to eliminate the district and split it among its Bay area neighbors, the better to help other Bay area Democrats; but probably too many people now live here for such a scheme to work. The current constituency or anything similar to it should not be considered safe for any party or candidate if McCloskey does not run. Most likely there will be seriously contested primaries in both parties and a general election in which either party would have a chance—the Republicans a better one if they nominate a McCloskey-like candidate; the Democrats, if the Republicans nominate a conservative. This district produced a larger vote for John Anderson than any other in California, and it is inclined always to environment-conscious candidates, so most likely whoever wins, he (or she) will be someone similar in basic attitudes to McCloskey.

Census Data Pop. (1980 final) 472,813, up 2% in 1970s. Median family income, 1970, $13,418, 140% of U.S.

The Voters

Employment profile 1970 White collar, 65%. Blue collar, 24%. Service, 10%. Farm, 1%.
Ethnic groups Black 1980, 5%. Hispanic 1980, 10%. Am. Ind. 1980, 1%. Asian 1980, 8%. Total foreign stock 1970, 25%. Canada, UK, Germany, Italy, 2% each.

Presidential Vote

1980	Reagan (R)	95,588	(46%)
	Carter (D)	72,649	(35%)
	Anderson (I)	32,926	(16%)
1976	Ford (R)	103,233	(52%)
	Carter (D)	89,818	(45%)

Rep. Paul N. McCloskey, Jr. (R) Elected Dec. 12, 1967; b. Sept. 29, 1927, San Bernardino; home, Portola Valley; Occidental Col., Cal. Inst. of Tech., 1945–46, Stanford U., B.A. 1950, LL.B. 1953.

Career Navy, 1945–47; USMC, Korea; Dpty. Dist. Atty., Alameda Co., 1953–54; Practicing atty., 1955–67.

Offices 205 CHOB, 202-225-5411. Also 305 Grant Ave., Palo Alto 94306, 415-326-7383.

Committees *Government Operations* (4th). Subcommittee: Manpower and Housing.

Merchant Marine and Fisheries (2d). Subcommittees: Fisheries and Wildlife Conservation and the Environment; Merchant Marine.

Group Ratings

	ADA	COPE	PC	LCV	CFA	RPN	NAB	NSI	NTU	ACA	ACU
1980	78	35	50	63	50	—	50	14	28	35	26
1979	58	39	38	63	19	—	—	—	35	48	48
1978	65	58	53	72	36	100	56	14	15	32	24

Key Votes

1) Draft Registn $	AGN	6) Fair Hsg DOJ Enfrc	FOR	11) Cut Socl Incr Dfns $	AGN
2) Ban $ to Nicrgua	AGN	7) Lim PAC Contrbtns	FOR	12) Hosptl Cost Controls	FOR
3) Dlay MX Missile	FOR	8) Cap on Food Stmp $	AGN	13) Gasln Ctrls & Allctns	AGN
4) Nuclr Mortorium	AGN	9) New US Dep Edcatn	—	14) Lim Wndfll Prof Tax	FOR
5) Alaska Lands Bill	FOR	10) Cut OSHA $	AGN	15) Chryslr Loan Grntee	—

Election Results

1980 general	Paul N. McCloskey, Jr. (R)	143,817	(72%)	($84,141)
	Kirsten Olsen (D)	37,009	(19%)	($7,016)
	Bill Evers (Libertarian)	15,073	(8%)	($15,688)
1980 primary	Paul N. McCloskey, Jr. (R)	51,688	(80%)	
	One other (R)	13,302	(20%)	
1978 general	Paul N. McCloskey, Jr. (R)	116,982	(73%)	($56,144)
	Kirsten Olsen (D)	34,472	(22%)	($54,203)

THIRTEENTH DISTRICT

Twenty years ago, what now is the 13th congressional district of California was for the most part acres of vineyards and fruit orchards below the mountains of the Coast Range near San Jose. This was one of the richest agricultural areas in the country, but it was also directly in the path of some of the most explosive suburban growth the nation has ever seen. Santa Clara County, which includes San Jose and the 13th district, grew from 290,000 people in 1950 to 1,064,000 in 1970 and 1,297,000 in 1980. In the 1960s and 1970s the 13th district just about tripled in population—a rate of growth exceeded by only a few other congressional districts in the United States.

Today the vineyards are almost all gone, their owners having prudently recultivated the grapes in more remote places before selling the land to developers. There is still some agriculture in the southern part of the district, but the 13th is now almost entirely suburban in character. The wealthier suburbs, as usual in California, are those higher up in the hills; here, Cupertino, Saratoga, Monte Sereno, and Los Gatos. Most of the district's population, 60%, lives in San Jose, technically a central city, but about as suburban in aspect as one could want: a vast, prosperous area of shopping centers and stucco homes, virtually all of them built in the last 20 years.

Ironically, the congressman from this fast-growing suburban district is the former mayor of San Jose, who finally insisted that the process of growth had to take second place to the process of orderly planning. When Norman Mineta was elected mayor in 1971, San Jose had grown from a small city of 95,000 in 1950 to a sprawling set of subdivisions of 445,000 in 1970. So rapid had been the growth that the city itself had difficulty maintaining, from day to day, a map that showed accurately all the streets that had been carved out by developers. Mineta said, in effect, "Enough," and pushed for zoning that would slow development to a pace that would allow the city to pay for the increased services new residents would require.

Mineta's policy was popular in San Jose, and in 1974, when Republican Congressman Charles Gubser decided to retire, Mineta was an obvious candidate. Gubser had been easily the most conservative member of the San Francisco Bay area delegation, a Republican who enjoyed baiting Pete McCloskey for his apostasy, a member of the Armed Services Committee who believed, and advanced his beliefs with some acerbity, in a large defense budget and most Pentagon policies. The Republicans ran a moderate former assemblyman, but this was the Watergate year, and Mineta won easily.

In Washington Mineta was recognized as one of the more promising members of the freshman class of 1974. He has high ratings from liberal and labor organizations, but he chose to concentrate on issues that have not historically attracted the attention of crusading Democrats. One of these is airline deregulation, which he has supported on the Public Works Aviation Subcommittee. Another is sunset legislation, which would require Congress to reauthorize federal programs or to let them die; he is one of the House's leading sponsors of this measure.

In the early months of the Reagan Administration, Mineta emerged as one of the leaders of the Democratic Party in fact, if not by virtue of position. He is a senior member of the Budget Committee and one of those who is considered flexible and open-minded on budget issues, willing to attack sacred cows if a good rationale is given, but also a believer in a compassionate approach to human needs.

Mineta seems to be in solid political shape back home. The continued population growth in his district means that it will be pared back for 1982, but no one doubts he will have a district from which he can easily win reelection.

Census Data Pop. (1980 final) 618,770, up 33% in 1970s. Median family income, 1970, $12,972, 135% of U.S.

The Voters

Employment profile 1970 White collar, 60%. Blue collar, 29%. Service, 10%. Farm, 1%.
Ethnic groups Black 1980, 3%. Hispanic 1980, 16%. Am. Ind. 1980, 1%. Asian 1980, 6%. Total foreign stock 1970, 22%. Italy, 3%; Canada, UK, Germany, 2% each.

Presidential Vote

1980	Reagan (R)	121,122	(53%)
	Carter (D)	73,035	(32%)
	Anderson (I)	29,470	(13%)
1976	Ford (R)	108,664	(53%)
	Carter (D)	91,620	(45%)

Rep. Norman Y. Mineta (D) Elected 1974; b. Nov. 12, 1931, San Jose; home, San Jose; U. of Cal., B.S. 1953.

Career Army, 1953–56; Owner/Agent, Mineta Ins. Agcy.; San Jose City Cncl., 1967–71, Vice Mayor, 1968–71, Mayor, 1971–74.

Offices 2352 RHOB, 202-225-2631. Also Golden Pacific Ctr., 1245 S. Winchester Blvd., Suite 310, San Jose 95128, 408-984-6045.

Committees *Budget* (5th).

Public Works and Transportation (5th). Subcommittees: Aviation (Chairman); Investigations and Oversight; Public Buildings and Grounds.

Select Committee on Intelligence (5th). Subcommittee: Program and Budget Authorization.

Group Ratings

	ADA	COPE	PC	LCV	CFA	RPN	NAB	NSI	NTU	ACA	ACU
1980	83	68	47	72	46	—	17	10	15	21	11
1979	79	85	48	72	71	—	—	—	17	13	8
1978	80	84	65	70	59	42	8	20	7	4	9

Key Votes

1) Draft Registn $	AGN	6) Fair Hsg DOJ Enfrc	FOR	11) Cut Socl Incr Dfns $	AGN
2) Ban $ to Nicrgua	AGN	7) Lim PAC Contrbtns	FOR	12) Hosptl Cost Controls	FOR
3) Dlay MX Missile	FOR	8) Cap on Food Stmp $	AGN	13) Gasln Ctrls & Allctns	AGN
4) Nuclr Mortorium	AGN	9) New US Dep Edcatn	FOR	14) Lim Wndfll Prof Tax	AGN
5) Alaska Lands Bill	FOR	10) Cut OSHA $	AGN	15) Chryslr Loan Grntee	FOR

1980 general	Norman Y. Mineta (D)..........	132,246	(59%)	($221,552)
	W. E. (Ted) Gagne (R)..........	79,766	(35%)	($9,439)
1980 primary	Norman Y. Mineta (D)..........	68,733	(100%)	
1978 general	Norman Y. Mineta (D)..........	100,809	(57%)	($176,628)
	Dan O'Keefe (R)..............	69,306	(40%)	($54,741)

FOURTEENTH DISTRICT

The 14th congressional district of California occupies a portion of the state's Central Valley, probably the world's most productive farmland. Only 50 miles from San Francisco Bay, the 14th is cut off from that cosmopolitan influence and, politically at least, the district is almost part of another world. The prosperity of the cities here, the most notable of which is Stockton, is rooted firmly in agriculture. The farms of the area—the district goes as far north in the Valley as the suburbs of Sacramento and as far south as Stanislaus County around Modesto—are not as often in the hands of the huge conglomerates as those in the southern reaches of the Valley. Many rather small, family-owned farms still exist in the 14th, on either side of the string of medium-sized cities along the Route 99 freeway. The district has a fair amount of industry, but agriculture is king.

Above the Valley, sometimes visible in the far distance, rises the Sierra Nevada, and the 14th has its share of the Mother Lode country and the mountains, going as far as Yosemite and Lake Tahoe. Ordinarily, except in years of drought, these mountains shed their snows down numerous rivers whose waters, carefully apportioned, irrigate the thirsty farms of the Valley. In the 1970s the Mother Lode country was suddenly, after more than a century of depopulation, the area of fastest population growth in California. Calaveras County has not had as many residents since the time when Mark Twain wrote about the jumping frog contest.

The political traditions of the Valley are Democratic—the result of the politics of some of its initial settlers from the South; of the Great Depression; and, to an unknown extent, of the Democratic politics of the McClatchy newspapers that dominate Valley journalism from Sacramento to Fresno. But while the Valley may be as Democratic as the San Francisco Bay area in partisan elections, during the 1970s it was not as liberal in its attitudes on cultural issues. These are measured with nice precision by the plethora of referenda on the California ballot. In 1978, for example, the Valley was evenly divided on the proposition, which was defeated, to bar homosexuals from teaching in schools; the Bay area, in contrast, voted 65% against. In the past the Valley has been the part of the state strongest for capital punishment, against coastal preservation, and against legalization of marijuana.

These differences foretold the sharp local shift to the Republicans in the off-year elections of 1978 and the presidential election of 1980. The 14th district, represented by a Democrat for 22 years, elected a Republican in 1978; and after years of favoring or coming close to favoring Democratic presidential nominees, it gave Ronald Reagan a 56%–34% margin over Jimmy Carter in 1980.

The change in congressional representation occurred in large part because of the Koreagate scandal. The incumbent, John McFall, was House Democratic whip in 1972–76 and had demonstrated the ability to funnel federal money to the district. But that was evidently less important to the migrants to this newly affluent area than the $3,000 McFall received from Tongsun Park in 1974. The money was deposited in his office account and used later for personal business.

But Koreagate was not the only factor that produced the victory of Republican Norman Shumway. Although his base is Stockton, he ran best in 1978 in the Mother Lode country — a sign that the new migrants were moving these counties away from the Democrats. In 1980 Shumway did not attract well-financed opposition and ran well ahead of Reagan. A member of the Banking and Merchant Marine Committees, he has a very solidly conservative voting record. Redistricting is going to realign congressional district boundaries significantly in the Valley, where a new district will probably be created, but in all likelihood Shumway will have a district in which he has great strength.

Census Data   Pop. (1980 final) 634,718, up 37% in 1970s. Median family income, 1970, $9,348, 98% of U.S.

The Voters

   Employment profile 1970   White collar, 44%. Blue collar, 33%. Service, 14%. Farm, 9%.
   Ethnic groups   Black 1980, 3%. Hispanic 1980, 15%. Am. Ind. 1980, 1%. Asian 1980, 4%. Total foreign stock 1970, 23%. Italy, 2%; Canada, UK, Germany, USSR, 1% each.

Presidential Vote

1980	Reagan (R)	128,907	(56%)
	Carter (D)	79,120	(34%)
	Anderson (I)	17,939	(8%)
1976	Ford (R)	92,163	(49%)
	Carter (D)	92,328	(49%)

Rep. Norman D. Shumway (R) Elected 1978; b. July 28, 1934, Phoenix, Ariz.; home, Stockton; U. of Utah, B.S. 1960, Hastings Col. of Law, J.D. 1963.

Career   Practicing atty., 1964–74; San Joaquin Co. Bd. of Supervisors, 1974–78, Chmn., 1978.

Offices   1228 LHOB, 202-225-2511. Also 1045 N. El Dorado, Stockton 95202, 209-464-7612.

Committees   *Banking, Finance and Urban Affairs* (10th). Subcommittees: Economic Stabilization; Financial Institutions Supervision, Regulation and Insurance; International Trade, Investment and Monetary Policy.

Merchant Marine and Fisheries (12th). Subcommittees: Coast Guard and Navigation; Fisheries and Wildlife Conservation and the Environment; Merchant Marine.

Select Committee on Aging (8th). Subcommittees: Human Services; Retirement Income and Employment.

Group Ratings

	ADA	COPE	PC	LCV	CFA	RPN	NAB	NSI	NTU	ACA	ACU
1980	0	7	13	17	14	—	100	100	65	95	86
1979	5	10	10	13	4	—	—	—	70	100	97

Key Votes

1) Draft Registn $	FOR	6) Fair Hsg DOJ Enfrc	AGN	11) Cut Socl Incr Dfns $	FOR
2) Ban $ to Nicrgua	FOR	7) Lim PAC Contrbtns	AGN	12) Hosptl Cost Controls	AGN
3) Dlay MX Missile	AGN	8) Cap on Food Stmp $	FOR	13) Gasln Ctrls & Allctns	AGN
4) Nuclr Mortorium	AGN	9) New US Dep Edcatn	AGN	14) Lim Wndfll Prof Tax	FOR
5) Alaska Lands Bill	FOR	10) Cut OSHA $	FOR	15) Chryslr Loan Grntee	AGN

Election Results

1980 general	Norman D. Shumway (R)	133,979	(61%)	($235,364)
	Ann Cerney (D)	79,883	(36%)	($65,486)
1980 primary	Norman D. Shumway (R)	51,599	(100%)	
1978 general	Norman D. Shumway (R)	95,962	(53%)	($251,948)
	John J. McFall (D).............	76,602	(43%)	($240,114)

FIFTEENTH DISTRICT

The 15th district of California is another Central Valley district, one of two dominated by the city and county of Fresno. Except for Sacramento, this is the part of the Valley that has most steadily maintained Democratic leanings. One reason is the large (15%) Mexican–American population here, the largest in the Valley except for the next-door 17th district. The Chicanos here are not migrants who pass through; they are often middle-class citizens with roots in their communities — and they vote. Moreover, the Fresno area has a more heterogeneous population than many parts of the Valley. There are especially large numbers of Armenian–Americans, such as novelist William Saroyan, who grew up and lived in Fresno. Another large group is made up of descendants of the original Okies, the people who left the dried-out fields of Oklahoma, Kansas, and Texas during the 1930s in search of the promised land of California. Here, as John Steinbeck chronicled in *The Grapes of Wrath,* these poor white people did backbreaking work in steamy hot fields for next to nothing and lived in miserable labor camps. Ironically, their sons and daughters are not particularly sympathetic — often are downright hostile — to the very similar plight of Mexican–Americans in the same fields today. Still, the 15th was by a considerable margin the most Democratic district in the Valley in the 1980 presidential election.

The congressman from this district, Democrat Tony Coelho, has strong roots in this part of the Central Valley and a solid knowledge of the world beyond as well. He served as an aide to B. F. Sisk, congressman for 24 years until his retirement in 1978; Sisk was an old-timer and a rather conservative Democrat, a migrant from Texas who often voted with southerners on the Rules Committee. Coelho's politics seems rather different. Like Sisk, he is protective of the landholding arrangements that have made the Central Valley one of the most productive farmlands in the world — and that have made some of the landowners here extremely wealthy. But his voting record on most issues is more closely in line with that of northern Democrats.

Coelho has also shown a great deal of political competence. In his first term he won a seat on the Agriculture Committee — a body of obvious importance to this district — and in his second term a seat on Interior as well. Moreover, when James Corman, the chairman of the House Democratic Campaign Committee, was defeated, Coelho moved in fast and got the post. He seems to have a good grasp on campaigning tactics and on the Democrats' need to match the Republicans' fund-raising and technological capacities. But it will take all his talents to get the Democrats off the defensive before the 1982 elections.

Coelho himself won his seat handily in 1978 — an impressive achievement for a man who for some years spent most of his time in Washington rather than the district. He will almost certainly get a safe Democratic seat out of the redistricting plan for 1982.

Census Data   Pop. (1980 final) 578,064, up 24% in 1970s. Median family income, 1970, $7,930, 83% of U.S.

The Voters

Employment profile 1970 White collar, 43%. Blue collar, 31%. Service, 14%. Farm, 12%.
Ethnic groups Black 1980, 5%. Hispanic 1980, 25%. Am. Ind. 1980, 1%. Asian 1980, 2%. Total foreign stock 1970, 21%. Germany, 2%; Canada, USSR, 1% each.

Presidential Vote

1980	Reagan (R)	79,871	(48%)
	Carter (D)	73,088	(44%)
	Anderson (I)	11,593	(7%)
1976	Ford (R)	66,972	(41%)
	Carter (D)	81,797	(54%)

Rep. Tony Coelho (D) Elected 1978; b. June 15, 1942, Los Banos; home, Merced; Loyola U., L.A., B.A. 1964.

Career Staff of U.S. Rep. B. F. Sisk, 1965–78, Admin. Asst., 1970–78.

Offices 216 LHOB, 202-225-6131. Also Fed. Bldg., 415 W. 18th St., Merced 95340, 209-383-4455.

Committees *Agriculture* (18th). Subcommittees: Cotton, Rice and Sugar; Domestic Marketing, Consumer Relations and Nutrition; Livestock, Dairy and Poultry.

Interior and Insular Affairs (23d). Subcommittees: Oversight and Investigations; Water and Power Resources.

Group Ratings

	ADA	COPE	PC	LCV	CFA	RPN	NAB	NSI	NTU	ACA	ACU
1980	72	71	47	45	71	—	8	40	14	9	11
1979	58	65	43	50	32	—	—	—	24	13	8

Key Votes

1) Draft Registn $	AGN	6) Fair Hsg DOJ Enfrc	AGN	11) Cut Socl Incr Dfns $	AGN
2) Ban $ to Nicrgua	AGN	7) Lim PAC Contrbtns	FOR	12) Hosptl Cost Controls	—
3) Dlay MX Missile	FOR	8) Cap on Food Stmp $	AGN	13) Gasln Ctrls & Allctns	FOR
4) Nuclr Mortorium	—	9) New US Dep Edcatn	FOR	14) Lim Wndfll Prof Tax	FOR
5) Alaska Lands Bill	FOR	10) Cut OSHA $	FOR	15) Chryslr Loan Grntee	FOR

Election Results

1980 general	Tony Coelho (D)	108,072	(72%)	($140,382)
	Ron Schwartz (R)	37,895	(25%)	($5,136)
1980 primary	Tony Coelho (D)	56,466	(100%)	
1978 general	Tony Coelho (D)	75,212	(60%)	($266,094)
	Chris Patterakis (R)	49,914	(40%)	($104,164)

SIXTEENTH DISTRICT

The 16th congressional district of California boasts some of the nation's most spectacular scenery, from the Monterey cypresses at Carmel's Pebble Beach, through the mountainous wild Big Sur coast, to William Randolph Hearst's San Simeon. Just a few miles from the ocean is some of the nation's richest farmland: the lettuce fields of the Salinas valley, the artichoke fields around Castroville. This is John Steinbeck country: he grew up in Salinas, and the Cannery Row he described in Monterey still exists, even if only as a tourist attraction.

The coastal counties over the years have tended to vote Republican. Landowners around Salinas and retirees in Santa Cruz and the Monterey peninsula tend to be conservative; the district's Mexican–Americans and its sprinklings of artists and writers are far outnumbered. But in the last decade, the 16th has moved noticeably to the left. A large part of the reason is the impact of environmental issues. It can be argued that there is no environment in America more worthy of protection, and people here have the examples of Los Angeles and the San Francisco Bay area to show what can happen. In addition, this district has an unusual number of students, more than 8% of the eligible electorate; those at the University of California's Santa Cruz branch are so liberal (97% for McGovern in 1972) that they have changed the voting balance of the whole county. Finally there seems to have been a notable generational change here, even more pronounced than in the state as a whole. The old electorate that went for Ronald Reagan in 1966 and Richard Nixon in 1968 is to a considerable extent gone, replaced by a group of voters for whom those men and those who followed them represent the enemy. Ronald Reagan did carry the district in 1980, but with a bare majority of the vote — nothing like 1966, when he carried all before him here.

The movement left has been reflected in the representation of the district. In the 1960s this was a safe seat for Republican Burt Talcott, a man so straitlaced that he made a speech chiding his colleagues for wearing sport coats on the House floor — too informal. Talcott was a faithful follower of the Nixon Administration, and his record on environmental issues got him put on the Dirty Dozen list. In 1972 and 1974 he was nearly beaten by a Mexican–American candidate, and in 1976 he was beaten conclusively.

The winner was Leon Panetta, a former Republican who resigned as head of the Office of Civil Rights of HEW in 1970, charging that the Nixon Administration was sacrificing school desegregation to its southern strategy. Panetta, who had grown up in the district, changed his party registration to Democratic and returned; after the 1974 election he was determined to run. He capitalized ably on the favorable trends in the district and at the same time avoided antagonizing local agricultural interests and shunned a United Farm Workers initiative that was on the ballot. Panetta has been one of those congressmen who pays close attention to his district, constantly attending meetings, bringing in disaster relief money, getting rid of a sand drift, and helping local sugar beet farmers.

Panetta's seat on the Agriculture Committee is an obvious asset in a district where agriculture is very much the primary industry. But nationally Panetta is more important as a member of the Budget Committee, where he is one of the bloc of Democrats inclined temperamentally to support government programs but willing as well to entertain intellectual arguments against them. Panetta thus has the potential to be one of the key members of Congress on important spending issues.

Electorally, Panetta seems to have had no problems in the 16th district, although to some extent his margin in 1980 may be due to weak opposition. Like most nonmetropolitan California districts, the 16th has increased in population in the 1970s and will have to be cut back by redistricting. Most likely Panetta would rather hold onto Santa Cruz at the northern edge of the district than the more Republican San Luis Obispo at the southern end.

Census Data Pop. (1980 final) 612,618, up 32% in 1970s. Median family income, 1970, $9,384, 98% of U.S.

The Voters

Employment profile 1970 White collar, 47%. Blue collar, 28%. Service, 16%. Farm, 9%.
Ethnic groups Black 1980, 4%. Hispanic 1980, 20%. Am. Ind. 1980, 1%. Asian 1980, 4%. Total foreign stock 1970, 25%. Canada, UK, Germany, Italy, 2% each.

Presidential Vote

1980	Reagan (R)	116,525	(50%)
	Carter (D)	79,073	(34%)
	Anderson (I)	25,921	(11%)
1976	Ford (R)	97,003	(49%)
	Carter (D)	95,482	(48%)

Rep. Leon E. Panetta (D) Elected 1976; b. June 28, 1938, Monterey; home, Carmel Valley; U. of Santa Clara, B.A. 1960, J.D. 1963.

Career Army, 1964–66; Legis. Asst. to U.S. Sen. Thomas Kuchel, 1966–69; Dir., U.S. Ofc. of Civil Rights, HEW, 1969–70; Exec. Asst. to the Mayor of New York City, 1970–71; Practicing atty., 1971–76.

Offices 431 CHOB, 202-225-2861. Also 380 Alvorado, Montercy 93940, 408-649-3555.

Committees *Agriculture* (14th). Subcommittees: Conservation, Credit and Rural Development; Domestic Marketing, Consumer Relations and Nutrition; Forests, Family Farms, and Energy.

Budget (9th).

Group Ratings

	ADA	COPE	PC	LCV	CFA	RPN	NAB	NSI	NTU	ACA	ACU
1980	67	58	60	63	50	—	25	10	24	29	24
1979	84	68	68	69	56	—	—	—	35	23	24
1978	50	63	75	65	36	36	58	10	24	50	22

Key Votes

1) Draft Registn $ AGN	6) Fair Hsg DOJ Enfrc FOR	11) Cut Socl Incr Dfns $ AGN
2) Ban $ to Nicrgua AGN	7) Lim PAC Contrbtns FOR	12) Hosptl Cost Controls FOR
3) Dlay MX Missile FOR	8) Cap on Food Stmp $ AGN	13) Gasln Ctrls & Allctns FOR
4) Nuclr Mortorium FOR	9) New US Dep Edcatn FOR	14) Lim Wndfll Prof Tax AGN
5) Alaska Lands Bill FOR	10) Cut OSHA $ AGN	15) Chryslr Loan Grntee AGN

Election Results

1980 general	Leon E. Panetta (D)	153,360	(71%)	($55,475)
	W. A. Jack Roth (R)	54,675	(25%)	($11,995)
1980 primary	Leon E. Panetta (D)	76,989	(100%)	
1978 general	Leon E. Panetta (D)	104,550	(61%)	($219,357)
	Eric Seastrand (R)	65,808	(39%)	($184,169)

SEVENTEENTH DISTRICT

The richest agricultural land in the United States lies in the southern part of California's Central Valley. The variety of crops grown here is impressive: grapes, cotton, alfalfa, canta-loupes, plums, peaches, lima beans, tomatoes, sugar beets, walnuts, olives, poultry, and dairy products. Fresno County each year produces the largest dollar volume of agricultural products in the United States, but other Valley counties are not far behind. This bounteous production is made possible by vast systems of irrigation, for a little more than a century ago nothing was grown here at all. Agriculture is naturally the central subject of politics in the Central Valley. Politicians built the irrigation systems and still control the critical price of water. Politicians decide on what basis farmworkers can bargain for their wages. And politicians tend to determine the support prices or conditions of sale of many of the products grown in the Valley.

This kind of politics tends to cross party lines, a fact pretty clearly shown by the history of representation of the 17th congressional district of California. In partisan terms, this has proved to be a volatile district. Its current boundaries cross the imaginary line halfway between Fresno and Bakersfield that separates traditional Democratic and traditional Republican territory. Three times in the past 14 years the district has defeated its incumbent congressman — an unusual record in an era when most incumbents are reelected easily. Yet all three followed roughly similar policies on agricultural issues, just as all three made a point of serving on the House Agriculture Committee.

The first of these incumbents to be defeated was Harlan Hagen, who lost in 1966. Hagen worked for the interests of the large growers here and was anything but a supporter of the United Farm Workers, which began strikes in this area as early as 1965. But he was caught up in the enthusiasm for Ronald Reagan and the strong local following of his Republican opponent. That was Bob Mathias, known internationally as the winner of the Olympic gold medal in the decathlon in 1948 and 1952. A native of Tulare County, Mathias was affable, attractive, and conservative. Even more than Hagen, he was supportive of the district's major agricultural interests.

Mathias, too, ultimately found himself in political trouble. He suffered particularly from a redistricting, which added much of Democratic Fresno County to the district for the 1974 election. His opponent that year was a member of the Fresno Board of Supervisors, John Krebs. An immigrant from Germany with a Kissingerian accent, Krebs was well known locally as an advocate of planned growth. He beat Mathias by a wide margin and proceeded to service on the Agriculture Committee himself.

Krebs's tenure in the House lasted only half as long as Mathias's. He was reelected easily in 1976 and seemed to be tending satisfactorily to district interests. But in 1978 he was upset by Republican Chip Pashayan. A native of Fresno of Armenian descent, Pashayan was able to cut Krebs's hometown majority to almost nothing, and he won big in Republican Tulare County. Pashayan attacked Krebs as a big spender and for his opposition to the Mineral King resort complex in the nearby Sierras. Pashayan spent much of his first term as spokesman for local farm interests on major legislation affecting water rights. He had only weak opposition in 1980 and was reelected with a stunningly large majority. Redistricting may change the shape of the district. If it moves north that will hurt Pashayan; if it moves south it will help him.

Census Data   Pop. (1980 final) 607,960, up 31% in 1970s. Median family income, 1970, $8,672, 90% of U.S.

The Voters

Employment profile 1970   White collar, 46%. Blue collar, 28%. Service, 12%. Farm, 14%.
Ethnic groups   Black 1980, 2%. Hispanic 1980, 27%. Am. Ind. 1980, 1%. Asian 1980, 3%. Total foreign stock 1970, 23%. USSR, 2%; Canada, 1%.

Presidential Vote

1980	Reagan (R)	108,148	(56%)
	Carter (D)	69,479	(36%)
	Anderson (I)	11,492	(6%)
1976	Ford (R)	87,145	(53%)
	Carter (D)	75,605	(46%)

Rep. Charles (Chip) **Pashayan, Jr.** (R) Elected 1978; b. Mar. 27, 1941, Fresno; home, Fresno; Pomona Col., B.A. 1963, U. of Cal., J.D. 1968, Oxford U., B. Litt. 1977.

Career Army, 1968–70; Practicing atty., 1969– ;Spec. Asst. to Gen. Counsel, HEW, 1973–75.

Offices 129 CHOB, 202-225-3341. Also 4114 Fed. Bldg., 1130 "O" St., Fresno 93721, 209-487-5487.

Committees *Interior and Insular Affairs* (8th). Subcommittees: Public Lands and National Parks; Water and Power Resources.

Post Office and Civil Service (6th). Subcommittees: Civil Service; Investigations.

Group Ratings

	ADA	COPE	PC	LCV	CFA	RPN	NAB	NSI	NTU	ACA	ACU
1980	11	21	23	28	7	—	80	100	52	77	71
1979	11	33	18	16	19	—	—	—	58	79	86

Key Votes

1) Draft Registn $	FOR	6) Fair Hsg DOJ Enfrc	AGN	11) Cut Socl Incr Dfns $	FOR
2) Ban $ to Nicrgua	FOR	7) Lim PAC Contrbtns	AGN	12) Hosptl Cost Controls	AGN
3) Dlay MX Missile	AGN	8) Cap on Food Stmp $	FOR	13) Gasln Ctrls & Alltns	AGN
4) Nuclr Mortorium	AGN	9) New US Dep Edcatn	AGN	14) Lim Wndfll Prof Tax	FOR
5) Alaska Lands Bill	AGN	10) Cut OSHA $	FOR	15) Chryslr Loan Grntee	AGN

Election Results

1980 general	Charles (Chip) Pashayan, Jr. (R) ..	129,159	(71%)	($482,896)
	Willard H. Johnson (D)	53,780	(29%)	($73,755)
1980 primary	Charles (Chip) Pashayan, Jr. (R) ..	47,953	(100%)	
1978 general	Charles (Chip) Pashayan, Jr. (R) ..	81,296	(54%)	($260,412)
	John Krebs (D)	67,885	(46%)	($156,932)

EIGHTEENTH DISTRICT

The Central Valley of California stands out clearly on a relief map—a swath of green down the central part of the state, from up near Oregon to a point only 100 miles north of Los Angeles, the green surrounded by the yellow and brown of the Coast Range and the Sierra Nevada. These flat, vast, heavily irrigated plains are probably the world's most productive farmland. The prosperity of the Central Valley has been built on the drive of agricultural entrepreneurs and the backs of migrant laborers. In the 1930s the workers were Okies forced off their land by swirling dust storms. Today they are mainly Mexican–Americans (including some who have come across the border illegally). Both groups started off with Democratic voting habits—to the extent that migrant workers vote at all. But underlying the common Democratic registration of the 1930s migrants and the Chicanos is a basic economic question: how shall the profits of the land be distributed?

The descendants of the Okies and others whose ancestors were more fortunate believe that the demands of today's farm workers, especially Cesar Chavez's United Farm Workers, will diminish the Anglos' share of the pie. For everyone in the Valley partakes of the profits of big farming, and nobody in the Valley thinks that the big companies that dominate agribusiness will absorb any losses caused by higher wages or better working conditions. So the politics in much of the Central Valley has come down to a conflict between the growers and farm laborers, with the vast majority on the side of the growers. You could have seen the same thing in the 1930s in towns dominated by the auto or steel industries; the only voters who supported the demands of the workers were the workers themselves.

In California so much was never plainer than in 1976, when the UFW placed Proposition 14 on the ballot. This was a measure to continue fully the compromise agricultural labor relations bill worked out by the UFW, the Teamsters, the growers, and Governor Jerry Brown—with a couple of changes in the rules. One feature of 14 seized upon by opponents was a provision that union organizers could conduct their drives on the property of the growers, which ads likened to the prospect of a homeowner having his property invaded by unwanted demonstrators. The result was unequivocal: Proposition 14 got only one out of three votes statewide, and in the Central Valley south from Sacramento 80% voted against it.

This kind of feeling is especially intense in Kern County around Bakersfield, which forms the heart of California's 18th congressional district. Kern is the southern end of the Valley and also the direct western terminus of the road from Oklahoma. It has an especially large number of descendants of the Dust Bowl migrants of the 1930s and more than an average number of Mexican–American farm workers: Kern County is the home of country singer Merle Haggard and the headquarters of Chavez's UFW. It was here that Chavez's first epic strike and boycott took place, against table grape producers in Delano, a dusty town some 25 miles north of Bakersfield, back in 1965. That was happening just as Kern County was trending strongly toward the Republicans, despite Democratic traditions and a heavy Democratic registration.

This area has had several congressmen, all conservative Republicans, in the last dozen years. The first was Bob Mathias, whose territory was gradually shifted north until he lost in 1974 from having too much of Democratic Fresno in his district. The second was William Ketchum, who was originally from Paso Robles near the coast; he was elected here in 1972 and moved his residence to Bakersfield in 1974. He seemed in good shape for reelection when he died suddenly of a heart attack in the summer of 1978.

To replace him on the ticket, the Republicans nominated Bakersfield Assemblyman Bill Thomas, who had campaigned as a strong backer of capital punishment. After a solid victory he got a seat on the House Agriculture Committee; he sat also as a freshman on the House ethics committee. His voting record is solidly conservative, and he seems entrenched in this district. Thomas seems sure to be reelected, whatever happens in redistricting, by a seat centered on Kern County.

Census Data   Pop. (1980 final) 572,865, up 24% in 1970s. Median family income, 1970, $9,300, 97% of U.S.

The Voters

Employment profile 1970 White collar, 44%. Blue collar, 32%. Service, 14%. Farm, 10%.
Ethnic groups Black 1980, 5%. Hispanic 1980, 19%. Am. Ind. 1980, 2%. Asian 1980, 2%. Total foreign stock 1970, 15%. Canada, UK, 1% each.

Presidential Vote

1980	Reagan (R)	114,504	(63%)
	Carter (D)	55,531	(30%)
	Anderson (I)	9,068	(5%)
1976	Ford (R)	89,166	(55%)
	Carter (D)	70,093	(43%)

Rep. William M. Thomas (R) Elected 1978; b. Dec. 6, 1941, Wallace, Idaho; home, Bakersfield; Santa Ana Community Col., San Fran. St. U., B.A., M.A. 1965.

Career Prof., Bakersfield Community Col., 1965–74; Cal. Assembly, 1974–78.

Offices 324 CHOB, 202-225-2915. Also 800 Truxtun, Bakersfield 93301, 805-323-8322.

Committees *Agriculture* (8th). Subcommittees: Cotton, Rice and Sugar; Department Operations, Research and Foreign Agriculture.

House Administration (5th). Subcommittees: Accounts; Office Systems; Policy Group on Information and Computers.

Group Ratings

	ADA	COPE	PC	LCV	CFA	RPN	NAB	NSI	NTU	ACA	ACU
1980	0	17	20	13	7	—	100	100	56	91	94
1979	5	5	15	13	11	—	—	—	59	100	97

Key Votes

1) Draft Registn $	FOR	6) Fair Hsg DOJ Enfrc	AGN	11) Cut Socl Incr Dfns $	FOR
2) Ban $ to Nicrgua	FOR	7) Lim PAC Contrbtns	AGN	12) Hosptl Cost Controls	AGN
3) Dlay MX Missile	—	8) Cap on Food Stmp $	FOR	13) Gasln Ctrls & Allctns	AGN
4) Nuclr Mortorium	AGN	9) New US Dep Edcatn	AGN	14) Lim Wndfll Prof Tax	FOR
5) Alaska Lands Bill	AGN	10) Cut OSHA $		FOR	15) Chryslr Loan Grntee	AGN

Election Results

1980 general	William M. Thomas (R)	126,046	(71%)	($192,111)
	Mary (Pat) Timmermans (D)	51,415	(29%)	($13,183)
1980 primary	William M. Thomas (R)	48,215	(86%)	
	One other (R)	8,127	(14%)	
1978 general	William M. Thomas (R)	85,663	(59%)	($166,534)
	Bob Sogge (D).................	58,900	(41%)	($142,280)

NINETEENTH DISTRICT

There are still parts of California that can make you understand what brought so many people — retirees, young families, hoboes, millionaires — out here 30 or 40 years ago: the soft climate, the mountains falling into the sea, the peaceful small towns, and the well-ordered smogless cities. One such area is the part of the state within the bounds of the 19th congressional district, which includes Santa Barbara County, much of Ventura County to the east, and a small part of San Luis Obispo County to the north. The Coast Range is as rugged, the Pacific as blue and warm, the towns—despite recent heavy growth—as pristine as any place on the coast.

This is also, for mystery fans, Ross Macdonald land. Macdonald lives here, in Santa Barbara, and most of his novels are set here or in other thinly disguised towns between here and Los Angeles. In one of the novels, *Sleeping Beauty,* Macdonald weaves the story around the famous Santa Barbara oil spill of 1969. The Interior Department had been allowing offshore oil drilling in the Santa Barbara Channel; something went wrong with the apparatus; oil gushed out, covering the beaches, destroying the birds, fouling the air. It was an incident that radicalized wealthy retirees and politicized young students—and, it can be argued, permanently shoved the Santa Barbara community at least a couple of notches leftward.

The tide has now, perhaps literally, turned. When oil was oozing into Santa Barbara Channel in 1969, the incoming Nixon Administration's Interior Secretary Walter Hickel helicoptered over the waters and ordered drilling stopped. The Reagan Administration's Interior Secretary, James Watt, as one of his first acts, issued an order allowing drilling to begin in the Santa Barbara Channel and other California coastal waters. Local protests arose, but only a murmur of dissatisfaction was heard in Washington.

Santa Barbara County, historically Republican, has moved toward the Democrats since 1969. Ventura County, with a large Mexican–American community in the industrial city of Oxnard and in the agricultural areas inland, has been moving in the other direction. The main reason is that the eastern part of the county has become increasingly an extension of the Los Angeles metropolitan area, a place where affluent people escape the smog and congestion of the San Fernando Valley. The 19th congressional district includes Santa Barbara County, a small part of San Luis Obispo to the north, and most of Ventura County. The district does not include most of the new suburbs of Ventura, but the Republican trend is nonetheless apparent.

The current congressman, Robert Lagomarsino, is an adept and intelligent politician who won the district under difficult circumstances and who has held it since with seeming ease. A Republican, he represented Ventura County (and ultimately Santa Barbara too) in the Assembly and Senate for 14 years. When the incumbent Republican congressman died in 1974, Lagomarsino was the obvious Republican candidate, and he was just about the only Republican in the nation to win a special election in the Watergate year of 1974. He had a good enough environmental record to propitiate Santa Barbara, and he was shrewd enough to make a point of saying that he would not support Richard Nixon and might even vote for impeachment. A member of the Interior and Foreign Affairs Committees, he is more liberal on environmental matters than on either foreign policy or defense issues.

Lagomarsino has been reelected with overwhelming margins; his 1980 Democratic opponent announced that she was withdrawing from the race. Redistricting will probably shift the district northward and might cost Lagomarsino the Democratic city of Oxnard.

Census Data　Pop. (1980 final) 565,413, up 22% in 1970s. Median family income, 1970, $10,241, 107% of U.S.

The Voters
　Employment profile 1970　White collar, 52%. Blue collar, 29%. Service, 14%. Farm, 5%.
　Ethnic groups　Black 1980, 3%. Hispanic 1980, 23%. Am. Ind. 1980, 1%. Asian 1980, 3%. Total foreign stock 1970, 24%. Canada, UK, Germany, 2% each.

Presidential Vote

1980	Reagan (R)	119,582	(54%)
	Carter (D)	72,903	(33%)
	Anderson (I)	22,713	(10%)
1976	Ford (R)	98,614	(50%)
	Carter (D)	95,297	(48%)

Rep. Robert J. Lagomarsino (R) Elected Mar. 5, 1974; b. Sept. 4, 1926, Ventura; home, Ventura; U. of Cal. at Santa Barbara, B.A. 1950, Santa Clara Law Sch., LL.B., 1953.

Career Navy, WWII; Practicing atty., 1954–74; Ojia City Cncl., 1958, Mayor, 1958–61; Cal. Senate, 1961–74.

Offices 2332 RHOB, 202-225-3601. Also Studio 121, 814 State St., Santa Barbara 93102, 805-963-1708.

Committees *Foreign Affairs* (6th). Subcommittees: Inter-American Affairs; International Economic Policy and Trade.

Interior and Insular Affairs (4th). Subcommittees: Insular Affairs; Public Lands and National Parks

Group Ratings

	ADA	COPE	PC	LCV	CFA	RPN	NAB	NSI	NTU	ACA	ACU
1980	11	16	20	43	7	—	92	100	59	83	84
1979	26	20	28	45	22	—	—	—	60	96	87
1978	5	5	13	27	14	83	100	100	31	96	92

Key Votes

1) Draft Registn $	AGN	6) Fair Hsg DOJ Enfrc	AGN	11) Cut Socl Incr Dfns $	FOR
2) Ban $ to Nicrgua	FOR	7) Lim PAC Contrbtns	FOR	12) Hosptl Cost Controls	AGN
3) Dlay MX Missile	AGN	8) Cap on Food Stmp $	FOR	13) Gasln Ctrls & Allctns	AGN
4) Nuclr Mortorium	FOR	9) New US Dep Edcatn	AGN	14) Lim Wndfll Prof Tax	FOR
5) Alaska Lands Bill	FOR	10) Cut OSHA $	FOR	15) Chryslr Loan Grntee	AGN

Election Results

1980 general	Robert J. Lagomarsino (R)	162,854	(78%)	($97,504)
	Carmen Lodise (D)	36,990	(18%)	($0)
	Jim Trotter (Libertarian).........	9,765	(5%)	($0)
1980 primary	Robert J. Lagomarsino (R)	53,285	(100%)	
1978 general	Robert J. Lagomarsino (R)	123,192	(72%)	($95,044)
	Jerome Zamos (D)	41,672	(24%)	($14,042)

TWENTIETH DISTRICT

What is now the 20th district of California is the lineal descendant of a seat that has been redistricted so many times since its initial creation in 1962 that it contains today virtually none of its original territory—and will probably lose that in redistricting before 1982.

As it is today, the 20th represents an attempt to create a political entity out of the people who have moved west from the San Fernando Valley, people trying to leapfrog the suburban sprawl of Los Angeles. Thus the district includes Malibu Beach and the rustic Topanga

114   CALIFORNIA

Canyon area along the ocean beyond the city limits; the towns of Newhall and Saugus above the mountains that are the northern boundary of the San Fernando Valley; and the fast-growing Ventura County suburbs of Simi Valley and Thousand Oaks (known locally as T.O.), connected by freeway to Los Angeles, over the mountains to the east.

The 20th also contains the western edge of Los Angeles's San Fernando Valley, where about 40% of its residents live. All these varied areas have in common a political affection for the conservative right; this is the first, numerically, of those suburban California districts that usually provide large margins for conservative candidates. The 20th and its various predecessors have had a number of different congressmen: a John Birch Society member; a Democratic Assembly veteran who ousted him and who then, disgusted with the pace of things in the House, retired; Ed Reinecke, who campaigned against obscenity, became lieutenant governor in 1969, and was convicted of perjury in 1974 while running for governor; and the present incumbent, the son of Mr. Conservative, Barry Goldwater, Jr.

Young Goldwater won the seat in a 1969 special election, largely because of his name, when he was just past 30. For a while his name was his only political asset, and he was not regarded highly in the House. But in recent years he has been both active and effective. Goldwater lobbied hard and effectively to save the Lockheed loan legislation and with then Congressman Ed Koch of New York worked to develop legislation to protect the privacy of citizens from the computerized lists that have proliferated in government and private business. Since Koch left the House to become mayor of New York, Goldwater has become indisputably the House's leading expert on privacy matters and deserves much credit for the bills on these matters passed in the 95th Congress. It is a classically conservative cause; but Goldwater was the first conservative in Congress to really pursue it.

Goldwater was urged to run for the Senate in 1976 and decided not to for personal reasons. In retrospect he might have won; there is no reason to suppose him politically much weaker than S. I. Hayakawa. There was talk that he would run against Alan Cranston in 1980, but it came to nothing. Then in early 1981 he announced he would run for the Senate seat held by Hayakawa. This is a chancy race, with a Republican primary that may have as many as six serious contenders and the likelihood of a strong Democratic candidate as well. In the meantime, the 20th district will probably be moved west a little more into Ventura County. It will remain a solidly Republican district and will presumably elect a new Republican congressman—or an incumbent, such as Robert Dornan, who may be in search of a new district.

Census Data   Pop. (1980 final) 640,635, up 37% in 1970s. Median family income, 1970, $13,583, 142% of U.S.

The Voters

Employment profile 1970   White collar, 62%. Blue collar, 26%. Service, 10%. Farm, 2%.
Ethnic groups   Black 1980, 1%. Hispanic 1980, 11%. Am. Ind. 1980, 1%. Asian 1980, 3%. Total foreign stock 1970, 22%. Canada, 3%; UK, Germany, Italy, 2% each; USSR, 1%.

Presidential Vote

1980	Reagan (R)	166,697	(63%)
	Carter (D)	67,044	(26%)
	Anderson (I)	20,802	(8%)
1976	Ford (R)	129,113	(59%)
	Carter (D)	86,610	(39%)

Rep. Barry M. Goldwater, Jr. (R) Elected Apr. 29, 1969; b. July 15, 1938, Los Angeles; home, Woodland Hills; U. of Colo., 1957–60, Ariz. St. U., B.A. 1962.

Career Stock broker, 1962–69.

Offices 2240 RHOB, 202-225-4461. Also 23421 Ventura Blvd., Suite 119, Woodland Hills 91364, 213-883-1233.

Committees *Public Works and Transportation* (5th). Subcommittees: Aviation; Investigations and Oversight.

Science and Technology (2d). Subcommittees: Energy Research and Production; Transportation, Aviation and Materials.

Group Ratings

	ADA	COPE	PC	LCV	CFA	RPN	NAB	NSI	NTU	ACA	ACU
1980	22	6	27	35	14	—	100	100	54	82	68
1979	21	5	20	26	4	—	—	—	62	100	97
1978	5	0	8	17	14	73	100	100	27	100	91

Key Votes

1) Draft Registn $	AGN	6) Fair Hsg DOJ Enfrc	AGN	11) Cut Socl Incr Dfns $	FOR
2) Ban $ to Nicrgua	FOR	7) Lim PAC Contrbtns	AGN	12) Hosptl Cost Controls	AGN
3) Dlay MX Missile	FOR	8) Cap on Food Stmp $	FOR	13) Gasln Ctrls & Allctns	AGN
4) Nuclr Mortorium	AGN	9) New US Dep Edcatn	—	14) Lim Wndfll Prof Tax	FOR
5) Alaska Lands Bill	FOR	10) Cut OSHA $		FOR	15) Chryslr Loan Grntee	AGN

Election Results

1980 general	Barry M. Goldwater, Jr. (R)	199,681	(79%)	($193,063)
	Matt Miller (D)	43,025	(17%)	($15,420)
1980 primary	Barry M. Goldwater, Jr. (R)	69,540	(100%)	
1978 general	Barry M. Goldwater, Jr. (R)	129,714	(66%)	($122,120)
	Pat Lear (D)	65,695	(34%)	($229,306)

TWENTY-FIRST DISTRICT

California's 21st congressional district is the heart of the San Fernando Valley. This vast expanse of land, surrounded on all sides by mountains, is almost entirely within the Los Angeles city limits. Annexed long ago, when it consisted of dusty fields and movie ranches — the movie *Chinatown* gives the details with fair accuracy — the Valley is now thoroughly filled up but still suburban in character. The straight streets go on for mile after mile, lined by neat stucco houses or by low-rise stores and offices. At major intersections there are great shopping centers. Hanging over all is the Los Angeles smog, a little less dismal there than in downtown L.A., but still a depressing part of life for those who came here looking for the Golden West.

The Valley has seen southern California's boom industries rise and fall — first agriculture, then the movie business, aerospace, and electronics. The boom-and-bust cycle is a common experience here, with the most notable recent bust in the early 1970s, when Lockheed lost some major government contracts. As the layoffs were being announced, the Valley was hit by the earthquake of 1971, which destroyed a veterans' hospital and threatened to crack the Van Norman Dam—a catastrophe that would have destroyed the homes of some 150,000 people. A period of disillusion set in. People began talking about moving back east, and indeed this period is the beginning of the great migrations of the 1970s to the Rocky Mountain states. The Valley is a happier, more confident place today: there have been no more major quakes, smog has decreased, and those most discontent have moved away. But in place of the euphoric optimism of the years after World War II one finds the cynical, jaded attitude of big city residents—and occasionally anger.

Anger is the main element that produced one of the major upsets of the 1980 congressional elections: the defeat of Congressman James Corman, a 20-year veteran and head of the Democratic Congressional Campaign Committee. Corman was beaten by Republican Bobbi Fiedler. This was not the result of some generalized rightward trend; the Valley, despite the sneers of comedians, is not a haven of right-wing racist suburbia. (This kind of disdain comes naturally to people in the entertainment business, who live in Beverly Hills or Bel Air south of the Santa Monica Mountains when they're making lots of money and the Valley north of the mountains when they are not.) The Valley politically is really the middle of the road. The 21st district occupies the northeast corner of the Valley and spreads out almost to the Santa Monica Mountains in the south and to within four or five miles of the mountains to the west. It includes Democratic North Hollywood with its large Jewish population, middle-class Van Nuys and Northridge, and Pacoima, with the Valley's small black ghetto. It does not include the Valley's highest-income areas—Woodland Hills, Encino, Sherman Oaks—which tend to be more Republican; and there is perhaps some trend to the Democrats here because of outmigration to farther suburbs of the kind of voters who simply dislike being in a central city.

The anger that produced Corman's defeat was anger against busing. The Los Angeles school system has been the subject of desegregation lawsuits for years, although of course there was never legal segregation here. In 1977 the state courts issued a districtwide busing order, which has produced some of the most absurd—and, for parents, maddening—results imaginable. The Los Angeles school district is vast, and San Fernando Valley grade school children found themselves under court order to attend schools in some cases more than 50 miles away. The natural reaction of any parent is to resist, and that is what happened here. Private schools sprang up, and antibusing majorities were quickly elected to the Los Angeles school board. One of their leaders was Bobbi Fiedler, a resident of the middle-income Northridge area in the Valley. She gained fame as one of the most outspoken opponents of busing.

Busing is not, strictly speaking, a congressional issue. Congress could vote a statute or a constitutional amendment forbidding busing in various circumstances, but it is a clumsy way to address what are inherently local situations. Busing in Los Angeles, as it turned out, was stopped by local political action: a state referendum was passed, bringing California in line with federal law. Despite the efforts of courts to preserve their jurisdiction when the law abolished it, busing was ordered stopped at the end of the 1980–81 school year when parents were allowed to withdraw their children from schools to which they were bused in April 1981. Nevertheless, busing inevitably became the major issue in the Corman–Fiedler race. Corman, who had moved to the Judiciary Committee despite constituency pressures in the early 1960s solely so he could support the civil rights bill, defended busing as a last resort means to desegregate schools. Only in late September did he declare his opposition to "massive forced busing." Fiedler, despite her claims that she was not a one-issue candidate and her general support of the Reagan platform, inevitably was seen as an antibusing candidate. As for the voters, what issue could be more important? The assumptions on which they built their lives, selected their neighborhoods, and planned their families were all under challenge, and they responded with rage.

What is perhaps surprising is not that Corman lost but that he came so close to winning. Many people think he would have won if Jimmy Carter had not conceded defeat when the polls in California were still open. There were stories of people leaving voting lines, and Corman lost by only 752 votes out of more than 150,000 cast. So the House lost one of its major advocates of tax reform and national health insurance and gained a new member whose chief policy goal has been achieved by the board of education on which she used to sit. For 1982 the major question is whether the Democrats, who control redistricting, will concede the seat to Fiedler, or whether they will try to draw as Democratic a seat as possible in the Valley, in the hopes of unseating her. The chances are that they will do the latter. She might run in the new 20th district, assuming that Barry Goldwater, Jr., tries for the Senate.

Census Data   Pop. (1980 final) 489,475, up 5% in 1970s. Median family income, 1970, $11,440, 119% of U.S.

The Voters

Employment profile 1970   White collar, 55%. Blue collar, 34%. Service, 11%. Farm, –%.
Ethnic groups   Black 1980, 5%. Hispanic 1980, 30%. Am. Ind. 1980, 1%. Asian 1980, 4%. Total foreign stock 1970, 30%. Canada, Italy, 3% each; UK, Germany, Italy, 2% each; Poland, 1%.

Presidential Vote

1980	Reagan (R)	80,766	(51%)
	Carter (D)	60,172	(38%)
	Anderson (I)	12,634	(8%)
1976	Ford (R)	73,773	(47%)
	Carter (D)	80,681	(51%)

Rep. Bobbi Fiedler (R) Elected 1980; b. Apr. 22, 1937, Santa Monica; home, Northridge; Santa Monica City Col.

Career   Housewife; Drugstore owner; Interior decorator; Organizer of BUSTOP, L.A. antibusing group, 1976; L.A. Sch. Bd., 1977–80.

Offices   1724 LHOB, 202-225-5811. Also 14600 Roscoe Blvd., Suite 506, Panorama City 91402, 213-787-1776.

Committee   *Budget* (12th).

Group Ratings and Key Votes: Newly Elected

Election Results

1980 general	Bobbi Fiedler (R)	74,843	(49%)	($560,492)
	James C. Corman (D)	74,091	(48%)	($905,231)

1980 primary	Bobbi Fiedler (R)	23,980	(74%)	
	Patrick L. O'Brien (R)	8,580	(26%)	($0)
1978 general	James C. Corman (D)...........	73,869	(60%)	($241,423)
	G. (Rod) Walsh (R)	44,519	(36%)	($25,429)

TWENTY-SECOND DISTRICT

Pasadena and Glendale, both with more than 100,000 people, are two Los Angeles area towns with well-established images. From sources as diverse as the mid-1960s rock song "Little Old Lady from Pasadena" and Raymond Chandler's description of the massive houses of wealthy recluses, one gets a picture that is still partially accurate. These are towns of large houses, of tree-shaded streets, of older, upper-income people whose basic instincts are profoundly conservative. All these adjectives apply also to California's 22d congressional district, of which Glendale and Pasadena and several adjacent suburbs are the major part. They include Burbank, the home, as almost everyone knows, of the NBC television studios; Altadena, a kind of upper Pasadena, just below the San Gabriel Mountains; LaCanada–Flintridge, and the Tujunga and Sunland neighborhoods of Los Angeles, highly conservative high-income neighborhoods, isolated and sandwiched between two mountain ridges. Each of these has a different personality. Pasadena has significant black and Mexican–American communities, each about one-fifth of the population; Pasadena has its own civic institutions, such as the Pasadena Playhouse and the Rose Bowl. More than the others, it is a city in its own right. Pasadena's well-to-do neighborhoods have also had an infusion of young whites in the 1970s. Glendale remains essentially elderly and not much changed from earlier years, physically not very far from some of Los Angeles's Mexican–American neighborhoods but determined to retain its distance. Burbank, also with an elderly population, is less set apart; physically it sits just at the eastern edge of the San Fernando Valley. LaCanada–Flintridge have younger populations, family people with good, often technical, jobs, determined that their children will have a good education, grounded in fundamentals.

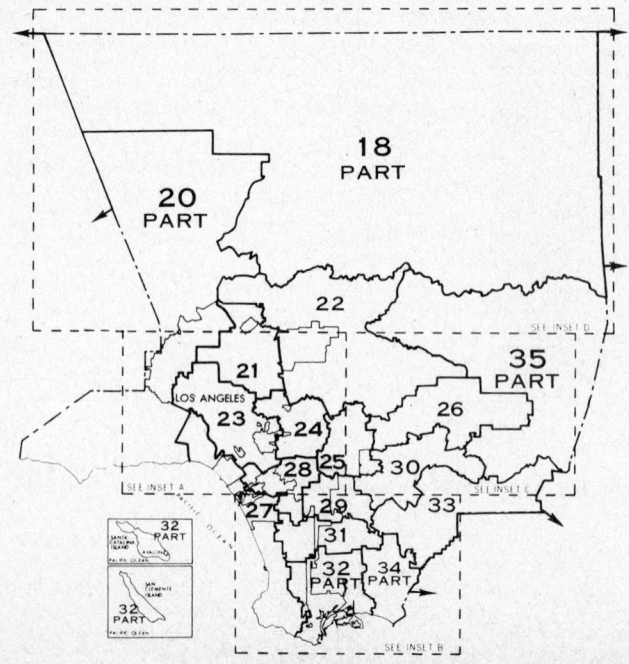

The 22d district has long been one of the most Republican districts in California. For a while in the 1970s it seemed to be trending Democratic, but that trend, if there was one, proved ephemeral. As economic issues came to the fore in state and national politics in the late 1970s, the 22d became again very dependably Republican.

This has been good news for the 22d's Congressman, Republican Carlos Moorhead. On his predecessor's retirement, Moorhead was first elected in 1972 with an uninspiring 57%; two years later, after he voted against the impeachment of Richard Nixon on the House Judiciary Committee, he was reelected with an undistinguished 56%. But with the change of issue focus, Moorhead's percentages rose to 65% in 1978 and 64% in 1980. In the House he is an earnest and faithful follower of conservative policies.

Census Data Pop. (1980 final) 467,466, up 1% in 1970s. Median family income, 1970, $11,741, 122% of U.S.

The Voters

Employment profile 1970 White collar, 53%. Blue collar, 36%. Service, 11%. Farm, –%.
Ethnic groups Black 1980, 9%. Hispanic 1980, 15%. Am. Ind. 1980, 1%. Asian 1980, 4%. Total foreign stock 1970, 27%. Canada, UK, Germany, 3% each; Italy, 2%.

Presidential Vote

1980	Reagan (R)	116,051	(61%)
	Carter (D)	56,067	(29%)
	Anderson (I)	13,815	(7%)
1976	Ford (R)	115,685	(61%)
	Carter (D)	71,648	(38%)

Rep. Carlos J. Moorhead (R) Elected 1972; b. May 6, 1922, Long Beach; home, Glendale; UCLA, B.A. 1943, USC, J.D. 1949.

Career Army, WWII; Practicing atty., 1950–72; Cal. Assembly, 1966–72.

Offices 2346 RHOB, 202-225-4176. Also Rm. 404, 420 N. Brand Blvd., Glendale 91203, 213-247-8445.

Committees *Energy and Commerce* (6th). Subcommittees: Energy Conservation and Power; Telecommunications, Consumer Protection and Finance.

Judiciary (5th). Subcommittees: Administrative Law and Governmental Regulations; Monopolies and Commercial Law.

Group Ratings

	ADA	COPE	PC	LCV	CFA	RPN	NAB	NSI	NTU	ACA	ACU
1980	11	16	23	35	7	—	91	100	60	96	89
1979	11	20	18	20	11	—	—	—	65	96	90
1978	5	0	13	16	14	64	100	100	47	100	92

Key Votes

1) Draft Registn $	AGN	6) Fair Hsg DOJ Enfrc	AGN	11) Cut Socl Incr Dfns $	FOR
2) Ban $ to Nicrgua	FOR	7) Lim PAC Contrbtns	AGN	12) Hosptl Cost Controls	AGN
3) Dlay MX Missile	AGN	8) Cap on Food Stmp $	FOR	13) Gasln Ctrls & Allctns	AGN
4) Nuclr Mortorium	AGN	9) New US Dep Edcatn	AGN	14) Lim Wndfll Prof Tax	FOR
5) Alaska Lands Bill	FOR	10) Cut OSHA $	FOR	15) Chryslr Loan Grntee	AGN

Election Results

1980 general	Carlos J. Moorhead (R)	115,241	(64%)	($124,297)
	Pierce O'Donnell (D)	57,477	(32%)	($171,977)
1980 primary	Carlos J. Moorhead (R)	54,760	(100%)	
1978 general	Carlos J. Moorhead (R)	99,502	(65%)	($56,371)
	Robert S. Henry (D)............	54,442	(35%)	($13,368)

TWENTY-THIRD DISTRICT

The 23d congressional district of Los Angeles is situated in one of the most prosperous — and most famous — parts of greater Los Angeles. It includes middle-class West Los Angeles and well-to-do Westwood, around the UCLA campus, and over the mountains in the San Fernando Valley, the communities of Sherman Oaks, Encino, Tarzana, and Reseda. Far better known is the separate city of Beverly Hills, one of the richest cities in the nation. Beverly Hills is still host every day to busloads of tourists gawking at the homes of the stars and to Mercedes-loads of the rich who shop at Beverly Hills's ultraexpensive and chic stores. There was a hubbub lately because a wealthy young Arab had painted the statues on his lawn and put plastic flowers in his pots; it is perhaps a measure of the progress of American civilization that most Beverly Hills residents now sternly uphold strict canons of good taste. Not far away is glittering Century City, the giant office and apartment development built on the former Twentieth Century–Fox backlot. Above in the mountains, in Laurel and Coldwater Canyons, are the overpriced rustic cabins and tree-secluded mansions of the would-be and genuinely rich.

The 23d is possibly the most heavily Jewish congressional district outside New York City, and of course many of its residents were lured here from New York by the entertainment business. It is also one of the most reliably Democratic high-income districts in the nation; Beverly Hills, with its large Jewish population, has the distinction of never having voted for Richard Nixon. This is also one of the half dozen or so districts where are concentrated most of the big contributors to national campaigns; even with the current limits on contributions, this is an especially important area for Democrats and for Republicans as well.

Curiously, until 1976 the 23d had never elected a Jewish congressman, although the area has been represented by a series of famous people. One was James Roosevelt (1955–65), son of FDR; the younger Roosevelt was a leading liberal in Congress but in 1972 endorsed Nixon at a time coinciding with the legal troubles of Bernard Cornfeld's Investors Overseas Service, of which Roosevelt had been vice president. Another was Sam Yorty (1951–55), the three-term mayor of Los Angeles (1961–73), a hawkish Democrat (in the 1972 New Hampshire presidential primary) turned Republican (after his 1973 loss to Tom Bradley) with a leftish political past. Going back a few more years, there was Helen Gahagan Douglas (1945–51), wife of actor Melvyn Douglas and once an actress herself; she was the target of Richard Nixon's famous 1950 Senate race, when he smeared her as the "pink lady."

The most recent ex-Congressman, Thomas Rees, was less well known at home and in Washington. He decided to quit in 1976, at 51, to practice law — one of many not-so-old congressmen who have been quitting these days. One reason is the redeye, the planes that leave the West Coast around midnight and arrive in Washington at seven in the morning. California congressmen have to ride them all the time, and no life-style, even one representing Beverly Hills in Congress, can be entirely pleasant under such circumstances.

The current congressman is Anthony Beilenson, a Beverly Hills state senator and assemblyman for 14 years who won the House seat with little difficulty. After two years of service,

Beilenson won a seat on the Rules Committee, where he is a supporter of the Democratic leadership and an intelligent and shrewd legislative strategist in his own right. He has been reelected easily and almost certainly has nothing to fear from redistricting.

Census Data Pop. (1980 final) 464,582, no change in 1970s. Median family income, 1970, $14,141, 148% of U.S.

The Voters

Employment profile 1970 White collar, 75%. Blue collar, 16%. Service, 9%. Farm, -%.
Ethnic groups Black 1980, 3%. Hispanic 1980, 8%. Asian 1980, 4%. Total foreign stock 1970, 39%.
USSR, 8%; Canada, 4%; UK, Germany, Poland, 3% each; Italy, Austria, 2% each; Hungary, 1%.

Presidential Vote

1980	Reagan (R)	100,601	(46%)
	Carter (D)	89,053	(41%)
	Anderson (I)	22,521	(10%)
1976	Ford (R)	106,129	(46%)
	Carter (D)	119,138	(52%)

Rep. Anthony C. Beilenson (D) Elected 1976; b. Oct. 26, 1932, New Rochelle, N.Y.; home, Sacramento; Harvard U., B.A. 1954, LL.B. 1957.

Career Practicing atty., 1957–59; Counsel, Cal. Assembly Com. on Finance and Insurance, 1960; Staff Atty., Cal. State Comp. and Insurance Fund, 1961–62; Cal. Assembly, 1963–66; Cal. Senate, 1971–77.

Offices 1025 LHOB, 202-225-5911. Also 11000 Wilshire Blvd., Los Angeles 90024, 213-824-7801.

Committee *Rules* (8th). Subcommittee: Rules of the House.

Group Ratings

	ADA	COPE	PC	LCV	CFA	RPN	NAB	NSI	NTU	ACA	ACU
1980	94	68	80	99	86	—	8	0	29	21	11
1979	100	83	85	89	75	—	—	—	27	8	15
1978	80	79	83	94	68	45	0	10	32	8	9

Key Votes

1) Draft Registn $	AGN	6) Fair Hsg DOJ Enfrc	FOR	11) Cut Socl Incr Dfns $	AGN
2) Ban $ to Nicrgua	AGN	7) Lim PAC Contrbtns	FOR	12) Hosptl Cost Controls	FOR
3) Dlay MX Missile	FOR	8) Cap on Food Stmp $	AGN	13) Gasln Cuts & Allctns	FOR
4) Nuclr Mortoriuim	FOR	9) New US Dep Edcatn	AGN	14) Lim Wndfll Prof Tax	AGN
5) Alaska Lands Bill	FOR	10) Cut OSHA $	AGN	15) Chryslr Loan Grntee	AGN

Election Results

1980 general	Anthony C. Beilenson (D)	126,020	(63%)	($61,194)
	Robert Winckler (R)	62,742	(32%)	($9,865)
	Jeffrey P. Lieb (Libertarian)	10,623	(5%)	($0)
1980 primary	Anthony C. Beilenson (D)	67,432	(85%)	
	One other (D)	11,588	(15%)	
1978 general	Anthony C. Beilenson (D)	117,498	(66%)	($47,776)
	Joseph Barbara (R)	61,496	(34%)	($9,170)

TWENTY-FOURTH DISTRICT

The heart of the entertainment business in the United States — of records and television as well as movies — remains where it has been for the last fifty years, on the west side of Los Angeles: from the old Hollywood neighborhood itself (it is not a separate city) down to Beverly Hills and Westwood and, over the mountains, in Universal City and downtown Burbank. Most of this territory, from Hollywood to the still gaudy Sunset Strip, lies within the bounds of the 24th congressional district of California. Here you will find Hollywood itself — a rather disappointing Hollywood Boulevard and tawdry stucco side streets. To the north, their precipitous rise dominating smogless days, are the Santa Monica Mountains; on the face of one of them is the Hollywood sign recently refurbished by show business celebrities. Among the mountains are picturesque houses built in steep canyons or on flat-topped mountains; yet from Hollywood the mountains look surprisingly desolate and wild. North of the mountains the 24th extends into the San Fernando Valley, including part of predominantly Jewish North Hollywood, and stretching to Sherman Oaks on the west and Burbank on the east. Here, within the 24th (or the 23d, just to the west) are the old movie and new TV studios, almost all the agents and production companies, and the homes of most of the stars.

Show business is in many ways a Jewish industry, and the 24th district, like the 23d, has a large Jewish population. Not everyone here lives in the well-manicured streets and spacious houses of Hancock Park or nearby Beverly Hills. There are also the middle-class streets of the Fairfax district, an older Jewish neighborhood, or of North Hollywood on the other side of the mountains. The southern edge of the district touches on Los Angeles's black ghetto, and there is a significant Mexican–American population also within the 24th's bounds. Here as well is the old, elegant Hancock Park neighborhood with its huge houses, where much of the non–show business elite of Los Angeles lives, and just to the south substantial Korean and Vietnamese neighborhoods. Indeed, Asians are the fastest-growing minority group in this part of Los Angeles, a group not politically significant today but likely to be of major importance in the near future.

This district was created quite anew by the court-ordered redistricting of 1973; before that its territory had been divided up between neighborhood constituencies. What is odd is that it was not created earlier, in 1972, by the then California Assembly Reapportionment Committee Chairman, Henry Waxman, who now represents it. That someone like Waxman should be a power in the Assembly says something about the fluidity and accessibility of power there and, in contrast, the inaccessibility of power in the Congress until the early 1970s. Waxman, elected to the Assembly at 29, had chosen the right side on a speakership fight and so got control of one of the Assembly's choicest committees. In Congress he continues to maintain close contact with a number of west Los Angeles state legislators, notably Howard Berman, who in 1975 became Assembly majority leader but in late 1980 was defeated for the speakership.

In Congress positions of power have become much more accessible since Waxman was first elected, as he himself has most vividly demonstrated. A decade ago a member with only two terms' seniority hardly rated a good-morning from a committee chairman; but Waxman successfully challenged the Democratic leadership and respected senior members for the chair of one of the House's most important subcommittees. This is the Energy and Commerce Committee's Health Subcommittee, which under Paul Rogers of Florida was a model of legislative competence. Rogers retired in 1978. In the past, the chair would have gone to the next senior Democrat, David Satterfield of Virginia; but his record was so reactionary that he was not even considered—another sign of how things have changed in the House. The next senior Democrat, Richardson Preyer, was highly respected and personally well liked, hardworking, and intelligent. Yet Waxman challenged and beat him. Preyer was hurt because he has substantial holdings in a major pharmaceutical company, although no one doubted his integrity; he was also hurt because, as a North Carolina congressman, he supported tobacco subsidies and opposed antismoking measures. Waxman was helped because he distributed over $24,000 of his own money in campaign funds to colleagues—a practice that is legal, but one engaged in only by senior House members until recently. Rules Chairman Richard Bolling attacked Waxman for trying to buy the chair, and the House leadership reportedly backed Preyer. But Waxman won among Commerce Committee Democrats 15–12.

This was a striking victory and makes Waxman one of the most important members of the House, although he does not have the power to impose his own views on other members. Waxman tends to favor national health insurance and health cost care containment measures; but just as he won his chair, the House generally was moving away from such measures and toward other, more voluntary programs. For 1981 most of his attention will probably be directed toward renewal of the Clean Air Act. Waxman has an obvious constituency interest here: although Los Angeles's air quality has improved in the last decade, voters here are strongly for air pollution control, and there is no local lobby against it. Los Angeles has an economic interest as well in preventing other parts of the country from using cheap but dirty fuels that will not in any circumstances be permitted in the Los Angeles Basin. The Clean Air Act is a complex and difficult piece of legislation, and Waxman can expect to come into conflict with some seasoned pros, including Energy and Commerce Chairman John Dingell of Michigan (who favors lower auto emission standards for automobiles) and Senate Environment ranking Democrat Jennings Randolph of West Virginia (who favors greater use of high-sulphur eastern coal). This legislation will be an exacting test of Waxman's legislative skill.

At home, Waxman faces another test—redistricting—which his experience and contacts should enable him to pass more easily, although he might have some trouble since his political ally Berman was defeated for speaker by Willie Brown. The odds are, however, that the legislature will not try to hurt as well-placed and skillful a legislator as Waxman.

Census Data Pop. (1980 final) 539,132, up 16% in 1970s. Median family income, 1970, $10,137, 106% of U.S.

The Voters

Employment profile 1970 White collar, 69%. Blue collar, 20%. Service, 11%. Farm, -%.
Ethnic groups Black 1980, 8%. Hispanic 1980, 27%. Am. Ind. 1980, 1%. Asian 1980, 13%. Total foreign stock 1970, 49%. USSR, 6%; Canada, UK, Germany, Poland, 3% each; Italy, 2%; Austria, Hungary, 1% each.

Presidential Vote

1980	Reagan (R)	65,890	(41%)
	Carter (D)	74,435	(47%)
	Anderson (I)	13,545	(9%)
1976	Ford (R)	74,042	(44%)
	Carter (D)	93,650	(56%)

Rep. Henry A. Waxman (D) Elected 1974; b. Sept. 12, 1939, Los Angeles; home, Los Angeles; UCLA, B.A. 1961, J.D. 1964.

Career Practicing atty., 1965–68; Cal. Assembly, 1968–74.

Offices 2418 RHOB, 202-225-3976. Also 8425 W. 3d St., Los Angeles 90048, 213-651-1041.

Committees *Energy and Commerce* (4th). Subcommittees: Health and the Environment (Chairman); Telecommunications, Consumer Protection and Finance.

Government Operations (13th). Subcommittees: Government Information and Individual Rights; Legislation and National Security.

Select Committee on Aging (21st). Subcommittee: Retirement Income and Employment.

Group Ratings

	ADA	COPE	PC	LCV	CFA	RPN	NAB	NSI	NTU	ACA	ACU
1980	83	89	73	94	78	—	0	13	19	22	14
1979	95	89	73	89	71	—	—	—	15	8	9
1978	90	90	88	91	73	33	0	10	12	13	9

1) Draft Registn $	AGN	6) Fair Hsg DOJ Enfrc	FOR	11) Cut Socl Incr Dfns $	AGN
2) Ban $ to Nicrgua	AGN	7) Lim PAC Contrbtns	FOR	12) Hosptl Cost Controls	FOR
3) Dlay MX Missile	FOR	8) Cap on Food Stmp $	AGN	13) Gasln Ctrls & Allctns	FOR
4) Nuclr Mortorium	FOR	9) New US Dep Edcatn	AGN	14) Lim Wndfll Prof Tax	AGN
5) Alaska Lands Bill	FOR	10) Cut OSHA $		AGN	15) Chryslr Loan Grntee	FOR

Election Results

1980 general	Henry A. Waxman (D)..........	93,569	(64%)	($32,391)
	Roland Cayard (R)	39,744	(27%)	($8,288)
1980 primary	Henry A. Waxman (D)..........	43,703	(100%)	
1978 general	Henry A. Waxman (D)..........	85,075	(63%)	($26,019)
	Howard G. Schaefer (R)........	44,423	(33%)	($48,400)
	Kevin Casey Peter (Peace & Frdm)	6,453	(5%)	

TWENTY-FIFTH DISTRICT

The 1980 census tells us 19% of Californians are of "Spanish origin." The vast majority of these people of course are Mexican–Americans who constitute the largest and, in many respects, the most hidden ethnic group in the state. Most Mexican–Americans do not live in well-defined ghettos; they are found all over the state (no congressional district has less than 5% "Spanish origin"). Chicanos can merge quite easily into the white Anglo middle class. And then there are illegal immigrants from Mexico, whose numbers are uncertain (they shun contact with officials, including census-takers) but have surely been growing in recent years.

Politically, Mexican–Americans have long been the most underrepresented group in the state. California sends three blacks to the House, but only one of its 43 congressmen is of Spanish origin, and only seven Mexican–Americans sit in the state legislature out of 120. Republicans have charged that Democrats slice up Mexican neighborhoods to add Democratic votes to districts dominated by other groups; there is some truth to that, but Republican plans would result in the election of more Chicanos and fewer Democrats, whom Chicano voters almost always prefer. But it is a mistake to suppose that Mexican–Americans' votes are as solidly Democratic as blacks'; Mexican voting behavior is really closer to what you would have seen in many immigrant neighborhoods fifty years ago: a preference for

Democrats, but a willingness to go Republican, particularly when personal economic circumstances become more comfortable.

The Mexican–Americans of California have been moving upward and outward in society, quietly and without much fanfare, much as Italian–Americans — another group that many said would never be assimilated into America — did 50 or 60 years ago.

In 1974, for the first time, the predominantly Mexican–American communities of eastern Los Angeles neighborhoods, e.g., Boyle Heights and Highland Park, have been put together with the suburb of East Los Angeles to form a single congressional district, the 25th, the first in California's history with a clear Mexican–American majority. The district also includes downtown Los Angeles — a more vital place than many people suppose — MacArthur Park, and Dodgers Stadium, and reaches west toward the seedy, once elegant Silver Lake district near Hollywood. Not surprisingly, the 25th is one of the poorest — and most Democratic — districts in California. Mexican–Americans, as they become better off and more assimilated, tend to move out, to the east and southeast, to working-class and middle-class suburbs.

For more than a decade one or another downtown Los Angeles district has been electing and reelecting Congressman Edward Roybal. Although of Spanish descent, Roybal is not directly from Mexico; he is from Albuquerque, New Mexico, where the Spanish-speaking community dates from before Plymouth Rock, and his ancestors have been living within the geographical bounds of this country probably for as long as those of any member of Congress.

The 95th Congress was not a pleasant session for Roybal. In September 1978, the House Ethics Committee recommended that he be censured for having lied about a $1,000 campaign contribution from Tongsun Park that he converted to his own use. Roybal admitted taking the money but said that he just made an error in judgment; his supporters persuaded the House that he should be only reprimanded, not censured. Some observers believe he would have been censured but for his minority status.

The political damage in Roybal's heavily Democratic district and in the House has been distinctly limited. His winning percentages dropped from 72% in 1976 to 68% in 1978 and 66% in 1980 but it is certain that the legislature will draw another Mexican–American majority district he can win. (Indeed, the 25th, unlike most inner-city districts, gained population in the 1970s, thanks to immigration from Mexico.) Roybal is the ninth-ranking Democrat on the Appropriations Committee, and in 1981 he won a subcommittee chairmanship — an elective post now — on the Treasury–Postal Service–General Government Subcommittee. That means that he will be responsible for preparing the appropriations for, among other agencies, the White House.

Census Data Pop. (1980 final) 547,997, up 13% in 1970s. Median family income, 1970, $7,804, 81% of U.S.

The Voters

Employment profile 1970 White collar, 39%. Blue collar, 48%. Service, 13%. Farm, –%.
Ethnic groups Black 1980, 4%. Hispanic 1980, 72%. Am. Ind. 1980, 1%. Asian 1980, 8%. Total foreign stock 1970, 55%. Canada, Germany, Italy, 1% each.

Presidential Vote

1980	Reagan (R)	27,630	(35%)
	Carter (D)	44,131	(56%)
	Anderson (I)	5,013	(6%)
1976	Ford (R)	30,106	(36%)
	Carter (D)	52,234	(62%)

Rep. Edward R. Roybal (D) Elected 1962; b. Feb. 10, 1916, Albuquerque, N.M.; home, Los Angeles; UCLA, Southwestern U.

Career Army, WWII; Dir of Health Educ., L.A. Co. Tuberculosis & Health Assn., 1945–49; L.A. City Cncl., 1949–62, Pres. Pro Tem, 1961–62.

Offices 2211 RHOB, 202-225-6235. Also New Fed. P.O. Bldg., 300 N. Los Angeles St., Los Angeles 90012, 213-688-4870.

Committees *Appropriations* (9th). Subcommittees: Labor, Health and Human Services, Education; Treasury, Postal Service, General Government (Chairman).

Select Committee on Aging (2d). Subcommittee: Housing and Consumer Interests (Chairman).

Group Ratings

	ADA	COPE	PC	LCV	CFA	RPN	NAB	NSI	NTU	ACA	ACU
1980	89	89	73	61	93	—	0	0	16	14	6
1979	84	94	73	79	81	—	—	—	21	5	6
1978	85	79	80	78	68	18	0	0	28	15	8

Key Votes

1) Draft Registn $	AGN	6) Fair Hsg DOJ Enfrc	FOR	11) Cut Socl Incr Dfns $	AGN
2) Ban $ to Nicrgua	—	7) Lim PAC Contrbtns	FOR	12) Hosptl Cost Controls	FOR
3) Dlay MX Missile	FOR	8) Cap on Food Stmp $	AGN	13) Gasln Ctrls & Allctns	FOR
4) Nuclr Mortorium	FOR	9) New US Dep Edcatn	FOR	14) Lim Wndfll Prof Tax	AGN
5) Alaska Lands Bill	FOR	10) Cut OSHA $	AGN	15) Chryslr Loan Grntee	FOR

Election Results

1980 general	Edward R. Roybal (D)	49,080	(66%)	($44,411)
	Richard E. Ferraro, Jr. (R)	21,116	(28%)	($14,751)
	William D. Mitchell (Libertarian) .	4,169	(6%)	($367)
1980 primary	Edward R. Roybal (D)	24,841	(100%)	
1978 general	Edward R. Roybal (D)	45,881	(67%)	($41,232)
	Robert K. Watson (R)	22,205	(33%)	

TWENTY-SIXTH DISTRICT

The mountains that encircle the Los Angeles basin are responsible for the area's mild climate; the desert to the north and east is usually 20 to 30 degrees hotter. But the mountains also bottle up the basin's air, allowing the sun to interact with automobile emissions to produce that typical Los Angeles product called photochemical smog. The same mountains provide a neat geographic barrier to dense settlement. North of the mountains there are 186,000 people in Los Angeles County; in the smaller area of land to the south, more than 7,000,000.

Partly because of the smog, it is considered more pleasant to live on the land slightly higher up close against the mountains than in the flatter, hotter, smoggier valley below. That is certainly the case in the part of the Los Angeles basin running east from the city toward San Bernardino, the area that 34 years ago first elected Richard Nixon to Congress. Here the lower suburbs are mainly inhabited by people with blue collar backgrounds and nominally Democratic allegiances, while the suburbs through which Foothill Boulevard passes — Sierra Madre, Arcadia, Monrovia, Bradbury, Duarte, Azusa, Glendora — are relatively high income and Republican. These latter communities form the heart of California's 26th congressional district, which also includes below them the smoggier suburbs of Temple City and San Gabriel and even working-class Baldwin Park. An exception to the rule just cited — not next to the mountains, but the most conservative of all suburbs — is the small community of San Marino, home of Los Angeles's wealthiest WASPs (such as the Chandlers of the *Los Angeles Times*), which seldom delivers a Republican vote below 80%.

San Marino also happens to be the home of the 26th district's Congressman, John Rousselot, who is not only a conservative Republican but was for years a proud member of that liberal bugbear, the John Birch Society. Membership has given him some trouble in his political career. Rousselot was first elected to Congress in 1960 but was beaten in 1962 after the Democrats went to great pains to draw him a district he couldn't win. (Too great pains, it turned out: the Democrats couldn't hold it either and lost it in 1966.) Rousselot went back on the JBS payroll for a while and in 1970, when a local congressman died, won his seat. The Birch Society provided him with some problems then; he defeated a moderate in the primary by only 127 votes. And in 1979, when he was considering running for the Senate, he finally resigned from the Society — and then decided not to run for other reasons.

Rousselot has a reputation in some quarters as a hard-eyed fanatic. Actually he is a pleasant, humorous man who will work for his ideas when they seem popular (he opposes the gasoline tax) or not (he opposes federal regulation of debt collectors). He is a man with a strong drive and energy that may come, as it did for Theodore Roosevelt, from having been crippled in childhood. In 1979 he won a seat on the Ways and Means Committee; and in his home district he is reelected easily.

Rousselot has had the satisfaction of seeing his views, once considered radical and unthinkable, now become something very close to the conventional wisdom. And he is likely to have the satisfaction of seeing a very winnable new district created in this general area in which he can continue to win reelection in the 1980s.

Census Data Pop. (1980 final) 469,700, up 1% in 1970s. Median family income, 1970, $11,668, 122% of U.S.

The Voters

Employment profile 1970 White collar, 59%. Blue collar, 31%. Service, 10%. Farm, –%.
Ethnic groups Black 1980, 2%. Hispanic 1980, 26%. Am. Ind. 1980, 1%. Asian 1980, 6%. Total foreign stock 1970, 25%. Canada, 3%; UK, Germany, Italy, 2% each.

Presidential Vote

1980	Reagan (R)	111,196	(64%)
	Carter (D)	47,638	(27%)
	Anderson (I)	11,573	(7%)
1976	Ford (R)	108,532	(61%)
	Carter (D)	66,151	(37%)

Rep. John H. Rousselot (R) Elected June 30, 1970; b. Nov. 1, 1927, Los Angeles; home, San Marino; Principia Col., B.A. 1949.

Career Pres. and Owner, John H. Rousselot & Assoc., pub. rel. consultants, 1954–58; Dir. of Pub. Info., Fed. Housing Admin., 1958–60; U.S. House of Reps. 1961–63; Management consultant, 1967–70.

Offices 2133 RHOB, 202-225-4206. Also 735 W. Duarte Rd., Arcadia 91006, 213-447-8125.

Committees *Ways and Means* (11th). Subcommittees: Public Assistance and Unemployment Compensation; Social Security.

Joint Economic Committee (3d) Subcommittees: Monetary and Fiscal Policy; Trade, Productivity and Economic Growth.

Group Ratings

	ADA	COPE	PC	LCV	CFA	RPN	NAB	NSI	NTU	ACA	ACU
1980	11	10	23	22	7	—	100	100	74	95	95
1979	5	12	13	5	0	—	—	—	74	100	100
1978	5	5	10	6	14	67	100	100	58	100	96

Key Votes

1) Draft Registn $	AGN	6) Fair Hsg DOJ Enfrc	AGN	11) Cut Socl Incr Dfns $	FOR
2) Ban $ to Nicrgua	—	7) Lim PAC Contrbtns	AGN	12) Hosptl Cost Controls	AGN
3) Dlay MX Missile	AGN	8) Cap on Food Stmp $	FOR	13) Gasln Ctrls & Allctns	AGN
4) Nuclr Mortorium	AGN	9) New US Dep Edcatn	AGN	14) Lim Wndfll Prof Tax	FOR
5) Alaska Lands Bill	AGN	10) Cut OSHA $		FOR	15) Chryslr Loan Grntee	AGN

Election Results

1980 general	John H. Rousselot (R)	116,715	(71%)	($92,824)
	Joseph Louis Lisoni (D)	40,099	(24%)	($41,082)
	William J. (B.J.) Wagener (Libert.)	7,700	(5%)	($1,120)
1980 primary	John H. Rousselot (R)	50,617	(100%)	
1978 general	John H. Rousselot (R)	113,059	(100%)	($54,386)

TWENTY-SEVENTH DISTRICT

The 27th congressional district of California is a long, thin swath of land along the Pacific Ocean, from Pacific Palisades in the north to Palos Verdes in the south. Between these two hilly, high-income prominences overlooking the ocean is a whole string of beach towns: sedate Santa Monica, with its own high-income areas and black ghetto; seedy Venice, its 1920s canals now in ruins, the home of Los Angeles's roller skating craze; flashy new Marina del Rey, where many of the apartment complexes allow singles only or ban children; Playa del Rey with Los Angeles International Airport right behind (the only airport referred to generally by its three-letter code, LAX); El Segundo and its oil refineries; Manhattan and Hermosa and Redondo Beaches, with their closely packed little houses and narrow streets.

These are exceedingly diverse areas, with different life-styles and different political habits. Historically Republican, the district now has a significant Democratic and liberal base — although not enough to dominate the entire constituency. Santa Monica has become the

home base of Tom Hayden and Jane Fonda, and their Committee for Economic Development; their forces have won control of the city government, based largely on the appeal of
their main plank, rent control, to the city's majority of renters. Venice, inhabited increasingly
by survivors of the counterculture, is Democratic as well; so, in its more glittering way, is
Marina del Ray. The beach towns in the 1970s have changed sharply in attitude. They used
to be the homes of old midwesterners, staunchly conservative on most issues; increasingly
they have become the homes of young people, conservative or simply undecided on economic issues but liberal on such cultural issues as marijuana, the Vietnam war, and abortion.

But there are spots of middle-class America here as well: the Westchester section of Los
Angeles, a subdivision built in the 1950s with an atmosphere still redolent of that era, and
Torrance, an upper-middle-income suburb south of and inland from the beach towns, a
place whose largest ethnic minority is Oriental. The Palos Verdes peninsula is one of the Los
Angeles area's highest-income areas, solidly conservative and Republican; it is, fittingly, the
home of economist Arthur Laffer, the inventor of the Laffer curve and one of the developers
of supply-side economics.

The demographic changes in the district in the 1970s have made for a turbulent politics,
made more turbulent because none of the major party candidates has been ideally suited to
the district — liberal on cultural issues, conservative on economics. The 27th has been held
since 1976 by Republican Robert Dornan, one of the most enthusiastic conservatives in the
House. Like Ronald Reagan, Dornan has a show business background; his uncle Jack Haley
was the tin woodman in *The Wizard of Oz,* and Dornan himself used to host a Los Angeles
television talk show. In three House races, he has now spent $2.5 million in campaigns and
won narrow victories each time against liberal Democrats. In 1976 he was outspent by his
opponent, a young millionaire from Beverly Hills; in 1978, he was outspent again by Carey
Peck, son of Gregory Peck, who came within 3,512 votes of beating him. In 1980, Dornan
himself spent $1.9 million, much of it on direct mail solicitations to raise money; as a result,
he was able to put on a substantial television advertising campaign and to amass as well a
nationwide list of contributors that should be invaluable to him in future campaigns. In two
of the last three elections, the district has had the most expensive House race in the country.

Why have elections here been so close? Essentially because Dornan has taken such conservative stands on cultural issues. A staunch backer of the Vietnam war, he invented the
POW bracelet. He was also involved in a campaign against certain textbooks in West Virginia. He was the Congress's most passionate backer of the B–1 bomber, a plane that would
have been built in the 27th district, although most of the workers at the North American
Aviation plant live farther inland. He opposes the Equal Rights Amendment. He is a particularly strenuous and dedicated opponent of abortion. Dornan had another problem in 1980:
a series of articles in the *Los Angeles Times* suggesting that he was seeking special treatment
of a convicted felon in return for testimony about illegal contributions the man made to
Peck's 1978 campaign and to the 1978 campaign of Alabama Senator Donald Stewart.

Nevertheless Dornan won a 51%–46% victory. His 2–1 margin in Palos Verdes almost
wiped out Peck's margins in Santa Monica, Venice, and Marina del Rey. Dornan also managed a narrow margin in the beach towns and a larger one in Torrance. He has had a certain
amount of luck: his first opponent, running at a time when national issues tended to favor
the Democrats, was weak; the most negative development for Dornan, the *Times* series,
came when opinion most strongly favored Republicans. But he also benefited from his undoubted enthusiasm and energy.

The question for 1982 is how long his luck will hold out. Redistricting poses a major problem. Los Angeles County gained less than the statewide average, and it would be possible to eliminate the 27th district altogether, giving various segments of it to adjacent districts. If that happened, Dornan would have the choice of running in a nearby Republican district, perhaps the 20th if that is abandoned by Barry Goldwater, Jr., or like Goldwater, running for the Senate himself. Dornan has one very considerable asset for either race: his mailing list, which should be capable of raising a substantial campaign budget for him. His hold on this seat has seemed precarious all along, but it is possible that he will stay in the House through the 1980s.

Census Data Pop. (1980 final) 463,584, no change in 1970s. Median family income, 1970, $13,625, 142% of U.S.

The Voters

Employment profile 1970 White collar, 67%. Blue collar, 23%. Service, 10%. Farm, –%.
Ethnic groups Black 1980, 2%. Hispanic 1980, 9%. Am. Ind. 1980, 1%. Asian 1980, 5%. Total foreign stock 1970, 27%. UK, 4%; Canada, 3%; Germany, USSR, 2% each.

Presidential Vote

1980	Reagan (R)	125,736	(57%)
	Carter (D)	66,220	(30%)
	Anderson (I)	20,616	(9%)
1976	Ford (R)	125,254	(59%)
	Carter (D)	82,854	(39%)

Rep. Robert K. Dornan (R) Elected 1976; b. Apr. 3, 1933, New York, N.Y.; home, Los Angeles; Loyola U., Westchester/Playa Del Rey, 1950–53.

Career Air Force, 1953–58; Freelance traveling journalist; Host, KTLA-TV talk show, 1969–73; TV producer and personality.

Offices 332 CHOB, 202-225-6451. Also 11000 Wilshire Blvd., Los Angeles 90024, 213-824-7222.

Committees *Foreign Affairs* (10th). Subcommittees: Asian and Pacific Affairs; Human Rights and International Organizations.

Select Committee on Aging (6th). Subcommittee: Housing and Consumer Interests.

Select Committee on Narcotics Abuse and Control (6th).

Group Ratings

	ADA	COPE	PC	LCV	CFA	RPN	NAB	NSI	NTU	ACA	ACU
1980	11	10	20	30	14	—	82	100	52	73	88
1979	16	12	23	38	15	—	—	—	51	88	89
1978	5	5	13	20	9	58	100	100	46	92	100

Key Votes

1) Draft Registn $	AGN	6) Fair Hsg DOJ Enfrc	AGN	11) Cut Socl Incr Dfns $	—
2) Ban $ to Nicrgua	FOR	7) Lim PAC Contrbtns	AGN	12) Hosptl Cost Controls	AGN
3) Dlay MX Missile	FOR	8) Cap on Food Stmp $	FOR	13) Gasln Ctrls & Allctns	AGN
4) Nuclr Mortorium	AGN	9) New US Dep Edcatn	FOR	14) Lim Wndfll Prof Tax	FOR
5) Alaska Lands Bill	FOR	10) Cut OSHA $	FOR	15) Chryslr Loan Grntee	AGN

Election Results

1980 general	Robert K. Dornan (R)	109,807	(51%)	($1,947,209)
	Carey Peck (D)	100,061	(47%)	($559,315)
1980 primary	Robert K. Dornan (R)	52,438	(100%)	
1978 general	Robert K. Dornan (R)	89,392	(51%)	($291,762)
	Carey Peck (D)	85,880	(49%)	($308,017)

TWENTY-EIGHTH DISTRICT

The 28th congressional district is one of two Los Angeles districts with a black majority. It lies southwest of downtown Los Angeles, southeast of Beverly Hills, northeast of the airport, northwest of the Watts Tower. The more middle class of the two black-majority districts, the 28th's demographic characteristics tell us something about the pace and nature of neighborhood change in Los Angeles in the 1970s and early 1980s. For this is not an area that has seen the kind of blockbusting and clearly defined racial neighborhoods that were the pattern in the 1940 and 1950s. One finds some all-black areas here, around the University of Southern California and to the south but also neighborhoods that have maintained biracial populations, such as the Crenshaw area where Mayor Thomas Bradley lives. To the west the district includes the mostly white Mar Vista section of Los Angeles and Culver City; to the south it includes the black majority suburb of Inglewood.

Someone looking at this area in 1970, when 40% of its residents were black and another 12% of Spanish origin, might have predicted rapid neighborhood turnover and the creation of new all-black neighborhoods. But that is not quite what has happened. The black percentage districtwide has risen from 40% to 50%—a change but scarcely an overwhelming one—and the Spanish origin percentage has risen almost as much, to 19%. But most Spanish origin people here are not clustered into a particular neighborhood and neither, to an increasing extent, are blacks. Culver City, once essentially all white, is now 8% black; but there is no established ghetto there. Inglewood is now 57% black, but there are no signs that the whites are about to move out en masse. This slower, more relaxed pace of neighborhood change seems to have prevented the rise of the sort of feverish politics sometimes seen in changing neighborhoods. In any case, this is a solidly Democratic area: not only the blacks, but a majority of the whites as well, regularly vote Democratic. With relatively little fuss the voters here have elected black Democrats: first Yvonne Brathwaite Burke, who left the House in 1978 to run unsuccessfully for attorney general of California, and then Julian Dixon, who had served six years in the California Assembly.

Dixon is considered a competent and politically shrewd congressman. In his first term he won a seat on the Appropriations Committee, and in his second he became chairman of the District of Columbia Appropriations Subcommittee—a body of not much importance in the national scheme of things, and indeed of somewhat less importance than it used to be now that Washington has home rule, but an office that is nevertheless of considerable importance to blacks. The 28th district has not lost population over the past ten years and is not likely to be changed markedly in redistricting.

Census Data   Pop. (1980 final) 469,346, up 1% in 1970s. Median family income, 1970, $9,942, 104% of U.S.

The Voters

Employment profile 1970   White collar, 54%. Blue collar, 31%. Service, 15%. Farm, –%.
Ethnic groups   Black 1980, 50%. Hispanic 1980, 19%. Am. Ind. 1980, 1%. Asian 1980, 6%. Total foreign stock 1970, 26%. Canada, Germany, 2% each; UK, Italy, USSR, 1% each.

Presidential Vote

1980	Reagan (R)	36,354	(24%)
	Carter (D)	102,516	(69%)
	Anderson (I)	7,733	(5%)
1976	Ford (R)	42,792	(29%)
	Carter (D)	104,135	(70%)

Rep. Julian C. Dixon (D) Elected 1978; b. Aug. 8, 1934, Washington, D.C.; home, Los Angeles; Cal. St. U. at L.A., B.S. 1962, Southwestern U., LL.B. 1967.

Career Army, 1957-60; Practicing atty.; Cal. Assembly, 1973-78.

Offices 423 CHOB, 202-225-7084. Also One La Brea Ave., Inglewood 90301, 213-678-5424.

Committee *Appropriations* (26th). Subcommittees: District of Columbia (Chairman); Foreign Operations.

Group Ratings

	ADA	COPE	PC	LCV	CFA	RPN	NAB	NSI	NTU	ACA	ACU
1980	94	88	70	62	86	—	9	0	11	10	6
1979	79	95	80	82	78	—	—	—	16	0	3

Key Votes

1) Draft Registn $	AGN	6) Fair Hsg DOJ Enfrc	FOR	11) Cut Socl Incr Dfns $	AGN
2) Ban $ to Nicrgua	AGN	7) Lim PAC Contrbtns	—	12) Hosptl Cost Controls	FOR
3) Dlay MX Missile	FOR	8) Cap on Food Stmp $	AGN	13) Gasln Ctrls & Allctns	FOR
4) Nuclr Mortorium	FOR	9) New US Dep Edcatn	FOR	14) Lim Wndfll Prof Tax	AGN
5) Alaska Lands Bill	FOR	10) Cut OSHA $	AGN	15) Chryslr Loan Grntee	—

Election Results

1980 general	Julian C. Dixon (D)	108,725	(79%)	($63,882)
	Robert Reid (R)	23,179	(17%)	($14,919)
1980 primary	Julian C. Dixon (D)	50,833	(100%)	
1978 general	Julian C. Dixon (D)	97,592	(100%)	($231,444)

TWENTY-NINTH DISTRICT

Watts has been a familiar American place name since the 1965 riot there put it in the national headlines. Although no longer in the headlines, Watts remains the heart of Los Angeles's black community, directly south of downtown. And, as official Los Angeles found out after

1965, despite its central location Watts is isolated from the mainstream of Los Angeles — off the principal bus lines, with no hospitals, few parks, and little in the way of municipal facilities. (Indeed, much of the territory around Watts isn't part of the city of Los Angeles at all, and the city has shown no inclination to annex it.) The area's most distinctive feature is the Watts Tower, a weird sculpture of bits of broken glass and scrap metal, assembled over some 30 years by Italian immigrant Simon Rodia. New York journalists sent to Watts in the wake of the riot were quick to write that the place didn't look like a ghetto. Actually more American blacks live in places like Watts — with its small frame double- or single-family houses along quiet streets — than in places like Harlem, with its five-story turn-of-the-century tenements.

Watts is also the heart of California's 29th congressional district, and the almost unanimously Democratic voting habits of the black areas inevitably place the district in the Democratic column. But there is another part of the 29th district, across Alameda Street, which is the unofficial eastern boundary of Watts. Alameda used to be an almost impenetrable racial barrier, separating blacks from working-class whites. In the 1970s, however, most of the working-class whites moved out (or died; the area was elderly) and were replaced by Mexican–Americans in the industrial suburbs of Huntington Park, Bell, Cudahy, and South Gate. In addition, Mexican–Americans moved into formerly black neighborhoods in the northern part of the district, near the Mexican concentration in East Los Angeles. In fact, during the 1970s, the 29th district slipped from majority (59%) to minority (49%) black; it lost 34,000 blacks and gained 120,000 Hispanics.

Neighborhood change here may someday produce a turbulent congressional politics; for the moment it has no more effect on House elections here than did the ill feelings between Watts blacks and the old South Gate whites (who trended Republican before they left). For the moment the 29th, and the similar successor district that will undoubtedly be drawn by redistricters, is disposed to reelect Congressman Augustus Hawkins. Now past 70, he is the premier black legislator in the nation, the senior member of the Congressional Black Caucus. For 28 years, from 1934 to 1962, he served in the California Assembly, and for most of that time was its only black member; in 1959 he was nearly elected speaker. But California was apparently not ready for that then, and so Hawkins had to settle for a seat in Congress. His experience has not been of the kind to produce verbal militance, and he has not been a favorite of some of the more voluble members of the Black Caucus.

Hawkins has been as productive a legislator as any current black member. He chairs an Education and Labor subcommittee and was the chief House sponsor of the Humphrey–Hawkins bill. Humphrey–Hawkins was intended to attack what anyone must admit is a severe problem: the persistently high rates of unemployment among blacks and other poor people, particularly young blacks. In its original form, the bill would have required the federal government to create jobs, at prevailing wage rates, until unemployment dropped to a set figure. In the 1976 campaign Humphrey–Hawkins became a kind of litmus test for Democratic candidates; Jimmy Carter eventually endorsed it, but in lukewarm terms, leaving little doubt he considered it impractical. Opponents of the measure charged that it would be inflationary and would produce make-work jobs, and in the inflation-conscious 95th Congress it was inevitable that the measure would be watered down or defeated. After Hubert Humphrey's death, there was a sentimental push to enact something with the Humphrey–Hawkins label on it. But the bill that was passed did not require the government to do anything, and it bears little relation to the measure Hawkins first proposed.

The fate of Humphrey–Hawkins must have been a disappointment to Hawkins, but it cannot have been the first he has suffered in a legislative career of 45 years. He is an authentic trailblazer who has seen much history and made some—and who has the capacity, if he wishes to stay in Congress a while longer, to do more.

Census Data   Pop. (1980 final) 488,347, up 5% in 1970s. Median family income, 1970, $7,359, 77% of U.S.

The Voters

Employment profile 1970   White collar, 36%. Blue collar, 46%. Service, 18%. Farm, –%.
Ethnic groups   Black 1980, 50%. Hispanic 1980, 39%. Am. Ind. 1980, 1%. Asian 1980, 8%. Total foreign stock 1970, 15%.

Presidential Vote

1980	Reagan (R)	17,564	(17%)
	Carter (D)	80,696	(80%)
	Anderson (I)	2,255	(2%)
1976	Ford (R)	19,596	(19%)
	Carter (D)	83,291	(80%)

Rep. Augustus F. Hawkins (D) Elected 1962; b. Aug. 31, 1907, Shreveport, La.; home, Los Angeles; UCLA, A.B. 1931; USC Institute of Govt.

Career   Real estate business; Cal. Assembly, 1935–62.

Offices   2371 RHOB, 202-225-2201. Also 936 W. Manchester St., Los Angeles 90044, 213-750-0260.

Committees   *House Administration* (Chairman).

Education and Labor (2d). Subcommittees: Elementary, Secondary and Vocational Education; Employment Opportunities (Chairman).

Joint Printing Committee (Vice-chairman).

Joint Library Committee (Chairman).

Group Ratings

	ADA	COPE	PC	LCV	CFA	RPN	NAB	NSI	NTU	ACA	ACU
1980	89	88	73	70	79	—	0	11	11	6	11
1979	74	93	73	84	70	—	—	—	15	0	3
1978	75	82	65	68	59	30	0	0	6	16	12

Key Votes

1) Draft Registn $	AGN	6) Fair Hsg DOJ Enfrc	FOR	11) Cut Socl Incr Dfns $	AGN
2) Ban $ to Nicrgua	AGN	7) Lim PAC Contrbtns	FOR	12) Hosptl Cost Controls	FOR
3) Dlay MX Missile	FOR	8) Cap on Food Stmp $	AGN	13) Gasln Ctrls & Allctns	FOR
4) Nuclr Mortorium	—	9) New US Dep Edcatn	FOR	14) Lim Wndfll Prof Tax	—
5) Alaska Lands Bill	FOR	10) Cut OSHA $	AGN	15) Chryslr Loan Grntee	FOR

Election Results

1980 general	Augustus F. Hawkins (D)........	80,095	(86%)	($33,711)
	Michael Arthur Hirt (R).........	10,282	(11%)	($0)
1980 primary	Augustus F. Hawkins (D)........	38,053	(100%)	
1978 general	Augustus F. Hawkins (D)........	65,214	(85%)	($13,887)
	Uriah J. Fields (R)	11,512	(15%)	($6,602)

THIRTIETH DISTRICT

The 30th congressional district of California is a string of suburbs in the San Gabriel Valley just east of downtown Los Angeles. While the wealthy and comfortable suburban towns of the next-door 26th district hug the mountains, those of the 30th are in the lower part of the valley, below the San Bernardino Freeway, where the smog fills the air from 7:30 in the morning on, and the Los Angeles and San Gabriel Rivers flow (when any water flows in them at all) through open concrete conduits. What makes these suburbs interesting is not smog or concrete river bottoms, but rather the fact that they are becoming increasingly the home of the Los Angeles area's middle-income Mexican–American population. Places such as Monterey Park and Montebello, built as comfortable Anglo suburbs in the 1940s and 1950s, lie only a few miles from the Los Angeles barrio; and it is here, as well as to the industrial suburbs farther east, such as El Monte and La Puente, that people from the barrio are moving. The residential migration pattern here is not the kind of white flight and wholesale change in neighborhood complexion one sees when a white neighborhood suddenly becomes black; the process is slower, and more amiable. Essentially, the Mexican–Americans are moving up, as Italian–Americans did; they still tend to some extent to cluster (as Americans of most ethnic backgrounds do) but are also living comfortably in neighborhoods with many people of different backgrounds.

Politically, Mexican–Americans tend to vote Democratic, as do most members of minorities who feel they suffer from discrimination or who feel that they benefit from programs to help the poor. But the Democratic percentages among Mexican–Americans, while still well above those of Anglo whites, are also notably below those of blacks. The logical conclusion is that Mexican–Americans are less likely to feel discriminated against or poor than they used to or than blacks now do. The Democratic percentage is indeed higher in the 30th district that it once was: George McGovern lost this district in 1972 while Jimmy Carter carried it in 1980 (albeit with less than a majority, and a percentage not much higher than McGovern's). But there is now less of a tendency than in the early 1970s for Mexican–Americans to feel that they will not be properly represented except by a Mexican–American congressman.

That is the conclusion, anyway, that one must draw from the congressional politics of the 30th district and the career of Congressman George Danielson. In 1974 Danielson had tough opposition from two Mexican–Americans in the Democratic primary and won with just 53% of the vote. But since then, despite the rising Mexican percentage, no Mexican competition has surfaced. One reason may be that Danielson, a member of the Judiciary Committee who made a creditable case for impeaching Richard Nixon, became better known to his constituents. Another may be Danielson's own campaigning; he speaks a somewhat wooden but ready Spanish and has always had Mexican–American constituents. Indeed, Danielson's whole career has been representing the edge of Mexican–American communities, from the time he was elected to the Assembly from Los Angeles in 1962 to his representation of this all-suburban district. But one must simply conclude that the ambitious local Mexican–American politicians — and there are a number of them — calculated that not much demand existed for a congressman who would be little different from Danielson except for a Mexican heritage.

Thus Danielson seems likely to prolong his legislative career for at least another several years. Redistricting should not change the boundaries of the 30th much, and he has proven the capacity to win reelection. He serves now not only on the Judiciary Committee, on which he chairs the subcommittee on Administrative Law and Governmental Relations, but also on Post Office and Civil Service and Veterans' Affairs. None of these is a particularly popular assignment; Danielson seems willing to do the hard work and take on the unpleasant assignments that other members shun and only seldom, as in the case of the impeachment hearings, pay off in significant publicity and renown.

Census Data Pop. (1980 final) 504,331, up 8% in 1970s. Median family income, 1970, $10,121, 106% of U.S.

The Voters

Employment profile 1970 White collar, 42%. Blue collar, 48%. Service, 10%. Farm, –%.
Ethnic groups Black 1980, 1%. Hispanic 1980, 62%. Am. Ind. 1980, 1%. Asian 1980, 7%. Total foreign stock 1970, 34%. Canada, Italy, 2% each; UK, Germany, USSR, 1% each.

Presidential Vote

1980	Reagan (R)	48,350	(44%)
	Carter (D)	52,905	(48%)
	Anderson (I)	6,550	(6%)
1976	Ford (R)	46,152	(39%)
	Carter (D)	69,424	(59%)

Rep. George E. Danielson (D) Elected 1970; b. Feb. 20, 1915, Wausa, Neb.; home, Monterey Park; U. of Neb., B.A. 1937, J.D. 1939.

Career Practicing atty.; FBI Agent 1939–44; Navy, WWII; Asst. U.S. Atty., So. Dist. of Cal, 1949–51; Cal. Assembly 1962–66; Cal. Senate. 1966–70.

Offices 2265 RHOB, 202-225-5464. Also 8873 E. Valley Rd., Rosemead 91770, 213-287-1134.

Committees *Judiciary* (7th). Subcommittees: Administrative Law and Governmental Regulations (Chairman); Courts, Civil Liberties and the Administration of Justice.

Post Office and Civil Service (12th). Subcommittees: Civil Service; Compensation and Employee Benefits; Human Resources.

Veterans' Affairs (3d). Subcommittees: Compensation, Pension and Insurance; Oversight and Investigations.

Group Ratings

	ADA	COPE	PC	LCV	CFA	RPN	NAB	NSI	NTU	ACA	ACU
1980	67	88	47	52	71	—	17	10	13	18	11
1979	84	85	70	78	63	—	—	—	19	0	0
1978	60	85	65	61	68	22	0	50	6	4	17

Key Votes

1) Draft Registn $	FOR	6) Fair Hsg DOJ Enfrc	FOR	11) Cut Socl Incr Dfns $	AGN
2) Ban $ to Nicrgua	AGN	7) Lim PAC Contrbtns	FOR	12) Hosptl Cost Controls	FOR
3) Dlay MX Missile	AGN	8) Cap on Food Stmp $	AGN	13) Gasln Ctrls & Allctns	FOR
4) Nuclr Mortorium	AGN	9) New US Dep Edcatn	FOR	14) Lim Wndfll Prof Tax	AGN
5) Alaska Lands Bill	FOR	10) Cut OSHA $	AGN	15) Chryslr Loan Grntee	FOR

Election Results

1980 general	George E. Danielson (D)	74,119	(72%)	($79,852)
	J. Arthur (Art) Platten (R)	24,136	(24%)	($5,006)

1980 primary	George E. Danielson (D)	33,564	(100%)	
1978 general	George E. Danielson (D)	66,241	(71%)	($98,834)
	Henry Ares (R)	26,511	(29%)	($50,823)

THIRTY-FIRST DISTRICT

The 31st district of California is a patch of fairly typical 1940s and 1950s Los Angeles County suburban territory, about 10 to 15 miles south of downtown Los Angeles and Beverly Hills. Most of it is made up of neat single-family pastel stucco houses, often with an above-ground backyard swimming pool and some slightly shabby lawn furniture. There are parcels of still vacant land here and newly laid-out subdivisions, and next to them the overgrown lots of factory workers' widows who are just getting by on Social Security. The 31st also contains sparkling steel and glass shopping centers and the fading pink stucco commercial strips of the late 1940s. Undergirding the economy are huge defense and auto assembly plants to the east and west.

The 31st sits directly south of the Watts black ghetto, and over the past few decades it has become increasingly black. The suburb of Compton has turned from all white to 75% black in 20 years; blacks also form substantial minorities in the working-class suburbs of Lynwood, Hawthorne, and Gardena. (Gardena has two other distinctions: it has a large Japanese–American community, and it is permitted by California law to license poker clubs at which some of the most cutthroat poker in the country is played.) This part of Los Angeles County has been solidly Democratic from the 1930s, when it was all white, and the persuasion is stronger, now that it is 36% black and 27% Hispanic.

Some of the suburbs were part of the assembly district that first sent Jess Unruh to the California Assembly in 1954 and served as his ultimate electoral base during his terms as speaker from 1961 to 1968. (He is now living in semiretirement as state treasurer.) Among Unruh's friends and allies rewarded with a congressional district come redistricting time was Charles Wilson, for 18 years the congressman from the 31st. His service in Washington for years attracted little notice. He managed a few postal bills on the Post Office and Civil Service Committee, chaired the subcommittee on the census for a while, and was an advocate of aid to South Korea on Armed Services. In 1978 he finally achieved some notice when he was reprimanded by the House for lying about a $600 wedding gift he had received from Tongsun Park. Fortunately for Wilson, the Democratic primary had already been held, and the district is heavily enough Democratic that he won reelection easily. Unfortunately for Wilson, House terms are only two years long.

This is the kind of district where people get elected to legislative office by putting up billboards that say things like "Charles Wilson is a good guy." Most voters have no idea what House, state Senate, Assembly, and county supervisor district they live in; they know little about the roles their representatives play; and they vote, for want of a better reason, for familiar names. Wilson's performance in the 1980 primary suggests that that is how he hung on to his seat for nine terms; running for a tenth, when he was finally known for something —the Tongsun Park connection— he was not only defeated but received only 15% of the vote in the primary. Ahead of him were two politicians trying for comebacks, former 34th district Congressman Mark Hannaford and former Lieutenant Governor Mervyn Dymally. Dymally received just under half the votes in the primary, enough for a solid win and had no trouble winning the general election.

Dymally is a man of undoubted talents and some political liabilities. He is intelligent and witty, with a distinctive speaking style and accent from his native Trinidad. But he has a reputation for being a wheeler-dealer which, deserved or not, resulted in his defeat for reelection as lieutenant governor by Mike Curb in 1978. Perhaps Dymally thinks he lost because of his race—although that does not explain his statewide victory in 1974. With his statewide ambitions gone, he seems to have a long legislative career ahead. He has already proved that he can win an election in a district where blacks are still very much a minority. Redistricting should pose no great problems.

Census Data   Pop. (1980 final) 463,513, no change in 1970s. Median family income, 1970, $10,042, 105% of U.S.

The Voters

  Employment profile 1970   White collar, 44%. Blue collar, 44%. Service, 12%. Farm, -%.
  Ethnic groups   Black 1980, 36%. Hispanic 1980, 27%. Am. Ind. 1980, 1%. Asian 1980, 7%. Total foreign stock 1970, 20%. Canada, 2%; UK, Germany, Italy, 1% each.

Presidential Vote

1980	Reagan (R)	39,927	(35%)
	Carter (D)	68,544	(59%)
	Anderson (I)	5,242	(5%)
1976	Ford (R)	38,052	(34%)
	Carter (D)	72,775	(65%)

Rep. Mervyn M. Dymally (D) Elected 1980; b. May 12, 1926, Trinidad, British West Indies; home, Compton; Cal. St. U., B.A. 1954, M.A. 1969, U.S. Internat. U., Ph.D. 1978.

Career Teacher, L.A. Schools, 1955–61; Coord., Cal. Disaster Ofc., 1961–62; Cal. Assembly, 1963–67; Cal. Senate, 1967–75; Lt. Gov. of Cal., 1975–79.

Offices 1116 LHOB, 202-225-5425. Also 2W30 Fed. Bldg., 15000 Aviation Blvd., Lawndale 90261, 213-536-6680, and City Hall, 2d Fl., 4455 W. 126th St., Hawthorne 90250, 213-536-6772.

Committees *Foreign Affairs* (18th). Subcommittees: Asian and Pacific Affairs; Human Rights and International Organizations.

Science and Technology (23d). Subcommittees: Science, Research and Technology; Transportation, Aviation and Materials.

District of Columbia (8th). Subcommittee: Judiciary and Education (Chairman).

Group Ratings and Key Votes: Newly Elected

Election Results

1980 general	Mervyn M. Dymally (D)	69,146	(64%)	($617,007)
	Don Grimshaw (R)	38,203	(36%)	($3,750)
1980 primary	Mervyn M. Dymally (D)	29,916	(49%)	
	Mark W. Hannaford (D)	14,512	(24%)	
	Charles H. Wilson (D)	9,320	(15%)	
	Two others (D)	7,192	(12%)	
1978 general	Charles H. Wilson (D)	55,667	(68%)	($139,728)
	Don Grimshaw (R)	26,490	(32%)	

THIRTY-SECOND DISTRICT

The 32d is one of 16 congressional districts wholly or partially within Los Angeles County. The focus of the 32d is the busy port area of Los Angeles — San Pedro, Wilmington, and Long Beach — and the nearby suburbs of Carson (blue collar) and Torrance (white collar). This is one of the working-class districts of the Los Angeles area; people here tend to work on the docks or in fishing boats, in one of the area's huge aircraft plants, or in the factories found in the industrial corridor to the northeast. In the 1970s the percentage of blacks in the district rose from 8% to 14% as some blacks moved south from Watts and Compton into the industrial suburb of Carson, but there has been nothing like the blockbusting and mass movements that occurred in the 1950s and 1960s. The 32d also includes near the port a sizable Yugoslav-American community — proof that Los Angeles is by no means without ethnic variety.

Most of the residents of the 32d are traditional Democrats, union members who supported the programs of Franklin D. Roosevelt and John F. Kennedy, but who have felt threatened by social trends not to their liking. On a few occasions this district has even gone Republican — for Ronald Reagan in 1966 and 1980 and Richard Nixon in 1972. In the latter case this was the California district with the greatest defection from normal Democratic allegiance.

The 32d has a congressman who seems to fit it like a glove: a Democrat who is a veteran public official, long considered very close to organized labor. He is Glenn Anderson, whose greatest fame came when, as lieutenant governor under Pat Brown, he was unlucky enough to have been acting governor when the Watts riot broke out. Afterward some people accused Anderson of waiting too long before dispatching the National Guard, and in the 1966 election he was badly beaten for reelection by Republican Robert Finch. Anderson ran for the House in 1968, when Cecil King, sponsor of Medicare, retired; although Republican Joseph Blatchford put on a strong campaign, Anderson was elected.

In the House Anderson received the kind of mundane committee assignments that tend to go to representatives of working-class port areas: Public Works and Merchant Marine and Fisheries. On both he is now high in seniority: second on Public Works and Transportation, as it is now called, and third on Merchant Marine. He chairs the subcommittee on Surface Transportation, which has jurisdiction over railroads.

Anderson's chances for reelection are assumed to be good. Presumably he will get another district very similar to this one. However, recent electoral trends in the area have not been favorable. The number of white working-class voters in San Pedro and Wilmington is declining; and in the surrounding areas, such as Palos Verdes (not in the current 32d but which might be added in redistricting) live a growing number of affluent, Republican-minded voters. That demographic change caused the upset defeat in 1978 of Assemblyman Vincent Thomas, who had represented San Pedro for 40 years; and it could conceivably threaten Anderson's tenure.

Census Data Pop. (1980 final) 474,215, up 2% in 1970s. Median family income, 1970, $9,873, 103% of U.S.

The Voters

Employment profile 1970 White collar, 46%. Blue collar, 41%. Service, 13%. Farm, -%.
Ethnic groups Black 1980, 14%. Hispanic 1980, 27%. Am. Ind. 1980, 1%. Asian 1980, 9%. Total foreign stock 1970, 26%. Canada, UK, Germany, Italy, 2% each; Yugoslavia, 1%.

Presidential Vote

1980	Reagan (R)	64,967	(48%)
	Carter (D)	58,065	(43%)
	Anderson (I)	8,728	(7%)
1976	Ford (R)	58,147	(44%)
	Carter (D)	72,386	(54%)

Rep. Glenn M. Anderson (D) Elected 1968; b. Feb. 21, 1913, Hawthorne; home, Harbor City; UCLA, B.A. 1936.

Career Mayor of Hawthorne, 1940–43; Cal. Assembly, 1943, 1945–51; Army, WWII; Lt. Gov. of Cal., 1958–67.

Offices 2329 RHOB, 202-225-6676. Also 300 Long Beach Blvd., Long Beach 90801, 213-548-2721.

Committees *Merchant Marine and Fisheries* (3d). Subcommittees: Fisheries and Wildlife Conservation and the Environment; Merchant Marine.

Public Works and Transportation (2d). Subcommittees: Aviation; Surface Transportation (Chairman).

Group Ratings

	ADA	COPE	PC	LCV	CFA	RPN	NAB	NSI	NTU	ACA	ACU
1980	72	64	53	44	64	—	33	40	23	33	21
1979	63	61	38	59	48	—	—	—	25	38	26
1978	60	80	60	43	55	18	17	50	17	41	26

Key Votes

1) Draft Registn $	FOR	6) Fair Hsg DOJ Enfrc	FOR	11) Cut Socl Incr Dfns $	AGN
2) Ban $ to Nicrgua	AGN	7) Lim PAC Contrbtns	FOR	12) Hosptl Cost Controls	FOR
3) Dlay MX Missile	AGN	8) Cap on Food Stmp $	AGN	13) Gasln Ctrls & Allctns	AGN
4) Nuclr Mortorium	AGN	9) New US Dep Edcatn	FOR	14) Lim Wndfll Prof Tax	FOR
5) Alaska Lands Bill	AGN	10) Cut OSHA $	AGN	15) Chryslr Loan Grntee	FOR

Election Results

1980 general	Glenn M. Anderson (D)	84,057	(66%)	($153,001)
	John R. Adler (R)	39,260	(31%)	($33,878)
1980 primary	Glenn M. Anderson (D)	43,475	(85%)	
	One other (D)	7,911	(15%)	
1978 general	Glenn M. Anderson (D)	74,004	(71%)	($109,228)
	Sonya Mathison (R)	23,242	(22%)	
	Ira Bader (Amer. Ind.)	6,363	(6%)	

THIRTY-THIRD DISTRICT

The 33d district of California, the end result of several redistrictings, centers on the southeast Los Angeles County suburbs of Norwalk, Downey, and Whittier. The last of these of course is the most famous: the boyhood home of Richard Nixon, the place founded by Quakers and named after the New England poet, and the profoundly conservative little town in sunny California. But the image created by the media is not quite right anymore, for Whittier has long since been swallowed up—and its own size swollen—by the advancing suburban tide of Los Angeles, and its special qualities have been diluted or lost. The function that Whittier, with the other suburbs of the 33d, serves is to house factory and lower- and middle-level white collar workers, people who in just about every way exemplify what we mean by middle class.

On paper this is a Democratic district, and in fact the 33d shows a healthy Democratic registration edge. But numbers often mean far less than many political writers assume, for ordinary voters feel no obligation to vote the way they register. Between 1958 and 1974 the 33d voted solidly Republican in every statewide election—for Barry Goldwater as well as Richard Nixon, for Ronald Reagan as well as Thomas Kuchel. Indeed, right-wing Republicanism has more strength here—certainly more enthusiasm and overt support—than the moderate Republicans who are supposed to be the party's strongest candidates in areas like this.

To understand why this should be so, go back to the early 1960s, when the smog was getting worse every year, taxes were rising as welfare costs went up, and students and blacks were rioting in Berkeley and Watts. With their values—and perhaps their savings—under attack, the middle-class people in places like the 33d felt that things were going sour, and it did not help that Watts was only a few miles away. It was then, after a conservative Democratic congressman died, that conservative Republican Del Clawson won a special election in June 1963 in an area that included much of what is now the 33d. President Kennedy was then preparing his civil rights bill and Martin Luther King, Jr., was planning the march on Washington—a time of turmoil and uncertainty, a time when the people of the 33d wanted a politics rooted in old-fashioned values.

And that is what conservatives like Clawson, Goldwater, and, later, Ronald Reagan offered—not so much tax relief as psychological assurance, assurance that their threatened way of life was the right one and that the things they had worked so hard for should not be scorned. Reagan in particular has excelled at soothing and reassuring middle-class people that they, not their fashionable detractors, are right about what is good for society.

Through shifting tides of redistricting, Clawson was reelected every two years. His conservative regularity helped him win a seat on the House Rules Committee, where he usually reflected the wishes of the House leadership. He was not a productive legislator, but then he did not go to Washington to pass new laws, rather to prevent bad ones from passing. At home his percentages were declining, but he didn't seem in danger of losing. In 1978, at 64, Clawson decided to retire.

No fewer than seven Republicans and ten Democrats competed to represent the 33d in his place. The winner was 55-year-old La Mirada Councilman Wayne Grisham, who attacked his Democratic opponent as a carpetbagger and who stressed the need to hold down taxes and government spending. He promised to follow in Clawson's footsteps, and there is no reason to believe he has not. In his brief House career, Grisham has served on four committees: Government Operations and Veterans' Affairs in his first term, Post Office and Civil Service and Public Works and Transportation in his second. He seems solidly entrenched politically and unlikely to be hurt by redistricting.

Census Data   Pop. (1980 final) 521,986, up 12% in 1970s. Median family income, 1970, $12,340, 129% of U.S.

The Voters

   Employment profile 1970   White collar, 54%. Blue collar, 36%. Service, 10%. Farm, –%.
   Ethnic groups   Black 1980, 2%. Hispanic 1980, 26%. Am. Ind. 1980, 1%. Asian 1980, 6%. Total foreign stock 1970, 22%. Canada, 3%; UK, Germany, Italy, 2% each.

Presidential Vote

1980	Reagan (R)	114,895	(63%)
	Carter (D)	53,102	(29%)
	Anderson (I)	11,464	(6%)
1976	Ford (R)	99,127	(56%)
	Carter (D)	75,709	(43%)

Rep. Wayne Grisham (R) Elected 1978; b. Jan. 10, 1923, Lamar, Colo.; home, La Mirada; Long Beach City Col., A.A. 1947, Whittier Col., B.A. 1947, USC, 1950–51.

Career Army Air Corps, WWII; Realtor; La Mirada City Cncl., 1970–79, Mayor, 1973–74, 1977–78.

Offices 120 CHOB, 202-225-3576. Also Suite 100, 13601 E. Whittier Blvd., Whittier 90605, 213-945-3061.

Committees *Post Office and Civil Service* (9th). Subcommittees: Census and Population; Investigations; Postal Personnel and Modernization.

Public Works and Transportation (13th). Subcommittees: Aviation; Water Resources.

Group Ratings

	ADA	COPE	PC	LCV	CFA	RPN	NAB	NSI	NTU	ACA	ACU
1980	6	6	20	30	7	—	100	88	61	90	88
1979	5	5	20	17	7	—	—	—	60	92	100

Key Votes

1) Draft Registn $	FOR	6) Fair Hsg DOJ Enfrc	AGN	11) Cut Socl Incr Dfns $	—
2) Ban $ to Nicrgua	FOR	7) Lim PAC Contrbtns	AGN	12) Hosptl Cost Controls	AGN
3) Dlay MX Missile	AGN	8) Cap on Food Stmp $	FOR	13) Gasln Ctrls & Allctns	AGN
4) Nuclr Mortorium	AGN	9) New US Dep Edcatn	AGN	14) Lim Wndfll Prof Tax	FOR
5) Alaska Lands Bill	AGN	10) Cut OSHA $	FOR	15) Chryslr Loan Grntee	AGN

Election Results

1980 general	Wayne Grisham (R)	122,439	(71%)	($103,423)
	Fred L. Anderson (D)	50,365	(29%)	($0)
1980 primary	Wayne Grisham (R)	39,301	(76%)	
	Mike Manicone (R)	12,736	(24%)	($27,231)
1978 general	Wayne Grisham (R)	79,533	(56%)	($162,423)
	Dennis S. Kazarian (D)	62,540	(44%)	($109,248)

THIRTY-FOURTH DISTRICT

Long Beach, with 361,000 people, is one of the few parts of suburban Los Angeles County with an urban character of its own. Long Beach has a man-made harbor competitive with L.A.'s San Pedro next door, which makes it one of the nation's major ports. There is also the beach, which gave the city its name; back in the 1920s and 1930s it helped to draw thousands of midwestern migrants to Long Beach, and the city built its own downtown and boardwalk-cum-amusement-park. In the 1930s the large number of retirees here contributed to California's zany political reputation; they were the strongest supporters of such welfare schemes as the Townsend Plan and the Ham 'n' Eggs movement (the latter helped to elect Earl Warren governor in 1942). Oldtimers can still recall when the Iowa picnics of the same period drew more than 50,000 people to Long Beach.

Today the atmosphere of Long Beach is different. Most of the town is filled with ordinary middle-class families. Retirees are just as likely to live in developments like the self-contained Rossmoor Leisure World, just across the line in Orange County, as in the stucco walkup apartments a couple of blocks from the ocean. Suburbia has grown out to Long Beach and absorbed it.

This newer Long Beach is still the largest single part, despite several boundary changes, of the 34th congressional district of California. The district now extends into Orange County, including half of Huntington Beach as well as Leisure World; in Los Angeles County the district includes half of Long Beach — generally speaking, the city's more prosperous part — and the middle-income suburbs of Lakewood and Bellflower. Overall the 34th is basically a Republican district, delivering solid Republican margins in statewide elections; but in its brief history it has elected a Democratic as well as a Republican congressman.

The Democratic congressman was Mark Hannaford, a professor at Long Beach City College and mayor of Lakewood. He was first elected in an upset over a Long Beach assemblyman in 1974, the Watergate year. Two years later, he was able to beat Republican Daniel Lungren, a young lawyer whose father was Richard Nixon's personal physician. Hannaford fought hard and did just about everything possible to hold the district.

But none of it was enough. Lungren, in 1978, was determined to avoid the mistakes of his previous campaign. He also had the advantage on the tax and spending issue since Hannaford, like many local government officials, had opposed Proposition 13. Lungren's conclusive victory here makes it about as clear as can be that this is a district that no Democrat could hold against a competent Republican challenger. In 1980 he was blessed with a Democratic opponent whose name is, simply, Simone. Lungren is the proud possessor of one of the House's most conservative voting records. He serves on the Judiciary Committee and, as a member of the Civil and Constitutional Rights Subcommittee, is on the front lines in the battle for constitutional amendments to outlaw abortion, impose prayer in schools, and prohibit busing. For 1982 he is likely to receive a district that is even more Republican and that should reelect him easily.

Census Data Pop. (1980 final) 475,676, up 2% in 1970s. Median family income, 1970, $11,831, 123% of U.S.

The Voters

Employment profile 1970 White collar, 57%. Blue collar, 32%. Service, 11%. Farm, –%.
Ethnic groups Black 1980, 2%. Hispanic 1980, 11%. Am. Ind. 1980, 1%. Asian 1980, 4%. Total foreign stock 1970, 20%. Canada, 3%; UK, Germany, 2% each; Italy, Netherlands, 1% each.

Presidential Vote

1980	Reagan (R)	123,748	(61%)
	Carter (D)	58,974	(29%)
	Anderson (I)	15,573	(8%)
1976	Ford (R)	112,251	(56%)
	Carter (D)	84,977	(42%)

Rep. Daniel E. (Dan) **Lungren** (R) Elected 1978; b. Sept. 22, 1946, Long Beach; home, Long Beach; Notre Dame U., B.A. 1964, USC, Georgetown U., J.D. 1971.

Career Staff of U.S. Sen. George Murphy, 1969–70; Staff of U.S. Sen. Bill Brock of Tenn., 1971; Spec. Asst., Repub. Natl. Comm., 1971–72; Practicing atty., 1973–78.

Offices 328 CHOB, 202-225-2415. Also 5514 Britton Dr., Long Beach 90815, 213-594-9761.

Committees *Judiciary* (10th). Subcommittees: Civil and Constitutional Rights; Immigration, Refugees and International Law.

Select Committee on Aging (10th). Subcommittees: Health and Long-Term Care; Human Services.

Group Ratings

	ADA	COPE	PC	LCV	CFA	RPN	NAB	NSI	NTU	ACA	ACU
1980	6	10	30	31	7	—	100	100	65	100	83
1979	0	10	13	14	7	—	—	—	69	100	97

Key Votes

1) Draft Registn $	FOR	6) Fair Hsg DOJ Enfrc	AGN	11) Cut Socl Incr Dfns $	FOR
2) Ban $ to Nicrgua	FOR	7) Lim PAC Contrbtns	AGN	12) Hosptl Cost Controls	AGN
3) Dlay MX Missile	AGN	8) Cap on Food Stmp $	FOR	13) Gasln Ctrls & Allctns	AGN
4) Nuclr Mortorium	AGN	9) New US Dep Edcatn	AGN	14) Lim Wndfll Prof Tax	FOR
5) Alaska Lands Bill	AGN	10) Cut OSHA $	FOR	15) Chryslr Loan Grntee	AGN

Election Results

1980 general	Daniel E. (Dan) Lungren (R)	138,024	(72%)	($235,834)
	Simone (D)	46,351	(24%)	($12,082)
1980 primary	Daniel E. (Dan) Lungren (R)	49,264	(100%)	
1978 general	Daniel E. (Dan) Lungren (R)	90,554	(54%)	($268,604)
	Mark W. Hannaford (D)	73,608	(44%)	($329,904)

THIRTY-FIFTH DISTRICT

It is hard to say which suburban Los Angeles County congressional district is the lineal descendant of the one represented by Richard Nixon from 1947 to 1951. There have since been five redistrictings, and the territory included in Nixon's 12th district, much more populous today than it was then, is divided among several seats now. The 26th has a reasonable claim to be the Nixon district, but so do the 33d that contains Whittier, Nixon's hometown, and the 35th that probably contains more of the acreage of Nixon's old 12th—plus the hometown of Jerry Voorhis, the liberal Democrat Nixon beat—than any of the others.

At any rate the 35th includes the eastern Los Angeles County suburbs of West Covina (which is much larger than neighboring Covina) and Pomona and Claremont that between them contain several high-quality small colleges. Also just across the San Bernardino County line the district includes some other comfortable suburbs: Ontario (with its own airport, now a major regional field for jets), Montclair, and Upland.

Just as Richard Nixon's capture of the old 12th district from liberal Democrat Jerry Voorhis was one of the victories that gave Republicans control of the House in 1946, the defeat of moderate Democrat Jim Lloyd here by Republican David Dreier was one of the victories that gave the Republicans major gains in the House elections in 1980. Lloyd won his seat, which had no incumbent when it was created by redistricting in 1974, by 735 votes; he increased his margins somewhat in 1976 and 1978 by stressing his moderate record, his aggressive views on defense (a 21-year Navy pilot, he backed higher defense spending), and his constituency services. Through the 1970s this formula was enough for victory, but in 1980 it was not. Dreier, who was beaten by Lloyd in 1978, beat him by almost exactly the same margin two years later.

Dreier is one of the youngest of the new House Republicans. He has been associated with the Claremont Colleges group, a conservatively inclined set of institutions (a think tank here is preparing redistricting plans for Republicans across the country); he was reportedly influenced in his attitudes by problems his small businessman father had with labor unions back in Kansas City. In any case, Dreier is one of the most conservative of the new House members, a man whose devotion to the principles of free enterprise probably exceeds his experience with the actual operation of the free enterprise system. He serves on the Government Operations and Small Business Committees.

Dreier's district is one of the few in Los Angeles County that had substantial population growth in the 1970s, and he should not have much trouble with redistricting. The more interesting question, during the 1980s, is whether the apparently rising number of Mexican–Americans here will shift the district's political allegiance to the left, and whether they, in their newly found middle-class circumstances, will shift toward the right.

Census Data Pop. (1980 final) 610,041, up 31% in 1970s. Median family income, 1970, $11,265, 118% of U.S.

The Voters

Employment profile 1970 White collar, 52%. Blue collar, 34%. Service, 12%. Farm, 2%.
Ethnic groups Black 1980, 6%. Hispanic 1980, 21%. Am. Ind. 1980, 1%. Asian 1980, 3%. Total foreign stock 1970, 20%. Canada, 3%; UK, Germany, Italy, 2% each.

Presidential Vote

1980	Reagan (R)	124,297	(62%)
	Carter (D)	58,017	(29%)
	Anderson (I)	14,318	(7%)
1976	Ford (R)	90,929	(55%)
	Carter (D)	72,664	(44%)

Rep. David Dreier (R) Elected 1980; b. July 5, 1952, Kansas City, Mo.; home, La Verne; Claremont Men's Col., B.A. 1973, M.A. 1975.

Career Dir., Corp. Relations, Claremont Men's Col., 1975–79; Rep. nominee for U.S. House, 1978; Dir., Pub. Affairs, Industrial Hydrocarbons, 1979–80.

Offices 1641 LHOB, 202-225-2305. Also 917 Village Oaks Dr., Covina 91724, 213-339-9078 and 714-592-2857.

Committees *Government Operations* (14th). Subcommittees: Environment, Energy and Natural Resources; Manpower and Housing.

Small Business (16th). Subcommittees: Export Opportunities and Special Small Business Problems; General Oversight.

Election Results

1980 general	David Dreier (R)	100,743	(52%)	($379,325)
	Jim Lloyd (D)	88,279	(45%)	($237,886)
1980 primary	David Dreier (R)	32,189	(53%)	
	Russ Blewett (R)	8,720	(14%)	($44,440)
	Frances M. Livingston (R)	8,036	(13%)	($49,963)
	Three others (R)	11,597	(19%)	
1978 general	Jim Lloyd (D)	80,388	(54%)	($147,556)
	David Dreier (R)	68,442	(46%)	($152,315)

THIRTY-SIXTH DISTRICT

Congressman George Brown of the 36th district of California is one of the Horatio Algers of the Congress. In the early 1950s Brown was an industrial physicist living in Monterey Park, a middle-class suburb east of Los Angeles. With his crew cut and slight paunch, Brown was scarcely distinguishable from tens of thousands of Los Angeles area scientists and engineers —but for his Quaker upbringing, a strong belief in disarmament and peace, and nascent political yearnings. In 1954 he ran for and won a seat on the Monterey Park City Council. His interest in government whetted, he tried for the state legislature and in the very Democratic year of 1958 was elected. Three years later the legislature was charged with drawing the state's congressional district lines and allotting the eight new districts California had gained in the 1960 census—the largest number of new districts any American legislature has had to deal with. George Brown served on the appropriate committee, and one of the districts came to be centered on Monterey Park. He was elected to Congress in 1962.

The story doesn't end there. In the House, Brown was one of the original peaceniks, even before the big escalation of the Vietnam war in 1965. Because many of his constituents considered his positions on issues far out, he had to fight every two years to win reelection. But he did win and in 1970 decided to make a try for the Senate. It looked like a dubious move at first. But Republican Senator George Murphy got into serious trouble when it was revealed that Technicolor was paying him $20,000 a year while he was serving in the Senate. Then just a month before the primary Richard Nixon invaded Cambodia, and a strong wave of antiwar feeling propelled Brown upward in the polls. His underfinanced campaign brought him nearly even with the favorite, Congressman John Tunney, and a switch of 99,000 votes out of 2.4 million cast would have given the peacenik the nomination and—judging from the size of Tunney's 1970 victory—the Senate seat as well.

There is more. Relatively few former congressmen make it back to Capitol Hill nowadays; it is just too wrenching to return without all that seniority you once had. But Brown, motivated more by a desire for peace than a hunger for power, decided to try anyway. Once again redistricting gave him his chance. In 1971 the legislature created a new district in the eastern end of the Los Angeles basin, at the intersection of Los Angeles, San Bernardino, and Riverside Counties. The district included all the most Democratic parts of San Bernardino and Riverside —the Mexican–American areas, the local University of California campus, and the working-class subdivisions around the Kaiser Steel plant in Fontana. Everyone assumed it would go Democratic in November. In an eight-candidate field Brown won the nomination with 28% of the vote; in the general he won with 56%, although Nixon was carrying the district.

Brown returned to serve on the Science Committee, as he had before, and also got a seat on Agriculture (this district has a large agricultural economy, although most of its residents live in suburban settings). He made relatively few waves this time, and his very liberal voting record was not as distinctive as it had been in the early 1960s. He has not had significant opposition since 1972. Thanks to the retirements, deaths, or defeats of more senior (and usually more conservative) Democrats, Brown now has impressive seniority: he is the fifth-ranking Democrat on Agriculture and the third-ranking on Science. He serves as chairman of the Department Operations, Research, and Foreign Agriculture Subcommittee.

Brown is now preparing for his third congressional redistricting. His district has gained population and, with a sympathetic Democratic legislature in Sacramento, he seems likely to retain a similar Democratic district for the 1980s. His percentage did drop as Reagan carried the district in 1980. But most likely Brown's Horatio Alger career will continue.

Census Data Pop. (1980 final) 559,239, up 21% in 1970s. Median family income, 1970, $9,407, 98% of U.S.

The Voters

Employment profile 1970 White collar, 47%. Blue collar, 37%. Service, 14%. Farm, 2%.
Ethnic groups Black 1980, 8%. Hispanic 1980, 22%. Am. Ind. 1980, 1%. Asian 1980, 1%. Total foreign stock 1970, 19%. Canada, 2%; UK, Germany, 1% each.

Presidential Vote

1980	Reagan (R)	92,118	(53%)
	Carter (D)	65,274	(37%)
	Anderson (I)	13,171	(8%)
1976	Ford (R)	64,801	(43%)
	Carter (D)	82,538	(55%)

Rep. George E. Brown, Jr. (D) Elected 1972; b. Mar. 6, 1920, Holtville; home, Colton; UCLA, B.A. 1946.

Career Army, WWII; Monterey Park City Cncl., Mayor, 1954–58; Personnel, Engineering, and Management Consultant, City of Los Angeles, 1957–61; Cal. Assembly, 1959–62; U.S. House of Reps., 1963–71; Candidate for Dem. nomination for U.S. Senate, 1970.

Offices 2342 RHOB, 202-225-6161. Also 552 N. LaCadena St., Colton 92324, 714-825-2472.

Committees *Agriculture* (5th). Subcommittees: Department Operations, Research and Foreign Agriculture (Chairman); Forests, Family Farms and Energy.

Science and Technology (3d). Subcommittees: Natural Resources, Agriculture Research and Environment; Science, Research and Technology; Space Science and Applications.

Group Ratings

	ADA	COPE	PC	LCV	CFA	RPN	NAB	NSI	NTU	ACA	ACU
1980	94	82	63	72	64	—	9	13	14	10	11
1979	84	74	80	87	63	—	—	—	17	0	3
1978	70	79	65	81	64	50	10	10	23	8	17

Key Votes

1) Draft Registn $	AGN	6) Fair Hsg DOJ Enfrc	FOR	11) Cut Socl Incr Dfns $	AGN
2) Ban $ to Nicrgua	AGN	7) Lim PAC Contrbtns	FOR	12) Hosptl Cost Controls	FOR

3) Dlay MX Missile	FOR	8) Cap on Food Stmp $	AGN	13) Gasln Ctrls & Allctns	FOR
4) Nuclr Mortorium	FOR	9) New US Dep Edcatn	FOR	14) Lim Wndfll Prof Tax	AGN
5) Alaska Lands Bill	FOR	10) Cut OSHA $	AGN	15) Chryslr Loan Grntee	FOR

Election Results

1980 general	George E. Brown, Jr. (D)	88,634	(53%)	($66,917)
	John Paul Stark (R)	73,252	(43%)	($38,094)
1980 primary	George E. Brown, Jr. (D)	51,494	(74%)	
	Gary Anthony Wedge (D)	17,657	(26%)	($0)
1978 general	George E. Brown, Jr. (D)	80,448	(63%)	($39,914)
	Dana Warren Carmody (R)	47,417	(37%)	($11,179)

THIRTY-SEVENTH DISTRICT

In the 1920s, when California first became a noted retirement haven, most older people moving out here were looking for homes along the ocean. If they were poor they retired in Long Beach or one of the beach towns near Los Angeles; if they were rich, they might go to Santa Barbara or La Jolla. Retirees were a large percentage of California's population before World War II than they have been since; the state is now actually younger than the national average. But there are still plenty of retirees, and in the 1960s and 1970s they have been moving not to the seashore where it is crowded, smoggy, and urban — but to the desert.

This is the land of California's 37th congressional district, a seat that takes in territory from two counties, San Bernardino and Riverside, but covers most of California's desert lands — at least the parts where people live. The district's boundaries begin roughly at the eastern end of the Los Angeles basin: it includes some of San Bernardino and the surrounding area, including the Seventh Day Adventist town of Loma Linda and some of the territory around Riverside. But most of the district lies east of the mountains that stop — or at least hinder — the Los Angeles smog from reaching the desert. Here the days are crystal clear, with the reddish mountains always visible in the distance, and the sky usually blue and cloudless. The desert can be fertile farmland, as it is in the Coachella Valley, but it needs to be irrigated; without daily doses of water almost any plant will wilt and die in the heat. The first white settlers in the desert were prospectors, and some ghost towns still stand. These constitute quite a contrast to Palm Springs and Palm Desert, which are outposts of affluence (Palm Springs is more show business, Palm Desert more WASPy). It is too hot here in the summer for most people, even though the heat is dry, but the winter weather is almost ideal. Two presidents have retired within the confines of the district, Eisenhower in Palm Desert for the winters, Ford in nearby Rancho Mirage — which is also the home of Frank Sinatra and Spiro Agnew.

There are of course more modest retirement communities sprinkled here and there, all of them basically Republican. People who have enough money to move to a condominium or even a trailer when they are 65 are far more likely to be Republicans than not, and the 37th district, with one of the highest median ages of any California district, is definitely Republican.

That party preference has prevailed in both presidential and congressional elections. Representing the area from 1966 until his death in a plane crash was Jerry Pettis, a self-made millionaire, Seventh Day Adventist (the only one in Congress), and member of the Ways and Means Committee. He was succeeded by his widow Shirley, who won a full term in 1976 but surprised her constituents by declining to run in 1978. Her successor is San Bernardino area Assemblyman Jerry Lewis (no relation to the comedian), who like the Pettises is regarded as an independent-minded conservative. Lewis won the Republican primary without difficulty and had an impressive margin in the general election.

Lewis is reportedly interested in running for lieutenant governor in 1982 but would like to bequeath the 37th or something like it—the current district must lose some 125,000 residents to meet the equal population standard—to an aide. But in all likelihood there will be a spirited Republican primary for the succession in this heavily Republican district.

Census Data Pop. (1980 final) 650,999, up 41% in 1970s. Median family income, 1970, $8,794, 92% of U.S.

The Voters

Employment profile 1970 White collar, 49%. Blue collar, 30%. Service, 16%. Farm, 5%.
Ethnic groups Black 1980, 3%. Hispanic 1980, 16%. Am. Ind. 1980, 1%. Asian 1980, 2%. Total foreign stock 1970, 20%. Canada, UK, Germany, 2% each.

Presidential Vote

1980	Reagan (R)	149,780	(63%)
	Carter (D)	69,594	(29%)
	Anderson (I)	14,706	(6%)
1976	Ford (R)	101,935	(54%)
	Carter (D)	84,725	(45%)

Rep. Jerry Lewis (R) Elected 1978; b. Oct. 21, 1934, Seattle, Wash.; home, Highland; UCLA, B.A. 1956.

Career Life insurance agent, 1959–78; Field Rep. to U.S. Rep. Jerry Pettis, 1968; Cal. Assembly, 1968–78.

Offices 327 CHOB, 202-225-5861. Also 101 6th St., Redlands 92373, 714-862-6030.

Committee *Appropriations* (20th). Subcommittees: Agriculture, Rural Development and Related Agencies; Foreign Operations; Legislature.

Group Ratings

	ADA	COPE	PC	LCV	CFA	RPN	NAB	NSI	NTU	ACA	ACU
1980	11	21	13	40	14	—	90	90	52	75	94
1979	5	15	8	13	4	—	—	—	55	88	90

Key Votes

1) Draft Registn $	AGN	6) Fair Hsg DOJ Enfrc	AGN	11) Cut Socl Incr Dfns $	FOR
2) Ban $ to Nicrgua	FOR	7) Lim PAC Contrbtns	AGN	12) Hosptl Cost Controls	AGN
3) Dlay MX Missile	AGN	8) Cap on Food Stmp $	FOR	13) Gasln Ctrls & Allctns	AGN
4) Nuclr Mortorium	AGN	9) New US Dep Edcatn	FOR	14) Lim Wndfll Prof Tax	FOR
5) Alaska Lands Bill	AGN	10) Cut OSHA $	FOR	15) Chryslr Loan Grntee	AGN

Election Results

1980 general	Jerry Lewis (R)	166,640	(72%)	($54,448)
	Donald M. Rusk (D)	58,462	(25%)	($47,382)
1980 primary	Jerry Lewis (R)	67,694	(83%)	
	Three others (R)	13,879	(17%)	
1978 general	Jerry Lewis (R)	106,581	(61%)	($159,433)
	Dan Corcoran (D).............	60,463	(35%)	($50,005)

THIRTY-EIGHTH DISTRICT

"Orange County" are two words that have become synonymous with "conservative" in political discourse. Twenty years ago Orange County, California, had all the notoriety possessed by a few thousand acres of citrus trees; its 1950 population was 216,000. By 1980 that figure had grown to 1.9 million. As the population mushroomed, Orange County has consistently turned in the highest Republican percentages of any major California county and, in some elections, although by no means all, of any major county in the country. Yet Orange County is not as monolithically conservative and Republican as is generally supposed. Democrats currently hold two out of six Orange County Assembly seats, and since 1962 Democrats have held the congressional district currently numbered the 38th.

Roughly speaking, the district includes the central portion of the heavily populated western half of Orange County, halfway between the ocean and the hills that separate it from the San Gabriel Valley in Los Angeles County. In its current borders the 38th includes most of Santa Ana and the factory-worker suburbs of Buena Park, Stanton, and Westminster. These are places one could not mistake for high-income areas, whether one is speeding by at 70 on the freeway or driving down the little cul-de-sacs and curving streets favored by developers in the 1950s and 1960s for even the squarest tracts of land.

A large number of Mexican–Americans live in the district, not only in the identifiable Mexican community in Santa Ana, but scattered throughout the subdivisions of the district; the Hispanic percentage has risen from 16% to 25% in the 1970s. The percentage of Asians has risen as well, from 1% to 6%. This gives the 38th more ethnic variety than is ordinarily associated with Orange County, and perhaps some additional Democratic votes — although these new residents probably identify pretty closely with the middle-class values of the people into whose houses they have moved and with their new neighbors.

The Democratic congressman from the district is Jerry Patterson, a former mayor of Santa Ana, who first won the district in 1974 and seems in solid political shape. He serves on the Banking Committee, where he tends to favor the savings institutions. Savings and loans in California, unlike most states, may be investor-owned, and some of the great fortunes of the state have been made by S&L founders, who are also responsible for financing and often directing the development that made Orange County, among other places, what it is today. Patterson chairs a subcommittee on a subject somewhat far afield, International Trade, Investment, and Monetary Policy.

The Republicans do not seem to have contested this seat seriously since Patterson first won it. It is almost the perfect size for a new district, and it is almost certain that the Democratic legislature will create a new 38th that is almost precisely the same — perhaps a little more Democratic because of the addition of a precinct here and the subtraction of another there.

Census Data Pop. (1980 final) 531,321, up 15% in 1970s. Median family income, 1970, $11,367, 119% of U.S.

The Voters

Employment profile 1970 White collar, 48%. Blue collar, 39%. Service, 12%. Farm, 1%.
Ethnic groups Black 1980, 2%. Hispanic 1980, 25%. Am. Ind. 1980, 1%. Asian 1980, 6%. Total foreign stock 1970, 20%. Canada, 3%; UK, 2%; Germany, Italy, 1% each.

Presidential Vote

1980	Reagan (R)	109,167	(63%)
	Carter (D)	47,995	(28%)
	Anderson (I)	11,375	(7%)
1976	Ford (R)	85,873	(55%)
	Carter (D)	67,994	(43%)

Rep. Jerry M. Patterson (R) Elected 1974; b. Oct. 25, 1934, El Paso, Tex.; home, Santa Ana; Long Beach St. U., B.A. 1960, UCLA, J.D. 1966.

Career Coast Guard, 1953–57; Practicing atty., 1967–74; Santa Ana City Cncl., 1967–73, Mayor, 1973–74.

Offices 2238 RHOB, 202-225-2965. Also Suite 921, 34 Civic Ctr. Plaza, Santa Ana 92701, 714-835-3811.

Committees *Banking, Finance and Urban Affairs* (9th). Subcommittees: Housing and Community Development; International Development Institutions and Finance (Chairman); International Trade, Investment and Monetary Policy.

Interior and Insular Affairs (19th). Subcommittees: Oversight and Investigations; Water and Power Resources.

Group Ratings

	ADA	COPE	PC	LCV	CFA	RPN	NAB	NSI	NTU	ACA	ACU
1980	72	72	67	67	64	—	27	40	15	18	18
1979	63	72	48	70	48	—	—	—	17	5	6
1978	60	94	68	71	64	20	10	50	7	24	30

Key Votes

1) Draft Registn $	AGN	6) Fair Hsg DOJ Enfrc	FOR	11) Cut Socl Incr Dfns $	AGN
2) Ban $ to Nicrgua	—	7) Lim PAC Contrbtns	FOR	12) Hosptl Cost Controls	FOR
3) Dlay MX Missile	AGN	8) Cap on Food Stmp $	AGN	13) Gasln Ctrls & Allctns	FOR
4) Nuclr Mortorium	FOR	9) New US Dep Edcatn	FOR	14) Lim Wndfll Prof Tax	—
5) Alaska Lands Bill	FOR	10) Cut OSHA $	—	15) Chryslr Loan Grntee	FOR

Election Results

1980 general	Jerry M. Patterson (D)	91,880	(56%)	($199,521)
	Art Jacobson (R)	66,256	(40%)	($39,195)
1980 primary	Jerry M. Patterson (D)	47,929	(100%)	
1978 general	Jerry M. Patterson (D)	75,471	(59%)	($134,557)
	Don Goedeke (R)	53,298	(41%)	($61,319)

THIRTY-NINTH DISTRICT

The 39th congressional district of California is the northern section of the heavily populated part of Orange County, one of three districts wholly or primarily within the limits of this jurisdiction whose name has become synonymous with conservatism. It includes some of Orange County's most important landmarks. In Anaheim, there is Disneyland, the amusement park whose opening here in 1955 introduced millions to Orange County, and Angels Stadium. In Fullerton is the headquarters of Norton Simon's business empire—just one of dozens of successful enterprises that have helped to make Orange County so prosperous. And in tiny Yorba Linda, where the subdivisions thin out and the scrubby hills begin, is the birthplace of Richard Nixon, a man whose career has moved back and forth out of Orange County over the past several decades.

The 39th district is pretty solidly Republican territory; most of the Orange County precincts that sometimes go Democratic were placed in the 38th district next door. It was the most Republican district in California in the 1980 presidential election; in congressional elections it pretty much follows suit. For several years the district sent Charles Wiggins to Congress. Wiggins's performance at the House Judiciary Committee impeachment hearings will not be forgotten. Although he took the side that history will record as wrong, his defense of Richard Nixon was eloquent without being rhetorical, and persuasive without being hortatory. Wiggins talked calmly, reasonably, and with full command of the facts—a fine trial lawyer with the case of his life. His work came as little surprise to those who had watched him in the House: he was a thoughtful, convincing advocate usually, but not always, of conservative causes. By the time the impeachment hearings had ended, he had enough prestige that his assessment of the June 23 tape was enough to get Nixon to resign.

Like many congressmen, Wiggins tired of the pace of congressional work and the need to stay in touch with constituents so far away. In 1978, after 12 years of service, he decided to retire. The succession in the 39th district was determined when Assemblyman William Dannemeyer was left without opposition in the Republican primary. Dannemeyer has an unusual background for a Republican congressman: he served in the California Assembly in the middle 1960s as a Democrat and switched parties only after he lost a race for the state Senate. But his Republican credentials are in order today, and he is not a dissenter from Republican ranks in the House. Redistricting and reelection should prove no problem for him.

Census Data Pop. (1980 final) 592,845, up 28% in 1970s. Median family income, 1970, $12,749, 133% of U.S.

The Voters

Employment profile 1970 White collar, 60%. Blue collar, 28%. Service, 11%. Farm, 1%.
Ethnic groups Black 1980, 1%. Hispanic 1980, 15%. Am. Ind. 1980, 1%. Asian 1980, 4%. Total foreign stock 1970, 19%. Canada, 3%; UK, Germany, 2% each; Italy, 1%.

Presidential Vote

1980	Reagan (R)	170,015	(70%)
	Carter (D)	51,811	(21%)
	Anderson (I)	16,328	(7%)
1976	Ford (R)	131,577	(63%)
	Carter (D)	73,263	(35%)

Rep. William E. Dannemeyer (R) Elected 1978; b. Sept. 22, 1929, Long Beach; home, Fullerton; Valparaiso U., B.A. 1950; Hastings Col. of Law, J.D. 1952.

Career Army, Korea; Practicing atty.; Dpty. Fullerton Dist. Atty.; Cal. Assembly, 1963–66, 1976–78.

Offices 1032 LHOB, 202-225-4111. Also 1370 Brea Blvd., Suite 108, Fullerton 92632, 714-992-0141.

Committees *Energy and Commerce* (11th). Subcommittees: Fossil and Synthetic Fuels; Health and the Environment.

Post Office and Civil Service (7th). Subcommittees: Compensation and Employee Benefits; Postal Personnel and Modernization.

Group Ratings

	ADA	COPE	PC	LCV	CFA	RPN	NAB	NSI	NTU	ACA	ACU
1980	6	10	23	31	14	—	100	90	80	100	78
1979	5	10	18	10	4	—	—	—	77	100	97

Key Votes

1) Draft Registn $	FOR	6) Fair Hsg DOJ Enfrc	AGN	11) Cut Socl Incr Dfns $	FOR
2) Ban $ to Nicrgua	FOR	7) Lim PAC Contrbtns	AGN	12) Hosptl Cost Controls	AGN
3) Dlay MX Missile	AGN	8) Cap on Food Stmp $	FOR	13) Gasln Ctrls & Allctns	AGN
4) Nuclr Mortorium	AGN	9) New US Dep Edcatn	AGN	14) Lim Wndfll Prof Tax	AGN
5) Alaska Lands Bill	AGN	10) Cut OSHA $		FOR	15) Chryslr Loan Grntee	AGN

Election Results

1980 general	William E. Dannemeyer (R)	175,228	(76%)	($154,849)
	Leonard L. Lahtinen(D)	54,504	(24%)	($16,369)
1980 primary	William E. Dannemeyer (R)	62,081	(100%)	
1978 general	William E. Dannemeyer (R)	112,160	(64%)	($161,151)
	William E. Farris (D)	63,891	(36%)	($47,172)

FORTIETH DISTRICT

During the past two decades, no other congressional district has had the kind of population growth that has been seen in the 40th district of California. This area includes most of the geographical expanse of Orange County, where the flat land of the Los Angeles Basin meets the mountains that surround it and moves along the south coast to include the northern tip of San Diego County. Within the district lived 201,000 people in 1960, 464,000 in 1970, and 774,000 in 1980. There was a pause in the growth here in the early 1970s, because of a dip in the Los Angeles Basin's economy and because of delays in development of the Irvine Ranch property—the largest single tract of undeveloped land adjacent to a major metropolitan area. But the city of Irvine complete with university, has now sprung up where a few years ago there were only empty fields. The Orange County boom picked up steam in the late 1970s and was especially robust in the eastern edges of the county, from Orange and Villa

Park in the north to Irvine and Newport Beach on the coast, to Mission Viejo farther down the coast near San Clemente and San Juan Capistrano.

So great has been the demand for new houses and condominiums that developers have staged lotteries; the people who get the lucky numbers get to buy the houses.

Long before Watergate, Orange County entered our political vocabulary as a synonym for conservatism. As its population grew in the 1950s and 1960s its Republican margins grew even faster. The kind of people Orange County attracted were naturally inclined to favor Republicans, especially such candidates as Ronald Reagan and Richard Nixon. These are well-off people, although not usually the richest in the Los Angeles area; many are engineers, technicians, draftsmen—people who tend to be comfortable with technological precision and apprehensive about social change. They believe strongly in the free enterprise system, the work ethic, and traditional social mores.

Orange County, with its geometrically laid-out subdivisions, its clean shopping centers, and its seemingly homogeneous population, seemed to be the kind of place these people were looking for. Its developers have imposed a predictable order on the lush and unpredictable California landscape of mountain, coast, and desert. In the 1960s, when blacks in Watts and students in Berkeley noted and asserted other values, people in Orange County responded at the ballot box with huge margins for the politicians who upheld their own standards.

But as the 1970s went on, Republican allegiances became less solid in Orange County and the confidence and esprit of the conservative voters here seems to have been damaged. One reason is that in many ways their adversaries have prevailed: the life-style of most Californians today, including residents of Orange County, in some ways resembles more closely the counterculture heroes of a dozen years ago than it does the traditional model people here had in mind. Orange County has become younger, and as it has become larger it has become less homogeneous. Also Orange County's values seem to have been betrayed by some of its leaders. This was a county very much touched by Watergate: Richard Nixon was born here and his onetime San Clemente mansion sits within the 40th district; a few miles away on the Pacific Coast Highway is the gleaming high rise on whose top floor Nixon's personal lawyer, Herbert Kalmbach, had his offices and from which he went forth to distribute hush money. Nixon and his aides claimed to be representing the old morality; but they betrayed its most basic tenets. Ronald Reagan claimed that the Watergate defendants were "not criminals at heart." But they were criminals under the law and in the settled judgment of the American people.

Scandals and schisms for a time hurt conservative morale in the 40th congressional district. Congressman John Schmitz, a member of the John Birch Society, was defeated in his Republican primary in 1972 and became the presidential candidate of the American Independent Party, once George Wallace's vehicle. He got a negligible number of votes outside Idaho and a few Rocky Mountain enclaves. But he has made a local comeback and with his puckish good humor was elected to the California Senate in 1978. Schmitz's successor was the Orange County Assessor, Andrew Hinshaw, a man with a reputation for efficiency and honesty in a demanding job. But in 1976 Hinshaw was convicted of accepting bribes from Radio Shack.

In the past several years, Orange County seems to have recovered much of its old elan. To replace Hinshaw, the Republican primary voters in 1976 gave Assemblyman Robert Badham a 1% margin over Schmitz. Badham has since represented the 40th district with an impeccable conservative voting record. The shocks of changing life-styles, Vietnam, and Watergate have now been absorbed; the temporary economic pause of the early 1970s almost forgotten, while the Carter Administration's perceived dismal performance confirmed Orange Countians' worst expectations. In Ronald Reagan people here found a new hero who is also a comfortable old friend — in 1980, the 40th district gave Reagan 69% of its very large number of votes. This district will have to be sliced up for 1982, since it now contains enough people for 1½ districts. But there is no doubt that Badham will be reelected or that this part of Orange County will continue to be represented by conservative Republicans.

Census Data Pop. (1980 final) 774,539, up 67% in 1970s. Median family income, 1970, $12,093, 127% of U.S.

The Voters

Employment profile 1970 White collar, 64%. Blue collar, 23%. Service, 12%. Farm, 1%.
Ethnic groups Black 1980, 2%. Hispanic 1980, 10%. Am. Ind. 1980, 1%. Asian 1980, 4%. Total foreign stock 1970, 19%. Canada, UK, 3% each; Germany, 2%; Italy, 1%.

Presidential Vote

1980	Reagan (R)	225,599	(69%)
	Carter (D)	68,255	(21%)
	Anderson (I)	24,575	(8%)
1976	Ford (R)	167,203	(67%)
	Carter (D)	79,649	(32%)

Rep. Robert E. Badham (R) Elected 1976; b. June 9, 1929, Los Angeles; home, Newport Beach; Occidental Col., 1947–48, Stanford U., B.A. 1951.

Career Navy, Korea; Secy. and V.P., Hoffman Hardware, Los Angeles, 1954–69; Cal. Assembly, 1963–77.

Offices 1108 LHOB, 202-225-5611. Also 1649 Westcliff, Newport Beach 92660, 714-631-0040.

Committees *Armed Services* (11th). Subcommittees: Procurement and Military Nuclear Systems; Research and Development.

House Administration (3d). Subcommittee: Accounts.

Group Ratings

	ADA	COPE	PC	LCV	CFA	RPN	NAB	NSI	NTU	ACA	ACU
1980	0	11	13	12	7	—	100	89	66	95	88
1979	0	10	10	6	4	—	—	—	66	96	100
1978	10	21	10	0	0	73	100	100	53	100	85

Key Votes

1) Draft Registn $	FOR	6) Fair Hsg DOJ Enfrc	AGN
2) Ban $ to Nicrgua	FOR	7) Lim PAC Contrbtns	AGN
3) Dlay MX Missile	AGN	8) Cap on Food Stmp $	FOR
4) Nuclr Mortorium	AGN	9) New US Dep Edcatn	AGN
5) Alaska Lands Bill	AGN	10) Cut OSHA $	FOR

11) Cut Socl Incr Dfns $ FOR
12) Hosptl Cost Controls AGN
13) Gasln Ctrls & Allctns AGN
14) Lim Wndfll Prof Tax FOR
15) Chryslr Loan Grntee AGN

Election Results

1980 general	Robert E. Badham (R)	213,999	(70%)	($123,492)
	Michael P. Dow (D)	66,512	(22%)	($15,863)
	Dan Mahaffey (Libertarian)	24,486	(8%)	($34,285)
1980 primary	Robert E. Badham (R)	90,706	(76%)	
	Richard G. Gardner (R)	23,938	(20%)	
	One other (R)	5,435	(5%)	
1978 general	Robert E. Badham (R)	147,882	(66%)	($51,719)
	Jim McGuy (D)................	76,358	(34%)	($5,182)

FORTY-FIRST DISTRICT

Before World War II, San Diego was a sleepy resort town with a fine natural harbor and a few Navy installations. Then the United States fought a war in the Pacific, and San Diego was forever changed. It became the Navy's West Coast headquarters, and naval installations proliferated. In later years its pleasant climate — perhaps the most equable in the continental United States — made it a favorite retirement place for Navy officers and for others as well. But San Diego, like most Sun Belt cities, is far more than a collection of retirement villages. It has developed a major industrial base, largely on high-skill businesses; its metropolitan area population has reached more than 1.8 million.

Before World War II San Diego was evenly divided politically, split between the well-to-do Republican north side and the more Mexican–American Democratic south side. In the years following the war, the heavy in-migration gave both the city and county of San Diego a very Republican, conservative complexion. Richard Nixon for years regarded this as his "lucky city"—until the unfolding ITT scandal caused him to cancel plans to have the 1972 Republican National Convention here. Since Watergate San Diego seems to have become an area where the two parties are competitive; Democrats have even managed to capture most of the county's Assembly seats. The city has elected a moderate Republican, Pete Wilson, as mayor, who has turned around traditional attitudes by stressing that there should be limits on San Diego's growth.

The 41st congressional district includes most of the city's comfortable neighborhoods, for example, Mission Bay, and few of its black and Mexican–American areas; the affluent parts are full of Navy retirees, who often have strong right-wing views. But the 41st also includes a couple of local colleges and increasingly a younger population; the newer retirement subdivisions are being built in the hills of the city beyond the district or in the suburbs.

During the 1970s the 41st trended Democratic when cultural issues were at stake; an increasing proportion of voters here react against moves to crack down on recreational drugs or punish homosexuals. But they also react as high-income Americans traditionally do when economic issues are at stake, at which time the Democratic trend here disappears and San Diego's large Republican margins reemerge.

These countervailing trends buffeted the late career of Congressman Bob Wilson, a Republican first elected in 1952 who retired in 1980. Wilson was throughout the 1970s one of the most senior Republicans in the House and for most of that time was ranking Republican on the Armed Services Committee. As might be expected, he was a backer of increased defense budgets generally and of greater spending on the Navy in particular. Wilson had trouble in 1974, when cultural issues dominated; he was reelected rather easily, although still with less than 60%, in 1976 and 1978 when economic issues seemed more important. When Wilson retired in 1980, the election seemed confusing to many, since the Democratic candidate was another Bob Wilson, a state senator with a rather conservative record and proven vote-getting ability in northern San Diego. Wilson backed the Kemp–Roth plan and favored nuclear power—the latter a position likely to turn off many of the younger voters in the district.

The Republican candidate, Bill Lowery, had many of the same issue positions but a different reputation. A protege and former appointee of Mayor Pete Wilson, with the image of a moderate, Lowery won a tough Republican primary against the son of Congressman Bob Wilson's predecessor, who seemed more conservative, and he assailed his Democratic opponent for trading on the retiring congressman's good name. With economic issues clearly more important than cultural ones, and with the Democrat sacrificing some of his natural edge on the latter, Lowery won comparatively easily. Befitting his background in city government, he sits on the Banking Committee and also on Science and Technology; the other new Republican from the San Diego area, Duncan Hunter, got Bob Wilson's seat on Armed Services. With a moderate image and conservative economic record, Lowery seems well suited to this district, and he should have little problem with redistricting.

Census Data Pop. (1980 final) 509,713, up 10% in 1970s. Median family income, 1970, $11,118, 118% of U.S.

The Voters

Employment profile 1970 White collar, 64%. Blue collar, 23%. Service, 13%. Farm, –%.
Ethnic groups Black 1980, 3%. Hispanic 1980, 8%. Am. Ind. 1980, 1%. Asian 1980, 4%. Total foreign stock 1970, 21%. Canada, 3%; UK, Germany, 2% each; Italy, 1%.

Presidential Vote

1980	Reagan (R)	138,300	(57%)
	Carter (D)	68,347	(28%)
	Anderson (I)	27,803	(12%)
1976	Ford (R)	122,469	(56%)
	Carter (D)	90,795	(42%)

Rep. Bill Lowery (R) Elected 1980; b. May 2, 1947, San Diego; home, San Diego; San Diego St. Col.

Career Pub. Rel./Adv; San Diego City Cncl., 1977–80, Dpty. Mayor, 1980.

Offices 1331 LHOB, 202-225-3201. Also 880 Front St., Rm. 6-S-15, San Diego 92188, 714-231-0957.

Committees *Banking, Finance and Urban Affairs* (17th). Subcommittees: Domestic Monetary Policy; Financial Institutions Supervision, Regulation and Insurance; Housing and Community Development.

Science and Technology (17th). Subcommittees: Energy Research and Production; Space Science and Applications.

Group Ratings and Key Votes: Newly Elected

Election Results

1980 general	Bill Lowery (R)	123,187	(53%)	($213,099)
	Bob Wilson (D)	101,101	(43%)	($362,792)
1980 primary	Bill Lowery (R)	37,066	(50%)	
	Dan McKinnon (R)	34,236	(46%)	($169,090)
	Two others (R)	3,571	(5%)	
1978 general	Bob Wilson (R)	107,685	(58%)	($118,820)
	King Golden, Jr. (D)	77,540	(42%)	($26,331)

FORTY-SECOND DISTRICT

Like most Sun Belt cities, San Diego has a second side. To many San Diego evokes images of La Jolla, its shopping streets lined with boutiques and stockbrokers' offices, or Mission Bay, with its comfortable homes of retired Navy officers, or the magnificent Balboa Park Zoo. But just a few miles away is another San Diego, down by the harbor, along the hills running inland, and on the flat, dusty land going down to Tijuana. This is the south side, where the city's blacks live in neighborhoods stretching east from the city's gleaming downtown, and where Mexican–Americans are scattered somewhat more widely in parts of the city from Encanto and Chollas Park in the east down through the blue collar suburbs of National City and Chula Vista to the south. The San Diego metropolitan area as a whole is heavily Republican, but most of these areas are Democratic and form the heart of California's 42d congressional district. The district includes as well some more Republican areas: the high-income beachfront community of Coronado, the pleasant suburbs of Lemon Grove and Spring Valley in the hills east of the city.

The district was designed to be Democratic — and until 1980 it mostly was. For 18 years it was represented by Lionel Van Deerlin, a former television newscaster who had risen to what is potentially one of the most powerful positions in the House, chairman of the Communications Subcommittee. But Van Deerlin, in his middle 60s, seemed to have lost his edge. His proposals for reform of the communications laws attracted no support in Washington, and back home he seemed to take his district for granted. In the 1980 election most observers assumed his seat was safe. But they reckoned without the landslide for Ronald Reagan or the energy of 42d district Republican candidate Duncan Hunter.

Hunter was the first Republican to run a serious congressional campaign in this part of San Diego in years. A Vietnam veteran and lawyer in a storefront office in an area with a large Mexican–American population, Hunter had a career profile one might more readily associate with a Democrat. He shook thousands of hands while Van Deerlin remained in Washington, and he attacked the incumbent for opposing increases in defense spending. Hunter ran essentially even with Reagan in the district. He won more than one-quarter of the votes in black neighborhoods; he had large margins in the Republican areas, and carried a 61% majority in working-class Chula Vista. Perhaps most important in a district that sits on the Mexican border and has seen an increase of 60,000 in its Hispanic population in the 1970s, he did well among Mexican voters. Conventional wisdom has it that Mexican–Americans vote heavily Democratic, and in many elections they do; but not in all. Van Deerlin evidently took the Mexican–American vote for granted. Hunter went out and talked to Mexican–

American voters, in identifiably Mexican neighborhoods and in working- and middle-class neighborhoods where Hispanics live unobtrusively among people with English-speaking backgrounds; and so he won many of their votes. He carried National City, which is 38% Hispanic, and did well in other Hispanic areas.

Hunter serves on the Armed Services Committee, an assignment he received over fellow San Diego freshman Bill Lowery, who has a more Republican seat. In his first months, Hunter got some pet projects for the San Diego area—a shipbuilding contract for a 100-knot craft and stopping sale of a destroyer to Ecuador after Ecuador seized a San Diego fishing boat.

Redistricting is a subject of some interest in San Diego County. Democrats at least theoretically control the process. Some Democrats want to make Hunter's district more Democratic although it is hard to see how they can, except for dropping Coronado, which casts only 7,000 votes anyway; other Democrats want to create a central San Diego district. That seems hardly likely: the biggest population growth in the area has been in the eastern and northern suburbs, which are heavily Republican; and any new district would lose at least some Democratic territory to the 42d. In all likelihood there will be two districts pretty much resembling the current 41st and 42d; and while the Democrats will certainly give Hunter a strong challenge, he has significant assets and has a good chance of holding on.

Census Data Pop. (1980 final) 549,981, up 18% in 1970s. Median family income, 1970, $8,960, 93% of U.S.

The Voters

Employment profile 1970   White collar, 46%. Blue collar, 36%. Service, 17%. Farm, 1%.
Ethnic groups   Black 1980, 13%. Hispanic 1980, 27%. Am. Ind. 1980, 1%. Asian 1980, 8%. Total foreign stock 1970, 23%. Canada, 2%; UK, Germany, Italy, 1% each.

Presidential Vote

1980	Reagan (R)	79,670	(53%)
	Carter (D)	55,380	(37%)
	Anderson (I)	12,636	(8%)
1976	Ford (R)	62,460	(46%)
	Carter (D)	69,939	(52%)

Rep. Duncan L. Hunter (R) Elected 1980; b. May 31, 1948, Riverside; home, Coronado; U. of Mont., 1967-68, U. of Cal., Santa Barbara, 1968-69, Western St. U., J.D. 1976.

Career Army, Vietnam; Practicing atty., 1976-80.

Offices 415 CHOB, 202-225-5672. Also 2530 Highland Ave., National City 92050, 714-474-8554.

Committee *Armed Services* (17th). Subcommittees: Military Personnel and Compensation; Procurement and Military Nuclear Systems.

Group Ratings and Key Votes: Newly Elected

Election Results

1980 general	Duncan L. Hunter (R)	79,713	(53%)	($208,596)
	Lionel Van Deerlin (D)..........	69,936	(47%)	($140,557)
1980 primary	Duncan L. Hunter (R)	15,870	(52%)	
	Michael T. McGuillen (R)	14,681	(48%)	($0)
1978 general	Lionel Van Deerlin (D)..........	85,126	(74%)	($72,903)
	Lawrence C. Mattera (R)	30,319	(26%)	($16,833)

FORTY-THIRD DISTRICT

One of the fastest-growing metropolitan areas in the United States during the 1970s was San Diego. The nature of its growth is suggested by one of its most famous residents, Reagan top aide Edwin Meese. After Reagan finished his second term as governor, Meese, rather than return to the San Francisco Bay area, where he had deep roots, decided to move to a suburb of San Diego instead. Meese is a man passionately interested in law enforcement and deeply respectful of the military; the Bay area, in 1974, was a place that seemed contemptuous of such attitudes, while they were still the views of the solid majority in San Diego. The Bay Area had communities with their own little liberation movements, gay rights activists, militant labor unions, plus rainy winters. San Diego had and has the West Coast's Navy headquarters, pleasant suburbs nestled between mountains, one of the world's most famous zoos, and a warm, sunny climate year round. Meese settled in one of the inland suburbs — places if anything more conservative than the high-income neighborhoods near the ocean — and taught law enforcement at a local university. The calmness and certainty of Meese's conservative views may derive at least in part from the serene atmosphere of San Diego in the late 1970s.

Meese's San Diego is part of the 43d congressional district, now with the largest population in California, and one of the four largest in the nation. The 43d includes the eastern suburbs of San Diego, e.g., El Cajon, the high-income La Jolla neighborhood in the northern part of the city, and the retirement communities in the northern part of San Diego County, between the city and the Marine Corps's Camp Pendleton. The 43d also extends far into the desert, to take in Imperial County, an agricultural county dependent almost entirely on cheap federal irrigation water and cheap migrant Mexican labor.

This is a heavily Republican area, which during the 1970s betrayed no signs of drifting to the left. The vast migration here, which nearly doubled the district's population, was obviously made up of people like Edwin Meese, above average in income, articulate, secure in their Republicanism. The local congressman, since a suburban San Diego district was first created in 1972, is Clare Burgener, a Republican of pretty much impeccable conservative credentials. A member of the Appropriations Committee, he seems to specialize quietly in matters related to the environment and development of resources. Burgener appears to be well respected by colleagues and constituents and is reelected by huge margins.

In 1980 the congressional race here attracted some notice, when the Democratic nomination was won by a member of the Ku Klux Klan. Actually this was an event of no significance; the only thing it showed was that there is never any serious competition for the Democratic nomination in such a heavily Republican district. Burgener got somewhat more votes than usual, as well as the endorsement of Democrat Senator Alan Cranston, among others. To contend, however, that the votes cast for the Democratic nominee represented support of the Klan would be absurd. The 43d is large enough for 1.65 House districts, and so suburban San Diego County will in effect be given a second district in 1982. No one doubts that both seats will be very Republican.

Census Data Pop. (1980 final) 866,687, up 87% in 1970s. Median family income, 1970, $9,995, 104% of U.S.

The Voters

Employment profile 1970 White collar, 52%. Blue collar, 30%. Service, 13%. Farm, 5%.
Ethnic groups Black 1980, 2%. Hispanic 1980, 15%. Am. Ind. 1980, 1%. Asian 1980, 3%. Total foreign stock 1970, 22%. Canada, UK, Germany, 2% each.

Presidential Vote

1980	Reagan (R)	232,808	(66%)
	Carter (D)	83,335	(24%)
	Anderson (I)	28,281	(8%)
1976	Ford (R)	159,790	(59%)
	Carter (D)	106,706	(39%)

Rep. Clair W. Burgener (R) Elected 1972; b. Dec. 5, 1921, Vernal, Utah; home, Rancho Santa Fe; San Diego St. U., A.B. 1950.

Career Army Air Corps, WWII; Pres. and Owner, Clair W. Burgener, Realtors, 1947–72; San Diego City Cncl., 1953–57, Vice Mayor, 1955–56; Cal. Assembly, 1963–67; Cal. Senate, 1967–73.

Offices 343 CHOB, 202-225-3906. Also Rm. 5(S)35, 880 Front St., San Diego 92188, 714-231-1912.

Committee *Appropriations* (11th). Subcommittees: Energy and Water Development; Legislative; Military Construction.

Group Ratings

	ADA	COPE	PC	LCV	CFA	RPN	NAB	NSI	NTU	ACA	ACU
1980	6	10	20	26	14	—	92	100	54	86	89
1979	16	20	13	20	4	—	—	—	75	96	95
1978	10	11	5	23	9	60	100	100	24	88	86

Key Votes

1) Draft Registn $	FOR	6) Fair Hsg DOJ Enfrc	AGN	11) Cut Socl Incr Dfns $	FOR
2) Ban $ to Nicrgua	FOR	7) Lim PAC Contrbtns	AGN	12) Hosptl Cost Controls	AGN
3) Dlay MX Missile	AGN	8) Cap on Food Stmp $	FOR	13) Gasln Ctrls & Allctns	AGN
4) Nuclr Mortorium	AGN	9) New US Dep Edcatn	AGN	14) Lim Wndfll Prof Tax	FOR
5) Alaska Lands Bill	FOR	10) Cut OSHA $		FOR	15) Chryslr Loan Grntee	AGN

Election Results

1980 general	Clair W. Burgener (R)	299,037	(87%)	($175,009)
	Tom Metzger (D)	46,383	(13%)	($26,003)
1980 primary	Clair W. Burgener (R)	92,931	(100%)	
1978 general	Clair W. Burgener (R)	167,150	(69%)	($90,072)
	Ruben B. Brooks (D)	76,308	(31%)	($8,511)

COLORADO

For those who still, in days of 55-mile-per-hour speed limits and high gasoline prices, drive cars across the country, Colorado is an unforgettable experience. After days of traveling through flat, sometimes gently rolling plains, lands that grow drier and browner and emptier as you go west, you go around a curve and over a slight rise and suddenly there it is: the Front Range of the Rockies, towering nearly 10,000 feet over the brown plateau. The eastern half of Colorado is part of the High Plains, sparsely populated grazing land with low rainfall; the western half is part of the Rocky Mountains, with dozens of peaks over 10,000 feet and grimy mining towns and glistening resort villages nestled in the valleys. But neither of these forbidding terrains is home to the civilization Colorado has become; the culture and economy of Colorado are based on the thin margin of land where they collide, where the plains dramatically give way to the mountains. In a 30-mile strip directly east of the Front Range live more than two-thirds of the people of Colorado, and here is where people have been flocking in such numbers, to make Colorado one of the nation's fastest growing states in the 1970s, when the state's population rose by nearly 700,000 to nearly 3 million. Metropolitan Denver, with more than half of the state's population, is the center, but there is an urbanized strip moving north through Boulder to the smaller cities of Greeley and Fort Collins and south through Colorado Springs to the old steel mill town of Pueblo.

Some national commentators see Colorado as a kind of wave of the future. The economic growth that is so apparent in the gleaming high rises of Denver contrasts with the sagging condition of so many industrial cities in the East and Midwest. Denver has become, as much as Houston or Dallas, an energy center where one can find the services and tools necessary to drill for oil or process shale or mine uranium. Denver is also a city that has grown because of new technology, with little companies that no one has ever heard of, adding up to a critical mass that, if it does not rival the Silicon Valley south of San Francisco, nonetheless is of considerable national importance. Historically, much of Colorado politics has involved the farmers on the plains (the Eastern Slope of the Rockies) struggling to get water from the mountaineers of the Western Slope. The Eastern Slope's success is memorialized in the naming of Denver's airport for Ben Stapleton, who got Western Slope water for Denver. While such battles remain important—Colorado reacted angrily to President Carter's decision to cancel some water projects here in 1977—most Colorado residents no longer focus on such parochial matters. Their economic prosperity leaves them freer to look at national issues from a broader and more disinterested perspective. The result has been a politics that is ideological in tone, that tends to be dominated by citizen volunteers, and that sometimes anticipates national trends.

It is also a politics that has seemed to swing wildly from right to left and then back to the right. Colorado Republicans, for example, had a big year in 1962; but the national swing to the kind of Goldwater politics they favored did not materialize soon after. Democrats, with special emphasis on environmental issues, were able to win major victories in 1972 and 1974.

The initial impulse for this movement came from a referendum to cut off state funding for the Winter Olympics, scheduled for 1976; the referendum's organizers, including Sam Brown and David Mixner, argued that the Olympics would be too expensive, would destroy much of Colorado's environment, and would benefit only a few businessmen and developers. Voters agreed; the 1976 Winter Olympics were held in Innsbruck, Austria. In the same year as the referendum, 1972, Floyd Haskell, an antiwar-Republican-turned-Democrat, was elected to the Senate, and liberal Patricia Schroeder ousted a Republican from the House in Denver. Two years later, Democrats swept the state. Dick Lamm, a young state legislator, was elected governor; Sam Brown, one of the leaders of the antiwar moratorium and of the Colorado anti-Olympics movement, became state treasurer; Gary Hart, George McGovern's national manager in 1972, was elected U.S. senator.

All these Democratic victories represented the triumph of a particular kind of political activist. Lamm's background is typical: a backpacker and mountain climber, he was educated in Wisconsin and California, calls himself a Unitarian, and taught in a university. These are college-educated people, often from affluent backgrounds, for whom environmental issues are more important than New Deal economics. The young newcomers to Colorado, themselves affluent and attracted to the state by its opportunities for outdoor activity, identified with the young Democrats' positions on cultural issues. Gary Hart's 1974 slogan made the identification explicit: "They've had their turn; now it's our turn."

But it has not turned out to be their turn, at least not without some serious competition. In his first two years in office, Governor Lamm reversed himself on important issues and feuded with the legislature and the press; Republicans regained control of the legislature in 1976 and have held it ever since. Colorado went solidly for Gerald Ford (now a part-time resident of the ski resort of Vail) and soured quickly on President Carter. After his water projects veto, his popularity never recovered, and he won only 31% of the vote in 1980. The Democrats lost Senator Floyd Haskell's seat by a wide margin in 1978 and nearly lost two congressional seats as well. And Lamm held onto the governorship that year more because of his opponent's mistakes (he favored phasing out a Denver Air Force base and opposed locating a solar energy research center in Denver) than because of his own affirmative popularity.

Yet 1980, so disastrous to Democrats elsewhere, was not nearly so bad for them in Colorado. Senator Hart was reelected, albeit by a narrow margin, and the two congressmen nearly beaten in 1978 won by wide margins. Meanwhile, Democrats lost only one seat in the state legislature. Among the reasons: the strength of major Democratic candidates, who built up their own volunteer organizations; the fact that local Democrats had long since established distance from the Carter Administration; the fact that much of the energy of the state's leading Republicans, such as beer maker Joseph Coors and his wife Holly, was directed into the Reagan campaign; and the lack of enthusiasm among most Republicans for the party's Senate nominee, Mary Estill Buchanan. Still, this has to be counted a Republican state in national politics, and it appears that politicians who believe in Ronald Reagan's policies—a good example is the state's junior senator, Bill Armstrong—have succeeded in winning the battle of ideas among Colorado's young voters.

But the Republicans have failed to oust Dick Lamm, who epitomizes the state's younger Democrats. Lamm was one of the leaders of the anti-Olympics movement and was the sponsor of the liberalized abortion law Colorado passed before the Supreme Court assumed superintendency of such legislation. First elected at age 39, he took a while to grow into the office; and he did so largely by skirting controversy and muting his own strong stands on cultural issues. He was helped by the Carter Administration — helped, because he vigorously opposed some of its water and environmental policies and thus assumed the mantle of Colorado's fighter against the federal government. He won in 1978 because of his opponent's mistakes and perhaps because his opponent's background (born in Texas, Baptist, successful oil-related business, occasional Sunday preacher) is less congenial to most Coloradans than Lamm's. He is expected to seek a third term in 1982 and by 1981 seemed more popular and less controversial than he had been since taking office. This is a state where Republicans have considerable strength, however. A sizable field is expected to seek the Republican nomination against Lamm, and it is entirely possible that the winner of the state's September primary will be a formidable opponent.

Gary Hart is now Colorado's senior senator and one of the few Democratic survivors of the 1980 Reagan landslide. For a while in 1980 it appeared he might lose. His Republican opponent, Mary Estill Buchanan, had gotten on the primary ballot only at the last minute, mostly because, as a moderate, she could not win 20% of the support at the Republican state nominating convention. She thereby became a heroine to some, although why a politician should be admired for wanting to get on the ballot is unclear. Buchanan as a candidate was woefully unprepared to deal with the issues; yet as a moderate and a woman in a Republican year she had a certain appeal.

Hart won not so much because of last-minute campaigning but as the result of seven years of groundwork. Like many young congressmen, he had returned to the state many times. His issue positions were in line with Colorado's in most respects, not because he changed stands at the last minute, but because he had been developing for years a different philosophy from that of McGovern and other older liberals. Hart was against price controls on oil and gas, for example, and in favor of some lowering of taxes for business. He opposed cutting off Colorado water projects. Most interestingly for a senator whose major political activity was on behalf of opponents of the Vietnam war, Hart took a seat on the Senate Armed Services Committee and delved deep into military policy. He became a somewhat original thinker on the committee. He supported the SALT II and Panama Canal Treaties, for example, but, unlike other Democrats, seemed to spend more time on combat readiness and strengthening the Navy. He is one who argues that the military relies too much on overly sophisticated equipment and yet is greatly underfunded elsewhere. He favors a larger Navy composed of a large number of small ships with new-technology weapons. He is a strong supporter of vertical- and short-takeoff aircraft for aircraft carriers. He is the major proponent of a theory of warfare that emphasizes throwing the enemy's commanders off guard by harrying them constantly — the tactics of Hitler's Panzer divisions when they overran France —and he believes that military officers should spend less time on bureaucratic tactics and more time studying historic military strategy. After the 1980 election he took the unusual step of signing up, at age 43, in the Naval Reserve. He has displayed the same talent for getting at first principles in his work on subcommittees on intelligence and nuclear power. Like most of the Democratic activists from whose ranks he sprang, he is skeptical about nuclear power, but he is also well informed and prepared to admit that the case for nuclear power has much to say for it. He also is likely to take a major role in revising the Clean Air Act in 1981. Hart was chairman of the commission to set up to monitor the implementation of this complicated legislation and has wide knowledge in this field; Denver, as it happens, also has one of the nation's worst air pollution problems.

Hart's heterodox views were already apparent in Colorado in 1974, when he won with 57% against a Republican incumbent, and apparent also when he survived in 1980, although only by a 50%–49% margin over Buchanan. Now suddenly a minority senator, he will probably be less important legislatively than he has been, although his expertise on military and other issues should give him much to do. Hart is one of the more thoughtful senators and also one of the more ambitious; he is one of those Democrats who has the potential to become a presidential candidate. It should not be forgotten that Hart as much as anyone devised the strategy that won George McGovern the Democratic nomination in 1972, and he has shown himself well able to adapt to different circumstances.

Bill Armstrong, Colorado's other senator, bears superficial resemblances to Hart. His background is in the ideological part of his party, in his case Republican; he was born the same year, 1937; he also won his seat by beating an incumbent senator with 59% of the vote. More than that, Armstrong remains identified today with the wing of the party he began with; but, then, many if not most Coloradans remain conservative Republicans on the major issues as well. Armstrong ran as an advocate of lower federal spending and a stronger defense; he was not as strong a backer of environmental causes as most Colorado Democrats but claimed to be environmentally minded as well. Armstrong's campaign was smoothly and competently run, and while he had some disappointments in 1980 — he backed former Georgian and former Army Secretary Bo Callaway in the primary, then backed Buchanan in the general against Hart — he does not appear to be in political trouble in Colorado.

The Republican victories of 1980 have catapulted Armstrong from the position of a junior minority member to that of a middle seniority member of the majority. He is in fact the second ranking Republican on the Budget Committee — an excellent position to put into effect his cut-spending policies.

Armstrong is also a member of the Finance Committee and chairs its Social Security Subcommittee. This could be one of the Senate's most demanding assignments. Social Security's problems in early 1981 did not seem immediately pressing, but everyone knows that the program will be in serious financial problems sooner or later. Armstrong has a subcommittee filled with thoughtful and knowledgeable members; will this be one occasion when Congress acts in advance of crisis rather than afterward? Rounding out his committee assignments is Banking; this is one senator very definitely concentrating on economic issues.

Colorado's fast-increasing population has resulted in the state getting an additional House seat in 1982. The current members, to judge from 1980 results, seem to have made all their seats safe; but over a ten-year period even the safest of seats has been known to get unsteady, and that can easily happen in a state where the political fashion changes as quickly as it sometimes has in Colorado. With the legislature Republican and the governor Democratic, the likeliest result is a plan that safeguards all the incumbents and which makes the new district, probably centered in the Denver suburbs, up for grabs — although given the political complexion of the Denver suburbs, it will probably lean Republican.

Census Data   Pop. (1980 final) 2,888,834, up 31% in 1970s: 1.28% of U.S. total, 28th largest. Central city, 34%; suburban, 46%. Median 4-person family income, 1978, $21,778, 107% of U.S., 10th highest.

1979 Share of Federal Tax Burden $5,545,000,000; 1.23% of U.S. total, 26th largest.

1979 Share of Federal Outlays $6,210,679,000; 1.34% of U.S. total, 26th largest.

DOD	$1,510,544,000	23d	(1.42%)	HEW	$1,687,845,000	35th	(0.94%)
DOE	$284,338,000	17th	(2.41%)	ERDA	$65,031,000	10th	(2.39%)
HUD	$61,386,000	30th	(0.93%)	NASA	$60,247,000	14th	(1.29%)
VA	$275,695,000	30th	(1.33%)	DOT	$346,767,000	15th	(2.10%)
EPA	$59,667,000	28th	(1.12%)	DOC	$108,636,000	9th	(3.43%)
DOI	$347,624,000	5th	(6.26%)	USDA	$497,728,000	19th	(2.06%)

Economic Base   Finance, insurance, and real estate; agriculture, notably cattle, wheat, dairy products, and corn; food and kindred products; machinery, especially electronic computing equipment; electrical equipment and supplies, especially electronic measuring instruments; printing and publishing, especially newspapers; tourism.

Political Lineup   Governor, Richard D. Lamm (D). Senators, Gary W. Hart (D) and William L. Armstrong (R). Representatives, 5 (3 D and 2 R); 6 in 1982. State Senate, 35 (20 R and 15 D); State House of Representatives, 65 (38 R and 27 D).

The Voters

Registration   1,434,257 Total. 455,825 D (32%); 439,610 R (31%); 538,822 unaffiliated (38%).
Employment profile 1970   White collar, 54%. Blue collar, 28%. Service, 14%. Farm, 4%.
Ethnic groups   Total foreign stock 1970, 13%. Germany, 2%; UK, USSR, 1% each.
Presidential Vote

1980	Reagan (R)	652,264	(55%)
	Carter (D)	368,009	(31%)
	Anderson (I)	130,633	(11%)
1976	Ford (R)	584,278	(54%)
	Carter (D)	460,801	(43%)

SENATORS

Sen. Gary W. Hart (D) Elected 1974, seat up 1986; b. Nov. 28, 1937, Ottawa, Kans.; home, Denver; Bethany Col., Yale U., LL.B. 1964.

Career   Atty., U.S. Dept. of Justice; Special Asst. to U.S. Secy. of Interior; Practicing atty., 1967–74; Natl. Campaign Dir., McGovern for Pres., 1971–72.

Offices   221 RSOB, 202-224-5852. Also 1748 High St., Denver 80218, 303-837-4421, and 303 Fed. Bldg., Pueblo 81003, 303-544-5277, ext. 355.

Committees   *Armed Services* (6th). Subcommittees: Military Construction; Strategic and Theatre Nuclear Forces; Sea Power and Force Projection.

Budget (6th).

Environment and Public Works (4th). Subcommittees: Environmental Pollution; Nuclear Regulation.

Group Ratings

	ADA	COPE	PC	LCV	CFA	RPN	NAB	NSI	NTU	ACA	ACU
1980	61	47	70	73	53	—	42	30	48	36	35
1979	58	88	78	—	52	—	—	9	31	15	27
1978	65	78	70	93	55	67	27	10	—	17	8

Key Votes

1) Draft Registn $	AGN	6) Fair Housng Cloture	FOR	11) Cut Socl Incr Defns	FOR
2) Ban $ to Nicrgua	—	7) Ban $ Rape Abortns	AGN	12) Income Tax Indexing	FOR
3) Dlay MX Missile	—	8) Cap on Food Stmp $	AGN	13) Lim Spdg 21% GNP	AGN
4) Nuclr Mortorium	FOR	9) New US Dep Edcatn	FOR	14) Incr Wndfll Prof Tax	FOR
5) Alaska Lands Bill	—	10) Cut OSHA Inspctns	FOR	15) Chryslr Loan Grntee	AGN

Election Results

1980 general	Gary W. Hart (D)..............	590,501	(50%)	($1,142,304)
	Mary Estill Buchanan (R)	571,295	(49%)	($1,099,945)
1980 primary	Gary W. Hart (D)..............	105,592	(100%)	
1974 general	Gary W. Hart (D)..............	471,691	(57%)	($352,557)
	Peter H. Dominick (R)..........	325,508	(39%)	($502,343)

Sen. William L. Armstrong (R) Elected 1978, seat up 1984; b. Mar. 16, 1937, Fremont, Neb.; home, Aurora; Tulane U., U. of Minn.

Career Pres., KOSI Radio, Aurora; Colo. House of Reps., 1963–64; Colo. Senate, 1965–72, Major. Ldr., 1969–72; U.S. House of Reps., 1973–78.

Offices 1321 DSOB, 202-224-5941. Also Suite 736, 1450 S. Havana, Aurora 80012, 303-837-2655.

Committees *Banking, Housing, and Urban Affairs* (4th). Subcommittees: Housing and Urban Affairs; International Finance and Monetary Policy; Economic Policy (Chairman).

Budget (2d).

Finance (9th). Subcommittees: Taxation and Debt Management; International Trade; Social Security and Income Maintenance Programs (Chairman).

Group Ratings

	ADA	COPE	PC	LCV	CFA	RPN	NAB	NSI	NTU	ACA	ACU
1980	17	5	20	27	0	—	100	90	75	92	100
1979	11	0	26	—	10	—	—	—	72	100	91
1978	5	6	8	—	9	43	100	90	—	92	89

Key Votes

1) Draft Registn $	AGN	6) Fair Housng Cloture	AGN	11) Cut Socl Incr Defns	FOR
2) Ban $ to Nicrgua	AGN	7) Ban $ Rape Abortns	FOR	12) Income Tax Indexing	FOR
3) Dlay MX Missile	—	8) Cap on Food Stmp $	FOR	13) Lim Spdg 21% GNP	FOR
4) Nuclr Mortorium	AGN	9) New US Dep Edcatn	AGN	14) Incr Wndfll Prof Tax	AGN
5) Alaska Lands Bill	AGN	10) Cut OSHA Inspctns	FOR	15) Chryslr Loan Grntee	AGN

Election Results

1978 general	William L. Armstrong (R)	480,596	(59%)	($1,081,944)
	Floyd K. Haskell (D)	330,247	(40%)	($664,249)
1978 primary	William L. Armstrong (R)	109,021	(73%)	
	Jack Swigert (R)	39,415	(27%)	($321,545)
1972 general	Floyd K. Haskell (D)	457,545	(49%)	($176,234)
	Gordon Allott (R)..............	447,957	(48%)	($308,305)

GOVERNOR

Gov. Richard D. Lamm (D) Elected 1974, term expires Jan. 1983; b. Aug. 3, 1935, U. of Wis., B.B.A. 1957, U. of Cal., LL.B. 1961.

Career CPA, 1961–62; Atty., Colo. Anti-Discrimination Comm., 1962–63; Practicing atty., 1963–75; Colo. House of Reps., 1966–75, Major. Ldr., 1971–75; Assoc. Prof. of Law, U. of Denver, 1969–75.

Offices Rm. 136, State Capitol, Denver 80203, 303-866-2471.

Election Results

1978 gen.	Richard D. Lamm (D)	483,885	(59%)
	Ted Strickland (R)	317,232	(39%)
1978 prim.	Richard Lamm (D), unopp.		
1974 gen.	Richard D. Lamm (D)	444,199	(53%)
	John D. Vanderhoof (R) . . .	378,907	(46%)

FIRST DISTRICT

Within sight—except on days when the smog is bad—of the Front Range of the Rockies is the mile-high city of Denver. It got its start serving the needs of local gold miners and cattle ranchers; today it is the service and distribution center for the entire Rocky Mountain region and a major regional center for energy exploration and development. Denver is the largest metropolitan area in the Rocky Mountain states, in fact the largest, except for Houston and Dallas–Fort Worth, between the Mississippi River and the West Coast. Over the past several years downtown Denver has sprouted a dozen or more steel-and-glass high rises, and more seem to be going up all the time. Denver has an old stockyard, some grimy warehouse districts, and plenty of light manufacturing. It also has its unpleasant slums; but for the most part this seems to be a carefully manicured city, with neighborhoods of small, carefully tended houses on pleasant streets. One reason for its orderliness is the external environment: the high plains cannot be littered with jerry-built houses because you can build only where there is water, and water is very carefully allocated in Denver.

The same environment that imposes the form of Denver's development is also what attracts people most to the city. People here like to think of themselves as close to nature; they are weekend backpackers, winter skiers, and amateur mountain climbers. God's own environment here, after all, is closer than in most cities—as close as the mountains rising in the distance, or as close as the line dividing a grassy, treed subdivision from the brown, barren High Plains. The change from developed land to natural is so abrupt here that one can hardly fail to know what this place was like before man built on it; and, for many, from that knowledge comes the desire to preserve from development in the years ahead what is still pristine.

The environmental impulse is usually stronger in such cities as Denver than it is in smaller towns, where people feel they may gain economically from new development. And it is this impulse, as much as anything else, that is responsible for the election of Denver's Congresswoman Patricia Schroeder. For 20 years Denver was represented by a conventional Democrat, who was upset in the 1970 primary by one of those young environmental-minded, antiwar activists who have since become so prominent in Colorado politics. The Republican

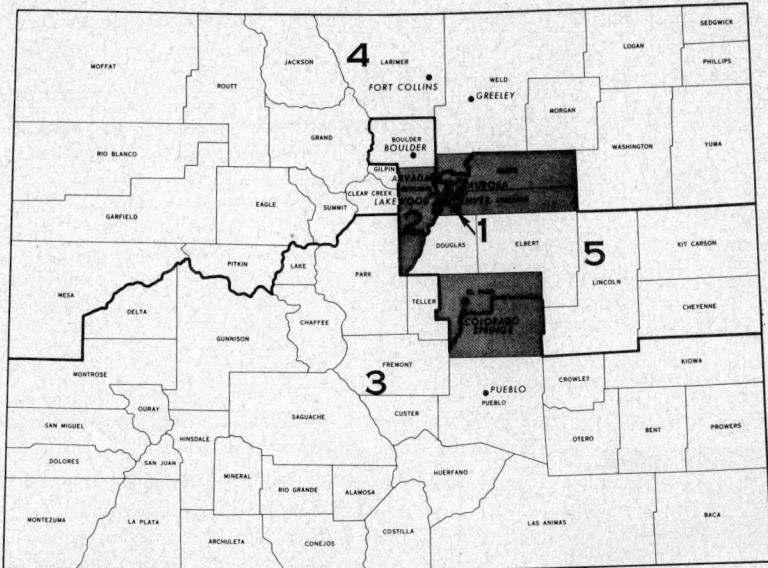

won the general election that year, in large part because of resentment over a busing order; but Schroeder came back and beat him in 1972. Her slogan — "If she wins, we win" — captured the identification with young Denverites who cared about issues other politicians seemed to shun.

Since 1972, despite the ups and downs of Colorado politics, Schroeder has won reelection by large margins (except for 1976, when she had 54%). Her district, the Colorado 1st, includes not quite all of the city of Denver; it is the most Democratic of the state's districts and went for Carter in 1976 (but not in 1980). In 1980 her opponent, a Republican woman who is part Mexican–American and part Indian, won less than 40% of the vote. What is likely to happen in redistricting is the addition to the district of the portion of the city of Denver that is now part of the 2d district, a heavily Democratic Chicano area the Republican legislature would probably like to take away from 2d district Democrat Tim Wirth; it will only make Schroeder's seat safer.

In Washington, Schroeder won a seat on the Armed Services Committee, initially over the objections of then Chairman F. Edward Hebert of Louisiana. Her inclination, stemming from her opposition to the Vietnam war, is to look on military expenditures skeptically and to seek ways they may be reduced. On this committee there has never been more than a small minority that has taken her view, and today they are a small body indeed, as national attention is directed at the question of how American military strength can be augmented. On Armed Services Schroeder concentrates on personnel matters, particularly those affecting women (such as military pensions); she has been active in efforts to get chemical weaponry out of the Rocky Mountain Arsenal near Denver.

Schroeder, like many other Democrats of her generation, is not necessarily a follower of the liberal position on every economic issue, and in the 96th Congress she was attacked by Ralph Nader for opposing what he considered to be consumer legislation. Such attacks do not seem to have diminished Schroeder's support among the voters of the 1st district or the allegiance she has from her core of volunteer supporters.

Census Data   Pop. (1980 final) 426,794, down 3% in 1970s. Median family income, 1970, $9,777, 104% of U.S.

The Voters

Employment profile 1970   White collar, 61%. Blue collar, 24%. Service, 15%. Farm, –%.
Ethnic groups   Black 1980, 14%. Hispanic 1980, 15%. Am. Ind. 1980, 1%. Asian 1980, 1%. Total foreign stock 1970, 17%. Germany, USSR, UK, 2% each.

Presidential Vote

1980	Reagan (R)	81,924	(43%)
	Carter (D)	76,017	(40%)
	Anderson (I)	27,046	(14%)
1976	Ford (R)	93,723	(48%)
	Carter (D)	93,764	(48%)

Rep. Patricia Schroeder (D) Elected 1972; b. July 30, 1940, Portland, Oreg.; home, Denver; U. of Minn., B.S. 1861, Harvard U., J.D. 1964.

Career   Field Atty., Natl. Labor Relations Bd., 1964–66; Practicing atty.; Lecturer and Law Instructor, Community Col. of Denver, 1969–70, U. of Denver, Denver Ctr., 1969, Regis Col., 1970–72; Hearing Officer, Colo. Dept. of Personnel, 1971–72; Legal Counsel, Colo. Planned Parenthood.

Offices   2410 RHOB, 202-225-4431. Also Denver Fed. Bldg., 1767 High St., Denver 80218, 303-837-2354.

Committees   *Armed Services* (12th). Subcommittees: Readiness; Research and Development.

Judiciary (12th). Subcommittees: Civil and Constitutional Rights; Immigration, Refugees and International Law.

Post Office and Civil Service (4th). Subcommittee: Civil Service (Chairwoman).

Group Ratings

	ADA	COPE	PC	LCV	CFA	RPN	NAB	NSI	NTU	ACA	ACU
1980	94	56	53	85	71	—	20	0	30	25	17
1979	79	65	53	74	33	—	—	—	63	42	25
1978	85	85	78	80	55	50	33	0	57	37	13

Key Votes

1) Draft Registn $	AGN	6) Fair Hsg DOJ Enfrc	FOR	11) Cut Socl Incr Dfns $	AGN
2) Ban $ to Nicrgua	AGN	7) Lim PAC Contrbtns	FOR	12) Hosptl Cost Controls	—
3) Dlay MX Missile	FOR	8) Cap on Food Stmp $	AGN	13) Gasln Ctrls & Allctns	AGN
4) Nuclr Mortorium	FOR	9) New US Dep Edcatn	AGN	14) Lim Wndfll Prof Tax	FOR
5) Alaska Lands Bill	FOR	10) Cut OSHA $	AGN	15) Chryslr Loan Grntee	AGN

Election Results

1980 general	Patricia Schroeder (D)	107,364	(60%)	($181,299)
	Naomi Bradford (R)	67,804	(38%)	($118,417)
1980 primary	Patricia Schroeder (D)	15,215	(100%)	
1978 general	Patricia Schroeder (D)	82,742	(62%)	($119,930)
	Gene Hutcheson (R)	49,845	(37%)	($146,210)

SECOND DISTRICT

In 1974 many districts that had regularly elected Republican congressmen chose Democrats instead. Most of these Democrats have been reelected, even in the Republican year of 1980, and they changed the partisan balance and tone of the House notably in the late 1970s. One such constituency is the 2d district of Colorado which in the past four elections has chosen Congressman Timothy Wirth, who was one of the original leaders of the 1974 freshman class and in many ways personifies it.

The 2d is a varied district, made up of three distinct parts. First there is Jefferson County, just west of Denver and its fastest-growing suburban area, a place where young engineers and accountants and office clerks and assembly line workers and their families have been settling within clear sight (on most days) of the Front Range. Affluent, upwardly mobile, home of the Reagan-boosting Coors brewery family, Jefferson County is usually solidly Republican. Second there is Boulder County, with the University of Colorado dominating the neat town just at the base of a mountain. In outward appearance Boulder is All-American enough to have been chosen as the home of *Mork and Mindy,* and is collegiate enough to be home to Celestial Seasonings tea; politically, it has been the scene of battles between Republicans, who traditionally carried it, and liberal Democrats, who can win when they mobilize and motivate the students. The third part of the district is a small Mexican–American neighborhood on the west side of Denver, which casts only 7% of the district's vote but produces large enough Democratic margins to make a political difference.

When Tim Wirth decided to run in 1974, it was apparent that the district was moving in his direction. Environmental issues — e.g., the 1972 referendum on the Winter Olympics — definitely favored the Democrats. With Boulder's newly enfranchised students suddenly capable of producing Democratic margins, the Republican incumbent was in trouble; and, although he knew it, there was not much he could do about it. Wirth, a 35-year-old management consultant and former White House fellow, was an attractive candidate and won.

Once elected, Wirth was one of the leaders of the 1974 Freshman Caucus. Previous freshman class organizations had been social; this one had a real effect. It insisted on better committee assignments and pushed for ouster of some committee chairmen. The effect continues to be felt in the House, even after the 1980 election; chairmen know that they are accountable to their fellow members and no longer feel free to act as arbitrarily as some did in the past.

Wirth, like many of the other 1974 freshmen, has not had the kind of voting record one expects from older northern Democrats. On cultural or noneconomic issues, he is more dependably on what is called the liberal side; but on economic issues, he questions liberal orthodoxy and can be convinced to line up with Republicans. Thus he has supported legislation backed by environmentalists, and he has also supported deregulation of oil and gas prices. He opposed President Carter's energy mobilization board, because it would override state decisions. He is one of the few members to have support from both environmental activists and oil company political action committees. Wirth has been attacked by some Democrats for his positions on economic issues, but he sees no apostasy on his part: his background is in business consulting, and he is quite prepared to believe that the free market may be the best means of allocating a scarce product.

Wirth's views on these matters are of considerable importance, because he holds a pivotal seat on the House Budget Committee. He is one of the younger Democrats who may or may not go along with the Republicans on a given issue and who thus tend to determine the outcome in the House and probably the whole Congress as well. Wirth is chairman of one of what Budget calls its task forces rather than subcommittees, on Energy and the Environment, obviously a popular subject back home.

Wirth has become one of the first 1974 freshmen to win a really important subcommittee chairmanship. He is fifth in rank among Democrats on the Commerce Committee—a body of great importance, and one on which his views on oil deregulation were tested—and after the 1980 election he unexpectedly succeeded to the chair of the Communications Subcommittee. This is the body that, with its Senate counterpart, writes the laws regulating the broadcast industry. It is subject to close scrutiny by many very smart people, for broadcast licenses, which are granted by the Federal Communications Commission under laws drafted by this subcommittee, are business assets worth hundreds of millions of dollars. One assumes that, as the news came in that Lionel Van Deerlin, the former chairman, was upset in his San Diego district, Wirth immediately started receiving invitations to broadcast industry banquets and weekend seminars. Van Deerlin had proposed a major revision of communications laws, a measure that went nowhere because it had no support except from the chairman. Wirth seems more interested in reorganizing the committee's work along functional lines, to take into account technological changes, such as the development of cable television, electronic record-keeping, and on-line computer systems.

Like most 1974 freshmen, Wirth has had to work hard to hold his seat, returning to the district often, handling constituency requests, and keeping in touch with local opinion. In 1976 and 1978 he won by an uninspiring margin; in 1980 he did better, beating an uncharacteristically (for Colorado) moderate Republican (a minister who opposes the death penalty) by a 56% to 41% margin. And for the first time, Wirth carried Jefferson County. Wirth's district has grown in population substantially since 1970, and he is going to have to lose some of his territory before 1982. Most likely the Denver portion of the district will go; and geographically it might be considered logical to let most of Boulder go as well. But that would leave Republican-leaning Jefferson as almost the entire district—a result Wirth would certainly fight and which would make it very difficult for him to have a secure seat in the 1980s. The alternative may be a plan more complex geographically but more congenial politically.

Census Data   Pop. (1980 final) 629,034, up 43% in 1970s. Median family income, 1970, $11,201, 117% of U.S.

The Voters

  Employment profile 1970   White collar, 60%. Blue collar, 28%. Service, 11%. Farm, 1%.
  Ethnic groups   Black 1980, 8%. Hispanic 1980, 9%. Am. Ind. 1980, 1%. Asian 1980, 2%. Total foreign stock 1970, 12%. Germany, 2%; UK, USSR, 1% each.

Presidential Vote

1980	Reagan (R)	145,045	(54%)
	Carter (D)	81,064	(30%)
	Anderson (I)	35,369	(13%)
1976	Ford (R)	137,501	(55%)
	Carter (D)	100,538	(41%)

Rep. Timothy E. Wirth (D) Elected 1974; b. Sept. 22, 1939, Santa Fe, N.M.; home, Denver; Harvard U., A.B. 1961, M.Ed. 1964, Stanford U., Ph.D. 1973.

Career White House Fellow, Spec. Asst. to Secy. of HEW, 1967–68; Dpty. Asst. Secy. of Educ., HEW, 1969–70; Businessman, Great Western United Corp.; Mgr., Rocky Mt. Ofc., Arthur D. Little, Inc., consultants.

Offices 2454 RHOB, 202-225-2161. Also 9485 W. Colfax, Lakewood 80215, 303-234-5200.

Committees *Budget* (8th).

Energy and Commerce (5th). Subcommittees: Fossil and Synthetic Fuels; Telecommunications, Consumer Protection and Finance (Chairman).

Group Ratings

	ADA	COPE	PC	LCV	CFA	RPN	NAB	NSI	NTU	ACA	ACU
1980	78	50	57	79	71	—	25	0	19	22	21
1979	74	63	58	68	37	—	—	—	31	16	23
1978	50	65	73	77	55	75	20	22	29	23	9

Key Votes

1) Draft Registn $	FOR	6) Fair Hsg DOJ Enfrc	FOR	11) Cut Socl Incr Dfns $	AGN
2) Ban $ to Nicrgua	AGN	7) Lim PAC Contrbtns	FOR	12) Hosptl Cost Controls	FOR
3) Dlay MX Missile	FOR	8) Cap on Food Stmp $	AGN	13) Gasln Ctrls & Allctns	AGN
4) Nuclr Mortorium	FOR	9) New US Dep Edcatn	FOR	14) Lim Wndfll Prof Tax	FOR
5) Alaska Lands Bill	FOR	10) Cut OSHA $	AGN	15) Chryslr Loan Grntee	AGN

Election Results

1980 general	Timothy E. Wirth (D)...........	153,550	(56%)	($548,261)
	John McElderry (R)	111,868	(41%)	($193,072)
1980 primary	Timothy E. Wirth (D)...........	17,132	(100%)	
1978 general	Timothy E. Wirth (D)...........	98,889	(53%)	($396,798)
	Ed Scott (R)	88,072	(47%)	($554,538)

THIRD DISTRICT

The 3d congressional district of Colorado is an odd geographical combination. It looks regular enough on the map, covering roughly the southern half of the state. But anyone who knows anything about Colorado knows that the 3d spans some of the most diverse terrain in the United States. The western half of the district is entirely mountainous. This is an area with its own special needs and inclinations and its own political traditions, the so-called Western Slope of the Rockies, where almost half the district's votes are cast. There is substantial variation here: there are skiing resorts, mining towns, Indian reservations, and places where Spanish is the most commonly spoken language. East of the Front Range the mountains suddenly cease; there begin the flat plains that slope imperceptibly down hundreds of miles to the Mississippi River. Most of the voters here are concentrated in Pueblo, one of

Colorado's least glamorous cities. Blessed with a major steel mill and very little else, Pueblo is a blue collar town with a substantial Hispanic minority. The 3d also includes a small portion of Colorado Springs, a much more affluent and fast-growing town, as well as some ranching territory to the east.

The 3d gained its present shape to suit the needs of a congressman who, after some unexpected trouble, decided to retire in 1978. In partisan terms, the district is fairly evenly divided; Gerald Ford carried it by a little more than 3,000 votes in 1976 and Hubert Humphrey edged Richard Nixon here by 95 votes in 1968. In 1980, however, Ronald Reagan ran away with the election here; Carter carried Pueblo and a few Hispanic counties narrowly.

The last two elections in this district have been seriously contested races between the same two men. Ray Kogovsek, the son of a Pueblo steelworker, was minority leader of the Colorado Senate when he entered the race in 1978 with strong labor support. Kogovsek was the initial favorite. But his opponent, a much older Republican state senator, Harold McCormick, traveled around the district in his car and talked about his expertise in water policy— always an important issue in Colorado. Kogovsek outspent McCormick; nevertheless he almost got caught napping. The Democrat won by only 366 votes, making this one of the closest races in the nation.

In Washington, Kogovsek got seats on Education and Labor (where he is a solid backer of unions) and on Interior (which controls federal water policy, among other things important to Colorado). McCormick ran again in 1980 and this time had greater support from national Republican groups. But Kogovsek has also worked the district hard (his family still lives in Pueblo, and he returns often), and the incumbent managed to win by what must be counted an impressive margin indeed.

What the redistricters will do with this district is hard to predict. They could just leave it alone, or take off the portion of Colorado Springs (which Kogovsek would like; it always goes Republican). Or they could take the northern Western Slope counties and attach them to this district, and subtract some of the territory to the east. This district would be somewhat more homogeneous geographically (although Pueblo and the Western Slope are quite different places) but would be more difficult for Kogovsek to win. His 1980 margin is his strongest club, for it suggests to the Republican legislature that they will have a hard time drawing district lines that will defeat him and might just as well leave him alone and concentrate on making the state's new 6th district Republican.

Census Data   Pop. (1980 final) 516,680, up 17% in 1970s. Median family income, 1970, $7,578, 80% of U.S.

The Voters

Employment profile 1970   White collar, 43%. Blue collar, 33%. Service, 16%. Farm, 8%.
Ethnic groups   Black 1980, 3%. Hispanic 1980, 21%. Am. Ind. 1980, 2%. Asian 1980, 1%. Total foreign stock 1970, 11%. Germany, 2%.

Presidential Vote

1980	Reagan (R)	106,515	(55%)
	Carter (D)	68,918	(36%)
	Anderson (I)	13,244	(7%)
1976	Ford (R)	88,106	(50%)
	Carter (D)	84,783	(47%)

Rep. Ray Kogovsek (D) Elected 1978; b. Aug. 19, 1941, Pueblo; home, Pueblo; Pueblo Jr. Col., 1960–62, Adams St. Col., B.S. 1964.

Career Pueblo Co. Chief Dpty. Clerk, 1964–72; Colo. House of Reps., 1969–71; Colo. Senate, 1971–78, Minor. Ldr., 1973–78.

Offices 430 CHOB, 202-225-4761. Also Rm. 425 United Bank Bldg., Pueblo 81003, 303-544-5277, ext. 313.

Committees *Education and Labor* (18th). Subcommittee: Health and Safety.

Interior and Insular Affairs (20th). Subcommittees: Mines and Mining; Public Lands and National Parks; Water and Power Resources.

Public Works and Transportation (27th). Subcommittee: Surface Transportation.

Group Ratings

	ADA	COPE	PC	LCV	CFA	RPN	NAB	NSI	NTU	ACA	ACU
1980	56	72	40	44	50	—	17	20	25	22	17
1979	68	80	65	69	70	—	—	—	11	8	15

Key Votes

1) Draft Registn $	FOR	6) Fair Hsg DOJ Enfrc	AGN	11) Cut Socl Incr Dfns $	AGN
2) Ban $ to Nicrgua	AGN	7) Lim PAC Contrbtns	AGN	12) Hosptl Cost Controls	FOR
3) Dlay MX Missile	AGN	8) Cap on Food Stmp $	AGN	13) Gasln Ctrls & Allctns	FOR
4) Nuclr Mortorium	AGN	9) New US Dep Edcatn	FOR	14) Lim Wndfll Prof Tax	AGN
5) Alaska Lands Bill	FOR	10) Cut OSHA $	AGN	15) Chryslr Loan Grntee	FOR

Election Results

1980 general	Ray Kogovsek (D)	105,820	(55%)	($301,626)
	Harold L. McCormick (R)	84,292	(44%)	($255,896)
1980 primary	Ray Kogovsek (D)	36,223	(100%)	
1978 general	Ray Kogovsek (D)	69,669	(49%)	($121,323)
	Harold L. McCormick (R)	69,303	(49%)	($81,500)

FOURTH DISTRICT

The 4th congressional district of Colorado, like the 3d, is a combination of counties on the plains east of the Front Range of the Rockies with counties west of the Front Range — on the Western Slope, as they say here. But while the balance between the Western and Eastern Slope is about even in the 3d district, in the 4th it is heavily weighted toward the Eastern Slope, which is to say the thin strip of settlement where the High Plains meet the Rockies, running north from the Denver city limit to the Wyoming state line. In the early 1970s, the congressional politics here was sometimes a kind of struggle between these two regions: the voters of the heavily populated Eastern Slope, with their desire to preserve the environment, outvoted people on the Western Slope, who wanted to see development in their often economically depressed communities. The loser was the Western Slope and its then congressman, Wayne Aspinall, for more than 20 years chairman of the House Interior Committee, who was beaten in the Democratic primary in 1972.

The Eastern Slope portion of the district, however, is much more Republican than Democratic. There are some industrial suburbs just north of Denver in the district, but as one goes north the country around the small cities of Greeley and Fort Collins is pretty solidly Republican; even more so is the grazing country of the High Plains running east to the Nebraska border. This is the area that produced Jim Johnson, the Republican who represented the district from the 1972 election until his retirement in 1980 — a generally faithful Republican who nonetheless opposed the Vietnam war and voted against many military spending programs.

There was never any really heated competition for Johnson's seat. Hank Brown, a former state senator who ran for lieutenant governor in 1978, was unopposed in the Republican primary. His general election opponent, Polly Baca Barragan, had the honor of being one of the four cochairpersons of the 1980 Democratic National Convention and was also a state senator herself from a suburban Denver district. But she was vastly outfinanced, and one suspects she ran primarily less out of any feeling that she could win than because her state senate seat was not up again until 1982. In any case, Brown won by a crushing margin. Brown, a solid conservative on economic issues, differs from many other Rocky Mountain Republicans in backing the Equal Rights Amendment and opposing constitutional amendments against abortion. He was nonetheless elected president of the Republican freshman class. He serves on the Interior Committee and on the Ethics Committee — the latter an unusual assignment for a freshman. He appears to be a respected and effective representative.

Census Data   Pop. (1980 final) 664,563, up 50% in 1970s. Median family income, 1970, $8,992, 94% of U.S.

The Voters

Employment profile 1970   White collar, 47%. Blue collar, 30%. Service, 14%. Farm, 9%.
Ethnic groups   Hispanic 1980, 10%. Am. Ind. 1980, 1%. Asian 1980, 1%. Total foreign stock 1970, 12%. USSR, 3%; Germany, 2%.

Presidential Vote

1980	Reagan (R)	155,774	(58%)
	Carter (D)	74,714	(28%)
	Anderson (I)	29,035	(11%)
1976	Ford (R)	130,713	(57%)
	Carter (D)	93,021	(40%)

Rep. Hank Brown (R) Elected 1980; b. Feb. 12, 1940, Denver; home, Greeley; U. of Colo., B.S. 1961, J.D. 1969.

Career   Navy, 1962–66; Colo. Senate, 1972–76, Asst. Major. Ldr., 1974; Rep. nominee for Lt. Gov. of Colo., 1978; Greeley City Planning Commission, 1979.

Offices   1319 LHOB, 202-225-4676. Also 1015 37th Ave. Ct., Suite 101A, Greeley 80631; 303-352-4112; 203 Fed. Bldg., Ft. Collins 80521, 303-493-9132; P.O. Box 767, Ft. Morgan 80701, 303-867-8909; and Fed. Bldg., Grand Junction 81501, 303-243-1736.

Committees   *Interior and Insular Affairs* (13th). Subcommittees: Oversight and Investigations; Public Lands and National Parks.

Standards of Official Conduct (5th).

Group Ratings and Key Votes: Newly Elected

Election Results

1980 general	Hank Brown (R)	178,221	(68%)	($233,857)
	Polly Baca Barragan (D)	76,849	(30%)	($116,186)
1980 primary	Hank Brown (R)	42,666	(100%)	
1978 general	James P. Johnson (R)...........	103,121	(61%)	($92,842)
	Morgan Smith (D)	65,241	(39%)	($160,520)

FIFTH DISTRICT

The 5th congressional district of Colorado is a combination of several disparate communities, a political constituency designed carefully by a Republican legislature in 1972. The bulk of the people live in the Denver suburbs north, east, and south of the city. As one proceeds clockwise in this manner, one goes from the more Democratic communities (Commerce City plus a small chunk of Denver itself) to the middle of the road (Aurora) to the wealthy and heavily Republican (Englewood and Littleton). To the south, after traveling Interstate 25 through some residential sprawl and then some arid, empty, mile-high plateau, there is Colorado Springs. This is a well-to-do, fast-growing city, known for its military installations (the Air Force Academy, Fort Carson) and tourist attractions (Pike's Peak, the Garden of the Gods). Politically Colorado Springs is staunchly Republican and goes Democratic only in the worst Republican years, such as 1974.

The 5th also moves east to the Kansas border. It was out in this vast country that Colorado boomers, in the wake of the Gold Rush of 1858, set the cavalry on defenseless Cheyenne families in the Sand Creek massacre. Today the appearance of this part of Colorado has scarcely changed: it is a region of large cattle ranches, tumbleweed, and gas station stop towns along Interstate 70. It is generally Republican and, after flirting with Jimmy Carter in 1976, turned against him, as did most of the High Plains area, in 1980.

The first congressman from this district was Bill Armstrong, a Republican leader in the legislature that drew the lines. Regarded as a strong conservative when he was first elected, Armstrong now seems — in the context of Rocky Mountain Republicans — to be a moderate. Elected to the Senate in 1978, he is considered a reasonable and skillful legislator.

The current congressman, Ken Kramer, has the reputation of being more ideological; in the Colorado legislature he was part of a group known as "The Crazies." He seems to be one of those Republicans willing to take liberals head-on on some of the tough issues: in the Colorado legislature he pushed an antipornography law and tried to get a right-to-work law passed. In the Congress he is one of the few Republicans still in a distinct minority, as a member of the still pro-labor House Education and Labor Committee. No one can be sure what will happen to the 5th district in redistricting, but it seems almost certain that Kramer, whose base is in Colorado Springs, will have as safe a Republican seat as this one in which to run for reelection.

Census Data Pop. (1980 final) 651,763, up 48% in 1970s. Median family income, 1970, $10,278, 107% of U.S.

The Voters

Employment profile 1970 White collar, 55%. Blue collar, 29%. Service, 13%. Farm, 3%.
Ethnic groups Black 1980, 3%. Hispanic 1980, 7%. Am. Ind. 1980, 1%. Asian 1980, 1%. Total foreign stock 1970, 11%. Germany, 2%; UK, 1%.

Presidential Vote

1980	Reagan (R)	157,035	(62%)
	Carter (D)	65,175	(26%)
	Anderson (I)	25,249	(10%)
1976	Ford (R)	124,534	(58%)
	Carter (D)	82,313	(39%)

Rep. Ken Kramer (R) Elected 1978; b. Feb. 19, 1942, Chicago, Ill.; home, Colorado Springs; U. of Ill., B.A. 1963, Harvard U., J.D. 1966.

Career Army, 1967–70; Dpty. Dist. Atty., 4th Judicial Dist., Colo. Springs, 1970–72; Practicing atty., 1972–78; Colo. House of Reps., 1973–78.

Offices 114 CHOB, 202-225-4422. Also Suite C & D, 1520 N. Union Blvd., Colorado Springs 80909, 303-632-8555.

Committees *Armed Services* (16th). Subcommittees: Military Installations and Facilities; Procurement and Military Nuclear Systems.

Education and Labor (6th). Subcommittees: Health and Safety; Labor–Management Relations.

Group Ratings

	ADA	COPE	PC	LCV	CFA	RPN	NAB	NSI	NTU	ACA	ACU
1980	0	12	20	22	7	—	91	100	68	91	88
1979	5	10	13	9	0	—	—	—	67	96	95

Key Votes

1) Draft Registn $	FOR	6) Fair Hsg DOJ Enfrc	AGN
2) Ban $ to Nicrgua	FOR	7) Lim PAC Contrbtns	AGN
3) Dlay MX Missile	AGN	8) Cap on Food Stmp $	FOR
4) Nuclr Mortorium	AGN	9) New US Dep Edcatn	AGN
5) Alaska Lands Bill	AGN	10) Cut OSHA $	FOR

11) Cut Socl Incr Dfns $	FOR
12) Hosptl Cost Controls	—
13) Gasln Ctrls & Allctns	AGN
14) Lim Wndfll Prof Tax	FOR
15) Chryslr Loan Grntee	FOR

Election Results

1980 general	Ken Kramer (R)	177,319	(72%)	($247,756)
	Ed Schreiber(D)	62,003	(25%)	($3,152)
1980 primary	Ken Kramer (R)	40,857	(100%)	
1978 general	Ken Kramer (R)	91,933	(60%)	($161,413)
	Gerry Frank (D)	52,914	(34%)	($63,325)
	L. W. Dan Bridges (I)	8,933	(6%)	($43,978)

CONNECTICUT

Connecticut is a state in political transition. There are still traces left of the "Connecticut Yankee" tradition celebrated by Mark Twain. If you drive around the state, you might even think it is dominated by small, neat cities and little saltbox colonial houses, by whaling ships and low green mountains, by old Yankees with slightly dry New England accents. That old

Connecticut was characterized by a taciturn contrariness — in manners and politics. In the early days of the Republic, Connecticut stayed with the Federalist Party after it had become extinct elsewhere, and in the earlier part of this century it was loyal enough to the Republican Party — the party of its Yankee majority — to support Herbert Hoover over Franklin Roosevelt in the Depression year of 1932.

Since that time two changes have overtaken Connecticut and have changed the style and tone of life here — and its politics — often in two contrary directions. The first of these was a change in the state's ethnic composition. The Yankees who formed a majority of the state's adult population in 1932 did not then form a majority of its population of children. The immigrants — Irish and Polish and especially Italians, almost all of them Catholic — had far more children; and those children, who grew up in the factory towns of New Haven, Hartford, Bridgeport, Waterbury, New Britain, and dozens of smaller places, are now the typical Connecticut residents of today. In New England for many years politics was a matter of religion, with Protestants voting Republican and Catholics voting Democratic. In the 1950s Catholics came to be the majority of Connecticut's adult population; and in the same decade Connecticut became a dependably Democratic state for the first time. Its status as such was confirmed in the 1960 election, and not only because John Kennedy easily carried this once obdurately Republican state, but also because its governor, Abraham Ribicoff, and its Democratic Party leader, John Bailey — a Jew and a Catholic — were among Kennedy's first major supporters and the first to recognize his appeal in such states as Connecticut.

The other change that has overtaken Connecticut is economic. In 1932 this was a state still made up of early 19th-century countryside and small towns and late 19th-century industrial towns. Since that time it has become increasingly suburban. Connecticut's central cities were never very large, and as the immigrants' children grew up they spilled over into adjoining towns. The state's economy developed comfortably, with high-paying factory jobs in such places as United Technology's Pratt & Whitney engine plant in East Hartford and at Electric Boat in New London (Connecticut is one of the biggest defense contract states) and high-paying white collar jobs in the new corporate headquarters being established in Greenwich, Stamford, and Fairfield, in the corner of the state nearest New York City. For many years in the 1960s and 1970s Connecticut had the nation's highest income levels. It still ranks near the top, and if its advantage over many of the booming Sun Belt states has been lessened by high fuel costs and taxes, it still is one of the minority of states with no income tax, and it has never spawned a government bureaucracy like those of Massachusetts or New York.

These two basic trends in Connecticut have led it in different political directions — the increasing Catholic population making it more Democratic, the increasing suburbanization making it Republican — at least sometimes. In practice it is more complicated than that because, while some ethnic groups have been heavily Democratic (the Irish), others, to some extent in reaction, have been Republicans (the Italians, the largest ethnic group in the state). And while some suburbs, notably such woodsy havens of New York commuters as New Canaan and Wilton, have been heavily Republican, others are often Democratic.

As late as the 1960s, Connecticut also had some of the strongest state party organizations in the nation. The straight party lever on Connecticut's voting machines helped: for many years in order to activate the machine you had to vote a straight ticket; then, if you wanted to and could figure out how, you could go to the trouble of splitting your ticket. For years few voters did. The result was that all politicians had a stake in the success of the top of their tickets and were willing to allow state party bosses, who had demonstrated their political sensitivity, to construct those tickets. The master was John Bailey, state Democratic chairman from 1946 until his death in 1975, who produced a string of ethnically balanced tickets and Democratic victories and who also produced such luminaries as Abraham Ribicoff and Chester Bowles. Bailey was his party's national chairman in the Kennedy and Johnson years, although his real power remained in Connecticut; Connecticut's Republican Party also produced a number of national chairmen in the two decades after World War II.

Since the late 1960s, however, Connecticut's strong parties have grown weaker. One reason is that the mandatory straight party lever was abolished, and slowly Connecticut voters learned to split their tickets as voters in most states long since learned to do. Second, the party organizations themselves tended to atrophy. Political patronage is not as attractive as it once was, and young people are simply not enlisting in party ranks. Republicans lost their stranglehold on the lower house of the legislature in a 1965 redistricting decision. Democrats in the late 1960s and early 1970s were split by such issues as the Vietnam war and crime. Party conventions no longer controlled nominations to statewide office. Without strong parties, Connecticut politics started to oscillate wildly between the parties, and the forces of ethnicity and suburbanization worked to produce results here that went against national trends. Thus Connecticut in 1968 went for Humphrey and in 1976 for Ford — one of the few states to support the losers in both of these close elections. It swept the Democrats out in 1970 — a pretty good Democratic year in most states — and in 1980 elected a new Democratic senator in a year in which Republicans gained 12 Senate seats nationwide.

It is only this kind of unusual politics that could have brought such a political maverick as Lowell Weicker to the U.S. Senate and made him dean of Connecticut's congressional delegation. Weicker was elected to the House in 1968, after service as first selectman (i.e., mayor) of Greenwich; he ran for the Senate in 1970 and won 42% of the vote. That was enough to win. The Democrats were split in Connecticut as never before. Antiwar activist Joseph Duffey had beaten John Bailey's candidate in the primary, but Senator Thomas Dodd — censured by the Senate, but still seeking vindication — ran as an Independent and did well among the Catholic ethnic communities, his traditional base.

Weicker proved to be anything but an orthodox Nixon Republican. On many issues he voted with Democrats but, more important, he became a member of the Senate Watergate Committee. He was the only member with his own personal investigating staff, and if he sometimes acted like the "excitable kid" John Ehrlichman said he was, he also expressed the indignation felt by many, including many of his fellow Republicans. Weicker's anger at Watergate has never abated; in 1981 he was one of the few senators to vote against the confirmation of Alexander Haig as secretary of state because of Haig's behavior during Watergate.

Weicker's party irregularity and lack of gravity make him a not especially powerful figure in the Republican Senate. He is the third-ranking member of the Senate Appropriations Committee — and chairman of the State, Commerce, and Justice Departments Subcommittee — and third-ranking on Energy as well. But he does not seem likely to be able to steer major legislation through to passage. Weicker evidently sees himself as a gadfly, as a Diogenes searching for honest men; perhaps he is not surprised that his stings evoke cries of protest and the glare of his lantern arouses resentment. His opinion of his own capacities is apparently not modest: in 1979 he announced he was running for president, and although he withdrew a few months later — the first official dropout in the 1980 presidential race — he did so only in the face of poll showings that he was trailing among Connecticut Republicans.

His own copartisans may indeed pose a greater threat to his political future than anyone else. In 1976 he rather handily beat Gloria Schaffer, a popular statewide official; he enters the Reagan Administration years the favorite to win the 1982 general election. The primary may be another matter. Some have suggested that Weicker might choose to avoid it altogether and run as an Independent, as his predecessor Thomas Dodd did, although with a negative result. The body of registered Republicans in Connecticut is small, only 26% of the electorate, and only 7% voted in the 1980 Republican Senate primary; those who did are inclined to conservatism on substantive issues and loyalty to major party figures. Weicker, with his high labor voting record and his maverick tendencies, could be offensive on both counts. Possible primary opponents include *Green Berets* author Robin Moore and Prescott Bush, Jr., son of the vice president. The best thing Weicker may have going among these voters is the argument that his vote may prove essential to the maintenance of Republican majorities in the Senate — although they may fear that, if reelected, he might someday choose to leave the party. And whoever wins the primary may have serious competition from Congressman Toby Moffett.

Weicker was in many ways overshadowed in the Senate for 10 years by his senior colleague, Abraham Ribicoff, who had become a kind of grand old man of Connecticut politics. First elected to Congress in 1948, elected governor in 1954 and 1958, he was widely popular and was able to avoid serious competition in the 1970s. In the Senate he was well positioned as a high-ranking Democrat on the Finance Committee and as chairman of Governmental Affairs, Ribicoff was always a skillful maker of alliances: he was the first major officeholder in the nation to endorse John Kennedy (who appointed him HEW secretary); he denounced Mayor Daley before the television cameras at the 1968 Democratic National Convention, earning him boos at the hall and plaudits in history; he was an ally of senators such as Russell Long and Robert Byrd and worked closely with the Carter Administration. He was also adept at choosing a time to leave: he decided to retire in 1980 at age 70, maintaining to the end a position of influence in the Senate, and the pride of having pulled out of the race before an aggressive young opponent might have emerged.

The man who replaces him is the son of former Senator Dodd, Christopher Dodd, a three-term congressman who, at age 36, was able to defeat as competent a candidate as former New York Senator James Buckley in what was, elsewhere in the nation, a heavily Republican year. Dodd had a number of advantages. One was a strong base in his congressional district, essentially the eastern four counties in the state, a collection of small towns and mill towns that ordinarily is politically marginal. As expected, he carried the 2d by a wide (62%–37%) margin. A second advantage was his pleasant, affable personality. Dodd is low-keyed, has a sense of humor, and is one of those relatively rare politicians who is genuinely liked by most of his colleagues. A third reason is probably the residual popularity of his late father and of the Dodd name among Connecticut's ethnic voters.

Thomas Dodd was one politician who did not make his career by climbing up the party ladder; rather, he made a record for himself as an opponent of communism, foreign and domestic, and a champion of the personal values of ethnic blue collar workers. Those were the votes he had carried in his last bitter race; those were votes Democratic presidential candidates had lost in Connecticut in the 1970s, thereby losing the state; and they were critical votes won by Christopher Dodd. James Buckley carried Fairfield County and did reasonably well in the western part of the state, which receives New York television and may have remembered him from his previous Senate campaigns. But Dodd carried not only the large cities (which have declining populations) but such second- and third-generation ethnic communities as Rocky Hill and Milford and Ansonia and Torrington. That was what enabled him to win a 56%–43% victory over a creditable opponent (although one whose Connecticut credentials were questioned) in a Republican year.

Dodd entered a Senate in which even Democrats with two years' seniority had a hard time holding onto committee seats because of the sudden Republican majority. Dodd has seats on the Banking Committee and on Foreign Relations — once considered a plum for Democrats, but now possibly a hot potato. Dodd is not a senator who needs to make headlines quickly, and he is one of a startlingly small number of younger Democrats whose prospects for a long Senate career are good. He is not likely to be an important senator in 1981 or 1982 but could be years from now.

In its last two state elections, Connecticut elected as its governor Ella Grasso, the first woman to win that office in her own right in any state. With parents who were Italian immigrants and an education at a Seven Sisters college, she was a natural bridge between ethnic and suburban Connecticut and between the machine and intellectual wings of the state's Democratic Party. She served three terms as secretary of state, two in Congress, and then was elected governor in 1974 by a comfortable margin. With a reputation as a liberal, she nonetheless produced austere budgets and lowered spending on some programs; she avoided the income tax, which has always been unpopular in Connecticut. Her finest hours perhaps came during the blizzard of 1978 when she set up a storm center, helicoptered through the state, and trudged through snowdrifts when her car got stuck. That performance helped "Mother Ella" win reelection that year and made this rumpled, hard-working woman the prototype of a governor most Connecticut voters of this generation will carry through life.

Forced to resign at the end of 1980 because of serious illness, Grasso was succeeded by her lieutenant governor, William O'Neill; she died in February 1981.

O'Neill is to most an unknown quantity politically: a man with a record in the state legislature but little executive experience. Faced with a difficult fiscal situation in early 1981, he had the potential for almost anything politically. Another little-known lieutenant governor, John Dempsey, had succeeded Ribicoff when he went off to Washington and ended up governing the state through the whole 1960s; there is no way of knowing whether O'Neill will be able to emulate Dempsey's example. As he took office, there seemed already to be a long line of potential competitors for his office, Democrats as well as Republicans.

Connecticut neither gained nor lost House seats in the 1980 census, and none of its current districts varies substantially from the statewide average. The redistricting process is in the hands of the Democrats, who will probably not change the boundaries much, except to move some of the very heavily Republican towns now in the marginal 5th district into the Republican 4th district, where they can do no harm.

Census Data   Pop. (1980 final) 3,107,576, up 2% in 1970s: 1.37% of U.S. total, 25th largest. Central city, 34%; suburban, 54%. Median 4-person family income, 1978, $22,278, 109% of U.S., 6th highest.

1979 Share of Federal Tax Burden $8,250,000,000; 1.83% of U.S. total, 20th largest.

1979 Share of Federal Outlays $8,267,940,000; 1.79% of U.S. total, 19th largest.

DOD	$4,001,938,000	8th	(3.77%)	HEW	$2,582,015,000	25th	(1.44%)
DOE	$41,149,000	28th	(0.35%)	ERDA	$11,517,000	27th	(0.42%)
HUD	$110,886,000	20th	(1.68%)	NASA	$98,369,000	9th	(2.10%)
VA	$214,639,000	35th	(1.03%)	DOT	$187,289,000	28th	(1.13%)
EPA	$52,548,000	31st	(0.99%)	DOC	$16,100,000	31st	(0.51%)
DOI	$10,752,000	46th	(0.19%)	USDA	$189,517,000	41st	(0.79%)

Economic Base Transportation equipment, especially aircraft and parts; finance, insurance, and real estate; machinery, especially general industrial machinery; fabricated metal products, especially cutlery, hand tools, and hardware; electrical equipment and supplies; primary metal industries, especially nonferrous rolling and drawing; printing and publishing, especially newspapers and commercial publishing.

Political Lineup Governor, William A. O'Neill (D). Senators, Lowell P. Weicker, Jr. (R) and Christopher J. Dodd (D). Representatives, 6 (4 D and 2 R); 6 in 1982. State Senate, 36 (22 D, 13 R, 1 vacancy); State House of Representatives, 151 (83 D and 68 R).

The Voters

Registration 1,706,361 Total. 669,131 D (39%); 449,548 R (26%); 586,660 unaffiliated (34%); 1022 other (0%).

Employment profile 1970 White collar, 52%. Blue collar, 36%. Service, 11%. Farm, 1%.

Ethnic groups Black 1980, 7%. Hispanic 1980, 4%. Asian 1980, 1%. Total foreign stock 1970, 32%. Italy, 8%; Canada, 4%; Poland, 3%; UK, Ireland, Germany, USSR, 2% each.

Presidential Vote

1980	Reagan (R)	677,210	(48%)
	Carter (D)	541,732	(39%)
	Anderson (I)	171,807	(12%)
1976	Ford (R)	719,261	(52%)
	Carter (D)	647,895	(47%)

1980 Democratic Presidential Primary			1980 Republican Presidential Primary		
Kennedy	98,662	(47%)	Bush	70,367	(39%)
Carter	87,207	(41%)	Reagan	61,735	(34%)
Two others	11,003	(5%)	Anderson	40,354	(22%)
Uncommitted	13,403	(6%)	Five others	5,572	(3%)
			Uncommitted	4,256	(2%)

SENATORS

Sen. Lowell P. Weicker, Jr. (R) Elected 1970, seat up 1982; b. May 16, 1931, Paris, France; home, Greenwich; Yale U., B.A. 1953, U. of Va., LL.B. 1958.

Career Army, 1953–55; Practicing atty.; Conn. Gen. Assembly, 1962–68; U.S. House of Reps., 1969–71.

Offices 313 RSOB, 202-224-4041. Also 102 U.S. Court House, 915 Lafayette Blvd., Bridgeport 06603, 203-579-5830.

Committees *Appropriations* (3d). Subcommittees: Defense; District of Columbia; HUD–Independent Agencies; Labor, Health and Human Services, Education; State, Justice, Commerce, and the Judiciary (Chairman).

Energy and Natural Resources (3d). Subcommittees: Energy Conservation and Supply (Chairman); Energy Research and Development; Water and Power.

Labor and Human Resources (6th). Subcommittees: Education;

Handicapped; Aging, Family and Human Services.

Select Committee on Small Business (Chairman). Subcommittees: Urban and Rural Economic Development; Government Procurement.

184   CONNECTICUT

Group Ratings

	ADA	COPE	PC	LCV	CFA	RPN	NAB	NSI	NTU	ACA	ACU
1980	72	81	63	87	73	—	38	38	27	43	20
1979	68	62	58	—	57	—	—	—	38	41	27
1978	60	87	50	72	55	100	22	33	11	20	29

Key Votes

1) Draft Registn $	FOR	6) Fair Housng Cloture	FOR
2) Ban $ to Nicrgua	FOR	7) Ban $ Rape Abortns	AGN
3) Dlay MX Missile	—	8) Cap on Food Stmp $	AGN
4) Nuclr Mortorium	AGN	9) New US Dep Edcatn	FOR
5) Alaska Lands Bill	FOR	10) Cut OSHA Inspctns	—

11) Cut Socl Incr Defns AGN
12) Income Tax Indexing AGN
13) Lim Spdg 21% GNP FOR
14) Incr Wndfll Prof Tax FOR
15) Chryslr Loan Grntee AGN

Election Results

1976 general	Lowell P. Weicker, Jr. (R)	785,683	(58%)	($480,709)
	Gloria Schaffer (D)	561,018	(41%)	($306,104)
1976 primary	Lowell P. Weicker, Jr. (R), nominated by convention			
1970 general	Lowell P. Weicker. Jr. (R)	443.008	(42%)	
	Joseph D. Duffey (D)	360,094	(34%)	
	Thomas J. Dodd (I)	260,264	(24%)	

Sen. Christopher J. Dodd (D) Elected 1980, seat up 1986; b. May 27, 1944, Willimantic; home, Norwich; Providence Col., B.A. 1966, U. of Louisville, J.D. 1972.

Career Peace Corps, Dominican Repub., 1966; Army, 1969; Practicing atty., 1972–74; U.S. House of Reps., 1974–80.

Offices 404 RSOB, 202-224-2823. Also 60 Washington St., Hartford 06106, 203-244-3470.

Committees *Banking, Housing, and Urban Affairs* (6th). Subcommittees: International Finance and Monetary Policy; Rural Housing and Development; Consumer Affairs.

Foreign Relations (8th). Subcommittees: International Economic Policy; African Affairs; Western Hemisphere Affairs.

Special Committee on Aging (7th).

Group Ratings (as Member of U.S. House of Representatives)

	ADA	COPE	PC	LCV	CFA	RPN	NAB	NSI	NTU	ACA	ACU
1980	72	81	43	79	50	—	0	11	21	24	—
1979	74	95	80	87	85	—	—	—	20	12	9
1978	80	90	65	81	59	42	0	44	13	8	9

Key Votes (as Member of U.S. House of Representatives)

1) Draft Registn $	AGN	6) Fair Hsg DOJ Enfrc	FOR
2) Ban $ to Nicrgua	AGN	7) Lim PAC Contrbtns	FOR
3) Dlay MX Missile	FOR	8) Cap on Food Stmp $	AGN
4) Nuclr Mortorium	FOR	9) New US Dep Edcatn	FOR
5) Alaska Lands Bill	FOR	10) Cut OSHA $	AGN

11) Cut Socl Incr Dfns $ AGN
12) Hosptl Cost Controls FOR
13) Gasln Ctrls & Allctns FOR
14) Lim Wndfll Prof Tax AGN
15) Chryslr Loan Grntee FOR

Election Results

1980 general	Christopher J. Dodd (D)	763,969	(56%)	($1,403,672)
	James L. Buckley (R)	581,884	(43%)	($1,652,120)
1980 primary	Christopher J. Dodd (D), nominated by convention			
1974 general	Abraham A. Ribicoff (D)	690,820	(64%)	($435,985)
	James H. Brannen III (R)	372,055	(34%)	($66,162)

GOVERNOR

Gov. William A. O'Neill (D) Appointed Jan. 1, 1981, term expires Jan. 1983; b. Aug. 11, 1930, Hartford; home, East Hampton; New Britain Teachers Col., U. of Hartford.

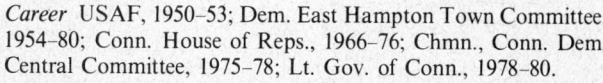

Career USAF, 1950–53; Dem. East Hampton Town Committee, 1954–80; Conn. House of Reps., 1966–76; Chmn., Conn. Dem. Central Committee, 1975–78; Lt. Gov. of Conn., 1978–80.

Offices State of Connecticut Executive Chambers, Hartford 06115, 203-566-4840.

Election Results

1978 gen.	Ella T. Grasso (D)	613,109	(59%)
	Ronald A. Sarasin (R)	422,316	(41%)
1978 prim.	Ella T. Grasso (D)	137,904	(67%)
	Robert K. Killian (D)......	66,924	(33%)
1974 gen.	Ella T. Grasso (D)	643,490	(59%)
	Robert H. Steele (R)	440,169	(41%)

FIRST DISTRICT

Hartford, for years Connecticut's largest city, is the state capital and the headquarters for many of the nation's largest insurance companies. Hartford and its suburbs also contain much of Connecticut's large defense industry—notably United Technology's big Pratt & Whitney aircraft engine factories. As with most of Connecticut's urban centers, people have long since moved out of Hartford into a string of comfortable suburbs. They range from working-class East Hartford and Windsor on the Connecticut River to the high-income Protestant and Jewish precincts of West Hartford and Bloomfield. Hartford itself, with the bulk of the area's poor and black residents, has many of the typical urban problems. But here in this small city, with its gleaming modern office buildings, its ornate state Capitol, and its high white collar employment, they do not seem as overwhelming as they do in New York or Philadelphia. There is a feeling here that problems can be solved, and that however unpleasant life may be other places it does not have to be unpleasant here.

The 1st congressional district, which includes Hartford and most of its suburbs, has long been the Democratic stronghold of the state. This is in large part due to the efforts of the late John Bailey, longtime state (1946–75) and national (1961–68) Democratic chairman. In year after year turnout and Democratic totals have been higher in the Hartford area than elsewhere in the state—a tradition that continues to this day. Not only in 1976, but in 1980 as well, the 1st congressional district gave Jimmy Carter pluralities.

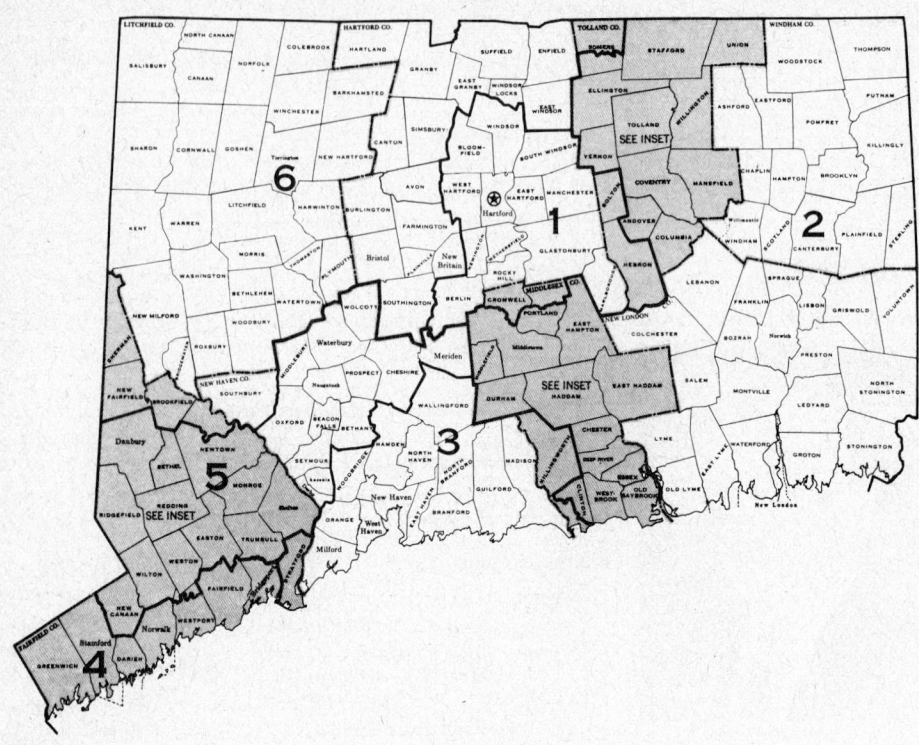

The 1st has had a Democratic congressman for more than 20 years. The current incumbent, William Cotter, was first elected in 1970, a difficult year for Democrats in this state, and had a tough primary and general election that year. Since then he has generally won easily. He has had a rather quiet career in the House. He is a member of the Ways and Means Committee, in many respects the most important committee in the House, and in 1981 became chairman of a Select Revenue Subcommittee. Cotter has a voting record that does not show him as falling within any well-defined camp, and he has generally voted with the majority of Democrats.

Census Data   Pop. (1980 final) 495,351, down 2% in 1970s. Median family income, 1970, $12,031, 126% of U.S.

The Voters

Employment profile 1970   White collar, 58%. Blue collar, 31%. Service, 11%. Farm, –%.
Ethnic groups   Black 1980, 12%. Hispanic 1980, 7%. Asian 1980, 1%. Total foreign stock 1970, 34%. Italy 7%; Canada, 6%; Poland, 4%; Ireland, 3%; USSR, UK, Germany, 2% each.

Presidential Vote

1980	Reagan (R)	89,511	(38%)
	Carter (D)	105,401	(46%)
	Anderson (I)	33,452	(15%)
1976	Ford (R)	108,585	(47%)
	Carter (D)	120,874	(52%)

Rep. William R. Cotter (D) Elected 1970; b. July 18, 1926, Hartford; home, Hartford; Trinity Col., Hartford, B.A. 1949.

Career Mbr., Court of Common Council, Hartford, 1953; Aide to Conn. Gov. Abraham Ribicoff, 1955–57; Dpty. Insurance Commissioner of Conn., 1957–64, Commissioner, 1964–70.

Offices 2134 RHOB, 202-225-2265. Also 450 Main St., Hartford 06101, 203-244-2383.

Committee *Ways and Means* (0th). Subcommittees: Select Revenue Measures (Chairman); Social Security.

Group Ratings

	ADA	COPE	PC	LCV	CFA	RPN	NAB	NSI	NTU	ACA	ACU
1980	44	68	47	28	71	—	33	44	29	25	29
1979	68	82	55	63	52	—	—	—	26	12	16
1978	50	63	48	45	35	27	10	56	10	28	29

Key Votes

1) Draft Registn $	AGN	6) Fair Hsg DOJ Enfrc	FOR	11) Cut Socl Incr Dfns $	AGN
2) Ban $ to Nicrgua	FOR	7) Lim PAC Contrbtns	AGN	12) Hosptl Cost Controls	FOR
3) Dlay MX Missile	AGN	8) Cap on Food Stmp $	AGN	13) Gasln Ctrls & Allctns	FOR
4) Nuclr Mortorium	FOR	9) New US Dep Edcatn	AGN	14) Lim Wndfll Prof Tax	AGN
5) Alaska Lands Bill	FOR	10) Cut OSHA $	FOR	15) Chryslr Loan Grntee	FOR

Election Results

1980 general	William R. Cotter (D)...........	137,849	(63%)	($127,447)
	Marjorie D. Anderson (R)	80,816	(37%)	($27,713)
1980 primary	William R. Cotter(D), nominated by convention			
1978 general	William R. Cotter (D)...........	102,749	(60%)	($96,791)
	Ben F. Andrews, Jr. (R)	67,828	(39%)	($54,733)

SECOND DISTRICT

The 2d district is the eastern half, geographically, of Connecticut. The district has Yankee villages and high-income summer and retirement colonies with such names as Old Saybrook and Old Lyme. It also has small and middle-sized towns such as Norwich, Danielson, and Putnam, with heavily Catholic and ethnic populations. Traditional Yankee Republicanism still has some strength here, but the political balance lies in the second- and third-generation ethnics in such places as Middletown and New London, the latter the site of the Electric Boat Company, a major defense contractor. This mix makes the 2d a middle-of-the-road, bellwether district in national and state elections and often a closely contested district in congressional elections.

As a result the 2d has had a succession of congressmen. None was actually defeated, and some have gone on to other things—Chester Bowles, for example, after one term in the

House, became number two man in the Kennedy State Department. Others have built up enough strength here to be plausible candidates statewide, including Horace Seely-Brown, Jr., who nearly beat Abraham Ribicoff for the Senate in 1962, and Bob Steele, who ran a strong but losing gubernatorial race against Ella Grasso in 1974. The most recent incumbent here, Christopher Dodd, had better fortune: he ran for the Senate seat vacated by Abraham Ribicoff in 1980, and won handily, even though he was a generally liberal Democrat running in a Republican year. Helping him was his 62%–37% margin in the 2d district.

That margin also helped the Democratic candidate for Congress, Sam Gejdenson (pronounced gay-den-son). He was not expected to be the winner at first: a state representative with a reputation as a liberal who quit the legislature to run. But he proved to have the affability and political skill to win. The Democratic district convention—an artifact of Connecticut's strong party system—favored another nominee, John Dempsey, son of a former governor. But Gejdenson literally outcampaigned Dempsey and beat him in virtually every city and town in the district. The Republican nominee, Tony Gugielmo, had become the party's choice only after the favorite, A. Searle Field, left the race before the district convention; Gugielmo barely survived a primary challenge and was not a strong campaigner. Even in these circumstances, and with Dodd on the ticket, Gejdenson won by a less than overwhelming margin—but that is mainly evidence of the strength of the Republican tide on issues that was decisive in so many other congressional districts. Gejdenson can be expected to be the same kind of hard-driving, liberal-oriented congressman as the 6th district's Toby Moffett and, having won in 1980, he must surely be the favorite to win in years hence.

Census Data   Pop. (1980 final) 537,988, up 6% in 1970s. Median family income, 1970, $10,885, 114% of U.S.

The Voters

Employment profile 1970   White collar, 48%. Blue collar, 39%. Service, 12%. Farm, 1%.
Ethnic groups   Black 1980, 3%. Hispanic 1980, 2%. Asian 1980, 1%. Total foreign stock 1970, 26%. Canada, 6%; Italy, 4%; Poland, 3%; UK, Germany, 2% each; USSR, Ireland, 1% each.

Presidential Vote

1980	Reagan (R)	108,219	(46%)
	Carter (D)	89,252	(38%)
	Anderson (I)	33,388	(14%)
1976	Ford (R)	110,616	(50%)
	Carter (D)	111,161	(50%)

Rep. Samuel Gejdenson (D) Elected 1980; b. May 20, 1948, Eshwege, Germany; home, Bozrah; Mitchell Col., A.S., U. of Conn., B.A. 1970.

Career   Conn. House of Reps., 1974–78; Coal Co. Consultant, 1978; Legislative Liaison to Gov. of Conn., 1979–80.

Offices   1503 LHOB, 202-225-2076. Also P.O. Box 2000, Norwich 06360, 203-886-0139, and 29 Court St., Middletown 06457, 203-346-1123.

Committees   *Foreign Affairs* (17th). Subcommittees: Human Rights and International Organizations; Inter-American Affairs.

Interior and Insular Affairs (26th). Subcommittees: Energy and the Environment; Oversight and Investigations; Public Lands and National Parks.

Group Ratings and Key Votes: Newly Elected

Election Results

1980 general	Samuel Gejdenson (D)	119,176	(53%)	($217,724)
	Tony Guglielmo (R)	104,107	(47%)	($141,682)
1980 primary	Samuel Gejdenson (D)	18,746	(62%)	
	John N. Dempsey (D)...........	11,654	(38%)	($156,073)
1978 general	Christopher J. Dodd (D)	116,624	(70%)	($125,326)
	Thomas H. Connell (R)	50,167	(30%)	($17,714)

THIRD DISTRICT

The 3d congressional district of Connecticut centers on the city of New Haven, once the state's largest and most industrialized major city and home of the state's best-known institution, Yale University. At the turn of the century, New Haven was the most important factory town in Connecticut, and it attracted thousands of Irish, Italian, and Polish immigrants. Today their descendants have spread out, from the old neighborhoods of frame houses huddled within walking distance of the factories to suburbs such as West Haven, East Haven, and Hamden. Founded by WASPs in the 16th century, and still WASP-dominated at the upper reaches of society, Greater New Haven is essentially an ethnic town. Yale, despite its national reputation, is a small university in enrollment and, except for a few blocks near the campus, New Haven is not really a college town.

New Haven's sociology might suggest that this is a heavily Democratic area, but the truth is more complicated. As in most American cities of the 19th century, an even–odd pattern prevailed. The native Yankees were usually Republican, and the first-arriving immigrant group, here as usual the Irish, were Democrats. The next immigrant group to arrive, slighted by the Irish and on occasion wooed by the WASPs, turned to the Republican Party, and so on. In New Haven, Italian–Americans were the second ethnic group to arrive, and the very large number of Italian–Americans made the Republican Party competitive with the Democrats. The city of New Haven, its population shrunk by urban renewal and the natural movement of young people to newer neighborhoods farther out, is more heavily Democratic than ever today. But the whole New Haven area, of which the 3d congressional district is a good approximation, was never overwhelmingly Democratic, even in New Deal days, and today seems to be moving away from the Democrats and toward the Republicans.

That is certainly the case in congressional elections. The 3d district was represented for 22 years by Robert Giaimo, a Democrat known for his conservative views on some cultural issues but also a leader of his national party in the 1970s. Giaimo was chairman of the House Budget Committee from 1976 to 1980 — a position he won in spirited competition in the Democratic Caucus. He fought hard battles against Republicans, who lined up unanimously against the Democrats on the committee, and was in effect a fighter for the Carter Administration, although usually without very much cooperation from the administration itself, against both those who wanted tighter budgets and those who wanted more spending on domestic programs. Giaimo's performance was good enough that Democrats changed their rule after the 1978 election and allowed him to seek a second term; the job was exhausting enough that he decided to quit.

Another reason might have been his showings in the 3d district. In 1976 and 1978 a Republican challenger, never lavishly financed, held him under 60% of the vote; and although Giaimo kept in touch with New Haven he did not spend much time campaigning there. So in 1980, at age 61, he decided to retire.

The choice in 1980 boiled down to a Jewish Democrat and an Italian Republican and, in the year of the Reagan sweep, the Republican won—although he is not exactly a Reagan Republican. Joseph Lieberman, the Democrat, represented New Haven in the state Senate and was considered a comer in state politics; he had also distinguished himself as the biographer of John Bailey, longtime Connecticut Democratic chairman. Lawrence DeNardis, a state senator from suburban Hamden, antagonized some Republicans by supporting the Equal Rights Amendment and a state income tax but won the nomination nevertheless. Lieberman held his own in New Haven and got almost all the votes Giaimo could in high-income WASPy suburbs. But in such places as Hamden and East Haven DeNardis made major gains. Indeed, he carried every city and town in the district except for New Haven and West Haven and won a solid, although hardly overwhelming, 52%–46% victory. It should not be dismissed as simply the result of the Republican sweep in 1980—which, after all, did not affect every contest in Connecticut. Much of the reason for the result lies in the Italian ethnic heritage that is so important to this area and the Republican leanings of so many Italian–American voters.

Census Data   Pop. (1980 final) 513,057, up 2% in 1970s. Median family income, 1970, $11,463, 120% of U.S.

The Voters

Employment profile 1970   White collar, 53%. Blue collar, 35%. Service, 11%. Farm, 1%.
Ethnic groups   Black 1980, 10%. Hispanic 1980, 3%. Asian 1980, 1%. Total foreign stock 1970, 31%. Italy, 10%; Poland, Ireland, UK, Canada, USSR, Germany, 2% each.

Presidential Vote

1980	Reagan (R)	117,043	(50%)
	Carter (D)	90,454	(39%)
	Anderson (I)	23,103	(10%)
1976	Ford (R)	121,685	(53%)
	Carter (D)	105,602	(46%)

Rep. Lawrence J. DeNardis (R) Elected 1980; b. Mar. 18., 1938, New Haven; home, Hamden; Holy Cross Col., B.A., 1960, NYU, M.A. 1964.

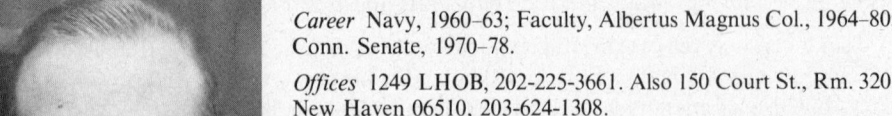

Career Navy, 1960–63; Faculty, Albertus Magnus Col., 1964–80; Conn. Senate, 1970–78.

Offices 1249 LHOB, 202-225-3661. Also 150 Court St., Rm. 320, New Haven 06510, 203-624-1308.

Committees *Education and Labor* (12th). Subcommittees: Elementary, Secondary and Vocational Education; Employment Opportunities; Postsecondary Education.

Government Operations (16th). Subcommittee: Intergovernmental Relations and Human Resources.

Select Committee on Narcotics Abuse and Control (7th).

Group Ratings and Key Votes: Newly Elected

Election Results

1980 general	Lawrence J. DeNardis (R)	117,024	(52%)	($185,799)
	Joseph I. Lieberman (D).........	103,903	(46%)	($302,054)
1980 primary	Lawrence J. DeNardis (R)	8,749	(61%)	
	Henry A. Povinelli (R)	5,679	(39%)	($18,237)
1978 general	Robert N. Giaimo (D)	96,830	(58%)	($157,304)
	John G. Pucciano (R)	66,663	(40%)	($102,667)

FOURTH DISTRICT

If Hartford County has been the traditional home of Connecticut's Democrats, then Fairfield County has been the bedrock of the state's Republicans. Fairfield is one of the richest counties in the nation, a land of broad, well-manicured lawns sweeping down to Long Island Sound, of woodsy New Canaan and artsy-craftsy Westport, of commuters driving down to the station to take the bedraggled New Haven Railroad into Manhattan. Unlike the rest of Connecticut, Fairfield County is in many ways an extension of New York City, economically and culturally. People watch New York, not Connecticut, television; they are Yankees, not Red Sox, fans; and their political attitudes, more than in other parts of this small state, are shaped by what is happening in the City. Indeed, people here often have little idea at all of what is happening in Connecticut.

Most of the people in Fairfield County live in the 4th congressional district—a string of high-income, traditionally Republican towns along Long Island Sound: Greenwich, Stamford, Darien, Norwalk, Westport, Fairfield. But it would be inaccurate to say that the harried advertising executive on a long commute is the typical 4th district voter. For the 4th also takes in the industrial city of Bridgeport as well as the affluent towns. Bridgeport is nothing like the South Bronx: it has a bounteous system of parks and its old ethnic neighborhoods are pleasant and unimperiled. But it is a large industrial town, quite separate from the commuter towns; and even there, below the railroad station or in the old downtown, you can see the slightly shabby small houses where the district's poorer voters live.

The two segments of the 4th—Bridgeport and the Republican towns—perform a kind of political counterpoint. Westport, for example, which went 36% for Kennedy in 1960, was 41% for McGovern in 1972, and back down to 30% for Carter in 1980 (with 14% for John Anderson). Moving in the opposite direction was Bridgeport. The Catholic Kennedy got 61% there in 1960, while the leftish McGovern got only 45%; Carter managed 56% in 1976 and 51% in 1980.

The 4th is, on balance, a Republican district, when the Democrats do better in the commuter towns they will likely do worse in Bridgeport. An exception was the Watergate year of 1974, when incumbent Republican Congressman Stewart McKinney was reelected with 54% of the vote. First elected in 1970, when Lowell Weicker left to run for the Senate, McKinney has concentrated on energy bills, reflecting the views more often of energy-poor New England than of free-market Republicans, and has devoted considerable attention to the thankless task of overseeing District of Columbia affairs. On most issues he tends to take positions typical of that not-quite-extinct breed, the moderate Republican.

McKinney is generally reelected with good margins and did as well in 1980 as he has in his career. His opponent, incidentally, was the young man who, as a Princeton undergraduate, designed an atomic bomb. After winning the primary in an upset he made no great impact in the general. Redistricting, even by a Democratic legislature, should be kind to McKinney. The district has lost population and the natural places to add are such heavily Republican towns as Weston and Wilton now in the 5th district.

Census Data   Pop. (1980 final) 478,265, down 5% in 1970s. Median family income, 1970, $12,692, 132% of U.S.

The Voters

Employment profile 1970   White collar, 56%. Blue collar, 33%. Service, 11%. Farm, –%.
Ethnic groups   Black 1980, 12%. Hispanic 1980, 8%. Asian 1980, 1%. Total foreign stock 1970, 35%. Italy, 8%; Poland, UK, 3% each; Canada, Ireland, Germany, USSR, 2% each.

Presidential Vote

1980	Reagan (R)	110,273	(53%)
	Carter (D)	76,569	(37%)
	Anderson (I)	20,723	(10%)
1976	Ford (R)	118,716	(56%)
	Carter (D)	91,058	(43%)

Rep. Stewart B. McKinney (R) Elected 1970; b. Jan. 30, 1931, Pittsburgh, Pa.; home, Fairfield; Princeton U., 1949–51, Yale U., B.A. 1958.

Career Air Force, 1951–55; Pres., CMF Tires, Inc.; Real estate development; Conn. House of Reps., 1967–70.

Offices 106 CHOB, 202-225-5541. Also Fed. Bldg., Lafayette Blvd., Bridgeport 06604, 203-384-2286.

Committees *Banking, Finance and Urban Affairs* (3d). Subcommittees: Economic Stabilization; Financial Institutions Supervision, Regulation and Insurance; Housing and Community Development.

District of Columbia (Ranking Member). Subcommittees: Fiscal Affairs and Health; Government Operations and Metropolitan Affairs.

Group Ratings

	ADA	COPE	PC	LCV	CFA	RPN	NAB	NSI	NTU	ACA	ACU
1980	78	57	30	62	42	—	36	13	28	41	13
1979	53	65	28	65	26	—	—	—	21	30	28
1978	55	55	48	50	41	83	20	0	15	26	35

Key Votes

1) Draft Registn $	AGN	6) Fair Hsg DOJ Enfrc	—	11) Cut Socl Incr Dfns $	AGN
2) Ban $ to Nicrgua	AGN	7) Lim PAC Contrbtns	FOR	12) Hosptl Cost Controls	AGN
3) Dlay MX Missile	FOR	8) Cap on Food Stmp $	AGN	13) Gasln Ctrls & Allctns	AGN
4) Nuclr Mortorium	AGN	9) New US Dep Edcatn	AGN	14) Lim Wndfll Prof Tax	FOR
5) Alaska Lands Bill	FOR	10) Cut OSHA $	AGN	15) Chryslr Loan Grntee	FOR

Election Results

1980 general	Stewart B. McKinney (R)........	124,285	(63%)	($220,183)
	John A. Phillips (D)	74,326	(37%)	($155,631)
1980 primary	Stewart B. McKinney (R), nominated by convention			
1978 general	Stewart B. McKinney (R)........	83,990	(58%)	($123,628)
	Michael G. Morgan (D)	59,918	(42%)	($51,744)

FIFTH DISTRICT

The 5th district is an amalgam of Connecticut's lesser-known cities and towns that are spread out over the hills just north of Long Island Sound. The district includes the industrial city of Waterbury and the decaying mill towns of the Naugatuck Valley; the relatively prosperous working-class town of Meriden to the east; and Danbury, the onetime hat manufacturing center, in the west. The industrial cities and towns are all traditionally Democratic; among them are the smaller, Yankee towns that are inevitably more Republican. Included also in the 5th in the 1972 redistricting were the heavily Republican towns of New Canaan, Wilton, and Weston—woodsy commuter towns where well-to-do executives from New York City or Fairfield County's burgeoning office parks live. The result is a district that is finely balanced on the partisan scale. In four of the five elections since the current boundaries were drawn—the exception was 1976—the 5th has been a very closely contested district.

It has also been a district that has switched between the parties. It unexpectedly dumped a veteran Democratic congressman in 1972 and has now been carried by Republican Ronald Sarasin three times and Democrat William Ratchford twice. Ratchford, with a political base in Danbury, four years of experience as speaker of the Connecticut House, and service in the administration of Governor Ella Grasso, might seem to have a natural advantage here. But he lost to Sarasin by a 50%–48% margin in 1974, and he has won by only narrow margins in 1978 and 1980. In 1978 his problem was the well-financed campaign of state Senator George Guidera, who had a base in Weston and a moderate image; in 1980 his problem was the Republican tide, which nearly brought a weaker Republican, Edward Donahue, into the Congress.

In both cases Ratchford lost the high-income commuter towns by very large margins. Without them he would have won 55%–45% in 1978 and 52%–48% in 1980. The trend districtwide is down for Democrats; not only did Jimmy Carter lose the district in 1980, but so did Senator Christopher Dodd, and in general the mill towns seem to be losing population while the Republican villages are gaining. Nevertheless, Ratchford stands to gain from redistricting, since the 5th will almost certainly lose Weston, Wilton, and New Canaan to the now underpopulated 4th district; that will make the district 2% to 3% more Democratic. But one must also expect Republicans to continue to target this district which, despite Ratchford's abilities, seems to be marginal indeed.

Census Data Pop. (1980 final) 542,298, up 7% in 1970s. Median family income, 1970, $12,200, 127% of U.S.

The Voters

Employment profile 1970 White collar, 51%. Blue collar, 39%. Service, 10%. Farm, –%.
Ethnic groups Black 1980, 4%. Hispanic 1980, 3%. Asian 1980, 1%. Total foreign stock 1970, 34%. Italy, 9%; Canada, 4%; Poland, 3%; UK, Ireland, Germany, 2% each; USSR, 1%.

Presidential Vote

1980	Reagan (R)	133,228	(54%)
	Carter (D)	83,705	(34%)
	Anderson (I)	26,998	(11%)
1976	Ford (R)	133,654	(56%)
	Carter (D)	104,081	(43%)

Rep. William R. Ratchford (D) Elected 1978; b. May 24, 1934, Danbury; home, Danbury; U. of Conn., B.A. 1956, Georgetown U., LL.B. 1959.

Career Conn. House of Reps., 1962–74, Spkr., 1969–72, Minor. Ldr., 1972–74; Dem. nominee for U.S. House of Reps., 1974; Chmn., Conn. Blue Ribbon Commission to Investigate Nursing Home Industry, 1975–76; Commissioner, Conn. Dept. of Aging, 1977–78.

Offices 432 CHOB, 202-225-3822. Also 135 Grand St., Waterbury 06701, 203-573-1418.

Committees *Education and Labor* (17th). Subcommittees: Elementary, Secondary and Vocational Education; Labor Standards.

House Administration (9th). Subcommittees: Accounts; Personnel and Police.

Select Committee on Aging (19th). Subcommittees: Health and Long-Term Care; Human Services.

Group Ratings

	ADA	COPE	PC	LCV	CFA	RPN	NAB	NSI	NTU	ACA	ACU
1980	83	72	67	87	75	—	0	0	18	19	14
1979	95	90	88	83	85	—	—	—	21	12	3

Key Votes

1) Draft Registn $	AGN	6) Fair Hsg DOJ Enfrc	FOR	11) Cut Socl Incr Dfns $	AGN
2) Ban $ to Nicrgua	AGN	7) Lim PAC Contrbtns	FOR	12) Hosptl Cost Controls	FOR
3) Dlay MX Missile	FOR	8) Cap on Food Stmp $	AGN	13) Gasln Ctrls & Allctns	FOR
4) Nuclr Mortorium	FOR	9) New US Dep Edcatn	FOR	14) Lim Wndfll Prof Tax	AGN
5) Alaska Lands Bill	FOR	10) Cut OSHA $	AGN	15) Chryslr Loan Grntee	FOR

Election Results

1980 general	William R. Ratchford (D)	117,316	(50%)	($150,570)
	Edward M. Donahue (R)	115,614	(50%)	($52,740)
1980 primary	William R. Ratchford (D), nominated by convention			
1978 general	William R. Ratchford (D)	96,738	(52%)	($139,778)
	George C. Guidera (R)	88,162	(48%)	($245,933)

SIXTH DISTRICT

Some congressional districts seem to be made up of territory left over after everyone else has constructed his own constituency. Such a district is the 6th of Connecticut. Its population concentrations are widely dispersed, at just about the opposite ends of the district. Enfield and Windsor Locks, in the far northwest corner, are predominantly Italian–American and part of the Hartford-to-Springfield, Massachusetts, industrial corridor. In the southeast corner of the 6th are Bristol and New Britain, the latter the city with the state's largest concentration of Polish–Americans. In the north central part of the district, amid the gentle mountains, are the mill towns of Torrington and Winsted, the latter of which is Ralph Nader's hometown. In among these Democratic areas are the Yankee Republican towns (e.g., Sharon, home of the Buckley clan) and such posh Republican suburbs of Hartford as Farmington, Avon, and Simsbury.

The 1964 legislature, which drew the district's lines (they have been altered only slightly since), expected the 6th to elect a Democrat, and generally it has. But overall the district must be classified as marginal. It has on occasion gone Republican in House elections (in 1966 and 1968), and over the long term its mill towns are tending to lose population while the affluent suburbs and Yankee towns are tending to gain. The district currently elects Toby Moffett, a Democrat who in many ways personifies the class of 1974, the year in which he was first elected. While still in his 20s he had worked in the executive branch and for Senator Walter Mondale, and then had gone back home to Connecticut to form and run his own Nader-style citizens' action group. Aggressive, energetic, working to solve people's problems — he was, even before he was elected to Congress, the image of the activist congressman-ombudsman. He was elected by a striking margin in 1974 at age 30 and reelected without great difficulty in 1976, 1978, and 1980.

Moffett is the kind of politician who is naturally bubbling over with ideas and with ideas on how they can be put into practice. Unfortunately, the ideas that he has championed did not fare especially well in the late 1970s. He was among the strongest of New England voices in favor of price controls on oil and natural gas — at a time when Congress, painfully and against its natural predilections and those of the Carter Administration, decided that controls had to go. The attempt to maintain low fuel prices for people in the Northeast simply could not prevail when world petroleum prices were going up sharply; and members such as Moffett never really had a convincing answer to the position that controlled domestic oil prices discouraged energy conservation. Since 1979 Moffett has chaired a Government Operations's Environment, Energy and Natural Resources Subcommittee (he won election to that post over three fellow 1974 freshmen who, by luck of the draw, had greater seniority), and there is hope among many young liberals that Moffett can expose wrongdoing by the oil companies and can help point the way to a more equitable energy policy. But in the meantime other initiatives, notably the moves of the Reagan Administration toward an end to controls, have the headlines.

Moffett's obvious talents have made him a natural competitor for one of Connecticut's Senate seats, and many thought he would run in 1980 for Abraham Ribicoff's seat; instead, he decided to avoid what would have been a difficult, although not necessarily impossible, primary against Christopher Dodd and to run for reelection to the House instead. Many have assumed that he will run for Lowell Weicker's seat in 1982, and the outcome of such a race must be considered problematical: Weicker could have problems with his own Republicans; while Weicker was strong in the 1976 general election, Moffett has his own strong following. Or he could run for governor, presumably by challenging William O'Neill in the convention and primary.

Census Data Pop. (1980 final) 540,617, up 7% in 1970s. Median family income, 1970, $11,898, 124% of U.S.

The Voters

Employment profile 1970 White collar, 50%. Blue collar, 40%. Service, 9%. Farm, 1%.
Ethnic groups Black 1980, 2%. Hispanic 1980, 2%. Total foreign stock 1970, 32%. Italy, 6%; Canada, Poland, 5% each; Germany, UK, 2% each; Ireland, 1%.

Presidential Vote

1980	Reagan (R)	118,936	(47%)
	Carter (D)	96,351	(38%)
	Anderson (I)	34,143	(14%)
1976	Ford (R)	126,005	(52%)
	Carter (D)	115,119	(48%)

Rep. Anthony Toby Moffett (D) Elected 1974; b. Aug. 18, 1944, Holyoke, Mass.; home, Unionville; Syracuse U., A.B. 1966, Boston Col., M.A. 1968.

Career Dir., Ofc. of Students and Youth, Ofc. of the U.S. Commissioner of Educ., 1969–70; Staff Aide to U.S. Sen. Walter Mondale of Minn., 1970–71; Dir., Conn. Citizens Action Group, 1971–74.

Offices 127 CHOB, 202-225-4476. Also 160 Farmington Ave., Bristol 06010, 203-589-5750.

Committees *Energy and Commerce* (8th). Subcommittees: Commerce, Transportation and Tourism; Energy Conservation and Power; Fossil and Synthetic Fuels; Health and the Environment.

Government Operations (12th). Subcommittee: Environment, ergy and Natural Resources (Chairman).

Group Ratings

	ADA	COPE	PC	LCV	CFA	RPN	NAB	NSI	NTU	ACA	ACU
1980	94	89	80	94	93	—	0	0	23	50	11
1979	100	94	93	89	96	—	—	—	31	4	3
1978	95	89	93	93	82	50	0	0	36	16	4

Key Votes

1) Draft Registn $	AGN	6) Fair Hsg DOJ Enfrc	FOR	11) Cut Socl Incr Dfns $	AGN
2) Ban $ to Nicrgua	AGN	7) Lim PAC Contrbtns	FOR	12) Hosptl Cost Controls	FOR
3) Dlay MX Missile	FOR	8) Cap on Food Stmp $	AGN	13) Gasln Ctrls & Allctns	FOR
4) Nuclr Mortorium	FOR	9) New US Dep Edcatn	FOR	14) Lim Wndfll Prof Tax	AGN
5) Alaska Lands Bill	FOR	10) Cut OSHA $	AGN	15) Chryslr Loan Grntee	FOR

Election Results

1980 general	Anthony Toby Moffett (D)	142,685	(59%)	($190,266)
	Nicholas Schaus (R)	98,331	(41%)	($125,137)
1980 primary	Anthony Toby Moffett (D), nominated by convention			
1978 general	Anthony Toby Moffett (D)	119,537	(64%)	($162,006)
	Daniel F. MacKinnon (R)	66,664	(36%)	($83,896)

DELAWARE

Delaware likes to boast that this was the "First State" because it ratified the Constitution before any other in 1787. But this tiny state's place in our national life depends much less on such history than on the fact that, because of its liberal incorporation laws and low taxes, it is the technical home of most of the nation's large corporations and the fact that it is the physical home of the DuPont Company. DuPont, with annual revenues of more than $12 billion, clearly dominates the state of Delaware, whose revenues are around $600 million. Wealthy members of the DuPont family—there are about 2,000 living DuPonts—and corporate executives of course have considerable say in what happens here. A few years ago a group of Naderites wrote a book about Delaware called *The Company State;* while it stumbles over itself in a rush to condemn the DuPonts, its basic point — that the DuPonts tend to run things — is sound. As if to make the Naderites' point, Delaware voters have elected a DuPont as governor in 1976 and 1980; but it should be noted that this DuPont has taken care throughout his political career to criticize the company. And those who think the family runs everything should reflect on the fact that DuPont's president is Irving Shapiro, a one-time government lawyer who is himself a Democrat and was a strong Carter supporter.

The politics of this small state (the second smallest in area, fourth smallest in population) has infrequently engaged the attention of commentators. Technically Delaware has as much clout in the U.S. Senate as California and New York; historically, however, it has not produced important senators for a long time, although both incumbents have attracted some favorable attention. Over the years Delaware has wavered between the Democrats and Republicans, with the DuPonts (the company owned the Wilmington newspapers for years) entrenched in both parties. In the 1960s the Republicans seemed to gain an edge, in part because of the increasing importance of fast-growing suburbs of New Castle County (the Wilmington suburbs). But Delaware still is capable of electing Democrats, and in 1980 it came within 2% of going for Jimmy Carter.

Delaware's senior statewide official is Senator William Roth, a Republican first elected to the House in 1966 and the Senate in 1970. During the first decade of his congressional career Roth enjoyed anonymity, but in the late 1970s he emerged as the leading Senate sponsor of several important pieces of legislation: a case in point for the proposition that Republicans seized the legislative initiative and won the battle of ideas with the Democrats during the years of the Carter presidency. Roth's first major initiative was the tuition tax credit, a proposal he pushed to provide parents with a tax credit of $250 per student for college tuitions. The idea was attacked by some as aid to the rich and by others as an end run around the First Amendment, but it does have undeniable political appeal.

Roth is also the Roth of the Kemp–Roth tax cut proposal (referred to by all Republican senators as the Roth–Kemp in deference to their colleague). Although Congressman Jack Kemp has received more publicity, Roth is an equally active proponent of this measure. The idea, as is well known now, is to cut federal tax rates by 10% each year for three successive years. Kemp–Roth backers argue that this would so stimulate the economy that government revenues would actually grow, a claim that is less preposterous than it seems at first. This was what seemed to happen when the tax rates were cut in the Kennedy–Johnson Administration. The difference, of course, is that ours is an inflationary time and that was not; many economists — and voters — fear that Kemp–Roth, if enacted, would feed inflation. There is an air of a campaign gimmick to the proposal: Republicans in Congress supported it, virtually unanimously, in the inflationary atmosphere of 1978 and the recessionary times of the spring of 1980. But if Kemp–Roth is not the panacea for our economic ills, it almost certainly has some capacity to stimulate a stagflated economy and has the virtue of originality in a time when most voters, consumers, and investors have grown used to incomes that do not keep up with inflation. No one claims that Roth himself has done all the thinking that went into the idea, but he has worked for passage of the bill doggedly and if it succeeds in some or all of its aims he will deserve considerable credit.

Roth is the third-ranking Republican on the Finance Committee, a position of considerable importance; but he cannot expect to become chairman soon, since the two senior Republicans (Bob Dole and Bob Packwood) are both younger and both well entrenched in their states. Roth is chairman of the Governmental Affairs Committee, a body that has been of varying importance in our recent history. It has the power to oversee virtually any aspect of the government and, through its Permanent Investigations Subcommittee which Roth also chairs, it can investigate almost anything. This is the subcommittee through which Joe McCarthy investigated the Army and John Kennedy investigated the Teamsters. The committee also handles government reorganization and regulatory reform—technical matters that can have enormous ramifications. Roth had to fight Paul Laxalt in early 1981 for jurisdiction over regulatory reform, an issue first raised by the Carter Administration and seen by the business community as a chance to rationalize obstructive and counterproductive government regulations. Roth and Laxalt agreed that Governmental Affairs and Laxalt's Judiciary Subcommittee would both submit bills to the floor, therefore preserving Roth's role in what is likely to be his committee's most important legislation in the 97th Congress.

As for investigations, for the moment Roth seems unlikely to make many headlines. The committee is most active when it is headed by a senator at odds with the administration; and the Reagan Administration and Senate Republicans like Roth seemed, at least at the outset, to be working pretty much in tandem. If only for that reason, Roth seems likely to play a quieter role in the Senate for the next few years. It seems unlikely that he will have great difficulty winning reelection in 1982, barring a sudden drop of popularity for Reagan and the Republicans; indeed, he may not attract significant opposition.

Delaware's junior senator, Joseph Biden, is seen by many, and especially by himself, as one of the leaders of the Democratic Party in the future. He may in time become the first Delaware Democrat since Thomas Bayard (Cleveland's first secretary of state) to be a serious candidate for president. Biden was elected to the Senate in 1972 when he was 29 (although he turned 30 by the time his term began); he campaigned against an incumbent who, the voters sensed accurately, would have been happier to retire. Biden had the advantages of energy, a skillful handling of issues, and an attractive family; tragically his wife and daughter were killed in an auto accident just after the election.

Biden is considered brash and aggressive, unashamed of his own ambitions and intelligent enough to realize them. He was the first incumbent senator to back Jimmy Carter in 1976, but he was willing to criticize Carter later when things were not working out well. Early in his Senate career he won seats on the committees that seemed most important at that time—Foreign Relations and Judiciary—and has used their platforms well. On Foreign Relations, Biden became an authentic expert on (and supporter of) the SALT II Treaty, and even those who do not care for him had to admit that he was well prepared and incisive. After the 1980 elections, Biden stood behind only Claiborne Pell among Democrats on Foreign Relations; he is much younger and stands a good chance to become chairman of the full committee someday.

On Judiciary he also ranks high, behind only former Chairman Edward Kennedy and Minority Leader Robert Byrd. In 1981 Kennedy chose the ranking minority position on Labor and Public Welfare, and so Biden became ranking Democrat on Judiciary. One of Biden's major projects on this committee is to limit the ability of federal courts to order schoolchildren bused. He has worked with Roth on this ever since a major busing plan was ordered for New Castle County. Some claim that Biden's stand is an example of opportunism, but it is intellectually supportable; and Biden argues strenuously that he is not an old-fashioned liberal, but an up-to-date Democrat who considers issues on their merits. Biden was reelected with ease against a weak opponent in 1978, a year disastrous for many other Democrats. Most observers expect him to try for the presidency sooner or later, if not in 1984 (when he might have to give up his Senate seat to run) then some time thereafter. That may be a little late for Biden, however. He is a master at the kind of campaigning that involves directly impressing the voters and that was so pivotal in the primaries of the 1970s; but the Democratic Party may move away from primaries and back to having professional politicians select more of its delegates, and it is not clear how well Biden can do at gathering the support of his peers. Temperamentally he is a man who runs against the establishment, even though he occupies a high place in the Senate himself; so it is not clear whether he can make the transition to a different kind of politics.

Delaware's governor is Pierre S. DuPont IV, who understandably prefers to be called Pete. He left the Congress with apparently no place to go but here: as a moderate Republican, he was unlikely to become a power in the House; as for the Senate, Biden seemed too formidable to beat and the Roth seat was unavailable. So in 1976 DuPont ran for governor and beat a Democratic incumbent inclined to malapropisms. DuPont is interested in environmental issues, which on occasion may pit him against the company; but he is not going to be some kind of revolutionary in Delaware. One big achievement of his administration is to revise Delaware's banking laws to encourage out-of-state banks to move some of their operations here. In personal style, DuPont might come directly from the pages of *The Preppy Handbook,* with his button-down collars and frayed shirts. His leadership style and character have worn well with the voters; he was reelected with 71% of the vote in 1980.

Delaware's one House seat is held by Republican Thomas Evans, a man whose power — and problems — come more from his personal character than from his professional positions. As a moderate Republican, he is not a particular power in the House; on the Merchant Marine Committee, he is part of the small minority that has voted against subsidies. But he was well connected with the Ford White House, and he did have the good fortune to be one of the first eastern Republicans to endorse Ronald Reagan for 1980. More than that, he became a genuinely close friend of the president — one of the few members of Congress Nancy Reagan invited to her husband's 70th birthday party in February 1981. A position was created for him — vice chairman of the campaign committee for presidential liaison — to make him part of the House Republican leadership. Although not as close to the Reagans as Senator Paul Laxalt, he seemed in early 1981 to be playing in the House the same role Laxalt was in the Senate — being the eyes and ears of the president, serving as a channel of communication, but at the same time being careful not to upstage his colleagues.

Then in March 1981 Evans admitted to having an "association" with Paula Parkinson, the lobbyist whose picture appeared in *Playboy* magazine and who was rumored to have had videotaped affairs with 17 congressmen. This was obviously a serious embarrassment and presumably will have some effect on his White House social life; how much, if any, it will reduce his political effectiveness is less clear. Nor is it clear how Evans will fare with Delaware voters. His association with Parkinson is over, and he is a man of some ability and charm; will he be forgiven?

Census Data Pop. (1980 final) 595,225, up 9% in 1970s: 0.26% of U.S. total, 47th largest. Central city, 12%; suburban, 55%. Median 4-person family income, 1978, $21,194, 104% of U.S., 14th highest.

1979 Share of Federal Tax Burden $1,443,000,000; 0.32% of U.S. total, 45th largest.

1979 Share of Federal Outlays $1,029,034,000; 0.22% of U.S. total, 49th largest.

DOD	$235,624,000	45th	(0.22%)	HEW	$433,060,000	48th	(0.24%)
DOE	$1,644,000	49th	(0.01%)	ERDA	$2,669,000	37th	(0.09%)
HUD	$15,590,000	47th	(0.24%)	NASA	$680,000	39th	(0.01%)
VA	$55,176,000	48th	(0.27%)	DOT	$56,202,000	48th	(0.34%)
EPA	$23,201,000	45th	(0.44%)	DOC	$6,971,000	46th	(0.22%)
DOI	$8,219,000	49th	(0.50%)	USDA	$35,284,000	50th	(0.15%)

200   DELAWARE

Economic Base   Finance, insurance, and real estate; chemicals and allied products, especially plastics materials and synthetics; food and kindred products, especially poultry dressing and canned fruits and vegetables; agriculture, notably broilers, corn, dairy products, and soybeans; apparel and other textile products.

Political Lineup   Governor, Pierre S. du Pont IV (R). Senators, William V. Roth, Jr. (R) and Joseph R. Biden, Jr. (D). Representatives, 1 R at large; 1 in 1982. State Senate, 21 (12 D and 9 R); State House of Representatives, 41 (25 R and 16 D).

The Voters

   Registration   300,600 Total. 131,990 D (44%); 98,139 R (33%); 159 American (0%); 70,312 other (23%).
   Employment profile 1970   White collar, 51%. Blue collar, 34%. Service, 13%. Farm, 2%.
   Ethnic groups   Black 1980, 16%. Hispanic 1980, 2%. Asian 1980, 1%. Total foreign stock 1970, 12%.

Presidential Vote

1980	Reagan (R)	111,252	(47%)
	Carter (D)	105,754	(45%)
	Anderson (I)	16,288	(7%)
1976	Ford (R)	109,780	(47%)
	Carter (D)	122,559	(52%)

SENATORS

Sen. William V. Roth, Jr. (R) Elected 1970, seat up 1982; b. July 22, 1921, Great Falls, Mont.; home, Wilmington; U. of Oreg., B.A. 1944, Harvard U., M.B.A. 1947, LL.B. 1947.

Career Army, WWII; Practicing atty.; Chmn., Del. Rep. State Comm., 1961–64; U.S. House of Reps., 1967–71.

Offices 3215 DSOB, 202-224-2441. Also 3021 Fed. Bldg., 844 King St., Wilmington 19801, 302-573-6291, and 200 U.S.P.O. Bldg., Georgetown 19947, 302-856-7690.

Committees *Finance* (3d). Subcommittees: International Trade; Savings, Pensions, and Investment Policy; Economic Growth, Employment, and Revenue Sharing.

Governmental Affairs (Chairman). Subcommittee: Permanent Subcommittee on Investigations (Chairman).

Joint Economic Committee (2d).

Select Committee on Intelligence (7th). Subcommittee: Budget.

Joint Committee on Taxation (3d).

Group Ratings

	ADA	COPE	PC	LCV	CFA	RPN	NAB	NSI	NTU	ACA	ACU
1980	22	21	27	65	0	—	100	90	69	73	81
1979	21	21	43	—	24	—	—	—	63	70	72
1978	15	11	25	44	20	60	82	78	50	83	88

Key Votes

1) Draft Registn $	AGN	6) Fair Housng Cloture	AGN	11) Cut Socl Incr Defns	FOR
2) Ban $ to Nicrgua	FOR	7) Ban $ Rape Abortns	FOR	12) Income Tax Indexing	FOR
3) Dlay MX Missile	AGN	8) Cap on Food Stmp $	FOR	13) Lim Spdg 21% GNP	FOR
4) Nuclr Mortorium	AGN	9) New US Dep Edcatn	FOR	14) Incr Wndfll Prof Tax	FOR
5) Alaska Lands Bill	FOR	10) Cut OSHA Inspctns	FOR	15) Chryslr Loan Grntee	FOR

DELAWARE 201

Election Results

1976 general	William V. Roth, Jr. (R)	125,454	(56%)	($322,080)
	Thomas Maloney (D)	98,042	(44%)	($211,258)
1976 primary	William V. Roth, Jr. (R), nominated by convention			
1970 general	William V. Roth, Jr. (R)	96,021	(59%)	
	Jacob W. Zimmerman (D)	64,835	(40%)	

Sen. Joseph R. Biden, Jr. (D) Elected 1972, seat up 1984; b. Nov. 20, 1942, Scranton, Pa.; home, Wilmington; U. of Del., B.A. 1965, Syracuse U., J.D. 1968.

Career Practicing atty., 1968–72; New Castle Co. Cncl., 1970–72.

Offices 456 RSOB, 202-224-5042. Also 6021 Fed. Bldg., Wilmington 19801, 302-573-6345.

Committees *Budget* (3d).

Foreign Relations (2d). Subcommittees: International Economic Policy; European Affairs.

Judiciary (Ranking Member). Subcommittees: Criminal Law; Security and Terrorism.

Select Committee on Intelligence (3d). Subcommittee: Collection and Foreign Operations.

Group Ratings

	ADA	COPE	PC	LCV	CFA	RPN	NAB	NSI	NTU	ACA	ACU
1980	67	76	80	71	67	—	17	33	35	18	31
1979	53	86	75	—	67	—	—	—	30	20	21
1978	50	61	70	92	60	63	30	0	24	27	30

Key Votes

1) Draft Registn $	—	6) Fair Housng Cloture	FOR	11) Cut Socl Incr Defns	FOR
2) Ban $ to Nicrgua	FOR	7) Ban $ Rape Abortns	FOR	12) Income Tax Indexing	AGN
3) Dlay MX Missile	—	8) Cap on Food Stmp $	AGN	13) Lim Spdg 21% GNP	AGN
4) Nuclr Mortorium	FOR	9) New US Dep Edcatn	FOR	14) Incr Wndfll Prof Tax	—
5) Alaska Lands Bill	FOR	10) Cut OSHA Inspctns	AGN	15) Chryslr Loan Grntee	FOR

Election Results

1978 general	Joseph R. Biden, Jr. (D)	93,930	(58%)	($487,504)
	James H. Baxter, Jr. (R)	66,479	(41%)	($206,250)
1978 primary	Joseph R. Biden, Jr. (D), nominated by convention			
1972 general	Joseph R. Biden, Jr. (D)	116,006	(50%)	($260,699)
	J. Caleb Boggs (R)	112,844	(49%)	($167,657)

GOVERNOR

Gov. Pierre S. du Pont IV (R) Elected 1976, term expires Jan. 1985; b. Jan. 22, 1935, Wilmington; Princeton U., B.S.E. 1956, Harvard U., LL.B. 1963.

Career Navy, 1957–60; Business exec., Photo Products Div., E.I. du Pont Co., 1963–70; Del. House of Reps., 1968–70; U.S. House of Reps., 1971–77.

Offices Legislative Hall, Dover 19001, 302-736-4101.

Election Results

1980 gen.	Pierre S. du Pont IV (R) ...	159,004	(71%)
	William J. Gordy (D)	64,217	(29%)
1980 prim.	Pierre S. du Pont IV (R), nominated by convention		
1976 gen.	Pierre S. du Pont IV (R) ...	130,531	(57%)
	Sherman W. Tribbitt (D) ...	97,480	(42%)

Rep. Thomas B. Evans, Jr. (R) Elected 1976; b. Nov. 5, 1931, Nashville, Tenn.; home, Wilmington; U. of Va., B.A. 1951, LL.B. 1953.

Career Pres., Evans and Assoc., Inc., insurance and employee benefits, 1964– ; Partner, Evans, Steffey and Assoc., mortgage brokers; Dir., Del. State Development Dept., 1969–70.

Offices 316 CHOB, 202-225-4165. Also Fed. Ofc. Bldg., Wilmington 19801, 302-571-6181.

Committees *Banking, Finance and Urban Affairs* (7th). Subcommittees: Consumer Affairs and Coinage; Housing and Community Development; International Development Institutions and Finance.

Merchant Marine and Fisheries (8th). Subcommittees: Coast Guard and Navigation; Fisheries and Wildlife Conservation and the Environment.

Group Ratings

	ADA	COPE	PC	LCV	CFA	RPN	NAB	NSI	NTU	ACA	ACU
1980	56	20	43	—	29	—	50	100	38	65	33
1979	26	15	25	50	19	—	—	—	38	81	79
1978	15	21	20	47	23	70	92	89	23	76	83

Key Votes

1) Draft Registn $	AGN	6) Fair Hsg DOJ Enfrc	AGN	11) Cut Socl Incr Dfns $	—
2) Ban $ to Nicrgua	FOR	7) Lim PAC Contrbtns	AGN	12) Hosptl Cost Controls	AGN
3) Dlay MX Missile	FOR	8) Cap on Food Stmp $	AGN	13) Gasln Ctrls & Allctns	AGN
4) Nuclr Mortorium	FOR	9) New US Dep Edcatn	AGN	14) Lim Wndfll Prof Tax	FOR
5) Alaska Lands Bill	FOR	10) Cut OSHA $	FOR	15) Chryslr Loan Grntee	FOR

Election Results

1980 general	Thomas B. Evans, Jr. (R)	133,842	(62%)	($340,383)
	Robert L. Maxwell (D)	81,227	(38%)	($86,038)
1980 primary	Thomas B. Evans, Jr. (R), nominated by convention			
1978 general	Thomas B. Evans, Jr. (R)	91,689	(58%)	($241,410)
	Gary E. Hindes (D)	64,863	(41%)	($57,252)

DISTRICT OF COLUMBIA

Washington, D.C., is a political paradox: the capital of the federal government and a city that, until 1974, had not been allowed to choose its own mayor and council for 100 years; a black-majority capital in a white-majority nation; a city whose most prominent citizens make their livings in public affairs but know little or nothing about the public affairs of their own city. It is probably true that those involved in national politics in any great nation know or care little about the local politics of the capital. But in the United States the phenomenon is more noticeable and pronounced than in Britain or France, because our capital is a city whose only significant business is government; it is not a commercial and cultural center like London or Paris. And the separation between national and local politics is particularly notable in Washington because of race.

For Washington, from the days before the Civil War, has been a special city for blacks. The slave trade was abolished here as part of the Compromise of 1850, and the city became a haven for free Negroes, who heavily outnumbered its slaves by the time Lincoln became president. Blacks formed more than one-quarter of the electorate that installed Governor Alexander Sheppard, the last elected head of the D.C. government in the 19th century, whose profligate spending led Congress to revoke the city's system of home rule. And blacks held high office in the District through the rest of the 19th century under Republican administrations. At the northern edge of the South, Washington always had a higher percentage of blacks than most major cities; and when the city's metropolitan population ballooned in the years after the New Deal and World War II, it was inevitable that, with the suburbs restricted to whites, the District would quickly have a black majority. It was fear of this majority, more than anything else, that kept Congress from granting the District self-government, even though the same Congress had helped establish some of the institutions — Howard University, Freedmen's Hospital — that made Washington so important to blacks all over the nation.

Washington officially got its black majority in the 1960 census; by 1970 the District was 71% black, a figure that has remained the same in the 1980 counts. Washington is now our only major city without a white working class. Its affluent whites live mostly in areas west of Rock Creek Park, in such redeveloped (or "gentrified") neighborhoods as Capitol Hill, and other neighborhoods (e.g., Adams–Morgan and Mount Pleasant) that are fast being gentrified but for the moment are very proud of what some citizens call their Third World atmosphere (to which many illegal immigrants from Latin America contribute). The white population is almost entirely highly educated and high income; the poor elderly whites who once lived in fear in newly black neighborhoods are now almost all gone. There are many well-to-do blacks in the District, too, although the outmigration of middle-income blacks to Prince Georges County, Maryland, and, less frequently, to other suburbs, has deprived the city of an important segment of its black middle class.

The development of politics in the District has been stunted by the long time it took to develop home rule. Not until 1964 could the residents of the District vote for president; not until 1968 could they elect their own school board; not until 1971 did Washington get a nonvoting delegate in the House of Representatives. Only in 1974 was the District able to elect its mayor and council. Until home rule, control of the District's budget and lawmaking processes were in the hands of Congress, and for 22 years (1949–53, 1955–73) that meant mostly in the hands of South Carolina Congressman John McMillan, chairman of the House District of Columbia Committee. McMillan and his fellow Dixiecrats on the House Committee were considered implacably hostile to the District's black majority and provided the city with many of the worst aspects of colonial government. Their power collapsed suddenly in 1972, when McMillan was defeated in his primary in South Carolina (in a district with a large black percentage) and several other southern committee members retired.

Yet even today Congress inevitably retains much power over the District. It is the power of the purse—Congress every year votes the District a federal payment, in lieu of the taxes federal buildings might pay if they were not tax exempt. The question is how much the federal payment should be. District officials inevitably argue for enough money to cover whatever budget they propose. Some members of Congress, for example, William Natcher who for years chaired the House Appropriations subcommittee on the District, claimed the D.C. government was squandering money and could live with much less. The federal payment gives Congress the same kind of power over Washington that most state legislatures get from the aid they provide large city governments; and while most big city mayors are used to going up to the capital with hat in hand, local Washington politicians assumed those days were over when home rule came. The disappointment is great, particularly since in the early 1980s the District seemed unable to maintain its level of expenditures and was forced to cut many services. Congress was also threatening to override a District referendum that would allow casino gambling in Washington— a clear violation of the idea of home rule, but one that is entirely within the powers of Congress.

At the head of the District government today is Mayor Marion Barry, who not so long ago was known as a militant who started an organization called Pride, Inc. He ran for the school board and got citywide recognition; in 1978 he entered the mayoral primary against incumbent Walter Washington and Council President Sterling Tucker. Each had his problems. Washington had been appointed mayor by Presidents Johnson and Nixon; he had worked ably with Congress to get money for the District; he had been known as the "walking mayor" for his efforts during the 1968 riots. But by 1978 his administration was beset by scandal and he was virtually incommunicado to the political and journalistic community. Tucker was judged competent and was well connected with the class of black businessmen and professionals; but he lacked charisma and magnetism.

Ironically, Barry's margin in the virtually even three-way primary probably came from affluent white voters, who saw in him the kind of outspoken, stylish leader they thought most blacks wanted. But it does not make too much sense to speak of racial patterns in Washington voting; the percentage in both 1974 and 1978 mayoral primaries among whites and blacks differed by only a few points. Age and cultural attitudes are more important in determining choices, and Washington has never had an electoral struggle here of the kind seen in so many cities between blacks and whites for control of the city government. Many blacks see in gentrification the possibility of a rise in the white percentage in the city, a white takeover of its government. But whites in Washington think that blacks ought to be in control here and are less than eager to take over a government that does not much impinge on their lives anyway.

By 1982, when the next mayoral primary will be held, Washington will have had home rule for almost ten years; and while Marion Barry will probably remain popular, he may have serious competition from Sterling Tucker or current Council President Arrington Dixon. The problem is that the District government has not performed up to expectations.

Economically much of Washington is booming. People are renovating houses and apartments; the business district is thriving and moving eastward into territory land developers once shunned; property values are still climbing not only in affluent white areas but in many of the city's comfortable black neighborhoods as well. But the city government is chronically broke. There is a tendency, natural in a city that so long lacked self-government, to blame others for its problems. Marion Barry likes to cite the fact that the city is prohibited from taxing the incomes of people who work in the District and live in the suburbs. But this is an unchangeable fact of life any District government must face; suburbanites on the congressional District committees will never allow their constituents to be taxed by D.C., and many other central cities labor under similar prohibitions. Congress is also portrayed as stingy. But no one denies that there is plenty of waste in the District government, and no responsible member of Congress wants to see it perpetuated. The District government performs many services better than it is given credit for. But voters in Washington are getting used to the fact that there are no longer any good alibis for the failings of local government here.

The District has one member of Congress, Delegate Walter Fauntroy, who necessarily spends a lot of time on District affairs. Like other nonvoting members, he can vote in committee, and he is now the number two Democrat on the House District of Columbia Committee. He first won his seat in a special 1971 election, and the real contest was in the Democratic primary; he has had no serious opposition since. Fauntroy gets on fairly well now with Mayor Barry, although he supported Tucker in the last election. He seems not to have any ambition to run for mayor himself. A minister with a proud past in the civil rights movement, he is also a fine tenor and does a fine rendition of "The Impossible Dream."

Fauntroy has not had particularly good fortune when he has ventured beyond local matters, however. In 1978 he got the Congress to approve a constitutional amendment giving the District full representation in the Congress, which in practical terms would mean the addition of two senators and a vote as well as a voice for the city's congressman. Fauntroy himself would obviously have a good chance to be elected to the Senate if this were passed. But as of early 1981 only a handful of states had ratified the amendment, and some — prompted by a right-wing movement interested in squelching both this measure and the Equal Rights Amendment — have explicitly disapproved it. It seems almost certain to join the list of constitutional amendments that have never been passed.

Census Data   Pop. (1980 final) 637,651, down 16% in 1970s: 0.28% of U.S. total. Central city, 100%. Median 4-person family income, 1978, $16,769, 82% of U.S..

1979 Share of Federal Tax Burden $1,938,000,000; 0.43% of U.S. total.

1979 Share of Federal Outlays $15,435,271,000; 3.33% of U.S. total, 8th largest.

DOD	$1,985,834,000	17th	(1.87%)	HEW	$2,840,984,000	22d	(1.59%)
DOE	$383,270,000	11th	(3.26%)	ERDA	$39,967,000	15th	(1.47%)
HUD	$290,887,000	8th	(4.41%)	NASA	$68,529,000	13th	(1.47%)
VA	$533,495,000	12th	(2.57%)	DOT	$1,705,711,000	1st	(10.34%)
EPA	$317,085,000	3d	(5.97%)	DOC	$446,303,000	2d	(14.09%)
DOI	$591,476,000	1st	(10.65%)	USDA	$456,508,000	20th	(1.90%)

Political Lineup   Representative, 1 D at large; 1 in 1982.

The Voters

   Registration   288,837 Total. 221,864 D (77%); 25,634 R (9%); 37,685 I (13%); 1,629 Other (1%); 105 U.S. Labor (0%); 143 Socialist Workers (0%).

Employment profile 1970   White collar, 51%. Blue collar, 34%. Service, 13%. Farm, 2%.
Ethnic groups   Black. 1980, 70%. Hispanic 1980, 3%. Total foreign stock 1970, 12%.

Presidential Vote

1980	Reagan (R)	23,313	(13%)
	Carter (D)	130,231	(75%)
	Anderson (I)	16,131	(9%)
1976	Ford (R)	27,873	(17%)
	Carter (D)	137,818	(82%)

Rep. Walter E. Fauntroy (D) Elected Mar. 23, 1971; b. Feb. 6, 1933, Washington, D.C.; Va. Union U., A.B. 1955, Yale U., B.D. 1958.

Career Pastor, New Bethel Baptist Church, 1958–; Founder and former Dir., Model Inner City Community Org.; Dir., Washington Bureau, SCLC, 1961–71, Coordinator, Selma to Montgomery March, 1965; Vice Chmn., D.C. City Cncl., 1967–79; Natl. Coordinator, Poor Peoples Campaign, 1969; Chmn., Bd. of Dirs., Martin Luther King, Jr., Ctr. for Social Change, 1969–.

Offices 2350 RHOB, 202-225-8050. Also 350 G St. N.W., Washington 20548, 202-275-0171.

Committees *Banking, Finance, and Urban Affairs* (7th). Subcommittees: Domestic Monetary Policy (Chairman); Economic Stabilization; General Oversight and Negotiation; Housing and Community Development.

District of Columbia (2d). Subcommittee: Fiscal Affairs and Health.

Group Ratings and Key Votes: Does Not Vote

Election Results

1980 general	Walter E. Fauntroy (D)	111,631	(74%)	
	Robert J. Roehr	21,021	(14%)	
	Josephine D. Butler.............	14,325	(10%)	
1980 primary	Walter E. Fauntroy (D), unopposed			
1978 general	Walter E. Fauntroy (D)	76,557	(87%)	($95,668)
	Jackson Champion (R)	11,667	(13%)	

FLORIDA

No southern state has changed more in the last generation than Florida. Like other southern states, it was changed by the civil rights revolution. But it has also been changed by an in-migration unique in American history. Back in 1950 Florida had 2.5 million residents; by the time the 1980 census was taken, the total was nearly 10 million. Just in the 1970s Florida's population grew by more than 3 million people, in search of sunshine and warmth, of year-round golf and swimming. Many of course are old people who want to spend their last years in a warm climate and enjoy the last of their money in a state with no income or inheritance tax. But there are also plenty of younger migrants with families flocking to such places as Orlando, with Disney World nearby, and West Palm Beach and Jacksonville.

Florida's politics has a peculiar instability for two reasons. The first is that so many citizens are recent arrivals—and so many of them are elderly. The majority of voters in Florida partake of no Florida tradition, indeed partake of no single political tradition at all: they come from all parts of the East, Midwest, and South. There are Jews from the Bronx and WASPs from Wilmette, well-to-do country club members from the South and retired factory workers from Pittsburgh who are just scraping by in trailer parks. Most of Florida's voters, however, have some kind of southern background, but there is no common frame of reference to organize and make sense of state politics. Moreover, the fact that so many new Floridians are elderly means that there is a greater turnover among the electorate than in other fast-growing states. The state's elderly voters in the early 1960s were mostly Republicans, from relatively affluent background; the retirees of the early 1980s are much more likely than before to come from blue collar backgrounds, and to vote Democratic.

The second reason for the instability of Florida politics is that this is a state like Ohio with many metropolitan areas, not one like New York or Illinois with one dominant metropolitan area. Miami's Dade County, for example, casts only 14% of the state's votes; even taking together the three counties of the Gold Coast — Dade, Broward, and Palm Beach — you have only 32% of the electorate. Another major metropolitan area has two central cities that could not be more unalike: working-class Tampa and retiree haven St. Petersburg. Jacksonville is big enough to be significant in the state's economy and politics, and so increasingly is Orlando, the home of Disney World now as well as the center of the state's citrus industry. There are literally dozens of smaller communities, from Naples to Pensacola which, for most of their residents, are Florida. Florida has eight major television markets, which means that a politician who wants to get known statewide must fly around constantly if he wants to get on local newscasts. Meanwhile, there is no dominant statewide newspaper, and the state capital, Tallahassee, is a small city tucked away almost in a corner of the state, more than a comfortable day's drive from where most Floridians live.

All these factors make Florida elections unpredictable and subject to startling fluctuations. In presidential elections, it trended Republican in the years after World War II but went for Jimmy Carter in 1976, then turned sharply against him in 1980. The Republicans captured the governorship here as long ago as 1966, but their governor, Claude Kirk, was so erratic that he lost his bid for reelection and indeed was nearly beaten in his primary in 1970. Since then the state has had two Democratic governors, both unknown state legislators who were able to run second in the initial primary, to beat better-known but more controversial Democrats in the runoff, and then to cruise to relatively easy general election victories: Reubin Askew in 1970 and Bob Graham in 1978. Florida, represented by the same two U.S. senators for 18 years in the 1950s and 1960s, has changed senators often since: it has reelected a senator only once since 1964. The state's delegation to the House had only six members, all conservative Democrats, in 1950. For 1982, Florida will increase its number of congressmen from the current 15 to 19; and while the redistricting process is controlled by Democrats, the Republicans will almost certainly gain at least two of the seats.

The instability of Florida politics was never illustrated better than in the 1980 elections. This had been one of Jimmy Carter's most important states. Next door to south Georgia, Florida was a place where he campaigned intensively before the 1976 primary, and he ended up winning despite challenges from George Wallace, with his appeal to white southerners, and Henry Jackson, with his appeal to transplanted northerners. Carter carried Florida in the general election that year as well, with pluralities in most parts of the state. In the 1980 primary, he held the state easily against Edward Kennedy (although he had been pressed closely in a straw poll of Democrats in the fall of 1979). Then came the influx of Cuban refugees, with more than 125,000 pouring into Florida during a period of 10 weeks.

Florida has had a Cuban exile community for some time, and Cubans are now both numerous and successful in the Miami area. But the state was unprepared for what happened in the spring and early summer of 1980, when Miami was bursting with refugees. Stories began to circulate about the behavior of the new arrivals: they were criminals; they had organized gangs preying on everyone in the streets; they lived in indescribably filthy conditions —stories that would surely be familiar to anyone who lived in New York in 1907, the year when 1.7 million immigrants came to the United States. The impression quickly grew that the national administration was mismanaging the crisis; and indeed the response of the Carter Administration was unsure—sometimes welcoming refugees from Castro's "paradise," sometimes sternly promising that no more would be allowed in and then declining to turn them back.

This Cuban influx came on top of other disturbing developments in the Miami area. The original Cuban refugees had helped to make Miami in many ways the economic capital of Latin America, the Latin American headquarters for major businesses and a shopping center free of high import taxes for affluent Latin Americans from many countries. Unfortunately, Miami also became the headquarters for much of America's drug business. By 1980 the city was awash in illegal drugs, marijuana from Colombia and Jamaica, cocaine from Peru and Bolivia. Law enforcement authorities estimated Miami's drug business at $7 billion annually, and Miami banks handled the large majority of America's $100 bills—a sure sign of illegal cash transactions. Naturally there were rashes of killings of Colombian couriers and Cuban dealers in the drug business. Many Floridians associated these developments with the Cuban influx. On top of that, there were a number of refugees coming in from Haiti, the Americas' least developed country, and riots in the Liberty City black neighborhood, along with angry talk from black militants that the Cubans (many of them, incidentally, black themselves) were being favored over black Americans. The political result was that by early fall the bottom had fallen out of Jimmy Carter's campaign in south Florida. The counties most affected, Dade and Broward, had given Carter a 106,000-vote plurality over Ford in 1976; in 1980 both ended up going for Reagan, by a total of 138,000 votes. If the Gold Coast had given Carter as high a percentage in 1980 as in 1976, he would have lost the state by only a 50%–44% margin, rather than the huge 56%–39% margin Reagan actually received.

At the same time, Carter lost ground in the rest of the state as well. In 1980 he failed to carry Jacksonville and Tampa, with their large white southern working-class vote, and he trailed badly in the hawkish Panhandle area. The only part of the state he carried was northeastern Florida, directly south of Georgia.

The Cuban refugee influx affected the state's other major contest, for U.S. senator, as well. This was one of Florida's complicated political races. The Democratic primary was a rematch between Senator Richard Stone and state Insurance Commissioner (and former Congressman) Bill Gunter; Stone had upset Gunter in the runoff in 1974 by only 10,000 votes and had won a narrow plurality in the general, which featured a significant American Independent candidate as well as a Republican. Stone had distinguished himself in the Senate by his support of the state's citrus industry on the Agriculture Committee and his support of Israel on Foreign Relations; he felt particularly strongly about the latter issue and had strong support from around the country because of it. But he had never succeeded in getting very well known in Florida. Meanwhile, Gunter had become known largely by running for various offices. After losing the Senate race in 1974, he ran to fill a vacancy as insurance commissioner and considered running for governor in 1978, although he decided not to. A politically adept Orlando native with a southern accent and plenty of charm, Gunter had natural appeal in the northern and central parts of the state; and he was able to prevent Stone from making the inroads he had in 1974 in the Panhandle. Stone's 100,000-vote edge in the Gold Coast was not enough to prevent Gunter from eking out a 52%–48% victory in the runoff.

But Gunter faced serious problems and, because Florida's runoff occurs in early October, had little time to solve them. His first problem was the fact that he had a solid and popular Republican opponent, Paula Hawkins. As public service commissioner, she had won a reputation of fighting for the consumer against the utilities; she was also well known statewide and had antagonized few voters. Moreover, she was from the Orlando area and thus eliminated Gunter's hometown advantage there. The Democrat's second problem was south Florida. The Gold Coast was still furious about the refugee issue and was also resentful of Gunter as the man who had defeated its candidate, Stone. Jewish voters, who are important indeed in the Gold Coast, were at best lukewarm toward Gunter. The result: Hawkins carried not only central Florida, as expected, but prevailed in the Gold Coast as well. Gunter's margins in many rural counties did not overcome Hawkins's victories in just about every county with a sizable portion of in-migrants from the North.

This makes Paula Hawkins Florida's first woman senator. She became known as an outspoken and unpredictable conservative; she won attention in early 1981 when she held a luncheon to protest food stamp fraud and served New York steaks and fresh asparagus. She is likely to blend in fairly easily with the new Republican majority at first, but she has earned a reputation as a political maverick and could be an unpredictable member of the majority as time goes on.

Florida's senior senator is Lawton Chiles, a Democrat who was first elected in 1970. Chiles was the originator of the walk as a campaign tactic, and as a little-known state senator he walked the length of Florida talking with voters in 1970. His pleasant demeanor, good looks, friendliness, and willingness to listen helped him to an upset victory in the Democratic runoff. In the general election, he rather easily beat Congressman William Cramer, a Republican who called loudly for the death penalty and is now a successful Washington lawyer–lobbyist. Before 1970, Democrats in Florida had been having problems straddling the gap between the national party (still popular on the Gold Coast but anathema elsewhere) and southern quasi-segregationists (still popular in many areas, but not among blacks and transplanted northerners). Chiles was one of the "New South" Democrats who bridged that gap in 1970. (Others included Reubin Askew and Jimmy Carter.) From the small citrus town of Lakeland, Chiles was obviously not a northern liberal, but he was not a vocal segregationist either. He won that election with comparative ease and was reelected by a wide margin in 1976. Although he may have a serious Republican opponent in 1982, he seems likely to be a strong candidate for reelection, if only because he has not antagonized any important segment of the electorate.

Chiles is a member of the Appropriations and Governmental Affairs Committees, and when Democrats controlled the Senate he made headlines as a subcommittee chairman investigating the GSA and government purchasing practices. He is not vocal on many national issues but swings into action when Florida's interests are threatened, as when he almost single-handedly defeated a Pentagon proposal to consolidate helicopter training in Alabama and phase out operations in Florida. He also is the ranking Democrat on the Special Committee on Aging—an important post, presumably, for Florida. Chiles is one of the most active members of the Senate's prayer breakfast group, a deeply religious man who has close relationships with like-minded colleagues on both sides of the aisle.

Florida's governor is another Democrat who likes to paint himself as a rural Floridian, but in fact he is also the first Florida governor to hail from Dade County. Bob Graham's rural credentials are legitimate, however. He is from a prominent Florida family, and he did indeed have a farm, most of which he subdivided and made into a model community called Miami Lakes. Graham made a liberal record in the state Senate, but he played that down during the 1978 campaign. Instead, he worked at 100 different jobs throughout the state and ran television advertisements asserting that he was in touch with the ordinary person. His main Democratic opponent, Attorney General Robert Shevin, had a record of stern law enforcement and support of capital punishment and a strong consumer protection record as well. He had hoped to be the state's first Jewish governor but was unable to expand his appeal sufficiently beyond the "condo belt" of the Gold Coast. In the general election, Graham faced and beat Jack Eckerd, a very wealthy drugstore chain owner, who has run for office several times in Florida and always lost. Eckerd ran well in the area covered by Tampa and St. Petersburg television stations, along the Gulf Coast, which contains about one-quarter of the state's voters, and he nearly carried Jacksonville, where he had the support of former Mayor Hans Tanzler, a born-again Christian who lost in the Democratic primary. But Eckerd was not able to carry the northern and Panhandle counties; he trailed in the Orlando area which usually goes Republican; and Graham won by huge margins in the Gold Coast.

Graham has been by most accounts a reasonably successful governor. He was able, for example, to secure the passage of a number of state constitution amendments in the 1980 general election. He has been less successful, however, in influencing Florida voters' attitudes toward national issues. He was a strong backer of Jimmy Carter, early and late, and gave Carter's nominating speech at New York; but he was unable to prevent the precipitous drop in Carter's vote from 52% in 1976 to 39% in 1980. Graham is eligible for a second term and is unlikely to be opposed seriously in the Democratic primary. He might, however, have trouble in the general election, if the gains the Republicans made in the Gold Coast in 1980 turn out to be a continuing shift away from the Democrats rather than just a one-time reaction to a sudden influx of Cuban refugees.

Census Data   Pop. (1980 final) 9,739,992, up 43% in 1970s: 4.30% of U.S. total, 7th largest. Central city, 26%; suburban, 59%. Median 4-person family income, 1978, $18,118, 89% of U.S., 42d highest.

1979 Share of Federal Tax Burden $16,906,000,000; 3.75% of U.S. total, 9th largest.

1979 Share of Federal Outlays $19,647,727,000; 4.24% of U.S. total, 6th largest.

DOD	$4,314,756,000	5th	(4.07%)	HEW	$9,170,765,000	4th	(5.13%)
DOE	$71,033,000	24th	(0.60%)	ERDA	$14,427,000	25th	(0.53%)
HUD	$186,583,000	11th	(2.83%)	NASA	$442,724,000	2d	(9.47%)
VA	$1,093,581,000	4th	(5.27%)	DOT	$701,994,000	7th	(4.25%)
EPA	$195,585,000	7th	(3.68%)	DOC	$63,534,000	12th	(2.01%)
DOI	$74,692,000	22d	(1.35%)	USDA	$719,425,000	8th	(2.99%)

Economic Base   Finance, insurance, and real estate; agriculture, notably oranges, cattle, dairy products, and grapefruit; food and kindred products, especially canned, cured, and frozen foods; tourism; transportation equipment, especially aircraft and parts, and ship and boat building and repairing; electrical equipment and supplies, especially communication equipment.

Political Lineup   Governor, Robert (Bob) Graham (D). Senators, Lawton Chiles (D) and Paula Hawkins (R). Representatives, 15 (11 D and 4 R); 19 in 1982. State Senate, 40 (27 D and 13 R); State House of Representatives, 120 (81 D and 39 R).

The Voters

   Registration   4,809,721 Total. 3,087,427 D (64%); 1,429,645 R (30%); 292,649 others (6%).

   Employment profile 1970   White collar, 50%. Blue collar, 32%. Service, 15%. Farm, 3%.

   Ethnic groups   Black 1980, 14%. Hispanic 1980, 9%. Asian 1980, 1%. Total foreign stock 1970, 18%. Germany, UK, Canada, 2% each; Italy, USSR, 1% each.

Presidential Vote

1980	Reagan (R)	2,046,951	(56%)
	Carter (D)	1,419,475	(39%)
	Anderson (I)	189,692	(5%)
1976	Ford (R)	1,469,531	(47%)
	Carter (D)	1,636,000	(52%)

1980 Democratic Presidential Primary			*1980 Republican Presidential Primary*		
Carter	666,321	(61%)	Reagan	345,699	(56%)
Kennedy	254,727	(23%)	Bush	185,996	(30%)
Two others	72,634	(7%)	Anderson	56,636	(9%)
No preference	104,321	(10%)	Six others	26,664	(4%)

SENATORS

Sen. Lawton Chiles (D) Elected 1970, seat up 1982; b. Apr. 3, 1930, Lakeland; home, Lakeland; U. of Fla., B.S. 1952, LL.B. 1955.

Career Army, Korea; Practicing atty., 1955-71; Instructor, Fla. Southern Col., 1955-57; Fla. House of Reps., 1958-66; Fla. Senate, 1966-70.

Offices 437 RSOB, 202-224-5274. Also Fed. Bldg., Lakeland 33801, 813-688-6681, and 931 Fed. Bldg., P.O. Box 79, 51 S.W. 1st Ave., Miami 33130, 305-350-4891.

Committees *Appropriations* (7th). Subcommittees: Agriculture and Related Agencies; Defense; Labor, Health and Human Services, Education; Transportation.

Budget (2d).

Governmental Affairs (3d). Subcommittees: Permanent Subcommittee on Investigations; Federal Expenditures, Research and Rules.

Special Committee on Aging (Ranking Member).

Group Ratings

	ADA	COPE	PC	LCV	CFA	RPN	NAB	NSI	NTU	ACA	ACU
1980	50	52	40	33	13	—	33	40	41	38	42
1979	42	47	38	—	38	—	—	—	25	26	21
1978	35	32	30	51	25	50	75	50	14	36	33

Key Votes

1) Draft Registn $	FOR	6) Fair Housng Cloture	FOR	11) Cut Socl Incr Defns	FOR
2) Ban $ to Nicrgua	AGN	7) Ban $ Rape Abortns	AGN	12) Income Tax Indexing	AGN
3) Dlay MX Missile	AGN	8) Cap on Food Stmp $	AGN	13) Lim Spdg 21% GNP	AGN
4) Nuclr Mortorium	AGN	9) New US Dep Edcatn	FOR	14) Incr Wndfll Prof Tax	FOR
5) Alaska Lands Bill	FOR	10) Cut OSHA Inspctns	FOR	15) Chryslr Loan Grntee	FOR

Election Results

1976 general	Lawton Chiles (D)..............	1,799,518	(63%)	($362,235)
	John Grady (R)................	1,057,886	(37%)	($394,574)
1976 primary	Lawton Chiles (D), unopposed			
1970 general	Lawton Chiles (D)..............	902,438	(54%)	
	William C. Cramer (R)	772,817	(46%)	

Sen. Paula Hawkins (R) Elected 1980, seat up 1986; b. Jan. 24, 1927, Salt Lake City, Utah; home, Winter Park; Utah St. U.

Career Rep. Nat. Committee, 1968; Spec. Advis. Committee, Consum. Affairs, Fed. Energy Admin., 1968; Pres. Commission on White House Fellowships, 1968; Fla. Pub. Svc. Commissioner, 1973–79.

Offices 1327 DSOB, 202-224-3041. Also 701 Semoran Blvd., Rm. 200, Altamonte Springs 32701, 305-339-1980, and 604 Lewis State Bank Bldg., Tallahassee 32301, 904-224-5748.

Committees *Agriculture, Nutrition and Forestry* (8th). Subcommittees: Agricultural Credit and Rural Electrification (Chairwoman); Agricultural Production, Marketing and Stabilization of Prices; Foreign Agricultural Policy; Nutrition.

Labor and Human Resources (4th). Subcommittees: Labor; Employment and Productivity; Investigations and General Oversight (Chairwoman).

Joint Economic Committee (5th).

Group Ratings and Key Votes: Newly Elected
Election Results

1980 general	Paula Hawkins (R)	1,822,460	(52%)	($696,969)
	Bill Gunter (D)	1,705,409	(48%)	($2,164,560)
1980 runoff	Paula Hawkins (R)	293,600	(62%)	
	Lou Frey, Jr. (R)	182,911	(38%)	($320,489)
1980 primary	Paula Hawkins (R)	209,856	(48%)	
	Lou Frey, Jr. (R)	119,834	(27%)	
	Ander Crenshaw (R)	54,767	(13%)	($71,626)
	Three others (R)	51,505	(12%)	
1974 general	Richard (Dick) Stone (D)	781,031	(43%)	($919,787)
	Jack Eckerd (R)	736,674	(41%)	($421,169)
	John Grady (AI)	282,659	(16%)	($148,495)

GOVERNOR

Gov. Robert (Bob) **Graham** (D) Elected 1978, term expires Jan. 1983; b. Nov. 9, 1936, Miami; U. of Fla., B.A. 1959, Harvard U., J.D. 1962.

Career V.P., Graham Co., cattle and dairy production; Chmn. of Bd., Sengra Development Corp., land developers; Fla. House of Reps., 1967–71; Fla. Senate, 1971–78.

Offices The Capitol, Tallahassee 32304, 904-488-1234.

Election Results

1978 gen.	Robert (Bob) Graham (D) . .	1,406,580	(56%)
	Jack M. Eckerd (R)	1,123,888	(44%)
1978 runoff	Robert (Bob) Graham (D) . .	482,535	(54%)
	Robert L. Shevin (D)	418,636	(46%)
1978 prim.	Robert L. Shevin (D)	364,732	(35%)
	Robert (Bob) Graham (D) . .	261,972	(25%)
	Hans G. Tanzler (D)	124,706	(12%)
	Jim Williams (D)	124,427	(12%)
	Three others (D)	161,696	(16%)
1974 gen.	Reubin Askew (D)	1,118,954	(61%)
	Jerry Thomas (R)	709,438	(39%)

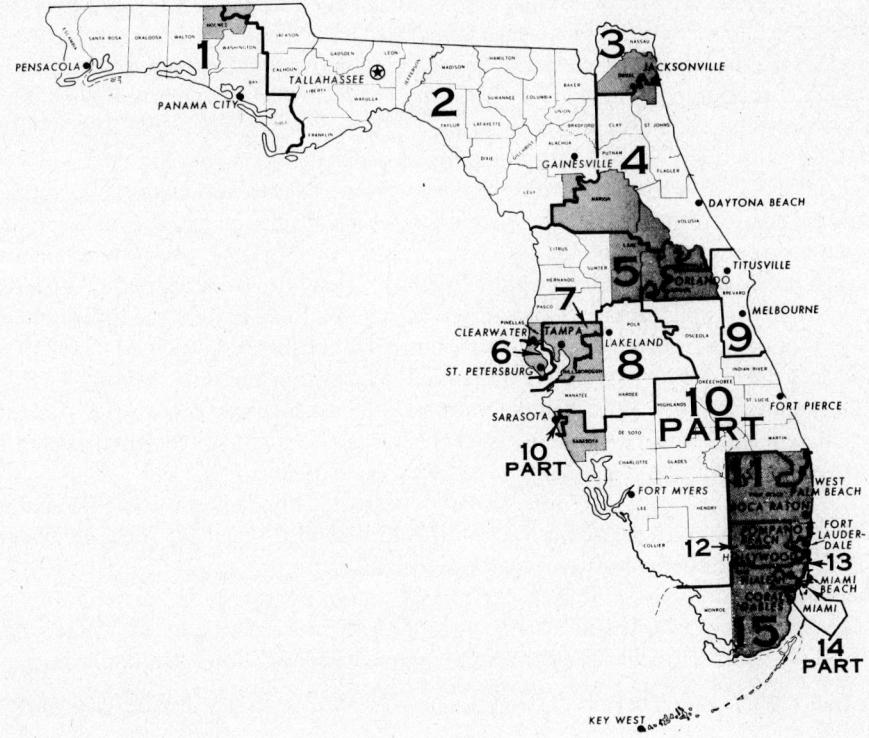

FIRST DISTRICT

One of the heaviest concentrations of military bases and installations in the nation can be found in the northern Panhandle counties that make up Florida's 1st congressional district. There are many reasons for this concentration. Pensacola, the district's largest city, is an old Gulf of Mexico port, and there has been a naval station here for just about as long as the United States has held the territory. There are more than 100 miles of coastline along the Gulf here, with a good port at Panama City as well as Pensacola. The climate is mild, the terrain inland flat and, where swampy, reclaimable. These characteristics have helped to bring to this area such huge facilities as Eglin Air Force Base, which spreads over the lion's share of three counties. There is another reason the Defense Department spends more than $900 million yearly around here, and that is the fact that for 12 years, from 1965 to 1977, Congressman Bob Sikes of the 1st district was chairman of the House Appropriations Sub-committee on Military Construction.

Sikes's philosophy and the interests of his district happily coincided. First elected in 1940, he was one of those southern Democrats who stood with Franklin Roosevelt when he was pushing Lend–Lease and instituting the draft. For his congressional career—the longest in Florida history—Sikes continued to believe that it was better to risk spending too much than to spend too little on military preparedness. Naturally a lot of that spending was done in the 1st district. When Sikes was first elected, this area was literally a backwater, with one of the lowest standards of living in the country. Today, thanks in part to his efforts, it is prosperous and booming, with income levels, after adjustment for local taxes and cost of living, at or above the national average. Sikes also found ways to help himself financially. In 1976 it was revealed that he failed to disclose that he used his committee position to get the government to allow development on land he owned, that he owned 1,000 shares of Fairchild Industries while voting for a bill granting them a $73 million contract, and that he had an interest in a Florida bank and tried to get a branch approved at the Pensacola Naval Air Station.

Every scrap of evidence indicates that the voters of the 1st district approve of Sikes's politics. This is a district with a Democratic heritage and a few blacks, and most of its voters are southern-born whites who tend to be even more supportive of the military and of an aggressive foreign policy than are southern whites generally. This is also a district that gave a large majority to that most pugnacious of candidates, George Wallace, in 1968 and in several primaries in Florida; and it is a district that gave fully 84% of its votes to Richard Nixon over George McGovern in 1972. It gave Gerald Ford only a razor-thin margin over Georgia neighbor Jimmy Carter in 1976. But when the (mostly) unhawkish character of Carter's foreign and defense policies became evident, the 1st district turned stoutly against him and, neighbor or no, gave him far fewer votes than Ronald Reagan in 1980.

The 1st district stuck with Sikes after he was reprimanded by the House in 1976, but in 1977 he was stripped of his chairmanship by a 189–93 vote. In 1978, at age 72, he decided to retire. Since then the district has been won twice by Earl Hutto, a Democratic legislator from Panama City who once was a TV newscaster there and in Pensacola. Hutto, who emphasized his religious background and is definitely in line with the district's hawkish instincts, has won two convincing victories over a formidable opponent who was once mayor of Pensacola.

Census Data   Pop. (1980 final) 555,343, up 23% in 1970s. Median family income, 1970, $7,621, 79% of U.S.

The Voters

   Employment profile 1970   White collar, 48%. Blue collar, 36%. Service, 15%. Farm, 1%.
   Ethnic groups   Black 1980, 14%. Hispanic 1980, 2%. Am. Ind. 1980, 1%. Asian 1980, 1%. Total foreign stock 1970, 5%.

Presidential Vote

1980	Reagan (R)	126,062	(54%)
	Carter (D)	99,637	(43%)
	Anderson (I)	4,762	(2%)
1976	Ford (R)	91,674	(50%)
	Carter (D)	89,170	(49%)

Rep. Earl Dewitt Hutto (D) Elected 1978; b. May 12, 1926, Midland City, Ala.; home, Panama City; Troy St. U., B.S. 1949, Northwestern U., 1951.

Career   Navy, WWII; Pres., Earl Hutto Advertising Agency; Fla. House of Reps., 1972–78.

Offices   330 CHOB, 202-225-4136. Also Fed. Bldg., Panama City 32401, 904-234-8933.

Committees   *Armed Services*   (19th). Subcommittees: Military Installations and Facilities; Research and Development; Seapower and Strategic and Critical Materials.

   Merchant Marine and Fisheries   (14th). Subcommittees: Coast Guard and Navigation; Fisheries and Wildlife Conservation and the Environment.

Group Ratings

	ADA	COPE	PC	LCV	CFA	RPN	NAB	NSI	NTU	ACA	ACU
1980	22	50	30	35	36	—	75	100	36	48	56
1979	21	35	23	24	23	—	—	—	32	36	49

Key Votes

1) Draft Registn $	FOR	6) Fair Hsg DOJ Enfrc	AGN	11) Cut Socl Incr Dfns $	FOR
2) Ban $ to Nicrgua	FOR	7) Lim PAC Contrbtns	FOR	12) Hosptl Cost Controls	FOR
3) Dlay MX Missile	AGN	8) Cap on Food Stmp $	AGN	13) Gasln Ctrls & Allctns	FOR
4) Nuclr Mortorium	AGN	9) New US Dep Edcatn	FOR	14) Lim Wndfll Prof Tax	FOR
5) Alaska Lands Bill	AGN	10) Cut OSHA $		FOR	15) Chryslr Loan Grntee	FOR

Election Results

1980 general	Earl Dewitt Hutto (D)	119,829	(61%)	($63,451)
	Warren Briggs (R)	75,939	(39%)	($227,563)
1980 primary	Earl Dewitt Hutto (D), unopposed			
1978 general	Earl Dewitt Hutto (D)	85,608	(63%)	($118,847)
	Warren Briggs (R)	49,715	(37%)	($186,711)

SECOND DISTRICT

The 2d congressional district of Florida is the part of the state that is most like the Deep South. This is really the southernmost extension of Dixie; sociologically and politically it is not very different from neighboring south Georgia. This is the part of Florida with the greatest concentration of blacks — more than one-quarter of the population — and most of them are not residents of black neighborhoods in the district's largest cities, Tallahassee and Gainesville, but rather live in proximity to whites in small towns and in small frame farmhouses in the flat, sometimes swampy countryside. This part of Florida was also the heart of the state 40 years ago, in the days before air conditioning when there were few northern migrants. Politically, its domination of the state lasted longer: north Florida's rural legislators, known as the Pork Chop Gang, controlled the legislature for years and still have influence there beyond their numbers. Even today, a disproportionate number of Florida's state institutions are located in this area, including the state capital at Tallahassee, state universities at Gainesville and Tallahassee, and the state prison at Raiford.

The 2d district was one part of Florida that stayed true to Jimmy Carter in 1980. The political terrain has been extremely important to Carter's political career: south Georgia volunteers fanned out here in 1975 and 1976 and took crucial votes away from George Wallace — the favorite in this part of Florida — in the 1976 primary. It was one of Carter's best Florida districts in the 1976 general election. In 1980 it again delivered solidly for him in the primary and, unlike all but two other Florida districts, gave him a majority in the general election.

The 2d district has stayed solidly Democratic in House elections, and since 1962 has elected Democratic Congressman Don Fuqua. His record has been in line with the tradition of southern Democrats representing rural and small-town districts; he favors strong defense measures and opposes many but by no means all federal domestic spending programs. He has risen in seniority to become chairman of the Science and Technology Committee, a body with potentially fascinating jurisdiction but relatively little political controversy today. Fuqua's subcommittee has jurisdiction over government research and development efforts in the Energy Department (outside defense and nuclear), including fossil fuels, solar energy, conservation, geothermal energy, biomass, and basic energy sciences. This is an area where many congressmen would like to make a mark. Fuqua has had one political scare, in the 1976 primary, when two opponents came within 355 votes of forcing him into a runoff. His problem then was lack of solid support in Tallahassee and Gainesville. He has evidently remedied that; at least no significant primary or general election opposition has emerged since then. He is young for a committee chairman—not yet 50—and may very well have a long congressional career ahead. Because of the geographical position of the district, Fuqua's chances should not be altered significantly by redistricting.

Census Data   Pop. (1980 final) 612,964, up 35% in 1970s. Median family income, 1970, $7,071, 74% of U.S.

The Voters

   Employment profile 1970   White collar, 49%. Blue collar, 28%. Service, 16%. Farm, 7%.
   Ethnic groups   Black 1980, 25%. Hispanic 1980, 2%. Asian 1980, 1%. Total foreign stock 1970, 4%.

Presidential Vote

1980	Reagan (R)	91,349	(42%)
	Carter (D)	115,951	(53%)
	Anderson (I)	9,141	(4%)
1976	Ford (R)	71,806	(37%)
	Carter (D)	120,425	(61%)

Rep. Don Fuqua (D) Elected 1962; b. Aug. 20, 1933, Jacksonville; home, Alta; U. of Fla., B.S. 1957.

Career Army, Korea; Fla. House of Reps., 1958–62.

Offices 2268 RHOB, 202-225-5235. Also 100 P.O. Bldg., Tallahassee 32302, 904-224-1152.

Committees *Science and Technology* (Chairman). Subcommittee: Energy Development and Applications (Chairman).

Government Operations (5th). Subcommittee: Legislation and National Security.

Group Ratings

	ADA	COPE	PC	LCV	CFA	RPN	NAB	NSI	NTU	ACA	ACU
1980	33	44	40	26	57	—	67	63	32	29	44
1979	32	39	33	54	15	—	—	—	29	18	32
1978	20	30	30	54	9	30	100	90	18	58	63

Key Votes

1) Draft Registn $	FOR	6) Fair Hsg DOJ Enfrc	AGN	11) Cut Socl Incr Dfns $	AGN
2) Ban $ to Nicrgua	—	7) Lim PAC Contrbtns	FOR	12) Hosptl Cost Controls	AGN
3) Dlay MX Missile	AGN	8) Cap on Food Stmp $	AGN	13) Gasln Ctrls & Allctns	FOR
4) Nuclr Mortorium	AGN	9) New US Dep Edcatn	FOR	14) Lim Wndfll Prof Tax	FOR
5) Alaska Lands Bill	FOR	10) Cut OSHA $	AGN	15) Chryslr Loan Grntee	FOR

Election Results

1980 general	Don Fuqua (D)	138,252	(71%)	($131,165)
	John R. LaCapra (R)	57,588	(29%)	($47,786)
1980 primary	Don Fuqua (D), unopposed			
1978 general	Don Fuqua (D)	112,649	(82%)	($88,381)
	Peter Brathwaite (R)	25,148	(18%)	($19,379)

THIRD DISTRICT

Jacksonville is a border city—on the border between the Old South and the new boom lands of central Florida. It was long Florida's largest city and, on paper, it retains that status because it has annexed most of surrounding Duval County. But Jacksonville's metropolitan population, although still considerable, has been eclipsed by Miami, Fort Lauderdale, St. Petersburg, Tampa, and even Orlando. Jacksonville remains an important port, paper manufacturer, and banking and insurance center; and if the central city has not grown much in the 1970s, the surrounding areas within commuter distance have. Because of its coolish winter climate, Jacksonville has not attracted the retirees or northern migrants who have flocked to Florida cities and condominium villages farther south. But it does have the largest black percentage of any major Florida city and a large population of southern white origin. It was the largest Florida city to go for George Wallace in 1968; it delivered a sizable margin for Jimmy Carter in 1976 and came close to backing him in 1980. A recent mayor, Hans Tanzler, an enthusiastic born-again Christian, had a local following of sufficient fervor to carry Jacksonville in the 1978 Democratic gubernatorial primary.

The 3d congressional district of Florida includes almost all of Jacksonville and one small county to the north. Its congressman since 1948, Democrat Charles Bennett, enjoys a reputation for probity and attention to duty that is second to none in the House. He was stricken with polio while serving in the Army during World War II, and in his first campaign it was suggested that he was not physically up to representing the district. Perhaps to refute that, Bennett prided himself on being present for every roll call vote and in the late 1960s broke the House record for consecutive attendance. After a while it got to the point that roll calls were sometimes delayed to accommodate Bennett; finally in 1972 he missed one.

Bennett is now one of the most senior members of the House. On the Armed Services Committee he ranks just behind Chairman Mel Price. He chairs a subcommittee on seapower; Jacksonville, as it happens, has major Navy facilities, including the giant base at Mayport, just outside the district boundaries but a major contributor to its economy. He is part of the Armed Services majority that has generally favored strong defense measures and has by and large supported established military policy as the best way to achieve them. He is considered a very strong supporter of the Navy, its most important advocate in the House. On domestic issues he votes sometimes but by no means always with northern Democrats— which makes him a crucial vote in this House. His toughest assignment has been as chairman of the House ethics committee (its official name is a mouthful: the Committee on Standards of Official Conduct). Bennett was passed over for this chair in the early 1970s; there was a feeling that he was too much of a stickler for propriety. But in 1978, with Bennett the most senior member and the House under examination in the Koreagate scandal, the chair could not be denied him. He oversaw the Abscam case and was part of the 10–2 majority that recommended and secured the expulsion of Congressman Ozzie Myers from the House. He also handled the investigation of the interesting question of how Congressman Morgan Murphy's electronic voting card had activated the House voting machine when Murphy, by his own admission, was at home in Chicago. In the 97th Congress, Bennett was relieved of the ethics assignment by a Democratic caucus rule that allows members to serve no more than two consecutive terms.

Bennett has for all practical purposes been unopposed for reelection for many years and can probably serve as long as he wants. The 3d is the Florida congressional district that has had the least population growth in the 1970s, and as a result its boundaries can and probably will be left pretty much alone.

Census Data   Pop. (1980 final) 469,156, up 4% in 1970s. Median family income, 1970, $8,252, 86% of U.S.

The Voters

   Employment profile 1970   White collar, 50%. Blue collar, 34%. Service, 15%. Farm, 1%.
   Ethnic groups   Black 1980, 29%. Hispanic 1980, 2%. Asian 1980, 1%. Total foreign stock 1970, 6%.

Presidential Vote

1980	Reagan (R)	72,378	(46%)
	Carter (D)	79,369	(51%)
	Anderson (I)	3,497	(2%)
1976	Ford (R)	48,756	(35%)
	Carter (D)	87,760	(64%)

Rep. Charles E. Bennett (D) Elected 1948; b. Dec. 2, 1910, Canton, N.Y.; home, Jacksonville; U. of Fla., B.A., J.D.

Career Practicing atty., 1934–42, 1947–48; Fla. House of Reps., 1941–42; Army, WWII.

Offices 2107 RHOB, 202-225-2501. Also Suite 352, Fed. Ofc. Bldg., 400 W. Bay St., Jacksonville 32202, 904-791-2587.

Committee *Armed Services* (2d). Subcommittees: Military Installations and Facilities; Military Personnel and Compensation; Seapower and Strategic and Critical Materials (Chairman).

Group Ratings

	ADA	COPE	PC	LCV	CFA	RPN	NAB	NSI	NTU	ACA	ACU
1980	22	42	43	30	21	—	92	70	42	42	58
1979	42	50	40	38	29	—	—	—	45	54	59
1978	30	25	45	53	27	50	100	90	44	85	63

Key Votes

1) Draft Registn $	FOR	6) Fair Hsg DOJ Enfrc	AGN	11) Cut Socl Incr Dfns $	FOR
2) Ban $ to Nicrgua	FOR	7) Lim PAC Contrbtns	FOR	12) Hosptl Cost Controls	AGN
3) Dlay MX Missile	AGN	8) Cap on Food Stmp $	AGN	13) Gasln Ctrls & Allctns	FOR
4) Nuclr Mortorium	AGN	9) New US Dep Edcatn	AGN	14) Lim Wndfll Prof Tax	AGN
5) Alaska Lands Bill	FOR	10) Cut OSHA $	FOR	15) Chryslr Loan Grntee	AGN

Election Results

1980 general	Charles E. Bennett (D)	104,672	(77%)	($39,318)
	Harry Radcliffe (R)	31,208	(23%)	($0)
1980 primary	Charles E. Bennett (D), unopposed			
1978 general	Charles E. Bennett (D), unopposed			

FOURTH DISTRICT

The 4th congressional district is part of transitional Florida. Occupying the territory south of Jacksonville and including about 100,000 residents of the city itself, the 4th sits at the divide of Old Dixie—north Florida—and the boom land to the south. The terrain here is just below the normal reach of wintertime frost—a fact of significance not only to the tourist trade but also for the area's big orange crop. The 4th also embodies Florida's transitional politics. Its northern counties went for George Wallace in the 1968 general election and the 1972 and 1976 primaries. The southern counties of Lake and Seminole, near Orlando, are both solidly Republican. In the middle of the district, both geographically and politically, is Daytona Beach, famous for its rock-hard sand beach. Like much of Florida this is a land of political contradictions: it can elect black city councilmen and vote for George Wallace in the same year. The district went narrowly for Jimmy Carter in 1976 and gave a larger margin to Ronald Reagan in 1980—a political performance very close to the statewide, and indeed national, average.

The 4th's congressman, Democrat Bill Chappell, may also be described as a transitional figure. Chappell was speaker of the Florida House back in the early 1960s when the legislature was still dominated by Old South conservatives—the Pork Chop Gang—from the northern part of the state. In the House he has been a member of the conservative southern bloc, one of that breed of Democrats who often vote like Republicans—and who will be crucial in 1981 and 1982 when the Republicans are only 26 votes shy of a majority.

Chappell occupies a critical committee position in the House, as second-ranking member of the House Defense Appropriations Subcommittee. This may not sound particularly important, but that is the body that passes on all defense appropriations (except for military construction, which has its own appropriations subcommittee) and so it can make crucial policy and dollar decisions. The chairmanship after the 1978 elections went to Joseph Addabbo, a New York City Democrat who had opposed the Vietnam war and questioned many defense programs; just as the House was moving toward spending more money on defense, the subcommittee seemed to be moving away from it. Chappell as senior Democrat ended up as sponsor of measures to spend more on such defense systems as the B-1 bomber and the nuclear aircraft carrier. In the 97th Congress Chappell is likely to have more success. Addabbo is still chairman, but the committee's new members include three southern Democrats and an additional Republican, which should effectively give control to those favoring more defense spending. The tougher question is what that spending will go for—how to get a more effective as well as a more expensive defense capability. On that issue Chappell is very much a Navy man and one who supports the large ships admirals have traditionally sought. It is worth noting that the district includes the Mayport Naval Base, the Navy's biggest East Coast installation outside the Norfolk area.

Chappell was first elected to Congress in 1968 but did not really win solidly until 1974; he has had little trouble since then. Redistricting will change the boundaries of the district con-

220   FLORIDA

siderably; indeed, because of fast growth in Florida what is now the 4th district is likely to be split evenly between the two new districts, one centered around Ocala and Gainesville (the latter now in the 2d district), the other centered around Daytona Beach. Since Chappell is from Ocala, he will probably choose to run in the former district; there is less likelihood also of Republican opposition there (although the university town of Gainesville may generate a primary opponent some year). The Daytona Beach district should be considered entirely up for grabs. The Democratic legislature and governor will try to make sure it leans Democratic, but they cannot put it entirely out of the reach of the Republicans, and the kind of Democrat it would nominate is entirely unclear. Presumably some local legislators will be fashioning the boundaries very carefully, and no one would be surprised to see one of them end up in Congress.

Census Data   Pop. (1980 final) 715,027, up 58% in 1970s. Median family income, 1970, $7,719, 81% of U.S.

The Voters

Employment profile 1970   White collar, 51%. Blue collar, 30%. Service, 15%. Farm, 4%.
Ethnic groups   Black 1980, 12%. Hispanic 1980, 2%. Asian 1980, 1%. Total foreign stock 1970, 11%. UK, Germany, Canada, 2% each.

Presidential Vote

1980	Reagan (R)	149,231	(57%)
	Carter (D)	104,021	(39%)
	Anderson (I)	8,281	(3%)
1976	Ford (R)	100,991	(46%)
	Carter (D)	115,332	(53%)

Rep. Bill Chappell, Jr. (D) Elected 1968; b. Feb. 3, 1922, Kendrick; home, Ocala; U. of Fla., B.A. 1947, LL.B. 1949.

Career Navy, WWII; Marion Co. Prosecuting Atty., 1950–54; Fla. House of Reps., 1955–64, 1967–68, Spkr., 1961–63.

Offices 2468 RHOB, 202-225-4035. Also Rm. 258 Fed. Bldg., Ocala 32670, 904-629-0039.

Committee *Appropriations* (12th). Subcommittees: Defense; Energy and Water Development; Military Construction.

Group Ratings

	ADA	COPE	PC	LCV	CFA	RPN	NAB	NSI	NTU	ACA	ACU
1980	6	26	23	13	7	—	82	88	43	63	67
1979	11	21	8	16	4	—	—	—	42	77	74
1978	5	25	20	23	9	36	100	100	18	84	88

Key Votes

1) Draft Registn $	FOR	6) Fair Hsg DOJ Enfrc	AGN	11) Cut Socl Incr Dfns $	FOR
2) Ban $ to Nicrgua	AGN	7) Lim PAC Contrbtns	AGN	12) Hosptl Cost Controls	AGN
3) Dlay MX Missile	AGN	8) Cap on Food Stmp $	FOR	13) Gasln Ctrls & Allctns	AGN
4) Nuclr Mortorium	AGN	9) New US Dep Edcatn	AGN	14) Lim Wndfll Prof Tax	FOR
5) Alaska Lands Bill	AGN	10) Cut OSHA $	FOR	15) Chryslr Loan Grntee	FOR

Election Results

1980 general	Bill Chappell, Jr. (D)	147,775	(66%)	($100,668)
	Barney E. Dillard, Jr. (R)	76,924	(34%)	($8,750)
1980 primary	Bill Chappell, Jr. (D), unopposed			
1978 general	Bill Chappell, Jr. (D)	113,302	(73%)	($87,346)
	Tom Boney (R)	41,647	(27%)	($9,118)

FIFTH DISTRICT

The 5th congressional district of Florida is one of those seats that makes no sense except as a political unit. It includes parts, but not all, of two diverse metropolitan areas plus a lot of rural acreage that has little in common with either. It stretches from the fast-growing city of Orlando in central Florida west to the Gulf and, bypassing Tampa, down to Clearwater and nearly to St. Petersburg. It was designed to suit the political purposes of Bill Gunter, a Democrat from Orlando, who managed to get elected to Congress in 1972 despite the area's Republican leanings and with the help of the 5th's intricately crafted boundaries. Gunter went on to other things — unsuccessful races for the Senate in 1974 and 1980 and election as Florida's insurance commissioner — and so the seat was picked up by the Republicans in 1974, and they have held it since. It will be known in history, however, not as Gunter's seat nor for being Republican, but as the district in the nation that gave us Congressman Richard Kelly.

There was something fishy about Kelly from the beginning. He is from Pasco County, an area just north of Clearwater, where people have been moving north of the Tampa–St. Petersburg area into condominiums and subdivisions raised from swamp in almost incredible numbers in the 1970s. Most of these people have little background in Florida politics, and they may have been attracted by Kelly's voluble conservatism; the fact that, as a local judge, he had been impeached a few years before, evidently meant little to them. Kelly won three general elections here, two by very narrow margins, and until the Abscam case broke he distinguished himself mainly by the vehemence with which he denounced aid to New York City, and by the tenuousness of his hold on his seat.

Then came Abscam. Kelly was the only Republican involved, the congressman who was videotaped stuffing $50,000 in cash into his pockets. He had his own story to tell: that he had been conducting his own investigation into bribery and corruption and had taken the money in the course of it. He went on NBC News to tell his story; David Brinkley manfully managed to avoid laughing on the air. Stripped of the obscurity most congressmen enjoy, Kelly was revealed mercilessly as a buffoon. The House Republican Conference quickly moved to expel him from its ranks; Kelly wisely resigned before it could act. He was defeated in the Republican primary, and not just narrowly either; in a three-way race the best he could manage was 18% of the vote. Even in Pasco County the voters, now with plenty of information about him, placed him third.

Both parties had seriously contested primaries. Democrats nominated David Best, who had nearly beaten Kelly in 1978; Republicans actually had a runoff, the winner of which was Bill McCollum, an Orlando area lawyer who had support districtwide except in his opponent's home county. The district had been trending Republican in local elections; the Democratic precincts of Orlando and Clearwater carefully included in the 1972 redistricting became less important as the district's population increased, mainly in Pasco County and other suburban areas, from 452,000 to more than 750,000 in ten years. So McCollum won the general election decisively, although not overwhelmingly.

The 5th district was one of the six fastest-growing districts in the nation in the 1970s, and because of this and the odd shape of the district, there is unlikely to be anything resembling the current 5th district when the 1982 elections come around. Instead, there are likely to be two districts that will include most of the territory now within the 5th. One district will likely include Pasco County, perhaps the Gulf counties just to the north (which are likely to experience as rapid growth in the 1980s as Pasco had in the 1970s), and parts of Pinellas County (Clearwater and the suburbs north of St. Petersburg) and Hillsborough County (the Tampa area) to the south. There are powerful Democratic state legislators from this area who will make efforts to assure that the district leans Democratic. But Pasco County has gone heavily Republican not only for Ronald Reagan but in elections for the state Senate and House in 1980; and the Republicans can be expected to contest this seat seriously.

The other new seat is likely to center around the Orlando area. Here there may be a wholesale redrawing of lines. The Democratic legislature may assume that, with all the Republican votes in the Orlando area, it may not be possible to defeat McCollum; in that case, they would give him the more Republican areas, some of them now in the 9th and even the 4th districts, and place Democratic precincts in the 9th, represented at the time of the last redistricting by a Republican but now by a Democrat, Bill Nelson. The result in that case would be a safe seat for McCollum; otherwise, he may face serious Democratic opposition again.

Census Data   Pop. (1980 final) 880,078, up 94% in 1970s. Median family income, 1970, $6,910, 73% of U.S.

The Voters

Employment profile 1970   White collar, 44%. Blue collar, 35%. Service, 14%. Farm, 7%.
Ethnic groups   Black 1980, 11%. Hispanic 1980, 2%. Total foreign stock 1970, 12%. Germany, UK, Canada, 2% each.

Presidential Vote

1980	Reagan (R)	201,043	(59%)
	Carter (D)	125,344	(37%)
	Anderson (I)	13,042	(4%)
1976	Ford (R)	126,229	(50%)
	Carter (D)	125,649	(50%)

Rep. Bill McCollum (R) Elected 1980; b. July 12, 1944, Brooksville; home, Altamonte Springs; U. of Fla., B.A. 1965, J.D. 1968.

Career Navy, 1969–72; Practicing atty., 1973–80; Chmn., Seminole Co. Rep. Exec. Committee, 1976.

Offices 1313 LHOB, 202-225-2176. Also 5800 U.S. Hwy. 19 N., Suite 224, Holiday 33590, 813-937-4231, and 701 E. Altamonte Dr., Suite 345, Altamonte Springs 32701, 305-830-6655.

Committees *Banking, Finance and Urban Affairs* (13th). Subcommittees: Domestic Monetary Policy; Financial Institutions Supervision, Regulation and Insurance; General Oversight and Renegotiation; Housing and Community Development.

Judiciary (12th). Subcommittees: Criminal Justice; Immigration, Refugees and International Law.

Group Ratings and Key Votes: Newly Elected

Election Results

1980 general	Bill McCollum (R)	177,603	(56%)	($278,664)
	David Best (D)	140,903	(44%)	($187,121)
1980 runoff	Bill McCollum (R)	34,875	(54%)	
	Vince Fechtel, Jr. (R)	29,229	(46%)	($86,197)
1980 primary	Bill McCollum (R)	26,152	(43%)	
	Vince Fechtel, Jr. (R)	23,942	(39%)	
	Richard Kelly (R)	10,889	(18%)	($148,154)
1978 general	Richard Kelly (R)	106,319	(51%)	($182,197)
	David Best (D)	101,867	(49%)	($149,383)

SIXTH DISTRICT

When somebody mentions St. Petersburg, almost everyone has an image of elderly retirees sitting on park benches in the Florida sun. The cliche has considerable validity. To be sure, St. Petersburg and its suburbs to the north and west do have some light manufacturing, and there are young families here with children. But this is largely a community of older people. The median age of Florida's 6th congressional district, which includes St. Petersburg and most of suburban Pinellas County, was in 1970 (and undoubtedly is today) the highest of any district in the nation. Some 50% of the 6th's eligible voters were 58 or over and fully 39% were 65 or older. In no other congressional district was the median age nearly so high.

Most of these people were not born in St. Petersburg, where there were not many people at all 65 years ago. They are immigrants from some other part of the South or, more frequently, from the North. The large Yankee concentration here produced the state's first center of Republican strength. The migrants of the 1940s and 1950s were people of at least modest affluence — blue collar workers of the time did not get much in the way of pensions — and the new residents continued to vote in St. Petersburg as they had back in Oak Park or Garden City. They carried Pinellas County for Eisenhower and in 1954 elected a Republican congressman, William Cramer. A tireless and effective partisan, Cramer built Florida's Republican Party and ultimately ran for the Senate, only to be beaten by Lawton Chiles in 1970.

Former Cramer aide and state Senator Bill Young had no trouble stepping into the seat, and he still holds it today. But St. Petersburg has been moving more into the Democratic column in recent elections. In 1976 Pinellas County and the 6th district almost went for Jimmy Carter, and in 1980 even 69-year-old Ronald Reagan did not do as well as his Florida statewide average here. The Democratic trend is the result of the increasing affluence of America's blue collar class. There is inevitably a considerable turnover in the 6th district's elderly population — very few of the voters who made this district Republican in the 1950s are still alive today — and many of the people who settled here in the later 1960s and the 1970s were from blue collar — and Democratic — backgrounds.

The trend has not created any trouble for Congressman Young. He is an affable man who provides good constituency services and wins by overwhelming margins. He is a member of the Appropriations Committee and was, until 1981, ranking minority member on the Foreign Operations Subcommittee. He made the unusual decision to give up that position in favor of a lower rank on the Defense Appropriations Subcommittee. One reason was probably that Defense is more important, but another may have been that Foreign Operations is not a pleasant assignment. Its job is to steer the unpopular foreign aid bill to passage, and Young had become involved in the fight to place restrictions on where international banking agencies can send money—a sticky issue with little payoff at home. His work on the HUD Subcommittee is probably more appreciated in St. Petersburg; one of the most successful HUD programs has been housing for senior citizens, for which St. Petersburg has a ready market. Young has been mentioned as a possible candidate in 1982 for the Senate seat held by Lawton Chiles.

Census Data   Pop. (1980 final) 600,088, up 33% in 1970s. Median family income, 1970, $7,657, 80% of U.S.

The Voters
 Employment profile 1970   White collar, 55%. Blue collar, 28%. Service, 17%. Farm, -%.
 Ethnic groups   Black 1980, 8%. Hispanic 1980, 1%. Asian 1980, 1%. Total foreign stock 1970, 22%. Germany, UK, 4% each; Canada, 3%; Italy, Ireland, Sweden, 1% each.

Presidential Vote

1980	Reagan (R)	146,473	(53%)
	Carter (D)	114,195	(42%)
	Anderson (I)	14,395	(5%)
1976	Ford (R)	118,337	(50%)
	Carter (D)	115,795	(49%)

Rep. C. W. Bill Young (R) Elected 1970; b. Dec. 16, 1930, Harmarsville, Pa.; home, Seminole.

Career   Aide to U.S. Rep. William C. Cramer of Fla., 1957–60; Fla. Senate, 1960–70, Minor. Ldr., 1966–70.

Offices   2266 RHOB, 202-225-5961. Also 627 Fed. Bldg., 144 1st Ave. S., St. Petersburg 33701, 813-893-3191.

Committees   *Appropriations* (8th). Subcommittees: Defense; HUD–Independent Agencies.

Select Committee on Intelligence (5th). Subcommittees: Oversight and Evaluation; Program and Budget Authorization.

Group Ratings

	ADA	COPE	PC	LCV	CFA	RPN	NAB	NSI	NTU	ACA	ACU
1980	11	10	37	30	14	—	8	100	54	88	84
1979	11	26	18	10	4	—	—	—	57	92	92
1978	10	15	25	27	23	58	100	100	31	93	88

Key Votes

1) Draft Registn $	FOR	6) Fair Hsg DOJ Enfrc	AGN	11) Cut Socl Incr Dfns $	FOR
2) Ban $ to Nicrgua	FOR	7) Lim PAC Contrbtns	AGN	12) Hosptl Cost Controls	AGN
3) Dlay MX Missile	AGN	8) Cap on Food Stmp $	FOR	13) Gasln Ctrls & Allctns	AGN
4) Nuclr Mortorium	AGN	9) New US Dep Edcatn	AGN	14) Lim Wndfll Prof Tax	FOR
5) Alaska Lands Bill	FOR	10) Cut OSHA $	FOR	15) Chryslr Loan Grntee	AGN

Election Results

1980 general	C. W. Bill Young (R), unopposed .			($61,313)
1980 primary	C. W. Bill Young (R), unopposed			
1978 general	C. W. Bill Young (R)	150,964	(79%)	($57,482)
	Jim Christison (D).............	40,654	(21%)	($128,579)

SEVENTH DISTRICT

Tampa, with more than 250,000 people, dominates the 7th congressional district of Florida. This is a very different city from St. Petersburg, which is about the same size, shares the same airport, and is just over the bridge across Tampa Bay. If St. Petersburg is known for its many retirees, Tampa is almost as well known for its large and established Cuban–American community and as the nation's leading manufacturer of cigars. Tampa's Cuban community dates from long before Castro and is much older than Miami's; it is also different politically. The anti-Castro Cubans of Miami tend toward free-market Republicanism; the Cuban–Americans of Tampa are traditional working-class Democrats. Beyond the Cuban community in Ybor City, Tampa is as much a white working-class city as there is in Florida. The 1968 election results suggest the split then and now as well: 35% for Nixon (roughly corresponding to the proportion of affluent or Yankee whites), 33% for Humphrey (Cubans, blacks, white union members), and 32% for Wallace (southern-origin whites). Eight years later most of the Wallace group went for Jimmy Carter, giving him a solid victory here; in 1980, Carter slipped here as elsewhere but still did better in this district than his Florida average.

Until 1962, Tampa was in the same district as St. Petersburg. Then, after the 1960 census, a Tampa district was created, and its congressman since that time has been Democrat Sam Gibbons. Unlike traditional Florida Democrats, Gibbons supported civil rights legislation and had a strong pro-labor voting record. In his early career he was one of an outnumbered group of liberals pushing for institutional reforms; most of those proposals have now become established.

In the early 1970s Gibbons was one of the major rebels in the House. After serving for several years on Education and Labor, he won a seat on Ways and Means, where he championed progressive tax reform and frequently disagreed with Chairman Wilbur Mills. After the 1972 election he made a brief race for the majority leadership but withdrew as it became clear that Tip O'Neill had the votes. Since the middle 1970s, Gibbons's legislative career has taken another direction. Instead of pushing measures to increase the tax bite on the wealthy, he has strongly supported measures to cut the capital gains tax. His voting record on other issues has moved to the right as well. But his influence does not seem to have increased — even though the House as a whole seems to have moved, albeit not so suddenly, in the same direction. Gibbons has never been a favorite of the House speaker and, although he is second-ranking Democrat on Ways and Means, he is overshadowed by Chairman Dan Rostenkowski, who is both a strong force himself and younger. That makes it unlikely that Gibbons will become chairman (unless Rostenkowski should become speaker himself someday), although on a given issue he might turn out to have the key vote.

Gibbons's most important post is as chairman of the Trade Subcommittee. Here he will be subject to pressures to increase protection for U.S. industries and jobs. The southern Democratic tradition is in support of free trade, and that is probably in the interest of a growing commercial center like Tampa. Gibbons is himself very much a supporter of free trade, a vigilant opponent of trade barriers and restrictions. He is a stalwart supporter of multilateral trade agreements and liberalized trade laws. Politically shrewd, in a post where he can make full use of his talents in a cause he believes in, he is in a strong position to be a major force for free trade and for shaping American trade policy for some years to come.

Census Data   Pop. (1980 final) 595,159, up 31% in 1970s. Median family income, 1970, $8,256, 86% of U.S.

The Voters

Employment profile 1970   White collar, 49%. Blue collar, 36%. Service, 13%. Farm, 2%.
Ethnic groups   Black 1980, 13%. Hispanic 1980, 10%. Asian 1980, 1%. Total foreign stock 1970, 14%. Italy, 2%; Germany, Canada, UK, 1% each.

Presidential Vote

1980	Reagan (R)	100,582	(52%)
	Carter (D)	82,344	(43%)
	Anderson (I)	8,726	(5%)
1976	Ford (R)	74,570	(45%)
	Carter (D)	88,612	(54%)

Rep. Sam Gibbons (D) Elected 1962; b. Jan. 20, 1920, Tampa; home, Tampa; U. of Fla., LL.B., 1947.

Career Army, WWII; Practicing atty., 1947–62; Fla. House of Reps., 1952–58; Fla. Senate, 1958–62.

Offices 2204 RHOB, 202-225-3376. Also 510 Fed. Bldg., 500 Zack St., Tampa 33602, 813-228-2101.

Committees *Ways and Means* (2d). Subcommittees: Oversight; Trade (Chairman).

Joint Committee on Taxation (2d).

Group Ratings

	ADA	COPE	PC	LCV	CFA	RPN	NAB	NSI	NTU	ACA	ACU
1980	39	50	53	26	50	—	33	56	27	30	32
1979	32	44	48	51	28	—	—	—	37	48	50
1978	10	26	48	58	27	70	91	60	23	67	55

Key Votes

1) Draft Registn $	FOR	6) Fair Hsg DOJ Enfrc	FOR	11) Cut Socl Incr Dfns $	AGN
2) Ban $ to Nicrgua	AGN	7) Lim PAC Contrbtns	AGN	12) Hosptl Cost Controls	—
3) Dlay MX Missile	AGN	8) Cap on Food Stmp $	FOR	13) Gasln Ctrls & Allctns	AGN
4) Nuclr Mortorium	—	9) New US Dep Edcatn	AGN	14) Lim Wndfll Prof Tax	AGN
5) Alaska Lands Bill	FOR	10) Cut OSHA $	AGN	15) Chryslr Loan Grntee	AGN

Election Results

1980 general	Sam Gibbons (D)	132,529	(72%)	($43,410)
	Charles P. Jones (R)	52,138	(28%)	($56)
1980 primary	Sam Gibbons (D), unopposed			
1978 general	Sam Gibbons (D), unopposed			

EIGHTH DISTRICT

Florida's 8th congressional district is made up of two distinct areas. More than two-thirds of the population lives along the Gulf Coast in such towns as Bradenton and Sarasota. These are, to varying degrees, well-off, sunbaked communities with lots of migrants and retirees from the North; Sarasota is especially affluent. The voters here, when they are not busy enjoying golf courses and yacht basins and pleasant condominiums, are likely to be reading *Barron's* and muttering about the crazy ways of the federal government. Needless to say, this is very Republican territory — Sarasota is often the most Republican part of Florida and in 1980 gave Ronald Reagan 69% of its votes.

Separated from the Gulf Coast by miles of swampland is the citrus-growing country in and around Polk County. Here the towns are smaller and older, with few of the glittering high rises that tower along the coast. The interior economy is geared more to agriculture than to wealthy retirees and tourists. Incongruously set amid the boom cities of central Florida, Polk County remains a part of Old Dixie politically. In 1968, Polk preferred George Wallace to Richard Nixon, while Nixon was carrying Sarasota County; in 1976 Jimmy Carter carried Polk while losing Sarasota. For more than 30 years Polk County has been the home of one of Florida's U.S. senators: Bartow native Spessard Holland, long unbeatable, gave valuable help to Lakeland lawyer Lawton Chiles in his upset victory in 1970.

The 8th is one of those districts national Republican congressional strategists have rightly had their eyes on for a long time — and have never won. The area has not supported a Democratic candidate for president since the 1940s and has gone Republican in statewide elections as well. The main reason is the strong Republican preference of the Gulf Coast area, and the fact that this is part of the district that has had by far the most rapid growth. But the Republicans have had problems winning the district. They were unable to beat longtime incumbent Democrat James Haley, a member of the family that owns the Ringling Brothers–Barnum & Bailey Circus, who was chairman of the House Interior Committee when he retired voluntarily in 1976. And that was the year when Jimmy Carter was running pretty strongly in the South — a run that probably helped the Democratic candidate for Congress in the 8th, Andy Ireland.

Ireland had other assets. He outspent the Republican nominee by a 2-to-1 margin in 1976. He had solid roots in Polk County plus the kind of educational and business background that made him attractive to upper-income Gulf Coast residents. In office, Ireland has had a record much more in line with traditional southern conservatives than with northern Democrats. No one can be sure what will happen in redistricting, but the Democratic legislature will probably detach Sarasota from the district and thus make the 8th (or whatever its new number is) even safer for Ireland than it was in 1980, when he won 69% of the vote, including 78% in Polk County.

Census Data   Pop. (1980 final) 646,104, up 43% in 1970s. Median family income, 1970, $7,341, 77% of U.S.

The Voters

Employment profile 1970   White collar, 43%. Blue collar, 35%. Service, 14%. Farm, 8%.
Ethnic groups   Black 1980, 13%. Hispanic 1980, 3%. Total foreign stock 1970, 10%. Germany, Canada, 2% each; UK, 1%.

Presidential Vote

1980	Reagan (R)	142,061	(60%)
	Carter (D)	86,314	(36%)
	Anderson (I)	8,614	(4%)
1976	Ford (R)	103,271	(52%)
	Carter (D)	93,597	(47%)

Rep. Andy Ireland (D) Elected 1976; b. Aug. 23, 1930, Cincinnati, Ohio; home, Winter Haven; Yale U., B.S. 1952, Columbia Business Sch., 1953–54, La. St. U.

Career Chmn. of the Bd., Barnett Banks of Winter Haven, Cypress Gardens, and Auburndale; Mbr., Winter Haven City Commission, 1966–68.

Offices 1124 LHOB, 202-225-5015. Also 519 W. Central Ave., Winter Haven 33880, 813-299-4041.

Committees *Foreign Affairs* (11th). Subcommittees: Asian and Pacific Affairs; International Operations.

Small Business (10th). Subcommittee: Export Opportunities and Special Small Business Problems (Chairman).

Group Ratings

	ADA	COPE	PC	LCV	CFA	RPN	NAB	NSI	NTU	ACA	ACU
1980	6	11	27	31	21	—	75	88	43	46	75
1979	16	10	18	42	4	—	—	—	44	50	62
1978	20	21	20	41	5	40	100	67	20	78	57

Key Votes

1) Draft Registn $	FOR	6) Fair Hsg DOJ Enfrc	AGN	11) Cut Socl Incr Dfns $	FOR
2) Ban $ to Nicrgua	AGN	7) Lim PAC Contrbtns	AGN	12) Hosptl Cost Controls	AGN
3) Dlay MX Missile	AGN	8) Cap on Food Stmp $	FOR	13) Gasln Ctrls & Allctns	AGN
4) Nuclr Mortorium	AGN	9) New US Dep Edcatn	FOR	14) Lim Wndfll Prof Tax	FOR
5) Alaska Lands Bill	FOR	10) Cut OSHA $	AGN	15) Chryslr Loan Grntee	FOR

Election Results

1980 general	Andy Ireland (D)	151,613	(69%)	($221,103)
	Scott Nicholson (R)	61,820	(28%)	($12,460)
1980 primary	Andy Ireland (D), unopposed			
1978 general	Andy Ireland (D), unopposed			($102,265)

NINTH DISTRICT

One of the fastest-growing parts of Florida in the 1970s has been the central Florida area around Orlando. This region is not endowed with great natural advantages; it has neither the beaches that brought so many people to Florida's Gold Coast (much of the beach here, around the Kennedy Space Center, is government property) nor the bays and over-the-water sunsets of the Gulf Coast. Central Florida, hot and muggy in the summer, is not often warm enough for swimming in the winter. There are many small lakes here, but the land is naturally swampy. This is good land for growing oranges, but orange groves do not by themselves attract large influxes of people.

The appeal of central Florida is not so much natural as man-made. The main attractions are the Kennedy Space Center on the coast in Brevard County and Disney World near Orlando in Orange County. They are the products of the 1960s and 1970s, respectively, and have helped to make central Florida perhaps the number one tourist destination in the United States. And they have done more than that. For this is not an area that has turned out to be overly dependent on tourist dollars or government spending—although both are very important. Central Florida has generated a metropolitan economy of its own that has attracted in-migrants from all over the country. Not a land of retirees thinking about the homes they have left, this is an area dominated by young families looking forward to the future.

As with much of Florida, the initial in-migration here seemed to produce a Republican trend and further in-migration seemed to make it more Democratic. This was one of the first parts of Florida to elect a Republican congressman, when Edward Gurney won in 1962. A silver-haired conservative with a Maine accent, Gurney became known to national audiences as the closest thing to a defender Richard Nixon had on the Senate Watergate Committee. He was later accused of accepting bribes and, although acquitted, did not seek reelection to the Senate in 1974. His House seat had been taken by his law partner, Louis Frey, who also had statewide ambitions but never realized them, losing for governor in 1978 and senator in 1980.

When the seat opened up again in 1978, Gurney ran again; it was almost the same constituency—Brevard County and most of Orange—that had elected him to the House in the 1960s. But now in the 1970s the district had a strong Democratic candidate in Bill Nelson, a young state legislator from Brevard County. Nelson had enough personal wealth to help finance his campaign and enough interest in process issues to renounce special-interest contributions. He won an easy 61% victory over Gurney and, two years later, won by even more. Nelson's committee assignments show his political savvy and ability: he has seats on the Budget Committee, which is in charge of holding down the federal budget, and chairs its task force on Tax Policy, and on the Science and Technology Committee, which is of great importance to the district that includes Cape Canaveral.

The 9th district need not be changed much by redistricting. It may end up trading some precincts with the 5th district, giving Nelson more Democratic votes in the city of Orlando—which will simply make his seat safer.

Census Data   Pop. (1980 final) 567,309, up 25% in 1970s. Median family income, 1970, $10,267, 107% of U.S.

The Voters

   Employment profile 1970   White collar, 60%. Blue collar, 27%. Service, 12%. Farm, 1%.
   Ethnic groups   Black 1980, 9%. Hispanic 1980, 3%. Asian 1980, 1. Total foreign stock 1970, 11%. UK, Germany, Canada, 2% each.

Presidential Vote

1980	Reagan (R)	126,606	(62%)
	Carter (D)	66,280	(32%)
	Anderson (I)	9,457	(5%)
1976	Ford (R)	95,392	(54%)
	Carter (D)	82,809	(46%)

Rep. Bill Nelson (D) Elected 1978; b. Sept. 29, 1942, Miami; home, Melbourne; Yale U., B.A. 1965, U. of Va., J.D. 1968.

Career Army, 1968–70; Practicing atty.; Fla. House of Reps., 1972–78.

Offices 307 CHOB, 202-225-3671. Also Suite 202 Goldfield Bldg., 65 E. NASA Blvd., Melbourne 32901, 305-724-1978.

Committees *Budget* (11th).

Science and Technology (17th). Subcommittees: Energy Development and Applications; Space Science and Applications.

Group Ratings

	ADA	COPE	PC	LCV	CFA	RPN	NAB	NSI	NTU	ACA	ACU
1980	33	37	33	48	43	—	67	78	28	46	33
1979	11	30	30	35	8	—	—	—	38	64	69

Key Votes

1) Draft Registn $	FOR	6) Fair Hsg DOJ Enfrc	FOR	11) Cut Socl Incr Dfns $	AGN
2) Ban $ to Nicrgua	FOR	7) Lim PAC Contrbtns	AGN	12) Hosptl Cost Controls	AGN
3) Dlay MX Missile	AGN	8) Cap on Food Stmp $	AGN	13) Gasln Ctrls & Allctns	AGN
4) Nuclr Mortorium	AGN	9) New US Dep Edcatn	AGN	14) Lim Wndfll Prof Tax	FOR
5) Alaska Lands Bill	FOR	10) Cut OSHA $	FOR	15) Chryslr Loan Grntee	FOR

Election Results

1980 general	Bill Nelson (D)	139,468	(70%)	($267,457)
	Stan Dowiat (R)	58,734	(30%)	
1980 primary	Bill Nelson (D), unopposed			
1978 general	Bill Nelson (D)	89,543	(61%)	($313,325)
	Edward J. Gurney (R)	56,074	(39%)	($212,679)

TENTH DISTRICT

The 10th congressional district includes, geographically, most of south Florida; and if most of its territory is made up of swamps and alligators, it nonetheless is one of the fastest-growing areas in population in the nation. This district was created in 1972 because of growth registered in the 1970 census, and it will probably be divided into essentially two new districts as a result of the 1980 census. The district, in its current boundaries, sweeps across the Florida peninsula, fronting on the Atlantic north of Palm Beach and on the Gulf of Mexico south from Sarasota to Naples. Accordingly its population centers are widely dispersed. It goes as far north as Disney World near Orlando; it takes in some of the fast-growing suburban territory west of West Palm Beach; it includes on the Gulf Coast the fast-growing areas around Port Charlotte, Fort Myers, and Naples. In between there are mainly the Everglades, the Sebring grand prix race course, and thousands of acres of orange groves and vegetable fields.

It is dangerous to generalize about such a vast area, and one with a population that has risen from one-quarter of a million 20 years ago to three-quarters of a million today. But it is fairly safe to say that the paradigmatic community here was swampland then and has been converted now to a tasteful. restrained stucco low-rise condominium community, with luxuriant vegetation and, of course, a pleasant climate most of the year. The residents are people who were successful up North — businessmen, professionals, and well-provided-for widows — who spend most of the year (but not necessarily the hottest summer months) in comfortable apartments. There are few Jews on the Gulf Coast or on the Gold Coast as far north as the area north of Palm Beach; these are people who feel at home in any midwestern or East Coast WASP or perhaps Catholic country club. These are people whose tastes in furniture run to Early American, although in deference to Florida they may have rattan; their tastes in politics are almost certainly Republican. Some of the Gulf Coast counties, for example, were over 70% for Ronald Reagan in 1980.

The congressman from this district since its creation is Republican L. A. (Skip) Bafalis. A former state legislator who ran for governor unsuccessfully in 1970 (he was defeated in the primary), Bafalis won the Republican nomination in the 10th in 1972 without much fuss and won the election easily. He has not had a serious challenge since. He is a party loyalist who makes few waves in the House or on the Ways and Means Committee; he actively pursued charges of tomato dumping, a source of concern in this district, which produces a large percentage of U.S. tomatoes. Since the district is likely to be split roughly evenly between two new districts for 1982, Bafalis will have the option of running where he wants. Probably he will choose to run from a district centered on Fort Myers and Naples. Another district, probably to include Sarasota and Port Charlotte, will almost certainly elect another Republican of similar views.

Census Data   Pop. (1980 final) 878,067, up 94% in 1970s. Median family income, 1970, $7,323, 76% of U.S.

The Voters

   Employment profile 1970   White collar, 43%. Blue collar, 33%. Service, 15%. Farm, 9%.
   Ethnic groups   Black 1980, 9%. Hispanic 1980, 3%. Total foreign stock 1970, 13%. Germany, UK, Canada, 2% each.

Presidential Vote

1980	Reagan (R)	241,648	(64%)
	Carter (D)	115,194	(31%)
	Anderson (I)	15,820	(4%)
1976	Ford (R)	146,879	(54%)
	Carter (D)	122,899	(46%)

Rep. L. A. (Skip) **Bafalis** (R) Elected 1972; b. Sept. 28, 1929, Boston, Mass.; home, Fort Myers Beach; St. Anselm's Col., A.B. 1952.

Career Army, Korea; Banker; Fla. House of Reps , 1964–65; Fla. Senate, 1966–70, Minor. Ldr., 1968; Cand. for Gov., 1970.

Offices 2433 RHOB, 202-225-2536. Also Room 106 Fed. Bldg., Fort Myers 33901, 813-334-4424.

Committee *Ways and Means* (8th). Subcommittees: Public Assistance and Unemployment Compensation; Trade.

232   FLORIDA

Group Ratings

	ADA	COPE	PC	LCV	CFA	RPN	NAB	NSI	NTU	ACA	ACU
1980	6	11	31	17	8	—	100	100	57	95	89
1979	0	16	10	10	4	—	—	—	63	100	95
1978	10	10	10	30	18	64	100	100	33	100	96

Key Votes

1) Draft Registn $	FOR	6) Fair Hsg DOJ Enfrc	AGN	11) Cut Socl Incr Dfns $	FOR
2) Ban $ to Nicrgua	FOR	7) Lim PAC Contrbtns	AGN	12) Hosptl Cost Controls	AGN
3) Dlay MX Missile	AGN	8) Cap on Food Stmp $	FOR	13) Gasln Ctrls & Allctns	AGN
4) Nuclr Mortorium	AGN	9) New US Dep Edcatn	AGN	14) Lim Wndfll Prof Tax	FOR
5) Alaska Lands Bill	AGN	10) Cut OSHA $	FOR	15) Chryslr Loan Grntee	AGN

Election Results

1980 general	L. A. (Skip) Bafalis (R)	272,393	(79%)	($128,953)
	Richard D. Sparkman (D)	72,646	(21%)	($26,963)
1980 primary	L. A. (Skip) Bafalis (R), unopposed			
1978 general	L. A. (Skip) Bafalis (R), unopposed			($22,007)

ELEVENTH DISTRICT

Fifty years ago Palm Beach was already a fashionable resort for the extremely rich. Across Lake Worth, West Palm Beach was a small town, a large percentage of whose residents devoted themselves to ministering to the needs of Palm Beach. There has been little change in Palm Beach since then, but West Palm Beach, near the northern end of the Gold Coast that runs all the way to Miami, has been altered beyond recognition. High-rise apartment houses and condominiums practically form a wall that blocks the mainland from the Atlantic. Jai alai frontons vie with gaudy bars for tourists' money, and the small hotels of the 1940s have been replaced with giant motor inns.

The northern end of the Gold Coast — in rough terms from Pompano Beach in Broward County to West Palm Beach in Palm Beach County — is the 11th congressional district of Florida. Like Fort Lauderdale, which is some 40 miles to the south, the 11th during the 1950s and 1960s became more Republican as more and more people moved here from the WASPy, well-to-do suburbs of the East and Midwest. Now it appears that the migration is becoming more Democratic, with more Jews and people with blue collar backgrounds in the big condominiums that are increasingly important politically here. This is a district that went for Nixon solidly over Humphrey (55%–28%) in 1968 and that was 74% for Nixon in 1972. But in 1976 Jimmy Carter got 50% of the vote here; and although he did not do as well in 1980 other Democrats have carried the area.

For more than 30 years the Palm Beach area was represented by the Rogers family, most of that by Paul Rogers (1954–79), who made an outstanding record as chairman of the Health Subcommittee of the Commerce Committee. When Rogers retired in 1978, he was succeeded ultimately by an aide, Dan Mica. But the succession was anything but automatic. Indeed, if Rogers had retired a few years before, the Republicans would probably have taken the seat, and as it was they made a major effort.

The Republican, Bill James, was his party's leader in the state legislature and had represented Palm Beach County there for 12 years. He outspent Mica by a considerable margin, and in a year when Republicans generally seemed to be on the offensive on issues. But Mica had the advantage of his association with Rogers, and solid support as well from condominium associations. On the Gold Coast today, the biggest political power brokers are people who organize their condominiums for one or another candidate. Usually they are the people who are veterans of campaigns up North, who have lots of time on their hands and little to do, and who are tenacious in grasping and milking grievances against the often unscrupulous condominium developers. That kind of support helped Mica win 55% in the 1978 primary, 55% in the 1978 general election, and 59% in the 1980 general election—although other Democrats were doing poorly in south Florida that year.

Mica is one of the less liberal Democrats from urban Florida. He serves on Foreign Affairs and Veterans' Affairs, and in early 1981 sought not one but two subcommittee chairs in vain. First he was beaten, among Foreign Affairs Democrats, by Michael Barnes for the Latin–American Subcommittee and then by Howard Wolpe for the Africa Subcommittee. Mica lost although, by virtue of a coin toss, he had seniority over the other two fellow 1978 freshmen; he ascribed his defeat to a liberal power play and said it was "a last flicker in this House of extremist attitudes." He is the kind of Democrat who can be expected to dissent from liberal positions in 1981 and 1982.

Census Data   Pop. (1980 final) 843,299, up 87% in 1970s. Median family income, 1970, $8,995, 94% of U.S.

The Voters

Employment profile 1970   White collar, 49%. Blue collar, 31%. Service, 16%. Farm, 4%.
Ethnic groups   Black 1980, 12%. Hispanic 1980, 4%. Total foreign stock 1970, 21%. Germany, UK, Canada, 3% each; Italy, 2%; Ireland, 1%.

Presidential Vote

1980	Reagan (R)	197,972	(57%)
	Carter (D)	125,797	(36%)
	Anderson (I)	22,713	(7%)
1976	Ford (R)	130,829	(49%)
	Carter (D)	128,416	(49%)

Rep. Dan Mica (D) Elected 1978; b. Feb. 4, 1944, Binghamton, N.Y.; home, West Palm Beach; U. of Fla., 1961–62, Miami Dade Jr. Col., A.A. 1965, Fla. Atlantic U., B.A. 1966.

Career Public school teacher, 1966–68; Admin. Asst. to U.S. Rep. Paul Rogers, 1968–78.

Offices 131 CHOB, 202-225-3001. Also 321 Fed. Bldg., West Palm Beach 33401, 305-832-6424.

Committees *Foreign Affairs* (12th). Subcommittees: Inter-American Affairs; International Operations.

Veterans' Affairs (12th). Subcommittees: Hospitals and Health Care; Housing and Memorial Affairs; Oversight and Investigations.

Group Ratings

	ADA	COPE	PC	LCV	CFA	RPN	NAB	NSI	NTU	ACA	ACU
1980	33	41	43	42	36	—	33	80	36	52	56
1979	53	35	55	53	40	—	—	—	34	32	38

Key Votes

1) Draft Registn $	FOR	6) Fair Hsg DOJ Enfrc	AGN	11) Cut Socl Incr Dfns $	FOR
2) Ban $ to Nicrgua	FOR	7) Lim PAC Contrbtns	FOR	12) Hosptl Cost Controls	FOR
3) Dlay MX Missile	—	8) Cap on Food Stmp $	AGN	13) Gasln Ctrls & Allctns	FOR
4) Nuclr Mortorium	AGN	9) New US Dep Edcatn	FOR	14) Lim Wndfll Prof Tax	AGN
5) Alaska Lands Bill	FOR	10) Cut OSHA $	FOR	15) Chryslr Loan Grntee	AGN

Election Results

1980 general	Dan Mica (D)	201,713	(59%)	($265,177)
	Al Coogler (R)	137,520	(41%)	($201,217)
1980 primary	Dan Mica (D), unopposed			
1978 general	Dan Mica (D)	123,346	(55%)	($158,573)
	Bill James (R)	99,757	(45%)	($228,969)

TWELFTH DISTRICT

For some people Fort Lauderdale evokes memories of college sand-and-beer vacations in the spring (they have made a comeback) or perhaps scenes from an Annette Funicello and Frankie Avalon movie. The city fathers would have you take back a different vision: a cosmopolitan, canalled city with a pleasant climate, with miles of wide beach, lilting palm trees, and cultural attractions and shopping you would expect from a major metropolitan area. There is some truth in this: Fort Lauderdale itself is just one city in the middle of literally dozens of communities in Florida's Gold Coast, a strip seldom more than six miles wide running from south of Miami to north of Palm Beach and with a population of more than 2.5 million. This land, dredged from swamp and muck, is some of the most valuable real estate in the country.

Fort Lauderdale and most of surrounding Broward County make up Florida's 12th congressional district. Most of the first immigrants here were from the upper-income suburbs of the East and Midwest, the Locust Valleys and Winnetkas of America. It was generally felt that the Fort Lauderdale area in the 1950s and much of the 1960s discouraged Jews from moving in; this was the WASPy part of Florida. Its politics was straight out of the old *Chicago Tribune:* solidly Republican, conservative, unchanging. It was fitting then that when the Fort Lauderdale area first got its own congressman in 1966, it elected a Republican brought up in Chicago, an overweight, affable man named J. Herbert Burke.

Since the late 1960s and early 1970s, Fort Lauderdale and Broward County have been changing politically, due largely to a second wave of migration. There has been an increasing number of Jewish voters here, first just across the county border from Miami in Hallandale and Hollywood, and later in Fort Lauderdale itself. Most of the old restrictions have disappeared, and those who want a purely WASP community have been moving elsewhere, often to the Gulf Coast. The result is that Broward County and the 12th district have become notably more Democratic. Back in 1964 Broward had gone for Barry Goldwater; by 1970 it gave a majority to Reubin Askew. In 1976 Broward was 52% for Jimmy Carter—the first time it had gone Democratic for president since 1944. A third migration seems to have moved it into the Republican column in 1980 — the influx of Cuban refugees into Florida that stirred so many fears and so much disgust with the Carter Administration; but it remains to be seen whether the effect is ongoing or only momentary.

This rapid change in population has made the politics of the 12th district highly unstable: in the last three elections it has elected three different congressmen. Congressman Burke had tough challenges in 1974 and 1976; when he was arrested for being disorderly in front of a nude go-go club in Fort Lauderdale in May 1978, it was clear he was in serious trouble. The Democrats have a history of fractious primaries here, and they had one in 1978; the winner, Ed Stack, had only 53% of the vote but was strong enough to oust the incumbent. Stack was an unusual freshman congressman: 68 years old, a former Republican, a veteran of 10 years as Broward County sheriff, a law-and-order man as the representative of a party whose voters historically at least were more sensitive to civil liberties than the needs of law enforcement.

As it turned out, Stack compiled a rather liberal record in Congress; nonetheless, he was vulnerable in the 1980 Democratic primary. He was beaten 58%–42% by Alan Becker, a former state legislator who had run an expensive statewide primary race for attorney general in 1978. But Becker found himself in trouble in the general election. Anger at the Carter Administration for both its Cuban and Middle East policies was eroding the Democratic base — and this was not simple disaffection; it was something close to rage. And the Republicans had a good candidate; Clay Shaw, the mayor of Fort Lauderdale, who had good access to Republican funds and used national Republican economic issues. Becker, in contrast, had spent most of his money in the September primary and, since he had only recently moved into the district from north Miami, had to face carpetbagger charges (although it is unclear why that should matter in a district in which almost none of its voters grew up). Becker's big advantage was support from condominium associations. But in the Republicans' best year in south Florida since the Eisenhower landslide of 1956, that was not enough. Shaw was victorious with a solid 55%. Having tied himself to the national Republican economic policies, Shaw admits his own fate will probably depend on their success or failure; certainly a district that has ousted incumbents in each of the last two elections cannot be considered a safe seat for anybody.

Population growth will require the creation of another congressional seat in the Gold Coast for 1982, and that will probably give Shaw a choice of districts. One district will probably extend north from Fort Lauderdale up into Palm Beach County, including the millionaires' town of Boca Raton. This would be a district less Jewish and more Republican than the current 12th and would be much safer for Shaw. The other district would extend from Fort Lauderdale southward to include Hollywood, Hallandale, and part of north Dade County. This seat would be more Democratic than the current 12th. In all likelihood, if this is how the seats are drawn, this new district would attract Becker and a host of competitors in the Democratic primary, and the winner of the October runoff would be the new congressman.

Census Data   Pop. (1980 final) 638,897, up 41% in 1970s. Median family income, 1970, $9,717, 101% of U.S.

The Voters

Employment profile 1970   White collar, 53%. Blue collar, 31%. Service, 15%. Farm, 1%.
Ethnic groups   Black 1980, 13%. Hispanic 1980, 4%. Asian 1980, 1%. Total foreign stock 1970, 25%. Italy, 4%; Germany, Canada, UK, 3% each; USSR, 2%; Poland, Ireland, 1% each.

236   FLORIDA

Presidential Vote

1980	Reagan (R)	140,464	(56%)
	Carter (D)	90,856	(36%)
	Anderson (I)	19,259	(8%)
1976	Ford (R)	97,867	(46%)
	Carter (D)	112,477	(53%)

Rep. E. Clay Shaw, Jr. (R) Elected 1980; b. Apr. 19, 1939, Miami; home, Ft. Lauderdale; Stetson U., B.A. 1961, U. of Ala., M.A. 1963, Stetson U., J.D. 1966.

Career Practicing atty., 1966–68; Ft. Lauderdale Chf. City Prosecutor, 1968–69, Assoc. Munic. Judge, 1969–71, City Commissioner, 1971–73, Vice Mayor, 1973–75, Mayor, 1975–80; Pres., Nat. Conf. of Rep. Mayors, 1979–80.

Offices 1213 LHOB, 202-225-3026. Also Broward Fed. Bldg., 299 E. Broward Blvd., Ft. Lauderdale 33301, 305-527-7253.

Committees *Merchant Marine and Fisheries* (15th). Subcommittees: Coast Guard and Navigation; Merchant Marine.

Public Works and Transportation (17th). Subcommittees: Surface Transportation; Water Resources.

Group Ratings and Key Votes: Newly Elected

Election Results

1980 general	E. Clay Shaw, Jr. (R)	128,561	(55%)	($423,603)
	Alan S. Becker (D)	107,164	(45%)	($117,264)
1980 primary	E. Clay Shaw, Jr. (R), unopposed			
1978 general	Edward J. Stack (D)	107,037	(62%)	($133,351)
	J. Herbert Burke (R)	66,610	(38%)	($74,697)

THIRTEENTH DISTRICT

Even as cities outwardly stay the same, they change internally, as old residents move out and new residents move in. That is what has been happening in Miami and its Dade County suburbs. This is an area whose total population has changed less than that of almost any of Florida's other major metropolitan counties. Yet there have actually been vast population movements. Of the two ethnic groups that seem increasingly to dominate Miami's politics, one was hardly present 20 years ago (the Cubans) and the other does not comprise much more than 15% of Dade County's population (the Jews). Yet each seems dominant in one of Dade County's three congressional districts.

The 13th district, which includes the northern third of Dade County plus the southern edge of Broward, is the one where Jews are particularly important. That is not because there is a Jewish majority here; there are no precise figures available, but probably only two districts in the nation, both in Brooklyn, have Jewish majorities. Only 4% of the residents of the 13th in 1970 had Yiddish as their mother tongue, and there are plenty of other ethnic concentrations: WASPs in Miami Shores, blacks on the north side of Miami in the area known as Liberty City (the site of riots as the Cuban refugees came in), and white southerners in Hialeah. Jews probably do not comprise more than 20% of the residents of the district. But because they are older and more likely to vote than the average, they probably include more than 30% of the voters and more than 40% of the Democratic primary voters. Since the 13th district was created for the 1972 election, all the leading congressional candidates here have been Jewish; and the Jewish voting habits make this Florida's most liberal district and the one most supportive of national Democratic candidates. It was one of only three Florida districts to give Jimmy Carter a majority in 1980; the others were the Dixie-dominated 2d and 3d districts in north Florida.

This ethnic background makes for a special kind of politics, one familiar to observers of the New York political scene. There are many interlocking alliances and a great deal of king-making in Miami politics, much of it done at the Tiger Bay Club organized by some politicos; and there are plenty of state and local offices in Dade County to keep people busy filing slates and making endorsements. Particularly important in primary elections here are the condominium associations. The large condominiums have brought together into one location — access to which can easily be controlled — many articulate people with organizational literacy, a knack for politics, and plenty of time on their hands. Properly organized, a single condominium can provide a candidate with an advantage of several hundred votes over his rivals — more than many Chicago precinct leaders can deliver.

William Lehman, the 13th's congressman, has had an interesting and somewhat unusual career. Lehman got his start in business as a used car dealer, known widely as "Alabama Bill." He reportedly developed the reputation, unusual in the trade, for reliability and honesty. Politics was obviously the next step. Lehman got himself elected to the school board and then, in 1972, to Congress when the 13th district was newly created. Lehman has not had tough opposition since — testimony to his acceptability in a district that sometimes seems supersaturated with politics. Lehman has a generally liberal voting record and a seat on the Appropriations Committee; he makes few political or legislative waves in Washington.

Census Data   Pop. (1980 final) 586,114, up 29% in 1970s. Median family income, 1970, $9,411, 98% of U.S.

The Voters

Employment profile 1970   White collar, 49%. Blue collar, 34%. Service, 16%. Farm, 1%.
Ethnic groups   Black 1980, 26%. Hispanic 1980, 23%. Asian 1980, 1%. Total foreign stock 1970, 32%. USSR, 4%; Italy, 3%; Canada, Germany, Poland, UK, 2% each; Austria, 1%.

Presidential Vote

1980	Reagan (R)	79,330	(42%)
	Carter (D)	95,384	(50%)
	Anderson (I)	15,160	(8%)
1976	Ford (R)	65,888	(33%)
	Carter (D)	130,805	(66%)

Rep. William Lehman (D) Elected 1972; b. Oct. 5, 1913, Selma, Ala.; home, North Miami Beach; U. of Ala., B.S. 1934, U. of Miami, Teaching Certif. 1963. Additional studies at Oxford U., Cambridge U., U. of Edinburgh, Harvard U., and Middlebury Col.

Career   Auto dealer, 1936–42, 1946–72; Army Air Corps, WWII; Teacher, Pub. Schools, 1963, Miami Dade Jr. Col., 1964–66; Dade Co. Sch. Bd., 1964–70, Chmn., 1971.

Offices   2347 RHOB, 202-225-4211. Also 2020 N.E. 163d St., Suite 108, North Miami Beach 33162, 305-945-7518.

Committee   *Appropriations* (23d). Subcommittees: District of Columbia; Foreign Operations; Transportation.

238   FLORIDA

Group Ratings

	ADA	COPE	PC	LCV	CFA	RPN	NAB	NSI	NTU	ACA	ACU
1980	83	72	67	54	71	—	17	0	14	17	11
1979	89	80	60	63	42	—	—	—	22	8	8
1978	80	85	69	77	55	55	18	30	14	12	5

Key Votes

1) Draft Registn $	FOR	6) Fair Hsg DOJ Enfrc	FOR	11) Cut Socl Incr Dfns $	AGN
2) Ban $ to Nicrgua	AGN	7) Lim PAC Contrbtns	FOR	12) Hosptl Cost Controls	FOR
3) Dlay MX Missile	FOR	8) Cap on Food Stmp $	AGN	13) Gasln Ctrls & Allctns	AGN
4) Nuclr Mortorium	AGN	9) New US Dep Edcatn	FOR	14) Lim Wndfll Prof Tax	AGN
5) Alaska Lands Bill	FOR	10) Cut OSHA $	AGN	15) Chryslr Loan Grntee	—

Election Results

1980 general	William Lehman (D)............	127,828	(75%)	($208,900)
	Alvin E. Entin (R).............	42,830	(25%)	($63,434)
1980 primary	William Lehman (D), unopposed			
1978 general	William Lehman (D), unopposed..			($70,087)

FOURTEENTH DISTRICT

Claude Pepper is the grand old man of Florida politics. Back in 1936 he first went to Capitol Hill as a 36-year-old U.S. senator. He was known even then for his old-fashioned southern style oratory, and once in the Senate he became a member of the southern establishment. But when other senators from Dixie began to sour on the New Deal, Pepper remained as loyal to FDR's domestic policies as he did to Roosevelt's conviction that the United States should be fully prepared for another war in Europe. For these stands and for his devotion to civil liberties, the young senator came to be called "Red Pepper." In 1950, during the era of Joe McCarthy, Pepper was defeated in a bitter Senate primary by Congressman George Smathers, and he retired to a Miami law practice.

Today Smathers himself has long since (1968) retired to a lucrative position as a Washington lobbyist, and Claude Pepper is back in Congress. After the 1960 census, when the Florida legislature was compelled to create a second Miami area House seat, Pepper was the logical choice to fill it. He won a solid majority in the 1962 Democratic primary and has since retained the seat with little difficulty. The congressman's oratorical style is still out of Dixie, but his record is such that he is a favorite of his black, Jewish, and poor elderly constituents.

If Pepper had won his 1950 Senate race against Smathers, he would have become chairman of the Senate Foreign Relations Committee (and, assuming reelection, would have held that position from 1958 to 1981). As things are, he cuts a lesser figure. But his years of experience on Capitol Hill count for something; only one member of either house, Senator Jennings Randolph of West Virginia, preceded Pepper to Congress. He holds a seat on the sometimes critical Rules Committee, where he usually advances the views of the House leadership and House liberals. Pepper has also been something of an aficionado of special committees. He set up a special committee on crime, which finally folded, and a special committee on aging. Often special committees are just a device for publicizing the chairman, but in the case of the special committee on aging Pepper actually advanced an idea with major implication for our whole society: eliminating the mandatory retirement age. Pepper succeeded in pushing through a bill to change the mandatory retirement age from 65 to 70 for most jobs. This was hailed as a major liberating force for many older people, although in fact there are more people who would prefer retiring at a younger age than are eager to hold onto their jobs past 65. The law will have a major effect when Pepper is no longer with us, particularly when the baby boom generation passes 65; can we be sure that there will be enough jobs for everyone then? The counterargument is that with more people available to work, there will be a more productive economy, and that in any case people should have the choice of whether they want to work or retire. Pepper, who has many elderly constituents, passionately supports the law; one reason may be that he himself is the oldest member of Congress and has served half his congressional career when past the age of 65.

When Pepper was first elected to the House, the most important voting bloc in his district was Jewish. Then his district included the whole northern half of Dade County, and much of central Miami was predominantly Jewish; today the district includes the central third of the county, and the predominant ethnic group in much of the area is Cuban. The central city of Miami has come to have a definite Latin flavor. Spanish is the language on Southwest 8th and other shopping streets. Miami has become the major center in the United States for Latin American trade and travel; Latins fly up to Miami to shop for consumer goods (most Latin nations have high tariffs), and the clientele of many Miami hotels is mainly Latin. Many American businesses find that Miami, rather than a site in Mexico or South America, is the best location for a Latin American office; it is easier to fly to most parts of Latin America from here than from any other place.

The Cuban community in Miami has helped to make the city a major Latin center. At the beginning of 1980 there were about 400,000 Cubans in Pepper's 14th congressional district, which includes most of Miami and part of Miami Beach and such other suburbs as Coral Gables. The Cubans are a diverse group politically, representing all types of opposition to Castro from right-wingers who would like a return to a Batista-style dictatorship to mild socialists who oppose Castro's eradication of civil liberties. Virtually every segment of the Cuban community responded positively when Fidel Castro announced, in the late spring of 1980, that he was letting more Cubans emigrate; the Cuban community chartered the boats that set out to carry Cubans from the port of Mariel. Through the summer, until the flow of emigration was cut off, more than 100,000 Cubans left their native land, and some 60,000 Cubans came to settle in Florida. There were lurid stories of crimes and misdeeds, and many of the new migrants were in fact from the criminal subculture. But many of the stories were simply the result of the suddenness of the Cuban influx and of the human tendency to assume the worst of the unknown.

The Jews and other northern migrants who came to the Miami area after World War II made this the one part of the state hospitable to Democratic liberalism. The Cubans' political philosophy has been different. Many of these people come from Cuba's old middle class, and although they eagerly accepted menial jobs on arriving in Miami they rapidly moved up in social status and income. Their opposition to Fidel Castro tends to make them hard-line anti-Communists; their experience of working their way up through the free enterprise system tends to make them appreciate its workings. As a result, the Cubans are much more likely to be Republicans than are other ethnic groups, although they do not always produce majorities for Republican candidates. As a result, the long-term trend in the 14th — in contrast to many Florida districts — has been away from the Democrats and toward the Republicans.

That long-term trend has not yet caught up with Claude Pepper. He had a serious opponent in 1978, a 30-year-old Cuban–American whose campaign was well financed and who raised some ethical issues against Pepper. Nevertheless Pepper won by nearly a 2-to-1 margin; and in 1980, at age 80, Pepper did even better. Pepper has not really slowed down or ceased the zestful pursuit of political objectives; he seems undaunted by the setbacks he has suffered and full of eagerness for the fights ahead.

Redistricting will shift the Pepper seat slightly southward, which probably means that there will be more Cubans here. For 1982 or even 1984 that is not too important; but in the long run in the 1980s this might turn out to be a Cuban—and perhaps even a Republican—seat.

Census Data   Pop. (1980 final) 505,623, up 12% in 1970s. Median family income, 1970, $8,203, 86% of U.S.

The Voters

Employment profile 1970   White collar, 46%. Blue collar, 37%. Service, 17%. Farm, -%.
Ethnic groups   Black 1980, 14%. Hispanic 1980, 55%. Asian 1980, 1%. Total foreign stock 1970, 56%. USSR, 4%; Poland, Germany, Canada, Italy, Austria, UK, 1% each.

Presidential Vote

1980	Reagan (R)	73,790	(55%)
	Carter (D)	50,720	(38%)
	Anderson (I)	9,211	(7%)
1976	Ford (R)	58,863	(43%)
	Carter (D)	76,357	(56%)

Rep. Claude Pepper (D) Elected 1962; b. Sept. 8, 1900, near Dudleyville, Ala.; home, Miami; U. of Ala., A.B. 1921, Harvard U., LL.B. 1924.

Career Instructor in Law, U. of Ark., 1924–25; Practicing atty., 1925–36, 1951–62; Fla. House of Reps., 1929–30; Fla. Bd. of Pub. Welfare, 1931–32; Fla. Bd. of Law Examiners, 1933–34; U.S. Senate, 1937–51; Candidate for Dem. nomination for U.S. Senate, 1950, 1958.

Offices 2239 RHOB, 202-225-3931. Also 823 Fed. Bldg., 51 S.W. 1st Ave., Miami 33130, 305-350-5565.

Committees *Rules* (2d). Subcommittee: Rules of the House.

Select Committee on Aging (Chairman). Subcommittee: Health and Long-Term Care (Chairman).

Group Ratings

	ADA	COPE	PC	LCV	CFA	RPN	NAB	NSI	NTU	ACA	ACU
1980	61	95	55	29	57	—	8	33	8	19	7
1979	58	79	50	58	44	—	—	—	14	5	3
1978	50	90	63	61	36	50	0	56	8	12	5

Key Votes

1) Draft Registn $	—	6) Fair Hsg DOJ Enfrc	FOR	11) Cut Socl Incr Dfns $	AGN
2) Ban $ to Nicrgua	—	7) Lim PAC Contrbtns	FOR	12) Hosptl Cost Controls	FOR
3) Dlay MX Missile	AGN	8) Cap on Food Stmp $	AGN	13) Gasln Ctrls & Allctns	FOR
4) Nuclr Mortorium	AGN	9) New US Dep Edcatn	FOR	14) Lim Wndfll Prof Tax	AGN
5) Alaska Lands Bill	FOR	10) Cut OSHA $	AGN	15) Chryslr Loan Grntee	—

Election Results

1980 general	Claude Pepper (D)	95,820	(75%)	($211,659)
	Evelio S. Estrella (R)	32,027	(25%)	($50,620)
1980 primary	Claude Pepper (D)	26,800	(79%)	
	One other (D)	7,012	(21%)	
1978 general	Claude Pepper (D)	65,202	(63%)	($239,864)
	Al Cardenas (R)	38,081	(37%)	($242,131)

FIFTEENTH DISTRICT

The suburbs south of Dade County are the fastest-growing part of the Miami metropolitan area. With relatively few Latins or blacks, these places lack the special character of Miami, and the area's physical ambience is not so different from that of Orange County, California. But while the people in California are bounded by ocean and mountains, the people here are hemmed in mainly by a giant swamp, the Everglades, from which their often valuable property was reclaimed. South Dade County is middle-class, middle- to upper-income territory that stretches out on both sides of U.S. 1 as it heads toward the Florida Keys.

The bulk of Florida's 15th congressional district lies in these southwest suburbs of Miami. Also in the district are the Keys (Monroe County) and some other territory obviously included for political reasons. For example, the 15th includes the University of Miami in Coral Gables and the nearby Coconut Grove section of Miami, both of them packed with liberal Democratic votes. The district also takes in a couple of blocks of downtown Miami, which connects the mainland with the 15th's section of Miami Beach.

This part of Miami Beach is the older, poorer, and almost entirely Jewish South Beach section and includes the hall where both parties' 1972 national conventions were held. The South Beach has on occasion played a crucial role in the politics of the district, as in 1972, when it provided virtually all of Congressman Dante Fascell's margin in an otherwise Republican year.

This has not been Fascell's usual experience; ordinarily he wins easily. First elected in 1954, Fascell is considered not quite so liberal as the 14th district's Claude Pepper, but he votes far more often with northern Democrats than white conservative southerners. For many years Fascell chaired a subcommittee on Latin American affairs — an important subject in Miami, which is the nation's leading center for Latin American trade. He now chairs the International Operations Subcommittee, in which capacity he manages sensitive legislation such as the State Department authorization bill — sensitive because it attracts mischievous amendments directed at members' pet causes in foreign policy. Fascell is the number three Democrat on Foreign Affairs, behind 70-year-old Clement Zablocki and 69-year-old L. H. Fountain, and he has a good chance of becoming chairman someday.

He is also number three on Government Operations and while he is not going to overshadow the colorful chairman, Jack Brooks of Texas, he is not afraid to stand up to Brooks when he disagrees with him. Indeed, Fascell is one of the most fearless members of the House and will not turn away from a fight with even the most formidable opponent. Thus he took on Brooks when Brooks opposed Jimmy Carter's government reorganization authorization bill, just as a few years before he had taken on Wayne Hays when Hays opposed certain aspects of campaign finance reform. Fascell is considered by some observers of the House to be one of its most competent and sensitive legislative craftsmen—a man who can put together a piece of legislation, explain it, and get it passed without having it watered down in the process. With considerable seniority and still short of retirement age, he should be in peak form over the next few years.

Census Data Pop. (1980 final) 646,764, up 43% in 1970s. Median family income, 1970, $9,909, 103% of U.S.

The Voters

Employment profile 1970 White collar, 60%. Blue collar, 24%. Service, 14%. Farm, 2%.
Ethnic groups Black 1980, 10%. Hispanic 1980, 27%. Asian 1980, 1%. Total foreign stock 1970, 31%. USSR, 5%; Poland, UK, Germany, Canada, 2% each; Italy, Austria, 1% each.

Presidential Vote

1980	Reagan (R)	119,317	(55%)
	Carter (D)	73,261	(34%)
	Anderson (I)	21,548	(10%)
1976	Ford (R)	91,053	(45%)
	Carter (D) .....,........	108,295	(53%)

Rep. Dante B. Fascell (D) Elected 1954; b. Mar. 9, 1917, Bridgehampton, L.I., N.Y.; home, Miami; U. of Miami, J.D. 1938.

Career Practicing atty., 1938–42, 1946–54; Army, WWII; Legal Attache, Dade Co. St. Legislative Del., 1947–50; Fla. House of Reps., 1950–54; Mbr., U.S. Delegation to U.N., 1969.

Offices 2354 RHOB, 202-225-4506. Also 904 Fed. Bldg., 51 S.W. 1st Ave., Miami 33130, 305-350-5301.

Committees *Foreign Affairs* (3d). Subcommittees: International Operations (Chairman); International Security and Scientific Affairs.

Government Operations (3d). Subcommittee: Legislation and National Security.

Group Ratings

	ADA	COPE	PC	LCV	CFA	RPN	NAB	NSI	NTU	ACA	ACU
1980	83	83	70	43	79	—	18	10	13	25	16
1979	74	68	60	57	63	—	—	—	20	4	0
1978	65	85	70	66	68	36	0	33	16	17	4

Key Votes

1) Draft Registn $	FOR	6) Fair Hsg DOJ Enfrc	FOR	11) Cut Socl Incr Dfns $	AGN
2) Ban $ to Nicrgua	AGN	7) Lim PAC Contrbtns	FOR	12) Hosptl Cost Controls	FOR
3) Dlay MX Missile	AGN	8) Cap on Food Stmp $	AGN	13) Gasln Ctrls & Allctns	FOR
4) Nuclr Mortorium	—	9) New US Dep Edcatn	FOR	14) Lim Wndfll Prof Tax	AGN
5) Alaska Lands Bill	FOR	10) Cut OSHA $	AGN	15) Chryslr Loan Grntee	FOR

Election Results

1980 general	Dante B. Fascell (D)	132,952	(65%)	($73,971)
	Herbert J. Hoodwin (R)	70,433	(35%)	($34,172)
1980 primary	Dante B. Fascell (D), unopposed			
1978 general	Dante B. Fascell (D)	108,837	(74%)	($47,724)
	Herbert J. Hoodwin (R)	37,897	(26%)	($69,590)

GEORGIA

It was one of the few moving tableaux in recent American politics. Jimmy Carter, his family, all kinds of prominent Democrats stood on the platform as the 1976 Democratic National Convention was ending, their heads bowed, listening to the impassioned oration-in-the-form-of-benediction delivered by the Rev. Martin Luther King, Sr. The father of the greatest leader of the civil rights movement was giving his blessing to the first white from the Deep South nominated for president in a century. It symbolized the changes that had been achieved in the nation, in the South, and in the state that increasingly has become the heart of the South, Georgia.

For until Jimmy Carter was elected governor in 1970, the politics of Georgia — like politics in most southern states — either turned entirely on race or threatened to. The great symbol of southern populism, Georgia's Tom Watson, had ended his political career in the 1920s as a raving racist. Georgia's most successful political family, the Talmadges — father Eugene was elected governor four times, son Herman was governor himself and served in the Senate for 24 years — gained most of their victories by posing as champions of rural whites and segregation and the opponents of Atlanta sophisticates and race-mixing. Georgia has had some very distinguished senators: Walter George who served more than 30 years and chaired Foreign Relations in the 1950s, Richard Russell who served 38 years and chaired Armed Services and Appropriations. Both devoted important parts of their careers to opposing civil rights bills, both for political reasons and out of genuine conviction. And virtually every successful Georgia politician has made the point that he comes from rural Georgia, not cosmopolitan Atlanta. The only major exception was the man who appealed most explicitly to rural Georgia, Lester Maddox.

The year 1980 was not good for Georgia's best-known politicians. Jimmy Carter, after working his way to the White House four years before, was beaten and beaten badly; Georgia was in fact the only state in the Union where he won an absolute majority of the votes. And Herman Talmadge, never a political ally of Carter, was beaten also; the financial improprieties that had caused the Senate to formally "denounce" him also apparently lowered his standing with the voters sufficiently to enable Republican Mack Mattingly to upset him. But it was Carter's defeat that really stung. It was not so much a matter of personal popularity. Indeed, Carter had won the governorship in 1970 with only 59% of the vote and might very well have had difficulty winning a second term in 1974 had he been eligible to run. But Carter remained an important symbol — to the South generally and to Georgia in particular. He represented the emergence of a "new South," purged of racial segregation and bitter strife, economically buoyant, while still maintaining its unique cultural style.

Carter's election as governor was the turning point. He ran for the office, as he had in 1966 and as dozens of Georgians had before him, as the champion of rural "rednecks" and as the implied opponent of civil rights measures and wicked Atlanta. Yet in his inaugural address Carter proclaimed that the days of racial segregation were over, and he hung the portrait of Martin Luther King, Jr., in the state Capitol. On another issue, in another place, such a political about-face would be seen as run-of-the-mill hypocrisy. But in Georgia in 1970 and 1971, it turned out to be an expression of a change that most white Georgians wanted to make and most black Georgians welcomed. Before Carter's election support from blacks almost ensured that a candidate could not get support from whites; Carter himself circulated a picture of his runoff opponent, Carl Sanders, with black members of the Atlanta basketball team. Since 1970, support from blacks has no longer been the kiss of death, and a politician can even hope to win with the support of Atlanta. The political life of the state has grown calmer and more peaceful. Furthering this trend has been strong economic growth. Rural Georgia, which for years exported its young people (especially blacks) to Atlanta and the North, now has factories and textile mills springing up and enough jobs for its fast-growing population. Metropolitan Atlanta has grown at an exceedingly rapid pace, stepping outside the bounds of the old metropolitan area and filling up once rural and small-town counties 50 and 75 miles away from Peachtree Street.

The current governor, George Busbee, has turned out to be more popular and less controversial than Carter, not to mention Carter's predecessor, Lester Maddox, whom Busbee beat in the 1974 runoff. One reason may be that there is less to be controversial about these days. Racial questions have long since been settled, and Busbee, like Carter a product of rural south Georgia, stands foursquare for integration. Meanwhile, the state's prosperity means that there are few fiscal problems. Busbee is the first Georgia governor eligible to serve two four-year terms, but he cannot run again in 1982. In all likelihood any number of Democrats will run for the nomination. Possibilities include Zell Miller, the lieutenant governor defeated by Talmadge in the 1980 Senate runoff; Jack Watson, one of Carter's top aides in the White House; and others. The Carter credential may or may not be an advantage; it, and quite a lot of money besides, were not enough to enable Bert Lance to make the runoff in 1974, and while the president carried the state in 1980 it is not clear how many Georgia voters really feel warmly about him. The Republicans can be expected to make a serious effort too, if only because they won the Senate seat in 1980 and may have their strongest chance at the governorship since they ran an Atlanta television newscaster against Carter in 1970.

The defeat of Herman Talmadge was predictable from the time his personal and financial problems were revealed; but the fact that he lost to a Republican rather than in the Democratic Party tells us much about the wide range of possible outcomes in Georgia politics today. Talmadge, elected governor in 1948 and 1950, first elected to the Senate in 1956, was one of the mainstays of Georgia politics, and one of the last of the old southern conservative Democrats in the Senate. He had had an image of rigor and integrity and indeed was one of the Democratic members of the Senate Watergate Committee. But in April 1978 he was accused by a former aide of using official funds for personal purposes; it was revealed, embarrassingly, that he never withdrew cash from his own checking account but relied, he said, on small gifts of spending money from constituents. Talmadge denied any improprieties but admitted that he suffered from alcoholism. After extensive investigation, the Senate formally denounced him in 1979.

Such revelations would end the careers of most senators. Talmadge, for the first time since 1950, had serious primary opposition. In the first primary Talmadge was unable to win an absolute majority—a sure sign of trouble —but he was able to eliminate some candidates with rural Georgia bases. In the runoff Talmadge succeeded in painting his opponent, Lieutenant Governor Zell Miller, as a liberal and confined him to carrying Atlanta and a few scattered counties around the state. Talmadge increased his percentage from 42% in the primary to 59% in the runoff.

The general election was expected to be easier. The Republican, Mack Mattingly, had been state Republican chairman, but he was by birth a Yankee and by residence, on St. Simons Island, epitomized the wealthy country club crowd. Mattingly was one Republican who could not expect to benefit from a Reagan landslide. He was, however, well financed, thanks in large part to the national Republican Party, and he could benefit from the ideas that the national party was propagating. More important, he benefited from Talmadge's problems. Metropolitan Atlanta, so long the target of such politicians as Talmadge, now had all of Talmadge's attention; he campaigned hard for votes among blacks. Talmadge still had great appeal in the rural areas; outside Georgia's metropolitan areas he won 61% of the vote. But in the 12 counties within a 60-mile circle around Atlanta, where 40% of the state's votes are cast, the verdict went crushingly the other way; 63% for Mattingly. Mattingly also carried the state's minor metropolitan areas by a small margin; indeed, almost everywhere there has been enough economic activity to generate a significant country club class—from the Chattanooga suburbs in the north to Valdosta in the south—Mattingly carried.

So after 24 years Talmadge lost the chair of the Agriculture Committee and the number two position on Finance. Mattingly is not likely to be as influential as was Talmadge before his troubles. But Georgians may have concluded that Talmadge would not have been either —even before they knew that Democrats would lose control of the Senate. Mattingly now has seats on the Appropriations and Governmental Affairs Committees and some time to let Georgians know what kind of senator he will be.

Georgia's senior senator is a man unknown to most Americans who nonetheless plays— even in a Republican Senate—an important role in American foreign and military policy. This is Sam Nunn who, as a 34-year-old state representative from south Georgia, was elected to Richard Russell's Senate seat in 1972. Nunn's campaign gave less indication of the kind of senator he would become than did his lineage; he is the grandnephew of former Congressman (1914–65) Carl Vinson, longtime chairman of the House Armed Services Committee. Nunn got Russell's seat on Armed Services and impressed Chairman John Stennis and others with his careful preparation and willingness to question old assumptions. Nunn is interested in cutting costs when possible, but he is more concerned with maintaining a strong defense; he has found himself at odds, at one time or another, with conventional wisdom both at the Pentagon and among defense spending critics. He was anything but an apologist for the Carter Administration. Indeed, he was critical from the moment Carter appointed Paul Warnke as his chief disarmament aide. He resisted what were once popular cries to cut American forces in Europe and South Korea and he thinks that the volunteer army has not worked well and that we should prepare ourselves to return to the draft.

Stennis has been replaced as chairman of Armed Services by John Tower, who has his own strong ideas about defense, and Nunn is now a member of the minority party. He ranks fifth in seniority among committee Democrats. But Nunn remains respected for his expertise and his candor and for his seriousness and refusal to engage in cheap shots.

Nunn's political strength in Georgia can be gauged by the 1978 election results. He got 80% in a six-candidate Democratic primary and 83% in the general election. Even if he had attracted more formidable opposition, he would have won easily. At 42, Nunn can look forward to a long Senate career and to the possibility, although it now may seem distant, of being chairman of the Armed Services Committee.

Redistricting does not pose serious problems for Georgia or its congressmen. The Atlanta-based 5th district, which currently has a black majority and a white congressman, needs to be expanded significantly in size, but there are adjacent fast-growing suburban areas available for that purpose which in some cases their current congressmen would be delighted to lose. The state's one Republican congressman, Newt Gingrich, could be hurt somewhat by redistricting; but he has considerable strength of his own, and it is not clear that the nearly all-Democratic legislature cares that much about party labels anyway. All but one of Georgia's congressmen were first elected in the 1970s, which means that there is not much seniority at stake here.

Census Data   Pop. (1980 final) 5,464,265, up 19% in 1970s: 2.41% of U.S. total, 13th largest. Central city, 18%; suburban, 40%. Median 4-person family income, 1978, $19,676, 96% of U.S., 29th highest.

1979 Share of Federal Tax Burden $8,430,000,000; 1.87% of U.S. total, 18th largest.

1979 Share of Federal Outlays $9,727,031,000; 2.10% of U.S. total, 17th largest.

DOD	$2,590,885,000	13th	(2.44%)	HEW	$3,490,531,000	16th	(1.95%)
DOE	$16,891,000	32d	(0.14%)	ERDA	$19,911,000	23d	(0.73%)
HUD	$141,364,000	13th	(2.14%)	NASA	$7,438,000	25th	(0.16%)
VA	$562,450,000	10th	(2.71%)	DOT	$451,712,000	12th	(2.74%)
EPA	$89,642,000	20th	(1.69%)	DOC	$24,783,000	23d	(0.78%)
DOI	$99,021,000	15th	(1.78%)	USDA	$600,247,000	10th	(2.50%)

Economic Base   Textile mill products, especially cotton textile mills and floor covering mills; finance, insurance, and real estate; agriculture, notably broilers, peanuts, eggs, and cattle; apparel and other textile mill products, especially men's and boys' furnishings; food and kindred products; transportation equipment, especially motor vehicles and equipment.

Political Lineup   Governor, George Busbee (D). Senators, Sam Nunn (D) and Mack Mattingly (R). Representatives, 10 (9 D and 1 R); 10 in 1982. State Senate, 56 (51 D and 5 R); State House of Representatives, 180 (157 D and 23 R).

The Voters

Registration   2,466,786 Total. No party registration.
Employment profile 1970   White collar, 44%. Blue collar, 40%. Service, 13%. Farm, 3%.
Ethnic groups   Black 1980, 27%. Hispanic 1980, 1%. Total foreign stock 1970, 2%.

Presidential Vote

1980	Reagan (R)	654,168	(41%)
	Carter (D)	890,733	(56%)
	Anderson (I)	36,055	(2%)
1976	Ford (R)	483,743	(33%)
	Carter (D)	979,409	(67%)

1980 Democratic Presidential Primary			*1980 Republican Presidential Primary*		
Carter	338,772	(88%)	Reagan	146,500	(73%)
Kennedy	32,315	(8%)	Bush	25,293	(13%)
Four others........	9,986	(3%)	Anderson	16,853	(8%)
Uncommitted pref....	3,707	(1%)	Six others	11,525	(6%)

SENATORS

Sen. Sam Nunn (D) Elected 1972, seat up 1984; b. Sept. 8, 1938, Perry; home, Perry; Emory U., A.B. 1960, LL.B. 1962.

Career Coast Guard, 1959–60; Legal Counsel, U.S. House of Reps. Armed Services Comm., 1962–63; Farmer; Practicing atty., 1963–72; Ga. House of Reps., 1968–72.

Offices 3241 DSOB, 202-224-3521. Also Rm. 430, 275 Peachtree St. N.E., Atlanta 30303, 404-221-4811, and 915B Main St., Perry 31069, 912-987-1458.

Committees *Armed Services* (5th). Subcommittees: Strategic and Theatre Nuclear Forces; Sea Power and Force Projection; Manpower and Personnel.

Governmental Affairs (4th). Subcommittees: Permanent Subcommittee on Investigations; Intergovernmental Relations.

Select Committee on Small Business (Ranking Member). Subcommittee: Capital Formation and Retention.

Group Ratings

	ADA	COPE	PC	LCV	CFA	RPN	NAB	NSI	NTU	ACA	ACU
1980	56	26	37	40	7	—	75	60	48	54	38
1979	11	32	32	—	24	—	—	—	41	40	39
1978	25	26	20	36	20	70	100	50	28	67	46

Key Votes

1) Draft Registn $	FOR	6) Fair Housng Cloture	AGN	11) Cut Socl Incr Defns	FOR
2) Ban $ to Nicrgua	FOR	7) Ban $ Rape Abortns	AGN	12) Income Tax Indexing	AGN
3) Dlay MX Missile	AGN	8) Cap on Food Stmp $	FOR	13) Lim Spdg 21% GNP	AGN
4) Nuclr Mortorium	AGN	9) New US Dep Edcatn	FOR	14) Incr Wndfll Prof Tax	FOR
5) Alaska Lands Bill	FOR	10) Cut OSHA Inspctns	FOR	15) Chryslr Loan Grntee	AGN

Election Results

1978 general	Sam Nunn (D)	536,320	(83%)	($548,814)
	John W. Stokes (R)	108,808	(17%)	
1978 primary	Sam Nunn (D)	525,703	(80%)	
	Five others (D)	131,584	(20%)	
1972 general	Sam Nunn (D)	635,970	(54%)	($567,968)
	Fletcher Thompson (R)	542,331	(46%)	($444,635)

Sen. Mack Mattingly (R) Elected 1980, seat up 1986; b. Jan. 7, 1931, Anderson, Ind.; home, St. Simon; Indiana U., B.A. 1957.

Career Air Force, 1955; IBM Sales, 1960–80; Pres., Mattingly's Office Products, 1965–80; Member, Rep. Nat. Comm. Econ Affairs Cncl., 1977–78, Energy Advisory Committee, 1978–79, Foundation for Defense Analysis, 1979–80.

Offices 6239 DSOB, 202-224-3643. Also 260 Capitol Ave. S.E., Atlanta 30334, 404-221-3898.

Committees *Appropriations* (13th). Subcommittees: Agriculture and Related Agencies; Energy and Water Development; Legislative Branch (Chairman); Military Construction; Treasury, Postal Service, and General Government.

Governmental Affairs (8th). Subcommittees: Energy, Nuclear Proliferation, and Government Processes; Intergovernmental Relations; Congressional Operations and Oversight.

Joint Economic Committee (6th).

Select Committee on Ethics (3d).

Group Ratings and Key Votes: Newly Elected

Election Results

1980 general	Mack Mattingly (R)	803,677	(51%)	($504,016)
	Herman E. Talmadge (D)........	776,025	(49%)	($2,213,289)
1980 primary	Mack Mattingly (R)	28,191	(60%)	
	Five others (R)	18,947	(40%)	
1974 general	Herman E. Talmadge (D)........	627,376	(72%)	($65,207)
	Jerry Johnson (R)	246,866	(28%)	($12,856)

GOVERNOR

Gov. George Busbee (D) Elected 1974, term expires Jan. 1983; b. Aug. 7, 1927, Vienna; Abraham Baldwin Ag. Col., Duke U., U. of Ga., A.B. 1949, LL.B. 1952.

Career Navy, WWII; Practicing atty., 1952–75; Ga. House of Reps., 1957–75, Asst. Admin. Flr. Ldr., 1963–65, Admin. Flr. Ldr., 1966, Major. Ldr. 1967–75.

Offices State Capitol, Atlanta 30334, 404-656-1776.

Election Results

1978 gen.	George Busbee (D)	534,572	(81%)
	Rodney M. Cook (R)......	128,139	(19%)
1978 prim.	George Busbee (D)	503,875	(72%)
	Roscoe Emory Dean, Jr. (D)	111,901	(16%)
	Four others (D)	80,135	(12%)
1974 gen.	George Busbee (D)	646,777	(69%)
	Ronnie Thompson (R).....	289,113	(31%)

FIRST DISTRICT

The 1st congressional district of Georgia is the southeastern part of the state, the portion lying along the Atlantic Ocean and proceeding several counties inland. The major city here is Savannah, the first major city in Georgia. It was laid out carefully in colonial days and contains dozens of parks. Many of the houses in the older section of the city have been restored, and much of Savannah has the sort of tree-shaded elegance that its founders envisaged. South of Savannah are the city of Brunswick and the resorts of St. Simons Island and Sea Island. Inland is rural territory: cotton, peanuts, and piney woods.

Georgia, although originally founded as a haven for convicts and poor white people, soon became slave territory, and southeast Georgia came to have a substantial slave population. Today one-third of the residents of the 1st congressional district are black. They played little role in the politics of the area in the 1950s or 1960s, but in the 1970s their votes have become important in local elections and at the one time during the decade when the House seat was seriously contested.

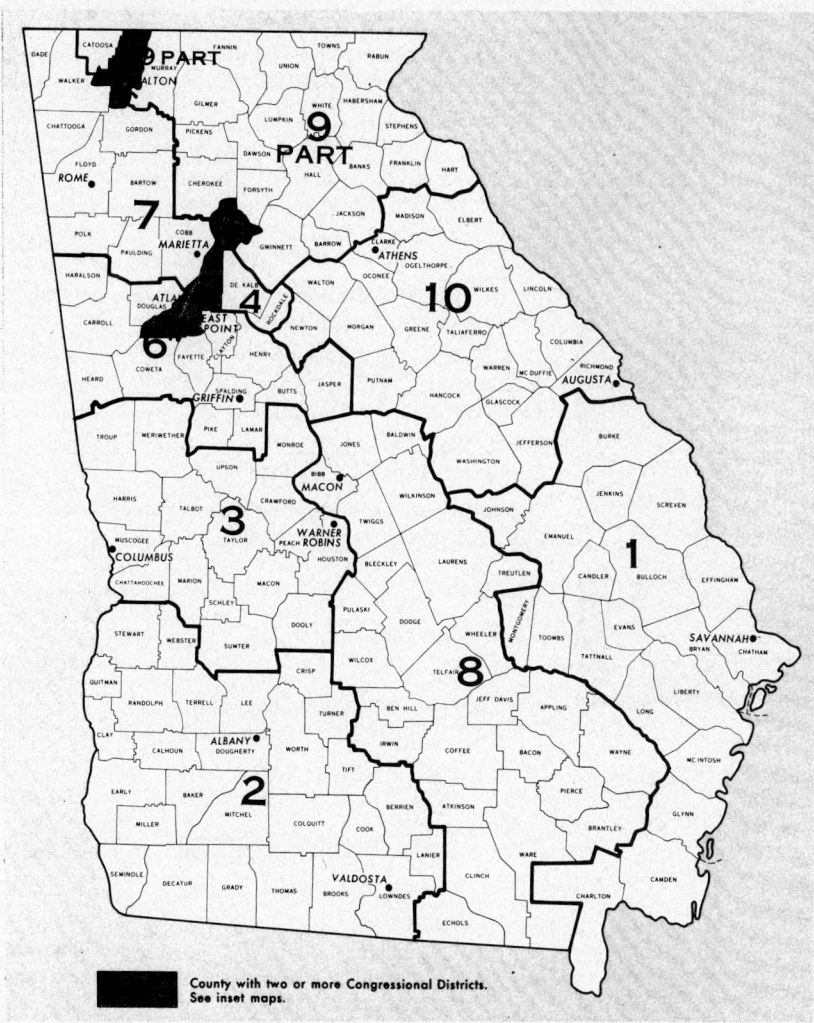

County with two or more Congressional Districts.
See inset maps.

Black voters provided part of the backing for Democrat Bo Ginn, the current congressman, when he ran against G. Elliott Hagan in 1972. Hagan had been in office for 10 years,
and Ginn had worked on his staff; but the incumbent was weak in Savannah and among
blacks. Apparently the former aide knew his boss's weaknesses well. After winning that primary handily, he has been reelected without difficulty ever since. He has moved upward
quietly on the Appropriations Committee and now chairs its Military Construction Subcommittee. This body does not allocate the lion's share of the Pentagon budget, but it is of
importance to districts which, like the 1st of Georgia, have substantial military bases and
whose economy is helped by continuing military construction.

Census Data   Pop. (1980 final) 527,732, up 16% in 1970s. Median family income, 1970, $7,102,
75% of U.S.

The Voters

Employment profile 1970   White collar, 39%. Blue collar, 40%. Service, 15%. Farm, 6%.
Ethnic groups   Black 1980, 34%. Hispanic 1980, 1%. Asian 1980, 1%. Total foreign stock 1970, 3%.

Presidential Vote

1980	Reagan (R)	61,810	(43%)
	Carter (D)	79,860	(55%)
	Anderson (I)	2,349	(2%)
1976	Ford (R)	49,282	(36%)
	Carter (D)	88,992	(64%)

Rep. Bo Ginn (D) Elected 1972; b. May 31, 1934, Morgan; home, Millen; Abraham Baldwin Ag. Col., 1951–53, Ga. Southern Col., B.S. 1956.

Career High school teacher; Asst. Mgr., Planters Electric Membership Corp., 1947–61; Admin. Asst. to U.S. Sen. Herman E. Talmadge, 1961–71; Cattle farmer and businessman, 1971–72.

Offices 2135 RHOB, 202-225-5831. Also Rm. 304 Fed. Bldg., Brunswick 31520, 912-264-4040.

Committee *Appropriations* (22d). Subcommittees: Defense; Military Construction (Chairman).

Group Ratings

	ADA	COPE	PC	LCV	CFA	RPN	NAB	NSI	NTU	ACA	ACU
1980	33	44	30	22	59	—	50	60	31	30	47
1979	21	45	28	41	15	—	—	—	28	59	43
1978	20	55	23	47	23	50	83	90	17	63	50

Key Votes

1) Draft Registn $	FOR	6) Fair Hsg DOJ Enfrc	AGN	11) Cut Socl Incr Dfns $	AGN
2) Ban $ to Nicrgua	AGN	7) Lim PAC Contrbtns	AGN	12) Hosptl Cost Controls	AGN
3) Dlay MX Missile	AGN	8) Cap on Food Stmp $	AGN	13) Gasln Ctrls & Allctns	FOR
4) Nuclr Mortorium	AGN	9) New US Dep Edcatn	FOR	14) Lim Wndfll Prof Tax	FOR
5) Alaska Lands Bill	FOR	10) Cut OSHA $		FOR	15) Chryslr Loan Grntee	—

Election Results

1980 general	Bo Ginn (D)	82,145 (100%)	($32,902)
1980 primary	Bo Ginn (D)	65,050 (100%)	
1978 general	Bo Ginn (D), unopposed		($58,340)

SECOND DISTRICT

The 2d congressional district is the southwestern corner of Georgia. It is the most agricultural, the least affluent, and, with the exception of the 5th district (Atlanta), the most heavily black district in the state. This area has always been part of the Deep South, which means that it has changed vastly since the middle 1960s. Then it was an area where racial segregation was very much the rule and where there were few jobs; young people regularly migrated north to Atlanta to get work. But times have changed here. The civil rights revolution, so bitterly resisted, has turned out to be very good for south Georgia, and most south Georgians think so. Blacks now vote, and black support is no longer the kiss of political death among whites. This part of the Deep South has grown more prosperous in the 1970s; there have been new plants and new jobs, enough for most of the young people who want to stay. One result of this is that districts like this are, for the first time in a century, getting more rather than less black. This is because southern blacks tend to have more children than southern whites, and now that most people remain in the area there is a natural increase in black percentage.

The 2d has been the scene of spirited congressional elections twice in 10 years, both times when an incumbent did not seek reelection. In 1970, Albany newscaster Dawson Mathis won the seat; he held it until he ran, unsuccessfully, against Herman Talmadge in the 1980 Senate primary. The 1980 Democratic primary was a kind of friends-and-neighbors contest, between candidates based in Albany, Thomasville, Valdosta, Tifton, and two mostly rural counties. The candidate from Albany, the district's largest city, led: state Representative Charles Hatcher. With 38% of the vote to the runner-up's 15% (there was a recount, to determine who finished second), Hatcher seemed clearly ahead. But runoffs have a certain momentum of their own, and defeated candidates will often support the second place finisher against the leader. Hatcher won the runoff, but with just 53% of the vote. He had less trouble with the Republican, whom he beat by a 3-to-1 margin.

Hatcher is a political ally of Governor George Busbee, who comes from Albany and is popular in this part of the state. Hatcher can be expected to vote with southern conservatives, like most of the other Democrats who represent rural Georgia. With the Republicans not too far from actual control, Hatcher could be an important figure, since he might supply them with votes they need on crucial and closely contested issues.

Census Data Pop. (1980 final) 522,952, up 14% in 1970s. Median family income, 1970, $6,238, 66% of U.S.

The Voters

Employment profile 1970 White collar, 36%. Blue collar, 38%. Service, 14%. Farm, 12%.
Ethnic groups Black 1980, 37%. Hispanic 1980, 2%. Total foreign stock 1970, 1%.

Presidential Vote

1980	Reagan (R)	57,604	(42%)
	Carter (D)	78,073	(57%)
	Anderson (I)	1,363	(1%)
1976	Ford (R)	39,456	(31%)
	Carter (D)	88,250	(69%)

Rep. Charles F. Hatcher (D) Elected 1980; b. July 1, 1939, Colquitt; home, Albany; Ga. Southern Col., B.S. 1965, U. of Ga., J.D. 1969.

Career Air Force, 1958–62; Practicing atty.; Ga. House of Reps., 1973–80, Asst. Flr. Ldr.

Offices 1726 LHOB, 202-225-3631. Also 225 Pine Ave., Albany 31701, 912-439-8067.

Committees *Agriculture* (23d). Subcommittees: Cotton, Rice and Sugar; Livestock, Dairy and Poultry; Tobacco and Peanuts.

Small Business (17th). Subcommittees: Energy, Environment and Safety Issues Affecting Small Business; SBA and SBIC Authority, Minority Enterprise and General Small Business Problems.

Group Ratings and Key Votes: Newly Elected

Election Results

1980 general	Charles F. Hatcher (D)	92,264	(74%)	($242,960)
	Jack E. Harrell, Jr. (R)	33,107	(26%)	($23,478)
1980 runoff	Charles F. Hatcher (D)	49,144	(53%)	
	Julian Holland (D)	44,397	(47%)	($88,290)
1980 primary	Charles F. Hatcher (D)	40,315	(38%)	
	Julian Holland (D)	15,976	(15%)	
	Hanson Carter (D)	15,747	(15%)	($56,972)
	J. David Halstead (D)	13,119	(12%)	
	Walter Stephens (D)	8,520	(8%)	($94,264)
	Wesley Patrick (D)	6,032	(6%)	($3,989)
	Three others (D)	6,122	(6%)	
1978 general	Dawson Mathis (D), unopposed ..			($100,914)

THIRD DISTRICT

The 3d congressional district is one of several south Georgia districts. It has one good-sized city, Columbus, which is largely a creation of one of the nation's largest military installations, Fort Benning. Columbus is very much an Army town: girls grow up here aspiring to marry young officers, and haircuts tend always to be short. Fort Benning is also the site of some history. It was here in the 1930s that Colonel George C. Marshall staged the maneuvers that anticipated so much of the kind of fighting that was to occur in World War II — showing the rare foresight of making ready to fight the next, rather than the last, war. It was also at Fort Benning, in the 1970s, that the Army tried Lieutenant William Calley on charges of leading the My Lai massacre in Vietnam.

Benning is only one of the military installations here. Another is Warner Robins Air Materiel Command in the eastern end of the 3d. Both, naturally, are of substantial economic importance to what was, until the 1970s, an economically backward area. Benning may have been placed here initially on the theory that the excruciatingly hot, humid Georgia summers would best condition soldiers for the rigors of combat in the tropics. But it did not hurt that Georgia was represented for years by Richard Russell and Carl Vinson, chairmen for years of the Senate and House Armed Services Committees, respectively.

The 3d also has the distinction of being the home district of former President Jimmy Carter. You don't have to look very far into the politics of the 3d to find out just how far Carter came in the last 15 years. Back in the middle 1960s, when Carter represented part of the 3d in the Georgia Senate, the small city of Americus was one of the parts of the South least hospitable to civil rights activities. Against this background it is not hard to understand how the Carter family's stand against segregation in their church and community was courageous indeed — especially for a politician and businessman who depended on white neighbors for his career and his livelihood. Carter was fortunate enough to avoid direct involvement in the civil rights revolution; he was elected to the state Senate before it started and campaigned as a rural Georgian (a "redneck," he said) rather than as a segregationist in his 1966 and 1970 gubernatorial campaigns.

Carter probably could have gone to Congress if he had wanted to: in 1966, when he ran for governor, the seat was open, and as a local officeholder he would have been a strong competitor for it. Instead, another young state legislator won the House seat: Jack Brinkley from Columbus. Brinkley's voting record — very conservative on cultural issues, middle of the road in economic issues — is probably what Carter would have compiled, given the political realities of the time; and it is a record that would effectively have disqualified him, in a way that his record as governor did not, from winning a national Democratic nomination. Carter went on to world fame; Brinkley, seldom encountering opposition, has continued to win reelection and is still in office. Indeed, he is the senior member now of the Georgia congressional delegation, sixth-ranking Democrat on the Armed Services Committee, and — of obvious import to the 3d district — on the new Military Installations and Facilities Subcommittee. He is also a senior member of the Veterans' Affairs Committee and one whose stance on the differences between traditional and innovative approaches to veterans' problems is not predictable. In seniority he ranks behind three somewhat older Democrats and so might be chairman someday.

Census Data   Pop. (1980 final) 500,940, up 9% in 1970s. Median family income, 1970, $7,550, 79% of U.S.

The Voters

Employment profile 1970   White collar, 41%. Blue collar, 40%. Service, 15%. Farm, 4%.
Ethnic groups   Black 1980, 35%. Hispanic 1980, 2%. Asian 1980, 1%. Total foreign stock 1970, 4%.

Presidential Vote

1980	Reagan (R)	47,356	(37%)
	Carter (D)	77,017	(60%)
	Anderson (I)	2,173	(2%)
1976	Ford (R)	36,878	(31%)
	Carter (D)	82,639	(69%)

Rep. Jack Brinkley (D) Elected 1966; b. Dec. 22, 1930, Faceville; home, Columbus; Young Harris Col., B.A. 1949, U. of Ga., J.D. 1959.

Career   Public school teacher, 1949–51; Air Force, 1951–56; Practicing atty., 1959–67; Ga. House of Reps., 1965–66.

Offices   2470 RHOB, 202-225-5901. Also 2429 Norris Rd., Columbus 31907, 404-568-3330.

Committees   *Armed Services* (6th). Subcommittees: Investigations; Military Installations and Facilities (Chairman).

Veterans' Affairs (4th). Subcommittees: Compensation, Pension and Insurance; Housing and Memorial Affairs.

Group Ratings

	ADA	COPE	PC	LCV	CFA	RPN	NAB	NSI	NTU	ACA	ACU
1980	11	27	27	61	14	—	83	100	36	59	79
1979	16	30	18	24	7	—	—	—	39	57	65
1978	15	35	35	47	14	75	92	90	22	70	42

Key Votes

1) Draft Registn $	FOR	6) Fair Hsg DOJ Enfrc	—	11) Cut Socl Incr Dfns $	FOR
2) Ban $ to Nicrgua	FOR	7) Lim PAC Contrbtns	AGN	12) Hosptl Cost Controls	AGN
3) Dlay MX Missile	AGN	8) Cap on Food Stmp $	AGN	13) Gasln Ctrls & Allctns	AGN
4) Nuclr Mortorium	AGN	9) New US Dep Edcatn	FOR	14) Lim Wndfll Prof Tax	FOR
5) Alaska Lands Bill	FOR	10) Cut OSHA $	FOR	15) Chryslr Loan Grntee	FOR

Election Results

1980 general	Jack Brinkley (D)	89,040 (100%)	($29,043)
1980 primary	Jack Brinkley (D)	66,410 (100%)	
1978 general	Jack Brinkley (D), unopposed		($14,531)

FOURTH DISTRICT

Stuck smack in the middle of the Deep South is the booming metropolis of Atlanta — "the city," it used to boast, "too busy to hate." The slogan grew out of Atlanta's reputation for racial tolerance and moderation, which it earned back in the 1950s and 1960s. But if Atlanta has practiced little overt segregation and if it has gained the sophistication of most northern cities, it has also developed some of the problems of urban life. Crime rates have been high, and especially appalling is the large number of black children who have been the victims of one or more murderers. Atlanta has a black majority now and black city officials; it has a thriving downtown and, despite the dispersion of population, a solid tax base. Dispersion has also separated the races more effectively in some respects than segregation used to. Children growing up in metropolitan Atlanta — black or white — may have less contact with members of the other race than they would have 20 years ago, or than they would now in the integrated schools of the small towns and rural counties of south Georgia.

Metropolitan Atlanta has spread far out into what used to be countryside, and the suburbs have a substantially greater population than does the city itself. About half the residents of suburban Atlanta live in DeKalb County, just to the east of the city. With a small part of the city and small just-suburbanizing Rockdale County, DeKalb makes up the 4th congressional district of Georgia. This area is the home of higher-income, better-educated Atlanta suburbanites (although the really rich in Atlanta live in mansions on the city's north side). Statistically the 4th is far closer to many similar northern areas than to south Georgia. Politically DeKalb and the 4th often behave more like a northern constituency than the non-Atlanta Georgia districts. When it was first created in 1964, the result of a landmark Supreme Court case, the 4th went for Lyndon Johnson and elected a liberal Democratic congressman, while the rest of Georgia switched from its traditional Democratic allegiance to the Republicanism of Barry Goldwater. In 1966, like many northern districts, the 4th elected a Republican congressman, and in the state election gave a big majority to Republican Bo Callaway over Democrat Lester Maddox. In the years that followed DeKalb voters generally preferred the Republicans' smooth, neutral-accented candidates to the rural-oriented, southern-accented candidates nominated by the Democrats. This is the only part of the state that has consistently elected a significant number of Republican legislators.

But suddenly in 1974, paralleling the North again, the 4th shifted back to the Democrats. Elliott Levitas, the new congressman elected that year, was in some respects a liberal: a supporter of civil rights, a frequent supporter of measures backed by organized labor, an opponent of bans on abortions. But once in Congress, he has also been a man who seeks to restrain the power of government; he was a major supporter of deregulation of the airlines and has pushed a bill to allow Congress to reject all rules and regulations issued by government agencies. This combination, plus plenty of hard work, has made Levitas very popular here, and he has been reelected with overwhelming margins. Even in 1980, when Jimmy Carter carried this district only narrowly and Republicans made a concerted effort here, Levitas was re-elected with 69% of the vote.

In the 1960s, DeKalb was the fastest-growing part of Georgia; in the 1970s the fastest growth has taken place farther out. The 4th district, however, has increased somewhat in population and has about the size that is required for a single congressional district. Its contours are likely to be changed significantly only if the legislature decides to include part of the 4th, rather than other adjacent districts, in the population-losing 5th district next door to Atlanta.

Census Data Pop. (1980 final) 543,954, up 18% in 1970s. Median family income, 1970, $11,750, 123% of U.S.

The Voters

Employment profile 1970 White collar, 66%. Blue collar, 25%. Service, 9%. Farm, -%.
Ethnic groups Black 1980, 28%. Hispanic 1980, 2%. Asian 1980, 1%. Total foreign stock 1970, 5%.

Presidential Vote

1980	Reagan (R)	81,516	(44%)
	Carter (D)	93,288	(50%)
	Anderson (I)	7,660	(4%)
1976	Ford (R)	70,912	(43%)
	Carter (D)	94,920	(57%)

Rep. Elliott H. Levitas (D) Elected 1974; b. Dec. 26, 1930, Atlanta; home, Atlanta; Emory U., B.S., LL.B., Rhodes Scholar, Oxford U., M.A., U. of Mich.

Career Practicing atty., 1955-75; Air Force; Ga. House of Reps., 1965-75.

Offices 2416 RHOB, 202-225-4272. Also 141 E. Trinity Pl., Decatur 30030, 404-377-1717.

Committees *Government Operations* (10th). Subcommittees: Intergovernmental Relations and Human Resources; Legislation and National Security.

Public Works and Transportation (6th). Subcommittees: Aviation; Investigations and Oversight (Chairman); Public Buildings and Grounds.

Group Ratings

	ADA	COPE	PC	LCV	CFA	RPN	NAB	NSI	NTU	ACA	ACU
1980	28	41	23	63	43	—	58	90	40	48	72
1979	21	37	45	52	22	—	—	—	37	46	56
1978	20	60	38	67	46	33	100	70	24	65	29

Key Votes

1) Draft Registn $	FOR	6) Fair Hsg DOJ Enfrc	FOR	11) Cut Socl Incr Dfns $	FOR
2) Ban $ to Nicrgua	FOR	7) Lim PAC Contrbtns	AGN	12) Hosptl Cost Controls	AGN
3) Dlay MX Missile	AGN	8) Cap on Food Stmp $	AGN	13) Gasln Ctrls & Allctns	FOR
4) Nuclr Mortorium	AGN	9) New US Dep Edcatn	FOR	14) Lim Wndfll Prof Tax	FOR
5) Alaska Lands Bill	FOR	10) Cut OSHA $	FOR	15) Chryslr Loan Grntee	AGN

Election Results

1980 general	Elliott H. Levitas (D)	117,091	(69%)	($142,342)
	Barry Billington (R)	51,546	(31%)	($84,355)
1980 primary	Elliott H. Levitas (D)	55,806	(100%)	
1978 general	Elliott H. Levitas (D)	60,284	(81%)	($94,745)
	Homer Cheung (R)	14,221	(19%)	

FIFTH DISTRICT

In the early 1960s Atlanta was just one of several southern cities most people had heard of. In the national consciousness, it was no more important than New Orleans, Miami, Memphis, Birmingham, or Richmond. By the late 1970s Atlanta had become the capital of the South — not just the economic capital but the recognized focal point of a great region. How has this come about? Part of the reason is the central role air travel plays today in business communication. Atlanta's airport, like Chicago's O'Hare, claims to be the busiest in the world; the saying is that you can't go anywhere in the South without going through Atlanta first. Naturally businesses tend to locate their southern headquarters in Atlanta. The city has also given birth to a number of small businesses that have become exceedingly successful giants, notably Coca-Cola and Delta Airlines.

But probably more than anything else, Atlanta's response to the civil rights revolution established the city as the capital of the South. The city's two longtime white mayors, William Hartsfield and Ivan Allen, were always far ahead of other southern leaders in their opposition to massive resistance to integration and their support of civil rights; Allen went so far as to testify in support of the Civil Rights Act of 1964, one of the few southern officials to do so. Hartsfield and Allen also got their city's business community together to discourage any violent resistance to civil rights legislation. Atlanta was determined to obey the law, and to obey quietly, so as not to discourage northern investors, who never liked the uncertainty and unpredictability of either civil rights demonstrations or violent white resistance. Atlanta liked to call itself "the city too busy to hate," and to a considerable extent it earned that reputation.

Blacks played as large a part as whites in making Atlanta capital of the South. Although Martin Luther King, Jr., led his first major civil rights movement in Montgomery, Alabama, his roots were in Atlanta; and although civil rights demonstrations occurred in countless cities and towns all over the South, the organizations and individuals who planned, coordinated, or financed them were headquartered, more often than not, in Atlanta. Atlanta has had a strong and vital black community since Reconstruction, and so a set of strong black institutions — colleges, churches, social groups — were there ready to play an important part in the civil rights struggle.

The 5th congressional district of Georgia includes most of Atlanta and some of the city's wealthy suburbs to the north. Less than half its residents were black in 1970, but a majority are black today. It includes most of the black neighborhoods on the west and south sides of the city, as well as the rich white residential neighborhood on the north side. Most of Atlanta's white establishment and most of its black leaders live in the 5th district.

The 5th congressional district has had a turbulent political history. It elected a liberal white Democrat in 1964; a conservative Republican in 1966, 1968, and 1970 who declined to provide constituency services for blacks; and then the now world famous Andrew Young in 1972, 1974, and 1976. Young was a successful congressman, but he became an important national figure because he had provided Jimmy Carter with support and testimony early, when Carter most needed support from a prominent Georgia black. For reward, Young got the ambassadorship to the United Nations, and fame as an advocate of closer ties between the United States and Third World nations. He achieved undeniable success in Africa, particularly in securing good U.S.–Nigerian relations. But his apparent tendency to identify Third World countries with the civil rights movements in the South got him into trouble when, in the face of orders and a presidential commitment to the contrary, he conducted direct negotiations with a representative of the Palestine Liberation Organization. That got him fired in August 1979. Since then he has returned at least part time to Atlanta and has continued to make the kind of controversial statements that got him into trouble when he was in office (e.g., that the Ayatollah Khomeini of Iran was "a kind of saint").

Young's seat in the House has been taken not by another black but by an ambitious white politician, Wyche Fowler. A former congressional aide and head of the Atlanta council, Fowler has solid liberal and civil rights credentials. Against a strong black candidate in the 1977 special election he won many black votes; Republicans are no longer competitive in the 5th. His voting record is liberal, although not so liberal as Young's, and he has political savvy enough to have gotten a seat on the Ways and Means Committee. Fowler was mentioned as a possible candidate for Herman Talmadge's Senate seat in 1980; he passed that race up but could be a statewide candidate in 1982 or later.

Fowler is one inner-city politician whom redistricting will almost certainly help. The 5th district lost population in the 1970s, as some slum neighborhoods were abandoned and as families in other neighborhoods grew older and children moved away. The result is that the district is more than 100,000 shy of the statewide average. Voters could be added from the southern Fulton County suburbs, near the airport; from suburban DeKalb County, a relatively high-income area; or from some of the adjoining counties that have fast been filling up with garden apartments, subdivisions bare of trees, and shopping centers. None of these areas has as large a black percentage as the current 5th district, which will help Fowler in the primary; and none has a really substantial Republican edge, which helps him deter the Republicans from a serious challenge in the general.

Census Data Pop. (1980 final) 420,474, down 9% in 1970s. Median family income, 1970, $9,050, 94% of U.S.

The Voters

Employment profile 1970 White collar, 55%. Blue collar, 28%. Service, 17%. Farm, –%.
Ethnic groups Black 1980, 51%. Hispanic 1980, 1%. Asian 1980, 1%. Total foreign stock 1970, 4%.

Presidential Vote

1980	Reagan (R)	51,201	(35%)
	Carter (D)	88,548	(60%)
	Anderson (I)	5,883	(4%)
1976	Ford (R)	47,204	(32%)
	Carter (D)	98,102	(68%)

Rep. Wyche Fowler, Jr. (D) Elected Apr. 5, 1977; b. Oct. 6, 1940, Atlanta; home, Atlanta; Davidson Col., B.A. 1963, Emory U., Atlanta, LL.B. 1969.

Career Army, 1963–65; Chief Asst. to U.S. Rep. Charles Weltner, 1965–66; Night Mayor for the City of Atlanta, 1966–69; Mbr., Atlanta Bd. of Aldermen, 1969–73; Pres., Atlanta City Cncl., 1973–77; Practicing atty., 1970–77.

Offices 1504 LHOB, 202-225-3801. Also Rm. 425 Wm. Oliver Bldg., 32 Peachtree St., Atlanta 30303, 404-688-8207.

Committees *Ways and Means* (16th). Subcommittees: Oversight; Select Subcommittee on Revenue Measures.

Select Committee on Intelligence (6th). Subcommittees: Legislation; Oversight and Evaluation.

Group Ratings

	ADA	COPE	PC	LCV	CFA	RPN	NAB	NSI	NTU	ACA	ACU
1980	61	71	43	80	50	—	25	50	28	48	16
1979	68	65	53	70	40	—	—	—	24	27	19
1978	45	58	55	68	55	27	50	86	17	36	17

Key Votes

1) Draft Registn $	FOR	6) Fair Hsg DOJ Enfrc	FOR	11) Cut Socl Incr Dfns $	AGN
2) Ban $ to Nicrgua	AGN	7) Lim PAC Contrbtns	FOR	12) Hosptl Cost Controls	FOR
3) Dlay MX Missile	FOR	8) Cap on Food Stmp $	AGN	13) Gasln Ctrls & Allctns	FOR
4) Nuclr Mortorium	FOR	9) New US Dep Edcatn	FOR	14) Lim Wndfll Prof Tax	AGN
5) Alaska Lands Bill	FOR	10) Cut OSHA $	FOR	15) Chryslr Loan Grntee	FOR

Election Results

1980 general	Wyche Fowler, Jr. (D)	101,646	(74%)	($141,037)
	F. William Dowda (R)	35,640	(26%)	($48,856)
1980 primary	Wyche Fowler, Jr. (D)	52,547	(86%)	
	One other (D)	8,760	(14%)	
1978 general	Wyche Fowler, Jr. (D)	52,739	(75%)	($142,684)
	Thomas P. Bowles, Jr. (R)	17,132	(25%)	($27,374)

SIXTH DISTRICT

The 6th congressional district of Georgia presents a nice example of demographic and political change in the South. Ten years ago this was a Deep South seat, made up of rural and small-town counties with one larger city, Macon. Politically, it was dependably Democratic in congressional elections, and without serious contest reelected a congressman first elected in the 1950s who had accumulated considerable seniority on the House Appropriations Committee and was also chairman of the House committee on ethics. He was the kind of politician who seemed impervious to change. Ten years later he was gone, technically by voluntary retirement but actually under direct threat of defeat.

The first step in how this came about was the redistricting mandated after the 1970 census. During the 1950s and 1960s rural Georgia had consistently lost population while metropolitan Atlanta gained. As a result, the 6th district had to be moved north: Macon was removed and several south Fulton County suburbs just south of Atlanta added. After redistricting, 48% of the district's population was in metropolitan Atlanta. These were not elite suburbs; they were instead the home of what might be called the uncomfortable middle class: people not quite secure in their pleasant status and fearful of the blacks and poor they left behind in Atlanta. Residents of the suburbs of East Point and College Park in south Fulton County were somewhat older; suburbs in Clayton and Fayette Counties, south of the airport, were full of young families in spanking new subdivisions. These are areas that have gone Republican on occasion, and which were also attracted by the segregationist appeals of Lester Maddox and George Wallace.

This is the district that the old congressman from the 6th, John Flynt, inherited. He had additional problems. He was accused of profiting from renting land to an auto company and then supporting the auto companies on emission standards. And he attracted a pesky, persistent Republican opponent, a young professor from one of the smaller counties in the district, Newt Gingrich. In that very Democratic year of 1974 Gingrich got 49% of the vote against Flynt; in 1976 he tried again and got 48%. In 1978 Flynt got the message and retired. Gingrich, still running hard, defeated state Senator Virginia Shapard 54%–46% and finally got his seat in Congress.

There he became a leader and activist among the freshmen Republicans — who for the first time in years outnumbered freshmen Democrats. His goal is ambitious: to try to establish a Republican majority in the House. It seems a lot closer now than it did in early 1979. Gingrich can be a tough partisan, but he also has a sense of the flow of history that is unusual in a young politician. He won reelection in 1980 with a solid 59% of the vote. Redistricting will affect him, and probably not too negatively unless the legislature takes special pains. He will probably lose the south Fulton County suburbs, which Gingrich carried only narrowly anyway; otherwise the boundaries need not change much since the district gained so much population in the 1970s. The district and the congressman will probably continue to be what emerged from the transformation of the 1970s.

Census Data   Pop. (1980 final) 626,354, up 37% in 1970s. Median family income, 1970, $9,284, 97% of U.S.

The Voters

Employment profile 1970   White collar, 44%. Blue collar, 44%. Service, 11%. Farm, 1%.
Ethnic groups   Black 1980, 23%. Hispanic 1980, 1%. Total foreign stock 1970, 2%.

Presidential Vote

1980	Reagan (R)	86,752	(40%)
	Carter (D)	122,387	(57%)
	Anderson (I)	4,144	(2%)
1976	Ford (R)	51,181	(32%)
	Carter (D)	106,430	(68%)

Rep. Newt Gingrich (R) Elected 1978; b. June 17, 1943, Harrisburg, Pa.; home, Carrollton; Emory U., B.A. 1965, Tulane U., M.A. 1967, Ph.D. 1970.

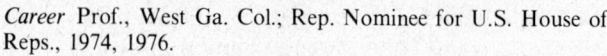

Career Prof., West Ga. Col.; Rep. Nominee for U.S. House of Reps., 1974, 1976.

Office 1005 LHOB, 202-225-4501.

Committees *House Administration* (4th). Subcommittee: Contracts and Printing.

Public Works and Transportation (8th). Subcommittees: Aviation; Investigations and Oversight; Surface Transportation.

Joint Committee on the Library (Ranking Member).

Joint Committee on Printing (Ranking Member).

Group Ratings

	ADA	COPE	PC	LCV	CFA	RPN	NAB	NSI	NTU	ACA	ACU
1980	11	10	23	50	14	—	92	100	50	91	76
1979	11	5	20	39	4	—	—	—	56	92	89

Key Votes

1) Draft Registn $	FOR	6) Fair Hsg DOJ Enfrc	—	11) Cut Socl Incr Dfns $	FOR
2) Ban $ to Nicrgua	FOR	7) Lim PAC Contrbtns	AGN	12) Hosptl Cost Controls	AGN
3) Dlay MX Missile	AGN	8) Cap on Food Stmp $	FOR	13) Gasln Ctrls & Allctns	AGN
4) Nuclr Mortorium	AGN	9) New US Dep Edcatn	FOR	14) Lim Wndfll Prof Tax	FOR
5) Alaska Lands Bill	FOR	10) Cut OSHA $	FOR	15) Chryslr Loan Grntee	AGN

Election Results

1980 general	Newt Gingrich (R).............	96,071	(59%)	($397,557)
	Dock H. Davis (D)............	66,606	(41%)	($72,962)
1980 primary	Newt Gingrich (R).............	4,963	(100%)	
1978 general	Newt Gingrich (R).............	47,078	(54%)	($219,336)
	Virginia Shapard (D)	39,451	(46%)	($313,056)

SEVENTH DISTRICT

The 7th congressional district of Georgia covers the northwest corner of the state. On the southeast the district touches the Atlanta city limits; on the northwest it reaches the bounds of Chattanooga, Tennessee. (There is some dispute here about the state line—some Georgians insist that the suburb and battle site of Lookout Mountain is not really in Tennessee.) Most of the 7th's recent population growth has occurred in the fringe of counties outside Atlanta, around Marietta, home of the Lockheed Corporation. Because there have been few blacks this far north in Georgia—no more than 5% of the electorate—racial issues never used to play as big a role here as in south Georgia. This is upcountry Piedmont, an area laden with textile and carpet mills, with plenty of low-wage jobs for men and women from the hills and the southern flatlands.

The 7th district has one of the nation's most unusual congressmen and the Congress's only urologist: Larry McDonald, a Democrat, and also a member of the John Birch Society. McDonald got in more or less by fluke: in 1974 he beat an incumbent Democrat who had a long-standing drinking problem. McDonald was nearly beaten several times since: in the 1974 general, the 1976 primary, the 1976 general, in the 1978 primary and runoff. In 1980 he ran much stronger, winning 68% in both the primary and the general election. One reason may be the increasing popularity of conservative ideas, bringing McDonald closer to respectability. Another may be the lack of pull by the Carter ticket. President Carter barely carried the district in 1980, a sharp decline from his 1976 performance here. There were rumors that the president's son Jack, who lives in Calhoun (also the home of Bert Lance) in the district, might run against McDonald; but he never did so.

Census Data   Pop. (1980 final) 605,750, up 32% in 1970s. Median family income, 1970, $9,223, 96% of U.S.

The Voters

Employment profile 1970   White collar, 43%. Blue collar, 47%. Service, 9%. Farm, 1%.
Ethnic groups   Black 1980, 7%. Hispanic 1980, 1%. Total foreign stock 1970, 2%.

Presidential Vote

1980	Reagan (R)	85,837	(47%)
	Carter (D)	90,632	(50%)
	Anderson (I)	4,532	(3%)
1976	Ford (R)	56,820	(36%)
	Carter (D)	102,093	(64%)

Rep. Larry P. McDonald (D) Elected 1974; b. Apr. 1, 1935, Atlanta; home, Marietta; Davidson Col., Emory U., M.D. 1957.

Career   U.S. Navy Physician and Overseas Flight Surgeon; Residency, Grady Mem. Hosp., Atlanta, and U. of Mich. Hosp., Ann Arbor, Mich.; Jr. Mbr., McDonald Urology Clinic, Atlanta.

Offices   103 CHOB, 202-225-2931. Also 100 Cherokee St., Marietta 30060, 404-422-4480.

Committee   *Armed Services* (15th). Subcommittees: Research and Development; Seapower and Strategic and Critical Materials.

Group Ratings

	ADA	COPE	PC	LCV	CFA	RPN	NAB	NSI	NTU	ACA	ACU
1980	6	5	20	39	7	—	100	100	86	100	100
1979	5	5	15	17	7	—	—	—	83	100	100
1978	15	5	18	23	18	70	100	100	88	100	95

Key Votes

1) Draft Registn $	FOR	6) Fair Hsg DOJ Enfrc	AGN	11) Cut Socl Incr Dfns $	FOR
2) Ban $ to Nicrgua	FOR	7) Lim PAC Contrbtns	AGN	12) Hosptl Cost Controls	AGN
3) Dlay MX Missile	AGN	8) Cap on Food Stmp $	FOR	13) Gasln Ctrls & Allctns	AGN
4) Nuclr Mortorium	AGN	9) New US Dep Edcatn	AGN	14) Lim Wndfll Prof Tax	FOR
5) Alaska Lands Bill	AGN	10) Cut OSHA $	FOR	15) Chryslr Loan Grntee	AGN

Election Results

1980 general	Larry P. McDonald (D)	115,892	(68%)	($276,449)
	Richard Castellucis (R)	54,242	(32%)	($6,292)

1980 primary	Larry P. McDonald (D)	67,463	(68%)	
	Jack Bade (D)	31,729	(32%)	($0)
1978 general	Larry P. McDonald (D)	47,090	(67%)	($331,925)
	Ernie Norsworthy (R)	23,698	(33%)	($9,767)

EIGHTH DISTRICT

The 8th congressional district is an elongated section of central and south Georgia. With the major exception of Macon — the only city above 100,000 in these parts — the 8th is mostly a rural area that was once devoted to cotton but is now mainly in peanuts, tobacco, chickens, and lumber. The once fertile soil here has been exhausted for years, and for years the area exported people — poor blacks and whites who left for the North or Atlanta to make a living. Some of this area once had black majorities, but until the 1960s the blacks here did not vote, and they have become a force in politics only within recent memory.

Like so many parts of the Deep South, the 8th district has had its partisan leanings reversed by the 1976 presidential campaign of Jimmy Carter. This territory was solid for John Kennedy in 1960, and even more solid for Barry Goldwater four years later, after the Democratic administration had pushed through the Civil Rights Act but before it passed the Voting Rights Act. With blacks voting but the vote split three ways, the area gave George Wallace a solid plurality in 1968, and it was overwhelmingly for Richard Nixon in 1972. In those two elections, whites voted almost unanimously for the candidates whom blacks passionately and almost unanimously opposed. Division was essentially along racial lines. Then Jimmy Carter became the Democratic nominee in 1976 and carried every county in this district. Division, to the extent there was any, was now along economic rather than racial lines. And because hard-pressed small farmers and blue collar workers vastly outnumber the country club set even among whites, this became prime Democratic country. Carter carried the district again with a solid majority in 1980.

For ten years before Carter's 1976 victory the congressman here was W. S. "Bill" Stuckey IV, a member of the family that started the pecan candy and gift shops that can be seen at interstate highway interchanges all over the country. Stuckey's most memorable race was in 1972, when he faced Macon Mayor Ronnie "Machine Gun" Thompson. Stuckey voted as one would expect a major stockholder of a food products conglomerate to vote; at 41, with an apparently safe seat, he decided to retire from Congress.

The current congressman is a man with a country boy name and a capacity for adroit political maneuvers. After serving six years in the legislature as a Republican, Billy Lee Evans found his Macon constituency redistricted in 1974 and promptly became a Democrat. Two years later he won the Democratic congressional primary with a base of support from Maconites and blacks. He turned around and won the general election against a former state senator with heavy margins in rural counties. Since 1976 he has not been seriously challenged. In Congress he has maintained a moderate to conservative voting record. Like almost all other members of the Georgia delegation, he was never particularly close personally or politically to Jimmy Carter or his administration.

Census Data   Pop. (1980 final) 508,028, up 11% in 1970s. Median family income, 1970, $6,836, 71% of U.S.

The Voters

Employment profile 1970   White collar, 37%. Blue collar, 42%. Service, 15%. Farm, 6%.
Ethnic groups   Black 1980, 31%. Hispanic 1980, 1%.

Presidential Vote

1980	Reagan (R)	53,197	(34%)
	Carter (D)	100,073	(64%)
	Anderson (I)	2,068	(1%)
1976	Ford (R)	37,348	(25%)
	Carter (D)	110,789	(75%)

Rep. Billy Lee Evans (D) Elected 1976; b. Nov. 10, 1941, Tifton; home, Macon; U. of Ga., B.A. 1963, LL.B. 1965.

Career Practicing atty., 1965–77; Ga. House of Reps., 1969–76.

Offices 113 CHOB, 202-225-6531. Also Rm. 331 Fed. Bldg., Macon 31208, 912-742-5753.

Committees *Judiciary* (13th). Subcommittees: Administrative Law and Governmental Regulations; Monopolies and Commercial Law.

Public Works and Transportation (14th). Subcommittees: Surface Transportation; Water Resources.

Small Business (12th). Subcommittee: Tax, Access to Equity Capital and Business Opportunities.

Select Committee on Narcotics Abuse and Control (6th).

Group Ratings

	ADA	COPE	PC	LCV	CFA	RPN	NAB	NSI	NTU	ACA	ACU
1980	6	52	17	26	29	—	63	67	42	70	61
1979	21	44	23	13	15	—	—	—	29	41	49
1978	15	32	18	50	9	45	40	80	32	65	65

Key Votes

1) Draft Registn $	FOR	6) Fair Hsg DOJ Enfrc	AGN	11) Cut Socl Incr Dfns $	FOR
2) Ban $ to Nicrgua	AGN	7) Lim PAC Contrbtns	AGN	12) Hosptl Cost Controls	AGN
3) Dlay MX Missile	AGN	8) Cap on Food Stmp $	AGN	13) Gasln Ctrls & Allctns	FOR
4) Nuclr Mortorium	AGN	9) New US Dep Edcatn	FOR	14) Lim Wndfll Prof Tax	FOR
5) Alaska Lands Bill	FOR	10) Cut OSHA $		FOR	15) Chryslr Loan Grntee	FOR

Election Results

1980 general	Billy Lee Evans (D).............	91,103	(75%)	($107,743)
	Darwin Carter (R)..............	31,033	(25%)	($44,034)
1980 primary	Billy Lee Evans (D).............	74,635	(100%)	
1978 general	Billy Lee Evans (D), unopposed ...			($186,027)

NINTH DISTRICT

The northeastern corner of Georgia is hundreds of miles from the cotton, peanut, and tobacco farmlands of Confederate south Georgia. Into this remote part of the state cut the southernmost ridges of the Appalachians, and the culture here is more of the mountains than the Deep South. In some mountain counties a Republican tradition lives on from the days of the Civil War when this area opposed slavery and secession. And other mountain traditions survive: the red clay hills here are reputed to contain more moonshine stills than any other part of the United States.

This bit of Appalachia forms about half of the 9th congressional district of Georgia. The other half is part of the region known as the Piedmont, the gently rolling upland above the fall line where so much of the nation's textile industry is located. Interstate 85, which begins in Durham, North Carolina, and goes to Atlanta, is the main street of the textile industry; and in the 1970s this has been a boom area. Its low wages and low strike rate have attracted other industries besides textiles to this region, including some from Europe. Interstate 85, as it proceeds northeast from Atlanta, also serves another function; and that is that it has enabled tens of thousands of people who work in the Atlanta metropolitan area to live farther out, in Gwinnett County that adjoins Atlanta on the northeast, or even farther. The fact is that most Americans do not want to live in or near big cities, and the prosperity of Greater Atlanta in the 1970s has enabled many people to move out beyond what used to be considered the limits of the metropolitan area. Gwinnett County is more rural in appearance, more small town in atmosphere, more devoted to traditional values. This is what many Georgians want, and the rapid population growth here has made the 9th Georgia's fastest-growing congressional district in the 1970s.

Overall the Dixie Democrats of the Piedmont and foothills far outnumber the mountain Republicans in the 9th. Democrats have lost this district only twice in national elections. In congressional politics there is seldom any significant contest. For 24 years, until his retirement in 1976, Phil Landrum, a Democrat known as the leading congressional voice of the textile industry, represented the district. Textiles are one of the least unionized industries in the nation, and Landrum coauthored the 1959 Landrum–Griffin Act, the last piece of major labor legislation Congress has passed.

After encountering some opposition in the 1974 primary, Landrum decided to retire in 1976. He was able to pass the district along to a former aide, Ed Jenkins. But Jenkins first had to win a multicandidate primary and then a runoff as well as a general election that year. Even two years later he was still encountering some trouble in the primary from an opponent who was able to carry Gwinnett County. The fast population growth in the district means that it will lose some territory, probably Gwinnett County, for 1982; this can only help to insulate Jenkins against this kind of opposition in the future. Jenkins has taken Landrum's seat on the Ways and Means Committee and supports trade restrictions on imports of textiles, apparel, and carpeting.

Census Data   Pop. (1980 final) 660,892, up 45% in 1970s. Median family income, 1970, $7,657, 80% of U.S.

The Voters

  Employment profile 1970   White collar, 34%. Blue collar, 53%. Service, 9%. Farm, 4%.
  Ethnic groups   Black 1980, 5%. Hispanic 1980, 1%.

Presidential Vote

1980	Reagan (R)	88,673	(42%)
	Carter (D)	114,933	(55%)
	Anderson (I)	3,870	(2%)
1976	Ford (R)	48,169	(29%)
	Carter (D)	117,461	(71%)

Rep. Ed Jenkins (D) Elected 1976; b. Jan. 4, 1933, Young Harris; home, Jasper; Young Harris Col., A.A. 1951, Emory U., U. of Ga., LL.B. 1959.

Career Coast Guard, 1952–55; Admin. Asst. to U.S. Rep. Phil Landrum, 1959–62; Asst. U.S. Atty., No. Dist. of Ga., 1962–64; Practicing atty., 1964–76; Jasper City Atty.; Pickens Co. Atty.

Offices 217 CHOB, 202-225-5211. Also P.O. Box 70, Jasper 30143, 404-692-2022.

Committees *Ways and Means* (12th). Subcommittees: Select Revenue Measures; Trade.

Group Ratings

	ADA	COPE	PC	LCV	CFA	RPN	NAB	NSI	NTU	ACA	ACU
1980	6	33	20	41	29	—	75	80	56	60	74
1979	11	44	30	24	15	—	—	—	39	64	51
1978	5	18	33	32	23	43	80	86	47	73	50

Key Votes

1) Draft Registn $	FOR	6) Fair Hsg DOJ Enfrc	AGN	11) Cut Socl Incr Dfns $	—
2) Ban $ to Nicrgua	AGN	7) Lim PAC Contrbtns	AGN	12) Hosptl Cost Controls	AGN
3) Dlay MX Missile	AGN	8) Cap on Food Stmp $	AGN	13) Gasln Ctrls & Allctns	FOR
4) Nuclr Mortorium	AGN	9) New US Dep Edcatn	FOR	14) Lim Wndfll Prof Tax	FOR
5) Alaska Lands Bill	FOR	10) Cut OSHA $	FOR	15) Chryslr Loan Grntee	FOR

Election Results

1980 general	Ed Jenkins (D)	115,576	(68%)	($115,012)
	David Ashworth (R)	54,341	(32%)	($0)
1980 primary	Ed Jenkins (D)	102,134	(100%)	
1978 general	Ed Jenkins (D)	47,264	(77%)	($127,124)
	David Ashworth (R)	14,172	(23%)	($16,163)

TENTH DISTRICT

The 10th congressional district of Georgia is a group of 21 counties in the northern part of the state. The district is anchored by the cities of Athens in the northwest and Augusta in the east. Athens, site of the "How About Them Dogs?" University of Georgia and home of former Secretary of State Dean Rusk, and Augusta, home of the formerly all-white Masters golf tournament, have over the years tended to vote like metropolitan Atlanta, opposing candidates supported by rural Georgia; in 1980 they both rejected Senator Herman Talmadge in favor of his successful Republican challenger, Mack Mattingly.

The rest of the 10th district, primarily rural and small-town counties, has a completely different political tradition, akin to what is found in south Georgia. There are a few black majority counties, and one with a black-controlled local government. But most of this area was in open rebellion against the national Democratic Party from the passage of the Civil Rights Act of 1964 until the nomination of Jimmy Carter 12 years later.

The congressman from the 10th, Doug Barnard, was first elected in 1976, and like his predecessor in the House is a banker by trade; although why an area like this should favor bankers is unclear. Barnard also has a political background: he was once an aide to Governor Carl Sanders, who was elected in 1962 and was considered a moderate in his time; Sanders was Jimmy Carter's opponent in the 1970 runoff and carried Atlanta and his hometown of Augusta. To win the seat, Barnard had to beat a former aide of Lester Maddox; he prevailed in the Democratic runoff with 52%. So by background Barnard is a moderate, but nothing like an intimate of Jimmy Carter; his record in the House by and large has been as close to the Republican as the Democratic mainstream. He was reelected without serious opposition in 1978 and 1980.

Census Data   Pop. (1980 final) 547,218, up 19% in 1970s. Median family income, 1970, $7,307, 76% of U.S.

The Voters

Employment profile 1970   White collar, 39%. Blue collar, 43%. Service, 15%. Farm, 3%.
Ethnic groups   Black 1980, 34%. Hispanic 1980, 1%. Total foreign stock 1970, 3%.

Presidential Vote

1980	Reagan (R)	60,334	(41%)
	Carter (D)	83,867	(56%)
	Anderson (I)	3,020	(2%)
1976	Ford (R)	46,493	(34%)
	Carter (D)	89,733	(66%)

Rep. Doug Barnard, Jr. (D) Elected 1976; b. Mar. 20, 1922, Augusta; home, Augusta; Augusta Col., Mercer U., B.A. 1943, LL.B. 1948.

Career Army, WWII; Banker, Ga. Railroad Bank and Trust, 1948–49, 1950–62, 1966–76; Fed. Resv. Bank of Atlanta, 1949–50; Exec. Secy. to the Gov. of Ga., 1963–66.

Offices 236 CHOB, 202-225-4101. Also Fed. Bldg., Athens 30603, 404-546-2194.

Committees *Banking, Finance and Urban Affairs* (19th). Subcommittees: Domestic Monetary Policy; Financial Institutions Supervision, Regulation and Insurance; International Trade, Investment and Monetary Policy.

Governmental Operations (19th). Subcommittee: Commerce, Consumer and Monetary Affairs.

Group Ratings

	ADA	COPE	PC	LCV	CFA	RPN	NAB	NSI	NTU	ACA	ACU
1980	11	16	17	17	14	—	73	75	41	63	61
1979	5	5	23	24	7	—	—	—	47	72	68
1978	10	5	18	40	9	60	83	90	27	75	63

Key Votes

1) Draft Registn $	FOR	6) Fair Hsg DOJ Enfrc	AGN	11) Cut Socl Incr Dfns $	FOR
2) Ban $ to Nicrgua	AGN	7) Lim PAC Contrbtns	AGN	12) Hosptl Cost Controls	AGN
3) Dlay MX Missile	AGN	8) Cap on Food Stmp $	AGN	13) Gasln Ctrls & Allctns	AGN
4) Nuclr Mortorium	AGN	9) New US Dep Edcatn	FOR	14) Lim Wndfll Prof Tax	FOR
5) Alaska Lands Bill	FOR	10) Cut OSHA $	FOR	15) Chryslr Loan Grntee	AGN

Election Results

1980 general	Doug Barnard, Jr. (D)	102,177	(80%)	($57,866)
	Bruce J. Neubauer (R)	25,194	(20%)	($4,431)
1980 primary	Doug Barnard, Jr. (D)	73,333	(100%)	
1978 general	Doug Barnard, Jr. (D), unopposed			($41,709)

HAWAII

Of all the islands and colonies acquired by the western powers in the late 19th century, only one has become an integral part of the country that acquired it: Hawaii. This outcome was far from obvious in the 1890s, when the last Hawaiian monarch, Queen Liliuokalani, was ousted from power and the Islands were annexed by the United States. One reason Hawaii has developed as it has is that there were close ties between the United States and Hawaii long before those events. American missionaries had been proselytizing in the Islands since the 1820s, and missionary families, as readers of James Michener know, had also become profitably involved in trade. Most Americans today think of Hawaii as a vacation paradise, not realizing that these volcanic islands have incredibly rich farmland. Well before annexation Hawaii was a major producer of sugar and later of pineapple for the American market.

But intensive farming and trade with advanced nations are not enough to develop the kind of advanced society and affluent standard of living Hawaii has today. If that were the case, there would not be much poverty left in the world. An economy also needs creative, hardworking people to establish businesses and provide labor. Hawaii has gotten most of its people from successive waves of immigration. The missionary families built the big trading businesses — the Big Five — which have dominated shipping and trading here; with the estate of the last surviving member of the royal family, the old Yankee families and their companies still control a huge percentage of Hawaii's land. But there were never enough native Hawaiians here — particularly after their numbers were reduced by disease — to provide the hard labor these operations needed. So labor was imported. People were brought in systematically, first from Japan, then later from China, the Philippines, Korea, Spain, and Portugal. Native Hawaiians were outnumbered as early as the turn of the century (although their percentage of the Islands' population is increasing today because of their high birth rate).

So Hawaii has become one of the most polyglot places in the world. Although there is plenty of intermarriage between groups and no overt segregation, many of the original traditions and ways of each group remain evident. The Japanese, the largest single migrant group after whites (who are sometimes called haoles), are by most measures the most successful, achieving success in the professions and in organizations such as unions, government, and the Democratic Party. But they have not developed a class of big entrepreneurs and businessmen, as the Chinese-Americans have; notable examples include the millionaire Chin Ho and former Senator Hiram Fong. Whites still tend to have the highest incomes; many come to Hawaii after they have been successful on the Mainland. Filipinos are more likely to be manual laborers. Native Hawaiians, from a culture that lived easily and well off a bounteous physical environment, also tend toward the lower end of the income scale, and some have mounted protest movements similar to those launched in the 1960s by American Indians.

Hawaii's ethnic mix seems a recipe for discord, and in fact ethnic differences do play some part in political preference here. But on the whole Hawaii is a good example of how people from diverse origins can live together. There is a distinctive form of pidgin spoken here, and there is as well a special kind of Hawaiian cultural provinciality—not an uncommon phenomenon on islands throughout the world. In any case, Hawaiians are proud of their tradition of tolerance (one meaning of the word aloha), and any form of racial segregation or discrimination is repugnant. Those attitudes delayed Hawaii's admission into the Union for some time; southern Democrats objected so much that Hawaii voted Republican for many years.

Hawaii has a standard of living today that matches the Mainland states. Its economy is still not self-sufficient, however; even today, after three decades of explosive growth, the Islands still have fewer than one million people, not really enough of a market to justify major capital expenditures. Agriculture continues to be very important to the economy here. Another major industry is tourism. The jet plane has done amazing things for Hawaii's economy but has made the state dependent in the process, producing a sense of near calamity when for the first time in years the number of tourists dropped in 1980 because of sharp increases in jet fuel and airfares. Thus a revolution in Iran and war in Iraq affect the life of an American state.

Another major component of the Hawaiian economy leaving the state economically dependent is the military. The Navy built fortifications and a huge drydock at Pearl Harbor as long ago as 1919, and since then Hawaii has been the center of American military power in the Pacific; the Japanese attack on Pearl Harbor in 1941 struck not just a peripheral outpost but the heart of the U.S. Navy. There are now more than 62,000 military personnel stationed in Hawaii, and this is not a state where antimilitary or antiwar attitudes ever made much headway. Finally, Hawaii, where the cost of living is very high, remains dependent on the Mainland for much of its food and manufactured products; shipping and warehousing remain major industries here, and the big unions—the International Longshoremen's and Warehousemen's Union (ILWU) and the Teamsters—are those associated with these industries.

Demographically, Hawaii is essentially a city–state, with about three-quarters of its population concentrated in and near Honolulu, on the island of Oahu. The other islands, however, have distinct personalities. Hawaii, the Big Island, is large enough to boast huge cattle ranches and has in Mauna Kea the highest mountain in the world if you count from its base far under the ocean to the peak that rises in a seemingly slow, endless way from Hilo or, on the other side of the island, from the Kona (western) Coast. On the north shore, with heavy rainfall and tropical foliage, are the old port of Hilo and Hawaii's macadamia nut industry; this is a blue collar, heavily Democratic area. On the Kona Coast, where there is little rainfall and the landscape is dominated by lava flows, there are retirement condominiums and a higher-income, more Republican population. Maui, at the beginning of the 1980s, was the fastest developing island, with dozens of luxury condominiums and rapidly rising real estate prices. Kauai, west of Oahu, is perhaps the least developed and most agricultural island; its large farm work force makes it the most Democratic of the islands.

Oahu itself has about the same land area as the city of Los Angeles, and perhaps even more diversity. The tourist usually sees Waikiki, with its 40-story hotels rising within a few feet of each other, its restaurants and souvenir shops—a place more to the taste of conventioneers, one would think, than to people looking for a place to relax. There are high-income neighborhoods past Waikiki, around Diamond Head and out to the Kahala and Koko Head beach areas; these places delivered large enough majorities for Ronald Reagan in 1980 to enable him almost to carry the state. Honolulu's other neighborhoods are politically more Democratic but ethnically diverse; there are no real slums here, but incomes are lower near the city's downtown and the military bases and airports to the west. The area around Pearl Harbor is middle class, with many military families; farther out the island, between the two jagged chains of mountains that lift it out of the sea, are some of Hawaii's best farmlands. Over the mountains to the west is the Leeward Coast, calm, sultry, and lightly populated; over the mountains to the northeast is the Windward Coast, windy as its name implies, with many prosperous and spanking new subdivisions.

Hawaii is the only state that was once a monarchy, but it has had no trouble accepting the Mainland parties. For the first couple of years after statehood, Hawaii tended to vote Republican. But soon a remarkable Democratic organization took control of the state's politics —and, despite challenges and some internal feuds, has never really relinquished it. One of its leaders was John Burns, who was elected governor in 1962 and remained in office until he retired because of illness in 1974.

Another leader of this group was Daniel Inouye, the state's first congressman-at-large and senator since 1962. Inouye was a distinguished member of the group of Japanese–Americans who fought in the Nisei 442d Infantry Regimental Command Team, the most decorated and perhaps most celebrated American military unit in World War II. Returning to Hawaii after the war, Inouye and other 442d veterans, like Hawaii's other senator, Spark Matsunaga, moved into the empty ranks of the territorial Democratic Party—and soon came to dominate it. The other major component of Hawaii's Democratic organization is the ILWU. This is the largest union in Hawaii, and an organization with a stormy radical past; its president still is Harry Bridges, who used to be denounced as a Communist and later dealt amicably with the big shipowners. The ILWU's clout in Hawaii politics is legendary; for 12 years (1960–72) no major candidate endorsed by the ILWU lost an election, and few have since.

Daniel Inouye is now Hawaii's senior elected official, the only person who has held major statewide office throughout the 20-plus years since statehood. He is also probably the most popular politician in Hawaii; he won more than 80% of the vote in his last three elections. He is also a national figure of some prominence. He keynoted the 1968 Democratic National Convention, but his greatest notice came when he served on the Senate Watergate Committee in 1973. His dignified, well-prepared performance contrasted crisply with the performance of some of the witnesses and of Haldeman and Ehrlichman lawyer John J. Wilson.

Inouye is known in the Senate as a loyal Democrat and a strong believer in the policies associated historically with Democratic administrations. He steadfastly supported President Johnson's domestic and Vietnam war policies; and on defense issues, unlike most other non-Dixie Democrats, he has never wavered in his support for strong defense policies and has no strong leaning toward any one of the services. Inouye's party regularity and competence won him seats on some of the Senate's big money committees—Appropriations and Commerce—and today he is the fourth-ranking Democrat on both of them. Inouye is one of those senators—a minority, certainly, since 1980—who believe strongly that the federal government can solve domestic and foreign problems; on Commerce he favors such programs as maritime subsidies and on Appropriations he tends usually to favor a larger federal role and more spending. This does not mean that he approves budget requests uncritically; he is too well prepared for that. But when questions are raised as to whether a given appropriation should be somewhat higher or lower, Inouye tends to favor the higher one. In a Democratic Senate Inouye would stand a good chance of chairing one of these committees one day; the present outlook, with the Republican majority, is more clouded. Inouye has been mentioned as a vice presidential candidate, and that is a possibility. But with his strong political standing in Hawaii — he easily won reelection in 1980 to a fourth term at age 56 — he is likely to be a power in the Senate for many years to come.

Hawaii's other senator, Spark Matsunaga, is less senior and less well known, although he is older than Inouye. Matsunaga sat in the House for 14 years, and he won his Senate seat in a 1976 primary fight with his fellow representative, Patsy Mink. Despite their similar voting records, there was a contrast between them. Mink was somewhat a rebel — an early opponent of the Vietnam war, for example. Matsunaga, on the other hand, was close to the House leadership and not a boat-rocker of any sort. Matsunaga won the October primary by a 52%–40% margin, and the general election was anticlimactic. The Republican candidate, the state's first governor, William Quinn, came out against heavy federal spending; but Hawaii, with its large military installations, federal aid to impacted areas, and so on, was not particularly interested in the theme. Matsunaga, with seats on the Finance and Energy Committees, has one of the more liberal voting records in the Senate. Second-ranking Democrat on the Trade Subcommittee, he is basically a free trader but is concerned about imported pineapples and macadamia nuts. He seems to be one of the most politically secure of the Democrats up for reelection in 1982, and it would be a surprise if the Republicans make a serious challenge for this seat.

For nearly a dozen years after its first big victory in 1962, the Democratic machine built by Burns, Inouye, and the ILWU dominated the state's politics. Since Burns's retirement, there has been factional strife; but the Republicans have failed despite a number of serious efforts to win major office, and the heir Burns left behind, George Ariyoshi, has proved successful in major contests. The biggest and most bitter struggle has been between Ariyoshi and longtime Honolulu Mayor Frank Fasi. In 1974 and 1978 Fasi challenged Ariyoshi for the governorship, and the fighting was brutal. They disagreed on issues, with Ariyoshi suggesting there should be limits on growth (he once proposed limiting the number of people who can move to the Islands) and Fasi arguing that development was good.

There were also contrasts in character and style. Ariyoshi is by no means a charismatic figure; "quiet but effective" was his 1978 campaign slogan. His speaking style is such that a half-hour documentary campaign film featured little footage of the governor talking and employed an actor to play him as a young man. Fasi in contrast is dynamic and flamboyant. He is also, in the opinion of some, somewhat less than honest. In 1977 he was charged with accepting bribes by a prosecutor employed by the Ariyoshi Administration. Eventually the charges were dropped, but the controversy continued. The ethnic differences between the two are reflected in their constituencies. Ariyoshi has a strong following among Japanese–Americans, who are the largest single ethnic group in the electorate — they were 28% of the state's population in 1970 but probably more than one-third of the Democratic primary electorate. Fasi has strong support from Chinese, Filipinos, and haoles. Ariyoshi beat Fasi by tantalizingly narrow margins in 1974 and 1978; and Eileen Anderson, a former Ariyoshi aide, beat Fasi in the 1980 primary for mayor of Honolulu. Whether that will remove Fasi from the political scene or end the Ariyoshi–Fasi rivalry is unclear. It is entirely possible that Ariyoshi will face a serious challenge in the 1982 gubernatorial primary.

Hawaii has two congressional districts: the 1st is bounded by the historic city limits of Honolulu (although the mayor's election includes the entire island of Oahu), and the 2d includes all the rest of Oahu and the Neighbor Islands. Hawaii has never elected a Republican to the House. It came closest to doing so in 1976, when Matsunaga and Mink relinquished their seats, and the Republicans made a serious attempt in the 1st district, which has a larger high-income and haole population and is slightly more Republican (it went for Reagan in 1980, for example, while the 2d by a larger margin went for Carter). The winner in the 1st district was Cecil Heftel, a millionaire broadcaster who had nearly beaten Hiram Fong in the 1970 Senate race. Heftel spent more than $300,000 of his own money in the race; he had a bitter primary, supported by Inouye but fiercely opposed by Ariyoshi; and he had a close race in the general election. In the 2d district, the contest was determined in the Democratic primary, which was won by Daniel Akaka, an Ariyoshi appointee. Neither has had significant opposition for election to the House.

Both Heftel and Akaka are pretty solid Democratic loyalists. Heftel serves on the Ways and Means Committee and thus has a voice on the major national issues of taxes, trade, and health care. Akaka serves on Appropriations and its Agriculture Subcommittee — bodies with practical concerns that are especially important to Hawaii.

Hawaii was one of only six states to be carried by President Carter in 1980, and the only one west of Minnesota. Two factors seem to have combined to produce the Carter victory and to make Hawaii so atypical to the rest of the nation in this contest: a strong leaning toward Democrats generally, combined with a strong inclination to support presidential candidates of the party in power. These two factors explain Hawaii's other presidential results, including its narrow margin for winning Democratic candidates in years in which Republicans were in power (1976 and 1960), its landslide margins for incumbents in 1972 and 1964, and its far higher than average Democratic percentages in years when the Democrats were in power (1980 and 1968). The inclination toward incumbents may be explained by the fact that this is a state that takes its patriotism very seriously, in part because the patriotism of some of its citizens was, unjustly, doubted within living memory, and in part because this is the only state whose population center has been under direct foreign attack since the War of 1812. This analysis would suggest that the Republicans have a chance of carrying Hawaii in 1984, although the state is likely to remain solidly Democratic in elections for state and congressional offices.

Census Data   Pop. (1980 final) 965,000, up 25% in 1970s: 0.43% of U.S. total, 39th largest. Central city, 38%; suburban, 41%. Median 4-person family income, 1978, $22,475, 110% of U.S., 3d highest.

1979 Share of Federal Tax Burden $2,029,000,000; 0.45% of U.S. total, 37th largest.

1979 Share of Federal Outlays $2,659,230,000; 0.57% of U.S. total, 39th largest.

DOD	$1,371,860,000	25th	(1.29%)	HEW	$602,208,000	42d (0.34%)
DOE	$3,815,000	41st	(0.03%)	ERDA	$2,139,000	39th (0.07%)
HUD	$22,075,000	42d	(0.33%)	NASA	$2,658,000	31st (0.06%)
VA	$61,940,000	46th	(0.30%)	DOT	$109,712,000	39th (0.66%)
EPA	$30,896,000	38th	(0.58%)	DOC	$15,799,000	32d (0.50%)
DOI	$16,059,000	44th	(0.29%)	USDA	$83,362,000	45th (0.35%)

Economic Base   Finance, insurance, and real estate; agriculture, notably sugarcane, pineapples, cattle, and dairy products; food and kindred products; tourism; apparel and other textile products, especially women's and misses' outerwear; printing and publishing, especially newspapers; stone, clay, and glass products, especially concrete, gypsum, and plaster products.

Political Lineup   Governor, George Aryioshi (D). Senators, Daniel K. Inouye (D) and Spark M. Matsunaga (D). Representatives, 2 D; 2 in 1982. State Senate, 25 (17 D and 8 R); State House of Representatives, 51 (39 D and 12 R).

The Voters

Registration   402,795 Total. No party registration.
Employment profile 1970   White collar, 50%. Blue collar, 31%. Service, 16%. Farm, 3%.
Ethnic groups   Black 1980, 2%. Hispanic 1980, 7%. Asian 1980, 60%. Total foreign stock 1970, 33%.

Presidential Vote

1980	Reagan (R)	130,112	(43%)
	Carter (D)	135,879	(45%)
	Anderson (I)	32,021	(11%)
1976	Ford (R)	139,969	(48%)
	Carter (D)	147,351	(51%)

SENATORS

Sen. Daniel K. Inouye (D) Elected 1962, seat up 1986; b. Sept. 7, 1924, Honolulu; home, Honolulu; U. of Hawaii, B.A. 1950, Geo. Wash. U., J.D. 1952.

Career Army, WWII; Honolulu Asst. Prosecuting Atty., 1953–54; Practicing atty., 1954–59; Hawaii Territorial House of Reps., 1954–58, Major. Ldr.; Hawaii Territorial Senate, 1958–59; U.S. House of Reps., 1959–63.

Offices 105 RSOB, 202-224-3934. Also 300 Ala Moana Blvd., Honolulu 96850, 808-546-7550.

Committees *Appropriations* (4th). Subcommittees: Defense; Foreign Operations; Labor, Health and Human Services, Education; Military Construction; State, Justice, Commerce, and the Judiciary.

Commerce, Science, and Transportation (4th). Subcommittees: Aviation; Communications; Merchant Marine and Tourism.

Select Committee on Indian Affairs (2d).

Select Committee on Intelligence (4th). Subcommittees: Budget; Collection and Foreign Operations.

Group Ratings

	ADA	COPE	PC	LCV	CFA	RPN	NAB	NSI	NTU	ACA	ACU
1980	67	75	40	33	60	—	0	14	24	23	11
1979	37	66	40	—	43	—	—	—	12	6	9
1978	60	81	45	54	25	50	11	25	6	19	0

Key Votes

1) Draft Registn $	FOR	6) Fair Housng Cloture	FOR	11) Cut Socl Incr Defns	FOR
2) Ban $ to Nicrgua	FOR	7) Ban $ Rape Abortns	AGN	12) Income Tax Indexing	AGN
3) Dlay MX Missile	AGN	8) Cap on Food Stmp $	—	13) Lim Spdg 21% GNP	AGN
4) Nuclr Mortorium	AGN	9) New US Dep Edcatn	—	14) Incr Wndfll Prof Tax	FOR
5) Alaska Lands Bill	—	10) Cut OSHA Inspctns	AGN	15) Chryslr Loan Grntee	FOR

Election Results

1980 general	Daniel K. Inouye (D)	224,485	(78%)	($480,113)
	Cooper Brown (R)	53,068	(18%)	($14,382)
1980 primary	Daniel K. Inouye (D)	198,467	(88%)	
	Two others (D)	28,291	(12%)	
1974 general	Daniel K. Inouye (D)	207,454	(83%)	($205,265)
	James D. Kimmel (People's Party)	42,767	(17%)	

Sen. Spark M. Matsunaga (D) Elected 1976, seat up 1982; b. Oct. 8, 1916, Kukuiula; home, Honolulu; U. of Hawaii, B.Ed. 1941, Harvard U., J.D. 1951.

Career Public school teacher, 1941; Army, WWII; Vets. Counselor, Surplus Prop. Ofc., U.S. Dept. of Interior, 1945–47; Chf., Priority Claimants' Div., War Assets Admin., 1947–48; Honolulu Asst. Pub. Prosecutor, 1952–54; Practicing atty., 1954–63; Hawaii Territorial House of Reps., 1954–59, Major. Ldr.; U.S. House of Reps., 1963–77.

Offices 5121 DSOB, 202-224-6361. Also 300 Ala Moana Blvd., Honolulu 96850, 808-546-7555.

Committees *Energy and Natural Resources* (6th). Subcommittees: Energy Conservation and Supply; Energy and Mineral Resources; Public Lands and Reserved Water.

Finance (4th). Subcommittees: Taxation and Debt Management; International Trade; Savings, Pensions, and Investment Policy.

Veterans' Affairs (3d).

Group Ratings

	ADA	COPE	PC	LCV	CFA	RPN	NAB	NSI	NTU	ACA	ACU
1980	78	83	47	51	53	—	0	14	21	13	0
1979	53	79	52	—	52	—	—	—	15	8	11
1978	70	89	58	67	50	78	0	20	4	5	0

Key Votes

1) Draft Registn $	AGN	6) Fair Housng Cloture	FOR	11) Cut Socl Incr Defns	AGN
2) Ban $ to Nicrgua	FOR	7) Ban $ Rape Abortns	—	12) Income Tax Indexing	AGN
3) Dlay MX Missile	AGN	8) Cap on Food Stmp $	AGN	13) Lim Spdg 21% GNP	AGN
4) Nuclr Mortorium	FOR	9) New US Dep Edcatn	FOR	14) Incr Wndfll Prof Tax	FOR
5) Alaska Lands Bill	FOR	10) Cut OSHA Inspctns	AGN	15) Chryslr Loan Grntee	FOR

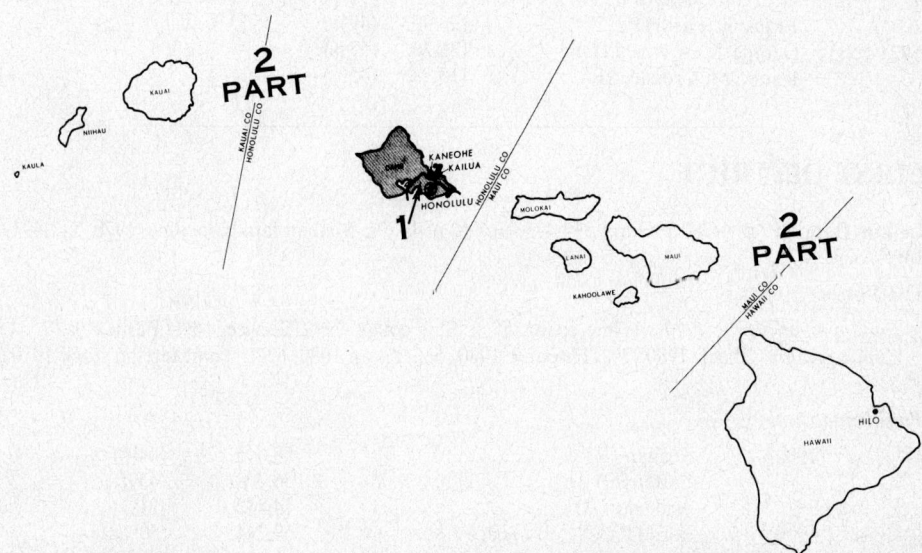

Election Results

1976 general	Spark M. Matsunaga (D)	162,305	(54%)	($435,130)
	William Quinn (R)	122,724	(41%)	($415,138)
	Tony Hodges (People's Party)	14,223	(5%)	
1976 primary	Spark M. Matsunaga (D)	109,731	(52%)	
	Patsy Mink (D)	84,732	(40%)	
	Three others (D)	16,697	(8%)	
1970 general	Hiram L. Fong (R)	124,163	(52%)	
	Cecil Heftel (D)	116,597	(48%)	

GOVERNOR

Gov. George R. Ariyoshi (D) Elected 1974, after serving as Acting Gov. since Oct. 1973, term expires Dec. 1982; b. Mar. 12, 1926, Honolulu; U. of Hawaii, U. of Mich., B.A. 1949, J.D. 1952.

Career Army, WWII; Practicing atty., 1953–70; Hawaii Territorial House of Reps. 1954–58; Hawaii Territorial Senate, 1958–59, State Senate, 1959–70, Major. Ldr., 1965–66, Major. Flr. Ldr., 1969–70; Lt. Gov. of Hawaii, 1970–74.

Offices Executive Chambers, State Capitol, Honolulu 96813, 808-548-5428.

Election Results

1978 gen.	George R. Ariyoshi (D)	153,394	(55%)
	John R. Leopold (R)	124,610	(44%)
1978 prim.	George R. Ariyoshi (D)	130,527	(51%)
	Frank F. Fasi (D).........	126,903	(49%)
1974 gen.	George R. Ariyoshi (D)	136,262	(55%)
	Randolph Crossley (R).....	113,388	(45%)

FIRST DISTRICT

Census Data Pop. (1980 prelim.) 394,423, up 9% in 1970s. Median family income, 1970, $12,491, 130% of U.S.

The Voters

Employment profile 1970 White collar, 55%. Blue collar, 29%. Service, 16%. Farm, –%.
Ethnic groups Black 1980, 2%. Hispanic 1980, 5%. Asian 1980, 63%. Total foreign stock 1970, 35%.

Presidential Vote

1980	Reagan (R)	58,045	(44%)
	Carter (D)	56,298	(43%)
	Anderson (I)	14,842	(11%)
1976	Ford (R)	67,234	(50%)
	Carter (D)	65,337	(49%)

Rep. Cecil Heftel (D) Elected 1976; b. Sept. 30, 1924, Cook Co., Ill.; home, Honolulu; Ariz. St. U., B.S. 1951, U. of Utah, NYU.

Career Army, WWII; Pres., Heftel Broadcasting, 1964– ; Dem. nominee for U.S. Senate, 1970.

Offices 1030 LHOB, 202-225-2726. Also Rm. 4104, 300 Ala Moana Blvd. Honolulu 96850, 808-546-8997.

Committee *Ways and Means* (15th). Subcommittees: Health; Oversight.

Group Ratings

	ADA	COPE	PC	LCV	CFA	RPN	NAB	NSI	NTU	ACA	ACU
1980	50	67	59	49	64	—	30	40	21	29	39
1979	42	65	33	44	28	—	—	—	29	13	17
1978	35	53	38	40	36	50	25	40	13	15	21

Key Votes

1) Draft Registn $	FOR	6) Fair Hsg DOJ Enfrc	FOR	11) Cut Socl Incr Dfns $	AGN
2) Ban $ to Nicrgua	AGN	7) Lim PAC Contrbtns	FOR	12) Hosptl Cost Controls	AGN
3) Dlay MX Missile	AGN	8) Cap on Food Stmp $	AGN	13) Gasln Ctrls & Allctns	FOR
4) Nuclr Mortorium	—	9) New US Dep Edcatn	FOR	14) Lim Wndfll Prof Tax	FOR
5) Alaska Lands Bill	FOR	10) Cut OSHA $	AGN	15) Chryslr Loan Grntee	AGN

Election Results

1980 general	Cecil Heftel (D)	98,256	(80%)	($340,023)
	Noble Aloma Keen (R)	19,819	(16%)	
1980 primary	Cecil Heftel (D)	73,162	(72%)	
	Charles M. Campbell (D)	26,024	(26%)	($17,684)
	One other (D)	2,031	(2%)	
1978 general	Cecil Heftel (D)	84,552	(78%)	($174,306)
	William D. Spillane (R)	24,470	(22%)	($18,694)

SECOND DISTRICT

Census Data   Pop. (1980 final) 570,577, up 40% in 1970s. Median family income, 1970, $10,848, 113% of U.S.

The Voters

Employment profile 1970   White collar, 44%. Blue collar, 35%. Service, 15%. Farm, 6%.
Ethnic groups   Black 1980, 2%. Hispanic 1980, 9%. Asian 1980, 59%. Total foreign stock 1970, 32%.

Presidential Vote

1980	Reagan (R)	72,067	(42%)
	Carter (D)	79,581	(46%)
	Anderson (I)	17,119	(10%)

| 1976 | Ford (R) .... | 72,769 | (46%) |
| | Carter (D) .... | 82,018 | (52%) |

Rep. Daniel K. Akaka (D) Elected 1976; b. Sept. 11, 1924, Honolulu; home, Honolulu; U. of Hawaii, B.Ed. 1952, M.Ed. 1966.

Career Welder, mechanic, and engineer, U.S. Army Corps of Engineers, WWII; Public school teacher and principal, 1953–71; Dir., Hawaii Ofc. of Econ. Opp., 1971–74; Spec. Asst. to the Gov. of Hawaii in Human Resources, 1975–76; Dir. Progressive Neighborhoods Program, 1975–76,

Offices 1510 CHOB, 202-225-4906. Also Rm. 5104 Kuhio Fed. Bldg., Honolulu 96813, 808-546-8952.

Committees *Appropriations* (30th). Subcommittees: Agriculture, Rural Development and Related Agencies; Treasury–Postal Service–General Government.

Select Committee on Narcotics Abuse and Control (9th).

Group Ratings

	ADA	COPE	PC	LCV	CFA	RPN	NAB	NSI	NTU	ACA	ACU
1980	72	74	63	35	71	—	0	25	14	25	16
1979	68	65	43	56	42	—	—	—	14	8	6
1978	55	80	50	63	50	27	9	40	4	7	21

Key Votes

1) Draft Registn $	FOR	6) Fair Hsg DOJ Enfrc	FOR	11) Cut Socl Incr Dfns $	AGN
2) Ban $ to Nicrgua	AGN	7) Lim PAC Contrbtns	FOR	12) Hosptl Cost Controls	FOR
3) Dlay MX Missile	AGN	8) Cap on Food Stmp $	AGN	13) Gasln Ctrls & Allctns	FOR
4) Nuclr Mortorium	FOR	9) New US Dep Edcatn	FOR	14) Lim Wndfll Prof Tax	FOR
5) Alaska Lands Bill	FOR	10) Cut OSHA $	AGN	15) Chryslr Loan Grntee	FOR

Election Results

1980 general	Daniel K. Akaka (D)	141,477	(90%)	($96,774)
	Smith D. Gordon (R)	15,903	(10%)	
1980 primary	Daniel K. Akaka (D)	113,552	(100%)	
1978 general	Daniel K. Akaka (D)	118,272	(86%)	($208,958)
	Charles Isaak (R)	15,697	(11%)	($7,016)

IDAHO

Idaho, like most of the other Rocky Mountain states, came into existence because of the mining business. In 1890, when it became a state, its major product was silver, and it was one of the strongest supporters of William Jennings Bryan's free silver program. But beginning early in the 20th century, Idaho became predominantly an agricultural state. The fertile lands along the Snake River Valley were irrigated, often thanks to federal reclamation projects, and the Idaho potato became famous across the nation. As a result, Idaho is different from the other fast-growing Rocky Mountain states. The population is not concentrated here as Colorado's is in metropolitan Denver and Arizona's in metropolitan Phoenix. Peo-

ple are spread fairly evenly across Idaho, from the Panhandle with its grimy mining towns and lumber mills in the north, through the Snake River Valley from Boise and Nampa in the west, to Pocatello and Idaho Falls in the east. Boise, which in 1980 for the first time recorded a population over the 100,000 mark, is a city of some dynamism — the home of such important companies as Boise Cascade (paper and lumber) and Morrison Knudsen (construction). The city's several gleaming towers and its proud older high rises shine against the backdrop of the mountains; its tree-shaded streets and Spanish-style railroad station bespeak a comfortable style of life that contrasts with the arid expanse of plains beyond the city.

Idaho's booming economy and its physical attractions and life-style have made it one of the fastest-growing states in the nation. The population here rose by one-third in the 1970s. But with the exception of a few places, such as the resort town of Sun Valley, the influx has not been like Colorado's — environmentalists with liberal attitudes on cultural issues — but of family people interested in a less hurried but still affluent way of life in a place with a small-town atmosphere where traditional values are accorded more respect than they are in big metropolitan areas. For every Carole King (the singer who moved to Idaho because she loves the environment) there are a dozen new Idahoans who left California because they thought Orange County was not conservative enough.

The great influx of the 1970s has strengthened the political trend that was already in evidence here a decade ago: a decided shift from Democratic to Republican. Idaho favored Bryan at the turn of the century, Wilson a few years later, and was solidly for Franklin Roosevelt and Harry Truman. As late as 1960 John Kennedy was able to win 46% of the vote here. But in the 1960s Idaho began to change course. People began thinking of themselves less as downtrodden employees of big corporations who need the federal government on their side and more as pioneering entrepreneurs who need to get the federal government off their backs. The federal government is a real presence here, as it is in most western states, and when it blocks exploitation of resources, as it frequently does in the interest of preserving the environment, it often arouses stronger resentment in the locality directly affected than gratitude in the broader area indirectly benefited. Idahoans do have a strong feeling for their land, as they evidenced when they ousted a Republican governor and elected Cecil Andrus in 1970 in an election that revolved around a proposal — which Andrus eventually killed — to mine molybdenum in the White Cloud Mountains. But they are also people who believe strongly in the free enterprise system and in traditional values — and they came to see the national Democrats as their adversaries.

Few people took much notice when Barry Goldwater nearly carried Idaho in 1964, but that was a signal that the state was moving to the right. By 1968 Hubert Humphrey could win only 31% of the vote here (George Wallace's best state west of Texas), and even as he was winning the presidency Jimmy Carter took only 37% in 1976. By 1980 Carter was exceedingly unpopular here — although Andrus, his Secretary of the Interior, retains a following back home — and Ronald Reagan carried the state 66% to 25%, his best showing in any state except Utah.

So what is surprising about Idaho politics is not that the Republicans have won most elections, but that they have not done better than they have. Indeed, in 1978 the state elected a Democratic governor for the third time in a row. John Evans, from a small town in the heavily Mormon southeastern corner of the state, was Andrus's lieutenant governor and succeeded to the governorship when Andrus went to Interior in 1977. Evans lacked Andrus's political style, but he managed state affairs in a manner satisfactory to voters. On issues, he has been

values and his stands on such issues as abortion were consistent with the conservative moral tone that prevails in Idaho. But his record on foreign policy issues and his general support of Democratic programs proved a burden too great to bear.

The result was the second closest Senate race in the nation. Symms won by exactly 4,262 votes. Church got nearly twice as many votes as Jimmy Carter, but in Idaho that was not enough to win. Symms was helped by a strong showing in his home area, Canyon County, a prosperous agricultural area just west of Boise. Church, meanwhile, given the national results, would have lost his cherished chairmanship even if he had won the election. Symms, elected at age 42, has what must be considered one of the safer Senate seats, given Idaho's feelings on issues; he has had no previous trouble winning reelection in his congressional district. The new senator has seats on the Budget, Finance, and Public Works Committees. The last will enable him to attend to Idaho's needs; the former probably will give him little power now but has the potential of major influence on economic policy sometime in the future.

Idaho has two seats in the House. The 1st district is the western geographical half of the state, including the Panhandle, Canyon County, and most of Boise. This seat was held by Symms and by McClure before him. The new congressman, Larry Craig, was a member of the state Senate and after he beat a state attorney general in the primary he was expected to have an easy time in the general election. Actually, the result was rather close. Democrat Glenn Nichols, who walked the length of the state, attacked Craig for his sympathies with the Sagebrush Rebellion and carried the sometimes Democratic Panhandle; most of Craig's margin came from the Boise area and Canyon County. Craig is expected to be a solidly conservative member of the cohesive Republican minority in the House; he is not, however, expected to be as close to the New Right as Symms or the 2d district's congressman, George Hansen.

Hansen is one of the authentic zanies in the Congress. His district is about as solidly Republican and conservative as any in the nation; and this, more than anything else, accounts for his continued political survival. The 2d district includes Sun Valley, the Craters of the Moon National Monument, Idaho's small slice of Yellowstone National Park, and the remains of the Teton Dam, which gave way in 1976 and caused great loss of life and property. Much of this area is Mormon and, except for the old railroad town of Pocatello, is strongly Republican.

George Hansen has always been known as one of the most conservative members of Congress. He was first elected in 1964, an upset winner in a year that was more Republican in Idaho than almost anywhere else. He lost his House seat when he ran against Frank Church in 1968 and won it again by defeating a relatively moderate Republican, Orval Hansen, in the 1974 primary. George Hansen has had a number of problems in recent years. In 1975 he pleaded guilty to campaign law violations and was sentenced to two months in jail—a sentence changed, after pleading by his lawyer, to a $42,000 fine. Hansen was nearly beaten by an underfinanced Democrat in 1976 but beat the same man by a wider margin in 1978.

After American embassy personnel were taken hostage in Iran in 1979, Congressman Hansen made two separate trips to Tehran and tried to negotiate their release. Despite his longtime hawkish position, he offered to set up a congressional commission of inquiry of past American actions—a position more craven than the Carter Administration ever adopted. It is possible that Hansen's actions prolonged the hostages' captivity; some Iranians

ple are spread fairly evenly across Idaho, from the Panhandle with its grimy mining towns and lumber mills in the north, through the Snake River Valley from Boise and Nampa in the west, to Pocatello and Idaho Falls in the east. Boise, which in 1980 for the first time recorded a population over the 100,000 mark, is a city of some dynamism — the home of such important companies as Boise Cascade (paper and lumber) and Morrison Knudsen (construction). The city's several gleaming towers and its proud older high rises shine against the backdrop of the mountains; its tree-shaded streets and Spanish-style railroad station bespeak a comfortable style of life that contrasts with the arid expanse of plains beyond the city.

Idaho's booming economy and its physical attractions and life-style have made it one of the fastest-growing states in the nation. The population here rose by one-third in the 1970s. But with the exception of a few places, such as the resort town of Sun Valley, the influx has not been like Colorado's — environmentalists with liberal attitudes on cultural issues — but of family people interested in a less hurried but still affluent way of life in a place with a small-town atmosphere where traditional values are accorded more respect than they are in big metropolitan areas. For every Carole King (the singer who moved to Idaho because she loves the environment) there are a dozen new Idahoans who left California because they thought Orange County was not conservative enough.

The great influx of the 1970s has strengthened the political trend that was already in evidence here a decade ago: a decided shift from Democratic to Republican. Idaho favored Bryan at the turn of the century, Wilson a few years later, and was solidly for Franklin Roosevelt and Harry Truman. As late as 1960 John Kennedy was able to win 46% of the vote here. But in the 1960s Idaho began to change course. People began thinking of themselves less as downtrodden employees of big corporations who need the federal government on their side and more as pioneering entrepreneurs who need to get the federal government off their backs. The federal government is a real presence here, as it is in most western states, and when it blocks exploitation of resources, as it frequently does in the interest of preserving the environment, it often arouses stronger resentment in the locality directly affected than gratitude in the broader area indirectly benefited. Idahoans do have a strong feeling for their land, as they evidenced when they ousted a Republican governor and elected Cecil Andrus in 1970 in an election that revolved around a proposal — which Andrus eventually killed — to mine molybdenum in the White Cloud Mountains. But they are also people who believe strongly in the free enterprise system and in traditional values — and they came to see the national Democrats as their adversaries.

Few people took much notice when Barry Goldwater nearly carried Idaho in 1964, but that was a signal that the state was moving to the right. By 1968 Hubert Humphrey could win only 31% of the vote here (George Wallace's best state west of Texas), and even as he was winning the presidency Jimmy Carter took only 37% in 1976. By 1980 Carter was exceedingly unpopular here — although Andrus, his Secretary of the Interior, retains a following back home — and Ronald Reagan carried the state 66% to 25%, his best showing in any state except Utah.

So what is surprising about Idaho politics is not that the Republicans have won most elections, but that they have not done better than they have. Indeed, in 1978 the state elected a Democratic governor for the third time in a row. John Evans, from a small town in the heavily Mormon southeastern corner of the state, was Andrus's lieutenant governor and succeeded to the governorship when Andrus went to Interior in 1977. Evans lacked Andrus's political style, but he managed state affairs in a manner satisfactory to voters. On issues, he has been

values and his stands on such issues as abortion were consistent with the conservative moral tone that prevails in Idaho. But his record on foreign policy issues and his general support of Democratic programs proved a burden too great to bear.

The result was the second closest Senate race in the nation. Symms won by exactly 4,262 votes. Church got nearly twice as many votes as Jimmy Carter, but in Idaho that was not enough to win. Symms was helped by a strong showing in his home area, Canyon County, a prosperous agricultural area just west of Boise. Church, meanwhile, given the national results, would have lost his cherished chairmanship even if he had won the election. Symms, elected at age 42, has what must be considered one of the safer Senate seats, given Idaho's feelings on issues; he has had no previous trouble winning reelection in his congressional district. The new senator has seats on the Budget, Finance, and Public Works Committees. The last will enable him to attend to Idaho's needs; the former probably will give him little power now but has the potential of major influence on economic policy sometime in the future.

Idaho has two seats in the House. The 1st district is the western geographical half of the state, including the Panhandle, Canyon County, and most of Boise. This seat was held by Symms and by McClure before him. The new congressman, Larry Craig, was a member of the state Senate and after he beat a state attorney general in the primary he was expected to have an easy time in the general election. Actually, the result was rather close. Democrat Glenn Nichols, who walked the length of the state, attacked Craig for his sympathies with the Sagebrush Rebellion and carried the sometimes Democratic Panhandle; most of Craig's margin came from the Boise area and Canyon County. Craig is expected to be a solidly conservative member of the cohesive Republican minority in the House; he is not, however, expected to be as close to the New Right as Symms or the 2d district's congressman, George Hansen.

Hansen is one of the authentic zanies in the Congress. His district is about as solidly Republican and conservative as any in the nation; and this, more than anything else, accounts for his continued political survival. The 2d district includes Sun Valley, the Craters of the Moon National Monument, Idaho's small slice of Yellowstone National Park, and the remains of the Teton Dam, which gave way in 1976 and caused great loss of life and property. Much of this area is Mormon and, except for the old railroad town of Pocatello, is strongly Republican.

George Hansen has always been known as one of the most conservative members of Congress. He was first elected in 1964, an upset winner in a year that was more Republican in Idaho than almost anywhere else. He lost his House seat when he ran against Frank Church in 1968 and won it again by defeating a relatively moderate Republican, Orval Hansen, in the 1974 primary. George Hansen has had a number of problems in recent years. In 1975 he pleaded guilty to campaign law violations and was sentenced to two months in jail — a sentence changed, after pleading by his lawyer, to a $42,000 fine. Hansen was nearly beaten by an underfinanced Democrat in 1976 but beat the same man by a wider margin in 1978.

After American embassy personnel were taken hostage in Iran in 1979, Congressman Hansen made two separate trips to Tehran and tried to negotiate their release. Despite his longtime hawkish position, he offered to set up a congressional commission of inquiry of past American actions — a position more craven than the Carter Administration ever adopted. It is possible that Hansen's actions prolonged the hostages' captivity; some Iranians

ple are spread fairly evenly across Idaho, from the Panhandle with its grimy mining towns and lumber mills in the north, through the Snake River Valley from Boise and Nampa in the west, to Pocatello and Idaho Falls in the east. Boise, which in 1980 for the first time recorded a population over the 100,000 mark, is a city of some dynamism — the home of such important companies as Boise Cascade (paper and lumber) and Morrison Knudsen (construction). The city's several gleaming towers and its proud older high rises shine against the backdrop of the mountains; its tree-shaded streets and Spanish-style railroad station bespeak a comfortable style of life that contrasts with the arid expanse of plains beyond the city.

Idaho's booming economy and its physical attractions and life-style have made it one of the fastest-growing states in the nation. The population here rose by one-third in the 1970s. But with the exception of a few places, such as the resort town of Sun Valley, the influx has not been like Colorado's — environmentalists with liberal attitudes on cultural issues — but of family people interested in a less hurried but still affluent way of life in a place with a small-town atmosphere where traditional values are accorded more respect than they are in big metropolitan areas. For every Carole King (the singer who moved to Idaho because she loves the environment) there are a dozen new Idahoans who left California because they thought Orange County was not conservative enough.

The great influx of the 1970s has strengthened the political trend that was already in evidence here a decade ago: a decided shift from Democratic to Republican. Idaho favored Bryan at the turn of the century, Wilson a few years later, and was solidly for Franklin Roosevelt and Harry Truman. As late as 1960 John Kennedy was able to win 46% of the vote here. But in the 1960s Idaho began to change course. People began thinking of themselves less as downtrodden employees of big corporations who need the federal government on their side and more as pioneering entrepreneurs who need to get the federal government off their backs. The federal government is a real presence here, as it is in most western states, and when it blocks exploitation of resources, as it frequently does in the interest of preserving the environment, it often arouses stronger resentment in the locality directly affected than gratitude in the broader area indirectly benefited. Idahoans do have a strong feeling for their land, as they evidenced when they ousted a Republican governor and elected Cecil Andrus in 1970 in an election that revolved around a proposal — which Andrus eventually killed — to mine molybdenum in the White Cloud Mountains. But they are also people who believe strongly in the free enterprise system and in traditional values — and they came to see the national Democrats as their adversaries.

Few people took much notice when Barry Goldwater nearly carried Idaho in 1964, but that was a signal that the state was moving to the right. By 1968 Hubert Humphrey could win only 31% of the vote here (George Wallace's best state west of Texas), and even as he was winning the presidency Jimmy Carter took only 37% in 1976. By 1980 Carter was exceedingly unpopular here — although Andrus, his Secretary of the Interior, retains a following back home — and Ronald Reagan carried the state 66% to 25%, his best showing in any state except Utah.

So what is surprising about Idaho politics is not that the Republicans have won most elections, but that they have not done better than they have. Indeed, in 1978 the state elected a Democratic governor for the third time in a row. John Evans, from a small town in the heavily Mormon southeastern corner of the state, was Andrus's lieutenant governor and succeeded to the governorship when Andrus went to Interior in 1977. Evans lacked Andrus's political style, but he managed state affairs in a manner satisfactory to voters. On issues, he has been

more conservative than his predecessor but has not dropped environmental considerations from his agenda. Evans was blessed in the 1978 election with an opponent whose strategy backfired. Allen Larsen, a Republican legislative leader, is a Mormon, like Evans; but unlike Evans he believes that the state should legislate Mormon rules of morality. His proposals to restrict liquor sales stirred great opposition in a state where more than 70% of the voters are not Mormons; hurting him even more was a feeling that Mormons were trying to take over the state. Evans won the election with a solid margin, doing especially well in the Panhandle where there are few if any Mormons.

The outlook for 1982 is not clear. Evans will probably run again, and he has not gotten himself into any political trouble. But this is a Republican state, and if the Republican primary should produce a stronger candidate than Larsen — who won with a minority, heavily Mormon vote in a multicandidate field — Republicans could capture the governorship for the first time since 1966.

Republicans now hold all four seats in Idaho's congressional delegation; but none of them won his seat initially with a large margin, and taken together the delegation is not as strong as several other Republican delegations from Rocky Mountain states. Its leading and most senior member is Senator James McClure, first elected to the House in 1966 and to the Senate in 1972. McClure is very much in line with the New Right consensus that predominates among Rocky Mountain Republicans. He is for a tougher military stance, reliance on the free market rather than government action, and for enforcement of moral positions such as opposition to abortion through federal legislation.

When the Republicans took over the Senate, McClure became chairman of the Energy and Natural Resources Committee. This gives him great power over national energy policy, which he will use to remove controls over the price and production of oil and natural gas, to encourage energy development on public lands, and to promote nuclear and geothermal power. It is also a position of great importance to Idaho. This body used to be known as the Interior Committee, and it has jurisdiction over all the federal lands except national forests, over mining and national parks, and over reclamation and water rights. McClure, who also chairs the Interior Appropriations Subcommittee, can be expected to act in behalf of the interests of Idaho's business community and its farmers, to restrict federal involvement except when (as in the case of reclamation and irrigation) it directly helps Idaho's economic interests. McClure is sympathetic to the goals of the Sagebrush Rebellion, the movement to give federal lands to the states. Opponents charge such a move would result in overdevelopment, because the states could not afford to spend as much on land management as the federal government can; McClure and others argue that the feds are unduly restricting development of lands, preventing beneficial economic growth and obstructing the exploitation of mineral resources the nation needs.

McClure is also a member of the Appropriations Committee. He has enough of a profile on foreign affairs to have been chosen to introduce Henry Kissinger at the 1980 Republican National Convention. A decade ago Kissinger did not need the protection of a New Right senator like McClure to prevent booing and hissing; indeed, Kissinger probably did not know then who McClure was. Now the Idahoan is potentially one of the more important members of the U.S. Senate.

Until 1980 McClure was certainly overshadowed by his senior colleague, Democrat Frank Church. First elected to the Senate in 1956 at age 32, Church became a favorite of Majority Leader Lyndon Johnson and won seats on Foreign Relations (where he supported arms control and opposed the Vietnam war) and Interior (on which he paid close attention to Idaho water interests). Many thought that Church's anti-Vietnam war stand would defeat him in hawkish Idaho in 1968. But a California-financed recall effort the year before stirred resentment against outside intrusion, and Church was fortunate enough to draw as his opponent Congressman George Hansen, not one of the Republicans' strongest candidates. Church won with 60% of the vote, and in the 1970s went on to be a powerful and productive legislator. On Interior, he locked up Idaho's water rights; on Foreign Relations, he led the movement to stop the bombing of Cambodia and get the United States to withdraw from Vietnam. In 1975 and 1976 he chaired a special committee to investigate the CIA and drew up the legislation limiting its powers and making it more accountable to Congress. In 1975–78, when the elderly John Sparkman was chairing Foreign Relations, Church was its real intellectual and political leader. It was also at this time, in 1976, that he ran for president and made a creditable showing. As a westerner, he opposed Jimmy Carter in some late primaries and won in Nebraska, Montana, Oregon, and Idaho. Defeated in Ohio on the last day of primaries, Church was one of the finalists in Jimmy Carter's choice for the vice presidency.

After the 1978 election, Church achieved his longtime goal: the chairmanship of the Senate Foreign Relations Committee. But many of the issues he had been so deeply interested in had passed by, and on other issues he found himself running against the tide of opinion. On the Middle East, he was able to play a constructive role as a supporter of Israel and of the Camp David peace accords. In other areas he was less successful. The SALT II Treaty was reported out eventually by the Foreign Relations Committee but died on the floor of the Senate in 1980; ironically, Church himself, always a backer of arms control, helped produce a critical delay in the consideration of SALT when he revealed, in August 1979 in Idaho, that the administration had discovered that there was a Soviet combat brigade in Cuba.

Church was successful in getting the Senate, by the narrowest of margins, to ratify the Panama Canal Treaties in 1978. But politically at least that was a Pyrrhic victory; the treaties, unpopular everywhere, had virtually no support in Idaho and had many vehement opponents.

The contest between Church and Congressman Steven Symms in the 1980 election was as much a battle of opposites as any race in the country. Symms was generally counted as one of the most right-wing members of the House; Church was considered one of the more left-wing members of the Senate. Symms, an apple rancher, opposes the federal government and almost all of its works; he is, therefore, sympathetic to the Sagebrush Rebellion. On foreign policy, the challenger favored more defense spending and accused Church of crippling the CIA. Oddly, Symms was also willing to lend a sympathetic ear to the government of Libya, at least when Libyans evinced an interest in buying Idaho products, despite Libya's ties to Russia and support of terrorism. During 1979, Church was attacked by the New Right-financed Anyone But Church committee; and during 1980, Symms launched similar attacks himself. But Symms also had his problems as a candidate, notably his close ties with Nelson Bunker Hunt, the Texas millionaire whose speculations in silver ended in disaster; Hunt was Symms's finance chairman, and Symms supported legislation that would have benefited Hunt. Symms was also faced with rumors that he was a womanizer.

This was one of the most bitterly contested Senate races in the country, and one in which few voters were neutral or had mild feelings. Church had accumulated much support over the years for his work on water rights, his support of wilderness legislation, and his attention to constituents' needs; unlike some other Democrats, he continued to enjoy returning to his home state and even was willing to ride a bucking bronco at a rodeo. Moreover, his personal

values and his stands on such issues as abortion were consistent with the conservative moral tone that prevails in Idaho. But his record on foreign policy issues and his general support of Democratic programs proved a burden too great to bear.

The result was the second closest Senate race in the nation. Symms won by exactly 4,262 votes. Church got nearly twice as many votes as Jimmy Carter, but in Idaho that was not enough to win. Symms was helped by a strong showing in his home area, Canyon County, a prosperous agricultural area just west of Boise. Church, meanwhile, given the national results, would have lost his cherished chairmanship even if he had won the election. Symms, elected at age 42, has what must be considered one of the safer Senate seats, given Idaho's feelings on issues; he has had no previous trouble winning reelection in his congressional district. The new senator has seats on the Budget, Finance, and Public Works Committees. The last will enable him to attend to Idaho's needs; the former probably will give him little power now but has the potential of major influence on economic policy sometime in the future.

Idaho has two seats in the House. The 1st district is the western geographical half of the state, including the Panhandle, Canyon County, and most of Boise. This seat was held by Symms and by McClure before him. The new congressman, Larry Craig, was a member of the state Senate and after he beat a state attorney general in the primary he was expected to have an easy time in the general election. Actually, the result was rather close. Democrat Glenn Nichols, who walked the length of the state, attacked Craig for his sympathies with the Sagebrush Rebellion and carried the sometimes Democratic Panhandle; most of Craig's margin came from the Boise area and Canyon County. Craig is expected to be a solidly conservative member of the cohesive Republican minority in the House; he is not, however, expected to be as close to the New Right as Symms or the 2d district's congressman, George Hansen.

Hansen is one of the authentic zanies in the Congress. His district is about as solidly Republican and conservative as any in the nation; and this, more than anything else, accounts for his continued political survival. The 2d district includes Sun Valley, the Craters of the Moon National Monument, Idaho's small slice of Yellowstone National Park, and the remains of the Teton Dam, which gave way in 1976 and caused great loss of life and property. Much of this area is Mormon and, except for the old railroad town of Pocatello, is strongly Republican.

George Hansen has always been known as one of the most conservative members of Congress. He was first elected in 1964, an upset winner in a year that was more Republican in Idaho than almost anywhere else. He lost his House seat when he ran against Frank Church in 1968 and won it again by defeating a relatively moderate Republican, Orval Hansen, in the 1974 primary. George Hansen has had a number of problems in recent years. In 1975 he pleaded guilty to campaign law violations and was sentenced to two months in jail—a sentence changed, after pleading by his lawyer, to a $42,000 fine. Hansen was nearly beaten by an underfinanced Democrat in 1976 but beat the same man by a wider margin in 1978.

After American embassy personnel were taken hostage in Iran in 1979, Congressman Hansen made two separate trips to Tehran and tried to negotiate their release. Despite his longtime hawkish position, he offered to set up a congressional commission of inquiry of past American actions—a position more craven than the Carter Administration ever adopted. It is possible that Hansen's actions prolonged the hostages' captivity; some Iranians might have been led to believe that they could get better terms from a Republican of Hansen's stripe than from Carter. But no one supposes that Hansen had any evil intent; even his fellow Republicans admit he is far from the most cerebral member of the House.

The 1980 Republican sweep and the strong Republican leanings of his district were enough to give him a decisive victory in the most recent election. How long the sternly moral people of the 2d district will feel comfortable being represented by a convicted misdemeanant is unclear. Hansen seems unlikely to lose a general election, but in the last two election years he has been held to 56% and 58% by primary opponent Jim Jones, and it is entirely conceivable that sooner or later Hansen will lose a primary.

Redistricting presents no problem to Idaho. Currently the two districts split the city of Boise and the surrounding suburban area, and for 1982 the legislature will likely just shift a few Boise precincts from the 1st district to the 2d, with a negligible effect on the political leanings of either one.

Census Data   Pop. (1980 final) 943,935, up 32% in 1970s: 0.42% of U.S. total, 41st largest. Central city, 11%; suburban, 7%. Median 4-person family income, 1978, $19,042, 93% of U.S., 34th highest.

1979 Share of Federal Tax Burden $1,443,000,000; 0.32% of U.S. total, 44th largest.

1979 Share of Federal Outlays $1,837,989,000; 0.40% of U.S. total, 43d largest.

DOD	$181,917,000	48th	(0.17%)	HEW	$522,306,000	45th	(0.29%)
DOE	$287,885,000	16th	(2.45%)	ERDA	$122,628,000	8th	(4.52%)
HUD	$15,762,000	46th	(0.24%)	NASA	$29,000	48th	(0.00%)
VA	$71,831,000	44th	(0.35%)	DOT	$64,249,000	45th	(0.39%)
EPA	$29,034,000	39th	(0.55%)	DOC	$7,387,000	44th	(0.23%)
DOI	$150,124,000	9th	(2.70%)	USDA	$269,464,000	37th	(1.12%)

Economic Base   Agriculture, notably cattle, potatoes, dairy products, and wheat; food and kindred products, especially canned, cured, and frozen foods; lumber and wood products, especially general sawmills and planing mills; finance, insurance, and real estate; chemicals and allied products, especially industrial chemicals; trailer coaches and other transportation equipment.

Political Lineup   Governor, John V. Evans (D). Senators, James A. McClure (R) and Steven D. Symms (R). Representatives, 2 R; 2 in 1982. State Senate, 35 (23 R and 12 D); State House of Representatives, 71 (56 R and 15 D).

The Voters

Registration   581,006 Total. No party registration.
Employment profile 1970   White collar, 43%. Blue collar, 33%. Service, 13%. Farm, 11%.
Ethnic groups   Hispanic 1980, 4%. Am. Ind. 1980, 1%. Asian 1980, 1%. Total foreign stock 1970, 10%.

Presidential Vote

1980	Reagan (R)	290,699	(66%)
	Carter (D)	110,192	(25%)
	Anderson (I)	27,058	(6%)
1976	Ford (R)	204,151	(59%)
	Carter (D)	126,549	(37%)

1980 Democratic Presidential Primary			*1980 Republican Presidential Primary*		
Carter	31,383	(62%)	Reagan	111,868	(83%)
Kennedy	11,087	(22%)	Anderson	13,130	(10%)
Uncommitted	5,934	(12%)	Uncommitted	3,441	(3%)
One other	2,078	(4%)	Two others	6,440	(5%)

SENATORS

Sen. James A. McClure (R) Elected 1972, seat up 1984; b. Dec. 27, 1924, Payette; home, Payette; U. of Idaho, J.D. 1950.

Career Practicing atty., 1950–66; Payette Co. Atty., 1950–56; Payette City Atty., 1953–66; Idaho Senate, 1960–66; U.S. House of Reps., 1967–73.

Offices 3121 DSOB, 202-224-2752. Also 304 N. 8th St., Rm. 434, Boise 83708, 208-384-1560, and 305 Fed. Bldg., Coeur d'Alene 83814, 208-664-3086.

Committees *Appropriations* (4th). Subcommittees: Agriculture and Related Agencies; Defense; Energy and Water Development; Interior (Chairman).

Energy and Natural Resources (Chairman). *Ex officio* member of all subcommittees.

Rules and Administration (4th).

Group Ratings

	ADA	COPE	PC	LCV	CFA	RPN	NAB	NSI	NTU	ACA	ACU
1980	17	11	13	6	0	—	92	100	64	92	100
1979	0	0	15	—	0	—	—	—	64	85	94
1978	0	6	13	16	5	40	100	100	32	91	96

Key Votes

1) Draft Registn $	AGN	6) Fair Housng Cloture	AGN	11) Cut Socl Incr Defns	FOR
2) Ban $ to Nicrgua	AGN	7) Ban $ Rape Abortns	FOR	12) Income Tax Indexing	FOR
3) Dlay MX Missile	—	8) Cap on Food Stmp $	FOR	13) Lim Spdg 21% GNP	FOR
4) Nuclr Mortorium	AGN	9) New US Dep Edcatn	FOR	14) Incr Wndfll Prof Tax	AGN
5) Alaska Lands Bill	—	10) Cut OSHA Inspctns	FOR	15) Chryslr Loan Grntee	AGN

Election Results

1978 general	James A. McClure (R)	194,412	(68%)	($385,536)
	Dwight Jensen (D)	89,635	(32%)	($55,163)
1978 primary	James A. McClure (R), unopposed			
1972 general	James A. McClure (R)	161,804	(52%)	($405,788)
	William E. Davis (D)	140,913	(47%)	($204,878)

Sen. Steven D. Symms (R) Elected 1980, seat up 1986; b. Apr. 23, 1938, Nampa; home, Caldwell; U. of Idaho, B.S. 1960.

Career USMC, 1960–63; Personnel and Production Mgr., V.P., Symms Fruit Ranch, Inc., 1963–72, Mbr., Bd. of Dirs., 1967– ; U.S. House of Reps., 1972–80.

Offices 452 RSOB, 202-224-6142. Also Lewiston, 208-743-1492; Moscow, 208-882-5560; Coeur d'Alene, 208-664-5490; Twin Falls, 208-734-2515; Idaho Falls, 208-522-9779; Lewiston, 208-233-5089.

Committees *Budget* (8th).

Environment and Public Works (7th). Subcommittees: Transportation (Chairman); Nuclear Regulation; Environmental Pollution.

Finance (10th). Subcommittees: International Trade; Energy and Agricultural Taxation; Estate and Gift Taxation.

Joint Economic Committee (4th).

Group Ratings (as Member of U.S House of Representatives):

	ADA	COPE	PC	LCV	CFA	RPN	NAB	NSI	NTU	ACA	ACU
1980	0	13	10	6	14	—	100	100	72	83	87
1979	5	6	18	12	4	—	—	—	78	100	100
1978	10	5	13	12	23	82	100	100	64	96	96

Key Votes (as Member of U.S House of Representatives):

1) Draft Registn $	—	6) Fair Hsg DOJ Enfrc	—	11) Cut Socl Incr Dfns $	FOR
2) Ban $ to Nicrgua	FOR	7) Lim PAC Contrbtns	AGN	12) Hosptl Cost Controls	AGN
3) Dlay MX Missile	AGN	8) Cap on Food Stmp $	FOR	13) Gasln Ctrls & Allctns	AGN
4) Nuclr Mortorium	—	9) New US Dep Edcatn	AGN	14) Lim Wndfll Prof Tax	FOR
5) Alaska Lands Bill	AGN	10) Cut OSHA $	FOR	15) Chryslr Loan Grntee	AGN

Election Results

1980 general	Steven D. Symms (R)	218,701	(50%)	($1,780,777)
	Frank Church (D)	214,439	(49%)	($1,931,487)
1980 primary	Steven D. Symms (R)	108,813	(100%)	
1974 general	Frank Church (D)	145,140	(56%)	($300,300)
	Robert L. Smith (R)	109,072	(42%)	($127,926)

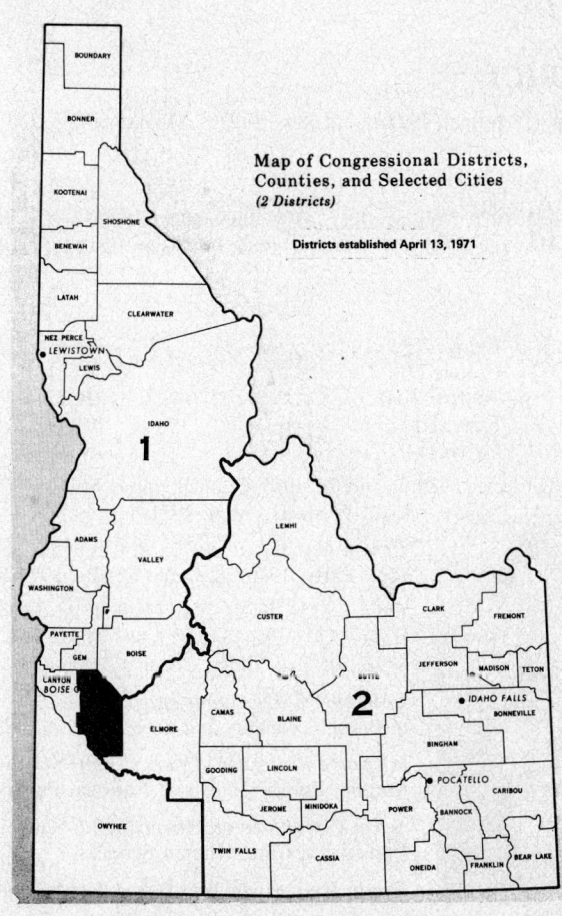

Map of Congressional Districts,
Counties, and Selected Cities
(2 Districts)

Districts established April 13, 1971

GOVERNOR

Gov. John V. Evans (D) Succeeded Gov. Cecil D. Andrus, Jan. 24, 1977, term expires Jan. 1983; b.

Jan. 18, 1925; Idaho St. U., Stanford U., B.A. 1951.

Career Army, WWII; Rancher and banker; Idaho Senate, 1953–57, 1967–73, Major. Ldr., 1957, Minor. Ldr. 1969–74; Mayor of Malad City, 1960–66.

Offices State House, Boise 83720, 208-384-2100.

Election Results

1978 gen.	John V. Evans (D)	169,540	(59%)
	Allan E. Larsen (R)	114,149	(40%)
1974 gen.	Cecil Andrus (D)	184,242	(71%)
	Jack Murphy (R)	68,731	(26%)

FIRST DISTRICT

Census Data   Pop. (1980 final) 492,688, up 38% in 1970s. Median family income, 1970, $8,466, 88% of U.S.

The Voters

Employment profile 1970   White collar, 43%. Blue collar, 34%. Service, 14%. Farm, 9%.
Ethnic groups   Hispanic 1980, 1%. Am. Ind. 1980, 1%. Asian 1980, 1%. Total foreign stock 1970, 11%.

Presidential Vote

1980	Reagan (R)	141,434	(62%)
	Carter (D)	66,316	(29%)
	Anderson (I)	16,754	(7%)
1976	Ford (R)	101,793	(58%)
	Carter (D)	68,459	(39%)

Rep. Larry Craig (R) Elected 1980; b. July 20, 1945, Council; home, Midvale; U. of Idaho, B.A. 1969, Geo. Wash. U., M.A. 1971.

Career Nat. Guard, 1970–74; Chmn., State Senate Races, Idaho Rep. Party, 1976–78; Idaho Senate, 1973–81.

Offices 515 CHOB, 202-225-6611. Also 304 N. 8th St., Rm. 134, Boise 83702, 208-334-9046; 903 D St., Lewiston 83501, 208-743-0792; 305 Fed. Bldg., Coeur d'Alene 83814, 208-667-6130.

Committees *Education and Labor* (13th). Subcommittees: Elementary, Secondary and Vocational Education; Health and Safety.

Interior and Insular Affairs (11th). Subcommittees: Mines and Mining; Public Lands and National Parks.

Select Committee on Aging (20th). Subcommittees: Health and Long-Term Care; Human Services.

Group Ratings and Key Votes: Newly Elected

Election Results

1980 general	Larry Craig (R)	116,845	(54%)	($306,910)
	Glenn Nichols (D)	100,697	(46%)	($92,124)
1980 primary	Larry Craig (R)	29,525	(53%)	
	Wayne Kidwell (R)	26,454	(47%)	
1978 general	Steven D. Symms (R)	86,680	(60%)	($278,503)
	Roy Truby (D)	57,972	(40%)	($112,361)

SECOND DISTRICT

Census Data   Pop. (1980 final) 451,247, up 27% in 1970s. Median family income, 1970, $8,280, 86% of U.S.

The Voters

Employment profile 1970   White collar, 43%. Blue collar, 31%. Service, 12%. Farm, 14%.
Ethnic groups   Hispanic 1980, 4%. Am. Ind. 1980, 1%. Asian 1980, 1%. Total foreign stock 1970, 10%.

Presidential Vote

1980	Reagan (R)	149,265	(72%)
	Carter (D)	43,876	(21%)
	Anderson (I)	10,304	(5%)
1976	Ford (R)	102,358	(62%)
	Carter (D)	58,090	(35%)

Rep. George Hansen (R) Elected 1974; b. Sept. 14, 1930, Tetonia; home, Pocatello; Ricks Col., B.A. 1956, Idaho St. U.

Career Air Force; High school teacher; Insurance and retailing business; Mayor of Alameda, 1961–62; Pocatello City Commissioner, 1962–65; U.S. House of Reps., 1965–69; Rep. nominee for U.S. Senate, 1968; Dpty. Under Secy., U.S. Dept. of Agriculture, 1969–71.

Offices 1125 LHOB, 202-225-5531. Also 211 Fed. Bldg., Box 740, Idaho Falls 83401, 208-523-5341.

Committees *Agriculture* (9th). Subcommittees: Domestic Marketing, Consumer Relations and Nutrition; Livestock, Dairy and Poultry.

Banking, Finance and Urban Affairs (4th). Subcommittees: Domestic Monetary Policy; Financial Institutions Supervision, Regulation and Insurance; International Trade, Investment and Monetary Policy.

Group Ratings

	ADA	COPE	PC	LCV	CFA	RPN	NAB	NSI	NTU	ACA	ACU
1980	6	18	7	5	14	—	100	100	73	95	88
1979	0	5	15	5	7	—	—	—	77	95	93
1978	5	6	15	19	23	50	100	100	69	96	95

Key Votes

1) Draft Registn $	AGN	6) Fair Hsg DOJ Enfrc AGN	11) Cut Socl Incr Dfns $ FOR
2) Ban $ to Nicrgua	—	7) Lim PAC Contrbtns AGN	12) Hosptl Cost Controls AGN

3) Dlay MX Missile AGN	8) Cap on Food Stmp $ —	13) Gasln Ctrls & Allctns AGN
4) Nuclr Mortorium AGN	9) New US Dep Edcatn AGN	14) Lim Wndfll Prof Tax FOR
5) Alaska Lands Bill AGN	10) Cut OSHA $ FOR	15) Chryslr Loan Grntee AGN

Election Results

1980 general	George Hansen (R)	116,196	(59%)	($222,447)
	Diane Bilyeu (D)	81,364	(41%)	($32,355)
1980 primary	George Hansen (R)	41,478	(58%)	
	Jim Jones (R)	30,729	(42%)	
1978 general	George Hansen (R)	80,591	(57%)	($282,203)
	Stan Kress (D)	60,040	(43%)	($150,956)

ILLINOIS

Illinois is one of those states whose growth and prosperity are the result almost entirely of the strength and growth of its private economy. It likes to boast of Abraham Lincoln, the most important politician Illinois has produced; but Lincoln's greatest contribution to Illinois (dwarfed, to be sure, by his contributions to the nation) was his work as a railroad lawyer, helping the railroads to connect the East and West. When white men first came to Illinois, they saw a vast, treeless prairie, an incredibly rich land; the topsoil can still be measured in feet, not inches. This vacant, flat land was also in an important geographic position—the closest connection between the Mississippi River Valley and the Great Lakes, directly aligned with the most level route from the American West to the East Coast and the outer world. It was the natural focus for the nation's rail network, and the natural place also for processing the agricultural products of the Midwest for use in the East and in Europe. Chicago was a frontier village in the 1830s; by 1890 it was a city of millions, one of the great metropolitan areas of the world, with a huge immigrant population drawn from all quarters of the world, and cultural institutions of the first magnitude. Downstate Illinois, in which Lincoln as a young man had seen an Indian uprising, was by the same time well established as one of the richest agricultural regions in the world.

This bustling and muscular Illinois has never been hospitable to political idealists. Politics has always been a business here; politicians have had the unglamorous job of managing the governmental institutions and, for the most part, seeing that they stay out of the way of commerce and industry. Chicago has had a political machine of note since before the turn of the century, a machine whose function has been to modulate the demands of the city's many ethnic groups and to maintain municipal services in the city. Businesses have always considered a certain amount of inefficiency and graft as a reasonable price to pay for these services, particularly since it has usually been possible to arrange for low property tax assessments. Of course most of Chicago's business leaders have been Republicans and boosters of the free enterprise system, but most of them also supported the late Mayor Richard J. Daley, because he did his job efficiently and because he built great structures, from McCormick Place to O'Hare Airport, which helped Chicago retain its status as a national center of commerce and world class city.

The Democrats are not the only party to practice machine politics here; the Republicans, while not as picturesque, are hardheaded professionals with little time for sentimentality or idealism. Politics is a business in Illinois, and while it is by no means the most important business in the state it is still pursued seriously and with the ends clearly in mind. *Don't Back No Losers* is the title of a recent book on Illinois politics.

The profit motive is an integral part of Illinois politics, which means a certain amount of corruption. There was a secretary of state who died leaving $800,000 in cash in shoeboxes in his dingy Springfield motel room; one of the state's recent governors, the late Otto Kerner, ended up in jail. For years there were stories of vote-stealing, and many Republicans are still convinced that Daley stole the state's electoral votes for John Kennedy in 1960. But vote fraud was pretty well stamped out by the *Chicago Tribune* and the Better Government Association in 1972, and even the counts in Chicago's West Side wards can now be considered accurate. There are still lots of ward and precinct leaders in Chicago—and in some down-state areas as well—that depend on public patronage jobs for their livings. But the fact is that these plums are no longer so attractive when salaries in private business have risen faster and civil service protections insulate many public employees from political retaliation. The Chicago Democratic machine is indeed eroding, although it has not vanished yet, and the main reason is that it simply cannot make it worthwhile for people in hardheaded Illinois to do all the hard work that is required of a precinct leader. There are still, however, ample rewards for those who win contracts to provide insurance or other professional services to government agencies—as some of Richard Daley's sons have.

The people who run Illinois's politics are realistic enough to understand that, in most circumstances, voters do not want to elect people of their backgrounds and characteristics. Accordingly, for the top statewide positions, both parties have usually nominated what are called blue ribbon candidates, people of impeccable backgrounds who never would have come up the usual routes of Illinois politics. Blue ribbon slates have given the nation such leaders as Adlai Stevenson and Paul Douglas in 1948, Charles Percy in 1966, Adlai Stevenson III in 1970, and James Thompson in 1976. Illinois has also produced enough good officeholders that its congressional delegation in recent years was probably the best and most powerful of any major state's, and included such members as John Anderson (who gave up his seat and ran for president in 1980), Dan Rostenkowski (now chairman of Ways and Means), Abner Mikva (appointed a federal judge by President Carter), Philip Crane (back after his losing presidential candidacy), Robert Michel (the new Republican leader in the House), Mel Price (chairman of Armed Services), and Paul Simon (one of the most thoughtful liberals in the House).

In national politics Illinois is a state that comes very close to the national average. It has backed only one losing presidential candidate since 1916 (Gerald Ford in 1976) and in 1980 came within 1% of the national results. Over the years Illinois has split fairly evenly between Republicans and Democrats. Republicans have the edge today; they have the governorship, a senior U.S. senator, a healthy majority (14–10) in the state's House delegation, and they have carried the state in the four most recent presidential elections. But they do not have complete control. The Republicans have a five-vote margin in the state House, but Democrats have a one-vote edge in the state Senate—which means that Republicans do not have complete control of redistricting. The new U.S senator elected in 1980, Alan Dixon, is a Democrat, and he won by a big margin. Democrats regained the post of Cook County state's attorney in 1980 (in the person of state Senator Richard M. Daley), and in a state where leading politicians have been indicted frequently, the power to prosecute is an important one. Republicans also had the embarrassment of seeing their attorney general, William Scott, convicted in 1980 of filing a false income tax return, even as he was seeking the party's nomination for U.S. senator.

Illinois's most nationally prominent politician today is Senator Charles Percy. Yet he came to his current position, chairman of the Senate Foreign Relations Committee, unexpectedly, and at a time when his career seemed to be in some eclipse. Percy first gained notice in politics as the boy wonder president of Bell & Howell who was head of the platform-drafting committee at the 1960 Republican National Convention; he was tabbed as a moderate Republican then because he cooperated with the agreement on the platform hammered out by Richard Nixon and Nelson Rockefeller. Percy went on to run for governor in 1964 and was defeated by the Democratic incumbent, a defeat some attributed to the Lyndon Johnson landslide but which more likely resulted from the fact that Percy had shown little interest in state politics before that year. Indeed, national journalists were already writing him up as a candidate for the presidency — although he wouldn't even have won the Republican nomination if the favorite, a conservative state officeholder, had not died of a heart attack before the primary. In 1966 Percy, still touted as a presidential candidate although he had never held elective office, ran for senator against Paul Douglas. He defeated the veteran liberal, who had been Percy's economics teacher at the University of Chicago, by an impressive margin and, at age 47, became hailed as a youthful hope for the Republicans.

But his presidential ambitions never materialized. Although he distingushed himself by offering an original plan for ending the Vietnam war, he was not a factor in the race for the 1968 Republican nomination. In 1972, like almost all other Republicans, he supported Nixon. As the Watergate scandal began to break, he geared up for 1976 and hired the highly competent Bailey Deardourff organization. But the elevation of Gerald Ford to the presidency ended Percy's hopes. He had been reelected easily to the Senate in 1972 against an underfinanced challenge from Congressman Roman Pucinski. But in 1978 he was nearly defeated by attorney Alex Seith, who criticized Percy for not supporting a more aggressive foreign policy and for not supporting income tax indexing. Percy had to scramble and seized on a negative ad in which Seith overstated his case; he also had great help from the Chicago media, which disliked Seith. The result was an unimpressive margin and a revelation that Percy was indeed vulnerable in Illinois.

So it appeared that the onetime boy wonder, now past 60, would serve out his term as a somewhat senior member of the minority party and either retire or face stiff competition. Instead, the 1980 elections brought him good fortune. Senator Jacob Javits of New York was defeated in the Republican primary, which made Percy the most senior Republican on the Foreign Relations Committee. And the Republicans won control of the Senate, which made Percy chairman. As such, he is expected by his Republican colleagues to work in tandem with a new administration for whose hard-line policies he has previously shown little enthusiasm. In his first days as chairman, Percy did take the trouble to document his previous support of tough foreign policy measures. But the fact is that on issues ranging from the Vietnam war to arms expenditures, he is one of those Republicans whose votes liberal Democrats had a chance of winning. He is also out of step with the Reagan Administration on another important issue: the Middle East. He has been sympathetic to the Palestine Liberation Organization's claims and is regarded as a foe of aid to Israel. Even before the Reagan Administration took office, Percy embarrassed it when the *New York Times* reported he told Andrei Gromyko that he favored creation of a demilitarized Palestinian state to permit Yasir Arafat to realize his wish to be a chief of state before he dies.

It is not clear in what direction Percy will lead Foreign Relations. He will surely work to confirm Reagan appointees, as he did Secretary of State Alexander Haig (although he agreed with Democrats to subpoena the index of Watergate tapes). The Republicans just behind him in seniority — Baker, Helms, Hayakawa, Lugar — are all likely to be more in line with Reagan policies than Percy, and they are likely to exert pressure on Percy to keep him in that direction. The Democratic minority, split between old opponents of the Vietnam war and those more sympathetic to the military, is unlikely to bring much pressure to bear. His staff choices may turn out to be critical, and initial indications are that foreign policy professionals will predominate.

Illinois's other senator, Alan Dixon, is that rarest of species, a 1980 Democratic freshman. His seat was held for 10 years by Adlai Stevenson III, who could probably have won another term. But Stevenson was tired of the Senate; he found himself increasingly differing from other Democrats in pursuing lines of attack on issues, and for months as Ethics Committee chairman, he had to preside over hearings on Herman Talmadge and other allegedly erring colleagues. When he announced his retirement from the Senate, Stevenson said he might be interested in running for president; no one took him up on it.

Dixon's success was reasonably well assured in Illinois's March primary — the earliest in the nation. As secretary of state and treasurer before that, Dixon had a name that was well known and a reputation for honesty and efficiency. He beat 1978 Senate candidate Seith easily in the primary; the same day, the Republicans nominated Lieutenant Governor Dave O'Neal (curiously, he and Dixon are from the same small town). Probably their strongest candidate would have been Attorney General Scott, but just as the primary was held Scott was on trial (he was ultimately convicted). A pharmacist and former downstate sheriff, O'Neal had a reputation as a conservative and as one who shoots from the hip; he never really overcame it. Dixon won by a comfortable margin. He carried not only Chicago but actually ran ahead in the usually Republican suburbs (suburban Cook County and the "collar counties," the five counties lying just outside of Cook) and in downstate Illinois as well.

Perhaps his lack of a record on national issues helped Dixon in a year when Democratic issue stands were not a political asset. He enters the Senate with 30 years of experience in state office and none in Washington, and if he is not likely to make a national name quickly he will probably be the Illinois senator who will look after the state's interests and problems more closely. He has seats on committees that oversee farming and housing — something for downstate, something for Chicago.

Illinois's governor, James Thompson, is a man of considerable personal force and attraction. He is an Illinois original, a young lawyer who made his career as a prosecutor. During the Nixon years he made an outstanding record as U.S. attorney in Chicago. He jailed some of Illinois's most important politicians (not all of them Democrats, by the way) and his conviction rate showed that he did not bring cases without solid evidence. He was elected governor in 1976 over an honest, jowly Chicago Democrat, and was easily reelected in 1978 (the state switched its gubernatorial elections to the off year) against a much younger and more articulate opponent. As governor, Thompson has been controversial on occasion, and he does not have firm control of the legislature — one house is Democratic, and many Republicans have their own base. Nevertheless, he seems firmly in command and has not made any major mistakes in four years.

Thompson appears to be in good shape for reelection in 1982, even if a name Democrat—e.g., Adlai Stevenson, who has returned to Chicago—should run. He has also been mentioned on numerous occasions for national office. But he has always had the reputation of being a moderate, which is no advantage in Republican circles these days, and he did not play an adroit role in the manuevering to the 1980 nomination. With a Republican president and numerous Republicans making national names for themselves, Thompson is unlikely to be a serious contender for national office in the near future. Still, he is young (46 in 1982), and who can know what is in the future?

The other major political figure in Illinois these days is Chicago's Mayor Jane Byrne. Her election in 1979 was considered somewhat a fluke: she defeated the machine-backed incumbent, Michael Bilandic, primarily because Bilandic did not do a good enough job of clearing snow from Chicago's streets during an especially harsh winter. In office, Byrne has been nothing if not controversial. She hinted in October 1979 that she would support President Carter for reelection and then the next month endorsed Edward Kennedy; she was then embarrassed when Kennedy did very poorly in Illinois's primary in March 1980. She has carried on a feud with the *Chicago Tribune* and even had her press secretary (who is also her husband) expel the *Trib*'s reporters from City Hall. Byrne does not have the iron control over the Chicago Democratic machine that Mayor Daley did; but then no one else could. And while she would like to assume the late mayor's mantle, she opposed his son, Richard M. Daley, in his successful race for Cook County state's attorney (prosecutor) in the 1980 primary. All this said, it should also be pointed out that Mayor Byrne is scrupulously honest, brainy, and that she has had her political successes as well; and no one would want to bet against her without some favorable odds when her term expires in 1983.

Illinois will have some serious redistricting to do before the 1982 elections. The state lost two seats in the 1980 census, and in all likelihood one of the losses will come in the city and one downstate. But nothing is certain. Neither party has control, although the Republicans are in stronger shape. They have the governor's veto and a firm majority in the state House. The Democrats have only a one-vote margin in the state Senate—a margin that disappeared momentarily when state Senator Harold Washington, elected to Congress, refused either to resign his seat or to fill it until Chicago Democrats agreed to select a successor to his liking. The Republicans in comic opera fashion organized the Senate for a while, although their gesture was futile: constitutionally, 30 votes are required to pass a bill and they have only 29. All that was soon resolved, and the Democrats returned to technical control. But it is not out of the question that they could lose one or more votes—and therefore their leverage—on redistricting matters. One possibility is that black Democrats will make a deal with Republicans, giving the latter a free hand in most parts of the state in return for the creation of three safely black districts. Another possibility is that Democrats will bargain away seats of older incumbents likely to retire—John Fary in Chicago and Mel Price downstate—and thus incumbents of both parties would be protected.

Census Data   Pop. (1980 final) 11,418,461, up 3% in 1970s: 5.04% of U.S. total, 5th largest. Central city, 33%; suburban, 48%. Median 4-person family income, 1978, $20,081, 108% of U.S., 8th highest.

1979 Share of Federal Tax Burden $27,274,000,000; 6.05% of U.S. total, 3d largest.

1979 Share of Federal Outlays $20,785,002,000; 4.49% of U.S. total, 5th largest.

DOD	$1,907,552,000	18th	(1.80%)	HEW	$8,764,306,000	5th	(4.90%)
DOE	$410,585,000	10th	(3.49%)	ERDA	$174,841,000	5th	(6.45%)
HUD	$354,369,000	4th	(5.38%)	NASA	$12,166,000	23d	(0.26%)

VA	$771,383,000	7th	(3.72%)	DOT	$982,347,000	4th	(5.95%)
EPA	$195,092,000	8th	(3.67%)	DOC	$21,273,000	25th	(0.67%)
DOI	$35,753,000	35th	(0.64%)	USDA	$839,441,000	6th	(3.49%)

Economic Base Finance, insurance, and real estate; machinery, especially construction and related machinery; electrical equipment and supplies, especially communication equipment; fabricated metal products; agriculture, notably corn, soybeans, hogs, and cattle; food and kindred products; printing and publishing, especially commercial printing; primary metal industries, especially blast furnaces and basic steel products.

Political Lineup Governor, James R. Thompson (R). Senators, Charles H. Percy (R) and Alan J. Dixon (D). Representatives, 24 (14 R and 10 D); 22 in 1982. State Senate, 59 (30 D and 29 R); State House of Representatives, 177 (91 R and 86 D).

The Voters

Registration 6,230,332 Total. No party registration.
Employment profile 1970 White collar, 49%. Blue collar, 37%. Service, 12%. Farm, 2%.
Ethnic groups Black 1980, 15%. Hispanic 1980, 6%. Asian 1980, 1%. Total foreign stock 1970, 20%. Germany, Poland, 3% each; Italy, 2%; UK, 1%.

Presidential Vote

1980	Reagan (R)	2,358,094	(50%)
	Carter (D)	1,981,413	(42%)
	Anderson (I)	346,754	(7%)
1976	Ford (R)	2,384,269	(50%)
	Carter (D)	2,271,295	(48%)

1980 Democratic Presidential Primary			*1980 Republican Presidential Primary*		
Carter	780,787	(65%)	Reagan	547,355	(48%)
Kennedy	359,875	(30%)	Anderson	415,193	(37%)
Two others & write-ins	60,405	(5%)	Bush	124,057	(11%)
			Five others & write-ins	43,476	(4%)

SENATORS

Sen. Charles H. Percy (R) Elected 1966, seat up 1984; b. Sept. 27, 1919, Pensacola, Fla.; home, Wilmette; U. of Chi., B.A. 1941.

Career Navy, WWII; Corp. Exec., Bell & Howell Co., Pres. and Chf. Exec. Officer, 1949–61, Bd, Chmn., 1961–66; Rep. of Pres. Eisenhower to pres. inaugurations in Peru and Bolivia, 1956; Rep. nominee for Gov., 1964.

Offices 4321 DSOB, 202-224-2152. Also 230 S. Dearborn St., Rm. 3859, Chicago 60604, 312-353-4952, and 117 P.O. Bldg., Springfield 62701, 217-515-4442.

Committees *Foreign Relations* (Chairman). Subcommittees: International Economic Policy; Arms Control, Oceans and International Operations and Environment.

Governmental Affairs (2d). Subcommittees: Permanent Subcommittee on Investigations; Federal Expenditures, Research, and Rules; Energy, Nuclear Proliferation, and Government Processes (Chairman).

Special Committee on Aging (3d).

Group Ratings

	ADA	COPE	PC	LCV	CFA	RPN	NAB	NSI	NTU	ACA	ACU
1980	39	41	40	77	40	—	50	50	48	64	40
1979	47	47	55	—	48	—	—	—	26	19	28
1978	50	47	43	62	35	90	57	11	13	18	20

Key Votes

1) Draft Registn $	FOR	6) Fair Housng Cloture	FOR	11) Cut Socl Incr Defns	FOR
2) Ban $ to Nicrgua	FOR	7) Ban $ Rape Abortns	AGN	12) Income Tax Indexing	FOR
3) Dlay MX Missile	AGN	8) Cap on Food Stmp $	AGN	13) Lim Spdg 21% GNP	FOR
4) Nuclr Mortorium	FOR	9) New US Dep Edcatn	FOR	14) Incr Wndfll Prof Tax	FOR
5) Alaska Lands Bill	FOR	10) Cut OSHA Inspctns	FOR	15) Chryslr Loan Grntee	FOR

Election Results

1978 general	Charles H. Percy (R)	1,698,711	(53%)	($2,163,555)
	Alex R. Seith (D)	1,448,187	(46%)	($1,371,478)
1978 primary	Charles H. Percy (R)	401,409	(84%)	
	One other (R)	74,739	(16%)	
1972 general	Charles H. Percy (R)	2,867,078	(62%)	($1,408,822)
	Roman Pucinski (D)	1,721,031	(37%)	($335,482)

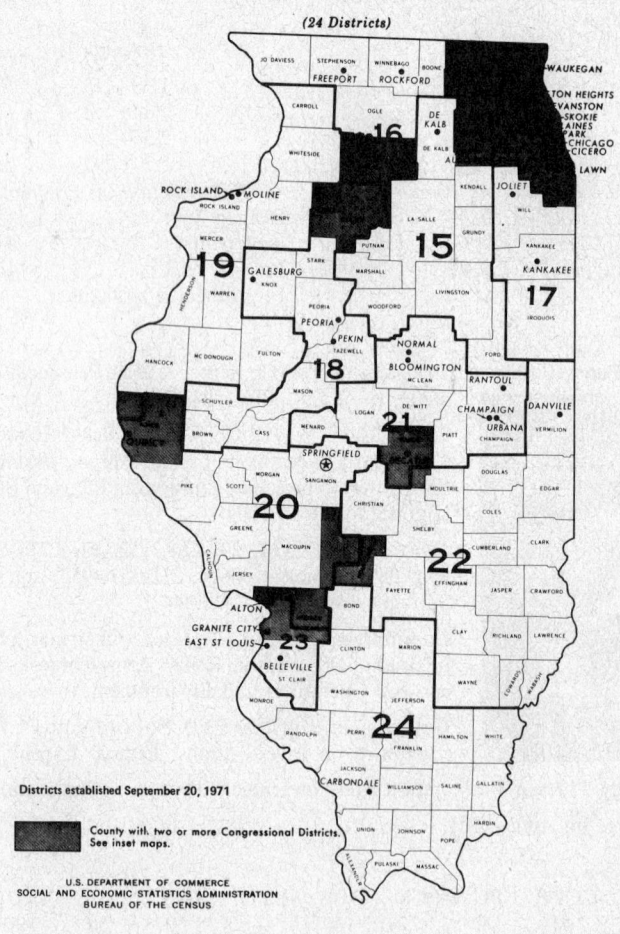

(24 Districts)

Districts established September 20, 1971

County with two or more Congressional Districts.
See inset maps.

U.S. DEPARTMENT OF COMMERCE
SOCIAL AND ECONOMIC STATISTICS ADMINISTRATION
BUREAU OF THE CENSUS

Sen. Alan J. Dixon (D) Elected 1980, seat up 1986; b. July 7, 1927, Belleville; home, Belleville; U. of Ill., B.S. 1949, Wash. U., St. Louis, LL.B. 1949.

Career Belleville Police Magistrate, 1948; Ill. House of Reps, 1951–63; Ill. Senate, 1963–71; Treas. of Ill, 1971–77; Sec. of State of Ill., 1977–81.

Offices 4203 DSOB, 202-224-2854. Also 230 S. Dearborn St., Chicago 60604, 312-353-5420; 108 P.O. Bldg., Springfield 62701, 217-492-4126; 227 Fed. Bldg., Mt. Vernon 62864, 618-244-6703.

Committees *Agriculture, Nutrition, and Forestry* (7th). Subcommittees: Agricultural Production, Marketing, and Stabilization of Prices; Foreign Agricultural Policy; Nutrition.

Banking, Housing, and Urban Affairs (7th). Subcommittees: Financial Institutions; Rural Housing and Development; Consumer Affairs.

Select Committee on Small Business (8th). Subcommittee: Urban and Rural Economic Development.

Group Ratings and Key Votes: Newly Elected

Election Results

1980 general	Alan J. Dixon (D)	2,565,302	(56%)	($2,346,897)
	David C. O'Neal (R)	1,946,296	(42%)	($1,293,991)
1980 primary	Alan J. Dixon (D)	671,746	(67%)	
	Alex Seith (D)	190,339	(19%)	($146,402)
	Three others & write-ins (D)	142,289	(14%)	
1974 general	Adlai E. Stevenson III (D)	1,811,496	(62%)	($757,329)
	George M. Burditt (R)	1,084,884	(37%)	($488,556)

GOVERNOR

Gov. James R. Thompson (R) Elected 1976, term expires Jan. 1983; b. May 8, 1936, Chicago; U. of Ill., Chicago, Washington U., St. Louis, Northwestern U., J.D. 1959.

Career Prosecutor for Cook Co. State's Atty., 1959–64; Assoc. Prof., Northwestern Law Sch., 1964–69; Chief, Dept. of Law Enforcement and Pub. Protection, Ill. Atty. Gen's. Ofc., 1969; 1st Asst. U.S. Atty., No. Dist. of Ill., 1970; U.S. Atty., 1971–75.

Offices State House, Springfield 62706, 217-782-6830.

Election Results

1978 gen.	James R. Thompson (R) . . .	1,859,684	(59%)
	Michael J. Bakalis (D)	1,263,134	(40%)
1976 gen.	James R. Thompson (R) . . .	3,000,395	(65%)
	Michael J. Howlett (D)	1,610,258	(35%)

FIRST DISTRICT

The most stable and longest-lived urban black community in the United States can be found on Chicago's South Side. Here, as long ago as the turn of the century, was a substantial community of blacks in the vicinity of 63d and Cottage Grove. There have always been poor people in the South Side ghetto, but there have been middle-class and prosperous blacks as well; this is the home of the nation's first black bourgeoisie. The South Side has been a center of black culture since before the jazz age, and there have always been more blacks here — at least half a million today — than in New York's Harlem.

The South Side has also furnished political leadership for blacks. Illinois's 1st congressional district, almost entirely black today, includes most of the South Side black community. It first elected a black congressman, Oscar DePriest, in 1928. DePriest was a Republican, for in those days black voters were still faithful to the party of Lincoln; they even stayed with Herbert Hoover in the depths of the Depression in 1932. But the New Deal and the racial liberalism of Eleanor Roosevelt attracted blacks to the Democratic Party in the 1930s. DePriest was beaten by a black Democrat, Arthur Mitchell, in 1934; Mitchell was succeeded in 1942 by another black Democrat, William Dawson.

Just about forgotten today, Dawson was the first American black since Reconstruction to be a major power in electoral politics. He was the undisputed political boss of the South Side, and he was consulted regularly by Mayor Daley and the bosses before him, just like ward leaders of other ethnic groups. Dawson for his part was not a boat-rocker. He endorsed civil rights measures, but in contrast to such leaders as A. Philip Randolph — who pressed hard for fair employment measures in the midst of World War II — Dawson was firmly committed to working within the conventional political system. His goals were to provide patronage jobs, Democratic nominations, and public services to the South Side's blacks, and to make sure that everyone knew they came courtesy of William Dawson. Generally he delivered. Dawson continued to serve in Congress until long after his health no longer permitted him to be effective. He finally retired in 1970 and died late in the year at age 84.

Dawson's black Democratic machine leaders delivered votes like almost no one else in Chicago. The turnout in the 1st district was — and is — always high. Through the early 1970s it was always promachine in the primary and nearly unanimously Democratic in the general. Dawson's black constituency was single-handedly responsible for keeping Mayor Daley in office in 1963, when he was opposed by a Polish Republican.

But all this changed when Dawson stepped down. His successor, Ralph Metcalfe, a one-time Olympic sprinter, was elected as a machine man, but he broke with Daley in 1972 when two prominent black dentists were beaten by Chicago police and the mayor refused to come to the congressman's office and discuss the matter. The South Side remains one of the two or three most Democratic districts in the nation in presidential elections, but in 1972 and 1978 there was massive ticket-splitting in favor of Republican Senator Charles Percy, and the area also backed Republicans for Cook County state's attorney. Metcalfe won reelection easily over machine-backed primary opponents. The machine did win back the seat in 1978, when Metcalfe died in October and Bennett Stewart was chosen by party committeemen; nevertheless, an insurgent Democrat nominated by the Republicans won 41% of the vote. Stewart in turn was soundly beaten in the 1980 primary by Harold Washington, a nonmachine politician who had run for mayor in 1979. Washington had nearly half the vote in a four-candidate field; Stewart got only 17%.

Chicago is a city where some consider it a demotion to move from the Board of Aldermen to the U.S. House of Representatives. At the time of his election, Washington was serving in Springfield in the state Senate; he kicked up a fuss for a while by refusing to resign that position until he was satisfied with the choice to succeed him. He may very well retain ambitions to be mayor. If so, he is likely to direct most of his attention over the next few years to city politics to prepare for the primary that comes in early 1983. This will cause some problems, since he is assigned to no less than three committees in the House—Education and Labor, Government Operations, Judiciary—and some key subcommittees, including the one that has kept bottled up proposed constitutional amendments such as abortion. Presumably Washington will leave his proxy with like-minded members.

Census Data   Pop. (1980 final) 369,901, down 20% in 1970s. Median family income, 1970, $8,373, 87% of U.S.

The Voters

Employment profile 1970   White collar, 46%. Blue collar, 35%. Service, 19%. Farm, -%.
Ethnic groups   Black 1980, 91%. Hispanic 1980, 1%. Asian 1980, 1%. Total foreign stock 1970, 5%.

Presidential Vote

1980	Reagan (R)	6,633	(5%)
	Carter (D)	128,426	(91%)
	Anderson (I)	3,092	(2%)
1976	Ford (R)	13,817	(10%)
	Carter (D)	130,882	(90%)

Rep. Harold Washington (D) Elected 1980; b. Apr. 15, 1922, Chicago; home, Chicago; Roosevelt U., B.A. 1949, Northwestern U., J.D. 1952.

Career Air Force Engineers, WWII; Lecturer in urban politics, Roosevelt U., 1975–77 ; Practicing atty., 1952–80; Asst. City Prosecutor, Chicago, 1954–58; Ill. House of Reps., 1965–76; Ill. Senate, 1977–80; Founder, Ill. Legislature Black Caucus.

Offices 1610 LHOB, 202-225-4372. Also 7801 S. Cottage Grove, Chicago 60619, 312-783-6800.

Committees *Education and Labor* (19th). Subcommittees: Elementary, Secondary and Vocational Education; Employment Opportunities; Health and Safety.

Government Operations (22d). Subcommittee: Manpower and Housing.

Judiciary (15th). Subcommittee: Civil and Constitutional Rights.

Group Ratings and Key Votes: Newly Elected

Election Results

1980 general	Harold Washington (D)	119,562	(95%)	($72,716)
	George Williams (R)	5,660	(5%)	($0)
1980 primary	Harold Washington (D)	30,522	(48%)	
	Ralph H. Metcalfe, Jr. (D)	12,356	(19%)	($782)
	Bennett M. Stewart (D)	10,810	(17%)	($52,061)
	John H. Stroger, Jr. (D)	10,284	(16%)	
1978 general	Bennett M. Stewart (D)	47,581	(59%)	($18,471)
	A. A. Rayner (R)	33,540	(41%)	($13,622)

SECOND DISTRICT

On the far South Side of Chicago, where the Calumet River has been deepened to accommodate the huge freighters of the Great Lakes, are the city's giant steel mills, ones that rival those in nearby Gary in size and stark grandeur. This part of Chicago is the heart of the city's heavy industry and has been ever since the Industrial Revolution came to the Midwest. The same area was the site of the Pullman strike of 1893, during which the laissez-faire President Cleveland sent in federal troops to uphold the rights of private capital. To the east, along the lakefront, are the large apartments and, behind them, the comfortable houses in what used to be a Jewish neighborhood; to the north is the South Side black ghetto. West of the steel mills are middle-class neighborhoods, most of them inhabited by members of the various ethnic groups that have for so long supplied most of the labor to keep the steel mills going.

Both parts of the 2d district have one thing in common: they have been the site of Chicago's—and the nation's—most massive neighborhood racial change in recent years. In 1960 less than 20% of the population within the current bounds of the 2d was black; in 1970 it was 40%, and by 1980 blacks formed 77% of the district's population. Blockbusting tactics have been a way of life here, and the first For Sale sign on a white block can often trigger a spasm of panic selling. Naturally the change has had an effect on the area's politics. Typically, just before blacks start moving into a neighborhood the whites become more Republican, or spawn a local conservative movement. Then blacks move in, and the area's Democratic percentages rise precipitously.

This is what happened to the politics of the 2d district as a whole. This area has traditionally elected Democrats to Congress, but in 1966, when black movement into the area was starting, it nearly elected a Republican. Then Democratic percentages began rising abruptly, as more blacks moved in, from 56% in the 1968 presidential election to 66% in 1972 and 83% in 1976. In 1970 the district elected Morgan Murphy, a well-connected adherent of the Daley machine, to Congress; his percentages rose to sky-high figures in the 1970s. He also rose in seniority, to the number three position on the Rules Committee. But in 1980 he decided to retire at age 48: he had suffered serious illnesses, he had been embarrassed by the fact that his electronic card had been used and his vote cast in the House's voting machine when he was in Chicago, and he was unwilling to live within the House's self-imposed limits on outside income.

The new congressman, Gus Savage, is a man Murphy beat in the 1970 primary. Savage is black, a publisher of community newspapers, and a decade ago he was regarded as an insurgent in Chicago. He is still not a follower of the Democratic machine but is considered less of a rebel than he used to be; or perhaps Chicago, with the fragmenting of the Daley machine, now has a politics more tolerant of diversity. In any case, Savage won his primary handily and white candidates do not seem to be a major factor in the politics of the district as currently defined.

That definition, however, will change with redistricting. Chicago currently has three black-majority districts, all represented by blacks; but each of them has lost population in the 1970s, and technically they have only enough people now for 2½ districts. Redistricters may try to maintain the current level of black representation, which means that Savage would definitely have more white constituents and conceivably a tougher race; or they could decide that the seat Chicago has to lose will be one of the black districts, in which case Savage might find himself in the same district with Harold Washington or Cardiss Collins. Few states in recent years have acted to force a reduction in black representation, but in Chicago the ethnic constituencies of each of the city's other congressmen all have plenty of clout, and it is not clear what is going to happen.

Census Data   Pop. (1980 final) 465,535, no change in 1970s. Median family income, 1970, $11,147, 116% of U.S.

The Voters

Employment profile 1970   White collar, 48%. Blue collar, 39%. Service, 13%. Farm, –%.
Ethnic groups   Black 1980, 77%. Hispanic 1980, 8%. Total foreign stock 1970, 25%. Poland, 4%; Italy, Ireland, Germany, 2% each; Yugoslavia, Sweden, 1% each.

Presidential Vote

1980	Reagan (R)	20,946	(12%)
	Carter (D)	145,205	(84%)
	Anderson (I)	3,612	(2%)
1976	Ford (R)	28,498	(17%)
	Carter (D)	137,384	(83%)

Rep. Gus Savage (D) Elected 1980; b. Oct. 30, 1925, Detroit, Mich.; home, Chicago; Roosevelt U., B.A. 1951, Kent Col. of Law, 1952–53.

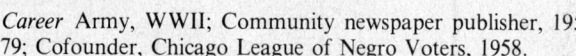

Career Army, WWII; Community newspaper publisher, 1954–79; Cofounder, Chicago League of Negro Voters, 1958.

Offices 1233 LHOB, 202-225-0773. Also 1743 E. 87th St., Chicago 60617, 312-374-5000.

Committees *Post Office and Civil Service* (16th).

Public Works and Transportation (23d). Subcommittees: Economic Development; Investigations and Oversight; Surface Transportation.

Small Business (21st). Subcommittees: SBA and SBIC Authority, Minority Enterprise and General Small Business Problems; Tax, Access to Equity Capital and Business Opportunities.

Group Ratings and Key Votes: Newly Elected

Election Results

1980 general	Gus Savage (D)	129,771	(88%)	($80,213)
	Marsha A. Harris (R)	17,428	(12%)	($11,033)
1980 primary	Gus Savage (D)	28,359	(45%)	
	Reginald V. Brown, Jr. (D)	21,243	(33%)	($50,455)
	Two others (D)	13,993	(22%)	
1978 general	Morgan F. Murphy (D)	80,906	(86%)	($43,328)
	James Wognum (R)	11,104	(12%)	

THIRD DISTRICT

The 3d congressional district of Illinois consists of the close-in southwest suburbs of Chicago plus about two wards worth of the city itself. If one had to generalize about the area, one might say that this is the place where the whites from the older ethnic neighborhoods of South Side Chicago have gone, either in flight as blacks have moved into their old neighborhoods, or simply as they grow up and have to move someplace to start their own families. There are small black ghettos here in the towns of Markham and Harvey, and in the 1970s blacks moved in small numbers to almost all parts of the district, but the overall ethnic tone is Irish–American, the group that always dominated southwest Chicago until the blacks moved in. But not everyone is Irish: the area is an ethnic olio with Polish–, Italian–, Lithuanian–, German–, Dutch–, Swedish–, and Czech–Americans represented in significant numbers. The people here are much more likely to hold white collar than blue collar jobs, but one

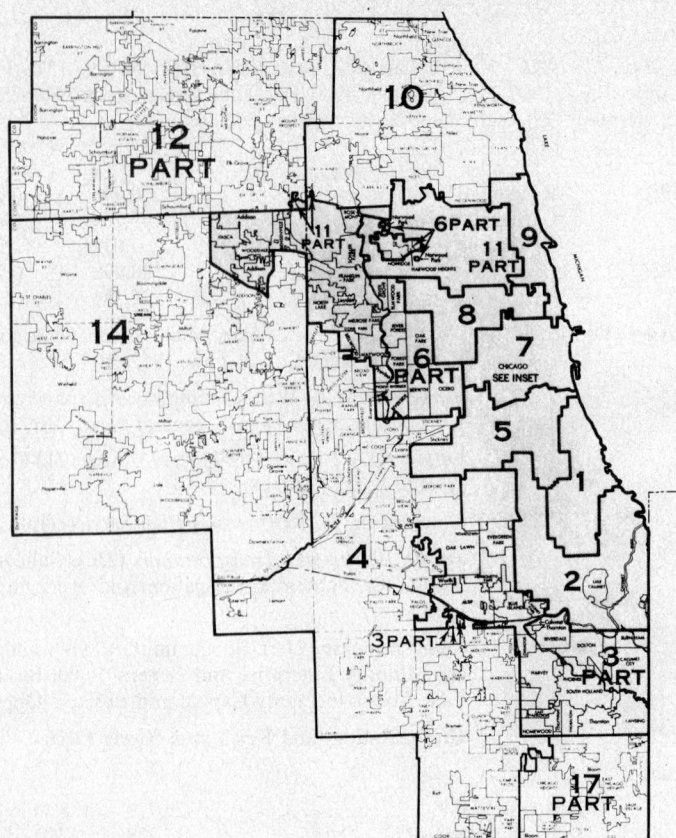

suspects that the situation for their parents was just the opposite. These are people whose hold on middle-class status is a little precarious, their recent prosperity notwithstanding.

The 3d district is one of those areas which are crucial to the outcome of Cook County elections which, contrary to outsiders' preconceptions, is not automatically won by the Democratic machine. Indeed, the Chicago suburbs as a whole are more Republican and conservative than those of any major city except Los Angeles. Many times Republicans, with huge suburban majorities, have been able to beat Daley Democrats in races for patronage—rich county offices as well as statewide elections—with such areas as the 3d district making the big difference. Most people here have Democratic backgrounds, but their comparative affluence tends to make Republicans out of them; they are, in short, classic ticket-splitters.

When the 3d district was first created, it was won by a Republican who had proved his mettle in winning a countywide election. But he was defeated two years later, in 1974, in somewhat of an upset. The winner was Martin Russo, a 30-year-old Democrat. With experience in the Cook County state's attorney's office, he had organization Democratic credentials. But unlike congressmen from the city of Chicago, he does not run as a machine candidate; he has been unopposed in primaries, and his real contest occurs in the general election.

In the House, Russo is not as liberal on noneconomic issues as most 1974 Democratic freshmen. Here he seems definitely to reflect the predilections of his constituents, who are tough on crime and not sympathetic to what they consider trends contrary to traditional morality. On economic issues, he generally votes with other Democrats. For example, he stood with the Carter Administration in opposing total deregulation of natural gas. But he also played a key role in killing the administration's proposal for hospital cost controls. In 1978, as a member of the Commerce Committee, Russo cast decisive votes against the proposal.

In 1979 Russo moved from Commerce to the Ways and Means Committee. He holds a key position on the Public Assistance Subcommittee, which handles the programs that received the lion's share of the Reagan–Stockman early 1981 budget cuts. Russo's vote will likely give the liberal Democrats a 6–5 margin on the subcommittee; if he goes with the Republicans, they will prevail. Russo himself seems to have no strong feelings on these issues, except a general Democratic orientation and an inclination not to go against established powers. In this regard he is similar to the committee's chairman, Dan Rostenkowski of Chicago.

In Cook County politics, Russo is an organization man, an opponent of Mayor Jane Byrne and a close ally of Richard M. Daley, the former mayor's son, who was elected Cook County state's attorney (i.e., prosecutor) by a close margin in 1980 with Byrne's strong opposition. Russo's percentage of the vote continued on the rise even in the Republican year of 1980; he simply has not been attracting significant opposition. He will have a problem, however, if redistricting puts the 3d district too far out in the suburbs. That could happen if the Illinois legislature tries to construct three black-majority districts in Chicago. If, however, as seems demographically easier given the census returns, there are to be just two black-majority districts, then the 3d will probably not be changed much in the districting process, and Russo should be in good electoral shape.

Census Data   Pop. (1980 final) 457,236, down 1% in 1970s. Median family income, 1970, $12,762, 133% of U.S.

The Voters

Employment profile 1970   White collar, 53%. Blue collar, 37%. Service, 10%. Farm, –%.
Ethnic groups   Black 1980, 11%. Hispanic 1980, 4%. Total foreign stock 1970, 28%. Poland, 4%; Ireland, Germany, Italy, 3% each; Lithuania, UK, 2% each; Netherlands, Sweden, Czechoslovakia, 1% each.

Presidential Vote

1980	Reagan (R)	109,179	(52%)
	Carter (D)	87,091	(41%)
	Anderson (I)	12,594	(6%)
1976	Ford (R)	121,448	(57%)
	Carter (D)	88,240	(42%)

Rep. Martin A. (Marty) **Russo** (D) Elected 1974; b. Jan. 23, 1944, Chicago; home, South Holland; De Paul U., B.S. 1965, J.D. 1967.

Career Law Clerk for Ill. Appellate Ct. Judge John V. McCormack, 1967–68; Practicing atty.; Cook Co. Asst. States Atty., 1971–73.

Offices 206 CHOB, 202-225-5736. Also 12526 S. Ashland Ave., Calumet Park 60643, 312-353-0439.

Committee *Ways and Means* (19th). Subcommittees: Public Assistance and Unemployment Compensation; Select Subcommittee on Revenue Measures.

Group Ratings

	ADA	COPE	PC	LCV	CFA	RPN	NAB	NSI	NTU	ACA	ACU
1980	50	68	57	72	64	—	80	10	44	39	33
1979	53	70	53	51	56	—	—	—	40	20	14
1978	35	63	40	66	36	42	46	56	39	50	30

Key Votes

1) Draft Registn $	FOR	6) Fair Hsg DOJ Enfrc	AGN	11) Cut Socl Incr Dfns $	AGN
2) Ban $ to Nicrgua	AGN	7) Lim PAC Contrbtns	FOR	12) Hosptl Cost Controls	AGN
3) Dlay MX Missile	FOR	8) Cap on Food Stmp $	AGN	13) Gasln Ctrls & Allctns	FOR
4) Nuclr Mortorium	AGN	9) New US Dep Edcatn	FOR	14) Lim Wndfll Prof Tax	AGN
5) Alaska Lands Bill	FOR	10) Cut OSHA $	AGN	15) Chryslr Loan Grntee	FOR

Election Results

1980 general	Martin A. (Marty) Russo (D)	137,283	(69%)	($211,989)
	Lawrence C. Sarsoun (R)	61,955	(31%)	($0)
1980 primary	Martin A. (Marty) Russo (D)	49,248	(100%)	
1978 general	Martin A. (Marty) Russo (D)	95,701	(65%)	($219,377)
	Robert L. Dunne (R)	51,098	(35%)	($113,083)

FOURTH DISTRICT

The 4th congressional district of Illinois is the southwestern corner of Cook County. The district includes some of the most Republican parts of what is supposed to be one of the nation's prime Democratic counties. It really isn't, because the usually Republican suburbs now cast 43% of the county's total votes; and as Chicago's population continues to move from city to suburbs, that percentage will continue to rise. Chicago's suburbs radiate from the city like spokes from the hub of a wheel, and the 4th district contains two widely separated built-up areas, one of which extends almost due south from the city, the other directly west. Nevertheless, the 4th is an area of rather homogeneous political complexion. By most social and economic indicators, it resembles the neighboring and closer-in 3d district; the 4th is just a shade richer and less ethnic and black. People here are several miles and another generation removed from the immigrants who filled up Chicago during its years of explosive growth, 1880–1930. They and their parents worked hard for what they have, and they intend to keep it. They have cut their ties with the city—an increasing number work as well as live in the suburbs—and with the Democratic Party.

As a result, the 4th is a very Republican district—one of about 65 of the current House seats that went for Barry Goldwater in 1964. Its congressman since 1958, Edward Derwinski, is a conservative proudly in the Goldwater mold. He was a young man when first elected (32), in the crew cut style of the day, and he is one of the few congressmen who still wears the style. His crusty, pungent personality leaves no doubt about where he stands. A proud Polish–American, Derwinski came to Congress when many politicians were talking about rolling the Iron Curtain back in Eastern Europe. He remains a staunch anti-Communist and high-ranking member of the Foreign Affairs Committee. To a considerable extent, he keeps alive the congressional tradition of bipartisan foreign policy more than anyone else in the House or certainly the Senate. He opposed the Panama Canal Treaties, for example, but once they were passed insisted that the Congress provide funding to carry out their terms. He was not against extending aid to Nicaragua's Sandinista government so long as it did not act like an ally of the Cubans, but at the same time he recognized that the policy was a gamble and might have to be abandoned. Behind his bluff exterior, Derwinski is one of the smartest operators on the Hill. He undoubtedly feels more comfortable with the Reagan Administration and its policies than he did with Carter's. But he will probably play something like the same role he played during the Carter Administration: making sure that American foreign policy actually works.

Derwinski has had achievements in other areas as well. By virtue of his position as ranking minority member of the Post Office and Civil Service Committee, he worked closely in 1978 with the committee's chairman, Morris Udall, and prolabor Democrat William Ford in working out a compromise version of the Carter Administration's civil service reform bill. Without Derwinski's work, this bill — which for the first time moves in the direction of making civil servants more responsible to the elected officials and the public they are supposed to serve — would never have received enough votes to pass. It was one of the major legislative achievements of the 95th Congress, for which Derwinski deserves much credit.

Derwinski should have no problem winning reelection. The 4th district gained population in the 1970s and is above the statewide average for new districts; any district created in this area would be so strongly Republican that the election would be essentially uncontested.

Census Data   Pop. (1980 final) 540,537, up 16% in 1970s. Median family income, 1970, $13,451, 140% of U.S.

The Voters

Employment profile 1970   White collar, 56%. Blue collar, 35%. Service, 9%. Farm, –%.
Ethnic groups   Black 1980, 6%. Hispanic 1980, 2%. Asian 1980, 1%. Total foreign stock 1970, 23%. Poland, Germany, Italy, 3% each; Czechoslovakia, 2%; UK, Ireland, Canada, 1% each.

Presidential Vote

1980	Reagan (R)	130,344	(57%)
	Carter (D)	76,622	(34%)
	Anderson (I)	18,017	(8%)
1976	Ford (R)	131,038	(61%)
	Carter (D)	80,530	(37%)

Rep. Edward J. Derwinski (R) Elected 1958; b. Sept. 15, 1926, Chicago; home, Flossmoor; Loyola U., B.S. 1951.

Career   Ill. House of Reps., 1957–58; Mbr., U.S. Delegation to U.N., 1971.

Offices   1401 LHOB, 202-225-3961. Also 12236 S. Harlem Ave., Palos Heights 60463, 312-448-3500.

Committees   *Foreign Affairs* (2d). Subcommittees: International Operations; International Security and Scientific Affairs.

Post Office and Civil Service (Ranking Member). Subcommittee: Investigations.

Group Ratings

	ADA	COPE	PC	LCV	CFA	RPN	NAB	NSI	NTU	ACA	ACU
1980	11	16	30	55	14	—	83	88	52	74	61
1979	11	40	18	41	15	—	—	—	50	73	82
1978	20	20	20	37	14	50	92	90	45	78	83

Key Votes

1) Draft Registn $	—	6) Fair Hsg DOJ Enfrc	AGN	11) Cut Socl Incr Dfns $	FOR
2) Ban $ to Nicrgua	FOR	7) Lim PAC Contrbtns	AGN	12) Hosptl Cost Controls	AGN
3) Dlay MX Missile	FOR	8) Cap on Food Stmp $	FOR	13) Gasln Ctrls & Allctns	AGN
4) Nuclr Mortorium	AGN	9) New US Dep Edcatn	AGN	14) Lim Wndfll Prof Tax	FOR
5) Alaska Lands Bill	AGN	10) Cut OSHA $	AGN	15) Chryslr Loan Grntee	FOR

Election Results

1980 general	Edward J. Derwinski (R)	152,377	(68%)	($108,597)
	Richard S. Jalovec (D)	71,814	(32%)	($63,686)
1980 primary	Edward J. Derwinski (R)	40,593	(83%)	
	One other (R)	8,118	(17%)	
1978 general	Edward J. Derwinski (R)	94,435	(67%)	($72,941)
	Andrew D. Thomas (D)	46,788	(33%)	($73,437)

FIFTH DISTRICT

In an unpretentious but reportedly comfortable house on the 3500 block of South Lowe Avenue in the 11th ward and the 5th congressional district in Chicago lived the most powerful ward committeeman in the United States. He was a man whose advice was routinely sought by presidents and senators and governors. For more than 20 years he held other important offices, such as chairman of the Cook County Democratic Committee and mayor of Chicago. His name was Richard J. Daley, and no matter how scorned or ridiculed he was elsewhere, he was loved and admired in the 11th ward of Chicago.

Chicago is a city of neighborhoods, and Daley's neighborhood, Bridgeport, is typical both of the 11th ward and the 5th district of which it is a part. Some 30% of the 5th's residents are black, but virtually all of them live in the fringes of the district, in the South Side or West Side ghettos. The heart of the 5th, neighborhoods such as Bridgeport, are all white. The people here live, as Daley did all his life, on these streets with dumpy-looking frame houses and sparkling clean sidewalks. On a nice day a visitor driving down South Lowe can see dozens of children with crisp Irish faces playing noisily but taking care not to injure the carefully manicured lawns. Blacks moving out from the center of the city have not found such neighborhoods as Bridgeport hospitable (to say the least) and have avoided them and moved farther out to places where the whites do not have such deep roots.

This choice urban property, not far from the Loop (Daley was known to ride a bicycle to work on occasion), thus remains the province of a tight-knit populace which, it seems, has always lived here. If there is something insular and anachronistic about these neighborhoods and something intolerant, there is also a vitality and a rootedness unknown in the shopping center land of suburban America.

Very early in life children in Bridgeport are taught their basic loyalties: the United States of America, the Roman Catholic Church, and the Democratic Party. If Bridgeport has not produced a president or a pope, it has produced the last four mayors of Chicago, from Ed Kelly, who took office in 1933, to Martin Kennelly, who was ousted in 1955 by Richard J. Daley, to Daley's hand-picked successor, Michael Bilandic, who was finally defeated in the 1979 primary—after he moved out of Bridgeport. No other neighborhood has ever dominated the government of a great city in this way. On occasion some of these loyalties have been called into doubt. The 5th district reacted negatively to blacks and peace demonstrators and gave Republicans unusually high percentages, although never majorities, in the period between 1966 and 1972. More recently, one suspects that Republican-inclined voters here have moved out to the suburbs, and Bridgeport continues as Democratic as ever.

The congressional succession in this district is a good example of how business is done in Chicago. Incumbent Congressman John Kluczynski died in 1975 at age 78. A few days later, state Representative John Fary was called into Mayor Daley's office. At 65, Fary had been a faithful machine officeholder for nearly 25 years. He thought the mayor was going to tell him it was time to retire; instead he was told he was going to Congress. The voters of the 5th have ratified the choice ever since. Fary has the kind of voting record and performance one would expect from a member with his background; and if he is advanced in years, he is still younger than the president and may well serve a few more terms in the House.

Census Data   Pop. (1980 final) 397,817, down 15% in 1970s. Median family income, 1970, $9,881, 103% of U.S.

The Voters

Employment profile 1970   White collar, 40%. Blue collar, 47%. Service, 13%. Farm, –%.
Ethnic groups   Black 1980, 30%. Hispanic 1980, 17%. Asian 1980, 1%. Total foreign stock 1970, 30%. Poland, 10%; Italy, Czechoslovakia, Lithuania, Germany, Ireland, 2% each; Yugoslavia, 1%.

Presidential Vote

1980	Reagan (R)	44,940	(28%)
	Carter (D)	106,568	(67%)
	Anderson (I)	6,096	(4%)
1976	Ford (R)	57,147	(33%)
	Carter (D)	113,899	(67%)

Rep. John G. Fary (D) Elected July 8, 1975; b. Apr. 11, 1911, Chicago; home, Chicago; Loyola U.

Career Businessman, 1931–76; Real estate broker; Ill. House of Reps., 1952–75.

Offices 1121 LHOB, 202-225-5701. Also 3968 Fed. Bldg., 230 S. Dearborn St., Chicago 60604, 312-353-7251.

Committees *Public Works and Transportation* (11th). Subcommittees: Aviation; Investigations and Oversight; Public Buildings and Grounds (Chairman); Water Resources.

Small Business (23d). Subcommittee: Tax, Access to Equity Capital and Business Opportunities.

Group Ratings

	ADA	COPE	PC	LCV	CFA	RPN	NAB	NSI	NTU	ACA	ACU
1980	44	79	57	26	79	—	18	20	13	21	11
1979	53	90	50	50	52	—	—	—	16	12	11
1978	40	80	50	47	55	20	0	50	17	22	9

Key Votes

1) Draft Registn $	FOR	6) Fair Hsg DOJ Enfrc	AGN	11) Cut Socl Incr Dfns $	AGN
2) Ban $ to Nicrgua	AGN	7) Lim PAC Contrbtns	FOR	12) Hosptl Cost Controls	—
3) Dlay MX Missile	AGN	8) Cap on Food Stmp $	AGN	13) Gasln Ctrls & Allctns	FOR
4) Nuclr Mortorium	AGN	9) New US Dep Edcatn	FOR	14) Lim Wndfll Prof Tax	AGN
5) Alaska Lands Bill	FOR	10) Cut OSHA $	AGN	15) Chryslr Loan Grntee	FOR

Election Results

1980 general	John G. Fary (D)	106,142	(80%)	($66,952)
	Robert V. Kotowski (R)	27,136	(20%)	($6,925)
1980 primary	John G. Fary (D)	51,281	(72%)	
	Melanie Kluczynski (D)	19,510	(28%)	($67,214)
1978 general	John G. Fary (D)	98,702	(84%)	($37,315)
	Joseph A. Barracca (R)	18,802	(16%)	

SIXTH DISTRICT

The 6th congressional district of Illinois is a suburban Chicago constituency. These are not the new suburbs, with their gleaming but pasteboardy houses stuck up on treeless lots one after another. The 6th is mostly a series of older, more established communities west and northwest of Chicago. Oak Park, for one, was the boyhood home of Ernest Hemingway; it is still a quiet middle-class community just across the city limits from the West Side Chicago black ghetto, and a town distinguished by its many Frank Lloyd Wright houses and by the way it has encouraged racial integration. To the south the very different town of Cicero has scarcely changed since the 1920s, when it was a Syndicate stronghold and bedroom community for Czechs and other Eastern European workers. In the middle 1960s, Cicero made headlines and TV footage when its citizens forcibly resisted the efforts of Martin Luther King, Jr., to integrate the city. Cicero's politics is dominated by an anachronism from the 1920s: a working-class, ethnic-based Republican machine. In just about every respect Cicero resembles Chicago neighborhoods like Bridgeport, but for some reason — perhaps just because this is a suburb and Bridgeport is part of the city — the partisan preferences are exactly the opposite.

On the map the remainder of the 6th district looks like a patchwork quilt of towns whose names are various combinations of "Park," "River," and "Forest," sometimes appended to more distinctive names. Most of these communities have some special quality. Maywood, for example, has a large black community, and Melrose Park is predominantly Italian-American; both are more Democratic than the district average. (Indeed, this is the most Italian of Illinois's districts. In the East, Italians have tended to stay in the central cities, but here they have long since moved to the suburbs.) Then there is Rosemont, a tiny place 35 years ago situated near a dusty airfield named after someone called O'Hare. Since that time, primarily through the efforts of Mayor Daley, O'Hare has become the busiest airport in the world — a claim contested by Atlanta's airport — and little Rosemont has sprouted a couple of dozen high-rise motels and office buildings. It is a premier example of the kind of businessmen's meeting culture that has grown up around our major airports. Also in the district are River Forest, Forest Park, and Riverside, older upper-middle-income suburbs that are strongholds of Illinois's Republican Party.

The 6th district has always been a Republican area and has always elected a Republican congressman since it was created in 1948. The incumbent, Henry Hyde, attracted little attention when he was first elected in 1974, but he has had plenty of legislative impact since. For he has been the prime sponsor of a series of Hyde Amendments to prohibit the use of federal funds for abortions. Hyde approaches that issue with the deep conviction that abortion of any kind is morally wrong and amounts to murder; he will not even make exceptions for pregnancies resulting from rape or incest. He has pursued the issue with great ingenuity and persistence, having sought out not only the obvious targets — abortions financed by Medicaid — but also less obvious ones — abortions for members of the Armed Forces and their dependents.

Hyde has been able to win solid majorities in the House for his amendments. The majority in the Senate up through 1980 went the other way, but in conference committee Hyde has proved largely victorious — partly because he has made it clear he will tack his amendments onto any conceivable piece of legislation, including appropriations bills, until they are passed. The federal government now pays for abortions in only the most limited of circumstances, and in fact today there is only a tiny percentage of the number of federally financed abortions than there used to be.

That is not enough for Hyde, of course. He sees the matter as a moral issue and is unwilling to settle for even nine-tenths of a loaf. With the changes in composition of the House and the new Republican majority in the Senate, Hyde can be expected to move not only for the extension of the Hyde Amendment but also for a constitutional amendment to restrict abortions. The key question for abortion foes is how far they should go. They might simply allow states to outlaw abortion, which means that some states would undoubtedly allow it; a few states even today volunteer to pay for Medicaid abortions themselves. The other choice is to outlaw abortion completely. But this is an amendment that would be much more difficult to pass, both in the Congress and, if it ever got there, in the state legislatures. Hyde's moral principles would lead him to go one way; his political realism — and he has proved that he is an intelligent legislative strategist — might lead him in the other. In any case, it is clear that he has become a major legislative force not through committee position or clout, but on the basis of strong convictions and political skill.

Now Hyde serves on the subcommittee that can do even more to ban abortions, if it wants to. That is the Civil and Constitutional Rights Subcommittee of the Judiciary Committee. Hyde should have solid support from the other three Republicans, but Chairman Don Edwards seems to have four solid votes against reporting out any constitutional amendment on abortion, and he is evidently determined to see that none is reported out. Hyde also disagrees with Edwards on other important issues that are likely to come before the subcommittee, such as extension of the Voting Rights Act of 1965. Liberals do not want to see the single most effective civil rights law diluted; conservatives such as Hyde argue that the problem the law was aimed at has been largely solved.

Hyde has not had any trouble winning reelection in the 6th district, and although the district's boundaries may very well be altered he is likely to win easily in 1982.

Census Data Pop. (1980 final) 425,111, down 8% in 1970s. Median family income, 1970, $12,700, 132% of U.S.

The Voters

Employment profile 1970 White collar, 55%. Blue collar, 36%. Service, 9%. Farm, -%.
Ethnic groups Black 1980, 8%. Hispanic 1980, 5%. Asian 1980, 1%. Total foreign stock 1970, 34%. Italy, 7%; Poland, Germany, Czechoslovakia, 4% each; Ireland, 2%; UK, Canada, Austria, 1% each.

Presidential Vote

1980	Reagan (R)	91,766	(52%)
	Carter (D)	69,003	(39%)
	Anderson (I)	14,505	(8%)
1976	Ford (R)	116,398	(59%)
	Carter (D)	78,144	(40%)

Rep. Henry J. Hyde (R) Elected 1974; b. Apr. 18, 1924, Chicago; home, Park Ridge; Georgetown U., B.S. 1947, Loyola U., J.D. 1949.

Career Navy, WWII; Practicing atty., 1950–75; Ill. House of Reps., 1967–74, Major. Ldr., 1971–72.

Offices 1203 LHOB, 202-225-4561. Also Rm. 220, Oak Park P.O. Bldg., 901 Lake St., Oak Park 60301, 312-383-6881.

Committees *Banking, Finance and Urban Affairs* (5th). Subcommittees: Financial Institutions Supervision, Regulation and Insurance; International Development Institutions and Finance; International Trade, Investment and Monetary Policy.

Judiciary (7th). Subcommittees: Civil and Constitutional Rights; Monopolies and Commercial Law.

Group Ratings

	ADA	COPE	PC	LCV	CFA	RPN	NAB	NSI	NTU	ACA	ACU
1980	28	26	30	43	21	—	67	80	38	74	47
1979	5	25	8	18	7	—	—	—	43	77	82
1978	10	5	15	33	18	83	75	100	22	70	87

Key Votes

1) Draft Registn $	FOR	6) Fair Hsg DOJ Enfrc	AGN	11) Cut Socl Incr Dfns $	FOR
2) Ban $ to Nicrgua	AGN	7) Lim PAC Contrbtns	AGN	12) Hosptl Cost Controls	—
3) Dlay MX Missile	AGN	8) Cap on Food Stmp $	FOR	13) Gasln Ctrls & Allctns	AGN
4) Nuclr Mortorium	AGN	9) New US Dep Edcatn	AGN	14) Lim Wndfll Prof Tax	FOR
5) Alaska Lands Bill	AGN	10) Cut OSHA $	FOR	15) Chryslr Loan Grntee	FOR

Election Results

1980 general	Henry J. Hyde (R)	123,593	(67%)	($144,469)
	Mario Raymond Reda (D).......	60,951	(33%)	($30,049)
1980 primary	Henry J. Hyde (R)	40,978	(100%)	
1978 general	Henry J. Hyde (R)	87,193	(66%)	($153,066)
	Jeanne P. Quinn (D)............	44,543	(34%)	($6,834)

SEVENTH DISTRICT

The Loop is what you think of when you think of Chicago. Here, where high-rise construction was pioneered, stand the city's giant skyscrapers, including the new Sears Tower, the world's tallest. Chicago also means the Near North Side, with its huge, classically designed high-rise apartments along Lake Michigan and, behind them, alternately smart and raunchy shopping streets. This is all part of Illinois's 7th congressional district—the glamorous part, the part best known to the outside world. But to the west beyond the Chicago River and the miles of railroad track—Chicago is still the nation's biggest rail center—lies the grim West Side ghetto. As you go inland from the lakefront, the territory is at first a potpourri: the nation's largest skid row on West Madison, followed by odd settlements of American Indians and Appalachians. Then comes the West Side ghetto, which casts the bulk of the votes here in the 7th district.

The West Side has traditionally been machine country. The black community here is more newly arrived, less middle class, less well organized—less of a community—than the blacks on the South Side in the 1st district. Some wards here that are virtually 100% black still elect Jewish or Italian ward committeemen — the last vestige of their onetime ethnic composition. Although the South Side black wards have broken party lines and voted Republican, the West Side has stayed true to the machine and casts huge Democratic majorities for all candidates.

Of all of Chicago's 50 wards, the 24th on the far West Side usually turns in the highest Democratic percentages — 97% for Jimmy Carter in 1980, for example. (Interestingly, the all-black 24th is right next to the all-white, heavily Republican suburb of Cicero.) This is the part of the city where voting irregularities used to occur when the machine needed votes; it is the West Side wards that Republicans are talking about when they say that Richard Daley stole the 1960 election for John Kennedy. Massive vote fraud is now a thing of the past, not because the machine might not like to steal some votes, but because too many people — the Better Government Association, the *Chicago Tribune,* Republican prosecutors — are watching.

The 24th ward was the political base for Jacob Arvey, the leading Democratic pol in Illinois during Adlai Stevenson's governorship and one of the men who made Richard Daley mayor in 1955; his power declined sharply after Daley took office. The 24th's more recent history is more violent. One alderman here was murdered, no one is saying by whom, in 1969. The next alderman, George Collins, was elected to Congress in 1970; he was killed in the December 1972 plane crash that also took the life of Mrs. Howard Hunt.

The current representative, Cardiss Collins, succeeded to her husband's seat in 1973. During her first years in Congress she seemed to be a cipher: she voted predictably with most Democrats and was reelected routinely by overwhelming margins. More recently she has distinguished herself as chairwoman of the Congressional Black Caucus and as an articulate and thoughtful advocate of policies to help blacks. She has a subcommittee chair that allows her to investigate and therefore affect housing programs, the Community Services Administration, and CETA. She is respected widely; politically she has grown more independent of the machine which is not the all-powerful force it was once on the West Side (although still more powerful than on the South Side). It seems unlikely that her seat will be redistricted out of existence for 1982; she has built up enough of a position and is still regular enough to have some friends in Springfield. If one of the city's three black districts is eliminated it will probably be one of the other two, both of which are represented by freshmen who are rebels against the organization. Collins, therefore, is likely to survive politically into what she undoubtedly hopes are more congenial times politically than the early 1980s.

Census Data   Pop. (1980 final) 372,353, down 20% in 1970s. Median family income, 1970, $7,536, 79% of U.S.

The Voters

Employment profile 1970   White collar, 35%. Blue collar, 49%. Service, 16%. Farm, %.
Ethnic groups   Black 1980, 50%. Hispanic 1980, 28%. Asian 1980, 2%. Total foreign stock 1970, 22%. Poland, 4%; Italy, 2%; USSR, 1%.

Presidential Vote

1980	Reagan (R)	17,988	(17%)
	Carter (D)	85,999	(79%)
	Anderson (I)	3,188	(3%)
1976	Ford (R)	21,836	(19%)
	Carter (D)	91,956	(81%)

Rep. Cardiss Collins (D) Elected June 5, 1973; b. Sept. 24, 1931, St. Louis, Mo.; home, Chicago; Northwestern U.

Career Stenographer, Ill. Dept. of Labor; Secy., accountant, and revenue auditor, Ill. Dept. of Revenue.

Offices 2438 RHOB, 202-225-5006. Also 230 S. Dearborn St., Chicago 60604, 312-353-5754.

Committees *Energy and Commerce* (20th). Subcommittees: Energy Conservation and Power; Fossil and Synthetic Fuels; Telecommunications, Consumer Protection and Finance.

Government Operations (7th). Subcommittee: Manpower and Housing (Chairwoman).

Select Committee on Narcotics Abuse and Control (8th).

Group Ratings

	ADA	COPE	PC	LCV	CFA	RPN	NAB	NSI	NTU	ACA	ACU
1980	89	94	77	81	64	—	0	13	18	20	7
1979	79	100	68	71	56	—	—	—	19	5	0
1978	65	85	73	61	59	38	0	13	21	14	12

Key Votes

1) Draft Registn $	AGN	6) Fair Hsg DOJ Enfrc	FOR
2) Ban $ to Nicrgua	AGN	7) Lim PAC Contrbtns	—
3) Dlay MX Missile	FOR	8) Cap on Food Stmp $	AGN
4) Nuclr Mortorium	FOR	9) New US Dep Edcatn	—
5) Alaska Lands Bill	FOR	10) Cut OSHA $	AGN

11) Cut Socl Incr Dfns $	AGN
12) Hosptl Cost Controls	FOR
13) Gasln Ctrls & Allctns	FOR
14) Lim Wndfll Prof Tax	AGN
15) Chryslr Loan Grntee	FOR

Election Results

1980 general	Cardiss Collins (D)	80,056	(85%)	($19,409)
	Ruth R. Hooper (R)	14,041	(15%)	($7,255)
1980 primary	Cardiss Collins (D)	29,420	(78%)	
	One other (D)	8,306	(22%)	
1978 general	Cardiss Collins (D)	64,716	(86%)	($34,857)
	James C. Holt (R)..............	10,273	(14%)	($13,610)

EIGHTH DISTRICT

The undisputed leader of the Chicago delegation in Congress and perhaps the strongest political force in Chicago itself is Congressman Dan Rostenkowski of the 8th district of Illinois. At the opening of the 97th Congress, when Democrats generally were in trouble, Rostenkowski had an embarrassment of riches: he had to choose between becoming majority whip (by appointment of Speaker O'Neill and Majority Leader Jim Wright) or chairman of the Ways and Means Committee. Given the choice, Rostenkowski picked Ways and Means. It is not a post that puts him directly in line for the speakership, but it is one in which he can pretty well be his own man — probably an important attraction for a man who served many years as Mayor Daley's chief lieutenant in Congress. While Democrats do in fact vote on committee chairmanships, Rostenkowski is the senior Democrat on the committee and he is not so far ideologically from just about any Democrat as to be objectionable; and his reputation for political astuteness deters opposition. For practical purposes, then, the Ways and Means post is one in which Rostenkowski is his own boss.

It is also a position where one has great power to influence the substance of legislation. Tax laws have to be initiated in the House, not the Senate, and that means they have to be initiated in Ways and Means. It was mastery of the complexity of tax law that, more than anything else, made Wilbur Mills such a powerful Ways and Means chairman from 1958 to 1974; and if Rostenkowski is not as knowledgeable, he is still competent and able to manage difficult legislation without getting into trouble. He is also, as Mills was, flexible on the issues. While other northern Democrats tended to support national health insurance, for example, Rostenkowski had his doubts; he also helped to torpedo the Carter Administration's program for controlling health care costs. He has not been interested in trade issues in the abstract; but he was concerned when imports threatened the American television manufacturers (they ultimately wiped out TV assembly in the United States, including a Zenith plant in the 8th district), and he may become concerned about other concrete examples of allegedly inadequate enforcement of trade laws. Critics charge that Rostenkowski is too responsive to business and hospital lobbyists; his boosters say he is ready to listen to all points of view and does not believe that Democratic orthodoxy holds all the answers. In the 97th Congress Ways and Means will be busy. It will deliberate on whatever tax cuts the Reagan Administration proposes, and it will have to deal with Republican proposals to cut business taxes by revising depreciation schedules. It must also rule on any proposal to revise Social Security. Moreover, it votes on health care legislation proposals. It handles trade proposals, such as the moves by steel and auto companies and unions to restrict imports. On none of these issues does Rostenkowski have a rock-hard position. On the resolution of most if not all of them he is likely to be a very influential actor.

And he still has potential for leadership positions as well. He took the Ways and Means chair at age 52, and it is not inconceivable that Democrats in some future Congress may choose to make him speaker (or, if the Republicans have their way, minority leader). Rostenkowski would have several advantages: while he is not a southern conservative, he is not a doctrinnaire liberal either; he is a politician who knows how to go along and get along, yet he is aggressive and likes to win; he presents an acceptable appearance to the outside world and has the additional advantage of representing an important ethnic group.

How did Dan Rostenkowski attain such a position? The most important step was one taken long ago and that was his election to Congress at age 30 in 1958. He was already a six-year veteran of the legislature, and one can only conjecture that Mayor Daley (then in his first term) and other machine leaders decided that this was a young man who had real potential. Usually the machine sends to Congress older followers, as a kind of reward; they are not expected to be particularly powerful in Washington. But in sending a politically talented 30-year-old to Washington, Daley was obviously betting on the future; and today the wager has paid off. Rostenkowski got a seat on Ways and Means early, and although he made some missteps on the way up (losing the caucus chairman post in 1970) he was early recognized as a comer. In 1980 the defeat of Al Ullman put him in the position to be Ways and Means chairman, and the defeat of John Brademas presented the option of the whip post.

Rostenkowski has also had the advantage of holding a very safe seat. The 8th congressional district of Illinois is part of the North and Northwest Side of Chicago, extending from the western city limits almost to Lake Michigan. This is middle- and lower-middle-class country, some of it in decline, with commercial strip developments and neighborhoods of one- and two-family houses. The overall impression is rather depressing, although many of the blocks are maintained with meticulous care. Most of the district is resolutely all white, although it does include part of the West Side black ghetto. The atmosphere here is decidedly ethnic, and the 8th is the heart of Chicago's large North Side Polish community. (Altogether, the 8th has the fourth largest Polish–American population of any district in the nation.) Its residents, less prosperous than their cousins in the adjoining 11th district, are closer to Old Country ways and more dependent on their ward organizations. This is the kind of urban area that many young middle-income Americans, in their rush to the curved-street subdivisions and shopping centers of the suburbs, are leaving behind. In fact, the 8th had as large a population loss as any Illinois district in the 1970s, as the area became increasingly elderly and childless. Theoretically, that would make the 8th a candidate for redistricting; but in fact no one doubts that the legislature will create a district that is safe for Rostenkowski.

Census Data   Pop. (1980 final) 429,120, down 7% in 1970s. Median family income, 1970, $9,867, 103% of U.S.

The Voters

Employment profile 1970   White collar, 39%. Blue collar, 49%. Service, 12%. Farm, –%.
Ethnic groups   Black 1980, 35%. Hispanic 1980, 27%. Asian 1980, 2%. Total foreign stock 1970, 35%. Poland, 9%; Italy, 6%; Germany, 3%; Ireland, 2%; Greece, 1%.

Presidential Vote

1980	Reagan (R)	32,694	(24%)
	Carter (D)	97,057	(70%)
	Anderson (I)	5,842	(4%)
1976	Ford (R)	43,152	(30%)
	Carter (D)	100,266	(70%)

Rep. Dan Rostenkowski (D) Elected 1958; b. Jan. 2, 1928, Chicago; home, Chicago; Loyola U., 1948–51.

Career Army, Korea; Ill. House of Reps., 1953–55; Ill. Senate, 1955–59.

Offices 2111 RHOB, 202-225-4061. Also 2148 N. Damen Ave., Chicago 60647, 312-431-1111.

Committees *Ways and Means* (Chairman). Subcommittee: Trade.

Joint Taxation Committee (Chairman).

Group Ratings

	ADA	COPE	PC	LCV	CFA	RPN	NAB	NSI	NTU	ACA	ACU
1980	50	87	53	24	79	—	18	25	17	17	12
1979	63	80	45	41	38	—	—	—	16	4	5
1978	50	63	45	46	41	44	9	38	8	21	18

Key Votes

1) Draft Registn $	FOR	6) Fair Hsg DOJ Enfrc	FOR	11) Cut Socl Incr Dfns $	AGN
2) Ban $ to Nicrgua	AGN	7) Lim PAC Contrbtns	FOR	12) Hosptl Cost Controls	FOR
3) Dlay MX Missile	AGN	8) Cap on Food Stmp $	AGN	13) Gasln Ctrls & Allctns	FOR
4) Nuclr Mortorium	—	9) New US Dep Edcatn	FOR	14) Lim Wndfll Prof Tax	AGN
5) Alaska Lands Bill	FOR	10) Cut OSHA $	AGN	15) Chryslr Loan Grntee	FOR

Election Results

1980 general	Dan Rostenkowski (D)	98,524	(85%)	($170,056)
	Walter F. Zilke (R)	17,845	(15%)	($0)
1980 primary	Dan Rostenkowski (D)	43,081	(89%)	
	One other (D)	5,286	(11%)	
1978 general	Dan Rostenkowski (D)	81,457	(86%)	($150,266)
	Carl C. LoDico (R)	13,302	(14%)	

NINTH DISTRICT

Along Chicago's Lake Shore Drive, overlooking Lake Michigan, are some of the nation's architecturally most distinguished high-rise buildings. There are more classic modern buildings of the International School here, probably, than anywhere else in the world. This is the face the nation's second largest city likes to show to the world: affluent, elegant, massive. Behind the apartment towers, however, lies another Chicago — an incredibly varied, sometimes funky, sometimes posh city. There are Appalachians, Italians, Mexicans, American Indians, and blacks — all just a few blocks from the row of high rises. This is the Chicago of Studs Terkel's Division Street, a city full of life's losers and winners; the Chicago of Saul Bellow, a city of successful small businessmen and irrationally vengeful hoodlums. To the north, behind the lakefront, are more conventional neighborhoods, mostly Catholic, but also including Chicago's largest Jewish community, just south of the suburbs of Evanston and Skokie. The lakefront and the territory a mile behind it form Illinois's 9th congressional district, which stretches from the Near North Side to the northern city limits.

Politically, the 9th has been one of the more liberal parts of the city — Democratic in general elections, often supporting antimachine candidates in the primary. It was the lakefront wards that were the political base of William Singer, who led the delegation that unseated Mayor Daley at the 1972 Democratic National Convention; more recently, however, machine-supporting candidates have recaptured many of the posts they lost in these wards when Daley was still alive. Mayor Jane Byrne did very well in the lakefront wards in 1979; whether she will do so again in 1983 is uncertain.

Except for two years, most of the area in the 9th district has been represented by the same congressman for more than three decades — Sidney Yates, a liberal Democrat who even at Mayor Daley's zenith of power was not counted as a machine loyalist. Yates is a scholarly man, a Jewish lawyer who did well in college and law school at a time when most Jewish parents were unschooled immigrants. He first won the seat in 1948, gave it up in 1962 to run an almost successful race against Senator Everett Dirksen, and then regained it in 1964. He has been reelected ever since without difficulty.

Had Yates remained in the House rather than run for the Senate in 1962, he would be the number two Democrat on the Appropriations Committee today, behind Jamie Whitten of Mississippi; instead, he is seventh-ranking Democrat and chairman of the Interior Subcommittee. This is a body that has jurisdiction over many federal environmental programs, and Yates has been counted as a friend of environmental causes; he is interested as well in federal support for the arts and sciences. He is not one of those Chicago members who are known for their clout, although he is an effective advocate when he is concerned about an issue.

The 9th district is, theoretically, one that could be eliminated by redistricting. That might happen if Yates is interested in retiring. But it is not clear that Dan Rostenkowski and Frank

Annunzio would like having sometimes insurgent lakefront wards in their districts; they might prefer to extend the 8th and 11th districts into the suburbs instead. Another plan might be to give Evanston or Skokie, both Democratic, to the 9th; the Republican incumbent from the 10th probably would not mind that. The actual redistricting plan will be the result of complicated negotiations, and the impact on this district is not yet clear.

Census Data   Pop. (1980 final) 419,088, down 10% in 1970s. Median family income, 1970, $10,966, 114% of U.S.

The Voters

Employment profile 1970   White collar, 64%. Blue collar, 25%. Service, 11%. Farm, –%.
Ethnic groups   Black 1980, 10%. Hispanic 1980, 14%. Am. Ind. 1980, 1%. Asian 1980, 7%. Total foreign stock 1970, 41%. USSR, 6%; Germany, 5%; Poland, 3%; Ireland, Sweden, Italy, UK, 2% each; Austria, Canada, Yugoslavia, Greece, 1% each.

Presidential Vote

1980	Reagan (R)	57,063	(33%)
	Carter (D)	95,175	(55%)
	Anderson (I)	18,346	(11%)
1976	Ford (R)	77,057	(42%)
	Carter (D)	105,493	(58%)

Rep. Sidney R. Yates (D) Elected 1964; b. Aug. 27, 1909, Chicago; home, Chicago; U. of Chi., Ph.B. 1931, J.D. 1933.

Career Practicing atty.; Asst. Atty. for Ill. St. Bank Receiver, 1935–37; Asst. Atty. Gen. attached to Ill. Commerce Comm., 1937–40; Navy, WWII; U.S. House of Reps., 1949–63; Dem. nominee for U.S. Senate, 1962.

Offices 2234 RHOB, 202-225-2111. Also 230 S. Dearborn St., Chicago 60604, 312-353-4596.

Committee *Appropriations* (7th). Subcommittees: Foreign Operations; Interior (Chairman); Treasury–Postal Service–General Government.

Group Ratings

	ADA	COPE	PC	LCV	CFA	RPN	NAB	NSI	NTU	ACA	ACU
1980	100	83	90	79	100	—	9	0	22	17	7
1979	95	95	85	90	93	—	—	—	24	4	11
1978	100	85	95	93	91	55	9	20	27	7	4

Key Votes

1) Draft Registn $	AGN	6) Fair Hsg DOJ Enfrc	FOR	11) Cut Socl Incr Dfns $	AGN
2) Ban $ to Nicrgua	AGN	7) Lim PAC Contrbtns	FOR	12) Hosptl Cost Controls	FOR
3) Dlay MX Missile	FOR	8) Cap on Food Stmp $	AGN	13) Gasln Ctrls & Allctns	FOR
4) Nuclr Mortorium	FOR	9) New US Dep Edcatn	AGN	14) Lim Wndfll Prof Tax	AGN
5) Alaska Lands Bill	FOR	10) Cut OSHA $	AGN	15) Chryslr Loan Grntee	—

Election Results

1980 general	Sidney R. Yates (D)	106,543	(73%)	($63,024)
	John D. Andrica (R)............	39,244	(27%)	($12,212)
1980 primary	Sidney R. Yates (D)	44,341	(87%)	
	One other (D)	6,608	(13%)	

1978 general	Sidney R. Yates (D)	87,543	(75%)	($14,870)
	John M. Collins (R)	28,673	(25%)	

TENTH DISTRICT

The 10th district of Illinois could be called the North Shore district. Its best-known towns include Evanston, home of Northwestern University and for many years of the Women's Christian Temperance Union. Above Evanston, along Lake Michigan are Wilmette, Winnetka, and Glencoe, whose New Trier Township High School likes to think of itself as (and perhaps is) the most academically distinguished public high school in the country. These suburbs along the lake shore were settled long ago, pioneered by commuters on Chicago's efficient railroad lines. The large houses and shady streets have a comfortable, lived-in look, and not a trace of shabbiness; this is the land of the book and movie *Ordinary People,* a place where pleasant, affluent people live in an environment that seems very different from the clamorous ethnic neighborhoods of Chicago.

The 10th district also extends inward from the lake, to newer communities: the primarily Jewish suburb of Skokie, where a group of local Nazis insisted on marching; and places such as Niles, Des Plaines, Glenview, and Northbrook, situated on the northwest rail lines and freeways, right in the path of the great suburban expansion of the 1960s. These places are not as rich as the lakefront communities, but they are, paradoxically perhaps, more Republican; there are fewer fashionable liberals and chic radicals here, and more people who have worked themselves up to affluence in small businesses and large corporations, and who see high taxes and government bureaucracy as enemies that can destroy the prosperity they have come to value by their own experience.

From the description it is apparent that the 10th district is rich. Indeed, the 1970 census found that it had the second highest median family income in the nation, exceeded only in the 8th district of Maryland, where incomes depend in large part on taxes that the federal government will use force, if necessary, to extract from its citizens. The people of the 10th, in contrast, tend to make their money producing goods and services that people buy voluntarily. The 10th's wealth, then, is firmly based on the private sector; yet this district has not been reliably Republican. It has its Democratic pockets: Skokie almost always goes Democratic and Evanston, with its large university vote, usually does now, although historically it was a bastion of Republicanism. On economic issues, the 10th on balance does come down on the Republican side. But on cultural issues—whether one is talking about the Vietnam war or women's rights or civil liberties—the 10th will often go with the Democrats.

The 10th is also attracted by politicians of obvious brainpower. That, and the importance of cultural issues, are probably the main reasons why this basically Republican district elected Abner Mikva, a liberal Democrat, as its congressman in 1974, 1976, and 1978. Mikva had been elected in 1968 and 1970 to represent a Democratic district on the South Side of Chicago which was then eliminated in redistricting; an antimachine Democrat, he moved to Evanston and ran there in a seat with no incumbent. In 1972 he was beaten, barely, by Republican Sam Young; in the next three elections, Mikva won, although never by much. He built a massive enthusiastic organization of students, housewives, and activists; he made sure that students with legal residences in the 10th district were contacted at their colleges and voted absentee back home. Plenty of money was spent as well: in 1978 Mikva spent nearly $400,000 and his Republican opponent, John Porter, spent more than $500,000. After winning three races by an aggregate of 3,634 votes, Mikva was appointed a judge on the prestigious District of Columbia Circuit Court of Appeals in 1979.

Predictably, the district went Republican on his departure. John Porter, his 1978 opponent, was well suited to the district: a thoughtful Republican with a reputation as a moderate, comparatively liberal on cultural issues, safely conservative on economic matters. He won the special election easily and won the full term in 1980 with 61% of the vote. He can be expected to hold this district for some time to come, in elections much less strenuously contested than it saw in 1980; the district boundaries will probably change somewhat due to redistricting, but the basic character of the North Shore district will remain.

Census Data   Pop. (1980 final) 435,596, down 6% in 1970s. Median family income, 1970, $16,576, 173% of U.S.

The Voters

Employment profile 1970   White collar, 74%. Blue collar, 18%. Service, 8%. Farm, -%.
Ethnic groups   Black 1980, 4%. Hispanic 1980, 2%. Asian 1980, 4%. Total foreign stock 1970, 31%. USSR, Germany, Poland, 4% each; Italy, UK, Sweden, Canada, 2% each; Austria, 1%.

Presidential Vote

1980	Reagan (R)	120,146	(52%)
	Carter (D)	78,426	(34%)
	Anderson (I)	28,394	(12%)
1976	Ford (R)	138,449	(59%)
	Carter (D)	89,608	(39%)

Rep. John E. Porter (R) Elected 1980; b. June 1, 1935, Evanston; home, Evanston; Northwestern U., B.A. 1957, U. of Mich., J.D. 1961.

Career Atty., U.S. Dept. of Justice, 1961–63; Practicing atty., 1963–80; Ill. House of Reps., 1972–78.

Offices 1529 LHOB, 202-225-4835. Also Evanston Civic Center, 2100 Ridge Ave., Evanston 60204, 312, 491-0101, and Des Plaines Civic Center, 1420 Miner St., Des Plaines 60016, 312-655-8787.

Committees *Appropriations* (22d). Subcommittees: District of Columbia; Foreign Operations; Labor–Health and Human Services–Education.

Group Ratings

	ADA	COPE	PC	LCV	CFA	RPE	NAB	NSI	NTU	ACA	ACU
1980	39	20	30	—	21	—	100	100	—	71	—

Key Votes

1) Draft Registn $	AGN	6) Fair Hsg DOJ Enfrc	AGN	11) Cut Socl Incr Dfns $	FOR
2) Ban $ to Nicrgua	—	7) Lim PAC Contrbtns	—	12) Hosptl Cost Controls	—
3) Dlay MX Missile	FOR	8) Cap on Food Stmp $	—	13) Gasln Ctrls & Allctns	—
4) Nuclr Mortorium	—	9) New US Dep Edcatn	—	14) Lim Wndfll Prof Tax	—
5) Alaska Lands Bill	—	10) Cut OSHA $	—	15) Chryslr Loan Grntee	—

Election Results

1980 general	John E. Porter (R)	137,707	(61%)	($677,662)
	Robert A. Weinberger (D)	89,008	(39%)	
1980 primary	John E. Porter (R)	62,266	(100%)	
1/22/80 spc. gen.	John E. Porter (R)	36,981	(54%)	($677,662)
	Robert A. Weinberger (D)	30,929	(46%)	($283,170)
12/79 spc. prim.	John E. Porter (R)	18,423	(71%)	
	John Nunrod (R)	7,505	(29%)	($25,190)
1978 general	Abner J. Mikva (D)	89,479	(50%)	($385,007)
	John E. Porter (R)	88,829	(50%)	($536,515)

ELEVENTH DISTRICT

The 11th congressional district of Illinois is the northwest corner of the city of Chicago. Made up of comfortable middle-class neighborhoods, the 11th has a higher percentage of families with relatively high incomes than any other Chicago district. It is also the Chicago district with the lowest percentage of blacks and the highest proportion of people of foreign stock. When second- or third-generation ethnics were able to afford to leave their old neighborhoods, they tended to move here to the northwest side. Almost all of Chicago's ethnic groups are well represented in these middle-class wards, especially Poles, Germans, Italians, Jews, Irish, and Greeks.

These are not people particularly attracted by WASP suburbs; indeed, they seem to consider them cold and inhospitable — and Republican. For these are ancestral Democrats, people who grew up revering Franklin D. Roosevelt and who think of the Chicago Democratic machine not as a group of crooks living off their tax dollars but as friendly people who can help you out when you need something from the city or county. They are also the kind of Democrats who don't especially like seeing their tax money spent on welfare mothers and food stamps.

The 11th district's congressman during most of the 1970s was Frank Annunzio, a Democrat originally elected from a Loop-based district that was eliminated by redistricting in 1972. He moved out to the 11th, which was being vacated by Roman Pucinski, the unsuccessful challenger of Senator Charles Percy that year. (Pucinski has gone on to a position of real power in Chicago: alderman.) In some elections in the 1970s, the voters of the 11th showed Republican proclivities, but not in local contests: indeed, Republicans lost their last alderman from the area. Nor has Annunzio had any great difficulty winning reelection.

Annunzio is a faithful follower of the Chicago Democratic machine and generally votes with most Democrats and organized labor in the House. He is chairman of a Banking subcommittee on Consumer Finance and has pushed forward a number of measures that are regarded as keeping businesses from hurting consumers. There are those who instinctively regard him, an Italian–American originally representing some of Chicago's tougher wards, as somehow unsavory; but in fact he has represented his district honestly and reasonably energetically. The only real threat to his incumbency is redistricting, which has caused him to move once; the 11th district's population is below the state average, and some adjustment of its boundaries will be necessary.

Census Data Pop. (1980 final) 430,754, down 7% in 1970s. Median family income, 1970, $12,005, 125% of U.S.

The Voters

Employment profile 1970   White collar, 53%. Blue collar, 37%. Service, 10%. Farm, –%.
Ethnic groups   Hispanic 1980, 8%. Asian 1980, 4%. Total foreign stock 1970, 47%. Poland, 10%;
Germany, 7%; Italy, 5%; USSR, 3%; Ireland, Greece, Czechoslovakia, Hungary, 1% each.

Presidential Vote

1980	Reagan (R)	91,388	(45%)
	Carter (D)	95,039	(47%)
	Anderson (I)	14,515	(7%)
1976	Ford (R)	111,064	(52%)
	Carter (D)	103,637	(48%)

Rep. Frank Annunzio (D) Elected 1964; b. Jan. 12, 1915, Chicago; home, Chicago; De Paul U., B.S.
1940; M.A. 1942.

Career Public school teacher, 1935–43; Legis. and Ed. Dir., United Steelworkers of Amer., Chicago, Calumet Region Dist. 31, 1943–49; Dir, Ill. Dept. of Labor, 1949–52; Private businessman, 1952–64.

Offices 2303 RHOB, 202-225-6661. Also Suite 201, 4747 W. Peterson Ave., Chicago 60646, 312-736-0700.

Committees *Banking, Finance and Urban Affairs* (5th). Subcommittees: Consumer Affairs and Coinage (Chairman); Economic Stabilization; Financial Institutions Supervision, Regulation and Insurance; General Oversight and Renegotiation.

House Administration (2d). Subcommittees: Accounts (Chairman); Personnel and Police.

Group Ratings

	ADA	COPE	PC	LCV	CFA	RPN	NAB	NSI	NTU	ACA	ACU
1980	56	79	57	26	79	—	25	33	13	18	11
1979	63	90	48	48	63	—	—	—	18	12	18
1978	40	79	45	51	46	36	17	50	7	22	23

Key Votes

1) Draft Registn $	AGN	6) Fair Hsg DOJ Enfrc	AGN	11) Cut Socl Incr Dfns $	AGN
2) Ban $ to Nicrgua	AGN	7) Lim PAC Contrbtns	FOR	12) Hosptl Cost Controls	FOR
3) Dlay MX Missile	AGN	8) Cap on Food Stmp $	AGN	13) Gasln Ctrls & Allctns	FOR
4) Nuclr Mortorium	AGN	9) New US Dep Edcatn	AGN	14) Lim Wndfll Prof Tax	AGN
5) Alaska Lands Bill	FOR	10) Cut OSHA $	AGN	15) Chryslr Loan Grntee	FOR

Election Results

1980 general	Frank Annunzio (D)	121,166	(70%)	($59,436)
	Michael R. Zanillo (R)	52,417	(30%)	($0)
1980 primary	Frank Annunzio (D)	63,147	(100%)	
1978 general	Frank Annunzio (D)	112,365	(74%)	($82,201)
	John Hoeger (R)	40,044	(26%)	($6,164)

TWELFTH DISTRICT

By far the fastest-growing part of Illinois during the 1960s and the 1970s is that portion of the
northwest Chicago suburbs that is the 12th congressional district of Illinois. In the 1960s this
area more than doubled in population, making it one of the four fastest-growing districts in
the nation; in the 1970s, while the Chicago metropolitan area's population stayed about

even, the 12th increased by 33%, making it, with the 14th district, by a considerable margin the fastest-growing congressional districts in the Midwest. The fact that this is the fastest-growing part of the metro area tells us something about the changing character of Greater Chicago: it is becoming more affluent and white collar, and less dependent on low-wage and factory jobs.

The suburbs strung out along the railroad lines radiating northwest from Chicago are mostly white collar and mostly affluent. They are not like the long-established lakefront suburbs where Chicago's richest and most prominent people live; they are the home of people who are disproportionately young, upper income, well educated — the people up toward the top, but not at the very top of Metro Chicago's social pyramid. Because they tend to be young, the swelling population figures here are heavy with children.

The residents of the 12th also tend to be very conservative politically. The word "conservative" is probably a misnomer, for these are people who want to see major change in the way our system works. They want less government, lower taxes, fewer regulations, and fewer government programs. But unlike some conservatives, the Republicans here are not necessarily interested in enforcing through government action their own ideas of personal morality.

This is the district that elects Philip Crane, the ultraconservative Republican who ran for president in 1980 in the hope of being considered a young Ronald Reagan. Crane won this seat, when the district was very much larger, in a 1969 special election; he has been reelected easily ever since (and was able to run for president and congressman simultaneously in Illinois in 1980). He comes by his conservatism from his father, a doctor with a radio advice program; he has a brother who is a congressman from Illinois's 22d district and another who has run three times in Indiana's 6th. Philip Crane has been head of the American Conservative Union, an organization that fears that congressional Republicans will sell out conservative principles; and he is one of those Republicans who believe their principles have been betrayed time and again by Republicans of the stripe of Gerald Ford and George Bush.

Crane's 1980 presidential campaign was something of a fiasco. He got started early but had severe staff problems in 1979; he spent weeks in New Hampshire campaigning personally but never really caught on. He argued that people should regard him as a kind of second choice to Ronald Reagan, but once Reagan won the New Hampshire primary and was ahead in almost all the others the strategy didn't make much sense. Crane is a genial and articulate man, yet one who does not surrender his deep beliefs. Withal, he seems to have been unable to convince people that he was of presidential stature. One problem for Crane is that he could not demonstrate his own effectiveness; and in his congressional career he has aimed at the propagation of ideas considerably at odds with the conventional wisdom rather than the achievement of incremental change. Evidently he did not much impress his successful rival: Crane complained at the Republican Convention that he, unlike other Republican candidates, did not get a speaking slot, and Reagan has made no other gestures to him. Still, Crane pretty accurately and with occasional flair represents views with considerable currency in the 12th district, and he is likely to go on doing so for some time.

Census Data   Pop. (1980 final) 611,505, up 33% in 1970s. Median family income, 1970, $15,173, 158% of U.S.

The Voters

   Employment profile 1970   White collar, 67%. Blue collar, 25%. Service, 8%. Farm, –%.
   Ethnic groups   Black 1980, 2%. Hispanic 1980, 3%. Asian 1980, 2%. Total foreign stock 1970, 20%. Germany, 4%; Italy, Poland, 2% each; Canada, UK, Sweden, USSR, 1% each.

Presidential Vote

1980	Reagan (R)	158,516	(62%)
	Carter (D)	65,143	(26%)
	Anderson (I)	28,616	(11%)
1976	Ford (R)	157,389	(68%)
	Carter (D)	70,460	(30%)

Rep. Philip M. Crane (R) Elected Nov. 25, 1969; b. Nov. 3, 1930, Chicago; home, Mt. Prospect; De Paul U., Hillsdale Col., B.A., Ind. U., M.A., Ph.D., U. of Mich., U. of Vienna.

Career Instructor, Ind. U., 1960–63; Asst. Prof., Bradley U., 1963–67; Dir. of Schools, Westminster Acad., 1967–68.

Offices 1035 LHOB, 202-225-3711. Also Suite 101, 1450 S. New Wilke Rd., Arlington Heights 60005, 312-394-0790.

Committee *Ways and Means* (5th). Subcommittees: Health; Oversight; Social Security.

Group Ratings

	ADA	COPE	PC	LCV	CFA	RPN	NAB	NSI	NTU	ACA	ACU
1980	6	5	13	20	7	—	100	100	87	95	100
1979	5	6	5	0	0	—	—	—	85	100	100
1978	5	6	10	10	9	67	100	100	70	100	95

Key Votes

1) Draft Registn $	AGN	6) Fair Hsg DOJ Enfrc	AGN	11) Cut Socl Incr Dfns $	FOR
2) Ban $ to Nicrgua	FOR	7) Lim PAC Contrbtns	AGN	12) Hosptl Cost Controls	—
3) Dlay MX Missile	AGN	8) Cap on Food Stmp $	—	13) Gasln Ctrls & Allctns	AGN
4) Nuclr Mortorium	—	9) New US Dep Edcatn	AGN	14) Lim Wndfll Prof Tax	FOR
5) Alaska Lands Bill	AGN	10) Cut OSHA $	FOR	15) Chryslr Loan Grntee	AGN

Election Results

1980 general	Philip M. Crane (R)	185,080	(74%)	($191,160)
	David McCartney (D)	64,729	(26%)	($9,424)
1980 primary	Philip M. Crane (R)	61,804	(100%)	
1978 general	Philip M. Crane (R)	110,503	(80%)	($191,075)
	Gilbert Bogen (D)	28,424	(20%)	

THIRTEENTH DISTRICT

The 13th congressional district of Illinois is part of the Chicago metropolitan area far beyond the range of the late Mayor Daley's machine, but well within the reach of the *Chicago Tribune*. The district forms a kind of half circle around the northern and western parts of the metropolitan area, as it stretches from the industrial town of Waukegan on Lake Michigan to a point below the German Catholic town of Aurora, due west of the Chicago Loop. Not quite as prosperous as the suburbs closer to Chicago, this area contains pockets of urban poverty and rural shabbiness, as well as some working-class neighborhoods and middle-class towns. The suburban building boom invaded the district's cornfields with real force in the late 1960s, but it slowed down abruptly in the late 1970s; and in general growth has not been as explosive as in the neighboring 12th or 14th districts.

In 1964 what is now the 13th district was a belt of suburban Cook County and collar county area that went for Barry Goldwater. Extending around the city at a radius from 20 to 60 miles, this area roughly coincided with the *Tribune*'s major circulation zone; and the *Tribune* Belt's preference for Goldwater was notable at a time when suburbs of other Great Lakes metropolitan areas went for Johnson. The *Tribune* was for many years the voice of mid-western Republicanism. It had few pretensions to objectivity. The *Tribune*'s longtime publisher, Colonel Robert McCormick, believed he knew the answer to the nation's problems and believed he had the obligation to use all his paper's columns in furtherance of what he believed. In the *Tribune* Belt around Chicago, where some people still had ties to the land and others had worked their way upward in the free enterprise system, Colonel McCormick's view of the world made sense, and his paper helped to strengthen the area's traditional Republicanism. In recent years the *Tribune* has changed; its news columns are objective in the tradition of the *New York Times,* and its editorial page does not necessarily breathe Republican fire. The nation has changed, too. The *Tribune* Belt in 1980 gave Ronald Reagan a large majority of its votes; but it did not find itself out of step with other suburban areas, or even with the nation as a whole.

The tenure of the 13th district's congressman dates from 1962, when the *Tribune* was becoming less slanted. He is a somewhat middle-of-the-road Republican, more inclined to agree with the Democrats than were the men who represented suburban and Downstate Illinois when he first went to the House or the young men who got elected in the Reagan sweep of 1980. This is Robert McClory, who still may be familiar to many for his role in the House Judiciary Committee impeachment hearings. McClory was then the second-ranking Republican on the committee—he lost the top slot by the flip of a coin 12 years before, which gave Edward Hutchinson, now retired, more seniority. A thin, nervous-seeming man, McClory was constantly commenting on the evidence, often with disapproval. He finally came out for impeaching Nixon for abuse of power but not for complicity in the coverup, for which he felt the evidence was insufficient.

McClory had some tough opposition in those Watergate days, both in primary and general elections. He survived that but has had more trouble since. In 1978 a primary challenger held him to 59%, in 1980 to 60%—neither margin showing great strength. He has won more easily in general elections. In 1982, at age 74, he will be one of the oldest members of the House, and he may face serious competition again if he decides to run. An additional complication: redistricting will almost certainly change the composition, although not the political complexion, of this district.

Census Data   Pop. (1980 final) 116,322, up 14% in 1970s. Median family income, 1970, $11,994, 125% of U.S.

The Voters

  Employment profile 1970   White collar, 47%. Blue collar, 40%. Service, 12%. Farm, 1%.
  Ethnic groups   Black 1980, 6%. Hispanic 1980, 5%. Asian 1980, 1%. Total foreign stock 1970, 18%. Germany, 4%; Poland, UK, Sweden, Canada, 1% each.

320   ILLINOIS

Presidential Vote

1980	Reagan (R)	116,322	(61%)
	Carter (D)	53,507	(28%)
	Anderson (I)	17,978	(9%)
1976	Ford (R)	109,215	(62%)
	Carter (D)	64,623	(37%)

Rep. Robert McClory (R) Elected 1962; b. Jan. 31, 1908, Riverside; home, Lake Bluff; Dartmouth Col., 1926–28, Chicago-Kent Col. of Law, LL.B. 1932.

Career Practicing atty.; Ill. House of Reps., 1951–53; Ill. Senate, 1953–63.

Offices 2109 RHOB, 202-225-5221. Also Kane County Municipal Bldg., 150 Dexter Ct., Elgin 60120, 312-697-5005.

Committees *Judiciary* (Ranking Member). Subcommittees: Administrative Law and Governmental Relations; Monopolies and Commercial Law.

Select Committee on Intelligence (3d). Subcommittee: Legislation.

Group Ratings

	ADA	COPE	PC	LCV	CFA	RPN	NAB	NSI	NTU	ACA	ACU
1980	17	25	50	32	36	—	75	88	42	67	47
1979	16	21	15	20	11	—	—	—	49	81	79
1978	45	21	20	34	18	91	91	89	21	73	70

Key Votes

1) Draft Registn $	AGN	6) Fair Hsg DOJ Enfrc	FOR	11) Cut Socl Incr Dfns $	FOR
2) Ban $ to Nicrgua	FOR	7) Lim PAC Contrbtns	AGN	12) Hosptl Cost Controls	AGN
3) Dlay MX Missile	AGN	8) Cap on Food Stmp $	AGN	13) Gasln Ctrls & Allctns	AGN
4) Nuclr Mortorium	AGN	9) New US Dep Edcatn	AGN	14) Lim Wndfll Prof Tax	FOR
5) Alaska Lands Bill	FOR	10) Cut OSHA $	FOR	15) Chryslr Loan Grntee	—

Election Results

1980 general	Robert McClory (R)	131,448	(72%)	($96,805)
	Michael Reese (D).............	52,000	(28%)	
1980 primary	Robert McClory (R)	40,335	(60%)	
	Cal Skinner, Jr. (R)	26,668	(40%)	($26,669)
1978 general	Robert McClory (R)	64,060	(61%)	($111,477)
	Frederick J. Steffen (D)	40,675	(39%)	($82,216)

FOURTEENTH DISTRICT

To judge from census figures on median family income, three of the nation's five most affluent congressional districts are in the suburbs of Chicago. One of them is the 14th of Illinois. And of all the richest districts, this is undoubtedly the most Republican and conservative. The district includes practically all of DuPage County, a fast-growing, affluent group of suburbs west of Chicago, that regularly produces higher Republican percentages than Orange

County, California. Appropriately, DuPage County was the site of the palatial estate of Colonel Robert McCormick, longtime publisher of the *Chicago Tribune;* for almost 50 years McCormick's paper was the house organ for his brand of conservative, isolationist Republicanism. If DuPage County has long since ceased to be isolationist, it must still be counted as conservative. People here have seen the free enterprise system work; it has made their lives comfortable and built pleasant communities all around them. They have also seen the corruption and the seaminess of the parts of life in Chicago they associate with the Democratic Party and its programs, and they want none of it. DuPage County back in 1964 went 60% for Barry Goldwater; in 1976 it was 69% for Gerald Ford, giving him a plurality of more than 100,000 votes and wiping out more than half of Jimmy Carter's margin in Cook County. In 1980, John Anderson cut into the Republican vote a little but Ronald Reagan still had 64% here and a margin above 100,000.

The suburbs of Chicago, led by DuPage County, have become the heartland of Illinois Republicanism, producing larger percentages and more votes for Republican candidates than historically Republican Downstate Illinois. Without the suburban vote in 1980, Ronald Reagan could not have carried Illinois.

The 14th district's congressman, John Erlenborn, has been witness to the changes in national political attitudes from the Goldwater defeat to the Reagan victory. He was first elected to the House in 1964 and as a freshman Republican had to stand by and watch as the Democrats enacted almost all the Great Society legislation into law. He has served, moreover, on the House Education and Labor Committee, a body which, even as Democratic programs became less popular, never lost a prolabor and pro–Great Society majority. It must have been lonely duty. Erlenborn has always been a pretty regular and conservative Republican, and for many years, even as he climbed in seniority, he had few successful legislative fights. He was one of those Republicans, however, who helped to lay the groundwork for the defeat of the Carter Administration and organized labor on two bills—common situs picketing and labor law reform—that have permanently reduced the clout of the AFL–CIO as a lobby, even at a time when Democrats still controlled the White House and both houses of Congress. (The measures passed the House after some controversy and were beaten in the Senate.)

Now that Republicans control the White House and the Senate, Erlenborn is in a more powerful position in the House. He is still only the number two Republican on Education and Labor; the ranking minority position is occupied by John Ashbrook of Ohio, a dreamy sort who specializes in lost causes. But for practical purposes, Erlenborn is the Republican leader on many Education and Labor issues. In the 1980s he has considerably more allies and more clout than he had in the past, and his role may be crucial if the Reagan Administration is to realize its apparent goal of reducing entitlement programs.

Erlenborn has no trouble winning reelection, the 14th district, its population having increased, will be altered by redistricting, but there will always be a solid Republican district centered in DuPage County.

Census Data   Pop. (1980 final) 625,629, up 35% in 1970s. Median family income, 1970, $14,527, 151% of U.S.

The Voters

Employment profile 1970   White collar, 65%. Blue collar, 27%. Service, 8%. Farm, –%.
Ethnic groups   Black 1980, 1%. Hispanic 1980, 2%. Asian 1980, 3%. Total foreign stock 1970, 21%. Germany, 4%; Italy, Poland, UK, 2% each; Czechoslovakia, Canada, Sweden, 1% each.

Presidential Vote

1980	Reagan (R)	182,308	(64%)
	Carter (D)	68,991	(24%)
	Anderson (I)	29,801	(11%)
1976	Ford (R)	168,314	(69%)
	Carter (D)	68,222	(28%)

Rep. John N. Erlenborn (R) Elected 1964; b. Feb. 8, 1927, Chicago; home, Elmhurst; U. of Notre Dame, 1944, Ind. St. Teachers Col., 1944–45, Loyola U., LL.B. 1949.

Career Navy, WWII; Practicing atty., 1949–50, 1952–64; Asst. States Atty., DuPage Co., 1950–52; Ill. House of Reps., 1957–65.

Offices 2265 RHOB, 202-225-3515. Also DuPage Co. Ctr., 421 N. County Farm Rd., Wheaton 60187, 312-668-1417.

Committees *Education and Labor* (2d). Subcommittees: Labor–Management Relations; Labor Standards; Post Secondary Education.

Government Operations (2d). Subcommittees: Government Information and Individual Rights; Legislation and National Security.

Group Ratings

	ADA	COPE	PC	LCV	CFA	RPN	NAB	NSI	NTU	ACA	ACU
1980	11	11	30	39	7	—	70	44	54	85	74
1979	26	20	15	21	7	—	—	—	48	68	69
1978	30	10	20	30	18	90	100	80	26	69	76

Key Votes

1) Draft Registn $	FOR	6) Fair Hsg DOJ Enfrc	AGN	11) Cut Socl Incr Dfns $	FOR
2) Ban $ to Nicrgua	AGN	7) Lim PAC Contrbtns	AGN	12) Hosptl Cost Controls	AGN
3) Dlay MX Missile	AGN	8) Cap on Food Stmp $	FOR	13) Gasln Ctrls & Allctns	AGN
4) Nuclr Mortorium	AGN	9) New US Dep Edcatn	AGN	14) Lim Wndfll Prof Tax	FOR
5) Alaska Lands Bill	AGN	10) Cut OSHA $	FOR	15) Chryslr Loan Grntee	AGN

Election Results

1980 general	John N. Erlenborn (R)	202,583	(77%)	($66,340)
	LeRoy E. Kennel (D)	61,224	(23%)	($0)
1980 primary	John N. Erlenborn (R)	73,801	(81%)	
	One other (R)	16,938	(19%)	
1978 general	John N. Erlenborn (R)	118,741	(75%)	($52,212)
	James A. Romanyak (D)	39,438	(25%)	

FIFTEENTH DISTRICT

The 15th congressional district of Illinois is where the Chicago metropolitan area meets the corn-growing prairie that stretches west toward the Rocky Mountains more than a thousand miles away. This is some of the richest farmland in the nation, crisscrossed by railroads and highways that lead to the huge market town of Chicago. Part of the 15th, the small conservative city of Aurora, is only 30 miles from Chicago; from there one can proceed west to DeKalb, site of Northern Illinois University, or south to the small industrial towns of Ottawa and Streator, on the way to Peoria. With its fertile soil and prosperous farmers, the 15th has historically been one of the most solidly Republican constituencies in the nation; only LaSalle County here turns in a Democratic majority now and then. Yet over the last 11 years the district has had five different congressmen — and one of them was a Democrat.

Part of the reason for the political volatility was redistricting. The old districts represented by Republicans Charlotte Reid (former vocalist on Don McNeill's Breakfast Club) and Leslie Arends were combined; Reid resigned to take a place on FCC, and the seat was won by Cliffard Carlson, who declined to oppose Arends in the 1972 general election. Arends was one of the grand old men of the Republican Party, first elected to Congress in 1934, House Republican whip since 1943. With his long white hair curling up under his collar, Arends remained a familar figure in the House until he was almost 80, eagerly gladhanding his colleagues with the joviality one encounters at a small-town Rotary luncheon. But Arends's performance in 1972 was disappointing, and he retired two years later. This set the stage for the Democrats; with the lackluster former Congressman Carlson as their candidate, the Republicans lost to a 49-year-old teacher named Tim Hall. Hall did not have much of the political savvy shown by so many other Democrats elected in 1974, and he was one of two members of that freshman class to be defeated in 1976.

The winner, and current congressman, is Tom Corcoran, personable, articulate, and well organized. His credentials included private industry (the Chicago & North Western Railway) and government (Washington representative of the state of Illinois). He serves on the Energy and Commerce Committee and has shown great competence in winning votes: in 1980 he was reelected with 77%. The only danger he faces is redistricting. This area, at the juncture of suburban Chicago and Downstate Illinois, was sliced up pretty badly in the redistricting 10 years ago, and the 15th could be the Downstate district that gets eliminated (although its population has increased slightly). Corcoran's problem, in that case, would be the Republican primary.

Census Data Pop. (1980 final) 495,322, up 7% in 1970s. Median family income, 1970, $10,619, 111% of U.S.

The Voters

Employment profile 1970 White collar, 41%. Blue collar, 42%. Service, 12%. Farm, 5%.
Ethnic groups Black 1980, 3%. Hispanic 1980, 5%. Total foreign stock 1970, 14%. Germany, 3%; Italy, UK, Sweden, 1% each.

Presidential Vote

1980	Reagan (R)	141,134	(64%)
	Carter (D)	57,919	(26%)
	Anderson (I)	19,477	(9%)
1976	Ford (R)	115,849	(59%)
	Carter (D)	78,766	(40%)

Rep. Tom Corcoran (R) Elected 1976; b. May 23, 1939, Ottawa; home, Ottawa; U. of Notre Dame, B.A. 1961, U. of Ill., U. of Chi., Northwestern U.

Career Army, 1963–65; Staff Dir. for Ill. Senate Pres. pro tem, W. Russell Arrington, 1966–69; Dir. of the State of Ill. Ofc., Wash., D.C., 1969–72; Admin. Asst. to Ill. Senate Pres. William C. Harris, 1972–74; V.P., Chicago and Northwestern Transportation Co., 1974–76.

Offices 1107 LHOB, 202-225-2976. Also 436 N. Lake St., Aurora 60506, 312-897-2220.

Committees *Energy and Commerce* (9th). Subcommittees: Energy Conservation and Power; Fossil and Synthetic Fuels.

Post Office and Civil Service (4th). Subcommittees: Human Resources; Postal Operations and Services.

Group Ratings

	ADA	COPE	PC	LCV	CFA	RPN	NAB	NSI	NTU	ACA	ACU
1980	6	5	27	36	7	—	—	100	54	96	33
1979	16	10	25	33	11	—	—	—	56	96	86
1978	25	10	18	44	23	70	100	70	24	88	87

Key Votes

1) Draft Registn $	FOR	6) Fair Hsg DOJ Enfrc	AGN	11) Cut Socl Incr Dfns $	FOR
2) Ban $ to Nicrgua	FOR	7) Lim PAC Contrbtns	AGN	12) Hosptl Cost Controls	AGN
3) Dlay MX Missile	AGN	8) Cap on Food Stmp $	FOR	13) Gasln Ctrls & Allctns	—
4) Nuclr Mortorium	—	9) New US Dep Edcatn	FOR	14) Lim Wndfll Prof Tax	FOR
5) Alaska Lands Bill	FOR	10) Cut OSHA $		FOR	15) Chryslr Loan Grntee	AGN

Election Results

1980 general	Tom Corcoran (R)	150,898	(77%)	($97,859)
	John P. Quillin (D)	45,721	(23%)	($0)
1980 primary	Tom Corcoran (R)	49,830	(100%)	
1978 general	Tom Corcoran (R)	80,856	(62%)	($180,076)
	Tim L. Hall (D)	48,756	(38%)	($21,368)

SIXTEENTH DISTRICT

The northwestern corner of Illinois, which forms the state's 16th congressional district, is slightly different politically from the rest of the state. A little like Wisconsin or Iowa, this part of Illinois has a larger number of Scandinavian–Americans and a stronger good government tradition than the patronage-rich precincts of Chicago or the businesslike precincts of the rest of Downstate Illinois. The political tradition here is, if anything, more Republican than the rest of Downstate; but it is a Republicanism that has been inclined on occasion toward maverick tendencies. The 16th district includes the town of Freeport, site of the most famous of the Lincoln–Douglas debates, and Galena, the home of President U. S. Grant, once a thriving commercial center but now a Mississippi River backwater. Its largest city is Rockford, which is actually the second largest city in Illinois; but its metropolitan area population is only 278,000, which is pretty insignificant next to Chicago's six million plus.

The 16th district turned out to have a special distinction in 1980: in it are the childhood homes of two of the three major presidential candidates in the general election, Ronald Reagan and John Anderson. Reagan's connection with the district is historic; although he retains happy memories, he left the town of Dixon in 1932. Anderson's relationship has been closer. He returned to Rockford after time in the military and Foreign Service and eventually was elected to Congress in 1960. He represented the district for 20 years, the first few years as a conventional conservative Republican (he even introduced a constitutional amendment to make the nation explicitly Christian), and later as a kind of liberal maverick. He cosponsored campaign finance reforms and condemned the Nixon Administration early in the Watergate crisis; for these and other sins he was nearly ousted from his leadership position (chairman of the House Republican Conference) in 1971 and 1975. His record eventually inspired conservative primary opposition, in the person of right-wing minister Don Lyon, in 1978; and after intensive campaigning Anderson was able to win only 58% of the vote. That did it: he decided to retire from the House, and after toying a moment with the idea of running for the Senate (the incumbent, Adlai Stevenson, was retiring), he decided to seek the Republican presidential nomination instead. He got a lot of attention from the national news media, which seemed fascinated with the idea of a moderate Republican even in a year when the Republican mood was clearly conservative. Anderson also began to appear a lot in *Doonesbury*—and the comic strip may have convinced many young voters with liberal views on cultural issues that Anderson was their kind of candidate. But he never actually won any Republican primaries. After coming close in Vermont and Massachusetts, he trailed Ronald Reagan in his native Illinois. Facing the choice of a hopeless race for the Republican nomination or an almost certainly unsuccessful independent candidacy, he chose the latter. There was a legitimate opening: neither Carter nor Reagan was seen as conservative on economic issues and liberal on cultural issues, while Anderson could be so depicted; and an increasing number of voters in the 1970s had been looking for just such a candidate. However, Anderson's candidacy never achieved its potential. The summer months were devoted to qualifying Anderson on the ballot in 50 states—something George Wallace accomplished eight years before in a less favorable legal framework with much less ballyhoo—and not until late in the fall did Anderson television advertisements begin to appear. He ended up with an uninspiring 7% of the vote—enough, however, to qualify him for some federal matching funds.

People in the 16th district knew long before 1980 that Anderson was not going to run for Congress again, and a spirited primary developed to succeed him. Don Lyon, the same right winger who had gotten 42% in the 1978 primary ran again; this time he had only 26%, an indication that some of his earlier support consisted of anti-Anderson votes. The winner was Lynn Martin, a state senator from Rockford. With the Republican nomination in hand and the reputation of a moderate (largely because she supports the Equal Rights Amendment in a state whose legislature has adamantly refused to ratify it), Martin was the clear favorite. The Democrat, Douglas Aurand, the county treasurer in Rockford, could not even come close; Martin won with 67% of the vote. Ironically, she will probably provide the district the kind of representation Anderson did during most of his congressional career, even though Anderson himself was deterred from running here again by the prospect of a tough race and, as a presidential candidate, finished third with 12% of the vote in a constituency he represented for 20 years. Still, Anderson has the option of running again in 1984, since he is entitled to federal funding and has a good mailing list of contributors. Meanwhile, he has returned to live in Rockford, where his youngest daughter is in school, while he makes his living lecturing and reflects on his options. It was Ronald Reagan, the native son who left 48 years ago, who carried the district with an absolute majority of the vote.

Census Data   Pop. (1980 final) 486,845, up 5% in 1970s. Median family income, 1970, $10,668, 111% of U.S.

The Voters

Employment profile 1970   White collar, 41%. Blue collar, 43%. Service, 11%. Farm, 5%.
Ethnic groups   Black 1980, 5%. Hispanic 1980, 2%. Total foreign stock 1970, 14%. Germany, Sweden, 3% each; Italy, 2%; UK, 1%.

Presidential Vote

1980	Reagan (R)	184,821	(64%)
	Carter (D)	65,855	(23%)
	Anderson (I)	35,622	(12%)
1976	Ford (R)	108,790	(58%)
	Carter (D)	76,448	(41%)

Rep. Lynn M. Martin (R) Elected 1980; b. Dec. 26, 1939, Chicago; home, Rockford; U. of Ill., B.A. 1960.

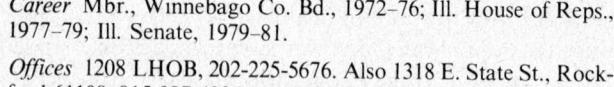

Career Mbr., Winnebago Co. Bd., 1972–76; Ill. House of Reps., 1977–79; Ill. Senate, 1979–81.

Offices 1208 LHOB, 202-225-5676. Also 1318 E. State St., Rockford 61108, 815-987-4326, and 3424 W. Elm St., McHenry 60050, 815-344-3939.

Committees Budget (9th).

House Administration (8th). Subcommittees: Accounts; Contracts and Printing.

Joint Committee on Printing.

Group Ratings and Key Votes: Newly Elected

Election Results

1980 general	Lynn M. Martin (R)	132,905	(67%)	($318,791)
	Douglas R. Aurand (D)	64,224	(33%)	($41,535)
1980 primary	Lynn M. Martin (R)	36,291	(45%)	
	Don Lyon (R)	20,643	(26%)	($383,221)
	Dick Crosby (R)	9,493	(12%)	($75,325)
	Steve Anderson (R)...........	9,294	(12%)	($29,314)
	One other (R)	4,975	(6%)	
1978 general	John B. Anderson (R)	76,752	(65%)	($232,379)
	Ernest W. Dahlin (D)	40,471	(35%)	($17,257)

SEVENTEENTH DISTRICT

The 17th congressional district of Illinois combines the southern edge of the Chicago metropolitan area with the fertile farmland of the central Illinois prairie. The district's largest city is Joliet, with less than 100,000 people, an economically healthy manufacturing city 50 miles southwest of Chicago. Somewhat less prosperous and considerably smaller is Kankakee, on the river and in the county of the same name, some 80 miles from Chicago and smack in the middle of farmland. Taken together, this territory is politically marginal in most years, although in 1980 it delivered healthy majorities for Ronald Reagan. Agricultural Iroquois County, in the southern part of the district, is one of the most Republican in the state (73%

for Reagan). In the northern part of the district Chicago Heights and Park Forest are swing suburbs, likely to go with the winner of any statewide election.

This district was established by the 1971 redistricting and has had only one congressman, Republican George O'Brien. A one-term member of the Illinois House, O'Brien got the nomination in 1972 when the House speaker, daunted by criticism that he had drawn the district's boundaries so he could run himself, decided not to make the race. O'Brien has had trouble in two general elections: in 1974, when Watergate helped the Democrats, and in 1976, when his opponent spent some $390,000 on billboards, newspaper ads, and red, white, and blue station wagons touring rural areas to publicize his candidacy. O'Brien survived this assault of hoopla with a solid 58% and has had no trouble since. He serves quietly in the House and on the Appropriations Committee.

Redistricting could change the shape of this district or, conceivably, eliminate it altogether. This is true although it now has one of the largest populations of Illinois districts, because it is poised on the boundary between Chicago suburbs and Downstate, and also because O'Brien may not have many friends when the redistricting plans are drawn up in Springfield.

Census Data Pop. (1980 final) 540,479, up 17% in 1970s. Median family income, 1970, $11,286, 118% of U.S.

The Voters

Employment profile 1970 White collar, 41%. Blue collar, 43%. Service, 21%. Farm, 3%.
Ethnic groups Black 1980, 12%. Hispanic 1980, 4%. Asian 1980, 1%. Total foreign stock 1970, 16%. Germany, Italy, 1% each.

Presidential Vote

1980	Reagan (R)	120,293	(58%)
	Carter (D)	72,365	(35%)
	Anderson (I)	12,138	(6%)
1976	Ford (R)	110,999	(55%)
	Carter (D)	88,195	(44%)

Rep. George M. O'Brien (R) Elected 1972; b. June 17, 1917, Chicago; home, Joliet; Northwestern U., A.B. 1939, Yale U.. J.D. 1947.

Career Air Force, WWII; Practicing atty.; Will Co. Bd. of Supervisors, 1956–64; Ill. House of Reps., 1971–72.

Offices 2439 RHOB, 202-225-3635. Also 101 N. Joliet St., Joliet 60431, 815-740-2040.

Committee *Appropriations* (12th). Subcommittees: Commerce, Justice, State and Judiciary; Labor–Health and Human Services–Education.

Group Ratings

	ADA	COPE	PC	LCV	CFA	RPN	NAB	NSI	NTU	ACA	ACU
1980	22	23	23	28	21	—	55	75	55	77	68
1979	11	20	10	24	7	—	—	—	51	73	86
1978	25	15	20	40	23	70	91	100	19	77	81

Key Votes

1) Draft Registn $	AGN	6) Fair Hsg DOJ Enfrc	AGN	11) Cut Socl Incr Dfns $	—
2) Ban $ to Nicrgua	FOR	7) Lim PAC Contrbtns	AGN	12) Hosptl Cost Controls	AGN
3) Dlay MX Missile	AGN	8) Cap on Food Stmp $	FOR	13) Gasln Ctrls & Allctns	AGN
4) Nuclr Mortorium	—	9) New US Dep Edcatn	AGN	14) Lim Wndfll Prof Tax	FOR
5) Alaska Lands Bill	FOR	10) Cut OSHA $	FOR	15) Chryslr Loan Grntee	FOR

Election Results

1980 general	George M. O'Brien (R)	125,806	(66%)	($132,147)
	Michael A. Murer (D)	65,305	(34%)	($29,724)
1980 primary	George M. O'Brien (R)	38,455	(100%)	
1978 general	George M. O'Brien (R)	94,375	(71%)	($112,346)
	Clifford J. Sinclair (D)	39,260	(29%)	($14,808)

EIGHTEENTH DISTRICT

"Will it play in Peoria?" was a favorite question among Nixon White House aides, believing as they did that they had a special and superior understanding of the thinking of Middle America. For them the country was personified by Peoria, a place where market researchers test commercial products and where the voters have usually produced comfortable margins for Republican candidates. Actually, it can be argued that Peoria is not all that typical. Its economy is not nearly so diversified as those of many Illinois cities, since it depends heavily on the Caterpillar farm machinery company; nor can its Republican voting behavior be described as all that typical of a nation that has, for most of the last 50 years, voted Democratic. Peoria today is a more varied and cosmopolitan place than the Nixon people might have supposed and indeed did turn pretty heavily against Nixon during Watergate. Earlier it had proven its capacity to produce unusual people, from Senator Everett McKinley Dirksen (who actually came from Pekin, across the Illinois River) to writer Betty Friedan.

Peoria is the nucleus of Illinois's 18th congressional district, the district now represented by the House's Republican Leader, Robert Michel (he dislikes the title minority leader). The successor-but-one of Dirksen in the House seat, Michel has been congressman here since the 1956 election and served as a congressional aide before that; although not yet 60, he is one of the most senior and most experienced congressional Republicans. For many of those years he was known less for his political acumen than for the facts that he was a star pitcher on the House Republican softball team and that he had a fine singing voice. But as he moved up slowly in seniority (he would be ranking minority member on Appropriations but for his leadership post), he also showed considerable political ability as well.

Michel's first leadership post was as chairman of the Republican Congressional Campaign Committee; he got that in 1973, when House Republicans rebelled against the choice dictated by the Nixon politicos. After the 1974 election, he became Republican whip, replacing fellow Illinoisan Leslie Arends. When Michel first took that position, his main job was to work with Minority Leader John Rhodes to round up enough votes to sustain Gerald Ford's vetoes; the Republicans were very much on the defensive. But over the next several years, and even though Republicans gained few seats in the House until 1980, House Republicans gained the initiative, and some of the credit for that should go to Michel. Not all: he is not a man who comes up with innovative policy ideas, like Jack Kemp or David Stockman. But he is politically shrewd, a man who is affable enough to get along with all his Republican colleagues and many Democrats as well and smart enough to frame issues in terms that give the maximum advantage to his side. In the Carter years, Republicans defeated the

Democrats on some notable issues, such as the proposed consumer protection agency, and became united around Republican initiatives that, at the least, embarrassed the Democrats, like the Kemp–Roth tax cut plan.

Many younger House Republicans thought John Rhodes was insufficiently aggressive as party leader, and before the 1980 elections Rhodes announced he would not run for minority leader again. The two main competitors for the post were Michel and Campaign Committee Chairman Guy VanderJagt. VanderJagt had the advantage of having worked directly for the election of many junior members and the exposure of having been keynoter at the 1980 Republican National Convention; he had the disadvantage of knowing relatively little about the nuts and bolts of legislation and House procedures. Both candidates claimed enough votes to win, but Michel turned out to be the better nose-counter and prevailed by a 103 to 87 vote margin. As Republican Leader Michel has the potential to be a man of national prominence; more important, he is also in a position to weld together a more or less permanent working majority of Republicans and conservative Democrats in the House. This means holding together the Republicans, which is easier when the party is a small minority without the burden of governing, and attracting some Democratic votes as well. Michel is probably as capable as any House Republican of achieving these goals.

Michel is reelected in the 18th district routinely every two years, although by less than stunning margins; one gathers that his interest in national legislation prevents him from paying as close attention to the district as those congressmen who end up winning by 3–1 margins. Michel's only real scare was in the Watergate year of 1974, when he was held to 55%; it seems hardly likely that the House Republican leader will have difficulty winning reelection in Peoria during the next few years.

Census Data   Pop. (1980 final) 486,948, up 5% in 1970s. Median family income, 1970, $10,096, 105% of U.S.

The Voters
Employment profile 1970   White collar, 44%. Blue collar, 38%. Service, 13%. Farm, 5%.
Ethnic groups   Black 1980, 5%. Hispanic 1980, 1%. Total foreign stock 1970, 9%. Germany, 2%; UK, 1%.

Presidential Vote

1980	Reagan (R)	135,243	(60%)
	Carter (D)	73,463	(33%)
	Anderson (I)	14,381	(6%)
1976	Ford (R)	113,592	(56%)
	Carter (D)	88,371	(43%)

Rep. Robert H. Michel (R) Elected 1956; b. Mar. 2, 1923, Peoria; home, Peoria; Bradley U., B.S. 1948.

Career Army, WWII; Admin. Asst., U.S. Rep. Harold Velde, 1949–56.

Offices 2112 RHOB, 202-225-6201. Also 1007 1st Natl. Bank Bldg., Peoria 61602, 309-673-6358.

Committees *Minority Leader.*

Group Ratings

	ADA	COPE	PC	LCV	CFA	RPN	NAB	NSI	NTU	ACA	ACU
1980	6	10	30	22	14	—	100	89	63	82	71
1979	5	10	3	5	0	—	—	—	55	87	92
1978	15	5	15	20	14	92	100	100	24	75	91

Key Votes

1) Draft Registn $	—	6) Fair Hsg DOJ Enfrc	AGN	11) Cut Socl Incr Dfns $	FOR
2) Ban $ to Nicrgua	FOR	7) Lim PAC Contrbtns	AGN	12) Hosptl Cost Controls	AGN
3) Dlay MX Missile	AGN	8) Cap on Food Stmp $	FOR	13) Gasln Ctrls & Allctns	AGN
4) Nuclr Mortorium	AGN	9) New US Dep Edcatn	AGN	14) Lim Wndfll Prof Tax	FOR
5) Alaska Lands Bill	AGN	10) Cut OSHA $	FOR	15) Chryslr Loan Grntee	AGN

Election Results

1980 general	Robert H. Michel (R)	125,561	(62%)	($134,540)
	John L. Knoppel (D)	76,471	(38%)	($43,483)
1980 primary	Robert H. Michel (R)	37,154	(100%)	
1978 general	Robert H. Michel (R)	85,973	(66%)	($57,439)
	Virgil R. Grunkemeyer (D).......	44,527	(34%)	

NINETEENTH DISTRICT

Tom Railsback is one of forty-odd Republican congressmen who were elected in previously Democratic districts in 1966—the best Republican year between the Eisenhower and the Reagan landslides. As such he is now one of the more senior Republicans in the House and one of the men the Reagan Administration must depend on to carry its legislation in the one still Democratic branch of government. Railsback is in many ways typical of those 1966 Republicans, and the kind of politics he has developed in 15 years in Washington gives us some suggestions of the potential the Reaganites have—and the problems they face—on Capitol Hill.

When Railsback was coming to political maturity, the Illinois Republican Party was still run by men out of the Everett Dirksen era—men who had followed Robert Taft in his battles against the internationalist Republicanism of the East and the New Deal Democratic politics of the national administration and the big industrial unions. These men had lost the great national battles, but they were still the dominant force in small-town Illinois Rotary clubs, and they were looking around for young men to take their places. Railsback was then 34, an attorney from Moline who had been in practice for less than 10 years, and a four-year veteran of the Illinois legislature. He was the kind of bright young man they were looking for: a young lawyer who could stay in Congress for many years and accumulate seniority and power, and who was noticeably brighter and more personable than the average Illinois small-city Republican lawyer. Their hope was that he would be a solid bulwark of conservative Republicanism, a loyal foot soldier in his first years and someday perhaps a leader in Republican ranks.

In some respects Tom Railsback has fulfilled these hopes. He has indeed gained seniority, and he is the second-ranking Republican on the Judiciary Committee, behind the much older Robert McClory from the Chicago suburbs. On most economic issues he has been at one with the body of House Republicans. On foreign policy as well he is definitely within the Republican mainstream. On a number of important issues, however, he has gone against what most House Republicans favor; and, more important, on these issues he has been a real leader in the House. The most famous of these is the question of the impeachment of

Richard Nixon. Early in the impeachment hearings, he decided he would vote against Nixon, and he began gathering together likeminded Republicans and conservative Democrats from the Judiciary Committee to agree on strategy and draft articles of impeachment. These, of course, were the crucial votes, and one can argue that Railsback was the crucial actor in bringing Nixon down.

More recently, Railsback has been the Republican leader in the bipartisan effort to reduce the influence and campaign spending of political action committees. PAC spending increasingly has favored Republicans, as more and more corporations form PACs and as PACs no longer believe that they must give to Democrats because Democrats are going to control things anyway. The major effort to curb PACs in 1980 was the Obey–Railsback amendment, a measure that was lobbied furiously by Common Cause among other groups but still fell short of passage. Its prospects in the Reagan years seem dismal.

If Railsback's record must often be disappointing to some of his original backers, it has met with general approval from his constituents. Railsback never suffered for his opposition to Nixon; indeed, he has not had primary opposition since the impeachment vote. In the general election, he has had widespread support, including the endorsement of the United Auto Workers, an important factor in the politics of the industrial cities of Rock Island and Moline, the largest urban area in the district. Rock Island and Moline sometimes go Democratic but deliver large margins to Railsback; the rest of the district, rich agricultural counties to the north and south of Rock Island along the Mississippi River, is very heavily Republican. While redistricting will probably change the boundaries of the district somewhat, it should not affect Railsback's chances for reelection.

Census Data   Pop. (1980 final) 474,872, up 3% in 1970s. Median family income, 1970, $9,579, 100% of U.S.

The Voters

Employment profile 1970   White collar, 39%. Blue collar, 39%. Service, 14%. Farm, 8%.
Ethnic groups   Black 1980, 3%. Hispanic 1980, 3%. Total foreign stock 1970, 11%. Germany, Sweden, 2% each.

Presidential Vote

1980	Reagan (R)	117,933	(57%)
	Carter (D)	72,573	(35%)
	Anderson (I)	13,176	(6%)
1976	Ford (R)	105,234	(53%)
	Carter (D)	90,524	(46%)

Rep. Tom Railsback (R) Elected 1966; b. Jan. 22, 1932, Moline home, Moline; Grinnell Col., B.A. 1954, Northwestern U., J.D. 1957.

Career Army, 1957–59; Practicing atty., 1957–67; Ill. House of Reps., 1963–67.

Offices 2104 RHOB, 202-225-5905. Also Rm. 228 Fed. Bldg., 211 19th St., Rock Island 61201, 309-794-1681.

Committees *Judiciary* (2d). Subcommittees: Courts, Civil Liberties and the Administration of Justice; Monopolies and Commercial Law.

Select Committee on Narcotics Abuse and Control (Ranking Member).

Group Ratings

	ADA	COPE	PC	LCV	CFA	RPN	NAB	NSI	NTU	ACA	ACU
1980	44	39	30	49	21	—	36	50	34	52	26
1979	26	55	25	28	19	—	—	—	35	50	42
1978	20	25	45	41	27	92	100	67	16	56	65

Key Votes

1) Draft Registn $	AGN	6) Fair Hsg DOJ Enfrc	FOR
2) Ban $ to Nicrgua	AGN	7) Lim PAC Contrbtns	FOR
3) Dlay MX Missile	FOR	8) Cap on Food Stmp $	AGN
4) Nuclr Mortorium	AGN	9) New US Dep Edcatn	AGN
5) Alaska Lands Bill	AGN	10) Cut OSHA $	AGN

11) Cut Socl Incr Dfns $	—
12) Hosptl Cost Controls	AGN
13) Gasln Ctrls & Allctns	AGN
14) Lim Wndfll Prof Tax	FOR
15) Chryslr Loan Grntee	FOR

Election Results

1980 general	Tom Railsback (R)	142,616	(73%)	($78,384)
	Thomas J. Hand (D)	51,753	(27%)	($0)
1980 primary	Tom Railsback (R)	43,740	(100%)	
1978 general	Tom Railsback (R), unopposed . . .			($28,647)

TWENTIETH DISTRICT

The 20th district of Illinois is a descendant of the district that sent Abraham Lincoln, then a young Springfield lawyer and Whig politician, to the House of Representatives in 1846. The western part of the district, at least, sometimes seems to have changed little since the 19th century. It remains a land of fertile prairies, the bottomlands of the Mississippi and Illinois Rivers, farm marketing towns, and courthouse villages. The river port of Quincy on the Mississippi River has not grown much since the turn of the century, nor has the little village of Nauvoo, from which the Mormons were expelled in 1846 and led by Brigham Young to their promised land in Utah.

The largest city in the 20th district is Springfield, with 99,000 people. It must have been a bustling, perhaps even a gracious town in Abe Lincoln's and Mary Todd's time. Today it is a typical state capital: a middle-sized city with an old Capitol building, several not-so-elegant hotels, a small black ghetto, a little bit of industry, and a few shopping centers on the edge of town. Next to state government, the Lincoln tourist business seems to be the mainstay of the local economy.

On paper the 20th is a politically marginal district. It sits right on the traditional boundary separating the Democratic counties to the south (which Lincoln never carried) and the Republican counties to the north. The persistence of these party preferences is astonishing: practically the same pattern was visible in the contest between Gerald Ford and Jimmy Carter in 1976. Here, as elsewhere, Carter was soundly beaten in 1980.

But the 20th was still, for the first time in 18 years, the site of a seriously contested race, indeed two seriously contested races, in both the Republican primary and the general election. On the surface, there seemed to be no major reason why Congressman Paul Findley should find himself in such trouble. First elected in 1960, he had been returned routinely for years. His voting record on most issues was in line with the Republican conservatism that was endorsed by such large margins here in Ronald Reagan's primary and general election victories. But Findley has not been an ordinary congressman. He fancies himself an expert and original thinker in a number of areas and sometimes leads lonely fights on issues. As a member of the Agriculture Committee, he opposed sugar price supports; as a member of Foreign Affairs, he has supported United States contacts with the Palestine Liberation Organization and even sat down and talked with PLO leader Yasir Arafat. In the late 1970s, Findley became increasingly preoccupied with the Middle East, and he has characterized himself as Arafat's best friend in Congress.

That, as much as anything else, sparked the competition here in 1980. In the Republican primary, David Nuessen won 44% against him; in the general election, Democrat David Robinson also won 44%. Both used Findley's support for the goals of what they described as a Soviet-backed terrorist organization against him. Although he survived, the high percentages his challengers achieved show that he is certainly vulnerable in a future election. Ironically, on the stands that he was attacked for—and on other issues on which he takes distinctive positions—Findley is not very influential with other members. He makes his speeches, argues his case, and almost no one pays any attention: he is a leader without followers.

Census Data   Pop. (1980 final) 486,141, up 5% in 1970s. Median family income, 1970, $9,269, 97% of U.S.

The Voters

Employment profile 1970   White collar, 46%. Blue collar, 33%. Service, 14%. Farm, 7%.
Ethnic groups   Black 1980, 5%. Hispanic 1980, 1%. Total foreign stock 1970, 8%. Germany, 2%; Italy, UK, 1% each.

Presidential Vote

1980	Reagan (R)	169,853	(58%)
	Carter (D)	104,156	(36%)
	Anderson (I)	13,697	(5%)
1976	Ford (R)	99,738	(52%)
	Carter (D)	89,300	(47%)

Rep. Paul Findley (R) Elected 1960; b. June 23, 1921, Jacksonville; home, Pittsfield; Ill. Col. in Jacksonville, B.A. 1943.

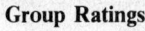

Career   Navy, WWII; Pres., Pike Press, Inc., 1947–60.

Offices   2113 RHOB, 202-225-5271. Also 205 Fed. Bldg., Springfield 62701, 217-525-4062.

Committees   *Agriculture* (2d). Subcommittees: Domestic Marketing, Consumer Relations and Nutrition; Wheat, Soybeans and Feed Grains.

Foreign Affairs (3d). Subcommittee: Europe and the Middle East.

Group Ratings

	ADA	COPE	PC	LCV	CFA	RPN	NAB	NSI	NTU	ACA	ACU
1980	28	17	30	48	21	—	64	44	39	70	37
1979	42	50	23	53	7	—	—	—	46	54	56
1978	35	15	45	34	32	80	83	75	21	79	59

Key Votes

1) Draft Registn $	FOR	6) Fair Hsg DOJ Enfrc	AGN	11) Cut Socl Incr Dfns $	FOR
2) Ban $ to Nicrgua	AGN	7) Lim PAC Contrbtns	AGN	12) Hosptl Cost Controls	AGN
3) Dlay MX Missile	AGN	8) Cap on Food Stmp $	FOR	13) Gasln Ctrls & Allctns	AGN
4) Nuclr Mortorium	AGN	9) New US Dep Edcatn	AGN	14) Lim Wndfll Prof Tax	FOR
5) Alaska Lands Bill	FOR	10) Cut OSHA $	AGN	15) Chryslr Loan Grntee	AGN

Election Results

1980 general	Paul Findley (R)	123,427	(56%)	($530,568)
	David Robinson (D)	96,950	(44%)	($674,974)
1980 primary	Paul Findley (R)	31,894	(56%)	
	David Nuessen (R)	25,499	(44%)	($127,681)
1978 general	Paul Findley (R)	111,054	(70%)	($117,721)
	Victor W. Roberts (D)	48,426	(30%)	($7,318)

TWENTY-FIRST DISTRICT

Downstate Illinois has always been one of the heartlands of the Republican Party. The stereotypical image is that Downstate is full of Republican farmers. Indeed it does have some of the richest farmlands in the nation, but the fact is that there are relatively few farmers: those that are here tend to live on giant farms, like the 3,000 acres Agriculture Secretary John Block owns. Actually, Downstate Illinois's population is mostly urban, clustered in small, industrial Decatur and in a white collar university town, Champaign–Urbana. These are the main population centers of the 21st congressional district of Illinois, a House seat that has gone Republican since 1938. This has not happened simply because people here are overwhelmingly Republican. Decatur, for example, often goes Democratic in elections; Champaign–Urbana, during the early 1970s and the protest against the Vietnam war, was trending toward the Democrats. The smaller counties, it is true, tend to tilt the district toward the Republicans in close national elections. But the continued and largely unchallenged Republican representation here seems to result as much from the area's social structure as from its party preference.

For this is an area that once, before the New Deal, was more heavily Republican than it is now. In those days the voters naturally elected the leading men in the community — successful lawyers, prominent businessmen, men active in the leading community organizations. They were intelligent, honest, and personable. The 21st district and other parts of Downstate Illinois have essentially continued this tradition, to the immense benefit of the Republican Party, since virtually anyone who fits this description in Downstate Illinois communities is a Republican.

Such a man is Congressman Edward Madigan of the 21st congressional district of Illinois. First elected in 1972, he was a successful businessman in Lincoln, one of the district's smaller cities. In the House he has a conservative voting record occasionally tempered by liberalism. He serves on the Energy and Commerce Committee, where he tends to support deregulation (of energy prices, railroad rates) and to back free-market approaches to problems. In 1981 he became ranking minority member on the Health Subcommittee, which has a wide and fascinating jurisdiction. Its primary business in 1981, for example, is passage of a revised Clean Air Act, which has ramifications for many important industries. Madigan has not projected a strong image on national issues. He seems more inclined to offer thoughtful solutions to less central problems, such as his proposal to allow the prescription of heroin to terminal cancer patients.

Madigan has grown very popular in his district and is regularly reelected by overwhelming majorities. His only problem is redistricting; there is an off chance that his would be the Downstate Illinois district to be lost when the new lines are drawn.

Census Data Pop. (1980 final) 490,872, up 6% in 1970s. Median family income, 1970, $10,043, 105% of U.S.

The Voters

Employment profile 1970 White collar, 51%. Blue collar, 29%. Service, 15%. Farm, 5%.
Ethnic groups Black 1980, 7%. Hispanic 1980, 1%. Asian 1980, 1%. Total foreign stock 1970, 7%. Germany, 2%.

Presidential Vote

1980	Reagan (R)	113,029	(50%)
	Carter (D)	87,652	(39%)
	Anderson (I)	21,996	(10%)
1976	Ford (R)	106,554	(55%)
	Carter (D)	85,545	(44%)

Rep. Edward R. Madigan (R) Elected 1972; b. Jan. 13, 1936, Lincoln; home, Lincoln; Lincoln Col.

Career Owner, taxi and car leasing co.; Lincoln Bd. of Zoning Appeals; Ill. House of Reps., 1967–72.

Offices 2457 RHOB, 202-225-2371. Also 202 W. Church St., Champaign 61820, 217-398-5516.

Committee *Energy and Commerce* (5th). Subcommittees: Commerce, Transportation and Tourism; Health and the Environment.

Group Ratings

	ADA	COPE	PC	LCV	CFA	RPN	NAB	NSI	NTU	ACA	ACU
1980	11	23	37	39	14	—	55	78	49	76	63
1979	37	32	18	35	19	—	—	—	40	68	59
1978	30	25	30	38	23	82	80	89	17	80	72

Key Votes

1) Draft Registn $	AGN	6) Fair Hsg DOJ Enfrc	AGN	11) Cut Socl Incr Dfns $	FOR
2) Ban $ to Nicrgua	FOR	7) Lim PAC Contrbtns	FOR	12) Hosptl Cost Controls	AGN
3) Dlay MX Missile	AGN	8) Cap on Food Stmp $	FOR	13) Gasln Ctrls & Allctns	AGN
4) Nuclr Mortorium	AGN	9) New US Dep Edcatn	FOR	14) Lim Wndfll Prof Tax	FOR
5) Alaska Lands Bill	FOR	10) Cut OSHA $	AGN	15) Chryslr Loan Grntee	FOR

Election Results

1980 general	Edward R. Madigan (R).........	132,186	(68%)	($148,147)
	Penny L. Severns (D)	63,476	(32%)	($27,577)
1980 primary	Edward R. Madigan (R).........	54,071	(100%)	
1978 general	Edward R. Madigan (R).........	97,473	(78%)	($78,219)
	Kenneth E. Baughman (D)	27,054	(22%)	

TWENTY-SECOND DISTRICT

The 22d congressional district of Illinois is geographically the largest district in the state, a collection of 20 predominantly rural Downstate counties. Its largest city, Danville, with 38,000 people, makes its living manufacturing farm equipment and otherwise serving as a trading center for the rural vicinity. This part of the Illinois prairie is prime agricultural country. The topsoil goes down deeper than just about anywhere else in the world, and the productivity of the farmland here is very high.

This district is, however, not of a piece politically. Across its midsection runs the Old National Road — now U.S. 40, paralleled by Interstate 70 — which is the approximate boundary of sociocultural influence in Downstate Illinois. North of this imaginary line is Yankee country, settled originally by farmers from northern Ohio or Indiana or Pennsylvania or Upstate New York. The accents are hard, and the politics has traditionally been Republican. Thus Danville, which is in the northern part of the district, used to elect as its congressman Joseph Cannon, the powerful speaker of the House against whom the progressives revolted in 1911. South of this imaginary line the land was settled by farmers from Kentucky, Virginia, and Tennessee. The accent here is softer and more drawling, and the politics traditionally more Democratic. Voters here had little use for the national Democratic politics of Hubert Humphrey or George McGovern, but many of them voted for Jimmy Carter in 1976. The close division of the 22d between these two segments can be seen in the 1976 presidential results: Gerald Ford carried this Downstate district, but with only 51% of the vote.

For 20 years the congressman from this district was George Shipley, a Democrat elected by a narrow margin in 1958 and reelected every two years, usually with percentages just above 50%. Shipley was the kind of Democrat in line with his district's thinking and by no means advanced on cultural issues. He won a seat on the Appropriations Committee and advanced to the eighth-ranking seniority position and a subcommittee chair. But he was in poor health, and in 1978 he decided at 50 to retire.

Shipley hoped to pass the seat on to his administrative assistant and brother-in-law, Don Watson. But experience on a Capitol Hill staff is not necessarily a good way to learn to run campaigns, and Watson was beaten in the Democratic primary by 34-year-old state Senator Terry Bruce. There was also an upset of sorts in the Republican primary. The early favorite was state legislator Roscoe Cunningham, a middle-aged veteran with an Everett Dirksen manner. But Cunningham was beaten by Daniel Crane, brother of 12th district Congressman Philip Crane and a Danville dentist. What Crane lacked in oratorical ability he made up in the capacity to raise funds and run a shrewd direct mail campaign.

The general election looked like a pretty even contest. But Crane was able to win a solid victory. Again money and organization seem to have made the difference. Philip Crane has access to national fund-raising direct mail lists, and from conservatives all over the country Daniel Crane was able to raise about four times as much money as Bruce. Again Crane relied heavily on direct mail, and again he won by a solid margin. Crane did even better in 1980, winning with 69% of the vote — the largest percentage ever recorded in this district. He seems in fine shape for 1982, although there is an outside chance the district could be split up by redistricting. Crane sits on the Post Office and Civil Service Committee, a good place to fight the evils of big government, and on the Small Business Committee.

Census Data   Pop. (1980 final) 490,731, up 6% in 1970s. Median family income, 1970, $8,350, 87% of U.S.

The Voters

Employment profile 1970   White collar, 37%. Blue collar, 40%. Service, 13%. Farm, 10%.
Ethnic groups   Black 1980, 2%. Hispanic 1980, 1%. Total foreign stock 1970, 4%. Germany, 1%.

Presidential Vote

1980	Reagan (R)	137,079	(60%)
	Carter (D)	80,436	(35%)
	Anderson (I)	9,176	(4%)
1976	Ford (R)	111,465	(51%)
	Carter (D)	104,967	(48%)

Rep. Daniel B. Crane (R) Elected 1978; b. Jan. 10, 1936, Chicago; home, Danville; Hillsdale Col., A.B. 1958, Ind. U., D.D.S. 1963, U. of Mich., 1964–65.

Career Army, Vietnam; Dentist, Dir., Crane Clinic, 1963–67.

Offices 115 CHOB, 202-225-5001. Also 426 Whittle Ave., Olney 62450, 618-395-2171.

Committees *Post Office and Civil Service* (8th). Subcommittees: Census and Population; Compensation and Employee Benefits.

Small Business (9th). Subcommittee: Tax, Access to Equity Capital and Business Opportunities.

Group Ratings

	ADA	COPE	PC	LCV	CFA	RPN	NAB	NSI	NTU	ACA	ACU
1980	11	10	20	39	7	—	100	100	86	96	100
1979	5	5	20	5	7	—	—	—	82	100	100

Key Votes

1) Draft Registn $	—	6) Fair Hsg DOJ Enfrc	AGN	11) Cut Socl Incr Dfns $	FOR
2) Ban $ to Nicrgua	FOR	7) Lim PAC Contrbtns	AGN	12) Hosptl Cost Controls	AGN
3) Dlay MX Missile	AGN	8) Cap on Food Stmp $	FOR	13) Gasln Ctrls & Allctns	AGN
4) Nuclr Mortorium	AGN	9) New US Dep Edcatn	AGN	14) Lim Wndfll Prof Tax	FOR
5) Alaska Lands Bill	AGN	10) Cut OSHA $	FOR	15) Chryslr Loan Grntee	AGN

Election Results

1980 general	Daniel B. Crane (R)	146,014	(69%)	($165,236)
	Peter M. Voelz (D)	66,065	(31%)	($19,691)
1980 primary	Daniel B. Crane (R)	44,476	(100%)	
1978 general	Daniel B. Crane (R)	86,051	(54%)	($438,764)
	Terry L. Bruce (D) ... .,,.....	73,331	(46%)	($107,281)

TWENTY-THIRD DISTRICT

The 23d congressional district of Illinois is the area across from St. Louis's Gateway Arch, where one can see East St. Louis, Belleville, and Granite City through the smog across the Mississippi River. These are not verdant St. Louis suburbs but grimy industrial towns crisscrossed by miles of railroad tracks. They have all the problems associated with core city areas: air pollution, inadequate housing, crime, and a declining tax base. East St. Louis became a black-majority town in the 1960s, but when blacks took over city hall, they found the treasury virtually bare — and the city lacking the resources to refill it. The Illinois side of the St. Louis metropolitan area has a disproportionate share of its poor and low-income working-class residents; the rich stay on the Missouri side of the river.

The 23d is easily the most Democratic of all the Downstate Illinois districts. It went for Stevenson in both Eisenhower landslides and came close to going for McGovern and Carter in 1972 and 1980 respectively. Local elections are almost always won by Democrats — the one notable exception being former St. Clair County Sheriff Dave O'Neal, who is now lieutenant governor of Illinois and was the Republican candidate for the U.S. Senate in 1980. The last time a Republican was elected to Congress here was in 1942. He was defeated in 1944 by Democrat Mel Price, who has been reelected ever since — usually by margins of better than 2-to-1. In Congress Price has held two positions with great importance for the federal budget — and national security. One was the chairmanship of the old Joint Committee on Atomic Energy, which for more than 25 years after World War II worked closely with the Atomic Energy Commission to develop nuclear weapons and nuclear power. Price was always a strong booster of nuclear power and was one of the authors of the Price–Anderson Act, which by providing federal insurance for nuclear power plant accidents tends to encourage the development of nuclear power.

Price's other important position is the chairmanship of the House Armed Services Committee. He assumed this position after the 1974 elections, when the new freshman Democrats dumped Edward Hebert of Louisiana and installed Price, the next most senior member. Ironically, Price does not share the younger Democrats' skepticism toward military spending; the history that has made an impression on him is the unpreparedness of the United States for war in the years before Pearl Harbor. His tendency has been to defer to the policies of successive administrations. In any case, the tide of opinion since Price became chairman has been moving pretty steadily toward the view that defense expenditures should be raised, not lowered, and the majority of the committee has always taken that view anyway. Price has accordingly had a more placid tenure than his immediate predecessors.

Price is now one of the oldest members of Congress. He turns 77 in 1982, and in 1980, for the first time in 20 years, he was held below a 2-to-1 margin by his Republican opponent. No one expects him to be beaten in this district, but it could be abolished in redistricting. So there is a good chance Price might face a tough race in the near future or might choose to retire.

Census Data   Pop. (1980 final) 441,876, down 5% in 1970s. Median family income, 1970, $9,872, 103% of U.S.

The Voters

Employment profile 1970   White collar, 45%. Blue collar, 41%. Service, 13%. Farm, 1%.
Ethnic groups   Black 1980, 19%. Hispanic 1980, 1%. Total foreign stock 1970, 8%. Germany, 2%.

Presidential Vote

1980	Reagan (R)	80,832	(47%)
	Carter (D)	82,375	(48%)
	Anderson (I)	6,836	(4%)
1976	Ford (R)	69,486	(40%)
	Carter (D)	100,616	(58%)

Rep. Melvin Price (D) Elected 1944; b. Jan. 1, 1905, E. St. Louis; home, E. St. Louis; St. Louis U., 1923-25.

Career Newspaper correspondent, E. St. Louis *Journal*, St. Louis *Globe-Democrat*; Sports ed., E. St. Louis *News-Review*; St. Clair Co. Bd. of Supervisors, 1929-31; Secy. to U.S. Rep. Edwin M. Schaefer, 1933-43; Army, WWII.

Offices 2110 RHOB, 202-225-5661. Also Fed. Bldg., 690 Missouri Ave., E. St. Louis 62201, 618-274-2200.

Committee *Armed Services* (Chairman). Subcommittees: Research and Development (Chairman); Procurement and Military Nuclear Systems.

Group Ratings

	ADA	COPE	PC	LCV	CFA	RPN	NAB	NSI	NTU	ACA	ACU
1980	56	89	57	44	86	—	8	22	8	13	5
1979	68	89	55	48	63	—	—	—	13	12	8
1978	45	85	60	47	64	36	9	38	6	23	13

Key Votes

1) Draft Registn $	FOR	6) Fair Hsg DOJ Enfrc	FOR	11) Cut Socl Incr Dfns $	AGN
2) Ban $ to Nicrgua	AGN	7) Lim PAC Contrbtns	FOR	12) Hosptl Cost Controls	FOR
3) Dlay MX Missile	AGN	8) Cap on Food Stmp $	AGN	13) Gasln Ctrls & Allctns	FOR
4) Nuclr Mortorium	AGN	9) New US Dep Edcatn	FOR	14) Lim Wndfll Prof Tax	AGN
5) Alaska Lands Bill	FOR	10) Cut OSHA $	AGN	15) Chryslr Loan Grntee	FOR

Election Results

1980 general	Melvin Price (D)	107,786	(64%)	($42,718)
	Ronald L. Davinroy (R)	59,644	(36%)	($23,683)
1980 primary	Melvin Price (D)	39,193	(86%)	
	Two others (D)	6,444	(14%)	
1978 general	Melvin Price (D)	74,247	(74%)	($42,416)
	Daniel J. Stack (R)	25,858	(26%)	($12,298)

TWENTY-FOURTH DISTRICT

Little Egypt is the name given the southernmost part of Illinois — the flat, fertile farmland where the Ohio River joins the Mississippi. This is low, alluvial land, subject to floods almost as often as ancient Egypt itself. The countryside is protected by giant levees that rise above the fields and hide any view of the waters. There is more than a touch of Dixie here: the southern tip of Illinois is geographically closer to Jackson, Mississippi, than to Chicago. The unofficial capital of Little Egypt is Cairo (pronounced KAYroh), a declining town at the exact confluence of the two rivers. Not so many years ago Cairo was the scene of a virtual war between its white majority and its large black minority; it must surely be one of the grimmest small towns in the United States.

There are no official boundaries to Little Egypt, but it is safe to say that the 24th congressional district goes north considerably beyond them. The district takes in the coal mining area around West Frankfort and Marion — one of the most heavily strip mined areas in the country. It extends to a point near the St. Louis suburbs and includes Carbondale, the site of Southern Illinois University. Nearly all this territory is Democratic in most elections, because of ancestral southern allegiance (this is southern-drawl, not midwestern hard-R, territory) or because of coal miners' preferences. But the district has not been reliably Democratic in recent presidential elections. It went against the Catholic John Kennedy in 1960 and the Great Society's Hubert Humphrey in 1968; while it gave southerner Jimmy Carter 54% of the vote in 1976, it turned against him sharply in 1980, as did many border areas, and gave him only 37%.

The 24th district also turned sharply, and rather unexpectedly, against its congressman, Paul Simon. This district has been represented by Democrats since 1954, and Simon, first elected in 1974, was not thought to be in trouble. Simon by common consent is one of the House's most thoughtful liberal Democrats, a man who wrote a book lamenting Americans' lack of knowledge of foreign languages and who is an expert in such an arcane field as adoption law. Admittedly, his cerebral liberalism might seem to be a little out of line with the rough-hewn drawls of Little Egypt, but in fact he is also a man well schooled in that most practical of politics, that of Illinois. As a small-town newspaper editor he was elected to the legislature, where he became known both for his support of reform and for his effectiveness — usually two mutually exclusive attributes in Illinois. He was elected lieutenant governor in 1968 and ran for governor in 1972; he lost the Democratic nomination because he had won the uneasy support of the Daley organization and his opponent, Daniel Walker, combined Downstate economy-minded support with last-minute votes from nonregistered Democrats who were suddenly allowed by the courts to vote in the primary. Simon has stayed out of statewide politics since and seemed to have made the 24th a safe district for himself.

On substantive matters Simon is both thoughtful and busy. He is chairman now of a major subcommittee on Postsecondary Education, the body that handles virtually all aid to higher education and most student loans, as well as federal aid to libraries, the arts and humanities, and museums. He serves on the Budget Committee and chairs its task force on Entitlements, Uncontrollables, and Indexing. He is well prepared, good humored, and generally respected.

Why was he in such trouble in 1980 then, against a man he had beaten easily two years before? One reason was that he spent a lot of time in national politics. He was an early supporter of Edward Kennedy for the presidency — a position that soon became very unpopular in southern Illinois. He spent considerable time working on legislative issues in Washington. And, one cannot help thinking, he simply got caught up in the unpopularity of the liberal programs with which he has been associated. Ironically, Simon is one of those liberals who can be persuaded to take a second look at liberal programs; he supports the below-minimum wage for teenagers, for example. Simon lost several traditionally Republican counties, as might be expected, but he also lost two big counties in the coal mining area that are ordinarily Democratic. He can be expected to work hard to get in better graces with the district's voters for 1982, but he can also be reasonably sure that the Republicans will contest this seat as seriously as they have done at any time in the last 30 years.

Census Data   Pop. (1980 final) 517,190, up 11% in 1970s. Median family income, 1970, $7,501, 78% of U.S.

The Voters

Employment profile 1970   White collar, 38%. Blue collar, 40%. Service, 15%. Farm, 7%.
Ethnic groups   Black 1980, 4%. Hispanic 1980, 1%. Total foreign stock 1970, 5%. Germany, 1%.

Presidential Vote

1980	Reagan (R)	131,012	(57%)
	Carter (D)	89,611	(39%)
	Anderson (I)	8,745	(4%)
1976	Ford (R)	109,391	(46%)
	Carter (D)	127,696	(53%)

Rep. Paul Simon (D) Elected 1974; b. Nov. 29, 1928, Eugene, Oreg.; home, Carbondale; U. of Oreg., 1945–46, Dana Col., 1946–48.

Career Editor–Publisher, Troy *Tribune,* and newspaper weekly chain owner, 1948–66; Army, 1951–53; Ill. House of Reps., 1955–63; Ill. Senate, 1963–69; Lt. Gov. of Ill., 1969–73; Candidate for Dem. nomination for Gov., 1972; Instructor, Sangamon St. U., 1973.

Offices 227 CHOB, 202-225-5201. Also 107 Glenview Dr., Carbondale 62901, 618-457-4171.

Committees *Budget* (4th).

Education and Labor (9th). Subcommittees: Employment Opportunities; Postsecondary Education (Chairman); Select Education.

Group Ratings

	ADA	COPE	PC	LCV	CFA	RPN	NAB	NSI	NTU	ACA	ACU
1980	78	72	63	72	64	—	17	0	18	24	40
1979	74	72	75	84	67	—	—	—	21	0	3
1978	65	83	78	87	73	63	13	11	12	10	0

Key Votes

1) Draft Registn $	FOR	6) Fair Hsg DOJ Enfrc	FOR	11) Cut Socl Incr Dfns $	AGN
2) Ban $ to Nicrgua	—	7) Lim PAC Contrbtns	FOR	12) Hosptl Cost Controls	FOR
3) Dlay MX Missile	FOR	8) Cap on Food Stmp $	AGN	13) Gasln Ctrls & Allctns	FOR
4) Nuclr Mortorium	FOR	9) New US Dep Edcatn	FOR	14) Lim Wndfll Prof Tax	FOR
5) Alaska Lands Bill	FOR	10) Cut OSHA $	AGN	15) Chryslr Loan Grntee	FOR

Election Results

1980 general	Paul Simon (D)	112,134	(49%)	($217,098)
	John T. Anderson (R)	110,176	(48%)	($42,494)
1980 primary	Paul Simon (D)	38,005	(73%)	
	Edwin Arentsen (D)	14,183	(27%)	
1978 general	Paul Simon (D)	110,298	(66%)	($99,017)
	John T. Anderson (R)	57,763	(34%)	($13,998)

INDIANA

The image of the political machine in most Americans' minds is that suggested by the operation run by the late Richard J. Daley: a political machine is a big city Democratic organization that lives on political patronage jobs and is thought, at least by its adversaries, to tolerate a good bit of corruption as well as what George Washington Plunkitt called "honest graft." But the most successful and thriving political machine in America today has none of these characteristics. This is the Republican organization in the state of Indiana. It is based not so much on city as on state politics, it staffs hundreds of patronage jobs but also represents a rather specific set of ideas of what government should do, and it is not known to be engaged in illegal practices in any major way. Yet it is a machine and it is successful. Republicans have held the governorship of Indiana since 1968, and they hold all the other statewide offices as well. They hold both U.S. Senate seats and large majorities in the state legislature; their minority position in the state's U.S. House delegation may be altered because of redistricting. Republicans hold the mayoralty in Indianapolis and patronage-rich county offices in most of the state's large counties.

No similar machine exists in any of the surrounding states, yet Indiana is in most respects no different from them. Physically it is part of the limestone-bottomed plain that starts where the hills west of Pittsburgh level off and continues west across the Mississippi River and ultimately to the Rocky Mountains. The land is well watered and fertile, but as long as 100 years ago Indiana became more industrial than agricultural. The state sits astride the great east–west transportation routes, accessible to the Great Lakes and the Mississippi and Ohio River systems. Its boundaries to the east and west are nothing more than dotted lines on the map, but in people's minds Indiana has been a separate and distinct place for many years now. Few other states have as unusual and creative a word as "Hoosier" to describe their residents, few others have had a writer who assumed the role of state poet laureate like James Whitcomb Riley. Indiana's political traditions have also contributed to its distinctiveness. Its heavy partisanship, going back to Civil War divisions; its practice of requiring patronage employees to contribute 2% of their salaries to their political parties—these were commonplace in all the lower midwestern states in the 1890s, but only in Indiana have they survived in such uninhibited fashion.

Indiana politics has long been a battle of allegiances rather than of ideas. For years the southern part of the state below U.S. 40, the Old National Road, where people speak with something like a southern drawl, was basically Democratic; while northern Indiana, where people talk with midwestern hard Rs and flat As, was heavily Republican. During the Depression years there developed in the small factory towns and the industrial complex around Gary a politics of working-class Democrats versus upper-class Republicans, but the difference was less a matter of dispute about how society should be governed—Indiana has never had much stomach for talk about income redistribution—than it was a matter of whose side you were on, the union's or management's.

The businesslike conduct of Indiana's political machines for many years gave the state an intensively competitive politics, even when one party or the other's national candidates were heavily beaten here. Thus Democrats held the governorship for most of the 1960s and held both of the state's U.S. Senate seats from 1962 to 1976. Little camaraderie exists between politicians of the two parties in Indiana; there is little appreciation of the merits of the other side; elections are a serious business, and the enemy's weaknesses are not indulged. Campaigns in Indiana have been among the most bitter and most closely contested in the nation, the champion probably being the contest between Senator Vance Hartke and Congressman Richard Roudebush in 1970. Nor is there any pretense of impartiality among the state's major institutions. The newspapers, especially those in Indianapolis, are strongly Republican. The two biggest banks in the state, one Republican and one Democratic, stand glaring at each other across the circle in the center of Indianapolis.

The two parties are not competitively balanced today, however, as was apparent in the 1980 election for governor. The incumbent, Dr. Otis Bowen, was the first Indiana governor eligible for two consecutive terms and was popular enough to have won a third, but he was barred from running. The Republican nominee — and it is a sign of the strength of the Republican party organization that there was no opposition in the primary — was Lieutenant Governor Robert Orr. The Democratic nominee, businessman John Hillenbrand, was a conservative from the southern part of the state, seemingly the kind of candidate best able to maximize the traditional Indiana Democratic vote. But he had a bruising primary and nearly lost to labor-backed state Senator Wayne Townsend, and in the end Hillenbrand ran behind liberal Senator Birch Bayh. Orr promised more of the kind of leadership Bowen provided, and voters responded by giving him 58% of the vote. He is likely to be a business-oriented governor, a conservative who is nonetheless concerned at least a little by the movement of jobs away from Indiana — the auto and steel industries have always been big employers here — toward the Sun Belt.

Both of Indiana's senators now are Republicans, for the first time in 22 years. They are men of very similar voting records, but of sharply different temperaments. Senator Richard Lugar is a man who has succeeded in politics although he lacks many of the character traits usually associated with politicians; he is not gregarious, he has little sense of humor, and his appearance is not striking. He is undeniably bright: a Rhodes Scholar who has worked his way up through brains and hard work. His brilliance had led Republican Party leaders to slate him for mayor of Indianapolis in 1967, when he was only 35. His major accomplishment there was a consolidation of Indianapolis and surrounding Marion County into something called Unigov (which had the happy effect of adding Republican votes to city elections); Indianapolis, as a result, is more prosperous and less burdened with the problems of aging than many other central cities. Lugar bucked the fashion among mayors and called for fewer rather than more federal programs; despite that, he beat New York City's John Lindsay for the vice presidency of the National League of Cities in 1969. The White House let it be known that Lugar was President Nixon's favorite mayor, and he played a prominent role at the 1972 Republican National Convention. Lugar ran twice for the Senate before he won: in the Democratic year of 1974 against Birch Bayh, and in 1976 against the then highly unpopular Vance Hartke. He must stand for reelection in 1982, but unless some major shift in Indiana politics occurs he is likely to be reelected without difficulty. Indeed, this will probably be the first time since 1964 that an Indiana Senate seat is not furiously contested.

Lugar entered a Senate in which Democrats had not only a numerical advantage but, it seemed, an even greater preponderance in the battle of ideas. Yet in the intervening years it has been the Republicans who have come forward most often with cogent analysis of and creative responses to the nation's problems, and Lugar is one of the reasons why. He is a scholarly man who likes to reserve an hour a day for reading and reflection; he is also a tough advocate and one who presses his opinions as far as he can. Lugar's first mark was made as a leader in the move to beat organized labor's law reform; he helped make sure that labor never got the needed 60 votes for cloture. On the Foreign Relations Committee, Lugar became one of the most articulate critics of the Carter Administration's SALT Treaty and he opposed the Panama Canal Treaties as well. The addition of such Republicans as Lugar, Jesse Helms, and S. I. Hayakawa in 1979 changed the once dovish, intellectual tone of this committee even before Republicans took control of the Senate.

Lugar is also a member of the Banking Committee, where he tends to side with commercial banks in their endless fights with the now beleagured thrift institutions, and of the Agriculture Committee. More than most Agriculture Committee members, he has a constituency with relatively few actual farmers and many more people involved in food processing and distribution; he heads one of the most important subcommittees, Research and General Legislation. On Banking he chairs the subcommittee on housing, but full committee Chairman Jake Garn refused to let Lugar appoint as head staffer the man he wanted. He was a leading sponsor of the bill to provide loan guarantees to Chrysler—a major Indiana employer—in 1980. Lugar has had at least a moment in the national spotlight, when he was under consideration for the vice presidency at the 1980 Republican National Convention. His ideas are now in the mainstream of Republican politics and arguably national politics as well; but evidently his political style and personality did not make a strongly positive impression on Reagan and his inner circle.

If Lugar is a kind of class intellectual and valedictorian, Indiana's other senator, Dan Quayle, is the class athlete and student body president—one the favorite of the teachers and the other the favorite of the students. Quayle in fact comes to the Senate at an early age (33) and without much experience. He did spend four years in the House, after he upset a Democratic incumbent in 1976, but he played little legislative role. Quayle comes from a family prominent in publishing; his father had a newspaper in the small town of Huntington and his grandfather was Eugene Pulliam, publisher of the *Indianapolis Star*. Quayle himself seemed destined for the life of the small-town grandee—successful business ventures, community service organizations, a nice family and pleasant vacations, and plenty of golf. His election to Congress changed most of that. He has voted a solidly conservative line and has not really had occasion to take the lead on legislation; he was part of a Republican minority in the House and is a very junior member of the Republican majority in the Senate. He does not seem to burn with any passion to reform society or dismantle government.

If Quayle's elevation seems fortuitous, it was, in at least one sense: Governor Bowen could have had this nomination for the asking but declined it because of his wife's health. It is a measure of how Republican the year was that Quayle could defeat, with a respectable 54%, one of the most gifted natural politicians in our recent history, Birch Bayh. There were surface similarities to their careers: Bayh at age 34 defeated a three-term incumbent senator at a time when his party nationally was on the rise. Bayh went on to some solid legislative accomplishments: constitutional amendments outlawing the poll tax, establishing the 18-year-old vote, and arranging the presidential succession (so that Gerald Ford, not Speaker Carl Albert, became president on the resignation of Richard Nixon). He led the successful fights to block the Supreme Court nominations of Clement Haynsworth and G. Harrold Carswell. He ran for president twice, in 1971 and again in 1976. He also squeaked through to reelection twice, in the Republican year of 1968 and in the Democratic year of 1974, when he was already under attack for blocking constitutional amendments to ban busing and abortion. By 1980 the baggage of his liberalism had become too heavy in conservative Indiana, even for a candidate as gifted at aw-shucksing as Bayh.

Whether Quayle will make as distinguished a record in the Senate remains to be seen. He should not be dismissed yet as a dilettante; for the first time in his brief career he has the position and the time to establish a genuine record of accomplishment. He is likely initially, in his votes on the floor and in the Budget and Armed Services Committees, to stick pretty closely to the Reagan Administration. His chairmanship of the Employment and Productivity Subcommittee on Labor and Public Welfare may put him in the spotlight on some issues that are high on the list of conservative priorities; he has a definite 4–3 conservative edge. Politically, it is a long time to 1986, but Quayle seems to have a constituency much more congenial to his views than Bayh ever did, and he (or Lugar) may be able to do what neither Bayh nor any other senator from the closely contested politics of Indiana has ever done: win a fourth term.

Indiana, like all the Great Lakes states, gained population at less than the national average during the 1970s, and as a result its current allotment of 11 seats in the House will be reduced to 10 in 1982. The Republican Party here has absolute control over the redistricting process and is not likely to give the Democrats any quarter. Democrats currently hold six House seats — dividends, mostly, of their good years of 1964 and 1974 — and that number will almost certainly be reduced by one, two, or perhaps three in the next election. The prime candidate for elimination is 2d district Democrat Floyd Fithian, although ironically his district currently has a higher population than any other in the state. But the redistricters will probably draw tough districts for at least two other Democrats, probably David Evans of the 6th district and Philip Sharp of the 10th district.

Census Data   Pop. (1980 final) 5,490,179, up 6% in 1970s: 2.42% of U.S. total, 12th largest. Central city, 33%; suburban, 37%. Median 4-person family income, 1978, $20,566, 101% of U.S., 22d highest.

1979 Share of Federal Tax Burden $11,045,000,000; 2.45% of U.S. total, 11th largest.

1979 Share of Federal Outlays $7,933,813,000; 1.71% of U.S. total, 20th largest.

DOD	$1,654,429,000	20th	(1.56%)	HEW	$3,820,599,000	14th	(2.14%)
DOE	$11,405,000	35th	(0.10%)	ERDA	$3,548,000	35th	(0.13%)
HUD	$108,485,000	21st	(1.65%)	NASA	$16,966,000	21st	(0.42%)
VA	$359,188,000	22d	(1.73%)	DOT	$237,227,000	23d	(1.44%)
EPA	$83,220,000	21st	(1.57%)	DOC	$45,380,000	15th	(1.43%)
DOI	$29,252,000	39th	(0.53%)	USDA	$371,358,000	27th	(1.55%)

Economic Base   Primary metal industries, especially blast furnaces and steel mills; electrical equipment and supplies, especially radio and television receiving equipment; finance, insurance, and real estate; transportation equipment, especially motor vehicles and equipment; agriculture, notably hogs, corn, soybeans, and cattle; machinery, especially general industrial machinery; fabricated metal products, especially structural metal products.

Political Lineup   Governor, Robert Orr (R). Senators, Richard G. Lugar (R) and J. Danforth (Dan) Quayle (R). Representatives, 11 (6 D and 5 R); 10 in 1982. State Senate, 50 (35 R and 15 D); State House of Representatives, 100 (63 R and 37 D).

The Voters

Registration   2,944,311 Total.
Employment profile 1970   White collar, 42%. Blue collar, 43%. Service, 12%. Farm, 3%.
Ethnic groups   Black 1980, 8%. Hispanic 1980, 2%. Total foreign stock 1970, 7%. Germany, 1%.

346 INDIANA

Presidential Vote

1980	Reagan (R)	1,255,656	(56%)
	Carter (D)	844,197	(38%)
	Anderson (I)	111,639	(5%)
1976	Ford (R)	1,183,958	(53%)
	Carter (D)	1,014,714	(46%)

1980 Democratic Presidential Primary

Carter	398,949	(68%)
Kennedy	190,492	(32%)

1980 Republican Presidential Primary

Reagan	419,016	(74%)
Bush	92,955	(16%)
Anderson	56,344	(10%)

SENATORS

Sen. Richard G. Lugar (R) Elected 1976, seat up 1982; b. Apr. 4, 1932, Indianapolis; home, Indianapolis; Denison U., B.A. 1954, Rhodes Scholar, Oxford U., B.A. and M.A., 1956.

Career Navy, 1957–60; V.P. and Treasurer, Thomas L. Green & Co., banking equip., 1960–67, Pres., 1968–77; Treasurer, Lugar Stock Farms, Inc., 1960–77; Mayor of Indianapolis, 1968–76; Rep. nominee for U.S. Senate, 1974.

Offices 1113 DSOB, 202-224-4814. Also 447 Fed. Bldg., Indianapolis 46204, 317-269-5555.

Committees *Agriculture, Nutrition, and Forestry* (4th). Subcommittees: Agricultural Research and General Legislation (Chairman); Rural Development, Oversight, and Investigation; Foreign Agricultural Policy; Nutrition.

Banking, Housing and Urban Affairs (5th). Subcommittees:

Housing and Urban Affairs (Chairman); Financial Institutions; Economic Policy; Rural Housing and Development.

Foreign Relations (5th). Subcommittees: International Economic Policy; European Affairs (Chairman); Western Hemisphere Affairs.

Select Committee on Intelligence (4th). Subcommittees: Analysis and Production; Collection and Foreign Operations.

Group Ratings

	ADA	COPE	PC	LCV	CFA	RPN	NAB	NSI	NTU	ACA	ACU
1980	17	11	17	30	7	—	91	80	53	83	76
1979	11	0	20	—	5	—	—	—	54	89	82
1978	10	11	30	24	25	70	83	100	32	92	92

Key Votes

1) Draft Registn $	FOR	6) Fair Housng Cloture	AGN	11) Cut Socl Incr Defns	FOR
2) Ban $ to Nicrgua	FOR	7) Ban $ Rape Abortns	FOR	12) Income Tax Indexing	FOR
3) Dlay MX Missile	AGN	8) Cap on Food Stmp $	FOR	13) Lim Spdg 21% GNP	FOR
4) Nuclr Mortorium	AGN	9) New US Dep Edcatn	AGN	14) Incr Wndfll Prof Tax	AGN
5) Alaska Lands Bill	FOR	10) Cut OSHA Inspctns	FOR	15) Chryslr Loan Grntee	FOR

Election Results

1976 general	Richard G. Lugar (R)	1,275,833	(59%)	($727,720)
	Vance Hartke (D)	868,522	(40%)	($654,729)

1976 primary	Richard G. Lugar (R)	393,064	(65%)
	Edgar Whitcomb (R)	179,203	(30%)
	One other (R)	28,790	(5%)
1970 general	Vance Hartke (D)	870,990	(50%)
	Richard L. Roudebush (R).......	866,707	(50%)

Sen. J. Danforth (Dan) **Quayle** (R) Elected 1980, seat up 1986; b. Feb. 4, 1947, Indianapolis; home, Huntington; Depauw U., B.A. 1969, Ind. U., J.D. 1974.

Career Admin. Asst. to the Gov. of Ind., 1971–73; Dir., Inheritance Tax Div., St. of Ind., 1973; Practicing atty.; Gen. Mgr. and Assoc. Publ., *Huntington Herald-Press,* 1974–76; U.S. House of Reps., 1976–80.

Offices 254 RSOB, 202-224-5623. Also 46 E. Ohio St., Rm. 447, Indianapolis 46204, 317-269-5555, and 5530 Fohl Ave., Hammond 46320, 219-932-5500, ext. 380-1.

Committees *Armed Services* (8th). Subcommittees: Strategic and Theatre Nuclear Forces; Sea Power and Force Projection; Manpower and Personnel.

Budget (11th).

Labor and Human Resources (3d). Subcommittees: Labor; Education; Employment and Productivity (Chairman).

Group Ratings (as Member of U.S. House of Representatives)

	ADA	COPE	PC	LCV	CFA	RPN	NAB	NSI	NTU	ACA	ACU
1980	0	13	23	37	14	—	91	100	56	90	77
1979	11	16	18	28	4	—	—	—	62	91	85
1978	15	11	28	23	27	91	100	78	46	81	77

Key Votes (as Member of U.S. House of Representatives)

1) Draft Registn $	FOR	6) Fair Hsg DOJ Enfrc	AGN	11) Cut Socl Incr Dfns $	FOR
2) Ban $ to Nicrgua	FOR	7) Lim PAC Contrbtns	AGN	12) Hosptl Cost Controls	AGN
3) Dlay MX Missile	AGN	8) Cap on Food Stmp $	FOR	13) Gasln Ctrls & Allctns	AGN
4) Nuclr Mortorium	AGN	9) New US Dep Edcatn	AGN	14) Lim Wndfll Prof Tax	FOR
5) Alaska Lands Bill	AGN	10) Cut OSHA $	FOR	15) Chryslr Loan Grntee	FOR

Election Results

1980 general	J. Danforth (Dan) Quayle (R)	1,182,414	(54%)	($2,430,878)
	Birch E. Bayh, Jr. (D)..........	1,015,922	(46%)	($2,773,254)
1980 primary	J. Danforth (Dan) Quayle (R)	397,453	(77%)	
	Roger Marsh (R)..............	118,273	(23%)	($173,712)
1974 general	Birch E. Bayh, Jr. (D)..........	889,269	(51%)	($1,024,486)
	Richard G. Lugar (R)	814,117	(46%)	($619,678)

GOVERNOR

Gov. Robert Orr (R) Elected 1980, term expires Jan. 1985; b. Nov. 17, 1917, Ann Arbor, Mich.; homes, Indianapolis and Evansville; Yale U., B.A., 1940, Harvard U. Bus. Sch., 1940–42

Career Army, WWII; Businessman, Orr Iron Co., 1946–73; Chmn., Vandenburgh Co. Rep. Party, 1965–69; Ind. Senate, 1968–72; Lt. Gov. of Ind., 1972–80.

Offices Rm. 206 State House, Indianapolis 46204, 317-633-4567.

Election Results

1980 gen.	Robert Orr (R)	1,257,383	(58%)
	John A. Hillenbrand (D) . . .	913,116	(42%)
1980 prim.	Robert Orr (R)	483,952	(100%)
1976 gen.	Otis R. Bowen (R)	1,236,555	(57%)
	Larry A. Conrad (D)	927,243	(43%)

FIRST DISTRICT

Anyone who has driven west on the Indiana Turnpike toward Chicago has seen it. Between the highway and the invisible shores of Lake Michigan is some of the most impressive and most polluted industrial landscape in the country. These are some of the nation's largest steel mills; from their chimneys and smokestacks come sulphrous fumes by day and the flare of flames at night. This is the heart of the 1st congressional district of Indiana, the northwestern corner of Hoosier America.

Without the giant steel mills, there would be no 1st district as we know it. The district's largest city, Gary, was founded in 1906 by J. P. Morgan's colossal United States Steel Corporation and named for one of Morgan's partners, Chicago lawyer and U. S. Steel Chairman Elbert Gary. The site chosen was ideal. Iron ore from the Lake Superior ranges could be carried by Great Lakes freighters into the huge man-made port at the southern tip of Lake Michigan. Coal from Pennsylvania and West Virginia could be transported to the mills on the great east–west rail lines as they pass through Gary, Hammond, and East Chicago on their way to Chicago. Today no less than five of the great steel manufacturers have mills here, and the local economy is totally dominated by steel.

In the last 70 years the steel mills have attracted thousands of immigrants to Gary and vicinity—Irish, Poles, Czechs, Ukrainians, and blacks from the American South. These groups live in uneasy proximity. In 1967 Richard Hatcher, a black, won the Democratic nomination and was elected mayor of Gary; he has been reelected ever since. But his victories were due almost entirely to the fact that Gary had become a black-majority city; he won very few white votes. Meanwhile, the Lake County Democratic machinery, as well as most of the county offices, have remained in the control of whites of diverse ethnic origin united in hostility to Hatcher. Lake County has for years been the scene of considerable political corruption, and sometimes of corrupt inertia. The Democrats, elected with the votes of the workers, have always permitted the steel companies to determine the assessed value of their own mills for property tax purposes.

As the 1970s passed, Gary became increasingly a black city. Hammond and East Chicago, just to the east, remain heavily white and ethnic. To the south there are newer suburban communities, populated by younger steelworkers and their families. Here the old ethnic

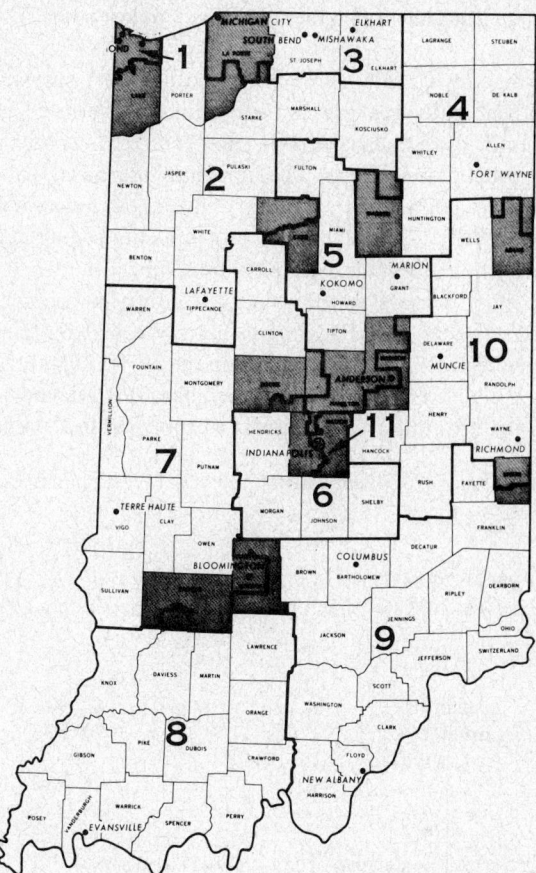

tradition and Democratic Party allegiance are much weaker than in the old neighborhoods, and white hostility to blacks has worked somewhat in the Republicans' favor. The 1st congressional district includes all of the older communities of Lake County and some of the newer suburbs.

It is a district of more than ordinary political turbulence, of feuds and battles and sacks full of cash. Yet for 24 years the 1st district sent the same man to Congress, Democrat Ray Madden. For years Madden held his ethnic audiences spellbound by telling how he uncovered the Katyn Forest massacre of 1940. In 1973, at the age of 80, he became chairman of the House Rules Committee. He was the first prolabor chairman in 20 years, but he was long past the point of effectiveness. He was also in trouble in the 1st district. In 1972 he was challenged by a young state Senator, Adam Benjamin, and nearly lost.

Four years later Benjamin ran again. Madden again had the support of the Democratic organization, of the big labor unions, and of Mayor Hatcher and his organization—as mutually mistrustful a group of allies as has ever been assembled. They supported Madden to maintain the district's national clout, but the voters didn't seem to care. Benjamin won by a stunning 56%-34% margin; the only other incumbent to lose so badly that year had been convicted of bribery.

Benjamin is considered politically shrewd—innocents don't survive 15 years of Lake County politics and beat all the big powers there. In his first term he gained a seat on the Appropriations Committee, an unusual feat. In his second term he became a subcommittee chairman, something even more unusual. The subcommittee, on legislative appropriations, is one that has little direct impact on the ordinary citizen; but it does control the budget of Congress, which makes Benjamin potentially a very influential figure in the House. In 1981 Benjamin succeeded to the chair of the Transportation Subcommittee. Benjamin is reelected every two years without difficulty even though Lake County has become less Democratic in other contests (it favored Carter over Reagan by only a 49%-46% margin). Redistricting will expand the district somewhat (it lost population in the 1970s) slightly beyond the borders of Lake County, but it is highly unlikely that the Republicans will do anything but quarantine this heavily Democratic area into a single district, keeping political damage to a minimum.

Census Data   Pop. (1980 final) 426,542, down 10% in 1970s. Median family income, 1970, $10,706, 112% of U.S.

The Voters

Employment profile 1970   White collar, 37%. Blue collar, 50%. Service, 13%. Farm, -%.
Ethnic groups   Black 1980, 29%. Hispanic 1980, 10%. Total foreign stock 1970, 20%. Poland, 3%; Germany, 2%.

Presidential Vote

1980	Reagan (R)	68,293	(41%)
	Carter (D)	90,663	(54%)
	Anderson (I)	6,357	(4%)
1976	Ford (R)	68,428	(38%)
	Carter (D)	108,388	(61%)

Rep. Adam Benjamin, Jr. (D) Elected 1976; b. Aug. 6, 1935, Gary; home, Hobart; U.S. Mil. Acad., West Point, B.S. 1958, Valparaiso U., J.D. 1968.

Career USMC, Korea; Army, 1958–61; High school teacher, 1961; Computer analyst, 1962–64; Zoning Admin., City of Gary, 1964–65; Exec. Secy. to the Mayor of Gary, 1965–67; Ind. House of Reps., 1967–71; Ind. Senate, 1971–77.

Offices 410 CHOB, 202-225-2461. Also 610 Connecticut St., Gary 46402, 219-886-2411.

Committees *Appropriations* (19th). Subcommittees: Energy and Water Development; Legislation; Transportation (Chairman).
Budget (15th).

Group Ratings

	ADA	COPE	PC	LCV	CFA	RPN	NAB	NSI	NTU	ACA	ACU
1980	61	74	50	30	64	—	42	40	31	33	32
1979	47	80	53	41	67	—	—	—	31	19	26
1978	65	80	65	53	59	17	8	50	18	22	17

Group Ratings

	ADA	COPE	PC	LCV	CFA	RPN	NAB	NSI	NTU	ACA	ACU
1980	56	63	53	75	57	—	50	33	30	27	12
1979	53	80	53	66	59	—	—	—	31	23	26
1978	25	50	53	63	32	36	55	50	28	58	46

Key Votes

1) Draft Registn $	AGN	6) Fair Hsg DOJ Enfrc	AGN
2) Ban $ to Nicrgua	FOR	7) Lim PAC Contrbtns	FOR
3) Dlay MX Missile	FOR	8) Cap on Food Stmp $	AGN
4) Nuclr Mortorium	AGN	9) New US Dep Edcatn	FOR
5) Alaska Lands Bill	FOR	10) Cut OSHA $	AGN

11) Cut Socl Incr Dfns $	AGN
12) Hosptl Cost Controls	AGN
13) Gasln Ctrls & Allctns	FOR
14) Lim Wndfll Prof Tax	AGN
15) Chryslr Loan Grntee	FOR

Election Results

1980 general	Floyd J. Fithian (D)	122,326	(54%)	($280,192)
	Ernest Nienmeyer (R)	103,757	(46%)	($53,426)
1980 primary	Floyd J. Fithian (D)	41,435	(100%)	
1978 general	Floyd J. Fithian (D)	82,402	(57%)	($196,945)
	J. Philip Oppenheim (R).........	52,842	(36%)	($136,475)
	William Costas (I)	9,368	(6%)	($47,312)

THIRD DISTRICT

The headlines of 1980 were full of news of the collapse of the American automobile industry and of the massive unemployment in towns heavily dependent on the auto factories. It must have made familiar reading to people in South Bend, Indiana. For South Bend suffered, many years ago and without much national notice, the same kind of catastrophe currently afflicting such auto centers as Flint and such steel centers as Youngstown in the early 1980s. In the late 1960s and early 1970s, the Studebaker Corporation went out of the automobile manufacturing business, and South Bend lost its largest employer. The population loss or stagnation that is beginning to be noticed around the Great Lakes region was apparent in South Bend back then. It is suffering again today from the further deterioration of the auto industry, since there are still a number of auto supplies businesses here.

Politically, South Bend is one of those ethnic, heavily Catholic cities, set in the midst of Republican farm territory, that have formed much of the Democratic base in the Midwest since the days of the New Deal. It is also, as almost everyone must know, the home of one of America's preeminent Catholic institutions, the University of Notre Dame. South Bend is also the largest, but not necessarily the politically dominant, city in the 3d congressional district of Indiana. The district also includes Michigan City, a grimy industrial community on the shores of Lake Michigan, and Elkhart, a manufacturing town east of South Bend that is more prosperous (its products include electronic components and musical instruments as well as auto parts) and much more Republican.

The 3d is one of those congressional districts that switched from Democratic to Republican in 1980 and in the process ousted one of the Congress's leading Democrats. He was John Brademas, first elected in 1958 and as House Democratic whip, the number three person in the Democratic leadership. The wonder, in retrospect, is not so much that Brademas was defeated but that he hung on so long. A cerebral Rhodes Scholar of Greek descent, he never seemed entirely at home in gritty South Bend. He did struggle to keep in touch with the district, however, which is not easy—there is no direct plane service to Washington, and it takes longer to get here from the capital than it does to get to Denver. Brademas made major legislative contributions in the fields of higher education and the arts; it is appropriate that after his defeat he was named president of New York University.

The new congressman, John Hiler, was elected at age 27 with little political experience; he had been defeated in a primary for the state legislature two years before. What he had going for him were national issues and national money. Republicans on the national level had developed a devastating critique of the Democratic programs that Brademas had supported; they learned from polling that Brademas was vulnerable, and they targeted his district. It paid off. Hiler can be expected to be a reliable member of the augmented Republican minority and he undoubtedly hopes to become part of a Republican majority soon. The Republican legislature will probably add Republican territory to the 3d; indeed, the district is underpopulated and the entire surrounding area is all more Republican.

Census Data   Pop. (1980 final) 481,917, up 2% in 1970s. Median family income, 1970, $10,606, 111% of U.S.

The Voters

   Employment profile 1970   White collar, 44%. Blue collar, 43%. Service, 12%. Farm, 1%.
   Ethnic groups   Black 1980, 7%. Hispanic 1980, 1%. Total foreign stock 1970, 13%. Poland, 3%; Germany, 2%.

Presidential Vote

1980	Reagan (R)	122,484	(54%)
	Carter (D)	88,535	(39%)
	Anderson (I)	14,122	(6%)
1976	Ford (R)	98,139	(53%)
	Carter (D)	84,017	(46%)

Rep. John P. Hiler (R) Elected 1980; b. Apr. 24, 1953, Chicago, Ill.; home, LaPorte; Williams Col., B.A. 1975, U. of Chicago, M.B.A. 1977.

Career   Foundry exec., family business; LaPorte Rep. City Chmn.; Delegate, White House Conf. on Small Business.

Offices   1338 LHOB, 202-225-3915. Also 120 River Glenn Ofc. Plaza, 501 E. Monroe, South Bend 46601, 219-234-4431.

Committees   *Government Operations* (13th). Subcommittees: Commerce, Consumer and Monetary Affairs; Environment, Energy and Natural Resources.

Small Business (10th). Subcommittees: Energy, Environment and Safety Issues Affecting Small Business; SBA and SBIC Authority, Minority Enterprise and General Small Business Problems.

Group Ratings and Key Votes: Newly Elected

Election Results

1980 general	John P. Hiler (R)	103,972	(55%)	($407,979)
	John Brademas (D)	85,136	(45%)	($744,068)
1980 primary	John P. Hiler (R)	23,548	(58%)	
	Richard Pfeil (R)	15,567	(38%)	($59,567)

| 1978 general | John Brademas (D) .... | 64,336 | (56%) | ($251,394) |
| | Thomas L. Thorson (R) .... | 50,145 | (43%) | ($102,766) |

FOURTH DISTRICT

The 4th congressional district of Indiana centers on Fort Wayne, the state's second largest city (although it is nowhere near as big as Indianapolis). More than half the district's votes are cast here and in surrounding Allen County. Fort Wayne is a typical medium-sized mid-western community, with a small black ghetto, nondescript frame houses that belong to the people who work in the factories and other local businesses.

The counties around Fort Wayne in the district are mostly agricultural flatland. Those to the south and west of the city have a Democratic tradition, but none went for Jimmy Carter, who did not strike a chord in this hard-R, northern-accented part of the state. The counties north and east of Fort Wayne are heavily Republican. Any sophisticated public opinion survey of the area would probably disclose little difference between these two areas on major issues; their differing party identifications are largely a matter of upbringing and tradition, traceable ultimately to differences in attitude toward the Civil War. The 4th district for a period of ten years was probably the most marginal district in Indiana, with no candidate receiving more than 55% in a general election.

That pattern ended abruptly with the election of Republican J. Danforth Quayle III in 1976. He brought to the district the conservative heritage inherent in being a grandson of *Indianapolis Star* publisher Eugene Pulliam and the advantage of having the ability to raise a large campaign treasury. He assembled his own organization and upset a Democratic incumbent. The district was used to older, dowdier congressmen; Quayle, handsome and in his early thirties, was quite a contrast. He won reelection with a stunning margin, carried the district easily in his successful race for the Senate in 1980, and in the same year saw his chief district aide, Daniel Coats, elected to the House in his place.

Coats campaigned as a Quayle follower and was elected easily; he can be expected to follow Quayle's conservative policies in the House. Redistricting is not too threatening. Republicans control the process and, whoever draws the lines, there must be a Fort Wayne–centered district in the northeastern corner of the state, and its basic partisan composition will not vary much.

Census Data   Pop. (1980 final) 506,982, up 7% in 1970s. Median family income, 1970, $10,443, 109% of U.S.

The Voters

Employment profile 1970   White collar, 44%. Blue collar, 42%. Service, 11%. Farm, 3%.
Ethnic groups   Black 1980, 5%. Hispanic 1980, 1%. Total foreign stock 1970, 6%. Germany, 2%.

Presidential Vote

1980	Reagan (R)	125,737	(58%)
	Carter (D)	70,264	(33%)
	Anderson (I)	15,859	(7%)
1976	Ford (R)	118,239	(59%)
	Carter (D)	79,908	(40%)

Rep. Daniel R. Coats (R) Elected 1980; b. May 16, 1943, Jackson, Mich.; home, Fort Wayne; Wheaton Col., B.A. 1965, Indiana U., J.D. 1971.

Career Army, 1966–68; Econ. consult. firm, 1968–70; Legal Intern, American Fletcher Nat. Bank, 1970–72; Asst. V.P. & Legal Counsel, Mutual Security Life Ins. Co., 1972–76; Dist. Rep. for U.S. Rep. J. Danforth (Dan) Quayle, 1976–80.

Offices 1427 LHOB, 202-225-4436. Also 326 Fed. Bldg., Ft. Wayne 46802, 219-424-3040.

Committees *Energy and Commerce* (17th). Subcommittees: Fossil and Synthetic Fuels; Oversight and Investigations.

Select Committee on Aging (17th). Subcommittee: Retirement Income and Employment.

Group Ratings and Key Votes: Newly Elected

Election Results

1980 general	Daniel R. Coats (R)	120,055	(61%)	($223,695)
	John D. Walda (D).............	77,542	(39%)	($126,520)
1980 primary	Daniel R. Coats (R)	35,138	(58%)	
	Paul Helmke (R)	14,550	(24%)	($102,989)
	Elmer MacDonald (R)	10,808	(18%)	($43,944)
1978 general	J. Danforth (Dan) Quayle (R)	80,527	(64%)	($142,446)
	John D. Walda (D).............	42,238	(34%)	($59,155)

FIFTH DISTRICT

The 5th congressional district lies smack in the middle of Indiana, which is to say in the middle of Middle America. The rich Hoosier farmland here is Farm Bureau country and politically very conservative. There are also three medium-sized factory towns, Anderson, Kokomo, and Marion, as well as Peru, the boyhood home of Cole Porter. The district also dips south to include a portion of the city of Indianapolis (an integrated Democratic neighborhood, placed in this Republican district to render it politically harmless). Just to the north of the city are the political poles of the district: Hamilton County, high-income, exurban Indianapolis, full of people who left the bland, uncrowded city because it was too urban for them, and very Republican; and Anderson, with its huge General Motors plant and thousands of UAW members, which is usually solidly Democratic.

This district has been hit especially hard by the depression in the auto industry. General Motors has major facilities not only in Anderson, but also in Marion and Kokomo, and Chrysler has — or had — one of its largest plants outside Michigan in Kokomo. There have been many layoffs and many more seem threatened. Yet there has been no movemenent in the 5th district toward the political party historically associated with alleviating unemployment, the Democrats. If anything, the movement was in the other direction. Hard-hit Kokomo, for instance, went for Reagan over Carter by a 59%–36% margin. It preferred Republican Dan Quayle to heavily labor-backed Senator Birch Bayh. And it helped to reelect Republican Congressman Elwood Hillis.

First elected in 1970, Hillis has had few problems electorally in the years since. His voting record makes some bows to Anderson and Kokomo as well as to Hamilton County: he has higher ratings from organized labor than most Indiana Republicans. Hillis had a stronger than usual opponent in 1980 but has never really been targeted by Democrats; and it is likely that the Republican legislators will give him a pretty favorable district for 1982.

For a representative of such a land-bound district of Middle America, Hillis has unusual committee assignments, Armed Services and Veterans' Affairs. This district does not have substantial military installations or much in the way of defense contracts (the same is true of Indiana generally); one must conclude that Hillis serves on these bodies because he is concerned about their work. A veteran of the Army, he is generally considered a partisan of the Army when the interests of the services collide, and he generally backs increased defense spending.

Census Data   Pop. (1980 final) 501,096, up 6% in 1970s. Median family income, 1970, $10,314, 108% of U.S.

The Voters

  Employment profile 1970   White collar, 41%. Blue collar, 44%. Service, 12%. Farm, 3%.
  Ethnic groups   Black 1980, 8%. Hispanic 1980, 1%. Total foreign stock 1970, 4%.

Presidential Vote

1980	Reagan (R)	127,587	(63%)
	Carter (D)	63,911	(32%)
	Anderson (I)	9,496	(5%)
1976	Ford (R)	119,475	(57%)
	Carter (D)	89,307	(42%)

Rep. Elwood R. Hillis (R) Elected 1970; b. Mar. 6, 1926, Kokomo; home, Kokomo; Ind. U., B.S. 1949, J.D. 1952.

Career Army, WWII; Practicing atty., 1952–71; Ind. House of Reps., 1967–71.

Offices 2336 RHOB, 202-225-5037. Also 518 N. Main St., Kokomo 46901, 317-457-4411.

Committees *Armed Services* (8th). Subcommittees: Military Personnel and Compensation; Procurement and Military Nuclear Systems; Readiness.

Veterans' Affairs (4th). Subcommittees: Hospitals and Health Care; Oversight and Investigations.

Group Ratings

	ADA	COPE	PC	LCV	CFA	RPN	NAB	NSI	NTU	ACA	ACU
1980	22	35	37	27	29	—	73	88	39	70	82
1979	11	17	10	32	4	—	—	—	46	83	68
1978	10	35	13	38	14	64	100	78	21	69	71

Key Votes

1) Draft Registn $	—	6) Fair Hsg DOJ Enfrc	AGN	11) Cut Socl Incr Dfns $	AGN
2) Ban $ to Nicrgua	FOR	7) Lim PAC Contrbtns	AGN	12) Hosptl Cost Controls	AGN
3) Dlay MX Missile	AGN	8) Cap on Food Stmp $	FOR	13) Gasln Ctrls & Allctns	AGN
4) Nuclr Mortorium	AGN	9) New US Dep Edcatn	FOR	14) Lim Wndfll Prof Tax	FOR
5) Alaska Lands Bill	FOR	10) Cut OSHA $	FOR	15) Chryslr Loan Grntee	FOR

Election Results

1980 general	Elwood R. Hillis (R)............	129,474	(62%)	($185,414)
	Nels J. Ackerson (D)	80,378	(38%)	($115,086)
1980 primary	Elwood R. Hillis (R)............	55,392	(100%)	
1978 general	Elwood R. Hillis (R)............	94,950	(68%)	($72,873)
	Max E. Heiss (D)	45,479	(32%)	

SIXTH DISTRICT

The 6th congressional district of Indiana takes in about one-third of the geographically sprawling city of Indianapolis, four suburban counties, and a couple of townships in another county. Over all, metropolitan Indianapolis has been one of our most Republican cities. It has never had the really large influxes of Eastern European immigrants who provided so many of the traditional Democratic votes in Chicago and Detroit and Cleveland, and its economic base is decidedly white collar, with banks, insurance companies, and state government the major employers. Beyond that there is an ethos here that is profoundly conservative. This is the headquarters of the American Legion, the hometown of James Whitcomb Riley and Benjamin Harrison, the base of the Pulliam newspaper chain.

The 6th district by and large is the more Republican part of the Indianapolis area. It does have some Democratic precincts: some of the black neighborhoods of Indianapolis and the white working-class areas around the Indianapolis Speedway where the 500 is held every Memorial Day. Most of the 6th consists of comfortable white collar neighborhoods, where Republican orthodoxy was never questioned long before the current renaissance of Republican thinking.

Yet, in congressional elections, this district has gone Democratic since 1974. The main reason is the energy, resourcefulness, and, it must be added, luck of Democratic Congressman David Evans. In 1974 he beat a 24-year incumbent by, among other things, standing beside a highway with a sign asking for votes. In 1976, 1978, and 1980, he faced Republican David Crane, brother of Illinois Congressman and presidential candidate Philip Crane and Downstate Illinois Congressman Daniel Crane. Crane is earnest, accomplished (a lawyer and a physician) and has been able to raise, with the help of his famous brother's mailing list, large sums of money, but he has never been able to win. One reason may be that Evans's voting record has turned more conservative in his years in office. Another is that he has obviously become adept in the use of the advantages of incumbency.

Evans could be running out of luck, however. The Republicans have control of the redistricting process and in the Indianapolis area the census figures give them plenty of leeway to redraw district lines. One likely strategy would be for them in effect to concede the 11th district to Andrew Jacobs, a Democrat so maverick these days that to some Republicans he is almost as good as a Republican. Thus Evans's 6th district would lose the Democratic black and Speedway areas; in compensation, it would gain, say, suburban Hamilton County, which gave Ronald Reagan a 74%–20% margin over Jimmy Carter in 1980. It is hard to see how Evans, for all his personal popularity, could carry such a district against a respectable Republican. He might choose, indeed, to contest the other, much more Democratic Indianapolis area district, even if it means a primary against Jacobs.

Census Data   Pop. (1980 final) 512,727, up 9% in 1970s. Median family income, 1970, $10,497, 110% of U.S.

The Voters

Employment profile 1970   White collar, 45%. Blue collar, 42%. Service, 11%. Farm, 2%.
Ethnic groups   Black 1980, 4%. Hispanic 1980, 1%. Total foreign stock 1970, 4%.

Presidential Vote

1980	Reagan (R)	123,538	(62%)
	Carter (D)	64,836	(33%)
	Anderson (I)	8,513	(4%)
1976	Ford (R)	113,083	(58%)
	Carter (D)	80,098	(41%)

Rep. David W. Evans (D) Elected 1974; b. Aug. 17, 1946, Lafayette; home, Indianapolis; Ind. U., B.A. 1967, 1967–70, Butler U., 1970–72.

Career Parochial school teacher and asst. principal, 1967–74; Dem. nominee for U.S. House of Reps., 1972.

Offices 438 CHOB, 202-225-2276. Also 4th Flr., Admin. Bldg., Weir Cook Airport, Indianapolis 46241, 317-269-7364.

Committees *Banking, Finance and Urban Affairs* (13th). Subcommittees: Economic Stabilization; Financial Institutions Supervision, Regulation and Insurance; Housing and Community Development.

Government Operations (11th). Subcommittees: Government Activities and Transportation; Legislation and National Security.

Select Committee on Aging (13th). Subcommittees: Health and Long-Term Care; Retirement Income and Employment.

Group Ratings

	ADA	COPE	PC	LCV	CFA	RPN	NAB	NSI	NTU	ACA	ACU
1980	28	53	30	52	29	—	92	70	58	63	42
1979	32	63	40	60	44	—	—	—	53	56	56
1978	25	55	45	48	32	18	73	78	55	63	50

Key Votes

1) Draft Registn $ FOR	6) Fair Hsg DOJ Enfrc FOR	11) Cut Socl Incr Dfns $ FOR
2) Ban $ to Nicrgua FOR	7) Lim PAC Contrbtns AGN	12) Hosptl Cost Controls AGN
3) Dlay MX Missile AGN	8) Cap on Food Stmp $ FOR	13) Gasln Ctrls & Allctns FOR
4) Nuclr Mortorium AGN	9) New US Dep Edcatn FOR	14) Lim Wndfll Prof Tax AGN
5) Alaska Lands Bill FOR	10) Cut OSHA $ AGN	15) Chryslr Loan Grntee FOR

Election Results

1980 general	David W. Evans (D)	99,089	(50%)	($311,007)
	David G. Crane (R)	98,302	(50%)	($595,637)
1980 primary	David W. Evans (D)	32,602	(93%)	
	One other (D)	2,364	(7%)	
1978 general	David W. Evans (D)	66,421	(52%)	($180,870)
	David G. Crane (R)	60,630	(48%)	($431,943)

SEVENTH DISTRICT

Like the old Wabash Cannonball—one of the most famous of the vanished combination passenger and freight trains—the Wabash River flows across the rolling farmland of western Indiana on its way to meet the Ohio and Mississippi Rivers. And in a nearly straight line from Indianapolis to St. Louis runs the Old National Road (now U.S. 40), closely paralleled by Interstate 70. The river and the road intersect in Terre Haute, which with fewer than 100,000 people is still the largest city in the 7th congressional district of Indiana. Terre Haute, despite its elegant French name, is a rough and crude place, once known for gambling and vice; it has the look of a rundown factory town. Politically Terre Haute has always had a strong Democratic machine (although it was the hometown of the great Socialist Eugene Debs), which more often than not has controlled the Vigo County courthouse.

The Wabash Cannonball traversed, in its day, both Democratic and Republican territory, and the dividing line, roughly, was at Terre Haute and the Old National Road. To the north the people speak with the hard-edged accent of the Midwest; to the south, they drawl in a manner reminiscent of Dixie. The counties to the north are traditionally Republican; those to the south traditionally Democratic. You can see the same demarcation in maps of the political preference of the 1860s. And although the preferences were submerged in the politics of the late 1960s and early 1970s, when all those rural counties went heavily Republican, they emerged again when Jimmy Carter of Plains, Georgia, faced Gerald Ford of Grand Rapids, Michigan, in 1976. Carter carried Terre Haute and the southern counties of the district and, although he didn't carry the 7th, did strikingly better than Hubert Humphrey had in 1968. Even in 1980 Carter carried the part of the district south of the Old National Road, but lost the northern portion by a 2–1 margin.

The 7th district was created in basically its present form in 1965 by a Democratic legislature that thought it was creating a Democratic district. It was a classic example of foiled redistricting. The year 1966 was a good one for Republicans and the Republican candidate, a young banker named John Myers, won the seat. And Myers has won ever since. He has often been helped by weak opposition. Eldon Tipton, the man he beat in 1966, ran again in 1968 and 1974; his son was Myers's opponent in 1976. Neither proved to be formidable competition. Probably his toughest opponent was Charlotte Zietlow, a councilwoman from the university town of Bloomington. But she ran in the not very Democratic year of 1978 and although she lowered Myers's percentage, Zietlow didn't come close to unseating him. Myers has a record of Republican regularity on most issues. He sits on the Appropriations Committee, where he serves as the ranking Republican on the Public Works Subcommittee, which parcels out money for post offices, dams, and the like. This was once an important post when congressmen depended on such goodies for reelection; now that they depend more on casework and franked mail it is less important, but not negligible. If the Republicans should win control of the House, Myers would become chairman of this subcommittee.

Census Data   Pop. (1980 final) 506,123, up 7% in 1970s. Median family income, 1970, $8,808, 92% of U.S.

The Voters

Employment profile 1970   White collar, 42%. Blue collar, 39%. Service, 14%. Farm, 5%.
Ethnic groups   Black 1980, 2%. Hispanic 1980, 1%. Total foreign stock 1970, 4%.

Presidential Vote

1980	Reagan (R)	113,098	(57%)
	Carter (D)	73,774	(37%)
	Anderson (I)	10,263	(5%)
1976	Ford (R)	111,589	(52%)
	Carter (D)	100,362	(47%)

Rep. John T. Myers (R) Elected 1966; b. Feb. 8, 1927, Covington; home, Covington; Ind. St. U., B.S. 1951.

Career Army, WWII; Cashier and Trust Officer, Foundation Trust Co., 1954–66.

Offices 2301 RHOB, 202-225-5805. Also Fed. Bldg., Terre Haute 47808, 812-238-1619.

Committees *Appropriations* (4th). Subcommittees: Agriculture, Rural Development and Related Agencies; Energy and Water Development.

Standards of Official Conduct (3d).

Group Ratings

	ADA	COPE	PC	LCV	CFA	RPN	NAB	NSI	NTU	ACA	ACU
1980	11	14	30	13	14	—	100	100	55	75	84
1979	0	17	5	5	4	—	—	—	58	91	84
1978	10	10	15	13	18	64	92	100	29	81	96

Key Votes

1) Draft Registn $	AGN	6) Fair Hsg DOJ Enfrc	AGN	11) Cut Socl Incr Dfns $	FOR
2) Ban $ to Nicrgua	FOR	7) Lim PAC Contrbtns	AGN	12) Hosptl Cost Controls	AGN
3) Dlay MX Missile	AGN	8) Cap on Food Stmp $	FOR	13) Gasln Ctrls & Allctns	AGN
4) Nuclr Mortorium	AGN	9) New US Dep Edcatn	AGN	14) Lim Wndfll Prof Tax	FOR
5) Alaska Lands Bill	AGN	10) Cut OSHA $	FOR	15) Chryslr Loan Grntee	AGN

Election Results

1980 general	John T. Myers (R)	137,604	(66%)	($142,908)
	Patrick D. Carroll (D)	69,051	(33%)	($51,232)
1980 primary	John T. Myers (R)	51,576	(100%)	
1978 general	John T. Myers (R)	86,955	(56%)	($136,796)
	Charlotte Zietlow (D)	67,469	(44%)	($161,992)

EIGHTH DISTRICT

The 8th congressional district of Indiana is the southwestern corner of the state. It contains the city of Evansville on the Ohio River and several river counties so hilly that they might be considered mountainous by midwestern standards. This part of Indiana was the first to be settled by white men. Vincennes, now a small town on the Wabash River, was once the metropolis of Indiana, and Robert Owen, the Scottish philanthropist, established the town of New Harmony downstream. (Owen's son was one of the first congressmen from the area, elected in 1842 and 1844.) Today Evansville is a reasonably prosperous city (fourth largest in the state), but much of the rest of the district has suffered ever since the railroads took most of the freight business away from Ohio River steamboats.

Much of southwestern Indiana was settled by German Catholics, who have traditionally voted Democratic. During the Civil War most of this area was copperhead country, friendly to the South and hostile to Mr. Lincoln's war. Today, although the issues have changed, the 8th remains generally Democratic. It has gone Democratic in most recent Senate elections and, although it did not cotton to the liberalism of Hubert Humphrey or George McGovern, it went Democratic for Jimmy Carter in 1976, and again in 1980.

With a Democratic tradition and recent shifts toward the Republicans, the 8th has been a marginal district, and it elected four different congressmen in four elections in the 1970s — the only district in the nation to do so. The first was Roger Zion, a Republican first elected in 1966, reelected easily in 1968, with difficulty in 1970, and easily in 1972. A member of the Public Works Committee who favored extensive road-building projects, Zion was slated as one of Environmental Action's Dirty Dozen three times. He lost finally in 1974.

The winner was Democrat Philip Hayes, a state senator who liked Evansville and Indianapolis better than Washington. Hayes decided that if he had to remain in Washington it might as well be as a senator, and so he ran against Vance Hartke in the 1976 Democratic primary. His almost entirely negative campaign nearly beat the unpopular incumbent. He was the only 1974 freshman to give up his seat voluntarily and one of only three who were not reelected in 1976.

Hayes was succeeded by David Cornwell, a Democrat who had been beaten in the 1974 primary. Cornwell had a number of weaknesses: he was from a small rural county, not Evansville, he had a very youthful appearance, and his voting record was not too far from the Democratic mainstream. These handicaps proved too much to overcome, and he was beaten in 1978.

The present incumbent is Joel Deckard, a former state legislator, solar heating contractor, and cable television executive. He beat a more moderate Republican in the primary and was expected to join the growing bloc of conservative Republicans in the House. Deckard received surprisingly tough opposition from a Democrat in 1980 who campaigned from a helicopter and derided Deckard's opposition to nuclear power. The Republican nevertheless survived, although he was one of the few members of his party in Indiana not in a position to benefit from Reagan's coattails. In all likelihood the district boundaries will not change much for 1982; the question is whether this district will once again be seriously contested.

Census Data   Pop. (1980 final) 508,397, up 8% in 1970s. Median family income, 1970, $8,557, 89% of U.S.

The Voters

Employment profile 1970   White collar, 38%. Blue collar, 44%. Service, 13%. Farm, 5%.
Ethnic groups   Black 1980, 3%. Total foreign stock 1970, 2%. Germany, 1%.

Presidential Vote

1980	Reagan (R)	124,107	(53%)
	Carter (D)	98,026	(42%)
	Anderson (I)	9,788	(4%)
1976	Ford (R)	110,108	(50%)
	Carter (D)	110,693	(50%)

Rep. H. Joel Deckard (R) Elected 1978; b. Mar. 7, 1942, Vandalia, Ill.; home, Evansville; U. of Evansville, 1962–67.

Career Radio newscaster, 1961–74; Ind. House of Reps., 1966–74; Div. Mgr., Cable TV Co., 1974–77; Builder, 1977–78.

Offices 125 CHOB, 202-225-4636. Also 210 S.E. 6th St., Evansville 42708, 812-423-4279.

Committees *Government Operations* (9th). Subcommittee: Environment, Energy and Natural Resources.

Public Works and Transportation (12th). Subcommittees: Aviation; Economic Development; Surface Transportation.

Group Ratings

	ADA	COPE	PC	LCV	CFA	RPN	NAB	NSI	NTU	ACA	ACU
1980	22	11	33	72	29	—	92	100	46	74	71
1979	21	26	33	56	11	—	—	—	61	88	82

Key Votes

1) Draft Registn $	AGN	6) Fair Hsg DOJ Enfrc	AGN	11) Cut Socl Incr Dfns $	FOR
2) Ban $ to Nicrgua	FOR	7) Lim PAC Contrbtns	AGN	12) Hosptl Cost Controls	AGN
3) Dlay MX Missile	AGN	8) Cap on Food Stmp $	FOR	13) Gasln Ctrls & Allctns	AGN
4) Nuclr Mortorium	FOR	9) New US Dep Edcatn	AGN	14) Lim Wndfll Prof Tax	FOR
5) Alaska Lands Bill	FOR	10) Cut OSHA $	FOR	15) Chryslr Loan Grntee	—

Election Results

1980 general	H. Joel Deckard (R)	119,415	(55%)	($222,543)
	Kenneth C. Snider (D)	97,059	(45%)	($137,761)
1980 primary	H. Joel Deckard (R)	34,665	(100%)	
1978 general	H. Joel Deckard (R)	83,019	(52%)	($231,632)
	David L. Cornwell (D)	76,654	(48%)	($112,985)

NINTH DISTRICT

The 9th congressional district of Indiana is the southeastern corner of the state. The southern part of the district, along the Ohio River, is hilly land, green and well watered but difficult to farm. This was one of the first parts of Indiana to be settled, and in a old river town such as Madison one can still see the homes of the 19th-century notables built when this was one of the leading cities in the state. History has passed it by: there was never much industrialization here, the major transportation routes pass elsewhere, and even the Ohio River barges do not bother to stop. Farther down the river, opposite Louisville, Kentucky, are the old towns of New Albany and Jeffersonville, small cities that are part of a much larger metropolitan area. This part of Indiana was first settled by southerners, people who came across the river from Kentucky; and it retains a Democratic political preference. In the strongly contested 1980 Senate race, for instance, Democrat Birch Bayh carried almost all the river counties and those immediately to the north — much as Democrats carried them in the closely contested elections of the 1860s.

To the north one comes to a physical divide, between the hilly land to the south and the limestone-based plain of the north. The major town here is Columbus, a company town whose company, Cummins Engine, has commissioned major international architects to design most of the city's schools, public buildings, and churches—making for startling effects in this environment. This part of the state is ancestrally more Republican and was solidly Republican in the 1980 elections.

The 9th district has, at various stages in its history, been seriously contested; in the ordinary course of things, it has elected Republican congressmen, but it has also elected Democrats in years in which the party's national ticket has been led by men with southern backgrounds, as in 1948 or 1964. That accounts for the election of Democratic Congressman Lee Hamilton in 1964, when he upset a Republican incumbent. But it does not explain Hamilton's continued reelection; that is a result of his moderate image on issues, his hard work in the district, and the fact that after a few elections hardheaded Indiana Republicans have given up on this seat and have moved on to contest seriously other Indiana districts where their chances are better. Hamilton was mentioned as a possible candidate for statewide office several times, but in 1976 he had to make a definite choice: oppose the unpopular Senator Vance Hartke in a primary or stay in the House. He chose the House and has concentrated increasingly on his work there.

Hamilton's decision not to challenge Hartke seems characteristic of his approach to difficult decisions: he is a man who seems reluctant to go against established authority, although he will do so when he feels he must. He was, for example, a supporter of the Vietnam war effort during the Johnson and most of the Nixon years. He has supported defense spending increases but, as a member of the ethics committee, was willing to threaten to cut off aid to South Korea unless it cooperated with the Tongsun Park investigation. Hamilton is a high-ranking member of the Foreign Affairs Committee and chairman of its subcommittee on Europe and the Middle East—important jurisdiction obviously. His is a voice highly respected and listened to on matters of difficult policy affecting the Middle East or Europe. He is aligned with no particular camp but has the respect—and the attention— of virtually everyone.

Although redistricting is in Republican hands, it seems unlikely that any major attempt will be made to defeat Hamilton. It is difficult, for one thing, to substantially redraw a district in the corner of a state; and Hamilton's popularity in his existing district suggests that even the addition of some heavily Republican counties would not tip the balance against him. The more likely result is that Republicans will put all possible Democratic territory in southern Indiana into the 9th, in effect conceding the district to Hamilton for the 1980s.

Census Data Pop. (1980 final) 544,023, up 15% in 1970s. Median family income, 1970, $9,001, 94% of U.S.

The Voters

Employment profile 1970 White collar, 37%. Blue collar, 47%. Service, 11%. Farm, 5%.
Ethnic groups Black 1980, 2%. Hispanic 1980, 1%. Total foreign stock 1970, 2%.

Presidential Vote

1980	Reagan (R)	117,173	(54%)
	Carter (D)	89,450	(41%)
	Anderson (I)	7,902	(4%)
1976	Ford (R)	101,335	(49%)
	Carter (D)	105,561	(51%)

Rep. Lee H. Hamilton, Jr. (D) Elected 1964; b. Apr. 20, 1931, Daytona Beach, Fla.; home, Columbus; DePauw U., B.A. 1952, Goethe U., Frankfort, Germany, 1952–53, Ind. U., J.D. 1956.

Career Practicing atty., 1956–64; Instructor, Amer. Banking Inst., 1960–61.

Offices 2187 RHOB, 202-225-5315. Also U.S.P.O., Columbus 47201, 812-372-2571.

Committees *Foreign Affairs* (5th). Subcommittees: Europe and the Middle East (Chairman); International Security and Scientific Affairs.

Joint Economic Committee (3d). Subcommittees: Economic Goals and Intergovernmental Policy (Chairman); Monetary and Fiscal Policy.

Select Committee on Intelligence (2d). Subcommittee: Legislation.

Group Ratings

	ADA	COPE	PC	LCV	CFA	RPN	NAB	NSI	NTU	ACA	ACU
1980	44	47	53	61	57	—	50	22	25	46	11
1979	53	70	53	55	38	—	—	—	30	27	23
1978	35	50	65	83	55	55	55	70	14	31	21

Key Votes

1) Draft Registn $	FOR	6) Fair Hsg DOJ Enfrc	FOR	11) Cut Socl Incr Dfns $	AGN
2) Ban $ to Nicrgua	AGN	7) Lim PAC Contrbtns	FOR	12) Hosptl Cost Controls	AGN
3) Dlay MX Missile	AGN	8) Cap on Food Stmp $	AGN	13) Gasln Ctrls & Allctns	AGN
4) Nuclr Mortorium	AGN	9) New US Dep Edcatn	AGN	14) Lim Wndfll Prof Tax	FOR
5) Alaska Lands Bill	FOR	10) Cut OSHA $	AGN	15) Chryslr Loan Grntee	FOR

Election Results

1980 general	Lee H. Hamilton, Jr. (D)	136,574	(64%)	($122,674)
	George Meyer, Jr. (R)...........	75,601	(36%)	($0)
1980 primary	Lee H. Hamilton, Jr. (D)	62,160	(90%)	
	One other (D)	6,883	(10%)	
1978 general	Lee H. Hamilton, Jr. (D)	99,727	(66%)	($111,793)
	Frank I. Hamilton, Jr. (R)	52,218	(34%)	($48,720)

TENTH DISTRICT

Before Robert and Helen Lynd published *Middletown* in the 1930s, many Americans imagined that small midwestern cities were tightly knit, homogeneous communities. What the Lynds discovered in Middletown—actually Muncie, Indiana—was something very different: a factory town divided sharply along class lines, with local affairs firmly controlled by a small business elite. Since the 1930s the General Motors and other major plants here have been unionized and blue collar wages have risen greatly. But the basic class divisions remain, more pronounced than in just about any other part of the country. Life-and-death economic power remains in the hands of businessmen, which means faraway GM executives in Detroit and New York as well as the Ball family in Muncie.

Nowhere are the class divisions so clearly expressed as in politics. A *New York Times* article quoted a member of the Muncie elite who thought that everyone in the town was a Republican. That is true of the great majority of members of the country club, but it is hardly an accurate picture of the city's voting habits. In fact Muncie votes for Democrats as often as for Republicans, and the working-class neighborhoods of the city almost always give Democrats big majorities. But there is little contact between people from these different strata and little sense of what the other is like. They know each other better through television programs than from personal experience.

Muncie lies roughly in the middle of Indiana's 10th congressional district, and with less than 100,000 is still the district's largest city. The only other sizable town, Richmond, is quite a different kind of place. It has a long-standing Quaker tradition and is the site of the Friends' Earlham College. But the Quakerism of this part of Indiana is closer to that of Richard Nixon's Whittier, California, than to that of Philadelphia's American Friends Service Committee. Richmond has kept strong Republican voting habits from its antislavery days before the Civil War.

The 10th district was the creation of a Republican redistricting; yet today the seat is held by a Democrat, Philip Sharp, a former professor at Ball State University. He was so typical of the 1974 Democratic freshmen that the *Washington Post* chose him as the subject for a series of profiles through the life of the 94th Congress. Sharp's political secret is hard work. He ran for Congress twice, in 1970 and 1972, before winning in 1974; 1982, assuming he runs, will be his seventh congressional campaign. His earlier races laid the groundwork for his 1974 defeat of Republican David Dennis, although it helped that Dennis, a peppery, combative man, was one of the most visible of Richard Nixon's defenders in the House Judiciary Committee's impeachment hearings. Sharp's attention to constituency service and frequent trips to the district as an incumbent have helped him to win reelection in 1976, 1978, and 1980. Certainly Sharp has used the advantages of incumbency more effectively than the Democrat elected here in 1958 who rented his front porch to the government as his district office and was defeated for reelection.

In his half-dozen years in Congress, Sharp has emerged as one of the real leaders of the House. He was not a flashy freshman, but he was one who, because of his steady hard work and ability to fashion compromise, soon attracted tough assignments from elders. He has worked especially hard on energy issues. In 1977 and 1978 he chaired an energy task force by appointment of Speaker O'Neill and he helped to fashion the compromise that phased out price controls on oil and natural gas over several years. In 1981 he became chairman of the Energy and Commerce subcommittee on Fossil and Synthetic Fuels. Despite its technical-sounding title, this is one of the most important subcommittees in the House. It has jurisdiction over coal, oil, natural gas, and synthetic fuels. The hard work of deregulation has mostly been done. But there are plenty of tough decisions left on synthetic fuels, coal slurry pipelines, coal severance taxes, and the strategic petroleum reserve. Sharp does not have majorities on his subcommittee or on the full Energy and Commerce Committee for traditional Democratic liberal positions. But he does have the ability to put together constructive legislation and an important position from which to do so.

Sharp will have to work hard to seek reelection in 1982. His district is already the product of a Republican legislature that tried to make it safely Republican, so the possibilities for making it more Republican are limited. But there are some. Most likely he will get some of the Indianapolis suburban counties that are among the most heavily Republican in the state. He will also get some rural Republican counties he has never represented, and he may be thrown into the same seat as another Democratic incumbent. His recent reelections suggest he is well established with his constituents. But he will have to continue working hard nonetheless.

Census Data   Pop. (1980 final) 487,803, up 3% in 1970s. Median family income, 1970, $9,635, 100% of U.S.

The Voters

Employment profile 1970 White collar, 37%. Blue collar, 47%. Service, 12%. Farm, 2%.
Ethnic groups Black 1980, 3%. Hispanic 1980, 1%. Total foreign stock 1970, 3%.

Presidential Vote

1980	Reagan (R)	132,498	(59%)
	Carter (D)	80,620	(36%)
	Anderson (I)	10,126	(5%)
1976	Ford (R)	105,448	(55%)
	Carter (D)	86,375	(45%)

Rep. Philip R. Sharp (D) Elected 1974; b. July 15, 1942, Baltimore, Md.; home, Muncie; DePauw U., Georgetown Sch. of Foreign Svc., B.S. 1964, Oxford U., 1966, Georgetown U., Ph.D. 1974.

Career Legis. Aide to U.S. Sen. Vance Hartke, 1964–69; Asst. and Assoc. Prof. of Poli. Sci., Ball St. U., 1969–74; Dem. nominee for U.S. House of Reps., 1970, 1972.

Offices 2452 RHOB, 202-225-3021. Also Fed. Bldg., 401 S. High St., Muncie 47305, 317-289-7948.

Committees *Energy and Commerce* (6th). Subcommittee: Fossil and Synthetic Fuels (Chairman).

Interior and Insular Affairs (12th). Subcommittee: Energy and the Environment.

Group Ratings

	ADA	COPE	PC	LCV	CFA	RPN	NAB	NSI	NTU	ACA	ACU
1980	50	63	53	61	57	—	58	33	38	29	21
1979	53	70	58	62	56	—	—	—	36	28	21
1978	50	70	83	83	64	58	50	40	21	26	8

Key Votes

1) Draft Registn $	AGN	6) Fair Hsg DOJ Enfrc	FOR	11) Cut Socl Incr Dfns $	AGN
2) Ban $ to Nicrgua	AGN	7) Lim PAC Contrbtns	FOR	12) Hosptl Cost Controls	AGN
3) Dlay MX Missile	FOR	8) Cap on Food Stmp $	AGN	13) Gasln Ctrls & Allctns	FOR
4) Nuclr Mortorium	AGN	9) New US Dep Edcatn	FOR	14) Lim Wndfll Prof Tax	AGN
5) Alaska Lands Bill	FOR	10) Cut OSHA $	AGN	15) Chryslr Loan Grntee	FOR

Election Results

1980 general	Philip R. Sharp (D)	103,083	(53%)	($165,181)
	William C. Frazier (R)	90,051	(47%)	($279,789)
1980 primary	Philip R. Sharp (D)	43,142	(90%)	
	One other (D)	5,057	(10%)	
1978 general	Philip R. Sharp (D)	73,343	(56%)	($107,372)
	William G. Frazier (R)	55,999	(43%)	($129,665)

ELEVENTH DISTRICT

The 11th district of Indiana includes most of the city of Indianapolis, which in the late 1960s annexed almost all of its Marion County suburbs to provide more rational local government and also to help preserve Republican control of city hall. There are plenty of factories here, but Indianapolis is more of an office town than most major cities in the Midwest, with major banks, insurance companies, and the state government. Like Columbus, the capital of Ohio, it never had the kind of migration of Eastern European ethnics that shaped the politics of the Great Lakes industrial cities; like Columbus, it has prospered and grown in recent years with the expansion of the white collar economy. Cleveland and Detroit and Gary and Chicago are heavily Democratic. Indianapolis remains almost as strongly Republican as it was in the 1920s.

As in all of Indiana, politics is a serious business here. Of the two major banks, for example, one is Republican and the other Democratic; naturally both have an interest in which party wins the state treasurer's office. Patronage is an integral part of politics and civil servants virtually unheard of. Most state, county, and city employees traditionally have had to "contribute" 2% of their paychecks to the party that got them their jobs. The national headquarters of the American Legion stares down toward the federal building and the state Capitol; this is a serious town, without much sense of humor.

Yet Indianapolis sends to Congress one of its funniest members, 11th district Congressman Andrew Jacobs. Jacobs is a liberal Democrat—although the adjective must be qualified—from a conservative Republican city; he approaches politics with an attitude less than stern. He has a fatalistic approach to things: in 1975 he refused to board an Indianapolis-to-Washington plane because only first class seats were available; it crashed, killing all aboard. His fearlessness in flouting tradition was shown in 1975 when he married Congresswoman Martha Keys of Kansas. They had met in that most unromantic of environments, the House Ways and Means Committee; and although their voting records were not identical, they decided to marry. On weekends Jacobs flew to Indianapolis and Keys took the plane on to Kansas City—at least until she was defeated in the 1978 election.

Jacobs has proved to be a durable part of the Indianapolis political scene. He was first elected to Congress in 1964—a Democratic year that coincided with the retirement of a Republican incumbent—and despite redistrictings, he won reelection three times. In those days he was a strong supporter of Great Society programs and had a standard Democratic voting record. In 1972 Jacobs was beaten by Protestant minister, William Hudnut III. Jacobs beat him in turn in 1974, leaving Hudnut to go on to be Richard Lugar's hand-picked successor as mayor of Indianapolis.

Jacobs was reelected by solid margins in 1976, 1978, and 1980. One reason undoubtedly was familiarity with and careful use of the advantages of incumbency. Another may have been Jacobs's increasingly independent voting record. On economic issues particularly he has been parting company with his liberal friends. He was one of the first Democrats to oppose the Carter Administration's $50 rebate, and his labor voting record is not much higher than that of 5th district Republican Elwood Hillis. Jacobs is a member of the House Ways and Means Committee and is one reason why the Democrats' large margin on that body (23–12) does not mean automatic support for liberal measures. On tax issues Jacobs is considered independent by those who admire him, and flaky by those who do not. In 1981 he got the chair of the Health Subcommittee, whose jurisdiction is limited to Medicare; with characteristic frankness, he let everyone know that he was not much interested in its work and took the post only because every other subcommittee chair was taken.

Republican legislatures used to redraw district lines in a way to defeat Jacobs and on one occasion (1972) succeeded. Given his local popularity and his recent voting record, however, the Republicans in control of the Indiana redistricting process now are unlikely to try to de-

feat him. Rather, they will probably try to concentrate all the Democratic parts of Indianapolis in his district, on the theory that they will do the least damage there. That might
mean that 6th district Democrat David Evans will choose to run against Jacobs in a primary;
but almost certainly, if this kind of plan is enacted, Jacobs will win again.

Census Data Pop. (1980 final) 442,998, down 6% in 1970s. Median family income, 1970, $10,785,
113% of U.S.

The Voters

Employment profile 1970 White collar, 53%. Blue collar, 34%. Service, 13%. Farm, –%.
Ethnic groups Black 1980, 26%. Hispanic 1980, 1%. Asian 1980, 1%. Total foreign stock 1970, 6%.
Germany, 1%.

Presidential Vote

1980	Reagan (R)	99,256	(54%)
	Carter (D)	76,146	(41%)
	Anderson (I)	8,781	(5%)
1976	Ford (R)	104,572	(55%)
	Carter (D)	86,916	(45%)

Rep. Andrew Jacobs, Jr. (D) Elected 1974; b. Feb. 24, 1932, Indianapolis; home, Indianapolis; Ind.
U., B.S. 1955, LL.B. 1958.

Career USMC, Korea; Practicing atty., 1958–65, 1973–74; Ind.
House of Reps., 1959–60; U.S. House of Reps., 1965–73.

Offices 1533 LHOB, 202-225-4011. Also 441 A Fed. Bldg., 46 E.
Ohio St., Indianapolis 46204, 317-269-7331.

Committee *Ways and Means* (8th). Subcommittees: Health
(Chairman); Social Security.

Group Ratings

	ADA	COPE	PC	LCV	CFA	RPN	NAB	NSI	NTU	ACA	ACU
1980	50	53	47	48	50	—	82	44	67	63	37
1979	68	55	68	60	52	—	—	—	63	60	53
1978	50	50	58	70	46	75	75	40	53	59	42

Key Votes

1) Draft Registn $	AGN	6) Fair Hsg DOJ Enfrc	FOR	11) Cut Socl Incr Dfns $	AGN
2) Ban $ to Niergua	FOR	7) Lim PAC Contrbtns	FOR	12) Hosptl Cost Controls	FOR
3) Dlay MX Missile	FOR	8) Cap on Food Stmp $	AGN	13) Gasln Ctrls & Allctns	AGN
4) Nuclr Mortorium	FOR	9) New US Dep Edcatn	AGN	14) Lim Wndfll Prof Tax	AGN
5) Alaska Lands Bill	FOR	10) Cut OSHA $	FOR	15) Chryslr Loan Grntee	FOR

Election Results

1980 general	Andrew Jacobs, Jr. (D)	105,468	(57%)	($39,581)
	Sheila Suess (R)	78,743	(43%)	($437,871)
1980 primary	Andrew Jacobs, Jr. (D)	31,964	(100%)	
1978 general	Andrew Jacobs, Jr. (D)	61,504	(57%)	($18,394)
	Charles F. Bosma (R)	45,809	(43%)	($55,971)

IOWA

Iowa brings to mind farms — some of the greenest, most fertile, best-tended farms known to men. Iowa was first settled in the years before the Civil War and filled up rapidly in the years afterward; it has never really grown much since and has sent many of its young people off to make their livings in the East or West. Superficially, there has been little change here since the turn of the century. Most Iowans still live on farms or in small towns, not in large cities or surrounding suburbs. The state has no military installations and very little defense industry — no reminder that this heartland of America has become more entangled with the outside world since the days of the Spanish–American War. Iowa has never experienced rapid urbanization nor has it had the kind of politics attendant upon it, not the equivalent of the Chicago machine nor of the conservatism of Orange County, California.

But Iowa has changed — indeed, has changed more dynamically than many parts of urban America — since the turn of the century. The key change has been in the productivity of agriculture. Technology in the late 19th century — the railroads, refrigeration — made possible the market agriculture we know today, and Iowa has been a leader in making it more productive. It is hard to overstate how great that increase in productivity has been. At the turn of the century, when the railroad network was already complete and food was already a big industry, nearly half of all Americans lived on farms and produced among them enough to feed a nation of 76 million and to export some besides; today only 3% of Americans are farmers, but they produce enough to feed a nation of 226 million and export enough to feed almost half the rest of the world as well.

Iowa is responsible for that, not only because it has some of America's richest farmland, but also because it has produced some of the most important crop hybrids and improved management and marketing techniques. This is a state where the houses and the values seem old, but where most citizens are innovators in their businesses. Far from being closed to the outside world, it is probably more open to it than are most residents of New York City. Iowans are acutely conscious that their own prosperity depends in large part on exports and world crop markets; they are acutely aware of the importance to their own lives of government regulations in Washington and the fluctuations of prices on the Chicago Board of Trade. Iowans are served by sophisticated newspapers, led by the *Des Moines Register,* which is one of the few papers in the nation with genuine statewide circulation. The state also has advanced university communities in Iowa City and Ames and many small college towns. Around the turn of the century, most Iowans seldom left their home county and only on rare occasions left the state. Today, the farthest reaches of the world are only a few hours' plane ride away from O'Hare Airport.

The changes that have come to Iowa have come largely because of the changes in agriculture, and the prosperity of Iowa remains very dependent on the success of agriculture — particularly corn, hogs, wheat, dairy and beef cattle. Like all farm states, it has always considered itself terribly vulnerable to downturns in agricultural prices; so, in 1980, it was extracting from most candidates in its presidential caucuses — the first major contest in the nation, held in January 1980 — a promise to oppose President Carter's embargo on Soviet grain shipments. But in fact agriculture has been pretty prosperous in Iowa in the 1970s and promises to be so in the future; the grain embargo, while it had some impact has not precipitated anything like the number of farm bankruptcies and foreclosures that Iowa has seen in the past. The fact is that agriculture is one of the healthiest segments of America's economy, one that continues to grow more productive while heavy industry stagnates, one that produces exports and foreign exchange while much of the nation is worried about competition from imports. Iowa has not grown at about the national average since the 1870s, which means that there has been massive migration out of this state, although the rate of out-migration slackened in the 1970s. The fact of previous migrations is apparent in the age structure of Iowa's population— only Florida and two other states have more elderly— but more room and more opportunity seem to exist for young people in Iowa than has been the case for many decades.

Political attitudes in Iowa have been shaped by the state's experience; and while they are less parochially concerned with agricultural issues than they used to be, they are still distinctive. Iowa has a certain orneriness, born perhaps in the numberless farm rebellions against national administrations, nurtured in the heritage of Germans and Scandinavians and Yankees who moved here precisely because they were unwilling to conform to the traditions of their native lands, which leads Iowa to be one of our most countercyclical of states. It seems to react, often harshly, against any national administration, not only angrily denouncing its farm programs but more recently sternly denouncing its foreign and domestic policies. Iowa is particularly stern in response to corruption. It is one of the handful of states that gave Nixon in 1972, when Watergate was still only a minor issue, a lower percentage than it had given him in 1968. The fierceness with which Iowa turned against Jimmy Carter and his Democrats is more well known. After the 1976 election, Democrats still controlled the Iowa legislature and held both of the state's Senate seats and four of its six House seats. Four years later, both Senate seats had gone Republican, the legislature was overwhelmingly Republican, and only the personal popularity of some incumbents had enabled the Democrats to hold onto three of the House seats.

The 1970s thus saw the rise and fall of a liberal Democratic Party in historically conservative Republican Iowa. The high point for the Democrats was probably in 1976, when they had been out of power for eight years; in that year Jimmy Carter came within 13,000 votes of carrying this historically Republican state running against a midwestern Republican incumbent president. In the middle 1970s the liberal Democrats in Iowa got many of their votes from a traditional party base— blue collar workers, some farmers, Catholics who in Iowa are more heavily Democratic than Catholics in Massachusetts— but they got the additional votes they needed for a majority on the new cultural, not the traditional Democratic economic issues. Opposition to the Vietnam war, skepticism about military spending programs, opposition to Watergate and other Nixon Administration corruption, opposition to tax breaks for big businesses— these were the kinds of issues that helped elect Dick Clark to the Senate in 1972 and John Culver in 1974. They had similar backgrounds: Clark had been Congressman Culver's administrative assistant and ran only when Culver declined to challenge incumbent Jack Miller in 1972; Clark's walk across the state that year attracted attention but it was the tax issue that probably enabled him to win. Culver then ran and won statewide in the Watergate year of 1974 when incumbent Harold Hughes decided to retire.

Each of these senators distinguished himself on Iowa issues such as agriculture and soil conservation but also in matters traditionally considered by outsiders to be of little interest to Iowans, but actually of great concern to what is one of the least parochial of states. Clark devoted much attention to African affairs and was the author of the amendment forbidding

U.S. military involvement in Angola, one sniped at occasionally by more bellicose types who have never, however, presented a case for Angola's strategic importance to the United States. Clark also provided crucial support for U.S. moves to help settle the crisis in Zimbabwe–Rhodesia. Culver specialized in military affairs as a member of the Armed Services Committee and was one of the Senate's best informed and most articulate defenders of arms control. No man as forceful and determined as this former Marine can be accused plausibly of being soft on the Russians or anyone else. Culver was the subject of Elizabeth Drew's book, *Senator,* which followed his exhausting activities for several days.

Despite their achievements, neither Clark nor Culver was able to win reelection to a full term; indeed, no Democratic senator from Iowa ever has. Clark was upset in 1978 by Republican Roger Jepsen in an election in which the abortion issue played a critical role; right-to-life opposition to Clark eroded his majorities to nothing in Catholic counties and neighborhoods, and he was not able to run strongly enough elsewhere to win. By 1980 it was obvious that Culver was in real trouble: opinion in the state had turned against him on major foreign and spending issues, the New Right launched a negative television advertising campaign against him, and the Republicans nominated a respectable conservative, Congressman Charles Grassley, to oppose him. Culver characteristically came back fighting, refusing to compromise his liberal beliefs or even to make rhetorical bows to the opposition. He ran about as effective a campaign as could have been run but lost by a decisive although not overwhelming majority.

Thus in two years one of the most liberal pairs of senators was replaced by one of the most conservative pairs. Jepsen and Grassley have rather different backgrounds and personal styles. Jepsen, with his white hair and dignified appearance, looks as much like the stereotype of a senator as any current member. Politically, he is something of a loner: he served as Robert Ray's lieutenant governor for four years but was not his political ally and indeed considered running against him; he got his nomination in 1978 against a Ray-backed moderate in large part because no other conservative bothered to compete for what seemed like a losing position. Jepsen is a member of the Agriculture and Armed Services Committees and generally can be counted on as one of the solidly conservative Republican votes; he has not taken a leadership position yet on any major issue. One subcommittee he heads must decide whether there is to be a military draft; he does not favor one but questions the competence of the volunteer army. He is up for reelection in 1984, and his fortunes may depend on whether Iowa reacts in a countercyclical manner to the Reagan Administration.

Charles Grassley is somewhat a contradiction: a man with a kind of hayseed manner who is in fact a competent professional legislator. He was in the Iowa legislature for 16 years before he was elected to the House in 1974, the only Republican to win in that Democratic year in Iowa. He built up strong loyalty in his north central Iowa district, which gave him nearly half his statewide margin over Culver in 1980. Grassley was on the Agriculture Committee in the House and also emphasized his work on senior citizen programs. Now he sits on the Budget and Finance Committees, which in 1981 promise to be the major focuses of legislative activity in the Senate. Grassley succeeded H. R. Gross in the House, a man who was known as the quintessential conservative nitpicker, and he has some of the same reputation himself. But in fact he avoids some of the more extreme positions of the New Right and is no more eager to be associated with those who want to do away with a program such as Social Security than is Ronald Reagan. He spent much time in the House calling for reduction in the national debt, yet on his first substantive vote in the Senate voted to raise the debt ceiling.

Iowa has one of the most perdurable and popular of state governors, Robert Ray. He was first elected in 1968 and has never really been challenged seriously yet; his margins, although healthy, tend to understate his political health. Ray's assets include an even temperament, complete honesty, a reputation for moderation, and basic competence. He is exactly the kind of governor people in a state like Iowa want. He has not been entirely successful, however, and in party matters he has almost completely failed to persuade the once moderate Iowa Republican Party to follow him on issues. The state's two senators were both elected after trouncing primary opponents associated with Ray, and the new state party chairman elected in 1981 is a conservative adversary of Ray's. The New Right correctly regards Ray as an obstacle to their complete political success in Iowa; but how lasting that success would be without a leader in Ray's mold is unclear. It may be that in 1982 Ray would decide, after 14 years in office, that he is tired of being governor; but if he runs he will surely be reelected. If he does not, conservative Republicans will make a major effort to win the post and may succeed; but their very efforts are likely to open a more turbulent new era in Iowa state politics. The prime Democratic contenders would be Attorney General Tom Miller, an ally of Culver and Clark, and Congressman Tom Harkin; leading Republicans include conservative Lieutenant Governor Terry Branstad.

Iowa does not have a presidential primary, but it does have what has become the first entry in the primary season each year: the Iowa precinct caucuses. In each of thousands of precincts across the state, on a frigid January night, a school, public building, or more usually a house is designated the Republican or Democratic precinct caucus site; and neighbors troop in to register their votes. The date was set at January in the 1970s by liberals who noted that George McGovern did well in Iowa's precinct caucuses in 1972 and wanted to have them come early in the primary season and give maximum attention to what they hoped would be liberal victories. National reporters did start paying attention to the Iowa caucuses in 1976, and in 1980 they attracted as much television and newspaper coverage as any primary. But liberal hopes were never realized.

Jimmy Carter led the Iowa Democratic caucuses in 1976, in part because he managed to win support from Democrats on both sides of the abortion issue, in part because supporters of some liberal candidates stayed cagily uncommitted in order to preserve their chances of going on to the state and national conventions. Four years later Carter benefited from having maintained his Iowa contacts during his three years in the White House but, more than that, he was helped by the tide of public opinion running, if not for him, then at least against Senator Edward Kennedy. Caucus turnout approached that of some primaries, and the verdict was unequivocal. On the Republican side, George Bush scored an upset victory over Ronald Reagan, in part because the Bush people organized the state ably, in part because Reagan had refused to show up for a candidates' debate in Iowa.

Census Data   Pop. (1980 final) 2,913,387, up 3% in 1970s: 1.29% of U.S. total, 27th largest. Central city, 24%; suburban, 16%. Median 4-person family income, 1978, $20,800, 102% of U.S., 20th highest.
1979 Share of Federal Tax Burden $5,951,000,000; 1.32% of U.S. total, 23d largest.
1979 Share of Federal Outlays $4,649,958,000; 1.00% of U.S. total, 33d largest.

DOD	$384,768,000	42d	(0.36%)	HEW	$2,293,050,000	26th (1.28%)
DOE	$15,703,000	34th	(0.13%)	ERDA	$12,365,000	26th (0.45%)
HUD	$61,738,000	29th	(0.94%)	NASA	$3,349,000	29th (0.07%)
VA	$245,727,000	32d	(1.18%)	DOT	$140,523,000	34th (0.85%)
EPA	$50,972,000	32d	(0.96%)	DOC	$7,279,000	45th (0.23%)
DOI	$13,122,000	45th	(0.24%)	USDA	$807,304,000	7th (3.36%)

Economic Base   Agriculture, notably cattle, hogs, corn, and soybeans; food and kindred products, especially meat products; finance, insurance, and real estate; machinery, especially farm machinery; electrical equipment and supplies, especially household appliances; printing and publishing, especially newspapers; fabricated metal products, especially structural metal products.

Political Lineup   Governor, Robert D. Ray (R). Senators, Roger W. Jepsen (R) and Charles E. Grassley (R). Representatives, 6 (3 R and 3 D); 6 in 1982. State Senate, 50 (29 R and 21 D); State House of Representatives, 100 (58 R and 42 D).

The Voters

   Registration   1,746,725 Total. 566,683 D (32%); 551,322 R (32%); 628,720 no party (36%).
   Employment profile 1970   White collar, 43%. Blue collar, 31%. Service, 14%. Farm, 12%.
   Ethnic groups   Black 1980, 1%. Hispanic 1980, 1%. Total foreign stock 1970, 11%. Germany, 4%.
   Presidential Vote

1980	Reagan (R)	676,026	(51%)
	Carter (D)	508,672	(39%)
	Anderson (I)	115,633	(9%)
1976	Ford (R)	632,863	(49%)
	Carter (D)	619,931	(48%)

1980 Democratic Presidential Caucuses		*1980 Republican Presidential Caucuses*		
Carter	(59%)	Bush	33,530	(32%)
Kennedy	(31%)	Reagan	31,348	(29%)
Uncommitted	(10%)	Baker	16,216	(15%)
		Connally	9,861	(9%)
		Crane	7,135	(7%)
		Two others	6,161	(6%)
		Undecided	1,800	(2%)

SENATORS

Sen. Roger W. Jepsen (R) Elected 1978, seat up 1984; b. Dec. 23, 1928, Cedar Falls; home, Davenport; U. of No. Ia., 1945–46, Ariz. St. U., B.S. 1950, M.A. 1953.

Career   Army, 1946–47; Counselor, Ariz. St. U., 1950–53; Farmer and insurance agent, 1954–55; Branch Mgr., Conn. General Life Ins. Co., 1956–72; Scott Co. Supervisor, 1962–65; Ia. Senate 1966–68; Lt. Gov. of Ia., 1968–72; Exec. V.P., Agridustrial Electronics Co., 1973–76; Pres. of Marketing Co., 1976–78.

Offices   110 RSOB, 202-224-3254. Also 1416 W. 16th St., Davenport 52804, 319-322-0120.

Committees   *Agriculture, Nutrition and Forestry* (7th). Subcommittees: Soil and Water Conservation (Chairman); Agricultural Credit and Rural Electrification; Foreign Agricultural Policy.

Armed Services (7th). Subcommittees: Tactical Warfare; Preparedness; Manpower and Personnel (Chairman).

Joint Economic Committee (Vice-chairman).

Group Ratings

	ADA	COPE	PC	LCV	CFA	RPN	NAB	NSI	NTU	ACA	ACU
1980	22	16	20	41	7	—	80	100	58	77	90
1979	0	0	18	—	5	—	—	—	63	92	96

Key Votes

1) Draft Registn $	AGN	6) Fair Housng Cloture	AGN	11) Cut Socl Incr Defns	FOR
2) Ban $ to Nicrgua	AGN	7) Ban $ Rape Abortns	FOR	12) Income Tax Indexing	—
3) Dlay MX Missile	AGN	8) Cap on Food Stmp $	FOR	13) Lim Spdg 21% GNP	FOR
4) Nuclr Mortorium	AGN	9) New US Dep Edcatn	AGN	14) Incr Wndfll Prof Tax	AGN
5) Alaska Lands Bill	FOR	10) Cut OSHA Inspctns	FOR	15) Chryslr Loan Grntee	AGN

Election Results

1978 general	Roger W. Jepsen (R)	421,598	(51%)	($728,268)
	Dick Clark (D)	395,066	(48%)	($860,774)
1978 primary	Roger W. Jepsen (R)	87,397	(57%)	
	Maurice Van Nostrand (R)	54,189	(36%)	($68,594)
	One other (R)	10,860	(7%)	
1972 general	Dick Clark (D)	662,637	(55%)	($241,803)
	Jack Miller (R)	530,525	(44%)	($328,263)

Sen. Charles E. Grassley (R) Elected 1980, seat up 1986; b. Sept. 17, 1933, New Hartford; home, New Hartford; U. of No. Ia., B.A. 1955, M.A. 1956, U. of Ia., 1957–58.

Career Farmer; Ia. House of Reps., 1959–74; U.S. House of Reps., 1975–80.

Offices 232 RSOB, 202-224-3744. Also 210 Waterloo Bldg., 531 Commercial St., Waterloo 50701, 319-232-6657; 721 Fed. Bldg., 210 Walnut St., Des Moines 50309, 515-284-4890; and 228 P.O. and Court House Bldg., Sioux City 51101, 712-233-3331.

Committees *Budget* (9th).

Finance (11th). Subcommittees: International Trade; Estate and Gift Taxation; Oversight of the Internal Revenue Service (Chairman).

Judiciary (8th). Subcommittees: Agency Administration (Chairman); Constitution; Immigration and Refugee Policy.

Special Committee on Aging (7th).

Group Ratings (as Member of U.S. House of Representatives)

	ADA	COPE	PC	LCV	CFA	RPN	NAB	NSI	NTU	ACA	ACU
1980	17	17	3	35	14	—	100	100	60	74	71
1979	11	20	13	20	7	—	—	—	57	88	83
1978	5	10	18	27	18	50	100	100	33	93	96

Key Votes (as Member of U.S. House of Representatives)

1) Draft Registn $	AGN	6) Fair Hsg DOJ Enfrc	AGN	11) Cut Socl Incr Dfns $	FOR
2) Ban $ to Nicrgua	FOR	7) Lim PAC Contrbtns	AGN	12) Hosptl Cost Controls	AGN
3) Dlay MX Missile	FOR	8) Cap on Food Stmp $	FOR	13) Gasln Ctrls & Allctns	AGN
4) Nuclr Mortorium	AGN	9) New US Dep Edcatn	AGN	14) Lim Wndfll Prof Tax	FOR
5) Alaska Lands Bill	FOR	10) Cut OSHA $	AGN	15) Chryslr Loan Grntee	FOR

Election Results

1980 general	Charles E. Grassley (R)	683,014	(53%)	($2,183,028)
	John C. Culver (D)	581,545	(46%)	($1,750,680)
1980 primary	Charles E. Grassley (R)	170,120	(66%)	
	Tom Stoner (R)	89,409	(34%)	($1,895,551)
1974 general	John C. Culver (D)	462,947	(52%)	($470,970)
	David M. Stanley (R)	420,546	(47%)	($336,067)

GOVERNOR

Gov. Robert D. Ray (R) Elected 1968, term expires Jan. 1983; b. Sept. 26, 1928, Des Moines; Drake U., B.A., LL.B.

Career Practicing atty.; Law and Reading Clerk, Ia. Senate; Chmn., Ia. Rep. St. Central Comm., 1965–68.

Offices State Capitol, Des Moines 50319, 515-281-5211.

Election Results

1978 gen.	Robert D. Ray (R)	491,713	(58%)
	Jerome Fitzgerald (D)	345,519	(41%)
1978 prim.	Robert D. Ray (R)	136,517	(88%)
	One other (R)	19,486	(12%)
1974 gen.	Robert D. Ray (R)	434,518	(58%)
	James F. Schaben (D)	377,553	(41%)

FIRST DISTRICT

The 1st congressional district of Iowa is the southeastern corner of the state. To a visitor from New York or California, this must look like a rather ordinary, sleepy part of the midwestern farm belt. But the 1st does have distinctive features. The little city of Burlington hardly seems important, but it has given its name to one of the nation's largest railroads (formerly the Chicago, Burlington & Quincy and now the Burlington Northern). Davenport is the home of the Palmer School of Chiropractic, the leading such institution in the nation.

Iowa City is the site of the State University of Iowa, among whose programs is a distinguished writers' workshop. The Amana colonies, known for their appliances and also for their preservation of a communal way of life that originated in Germany, are in the 1st. Not far away (although in another district) is West Branch, the birthplace of Herbert Hoover.

This is also a district that has had a fiercely contested congressional politics for most of the past 20 years. The partisan balance is relatively even here: Iowa City and Burlington are Democratic, Davenport marginal, and most of the rural counties Republican. And for years the district's congressmen seemed unable to use the advantages of incumbency effectively. Fred Schwengel, a moderate Republican who represented the district in 1955-65 and 1967-73, was president of the National Capital Historical Society and a Lincoln buff. He was beaten in 1964, nearly beaten in both the primary and the general election in 1970, and beaten again in 1972. His successor, Democrat Edward Mezvinsky, served on the House Judiciary Committee during the Nixon impeachment hearings and apparently made a good enough impression to win reelection in 1974, although his motion to impeach Nixon for misuses of government funds did not carry. But his marriage to a reporter for one of the local Washington television stations may have kept him from returning to the district often enough, and he was defeated in 1976.

The current congressman, Jim Leach, seems to be a man who, at last, has the knack of holding onto this district. He has a wide-ranging background, including stints on the staff of Donald Rumsfeld and in the foreign service. But when he was elected, he was the head of the family propane gas business — a down-to-home credential at a time when voters wanted responsiveness more than high-level experience in their elected officials. Leach is a kind of Robert Ray Republican. His record on economic issues is in line with the party's support for free enterprise and suspicion of or even hostility toward government regulation. But he is considerably more liberal on noneconomic and cultural issues. It is a combination that seems eminently salable in Iowa, and Leach has been able to carry Iowa City's Johnson County, whose liberalism tends to be concerned with cultural issues, as well as the better-off neighborhoods in Davenport and the traditionally Republican rural counties.

In the last two elections, against respectable opposition, Leach has won by nearly 2-to-1 margins — the best showings for any candidate since 1920 in this chronically marginal district. His popularity has not been translated into a statewide candidacy, and with both of Iowa's Senate seats now in Republican hands he seems to have lost his chance. Leach has a relatively high seniority seat on the Banking Committee and in 1981 gained a seat on Foreign Affairs.

Census Data Pop. (1980 final) 505,896, up 7% in 1970s. Median family income, 1970, $9,594, 100% of U.S.

The Voters

Employment profile 1970 White collar, 45%. Blue collar, 33%. Service, 14%. Farm, 8%.
Ethnic groups Black 1980, 3%. Hispanic 1980, 2%. Asian 1980, 1%. Total foreign stock 1970, 9%. Germany, 3%.

Presidential Vote

1980	Reagan (R)	105,371	(47%)
	Carter (D)	97,431	(41%)
	Anderson (I)	22,218	(10%)
1976	Ford (R)	105,060	(49%)
	Carter (D)	104,675	(49%)

Rep. James A. S. (Jim) **Leach** (R) Elected 1976; b. Oct. 15, 1942, Davenport; home, Davenport; Princeton U., B.A. 1964; Johns Hopkins U., M.A. 1966, London Sch. of Econ., 1966–68.

Career Staff Mbr., U.S. Rep. Donald Rumsfeld of Ill., 1965–66; U.S. Foreign Svc., 1968–69, 1971–72; Admin. Asst. to the Dir. of OEO, 1969–70; Pres., Flamegas Co., Inc., propane gas marketers, 1973– ; Rep. nominee for U.S. House of Reps., 1974.

Offices 1406 LHOB, 202-225-6576. Also 234 Fed. Bldg., 322 W. 3d St., Davenport 52801, 319-326-1841.

Committees *Banking, Finance and Urban Affairs* (6th). Subcommittees: Housing and Community Development; Financial Institutions Supervision, Regulation and Insurance; International Trade, Investment and Monetary Policy.

Foreign Affairs (11th). Subcommittees: Asian and Pacific Affairs; Human Rights and International Organizations.

Group Ratings

	ADA	COPE	PC	LCV	CFA	RPN	NAB	NSI	NTU	ACA	ACU
1980	61	37	60	63	51	—	58	40	38	58	37
1979	37	30	40	51	38	—	—	—	46	56	59
1978	35	25	40	47	18	92	92	50	25	63	75

Key Votes

1) Draft Registn $	AGN	6) Fair Hsg DOJ Enfrc	FOR	11) Cut Socl Incr Dfns $	AGN
2) Ban $ to Nicrgua	AGN	7) Lim PAC Contrbtns	FOR	12) Hosptl Cost Controls	AGN
3) Dlay MX Missile	FOR	8) Cap on Food Stmp $	FOR	13) Gasln Ctrls & Allctns	AGN
4) Nuclr Mortorium	—	9) New US Dep Edcatn	FOR	14) Lim Wndfll Prof Tax	FOR
5) Alaska Lands Bill	FOR	10) Cut OSHA $	FOR	15) Chryslr Loan Grntee	FOR

Election Results

1980 general	James A. S. (Jim) Leach (R)	133,349	(64%)	($235,933)
	Jim Larew (D)	72,602	(35%)	($46,834)
1980 primary	James A. S. (Jim) Leach (R)	30,383	(100%)	
1978 general	James A. S. (Jim) Leach (R)	79,940	(64%)	($241,356)
	Dick Myers (D)	45,037	(36%)	($123,626)

SECOND DISTRICT

The 2d congressional district of Iowa is the northeastern corner of the state. The district's largest city is Cedar Rapids, Iowa's second largest city, a manufacturing town whose current largest employer is the high technology firm of Collins Radio. Politically, Cedar Rapids and surrounding Linn County in recent years have become a kind of bellwether; they gave Jimmy Carter a small margin in 1976 and Ronald Reagan a somewhat larger one in 1980. The other parts of the district tend to balance out politically. There are two other fair-sized cities on the Mississippi River: Clinton, populated by German Protestants, tends to be Republican; Dubuque, almost entirely German Catholic, is heavily Democratic in most, although these days not all, elections. (This city, made famous by Harold Ross's remark that his *New Yorker* was not edited for "the little old lady in Dubuque," produced a large margin for George McGovern in 1972.) The knobby hills that flank the Mississippi are less suitable for corn, hogs, wheat, and cattle than the rolling plains farther west, but this part of Iowa provided the inspiration for much of the work of Grant Wood and its scenery is some of the most beautiful in the Midwest.

The 2d district is one that, in the 1970s, has run close to the state and national averages: it just missed going for Carter in 1976 and was within 2% of the national percentages in the 1980 presidential election. In House elections it has been seriously contested as often as not over the last 20 years. This was the House seat won by John Culver in the 1964 Johnson landslide; Culver became the only 1964 freshman in Iowa to hold onto his seat in 1966 and, despite several tough challenges, held on and was elected to the Senate in 1974. That was a good Democratic year, and another Democrat, Michael Blouin, won the seat that year. Blouin's margin, however, was uninspiring, and he did worse in 1976 against the same opponent, Tom Riley, who had also given Culver a tough race.

In 1978, the Republicans ran a different kind of candidate. Tom Tauke was only 28 years old, a Catholic from Dubuque, and already a four-year veteran of the Iowa legislature when he ran that year. His background helped him eat into the Catholic/Dubuque Democratic base here, at the same time as the abortion issue was hurting such Democrats as Senator Dick Clark among the same constituency. Tauke spent some $250,000 and beat Blouin by a larger margin than the Democrat had ever enjoyed and in the process became the youngest Republican in the House. During his first term, Tauke displayed considerable political acuity and compiled a voting record that went over well in the district, and in 1980 he was able to increase his margin. Democrat Steve Sovern was able in his Linn County base to hold Tauke even but Tauke won a large percentage (57%) in Dubuque County. That gave Tauke a solid margin, but not the kind of overwhelming one young congressmen like to win by in order to deter opposition. This district, which is not likely to be changed substantially by redistricting, has seen close contests in each of the last four elections, and it may be seriously contested again in 1982.

Census Data Pop. (1980 final) 484,684, up 3% in 1970s. Median family income, 1970, $9,511, 99% of U.S.

The Voters
Employment profile 1970 White collar, 41%. Blue collar, 34%. Service, 13%. Farm, 12%.
Ethnic groups Black 1980, 1%. Hispanic 1980, 1%. Total foreign stock 1970, 10%. Germany, 4%.

Presidential Vote

1980	Reagan (R)	106,149	(49%)
	Carter (D)	85,681	(40%)
	Anderson (I)	20,023	(9%)
1976	Ford (R)	103,383	(49%)
	Carter (D)	101,530	(49%)

Rep. Thomas J. (Tom) **Tauke** (R) Elected 1978; b. Oct. 11, 1950, Dubuque; home, Dubuque; Loras Col., B.A. 1972, U. of Ia., J.D. 1974.

Career Practicing atty.; Ia. House of Reps., 1975 78.

Offices 319 CHOB, 202-225-2911. Also 222 Fed. Bldg., Dubuque 52001, 319-557-7740.

Committees *Energy and Commerce* (13th). Subcommittees: Fossil and Synthetic Fuels; Telecommunications, Consumer Protection and Finance; Energy Conservation and Power.

Select Committee on Aging (14th). Subcommittee: Human Services.

Group Ratings

	ADA	COPE	PC	LCV	CFA	RPN	NAB	NSI	NTU	ACA	ACU
1980	33	—	30	59	36	—	91	60	49	61	47
1979	32	22	30	41	11	—	—	—	57	77	69

Key Votes

1) Draft Registn $	AGN	6) Fair Hsg DOJ Enfrc	FOR	11) Cut Socl Incr Dfns $	AGN
2) Ban $ to Nicrgua	AGN	7) Lim PAC Contrbtns	FOR	12) Hosptl Cost Controls	AGN
3) Dlay MX Missile	AGN	8) Cap on Food Stmp $	AGN	13) Gasln Ctrls & Allctns	AGN
4) Nuclr Mortorium	AGN	9) New US Dep Edcatn	AGN	14) Lim Wndfll Prof Tax	FOR
5) Alaska Lands Bill	FOR	10) Cut OSHA $		FOR	15) Chryslr Loan Grntee	AGN

Election Results

1980 general	Thomas J. (Tom) Tauke (R)	117,631	(57%)	($307,972)
	Steve Sovern (D)	87,131	(42%)	($129,815)
1980 primary	Thomas J. (Tom) Tauke (R)	28,924	(100%)	
1978 general	Thomas J. (Tom) Tauke (R)	72,644	(52%)	($250,432)
	Michael T. Blouin (D)	65,450	(47%)	($141,533)

THIRD DISTRICT

Iowa's 3d congressional district, in the north central part of the state, is almost perfectly square, a chunk of fertile Iowa farmland with several small industrial cities. The largest is Waterloo, a gritty factory town, with big meat packing and farm machinery plants; this is a place that has had its economic problems lately, and the Rath meat packing plant has been sold to its employees, who hope to run it at least at breakeven point in order to save their jobs. Smaller and less troubled is Mason City, up in the northern part of the district near the Minnesota border. Marshalltown, hometown of Meredith Willson (*The Music Man*) and Merle Miller (*Plain Speaking*), is a neat, pleasant courthouse town halfway between Des Moines and Waterloo. The land here is bounteous and serene, but it is also a difficult taskmaster, with its long, bone-chilling winters, its sometime dry summers, its tornadoes and unannounced storms.

The 3d district in its congressional representation and its voting habits is perhaps the best exemplar of Iowa's conservative Republican tradition—and of the fact that that tradition has often been seriously challenged. It was personified in H. R. Gross, who for 26 years (1949–75) represented the district. Spending most of his time on the floor, objecting to unanimous consent requests, decrying what he considered wasteful spending, asking for quorum calls, Gross was the undisputed curmudgeon of the House. Many considered him a pain in the neck, but his positions appear today more reasonable than they did to most members when he was enunciating them, and he exerted a kind of discipline on the legislative process that on balance was probably useful. On his retirement in 1974, Gross was succeeded by Charles Grassley, now Iowa's junior senator, a man who likes to speak of his background as a farmer and his opposition to government spending. Grassley did not station himself on the House floor as Gross did, preferring to do some of his work in committee and also returning more often to the district.

When Grassley ran for the Senate, he was succeeded by Republican Cooper Evans, a wealthy Grundy County farmer. But the succession was not automatic. Grassley himself had won his first election over 25-year-old Democrat Steve Rapp with only 51% of the vote.

And Evans, running in a heavily Republican year, took only 51% against Democrat Lynn Cutler. One reason for the closeness of the election is that Cutler, a Black Hawk County commissioner from Waterloo, was a strong candidate and, as a woman, was able to attract attention in the district and campaign contributions from outsiders. Another reason was the economic situation in Waterloo. Cutler carried 53% of the vote in Black Hawk County and carried the county that includes Mason City as well. But Evans, who spent liberally of his own personal wealth, carried Marshalltown and got small but sufficient margins in most of the rural counties as well, for a narrow victory. This is a district which, in a less Republican year, would probably have gone Democratic; the failure to pick up Republican districts like this, as much as anything else, is responsible for the Democrats' loss of 33 seats in the House in 1980.

Evans should by all standards be able to increase his margins. He serves on the Agriculture Committee and can be expected to support the Reagan Administration's programs strongly (although not the Russian grain embargo). That might, however, leave him vulnerable if the Reagan Administration's programs fail to live up to the public's expectations, and the Cutler candidacy shows that the Democrats here are still capable of putting on a strong campaign.

Census Data Pop. (1980 final) 477,736, up 1% in 1970s. Median family income, 1970, $8,911, 93% of U.S.

The Voters

  Employment profile 1970 White collar, 40%. Blue collar, 32%. Service, 14%. Farm, 14%.
  Ethnic groups Black 1980, 2%. Hispanic 1980, 1%. Total foreign stock 1970, 12%. Germany, 5%.

Presidential Vote

1980	Reagan (R)	115,682	(53%)
	Carter (D)	83,485	(38%)
	Anderson (I)	17,496	(8%)
1976	Ford (R)	108,563	(51%)
	Carter (D)	101,443	(48%)

Rep. Cooper Evans (R) Elected 1980; b. May 26, 1924, Cedar Rapids; home, Grundy Center; Ia. St. U., B.S. 1949, M.S. 1954, Oak Ridge Sch. of Reactor Technology, Deg. in Nuc. Engineering, 1956.

Career Army, 1947–65; Corn farmer, 1965–80; Commodities trader, 1968–80; Ia. House of Reps., 1974–79.

Offices 317 CHOB, 202-225-3301. Also 162 W. 4th St., Waterloo 50704, 319-234-3295; 309 P.O. Bldg., Mason Coty 50401, 515-424-3613; and 13 W. Main St., Marshalltown 50158, 515-753-3172.

Committee *Agriculture* (18th). Subcommittees: Conservation, Credit, and Rural Development; Department Operations, Research and Foreign Agriculture; Wheat, Soybeans and Feed Grains.

Group Ratings and Key Votes: Newly Elected

Election Results

1980 general	Cooper Evans (R)	107,869	(51%)	($575,496)
	Lynn G. Cutler (D)	101,735	(48%)	($227,543)

1980 primary	Cooper Evans (R)	26,480	(45%)	
	James West (R)	20,460	(35%)	($61,262)
	W. Richard Hansen (R)	10,871	(18%)	($44,285)
	One other (R)	1,372	(2%)	
1978 general	Charles E. Grassley (R)..........	103,659	(75%)	($160,100)
	John Knudson (D)	34,880	(25%)	($11,581)

FOURTH DISTRICT

The 4th congressional district of Iowa is the south central region of the state. More than half its votes are cast in Des Moines and surrounding Polk County, and Des Moines is the focus of this district in every respect but geographical. It is the state capital, for one thing, but it is also the largest financial and commercial center of Iowa; it is a significant manufacturing center as well, with the main product of course being farm machinery. It is also the home of the *Des Moines Register and Tribune,* one of the nation's few newspapers with genuine statewide circulation and one that is in many ways an intellectual leader in the state. Des Moines is essentially a Democratic town in a historically Republican state, the most Democratic part of Iowa in most elections except for Dubuque and scattered Catholic rural counties. South of Des Moines is farm country. The settlers here were primarily Protestant, some from points east in the Midwest, some from the South. The political map of the area looks like a quilt, with Democratic and Republican areas alternating with no apparent design. This results from settlement patterns and ancestral preferences, with little change in partisan preferences over time.

Representing the 4th district in the House is Neal Smith, a Democrat first elected in 1958. Caught on the wrong side of a political generation gap, he began to enjoy significant seniority just as seniority was being devalued by the 1974 freshmen. A moderate-to-liberal Democrat, he found himself to the right of other Iowa Democrats — after spending most of his political life to the left of most Iowans. In 1975 Smith sought to be the first chairman of the Budget Committee; he came close but lost to Brock Adams, who later became Jimmy Carter's first secretary of transportation. Smith chaired the Small Business Committee, a body with many members but fewer ongoing legislative responsibilities than most House standing committees. He gave up that chair in 1980 to become chairman of the State, Justice, Commerce and Judiciary Subcommittee of the Appropriations Committee — at just the time when Appropriations was losing some of its power to set federal spending levels to the reconciliation process that is in the hands of the Budget Committee.

From all these facts one might conclude that Neal Smith is hardworking but not flashy, capable but not possessed of that ambition that makes so many politicians unpleasant and also successful, and that would be pretty close to the truth. For many years Smith was reelected without significant opposition and carried not only Polk County but all the rural counties in the district as well. In 1980, for the first time in years, he had an aggressive and well-financed opponent, Don Young, a physician from Des Moines. Young held Smith to 54% of the vote — a sharp change from previous elections — and the Republican even managed to carry a couple of the smaller counties. This result may very well encourage Republicans to run a serious challenge again in 1982. The 4th in its current boundaries is the most Democratic of Iowa's districts on paper but even so is not much more than 4% more Democratic than the state average in most elections. It went for Reagan over Carter in 1980. Smith is not without his own resources, however; he has a record and a personality that have worn well for many years and committee positions which, if not as powerful as they once were, are nevertheless of considerable national importance.

Census Data   Pop. (1980 final) 489,070, up 4% in 1970s. Median family income, 1970, $9,589, 100% of U.S.

The Voters

Employment profile 1970   White collar, 51%. Blue collar, 30%. Service, 14%. Farm, 5%.
Ethnic groups   Black 1980, 3%. Hispanic 1980, 2%. Asian 1980, 1%. Total foreign stock 1970, 9%. Germany, 1%.

Presidential Vote

1980	Reagan (R)	105,520	(46%)
	Carter (D)	98,326	(43%)
	Anderson (I)	21,354	(9%)
1976	Ford (R)	98,765	(45%)
	Carter (D)	116,438	(53%)

Rep. Neal Smith (D) Elected 1958; b. Mar. 23, 1920, Hendrick; home, Altoona; U. of Mo., 1945–46, Syracuse U., 1946–47, Drake U., LL.B. 1950.

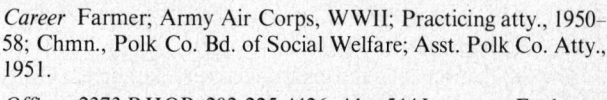

Career Farmer; Army Air Corps, WWII; Practicing atty., 1950–58; Chmn., Polk Co. Bd. of Social Welfare; Asst. Polk Co. Atty., 1951.

Offices 2373 RHOB, 202-225-4426. Also 544 Insurance Exchange Bldg., Des Moines 50309, 515-284-4634.

Committees *Appropriations*(4th). Subcommittees: Commerce, Justice, State and Judiciary; Labor–Health and Human Services–Education.

Small Business (2d). Subcommittees: Export Opportunities and Special Issues Affecting Small Business; SBA and SBIC Authority, Minority Enterprise and General Small Business Problems.

Group Ratings

	ADA	COPE	PC	LCV	CFA	RPN	NAB	NSI	NTU	ACA	ACU
1980	72	61	53	44	57	—	10	13	20	14	5
1979	42	53	28	39	19	—	—	—	19	21	24
1978	60	65	53	59	46	75	17	40	8	11	13

Key Votes

1) Draft Registn $	AGN	6) Fair Hsg DOJ Enfrc	FOR	11) Cut Socl Incr Dfns $	AGN
2) Ban $ to Nicrgua	—	7) Lim PAC Contrbtns	FOR	12) Hosptl Cost Controls	AGN
3) Dlay MX Missile	FOR	8) Cap on Food Stmp $	AGN	13) Gasln Ctrls & Allctns	AGN
4) Nuclr Mortorium	AGN	9) New US Dep Edcatn	FOR	14) Lim Wndfll Prof Tax	FOR
5) Alaska Lands Bill	FOR	10) Cut OSHA $	AGN	15) Chryslr Loan Grntee	FOR

Election Results

1980 general	Neal Smith (D)	117,896	(54%)	($87,813)
	Donald C. Young (R)	100,335	(46%)	($240,518)
1980 primary	Neal Smith (D)	19,183	(100%)	
1978 general	Neal Smith (D)	88,526	(65%)	($43,447)
	Charles E. Minor (R)	48,308	(35%)	($9,615)

FIFTH DISTRICT

The 5th congressional district of Iowa is the southwestern corner of the state. This is where the plains, as they roll toward the Missouri River, become more brown and less green than they are farther east; the towns become less frequent and less thickly settled; the spaces seem to grow more wide open. In eastern Iowa farmers raise corn and feed grain to fatten hogs; farther west, you begin to see more cattle and wheat.

There are some slight political differences also between this part of Iowa and the rest of the state, for the 5th district is one of the more Republican parts of Iowa. Its largest city, Council Bluffs, directly across the Missouri River from Omaha, Nebraska, is ordinarily Republican and has gone Republican in every presidential election since 1964. Ames, the district's only other city of any size, contains Iowa State University and casts a liberal vote; it went 55% for Senator John Culver in his losing race in 1980, for instance, and at the same time gave John Anderson 19% of its votes — one of his highest percentages anywhere in the country. The rural counties are more varied politically than they are agriculturally. The Catholic counties are Democratic, the more numerous Yankee Protestant counties Republican. The counties along the Missouri border have some affinity for the kind of southern Democrats rural Missourians favor; that was evident in their support of Jimmy Carter in 1976, although not in 1980.

The 5th district is a good example of why the current House has stayed Democratic through the Republican trend evident in the 1980 election results — and, indeed, why it has continued to elect a Democrat who is on some issues considered one of the liberal leaders of the House. That is Tom Harkin, one of those Democrats first elected in 1974 and who has returned ever since with large margins. One of Harkin's secrets is hard work. He first ran in this district in 1972, and in that year of Nixon's landslide got 49% against a Republican incumbent. For the next two years he campaigned practically nonstop, and in 1974 it paid off, and the incumbent was beaten. Another reason for his victories is that he has identified himself with the way of life of people in the district. In his 1974 campaign he set aside one day a week on which he could work at some ordinary, often menial job in the district. These work days got the candidate positive television coverage and provided some good footage for television commercials, one of which showed Harkin literally shoveling manure.

A third secret of Harkin's success is that he has continued to focus on the cultural and nonmacroeconomic issues that helped him get elected in the first place. He continues to serve on the Agriculture Committee, where he supports price support programs and food stamps. In 1981 he became chairman of the Livestock, Dairy, and Poultry Subcommittee — a body of obvious importance to this district and a post that is liable to be a political asset to Harkin for years to come. In that capacity he has generally favored high dairy price supports and was the leader in early unsuccessful attempts to circumvent the Reagan Administration cuts in that program. He favors tougher requirements for labeling imported meat and inspecting the American meat industry. He also took the initiative and was the main sponsor of legislation to prevent international banks from lending money to governments that violate human rights. He moved to cut military aid to South Korea at one point because of human rights violations — at a time when South Korea was in the spotlight in the Koreagate scandal. That probably struck a chord in Iowa, where voters abhor scandals. He strongly opposed the Clinch River breeder reactor. He argued strongly against a bill that would relax clean air standards in rural areas that now have little pollution. Not all of these moves have been successful, but they have been seriously pursued, and they have probably succeeded in highlighting Harkin's legislative agenda to his constituents—at the expense of the Republican agenda of cutting government spending and increasing defense.

That has paid off politically. Harkin won by nearly a 2-to-1 margin, and he survived with a smaller but still impressive margin in 1978. In 1980, when Jimmy Carter could manage to win only 35% of the votes in the 5th district, and when Harkin had serious and well-financed opposition in the person of state Senator Calvin Hultman, Harkin still won reelection with 60% of the vote. It was a signal achievement, and one that suggests that this congressman has achieved a rapport with his constituency that goes far beyond normal attachments. It is possible that the Republican legislature will attempt to hurt Harkin by removing Ames from the district, although doing so would hurt Republican chances in at least one other district; but in 1980 Harkin would have won with 59% even without Ames. There have also been rumors that Harkin may run for governor.

Census Data Pop. (1980 final) 491,384, up 5% in 1970s. Median family income, 1970, $8,338, 87% of U.S.

The Voters

Employment profile 1970 White collar, 40%. Blue collar, 28%. Service, 14%. Farm, 18%.
Ethnic groups Hispanic 1980, 1%. Total foreign stock 1970, 9%. Germany, 3%.

Presidential Vote

1980	Reagan (R)	122,135	(55%)
	Carter (D)	77,523	(35%)
	Anderson (I)	19,660	(9%)
1976	Ford (R)	107,605	(50%)
	Carter (D)	103,483	(48%)

Rep. Tom Harkin (D) Elected 1974; b. Nov. 19, 1939, Cumming; home, Ames; Ia. St. U., B.S. 1962; Catholic U., J.D. 1972.

Career Navy, 1962–67; Staff Aide to U.S. Rep. Neal Smith, 1969–70; Dem. nominee for U.S. House of Reps., 1972; Atty., Polk Co. Legal Aid Society, 1973–74.

Offices 2411 RHOB, 202-225-3806. Also P.O. Box 264, 213 P.O. Bldg., Ames 50010, 515-232-6111.

Committees *Agriculture* (10th). Subcommittees: Conservation, Credit and Rural Development; Domestic Marketing, Consumer Relations and Nutrition; Livestock, Dairy, and Poultry (Chairman).

Science and Technology (6th). Subcommittees: Energy Development and Applications; Transportation, Aviation and Materials.

Group Ratings

	ADA	COPE	PC	LCV	CFA	RPN	NAB	NSI	NTU	ACA	ACU
1980	78	47	70	94	71	—	9	0	23	33	11
1979	74	79	68	83	52	—	—	—	28	15	23
1978	60	70	80	83	77	42	46	0	39	26	8

Key Votes

1) Draft Registn $	AGN	6) Fair Hsg DOJ Enfrc	FOR	11) Cut Socl Incr Dfns $	AGN
2) Ban $ to Nicrgua	AGN	7) Lim PAC Contrbtns	FOR	12) Hosptl Cost Controls	AGN
3) Dlay MX Missile	FOR	8) Cap on Food Stmp $	AGN	13) Gasln Ctrls & Allctns	AGN
4) Nuclr Mortorium	FOR	9) New US Dep Edcatn	FOR	14) Lim Wndfll Prof Tax	FOR
5) Alaska Lands Bill	FOR	10) Cut OSHA $	AGN	15) Chryslr Loan Grntee	AGN

Election Results

1980 general	Tom Harkin (D)	127,895	(60%)	($314,334)
	Cal Hultman (R)	84,472	(40%)	($309,325)
1980 primary	Tom Harkin (D)	16,267	(100%)	
1978 general	Tom Harkin (D)	82,333	(59%)	($144,160)
	Julian B. Garrett (R)	57,377	(41%)	($64,680)

SIXTH DISTRICT

The 6th congressional district of Iowa is the northwestern corner of the state where water and trees begin to get scarce and the sky seems to get bigger. Except for Sioux City, an old river city that is larger than neighboring Sioux Falls, South Dakota, the 6th is almost entirely rural in character, with small farm market towns and grain elevators towering here and there in the distance. The district has traditionally been Republican, like most of Iowa, but with some exceptions—the kind of political divergences from normality that dot the maps of all the Great Plains states. These usually stem from their initial settlement by different ethnic or religious groups. A colony of German Catholics or Norwegians, to name only one usually Democratic and one usually Republican group, would send encouraging letters back to the Old Country and sometimes would forward steamship passage and railroad fare so that relatives or friends could make their way to new homes in Iowa or Kansas or the Dakotas. Such history makes sense of the Republican sentiments of Sioux County, Iowa (settled by Dutch Protestants and 79% for Ronald Reagan in 1980), or the Democratic leanings of nearby Palo Alto County (settled by German Catholics and 55% for Jimmy Carter in 1976). Palo Alto has a further distinction: it is one of three American bellwether counties that has never voted for a loser in a presidential election; the other two are Coos County, New Hampshire, and Crook County, Oregon.

The 6th district currently has a Democratic congressman, elected in that surge of Democratic strength in Iowa in the early 1970s and strong enough to hold onto the seat in more Republican times. He is Berkley Bedell, an attractive candidate wholly apart from partisan considerations. He grew up a fishing enthusiast in the town of Spirit Lake, near the Minnesota border. World War II intervened and he never finished college, but he started his own business manufacturing fishing tackle. This was not ordinary stuff: it was the monofilament line that revolutionized fishing habits, and Bedell became a millionaire. A deeply religious man, he also became a friend of Governor and Senator Harold Hughes, and Hughes—himself from a small town in the 6th district—convinced Bedell he should enter politics. He became a Democrat, ran for Congress in 1972 and got 48% against Republican incumbent Wiley Mayne. Bedell ran again in 1974. In the meantime, Mayne had voted against the impeachment of Richard Nixon, an act of political courage for which he never received much credit; and Bedell easily won the general election.

Bedell has proved to be a popular congressman. He has seats on the Agriculture and Small Business Committees, both of importance to the district, although Agriculture is much more important legislatively. He is chairman of an artfully named subcommittee: Energy, Environment, and Safety Issues Affecting Small Business, which concerns itself with such matters as gasoline marketing practices and gasohol production. Bedell has proved to be very popular in his district. Some thought he might be in trouble in 1980 because his fishing tackle company was being investigated on charges that it imported products from its Taiwan subsidiary at artificially low prices to avoid payment of customs duties. But nothing adverse was ever proved, and Bedell's reputation for honesty and probity did not suffer. He was reelected in 1980 with 64% of the vote — the highest percentage of any congressman in Iowa — and in a district where his party's presidential candidate received only 34%. Given that kind of performance, Bedell seems to have made this a safe seat; and it is hard to see how redistricting can change that in any significant way.

Census Data   Pop. (1980 final) 464,617, down 1% in 1970s. Median family income, 1970, $8,314, 87% of U.S.

The Voters

Employment profile 1970   White collar, 40%. Blue collar, 28%. Service, 14%. Farm, 18%.
Ethnic groups   Hispanic 1980, 1%. Total foreign stock 1970, 16%. Germany, 5%.

Presidential Vote

1980	Reagan (R)	121,169	(58%)
	Carter (D)	71,226	(34%)
	Anderson (I)	14,882	(7%)
1976	Ford (R)	109,482	(54%)
	Carter (D)	92,362	(45%)

Rep. Berkley Bedell (D) Elected 1974; b. Mar. 5, 1921, Spirit Lake; home, Spirit Lake; Ia. St. U., 1940–42.

Career Army Air Corps, WWII; Founder and Chmn., Berkley & Co., fishing tackle mfrs.; Dem nominee for U.S. House of Reps., 1972.

Offices 2440 CHOB, 202-225-5476. Also 406 Fed. Bldg., Fort Dodge 50501, 515-573-7169.

Committees *Agriculture* (11th). Subcommittees: Conservation, Credit and Rural Development; Forests, Family Farms and Energy; Wheat, Soybeans and Feed Grains.

Small Business (6th). Subcommittees: Antitrust and Restraint of Trade Activities Affecting Small Business; Energy, Environment and Safety Issues Affecting Small Business (Chairman).

Group Ratings

	ADA	COPE	PC	LCV	CFA	RPN	NAB	NSI	NTU	ACA	ACU
1980	72	44	67	88	64	—	0	0	27	13	11
1979	79	70	58	82	42	—	—	—	32	23	24
1978	70	53	87	96	77	67	36	0	34	22	22

Key Votes

1) Draft Registn $	AGN	6) Fair Hsg DOJ Enfrc	FOR	11) Cut Socl Incr Dfns $	AGN
2) Ban $ to Nicrgua	AGN	7) Lim PAC Contrbtns	FOR	12) Hosptl Cost Controls	AGN
3) Dlay MX Missile	FOR	8) Cap on Food Stmp $	AGN	13) Gasln Ctrls & Allctns	AGN
4) Nuclr Mortorium	FOR	9) New US Dep Edcatn	FOR	14) Lim Wndfll Prof Tax	AGN
5) Alaska Lands Bill	FOR	10) Cut OSHA $	FOR	15) Chryslr Loan Grntee	—

Election Results

1980 general	Berkley Bedell (D)	129,460	(64%)	($200,428)
	Clarence S. Carney (R)	71,866	(36%)	($250,335)
1980 primary	Berkley Bedell (D)	14,719	(100%)	
1978 general	Berkley Bedell (D)	87,139	(66%)	($93,188)
	Willis E. Junker (R)	44,320	(34%)	($14,477)

KANSAS

The political history of Kansas began with a rush in the 1850s, and the outcome of the struggle of that decade has pretty much shaped the state's politics since. The land here was virtually unsettled in 1850, and by the terms of the Kansas–Nebraska Act of 1854 the question of whether Kansas would be a free or slave state would be decided by its voters — a system known to its proponents as popular sovereignty and to its detractors as squatter sovereignty. Everyone assumed that Nebraska would be free soil, but Kansas — just west of slaveholding Missouri — was in doubt. Almost immediately proslavery southerners and abolitionist New Englanders were financing likeminded settlers and moving them to Kansas; soon armed fighting broke out between Democratic "bushwhackers" and free-soil "jayhawkers." Proslavery raiders from Missouri rode into the territory, and John Brown massacred antiabolitionists at Pottawatomie Creek. This was "bleeding Kansas"—a major national issue and one of the direct causes of the Civil War. When the South seceded in 1862, Kansas was admitted to the Union as a free state, with a solid Republican majority. It has remained pretty solidly Republican ever since.

The major exception to Republican hegemony came during the depression of the 1890s — the Populist revolt. During the previous decade, years of unusually high rainfall on the plains, Kansas had attracted hundreds of thousands of new settlers. Suddenly the rain all but stopped; and that, together with a worldwide drop in wheat prices, showed that the Kansas plains could not support all who had come to depend on them. The state's boom had gone bust; some Kansas counties have never again reached the population levels recorded in the 1890 census.

Suddenly Populists were beating Republicans in Kansas. They were politicians such as Mary Ellen Lease ("What you farmers should do is to raise less corn and more hell") and "Sockless Jerry" Simpson, who served as an impoverished congressman. Lease, Simpson, and the farmers of the Populist Party became advocates of arcane doctrines of free silver and commodity credit programs. William Jennings Bryan, the lion of the prairies, was their man, and he swept Kansas in 1896. The period of Populist dominance — colorful, revivalistic, desperate — was soon over. Around 1900 the nation began to enjoy a period of agricultural prosperity so great that parity prices are still based on those years. With small-town Republicans back in control, Bryan failed to carry Kansas in 1900 or 1908, William Allen White, the progressive Republican editor of the *Emporia Gazette,* was the closest thing in the state's politics to a radical.

But echoes of the farm revolt of the 1890s can still be heard in Kansas politics. Fewer Kansans than ever are actually farmers, but the state's economy still depends heavily on agriculture. For years agriculture has been one of the most heavily regulated and subsidized businesses in the nation, the very definition of a special interest; yet there remains an assumption, held not just among farmers, that any government action that helps farmers is in the public interest. Whether or not our agriculture policy can be defended on logical grounds, the fact is that it works: American farmers produce so efficiently that this country can feed almost half the world, and agriculture has become our biggest foreign exchange earner. In any case, Kansas voters are always ready to react angrily against the party in power if they feel that farm policy is not being properly managed. There were farm revolts against the Republicans in the late 1950s and again around the Watergate year of 1974; there were farm revolts against the Democrats in the late 1960s and again in the late 1970s.

Kansas's basic leanings are so heavily Republican, however, that even revolts against a Republican administration do not necessarily produce Democratic victories. In 1974, for example, Democrat Bill Roy came close to beating Senator Robert Dole but still fell short and Democrats did not capture any previously Republican House seats (although they did take one in 1976). In contrast, in 1980, when the tide was running strongly against the national Democratic administration, Kansas gave Reagan a 58%–33% victory over Carter; the president carried only one of the state's 105 counties, the one containing the industrial city of Kansas City, Kansas.

These tides do not necessarily affect Kansas's state elections. In fact, this Republican state has had Democratic governors for 16 of the last 26 years. The current Democratic incumbent, John Carlin, was elected at 38 in 1978 after two years as speaker of the state House. A dairy farmer from a rural county, he seemed more in line with Kansas mores than did the incumbent, Robert Bennett, who sported a beard and came from the affluent Kansas City suburbs. Carlin, however, has a Republican legislature to contend with; he achieved his greatest national notice when he came out against the binding rule sought by his fellow Carter supporters at the 1980 Democratic National Convention. In Kansas he surprised many by vetoing a death penalty bill after promising in his campaign to sign it. He is up for reelection in 1982.

Kansas's leading politician today is Senator Bob Dole. He is a national figure as well, known to the public for having been Gerald Ford's running mate in 1976, and known now in Washington as Russell Long's successor as chairman of the Senate Finance Committee. Dole is a man with an acid wit and a nimble brain, a knowledge of Washington and some feeling still for the central Kansas plains where he grew up. He is also a bitter partisan on occasion and a man whose political career has had a number of ups and downs.

Dole is a Washington veteran now: first elected to the House in 1960 and the Senate in 1968. He distinguished himself there, at a time when members of the Republican minority regularly were deserting the Nixon cause, as the Nixon Administration's staunchest — and self-appointed — defender. That led to his selection as Republican national chairman, a job he served in from 1971 to 1973; cut off from almost any contact with the Committee to Re-elect the President, he was nonetheless expected to defend the President against charges arising from the Watergate break-in. Dole thus achieved national notice; but he also got himself in trouble back in Kansas. During the 1974 campaign, he was trailing Congressman Bill Roy, a doctor–lawyer from Topeka, and it looked as if Dole were going to lose. Then he counterattacked, with a commercial showing mud being thrown on a Dole poster and attacking his opponent for having performed therapeutic abortions. It was both a brilliant and vicious campaign — and characteristic of the best and worst of Bob Dole.

Safe in office for a second term, Dole mellowed and became more interested in legislation. With a seat on the Agriculture Committee and an interest in promoting Kansas wheat interests, Dole also became one of the architects of the food stamp program, working with George McGovern to produce a plan that would be both more generous and fiscally less expensive. On the Finance Committee, Dole mastered some tough issues and played a constructive role.

Dole also became somewhat of a national political personality — and not a particularly successful one. He was chosen, late at night, as Gerald Ford's vice presidential candidate in 1976. And if he did not prove himself unqualified for the position, he did not really distinguish himself either. His partisan slips—"Democrat wars"— did not help the Ford–Dole ticket win the Democratic votes they needed, and he was clearly the loser in the Dole–Mondale debate. His sense of humor, or what was left of it as the campaign went on, seemed aimed in a self-deprecating, almost cruel way against himself. In the end, Dole's presence on the ticket did not seem to help the Republicans, and the Ford–Dole ticket won by an unimpressive margin in safely Republican Kansas.

Dole's 1980 presidential campaign was even sadder. He never really amassed an organization or raised much money; his witty comments ended up being addressed mainly at himself. He seemed, as he increasingly has in the late 1970s, to see himself as a Washington insider, an ambassador from the complicated inside world of government to the ignorant voters out there. There is something to this view. Dole has been in Washington 20 years, he does know a lot about government, and many of the easy answers voters are accustomed to getting from candidates have little relationship to how things happen once they get in office. But it is not a very good way to go about winning votes in New Hampshire, and the best that can be said about Dole's presidential race is that it was over mercifully soon.

After the Republicans' unexpected capture of the Senate in 1980, Dole suddenly found himself, after only 12 years, a very senior member. He became chairman of the Senate Finance Committee, one of the key positions in the Congress. Dole has a hard act to follow: Russell Long knew the substance of the tax laws and knew the politics of the committee better than anyone else, and he was the master of the art of keeping all major issues unresolved until an all-night session at the end of the year, when he could wear down his opponents and sneak through his pet projects. Dole's knowledge is not yet as great and his capacity for craftiness is uncertain; but he does have great native ability and has shown that he can grow into being a constructive legislator. If he can use his brains and sense of humor, and curb his bitterness and his partisan tendencies, he has the potential of being an effective Finance chairman. His years in the Senate have left their imprint on his positions on issues. He is not an enthusiast for the Kemp–Roth tax cut, although he does support it, nor for supply-side economics generally. He continues to favor federal catastrophic health insurance, an idea long championed by Russell Long as an alternative to Edward Kennedy's national health insurance, rather than the competition bill backed by Senator David Durenberger and, when he was a congressman, by David Stockman. He is much more favorable toward the food stamp program than is Agriculture Chairman Jesse Helms. He is a strong supporter of free trade and particularly concerned about encouraging agricultural exports. There is another element in Dole's politics: for all his vitriolic humor, he is one Republican who, in the opinion of some Washington observers, really does have compassion for the poor and those with difficulties. Dole was reelected without difficulty in Kansas in 1980, and presumably can hold the seat for many years unless the political climate turns strongly against the Republicans.

Kansas's other senator is Nancy Landon Kassebaum, elected in 1978 and at that time the only woman in the Senate. She has a fine Kansas heritage, for she is the daughter of Alf Landon, onetime governor and the Republican nominee against Franklin Roosevelt in 1936— Landon in his nineties saw his daughter elected to the Senate. She was not the initial favorite in the race; she had little political experience, and the only elective office she had held was a membership on a local school board. But in a nine-candidate field she won the Republican primary with 31% of the vote; and her upset win made her the favorite over Bill Roy, who even in that Republican year had enough popularity to beat the male Republican candidates. Kassebaum is considered a somewhat moderate Republican, but one who is not inclined to be a maverick or troublemaker to party leaders. She has plummy committee assignments: Commerce, Foreign Relations, and the third-ranking seat on the Budget Committee.

Kansas is a state that should not have too much trouble redistricting its congressional seats. All five districts have populations pretty close to the state average. One possible change is to have more of industrial Kansas City in the 2d district, which would make it more Democratic (which would please the governor and displease only the incumbent who is not well thought of even by Republicans) and would make the 3d district safer for Republican Larry Winn. But the easier course is inertia, to leave the district lines pretty much where they are.

Census Data   Pop. (1980 final) 2,363,208, up 5% in 1970s: 1.04% of U.S. total, 32d largest. Central city, 19%; suburban, 28%. Median 4-person family income, 1978, $19,792, 97% of U.S., 27th highest.

1979 Share of Federal Tax Burden $4,914,000,000; 1.09% of U.S. total, 29th largest.

1979 Share of Federal Outlays $4,731,184,000; 1.02% of U.S. total, 32d largest.

DOD	$1,176,167,000	27th	(1.11%)	HEW	$1,790,248,000	33d	(1.00%)
DOE	$1,793,000	48th	(0.02%)	ERDA	$1,133,000	42d	(0.04%)
HUD	$61,284,000	31st	(0.93%)	NASA	$1,689,000	33d	(0.04%)
VA	$227,991,000	34th	(1.10%)	DOT	$142,776,000	33d	(0.87%)
EPA	$33,364,000	37th	(0.63%)	DOC	$10,458,000	38th	(0.33%)
DOI	$39,864,000	31st	(0.72%)	USDA	$599,937,000	11th	(2.50%)

Economic Base   Agriculture, especially cattle, wheat, hogs, and sorghum grain; finance, insurance, and real estate; transportation equipment, especially aircraft and parts; food and kindred products; machinery; printing and publishing, especially newspapers; oil and gas extraction, especially crude petroleum and natural gas.

Political Lineup   Governor, John W. Carlin (D). Senators, Robert Dole (R) and Nancy Landon Kassebaum (R). Representatives, 5 (4 R and 1 D); 5 in 1982. State Senate, 40 (24 R and 16 D); State House of Representatives, 125 (72 R and 53 D).

The Voters

   Registration   1,290,539 Total. 313,890 D (24%); 407,613 R (32%); 569,036 unaffiliated (44%)
   Employment profile 1970   White collar, 48%. Blue collar, 31%. Service, 13%. Farm, 8%.
   Ethnic groups   Black 1980, 5%. Hispanic 1980, 3%. Am. Ind. 1980, 1%. Asian 1980, 1%. Total foreign stock 1970, 8%. Germany, 2%.

Presidential Vote

1980	Reagan (R)	566,812	(58%)
	Carter (D)	326,150	(33%)
	Anderson (I)	68,231	(7%)
1976	Ford (R)	502,752	(52%)
	Carter (D)	430,421	(45%)

1980 Democratic Presidential Primary			*1980 Republican Presidential Primary*		
Carter	109,807	(57%)	Reagan	179,739	(63%)
Kennedy	61,318	(32%)	Anderson	51,924	(18%)
Brown	9,434	(5%)	Bush	35,838	(13%)
Four others........	2,196	(1%)	Nine others	11,171	(4%)
None	11,163	(6%)	None	6,726	(2%)

SENATORS

Sen. Robert Dole (R) Elected 1968, seat up 1986; b. July 22, 1923, Russell; home, Russell; U. of Kans., 1941–43, Washburn Municipal U., B.A., LL.B. 1952.

Career Army, WWII; Kans. House of Reps., 1951–53; Russell Co. Atty., 1953–61; U.S. House of Reps., 1961–69; Chmn., Rep. Natl. Comm., 1971–73; Rep. nominee for V.P., 1976.

Offices 2213 DSOB, 202-224-6521. Also 4601 State Ave., Kansas City 66102, 913-287-4545, and Fed. Ofc. Bldg., 444 S.E. Quincy St., Topeka 66683, 913-295-2745.

Committees *Agriculture, Nutrition and Forestry* (2d). Subcommittees: Agricultural Research and General Legislation; Foreign Agricultural Policy; Nutrition (Chairman).

Finance (Chairman). Subcommittees: Health; Social Security and Income Maintenance Programs; Oversight of the Internal Revenue Service.

Judiciary (5th). Subcommittees: Courts (Chairman); Criminal Law; Regulatory Reform.

Rules and Administration (7th).   *Joint Committee on Taxation* (Vice-chairman).

Group Ratings

	ADA	COPE	PC	LCV	CFA	RPN	NAB	NSI	NTU	ACA	ACU
1980	22	28	33	49	20	—	75	100	44	77	67
1979	21	21	29	—	24	—	—	—	36	64	75
1978	20	22	28	20	25	50	58	100	18	58	88

Key Votes

1) Draft Registn $	AGN	6) Fair Housng Cloture	AGN	11) Cut Socl Incr Defns	FOR
2) Ban $ to Nicrgua	AGN	7) Ban $ Rape Abortns	FOR	12) Income Tax Indexing	FOR
3) Dlay MX Missile	AGN	8) Cap on Food Stmp $	AGN	13) Lim Spdg 21% GNP	FOR
4) Nuclr Mortorium	AGN	9) New US Dep Edcatn	AGN	14) Incr Wndfll Prof Tax	AGN
5) Alaska Lands Bill	AGN	10) Cut OSHA Inspctns	FOR	15) Chryslr Loan Grntee	FOR

Election Results

1980 general	Robert Dole (R)	598,686	(64%)	($1,226,188)
	John Simpson (D).............	340,271	(36%)	($323,792)
1980 primary	Robert Dole (R)	201,484	(82%)	
	One other (R)	44,674	(18%)	
1974 general	Robert Dole (R)	403,983	(51%)	($1,110,024)
	Bill Roy (D)..................	390,451	(49%)	($836,927)

Sen. Nancy Landon Kassebaum (R) Elected 1978, seat up 1984; b. July 29, 1932, Topeka; home, Wichita; U. of Kans., B.A. 1954, U. of Mich., M.A. 1956.

Career Staff of U.S. Sen. James B. Pearson, 1975.

Offices 304 RSOB, 202-224-4774. Also Fed. Ofc. Bldg., Box 51, 444 S.E. Quincy St., Topeka 66683, 913-295-2888.

Committees *Budget* (3d).

Commerce, Science, and Transportation (5th). Subcommittees: Aviation (Chairman); Science, Technology and Space; Surface Transportation.

Foreign Relations (7th). Subcommittees: International Economic Policy; African Affairs (Chairman); Western Hemisphere Affairs.

Special Committee on Aging (4th).

Group Ratings

	ADA	COPE	PC	LCV	CFA	RPN	NAB	NSI	NTU	ACA	ACU
1980	44	25	27	48	7	—	90	60	44	70	52
1979	37	22	29	—	19	—	—	—	52	63	64

Key Votes

1) Draft Registn $	AGN	6) Fair Housng Cloture	AGN	11) Cut Socl Incr Defns	FOR
2) Ban $ to Nicrgua	FOR	7) Ban $ Rape Abortns	AGN	12) Income Tax Indexing	FOR
3) Dlay MX Missile	FOR	8) Cap on Food Stmp $	FOR	13) Lim Spdg 21% GNP	FOR
4) Nuclr Mortorium	AGN	9) New US Dep Edcatn	AGN	14) Incr Wndfll Prof Tax	AGN
5) Alaska Lands Bill	FOR	10) Cut OSHA Inspctns	—	15) Chryslr Loan Grntee	AGN

Election Results

1978 general	Nancy Landon Kassebaum (R) ...	403,354	(54%)	($856,644)
	Bill Roy (D)................	317,602	(42%)	($813,754)
1978 primary	Nancy Landon Kassebaum (R) ...	67,324	(31%)	
	Wayne Angell (R)	54,161	(25%)	($388,334)
	Sam Hardage (R)	30,248	(14%)	($489,983)
	Jan Meyers (R)	20,933	(10%)	($72,307)
	Five others (R)	47,476	(22%)	
1972 general	James B. Pearson (R)	622,591	(71%)	($109,651)
	Arch O. Tetzlaff (D)	200,764	(23%)	($6,742)

GOVERNOR

Gov. John W. Carlin (D) Elected 1978, term expires Jan. 1983; b. Aug. 3, 1940, Salina; Kans. St. U., B.S.

Career Dairy farmer, cattle sales mgr.; Kans. House of Reps., 1971–79, Minor. Ldr., 1975–77, Spkr., 1977–79.

Offices 2d Flr., State Capitol, Topeka 66612, 913-296-3232.

Election Results

1978 gen.	John W. Carlin (D)	363,835	(49%)
	Robert F. Bennett (R)	348,015	(47%)
1978 prim.	John W. Carlin (D)	71,366	(55%)
	Bert Chaney (D)	34,132	(26%)
	Harry Wiles (D)	23,762	(18%)
1974 gen.	Robert F. Bennett (R)	387,792	(49%)
	Vern Miller (D)...........	384,115	(49%)

FIRST DISTRICT

The 1st congressional district of Kansas covers more than half the state's land area. It contains more counties (57) than any other congressional district in the country except the state of North Dakota, which elects one congressman-at-large. This fact is not just a bit of trivia; it tells us a good deal about the expectations of the people who first settled this part of Kansas. Most of them came here in the 1880s from such states as Illinois and Iowa and Missouri. When they organized counties, as they quickly did, they made them 36 miles square, just as they had in the old Midwest. Deceived by a few years of unusually heavy rainfall, the settlers expected that the new counties would eventually contain as many people as the old ones back home; hence they were made the same size. Not only the small size of the counties, but

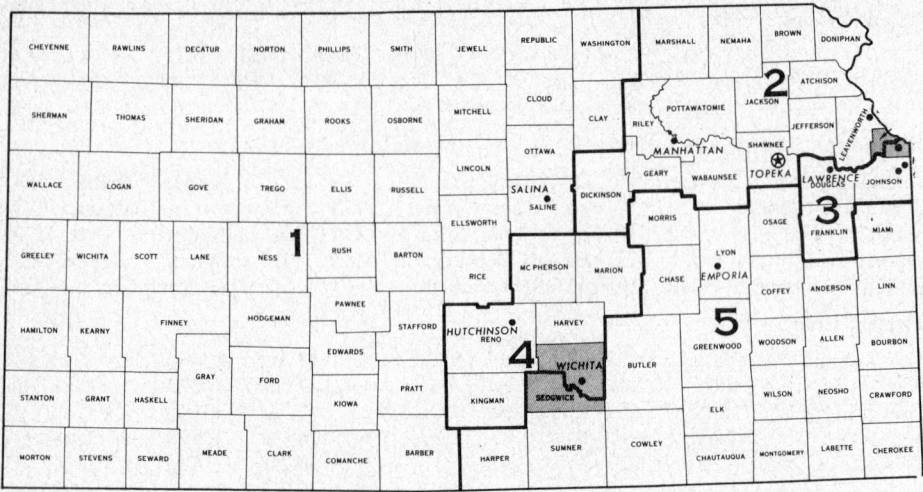

the grandiose place names (Concordia, Minneapolis, Montezuma) testify to the settlers' hopes, dreams, and ambitions.

But they never materialized. Out here past 98° longitude, rainfall is normally half what it is in Illinois. In the early years of the 19th century, this part of the country had been called the Great American Desert—a howling wilderness of arid, treeless land and blowing soil. The early settlers worked hard to prove the image wrong, but they never entirely succeeded. So the thousands more who were expected to come never arrived; today the average population of the district's 57 counties is about 8,000.

Most are far less populous than that because the average is inflated by the district's "urban" concentrations. The largest city, Salina, has only 41,000 people; Dodge City, terminus of the old cattle drives and once the home of Wyatt Earp, has just 17,000 people; Holcomb, made famous by Truman Capote's *In Cold Blood*, has less than 1,000. Hays, a German Catholic town of 16,000, is one part of the district that goes Democratic; so too sometimes do some counties along the Arkansas River first settled by southerners. But the real 1st cannot be found in the towns. This is livestock and wheat country, one of the most agricultural districts in the nation. For miles on end you can see nothing but rolling brown fields, sectioned off here and there by barbed wire fence, and in the distance a grain elevator towering over a tiny town. The winds and rain and tornadoes that come suddenly out of the sky remind you that the original settlers likened this part of Kansas to an ocean and thought themselves in their wooden wagons almost as helpless as passengers at sea in a wooden rowboat.

This 1st district is Republican basically, but like most of the agricultural Great Plains area it has a tendency to go against the party in power. The last time it elected a Democratic congressman was in 1960; his district was combined with another represented by Bob Dole in 1962, and Republicans have won there ever since. In 1980 its two political tendencies worked in tandem to produce a rousing 66%–26% margin for Ronald Reagan over Jimmy Carter. Dole represented western Kansas for eight years in the House and was followed in the 1st district by Republican Keith Sebelius. After 12 years, having reached the position of ranking minority member of the House Agriculture Committee, Sebelius retired in 1980 at age 64.

The succession was determined essentially in the Republican primary. The leading candidate was Pat Roberts, Sebelius's top aide for 12 years. Although he was attacked for changing his residence from Topeka to the 1st congressional district only in 1980, he won a convincing 56% in a three-candidate Republican primary. The general election was easier. The Democrat, state legislator, Phil Martin, carried Hays and his own home area but could do no better than hold Roberts to 62% of the vote. This appears to be a safe Republican seat—unless the Reagan Administration should get into terrible trouble in the farm belt.

Census Data Pop. (1980 final) 448,824, no change in 1970s. Median family income, 1970, $7,820, 82% of U.S.

The Voters

Employment profile 1970 White collar, 40%. Blue collar, 27%. Service, 14%. Farm, 19%.
Ethnic groups Black 1980, 1%. Hispanic 1980, 3%. Total foreign stock 1970, 9%. Germany, 3%.

Presidential Vote

1980	Reagan (R)	134,777	(66%)
	Carter (D)	53,845	(26%)
	Anderson (I)	11,995	(6%)
1976	Ford (R)	106,533	(53%)
	Carter (D)	91,355	(45%)

Rep. Pat Roberts (R) Elected 1980; b. Apr. 20, 1936, Topeka; home, Dodge City; Kans. St. U., B.A. 1968.

Career USMC, 1958–62; Coowner, editor, Ariz. newspaper, 1962–67; Admin. Asst., Press Secy. to U.S. Sen. Frank Carlson, 1967–69; Admin. Asst. to U.S. Rep. Keith G. Sebelius, 1969–80.

Offices 1428 LHOB, 202-225-2715. Also P.O. Box 550, Dodge City 67801, 316-227-2244; P.O. Box 128, Norton 67654, 913-877-2454; and P.O. Box 1224, Salina 67401, 913-825-5409.

Committees Agriculture (11th). Subcommittees: Conservation, Credit and Rural Development; Department Operations, Research and Foreign Agriculture; Wheat, Soybeans, and Feed Grains.

Select Committee on Aging (21st). Subcommittee: Health and Long-Term Care.

Group Ratings and Key Votes: Newly Elected

Election Results

1980 general	Pat Roberts (R)...............	121,545	(62%)	($229,593)
	Phil Martin (D) .,.............	73,586	(38%)	($63,232)
1980 primary	Pat Roberts (R)...............	37,389	(56%)	
	Steve Pratt (R)	24,231	(36%)	($536,608)
	One other (R)	5,649	(8%)	
1978 general	Keith G. Sebelius (R), unopposed .			($52,986)

SECOND DISTRICT

Topeka is the capital of Kansas and one of those prosperous, progressive midwestern cities that have provided much of the dynamism of the region. The economy is based first on state government, but Topeka is also an important agricultural center. There are big new buildings downtown; cleancut, pleasant neighborhoods in all directions. This is the hometown of Alf Landon, the still vigorous and progressive Republican who carried Maine and Vermont in the 1936 Roosevelt landslide; and the home as well of the Menninger Psychiatric Clinic. And although Topeka does not like to remember it, this is the city where the lawsuit *Brown* v. *Board of Education* was filed; the eventual decision declared segregation in public schools to be unconstitutional.

Topeka casts about 40% of the votes in the 2d congressional district of Kansas. Other important concentrations of population are Manhattan, site of Kansas State University and not far from the Army's Fort Riley; Leavenworth, where set on the bluffs above the Missouri River is the Army's famous prison; and Kansas City, a small portion of which is included in the district. Otherwise, the district is rural agricultural country. Politically this is basically a Republican area; only Kansas City regularly votes Democratic. But it is less heavily Republican than western Kansas and on occasion is willing to split tickets. As a result the district has had Democratic congressmen for eight of the last 12 years: Bill Roy, the doctor–lawyer who was enormously popular and ran strong races for both of Kansas's Senate seats, in 1974 and 1978; and Martha Keys, wife of a Kansas State professor who got her start in the McGovern campaign and won notoriety in Washington for divorcing her husband and marrying fellow Representative Andrew Jacobs (they met in the Ways and Means Committee).

Keys was never as secure politically as Roy, and her remarriage hurt her much more than it did Jacobs. She was defeated in 1978 by Republican Jim Jeffries, a man identified with the New Right, who was able to win again in 1980 against Keys's former husband, Sam Keys. Campaigns in which Jeffries has been involved have a way of getting nasty. Martha Keys's supporters charged that Jeffries misrepresented her record and spied on her campaign. A 1980 Republican opponent called him a captive of New Right fringe groups. Jeffries himself has not yet won by an impressive margin. He could not carry Topeka, Manhattan, or Kansas City against Martha Keys and won solely on the basis of strength in the rural counties. In 1980 he had serious primary competition—an oddity for an incumbent Republican—and was able to win only 49% against two opponents. This is a pretty good sign that even Republicans would rather have someone else. And against Sam Keys in the fall of 1980, Jeffries again lost Topeka and Kansas City and won by carrying the rural areas by a good margin.

During the 1980 campaign Sam Keys called Jeffries incompetent and an embarrassment to Kansas and played a tape of Jeffries appearing before the Kansas Farm Bureau and laughing uncontrollably. Republicans privately will admit that Jeffries is a bit of a flake—and the election results indicate that his constituents tend to feel the same way. It is possible that he will win another term in Republican Kansas, but he is vulnerable in the primary and could be beaten in the general by a good Democratic candidate if opinion moves even slightly against the Republicans generally. He is not considered one of the stronger legislators in the House.

Census Data   Pop. (1980 final) 474,814, up 5% in 1970s. Median family income, 1970, $8,680, 91% of U.S.

The Voters

   Employment profile 1970   White collar, 49%. Blue collar, 30%. Service, 14%. Farm, 7%.
   Ethnic groups   Black 1980, 8%. Hispanic 1980, 3%. Am. Ind. 1980, 1%. Asian 1980, 1%. Total foreign stock 1970, 9%. Germany, 3%.

Presidential Vote

1980	Reagan (R)	102,325	(57%)
	Carter (D)	62,464	(35%)
	Anderson (I)	13,040	(7%)
1976	Ford (R)	97,156	(54%)
	Carter (D)	78,881	(44%)

Rep. Jim Jeffries (R) Elected 1978; b. June 1, 1925, Detroit, Mich.; home, Atchison; Mich. St. U., 1945–47.

Career Army Air Corps, WWII; Farmer, 1947–49; Market research, sales, and investment business, 1949–.

Offices 424 CHOB, 202-225-6601. Also Fed. Ofc. Bldg., 444 S.E. Quincy St., Topeka 66683, 913-295-2811.

Committees *Public Works and Transportation* (14th). Subcommittees: Public Buildings and Grounds; Water Resources.

Veterans' Affairs (7th). Subcommittees: Education, Training and Employment; Oversight and Investigations.

Group Ratings

	ADA	COPE	PC	LCV	CFA	RPN	NAB	NSI	NTU	ACA	ACU
1980	6	10	17	30	14	—	100	100	69	96	95
1979	0	10	15	1	7	—	—	—	71	100	100

Key Votes

1) Draft Registn $	FOR	6) Fair Hsg DOJ Enfrc	AGN	11) Cut Socl Incr Dfns $	FOR
2) Ban $ to Nicrgua	FOR	7) Lim PAC Contrbtns	AGN	12) Hosptl Cost Controls	AGN
3) Dlay MX Missile	AGN	8) Cap on Food Stmp $	FOR	13) Gasln Ctrls & Allctns	AGN
4) Nuclr Mortorium	AGN	9) New US Dep Edcatn	AGN	14) Lim Wndfll Prof Tax	FOR
5) Alaska Lands Bill	AGN	10) Cut OSHA $	FOR	15) Chryslr Loan Grntee	AGN

Election Results

1980 general	Jim Jeffries (R)	92,107	(54%)	($249,144)
	Sam Keys (D)	78,859	(46%)	($117,796)
1980 primary	Jim Jeffries (R)	26,269	(49%)	($46,296)
	Bill McCormick (R)	16,901	(32%)	($0)
	Larry Abelt (R)	10,318	(19%)	
1978 general	Jim Jeffries (R)	76,419	(52%)	($332,482)
	Martha Keys (D)	70,460	(48%)	($145,473)

THIRD DISTRICT

The 3d congressional district is not a very typical hunk of Kansas. It lies almost entirely within the Kansas City metropolitan area and contains most or all of two counties that regularly produce the state's largest Democratic and Republican majorities. More than 80% of the district's residents live in either Democratic Wyandotte County (Kansas City, much smaller than its sophisticated Missouri neighbor) or in Republican Johnson County (prosperous

Kansas City suburbs, including Overland Park, Prairie Village, and Shawnee Mission). On the Kansas side of the small street that separates Johnson County from Missouri live a disproportionate number of the metropolitan area's richest and most conservative citizens. Wyandotte County—industrial, redolent of meat packing plants—has had little growth in recent decades. Johnson County—a land of new subdivisions and country clubs—is booming. As recently as 1960 Wyandotte was the larger county; now Johnson casts twice as many votes as Wyandotte.

Johnson County's growth has made for increasing Republican dominance in the 3d district, and by all odds this should be a safe Republican district by now. A Democrat raised a serious challenge here in 1970, but for the rest of the 1970s Congressman Larry Winn was able to win reelection without serious competition. But in 1980 Winn suddenly found that he did have opposition, in the person of 32-year-old Dan Watkins, one of the strategists behind Governor John Carlin's upset victory in 1978.

Watkins's argument was simple: Winn hadn't done much in 14 years in Congress. There was supporting evidence, including Winn's unusually low 67% attendance record. Winn is now the ranking Republican on the Science Committee and fourth-ranking Republican on Foreign Affairs, but the fact is that he is not known as a legislative craftsman or indeed as someone who is particularly active on legislation. In his defense he argues plausibly that Republicans are not going to pass much legislation in a Democrat-controlled House and that his low attendance record one year was due to his service as an appointed congressional representative at the United Nations. Nonetheless, the picture one has is of a congressman with some seniority who, aside from his work on the Science Committee, is not particularly aggressive or hard-charging.

Winn's biggest political advantage in 1980 was the basic congressional district leaning of Johnson County. He ran behind Ronald Reagan there but still had 62% of the vote in the county where most of the district's votes are cast. Watkins carried the university town of Lawrence and carried Kansas City, but Winn may have held his margin down in the latter because he keeps his constituency service operations in Kansas City rather than Johnson County. Although Winn won with a solid majority, the result does disclose a certain weakness on the incumbent's part—a weakness that might be exploited by a Democrat if somehow national issues dented Republican strength in Johnson County, or that might be exploited by a Republican in the primary.

Census Data   Pop. (1980 final) 492,551, up 10% in 1970s. Median family income, 1970, $10,928, 114% of U.S.

The Voters

Employment profile 1970   White collar, 58%. Blue collar, 29%. Service, 11%. Farm, 2%.
Ethnic groups   Black 1980, 9%. Hispanic 1980, 3%. Am. Ind. 1980, 1%. Asian 1980, 1%. Total foreign stock 1970, 8%. Germany, 1%.

Presidential Vote

1980	Reagan (R)	112,391	(55%)
	Carter (D)	70,039	(34%)
	Anderson (I)	18,272	(9%)
1976	Ford (R)	110,829	(58%)
	Carter (D)	79,674	(42%)

Rep. Larry Winn, Jr. (R) Elected 1966; b. Aug. 22, 1919, Kansas City, Mo.; home, Overland Park; U. of Kans., A.B. 1941.

Career Radio announcer, WHB, Kansas City, Mo.; North American Aviation; Pub. Rel. Dir., Amer. Red Cross, Kansas City, Mo.; Builder; V.P., Winn-Rau Corp., 1950-.

Offices 2268 RHOB, 202-225-2865. Also 204 Fed. Bldg., Kansas City 66101, 913-621-0832.

Committees *Foreign Affairs* (4th). Subcommittees: International Operations; International Security and Scientific Affairs.

Science and Technology (Ranking Member).

Group Ratings

	ADA	COPE	PC	LCV	CFA	RPN	NAB	NSI	NTU	ACA	ACU
1980	11	14	20	26	14	—	67	100	45	79	53
1979	0	11	3	12	0	—	—	—	48	86	79
1978	10	17	10	18	14	73	100	90	20	88	91

Key Votes

1) Draft Registn $	FOR	6) Fair Hsg DOJ Enfrc	AGN	11) Cut Socl Incr Dfns $	FOR
2) Ban $ to Nicrgua	FOR	7) Lim PAC Contrbtns	—	12) Hosptl Cost Controls	—
3) Dlay MX Missile	AGN	8) Cap on Food Stmp $	FOR	13) Gasln Ctrls & Allctns	—
4) Nuclr Mortorium	—	9) New US Dep Edcatn	AGN	14) Lim Wndfll Prof Tax	FOR
5) Alaska Lands Bill	AGN	10) Cut OSHA $		FOR	15) Chryslr Loan Grntee	FOR

Election Results

1980 general	Larry Winn, Jr. (R).............	109,294	(55%)	($199,677)
	Dan Watkins (D)	82,414	(42%)	($123,494)
1980 primary	Larry Winn, Jr. (R).............	36,123	(100%)	
1978 general	Larry Winn, Jr. (R), unopposed ..			($17,691)

FOURTH DISTRICT

Before World War II, Wichita, Kansas, was a small city, a trading center for farm commodities, depending for its livelihood on the agricultural yield of the surrounding counties. Today Wichita is a substantial city, with a metropolitan population of 410,000; it is, one might say, the Sun Belt city farthest north. Wichita owes much of its prosperity to the general aviation industry. During World War II and the years immediately after, aircraft manufacturing caused major growth around the city. Boeing has a big plant here; so do Cessna, Beechcraft, Piper. Wichita is far and away the nation's leading center for producing airplanes — anything short of jetliners. This is a cyclical business. When the kinds of small businesses that buy most of these planes encounter a profit squeeze, one of the easiest ways to economize is to not buy a plane; and Wichita falls on bad times. But when small businesses prosper, so does Wichita. During most of the 1970s it has done well. The market for small planes has stayed robust, and the rise in oil prices has made the stripper wells around Wichita of economic importance again.

Wichita's politics reflects two conflicting tendencies. On the one hand, this is a newly prosperous city that believes in free enterprise and economic growth and is suspicious of government regulation; such feelings tend to make Wichita Republican, and it has gone Republican
in most state and national elections. But at the same time Wichita is a city that seems more
than half southern, with many residents from Arkansas, Oklahoma, and southern Kansas.
People here often speak with a southern drawl, and Wichita would just as soon look south
to Texas as north to Kansas City. This kind of background inclines Wichita toward the
Democrats. In 1976 Wichita delivered a near majority for Jimmy Carter, and even in 1980 it
gave Carter a better percentage than almost any other part of Kansas.

The 4th congressional district of Kansas includes all of Wichita, most of surrounding
Sedgwick County, and several other counties, including the city of Hutchinson; two-thirds
of the votes are cast in Wichita and Sedgwick County. The 4th district is represented in the
House by a man with a rather unusual background for a Kansas congressman. He is Dan
Glickman, a Wichita Democrat, first elected at age 31 in 1976 when he defeated a 16-year
Republican incumbent. Glickman was well known locally for his service on the Wichita
school board, at a time when voters valued local experience more than years in Washington.
Glickman's views are not far out of line with Wichita's attitudes. He had once worked for a
Republican senator, and he is skeptical about many government programs and wants to cut
spending. At a time when much of the creative thought in our politics comes from Republicans, Glickman is crackling with ideas on how government can be made to work better—or
can be done without.

Glickman won seats on the Agriculture and Science Committees—something for the
rural counties, something for Wichita's aviation industry. On Science, he heads the subcommittee that handles research and development funds for the Federal Aviation Administration (about $500 million), an area of obvious interest to Wichita, and R&D for NASA aero-
nautics and transportation, including electric automobiles. He has won reelection twice with
margins of greater than 2-to-1. As an energetic and newsmaking congressman from Wichita,
Glickman has become a familiar figure in half of Kansas. He decided not to make the race
against Bob Dole in 1980, and for a statewide opportunity he must wait at least until 1984
when Nancy Landon Kassebaum's seat is open to contest; his major problem is that, in a
Republican state, both incumbent Republican senators seem popular and vigorous.

Census Data   Pop. (1980 final) 466,412, up 4% in 1970s. Median family income, 1970, $9,970, 95%
of U.S.

The Voters

   Employment profile 1970   White collar, 51%. Blue collar, 32%. Service, 14%. Farm, 3%.
   Ethnic groups   Black 1980, 7%. Hispanic 1980, 3%. Am. Ind. 1980, 1%. Asian 1980, 1%. Total foreign stock 1970, 7%. Germany, 2%.

Presidential Vote

1980	Reagan (R)	109,579	(53%)
	Carter (D)	74,935	(36%)
	Anderson (I)	15,799	(8%)
1976	Ford (R)	89,201	(50%)
	Carter (D)	85,681	(48%)

Rep. Dan Glickman (D) Elected 1976; b. Nov. 24, 1944, Wichita; home, Wichita; U. of Mich., B.A. 1966; Geo. Wash. U., J.D. 1969.

Career Trial Atty., SEC, Washington, D.C., 1969–70; Practicing atty., 1970–77.

Offices 1507 LHOB, 202-225-6216. Also Box 403, Wichita 67201, 316-262-8396.

Committees *Agriculture* (16th). Subcommittees: Conservation, Credit and Rural Development; Domestic Marketing, Consumer Relations and Nutrition; Wheat, Soybeans and Feed Grains.

Judiciary (14th). Subcommittee: Administrative Law and Governmental Relations.

Science and Technology (11th). Subcommittee: Transportation, Aviation and Materials (Chairman).

Group Ratings

	ADA	COPE	PC	LCV	CFA	RPN	NAB	NSI	NTU	ACA	ACU
1980	56	37	53	81	50	—	50	56	32	33	21
1979	47	70	60	47	48	—	—	—	37	31	36
1978	50	50	53	60	32	67	75	30	23	48	29

Key Votes

1) Draft Registn $	AGN	6) Fair Hsg DOJ Enfrc	FOR	11) Cut Socl Incr Dfns $	FOR
2) Ban $ to Nicrgua	FOR	7) Lim PAC Contrbtns	FOR	12) Hosptl Cost Controls	AGN
3) Dlay MX Missile	FOR	8) Cap on Food Stmp $	AGN	13) Gasln Ctrls & Allctns	FOR
4) Nuclr Mortorium	—	9) New US Dep Edcatn	AGN	14) Lim Wndfll Prof Tax	FOR
5) Alaska Lands Bill	FOR	10) Cut OSHA $		AGN	15) Chryslr Loan Grntee	AGN

Election Results

1980 general	Dan Glickman (D)	124,014	(69%)	($122,894)
	Clay Hunter (R)	55,899	(31%)	($42,466)
1980 primary	Dan Glickman (D)	23,841	(100%)	
1978 general	Dan Glickman (D)	100,139	(70%)	($90,827)
	Jim Litsey (R)	43,854	(30%)	($73,264)

FIFTH DISTRICT

The southeastern corner of Kansas has been nicknamed "the Balkans"—a reference to the Eastern European origin of some of the area's residents and to its low hill country, the outer fringe of the Ozarks. The hills here contain some coal, and the main town was named Pittsburg—another example of the unrealistic optimism of the people who first settled Kansas. This part of the state never became a notable coal or manufacturing center, and for many years it was in unmistakable decline. Only in the 1970s has its population increased slightly, and that largely because of retirees and others moving to small towns near the hills. This southeastern corner of Kansas is the heart of the state's 5th congressional district, which stretches south to a point near Kansas City and west past Wichita and Sumner County, Kansas's number one wheat county, and beyond.

Emporia is one of the larger towns in the district, and the home of William Allen White, the newspaper editor whose name was a household word 40 years ago but draws a blank today. White was the voice of progressive midwestern Republicanism. Horrified by the

Populists of his youth, as were most townspeople in the Midwest, White was enchanted by Theodore Roosevelt and came to care about the plight of society's unfortunates. Although a native of one of the nation's most isolationist regions, White was a leading spokesman for American aid to the British during the ominous days before Pearl Harbor.

The 5th district's politics has been pretty consistently Republican, and it has never had a congressman who has attracted national attention. In 1978, when Congressman Joe Skubitz retired, there was a spirited competition for the seat, with five Democrats and six Republicans running. The Republican primary was won by a dark horse, optometrist Robert Whittaker. A friendly man who had served one term in the state legislature, Whittaker went door to door talking with voters and worked at various jobs around the district for a day at a time. His record in the House has been pretty solidly conservative, and he was reelected in 1980 with an overwhelming margin—running well ahead of Ronald Reagan in the district. He appears to have a very safe seat.

Census Data   Pop. (1980 final) 480,607, up 8% in 1970s. Median family income, 1970, $7,450, 78% of U.S.

The Voters

   Employment profile 1970   White collar, 40%. Blue collar, 36%. Service, 14%. Farm, 10%.
   Ethnic groups   Black 1980, 2%. Hispanic 1980, 2%. Am. Ind. 1980, 1%. Total foreign stock 1970, 6%. Germany, 1%.

Presidential Vote

1980	Reagan (R)	115,495	(59%)
	Carter (D)	68,847	(35%)
	Anderson (I)	9,894	(5%)
1976	Ford (R)	95,763	(50%)
	Carter (D)	92,164	(48%)

Rep. Robert (Bob) **Whittaker** (R) Elected 1978; b. Sept. 18, 1939, Eureka; home, Augusta; Ill. Col. of Optometry, B.S. 1961, Dr. of Optometry 1962.

Career Optometrist; Kans. House of Reps., 1975–77.

Offices 516 CHOB, 202-225-3911. Also 109 W. 5th St., Pittsburg 66762, 316-323-2320.

Committee *Energy and Commerce* (12th). Subcommittees: Energy Conservation and Power; Health and the Environment; Oversight and Investigations.

Group Ratings

	ADA	COPE	PC	LCV	CFA	RPN	NAB	NSI	NTU	ACA	ACU
1980	11	10	27	48	14	—	92	100	53	88	95
1979	0	10	15	21	11	—	—	—	53	96	92

Key Votes

1) Draft Registn $	FOR	6) Fair Hsg DOJ Enfrc	AGN	11) Cut Socl Incr Dfns $	FOR
2) Ban $ to Nicrgua	FOR	7) Lim PAC Contrbtns	AGN	12) Hosptl Cost Controls	AGN
3) Dlay MX Missile	AGN	8) Cap on Food Stmp $	FOR	13) Gasln Ctrls & Allctns	AGN

4) Nuclr Mortorium	AGN	9) New US Dep Edcatn	AGN	14) Lim Wndfll Prof Tax	FOR
5) Alaska Lands Bill	AGN	10) Cut OSHA $	FOR	15) Chryslr Loan Grntee	AGN

Election Results

1980 general	Robert (Bob) Whittaker (R)	141,029	(74%)	($113,716)
	David L. Miller (D)	45,676	(24%)	($1,204)
1980 primary	Robert (Bob) Whittaker (R)	45,550	(100%)	
1978 general	Robert (Bob) Whittaker (R)	86,011	(57%)	($259,120)
	Don Allegrucci (D)	62,402	(41%)	($114,247)

KENTUCKY

In 1775 Daniel Boone made his way through the Cumberland Gap in the Appalachian Mountains and came upon what we now know as Kentucky—a fertile, virgin land of gently rolling hills. After the Revolutionary War, streams of people from Virginia traveled Boone's Wilderness Road and settled in the hills and countryside around Lexington. The exodus was the new nation's first frontier boom and, up to that time, one of the most extensive mass migrations in western history. No more than a few dozen whites lived in Kentucky before the war; the 1790 census counted 73,000; by 1820 there were 564,000 Kentuckians, making the state the sixth largest in the nation. In those days Kentucky was the frontier, its communities full of opportunity and unburdened by the hierarchies that structured the societies of coastal America. Henry Clay, to take the most famous example, came to Kentucky from Virginia as a penniless youth. By the time he was 30 he had done well enough in law and land speculation to build a mansion with silver doorknobs and well enough in politics to become a United States senator.

In some respects Kentucky has not changed much since Clay's time. The state is still largely rural: only 21% of its residents live in Greater Louisville and only 7% in the Kentucky suburbs of Cincinnati, the state's only major metropolitan areas. During the 1950s and 1960s many people migrated out of the state; Kentuckians looking for jobs left the hills for the industrial cities of the Midwest, California, and Texas. In the 1970s, the trend was reversed, and most younger people now remain in Kentucky and find jobs here rather than seek them elsewhere.

But recent prosperity has not changed the local landscape much. The tobacco fields, the thoroughbred horse country of the Blue Grass region, and the cotton fields of western Kentucky are pretty much the same as they have been for years. Coal has brought more changes. Always a major coal producer, Kentucky has major fields in the eastern mountains and in the western part of the state as well. Coal used to be mined mostly underground, by union miners who worked in inherently hazardous conditions and lived in grimy, isolated villages. But the 1970s boom in coal has been a strip mining boom. More of the work is done by machines and less and less by union members. The extraction is all done under the sky, making for relatively safe working conditions and reduced capital costs. Hence small companies find it easier to enter the business. So the coal counties of Kentucky are now filled with new coal millionaires with fleets of Rolls-Royces, plenty of jobs with good wages, and, since Kentucky does not regulate strip mining strictly, ugly scars across the hills and valleys.

Politics in Kentucky also seems caught in some kind of time warp. As in many border states, in Kentucky political divisions are still based on the splits caused by the Civil War. Although Kentucky was a slave state—it voted to stay with the Union—there were, to say the least, strong feelings on both sides of the conflict. Most of the hill country was pro-Union and remains Republican today; the major change occurred in counties where coal miners joined the United Mine Workers in the 1930s and became Democrats. The Blue Grass region and the western part of the state, sometimes called the Pennyrile, were more likely to be slaveholding territory, and today remain mostly Democratic, except for the rapidly growing small city of Lexington. Louisville, first settled and influenced by German immigrants, was an antislavery river town, and for years supported a strong Republican organization. These patterns, which have prevailed now for more than 100 years, were as apparent as ever in the last two presidential elections. Both times Jimmy Carter lost by a narrow margin the county that contains Louisville, lost the Cincinnati suburbs and the mountain counties in the southeast, and carried the mining counties in the east, the Blue Grass country around Lexington, and the Pennyrile. Slightly smaller margins in the rural area in 1980 transformed Carter's fairly comfortable victory in Kentucky in 1976 to a razor's-edge defeat four years later, but the basic patterns of support were the same—which was not true in much of the rest of the country.

In most Kentucky elections over the years, Democrats have outvoted Republicans, although not by the kind of overwhelming margins found farther south. Thus for years major electoral decisions were made in the Democratic primary. The most famous figure to come out of this era was Alben Barkley, who was congressman from Paducah (1913–27), U.S. senator (1927–49), vice president under Harry Truman, and senator again until his death in 1956. But by the 1960s Kentucky had been moving slowly toward the Republicans as so many rural-oriented states did during the Kennedy–Johnson Administration, and for one four-year period (1967–71) Republicans held the governorship and both Senate seats.

The first Republican victories were won by moderates from areas of the party's traditional strength, the Cumberland plateau and Louisville. The moderates included Senator John Sherman Cooper who between Senate terms (he kept winning special elections to fill vacancies but for a long time lost the full terms) served as ambassador to India. An opponent of American involvement in Southeast Asia, Cooper retired voluntarily, still popular, in 1972. Another Republican moderate was Senator (1957–69) Thruston Morton, onetime chairman of the Republican National Committee.

The late 1960s saw Kentucky's political parties take positions more in line with those of national leaders. Under Governor Bert Combs (1959–63) the Democrats were more attentive to the problems of the black and the poor than was traditional in Kentucky. As if in response, the Republicans moved in the direction of Barry Goldwater and Richard Nixon. The key figure here was Louie Nunn, who nearly won the governorship in 1963, did win in 1967, and saw a protege—Kentucky does not allow its governors to serve consecutive full terms and also requires them to swear that they have never participated in a duel—come reasonably close to winning in 1971.

Now that era of competition along national lines seems over. Democrats, with margins almost entirely from rural areas, have won and held the governorship and both Senate seats in the last decade. The governorship has traditionally been the major prize in Kentucky politics; the governor has unusually wide powers, and most Kentucky politicos do not care much about what is happening in Washington. The crucial election was in 1971. Facing Nunn's candidate was Lieutenant Governor Wendell Ford, a Democrat whose economic policies gave him support from teachers' groups and organized labor but whose Owensboro accent and conservative attitude on cultural issues made him acceptable to traditional rural Democrats who found their party's national candidates objectionable. Nunn had won his election on cultural issues; Ford's major plank was repeal of the sales tax on food. The Democrat was elected by a fair margin and promptly made good on his promise.

Ford was elected to the Senate in 1974 and was succeeded by Lieutenant Governor Julian Carroll. Like Ford, he had roots in the southwestern part of the state, in his case in Paducah; and although he and Ford were not political allies their support came from the same voters. Carroll was considered a strong governor indeed, and won a full term in 1975. He dominated the legislature and presided over a period of economic growth for Kentucky; he probably could have won reelection in 1979 if he had been eligible to run. Instead there was a large field of serious Democratic candidates: Lieutenant Governor Thelma Stovall; Commerce Commissioner Terry McBrayer, Carroll's choice; 1st district Congressman Carroll Hubbard; former Louisville Mayor Harvey Sloane, the only candidate with an urban rather than a rural base, who walked across the state to publicize his campaign; and a late entry, John Y. Brown, Jr., who made many millions off Kentucky Fried Chicken. In a six-week primary campaign, Brown spent $2 million, buying television ads in markets as remote as Indianapolis, and getting much free notice from the activities of his wife, sometime sportscaster Phyllis George. That was enough to give him a narrow victory over Sloane. Sloane won big in Louisville and surrounding counties; McBrayer did well in the eastern mountain areas and in counties where Carroll had strong organization; Hubbard carried, although only barely, his own congressional district in the western end of the state; and Brown, with his saturation television campaign, carried everything else and got enough second place votes to win. He did especially well in bigger cities such as Lexington and Owensboro, where political organization and personal contacts are less important than media.

In the general election Brown faced none other than Louie Nunn, trying for a comeback. But Brown beat him with a showing typical of the divisions in Kentucky politics. Brown has been mentioned as a possible presidential candidate, and his picture has been featured in a lavish advertising campaign for the state. But first he must prove himself, as a neophyte, in the complex business of Kentucky state politics. He cannot run for governor again in 1983, although he is trying to change that, and neither of the Senate seats is likely to be open to a Democrat for some time. Most of Brown's defeated rivals still have ambitions for the governorship, and less than halfway into his term some were preparing for the campaign.

Wendell Ford ran for the Senate with some reluctance. In Kentucky one hesitates before giving up one year of a governorship even for what could turn out to be a lifetime Senate seat. Ford also had a tough race that year, against Republican incumbent Marlow Cook. But the Democrat won and went on to become an important senator. He has been a critical member of the Commerce Committee, because he cannot be counted on as voting consistently with either liberal or conservative, proregulation or antiregulation blocs. He gets high ratings from organized labor, with much lower ratings from liberal groups more concerned with cultural issues. He was not always a solid supporter of the Carter Administration, opposing the Panama Canal Treaties, for example, despite intensive lobbying.

Ford has managed to win more support from both labor and business for his own campaigns and as chairman of the Senate Democratic Campaign Committee. He has had more success in the former than in the latter. In 1980 he drew a bye: his Republican opponent was

70-year-old Mary Louise Foust, a perennial candidate with little financial support or public recognition. He won that race by nearly a 2-to-1 margin, with the highest percentage ever won by a candidate in a Senate election in Kentucky. As campaign committee chairman, however, Ford presided over a net loss of 12 seats for the Democrats and saw the Republicans win control of the Senate for the first time since 1952. Of course not all — or even very much — of the blame for these losses should go to Ford, but the fact is that the Democratic campaign committees provide far less aid, financial and technical, to their candidates than do their Republican counterparts.

Kentucky's senior senator is Walter "Dee" Huddleston. To a considerable extent he owes his initial election to Ford: Huddleston was the hand-picked choice for the Democratic nomination in 1972, Ford's first year as governor, and he won the general election narrowly over Louie Nunn. In the Senate he serves quietly on the Agriculture and Appropriations Committees; if the Democrats had retained control of the Senate, he would have become chairman of Agriculture in 1981. Huddleston votes more often with northern Democrats than with Republicans, but his vote cannot be taken for granted by the liberals or the leadership; he is closer to traditional southern Democrats in sentiment than is Ford. But not on all issues. He voted for the Panama Canal Treaties in 1978 — an act of some political courage for a senator up for reelection in a state such as Kentucky that year. And he has handled some difficult legislative problems, such as the proposed charter for the intelligence agencies.

As it turned out, reelection was no problem for Huddleston. He did not have significant opposition and won by a wide margin. It is far too early to tell for sure whether he will be as lucky in 1984. One thing to keep in mind is that the Republicans, if they win the governorship, will be able to finance a serious candidacy and almost surely will give Huddleston a tougher time than he had in 1978.

In the censuses after the 1940s and 1950s Kentucky lost House seats because so many of its children had grown up and moved elsewhere. More recently, with less outmigration, there have been no such losses: for 1982 Kentucky will again elect seven congressmen. In only one instance will a district have to be substantially altered: the 3d district, which consists primarily of the city of Louisville, lost population in the 1970s and will have to have some suburban (and presumably more Republican) territory added. Adjustments to other districts will have to be made but will probably be relatively minor. Given the census results and the attitudes of the voters, there is little the Democratic governor and legislature can do to unseat any of the state's three Republican congressmen.

Census Data   Pop. (1980 final) 3,661,433, up 14% in 1970s: 1.62% of U.S. total, 23d largest. Central city, 17%; suburban, 28%. Median 4-person family income, 1978, $17,924, 88% of U.S., 44th highest.

1979 Share of Federal Tax Burden $5,680,000,000; 1.26% of U.S. total, 25th largest.

1979 Share of Federal Outlays $6,603,512,000; 1.42% of U.S. total, 25th largest.

DOD	$1,092,164,000	30th	(1.03%)	HEW	$2,711,490,000	24th	(1.52%)
DOE	$451,101,000	9th	(3.83%)	ERDA	$63,084,000	11th	(2.32%)
HUD	$95,048,000	24th	(1.44%)	NASA	$917,000	37th	(0.02%)
VA	$342,654,000	24th	(1.65%)	DOT	$210,800,000	27th	(1.28%)
EPA	$55,915,000	29th	(1.05%)	DOC	$18,896,000	26th	(0.60%)
DOI	$37,785,000	34th	(0.68%)	USDA	$408,128,000	26th	(1.70%)

Economic Base   Agriculture, notably tobacco, cattle, dairy products, and hogs; finance, insurance, and real estate; electrical equipment and supplies, especially household appliances; machinery; bituminous coal mining; apparel and other textile products, especially men's and boys' furnishings; food and kindred products, especially distilled liquor and other beverages.

Political Lineup   Governor, John Y. Brown, Jr. (D). Senators, Walter D. (Dee) Huddleston (D) and Wendell H. Ford (D). Representatives, 7 (4 D and 3 R); 7 in 1982. State Senate, 38 (28 D and 10 R); State House of Representatives, 100 (74 D and 26 R).

The Voters

Registration   1,824,455 Total. 1,238,317 D (68%); 521,127 R (29%); 65,011 other (3%).
Employment profile 1970   White collar, 40%. Blue collar, 41%. Service, 13%. Farm, 6%.
Ethnic groups   Black 1980, 7%. Hispanic 1980, 1%. Total foreign stock 1970, 2%.

Presidential Vote

1980	Reagan (R)	635,274	(49%)
	Carter (D)	617,417	(48%)
	Anderson (I)	31,127	(2%)
1976	Ford (R)	531,852	(46%)
	Carter (D)	615,717	(53%)

1980 Democratic Presidential Primary			*1980 Republican Presidential Primary*		
Carter	106,819	(67%)	Reagan	78,072	(82%)
Kennedy	55,167	(23%)	Bush	6,861	(7%)
Uncommitted	19,219	(8%)	Anderson	4,791	(5%)
Two others	5,126	(2%)	Uncommitted	3,084	(3%)
			Two others	1,987	(2%)

SENATORS

Sen. Walter D. (Dee) **Huddleston** (D) Elected 1972, seat up 1984; b. Apr. 15, 1926, Cumberland Co.; home, Elizabethtown; U. of Ky., B.A. 1949.

Career   Army, WWII; Sports and Program Dir., WKCT Radio, Bowling Green, 1949–52; Gen. Mgr., WIEL Radio, Elizabethtown, 1952–72; Partner and Dir., WLBN Radio, Lebanon, 1957–72; Ky. Senate, 1965–72, Major. Flr. Ldr., 1970, 1972.

Offices   2121 DSOB, 202-224-2451. Also 136-C New Fed. Bldg., 600 Federal Pl., Louisville 40202, 502-582-6304, and 220 W. Dixie Ave., Elizabethtown 42701, 502-769-6316.

Committees   *Agriculture, Nutrition, and Forestry* (Ranking Member). Subcommittees: Soil and Water Conservation; Agricultural Production, Marketing, and Stabilization of Prices; Agricultural Research and General Legislation.

Appropriations (9th). Subcommittees: Defense; Energy and Water Development; HUD–Independent Agencies; Interior.

Select Committee on Intelligence (2d). Subcommittees: Legislation and the Rights of Americans; Collection and Foreign Operations.

Select Committee on Small Business (2d). Subcommittees: Government Regulation and Paperwork, Export Promotion and Market Development.

Group Ratings

	ADA	COPE	PC	LCV	CFA	RPN	NAB	NSI	NTU	ACA	ACU
1980	44	61	23	19	13	—	33	44	29	26	21
1979	37	61	38	—	43	—	—	—	18	26	23
1978	30	67	35	41	10	56	55	50	15	27	17

Key Votes

1) Draft Registn $	FOR	6) Fair Housng Cloture	AGN	11) Cut Socl Incr Defns	FOR
2) Ban $ to Nicrgua	FOR	7) Ban $ Rape Abortns	FOR	12) Income Tax Indexing	AGN

3) Dlay MX Missile	AGN	8) Cap on Food Stmp $	AGN	13) Lim Spdg 21% GNP	AGN
4) Nuclr Mortorium	AGN	9) New US Dep Edcatn	FOR	14) Incr Wndfll Prof Tax	FOR
5) Alaska Lands Bill	FOR	10) Cut OSHA Inspctns	FOR	15) Chryslr Loan Grntee	FOR

Election Results

1978 general	Walter D. (Dee) Huddleston (D) ..	290,730	(61%)	($456,432)
	Louie Guenthner, Jr. (R)	175,766	(37%)	($76,445)
1978 primary	Walter D. (Dee) Huddleston (D) ..	89,333	(76%)	
	Three others (D)	28,808	(24%)	
1972 general	Walter D. (Dee) Huddleston (D) ..	528,550	(51%)	($658,590)
	Louis B. Nunn (R)	494,337	(48%)	($603,649)

Sen. Wendell H. Ford (D) Elected 1974, seat up 1986; b. Sept. 8, 1924, Daviess Co.; home, Owensboro; U. of Ky., Md. School of Insurance.

Career Army, WWII; Family insurance business; Chf. Admin. Asst. to Gov. Bert Combs; Ky. Senate, 1965–67; Lt. Gov. of Ky., 1967–71; Gov. of Ky., 1971–74.

Offices 363 RSOB, 202-224-4343. Also 172-C New Fed. Bldg., 600 Federal Pl., Louisville 40202, 502-582-6251.

Committees *Commerce, Science, and Transportation* (5th). Subcommittees: Communications; Consumer; Science, Technology, and Space.

Energy and Natural Resources (4th). Subcommittees: Energy Regulations; Energy Research and Development; Water and Power.

Rules and Administration (Ranking Member).

Joint Committee on Printing (2d).

Group Ratings

	ADA	COPE	PC	LCV	CFA	RPN	NAB	NSI	NTU	ACA	ACU
1980	78	73	40	33	40	—	46	70	29	27	19
1979	32	60	38	—	33	—	—	—	27	46	32
1978	45	68	43	30	25	60	40	70	14	42	52

Key Votes

1) Draft Registn $	FOR	6) Fair Housng Cloture	FOR	11) Cut Socl Incr Defns	FOR
2) Ban $ to Nicrgua	FOR	7) Ban $ Rape Abortns	FOR	12) Income Tax Indexing	AGN
3) Dlay MX Missile	AGN	8) Cap on Food Stmp $	FOR	13) Lim Spdg 21% GNP	AGN
4) Nuclr Mortorium	FOR	9) New US Dep Edcatn	FOR	14) Incr Wndfll Prof Tax	FOR
5) Alaska Lands Bill	FOR	10) Cut OSHA Inspctns	AGN	15) Chryslr Loan Grntee	FOR

Election Results

1980 general	Wendell H. Ford (D)	720,891	(65%)	($491,522)
	Mary Louise Foust (R)..........	386,029	(35%)	($7,406)
1980 primary	Wendell H. Ford (D)	188,047	(87%)	
	Flora T. Stuart (D)	28,202	(13%)	
1974 general	Wendell H. Ford (D)	399,406	(54%)	($1,006,670)
	Marlow W. Cook (R)..........	328,982	(44%)	($524,569)

GOVERNOR

Gov. John Young Brown, Jr. (D) Elected 1979, term expires Dec. 1983; b. Dec. 28, 1933, Lexington; home, Lexington; U. of Ky., B.A. 1957, J.D. 1960.

Career Businessman; Practicing atty.; Hon. Treas., Dem. Party, 1972; Chmn., Dem. Nat. Com. Young Ldrshp. Cncl.; Chmn., Nat. Gov. Assn. Task Force on Small Business, 1980.

Offices Office of the Governor, State Capitol, Frankfort 40601, 502-564-2611.

Election Results

1979 gen.	John Young Brown, Jr. (D)	588,088	(59%)
	Louie B. Nunn (R)	381,278	(41%)
1979 prim.	John Young Brown, Jr. (D)	165,158	(29%)
	Harvey Sloane (D)	139,713	(25%)
	Terry McBrayer (D)	131,530	(23%)
	Carroll Hubbard, Jr. (D) . . .	68,577	(12%)
	Thelma L. Stovall (D)	47,633	(8%)
	Four others (D)	14,175	(3%)
1975 gen.	Julian M. Carroll (D)	470,159	(63%)
	Robert E. Gable (R)	277,998	(37%)

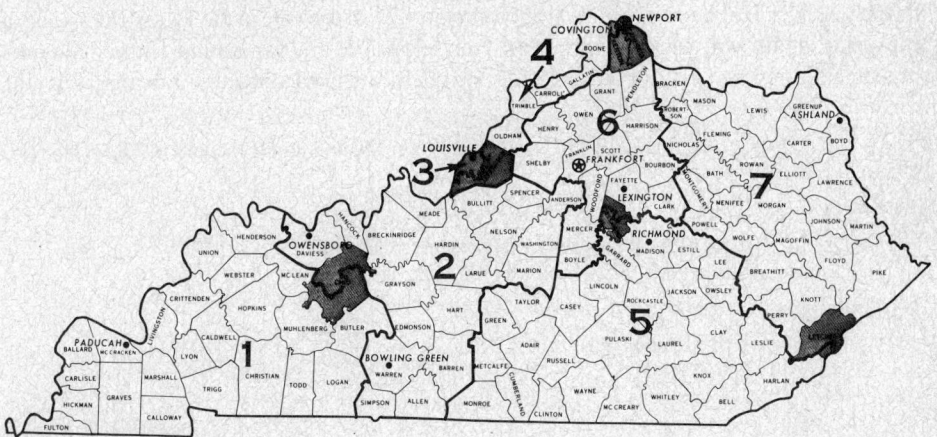

FIRST DISTRICT

The western end of Kentucky, known historically as the Jackson Purchase, almost seems to be part of another state — of west Tennessee or the lowlands of the Bootheel of Missouri or even the Mississippi Delta. This is low lying land, protected from the great muddy river by levees and cut off from the rest of Kentucky by the dammed-up Tennessee and Cumberland Rivers. Economically and politically, the area resembles the Deep South. It is the northern-most point of extensive cotton cultivation, although tobacco is actually a more important crop here, as it is in much of Kentucky. There are a considerable number of blacks here, in contrast to the rest of Kentucky, where there are few outside Louisville. And this is an area that went solidly for Jimmy Carter in 1976 and 1980 (albeit more solidly in the earlier year) and was carried by George Wallace in 1968.

Just to the east of the Tennessee and Cumberland Rivers is a region called the Pennyrile (after pennyroyal, a prevalent variety of wild mint). Here one finds a land of low hills and small farms. It is also the home of the west Kentucky coalfields, the site of much strip mining in recent years. Like the Jackson Purchase, the Pennyrile is ancestrally Democratic and, with the exception of a few counties, continues to vote that way in almost every election.

These two parts of Kentucky form the state's 1st congressional district, the area that first elected Alben Barkley to Congress back in 1912. It has elected Democrats ever since. The current incumbent, Carroll Hubbard, was first elected in 1974 after he had the foresight to challenge a weak incumbent in the primary. On arrival in Washington, Hubbard was chosen chairman of the Freshman Caucus, the very existence of which was somewhat an innovation. Actually Hubbard turned out to be not very typical of the Democrats first elected that year. His record on noneconomic issues is uniformly conservative; on economic issues his record is mixed. Hubbard's ambitions do not seem centered on Capitol Hill. He ran for governor in 1979 and made a creditable showing in a multicandidate primary; he could very well try again in 1983. He is aligned with none of the major factions in the state's Democratic party (those led by former governors Wendell Ford and Julian Carroll) nor with incumbent Governor John Y. Brown, Jr.; he will have to depend, in the first instance at least, on support from his own constituents in the Pennyrile and the Jackson Purchase. But in 1979, his support was far from unanimous in his home district. In fact Julian Carroll, the outgoing governor, managed to carry his hometown of Paducah for his hand-picked candidate, Terry McBrayer, over Hubbard. Overall, Hubbard won 33% of the vote in the 1st district — only a hair ahead of Brown, who relied primarily on television, and far behind Harvey Sloane's showing in his home territory of Louisville. Hubbard will need a stronger base than this if he is to win in 1983.

Census Data Pop. (1980 final) 517,137, up 12% in 1970s. Median family income, 1970, $6,788, 71% of U.S.

The Voters

Employment profile 1970 White collar, 33%. Blue collar, 46%. Service, 13%. Farm, 8%.
Ethnic groups Black 1980, 9%. Hispanic 1980, 1%. Total foreign stock 1970, 1%.

Presidential Vote

1980	Reagan (R)	81,192	(44%)
	Carter (D)	101,091	(54%)
	Anderson (I)	2,500	(1%)
1976	Ford (R)	55,462	(33%)
	Carter (D)	110,686	(66%)

Rep. Carroll Hubbard, Jr. (D) Elected 1974; b. July 7, 1937, Murray; home, Mayfield; Georgetown Col., Georgetown, Ky., B.A. 1959, U. of Louisville, J.D. 1962.

Career Practicing atty., 1962–74; Ky. Senate, 1967–75.

Offices 2244 RHOB, 202-225-3115. Also 145 E. Center St., McCoy Bldg., Madisonville 42431, 502-825-1371.

Committees *Banking, Finance and Urban Affairs* (11th). Subcommittees: Domestic Monetary Policy; Financial Institutions Supervision, Regulation and Insurance; Housing and Community Development.

Merchant Marine and Fisheries (7th). Subcommittees: Merchant Marine; Panama Canal and Outer Continental Shelf (Chairman).

Group Ratings

	ADA	COPE	PC	LCV	CFA	RPN	NAB	NSI	NTU	ACA	ACU
1980	22	58	27	31	29	—	73	70	44	46	63
1979	21	33	18	10	22	—	—	—	46	54	54
1978	10	65	30	13	27	50	67	100	17	68	65

Key Votes

1) Draft Registn $	FOR	6) Fair Hsg DOJ Enfrc	AGN	11) Cut Socl Incr Dfns $ AGN
2) Ban $ to Nicrgua	FOR	7) Lim PAC Contrbtns	FOR	12) Hosptl Cost Controls FOR
3) Dlay MX Missile	AGN	8) Cap on Food Stmp $	—	13) Gasln Ctrls & Allctns FOR
4) Nuclr Mortorium	AGN	9) New US Dep Edcatn	AGN	14) Lim Wndfll Prof Tax FOR
5) Alaska Lands Bill	—	10) Cut OSHA $	AGN	15) Chryslr Loan Grntee FOR

Election Results

1980 general	Carroll Hubbard, Jr. (D)	118,565	(100%)	($95,581)
1980 primary	Carroll Hubbard, Jr. (D)	35,708	(83%)	
	Two others (D)	7,571	(17%)	
1978 general	Carroll Hubbard, Jr. (D), unopp. .			($79,097)

SECOND DISTRICT

The 2d congressional district of Kentucky is a sprawling, largely rural area extending from the Blue Grass country not too far from Lexington to the hilly Pennyrile area around Bowling Green. Its largest city is the prosperous factory town of Owensboro on the Ohio River, which has only 53,000 people. The best-known features of the district are Fort Knox, where the nation's gold bullion is kept, and Bardstown, where one can find Stephen Collins Foster's "Old Kentucky Home." Bardstown is also a town that suffered disproportionately from the Vietnam war. Sixteen of its sons died there, five of them within two weeks of each other. Also in the district is the birthplace and boyhood home of Abraham Lincoln.

Kentucky was a slave state that was sharply divided when the South seceded; for a while it said that it was remaining neutral but finally sided with the Union. Much of the current 2d district was sympathetic to the South, and most of it still votes Democratic today—at least in state elections. This is a district that went for Dixie's Jimmy Carter in 1976; after four years of the Carter Administration it shifted to Ronald Reagan in 1980.

William Natcher, generally considered a conservative Democrat, has represented this district since a special election in 1953. He is now the third-ranking Democrat on the House Appropriations Committee. In Washington he was known for years for his service as chairman of the District of Columbia Appropriations Subcommittee; in that capacity he had charge of the city's budget. Natcher was attacked for being tightfisted and for being prejudiced against the District's black majority, but the progress of the D.C. government since it gained home rule suggests that his actions resulted from different motivations. He is a man who abhors waste, who is meticulous and attentive to detail, and who works very hard. If he sometimes acted autocratically and seemed to substitute his own judgment for that of the people of Washington (as when he insisted on the building of an unwanted freeway), he also imposed some discipline on the city government and its budget.

In 1979 Natcher succeeded to a potentially far more powerful position, the chairmanship of the Labor–HEW (now Labor–HHS–Education) Appropriations Subcommittee, a body that passes on a huge percentage of the federal budget—and most of President Reagan's budget cuts. His predecessor, Daniel Flood, had a reputation of generosity toward govern-

ment programs; Natcher was expected to be more tightfisted. Certainly he has been consci-
entious. He is proud that he has never missed a roll call vote or quorum call on the floor of
the House since he was elected in 1953 — surpassing the old attendance record set by Charles
Bennett of Florida. Natcher is one of those old-fashioned congressmen who does his own
reading and research and prides himself on being well prepared. That is a hard task on the
Labor–HEW Subcommittee, one that is perhaps beyond the capacity of any one man. In
his first term as chairman, Natcher did not really make a dent in the domestic programs'
budget, primarily because of the difficulty of the task, but also because he is somewhat more
generously inclined than his reputation, as his voting record shows. Another factor is that
increasingly higher budget levels are being set as part of the budget process, and the Appropriations subcommittees are simply left to fill in the details. This is important work, and it is
what Natcher is temperamentally suited for; but it is not going to make vast differences in
the flow of money in our society nor the balance between the public and the private sectors.

Natcher's conscientiousness might not serve him well politically if he should ever get serious opposition; his insistence on a perfect attendance record and his refusal to spend any
money but his own on campaigns make it difficult for him to stage a campaign that will effectively communicate with voters. Nonetheless, now past 70, he is not about to change his
ways, and the best anyone has done against him lately is the 40% a Republican got here in
1976.

Census Data   Pop. (1980 final) 541,969, up 18% in 1970s. Median family income, 1970, $7,042, 73%
of U.S.

The Voters

Employment profile 1970   White collar, 35%. Blue collar, 42%. Service, 12%. Farm, 11%.
Ethnic groups   Black 1980, 6%. Hispanic 1980, 1%. Total foreign stock 1970, 2%.

Presidential Vote

1980	Reagan (R)	88,017	(50%)
	Carter (D)	82,335	(47%)
	Anderson (I)	3,142	(2%)
1976	Ford (R)	65,476	(44%)
	Carter (D)	81,529	(55%)

Rep. William H. Natcher (D) Elected Aug. 1, 1953; b. Sept. 11, 1909, Bowling Green; home, Bowling
Green; W. Ky. St. Col., B.A. 1930, Ohio St. U., LL.B. 1933.

Career   Practicing atty., 1934–53; Fed. Conciliation Commissioner, W. Dist. of Ky., 1936–37; Warren Co. Atty., 1937–49;
Navy, WWII; Commonwealth Atty., 8th Judicial Dist. of Ky.,
1951–53.

Offices   2333 RHOB, 202-225-3501. Also 414 E. 10th St., Bowling
Green 42101, 502-842-7376.

Committee   *Appropriations* (3d). Subcommittees: Agriculture,
Rural Development and Related Agencies; District of Columbia;
Labor–Health and Human Services–Education (Chairman).

Group Ratings

	ADA	COPE	PC	LCV	CFA	RPN	NAB	NSI	NTU	ACA	ACU
1980	50	47	47	30	50	—	50	60	31	29	29
1979	42	50	25	34	22	—	—	—	25	15	31
1978	35	60	43	57	41	33	33	60	4	26	29

Key Votes

1) Draft Registn $	AGN	6) Fair Hsg DOJ Enfrc	AGN	11) Cut Socl Incr Dfns $	AGN
2) Ban $ to Nicrgua	AGN	7) Lim PAC Contrbtns	FOR	12) Hosptl Cost Controls	AGN
3) Dlay MX Missile	AGN	8) Cap on Food Stmp $	AGN	13) Gasln Ctrls & Alletns	FOR
4) Nuclr Mortorium	AGN	9) New US Dep Edcatn	FOR	14) Lim Wndfll Prof Tax	FOR
5) Alaska Lands Bill	FOR	10) Cut OSHA $	AGN	15) Chryslr Loan Grntee	FOR

Election Results

1980 general	William H. Natcher (D)	99,670	(66%)	($3,145)
	Mark T. Watson (R)............	52,110	(34%)	($7,425)
1980 primary	William H. Natcher (D), unopposed			
1978 general	William H. Natcher (D), unopposed			

THIRD DISTRICT

The 3d congressional district of Kentucky is made up of the city of Louisville and a few of its suburbs to the south and west. Despite the local pronunciation (LOOuhvul) and southern traditions — Alistair Cooke calls Kentucky the most self-consciously southern of states, although it never seceded — Louisville is really less of a southern town than it likes to think. It is closer in spirit to other old river ports, e.g., Cincinnati and St. Louis, which, although larger, sprang up at about the same time in locations that are similar. All three cities, and particularly their large German–American communities, were hostile to the southern-leaning politics of their slaveholding rural neighbors at the time of the Civil War, and all three had long-standing Republican traditions, among blacks as well as whites. St. Louis turned Democratic in the 1930s, Cincinnati is still decidedly Republican, and Louisville moves back and forth.

The 1960s was a good decade for the Republicans here, while the 1970s was a good decade for the Democrats. The two major offices are the mayoralty of Louisville and the Jefferson County judgeship, the administrative position at the head of county government. Democrats have held the mayor's office since 1968; as a central city Louisville is probably too Democratic for the Republicans to make a strong effort. But Republican Mitch McConnell did win the county judge's office in 1978 and, as such, becomes a contender for a statewide office, perhaps Huddleston's Senate seat (County Judge Marlow Cook was elected U.S. senator in 1968); and the current mayor, William Stansbury, was seriously embarrassed when an emergency developed over a weekend and it was discovered that he was out of town with a female aide. He will likely be succeeded in 1981 by Harvey Sloane, a doctor who was a widely popular mayor in 1973–77 and who nearly won the Democratic nomination for governor in 1979.

One of the beneficiaries of the Democrats' surge here in the early 1970s was Congressman Romano Mazzoli. He defeated Republican incumbent William Cowger, a former Louisville mayor, in 1970 in one of the closest races in the country and has, with one major exception, held the seat easily ever since. The exception was in 1976, when Louisville had been under a federal court busing order for a year, and Mazzoli, as a member of the Judiciary Committee, had not voted to report out an antibusing constitutional amendment. He had to weather tough challenges in both the primary and the general election. But by 1978 his problems seem to have vanished. Busing had become less important to voters, and Mazzoli won both primary and general election with ease. He did as well in 1980.

If busing was one hot potato Mazzoli had to field in his capacity as a member of the Judiciary Committee, the issue of immigration may be another. He chairs the subcommittee on Immigration, Refugees, and International Law, which is under heavy pressure to act to tighten up immigration laws, although it is probably unwilling to use the means best able to accomplish that end—a national identity card. Fortunately for Mazzoli, immigration has not been a pressing problem in Louisville since the Germans stopped coming over late in the 1800s, and he will not be under heavy local pressures here as he was on busing.

For 1982 his major problem will be redistricting. The 3d district, like most central city constituencies, lost population in the 1970s and will have to be expanded by about 100,000 people. They will almost certainly come from the Louisville suburbs, some of which are Democratic (those directly south of the city; those to the east are high income and Republican). But however the legislature draws the lines, and it is likely to be favorable to Mazzoli since both houses and the governorship are controlled by Democrats, the district is likely to be at least a little less Democratic—which could spell trouble for the congressman sometime in the 1980s, particularly if the Republicans are able to build on their local victories in Jefferson County.

Census Data   Pop. (1980 final) 393,352, down 15% in 1970s. Median family income, 1970, $8,902, 93% of U.S.

The Voters

Employment profile 1970   White collar, 44%. Blue collar, 42%. Service, 14%. Farm, –%.
Ethnic groups   Black 1980, 25%. Hispanic 1980, 1%. Total foreign stock 1970, 4%.

Presidential Vote

1980	Reagan (R)	56,932	(40%)
	Carter (D)	80,370	(56%)
	Anderson (I)	4,882	(3%)
1976	Ford (R)	63,690	(43%)
	Carter (D)	79,407	(53%)

Rep. Romano L. Mazzoli (D) Elected 1970; b. Nov. 2, 1932, Louisville; home, Louisville; Notre Dame U., B.S. 1954, U. of Louisville, J.D. 1960.

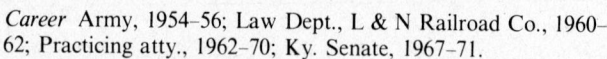

Career   Army, 1954–56; Law Dept., L & N Railroad Co., 1960–62; Practicing atty., 1962–70; Ky. Senate, 1967–71.

Offices   2246 RHOB, 202-225-5401. Also 551 New Fed. Bldg., 600 Federal Pl., Louisville 40202, 502-582-5129.

Committees   District of Columbia (3d). Subcommittee: Judiciary and Education.

Judiciary (8th). Subcommittees: Immigration, Refugees and International Law (Chairman); Monopolies and Commercial Law.

Small Business (14th). Subcommittee: General Oversight.

Select Committee on Intelligence (4th). Subcommittee: Legislation (Chairman).

Group Ratings

	ADA	COPE	PC	LCV	CFA	RPN	NAB	NSI	NTU	ACA	ACU
1980	33	46	47	54	43	—	55	33	31	33	17
1979	42	74	35	28	24	—	—	—	29	16	24
1978	40	50	50	62	32	82	46	30	16	31	36

Key Votes

1) Draft Registn $	AGN	6) Fair Hsg DOJ Enfrc	FOR	11) Cut Socl Incr Dfns $	—
2) Ban $ to Nicrgua	AGN	7) Lim PAC Contrbtns	AGN	12) Hosptl Cost Controls	—
3) Dlay MX Missile	FOR	8) Cap on Food Stmp $	AGN	13) Gasln Ctrls & Allctns	FOR
4) Nuclr Mortorium	AGN	9) New US Dep Edcatn	AGN	14) Lim Wndfll Prof Tax	FOR
5) Alaska Lands Bill	AGN	10) Cut OSHA $	AGN	15) Chryslr Loan Grntee	FOR

Election Results

1980 general	Romano L. Mazzoli (D).........	85,873	(64%)	($94,674)
	Richard Cesler (R)	46,681	(35%)	($18,449)
1980 primary	Romano L. Mazzoli (D).........	18,734	(79%)	
	Three others (D)	4,898	(21%)	
1978 general	Romano L. Mazzoli (D).........	37,346	(66%)	($110,638)
	Norbert D. Leveronne (R)	17,785	(31%)	

FOURTH DISTRICT

The 4th congressional district of Kentucky is a geographical oddity—the result of the state's loss of a congressional district in the 1960 census and three subsequent redistrictings. The 4th today consists of two nearly equal-sized suburban areas connected by a thin strip of rural counties that run 120 miles along the Ohio River. The first and larger of these suburban areas is Jefferson County, excluding the city of Louisville and a few adjacent suburbs that make up the 3d district. This part of the 4th is prosperous and growing fairly rapidly; like most affluent suburbs, it tends to vote Republican. The tendency has been fortified of late by the rural and countrified background of most of Kentucky's leading Democratic politicians, who have won statewide elections easily but have sometimes failed to carry suburban Jefferson County. The other suburban part of the 4th district lies across the Ohio River from Cincinnati. About half the voters here live in the old, decaying cities of Covington and Newport on the river; like Cincinnati, they usually go Republican. The other half live in the prosperous suburbs on the heights; these areas are quite heavily Republican.

The connecting counties along the river are part of an older Kentucky. Bypassed by Interstate 71, the little tobacco towns here retain the 19th-century Democratic voting habits, although the few ballots cast get lost in the districtwide totals.

Since 1966 the congressman from the 4th has been Republican Gene Snyder, who also represented the 3d district for one term until he was swept out by the Johnson landslide of 1964. Snyder has had only two tough races since then: the 1966 primary, when he beat one-time Cleveland Browns quarterback George Ratterman, and the 1974 general, when he beat Kyle Hubbard, brother of 1st district Congressman Carroll Hubbard. For many years Snyder was the most conservative member of the Kentucky delegation, although his voting record does not show the kind of orthodoxy one would expect of a politician who began his career as an admirer of Barry Goldwater. He is one of the leading Republicans on the Merchant Marine and Public Works Committees—odd assignments for a free-market conservative, since most of their work is supervising the spending of large sums of public monies.

But Snyder is by no means opposed to all spending projects and has supported subsidies for shipyards. There are shipyards in the district that can build the barges that ply the Ohio and Mississippi Rivers with cargoes of coal and other bulky and messy commodities.

Snyder was first elected to Congress in 1962 at age 34 and has the prospect of a long career. Redistricting should pose few problems for him; he will probably lose some of the more Democratic Jefferson County precincts to the 3d district, which will make the 4th even more Republican. If his district is expanded to include some of the heavily Democratic rural counties in the Blue Grass area, he should survive handily.

Census Data Pop. (1980 final) 534,324, up 16% in 1970s. Median family income, 1970, $10,359, 109% of U.S.

The Voters

Employment profile 1970 White collar, 51%. Blue collar, 37%. Service, 10%. Farm, 2%.
Ethnic groups Black 1980, 4%. Hispanic 1980, 1%. Total foreign stock 1970, 5%.

Presidential Vote

1980	Reagan (R)	116,003	(57%)
	Carter (D)	78,914	(39%)
	Anderson (I)	7,501	(4%)
1976	Ford (R)	104,266	(57%)
	Carter (D)	77,963	(43%)

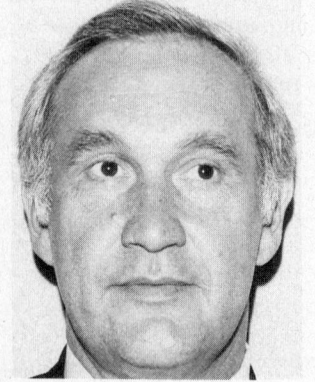

Rep. Gene Snyder (R) Elected 1966; b. Jan. 26, 1928, Louisville; home, Jefferson Co.; Jefferson School of Law, LL.B. 1950.

Career Practicing atty., 1950–67; Realtor and builder; Jeffersontown City Atty., 1954–58; Jefferson Co. 1st Dist. Magistrate, 1957–65.

Offices 2185 RHOB, 202-225-3465. Also 125 Chenoweth Ln., St. Matthews 40207, 502-895-6949.

Committees *Merchant Marine and Fisheries* (Ranking Member).

Public Works and Transportation (2d). Subcommittees: Aviation; Surface Transportation; Water Resources.

Group Ratings

	ADA	COPE	PC	LCV	CFA	RPN	NAB	NSI	NTU	ACA	ACU
1980	11	21	27	13	21	—	100	100	60	71	89
1979	5	15	10	10	7	—	—	—	55	81	82
1978	15	20	20	20	27	42	83	100	38	96	88

Key Votes

1) Draft Registn $	AGN	6) Fair Hsg DOJ Enfrc	AGN	11) Cut Socl Incr Dfns $	FOR
2) Ban $ to Nicrgua	FOR	7) Lim PAC Contrbtns	AGN	12) Hosptl Cost Controls	AGN
3) Dlay MX Missile	AGN	8) Cap on Food Stmp $	FOR	13) Gasln Ctrls & Allctns	FOR
4) Nuclr Mortorium	AGN	9) New US Dep Edcatn	AGN	14) Lim Wndfll Prof Tax	FOR
5) Alaska Lands Bill	AGN	10) Cut OSHA $	FOR	15) Chryslr Loan Grntee	AGN

Election Results

1980 general	Gene Snyder (R)	126,049	(67%)	($83,015)
	Phil M. McGary (D)............	62,138	(33%)	($38,005)
1980 primary	Gene Snyder (R), unopposed			
1978 general	Gene Snyder (R)	62,067	(66%)	($122,834)
	George C. Martin (D)	32,212	(34%)	($30,231)

FIFTH DISTRICT

If you are looking for evidence that political preference in the United States is not simply the result of economic status, the results of any recent presidential election provide the proof. For in 1980, as in 1976, 1972, and 1968, the precincts of the richest people in the country — the Upper East Side of Manhattan and the area around Beverly Hills, California — went for the Democrat. Meanwhile, the Republicans, supposedly the party of the rich, were carrying by a solid margin, as they have in the past three elections, the 5th congressional district of Kentucky, a district with a median income in 1970 (the last year for which figures for congressional districts are available) several hundred dollars lower than that of any other in the nation. Very few of the nation's 435 districts regularly produce such high Republican percentages.

Reagan's performance here was, if anything, a little below the usual levels of Republican support. The hills and hollows of the Cumberland plateau in south central Kentucky have consistently delivered some of the largest Republican percentages in the United States for more than a century. The nomination of a southerner by the Democratic Party did not change that. The small farmers here were hostile to the slaveholding South and to the uppity proslavery Blue Grass region to the north in the years around the Civil War. The people here live in one of the most isolated and provincial areas of the United States, and they have had little trouble maintaining their party identification ever since.

Only in places where the United Mine Workers organized successfully in the 1930s have the mountain people switched to the Democrats. But there are fewer mines and miners here than in the adjacent 7th district. About the only consistently Democratic county in the 5th is "bloody Harlan," where in the 1930s the mine owners' men and the UMW members shot and killed each other in pitched battles. For years thereafter Harlan County, like the coal industry, was in decline; its population fell from 64,000 in 1940 to 36,000 in 1970. Now it is up again, to 41,000, and Rolls-Royces can be seen in some towns.

The 5th district is one part of southern-accented America where winning the Republican primary is tantamount to election. In 1980 Republican Congressman Tim Lee Carter retired, after 16 years of service; a physician, he made his greatest mark as a member of the Health Subcommittee. The succession was determined in the 11-candidate primary field, the winner of which, Hal Rogers, had just 23% of the vote. Rogers was a supporter of Dr. Carter's, the Republican candidate for lieutenant governor in 1979, and a party activist associated with the Gerald Ford rather than the Ronald Reagan wing of the party. As such, he can be expected to continue Dr. Carter's tradition: a voting record basically conservative but with a fair number of bows to compassion and generosity on economic issues.

Census Data Pop. (1980 final) 559,778, up 11% in 1970s. Median family income, 1970, $4,669, 49% of U.S.

The Voters

Employment profile 1970   White collar, 33%. Blue collar, 43%. Service, 12%. Farm, 12%.
Ethnic groups   Black 1980, 2%. Hispanic 1980, 1%.

Presidential Vote

1980	Reagan (R)	121,708	(60%)
	Carter (D)	75,712	(38%)
	Anderson (I)	2,581	(1%)
1976	Ford (R)	97,001	(56%)
	Carter (D)	73,330	(43%)

Rep. Harold Rogers (R) Elected 1980; b. Dec. 31, 1937, Barrier; home, Somerset; U. of Ky., B.A. 1962, J.D. 1964.

Career Nat. Guard, 1956–64; Newsman, radio announcer, 1955–62; Practicing atty., 1964–69; States Atty., Pulaski and Rockdale Cos., 1969–81; Rep. nominee for Lt. Gov. of Ky., 1979.

Offices 413 CHOB, 202-225-4601. Also 210 E. Mt. Vernon St., Somerset 42501, 606-679-8346.

Committee *Energy and Commerce* (15th). Subcommittees: Energy, Conservation and Power; Fossil and Synthetic Fuels; Oversight and Investigations.

Group Ratings and Key Votes: Newly Elected

Election Results

1980 general	Harold Rogers (R)	112,093	(67%)	($313,974)
	Ted R. Marcum (D)	54,027	(33%)	($4,788)
1980 primary	Harold Rogers (R)	13,266	(23%)	
	Tom Emberton (R)	10,576	(19%)	($132,544)
	Gene Huff (R)	9,595	(17%)	($44,390)
	John D. Rogers (R)	7,439	(13%)	($182,051)
	Seven others (R)	15,877	(28%)	
1978 general	Tim Lee Carter (R)	59,743	(79%)	($44,631)
	Jesse M. Ramey (D)	15,714	(21%)	

SIXTH DISTRICT

The 6th congressional district of Kentucky, although geographically compact, can be divided into two politically distinct parts. The first can be called the Blue Grass country. This is our traditional picture of Kentucky: the rolling green meadows where, behind the white wooden fences, thoroughbreds graze; the stately white mansion on the hillock overlooking the fields; the colonel sitting on the mansion's front porch, dressed in a white suit and sipping a mint julep. There actually are places like this in the 6th district, for it contains most of the beautiful horse country around Lexington, and it was the residence of the late Colonel Harland Sanders himself.

But few of the residents of the Blue Grass are so rich. More typical are the small towns with houses built as long ago as the 1810s—this part of Kentucky was the first part of the United States settled by migrants from across the Appalachians—or the small, poorer farms with their frame houses. The spiritual capital of this part of the 6th district is not Lexington, but Frankfort, the small and surprisingly industrial capital city. Frankfort and Franklin County lead the district in Democratic allegiance (it was 63% for Carter in 1980); the town's usual preference is strengthened by the fact that Kentucky is a patronage state and the Democrats have held the governor's office for all but eight of the last 50 years. Overall, the traditional Blue Grass part of the 6th district almost always delivers Democratic majorities—enough to enable Jimmy Carter to carry this district in both 1976 and 1980.

The other part of the 6th district is modern Lexington. This is a far bigger town than the city Henry Clay knew, although it retains a few historic structures. Its downtown is hardly picturesque, but it is a place of real prosperity, largely because of the main IBM typewriter plant that is located here. IBM's presence has made Lexington a major center for high technology industry and white collar employment. The Lexington area's population has grown an unusual 18% in the 1970s, and most of that growth has been in the kind of affluent neighborhoods that tend to favor Republicans. These newly affluent, technology-minded voters find the rural-oriented Democrats, who are usually the party's statewide candidates, particularly uncongenial. While the 6th as a whole went for Carter in 1980, Lexington delivered nearly a 5,000-vote margin for Ronald Reagan.

The 6th district is represented in the House by a Republican, and the way the Republicans took the district is a lesson in fast political footwork. In 1976 they didn't even have a candidate here; John Breckinridge, a conservative Democrat from a fine old Kentucky family (one ancestor was Jefferson's attorney general, another was Buchanan's vice president), was reelected with 94% of the vote. But Breckinridge was upset in the 1978 primary by state Senator Tom Easterly, a former AFL–CIO staffer with strong labor support. Easterly won almost entirely because of his margins in Frankfort.

The Republicans saw their chance. They persuaded their nominee, 68-year-old Marie Louise Foust, to withdraw from the race and substituted 45-year-old Larry Hopkins of Lexington. They poured plenty of money into Hopkins's race — he spent nearly $300,000 — and attacked Easterly as a supporter of big government, big labor, and big spending. Hopkins won with a 2-to-1 margin in Lexington, more than enough to overcome Easterly's edge in the traditional Blue Grass counties. In his first term, Hopkins worked hard on constituency service and compiled a solid Republican voting record. Easterly ran again in 1980, and this time he lost by a bigger margin. Hopkins carried 68% of the vote in Lexington (compared to 49% for Reagan) and carried the Blue Grass area as well; only Frankfort and three small counties stayed with Easterly. Given the advantages accruing to incumbents, Hopkins seems a good bet to stay in the House for some time. The Democratic legislature may try to hurt him in redistricting, but it is hard to see how they can damage him much, short of dividing Lexington between two districts — which seems unlikely. The adjacent counties to the south and north are heavily Republican; to the west are the heavily Republican Louisville suburbs. The territory to the east is heavily Democratic, but it is unlikely that 7th district Congressman Carl Perkins, a real asset to Kentucky as chairman of the Education and Labor Committee, is going to allow some of his Democratic counties to be taken away.

Census Data Pop. (1980 final) 548,417, up 19% in 1970s. Median family income, 1970, $8,678, 91% of U.S.

The Voters

Employment profile 1970 White collar, 46%. Blue collar, 34%. Service, 13%. Farm, 7%.
Ethnic groups Black 1980, 8%. Hispanic 1980, 1%. Total foreign stock 1970, 2%.

420   KENTUCKY

Presidential Vote

1980	Reagan (R)	89,167	(46%)
	Carter (D)	93,179	(48%)
	Anderson (I)	8,063	(4%)
1976	Ford (R)	77,765	(46%)
	Carter (D)	88,195	(52%)

Rep. Larry J. Hopkins (R) Elected 1978; b. Oct. 25, 1933, Winyo; home, Lexington; Murray St. U., So. Meth. U., Purdue U.

Career USMC, Korea; Stockbroker; Ky. House of Reps., 1972–77; Ky. Senate, 1978.

Offices 331 CHOB, 202-225-4706. Also 400 E. Main, Lexington 40507, 606-233-2848.

Committees *Agriculture* (7th). Subcommittees: Livestock, Dairy and Poultry; Tobacco and Peanuts.

Armed Services (14th). Subcommittees: Investigations; Military Personnel and Compensation.

Group Ratings

	ADA	COPE	PC	LCV	CFA	RPN	NAB	NSI	NTU	ACA	ACU
1980	6	22	30	31	14	—	100	100	56	87	89
1979	16	22	23	17	19	—	—	—	57	85	82

Key Votes

1) Draft Registn $	FOR	6) Fair Hsg DOJ Enfrc	AGN	11) Cut Socl Incr Dfns $	FOR
2) Ban $ to Nicrgua	FOR	7) Lim PAC Contrbtns	FOR	12) Hosptl Cost Controls	AGN
3) Dlay MX Missile	AGN	8) Cap on Food Stmp $	FOR	13) Gasln Ctrls & Allctns	FOR
4) Nuclr Mortorium	FOR	9) New US Dep Edcatn	AGN	14) Lim Wndfll Prof Tax	FOR
5) Alaska Lands Bill	AGN	10) Cut OSHA $	FOR	15) Chryslr Loan Grntee	AGN

Election Results

1980 general	Larry J. Hopkins (R)	105,376	(59%)	($300,296)
	Tom Easterly (D)	72,473	(40%)	($79,344)
1980 primary	Larry J. Hopkins (R), unopposed			
1978 general	Larry J. Hopkins (R)	52,092	(51%)	($291,920)
	Tom Easterly (D)	47,436	(46%)	($134,770)

SEVENTH DISTRICT

The 7th congressional district of Kentucky is part — some would say the heart — of Appalachia. Although the 5th district is officially the state's (and the nation's) lowest-income district, the 7th has long been considered one of the most poverty-stricken and isolated places in the country. The only city here of any size is Ashland (home of Ashland Oil) on the Ohio River near Huntington, West Virginia, and that has only 27,000 people. The rural hills and hollows of the district, however, are some of the most densely populated rural areas in the United States. Coal has been the region's economic mainstay — its sustenance in good years and its scourge in bad. The 1950s and 1960s were generally bad times for coal: oil was replacing it as a heating and industrial fuel, and machines were replacing miners in the mines that were operating. For more than a quarter century, eastern Kentucky was exporting its young men and women to the industrial cities of the North, although most of them continued to think of this mountainous country as "home."

Now many of these people are returning home for good, and the stream of migration north has stopped. Coal is back in demand, and there are suddenly new millionaires and visible prosperity in the Appalachians. Affluence is not yet universal here. Employment in mining is far below 1940s levels, since so much of the coal today is strip mined; and many of the new mines do not pay union wages. But the boom in coal seems to have had its effect on the economy of eastern Kentucky generally, and jobs seem more plentiful here than they have in decades. In contrast, the industrial cities of the Great Lakes now have little to offer. The story is told as well as anywhere in the census figures: the 7th district lost population consistently from 1940, when this area had 579,000 people, to 1970, when it had 459,000. Now in the 1970s it has risen, not all the way back to the 1940 level, but to 564,000, a sharp reversal of the trend.

The problems of the coal industry have played a major role in shaping political attitudes here, and what the Civil War was for most of Kentucky the struggles of the 1930s were for the 7th district. Many counties here were the scene then of pitched battles between mine owners' men and United Mine Workers organizers; there were shootings and killings aplenty in this area that was so isolated then that it seldom attracted the attention of the national press. Out of these struggles most of the people here came to feel an allegiance to the party of Franklin Roosevelt, and that allegiance has remained unabated through the rises and the various falls of the fortunes of the coal industry in the years since. Today there are a few Republican counties left in the 7th, places with little coal where Unionist sentiment from the Civil War days still prevails, but the district as a whole is solidly Democratic. Each county, however, has a story of its own, and these are still places that are difficult to get to and are out of contact, except for television, with even close neighbors. Thus Knott County, to take one example, was 77% for Carter in the 1980 election, while Jackson County, 20 miles away and quite similar in outward appearance, was 82% for Reagan.

Knott County is the home of the district's congressman, Carl Perkins, and not surprisingly he is a Democrat. For some years now he has been reelected by better than 2-to-1 margins. First elected in 1948, Perkins has been, since the ouster of Adam Clayton Powell in 1967, chairman of the House Education and Labor Committee. At that time Perkins was a firm supporter of Lyndon Johnson's Great Society programs, and Education and Labor was a glamor committee, with jurisdiction over federal aid to education, the antipoverty programs, and other innovative social programs. Today those programs have lost much of their glamor. Most are under attack by the Republicans, and few Democrats can summon up much enthusiasm in their defense. Carl Perkins is one who can, and his inclination is not to compromise nor surrender an inch; he will fight to save whatever he can. He will have considerable support on his committee, almost all of whose Democratic members are inclined to share his feelings; organized labor, after it was beaten on a major labor bill in 1959, vowed that it would pack Education and Labor with a prolabor majority, and it has. Perkins has iron control of the committee's staff and holds the chairmanship of the subcommittee that handles the lion's share of aid to education, from preschool through elementary and secondary to vocational, and including school lunches.

This has not meant, however, that the committee has been able to control the legislative process. During the Carter Administration, it reported out labor law reform and common situs picketing bills, only to see them stopped elsewhere in the Congress. In the Reagan years, the committee may be in effect bypassed on issues such as repeal of Davis–Bacon (the law that effectively requires the federal government to pay union wages for construction work). Perkins is an effective chairman, but on these and other issues it appears that he simply lacks the votes to prevail.

Census Data   Pop. (1980 final) 566,456, up 23% in 1970s. Median family income, 1970, $5,528, 58% of U.S.

The Voters

Employment profile 1970   White collar, 34%. Blue collar, 47%. Service, 12%. Farm, 7%.
Ethnic groups   Black 1980, 1%. Hispanic 1980, 1%.

Presidential Vote

1980	Reagan (R)	81,842	(43%)
	Carter (D)	104,596	(55%)
	Anderson (I)	2,409	(1%)
1976	Ford (R)	66,890	(39%)
	Carter (D)	104,213	(60%)

Rep. Carl D. Perkins (D) Elected 1948; b. Oct. 15, 1912, Hindman; home, Hindman; Caney Jr. Col., Lees Jr. Col., U. of Louisville, Jefferson School of Law, LL.B. 1935.

Career   Practicing atty., 1935–48; Ky. House of Reps., 1940; Knott Co. Atty., 1941–48; Army, WWII.

Offices   2328 RHOB, 202-225-4935. Also P.O. Bldg., Ashland 41101, 606-325-8530.

Committee   *Education and Labor* (Chairman). Subcommittee: Elementary, Secondary and Vocational Education (Chairman).

Group Ratings

	ADA	COPE	PC	LCV	CFA	RPN	NAB	NSI	NTU	ACA	ACU
1980	56	83	47	39	64	—	17	60	21	29	37
1979	58	70	40	43	48	—	—	—	18	15	17
1978	45	67	55	52	59	27	17	50	10	23	17

Key Votes

1) Draft Registn $	AGN	6) Fair Hsg DOJ Enfrc	AGN	11) Cut Socl Incr Dfns $	AGN
2) Ban $ to Nicrgua	AGN	7) Lim PAC Contrbtns	FOR	12) Hosptl Cost Controls	FOR
3) Dlay MX Missile	AGN	8) Cap on Food Stmp $	AGN	13) Gasln Ctrls & Allctns	FOR
4) Nuclr Mortorium	AGN	9) New US Dep Edcatn	FOR	14) Lim Wndfll Prof Tax	FOR
5) Alaska Lands Bill	FOR	10) Cut OSHA $	AGN	15) Chryslr Loan Grntee	FOR

Election Results

1980 general	Carl D. Perkins (D)	117,665	(100%)	($0)
1980 primary	Carl D. Perkins (D)	30,722	(86%)	
	One other (D)	5,056	(14%)	
1978 general	Carl D. Perkins (D)	51,559	(76%)	
	Grandville Thomas (R)	15,861	(24%)	

LOUISIANA

Louisiana was described by A. J. Liebling as an outpost of the Levant along the Gulf of Mexico, and there is indeed something foreign in the state's culture and physical environment. While most of the United States faces east toward the Atlantic Ocean or west toward the Pacific, Louisiana faces resolutely south, to the Gulf of Mexico and the steamy heat and disorganized societies of Latin America beyond. New Orleans is our one major city that still preserves the look and feel it had as a Spanish outpost in the New World, and Louisiana is the only state whose legal system comes not from British common law but from the code of continental Europe. About half of Louisiana is nothing more than delta land, the deposits of soil brought downstream by the Mississippi River and accumulated at its mouth. Once the Mississippi emptied into the Gulf in what is now northern Louisiana, and the land below is soggy, swampy delta, laced with tributaries and offshoots of the Mississippi, bayous and such major rivers as the Atchafalaya.

Southern Louisiana is not easy land to settle. The Mississippi is held between giant levees, high above the surrounding land. It is possible to farm some of this land, but much is nearly under water; looking out over a distance one can hardly tell where the land ends and water begins. At the edge of settlement of New Orleans and other urban areas, the swamp abruptly begins; people in the subdivisions at the edge sometimes find alligators in their yards. Houses do not have basements, and in New Orleans even the cemeteries, with their ornate 19th-century headstones, are above ground.

Louisiana was the site of an advanced civilization when almost all the rest of the South was still Indian territory (although some of the Indians were pretty advanced themselves). New Orleans was one of the five largest cities at the outbreak of the Civil War and the only significant urban center in the Confederacy by modern industrial standards. Yet in the years after the Civil War Louisiana became one of the poorest of states. There was always a large black population here, because the sugar, rice, and cotton plantations required large numbers of slaves. War and emancipation destroyed the wealth of the plantations, and while New Orleans remained a great port — its position at the mouth of the Mississippi and the terminus of the Illinois Central Railroad guaranteed that — it was also very much a low-wage labor town. In its rickety frame houses, not always strong enough to keep the rain out and never tight enough to keep out the summer humidity or a winter chill, lived New Orleans's working class, blacks often living close by whites. New Orleans was one of the most corrupt of American cities in the years of Reconstruction, when its votes were regularly purchased and bid for; and like other southern cities it became rigidly segregated in the years after 1890.

The Louisiana of the 1920s was a place with enough vitality to give jazz to America and the world, but it also remained desperately poor. As in underdeveloped nations, a thin stratum of people managed to become very rich and a large majority stayed dirt poor and seemingly without prospects of improving their conditions. One out of four Louisianans was illiterate; while there were streetcar scandals in New Orleans most of the parishes (the Louisiana name for county) of the state had never had a paved road. That was the situation when Huey P. Long became governor in 1928. Perhaps no other politician has had as great and enduring an effect on the life of a state as the Kingfish. Although he was governor for only four years and senator for three more, he ruled Louisiana with an iron hand; if his political enemies were willing to bribe and cheat to get their way, he proved over and over that he could beat them at their own game. In his short period in office Long built the state's skyscraper Capitol and Louisiana State University, he built a network of concrete roads and instituted an old age pension. Long was a serious national figure as well. His nebulous "share the wealth" program generated enough pressure to move Franklin Roosevelt to support Social Security and the Wagner Act in 1935. Roosevelt believed that Long would have been his most dangerous opponent in 1936, and many Americans believed it was only a matter of time before Long would be president. Instead, he was murdered in the halls of the Capitol in Baton Rouge in 1935 at the age of 42.

Ever since, proteges of Huey and members of the Long family have held high political office in Louisiana; elections for 30 years have split along pro- and anti-Long lines. For the most part Huey Long built a coalition of the poor, blacks as well as whites, against the rich and better off (although one should add that the Long faction was never powerful in New Orleans, even in its poor neighborhoods). What is so amazing is that this structure of politics was built on top of a state that was already divided in two other ways. First was the division by race, familiar enough to those who know the pre–civil rights South. In Louisiana, though, it should be noted that despite its high black percentage (in 1980 the third highest in the nation) many blacks, notably in New Orleans, were always allowed to vote, which was definitely not the case in such places as Mississippi and South Carolina. The other bifurcation is between Catholic and Protestant, between Cajuns and Baptists. The Cajun population of Louisiana is descended from the Acadians, French settlers of Nova Scotia who were driven away when the British took over the territory in 1755.

The Cajuns were settled in Louisiana, and were then and are now the only major settlement of French-speaking people in the United States. About one out of six Louisianans today has French as his or her native tongue, and at least as many more have French names or (as in the case of former Governor Edwin Edwards) French blood, and more than one in three Louisianans is Catholic. Catholicism is the most prevalent religion in the New Orleans metropolitan area, but the real Cajun country is farther west, among the bayous and crawfish-laden swamps of southern Louisiana. There is a different culture here, valued more during a revival in the 1970s than in the past. French is spoken regularly and English is spoken with a particular accent; the cuisine, spicy and laced with shellfish, is unique. Many cultural differences exist between the teetotaling Baptists of northern Louisiana and the beer-drinking Cajuns of the south, and those differences have come out from time to time in politics, usually in no more threatening form than a preference for a candidate of one religious background or another.

The Cajuns have been helped in their determination to preserve their heritage by the major economic development in Louisiana since Huey Long's time — the rise of the oil industry.

Oil had already been discovered in Long's time, and although he fought the big oil companies he was also something of an investor in oil himself (as is his son, Senator Russell Long).
Louisiana has long been the nation's second leading oil producing state, after Texas, and it
has also been one of the major refiners; the Exxon refinery in Baton Rouge, a giant installation, has long had a tradition of producing the largest oil company's chief executives. Oil has
by and large been good to Louisiana. If it has polluted some bayous, it has also brought jobs,
and well-paying ones, to rural parts of the state that otherwise would have lost their children
to the big cities of the north. Much oil production is in the Cajun region, and the resultant
prosperity—much of it from recent finds in the Tuscaloosa Trench—has enabled the Cajuns to remain in the area and to prosper. Voters in most states usually regard oil companies
as ogres; voters in Louisiana, in Levantine fashion, regard the big companies as their friends.
   Indeed, this feeling that large businesses help the state has intensified despite the populist
teachings of Huey Long to which people still pay tribute; the contradiction is personified in
Russell Long, who sees himself as both the friend of the little man and of large productive
enterprises. In Levantine fashion Louisianans have always been inclined to believe that the
end justifies the means; they tolerated the corruption of the Huey Long period or the wheeling and dealing of an Edwin Edwards as a necessary and entirely unnoteworthy means to
the end of building a commonwealth that works. Louisianans still treasure their state pension checks even as they root for Exxon, and while the rest of America seems to be in economic doldrums, Louisiana in its sweaty, bustling way seems to be moving ahead.
   Louisiana's foremost politician today is Russell Long. He was first elected to the Senate in
1948 at age 30, with every prospect of holding a lifetime seat. His chief political asset at that
time was the memory of his father. In the years since he has gained the reputation of being a
political operator second to none, a virtuoso as chairman of the Senate Finance Committee.
But the road has been rocky on the way. He was Senate majority whip for a while, elected in
1965 by an odd coalition of southerners and liberals; but after four stormy years and some
personal problems he managed to overcome, Long lost the post to Edward Kennedy in an
upset.
   Long was chairman of the Senate Finance Committee from 1965 until the Democrats lost
control of the Senate in the 1980 elections. In his first years, Long acted like an old-fashioned
committee chairman, monopolizing staff resources by refusing to create subcommittees and
conducting much of the committee's business in secret sessions. But over the years he had to
abandon such devices and came to dominate the committee more through his mastery of its
subject matter and his sensitivity to the rhythm of the legislative process. Although he is now
no more than ranking minority member, he still has a great deal of leverage, and the new
chairman, Robert Dole of Kansas, at least early in his term could not prevent himself from
deferring to Long.
   Finance has an impressive jurisdiction: all tax measures, including Social Security and
Medicare, and international trade matters as well. In early 1981 it appeared that Finance
would be one of the crucial committees for Ronald Reagan's economic programs, at least
on the tax side. Long's own views are difficult to categorize. He has come forward over the
years with some original ideas and initiatives: the $1 checkoff on the income tax form for
presidential campaign financing and encouraging, through the tax code, employee stock
ownership. He has also exerted his power negatively; it was Senate Finance that killed Richard Nixon's family assistance plan. Although his father was an opponent of the oil companies, Russell Long has been a champion of measures they back. His sagacity has often been

praised, but it has to be said as well that he presided over Social Security benefit and tax increases that now seem excessively—and dangerously—generous. Rather than revising income tax rates downward as inflation pushed people into higher brackets, he specialized in providing ad hoc tax cuts every year, usually just around adjournment time—a process that gave Russell Long maximum leverage over Congress. On trade issues Long defies characterization. He has been a strong supporter of multilateral trade agreements, but he has been very concerned about imports of sugar and rice, both of them of course Louisiana products. On the Merchant Marine Subcommittee he is a strong supporter of maritime subsidies.

Good humored, smart, cagey, and full of good intentions he is; but Long has been more inclined to ad hoc remedies than to systemic reform. He will probably not be chairman again in the next few years, but no one doubts he will continue to be a major force, and few people doubt that he can be reelected indefinitely.

Actually, the latter assumption is open to at least some question. For years Long had no significant opposition in Louisiana, and he has never really been given any reason to learn how to conduct a vigorous campaign in this media age. In 1980 he did have a somewhat serious challenge in the state's primary. Louisiana has a peculiar election system, instituted by Edwin Edwards after he was forced to win a primary, a Democratic runoff, and a general election, while his Republican opponent had to fight only the last. There is a September primary (October in gubernatorial elections) in which candidates of all parties run with party designations. If any candidate gets 50% of all votes cast for the office, he or she is elected; if not, the top two candidates (even if they are of the same party) face off in a runoff several weeks later. Thus the election for Long's seat and most House seats in Louisiana in 1980 was effectively held in September; only one runoff, and the presidential contest, were held in November.

Long had one opponent, Democratic state legislator Louis (Woody) Jenkins, who had also run against Senator Bennett Johnston in 1978. Jenkins attacked Long as a left winger, citing his vote for the Panama Canal Treaties and charging that he had not cut taxes and government spending enough. A similar platform had gotten Jenkins 41% of the vote against Johnston in a two-candidate race; he lost to Long by almost the same margin, 58%-39%. Long, as might be expected of a canny Finance chairman, had been able to raise much more money than Jenkins; but his margin, while decisive, cannot be called overwhelming. It certainly seems likely that he can win at least one more full term, although it is possible that the Republican Party will make a serious challenge against him someday.

Bennett Johnston, Louisiana's other senator, is a man who has a similar reputation for political and legislative ability. Johnston did not come by his seat automatically but was favored by circumstance. In 1972, after a nearly successful race for governor, he ran for the U.S. Senate against incumbent Allen Ellender, who died suddenly at age 82 after the filing deadline and before the primary. Johnston was the only candidate who filed against him, and he won the Democratic nomination easily; in the general election he faced the independent candidacy of former Governor John McKeithen but again won handily. At age 40 Johnston had won a seat that his predecessor had held for 36 years.

Johnston is a man with that easy charm that so many southern politicians seem born with. He is popular with his colleagues and served as Democratic campaign chairman during his first term. His voting record has generally been what one would expect from a man from the comfortable, country club precincts of Shreveport who wants to get on with Senate Democrats. He has a seat on the Appropriations Committee but has made his greatest mark so far as a member of the Energy Committee. Johnston has proved to be an extremely active and competent advocate of positions backed by oil companies. On the long-stalled major energy bill, he was the Senate's main advocate of deregulation of natural gas, and he has mastered the minutiae of deregulation issues to the point that even those on the other side rely on his expertise. Now that deregulation has been achieved in major part, Johnston may find himself concentrating more on other aspects of the committee's jurisdiction, including environmental matters. He is currently the second-ranking Democrat on the Energy Committee but will likely become the ranking Democrat in 1983, since Henry Jackson, who currently holds that position, will probably take it on Armed Services on the expected retirement of John Stennis. In addition, Johnston is ranking Democrat on the Energy and Interior Appropriations Subcommittee.

Johnston's 59% of the vote when he ran for reelection in 1978 was a little below expectations, since most observers had written off his opponent as a right-wing nut. Johnston's performance seems now a gauge of the strength of conservative views on national issues in Louisiana. The state has had close races in the last two presidential elections, but this is more because of Jimmy Carter's southern origins and his near-unanimous support from blacks than because any form of national liberalism has anything close to a majority constituency in this state. In House elections Louisiana tends mostly toward conservatives, although there are some notable exceptions (Lindy Boggs, Gillis Long) and a number of other recent Louisiana congressmen have shown the same degree of pragmatism and ability to get along with other Democrats as have Senators Long and Johnston. This is not a state that admires impractical idealism or places a high premium on ideological purity.

Yet Louisiana does have a governor who has exhibited some of these qualities, Republican David Treen. He has been running for office, first unsuccessfully, then successfully, for years. He ran against Congressman Hale Boggs in 1964 and 1968 when Boggs's support of civil rights acts got him in trouble; he ran for governor in 1972 and came close to beating Edwin Edwards. Then he was elected to Congress later in that year; his political base is in Metairie, the high-income suburb in Jefferson Parish just west of New Orleans. He ran again for governor in 1979, this time coming in first in the initial primary and holding on for a narrow victory over Democrat Louis Lambert in December 1979. It helped that Lambert had finished second only after a protracted dispute with Lieutenant Governor James Fitzmorris, and that most of the other half dozen Democrats in the race, some of them pretty liberal, endorsed the ultraconservative Treen rather than the heavy-spending (more than $4 million) Lambert. Indeed, the entire gubernatorial contest was characterized by heavy spending, and candidates who could raise only $1 million in effect lost by default. In this respect the race was closer in spirit to presidential elections in oil-rich Venezuela, where vast sums are spent, than it was to most elections in the United States.

Treen is generally conceded to be honest and well intentioned, and the rigidity of conservative views that seemed apparent in his congressional voting record have not prevented him from accommodating himself to the twists and turns of Louisiana politics.

Treen is not the dominant figure in state politics, however. That title still belongs to Edwin Edwards. First elected in 1972, Edwards has dominated the state's politics as no governor since Huey Long. He was fortunate enough to inherit a state that suddenly was no longer concerned with the issues of racial segregation, and a state that was in line for economic health as the price of oil rose. He added to that good fortune a consummate ability to deal with the legislature and a total lack of embarrassment over charges of scandal that have been made against him. Edwards's argument to the people of Louisiana is that he gets things done, and if he likes wearing expensive clothes and gambling in Las Vegas, fine. Most Louisianans buy the argument and indulge him such eccentricities as his nominating speech for Jerry Brown at the 1976 Democratic national convention. It is generally conceded that Edwards could have won another term as governor in 1979 if he had been eligible to run, and he has let it be known that he will be running again when Treen comes up for reelection in 1983. Meanwhile he holds court in Baton Rouge as if he still held office. It may be that the luster will come off Edwards's record once he is out of office for a while or that Treen will establish himself as entitled to another term; but Edwards has a chance for the kind of comeback few southern governors achieve.

Louisiana has eight congressional districts and neither gains nor loses any as a result of the 1980 census. With one exception, the state could redistrict with only minor changes in the boundary lines; and given a Republican governor and a large number of factions among Democratic legislators, few changes appear likely. The one possible change that may have political impact is that Lindy Boggs's 2d congressional district might have to include 60,000-odd additional suburbanites, in precincts that tend to go heavily Republican and whose presence in the district might stimulate a serious Republican candidacy.

Census Data Pop. (1980 final) 4,203,972, up 15% in 1970s: 1.86% of U.S. total, 19th largest. Central city, 29%; suburban, 34%. Median 4-person family income, 1978, $18,691, 91% of U.S., 37th highest.

1979 Share of Federal Tax Burden $6,852,000,000; 1.52% of U.S. total, 22d largest.

1979 Share of Federal Outlays $7,499,840,000; 1.62% of U.S. total, 21st largest.

DOD	$1,129,964,000	28th	(1.06%)	HEW	$2,747,666,000	23d	(1.54%)
DOE	$875,315,000	5th	(7.44%)	ERDA	$1,358,000	41st	(0.05%)
HUD	$106,012,000	22d	(1.61%)	NASA	$133,362,000	8th	(2.85%)
VA	$364,943,000	21st	(1.76%)	DOT	$221,206,000	24th	(1.34%)
EPA	$69,733,000	24th	(1.31%)	DOC	$377,689,000	3d	(11.93%)
DOI	$38,120,000	33d	(0.69%)	USDA	$532,652,000	17th	(2.22%)

Economic Base Finance, insurance, and real estate; agriculture, notably cattle, soybeans, rice, and dairy products; oil and gas extraction, especially oil and gas field services; food and kindred products; chemicals and allied products, especially industrial chemicals; transportation equipment, especially ship building and repairing.

Political Lineup Governor, David C. Treen (R). Senators, Russell B. Long (D) and J. Bennett Johnston, Jr. (D). Representatives, 8 (6 D and 2 R); 8 in 1982. State Senate, 39 D; State House of Representatives, 105 (95 D and 10 R).

The Voters

  Registration 2,015,402 Total. 1,744,465 D (87%); 149,903 R (7%); 121,034 other (6%).
  Employment profile 1970 White collar, 45%. Blue collar, 36%. Service, 16%. Farm, 3%.
  Ethnic groups Black 1980, 29%. Hispanic 1980, 2%. Asian 1980, 1%. Total foreign stock 1970, 4%

French-speaking, 16%.

Presidential Vote

1980	Reagan (R)	792,853	(51%)

	Carter (D)	708,453	(46%)
	Anderson (I)	26,345	(2%)
1976	Ford (R)	587,446	(46%)
	Carter (D)	661,365	(52%)

1980 Democratic Presidential Primary				*1980 Republican Presidential Primary*		
Carter	199,956	(56%)		Reagan	31,212	(75%)
Kennedy	80,797	(23%)		Bush	7,818	(19%)
Brown	16,774	(5%)		Four others.........	432	(1%)
Four others........	19,600	(5%)		Uncommitted	2,221	(5%)
Uncommitted	41,614	(12%)				

SENATORS

Sen. Russell B. Long (D) Elected 1948, seat up 1986; b. Nov. 3, 1918, Shreveport; home, Baton Rouge; La. St. U., B.A. 1941, LL.B. 1942.

Career Navy, WWII; Practicing atty., 1945–57.

Offices 217 RSOB, 202-224-4623. Also 220 Fed. Bldg., 750 Fla. Blvd., Baton Rouge 70801, 504-387-0181 ext. 445.

Committees *Commerce, Science and Transportation* (2d). Subcommittees: Merchant Marine and Tourism; Surface Transportation.

Finance (Ranking Member). Subcommittees: Taxation and Debt Management; Health; Social Security and Income Maintenance Programs.

Joint Committee on Taxation (Ranking Member).

Group Ratings

	ADA	COPE	PC	LCV	CFA	RPN	NAB	NSI	NTU	ACA	ACU
1980	28	50	23	7	27	—	50	83	35	29	56
1979	11	62	23	—	19	—	—	—	29	32	43
1978	25	28	28	12	35	40	40	44	12	47	19

Key Votes

1) Draft Registn $	—	6) Fair Housng Cloture	AGN	11) Cut Socl Incr Defns	FOR
2) Ban $ to Nicrgua	AGN	7) Ban $ Rape Abortns	—	12) Income Tax Indexing	AGN
3) Dlay MX Missile	AGN	8) Cap on Food Stmp $	FOR	13) Lim Spdg 21% GNP	AGN
4) Nuclr Mortorium	—	9) New US Dep Edcatn	FOR	14) Incr Wndfll Prof Tax	AGN
5) Alaska Lands Bill	AGN	10) Cut OSHA Inspctns	—	15) Chryslr Loan Grntee	FOR

Election Results

1980 primary	Russell B. Long (D)	484,770	(58%)	($2,166,838)
	Louis (Woody) Jenkins (D)	325,922	(39%)	
	Three others, (D, R, No Party) ...	30,321	(4%)	
1974 general	Russell B. Long (D)	434,643	(100%)	($498,774)

Sen. J. Bennett Johnston, Jr. (D) Elected 1972, seat up 1984; b. June 10, 1932, Shreveport; home, Shreveport; Wash. & Lee U., La. St. U., LL.B. 1956.

Career Army, 1956–59; Practicing atty.; La. House of Reps., 1964–68, Flr. Ldr.; La. Senate, 1968–72.

Offices 421 RSOB, 202-224-5824. Also Rm. 1010 Hale Boggs Fed. Bldg., 500 Camp St., New Orleans 70130, 504-589-2427, and 7A12 New Fed. Bldg, and Courthouse, 500 Fannin St., Shreveport 71102, 318-226-5085.

Committees *Appropriations* (8th). Subcommittees: Defense; Energy and Water Development; Foreign Operations; Interior.

Budget (4th).

Energy and Natural Resources (2d). Subcommittees: Energy Regulation; Energy Research and Development; Energy and Mineral Resources.

Group Ratings

	ADA	COPE	PC	LCV	CFA	RPN	NAB	NSI	NTU	ACA	ACU
1980	33	41	27	13	7	—	40	60	35	29	38
1979	16	42	18	—	14	—	—	—	30	37	33
1978	15	13	18	26	15	20	64	78	16	60	65

Key Votes

1) Draft Registn $	FOR	6) Fair Housng Cloture	AGN	11) Cut Socl Incr Defns	FOR
2) Ban $ to Nicrgua	FOR	7) Ban $ Rape Abortns	FOR	12) Income Tax Indexing	AGN
3) Dlay MX Missile	AGN	8) Cap on Food Stmp $	AGN	13) Lim Spdg 21% GNP	AGN
4) Nuclr Mortorium	AGN	9) New US Dep Edcatn	FOR	14) Incr Wndfll Prof Tax	AGN
5) Alaska Lands Bill	AGN	10) Cut OSHA Inspctns	—	15) Chryslr Loan Grntee	FOR

Election Results

1978 primary	J. Bennett Johnston, Jr. (D)	498,773	(59%)	($857,860)
	Louis (Woody) Jenkins (D)	340,896	(41%)	($327,340)
1972 general	J. Bennett Johnston, Jr. (D)	598,987	(55%)	($511,616)
	John J. McKeithen (I)	250,161	(23%)	($394,510)
	Ben C. Toledano (R)	206,846	(19%)	($116,347)

GOVERNOR

Gov. David C. Treen (R) Elected 1979, term expires March 1984; b. July 16, 1928, Baton Rouge; home, Metairie; Tulane U., B.A. 1948; LL.B. 1950.

Career Air Force, 1950–52; Practicing atty., 1950–51, 1957–72; V.P. and Legal Counsel, Simplex Manufacturing Corp., 1952–57; Rep. nominee for U.S. House of Reps., 1962, 1964, 1968; Rep. nominee for Gov., 1972; U.S. House of Reps., 1972–80.

Offices P.O. Box 44004, Baton Rouge 70804, 504-342-7015.

Election Results

1979 gen.	David C. Treen (R)	690,691	(50%)
	Louis Lambert (D)	681,134	(50%)
1979 prim.	David C. Treen (R)	297,469	(22%)
	Louis Lambert (D)	283,266	(21%)
	James E. Fitzmorris (D)....	280,760	(20%)
	Paul Hardy (D)	227,026	(17%)
	E. L. (Bubba) Henry (D) ...	135,769	(10%)
	Edgar G. Mouton, Jr. (D) ..	124,333	(9%)
	Three others (D, D, I)	17,052	(1%)
1975 gen.	Edwin W. Edwards (D)	430,095	(100%)
1975 prim.	Edwin W. Edwards (D)	750,107	(62%)
	Robert G. Jones (D)	292,220	(24%)
	Wade O. Martin, Jr. (D) ...	146,368	(12%)
	Three others (D)	14,309	(1%)

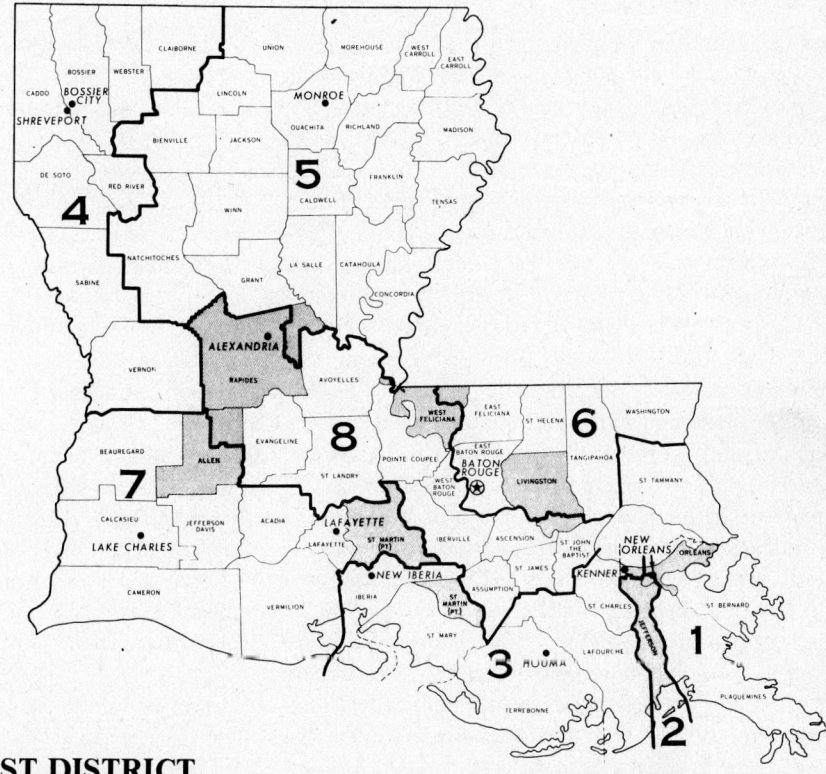

FIRST DISTRICT

The 1st congressional district of Louisiana includes the northern and eastern parts of New Orleans; two parishes astride the Mississippi River, and one once rural and now suburbanized parish north of Lake Pontchartrain. This is not the picturesque, tourist's part of New Orleans. The district's boundary passes just north of the French Quarter and includes most of the city's port facilities; it is otherwise almost entirely residential. These are neighborhoods of basementless houses, built on oozy land below sea level, where the ordinary people of New Orleans live. Some, on streets stretching to Lake Pontchartrain, are modern 1950s houses, the homes of the city's solid middle class; others are the rickety frame houses of poor blacks or whites. (New Orleans has no well-defined black ghetto; blacks live in most parts of the city.) Farther east, but still within the city limits, is a swamp that reaches to the Mississippi state border; the swamp is just beginning to be reclaimed and to be populated with giant apartment complexes and shopping centers.

A more famous part of the 1st are the two small river parishes, St. Bernard and Plaquemines. Much of St. Bernard is now suburbanized, but just downriver in the delta lands of the Mississippi River are insular communities of French-speaking river pilots and shrimp fishermen. Politics is a serious business here. For years Plaquemines was controlled by Leander Perez. Once a Huey Long supporter, Perez was such an ardent segregationist that he was excommunicated by the Catholic Church. But he could still deliver virtually all the votes in Plaquemines. The deliverability of the vote is shown by the varying percentages received by the same candidate, Republican Robert Livingston: 74% in the 1976 general election, 23% in the 1977 primary, and 95% in the September 1978 primary.

What is at stake in Plaquemines is no longer segregration. This is rich oil and sulphur country, with large offshore deposits; local landowners, among them the Perezes, are in a position to become very rich indeed. Obviously it is convenient in such circumstances to have iron control of the local government. In 1981 the sons of Leander Perez encountered some problems: Chalin Perez, president of the parish council, was indicted on charges of stealing $19.5 million from the parish, and Leander Perez, Jr., as district attorney, managed to block an indictment of him for stealing $43 million. St. Bernard Parish used to have machine control almost as solid as Plaquemines; but there has been too much suburban growth now, diluting the voting power of the small communities that are the bulwark of the machine. The people who have moved in are from white working-class communities in New Orleans, the kind of Democrats who used to support George Wallace.

For 36 years the 1st district was represented by F. Edward Hebert, who served for four years (1970–74) as chairman of the House Armed Services Committee. A hawkish exponent of military spending, Hebert had his pet projects in New Orleans, including a military hospital closed after his retirement for lack of use. After the 1974 elections he was voted out of his chairmanship by the Democratic Caucus and he chose to retire in 1976. For the next year the district experienced turbulent congressional politics. Richard Tonry, a St. Bernard legislator who won an upset victory in 1976, was accused of massive vote fraud, resigned in the spring of 1977, and was convicted a year later of misuse of campaign funds. The Republican who was beaten in 1976, Robert Livingston, won the 1977 special election; he ultimately spent more than one million dollars in the 1976–78 period.

Once in office, Livingston has seemed politically secure. The bearer of a proud old Louisiana name, he has voted with most Republicans on most issues and has attended well to local matters. Under Louisiana's new electoral system, he takes on all comers in the September primary and, if he wins 50% of the vote, he wins the election right there. In 1978 and 1980 he won 86% and 88% against weak Democrats. In 1981 Livingston moved from the Public Works to the Appropriations Committee and, still under 40, seems to be in good shape to enjoy a long congressional career.

Census Data   Pop. (1980 final) 523,320, up 15% in 1970s. Median family income, 1970, $8,655, 90% of U.S.

The Voters

Employment profile 1970 White collar, 52%. Blue collar, 34%. Service, 14%. Farm, -%.
Ethnic groups Black 1980, 37%. Hispanic 1980, 4%. Asian 1980, 1%. Total foreign stock 1970, 7%. Italy, 2%; French-speaking, 8%.

Presidential Vote

1980	Reagan (R)	100,436	(51%)
	Carter (D)	90,636	(46%)
	Anderson (I)	3,794	(2%)
1976	Ford (R)	78,928	(47%)
	Carter (D)	83,061	(50%)

Rep. Robert L. (Bob) Livingston (R) Elected Aug. 27, 1977; b. Apr. 30, 1943, Colorado Springs, Col.; home, New Orleans; Tulane U., B.A. 1967, J.D. 1968.

Career Practicing atty.; Asst. U.S. Atty., 1970–73; Chf. Spec. Prosecutor, Orleans Parish Dist. Atty.'s Ofc., 1974–75; Chf. Prosecutor, La. Atty. Gen.'s Ofc. Organized Crime Unit, 1975–76.

Offices 206 CHOB, 202-225-3015. Also 742 F. Edward Hebert Bldg., 610 South St., New Orleans 70130, 504-589-2753.

Committee *Appropriations* (17th). Subcommittees: Foreign Operations; Labor–Health and Human Services–Education.

Group Ratings

	ADA	COPE	PC	LCV	CFA	RPN	NAB	NSI	NTU	ACA	ACU
1980	11	5	17	35	36	—	91	90	47	83	82
1979	11	10	13	17	0	—	—	—	56	83	92
1978	10	15	10	3	23	60	71	100	26	92	96

Key Votes

1) Draft Registn $	FOR	6) Fair Hsg DOJ Enfrc	AGN	11) Cut Socl Incr Dfns $	FOR
2) Ban $ to Nicrgua	FOR	7) Lim PAC Contrbtns	AGN	12) Hosptl Cost Controls	AGN
3) Dlay MX Missile	AGN	8) Cap on Food Stmp $	FOR	13) Gasln Ctrls & Allctns	AGN
4) Nuclr Mortorium	AGN	9) New US Dep Edcatn	AGN	14) Lim Wndfll Prof Tax	FOR
5) Alaska Lands Bill	AGN	10) Cut OSHA $	FOR	15) Chryslr Loan Grntee	AGN

Election Results

1980 primary	Robert L. (Bob) Livingston (R) ...	81,777	(88%)	($138,724)
	Two others (D, No Party)	10,778	(12%)	
1978 primary	Robert L. (Bob) Livingston (R) ...	89,469	(86%)	($347,844)
	Sanford Krasnoff (D)	14,373	(14%)	
1977 spec. elect.	Robert L. (Bob) Livingston (R) ...	56,121	(51%)	
	Ron Faucheux (D)	40,802	(37%)	
	Sanford Krasnoff (I)	12,665	(12%)	
1977 primary	Robert L. (Bob) Livingston (R) ...	5,551	(88%)	
	James A. Moreau (R)	776	(12%)	

SECOND DISTRICT

Since New Orleans fell into American hands with the Louisiana Purchase of 1803, it has been one of the nation's most distinctive cities. The heritage of the city's French and Spanish past can still be seen in the French Quarter, where carefully preserved old houses with their iron balconies exist amid the squalor of tourist-packed bars and some of the nation's finest restaurants. New Orleans remains our second busiest port, adding the new function of sending out Louisiana's oil and petroleum products in huge tankers to its historic role as the outlet of the Mississippi Valley and entrepot of Latin American trade.

It is the older, more distinctive parts of New Orleans that make up most of Louisiana's 2d congressional district. It begins at the French Quarter, its 19th-century homes still intact because the Americans preferred to build a new downtown west of its boundary at Canal Street, away from the snobbish Creoles. Beyond is the slum known as the Irish Channel — New Orleans had more European immigrants than any other part of the South — and the Garden District, with its antebellum houses covered with tangles of vines and Spanish moss. Some of the country's last trolley cars still run out St. Charles Avenue to the Uptown section of large houses near Tulane University. The 2d district includes most of New Orleans's richest citizens, but more than half the residents of this part of the city are black; and the blacks here, unlike those in rural northern Louisiana, have a long steady tradition of voting on election day. They have provided most of the votes to elect the city's first black mayor, Ernest "Dutch" Morial, as well as his white predecessor, Moon Landrieu.

Besides this part of New Orleans, the 2d district takes in part of suburban Jefferson Parish. The parish extends south through the swamps to Barataria Bay, where the pirate Jean Lafitte hung out before he ventured forth to help Andrew Jackson whip the British in 1815. The 2d's portion of Jefferson includes the old, small cities along the banks of the Mississippi River, which once upon a time had a reputation for vice and corruption and more recently have been the scene of disastrous grain elevator explosions. But the district does not include the prosperous, fast-growing, politically conservative suburb of Metairie just south of Lake Pontchartrain.

From 1941 to 1943 and 1947 to 1972 — 28 years altogether — the 2d district was represented by Hale Boggs. He won his first race as a rebel against the local machine; and after a spirited struggle in 1971 became House majority leader — just a step away from the speaker's chair. Boggs's career ended suddenly in October 1972, when he was lost in a plane crash while campaigning with freshman Nick Begich of Alaska. Boggs was a mercurial man: a stirring oldtime orator, a gifted trader of votes, a southerner who had a strong liberal record and had even dared to support the Civil Rights Acts of 1965 and 1968. Ironically, Boggs died just as the Louisiana legislature had finally drawn a safe district for him. In 1964 and 1968 he had barely survived strong challenges from Republican David Treen, who is now governor; in the latter year his civil rights votes hurt him so much in the white neighborhoods of New Orleans and Jefferson Parish that he won with only 51%. The current 2d, where 33% of the registered voters are black, reelected him posthumously.

The majority leader's successor in the 2d district is his widow, Corinne Claiborne Boggs, universally known as Lindy, who won a 1973 special election with 81%. Sometimes when a congressman dies, his widow is elected as a temporary expedient; that is not the case here. For many years Lindy Boggs was considered one of the most knowledgeable of congressional wives and enjoyed wide respect in Washington and New Orleans. The worst that anyone had to say about her was that she sometimes seemed just a little too nice. She has the manners of a girl raised on a plantation (which she was), the panache of someone with an elegant old house in the French Quarter (which she has), and the political savvy of one who has waged some tough campaigns and has moved in the highest circles of Washington for years (which she has). Her talents were on view to the nation when she served as permanent chairman of the 1976 Democratic National Convention.

Lindy Boggs in her own right now has more seniority than most House Democrats. She has a seat on the House Appropriations Committee and serves on the HUD–Independent Agencies and Energy and Water Development Subcommittees. On major issues she seems inclined to support the House leadership, but she is not a doctrinnaire liberal on all issues. She has been reelected with large margins in the 1970s, against desultory opposition; in 1980, against a tougher Republican and a weak Democrat, she won 61% of the vote in Louisiana's September primary and was thereby reelected. That is a strong enough showing to suggest she is not particularly vulnerable, although redistricting will probably result in the addition of some precincts from Republican Metairie into the district, and that may stimulate the Republicans into giving her serious opposition.

Census Data Pop. (1980 final) 462,641, up 2% in 1970s. Median family income, 1970, $7,611, 79% of U.S.

The Voters
Employment profile 1970 White collar, 47%. Blue collar, 35%. Service, 18%. Farm, –%.
Ethnic groups Black 1980, 41%. Hispanic 1980, 4%. Asian 1980, 1%. Total foreign stock 1970, 8%. Italy, 1%; French-speaking, 11%.
Presidential Vote

1980	Reagan (R)	63,625	(43%)
	Carter (D)	75,187	(51%)
	Anderson (I)	3,527	(2%)
1976	Ford (R)	54,014	(43%)
	Carter (D)	67,964	(55%)

Rep. Lindy (Mrs. Hale) **Boggs** (D) Elected Mar. 20, 1973; b. Mar. 13, 1916, Brunswick Plantation; home, New Orleans; Sophie Newcomb Col. of Tulane U., B.A. 1935.

Career Public school teacher; Gen. Mgr., campaigns of U.S. Rep. Hale Boggs; Cochwmn., Presidential Inaugural Balls, 1961, 1965.

Offices 2353 RHOB, 202-225-6636. Also 1012 Hale Boggs Bldg., 500 Camp St., New Orleans 70130, 504-589-2274.

Committee *Appropriations* (18th). Subcommittees: Energy and Water Development; HUD–Independent Agencies.

Group Ratings

	ADA	COPE	PC	LCV	CFA	RPN	NAB	NSI	NTU	ACA	ACU
1980	50	50	37	40	71	—	10	44	11	30	31
1979	42	61	20	40	19	—	—	—	13	20	30
1978	45	65	43	37	50	50	0	70	4	31	36

Key Votes

1) Draft Registn $	FOR	6) Fair Hsg DOJ Enfrc	FOR	11) Cut Socl Incr Dfns $	AGN
2) Ban $ to Nicrgua	AGN	7) Lim PAC Contrbtns	AGN	12) Hosptl Cost Controls	AGN
3) Dlay MX Missile	AGN	8) Cap on Food Stmp $	AGN	13) Gasln Ctrls & Allctns	—
4) Nuclr Mortorium	AGN	9) New US Dep Edcatn	AGN	14) Lim Wndfll Prof Tax	FOR
5) Alaska Lands Bill	—	10) Cut OSHA $	AGN	15) Chryslr Loan Grntee	FOR

Election Results

1980 primary	Lindy Boggs (D)	45,091	(61%)	($571,673)
	Rob Couhig (R)	25,521	(34%)	($130,210)
	One other (D)	3,571	(5%)	
1978 primary	Lindy Boggs (D)	57,056	(87%)	($60,404)
	Two others (No Party)	8,411	(13%)	

THIRD DISTRICT

The 3d congressional district is made up of two quite different parts of southern Louisiana —different economically, culturally, and politically. Most of the physical expanse of the district is part of Louisiana's Cajun country—miles of bayou and swamp giving way from time to time to little roads and crossroads towns where French remains the first language and roadside diners feature crawfish etouffe. But Cajun country looks not just to tradition. It has become one of the nation's major oil-producing areas, and many of the people here work in local oil production or on offshore oil rigs. The oil industry indirectly and inadvertently may be responsible for preserving Cajun culture, for people here, unlike those in many other southern rural areas, have not had to migrate north to find well-paying jobs and opportunities for advancement.

The Cajun country is traditionally Democratic, but the influence of the oil industry—not heavy-handed propaganda by the oil companies, but rather the example of success and prosperity oil production has brought here—has made this area more Republican in recent years. In the 1980 presidential the Cajun counties of the 3d district, on balance, went for Ronald Reagan over Jimmy Carter.

The other part of the 3d district is suburban Jefferson Parish outside of New Orleans. Some 40% of the voters in the current 3d district live in the upper-income suburbs of Metairie and Kenner. Here the lowlands between the Mississippi River and Lake Pontchartrain have been drained and subdivided and occupied by the kind of middle-income people who have little use for either the charms or the drawbacks of New Orleans. As an answer to the French Quarter, it even has its own shopping center of night clubs, Fat City. This is not the most exclusive part of the New Orleans area but it is, on the average, the most prosperous. It is also exceedingly conservative. In national and statewide elections, this part of Jefferson Parish typically delivers the largest Republican margins in the state.

These two disparate parts of the state were joined together by the requirements of the one-person-one-vote doctrine. In the past decade, the 3d has elected congressmen of both major parties. David Treen, a Republican fresh from a narrow defeat in the race for governor, ran here and carried the district in 1972; he is from Jefferson Parish and got 73% of the vote in that crucial election. Treen had a doctrinaire conservative voting record in Congress, but in Louisiana he was able to get along with a wide range of people; and he was reelected easily in the district. He ran for governor in 1979 and, with a strong base in Jefferson Parish, finished first in the initial primary; in the runoff, against a Democrat with serious problems, he was elected. That left the district open and, much to Republicans' surprise, it was captured by a Democrat, W. J. (Billy) Tauzin. As his name suggests, he is of Cajun background, from Thibodaux in Lafourche Parish; he had the strong backing of outgoing Governor Edwin Edwards, himself a Cajun, and won the May special election runoff by a wide enough margin that the Republicans did not even field a candidate in the September primary.

Treen was a congressman with his eye on the politics of the governorship; Tauzin, to judge from his committee assignments, seems to be more interested in local matters. He serves on the Energy and Merchant Marine Committees, both bodies of great importance to the district. He can be counted on to favor decontrols of oil and natural gas prices and to oppose environmental measures that the oil industry feels will cripple its exploration and recovery efforts. He can also be expected to back the current subsidies of the maritime industry.

Census Data Pop. (1980 final) 570,243, up 25% in 1970s. Median family income, 1970, $9,146, 95% of U.S.

The Voters

Employment profile 1970 White collar, 50%. Blue collar, 37%. Service, 11%. Farm, 2%.
Ethnic groups Black 1980, 14%. Hispanic 1980, 4%. Am. Ind. 1980, 1%. Asian 1980, 1%. Total foreign stock 1970, 5%. Italy, 1%; French-speaking, 29%.

Presidential Vote

1980	Reagan (R)	124,949	(60%)
	Carter (D)	74,724	(36%)
	Anderson (I)	4,422	(2%)
1976	Ford (R)	92,277	(54%)
	Carter (D)	76,664	(44%)

Rep. Wilbert J. (Billy) **Tauzin** (D) Elected May 22, 1980; b. June 14, 1943, Chackbay; home, Thibodaux; Nicholls St. U., B.A. 1964, La. St. U., J.D. 1967.

Career Legis. Aide, La. Sen., 1964–68; Practicing atty., 1968–80; La. House of Reps., 1971–79.

Offices 222 CHOB, 202-225-4051. Also Dist. Off. 4900, Veterans Memorial Blvd., Metairie 70002, 504-889-2303; Fed. Bldg., Suite 107, Houma 70360, 504-876-3033; and 210 E. Main St., New Iberia 70560, 318-367-8231.

Committees *Energy and Commerce* (22d). Subcommittees: Fossil and Synthetic Fuels; Oversight and Investigations; Telecommunications, Consumer Protection and Finance.

Merchant Marine and Fisheries (16th). Subcommittees: Coast Guard and Navigation; Fisheries and Wildlife Conservation and the Environment.

Group Ratings

	ADA	COPE	PC	LCV	CFA	RPN	NAB	NSI	NTU	ACA	ACU
1980	—	67	25	20	25	—	67	100	23	42	43

Key Votes

1) Draft Registn $	—	6) Fair Hsg DOJ Enfrc	AGN	11) Cut Socl Incr Dfns $	—
2) Ban $ to Nicrgua	—	7) Lim PAC Contrbtns	—	12) Hosptl Cost Controls	—
3) Dlay MX Missile	—	8) Cap on Food Stmp $	—	13) Gasln Ctrls & Allctns	—
4) Nuclr Mortorium	—	9) New US Dep Edcatn	—	14) Lim Wndfll Prof Tax	—
5) Alaska Lands Bill	—	10) Cut OSHA $	—	15) Chryslr Loan Grntee	—

Election Results

1980 primary	Wilbert J. (Billy) Tauzin (D)	80,455	(85%)	($684,431)
	One other (D)	14,074	(15%)	
5/17/80 spc. elc..	Wilbert J. (Billy) Tauzin (D)	62,108	(53%)	
	James Donelon (R)	54,815	(47%)	($534,891)
4/80 spec. prim.	James Donelon (R)	37,191	(45%)	
	Wilbert J. (Billy) Tauzin (D)	35,384	(43%)	
	Two others (D, D)	9,887	(12%)	
1978 general	David C. Treen (R), unopposed ...			($48,855)

FOURTH DISTRICT

Northern Louisiana is part of the Deep South, with none of the Creole ambience of New Orleans or the French accents of the Cajun country. For 150 years Baptist farmers have worked the upcountry hills around Shreveport, the commercial center of the area and the largest city in the 4th congressional district. Shreveport and the adjacent suburban areas form almost precisely one-half of the 4th district, and in recent years they have become rather different in political attitudes from the rest of the district.

For the rural parishes remain wedded to a kind of Deep South attachment to the Democratic Party. To be sure, they were unhappy enough with civil rights and the Great Society to have abandoned such candidates as Hubert Humphrey and George McGovern; but they were Democratic enough to have supported George Wallace rather than Richard Nixon and to have voted not just once but twice for Jimmy Carter.

Shreveport started off as part of the same culture, simply the market town for the adjacent agricultural parishes. But in the 1940s oil was found here and population grew substantially, and today Shreveport is more like the small oil towns of east Texas than the rural territory that surrounds it. The newly rich are closely acquainted with the virtues of the free enterprise system (little attention is given the government subsidies the oil industry has received over the years) and they bring a doctrinaire free-market philosophy to politics. Traditional Democratic allegiance means nothing to them, although they are willing to support like-minded Democrats. But just as they are economically more conservative than their rural neighbors they are in cultural style more advanced and urbane. They wait not only for the latest issue of *Human Events* but for the latest Neiman Marcus catalogue.

In presidential elections Shreveport and nearby parishes have been heavily Republican, favoring Gerald Ford in 1976 and Ronald Reagan in 1980. In congressional elections for 16 years the district supported Joe Waggoner, a country Democrat who was for some years the effective leader of the coalition of Republicans and southern Democrats in the House Ways and Means Committee and on the floor of the House. But in 1978 Waggoner retired, and the 4th district has seen since a kind of turbulent politics, with three high-spending candidates representing each of the major tendencies in the district. They are:

• Jimmy Wilson, a Republican. His natural base is in the Shreveport area, in Caddo and Bossier Parishes. Wilson was the first Republican to make a major effort here, and in the 1978 primary, in which three candidates split 100,000 votes almost evenly, he finished second. In the November general, he lost to Democrat Claude (Buddy) Leach by 266 votes. Wilson charged Leach with vote fraud and attempted to have him unseated by the House.

Presented with its second vote fraud case from Louisiana in two years, the House declined to unseat a Democrat for a Republican; Leach was indicted but ultimately acquitted. Wilson ran again in 1980, and this time in another close three-way primary he finished third, behind Leach and Buddy Roemer. Under Louisiana's unique electoral law, that meant he was eliminated from the race, although both Leach and Roemer ran as Democrats. As might have been expected, Wilson endorsed Roemer.

• Claude (Buddy) Leach is the only one of the three major candidates who has a base in the rural southern part of the district. In style and voting record he is a solidly conservative Democrat, of the Joe Waggoner type, yet he draws his votes from the parishes that preferred Carter over Ford or Reagan. In 1980 — after the vote fraud charges had been aired for almost two years — Leach still was able to win, against Wilson, Roemer, and three other Democrats, 55% of the vote in the four southern parishes that all went for Carter, while he was getting only 20% in Caddo and Bossier Parishes around Shreveport. That southern base was enough to get him into the general election. But he was not able to build on it, and he received only 36% of the vote against Roemer. Essentially supporters of all the other candidates ganged up on Leach. His showing is all the more striking considering the vast amounts of money — probably more than $1 million — his campaigns have spent in this district over two elections.

• Buddy Roemer looks like the Louisiana version of a liberal, or at least a city slicker: he is young, Harvard-educated, and his father was a leading operative in Governor Edwin Edwards's administration (and later had legal problems of his own). Neither Roemer is actually from Shreveport, but Buddy Roemer moved there after school and obviously built some kind of political base. He spent more than $500,000 in 1978 only to finish third in the initial primary, missing the second spot by 1,539 votes; in 1980 he ran second to Buddy Leach and then pulverized him in the general. Roemer's advantage was strong support from the Shreveport newspapers and big margins in Caddo and Bossier Parishes. He is an articulate candidate, but not a liberal one; he threatened to vote against Tip O'Neill for speaker, until someone pointed out to him that that vote could destroy his claims to membership in the Democratic Caucus and cost him the committee positions he wanted. He supported O'Neill.

How strong a hold will Roemer have on this district? One might as well ask, why have these three men been fighting with such energy, so much money, and, if one believes indictments, so much chicanery in one case, for a seat in the House of Representatives? Unlike some public offices in Louisiana, a House seat does not give a freshman member great clout or patronage; he is not likely to be feted at home or sought out in Washington. Leach in his single term sat on Armed Services, an appropriate body since the Army's Fort Polk is in his end of the district; Roemer sits on Public Works, the old pork barrel committee, although he made a point of opposing a canal between the Red and Mississippi Rivers (he might have argued that nature has already seen that the two rivers are connected). There is always the possibility of running for statewide office some time in the future, and probably each of these candidates has seen in the mirror a possible future governor of Louisiana; and there is the honor and satisfaction, presumably, of serving in Congress.

But one cannot help thinking that the major attraction of these two races was the fight itself. Louisiana politics, with its uninhibited money raising and its charges of vote stealing and fraud, may be the closest thing after professional football to armed conflict our society sanctions; and the pull of battle may simply be irresistible. It is possible that the battle may now be over in the 4th district, and Roemer could win another term without significant opposition. (Redistricting will not be a problem most likely, since the district can reach the required population by swapping one town with the 7th.) But it is also entirely possible that Leach, Wilson, or some other candidates will again come out swinging and the 4th district will see its third furiously contested election in a row.

Census Data   Pop. (1980 final) 508,593, up 12% in 1970s. Median family income, 1970, $7,336, 77% of U.S.

The Voters

Employment profile 1970   White collar, 44%. Blue collar, 37%. Service, 17%. Farm, 2%.
Ethnic groups   Black 1980, 32%. Hispanic 1980, 3%. Total foreign stock 1970, 3%.

Presidential Vote

1980	Reagan (R)	96,750	(54%)
	Carter (D)	78,745	(44%)
	Anderson (I)	1,945	(1%)
1976	Ford (R)	78,365	(53%)
	Carter (D)	66,125	(45%)

Rep. Buddy Roemer (D) Elected 1980; b. Oct. 4, 1943, Shreveport; home, Bossier City; Harvard U., B.A. 1964, M.B.A. 1967.

Career   Businessman, Farmer, Banker, 1967–80; Delegate, La. Const. Conv., 1972.

Offices   1725 LHOB, 202-225-2777. Also P.O. Drawer 5100, Bossier City 71111, 318-797-9000.

Committees   *Public Works and Transportation* (25th). Subcommittees: Aviation; Investigations and Oversight; Water Resources.

Small Business (22d). Subcommittees: General Oversight; Tax, Access to Equity Capital and Business Opportunities.

Group Ratings and Key Votes: Newly Elected

Election Results

1980 general	Buddy Roemer (D)	103,625	(64%)	($693,859)
	Claude (Buddy) Leach (D)	58,705	(36%)	($643,639)
1980 primary	Claude (Buddy) Leach (D)	35,847	(29%)	
	Buddy Roemer (D)	33,049	(27%)	
	Jimmy Wilson (R).............	29,992	(24%)	($106,800)
	Three others (D, D, D)..........	24,203	(20%)	
1978 general	Claude (Buddy) Leach (D)	65,583	(50%)	($771,303)
	Jimmy Wilson (R).............	65,317	(50%)	($402,713)

FIFTH DISTRICT

The upcountry 5th congressional district of Louisiana, the state's most rural, is part of the Deep South. Aside from the small city of Monroe, the 5th has no urban center of any consequence. The agricultural establishments in this cotton and piney woods country range from large plantations along the Mississippi River to small, poor hill farms in such places as Winn Parish, the boyhood home of Huey P. Long. The 5th has one of the highest black populations, but black voter registration lags somewhat behind — a remnant of the days when few blacks in this part of Louisiana dared to vote.

For 30 years the 5th district was represented by Congressman Otto Passman, who made a name for himself as long ago as the 1950s as the scourge of the foreign aid program. A member of the so-called "college of cardinals," i.e., the chairmen of the House Appropriations subcommittees, Passman was actually playing more complicated games. In 1976 he was indicted for extorting lucrative foreign aid and shipping contracts from foreign governments for a favored agent; pleading bad health, he delayed his trial and ultimately was acquitted by a hometown jury. What is surprising is that Passman's career lasted as long as it did. A challenger came within 11% of forcing him into a runoff in 1972, and when he finally faced a serious primary challenger in 1976 he lost.

The winner was Jerry Huckaby, a dairy farmer and former Western Electric management employee. The Republicans seriously contested this district and in a pattern often seen in the South were able to carry the urban area, Monroe, with its newly affluent and upwardly mobile population, but were not able to carry the culturally more traditional rural parishes. The trend in national contests has been conservative; Jimmy Carter nearly carried the district in 1976 but fell far short in 1980. The trend in congressional elections has been the opposite for Huckaby. In Louisiana's unique electoral system, in which a candidate who wins 50% against all opponents in the September primary wins the election, Huckaby has done better and better. Against a serious Democratic opponent he won 52% of the vote in 1978, after spending large sums indeed; against a nuisance candidate in 1980 he had 89%. Huckaby is unlikely to be affected in any significant way by redistricting.

In Washington Huckaby sits on the Agriculture and Interior Committees. The former is of clear importance to this rural district; the latter is of obvious importance to Louisiana, particularly since Huckaby sits on the subcommittees affecting energy and environment — which is to say that he has something to say about the conditions under which mineral exploration takes place.

Census Data   Pop. (1980 final) 507,333, up 11% in 1970s. Median family income, 1970, $5,762, 60% of U.S.

The Voters
  Employment profile 1970   White collar, 40%. Blue collar, 37%. Service, 16%. Farm, 7%.
  Ethnic groups   Black 1980, 32%. Hispanic 1980, 1%. Total foreign stock 1970, 1%.

Presidential Vote

1980	Reagan (R)	107,171	(55%)
	Carter (D)	81,524	(42%)
	Anderson (I)	1,628	(1%)
1976	Ford (R)	84,131	(50%)
	Carter (D)	81,204	(48%)

Rep. Jerry Huckaby (D) Elected 1976; b. July 19, 1941, Jackson Parish; home, Ringgold; La. St. U., B.S. 1963, Ga. St. U., M.B.A. 1968.

Career Mgmt. position, Western Electric, 1963–73; Dairy farmer, 1963–76.

Offices 228 CHOB, 202-225-2376. Also 1200 N. 18th St., Monroe 71201, 318-387-2244.

Committees *Agriculture* (15th). Subcommittees: Cotton, Rice and Sugar; Forests, Family Farms and Energy; Wheat, Soybeans and Feed Grains.

Interior and Insular Affairs (18th). Subcommittees: Energy and the Environment; Mines and Mining.

Group Ratings

	ADA	COPE	PC	LCV	CFA	RPN	NAB	NSI	NTU	ACA	ACU
1980	11	21	20	39	14	—	92	100	36	58	89
1979	11	21	13	13	4	—	—	—	49	76	76
1978	25	30	18	10	23	69	75	100	19	88	87

Key Votes

1) Draft Registn $	FOR	6) Fair Hsg DOJ Enfrc	AGN	11) Cut Socl Incr Dfns $	FOR
2) Ban $ to Nicrgua	FOR	7) Lim PAC Contrbtns	AGN	12) Hosptl Cost Controls	AGN
3) Dlay MX Missile	AGN	8) Cap on Food Stmp $	AGN	13) Gasln Ctrls & Allctns	AGN
4) Nuclr Mortorium	AGN	9) New US Dep Edcatn	FOR	14) Lim Wndfll Prof Tax	FOR
5) Alaska Lands Bill	AGN	10) Cut OSHA $	FOR	15) Chryslr Loan Grntee	FOR

Election Results

1980 primary	Jerry Huckaby (D)	93,519	(89%)	($60,316)
	One other (D)	11,748	(11%)	
1978 primary	Jerry Huckaby (D)	66,276	(52%)	($384,207)
	Jim Brown (D)	38,969	(31%)	($117,800)
	Three others (D)	22,049	(17%)	

SIXTH DISTRICT

When Governor-elect Huey P. Long moved himself and his belongings to Baton Rouge in 1928, the Louisiana capital was a small, sleepy southern town with a population of 30,000. Today Baton Rouge is a bustling city of 219,000, with its population up 32% in the 1970s — and the change is thanks both to the Kingfish and to his bitterest political enemies. Long built a major university in Baton Rouge (Louisiana State) and vastly increased the size and scope of state government. And his old enemies the oil companies, primarily Standard of New Jersey (now Exxon), built the big refineries and petrochemical plants that are the other base of Baton Rouge's prosperity. For Exxon, now the nation's largest industrial corporation, Baton Rouge is an especially important town; management at the big Exxon refinery here has produced several of Exxon's chief executives.

Baton Rouge and its suburban fringe make up almost two-thirds of Louisiana's 6th congressional district and cast an even larger percentage of its votes. The remainder of the district is to the east, in farming and piney woods country; the most notable town here is Boga-lusa, a lumber mill town on the Mississippi line and the scene of Ku Klux Klan activity over the years. This area is known as the Florida Parishes, for its acquisition by the United States was accomplished when West Florida was annexed in 1810.

The district is traditionally Democratic but has been moving in a definitely Republican direction in recent years. It favored Jimmy Carter by a solid margin in 1976 but went for Ronald Reagan in 1980. Carter's southern origin and his ambiguity on oil issues probably helped him win here in 1976; four years later he was identified as an opponent of decontrol (although he finally favored it) and lost Baton Rouge quite heavily. In congressional politics, the 6th has been a Republican district since 1975 and perhaps 1974. The reason for the am-biguity is that the 1974 election had to be rerun, because the results from one Democratic precinct were not recorded; most likely the Democratic nominee, a young liberal who had beaten right-wing incumbent John Rarick in the primary, would have won in that event. But in the January 1975 rerun the Republican, Henson Moore, ran a strong campaign and was elected.

Moore has represented the district ever since and appears to have built up great popularity. In the last two election years, he has received 91% of the votes in Louisiana's September all-candidate primary, which meant that he was elected twice without having to run in November. Moore is an aggressive member of the House Ways and Means Committee, charging the Democrats with trying to stack the committee and attacking them vigorously on a variety of issues. He can be counted on to defend and advance the interests of oil producers; he strongly supports the kind of supply-side economics championed by the Reagan Administration. He is an ardent free trader, interested in agricultural exports. If the Reagan–Republican economic policies fulfill their promises, Moore could have a bright future indeed. He has been mentioned as a candidate for statewide office, but with the governorship effectively foreclosed to him until at least 1987, he might end up running for one of the state's Senate seats. The level of popularity he has earned in Baton Rouge and the Florida Parishes sug-gests that he would wear well under statewide exposure.

The 1980 census showed the 6th to be the largest of Louisiana's congressional districts, and it will have to be pared down in size for the 1982 election. Most likely it will trade terri-tory with the current 8th district, which is much more Democratic. If Baton Rouge is left entirely in the 6th, this district, if anything, will be more Republican than it is now.

Census Data Pop. (1980 final) 577,140, up 27% in 1970s. Median family income, 1970, $8,230, 86% of U.S.

The Voters

Employment profile 1970 White collar, 48%. Blue collar, 34%. Service, 15%. Farm, 3%.
Ethnic groups Black 1980, 30%. Hispanic 1980, 2%. Total foreign stock 1970, 3%. French-speak-ing, 4%.

Presidential Vote

1980	Reagan (R)	109,692	(50%)
	Carter (D)	101,252	(46%)
	Anderson (I)	4,353	(2%)
1976	Ford (R)	74,781	(44%)
	Carter (D)	90,224	(53%)

Rep. W. Henson Moore (R) Elected Jan. 7, 1975; b. Oct. 4, 1939, Lake Charles; home, Baton Rouge; La. St. U., B.A. 1961, J.D. 1965, M.A. 1973.

Career Army, 1965–67; Practicing atty., 1967–74.

Offices 2444 RHOB, 202-225-3901. Also 236 Fed. Bldg., 750 Fla. Blvd., Baton Rouge 70801, 504-344-7679.

Committee *Ways and Means* (12th). Subcommittees: Oversight; Public Assistance and Unemployment Compensation; Select Subcommittee on Revenue Measures.

Group Ratings

	ADA	COPE	PC	LCV	CFA	RPN	NAB	NSI	NTU	ACA	ACU
1980	11	0	23	30	14	—	100	100	49	79	74
1979	11	16	15	17	0	—	—	—	56	92	97
1978	5	0	15	17	23	58	100	100	25	96	96

Key Votes

1) Draft Registn $	AGN	6) Fair Hsg DOJ Enfrc	AGN	11) Cut Socl Incr Dfns $	FOR
2) Ban $ to Nicrgua	FOR	7) Lim PAC Contrbtns	AGN	12) Hosptl Cost Controls	AGN
3) Dlay MX Missile	AGN	8) Cap on Food Stmp $	FOR	13) Gasln Ctrls & Allctns	AGN
4) Nuclr Mortorium	AGN	9) New US Dep Edcatn	AGN	14) Lim Wndfll Prof Tax	FOR
5) Alaska Lands Bill	AGN	10) Cut OSHA $	FOR	15) Chryslr Loan Grntee	AGN

Election Results

1980 primary	W. Henson Moore (R)	118,540	(91%)	($88,376)
	One other (D)	12,149	(9%)	
1978 primary	W. Henson Moore (R)	102,430	(91%)	($78,680)
	Bobby G. Pailette, Sr. (D)	10,256	(9%)	

SEVENTH DISTRICT

The 7th congressional district of Louisiana is one of very few in the nation where nearly half the population grew up speaking a language other than English. Here the language is French, Cajun style, and it was the mother tongue of 44% of the 7th's population in 1970 (the 1980 census figures have not yet been tabulated). This district is the southwestern part of Louisiana, which hugs the Gulf Coast, from the swamps of the Atchafalaya River in the east through the medium-sized city of Lafayette, the unofficial capital of the Cajun country, west to Lake Charles and the Texas border.

Many rural backwaters like this have died in the last 25 years; not so the Cajun country of Louisiana. What has kept people here is petroleum, in plenteous quantities under the swampy soil, with even more below the Gulf a few miles out to sea. Oil and attendant industries provide jobs here while the rest of the country suffers through recession, and they have provided money to keep all the Cajuns who wish to remain in their homeland. Cajun culture remains healthy as well. The Cajuns are working to promote the use of French and to hold onto other regional—especially culinary—traditions.

The congressman from the 7th, John Breaux, is a practical-minded legislator who is having a substantial effect on important legislation. When he was first elected in September 1972, to replace his former boss, Edwin Edwards, who had been elected governor, Breaux was the youngest member of Congress. It was before the time when House freshmen were important, and Breaux attracted little notice. He did make a point of winning seats on the Public Works and Merchant Marine Committees—two prosaic bodies of importance to this coastal district. Traditionally, they have handled matters like dredging swamps and building levees, the kind of labor-intensive projects that were so helpful to the 7th before the boom in the oil industry. More recently they have also been considering broader environmental policy questions.

Here Breaux has played an important role. Generally he votes on the side of those who favor more economic development even at the risk of some degredation of the environment. Thus he was the major sponsor of an amendment to relax federal control over landfill and dumping operations in marshes and swamps. He sponsored a successful amendment to relax clean air standards in areas whose air currently is reasonably clean; an earlier law tended to prohibit even tiny increments of pollution in such areas, thus discouraging any industrial development there at all, even of a kind that would be allowed in a built-up area. With David Treen, then of the 3d district and now Edwards's successor as governor, Breaux sponsored a measure to change leasing procedures in the continental shelf in ways favored by the oil companies. On the Maritime Committee he generally supports maritime subsidies but looks out first of all for the interests of oil companies; he opposed oil cargo preference on the floor of the House.

On issues that are likely to come up in 1981 and 1982, Breaux could play a major role. His positions on the Clean Air Act, which comes up for renewal in September 1981, suggest that he will back relaxation of some standards. He is known as one of the leading congressional opponents of the law of the sea convention negotiated by the Carter Administration, arguing that it gives foreign nations too much control over undersea resources that could be exploited by American corporations. Critics of Breaux would probably charge that he works primarily for the interests of big businesses. He would probably reply that increased economic development improves the lives of ordinary people, and he could cite the experience of his home district as evidence for that proposition. Breaux seems to have much the same kind of political savvy as Edwards. But he has shown no interest in statewide office and has concentrated instead on his congressional career. He repelled a serious challenge by a Republican in 1978, and while there is a Republican trend in the district (particularly in Lafayette, which may have more new millionaires per capita than any other city in the country), he seems to be well entrenched. Redistricting will likely result in only the most minor alteration of the 7th district's boundaries.

Census Data   Pop. (1980 final) 543,235, up 19% in 1970s. Median family income, 1970, $7,197, 76% of U.S.

The Voters

   Employment profile 1970   White collar, 42%. Blue collar, 38%. Service, 15%. Farm, 5%.
   Ethnic groups   Black 1980, 20%. Hispanic 1980, 2%. Total foreign stock 1970, 2%. French-speaking, 44%.

Presidential Vote

1980	Reagan (R)	103,149	(49%)
	Carter (D)	98,122	(47%)
	Anderson (I)	4,200	(2%)
1976	Ford (R)	65,387	(38%)
	Carter (D)	101,186	(59%)

Rep. John B. Breaux (D) Elected Sept. 30, 1972; b. Mar. 1, 1944, Crowley; home, Crowley; U. of S.W. La., B.A. 1964, La. St. U., J.D. 1967.

Career Practicing atty., 1967–68; Legis. Asst., Dist. Mgr. to U.S. Rep. Edwin W. Edwards, 1968–72.

Offices 2159 RHOB, 202-225-2031. Also 2530 P.O. and Fed. Bldg., Lake Charles 70601, 318-433-1122.

Committees *Merchant Marine and Fisheries* (4th). Subcommittees: Fisheries and Wildlife Conservation and the Environment (Chairman); Merchant Marine; Panama Canal and Outer Continental Shelf.

Public Works and Transportation (4th). Subcommittees: Surface Transportation; Water Resources.

Group Ratings

	ADA	COPE	PC	LCV	CFA	RPN	NAB	NSI	NTU	ACA	ACU
1980	11	28	13	22	21	—	83	80	28	48	33
1979	5	30	5	7	4	—	—	—	39	54	75
1978	5	5	15	5	18	30	91	100	21	86	86

Key Votes

1) Draft Registn $	FOR	6) Fair Hsg DOJ Enfrc	AGN	11) Cut Socl Incr Dfns $	AGN
2) Ban $ to Nicrgua	FOR	7) Lim PAC Contrbtns	AGN	12) Hosptl Cost Controls	—
3) Dlay MX Missile	—	8) Cap on Food Stmp $	AGN	13) Gasln Ctrls & Allctns	AGN
4) Nuclr Mortorium	—	9) New US Dep Edcatn	AGN	14) Lim Wndfll Prof Tax	FOR
5) Alaska Lands Bill	AGN	10) Cut OSHA $	FOR	15) Chryslr Loan Grntee	FOR

Election Results

1980 primary	John B. Breaux (D), unopposed			($89,822)
1978 primary	John B. Breaux (D)	78,297	(60%)	($183,424)
	Mike Thompson (R)	42,247	(33%)	($120,978)
	One other (D)	9,126	(7%)	

EIGHTH DISTRICT

After the lines for seven of Louisiana's eight congressional districts were drawn, the territory remaining became the steamshovel-shaped 8th district—or so, at least, it seems. This is a seat with no real common sense of common identity and which crosses the state's long-acknowledged regional borders; it contains one parish where 96% of the churchgoers are Catholic and another where Catholics are heavily outnumbered by Baptists. Geographically, the 8th is bounded on the east by Lake Pontchartrain; on the west it moves along the Mississippi and Red Rivers to a point within 30 miles of the Texas border.

Three factors explain the district's rather unusual political behavior. The first of these is the large black population. In 1980 29% of the voters here were black — the second highest figure in the state. In the days before the Civil War, the old sugar and cotton plantations along the Mississippi required hundreds of slaves to do the work; today, blacks form majority voting blocs in a few parishes and large minorities in many others. Second, the district has a high Cajun concentration, particularly in the southern parishes of Evangeline and St. Landry. Third, there is the legacy of the Long family. A decade ago, the 8th still contained Huey Long's home parish of Winn; that now is in the 5th district. But this is still very much Kingfish country.

These three factors combine to make the 8th district pretty solidly Democratic in national politics and a very solid base for Congressman Gillis Long, an important Democratic leader in the House of Representatives. It was not always so. During the days when racial segregation was the main political issue in Louisiana, a conservative member of the Long family, Speedy Long, was elected here (from 1964 to 1970), as the district also went for George Wallace and Richard Nixon. But the civil rights revolution was ultimately accepted, and the district went back to voting on its traditional patterns. Gillis Long, first elected in 1962 and defeated two years later in the Democratic primary, won the district rather easily in 1972 and has held it ever since. It was one of two in Louisiana (the other was Lindy Boggs's 2d district) that went for Jimmy Carter both in 1976 and 1980.

Gillis Long is a talented politician and one of the House's ablest legislators. He is currently the third-ranking Democrat on the House Rules Committee, behind Chairman Richard Bolling and octogenarian Claude Pepper. Rules has a peculiar function in the House: it sets the limits of debate and the degree of amendment permitted for almost every measure that comes to the floor (an important exception: budget reconciliation matters). By limiting amendment or by sometimes not reporting out a measure at all, Rules can determine the substantive outcome on issues even though it is supposed to be a purely procedural body. In the 1950s and 1960s a bipartisan conservative majority on the committee used its power to defeat liberal measures; in the early 1970s, under elderly chairmen, Rules became chaotic and uncontrollable. Under Bolling and with the assistance of men like Long (who is Bolling's close ally and friend), Rules has become, as it should be, a working arm of the Democratic majority. To a substantial extent, Rules may tend to determine whether the Reagan Administration gets what it wants in the House. This makes Gillis Long a pivotal legislator, one of the key figures in the Congress.

On substantive issues Long is that rarity, a genuine, humane southern populist; his ratings from liberal organizations are not particularly high but he works closely with the Democratic leadership. He gave up on his dream of running for governor in 1979 and, shortly afterward, suffered a heart attack; when his health returned, his colleagues gave him a warm welcome back. He is one of those congressmen who is both admired and generally liked. Long has had little trouble winning reelection in the 8th, and against a more serious Republican challenge than usual in 1980 he won 69% of the vote. Redistricting could conceivably pose a problem: the 8th must add a little territory to meet the population standard, and it might have to give up a little of what it has now to the 5th district. But unless the legislature decides to radically alter the state's districts, Long is probably assured of a solid political base.

Census Data   Pop. (1980 final) 511,467, up 12% in 1970s. Median family income, 1970, $6,092, 64% of U.S.

The Voters

Employment profile 1970   White collar, 36%. Blue collar, 39%. Service, 17%. Farm, 8%.
Ethnic groups   Black 1980, 33%. Hispanic 1980, 2%. Total foreign stock 1970, 2%. French-speaking, 28%.

Presidential Vote

1980	Reagan (R)	89,730	(45%)
	Carter (D)	105,241	(53%)
	Anderson (I)	2,476	(1%)
1976	Ford (R)	59,137	(38%)
	Carter (D)	94,900	(60%)

Rep. Gillis W. Long (D) Elected 1972; b. May 4, 1923, Winnfield; home, Alexandria; La. St. U., B.A. 1959, J.D. 1951.

Career Army, WWII; Legal Counsel, U.S. Senate Comm. on Small Business, 1951; Chf. Counsel, U.S. House of Reps. Spec. Comm. on Campaign Expenditures; U.S. House of Reps., 1963–65; Asst. Dir., U.S. Ofc. of Econ. Opp., 1965–66; Legis. Counsel, Natl. Commission of Urban Growth Policy, 1968–69; Practicing atty., 1970–72.

Offices 2311 RHOB, 202-225-4926. Also P.O. Box 410, Alexandria 71301, 318-487-4595.

Committees *Rules* (3d). Subcommittee: The Legislative Process (Chairman).

Joint Economic Committee (4th). Subcommittee: International Trade, Finance and Security Economics (Chairman).

Group Ratings

	ADA	COPE	PC	LCV	CFA	RPN	NAB	NSI	NTU	ACA	ACU
1980	50	63	40	39	79	—	10	60	13	21	26
1979	26	50	20	37	19	—	—	—	17	24	43
1978	50	63	43	44	46	55	25	67	10	21	19

Key Votes

1) Draft Registn $	FOR	6) Fair Hsg DOJ Enfrc	FOR	11) Cut Socl Incr Dfns $	AGN
2) Ban $ to Nicrgua	FOR	7) Lim PAC Contrbtns	FOR	12) Hosptl Cost Controls	AGN
3) Dlay MX Missile	AGN	8) Cap on Food Stmp $	—	13) Gasln Ctrls & Allctns	AGN
4) Nuclr Mortorium	AGN	9) New US Dep Edcatn	FOR	14) Lim Wndfll Prof Tax	FOR
5) Alaska Lands Bill	—	10) Cut OSHA $	AGN	15) Chryslr Loan Grntee	—

Election Results

1980 primary	Gillis W. Long (D)	75,433	(69%)	($223,493)
	Clyde C. Holloway (R)	27,816	(25%)	($44,635)
	One other (R)	6,243	(6%)	
1978 primary	Gillis W. Long (D)	80,666	(80%)	($189,507)
	Robert Mitchell (R)	20,547	(20%)	($7,106)

MAINE

"As Maine goes, so goes the nation," our best-known political rule of thumb, is also one of the least accurate. Almost everyone knows James Farley's variation, enunciated after FDR's landslide, "As Maine goes, so goes Vermont." Actually, the saying got started not because Maine was an accurate bellwether but because up through the 1950s the state held its general elections in September, on the sensible theory that they should not be conducted at a time of the year when the weather is likely to be inclement and the sky is certain to be dark before five o'clock.

In any case, Farley's description has turned out to be closer to the truth than the old saying. In recent years, Maine's political behavior has been countercyclical. It voted for the losers in the last four close presidential elections—for Dewey in 1948, Nixon in 1960, Humphrey in 1968, and Ford in 1976. And, although no one noticed it much in the Republican landslide, it came very close to going for the loser again in 1980, giving Reagan only a 46%–42% margin over Carter, with 10% for John Anderson. In local elections, Maine has also produced a countercyclical pattern. Its Democrats captured the governorship and both the state's congressional seats in 1966, a Republican year elsewhere; and in Democratic 1974, Maine elected two Republican congressmen and the Democrats lost the governorship to a Republican running as an Independent. In 1978 Maine followed the national pattern and elected a Republican senator, but it also elected a Democratic governor.

For most of its history, Maine was one of our most Republican states. Set far east and north of the rest of the country, it was not admitted to the Union until 1820 (it was part of Massachusetts before that) and did not experience its greatest growth until the 1830s. During most of the 19th century, Maine was as much a frontier state as Illinois or Iowa. Settlers moved not only west but northeast in search of new land and more space, and they found it—can still find it—in Maine. Maine does, in fact, have as much land area as the rest of New England put together. It has been a significant agricultural state; although the lands in the southern part of the state are stony and not especially productive, Aroostook County in northern Maine is still one of our major producers of potatoes (despite tough competition from Idaho and Canada).

There were limits ultimately to the settlement of Maine, however—limits imposed more by the land than anything else; the land is not very fertile as one goes north, the weather is too cold, and the one product most of Maine can easily produce—lumber—does not require large settlements of people. Maine reached a population of 600,000 before 1860, 700,000 about 1905, and 800,000 in the 1930s—extraordinarily low population growth that resulted from the outmigration of young people and a steady aging of the population.

In the 1970s Maine has had its highest rate of population growth since the 1840s. But this growth has not really resulted in—or reflected—a buoyant local economy. Rather, it is part of a nationwide movement of retirees and younger people willing to settle for lower dollar incomes into what used to be primarily resort and vacation areas. The fastest population gains in Maine have been in counties along the coast, not inland in farming areas or in the old mill towns; the people who have come in are looking more for the physical environment and cultural attitudes that life in Maine can supply than they are for some chance at fast economic gain. When one takes into account local taxes and cost of living (which includes the very high cost of oil or other petroleum-based heating fuels), Maine can be said to have the lowest level of income in the country.

In its frontier days, Maine was settled mostly by Yankees from farther south in New England and that accounts for the Republican preference that has characterized most of its political history. Later, in the 20th century, as the Yankee stock aged, Maine had other immigrants: French Canadians from Quebec especially, Irish from Ireland and Boston, Greeks attracted perhaps from their own rocky coasts to the much colder rocky coasts of Maine. As the years went by, Maine became increasingly less Protestant and less Republican, until finally the Democrats became competitive here. The moment can be pinpointed: when Edmund Muskie was elected governor in 1954.

Muskie still remains the dominant figure in Maine politics, although he has not served in elective office since he resigned from the Senate to become Jimmy Carter's secretary of state in May 1980. Muskie's immigrant background—his father was a tailor from Poland—made him a natural champion of Maine's Democratic Party; his taciturn manner and craggy honesty gave him appeal among Yankees as well. Muskie was elected to the Senate in 1958 and there concentrated on seemingly dull issues but ones full of meaning for both Maine and the nation: reconciling the need to cut down on air and water pollution with a need for economic growth. He is the father of the nation's major antipollution legislation which by and large has achieved its goals—cleaner air and water at a pretty reasonable cost. He was the first chairman of the Senate Budget Committee. He became a national figure in 1968 as Hubert Humphrey's choice for the vice presidency; he was the front-runner for, although not the winner of, the 1972 Democratic presidential nomination. Muskie's strength as a national leader was his patience and skill in reconciling divergent goals; his weakness, more than his well-publicized temper, was his tendency to go along with the conventional wisdom on many issues. Muskie's popularity remained high in Maine; it helped to carry the state for Humphrey in 1968 and nearly carried it for Carter in 1980. It helped elect Democratic congressmen and it helped Democrat William Hathaway unseat Senator Margaret Chase Smith in 1972. Muskie himself was reelected with a solid margin (although not his largest) in 1976 against a free-spending opponent; it was generally assumed that he would retire at age 68 in 1982 when his term was up.

By the time Muskie left the Senate, his Maine Democrats, who had been so successful for so many years, were back on the defensive. The state's other Senate seat was captured in 1978 by Republican William Cohen and he won, over Democratic incumbent Hathaway, by a runaway margin. When he was first elected to the House in 1972, Cohen was the only Republican in the Maine congressional delegation. His election was the triumph of a pleasant, unusual young mayor of Bangor over a lackluster Democrat. In his first term Cohen became well known in his district and nationally as a member of the House Judiciary Committee considering the impeachment of Richard Nixon. He was one of the Republicans who supported impeachment, and his able presentation made a good impression.

Cohen was counted as a liberal Republican in the House; he tended to have 50% ratings from nearly every group. Cohen charged in 1978 that Hathaway was a doctrinaire liberal and, although Cohen himself had no military record and had not concentrated on military issues in the House, charged that Hathaway was not strong enough on defense. The Republican also had some local issues working for him. One was the Lincoln–Dickey—a proposal that had been around for at least 20 years to build a hydroelectric power generating facility on the St. Johns River. Democrats and unions have supported it because it would advance public power in the East and provide cheap power and construction jobs in a chronically depressed area. Republicans have tended to oppose it on the grounds that it is not necessary and would damage the environment. The other local issue was the question of Indian land claims. Various tribes had filed lawsuits claiming that they still owned most of the state, and while the cases were in court the congressional delegation tried to work out compromise proposals, extinguishing the Indians' claim in return for federal payments. Hathaway supported and Cohen opposed the Carter Administration compromise proposal. Opinion in the state was, to say the least, hostile to the Indians' claims, and Cohen's position was clearly a political asset.

In the Senate Cohen has voted more often with other Republicans than he did in the House. This may reflect as much as anything else the degree of cohesion Republicans were able to achieve in the second half of the Carter term; but it also seems to have reflected a genuine shift in philosophy or perspective. He serves on the Armed Services Committee where he is on the side of spending more for defense. He chairs the Seapower Subcommittee and has emerged, in alliance with Democrat Gary Hart of Colorado, as the chief proponent of building a larger Navy of smaller ships rather than concentrating on the huge ships that the Navy has sought in both the Carter and Reagan Administrations. He is also concerned, as any senator from Maine would be, to see that the Bath Iron Works in Bath, Maine, gets its share of shipbuilding contracts and he is ready to point out that Bath has an excellent record. Cohen votes with Republicans on tax and many spending cuts. One might say that Cohen shifted toward these positions, as his 1978 campaign shows, well before the nation's voters did, that he anticipated rather than responded to the change in national mood. In any case, he seems popular in Maine and in line with what is now the majority feeling in the Senate.

It is possible that Cohen will be joined by another Maine Republican in the Senate after 1982. After Muskie's resignation, Governor Joseph Brennan, a Democrat, appointed George Mitchell to fill the vacancy. Mitchell is about as closely associated with Muskie as it is possible to be; he served on his staff, was his appointee to political and governmental posts, and was his choice for at least one other top elective office (the governorship, which he lost to Independent James Longley in 1974). Mitchell's Senate record is in line with Muskie's; indeed, he serves on Environmental Pollution, the successor to the subcommittee on which Muskie made so much antipollution law. Mitchell is perhaps a little more conservative than Muskie on some issues; of course, as a junior member of what is now the minority party he is not in a position to attach his name to major legislation or to get much national press coverage.

Mitchell is certain to have tough competition for the seat—indeed, there is talk that he might be opposed by former Democratic Governor Kenneth Curtis as well as by Republicans. Maine has only two House seats and each congressman is effectively a statewide political figure; the temptation in these circumstances to run for the Senate is considerable. Maine currently has two Republican House members, both, to judge from recent election returns, extremely popular. David Emery, from the southern 1st district, was one of the few Republicans to unseat an incumbent Democrat in the Watergate year of 1974, and he did it at age 26—after four years of service in the Maine legislature. He is not charismatic in appearance, but he seems to have natural political talents. In 1980 he was reelected with a thundering 68% of the vote against a creditable opponent; just afterward, the Republican Conference elected him their deputy whip—the number three position in the Republican leadership. He serves on Armed Services, where he is regarded as pro-Navy and supports shipbuilding contracts for the Bath Iron Works. At age 34 in 1982, Emery faces a difficult choice: an iffy race for a Senate seat, or a safe House seat with the prospect of a major leadership position.

Iron Works. At age 34 in 1982, Emery faces a difficult choice: an iffy race for a Senate seat, or a safe House seat with the prospect of a major leadership position.

One reason Emery might have trouble in the Senate race is the appeal of the 2d district's Congressman Olympia Snowe. She is more distinctive in personality and appearance and she was reelected with 79% in 1980. Like Emery, she is an aggressively partisan Republican but also one with a record that is sometimes agreeable to liberal groups as well as conservative. One reason is that both tend to support measures that would help depressed and energy-poor regions like Maine; it is still an open question whether those natural tendencies of a Republican in this state will not be overshadowed by the performance of a Republican national administration determined to cut spending. In any case, the prospects are for a very strenuous primary between these two young Republicans, to be followed by a very seriously contested general election—as tough a Senate race as any state will see in 1982.

That will leave Maine's two House seats open. The current boundaries will have to be altered slightly because the northern half of the state has not grown quite as fast as the southern. The current districts each almost precisely replicate the state's overall political divisions, because a previous Republican legislature divided the Democratic areas—Portland on the one hand and Lewiston–Auburn on the other—in the southeastern portion of the state between the two districts. That division will probably not be disturbed, since Democrats hold the governorship and one house of the legislature and the Republicans have a one-vote margin in the state Senate. If the districts are left pretty much as is, both districts, if no incumbent is running, must be considered marginal.

The current governor, Joseph Brennan, owes much of his victory in 1978 to the Indian claims issue. He had been attorney general the preceding four years and in that office opposed all Indian land claims and argued strongly against compromise of any kind. That is a position most people would call conservative; ironically, the most national attention directed at Brennan came when he became the only governor to support the presidential campaign of Edward Kennedy, who is usually termed a liberal. This combination of liberal stands on economic issues and conservative stands on what might be called a cultural issue seems to work well in Maine, with its struggling economy and its changing ethnic mix.

Census Data   Pop. (1980 final) 1,124,660, up 13% in 1970s: 0.50% of U.S. total, 38th largest. Central city, 11%; suburban, 12%. Median 4-person family income, 1978, $16,885, 83% of U.S., 48th highest.

1979 Share of Federal Tax Burden $1,758,000,000; 0.39% of U.S. total, 40th largest.

1979 Share of Federal Outlays $2,263,279,000; 0.48% of U.S. total, 40th largest.

DOD	$579,576,000	35th	(0.55%)	HEW	$944,866,000	37th	(0.53%)
DOE	$2,063,000	47th	(0.02%)	ERDA	$395,000	48th	(0.01%)
HUD	$36,130,000	37th	(0.55%)	NASA	$334,000	42d	(0.01%)
VA	$131,834,000	38th	(0.64%)	DOT	$72,335,000	43d	(0.44%)
EPA	$39,976,000	35th	(0.75%)	DOC	$16,507,000	30th	(0.52%)
DOI	$9,894,000	47th	(0.18%)	USDA	$105,985,000	44th	(0.44%)

Economic Base   Leather footwear, and other leather and leather products; paper and allied products, especially paper mills other than building paper; agriculture, notably potatoes, eggs, broilers, and dairy products; finance, insurance, and real estate; food and kindred products; lumber and wood products.

Political Lineup   Governor, Joseph E. Brennan (D). Senators, William S. Cohen (R) and George J. Mitchell (D). Representatives, 2 R; 2 in 1982. State Senate, 33 (17 R and 16 D); State House of Representatives, 151 (84 D and 67 R).

The Voters

Registration   759,978 Total. 242,209 D (32%); 218,556 R (29%).
Employment profile 1970   White collar, 41%. Blue collar, 44%. Service, 12%. Farm, 3%.
Ethnic groups   Total foreign stock 1970, 19%. Canada, 14%.

Presidential Vote

1980	Reagan (R)	238,522	(46%)
	Carter (D)	220,974	(42%)
	Anderson (I)	53,450	(10%)
1976	Ford (R)	236,320	(49%)
	Carter (D)	232,279	(48%)

SENATORS

Sen. William S. Cohen (R) Elected 1978, seat up 1984; b. Aug. 28, 1940, Bangor; home, Bangor; Bowdoin Col., B.A. 1962, Boston U., LL.B. 1965.

Career Practicing atty., 1965–72; Asst. Penobscot Co. Atty., 1968; Instructor, Husson Col., 1968, U. of Maine, 1968–72; Bangor City Cncl., 1969–72, Mayor, 1971–72; U.S. House of Reps., 1973–78.

Offices 1251 DSOB, 202-224-2523. Also Fed. Bldg., Bangor 04401, 207-947-6504.

Committees *Armed Services* (6th). Subcommittees: Strategic and Theatre Nuclear Forces; Sea Power and Force Projection (Chairman); Manpower and Personnel.

Governmental Affairs (6th). Subcommittees: Permanent Subcommittee on Investigations; Energy, Nuclear Projection, and Government Processes; Oversight of Government Management (Chairman).

Select Committee on Indian Affairs (Chairman).

Special Committee on Aging (5th).

Group Ratings

	ADA	COPE	PC	LCV	CFA	RPN	NAB	NSI	NTU	ACA	ACU
1980	33	22	37	82	20	—	91	80	46	68	48
1979	42	38	66	—	62	—	—	—	37	62	61
1978	30	21	35	79	41	50	55	78	—	58	67

Key Votes

1) Draft Registn $	AGN	6) Fair Housng Cloture	AGN	11) Cut Socl Incr Defns	FOR
2) Ban $ to Nicrgua	AGN	7) Ban $ Rape Abortns	AGN	12) Income Tax Indexing	FOR
3) Dlay MX Missile	—	8) Cap on Food Stmp $	AGN	13) Lim Spdg 21% GNP	FOR
4) Nuclr Mortorium	FOR	9) New US Dep Edcatn	AGN	14) Incr Wndfll Prof Tax	FOR
5) Alaska Lands Bill	FOR	10) Cut OSHA Inspctns	FOR	15) Chryslr Loan Grntee	AGN

Election Results

1978 general	William S. Cohen (R)	212,294	(57%)	($648,739)
	William D. Hathaway (D)	127,327	(34%)	($423,027)
	Hayes Gahagan (I)	27,824	(7%)	($115,901)
1978 primary	William S. Cohen (R), unopposed			
1972 general	William D. Hathaway (D)	224,270	(53%)	($202,208)
	Margaret Chase Smith (R)	197,040	(47%)	($14,950)

Sen. George J. Mitchell (D) Appointed May 1980, seat up 1982; b. Aug. 20, 1933, Waterville; home, Waterville; Bowdoin Col., B.A. 1954, Georgetown U., J.D. 1960.

Career Army Counterintelligence, 1954–56; U.S. Dept. of Justice, 1960–62; Asst. Atty., Cumberland Co., 1971; U.S. Atty. for Me., 1977–79; U.S. Dist. Judge for Me., 1979–80.

Offices 344 RSOB, 202-224-5344. Also P.O. Box 8300, 151 Forest Ave., Portland 01401, 207-722-1226; 5 Washington St., Biddeford 04005, 207-282-4144; 8 Lisbon St., Lewiston 04240, 207-784-0163; P.O. Box 1237, 202 Harlow St., Bangor 04401, 207-945-6024; P.O. Box 786, Fed. Bldg., 33 College Ave., Waterville 04901, 207-873-3361; 387 Main St., Rockland 04841, 207-596-0311; and 6 Church St., Presque Isle 04769, 207-833-7313.

Committees *Environment and Public Works* (6th). Subcommittees: Environmental Pollution; Nuclear Regulation.

Finance (9th). Subcommittees: Savings, Pensions, and Investment Policy; Economic Growth, Employment, and Recenue Policy; Energy and Agricultural Taxation.

Veterans' Affairs (5th).

Group Ratings

	ADA	COPE	PC	LCV	CFA	RPN	NAB	NSI	NTU	ACA	ACU
1980	67	78	82	69	80	—	75	0	38	18	8

Key Votes

1) Draft Registn $	AGN	6) Fair Housng Cloture	FOR	11) Cut Socl Incr Defns	—
2) Ban $ to Nicrgua	FOR	7) Ban $ Rape Abortns	FOR	12) Income Tax Indexing	—
3) Dlay MX Missile	AGN	8) Cap on Food Stmp $	—	13) Lim Spdg 21% GNP	—
4) Nuclr Mortorium	—	9) New US Dep Edcatn	—	14) Incr Wndfll Prof Tax	—
5) Alaska Lands Bill	FOR	10) Cut OSHA Inspctns	AGN	15) Chryslr Loan Grntee	—

Election Results

1976 general	Edmund S. Muskie (D)	292,704	(60%)	($320,427)
	Robert A. G. Monks (R)	193,489	(40%)	($598,490)
1976 primary	Edmund S. Muskie (D), unopposed			
1970 general	Edmund S. Muskie (D)	199,954	(62%)	
	Neil S. Bishop (R)	123,906	(38%)	

GOVERNOR

Gov. Joseph E. Brennan (D) Elected 1978, term expires Jan. 1983; b. Nov. 2, 1934, Portland; Boston Col., B.A., U. of Maine, J.D.

Career Practicing atty.; Maine House of Reps., 1965–71; Cumberland Co. Atty., 1971–73; Maine Senate, 1973–75, Dem. Flr. Ldr; Atty. Gen. of Maine, 1975–78.

Offices Augusta 04880, 207-289-3531.

Election Results

1978 gen.	Joseph E. Brennan (D)	176,493	(48%)
	Linwood E. Palmer, Jr. (R).	126,862	(34%)
	Herman C. Frankland (I)...	65,889	(18%)
1978 prim.	Joseph E. Brennan (D)	38,361	(52%)
	Philip L. Merrill (D)	26,803	(36%)
	Richard J. Carey (D)	8,588	(12%)
1974 gen.	James J. Longley (I).......	142,464	(40%)
	George J. Mitchell (D).....	132,219	(37%)
	James S. Erwin (R)	84,176	(23%)

FIRST DISTRICT

Census Data Pop. (1980 final) 581,185, up 17% in 1970s. Median family income, 1970, $8,688, 91% of U.S.

The Voters

Employment profile 1970 White collar, 44%. Blue collar, 42%. Service, 12%. Farm, 2%.
Ethnic groups Total foreign stock 1970, 18%. Canada, 11%.

Presidential Vote

1980	Reagan (R)	126,274	(45%)
	Carter (D)	117,613	(42%)
	Anderson (I)	30,889	(11%)
1976	Ford (R)	127,019	(49%)
	Carter (D)	123,598	(47%)

Rep. David F. Emery (R) Elected 1974; b. Sept. 1, 1948, Rockland; home, Rockland; Worcester Polytechnic Inst., B.S. 1970.

Career Maine House of Reps., 1971–74.

Offices 2437 RHOB, 202-225-6116. Also 46 Sewall St., Augusta 04330, 207-775-3131.

Committees *Armed Services* (9th). Subcommittees: Research and Development; Seapower and Strategic and Critical Material.

Merchant Marine and Fisheries (7th). Subcommittees: Fisheries and Wildlife Conservation and the Environment; Oceanography.

Group Ratings

	ADA	COPE	PC	LCV	CFA	RPN	NAB	NSI	NTU	ACA	ACU
1980	39	21	37	77	36	—	75	70	43	67	58
1979	26	37	40	59	15	—	—	—	45	75	70
1978	25	35	45	70	32	45	75	80	25	69	83

Key Votes

1) Draft Registn $	FOR	6) Fair Hsg DOJ Enfrc	FOR
2) Ban $ to Nicrgua	AGN	7) Lim PAC Contrbtns	FOR
3) Dlay MX Missile	FOR	8) Cap on Food Stmp $	AGN
4) Nuclr Mortorium	FOR	9) New US Dep Edcatn	—
5) Alaska Lands Bill	FOR	10) Cut OSHA $	—

11) Cut Socl Incr Dfns $	FOR
12) Hosptl Cost Controls	AGN
13) Gasln Ctrls & Allctns	AGN
14) Lim Wndfll Prof Tax	FOR
15) Chryslr Loan Grntee	AGN

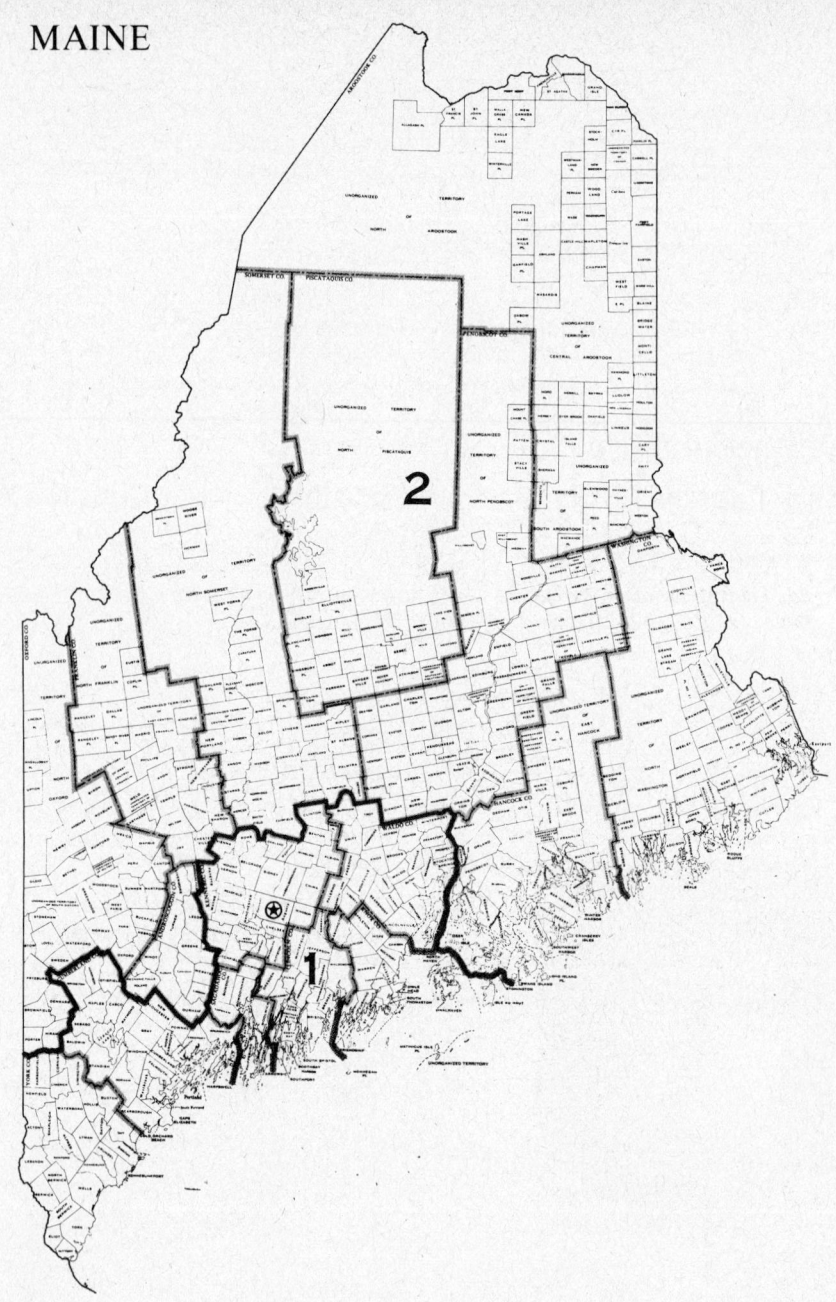

Election Results

1980 general	David F. Emery (R)	188,667	(68%)	($247,509)
	Harold C. Pachios (D)	86,819	(32%)	($141,864)
1980 primary	David F. Emery (R)	29,257	(100%)	
1978 general	David F. Emery (R)	120,791	(61%)	($200,480)
	John Quinn (D)................	70,348	(36%)	($73,755)

SECOND DISTRICT

Census Data   Pop. (1980 final) 543,475, up 9% in 1970s. Median family income, 1970, $7,733, 81% of U.S.

The Voters

Employment profile 1970   White collar, 37%. Blue collar, 47%. Service, 12%. Farm, 4%.
Ethnic groups   Amer. Ind. 1980, 1%. Total foreign stock 1970, 20%. Canada, 16%.

Presidential Vote

1980	Reagan (R)	112,248	(46%)
	Carter (D)	103,361	(43%)
	Anderson (I)	22,438	(9%)
1976	Ford (R)	109,301	(49%)
	Carter (D)	108,681	(48%)

Rep. Olympia J. Snowe (R) Elected 1978; b. Feb. 21, 1947, Augusta; home, Auburn; U. of Maine, B.A. 1969.

Career Dist. Ofc. Mgr. for U.S. Rep. William S. Cohen, 1973; Maine House of Reps., 1973–76; Maine Senate, 1977–78.

Offices 130 CHOB, 202-225-6306. Also Rm. 232 Fed. Bldg., Bangor 04401, 207-942-4198.

Committees *Foreign Affairs* (14th). Subcommittees: Africa; Europe and the Middle East.

Select Committee on Aging (9th). Subcommittee: Human Services.

Small Business (7th). Subcommittee: Tax, Access to Equity Capital and Business Opportunities.

Group Ratings

	ADA	COPE	PC	LCV	CFA	RPN	NAB	NSI	NTU	ACA	ACU
1980	28	33	40	57	36	—	73	67	37	75	47
1979	39	60	45	48	36	—	—	—	44	62	49

Key Votes

1) Draft Registn $	FOR	6) Fair Hsg DOJ Enfrc	AGN	11) Cut Socl Incr Dfns $	AGN
2) Ban $ to Nicrgua	AGN	7) Lim PAC Contrbtns	FOR	12) Hosptl Cost Controls	AGN
3) Dlay MX Missile	AGN	8) Cap on Food Stmp $	AGN	13) Gasln Ctrls & Allctns	FOR
4) Nuclr Mortorium	AGN	9) New US Dep Edcatn	AGN	14) Lim Wndfll Prof Tax	AGN
5) Alaska Lands Bill	FOR	10) Cut OSHA $		15) Chryslr Loan Grntee	AGN

Election Results

1980 general	Olympia J. Snowe (R)	186,406	(79%)	($187,934)
	Harold J. Silverman (D)	51,026	(21%)	($20,947)
1980 primary	Olympia J. Snowe (R)	23,234	(100%)	
1978 general	Olympia J. Snowe (R)	87,939	(51%)	($220,981)
	Markham L. Gartley (D)	70,691	(41%)	($132,156)

MARYLAND

Maryland's attenuated shape reflects the fact that this is one of the most diverse states. Although it ranks only 42d in area, you can drive 350 miles wholly within its boundaries. In that distance you move from the south-of-the-Mason–Dixon-Line Eastern Shore, through the booming suburbs (and some declining ones) of Baltimore and Washington, and up into the Appalachian Mountains. Tiny Maryland has just about every kind of people — northerners and southerners, blacks and ethnics, civil servants and Chesapeake Bay watermen, almost all the diversity of the entire United States compressed into one small package.

The very diversity of this state has made it difficult to maintain a single identity. It was more successful in so doing 50 years ago, when H. L. Mencken was extolling the virtues of the pleasant life of his native city in the *Baltimore Sun*. Maryland was then a kind of city–state: 49% of its residents lived in the closely packed, rowhouse-lined streets of Baltimore, with most of the rest spread in two diverse hinterlands, the southern-oriented counties on both shores of Chesapeake Bay and the northern-accented wheat-growing country around the antique small cities of Frederick and Hagerstown and the mountain-bound industrial city of Cumberland. Maryland was then a place tolerant of its regional eccentricities: Prohibition was enforced only laxly in Baltimore; the state's old law guaranteeing blacks equal access to public accommodations specifically excluded the Eastern Shore.

Today Maryland is quite different. Only 19% of its people live in the city of Baltimore, and the Eastern Shore and western counties include a much smaller percentage of the state's population than they did 50 years ago. Most Marylanders now live in suburban communities, 52% in suburban counties around Baltimore and 29% in the two suburban counties around Washington, D.C. Just 40 miles apart, these two metropolitan areas could hardly be more different. Baltimore is a major port with big shipbuilding companies and the nation's largest steel mill. Its heavy industries have attracted the kind of ethnic migration common to the big cities of the East Coast, as well as a large black migration from the South, although Baltimore today is in better economic shape than the cities to the northeast. Washington, whose economy is of course based on government, has been something of a boom town in the 1960s and 1970s. As civil service salaries have risen, the Washington suburbs in Montgomery County have come to have the highest median incomes in the country; as government has grown bigger, Washington has developed a vigorous private economy of lawyers, lobbyists, consultants, trade associations, government contractors, all paying high professional salaries. Much of the growth of Washington has taken place in the Maryland suburbs, where high-rise office building and apartment complexes stand in what was pasture land a few years ago.

Maryland's diversity made the state a pretty good indicator of national trends in presidential elections from 1960 to 1976, coming as close as any state to duplicating the national results. Yet in 1980 Maryland was one of the six states that backed Jimmy Carter. One reason was the southern white vote, not only on the Eastern Shore but in many suburban areas as well; while Carter did not get enough of them to carry more than one rural county, he did do better here than among similar voters of Yankee origins in the other East Coast states. A second reason for Carter's better showing here is Maryland's relatively large number of blacks. This is one state where the black percentage has been increasing (it is now 23%), largely because many Washington area blacks have been moving out from the District of Columbia to Prince Georges County and, although much less often, to Montgomery County as well. As a result, Carter got an absolute majority of the votes in Prince Georges in 1980—one of the few suburban counties in the nation where he was able to do so. And in Baltimore's black-majority 7th congressional district, Carter had nearly a 100,000-vote plurality over Reagan —far exceeding his statewide plurality. Finally, there is a white working-class vote in Baltimore and its suburbs that went to Carter in 1976 and again in 1980. It is worth noting, finally, one factor that apparently was not of great help to Carter: Maryland's large number of federal employees. There is little evidence in the election returns that the prospect of Reagan's cutting government spending led bureaucrats to vote Democratic. Carter failed to carry Montgomery County and probably lost the white vote in Prince Georges to Reagan as well. Moreover, in the presidential primary voters in the Washington suburbs (like those in the District itself) rejected Carter in favor of Edward Kennedy.

Maryland's growth and the lack of roots here for so many of its suburban citizens have contributed to an unfortunate aspect of the state's public life: its sometimes widespread corruption. Two of its recent governors have been disgraced: Spiro Agnew, who, it turns out, was pocketing payoffs in the vice president's office even as he was excoriating adversaries for immoral behavior; and Marvin Mandel, his canny successor, who was convicted on federal charges of fraud for receiving favors from a few well-placed cronies and doing favors for them in return. Mandel would like to be remembered as a competent manager and a sometimes gifted conductor of the legislature; and it must be said that he was convicted on some novel theories of law and after undergoing scrutiny that many current officials in many states could not withstand.

Nevertheless, the legacy of Mandel and Agnew—and the feelings aroused by the convictions of many local officials—left Maryland voters with a taste for something new in the 1978 gubernatorial election. The acting governor, on Mandel's conviction, was Blair Lee III, bearer of a proud family name—he is related to the Lees of Virginia and the Blairs of Blair House, and his family owned most of what is now downtown Silver Spring—and a man with a candid, crusty personality and an unsmirched reputation for honesty. He was the initial favorite in the Democratic primary, but voters were looking for something new. They found it in a candidate who began almost unknown to the voters, Harry Hughes. He had a competent record in state government, first in the legislature and then as head of Mandel's transportation department—a position he resigned in protest because, he said, of tampering with the process for selecting state contractors. Hughes was from the conservative Eastern Shore but had put together Maryland's one major tax reform and had supported civil rights measures in the 1960s. But all these credentials helped him little until he received the endorsement of the *Baltimore Sun*. In our times newspaper endorsements are seldom influential, but this was different; voters went for Hughes not because they looked to the *Sun* for political advice, but because the *Sun*'s editorial was evidence that Hughes was the kind of man they were looking for.

Hughes won the primary solidly and had little trouble in the general election. Republicans have often won the governorship in Maryland but usually only when the Democratic candidate has had some special problem, and Hughes had none. In office Hughes has generated little controversy; Maryland's prosperity and growth have not presented him with grave fiscal problems. The most interesting aspect of his administration may be his struggle to keep quiet his lieutenant governor, an obscure Prince Georges County council member who was recruited for the ticket when Hughes seemed to have no chance; this man is painfully inarticulate and at the same time fervently opposed to abortion, and it is certain that Hughes will drop him in 1982. Otherwise, it is possible that Hughes will win reelection without strenuous competition.

The money in Maryland politics is in state and local office. There have been no allegations of corruption or even patronage-oriented politics about the members of the state's congressional delegation. Its senior member, Senator Charles Mathias, is a model of probity and integrity. From an old family in Frederick County, in the hills west of Washington and Baltimore, he served as a liberal Republican congressman from a district including Montgomery County in the 1960s and was elected to the Senate in 1968. Mathias is the old-fashioned kind of Republican for whom one of the party's main attractions is its historic record on civil rights and he was not pleased to see his party dominated by civil rights legislation foes such as Barry Goldwater. Mathias is the second-ranking Republican on the Judiciary Committee, which handles civil rights; in 1979, when Republicans were still far from a Senate majority, Strom Thurmond made a point of exercising his seniority and taking the ranking chair on Judiciary rather than on Armed Services, as he could have, precisely to prevent Mathias from getting it. As a result, Thurmond is now chairman of the Judiciary Committee and was able to abolish the Antitrust Subcommittee Mathias would have headed; Mathias has no power to hire staff and may end up as part of the committee's minority on many votes.

Mathias was not part of the Republican unity so apparent in 1980. He endorsed Ronald Reagan only perfunctorily and made it clear that he viewed the prospect of a Reagan presidency with some distaste. As a result, he is not a particular favorite among many Senate Republicans. Not only is he not chairman of Judiciary (although he does chair the Subcommittee on Criminal Justice) but he was persuaded to give up a high-ranking seat on the Appropriations Committee (behind Chairman Mark Hatfield and Republican Whip Ted Stevens) and to take a middle-ranking position on Foreign Relations in return. He also got to chair the Rules and Administration Committee, a body that is not especially important unless something unusual comes along (such as the nomination of a new vice president). That post was open because all of its Republican members in the previous Congress had better chairmanships or in one case a Cabinet position; even the most conservative members could hardly deny it to Mathias, who after all is tied for eighth in seniority among Senate Republicans. He chairs the subcommittee with jurisdiction over the District of Columbia — still an important post for a Maryland senator.

As a member of the minority party during the partisan struggles of the Nixon Administration, Mathias was often in a key position, sometimes going along with Democrats, sometimes sticking with Republicans. He is one of those senators whose views are considered sound and whose judgment on difficult issues is respected and sought. How he will fare as one of the few members of an otherwise cohesive majority inclined to dissent from his party's orthodoxy is less clear. Mathias has high ratings from liberal and labor organizations, and conservative groups definitely feel he is not one of their own. Yet he does have a greater respect for the free-market system than do most Democrats. In all, he seems a man more temperamentally suited to careful, judicious opposition than to strong advocacy of any establishment's program.

Mathias seemed threatened for a while with opposition in the Republican primary in 1980, and a few years earlier even toyed with the idea of running as an independent. Primary opposition from someone like Robert Bauman—the congressman who later got in trouble for personal reasons—could have hurt or even defeated Mathias in a primary limited to a relatively small number of registered Republicans. As it was, against five little-known opponents, the senator won with just 55% of the vote. In the general election, against a Prince Georges County legislator who campaigned most heatedly on the abortion issue, Mathias carried Baltimore city and every county and won 66% of the vote.

The state's other senator, Paul Sarbanes, is a Democrat from Baltimore in his first term. He won his seat in 1976 rather easily, despite prominent opposition, beating former Senator Joseph Tydings in the Democratic primary and incumbent Senator Glenn Beall in the general election. Sarbanes's voting record is generally considered liberal, but temperamentally he is even more cautious than Mathias and seldom lets others know what he is thinking until he has made up his mind. In a state where Democratic politicians usually get ahead in a gregarious, back-slapping environment, Sarbanes has always been something of a loner: a rebel against Marvin Mandel in the state Assembly, an insurgent who took on an incumbent U.S. congressman and committee chairman in the 1970 primary, a House Judiciary Committee member who was expected all along to support Nixon's impeachment but who did not commit himself until he had digested all the evidence. Sarbanes has come out a winner from all these situations not because he has made friends but because he works hard and knows his stuff.

Now Sarbanes is part of the minority. He has a seat on the Banking Committee but gets most notice on Foreign Relations, where he is an intellectual leader of the now heavily outnumbered liberals wary of arms spending and of situations that could prove to be more Vietnams. He is of Greek descent, and he spent much time and effort maintaining for some years the embargo on arms sales to Turkey in retaliation for Turkey's invasion of Cyprus.

Sarbanes's seat is up in 1982, and he has been named to some right-wing hit lists. By the kind of conventional analysis that made sense until the Democrats lost the Senate, he should not be in any kind of trouble; he has not offended any significant segment of voters, his Democratic label is still an asset here rather than a liability as Jimmy Carter has proved, and there are no obvious prominent Republican candidates. But in early 1981 the New Right group, NCPAC, ran a series of TV ads against Sarbanes, and suddenly everyone began expecting a seriously contested race. One possible opponent is Republican Congresswoman Marjorie Holt.

Maryland has a rather odd history of Democratic presidential primaries. George Wallace nearly won in 1964, at which point the legislature abolished the primary; it was revived for 1972, when Wallace did win, the day after he was shot in a Prince Georges County shopping center. In 1976 this was the first primary Jerry Brown contested and, in alliance with such distinctly non-New Politics leaders as Marvin Mandel, he managed to beat Jimmy Carter here. Brown took that to mean that his philosophy could attract many votes; more likely it meant that voters, in the knowledge that Jimmy Carter would be nominated anyway, were willing to give some encouragement to a more interesting and entertaining candidate. In the 1980 Maryland primary, held after Brown had withdrawn his candidacy, he got only 3% of the vote, while Carter was beating Kennedy by 47%–38%.

The continuing shift of population to the suburbs — or at least some of the suburbs — has required considerable redistricting, but it is possible to adjust the lines with minimal damage to any of the state's incumbent House members. Possibly the Democratic legislature and governor would like to cause some damage to Marjorie Holt, the one Republican in the delegation, but, given the demographics and her strong base in Anne Arundel County, it will be difficult to do so.

Census Data   Pop. (1980 final) 4,216,446, up 7% in 1970s: 1.86% of U.S. total, 18th largest. Central city, 19%; suburban, 65%. Median 4-person family income, 1978, $23,461, 115% of U.S., 2d highest.

1979 Share of Federal Tax Burden $9,602,000,000; 2.13% of U.S. total, 13th largest.

1979 Share of Federal Outlays $11,649,092,000; 2.51% of U.S. total, 14th largest.

DOD	$3,375,777,000	10th	(3.18%)	HEW	$3,802,481,000	15th	(2.13%)
DOE	$494,918,000	8th	(4.21%)	ERDA	$24,989,000	19th	(0.92%)
HUD	$121,130,000	17th	(1.84%)	NASA	$394,648,000	4th	(8.44%)
VA	$305,646,000	27th	(1.47%)	DOT	$399,389,000	14th	(2.42%)
EPA	$124,507,000	15th	(2.34%)	DOC	$465,311,000	1st	(14.69%)
DOI	$48,561,000,000	27th	(0.87%)	USDA	$307,445,000	34th	(1.28%)

Economic Base   Finance, insurance, and real estate; primary metal industries, especially blast furnaces and steel mills; food and kindred products; agriculture, notably dairy products, broilers, cattle, and corn; electrical equipment and supplies, especially communication equipment; transportation equipment, especially motor vehicles and equipment and ship building and repairing; apparel and other textile products.

Political Lineup   Governor, Harry R. Hughes (D). Senators, Charles McC. Mathias, Jr, (R) and Paul S. Sarbanes (D). Representatives, 8 (7 D and 1 R); 8 in 1982. State Senate, 47 (40 D and 7 R); State House of Delegates, 141 (125 D and 16 R).

The Voters

Registration   2,064,883 Total. 1,431,339 D (69%); 482,955 R (23%); 160,582 other (8%).
Employment profile 1970   White collar, 41%. Blue collar, 44%. Service, 12%. Farm, 3%.
Ethnic groups   Black 1980, 23%. Hispanic 1980, 2%. Asian 1980, 2%. Total foreign stock 1970, 12%. Germany, 2%; Italy, USSR, UK, Poland, 1% each.

Presidential Vote

1980	Reagan (R)	680,606	(44%)
	Carter (D)	726,161	(47%)
	Anderson (I)	119,537	(8%)
1976	Ford (R)	672,661	(47%)
	Carter (D)	759,612	(53%)

1980 Democratic Presidential Primary			*1980 Republican Presidential Primary*		
Carter	226,528	(47%)	Reagan	80,557	(48%)
Kennedy	181,091	(38%)	Bush	68,389	(41%)
Three others	23,592	(5%)	Anderson	16,244	(10%)
Uncommitted	45,879	(10%)	One other	2,113	(1%)

SENATORS

Sen. Charles McC. Mathias, Jr, (R) Elected 1968, seat up 1986; b. July 24, 1922, Frederick; home, Frederick; Haverford Col., B.A. 1944, U. of Md., LL.B. 1949.

Career Navy, WWII; Asst. Atty. Gen. of Md., 1953–54; Frederick City Atty., 1954–59; Md. House of Delegates, 1959–60; U.S. House of Reps., 1961–69.

Offices 358 RSOB, 202-224-4654. Also 1616 Fed. Ofc. Bldg., 31 Hopkins Plaza, Baltimore 21201, 301-962-4850.

Committees *Foreign Relations* (6th). Subcommittees: International Economic Policy (Chairman); African Affairs; European Affairs.

Governmental Affairs (4th). Subcommittees: Permanent Subcommittee on Investigations; Governmental Efficiency and the District of Columbia (Chairman); Civil Service, Post Office, and General Services.

Judiciary (2d). Subcommittees: Criminal Law (Chairman); Juvenile Justice; Regulatory Reform.

Rules and Administration (Chairman).

Joint Committee on the Library (Vice-chairman).

Joint Committee on Printing (Chairman).

Group Ratings

	ADA	COPE	PC	LCV	CFA	RPN	NAB	NSI	NTU	ACA	ACU
1980	72	100	53	62	60	—	0	33	18	8	7
1979	63	79	52	—	62	—	—	—	18	15	0
1978	50	76	53	68	30	100	18	13	9	22	5

Key Votes

1) Draft Registn $	AGN	6) Fair Housng Cloture	FOR	11) Cut Socl Incr Defns	—
2) Ban $ to Nicrgua	FOR	7) Ban $ Rape Abortns	AGN	12) Income Tax Indexing	AGN
3) Dlay MX Missile	—	8) Cap on Food Stmp $	AGN	13) Lim Spdg 21% GNP	FOR
4) Nuclr Mortorium	AGN	9) New US Dep Edcatn	FOR	14) Incr Wndfll Prof Tax	FOR
5) Alaska Lands Bill	FOR	10) Cut OSHA Inspctns	AGN	15) Chryslr Loan Grntee	FOR

Election Results

1980 general	Charles McC. Mathias, Jr, (R)....	850,970	(66%)	($848,456)
	Edward T. Conroy (D)	435,118	(34%)	($162,966)
1980 primary	Charles McC. Mathias, Jr, (R)....	82,430	(55%)	
	John M. Brennan (R)	24,848	(17%)	($73,338)
	V. Dallas Merrell (R)	23,073	(13%)	($71,448)
	Three others (R)	19,622	(13%)	
1974 general	Charles McC. Mathias, Jr, (R)....	503,223	(57%)	($329,845)
	Barbara A. Mikulski (D)	374,563	(43%)	($74,311)

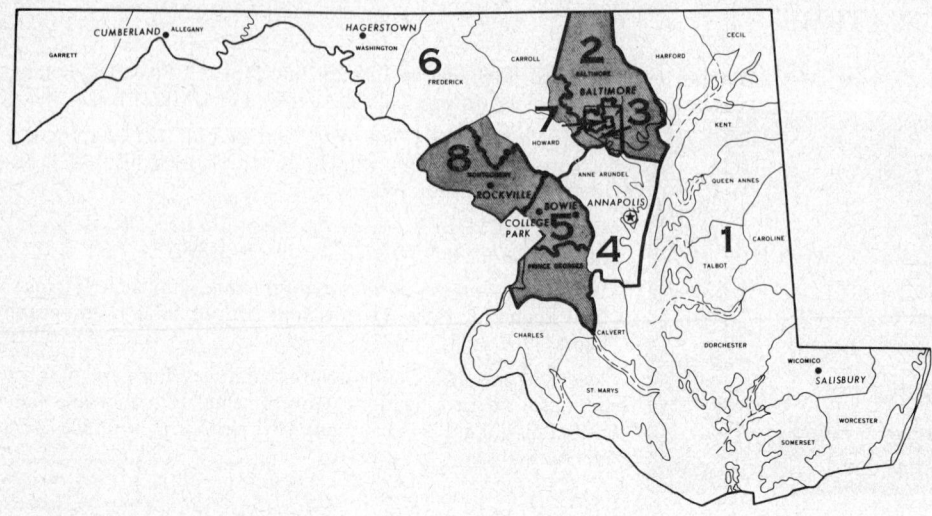

Sen. Paul S. Sarbanes (D) Elected 1976, seat up 1982; b. Feb. 3, 1933, Salisbury; home, Baltimore; Princeton U., A.B. 1954, Rhodes Scholar, Oxford U., B.A. 1957, Harvard U., LL.B., 1960.

Career Law Clerk to Judge Morris A. Soper, U.S. 4th Circuit Ct. of Appeals, 1960–61; Practicing atty., 1961–62, 1965–71; Admin. Asst. to Chmn. Walter W. Heller of the Pres. Cncl. of Econ. Advisers, 1962–63; Exec. Dir., Baltimore Charter Revision Comm., 1963–64; Md. House of Delegates, 1969–70; U.S. House of Reps., 1971–77.

Offices 2327 DSOB, 202-224-4524. Also 1518 Fed. Ofc. Bldg., Baltimore 21201, 301-962-4436, and 344 E. 33d St., Baltimore 21218, 301-962-4436.

Committees *Banking, Housing, and Urban Affairs* (5th). Subcommittees: Housing and Urban Affairs; Economic Policy; Securities.

Foreign Relations (4th). Subcommittees: International Economic Policy; European Affairs; Near Eastern and South Asian Affairs.

Joint Economic Committee (4th).

Group Ratings

	ADA	COPE	PC	LCV	CFA	RPN	NAB	NSI	NTU	ACA	ACU
1980	83	94	80	85	87	—	8	10	16	0	0
1979	79	100	83	—	86	—	—	—	17	15	6
1978	90	95	90	86	80	60	8	20	6	8	4

Key Votes

1) Draft Registn $	AGN	6) Fair Housng Cloture	FOR	11) Cut Socl Incr Defns	AGN
2) Ban $ to Nicrgua	FOR	7) Ban $ Rape Abortns	AGN	12) Income Tax Indexing	AGN
3) Dlay MX Missile	AGN	8) Cap on Food Stmp $	AGN	13) Lim Spdg 21% GNP	AGN
4) Nuclr Mortorium	FOR	9) New US Dep Edcatn	FOR	14) Incr Wndfll Prof Tax	FOR
5) Alaska Lands Bill	FOR	10) Cut OSHA Inspctns	AGN	15) Chryslr Loan Grntee	FOR

Election Results

1976 general	Paul S. Sarbanes (D)	772,101	(57%)	($891,533)
	J. Glenn Beall, Jr. (R)	530,439	(39%)	($572,016)
	Bruce Bradley (I)	62,750	(5%)	
1976 primary	Paul S. Sarbanes (D)	302,983	(55%)	
	Joseph D. Tydings (D)	191,875	(35%)	
	Six others (D)	52,896	(10%)	
1970 general	J. Glenn Beall, Jr. (R)	484,960	(51%)	
	Joseph D. Tydings (D)	460,422	(48%)	

GOVERNOR

Gov. Harry R. Hughes (D) Elected 1978, term expires Jan. 1983; b. Nov. 13, 1926, Easton; U. of Md., B.S. 1949, Geo. Wash. U., LL.B. 1952.

Career Navy Air Corps, WWII; Practicing atty.; Md. House of Delegates, 1955–58; Md. Senate, 1959–70, Major. Ldr., 1965–70; Chmn., Dem. Party of Md., 1969–70; Dir., Md. Dept. of Transportation, 1971–77.

Offices Executive Dept., State House, Annapolis 21404, 301-269-3591.

Election Results

1978 gen.	Harry R. Hughes (D)	718,328	(71%)
	J. Glenn Beall, Jr. (R)	293,635	(29%)
1978 prim.	Harry R. Hughes (D)	213,457	(37%)
	Blair Lee (D)	194,236	(34%)
	Ted Venetoulis (D)	140,486	(25%)
	One other (D)	25,200	(4%)
1974 gen.	Marvin Mandel (D)	602,648	(63%)
	Louise Gore (R)	346,449	(37%)

FIRST DISTRICT

Until the completion of the Chesapeake Bay Bridge in 1952, the Eastern Shore of Maryland was virtually cut off from the rest of the state. The "Eastern" refers to the east shore of the Chesapeake, a part of Maryland that remains almost a world unto itself—a region of southern drowsiness, chicken farms, and fishing villages. Its history has been told in James Michener's best-seller *Chesapeake*. Before the Civil War, the Eastern Shore was very much slaveholding country. Up through the 1960s, attachment to the mores of the South persisted; until 1964 Maryland had a public accommodations law that explicitly excluded the Eastern Shore counties. Mostly rural still, the economy of the region is buoyed by tourists, summer people, and the rich who have built big estates here.

The Eastern Shore bulks larger than its numbers in Maryland politics. It continues to produce important state legislators and has given the state two of its last four governors—J. Millard Tawes (1959–67) and the current incumbent Harry Hughes. But because its population has not grown much—slightly more than doubling between 1790 and 1970, although it has grown more rapidly since—the Shore is less and less important electorally. The 1st congressional district is, by reputation, the Eastern Shore district, although only 49% of its current population actually lives east of the Bay. The rest are found in two entirely separate areas. The first is Harford County, a northern extension of the Baltimore metropolitan area; the second is Charles, St. Mary's, and Calvert Counties south of Annapolis. The latter are where Lord Baltimore's Catholics first settled Maryland, and there is a substantial rural Catholic population there still. This part of the state is also known for having had until the 1960s the East Coast's last legal slot machines before the legalization of gambling in Atlantic City.

Both the Eastern Shore and the two western shore parts of the 1st have a deceptively high Democratic registration. Although Democrats still win local and state elections here, the district has been Republican in national elections pretty consistently for 30 years. Among white voters, the Republican preference is pretty strong; one-fifth of the district's residents are black, and they are almost unanimously Democratic. The 1st district has gone Democratic in House races only three times since World War II, and the most recent Democratic victory, in 1980, came under the most unusual of circumstances.

That was the defeat by Democrat Roy Dyson of incumbent Republican Congressman Robert Bauman. Until early October Bauman seemed headed for an easy victory over Dyson, whom he had beaten 54%–46% four years before. Bauman was one of the most vociferous and politically adept conservatives in Congress, a man who had mastered House rules and from his seat on the Rules Committee or his vigilance on the floor made life difficult and sometimes impossible for the Democratic leadership. Acerbic, aggressive, sternly righteous, occasionally capable of humor, Bauman by sheer force of character had made himself a force in the House; in his district, by hard work he had made safe a seat he had first won in a 1973 special election.

Then, on October 3, Bauman was charged in Washington with soliciting sex from a 16-year-old boy. There was shock in the 1st district and in the conservative movement as well. Bauman had been a supporter of "pro-family" causes and had ridiculed supporters of gay rights legislation; it now became apparent that he had been involved with great frequency in homosexual acts. Bauman pleaded the bottle; he said that the incident for which he was charged, which had occurred in March, had resulted from acute alcoholism, which he had overcome with the aid of counseling. And indeed Bauman was very active at the Republican National Convention and had the look of a man somehow liberated; he even showed considerable humor and forbearance. Unfortunately, there was little to corroborate Bauman's claim of alcoholism; he had not been known to drink to excess, and such conduct seemed uncharacteristic of him. Moreover, the *Washington Star* reported an FBI charge that a Maryland woman had threatened to accuse Bauman publicly of homosexuality unless he secured an honorable discharge of the woman's son from the Navy. Navy documents obtained by the FBI, according to the report, noted that the sailor had been discharged "at the request of the congressman." This charge was never confirmed, but if true it might persuade voters that Bauman had misused his office — although he denied that his official conduct had been in any way affected by his personal problems.

Conservative groups faced a quandary. The American Conservative Union, which Bauman had headed, supported him. But the Committee for the Survival of a Free Congress and its head, Paul Weyrich, called on him to resign. The latter were willing to repudiate a friend and ally because he had transgressed against what they had supposed were their shared and deeply felt principles. Bauman also lost support in his district, including that of the *Salisbury Times,* the local newspaper. Many of his other supporters were in consternation.

As it turned out, Bauman did not lose all his support, but he did lose enough to lose the election. Bauman carried the northern and central Eastern Shore counties, an area where he lived and which he had represented in the state Senate as well as in Congress. Dyson carried the southern Eastern Shore area around Salisbury and carried Charles, Calvert, and St. Mary's Counties by wide margins. With only 52% of the vote, and a victory in such unusual circumstances, Dyson cannot be considered the holder of a safe seat; and most likely the Republicans (and possibly even Bauman) will contest the seat seriously in 1982. Interestingly, House Republicans have engaged Bauman as a consultant; although they did not by and large conspicuously support him during the campaign, they still value his knowledge of parliamentary tactics.

Census Data   Pop. (1980 final) 609,837, up 25% in 1970s. Median family income, 1970, $8,295, 93% of U.S.

The Voters
   Employment profile 1970   White collar, 42%. Blue collar, 40%. Service, 13%. Farm, 5%.
   Ethnic groups   Black 1980, 17%. Hispanic 1980, 1%. Asian 1980, 1%. Total foreign stock 1970, 5%. Germany, 1%.

Presidential Vote	1980	Reagan (R)	104,227	(52%)
		Carter (D)	83,894	(42%)
		Anderson (I)	11,398	(6%)
	1976	Ford (R) `................	87,481	(51%)
		Carter (D)	85,106	(49%)

Rep. Roy Dyson (D) Elected 1980; b. Nov. 15, 1948, Great Mills; home, Great Mills; U. of Baltimore, 1970, U. of Md, 1971.

Career Legis. Asst., Agr.–Labor Subcom., U.S. House of Reps., 1973–74; Md. House of Del., 1974–80; Dem. nominee for U.S. House of Reps., 1976.

Offices 1020 LHOB, 202-225-5311. Also 20 E.Fulford Ave., Bel Air 21014, 301-838-2063; 1 Plaza E., Suite 703, Salisbury 21801, 301-742-9070; Waldorf Five Ctr., Suite 105, Rte. 5, Waldorf 20601, 301-645-4844.

Committees *Armed Services* (24th). Subcommittees: Military Installations and Facilities; Seapower and Strategic and Critical Materials.

Merchant Marine and Fisheries (21st). Subcommittees: Coast Guard and Navigation; Fisheries and Wildlife Conservation and the Environment; Oceanography.

Group Ratings and Key Votes: Newly Elected

Election Results

1980 general	Roy Dyson (D)	97,743	(52%)	($162,017)
	Robert E. Bauman (R)	91,143	(48%)	($358,926)
1980 primary	Roy Dyson (D)	26,585	(69%)	
	Donald M. DeArmon (D)	11,833	(31%)	
1978 general	Robert E. Bauman (R)	80,202	(64%)	($220,076)
	Joseph D. Quinn (D)	46,093	(36%)	($88,759)

SECOND DISTRICT

Baltimore County, as anyone who lives there will tell you, is entirely separate from the city of Baltimore. It is, by definition of the Census Bureau, totally suburban, but it is far from homogeneous. In the north of the county are verdant horse farms; just northwest of the city is the predominantly Jewish suburb of Pikesville; due north of Baltimore is WASPy, well-to-do Towson; east of Baltimore are the working-class suburbs of Dundalk and Sparrows Point. In one respect, however, Baltimore County is not diverse; while 55% of the residents of Baltimore city are black, just 8% of county residents are.

This is the place that gave us Spiro Agnew. Like most of Maryland, Baltimore County registers and, in local elections, usually votes Democratic. But in 1962 the Democrats had scandal problems and, to everyone's surprise, the Republican nominee for county executive — former zoning board member Agnew — actually won. Doubtful of reelection four years later, Agnew got his party's nomination for governor, which became worth something when Democrats chose the eccentric George P. ("your home is your castle") Mahoney as their nominee. From county executive to vice president, Agnew provided mediocre service and was rewarded with immediate advancement — and with a regular series of bribes and payoffs. Agnew's Democratic successor, Dale Anderson, committed the same crimes; unfortunate enough not to have been governor or vice president, he went to jail.

In Congress Baltimore County has been represented ever since by a professor whose honesty is above reproach. In 1962 the Democrats in the 2d congressional district, which then included all of Baltimore County, nominated Clarence D. Long, Ph.D., professor of economics at Johns Hopkins University, as their candidate for Congress. A blue ribbon candidate in a year of scandals, Long won that election and, through a series of redistrictings, has been reelected for every term up to the present. Currently the 2d district includes most of Baltimore County, including such diverse areas as Dundalk, Towson, and Pikesville, plus a small Jewish neighborhood in Baltimore city. The secret of Long's political success over the years has been close attention to his constituents. He returns home from Washington every night and throughout the year rides around in a trailer to meet constituents and handle the problems they bring to him.

In Washington many oldtime members of Congress regarded Long — universally referred to as "Doc" — with the suspicion men of the world traditionally have reserved for professors. Younger members, although they may respect him more, regard him as part of another generation. Legislatively, Long has in effect become a kind of specialist. Since 1977 he has chaired the Appropriations subcommittee on Foreign Operations, which in effect means that he passes on all bills for foreign aid. This is a burdensome job. It means steering the always unpopular foreign aid bill to passage, and it also means protecting it against various kinds of riders that congressmen of the right and the left, or this and that ethnic or national pressure group, want to attach. Long was one of the few members of Congress with a son who served in Vietnam; he switched from hawk to dove in 1970, and later in the decade became one of Capitol Hill's leading exponents of the importance of human rights in foreign policy. He has at various times, for example, favored cutting off aid to South Korea and Chile. In 1981, after a trip to El Salvador, he argued for cutting off military aid to that country, and missed getting his subcommittee to agree by only an 8–7 margin.

Long is not the most adept of legislators, but the foreign aid bills have gotten through in reasonably orderly fashion. In the 2d district, he had become accustomed to winning without serious opposition until, in 1980, he faced an opponent who made a real effort: Helen Delich Bentley, a newspaper reporter who became head of the Maritime Administration in the Nixon Administration. Bentley did not win, but she held Long to 57% of the vote — his lowest percentage since his first election. Redistricting will undoubtedly shuffle the district's boundaries, presumably in a manner maximally helpful to Democrats, without hurting the two Baltimore city Democrats, both of whom must add suburban territory. Whether Doc Long, who turns 74 in 1982, will seek another term is unclear.

Census Data   Pop. (1980 final) 521,905, up 6% in 1970s. Median family income, 1970, $12,140, 127% of U.S.

The Voters

Employment profile 1970   White collar, 59%. Blue collar, 32%. Service, 8%. Farm, 1%.
Ethnic groups   Black 1980, 9%. Hispanic 1980, 1%. Asian 1980, 1%. Total foreign stock 1970, 17%. USSR, 4%; Poland, Germany, Italy, 2% each; UK, 1%.

Presidential Vote

1980	Reagan (R)	103,501	(46%)
	Carter (D)	102,508	(45%)
	Anderson (I)	18,928	(5%)
1976	Ford (R)	109,176	(52%)
	Carter (D)	101,830	(48%)

Rep. Clarence D. Long (D) Elected 1962; b. Dec. 11, 1908, South Bend, Ind.; home, Ruxton; Wash. and Jeff. Col., B.A.; Princeton U., M.A., Ph.D.

Career   Navy, WWII; Prof. of Econ., Johns Hopkins U., 1946–64; Sr. Staff Mbr., Pres. Cncl. of Econ. Advisers, 1953–54, 1956–57; Acting Chmn., Md. Dem. St. Central Comm., 1961–62.

Offices   2405 RHOB, 202-225-3061. Also Rm. 200 P.O. Bldg., Towson 21204, 301-828-6616.

Committee   *Appropriations* (6th). Subcommittees: Foreign Operations (Chairman); Interior; Military Construction.

Group Ratings

	ADA	COPE	PC	LCV	CFA	RPN	NAB	NSI	NTU	ACA	ACU
1980	83	53	67	60	79	—	42	30	22	25	21
1979	74	65	63	70	48	—	—	—	30	36	29
1978	40	42	65	83	55	42	42	67	13	37	33

Key Votes

1) Draft Registn $	AGN	6) Fair Hsg DOJ Enfrc	FOR	11) Cut Socl Incr Dfns $	AGN
2) Ban $ to Nicrgua	AGN	7) Lim PAC Contrbtns	FOR	12) Hosptl Cost Controls	FOR
3) Dlay MX Missile	FOR	8) Cap on Food Stmp $	AGN	13) Gasln Ctrls & Allctns	AGN
4) Nuclr Mortorium	FOR	9) New US Dep Edcatn	AGN	14) Lim Wndfll Prof Tax	AGN
5) Alaska Lands Bill	FOR	10) Cut OSHA $	AGN	15) Chryslr Loan Grntee	AGN

Election Results

1980 general	Clarence D. Long (D)	121,017	(57%)	($153,619)
	Helen Delich Bentley (R)	89,961	(43%)	($252,871)
1980 primary	Clarence D. Long (D)	44,280	(57%)	
	Thomas B. Kernan (D)	30,335	(39%)	($79,507)
	One other (D)	3,217	(4%)	
1978 general	Clarence D. Long (D)	98,601	(66%)	($61,863)
	Malcolm M. McKnight (R)	49,886	(34%)	($30,777)

THIRD DISTRICT

At the beginning of the 1970s, Baltimore seemed to be a city in trouble. Like other cities farther up on the East Coast, its housing was aging, its population was declining, and its economy seemed to be sagging. But the 1970s have turned out to be good for Baltimore. Its diversified economy has not collapsed but rather has at least kept up with the effects of inflation. Both low-wage and high-wage jobs are being generated, and the city's downtown and some of its neighborhoods have been revitalized with new building that at the same time is respectful of the old. The city government under Mayor Donald Schaefer—quite possibly the best mayor in the country today—has managed to work well in the estimation of both black and white Baltimoreans, a fact that has made for civic peace at a time when the city's population is about equally divided between the two races. And, if Baltimore's population is declining, that is largely due to the lower number of children people are having these days and the aging of much of the white population—neither a development that suggests collapse of the city.

The 3d congressional district is centered on the east side of Baltimore, a place that has become a favorite of political sociologists. This is an area of ethnic communities—Irish, Italian, German, Greek, and especially Polish—that have kept their vitality even as, outwardly, they seem to have changed little in the 1960s and 1970s. The unique Baltimore row houses stand here as carefully maintained as ever, and the streets are spotless and still often filled with children. The district proceeds west from east Baltimore to the city's revitalized downtown and the old neighborhoods near the harbor, including the one that contains Francis Scott Key's Fort McHenry. Still farther west are the middle-class suburbs of Catonsville and Arbutus, where the row houses thin out to become detached homes. The 3d also proceeds north from east Baltimore to take in the largely Catholic neighborhoods in the northeastern part of the city, Johns Hopkins University, and a small chunk of suburban Baltimore County.

East Baltimore and the 3d district are traditional Democratic territory, although they turned against the party's national ticket in 1968 (41% for Humphrey) and 1972 (33% for McGovern). Locally, Democrats are always elected. Baltimore never really has had the kind of centrally structured political machines that some cities have; at most, there have been confederations of neighborhood organizations. In the 1970s this part of Baltimore produced a number of bright young politicians who came up not so much in rebellion against an organization as they did by creating new-styled organizations of their own supporters. One such was Paul Sarbanes, elected congressman here in 1970, by beating incumbent George Fallon, chairman of the House Public Works Committee; Sarbanes went on to the Senate in 1976. Another is Barbara Mikulski. She got her start in local politics in Polish east Baltimore, then was chosen as head of the national Democratic Party's commission on delegate selection at a time when women and big-city ethnics sympathetic with party reform were scarce. She performed creditably, with characteristic zest and rapid-fire humor. Although she has become a national figure, she remains close to her district, and she is still more comfortable in east Baltimore than she is in Georgetown—or, these days, on Capitol Hill.

For on policy issues Mikulski is very much at odds with the national trends. So, for that matter, is the 3d district, which gave Carter a majority of its votes in 1976 and increased his share to 55% in 1980 rather than decreasing it (probably because of an increased black population in some portions of the district). Mikulski was herself a strong Edward Kennedy supporter in the primaries, and she would have placed his name in nomination in New York had he not withdrawn from the race the morning before.

Like most central city districts, the 3d lost population in the 1970s, because of the smaller number of children living in the district's row houses. That means that the 3d will have to add on about 95,000 people in the suburbs; probably the district will not expand in the city, because that would hurt Parren Mitchell of the 7th district. The 3d could add on people in northern Anne Arundel County, which is somewhat more Republican an area than any now in the district; or it could take Democratic suburbs of Baltimore County directly to the east, a less likely course since it would make the suburban 2d district dangerously Republican.

Census Data Pop. (1980 final) 431,532, down 12% in 1970s. Median family income, 1970, $10,022, 105% of U.S.

The Voters

Employment profile 1970 White collar, 54%. Blue collar, 35%. Service, 11%. Farm, –%.

Ethnic groups Black 1980, 22%. Hispanic 1980, 2%. Asian 1980, 1%. Total foreign stock 1970, 15%. Germany, 3%; Italy, Poland, 2% each.

Presidential Vote

1980	Reagan (R)	59,589	(37%)
	Carter (D)	87,965	(55%)
	Anderson (I)	10,647	(7%)
1976	Ford (R)	78,442	(48%)
	Carter (D)	83,341	(52%)

Rep. Barbara A. Mikulski (D) Elected 1976; b. July 20, 1936, Baltimore; home, Baltimore; Mt. St. Agnes Col., Baltimore, B.A. 1958; U. of Md., M.S.W. 1965.

Career Admin., Baltimore Dept. of Soc. Svcs.; Caseworker; Teacher; Adjunct Prof., Loyola Col., 1972–76; Chwmn., Dem. Natl. Com. Commission on Delegate Selection and Party Structure, 1973; Dem. nominee for U.S. Senate, 1974.

Offices 407 CHOB, 202-225-4016. Also 1414 Fed. Bldg., Baltimore 21201, 301-962-4510.

Committees *Energy and Commerce* (14th). Subcommittees: Commerce, Transportation and Tourism; Health and the Environment.

Merchant Marine and Fisheries (12th). Subcommittees: Coast Guard and Navigation; Merchant Marine; Oceanography.

Group Ratings

	ADA	COPE	PC	LCV	CFA	RPN	NAB	NSI	NTU	ACA	ACU
1980	89	83	60	74	71	—	9	20	16	27	11
1979	84	100	70	81	74	—	—	—	22	12	8
1978	85	85	83	83	91	33	0	11	10	7	13

Key Votes

1) Draft Registn $	FOR	6) Fair Hsg DOJ Enfrc	FOR	11) Cut Socl Incr Dfns $	AGN
2) Ban $ to Nicrgua	AGN	7) Lim PAC Contrbtns	FOR	12) Hosptl Cost Controls	FOR
3) Dlay MX Missile	FOR	8) Cap on Food Stmp $	AGN	13) Gasln Ctrls & Allctns	FOR
4) Nuclr Mortorium	FOR	9) New US Dep Edcatn	AGN	14) Lim Wndfll Prof Tax	AGN
5) Alaska Lands Bill	FOR	10) Cut OSHA $	AGN	15) Chryslr Loan Grntee	FOR

Election Results

1980 general	Barbara A. Mikulski (D)	102,293	(76%)	($39,353)
	Russell T. Schaffer (R)	32,074	(24%)	($0)
1980 primary	Barbara A. Mikulski (D)	40,928	(75%)	
	Four others (D)	13,609	(25%)	
1978 general	Barbara A. Mikulski (D), unopp. .			($38,333)

FOURTH DISTRICT

The 4th congressional district of Maryland runs from the Baltimore city limits to the District of Columbia line. It includes all of Anne Arundel County (Annapolis and Baltimore suburbs) and part of Prince Georges County (near Washington). These are suburban areas that boomed in the 1960s and 1970s, with the population growing at the rate of about 100,000 in each decade. In the middle of the district is Annapolis, the quaint 18th-century town that contains Maryland's State House — the oldest Capitol in the nation still in use — and the United States Naval Academy. Moving inexorably over the low-lying hills and around the wide Chesapeake inlets toward Annapolis are the not-so-fashionable suburbs of Baltimore where many of the 4th district's residents live: Linthicum, Glen Burnie, Severna Park. On the other side of the district, near Washington, are the fast-growing community of Oxon Hill and the older working-class suburbs of Suitland and Camp Springs. Near Annapolis, but stuck in the middle of the rural countryside, is the new townhouse and shopping center suburb of Crofton, where Spiro Agnew first settled after his resignation as vice president.

This is a district where two-thirds of the voters register Democratic but which is sometimes carried by Republicans in close elections. Jimmy Carter won a 180-vote plurality here in 1976, and it was carried comfortably by Ronald Reagan in 1980. The only representative the district has ever had is a very solidly conservative Republican, Marjorie Holt. She was the Anne Arundel county clerk when the district was created in 1972 — the first time this county has ever so dominated a congressional district. She has been elected with ease against both liberal and conservative Democrats and is considered to have a good constituency service operation — vital in a district where many voters are federal employees.

In the heavily Democratic Congresses in which she first served, Mrs. Holt was anonymous. But in recent years she has become rather prominent. As a member of the Budget Committee, she has been the prime sponsor of Republican amendments to make deeper cuts in nonmilitary spending than the Democrats want. As member of Armed Services, she has tended to support higher military spending. She is not flashy, but she has a certain dogged persistence that one might expect of a woman who entered law school in 1946, a year that law schools were flooded with male veterans returning from war.

The 4th district now has a higher population than the state average and must lose some territory. One solution would be for some of the northern Anne Arundel suburbs to be absorbed in one of the Baltimore area districts and for the 4th to push south into Charles and Calvert Counties — fast-growing areas filled up in large parts with former residents of the 4th anyway. Mrs. Holt might resist this, since she would lose some of her Anne Arundel base, but as a Republican in a state where Democrats control the redistricting process, she may have little to say. Whatever happens, she is likely to win reelection easily.

Census Data Pop. (1980 final) 585,036, up 18% in 1970s. Median family income, 1970, $11,892, 125% of U.S.

The Voters

Employment profile 1970 White collar, 60%. Blue collar, 28%. Service, 11%. Farm, 1%.
Ethnic groups Black 1980, 22%. Hispanic 1980, 1%. Asian 1980, 2%. Total foreign stock 1970, 10%. Germany, 2%; Italy, UK, 1% each.

Presidential Vote

1980	Reagan (R)	94,648	(50%)
	Carter (D)	80,702	(42%)
	Anderson (I)	13,422	(7%)
1976	Ford (R)	86,352	(50%)
	Carter (D)	86,532	(50%)

Rep. Marjorie S. Holt (R) Elected 1972; b. Sept. 17, 1920, Birmingham, Ala.; home, Severna Park; Jacksonville U., B.A. 1946, U. of Fla., J.D. 1949.

Career Practicing atty., 1950–66; Anne Arundel Co. Supervisor of Elections, 1963–65; Anne Arundel Co. Clk. of Circuit Ct., 1966–72.

Offices 2434 RHOB, 202-225-8090. Also 95 Aquahart Rd., Glen Burnie 21061, 301-768-8050.

Committees *Armed Services* (6th). Subcommittees: Military Personnel and Compensation; Procurement and Military Nuclear Systems.

District of Columbia (4th). Subcommittees: Government Operations and Metropolitan Affairs; Judiciary and Education.

Group Ratings

	ADA	COPE	PC	LCV	CFA	RPN	NAB	NSI	NTU	ACA	ACU
1980	6	16	23	38	0	—	100	100	60	86	100
1979	0	16	18	7	7	—	—	—	63	100	97
1978	5	20	13	27	14	45	100	100	50	85	100

Key Votes

1) Draft Registn $	FOR	6) Fair Hsg DOJ Enfrc	AGN	11) Cut Socl Incr Dfns $	FOR
2) Ban $ to Nicrgua	—	7) Lim PAC Contrbtns	AGN	12) Hosptl Cost Controls	AGN
3) Dlay MX Missile	AGN	8) Cap on Food Stmp $	FOR	13) Gasln Ctrls & Allctns	AGN
4) Nuclr Mortorium	AGN	9) New US Dep Edcatn	AGN	14) Lim Wndfll Prof Tax	FOR
5) Alaska Lands Bill	AGN	10) Cut OSHA $	FOR	15) Chryslr Loan Grntee	—

Election Results

1980 general	Marjorie S. Holt (R)	120,985	(72%)	($147,170)
	James I Riley (D)	47,375	(28%)	($9,225)
1980 primary	Marjorie S. Holt (R), unopposed			
1978 general	Marjorie S. Holt (R)	71,374	(62%)	($107,607)
	Sue F. Ward (D)	43,663	(38%)	($37,478)

FIFTH DISTRICT

The 5th congressional district of Maryland includes most of Prince Georges County, the largest suburban county in the state. Situated just north and east of Washington, D.C., Prince Georges is somewhat less white collar and less affluent than neighboring Montgomery County, and it is regarded by Washington area residents as a kind of working-class community. Fortifying the image is the fact that fully 37% of Prince Georges's residents now are black. But compared to national averages, Prince Georges is very affluent indeed. The main reason is the high salaries and wages paid by the federal government. In 1970 38% of the work force here was employed by Uncle Sam — the highest such figure for any congressional district in the nation — and the figure today (not available from the census at this writing) may well be higher. The difference between Montgomery and Prince Georges is not only money but the way one regards one's status in society. Prince Georges has many comfortable and pleasant neighborhoods, but you will not find many people here who make the gossip columns. P.G. residents are the bureaucrats who keep all those offices in Washington and the suburbs filled, who keep the memos and agendas churning out of photocopy machines, regardless of who is president or who controls Congress.

Over the past 20 years the 5th has experienced major population change. In the 1960s the pattern was growth: the area's population shot up 69% in 10 years, making it one of the fastest-growing congressional districts in the nation. The rapid growth began here in the 1950s, when Metropolitan Washington's population burst outside the District line; the rush to the suburbs may have been accelerated but would have happened anyway, when the District's schools were integrated in 1955. This movement has been portrayed as white flight, but to a large extent it simply reflected the fact that the entire Washington area's population was increasing rapidly, and there simply wasn't room for any more people in the District. Young people with families sought neighborhoods with people in similar situations, as people always do, and many found them in Prince Georges; for a while P.G. had the nation's tenth largest school system.

Then, around the end of the 1960s, another population movement began. This time it was a movement of middle- and sometimes lower-income blacks out from the District into many of the closer-in suburbs in Prince Georges. Once again the major reason was the huge population gains of the whole metro area — during the 1960s it grew at a faster rate than any other major metro area except Houston. In the early 1970s, there was little sewer capacity in low-lying Prince Georges and hence little new construction; as a result, when blacks moved in, whites moved out, often to farther-out new suburban communities in Anne Arundel or Charles Counties. The 5th district was 16% black in 1970 and 35% in 1980.

The changing racial composition of the area has caused many of the same problems such population shifts cause in central cities. The political powers in Prince Georges County have traditionally been what one would expect in a rural semisouthern area where the Democratic Party is as likely to mean George Wallace as George McGovern. There have been more up-to-date Democratic machines, which definitely include blacks, although Democrats do not now control the county executive's office. Blacks have charged that P.G. police have harassed and beaten them, and such things have doubtless occurred. There was a major court busing order here, which resulted in a lot of school buses traveling around, some antibusing politicking by whites, and withdrawal of many whites from the county's public schools.

Since the 1974 election the district's representative in the House has been Gladys Spellman, a Democrat who got her start as a reformer in county government. Spellman's major assets have been hard work and constituency service — vital where there are so many federal employees. On the Post Office and Civil Service Committee she steadfastly opposed all laws that would make government employees more accountable. She is concerned about the image of government workers as well and has regularly issued a "beautiful bureaucrat" award.

Spellman was headed for easy reelection in late October 1980 when she suddenly collapsed with a heart attack. In a comatose state, she was reelected with 80% of the vote. When it became apparent her condition was not improving, Speaker O'Neill had the House declare the seat vacant, and Maryland set the primary for April 7 and the general election for May.

For a moment, the election to succeed her put Prince Georges County in the national spotlight. There was a crowded Democratic primary, and one of the leading candidates was Gladys Spellman's husband Reuben; if he had won, it would have been the first instance of a husband replacing his wife in Congress. But Spellman had little of his wife's political skill, and he was beaten by Steny Hoyer, a former state senator of great ambitions who as Blair Lee's candidate for lieutenant governor in the 1978 primary went down to defeat when Lee was upset by Harry Hughes. Hoyer was pressed hard in the general election by Republican Audrey Scott, the mayor of Bowie. She emphasized her support of Ronald Reagan's economic programs, while Hoyer was skeptical. The Democrat's victory was hailed by some as an endorsement of his party, but given the narrowness of the margin it seems likely he would have been defeated if the district did not have such a large black population. But having won, he does not seem to be a particularly inviting target for the Republicans in 1982, since by then he will have been providing constituency services to residents of the 5th district for more than 1½ years. Redistricting will likely add some territory, probably from southern Prince Georges County, to the district.

Census Data Pop. (1980 final) 469,179, down 3% in 1970s. Median family income, 1970, $12,286, 128% of U.S.

The Voters

Employment profile 1970 White collar, 67%. Blue collar, 23%. Service, 10%. Farm, -%.
Ethnic groups Black 1980, 35%. Hispanic 1980, 3%. Asian 1980, 3%. Total foreign stock 1970, 13%. Italy, 2%; Germany, UK, 1% each.

Presidential Vote

1980	Reagan (R)	55,344	(40%)
	Carter (D)	71,759	(51%)
	Anderson (I)	11,765	(8%)
1976	Ford (R)	58,086	(41%)
	Carter (D)	82,660	(59%)

Rep. Steny H. Hoyer (D) Elected May 19, 1981; b. June 14, 1939, New York City; home, Berkshire; U. of Md., B.S. 1963, Georgetown U., J.D. 1966.

Career Practicing atty., 1966–80; Md. Senate, 1966–79, Pres., 1975–79; Mbr., Md. Bd. for Higher Education, 1978–.

Office 1513 LHOB, 202-225-4131.

Committees *Banking, Finance and Urban Affairs* (26th).

Post Office and Civil Service (16th).

Group Ratings and Key Votes: Newly Elected

Election Results

5/19/81 spc. elct.	Steny H. Hoyer (D)	42,573	(55%)	
	Audrey Scott (R)	33,708	(44%)	
4/7/81 spc. prm.	Steny H. Hoyer (D)	14,127	(30%)	
	Reuben Spellman (D)	12,474	(27%)	
	Edward T. Conroy (D)	6,190	(13%)	
	Stewart Bainum, Jr. (D)	5,882	(13%)	
	Sue V. Mills (D)	4,392	(9%)	
	Thomas Patrick O'Reilly (D)	2,526	(5%)	
	Thirteen others (D)	964	(2%)	
1980 general	Gladys Noon Spellman (D)	106,035	(80%)	($96,646)
	Kevin R. Igoe (R)	25,693	(20%)	($24,333)
1980 primary	Gladys Noon Spellman (D)	33,244	(88%)	
	One other (D)	4,518	(12%)	
1978 general	Gladys Noon Spellman (D)	64,868	(77%)	($72,520)
	Saul J. Harris (R)	19,160	(23%)	($32,209)

SIXTH DISTRICT

West of Baltimore and Washington a series of gentle Maryland hills rise to the low mountains of the Catoctins and the Appalachian ridges. Here is a land known for its fertile valleys and its antique cities, e.g., Frederick, where Barbara Fritchie supposedly reared her old gray head. Also here are the small industrial cities of Hagerstown and, high in the mountains, Cumberland. The mountain folk and Pennsylvania Dutch who settled western Maryland left behind a Republican heritage, unusual in a state that is Democratic by tradition and custom. Nevertheless, a majority of the voters here, as in the rest of the state, are registered Democrats, simply because the Democratic primary is almost always where the action is. Come November, these "Democrats" are ready to vote Republican once again. In 1980, for example, Ronald Reagan carried western Maryland easily.

The 6th congressional district includes all of western Maryland and a portion of suburban Baltimore County. The only part of the 6th markedly out of step with the conservative, rural mores of the district is the much-heralded "new town" of Columbia in Howard County. It is a planned, integrated development that had 8,000 people in 1970 and 57,000 in 1980. Columbia is not as great a departure from other large suburban developments as it would like to think, but its new town atmosphere did have the politically significant effect of attracting a disproportionate number of voters with liberal cultural values who otherwise would probably live in Baltimore County.

Beverly Byron, the representative from this district, is the fourth Byron elected to Congress by western Maryland. Her husband's father and mother served in the 1940s, and her husband, Goodloe Byron, was congressman from the 1970 election until his death in October 1978. Mrs. Byron was substituted as the Democratic candidate, although another Democrat, Dan Rupli, had used environmental issues to make strong showings against the late congressman in the 1976 and 1978 primaries. The Republican candidate lived in the hotel that was the model for the Broadway and television show, *The Hot L Baltimore,* and had been jailed for assaulting a woman bus driver; when he heard that Byron had died, he went to the Capitol and demanded to be seated.

With that kind of opposition, Mrs. Byron was elected easily. She made a record that leaned heavily toward the conservative side, as had her husband's; but she did support the Alaska lands bill, a major priority for environmentalists, and perhaps for that reason she did not get opposition from Rupli or anyone but nuisance candidates in the Democratic primary. In the general election, against a Republican who made a real effort, Mrs. Byron won 70% of the vote, carrying even her opponent's usually Republican county. She can be considered now to have a safe seat.

Census Data Pop. (1980 final) 631,322, up 28% in 1970s. Median family income, 1970, $9,749, 102% of U.S.

The Voters

Employment profile 1970 White collar, 46%. Blue collar, 39%. Service, 11%. Farm, 4%.
Ethnic groups Black 1980, 6%. Hispanic 1980, 1%. Asian 1980, 1%. Total foreign stock 1970, 5%.

Presidential Vote

1980	Reagan (R)	128,716	(55%)
	Carter (D)	86,833	(37%)
	Anderson (I)	17,471	(7%)
1976	Ford (R)	112,380	(55%)
	Carter (D)	92,682	(45%)

Rep. Beverly B. Byron (D) Elected 1978; b. July 27, 1932, Baltimore; home, Frederick; Hood Col., 1963–64.

Career Campaign Asst., U.S. Rep. Goodloe E. Byron.

Offices 1216 LHOB, 202-225-2721. Also Fredericktown Mall, Frederick 21701, 301-662-8622.

Committees Armed Services (17th). Subcommittees: Military Personnel and Compensation; Procurement and Military Nuclear Systems.

Interior and Insular Affairs (24th). Subcommittees: Mines and Mining; Oversight and Investigations; Public Lands and National Parks.

Select Committee on Aging (18th). Subcommittee: Housing and Consumer Interests.

Group Ratings

	ADA	COPE	PC	LCV	CFA	RPN	NAB	NSI	NTU	ACA	ACU
1980	22	32	30	67	14	—	73	78	41	65	63
1979	16	45	28	41	12	—	—	—	42	58	71

Key Votes

1) Draft Registn $	FOR	6) Fair Hsg DOJ Enfrc	AGN	11) Cut Socl Incr Dfns $	FOR
2) Ban $ to Nicrgua	FOR	7) Lim PAC Contrbtns	AGN	12) Hosptl Cost Controls	AGN
3) Dlay MX Missile	AGN	8) Cap on Food Stmp $	AGN	13) Gasln Ctrls & Allctns	AGN
4) Nuclr Mortorium	AGN	9) New US Dep Edcatn	AGN	14) Lim Wndfll Prof Tax	AGN
5) Alaska Lands Bill	FOR	10) Cut OSHA $	AGN	15) Chryslr Loan Grntee	FOR

Election Results

1980 general	Beverly B. Byron (D)	146,101	(70%)	($163,168)
	Raymond E. Beck (R)	62,913	(30%)	($73,203)
1980 primary	Beverly B. Byron (D)	38,842	(71%)	
	Five others (D)	15,827	(29%)	
1978 general	Beverly B. Byron (D)	126,196	(90%)	($1,542)
	Melvin Perkins (R)	14,545	(10%)	

SEVENTH DISTRICT

Baltimore has always had a large black community. In 1960, 35% of its citizens were black; in 1970, 46%; in 1980, 55%. Yet blacks have never been the kind of force in Baltimore politics that they have been in such diverse cities as Cleveland, Atlanta, and Oakland. One reason may be Baltimore's accommodating political tradition; oldtime white Democrats here have always dealt with their black counterparts across town, and mutual benefits could be arranged. "Walking-around money" has always been an important factor in Baltimore's black precincts on election days, even though it is no longer clear what it buys; but one thing it does do is to prevent a black-power sort of politics. The major reason there is no black mayor in this black-majority city is the performance of Mayor Donald Schaefer, who lives in a black neighborhood himself and has such strong support from blacks that when he was up for re-election in 1979 no black filed against him. Schaefer may be part of the wave of the future — a group of mayors of both races who hold their offices regardless of the complexion of their constituents, solely because the voters think they are doing a good job. There is a lack of urgency in black politics, a lack of the sense that things will be disastrous if they do not organize and elect black officeholders. So blacks have simply declined to take political control of Baltimore.

They have, however, got hold of Maryland's 7th congressional district, which contains almost all of Baltimore's predominantly black neighborhoods, including in 1980 77% of the city's blacks and 24% of its whites. The incumbent congressman, Parren Mitchell, was first elected in 1970 when he beat a white incumbent in the primary by exactly 38 votes; the district then included part of the Baltimore suburbs and had a large Jewish population. Mitchell had one more tough race, a 1972 primary challenge from another black. After that he has won easily.

Mitchell began his career in Congress technically as a political novice. He had been a professor at Morgan State University and had not held public office before. But he is from an important political family. His older brother, Clarence Mitchell, was for many years the canny Washington lobbyist for the NAACP; his nephew served in the Maryland Senate. Parren Mitchell became the first black member of the Banking Committee, which handles housing programs; and initially he was expected to concentrate in that field. But housing was not a growth federal field in the 1970s (although Baltimore has some innovative programs). Mitchell used to chair a subcommittee on domestic and monetary policy. In practice this means overseeing the work of the Federal Reserve and absorbing various theories of monetarism and disintermediation, and by all accounts Mitchell has performed creditably in that capacity.

Now he is chairman of the Small Business Committee, a body that by virtue of its name and jurisdiction is very popular among congressmen but which in fact has a very constricted legislative jurisdiction. Mostly it deals with the Small Business Administration, a body that gives below-market-interest-rate loans to some small businesses; the whole concept of the SBA has been questioned by high officials in the Reagan Administration, who argue that it simply sops up capital, wastes some, and gives the rest to enterprises that are not necessarily creditworthy. Mitchell, who comes from a community where people who deemed themselves creditworthy were often unable to obtain commercial financing because of their race, presumably has different ideas.

Census Data   Pop. (1980 final) 420,492, down 14% in 1970s. Median family income, 1970, $7,841, 82% of U.S.

The Voters

Employment profile 1970 White collar, 37%. Blue collar, 40%. Service, 23%. Farm, –%.
Ethnic groups Black 1980, 79%. Hispanic 1980, 1%. Total foreign stock 1970, 5%.

Presidential Vote

1980	Reagan (R)	14,103	(11%)
	Carter (D)	111,554	(85%)
	Anderson (I)	4,232	(3%)
1976	Ford (R)	22,795	(18%)
	Carter (D)	101,341	(82%)

Rep. Parren J. Mitchell (D) Elected 1970; b. Apr. 29, 1922, Baltimore; home, Baltimore; Morgan St. Col., B.A. 1950, U. of Md., M.A. 1952, U. of Conn., 1960.

Career Army, WWII; Prof. and Asst. Dir. of the Urban Studies Institute, Morgan St. Col.; Exec. Secy., Md. Comm. on Interracial Problems and Relations, 1963–65; Exec. Dir., Baltimore Community Action Agcy, 1965–68.

Offices 2367 RHOB, 202-225-4741. Also Rm. 1018 Geo. Fallon Fed. Ofc. Bldg., 31 Hopkins Plaza, Baltimore 21201, 301-962-3223.

Committees *Banking, Finance and Urban Affairs* (6th). Subcommittees: Domestic Monetary Policy; General Oversight and Renegotiation; Housing and Community Development.

Small Business (Chairman). Subcommittee: SBA and SBIC Authority, Minority Enterprise and General Small Business Problems (Chairman).

Joint Economic Committee (5th). Subcommittees: Investment, Jobs and Prices; Trade, Productivity and Economic Growth.

Group Ratings

	ADA	COPE	PC	LCV	CFA	RPN	NAB	NSI	NTU	ACA	ACU
1980	89	89	76	84	93	—	0	11	20	9	11
1979	100	100	88	97	89	—	—	—	24	0	3
1978	90	95	93	75	91	40	0	10	24	8	8

Key Votes

1) Draft Registn $	AGN	6) Fair Hsg DOJ Enfrc	FOR	11) Cut Socl Incr Dfns $	AGN
2) Ban $ to Nicrgua	AGN	7) Lim PAC Contrbtns	FOR	12) Hosptl Cost Controls	FOR
3) Dlay MX Missile	FOR	8) Cap on Food Stmp $	AGN	13) Gasln Ctrls & Allctns	FOR
4) Nuclr Mortorium	FOR	9) New US Dep Edcatn	AGN	14) Lim Wndfll Prof Tax	AGN
5) Alaska Lands Bill	FOR	10) Cut OSHA $	AGN	15) Chryslr Loan Grntee	FOR

Election Results

1980 general	Parren J. Mitchell (D)	97,104	(88%)	($104,567)
	Victor Clark, Jr. (R)	12,650	(12%)	($0)
1980 primary	Parren J. Mitchell (D)	33,747	(81%)	
	One other (D)	7,681	(19%)	
1978 general	Parren J. Mitchell (D)	51,996	(89%)	($93,693)
	Debra Hanania Freeman (I)	6,626	(11%)	($7,052)

EIGHTH DISTRICT

By most measures one cares to use, the 8th congressional district of Maryland has been the richest in the nation. It includes just about all of Maryland's Montgomery County—the hunk of valuable suburban and county real estate immediately northeast of Washington, D.C. Like Prince Georges County to the east, Montgomery experienced vast population increases in the 1950s and 1960s; unlike Prince Georges, the increase continued, at least in certain outlying parts of the county, in the 1970s. The migrants here are of a rather different sort. They tend to have higher incomes and more education, and they are more likely to hold white collar, professional, or executive jobs. The typical resident of the 8th is a high-ranking GS-15 civil servant or perhaps a lawyer in private practice; a person as likely as not to have a graduate school degree, and one who professes a vaguely liberal sort of politics. Montgomery voters are usually willing to go with Democrats, but their favorite kind of candidate has been the liberal Republican who cares deeply about the political process, like Senator Charles Mathias.

In 1980, faced with the unpalatable alternatives of a conservative Republican, a Democrat who seemed simply incompetent to many of these insiders, and an Independent with appeal on the issues but no chance of winning, the 8th district gave no one a majority; although it is significant to note that Ronald Reagan did have a 47%–40% edge. Evidently these canny voters do not believe he is going to dismantle the federal government that in most cases has been so good to them. Montgomery County was never characterized by the radical chic; what shows is that Ronald Reagan's Republicanism has become respectable for these League of Women Voters liberals.

That may end up signaling a kind of revolution in Montgomery County politics. In the 1960–76 period, Montgomery voted for Democrats in all close presidential elections but consistently elected liberal Republican congressmen: first Mathias, then Gilbert Gude, and in 1976 Newton Steers. Yet now Montgomery gives a plurality to a conservative Republican for president and—against the national trend—elects a Democrat to the House. Perhaps the same Montgomery liberals who calculated that they needed a Republican check on Democratic presidents now calculate that they need a Democratic check on a Republican president.

Part of the reason for that shift is the hard work and competence of the new congressman, Michael Barnes. He had served on the Maryland public service commission and on Senator Edmund Muskie's staff, and he got it into his head that he could challenge and defeat Newton Steers in 1978. The odds seemed forbidding: incumbents are usually reelected, and Steers was not really out of line with the district on issues. But Steers is somewhat more brash than his Republican predecessors, and Barnes simply worked harder. He was able to win with 51% in 1978. In 1980 there was a rematch, and Steers was determined not to be outcampaigned. But Barnes had been working the district carefully and thoughtfully, providing constituency services well and also taking the trouble to meet with and listen to constituents constantly. It paid off: Barnes won reelection with 59% in a year when Democrats with supposedly safe seats were losing all over the country.

Shortly afterward, he also won a subcommittee chair that may turn out to be one of the most important posts in the 97th Congress. This was the chairmanship of the Inter-American Affairs Subcommittee of Foreign Affairs. The incumbent, Gus Yatron of Pennsylvania, was voted out by committee Democrats for being too conservative on human rights issues and for being inactive. Barnes had a strong background in Latin American affairs and a commitment to human rights stances the majority of committee Democrats—although not necessarily a majority of the House—supports. He beat Dan Mica of Florida, although Mica, by virtue of a coin toss, is technically more senior. Almost as soon as Barnes won the position, the Reagan Administration began pushing for military aid for El Salvador, a policy about which Barnes had doubts. Suddenly this product of what Alan Ehrenhalt of *Congressional Quarterly* called the juniority system was the major Democratic spokesman on an important area of national policy. That stature, plus his continued hard work in Montgomery County, should leave him in good shape for the 1982 election.

Census Data   Pop. (1980 final) 547,176, up 11% in 1970s. Median family income, 1970, $17,102, 178% of U.S.

The Voters

   Employment profile 1970   White collar, 79%. Blue collar, 13%. Service, 7%. Farm, 1%.
   Ethnic groups   Black 1980, 9%. Hispanic 1980, 4%. Asian 1980, 4%. Total foreign stock 1970, 21%. USSR, 3%; Germany, UK, 2% each; Canada, Poland, Italy, 1% each.

Presidential Vote

1980	Reagan (R)	120,478	(47%)
	Carter (D)	100,946	(40%)
	Anderson (I)	31,674	(12%)
1976	Ford (R)	117,949	(48%)
	Carter (D)	126,116	(52%)

Rep. Michael D. Barnes (D) Elected 1978; b. Sept. 3, 1943, Washington, D.C.; home, Kensington; U. of N.C., B.A. 1965, Inst. of Higher Internatl. Studies, Geneva, Switz., 1965–66, Geo. Wash. U., J.D. 1972.

Career Spec. Asst. to U.S. Sen. Edmund S. Muskie of Maine, 1970–72; Practicing atty., 1972– ; Md. Pub. Svc. Comm., 1975–78; Vice-Chmn., Wash. Metro Area Transit Comm., 1976–78.

Office 1607 LHOB, 202-225-5341.

Committees *District of Columbia* (7th). Subcommittee: Government Operations and Metropolitan Affairs; Judiciary and Education.

Foreign Affairs (13th). Subcommittees: Human Rights and International Organizations; Inter-American Affairs (Chairman).

Group Ratings

	ADA	COPE	PC	LCV	CFA	RPN	NAB	NSI	NTU	ACA	ACU
1980	94	82	77	91	86	—	0	0	17	13	6
1979	89	95	90	95	89	—	—	—	17	8	13

Key Votes

1) Draft Registn $	AGN	6) Fair Hsg DOJ Enfrc	FOR	11) Cut Socl Incr Dfns $	AGN
2) Ban $ to Nicrgua	AGN	7) Lim PAC Contrbtns	FOR	12) Hosptl Cost Controls	FOR
3) Dlay MX Missile	FOR	8) Cap on Food Stmp $	AGN	13) Gasln Ctrls & Allctns	FOR
4) Nuclr Mortorium	FOR	9) New US Dep Edcatn	AGN	14) Lim Wndfll Prof Tax	AGN
5) Alaska Lands Bill	FOR	10) Cut OSHA $	AGN	15) Chryslr Loan Grntee	AGN

Election Results

1980 general	Michael D. Barnes (D)	148,301	(59%)	($349,924)
	Newton I. Steers, Jr. (R)	101,659	(41%)	($565,952)
1980 primary	Michael D. Barnes (D), unopposed			
1978 general	Michael D. Barnes (D)	81,851	(51%)	($134,588)
	Newton I. Steers, Jr. (R)	77,807	(49%)	($162,980)

MASSACHUSETTS

Massachusetts politics is full of seeming paradoxes. This is the state that gives us Edward Kennedy, the leading spokesman for what is known as liberalism today, but in 1980 it went for Ronald Reagan and in 1978 elected as its governor a man whose campaign manager said he won the primary by putting all the hate groups in a cauldron and letting them boil. It is the only state that went for dovish George McGovern in 1972, but it is also the only state besides New York to go for hawkish Henry Jackson in the 1976 presidential primary. Such paradoxes cannot be explained on the basis of the recent results alone. To resolve them it is necessary to go back into history, to see how Massachusetts politics developed.

The crucial event that structured electoral politics here was not, as it was in so many states, the Civil War — it was instead the Irish potato famine of the 1840s. That blight forced hundreds of thousands of Irish to immigrate to the United States, to the point where there are far more people of Irish descent here than in Ireland today. Nowhere did these new Americans make a greater impact than in Boston and Massachusetts. They found a thriving Yankee economic and political culture whose hostility was symbolized by "No Irish need apply" signs. And ever since, much of politics in Massachusetts has been a struggle between Yankee and Irish for domination.

That ethnic conflict was very much reflected in party politics. The Yankees of the 1840s, not long removed from Federalism, were solid Whigs, who would later become one of the bulwarks of the Republican Party when it was formed a decade later. The Whigs and Republicans had policies that appealed to the Yankees: promotion of public works to help business (the Yankees were busy building roads and textile mills), protective tariffs, sympathy for suitably distant oppressed people such as the blacks of the South and for such uplifting social movements as temperance. The Irish knew from the beginning that they were not going to get very far in the party of the Yankees, and they found the Democrats of the 19th century more congenial. We now think of the Democrats as a party promoting government action, but in those days the Democracy represented laissez-faire — which was fine with the Irish. They came from a place where the government was the enemy; they didn't want the government spending money to help the rich, they didn't want it to regulate immigration, they didn't want it to promote the cause of blacks who might compete with them in the labor market, and they didn't want it to prohibit liquor. They were people familiar with competing hierarchies — the hierarchy of the hated English lords and the hierarchy of their own, often suppressed, Roman Catholic Church. The Democratic Party, with its ward organizations and rituals, seemed like a sympathetic hierarchy. So the Irish went into politics, determined to beat the Protestants.

And that is pretty much the story of a century of Massachusetts politics. Throughout, the Irish share of the population continually rose — and there were other immigrants, who usually became Democrats, too — while the Yankee share of the population declined. Yankees had smaller families, they moved out west; the Irish stayed put and eventually ruled as Massachusetts very slowly moved from being one of our most Republican states to becoming one of our most Democratic. The state gave Republicans majorities in every presidential election from the Civil War to 1924; in 1928, when the Democrats nominated an Irish Catholic, Al Smith, Massachusetts went Democratic. In 1918 the state had elected a Democratic senator, but Republicans won as many congressional seats as Democrats in the years to come. In the 1920s, 1930s, 1940s, and 1950s, a pretty close balance existed between Yankee Republicans and Irish Democrats; the Democrats were making headway, but the Republicans fielded candidates who were smarter or more honest. The state's preference in presidential elections shifted very little in this period. While the nation oscillated between Roosevelt and Eisenhower, in Massachusetts it was the balance between Yankee and Irish, not the programs of the New Deal or the popularity of individual candidates that usually made the difference.

Thus political conflict in Massachusetts never really fell into the liberal vs. conservative lines of the New Deal. The Republicans here retained a kind of Yankee interventionism, strongly favoring civil rights, pushing an anti-isolationist foreign policy, opposing the excesses of Joe McCarthy. Massachusetts Democrats, on the other hand, like the Republic of Ireland, were hostile to the British and cheered Joe McCarthy after World War II as one of their own. (Joseph Kennedy used to invite him to Hyannisport.) The Republicans promised to root out corruption. The Democrats had the more complacent attitude typical of an ethnic group only recently able to aspire to public office.

In the 1960s and 1970s, for the first time in Massachusetts history, the Irish Democrats and the Yankee Republicans began moving in the same direction. The key figure is Senator Edward Kennedy. More even than his brother the president, he has by personal example helped to shape attitudes in the state; after all, he has been the leading public figure here for nearly 20 years. On a whole series of issues, Kennedy as well as the national Democratic Party took positions that in Massachusetts had been more typical of interventionist Yankees than laissez-faire Irish. Kennedy strongly supported civil rights, he favored helping people who were impoverished or starving, he opposed the war in Vietnam, he stood against the excesses of Watergate. He was also indubitably against corruption. Kennedy's stands made such positions respectable, even mandatory, among Democratic politicians and among the Catholic majority of voters in Massachusetts. And his stands led the Yankee minority to vote more and more often for the Democratic Party. It was no accident then, and not simply the result of local recession, that Massachusetts voted for McGovern in 1972. It represented a kind of reconciliation here, which saw the upper-crust Yankee suburb of Lincoln and the lower-income Irish city of Somerville going for the same candidate.

But that does not mean that Yankee and Irish conflicts have ended. On the contrary, they emerged in classic form in the 1978 gubernatorial election. The incumbent governor, Michael Dukakis, had been elected in 1974 as a kind of cerebral liberal. He had attracted attention early by his personal austerity (riding to work on the subway) and by cutting the state budget drastically. His actions probably had majority support, but nobody really felt he was their man. The liberals felt betrayed by the budget cuts, while Irish and other ethnics found him cold and unwilling to wheel and deal politically. Almost everyone was unhappy when he raised taxes after promising not to do so. As a result, Dukakis was more vulnerable in the Democratic primary than he supposed, and he was beaten by one Edward King.

If Ted Kennedy represents the liberal and humanitarian side of Massachusetts Irish politics, King represents the conservative and resentful side. Kennedy the millionaire makes a point of flying tourist on scheduled airlines; King, the self-made man, loves expense account living. In his primary campaign King emphasized his support of capital punishment, mandatory prison sentences for drug dealers, raising the drinking age to 21, building nuclear power plants, downplaying environmental concerns, and spurring economic growth. King was opposed by a Republican who was a quintessential Yankee: Francis Hatch, a rich North Shore state legislator, who inherited liberal support when Dukakis lost the primary. House Speaker Tip O'Neill tried to persuade King to downplay his cultural issues and to emphasize that he stood in the Democratic economic tradition of helping the little guy. O'Neill had a special interest in the election: his son, Thomas O'Neill III, was the incumbent lieutenant governor, who was tied to King's ticket and would lose if King did. King ended up prevailing by a small margin. Examination of the election returns shows that the outcome was nothing other than the standard triumph of Irish over Yankee. Hatch made big gains in university towns and well-to-do areas where McGovern had done well, but he could not crack the solidly Catholic middle-class suburbs of Boston. The result was not so much a repudiation of liberalism in Massachusetts as it was an assertion of the commonwealth's traditional ethnic politics.

Nevertheless, King's administration has made a difference in the way this state is governed. In the early 1970s, under liberal Republican Governor Francis Sargent, government had grown like wildfire in Massachusetts, and its taxes became the highest in the nation. King vowed to change that. He acted clumsily, made enemies, made bad appointments, on occasion looked foolish — but to some extent he succeeded in what he set out to do. State taxes were lowered, and in a referendum called Proposition 2½ voters put a cap on local property taxes. King's policies seemed to bear fruit. In 1980 and in early 1981 Massachusetts had a much lower rate of unemployment and a much more buoyant economy than other northeastern states, while in the middle 1970s it had lagged behind. Supply-side economists claimed that lower taxes had stimulated entrepreneurial energy and economic growth. Others said that Massachusetts economy had finally shed its heritage of low-wage jobs to be one based on high wages and high technology growth — a development having nothing to do with King.

King is sure to have plenty of opposition in 1982. Most politically active Democrats consider him anathema. Tom O'Neill is likely to be a candidate, and Michael Dukakis might run again. The Republicans will probably also try to field a significant candidate. The economic condition of the state, and the condition of its less fortunate citizens in the Reagan years, are sure to be central subjects in the campaign. But the chances are that it will come down, in the end, to something like the old battle of Yankee versus Irish.

That is the prospect as well for the 1982 Senate race, in which Edward Kennedy will run for his seat again. Some speculate that Kennedy may be vulnerable, and he has been targeted by New Right groups. But there is no reason to believe that he can be beaten in Massachusetts. He won the 1980 presidential primary here by an impressive margin, even when he was losing in most other states. President Carter's weak Massachusetts showing — his 42% was 12% below George McGovern's percentage — does not tell us much about Kennedy's appeal. Kennedy has consistently been winning most of the 15% of the votes that went to John Anderson and even some of the 42% that went for his fellow Irishman, Ronald Reagan.

Kennedy is still regarded by most Massachusetts voters as a member of a kind of royal family. He was elected originally at age 30, when he had no substantial credentials of his own. He was reelected by a substantial majority here one year after the Chappaquiddick accident. Even today pictures of his brother still hang on walls in living rooms and bars all over Massachusetts. Kennedy also has substantial accomplishments in the Senate, from the work he did in leading revision of the immigration bills in 1965 to his work, unlikely to meet success soon, seeking a national health care program.

Kennedy's record, indeed, would be a formidable asset to any senator. Considered by many a doctrinaire liberal, he was nonetheless the first politician seriously to press for airline deregulation, and despite the opposition of most of the airlines and such well-positioned committee chairmen as Howard Cannon of Nevada, Kennedy (allied on the issue with the Carter Administration) was successful. He also obtained some measure of success deregulating the trucking industry. As chairman of the Senate Judiciary Committee in 1979 and 1980, he worked with his Republican counterpart (and, although no one knew it at the time, successor) Strom Thurmond to reform the federal criminal code. This is all highly technical business and Edward Kennedy, who has the reputation in some quarters as a playboy, is in fact a very hard worker who masters details and outargues the opposition. He could not in any other way have achieved the legislative successes he has.

In 1981, with the Democrats in the minority, Kennedy abandoned his top position on Judiciary to become ranking minority member of the Labor and Public Welfare Committee. He evidently felt that Labor is where many of the important fights of the next two years were to be fought. Labor has jurisdiction over many of the social programs Kennedy wants to keep and Reagan wants to kill; over some difficult cultural issues; and over the labor laws, about which organized labor is very worried indeed. Kennedy, who spent much of his earlier Senate career in careful deference to his elders, now finds that after 18 years he is the ranking minority member on a committee chaired by Orrin Hatch of Utah, who was first elected to the Senate in 1976. Kennedy's switch from concentrating on Judiciary to concentrating on Labor relieves him from a position where his stands on controversial issues — constitutional amendments on abortion and balancing the budget, busing, capital punishment — were either unpopular or politically dangerous. But it also suggests that he is gambling that the positions he took on economic issues that proved to be so unhelpful in his 1980 presidential campaign will be more popular in the future.

The 1980 campaign must have been a profoundly unnerving experience for Kennedy, a man who many have assumed will just naturally be president. He turned down nominations he probably could have had in 1968 and 1972; he refused to run, and made that refusal stick, in 1976. For a while, even while the polls showed him way ahead of President Carter and the Republicans, it looked as if he would not run in 1980. Then, during the summer of 1979, he evidently changed his mind. Carter's much publicized Camp David domestic energy summit and his malaise speech both fell flat. The president himself had adopted a truculent attitude; if Kennedy runs, he made sure reporters heard, "I'll whip his ass," even though Kennedy, one of the best-known figures in American politics, was way ahead in the polls at the time.

Why did Kennedy's standing decline so suddenly and disastrously in the fall of 1979? First of all, there was what some called the character factor and others called Chappaquiddick. Although the incident was known to everyone for ten years before Kennedy ran, the impact undoubtedly increased when he entered the race. Stories were circulating depicting Kennedy as some kind of roue, although he is a more devoted family man than many of those politicians who are always talking about family values; of all senators with adolescent children,

Kennedy probably spends more time with his own. A second factor was his halting performance in the Roger Mudd interview, where he seemed unable to articulate any rationale for running. Third, there was the Iran crisis. Kennedy had the misfortune to announce his candidacy (as did Jerry Brown) the week the hostages were seized in Tehran. In early December he made statements criticizing the Shah for "running one of the most violent regimes in the history of mankind" and the administration for letting the Shah into the United States. Although many voters agreed with his assessments, even more felt that this was not an appropriate time to say things that might suggest that the Iranian terrorists had a legitimate reason for their acts. Kennedy was undoubtedly hurt by the tendency of voters to rally around the president in a time of crisis. But his own actions and comments accelerated his drop in the polls.

So by the beginning of 1980 Kennedy was far behind Carter among Democratic primary voters, and he never really recovered. In January he lost by more than 2–1 in the Iowa caucuses, where there was a record turnout. In February he lost in the New Hampshire primary, right next door to Massachusetts, a contest in which a large majority of the voters are Catholic. He won impressively in Massachusetts. And, just as his campaign seemed about to collapse, he won in New York, where he was helped by the Carter Administration's vote against Israel the week before in the United Nations. Kennedy won other primaries, mostly in eastern states, but a few elsewhere: Massachusetts, New York, New Jersey, Pennsylvania, the District of Columbia, South Dakota, New Mexico, and California. He won the Arizona caucuses. But most of these victories were achieved only after it was evident that he could not win the nomination. Kennedy stayed in the race after the primaries because, he said, the president refused to debate him; and Carter in fact made no overtures to his beaten opponent. The result was that the August convention in New York nominated Carter but was controlled by Kennedy. Conventions have become a form of television advertisement for the majority candidate but a minority candidate with a cohesive following greater than one-third of the delegates can, by use of the rules and delaying tactics, keep the majority candidate off prime time. Kennedy had 40% of the votes, and as his price for maintaining the schedule Carter wanted, he extracted platform planks and the right to make a speech Tuesday night. When Kennedy began to speak, it became evident why he had remained in the race (although he had formally withdrawn by that time). This is his metier: a rousing inspirational speech to a huge, enthusiastic audience, the words beautifully crafted, the lines stirringly delivered: "For all those whose cares have been our concern, the work goes on, the cause endures, the hope still lives, and the dream shall never die." Nothing Carter did could come close to matching this performance.

Many Kennedy supporters assume it is just a matter of time before he is the Democratic nominee in 1984 and then president. But 1980 suggests some reasons for caution. The character factors that hurt him will still be around. His issue stands — his support of more government protection for the poor and the middle class — were a liability in 1980 and, unless opinion changes, will be a liability in 1984. Kennedy believes strongly in an expansion of the government's role, in national health insurance, in a bigger government jobs program; he seems to see a nation where millions are economically deprived and desperately in need of help. The problem is that most American voters today don't believe that Kennedy's picture is accurate any longer. Since 1964 they have not given a majority of their votes to a candidate who unequivocally backed an expansion of government's role, and they certainly did not in 1980. It is possible that the Reagan's Administration's programs could fail, the economy could shift into a depression, many more poor and deprived people could suddenly start voting, and Kennedy's ideas could become much more popular. But the fact is that those who back those ideas had hoped to get into the White House in 1980 more from Kennedy's personal popularity than from the popularity of those ideas. Now they must do the hard slogging work of persuading people that their vision is accurate and their programs desirable.

If Kennedy should show any weakness in Massachusetts in 1982, it will be because of his stands on issues. This is perhaps the last state that would abandon the idea of a large, compassionate government. But the current of ideas, even in Massachusetts, seems to be moving in the other direction. Do all the Anderson voters share Kennedy's economic views? Do people in this increasingly high-wage state see themselves as part of a society where millions remain poor and helpless? Kennedy will almost surely avoid really serious opposition and should win by a big margin. But the Massachusetts Senate race will be worth watching for what it tells us about the strength of his ideas and of his likely presidential candidacy in 1984.

Kennedy must have supposed that when young Democratic Congressman Paul Tsongas beat Republican Edward Brooke for the state's other Senate seat that he finally had a colleague who would tend industriously to Massachusetts matters and leave him freer to concentrate on broad national issues. Tsongas, after all, had been a congressman from Lowell for two terms and had spent much effort on the renewal program in that old, but now once again prosperous, industrial city. Tsongas's campaign in the crowded Democratic primary had emphasized his difficult-to-pronounce name. In the general election the dominant figure was that of Brooke: a talented and articulate man in terrible trouble because of a bitter divorce and a disputed property settlement. Tsongas tastefully avoided that whole matter and emphasized that he was closer to Edward Kennedy's views on economic issues than Brooke was. The result was that Brooke was narrowly defeated. He was the first (and so far only) black elected to the Senate by popular vote; he was a leader on a variety of legislative issues including abortion, on which he courageously led the opposition to cutting off government funding for abortion.

Tsongas has proved also to be a senator more interested in national than local issues. In his first year he tried to get on the Foreign Relations Committee; but that would have put two Greek–Americans on that body just as the Carter Administration was trying to resume military aid to Turkey. He served instead on Energy, where as a northeasterner he tended to oppose all attempts to end energy price controls, and on Banking. In 1980 he succeeded in moving from Banking to Foreign Relations. Tsongas attracted the most attention when, at the 1980 ADA convention, he made a speech saying that Democrats were going to have to rethink their programs and come up with new ideas. The reception, even from ADAers and even before the November 1980 election, was favorable. Tsongas had articulated the sense that many Democrats had that their programs had become disconnected from reality and that their list of goals had become more a theological litany than a program for action. On specifics, Tsongas seems not quite so ready to depart from the standard Democratic agenda. But he has succeeded in establishing himself as a thoughtful national figure and as advancing the public discussion in a direction that seems inevitable now but was not where it was going before.

Massachusetts loses one of its 12 congressional seats for 1982. In this heavily Democratic state the likely victim of the redistricting process is one of the state's two Republican members of Congress, Margaret Heckler. Her long, thin, attenuated 10th district seems likely to be combined with the 4th of freshman liberal Democrat Barney Frank, with Frank favored to prevail in the election. The other possible victim is 7th district Democrat Edward Markey.

Census Data   Pop. (1980 final) 5,737,037, up 1% in 1970s: 2.53% of U.S. total, 11th largest. Central city, 28%; suburban, 58%. Median 4-person family income, 1978, $20,512, 100% of U.S., 23d highest.

1979 Share of Federal Tax Burden $12,172,000,000; 2.70% of U.S. total, 10th largest.

1979 Share of Federal Outlays $13,711,030,000; 2.96% of U.S. total, 11th largest.

DOD	$3,614,664,000	9th	(3.41%)	HEW	$5,718,032,000	10th	(3.20%)
DOE	$119,949,000	23d	(1.02%)	ERDA	$40,417,000	14th	(1.49%)
HUD	$300,721,000	7th	(4.56%)	NASA	$51,853,000	16th	(1.11%)
VA	$641,001,000	8th	(3.09%)	DOT	$667,712,000	8th	(4.03%)
EPA	$170,410,000	10th	(3.21%)	DOC	$59,234,000	13th	(1.87%)
DOI	$58,678,000	24th	(1.06%)	USDA	$287,770,000	36th	(1.20%)

Economic Base   Finance, insurance, and real estate; electrical equipment and supplies, especially communication equipment; machinery, especially special industry machinery; apparel and other textile products, especially women's and misses' outerwear; printing and publishing, especially newspapers and commercial printing; fabricated metal products; food and kindred products.

Political Lineup   Governor, Edward J. King (D). Senators, Edward M. Kennedy (D) and Paul E. Tsongas (D). Representatives, 12 (10 D and 2 R); 11 in 1982. State Senate, 40 (32 D, 7 R, and 1 I); State House of Representatives, 160 (128 D, 31 R, and 1 I).

The Voters

Registration   3,156,672 Total.

Employment profile 1970   White collar, 53%. Blue collar, 34%. Service, 13%. Farm, –%.
Ethnic groups   Black 1980, 4%. Hispanic 1980, 2%. Asian 1980, 1%. Total foreign stock 1970, 33%. Canada, 8%; Italy, 5%; Ireland, 4%; UK, 3%; Poland, USSR, 2% each; Portugal, 1%.

Presidential Vote

1980	Reagan (R)	1,056,223	(42%)
	Carter (D)	1,053,802	(42%)
	Anderson (I)	382,539	(15%)
1976	Ford (R)	1,030,276	(40%)
	Carter (D)	1,429,475	(56%)

1980 Democratic Presidential Primary			*1980 Republican Presidential Primary*		
Kennedy	590,393	(65%)	Bush	124,365	(31%)
Carter	260,401	(29%)	Anderson	122,987	(31%)
Others	36,866	(4%)	Reagan	115,334	(29%)
No preference	19,663	(2%)	All others	35,897	(9%)
			No preference	2,243	(0%)

SENATORS

Sen. Edward M. Kennedy (D) Elected 1962, seat up 1982; b. Feb. 22, 1932, Boston; home, Boston; Harvard U., A.B. 1956, Acad. of Internatl. Law, The Hague, The Netherlands, 1958, U. of Va., LL.B. 1959.

Career   Army, 1951–53; Asst. Dist. Atty., Suffolk Co., 1961–62.

Offices   109 RSOB, 202-224-4543. Also Rm. 2400A JFK Fed. Bldg., Boston 02203, 617-223-2826.

Committees   *Judiciary* (2d). Subcommittees: Immigration and Refugee Policy; Juvenile Justice.

Labor and Human Resources (Ranking Member). Subcommittees: Labor; Education; Employment and Productivity; Investigations and General Oversight.

Joint Economic Committee (3d).

Group Ratings

	ADA	COPE	PC	LCV	CFA	RPN	NAB	NSI	NTU	ACA	ACU
1980	33	100	17	77	27	—	0	0	21	20	0
1979	79	94	49	—	81	—	—	—	17	5	0
1978	95	95	93	96	80	56	9	0	9	4	4

Key Votes

1) Draft Registn $	AGN	6) Fair Housng Cloture	FOR	11) Cut Socl Incr Defns	—
2) Ban $ to Nicrgua	—	7) Ban $ Rape Abortns	AGN	12) Income Tax Indexing	—
3) Dlay MX Missile	FOR	8) Cap on Food Stmp $	AGN	13) Lim Spdg 21% GNP	—
4) Nuclr Mortorium	FOR	9) New US Dep Edcatn	FOR	14) Incr Wndfll Prof Tax	FOR
5) Alaska Lands Bill	FOR	10) Cut OSHA Inspctns	—	15) Chryslr Loan Grntee	FOR

Election Results

1976 general	Edward M. Kennedy (D)	1,726,657	(69%)	($896,196)
	Michael S. Robertson (R)	722,641	(29%)	($168,854)
1976 primary	Edward M. Kennedy (D)	534,725	(75%)	
	Two others (D)	176,811	(25%)	
1970 general	Edward M. Kennedy (D)	1,202,856	(62%)	
	Josiah Spaulding (R)............	715,978	(37%)	

Sen. Paul E. Tsongas (D) Elected 1978, seat up 1984; b. Feb. 14, 1941, Lowell; home, Lowell; Dartmouth Col., B.A. 1962, Yale U., LL.B. 1967, Harvard U., 1973.

Career Peace Corps Volunteer, Ethiopia, 1962–64, Trng. Coord., West Indies, 1967–68; Mbr., Governor's Comm. on Law Enforcement, 1968–69; Mass. Dpty. Asst. Atty. Gen., 1969–71; Practicing atty., 1971–74; U.S. House of Reps., 1975–78.

Offices 362 RSOB, 202-224-2742. Also 325 Merrimack St., Lowell 01852, 617-459-0101.

Committees *Energy and Natural Resources* (8th). Subcommittees: Energy Conservation and Supply; Energy Research and Development; Water and Power.

Foreign Relations (6th). Subcommittees: African Affairs; East Asian and Pacific Affairs; Western Hemisphere Affairs.

Select Committee on Small Business (7th). Subcommittee: Advocacy and the Future of Small Business.

Group Ratings

	ADA	COPE	PC	LCV	CFA	RPN	NAB	NSI	NTU	ACA	ACU
1980	89	84	77	82	93	—	9	0	22	12	5
1979	74	100	75	—	86	—	—	—	21	11	6
1978	50	88	50	78	32	50	0	0	13	18	0

Key Votes

1) Draft Registn $	AGN	6) Fair Housng Cloture	FOR	11) Cut Socl Incr Defns	AGN
2) Ban $ to Nicrgua	FOR	7) Ban $ Rape Abortns	AGN	12) Income Tax Indexing	FOR
3) Dlay MX Missile	FOR	8) Cap on Food Stmp $	AGN	13) Lim Spdg 21% GNP	AGN
4) Nuclr Mortorium	—	9) New US Dep Edcatn	FOR	14) Incr Wndfll Prof Tax	FOR
5) Alaska Lands Bill	FOR	10) Cut OSHA Inspctns	AGN	15) Chryslr Loan Grntee	FOR

Election Results

1978 general	Paul E. Tsongas (D)	1,093,283	(55%)	($768,383)
	Edward W. Brooke (R)	890,584	(45%)	($1,284,855)

1978 primary	Paul E. Tsongas (D)	296,915	(36%)	
	Paul Guzzi (D)	258,960	(31%)	($301,747)
	Kathleen Sullivan Alioto (D)	161,036	(19%)	($143,777)
	Two others (D)	117,861	(14%)	
1972 general	Edward W. Brooke (R)	1,505,932	(64%)	($368,038)
	John J. Droney (D)	823,278	(35%)	($82,888)

GOVERNOR

Gov. Edward J. King (D) Elected 1978, term expires Jan. 1983; b. May 11, 1925, East Boston; Boston Col., B.A. 1948, Bentley Col., 1951–53.

Career Navy, WWII; Pro Football Player, Buffalo Bills 1948–49, Baltimore Colts 1950–51; Accountant, 1953–56; Asst. Dir. and Comptroller, Boston Museum of Science, 1956–59; Mass. Port Authority Comptroller, 1959, Secy.–Treas., 1960–63, Dir., 1963–74; Pres., New England Cncl., 1975–77.

Offices Rm. 360 State House, Boston 02133, 617-727-3600.

Election Results

1978 gen.	Edward J. King (D)	1,030,294	(53%)
	Francis W. Hatch, Jr. (R) ..	926,072	(47%)
1978 prim.	Edward J. King (D)	442,174	(51%)
	Michael S. Dukakis (D)	365,417	(42%)
	One other (D)	58,220	(7%)
1974 gen.	Michael S. Dukakis (D)	992,284	(54%)
	Francis W. Sargent (R)	784,353	(42%)

FIRST DISTRICT

The 1st congressional district of Massachusetts is the western end of the state: the Berkshire Mountains and most of the Massachusetts portion of the Connecticut River valley. The Berkshires are known as a summer resort and for such picturesque towns as Lenox, home of the Tanglewood music festival. More important politically are the old mill towns and manufacturing centers nestled in the mountains, such as Pittsfield, the district's largest city, and North Adams. The second- and third-generation immigrants packed into these tiny mill towns almost inevitably outvote the small-town and farm Yankee Republicans by substantial margins. The Connecticut valley (called the Pioneer Valley here in Massachusetts) is a similar place politically: small Republican towns that are more than offset by the occasional Democratic mill towns. In the middle of the valley are the college towns of Amherst, with Amherst College and the University of Massachusetts, and Northampton, home of Smith College and of Calvin Coolidge. To the south are industrial and residential suburbs of Springfield: Holyoke, Westfield, and West Springfield.

In national elections, the 1st almost always votes Democratic: it went for McGovern in 1972 and comfortably for Carter in 1976. But in congressional races it is still Republican as it has been since Yankees were a clear majority here. Congressman Silvio Conte has become so entrenched that he seldom has opposition and, when he does, he wins with something like the 64% he received in 1976. Conte's most notable challenge occurred in 1958, his first House race, when he faced Williams College political scientist James MacGregor Burns. The professor got the national publicity but Conte, who had represented Berkshire County in the

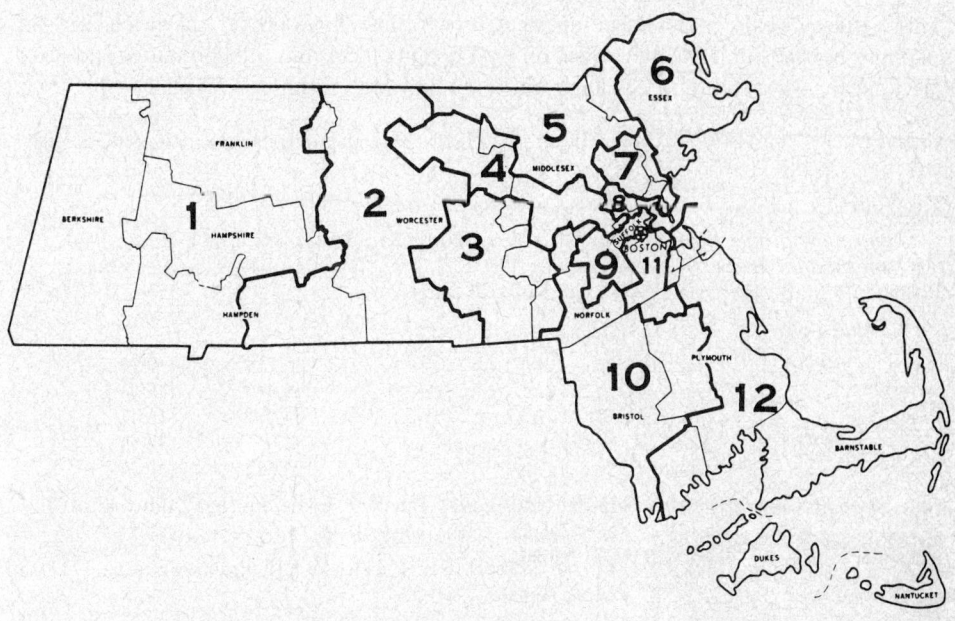

state Senate for eight years, got the local votes. So Burns went on to finish his Roosevelt biography, and Conte went to Washington.

Conte is considered very affable and politically very shrewd. Early in his House career he won a seat on the Appropriations Committee. His voting record gave him the reputation of being one of the most liberal Republicans in the House, but that is not necessarily because he is always in favor of spending federal money. On the contrary, on many of the issues on which he has dissented from Republican orthodoxy he has favored less spending—the supersonic transport, defense spending, the B–1 bomber. For years he led moves to put ceilings on farm subsidy payments and has succeeded in having a $20,000 ceiling imposed on payments to any one owner. He supported the Carter Administration's proposal to cut spending on federal water projects.

Yet Conte does not hesitate to take care of his district (there have been no cuts in Amtrak lines there, for example) and is not regarded as quixotic. Given his voting record, many conservatives wanted to keep him from becoming ranking Republican on Appropriations in 1979. But Conte had the strong support of Robert Michel, Republican whip and an Appropriations member himself, and the conservative challenge was overcome with ease. Appropriations is a committee in danger of being bypassed on major budget decisions by the Budget Committee and its reconciliation process. Conte's inclination probably is to maintain a major role for Appropriations, and while he is likely to be a team player for the Republican program, he also has tended to support the major spending decisions and priorities currently under attack. On the Labor–Health and Human Services–Education Subcommittee, which has jurisdiction over most of the programs the Reagan budget cutters want to slash, Conte has a critical vote. With his support, subcommittee liberals can prevail, even without their own chairman, William Natcher of Kentucky; but if Conte sticks with the Republicans and can win support from the careful Natcher, the administration will win just about every fight.

This is true as well on other subcommittees, on which he sits ex officio. In March 1981, for example, he and Jamie Whitten voted on the Foreign Operations Subcommittee and saved the Reagan Administration's military aid to El Salvador by an 8–7 margin.

Census Data   Pop. (1980 final) 489,401, up 4% in 1970s. Median family income, 1970, $10,311, 108% of U.S.

The Voters

Employment profile 1970   White collar, 49%. Blue collar, 36%. Service, 14%. Farm, 1%.
Ethnic groups   Black 1980, 1%. Hispanic 1980, 2%. Total foreign stock 1970, 27%. Canada, 7%; Poland, 5%; Italy, 3%; Ireland, UK, Germany, 2% each.

Presidential Vote

1980	Reagan (R)	85,268	(39%)
	Carter (D)	93,495	(43%)
	Anderson (I)	34,431	(16%)
1976	Ford (R)	88,051	(40%)
	Carter (D)	124,042	(56%)

Rep. Silvio O. Conte (R) Elected 1958; b. Nov. 9, 1921, Pittsfield; home, Pittsfield; Boston Col., Boston Col. Law Sch., LL.B. 1949.

Career Seabees, SW Pacific, WWII; Practicing atty., 1949–58; Mass. Senate, 1951–59.

Offices 2300 RHOB, 202-225-5335. Also 78 Center St., Pittsfield 01201, 413-442-0946.

Committees *Appropriations* (Ranking Member). Subcommittees: Labor–Health and Human Services–Education; Legislative; Transportation.

Small Business (2d). Subcommittee: Energy, Environment and Safety Issues Affecting Small Business.

Group Ratings

	ADA	COPE	PC	LCV	CFA	RPN	NAB	NSI	NTU	ACA	ACU
1980	83	68	60	76	71	—	17	30	23	30	17
1979	53	90	73	79	67	—	—	—	25	23	23
1978	50	55	55	77	50	58	50	50	16	26	25

Key Votes

1) Draft Registn $	AGN	6) Fair Hsg DOJ Enfrc	FOR	11) Cut Socl Incr Dfns $	AGN
2) Ban $ to Nicrgua	AGN	7) Lim PAC Contrbtns	FOR	12) Hosptl Cost Controls	FOR
3) Dlay MX Missile	—	8) Cap on Food Stmp $	AGN	13) Gasln Ctrls & Allctns	FOR
4) Nuclr Mortorium	FOR	9) New US Dep Edcatn	FOR	14) Lim Wndfll Prof Tax	AGN
5) Alaska Lands Bill	FOR	10) Cut OSHA $	AGN	15) Chryslr Loan Grntee	FOR

Election Results

1980 general	Silvio O. Conte (R)	156,415	(75%)	($80,126)
	Helen Poppy Doyle (D)	52,457	(25%)	($14,464)
1980 primary	Silvio O. Conte (R), unopposed			
1978 general	Silvio O. Conte (R), unopposed ...			($5,771)

SECOND DISTRICT

The 2d congressional district of Massachusetts includes the city of Springfield, many of its suburbs, and a collection of rural and small industrial towns to the east. Springfield and Chicopee, which together have about one-half of the district's population, are its Democratic bastions, although most of the rest of the 2d often produces Democratic margins as well. The image of the small New England town is of a clapboard village peopled by taciturn Yankees. But in fact many of the old Protestants have died off or long since moved west, and in their place are people more likely to be of Irish, Italian, or Polish descent. The storefronts here may have New England Yankee facades, but hanging above are signs with names of Italian or Polish proprietors.

Springfield is the hometown of several famous political pros: Lawrence O'Brien, the Democratic national chairman whose telephone was the target of the Watergate burglars; the well-known campaign consultant Joseph Napolitan, who still maintains an office here; and Alaska's former Senator Mike Gravel. All grew up and learned their first political lessons in Springfield's wards and precincts; their own ethnic origins — Irish, Italian, French Canadian — suggest the variety of this small city.

Another Springfield political pro is 2d district Congressman Edward Boland, a Democrat with more than a quarter century of service in the House. For many years Boland, long a bachelor, roomed with Tip O'Neill, whose wife remained in Cambridge; they have ended that relationship but remain close. Like O'Neill, Boland for years was a politician who could bridge the gap between the senior big city politicians — a group to which he temperamentally belongs — and the younger, more ideological liberals in the Democratic Caucus. Now he is one of the most senior members of the Congress himself, and his career is likely to be much more visible than it has been.

One reason is that Boland chairs the permanent Intelligence Committee in the House. This is a sensitive assignment. Boland has supported some defense budget cuts and questioned some intelligence practices, but he does not share the suspicion of the national security bureaucracies that characterizes many of the liberals coming out of the Vietnam war era.

Boland's other major position of power is on the House Appropriations Committee. He ranks second among committee Democrats in seniority. At the beginning of the 96th Congress there was a move to elect Boland chairman. He declined to support it; he has always been a team player, and presumably he and O'Neill had assurances from Jamie Whitten of Mississippi, the most senior member, that he would not use the chair to frustrate the wishes of the Democratic majority. Nonetheless, Boland received 88 votes to Whitten's 157 — not quite so much a loss as first appears, since a switch of just 35 votes would have made Boland chairman.

The difference, in any case, would probably have been less dramatic than the difference between the ADA ratings of the two men. Appropriations historically has been a committee more cautious on domestic spending than the House, and in the antispending environment of 1979 Boland would not have tried to make major changes. Moreover, much of the real work is done in subcommittees, and the real powers are the subcommittee chairmen — the so-called college of cardinals. Boland, as a longtime subcommittee chairman, would not have been likely to challenge them directly. He himself chairs the subcommittee on HUD–Independent Agencies, a body that, with the effective demise of many public housing programs, is less important than it once was.

Boland should have no trouble winning reelection in the 1980s, and redistricting will not likely alter the shape or the political leanings of the district substantially.

Census Data Pop. (1980 final) 466,126, down 1% in 1970s. Median family income, 1970, $10,268, 107% of U.S.

The Voters

Employment profile 1970 White collar, 45%. Blue collar, 42%. Service, 12%. Farm, 1%.
Ethnic groups Black 1980, 6%. Hispanic 1980, 4%. Total foreign stock 1970, 31%. Canada, 9%; Poland, 5%; Italy, 3%; Ireland, UK, 2% each; USSR, Germany, 1% each.

Presidential Vote

1980	Reagan (R)	86,646	(42%)
	Carter (D)	87,560	(43%)
	Anderson (I)	28,211	(14%)
1976	Ford (R)	74,953	(38%)
	Carter (D)	116,757	(59%)

Rep. Edward P. Boland (D) Elected 1952; b. Oct. 1, 1911, Springfield; home, Springfield; Boston Col. Law Sch.

Career Mass. House of Reps., 1935–41; Hampton Co. Register of Deeds, 1941–42, 1946–49; Army, WWII; Military Aide to Gov. Paul A. Dever, 1949–52.

Offices 2426 RHOB, 202-225-5601. Also 1883 Main St., Springfield 01103, 413-733-4127.

Committees *Appropriations* (2d). Subcommittees: Energy and Water Development; HUD–Independent Agencies (Chairman).

Select Committee on Intelligence (Chairman). Subcommittee: Program and Budget Authorization (Chairman).

Group Ratings

	ADA	COPE	PC	LCV	CFA	RPN	NAB	NSI	NTU	ACA	ACU
1980	78	63	67	63	86	—	0	20	18	21	5
1979	68	90	70	70	74	—	—	—	21	9	16
1978	50	75	65	65	73	27	9	56	9	15	13

Key Votes

1) Draft Registn $	FOR	6) Fair Hsg DOJ Enfrc	FOR	11) Cut Socl Incr Dfns $	AGN
2) Ban $ to Nicrgua	AGN	7) Lim PAC Contrbtns	FOR	12) Hosptl Cost Controls	FOR
3) Dlay MX Missile	FOR	8) Cap on Food Stmp $	AGN	13) Gasln Ctrls & Allctns	FOR
4) Nuclr Mortorium	FOR	9) New US Dep Edcatn	AGN	14) Lim Wndfll Prof Tax	AGN
5) Alaska Lands Bill	FOR	10) Cut OSHA $	AGN	15) Chryslr Loan Grntee	FOR

Election Results

1980 general	Edward P. Boland (D)	120,711	(67%)	($28,553)
	Thomas P. Swank (R)	38,672	(22%)	($0)
	John B. Aubuchon (I)	20,247	(11%)	
1980 primary	Edward P. Boland (D)	38,811	(71%)	
	Paul M. Kozikowski (D)	11,999	(22%)	($0)
	One other (D)	3,784	(7%)	
1978 general	Edward P. Boland (D)	101,570	(73%)	
	Thomas P. Swank (R)	37,881	(27%)	

THIRD DISTRICT

Worcester, the second largest city in Massachusetts with 161,000 people, is a manufacturing town that lies roughly in the geographical center of the state. Worcester is surrounded by an almost random assortment of comfortable suburbs and tiny mill towns. The thin New England soil only barely covers here, and layers of rock undergird everything. Although there are a number of colleges and universities about, they do not, as in the Boston area, have a major effect on the culture of the entire community. Nor is there here a leftish, culturally sophisticated Yankee upper class. This is nitty-gritty New England, where the Democratic majorities come almost entirely from the all but genetically ingrained voting habits of middle- and lower-class voters of varied ethnic backgrounds.

In congressional elections, the Worcester-based 3d district has been strongly Democratic for about as long as anyone can remember. From 1946 to 1972 it regularly elected and re-elected Democrat Harold Donohue, one of the senior members of the House Judiciary Committee that voted to impeach Richard Nixon. Donohue had had at least one close call at the polls and had stayed in the House after many of his contemporaries had left; he retired in 1974.

There was an unusually serious contest here to replace Donohue. The favorite, Democrat Joseph Early, won, but with only 50%; the energetic Republican had 38%, and an Independent 12%. Early won a seat on the Appropriations Committee once in the House — the kind of reward Tip O'Neill likes to give members of the Massachusetts delegation. On noneconomic issues, he is perhaps the most conservative member of the Massachusetts delegation — but by national standards that is not very conservative at all.

Early is not likely to have political difficulty, either in redistricting or in the 1982 election.

Census Data Pop. (1980 final) 472,767, up 1% in 1970s. Median family income, 1970, $10,863, 113% of U.S.

The Voters

    Employment profile 1970 White collar, 49%. Blue collar, 38%. Service, 13%. Farm, –%.
    Ethnic groups Black 1980, 1%. Hispanic 1980, 2%. Asian 1980, 1. Total foreign stock 1970, 32%. Canada, 8%; Italy, 5%; Ireland, 3%; UK, Poland, Sweden, 2% each; USSR, Lithuania, 1% each.

Presidential Vote

1980	Reagan (R)	81,551	(41%)
	Carter (D)	85,914	(44%)
	Anderson (I)	27,858	(14%)
1976	Ford (R)	80,584	(38%)
	Carter (D)	125,450	(59%)

Rep. Joseph D. Early (D) Elected 1974; b. Jan. 31, 1933, Worcester; home, Worcester; Col. of the Holy Cross, B.S. 1955.

Career Navy, 1955–57; High school teacher and coach, 1959–63; Mass. House of Reps., 1963–74.

Offices 2349 RHOB, 202-225-6101. Also 34 Mechanic St., Rm. 203, Worcester 01608, 617-752-6718.

Committee *Appropriations* (16th). Subcommittees: Commerce, Justice, State and Judiciary; Labor–Health and Human Services–Education.

Group Ratings

	ADA	COPE	PC	LCV	CFA	RPN	NAB	NSI	NTU	ACA	ACU
1980	67	71	57	79	86	—	27	20	30	20	31
1979	74	84	78	79	74	—	—	—	41	24	32
1978	70	68	73	97	68	36	30	22	37	23	9

Key Votes

1) Draft Registn $	AGN	6) Fair Hsg DOJ Enfrc	FOR	11) Cut Socl Incr Dfns $	AGN
2) Ban $ to Nicrgua	FOR	7) Lim PAC Contrbtns	FOR	12) Hosptl Cost Controls	FOR
3) Dlay MX Missile	FOR	8) Cap on Food Stmp $	FOR	13) Gasln Ctrls & Allctns	FOR
4) Nuclr Mortorium	FOR	9) New US Dep Edcatn	AGN	14) Lim Wndfll Prof Tax	AGN
5) Alaska Lands Bill	FOR	10) Cut OSHA $	AGN	15) Chryslr Loan Grntee	AGN

Election Results

1980 general	Joseph D. Early (D)	141,560	(72%)	($71,210)
	David G. Skehan (R)	54,213	(28%)	($0)
1980 primary	Joseph D. Early (D)	31,515	(100%)	
1978 general	Joseph D. Early (D)	119,337	(75%)	($50,609)
	Charles Kevin McLeod (R)	39,259	(25%)	($8,645)

FOURTH DISTRICT

The 4th congressional district of Massachusetts is a geographical oddity, a thin corridor extending from near Boston's Kenmore Square more than 100 miles out into the rocky Massachusetts countryside to the mill town of Gardner. This district is almost as varied as Massachusetts itself. The innermost part of the district, the Boston suburbs of Brookline and Newton, are long-settled communities with above-average incomes and comfortable sprawling houses. Each also has a substantial Jewish population; indeed, this is the most Jewish of the Massachusetts congressional districts. Just the other side of the Massachusetts Turnpike from Newton is the suburb of Waltham, an entirely different place. Waltham got its start as an old cotton mill town, and, although it now sits at the edge of the Route 128 electronics corridor, it still has very much the mill town atmosphere. The population is heavily Catholic, with many French Canadians, low income, and increasingly elderly. Farther out are varied suburbs: woodsy Weston and preppy Lincoln, rustic Wayland, working-class Framingham. The district moves farther northwest, through sparsely settled land, past the Army's Fort Devens, to the mill towns of Fitchburg and Leominster (pronounced as if there were no o). Here Boston and its East Coast sophistication seem a long way away. People are close to their community institutions, especially their churches, and to their families; their way of life is threatened economically (because mills have been closing down for 80 years now) and culturally (where else can one find this kind of community anymore?).

This district has been electing some of the most liberal members of Congress for more than a decade, but only after major struggles that sometimes seemed to be more battles of life-style than of politics. For 10 years here the congressman was Robert Drinan, S.J., the first Roman Catholic priest elected to be a member of the House of Representatives in American history. Drinan, the longtime dean of Boston College Law School, first won in 1970 by beating an elderly incumbent, Philip Philbin, a white-maned Irishman who voted liberal on domestic issues and with the Pentagon on the House Armed Services Committee. Drinan had four tough general elections after that. His candidacy had its beginnings in opposition to the Vietnam war, and his career had its greatest intensity in his opposition to Richard Nixon and all his works. His original political base was in Newton and Brookline, where he became very popular with Jewish constituents for his stands on a wide variety of issues, including his strong support of Israel. Many Catholics, in working-class Waltham and Framingham, and in the western end of the district, were more hostile; a strong feeling exists among many Catholics against a priest being in politics. Also troublesome to some was his stand on abortion, or rather his opposition to antiabortion amendments.

As the 1970s went on, Drinan built up a strong base in the western end through constituency service and was reelected without difficulty in 1978. But his political career was ended suddenly in 1980 when the Church ruled that such orders as the Jesuits could not exempt their members from the general prohibition against priests seeking public office. Some suspected that the Pope or Humberto Cardinal Medeiros of Boston wanted Drinan out of Congress because of his refusal to support right-to-life measures. Whatever the reasons for the change in Church position, Drinan obeyed without complaint.

The people who had backed Drinan had a successor in mind, state Representative Barney Frank. He moved from Boston into the district and managed to persuade other liberals not to run. Frank, once a tutor at Harvard and aide to Congressman Michael Harrington, is a fast-talking raconteur with a Jersey City accent. He is the closest thing there is to a natural politician. In a conservative year, he remained a zestful liberal. Like Drinan, he had vehement opposition in his first election. In the primary, Waltham Mayor Arthur Clark waged a strong campaign and was aided as the primary approached by a statement from Cardinal Medeiros recommending that Catholics vote against candidates who do not favor right-to-life measures. This was understood as a message to vote against Frank and Congressman James Shannon in the adjoining 5th district, and in these Catholic majority constituencies both were nearly defeated. Frank carried Newton, Brookline, and the high-income suburbs with better than 70%; Clark got 82% in Waltham and carried the western end 60%–37%. The result was a narrow Frank victory.

The general election, against Republican Richard Jones, showed a similar split. Frank carried Newton and Brookline by 2–1 and ran ahead of the Democratic ticket in other high-income suburbs. In Waltham, however, a town that Jimmy Carter carried, Frank got only 40% of the vote, and in the western towns he got only 41%. Again, Frank won with 52%.

If this were not a redistricting year, the course for the next two years would be quite clear. Frank would use the advantages of incumbency to augment his standing in the western end of the district, as Drinan did, and would attempt to increase his standing in Waltham while keeping in touch with his base in Newton and Brookline. But redistricting means that Massachusetts must lose one of its congressional districts, and the predictions in early 1981 were that the overwhelmingly Democratic legislature would take the two geographically attenuated districts, Frank's 4th and Republican Margaret Heckler's 10th, give some of their far-flung parts to other population-light districts, and combine their main areas in the Boston suburbs. Frank would presumably not be unhappy to lose the western towns, which he has yet to carry; he can be reasonably sure that the Democratic legislature will give him both Newton and Brookline, which he definitely needs, and he probably wants both Framingham and Waltham, since in a race between a Democrat and an upper-income Republican such as Heckler both would probably go Democratic. Frank is generally considered to be the favorite in this situation, and there is some talk that Heckler, who once served on a unique Massachusetts institution called the Governor's Council, might run for governor.

Although redistricting and the 1982 election will necessarily take up much of his time and energy, Frank still manages to serve on no less than three House committees: Banking, Government Operations, and Judiciary. He has the potential to be one of the constructive legislators and one of the most vivid personalities in the House in the 1980s, whatever the national ideological trend, provided he can get past the 1982 election.

Census Data   Pop. (1980 final) 459,878, down 4% in 1970s. Median family income, 1970, $12,409, 129% of U.S.

The Voters
  Employment profile 1970   White collar, 62%. Blue collar, 27%. Service, 11%. Farm, –%.
  Ethnic groups   Black 1980, 2%. Hispanic 1980, 2%. Asian 1980, 2%. Total foreign stock 1970, 37%. Canada, 11%; Italy, USSR, 5% each; Ireland, 3%; UK, Poland, 2% each; Germany, 1%.

Presidential Vote	1980	Reagan (R)	83,686	(40%)
		Carter (D)	88,488	(42%)
		Anderson (I)	34,803	(17%)
	1976	Ford (R)	88,613	(42%)
		Carter (D)	117,919	(58%)

Rep. Barney Frank (D) Elected 1980; b. Mar. 31, 1940, Bayonne, N.J.; home, Newton Highlands; Harvard Col., B.A. 1962; Harvard U., 1962–67, J.D. 1977.

Career   Chf. of Staff to Boston Mayor Kevin White, 1967–76; Admin. Asst. to U.S. Rep. Michael Harrington, 1971–72; Mass. House of Reps., 1973–80; Lecturer on Pub. Policy, Harvard JFK Sch. of Govt., 1979–80.

Offices   1609 LHOB, 202-225-5931. Also 400 Totten Pond Rd., Waltham 02154, 617-890-9455, and Philip T. Philbin Fed. Bldg., 881 Main St., Fitchburg 01420, 617-342-8722.

Committees   *Banking, Finance and Urban Affairs* (23d). Subcommittees: General Oversight and Renegotiation; Housing and Community Development; International Trade, Investment and Monetary Policy.

Government Operations (21st). Subcommittees: Environment, Energy and Natural Resources; Intergovernmental Relations and Human Resources.

Judiciary (16th). Subcommittees: Courts, Civil Liberties and the Administration of Justice; Immigration, Refugees and International Law.

Select Committee on Aging (26th). Subcommittee: Retirement Income and Employment.

Group Ratings and Key Votes: Newly Elected

Election Results

1980 general	Barney Frank (D)	103,446	(52%)	($446,826)
	Richard A. Jones (R)	95,898	(48%)	($53,481)
1980 primary	Barney Frank (D)	42,612	(52%)	
	Arthur S. Clark (D)	37,694	(47%)	($110,851)
1978 general	Robert F. Drinan (D), unopposed .			($149,345)

FIFTH DISTRICT

The 5th congressional district of Massachusetts centers on two transportation arteries that have, in their times, been vital to the state's economic development. The first is the Merrimack River, whose falls provided the power for the great textile mills built by Boston Brahmins in company towns they named for themselves, Lowell and Lawrence. Back in the mid-

19th century, the New England textile business was a boom industry that first employed local farm girls and then went on to hire hundreds of thousands of immigrants from Ireland and French Canada. Virtually all the New England textile firms have long since moved south and even abroad in search of lower wages; and with the mills of Lowell and Lawrence quiet, these cities suffered through a local depression that lasted something like forty years.

In the 1960s both cities perked up a bit, largely because of the peripheral influence of the area's other major artery, Route 128, a circumferential highway around Greater Boston. Dozens of the nation's leading electronics and defense research firms, drawing brainpower from the area's universities, have located along both sides of the roadway. They have also had their ups and downs. Some defense contractors found the political climate in Massachusetts unfavorable during the Vietnam war, and in the middle 1970s the state's economy seemed to be in trouble. More recently, Route 128 has been booming. The microchip industry has its outposts here, new inventions are being developed, and there seems to be a psychological and investment climate hospitable to entrepreneurial innovation. Some would argue that recent tax cuts have made the state all that much more hospitable. The prosperity has spread from the 128 suburbs even to Lowell and Lawrence. Lowell in particular has benefited from the recycling of its old brick mills and federal aid first obtained by then 5th district Congressman and now Senator Paul Tsongas.

The 5th district is historically a Republican district; Tsongas, first elected in 1974, was the first Democrat ever to represent it. His election was the culmination of a shift in opinion toward Democrats here; voters in the suburbs were increasingly repelled by Republicans as noneconomic issues like the Vietnam war came to the fore. Now it may be that they are turning back, as economic issues become more important. The 5th district cast a rather sizable plurality of its votes for Ronald Reagan in 1980, a man it would not have found palatable a few years ago. Possibly the apparent success of local tax cuts in stimulating the recent boom made Reagan less unacceptable; in any case, he got the kind of margins Republicans used to get in the suburbs to swamp the Democratic margins in Lowell and Lawrence.

After Tsongas ran for the Senate, two spirited congressional elections followed in the 5th. In the six-candidate Democratic primary the winner was 26-year-old James Shannon, whose votes came mostly from his local base in Lawrence but who got enough support in the rest of the district to beat a Lowell-based conservative. The Republicans fielded an interesting candidate, Middlesex County Sheriff John Buckley, but he evidently confused voters by underplaying his support of decriminalization of marijuana and gun control and emphasizing economic issues instead. A conservative Independent candidate got nearly as many votes as Buckley, and with 52% of the votes Shannon became, for a while, the youngest member of Congress.

With the help of Speaker O'Neill, Shannon got a seat on the Ways and Means Committee, and shortly thereafter earned a reputation for political acumen. Nevertheless Shannon had problems in the 1980 primary when Humberto Cardinal Medeiros called on Catholics to vote against candidates who would not support right-to-life measures. Shannon, a Catholic, was one such candidate and was thrown sharply on the defensive. Yet the election returns suggest that he had trouble more because his opponent, who had come within 2% of his total in the 1978 primary, had a strong base in Lowell and the towns immediately surrounding. Shannon won by combining his Lawrence base with majorities in the high-income suburbs and in the rural towns in the western end of the district. The general election was not nearly so difficult for Shannon.

500 MASSACHUSETTS

Shannon has the potential someday to be one of the most powerful members of the House. He is by a considerable margin the youngest member of Ways and Means and sits on two important subcommittees, Trade and Social Security. On the latter, he is a member inclined to be liberal with benefits; on Trade, he tends to be protective toward industries in his district that are in trouble, such as shoes, leather goods, and textiles. This is the traditional Massachusetts position, although these industries are by now less important than they once were and are not generating the recent economic growth of Massachusetts.

Shannon must still worry at least a little about redistricting for 1982. The chances are that the legislature will not change the boundaries of his district substantially. The worst it could do to Shannon is to remove his Lawrence base, which is unlikely; more probably it will add some of the towns in the western end of the current 4th district.

Census Data Pop. (1980 final) 495,675, up 5% in 1970s. Median family income, 1970, $11,532, 120% of U.S.

The Voters

Employment profile 1970 White collar, 52%. Blue collar, 36%. Service, 11%. Farm, 1%.
Ethnic groups Black 1980, 1%. Hispanic 1980, 4%. Asian 1980, 1%. Total foreign stock 1970, 31%. Canada, 10%; Italy, 4%; UK, Ireland, 3% each; Poland, Greece, Germany, 1% each.

Presidential Vote

1980	Reagan (R)	97,018	(44%)
	Carter (D)	86,302	(39%)
	Anderson (I)	33,201	(15%)
1976	Ford (R)	87,340	(40%)
	Carter (D)	125,892	(57%)

Rep. James M. Shannon (D) Elected 1978; b. Apr. 4, 1952, Lawrence; home, Lawrence; Johns Hopkins U., B.A. 1972, Geo. Wash. U., J.D. 1975.

Career Aide to U.S. Rep. Michael Harrington; Practicing atty.

Offices 224 CHOB, 202-225-3411. Also 325 Merrimack St., Lowell 01852, 617-459-0101.

Committee *Ways and Means* (18th). Subcommittees: Social Security; Trade.

Group Ratings

	ADA	COPE	PC	LCV	CFA	RPN	NAB	NSI	NTU	ACA	ACU
1980	94	89	80	88	93	—	0	10	19	14	6
1979	95	95	93	87	96	—	—	—	20	4	5

Key Votes

1) Draft Registn $	AGN	6) Fair Hsg DOJ Enfrc	FOR
2) Ban $ to Nicrgua	AGN	7) Lim PAC Contrbtns	FOR
3) Dlay MX Missile	FOR	8) Cap on Food Stmp $	AGN
4) Nuclr Mortorium	FOR	9) New US Dep Edcatn	FOR
5) Alaska Lands Bill	FOR	10) Cut OSHA $	AGN

11) Cut Socl Incr Dfns $	AGN
12) Hosptl Cost Controls	FOR
13) Gasln Ctrls & Allctns	FOR
14) Lim Wndfll Prof Tax	AGN
15) Chryslr Loan Grntee	FOR

Election Results

1980 general	James M. Shannon (D)	136,758	(66%)	($326,587)
	William C. Sawyer (R)	70,547	(34%)	($110,365)
1980 primary	James M. Shannon (D)	41,207	(54%)	
	Robert F. Hatem (D)	34,573	(46%)	($53,045)
1978 general	James M. Shannon (D)	90,156	(52%)	($180,667)
	John J. Buckley (R)	48,685	(28%)	($97,637)
	James J. Gaffney III (I)	33,835	(20%)	($17,740)

SIXTH DISTRICT

The 6th congressional district of Massachusetts is the North Shore district. Along and just back of the rocky coast north of Boston are the estates of some of the commonwealth's oldest families, including—to name some still important politically—the Saltonstalls, the Lodges, and the Hatches. Only a few miles away are the fishermen of Gloucester, who suffered in recent years from the encroachment of Russian trawlers until the United States extended its territorial waters to 200 miles. Here also are the textile mill workers in Haverhill and Newburyport on the Merrimack River—or people who used to be textile workers, since most of the mills have closed—and the artists and summer people of Rockport. To the south is Salem, where twenty witches were once hanged and pressed to death, and where Nathaniel Hawthorne's house of seven gables still stands in a neighborhood of neat 19th-century homes. Also in the southern part of the district is the boating suburb of Marblehead, which Jews now share with WASPs; Lynn, whose troubled shoe industry has been pressing for years for protection against imports; and Peabody, a newer city inland, with a large shopping center and a middle-income population.

The 6th district is the site of the original gerrymander, named for the desire of its perpetrator, Elbridge Gerry, to corral all the area's Federalist voters into one misshapen seat. Since then the North Shore's wealthy towns and Brahmin families have given the area a reputation for Republicanism it has for some time ceased to deserve. Republican representation of the district continued through personal popularity of Congressman William Bates, until his death in 1969.

The result of the special election to replace him showed the way things were going in Massachusetts. Republican William Saltonstall was beaten by Democrat Michael Harrington. A hot-tempered opponent of the Vietnam war, Harrington never found a comfortable niche in the House. In the 94th Congress there was a move to censure him for disclosing classified information on American aid to the Chilean junta, although the material was true and government officials were lying about it; Harrington got off on a technicality. He seems to have been the only member of Congress concerned about what this country did in Chile. In 1976 several ballot measures he was strongly backing were defeated in Massachusetts, and his own percentage was sharply reduced. He decided to retire in 1978 and, at 42, to return to Massachusetts.

When he left the race, Harrington was already being challenged by Peabody Mayor Nicholas Mavroules, a more traditional kind of Democrat. A local officeholder for twenty years, Mavroules was no ideologue; he won the three-candidate primary with little difficulty. The Republican candidate, airline pilot Bill Bronson, had run against Harrington in 1976 and was primed to run an anti-Harrington campaign again. Mavroules left him off balance and exposed Bronson's own peculiar views, such as a proposal to return most welfare programs to churches and other private institutions. Nevertheless Bronson got a better percentage against Mavroules than he had against Harrington and ran quite a creditable race.

Mavroules had even greater difficulties in 1980. The district seemed to be returning to its Republican tradition. Ronald Reagan carried it and Jimmy Carter got only 38% of the vote here. Mavroules was being investigated on charges of influence peddling while mayor (he was cleared on these during the campaign season) and on income tax questions. Republican Thomas Trimarco emphasized his opposition to high federal spending and managed to win 47% of the vote to Mavroules's 51%. This was close enough to an upset that it is almost certain the Republicans will try hard again, particularly if Mavroules's legal troubles continue. There may also be a serious Democratic primary challenge to the incumbent. Redistricting could add a few towns at the edges to this district and change the political balance very slightly in the Republican direction—but slightly could be enough.

Census Data   Pop. (1980 final) 471,373, down 1% in 1970s. Median family income, 1970, $10,904, 114% of U.S.

The Voters

Employment profile 1970   White collar, 52%. Blue collar, 36%. Service, 12%. Farm, -%.
Ethnic groups   Black 1980, 2%. Hispanic 1980, 1%. Total foreign stock 1970, 31%. Canada, 10%; Italy, 4%; Ireland, UK, 3% each; USSR, Poland, Greece, 2% each.

Presidential Vote

1980	Reagan (R)	97,969	(44%)
	Carter (D)	86,256	(38%)
	Anderson (I)	38,271	(17%)
1976	Ford (R)	97,834	(44%)
	Carter (D)	119,963	(53%)

Rep. Nicholas Mavroules (D) Elected 1978; b. Nov. 1, 1929, Peabody; home, Peabody; M.I.T., night courses.

Career Peabody Ward Cncl., 1958–61, Councillor-at-Large, 1964–65, Mayor, 1967–78.

Offices 1204 LHOB, 202-225-8020. Also 99 Washington St., Salem 01970, 617-745-5800.

Committees *Armed Services* (18th). Subcommittees: Investigations; Procurement and Military Nuclear Systems.

Small Business (15th). Subcommittee: Energy, Environment, and Safety Issues Affecting Small Business.

Group Ratings

	ADA	COPE	PC	LCV	CFA	RPN	NAB	NSI	NTU	ACA	ACU
1980	72	77	60	85	58	—	0	50	18	15	7
1979	63	95	70	85	70	—	—	—	18	8	14

Key Votes

1) Draft Registn $	AGN	6) Fair Hsg DOJ Enfrc	—	11) Cut Socl Incr Dfns $	AGN
2) Ban $ to Nicrgua	FOR	7) Lim PAC Contrbtns	FOR	12) Hosptl Cost Controls	—

3) Dlay MX Missile	FOR	8) Cap on Food Stmp $	AGN	13) Gasln Ctrls & Allctns	FOR
4) Nuclr Mortorium	FOR	9) New US Dep Edcatn	FOR	14) Lim Wndfll Prof Tax	AGN
5) Alaska Lands Bill	FOR	10) Cut OSHA $	AGN	15) Chryslr Loan Grntee	FOR

Election Results

1980 general	Nicholas Mavroules (D)	111,393	(51%)	($360,960)
	Thomas H. Trimarco (R)	103,192	(47%)	($250,061)
1980 primary	Nicholas Mavroules (D)	32,177	(69%)	
	Kenneth G. Bellevue (D).........	14,405	(31%)	($6,653)
1978 general	Nicholas Mavroules (D)	97,099	(54%)	($290,331)
	William E. Bronson (R)	83,511	(46%)	($185,029)

SEVENTH DISTRICT

The 7th congressional district of Massachusetts is a collection of suburbs just north of Boston. Its sociological range extends from Chelsea, where Jewish immigrants first disembarked more than 80 years ago, to Melrose, a comfortable and still distinctly Yankee (and Republican) town. Most of the communities here lie somewhere in between these two extremes and contain many descendants of Irish and Italian immigrants who have reached some degree of financial security if not affluence.

The political trends over the last 30 years here illustrate the change in ethnic composition in the area and shifts in basic attitudes. In the 1950s this was considered a Republican district, and in 1960 John Kennedy was thought to have done unusually well when he carried the area with 57% of the vote. But the Kennedy aura made Democratic politics more popular even as the percentage of Catholics was increasing. So in 1968 Hubert Humphrey, although not himself of Irish stock, got 66% of the vote. Four years later George McGovern, although he lost nationally, did as well as Kennedy; in other words, Democrats were running about 20% ahead of their national standing here. Then the gap narrowed. Jimmy Carter got 57% here in 1976, 7% ahead of his national percentage, and in 1980 Carter came within 463 votes of losing the district and carried it with a 42% plurality, only 1% ahead of his national average. Undoubtedly some of this trend represents the cultural difference between south Georgia and Massachusetts and the fact that Carter was opposed by Massachusetts's own Edward Kennedy in the primaries. Nevertheless, the change is striking. It suggests that an area that was once solidly liberal on both economic and cultural issues is now conservative on economic issues and by no means convinced that cultural issues are important.

The Democratic trend continues, however, in congressional elections. Until 1954 this was a Republican district with a Republican congressman. That year, two years after John Kennedy was elected to the Senate, one of his college roommates, Torbert Macdonald, was elected to the House as a Democrat in the 7th district. Macdonald was reelected without difficulty until his death in May 1976.

The transformation of the district's politics was reflected in the field of candidates to succeed Macdonald. There were twelve Democrats in the primary and no Republican; 105,000 voters participated in the Democratic primary, 10,000 in the Republican. The winner was 30-year-old state Representative Edward Markey, who beat Macdonald's administrative assistant and ten minor candidates. Markey had a maverick record in the legislature that earned him a legislator of the year award from the bar association; he also had the endorsement of 6th district Congressman Michael Harrington. What he didn't have, in a year when voters didn't want it anyway, was Washington experience. It turned out that he had never been in Washington at all; reporters took to writing "Mr. Smith goes to Washington" stories about him as soon as he came to serve out the rest of Macdonald's term.

Markey has not behaved like a neophyte politically. He won seats on the Commerce and Interior Committees and in 1981 won the chair of the Oversight and Investigations Subcommittee of Interior. Markey hoped to use this to spotlight misdeeds of the oil companies and to demonstrate the dangers and impracticalities of nuclear power. He must proceed with some caution, however, since at least one of the Democrats on the subcommittee, Beverly Byron, often votes with Republicans.

Markey has been reelected either by a spectacular margin or has been unopposed. His one serious problem could be redistricting. His district is one that, by virtue of its geographic position and population, could easily be eliminated, and reportedly he does not have many powerful friends in the Massachusetts State House. His best hopes are that the legislators will be persuaded to target Republican Margaret Heckler instead, and this seems more likely; even so, Markey will at the least gain new territory that may contain ambitious young Democratic politicians, or perhaps even a Republican.

Census Data   Pop. (1980 final) 451,683, down 5% in 1970s. Median family income, 1970, $11,406, 119% of U.S.

The Voters

  Employment profile 1970   White collar, 57%. Blue collar, 32%. Service, 11%. Farm, –%.
  Ethnic groups   Black 1980, 1%. Hispanic 1980, 2%. Asian 1980, 1%. Total foreign stock 1970, 37%. Italy, 12%; Canada, 9%; Ireland, 4%; USSR, UK, 3% each; Poland, 1%.

Presidential Vote

1980	Reagan (R)	90,726	(42%)
	Carter (D)	91,189	(42%)
	Anderson (I)	30,656	(14%)
1976	Ford (R)	86,572	(39%)
	Carter (D)	126,935	(57%)

Rep. Edward J. Markey (D) Elected 1976; b. July 11, 1946, Malden; home, Malden; Boston Col., B.A. 1968, J.D. 1972.

Career   Mass House of Reps., 1973–76.

Offices   403 CHOB, 202-225-2836. Also 2100A JFK Fed. Bldg., Boston 02203, 617-223-2781.

Committees   *Energy and Commerce* (10th). Subcommittees: Energy Conservation and Power; Fossil and Synthetic Fuels; Telecommunications, Consumer Protection and Finance.

Interior and Insular Affairs (13th). Subcommittees: Energy and the Environment; Oversight and Investigations (Chairman).

Group Ratings

	ADA	COPE	PC	LCV	CFA	RPN	NAB	NSI	NTU	ACA	ACU
1980	83	84	83	100	93	—	0	0	23	22	11
1979	95	95	88	97	93	—	—	—	25	8	8
1978	90	85	85	94	96	42	0	0	31	7	8

Key Votes

1) Draft Registn $	AGN	6) Fair Hsg DOJ Enfrc	FOR	11) Cut Socl Incr Dfns $	AGN
2) Ban $ to Nicrgua	AGN	7) Lim PAC Contrbtns	FOR	12) Hosptl Cost Controls	FOR
3) Dlay MX Missile	FOR	8) Cap on Food Stmp $	AGN	13) Gasln Ctrls & Allctns	FOR
4) Nuclr Mortorium	FOR	9) New US Dep Edcatn	FOR	14) Lim Wndfll Prof Tax	AGN
5) Alaska Lands Bill	FOR	10) Cut OSHA $	AGN	15) Chryslr Loan Grntee	FOR

Election Results

1980 general	Edward J. Markey (D)	155,759	(100%)	($67,173)
1980 primary	Edward J. Markey (D)	29,190	(85%)	
	James J. Murphy (D)	5,247	(15%)	($0)
1978 general	Edward J. Markey (D)	145,615	(85%)	($60,542)
	James J. Murphy (I)	26,017	(15%)	

EIGHTH DISTRICT

The 8th of Massachusetts is a congressional district with a number of distinctive features. It is the home of no less than three major universities — Harvard, MIT, and Boston University — and of dozens of small colleges; in all, the 8th has the second highest proportion of college students (15% of the potential electorate in 1970) in the nation. The 8th is distinctive physically: it includes most of Boston's downtown, with its 1920s buildings alternating with modern architecture and Faneuil Hall and the restored 1820s Quincy Market. It has literally dozens of distinctive neighborhoods, from the Italian quarter in Boston's North End to the insular Irish community of Charlestown, the newer Portuguese community in Cambridge, the Armenians in Watertown, the elderly Jews of Brighton, and the upper-income Yankees and professors of Belmont. And it is distinctive in its congressional representation. This heavily Democratic part of heavily Democratic Massachusetts has been represented successively by a president of the United States and a speaker of the House of Representatives — the only district in American history with such a record.

The president of course was John Kennedy, who won this seat in 1946 as a rich young veteran and held it for six years while waiting to run for the Senate; and the speaker is Thomas "Tip" O'Neill, elected here in 1952 after serving as the first Democratic speaker of the Massachusetts house, and speaker of the House in Washington since the beginning of 1977.

O'Neill is a man of town, not gown, politics, and he still feels most comfortable in the company of experienced Irish pols. In his first years in the House, he was a man who got along by going along — and got a seat on the Rules Committee out of it. In 1967, however, he took the step — rare at the time — of coming out publicly against Lyndon Johnson's policy in Vietnam. This was long before the university vote was important in the district; O'Neill had been persuaded by his children that the war was wrong. As an Irish big city pol who supported the antiwar position, he was a natural bridge between different segments of the Democratic Caucus in the late 1960s and early 1970s.

He also knew how to count. In 1971 he supported Hale Boggs's candidacy for majority leader and brought a number of eastern votes along with him. Boggs won, and O'Neill was appointed whip. When Boggs was lost in a plane crash in 1972, O'Neill succeeded to the majority leadership essentially without opposition. The succession to the speakership, after Carl Albert retired in 1976, was even easier.

How has O'Neill stacked up as speaker? First, he is in fact the functioning leader of the Democratic majority in the House — something that could not really be said of his two predecessors and indeed was seldom true of the fabled Sam Rayburn in his later years. Part of the reason for O'Neill's effectiveness is lack of competing power centers. The Rules Committee, no longer chaired by southern conservatives, is responsive to the speaker's wishes. Such committee chairmen as Wilbur Mills of Ways and Means and Wayne Hays of House Administration are gone. Phillip Burton, defeated in 1976 for majority leader by one vote, is not a close O'Neill friend; Jim Wright, the man who did win, does not have as much of a personal power base. If power in the House today is diffused among dozens of subcommittee chairmen and activist members of both parties, it is also concentrated to a greater extent than it used to be at the top, in the hands of the speaker. Some of those who complain that there are no strong leaders in the House anymore are columnists who used to have good sources on the Hill but who now do not get the inside story and scoop from O'Neill. Instead, the speaker is candid about his plans and strategies in open press conference.

O'Neill is a highly partisan man, and unlike some of his predecessors, he has no great affection for his Republican counterparts. Republicans are the enemy, and the speaker sees his job as getting legislation through with Democratic votes. His task will be more difficult now that there are only 242 Democratic votes — just 26 more than the majority of 218 — than it was when there were 290, as there were just after the 1974 elections. O'Neill's job will be even more difficult since President Reagan, at least at the beginning of his term, seemed to be doing a fine job of defining the issues and controlling the dialogue. O'Neill has shown, however, that he can be a legislative strategist of great talent. The best example is the energy bill in the 95th Congress. When the Carter Administration advanced its proposals, O'Neill's impulse was to help get them through the House. But it would be difficult. Various committees had jurisdiction over different parts of the program, and they had different policy preferences; the House had failed to report out anything at all when President Ford submitted an energy bill. So O'Neill set up an ad hoc committee, including members from all the relevant committees that had to pass on the substantive legislation. He chose as its chairman Thomas Ashley of Ohio, a competent worker with few personal enemies and without the sort of ambition that makes other members nervous or jealous. He got the main problems thrashed out in that committee and then got the legislative committees to report out the bill. Most of the points in the program he put into one major bill, which members had to vote up or down; there would be no piece-by-piece dismemberment of the legislation on the floor. Certain particularly important and controversial provisions — notably the question of deregulation of natural gas — were to be voted on separately. Then the bill passed the House. It was quite a contrast with the Senate's approach to the same legislation, which featured lengthy and often frivolous filibustering, endless nonbargaining at conference committee. O'Neill framed the issues, got an up-or-down vote, and passed a major bill. There had not been a performance like this in the House for a long, long time.

But this episode also shows what has turned out to be O'Neill's greatest weakness: he does not set goals on major issues himself. When he became speaker, he expected the national administration of his party to establish its priorities on issues and to come up with specific programs; when the Carter Administration did this, as on energy, O'Neill performed ably. But too often the Carter Administration had no priorities or sent up legislation, such as its welfare and tax reforms, about which it soon became clear that the president really cared very little. O'Neill is the old-fashioned kind of Democrat who believes in generous aid to the poor and the helpless. The Carter Administration kept sending him conflicting signals — or no signals at all — and as a result his legislative talents were seldom brought into play.

MASSACHUSETTS 507

O'Neill is now faced with an entirely different situation, and like many other Democrats he is not sure what course to follow. Priorities were set very clearly at the start of the Reagan Administration, and Democrats could not decide whether to put up a probably futile fight against the Reagan budget cuts or whether to go along and concede the issue to Reagan. O'Neill the partisan Democrat may be torn one way and O'Neill the leader of one branch of government the other. Presumably he will lead a fight on at least some points, but choosing that ground is difficult and there is no national administration and there are no nationally respected leaders to give guidance. O'Neill, after 44 years as a legislator — 16 in Massachusetts and 28 in Washington — is now forced to make the kind of decisions on which he and all other legislative leaders have been accustomed to deferring to others. His task is all the more difficult because House Democrats so obviously do not agree among themselves on either strategy or tactics — not to speak of issue positions. O'Neill may have control of procedure in the House; he has a substantial majority on the Rules Committee and a strong ally in Chairman Richard Bolling. But on most issues the traditional Democratic position probably does not command a majority on the House floor. O'Neill can use procedure to help him win a few additional votes here and there, or to prevent Republicans from framing the issue most favorably to their cause. But he is the kind of leader who tends to allow up-or-down votes on major substantive issues, and he seems unlikely to control many outcomes through procedural legerdemain.

O'Neill must in some respects be a frustrated man: he is the best speaker the House has had for some time, and yet his party has steadily lost members since he assumed that post. Those losses result largely from issues beyond his ability to control. But the fact is that he does not present the kind of image that voters seem to want; he is part of an older, backroom tradition of politics, and he does not have the smooth, soft-toned television delivery of a Howard Baker. O'Neill did display a mastery of the proceedings at the 1980 Democratic National Convention, which would have gotten out of control if the Carter forces had been able to do what they wanted unhampered by the calm and independent force of the speaker; but this is a subtle kind of performance that few television viewers were able to appreciate. Their image of O'Neill is probably more like that of the careless white-maned driver of the car that runs out of gas in the very effective Republican television ad.

There have been rumors that O'Neill will retire, and he turns 70 in 1982. But he is still a year younger than President Reagan, and he still seems to have a taste for the fray. He would not, one assumes, like to be minority leader, a position he last held in the Massachusetts House in 1947 and 1948. But he probably will run again. The 8th district has had considerable population loss since 1970, which means that the boundaries of the district will have to be changed, but the Democratic legislature back home will certainly draw him a district he can easily win.

Census Data Pop. (1980 final) 435,160, down 8% in 1970s. Median family income, 1970, $10,317, 108% of U.S.

The Voters

Employment profile 1970 White collar, 63%. Blue collar, 24%. Service, 13%. Farm, -%.
Ethnic groups Black 1980, 4%. Hispanic 1980, 3%. Asian 1980, 3%. Total foreign stock 1970, 41%. Italy, 10%; Canada, 8%; Ireland, 6%; UK, USSR, 2% each; Portugal, Greece, Germany, Poland, 1% each.

Presidential Vote

1980	Reagan (R)	56,312	(31%)
	Carter (D)	92,707	(51%)
	Anderson (I)	28,822	(16%)
1976	Ford (R)	62,247	(35%)
	Carter (D)	117,446	(65%)

Rep. Thomas P. (Tip) **O'Neill, Jr.** (D) Elected 1952; b. Dec. 9, 1912, Cambridge; home, Cambridge; Boston Col., A.B. 1936.

Career Insurance business; Mass. House of Reps., 1936–52, Minor. Ldr., 1947–48, Spkr., 1948–52; Cambridge School Comm., 1946–47.

Offices 2231 RHOB, 202-225-5111. Also 2200A JFK Fed. Bldg., Boston 02203, 617-223-2784.

Committees *The Speaker of the House.*

Group Ratings and Key Votes: Speaker does not usually vote

Election Results

1980 general	Thomas P. (Tip) O'Neill, Jr. (D) ..	128,689	(78%)	($62,837)
	William A. Barnstead (D)........	35,477	(22%)	($4,829)
1980 primary	Thomas P. (Tip) O'Neill, Jr. (D) ..	41,782	(100%)	
1978 general	Thomas P. (Tip) O'Neill, Jr. (D) ..	102,160	(75%)	($16,274)
	William A. Barnstead (R)........	28,566	(21%)	

NINTH DISTRICT

Boston is the most political of cities. Boston malcontents did more than anyone else to start the American Revolution, and Boston was the hotbed of the abolitionist movement that had so much to do with igniting the Civil War. Boston is also, and this is no coincidence, the nation's most Irish city, for the Irish seem to have some magical aptitude for politics. The proportion of Irish–Americans who live here does not really show up in the census figures, which show only the 7% who came themselves or whose parents came from Ireland; the fact is that there has been heavy Irish immigration here since 1845, and that the Boston Irish are remarkably unassimilated. In the old Irish neighborhoods of South Boston and Charlestown, people keep their ethnic identity although their ancestors may have stepped off the boat more than a century ago. This is not a city where Irish identity is forgotten.

The Irish remain the most important ethnic group in Boston; they have held the mayor's office without substantial interruption from 1906 to the present day. Much of the older Boston wealth, it is true, is still in Yankee Protestant hands, controlled by the kind of people who preserve such Boston institutions as the Athenaeum and the Somerset Club and live in old town houses in Louisburg Square on Beacon Hill. And much of the attention in Boston in recent years has gone to people who are in many ways, the spiritual (and sometimes the lineal) descendants of Samuel Adams and his raucous friends: the leftish, recent/former/ present students, the young liberated people who make up an increasing percentage of the population here. For Boston is, if you look at it that way, the nation's largest college town, not just because of Harvard and MIT across the river in Cambridge, but because of literally hundreds of other schools of all kinds and all levels of repute. Boston is one of the few American cities where the local media, the big retailers, even the banks cater to a market of this sort.

So we have this arresting paradox. Boston, which by some indications is solidly to the left politically (more than 60% for McGovern in 1972), is also the site of the nation's longest-lasting and most bitter antibusing protest (the city went for George Wallace in the 1976 presidential primary). The way to explain the contradiction is to look at just who is upset, and at what. The antiwar movement had its constituency in the post–student generation here; the Irish neighborhoods, after initial hostility and on prompting by Edward Kennedy, concurred. Busing is a problem that troubles almost exclusively the Irish ghettos, such as South Boston, where most of the violence took place. The post–student generation has never been part of the busing controversy.

Moreover, the long-term impact of the busing controversy seems limited. The number of people whose children were affected is not all that great. Many of the whites in the city have always sent their children to Catholic schools; many others are too old to have children of school age. The busing orders that began when blacks formed only a minority of the school population have produced enough white flight that relatively few whites are left in the public school system; many have left for the suburbs, where indeed they might have moved in the natural course of things even without busing.

Certainly the evidence of election returns shows that busing is the concern of a minority. Wallace won here in 1976, but with only 25% of the vote. Mayor Kevin White twice beat Louise Day Hicks, the school committee member closely identified with opposition to busing; and the current school committee does not have a strong antibusing majority. Mrs. Hicks was elected to Congress in 1970, but with minorities in both the primary and general election. She had a minority again in the 1972 primary and lost the general election to a Democratic state senator who was running as an Independent.

That was Joseph Moakley, and he remains the congressman from the 9th district. After his initial victory, he has had no problem winning reelection. Succeeding to a seat once held by a recent Speaker, John McCormack, who served here from 1928 until his retirement in 1970, he was helped by the current Speaker, Tip O'Neill, to a seat on the House Rules Committee. Predictably his votes are in line with the wishes of the House leadership.

Moakley's district will have to be changed somewhat in redistricting. Tip O'Neill's district will probably include more of Boston that it now does, and the 9th will have to go out into more suburbs. Technically, this might put Moakley in the same district with 11th district Congressman Brian Donnelly, but in that event the chances are that Donnelly would move his residence farther out and run in the new 11th.

Census Data Pop. (1980 final) 425,958, down 10% in 1970s. Median family income, 1970, $10,144, 106% of U.S.

The Voters

Employment profile 1970 White collar, 55%. Blue collar, 28%. Service, 17%. Farm, –%.
Ethnic groups Black 1980, 20%. Hispanic 1980, 6%. Asian 1980, 2%. Total foreign stock 1970, 34%. Ireland, 7%; Italy, Canada, 5% each; UK, USSR, 2% each; Poland, Germany, 1% each.

510   MASSACHUSETTS

Presidential Vote

1980	Reagan (R)	64,451	(40%)
	Carter (D)	73,906	(46%)
	Anderson (I)	21,685	(13%)
1976	Ford (R)	69,631	(44%)
	Carter (D)	90,048	(56%)

Rep. John Joseph (Joe) **Moakley** (D) Elected 1972 as Independent, seated in Congress as Democrat, Jan. 3, 1973; b. Apr. 27, 1927, Boston; home, Boston; U. of Miami, B.A., Suffolk U., LL.B. 1956.

Career Navy, WWII; Mass. House of Reps., 1953–65, Major. Whip, 1957; Practicing atty., 1957–72; Mass. Senate, 1965–69; Boston City Cncl., 1971.

Offices 221 CHOB, 202-225-8273. Also 1900C JFK Fed. Bldg., Boston 02203, 617-223-5715.

Committee *Rules* (4th). Subcommittee: Rules of the House (Chairman).

Group Ratings

	ADA	COPE	PC	LCV	CFA	RPN	NAB	NSI	NTU	ACA	ACU
1980	72	82	60	89	79	—	0	20	10	10	12
1979	79	85	75	83	78	—	—	—	16	8	11
1978	75	90	70	91	68	36	0	10	8	4	8

Key Votes

1) Draft Registn $	FOR	6) Fair Hsg DOJ Enfrc	FOR	11) Cut Socl Incr Dfns $	AGN
2) Ban $ to Nicrgua	AGN	7) Lim PAC Contrbtns	FOR	12) Hosptl Cost Controls	FOR
3) Dlay MX Missile	FOR	8) Cap on Food Stmp $	AGN	13) Gasln Ctrls & Allctns	FOR
4) Nuclr Mortorium	FOR	9) New US Dep Edcatn	FOR	14) Lim Wndfll Prof Tax	AGN
5) Alaska Lands Bill	FOR	10) Cut OSHA $	AGN	15) Chryslr Loan Grntee	FOR

Election Results

1980 general	John Joseph (Joe) Moakley (D)...	104,010	(100%)	($81,938)
1980 primary	John Joseph (Joe) Moakley (D)...	27,162	(100%)	
1978 general	John Joseph (Joe) Moakley (D)...	106,805	(92%)	($46,217)
	Brenda L. M. Franklin (Soc. Wrkrs.)	6,794	(6%)	

TENTH DISTRICT

The 10th congressional district of Massachusetts is one example of a geographical monstrosity tailored to the political needs of one longtime incumbent and now serving those of another in equally good fashion. The 10th is made up of two quite different parts. In the north are the Boston suburbs: posh, WASPy Wellesley and the more middle-class Natick next door. This remains one of the most Republican areas in the state. In the south is the city of Fall River, the district's largest city; it is an aging mill town that never really recovered from the southward flight of its 110 cotton mills. The huge granite and brick structures are now occupied, if at all, with marginal dress and curtain sweatshops that pay the French

Canadian and Portuguese workers (most of the latter from the Azores) minimal wages. This end of the 10th is dominated politically by voters of Portuguese, French Canadian, and Italian descent who ordinarily vote Democratic. The middle of the 10th, between the two ends of the district, is composed of sparsely populated towns spread over the rolling hills between Boston and Providence. Among them are Foxboro, home of the New England Patriots, and North Attleboro, home of the district's longtime (1925-67) Congressman, Joseph W. Martin Jr.

For many years the district's boundaries were drawn to provide a safe seat for Martin, who was speaker of the House following the Republican congressional victories of 1946 and 1952. But by the 1960s Martin had been ousted from the leadership and, past 80, was no longer capable of campaigning. Challenged in the primary, he was defeated by Margaret Heckler, a Wellesley attorney, who was then the only Republican member of the Governor's Council—an antique institution that survives from colonial days only in Massachusetts, New Hampshire, and Maine.

Heckler has not really had much difficulty winning election since 1966. Her reputation as a liberal Republican helps her in the district, and generally she does score higher ratings from liberal than conservative groups. At the same time, she has been willing to help the Republican leadership when it really needs it. She has a reputation among her colleagues of agonizing over issues before deciding how to cast her vote; it is easier to figure out what to do when you are a Massachusetts Democrat than when you are a Massachusetts Republican. Despite her seniority, she does not have high positions on major committees. She is ranking minority member of the Veterans' Affairs subcommittee on Education, Training, and Employment. She devotes much of her time and energy to veterans' issues and is one of the committee's most vocal supporters of what is considered the innovative approach to veterans' issues—supporting more generous benefits for non–service-connected disabilities, counseling centers and other readjustment programs for Vietnam veterans, and opposing cuts in VA health programs. This has been the minority position on the committee, however, and since veterans' bills are normally considered in the House under a rule that allows no amendments, they are for the most part never even considered on the floor. In 1981 Mrs. Heckler switched from the Agriculture Committee to Science and Technology, usually considered a minor assignment, although it may have a lot of importance for a high tech state such as Massachusetts.

Mrs. Heckler probably faces a tough election in 1982, not because of any great political weakness on her part but because of redistricting. Massachusetts must lose one congressional district, and as one of the two Republicans from a state whose legislature is overwhelmingly Democratic, and a Republican moreover whose district is attenuated and easily divisible among its neighbors, she is an obvious target.

The betting in early 1981 was that the northern part of the 10th (Wellesley, Natick, the Foxboro area) would be combined with the eastern end of the 4th (Brookline, Newton, and Waltham). That would mean a general election battle between Heckler and 4th district freshman Democrat Barney Frank. It would be an interesting clash of personalities and contrast of temperaments: the rapid-fire Frank versus the fluent Mrs. Heckler. Frank will presumably have one of the most liberal records in Congress, Mrs. Heckler one of the most liberal among Republicans. The demography of the new district and its previous representation will probably favor Frank, but no one should rule out Margaret Heckler, a Republican who has held high office in Democratic Massachusetts for 20 years. Another possibility is for Mrs. Heckler to run for governor—a possibility that has many Democrats scared.

Census Data   Pop. (1980 final) 523,101, up 10% in 1970s. Median family income, 1970, $10,747, 112% of U.S.

The Voters

Employment profile 1970   White collar, 46%. Blue collar, 41%. Service, 12%. Farm, 1%.
Ethnic groups   Black 1980, 1%. Hispanic 1980, 1%. Total foreign stock 1970, 32%. Canada, 8%; Portugal, 6%; UK, 3%; Italy, Ireland, Poland, 2% each; USSR, 1%.

Presidential Vote

1980	Reagan (R)	67,592	(45%)
	Carter (D)	57,584	(38%)
	Anderson (I)	23,055	(15%)
1976	Ford (R)	95,210	(43%)
	Carter (D)	118,890	(54%)

Rep. Margaret M. Heckler (R) Elected 1966; b. June 21, 1931, Flushing, N.Y.; home, Wellesley; Albertus Magnus Col., A.B. 1953, Boston Col., LL.B. 1956.

Career Mbr., Mass. Governors Cncl., 1962–66.

Offices 2312 RHOB, 202-225-4335. Also One Washington St. Wellesley Hills 02181, 616-235-3350.

Committees *Science and Technology* (9th). Subcommittee: Science, Research and Technology.

Veterans' Affairs (2d). Subcommittees: Education, Training and Employment; Hospitals and Health Care.

Joint Economic Committee(2d). Subcommittees: Agriculture and Transportation (Vice-chairwoman); Investment, Jobs and Prices.

Group Ratings

	ADA	COPE	PC	LCV	CFA	RPN	NAB	NSI	NTU	ACA	ACU
1980	67	74	70	74	86	—	27	60	25	23	18
1979	47	75	65	72	67	—	—	—	31	38	32
1978	55	70	53	86	64	40	25	63	17	22	42

Key Votes

1) Draft Registn $	AGN	6) Fair Hsg DOJ Enfrc	FOR	11) Cut Socl Incr Dfns $	AGN
2) Ban $ to Nicrgua	FOR	7) Lim PAC Contrbtns	FOR	12) Hosptl Cost Controls	FOR
3) Dlay MX Missile	FOR	8) Cap on Food Stmp $	AGN	13) Gasln Ctrls & Allctns	FOR
4) Nuclr Mortorium	AGN	9) New US Dep Edcatn	FOR	14) Lim Wndfll Prof Tax	AGN
5) Alaska Lands Bill	FOR	10) Cut OSHA $	AGN	15) Chryslr Loan Grntee	FOR

Election Results

1980 general	Margaret M. Heckler (R)	131,794	(61%)	($264,688)
	Robert E. McCarthy (D)	85,629	(39%)	($158,110)
1980 primary	Margaret M. Heckler (R)	4,829	(100%)	
1978 general	Margaret M. Heckler (R)	102,080	(61%)	($210,730)
	John J. Marino (D)	64,868	(39%)	($78,848)

ELEVENTH DISTRICT

The 11th congressional district of Massachusetts includes the southern third of Boston, most of the city's South Shore suburbs, and more suburban territory stretching south to include the shoe manufacturing city of Brockton. With few exceptions, the 11th district's Dorchester and Hyde Park wards of Boston and its suburban towns — Quincy, Braintree (the ancestral home of the Adamses), and the newer Holbrook, Stoughton, and Randolph, away from the Shore — are filled with sons and daughters of Irish, Italian, and Jewish immigrants. Because most of these residents have remained loyal to their forebears' Democratic voting habits, the 11th has been heavily Democratic in recent years. Its Yankee minority, whose ancestors sent John Quincy Adams to the House for the last years of his life (1831–48), has been steadily abandoning the Republican Party, thus adding to the Democratic majorities — at least until the 1980 presidential election.

The succession of congressmen from this district points up the changes that have occurred in the last two generations of Massachusetts politics. For 30 years, from 1929 to 1959, the district's congressman was a Brahmin Republican with the imposing name of Richard Wigglesworth. His successor for 20 years, from 1959 to 1979, was James Burke, whose name and visage mirror his Irish descent. A loyal follower of the Democratic leadership, Burke epitomized old-fashioned Boston Irish politics. He was a member of the Ways and Means Committee, and as head of the subcommittee on Social Security, he was always generous about increasing benefits. Concerned about the plight of shoe workers in his district, Burke sponsored a major bill backed by the AFL–CIO to put restrictions on imports. A congressman with a near-perfect labor record, he joined other Massachusetts Democrats in opposing the Vietnam war. But Burke's approach to politics was always practical rather than idealistic. He is supposed to have advised a young colleague that "you only have to worry about two things around here — Social Security and shoes."

Burke's health deteriorated, and in 1976 he was nearly beaten in the Democratic primary by Patrick McCarthy, who despite his name was a native of California, not Massachusetts. At 68, Burke retired at the end of the term; still bitter about 1976, he and other local politicians backed Brian Donnelly. At 31, he was already a three-term veteran of the state legislature; with deep roots in the district, he easily beat McCarthy and other opponents. The general election was anticlimactic. This district, which had never had a Democratic congressman before Burke, had no Republican candidate at all. Donnelly has seats on the Public Works and Merchant Marine Committees, suggesting that he, like his predecessor, is more interested in bread-and-butter issues than in starry-eyed causes.

In his second term Donnelly got a seat on the Budget Committee, where he is expected to vote in accordance with the wishes of the Democratic leadership. Redistricting will probably move the 11th district southward, because of population loss in Boston and the close-in suburbs and population gain farther south and in Plymouth County. In that event, Donnelly will have the choice between a primary with 9th district incumbent Joseph Moakley or — and this is probably what he will choose — moving his residence into one of the suburbs.

Census Data   Pop. (1980 final) 461,396, down 3% in 1970s. Median family income, 1970, $11,052, 115% of U.S.

The Voters

Employment profile 1970   White collar, 54%. Blue collar, 33%. Service, 13%. Farm, –%.
Ethnic groups   Black 1980, 9%. Hispanic 1980, 2%. Asian 1980, 1%. Total foreign stock 1970, 35%. Ireland, Canada, 7% each; Italy, 6%; UK, USSR, 3% each; Poland, Lithuania, 1% each.

Presidential Vote

1980	Reagan (R)	84,624	(44%)
	Carter (D)	82,538	(42%)
	Anderson (I)	25,285	(13%)
1976	Ford (R)	80,004	(41%)
	Carter (D)	113,549	(59%)

Rep. Brian J. Donnelly (D) Elected 1978; b. Mar. 2, 1946, Boston; home, Boston; Boston U., B.S. 1970.

Career Dir. of Youth Activities, Dorchester YMCA, 1968–70; High school and trade school teacher and coach, 1969–72; Mass. House of Reps., 1973–79.

Offices 1019 LHOB, 202-225-3215. Also 47 Washington St., Quincy 02169, 617-472-1314.

Committees *Budget* (16th).

Merchant Marine and Fisheries (15th). Subcommittees: Fisheries and Wildlife Conservation and the Environment; Merchant Marine.

Public Works and Transportation (26th). Subcommittees: Economic Development; Public Buildings and Grounds; Surface Transportation.

Group Ratings

	ADA	COPE	PC	LCV	CFA	RPN	NAB	NSI	NTU	ACA	ACU
1980	72	71	53	76	50	—	8	50	18	24	16
1979	63	74	75	69	81	—	—	—	30	28	38

Key Votes

1) Draft Registn $	AGN	6) Fair Hsg DOJ Enfrc	—	11) Cut Socl Incr Dfns $	AGN
2) Ban $ to Nicrgua	AGN	7) Lim PAC Contrbtns	FOR	12) Hosptl Cost Controls	FOR
3) Dlay MX Missile	FOR	8) Cap on Food Stmp $	AGN	13) Gasln Ctrls & Allctns	FOR
4) Nuclr Mortorium	AGN	9) New US Dep Edcatn	AGN	14) Lim Wndfll Prof Tax	AGN
5) Alaska Lands Bill	FOR	10) Cut OSHA $	AGN	15) Chryslr Loan Grntee	FOR

Election Results

1980 general	Brian J. Donnelly (D)	137,066	(100%)	($60,806)
1980 primary	Brian J. Donnelly (D)	42,310	(100%)	
1978 general	Brian J. Donnelly (D)	133,644	(92%)	($184,204)
	H. Graham Lowry (U.S. Labor) ..	12,044	(8%)	

TWELFTH DISTRICT

The 12th congressional district of Massachusetts is one of those seats that was originally designed to elect a Republican congressman and now elects a Democrat. The heavily Democratic city of New Bedford, an old whaling port where the hard-pressed fishing industry is still important, was combined with traditionally Republican territory. This includes some of the more well-to-do South Shore suburbs of Boston (Cohasset, Hingham), most of Plymouth County, Cape Cod, and the two resort islands of Martha's Vineyard and Nantucket. The last was the whaling port from which Herman Melville's Captain Ahab sailed in pursuit of Moby Dick; today, like the Vineyard, Nantucket is a place for rich and trendy summer people, with quaint old New England houses carefully restored. Both islands are upset about losing their seat in the Massachusetts legislature and once threatened to secede or join New Hampshire or Vermont.

This is still the closest thing to a dependably Republican district in Massachusetts, the only Massachusetts district to favor Richard Nixon over George McGovern in 1972, and its majority for Jimmy Carter in 1976 was the state's smallest. In 1980, it favored Reagan over Carter by a 46%–37% margin, again the most Republican in the state. The 12th is also the fastest-growing and perhaps the most prosperous district in Massachusetts. The Cape is changing from a seasonal resort area to a year-round residence for the affluent retired; Plymouth County, meanwhile, is filling up with people who want to live a little farther out from Boston.

The 12th has now broken with years of Republican tradition and regularly elects a Democratic Congressman, Gerry Studds. (His first name, a reminder that he is distantly related to Elbridge Gerry, vice president under Madison and drafter of the original gerrymander, is pronounced with a hard g.) Studds first ran in 1970 and nearly beat the Republican incumbent; during the next two years he learned Portuguese and studied the problems of the local fishing industry. Even against a heavy-spending Republican in 1972, he won.

Much of the fervor behind Studds's first two campaigns came from his opposition to the war in Southeast Asia. But his record in the House shows a concentration on the practical problems of the 12th district. He has switched now from Public Works to the Foreign Affairs Committee, and he has advanced amendments to prohibit sale of the AWACs weapon system to Iran and to cut military aid to Argentina. But he has also stayed on the Merchant Marine and Fisheries Committee where he supports maritime subsidies but occasionally shows a streak of independence. In his first term he succeeded in pushing through a bill to extend the territorial waters of the United States to 200 miles from shoreline. More recently he has worked on the continental shelf bill, looking out for the interests of small fishermen and has sponsored a bill to protect local businesses from losses due to oil spills. Concentration on such matters has paid off politically. Since 1972 he has had only nuisance opposition, with no Republican opponents whatever in two of the last three elections. The district must lose some territory in redistricting, but that should pose no major difficulty for Studds.

Census Data Pop. (1980 final) 584,879, up 23% in 1970s. Median family income, 1970, $10,132, 106% of U.S.

The Voters

Employment profile 1970 White collar, 48%. Blue collar, 38%. Service, 13%. Farm, 1%.
Ethnic groups Black 1980, 1%. Hispanic 1980, 1%. Total foreign stock 1970, 31%. Canada, 7%; Portugal, 5%; UK, 4%; Italy, Ireland, 2% each; Poland, 1%.

Presidential Vote

1980	Reagan (R)	161,788	(46%)
	Carter (D)	127,873	(37%)
	Anderson (I)	56,261	(16%)
1976	Ford (R)	119,237	(46%)
	Carter (D)	132,554	(51%)

Rep. Gerry E. Studds (D) Elected 1972; b. May 12, 1937, Mineola, N.Y.; home, Cohasset; Yale U., B.A. 1959, M.A.T. 1961.

Career U.S. Foreign Svc., 1961–63; Exec. Asst. to William R. Anderson, Pres. Consultant for a Domestic Peace Corps, 1963; Legis. Asst. to U.S. Sen. Harrison J. Williams of N.J., 1964; Prep. sch. teacher, 1965–69.

Offices 1501 LHOB, 202-225-3111. Also 243 P.O. Bldg., New Bedford 02740, 617-999-1251.

Committees *Foreign Affairs* (10th). Subcommittees: Africa; Inter-American Affairs.

Merchant Marine and Fisheries (5th). Subcommittees: Coast Guard and Navigation (Chairman); Fisheries and Wildlife Conservation and the Environment; Oceanography.

Group Ratings

	ADA	COPE	PC	LCV	CFA	RPN	NAB	NSI	NTU	ACA	ACU
1980	100	84	80	96	86	—	0	0	22	17	11
1979	100	95	95	93	96	—	—	—	21	4	5
1978	95	90	93	97	86	42	0	0	27	7	8

Key Votes

1) Draft Registn $	AGN	6) Fair Hsg DOJ Enfrc	FOR	11) Cut Socl Incr Dfns $	AGN
2) Ban $ to Nicrgua	AGN	7) Lim PAC Contrbtns	FOR	12) Hosptl Cost Controls	FOR
3) Dlay MX Missile	FOR	8) Cap on Food Stmp $	AGN	13) Gasln Ctrls & Allctns	FOR
4) Nuclr Mortorium	FOR	9) New US Dep Edcatn	FOR	14) Lim Wndfll Prof Tax	AGN
5) Alaska Lands Bill	FOR	10) Cut OSHA $	AGN	15) Chryslr Loan Grntee	FOR

Election Results

1980 general	Gerry E. Studds (D)	195,791	(73%)	($78,937)
	Paul V. Doane (R)	71,620	(27%)	($47,490)
1980 primary	Gerry E. Studds (D)	50,248	(100%)	
1978 general	Gerry E. Studds (D), unopposed . .			($20,889)

MICHIGAN

As the 1980s began, no state was more sorely troubled by the nation's economic situation than Michigan. While most of the nation was preparing for a nasty but quick recession, people in Michigan began to fear that the way of life they had labored for years to build was about to vanish. The basic problem was one that had been apparent for years: Michigan was overly dependent on one industry, automobiles. It is an industry that has always been sensitive to ups and downs of the economy: cars, after all, are one of the easiest purchases to postpone. Metropolitan Detroit was a boom town in the years between 1910 and 1930 when the auto industry grew from a gadgets and luxury trade to the nation's largest mass production industry. Accordingly, the population of the three-county metro area increased from 613,000 in 1910 to 2,177,000 in 1930. Then, in a pattern common to one-industry boom towns, the bustling growth of one era was matched by stagnation a half century later. The problem, as Jane Jacobs has pointed out, is that successful, efficient giant firms — the General Motors, Ford, and Chrysler of the 1925-75 period — squeeze out innovative small businesses and create a climate hostile to economic innovation. Then they themselves become less successful.

The automobile industry prospered in the years following World War II because it persuaded Americans constantly to trade in their cars for larger, differently designed models and because it succeeded in making the two-car rather than the one-car family the norm. But by the 1970s the possibilities for continued expansion of this market were limited. Consumers with tastes for gaudy new models were being replaced by younger people with a taste for the more austere styling of foreign cars, and about as many families had bought a second or third car as were likely to do so.

Yet the people who ran the auto companies seemed to assume that things could go on as they had. By 1980 they were blaming government regulations — increased fuel efficiency requirements, mandated safety equipment — for their problems. But the marginal cost of the safety equipment was small, and the efficiency requirements had stimulated the first innovative engineering advances the American auto industry had produced since it developed the automatic transmission in 1938. Meanwhile, carmakers poured huge amounts into annual styling changes. A greater problem was the fact that the government kept price controls on gasoline through the 1970s, stimulating higher sales of big cars after the 1974 gas crisis and persuading Ford and Chrysler managements not to invest heavily in tooling for small cars — which would have sold much better than the big models they had in stock when the gas crisis of 1979 hit.

But even without these developments, it is apparent now that by 1970 American automakers had to look for foreign growth or product diversification for growth. Instead they continued to pursue business as usual. They accepted without much more than a show of protest or a short strike the United Auto Workers' demands for high wages and fringe benefits, which made auto workers the best-paid mass production workers in America. They assumed evidently that they could pass these costs along forever to the American consumer. But in an era of inflation, with strong foreign competition, they could no longer do so; and they made no effort at all to develop an export business, which might have made sense in a world where wages in other countries were rising rapidly too. So by the end of the 1970s Chrysler was in such bad financial shape that it had to seek government loan guarantees to keep out of bankruptcy; Ford was shaky; American Motors was about to be purchased, in effect, by Renault; only General Motors was still solid. And Michigan was in deep trouble.

It would be a mistake to say that all of Michigan was in trouble, or that every part of the state was dependent on the auto industry. There is a pretty clear divide here between the Metro Detroit area and outstate Michigan; and, although some outstate cities, such as Flint, Saginaw, and to some extent Lansing, are heavily dependent on autos, outstate Michigan as a whole is much more diversified and economically healthy than Metro Detroit. Indeed, the three major counties of the metro area — Wayne, Oakland, and Macomb — have on balance had little growth from 1960 (3.7 million) to 1980 (4.0 million), partly because some people who work in the Detroit metro area have moved to counties farther out, but mostly because the auto-based economy of Detroit did not expand much or increase its number of jobs in the 1960s and 1970s. Outstate Michigan, in contrast, has done much better. Its small metro areas — such places as Grand Rapids, Kalamazoo, Lansing — are much more like the small-town ideal most Americans have than are even the more pleasant suburbs of Detroit. Their economies are somewhat more diversified, and some of them have benefited as well from the growth of state government and especially Michigan's outstanding university system. There has been a particular boom in the northern part of Michigan's Lower Peninsula, which had some of the nation's largest population gain percentages in the 1970s; retirees and younger people as well, willing to settle for lower wages in a lower cost of living environment, have been moving to this vacation and resort area from the Detroit area and from other industrial states to the south.

Still, the auto industry does affect the whole state, and its problems in the late 1970s definitely affected state government and politics. With Chrysler laying off literally tens of thousands of workers, unemployment reached figures around 15%, and state government found itself spending $700 million more than it took in. The city government of Detroit was in worse shape. Not only government activity felt the impact. State employees and Chrysler workers took explicit pay cuts; others, through loss of overtime or because of lack of business, took what in effect were cuts. Michigan, which had managed to build one of the highest levels of income in the nation on a heavily blue collar work base suddenly found itself having its income reduced at a time when inflation was over 10%.

In previous recessions, in 1958 or 1970, Michigan had suffered high unemployment but had looked forward to a time when its economy would revive. At the beginning of the 1980s the future looked even bleaker than the present. It became clear, finally, that the domestic auto market would not support ever-increasing payrolls. Chrysler, if it survived, would do so as a much smaller company; Ford was clearly due for serious trimming as well. The whole network of businesses that depend on the auto companies are never likely to be as strong as they were. Metro Detroit, which has depended so long on the auto industry, now must do what that dependence has made very difficult—diversify—or else watch itself shrink. The latter course is more likely. Radio stations in Detroit advertise job vacancies in Houston, and outmigration, already a factor in the 1960s and 1970s, was by 1980 a steady stream.

The crisis had called into question the basis of the good life that people had been building for decades. Michigan's superior system of public education, its physical environment, its generous government protections—all were threatened.

The economic situation in Michigan has produced a politics of turmoil. More than anywhere else in the nation, people here are uncertain about their future and the future of their communities and previous political allegiances have become less important than they were. On the one hand, one might expect Michigan, long considered a Democratic state, to move even closer to the Democrats on the theory that the party would be more generous with government aid. But in fact Michigan went for Ronald Reagan for president in 1980, by almost as large a margin as he won nationwide. One reason was a steady diminution in the Democratic base among Detroit area auto and other blue collar workers. In 1960, John F. Kennedy came to Cadillac Square in Detroit on Labor Day for the traditional opening of the Democratic presidential campaign. More than 60,000 people came there to hear him. Eight years later, Hubert Humphrey decided to begin his campaign elsewhere; labor leaders had informed him that they simply could not get a big crowd together over a holiday weekend. Metro Detroit, filled with auto workers from Poland and Alabama, southern Italy and eastern Kentucky and rural Ontario, and with the very political United Auto Workers Union, gave Kennedy a 62%–38% margin over Richard Nixon in 1960—enough, because Metro Detroit cast almost half the state's votes, but just barely enough, to overcome Nixon's 60%–40% margin outstate. In Wayne County, which includes Detroit, nearly 1.2 million people voted, and they gave Kennedy a 773,000 to 394,000 margin.

By 1980, the Democratic margins in the Detroit area had vanished. In Wayne County only 890,000 people voted, and they gave Carter only a 206,000-vote margin. The suburbs of Oakland County and once heavily Democratic Macomb County both went for Reagan, who lost Metro Detroit by only a 49%–44% margin. Moreover, the metro area, with its sluggish growth, now casts only 42% of the state's votes—despite a rise in turnout that must be attributed to uneasiness over the auto industry's plight and the economic future of the state. Outstate Michigan, despite its Republican traditions, showed little enthusiasm for Reagan and gave him only 53% of its votes. But Carter got a lower percentage here than George McGovern had eight years before. Outstate Michigan, to the extent it is not preoccupied with the problems of the auto industry, is basically part of the Upper Midwest bloc, similar to Wisconsin and Minnesota with their progressive traditions—an area essentially conservative on economic issues but inclined to be liberal on noneconomic, cultural issues. The Democrats would by now have become the clear minority party in Michigan if they could do no better outstate than they did in 1960; instead, at least some Democrats have carried districts here and there outside Metro Detroit and the state's two Democratic senators won not only because they had big majorities in Metro Detroit but also because they held Republicans nearly even outstate.

The most popular politician in the state, however, is a Republican, Governor William Milliken. He is a mild, pleasant man who seems to lack the ambition to have reached this position on his own; in fact, he was George Romney's lieutenant governor and became governor when disappointed presidential candidate Romney became Richard Nixon's first secretary of Housing and Urban Development. Once in office Milliken has proved unacceptable to virtually no one and inspires considerable enthusiasm among at least some voters —especially the well-educated affluent voters of the high-income suburbs. He has made inroads among Catholic voters in the Detroit area, at first because he supported aid for parochial schools and later in spite of his support of state aid for abortions for the indigent; he has generally supported the expansion of state government of the 1970s, although Republicans are confident he was less profligate than a Democrat would have been; he has adjusted to the tax cut measure passed by voters in 1978. Milliken's one major default in office was his failure to act aggressively enough to protect the state from contamination by PBB, a flame retardant placed in cattle feed by mistake and fed to dairy cattle; it is a poison that cannot be expelled from the system and is present in the bodies of virtually everyone in the state —and no one knows with what ill effects. There has been considerable dispute over whether the state acted fast enough to get infected cattle and dairy products off the market and acted carefully enough in disposing of the carcasses of the infected animals.

Milliken won reelection by narrow margins over Sander Levin in 1970 and 1974 and by a larger margin against state Senator Bill Fitzgerald in 1978. By 1982, he will have been governor for 14 years. In the future he is not especially likely to get an administration appointment. Milliken was a strong supporter of George Bush in Michigan's presidential primary and was largely responsible for Bush's showing; he supported Reagan volubly in the general election, although there is some dispute as to how wholeheartedly. Milliken could run again and would be a very strong candidate, if only because people might feel his familiarity comforting in a turbulent time. If he retires there is no clear successor. His lieutenant governor, James Brickley, is not particularly well known statewide; Frank Kelley, who will have been the state's attorney general for more than 20 years, may find that position more comfortable than the risks of seeking the governorship. There are large numbers of Democrats and some Republicans in the legislature, in local government, and in private life who would like to run. Michigan will, if Milliken retires, have as wide open a gubernatorial race as any large state in 1982..

The state's senior senator, Donald Riegle, is still in his early 40s and has already had a long and sometimes colorful career. He started off as a Republican, and in 1966 won an upset victory in the Flint congressional seat; soon he was winning votes from blacks and endorsements from the UAW as well as enjoying the usual management-oriented Republican base. An opponent of the Vietnam war, Riegle campaigned for Pete McCloskey in the 1972 New Hampshire presidential primary and switched to the Democratic Party in early 1973. When Senator Philip Hart decided to retire in 1976, Riegle was the least known of the three major Democrats running for the seat; he outcampaigned the other two and won the nomination. The general election contest was bizarre. In mid-October the *Detroit News* reported that Riegle had had sexual relations with a woman and that the sessions had been taped. Not only that, the *News* printed transcripts. The paper wanted to beat Riegle in the worst way, but their tactic backfired. Voters who might have thought Riegle indiscreet or ridiculous after the first article were revolted after the transcripts were printed. After all, one of the few things most voters have in common is that they have had intimate sexual experiences, and no one wants transcripts of such experiences printed in a newspaper. Lost in all the commotion was Riegle's opponent, Republican Congressman Marvin Esch, who had been elected the same year as Riegle and had a similar voting record — without the urge toward rebellion. Riegle won the election by a small but solid plurality.

Riegle's term in the Senate has been characterized not by high jinks but by hard work. He has seats on the leading economic committees — Banking, Commerce, and Human Resources — which are more important to Michigan now than they were even in 1976. On Human Resources he can be counted on to oppose moves to weaken labor legislation — which is important to heavily unionized Michigan. He was the Senate's leading advocate of reducing clean air standards, a move supported both by the auto companies and the United Auto Workers. As chairman of the Consumer Affairs Subcommittee of Banking, he managed two significant pieces of legislation, one on debt collection and the other safeguarding consumers' rights in electronic banking and funds transfers. And he was the leader of the successful fight in the Senate to get the federal government to issue loan guarantees for Chrysler. At this writing, Chrysler's fate is not clear; but it is clear that if Riegle had not been successful in what was at the beginning by no means an easy fight, Michigan would have lost many more jobs than it did in 1979 and 1980. Riegle is indeed an appropriate person to lead these fights in which Michigan's leading business and union figures are on the same side. Riegle's initial career was in business, with IBM, and he can still talk business school language. But he also has one of the most solid prolabor records in the Senate. Riegle's party switch, which put him with the Democrats when they made their big Watergate gains, now leaves him a member of the minority (which he was for most of his career in the House). But he has proved himself to be a tenacious, hard-working fighter, and also one capable of assembling a majority in difficult circumstances.

Riegle will likely face a tough fight for reelection in 1982. Michigan Senate elections lately have been close, and a creditable Republican challenger is likely to emerge. At the beginning of 1981, however, it was not clear who that would be; one possibility, Congressman David Stockman, the only member of the state's delegation to vote against the Chrysler loan guarantee, became President Reagan's OMB director instead. Riegle has a solid base in Flint, but that is only a small city; and a senator from a big state like Michigan cannot hope to have the close personal contact with constituents a senator from a small state like Wyoming can establish. Much will depend on the state of Michigan's economy, and whether voters here think they need more assistance from the federal government (as Democrats have been arguing) or less interference from federal regulations (as Ronald Reagan argued here in 1980).

Michigan's other senator is Carl Levin, former president of the Detroit city council and brother of 1970 and 1974 gubernatorial nominee Sander Levin. His record in Detroit was one of constructive cooperation with, but independence from, Mayor Coleman Young. While Young is very popular with blacks and distrusted by some whites, Levin was one figure who in times of racial turbulence earned the trust and votes of Detroiters of both races. His own attractive record helped him to a substantial victory in a multicandidate Democratic primary in 1978, and he went into the general election with what appeared to be enough strength to win. He had additional help, however, from his opponent, Senator Robert Griffin. Over the years Griffin had proved himself one of the canniest politicians Michigan has ever produced: he pushed the Landrum–Griffin labor bill through a heavily Democratic House in 1959 over the opposition of organized labor; he won a Senate seat in 1966 over six-term former Governor G. Mennen Williams; he singlehandedly kept Abe Fortas from being chief justice of the U.S. Supreme Court; he held his seat in 1972 by cleverly exploiting the busing issue when Detroit and its suburbs were under a federal court busing order; he was a close ally of President Ford.

Then in late 1976 and early 1977 Griffin suffered a number of setbacks. Ford was beaten, which meant that Griffin lost all hope of a Supreme Court appointment; then Griffin himself was beaten, unexpectedly, in his race to succeed Hugh Scott as Senate Republican leader. The new senators preferred the more photogenic, more presentable Howard Baker. So early in 1977 Griffin announced he would retire in 1978, and this usually diligent senator missed 216 roll call votes. A year later he reconsidered and decided to run. But Levin peppered him with charges of absenteeism and lack of enthusiasm. In a state where 40% of the work force belongs to unions and most working adults have to punch a time clock if they want to get paid, the absenteeism issue worked well. Levin won a victory similar in support levels to Rie-gle's, with a solid 3–2 edge in Metro Detroit and a very respectable 48% in outstate Michigan. He was helped by the increasing migration from the Detroit area to the northern part of the Lower Peninsula; he carried many counties that never used to go Democratic, as well as such industrial areas as Flint, Bay City, Port Huron, and the old mining country of the Upper Peninsula.

Levin has committee assignments that show an interest in broad national policies: Armed Services and Governmental Affairs. Michigan is a state that receives little defense money, and Levin by convictions is one of the Senate's greatest skeptics about the work of strategic nuclear weapons; he believes in modernization of the Army; he is a strong believer in arms control agreements. For the time being, at least, he seems clearly in a minority position on most of these issues. On Governmental Affairs, he has been working closely with David Boren, a much more conservative Oklahoma Democrat also elected in 1978, to fashion a bill to allow Congress to veto regulations adopted by administrative agencies; Levin feels some go too far and undermine good programs. Levin will have a hard time making his views prevail in a Senate where Republicans have the majority; but he is a man of passionate convictions who is also capable of understanding the contrary passions of others — which is to say a natural creative legislator. He has the luxury of not having his seat come up for reelection until 1984.

Michigan has lost one congressional seat in reapportionment in the 1980 census — ironically, a seat it had gained in the 1960 census, after the last decade of above-national-average growth in the industrial Great Lakes region. The loss must come out of the Detroit metro area, although a reshuffling of boundaries may make the loser in the inevitable game of musical chairs someone as far afield from Detroit as Carl Pursell of the 2d district. The legislature is solidly Democratic — in all the recent years of national Republican trends, Republicans have made no significant gains in elections for state legislative seats here — and, while Governor Milliken has a veto, his leverage is not too great. Neither the governor nor the legislature will eliminate the state's two black-dominated districts, which means that one of the white congressmen representing Wayne, Oakland, or Macomb Counties will be eliminated. Almost all are Democrats, some of them quite powerful in Washington — e.g., John Dingell and William Ford, who are sure to survive. There are too many high-income, heavily

Republican precincts in Oakland County to eliminate Republican veteran William Broomfield. That leaves as likely targets the two relatively junior members from the east side suburbs, or one of the less senior members from the west side suburbs (including the one Republican in the group, Pursell). Outstate congressional districts, however, are not likely to be fundamentally altered; and while the legislature would like to help Democrats, it is not clear whether this is best done by weakening a Republican incumbent in one district or strengthening the Democrat in the district next door. This will be one of the more complex of the redistrictings for 1982.

Census Data   Pop. (1980 final) 9,258,344, up 4% in 1970s: 4.09% of U.S. total, 8th largest. Central city, 24%; suburban, 57%. Median 4-person family income, 1978, $22,063, 108% of U.S., 9th highest.

1979 Share of Federal Tax Burden $20,737,000,000; 4.60% of U.S. total, 7th largest.

1979 Share of Federal Outlays $14,327,799,000; 3.09% of U.S. total, 10th largest.

DOD	$2,102,734,000	16th	(1.98%)	HEW	$7,559,697,000	8th	(4.22%)
DOE	$33,975,000	29th	(0.29%)	ERDA	$9,815,000	29th	(0.36%)
HUD	$239,862,000	9th	(3.64%)	NASA	$14,588,000	22d	(0.31%)
VA	$600,794,000	9th	(2.90%)	DOT	$338,186,000	16th	(2.05%)
EPA	$191,726,000	9th	(3.61%)	DOC	$30,720,000	19th	(0.97%)
DOI	$45,743,000	28th	(0.82%)	USDA	$517,789,000	18th	(2.15%)

Economic Base   Motor vehicles and equipment, and other transportation equipment; machinery, especially metalworking machinery; finance, insurance, and real estate; fabricated metal products, especially metal stampings; primary metal industries, especially iron and steel foundries; agriculture, notably dairy products, cattle, dry beans, and corn; food and kindred products.

Political Lineup   Governor, William G. Milliken (R). Senators, Donald W. Riegle, Jr. (D) and Carl Levin (D). Representatives, 19 (12 D and 7 R); 18 in 1982. State Senate, 38 (24 D and 14 R); State House of Representatives, 110 (64 D and 46 R).

The Voters

Registration 5,730,048 Total. No party registration.
Employment profile 1970 White collar, 45%. Blue collar, 41%. Service, 13%. Farm, 1%.
Ethnic groups Black 1980, 13%. Hispanic 1980, 2%. Asian 1980, 1%. Total foreign stock 1970, 19%. Canada, 4%; Poland, Germany, UK, 2% each; Italy; 1%.

Presidential Vote

1980	Reagan (R)	1,915,225	(49%)
	Carter (D)	1,661,532	(42%)
	Anderson (I)	275,223	(7%)
1976	Ford (R)	1,893,742	(52%)
	Carter (D)	1,696,714	(46%)

1980 Democratic Presidential Primary
This primary did not affect delegate selection.

Brown............	23,043	(29%)
One other	8,948	(11%)
Scattering	10,048	(13%)
Uncommitted	36,385	(46%)

1980 Republican Presidential Primary

Bush	341,998	(57%)
Reagan	189,184	(32%)
Anderson	48,947	(8%)
Two others & scattering	4,782	(1%)
Uncommitted	10,265	(2%)

SENATORS

Sen. Donald W. Riegle, Jr. (D) Elected 1976, seat up 1982; b. Feb. 4, 1938, Flint; home, Flint; Flint Jr. Col., W. Mich. U., U. of Mich., B.A. 1960, Mich. St. U., M.B.A. 1961.

Career Consultant, IBM Corp., 1961–64; Faculty Mbr., Mich. St. U., Boston U., Harvard U.; U.S. House of Reps., 1967–77, first elected as Repub., switched to Dem. Party Feb. 27, 1973.

Offices 1207 DSOB, 202-224-4822. Also 477 Michigan Ave., 18th Flr., Detroit 48226, 313-226-3188, and Genesee Towers, 1st and Harrison Sts., Flint 48502, 313-234-5621.

Committees *Banking, Housing, and Urban Affairs* (4th). Subcommittees: Housing and Urban Affairs; Economic Policy; Securities.

Budget (8th).

Commerce, Science and Transportation (6th). Subcommittees: Science, Technology, and Space; Surface Transportation.

Labor and Human Resources (6th). Subcommittees: Labor; Alcoholism and Drug Abuse.

Group Ratings

	ADA	COPE	PC	LCV	CFA	RPN	NAB	NSI	NTU	ACA	ACU
1980	83	100	73	96	67	—	8	0	20	4	0
1979	84	94	69	—	86	—	—	—	20	15	6
1978	85	89	80	71	70	67	11	20	7	0	8

Key Votes

1) Draft Registn $	AGN	6) Fair Housng Cloture	FOR	11) Cut Socl Incr Defns	AGN
2) Ban $ to Nicrgua	FOR	7) Ban $ Rape Abortns	AGN	12) Income Tax Indexing	FOR
3) Dlay MX Missile	FOR	8) Cap on Food Stmp $	AGN	13) Lim Spdg 21% GNP	AGN
4) Nuclr Mortorium	FOR	9) New US Dep Edcatn	FOR	14) Incr Wndfll Prof Tax	FOR
5) Alaska Lands Bill	FOR	10) Cut OSHA Inspctns	AGN	15) Chryslr Loan Grntee	FOR

Election Results

1976 general	Donald W. Riegle, Jr. (D)	1,831,031	(52%)	($795,821)
	Marvin L. Esch (R)	1,635,087	(47%)	($809,564)
1976 primary	Donald W. Riegle, Jr. (D)	325,705	(44%)	
	Richard A. Austin (D)	208,310	(28%)	
	James G. O'Hara (D)	170,473	(23%)	
	One other (D)	30,655	(4%)	
1970 general	Philip A. Hart (D)	1,744,672	(67%)	
	Lenore Romney (R)	858,438	(33%)	

Sen. Carl Levin (D) Elected 1978, seat up 1984; b. June 28, 1933, Detroit; home, Detroit; Swarthmore Col., B.A. 1956, Harvard U., J.D.

Career Practicing atty.; Asst. Atty. Gen. of Mich and Gen. Counsel for the Mich. Civil Rights Comm., 1964–67, Spec. Asst. Atty. Gen. of Mich. and Chief Appellate Defender for the City of Detroit, 1968–69; Detroit City Cncl., 1969–78, Pres., 1973–78.

Offices 140 RSOB, 202-224-6221. Also 18th Flr., McNamara Bldg., Detroit 48226, 313-226-6020.

Committees *Armed Services* (8th). Subcommittees: Tactical Warfare; Preparedness.

Governmental Affairs (8th). Subcommittees: Energy, Nuclear Proliferation, and Government Processes; Oversight of Government Management.

Select Committee on Small Business (6th). Subcommittee: Innovation and Technology.

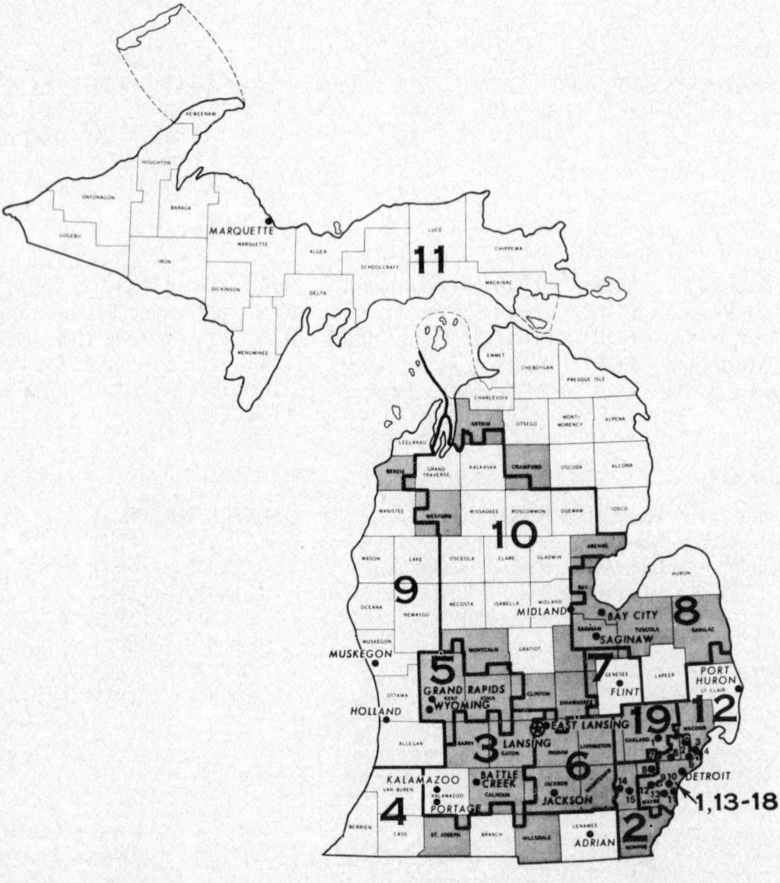

Group Ratings

	ADA	COPE	PC	LCV	CFA	RPN	NAB	NSI	NTU	ACA	ACU
1980	94	94	77	80	80	—	0	10	16	12	0
1979	74	95	72	—	86	—	—	—	16	11	9

Key Votes

1) Draft Registn $	AGN	6) Fair Housng Cloture	FOR
2) Ban $ to Nicrgua	—	7) Ban $ Rape Abortns	AGN
3) Dlay MX Missile	FOR	8) Cap on Food Stmp $	AGN
4) Nuclr Mortorium	FOR	9) New US Dep Edcatn	FOR
5) Alaska Lands Bill	FOR	10) Cut OSHA Inspctns	AGN

11) Cut Socl Incr Defns	AGN
12) Income Tax Indexing	AGN
13) Lim Spdg 21% GNP	AGN
14) Incr Wndfll Prof Tax	FOR
15) Chryslr Loan Grntee	FOR

Election Results

1978 general	Carl Levin (D)	1,484,193	(52%)	($971,775)
	Robert P. Griffin (R)	1,362,165	(48%)	($1,681,550)
1978 primary	Carl Levin (D)	226,584	(39%)	
	Phil Power (D)	115,117	(20%)	($943,500)
	Richard Vander Veen (D)........	89,257	(15%)	($264,217)
	Anthony Derezinski (D)	53,696	(9%)	($63,917)
	John Otterbacher (D)	50,860	(9%)	($152,498)
	Paul Rosenbaum (D)	46,896	(8%)	($153,189)
1972 general	Robert P. Griffin (R)	1,781,065	(52%)	($1,394,927)
	Frank J. Kelly (D)	1,577,178	(47%)	($547,819)

GOVERNOR

Gov. William G. Milliken (R) Appointed 1969, elected 1970, term expires Jan. 1983; b. Mar. 26, 1922; Yale U., B.A.

Career Army Air Corps, WWII; Pres.., J.W. Milliken, Inc., Dept. Store Chain; Mich. Senate, 1961–65, Major. Flr. Ldr., 1963; Lt. Gov. of Mich., 1965–69.

Office State Capitol Box 30013, Lansing 48909, 517-373-3430.

Election Results

1978 gen.	William G. Milliken (R)....	1,628,485	(57%)
	William B. Fitzgerald (D) ..	1,237,256	(43%)
1978 prim.	Wm. G. Milliken (R), unopp.		
1974 gen.	William G. Milliken (R)....	1,365,865	(51%)
	Sander M. Levin (D)	1,242,247	(47%)

FIRST DISTRICT

The 1st congressional district of Michigan includes the north and near northwest sides of Detroit, plus the enclave–suburb of Highland Park. This area is a good example of the pace of neighborhood change in 20th-century America. Sixty-odd years ago the land here was given over completely to Michigan farms; at that time Detroit's growth had not yet reached the southern boundary of the 1st, five miles north of the Detroit River. Then, in 1910, Henry Ford built his first big auto plant in Highland Park. At that time, as now, manufacturers located their factories at the edge of urban settlement, where a labor force is at hand, land prices are cheap, and room to expand is available. In the years that followed, mile after mile of closely spaced one- and two-family houses were built in subdivisions geared to scale imposed by the automobile. Ethnic neighborhood patterns emerged: Polish in the eastern and southern parts of the current 1st; Jewish in the middle; and a rich WASP section north of Highland Park. During the 1910–30 period population growth here was as rapid as anywhere in the country, and even today most of the 1st's housing units were built in those two decades.

In the years that followed World War II another kind of change took place. In 1945 there were few black enclaves within the lines of the current 1st; even in 1950 less than 5% of the residents of the area were black. By 1970 that figure had risen to 70% and by 1980 it was 87%. The first white exodus — or, rather, the first black movement in — occurred during the late 1940s and early 1950s. Thousands of blacks who had come to Detroit during the war left the small ghettos in which they had been confined, while whites fled to the outer limits of the city or to the FHA-financed suburbs. Whole square miles of Detroit changed racial complexion within a year or two. Later, in the wake of the 1967 riot, another particularly rapid racial transformation took place. What was previously Detroit's Jewish neighborhood along Seven Mile Road soon became heavily black. Around the same time the city's most affluent area opened up to blacks; today some of the most elegant housing in the Detroit area — the kind they don't build anymore — can be found in black or integrated neighborhoods. Population declined here in the 1970s, but not at the high rates associated with social disorganization and rampant crime, as in the 13th district; the change here is mostly the result of people having fewer children and therefore smaller households.

There are still pockets of all-white territory in the 1st, particularly in the Polish neighborhoods that resist change of any sort. Generally speaking, the blacks in the 1st are more affluent and better educated than those in the nearby 13th district; most people here own their own homes, and they are also more likely to vote. Some analysts have speculated that blacks, as they grow more affluent, will grow more conservative and Republican. Maybe so, but the evidence here is quite to the contrary. In the 1972, 1976, and 1980 presidential races this was one of the two or three most Democratic congresssional districts in the country.

The 1st district's congressman is John Conyers, a Democrat who has always been regarded as outspoken. In 1964, when he was first elected to the House, there were only four other blacks there, and he was by far the most militant. From the beginning, for example, he spoke and voted against the Vietnam war. He was instrumental in setting up the Congressional Black Caucus, in part to get around the mellow ways of older black members; now, ironically, it is some of the younger blacks who are more prone to work quietly within the system. As a member of the Judiciary Committee, Conyers voted for the impeachment of Richard Nixon; indeed, he had called for Nixon's impeachment in 1972 for what he regarded as his illegal warmaking activities.

Conyers seems to regard his job as expressing a point of view and seems to care less about being effective. Thus in early 1979 he made a point of walking out of a White House meeting with President Carter in disgust. That didn't accomplish much, and it probably reduced Conyers's effectiveness; but as poll evidence showed some weeks later, it did accurately reflect the attitude of many blacks and white liberals toward Carter's proposed budget cuts. His relations with the Reagan Administration are likely to be as distant as those of any member of Congress. Conyers is now fifth-ranking Democrat on the Judiciary Committee and chairman of the Criminal Justice Subcommittee. He has done a competent job of managing legislation on the floor despite his firebrand reputation. His district is safe — he has never received less than 85% in a primary or general election since 1964 — and he has at least an outside chance of being chairman of the Judiciary Committee someday. Redistricting will probably move the 1st district out farther northwest, following black population movement, and it is almost certain that Conyers will have a safe seat.

Census Data   Pop. (1980 final) 393,444, down 16% in 1970s. Median family income, 1970, $9,997, 104% of U.S.

The Voters

Employment profile 1970   White collar, 41%. Blue collar, 42%. Service, 17%. Farm, –%.
Ethnic groups   Black 1980, 87%. Hispanic 1980, 1%. Total foreign stock 1970, 15%. Canada, Poland, 2% each; USSR, UK, Germany, 1% each.

Presidential Vote

1980	Reagan (R)	5,867	(5%)
	Carter (D)	112,907	(93%)
	Anderson (I)	1,402	(1%)
1976	Ford (R)	12,618	(10%)
	Carter (D)	121,815	(89%)

Rep. John Conyers, Jr. (D) Elected 1964; b. May 16, 1929, Detroit; home, Detroit; Wayne St. U., B.A. 1957, LL.B. 1958.

Career Army, Korea; Legis. Asst. to U.S. Rep. John Dingell, 1958–61; Practicing atty., 1959–61; Referee, Mich. Workmen's Comp. Dept., 1961–63.

Offices 2313 RHOB, 202-225-5126. Also 305 Fed. Bldg., 231 W. Lafayette St., Detroit 48226, 313-226-7022.

Committees Government Operations (6th). Subcommittees: Commerce, Consumer and Monetary Affairs; Manpower and Housing.

Judiciary (5th). Subcommittees: Crime; Criminal Justice (Chairman).

Group Ratings

	ADA	COPE	PC	LCV	CFA	RPN	NAB	NSI	NTU	ACA	ACU
1980	78	89	97	81	86	—	25	0	26	25	18
1979	79	100	65	81	56	—	—	—	33	13	12
1978	45	94	73	63	64	25	0	0	57	11	7

Key Votes

1) Draft Registn $	AGN	6) Fair Hsg DOJ Enfrc	FOR	11) Cut Socl Incr Dfns $	AGN
2) Ban $ to Nicrgua	—	7) Lim PAC Contrbtns	FOR	12) Hosptl Cost Controls	FOR
3) Dlay MX Missile	FOR	8) Cap on Food Stmp $	—	13) Gasln Ctrls & Allctns	FOR
4) Nuclr Mortorium	FOR	9) New US Dep Edcatn	AGN	14) Lim Wndfll Prof Tax	AGN
5) Alaska Lands Bill	FOR	10) Cut OSHA $	AGN	15) Chryslr Loan Grntee	FOR

Election Results

1980 general	John Conyers, Jr. (D)	123,286	(95%)	($20,543)
	William M. Bell (R)	6,244	(5%)	($0)
1980 primary	John Conyers, Jr. (D)	26,251	(100%)	
1978 general	John Conyers, Jr. (D)	89,646	(93%)	($23,759)
	Robert S. Arnold (R)	6,878	(7%)	

SECOND DISTRICT

The 2d congressional district of Michigan is an odd amalgam: a collection of university campuses, burgeoning suburbs, and aging factories. The district takes in the western and southern edges of the Detroit metropolitan area and lies entirely within the Detroit television market. But the 2d's most important city, Ann Arbor, sets itself apart from what it considers a grimy and industrial Detroit. Ann Arbor, with 100,000 residents, is the home of the University of Michigan, with 43,000 students, one of the nation's largest and most prestigious universities. This institution, along with Eastern Michigan University and its 18,000 students, in nearby Ypsilanti, gives the 2d district the largest proportion of college students among eligible voters — 15% in 1970 — of any congressional district in the nation. Indeed the student vote here is so large that in Ann Arbor it spawned a Human Rights Party that enjoyed some vitality in the partisan and fiercely contested city elections.

Until the early 1970s Ann Arbor was a conservative Republican town. Its heritage came from its large German-American population, many of them descended from immigrants fleeing from the failures of the revolution of 1848. Democratic strength lay in the working-class wards of Ypsilanti, near the giant Willow Run plant, and in Monroe County, to the south along Lake Erie. Then, with the student vote, things changed sharply. In 1972 Washtenaw County, which includes Ann Arbor and Ypsilanti, was one of four Michigan counties to go for George McGovern. By 1976, with the Vietnam war over and Richard Nixon out of office, Washtenaw went for U of M graduate Gerald Ford; it was the only major county in the country to have favored McGovern and then Ford.

Aligned consistently against Washtenaw County in the politics of the 2d district is the portion of the district in the Detroit suburbs. The largest town here is Livonia, with more people but fewer votes than Ann Arbor (more of its residents are children under 18). Despite the presence of a couple of General Motors plants, Livonia is middle income and up, and Republican in national and congressional elections. It is one of those places that ballooned with instant subdivisions; its population rose from 17,000 in 1950 to 110,000 in 1970; now that its children are growing up, its population fell to 104,000 in 1980.

In the early and middle 1970s, the 2d district was the scene of pitched congressional battles, both in the Democratic primary — which tended to feature battles between Livonia and Ann Arbor candidates — and in the general election. But the Democrats never won; the district was held by Marvin Esch, a Republican with a voting record acceptable to every rating group and a man adroit enough to appeal to every part of the district. With tough races every two years, he decided that he might as well run for the Senate in 1976; he did so and almost won. Succeeding him was another Republican, Carl Pursell, who had represented Livonia in the state Senate; by 344 votes Pursell edged out a liberal doctor from Ann Arbor.

In the less turbulent politics of the late 1970s, Pursell had less trouble holding onto the district. He won a seat on the Education and Labor Committee; his overall voting record was rated better by liberal than conservative groups; his record on committee issues was good enough that he was endorsed for reelection by the United Auto Workers in 1978. Two years later, Pursell had significant opposition in the person of Kathleen O'Reilly, former head of the Consumer Federation of America. But Pursell was able to carry even Washtenaw County and won a 57%–41% victory. If there were a Democratic governor as well as a Democratic legislature here, this is the Michigan district that might disappear in the redistricting process. But Governor William Milliken will probably protect it by threat of veto, and the 2d will probably survive in something like its present form, perhaps without Livonia. That will make elections closer, perhaps, but still should give Pursell an edge.

Census Data   Pop. (1980 final) 505,001, up 8% in 1970s. Median family income, 1970, $12,908, 135% of U.S.

The Voters

Employment profile 1970   White collar, 53%. Blue collar, 33%. Service, 13%. Farm, 1%.
Ethnic groups   Black 1980, 6%. Hispanic 1980, 1%. Asian 1980, 1%. Total foreign stock 1970, 17%. Canada, 4%; Germany, UK, 2% each; Poland, Italy, 1% each.

Presidential Vote

1980	Reagan (R)	100,535	(48%)
	Carter (D)	82,977	(40%)
	Anderson (I)	20,055	(10%)
1976	Ford (R)	109,460	(53%)
	Carter (D)	90,984	(45%)

Rep. Carl D. Pursell (R) Elected 1976; b. Dec. 19, 1932, Imlay City; home, Plymouth; E. Mich. U., B.A. 1957, M.A. 1962.

Career Army, 1957–59; Army Reserve, 1959–65; Teacher; Businessman; Mbr., Wayne Co. Bd. of Comm., 1969–70; Mich. Senate, 1971–76.

Offices 1414 LHOB, 202-225-4401. Also 15273 Farmington Rd., Livonia 48154, 313-427-1081.

Committee *Appropriations* (15th). Subcommittees: Labor–Health and Human Services–Education; Transportation.

Group Ratings

	ADA	COPE	PC	LCV	CFA	RPN	NAB	NSI	NTU	ACA	ACU
1980	89	71	60	77	64	—	40	25	25	36	18
1979	53	65	48	76	32	—	—	—	38	38	28
1978	60	56	45	69	46	70	46	33	44	31	38

Key Votes

1) Draft Registn $	AGN	6) Fair Hsg DOJ Enfrc	FOR	11) Cut Socl Incr Dfns $	AGN
2) Ban $ to Nicrgua	AGN	7) Lim PAC Contrbtns	FOR	12) Hosptl Cost Controls	AGN
3) Dlay MX Missile	FOR	8) Cap on Food Stmp $	AGN	13) Gasln Ctrls & Allctns	FOR
4) Nuclr Mortorium	FOR	9) New US Dep Edcatn	FOR	14) Lim Wndfll Prof Tax	FOR
5) Alaska Lands Bill	FOR	10) Cut OSHA $	AGN	15) Chryslr Loan Grntee	FOR

Election Results

1980 general	Carl D. Pursell (R)	115,562	(57%)	($143,576)
	Kathleen F. O'Reilly (D)	83,550	(41%)	($129,805)
1980 primary	Carl D. Pursell (R)	11,496	(90%)	
	One other (R)	1,383	(10%)	
1978 general	Carl D. Pursell (R)	97,503	(68%)	($94,764)
	Earl Greene (D)	45,631	(32%)	($27,212)

THIRD DISTRICT

The 3d congressional district of Michigan is in the south central part of the state. Its three major urban areas have a thriving and variegated economy. Battle Creek is known as the cereal city; it was at a tuberculosis sanitarium here that the first cold breakfast cereal was concocted. Both Kellogg's and Post have plants here now. Not far to the west is Kalamazoo, the headquarters of the Upjohn pharmaceutical firm and of the Checker cab manufacturing company. Finally the 3d includes the Eaton County suburbs of Lansing, a city that is the home both of Oldsmobile and of the Michigan state government.

This is a prosperous, stable part of the state, and one that has always been attached to the Republican Party. Indeed, Republicanism got its start in 1854 just east of here, in Jackson. Yet Republicanism is on a definite decline in this area. Both Kalamazoo and Battle Creek have elected some Democratic legislators in the 1970s — something that never used to happen. Republican margins in statewide elections have grown smaller. Now the 3d district has a Democratic congressman.

He replaces a Republican elected in 1966 — a year when the Republicans gained five Michigan House seats from the Democrats. Garry Brown was a popular and hardworking congressman here for some years. But as time went on, he seemed busier in Washington defending business interests on the Banking Committee than he was in providing services to people in the district. And active young Democrats were showing that they could do a better job in this regard.

One of them was Howard Wolpe, the first Democrat ever elected to the state legislature from Kalamazoo. Brown's weakness became obvious in 1974, when he won with only 52%, and Wolpe ran in 1976. He fell just short that year but never stopped running. Wolpe had run poorly in Eaton County; in 1977 Senator Donald Riegle hired him to run his Lansing office, and he moved into Eaton. It paid off: he increased his Eaton County percentage from 40% to 46% and held his own in Kalamazoo and Battle Creek. It was enough to make the difference, and to make the district Democratic. Despite the national Republican trend and a strong, self-financed Republican opponent, Wolpe was able to maintain 45% in Eaton County which, with his margins in Kalamazoo and Battle Creek, gave him a 52% victory. Redistricting will probably not present a major problem; the district has just about the state average in population, and the Democratic legislature should see to it that the details are favorable to Wolpe. He might even get some Democratic precincts in Lansing from the 6th district, which since 1980 is represented by a Republican.

Wolpe's energy has shown up not only in campaigns but in his performance in Congress. In 1981, after only two years' service, he won a major subcommittee chairmanship, on the Africa Subcommittee of Foreign Affairs. This is a potential hot spot, given the volatility of African affairs, and Wolpe is likely to take a very different approach from his Senate counterpart, Nancy Landon Kassebaum, or the Reagan Administration. The Republicans want less disapproving relations with South Africa and look unkindly on African nations that have cordial relations with Cuba and the Soviet Union. Wolpe, who lived for two years in Nigeria, is more sympathetic to the views of the black African leaders and will be a major force in government for the propagation of such views. In the race for the subcommittee chair he beat Dan Mica of Florida, who was technically more senior by virtue of a coin toss, among Foreign Relations Committee Democrats; but Wolpe had the endorsement of the Congressional Black Caucus.

Census Data Pop. (1980 final) 506,935, up 8% in 1970s. Median family income, 1970, $10,913, 114% of U.S.

The Voters

Employment profile 1970 White collar, 46%. Blue collar, 39%. Service, 13%. Farm, 2%.
Ethnic groups Black 1980, 6%. Hispanic 1980, 1%. Total foreign stock 1970, 10%. Netherlands, Canada, 2% each; Germany, UK, 1% each.

Presidential Vote

1980	Reagan (R)	116,500	(53%)
	Carter (D)	78,228	(36%)
	Anderson (I)	20,525	(9%)
1976	Ford (R)	119,812	(59%)
	Carter (D)	80,137	(39%)

Rep. Howard Wolpe (D) Elected 1978; b. Nov. 2, 1939, Los Angeles, Cal.; home, Lansing; Reed Col., B.A. 1960, M.I.T., Ph.D. 1967.

Career Consultant, U.S. Peace Corps, 1966–67, U.S. State Dept. Foreign Svc. Inst., 1967–72; Prof., W. Mich. U., 1967–72; Kalamazoo City Cncl., 1969–73; Mich. House of Reps., 1973–76; Dem. nominee for U.S. House of Reps., 1976; Regional Rep. and State Liaison to U.S. Sen. Donald W. Riegle, Jr., 1977–78.

Offices 1118 LHOB, 202-225-5011. Also 142 N. Kalamazoo Mall, Kalamazoo 49007, 616-385-0039.

Committees *Foreign Affairs* (14th). Subcommittees: Africa (Chairman); International Economic Policy and Trade.

Science and Technology (16th). Subcommittees: Energy Development and Applications; Energy Research and Production.

Group Ratings

	ADA	COPE	PC	LCV	CFA	RPN	NAB	NSI	NTU	ACA	ACU
1980	94	79	80	99	79	—	0	0	18	30	17
1979	100	90	88	93	89	—	—	—	21	8	5

Key Votes

1) Draft Registn $	AGN	6) Fair Hsg DOJ Enfrc	FOR	11) Cut Socl Incr Dfns $	AGN
2) Ban $ to Nicrgua	AGN	7) Lim PAC Contrbtns	FOR	12) Hosptl Cost Controls	FOR
3) Dlay MX Missile	—	8) Cap on Food Stmp $	AGN	13) Gasln Ctrls & Allctns	FOR
4) Nuclr Mortorium	FOR	9) New US Dep Edcatn	FOR	14) Lim Wndfll Prof Tax	AGN
5) Alaska Lands Bill	FOR	10) Cut OSHA $	AGN	15) Chryslr Loan Grntee	FOR

Election Results

1980 general	Howard Wolpe (D).............	113,080	(52%)	($341,910)
	James S. Gilmore (R)	102,591	(47%)	($702,649)
1980 primary	Howard Wolpe (D).............	7,680	(100%)	
1978 general	Howard Wolpe (D).............	83,932	(51%)	($219,397)
	Garry Brown (R)..............	79,572	(49%)	($242,768)

FOURTH DISTRICT

The 4th congressional district of Michigan is shaped like a very short capital L. It includes Michigan's southwestern corner plus a string of counties along the state's border with Indiana and Ohio. The district's main urban concentration is the Benton Harbor–St. Joseph area on Lake Michigan. These two next-door cities could hardly be less alike. Benton Harbor is industrial, with a big Whirlpool plant, and a majority of its citizens are black, while St. Joseph is virtually all white and has the air of a prosperous suburb. Besides Benton Harbor there is also a black community of some size in and near Cassopolis and Dowagiac—descendants of slaves who found their way to these stations on the underground railroad. For the most part the 4th is agricultural and small town, with rolling hills, occasional lakes, and many dairy farms. The district has a relatively large number of German–Americans; in ethnic composition it is more like northern Indiana or Ohio than outstate Michigan. The 4th is also disconnected from Michigan in another way: most of it lies within the Chicago, South Bend, or Toledo media markets.

If you want to understand the political background of this part of America, a good place to visit is the county seat of Hillsdale. Here the courthouse and the local college were built when the Republican Party was young, and the college in particular epitomized the things Republicans then stood for. It believed in absolute honesty and was inclined toward temperance; it was one of the first American colleges to admit women or blacks and was strongly opposed to slavery. These were the principles that inspired the Republicans of the late 19th century. Now, in the late 20th century, things in Hillsdale haven't changed much. This was one of the few Michigan colleges where there was no protest against the Vietnam war; hair always remained short and skirts long; temperance is still encouraged (the longtime Prohibition Party presidential candidate, E. Harold Munn, comes from Hillsdale). College administrators have turned down federal funds and refused to file compliance reports of their admissions or hiring practices; they say that they have been admitting blacks and women for 100 years and don't need the federal government to tell them what to do.

The 4th has always been a Republican district. One recent congressman was Edward Hutchinson, the ranking minority member of the House Judiciary Committee during the impeachment hearings, whose support of Richard Nixon illustrated the steadfastness or stubbornness of a small-town lawyer. His successor was a man with a similar voting record but a very different temperament. At 29, when he ran for Congress, David Stockman was already a Capitol Hill veteran as director of the House Republican Conference. He was a protege of John Anderson of Illinois. On the Hill, Stockman provided congressional conservatives with some of their freshest thinking and strongest advocacy in some time.

Within weeks of the 1980 election, Stockman went from being a junior member of the party out of power—albeit an important member, given the force of his ideas and the strength of his advocacy—to being perhaps the most powerful man in the federal government after the president. He had served as a stand-in for John Anderson and later Jimmy Carter when Reagan prepared for his television debates, and Stockman's brains and quickness obviously impressed Reagan. So, we must assume, did his willingness to question the conventional wisdom, his knowledge of the federal government, and his determination to stem its growth. As Director of the Office of Management and the Budget, Stockman is by far the youngest member of the Reagan Cabinet, the least conventional, and, initially at least, the busiest—cutting the federal budget in almost every area before the new department heads could find out much of what was going on. Stockman dazzled official Washington with his knowledge of detail and his self-assurance, but he himself recognized that he was well positioned to be the scapegoat if the budget cuts and supply-side economics of the Reagan program do not work.

To fill Stockman's seat in the 4th, a special Republican primary was held on March 24, 1981. This was basically a three-way contest between a candidate based in Adrian, a candidate backed by fundamentalist Christian groups, and Stockman's former campaign chairman who had Stockman's endorsement. The latter was the favorite; however, the winner, by a 38% to 36% margin, was the man backed by the fundamentalists, 29-year-old state Representative Mark Siljander, who had also gained fame for trying unsuccessfully to get a property tax limit referendum on the ballot in 1980. His primary triumph shows the strength of cultural issues among Republican primary voters as compared with the economic issues emphasized by Stockman. Siljander won the April 21 general election easily; this is a far more Republican district than the outstate Michigan districts that went Democratic in special elections when Richard Nixon was under attack during the Watergate crisis.

Census Data   Pop. (1980 final) 515,197, up 10% in 1970s. Median family income, 1970, $9,693, 101% of U.S.

The Voters

  Employment profile 1970   White collar, 37%. Blue collar, 47%. Service, 12%. Farm, 4%.
  Ethnic groups   Black 1980, 7%. Hispanic 1980, 2%. Total foreign stock 1970, 10%. Germany, 3%; Canada, 1%.

Presidential Vote

1980	Reagan (R)	122,398	(60%)
	Carter (D)	66,802	(33%)
	Anderson (I)	11,786	(6%)
1976	Ford (R)	111,830	(58%)
	Carter (D)	77,086	(40%)

Rep. Mark Siljander (R) Elected April 21, 1981; b. June 11, 1951, Chicago, Ill.; home, Three Rivers; W. Mich U., B.A. 1972, M.A. 1973.

Career Franchise for home building firm, 1973–76; Bonanza Restaurants, Inc., 1974–76; Mich. House of Reps., 1976–80.

Offices 1022 LHOB, 202-225-3761. Also 325 S. Main St., Adrian 49221, 517-265-1511; 815 Main St., Suite 3A, St. Joseph 49085, 616-982-0722; and 15788 W. Michigan Ave., Three Rivers 49093, 616-279-7125.

Committees *Small Business* (17th). Subcommittee: Antitrust and Restraint of Trade Activities Affecting Small Business.

Veterans' Affairs (13th). Subcommittees: Compensation, Pension, and Insurance; Education, Training and Employment.

Election Results

4/21/81 spc. elct.	Mark Siljander (R)	36,046	(73%)	
	Johnie A. Rodebush (D)	12,461	(25%)	
3/30/81 sp. prm.	Mark Siljander (R)	17,845	(38%)	
	John Globensky (R)	16,993	(36%)	
	John Mowat (R)	10,385	(22%)	
	Four others (R)	2,352	(5%)	
1980 general	David (Dave) Stockman (R)	148,950	(75%)	($90,721)
	Lyndon G. Furst (D)	47,777	(24%)	($14,235)
1980 primary	David (Dave) Stockman (R)	31,391	(100%)	
1978 general	David (Dave) Stockman (R)	95,440	(71%)	($62,211)
	Morgan L. Hager, Jr. (D)	38,204	(28%)	

FIFTH DISTRICT

The 5th congressional district of Michigan is the seat that gave us our 40th Vice President, Gerald Ford, and which by electing a member of the opposite party as his successor in the House helped to make Ford our 38th president. The center of the district is Grand Rapids, a medium-sized city that was Ford's boyhood home and the place where he practiced law just before and after World War II. After his election to Congress in 1948 he moved to the Washington area, and after his defeat in 1976 he moved to Rancho Mirage, California. Yet there has always been a warm feeling here for Ford: high schools were named for him while he was still in Congress, and his appearance in downtown Grand Rapids in the last days before the 1976 election was a moment of genuine emotion.

The Grand Rapids that first elected Ford was a solidly Republican town, faithful to the party through all the New Deal years. It had a heritage of Yankee Republicanism and, perhaps more important, of Dutch conservatism. This is the heart of the nation's largest concentration of Dutch–Americans, as a glance at the phone book's list of Vander . . .s will show. The Dutch in Holland may be liberal on many issues; but when Dutch migrate, whether to South Africa or western Michigan, they are rigidly conservative, in personal habits as well as political preference. The Dutch gave us, before Ford, Senator Arthur Vandenberg, the founder of the now-abandoned tradition of bipartisan foreign policy. Vandenberg helped Ford win the nomination in 1948 because the local congressman remained an isolationist. Ford's career was helped later on by others when he was a useful instrument to seek their ends, from the group of young Republican congressmen who made him minority leader in 1965 to the Richard Nixon who needed a vice presidential nominee who would be confirmed by a Democratic Congress.

As Gerald Ford advanced as a national Republican, the 5th district was slowly moving away from its old party. Ford's seat was safe enough that the slippage didn't need his attention; and he didn't seem concerned when in his last two congressional elections, 1970 and 1972, his percentage declined to 61%—the lowest in his congressional career. This was part of the Democratic trend in the Upper Midwest that occurred even as Nixon was making gains in the South and the Sun Belt. So Ford was stunned when, in the spring 1974 special election to succeed him, the 5th district was won by Democrat Richard VanderVeen. The theme of the VanderVeen campaign was simple: Gerald Ford, not Richard Nixon, should be president. For once voters could do something to get rid of an unpopular president, and 53% of them voted for VanderVeen.

VanderVeen had the additional advantage of being a presentable candidate, a successful lawyer of quiet, conservative demeanor. His special election victory was followed by another in the 1974 general election. But 1976 proved too much for him. The Republicans had two advantages: a local hero running for president and a strong congressional candidate. Ford received 68% in Grand Rapids's Kent County and a higher percentage for president than he had ever received for Congress in his old district. Harold Sawyer, the new congressman, had had a lucrative law practice and had become Kent County prosecutor; in that office he gained a lot of headlines and popularity. He beat VanderVeen by a clean 54%–46% margin.

Sawyer proved to be a somewhat controversial congressman in Washington, serving on the ethics committee and pushing for an investigation of South Korean lobbying. He had been expected to win reelection easily. But like Ford he was surprised by the Democratic trend in the district. Grand Rapids lawyer Dale Sprik came within 1% of winning; indeed, he carried Kent County and lost the election only in the small outlying counties in the district.

The national Republican trend was apparent here as elsewhere in 1980, and Sawyer this time beat Sprik by a larger, but not huge, margin. But it remains to be seen whether Gerald Ford's hometown will be captivated by the politics of Ronald Reagan.

Census Data   Pop. (1980 final) 509,317, up 9% in 1970s. Median family income, 1970, $10,550, 110% of U.S.

The Voters

Employment profile 1970   White collar, 46%. Blue collar, 40%. Service, 12%. Farm, 2%.
Ethnic groups   Black 1980, 7%. Hispanic 1980, 2%. Total foreign stock 1970, 17%. Netherlands, 7%; Poland, Canada, Germany, 2% each.

Presidential Vote

1980	Reagan (R)	127,736	(55%)
	Carter (D)	81,566	(35%)
	Anderson (I)	19,696	(9%)
1976	Ford (R)	141,655	(67%)
	Carter (D)	67,423	(32%)

Rep. Harold S. Sawyer (R) Elected 1976; b. Mar. 21, 1920, San Francisco, Cal.; home, Rockford; U. of Cal., LL.B., 1945.

Career   Navy, WWII; Practicing atty., 1945–75; Kent Co. Prosecutor, 1975–77.

Offices   123 CHOB, 202-225-3831. Also Fed. Bldg., 110 Michigan N.W., Grand Rapids 49503, 616-451-8383.

Committees   *Judiciary* (9th). Subcommittees: Courts, Civil Liberties and the Administration of Justice; Crime.

Veterans' Affairs (5th). Subcommittees: Education, Training and Employment; Oversight and Investigations.

Group Ratings

	ADA	COPE	PC	LCV	CFA	RPN	NAB	NSI	NTU	ACA	ACU
1980	11	24	23	52	21	—	73	78	49	83	58
1979	16	25	23	28	7	—	—	—	54	85	82
1978	25	11	20	43	14	70	86	67	26	79	67

Key Votes

1) Draft Registn $	FOR	6) Fair Hsg DOJ Enfrc	AGN	11) Cut Socl Incr Dfns $	AGN
2) Ban $ to Nicrgua	FOR	7) Lim PAC Contrbtns	AGN	12) Hosptl Cost Controls	—
3) Dlay MX Missile	AGN	8) Cap on Food Stmp $	FOR	13) Gasln Ctrls & Allctns	AGN
4) Nuclr Mortorium	AGN	9) New US Dep Edcatn	AGN	14) Lim Wndfll Prof Tax	—
5) Alaska Lands Bill	FOR	10) Cut OSHA $	FOR	15) Chryslr Loan Grntee	FOR

Election Results

1980 general	Harold S. Sawyer (R)	118,061	(53%)	($366,147)
	Dale R. Sprik (D)	101,737	(46%)	($201,895)
1980 primary	Harold S. Sawyer (R)	23,970	(81%)	
	One other (R)	5,484	(19%)	
1978 general	Harold S. Sawyer (R)	81,794	(49%)	($134,454)
	Dale R. Sprik (D)	80,622	(49%)	($69,641)

SIXTH DISTRICT

The 6th congressional district of Michigan is a Middle America chunk of outstate Michigan, a district that in the 1970s switched from a Republican congressman to a Democrat and then back to a Republican again. Up through the late 1970s, this was an area that seemed to have a strong economic base. In the 1960s and 1970s, under Republican Governors George Romney and William Milliken, state government had been a growth industry. Lansing, the major city in the 6th district, is the state capital and, in addition, right next door is East Lansing, home of Michigan State University, with more than 40,000 students. Lansing is also the site of the main Oldsmobile factory, whose prosperity seemed assured in the years when Cutlasses outsold all other models. But Cutlass sales are down — although not as disastrously as sales of Chrysler and Ford cars — and state government receipts declined disastrously in 1980 and 1981. Lansing, which once seemed impervious to economic distress, is now a metropolitan area in considerable trouble.

The other major city in the district is Jackson, an old industrial town and site of the state prison, one of the nation's largest. Back in 1854, the Republican Party got its start here in Jackson (a town named for the first president who called himself a Democrat). Aside from these urban areas, the 6th is a collection of small towns and rural townships. Some, such as Stockbridge and Mason, are old towns whose architecture is reminiscent of the Yankee migrants from Upstate New York who first settled them. Others — for example, Howell — are the sites of new subdivisions to which former residents of metropolitan Detroit, unhappy with the city's crime rate and high black population, have been moving.

Politically, Lansing is about evenly divided between the parties; East Lansing, a high-income, heavily Republican suburb until students got the vote, is now generally Democratic. Jackson tends to go Republican and the older rural areas are solidly Republican. Voters around Howell have, in many cases, Democratic backgrounds; but they also have the most conservative attitudes in the district on cultural issues and they gave Ronald Reagan a large majority.

At the beginning of the 1970s the 6th had a short-tempered Republican congressman who had served since the 1950s; he lobbied actively in Washington for the auto companies but spent little time in the district and was totally out of touch with the newly enfranchised students. Confident of a Republican landslide, he didn't campaign much, and he was nearly beaten by 29-year-old Democrat Bob Carr, an assistant attorney general with a Mark Spitz mustache. Carr kept running after the election, and the Republican retired. Against a conservative Republican his own age, Carr barely won; he beat him by a better margin in 1976. He won comfortably in 1978.

Carr was an important part of the freshman class of 1974. He got a seat on the House Armed Services Committee, a body usually shunned by young liberals because of its uncongenial membership. But Carr is a qualified pilot himself and seemed not to be inhibited by stars or medals. He worked for the Carter Administration position on some defense bills, notably on the B-1 bomber, which he helped to kill, and the neutron bomb. Probably his greatest achievement in Congress so far was in his first term, in early 1975. President Ford and Secretary of State Kissinger were pressing Congress hard for aid to Cambodia as the Khmer Rouge seemed to be closing in on Phnom Penh. Many congressional veterans had a sort of reflexive instinct to compromise — the same instinct that had got us into the Vietnam war in the first place. Carr felt that was a mistake. At just the right moment he demanded a

Democratic Caucus vote on the issue. The result, when people had to be put on record, was a 189–49 vote against the administration proposal. It was clear Ford could not get approval for any Cambodian intervention from Congress, and the idea was dropped.

The election of Republican Jim Dunn in 1980 cannot be ascribed to Carr's laziness; he continued to fly his own plane back to the district almost every weekend. Nor was it a matter of coattails; voters here are perfectly capable of splitting their tickets and Reagan's margin in the district was less than overwhelming. Dunn did have the advantages of plentiful self-financing (his campaign spent $294,000 in all), and he astutely concentrated heavily on Jackson County. But what really seems to have worked for Dunn is the same set of issues that had once helped Carr—defense and the military. Carr's reputation as a military budget-cutter was well established and, in the context of the Soviet invasion of Afghanistan, the seizure of the hostages in Iran, and the Iran–Iraq War, became a liability rather than an asset.

Dunn hit hard on the issue of increased military spending and made particular gains in the areas around Jackson and Howell. Dunn now sits as part of the still cohesive Republican minority and as a member of the Science and Veterans' Affairs Committees. The major question for 1982 is whether the Democratic legislature will in effect concede the 6th and put some of its more Democratic precincts in the 3d district to help Howard Wolpe, or whether the Democrats will try to make it a little less Republican than it is now in the hope that a Democrat makes a strong challenge here in 1982.

Census Data   Pop. (1980 final) 520,542, up 11% in 1970s. Median family income, 1970, $11,105, 116% of U.S.

The Voters

Employment profile 1970   White collar, 50%. Blue collar, 34%. Service, 14%. Farm, 2%.
Ethnic groups   Black 1980, 6%. Hispanic 1980, 3%. Asian 1980, 1%. Total foreign stock 1970, 12%. Canada, Germany, 2% each; UK, Poland, 1% each.

Presidential Vote

1980	Reagan (R)	114,648	(50%)
	Carter (D)	84,771	(37%)
	Anderson (I)	24,499	(11%)
1976	Ford (R)	120,079	(57%)
	Carter (D)	84,753	(40%)

Rep. Jim Dunn (R) Elected 1980; b. July 12, 1943, Detroit; home, East Lansing; Mich. St. U., B.A. 1967.

Career   Painting contractor, 1967–69; Pres., Dunn & Fairmont, bldg. contractor, 1969–81; Mich. Small Bus. Advisory Cncl.

Offices   1630 LHOB, 202-225-4872. Also 245 Fed. Bldg., Lansing 48933, 517-377-1893, and City Hall, 161 W. Michigan Ave., Jackson 49201, 517-787-4323.

Committees   *Science and Technology* (16th). Subcommittees: Energy Development and Applications; Transportation, Aviation and Materials.

Veterans' Affairs (9th). Subcommittees: Hospitals and Health Care; Housing and Memorial Affairs.

Group Ratings and Key Votes: Newly Elected

Election Results

1980 general	Jim Dunn (R)	111,272	(51%)	($345,127)
	Bob Carr (D)	108,548	(49%)	($146,725)
1980 primary	Jim Dunn (R)	21,270	(81%)	
	One other (R)	5,063	(19%)	
1978 general	Bob Carr (D)	97,971	(57%)	($174,104)
	Mike Conlin (R)	74,718	(43%)	($145,074)

SEVENTH DISTRICT

With five major General Motors plants and a metropolitan population of 521,000, Flint is probably the nation's largest company town. Some 60% of metropolitan Flint's wage earners are on the GM payroll, and although there is some GM white collar employment here, this is mainly the Chevrolet and Buick factory town. Flint has no five o'clock rush hour; its traffic jams come at three-thirty when the shifts break. Even those who have profited most handsomely from the auto industry have not taken themselves out of Flint; the plushest residential district here has a panoramic view of a Chevrolet plant. For years civic life in Flint was dominated by Charles Stewart Mott, a member of the General Motors board of directors for 60 years and for most of that time the largest individual shareholder in the corporation; the old man ran his Mott Foundation, one of the nation's largest, out of Flint and concentrated on local projects until his death a few years ago at 97.

As the 1980s began Flint was a city in economic trouble. It had the nation's highest unemployment rate. Even though General Motors was not in as bad shape as Chrysler or Ford, it nonetheless had to lay off thousands of workers, and in a town as undiversified economically as Flint the impact was speedily felt. Unemployment in early 1981 was closer to 20% than 10%, business at stores and shopping centers was down, and some — especially younger people without firmly established households — were leaving. There was talk that the wage levels in union contracts would be scaled back. The high wages in the auto industry that had produced such a good life for so many here in the 1970s seemed to be coming abruptly to an end. Flint's condition made it almost an obligatory stop on presidential campaigns, and Ronald Reagan spent plenty of time here. Still, the Flint area delivered a sizable plurality for Jimmy Carter in 1980 as it had in 1976.

Flint should be used to booms and busts; it owes its present existence to the boom years of the auto industry, the two decades between 1910 and 1930 and grew during the war and postwar booms of the 1940s. During both these periods Flint attracted tens of thousands of immigrants from the rural South — whites from the hills of Kentucky and Tennessee and blacks from the cotton fields of Alabama and Mississippi. Since the 1930s the politics of the migrants has been Democratic. Oldtimers here can still recall the sitdown strikes of the 1930s, led by young unionists Roy, Victor, and Walter Reuther; the United Auto Workers remains a major political and social force here today. In the late 1960s racial friction threatened to break the Democratic coalition. In 1968 George Wallace had the support of many white UAW members and a few local presidents; only a concerted union effort held him to 15% of the vote. But unlike Detroit, Flint had no major busing crisis; McGovern actually ran better here than Humphrey, as he did in outstate Michigan generally, and Carter carried the area with a fair majorities in 1976 and even 1980.

Flint is the nucleus of Michigan's 7th congressional district. The city's metropolitan area and its media market coincide almost perfectly with the district lines. This makes it ideal for an incumbent congressman. It is easy to communicate with voters: the local congressman is a celebrity; he is covered thoroughly by the local newspaper; he can easily get on the local television newscasts. His local staff is as large as that of any public official in the Flint area, and his ability to help citizens solve their problems with government is probably greater. For these reasons it is not surprising that the 7th district has had two extremely strong local congressmen, who began as members of different political parties.

The first was Donald Riegle, elected in 1966 at 28 as a Republican; he beat a Democrat who took the district for granted. Riegle worked hard and used all the advantages of incumbency; he established good relations with the black community and by 1970 was able to win the UAW endorsement—both unheard of in a town where Republicans spent time only with management and Democrats only with labor. Increasingly he was out of step with Republicans in the House. He opposed the Vietnam war and in early 1973 switched to the Democratic Party. He was reelected easily as a Democrat and ran successfully for the Senate in 1976.

The current congressman is Democrat Dale Kildee. First elected to the state House in 1964, he moved to the state Senate in 1974, beating a 26-year incumbent in the primary by a 3-1 margin. In 1976 he won the congressional primary easily over a UAW local president and got 71% in the general; in 1978 he did even better. Where Riegle had relied on expensive television advertising in his first races, Kildee has always relied on old-fashioned door-to-door campaigning; in his career he has probably knocked on every door in Flint.

With a background in education and experience in that area in the Michigan legislature, Kildee holds a seat on the Education and Labor Committee. In the 95th Congress he was the man who initiated and shepherded through the measure to make the use of children in pornography a federal crime, an unusually successful legislative effort by a freshman. He is part of the liberal majority on Education and Labor and is a member of its major education subcommittee and the subcommittee on Labor–Management Relations. Both bodies are likely to handle major Republican initiatives—education budget cuts and changes in the labor laws—and Kildee is likely to be part of the majorities that reject both, at least on the subcommittee and committee level. In addition he gained in 1981 a seat on the Interior Committee, which has the job of keeping an eye on Interior Secretary James Watt.

Census Data Pop. (1980 final) 478,093, up 3% in 1970s. Median family income, 1970, $11,207, 117% of U.S.

The Voters

Employment profile 1970 White collar, 37%. Blue collar, 50%. Service, 12%. Farm, 1%.
Ethnic groups Black 1980, 17%. Hispanic 1980, 2%. Am. Ind. 1980, 1%. Total foreign stock 1970, 12%. Canada, 3%; UK, 2%; Germany, 1%.

Presidential Vote

1980	Reagan (R)	84,272	(43%)
	Carter (D)	94,837	(49%)
	Anderson (I)	12,829	(7%)
1976	Ford (R)	84,998	(47%)
	Carter (D)	93,377	(52%)

Rep. Dale E. Kildee (D) Elected 1976; b. Sept. 16, 1929, Flint; home, Flint; Sacred Heart Sem., Detroit, B.A. 1952, U. of Mich., M.A. 1961, Rotary Fellow, U. of Peshawar, Pakistan.

Career High school teacher, 1954–64; Mich. House of Reps., 1965–75; Mich. Senate, 1975–77.

Offices 314 CHOB, 202-225-3611. Also 444 Church St., Flint 48502, 313-239-1437.

Committees *Education and Labor* (14th). Subcommittees: Elementary, Secondary and Vocational Education; Labor–Management Relations; Labor Standards.

Interior and Insular Affairs (22d). Subcommittees: Insular Affairs; Public Lands and National Parks.

Group Ratings

	ADA	COPE	PC	LCV	CFA	RPN	NAB	NSI	NTU	ACA	ACU
1980	89	84	77	83	71	—	0	10	15	21	11
1979	89	98	88	93	93	—	—	—	18	12	10
1978	80	95	78	87	77	42	0	0	13	7	8

Key Votes

1) Draft Registn $	AGN	6) Fair Hsg DOJ Enfrc	FOR	11) Cut Socl Incr Dfns $	AGN
2) Ban $ to Nicrgua	AGN	7) Lim PAC Contrbtns	FOR	12) Hosptl Cost Controls	FOR
3) Dlay MX Missile	FOR	8) Cap on Food Stmp $	AGN	13) Gasln Ctrls & Allctns	FOR
4) Nuclr Mortorium	FOR	9) New US Dep Edcatn	FOR	14) Lim Wndfll Prof Tax	AGN
5) Alaska Lands Bill	FOR	10) Cut OSHA $	AGN	15) Chryslr Loan Grntee	FOR

Election Results

1980 general	Dale E. Kildee (D)	147,280	(93%)	($32,391)
	Dennis L. Berry (Libertarian).....	11,507	(7%)	($0)
1980 primary	Dale E. Kildee (D)	31,504	(100%)	
1978 general	Dale E. Kildee (D)	105,402	(77%)	($46,558)
	Gale M. Kronk (R).............	29,958	(22%)	($23,487)

EIGHTH DISTRICT

To understand the geography of the 8th congressional district of Michigan, you must know that Michigan's Lower Peninsula is shaped like a mittened hand. The 8th district includes most of the Thumb (as it is called locally) and the bottom part of the index finger. The Thumb is almost entirely agricultural, tilled by descendants of the German and Canadian farmers who first settled the area more than a century ago. During that time the Thumb has been rock-solid Republican territory.

Where the index finger extends from the palm (this is not local nomenclature) are Saginaw, with 77,000 people, and Bay City, with about half as many. Both cities have been important since the 19th century when Michigan was the nation's leading lumber producer and the cities were major lumber ports. Today they are sustained in large part by auto plants, notably General Motors's Saginaw Steering, which makes more power steering equipment than any other plant in the world. Unlike most of the rest of outstate Michigan, the 8th district has few institutions of higher learning and has had relatively little growth in recent years.

This is the sort of area that ordinarily remains obscure to followers of national events. Although Bay City has been a Democratic town for many years, Saginaw has not, and the heavy Republican margins in the Thumb have made the area in the 8th district safely Republican for most of the 20th century. It had little impact on national politics since one of its congressmen coauthored the Fordney–McCumber tariff—until 1974. Then, suddenly, the calling of a special election here to replace a retiring Republican congressman made the 8th district the center of national attention. A Democrat had already captured the Gerald Ford seat around Grand Rapids by calling for the impeachment of Richard Nixon, and now the Democrats, in the person of state Representative Bob Traxler, were trying to make the 8th district race another referendum on the unpopular president. The Republican, James Sparling, who had the misfortune of having worked briefly in the Nixon White House, called on Nixon to campaign. That may have backfired; Traxler won, albeit by a narrow margin; and the move for impeachment grew stronger.

When Traxler won that election, he was an important enough national figure to have appeared on Face the Nation. But soon the 8th lapsed into its accustomed obscurity. Traxler eventually won a seat on House Appropriations and amassed considerable seniority on the Agriculture and HUD–Independent Agencies Subcommittees. He is currently second in seniority to the chairmen on both of these bodies, and since the chairmen were born in 1910 and 1911, Traxler's chance of joining the "college of cardinals"—the unofficial name for the chairmen of the appropriations subcommittees—is excellent. Of the two posts, the more powerful is probably Agriculture, through which Jamie Whitten has had a major hand in shaping American farm and food policy for nearly 30 years; on that subcommittee Traxler has been a major supporter of the food stamp program.

Traxler has been reelected every two years by comfortable margins. Redistricting will probably shift the district somewhat northward, but since many of these rural counties have been getting lots of new and mostly Democratic residents from the Detroit metropolitan area, that should not affect Traxler's chances significantly.

Census Data   Pop. (1980 final) 505,144, up 8% in 1970s. Median family income, 1970, $10,270, 107% of U.S.

The Voters

Employment profile 1970   White collar, 38%. Blue collar, 45%. Service, 13%. Farm, 4%.
Ethnic groups   Black 1980, 7%. Hispanic 1980, 4%. Total foreign stock 1970, 16%. Canada, 4%; Germany, 3%; Poland, 2%; UK, 1%.

Presidential Vote

1980	Reagan (R)	112,243	(53%)
	Carter (D)	85,019	(40%)
	Anderson (I)	13,473	(6%)
1976	Ford (R)	105,159	(55%)
	Carter (D)	84,198	(44%)

Rep. Bob Traxler (D) Elected Apr. 1974; b. July 21, 1931, Kawkawlin; home, Bay City; Mich. St. U., B.A. 1953, Detroit Col. of Law, LL.B. 1959.

Career Army, 1953–55; Asst. Bay Co. Prosecutor, 1960–62; Mich. House of Reps., 1963–74, Major. Flr. Ldr., 1965.

Offices 2448 RHOB, 202-225-2806. Also 62 New Fed. Bldg., 100 S. Warren, Saginaw 48606, 517-753-6444.

Committee *Appropriations* (15th). Subcommittees: Agriculture, Rural Development and Related Agencies; HUD–Independent Agencies; Legislative.

Group Ratings

	ADA	COPE	PC	LCV	CFA	RPN	NAB	NSI	NTU	ACA	ACU
1980	56	79	63	43	79	—	9	29	14	17	24
1979	47	85	53	52	67	—	—	—	19	13	21
1978	45	80	50	70	50	20	10	67	11	20	21

Key Votes

1) Draft Registn $	AGN	6) Fair Hsg DOJ Enfrc	FOR	11) Cut Socl Incr Dfns $	AGN
2) Ban $ to Nicrgua	AGN	7) Lim PAC Contrbtns	AGN	12) Hosptl Cost Controls	AGN
3) Dlay MX Missile	AGN	8) Cap on Food Stmp $	AGN	13) Gasln Ctrls & Allctns	FOR
4) Nuclr Mortorium	AGN	9) New US Dep Edcatn	FOR	14) Lim Wndfll Prof Tax	FOR
5) Alaska Lands Bill	AGN	10) Cut OSHA $	AGN	15) Chryslr Loan Grntee	FOR

Election Results

1980 general	Bob Traxler (D)	124,155	(61%)	($88,798)
	Norman R. Hughes (R)	77,009	(38%)	($25,075)
1980 primary	Bob Traxler (D)	21,059	(100%)	
1978 general	Bob Traxler (D)	103,346	(67%)	($97,020)
	Norman R. Hughes (R)	51,900	(33%)	($40,795)

NINTH DISTRICT

From Gary, Indiana, up through Chicago and Milwaukee, north to Sheboygan and Mani- towoc, Wisconsin, the western shore of Lake Michigan is heavily industrial. Behind the great sand dunes that line the eastern, Michigan, side of the lake there are a few grimy indus- trial towns such as Muskegon and old lumber ports such as Ludington. But most of the Michigan side of Lake Michigan is given over to farming; despite the northern weather, fruits and vegetables do well here within a few miles of the shore. The area around Traverse City is the chief cherry producing center in the United States.

Michigan's 9th congressional district covers most of the eastern shore of Lake Michigan. The 9th extends from Allegan County in the south to Leelanau in the north—the latter is the extended little finger of Michigan's mitten-shaped Lower Peninsula. Along with Grand Rapids, the southern portion of the district has the nation's largest concentration of Dutch– Americans. One of the cities here, Holland, holds a tulip festival every year, complete with people walking around in wooden shoes.

The Dutch are probably the most conservative and Republican of all identifiable American ethnic groups. Ottawa County, which contains Holland and Zeeland, was one of only three Michigan counties to go for Barry Goldwater in 1964. To the north the country is politically more varied. Industrial Muskegon is sometimes Democratic, but Republicans can also carry it. The smaller counties are mostly Republican; those with old lumber ports marginally so. An oddity here is tiny Lake County, a large number of whose residents are black and which always goes Democratic; here one may find one of the nation's first black resort areas, founded at the turn of the century by members of Chicago's black bourgeoisie.

The 9th has always been a Republican district. It was represented for ten years by Robert Griffin, until he went to the Senate in 1966; it has been represented for longer than that by his successor Guy VanderJagt. His background seems ideal for this seat: he comes originally from the northern part of the district, and his Dutch name is a considerable asset in the southern part. VanderJagt has had a number of interesting careers: he was a television newscaster and a practicing attorney, and he holds a divinity degree as well. He has shown an interest in environmental causes not always typical of Republicans and was largely responsible for the creation of the Sleeping Bear Dunes National Lakeshore in the northern part of the district.

After many years of laboring in obscurity, VanderJagt has become one of the best-known House Republicans. His greatest exposure to the public came when he served as keynoter of the 1980 Republican National Convention, although his speech was delayed a day so as to accommodate the large number of other speakers at the convention. VanderJagt displayed his rather old-fashioned oratorical style — his voice rising in a crescendo or falling to a whisper, his metaphors homey, his jokes corny, speaking all the while without notes or Teleprompter. His style comes from the grand old American tradition of Sunday afternoon oratory, from the days when people had no better entertainment than to listen to an inspirational orator go on for hours. VanderJagt made a strong case against the incumbent Democratic administration, but he evidently did not make an especially strong case for his own nomination for the vice presidency, for which he was reportedly under consideration.

If VanderJagt achieved his greatest notice orating, he achieved his greatest success as chairman of the House Republican Campaign Committee. For years this was a frustrating job, as Republicans seldom seemed able to come up with as many strong candidates as Democrats and counted themselves lucky if they managed to hold even. VanderJagt's two terms as chairman have produced very different results. Republicans gained 11 seats in 1978 and would have picked up more but for the weakness of some incumbents; and they captured an additional 33 seats in 1980, essentially wiping out all the gains the Democrats had made since Watergate. This put the Republicans within 26 seats of a formal majority in the House — and probably gave them a working majority on most issues. Under VanderJagt's leadership, the campaign committee made substantial contributions to the Republican resurgence. It raised money through direct mail far, far better than the Democrats; it targeted seats intelligently; it helped to recruit good candidates; it provided technical assistance from a wide variety of campaign professionals. The Democrats, stunned by their 1980 losses, are now trying to emulate what the Republicans have done.

Nothing could be sweeter for VanderJagt. He is, despite his moderate voting record on some issues, a tough partisan, and he seems to have gotten considerably more partisan in recent years. He hoped that his campaign committee chairmanship, which introduced him to so many of the new Republican members, would enable him to win the House Republican leadership. He argued as well that he would be more presentable to the general public than his competitor (and predecessor as campaign chairman), Robert Michel, and that he would cooperate less with the Democrats. But none of these arguments was able to overcome Michel's competence and his strongest talking point, the fact that he as minority whip knew the House, its rules, and its members far better than VanderJagt, who had been spending so much time on campaigns.

VanderJagt has been mentioned very occasionally as a possible candidate for statewide office in Michigan. But his voting record increasingly is geared to his Republican constituency, and it seems almost certain that he would prefer to stay in the House. Redistricting should be no problem for him, and barring unforeseen circumstances he should be able to look forward to a long House career.

Census Data   Pop. (1980 final) 537,268, up 15% in 1970s. Median family income, 1970, $9,474, 99% of U.S.

The Voters

Employment profile 1970   White collar, 37%. Blue collar, 46%. Service, 13%. Farm, 4%.
Ethnic groups   Black 1980, 4%. Hispanic 1980, 2%. Am. Ind. 1980, 1%. Total foreign stock 1970, 15%. Netherlands, 4%; Germany, Canada, 2% each; Poland, 1%.

Presidential Vote

1980	Reagan (R)	140,514	(60%)
	Carter (D)	76,224	(33%)
	Anderson (I)	14,592	(6%)
1976	Ford (R)	139,170	(63%)
	Carter (D)	78,084	(36%)

Rep. Guy Vander Jagt (R) Elected 1966; b. Aug. 26, 1931, Cadillac; home, Cadillac; Hope Col., B.A. 1953, Yale U., B.D., Rotary Fellow, Bonn U., Germany, 1956, U. of Mich., LL.B. 1960.

Career   Practicing atty., 1960–64; Mich. Senate, 1965–66.

Offices   2409 RHOB, 202-225-3511. Also 950 W. Norton Ave., Muskegon 49441, 616-733-3131.

Committee   *Ways and Means* (4th). Subcommittees: Select Revenue Measures; Trade.

Group Ratings

	ADA	COPE	PC	LCV	CFA	RPN	NAB	NSI	NTU	ACA	ACU
1980	22	11	30	35	14	—	82	100	48	79	69
1979	5	26	13	20	4	—	—	—	55	88	82
1978	10	5	5	23	9	70	88	100	20	79	100

Key Votes

1) Draft Registn $	—	6) Fair Hsg DOJ Enfrc AGN	11) Cut Socl Incr Dfns $ FOR
2) Ban $ to Nicrgua	FOR	7) Lim PAC Contrbtns AGN	12) Hosptl Cost Controls AGN
3) Dlay MX Missile	AGN	8) Cap on Food Stmp $ FOR	13) Gasln Ctrls & Allctns AGN
4) Nuclr Mortorium	AGN	9) New US Dep Edcatn AGN	14) Lim Wndfll Prof Tax FOR
5) Alaska Lands Bill	AGN	10) Cut OSHA $ FOR	15) Chryslr Loan Grntee FOR

Election Results

1980 general	Guy Vander Jagt (R)	168,713	(97%)	($185,491)
1980 primary	Guy Vander Jagt (R)	41,453	(100%)	
1978 general	Guy Vander Jagt (R)	122,363	(70%)	($197,290)
	Howard M. Leroux (D)	53,450	(30%)	($38,498)

TENTH DISTRICT

Draw a line on a map across Michigan's Lower Peninsula from Bay City to Muskegon. South of that line live 90% of the state's residents, almost half in the Detroit metropolitan area and the rest in and around the state's other industrial cities. North of the line, Michigan is covered with forests, and little of it has ever been farmed; the largest city in this part of the Lower Peninsula has a population of only 15,000. The forests here were ravaged by the lumber barons of the turn of the century, and only now are they growing back. More recently there has been another environmental disaster: the feeding of the poisonous flame retardant PBB to cattle. Many of this area's dairy herds have had to be slaughtered and people in the sparsely populated counties chosen for burial sites have protested loudly. PBB is known to be a poison; it has found its way through the food chain into the bodies of just about everyone in Michigan and cannot be expelled. But no one knows what its long-term effects are.

For years this northern part of the Lower Peninsula has depended economically on the tourist and recreation business. Every weekend during the summer, and during the hunting season in the fall and the skiing season in the winter, cars jam Interstate 75 as city people flee to cottages on Michigan lakes or resorts in the woods. The fishing here is excellent, as Ernest Hemingway learned as a boy during summer visits; it is even better now that the lakes have been stocked with the huge coho salmon. As the 1960s became 1970s, many people who had been coming up here for weekends or vacations decided to move to the area permanently. Wages are not as high as in the Detroit area, but neither is the cost of living, and the pace of life is slower and more pleasant. Today these north woods are in the middle of a population boom—something they haven't experienced since the 1890s.

The 10th congressional district spans the line across Lower Michigan. The district dips south to the Lansing city limit, and its lower counties are fairly thickly populated with small towns and farms. The largest city here is Owosso, the boyhood home of Thomas Dewey. Up north, where the farms become woods, the biggest towns are Midland, home of Dow Chemical Company, whose early commitment to energy efficiency earned it good publicity and whose production of napalm and Agent Orange generated publicity the company didn't want; Traverse City, which produced both Governor William Milliken and former Senator Robert Griffin; and Mount Pleasant, home of Central Michigan University.

Most of outstate Michigan has seen a Democratic trend in the 1970s, but nowhere has it been more notable—and would it have been more surprising ten years ago—than in the 10th district. This was once the safest of Republican territory. But the recent immigration into the area, much of it from the Democratic Detroit area, has been combined with a general trend toward the Democrats to produce a major change. Certainly among those who would have been most surprised to hear such a trend predicted was Elford Cederberg, for years the 10th district's congressman. First elected in 1952, he was one of a dwindling number of Republican congressmen who could remember when their party controlled the House.

But beginning in 1974, he began having trouble at home, and in 1978 he was defeated by Donald Albosta, a farmer who served in the Michigan legislature and had urged strong state government action against PBB.

Albosta is, by just about any measure, the most conservative Democrat in the Michigan delegation. He is not a particularly smooth speaker and has antagonized many of his copartisans. But he has done well enough with his constituents to have been elected to a second term over a creditable opponent, state Senator Richard Allen. He sits on the Public Works and Post Office Committees and does not cut an especially influential figure in Washington. Redistricting will change the shape of the district somewhat and cut it down in size; after the population gains of the 1970s it is one of the two largest in the state. It is likely to be seriously contested again in 1982; although the long-term trend here is to the Democrats, there are still plenty of Republican voters here, and Republicans may believe that the national trend is in their favor.

Census Data Pop. (1980 final) 580,061, up 24% in 1970s. Median family income, 1970, $9,299, 97% of U.S.

The Voters

Employment profile 1970 White collar, 41%. Blue collar, 41%. Service, 14%. Farm, 4%.
Ethnic groups Black 1980, 4%. Hispanic 1980, 1%. Total foreign stock 1970, 11%. Canada, 3%; Germany, 2%.

Presidential Vote

1980	Reagan (R)	136,702	(55%)
	Carter (D)	87,373	(35%)
	Anderson (I)	19,644	(8%)
1976	Ford (R)	129,329	(58%)
	Carter (D)	90,223	(41%)

Rep. Donald Joseph (Don) **Albosta** (D) Elected 1978; b. Dec. 5, 1925, Saginaw Co.; home, St. Charles; Delta Col.

Career Navy, WWII; Farmer; Saginaw Co. Comm., 1970–74; Mich. House of Reps., 1974–76.

Offices 1318 LHOB, 202-225-3561. Also 419 S. Saginaw Rd., Midland 48640, 517-839-0790.

Committees *Post Office and Civil Service* (8th). Subcommittees: Compensation and Employee Benefits; Postal Operations and Services.

Public Works and Transportation (20th). Subcommittees: Economic Development; Investigations and Oversight; Surface Transportation.

Select Committee on Aging (30th). Subcommittee: Human Services.

Group Ratings

	ADA	COPE	PC	LCV	CFA	RPN	NAB	NSI	NTU	ACA	ACU
1980	28	68	33	30	21	—	45	25	22	42	32
1979	58	80	45	55	41	—	—	—	31	12	22

Key Votes

1) Draft Registn $	AGN	6) Fair Hsg DOJ Enfrc	AGN	11) Cut Socl Incr Dfns $	AGN
2) Ban $ to Nicrgua	AGN	7) Lim PAC Contrbtns	AGN	12) Hosptl Cost Controls	AGN

3) Dlay MX Missile	AGN	8) Cap on Food Stmp $	FOR	13) Gasln Ctrls & Allctns	FOR
4) Nuclr Mortorium	AGN	9) New US Dep Edcatn	FOR	14) Lim Wndfll Prof Tax	FOR
5) Alaska Lands Bill	FOR	10) Cut OSHA $	AGN	15) Chryslr Loan Grntee	FOR

Election Results

1980 general	Donald Joseph (Don) Albosta (D)	126,962	(52%)	($355,147)
	Richard J. Allen (R)	111,496	(46%)	($410,995)
1980 primary	Donald Joseph (Don) Albosta (D)	15,240	(100%)	
1978 general	Donald Joseph (Don) Albosta (D)	94,913	(51%)	($258,244)
	Elford A. Cederberg (R)	89,451	(49%)	($146,993)

ELEVENTH DISTRICT

Michigan's Upper Peninsula (or the UP, as it is called here) is a world unto itself. It is isolated most of the year from the rest of the state by the elements, and for years travel here was discouraged by exorbitant ($3.75) tolls on the Mackinac Straits Bridge. The UP was first settled around the turn of the century, when the iron and copper mines were booming, and the place had a Wild West air about it. The population influx here was polyglot: Irish, Italians, Swedes, Norwegians, and Finns, the last of whom remain the largest ethnic group here. While working in the mines, the immigrants picked up some radical social ideas and Democratic voting habits; their descendants still retain the latter.

Some time ago the mines petered out, leaving the UP's stagnant economy dependent on summer tourists and fall hunters. Farming has never been important here; it has been known to snow in July and the growing season is too short for most crops. After World War II the young people of the Upper Peninsula left to move to Detroit, Chicago, and the West Coast. Since the 1940 census, the UP's population has hovered around 300,000 (it was 332,000 in 1920). In the 1970s, as metropolitan areas became more unattractive and job opportunities scarcer, the UP's population rose to 318,000; but there has not been the migration into the area that has been seen in the northern part of the Lower Peninsula. The closest thing to a city here is Marquette, with 23,000 people.

The Upper Peninsula forms about two-thirds of Michigan's 11th congressional district. The 11th altogether is a vast expanse, with 40% of Michigan's land area but only 6% of its population; geographically it is the second largest congressional district east of the Mississippi River. From Tawas City, in the southern part of the 11th in the Lower Peninsula, to Ironwood, at the western tip of the Upper, is a distance of 477 miles. Obviously any serious congressional candidate must travel by airplane.

The Lower Peninsula portion of the 11th, the area below the bridge, has neither the tradition of the mines nor the Democratic voting habits of the UP. It is a more prosperous area, with a big tourist trade and recently significant in-migration. As a whole, the 11th is politically marginal, although oddly the area has elected a Democrat to Congress only once since World War II. From 1966 to 1978 the congressman was Republican Philip Ruppe, scion of a rich Upper Peninsula brewing family. During that time he compiled a more mixed voting record than most Michigan Republicans and had received fairly high labor ratings.

The new Republican congressman, state Senator Robert Davis, had a strong base in the Lower Peninsula portion of the district. The Democrat, Keith McLeod, had little political background but was astute enough to beat more experienced primary opponents; his background as a banker and his stands on issues made him seem more like a Republican to many

Democratic insiders, however. The race was decided on regional, not economic, lines. This was one district that Republican Governor William Milliken failed to carry, and McLeod carried the Upper Peninsula portion of the district, which casts most of the votes. Davis however, won 64% of the vote below the bridge, which was enough to give him a decisive victory.

In his first two years in the House, Davis obviously worked effectively to strengthen his position in the UP, and by the time the 1980 election came around he was able to carry every county in the district by a wide margin. Like his predecessor, he has labor and liberal ratings well above those of most Republicans, but his conservative ratings are also high. He is more willing than most Republicans to support public spending, and particularly on military programs; he is a member of the Armed Services Committee, and the 11th has had a number of air force bases that have been threatened with being closed down.

Census Data   Pop. (1980 final) 518,732, up 11% in 1970s. Median family income, 1970, $7,884, 82% of U.S.

The Voters

Employment profile 1970   White collar, 41%. Blue collar, 40%. Service, 16%. Farm, 3%.
Ethnic groups   Black 1980, 1%. Am. Ind. 1980, 2%. Total foreign stock 1970, 23%. Canada, Finland, 5% each; Germany, Sweden, UK, 2% each; Italy, Poland, 1% each.

Presidential Vote

1980	Reagan (R)	121,678	(50%)
	Carter (D)	101,478	(42%)
	Anderson (I)	15,857	(7%)
1976	Ford (R)	103,331	(50%)
	Carter (D)	98,653	(48%)

Rep. Robert W. (Bob) Davis (R) Elected 1978; b. July 31, 1932, Marquette; home, Gaylord; No. Mich. U., 1950, 1952, Hillsdale Col., 1951–52, Wayne St. U., B.S. 1954.

Career Mortician, 1954–66; St. Ignace City Cncl., 1964–66; Mich. House of Reps., 1966–70; Mich. Senate, 1970–78, Minor. Whip, 1970–74, Minor. Ldr., 1974–78.

Offices 1224 LHOB, 202-225-4735. Also Rm. 102 Fed. Bldg., Alpena 49707, 517-356-2028.

Committees *Armed Services* (15th). Subcommittees: Investigations; Research and Development.

Merchant Marine and Fisheries (9th). Subcommittees: Coast Guard and Navigation; Fisheries and Wildlife Conservation and the Environment; Merchant Marine.

Group Ratings

	ADA	COPE	PC	LCV	CFA	RPN	NAB	NSI	NTU	ACA	ACU
1980	39	67	50	41	50	—	73	89	38	55	47
1979	6	55	25	24	23	—	—	—	42	76	61

Key Votes

1) Draft Registn $	FOR	6) Fair Hsg DOJ Enfrc	AGN	11) Cut Socl Incr Dfns $	AGN
2) Ban $ to Nicrgua	FOR	7) Lim PAC Contrbtns	AGN	12) Hosptl Cost Controls	AGN
3) Dlay MX Missile	AGN	8) Cap on Food Stmp $	FOR	13) Gasln Ctrls & Allctns	FOR
4) Nuclr Mortorium	AGN	9) New US Dep Edcatn	FOR	14) Lim Wndfll Prof Tax	FOR
5) Alaska Lands Bill	AGN	10) Cut OSHA $	FOR	15) Chryslr Loan Grntee	FOR

Election Results

1980 general	Robert W. (Bob) Davis (R)	146,205	(66%)	($121,198)
	Dan Dorrity (D)	75,515	(34%)	($42,578)
1980 primary	Robert W. (Bob) Davis (R)	39,210	(100%)	
1978 general	Robert W. (Bob) Davis (R)	96,351	(55%)	($158,755)
	Keith McLeod (D)	79,081	(45%)	($131,304)

TWELFTH DISTRICT

Macomb County, adjoining Detroit to the northeast, is an area of fast-growing suburban sprawl of the type found in many of the nation's metropolitan areas. In 1950 Macomb had 184,000 people; by 1970, 625,000—more than tripling its population in twenty years. The southern part of the county, near Detroit, has reached its population maximum and in the 1970s Macomb's population rose only to 694,000. The northern reaches of the county remain rural, but for twenty miles beyond Eight Mile Road, the Detroit city limit, Macomb is an agglomeration of neat suburbs, winding streets, thin-walled garden apartments, and gleaming new shopping centers. Unlike the residents of similar places in southern California, the people here have roots, most of them on the east side of Detroit. The descendants of Polish and Italian immigrants who came to man the east side auto plants have moved in just a generation to such suburbs as Warren, East Detroit, Roseville, St. Clair Shores, and Sterling Heights.

Macomb County is mainly a blue collar suburb; most people here earn their living in blue collar or service jobs. Thanks to high UAW wages, Macomb is also one of the highest-income counties in the nation, with a median family income that was 25% above the national average in 1970 and kept pace with inflation during most of the decade. Yet upward mobility has meant more in dollars and comfort than in status: even if you can buy a $75,000 house, it is still less than pleasant to work on an assembly line.

Macomb County residents got their politics from their parents back on the east side, and they were solidly Democratic. President Kennedy won 63% of the vote here in 1960—his best showing in any suburban county in the United States. But as the 1960s went on, the Democratic allegiance here faded. In state elections George Romney and then William Milliken carried Macomb. In national elections George Wallace won 14% here in 1968. Then in the early 1970s a federal court ordered busing from all of Detroit's suburbs to the city itself. Macomb County was the strongest area opposed: people didn't want their kids to go to school with blacks, to go to school where it might be dangerous, to go to school far away. Richard Nixon won 64% of the vote here, more than double his 1968 percentage. In the 1970s Democrats have hoped that Macomb would return to its old voting habits. But, except in local elections, it has not done so. Increasingly its new subdivisions are for the affluent; new immigration is probably more Republican than its earlier residents. But even more important, the Democrats' stands on the social issues of the 1966–72 period seem to have snapped the bonds of an allegiance that, after all, resulted from the struggle between labor and management 30 years ago. People in Macomb County no longer think of themselves as part of the downtrodden half of society; they see themselves as part of a large, comfortable, but put-upon middle class.

The 12th congressional district includes most of Macomb County. It has lost some of its most heavily Democratic areas—Warren, East Detroit—to neighboring districts and has added the fair-sized county that includes the old industrial city of Port Huron to the north; but it is still primarily a Macomb district. Given the changes in political attitudes here, it is not surprising that the 12th has experienced close congressional contests in three of the last four elections. The first was in 1972, when veteran Democrat James O'Hara, first elected in 1958, was nearly unseated because of the busing issue, even though he was solidly antibusing himself; that was how strong opinion was at that time. Once the busing order was overturned by the Supreme Court, the issue vanished and O'Hara was reelected easily in 1974. But in 1976 he decided to run for the Senate and lost in the primary to 7th district Congressman Donald Riegle.

The new congressman is Democrat David Bonior, a young veteran of the state legislature who has received high ratings from liberal and labor organizations. In the 1976 primary he barely beat a much older legislator who had always catered to the anti-Detroit feelings of many Macomb residents. Bonior has faced significant Republican challenges in all three general elections, and in years of a Republican national trend has not been able to win this historically Democratic district with more than 55% of the vote. That performance is almost certain to make him a Republican target again in 1982, but much will depend on redistricting. One proposal would essentially eliminate the 14th district on Detroit's east side; that would bring the 12th closer to Detroit, make it more Democratic, but also might put Bonior in a primary with the 14th's freshman congressman, Dennis Hertel, who has a strong base of his own. If the 14th is not eliminated, then the 12th will move farther out from Detroit, into yet more Republican territory; Republicans will then have their best chance since the busing crisis to carry this district.

Bonior has always had an interest in environmental issues and in his first two terms served on two committees that affect them, Public Works and Merchant Marine. In 1981 he moved to the Rules Committee. His appointment by the speaker (for this is how Democrats on Rules are chosen now) shows confidence that he will cooperate with the leadership in determining when and under what procedural terms legislation will be considered on the floor of the House. The Democratic leadership, which does not command majorities on many substantive issues on the floor of the House, does have a solid majority on Rules and will likely control procedural issues; the result will be a fascinating lesson in whether substantive or procedural majorities will prevail.

Census Data   Pop. (1980 final) 544,744, up 17% in 1970s. Median family income, 1970, $12,003, 125% of U.S.

The Voters

Employment profile 1970   White collar, 46%. Blue collar, 42%. Service, 11%. Farm, 1%.
Ethnic groups   Black 1980, 2%. Hispanic 1980, 1%. Total foreign stock 1970, 24%. Canada, 7%; Germany, Italy, 3% each; Poland, UK, 2% each.

Presidential Vote

1980	Reagan (R)	123,619	(54%)
	Carter (D)	86,172	(38%)

	Anderson (I)	15,321	(7%)
1976	Ford (R)	104,379	(53%)
	Carter (D)	87,787	(45%)

Rep. David E. Bonior (D) Elected 1976; b. June 6, 1945, Detroit; home, Mt. Clemens; U. of Ia., B.A. 1967, Chapman Col., M.A. 1972.

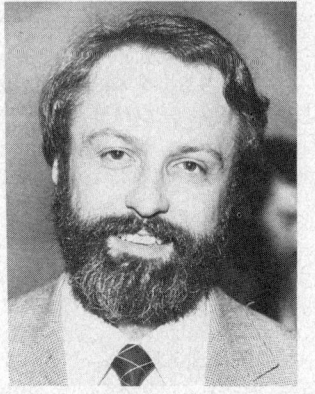

Career Probation officer and adoption caseworker, 1967–68; Air Force, 1968–72; Mich. House of Reps., 1973–77.

Offices 1130 LHOB, 202-225-2106. Also 85 N. Gratiot Ave., Mt. Clemens 48043, 313-469-3232.

Committee *Rules* (10th). Subcommittee: Rules of the House.

Group Ratings

	ADA	COPE	PC	LCV	CFA	RPN	NAB	NSI	NTU	ACA	ACU
1980	83	89	77	88	79	—	0	0	20	18	12
1979	89	95	80	98	67	—	—	—	18	0	5
1978	90	90	93	91	86	25	0	0	18	11	9

Key Votes

1) Draft Registn $	FOR	6) Fair Hsg DOJ Enfrc	FOR	11) Cut Socl Incr Dfns $	AGN
2) Ban $ to Nicrgua	AGN	7) Lim PAC Contrbtns	FOR	12) Hosptl Cost Controls	FOR
3) Dlay MX Missile	FOR	8) Cap on Food Stmp $	AGN	13) Gasln Ctrls & Allctns	FOR
4) Nuclr Mortorium	FOR	9) New US Dep Edcatn	FOR	14) Lim Wndfll Prof Tax	AGN
5) Alaska Lands Bill	FOR	10) Cut OSHA $	AGN	15) Chryslr Loan Grntee	FOR

Election Results

1980 general	David E. Bonior (D)	112,698	(55%)	($105,574)
	Kirk Walsh (R)	90,931	(45%)	($54,170)
1980 primary	David E. Bonior (D)	20,383	(82%)	
	Two others (D)	4,336	(18%)	
1978 general	David E. Bonior (D)	82,892	(55%)	($119,682)
	Kirby Holmes (R)	68,063	(45%)	($69,251)

THIRTEENTH DISTRICT

The 13th Congressional district of Michigan is Detroit's inner city, the only district completely inside the Detroit city limits. Most of the landmarks of Detroit, and most of the city's problems, are found within this area. The 13th includes Detroit's downtown and its new Renaissance Center on the riverfront; it includes the Joe Louis Convention Arena where the 1980 Republican National Convention was held. A few miles inland is the General Motors Building, the headquarters of Detroit's least unhealthy auto company, and only a few miles away from the Poletown area where GM, with city help and against local resistance, is tearing down old houses and building a new plant. Major auto plants were sited at the periphery of the 13th; this was the edge of settlement when they were built, mostly in the 1910–20 decade. Even the freeways' names remind one of the importance of the auto industry here: Edsel B. Ford, Walter P. Chrysler, and the Fisher brothers of General Motors.

The population patterns also tell a graphic story about what happens when one industry —even one as large and rich as the auto industry—comes to dominate the economic life of a large metropolitan area. For this has been the site of one of America's civic disasters in recent years. This is not because its residents are black. There are in fact many stable and pleasant black neighborhoods farther out in Detroit, and there are still pockets here and there (as in Poletown) of old white residential communities in the 13th. The problem, rather, is that this area has become rapidly depopulated. Within the bounds of the 13th district in 1960 lived 576,000 people. By 1970 that had declined to 465,000, the biggest percentage loss of population in the 1960s of any congressional district in the United States. But the decline had only begun. In the 1970s, the population of the 13th slipped to only 291,000 — only half the number of people who had lived there 20 years before.

Population loss does not always hurt a community. It may only reflect the fact that people are having fewer children or that elderly or single people can afford to live by themselves, leaving fewer people per dwelling unit. But the population loss in the 13th obviously goes far beyond that. In Detroit for 50 years there have always been rapid population movements out from the central city; this was a boom town for many years, and subdivisions first within the city limits and then in suburb after suburb would spring up in a single year. Typically, the most prosperous people would move farthest out; those with the lowest wages would stay behind. Blacks first appeared in Detroit in really substantial numbers in World War II, and until the late 1940s were pent up in a few neighborhoods by racial segregation and the housing shortage of the time that prevented almost everyone from moving. Then, when whites began moving farther out into newer suburbs, blacks essentially followed into their old neighborhoods. They were replaced, in the 1950s and 1960s, by new migrants, mostly blacks who came up from the South looking for opportunity and willing to work at low-wage jobs. But as the 1960s turned into the 1970s, the number of low-wage jobs fell. High wages at the auto companies meant that few jobs were available except in boom years. It was part of Detroit's historic pattern that so many people moved out of the 13th district in the 1960–80 period. What was not part of the pattern is that they were not replaced by anybody else.

This kind of population loss turned out to have grim results. The inner-city neighborhoods lost their natural leaders, the kind of people who nurture and maintain community institutions. Left were the violent young men who commit the lion's share of Detroit's crimes. After the 1967 riot, gun ownership became nearly universal in Detroit, and the city's murder rate was the highest in the country. That undoubtedly spurred further outmigration; the pressure was no longer the fact that newcomers were arriving, but that conditions in the inner city were so dangerous. Naturally there was a call for saving the old neighborhoods, but it was not clear that anybody really wanted them saved. The quality of the housing stock in this part of Detroit is generally low; these are frame houses built at the turn of the century for working people. In the past they were torn down for urban renewal projects, which were built years later; now many are still standing, occupied only by vandals, and many are being burned down with grim regularity by arsonists.

In such circumstances, the 13th district has naturally been coming apart as a political community. Voter turnout has been declining rapidly; the major black vote in Detroit now is farther out, in the 1st district. The electorate is more than three-quarters black, and this was one of the first northern constituencies to elect a black congressman, back in 1954. That was Charles Diggs, Jr., first elected at age 27, first chairman of the Congressional Black Caucus, chairman of the Africa Subcommittee of Foreign Affairs for many years, and chairman of the House District of Columbia Committee from 1973 to 1978. With these credentials, Diggs should have been a leader of national stature. But he lacked the drive and ambition that animate most politicians; indeed, he won his seat more because of his father's efforts than his own. Diggs also lacked a moral compass: beset by personal problems and debts, he diverted $60,000 in staff salaries to himself. He was convicted of this crime in October 1978 and sentenced to jail. The charges did not prevent him from winning renomination that year, and the conviction did not prevent him from winning reelection, but his congressional career was effectively over. He was stripped of his committee positions, and when his conviction was affirmed he resigned from Congress.

Naturally many competitors emerged for the seat in 1980, with 12 candidates in the Democratic primary. But it was a measure of the diminution of the political community here that only 21,000 voters bothered to participate in the Democratic primary to choose a new congressman for the first time in 26 years. Among the major candidates were one city councilman and the son of another and a state senator; but the easy winner, with 42% of the vote, was former Judge George Crockett. He was easily elected in November and became, at 71, the oldest freshman congressman since an 81-year-old West Virginian was elected in 1956.

Crockett is something of a folk hero in Detroit's black community. A veteran of left-wing politics, he was elected to Detroit's Recorder's Court (the criminal court) in the 1960s; he aroused great controversy in the late 1960s when he went down to the courthouse in the middle of the night, held hearings, and released on bail men arrested for killing a policeman. Whites launched a movement to recall him; but he had solid black support and was never defeated. Judge Crockett must be the new member least sympathetic to the ideology of the Reagan Administration and the New Right. He is a man of steely self-assurance, however, and has done what he has seen as his duty in much more unfriendly environments.

When a district loses population as rapidly as the 13th, the natural move is to eliminate it in redistricting. This will not happen, because both Democrats and Republicans in Michigan believe it is important to have two black-majority districts. That means that one of the white-majority districts in Metropolitan Detroit will have to be eliminated. A prime target is the 14th district, on the east side of Detroit; if it is sliced up, Crockett's district will receive quite a few white precincts. The alternative is to extend the district west and southwest, through a few black neighborhoods and into white ethnic communities. In either case, the prospect is for Crockett's margins to be lower, but that is not likely to affect his legislative conduct. He is in fine health and seems to have a solid hold on the district for now; but considering his age, there are many black politicians eyeing the 13th for some future election in the 1980s.

Census Data Pop. (1980 final) 291,394, down 37% in 1970s. Median family income, 1970, $7,770, 82% of U.S.

The Voters

Employment profile 1970 White collar, 32%. Blue collar, 48%. Service, 20%. Farm, -%.
Ethnic groups Black 1980, 79%. Hispanic 1980, 3%. Asian 1980, 1%. Total foreign stock 1970, 12%. Canada, Poland, 2% each; Germany, 1%.

Presidential Vote

1980	Reagan (R)	5,090	(6%)
	Carter (D)	73,593	(92%)
	Anderson (I)	1,113	(1%)
1976	Ford (R)	10,654	(13%)
	Carter (D)	82,895	(86%)

Rep. George W. Crockett, Jr. (D) Elected 1980; b. Aug. 10, 1909, Jacksonville, Fla.; home, Detroit; Morehouse Col., A.B. 1931, U. of Mich., J.D. 1934.

Career Practicing atty., 1934–39, 1947–65; Sr. Atty., U.S. Dept. of Labor, 1939–43; Founder–Dir., UAW Fair Practices Dept., 1944–46; Judge, Recorder's Ct., 1966–78; Visiting Judge, Mich. Ct. of Appeals, 1979; Acting Corp. Counsel, Detroit, 1980.

Offices 1531 LHOB, 202-225-2261. Also 8401 Woodward Ave., Suite 106, Detroit 48202, 313-874-4900, and 2866 E. Grand Blvd., Detroit 48202, 313-875-4225.

Committees *Foreign Affairs* (15th). Subcommittees: Africa; International Operations.

Small Business (16th). Subcommittees: Export Opportunities and Special Small Business Problems; General Oversight.

Select Committee on Aging (31st). Subcommittees: Housing and Consumer Interests; Human Services.

Group Ratings and Key Votes: Newly Elected

Election Results

1980 general	George W. Crockett, Jr. (D)	79,719	(92%)	($43,619)
	M. Michael Hurd (R)	6,473	(7%)	($0)
1980 primary	George W. Crockett, Jr. (D)	8,810	(42%)	
	David S. Holmes, Jr. (D)	4,187	(20%)	
	Clyde Cleveland (D)	3,373	(16%)	
	Nicholas Hood III (D)	3,364	(16%)	
	Eight others (D)	1,767	(8%)	
1978 general	Charles C. Diggs, Jr. (D)	44,771	(79%)	($6,700)
	Dovie T. Pickett (R)	11,749	(21%)	($7,959)

FOURTEENTH DISTRICT

The east side of Detroit is the heart of Michigan's 14th congressional district. It is composed of a series of residential neighborhoods of varying degrees of affluence, most of them all white and heavily Catholic. Suburban territory nicely brackets and defines the east side. To the east, along Lake St. Clair, are the five Grosse Pointes: wealthy, conservative, snobby. There used to be a "point system" here: potential residents were given points for undesirable characteristics, such as swarthy complexions or unusual names, and those with too many points could not buy houses. That is gone now, but the well-to-do Irish and Italian Catholic families who have worked their way here are as eager to maintain the area's exclusivity as the descendants of Michigan's old lumber families.

In the district's southwest corner is the enclave of Hamtramck, an almost entirely Polish–American city surrounded by Detroit. It was here that thousands of immigrants flocked to get jobs in the Dodge Main, Plymouth, and Packard auto plants; during the 1910s Hamtramck was the fastest-growing city in the nation. In 1930 as many as 56,000 people lived here. Today the population is down to 21,000, mostly old people, and Dodge Main has been torn down. Hamtramck has been the butt of dozens of Polish jokes, but anybody who takes the trouble to visit the city will find freshly painted houses and carefully tended lawns — evidence of the pride of ownership that still flourishes here and in so many Polish–American neighborhoods.

To the north of Detroit's east side is yet another suburban part of this district: half of Warren and all of East Detroit, both Macomb County suburbs, which were added to the district in 1972. These are working-class suburbs, in which people live in a prosperity that their grandparents in Hamtramck never anticipated. Altogether, the 14th has one of the highest proportions of Polish–Americans, as well as the highest proportion of Belgian–Americans.

For most of the 1960s and 1970s this district had a congressman who distinguished himself, but whose career was ultimately disappointing. Lucien Nedzi, a Democrat first elected in 1961, had a seat on the Armed Services Committee and in the late 1960s and early 1970s was one of its few members to oppose the Vietnam war. He rose in seniority and chaired an intelligence subcommittee; in 1975, at the height of suspicion of the CIA, it was revealed that he had not disclosed evidence he had heard in secret sessions on CIA illegal involvement in domestic affairs and assassination plots. That cost him the chair of a special committee on intelligence. For the next five years he was relatively inactive legislatively, and he decided to retire at age 55 in 1980.

That made for a spirited contest in the 14th district, which may determine the representation of this area for many years — or for just one term. This has been a Democratic district for years, but Republicans have occasionally made serious challenges, as in the 1961 special election and in 1972 when busing was a hot issue. In 1980 the Republican candidate was Vic Caputo, a local newscaster, who was well known and well financed. But he was not able ultimately to beat the Democrat, state Representative Dennis Hertel. Hertel is one of several political brothers (one is in the state Senate now, another replaced Dennis in the state House) who have built a solid organization on the east side, and Dennis Hertel won an eight-candidate Democratic primary with 62% of the vote. His percentage in the general election was just 53%, but in a Republican year against a serious Republican opponent, the figure was impressive.

The difficult problem for Hertel is redistricting. The Detroit metropolitan area must lose one congressional district, and there is a general consensus that neither of the black districts will be eliminated, although one of them, the 13th, lost nearly half its population in the 1970s. One solution would be to expand the 13th far into the east side, give some more of the east side to the 1st, and move the 12th southward in Macomb County to take the 14th's portion of that county. This would give Hertel the choice of running against a black incumbent in a black-majority district or against David Bonior of the 12th district, which is basically Macomb County. Presumably he would do the latter — or return to the east side turf that the Hertel brothers have cultivated so carefully.

Census Data   Pop. (1980 final) 412,244, down 12% in 1970s. Median family income, 1970, $12,394, 129% of U.S.

The Voters

Employment profile 1970   White collar, 50%. Blue collar, 39%. Service, 11%. Farm, –%.
Ethnic groups   Black 1980, 14%. Hispanic 1980, 1%. Asian 1980, 1%. Total foreign stock 1970, 37%. Poland, 9%; Italy, Canada, 6% each; Germany, 4%; UK, 2%; Austria, Yugoslavia, 1% each.

Presidential Vote

1980	Reagan (R)	79,304	(49%)
	Carter (D)	72,151	(44%)
	Anderson (I)	9,686	(6%)
1976	Ford (R)	87,498	(51%)
	Carter (D)	82,896	(48%)

Rep. Dennis M. Hertel (D) Elected 1980; b. Dec. 7, 1948, Detroit; home, Detroit; E. Mich. U., B.S. 1971, Wayne St. U., J.D. 1974.

Career Practicing atty.; Mich. House of Reps., 1974–1980.

Offices 1017 LHOB, 202-225-6246. Also 20491 Van Dyke, Detroit 48234, 313-892-4010.

Committees *Armed Services* (25th). Subcommittees: Procurement and Military Nuclear Systems; Seapower and Strategic and Critical Materials.

Merchant Marine and Fisheries (20th). Subcommittees: Fisheries and Wildlife Conservation and the Environment; Merchant Marine; Oceanography.

Group Ratings and Key Votes: Newly Elected

Election Results

1980 general	Dennis M. Hertel (D)	90,362	(53%)	($160,000)
	Vic Caputo (R)	78,395	(46%)	($211,590)
1980 primary	Dennis M. Hertel (D)	20,595	(62%)	
	John Kelly (D)	6,188	(19%)	($26,274)
	Walter J. Gajewski (D)	3,389	(10%)	($7,255)
	Helen M. Irving (D)	1,477	(4%)	($19,931)
	Four others (D)	1,381	(4%)	
1978 general	Lucien N. Nedzi (D)	84,032	(67%)	($23,898)
	John Edward Getz (R)	40,716	(33%)	($6,225)

FIFTEENTH DISTRICT

The 15th congressional district of Michigan is a collection of suburbs southwest of Detroit. This is the industrial part of the Detroit metropolitan area, an extremely flat plain that sweeps northwest from Lake Erie; across it are the freeways and railroads that connect the factories of southeastern Michigan with their markets. This is the part of the Detroit metropolitan area visitors who arrive by airplane see first: the little frame houses standing in clumps near the freeways, the clutter of commercial developments and small job shops on the major streets, the giant tire advertising sign on the Ford Freeway going into the city. None of Detroit's high-income suburbs are in this part of the metropolitan area; these are the bedroom communities occupied by people who keep the paperwork and assembly lines of the automobile companies moving.

Metropolitan growth has pushed out from Detroit into the 15th, first rapidly in the 1945–60 period when suburbs such as Dearborn Heights and Taylor grew from almost nothing to cities approaching 80,000 in population, and now more slowly. The only part of the 15th with really explosive growth in the 1970s was Canton Township, at the northwest corner of the district, which grew from 11,000 to 48,000. The biggest employer here is the Ford Motor Company, and the last period in which Ford's Michigan payrolls (and those of GM and

Chrysler as well) expanded substantially ended in the 1957–58 recession; since then, even in good years, the auto companies have put new plants in other states and have invested in labor-saving devices. By 1980 Ford was no longer profitable and looked to be facing the same kind of troubles Chrysler was going through. The economic basis of life in the blue collar suburbs — a life more economically bounteous than most people here had ever expected to live — was suddenly threatened with disaster.

The 15th district, and indeed most of the suburbs of Detroit, are historically Democratic and were once among the most heavily Democratic suburban parts of the country. But since the middle 1960s that has changed. George Wallace attracted 16% of the vote in this district in 1968, and in 1972 it was severely shaken when a federal court issued a cross-district busing order. That was later rescinded, and this almost all-white area (there is a black majority in the town of Inkster, and scattered blacks elsewhere) relaxed a little; but it never returned to its old Democratic leanings. Prosperity eroded the sense people had that they were part of a downtrodden working class needing protection from the federal government; they felt instead that bureaucrats and social engineers were trying to change their lives in ways they didn't like. Progressive tax rates, which had once seemed a good way to soak the rich, now began to attack their paychecks. Many white southerners live in this district, but Jimmy Carter could win only 53% of the vote here in 1976, and he lost the district to Ronald Reagan in 1980.

The 15th nonetheless has a Democratic congressman who seems strong at home and is fast becoming one of the most influential, if not one of the most famous, members of the House. He is William Ford — no relation to the car family or the former president — who as a young state legislator was elected when the district was first created in 1964. Ford's most noted achievement to date was probably his role in crafting the civil service reform bill. This measure was sent up by the Carter Administration with much ballyhoo, and then Congress was left to deal with it. Government unions wanted to emasculate it; Republicans were leery. Ford, always a strong union supporter himself, worked with Republican Edward Derwinski and Democrat Morris Udall, and fashioned a bill that, for the first time, moved in the direction of making government employees more accountable. Ford is now chairman of the Post Office and Civil Service Committee, a mostly thankless job, particularly when the Reagan Administration is bent on cutting back on federal spending and the government employee unions are determined to protect and extend every gain they have obtained.

That is not really Ford's main committee assignment, however, nor the one that will probably be most important in the future. He is now the third-ranking Democrat on the House Education and Labor Committee, notably younger than the two who outrank him (Chairman Carl Perkins and Californian Augustus Hawkins). This was once the glamor committee of the House, with jurisdiction over all the antipoverty programs; now it is a very practical body, on which organized labor and the education community are counting to keep the gains they have won in past administrations and which are threatened by the Reagan budget cuts. At the present time the committee has a solid prolabor and pro-education majority, but the margin could become very small — or disappear — if the Republicans should make major gains. Ford has a very solid labor voting record and can be counted on to support labor's positions in almost every case. He is also the second-ranking Democrat on the major education subcommittee that handles the big money bills, and next to Chairman Perkins he has a grasp of the details better than anyone else on the committee. Ford seems almost certain to be at the center of fights on these issues in the 1980s.

Meanwhile, Ford seems unlikely to be threatened seriously in his district. There was much to-do in 1980 when a Nazi won the Republican nomination against him. Of course this was meaningless: the handful of Republican primary voters here had no idea whom they were voting for; the man got even fewer votes than most Republicans in the general election; and when he ran in another Michigan district and spent money telling voters who he was, in the 4th district special election, he got only 2% of the votes cast. Redistricting will probably extend the 15th district out farther from Detroit, into Ypsilanti or Monroe County, both industrial areas similar in character to the towns of the current 15th and both Democratic in local elections if not always in national contests.

Census Data   Pop. (1980 final) 521,898, up 12% in 1970s. Median family income, 1970, $12,460, 130% of U.S.

The Voters

Employment profile 1970   White collar, 42%. Blue collar, 47%. Service, 11%. Farm, –%.
Ethnic groups   Black 1980, 6%. Hispanic 1980, 2%. Asian 1980, 1%. Total foreign stock 1970, 19%. Canada, 5%; Poland, 3%; UK, Germany, Italy, 2% each.

Presidential Vote

1980	Reagan (R)	89,981	(48%)
	Carter (D)	86,621	(45%)
	Anderson (I)	11,832	(6%)
1976	Ford (R)	81,619	(46%)
	Carter (D)	91,412	(52%)

Rep. William D. Ford (D) Elected 1964; b. Aug. 6, 1927, Detroit; home, Taylor; Neb. Teachers Col., 1946, Wayne St. U., 1947–48, U. of Denver, B.S. 1949, J.D. 1951.

Career   Practicing atty., 1951–64; Taylor Twnshp. J.P., 1955–57; Melvindale City Atty., 1957–59; Mich. Senate, 1963–65.

Offices   239 CHOB, 202-225-6261. Also Wayne Fed. Bldg., Wayne 48184, 313-722-1411.

Committees   *Education and Labor* (3d). Subcommittees: Elementary, Secondary and Vocational Education; Labor–Management Relations; Postsecondary Education.

Post Office and Civil Service (Chairman). Subcommittee: Investigations (Chairman).

Group Ratings

	ADA	COPE	PC	LCV	CFA	RPN	NAB	NSI	NTU	ACA	ACU
1980	78	95	53	53	79	—	29	11	10	5	6
1979	68	77	65	51	74	—	—	—	17	8	8
1978	60	100	60	76	50	10	9	22	7	14	14

Key Votes

1) Draft Registn $	AGN	6) Fair Hsg DOJ Enfrc	FOR	11) Cut Socl Incr Dfns $	AGN
2) Ban $ to Nicrgua	AGN	7) Lim PAC Contrbtns	FOR	12) Hosptl Cost Controls	FOR
3) Dlay MX Missile	FOR	8) Cap on Food Stmp $	AGN	13) Gasln Ctrls & Allctns	FOR
4) Nuclr Mortorium	AGN	9) New US Dep Edcatn	FOR	14) Lim Wndfll Prof Tax	AGN
5) Alaska Lands Bill	AGN	10) Cut OSHA $	AGN	15) Chryslr Loan Grntee	FOR

Election Results

1980 general	William D. Ford (D)............	113,492	(68%)	($83,295)
	Gerald R. Carlson (R)	53,046	(32%)	($0)
1980 primary	William D. Ford (D)............	22,171	(100%)	
1978 general	William D. Ford (D)............	95,137	(80%)	($61,157)
	Edgar Nieten (R)...............	23,177	(20%)	

SIXTEENTH DISTRICT

Michigan's 16th congressional district is an industrial part of the Detroit metropolitan area made up of three distinct areas of roughly equal population: the Delray section of Detroit, the Downriver suburbs, and the city of Dearborn. Delray, the southwest corner of Detroit, is an old ethnic neighborhood that looks much as it did in the 1920s. The Downriver suburbs grow more prosperous and modern as one proceeds south along the Detroit River, although an insular quality remains in such places as River Rouge and Ecorse, divided neatly into ethnic and racial sections by the railroad tracks. Dearborn is the district's most famous town. Here the Ford Motor Company has its headquarters and its giant Rouge plant; this is also the place where Henry Ford built his Greenfield Village.

The 16th is one of the nation's most heavily industrial districts. From the Interstate 75 bridge over the Rouge River, you can see the Ford Rouge plant and a couple of refineries on one side and the huge steel mills and chemical plants of the Downriver communities on the other. For the distinction of premier industrial landscape of America, this ranks with the view of Gary from the Indiana Turnpike and the spectacle of northern New Jersey from the Pulaski Skyway. Almost flush up against the industrial plants and well within range of their sulphurous odors are the neat, tightly packed houses of the old ethnic neighborhoods—still mostly Polish, Hungarian, and Italian, but now with considerable numbers of Mexican- and Arab-Americans. The 16th does contain a few high-income WASP enclaves in the western part of Dearborn and on the island of Grosse Ile in the Detroit River. Most of the district, however, is working-class and vintage Democratic country.

The congressman from this district is John Dingell, a Democrat who is one of the most important legislators in either house of Congress. In 1981 he became chairman of the House Energy and Commerce Committee, and for a number of years he has been one of the major forces in the House on energy legislation. Generally he has opposed positions taken by the oil companies. He was instrumental in getting the House to oppose decontrol of energy prices as long as it did, but his positions did not finally prevail. Dingell remains a powerful figure nevertheless. He is an aggressive advocate and a tough negotiator, a man known for his bursts of temper but who also is knowledgeable and well prepared. He has a good degree of control over his committee, which was the busiest House committee in the 96th Congress. He has good relations with the younger liberals who chair its important subcommittees, and he had no trouble reshuffling subcommittee jurisdictions in 1981; Dingell himself retains the chair of its Investigations Subcommittee.

Another area in which he has taken a major part is the question of air pollution. As one of the senior members of the Michigan delegation, Dingell has been the leader of moves supported by the auto industry and the United Auto Workers to relax the requirements of the Clean Air Act. Dingell was successful in the House by a narrow margin here the last time this issue came up; it will be considered again in 1981.

One thing that helped Dingell in this fight was his reputation as a conservationist. He comes to such issues from a different route than many environmentalists; he is an enthusiastic hunter (and opponent of gun controls) and avid outdoorsman. On the Merchant Marine and Fisheries Committee and on the floor he has pushed through numerous pieces of conservationist legislation, and his fervor here is just as great as when he opposes the oil companies on pricing matters.

Dingell holds a safe seat in the 16th. His father was first elected to Congress in 1932, and Dingell himself was elected on his father's death in 1955, before he was 30. He has had no trouble winning reelection since, with one exception. That was in 1964, when redistricting placed him in the same district with Congressman John Lesinski. Both were Democrats of Polish descent and both had succeeded fathers who had first been elected in 1932. The major difference was that Dingell had voted for the Civil Rights Act of 1964, while Lesinski was the one northern Democrat to vote against it. With the vigorous support of the United Auto Workers, Dingell won that election and has had no problems since.

The 16th district went for Jimmy Carter even in 1980, and while it will be moved out from Detroit somewhat by redistricting its basic political complexion should not be much different.

Census Data   Pop. (1980 final) 397,937, down 15% in 1970s. Median family income, 1970, $11,800, 124% of U.S.

The Voters

Employment profile 1970   White collar, 43%. Blue collar, 45%. Service, 12%. Farm, –%.
Ethnic groups   Black 1980, 8%. Hispanic 1980, 5%. Total foreign stock 1970, 31%. Poland, 7%; Canada, 5%; Italy, 3%; UK, Germany, Hungary, 2% each.

Presidential Vote

1980	Reagan (R)	76,947	(45%)
	Carter (D)	79,784	(47%)
	Anderson (I)	10,813	(6%)
1976	Ford (R)	75,048	(44%)
	Carter (D)	93,021	(54%)

Rep. John D. Dingell (D) Elected Dec. 13, 1955; b. July 8, 1926, Colorado Springs, Colo.; home, Trenton; Georgetown U., B.S. 1949, J.D. 1952.

Career   Army, WWII; Practicing atty., 1952–55; Research Asst. to U.S. Dist. Judge Theodore Levin, 1952–53; Wayne Co. Asst. Prosecuting Atty., 1953–55.

Offices   2221 RHOB, 202-225-4071. Also 4917 Schaefer Rd., Dearborn 48126, 313-846-1276.

Committee   *Energy and Commerce* (Chairman). Subcommittee: Oversight and Investigations (Chairman).

Group Ratings

	ADA	COPE	PC	LCV	CFA	RPN	NAB	NSI	NTU	ACA	ACU
1980	67	76	47	58	43	—	9	13	14	18	0
1979	58	80	55	51	38	—	—	—	23	17	21
1978	50	90	65	77	55	18	0	50	14	25	22

Key Votes

1) Draft Registn $	FOR	6) Fair Hsg DOJ Enfrc	AGN	11) Cut Socl Incr Dfns $	AGN
2) Ban $ to Nicrgua	AGN	7) Lim PAC Contrbtns	AGN	12) Hosptl Cost Controls	FOR
3) Dlay MX Missile	FOR	8) Cap on Food Stmp $	AGN	13) Gasln Ctrls & Allctns	FOR
4) Nuclr Mortorium	FOR	9) New US Dep Edcatn	AGN	14) Lim Wndfll Prof Tax	AGN
5) Alaska Lands Bill	AGN	10) Cut OSHA $	AGN	15) Chryslr Loan Grntee	FOR

Election Results

1980 general	John D. Dingell (D)	105,844	(70%)	($115,821)
	Pamella A. Seay (R)	42,735	(28%)	($1,541)
1980 primary	John D. Dingell (D)	21,780	(88%)	
	One other (D)	2,906	(12%)	
1978 general	John D. Dingell (D)	93,387	(76%)	($61,246)
	Melvin E. Heuer (R)	26,827	(22%)	

SEVENTEENTH DISTRICT

Northwest Detroit historically has been the middle-class and white collar part of the city. For mile after mile the straight streets here are lined with single-family homes; the factories responsible for their existence are many miles away. This area was almost entirely farmland in 1920; in the years just after World War II it was completely filled with houses. For many years this was the fulcrum of Michigan politics; as it went, so went the state. It was Republican in most elections until the early 1950s, then in 1954, as the children of Detroit's first auto workers moved out here, it went solidly Democratic. In the years since, northwest Detroit has sometimes gone Republican, but never by much; and as migration within the city continues, it has gotten more Democratic. In the 1970s, increasing numbers of blacks have been moving into northwest Detroit, adding to the Democratic percentages notably.

Northwest Detroit is the heart of the 17th congressional district of Michigan, a district that was once all in Detroit. Now, with population shifting out toward the suburbs, so has the district. It includes Redford Township, politically and sociologically just about indistinguishable from the northwest Detroit neighborhoods it adjoins; Southfield, with a large Jewish population, and with high-rise office buildings whose square footage now rivals downtown Detroit's; and Farmington Hills, west of Southfield, generally affluent and Protestant, the only reliably Republican part of the district.

The 1954 election gave the 17th a Democratic representative, Martha Griffiths, who became extremely popular in the district. She served on the Ways and Means Committee, but her most important achievement was persuading the House to pass the Equal Rights Amendment. Griffiths decided to retire in 1974, and the decision on her succesor was made in the Democratic primary.

The winner, by 256 votes, was state legislator William Brodhead, whose background was in the kind of politics produced by opponents of the Vietnam war. He had the support of the Liberal Conference, a group of volunteers capable of organizing most precincts in the district and squeezing a few extra votes out of each of them, as well as that of the United Auto Workers, the more traditional force in Democratic politics here.

Brodhead won Griffiths's old seat on the Ways and Means Committee and for the most part has joined the ranks of liberals there, that is, those who want the kind of tax reform that will plug loopholes and make the income tax more progressive. In 1981 he became head of the Democratic Study Group, the liberal organization that in the late 1960s and early 1970s was a driving force in the House, but that now has competition from many groups modeled after it. So in early 1981 Brodhead surprised just about everyone when he urged that the 70% marginal rate on "unearned" (i.e., nonsalary) income be lowered immediately to the 50% maximum on other kinds of income. This is a reform that works against progressivity and that even the Reagan White House hesitated to adopt. Brodhead's attitude may have been affected by the financial problems of the auto companies and of his home state of Michigan; he may be more likely to believe now than he was a few years ago that low levels of reward for invested capital is a problem for society.

Brodhead has had only one serious Republican opponent, in 1976, and he won easily. In 1980 his opponent was a mental patient whose name on the ballot resembled that of a well-known local official. The 17th district will probably be changed substantially by redistricting, although in effect all that will happen is that the constituency will follow its old residents out from Detroit into the northwest suburbs. There has been talk that Brodhead may run for governor, and if he does he has the potential to be a formidable candidate.

Census Data   Pop. (1980 final) 453,057, down 3% in 1970s. Median family income, 1970, $13,449, 140% of U.S.

The Voters

Employment profile 1970   White collar, 58%. Blue collar, 31%. Service, 11%. Farm, –%.
Ethnic groups   Black 1980, 30%. Hispanic 1980, 2%. Asian 1980, 1%. Total foreign stock 1970, 34%. Canada, 8%; Poland, UK, 4% each; Germany, USSR, 3% each; Italy, 2%.

Presidential Vote

1980	Reagan (R)	72,582	(41%)
	Carter (D)	89,835	(51%)
	Anderson (I)	11,878	(7%)
1976	Ford (R)	87,946	(50%)
	Carter (D)	87,311	(49%)

Rep. William M. Brodhead (D) Elected 1974; b. Sept. 12, 1941, Cleveland, Ohio; home, Detroit; John Carroll U., 1959–60, U. of Detroit, 1960–63, Wayne St. U., A.B. 1965, U. of Mich., J.D. 1967.

Career   Practicing atty., 1968–71; Mich. House of Reps., 1971–75.

Offices   1114 LHOB, 202-225-4961. Also 24261 Grand River Ave., Detroit 48219, 313-537-1400.

Committee   *Ways and Means* (11th). Subcommittees: Oversight; Public Assistance and Unemployment Compensation.

Group Ratings

	ADA	COPE	PC	LCV	CFA	RPN	NAB	NSI	NTU	ACA	ACU
1980	94	89	70	78	86	—	0	0	18	4	11
1979	100	95	90	93	89	—	—	—	24	4	3
1978	85	100	93	98	82	45	0	0	36	7	4

Key Votes

1) Draft Registn $	AGN	6) Fair Hsg DOJ Enfrc	FOR	11) Cut Socl Incr Dfns $	AGN
2) Ban $ to Nicrgua	AGN	7) Lim PAC Contrbtns	FOR	12) Hosptl Cost Controls	FOR
3) Dlay MX Missile	FOR	8) Cap on Food Stmp $	AGN	13) Gasln Ctrls & Allctns	FOR
4) Nuclr Mortorium	FOR	9) New US Dep Edcatn	FOR	14) Lim Wndfll Prof Tax	AGN
5) Alaska Lands Bill	FOR	10) Cut OSHA $	AGN	15) Chryslr Loan Grntee	FOR

Election Results

1980 general	William M. Brodhead (D)	127,525	(73%)	($18,539)
	L. Patterson (R)	44,313	(25%)	($0)
1980 primary	William M. Brodhead (D)	23,243	(100%)	
1978 general	William M. Brodhead (D)	106,303	(95%)	($12,158)
	Hector McGregor (AIP)	5,341	(5%)	

EIGHTEENTH DISTRICT

The 18th congressional district of Michigan combines two areas that until recently have had little in common and had never before been joined in the same constituency: parts of Oakland and Macomb Counties in suburban Detroit. Oakland is a county that traditionally has been as Republican as outstate Michigan. Indeed, it had its beginnings as a farm community, with Royal Oak, the largest city in the 18th district, as a small market town. Then the migration to the suburbs began. Oakland lay adjacent to northwest Detroit, the most affluent part of the city, and it attracted the highest-income and best-educated people in the metropolitan area. In Detroit, where politics very much resembled class warfare at the time, such people tended to vote heavily Republican. Southern Macomb County, in contrast, had little settlement of any kind and no significant villages. It attracted migrants from the east side of Detroit—factory workers primarily and people of Polish or other Eastern European descent. Their tradition was Democratic. The contrast between the counties can be seen in the 1960 election returns: Macomb was 63% for Kennedy, while Oakland was 54% for Nixon.

In the 1960s and 1970s the differences between Oakland and Macomb—especially those parts in the 18th district—have tended to fade. The 18th always included some working-class suburbs in Oakland, notably Hazel Park and Madison Heights, most of whose residents speak with the accents of the mountains of Kentucky and Tennessee. It also includes the Jewish and heavily Democratic suburb of Oak Park. And in recent years affluent, Republican-leaning voters have tended to move out from such suburbs as Royal Oak and Berkley to newer suburbs farther out; the trend is therefore toward the Democrats. In Macomb a different process has taken place. Working-class consciousness has been fading, as high auto worker wages have put blue collar workers definitely into the middle-income brackets. Now they have summer homes and can afford winter vacations; and they worry, as much as management personnel, about high taxes, inflation, and high levels of government spending. They have stopped thinking of themselves as beneficiaries of government action and have started thinking of themselves as people who finance it. The result is a trend toward the Republicans in Macomb. The convergence of the two counties can be seen from the 1980 election returns: Ronald Reagan's margin over Jimmy Carter was almost as large in Macomb (52%-40%) as in Oakland (55%-36%).

Still, in local elections this district leans Democratic. Much of its Oakland territory is Democratic, while its portion of Macomb County—Sterling Heights and half of Warren—has not been trending too strongly to the Republicans. In 1972, when there was no incumbent, the district did elect a Republican congressman; but he won solely because of the busing issue that was then raging. That faded, as the cross-district busing order was overruled, and the Republican lost in 1974. The current incumbent, Democrat James Blanchard, won a tough primary that year and has not had real difficulty in elections since. His voting record is in line with northern Democrats, but one of his chief legislative goals is not one traditionally associated with them. That is the so-called sunset bill, which would require every federal program to be reauthorized by Congress every five years or else go out of existence. He is the chief House backer of the measure. While no one knows exactly what its effect would be, it is one attempt to impose some discipline and order on the mass of government programs that exist today without abolishing the best of them.

Blanchard's other major endeavor was the Chrysler loan guarantee bill. As a member of the Banking Committee and a representative of Metropolitan Detroit, he was the logical chief sponsor of this measure in the House, and he showed the capacity for hard work and persuasion needed to get this measure—whose prospects initially seemed dim—passed into law.

Blanchard has not been targeted by Republicans, and his district does not seem especially menaced by redistricting, although it will likely have its boundaries changed somewhat.

Census Data   Pop. (1980 final) 489,346, up 5% in 1970s. Median family income, 1970, $13,627, 142% of U.S.

The Voters

Employment profile 1970   White collar, 57%. Blue collar, 34%. Service, 9%. Farm, -%.
Ethnic groups   Black 1980, 2%. Hispanic 1980, 1%. Asian 1980, 1%. Total foreign stock 1970, 29%. Canada, 7%; Poland, 4%; UK, 3%; Italy, Germany, USSR, 2% each.

Presidential Vote

1980	Reagan (R)	101,004	(49%)
	Carter (D)	85,575	(42%)
	Anderson (I)	15,430	(8%)
1976	Ford (R)	109,551	(53%)
	Carter (D)	93,705	(45%)

Rep. James J. (Jim) **Blanchard** (D) Elected 1974; b. Aug. 8, 1942, Detroit; home, Pleasant Ridge; Mich. St. U., B.A. 1964, M.B.A. 1965, U. of Minn., J.D. 1968.

Career   Practicing atty., 1968–74; Legal Aide, Mich. St. Election Bureau, 1968–69; Admin. Asst. to Mich. Atty. Gen. Frank J. Kelley, 1970–71; Asst. Atty. Gen. of Mich.; Legal Advisor to Mich. Depts. of Licensing and Regulation, Commerce, and Agriculture.

Offices   2453 RHOB, 202-225-2101. Also 26111 Woodward, Royal Oak 48070, 313-543-1106.

Committee   *Banking, Finance and Urban Affairs* (10th). Subcommittees: Domestic Monetary Policy; Economic Stabilization (Chairman); Housing and Community Development.

Science and Technology (8th). Subcommittees: Energy Development and Applications; Natural Resources, Agriculture Research and Environment.

Group Ratings

	ADA	COPE	PC	LCV	CFA	RPN	NAB	NSI	NTU	ACA	ACU
1980	72	89	60	52	79	—	0	0	11	13	18
1979	79	90	68	76	78	—	—	—	13	8	5
1978	65	95	68	83	59	42	0	0	17	15	9

Key Votes

1) Draft Registn $	AGN	6) Fair Hsg DOJ Enfrc	FOR	11) Cut Socl Incr Dfns $	AGN
2) Ban $ to Nicrgua	AGN	7) Lim PAC Contrbtns	FOR	12) Hosptl Cost Controls	FOR
3) Dlay MX Missile	AGN	8) Cap on Food Stmp $	AGN	13) Gasln Ctrls & Allctns	FOR
4) Nuclr Mortorium	—	9) New US Dep Edcatn	FOR	14) Lim Wndfll Prof Tax	AGN
5) Alaska Lands Bill	FOR	10) Cut OSHA $	AGN	15) Chryslr Loan Grntee	FOR

Election Results

1980 general	James J. (Jim) Blanchard (D)	135,705	(65%)	($101,378)
	Betty J. Suida (R)	68,575	(33%)	
1980 primary	James J. (Jim) Blanchard (D)	20,501	(100%)	
1978 general	James J. (Jim) Blanchard (D)	113,037	(74%)	($89,842)
	Robert J. Salloum (R)	36,913	(24%)	

NINETEENTH DISTRICT

Just under half of Oakland County, the second most populous county in Michigan, is in the state's 19th congressional district, which also includes a small portion of Livingston County. Technically, all of the district is in the Detroit metropolitan area; in fact, the picture is a little more complicated. For what is really happening in the 19th is that the most affluent parts of the Detroit metropolitan area are moving out, and when they do, they run into older, working-class communities. The most notable of these is Pontiac, an industrial city that produces Pontiac automobiles and GMC trucks. Pontiac has a large population of blacks from the Deep South and whites from the hills of Kentucky and Tennessee. In the early 1970s there was great resistance to a busing order here; to a significant extent, many whites responded by moving farther out, to Waterford Township (a suburb that casts as many votes as Pontiac now) or to one of the communities of summer cottages that line the inland lakes or one of the newer subdivisions near a ski resort resting on man-made hills. Scattered throughout northern Oakland County are a number of small working-class communities — Wixom, Walled Lake, Lake Orion — which are politically similar to Pontiac and Waterford Township: historically Democratic, but trending to Republicans on cultural issues.

Not more than a mile south of the Pontiac black ghetto is the Detroit suburb of Bloomfield Hills, which together with nearby Birmingham is the heart of the high-income suburban belt in Oakland County. Here most of Detroit's top auto executives live as well as middle management personnel and professionals. While downtown Detroit deteriorated, there was a great boom in both commercial and residential construction in Birmingham, Bloomfield Hills, and the similar communities of Troy, Rochester, and West Bloomfield. The museums and concert halls may remain in Detroit, but the stores and services that cater to the carriage trade are mostly out here now in Oakland County. These high-income suburbs are the heart of the 19th district; they outvote Pontiac, Waterford, and similar areas. And, almost needless to say, these high-income areas in this midwestern industrial community are heavily Republican—often on the order of 3-1 margins. While they have a certain tolerance for social liberalism (Birmingham passed an open housing ordinance by referendum, for example, although few blacks have chosen to move there), on economic issues the voters here have no doubt about which party is on their side.

That makes the 19th the only reliably Republican district in the Detroit metropolitan area and arguably the strongest Republican district in the state. The congressman is William Broomfield, a Republican who was first elected in the Republican year of 1956. That makes him one of the most senior Republicans in the House, and he is ranking minority member of the Foreign Affairs Committee. On that body he has been a strong supporter of Israel (there is a substantial Jewish population in Oakland County) and a backer of policies of the government generally. Broomfield, after all, had his first experience during the Eisenhower years, when there was a broad consensus on foreign policy and a vibrant tradition of bipartisanship. Temperamentally, he is a man who does not like to rock the boat and, despite his generally solid Republican views, he cooperated with the Carter Administration on many matters; in the 1980s he seems sure to go along with the national administration. His voting record, somewhat mixed over the years, is pretty orthodox Republican these days. Broomfield is not a mover and a shaker in the House; he is more a man who likes to go along with opinion generally accepted by the kind of voters who predominate in his district, and he seldom makes waves.

Back in the 1950s Broomfield was one of those young Republican congressmen who pioneered the techniques of using the advantages of incumbency to help them win reelection in possibly marginal districts. He survived the Democratic years of 1958 and 1964 without difficulty. In 1972 he beat another Republican incumbent in the primary when they were thrown in the same district with each other. Not yet 60, he seems able to continue winning without difficulty for as long as he chooses to run. Redistricting will probably affect this district very little.

Census Data   Pop. (1980 final) 577,989, up 24% in 1970s. Median family income, 1970, $13,405, 140% of U.S.

The Voters

Employment profile 1970   White collar, 53%. Blue collar, 35%. Service, 11%. Farm, 1%.
Ethnic groups   Black 1980, 6%. Hispanic 1980, 2%. Asian 1980, 1%. Total foreign stock 1970, 17%. Canada, 5%; UK, Germany, 2% each; Poland, 1%.

Presidential Vote

1980	Reagan (R)	156,066	(59%)
	Carter (D)	83,506	(32%)
	Anderson (I)	21,232	(8%)
1976	Ford (R)	132,349	(62%)
	Carter (D)	76,909	(36%)

Rep. William S. Broomfield (R) Elected 1956; b. Apr. 28, 1922, Royal Oak; home, Birmingham; Mich. St. U., B.A. 1951.

Career Mich. House of Reps., 1949–55, Spkr. Pro Tem, 1953; Mich. Senate, 1955–57; Mbr. U.S. Delegation to U.N., 1967.

Offices 2306 RHOB, 202-225-6135. Also 430 N. Woodward St., Birmingham 48011, 313-642-3800.

Committees *Foreign Affairs* (Ranking Member). Subcommittee: International Security and Scientific Affairs.

Small Business (4th). Subcommittee: Export Opportunities and Special Small Business Problems.

Group Ratings

	ADA	COPE	PC	LCV	CFA	RPN	NAB	NSI	NTU	ACA	ACU
1980	11	17	20	57	14	—	75	89	50	75	67
1979	16	32	20	31	11	—	—	—	52	76	86
1978	10	5	10	38	18	92	100	90	27	76	82

Key Votes

1) Draft Registn $	AGN	6) Fair Hsg DOJ Enfrc	AGN	11) Cut Socl Incr Dfns $	FOR
2) Ban $ to Nicrgua	FOR	7) Lim PAC Contrbtns	AGN	12) Hosptl Cost Controls	AGN
3) Dlay MX Missile	AGN	8) Cap on Food Stmp $	FOR	13) Gasln Ctrls & Allctns	AGN
4) Nuclr Mortorium	AGN	9) New US Dep Edcatn	AGN	14) Lim Wndfll Prof Tax	FOR
5) Alaska Lands Bill	FOR	10) Cut OSHA $	FOR	15) Chryslr Loan Grntee	FOR

Election Results

1980 general	William S. Broomfield (R)	168,530	(73%)	($83,608)
	Wayne E. Daniels (D)..........	60,100	(26%)	($9,608)
1980 primary	William S. Broomfield (R)	30,629	(100%)	
1978 general	William S. Broomfield (R)	117,122	(71%)	($41,916)
	Betty F. Collier (D).............	47,165	(29%)	

MINNESOTA

Over the years Minnesota has been one of the nation's leading exporters of iron ore, wheat, flour, and political talent. In the past two decades this not especially populous and geographically peripheral state has given us Hubert Humphrey, Walter Mondale, Eugene McCarthy, Orville Freeman, Warren Burger, and Harry Blackmun. There are still people who remember Minnesota in the 1930s when it produced such national figures as Harold Stassen (a very real presidential contender in 1940 and 1948) and Floyd Olson, the talented and promising Farmer–Labor governor who died prematurely in 1936. No other state of this size — or any size — has produced so many presidential candidates in recent years, and few have had congressional delegations of similar distinction.

Nor have many states experienced such sharp reversals of political fortune as Minnesota has in recent years. For most of the 1970s the Democratic–Farmer–Labor (DFL) Party here had been supreme, holding all the top offices, a majority of congressional seats, and large majorities in the state legislature. Recovering quickly from the 1968 division over the Vietnam war, the DFL had become the nation's best-organized political party. Yet in 1978 Minnesota's Republicans — officially renamed the Independent–Republicans — won both of the state's Senate seats and the governorship and made major gains in state legislative seats as well. It was a stunning victory for a party that had had few victories of any kind in the preceding ten years and a shocking defeat for the party that had just lost its greatest leader, Hubert Humphrey. Then, in 1980, Minnesota was one of six states to go for Jimmy Carter in the presidential election. One reason certainly was the presence of Walter Mondale on the Democratic ticket. But even so, the pattern by which the Democrats carried the state was sufficiently similar to pre-1978 voting patterns to suggest that Minnesota had returned its traditional DFL voting habits.

To put these developments in context we need to go back to the beginnings of Minnesota. This state was far north of the nation's great paths of East–West migration: Minneapolis and St. Paul are at the same latitude as Bangor, Maine, or Vancouver, Washington. In the mid-19th century Yankee immigrants who swelled the populations of Iowa, Nebraska, and Kansas bypassed Minnesota and left it to the Norwegians, Swedes, and Germans who were not deterred by its icy lakes and ferocious winters. These people were more interested in setting up communities that would retain at least some of the characteristics of their native lands. The nation was knit together in those days by the great East–West railroads, and the twin cities of Minneapolis and St. Paul sprang up almost at once at the confluence of the Minnesota and Mississippi Rivers as the center of a great agricultural empire stretching west from Minnesota through the Dakotas and eventually into Montana and beyond. The railroad magnates of St. Paul and the giant millers of Minneapolis seemed to absolutely govern the economic life of the vast Scandinavian–German province of America.

The various rebellions against this dominance have given the politics of Minnesota an almost Scandinavian ambience. As in Wisconsin and North Dakota, a strong third party developed here in the years after the Populist era; and that organization, the Farmer–Labor Party, dominated Minnesota politics in the 1930s. Its great leader was Floyd Olson, and it was beaten by Harold Stassen in 1938 — a year of Republican victory as great as 1978. Even in the 1940s the Farmer–Labor Party was still at least as important as the state's historically negligible Democrats when they merged to form the DFL in 1945; Hubert Humphrey was one of the architects of that merger. Idealistic, blessed with dozens of talented young men and women, the DFL, led by Humphrey, swept the election of 1948 and since then has been the most important political force in the state. Even when it has lost elections, as in 1966 and 1978, it has been the DFL's mistakes or internal discord as much as the Republicans' strength that have produced the outcome.

In 1976 the DFL was in a position of great strength. Senator Walter Mondale was chosen by Jimmy Carter as his running mate in July and was elected vice president of the United States in November; the Carter–Mondale ticket won with 55% of the vote in Minnesota. Senator Hubert Humphrey was reelected to a fifth term with 68% of the vote. The DFL increased its already large margins in the state legislature and reelected its five congressmen easily.

It was appropriate that Humphrey led the ticket that year. Just a month before the election, he underwent surgery for cancer, the disease from which he died in early 1978. But Minnesotans were prepared to reelect him whatever the condition of his health. His career here spanned the entire post–World War II era and the existence of the DFL Party. Some of Humphrey's eulogists would concentrate on his failure to become president. But more than any of the presidents of his time, Humphrey influenced the course of government and the thinking of the nation. He first became a national figure in 1948, with his speech before the Democratic National Convention urging a strong civil rights plank. He stayed with that cause and in 1964, as Senate majority whip, floor-managed the landmark Civil Rights Act. He was an early advocate of disarmament and saw his proposals of the 1950s become the policy of the 1960s and 1970s. He advocated expansionary fiscal policies, which became standard practice in the 1960s. More articulately than anyone else he urged a compassionate government that would reach out to help the poor, the helpless, and the ordinary person. The very balance between the public and private sectors, the size and scope of government activity, the array of government services—all of these today are pretty much what Humphrey had been advocating for 30 years.

Humphrey's career nicely illustrates the principle that achievement does not depend on title or position. He was Senate majority whip for four years, but he was never majority leader, although he ran for the office in 1976; he never chaired a standing committee, although he served 23 years in the Senate. His four years as vice president were not his happiest nor most productive, and he antagonized many of his natural allies by backing the administration's Vietnam war policy. His races for the presidency were not successful; he was underfinanced in 1960, he was disorganized and confronted with a divided party in 1968, and he was late in entering the race in 1972. But over the years he was more successful than any other politician as a purveyor of ideas, a framer of issues. It seems ironic that in the years after Humphrey's death, the quasi-welfare state and large government he had done so much to establish came under increasing attack from the politicians and the voters—and seemed to be repudiated in Ronald Reagan's election in 1980. But that in a way is evidence of the triumph of Humphrey's ideas, for it shows the extent to which they had become reality; and if American liberals seemed after Humphrey's death to have run out of ideas, it was largely because they had succeeded in putting most of their ideas into practice.

When Mondale became vice president, the vacancy he left in the Senate was filled by Governor Wendell Anderson, who resigned and let Lieutenant Governor Rudy Perpich appoint him. Humphrey's vacancy in the Senate was filled by his widow, Muriel Humphrey. In early 1978 the Republicans started making the point that all of Minnesota's top statewide positions were filled by people not elected to them—and all would be up in the 1978 elections. "The DFL is going to face something scary," said a billboard put up by Republican gubernatorial candidate Albert Quie, "an election."

It was not an entirely fair charge. Minnesotans had after all elected DFL candidates to all these posts. They had voted for the Carter–Mondale ticket, knowing that if it won, Mondale would be replaced in the Senate by someone else. They had voted for Hubert Humphrey, although they knew he was ill. What they had not known was that the governor would procure his own appointment to the Senate. That is what really crippled the DFL in the 1978 elections from the start. Since senators have been elected by popular vote, nine governors have had themselves appointed to the Senate; only one of them has been elected by the voters.

The race for the other seat was more turbulent. It seemed at first likely that it would be decided within the DFL, whose state party convention endorsed Congressman Donald Fraser. But self-made millionaire Bob Short, a longtime DFL fundraiser, took the unusual step of challenging the convention choice in the primary. He had a number of strong issues: Fraser's support of free choice in abortions; Fraser's leadership in setting up a Boundary Waters Canoe Area in northern Minnesota, which was strongly opposed by local residents and summer cottage owners; and Short's own promise to cut $100 billion from the budget and cut taxes by half that amount. On primary day Short won a narrow victory; Fraser supporters reacted bitterly and started a "Stop Short" movement. The Republican candidate, David Durenberger, was an attractive contender in his own right: a rather liberal Republican who nonetheless was much less sold on government programs than Fraser, and who was able effectively to contrast himself with the aggressive Short. With support from both liberals and conservatives, he was able to win 61% of the vote — virtually an unprecedented showing in Minnesota.

That was not the only reason the DFL lost, however. The other was that the voters here were moving in a Republican direction on many issues. Minnesota in the post–World War II era has been a state with sharp partisan divisions along economic lines; such rich suburbs of Minneapolis as Edina are overwhelmingly Republican, the poorer white working-class areas (there is only a handful of blacks in the state) are heavily DFL. The mining counties in northern Minnesota are heavily Democratic, the prosperous farm market towns in the southern part of the state solidly Republican, and the farm counties of western Minnesota — their economies heavily dependent on wheat prices and export policies — vary sharply from one election to another. The accomplishment of most of the Humphrey–DFL domestic program left working-class Democratic voters with little more to demand. At the same time, the inevitable failure of government to accomplish all its ends smoothly sparked dissatisfaction among all voters, especially Republicans but also those who continued to approve the basic outlines of the welfare state but disliked many of the details. As a state, Minnesota was becoming much more conservative on economic issues — that is, convinced that government should be cut back rather than expanded. On noneconomic or cultural issues, Minnesota has always been relatively liberal, as befits a state with a Scandinavian heritage, and during the Nixon years these cultural attitudes had helped make Minnesota one of the most Democratic states (it was McGovern's second best state in 1972, for example, just after Massachusetts). But with the Carter Administration in office, the Republican Party here broke loose from cultural issues and was able to campaign on basically economic issues. That, plus the peculiar circumstances of the 1978 election, produced the major Republican victory that year.

The self-appointment issue certainly helped Rudy Boschwitz defeat Wendell Anderson. Anderson was better known, but Boschwitz had some name recognition from television ads for his plywood company. Boschwitz tried to campaign as a liberal Republican, downplaying talk of tax cuts and avoiding an appearance with Ronald Reagan. He is a strong backer of Israel and a strong opponent of nuclear power; he chairs the Near Eastern Affairs Subcommittee. Boschwitz ended up winning his race rather easily, but it is not clear how much strength he really has in Minnesota. His voting record tends more toward that of most Republicans than his campaign message would seem to have implied. Boschwitz has a high-ranking seat on the Budget Committee and a seat on Agriculture as well — both positions that could help him back home. But it is too early to say how opinion will shake out in 1984, when Boschwitz's seat is up. He undoubtedly expects serious opposition.

Durenberger occupies the seat once held by Humphrey and is up for reelection in 1982. He is probably about as strong as a Republican could be in Minnesota. He is thoughtful and has a pleasant personality. His record makes concessions to liberals on cultural matters but is generally in line with Republicans' initiatives on economic issues. He will have plenty to say on them, since he sits on the Finance Committee. He is the chairman of Finance's subcommittee on Health, where he is the leading Senate sponsor of the competition bill. The idea is to give tax incentives to companies that give their employees a choice of medical plans, with cost figures plainly indicated, in the hope that health care consumers will opt for the cheaper plans and that insurers will therefore have an incentive to keep medical expenses down. Durenberger draws on the experience of Minnesota's HMOs (health maintenance organizations), which are more widespread here than in any other part of the country. Durenberger might prove vulnerable if Walter Mondale should come back, as Humphrey did in 1970, and run for the Senate again; but Mondale announced in early 1981 that he would not do so. A key question in this race will be the strength of the DFL challenge.

A Republican who will probably face a tough challenge in 1982 is Governor Albert Quie. The state has faced budget shortfalls after an initial tax cut. The Republicans were ecstatic when they held the DFL to a 67–67 tie in the state House in 1978; but in 1980 the DFL won control of the House again, and it had never come close to losing control of the Senate. One possible strong candidate against Quie is Attorney General Warren Spannaus. Quie is an unusual political quantity, a congressman for 20 years who returned home to run for state office (Donald Fraser, defeated for the Senate, has done the same thing; he was elected mayor of Minneapolis in 1979); he will fight hard to stay on and has not done anything really to antagonize voters. This is a race likely to be seriously contested, and at a high level on both sides.

Serious contests are also likely in two Minnesota House seats, the 6th and 7th, where margins were small in 1980. Republicans won both seats, picking up the 6th after a DFL incumbent retired; the DFL will almost surely counterattack in 1982. Minnesota neither gains nor loses seats for 1982, and redistricting should not be too difficult, despite some large population shifts away from the center of the Twin Cities areas and toward surrounding rural counties. The DFL legislature and Republican governor will probably agree simply to extend the Minneapolis and St. Paul districts outward and maintain the outstate districts within more or less their current boundaries. No incumbent will be seriously affected by such changes. The real question for Minnesota will be the impact of Reagan Administration programs. Success for the Republicans on economic issues and a downplaying of conservative stands on the cultural issues are the best formula for the Republicans here to maintain their 1978 and 1980 gains; failure on the economic front or strife on cultural issues will help the DFL win back the majority status they believe is really theirs in this state.

Census Data Pop. (1980 final) 4,077,148, up 7% in 1970s: 1.80% of U.S. total, 21st largest. Central city, 21%; suburban, 43%. Median 4-person family income, 1978, $21,455, 105% of U.S., 13th highest.

1979 Share of Federal Tax Burden $8,340,000,000; 1.85% of U.S. total, 19th largest.

1979 Share of Federal Outlays $7,314,432,000; 1.58% of U.S. total, 23d largest.

DOD	$1,125,678,000	29th	(1.06%)	HEW	$3,088,469,000	19th	(1.73%)
DOE	$15,875,000	33d	(0.13%)	ERDA	$7,984,000	31st	(0.29%)
HUD	$118,698,000	18th	(1.80%)	NASA	$10,679,000	24th	(0.23%)
VA	$372,229,000	20th	(1.79%)	DOT	$329,652,000	17th	(2.00%)
EPA	$114,600,000	16th	(2.16%)	DOC	$15,616,000	33d	(0.49%)
DOI	$78,619,000	21st	(1.42%)	USDA	$1,018,185,000	4th	(4.24%)

Economic Base   Agriculture, notably cattle, dairy products, corn, and hogs; finance, insurance, and real estate; machinery, especially electronic computing equipment; food and kindred products, especially meat products; printing and publishing, especially commercial printing; electrical equipment and supplies; fabricated metal products, especially structural metal products.

Political Lineup   Governor, Albert H. Quie (IR). Senators, David Durenberger (IR) and Rudy Boschwitz (IR). Representatives, 8 (5 IR and 3 DFL); 8 in 1982. State Senate, 67 (45 DFL and 22 IR); State House of Representatives, 134 (70 DFL and 64 IR).

The Voters

Registration   2,787,277 Total. No party registration.
Employment profile 1970   White collar, 49%. Blue collar, 31%. Service, 13%. Farm, 7%.
Ethnic groups   Black 1980, 1%. Hispanic 1980, 1%. Asian 1980, 1%. Am. Ind. 1980, 1%. Total foreign stock 1970, 19%. Germany, 4%; Sweden, Norway, 3%; Canada, 2%.

Presidential Vote

1980	Reagan (R)	873,268	(43%)
	Carter (D)	954,173	(47%)
	Anderson (I)	174,997	(9%)
1976	Ford (R)	819,395	(42%)
	Carter (D)	1,070,440	(55%)

SENATORS

Sen. David Durenberger (IR) Elected 1978, seat up 1982; b. Aug. 19, 1934, St. Cloud; home, Minneapolis; St. John's U., 1955, U. of Minn., J.D. 1959.

Career   Army, 1956; Practicing atty., 1959–66; Exec. Secy. to Gov. Harold LeVander. 1969–71; Counsel for Legal & Community Affairs, Corporate Secy., Mgr. Internatl. Licensing Div., H.B. Fuller Co., 1971–78.

Offices   353 RSOB, 202-224-3244. Also 174 Fed. Cts.Bldg., 110 S. 4th St., Minneapolis 55401, 612-725-6111.

Committees   *Finance* (8th). Subcommittees: Energy and Agricultural Taxation; Health (Chairman); Social Security and Income Maintenance Programs.

Governmental Affairs (7th). Subcommittees: Energy, Nuclear Proliferation, and Government Processes; Federal Expenditures, Research, and Rules; Intergovernmental Relations (Chairman).

Select Committee on Intelligence (6th). Subcommittees: Budget; Analysis and Production; Collection and Foreign Operations.

Special Committee on Aging (8th).

Group Ratings

	ADA	COPE	PC	LCV	CFA	RPN	NAB	NSI	NTU	ACA	ACU
1980	44	33	40	75	20	—	25	70	35	72	40
1979	53	66	60	—	52	—	—	—	26	36	45

Key Votes

1) Draft Registn $	FOR	6) Fair Housng Cloture	FOR	11) Cut Socl Incr Defns	FOR
2) Ban $ to Nicrgua	FOR	7) Ban $ Rape Abortns	FOR	12) Income Tax Indexing	FOR
3) Dlay MX Missile	AGN	8) Cap on Food Stmp $	AGN	13) Lim Spdg 21% GNP	FOR
4) Nuclr Mortorium	FOR	9) New US Dep Edcatn	FOR	14) Incr Wndfll Prof Tax	FOR
5) Alaska Lands Bill	FOR	10) Cut OSHA Inspctns	FOR	15) Chryslr Loan Grntee	AGN

Election Results

1978 general	David Durenberger (IR)	957,908	(61%)	($1,062,271)
	Robert E. Short (DFL)..........	538,675	(35%)	($1,972,060)
1978 primary	David Durenberger (IR)	139,187	(67%)	
	Malcolm Moos (IR)	32,314	(16%)	($25,889)
	Three others (IR)..............	35,419	(17%)	
1976 general	Hubert H. Humphrey (DFL)	1,290,736	(68%)	($618,878)
	Jerry Brekke (R)	478,602	(25%)	($43,912)
	Paul Helm (Amer.)	125,612	(7%)	
1976 primary	Hubert H. Humphrey (DFL)	317,632	(91%)	
	One other (DFL)..............	30,262	(9%)	
1970 general	Hubert H. Humphrey (DFL)	788,256	(58%)	
	Clark MacGregor (R)	568,025	(42%)	

Sen. Rudy Boschwitz (IR) Elected 1978, seat up 1984; b. 1930, Berlin, Germany; home, Plymouth; Johns Hopkins U., NYU., B.S. 1950, LL.B. 1953.

Career Army, 1953–55; Practicing atty.; Founder and Pres., Plywood Minnesota, 1963–78.

Offices 2317 DSOB, 202-224-5641. Also 210 Bremer Bldg., St. Paul 55101, 612-221-0905.

Committees *Agriculture, Nutrition, and Forestry* (6th). Subcommittees: Agricultural Production, Marketing, and Stabilization of Prices; Rural Development, Oversight, and Investigations; Foreign Agricultural Policy (Chairman); Agricultural Research and General Legislation.

Budget (4th).

Foreign Relations (8th). Subcommittees: European Affairs; East Asian and Pacific Affairs; Near Eastern and South Asian Affairs (Chairman).

Select Committee on Small Business (5th). Subcommittees: Capital Formation and Retention; Export Promotion and Market Development (Chairman).

Group Ratings

	ADA	COPE	PC	LCV	CFA	RPN	NAB	NSI	NTU	ACA	ACU
1980	28	10	37	67	7	—	55	89	53	96	55
1979	21	21	43	—	14	—	—	—	42	63	73

Key Votes

1) Draft Registn $	FOR	6) Fair Housng Cloture	FOR	11) Cut Socl Incr Defns	FOR
2) Ban $ to Nicrgua	FOR	7) Ban $ Rape Abortns	FOR	12) Income Tax Indexing	FOR
3) Dlay MX Missile	AGN	8) Cap on Food Stmp $	FOR	13) Lim Spdg 21% GNP	FOR
4) Nuclr Mortorium	FOR	9) New US Dep Edcatn	FOR	14) Incr Wndfll Prof Tax	AGN
5) Alaska Lands Bill	FOR	10) Cut OSHA Inspctns	FOR	15) Chryslr Loan Grntee	AGN

Election Results

1978 general	Rudy Boschwitz (IR)	894,092	(57%)	($1,870,163)
	Wendell Anderson (DFL)........	638,375	(40%)	($1,154,351)
1978 primary	Rudy Boschwitz (IR)	185,393	(87%)	
	Harold Stassen (IR)	28,170	(13%)	($139,230)
1972 general	Walter F. Mondale (DFL)	981,320	(57%)	($536,532)
	Phil Hansen (R)	742,121	(43%)	($304,750)

GOVERNOR

Gov. Albert H. Quie (IR) Elected 1978, term expires Jan. 1983; b. Sept. 18, 1923, near Dennison; St. Olaf Col., B.A. 1950.

Career Navy, WWII; Dairy farmer; Minn. Senate, 1954–58; U.S. House of Reps., 1958–78.

Offices State Capitol, St. Paul 55155, 612-296-3391.

Election Results

1978 gen.	Albert H. Quie (IR)	830,019	(54%)
	Rudy Perpich (DFL)	718,244	(46%)
1978 prim.	Albert H. Quie (IR)	174,999	(84%)
	One other (IR)	34,406	(16%)
1974 gen.	Wendell Anderson (DFL) ..	786,787	(63%)
	John W. Johnson (R)......	367,722	(29%)
	James G. Miles (I)	62,150	(5%)

FIRST DISTRICT

The 1st congressional district of Minnesota, the southeastern corner of the state, is a region of farms, grain elevator towns, and small, pleasant cities. This is the Minnesota district with the most in common with the rural Midwest farther south. In its ethnic and political traditions, it is more like Iowa—that is, more Yankee and more Republican—than Minnesota as a whole. The district's largest city, Rochester, is the home of the Mayo Clinic and, until 1971, of its onetime counsel and now U.S. Supreme Court Justice Harry Blackmun (whose reluctance to challenge doctors' judgments contributed to his 1973 opinion legalizing most abortions). Rochester is a comparatively rich, idyllic, white collar town; Olmsted County, of which it is a part, is the largest Minnesota county that is consistently Republican.

The northern end of the 1st district is rather different. Here, in Dakota County across the river from St. Paul and in Washington County just to the east of the capital, we pass from the rural and small-city atmosphere of southeastern Minnesota to the outskirts of the Twin Cities metropolitan area. These are working-class suburbs in most cases, where newly laid out subdivisions attract young families who grew up in the straighter streets and older houses of St. Paul.

These Dakota and Washington County suburbs tend to vote for DFL candidates, while the other part of the district tends to go Republican. Congressional elections, however, have not usually been so close. This district has been represented for more than 20 years by Republicans whose voting records make more than a bow toward the liberalism personified by the DFL's Hubert Humphrey, and they have regularly been reelected by margins larger than Republicans in statewide races can amass here. From 1958 until he was elected governor in 1978, Albert Quie represented this district—long enough to become ranking minority member of the House Education and Labor Committee. He picked what turned out to be a good Republican year to retire from Congress, and his successor was a similar-minded Republican, Arlen Erdahl. In another year he might not have been so successful in an open seat contest; he had lost the Republican nomination in 1974 in the 2d district, and he had been defeated as secretary of state later that year. But in 1978 Erdahl won a solid margin over a young DFL legislator from the St. Paul area, and in 1980 he was reelected with an overwhelming percentage. Like Quie, he got a seat on Education and Labor, and his voting record is notably more liberal than those of other Minnesota House Republicans. Redistricting will likely remove all or most of Dakota and Washington Counties from the district, which will only make Erdahl's seat safer.

Census Data Pop. (1980 final) 538,276, up 14% in 1970s. Median family income, 1970, $10,272, 107% of U.S.

The Voters

Employment profile 1970 White collar, 46%. Blue collar, 30%. Service, 15%. Farm, 9%.
Ethnic groups Hispanic 1980, 1%. Asian 1980, 1%. Total foreign stock 1970, 14%. Germany, 4%; Norway, 2%; Sweden, Canada, 1% each.

Presidential Vote

1980	Reagan (R)	118,530	(47%)
	Carter (D)	107,960	(43%)
	Anderson (I)	21,763	(9%)
1976	Ford (R)	117,565	(48%)
	Carter (D)	125,615	(49%)

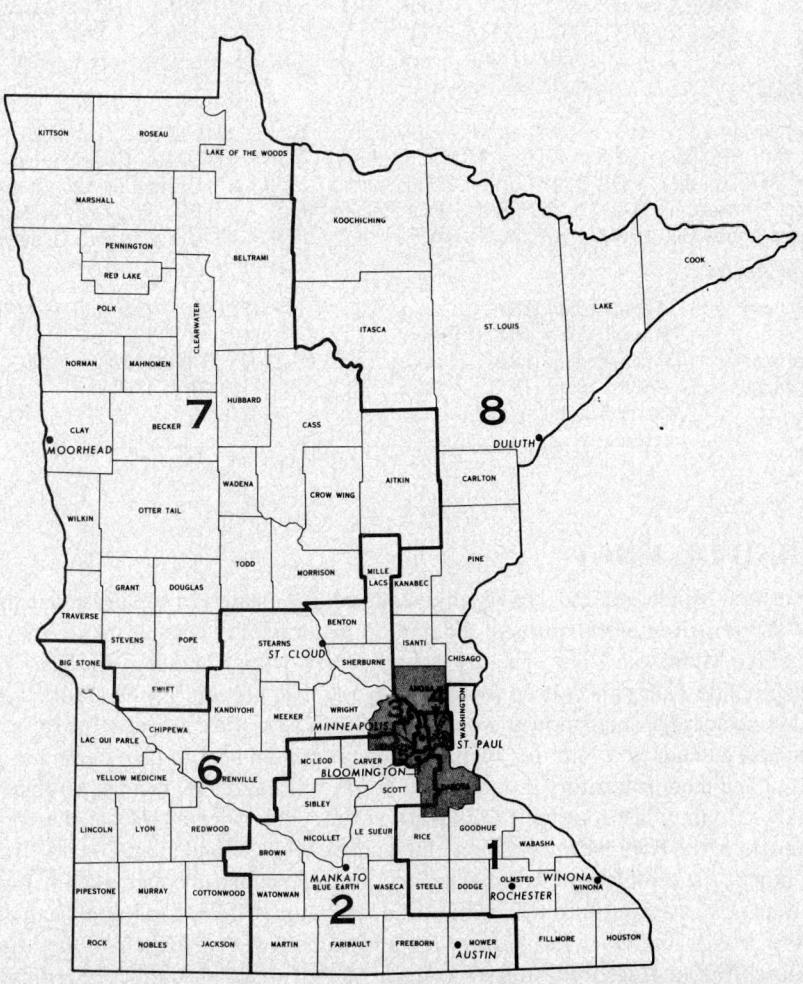

Rep. Arlen Erdahl (IR) Elected 1978; b. Feb. 27, 1931, Blue Earth; home, W. St. Paul; St. Olaf Col., B.A. 1953, Harvard U., M.P.A. 1966.

Career Minn. House of Reps., 1963–70; Secy. of State of Minn., 1970–74; Minn. Pub. Svc. Comm., 1975–78.

Offices 1518 LHOB, 202-225-2271. Also 33 Wentworth Bldg., W. St. Paul 55119, 612-725-7716.

Committees *Education and Labor* (7th). Subcommittees: Elementary, Secondary and Vocational Education; Postsecondary Education; Select Education.

Foreign Affairs (12th). Subcommittees: Africa; International Economic Policy and Trade.

Group Ratings

	ADA	COPE	PC	LCV	CFA	RPN	NAB	NSI	NTU	ACA	ACU
1980	56	21	37	58	21	—	73	56	39	54	37
1979	32	17	30	46	19	—	—	—	51	76	74

Key Votes

1) Draft Registn $	AGN	6) Fair Hsg DOJ Enfrc	FOR	11) Cut Socl Incr Dfns $	AGN
2) Ban $ to Nicrgua	AGN	7) Lim PAC Contrbtns	AGN	12) Hosptl Cost Controls	AGN
3) Dlay MX Missile	FOR	8) Cap on Food Stmp $	FOR	13) Gasln Ctrls & Allctns	AGN
4) Nuclr Mortorium	AGN	9) New US Dep Edcatn	FOR	14) Lim Wndfll Prof Tax	FOR
5) Alaska Lands Bill	FOR	10) Cut OSHA $	FOR	15) Chryslr Loan Grntee	AGN

Election Results

1980 general	Arlen Erdahl (IR)	171,099	(72%)	($100,621)
	Russell V. Smith (DFL)	67,279	(28%)	($0)
1980 primary	Arlen Erdahl (IR)	23,337	(100%)	
1978 general	Arlen Erdahl (IR)	110,090	(56%)	($194,363)
	Gerry Sikorski (DFL)	83,271	(43%)	($149,089)

SECOND DISTRICT

South central Minnesota, most of which is included in the state's 2d congressional district, is one of the most Republican parts of the state. A majority of the people in the 2d live in the valley of the Minnesota River. The towns here—New Ulm, Mankato, St. Peter—are old and their political allegiances deep rooted and mostly Republican. To the southeast, the district also includes the small industrial and usually DFL city of Austin, near the Iowa border. The 2d also extends well into the Twin Cities metropolitan area to take in the heavily Republican high-income territory around Lake Minnetonka and a politically marginal section of Dakota County, just south of St. Paul. The Democratic tide of 1974 was the acid test of the strength of the Republican tradition in the upper Midwest and in the 2nd district, unlike many others, the tradition prevailed. The incumbent Republican congressman, threatened more than he was accustomed to in 1972, decided to retire in 1974. The Republican nominee was 30-year-old Tom Hagedorn, one of the most conservative members of the Minnesota legislature. Half of Hagedorn's margin came from the two small counties he represented in the legislature, but nonetheless he won.

When Hagedorn entered Congress, the spotlight was on the Democratic freshmen elected in 1974 — a distinctive group and one that in succeeding years affected public policy in important ways. In that context Hagedorn seemed unimportant. But from the perspective on the far side of the 1980 elections, Hagedorn is a much more important figure. He is, in a sense, a precursor of the idealistic and aggressive young Republican conservatives, elected mostly in 1978 or 1980, who have in turn changed the tone of the Congress and the substance of its deliberations. Hagedorn, for example, has been one of the proponents of repeal of the Davis–Bacon Act, which requires the federal government to pay construction workers the prevailing wage in their area (which usually turns out to be the union wage). When Hagedorn came to Congress, no one seriously thought this law could be changed; by early 1981, it seemed likely to be repealed. Hagedorn is now the ranking Republican on Agriculture's Livestock, Dairy, and Poultry Subcommittee; he was the point man for the Reagan Administration's proposal to prevent an increase in dairy subsidies in April 1981. He has also fought the Department of Agriculture when, in the Carter Administration, it tried to ban nitrites in foods. He has pushed for deregulation of trucking, a proposal that never was thought politically feasible until recently.

Unheralded in 1974, Hagedorn could turn out to be one of the more important young members of the House in the 1980s, particularly if the Republicans achieve what seemed until recently to be their impossible dream and win a majority of House seats. Hagedorn is reelected by wide margins every two years, and redistricting should not substantially alter the Republican leanings of the district. The only political danger facing him is if Reagan policies on which he takes the lead (e.g., reducing milk subsidies) should prove unpopular in this agricultural district.

Census Data   Pop. (1980 final) 548,682, up 15% in 1970s. Median family income, 1970, $9,703, 101% of U.S.

The Voters

Employment profile 1970   White collar, 43%. Blue collar, 33%. Service, 12%. Farm, 12%.
Ethnic groups   Hispanic 1980, 1%. Asian 1980, 1%. Total foreign stock 1970, 14%. Germany, 5%; Norway, 2%; Sweden, 1%.

Presidential Vote

1980	Reagan (R)	134,627	(51%)
	Carter (D)	103,035	(39%)
	Anderson (I)	22,119	(8%)
1976	Ford (R)	123,435	(48%)
	Carter (D)	125,615	(49%)

Rep. Tom Hagedorn (IR) Elected 1974; b. Nov. 27, 1943, Blue Earth; home, Truman.

Career Farmer; Minn. House of Reps., 1970–74.

Offices 2344 RHOB, 202-225-2472. Also Box 3148, Mankato 56001, 507-388-4563.

Committees *Agriculture* (4th). Subcommittees: Livestock, Dairy and Poultry; Wheat, Soybeans and Feed Grains.

Public Works and Transportation (6th). Subcommittees: Aviation; Economic Development; Surface Transportation.

Group Ratings

	ADA	COPE	PC	LCV	CFA	RPN	NAB	NSI	NTU	ACA	ACU
1980	11	22	30	22	14	—	73	89	58	68	82
1979	0	5	15	5	7	—	—	—	54	100	89
1978	5	0	10	12	14	73	92	100	41	92	96

Key Votes

1) Draft Registn $	FOR	6) Fair Hsg DOJ Enfrc	AGN	11) Cut Socl Incr Dfns $	FOR
2) Ban $ to Nicrgua	FOR	7) Lim PAC Contrbtns	AGN	12) Hosptl Cost Controls	AGN
3) Dlay MX Missile	AGN	8) Cap on Food Stmp $	FOR	13) Gasln Ctrls & Allctns	AGN
4) Nuclr Mortorium	—	9) New US Dep Edcatn	AGN	14) Lim Wndfll Prof Tax	FOR
5) Alaska Lands Bill	AGN	10) Cut OSHA $	FOR	15) Chryslr Loan Grntee	AGN

Election Results

1980 general	Tom Hagedorn (IR)	158,082	(61%)	($196,870)
	Harold J. Bergquist (DFL)	102,586	(39%)	($31,651)
1980 primary	Tom Hagedorn (IR)	26,106	(100%)	
1978 general	Tom Hagedorn (IR)	145,415	(70%)	($172,482)
	John F. Considine (DFL)........	61,173	(30%)	($22,086)

THIRD DISTRICT

The natural pattern of urban development in America has been for population to spread out from a central city into ever less densely populated rings of suburbs. A good place to observe this phenomenon is in the Minneapolis–St. Paul metropolitan area, which has had substantial population growth and where this pattern of dispersal cannot be attributed to white flight from a black central city, since there are very few blacks in the Twin Cities. The economy here is diversified, with many old blue collar industries (the railroads, General Mills, Pillsbury) and many new, predominantly white collar businesses (Honeywell, 3M, Control Data,.Investors Diversified Services). There has been movement toward the blue collar suburbs around St. Paul and north and northwest of Minneapolis, around the major railroad lines; and many blue collar workers are moving even farther out, past the old limits of the Twin Cities metro area and into counties formerly classified as rural. With factories in the suburbs and freeways in every direction, it is possible to live 60 or 70 miles from downtown Minneapolis or St. Paul and still work in the metro area.

The white collar suburbs tend to be west and southwest of Minneapolis. Most of them are gathered into the 3d congressional district of Minnesota, which includes also some blue collar territory. At the northern edge of the district, along the Mississippi River as it flows into Minneapolis, are blue collar suburbs such as Brooklyn Park and Brooklyn Center. At the far southern end are such middle-income suburbs as Richfield and Bloomington, settled in the 1950s and with populations that are now aging. In the middle of the district are high-income WASP retreats: Plymouth, Golden Valley, and Minnetonka, along with Edina, probably the state's highest-income and most Republican town. Just north of Edina is the predominantly Jewish suburb of St. Louis Park.

This district is mixed enough in its demographic composition that it seldom gives large margins to statewide candidates of any party, but on balance the high-income Republican suburbs usually overcome the middle-income or Jewish DFL suburbs in major races, and the district has elected only Republican congressmen since 1960. The current incumbent,

Bill Frenzel, had a close race when he first ran in 1970, and in the early part of the decade he had a reputation as a somewhat liberal Republican. He played a major part in fashioning campaign finance reform, showing both a desire to pass constructive legislation and a desire to protect the interests of the Republican Party.

Frenzel is a man with the temperament of a fighter and a challenger of conventional wisdom. As his time in the House went on, his voting record began to change. Around 1975 his ratings from liberal and labor groups began to plunge and his ratings from conservative and business groups rose. His partisan instincts may have combined with his contentiousness, or perhaps he simply decided that, on economic issues particularly, the Republican prescriptions made more sense. In any case, as a high-ranking member of the Ways and Means Committee, he is firmly in the Republican corner on most major issues and has the potential at least of being a major fighter for the Republican position. He is a strong and consistent supporter of free trade, a member of the Trade Committee who is very knowledgeable and thoughtful about the issue and often takes the lead in opposing trade restrictions.

Frenzel has had no trouble winning reelection, even when it was reported he was more than a year late in filing his 1972 income tax return. He has declined to run for the Senate and has seen two younger Republicans win the state's Senate seats. He has the potential, however, to be a considerable power in the House. Redistricting here will probably follow the people, moving the boundaries outward, without shifting the political balance.

Census Data   Pop. (1980 final) 486,954, up 3% in 1970s. Median family income, 1970, $13,248, 138% of U.S.

The Voters

Employment profile 1970   White collar, 64%. Blue collar, 26%. Service, 10%. Farm, -%.
Ethnic groups   Black 1980, 1%. Hispanic 1980, 10%. Asian 1980, 2%. Total foreign stock 1970, 16%. Sweden, 3%; Norway, Germany, Canada, 2% each.

Presidential Vote

1980	Reagan (R)	118,227	(45%)
	Carter (D)	113,429	(43%)
	Anderson (I)	27,630	(10%)
1976	Ford (R)	124,439	(49%)
	Carter (D)	120,201	(48%)

Rep. Bill Frenzel (IR) Elected 1970; b. July 31, 1928, St. Paul; home, Golden Valley; Dartmouth Col., B.A. 1950, M.B.A. 1951.

Career Navy, Korea; Pres., Minn. Terminal Warehouse Co.; Minn. House of Reps., 1962–70.

Offices 1026 LHOB, 202-225-2871. Also 120 Fed. Bldg., 110 S. 4th St., Minneapolis 55401, 612-725-2173.

Committees *Budget* (4th).

House Administration (Ranking Member). Subcommittee: Accounts.

Ways and Means (6th). Subcommittee: Trade.

Group Ratings

	ADA	COPE	PC	LCV	CFA	RPN	NAB	NSI	NTU	ACA	ACU
1980	22	12	27	31	7	—	92	50	57	70	75
1979	21	25	5	16	4	—	—	—	56	64	65
1978	35	20	20	42	14	89	90	56	44	64	63

Key Votes

1) Draft Registn $	AGN	6) Fair Hsg DOJ Enfrc	AGN	11) Cut Socl Incr Dfns $	FOR
2) Ban $ to Nicrgua	AGN	7) Lim PAC Contrbtns	AGN	12) Hosptl Cost Controls	AGN
3) Dlay MX Missile	AGN	8) Cap on Food Stmp $	FOR	13) Gasln Ctrls & Allctns	—
4) Nuclr Mortorium	—	9) New US Dep Edcatn	AGN	14) Lim Wndfll Prof Tax	FOR
5) Alaska Lands Bill	AGN	10) Cut OSHA $	FOR	15) Chryslr Loan Grntee	AGN

Election Results

1980 general	Bill Frenzel (IR)	179,393	(76%)	($112,308)
	Joel Alexander Saliterman (DFL) .	57,868	(24%)	($0)
1980 primary	Bill Frenzel (IR), unopposed			
1978 general	Bill Frenzel (IR)	128,759	(66%)	($179,807)
	Michael O. Freeman (DFL)	67,120	(34%)	($154,738)

FOURTH DISTRICT

St. Paul, the smaller of Minnesota's Twin Cities, is an old river town with a history somewhat like that of St. Louis, hundreds of miles farther down the Mississippi River. Settled before Minneapolis, St. Paul was for some years the larger of the two, as well as the state capital. While Minneapolis was attracting Swedes and Yankees, St. Paul got more Irish and German Catholics; while Minneapolis was becoming the nation's largest grain milling center, St. Paul's economic role was that of a transportation hub: a railroad center and a river port. Long before the Democratic–Farmer–Labor Party was formed, St. Paul was one of the few places in Minnesota where Democrats sometimes won elections, and through all the changes that have occurred since, the city and its suburbs have remained staunchly DFL— with the single, and perhaps momentary, exception of 1978.

In these days when the one-person-one-vote rule requires intricately drawn congressional district borders, the 4th district of Minnesota is the closest thing in the nation to a district that is totally coincident with a single county: it includes all but the tiniest smidgin of St. Paul's Ramsey County. A solidly Democratic district, the 4th has been represented by Democrats for more than 30 years. Its most prominent congressman was Eugene McCarthy (1949–59), who in those days did not dabble much in poetry. He was a hardworking member of the Ways and Means Committee and one of the founders of the Democratic Study Group. Although he was happy with the pace of life in the House, McCarthy, perhaps contemplating an eventual presidential candidacy, ran for the Senate in 1958.

The succession here has been governed by the DFL convention ever since. Minnesota's political activists believe deeply in the idea of strong political parties, and in an effort to make their party organizations really mean something they tend to respect their decisions on nominations to office. Primaries are unusual, and it is very rare to see a party nominee defeated; when it does happen, as it did with Congressman Donald Fraser in the 1978 Senate race, the result is usually disaster for the party. Here in the 4th district, when Congressman Joseph Karth retired in 1976, the DFL nomination was decisive in choosing his successor. On the 13th ballot the nomination went to state legislator Bruce Vento. Later he was challenged in the primary, but he got a solid 52%–23% margin over his nearest opponent.

Vento went on to win his general election by a huge margin and to compile a record that earned top marks from labor and liberal organizations. In the ordinary course of things he could expect to hold the seat easily, but in 1978 Minnesota's Republican sweep was strong enough to carry Ramsey County out of the DFL column in both Senate races and the contest for governor. And the Republican Party, for the first time in years, spent a significant amount of money in the 4th district and held Vento to under 60%. In 1980 the Republicans tried even harder, and Vento was again held to less than 60%. The question now is whether the Republicans will target it again in 1982, when its boundaries will likely have been expanded to take in more Republican-inclined territory. They may be discouraged by their failure to raise the Republican percentage in 1980 even after spending more than $300,000.

Census Data Pop. (1980 final) 457,422, down 3% in 1970s. Median family income, 1970, $11,306, 118% of U.S.

The Voters

  Employment profile 1970 White collar, 56%. Blue collar, 31%. Service, 13%. Farm, –%.
  Ethnic groups Black 1980, 3%. Hispanic 1980, 2%. Am. Ind. 1980, 1%. Asian 1980, 1%. Total foreign stock 1970, 19%. Germany, 3%; Sweden, Canada, 2% each; Norway, 1%.

Presidential Vote	1980			
		Reagan (R)	78,432	(34%)
		Carter (D)	124,166	(54%)
		Anderson (I)	23,081	(10%)
	1976	Ford (R)	85,922	(38%)
		Carter (D)	133,051	(59%)

Rep. Bruce F. Vento (DFL) Elected 1976; b. Oct. 7, 1940, St. Paul; home, St. Paul; U. of Minn., A.A. 1962, Wis. St. U., River Falls, B.S. 1965.

Career Jr. high school teacher, 1965–76; Minn. House of Reps., 1971–77, Asst. Major. Ldr., 1974–76.

Offices 230 CHOB, 202-225-6631. Also Rm. 544 Fed. Cts. Bldg., St. Paul 55101, 612-725-7869.

Committees *Banking, Finance and Urban Affairs* (18th). Subcommittees: Economic Stabilization; Financial Institutions Supervision, Regulation and Insurance; Housing and Community Development.

Interior and Insular Affairs (17th). Subcommittees: Energy and the Environment; Public Lands and National Parks.

Select Committee on Aging (25th). Subcommittees: Human Services; Retirement Income and Employment.

Group Ratings

	ADA	COPE	PC	LCV	CFA	RPN	NAB	NSI	NTU	ACA	ACU
1980	100	84	73	90	86	—	8	0	19	9	11
1979	95	95	75	92	85	—	—	—	21	4	5
1978	65	95	83	78	82	33	0	10	26	7	4

Key Votes

1) Draft Registn $	AGN	6) Fair Hsg DOJ Enfrc	FOR	11) Cut Socl Incr Dfns $	AGN
2) Ban $ to Nicrgua	AGN	7) Lim PAC Contrbtns	FOR	12) Hosptl Cost Controls	FOR
3) Dlay MX Missile	FOR	8) Cap on Food Stmp $	AGN	13) Gasln Ctrls & Allctns	FOR
4) Nuclr Mortorium	FOR	9) New US Dep Edcatn	FOR	14) Lim Wndfll Prof Tax	AGN
5) Alaska Lands Bill	FOR	10) Cut OSHA $	AGN	15) Chryslr Loan Grntee	FOR

Election Results

1980 general	Bruce F. Vento (DFL)	119,182	(59%)	($128,032)
	John Berg (IR)	82,537	(41%)	($318,545)
1980 primary	Bruce F. Vento (DFL), unopposed			
1978 general	Bruce F. Vento (DFL)	95,989	(58%)	($80,225)
	John Berg (IR)	69,396	(42%)	($76,705)

FIFTH DISTRICT

The 5th congressional district of Minnesota is virtually all of the city of Minneapolis and a couple of blue collar suburbs in Anoka County to the north. Minneapolis is known as the nation's leading grain milling center and for its sophisticated white collar industries. But the great business interests do not account for its distinctive political tradition. This comes instead from the Swedish and other Scandinavian immigrants who started coming here in the 1880s. There were probably two reasons why they were attracted to Minnesota: first, from the resemblance of the American north country, with its hilly countryside, thousands of glacier-carved lakes, and long cold winters, to the Scandinavia they had known; and, second, because there were opportunities here that native-stock Americans, eager to head straight west out of Illinois and Missouri, failed to pursue. (The same opportunities seem to have attracted Minneapolis's latest ethnic group, the Hmongs from Indochina.) The Scandinavians have given Minneapolis a liberal political tradition, hospitable in turn to the Harold Stassens and David Durenbergers of the Republican Party as well as to the Hubert Humphreys and Walter Mondales of the DFL.

The 5th district has had a succession of congressmen of national stature, whose defeats have hurt the causes they held most dear. The first of these was Walter Judd, the 1960 Republican National Convention keynoter and longtime unofficial head of the China lobby. His defeat in his bid for reelection in 1962 did not destroy the lobby but did undermine the idea, prevalent in the 1950s, that most Americans were deeply devoted to the Nationalist Chinese regime on Taiwan. The second was the man who beat Judd, Donald Fraser. He was one of the leading liberals in the House, a hard worker who had no impulse to compromise his principles however much it might help him politically to do so. Fraser was national chairman of the ADA, and in his last terms investigated Korean lobbying in Congress and the Sun Myung Moon cult, and sponsored a controversial Boundary Waters Canoe Area that would prohibit motorboats in this northern Minnesota area. All these things, plus his refusal to back antiabortion laws and indulge in government antispending rhetoric, cost him votes when he ran for the Senate in 1978, and together they cost him enough that he lost the DFL primary to Robert Short. That defeat in liberal Minnesota led to national speculation that traditional liberal doctrine simply could not hold popular support—speculation that seems even harder to resist in light of the results of the 1980 elections.

Nonetheless, the 5th district continues to support liberal Democrats, both in statewide and congressional races. As many affluent and middle-class people have moved to the suburbs, the 5th has become a solidly Democratic district, delivering a healthy majority for George McGovern in 1972. The 1978 DFL nominee, Martin Olav Sabo—the middle name is a nice reminder of his Scandinavian background—was speaker of the Minnesota House; at age 40 he had 18 years of legislative experience. The Republicans, realizing that 1978 might be their best year in Minnesota in a generation, put on a real campaign, complete with television advertising, but were able to win only 38% of the vote. Redistricting will add quite a bit of suburban territory to this district, but it still should be solidly DFL.

The House Democratic leadership in Washington has a soft spot in its heart for former speakers—Tip O'Neill himself was speaker of the Massachusetts House before he came to Congress—and Sabo received a seat on the Appropriations Committee. He was one of only three freshmen to do so. He seems destined for a long congressional career and should have a record as liberal as any.

Census Data   Pop. (1980 final) 414,657, down 13% in 1970s. Median family income, 1970, $10,323, 108% of U.S.

The Voters

Employment profile 1970   White collar, 55%. Blue collar, 30%. Service, 15%. Farm, –%.
Ethnic groups   Black 1980, 7%. Hispanic 1980, 1%. Am. Ind. 1980, 2%. Asian 1980, 1%. Total foreign stock 1970, 23%. Sweden, 5%; Norway, 4%; Germany, 3%; Canada, 2%; Poland, 1%.

Presidential Vote

1980	Reagan (R)	63,830	(29%)
	Carter (D)	123,562	(57%)
	Anderson (I)	26,750	(12%)
1976	Ford (R)	76,940	(35%)
	Carter (D)	134,503	(61%)

Rep. Martin Olav Sabo (DFL) Elected 1978; b. Feb. 28, 1938, Crosby, N.D.; home, Minneapolis; Augsburg Col., B.A. 1959, U. of Minn.

Career   Minn House of Reps., 1961–78, Minor. Ldr., 1969–73, Spkr., 1973–78.

Offices   426 CHOB, 202-225-4755. Also Rm. 166, 110 S. 4th St., Minneapolis 55401, 612-725-2081.

Committee   *Appropriations* (25th). Subcommittees: Transportation; HUD–Independent Agencies.

Group Ratings

	ADA	COPE	PC	LCV	CFA	RPN	NAB	NSI	NTU	ACA	ACU
1980	94	79	73	74	79	—	17	0	18	9	11
1979	100	90	83	86	85	—	—	—	24	8	8

Key Votes

1) Draft Registn $	AGN	6) Fair Hsg DOJ Enfrc	FOR	11) Cut Socl Incr Dfns $	AGN
2) Ban $ to Nicrgua	AGN	7) Lim PAC Contrbtns	FOR	12) Hosptl Cost Controls	FOR
3) Dlay MX Missile	FOR	8) Cap on Food Stmp $	AGN	13) Gasln Ctrls & Allctns	FOR
4) Nuclr Mortorium	FOR	9) New US Dep Edcatn	AGN	14) Lim Wndfll Prof Tax	AGN
5) Alaska Lands Bill	FOR	10) Cut OSHA $	AGN	15) Chryslr Loan Grntee	FOR

Election Results

1980 general	Martin Olav Sabo (DFL)	126,451	(70%)	($83,547)
	John Doherty (IR)	48,200	(27%)	($0)
1980 primary	Martin Olav Sabo (DFL)	22,477	(100%)	
1978 general	Martin Olav Sabo (DFL)	91,673	(62%)	($84,652)
	Michael Till (IR)	55,412	(38%)	($129,487)

SIXTH DISTRICT

The 6th congressional district of Minnesota is farm country, the beginnings of the great wheat fields that sweep across Minnesota into the Dakotas and Montana. Long freight trains move through the landscape, on tracks first laid out by such empire builders as James J. Hill of the Great Northern Railway. The groaning diesels pull cars west to the Pacific or east to St. Paul or Chicago; engines and cars whiz through dozens of little crossroads towns, each with its grain elevator and antique depot. The voting patterns of the 6th — long Minnesota's most marginal district — reflect the ethnic groups Hill and other railroad barons attracted to this part of Minnesota: Republican Norwegians and Yankees, Democratic–Farmer–Labor Swedes, ticket-splitting German Catholics.

The German population here is most heavily concentrated in Stearns County, which contains St. Cloud, the largest town in the district, and Sauk Centre, the boyhood home of Sinclair Lewis and the setting for his novel *Main Street*. Until the outbreak of World War I, the Germans who settled here and elsewhere were regarded as the "best" of the immigrants: thrifty and hardworking, just like the old Yankee stock. But when the United States went to war with the Kaiser, these German–Americans found themselves the target of national hatred. The teaching of German was prohibited in many states; sauerkraut became liberty cabbage; the heritage that so many German–Americans had worked hard to protect was suddenly considered subversive.

That experience seems to have affected political attitudes among this group for decades. Not surprisingly, these people were very much against the idea of going to war against Germany in 1917, and 20 years later they again dreaded such a war. This was the part of Minnesota that sent the progressive, antiwar Charles A. Lindbergh, Sr., to Congress during World War I, and which produced his son, the aviator who became one of the most popular leaders in the fight to keep the United States out of World War II. As Samuel Lubell has pointed out, Stearns County and places like it were the heart of isolationist sentiment in this country, switching wildly from one party to the other in an effort to prevent future wars with Germany or to avenge past ones.

The 6th district has been one of the most marginal congresional districts in the nation. Since 1962, only once has a candidate here won reelection with more than 56% of the vote, and often the contest has been closer. In 1962 and 1964 DFLer Alec Olson won here; in 1966, 1968, 1970, and 1972 Republican John Zwach, a veteran of the state legislature; in 1974, 1976, and 1978 DFLer Richard Nolan. Nolan in many ways was typical of 1974 freshman Democrats: young (31 when first elected) but with much practical political experience; liberal but adept at appealing to district voters on local issues; hardworking and willing to return to the district constantly (Nolan lost to Zwach in 1972 and never stopped campaigning, more or less forcing the incumbent to retire). Nolan also had some of the problems that bedeviled liberal Democrats in the Upper Midwest in the late 1970s. His support for government spending programs was no longer popular. Farmers directed any discontent they had at Democrats. And the abortion issue cost him some votes, notably in heavily Catholic Stearns County.

His share of the vote cut to 55% in 1978, Nolan decided to retire from Congress at age 37 in 1980. He was already facing strenuous opposition: Vin Weber, a 28-year-old Republican who had helped put together Rudy Boschwitz's Senate campaign in 1978, was already running hard. Weber stressed his total opposition to abortion and argued for a free-market approach to agriculture. The DFL candidate, Archie Baumann, had been an aide to Nolan and stressed his support of government agriculture programs. He did manage to carry some agricultural counties. But Weber carried Stearns County by 2,000 votes and won almost double that margin in the district's portion of Hennepin County—some of the farther-out suburbs of Minneapolis, which are not necessarily heavily Republican in other contests.

It is almost certain that the DFL will be contesting this district seriously again in 1982; by now folks here must be used to the kind of closely contested House races that voters in most other districts see only about once in a generation. Weber seems to personify the new 1980 generation of Republicans as Nolan personified the 1974 generation of Democrats, and the new incumbent, like the old, will likely rise or fall on the success or failure of the ideas he represents.

Census Data   Pop. (1980 final) 554,522, up 16% in 1970s. Median family income, 197X, $7,984, 83% of U.S.

The Voters

Employment profile 1970   White collar, 38%. Blue collar, 30%. Service, 13%. Farm, 19%.
Ethnic groups   Total foreign stock 1970, 18%. Germany, 6%; Norway, Sweden, 3% each.

Presidential Vote

1980	Reagan (R)	131,735	(49%)
	Carter (D)	107,458	(40%)
	Anderson (I)	18,627	(7%)
1976	Ford (R)	104,667	(41%)
	Carter (D)	140,420	(55%)

Rep. Vin Weber (IR) Elected 1980; b. July 24, 1952, Slaton; home, St. Cloud; U. of Minn., 1970–73.

Career Pres., Weber Publ. Co., family business; Press Secy.–Researcher for U.S. Rep. Tom Hagedorn, 1974; Cmpgn. Mgr., Chf. Minn. Aide for Sen. Rudy Boschwitz, 1978–80.

Offices 514 CHOB, 202-225-2331. Also 720 St. Germain, Rm. 135, St. Cloud 56301, 612-252-7580, and 208 College Dr., Marshall 56258, 507-532-9611.

Committees *Science and Technology* (11th). Subcommittees: Energy Development and Applications; Science, Research and Technology.

Small Business (12th). Subcommittee: Tax, Access to Equity Capital and Business Opportunities.

Group Ratings and Key Votes: Newly Elected

Election Results

1980 general	Vin Weber (IR)	140,402	(53%)	($498,304)
	Archie Baumann (DFL)	126,173	(47%)	($188,181)
1980 primary	Vin Weber (IR)	18,154	(87%)	
	One other (IR)................	2,655	(13%)	
1978 general	Richard Nolan (DFL)	115,880	(55%)	($212,542)
	Russ Bjorhus (IR)	93,742	(45%)	($138,982)

SEVENTH DISTRICT

The 7th congressional district of Minnesota occupies the northwest quadrant of the state. This is the most sparsely populated part of Minnesota, with 32% of the state's land area but only 12% of its people. Along the Red River of the North, just next to North Dakota, are vast wheat fields; to the east are acres of lakes, forest, and occasional resort communities. This is the country of the legendary Paul Bunyan and his blue ox Babe, whose statues stand together in Bemidji, a small town on the shores of one of Minnesota's 10,000 lakes. Not far away is Lake Itasca, the headwater of the Mississippi River.

The district was first settled by hardy Swedish and Norwegian lumberjacks and farmers. The Republican stronghold is heavily Norwegian Otter Tail County, near the southern end of the district; the strongest DFL territory is at the edges of the district, in the counties nearest Minneapolis and St. Paul. The northern counties, which were Farmer–Labor Party strongholds in the 1930s, used to be heavily DFL but have been trending Republican in the late 1970s.

The 7th has had a rather colorful political history. It made national headlines in 1958 when Coya Knutson was the DFL congresswoman here; her husband Andy issued a plaintive statement urging her to come home and, among other things, make his breakfast again. Apparently many voters considered the request reasonable; Knutson was the only Democratic incumbent to lose in the heavily Democratic year of 1958. The man who beat her, an ultraconservative Republican, never demonstrated much popularity, and was finally beaten by DFL candidate Bob Bergland in 1970. Bergland became extremely popular, and made enough of a mark on the Agriculture Committee to be appointed secretary of Agriculture by President Carter.

So in February 1977 there was a special election to fill the seat. The DFL nominated a Bergland and Mondale staffer; the Republicans were wise enough to select a farmer of Scandinavian descent, Arlan Stangeland. He won by a stunning margin. In Congress he has turned out to be probably the most conservative member of the Minnesota delegation. The district has traditionally been close in statewide races, although it went solidly Republican in 1978 and did not go for the Carter–Mondale ticket in 1980. Nevertheless, a young DFL veteran of the legislature, Gene Wenstrom, has contested the seat very vigorously in the last two elections. He has criticized Stangeland's voting record and his refusal to take a seat on the Agriculture Committee. The incumbent was held to 52%–45% and 52%–48% wins in 1978 and 1980. Those are not good signs for any incumbent, particularly when national trends — e.g., the unpopularity of the Carter grain embargo — were working in his favor. We can expect a close race in this district again in 1982.

Census Data   Pop. (1980 final) 520,468, up 10% in 1970s. Median family income, 1970, $7,890, 74% of U.S.

The Voters

Employment profile 1970   White collar, 39%. Blue collar, 28%. Service, 15%. Farm, 18%.
Ethnic groups   Am. Ind. 1980, 3%. Total foreign stock 1970, 21%. Norway, 7%; Germany, Sweden, 4% each; Canada, 2%.

Presidential Vote

1980	Reagan (R)	132,532	(51%)
	Carter (D)	108,610	(42%)
	Anderson (I)	16,496	(6%)
1976	Ford (R)	102,502	(42%)
	Carter (D)	135,192	(55%)

Rep. Arlan Stangeland (IR) Elected Feb. 22, 1977; b. Feb. 8, 1930, Fargo, N.D.; home, Barnesville.

Career Farmer; Minn. House of Reps., 1966–74.

Offices 1519 LHOB, 202-225-2165. Also 403 Center Ave., Moorhead 56560, 218-233-8631.

Committees *Agriculture* (10th). Subcommittees: Cotton, Rice and Sugar; Forests, Family Farms and Energy; Wheat, Soybeans and Feed Grains.

Public Works and Transportation (7th). Subcommittees: Investigations and Oversight; Public Buildings and Grounds; Surface Transportation.

Group Ratings

	ADA	COPE	PC	LCV	CFA	RPN	NAB	NSI	NTU	ACA	ACU
1980	0	21	30	22	29	—	75	100	54	79	79
1979	5	25	13	17	8	—	—	—	56	88	87
1978	5	0	3	13	9	55	91	100	43	91	96

Key Votes

1) Draft Registn $	FOR	6) Fair Hsg DOJ Enfrc	AGN	11) Cut Socl Incr Dfns $	FOR
2) Ban $ to Nicrgua	FOR	7) Lim PAC Contrbtns	AGN	12) Hosptl Cost Controls	AGN

3) Dlay MX Missile	AGN	8) Cap on Food Stmp $	FOR	13) Gasln Ctrls & Allctns	AGN
4) Nuclr Mortorium	AGN	9) New US Dep Edcatn	AGN	14) Lim Wndfll Prof Tax	FOR
5) Alaska Lands Bill	AGN	10) Cut OSHA $	FOR	15) Chryslr Loan Grntee	FOR

Election Results

1980 general	Arlan Stangeland (IR)	135,084	(52%)	($267,705)
	Gene Wenstrom (DFL)..........	124,026	(48%)	($253,893)
1980 primary	Arlan Stangeland (IR)	27,979	(100%)	
1978 general	Arlan Stangeland (IR)	109,456	(52%)	($192,034)
	Gene Wenstrom (DFL)..........	93,055	(45%)	($112,549)

EIGHTH DISTRICT

The 8th congressional district of Minnesota is the northeast corner of the state. Like the 7th, most of the acreage here consists of lakes and forests. But the 8th has far fewer farmers, and most of its population is concentrated in a few essentially urban areas. Because of redistricting, the 8th currently (although it will probably not in 1982) reaches down to Anoka County —blue collar Democratic suburbs of Minneapolis and St. Paul. But the focus of the district —and most of its population— is in St. Louis County, in the Lake Superior port of Duluth, which contains 93,000 people after having almost exactly 100,000 for 50 years, and the towns of the Mesabi Range. This part of Minnesota has been the source of most of the nation's iron ore, which is scooped out of the low-lying hills of the Mesabi, transported by rail to Duluth, loaded on giant freighters, and shipped to Chicago, Gary, Detroit, Cleveland, and Pittsburgh.

Life has not been gentle here. The entrepreneurs who first began the iron ore operations, around the turn of the century, had little respect for the land, digging it up here and putting a factory or a loading dock there, and depositing the waste products of their works wherever they liked. Several years ago most Minnesotans wanted to stop Armco and Republic Steel from dumping taconite tailings with dangerous asbestoslike fibers into Lake Superior. But the companies said that if ordered to stop they would shut down the plant, and people in Silber Bay urged that the dumping be continued. More recently there was a controversy over a proposed Boundary Waters Canoe Area in the northern lakes. The legislation proposed by Minneapolis Congressman Donald Fraser would prohibit motorboats, to keep the lakes pristine; environmentalists loved it, but the local people, afraid of losing tourists and simply because they like motorboats, were furious. Their anger was one of the main reasons Fraser lost the 1978 Senate primary to Bob Short.

The congressman from this district, Democrat James Oberstar, seems to reflect district opinion closely. He has very high ratings from labor and liberal organizations and a strong Democratic Party support score. But he also stood up strongly against prohibiting motorboats in the Boundary Waters Area. He used to be an aide to John Blatnik, who represented the district for 28 years until his retirement in 1974 and was chairman of the House Public Works Committee. Oberstar was strong enough to win the primary that year over DFL convention winner Tony Perpich (brother of then Lieutenant Governor and later Governor Rudy Perpich) and state Senator Florian Chmielewski—names that suggest the ethnic variety of the district. Oberstar sits on the Public Works and Merchant Marine Committees— the kind of prosaic assignments that can mean bread and butter to the 8th district. On Public Works, he chairs the Economic Development Subcommittee, the body with jurisdiction over the EDA, a program threatened with extinction by the Reagan Administration. Oberstar's response was to show graphically how much development and private investment had been stimulated in Duluth because of EDA's work. He has broader interests as well, as indicated by his proposal to allow tax deductions for expenses in adopting a child. His competence has been rewarded with easy reelection victories. Redistricting may cost the district some of its southern counties, but it will remain very heavily Democratic.

Census Data   Pop. (1980 final) 556,150, up 16% in 1970s. Median family income, 1970, $9,393, 98% of U.S.

The Voters

Employment profile 1970   White collar, 41%. Blue collar, 42%. Service, 14%. Farm, 3%.
Ethnic groups   Am. Ind. 1980, 1%. Total foreign stock 1970, 24%. Sweden, 5%; Finland, 4%; Norway, 3%; Canada, Germany, 2% each.

Presidential Vote

1980	Reagan (R)	92,565	(35%)
	Carter (D)	148,783	(56%)
	Anderson (I)	18,524	(7%)
1976	Ford (R)	83,325	(33%)
	Carter (D)	161,172	(64%)

Rep. James L. Oberstar (DFL) Elected 1974; b. Sept. 10, 1934, Chisholm; home, Chisholm; Col. of St. Thomas, B.A. 1956, Col. of Europe, Bruges, Belgium, M.A. 1957.

Career Admin. Asst. to U.S. Rep. John A. Blatnik, 1965–74; Administrator, U.S. House of Reps. Comm. on Pub. Works, 1971–74.

Offices 2351 RHOB, 202-225-6211. Also 231 Fed. Bldg., Duluth 55802, 218-727-7474.

Committees *Merchant Marine and Fisheries* (10th). Subcommittees: Coast Guard and Navigation; Fisheries and Wildlife Conervation and the Environment.

Public Works and Transportation (7th). Subcommittees: Aviation; Economic Development (Chairman); Water Resources.

Group Ratings

	ADA	COPE	PC	LCV	CFA	RPN	NAB	NSI	NTU	ACA	ACU
1980	83	89	70	70	86	—	0	10	12	17	16
1979	79	95	78	76	81	—	—	—	14	4	8
1978	70	85	70	57	68	25	0	10	20	7	8

Key Votes

1) Draft Registn $	AGN	6) Fair Hsg DOJ Enfrc	FOR	11) Cut Socl Incr Dfns $	AGN
2) Ban $ to Nicrgua	AGN	7) Lim PAC Contrbtns	FOR	12) Hosptl Cost Controls	—
3) Dlay MX Missile	FOR	8) Cap on Food Stmp $	AGN	13) Gasln Ctrls & Allctns	FOR
4) Nuclr Mortorium	FOR	9) New US Dep Edcatn	FOR	14) Lim Wndfll Prof Tax	—
5) Alaska Lands Bill	AGN	10) Cut OSHA $	AGN	15) Chryslr Loan Grntee	FOR

Election Results

1980 general	James L. Oberstar (DFL)	182,228	(70%)	($188,096)
	Edward Fiore (IR)	72,350	(28%)	($18,673)
1980 primary	James L. Oberstar (DFL)	38,450	(56%)	
	Thomas E. Dougherty (DFL)	30,618	(44%)	($90,492)
1978 general	James L. Oberstar (DFL)	171,125	(87%)	($64,117)
	John W. Hull (Amer.)	25,015	(13%)	

MISSISSIPPI

Mississippi is the quintessential southern state, the place you think of when you hear southern cliches, from the magnolia blossom-strewn lawn of the antebellum mansion to the tarpaper shacks of black sharecroppers. Historically, it is the product of several streams of migration: land-hungry Jacksonian farmers settled the northeastern and central parts of the state, which are still heavily white and largely rural and small town; wealthy planters settled the Mississippi River valley, together with their slaves. Mississippi has had a sort of mystique about it, thanks to the work of its literary geniuses, such as William Faulkner and Eudora Welty. Mississippi has also been known for years as the state with the largest percentage of blacks, which it still is, and as the state with the lowest incomes and standard of living, which it probably is not.

For the fact is that Mississippi has changed immeasurably over the last 20 years — changed perhaps as much as any part of the country. In the late 1940s, Mississippi still seemed like another country to most Americans. Along its dusty roads leading from market towns were loose-jointed frame farmhouses, where people, white as well as black, lived without automobiles and farmed without machines; their isolation was more like the life of farmers in the early 19th century than like the life of Americans about to enter the freeway age. Many Mississippians were still sharecroppers, living in effect outside the money economy; and many others considered themselves lucky to make a few hundred dollars a month. There were successful businesses and plantations in Mississippi, but somehow the wealth here never seemed to trickle down, and many of the state's most talented young people left to make their livings elsewhere.

In that era Mississippi politics had no match in the nation for crudity and on occasion savagery. There was always an economic division between the rich white planters of the Delta and the River valley and the poor white farmers of the hillier north and east. But even more important was the division between the races. As recently as 1940, 49% of Mississippi's citizens were black, and white supremacy was maintained by a system as rigid and stern as South Africa's is today. Blacks were not allowed to vote; they could not of course mingle with whites in schools or public accommodations; they had to address whites with particular phrases. Infractions were sometimes punished by death; lynchings were not uncommon in the 1940s and occurred up through the 1950s, and as late as 1964 three civil rights activists were murdered in the town of Philadelphia.

With this grim background, Mississippi's economy languished and its politics attracted few top-notch people. Thus the state had as governor and senator Theodore Bilbo, who liked to compare blacks with monkeys, and Ross Barnett, the buffoonish governor who served when the University of Mississippi was integrated by federal troops in 1963. In national politics, Mississippi increasingly diverged from the rest of the country. In 1960 it backed an independent slate of electors — the only state to do so — and in 1964, when virtually no blacks voted, it went 87% for Goldwater. In 1968, with many blacks voting, it was still 63% for Wallace, and in 1972 it went for the winner, Richard Nixon, but gave him the biggest percentage he received in any state. In national elections, the candidacy of Jimmy Carter brought Mississippi back to the national mainstream; Carter narrowly carried the state in 1976 and narrowly lost it in 1980.

But other factors were much more important than the presence of a southerner on the national Democratic ticket in producing the metamorphosis of Mississippi. The first were the civil rights laws, particularly the Voting Rights Act of 1965, which gave blacks the right to vote and forever changed Mississippi politics. It did not, as some naive rural blacks hoped, give blacks majority control, because in the post–World War II era the black percentage of the population had been declining rapidly in the state: from 49% before the war to 35% in 1980. Moreover, a disproportionate number of blacks were children, which meant that the black percentage of the voting population was even lower; perhaps white Mississippians finally quit resisting black enfranchisement in part because they were confident that blacks could not suddenly take over the state.

Nevertheless, being a part of the electorate can make a difference. Blacks will not win very many races in Mississippi where all blacks vote one way and all whites another. But a state legislator or a city council member with a 10% or 20% or 30% black constituency is generally going to be interested in what they think and whom they will vote for — no politician likes to write off permanently a constituency of that size. This means that as Mississippi blacks have become more talented at exerting political pressure, they have — quietly and out of the national spotlight — been getting more of what they want. It is this kind of change more than the much publicized election of black mayors in tiny hamlets in the Delta (notably Charles Evers) that can make for real change in the way blacks live in Mississippi.

Moreover, since the beginning of the 1970s, black outmigration has slowed way down, and the long-term trend, for the first time since the 1870s, is for the black percentage in Mississippi to increase as the years grow on. The primary reason is that the state's economy has been taking off. Is this due to integration? No one is sure, but it is becoming increasingly clear that the number of jobs started rising just as Mississippi lost its segregationist ways. Part of the reason may be that investors don't like putting up plants and buildings where there is racial strife; part of the reason may be that people here have become better educated and more skilled; part of the reason may be that wage levels in many northern states got so much higher than those in the South that states like Mississippi became more attractive. Another reason — not mentioned by those who focus only on the motives of white businessmen and the performance of state government — is that Mississippi's blacks themselves, finally free to express themselves and to make their livings as they wish, have been more likely, if they are skilled, to stay in Mississippi and more likely, whether skilled or not, to work harder and to put out more effort than they were in the days when it seemed that anything they might accomplish would only be to the advantage of the white man.

The last time Mississippi elected a governor outspokenly opposed to civil rights was in 1967. The governorship races of 1971 and 1975 were conducted largely without explicit reference to the race issue, and the governor elected in 1979, William Winter, has a reputation dating back to the 1960s as a supporter of equal rights for blacks. Winter's winning of the governorship was probably delayed by this reputation (he had run and lost in 1967 and 1975), but by the time he won in 1979 other issues were more important — education, new jobs and industry, crime. Winter is by temperament more comfortable with tradition and stability, but by conviction he has found himself one of those people most responsible for changing Mississippi. In the 1979 election against a well-known Republican, Gil Carmichael, he was able to combine support from blacks and hill country whites — the same coalition that had carried the state for Carter in 1976 — with support from well-to-do whites in Jackson and other Mississippi cities. This last group has been the fastest-growing part of the electorate; as Mississippi has grown more prosperous its upper-income group has been growing, and as in other Sun Belt states its politics has been a mixture of laissez-faire economics and conservative cultural attitudes. Winter, a successful lawyer who himself lives on the lush north side of Jackson, can speak these people's language and win many of their votes.

He proved this not only in 1979 but in 1980, when he campaigned hard for Jimmy Carter—the first time a governor has stumped for a national Democratic nominee in living memory. Carter did lose the state, but only narrowly (49%-48%), and his share of the vote dropped only 1.5%—the lowest such drop in the country. Moreover, Carter's share of the vote in Jackson's Hinds County went up from 38% to 44%—a result matched in few places in the country. One reason was high turnout among blacks, stimulated by a black independent congressional candidacy; another was the increasing respectability Winter has won for the Democrats among higher-income voters.

Another sign of the change in Mississippi is congresssional redistricting. After the 1970 census, Mississippi legislators drew the boundaries of the state's five congressional districts carefully so that no district would have a black majority. But in 1980 at least a few white politicians were proposing that the state create a black-majority district. The issue is not, at this writing, decided, and there will probably be no black-majority district, if only because the legislature does not want to change vastly the districts of senior legislators such as Appropriations Chairman Jamie Whitten and Veterans' Affairs Chairman Sonny Montgomery. Redistricting is in abeyance anyway, pending the outcome of the July 1981 special election in the 4th district, for the seat vacated by the resignation of Jon Hinson after he was charged with a sexual offense. If the Republicans hold onto the seat, the Democratic legislators just might conclude that they would prefer a black Democrat to a white Republican and try to draw the lines to produce that result; if a white Democrat wins, the legislature will likely try to protect him (there is no major black candidate, although there is a large black majority in the current 4th district).

For 31 years Mississippi had the same two senators, James Eastland and John Stennis, both solidly conservative, both extremely powerful committee chairmen for many years—Eastland of Judiciary from 1955 to 1979 and Stennis of Armed Services from 1969 to 1981. Eastland will be remembered as the Senate's most implacable and, for years, most powerful opponent of civil rights; although toward the end, before he decided to retire, he had hired blacks on his staff and was making overtures to black community leaders. He would have had a tough race in 1978 and as soon as one formidable opponent entered he withdrew.

John Stennis is now the senior member of the Senate but, since the Democrats no longer have a majority, he is neither president pro tempore nor even a committee chairman. Where Eastland was gruff and uncommunicative, Stennis has always been gracious and devoted to duty. He is a man who remembers the lessons of World War II, and he has always favored a strong defense. At the same time, he has always been a senator inclined to support presidents of either party. Thus it was not surprising that Richard Nixon in 1973 chose Stennis to authenticate his versions of the Watergate tapes (Stennis may have been even more attractive to Nixon because at the time he was bedridden in a hospital and somewhat hard of hearing). Stennis has suffered some rebuffs in recent years. Not only did he lose the Armed Services chair, but when he did the new chairman, John Tower, reorganized the committee. The creation of new subcommittees to oversee intelligence can be interpreted as a rebuff; Stennis had chaired the Armed Services subcommittee which had the same function.

Stennis has also strongly backed the Tennessee–Tombigbee Waterway, a barge channel that would connect northern Mississippi directly with the Gulf of Mexico but has not been able to prevent the project from being subjected to critical scrutiny. Stennis came to the Senate at a time when senators showed deference to the president and to each other, and he must find the present atmosphere a little alien.

Stennis's seat is up in 1982, when he turns 81, and in Mississippi just about everyone expects him to retire. He won back in 1976 without significant opposition, but that may have resulted from the fact that he had been shot in Washington in 1973 by a burglar; his valiant recovery increased people's natural sympathy for him. The odds, at this writing, are that he will be succeeded by a Republican. The strongest candidate is probably Congressman Trent Lott, but he may not want to run because he is now Republican whip of the House. Another possibility is Charles Pickering who was almost elected state attorney general in 1979 — one of the very few Republicans in the South to come close to election to a statewide office below governor. On the Democratic side the picture is less clear; Governor Winter has no interest in the office.

Mississippi already has one Republican senator, Thad Cochran, elected to fill Eastland's seat in 1978. For six years he was congressman from the district that includes Jackson, and in personal demeanor as well as political attitudes he personifies the upwardly mobile, affluent voters of Mississippi's cities. He won the election with 45% because the opposition was split — just as he first won his congressional seat with less than a majority. His majorities came mainly from the cities, of which he carried every one. Cochran's Democratic opponent, Maurice Dantin, chosen after an arduous primary in which he defeated Governor Cliff Finch, carried the eastern hill counties and various rural counties with low black percentages, as well as his home area in the southern part of the state. His total came to 32% of the vote. The remaining 23% went to Charles Evers, brother of the slain civil rights leader, Medgar Evers, and mayor of a black-majority hamlet, who carried most of the black vote.

The national press was fascinated by Evers's platform: he was against busing, in favor of cracking down on welfare cheats, against the Panama Canal Treaty. He had backing from businessmen and oil millionaires. This is far different from the issue positions of most northern black politicians, but it was close to the platforms of Cochran and Dantin. If the Mississippi legislature does create a black congressional district, it could conceivably elect Evers — which would make for some interesting diversity of opinion in the Congressional Black Caucus.

Cochran is an engaging, articulate man with a soft-spoken manner and soft drawl reminiscent of Howard Baker. His voting record gives him solid ratings from conservative organizations, although New Right leaders do not regard him as one of their own. He certainly does not have a fanatic or frenzied air; and on occasion he takes positions that annoy some conservatives and even his constituents. He is not one of those Republican freshmen fortunate enough to have won a committee chair, but he does have seats on the Appropriations and Agriculture Committees. That suggests that he is more interested in representing the interests of Mississippi over the long run. Most likely he will have an opportunity to do that. He has very solid support from his upper-income base and has antagonized no significant group of voters. His seat is up in 1984.

Census Data   Pop. (1980 final) 2,520,638, up 14% in 1970s: 1.11% of U.S. total, 31st largest. Central city, 13%; suburban, 14%. Median 4-person family income, 1978, $16,586, 81% of U.S., 49th highest.

1979 Share of Federal Tax Burden $3,246,000,000; 0.72% of U.S. total, 33d largest.

594   MISSISSIPPI

1979 Share of Federal Outlays $5,036,200,000; 1.10% of U.S. total, 30th largest.

DOD	$1,339,867,000	26th	(1.26%)	HEW	$1,941,982,000	30th	(1.09%)
DOE	$7,557,000	38th	(0.06%)	ERDA	$5,777,000	33d	(0.21%)
HUD	$64,280,000	28th	(0.98%)	NASA	$29,180,000	18th	(0.62%)
VA	$279,136,000	29th	(1.35%)	DOT	$126,382,000	35th	(0.77%)
EPA	$59,927,000	27th	(1.13%)	DOC	$31,646,000	18th	(1.00%)
DOI	$45,480,000	29th	(0.82%)	USDA	$439,539,000	21st	(1.83%)

Economic Base   Agriculture, notably cattle, cotton lint, soybeans, and broilers; apparel and other textile products, especially men's and boys' furnishings; finance, insurance, and real estate; lumber and wood products, especially sawmills and planing mills; transportation equipment, especially motor vehicles and equipment, and ship building and repairing; food and kindred products.

Political Lineup   Governor, William Winter (D). Senators, John C. Stennis (D) and Thad Cochran (R). Representatives, 5 (3 D, 1 R, 1 seat vacant); 5 in 1982. State Senate, 47 (43 D and 4 R); State House of Representatives, 122 (116 D, 4 R, and 2 I).

The Voters

Registration   1,485,539 Total. No party registration.
Employment profile 1970   White collar, 39%. Blue collar, 41%. Service, 14%. Farm, 6%.
Ethnic groups   Black 1980, 35%. Hispanic 1980, 1%. Total foreign stock 1970, 1%.

Presidential Vote

1980	Reagan (R)	441,089	(49%)
	Carter (D)	429,281	(48%)
	Anderson (I)	12,036	(1%)
1976	Ford (R)	366,846	(48%)
	Carter (D)	381,309	(50%)

SENATORS

Sen. John C. Stennis (D) Elected Nov. 4, 1947, seat up 1982; b. Aug. 3, 1901, Kemper Co.; home, De Kalb; Miss. St. U., B.S. 1923, U. of Va., LL.B. 1928.

Career Miss. House of Reps., 1928–32; Dist. Prosecuting Atty., 16th Judicial Dist. 1931–37; Circuit Judge, 1937–47.

Offices 205 RSOB, 202-224-6253. Also 303 P.O. Bldg., Jackson 39205, 601-353-5494.

Committees *Appropriations* (2d). Subcommittees: Agriculture and Related Agencies; Defense; Energy and Water Development; HUD–Independent Agencies; Transportation.

Armed Services (Ranking Member).

Group Ratings

	ADA	COPE	PC	LCV	CFA	RPN	NAB	NSI	NTU	ACA	ACU
1980	17	37	40	0	33	—	73	50	47	43	50
1979	11	35	29	—	10	—	—	—	35	46	41
1978	10	6	28	23	10	50	73	80	20	73	50

Key Votes

1) Draft Registn $	FOR	6) Fair Housng Cloture	AGN	11) Cut Socl Incr Defns	FOR
2) Ban $ to Nicrgua	FOR	7) Ban $ Rape Abortns	—	12) Income Tax Indexing	AGN
3) Dlay MX Missile	AGN	8) Cap on Food Stmp $	FOR	13) Lim Spdg 21% GNP	AGN
4) Nuclr Mortorium	AGN	9) New US Dep Edcatn	FOR	14) Incr Wndfll Prof Tax	—
5) Alaska Lands Bill	AGN	10) Cut OSHA Inspctns	—	15) Chryslr Loan Grntee	AGN

Election Results

1976 general	John C. Stennis (D)	554,433	(100%)	($119,852)
1976 primary	John C. Stennis (D)	157,943	(85%)	
	One other (D)	27,016	(15%)	
1970 general	John C. Stennis (D)	286,622	(88%)	
	William R. Thompson (I)	37,593	(12%)	

Sen. Thad Cochran (R) Elected 1978, seat up 1984; b. Dec. 7, 1937, Pontotoc; home, Jackson; U. of Miss., B.A. 1959, J.D. 1965, Rotary Fellow, Trinity Col., Dublin, Ireland, 1963–64.

Career Navy, 1959–61; Practicing atty., 1965–72; U.S. House of Reps., 1973–78.

Offices 321 RSOB, 202-224-5054. Also Rm. 316 Fed. Bldg., Jackson 39205, 601-969-1353.

Committees *Agriculture, Nurtrition, and Forestry* (5th). Subcommittees: Soil and Water Conservation; Agricultural Production, Marketing, and Stabilization of Prices (Chairman); Foreign Agricultural Policy.

Appropriations (8th). Subcommittees: Agriculture and Related Agencies (Chairman); Energy and Water Development; Interior; State, Justice, Commerce, and the Judiciary; Transportation.

Group Ratings

	ADA	COPE	PC	LCV	CFA	RPN	NAB	NSI	NTU	ACA	ACU
1980	22	16	20	19	13	—	75	100	46	88	90
1979	5	16	38	—	19	—	—	—	47	70	76
1978	0	7	13	21	18	63	100	100	25	83	88

Key Votes

1) Draft Registn $	FOR	6) Fair Housng Cloture	AGN	11) Cut Socl Incr Defns	FOR
2) Ban $ to Nicrgua	AGN	7) Ban $ Rape Abortns	FOR	12) Income Tax Indexing	FOR
3) Dlay MX Missile	AGN	8) Cap on Food Stmp $	AGN	13) Lim Spdg 21% GNP	FOR
4) Nuclr Mortorium	AGN	9) New US Dep Edcatn	FOR	14) Incr Wndfll Prof Tax	AGN
5) Alaska Lands Bill	FOR	10) Cut OSHA Inspctns	FOR	15) Chryslr Loan Grntee	AGN

Election Results

1978 general	Thad Cochran (R).............	263,089	(45%)	($1,052,303)
	Maurice Danton (D)	185,454	(32%)	($873,518)
	Charles Evers (I)	133,646	(23%)	($135,119)
1978 primary	Thad Cochran (R).............	50,857	(69%)	
	Charles Pickering (R)	22,880	(31%)	($187,565)
1972 general	James O. Eastland (D)	375,102	(58%)	($410,221)
	Gil Carmichael (R)	249,779	(39%)	($154,913)

GOVERNOR

Gov. William F. Winter (D) Elected 1979, term expires Jan. 1984; b. Feb. 21, 1923, Grenada Co.; home, Jackson; U. of Miss., B.A. 1943, J.D. 1949.

Career Army, WWII; Miss. House of Reps., 1948–56; Miss. Tax Collector, 1956–64, Treasurer, 1964–68; Dem. nominee for Gov., 1967, 1975; Practicing atty., 1968–72, 1976–79; Lt. Gov. of Miss., 1972–76.

Offices The Capitol, Jackson 39205, 601-354-7575.

Election Results

1979 gen.	William F. Winter (D)	413,620	(61%)
	Gil Carmichael (R)	263,702	(39%)
1979 runoff	William F. Winter (D)	386,174	(57%)
	Evelyn Gandy (D)	295,835	(43%)
1979 prim.	Evelyn Gandy (D)	224,746	(30%)
	William F. Winter (D)	183,944	(25%)
	John Arthur Eaves (D)	143,411	(19%)
	Jim Herring (D)	135,812	(18%)
	Two others (D)	49,250	(7%)
1975 gen.	Cliff Finch (D)	369,568	(54%)
	Gil Carmichael (R)	319,632	(46%)

FIRST DISTRICT

The 1st congressional district of Mississippi occupies the northernmost section of the state and spans the gamut of Mississippi's terrain, from the cotton-rich Delta along the Mississippi River to Tishomingo County on the Tennessee River in the state's northeastern corner. The black majorities in some of the Delta counties have been politically active—and in some cases successful—since the early 1970s. As one moves east into the hill territory, there are fewer and fewer blacks; instead, one finds white farmers whose families have been working hardscrabble farms here for more than a century. This is not as poor a region as it used to be, however. Small businesses are growing up here and jobs, which if not high income by northern standards, are plentiful and afford a decent living in this low-cost part of the country. In the middle of the district is Oxford, site of Ole Miss and of the racial disorders accompanying the university's integration in 1962, and famous also as the lifelong home of William Faulkner.

The 1st district's boundaries were drawn a decade ago by a legislature that wanted to make sure that no Mississippi seat would ever have a black majority; accordingly, it is made up of two quite different kinds of areas. However, in the late 1970s they have been voting similarly: the black Delta counties and the northeastern hill counties have all given large majorities to Democrats generally and to Jimmy Carter in particular. There are few cities this far north in Mississippi with large affluent Republican areas.

The congressman from this district is Jamie Whitten, the chairman of the House Appropriations Committee. He was first elected in 1941, a month before Pearl Harbor; for years he of course voted for white supremacy and advanced steadily in seniority. Since 1949 (except for 1953–55 when Republicans had control) he has chaired the Agriculture Subcommittee of the Appropriations Committee. This has made him a kind of permanent secretary of agriculture; the top bureaucrats in the department have long believed that Whitten will outlast their titular bosses. Whitten has not been afraid to use his influence in the depart-

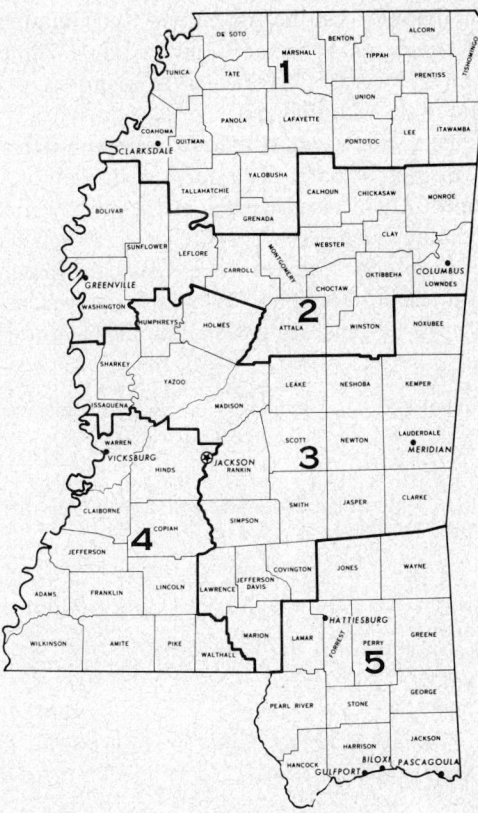

ment's affairs. He was a strong force for large subsidy payments to cotton farmers; for years the cotton program has been the most costly of any of Agriculture's crop subsidies. He has strongly backed attempts to increase production and kill vermin with pesticides and has been entirely unsympathetic to environmentalists' claims that such practices are damaging and self-defeating. Over the years Whitten has developed a network of friends in state agricultural departments and among county agricultural agents all over the country. A secretary of agriculture ignores him at his peril.

In 1979 Whitten obtained a position of greater note, as chairman of the full Appropriations Committee, although his power in that position is circumscribed by the views of the Democratic Caucus. There was a move by junior members in 1979 to pass over him for another Appropriations member; it was defeated 157–88, which is to say that a switch of 35 votes would have cost him the chair. Whitten had the support of Speaker O'Neill and of Edward Boland, the man proposed for the chair by the rebels; but one must assume that there were some assurances, explicit or otherwise, as to how he would conduct business on the committee. He has not acted, as some southern chairmen used to, in such a way as to promote his own views and defeat the goals of most Democrats. Indeed, Whitten's voting record is the best evidence that the possibility of ousting a committee chairman has real effect. After 1975, when that rule went into effect, Whitten's rating from organized labor jumped from the 10% level to about 40%. On the Agriculture Subcommittee he has successfully fought attempts to kill the food stamp program — not exactly a Whitten favorite in the years before 1975. Of course the emergence of black voters as an important force in the 1st district may have had something to do with that too.

The boundaries of the 1st district will have to be redrawn only if the legislature tries to create a new black majority district. In that case the northern district will consist almost entirely of heavily white hill counties. These have been among the most Democratic in the state, and Whitten shows every sign of remaining a strong vote-getter, although his percentage did dip to 63% in the 1980 general election. (One reason: a significant Republican vote in DeSoto County, the Mississippi suburbs of Memphis.) Whitten has served in the House longer than any other member, but he will be only 72 in 1982 and should have no trouble winning reelection if he wants it.

Census Data   Pop. (1980 final) 495,709, up 14% in 1970s. Median family income, 1970, $5,577, 58% of U.S.

The Voters

  Employment profile 1970   White collar, 34%. Blue collar, 45%. Service, 12%. Farm, 9%.
  Ethnic groups   Black 1980, 30%. Hispanic 1980, 1%.

Presidential Vote

1980	Reagan (R)	74,191	(42%)
	Carter (D)	97,650	(55%)
	Anderson (I)	3,073	(2%)
1976	Ford (R)	56,974	(37%)
	Carter (D)	91,615	(60%)

Rep. Jamie L. Whitten (D) Elected Nov. 4, 1941; b. Apr. 18, 1910, Cascilla; home, Charleston; U. of Miss.

Career   Practicing atty.; School principal; Miss. House of Reps., 1931; Dist. Prosecuting Atty., 17th Judicial Dist., 1933–41.

Offices   2314 RHOB, 202-225-4306. Also P.O. Bldg., Charleston 38921, 601-647-2413.

Committee   *Appropriations* (Chairman). Subcommittee: Agriculture, Rural Development and Related Agencies (Chairman).

Group Ratings

	ADA	COPE	PC	LCV	CFA	RPN	NAB	NSI	NTU	ACA	ACU
1980	28	29	23	27	29	—	75	90	35	57	68
1979	16	35	8	21	11	—	—	—	32	36	40
1978	20	39	13	7	18	73	60	100	17	55	75

Key Votes

1) Draft Registn $	FOR	6) Fair Hsg DOJ Enfrc	AGN	11) Cut Socl Incr Dfns $	AGN
2) Ban $ to Nicrgua	FOR	7) Lim PAC Contrbtns	AGN	12) Hosptl Cost Controls	AGN
3) Dlay MX Missile	AGN	8) Cap on Food Stmp $	AGN	13) Gasln Ctrls & Allctns	FOR
4) Nuclr Mortorium	AGN	9) New US Dep Edcatn	FOR	14) Lim Wndfll Prof Tax	FOR
5) Alaska Lands Bill	AGN	10) Cut OSHA $	AGN	15) Chryslr Loan Grntee	FOR

Election Results

1980 general	Jamie L. Whitten (D)	104,269	(63%)	($67,794)
	T. K. Moffett (R)	61,292	(37%)	($75,353)
1980 primary	Jamie L. Whitten (D), unopposed			
1978 general	Jamie L. Whitten (D)	57,358	(67%)	($87,331)
	T. K. Moffett (R)	26,734	(31%)	($71,620)

SECOND DISTRICT

The 2d congressional district of Mississippi, a belt of counties in the north central part of the state, stretches from the Mississippi River to the hill country along the Alabama border. The flat fertile land along the river is the Delta, an area not fully developed until well after the Civil War. This was originally swampy land, often flooded, traversed by many rivers that flow into the Mississippi. In the late 19th century the land was drained, the great river lined with levees, and the Illinois Central track laid down from Memphis to New Orleans. It was discovered then that the topsoil here, accumulated over centuries of Mississippi spring floods, reached depths of 25 feet. So the Delta wilderness of northern Mississippi, the destruction of which Faulkner laments in some of his stories, became the region of the state's largest and most productive cotton plantations.

That also meant that the Delta came to have Mississippi's largest concentration of blacks. Although slavery had been abolished, most blacks lived in great poverty at the turn of the century; as sharecroppers or tenant farmers they were essentially outside the cash economy. Serving as low-wage labor on the cotton plantations seemed not much different from slavery itself. Many Delta counties still have black majorities. The 2d district includes part of the Delta, including its leading city, Greenville; it also includes part of mostly white eastern Mississippi, and so does not have a black majority.

The congressman from the 2d district for five terms has been David Bowen, a Democrat first elected in 1972. A graduate of Harvard and Oxford, he has been considered a moderate by Mississippi standards, although in fact his voting record is not far out of line with traditional Mississippi conservatism, and his legislative interests — reflected in his committee assignments, Agriculture and Merchant Marine — are not far afield. Bowen has not attracted much attention in the House. Perhaps the newsworthy aspects of his career were the charges by one of his Republican opponents that Bowen, a bachelor who is a regular at Washington embassy parties had attended a party given by Tongsun Park and had been named bachelor of the month by *Cosmopolitan* magazine. He serves as chairman of the Rice, Sugar and Cotton Subcommittee of the Agriculture Committee, a body that has handled some of the most politically sensitive agricultural subsidy programs. In recent years the only one of these commodities that has received major subsidies is cotton — which is also the only one produced in commercially significant amounts in Bowen's district.

Bowen has been reelected with large majorities. The only threat to his tenure might be the creation of a black-majority House district, which would at the least cost him several of his counties and might force him to run in an almost entirely different district, perhaps one based primarily on Jackson.

Census Data Pop. (1980 final) 460,780, up 5% in 1970s. Median family income, 1970, $5,446, 57% of U.S.

The Voters

Employment profile 1970   White collar, 37%. Blue collar, 39%. Service, 15%. Farm, 9%.
Ethnic groups   Black 1980, 45%. Hispanic 1980, 1%. Total foreign stock 1970, 1%.

Presidential Vote

1980	Reagan (R)	70,194	(46%)
	Carter (D)	79,717	(52%)
	Anderson (I)	1,849	(1%)
1976	Ford (R)	61,511	(46%)
	Carter (D)	69,152	(51%)

Rep. David R. Bowen (D) Elected 1972; b. Oct. 21, 1932, Houston; home, Cleveland; Harvard U., A.B. 1954, Oxford U., M.A.

Career Asst. Prof., Miss. Col., 1958–59, Millsaps Col., 1959–64; U.S. Ofc. of Econ. Opp., 1966–67; Congressional Liaison Ofc., U.S. Chamber of Commerce, 1967–68; Miss. Fed.–State Coordinator for the Governor's. Ofc., 1968–72.

Offices 2421 RHOB, 202-225-5876. Also 101 S. Court St., Cleveland 38732, 601-846-1801.

Committees *Agriculture* (6th). Subcommittees: Conservation, Credit and Rural Development; Cotton, Rice and Sugar (Chairman); Department Operations, Research, and Foreign Agriculture.

Foreign Affairs (21st). Subcommittee: Asian and Pacific Affairs.

Merchant Marine and Fisheries (6th). Subcommittees: Fisheries and Wildlife Conservation and the Environment; Panama Canal and Outer Continental Shelf.

Group Ratings

	ADA	COPE	PC	LCV	CFA	RPN	NAB	NSI	NTU	ACA	ACU
1980	28	23	20	7	21	—	50	56	24	43	29
1979	11	26	13	13	4	—	—	—	34	70	68
1978	15	20	10	13	5	60	90	100	22	88	92

Key Votes

1) Draft Registn $	FOR	6) Fair Hsg DOJ Enfrc	AGN	11) Cut Socl Incr Dfns $	AGN
2) Ban $ to Nicrgua	AGN	7) Lim PAC Contrbtns	AGN	12) Hosptl Cost Controls	AGN
3) Dlay MX Missile	AGN	8) Cap on Food Stmp $	AGN	13) Gasln Ctrls & Allctns	AGN
4) Nuclr Mortorium	AGN	9) New US Dep Edcatn	FOR	14) Lim Wndfll Prof Tax	FOR
5) Alaska Lands Bill	AGN	10) Cut OSHA $	FOR	15) Chryslr Loan Grntee	AGN

Election Results

1980 general	David R. Bowen (D)............	96,750	(70%)	($56,912)
	Frank Drake (R)	42,300	(30%)	($21,573)
1980 primary	David R. Bowen (D), unopposed			
1978 general	David R. Bowen (D)............	57,678	(62%)	($90,850)
	Dr. Roland Byrd (R)	35,730	(38%)	($91,580)

THIRD DISTRICT

The 3d is one of three Mississippi districts that, in their current boundaries, stretch from the heavily black Delta across the hills of central Mississippi to the Alabama border. Like the others, the 3d was so constructed ten years ago as to prevent blacks from controlling the outcome of congressional elections here. Of all of Mississippi's districts, this is the most rural and agricultural. Its only urban areas of any size are the small city of Meridian and the part of Rankin County across the Pearl River from Jackson. More typical—and notorious—are towns such as Philadelphia in Neshoba County, where three civil rights workers were murdered in 1964, and in which Ronald Reagan unaccountably chose to make a campaign appearance in 1980.

The congressman from the 3d district is Sonny Montgomery. He is an exemplar of the traditional southern Democrat: devoted to his work, a delightful companion, dedicated to his principles but possessed of a fine sense of humor. A veteran of both World War II and Korea, Montgomery serves on the Armed Services and Veterans' Affairs Committees. In 1981 Montgomery became chairman of the House Veterans' Affairs Committee, a body led for years by conservative southerners sympathetic to the major veterans' organizations. He certainly falls under that description himself and has tended to oppose counseling programs and benefit extensions advanced in the name of Vietnam veterans. But those who favor the less traditional and more innovative approaches find him somewhat flexible and willing to listen. He is not considered likely to be one of the House committee chairmen who will fight against Reagan Administration budget cuts in his committee's programs. He has always been on the side of urging a strong defense and is an unabashed enthusiast for things military. He is Capitol Hill's strongest champion of the Reserves and the National Guard—bodies with much support in Congress, although they were used sparingly or not at all in the Vietnam war. On other issues Montgomery almost invariably votes with the bulk of Republicans and the still fairly significant number of conservative southern Democrats.

Montgomery occupies an important position in a House where Democrats have a relatively small majority. With the Republicans united as they were in the late 1970s, the Democrats can lose no more than 26 votes and still command a majority on a given issue. But men like Montgomery are not very likely to vote with most Democrats on the merits of most issues. Montgomery, however, does not seem temperamentally inclined to rebellion and appeals to party loyalty by senior Democrats could prevail with him.

Montgomery is regularly reelected by near-unanimous votes; the last time he had a Republican opponent, in 1978, he won 92% of the vote. His district could be altered considerably if the legislature creates a black-majority seat, but in all likelihood he will continue to win wherever the district lines go—even in Jackson, which has had Republican congressmen for 10 years now.

Census Data Pop. (1980 final) 514,218, up 15% in 1970s. Median family income, 1970, $5,320, 55% of U.S.

The Voters

Employment profile 1970 White collar, 33%. Blue collar, 44%. Service, 13%. Farm, 10%.
Ethnic groups Black 1980, 38%. Hispanic 1980, 1%. Am. Ind. 1980, 1%.

Presidential Vote

1980	Reagan (R)	98,438	(51%)
	Carter (D)	91,930	(47%)
	Anderson (I)	2,307	(1%)
1976	Ford (R)	82,515	(50%)
	Carter (D)	79,021	(48%)

Rep. G. V. (Sonny) **Montgomery** (D) Elected 1966; b. Aug. 5, 1920, Meridian; home, Meridian; Miss. St. U., B.S.

Career Army, WWII and Korea; Owner, Montgomery Insurance Agcy.; V.P., Greater Miss. Life Ins. Co.; Miss. Senate, 1956–66.

Offices 2184 RHOB, 202-225-5031 Also P.O. Box 5618, Meridian 39301, 601-693-6681.

Committees *Armed Services* (9th). Subcommittees: Military Installations and Facilities; Military Personnel and Compensation.

Veterans' Affairs (Chairman). Subcommittees: Compensation, Pension, and Insurance; Oversight and Investigations (Chairman).

Group Ratings

	ADA	COPE	PC	LCV	CFA	RPN	NAB	NSI	NTU	ACA	ACU
1980	0	6	17	17	14	—	91	100	55	58	95
1979	5	10	10	6	4	—	—	—	54	87	87
1978	5	15	10	14	9	50	100	89	30	85	88

Key Votes

1) Draft Registn $	FOR	6) Fair Hsg DOJ Enfrc	AGN	11) Cut Socl Incr Dfns $	FOR
2) Ban $ to Nicrgua	FOR	7) Lim PAC Contrbtns	AGN	12) Hosptl Cost Controls	AGN
3) Dlay MX Missile	AGN	8) Cap on Food Stmp $	FOR	13) Gasln Ctrls & Allctns	AGN
4) Nuclr Mortorium	AGN	9) New US Dep Edcatn	FOR	14) Lim Wndfll Prof Tax	FOR
5) Alaska Lands Bill	AGN	10) Cut OSHA $	FOR	15) Chryslr Loan Grntee	AGN

Election Results

1980 general	G. V. (Sonny) Montgomery (D) ..	128,035	(100%)	($9,909)
1980 primary	G. V. Montgomery (D), unopposed			
1978 general	G. V. (Sonny) Montgomery (D) ..	101,685	(92%)	($45,478)
	Dorothy Cleveland (R)	8,408	(8%)	

FOURTH DISTRICT

Mississippi's capital and largest city, Jackson, is the center of one of the state's two significant urban concentrations. It has experienced considerable growth in the 1960s and 1970s — aside from the Gulf Coast, more growth than any other part of the state. It is still only a small city by northern standards, but the boom atmosphere is apparent. Much of Jackson's growth has been accounted for by well-to-do whites; the city has its new subdivisions of pleasant, large colonial houses under huge, overhanging trees, inhabited by new Mississippi millionaires. Even the less well-to-do — people who grew up poor and now make $23,000 a year, more than they ever dreamed of — tend to think of themselves as new rich, and in fact money goes a good deal further in Jackson than it does in one of our major metropolitan areas.

As a result of this kind of growth, Jackson has become one of the most Republican parts of the state. The young, better-educated, upwardly mobile Jacksonites find great appeal in the crisp ideology of the Republican Party. There is a countervailing factor in politics here, however, and that is the appeal in Jackson of Governor William Winter. A Democrat with a background in the Jackson establishment, Winter was an early supporter of civil rights who also has an appeal to upper-income whites. Since his election in 1979, he has stumped hard for Democrats generally, and he is probably the major reason that Jackson is one of the few places in the South where Jimmy Carter did better in 1980 than in 1976.

The 4th congressional district of Mississippi contains Jackson, and Jackson together with suburban Hinds County casts about half its votes. The remainder of the district is the southwestern corner of the state, including Vicksburg, the site of the great Civil War battle; Natchez, with its well-preserved antebellum mansions; and several small counties with black majorities. The district also includes some white-majority counties directly south and slightly southeast of Jackson, going down to the Louisiana border.

The 4th district was the scene of one of the most bizarre congressional elections of 1980. For eight years it had been electing Republicans: Thad Cochran, who won in 1972 and was reelected twice, and Jon Hinson, a former aide to Cochran who won in 1978. Both won their initial victories with only about 50% of the vote, in situations where a white Democratic and black Independent candidate split the opposition. Both Cochran and Hinson depended for their bedrock support on the upper-income precincts of Jackson. In 1980, a similar race seemed to be shaping up. Hinson was opposed by Britt Singletary, a white Democrat who had once been an aide to Senator James Eastland and who had beaten a black in the primary, and by Leslie McLemore, a black Independent. The outcome seemed preordained.

Then on August 8 Hinson shocked everyone by announcing that he had been a survivor of a 1977 fire in a Washington homosexual movie house where several people were killed and that he had also paid a fine for creating a public nuisance after being arrested in a homosexual meeting place in suburban Washington the year before. Hinson claimed that he had since had a religious conversion experience, and his wife, whom he had recently married, stood by him and campaigned for him.

Some Republican leaders wanted Hinson to withdraw from the race, but he refused to do so. A few years ago, it would have seemed unthinkable that someone with such a record could win an election in Mississippi, but times evidently have changed. Hinson won considerable sympathy from voters, and many believed that he had worked hard and done a good job. His generally conservative voting record was in line with most local opinion; unlike Robert Bauman of Maryland, who had a somewhat similar problem, he had never made scathing denunciations of homosexuality.

But what really reelected Hinson was the split in the opposition. The incumbent had only 39% of the vote; indeed, he got an absolute majority only in his home county and had only 37% in Jackson's Hinds County. But Singletary, the Democrat, showed even greater weakness: he ran third, carrying not a single county, with only 29% of the vote. McLemore ran as good a race as any black candidate has in Mississippi, winning 30% of the vote and carrying three counties; he led Singletary by 656 votes.

Hinson shocked his constituents one final time on February 4, 1981, when he was arrested in a House office building men's room and charged with attempted oral sodomy. Immediately he came under intense pressure from his Republican supporters to resign; he retreated to a Washington hospital and announced in March that he would resign April 13. The special election was set for June 23. It is run under a system like that in Louisiana: candidates of all parties run in the primary election and, if none gets an absolute majority, the top two candidates, of whatever party, face each other in a runoff. The runoff provision, as perhaps was intended, discouraged an independent black candidacy; Singletary is running again and is seeking black support; and McLemore, perhaps spurred by the policies of the Reagan Administration, is promising to support the Democrat in the runoff. The Republican, 45-year-old Liles Williams, president of a construction company, first got local notice by organizing a major meeting of the Religious Roundtable; his victory would be seen as a triumph of the local Republican Party, which had been seriously embarrassed by Hinson, and for the religious right.

Census Data Pop. (1980 final) 500,329, up 13% in 1970s. Median family income, 1970, $6,802, 71% of U.S.

The Voters

   Employment profile 1970 White collar, 47%. Blue collar, 35%. Service, 15%. Farm, 3%.
   Ethnic groups Black 1980, 45%. Hispanic 1980, 1%. Total foreign stock 1970, 1%.
Presidential Vote

1980	Reagan (R)	94,921	(50%)
	Carter (D)	88,623	(47%)
	Anderson (I)	2,307	(1%)
1976	Ford (R)	86,002	(54%)
	Carter (D)	70,260	(44%)

Rep. Jon C. Hinson (R) Resigned April 13, 1981. Special election and runoff, scheduled for June 23 and July 7, 1981, respectively.

Election Results

1980 general	Jon C. Hinson (R)	69,321	(39%)	($252,966)
	Lester Burl McLemore (I)	52,959	(30%)	($43,198)
	Britt R. Singletary (D)	52,303	(29%)	($104,871)
1980 primary	Jon C. Hinson (R), unopposed			
1978 general	Jon C. Hinson (R)	68,225	(52%)	($249,548)
	John Hampton Stennis (D)	34,837	(26%)	($311,474)
	Evan Doss (I)	25,134	(19%)	($20,564)

FIFTH DISTRICT

The 5th congressional district of Mississippi is the state's Gulf Coast district. About half its residents live in and around the Gulf cities of Biloxi, Gulfport, Pascagoula, and Moss Point; together they constitute the only significant urban concentration in Mississippi outside Jackson. The remainder live inland, in farm counties or in the middle-sized cities of Hattiesburg and Laurel. Much of this land is piney woods and paper mill country and never contained many plantations. As a result there are relatively few blacks here—the lowest percentage of any congressional district in Mississippi.

The 5th district is a boom area economically and one whose residents are pleased with the free enterprise system and what it has produced for them and for the nation. They are mostly from the South, and mostly from less well-to-do surroundings than they now enjoy. They like to think of themselves as rugged individualists, people who have made their own way. Yet this area owes a fair amount of its prosperity and growth to the federal government. The Litton Shipyards in Pascagoula gets about $600 million a year in defense funds; Litton was an inexperienced but well-connected contractor when it won this plum in the Nixon Administration. There are indications that Litton simply bid low and assumed that it could get the Pentagon to fork over more money later, and there is considerable evidence that the shipyard's performance was at first below acceptable standards. The Gulf Coast was not deprived of this contract, though, not with the kind of political representation it has had, including Senate Armed Services Chairman John Stennis and former House Rules Chairman William Colmer. The 5th may have been rewarded for its electoral performance as well; this district gave Richard Nixon his largest percentage in 1972, a near-unanimous 87%.

The 5th district's current congressman, Trent Lott, is a young man with considerable accomplishments to his credit and every prospect of a bright political future. He served four years as an aide to Congressman Colmer, and when Colmer retired Lott ran for his seat—as a Republican. He won that race, and got a seat on the House Judiciary Committee, where he was a stout defender of President Nixon and also, as he enjoyed pointing out when the Democrats said young people mistrusted the president, the youngest member of the committee. In 1975 he got a seat on the Rules Committee and after the 1980 election he was elected House Republican whip—the number two position in the House Republican leadership.

Lott is a man who must make a big decision in 1982. He has an excellent chance to win the Senate seat likely to be vacated by John Stennis. He is pretty well known statewide, and as Ronald Reagan's state campaign chief, he spent much of 1980 getting known in other parts of Mississippi. He is a crisp speaker, and his views on issues give him no problems at all with the Mississippi electorate. Yet his future in the House may be even brighter. His seat is safe (he won 74% in 1980) and he has won a top leadership position before turning 40. If Republicans should succeed in gaining control or getting within striking distance of control of the House in 1982, he would have an excellent chance of being speaker someday, if history works out his way for a very long time. But he cannot know how well Republicans will do in the House until he has to make his decision. A Republican leadership position in a Democratic House or a junior Republican seat in a Republican Senate—this is an embarrassment of riches. Although each choice has its possible drawbacks, the very existence of this quandary shows how fast this young man's career has moved in a short time.

Census Data Pop. (1980 final) 549,602, up 22% in 1970s. Median family income, 1970, $7,053, 74% of U.S.

The Voters

Employment profile 1970 White collar, 42%. Blue collar, 43%. Service, 13%. Farm, 2%.
Ethnic groups Black 1980, 20%. Hispanic 1980, 1%. Asian 1980, 1%. Total foreign stock 1970, 3%.

Presidential Vote

1980	Reagan (R)	103,345	(58%)
	Carter (D)	71,281	(40%)
	Anderson (I)	2,500	(1%)
1976	Ford (R)	80,024	(51%)
	Carter (D)	71,261	(46%)

Rep. Trent Lott (R) Elected 1972; b. Oct. 9, 1941, Grenada; home, Pascagoula; U. of Miss., B.A. 1963, J.D. 1967.

Career Practicing atty., 1967–68; Admın. Asst. to U.S. Rep. Wıl-liam M. Colmer, 1968–72.

Offices 2400 RHOB, 202-225-5772. Also P.O. Box 1557, Gulfport 39501, 601-864-7670.

Committees *Minority whip.*

Rules (3d). Subcommittees: Rules of the House; The Legislative Process.

Group Ratings

	ADA	COPE	PC	LCV	CFA	RPN	NAB	NSI	NTU	ACA	ACU
1980	6	12	17	17	14	—	100	100	55	83	94
1979	0	0	5	14	0	—	—	—	60	92	92
1978	10	25	13	8	14	58	100	100	31	93	92

Key Votes

1) Draft Registn $	FOR	6) Fair Hsg DOJ Enfrc	AGN	11) Cut Socl Incr Dfns $	FOR
2) Ban $ to Nicrgua	FOR	7) Lim PAC Contrbtns	AGN	12) Hosptl Cost Controls	AGN
3) Dlay MX Missile	AGN	8) Cap on Food Stmp $	FOR	13) Gasln Ctrls & Allctns	AGN
4) Nuclr Mortorium	AGN	9) New US Dep Edcatn	FOR	14) Lim Wndfll Prof Tax	FOR
5) Alaska Lands Bill	AGN	10) Cut OSHA $	FOR	15) Chryslr Loan Grntee	AGN

Election Results

1980 general	Trent Lott (R)	131,559	(74%)	($163,118)
	Jimmy McVeay (D)	46,416	(26%)	($73,054)
1980 primary	Trent Lott (R), unopposed			
1978 general	Trent Lott (R), unopposed			($32,708)

MISSOURI

Missouri is a border state, admitted to the Union in 1821 as part of the compromise that bears its name—a state whose boundaries jutted far north into free territory; a state that sent proslavery raiders over the border into Kansas in the 1850s to fight settlers shipped in by abolitionists; a state that saw its own civil war, one separated geographically, although not spiritually, from the conflict east of the Mississippi River. Missouri was also a gateway to the American West, an avenue for the great Yankee migrations west from Ohio, Indiana, and Illinois, and the eastern terminus of the Pony Express and the Transcontinental Railroad. It is almost literally at the center of the country; the geographic center of the coterminous 48 states lies not far away in Kansas, and the population center is in Missouri itself, just southwest of St. Louis.

Politically Democrats have always been the dominant party in Missouri, but there has always been a Republican Party capable of winning at least some elections. The Democratic edge is the result of Missouri's slave state traditions; Missouri's most famous Democrat, Harry Truman, had a grandfather who fought in the Rebel army, and his mother, who lived to see her son president, remained a Confederate sympathizer all her life. Truman's background—southern rural and Kansas City urban—typified the tensions within Missouri's Democratic Party and also explains why Truman, who integrated the armed forces, could also react negatively to the civil rights movement of the 1960s. Truman's combination of liberalism on economic issues, a mixed response on cultural issues, and an affection for old political friends, still characterizes many Missouri politicians.

If Missouri is at the center of the nation demographically, it is also near the center politically. Presidential elections here over the past 30 years have always been close and have usually hewed closely to the national pattern (the one time Missouri hasn't supported the winning presidential candidate in this century was 1956, when it went for Adlai Stevenson). In half of the last eight elections, the winning candidate has carried the state by less than 30,000 votes; Jimmy Carter won here by 70,000 in 1976 and lost by 140,000 in 1980, with about two million votes cast each time. Carter's 1976 victory was probably due to his southern origin; he carried the state's rural counties, most of which have Democratic traditions and still vote Democratic for state and local office and even in House races, but which go Republican in statewide contests for governor and senator. In 1980, however, Reagan ran 8% ahead of Gerald Ford's showing outside the St. Louis and Kansas City metro areas, beating Carter there by a 56%–41% margin; Carter lost the Kansas City area and only narrowly carried Metropolitan St. Louis, the one area where Reagan ran behind Ford.

In 1980 Republicans in Missouri had overall as good a year as they have had in this state since 1946. They recaptured the governorship and took the important office of attorney general as well, and they came within 100,000 votes of upsetting incumbent Senator Thomas Eagleton. They held the two congressional districts they had and captured two others, and are well positioned for the redistricting that will reduce Missouri's ten districts to nine for the 1982 election. Missouri's traditional partisan leanings are still apparent in the lopsided Democratic margins in the legislature. But Republicans have eroded the Democrats' base in the St. Louis and Kansas City metropolitan areas and in traditionally Democratic rural areas such as the Bootheel in the southeast and Little Dixie in the northeast without having their own bases in affluent suburban areas and the Ozarks in the southwest weakened. None of this makes Missouri anything like an automatically Republican state. But just as there are suggestions that the nation no longer has a natural Democratic majority, so it seems in Missouri.

The Republicans' performance in the gubernatorial elections is particularly strong evidence. Christopher Bond, at age 41, in 1980 won his second term as governor in three elections, having lost only narrowly and in a startling upset in 1976. Although he comes from a small county in the central part of the state, Bond is not in the image of an old-fashioned rural Missouri politician. His family is rich and he went to eastern schools; at age 30 he went to work for John Danforth, then recently elected as state attorney general; in 1970, at 31, he was elected state auditor, a position in which he could investigate the shenanigans of some other Missouri politicians. Bond won a solid victory in 1972 and a kind of mandate for reform, and in fact did institute a number of reforms of the political process in the state. He was caught unprepared for the aggressive campaign of Kansas City prosecutor Joseph Teasdale in 1976 and, after basking in glory as the Republicans held their national convention in Kansas City, lost reelection by 13,000 votes. He avenged that defeat by a solid, although not overwhelming margin in 1980, managing to beat Teasdale even in the Kansas City area. Teasdale campaigned as the candidate of compassion and of vigilance against hazardous wastes; Bond campaigned as the candidate of efficiency and managerial competence, with a proposal of tax exemptions for the elderly to boot. That victory puts Bond in a position to dominate Missouri politics for some time to come; the state allows its governors to serve two consecutive four-year terms and, once burned, he is not likely to be overconfident again. If reelected in 1984, he might be a candidate against Thomas Eagleton in 1986 — but it is really too early for speculation on that.

Eagleton was nearly upset himself in 1980. He did, however, have an inkling of the trouble he faced and managed to respond with a more vigorous campaign than his reelection margin in 1974 might have led him to believe was necessary. The problem was not so much his opponent, St. Louis County Executive Gene McNary, a man with some local base in the St. Louis suburbs but no great personal magnetism. What McNary had going for him most of all was the set of ideas associated in 1980 with the Republican Party and with Ronald Reagan: that government needed to be made smaller, that inflation had to be attacked resolutely, that American defense forces had to be strengthened, and that the Democrats in their years in power had failed to do these things. Eagleton, with an impeccably Democratic record on most issues, was thrown on the defensive and had to depend on his considerable personal popularity to win. McNary's hometown advantage held Eagleton to virtually no edge in the St. Louis area and the senator lost the counties outside the metropolitan area; virtually his entire margin came from the Kansas City metropolitan area, where he scored a nearly 2-to-1 victory.

Eagleton remains at least vestigially famous nationally from 1972, when he was nominated for vice president on George McGovern's ticket and then dropped from the ticket several days after McGovern and the nation learned that Eagleton had been hospitalized and given electroshock treatment for depression some years before. Eagleton's career up to that time had been dazzling: he was circuit attorney in St. Louis at 27, attorney general at 31, lieutenant governor at 35, and U.S. senator at 39. He gave up a safe statewide office in 1968 to run against an incumbent Democrat, Edward Long, in the primary; he then beat a creditable Republican, suburban St. Louis Congressman Thomas Curtis, by a narrow margin in the general election. Reelected easily in 1974, Eagleton was expected to have an easy time in 1980, but instead he nearly got caught in the national Republican tide. He was one of the last Democratic senators to be targeted by the New Right groups and by national Republicans as it became clear to them that Republicans were in good shape throughout the country.

Eagleton, who chaired a minor and now abolished Senate committee (District of Columbia) as a freshman, probably expected to emerge from the 1980 election to a position of considerable power and influence in the Senate. He is in what should be his most productive years and is generally respected for his competence in the Senate. He must have looked forward to soon becoming the chairman of the Governmental Affairs Committee, a post that affords ample chance for publicized investigating, and to holding high-ranking seats on the Labor and Appropriations Committees. Eagleton is generally counted as a vote for organized labor and for government education and health programs on the Labor Committee. On Appropriations he is the ranking member on the Agriculture Subcommittee and also serves on Defense, where he sometimes joins William Proxmire in supporting cuts but also strongly backs the McDonnell–Douglas fighter plane programs. He still has his committee assignments, but with the Republicans in control of the Senate he has considerably less leverage than he must have expected. Eagleton has the capacity to be a strong legislator—the raw ability and a tendency to avoid sterotyped and uncompromisable positions—but he will have to look out to find issues that he can take the lead on.

Missouri's other senator, John Danforth, has had a somewhat similar career to Eagleton's. His family, which started Ralston Purina, is one of the nation's wealthiest and most philanthropic; he himself has a divinity degree and has sometimes approached politics with a churchy intensity. Danforth was elected state attorney general in 1968 at age 32 and nearly defeated Senator Stuart Symington two years later in a campaign in which he strongly supported the Nixon Administration. He has, however, generally been identified as a moderate Republican.

Danforth's victory in his 1976 Senate race turned out to be a comfortable one, but that had not been at all certain through the year. He had been expected to face tough competition from Congressman James Symington, son of the retiring senator; but Symington was overtaken by Congressman Jerry Litton, who featured his background as a farmer and won big majorities in the rural areas. Litton and his family were killed in a plane crash on primary night; the Democrats, after a period of mourning, nominated the man who edged Symington out of second place in the primary, former Governor Warren Hearnes. He had once been a big vote-getter, but he left office amid an odor of scandal and seemed to personify the kind of politician Danforth and Bond had been running against. Danforth made major inroads in Democratic areas both in and around St. Louis and in rural counties, and won with ease.

Danforth now has membership on the major committees concerned with economic issues, Finance and Commerce. He is a senator who has generally taken the lead on the side of the aging industrial states and in favor of energy consumers rather than energy producers. He chairs the subcommittee on Surface Transportation, with jurisdiction over trucking and the ailing railroads. He is also chairman of the International Trade Subcommittee, potentially one of the most important in Congress. In early 1981 he and the ranking Democrat, Lloyd Bentsen, came out for restrictions on foreign auto imports. There was speculation that this was just a ploy to get the Japanese to agree voluntarily to limit imports while the American auto industry retooled. Danforth himself seems to have no strong philosophic orientation either toward free trade or protection; and his vision of Missouri as an aging, energy-consuming state suggests that he may be hospitable to other forms of protection. This subcommittee could conceivably end up as a prorestriction counterweight to the pro–free trade Trade Subcommittee of the House Ways and Means Committee. That is somewhat ironic, given the free-trade views of most conservative Republicans today, in a Republican Senate; it is a reversion, perhaps, to the days when the Republicans were the party of tariffs and the Democrats the party opposed to them.

Danforth's seat is up in 1982 and going into the Reagan presidency he seemed to be a formidable favorite for reelection. He is sure to have a competent, well-financed campaign, and his record has done little to antagonize Missourians and much to reassure them that he is neither a flaming liberal nor a troglodyte conservative.

The Republicans finally made a breakthrough in Missouri House elections in 1980. From 1968 to 1974 Democrats had won nine of the state's ten seats; in 1976, when five incumbents retired, Republicans hoped to make major gains but captured just one district, when the incumbent Democrat made fraudulent statements about his background. In 1980, however, Republicans picked off two seats, one a Republican-leaning district where the incumbent retired, another where a seemingly invulnerable incumbent got into trouble and was knocked off by an enterprising challenger.

The Republicans have an additional opportunity now that Missouri loses one of its seats. The Democrats control the legislature, with enough votes theoretically to override the governor's veto, but in practice Missouri Democrats are a fractious lot, and the lines will probably not be drawn on party lines. The question is who will be left standing in the game of musical chairs. The obvious choice is Bill Clay of St. Louis, whose district has lost more population than any other, and who is not particularly popular with other politicians. But Clay is black, and many legislators will hesitate before eliminating the one black congressman when blacks form 10% of the state's population. Others whose districts have lost large numbers are Richard Bolling, chairman of the House Rules Committee, and Richard Gephardt, a young Democrat of great promise; few states would want to oust congressmen of this caliber. The districts at the periphery of the state will probably not be changed much, because that is difficult to do technically. That leaves two vulnerable members: Republican Wendell Bailey, a freshman, and Robert Young, a labor-oriented Democrat. The result is not predictable. Missouri's seats were redistricted several times in the 1960s and the legislature is difficult to control.

Census Data   Pop. (1980 final) 4,917,444, up 5% in 1970s: 2.17% of U.S. total, 15th largest. Central city, 24%; suburban, 39%. Median 4-person family income, 1978, $19,268, 94% of U.S., 32d highest.

1979 Share of Federal Tax Burden $9,512,000,000; 2.11% of U.S. total, 14th largest.

1979 Share of Federal Outlays $11,923,197,000; 2.60% of U.S. total, 13th largest.

DOD	$4,152,131,000	6th	(3.91%)	HEW	$4,066,765,000	11th	(2.27%)
DOE	$235,323,000	18th	(2.00%)	ERDA	$14,577,000	24th	(0.53%)
HUD	$164,941,000	12th	(2.50%)	NASA	$6,574,000	26th	(0.14%)
VA	$472,939,000	15th	(2.28%)	DOT	$315,966,000	18th	(1.91%)
EPA	$97,808,000	18th	(1.84%)	DOC	$27,519,000	21st	(0.87%)
DOI	$50,505,000	25th	(0.91%)	USDA	$578,390,000	14th	(2.41%)

Economic Base   Agriculture, notably cattle, hogs, soybeans, and dairy products; finance, insurance, and real estate; transportation equipment, especially motor vehicles and equipment; food and kindred products; printing and publishing; electrical equipment and supplies; apparel and other textile products, especially men's and boys' furnishings, and women's and misses' outerwear.

Political Lineup   Governor, Christopher Bond (R). Senators, Thomas F. Eagleton (D) and John C. Danforth (R). Representatives, 10 (6 D and 4 R); 9 in 1982. State Senate, 34 (23 D and 11 R); State House of Representatives, 163 (111 D and 52 R).

The Voters

  Registration   2,841,143 Total. No party registration.
  Employment profile 1970   White collar, 47%. Blue collar, 36%. Service, 13%. Farm, 4%.
  Ethnic groups   Black 1980, 10%. Hispanic 1980, 1%. Total foreign stock 1970, 7%. Germany, 2%.

Presidential Vote

1980	Reagan (R)	1,074,181	(51%)
	Carter (D)	931,182	(44%)
	Anderson (I)	77,920	(4%)
1976	Ford (R)	927,443	(47%)
	Carter (D)	998,387	(51%)

SENATORS

Sen. Thomas F. Eagleton (D) Elected 1968, seat up 1986; b. Sept. 4, 1929, St. Louis; home, St. Louis; Amherst Col., B.A. 1950, Harvard U., LL.B. 1953.

Career   Navy, 1948–49; Practicing atty.; St. Louis Circuit Atty., 1956–60; Atty. Gen. of Mo., 1961–65; Lt. Gov. of Mo., 1965–69.

Offices   1209 DSOB, 202-224-5721. Also 4039 Fed. Ofc. Bldg., St. Louis 63103, 314-425-5067, and Rm. 911 Fed. Bldg., 811 Grand Ave., Kansas City 64106, 816-374-2747.

Committees   *Appropriations* (6th). Subcommittees: Agriculture and Related Agencies; Defense; Labor, Health and Human Services, Education; Transportation.

Governmental Affairs (Ranking Member). Subcommittee: Governmental Efficiency and the District of Columbia.

Labor and Human Resources (5th). Subcommittees: Education; Handicapped; Aging, Family and Human Services.

Select Committee on Ethics (3d).

Group Ratings

	ADA	COPE	PC	LCV	CFA	RPN	NAB	NSI	NTU	ACA	ACU
1980	78	89	47	46	47	—	50	22	50	8	18
1979	58	95	49	—	57	—	—	—	31	19	17
1978	50	79	63	62	45	44	42	20	15	9	13

Key Votes

1) Draft Registn $	AGN	6) Fair Housng Cloture	FOR	11) Cut Socl Incr Defns	AGN
2) Ban $ to Nicrgua	AGN	7) Ban $ Rape Abortns	—	12) Income Tax Indexing	AGN
3) Dlay MX Missile	FOR	8) Cap on Food Stmp $	AGN	13) Lim Spdg 21% GNP	AGN
4) Nuclr Mortorium	—	9) New US Dep Edcatn	FOR	14) Incr Wndfll Prof Tax	FOR
5) Alaska Lands Bill	FOR	10) Cut OSHA Inspctns	AGN	15) Chryslr Loan Grntee	FOR

Election Results

1980 general	Thomas F. Eagleton (D).........	1,074,859	(52%)	($1,390,560)
	Gene McNary (R)	985,399	(48%)	($1,173,161)
1980 primary	Thomas F. Eagleton (D).........	553,392	(86%)	
	Two others (D)	91,957	(14%)	
1974 general	Thomas F. Eagleton (D).........	735,433	(60%)	($647,143)
	Thomas B. Curtis (R)	480,900	(39%)	($362,804)

Sen. John C. Danforth (R) Elected 1976, seat up 1982; b. Sept. 5, 1936, St. Louis; home, Flat; Princeton U., A.B. 1958, Yale U., B.D. and LL.B. 1963.

Career Practicing atty., 1963–69; Atty. Gen. of Mo., 1969–77; Rep. nominee for U.S. Senate, 1970.

Offices 460 RSOB, 202-224-6154. Also Suite 1867 Railway Exch. Bldg., 611 Olive St., St. Louis 63101, 314-425-6381, and Suites 943–945 Fed. Ofc. Bldg., 811 Grand Ave., Kansas City 64106, 816-374-6101.

Committees *Commerce, Science and Transportation* (4th). Subcommittees: Aviation; Consumer; Surface Transportation (Chairman).

Finance (4th). Subcommittees: Taxation and Debt Management; International Trade (Chairman); Social Security and Income Maintenance Programs.

Governmental Affairs (5th). Subcommittees: Permanent Subcommittee on Investigations; Federal Expenditures, Research, and Rules (Chairman); Intergovernmental Relations.

Group Ratings

	ADA	COPE	PC	LCV	CFA	RPN	NAB	NSI	NTU	ACA	ACU
1980	50	39	37	48	20	—	75	80	44	48	43
1979	16	42	35	—	33	—	—	—	37	52	42
1978	25	32	28	32	25	70	58	22	21	38	43

Key Votes

1) Draft Registn $	AGN	6) Fair Housng Cloture	AGN	11) Cut Socl Incr Defns	FOR
2) Ban $ to Nicrgua	AGN	7) Ban $ Rape Abortns	FOR	12) Income Tax Indexing	FOR
3) Dlay MX Missile	AGN	8) Cap on Food Stmp $	AGN	13) Lim Spdg 21% GNP	FOR
4) Nuclr Mortorium	AGN	9) New US Dep Edcatn	FOR	14) Incr Wndfll Prof Tax	FOR
5) Alaska Lands Bill	FOR	10) Cut OSHA Inspctns	FOR	15) Chryslr Loan Grntee	FOR

Election Results

1976 general	John C. Danforth (R)	1,090,067	(57%)	($741,465)
	Warren E. Hearnes (D)	813,571	(42%)	($660,953)
1976 primary	John C. Danforth (R)	284,025	(93%)	
	One other (R)	19,796	(7%)	
1970 general	Stuart Symington (D)	654,831	(51%)	
	John C. Danforth (R)	617,903	(48%)	

GOVERNOR

Gov. Christopher S. Bond (R) Elected 1980, term expires Jan. 1985; b. Mar. 6, 1939, St. Louis; home, Kansas City; Princeton U., B.A. 1960, U. of Va., J.D. 1963.

Career Clk. for U.S. Court of Appeals Chf. Judge Elbert P. Tuttle, 5th Ct., Atlanta, Ga., 1963–64; Practicing atty., 1964–69; Asst. Atty. Gen. of Mo., 1969; Mo. State Auditor, 1970–72; Gov. of Mo., 1973–77; Pres., Great Plains Legal Foundation, 1977–79.

Offices Exec. Ofc., State Capitol Bldg., Jefferson City 65101, 314-751-3222.

Election Results

1980 gen.	Christopher S. Bond (R) . . .	1,098,950	(53%)
	Joseph P. Teasdale (D)	981,884	(47%)
1980 prim.	Christopher S. Bond (R) . . .	223,678	(64%)
	William Phelps (R)	122,867	(35%)
	Two others (R)	5,534	(2%)
1976 gen.	Joseph P. Teasdale (D)	971,184	(50%)
	Christopher S. Bond (R) . . .	958,110	(50%)

FIRST DISTRICT

St. Louis is one of those American cities that have changed most in the last 30 years. In that time its population has declined from 856,000 to 450,000, and the city has changed from having a rather large black neighborhood to having a black majority. Some of these changes are essentially benign and normal in the course of metropolitan growth. Natural increase and migration during the 1950s meant that there would be larger and larger numbers of blacks, and for two reasons — because of the tendency of Americans of all kinds to move into neighborhoods of shared affinities and because of segregated housing practices — blacks clustered on the north side of St. Louis and in some adjacent suburbs. Young whites, in the natural course of things, tended to move to the suburbs rather than stay in the neighborhoods where they grew up: the latter were increasingly filled with old people, and the lion's share of suitable housing available at any given time was to be found in the suburbs.

These two trends have occurred in most major metropolitan areas. What is startling about St. Louis is the extent to which the central city has become depopulated. It was one of America's proudest metropolises in its day, the nation's fourth largest central city; and perhaps its decline now is due to the fact that most of its housing stock is old, built in the days before automobiles became the normal mode of transportation, and simply not very attractive to midcentury Americans, black or white. St. Louis has its fascinating neighborhoods — especially the old private streets with huge mansions near Forest Park — but much of the city is made of brick and frame houses packed into narrow streets. The riverfront is hidden mostly by railroads, warehouses, and factories; the center of the city, between downtown on the

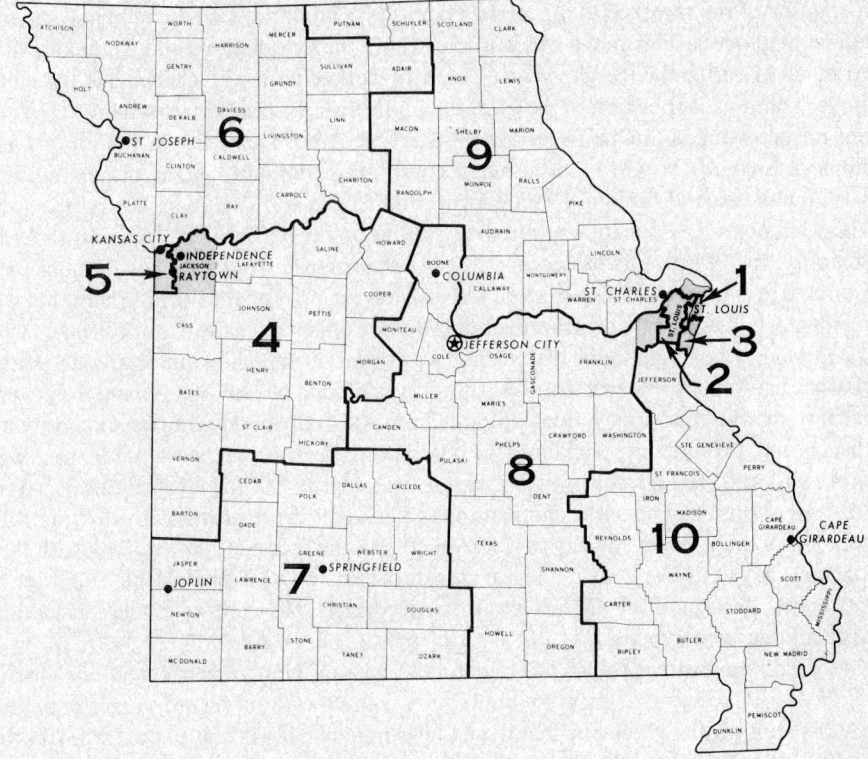

Mississippi and Forest Park near the western city limits, was torn down for public housing. Despite brave attempts — the Gateway Arch, the now dilapidated Gaslight Square area, the Busch Memorial Stadium — much of the action here has moved to the suburbs; the big new high-rise office area is in the suburb of Clayton, west of Forest Park.

The 1st congressional district of Missouri is the northern half of the city of St. Louis and a slice of suburban St. Louis County immediately west of the city limits. The north side of the city now is inhabited almost entirely by blacks, and the district was designed to contain a black majority. The suburbs include parts of Maplewood, Webster Groves, and Richmond Heights; white collar communities, University City, traditionally St. Louis's predominantly Jewish suburb, now with an increasing percentage of blacks; and the working class suburbs of Pagedale, Wellston, Pine Lawn, Northwoods, Normandy, and Bel-Ridge, originally all white but now increasingly black.

The 1st is consistently the most Democratic district in Missouri, by a considerable margin. Since 1968 it has been represented by Bill Clay, who got his political start as a union staffer and civil rights activist. When he was first elected, he was considered one of the most militant black members; only five years before, he had served 105 days in jail for participating in a civil rights demonstration.

Clay's record in the House is somewhat different, however. He is considered one of organized labor's most faithful supporters on the House Education and Labor Committee and on Post Office and Civil Service. From his seat on the latter body he has been the House's chief sponsor of the measure to repeal the Hatch Act's limitations on the political activities of federal employees. This move was unsuccessful in the Carter years and is unlikely to be heard much of during the Reagan years. Clay also worked hard with elements in the public employee unions in opposition to the Carter Administration's civil service reform act. Again he was unsuccessful, with Chairman Morris Udall, prolabor Democrat William Ford, and Republican Edward Derwinski fashioning a compromise despite Clay's efforts to scuttle it. Clay is now the second-ranking Democrat on Post Office and Civil Service and the sixth-ranking Democrat on Education and Labor. But his power may not be commensurate with his seniority. In 1981 he was passed over for the chairmanship of the Labor–Management Subcommittee in favor of Phillip Burton, who had less seniority on the subcommittee but who was evidently considered by organized labor to be a stronger advocate of its position in what were expected to be tough fights with Republicans bent on changing important labor laws.

Clay has had other problems. In 1976 it was revealed that he had been billing the government for numerous auto trips home, although he was actually purchasing less expensive airline tickets and, presumably, pocketing the difference. The next year he was under investigation for tax fraud. His administrative assistant was sent to jail for falsification of payroll records. All of this inspired some competition in the Democratic primary. In 1976 and 1978 six candidates each time held Clay to just over 60% of the primary vote; in 1980, with three opponents, Clay got 72%. Only in the last case did he receive a majority of the vote in the St. Louis County portion of the district, and then only barely. He seems to evoke considerable hostility among white voters.

This could be a greater problem for him in 1982. Missouri loses one congressional district, and if the legislature were to draw the boundaries entirely without regard to race or politics, Clay's district is probably the one that would be eliminated; it has only about three-quarters of its 1970 population. Certainly there will be some sentiment to draw a new district with a black majority; blacks make up 10% of Missouri's population and many white legislators feel they are entitled to one district that will elect a black congressman who does not have to cater to whites. But even a district drawn up to Clay's specifications will present some problems for him. New areas either in the suburbs or the city will inevitably contain white voting majorities, and Clay has never done well with white voters. If the district lines are drawn too far into the northwest St. Louis suburbs, Clay may be thrown into the same district with 2d district incumbent Bob Young, a canny politician with strong labor ties and the ability to mobilize a maximum anti-Clay vote if he has to. Clay does not have a network of strong personal or political supporters in the legislature, and so the outcome of his 1982 race seems unclear.

Census Data   Pop. (1980 final) 347,192, down 26% in 1970s. Median family income, 1970, $8,485, 89% of U.S.

The Voters

  Employment profile 1970   White collar, 46%. Blue collar, 33%. Service, 21%. Farm, –%.
  Ethnic groups   Black 1980, 65%. Hispanic 1980, 1%. Asian 1980, 1%. Total foreign stock 1970, 8%. Germany, 2%.

Presidential Vote

1980	Reagan (R)	31,649	(24%)
	Carter (D)	95,628	(72%)
	Anderson (I)	5,092	(4%)
1976	Ford (R)	38,903	(28%)
	Carter (D)	95,153	(70%)

Rep. William (Bill) **Clay** (D) Elected 1968; b. Apr. 30, 1931, St. Louis; home, St. Louis; St. Louis U., B.S. 1953.

Career Real estate broker; Life insurance business, 1959–61; St. Louis City Alderman, 1959–64; Business Rep., City Employees Union, 1961–64.

Offices 2264 RHOB, 202-225-2406. Also 5980 Delmar Blvd., St. Louis 63112, 314-725-5770.

Committees *Education and Labor* (6th). Subcommittees: Employment Opportunities; Labor–Management Relations.

Post Office and Civil Service (3d). Subcommittees: Civil Service; Investigations; Postal Operations and Services (Chairman).

Group Ratings

	ADA	COPE	PC	LCV	CFA	RPN	NAB	NSI	NTU	ACA	ACU
1980	83	89	73	87	79	—	0	11	20	16	6
1979	100	95	85	91	89	—	—	—	24	4	3
1978	85	95	78	69	82	33	0	0	24	12	4

Key Votes

1) Draft Registn $	AGN	6) Fair Hsg DOJ Enfrc	—	11) Cut Socl Incr Dfns $	AGN
2) Ban $ to Nicrgua	AGN	7) Lim PAC Contrbtns	FOR	12) Hosptl Cost Controls	FOR
3) Dlay MX Missile	FOR	8) Cap on Food Stmp $	AGN	13) Gasln Ctrls & Allctns	FOR
4) Nuclr Mortorium	FOR	9) New US Dep Edcatn	FOR	14) Lim Wndfll Prof Tax	AGN
5) Alaska Lands Bill	FOR	10) Cut OSHA $	AGN	15) Chryslr Loan Grntee	FOR

Election Results

1980 general	William (Bill) Clay (D)	91,272	(70%)	($102,908)
	Bill White (R)	38,667	(30%)	($0)
1980 primary	William (Bill) Clay (D)	37,611	(72%)	
	Three others (D)	14,436	(28%)	
1978 general	William (Bill) Clay (D)	65,950	(67%)	($91,254)
	Bill White (R)	30,995	(31%)	($40,834)

SECOND DISTRICT

The 2d congressional district of Missouri is the heart of St. Louis County, a jurisdiction that is adjacent to, but includes no part of, the city of St. Louis. The county originally was set apart so that its rural concerns would not be a drain on the treasury of booming St. Louis; now the city of St. Louis has about half the population and much less than half the wealth of the county. The 2d district runs the political gamut of suburbs. On its north side, north of Interstate 70, are blue collar communities such as Bellefontaine Neighbors, Jennings, Ferguson, Berkeley, and Hazelwood. Most of the people who live here grew up on the north side of St. Louis, which is now almost entirely black; many work in the giant McDonnell–Douglas aircraft plants located on the north side of the county. In the south end of the district are comfortable white collar, traditionally Republican suburbs such as Kirkwood and Webster Groves, now with some black population also, but nonetheless as Republican as ever. In the middle of the county, in University City and the towns to the west, Olivette and Creve Coeur, live most members of the Jewish community of metropolitan St. Louis. Just to the south, along the Daniel Boone Freeway, is Ladue, the home of most members of the St. Louis establishment and clearly the premier suburb in the metropolitan area. Farther out, beyond the Interstate 244 beltway, are the only parts of the metropolitan area that have been growing rapidly in the 1970s. These suburbs are high income, but not as prestigious as Ladue; their residents are somewhat younger; and they have been very heavily Republican in recent elections—the main reason the Democrats no longer take significant majorities out of the St. Louis metropolitan area in statewide elections.

Altogether the diverse makeup of the 2d district produces results that are often close to those of the state as a whole—although few other parts of Missouri resemble it much. Its congressmen tend to become well known in the St. Louis area and thus are natural candidates for statewide office; the last two congressmen here have run for the Senate and lost, Republican Thomas Curtis in 1968 and Democrat James Symington in 1976.

The current incumbent, Bob Young, may be in a different situation. He comes not from the blueblood background of his predecessors but from a blue collar neighborhood in the north side of the district. He was active in the pipefitters' union and served 20 years in the legislature before his election to Congress in 1976. That year he won a narrow victory over a well-financed Republican. Young's background and positions are classically crafted for assembling an old-fashioned Democratic coalition: he is a strong union man, he appeals to many Catholics as a strong opponent of abortion, and he is a strong supporter of Israel. He sits on nuts-and-bolts committees, Public Works and Transportation and Science and Technology. The latter is especially important to a district where McDonnell–Douglas is one of the largest employers.

Young had serious Republican competition in 1978 but managed to increase his percentage; in 1980, against a weaker opponent, he won easily. He may face greater problems in 1982, because of redistricting. Missouri lost a seat in the 1980 census, and Young could turn out to be the victim. Conceivably he could be thrown into the same district as either of the two congressmen based in the city of St. Louis, Bill Clay or Richard Gephardt; or he could have his district moved farther out into the suburbs or past St. Louis County into rural areas. If the latter happens, the district is likely to be more Republican. Young is well connected and will do his best to get a favorable district from the Democratic legislature. But demography and the political claims of some of the other members of the Missouri delegation may work against him.

Census Data   Pop. (1980 final) 467,710, no change in 1970s. Median family income, 1970, $12,597, 131% of U.S.

The Voters

Employment profile 1970   White collar, 63%. Blue collar, 28%. Service, 9%. Farm, –%.
Ethnic groups   Black 1980, 11%. Hispanic 1980, 1%. Asian 1980, 1%. Total foreign stock 1970, 12%. Germany, 2%; Italy, 1%.

Presidential Vote

1980	Reagan (R)	127,456	(55%)
	Carter (D)	91,777	(39%)
	Anderson (I)	12,813	(5%)
1976	Ford (R)	124,204	(56%)
	Carter (D)	95,108	(43%)

Rep. Robert A. Young (D) Elected 1976; b. Nov. 22, 1923, St. Louis; home, St. Ann.

Career Army, WWII; Pipefitter; Mo. House of Reps., 1957–63; Mo. Senate, 1963–77.

Offices 1317 LHOB, 202-225-2561. Also 4154 Cypress Rd., St. Ann 63074, 314-425-7200.

Committees *Public Works and Transportation* (12th). Subcommittees: Aviation; Surface Transportation; Water Resources.

Science and Technology (13th). Subcommittees: Energy Development and Applications; Energy Research and Production.

Group Ratings

	ADA	COPE	PC	LCV	CFA	RPN	NAB	NSI	NTU	ACA	ACU
1980	50	56	47	40	57	—	8	30	20	33	5
1979	53	82	45	42	63	—	—	—	25	16	18
1978	25	75	48	33	41	25	42	78	12	48	35

Key Votes

1) Draft Registn $	FOR	6) Fair Hsg DOJ Enfrc	AGN	11) Cut Socl Incr Dfns $	AGN
2) Ban $ to Nicrgua	AGN	7) Lim PAC Contrbtns	FOR	12) Hosptl Cost Controls	AGN
3) Dlay MX Missile	FOR	8) Cap on Food Stmp $	AGN	13) Gasln Ctrls & Allctns	FOR
4) Nuclr Mortorium	AGN	9) New US Dep Edcatn	FOR	14) Lim Wndfll Prof Tax	FOR
5) Alaska Lands Bill	AGN	10) Cut OSHA $		AGN	15) Chryslr Loan Grntee	FOR

Election Results

1980 general	Robert A. Young (D)	148,227	(64%)	($149,633)
	John O. Shields (R)	81,762	(36%)	($94,811)
1980 primary	Robert A. Young (D)	51,325	(86%)	
	One other (D)	8,175	(14%)	
1978 general	Robert A. Young (D)	102,911	(56%)	($158,326)
	Bob Chase (R)................	79,495	(44%)	($148,440)

THIRD DISTRICT

Missouri's 3d congressional district consists of the south side of the city of St. Louis and an adjacent portion of suburban St. Louis County. The line drawn through the middle of St. Louis to separate the 3d from the 1st district also neatly separates the black part of the city from the white. In the 1970s, blacks for the most part had been moving out from the north side of St. Louis to the suburbs nearby, leaving the south side of the city to whites. Here on the south side there are still signs of the German immigrants who made St. Louis one of the nation's bustling and progressive cities in the late 19th century; today, symbolically, an Altenheim (old people's home) still sits on the banks of the Mississippi River. The most famous of the St. Louis Germans was Carl Schurz, a friend of Lincoln, a Union Army officer in the Civil War, secretary of the Interior, and U.S. senator from Missouri.

Schurz was a Republican, and for years St. Louis was a Republican island in a Democratic sea. But with the New Deal, St. Louis became one of our most Democratic cities. This is an elderly district (the median age of eligible voters was 50 in 1970 and is probably higher today), and for many of the people here the 1930s remain a vivid memory. Most of them retain Democratic voting habits; in some of the traditionally better-off wards at the edge of the city, people tend to be Republican. The suburban area is a natural extension of the city. Most of the people there moved out along the radial avenues extending from the middle of St. Louis. The suburban voters, however, tend to be younger; the Depression is not an important part of their consciousness; their incomes are somewhat higher than those left behind in the city; and they are more Republican. Thus in 1980 the St. Louis city portion of the 3d district was 51% for Jimmy Carter, while the suburban portion was 60% for Reagan.

The 3d district has one of the most politically adept of the younger members of Congress, Democrat Richard Gephardt. When he first ran for the seat, in 1976, it was thought that the Republicans might make a real battle here. But Gephardt won an absolute majority in a four-candidate primary and got nearly a 2–1 victory over a well-known Republican in the general election. He proved able to campaign effectively personally, to put together a good organization, to raise money, and to stage a good media campaign. In his first term in the House he was assigned to the Ways and Means Committee and in the second to Budget as well—signs that he is well respected in the House. He is not necessarily a conventional Democrat. His views on substantive issues are not always those of liberal and labor organizations. Gephardt has taken a major role on health issues. He helped to defeat the Carter Administration's health care cost control bill, on the grounds that it would be bureaucratic and ineffective, and sponsored instead (with none other than David Stockman) what is known in health circles as the competition bill, a measure to use tax incentives to encourage employers to offer employees a range of health care plans, with clear price tags on each. The hope is that market mechanisms would then make the health care system work more effficiently and inexpensively.

On trade issues Gephardt is not enthusiastic about trade barriers but, like Missouri's senators, is concerned about the auto industry. On tax and economic issues he is open to arguments that taxes on investment and high incomes should be lower rather than higher. On some issues he has been allied with James Jones, the new chairman of the Budget Committee; on others, he has worked with more liberal Democrats. In the 97th Congress, he could well play a pivotal role. Ways and Means handles major tax legislation and Budget handles proposed budget cuts—in other words, the major legislative initiatives of the Reagan Administration all pass before committees on which Gephardt serves. To the extent that Gephardt goes along with such measures, he can help assure their passage; if he opposes them strongly, he may help to stop them in the House and in effect stymie Reagan's program.

Gephardt could theoretically face problems in redistricting, but it seems likely that a politician with this much ability can ensure his own political safety. His district will have to expand either to the north side of St. Louis, in which he might find himself in a primary fight with Bill Clay, or into the St. Louis County suburbs, where he might collide with Bob Young.

Census Data   Pop. (1980 final) 407,974, down 13% in 1970s. Median family income, 1970, $10,199, 106% of U.S.

The Voters

Employment profile 1970   White collar, 52%. Blue collar, 36%. Service, 12%. Farm, –%.
Ethnic groups   Black 1980, 7%. Hispanic 1980, 1%. Asian 1980, 1%. Total foreign stock 1970, 15%.
Germany, 4%; Italy, 2%.

Presidential Vote

1980	Reagan (R)	94,637	(51%)
	Carter (D)	81,774	(44%)
	Anderson (I)	8,191	(4%)
1976	Ford (R)	90,574	(50%)
	Carter (D)	85,741	(48%)

Rep. Richard A. Gephardt (D) Elected 1976; b. Jan. 31, 1941, St. Louis; home, St. Louis; Northwestern U., B.S. 1962, U. of Mich., J.D. 1965.

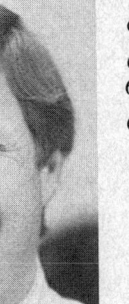

Career   Practicing atty., 1965–76; St. Louis City Alderman, 1971–76.

Offices   218 CHOB, 202-225-2671. Also 3470 Hampton, St. Louis 63109, 314-351-5100.

Committees   *Budget* (10th).

Ways and Means (13th). Subcommittee: Social Security.

Group Ratings

	ADA	COPE	PC	LCV	CFA	RPN	NAB	NSI	NTU	ACA	ACU
1980	56	61	57	65	43	—	42	10	30	33	6
1979	74	85	53	62	54	—	—	—	41	16	21
1978	35	75	63	60	41	27	50	60	58	48	33

Key Votes

1) Draft Registn $ —	6) Fair Hsg DOJ Enfrc AGN	11) Cut Socl Incr Dfns $ AGN
2) Ban $ to Nicrgua AGN	7) Lim PAC Contrbtns FOR	12) Hosptl Cost Controls AGN
3) Dlay MX Missile FOR	8) Cap on Food Stmp $ AGN	13) Gasln Ctrls & Allctns FOR
4) Nuclr Mortorium —	9) New US Dep Edcatn AGN	14) Lim Wndfll Prof Tax FOR
5) Alaska Lands Bill FOR	10) Cut OSHA $ AGN	15) Chryslr Loan Grntee FOR

Election Results

1980 general	Richard A. Gephardt (D)	143,132	(78%)	($198,785)
	Robert A. Cedarburg (R)	41,277	(22%)	($0)
1980 primary	Richard A. Gephardt (D)	65,901	(100%)	
1978 general	Richard A. Gephardt (D)	121,565	(82%)	($113,977)
	Lee Buchschacher (R)	26,881	(18%)	

FOURTH DISTRICT

The home congressional district of the late Harry Truman was the 4th district of Missouri. Truman's background—he never represented the district in the House but served in the Senate from 1935 to 1945—tells us a lot about the district, even today. Truman was born in the town of Lamar, in the southern end of the 4th, near the Oklahoma and Arkansas borders. His family was Democratic, which means in his mother's case at least that it cherished a lifelong sympathy for the cause of the Confederacy. The largest city in the 4th district, way at its other end, is Independence. It is an old courthouse town, where Truman lived on what is now Truman Road in a 19th-century Victorian house long in his wife's family. Just a few blocks away is the Jackson County Courthouse where Truman was county judge (an administrative position) before his election to the Senate. In those days Independence was a small town, the incongruous seat of a county that included bustling Kansas City. Today the suburban growth emanating from Kansas City has so ballooned the population of Independence that Truman's old Victorian neighborhood has nearly been engulfed by subdivisions.

The 4th district is a combination of rural Missouri counties, such as the one Truman grew up in, and part of the Kansas City metropolitan area, where he began his political career. Its political history is almost totally Democratic. The rural counties, although to a diminished extent in recent years, have clung to the party more sympathetic to the South—even though Jimmy Carter lost most of them to Ronald Reagan in 1980. Kansas City has been Democratic since the days of Tom Prendergast, the political boss who gave Truman his start and later ended up in jail. Truman himself had no part in Prendergast's graft (the boss was a cement contractor, and under him Kansas City built huge edifices), but Truman was a beneficiary of the fraudulently high number of votes the machine piled up. Jackson County was reported to have cast 295,000 votes in the 1936 election, Prendergast's last—more than it has ever since, despite a subsequent 31% growth in population. The 1980 total was 256,000.

The 4th's representation seems to have alternated between Jackson County, which casts 42% of its votes, and the rural areas. In 1976 Congressman William Randall retired after 17 years in office; a Democrat, he had previously been one of Truman's successors as Jackson County judge. Nine candidates entered the Democratic primary, and the winner, with 40%, was a state senator from a small county not too far from Kansas City, Ike Skelton. There was also a serious Republican effort here, from the mayor of Independence. But he was unable to carry Jackson County, and Skelton won big percentages in most of the rural counties. In his first term in the House Skelton acquired a seat on the Agriculture Committee and compiled a voting record fairly liberal on economic but not on cultural issues. He was reelected without difficulty in 1978 and 1980. After the 1980 election he switched committees from Agriculture to Armed Services, showing an increased interest in national issues. (This part of Missouri, and indeed most of the state except for the portion around Fort Leonard Wood, is not loaded with military installations.) At this point, it does not seem likely that the Republicans will target this seat.

Census Data   Pop. (1980 final) 541,810, up 16% in 1970s. Median family income, 1970, $8,740, 91% of U.S.

The Voters

Employment profile 1970   White collar, 42%. Blue collar, 38%. Service, 12%. Farm, 8%.
Ethnic groups   Black 1980, 2%. Hispanic 1980, 1%. Total foreign stock 1970, 4%. Germany, 1%.

Presidential Vote

1980	Reagan (R)	118,144	(52%)
	Carter (D)	96,968	(43%)
	Anderson (I)	7,558	(3%)
1976	Ford (R)	100,517	(48%)
	Carter (D)	108,477	(51%)

Rep. Ike Skelton (D) Elected 1976; b. Dec. 20, 1931, Lexington; home, Lexington; Wentworth Mil. Acad., U. of Mo., B.A. 1953, LL.B. 1956, U. of Edinburgh, Scotland, 1956.

Career Lafayette Co. Prosecuting Atty., 1957–60; Spec. Asst. Atty. Gen. of Mo., 1961–63; Practicing atty., 1964–71; Mo. Senate, 1971–76.

Offices 1404 LHOB, 202-225-2876. Also 219 Fed. Bldg., 301 W. Lexington, Independence 64050, 816-252-2560.

Committees *Armed Services* (20th). Subcommittees: Military Personnel and Compensation; Readiness.

Small Business (11th). Subcommittee: Export Opportunities and Special Small Business Problems.

Group Ratings

	ADA	COPE	PC	LCV	CFA	RPN	NAB	NSI	NTU	ACA	ACU
1980	17	58	30	31	29	—	58	78	31	42	53
1979	32	55	30	42	12	—	—	—	34	26	44
1978	20	61	30	30	14	56	64	90	21	68	50

Key Votes

1) Draft Registn $	FOR	6) Fair Hsg DOJ Enfrc	AGN	11) Cut Socl Incr Dfns $	FOR
2) Ban $ to Nicrgua	AGN	7) Lim PAC Contrbtns	FOR	12) Hosptl Cost Controls	AGN
3) Dlay MX Missile	AGN	8) Cap on Food Stmp $	AGN	13) Gasln Ctrls & Allctns	FOR
4) Nuclr Mortorium	AGN	9) New US Dep Edcatn	—	14) Lim Wndfll Prof Tax	AGN
5) Alaska Lands Bill	FOR	10) Cut OSHA $	AGN	15) Chryslr Loan Grntee	FOR

Election Results

1980 general	Ike Skelton (D)	151,459	(68%)	($115,981)
	Bill Baker (R)	71,869	(32%)	($1,921)
1980 primary	Ike Skelton (D)	63,567	(89%)	
	One other (D)	8,036	(11%)	
1978 general	Ike Skelton (D)	120,748	(73%)	($149,080)
	Bill Baker (R)	45,116	(27%)	

FIFTH DISTRICT

The 5th congressional district of Missouri includes the heart of Kansas City—the central portion of the city, including its downtown and most of its industrial area down by the river and the stockyards. This area is the focus of the Kansas City metropolitan area, an important manufacturing and commercial hub for the farmlands of western Missouri and most of Kansas—and a city with the air and assurance of one of the nation's major and growing metropolitan areas. "Everything's up to date in Kansas City," goes the song from *Oklahoma!*, which was set in 1907, and Kansas City indeed did have then all the modern accoutrements. It still does today. The 5th district includes the city's downtown skyscrapers sitting on the bluffs above the Missouri River and the Kansas City stockyards. Across a valley facing them is the luxurious Crown Center development started by Hallmark, the greeting card company that is one of the major employers and style-setters of the city. Here in the 5th are the city's black ghettos and some of its white working-class neighborhoods. It also includes the high-income neighborhoods around the County Club Plaza — the nation's first shopping center, built in the 1920s — just across the state line from the high-income suburbs of Johnson County, Kansas.

In 1948 a 32-year-old World War II veteran who had lived in Kansas City only a couple of years, Richard Bolling, was elected congressman from the 5th district. From the beginning he seemed likely to be an exceptional congressman, and he has been — although his career has had its ups and downs. In his first years he became one of Speaker Sam Rayburn's proteges and won a seat on the Rules Committee. But after Rayburn's death in 1961 he failed to get the leadership post he wanted; Speaker McCormack and Majority Leader Carl Albert picked Hale Boggs to be the Democratic whip. Frustrated, Bolling wrote two first-rate books analyzing and attacking the way things were done in the House, *House Out of Order* and *Power in the House.* He argued that the seniority system should not automatically determine committee chairmanships and that the Democratic Caucus should make committee chairmen accountable; in effect he set the agenda of reform for more than a dozen years and provided the impetus for reforms that would, in large part, be accomplished after the big Democratic victory of 1974 and the class of 75 reform-minded freshmen it brought in.

Bolling played an important, although not completely successful, role in this process. In 1974 and 1975 he presided over a major effort to reform the House committee structure, most of whose proposals were defeated, in large part because of opposition from Phillip Burton of California. After the 1976 election Bolling was a leading candidate for the majority leadership, to be decided by secret ballot in the Democratic Caucus. But on the second ballot, Jim Wright of Texas edged him out by 95-93, knocking him out of the race; had he gotten onto the final ballot against Burton he would have won (Wright defeated Burton by only one vote).

His position on the Rules Committee was challenging but also must have been frustrating. Under Speakers Albert and Tip O'Neill he has generally been the leadership's senior man on that body, but he did not become chairman until 1979. Southern conservatives, profoundly out of sympathy with most House Democrats, chaired the committee from 1955 to 1973; from 1958 to 1979 there was never a chairman under 74 years old. The power of the committee is, theoretically, great. Every bill that comes before the House (with certain exceptions that require unanimous consent or suspension of the rules) must have a rule, that is, a resolution that sets the length of debate and the extent to which a bill can be amended. Rules are obviously a necessity if business is to be conducted efficiently in a legislature with 435 members; but there is obviously a possibility of abuse. Some previous Rules chairmen, notably Howard Smith of Virginia, used their power to defeat measures that they didn't like but that could have won majority approval. Bolling has argued that Rules should be responsive to the speaker, as indeed it was until the speaker was shorn of his powers in 1911 (before that, the speaker was also chairman of Rules). After becoming chairman, Bolling got approved a procedure giving the speaker the right to appoint all majority party members of Rules. The result, likely to be tested in the 97th Congress, is a committee on which O'Neill and Bolling will have a majority for the positions they favor even when those positions may not command a majority on the floor.

This can be a mighty power. Typically the House has carefully limited the number of amendments that can be added to a bill on the floor, which makes good legislative sense generally: members should have the right to vote up or down on major changes in a bill but should not be able to clutter it with nongermane or crippling amendments. But limitations on amendment can also make it impossible for a majority in the House to write the bill it wants and can force a majority to take or leave a measure they do not really want. This could happen, for example, with legislation critical to the Reagan Administration. Bolling is not a man to engage in high-handed tactics arbitrarily. He is a scholar of the legislative process, a genial man who appreciates the talents and positions of his adversaries. But he is also a strong partisan Democrat, a greater believer than many of his younger colleagues in the economic programs of the party, although he never shared their opposition to the Vietnam war. He is working amiably and cooperatively not only with O'Neill but also with Burton and others whom he has opposed in the past. He is likely to be a critically important legislator in the 97th Congress.

Bolling has been reelected every two years by the 5th district with large majorities; in 1980, a bad Democratic year nationally, he won 70% of the vote. His district will have to be expanded significantly for 1982, but the likelihood is that it will absorb territory around its current periphery—more of Kansas City and perhaps the city of Independence, Harry Truman's old hometown, just to the east. Most of this area is marginally more Republican than the current 5th, although Bolling's district now already includes most of the really heavily Republican high-income precincts in the city.

Census Data Pop. (1980 final) 400,953, down 14% in 1970s. Median family income, 1970, $9,727, 101% of U.S.

The Voters

Employment profile 1970 White collar, 53%. Blue collar, 32%. Service, 15%. Farm, –%.

Ethnic groups Black 1980, 31%. Hispanic 1980, 3%. Asian 1980, 1%. Total foreign stock 1970, 9%. Germany, Italy, 1% each.

Presidential Vote

1980	Reagan (R)	56,925	(35%)
	Carter (D)	94,512	(59%)
	Anderson (I)	8,166	(5%)
1976	Ford (R)	60,538	(40%)
	Carter (D)	87,965	(58%)

Rep. Richard Bolling (D) Elected 1948; b. May 17, 1916, New York, N.Y.; home, Kansas City; U. of the South, B.A. 1937, M.A. 1939, Vanderbilt U., 1939 40.

Career Army, WWII; Teacher and coach, Sewanee Mil. Acad.; Vets. Advisor and Dir. of Student Activities, U. of Kansas City.

Offices 2365 RHOB, 202-225-4535. Also Fed. Ofc. Bldg., 811 Grand Ave., Kansas City 64106, 816-842-4798.

Committees *Rules* (Chairman).

Joint Economic Committee (2d). Subcommittees: Agriculture and Transportation; Economic Goals and Intergovernmental Policy.

Group Ratings

	ADA	COPE	PC	LCV	CFA	RPN	NAB	NSI	NTU	ACA	ACU
1980	72	83	63	57	71	—	10	29	14	23	6
1979	53	57	38	77	30	—	—	—	14	7	8
1978	65	94	68	57	55	50	0	33	8	9	5

Key Votes

1) Draft Registn $	FOR	6) Fair Hsg DOJ Enfrc	FOR	11) Cut Socl Incr Dfns $	AGN
2) Ban $ to Nicrgua	AGN	7) Lim PAC Contrbtns	FOR	12) Hosptl Cost Controls	FOR
3) Dlay MX Missile	—	8) Cap on Food Stmp $	—	13) Gasln Ctrls & Allctns	FOR
4) Nuclr Mortorium	AGN	9) New US Dep Edcatn	—	14) Lim Wndfll Prof Tax	—
5) Alaska Lands Bill	FOR	10) Cut OSHA $	—	15) Chryslr Loan Grntee	FOR

Election Results

1980 general	Richard Bolling (D)	110,957	(70%)	($113,299)
	Vincent E. Baker (R)	47,309	(30%)	($11,388)
1980 primary	Richard Bolling (D)	40,656	(82%)	
	One other (D)	9,110	(18%)	
1978 general	Richard Bolling (D)	82,140	(72%)	($66,241)
	Steven L. Walter (R)	30,360	(27%)	($9,096)

SIXTH DISTRICT

Northwest Missouri is mostly farmland, gentle rolling hill country above the bluffs that line the Missouri and other major rivers. In many ways this is a place left behind by the 20th century. The mechanization of the family farm has thinned out the population here, as young people seek a better way to make a living elsewhere. All the counties of northwest Missouri, except those in the Kansas City metropolitan area, had more people in 1900 than they do today; in 1900 they had a total population of 508,000 and in 1980, 301,000. Perhaps the most poignant story belongs to St. Joseph, once one of the leading ports of entry to the American West: it was here that the Pony Express riders first saddled up for their transcontinental sprints to Sacramento. In 1900 St. Joseph was a solid commercial competitor of Kansas City, with 102,000 people compared to Kansas City's 163,000. Today Metropolitan Kansas City has more than a million people, while St. Joseph's population has dwindled to 72,000 and is diminishing still.

The 6th congressional district covers almost precisely the northwestern corner of Missouri, the land north and east of the Missouri River, west of a line drawn north and south through the middle of the state. Although most of the expanse of the 6th is given over to agriculture, as it was at the turn of the century, most of its residents now live in metropolitan areas. Some are in St. Joseph, but by far the bulk of this population can be found in Clay and Platte Counties in metropolitan Kansas City. To give itself space to grow, Kansas City has been systematically annexing land in these two counties for 20 years; much of it has been bulldozed for subdivisions or to accommodate Kansas City's giant new airport. The Census Bureau considers Clay and Platte Counties as part of the central city, and technically they are; but their character is suburban or even rural. Travelers driving into town from Mid-Continent International, the new airport, pass through miles of dairy grazing land and cornfields — inside the city limits of Kansas City.

The 6th is one of those Missouri districts that in national and statewide elections trended Republican in the 1960s and 1970s; it didn't like Kennedy's Catholicism, Johnson's Great

Society, or Humphrey's or McGovern's liberalism. But there is still a Democratic tradition here, evident in the returns from local and state legislative elections, where most of the winners are Democrats, and in its initial reaction, if not its final verdict, on Jimmy Carter. This is one of the noncentral city districts that Carter carried in 1976, without which he would not have carried Missouri, and even in 1980 the 6th district gave him a percentage above his national average.

In congressional representation the district has moved slowly, and sometimes haltingly, from Democratic to Republican. It had an old-fashioned southern-style conservative Democrat in the 1960s; in 1972 and 1974, it elected Jerry Litton, a wealthy Charolais beef farmer who won the 1976 Democratic Senate primary and then died in a plane crash on primary night; then in 1976, when the district was shifting back to the Democrats in the presidential election, it elected Republican Tom Coleman to Congress.

Coleman's victory resulted in large part from the problems of his Democratic opponent, Morgan Maxfield. Maxfield was a protege of Lamar Hunt, owner of the Kansas City Chiefs, and he spent more than $200,000 on his own campaign. It was going swimmingly until an article about him appeared in the *Kansas City Star* in October. The paper had been doing some digging into Maxfield's background. Reporters found that although he claimed he grew up in poverty, his father was a prosperous doctor; although he said he was a graduate of Harvard Business School, he had actually taken only a six-week course there; although he said he was a bachelor, he had a wife and children back in Texas. Coleman, a veteran of the Missouri legislature and a respectable candidate, was able to take advantage of this opening and to win easily; the surprise is that Maxfield got as much as 41% of the vote.

Coleman's political progress can serve as an object lesson in the intelligent use of incumbency. He did a good job of keeping in touch with his constituents through franked mail and personal appearances. He got a seat on the House Agriculture Committee and made a major effort to identify himself with agricultural issues in the rural counties, where he was unknown initially. In 1978 he had serious competition from Kansas City area legislator Phil Snowden; the Republican managed a solid victory. In 1980, against a weaker opponent, he won more than 70% of the vote and carried every county in the district. He is reasonably high in seniority on both Agriculture and Education and Labor Committees and would become a subcommittee chairman if Republicans took control of the House. Redistricting may affect his district's boundaries somewhat, although, given his strong margin in 1980, it seems unlikely to threaten his tenure. This district, which gained population in the 1970s and is situated in a corner of the state, is not likely to be the Missouri district that will disappear in the redistricting process.

Census Data   Pop. (1980 final) 508,848, up 8% in 1970s. Median family income, 1970, $8,507, 89% of U.S.

The Voters

Employment profile 1970   White collar, 43%. Blue collar, 35%. Service, 12%. Farm, 10%.
Ethnic groups   Black 1980, 1%. Hispanic 1980, 1%. Total foreign stock 1970, 5%. Germany, 1%.

Presidential Vote

1980	Reagan (R)	112,712	(52%)
	Carter (D)	93,933	(43%)
	Anderson (I)	8,233	(4%)
1976	Ford (R)	99,618	(47%)
	Carter (D)	107,977	(52%)

Rep. E. Thomas (Tom) **Coleman** (R) Elected 1976; b. May 25, 1943, Kansas City; home, Kansas City; Wm. Jewell Col., B.A. 1965, NYU., M.A. 1969, Washington U., St. Louis, J.D. 1969.

Career Asst. Atty. Gen. of Mo., 1969–72; Mo. House of Reps., 1973–76.

Offices 1527 LHOB, 202-225-7041. Also 2701 Rock Creek Pkwy., Kansas City 64116, 816-474-9035.

Committees *Agriculture* (5th). Subcommittees: Conservation, Credit and Rural Development; Domestic Marketing, Consumer Relations and Nutrition.

Education and Labor (5th). Subcommittees: Elementary, Secondary and Vocational Education; Human Resources; Postsecondary Education.

Group Ratings

	ADA	COPE	PC	LCV	CFA	RPN	NAB	NSI	NTU	ACA	ACU
1980	6	10	13	31	7	—	91	100	49	87	67
1979	11	10	13	28	4	—	—	—	50	96	92
1978	20	11	15	40	18	50	92	100	33	93	83

Key Votes

1) Draft Registn $	FOR	6) Fair Hsg DOJ Enfrc	AGN
2) Ban $ to Nicrgua	FOR	7) Lim PAC Contrbtns	AGN
3) Dlay MX Missile	—	8) Cap on Food Stmp $	FOR
4) Nuclr Mortorium	AGN	9) New US Dep Edcatn	AGN
5) Alaska Lands Bill	FOR	10) Cut OSHA $	FOR

11) Cut Socl Incr Dfns $	FOR
12) Hosptl Cost Controls	AGN
13) Gasln Ctrls & Allctns	AGN
14) Lim Wndfll Prof Tax	FOR
15) Chryslr Loan Grntee	AGN

Election Results

1980 general	E. Thomas (Tom) Coleman (R) . . .	149,281	(71%)	($188,403)
	Vernon King (D)	62,048	(29%)	($22,751)
1980 primary	E. Thomas (Tom) Coleman (R) . . .	28,685	(100%)	
1978 general	E. Thomas (Tom) Coleman (R) . . .	96,574	(56%)	($274,804)
	Phil Snowden (D)	76,061	(44%)	($280,118)

SEVENTH DISTRICT

Mention the Ozarks and you evoke an image of rural poverty: people with quaint accents living in hillside shacks, cut off from the current of 20th-century America—a kind of Dogpatch. But for the Ozark Mountains of southwest Missouri, an area roughly coincident with the state's 7th congressional district, the Dogpatch image is far from accurate and is getting less accurate every year. Here you can find sizable and prosperous cities, such as Springfield, the third largest in the state, and Joplin. Outside the cities you can see how the landscape has been transformed in recent years, as people from St. Louis and Kansas City and even Chicago build vacation homes or even year-round residences in the pleasant green hills and along the large, often man-made, lakes. The climate here is relatively temperate, and the Ozarks are free of many of the stresses and strains of metropolitan life that so many Americans find unpleasant. The Ozarks, long a backwater, are now one of the fastest-growing parts of the country.

Many mountain areas — eastern Tennessee and central Kentucky as well as the Ozarks — have developed a politics contrary to that of the lowlands, politics that goes back more than a century. Most people here in the 1860s did not share the slaveholding habits or Confederate sympathies of most central Missourians, and during the Civil War they became staunch Republicans — and have stayed that way. During the 1960s the Republican inclination was strengthened by distaste for Democratic government programs and by the urban experiences of many of the area's new arrivals, who seemed to like the fact that there were few blacks and little evidence of the youth culture here. In close statewide elections every county of the 7th usually goes Republican; none, for example, voted to reelect Senator Thomas Eagleton in 1980. Jimmy Carter failed to carry the district not only in 1980 but in 1976 as well.

The 7th was for years the only Missouri district to send a Republican to Congress (although now there are three others). The current incumbent is Gene Taylor, a Sarcoxie auto dealer who was Republican National Committeeman when he first ran for the seat in 1972. His most difficult election was the first Republican primary, in which he narrowly defeated John Ashcroft, now Missouri's attorney general. Taylor was also pressed in the 1974 election, but since then has won easily. He sits on the Post Office and Civil Service Committee and after the 1980 election gave up a senior seat on Public Works in order to take a seat on the Rules Committee. There he can be expected to be a tough fighter for the aggressive Republican Conference. The 7th has gained population as fast as any Missouri district in the 1970s and has been getting even more Republican; redistricting, therefore, is unlikely to harm Taylor in the least.

Census Data   Pop. (1980 final) 570,244, up 22% in 1970s. Median family income, 1970, $6,832, 71% of U.S.

The Voters

   Employment profile 1970   White collar, 41%. Blue collar, 39%. Service, 13%. Farm, 7%.
   Ethnic groups   Black 1980, 1%. Hispanic 1980, 1%. Am. Ind. 1980, 1%. Total foreign stock 1970, 3%.

Presidential Vote

1980	Reagan (R)	146,971	(60%)
	Carter (D)	88,807	(36%)
	Anderson (I)	6,335	(3%)
1976	Ford (R)	114,881	(52%)
	Carter (D)	103,297	(47%)

Rep. Gene Taylor (R) Elected 1972; b. Feb. 10, 1928, near Sarcoxie; home, Sarcoxie; S.W. Mo. St. Col.

Career Public school teacher; Pres., Gene Taylor Ford Sales, Inc.; Mayor of Sarcoxie, 1954-60.

Offices 2430 RHOB, 202-225-6536. Also 314A Wilhoit Bldg., Springfield 65806, 417-862-4317.

Committees *Post Office and Civil Service* (2d). Subcommittees: Civil Service; Postal Operations and Services.

Rules (4th). Subcommittees: Rules of the House; The Legislative Process.

Group Ratings

	ADA	COPE	PC	LCV	CFA	RPN	NAB	NSI	NTU	ACA	ACU
1980	11	16	27	17	14	—	100	100	68	88	89
1979	0	10	8	3	0	—	—	—	65	100	97
1978	10	15	18	13	18	50	100	100	33	96	88

Key Votes

1) Draft Registn $	FOR	6) Fair Hsg DOJ Enfrc	AGN	11) Cut Socl Incr Dfns $	FOR
2) Ban $ to Nicrgua	FOR	7) Lim PAC Contrbtns	AGN	12) Hosptl Cost Controls	AGN
3) Dlay MX Missile	AGN	8) Cap on Food Stmp $	FOR	13) Gasln Ctrls & Allctns	AGN
4) Nuclr Mortorium	AGN	9) New US Dep Edcatn	AGN	14) Lim Wndfll Prof Tax	FOR
5) Alaska Lands Bill	AGN	10) Cut OSHA $	FOR	15) Chryslr Loan Grntee	—

Election Results

1980 general	Gene Taylor (R)	161,668	(68%)	($99,889)
	Ken Young (D)	76,844	(32%)	($0)
1980 primary	Gene Taylor (R)	71,052	(100%)	
1978 general	Gene Taylor (R)	104,566	(61%)	($104,612)
	Jim Thomas (D)	66,351	(39%)	($25,037)

EIGHTH DISTRICT

The 8th congressional district of Missouri occupies the central region, the geographical heart, of the state; only at one point, along the Arkansas border, does it touch the state's boundary. Yet it does not form much of a community; rather, it appears to include everything that was left over when the other districts, with their own distinct personalities, were drawn. At one point, Missouri underwent five redistrictings in 15 years, and the 8th's shape changed markedly, like a piece of modeling clay being shaped by a child. Today the district in outline looks like a chocolate rooster with a solid base. The comb includes Columbia, the district's largest city and the home of the University of Missouri. At just about where the ears would be, if chickens had ears, is Jefferson City, the sleepy little state capital. The tail feathers are in the western end of suburban St. Louis County; the feet or leg base is solidly in the Ozarks, extending to the Arkansas border.

There are areas of diverse political leanings. Columbia, with a Dixie Democratic heritage, also has a sizable university vote. The St. Louis County suburbs, during the 1970s areas of significant population growth in solid subdivisions with massive colonials, are staunchly Republican and getting more so. Probably the most interesting parts of the district are Jefferson City and the counties to the east, which have been strongly Republican since they were settled by antislavery German '48ers in the middle 19th century. Although the Ozark counties are Republican, most of the rural counties in the 8th are traditional Missouri Democratic. The most notable features south of Jefferson City are Fort Leonard Wood, long one of the Army's centers for basic training, and the resort area around Lake of the Ozarks.

Altogether, the district is increasingly Republican, not only in national elections (it went for Gerald Ford in 1976 and in 1980 was the second most Republican of all Missouri districts, after the 7th) but in statewide elections as well. In congressional elections until 1980, however, it elected a Democrat, Richard Ichord. His increasingly conservative record did not save him from political trouble here. He had the unique distinction in the House of having had a committee (the old House Un-American Activities Committee, which he renamed) abolished out from under him; it had never produced much legislation but had concentrated on sometimes spectacular investigations, and after the 1974 election it was abolished by a

parliamentary device engineered by Phillip Burton. Closer to home, Ichord was embarrassed by a Columbia newspaper series that suggested that he had few legislative accomplishments and could not handle crises well. Facing significant Republican opposition for the first time in years, Ichord was held to 60% of the vote; he decided to retire, at age 54, in 1980.

There were lively primaries in both parties in 1980. The winner in the Republican primary was Wendell Bailey, a homespun legislator from the southern end of the district, who ran an energetic campaign emphasizing national Republican themes on virtually all the issues and proudly mentioned his lack of Washington experience. The Democrat, St. Louis County state legislator Steve Gardner, had a tougher problem trying to balance a liberal base with the more conservative majority. Bailey won a convincing victory and lost only Columbia and the area around Fort Leonard Wood.

Bailey's main problem for 1982 is redistricting. Democrats have enough votes in the legislature to override Governor Christopher Bond's vetoes and so, theoretically at least, have control of the redistricting process. Missouri must lose one House seat. One obvious candidate for elimination, because of its geographical position and because it is now represented by a freshman Republican, is the 8th. Democrats Harold Volkmer of the 9th district and Ike Skelton of the 4th might want some of its Democratic counties in the north; Republicans Gene Taylor of the 7th and Bill Emerson of the 10th, although they do not wish to unseat Bailey, would like some of the Republican counties in the Ozarks and the old German areas along the Missouri River. The 8th is not the only candidate for elimination, and Bailey might end up with enough of his own district to run a strong race. But it is possible that this always oddly shaped district may vanish in the redistricting process.

Census Data   Pop. (1980 final) 563,716, up 21% in 1970s. Median family income, 1970, $7,743, 81% of U.S.

The Voters

Employment profile 1970   White collar, 46%. Blue collar, 37%. Service, 12%. Farm, 5%.
Ethnic groups   Black 1980, 4%. Hispanic 1980, 1%. Asian 1980, 1%. Total foreign stock 1970, 5%. Germany, 2%.

Presidential Vote

1980	Reagan (R)	129,726	(57%)
	Carter (D)	89,284	(39%)
	Anderson (I)	8,568	(4%)
1976	Ford (R)	105,449	(52%)
	Carter (D)	93,354	(46%)

Rep. Wendell Bailey (R) Elected 1980; b. July 31, 1940, Willow Springs; home, Willow Springs; S.W. Mo. St. U., B.S. 1962.

Career   Auto dealer, 1962–70; Mayor, City Cncl. Rep., Willow Springs, 1970–72; Mo. House of Reps., 1972–80.

Offices   504 CHOB, 202-225-5155. Also 105 W. High, Box 1806, Jefferson City 65102, 314-634-3331, and 1039 Kingshighway, Rolla 65401, 314-341-2520.

Committees   *Education and Labor* (14th). Subcommittees: Labor Standards; Postsecondary Education; Select Education.

Government Operations (15th). Subcommittees: Government Activities and Transportation; Government Information and Individual Rights.

Election Results

1980 general	Wendell Bailey (R)	127,675	(57%)	($254,341)
	Steve Gardner (D)	95,751	(43%)	($138,074)
1980 primary	Wendell Bailey (R)	17,741	(34%)	
	Paul Dietrich (R)	14,081	(27%)	($106,168)
	Larry R. Marshall (R)	10,017	(19%)	($73,516)
	Donald D. Meyer (R)	7,735	(15%)	($5,205)
	Two others (R)	3,089	(6%)	
1978 general	Richard H. Ichord (D)	96,509	(60%)	($120,482)
	Donald D. Meyer (R)	63,109	(40%)	($78,847)

NINTH DISTRICT

The part of rural Missouri that has most faithfuly sustained a Democratic tradition is not the southern part of the state; rather, it is the Little Dixie region, north of the Missouri River and across the Mississippi River from Illinois. The land here was settled early in the 19th century mainly by immigrants from Kentucky and Tennessee. During the Civil War some citizens of Little Dixie fought on the Confederate side, and at least one county declared itself independent of the unionist state of Missouri. Since then, not much urbanization has come to this part of Missouri—so little that Mark Twain would probably recognize his native Hannibal, one of Little Dixie's largest towns, were it not for the tourist traps that use Twain himself for bait. Nor have voting habits changed much. This part of the state continues to be more Democratic than Missouri as a whole. It gave Jimmy Carter a majority in 1976 (although not in 1980), and George McGovern even carried a county here.

Little Dixie was once a congressional district unto itself. Now, because of the one-person-one-vote requirement, the region has just a bare majority of the residents of Missouri's 9th congressional district. The rest of the 9th is the northern reaches of the St. Louis metropolitan area: fast-growing, increasingly Republican St. Charles County and a northern chunk of St. Louis County, which is predominantly blue collar and Democratic.

This district has had a succession of distinctive congressmen. For 40 years it was represented by Clarence Cannon, onetime parliamentarian of the House and chairman of the Appropriations Committee for two decades. During his last year he and his Senate counterpart, the late Carl Hayden, got into a monumental battle over which side of the Capitol should be the site of a conference meeting; this battle of octogenarians held up the whole federal budget for several months. Cannon's successor was William Hungate, a peppery and generally liberal Democrat who was one of the wittier members of the House Judiciary Committee. He retired young in 1976 to get away from the hassles of Congress to the pleasures of private law practice.

This was only the second time in 54 years that the 9th district had a race without an incumbent, and naturally there was considerable competition for the seat. Leading the eleven-candidate Democratic primary with 35% of the vote was Hannibal state legislator Harold Volkmer. In the old days, that would have been the end of it: a long congressional career would have ensued more or less automatically. But Volkmer has had serious competition from Republicans, in 1976 and again in 1980. Both times his opponents were based in the St. Louis area, and both times they held the Democrat close to even there. But his big margins in Little Dixie were enough to make the difference.

Volkmer could face more tough opposition in 1982, depending on the outcome of redistricting. What he would probably like is for the legislature to leave the boundaries of the 9th district alone — a possible outcome, since the district has gained population faster than the state average. But there will be a temptation to appropriate some of his Democratic precincts in St. Louis County to raise the population of the St. Louis-based districts that must expand. In that case, the best Volkmer could hope for would be the addition of Columbia to the district. A worse alternative, from his point of view, would be the addition of the St. Louis County suburbs now in the 8th district or the addition of the old German counties along the Missouri River — both areas heavily Republican.

Census Data   Pop. (1980 final) 553,948, up 18% in 1970s. Median family income, 1970, $9,573, 100% of U.S.

The Voters

  Employment profile 1970   White collar, 45%. Blue collar, 36%. Service, 11%. Farm, 8%.
  Ethnic groups   Black 1980, 4%. Hispanic 1980, 1%. Total foreign stock 1970, 5%. Germany, 2%.

Presidential Vote

1980	Reagan (R)	136,104	(55%)
	Carter (D)	100,392	(41%)
	Anderson (I)	7,930	(3%)
1976	Ford (R)	109,684	(50%)
	Carter (D)	108,189	(49%)

Rep. Harold L. Volkmer (D) Elected 1976; b. Apr. 4, 1931, Jefferson City; home, Hannibal; Jefferson City Jr. Col., St. Louis U., U. of Mo., LL.B. 1955.

Career Army, 1955–57; Practicing atty., 1957–60; Marion Co. Prosecuting Atty., 1960–66; Mo. House of Reps., 1967–77.

Offices 1007 LHOB, 202-225-2956. Also 316 Fed. Bldg., Hannibal 63401, 314-221-1200.

Committees *Agriculture* (22d). Subcommittees: Department Operations, Research and Foreign Agriculture; Livestock, Dairy and Poultry; Wheat, Soybeans and Feed Grains.

Science and Technology (15th). Subcommittees: Energy Development and Applications; Energy Research and Production; Investigations and Oversight.

Group Ratings

	ADA	COPE	PC	LCV	CFA	RPN	NAB	NSI	NTU	ACA	ACU
1980	39	58	47	39	36	—	42	30	29	29	26
1979	37	58	33	28	28	—	—	—	45	38	42
1978	45	65	53	40	36	25	75	40	28	54	33

Key Votes

1) Draft Registn $	FOR	6) Fair Hsg DOJ Enfrc	AGN	11) Cut Socl Incr Dfns $	AGN
2) Ban $ to Nicrgua	AGN	7) Lim PAC Contrbtns	AGN	12) Hosptl Cost Controls	AGN
3) Dlay MX Missile	AGN	8) Cap on Food Stmp $	AGN	13) Gasln Ctrls & Allctns	FOR
4) Nuclr Mortorium	AGN	9) New US Dep Edcatn	FOR	14) Lim Wndfll Prof Tax	AGN
5) Alaska Lands Bill	AGN	10) Cut OSHA $	AGN	15) Chryslr Loan Grntee	FOR

Election Results

1980 general	Harold L. Volkmer (D)	135,905	(56%)	($177,237)
	John W. Turner (R)	104,835	(44%)	($196,790)
1980 primary	Harold L. Volkmer (D)	73,258	(86%)	
	One other (D)	11,495	(14%)	
1978 general	Harold L. Volkmer (D)	135,170	(75%)	($101,375)
	Jerry Dent (R)	45,795	(25%)	

TENTH DISTRICT

The 10th congressional district of Missouri is roughly congruent with the southeastern corner of the state. The best-known part of the district is extreme southeastern Missouri, known commonly as the Bootheel. This part of the country was first settled by southerners coming up from Mississippi, looking for more fertile, moist, level land for growing cotton. They found it here, in the late 19th and early 20th centuries, and since then the Bootheel has had more of a Deep South feel to it than any other part of Missouri. The alluvial lands of the Bootheel have shifted mostly from cotton to soybeans in recent years, but the southern heritage still prevails. This is a basically Democratic part of Missouri: it contains the only county in the state that George Wallace carried in the 1968 general election, and it was carried solidly by Jimmy Carter both in 1976 and in 1980.

The rest of the district is somewhat different. The 10th goes westward to the Ozarks, although it does not reach to the really Republican counties here; its mountain areas are mostly Democratic. It reaches north also almost to St. Louis. The river counties here vary — Cape Girardeau is solidly Republican, St. Francois and Ste. Genevieve (pronounced with little hint of their French origin) are more evenly divided. One-quarter of the district's population is in Jefferson County, a portion of the St. Louis metropolitan area. This is one of those places within freeway commuting distance of the big city and its suburban factories that has retained much of its countrified air even as it has sprouted subdivisions filled with medium-sized tract houses or row-house condominiums. Jefferson County is ancestrally Democratic and it has attracted not the upper crust of St. Louis but a mixture of working-class and white collar people who find the ambience of a small southern town congenial. It retains a basic Democratic preference but can be converted; it went for Ronald Reagan over Jimmy Carter in 1980.

The 10th was the scene of the biggest upset in Missouri's congressional elections in 1980, the defeat of Democratic Congressman Bill Burlison by Republican challenger Bill Emerson. There was little in Burlison's outward statistics to suggest that he was vulnerable: he had been reelected with 65% of the vote in 1978, and he had never won with significantly less than that since 1972. He was, moreover, the second-ranking Democrat on the Agriculture Appropriations Subcommittee. Burlison was vulnerable in 1980 for two reasons. One was a personal scandal: he had appealed to the Postmaster General to abrogate the firing of a woman postal worker in the district, and her husband accused Burlison of having an affair with her. More important, Burlison had a record that was not far out of line with those of most northern Democrats. Many rural Missouri Democrats like to think of themselves as southern conservatives, but Burlison had ratings of about 50% from liberal and about 75% from labor organizations. Emerson, a native of the district, who had been a lobbyist in Washington, charged that Burlison was a sure vote for the Democratic leadership whenever needed, and he tried to link Burlison with national Democratic positions on government spending and benefits programs. Burlison evidently was unable to persuade the voters of this not very rich district that those programs were basically in their interest.

The result was no fluke: Emerson won a solid victory, losing only a few Bootheel and mountain counties and carrying Jefferson County solidly. Indeed, Emerson actually ran ahead of Ronald Reagan districtwide. He won a seat on the Agriculture Committee, always important to this area. The 10th will not likely be greatly altered by redistricting, and there is little that the Democratic legislature can do to make it more Democratic. Emerson, like many freshman Republicans, may find his fate hanging on the perceived success of the Reagan economic programs, but he has also shown the energy and initiative to suggest that he will use the advantages of incumbency to help make this Democratic-leaning area a safe Republican district.

Census Data   Pop. (1980 final) 555,049, up 19% in 1970s. Median family income, 1970, $7,048, 74% of U.S.

The Voters

   Employment profile 1970   White collar, 36%. Blue collar, 44%. Service, 13%. Farm, 7%.
   Ethnic groups   Black 1980, 4%. Hispanic 1980, 1%. Total foreign stock 1970, 2%.

Presidential Vote

1980	Reagan (R)	113,704	(53%)
	Carter (D)	95,288	(44%)
	Anderson (I)	4,561	(2%)
1976	Ford (R)	80,655	(43%)
	Carter (D)	108,223	(57%)

Rep. Bill Emerson (R) Elected 1980; b. Jan. 1, 1938, St. Louis; home, De Soto; Westminster Col., B.A. 1959, U. of Baltimore, LL.B. 1964.

Career   Air Force Reserve, 1964–; Spec. Asst. to U.S. Rep. Bob Ellsworth, Kans., 1961–67; Admin. Asst to U.S. Rep. Charles Mathias, 1968–69; Dir. of Govt. Relations, Fairchild Indust., 1970–74; Exec. Asst to Chmn. of Fed. Election Comm., 1975; Dir., Fed. Relations, TRW, Inc., 1976–79.

Offices   418 CHOB, 202-225-4404. Also 339 Broadway, Cape Girardeau 63701, 314-335-0101, and P.O. Box 242, Hillsboro 63050, 314-789-3561.

Committee   *Agriculture* (12th). Subcommittees: Cotton, Rice and Sugar; Department Operations, Research and Foreign Agriculture; Wheat, Soybeans and Feed Grains.

Group Ratings and Key Votes: Newly Elected

Election Results

1980 general	Bill Emerson (R)	116,167	(55%)	($282,494)
	Bill D. Burlison (D)	94,465	(45%)	($210,444)
1980 primary	Bill Emerson (R)	18,758	(77%)	
	James A. Weir (R)	5,573	(23%)	($0)
1978 general	Bill D. Burlison (D)	99,148	(65%)	($51,165)
	James A. Weir (R)	52,687	(35%)	

MONTANA

Montana is the nation's fourth largest state in area but only 44th in population. The name is not entirely accurate. There are indeed mountains, rugged chains of the Rockies, throughout the western half of the state; but eastern Montana is almost entirely a brown, treeless plain, rolling upward from the Missouri and Yellowstone Rivers undergirded, it turns out, by huge supplies of coal. Montana is the kind of place most Americans say they would like to live in. The state has no big cities—the largest metropolitan area, Billings, has little more than 100,000 people—and the opportunities for hunting, fishing, camping, and boating in unspoiled surroundings are plentiful, which means that wide open spaces abound: you can sometimes drive 40 miles down a road and not see another car. But life in Montana can also be physically harsh. During the winter the winds sweep down unimpeded from the Arctic, and snow is feet thick in the mountains; during the summer, the plains are often baked in heat unrelieved by rain.

Montana's first white settlers were the kind of men willing to go anywhere to get what they were after—they were miners—and they found large deposits of gold, silver, and copper in the mountains of Montana. Raucous mining towns sprang up, complete with outlaws and vigilantes. The largest such town, Butte, sitting on "the richest hill on earth," was for many years the state's largest city. Butte was known all over the country as a wild place, full of company goons and IWW organizers, a city with a Socialist mayor and with millionaires who bought and sold seats in the U.S. Senate. The early silver kings, Marcus Daly and William A. Clark, were also politicians and senators; their successors sold out to eastern interests who assembled all the state's mines into the Anaconda Corporation. Established by 1910, Anaconda exerted unparalleled power over the economic life of the state. It created the Montana Power Company to suit its needs. It bought up all of Montana's newspapers except the *Great Falls Tribune*. Even so, it did not win all its political battles. Montana elected many leading progressives, even in Anaconda's heyday, Republicans such as Joseph Dixon; Democrats such as Thomas Walsh (who exposed the Teapot Dome scandal); and young progressive Burton K. Wheeler. But Anaconda did see that it escaped significant state taxation and regulation. That increased Anaconda's profits; or as the company might also have said, it helped make its metal competitive in world markets and thus created more jobs and prosperity in Montana and the United States.

The old fights between Anaconda and the progressives cut across party lines, but the New Deal tended to organize the state's politics in a partisan manner. On the Republican side were Anaconda (although it became less interested in state politics when it bought copper mines in Chile), Montana Power, the Stockmen's Association of the eastern plains, and prosperous farmers of the Farm Bureau. On the Democratic side were most of the old progressives, labor unions (Montana has never passed a right to work law), small farmers groups such as the National Farmers' Union, and backers of New Deal programs (for a while in the 1930s Montana received more federal outlay per capita than almost any other state). Geographically, the eastern plains and Billings usually vote Republican and the western mountains and Butte, Great Falls, and Missoula usually go Democratic. The echoes of class warfare have grown dimmer over the years: Anaconda sold its newspapers in 1959 and in the

1970s was itself absorbed by Arco. But the divisions in politics here remain basically economic. Butte, now with less than half its 1920 population, and the town of Anaconda, about to become a ghost town as the mine shuts down and its real estate is rendered worthless, are still heavily Democratic; Billings, riding a local boom similar to those the Sun Belt cities enjoy, is heavily Republican.

In general Democrats have won the big elections here but seldom by very large margins. Montana has only once elected a Republican U.S. senator but came within a few percentage points of doing so half a dozen times. For 16 years it was represented by the Democratic pair of Mike Mansfield, the Senate majority leader for those 16 years, and Lee Metcalf, an old-fashioned liberal. Mansfield retired in 1976, and Metcalf died in early 1978, months before he was expected to retire also. Mansfield was always reelected with large margins; Metcalf always just squeaked by. The current senators, John Melcher and Max Baucus, have won impressive election victories in Montana. But in the increasingly conservative climate of the Rocky Mountain states, neither can be said to hold a safe seat.

John Melcher had the easier time. His succession to Mike Mansfield's seat was nearly automatic. A veterinarian and local officeholder, he had won the seat in the 2d district (the eastern, plains part of the state, including Great Falls and Billings) in a special election in 1969. The 2d is a vast expanse — the fourth largest district in the nation in area — where cattle ranches stretch as far as the eye can see and towering buttes rise over the magnificently eroded High Plains. This is the agricultural part of the state, and the part that has Montana's coal strip mines, but almost half its votes are cast in the two urban areas. Melcher became a strong vote-getter in this usually more Republican part of the state, and when Mansfield announced his retirement, Melcher found no serious opposition. The conservative Republican candidate was the beneficiary of much fund-raising by Jesse Helms and the like, but he was never able to translate his money into votes.

Melcher's committee assignments seem geared to the major day-to-day needs of the state. One is Agriculture; the plains here are wheat country, and Melcher has devoted much of his attention to wheat issues and to a related program, food stamps. The other is Energy and Natural Resources — what used to be known as the Interior Committee. This has always been a committee that westerners have sought, because it has jurisdiction over much that affects their communities: the vast amount of public lands in the western states, grazing and hunting rights on them, national parks and wilderness areas, Indian tribes, and — especially important to Montana these days — strip mining. On national issues, Melcher has been moving away from the national Democrats, as was apparent when he voted against the Panama Canal Treaties. On economic issues he still hews pretty closely to the Democratic line; on noneconomic issues he often parts company with his copartisans. Melcher must stand for reelection in 1982 and could face the most difficult race he has had in more than a decade. Republicans have by now won most of the Rocky Mountain Senate seats, and they know that the amount of money needed to run a respectable campaign here is, by national standards, very low. Meanwhile, Montana's receptivity to the message of the Republican right is suggested by Ronald Reagan's heavy 57%-32% victory over Jimmy Carter.

Another suggestion of the potential of Republican campaigns is the 1978 Senate race. By all odds the easy winner should have been the Democratic congressman from the 1st (western, mountain), Max Baucus — a young, attractive, hardworking public official with a proven vote-getting record. But Republican Larry Williams was able to make great headway with a saturation media campaign in September and October attacking Baucus for his attitudes on the Panama Canal Treaties and aid to Southeast Asia. Baucus's forces slowed Williams's momentum by printing an old promotion picture of the Republican, showing him with long curly hair and wearing love beads. Printed next to it was a picture of Baucus riding a bucking bronco. Baucus won with 55%. In the Senate he got committee assignments with national scope — Finance and Judiciary — as well as a seat on the more practical Environment and Public Works Committee. Health seems to be the area he has chosen for specialization. He is ranking Democrat on the Health Subcommittee on Finance, on which he takes special interest in rural health care delivery and long-term care, and on the Toxic Substances and Environmental Oversight Subcommittee of Environment. On the Trade Subcommittee he promotes North American trade, with Canada, Mexico, and the Caribbean; he is basically a free trader, interested in encouraging agricultural exports.

The 1st district seat that Baucus left behind is basically Democratic; Republicans have won it only four times since the 1920s. But from 1960 to 1972 it was the scene of constant close elections, largely because of the weakness of Arnold Olsen, a Democrat first elected in 1960 and defeated in 1970 and 1972. The district has some strong Democratic voting blocs: Butte, Anaconda, and their miners have been 2–1 Democratic for more than 50 years (although in 1900 they had 27% of the state's population and today they have only 6%); Missoula has become increasingly Democratic since students at the University of Montana got the vote; mining and Indian counties at various corners of the district produce Democratic majorities. The Republican strongholds — the new rich city of Kalispell, the state capital of Helena, the southwestern corner of the state near Yellowstone National Park and Chet Huntley's Big Sky development — are usually not enough to overcome the Democrats.

That was the case in 1978, when the seat was open and there was a spirited contest here. The Democratic nominee, state legislator Pat Williams, is close enough to organized labor that the state AFL–CIO director is godfather to one of his children. His Republican opponent, Jim Waltermire, surprised everyone by winning the primary over Tippy Huntley, the newscaster's widow, and proceeded to spend lots of money. But Waltermire was unable to break the Democratic strength in Missoula and Williams carried his hometown, usually Republican Helena. In 1980, in the face of a national Republican trend but against an eccentric Republican, Williams won reelection with 61%. He serves on the Interior Committee, of great importance to a district like this, and on Education and Labor, where he can be counted on to resist efforts to weaken the labor laws.

When Melcher ran for the Senate, the 2d district seat reverted to the normalcy of a Republican congressman. Ron Marlenee won with a convincing 55% over a strong Democratic opponent. Marlenee's record seems to be oriented more to district than to national concerns. He serves on the Agriculture and Interior Committees — the same assignments that Melcher has in the Senate. On farm programs he tends to support more generous payments to farmers than do many Republicans. His voting record generally follows Republican lines, but he is not one of the Rocky Mountain states' New Right conservatives.

Few people think that the actions of Montana state government or the policies of the governor of Montana are of much importance to the nation, and in most respects they are not. But the combination of a national energy problem and the presence of major coal deposits in Montana make certain state policies very important indeed. The key policy here is the 30% severance tax Montana places on coal — the highest such tax in the country. Officials in, of all places, Texas have complained bitterly that Montana is unfairly stripping consumer states of their wealth for its own greedy purposes. Naturally Montanans see it differently.

They argue that they are just getting back something they will need for land reclamation and other public purposes in return for giving up a depletable resource. If this appears to reverse Anaconda's old policy of avoiding state taxes, it is in one respect similar: the entity making the decision finds it in the public interest to keep more money for itself. Montana remains a state—one of the very few left—that sees as the centerpiece of its economy the exploitation of a nonrenewable resource.

The 30% severance tax was instituted under Governor Thomas Judge, a Democrat with a liberal reputation and a personality that did not, after two four-year terms, wear well. He was beaten in the 1980 Democratic primary by Lieutenant Governor Ted Schwinden, a folksy rancher with few enemies. The Republican candidate, Jack Ramirez, had one major issue going for him: he had pushed a tax cut through the legislature. But as a corporate lawyer from Billings (despite the name, he is blond and blue-eyed), Ramirez was vulnerable to attack as a city slicker and protector of moneyed interests. That kind of attack has not worked against other new-to-the-state, fresh-faced conservatives in the Rocky Mountain area (such as Senator Orrin Hatch of Utah), but it worked in Montana against Ramirez. Schwinden carried all but a few scattered counties and won with 55%. Democrats have now controlled the governorship since 1968, although Republicans control both houses of the legislature.

Congressional redistricting does not present much of a problem in Montana. The two districts are now close to the state population average, and the transfer of one of two small blocs of counties (either Liberty–Pondera–Toole or Park–Meagher) from the 1st to the 2d will even things out. Ironically, all these counties were removed from the 2d district and placed in the 1st ten years ago. Incidentally, Montana's districts, although they will remain among the nation's largest in area, will be the nation's smallest in population after the 1982 redistricting.

Census Data Pop. (1980 final) 786,690, up 13% in 1970s: 0.35% of U.S. total, 44th largest. Central city, 16%; suburban, 8%. Median 4-person family income, 1978, $17,878, 88% of U.S., 46th highest.

1979 Share of Federal Tax Burden $1,398,000,000; 0.31% of U.S. total, 46th largest.

1979 Share of Federal Outlays $1,753,966,000; 0.40% of U.S. total, 44th largest.

DOD	$193,434,000	47th	(0.18%)	HEW	$554,168,000	43d	(0.31%)
DOE	$41,747,000	27th	(0.35%)	ERDA	$654,000	46th	(0.02%)
HUD	$18,659,000	44th	(0.28%)	NASA	$3,000	50th	(0.00%)
VA	$77,307,000	43d	(0.37%)	DOT	$79,217,000	42d	(0.48%)
EPA	$22,371,000	47th	(0.42%)	DOC	$15,396,000	34th	(0.49%)
DOI	$128,925,000	13th	(2.32%)	USDA	$361,605,000	30th	(1.50%)

Economic Base Agriculture, notably cattle, wheat, barley, and dairy products; finance, insurance, and real estate; lumber and wood products, especially sawmills and planing mills; primary nonferrous metals, and other primary metal industries; food and kindred products; metal mining.

Political Lineup Governor, Ted Schwinden (D). Senators, John Melcher (D) and Max Baucus (D). Representatives, 2 (1 D and 1 R); 2 in 1982. State Senate, 50 (28 R and 22 D); State House of Representatives, 100 (57 R and 43 D).

The Voters

Registration 496,402 Total. No party registration.
Employment profile 1970 White collar, 45%. Blue collar, 28%. Service, 15%. Farm, 12%.
Ethnic groups Hispanic 1980, 1%. Am. Ind. 1980, 5%. Total foreign stock 1970, 17%.

Presidential Vote

1980	Reagan (R)	206,814	(57%)
	Carter (D)	118,032	(32%)
	Anderson (I)	29,281	(8%)

1976	Ford (R)	173,703	(53%)
	Carter (D)	149,259	(45%)

1980 Democratic Presidential Primary			*1980 Republican Presidential Primary*		
Carter	66,922	(51%)	Reagan	68,744	(87%)
Kennedy	47,671	(37%)	Bush	7,665	(10%)
No preference	15,466	(12%)	No preference	3,014	(4%)

SENATORS

Sen. John Melcher (D) Elected 1976, seat up 1982; b. Sept. 6, 1924, Sioux City, Ia.; home, Forsyth; U. of Minn., 1942–43, Ia. St. U., D.V.M., 1950.

Career Army, WWII; Veterinarian, 1950–69; Forsyth City Cncl., 1953–55, Mayor, 1955–61; Mont. House of Reps., 1961–63, 1969; Mont. Senate, 1963–67; U.S. House of Reps., 1969–77.

Offices 253 RSOB, 202-224-2644. Also 1016 Fed. Bldg., Billings 59102, 406-657-6644, and 12 6th St. South, Great Falls 59401, 406-452-9585.

Committees *Agriculture, Nutrition and Forestry* (4th). Subcommittees: Agricultural Production, Marketing, and Stabilization of Prices; Nutrition; Forestry, Water Resources, and Environment.

Energy and Natural Resources (7th). Subcommittees: Energy Regulation; Water and Power; Public Lands and Reserved Water.

Select Committee on Indian Affairs (Ranking Member).

Special Committee on Aging (3d).

Group Ratings

	ADA	COPE	PC	LCV	CFA	RPN	NAB	NSI	NTU	ACA	ACU
1980	50	88	47	44	47	—	33	50	25	13	21
1979	58	89	43	—	29	—	—	—	21	15	25
1978	45	63	58	51	40	25	17	50	13	39	26

Key Votes

1) Draft Registn $	AGN	6) Fair Housng Cloture	FOR	11) Cut Socl Incr Defns	AGN
2) Ban $ to Nicrgua	—	7) Ban $ Rape Abortns	FOR	12) Income Tax Indexing	AGN
3) Dlay MX Missile	AGN	8) Cap on Food Stmp $	AGN	13) Lim Spdg 21% GNP	AGN
4) Nuclr Mortorium	FOR	9) New US Dep Edcatn	FOR	14) Incr Wndfll Prof Tax	AGN
5) Alaska Lands Bill	AGN	10) Cut OSHA Inspctns	—	15) Chryslr Loan Grntee	FOR

Election Results

1976 general	John Melcher (D)	206,232	(64%)	($311,101)
	Stanley C. Burger (R)	115,213	(36%)	($563,543)
1976 primary	John Melcher (D)	89,413	(89%)	
	One other (D)	11,593	(11%)	
1970 general	Mike Mansfield (D)	150,060	(61%)	
	Harold E. Wallace (R)	97,809	(39%)	

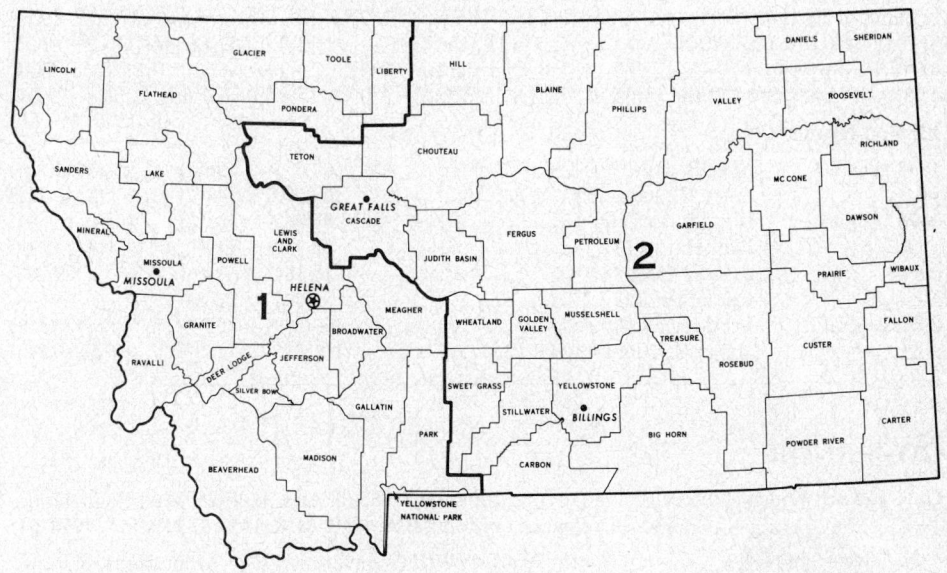

Sen. **Max Baucus** (D) Elected 1978, seat up 1984; b. Dec. 11, 1941, Helena; home, Missoula; Stanford U., B.A. 1964, LL.B. 1967.

Career Staff Atty., Civil Aeronautics Bd., 1967–68; Legal Staff, Securities and Exchange Comm., 1969–71, Legal Asst. to the Chmn., 1970–71; Practicing atty., 1971–75; Mont. House of Reps., 1973–75; U.S. House of Reps., 1975–78.

Offices 1107 DSOB, 202-224-2651. Also Fed. Bldg., Helena 59601, 406-443-4041.

Committees *Environment and Public Works* (7th). Subcommittees: Water Resources; Nuclear Regulation.

Finance (6th). Subcommittees: Health; International Trade; Oversight of the Internal Revenue Service.

Judiciary (7th). Subcommittees: Agency Administration; Courts; Separation of Power.

Select Committee on Small Business (5th). Subcommittee: Productivity and Competition.

Group Ratings

	ADA	COPE	PC	LCV	CFA	RPN	NAB	NSI	NTU	ACA	ACU
1980	72	82	63	78	60	—	25	10	29	16	0
1979	63	89	49	—	52	—	—	—	23	12	9
1978	40	79	68	52	50	55	17	40	18	35	17

Key Votes

1) Draft Registn $	FOR	6) Fair Housng Cloture	FOR	11) Cut Socl Incr Defns	AGN
2) Ban $ to Nicrgua	—	7) Ban $ Rape Abortns	AGN	12) Income Tax Indexing	AGN
3) Dlay MX Missile	AGN	8) Cap on Food Stmp $	—	13) Lim Spdg 21% GNP	AGN
4) Nuclr Mortorium	—	9) New US Dep Edcatn	FOR	14) Incr Wndfll Prof Tax	FOR
5) Alaska Lands Bill	FOR	10) Cut OSHA Inspctns	AGN	15) Chryslr Loan Grntee	FOR

Election Results

1978 general	Max Baucus (D)	160,353	(56%)	($653,756)
	Larry Williams (R)	127,589	(44%)	($346,721)
1978 primary	Max Baucus (D)	87,085	(65%)	
	Paul Hatfield (D)	25,789	(19%)	($124,412)
	John Driscoll (D)	18,184	(14%)	($29,720)
	One other (D)	2,404	(2%)	
1972 general	Lee Metcalf (D)	163,609	(52%)	($136,551)
	Henry S. Hibbard (R)...........	151,316	(48%)	($286,748)

GOVERNOR

Gov. Ted Schwinden (D) Elected 1980, term expires Jan. 1985; b. Aug. 31, 1925, Wolf Point; home, Helena; U. of Mont., B.A. 1949, M.A. 1950, U. of Minn., 1950–54.

Career Army, WWII; Grain farmer 1954–; Mont. House of Reps., 1958; Mont. Legis. Cncl., 1959–61, Commissioner of State Lands, 1969–76; Lt. Gov. of Mont., 1976–80.

Offices State Capitol, Office of the Governor, Helena 59601, 406-449-3111.

Election Results

1980 gen.	Ted Schwinden (D)	199,574	(55%)
	Jack Ramirez (R)	160,892	(45%)
1980 prim.	Ted Schwinden (D)	69,051	(51%)
	Thomas L. Judge (D)......	57,946	(42%)
	Two others (D)	9,367	(7%)
1976 gen.	Thomas L. Judge (D)......	195,420	(62%)
	Bob Woodahl (R).........	115,848	(37%)

FIRST DISTRICT

Census Data   Pop. (1980 final) 410,071, up 18% in 1970s. Median family income, 1970, $8,576, 89% of U.S.

The Voters

Employment profile 1970   White collar, 46%. Blue collar, 31%. Service, 15%. Farm, 8%.
Ethnic groups   Hispanic 1980, 1%. Am. Ind. 1980, 3%. Total foreign stock 1970, 16%.

Presidential Vote

1980	Reagan (R)	107,574	(55%)
	Carter (D)	64,393	(33%)
	Anderson (I)	16,316	(8%)
1976	Ford (R)	90,124	(53%)
	Carter (D)	77,885	(46%)

Rep. Pat Williams (D) Elected 1978; b. Oct. 30, 1937, Helena; home, Helena; U. of Mont., Wm. Jewell Col., U. of Denver, B.S. 1961, W. Mont. Col.

Career Public school teacher; Mont. House of Reps., 1966–68; Exec. Asst. to U.S. Rep. John Melcher, 1968–71; Mont. State Coord., Family Educ. Program, 1971–78.

Offices 1512 LHOB, 202-225-3211. Also 306 Steamboat Block, 616 Helena Ave., Helena 59601, 406-443-7878.

Committees *Education and Labor* (16th). Subcommittees: Elementary, Secondary and Vocational Education; Human Resources; Labor Standards.

Interior and Insular Affairs (21st). Subcommittees: Energy and the Environment; Public Lands and National Parks.

Group Ratings

	ADA	COPE	PC	LCV	CFA	RPN	NAB	NSI	NTU	ACA	ACU
1980	72	67	50	78	50	—	17	38	18	18	19
1979	79	80	68	65	67	—	—	—	26	25	26

Key Votes

1) Draft Registn $	FOR	6) Fair Hsg DOJ Enfrc	—	11) Cut Socl Incr Dfns $	AGN
2) Ban $ to Nicrgua	AGN	7) Lim PAC Contrbtns	FOR	12) Hosptl Cost Controls	FOR
3) Dlay MX Missile	FOR	8) Cap on Food Stmp $	AGN	13) Gasln Ctrls & Allctns	FOR
4) Nuclr Mortorium	FOR	9) New US Dep Edcatn	AGN	14) Lim Wndfll Prof Tax	AGN
5) Alaska Lands Bill	FOR	10) Cut OSHA $	AGN	15) Chryslr Loan Grntee	FOR

Election Results

1980 general	Pat Williams (D)	112,866	(61%)	($144,030)
	John K. McDonald (R)	70,874	(39%)	($35,717)
1980 primary	Pat Williams (D)	56,532	(75%)	
	Bill Hand (D)	18,620	(25%)	($38,372)
1978 general	Pat Williams (D)	86,016	(57%)	($177,536)
	Jim Waltermire (R)	64,093	(43%)	($241,888)

SECOND DISTRICT

Census Data Pop. (1980 final) 376,619, up 9% in 1970s. Median family income, 1970, $8,436, 88% of U.S.

The Voters

Employment profile 1970 White collar, 45%. Blue collar, 25%. Service, 14%. Farm, 16%.
Ethnic groups Hispanic 1980, 2%. Am. Ind. 1980, 6%. Total foreign stock 1970, 19%.

Presidential Vote

1980	Reagan (R)	99,240	(59%)
	Carter (D)	53,639	(32%)
	Anderson (I)	12,965	(8%)
1976	Ford (R)	83,579	(53%)
	Carter (D)	71,374	(45%)

Rep. Ron Marlenee (R) Elected 1976; b. Aug. 8, 1935, Scobey; home, Scobey; Mont. St. U., U. of Mont., Reisch Sch. of Auctioneering.

Career Farmer, rancher, and businessman.

Offices 409 CHOB, 202-225-1555. Also Fed. Bldg., 310 N. 26th St., Billings 59101, 406-585-6753.

Committees *Agriculture* (6th). Subcommittees: Forests, Family Farms and Energy; Wheat, Soybeans and Feed Grains.

Interior and Insular Affairs (6th). Subcommittees: Oversight and Investigations; Public Lands and National Parks.

Group Ratings

	ADA	COPE	PC	LCV	CFA	RPN	NAB	NSI	NTU	ACA	ACU
1980	22	32	23	41	14	—	100	100	56	83	18
1979	21	32	28	36	22	—	—	—	56	92	73
1978	25	26	28	42	27	50	91	78	24	85	78

Key Votes

1) Draft Registn $	FOR	6) Fair Hsg DOJ Enfrc	AGN	11) Cut Socl Incr Dfns $	FOR
2) Ban $ to Nicrgua	FOR	7) Lim PAC Contrbtns	FOR	12) Hosptl Cost Controls	AGN
3) Dlay MX Missile	AGN	8) Cap on Food Stmp $	FOR	13) Gasln Ctrls & Allctns	FOR
4) Nuclr Mortorium	FOR	9) New US Dep Edcatn	AGN	14) Lim Wndfll Prof Tax	FOR
5) Alaska Lands Bill	AGN	10) Cut OSHA $	FOR	15) Chryslr Loan Grntee	FOR

Election Results

1980 general	Ron Marlenee (R)	91,431	(59%)	($214,917)
	Thomas G. Monahan (D)	63,370	(41%)	($36,699)
1980 primary	Ron Marlenee (R)	31,146	(100%)	
1978 general	Ron Marlenee (R)	75,766	(57%)	($286,863)
	Thomas G. Monahan (D)	57,480	(43%)	($27,019)

NEBRASKA

Nebraska is a state that sprang suddenly into existence and has changed rather little in the years since. Its beginnings were in the great land rush of the 1880s, when nearly half a million people, most of them from the Republican Midwest, surged into Nebraska. At the beginning of that decade Nebraska had a population of 452,000; in 1890 it reached 1,062,000 — not far below the 1980 figure of 1,570,000. In the 1880s the patterns of Nebraska life became clear. Most of the state was devoted to farming: corn and hogs to the east, dry-land wheat farming and cattle grazing to the west. Omaha became a major regional center in the 1880s, and Lincoln was established as the state capital. No other major urban centers developed then or exist now.

Many of the people who first settled Nebraska assumed that it would grow as did the major states to the east, such as Missouri, Illinois, and Iowa. They thought that Nebraska county seats would become major manufacturing centers and that small Nebraska towns would become rivals of St. Louis or Chicago or Cleveland. After all, Chicago itself had grown from nothing to become one of the largest cities in the world in just 20 or 30 years. If that were to happen in Nebraska, land values would rise, many original settlers would get rich, and there would be plenty of work close to home for their children. But Nebraska did not become another Illinois. The 1880s were a time of plentiful rain here; the 1890s were a decade of drought. Nebraska stopped growing: many counties and Omaha itself lost population. More catastrophic for the Nebraskans of the day was that it became obvious that Nebraska's economy would never support all the children of the people who lived there. Most of Nebraska's settlers, like most migrants into most states were young people, optimistic and motivated, in search of opportunity, and with families full of children. Fully 48% of the one million Nebraskans of 1890 were children; a very large percentage of them moved elsewhere when they grew up. Since 1890, Nebraska has been a state that has exported people, to the west and to the great metropolitan areas of the Midwest and, more recently, to Texas. As a result, its population today and for years now has been disproportionately elderly (another reason is that Nebraskans tend to live longer than most Americans). Another result: many of the most talented people who grew up here have left, including President Kennedy's top assistant Theodore Sorenson and entertainer Johnny Carson.

It was the sudden boom of the 1880s and bust of the 1890s that produced the most colorful —and atypical—politics of Nebraska's history, the populist movement and William Jennings Bryan. Nebraska's settlers were mostly from Republican backgrounds, and for the most part this has been one of the most Republican of states. Yet the only serious presidential contender it produced was Bryan, "the silver-tongued orator of the Platte," a man considered a radical in his time—so much so that the incumbent Democratic president refused to support him. Bryan was only 36 when he delivered the famous Cross of Gold speech to the 1896 Democratic Convention, the speech that won him the party's nomination and helped him come close to the White House. Nebraskans supported Bryan, whose program may have been forward-looking, but whose purpose was essentially retrograde: to restore Nebraska to the prosperity and hopes it had had a decade before. Bryan won the Democratic nomination again in 1900 and 1908 but never came as close to winning as he did the first time. By then, Nebraska had already moved back to the Republicans, and Bryan himself eventually moved to Florida. Since Bryan's time, Nebraska's most notable lapse from conservatism was the career of George Norris, congressman (1903–13) and senator (1913–43). During the progressive era, Norris led the House rebellion against Speaker Joseph Cannon; during the 1930s he pushed through the Norris–LaGuardia Anti-Injunction Act, the first national pro-union legislation, and the Tennessee Valley Authority.

Since 1900 92% of Nebraska's population growth has been in and around Omaha and Lincoln; between them they now contain 43% of the state's people. Most of the immigrants to Omaha, a railroad, meatpacking, and manufacturing center, and Lincoln, the state capital and home of the University of Nebraska, come from the rural, Republican hinterland. There is also a sizable Eastern European community on the south side of Omaha which, like the city's small black neighborhood, usually votes Democratic; so too do a few isolated rural counties. But as a whole Nebraska is almost always solidly Republican in national elections. In the close elections of 1960, 1968, and 1976, the Republican nominee carried both big cities and lost only three or four counties out of 93; in 1980, Ronald Reagan carried every county, and some by enormous margins (e.g., 481 to 33).

Yet Nebraska today, for the first time in its history, has two Democratic U.S. senators. This has resulted not so much from a major shift in opinion as from special local circumstances. In 1975 the state had two Republican senators with more than 20 years of seniority and records of great party loyalty, Roman Hruska and Carl Curtis. Both had turned 70, and both had nearly lost their last elections. Hruska will be remembered by history for his argument, made in defense of the nomination of Judge Carswell, that mediocre people deserve representation on the Supreme Court. Curtis will be remembered for scurrying around to the morning interview programs after Richard Nixon released the June 23 tape transcript and asserting continued faith in the president. Obviously both were going to retire and in the normal course of things might have been replaced by the Republican congressmen from Omaha and the outstate areas — a geographical distribution that had become a Nebraska pattern. But in neither case did the succession go according to plan.

The problem in 1976 was that the state's Republicans preferred Omaha Congressman John McCollister to Omaha Mayor Edward Zorinsky, and Zorinsky refused to go along. But instead of running against McCollister in the Republican primary, he ran as a Democrat, beat the Democratic state chairman in the primary, and then beat the congressman in the general. Throughout, Zorinsky's views remained more Republican than Democratic and have ever since. He has always been a fiscal conservative; he advocated a free market in agriculture; he voted against the Panama Canal Treaties. Before the 1980 election there was talk that Zorinsky would switch to the Republicans if his vote made the difference between Republican and Democratic organization of the Senate; the point became moot when the Republicans won enough seats to control the Senate without him.

Zorinsky remains something of a wild card in the Senate, however, and in Nebraska. There was talk that he might run for reelection in 1982 as a Republican, which is after all the preferred party identification in Nebraska; but Republican leaders seemed no more welcoming in 1981 than in 1976. Most likely he will run as a Democrat, which means he is likely to get a good fight for the seat. Among the possible contenders: Governor Charles Thone, who himself spent four terms in the House; Representative Douglas Bereuter, from the Lincoln district; and freshman Representative Hal Daub, from Omaha.

The way the other seat came to be Democratic is a different story. Here it was the strength of the Democratic candidate, Goveror James Exon, that was decisive. The best candidate the Republicans could produce in 1978 was Donald Shasteen, a longtime aide to Curtis, who made some harsh charges against Exon. But Exon had solid popularity. He had first campaigned for the governorship in 1970 on a cut-spending program, and he had been reelected easily in 1974. In 1978 Exon carried 92 of 93 counties and 68% of the vote. In the Senate Exon is closer to the Democratic position on issues than Zorinsky but not as close as most other midwestern Democrats, most of whom have less Republican constituencies. Although not a power, Exon is regarded as solid and workmanlike. His strong home state standing apparently leaves him comfortable with committee assignments of national scope: Armed Services, Commerce, Budget. Few people doubt that he can win reelection easily in 1984.

Nebraska's Governor, Charles Thone, was elected in 1978 and restored the office to Republican hands; oddly, it had been held by Democrats for all but four of the preceding 20 years. Thone's victory was not overwhelming, but in office he has managed to avoid major controversies at a time when Nebraska is doing somewhat better economically than it has been accustomed to (and better economically than more industrial midwestern states). Under these circumstances, it seems likely he can win a second term.

Nebraska has a presidential primary that, on occasion, has attracted some attention. It comes in early May, after the run of major primaries in March and April and a month before the big state primaries of June. Curiously, it has been the Democrats who have livened things up here, although this is one of the very few states that has more registered Republicans than Democrats. In 1976 Idaho Senator Frank Church started his campaign here and described himself as a westerner, an opponent of gun control laws, as well as an opponent of the Vietnam war. His victory over Jimmy Carter made Church, for a while, a significant candidate. In 1968 another Democrat generally known as a liberal, Robert Kennedy, did well in this generally conservative state; his defeat of Eugene McCarthy here kept his campaign going. And in 1980 Edward Kennedy lost to Jimmy Carter, but by a relatively narrow 47%–38% margin.

Census Data   Pop. (1980 final) 1,570,006, up 6% in 1970s: 0.69% of U.S. total, 35th largest. Central city, 31%; suburban, 13%. Median 4-person family income, 1978, $19,319, 95% of U.S., 35th highest.

1979 Share of Federal Tax Burden $3,066,000,000; 0.68% of U.S. total, 35th largest.

1979 Share of Federal Outlays $3,310,602,000; 0.71% of U.S. total, 37th largest.

DOD	$442,995,000	39th	(0.42%)	HEW	$1,161,387,000	36th	(0.65%)
DOE	$1,070,000	50th	(0.01%)	ERDA	$341,000	49th	(0.01%)
HUD	$32,512,000	39th	(0.49%)	NASA	$144,000	46th	(0.00%)
VA	$153,303,000	36th	(0.74%)	DOT	$100,811,000	40th	(0.61%)
EPA	$17,175,000	49th	(0.32%)	DOC	$5,923,000	49th	(0.19%)
DOI	$29,244,000	40th	(0.53%)	USDA	$862,887,000	5th	(3.59%)

Economic Base   Agriculture, notably cattle, corn, hogs, and wheat; finance, insurance, and real estate; food and kindred products, especially meat products; electrical equipment and supplies; machinery, especially farm machinery; printing and publishing, especially newspapers; fabricated metal products, especially structural metal products.

Political Lineup   Governor, Charles Thone (R). Senators, Edward Zorinsky (D) and J. James Exon (D). Representatives, 3 R; 3 in 1982. Unicameral Legislature, 49 (33 R and 16 D).

The Voters

Registration   856,182 Total. 376,534 D (44%); 424,963 R (50%); 54,471 I (6%); 214 Libertarian (0%).

Employment profile 1970   White collar, 45%. Blue collar, 28%. Service, 14%. Farm, 13%.

Ethnic groups   Black 1980, 3%. Hispanic 1980, 2%. Am. Ind. 1980, 1%. Total foreign stock 1970, 14%. Germany, 4%.

Presidential Vote

1980	Reagan (R)	419,214	(66%)
	Carter (D)	166,424	(26%)
	Anderson (I)	44,854	(7%)
1976	Ford (R)	359,705	(59%)
	Carter (D)	233,692	(38%)

1980 Democratic Presidential Primary			1980 Republican Presidential Primary		
Carter	72,120	(47%)	Reagan	155,995	(76%)
Kennedy	57,826	(38%)	Bush	31,380	(15%)
Two others & write-ins	7,894	(5%)	Anderson	11,879	(6%)
Uncommitted	16,041	(10%)	Four others & write-ins	5,949	(3%)

SENATORS

Sen. Edward Zorinsky (D) Elected 1976, seat up 1982; b. Nov. 11, 1928, Omaha; home, Omaha; U. of Neb., B.A., Notre Dame U., Harvard U.

Career Tobacco wholesaler; Omaha Pub. Power District, 1969–73; Mayor of Omaha, 1973–77, elected as Repub., switched to Dem. Party, Dec. 1975.

Offices 431 RSOB, 202-224-6551. Also 8311 Fed. Bldg., Omaha 68102, 402-221-4381.

Committees *Agriculture, Nutrition, and Forestry* (3d). Subcommittees: Agricultural Credit and Rural Electrification; Agricultural Production, Marketing, and Stabilization of Prices; Foreign Agricultural Policy.

Foreign Relations (5th). Subcommittees: Arms Control, Oceans and International Operations, and Environment; European Affairs; Western Hemisphere Affairs.

Group Ratings

	ADA	COPE	PC	LCV	CFA	RPN	NAB	NSI	NTU	ACA	ACU
1980	22	31	30	33	13	—	100	60	56	62	70
1979	21	37	32	—	33	—	—	—	59	63	64
1978	25	16	38	51	45	40	58	80	29	74	78

Key Votes

1) Draft Registn $	FOR	6) Fair Housng Cloture	AGN	11) Cut Socl Incr Defns	FOR
2) Ban $ to Nicrgua	FOR	7) Ban $ Rape Abortns	FOR	12) Income Tax Indexing	FOR
3) Dlay MX Missile	AGN	8) Cap on Food Stmp $	FOR	13) Lim Spdg 21% GNP	FOR
4) Nuclr Mortorium	AGN	9) New US Dep Edcatn	FOR	14) Incr Wndfll Prof Tax	AGN
5) Alaska Lands Bill	FOR	10) Cut OSHA Inspctns	FOR	15) Chryslr Loan Grntee	AGN

Election Results

1976 general	Edward Zorinsky (D)	313,805	(53%)	($237,613)
	John Y. McCollister (R)	279,284	(47%)	($391,287)
1976 primary	Edward Zorinsky (D)	79,988	(49%)	
	Hess Dyas (D)	77,384	(47%)	
	One other (D)	7,194	(4%)	
1970 general	Roman L. Hruska (R)	240,894	(52%)	
	Frank B. Morrison (D)..........	217,681	(47%)	

Sen. J. James Exon (D) Elected 1978, seat up 1984; b. Aug. 9, 1921, Geddes, S.D.; home, Lincoln; U. of Omaha.

Career Army, WWII; Branch Mgr., Universal Finance Co., 1946–54; Pres., Exon's Inc., office equip. business, 1954–70; Vice Chmn., Neb. St. Central Comm., 1964–68; Gov. of Neb., 1970–78.

Offices 3313 DSOB, 202-224-4224. Also Fed. Bldg., Omaha 68102, 402-221-4665.

Committees *Armed Services* (7th). Subcommittees: Military Construction; Strategic and Theatre Nuclear Forces; Manpower and Personnel.

Budget (10th).

Commerce, Science, and Transportation (7th). Subcommittees: Aviation; Business, Trade, and Tourism.

Group Ratings

	ADA	COPE	PC	LCV	CFA	RPN	NAB	NSI	NTU	ACA	ACU
1980	39	37	43	33	20	—	73	60	57	44	58
1979	21	37	43	—	33	—	—	—	42	39	41

Key Votes

1) Draft Registn $	FOR	6) Fair Housng Cloture	AGN	11) Cut Socl Incr Defns	FOR
2) Ban $ to Nicrgua	AGN	7) Ban $ Rape Abortns	FOR	12) Income Tax Indexing	AGN
3) Dlay MX Missile	AGN	8) Cap on Food Stmp $	FOR	13) Lim Spdg 21% GNP	AGN
4) Nuclr Mortorium	AGN	9) New US Dep Edcatn	AGN	14) Incr Wndfll Prof Tax	FOR
5) Alaska Lands Bill	FOR	10) Cut OSHA Inspctns	FOR	15) Chryslr Loan Grntee	AGN

Election Results

1978 general	J. James Exon (D)	334,096	(68%)	($234,862)
	Don Shasteen (R)	159,706	(32%)	($218,148)
1978 primary	J. James Exon (D), unopposed			
1972 general	Carl T. Curtis (R)	301,841	(53%)	($250,392)
	Terry Carpenter (D)	265,922	(47%)	($38,629)

GOVERNOR

Gov. Charles Thone (R) Elected 1978, term expires 1983; b. Jan. 4, 1924, Hartington; U. of. Neb., J.D. 1950.

Career Army, WWII; Dpty. Secy. of State of Neb., 1950–51; Asst. Atty. Gen. of Neb., 1951–52; Asst. U.S. Dist. Atty., Lincoln Ofc., 1952–54; Admin. Asst. to U.S. Sen. Roman L. Hruska, 1954–59; Practicing atty., 1959–71; U.S. House of Reps., 1971–79.

Offices State Capitol, Lincoln 68509, 402-471-2224.

Election Results

1978 gen.	Charles Thone (R)	275,473	(56%)
	Gerald T. Whelan (D)	216,754	(44%)
1978 prim.	Charles Thone (R)	89,378	(45%)
	Robert A. Phares (R)......	48,402	(25%)
	Stan Juelfs (R)	43,828	(22%)
	Two others (R)	15,546	(8%)
1974 gen.	J. James Exon (D)	267,012	(59%)
	Richard D. Marvel (R)	159,780	(35%)
	Ernest Chambers (I)	24,320	(5%)

FIRST DISTRICT

The 1st congressional district of Nebraska is a band of 27 counties in the eastern part of the state. Outside of Lincoln, the district's largest city, the economy of the 1st is based almost entirely on agriculture. The political inclination of the region is Republican, of course, but there are a couple of counties with large German Catholic communities that have faithfully supported Democrats of such diverse origin as John Kennedy and Jimmy Carter (in 1976, but not 1980). Lincoln, the capital and — more important to people here — home of the University of Nebraska Cornhuskers, is traditionally Republican. The city's large number of state employees have sometimes joined members of the university community to swing Lincoln into the Democratic column. But on a number of occasions Lincoln, with all its state

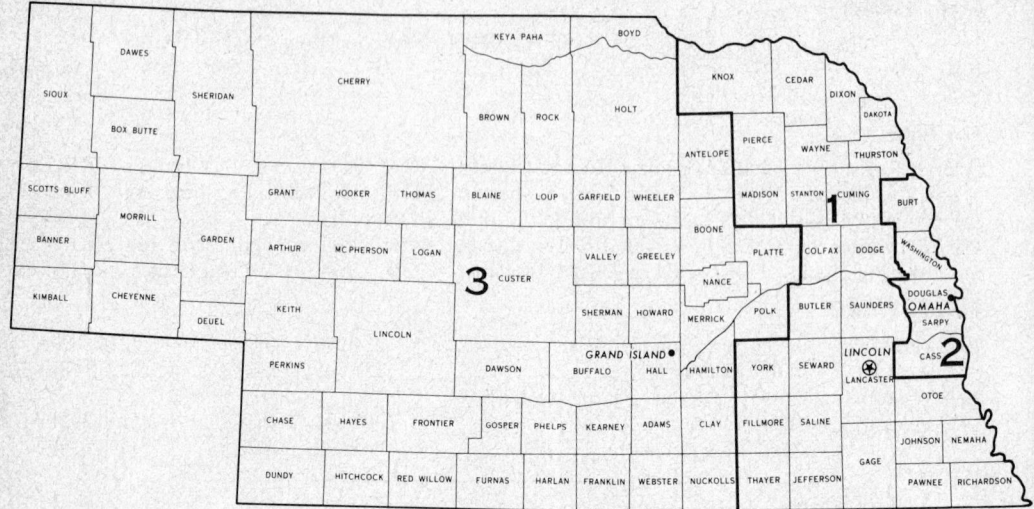

government employees, seems to have preferred Republicans to economy-minded Demo-crats. In 1970 this was one of the few parts of the state that did not favor Governor James Exon, and in 1978 it gave a solid margin to Charles Thone over Exon's Lieutenant Gover-nor, Gerald Whalen.

The 1st district saw a number of close congressional elections in the 1960s and 1970s but seems unlikely to have many in the 1980s. A Democrat actually captured the district in 1964 and came close to winning in 1966 and 1968; that Democrat ran as an Independent in 1970 and split the Democratic vote, helping to elect Thone. There was a close race again in 1974 and in 1978 when Thone stepped down to run for governor. The Democrat was state party chairman Hess Dyas, the Republican Douglas Bereuter, a top appointee of a Republican governor whose tax policies helped elect Exon in 1970. Bereuter, with the reputation of a thoughtful moderate, won in 1978 with an impressive 58%. In 1980 he won with a near-unanimous 79%. As a member of what is still the minority party in the House, Bereuter is not likely to play a major legislative role immediately. But he has a safe seat and excellent prospects for statewide office.

The 1980 census, incidentally, requires very little fiddling with Nebraska's House district boundaries and should have no political impact on its congressional delegation.

Census Data   Pop. (1980 final) 525,386, up 6% in 1970s. Median family income, 1970, $8,203, 86% of U.S.

The Voters

Employment profile 1970   White collar, 43%. Blue collar, 27%. Service, 15%. Farm, 15%.
Ethnic groups   Black 1980, 1%. Hispanic 1980, 1%. Am. Ind. 1980, 1%. Total foreign stock 1970, 14%. Germany, 6%.

Presidential Vote

1980	Reagan (R)	133,971	(63%)
	Carter (D)	59,729	(28%)
	Anderson (I)	17,612	(8%)
1976	Ford (R)	116,030	(57%)
	Carter (D)	81,590	(40%)

Rep. Douglas K. (Doug) **Bereuter** (R) Elected 1978; b. Oct. 6, 1939, York; home, Utica; U. of Neb., B.A. 1961, Harvard U., M.C.P. 1963, M.P.A. 1973.

Career Army, 1963–65; Residential and commercial development consultant; Neb. Legislature, 1975–78; Chmn., Urban Development Comm., Natl. Conf. of State Legislatures, 1977–78.

Offices 1314 LHOB, 202-225-4806. Also 1045 K St., Lincoln 68501, 402-471-5400.

Committees *Banking, Finance and Urban Affairs* (19th). Subcommittees: Economic Stabilization; General Oversight and Renegotiation; Housing and Community Development.

Interior and Insular Affairs (9th). Subcommittees: Energy and the Environment; Insular Affairs; Water and Power Resources.

Small Business (8th). Subcommittees: Energy, Environment and Safety Issues Affecting Small Business; General Oversight.

Select Committee on Aging (13th). Subcommittee: Housing and Consumer Interests.

Group Ratings

	ADA	COPE	PC	LCV	CFA	RPN	NAB	NSI	NTU	ACA	ACU
1980	33	32	40	52	36	—	83	80	41	74	58
1979	32	25	25	50	22	—	—	—	46	73	74

Key Votes

1) Draft Registn $	FOR	6) Fair Hsg DOJ Enfrc	FOR	11) Cut Socl Incr Dfns $	AGN
2) Ban $ to Nicrgua	FOR	7) Lim PAC Contrbtns	AGN	12) Hosptl Cost Controls	AGN
3) Dlay MX Missile	AGN	8) Cap on Food Stmp $	FOR	13) Gasln Ctrls & Allctns	AGN
4) Nuclr Mortorium	FOR	9) New US Dep Edcatn	AGN	14) Lim Wndfll Prof Tax	FOR
5) Alaska Lands Bill	FOR	10) Cut OSHA $		FOR	15) Chryslr Loan Grntee	FOR

Election Results

1980 general	Douglas K. (Doug) Bereuter (R) ..	160,705	(79%)	($175,876)
	Rex S. Story (D)	43,605	(21%)	($14,592)
1980 primary	Douglas K. (Doug) Bereuter (R) ..	59,290	(100%)	
1978 general	Douglas K. (Doug) Bereuter (R) ..	99,013	(58%)	($167,688)
	Hess Dyas (D)	71,311	(42%)	($164,227)

SECOND DISTRICT

The 2d congressional district of Nebraska is metropolitan Omaha and a couple of rural counties. The latter are not very important politically; nine-tenths of the district's votes are cast in Douglas County (Omaha) and Sarpy County (suburban overflow, plus Offutt Air Force Base, the home of the Strategic Air Command). Omaha, like most of Nebraska, sprang into existence suddenly in the 1880s, when it became a regional meatpacking and railroad center of considerable importance. In the nation's boom decades after World War II, Omaha had below-average growth; its major industries were not growing. More recently, it has been growing somewhat more rapidly than the larger metropolitan areas of the Midwest (although not nearly so fast as the metropolitan areas of the Sun Belt).

One reason is the general prosperity of American agriculture, for this is a city whose economy depends very heavily on farming; another may be the rather probusiness attitudes here. But more important perhaps is the fact that Omaha is closer, physically and culturally, to the kind of small-town life so many middle-class Americans are seeking. If it lacks the cultural glitter and size of Metro Kansas City, St. Louis, or Chicago, it also lacks to a considerable extent their crime, their racial antagonisms, and the sense of anonymity imposed on people who live in the miles-long, faceless middle-income subdivisions. Omaha has many of the assets of a major metropolitan area, along with a size that does not overwhelm and a hospitality to traditional family and religious values. That is what many Americans are seeking today, and that is one reason why fewer people seem to be choosing to leave Omaha today when hundreds of thousands are leaving Metro Chicago.

Omaha, although it sometimes votes Democratic, is essentially a Republican town; indeed, it seems to be getting more so. The 2d district has almost always elected Republican congressmen. The only recent exception was in 1976 and 1978, when Democrat John Cavanaugh was elected. Cavanaugh had several advantages: his father was a well-known local official, he was young (31 when he first ran) and personable, and once in office he worked hard at providing constituency services. Nevertheless, Republican Hal Daub was able to reduce his margin in 1978, and in 1980 Cavanaugh decided not to run for reelection. His decision a few years ago would have been uncharacteristic for a young congressman, and surely one reason for it was that Daub was running again and Cavanaugh clearly would have to fight hard to hold the seat — and might lose anyway. But another reason, which Cavanaugh himself cited, was a desire to spend more time with his wife and children. These days constituents expect a congressman to spend almost every weekend with them; with an arduous schedule in Washington, he (or she) is lucky to get in any family time at all. The result in many cases is divorce; in Cavanaugh's it was retirement. He has returned to Omaha to practice law; perhaps someday when his children have grown, he will again enter congressional politics.

Hal Daub entered the 1980 race with substantial advantages: good name identification from his 1978 race, excellent financing, a strong adherence to Republican tax- and spending-cut policies in what turned out to be a strong Republican year. His Democratic opponent, a county commissioner from Omaha, tried to argue that he was even more conservative than Daub but ran behind in Omaha and farther behind elsewhere. Even a last-minute charge that Daub gave beer to underage volunteers at a party failed to make the race close.

Daub is in many ways typical of the younger Republicans who were elected in 1978 and 1980 and who hope to be part of the majority party in the House after the 1982 election. He is young (elected when he was 39), hardworking, and ambitious enough to have run two campaigns against significant opponents. Most of the Democrats elected in 1974 and 1976 had backgrounds in law firms, government, or simply politics; Daub, like so many of the other young Republicans, has a background in business — not a bureaucratic position in a huge company but a management post in a small, entrepreneurial business. He was helped by his adherence to programs Republicans worked out at the national level, such as the Kemp-Roth tax cut; he was helped even more by the fund-raising mechanisms Republicans developed nationally. His voting record in the short term seems fairly predictable: he is likely to be a strong supporter of the Reagan Administration. In the longer term, it is not entirely clear how such Republicans as Daub will go and what issues they will concentrate on; nor is it clear whether they will, as they would like to, become the dominant force in the House. In any case, Daub's showings in 1978 and 1980 suggest that he should be a good bet for reelection in 1982, barring major problems for the Reagan Administration. Indeed, the question is whether Daub will attract significant Democratic opposition at all.

Census Data Pop. (1980 final) 528,517, up 7% in 1970s. Median family income, 1970, $10,163, 106% of U.S.

The Voters

Employment profile 1970 White collar, 53%. Blue collar, 31%. Service, 14%. Farm, 2%.
Ethnic groups Black 1980, 8%. Hispanic 1980, 2%. Asian 1980, 1%. Total foreign stock 1970, 14%. Germany, 3%.

Presidential Vote

1980	Reagan (R)	124,810	(61%)
	Carter (D)	61,448	(30%)
	Anderson (I)	15,958	(8%)
1976	Ford (R)	114,991	(59%)
	Carter (D)	75,884	(39%)

Rep. Harold J. (Hal) Daub (R) Elected 1980; b. Apr. 23, 1941, Fort Bragg, N.C.; home, Omaha; Washington U., St. Louis, B.S. 1963, U. of Neb., Lincoln, J.D. 1966.

Career Army, Korea; Practicing atty., 1968–71; V.P., Gen. Counsel, Standard Chemical Mfg. Co., 1971–80; Douglas Co. Rep. Chmn., 1974–77; Rep. nominee for U.S. House of Reps., 1978.

Offices 1008 LHOB, 202-225-4155. Also 8424 Fed. Bldg., 215 N. 17th St., Omaha 68102, 402-221-4216.

Committees *Government Operations* (12th). Subcommittees: Commerce, Consumer and Monetary Affairs; Government Activities and Transportation.

Small Business (13th). Subcommittees: Antitrust and Restraint of Trade Activities Affecting Small Business; SBA and SBIC Authority, Minority Enterprise and General Small Business Problems.

Select Committee on Aging (19th). Subcommittee: Health and Long-Term Care.

Group Ratings and Key Votes: Newly Elected

Election Results

1980 general	Harold J. (Hal) Daub (R)	107,736	(53%)	($337,833)
	Richard M. Fellman (D)	88,843	(44%)	($153,539)
1980 primary	Harold J. (Hal) Daub (R)	33,306	(61%)	
	Mike Albert (R)	17,874	(33%)	($176,304)
	Two others (R)	3,371	(6%)	
1978 general	John J. Cavanaugh (D)	77,135	(52%)	($144,071)
	Harold J. (Hal) Daub (R)	70,309	(48%)	($237,741)

THIRD DISTRICT

One-third of Nebraska's population is spread out over the western three-quarters of its land area—the 3d congressional district. As one drives west here, the rolling fields of corn and wheat give way to the sand hills and cattle country, much of it devoid of signs of human habitation for miles on end. This is the part of Nebraska to which settlers thronged during the unusually moist 1880s and which their descendants for years have been leaving, often reluctantly, ever since. Today most of the people here live along the Platte River or near such towns as Grand Island, Hastings, Kearney, and Scottsbluff—none with more than 35,000 people.

When one divides the country into regions, Nebraska is always part of the Midwest. But the part of the state that is the 3d congressional district is in many ways more similar to Wyoming, just to the west, than it is to Iowa to the east. Economically, grazing is more important than corn or wheat here; physically, the rainfall is usually low, not much more than on the high plains of Wyoming or Colorado. Politically, this region seems more western than midwestern as well. Twenty years ago western Nebraska was the scene of farm rebellions against the Eisenhower Administration, and Democrats even won House seats in this region. Now the area has become very heavily Republican, and the 3d district is one of the safest Republican seats in the House. Folks here proved to be about as hostile to the Carter Administration as voters anywhere; fully 73% of the votes here were cast for Ronald Reagan, and only 21% for Jimmy Carter in 1980.

There was a seriously contested House race here as recently as 1974, when a wealthy Democrat came within 737 votes of winning. But the successful Republican, Virginia Smith, has not had any trouble since. In 1980 she won with 84% of the vote — one of the strongest showings in the nation. Mrs. Smith's background suggests party regularity. For 20 years she chaired the American Farm Bureau Women; the Farm Bureau, of course, has been one of the pillars of Republican strength in American agriculture for many years. In what has become a cohesive Republican bloc Mrs. Smith has been a very reliable Republican vote. She has a seat on the Appropriations Committee and, although she has reached an age that might have suggested retirement a few years ago, she can reply that she was born in the same year as the newly elected president. For a person of her views, this must be an exciting time to serve in Congress. Why should she quit now?

Census Data   Pop. (1980 final) 516,103, up 4% in 1970s. Median family income, 1970, $7,549, 79% of U.S.

The Voters

Employment profile 1970   White collar, 38%. Blue collar, 27%. Service, 14%. Farm, 21%.
Ethnic groups   Hispanic 1980, 2%. Total foreign stock 1970, 13%. Germany, 4%.

Presidential Vote

1980	Reagan (R)	160,433	(73%)
	Carter (D)	45,247	(21%)
	Anderson (I)	11,284	(5%)
1976	Ford (R)	128,198	(61%)
	Carter (D)	75,813	(36%)

Rep. Virginia Smith (R) Elected 1974; b. June 30, 1911, Randolph, Ia.; home, Chappell; U. of Neb., B.A. 1934.

Career   Natl. Chwmn., Amer. Farm Bureau Women, 1955–74; Chwmn., Pres. Task Force on Rural Development, 1971–72.

Offices   2202 RHOB, 202-225-6435. Also P.O. Bldg., Main Fl., Grand Island 68801, 308-381-0505.

Committee   *Appropriations* (13th). Subcommittees: Agriculture, Rural Development and Related Agencies; Energy and Water Development.

Group Ratings

	ADA	COPE	PC	LCV	CFA	RPN	NAB	NSI	NTU	ACA	ACU
1980	11	6	33	26	14	—	100	100	51	78	68
1979	11	15	15	24	11	—	—	—	54	96	95
1978	10	5	13	34	9	91	92	90	25	78	88

Key Votes

1) Draft Registn $	FOR	6) Fair Hsg DOJ Enfrc	AGN	11) Cut Socl Incr Dfns $	FOR
2) Ban $ to Nicrgua	FOR	7) Lim PAC Contrbtns	AGN	12) Hosptl Cost Controls	AGN
3) Dlay MX Missile	AGN	8) Cap on Food Stmp $	FOR	13) Gasln Ctrls & Allctns	AGN
4) Nuclr Mortorium	AGN	9) New US Dep Edcatn	AGN	14) Lim Wndfll Prof Tax	FOR
5) Alaska Lands Bill	AGN	10) Cut OSHA $	FOR	15) Chryslr Loan Grntee	AGN

Election Results

1980 general	Virginia Smith (R).............	182,887	(84%)	($93,496)
	Stan Ditus (D)................	34,967	(16%)	($15,970)
1980 primary	Virginia Smith (R).............	77,383	(100%)	
1978 general	Virginia Smith (R).............	141,597	(80%)	($66,795)
	Marilyn Fowler (D)............	35,371	(20%)	($40,313)

NEVADA

The history of Nevada began in 1859 with the discovery of the Comstock Lode — one of those huge mineral finds that triggered a rush of prospectors, speculators, and the usual hangers-on. Suddenly there was a large town here, Virginia City, and a territorial government in Carson City; there were opera houses and even a United States Mint, to coin some of the silver from the mines. When Civil War Republicans thought (mistakenly, as it turned out) they desperately needed electoral votes to reelect Lincoln in 1864, they contrived to make these two towns, plus tens of thousands of square miles of the vacant, arid Great Basin to the north, west, and south, the state of Nevada. Statehood was achieved and the electoral votes cast in time, and Nevada thereby became our third western state.

But soon enough the veins of silver and gold petered out. The opera houses closed and the prospectors scattered — to Lead, South Dakota; Bisbee, Arizona; and the Klondike River in the Yukon Territory. Nevada, with fewer than 100,000 residents, was left in economic doldrums for decades. During the Depression of the 1930s the state government was on the verge of bankruptcy. So the legislature legalized gambling and liberalized its divorce laws at just about the same time the federal government was building Hoover Dam near Las Vegas. Without realizing it, Nevada had tied its economy to one of the leading growth industries of the next 40 years: tourism.

During that time, Nevada's population has exploded, and demographically the state bears little resemblance to its historical origins. Up to the end of World War II, the state's population was concentrated in and around Reno and Carson City. But Reno's dominance was challenged in 1947, when Bugsy Siegel opened the Flamingo, the first big casino hotel on the Las Vegas Strip. Las Vegas has since become the state's dominant city, and more than half of Nevada's residents live there or in surrounding Clark County. Reno has also grown rapidly, and in the 1970s Nevada's population increased by more than 60% — the highest percentage growth rate in the nation. Between them, the two metropolitan areas have more than three-quarters of the state's population; the rest of the state, known as the Cow Counties, remain as empty as they always have been or, in the cases of ghost towns, even emptier.

Politically, Nevada is a state that seems somewhat uncomfortable with what it has become. Like most of the Rocky Mountain states, it has moved increasingly toward Republicans in recent years: supporting candidates who backed Moral Majority positions and giving birth to the Sagebrush Rebellion—the move to force the federal government to yield most of the public lands to the states. Nevada was one of Ronald Reagan's best states; it gave him 83% of its votes in the Republican presidential primary and 63% in the general election. Yet Nevada's economy is based on two industries most of Reagan's followers disapprove of— gambling and government. The big casinos and the federal government's atomic proving grounds remain the state's two big employers; the federal government retains title to 87% of Nevada's land. On this base, Nevadans have built a buoyant private economy; but underneath, it is based on money that outsiders—gamblers, federal taxpayers—bring in.

Some of these contradictions are embodied in the man who, by 1980, had emerged as Nevada's leading political figure, Senator Paul Laxalt. He was Reagan's campaign chairman in both 1976 and 1980, a man of high moral standards; he has also been a casino owner and a tough and effective politician. He has had national prominence for only a few years; but in Nevada he has been a prominent figure for a long time, and more than anyone else he must be credited with the success of the state's Republican Party. Back in 1964, when Barry Goldwater was badly beaten here, Laxalt nearly upset Senator Howard Cannon, now his colleague; the Democrat's margin was only 48 votes. In 1966 Laxalt beat a two-term governor, and almost as soon as he took office Howard Hughes moved to Las Vegas and began buying casinos. Hughes was welcomed to the state, in large part because many people thought organized crime had an interest in the casinos until he bought them, and Laxalt was especially enthusiastic; indeed, Laxalt was the only man outside Hughes's entourage that the recluse actually spoke to. For personal reasons, Laxalt did not seek reelection in 1970; at that point Hughes left Nevada.

Laxalt's election to the Senate in 1974 was not automatic. He beat Democrat Harry Reid, then lieutenant governor, by only 624 votes. But that was a Democratic year; as more and more like-minded Republicans were elected to the Senate in 1976, 1978, and 1980, Laxalt became their natural leader. He is a man of strong views and easy affability—qualities that were very much in view when he led the unsuccessful opposition to the Panama Canal Treaties. He devoted much of 1979 and 1980 to the Reagan campaign and was for most of that period one of Reagan's closest advisors; their relationship goes back to the days when they governed adjacent states. But Laxalt also showed that he could hold a grudge. He was reportedly one of those who urged in Detroit that Republican National Chairman Bill Brock be dumped, apparently because Brock refused to use party funds raised by a Reagan letter to finance a campaign against the Canal Treaties. When Reagan chose George Bush as his vice presidential candidate, Laxalt was pointedly absent from the hall.

Nonetheless, no one doubts that Laxalt has great influence in the Reagan Administration. He has missed out on high positions himself: Reagan evidently felt that two conservative westerners on one ticket were one too many; and after the Republicans unexpectedly captured the Senate, Reagan came out for Howard Baker for majority leader so quickly that any chance of a move to put Laxalt in that position was squelched. But no one doubts that Laxalt is Reagan's man in the Senate. He is the only senator who does not hold a leadership position who regularly attends leadership meetings — recognition of his unofficial status as President Reagan's emissary to the Senate. He has a warm personal relationship with the president and Mrs. Reagan, and is well liked and trusted in the Senate as well. By early 1981 he developed an amicable and productive working relationship with Baker.

Legislatively, he has generally worked quietly, the notable exception being on the Panama Canal Treaties. But he will probably be more visible on major issues in the 97th Congress. He sits on Appropriations, which usually affects policy quietly. But he is chairman of the Military Construction Subcommittee, which has jurisdiction over the MX missile system. This has aroused much opposition in hawkish Nevada and Utah, because it would require literally tearing up much of the landscape of these two states and building construction boom towns in the process; Laxalt, as an advocate of strong defense and as a believer in state control over public lands is in an uncomfortable position on this one. Laxalt also chairs the Judiciary subcommittee that handles regulatory reform — a technical issue that was raised by the Carter Administration and in which business interests are seeking simplification of regulatory processes that can delay economically beneficial activity almost indefinitely under present rules. Laxalt fought with William Roth of the Governmental Affairs Committee regarding jurisdiction over this issue, and they agreed that both would report bills to the floor and attempt to reconcile them there — a method that could result in either quick resolution or a messy impasse.

Laxalt was not expected to have much trouble winning reelection; he spent more time on Reagan's campaign than on his own and in the end he did win convincingly, by a 59%–37% margin. Nonetheless, his opponent, Mary Gojack, is an interesting enough character to have earned some notice; and in fact she held the locally popular Laxalt to a percentage under Reagan's. A former manager of a gravel pit and a trailer park, she was a blackjack dealer at a casino while attending school. She is familiar with the less glamorous side of Nevada's boom. Her strong anti-Laxalt campaign was not enough, however, to enable her to carry Clark County, which once was the state's Democratic stronghold. Twenty years ago, Clark County's votes were enough to carry Nevada for John Kennedy; now, with the state's population almost triple what it was in 1960, even Clark County is solidly Republican in national and even some local elections.

Nevada's other Senate seat, however, still belongs to a Democrat whose politics has roots in an old tradition. For years Nevada had conservative Democratic senators, such men as Key Pittman, once chairman of the Foreign Relations Committee, and Pat McCarran, who wrote restrictive immigration and antisubversive acts. Howard Cannon, first elected in 1958, has carried on that tradition in modified form. He has often been one of the critical votes in the Senate; he has low ratings from liberal organizations but goes along with most Democrats on many key issues. Now that the Democrats are no longer in the majority, Cannon's vote may not be so critical. But if the badly outnumbered liberals should try to use the filibuster weapon, they may be able to count on his support; Democrats from Nevada have an old tradition of not voting for cloture, on the grounds that the filibuster is one of the major sources of clout for a small state.

Until the 1980 election, Cannon served as chairman of the Commerce Committee, and while he has been forced to give up that post to Bob Packwood of Oregon, the Nevadan is certainly not without influence. Commerce is a committee of great importance, with jurisdiction over most of the industries heavily regulated by the federal government: the airlines, the broacasting networks, the maritime industry, railroads, and trucking. Commerce has had a number of chairmen—Cannon was one, his predecessor Warren Magnuson was another—who have an instinctive knack for getting things done and getting along with people on Capitol Hill; for the stakes are high and not a comma is changed in Commerce's legislation without a battery of lobbyists hovering about.

Cannon was a key figure in some of the recent deregulation legislation. An expert on aviation, he had at first opposed deregulation of the airlines, which most of the airlines opposed as well; but when the law was largely put into effect administratively, Cannon supported it and fashioned the actual bill that was passed. Later, when the Carter Administration and liberal senators pushed for a tough trucking deregulation bill, Cannon proposed a milder version and was instrumental in pushing through the final compromise version. All of these measures were strongly opposed by most trucking companies (which could bar competitors from their routes under the old law) and the Teamsters Union.

This last situation nearly got Cannon into trouble. In 1980 the Justice Department investigated charges that he had gotten the Teamsters to raise the value of property he owned; he replied that he had simply been talking with Allen Dorfman, a Teamsters attorney, about trucking deregulation. The government decided that Cannon had done nothing to warrant prosecution. These charges arose from an investigation that produced, in 1981, the indictment of Dorfman and of incoming Teamsters president Roy Williams on charges that he tried to bribe Cannon. But Cannon was not indicted himself, and the indictment notes that the attempted bribe never in fact was given. And it should be noted that Cannon has a long record—going back to when he was district attorney in Las Vegas—of proven integrity in testing circumstances.

Cannon's other major legislative post is on the Armed Services Committee. He holds the rank of general in the Air Force and has always been a backer of generous defense expenditures and a proponent of the Air Force in particular. He is indeed an aviation expert and enthusiast, and at one time he chaired both the civil and military aviation subcommittees in the Senate. Today he ranks behind John Stennis and Henry Jackson in seniority among Armed Services Democrats.

Cannon's seat is up in 1982, and there is some question as to whether he will seek reelection. He turns 70 that year, and voters have retired many senators of that age recently; he cannot claim now, as he could in the past, that as a member of the majority party in the Senate and the president's party he has great clout. Laxalt, instead, is clearly the man with a pipeline to the White House. Cannon won convincingly in 1970 over a candidate backed strongly by Spiro Agnew; that was his last real test. He had weak opposition in 1976. While he certainly cannot be counted out, this is a seat that the Republicans will almost certainly contest vigorously. Probably their strongest candidate would be the current governor, Robert List.

So it is possible that Cannon, after 24 years and without the pleasures and prerogatives of a chairmanship, will choose to retire. In that case, there are a number of strong Democrats who might seek his seat. One is Mike O'Callaghan, who served as governor for eight years until he retired in 1978. O'Callaghan could easily have had a third term had he wanted it; but he honored the apparent intent of an ambiguous provision in the state constitution and did not run again. Out of office, he went to work for the *Las Vegas Sun,* a newspaper with a lively interest in politics; he broke party lines to endorse List for governor in 1978. Also popular, but not as well known to the voters, is the state's single congressman, Jim Santini. First elected in 1974, he has compiled a record that is sharply different from the western stereotype of an eastern liberal Democrat. On the Interior Committee, he has tended to concentrate on Nevada issues, such as tourism, preserving Lake Tahoe, responding to the Sagebrush Rebellion, and the MX missile system. Like Nevada's senators, he questions the need to excavate large parts of Nevada and neighboring Utah to build the system and does not support the MX in the form proposed by the Carter Administration. He chairs the Mines Subcommittee and has worked to open up more federal lands for mineral exploration. Santini has support from all segments of Nevada's population and has not had a well-financed opponent since he won the seat in 1974; he won reelection in 1980 with 68% of the vote, running nearly 100,000 votes ahead of President Carter. The third Democrat who might run is Harry Reid, Laxalt's 1974 opponent, who is now director of the state gaming commission — obviously one of the most sensitive jobs in Nevada.

For the first time in history, Nevada will have two congressmen after the 1982 election. Since more than half the state's population is in Clark County, the Las Vegas area will have to be split. The legislature might choose to create one district consisting of most of the Las Vegas area and one that would include the rest of the state. The political result, in that case, would depend on which part of the Las Vegas area is attached to the rest of the state — heavily Democratic North Las Vegas, with its large black population, some of the high-income precincts around the Las Vegas Strip, or some of the culturally conservative suburbs southeast of Las Vegas toward Hoover Dam. Santini, if he does not run for the Senate, would be a cinch to hold the Las Vegas seat for the Democrats; a possible successor would be Harry Reid. The other district will be up for grabs, with either party and a multitude of different candidates capable of winning.

Republican Robert List has been governor since the 1978 election and seems to have served without antagonizing voters. The national trends favor his party, and he seems likely to win a second term if he seeks it. The most sensitive duties of a Nevada governor, of course, involve supervision of the gambling industry; List faces a special problem since New Jersey's entry into the competition for legalized gambling dollars has coincided with higher air fares due to increased jet fuel prices. But the 1980 census seems to be telling us that Nevada is no longer entirely dependent on gambling; that it has reached the point of takeoff, a point where it is generating enough business activity to fill its own needs and to provide goods that previously were imported from elsewhere. If that is so, Nevada will continue to thrive for some time, with its Moral Majority politics and legalized prostitution (in some of the Cow Counties), its government payrolls and Sagebrush Rebellion.

Census Data Pop. (1980 final) 799,184, up 64% in 1970s: 0.35% of U.S. total, 43d largest. Central city, 33%; suburban, 49%. Median 4-person family income, 1978, $21,106, 103% of U.S., 15th highest.

1979 Share of Federal Tax Burden $1,623,000,000; 0.36% of U.S. total, 42d largest.

1979 Share of Federal Outlays $1,673,237,000; 0.36% of U.S. total, 45th largest.

DOD	$334,338,000	43d	(0.32%)	HEW	$426,290,000	49th	(0.24%)
DOE	$335,429,000	13th	(2.85%)	ERDA	$22,271,000	22d	(0.82%)
HUD	$14,960,000	48th	(0.23%)	NASA	$934,000	36th	(0.02%)
VA	$70,297,000	45th	(0.34%)	DOT	$95,513,000	41st	(0.58%)
EPA	$26,574,000	40th	(0.50%)	DOC	$7,781,000	42d	(0.25%)
DOI	$110,076,000	14th	(1.98%)	USDA	$33,648,000	51st	(0.14%)

Economic Base Tourism; finance, insurance, and real estate; agriculture, notably cattle, dairy products, hay, and sheep; metal mining, especially copper ores; paper and allied products; primary metal industries, especially nonferrous rolling and drawing.

Political Lineup   Governor, Robert F. List (R). Senators, Howard W. Cannon (D) and Paul Laxalt (R). Representatives, 1 D at large; 2 in 1982. State Senate, 20 (15 D and 5 R); State Assembly 40 (26 D and 14 R).

The Voters

Registration   297,318 Total. 168,617 D (53%); 115,182 R (39%); 676 Lib. (0%); 22,843 Nonpartisan (8%).

Employment profile 1970   White collar, 47%. Blue collar, 26%. Service, 25%. Farm, 2%.

Ethnic groups   Black 1980, 6%. Hispanic 1980, 7%. Am. Ind. 1980, 2%. Asian 1980, 2%. Total foreign stock 1970, 14%.

Presidential Vote

1980	Reagan (R)	155,017	(63%)
	Carter (D)	66,666	(27%)
	Anderson (I)	17,651	(7%)
	None of these candidates ...	4,193	(2%)
1976	Ford (R)	101,273	(50%)
	Carter (D)	92,479	(46%)

1980 Democratic Presidential Primary			*1980 Republican Presidential Primary*		
Carter	25,159	(38%)	Reagan	39,352	(83%)
Kennedy	19,296	(29%)	Bush	3,078	(6%)
None of these candidates	22,493	(34%)	None of these candidates	4,965	(10%)

SENATORS

Sen. Howard W. Cannon (D) Elected 1958, seat up 1982; b. Jan. 26, 1912, St. George, Utah; home, Las Vegas; Dixie Jr. Col., Ariz. St. Teachers Col., B.E. 1933, U. of Ariz., LL.B. 1937.

Career   Reference Atty., Utah Senate, 1938; Washington Co. Atty., 1940–41; Practicing atty., 1938–41, 1946–58; Army Air Corps, WWII; Las Vegas City Atty., 1949–58.

Offices   259 RSOB, 202-224-6244. Also 4602 U.S. Fed. Bldg., 300 Las Vegas Blvd. S., Las Vegas 89101, 702-385-6278, and 4024 U.S. Fed. Bldg., 300 Booth St., Reno 89502, 702-784-5544.

Committees   *Armed Services* (3d). Subcommittees: Military Construction; Strategic and Theatre Nuclear Forces; Tactical Warfare.

Commerce, Science, and Transportation (Ranking Member). Subcommittee: Aviation.

Rules and Administration (2d).

Joint Committee on Printing (4th).

Group Ratings

	ADA	COPE	PC	LCV	CFA	RPN	NAB	NSI	NTU	ACA	ACU
1980	33	41	50	23	47	—	33	89	32	39	33
1979	21	61	43	—	29	—	—	—	28	24	24
1978	30	33	45	36	45	60	46	67	18	43	46

Key Votes

1) Draft Registn $	—	6) Fair Housng Cloture	—	11) Cut Socl Incr Defns	FOR
2) Ban $ to Nicrgua	—	7) Ban $ Rape Abortns	AGN	12) Income Tax Indexing	AGN
3) Dlay MX Missile	AGN	8) Cap on Food Stmp $	AGN	13) Lim Spdg 21% GNP	AGN
4) Nuclr Mortorium	AGN	9) New US Dep Edcatn	FOR	14) Incr Wndfll Prof Tax	FOR
5) Alaska Lands Bill	AGN	10) Cut OSHA Inspctns	FOR	15) Chryslr Loan Grntee	FOR

Election Results

1976 general	Howard W. Cannon (D)	127,214	(63%)	($405,380)
	David Towell (R)	63,471	(31%)	($54,842)
1976 primary	Howard W. Cannon (D), unopposed			
1970 general	Howard W. Cannon (D)	85,187	(58%)	
	William J. Raggio (R)...........	60,838	(41%)	

Sen. Paul Laxalt (R) Elected 1974, seat up 1986; b. Aug. 2, 1922, Reno; home, Carson City; Santa Clara U., 1940–43; U. of Denver, B.S., LL.B. 1949.

Career Army, WWII; Ormsby Co. Dist. Atty., 1951–54; Practicing atty., 1954–66, 1970–74; Lt. Gov. of Nev., 1963–66; Gov. of Nev., 1966–70.

Offices 315 RSOB, 202-224-3542. Also U.S. Fed. Bldg., Rm. 2016, 300 Booth St., Reno 89502, 702-784-5568, and U.S. Fed. Bldg., Rm. 4626, 300 Las Vegas Blvd. S., Las Vegas 89101, 702-385-6547.

Committees *Appropriations* (5th). Subcommittees: HUD–Independent Agencies; Interior; Military Construction (Chairman); State, Justice, Commerce, and the Judiciary; Treasury, Postal Service, and General Government.

Judiciary (3d). Subcommittees: Agency Administration; Criminal Law; Regulatory Reform (Chairman).

Group Ratings

	ADA	COPE	PC	LCV	CFA	RPN	NAB	NSI	NTU	ACA	ACU
1980	11	5	20	16	13	—	90	100	56	100	100
1979	5	12	18	—	10	—	—	—	69	91	100
1978	5	18	20	16	20	57	75	100	56	81	100

Key Votes

1) Draft Registn $	FOR	6) Fair Housng Cloture	AGN	11) Cut Socl Incr Defns	FOR
2) Ban $ to Nicrgua	AGN	7) Ban $ Rape Abortns	—	12) Income Tax Indexing	FOR
3) Dlay MX Missile	—	8) Cap on Food Stmp $	—	13) Lim Spdg 21% GNP	FOR
4) Nuclr Mortorium	AGN	9) New US Dep Edcatn	AGN	14) Incr Wndfll Prof Tax	AGN
5) Alaska Lands Bill	AGN	10) Cut OSHA Inspctns	FOR	15) Chryslr Loan Grntee	AGN

Election Results

1980 general	Paul Laxalt (R)	144,224	(59%)	($1,126,826)
	Mary Gojack (D)..............	92,129	(37%)	($285,619)
	None of these candidates	3,163	(1%)	
1980 primary	Paul Laxalt (R)	45,857	(90%)	
	One other (R)	2,509	(5%)	
	None of these candidates	2,501	(5%)	
1974 general	Paul Laxalt (R)	79,605	(47%)	($385,861)
	Harry Reid (D)	78,981	(47%)	($400,553)
	Jack Doyle (Ind. Amer.).........	10,887	(5%)	

GOVERNOR

Gov. Robert F. List (R) Elected 1978, term expires Jan. 1983; b. Sept. 1, 1936, Visalia, Cal.; Utah St. U., B.S. 1959, U. of Cal., J.D. 1962.

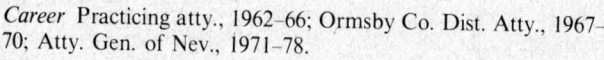

Career Practicing atty., 1962–66; Ormsby Co. Dist. Atty., 1967–70; Atty. Gen. of Nev., 1971–78.

Offices Governor's Mansion, Carson City 89701, 702-885-5670.

Election Results

1978 gen.	Robert F. List (R)	108,097	(56%)
	Robert E. Rose (D)	76,361	(40%)
1978 prim.	Robert F. List (R)	40,057	(89%)
	Three others (R)	5,000	(11%)
1974 gen.	Mike O'Callaghan (D)	114,114	(67%)
	Shirley Crumpler (R)	28,959	(17%)
	James Ray Houston (I)	26,285	(16%)

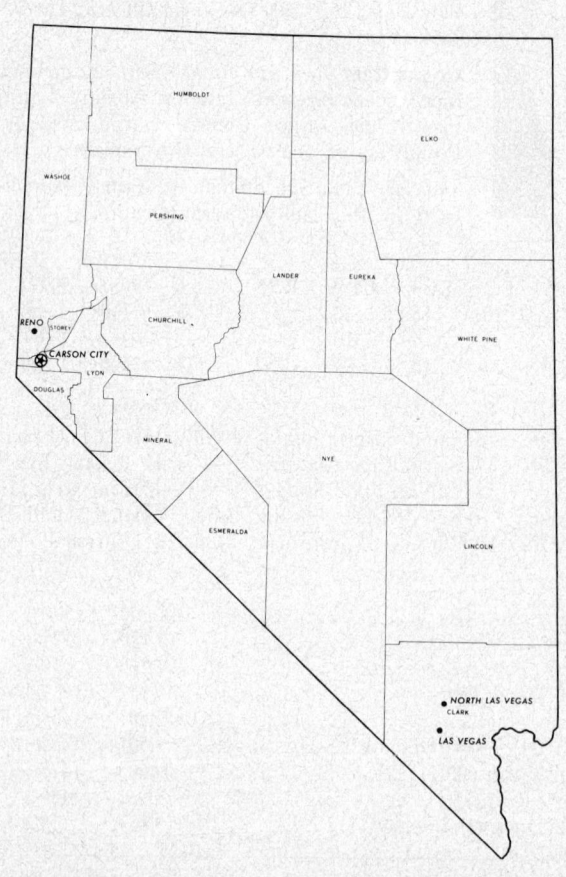

Rep. Jim Santini (D) Elected 1974; b. Aug. 13, 1937, Reno; home, Las Vegas; U. of Nev., B.S. 1959, Hastings Col. of Law, J.D. 1962.

Career Practicing atty.; Army, 1963–66; Clark Co. Dpty. Dist. Atty., 1968–69, Public Defender, 1968–70, J.P., 1970–72, Dist. Ct. Judge, 1972–74.

Offices 2429 RHOB, 202-225-5965. Also Suite 4-260 Fed. Bldg., 300 Las Vegas Blvd. S., Las Vegas 89101, 702-385-6575.

Committees *Energy and Commerce* (9th). Subcommittees: Commerce, Transportation and Tourism; Oversight and Investigations.

Interior and Insular Affairs (8th). Subcommittees: Mines and Mining (Chairman); Public Lands and National Parks.

Select Committee on Aging (12th). Subcommittee: Housing and Consumer Interests.

Group Ratings

	ADA	COPE	PC	LCV	CFA	RPN	NAB	NSI	NTU	ACA	ACU
1980	17	38	20	50	7	—	73	70	44	58	59
1979	16	30	30	28	31	—	—	—	46	61	58
1978	5	35	40	25	27	50	67	78	17	65	57

Key Votes

1) Draft Registn $	FOR	6) Fair Hsg DOJ Enfrc	—	11) Cut Socl Incr Dfns $	FOR
2) Ban $ to Nicrgua	FOR	7) Lim PAC Contrbtns	FOR	12) Hosptl Cost Controls	AGN
3) Dlay MX Missile	FOR	8) Cap on Food Stmp $	AGN	13) Gasln Ctrls & Allctns	AGN
4) Nuclr Mortorium	AGN	9) New US Dep Edcatn	FOR	14) Lim Wndfll Prof Tax	FOR
5) Alaska Lands Bill	AGN	10) Cut OSHA $	FOR	15) Chryslr Loan Grntee	AGN

Election Results

1980 general	Jim Santini (D)	165,107	(68%)	($392,583)
	Vince Saunders (R)	63,163	(26%)	($58,760)
	None of these candidates	8,558	(3%)	
1980 primary	Jim Santini (D)	54,495	(79%)	
	One other (D)	8,407	(12%)	
	None of these candidates	5,832	(8%)	
1978 general	Jim Santini (D)	132,513	(75%)	($204,389)
	Bill O'Mara (R)	44,425	(25%)	($34,543)

NEW HAMPSHIRE

Once every four years New Hampshire becomes the center of the nation's political attention. Presidential candidates trudge through the melting snow and gooey mud of the state's industrial cities and small New England towns, wooing the votes of about 111,000 Democrats and 147,000 Republicans. New Hampshire's primary is not quite the first event of the presidential campaign season; it was preceded in 1980 by the Iowa caucuses and (although no one paid much attention) the primary in Puerto Rico. But New Hampshire is still the first full-fledged state to hold a full-fledged primary election, and it is determined to keep things that way. So for more than 30 years this remote state has quadrennially attracted dozens of candidates, hundreds of journalists and, sometimes, thousands of enthusiastic volunteers.

New Hampshire has thus become our primary arena of what columnist Mark Shields calls retail politics—a candidate seeking votes from individual persons or small groups. Even with entourages of press and Secret Service, the candidates still come up here and talk —actually converse—with ordinary voters. It is just about the only place in the country that candidates seek the views of—and seek to impress—ordinary citizens. Retail campaigning is possible, and expected, here because the electorate is small and the state is a geographically manageable size; more than two-thirds of its citizens live clustered in the southern half of the state, not much more than an hour or two from the Boston airport. The importance of retail politics tends to hurt incumbent presidential candidates and front-runners, who are burdened with larger entourages; it gives tremendous advantages to the candidate who is not busy tending to the duties of public office—for example, Ronald Reagan in 1976 and 1980, Jimmy Carter in 1976, and George Bush in 1980. Retail politicking in New Hampshire does not involve only candidates. There is a terrific advantage in having a corps of enthusiastic volunteers, as Eugene McCarthy in 1968 and George McGovern in 1972 found. There is always speculation in the national press as to whether this or that former Republican governor (there are several of them still active) is going to support this or that candidate. On occasion, organizations have functioned without the presence of the candidate, as in the write-in effort for Henry Cabot Lodge that defeated retail campaigners Nelson Rockefeller and Barry Goldwater in 1964.

In contrast, television advertising is far less important here than in most campaigns. Voters are used to meeting candidates, or at least their volunteers. And buying television time on Boston stations (the only outlet for most of New Hampshire) is relatively expensive and counts against campaign spending limits (although candidates argue that these expenditures are really aimed at Massachusetts, which has a primary soon after).

The importance of retail politics in New Hampshire is one reason voters here have time and again fooled the soothsayers. There was the Lodge write-in in 1964; Eugene McCarthy's 42% against Lyndon Johnson in 1968, which destroyed the myth of an incumbent's invulnerability, and George McGovern's startlingly high 37% in 1972. Jimmy Carter's 28% victory here—achieved with just 23,373 votes—put him on the covers of two newsmagazines and gave him something close to front-runner status—although most voters in the 49 other states knew nothing whatever about him. Carter was as good a retail campaigner as New Hampshire has seen, sleeping in the houses of supporters and making his bed, talking quietly with voters and separating himself from the other liberal contenders, sending in his crews of Georgians to campaign. Some observers have argued that retail campaigning ability is a poor test for the presidency, but there are at least some talents it spotlights that are important for a president to have. The same talents that gave him his first New Hampshire primary victory also helped Carter produce the Israel–Egypt Camp David settlement. But there are limits as well to what retail campaigning shows. New Hampshire Democratic primary voters were willing to renominate Carter against Edward Kennedy of nearby Massachusetts in 1980, although they gave the president less than a majority. But in the general election they issued a grim verdict on the man that voters in this state, more than any other but Georgia and maybe Iowa, know better; they gave Jimmy Carter just 28% of their votes. True, New Hampshire has been trending toward Republicans generally and has reacted strongly against big government; but this is still as crushing a verdict on the Carter presidency as has been rendered.

About one-quarter of 1% of the nation's general election voters participate in the New Hampshire presidential primaries, and the question arises: is this anything like a representative group? On the Democratic side, the answer is almost certainly negative. The New Hampshire Democratic electorate is heavily Catholic, with large numbers of French Canadians, an ethnic group hardly seen in this country outside the three northern New England states. It includes many workers in such dying industries as textiles and is heavily influenced in its issue positions by the right-wing views of the *Manchester Union Leader,* the state's dominant newspaper. Indeed, the Democratic primary voters of Manchester, the state's largest city, regularly vote for Republican candidates in the general election. The Republican primary, however, has better claims for being representative. In fact, one could argue that the Republican electorate in New Hampshire is more representative of the body of people who actually vote Republican in general elections than are Republican electorates in much bigger primary states. This is one of the five states where one finds more registered Republicans than Democrats, and registered Republicans here come from all walks of life and all parts of the state — not just the country club set in metropolitan areas, as is true in most southern states, or just from a relatively nonurban part of the state, as is true in such places as New York and Illinois. And the Republican electorate here has been a rather accurate prognosticator of the final national Republican outcome: in 1976 Ford led Reagan in New Hampshire 49%–48%; in 1980 Reagan had 50%, far ahead of George Bush's 23%.

New Hampshire's primary now takes place in late February, and by the first of March the politicians and their camps of followers are gone. New Hampshire, which casts only four electoral votes, often never sees a national candidate again. Politics in the state returns to normal, dominated by fractious politicians and the irritable William Loeb, publisher of the *Union Leader,* the man who sets the political tone of the state although he actually lives in Massachusetts and is a legal resident of Nevada. The *Union Leader* is known as a right-wing paper, a champion of American strength abroad and an opponent of big government at home; and if it has not had much luck electing its favorites in years past it may have done better than it ever dreamed with Ronald Reagan in 1980. The paper did strongly support Reagan: it constantly ran front page articles praising him, on the slightest pretext; it ran negative articles on George Bush and raised the issue of his former membership in the Trilateral Commission; in 1979 it focused negative and, some said, scurrilous attention on Congressman Philip Crane, a conservative who many thought would take votes away from Reagan, but who ultimately won only 2% here despite heavy campaigning.

The *Union Leader* tends to set the agenda for state issues as well. In the early 1960s New Hampshire was one of several states that did not have either a sales or an income tax. Liberals and many respectable voices of the middle argued that these states needed broad based taxes to support necessary or beneficial state services. Other states eventually agreed, and by the early 1970s New Hampshire was left as the only state without a broad-based tax. But the *Union Leader* never wavered in its opposition to such taxes and in 1972, 1974, and 1976 was able to help elect as governor Meldrim Thomson, a zany conservative who promised to veto any tax bill. Thomson was sneered at by the outside journalists who came to cover the New Hampshire primary, but he achieved his objectives in New Hampshire. There still is no income or sales tax here, and the state has grown and prospered as no other in the East. Its population increased by 25% in the 1970s while that in next-door, heavily taxed Massachusetts increased by 1%; businesses came across the New Hampshire line or started up there; wages and salaries increased and even old factory towns such as Manchester and Nashua were growing.

But not everything is rosy in New Hampshire. The levels of public services are low indeed and, as former Massachusetts Governor Michael Dukakis noted, if you have a child with a serious physical handicap, you are not going to be happy in New Hampshire. The rapid growth has often spoiled the woodsy environment with ticky-tacky subdivision houses and storefronts, and the level of cultural achievement is not high.

Governor Thomson is now out of office, but his policies live on; in fact, New Hampshire seems farther today from enacting a broad-based tax than it was a dozen years ago. Ironically, Thomson lost in 1978 mostly because his policies for once cost New Hampshire citizens more than his opponent's policies did. The issue was whether a local utility could pass on to its customers a 17% surcharge for construction work in progress on the controversial Seabrook nuclear power plant. The utility claimed that it couldn't complete the plant without the surcharge and Thomson, a strong backer of nuclear power and opponent of the antinuclear Clamshell Alliance demonstrators, went along. Democrat Hugh Gallen opposed the surcharge and so, apparently, did most New Hampshire voters. They may favor nuclear power, but they don't want to pay for it until it is completed. New Hampshire is one of four states with gubernatorial elections every two years, and Gallen beat Thomson again in 1980, increasing his percentage to 59%. Gallen is aided by his opposition to a broad-based state tax—indeed, he almost certainly could not be elected if he felt differently.

Four years ago New Hampshire was represented by two Democrats in the U.S. Senate; now it is represented by two Republicans. The change is not too shocking in retrospect, given the conservative trend in New Hampshire's attitudes and the success of its no-tax state policies, but it came as something of a surprise to political observers anyway. Most surprising was the defeat of Senator Thomas McIntyre by airline pilot Gordon Humphrey in 1978. McIntyre had not seemed to be in any trouble. First elected in 1962, he beat Loeb-backed Republicans Harrison Thyng and Wesley Powell in 1966 and 1972. McIntyre was considered a moderate and was personally well liked. But in 1978 he seemed unconcerned about the election while Humphrey, although he began totally unknown, campaigned hard. He proved adept at raising money and outspent the incumbent. He attacked McIntyre vigorously for supporting the Panama Canal Treaties, food stamps, foreign aid, and federal funding of abortions. The *Union Leader* launched furious and effective attacks on McIntyre, who still believes they exceeded the bounds of fair comment. Humphrey won the election in one of the biggest upsets of 1978—and one that made the Republican capture of the Senate in 1980 possible. Humphrey made great gains over previous McIntyre opponents in his home area, the southwestern corner of the state, but most striking was McIntyre's failure to carry Manchester, which has more than a 2-1 Democratic registration edge. Loeb's editorials and news columns seem to have had a major impact in this working-class city.

Humphrey started his term by flouting tradition and refusing to be escorted down the center aisle by his then Democratic colleague John Durkin. On most issues Humphrey joined the bloc of New Right senators, most of whom are from the Rocky Mountain states. He has important committee assignments: Armed Services, where he is a strong backer of aggressive military action; Human Resources, where he stands with the bloc of Republicans opposed to organized labor; and Energy and Natural Resources, where he favors complete decontrol of energy prices. Humphrey has moved rapidly from the position of an outside conservative activist to that of a man in power; he retains his aggressive spirit and has not been domesticated by official Washington. Humphrey has the chance now to play a major role on some issues conservatives have been very concerned about. They have complained about the lack of readiness in the military, and he is chairman of the subcommittee on preparedness — although he seemed in his first two years more interested in strategic questions than in the mundane business of supplying spare parts and getting competent technicians. He must stand for reelection in 1984, and if the mood of New Hampshire does not change much he will probably be a favorite to win.

The state's other Senate seat changed hands in 1980, from Democrat John Durkin to Republican Warren Rudman, who are old political adversaries, and the race was a bitter one. Durkin, a former state insurance commissioner, ran for the Senate first in 1974 and ended up in what was ruled a tie with Congressman Louis Wyman. The secretary of state said Durkin was ahead by 10 votes, but the ballot commission (on which Rudman, as state attorney general, served) said Wyman won by 2. The Democratic Senate was inclined to accept Durkin but could not end a filibuster by the Republicans. The election was rerun in the summer of 1975, and Durkin won largely on an issue that had arisen in the previous campaign. Back in 1972 Wyman had introduced one Ruth Farkas to people at the Committee to Re-elect the President; she had contributed $250,000 after the election and had shortly afterwards been named ambassador to Luxembourg. Durkin made a name in the Senate as a vociferous opponent of removing price controls on oil and natural gas and in New Hampshire as a vociferous opponent of Jimmy Carter.

Meanwhile, after an 11-candidate primary Republicans managed to unite around Rudman, although he is not as militantly conservative as some would like. Rudman harbored an old grudge against Durkin, who prevented him from becoming chairman of the Interstate Commerce Commission in the Ford Administration. Rudman charged that Durkin was a creature of organized labor and benefited probably from the general Republican tide of opinion in the state. Durkin carried the western edge of the state along the Connecticut River and the southeastern corner around the industrial cities of Portsmouth and Dover. But, although Durkin carried Manchester, Rudman carried solidly most of central New Hampshire — the strongest circulation area of the *Union Leader.*

As a junior senator Rudman has a seat on the Appropriations Committee, traditionally the favorite of Senate insiders, and on Governmental Affairs, usually the Senate's leading investigative committee. He is expected to be less aggressive than Humphrey and somewhat more conventional in his views but will almost surely be a strong supporter of the Reagan Administration.

With only the slightest changes, New Hampshire's two congressional districts have had the same boundaries since 1881. The lines neatly separate the cities of Manchester and Nashua, both mill towns on the Merrimack River and the only two substantial urban concentrations in the state. Both have large numbers of Irish, Italian, and especially French Canadian immigrants and their offspring, who have historically provided the Democratic base in this usually Republican state. The purpose of the 1881 redistricting was to put both districts permanently out of reach of the Democrats, and for the most part it has worked: Democrats have won both districts only twice, in 1890 and 1912, and until the 1970s won the 1st district also on five separate occasions.

The 1st district's politics tend to be dominated by Manchester, the state's largest city. There are also significant concentrations of people in the Portsmouth area, on the Maine border, and along the Masschusetts border, where Boston area commuters, in search of life in the country and lower taxes, have been moving in great numbers. Commentators assume that these new New Hampshire residents vote like Massachusetts liberals, but that is not always true. Many left Massachusetts precisely because they disliked the politics there and are quite pleased with New Hampshire's antitax consensus.

The only Democrat left in the New Hampshire congressional delegation today is 1st district Congressman Norman D'Amours. He had the good fortune to be running in 1974, a heavily Democratic year when the incumbent here, Louis Wyman, ran for the Senate. D'Amours has the image of a moderate Democrat and is more comfortable with the party's working-class tradition and working-class cultural attitudes than he is with the liberal activists who have run the McCarthy, McGovern, Udall, and Kennedy campaigns in New Hampshire's presidential primaries. D'Amours was fortunate in 1976 and 1978 not to have serious competition. Against former state House speaker and Meldrim Thomson aide Marshall Cobleigh, D'Amours proved his strength, winning with 61% of the vote and running far ahead of Jimmy Carter, who had 27% in the 1st district. He was willing to sacrifice his party standing to do so; he told the *Manchester Union Leader* that if the election went into the House he would support the winner in the district. He must have known this would be Reagan and that he was committing himself to a vote that might cost him his membership in the Democratic Caucus and his committee positions. D'Amours sits now on the Banking and Merchant Marine Committees, two bodies generally more congenial to practical men of the world than to visionary idealists.

The 2d district is somewhat less urban than the 1st, although it does include Concord, the state capital, Salem, the most populous town on the Massachusetts border, and Nashua, a mill town on the Merrimack and the state's second largest city. For 18 years, until his retirement in 1980, the district was represented by James Cleveland, a mild-mannered, moderate Republican who suited his constituents well. He retired although he was next in line for the ranking minority positions on both the Public Works and House Administration Committees. The real election here, it turned out, was in the Republican primary. The winner was Judd Gregg, 33-year-old son of former Governor Hugh Gregg, who headed Ronald Reagan's campaign here in 1976 and George Bush's in 1980. Gregg beat Susan McLane, Charles Bakst, and eight other Republicans in the primary by outcampaigning them. He had a strong field organization—perhaps helped by his father's years of field work—and had a heavy personal campaign schedule. As in so many districts, the voters seemed to want a congressman who demonstrated the ability to stay close in touch with them. Gregg's Democratic opponent, the mayor of Nashua, never really had a chance, and in a Republican year this attractive young Republican carried almost every city and town in the district (the only exceptions: Nashua and the mill town of Berlin in the north). Gregg is on the Government Operations and Science Committees.

New Hampshire does not face a serious redistricting problem for 1982, since its two districts are only 10,500 voters off the statewide average. The transfer of a few small towns from the 1st district to the 2d will make up the difference without much effect on either D'Amours or Gregg.

Census Data　Pop. (1980 final) 920,610, up 25% in 1970s: 0.41% of U.S. total, 42d largest. Central city, 17%; suburban, 19%. Median 4-person family income, 1978, $20,247, 99% of U.S., 25th highest.

1979 Share of Federal Tax Burden　$1,713,000,000; 0.38% of U.S. total, 41st largest.

1979 Share of Federal Outlays $1,666,932,000; 0.36% of U.S. total, 46th largest.

DOD	$533,262,000	37th	(0.50%)	HEW	$648,451,000	41st	(0.36%)
DOE	$2,556,000	44th	(0.02%)	ERDA	$319,000	50th	(0.01%)
HUD	$22,357,000	41st	(0.34%)	NASA	$1,421,000	34th	(0.03%)
VA	$89,821,000	42d	(0.43%)	DOT	$60,068,000	47th	(0.36%)
EPA	$37,634,000	36th	(0.71%)	DOC	$7,753,000	43d	(0.24%)
DOI	$8,213,000	50th	(0.15%)	USDA	$44,327,000	47th	(0.18%)

Economic Base Leather footwear and other leather products; tourism; electrical equipment and supplies; finance, insurance, and real estate; machinery; textile mill products; rubber and plastics products not otherwise classified, especially miscellaneous plastics products.

Political Lineup Governor, Hugh J. Gallen (D). Senators, Gordon J. Humphrey (R) and Warren Rudman (R). Representatives, 2 (1 R and 1 D), 2 in 1982. State Senate, 24 (13 R, 10 D, and 1 vacancy); State House of Representatives, 400 (239 R, 160 D, and 1 vacancy).

The Voters

Registration 522,751 Total. 170,030 D (33%); 210,382 R (40%); 142,339 undeclared (27%).
Employment profile 1970 White collar, 45%. Blue collar, 42%. Service, 12%. Farm, 1%.
Ethnic groups Hispanic 1980, 1%. Total foreign stock 1970, 23%. Canada, 13%.

Presidential Vote

1980	Reagan (R)	221,705	(58%)
	Carter (D)	108,864	(28%)
	Anderson (I)	49,693	(13%)
1976	Ford (R)	185,935	(55%)
	Carter (D)	147,635	(43%)

1980 Democratic Presidential Primary			*1980 Republican Presidential Primary*		
Carter	52,692	(47%)	Reagan	72,983	(50%)
Kennedy	41,745	(37%)	Bush	33,443	(23%)
Brown	10,743	(10%)	Baker	18,943	(13%)
All others	6,750	(6%)	Anderson	14,458	(10%)
			All others	7,330	(4%)

SENATORS

Sen. Gordon J. Humphrey (R) Elected 1978, seat up 1984; b. Oct. 9, 1940, Briston, Conn.; home, Sunapee; Geo. Wash. U., U. of Md., Burnside-Off Aviation Inst. Flight Proficiency, Dallas Tex.

Career Air Force, 1958–62; Civilian ferry pilot, 1964–65; Universal Air Transport, Detroit, Mich., 1966–67; Pilot, Allegheny Airlines, 1967–78.

Offices 6205 DSOB, 202-224-2841. Also Rm. 730, 275 Chestnut St., Manchester 03103, 603-666-7691.

Committees *Armed Services* (5th). Subcommittees: Military Construction; Preparedness (Chairman); Sea Power and Force Projection.

Energy and Natural Resources (7th). Subcommittees: Energy Conservation and Supply; Energy Regulation (Chairman); Energy and Mineral Resources.

Labor and Human Resources (7th). Subcommittees: Alcoholism and Drug Abuse (Chairman); Aging, Family, and Human Services; Investigations and General Oversight.

Group Ratings

	ADA	COPE	PC	LCV	CFA	RPN	NAB	NSI	NTU	ACA	ACU
1980	6	5	17	27	0	—	100	100	74	96	100
1979	5	10	26	—	19	—	—	—	73	93	100

Key Votes

1) Draft Registn $	FOR	6) Fair Housng Cloture	AGN	11) Cut Socl Incr Defns	FOR
2) Ban $ to Nicrgua	AGN	7) Ban $ Rape Abortns	FOR	12) Income Tax Indexing	FOR
3) Dlay MX Missile	AGN	8) Cap on Food Stmp $	FOR	13) Lim Spdg 21% GNP	FOR
4) Nuclr Mortorium	AGN	9) New US Dep Edcatn	AGN	14) Incr Wndfll Prof Tax	AGN
5) Alaska Lands Bill	AGN	10) Cut OSHA Inspctns	FOR	15) Chryslr Loan Grntee	AGN

Election Results

1978 general	Gordon J. Humphrey (R)........	133,745	(51%)	($357,107)
	Thomas J. McIntyre (D)	127,945	(49%)	($289,628)
1978 primary	Gordon J. Humphrey (R)........	35,503	(50%)	
	James Massiello (R)	18,371	(26%)	($75,769)
	Alf E. Jacobson (R)	13,619	(19%)	
	One other (R)	2,885	(5%)	
1972 general	Thomas J. McIntyre (D)	184,495	(57%)	($82,800)
	Wesley Powell (R).............	139,852	(43%)	($104,779)

Sen. Warren Rudman (R) Elected 1980, seat up 1986; b. May 18, 1930, Boston, Mass.; home, Nashua; Syracuse U., B.S. 1952, Boston Col., J.D. 1960.

Career Army, Korea; Atty. Gen. of N.H., 1970–76; Pres. Nat. Assn. of Attys. Gen., 1975.

Offices 4104 DSOB, 202-224-3324. Also Fed. Bldg., 80 Daniels St., Portsmouth 03081, 603-431-5900; 125 N. Main St., Concord 03301, 603-225-7115; and Norris Cotton Fed. Bldg., 275 Chestnut St., Manchester 03101, 603-666-7591.

Committees *Appropriations* (14th). Subcommittees: Defense; Foreign Operations; Interior; Labor, Health and Human Services, Education; State, Justice, Commerce, and the Judiciary.

Governmental Affairs (9th). Subcommittees: Permanent Subcommittee on Investigations (Vice-chairman); Governmental Efficiency and the District of Columbia; Oversight of Government Management.

Select Committee on Small Business (8th). Subcommittees: Innovation and Technology (Chairman); Advocacy and the Future of Small Business.

Group Ratings and Key Votes: Newly Elected

Election Results

1980 general	Warren Rudman (R)............	195,559	(52%)	($585,926)
	John A. Durkin (D)	179,455	(48%)	($676,150)
1980 primary	Warren Rudman (R)............	20,206	(20%)	
	John Sununu (R)	16,885	(17%)	($187,595)
	Wesley Powell (R).............	14,861	(15%)	($0)
	Eight others (R)...............	147,607	(47%)	
1975 special	John A. Durkin (D)	140,778	(54%)	
	Louis C. Wyman (R)	113,007	(43%)	
1974 general	John A. Durkin (D)	110,924	(50%)	($128,389)
	Louis C. Wyman (R)	110,914	(50%)	($138,605)

1974 primary   John A. Durkin (D)   22,258   (50%)
                 Lawrence Radway (D)   14,646   (33%)
                 Two others (D)   7,615   (17%)

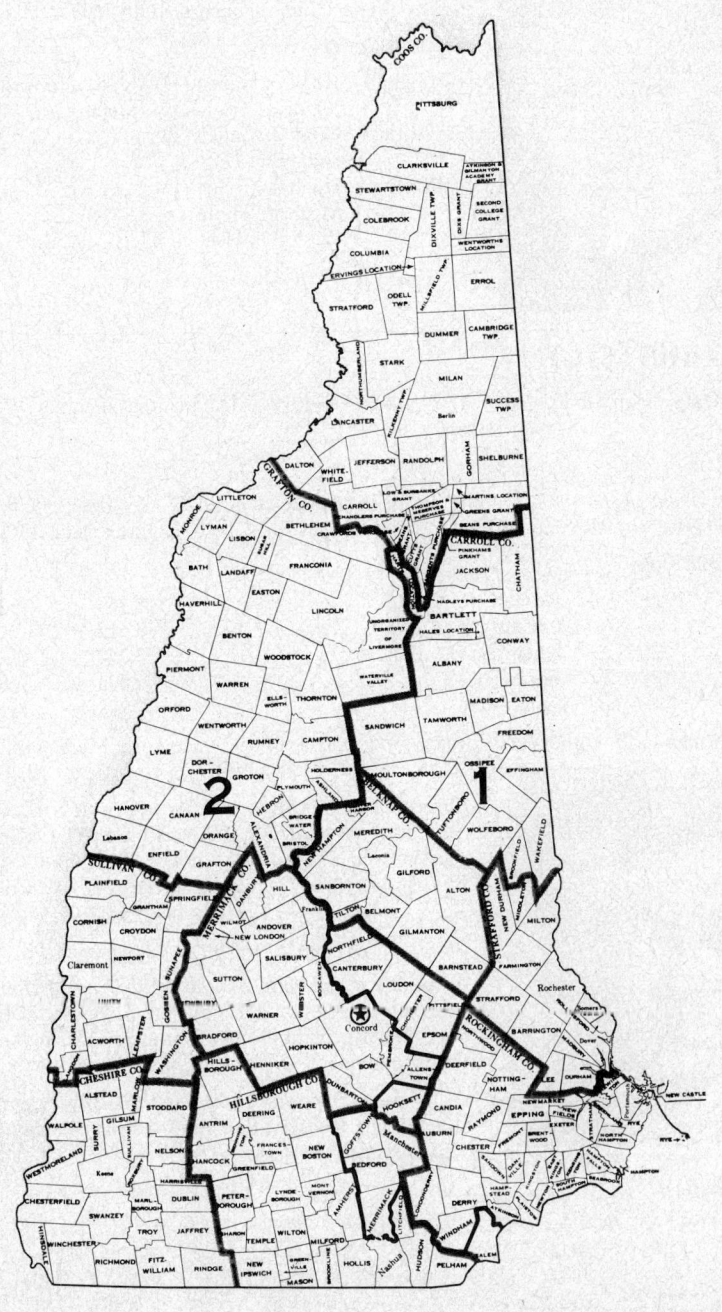

GOVERNOR

Gov. Hugh J. Gallen (D) Elected 1978, term expires Jan. 1983; b. July 30, 1924, Portland, Oreg.

Career Minor league baseball player; Car salesman, 1948–; Pres., Hugh J. Gallen, Inc., GM dealership; Dem. State Chmn., 1971–72.

Offices State House, Concord 03301, 603-271-1110.

Election Results

1980 gen.	Hugh J. Gallen (D)	226,436	(59%)
	Meldrim Thomson, Jr. (R) .	156,178	(41%)
1980 prim.	Hugh J. Gallen (D)	37,786	(81%)
	One other (D)	8,689	(19%)
1978 gen.	Hugh J. Gallen (D)	133,133	(49%)
	Meldrim Thomson, Jr. (R) .	122,464	(45%)
	Wesley Powell, Jr. (I)	12,349	(5%)

FIRST DISTRICT

Census Data Pop. (1980 final) 470,924, up 28% in 1970s. Median family income, 1970, $9,631, 100% of U.S.

The Voters

Employment profile 1970 White collar, 45%. Blue collar, 42%. Service, 12%. Farm, 1%.
Ethnic groups Hispanic 1980, 1%. Total foreign stock 1970, 23%. Canada, 13%.

Presidential Vote

1980	Reagan (R)	118,160	(60%)
	Carter (D)	53,617	(27%)
	Anderson (I)	23,754	(12%)
1976	Ford (R)	95,003	(56%)
	Carter (D)	72,778	(43%)

Rep. Norman E. D'Amours (D) Elected 1974; b. Oct. 14, 1937, Holyoke, Mass.; home, Manchester; Assumption Col., B.A. 1960, Boston U., LL.B. 1963.

Career Practicing atty.; Asst. Atty. Gen. of N.H., 1966–69; Criminal Law Instructor, St. Police Trng. Sch., 1967–69; Dir., Manchester Area Sch. for Police Prosecutors, 1970; Manchester City Prosecutor, 1970–72; Instructor, St. Anselm's Col., 1972–73.

Offices 2242 RHOB, 202-225-5456. Also 275 Chestnut St., Manchester 03101, 603-668-6800.

Committees *Banking, Finance and Urban Affairs* (14th). Subcommittees: Economic Stabilization; Financial Institutions Supervision, Regulation and Insurance; Housing and Community Development.

Merchant Marine and Fisheries (9th). Subcommittees: Fisheries and Wildlife Conservation and the Environment; Oceanography (Chairman).

Group Ratings

	ADA	COPE	PC	LCV	CFA	RPN	NAB	NSI	NTU	ACA	ACU
1980	56	58	57	72	57	—	45	40	26	38	11
1979	63	85	68	76	74	—	—	—	32	31	24
1978	45	80	65	73	50	20	25	70	21	42	25

Key Votes

1) Draft Registn $	FOR	6) Fair Hsg DOJ Enfrc	FOR	11) Cut Socl Incr Dfns $	FOR
2) Ban $ to Nicrgua	AGN	7) Lim PAC Contrbtns	FOR	12) Hosptl Cost Controls	FOR
3) Dlay MX Missile	AGN	8) Cap on Food Stmp $	AGN	13) Gasln Ctrls & Allctns	FOR
4) Nuclr Mortorium	AGN	9) New US Dep Edcatn	—	14) Lim Wndfll Prof Tax	AGN
5) Alaska Lands Bill	FOR	10) Cut OSHA $	FOR	15) Chryslr Loan Grntee	AGN

Election Results

1980 general	Norman E. D'Amours (D)	114,061	(61%)	($100,417)
	Marshall W. Cobleigh (R)	73,565	(39%)	($66,062)
1980 primary	Norman E. D'Amours (D), unopp.			
1978 general	Norman E. D'Amours (D)	82,697	(63%)	($92,791)
	Daniel M. Hughes (R)	49,131	(37%)	($48,897)

SECOND DISTRICT

Census Data Pop. (1980 final) 449,686, up 31% in 1970s. Median family income, 1970, $9,736, 102% of U.S.

The Voters

Employment profile 1970 White collar, 45%. Blue collar, 42%. Service, 12%. Farm, 1%.
Ethnic groups Hispanic 1980, 1%. Total foreign stock 1970, 23%. Canada, 13%.

Presidential Vote

1980	Reagan (R)	103,545	(56%)
	Carter (D)	55,242	(30%)
	Anderson (I)	25,939	(14%)
1976	Ford (R)	90,932	(54%)
	Carter (D)	74,857	(44%)

Rep. Judd Gregg (R) Elected 1980; b. Feb. 14, 1947, Nashua; home, Greenfield; Columbia U., A.B. 1969, Boston U., J.D. 1972.

Career Practicing atty., 1976–80; Chmn., Nashua Rep. Committee, 1976; N.H. State Exec. Cncl., 1978.

Offices 503 CHOB, 202-225-5206. Also Fed. Bldg., 55 Pleasant St., Concord 03301, 603-228-0315, and 1 Spring St., Nashua 03060, 603-883-0800.

Committees *Government Operations* (17th). Subcommittee: Environment, Energy and Natural Resources.

Science and Technology (12th). Subcommittees: Energy Development and Applications; Science, Research and Technology.

Select Committee on Aging (16th). Subcommittee: Retirement Income and Employment.

Group Ratings and Key Votes: Newly Elected

Election Results

1980 general	Judd Gregg (R)	113,304	(64%)	($122,167)
	Maurice L. Arel (D)	63,350	(36%)	($100,144)
1980 primary	Judd Gregg (R)	16,603	(34%)	
	Susan McLane (R)	12,064	(25%)	($90,263)
	Charlie Bass (R)	10,689	(22%)	($170,161)
	Six others (R)	84,535	(19%)	
1978 general	James C. Cleveland (R)	84,535	(68%)	($65,961)
	Edgar J. Helms (D)............	39,546	(32%)	($22,207)

NEW JERSEY

New Jersey is a much maligned state, an object of derision for New Yorkers and a place little known by everyone else. Its fate was evident even in colonial times, when it was remarked that New Jersey was a valley between two mountains of conceit. The reference of course was to Philadelphia and New York, which even then overshadowed what lay in between. New Jersey is a state with a clear geographic definition, bounded by the Hudson River and the Atlantic Ocean on the east and the Delaware River on the west. It is even a state of some physical beauty: to the west of the grimy New Jersey Turnpike corridor, the part of the state most people know best, are mountains of surprising height and bucolic countryside; to the east are the mysterious Pine Barrens, still as virgin as they were in colonial times, and the kaleidoscopic variety of the resort towns of the Jersey Shore.

New Jersey is the ninth largest state in the nation in population, and the most densely populated. It is a manufacturing center of great note and the home of numerous corporations; it has housed Thomas Edison and given birth to Frank Sinatra. Yet somehow it has never had its own identity. In an era of giant metropolitan areas, most residents of New Jersey think of themselves as citizens of Metropolitan New York or Greater Philadelphia. Downtown is across a state line; the local sports teams are in the big cities (except for the pro football Giants who moved from Yankee Stadium to Hackensack upon completion of the Meadowlands sports complex), and this is one of two states (Delaware is the other) that does not have its own VHF television station. For many New Jersey is a place of convenience—a good location for a plant, a pleasant suburb without New York or Pennsylvania income taxes—rather than a promised land.

The lack of state identity is increased by the variety and heterogeneity of the state itself. The outsider's image of New Jersey is of the industrial Turnpike corridor and the soot-blackened row houses that they see before entering the Lincoln or Holland Tunnels on their way to New York. But you can find practically any kind of neighborhood you want in New Jersey. Particularly in northern New Jersey, within 60 miles of New York, are many high-income suburbs, as well as the horse farm country around Far Hills and the university town of Princeton. There are the old row house communities of Hudson County as well—but they are being changed and often renovated by the new immigrants, Cubans and other Latins, who have been thronging to these once stagnant immigrant entrepots in the 1970s. There are old industrial towns, such as Paterson with its factories on the millrace of the Passaic River, and 1950s working-class suburbs, and those south of Elizabeth that line both sides of the Turnpike. There are retirement villages and old beach resorts and in south Jersey even a few small towns that have the southern atmosphere of Delaware or Maryland or maybe even Virginia.

New Jersey's politics has been shaped by these factors—by the lack of a real identity in the state and by its heterogeneity. The lack of identity has left New Jersey vulnerable to boss control and to swings of sudden enthusiasm for one politician or another who seems likely to be a savior. The lack of close identification with New Jersey affairs has also left the state with congressional delegations many of whose members are pleasant and unobjectionable to their constituents but not very effective in Washington. New Jersey's heterogeneity has left the state's politics in the hands of a small number of county political bosses, who until the 1970s dominated the legislature and tended to select candidates for governor — the only state office that is elective and therefore the one real prize in state politics. Voters ordinarily have little information on state politics, because the major medium, television, devotes little time to it; the only exception is during gubernatorial campaigns, and that primarily because they are held in off years (1977, 1981, 1985) and because a state public financing law ensures that any serious candidate will have enough money to get his message across. In fact New Jersey is the second most expensive media state, after only California, because candidates have to buy both New York and Philadelphia TV.

Another problem endemic to New Jersey politics is corruption. It is hard to know whether it runs in cycles or whether it is simply exposed every once in a while. One cycle of exposure occurred in the early 1970s, when U.S. attorneys appointed, in effect, by Senator Clifford Case, a liberal Republican with no organizational ties, began tough investigations and prosecutions of organized crime figures and public officials. The roster of convictions included the Democratic bosses of Hudson County (Jersey City), the then mayor of Newark, the 1970 Republican candidate for U.S. Senate, and leading officials in the administrations of Democratic Governor Richard Hughes (1961–69) and of Republican Governor William Cahill (1969–73). Then the news of corruption subsided. Cahill was beaten in the 1973 Republican primary, by Congressman Charles Sandman, a right-wing Republican; his nomination ensured the election of the Democratic nominee, Brendan Byrne, a judge who became famous when tapes of a Mafia boss's tapped telephone conversation had a don describing him as unbuyable. In fact there have been no major scandals in the Byrne administration — he was reelected in 1977 — and so the state may have been unprepared for the indictments in the Abscam case in 1980 of such prominent New Jersey politicians as Senator Harrison Williams, Congressman Frank Thompson, and Camden Mayor Angelo Errichetti.

Byrne has not been a popular governor, yet he can claim a number of accomplishments. One is to have conducted an administration free of major scandal. Another is the enactment of the state's first income tax. His predecessors Hughes and Cahill had each in turn sought such a tax and each had been rebuffed by the legislature; Byrne succeeded after several years of struggle and with some help from the state's activist Supreme Court. The third major accomplishment was the establishment of legalized gambling in Atlantic City — the first legalization of games of chance east of Nevada since Maryland outlawed St. Mary's County's slot machines in 1968. Gambling has turned that seedy resort center into one of the nation's leading tourist destinations. The move has also caused some problems and has led to some resignations from the state gambling board; but it has also produced new revenue for the state. None of these achievements succeeded in making Byrne popular, and one can see why. Running a scandal-free administration is a negative achievement in a sense, the income tax was not popular, and legalized gambling gave major benefits to only one small part of the state. Byrne was reelected in 1977 largely because there were four other serious candidates in the Democratic primary (he had only 30% of the vote, but there is no runoff here) and because an inept Republican opponent who, despite his anti–income tax campaign, had himself once voted for the income tax.

New Jersey elects a new governor in 1981. Byrne is ineligible for a third term. Altogether, eight Republicans and 15 Democrats ran in their parties' primaries in the spring of 1981 and spent liberally. The existence of public financing tends to encourage the entry of any candidate who has a local fund-raising base that can get him or her over the $50,000 threshold of private contributions needed to trigger matching payments from the state. The power of the New Jersey governor, and the prospect that the person elected in 1981 may serve eight years, encourages practically every aspirant to run lest he miss the one chance in his political generation. It is also the one chance media-starved New Jersey has to enjoy a constructive dialogue on the future of the state, although there is always the danger that the campaign will focus instead on negative charges or boasts that one candidate or another is freest of corruption.

The winners were Democratic Congressman James Florio, who managed to add to his south Jersey base significant numbers of votes in the northern media market, and Republican former Speaker Thomas Kean, a member of an old aristocratic New Jersey family who shed his liberal label, endorsed major tax cuts, and won the support of such supply-siders as 1978 Senate candidate Jeffrey Bell. Both men have the potential to be strong candidates in November, and each has legitimate claims to the office and a corruption-free record. Whatever complaints there may be about New Jersey's public financing, these results seem to argue that the system works well.

Neither party seems to hold a significant advantage here. The Democrats have held the governorship for all but four of the last 28 years, and so the Republicans would seem to be overdue. The Republicans also seem to have the clear balance in national elections; their presidential candidates have carried New Jersey every time out since 1964. Yet New Jersey has two Democratic senators and a majority Democratic House delegation, and despite determined efforts has elected Democratic majorities in the legislature throughout the 1970s. If one can draw a conclusion from this, it is that the Democrats have a larger number of talented political candidates, enough to overcome, in contests requiring many candidates, the edge Republicans may have on some of the major issues.

New Jersey's two Democratic senators are altogether unalike, in generational terms or for what they are known best. Senator Harrison Williams has been in office since he was first elected in 1958, yet he seems never to have made an impression outside the state until he was indicted in the Abscam scandal in 1980. In early May 1981, he was found guilty, and his conviction is under appeal at this writing, but, whatever the outcome, his political career seems likely to be finished. The charges that he promised legislative assistance in return for arranging a business deal are so serious that he would seem to have a hard time rehabilitating himself with the public even if it believes his claim that he never sought nor took a bribe himself, as seems likely. Williams's problems seem to have come after he married his second wife, when his standard of living suddenly rose; certainly he is a person who should know what he is doing on Capitol Hill, after 22 years in the Senate and three in the House before that.

Yet Williams has left few footprints in his career. He served for some years as chairman of the Labor and Public Welfare Committee, where he worked in tandem with lobbyists for organized labor; he leaves no major legislation resulting from creative impulse. He also chaired important subcommittees on securities and on mass transit, and made some legislative contributions in both areas. He is now the ranking Democrat on the Banking Committee. But overall he seems to have had little impact in the Senate. His most vivid impression on most voters in New Jersey came in 1970, when he admitted that he was an alcoholic; he had been censured earlier by the state NAACP for showing up incoherent at a breakfast meeting. He has kept his alcohol problem under control since but has never told his constituents much about the fires that may burn beneath his pleasant and impassive surface.

The succession to Williams's seat is even harder to predict than the outcome of the gubernatorial race. There have been suggestions that he might resign before the end of the term even if his conviction is reversed on appeal, or that the Senate might even oust him. So conceivably a special election may be held in the fall of 1981 (the state primary may have to be moved back in any case to accommodate the redistricting schedule). As in the governorship race, there are likely to be a lot of competitors, although here no public financing exists to subsidize the inevitably expensive media campaigns that will probably be necessary to win. Republicans will make a major effort to win here, and one interesting candidate would be Jeffrey Bell, the Republican nominee for the other seat in 1978, a onetime aide of Governor Ronald Reagan, and one of the first backers of the Kemp–Roth tax cut and supply-side economics. Reagan-minded Republicans are acutely aware that this state has not elected a senator with anything like their views since 1952 (Republican Senator Clifford Case, defeated by Bell in the 1978 primary, voted much more often with Democrats than Republicans).

The state's other Senate seat is held by Bill Bradley, known to most of the nation as the basketball star with Princeton and the New York Knicks. Bradley is a good deal more than that. At Princeton he was a scholar as well as an athlete and won a Rhodes Scholarship — passing up two lucrative years in professional basketball. Unlike other athletes, he refused to make commercial endorsements but did write a thoughtful book about his experiences. Bradley had also worked in New Jersey politics for several years and, when he decided to run for the Senate in 1978, won the Democratic nomination with ease. Meanwhile, the 74-year-old Clifford Case was beaten by Jeffrey Bell, who is even younger than Bradley and who had the advantage of an original program. But Bradley made sure that voters knew more about him than just his basketball career, and he showed that he could handle difficult issues with ease. He also showed more concern about keeping in touch with New Jersey than had the thoughtful Case or the aloof Williams, men who had been New Jersey's two senators for the preceding 20 years. The result was a 55% Bradley victory in what was nationally a rather Republican year.

Senators are often suspicious of new colleagues who begin their careers as celebrities. Bradley seems to have disarmed any such suspicions. In his first two years he generally avoided publicity and concentrated on winning choice committee assignments — Finance, Energy. He spent long hours learning the rules and tended to the kind of chores other senators like to be relieved of. He prepared himself well on the merits of the issues and studiously avoided grandstanding. Then, when he had done the groundwork and developed one issue thoroughly, he acted quickly and got the Senate to require the Carter Administration, against its wishes, to begin to fill the nation's strategic oil reserve — something Carter later bragged about doing after the outbreak of the Iran–Iraq war.

It is possible that Bradley may seek more visibility in the next four years. He no longer need defer to committee chairmen, since they are Republicans; and the ranks of more or less liberal Democrats who can develop an issue and push through a bill have been drastically thinned. He has been mentioned in some quarters as a possible presidential candidate, and he may run someday, although one would assume that it would be too soon in 1984, when he turns 41. Bradley is not likely to be interested merely in increasing his name recognition; he is already well known. What he needs, whether he simply intends to be an effective senator from New Jersey or whether he intends to run for president, is to become known for his work on issues of substance. That seems to suit his temperament in any case. He is not up for re-election until 1984, and in the meantime he is likely to be quiet, until he finds an issue on which he is prepared and on which he can make a difference.

Democrats hold an 8 7 edge on New Jersey's House delegation, which is scheduled to be reduced from 15 to 14 members for 1982. Democrats had an edge as high as 11–4 after the 1974 election, but it was eroded in years since, particularly in 1980, when Republicans defeated Frank Thompson, then indicted and later convicted in the Abscam scandal, and Andrew Maguire, one of the most talented and aggressive of the 1974 freshman Democrats. Redistricting will be controlled in 1981 by the Democrats, who have solid margins in the legislature and by Brendan Byrne in the governor's chair; it is a measure of how little that control can mean, however, that Republicans designed the last plan, which at one point gave the Democrats such a big margin. The state has to lose one district, out of the northeastern part of the state. It is reasonable to bet that Peter Rodino, the chairman of the House Judiciary Committee, will not be discommoded if he wants to run again, and that there will continue to be a Hudson County–dominated district like the 14th currently represented by Frank Guarini. In that case, the loser is likely to be one of the following four: Joseph Minish, Democrat of suburban Essex County; Robert Roe, Democrat of Passaic County; and Bergen County Republicans Harold Hollenbeck and Marge Roukema.

Census Data   Pop. (1980 final) 7,364,158, up 3% in 1970s: 3.25% of U.S. total, 9th largest. Central city, 16%; suburban, 75%. Median 4-person family income, 1978, $22,189, 109% of U.S., 7th highest.

1979 Share of Federal Tax Burden $18,168,000,000; 4.03% of U.S. total, 8th largest.

1979 Share of Federal Outlays $12,629,161,000; 2.73% of U.S. total, 12th largest.

DOD	$2,309,040,000	14th	(2.18%)	HEW	$6,213,313,000	9th	(3.48%)
DOE	$210,238,000	19th	(1.79%)	ERDA	$193,110,000	4th	(7.12%)
HUD	$236,465,000	10th	(3.59%)	NASA	$58,392,000	15th	(1.25%)
VA	$464,118,000	16th	(2.24%)	DOT	$461,621,000	10th	(2.80%)
EPA	$163,562,000	11th	(3.08%)	DOC	$68,374,000	11th	(2.16%)
DOI	$32,032,000	37th	(0.58%)	USDA	$339,137,000	32d	(1.41%)

Economic Base   Finance, insurance, and real estate; chemicals and allied products, especially industrial chemicals and drugs; electrical equipment and supplies, especially communication equipment; apparel and other textile products, especially women's and misses' outerwear; machinery; fabricated metal products; food and kindred products.

Political Lineup   Governor, Brendan T. Byrne (D). Senators, Harrison A. Williams, Jr. (D) and Bill Bradley (D). Representatives, 15 (8 D and 7 R); 14 in 1982. State Senate, 40 (25 D, 13 R, 2 vacancies); State Assembly, 80 (44 D and 36 R).

The Voters

Registration   3,764,369 Total. 1,232,755 D (33%); 783,304 R (21%).

Employment profile 1970   White collar, 53%. Blue collar, 36%. Service, 11%. Farm, –%.
Ethnic groups   Black 1980, 13%. Hispanic 1980, 7%. Asian 1980, 1%. Total foreign stock 1970, 30%. Italy, 7%; Germany, Poland, 3% each; UK; USSR, Ireland, 2% each; Austria, 1%.

Presidential Vote

1980	Reagan (R)	1,546,557	(52%)
	Carter (D)	1,147,364	(39%)
	Anderson (I)	234,632	(8%)
1976	Ford (R)	1,509,688	(50%)
	Carter (D)	1,444,653	(48%)

1980 Democratic Presidential Primary			*1980 Republican Presidential Primary*		
Kennedy	315,109	(56%)	Reagan	225,959	(81%)
Carter	212,387	(38%)	Bush	47,447	(17%)
Uncommitted	19,499	(3%)	One other	4,571	(2%)
One other	13,913	(2%)			

SENATORS

Sen. Harrison A. Williams, Jr. (D) Elected 1958, seat up 1982; b. Dec. 10, 1919, Plainfield; home, Bedminster; Oberlin Col., B.A. 1941, Georgetown U. Sch. of Foreign Svc., Columbia U., LL.B. 1948

Career Navy, WWII; Practicing atty.; U.S. House of Reps., 1953–57.

Offices 352 RSOB, 202-224-4744. Also Rm. 939A Fed. Bldg., 970 Broad St., Newark 07102, 201-645-3030.

Committees *Banking, Housing, and Urban Affairs* (Ranking Member). Subcommittees: Housing and Urban Affairs; Financial Institutions; International Finance and Monetary Policy.

Labor and Human Resources (3d). Subcommittees: Labor; Handicapped; Alcoholism and Drug Abuse.

Rules and Administration (5th).

Joint Committee on the Library (2d).

Group Ratings

	ADA	COPE	PC	LCV	CFA	RPN	NAB	NSI	NTU	ACA	ACU
1980	72	94	73	82	80	—	0	10	18	13	5
1979	74	95	69	—	76	—	—	—	13	0	0
1978	80	89	63	72	55	70	0	10	9	9	4

Key Votes

1) Draft Registn $	FOR	6) Fair Housng Cloture	FOR	11) Cut Socl Incr Defns	AGN
2) Ban $ to Nicrgua	—	7) Ban $ Rape Abortns	—	12) Income Tax Indexing	AGN
3) Dlay MX Missile	FOR	8) Cap on Food Stmp $	AGN	13) Lim Spdg 21% GNP	AGN
4) Nuclr Mortorium	FOR	9) New US Dep Edcatn	FOR	14) Incr Wndfll Prof Tax	FOR
5) Alaska Lands Bill	FOR	10) Cut OSHA Inspctns	AGN	15) Chryslr Loan Grntee	FOR

Election Results

1976 general	Harrison A. Williams, Jr. (D)	1,681,140	(61%)	($610,090)
	David F. Norcross (R)	1,054,508	(38%)	($73,499)
1976 primary	Harrison A. Williams, Jr. (D)	378,553	(85%)	
	One other (D)	66,178	(15%)	
1970 general	Harrison A. Williams, Jr. (D)	1,157,074	(54%)	
	Nelson A. Gross (R)	903,026	(42%)	

Sen. Bill Bradley (D) Elected 1978, seat up 1984; b. July 28, 1943, Crystal City, Mo.; home, Denville; Princeton U., B.A. 1965, Rhodes Scholar, Oxford U., 1965–68.

Career U.S. Olympic Team, 1964; Pro basketball player, New York Knicks, 1967–77.

Offices 2107 DSOB, 202-224-3224. Also 1605 Vauxhall Rd., Union 07083, 201-688-0960.

Committees *Energy and Natural Resources* (9th). Subcommittees: Energy Conservation and Supply; Energy and Mineral Resources; Water and Power.

Finance (8th). Subcommittees: International Trade; Energy and Agricultural Taxation; Health.

Special Committee on Aging (5th).

Group Ratings

	ADA	COPE	PC	LCV	CFA	RPN	NAB	NSI	NTU	ACA	ACU
1980	72	100	63	75	80	—	9	10	17	0	6
1979	68	95	66	—	76	—	—	—	20	4	6

Key Votes

1) Draft Registn $	AGN	6) Fair Housng Cloture	FOR	11) Cut Socl Incr Defns	AGN
2) Ban $ to Nicrgua	—	7) Ban $ Rape Abortns	AGN	12) Income Tax Indexing	AGN
3) Dlay MX Missile	AGN	8) Cap on Food Stmp $	AGN	13) Lim Spdg 21% GNP	AGN
4) Nuclr Mortorium	FOR	9) New US Dep Edcatn	FOR	14) Incr Wndfll Prof Tax	FOR
5) Alaska Lands Bill	—	10) Cut OSHA Inspctns	AGN	15) Chryslr Loan Grntee	FOR

Election Results

1978 general	Bill Bradley (D)	1,082,960	(56%)	($1,688,499)
	Jeffrey Bell (R)	844,200	(43%)	($1,418,931)
1978 primary	Bill Bradley (D)	217,502	(59%)	
	Richard C. Leone (D)	97,667	(26%)	($328,052)
	Alexander Menza (D)	32,386	(9%)	($65,154)
	Three others (D)	21,698	(6%)	
1972 general	Clifford P. Case (R)	1,743,854	(62%)	($145,275)
	Paul J. Krebs (D)	963,573	(35%)	

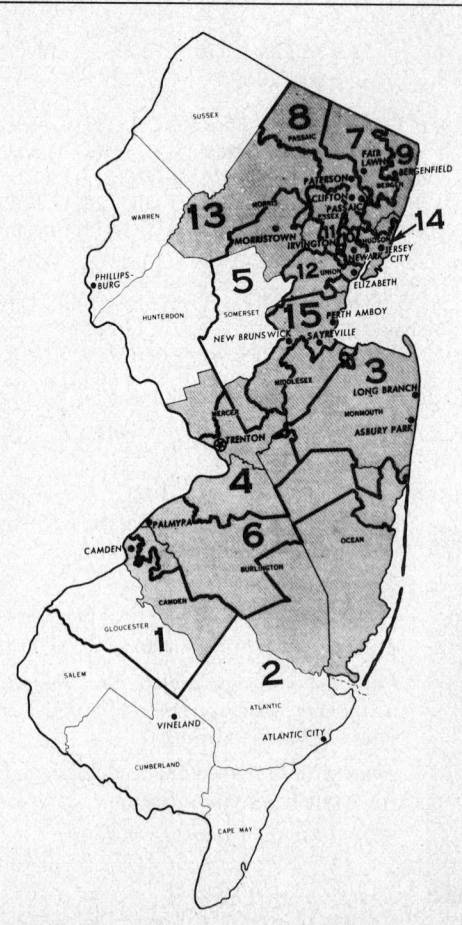

GOVERNOR

Gov. Brendan T. Byrne (D) Elected 1973, term expires Jan. 1982; b. Apr. 1, 1924, West Orange; Seton Hall U., Princeton U., A.B. 1949, Harvard U., LL.B. 1951.

Career Army Air Corps, WWII; Practicing atty.; Founder, Bd. Chmn., Intercontinental Ins. Co.; Asst. Counsel, Exec. Secy. to Gov. Robert B. Meyner, 1955–58; Dpty. Atty. Gen. in charge of Essex Co. Prosecutor's Ofc., 1958–59; Essex Co. Prosecutor, 1959–68; Pres., N.J. St. Bd. of Pub. Utilities, 1968–70; Superior Ct. Judge, 1970–72.

Offices Trenton 08625, 609-292-6000.

Election Results

1977 gen.	Brendan T. Byrne (D)	1,184,564	(56%)
	Raymond H. Bateman (R) .	888,880	(42%)
1977 prim.	Brendan T. Byrne (D)	175,448	(30%)
	Robert A. Roe (D)	134,116	(23%)
	Ralph C. DeRose (D)	99,948	(17%)
	James J. Florio (D)	87,743	(15%)
	Joseph A. Hoffman (D)	58,835	(10%)
	Six others (D)	22,908	(4%)
1973 gen.	Brendan T. Byrne (D)	1,414,613	(66%)
	Charles W. Sandman (R)...	676,235	(32%)

FIRST DISTRICT

The 1st congressional district of New Jersey is part of suburban Philadelphia, an area of the state more attuned to the city across the Delaware River than it is to Trenton or certainly Newark. The 1st takes in a cross-section of industrial America. Along the banks of the Delaware are the factories and oil tanks of such cities as Camden, the district's largest and the location of such American institutions as Walt Whitman's last home and the Campbell Soup Company. These are the places that are declining in population and suffering from the same ills that afflict much larger central cities — except that fewer people here seem to care. Southern New Jersey, with its petrochemical industry, appears to have the highest rates of some forms of cancer in America — but this is not the sort of thing that becomes a local political issue.

The industrial and suburban towns here fan out along the old rail lines running out of Camden and paralleling the river. Here on the flat plains of south Jersey are the subdivisions of the 1940s, 1950s, and 1960s, that thin out into the truck farming vegetable and fruit country. In general, the towns nearest the river, which are more industrial, vote Democratic, while those farther inland tend to go Republican. This is a land inhabited in large part by the third- and fourth-generation descendants of America's early 20th-century immigrants; Italian-Americans are the largest single group. Many of these people have their roots in old ethnic neighborhoods across the river in Philadelphia; they got better jobs than their parents, made more money, and moved across the Delaware. They grew up thinking of themselves as part of the great American working class, beneficiaries of programs such as Social Security and unemployment compensation. They supported the New Deal and tended to vote Democratic; when they backed a Republican, it was Senator Clifford Case or 1st district Congressman and later Governor William Cahill who backed New Deal measures and had a high labor voting record.

The last 15 years have seen a change in these attitudes and in the basic political orientation here. In the late 1960s, these people started thinking of themselves less as workingmen and more as hardworking taxpayers and upholders of traditional standards of morality that were under attack from demonstrating students and rioting blacks. The 1st district in that period had a congressman who exemplified these attitudes, a former sheriff and conservative Republican named John Hunt. He was destroyed politically by Watergate, which made a mockery of the moral pretensions of Richard Nixon and his followers. For voters in such places as New Jersey's 1st district, morality and traditional values ceased to be political issues, and they reverted to their ancestral Democratic preference. Their new congressman, who beat Hunt in 1974, was James Florio, a Democrat who has turned out to have a high liberal and labor voting record but who does nothing to offend people holding traditional cultural values.

Florio has been reelected with huge percentages; essentially he has been unopposed. Yet the district as a whole has been moving Republican at least in national elections. It embraced the cause of Ronald Reagan, not so much out of cultural issues (abortion, for one, is not a burning issue here) as they did out of a sense that the Carter Administration had failed on the basic economic and foreign policy issues.

Florio has had a successful career on Capitol Hill and one that may, in New Jersey politics, be more successful still. In June 1981 he won the Democratic nomination for governor, with 26% of the vote in a 13-candidate field. Florio had a strong local base, as indeed he had had four years before when he ran for the office; but in 1981 he was able as well to get significant percentages in all parts of the state. His prospects for the general election against Republican Thomas Kean are unclear. Kean has embraced the Reaganite cause of tax cuts; Florio favors more conventional policies. But Florio has the advantage of ethnic background. Kean is an aristocrat who speaks with what sounds like a Boston accent; Florio is an Italian–American in a state where Italians are the largest ethnic majority and that has never had an Italian–American governor.

Should Florio win, there would be a special election sometime in early 1982 to fill the House seat he would vacate; a Democrat would be favored to win, although Republicans might have a chance. If Florio loses the governorship he would of course continue in the House, where he has an important position. He chairs the Transportation Subcommittee of the Energy and Commerce Committee, an important body especially to southern New Jersey with its commuter and important freight rail lines. Energy and Commerce in 1979 was the busiest committee in the House, and Florio has the potential to be one of its more important legislators. He was the major force behind the "superfund" bill to clean up toxic wastes. His local base seems strong enough that he should have no trouble holding the district even if he cannot win statewide.

Census Data Pop. (1980 final) 524,125, up 10% in 1970s. Median family income, 1970, $10,314, 107% of U.S.

The Voters

Employment profile 1970 White collar, 46%. Blue collar, 42%. Service, 11%. Farm, 1%.
Ethnic groups Black 1980, 15%. Hispanic 1980, 4%. Asian 1980, 1%. Total foreign stock 1970, 18%. Italy, 5%; UK, Germany, Poland, 2% each; Ireland, 1%.

Presidential Vote

1980	Reagan (R)	92,376	(47%)
	Carter (D)	84,465	(43%)
	Anderson (I)	16,867	(9%)
1976	Ford (R)	82,661	(42%)
	Carter (D)	112,500	(58%)

Rep. James J. Florio (D) Elected 1974; b. Aug. 29, 1937, Brooklyn, N.Y.; home, Camden; Trenton St.

Col., B.A. 1962, Columbia U., 1962–63. Rutgers U., J.D. 1967.

Career Practicing atty., 1967–74; N.J. Gen. Assembly, 1969–75.

Offices 1740 LHOB, 202-225-6501. Also 23 S. White Horse Pike, Somerdale 08083, 609-627-8222.

Committees *Energy and Commerce* (7th). Subcommittees: Commerce, Transportation and Tourism (Chairman); Health and the Environment.

Interior and Insular Affairs (11th). Subcommittees: Oversight and Investigations; Public Lands and National Parks.

Select Committee on Aging (8th). Subcommittees: Health and Long-Term Care; Human Services.

Group Ratings

	ADA	COPE	PC	LCV	CFA	RPN	NAB	NSI	NTU	ACA	ACU
1980	72	89	67	81	79	—	8	44	18	13	16
1979	84	95	85	91	93	—	—	—	20	12	16
1978	55	75	73	87	77	42	18	57	13	22	17

Key Votes

1) Draft Registn $	FOR	6) Fair Hsg DOJ Enfrc	FOR	11) Cut Socl Incr Dfns $	AGN
2) Ban $ to Nicrgua	AGN	7) Lim PAC Contrbtns	FOR	12) Hosptl Cost Controls	FOR
3) Dlay MX Missile	FOR	8) Cap on Food Stmp $	AGN	13) Gasln Ctrls & Allctns	FOR
4) Nuclr Mortorium	FOR	9) New US Dep Edcatn	AGN	14) Lim Wndfll Prof Tax	AGN
5) Alaska Lands Bill	FOR	10) Cut OSHA $	AGN	15) Chryslr Loan Grntee	FOR

Election Results

1980 general	James J. Florio (D)............	147,352	(77%)	($143,463)
	Scott L. Sibert (R)	42,154	(22%)	($23,165)
1980 primary	James J. Florio (D)............	33,181	(100%)	
1978 general	James J. Florio (D)............	106,906	(79%)	($76,026)
	Robert M. Deitch (R)...........	26,853	(20%)	

SECOND DISTRICT

The 2d congressional district of New Jersey takes in Atlantic, Cape May, Cumberland, and Salem Counties, along with parts of Ocean and Burlington Counties. The 2d is geographically the largest and the most sparsely populated district in the state. The flat, often swampy lands of south Jersey are one of the premier vegetable farm areas of the country; and along the ocean are the beach resorts of Atlantic City, Wildwood, and Cape May. They run the gamut: Cape May was one of the original beach resorts in the United States and has many well-preserved Victorian houses; Atlantic City was the nation's leading resort between the two world wars, and its tawdry buildings have lately been spruced up — or torn down — for the influx of visitors enjoying America's first legalized casino gambling outside Nevada.

Cumberland and Salem Counties, like neighboring Delaware, have an almost southern atmosphere and an intermittent Democratic voting tradition that go back to the 19th century. That showed up when Jimmy Carter first ran for president; he did as well here in 1976 (although he failed to carry New Jersey) as any Democrat except Lyndon Johnson in the last 40 years. Cape May is a Republican bastion. Atlantic City, where most of the district's higher-than-average black population can be found, has been increasingly Democratic, although one can see from time to time evidence of the erstwhile dominance of the county by its old-fashioned Republican machine.

This was the district that elected Charles Sandman, the Republican congressman whose defense of Richard Nixon at the House Judiciary Committee recalled in tone if not in content the manner of the late Joseph McCarthy. That performance ended Sandman's political career; he lost that fall to Democrat William Hughes, who has represented the district ever since. As quiet as Sandman was noisy, Hughes has not attracted great publicity in the House. One of his pet causes is to prohibit people working for the government to move immediately into jobs in industries they used to regulate, and he has had at least one of his measures passed. He has also worked to get a share of revenues for the states from oil that is found offshore — undoubtedly because there has been much exploration, although no commercial discovery, of oil off the coast of New Jersey. Hughes's voting record is mixed: he gets almost as high ratings from conservative groups as from liberals. He has in any case proved very popular in the 2d district. He chairs a Judiciary subcommittee on crime.

That popularity was sorely tested in 1980, when Hughes had substantial opposition in the person of Cape May County Sheriff Beech Fox. Hughes lost Ocean County, the fastest-growing part of the district, where many residents are retirees or other newcomers from New York not familiar with New Jersey politics. But in the more settled southern part of the district, even in Cape May, Hughes was able to win solid majorities. Redistricting, controlled by Democrats, will probably help him marginally, since the natural thing to do, even apart from partisan considerations, is to remove some of Ocean County from the district. The question then is whether Republicans will target this district again.

Census Data   Pop. (1980 final) 610,529, up 28% in 1970s. Median family income, 1970, $9,039, 94% of U.S.

The Voters

Employment profile 1970   White collar, 42%. Blue collar, 41%. Service, 15%. Farm, 2%.
Ethnic groups   Black 1980, 12%. Hispanic 1980, 4%. Total foreign stock 1970, 20%. Italy, 5%; Germany, 3%; UK, USSR, 2% each; Poland, Ireland, 1% each.

Presidential Vote

1980	Reagan (R)	141,464	(55%)
	Carter (D)	94,184	(37%)
	Anderson (I)	17,210	(7%)
1976	Ford (R)	120,914	(49%)
	Carter (D)	123,144	(51%)

Rep. William J. Hughes (D) Elected 1974; b. Oct. 17, 1932, Salem; home, Ocean City; Rutgers U., A.B. 1955, J.D. 1968.

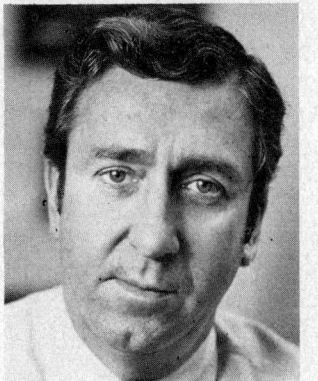

Career Practicing atty., 1959–74; Cape May Co. Asst. Prosecutor, 1960–70; Ocean City Solicitor, 1970–74.

Offices 436 CHOB, 202-225-6572. Also 2920 Atlantic Ave., Atlantic City 08401, 609-345-4844.

Committees *Judiciary* (9th). Subcommittees: Crime (Chairman); Monopolies and Commercial Law.

Merchant Marine and Fisheries (11th). Subcommittees: Coast Guard and Navigation; Fisheries and Wildlife Conservation and the Environment; Oceanography.

Select Committee on Aging (10th). Subcommittee: Human Services.

Group Ratings

	ADA	COPE	PC	LCV	CFA	RPN	NAB	NSI	NTU	ACA	ACU
1980	61	53	57	83	50	—	45	50	37	42	32
1979	58	80	65	72	63	—	—	—	38	27	16
1978	55	68	58	76	59	33	36	60	27	35	24

Key Votes

1) Draft Registn $	FOR	6) Fair Hsg DOJ Enfrc	FOR	11) Cut Socl Incr Dfns $	FOR
2) Ban $ to Nicrgua	AGN	7) Lim PAC Contrbtns	FOR	12) Hosptl Cost Controls	AGN
3) Dlay MX Missile	FOR	8) Cap on Food Stmp $	AGN	13) Gasln Ctrls & Allctns	FOR
4) Nuclr Mortorium	FOR	9) New US Dep Edcatn	FOR	14) Lim Wndfll Prof Tax	AGN
5) Alaska Lands Bill	FOR	10) Cut OSHA $		AGN	15) Chryslr Loan Grntee	AGN

Election Results

1980 general	William J. Hughes (D)	135,437	(57%)	($101,246)
	Beech N. Fox (R)	97,072	(41%)	($141,776)
1980 primary	William J. Hughes (D)	22,105	(100%)	
1978 general	William J. Hughes (D)	112,768	(66%)	($108,703)
	James H. Biggs (R)	56,997	(34%)	

THIRD DISTRICT

Monmouth County is a place with a name made notable by a Revolutionary War battle and a 20th-century racetrack. Here, around the turn of the century, some of America's first beach resorts were developed, to cater to the increasing number of people with time and money for summer vacations. Beach manners have changed a lot since the days of full-length swimsuits, but the Monmouth County shore still attracts hundreds of thousands of bathers every year. Its summer home areas, with houses ranging from shacks to mansions, have increasingly become year-round communities, with many residents commuting to jobs in north Jersey or even Manhattan, some on the rickety North Jersey Coast Line railroad but more on the Garden State Parkway. The flatlands behind the beaches are the areas of fastest growth; here retirement villages and subdivisions attract people from the outer Jersey reaches of the New York metropolitan area.

Virtually all of Monmouth County, plus Lakewood Township and Point Pleasant in Ocean County just to the south, make up New Jersey's 3d congressional district. By tradition Monmouth is a Republican stronghold, and it runs about 5% more Republican than the state as a whole. Thus it favored Gerald Ford in 1976 and Ronald Reagan in 1980 by comfortable margins, but it also went for Senator Bill Bradley in 1978 and Governor Brendan Byrne in 1977. In congressional elections it has been, at least on the surface, quite steady. It elected the same Republican from 1940 until he retired in 1964, and since that time it has elected Democrat James Howard.

Howard is one of the few members of the House who is chairman of a standing committee, the Public Works and Transportation Committee, a position to which he succeeded after its previous chairman, Harold Johnson of California, was defeated in the 1980 election. The committee is a body on which partisan differences are not always very important. One of its primary functions, and the one with which Howard has always been most associated, is the federal highway program. This has been financed largely by a gasoline tax of a fixed number of cents — a bonanza for roadbuilders in the old days, when construction costs were relatively low and gas prices were so low that an excise rather than a fixed tax would have produced very little. It is less bounteous today, since construction costs are far higher and the 4¢ gas tax is a small fraction of the money the public spends on gasoline. Nevertheless, there is great public resistance, given gas price rises in recent years, to any increase whatever in the tax. As a result, the government has had to forgo tying up the last loose threads of the interstate highway system, and the highway lobby is screaming that other revenue sources are needed to maintain current interstate and federal highways and bridges. Public Works also has responsibility for the nation's railroads — not a pleasant duty; it has traditionally also been the pork barrel committee, the body that passes around dams and other federal construction projects. Nowadays, however, relatively few members count these as great political assets and Howard is not a political horse trader like some of his predecessor chairmen. As for mass transit, Howard was unable to get his bill passed in the last-minute crunch in 1980 and scaled down his plans in 1981.

Voters imagine that they are electing a congressman who deals with all the problems of the world; in fact, congressmen inevitably have to specialize. In Howard the voters of the 3d district are electing a man who deals with difficult policy problems in which, by their nature, all desirable ends cannot be accomplished. Howard, by general consent, approaches these problems with honorable intentions and competence. It is not the stuff of which snappy campaign slogans are made, however, and Howard has occasionally been attacked by cheap shots: for example, for not improving conditions on the North Jersey Coast Line. The 3d is basically a Republican district; it has favored no Democratic presidential candidate except Johnson since New Jersey's own Woodrow Wilson ran. Republicans have targeted Howard several times, in 1966, 1970, 1972, 1978, and 1980, and in the last attempt nearly succeeded in beating him.

The Republican candidate was well chosen: Assemblywoman Marie Muhler, a fiscal conservative in line with national Republican economic policies, but a backer of the Equal Rights Amendment and unrestricted abortions. Muhler made her mark in the legislature as a backer of minimum competency standards of students — a move that aroused the opposition of the teachers' unions. Encouraged by the fact that Howard had won only 56% of the vote in 1978, Republicans poured money into this district and came within 1% of defeating the veteran incumbent.

Will Howard's committee position and seniority help him in 1982? Sometimes it works the other way around. Districts like the 3d of New Jersey are not indigents looking for federal boodle; pork barrel politics would not get Howard far. Moreover, sometimes a senior member's profile on national issues is far more controversial than a junior member's profile as his district's friendly ombudsman. Howard may need some help from the Democratic legislature as it redistricts in order to survive; but it will be difficult for them within the limits of the equal population rule to give him some Democratic territory in adjacent Middlesex County or indeed to raise the district's Democratic percentages without changing its boundaries markedly.

Census Data Pop. (1980 final) 525,767, up 11% in 1970s. Median family income, 1970, $11,291, 117% of U.S.

The Voters

Employment profile 1970 White collar, 56%. Blue collar, 31%. Service, 12%. Farm, 1%.
Ethnic groups Black 1980, 9%. Hispanic 1980, 3%. Asian 1980, 1%. Total foreign stock 1970, 25%. Italy, 5%; Germany, UK, 3% each; USSR, Poland, Ireland, 2% each.

Presidential Vote

1980	Reagan (R)	130,961	(57%)
	Carter (D)	76,116	(33%)
	Anderson (I)	18,440	(8%)
1976	Ford (R)	118,767	(56%)
	Carter (D)	93,283	(44%)

Rep. James J. Howard (D) Elected 1964; b. July 24, 1927, Irvington; home, Wall Twnshp.; St. Bonaventure U., B.A. 1952, Rutgers U., M.Ed. 1958.

Career Navy, WWII; Teacher and Acting Principal, Wall Township Sch. Dist., 1952–64.

Offices 2245 RHOB, 202-225-4671. Also 808 Belmar Plaza, Belmar 07719, 201-681-3321.

Committees *Public Works and Transportation* (Chairman).

Group Ratings

	ADA	COPE	PC	LCV	CFA	RPN	NAB	NSI	NTU	ACA	ACU
1980	83	74	57	52	79	—	0	50	12	14	0
1979	79	95	70	82	81	—	—	—	13	8	13
1978	60	84	65	62	68	17	0	33	5	9	5

Key Votes

1) Draft Registn $	FOR	6) Fair Hsg DOJ Enfrc	FOR	11) Cut Socl Incr Dfns $	AGN
2) Ban $ to Nicrgua	AGN	7) Lim PAC Contrbtns	FOR	12) Hosptl Cost Controls	FOR
3) Dlay MX Missile	—	8) Cap on Food Stmp $	AGN	13) Gasln Ctrls & Allctns	FOR
4) Nuclr Mortorium	FOR	9) New US Dep Edcatn	FOR	14) Lim Wndfll Prof Tax	AGN
5) Alaska Lands Bill	FOR	10) Cut OSHA $	AGN	15) Chryslr Loan Grntee	FOR

Election Results

1980 general	James J. Howard (D)	106,269	(50%)	($208,253)
	Marie S. Muhler (R)............	104,184	(49%)	($163,436)
1980 primary	James J. Howard (D)	20,522	(100%)	
1978 general	James J. Howard (D)	83,349	(56%)	($123,220)
	Bruce G. Coe (R)	64,730	(43%)	($145,048)

FOURTH DISTRICT

The 4th congressional district of New Jersey occupies a geographically central portion of the state. It cuts a swath across New Jersey from the capital in Trenton, along the Delaware River, to Cliffwood Beach, on Raritan Bay, across from Staten Island, New York. The New Jersey Turnpike runs through most of the district, starting in the south about 20 miles from center city Philadelphia, proceeding past industrial suburbs to the south side of Trenton, across flat marshy land to East Brunswick, where it expands to 12 lanes for its final miles, north of the 4th district to New York. All this terrain is essentially Democratic, the kind of place that is home to people who work in New Jersey's factories and hold down jobs in its offices.

This is the district that elected Frank Thompson, probably the most distinguished victim of the Abscam scandal. When the scandal broke, Thompson had been in Congress for 25 years; he was chairman of the House Administration Committee (the position from which Wayne Hays wielded so much power) and number two Democrat on Education and Labor; he was a smart, witty politician and a friend of organized labor. He was also a man, or so the government charged, who would accept a $50,000 bribe for helping a foreign businessman enter and remain in the United States. His involvement was perhaps the biggest surprise of Abscam, and his friends in organized labor and liberal movements put together a defense fund. What they could not put together is a rationale for why this talented and well-positioned man did what the government claimed.

Thompson's trial was not held until after the 1980 election, and he maintained his innocence all along. That did not help him, however, in the general election. He had beaten his Republican opponent, right-to-lifer Christopher Smith, decisively in 1978; he lost by almost as big a margin in 1980. Nor was this in any way because of coattails; this was not a majority Republican district even in 1980.

Smith's political fate hinges on redistricting as much as anything else. A district as elongated in shape as this is can be changed very substantially, particularly since it is in the center of the state. Trenton and surrounding Mercer County, the heart of the district, are heavily Democratic (they went for Carter in 1980); the somewhat less Democratic Middlesex County portion might be a welcome addition to beleaguered Democrat James Howard's 3d district. The likeliest change is that the legislature would shift the focus of the district south, which would not necessarily help Smith; the Democrats might add Democratic portions of the 6th district along the Delaware River across from Philadelphia. There is a general assumption in New Jersey that Smith has few political assets outside Thompson's Abscam problems and will turn out to be a one-term congressman.

Census Data   Pop. (1980 final) 487,962, up 2% in 1970s. Median family income, 1970, $11,086, 116% of U.S.

The Voters

Employment profile 1970   White collar, 49%. Blue collar, 38%. Service, 12%. Farm, 1%.
Ethnic groups   Black 1980, 14%. Hispanic 1980, 3%. Asian 1980, 1%. Total foreign stock 1970, 25%. Poland, 4%; Germany, 3%; UK, Hungary, USSR, 2% each; Ireland, Austria, 1% each.

Presidential Vote

1980	Reagan (R)	84,103	(47%)
	Carter (D)	78,828	(44%)
	Anderson (I)	14,056	(8%)
1976	Ford (R)	83,561	(46%)
	Carter (D)	97,112	(54%)

Rep. Christopher H. Smith (R) Elected 1980; b. Mar. 4, 1953, Rahway; home, Old Bridge; Worcester Col., England, 1974, Trenton St. Col., B.S. 1975.

Career Sales Exec., family-owned sporting goods business, 1975–80; Exec. Dir., N.J. Right to Life, 1977–78; Rep. nominee for U.S. House of Reps., 1978; Legis. Agent for N.J. Senate and Assembly, 1979.

Offices 513 CHOB, 202-225-3765. Also 2333 White Horse, Mercerville Rd., Suite H, Trenton 08619, 609-890-2800; Madison Arms Plaza, 18 Throckmorton La., Rm. 208; Old Bridge 08857, 201-679-7440; and 222 High St., Burlington City 08016, 609-386-5534.

Committees *Small Business* (14th). Subcommittees: General Oversight; SBA and SBIC Authority, Minority Enterprise and General Small Business Problems.

Veterans' Affairs (11th). Subcommittees: Hospitals and Health Care; Housing and Memorial Affairs.

Group Ratings and Key Votes: Newly Elected

Election Results

1980 general	Christopher H. Smith (R)........	95,447	(57%)	($79,069)
	Frank Thompson, Jr. (D)........	68,480	(41%)	($169,065)
1980 primary	Christopher H. Smith (R)........	8,121	(83%)	
	One other (R)	1,676	(17%)	
1978 general	Frank Thompson, Jr. (D)........	69,259	(61%)	($66,828)
	Christopher H. Smith (R)........	41,833	(37%)	($15,717)

FIFTH DISTRICT

Most people's image of New Jersey is the one they get from the drive from Newark Airport to Manhattan: factories spewing smoke into the already smoggy air, swampland pocked with truck terminals and warehouses, grim lines of Jersey City row houses, and the docks on the Hudson River. But there is another New Jersey — one that begins 40 or 50 miles outside Manhattan, past the first ridge of mountains west of Newark. Such is the area that is New Jersey's 5th congressional district. Out here the high-income suburbs fade into the elegant horse farm country around Morristown and Far Hills, Peapack and Bernardsville and Basking Ridge. The 5th also includes middle-class suburbs, places such as Parsippany–Troy Hills, where subdivisions of tightly grouped houses sell for prices considered modest these days.

But most of the 5th district, at least in area, from the horse country of Morris and Somerset Counties to the rich university town of Princeton, is high-income territory; in fact, in 1970 it ranked 11th in median family income of all the nation's 435 congressional districts.

It is appropriate, then, that the 5th district has a line of representatives going back more than 50 years from America's wealthiest and most aristocratic families. There was Charles Eaton, congressman from 1924 to 1952, a relative of the industrialist Cyrus Eaton. He was followed by Peter H. B. Frelinghuysen, descendant of a fire-breathing 18th-century Dutch preacher and scion of a family that has produced three U.S. senators, an unsuccessful candidate for vice president, and a secretary of state. A moderate Republican, Frelinghuysen lost a leadership post to Melvin Laird in 1965, but in 1974 became ranking Republican on the Foreign Affairs Committee. His support of Nixon and Ford foreign policies hurt him in the district, and he received stronger than usual competition from a Vietnam war opponent in 1972; perhaps that is why he retired in 1974.

Frelinghuysen's successor is another aristocrat, Millicent Fenwick of Bernardsville. She came to politics late, after such diverse activities as attending the New School for Social Research and working as an editor for *Vogue*. She is a person of definite and irresistible character. Tall and thin, she speaks with the kind of accent heard at the most fashionable girls' schools. At the end of a meeting she will take her pipe out of her purse and start puffing away.

Fenwick has had considerable impact on the House, although she remains a not very senior member of the minority party. In her first term she was not afraid to rise on the floor and take on Wayne Hays before his downfall. In her second term she served on the House ethics committee and was a major force for a thorough investigation of the Tongsun Park scandal. On a number of procedural issues—campaign finance, committee staffing—she has led strong attacks on the Democratic leadership. She is a fervent Republican, with a kind of noblesse-oblige liberalism; as a state official in New Jersey, she worked hard to help low-income consumers get more value for their money. Her zest for procedural reform is combined with caution on economic issues and some parsimony in spending government money.

Fenwick has not been one to wait to attain seniority on a committee; she has rather moved from one assignment to another. In 1979 she got off the Banking and ethics committees, and went on Foreign Affairs and the District of Columbia; in 1981 she stayed on Foreign Affairs and switched from D.C. to Education and Labor. It will be interesting to see how she responds to the battles on the latter committee between Reagan Republicans and organized labor on labor laws and on education and other spending programs. None of this switching around, indeed nothing she does, hurts her in the 5th district. Her kind of politics is the most popular politics possible in this district, and she has steadily increased her percentage to an enviable 78% in 1980. Redistricting is not likely to change this district significantly, since it is so heavily Republican and Fenwick is so popular that the Democratic legislature is unlikely to tamper with it.

Census Data   Pop. (1980 final) 473,351, down 1% in 1970s. Median family income, 1970, $14,218, 148% of U.S.

The Voters

   Employment profile 1970   White collar, 65%. Blue collar, 26%. Service, 9%. Farm, –%.
   Ethnic groups   Black 1980, 4%. Hispanic 1980, 2%. Asian 1980, 2%. Total foreign stock 1970, 29%. Italy, 6%; Germany, UK, Poland, 3% each; USSR, Ireland, 2% each; Austria, Canada, Hungary, 1% each.

Presidential Vote

1980	Reagan (R)	122,338	(56%)
	Carter (D)	70,704	(32%)
	Anderson (I)	22,523	(10%)
1976	Ford (R)	128,276	(59%)
	Carter (D)	88,004	(41%)

Rep. Millicent Fenwick (R) Elected 1974; b. Feb. 25, 1910, New York, N.Y.; home, Bernardsville; Columbia U., 1933, New Sch. for Soc. Research, 1942.

Career Assoc. Ed., Conde Nast Publications, 1938–52; Mbr., Bernardsville Borough Cncl., 1958–64; N.J. Gen. Assembly, 1969–72; Dir. N.J. Div. of Consumer Affairs, 1972–74.

Offices 1230 LHOB, 202-225-7300. Also 41 N. Bridge St., Somerville 08876, 201-722-8200.

Committees *Education and Labor* (9th). Subcommittees: Employment Opportunities; Labor–Management Relations; Labor Standards.

Foreign Affairs (9th). Subcommittee: Europe and the Middle East.

Select Committee on Aging (11th). Subcommittee: Health and Long-Term Care.

Group Ratings

	ADA	COPE	PC	LCV	CFA	RPN	NAB	NSI	NTU	ACA	ACU
1980	67	32	50	94	50	—	67	20	56	54	33
1979	53	42	40	69	23	—	—	—	53	48	34
1978	55	35	54	87	36	100	58	40	57	33	38

Key Votes

1) Draft Registn $	AGN	6) Fair Hsg DOJ Enfrc	FOR	11) Cut Socl Incr Dfns $	AGN
2) Ban $ to Nicrgua	AGN	7) Lim PAC Contrbtns	FOR	12) Hosptl Cost Controls	AGN
3) Dlay MX Missile	FOR	8) Cap on Food Stmp $	FOR	13) Gasln Ctrls & Allctns	AGN
4) Nuclr Mortorium	AGN	9) New US Dep Edcatn	AGN	14) Lim Wndfll Prof Tax	FOR
5) Alaska Lands Bill	FOR	10) Cut OSHA $	AGN	15) Chryslr Loan Grntee	AGN

Election Results

1980 general	Millicent Fenwick (R)	156,016	(78%)	($32,578)
	Kieran E. Pillion, Jr. (D)	41,269	(21%)	($7,177)
1980 primary	Millicent Fenwick (R)	23,419	(70%)	
	Larry (C. A.) Haverly (R)	10,080	(30%)	($4,358)
1978 general	Millicent Fenwick (R)	100,739	(73%)	($61,777)
	John T. Fahy (D)	38,108	(27%)	($43,509)

SIXTH DISTRICT

The 6th congressional district of New Jersey is weirdly shaped, spanning the entire state from the Delaware River to the Atlantic Ocean, and bringing into a single constituency people from sociologically diverse and geographically disparate communities. About half its residents live in the Philadelphia suburbs of Burlington and Camden Counties; important towns here include Cherry Hill and Willingboro (formerly Levittown). The heritage here may be Democratic, but the voting leans slightly Republican. The boom area in the 1970s is at the other end of the district, on or near the Jersey shore in Ocean County, which now has about one-quarter of the district's population; many of the new residents here are retirees from middle-class neighborhoods in New York and Philadelphia, fleeing from high taxes and crime. This is one of the most heavily Republican parts of New Jersey. Connecting these two regions — which have little in common — are the sparsely inhabited swamps and truck farms of south Jersey.

The 6th was created in close to its present form by the 1966 redistricting, and its first congressman was Republican William Cahill, who was elected governor in 1969 and defeated for renomination in 1973. The new congressman, elected in 1970, was Republican Edwin Forsythe. Despite six terms of service, Forsythe has little seniority on committees. He is a high-ranking Republican on the Merchant Marine Committee, on which he is one of the few members opposed to maritime subsidies, and a low-ranking Republican on the Science Committee, which he joined in 1977. His voting record does not follow any of the usual patterns in the House: he departs from Republican conservatism on many, although not all, cultural issues, and on a few economic issues. He appears to be a man with some interesting convictions but without the driving ambition that characterizes most of his colleagues in the House.

Redistricting will probably not prove troublesome for him. One reason is that his district has increased more than average, and another is its geographical position: to make it less Republican, the Democratic legislature would have to take from Democratic incumbents Democratic cities and townships they would rather hold onto.The focus of the district is likely to move a little south, taking in more of Ocean County. There is no reason to expect that Forsythe should not be reelected from such a district, although he might be vulnerable to a primary challenge someday.

Census Data Pop. (1980 final) 572,112, up 20% in 1970s. Median family income, 1970, $11,689, 122% of U.S.

The Voters

Employment profile 1970 White collar, 59%. Blue collar, 31%. Service, 9%. Farm, 1%.
Ethnic groups Black 1980, 7%. Hispanic 1980, 2%. Asian 1980, 2%. Total foreign stock 1970, 21%. Italy, 5%; Germany, UK, 3% each; Poland, USSR, 2% each; Ireland, 1%.

Presidential Vote	1980	Reagan (R)	131,054	(55%)
		Carter (D)	83,224	(35%)
		Anderson (I)	20,606	(9%)
	1976	Ford (R)	115,807	(52%)
		Carter (D)	108,251	(48%)

Rep. Edwin B. Forsythe (R) Elected 1970; b. Jan. 17, 1916, Westtown, Pa.; home, Moorestown.

Career Secy., Moorestown Bd. of Adjustment, 1948–52, Mayor, 1957–62; Chmn., Moorestown Twnshp. Planning Bd., 1962–63; N.J. Senate, 1963–69, Asst. Minor. Ldr., 1966, Minor. Ldr., 1967, Sen. Pres. and Acting Gov. of N.J., 1968, Pres. Pro Tem, 1969.

Offices 2210 RHOB, 202-225-4765. Also 3d and Mill Sts., Moorestown 08057, 609-235-6622.

Committees *Merchant Marine and Fisheries* (3d). Subcommittees: Fisheries and Wildlife Conservation and the Environment; Panama Canal and the Outer Continental Shelf.

Standards of Official Conduct (4th).

Science and Technology (7th). Subcommittees: Energy Research and Production; Science, Research and Technology.

Group Ratings

	ADA	COPE	PC	LCV	CFA	RPN	NAB	NSI	NTU	ACA	ACU
1980	50	28	30	70	36	—	80	25	56	83	68
1979	21	11	10	30	4	—	—	—	57	57	60
1978	40	16	23	27	18	82	80	28	51	70	83

Key Votes

1) Draft Registn $	AGN	6) Fair Hsg DOJ Enfrc	AGN	11) Cut Socl Incr Dfns $	AGN
2) Ban $ to Nicrgua	AGN	7) Lim PAC Contrbtns	AGN	12) Hosptl Cost Controls	AGN
3) Dlay MX Missile	FOR	8) Cap on Food Stmp $	AGN	13) Gasln Ctrls & Allctns	AGN
4) Nuclr Mortorium	AGN	9) New US Dep Edcatn	—	14) Lim Wndfll Prof Tax	—
5) Alaska Lands Bill	—	10) Cut OSHA $		15) Chryslr Loan Grntee	AGN

Election Results

1980 general	Edwin B. Forsythe (R)	125,792	(56%)	($109,593)
	Lewis M. Weinstein (D)	92,227	(41%)	($86,488)
1980 primary	Edwin B. Forsythe (R)	18,768	(90%)	
	One other (R)	2,126	(10%)	
1978 general	Edwin B. Forsythe (R)	89,446	(60%)	($87,804)
	W. Thomas McGann (D)	56,874	(38%)	($60,647)

SEVENTH DISTRICT

Bergen County, the northeast corner of New Jersey, is one of the nation's more comfortable and affluent suburban areas. Just across the George Washington Bridge from Manhattan, behind the Palisades that line the Hudson, are some of the nation's wealthier suburbs, sparsely settled (because of minimum acreage zoning), hilly, and tree-shaded. Most of them have the patina of age; the new, treeless subdivisions are going up farther south in New Jersey or to the north in what used to be called Upstate New York. Shopping centers, not skyscrapers, are the most prominent landmarks here, and although there are some out-of-gas industrial towns along the Passaic and Hackensack Rivers, the overall picture here is of settled affluence and neat prosperity.

Bergen County is divided into two congressional districts; the 7th occupies roughly the western half of it. Republicans drew the slightly irregular lines to split the county's centers of Democratic strength between the two seats: the 7th bulges south to take in industrial Hackensack and Jewish Teaneck to go with the generally Republican suburbs to the north and west. But redistricters' strategies do not always work. Entirely contrary to expectations, the 9th district in eastern Bergen County has gone Republican and the 7th district has gone Democratic in the majority of elections held under the current districting plan.

The Democrat who carried the 7th district was Andrew Maguire, and for a while at least he seemed tailored to this affluent, culturally liberal district. He had a Ph.D. from Harvard, a fellowship in England, a job with the Ford Foundation, and at age 37 in 1974 he was able to upset a liberal but elderly Republican who was not able to campaign vigorously. Maguire won a number of important fights in his House career: he got the House to consider conflict of interest charges against Bob Sikes, chairman of the Appropriations Military Construction Subcommittee, which ended the Floridian's career; he fought for tough clean air standards. Maguire also lost some: he wanted to ban saccharin after researchers found it caused cancer in animals, and he was one of the leading opponents of decontrol of oil prices. It was this kind of issue that probably got Maguire in trouble. The comfortable residents of the 7th were happy to have a procedural reformer, but they were less happy with a backer of government regulations and an outspoken critic of business.

The Republicans were fortunate to have a strong candidate here in Marge Roukema, a former school board member in Ridgewood (also Maguire's hometown). She won the Republican nomination with 39% of the primary vote in 1978, and got 47% against Maguire in the general. She never really stopped campaigning after that. She seemed more in line with district opinion. On cultural issues, she backed the Equal Rights Amendment and opposed curbs on abortion; there was no way Maguire could identify her with the Rev. Jerry Falwell. On economic issues, she attacked Maguire as antibusiness and overly enamored with government action—themes in line with both Republican doctrine and public thinking in 1980. Maguire put on a model intensive campaign, but he could not prevail, and Roukema won a 51%–47% victory.

As one of several new women (all Republicans) in the 97th Congress, Roukema attracted some attention. She also got seats on the Banking Committee and the Education and Labor Committee. To some extent her political fate will probably depend on the fortunes of the Reagan Administration's leading programs; Republicans are identified in voters' minds with a single set of coherent ideas, and they will probably rise and fall depending on how well those ideas do in practice.

Roukema has another problem: redistricting. North Jersey loses one of its congressional districts for 1982, and a Democratic legislature and governor will have a chance to draw the lines in 1981. What they may try to do is to squeeze two Bergen County Republicans—Roukema and Harold Hollenbeck—together into the same district, and let them fight it out in the primary. Another possibility is that Roukema may be thrown into the same district with Robert Roe of Passaic County, leaving her with some solid Democratic blue collar territory and a race that will be difficult to win (less difficult if Roe succeeds in getting himself elected as governor in 1981). It would be possible to draw Roukema a district that would cause her no problems, but the legislature is not likely to do that.

Census Data   Pop. (1980 final) 447,619, down 7% in 1970s. Median family income, 1970, $14,257, 148% of U.S.

The Voters

Employment profile 1970   White collar, 65%. Blue collar, 27%. Service, 8%. Farm, –%.
Ethnic groups   Black 1980, 4%. Hispanic 1980, 3%. Asian 1980, 2%. Total foreign stock 1970, 36%. Italy, 9%; Germany, 5%; Poland, UK, 3% each; USSR, Ireland, 2% each; Austria, Canada, Netherlands, 1% each.

Presidential Vote

1980	Reagan (R)	126,536	(57%)
	Carter (D)	71,849	(32%)
	Anderson (I)	21,619	(10%)
1976	Ford (R)	129,847	(58%)
	Carter (D)	93,764	(42%)

Rep. Margaret S. (Marge) **Roukema** (R) Elected 1980; b. Sept. 19, 1929, Newark; home, Ridgewood; Montclair St. Col., B.A. 1951, 1951–53.

Career High school teacher, 1951–55; Ridgewood Bd. of Educ., 1970–73; Cofounder, Ridgewood Sr. Citizens Housing Corp., 1973; Rep. nominee for U.S. House of Reps., 1978.

Offices 226 CHOB, 202-225-4465. Also 10 Forest Ave., Paramus 07652, 201-845-3335.

Committees *Banking, Finance and Urban Affairs* (16th). Subcommittees: Economic Stabilization; General Oversight and Renegotiation; Housing and Community Development.

Education and Labor (10th). Subcommittees: Elementary, Secondary and Vocational Education; Labor Standards.

Group Ratings and Key Votes: Newly Elected

Election Results

1980 general	Margaret S. (Marge) Roukema (R)	108,760	(51%)	($411,986)
	Andrew Maguire (D)	99,737	(47%)	($346,781)
1980 primary	Margaret S. (Marge) Roukema (R)	16,880	(100%)	
1978 general	Andrew Maguire (D)	78,358	(52%)	($202,210)
	Margaret S. (Marge) Roukema (R)	69,543	(47%)	($142,266)

EIGHTH DISTRICT

In the late 18th century Alexander Hamilton journeyed to the Great Falls of the Passaic River, some 20 miles west of the Hudson, and predicted major industrial development for the area around it. His prediction made sense: industry then depended on falling water for energy, and the Great Falls were 72 feet high, the highest in the East except for Niagara. Hamilton died—in a duel in nearby Weehawken—before his dream was fulfilled, but by the late 19th century Paterson, founded here at the Great Falls, became one of the major manufacturing cities in the United States. It developed major silk and locomotive factories and attracted immigrants from England, Ireland, and, after the turn of the century, Italy and Poland. Paterson was a tough town, and even as its town fathers were erecting imposing public buildings, its narrow streets were buzzing with rumor of anarchist plots. The great silk strike of 1913 here was led by the revolution-minded Industrial Workers of the World.

Today Paterson remains a manufacturing center, although neither silk nor locomotives are any longer its mainstay. Although more or less surrounded by suburbs of New York and Newark, it is resolutely nonsuburban—a small central city with its own little suburbs that just happens to be an easy freeway ride away from the George Washington Bridge. Paterson is the center of New Jersey's 8th congressional district, which includes most of surrounding Passaic County. To the south there is the old industrial city of Passaic and the larger, more middle-class Clifton; to the north and west are upper-income suburbs of Paterson, most notably Wayne Township. The political heritage of the 8th district is Democratic, a dim memory perhaps of its more radical past. But as in other factory towns there has been a shift away from the Democrats since 1960: the 8th went for Kennedy in 1960, Nixon in 1968, Ford in 1976, and Reagan in 1980.

The current congressman, Democrat Robert Roe, was the victor by only 960 votes in the 1969 special election that first sent him to Washington. Involved in local and state government before that, he serves on the Public Works and Science Committees. It is on the former that he has made his greatest mark. As chairman for some years of the Economic Development Subcommittee, he managed authorization for EDA, which provides aid to all kinds of city and other local governments. This program was slated for extinction by the incoming Reagan Administration, which argued that the programs do little but aid businessmen who would make investments anyway. Roe, however, maintains faith in such programs — and the faith, as well, of a man with a background and perhaps a future in state and local government. But by 1981 he had moved on to chair the Water Development Subcommittee, keeper of the traditional pork barrel.

For Roe has pretty clearly had his eyes on the governorship of New Jersey for the past half-dozen years. He ran in 1977 and raised the kind of substantial sums of money needed to run a media campaign in New Jersey. In an 11-candidate primary field, he won 86% of the vote in Passaic County, and did well enough elsewhere in north Jersey for 23% of the vote and a respectable second place finish to incumbent Brendan Byrne. In 1981 he ran again but made a major strategic error: he was the only one of the 13 Democrats running who declined New Jersey's generous public financing. Without that money he was unable to get his message across and finished a distant second with 16% of the vote. He has had no difficulty, even in Republican 1980, in winning reelection to Congress and will probably get a favorable district from the Democratic legislature.

Census Data   Pop. (1980 final) 462,340, down 3% in 1970s. Median family income, 1970, $10,783, 113% of U.S.

The Voters

Employment profile 1970   White collar, 46%. Blue collar, 44%. Service, 10%. Farm, –%.
Ethnic groups   Black 1980, 13%. Hispanic 1980, 14%. Asian 1980, 1%. Total foreign stock 1970, 38%. Italy, 10%; Poland, 5%; Germany, 3%; USSR, UK, Netherlands, Austria, Hungary, 2% each; Czechoslovakia, Ireland, 1% each.

Presidential Vote

1980	Reagan (R)	84,715	(52%)
	Carter (D)	65,102	(40%)
	Anderson (I)	9,487	(6%)
1976	Ford (R)	86,402	(52%)
	Carter (D)	79,546	(48%)

Rep. Robert A. Roe (D) Elected Nov. 4, 1969; b. Feb. 28, 1924, Wayne; home, Wayne; Oreg. St. U., Wash. St. U.

Career   Army, WWII; Wayne Twnshp. Committeeman, 1955–56; Mayor, 1956–61; Passaic Co. Bd. of Freeholders, 1959–63, Dir., 1962–63; Commissioner, N.J. Dept. of Conservation and Econ. Development, 1963–69.

Offices   2243 RHOB, 202-225-5751. Also U.S.P.O., 194 Ward St., Paterson 07510, 201-523-5152.

Committees   *Public Works and Transportation* (3d). Subcommittees: Economic Development; Investigations and Oversight; Water Resources (Chairman).

Science and Technology (2d). Subcommittees: Energy Development and Applications; Energy Research and Production.

Group Ratings

	ADA	COPE	PC	LCV	CFA	RPN	NAB	NSI	NTU	ACA	ACU
1980	67	85	53	61	57	—	0	38	11	17	17
1979	58	95	45	59	37	—	—	—	14	4	13
1978	35	85	48	60	50	25	90	33	7	19	25

Key Votes

1) Draft Registn $	FOR	6) Fair Hsg DOJ Enfrc	FOR	11) Cut Socl Incr Dfns $	AGN
2) Ban $ to Nicrgua	AGN	7) Lim PAC Contrbtns	FOR	12) Hosptl Cost Controls	FOR
3) Dlay MX Missile	FOR	8) Cap on Food Stmp $	AGN	13) Gasln Ctrls & Allctns	FOR
4) Nuclr Mortorium	AGN	9) New US Dep Edcatn	FOR	14) Lim Wndfll Prof Tax	AGN
5) Alaska Lands Bill	FOR	10) Cut OSHA $		AGN	15) Chryslr Loan Grntee	FOR

Election Results

1980 general	Robert A. Roe (D)	95,493	(67%)	($244,752)
	William R. Cleveland (R)	44,625	(31%)	($15,894)
1980 primary	Robert A. Roe (D)	14,662	(100%)	
1978 general	Robert A. Roe (D)	69,496	(75%)	($66,635)
	Thomas Melani (R).............	23,842	(25%)	($5,800)

NINTH DISTRICT

The 9th congressional district of New Jersey is, in rough terms, the eastern half of Bergen County plus the northern end of Hudson County. North of the George Washington Bridge and west of the Palisades that rise above the Hudson are the affluent, most heavily Republican parts of Bergen County: Tenafly, Dumont, Closter, Old Tappan. Near the Jersey end of the bridge are several predominantly Jewish and politically liberal suburbs. Atop the Palisades huge apartment towers overlook New York City, occupied by well-to-do people who want to escape the city and its taxes but who still want a view of Manhattan. South of the bridge, toward and into Hudson County, are older and less affluent suburbs, where people guard their suburban gentility as if it were their very lives and wear Republican party registration as a badge of their social distinction.

The Jersey Meadows separate the southern part of the 9th district—a section with about one-fifth of the district's population—from the rest. The Meadows are a swamp for which there are great plans. The new stadium for the New York (or Jersey) pro football Giants has been built, and other construction is taking place on this well-located land. But much of the Meadows is still pocked with gas stations and their giant signs, oil tank farms, truck terminals, and 12 lanes of New Jersey Turnpike. The 9th's southern towns, right next to the Meadows, are peopled with Polish–American and Italian–American citizens who usually vote Democratic. This is the part of the district that has produced its last two congressmen, Democrat Henry Helstoski and Republican Harold Hollenbeck.

Each in his own way was a political oddity. Helstoski won an upset victory in the Johnson landslide of 1964 and held on through a series of Republican redistrictings until in 1976 he was indicted for accepting bribes to help aliens stay in this country; he lost the seat that year to Hollenbeck. For his part, Hollenbeck had built a political career as a Republican from a Democratic town and, coming from an industrial corner of the district, was out of tune with the affluent suburbs that typically provide most of its Republican votes. He is an old-fashioned kind of liberal Republican, one of those who votes with Democrats more often on economic than noneconomic issues. He had a tough challenge in 1978 but was reelected with 49% while Helstoski, running as a candidate of the Always for People Party, won 13% of the vote. Helstoski lost the Democratic primary in 1980, but the nominee against Hollenbeck ran a quiet race, and this time Hollenbeck won with 59% of the vote — as convincing a victory as this district has seen since Helstoski's victory in the Watergate year of 1974 or, before that, Republican Frank Osmers's win in the 1956 Eisenhower landslide.

Hollenbeck's political fate is tied up with redistricting. North Jersey loses a seat, and the Democratic legislature has an opportunity to draw the lines in 1981. If most of Hudson County remains one district, that means that the 9th will have to be expanded westward into what now is the 7th. The problem for Hollenbeck is not necessarily that this territory will be less Republican, but that it might get him into a primary battle with Marge Roukema, a freshman but a Republican more in line with the upper-income attitudes that are dominant among Bergen County primary voters.

Census Data   Pop. (1980 final) 459,966, down 4% in 1970s. Median family income, 1970, $12,428, 130% of U.S.

The Voters

Employment profile 1970   White collar, 58%. Blue collar, 34%. Service, 8%. Farm, –%.
Ethnic groups   Black 1980, 3%. Hispanic 1980, 13%. Asian 1980, 3%. Total foreign stock 1970, 44%. Italy, 12%; Germany, 5%; Ireland, Poland, 3% each; UK, USSR, 2% each; Austria, 1%.

Presidential Vote

1980	Reagan (R)	117,284	(55%)
	Carter (D)	74,822	(35%)
	Anderson (I)	17,373	(8%)
1976	Ford (R)	116,058	(54%)
	Carter (D)	96,933	(46%)

Rep. Harold C. Hollenbeck (R) Elected 1976; b. Dec. 29, 1938, Passaic; home, East. Rutherford; Fairleigh Dickinson U., B.A. 1961; U. of Va., J.D. 1964.

Career   Practicing atty., 1965–77; Carlstadt Borough Prosecutor, 1966–67; East Rutherford Borough Cncl., 1967–69; N.J. Gen. Assembly, 1968–71; N.J. Senate, 1972–73.

Offices   1526 LHOB, 202-225-5061. Also 1550 Lemoine Ave., Ft. Lee 07024, 201-947-6868.

Committees   *Public Works and Transportation* (11th). Subcommittees: Aviation; Economic Development; Investigations and Oversight.

Science and Technology (5th). Subcommittees: Energy Research and Production; Space Science and Applications; Transportation, Aviation and Materials.

Select Committee on Aging (17th). Subcommittee: Retirement Income and Employment.

Group Ratings

	ADA	COPE	PC	LCV	CFA	RPN	NAB	NSI	NTU	ACA	ACU
1980	89	74	67	82	64	—	20	38	21	32	16
1979	63	85	60	79	74	—	—	—	27	38	16
1978	50	75	53	75	50	40	17	56	16	22	42

Key Votes

1) Draft Registn $	AGN	6) Fair Hsg DOJ Enfrc	FOR	11) Cut Socl Incr Dfns $	AGN
2) Ban $ to Nicrgua	—	7) Lim PAC Contrbtns	FOR	12) Hosptl Cost Controls	AGN

3) Dlay MX Missile	FOR	8) Cap on Food Stmp $	AGN	13) Gasln Ctrls & Allctns	FOR
4) Nuclr Mortorium	FOR	9) New US Dep Edcatn	FOR	14) Lim Wndfll Prof Tax	AGN
5) Alaska Lands Bill	FOR	10) Cut OSHA $	AGN	15) Chryslr Loan Grntee	FOR

Election Results

1980 general	Harold C. Hollenbeck (R)	116,128	(59%)	($145,586)
	Gabriel M. Ambrosio (D)........	75,321	(38%)	($182,804)
1980 primary	Harold C. Hollenbeck (R)	12,050	(100%)	
1978 general	Harold C. Hollenbeck (R)	73,478	(49%)	($84,548)
	Nicholas S. Mastorelli (D)	56,888	(38%)	($121,447)
	Henry Helstoski (Alws. for Pple.)	19,126	(13%)	($25,622)

TENTH DISTRICT

When it became clear that Peter Rodino, congressman from the 10th district of New Jersey, would chair the hearings on the impeachment of Richard Nixon, some House members were apprehensive. Rodino had become chairman of the Judiciary Committee only the year before, in 1973, after the defeat of New York's Emanuel Celler; and Celler, although 86 when he lost, was an assertive chairman who let Rodino take little responsibility. But these apprehensions proved ungrounded. Relying on the Judiciary staff assembled by Celler as well as on the more publicized services of impeachment counsel John Doar, Rodino was able to master the factual and legal case against Nixon and to get smoothly past the parliamentary difficulties as well. His chairing of the hearings was even-tempered and fair; he was careful to give the minority every opportunity to advance its views. But there could be little doubt of where Rodino stood in the face of the massive evidence and, to be a bit cynical about it, in light of the overwhelming sentiments of his constituency; he came out solemnly on the side that Richard Nixon should be removed from office.

One strength of the American political system is that it has produced people of extraordinary talent who have happened to find their way into crucial positions at critical times and who have performed far better than their records gave anyone the right to expect. Such leaders sometimes come from the most unlikely places: a Lincoln from the midwestern hick town of Springfield, Illinois; a Franklin Roosevelt from the aristocratic patroon families of the Hudson Valley. Within that tradition is Peter Rodino, from Newark, New Jersey—a place that some, including its mayor, have said will be the first American city to die.

Three decades ago, when Peter Rodino was first elected to Congress, Newark was a fairly prosperous industrial city with a large white collar employment base. With nearly half a million people, it was the financial center of New Jersey, a city proud of its tree-shaded middle-class neighborhoods. Today the downtown remains, although Prudential Insurance, the biggest employer there, is rapidly but quietly moving much of its operations to the suburbs. Much of the rest of Newark resembles Berlin after the war. With one notable exception, the middle class has left in search of nicer lawns and safer streets in the suburbs; most of the people remaining in Newark are here because they cannot get out. This is not just a matter of racial change, although Newark is now two-thirds black, for middle-income black people, like their white counterparts, are abandoning the city for the more comfortable suburbs. Newark suffered through organized crime control of its city government in the 1960s and a major riot in 1967. Now with the population more than 100,000 below what it was in 1950, much of it is simply being abandoned.

The one exception to that pattern is the community that Peter Rodino comes from, the Italian–Americans who remain in the North Ward. The Jews who once lived in Philip Roth's Weequahic Park have long since moved to such places as Maplewood or Short Hills; the

Irish have vanished beyond the city limits into Livingston or West Orange; the WASPs, to the extent there ever were any in Newark, are now far away in Morris or Somerset County. But many Italians remain, in close-knit neighborhoods where everybody knows everyone else, nobody steals or shoots anyone, and people speak Italian on the streets and in the shops.

The North Ward has steadily resisted black immigration, but within the city as a whole whites have been in the minority since before 1970. Kenneth Gibson, a black engineer with little political experience, was elected mayor in 1970; there have been black majorities on the council and school board since 1974. Many blacks are bitter that the city they finally inherited is financially in deep trouble; its tax base dwindles year by year, and it must go begging to the state and federal governments annually for the most basic city services. Newark in the late 1970s was getting more than half its budget from the federal government — which is all well and good except when the government threatens, as it did when Ronald Reagan came to office, to cut spending on those programs.

Newark makes up about three-quarters of the population of the 10th congressional district; the rest lies in East Orange — also with a black majority — and two tiny suburbs, one industrial and one high income. Not surprisingly, Rodino has had black opposition. In 1972, against a creditable candidate, Rodino's strong civil rights record and liberal views on issues helped him win 57% in the primary. He had no serious challenges in the latter 1970s, when memory of the impeachment hearings was strong; and apparently it had not weakened by 1980. Then, against three black opponents, Rodino won 62% of the vote in the primary. For 1982, the district will likely be expanded because of population loss; if Rodino retires, however, the district could be chopped up and distributed to other north Jersey districts, since the area must lose a seat in redistricting.

Census Data   Pop. (1980 final) 426,370, down 11% in 1970s. Median family income, 1970, $8,300, 86% of U.S.

The Voters

   Employment profile 1970   White collar, 39%. Blue collar, 46%. Service, 15%. Farm, –%.
   Ethnic groups   Black 1980, 60%. Hispanic 1980, 15%. Asian 1980, 1%. Total foreign stock 1970, 23%. Italy, 7%; Poland, 2%; Ireland, USSR, Germany, UK, 1% each.

Presidential Vote	1980			
		Reagan (R)	22,261	(22%)
		Carter (D)	73,860	(74%)
		Anderson (I)	3,490	(3%)
	1976	Ford (R)	31,267	(27%)
		Carter (D)	82,612	(73%)

Rep. Peter W. Rodino, Jr. (D) Elected 1948; b. June 7, 1909, Newark; home, Newark; Rutgers U., LL.B. 1937.

Career Army, WWII; Practicing atty.

Offices 2462 RHOB, 202-225-3436. Also Suite 1435A Fed. Bldg., 970 Broad St., Newark 07102, 201-645-3213.

Committees *Judiciary* (Chairman). Subcommittee: Monopolies and Commercial Law (Chairman).

Select Committee on Narcotics Abuse and Control (2d).

Group Ratings

	ADA	COPE	PC	LCV	CFA	RPN	NAB	NSI	NTU	ACA	ACU
1980	67	95	73	72	79	—	0	0	14	14	11
1979	63	100	70	85	56	—	—	—	17	0	3
1978	35	83	40	73	27	0	0	10	15	0	0

Key Votes

1) Draft Registn $	AGN	6) Fair Hsg DOJ Enfrc	FOR	11) Cut Socl Incr Dfns $	AGN
2) Ban $ to Nicrgua	AGN	7) Lim PAC Contrbtns	—	12) Hosptl Cost Controls	FOR
3) Dlay MX Missile	—	8) Cap on Food Stmp $	AGN	13) Gasln Ctrls & Allctns	FOR
4) Nuclr Mortorium	FOR	9) New US Dep Edcatn	—	14) Lim Wndfll Prof Tax	AGN
5) Alaska Lands Bill	—	10) Cut OSHA $	AGN	15) Chryslr Loan Grntee	FOR

Election Results

1980 general	Peter W. Rodino, Jr. (D)	76,154	(85%)	($212,925)
	Everett J. Jennings (R)	11,778	(13%)	($0)
1980 primary	Peter W. Rodino, Jr. (D)	26,943	(62%)	
	Donald M. Payne (D)..........	9,825	(23%)	($34,046)
	Golden E. Johnson (D).........	5,316	(12%)	($47,202)
	One other (D)	1,251	(3%)	
1978 general	Peter W. Rodino, Jr. (D)	55,074	(86%)	($46,110)
	John L. Pelt (R)	8,066	(13%)	

ELEVENTH DISTRICT

The 11th congressional district of New Jersey consists of most of suburban Essex County. This string of suburban towns around Newark is theoretically within commuting distance of New York, but the orientation here is really to northern New Jersey: people here tend to work in downtown Newark or, more frequently lately, in one of the suburban office complexes or factories. The ethnic origins of the different suburbs tend to follow the lines of the radial avenues coming out of the once ethnic neighborhoods of Newark. There is a definite Italian–American flavor to the towns of Belleville, Bloomfield, and Nutley, all adjoining Newark's heavily Italian North Ward. There is a substantial Jewish population in South Orange and Maplewood, adjacent to what was once the Jewish part of Newark. An anomaly is Montclair, situated on a ridge overlooking the Manhattan skyline; part of it is upper-income WASP, part middle-income black. Farther out are such comfortable upper-income places as Caldwell, Fairfield, and Essex Fells.

In the 1960s the 11th district included the Central Ward of Newark and the suburb of East Orange, both with black majorities by the end of the decade. But redistricting removed these areas and made the district entirely suburban and, in national elections, much less Democratic; the 11th went for Ford and Reagan, not for Carter, in the last two national elections. But that has posed no political problems for Congressman Joseph Minish. Back in 1962 Minish came out of the labor movement to replace Hugh Addonizio, who became mayor of Newark because, as he told a friend at the time, you could make a million dollars with the job. However much he made, Addonizio ended up in jail. Minish has seldom been seriously challenged and has had no trouble winning every two years. He is now the fourth-ranking Democrat on the Banking Committee and chairman of its General Oversight Subcommittee and of the House Administration Subcommittee on Personnel and Police. His major accomplishment, according to the Nader Congress Project several years ago, was a law setting up credit unions for servicemen living on bases overseas. Should he choose to retire, one possibility to succeed him is the very youthful Essex County Executive, Peter Shapiro, who is the most forceful politician in the Newark area today.

This is another one of the north Jersey seats vulnerable to elimination through redistricting. It is likely to survive in something not too dissimilar from its current form largely because a Democratic legislature is doing the redistricting and the 11th has demonstrated its willingness to reelect a Democratic congressman indefinitely.

Census Data   Pop. (1980 final) 449,556, down 5% in 1970s. Median family income, 1970, $12,508, 130% of U.S.

The Voters

Employment profile 1970   White collar, 60%. Blue collar, 30%. Service, 10%. Farm, —%.
Ethnic groups   Black 1980, 14%. Hispanic 1980, 3%. Asian 1980, 2%. Total foreign stock 1970, 38%. Italy, 11%; Poland, USSR, 4% each; Germany, UK, 3% each; Ireland, Austria, 2% each.

Presidential Vote

1980	Reagan (R)	95,919	(50%)
	Carter (D)	77,094	(40%)
	Anderson (I)	16,689	(9%)
1976	Ford (R)	104,888	(51%)
	Carter (D)	98,038	(49%)

Rep. Joseph G. Minish (D) Elected 1962; b. Sept. 1, 1916, Throop, Pa.; home, West Orange.

Career Army, WWII; Political Action Dir., AFL–CIO Dist. 4, 1953–54; Exec. Secy., Essex W. Hudson Labor Cncl., 1954–61, Treas., 1961–62.

Offices 2162 RHOB, 202-225-5035. Also 308 Main St., Orange 07050, 201-645-6363.

Committees *Banking, Finance and Urban Affairs* (4th). Subcommittees: Consumer Affairs and Coinage; Economic Stabilization; Financial Institutions Supervision, Regulation and Insurance; General Oversight and Renegotiation (Chairman).

House Administration (6th). Subcommittees: Contracts and Printing; Personnel and Police (Chairman).

Group Ratings

	ADA	COPE	PC	LCV	CFA	RPN	NAB	NSI	NTU	ACA	ACU
1980	72	78	67	87	71	—	8	40	24	23	21
1979	58	100	70	78	74	—	—	—	20	16	22
1978	35	85	75	83	77	17	17	44	14	21	17

Key Votes

1) Draft Registn $	FOR	6) Fair Hsg DOJ Enfrc	FOR	11) Cut Socl Incr Dfns $	AGN
2) Ban $ to Nicrgua	FOR	7) Lim PAC Contrbtns	AGN	12) Hosptl Cost Controls	FOR
3) Dlay MX Missile	FOR	8) Cap on Food Stmp $	AGN	13) Gasln Ctrls & Allctns	—
4) Nuclr Mortorium	FOR	9) New US Dep Edcatn	AGN	14) Lim Wndfll Prof Tax	AGN
5) Alaska Lands Bill	FOR	10) Cut OSHA $	AGN	15) Chryslr Loan Grntee	FOR

Election Results

1980 general	Joseph G. Minish (D)	106,155	(63%)	($77,750)
	Robert A. Davis (R)	57,772	(34%)	($17,068)
1980 primary	Joseph G. Minish (D)	28,491	(100%)	
1978 general	Joseph G. Minish (D)	88,294	(71%)	($71,900)
	Julius George Feld (R)	35,642	(28%)	

TWELFTH DISTRICT

The 12th congressional district of New Jersey consists of all of Union County except for one small city and two townships. For the most part the 12th is classic, if a little timeworn, suburban country. There are a few stereotyped WASP havens such as Summit, but more typical of the district are Cranford, Westfield, and Union—towns inhabited by the sons and daughters of Italian, Polish, and German immigrants, whose claim on prosperity is now more than a generation old but still, psychologically at least, a little precarious. Even the district's two most industrial cities, Elizabeth and Plainfield, although they have had crime, riots, and poverty, are not in as bad shape as Newark; Elizabeth indeed has been rejuvenated by a rapidly increasing Hispanic population. The district is bisected by perhaps the most garish strip highway in the East, U.S. 22, which gets less use now than in the 1960s. The new Interstate 78 that parallels it gets most of the truck traffic, and the teenagers who used to drag race and gather at the drive-in restaurants have grown up and moved to farther suburbs.

In Union County political preferences tend toward the middle of the road. Elizabeth and Plainfield are somewhat Democratic, Summit and Westfield Republican, and usually they cancel each other out. In the close national elections of 1960, 1968, and 1976, this New Jersey district came within a couple of percentage points of duplicating the national results for major party candidates—although it did go for the losers in two out of three. In 1980 it was 1% more for Reagan and 1% less for Carter than the national average. In the 1950s the 12th district produced two men who served the state as U.S. senators for more than 20 years each—Republican Clifford Case who served here from 1945 to 1953 and Democrat Harrison Williams who was elected in 1953 and 1954 and defeated in 1956. After long careers, both had political troubles. Case was beaten in the 1978 Republican primary, and Williams was indicted and convicted in the Abscam scandal.

The Republican who beat Williams in that 1956 election was Florence Dwyer, a liberal who won subsequent elections with record margins. The current congressman, Matthew Rinaldo, was elected when Dwyer retired in 1972. With experience in local government and the New Jersey Senate, Rinaldo was well known; his voting record, one of the most liberal of House Republicans, tends to protect him against Democratic challenges. He was one of two Republicans on the Commerce Committee, for example, to oppose deregulation of natural gas. Rinaldo has regularly been reelected by overwhelming margins and is mentioned on occasion as a candidate for national office. Given his strong Union County base, he seems unlikely to be hurt much by redistricting. There is some possibility that he will run for Williams's Senate seat in 1982, although he would certainly have primary competition from more conservative Republicans.

Census Data Pop. (1980 final) 443,033, down 7% in 1970s. Median family income, 1970, $12,787, 133% of U.S.

The Voters

Employment profile 1970 White collar, 56%. Blue collar, 34%. Service, 10%. Farm, –%.
Ethnic groups Black 1980, 15%. Hispanic 1980, 8%. Asian 1980, 1%. Total foreign stock 1970, 35%. Italy, 7%; Poland, Germany, 4% each; USSR, 3%; UK, Ireland, Austria, 2% each; Canada, 1%.

Presidential Vote

1980	Reagan (R)	100,488	(53%)
	Carter (D)	73,083	(38%)
	Anderson (I)	14,244	(7%)
1976	Ford (R)	106,127	(54%)
	Carter (D)	91,007	(46%)

Rep. Matthew J. Rinaldo (R) Elected 1972; b. Sept. 1, 1931, Elizabeth; home, Union; Rutgers U., B.S. 1953, Seton Hall U., M.B.A. 1959, NYU Sch. of Pub. Admin., 1969.

Career Pres., Union Twnshp. Zoning Bd. of Adjustment, 1962–63; Union Co. Bd. of Freeholders, 1963–64; N.J. Senate, 1967–72.

Offices 2338 RHOB, 202-225-5361. Also 1961 Morris Ave., Union 07083, 201-687-4235.

Committees *Energy and Commerce* (7th). Subcommittees: Energy Conservation and Power; Telecommunications, Consumer Protection and Finance.

Select Committee on Aging (Ranking Member). Subcommittee: Human Services.

Group Ratings

	ADA	COPE	PC	LCV	CFA	RPN	NAB	NSI	NTU	ACA	ACU
1980	61	84	57	57	79	—	33	90	26	38	44
1979	42	75	53	69	63	—	—	—	30	50	33
1978	50	80	53	80	73	36	18	70	14	33	50

Key Votes

1) Draft Registn $	AGN	6) Fair Hsg DOJ Enfrc	FOR
2) Ban $ to Nicrgua	FOR	7) Lim PAC Contrbtns	FOR
3) Dlay MX Missile	AGN	8) Cap on Food Stmp $	AGN
4) Nuclr Mortorium	AGN	9) New US Dep Edcatn	FOR
5) Alaska Lands Bill	FOR	10) Cut OSHA $	AGN

11) Cut Socl Incr Dfns $	AGN
12) Hosptl Cost Controls	FOR
13) Gasln Ctrls & Allctns	FOR
14) Lim Wndfll Prof Tax	AGN
15) Chryslr Loan Grntee	FOR

Election Results

1980 general	Matthew J. Rinaldo (R)	134,973	(77%)	($229,475)
	Rose Zeidwerg Monyek (D)	36,577	(21%)	($0)
1980 primary	Matthew J. Rinaldo (R)	17,431	(100%)	
1978 general	Matthew J. Rinaldo (R)	94,850	(73%)	($192,778)
	Richard McCormack (D)	34,423	(27%)	($13,556)

THIRTEENTH DISTRICT

The 13th congressional district of New Jersey is the northwestern part of the state. Historically, this is an area that was bypassed by westward migration. The land here is not the swamp or flatlands that you find in most of the rest of the state; it is mountainous, marked by one corduroylike ridge after another, running from Upstate New York in the northeast to Pennsylvania in the southwest. This was never good farming territory and nobody ever found much in the way of coal or other minerals here. The railroads had difficulty traversing this country, where all the ridges simply got in their way; it remained one of the most lightly populated parts of the East through 1950s. In the next 20 years, this area has seen its first boom, and for one basic reason: it is within an hour or so freeway ride from New York City and northern New Jersey. Once too far away to be urban, it now has its own office complexes and factories, and it has become a favored place for above-average-income but not really wealthy people who want to get away from the urban atmosphere — physical and cultural — of New York and its close-in New Jersey suburbs. The 13th congressional district, established in 1972, marked the first time in memory this area had its own congressional district — a recognition of the population growth that has, finally, been occurring here.

The 13th includes about half of Morris County, the less fashionable and less urbanized half of a relatively high-income county; and it includes as well the northwestern counties of New Jersey: rural Sussex; Warren with its industrial center of Phillipsburg, across the Delaware River from Easton, Pennsylvania; and Hunterdon, still a pleasant rural retreat but also the headquarters of some major corporations. It extends as far south as the borders of Trenton and includes some of the capital's suburbs.

The 13th was designed to be Republican, and by most measures is one of the most heavily Republican districts in New Jersey. Yet during the 1970s it elected three congressmen of both political parties. One reason was the unexpected exposure of Joseph Maraziti, the Republican elected in 1972, in the House Judiciary Committee impeachment hearings. Maraziti as a state legislator helped design the district, but his performance on television made him beatable. He was defeated in 1974 by Helen Stevenson Meyner, a cousin of the Adlai Stevensons and wife of former Governor Robert Meyner. She did as well as one could expect of a Democrat in this district, but she barely held on in 1976 and was defeated in 1978.

The current congressman, Republican Jim Courter, is one of that breed of young conservatives who have changed the tone and hope to change the substance of the House. Courter is a former Peace Corps volunteer and legal services attorney, but he is also a man who evidently feels that the nation's best interests are served by free-market capitalism and by limiting government spending and abolishing some government programs. He was one of the leaders of the fight — and one of the few from the Northeast to lead it — to decontrol gasoline prices. He had by far the most conservative voting record in the New Jersey delegation in the 96th Congress and can be expected to support the Reagan Administration — or oppose it from the right — in the 97th.

The 13th has continued to gain population at above the state average rate in the 1970s and as a result it is unlikely that Courter can be hurt much by redistricting.

Census Data   Pop. (1980 final) 577,078, up 21% in 1970s. Median family income, 1970, $11,730, 122% of U.S.

The Voters

Employment profile 1970   White collar, 51%. Blue collar, 37%. Service, 10%. Farm, 2%.
Ethnic groups   Black 1980, 2%. Hispanic 1980, 2%. Asian 1980, 1%. Total foreign stock 1970, 24% Italy, Germany, 4% each; UK, 3%; Poland, 2%; Hungary, Ireland, USSR, Austria, 1% each.

Presidential Vote

1980	Reagan (R)	138,364	(60%)
	Carter (D)	65,847	(29%)
	Anderson (I)	22,042	(10%)
1976	Ford (R)	127,723	(59%)
	Carter (D)	87,608	(41%)

Rep. James A. (Jim) **Courter** (R) Elected 1978; b. Oct. 14, 1941, Montclair; home, Hackettstown; Colgate U., B.A. 1963, Duke U., J.D. 1966.

Career Peace Corps, Venezuela, 1967–69; Practicing atty., 1969–70; Atty., Union Co. Legal Svcs., 1970–71; 1st Asst. Warren Co. Prosecutor, 1973–77.

Offices 325 CHOB, 202-225-5801.

Committees *Armed Services* (13th). Subcommittees: Procurement and Military Nuclear Systems; Research and Development.

Post Office and Civil Service (5th). Subcommittees: Census and Population; Civil Service.

Group Ratings

	ADA	COPE	PC	LCV	CFA	RPN	NAB	NSI	NTU	ACA	ACU
1980	11	16	33	46	21	—	83	100	56	83	68
1979	11	16	15	24	4	—	—	—	55	81	82

Key Votes

1) Draft Registn $	FOR	6) Fair Hsg DOJ Enfrc	AGN	11) Cut Socl Incr Dfns $	FOR
2) Ban $ to Nicrgua	FOR	7) Lim PAC Contrbtns	AGN	12) Hosptl Cost Controls	AGN
3) Dlay MX Missile	AGN	8) Cap on Food Stmp $	FOR	13) Gasln Ctrls & Allctns	AGN
4) Nuclr Mortorium	AGN	9) New US Dep Edcatn	FOR	14) Lim Wndfll Prof Tax	FOR
5) Alaska Lands Bill	FOR	10) Cut OSHA $	FOR	15) Chryslr Loan Grntee	AGN

Election Results

1980 general	James A. (Jim) Courter (R)	152,862	(72%)	($262,786)
	Dave Stickle (D)	56,251	(26%)	($18,474)
1980 primary	James A. (Jim) Courter (R)	25,779	(100%)	
1978 general	James A. (Jim) Courter (R)	77,301	(52%)	($330,688)
	Helen S. Meyner (D)	71,808	(48%)	($194,641)

FOURTEENTH DISTRICT

"I am the law," Frank Hague used to say, and in Hudson County, New Jersey, he was. Back in the 1930s, when Hague was at the peak of his powers as boss of the Hudson County Democratic machine, he chose governors and U.S. senators, prosecutors and judges, and even had some influence in the White House of Franklin D. Roosevelt. In Jersey City and other Hudson County towns — then and now the most densely populated part of the United States outside Manhattan — Hague controlled almost every facet of life. He determined who would stay in business and who would not; he controlled tax assessments and the issuance of parking tickets; he had the support of the workingman and kept the CIO out of town for years (resulting in a major Supreme Court case). Hague's power was firmly anchored in votes. Jersey City and Hudson County had huge payrolls, and every jobholder was expected to produce a certain number of votes on election day. Democratic candidates could expect a 100,000-vote margin in Hudson County and since they often lost the rest of the state by less than that, they were indebted indeed. Hague's power continued into the 1940s until some former allies turned on him and took over the machine. The history of Hudson County politics since that time has been a history of entangling alliances, occasional betrayals, indictments, and reform movements that quickly become the new machine.

To the naked eye Hudson County has not changed much since Frank Hague's time. It still consists of the same series of towns on the granite Palisades ridge between New York Harbor and the Jersey Meadows: Jersey City, Bayonne, Weehawken, Union City, and (below the ridge and just on the waterfront) Hoboken. To exploit the view of the Manhattan skyline some luxury high-rise apartments have been built in the northern end of the county, but most of Hudson County's residents live in the same cramped apartments and stone row houses that were aging even before the Great Depression.

Hudson County's function throughout its history has been to absorb some of America's millions of immigrants, to provide them with a community of people similar to them, to provide them with jobs, whether on the waterfront or in great factories or on the railroads or in Jersey City's city hall. Physically, it is a kind of island, cut off from New York (some Hudson Countians have never been to the city whose skyscrapers they see every day) and separated from the rest of New Jersey, not only its bucolic suburbs but industrial Newark as well, by the Jersey Meadows. Hudson County reached its peak population of 690,000 in 1930, just a few years after most immigration was cut off, when its row houses and apartments were filled with young foreigners who spoke broken English (or with a thick brogue) and had many children. In the years after, the children grew up; some stayed in Hudson County, but many moved away, to less distinctive suburban communities, to blend in with the great American middle class. Because immigration was restricted, there were fewer young families to replace the ones who grew up, and Hudson County's population fell to 555,000 in 1980.

Yet evidence of a contrary trend is evident. Hudson County's Irish and Italian population —there have never been many blacks here—is elderly and has almost as many deaths as births. But there is a new migration, of Spanish-speaking people from Latin America, to Hudson County. Union City has become predominantly Cuban-American, and Jersey City now has many neighborhoods where Spanish is regularly spoken. These new migrants, like those of the early 20th century, tend to be young people with many children; if they have entered the country illegally in many cases, they are paying their taxes (through withholding) and are raising children who will be able to pay taxes and support the millions of 1945–65 baby boom babies, who have had small families themselves, when they become elderly.

The Spanish migration has had only a limited impact on Hudson County politics thus far. Most of the voters here are elderly people from earlier migrations. In Hague's day they almost always voted Democratic (except when Hague was punishing some Democrat); so important was the machine in people's lives and so limited were their abilities to get by without its blessing that they were happy to help out on election day. By the 1960s the machine had become less important. Prosperity had come to Hudson County, at least to the extent that people no longer depended on the machine for jobs or coal; service in the machine's cadres came to be more of a burden with fewer rewards; people whose relatives and children had moved elsewhere no longer felt so confined or helpless. The result was increasing Republican sentiment in elections. The traditional Democrats of Hudson County, with their belief in church and family, had little use for McGovern's Democrats; terrified of street criminals, they were ready to vote for candidates who were tough on crime. Many of the new Spanish residents, particularly the Cubans, see their values reflected much more accurately in the Republican than the Democratic Party. The 100,000-vote-plus Democratic margins Hudson County in previous national and many statewide elections have vanished; Jimmy Carter carried the county by only 4,000 votes in 1980.

The Hudson County Democratic machine endorsement does still carry some weight on primary day, however, and the current congressman, from the 14th district, which includes almost all of Hudson County, Frank Guarini, was county Democratic chairman before his election in 1978. The decline in Democratic sentiment was shown in 1976, when incumbent Dominick Daniels retired, and the Democratic nominee, Assembly Speaker Joseph Le-Fante, was almost defeated. LeFante was persuaded by the machine to retire in 1978, at which point Guarini, who seems to have much more political clout, was elected by an overwhelming margin. Guarini presents the image of a polished, knowledgeable man with powerful political credentials. He is a member of the House Ways and Means Committee and of its Trade Subcommittee. He also led the House in 1980 in (perfectly legal) outside earnings, with more than $900,000 income from his law firm. Evidently there still is some advantage to associating oneself with the Hudson County Democratic machine.

Census Data Pop. (1980 final) 428,399, down 10% in 1970s. Median family income, 1970, $9,607, 100% of U.S.

The Voters

  Employment profile 1970 White collar, 45%. Blue collar, 43%. Service, 12%. Farm, –%.
  Ethnic groups Black 1980, 16%. Hispanic 1980, 23%. Asian 1980, 3%. Total foreign stock 1970, 39%. Italy, 10%; Poland, 5%; Ireland, UK, 3% each; Germany, USSR, 2% each; Austria, 1%.

Presidential Vote

1980	Reagan (R)	65,713	(43%)
	Carter (D)	76,679	(51%)
	Anderson (I)	6,595	(4%)
1976	Ford (R)	70,173	(43%)
	Carter (D)	91,375	(57%)

Rep. Frank J. Guarini (D) Elected 1978; b. Aug. 20, 1924, Jersey City; home, Jersey City; Dartmouth Col., Columbia U., NYU, J.D., LL.M., Acad. of Internatl. Law, The Hague, Holland.

Career Navy, WWII; Practicing atty.; N.J. Senate, 1965–72.

Offices 1530 LHOB, 202-225-2765. Also 910 Bergen Ave., Jersey City 07306, 201-659-7700.

Committees *Ways and Means* (17th). Subcommittees: Social Security; Trade.

Select Committee on Narcotics Abuse and Control (17th).

Group Ratings

	ADA	COPE	PC	LCV	CFA	RPN	NAB	NSI	NTU	ACA	ACU
1980	67	68	70	74	64	—	17	40	20	39	37
1979	74	95	73	81	78	—	—	—	19	8	10

Key Votes

1) Draft Registn $	—	6) Fair Hsg DOJ Enfrc	FOR	11) Cut Socl Incr Dfns $	AGN
2) Ban $ to Nicrgua	AGN	7) Lim PAC Contrbtns	FOR	12) Hosptl Cost Controls	FOR
3) Dlay MX Missile	AGN	8) Cap on Food Stmp $	AGN	13) Gasln Ctrls & Allctns	FOR
4) Nuclr Mortorium	FOR	9) New US Dep Edcatn	AGN	14) Lim Wndfll Prof Tax	AGN
5) Alaska Lands Bill	FOR	10) Cut OSHA $	AGN	15) Chryslr Loan Grntee	FOR

Election Results

1980 general	Frank J. Guarini (D)	86,921	(64%)	($182,622)
	Dennis Teti (R)	45,606	(34%)	($59,428)
1980 primary	Frank J. Guarini (D)	40,825	(100%)	
1978 general	Frank J. Guarini (D)	67,008	(64%)	($83,325)
	Henry J. Hill (R)...............	21,355	(20%)	($7,566)
	Thomas E. McDonough (I)	15,015	(14%)	($17,271)

FIFTEENTH DISTRICT

The 15th congressional district of New Jersey takes in most of Middlesex County, the state's fastest-growing Democratic area in the 1950s and 1960s. The 15th is the kind of place where ethnic Americans move when they have made good, gotten decent jobs, and can afford something better than the old row houses of places like Hudson County. The 15th has the largest concentration of Hungarian–Americans of any congressional district in the nation, in and around New Brunswick; it also has sizable neighborhoods of Polish–Americans in Woodbridge and Italian–Americans in Perth Amboy. From the old ethnic neighborhoods in these small central cities the children of the original immigrants have moved out into such places as Edison Township, Piscataway Township, and Sayreville, where they live in pleasant subdivisions. Middlesex County had its fastest growth in the 1950s, when the second generation of immigrants were having large numbers of babies themselves. That was the last decade in which New Jersey had large increases in the number of manufacturing jobs.

These suburban voters have not forgotten their Democratic heritage, but on occasion they are willing to ignore it. John Kennedy got a comfortable 58% in this heavily Catholic county in 1960, but Hubert Humphrey carried it with less than a majority in 1968. Now it votes at just about the national average: Jimmy Carter carried it narrowly in 1976 and lost it by a wider margin in 1980. As life in Middlesex County has become less distinctive and less visibly different from the experiences of other Americans, its political behavior has been, in the language of political scientists, regressing to the mean. Middlesex County and the 15th district have long had a well-known Democratic machine, run for many years by David Willentz, who first gained fame in the 1930s as the prosecutor of accused Lindbergh kidnapper Bruno Hauptmann and whose Perth Amboy law office in later years somehow always seemed to attract some of the nation's largest businesses as clients. Middlesex acquired its own congressional district in 1962, and the Willentz machine has in effect filled it ever since. In 1962 it picked Edward Patten, then an appointive statewide official, already 57 years old, a man with a puckish sense of humor and a loyalty to the Democratic Party. Patten never pretended to be one of the House's leading intellects but rose to a high position on the Appropriations Committee and made many friends. He also had his problems. In 1978 he was charged with claiming that a contribution to a county political organization had come from Patten himself when it had actually come from Tongsun Park. He won only 59% in the primary (before the ethics committee officially made the charge) and won only a 48%–46% victory in the general election. Patten decided to retire at age 75 in 1980.

The current congressman is Bernard Dwyer, elected at age 59, who was state Senate majority leader. The Middlesex machine persuaded Patten to retire and backed Dwyer strongly; he won a bruising primary with 32% of the vote. In the general election, the Republicans were handicapped by feuding between their nominee and his ultraconservative primary opponent. Dwyer, unlike most Democratic candidates in open seats these days, depended on his party organization and prevailed by a 53%–44% margin. He will likely be a solid Democratic vote in the House and will not be a member who makes waves; as a freshman, he won a seat on the Appropriations Committee.

The 15th district was whittled down from the whole of Middlesex County (as it was in the 1960s) to most of it in the 1970s. Now that there are no longer lots of new manufacturing jobs being created in this area, the district will have to be increased again in size, although it will not be as large as the whole county. Some other congressman, notably James Howard of the 3d district, might like some of the more Democratic chunks of Middlesex for his district; but the county machine here still has clout in the legislature and will likely insist on a Middlesex-only district, which in turn will almost certainly continue to reelect Dwyer for some time to come.

Census Data   Pop. (1980 final) 475,951, no change in 1970s. Median family income, 1970, $11,793, 123% of U.S.

The Voters

Employment profile 1970   White collar, 49%. Blue collar, 41%. Service, 10%. Farm, –%.
Ethnic groups   Black 1980, 8%. Hispanic 1980, 7%. Asian 1980, 2%. Total foreign stock 1970, 33%. Italy, Poland, 5% each; Hungary, 4%; Germany, 3%; USSR, UK, Czechoslovakia, Austria, 2% each; Ireland, 1%.

Presidential Vote

1980	Reagan (R)	93,625	(49%)
	Carter (D)	82,203	(43%)
	Anderson (I)	13,402	(7%)
1976	Ford (R)	87,830	(46%)
	Carter (D)	101,616	(54%)

Rep. Bernard J. Dwyer (D) Elected 1980; b. Jan. 24, 1921, Perth Amboy; home, Edison.

Career Navy, WWII; Insurance exec., 1945–80; Edison Twp. Cncl., 1958–70; Mayor, 1970–74; N.J. Senate, 1974–80.

Offices 437 CHOB, 202-225-6501. Also Perth Amboy Nat. Bank Bldg., 313 State St., Perth Amboy 08861, 201-826-4610, and P.O. Bldg., 86 Bayard St., New Brunswick 08901, 201-545-5655.

Committee Appropriations (33d). Subcommittees: Commerce, Justice, State and Judiciary; Labor–Health and Human Services–Education.

Group Ratings and Key Votes: Newly Elected

Election Results

1980 general	Bernard J. Dwyer (D)	92,457	(53%)	($149,141)
	William J. O'Sullivan, Jr. (R)	75,812	(44%)	($53,055)

1980 primary	Bernard J. Dwyer (D)	16,328	(32%)	
	David C. Schwartz (R)	12,800	(25%)	($91,497)
	George A. Spadoro (D)	12,329	(24%)	($71,365)
	Richard Pucci (D)	7,720	(15%)	($56,910)
	One other (D)	1,806	(4%)	
1978 general	Edward J. Patten (D)	55,944	(48%)	($50,407)
	Charles W. Wiley (R)	53,108	(46%)	($46,314)
	Ann Bastian (I)	5,396	(5%)	

NEW MEXICO

New Mexico is our most unusual state. The culture of every other state is based primarily on what the initial white settlers brought to the land; the original inhabitants (except in Hawaii) have either disappeared or no longer form a substantial part of the population. Not so in New Mexico. The American culture here is superimposed on a society whose written history dates back to 1609, when the first Spaniards established a settlement in Santa Fe, and to centuries long past when the Indians of the various pueblos set up agricultural societies on the sandy, rocky lands of northern New Mexico. A very substantial minority of New Mexicans are descendants of these Indians or the Spanish, or both. Nearly one-third of the people here in the ordinary course of things speak Spanish, and few of them are recent migrants from Mexico. This is the northernmost reach of the Indian civilizations of the Cordilleras, which extend south through Mexico, Central America, and down South America as far as Chile.

The Hispanic–Indian culture dominates most of northern and western New Mexico, except for enclaves — usually related to mining or, in the case of Los Alamos, atomic energy — where Anglos have settled. In vivid contrast to the Hispanic part of New Mexico is the area called Little Texas. With small cities, plenty of oil wells, vast cattle ranches, and desolate military bases, this region resembles, economically and culturally, the adjacent high plains of west Texas. Oil is important here but not as vital as the military presence: a couple of Air Force bases and the Army's White Sands Missile Range, near Alamogordo, where the first atomic bomb was detonated.

In the middle of the state is Albuquerque which, with the coming of the air conditioner, grew from a small desert town into a booming Sun Belt city. Albuqerque is also heavily dependent on the military and on the atomic energy establishment. There are two bases within the city limits and its largest employer is the Bell System's Sandia Laboratories, an atomic energy contractor. Metropolitan Albuquerque now has a little more than one-third of the state's population — about the same percentage as the Hispanic areas and Little Texas.

For many years New Mexico politics was a somnolent business. Local bosses — first Republican, then Democratic — controlled the large Hispanic vote. Elections in many counties featured irregularities that would have made a Chicago ward committeeman blush. New Mexico also had for years a balanced ticket: one Spanish and one Anglo senator, with the offices of governor and lieutenant governor split between the groups.

In the last few elections, a new pattern has emerged. The Republicans have pursued a conservative strategy in statewide contests, in effect conceding the Hispanic areas and hoping for compensating margins in Little Texas and Albuquerque. For the most part it has worked, although usually by narrow margins. Gerald Ford carried New Mexico in 1976—the first time in its history the state has voted for a losing candidate for president. In 1980 New Mexico went for Ronald Reagan by a solid 55%–37% margin. For the first time since 1917, Republicans hold the entire New Mexico congressional delegation—both Senate seats and the two House districts. Democrats hold onto the governorship, but their margins in the last two elections have totaled only 7,530 votes.

Moreover, the elections have produced two very different governors. Jerry Apodaca, elected in 1974, is a Hispanic who was a football star for the University of New Mexico; he was elected with 62% in the Hispanic areas—the best showing any Democrat has made for years. Bruce King, elected in 1970 and 1978, is a rancher from Santa Fe County in the northern part of the state. He too does well in Hispanic areas, but he also runs stronger than Apodaca in Little Texas. The reason for the alternation is that New Mexico does not allow its governors consecutive terms; the two men are not political allies.

Senator Pete Domenici is today the most prominent politician from New Mexico, but only a few years ago he labored in obscurity. He was first elected to the Senate only in 1972, and as a junior Republican his interests and predilections did not seem particularly important to anyone. Today they are. In 1981 he became chairman of the Senate Budget Committee—arguably the most important position in the Senate as incoming President Reagan set forth his budget-cutting goals. From the beginning Domenici was classed as a conservative Republican, and his attitude toward budget-cutting confirms this. He definitely would like to see the size and scope of the federal government reduced. At the same time, he is not considered one of the charter members of the New Right. A deeply religious man with a reputation for thoughtfulness, he came along before the New Right movement became important and he sets his priorities independently. Domenici was a member of the Budget Committee when ranking Republican Henry Bellmon worked closely with Chairman Edmund Muskie, and he seldom dissented from this bipartisan approach, although it was attacked shrilly by some conservatives. Domenici's iconoclasm was saved for other matters, such as his move (successful in large part because the *Washington Post* devoted a series of articles to it) to impose tolls on interstate river barge traffic.

Now Domenici has an opportunity to apply such skepticism and cerebration to all kinds of government activity. He has worked closely with Reagan's OMB director, David Stockman, and has a solid majority of conservative Republicans on the committee—Republicans who, moreover, have little if any Senate experience and are likely to defer at least for a while to his judgment. He at least began his service as chairman on good terms with James Jones, the Oklahoma Democrat who is chairman of the House Budget Committee. Domenici, however, has been known as a stormy participant in conference committees, and his sessions to settle the inevitable differences between the Republican Senate and the Democratic House may test his abilities to compromise, and know when not to compromise.

Domenici last won reelection in 1978, but by a smaller margin than expected—only 53% of the vote. Indeed, he might have been upset if his opponent, Democratic Attorney General Toney Anaya, had been able to raise a respectable campaign budget. Domenici got only 53% in Metropolitan Albuquerque—a poor showing for a Republican in that Sun Belt city and evidence that this part of the state may be moving away from the Republicans. Anaya carried the Hispanic areas, and Domenici was saved only by his large margin in Little Texas.

Domenici's national prominence makes it likely that he will be less vulnerable when he stands for reelection in 1984. But much will depend on the success of the Reagan economic programs, with which Domenici seems likely to become associated.

New Mexico's other senator, former astronaut Harrison Schmitt, is as unusual as the state. He is by profession a geologist with degrees from Caltech and Harvard; he got to be an astronaut not because he was an experienced pilot but because he was an expert on rocks. Schmitt grew up in New Mexico, in an out-of-the-way mining town. But he returned only when contemplating his Senate bid; he loaned $90,000 to his own campaign, but he seemed a man of the people when he drove around in his own red pickup truck (which he later brought to Washington).

Schmitt's 57% victory was less a measure of his own popularity than of the unpopularity of his opponent, Democratic incumbent Joseph Montoya. People wondered how Montoya accumulated a net worth of $4 million, although he began his public career without means and was seldom off the public payroll. They learned that he was half owner of a building in Santa Fe leased to the Post Office and that IRS officials had blocked an audit of his tax returns when he chaired an IRS subcommittee. Schmitt's slogan put it succinctly: "Honesty... for a change."

More than Domenici, Schmitt is a conservative Republican, part of that group of Rocky Mountain Republicans who have been aggressively and effectively attacking Democratic programs and precepts. He is undeniably brainy and, if his personality is not exactly magnetic, he seems to have good political instincts. Schmitt is particularly interested, as one might expect, in the space program and in such high technology items as lasers and space-based systems. He is able to devote some attention to these as a member of the Defense Subcommittee of Appropriations; he also chairs the Commerce subcommittee with jurisdiction over the space program. And he chairs the Labor–HHS–Education Appropriations Subcommittee. For years that was the preserve of Warren Magnuson of Washington, a generous old New Dealer who looked with fond affection on education programs, supported labor unions, and was a Medici-like patron of the various health research programs. Schmitt, with his technical background and conservative politics, is likely to have very different attitudes. In the short run, he will likely support the Reagan Administration's budget cuts; in the long run, if he remains in the Senate and in this position, he may have a major effect on many aspects of American life.

The circumstances of Schmitt's election and the Democratic trend in Albuquerque in 1978 and 1980 make it premature to say that Schmitt's seat is safe. He has major assets in his campaign for reelection but some liabilities too. For one thing he has not been in the state all that much for years, except during his 1976 campaign. A likely opponent for Schmitt is former Governor Jerry Apodaca, who left office popular (consecutive terms are not allowed). He is likely to have a strong base in the Hispanic areas and to lag behind Schmitt in Little Texas. The key will probably be Albuquerque. Although Schmitt begins with significant advantages, this is one of relatively few Republican seats that seems at all vulnerable to Democrats, so it is likely that the Democratic candidate will not lack for funds as Anaya did.

New Mexico is divisible into three almost precisely equal parts with different political leanings, and for 1982 the state will have, for the first time, three congressional districts. The current districts tend to cut across the natural regional lines. The current 1st district covers the northeastern and north central parts of the state, including Albuquerque and most of the Hispanic area. Santa Fe, the small state capital and a city of distinctive charm, is here, as is Taos, which has attracted artists and hangers-on since before D. H. Lawrence's sojourn here in the 1920s. The congressman here, Manuel Lujan, is the senior member of the New Mexico delegation. A member of a Hispanic family that has been active in politics for decades, he was first elected in 1968 and for many years thereafter was reelected easily. Recently he has had more trouble. In 1980 he came close to losing to Democrat Bill Richardson. Indeed, outside of Albuquerque, Lujan actually trailed. Richardson, a newcomer to the state, campaigned hard; despite his name, he is of Mexican descent on his mother's side and is fluent in Spanish.

The likelihood for 1982 is that Albuquerque and Bernalillo County will be set apart in a district of their own. This is good news for Lujan, since he has always carried the county; and although he might attract significant opposition (he got only 53% there against Richardson) he would be favored. He can make the kind of argument western Democrats have long used: that his committee positions — Interior and Science — are of vital importance to his district. He is currently the ranking Republican on Interior, which means he will be chairman if the Republicans win control and he is reelected; he is the fourth-ranking Republican on Science. His record on environmental issues is generally closer to that of the Reagan Administration than that of environmental activist groups; like all New Mexican congressmen, he favors further development of nuclear power.

That leaves a new district without an incumbent, which will consist essentially of the northern half of the state. The constituency will include Santa Fe and the Hispanic counties currently in the 1st; it will probably include Farmington, a very conservative uranium mining town in the northwestern corner of the state, and the counties immediately below, which abut on the Navajo reservation and have a large Indian population. This is about as Democratic a district as can be created in New Mexico. Richardson, after his strong showing in 1980, would have an excellent chance to carry the district although he may have competition from candidates with Hispanic names. Politics in a Democratic primary in northern New Mexico is hard to predict. There are people in some of the out-of-the-way towns, where only Spanish is spoken, who claim to control votes and whose support can be obtained for various considerations; there are personal rivalries and family loyalties that go back for decades. This could be one of the most interesting congressional races of 1982.

The current 2d congressional district includes most of Little Texas, the barren Rio Grande Valley, plus the Navajo country and Farmington, which it will probably lose for 1982. In 1980 the 2d was the scene of one of the most interesting and bizarre congressional races in the nation. The incumbent, Harold Runnels, a conservative Democrat from Little Texas, had been first elected in 1970 and had not had any political problems for years. His service on the Armed Services Committee helped to protect southern New Mexico's major military bases. Runnels was renominated with ease against a weak opponent in 1980 but died in the summer following the June primary. The Democratic state committee met to name a new nominee and decided on David King, then state finance secretary and also nephew of Governor Bruce King. The Republicans nominated Joe Skeen, their nearly successful gubernatorial candidate in 1974 and 1978. But Skeen was ruled off the ballot, on the plausible grounds that since the Republicans had never nominated a candidate in the first place there was no vacancy to fill. Meanwhile, King's nomination was greeted with scathing criticism, and the young Democrat sought to withdraw; but state elections officials ruled that it was past the withdrawal deadline. Both rulings are entirely defensible, but to many it looked as though state officials were trying to elect King without opposition. Skeen decided to run as a write-in candidate, and so did Dorothy Runnels, widow of the congressman, who had lost the Democratic nomination to King.

And so it happened that a Democratic candidate for Congress running unopposed in a Democratic district was able to win only 34% of the votes. Nearly two-thirds went to the two write-in candidates. Mrs. Runnels got a solid majority in her home county on the Texas border and carried one of the Navajo counties as well; Skeen did best in Roswell, one of the largest towns in Little Texas, near his home base. Altogether Skeen had 38% of the vote and Mrs. Runnels 28% — both substantial achievements given the write-in format. Skeen is now a member of the Agriculture and Science Committees (the latter is important in every part of New Mexico), has a reputation as a conservative, and seems likely to fit in well with other Sun Belt Republicans. The parts of the district likely to be removed do not change the partisan balance much, and Skeen is the favorite to win reelection — unless he runs for governor once again.

The race for governor is certainly difficult to predict, since many candidates are likely to run and the incumbent cannot. Bruce King, elected twice in the 1970s, was not helped by his nephew's defeat in 1980 and is in a poor position to name a successor. Well-known contenders otherwise are not apparent. This is an election that has been decided by very close margins for some time now and may well be again in 1982.

Census Data Pop. (1980 final) 1,299,968, up 28% in 1970s: 0.57% of U.S. total, 37th largest. Central city, 29%; suburban, 13%. Median 4-person family income, 1978, $18,738, 92% of U.S., 36th highest.

1979 Share of Federal Tax Burden $1,984,000,000; 0.44% of U.S. total, 38th largest.

1979 Share of Federal Outlays $3,893,826,000; 0.84% of U.S. total, 35th largest.

DOD	$814,070,000	33d	(0.77%)	HEW	$851,165,000	39th	(0.48%)
DOE	$893,838,000	4th	(7.60%)	ERDA	$153,998,000	6th	(5.68%)
HUD	$33,091,000	38th	(0.50%)	NASA	$17,100,000	20th	(0.37%)
VA	$150,760,000	37th	(0.73%)	DOT	$123,010,000	36th	(0.75%)
EPA	$17,817,000	48th	(0.34%)	DOC	$11,207,000	37th	(0.35%)
DOI	$344,045,000	6th	(6.20%)	USDA	$210,866,000	39th	(0.88%)

Economic Base Agricultural, notably cattle, dairy products, hay, and cotton lint; finance, insurance, and real estate; oil and gas extraction, especially oil and gas field services; metal mining, especially uranium–radium–vanadium ores; food and kindred products; tourism.

Political Lineup Governor, Bruce King (D). Senators, Peter V. (Pete) Domenici (R) and Harrison H. (Jack) Schmitt (R). Representatives, 2 R; 3 in 1982. State Senate, 42 (22 D and 20 R); State House of Representatives, 70 (41 D and 29 R).

The Voters

Registration 654,502 Total. 410,281 D (63%); 194,662 R (30%); 45,924 I (7%); 3,633 minor parties (0%)

Employment profile 1970 White collar, 51%. Blue collar, 30%. Service, 15%. Farm, 4%.

Ethnic groups Black 1980, 2%. Hispanic 1980, 37%. Am. Ind. 1980, 8%. Asian 1980, 1%. Total foreign stock 1970, 9%.

Presidential Vote

1980	Reagan (R)	250,779	(55%)
	Carter (D)	167,832	(37%)
	Anderson (I)	29,459	(6%)
1976	Ford (R)	211,419	(51%)
	Carter (D)	201,148	(48%)

1980 Democratic Presidential Primary		
Kennedy	73,721	(46%)
Carter	66,621	(42%)
Two others	9,288	(6%)
Uncommit. deleg.	9,734	(6%)

1980 Republican Presidential Primary		
Reagan	37,982	(64%)
Anderson	7,171	(12%)
Bush	5,892	(10%)
Crane	4,412	(7%)
Two others	2,742	(5%)
Uncommit. deleg.	1,347	(2%)

SENATORS

Sen. Peter V. (Pete) **Domenici** (R) Elected 1972, seat up 1984; b. May 7, 1932, Albuquerque; home, Albuquerque; U. of Albuquerque, 1950–52, U. of N.M., B.S. 1954, Denver U., LL.B. 1958.

Career Practicing atty., 1958–72; Mbr., Albuquerque City Commission, 1966–68, Mayor Ex-Officio, 1967–68; Rep. nominee for Gov., 1970.

Offices 4239 DSOB, 202-224-6621. Also New Postal Bldg., Santa Fe 87501, 505-988-6511, and Rm. 10013 Dennis Chavez New Fed. Bldg., 500 Gold Ave., S.W., Albuquerque 87102, 505-766-3481.

Committees *Budget* (Chairman).

Energy and Natural Resources (4th). Subcommittees: Energy Regulation; Energy Research and Development (Chairman); Public Lands and Reserved Water.

Environment and Public Works (3d). Subcommittees: Nuclear Regulation; Water Resources.

Special Committee on Aging (2d).

Group Ratings

	ADA	COPE	PC	LCV	CFA	RPN	NAB	NSI	NTU	ACA	ACU
1980	17	22	33	23	0	—	90	89	50	71	62
1979	5	26	20	—	5	—	—	—	44	69	77
1978	15	47	33	16	25	20	91	90	24	65	67

Key Votes

1) Draft Registn $	FOR	6) Fair Housng Cloture	AGN	11) Cut Socl Incr Defns	FOR
2) Ban $ to Nicrgua	FOR	7) Ban $ Rape Abortns	FOR	12) Income Tax Indexing	—
3) Dlay MX Missile	AGN	8) Cap on Food Stmp $	FOR	13) Lim Spdg 21% GNP	FOR
4) Nuclr Mortorium	AGN	9) New US Dep Edcatn	FOR	14) Incr Wndfll Prof Tax	AGN
5) Alaska Lands Bill	FOR	10) Cut OSHA Inspctns	FOR	15) Chryslr Loan Grntee	AGN

Election Results

1978 general	Peter V. (Pete) Domenici (R)	183,442	(53%)	($914,634)
	Toney Anaya (D)	160,045	(47%)	($175,633)
1978 primary	Peter V. Domenici (R), unopposed			
1972 general	Peter V. (Pete) Domenici (R)	204,253	(54%)	($517,310)
	Jack Daniels (D)	173,815	(46%)	($496,980)

Sen. Harrison H. (Jack) Schmitt (R) Elected 1976, seat up 1982; b. July 3, 1935, Santa Rita; home, Albuquerque; Cal. Tech., B.S. 1957, Fulbright Fellow, U. of Oslo, Norway, 1957–58, Harvard U., Ph.D. 1964.

Career Consulting geologist; NASA Scientist–Astronaut, 1965–73, Apollo 17 Lunar Module Pilot, 1972; Asst. Administrator for Energy Problems, NASA, 1974.

Offices 5513 DSOB, 202-224-5521. Also Rm. 9017 Dennis Chavez New Fed. Bldg., 500 Gold Ave., S.W., Albuquerque 87102, 505-766-3636, and U.S. Courthouse, Santa Fe 87501, 505-988-6647.

Committees *Appropriations* (7th). Subcommittees: Defense; Energy and Water Development; HUD–Independent Agencies; Interior; Labor, Health and Human Services, Education (Chairman).

Banking, Housing, and Urban Affairs (8th). Subcommittees: Consumer Affairs; Financial Institutions; Rural Housing and Development (Chairman); Securities.

Commerce, Science and Transportation (3d). Subcommittees: Communications; Science, Technology, and Space (Chairman); Surface Transportation.

Select Committee on Intelligence (8th). Subcommittees: Collection and Foreign Operations; Legislation and the Rights of Americans (Chairman).

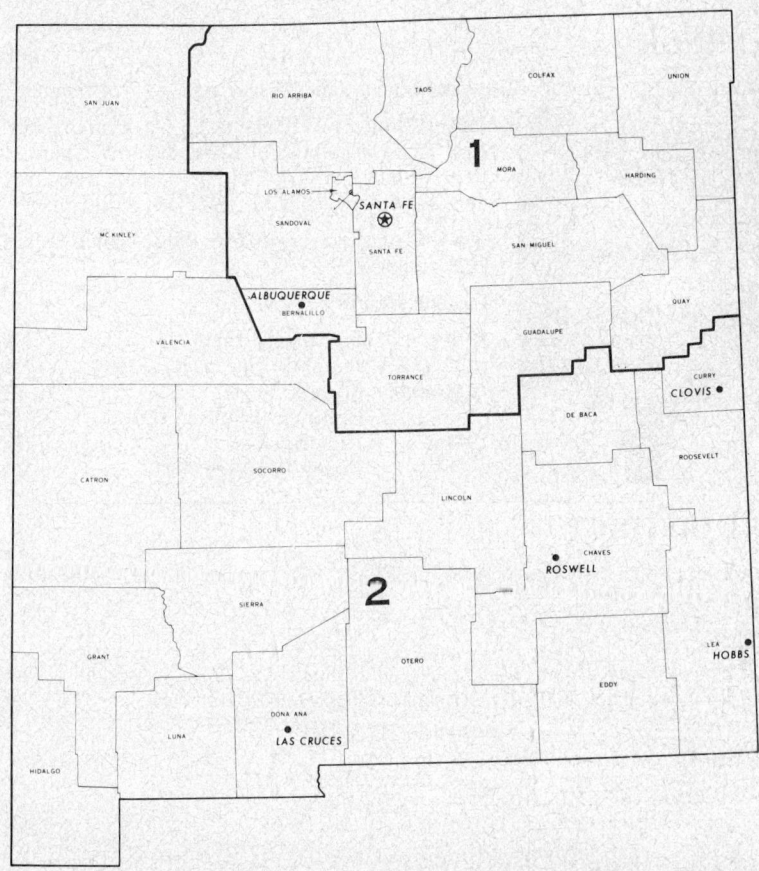

Group Ratings

	ADA	COPE	PC	LCV	CFA	RPN	NAB	NSI	NTU	ACA	ACU
1980	17	23	30	27	13	—	64	100	48	86	72
1979	16	16	20	—	19	—	—	—	46	78	82
1978	20	24	23	18	25	67	92	100	21	75	74

Key Votes

1) Draft Registn $	FOR	6) Fair Housng Cloture	AGN	11) Cut Socl Incr Defns	FOR
2) Ban $ to Nicrgua	—	7) Ban $ Rape Abortns	AGN	12) Income Tax Indexing	FOR
3) Dlay MX Missile	—	8) Cap on Food Stmp $	FOR	13) Lim Spdg 21% GNP	FOR
4) Nuclr Mortorium	AGN	9) New US Dep Edcatn	AGN	14) Incr Wndfll Prof Tax	AGN
5) Alaska Lands Bill	AGN	10) Cut OSHA Inspctns	FOR	15) Chryslr Loan Grntee	FOR

Election Results

1976 general	Harrison H. (Jack) Schmitt (R) . . .	234,681	(57%)	($441,309)
	Joseph Montoya (D).	176,382	(43%)	($451,111)
1976 primary	Harrison H. (Jack) Schmitt (R) . . .	34,074	(72%)	
	Eugene W. Peirce, Jr. (R).	10,965	(23%)	
	One other (R)	2,481	(5%)	
1970 general	Joseph Montoya (D).	151,486	(52%)	
	Anderson Carter (R)	135,004	(47%)	

GOVERNOR

Gov. Bruce King (D) Elected 1978, term expires Jan. 1983; b. Apr. 6, 1924, Stanley; U. of N.M.

Career Army, WWII; Santa Fe Co. Comm., 1954–58, Chmn., 1957–58; N.M. House of Reps., 1959–69, Spkr., 1963–69; State Dem. Chmn., 1968–69; Pres., N.M. State Constitutional Convention, 1969., Gov. of N.M., 1971–75; Cattle rancher.

Offices Executive Legislative Bldg., Santa Fe 87503, 505-827-2221.

Election Results

1978 gen.	Bruce King (D)	174,631	(51%)
	Joseph R. Skeen (R)	170,848	(49%)
1978 prim.	Bruce King (D)	92,432	(61%)
	Robert E. Ferguson (D). . . .	58,334	(39%)
1974 gen.	Jerry Apodaca (D)	164,177	(50%)
	Joseph R. Skeen (R)	160,430	(49%)

FIRST DISTRICT

Census Data Pop. (1980 final) 664,589, up 30% in 1970s. Median family income, 1970, $8,187, 85% of U.S.

The Voters

Employment profile 1970 White collar, 57%. Blue collar, 26%. Service, 15%. Farm, 2%.
Ethnic groups Black 1980, 2%. Hispanic 1980, 43%. Am. Ind. 1980, 4%. Asian 1980, 1%. Total foreign stock 1970, 7%.

Presidential Vote

1980	Reagan (R)	130,017	(51%)
	Carter (D)	97,809	(38%)
	Anderson (I)	22,201	(9%)

1976	Ford (R)	116,334	(50%)
	Carter (D)	113,197	(49%)

Rep. Manuel Lujan, Jr. (R) Elected 1968; b. May 12, 1928, San Ildefonso; home, Albuquerque; St. Mary's Col., San Francisco, Cal., Col. of Santa Fe., B.S. 1950.

Career Insurance agent; Vice. Chmn., N.M. Rep. Party.

Offices 1323 LHOB, 202-225-6316. Also Rm. 10001 Dennis Chavaz New Fed. Bldg., 500 Gold Ave., S.W., Albuquerque 87102, 505-766-2538.

Committees *Interior and Insular Affairs* (Ranking Member). Subcommittees: Energy and the Environment; Water and Power Resources.

Science and Technology (4th). Subcommittees: Energy Research and Production; Investigations and Oversight.

Group Ratings

	ADA	COPE	PC	LCV	CFA	RPN	NAB	NSI	NTU	ACA	ACU
1980	28	26	30	43	29	—	73	78	46	58	71
1979	11	25	15	20	4	—	—	—	54	84	83
1978	5	24	18	10	5	15	85	90	22	86	89

Key Votes

1) Draft Registn $	AGN	6) Fair Hsg DOJ Enfrc	AGN	11) Cut Socl Incr Dfns $	AGN
2) Ban $ to Nicrgua	FOR	7) Lim PAC Contrbtns	AGN	12) Hosptl Cost Controls	AGN
3) Dlay MX Missile	FOR	8) Cap on Food Stmp $	FOR	13) Gasln Ctrls & Allctns	AGN
4) Nuclr Mortorium	AGN	9) New US Dep Edcatn	AGN	14) Lim Wndfll Prof Tax	FOR
5) Alaska Lands Bill	FOR	10) Cut OSHA $	FOR	15) Chryslr Loan Grntee	AGN

Election Results

1980 general	Manuel Lujan, Jr. (R)	125,910	(51%)	($178,309)
	Bill Richardson (D)	120,903	(49%)	($230,955)
1980 primary	Manuel Lujan, Jr. (R)	28,961	(100%)	
1978 general	Manuel Lujan, Jr. (R)	118,075	(63%)	($121,421)
	Robert M. Hawk (D)	70,761	(37%)	($49,707)

SECOND DISTRICT

Census Data Pop. (1980 final) 635,379, up 26% in 1970s. Median family income, 1970, $7,551, 79% of U.S.

The Voters

Employment profile 1970 White collar, 45%. Blue collar, 35%. Service, 14%. Farm, 6%.

Ethnic groups Black 1980, 2%. Hispanic 1980, 30%. Am. Ind. 1980, 12%. Total foreign stock 1970, 10%.

Presidential Vote

1980	Reagan (R)	120,762	(60%)
	Carter (D)	70,011	(35%)
	Anderson (I)	7,528	(4%)
1976	Ford (R)	95,085	(52%)
	Carter (D)	87,951	(47%)

Rep. Joseph R. (Joe) **Skeen** (R) Elected 1980; b. June 30, 1927, Roswell; home, Picacho; Tex. A&M U., B.S. 1950.

Career Navy, WWII; Air Force Res., 1950–51; Sheep rancher, 1950–80; N.M. Senate, 1961–70; N.M. Rep. Chmn., 1962–65; Rep. nominee for Gov. of N.M., 1974, 1978.

Offices 1507 LHOB, 202-225-2365. Also E-306 Fed. Ofc. Bldg., 200 Griggs, Las Cruces 88001, 505-524-8022; Fed. Ofc. Bldg., 300 N. Richardson, Roswell 88201, 505-622-0055; and Kyser Ofc. Complex, 300 Arrington, Farmington 87401, 505-327-4933.

Committees *Agriculture* (14th). Subcommittees: Conservation, Credit, and Rural Development; Forests, Family Farms and Energy; Livestock, Dairy and Poultry.

Science and Technology (14th). Subcommittees: Energy Development and Applications; Science, Research and Technology.

Group Ratings and Key Votes: Newly Elected

Election Results

1980 general	Joseph R. (Joe) Skeen, write-in (R)	61,564	(38%)	($73,156)
	David King (D)	55,085	(34%)	($91,964)
	Dorothy Runnels, write-in	45,343	(28%)	($167,622)
1978 general	Harold Runnels (D), unopposed . .			($69,953)

NEW YORK

From the 1920s to the 1960s New York — the state and the city — earned the reputation of having the best and most innovative state and local government in the nation. New ideas were tried in New York first, and they worked. New York expected naturally to be leader and waited for others to follow. In the 1970s New York was a civic pioneer in another way — disaster. New York City's government was threatened with bankruptcy in 1975 and was forced to allow others — representatives of state government, the financial community, even the municipal unions — to control its finances and try to cut its bureaucracy. Hugh Carey, elected in 1974 as the state's first Democratic governor in a generation, was expected to follow in the expansive liberal tradition of Al Smith, Franklin Roosevelt, and Herbert Lehman. Instead Carey cut budgets and taxes; his major achievements were to help New York City avoid bankruptcy and to enable the state government escape the same perilous condition.

For generations New York had been the nation's leading port of entry for immigrants — welcoming millions of the poor and needy from Ireland, Italy, Germany, Eastern Europe, and, after World War II, from the black belts of the American South and from Puerto Rico. But in the 1970s New York state's population fell, for the first time in history, and not by just a little. The state lost about 700,000 people. There were charges that the Census Bureau undercounted blacks and Hispanics, but in fact they missed many more of them in 1970 than 1980, which means that the population loss was even greater than recorded. New York City's population, which had hovered at just below the eight million level since 1940, was suddenly reduced to seven million. The close-in suburbs of New York also lost population, as did the Buffalo metropolitan area and the industrialized Mohawk Valley of Upstate New York.

At the end of the 1970s the outlook for New York seemed bleak. Yet it may be that the developments that seem so dire were preparing New York for a better future. There were two major reasons for the population loss, neither of them necessarily damaging in the long run. The first is simply the aging of the population and the smaller number of children in families. Suburban Nassau County on Long Island, for example, which filled up with young families in the 15 years after World War II, is now a series of empty-nest communities, with older adults and fewer children; it had 20,000 more housing units in 1980 than 1970, but 109,000 fewer people. The same phenomenon is apparent in many of the middle-class residential neighborhoods of Brooklyn, Queens, and the Bronx — and there are far more such neighborhoods than most people in the rest of the country realize.

The second reason for the population loss is that in-migrations have largely ceased. It used to be that whole high school classes of blacks in the Carolinas would get on the bus for New York the day after graduation. Now they stay home; the South is more congenial (in large part because of the changes wrought by the civil rights revolution) and jobs in the South are more plentiful. In the 1950s it seemed to some New Yorkers that they were inundated by migration from Puerto Rico. But since 1965 the balance of the flow has been away from New York and back to Puerto Rico. The 21st congressional district in the south Bronx, the most heavily Puerto Rican in New York, lost 50% of its population in the 1970s. Some of these people moved farther out in New York City or the suburbs, but many more apparently moved back to Puerto Rico.

The slackening of in-migration parallels the sharply reduced number of manufacturing jobs in New York City. That reduction also is no disaster. Most of the jobs lost were low paying, and it has long been one of the goals of the labor movement to raise the level of wages in New York. They have been successful, and so low-wage occupations such as apparel have moved out of the city, to rural Pennyslvania, the coastal plains of the Carolinas, and Taiwan. The factories themselves were not giant buildings like steel mills or auto plants; they were floors in Manhattan buildings where clothing was stitched and electrical components assembled. That real estate is now worth much more as white collar office space or for residences; the hottest parts of Manhattan today are the Soho and Cast Iron Districts where old factory buildings are being converted into artists' lofts, and chic shops and restaurants are springing up where once there was nothing but trucks loading up with finished garments. There was a time lag between the sharp reductions in the number of low-wage jobs — apparent in the years of John Lindsay's mayoralty in the late 1960s — and the end of low-wage migration to New York, but the lag did not last as long as most people believe. And if, as conservatives believe, people were once induced to migrate here or were persuaded to stay because of generous welfare payments, that attraction was reduced when New York, threatened with bankruptcy, refused to raise its welfare payments between 1972 and 1981.

At the very same time that people were talking about New York City dying, it was obvious that in some important respects the city was thriving. The amount of office space in Manhattan has more than doubled since World War II. Record amounts of office construction are scheduled for completion in 1981 and 1982, and demand has pushed up rents to astronomic levels — far higher than any other city. While headlines screamed when New York lost a corporate headquarters with a few hundred jobs, Manhattan was simultaneously gaining hundreds more in small increments. New York's vitality as an office center — as a center of high-wage white collar employment — has never been greater. Despite predictions, the nation's financial community is still very much concentrated here; so is the management at least of the clothing, entertainment, media, and publishing industries. As a center of ideas in a society whose chief product increasingly is ideas, New York is thriving. The boom went on even as city government was on the point of collapse and as such services as the subways, street paving, and garbage collection visibly deteriorated. Even before the election of Ronald Reagan, New York had become what John Kenneth Galbraith described America as in the 1950s: a place of private affluence and public squalor.

There is an easy answer as to how this came about. State and local government in New York pioneered in providing public services and therefore in providing public employment. Their bureaucracies, often staffed with very talented people, grew with a reckless momentum to the point of absurdity. Today a city of seven million seems compelled to employ some 200,000 of public employees — about one for every 20 adults. Ironically, the chief buyers of the shakiest bonds the city government issued during its financial crisis are the pension funds of the city employees. Essentially, the unions were forced to make their members finance the very generous wages and fringe benefits that they enjoy. There is justice in that, but the fact remains that this bloated bureaucracy delivers very little in the way of service per employee. The thriving commercial center of New York — and the people in the rest of the nation who buy its products — are forced to pay tribute to a public work force that produces very little in return. The New York City financial crisis lowered the cost of this tribute, but it remains a dead weight on the vital high-wage economy of Manhattan.

Aside from Manhattan, New York City has another major economic asset: the city's strong middle-class neighborhoods in the outer four boroughs. There is a lot of talk about the problems of minorities in New York — every presidential candidate in the 1980 election seemed obliged to visit the south Bronx, where few people and virtually no voters live anymore. But the fact is that New York is one of the few central cities of the Northeast or Great Lakes area with a majority population that is white, non-Hispanic, and middle class. During the 1970s there was outmigration from the New York metropolitan area of Puerto Ricans and almost certainly of blacks; the only major minority in-migration was of Latin Americans, many of them illegal immigrants, who demand rather little in the way of public services. More than 70% of the population loss in the metropolitan area (not including New Jersey) in the 1970s came in the four of its 24 congressional districts with predominantly minority populations. In these districts population declined fully 31%; in other words, for every three people there in 1970 there were only two in 1980. Population loss was negligible in other areas. The largely Jewish middle-income congressional districts in the metropolitan area lost 6% of their population, a figure that is more than explained by smaller family sizes. In Manhattan the population in Harlem declined about 100,000 but actually increased in the rest of the island, with its large numbers of high-income and young single residents. In the area's predominantly Catholic congressional districts, which contain almost half the total population, the population drop in the 1970s was a minuscule 1%. Admittedly, the composition of some of these areas is changing. New immigrants — Colombians and Salvadorians, Greeks and Arabs, Koreans and Chinese — are moving into what used to be largely Irish and Italian neighborhoods. You find different names on the storefronts and different merchandise inside. But by and large these migrants seem to be moving on the same upward ladder that the Irish and Italians climbed 50 or 100 years ago. There are not nearly as many of them — reflecting the lower number of low-wage and entry-level jobs these days.

While the focus of national attention has been on New York City's economic problems, the fact is that the City has its own strong resources; of graver concern are the economic problems faced by Upstate New York. In the late 1800s this was one of the booming parts of the industrializing nation. The New York Central Railroad, running north along the Hudson and then west along the Mohawk and the route of the Erie Canal, was the great highway between the coast and the great inland plains; and Upstate New York was at the center of things. Its prosperous cities grew steadily, and the rich factory owners and their immigrant workers could all afford to build sturdy brick houses to keep out the cold during Upstate's long winters. Upstate New York was a kind of intellectual capital as well, with hundreds of small colleges, giving birth to such diverse movements as abolitionism, women's rights, and the Mormon Church.

Today Upstate New York is geographically a kind of backwater. None of its airports is very busy, passenger trains no longer run, and the freight lines here are bankrupt and poorly maintained. People seek the warmer environment of the Sun Belt in an air-conditioned age and care little for Upstate's green hills and majestic mountains, its plentiful water supply, its accessibility to supplies of coal and iron ore. Its largest city, Buffalo, is one of those Great Lakes metropolises whose economy is visibly sagging; old steel mills are being closed and there is little new investment. Albany, as the headquarters of state government, had a growth industry in the 1960–75 period, but no more. Even Rochester, a corporate headquarters town (Eastman Kodak and, until it moved to Connecticut, Xerox), is not really surging ahead. Upstate New York has problems similar to northeastern Ohio or western Pennsylvania, with a difference: it gets less attention.

Despite all the changes in the political economy of New York, there have been few outward changes in the electoral politics of the state. The conventional wisdom has it that New York is a Democratic state, and by and large it does elect Democrats: Governor Carey, Senator Daniel Patrick Moynihan, majorities of the U.S. House delegation and state Assembly. But Republicans carried the state, although narrowly, for Ronald Reagan in 1980 and elected a conservative Republican senator, Alfonse D'Amato, as well. Republicans also retain control of the state Senate and so have an effective veto over the redistricting process—something of vital importance for a state whose House delegation will be reduced from 39 to 34 for 1982. Upstate New York still generally votes Republican, and New York City generally votes Democratic. But underneath surface similarities with the past, New York politics is changing. The issues that are being decided are different, and so are the bases for party and candidate preference.

Yet an understanding of how New York politics works today is impeded by the prevalence of analysis based on how it used to work. Just as New York's earlier successes in state and local government prevented it from understanding its problems in the 1970s until it was almost too late, so the earlier structure of its politics still prevents people from understanding its elections as they occur today. That earlier structure comes from the age following the great immigrations of the 1890–1914 period. To understand it, a good place to start is 1910, when the population of immigrant-swollen Manhattan was 2.3 million (compared with 1.4 million today). Early- to middle-20th-century politics in New York was shaped in almost every respect by immigrants in a state where even today one-third of the people were either born abroad or had at least one parent who was. It was the immigrant population that produced the real strength of New York's political machines: Tammany Hall, the Manhattan machine, was led by Irish–Americans through the 1940s and by Italian–Americans thereafter, and the votes that the machine and its counterparts in the Bronx and Brooklyn could deliver were mainly those of Irish and Italian immigrants. Other immigrants, especially the Jews, never liked Catholic-dominated Tammany. In the 1910s they were electing Socialists to Congress; and in the 1930 and 1940s the American Labor and Liberal Parties were created so that Jewish immigrants who didn't read much English could vote for Roosevelt and Mayor Fiorello LaGuardia on the same party lever.

New York City was then (and is now) about one-quarter Jewish, and it was this leftish, anti-Tammany vote that became the fulcrum in state elections. In the 1920s and 1930s the progressive policies of Smith, Roosevelt, and Lehman helped Democrats to hold the governorship for 22 of 24 years. In the 1940s and 1950s, progressive Republican policies — which is to say basic acceptance of the New Deal — helped to win enough Jewish votes for statewide victories for Governors Thomas Dewey and Nelson Rockefeller and Senators Irving Ives, Jacob Javits, and Kenneth Keating.

From this basic picture of the New York electorate — machine Democrats and Upstate Yankee Republicans balanced off evenly, with a decisive, leftish bloc of primarily Jewish immigrants making the choice — grew whole national political strategies. Apparently on the theory that all big states were like New York (although none of the rest has nearly so large a Jewish population), the idea became established that Republicans couldn't win the presidency without appealing to big liberal independent blocs, and that they couldn't lose if they did so successfully. Unfortunately for this notion, Dewey in 1948 and Nixon in 1960 ran such campaigns and lost, while the Nixon of 1968 and 1972 and Ronald Reagan in 1980 ran very different campaigns and won.

Such is the conventional wisdom that developed about New York — and national — politics. It became fully articulated in the 1950s, just as the basic demographic conditions that produced it were disappearing. For New York was no longer a state dominated by self-conscious minorities as it was during the New Deal. Immigration was cut off almost completely by law in the early 1920s, and as New York's immigrants grew older they became less dependent on — and less close to — the political machines. It looked for a while as though the earlier immigrants' role would be taken over by blacks and Puerto Ricans. But machines were never really successful in bringing out their votes, and in the 1970s the number of black and Puerto Rican voters actually began to fall — particularly in the Democratic primary.

The result is that New York no longer has a left-wing vote larger than any other state's, just as it no longer has Democratic machines determining the outcomes of elections. The 1980 election showed just how weak the left had become in New York. The Democratic candidate, Jimmy Carter, won just 44% of the state's votes — only 3% better than George McGovern had done in 1972. And John Anderson took only 8% of the New York's votes, just about his national average. In New York City, which had given 14% of its votes to Communist-supported Henry Wallace in 1948, only 6% voted for John Anderson, although he was on the Liberal line on the ballot. Everyone had expected Carter to win New York, as he had in 1976, but his victory then seems in retrospect to have been due more to special circumstances than to the existence of an underlying Democratic majority.

The special circumstance was the issue of aid to New York City. President Ford, in the process of negotiating with Congress, had expressed opposition to the idea of providing New York City with federal loan guarantees in its financial crisis in 1975, although he ultimately signed the bill Congress passed. But the defensive attitude of New Yorkers in the unexpected crisis was summed up by a *Daily News* headline "Ford to City: Drop Dead." Although Ford had never used anything like those words, the Carter campaign printed millions of fliers with the headline and made the aid to New York City the central issue of the Democratic presidential campaign in the state. The result was that Carter in 1976 got a higher percentage of the votes in New York City and its suburbs than any presidential candidate since 1936 except for Lyndon Johnson in his landslide of 1964. This was not the result of cultural affinity between the south Georgia peanut farmers and the voters of New York; it stemmed from the single issue of aid to the city. Carter's lack of appeal to New Yorkers was evident in his 1976 showing Upstate, where he ran behind, not ahead of, previous Democrats who had carried the state.

Well into the 1970s political writers in New York concentrated on the doings of the city's Democratic bosses, the county chairmen in each of the four biggest boroughs. It should be apparent to anyone by now that these men have little to do with election outcomes. The machines are in another business now: the brokering of judicial patronage; a county chairman's endorsement is generally a liability rather than an asset. There have been bosses of other parties with much more influence, but all are more or less retired now: Joseph Margiotta, Republican chairman in Nassau County on Long Island, an astute leader who actually did control local politics with the help of county patronage, but who was sidelined by a trial in the spring of 1981; Alex Rose, the leader of the Liberal Party until his death in 1976, although he lived to see it finish far behind the Conservatives; and leaders of the Conservative Party who elected a U.S. senator (James Buckley in 1970) and achieved their goal of moving the Republican Party to the right.

The biggest power brokers in New York today are not party chairmen, but political consultants, and the most successful — he worked for Governor Carey and Mayor Edward Koch — is David Garth. Garth's television advertisements almost always show an aggressive, knowledgeable candidate, fighting the powers that be, and he seems to have a particularly good instinctive understanding of the New York electorate.

The basic constituencies in the New York electorate are now quite different from the 1940s model that still fascinates so many analysts. Instead of machine Democrats in New York City, we have their children and grandchildren — Catholic or Jewish, middle income, with a Democratic heritage, but hard-pressed financially and not pleased with the cultural liberalism that is so attractive to so many Manhattan voters. Instead of Upstate Yankee Republicans, we have an Upstate electorate that is heavily Catholic, that retains a Republican self-image because of its distrust of New York City, but which is willing on many occasions to support Democrats. Instead of a large leftish bloc of Jewish voters, we have very much smaller and more dispirited blocs of blacks and Puerto Ricans. And where there was no significant bloc before, today we have one-quarter of the electorate in the New York suburbs.

Thus New York City, without the aid issue, gave Jimmy Carter a much lower percentage (only 55%, down from 67% in 1976) than most Democrats have received here; in the last 50 years only McGovern and Stevenson did worse, and not by much (52%). Upstate Carter did almost as well in 1980 as he had in 1976 — a result seen in very few parts of the country; he lost this usually Republican area to Reagan by only a 48%-42% margin. The voters here, especially Catholics, seem to have a predilection for supporting incumbent presidents, a leaning that was apparent in 1972, 1964, 1956, and in the 1940s as well. In the New York City suburbs, where the tradition is Republican, Gerald Ford had won by only a 53%-47% margin; Ronald Reagan expanded that to 56%-34%. Reagan's carrying of New York was unexpected, and indeed it was one of his weakest states. Yet his chances for 1984 — assuming reasonable success for his programs — are good. If Upstate continues to lean to incumbents, he has a good chance to increase his edge there, and if he maintains his 1980 level in New York City he has excellent prospects for an absolute majority. Demographically as well the trend is in the Republicans' favor. Democratic New York City cast 42% of the state's votes in 1960 and only 31% in 1980, while the suburbs' share went up from 18% to 24% and Upstate's from 39% to 45%. Actually, the absolute number of votes cast in the suburbs and Upstate did not increase appreciably; but the number of votes cast in New York City declined from 3.1 million in 1960 to 1.9 million in 1980.

The 1980 election also saw another surprise in New York: the election of Republican Senator Alfonse D'Amato. D'Amato began the race almost entirely unknown outside Nassau County, where he was presiding supervisor of the Town of Hempstead. (He likes to point out that Hempstead had nearly 800,000 residents, but the duties of the office are limited.) His sole assets were the strong support of Joseph Margiotta's Nassau machine, a conservative stand on issues, and an Italian name. They were enough for him to defeat in the Republican primary Senator Jacob Javits, who has been winning statewide elections in New York for 26 years and was in Congress for eight years before that. Javits had an age problem (he was 76) and a health problem (he has a degenerative disease that is robbing him of physical coordination); but he still has the mental alertness and acuity that have led many to label him the brainiest senator. His greatest problem was the issues. For many years New York did not allow primaries for statewide office (Nelson Rockefeller vetoed several primary bills) and Javits had never faced a Republican primary electorate in the race for senator before. That electorate is relatively small, a majority of its voters live Upstate, and its New York City voters are mainly of Italian descent. But Javits was really overtaken in the suburbs. In Long Island's Nassau and Suffolk Counties, D'Amato got over 70% of the vote. The voters here, even if they once shared Javits's fervor for civil rights and his support of New Deal measures, were tired of big government and saw Javits as its champion.

D'Amato was still not favored in the general election; indeed, attention had been focused during the primary season on the Democrats' contest. The favorite there, former city Consumer Affairs Commissioner Bess Myerson — known also for being the first Jewish Miss America — was overtaken by Congresswoman Elizabeth Holtzman. Serious, hardworking, so liberal that she had voted against most defense appropriations bills, Holtzman overtook Myerson largely on the basis of a big margin in Manhattan. So in the general the contest was basically between a Manhattan candidate (although Holtzman is from Brooklyn, and had a strong base there as well) and a suburban candidate. Given the basic predilections of New York voters, the surprise is that the general was so close. And it wouldn't have been without the presence in the race, as the Liberal Party candidate, of Jacob Javits. He was urged by many, including, finally, his old backer the *New York Times,* to leave the race and help Holtzman; but he hesitated to declare himself politically dead, and he may have hoped for some credit from the forces of Ronald Reagan (whom he steadfastly supported, although the Liberal nominee was John Anderson). With any kind of plurality among Javits's supporters, Holtzman would have won. Instead she lost by some 80,000 votes, 1% of the total. She had a much larger margin than Carter in New York City and managed even to hold D'Amato to a 50%–40% margin in the suburbs. But in Upstate New York, where the incumbent president was running well, she trailed D'Amato by a 52%–36% margin. Holtzman was evidently too much of a city candidate for some Upstaters. New York voters have proved over and over, in James Buckley's election in 1970 and his defeat in 1976, and in presidential elections in 1960 and 1968 and 1976, that there is about a 45% vote base for a candidate representing the views of the national Republican Party. This is exactly the percentage that D'Amato got. Whether he can do better in 1986 is obviously an open question.

D'Amato thus unexpectedly became part of the unexpected Republican majority of the Senate. He seemed a rather unpleasant man during much of the campaign, charging that Javits was not physically up to the job and attacking Holtzman vitriolically for her stand on defense. Shortly after his election, he broke with Joseph Margiotta, who had been his political patron for his entire career. That means that, in a Republican administration, D'Amato thus is likely to have the say over all the federal patronage in New York. He will select three out of every four federal judges (Moynihan will choose the other, presumably with the help of the advisory panel he has used in the past), the federal marshals, U.S. attorneys (although he is letting the major U.S. attorneys in Manhattan and Brooklyn stay in until their terms expire), and the heads of the New York regional offices of the various federal bureaucracies. For a man who was toiling at the middle levels of a patronage-oriented county government, this must be heady stuff indeed, although he will have to defer to some extent to state Party Chairman George Clark, an early Reagan backer. Indeed, his influence on public policy may be greater in his role as patronage dispenser than in his work on the Appropriations and Banking Committees.

The senior senator from New York now is Daniel Patrick Moynihan, who although still in his early 50s has had as long and varied a public career as anyone in the Senate. He worked for Governor Averell Harriman in the 1950s, served as assistant secretary of labor in the Kennedy and Johnson Administrations, was chief domestic adviser to President Nixon and his ambassador to India, and was ambassador to the United Nations under President Ford. In all these jobs he displayed a talent for original thinking and, increasingly, a taste for controversy. Controversies were engendered by his report on the black family in the 1960s and his call for "benign neglect" of racial problems in the early 1970s. He struggled to put together the Nixon Administration's family assistance program but ultimately saw it torpedoed in the Senate Finance Committee. At the United Nations, Moynihan spoke out against Russia and for Israel and ignored the conventional wisdom that policymakers should accept the premises of Third World and Soviet demands and negotiate quietly for small concessions.

Moynihan's actions at the UN made him suddenly popular with Jewish and other voters in New York and, although he said on *Face the Nation* that it would be "dishonorable" to run for the Senate after serving in the UN, he did so. The race was a classic confrontation between those, such as Bella Abzug and his other opponents, who believed that America was generally in the wrong in foreign policy, and those who like Moynihan believed that although Vietnam had been a mistake America was generally right in foreign policy. Moynihan won over Abzug, but by just 10,000 votes out of 916,000 cast. In the general election he beat incumbent James Buckley by a solid margin; Buckley, a principled man who had won a three-way race with only 39% of the vote in 1970, had the misfortune to have expressed doubts about aid to New York City. This is the seat New York seems to reserve for outsiders: it was held by Robert Kennedy; Buckley before his election lived on the family estate in Sharon, Connecticut, and ran for the Senate in that state in 1980; Moynihan, although he had lived in New York for many years and ran for New York City Council president in 1965, was a Harvard professor when he ran in 1976.

When Moynihan entered the Senate, it seemed that he would be entering the least creative phase of his public career. A large part of the job of any representative of New York these days is to keep federal money flowing into the state and to maintain federal loan guarantees. Moynihan sought and obtained a seat on the Senate Finance Committee—an excellent position from which to do just that. But Senate service, rather than confining Moynihan to mundane tasks, seems to have liberated him to think about a range of public policy problems. His long essay on the SALT Treaty in the *New Yorker* was probably the most original contribution by a senator on that difficult issue — and one that left Moynihan not squarely committed in either camp. He is one senator who reads widely and — his ornate style leaves no doubt — writes his own speeches and articles. He was very much at odds with the Carter Administration, believing it too soft in foreign policy and insufficiently attentive to the problems of places like New York in domestic affairs. His relationship to the Reagan Administration might be closer, but in early 1981 he was making tough attacks on the Moral Majority and New Right. Moynihan is ranking minority member now on the Finance subcommittee that handles Social Security and welfare, but he no longer backs comprehensive welfare reform, with an explicit guaranteed minimum income, that he pushed for a decade ago. He also serves on the International Trade Subcommittee; his intellectual leanings incline him against import protections, but the needs of New York — the apparel industry in New York City, steel in Buffalo — may lead him to look with sympathy on protective measures.

Moynihan is one of those senators who seem to have national ambitions. To some extent he has already realized them: he has been a national figure for more than a decade now, and he has demonstrated again and again the ability to frame issues if not the ability to control entirely the flow of the public dialogue. He has not yet run for president, but he might very well do so in 1984, assuming reelection by a comfortable margin in 1982. His strengths are obvious: a broad range of experience and originality of thought, an unusual combination in any public man. He is intellectual, yet pugnacious. His weaknesses are less apparent these days, but there are: an eagerness sometimes to seek out quarrels, a tendency to personalize issues, a hot temper. He has an enthusiastic national constituency, similar to that of Henry Jackson (whom Moynihan supported in 1976); he has strong support in the Jewish community, in many quarters of organized labor, and among the group of intellectuals associated with such publications as *Commentary* and the *Public Interest*. His opposition comes from that segment of the liberal community for whom the Vietnam experience remains central or who consider Moynihan unsympathetic to blacks. Sometimes Moynihan and his supporters seem to see him as another Winston Churchill, warning the world of perils others ignore. They may remember uncomfortably that Churchill was not summoned to power until his nation was on the brink of ruin and its political establishment had no other choice.

Moynihan's supporters believe he is highly popular in New York and will win reelection with ease in 1982. But the possibility at least exists of significant opposition. Even in the primary, he may face an opponent on the left who could command a large percentage of the votes simply on the basis of opposition to Moynihan. In the general election there is the possibility of someone like Buffalo area Congressman Jack Kemp running for the Republicans — a man who has shown as much originality on occasions as Moynihan. New York is too big a constituency for any officeholder to establish a close relationship with his constituents and is too volatile to take for granted.

The other major election in New York in 1982 will be for governor. New York's state government has been dominated for 24 years now by two men. Nelson Rockefeller, elected governor four times, vastly expanded state government, increasing services and welfare payments, building a state university system almost from scratch, and leaving as his monument the giant Albany Mall — and a state government in serious financial problem. That became apparent only when Hugh Carey, the first Democrat elected in 20 years, succeeded Malcolm Wilson, Rockefeller's faithful conservative lieutenant governor who served himself as governor for a year. In his first year Carey faced the New York City financial crisis and found it necessary for the state to retrench as well. The major success of his governorship has been the rescue of the city government and the continued solvency of the state. Taxes have come down somewhat, economic activity is up, the growth of the bureaucracy has been stopped.

In the old days, Democrats in New York favored big government and generous aid for the City; the Republicans were opposed to both. In the Carey and Rockefeller years the truth was closer to the opposite. In Albany, Carey has worked on a bipartisan basis with the Republican leaders of the state Senate on all his major programs; in effect New York has coalition government. Yet every four years there is an election in which the City comes out heavily on the Democratic side and Upstate and the suburbs go Republican. In 1978 Carey narrowly beat Perry Duryea, then Republican leader of the Assembly. It is not clear whether Carey will run in 1982, but if he does, he will have problems because of his reclusiveness and his occasional erratic remarks (such as his assertion in 1980 that the Senate seat up that year is a "Jewish seat"). Carey does not devote much attention to what he considers the unimportant aspects of his job nor does he suffer fools gladly. He is unlikely to have primary opposition if he runs, but he will face a strong Republican challenge, perhaps from someone such as Senate Majority Leader Warren Anderson, perhaps from an outsider to state government such as Jack Kemp.

The other major office in New York is the mayoralty of New York City. For years the city budget was larger than the state's, and in many ways the mayor set the tone for public life in the greater part of this state. Mayor John Lindsay, for example, with his sympathy for blacks and Hispanics and evident disdain for nonaffluent whites, helped stir the resentment among middle-class New Yorkers that led to the election of Senator James Buckley and the development of the kind of Archie Bunker mentality that characterized attitudes in the outer boroughs in the late 1960s and early 1970s. The current mayor, Edward Koch, comes from a liberal background — he was a leader of the Greenwich Village reformers who fought Tammany Hall leader Carmine DeSapio in the late 1950s and early 1960s — and was a Manhattan congressman when he ran for mayor in 1977. Koch attracted attention by taking positions more characteristic of the outer boroughs than of Manhattan — favoring capital punishment, for example. He was tough on crime, opposed to racial quotas, and determined to cut the city budget. The battle was in the Democratic primaries, where he managed to force incumbent Mayor Abraham Beame into third place and then polished off Mario Cuomo in the primary. Cuomo, a civic leader in Queens who opposed the death penalty, is now Hugh Carey's lieutenant governor and a likely candidate for governor should Carey choose to retire.

In office Koch has restored New York City to something approaching financial health, has squared off with the municipal workers' unions, has lost the support of most black and Puerto Rican politicians, and has sparked all kinds of controversies. He has also become exceedingly popular among every segment of the electorate. As this is written, he is running for reelection in 1981, and the speculation is that he will have no significant opposition in the Democratic primary and may actually be awarded the Republican nomination as well. Koch may be abrasive, he may insert his personality too much into public affairs, but New Yorkers like his style and his accomplishments. Even among black and Puerto Rican voters, he has considerable popularity.

For many years New York was used to playing a major role in presidential politics. Until 1972 it had more electoral votes than any other state, and for years it produced far more than its share of presidential candidates. Three times in this century both major parties' candidates have come from New York. But more recently New York has produced few contenders. Governors Rockefeller and Harriman ran unsuccessful races for their parties' nominations; excepting Eisenhower and Nixon, who had legal residences in New York but never made political careers there, the last New Yorker nominated by a major party was Thomas Dewey in 1948. Senator Moynihan and Governor Carey, both mentioned in the past as possible candidates, have so far not run.

The New York presidential primary is held early enough in the primary season and covers enough delegates to be of truly national importance. Yet its relevance to the rest of the country seems limited. On the Democratic side, because of registration and turnout, Jewish voters comprise perhaps as much as one-third of the primary electorate. This is one reason for the outcome of the 1980 presidential primary here. Shortly before, the Carter Administration's UN representatives had voted for a resolution condemning Israel's occupation of the West Bank in terms referring to the crimes of Nazi Germany. It was all a mistake in communication, the State Department said, but the damage was done. Jewish voters, convinced that Carter was basically unsympathetic to them and would no longer support their causes if he were reelected, swung heavily to Edward Kennedy. Kennedy also benefited from New York's continued backing for expansive federal aid programs. The result was Kennedy's first big win outside Massachusetts — a result that kept him in the race, although he could never repeat it outside the Eastern Seaboard and in a few small states in the interior (South Dakota, New Mexico) that held their primaries late in the season after the nomination was already decided.

On the Republican side, primaries were never needed for years; the delegation was controlled by Nelson Rockefeller. But that is no longer the case, and no one should assume that conservatives cannot win a Republican primary these days in New York. In New York City and its suburbs the primary electorate is relatively small and quite conservative; Upstate, where Republican registration is more common and extends over a broader segment of society, the conservatives may not be quite as strong.

The New York legislature has the unpleasant task of drawing new boundaries for New York's congressional districts and reducing the number of districts from 39 to 34. This will have to be done on a bipartisan basis, since Democrats control the Assembly and Republicans the Senate. But it is clear from the demographics that Democrats will lose most of the districts. Four of the five districts to be eliminated must come out of New York City, and almost all the city districts are now held by Democrats. In a state as large and various as New York, there is plenty of leeway for redistricting, even within these political constraints and the limitations imposed by the equal population rule. If the districts with the largest population losses are the ones to go, then New York's minority representation will decrease, since it is the districts with black or Hispanic majorities that have had the greatest population losses (the 12th, 14th, 19th, and 21st districts). But in all likelihood the losers will be the districts currently represented by members with relatively few friends in Albany and relatively little influence on Capitol Hill. This means trouble for, among others, Democrat James Scheuer (who lost a seat through redistricting 10 years ago) and freshman Republican John LeBoutillier, among others. In the Upstate region, the districts that seem demographically the most desirable targets for redisricting are those in the Buffalo area. But the congressmen there all have strong political assets, and the legislature may choose instead to in effect combine the two Syracuse districts, both represented currently by recently elected Republicans. Almost certainly there will be a number of bitter primaries and hard-fought general elections pitting incumbent versus incumbent.

Census Data   Pop. (1980 final) 17,557,288, down 4% in 1970s: 7.75% of U.S. total, 2d largest. Central city, 47%; suburban, 41%. Median 4-person family income, 1978, $19,660, 96% of U.S., 30th highest.

1979 Share of Federal Tax Burden $39,266,000,000; 8.71% of U.S. total, 2d largest.

1979 Share of Federal Outlays $37,112,228,000; 8.02% of U.S. total, 2d largest.

DOD	$5,556,406,000	4th	(5.24%)	HEW	$18,013,672,000	1st	(10.08%)
DOE	$327,239,000	14th	(2.78%)	ERDA	$74,354,000	9th	(2.74%)
HUD	$806,496,000	1st	(12.23%)	NASA	$69,448,000	12th	(1.49%)
VA	$1,506,575,000	2d	(7.26%)	DOT	$1,129,396,000	2d	(6.84%)
EPA	$483,819,000	1st	(9.11%)	DOC	$223,328,000	4th	(7.05%)
DOI	$80,517,000	20th	(1.45%)	USDA	$1,907,232,000	1st	(7.94%)

Economic Base   Finance, insurance, and real estate; apparel and other textile products, especially women's and misses' outerwear; electrical equipment and supplies, especially communication equipment; printing and publishing, especially commercial printing and newspapers; machinery, especially office and computing machines; food and kindred products, especially bakery products and beverages; agriculture, especially dairy products, cattle, eggs, and greenhouse products.

Political Lineup   Governor, Hugh L. Carey (D). Senators, Daniel Patrick Moynihan (D) and Alfonse M. D'Amato (R). Representatives, 39 (22 D and 17 R); 34 in 1982. State Senate, 60 (35 R and 25 D); State Assembly, 150 (86 D and 64 R).

The Voters

   Registration   7,358,946 Total. 3,455,596 D (47%); 2,467,472 R (34%); 106,777 Conservative (1%); 70,010 Liberal (1%); 15,282 Right to Life (0%); 1,243,809 other (17%).
   Employment profile 1970   White collar, 55%. Blue collar, 31%. Service, 13%. Farm, 1%.
   Ethnic groups   Black 1980, 14%. Hispanic 1980, 9%. Asian 1980, 2%. Total foreign stock 1970, 33%. Italy, 7%; USSR, Poland, Germany, 3% each; Ireland, UK, Canada, 2% each; Austria, 1%.

Presidential Vote	1980	Reagan (R)	2,893,831	(47%)
		Carter (D)	2,728,372	(44%)
		Anderson (I)	467,801	(8%)
	1976	Ford (R)	3,100,791	(47%)
		Carter (D)	3,389,558	(52%)

1980 Democratic Presidential Primary		
Kennedy	582,757	(59%)
Carter	406,305	(41%)

SENATORS

Sen. Daniel Patrick Moynihan (D) Elected 1976, seat up 1982; b. Mar. 16, 1927, Tulsa, Okla.; home, New York City; CCNY, 1943, Tufts U., B.A. 1948, M.A. 1949, Ph.D. 1961.

Career   University professor; U.S. Asst. Secy. of Labor, 1963–65; Asst. to the Pres. for Urban Affairs, 1969–70; U.S. Ambassador to India, 1973–74; U.S. Ambassador to the U.N., 1975–76.

Offices   442 RSOB, 202-224-4451. Also 733 3d Ave., New York 10017, 212-661-5150, and Fed. Ofc. Bldg., Buffalo 14202, 716-842-3493.

Committees   *Budget* (9th).

Environment and Public Works (5th). Subcommittees: Environmental Pollution; Transportation; Water Resources.

Finance (5th). Subcommittees: Economic Growth, Employment, and Revenue Sharing; International Trade; Social Security and Income Maintenance Programs.

Select Committee on Intelligence (Vice-chairman).

Group Ratings

	ADA	COPE	PC	LCV	CFA	RPN	NAB	NSI	NTU	ACA	ACU
1980	72	100	77	71	73	—	36	10	22	8	0
1979	47	100	63	—	81	—	—	—	14	15	16
1978	60	89	60	65	45	67	9	30	8	4	9

Key Votes

1) Draft Registn $	FOR	6) Fair Housng Cloture	FOR	11) Cut Socl Incr Defns	AGN
2) Ban $ to Nicrgua	FOR	7) Ban $ Rape Abortns	AGN	12) Income Tax Indexing	AGN
3) Dlay MX Missile	AGN	8) Cap on Food Stmp $	AGN	13) Lim Spdg 21% GNP	AGN
4) Nuclr Mortorium	AGN	9) New US Dep Edcatn	AGN	14) Incr Wndfll Prof Tax	FOR
5) Alaska Lands Bill	FOR	10) Cut OSHA Inspctns	AGN	15) Chryslr Loan Grntee	FOR

Election Results

1976 general	Daniel Patrick Moynihan (D)	3,422,594	(54%)	($1,210,796)
	James L. Buckley (R)	2,836,633	(45%)	($2,101,424)
1976 primary	Daniel Patrick Moynihan (D)	333,697	(36%)	
	Bella S. Abzug (D)	323,705	(35%)	
	Ramsey Clark (D)	94,191	(10%)	
	Paul O'Dwyer (D)	82,689	(9%)	
	Abraham Hirshfeld (D)	82,331	(9%)	
1970 general	James L. Buckley (C)	2,288,190	(39%)	
	Richard L. Ottinger (D)	2,171,232	(37%)	
	Charles E. Goodell (R-L)	1,434,472	(24%)	

Sen. Alfonse M. D'Amato (R) Elected 1980, seat up 1986; b. Aug. 1, 1937, Brooklyn; home, Island Park; Syracuse U., B.S. 1959, J.D. 1961.

Career Island Pk. Atty., Asst. Hempstead Atty., 1965–68; Pub. Admin., Nassau Co., 1969; Hempstead Town Receiver of Taxes, 1969, Supervisor, 1971, Presiding Supervisor, 1977.

Offices 432 RSOB, 202-224-6542. Also 420 Leo O'Brian Fed. Bldg., Albany 12207, 518-463-2244; 111 W. Huron, Rm. 620, Buffalo 14202, 716-846-4112; and 1 Penn Plaza, Suite 1632, New York 10001, 212-947-7390.

Committees *Appropriations* (12th). Subcommittees: Defense; District of Columbia (Chairman); Foreign Operations; HUD–Independent Agencies; Transportation.

Banking, Housing, and Urban Affairs (6th). Subcommittees: Consumer Affairs; Financial Institutions; Housing and Urban Affairs; Securities.

Select Committee on Small Business (9th). Subcommittees: Government Regulation and Paperwork; Urban and Rural Economic Development (Chairman).

Group Ratings and Key Votes: Newly Elected

Election Results

1980 general	Alfonse M. D'Amato (R-C-RTL) .	2,699,652	(45%)	($1,699,709)
	Elizabeth Holtzman (D)	2,618,661	(44%)	($2,173,056)
	Jacob K. Javits (L)	664,544	(11%)	($1,846,313)
1980 primary	Alfonse M. D'Amato (R)	323,468	(56%)	
	Jacob K. Javits (R)	257,433	(44%)	
1974 general	Jacob K. Javits (R-L)	2,340,188	(45%)	($1,090,437)
	Ramsey Clark (D)	1,973,781	(38%)	($855,576)
	Barbara A. Keating (C)	822,584	(16%)	($192,462)

GOVERNOR

Gov. Hugh L. Carey (D) Elected 1974, term expires Jan. 1983; b. Apr. 11, 1919, Brooklyn; St. John's U., J.D. 1951.

Career Army, WWII; Family petroleum distrib. business, 1947–51; Practicing atty., 1951–61; U.S. House of Reps., 1961–75.

Offices Executive Chamber, State Capitol, Albany 12224, 518-474-8390.

Election Results

1978 gen.	Hugh L. Carey (D-L)	2,429,272	(51%)
	Perry B. Duryea (R-C)	2,156,404	(45%)
1978 prim.	Hugh L. Carey (D)	376,457	(52%)
	Mary Anne Krupsak (D) . . .	244,252	(34%)
	Jeremiah B. Bloom (D)	103,479	(14%)
1974 gen.	Hugh L. Carey (D-L)	3,028,503	(57%)
	Malcolm Wilson (R-C)	2,219,667	(42%)

FIRST DISTRICT

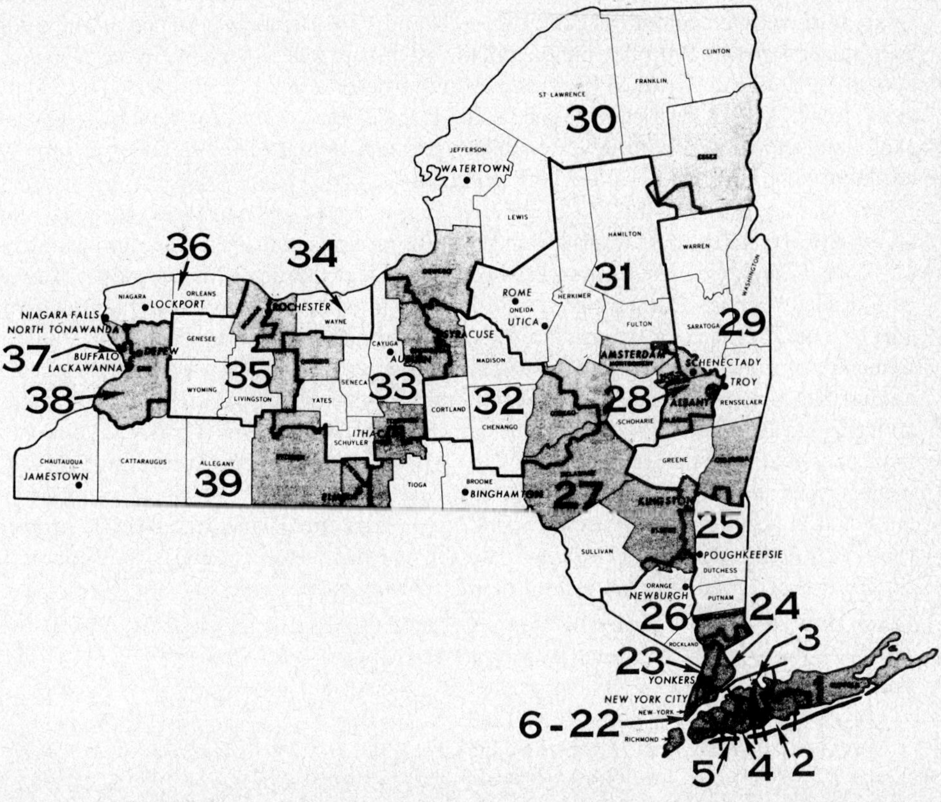

The 1st congressional district of New York includes the eastern end of Long Island, from 50 to 100 miles from Manhattan. The best-known part of the district is the eastern tip that juts out into the Atlantic Ocean; here rich New Yorkers flock each summer to the fashionable beach resorts of the Hamptons and Montauk. This is a lovely area, settled first by New Englanders and now maintained in the kind of pristine countrification made possible only from the interest taken by affluent outsiders. Inland and west of the Hamptons is the more typical rural Long Island: acres of potato fields, truck farms, rickety housing occupied by farm workers.

Before World War II virtually all of the current 1st district was agricultural, little changed from the 19th century. Today metropolitan New York has moved in inexorably. The area within the current 1st district has increased in population from 232,000 in 1960 to 467,000 in 1970 and 606,000 in 1980 — the largest population increases of any congressional district in the East.

As in fast-growing parts of the Sun Belt, the mood out here is very conservative. A correlation seems to exist between conservative political attitudes and the desire to move this far away from New York City — a fear of crime, a dislike of blacks and Puerto Ricans, a distaste for the moral tone of cosmopolitan life. There is a desire to leave behind the chaos and the corruption of the city for the supposedly simpler, less hectic pace of life on Long Island. The outcome is seldom so pleasing. The new subdivisions on eastern Long Island have houses larger and farther apart than those back in Brooklyn and Queens, but they also lack the cohesiveness of the old ethnic neighborhoods. Children are no more docile, adolescents no less rebellious out here. The economy is less diversified than New York's and sometimes less stable; among the biggest employers are Grumman and Republic Aviation, both of which have had big defense payrolls.

The conservatism of eastern Long Island has had its ebbs and flows. This was the part of New York state that most strongly supported Conservative candidate James Buckley in his successful Senate race in 1970. But after the Watergate crisis, the voters here seemed to revert to an ancestral Democratic allegiance. In 1974 and 1976 Democrats carried all three congressional districts in Suffolk County, and the 1st district was rather close in the 1976 presidential election. Four years of the Carter Administration seem to have reversed the Democratic trend. The 1st district went solidly for Ronald Reagan and for Republican Senate candidate Alfonse D'Amato. The Republican platform of more defense and lower domestic spending suits most of the voters here perfectly.

The 1st district's current Congressman, William Carney, was actually a registered Conservative when he first ran for this seat in 1978. The race was wide open, since the incumbent, Otis Pike, a witty, eloquent Democrat who had represented eastern Long Island for 18 years, had decided to retire. Carney received Republican organization support in the primary as part of a deal between the two parties. He won the general election by a substantial but not tremendously impressive margin. In 1980 his performance was not especially impressive. He got just 58% of the vote in the Republican primary and won the general election with a similar margin to 1978's — no evidence of the national conservative trend. Carney has one of the most conservative voting records in the New York area delegation. His committee assignments — Science and Technology, Merchant Marine and Fisheries — show a concern for the practical needs of the district. He is one New York congressman who faces no problem from redistricting. His district is larger than the new districts will be and, sitting out on the eastern end of Long Island, it cannot be joined with politically less favorable territory.

Census Data Pop. (1980 final) 603,787, up 29% in 1970s. Median family income, 1970, $11,643, 121% of U.S.

The Voters

Employment profile 1970 White collar, 55%. Blue collar, 30%. Service, 14%. Farm, 1%.
Ethnic groups Black 1980, 3%. Hispanic 1980, 3%. Asian 1980, 1%. Total foreign stock 1970, 28%. Italy, 7%; Germany, 4%; UK, Poland, Ireland, 2% each; USSR, 1%.

Presidential Vote

1980	Reagan (R)	124,331	(57%)
	Carter (D)	71,530	(33%)
	Anderson (I)	17,756	(8%)
1976	Ford (R)	117,277	(54%)
	Carter (D)	98,409	(45%)

Rep. William Carney (R) Elected 1978; b. July 1, 1942, Brooklyn; home, Hauppauge; Fla. St. U., 1960–61.

Career Army, 1961–64; Salesman, heavy equipment business, 1972–76; Suffolk Co. Legis., 1976–79.

Offices 1113 LHOB, 202-225-3826. Also 180 E. Main St., Smithtown 11787, 516-724-4888.

Committees *Merchant Marine and Fisheries* (10th). Subcommittees: Fisheries and Wildlife Conservation and the Environment; Oceanography.

Science and Technology (8th). Subcommittees: Natural Resources, Agriculture Research and Environment; Transportation, Aviation and Materials.

Group Ratings

	ADA	COPE	PC	LCV	CFA	RPN	NAB	NSI	NTU	ACA	ACU
1980	11	28	20	22	21	—	92	100	51	83	83
1979	0	15	10	17	4	—	—	—	57	85	92

Key Votes

1) Draft Registn $	FOR	6) Fair Hsg DOJ Enfrc	AGN	11) Cut Socl Incr Dfns $	FOR
2) Ban $ to Nicrgua	FOR	7) Lim PAC Contrbtns	AGN	12) Hosptl Cost Controls	AGN
3) Dlay MX Missile	AGN	8) Cap on Food Stmp $	FOR	13) Gasln Ctrls & Allctns	AGN
4) Nuclr Mortorium	—	9) New US Dep Edcatn	AGN	14) Lim Wndfll Prof Tax	FOR
5) Alaska Lands Bill	AGN	10) Cut OSHA $	FOR	15) Chryslr Loan Grntee	FOR

Election Results

1980 general	William Carney (R-C-RTL)	115,213	(56%)	($195,878)
	Thomas A. Twomey (D)	85,629	(42%)	($120,143)
1980 primary	William Carney (R).............	15,210	(58%)	
	J. J. Hart (R).................	11,102	(42%)	($66,464)
1978 general	William Carney (R-C)...........	90,155	(56%)	($130,642)
	John F. Randolph (D)	67,180	(42%)	($76,810)

SECOND DISTRICT

At the end of World War II, Suffolk County, which includes the eastern geographical half of Long Island, was largely given over to potato fields. It was also directly in the path of one of the major suburban migrations of our day. On the highways that Robert Moses built to connect his parks to the middle-class parts of New York City came tens of thousands of young veterans and their families, forsaking the row house neighborhoods where they had grown up for the comparatively spacious lots and single-family houses of Levittown and other Long Island subdivisions. The first wave of postwar migration moved into Nassau County, and it was a pretty accurate cross-section of all but the poorest New Yorkers: almost half Catholic, about one-quarter Jewish and one-quarter Protestant. Then, as Long Island developed an employment base of its own, the next wave of migration started, this time as far out as Suffolk County. This second wave was somewhat more Catholic and less Jewish, more blue collar (aircraft manufacturers were big Suffolk County employers) and less white collar, more Democratic perhaps in ancestral politics but fundamentally more conservative on most issues.

The 2d congressional district of New York covers the south shore suburban communities of Suffolk, from Amityville and Babylon east through Bay Shore and Islip to Sayville and Bayport — one community after another strung out along the Sunrise Highway. This is one of the lowest-income parts of Long Island, out past the fashionable and expensive suburbs with their minimum acreage zoning, far from the picturesque north shore and separated by the Great South Bay from the beaches of Fire Island. This area filled up with people in the 1950s and 1960s and has had little growth since; the modest homes in some cases are being upgraded by their owners and in some cases left with chipped paint and cracked shingle siding.

The current congressman from the 2d, Democrat Thomas Downey, won this seat in one of the biggest upsets of 1974. The Republican incumbent had won 66% two years before, and Downey was only a 25-year-old law student. But Downey was no political novice. He had served three years in the Suffolk County legislature and knew how to convince voters that he would give them more energetic representation and service than they were used to. That formula has served him well in elections since. He has never won in a real landslide. But despite the national Republican trend — evident in some of the results for other offices in the 2d — Downey has been reelected with percentages like the 56% he won in 1980.

For his first two terms in the House, Downey was a dovish member of the Armed Services Committee. In 1979 he switched to Ways and Means. Downey is inclined to be rather more generous than the Reaganites on welfare and income support programs; he brings to the issue both a fervor born of compassion for the poor and a knowledge of the substance of the issue grounded in hard work. On trade issues he has been sympathetic to claims for protection on some occasions, particularly when they come from unions, but cannot be classified as an all-out free trader or protectionist. He is also a member of the Budget Committee, on which he has been one of the most pugnacious critics of the Reagan Administration.

Downey is not threatened much by redistricting. The 2d may shift slightly to the east, but the legislature will probably see that he does not gain heavily Republican territory; enough New York incumbents will be unable to return without defeating one of the state's Ways and Means members as well.

Census Data Pop. (1980 final) 489,073, up 5% in 1970s. Median family income, 1970, $11,938, 125% of U.S.

The Voters

Employment profile 1970 White collar, 49%. Blue collar, 37%. Service, 14%. Farm, –%.
Ethnic groups Black 1980, 6%. Hispanic 1980, 7%. Asian 1980, 1%. Total foreign stock 1970, 28%. Italy, 9%; Germany, 3%; Ireland, UK, 2% each; Canada, Poland, 1% each.

Presidential Vote

1980	Reagan (R)	91,682	(58%)
	Carter (D)	52,068	(33%)
	Anderson (I)	10,830	(7%)
1976	Ford (R)	90,243	(54%)
	Carter (D)	75,033	(45%)

Rep. Thomas J. Downey (D) Elected 1974; b. Jan. 28, 1949, Ozone Park; home, West Islip; Cornell U., B.S. 1970, St. John's U. Law School, 1972–74.

Career Personnel mgmt. and labor relations, Macy's Dept. Store; Suffolk Co. Legislature, 1971–74.

Offices 303 CHOB, 202-225-3335. Also 4 Udall Rd., West Islip 11759, 516-661-8777.

Committees *Budget* (14th).

Ways and Means (14th). Subcommittee: Trade.

Select Committee on Aging (7th). Subcommittee: Retirement Income and Employment.

Group Ratings

	ADA	COPE	PC	LCV	CFA	RPN	NAB	NSI	NTU	ACA	ACU
1980	94	84	80	94	86	—	0	10	19	13	11
1979	89	88	83	89	85	—	—	—	23	0	3
1978	60	100	78	92	68	45	18	30	13	7	9

Key Votes

1) Draft Registn $	AGN	6) Fair Hsg DOJ Enfrc	FOR	11) Cut Socl Incr Dfns $	AGN
2) Ban $ to Nicrgua	AGN	7) Lim PAC Contrbtns	FOR	12) Hosptl Cost Controls	FOR
3) Dlay MX Missile	FOR	8) Cap on Food Stmp $	AGN	13) Gasln Ctrls & Allctns	FOR
4) Nuclr Mortorium	FOR	9) New US Dep Edcatn	FOR	14) Lim Wndfll Prof Tax	AGN
5) Alaska Lands Bill	FOR	10) Cut OSHA $	AGN	15) Chryslr Loan Grntee	FOR

Election Results

1980 general	Thomas J. Downey (D)	84,035	(56%)	($190,889)
	Louis J. Modica (R-C-RTL)	65,106	(44%)	($72,678)
1980 primary	Thomas J. Downey (D), unopposed			
1978 general	Thomas J. Downey (D)	64,807	(55%)	($149,400)
	Harold J. Withers, Jr. (R-C)	53,322	(45%)	($33,119)

THIRD DISTRICT

The 3d congressional district of New York is part of the Long Island suburbs of the city and straddles the line between Nassau County and Suffolk County. The expansion of the metropolitan area marched through here some time ago: the swiftest population rise in Nassau County was in the 1950s and in the farther-out Suffolk County portion it was in the 1960s. By the 1970s, as children grew up and moved out of their parents' homes, there was actually population decline in this area which had grown so explosively so recently.

Somewhat more than half the 3d district's citizens live in Nassau County, in areas as diverse as fashionable and high-income North Shore communities such as Locust Valley, less fashionable but nonetheless well-to-do Syosett in the middle of Long Island, and deeply conservative and middle-income Massapequa on the South Shore. The remainder of the district is just to the east, in Suffolk County; that portion is dominated by the middle-class town of Huntington but also includes the small black ghetto of Wyandanch.

The 3d district was created by a Republican legislature following the 1970 census and so far in its brief history has had five close elections and three congressmen. The first congressman was Angelo Roncallo, a faithful member of Joseph Margiotta's Nassau County Republican machine. He was indicted on conspiracy charges and, although acquitted, he lost the 1974 election. The winner, Joseph Ambro, was a local official in Huntington. He had an often liberal record on economic issues and a conservative record on cultural issues, but that was not enough to give him a safe seat; that required also the sort of ceaseless work that young bachelors such as Thomas Downey seem willing to do but about which seasoned family men like Ambro are understandably reluctant. In 1978, Gregory Carman, a member of one of the founding families of the small town of Farmingdale, ran as the Republican candidate. He raised a large campaign treasury and nearly won. Encouraged, he tried again in 1980. The national trend on issues and the strong campaign of Carman, ably assisted by Margiotta's organization, prevailed. Carman won a solid 53%–45% victory in Nassau, enough to overcome Ambro's almost identical margin in the less populous Suffolk portion of the district. Carman has solid Republican credentials and comes from a political tradition that encourages conformity. A member of the Banking Committee, he can be expected to back the Reagan Republican platform.

Redistricting will require some adjustment of the district's boundaries, although there is little chance that it will be eliminated or vastly changed in shape. It will have to take in some territory to the east, and certainly Carman and the Nassau Republicans will want to expand to heavily Republican Commack and Smithtown, north shore towns now in the 1st district, rather than into more marginal or even Democratic south shore places such as Amityville, Copiague, and Lindenhurst in the 2d. If a trade can be arranged with the 2d, giving up Wyandanch for some more Republican precincts, so much the better for the political security of both incumbents.

Census Data   Pop. (1980 final) 446,948, down 4% in 1970s. Median family income, 1970, $14,396, 150% of U.S.

The Voters

Employment profile 1970   White collar, 62%. Blue collar, 27%. Service, 11%. Farm, –%.
Ethnic groups   Black 1980, 6%. Hispanic 1980, 3%. Asian 1980, 1%. Total foreign stock 1970, 32%. Italy, 9%; Germany, 4%; USSR, 3%; UK, Poland, Ireland, 2% each; Canada, Austria, 1% each.

Presidential Vote

1980	Reagan (R)	106,282	(57%)
	Carter (D)	63,346	(34%)
	Anderson (I)	14,895	(8%)
1976	Ford (R)	105,322	(54%)
	Carter (D)	88,901	(46%)

Rep. Gregory W. Carman (R) Elected 1980; b. Jan. 31, 1937, Farmingdale; home, Farmingdale; St. Lawrence U., B.A. 1958, St. John's U., J.D. 1961.

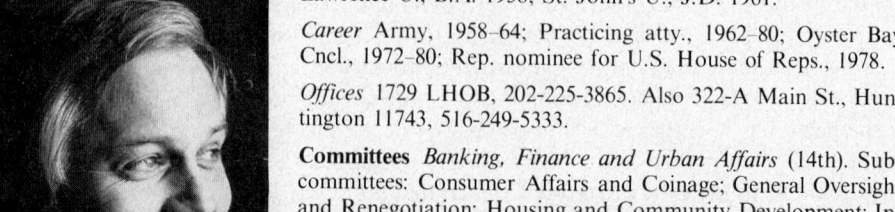

Career Army, 1958–64; Practicing atty., 1962–80; Oyster Bay Cncl., 1972–80; Rep. nominee for U.S. House of Reps., 1978.

Offices 1729 LHOB, 202-225-3865. Also 322-A Main St., Huntington 11743, 516-249-5333.

Committees *Banking, Finance and Urban Affairs* (14th). Subcommittees: Consumer Affairs and Coinage; General Oversight and Renegotiation; Housing and Community Development; International Trade, Investment and Monetary Policy.

Select Committee on Aging (23d). Subcommittees: Housing and Consumer Interests; Retirement Income and Employment.

Group Ratings and Key Votes: Newly Elected

Election Results

1980 general	Gregory W. Carman (R-C).......	87,952	(50%)	($1,038,125)
	Jerome A. Ambro, Jr. (D-RTL) ..	83,389	(47%)	($120,061)
1980 primary	Gregory W. Carman (R), unopposed			
1978 general	Jerome A. Ambro, Jr. (D)	70,526	(51%)	($80,256)
	Gregory W. Carman (R-C).......	66,458	(48%)	($311,390)

FOURTH DISTRICT

At the end of World War II, Nassau County, just beyond the New York City limits, consist-ed mostly of potato fields. Here and there, in this flat Long Island country 30 or 40 miles east of Manhattan, a few subdivisions had been laid out before the war. On the North Shore and in such places as Old Westbury sat the Gatsbyesque estates of some of New York's wealthiest families. But the vast center of Nassau County lay undeveloped. It did not stay that way for long. Just after the war, a young builder named Willam Levitt built an entire town full of small tract houses and named it for himself. Soon Levittown came to symbolize Long Island's vast postwar growth. Young married couples flocked out to the Island and created a new life-style very different from their own Depression childhoods pent up in the city.

So during the 1940s and 1950s Nassau County filled up and became the kind of metropol-itan community that is familiar today but was largely undreamed of by the veterans who re-turned to New York from World War II. In 1945 Nassau County had a population of about 450,000. By 1960 there were 1,300,000 people here. The number rose slightly to 1,428,000 in 1970 and then dropped to 1,319,000 in 1980. The reason is not that the area is deteriorating but simply that the population is aging. The baby boom babies have grown up, and most of them are not staying in Nassau. Not many houses are for sale here at any one time, so those who like the Long Island life-style move farther out the Island to Suffolk County, while those who want a more urban existence head into New York City. Some, who have difficulty finding jobs or who like other parts of the country better, have left the New York area entirely.

In the 1950s there was speculation that the new suburban life-style was creating new poli-tical attitudes, that when the young postwar marrieds left the New York City limits they dropped their Democratic habits and became Republicans. In retrospect this notion seems clearly wrong. It was not the county line that made the difference; many did register Repub-lican here, but that was because the Republican primary determined who held most local government positions, not because they necessarily thought of themselves as Republicans. But such movement as there was to the Republicans was part of a broader trend, away from the New Deal, toward the politics of the Eisenhower era. It was a response to times of unan-ticipated prosperity and affluence, not an attempt to blend into the local landscape.

The 4th congressional district of New York is one of two seats that lies entirely within Nassau County. The 4th includes many areas of the 1950s boom, including the original Levittown and next-door Hicksville. Both these places have lost population since 1960, as the children of the original settlers grew up and moved away. The district also includes posh Old Westbury and the black ghetto of New Cassel not far away. But the nucleus of the 4th, the part that connects it to predecessor districts, is a string of towns along the South Shore of Long Island. They include Oceanside, Freeport, and Merrick, where most residents come from older Jewish and Catholic neighborhoods in the city; these are marginal politically. Also here are Bellmore, Wantagh, and Seaford, more heavily Catholic and usually much more Republican. These were added in the 1972 redistricting, to help incumbent Republican Congressman Norman Lent.

Lent is the beneficiary of a couple of redistrictings. The first, in 1970, helped him beat Allard Lowenstein, elected two years before with the help of student volunteers after he helped to put together the campaign that ousted Lyndon Johnson from the presidency. The second, in 1972, made the district safely Republican in most contests. Since then his opposition has gotten weaker and his percentages have grown much higher.

Redistricting for 1982 will change the boundaries of the district yet again, with major additions made necessary by population loss (some 32,000) over the last ten years. The chances are that the Nassau County delegation to the legislature will see that Lent has a safe district.

In the House Lent is a reliable member of the Republican Party but is not closely identified with any particular issue. He is a member of the Energy and Commerce Committee, one of the most critical committees in the House — and in 1979 and 1980 the most hardworking. He serves on the subcommittee on Oversight and Investigations, which technically has broad jurisdiction but which has no direct legislative responsibilities. He is ranking minority member of the relatively uncontroversial subcommittee on Commerce, Transportation, and Tourism. In addition, Lent is a member of the Merchant Marine and Fisheries Committee, on which he is one of the few members who have opposed maritime subsidies. He does not attract great attention in the House but is considered competent and influential.

Census Data   Pop. (1980 final) 428,685, down 8% in 1970s. Median family income, 1970, $14,376, 150% of U.S.

The Voters

Employment profile 1970   White collar, 63%. Blue collar, 26%. Service, 11%. Farm, –%.
Ethnic groups   Black 1980, 6%. Hispanic 1980, 3%. Asian 1980, 1%. Total foreign stock 1970, 33%. Italy, 7%; USSR, 5%; Germany, 4%; Poland, Ireland, 3% each; UK, Austria, 2% each; Canada, 1%.

Presidential Vote

1980	Reagan (R)	111,230	(58%)
	Carter (D)	61,754	(32%)
	Anderson (I)	15,925	(8%)
1976	Ford (R)	103,663	(51%)
	Carter (D)	98,788	(49%)

Rep. Norman F. Lent (R) Elected 1970; b. Mar. 23, 1931, Oceanside; home, E. Rockaway; Hofstra Col., B.A. 1952, Cornell U., J.D. 1957.

Career Navy, Korea; Practicing atty., 1957–70; Asst. E. Rockaway Police Justice, 1960–62; N.Y. Senate, 1962–70.

Offices 2228 RHOB, 202-225-7896. Also Rm. 300, 2280 Grand Ave., Baldwin 11510, 516-223-1616.

Committees *Energy and Commerce* (4th). Subcommittees: Commerce, Transportation and Tourism; Oversight and Investigations.

Merchant Marine and Fisheries (6th). Subcommittees: Coast Guard and Navigation; Panama Canal and Outer Continental Shelf.

Group Ratings

	ADA	COPE	PC	LCV	CFA	RPN	NAB	NSI	NTU	ACA	ACU
1980	17	33	30	32	14	—	75	100	38	61	56
1979	0	40	23	28	15	—	—	—	41	68	76
1978	20	20	33	48	36	64	56	100	21	75	95

Key Votes

1) Draft Registn $	FOR	6) Fair Hsg DOJ Enfrc	AGN	11) Cut Socl Incr Dfns $	FOR
2) Ban $ to Nicrgua	FOR	7) Lim PAC Contrbtns	AGN	12) Hosptl Cost Controls	AGN
3) Dlay MX Missile	—	8) Cap on Food Stmp $	AGN	13) Gasln Ctrls & Allctns	AGN
4) Nuclr Mortorium	AGN	9) New US Dep Edcatn	AGN	14) Lim Wndfll Prof Tax	FOR
5) Alaska Lands Bill	AGN	10) Cut OSHA $	AGN	15) Chryslr Loan Grntee	FOR

Election Results

1980 general	Norman F. Lent (R-C-RTL)	117,455	(67%)	($161,941)
	Charles F. Brennan (D-L)	58,270	(33%)	($24,422)
1980 primary	Norman F. Lent (R-C), unopposed			
1978 general	Norman F. Lent (R-C)	94,711	(66%)	($83,658)
	Everett A. Rosenblum (D)	46,508	(33%)	($11,774)

FIFTH DISTRICT

The 5th congressional district of New York includes most of the older suburban parts of Long Island. In the northern part of the district is Garden City, a WASPy suburb laid out in the 1920s; it is, as it always has been, heavily Republican. To the south are places such as Hempstead, Rockville Centre, and Valley Stream, towns on the radial highways leading into Queens. These places were developed somewhat later, and each of them has its own, slightly different character. Politically, these towns are a little more Democratic than average in Nassau County and somewhat more Republican than New York state as a whole. At the southern end of the district, below Kennedy Airport and just north of the Atlantic, are Long Beach and the Five Towns — Lawrence, Inwood, Cedarhurst, Hewlett, and Woodmere — all developments that were begun in the 1920s, all heavily Jewish, and all solidly Democratic. Each of the towns so far mentioned together make for a marginal constituency; but the New York legislature, then solidly controlled by Republicans, was careful to add to them the heavily Republican suburbs of East Meadow and Uniondale, the latter the home of Nassau County Republican boss Joseph Margiotta.

Margiotta has controlled one of the few successful political machines in the America of the 1970s. His critics charge him with a variety of nefarious practices: giving favored insurance businesses big public contracts, giving county business to a variety of other firms owned by men faithful to the machine, extracting political contributions from public employees, dictating political nominations. Margiotta himself was indicted and stood trial on a variety of charges in the spring of 1981. But the practices of Margiotta's machine have been no secret, and the voters of Nassau County — with one of the highest levels of education in the United States — have voted again and again to give Margiotta's Republicans control of the local government and of most of the county's seats in the state legislature and Congress. They perhaps disapprove of the machine but are determined anyway to favor Republicans' national and state policies; or they perhaps approve of both.

In any case, the Margiotta machine works, and one of the clearest indications of that comes in the congressional election for the 5th district House seat. This was held for 18 years by John Wydler, a faithful Republican from Garden City who rose to become ranking minority member on the Science and Technology Committee. Wydler was a regional Republican whip and a dependable Republican on almost all issues. He was reelected easily and had his toughest challenge in 1976 when Allard Lowenstein, who had won once in a Long Island district in 1968 and had run in the meantime in Brooklyn, ran in the 5th. Wydler decided to retire at age 56 from the House in 1980.

His successor is a man who has worked his way up from the Nassau County parks department to congressman via faithful service in the Margiotta machine, Raymond McGrath. At age 38, he had no opposition for the Republican nomination in what was almost surely a safe Republican seat. His opponent in the general election, Karen Burstein, who represented the Five Towns and part of Queens in the state Senate, was better known and had more style. But McGrath had more votes, by a solid 58%–42% margin. In the House McGrath has the same committee assignments as Wydler had—Science and Technology and Government Operations—and will probably pursue the same kind of House career. First elected at age 38, he may be in the House a long time. Redistricting will certainly change the boundaries of the 5th district but should not significantly reduce McGrath's chances of reelection.

Census Data Pop. (1980 final) 436,801, down 7% in 1970s. Median family income, 1970, $14,102, 147% of U.S.

The Voters

Employment profile 1970 White collar, 65%. Blue collar, 24%. Service, 11%. Farm, –%.
Ethnic groups Black 1980, 13%. Hispanic 1980, 4%. Asian 1980, 1%. Total foreign stock 1970, 38%. Italy, 9%; USSR, 5%; Germany, 4%; Poland, Ireland, 3% each; UK, Austria, 2% each.

Presidential Vote

1980	Reagan (R)	101,877	(53%)
	Carter (D)	74,302	(39%)
	Anderson (I)	11,418	(6%)
1976	Ford (R)	107,909	(52%)
	Carter (D)	100,782	(48%)

Rep. Raymond J. McGrath (R) Elected 1980; b. Mar. 27, 1942, Valley Stream; home, Valley Stream; SUNY, Brockport, B.S. 1963; NYU; M.A. 1968.

Career High school phys. ed. teacher, 1963–65; Hempstead Dpty. Commissioner of Parks and Rec., 1969–76; N.Y. State Assembly, 1976–80.

Offices 506 CHOB, 202-225-5516. Also 175 N. Central Ave., Valley Stream 11580, 516-872-9550.

Committees *Government Operations* (11th). Subcommittees: Government Activities and Transportation; Intergovernmental Relations and Human Resources.

Science and Technology (13th). Subcommittees: Energy Development and Applications; Space Science and Applications.

Group Ratings and Key Votes: Newly Elected

Election Results

1980 general	Raymond J. McGrath (R-C-RTL).	105,140	(58%)	($265,777)
	Karen S. Burstein (D-L)	77,228	(42%)	($310,158)
1980 primary	R. J. McGrath (R-C-RTL), unopp.			
1978 general	John W. Wydler (R-C)	84,882	(58%)	($84,425)
	John W. Matthews (D-L)	60,519	(42%)	($34,334)

SIXTH DISTRICT

New York's 6th congressional district consists of almost equal parts of the North Shore of Long Island in Nassau County and the Borough of Queens in New York City. The North Shore has long been famous as the home of such rich and well-born aristocrats as Theodore Roosevelt as well as nouveaux riches such as the fictional Jay Gatsby who tried to imitate the life-style. Today huge WASPy estates still sit on peninsulas jutting out into Long Island Sound, as well as in such towns as Sands Point and Port Washington. But politically more significant in the 6th district portion of the North Shore are rich, predominantly Jewish suburbs such as Great Neck. Despite their wealth, Great Neck and the surrounding communities inevitably produce large Democratic majorities, even for McGovern in 1972. It is inland, to the south, in the less high-income, more Protestant suburbs that one finds Republican strength in the North Shore.

The boundaries of the Queens portion of the district were drawn by a Republican legislature to include all possible neighborhoods of conservative homeowners and to exclude housing projects and high-rise apartment complexes inhabited mainly by Democrats. In the late 1960s and early 1970s, this was a place where the politics of John Lindsay was exceedingly unpopular, and where the politics of Richard Nixon and James Buckley proved very popular—at least for a while.

The 6th district has generally been considered a Nassau County district and a Democratic one, with Great Neck the typical community. But in fact most of its residents live in Queens, and the more typical community is a place such as Douglaston, with its architecturally nondescript brick houses rising from street-level garages to living rooms with picture windows overlooking one of the less picturesque parts of Long Island Sound. The misleading impression of the district persists largely because this district was represented in the 1970s by Lester Wolff, a Nassau Democrat first elected in 1964.

Wolff parlayed that surprise victory into a long congressional career. He worked hard in his early years courting his constituents, and it paid off in 1972 when, after redistricting, he bluffed Queens Republican Congressman Seymour Halpern out of running here and then beat a Catholic assemblyman from Queens entirely on the basis of his Nassau margin. Wolff owed his large margins in the next three elections mostly to Watergate. The Queens portion of the district turned sharply against Richard Nixon's Republicans and returned to what was in many cases for many voters an ancestral Democratic allegiance. The aid to New York City issue strengthened this tendency, and the Republicans did not seriously contest this election after 1972. He became chairman of the Foreign Affairs subcommittee on Asia and the Pacific and spent much of his time investigating that area's problems firsthand.

Then in 1980 Wolff was upset by 27-year-old John LeBoutillier, the youngest Republican in the 97th Congress. LeBoutillier had already had an interesting career, as the author of a book called *Harvard Hates America*, based on his observations of other students at the college and business school, and a novel about a Saudi Arabian prince and various derring-do. Wolff must not have taken this challenger very seriously at first: LeBoutillier was not a product of (although he was supported by) Joseph Margiotta's Nassau County Republican machine, he was not well known in the district, and in a predominantly Catholic and Jewish district he had the demeanor and style of someone out of the *Preppy Handbook*. Yet LeBoutillier turned these characteristics into advantages. He raised large sums from Harvard classmates and admirers of his books. He benefited from the national Republican trend on issues, and he became well known by attacking Wolff for junketeering on his Asian and other trips. He concentrated not on Nassau County, where the votes were pretty well lined up on one side or the other, but in Queens, which was larger and more likely to switch. LeBoutillier ended up carrying Nassau by just 131 votes, but he had a solid 56%–44% margin in Queens. The 6th district finally went Republican, as it had been designed to do eight years before.

The question for 1982 is whether the 6th will go Republican again — or whether there will be a 6th district at all in 1982. Reapportionment will cost New York five districts, and while the 6th has not had substantial population losses, several circumstances combine to make it vulnerable to dismemberment in redistricting. Split almost evenly between Queens and Nassau, city and suburb, its retention is not a high priority for either county. The Nassau County Republican machine will probably concentrate on safeguarding the incumbents in the 3d, 4th, and 5th districts, all of whom are closer to the machine than LeBoutillier; Queens Republicans will have little impact on redistricting. LeBoutillier, as a newcomer to New York politics and a brash one at that, does not have any obvious protectors in Albany. He will need many of the political skills he has shown so far to protect his seat. But if he manages to obtain the creation of a seat similar to the current 6th he will almost certainly be the favorite to win it.

Census Data   Pop. (1980 final) 432,489, down 8% in 1970s. Median family income, 1970, $14,483, 151% of U.S.

The Voters

Employment profile 1970   White collar, 68%. Blue collar, 22%. Service, 10%. Farm, –%.
Ethnic groups   Black 1980, 4%. Hispanic 1980, 6%. Asian 1980, 4%. Total foreign stock 1970, 45%. Italy, 10%; USSR, Germany, 5% each; Poland, Ireland, 4% each; UK, 3%; Austria, 2%; Canada, Greece, 1% each.

Presidential Vote

1980	Reagan (R)	99,905	(54%)
	Carter (D)	65,996	(36%)
	Anderson (I)	14,497	(8%)
1976	Ford (R)	99,497	(50%)
	Carter (D)	97,676	(50%)

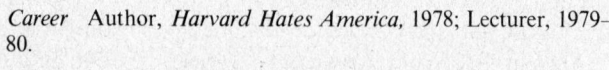

Rep. John Le Boutillier (R) Elected 1980; b. May 26, 1953, Glen Cove; home, Westbury; Harvard Col., B.A. 1977, Harvard Bus. Sch., M.B.A. 1979.

Career   Author, *Harvard Hates America,* 1978; Lecturer, 1979–80.

Offices   417 CHOB, 202-225-5956. Also 216–15 Northern Blvd., Bayside 11361, 212-225-1876, and 125 Plandome Rd., Manhasset 11030, 516-365-9420.

Committee   *Foreign Affairs* (15th). Subcommittees: Human Rights and International Organizations; International Security and Scientific Affairs.

Group Ratings and Key Votes: Newly Elected

Election Results

1980 general	John Le Boutillier (R-C-RTL)	89,762	(53%)	($490,121)
	Lester L. Wolff (D-L)	80,209	(47%)	($110,221)
1980 primary	John Le Boutillier (R), unopposed			
1978 general	Lester L. Wolff (D-L)	80,799	(60%)	($39,886)
	Stuart L. Ain (R)	44,304	(33%)	($77,565)
	Howard Horowitz (C)..........	9,503	(7%)	

SEVENTH DISTRICT

The 7th congressional district of New York in southern Queens takes in a series of middle-class neighborhoods of varying ethnic composition. Just north of Kennedy Airport is the two-family-house neighborhood of Ozone Park, with a large Italian–American population. To the north, along Queens Boulevard, are the high-rise apartments of Rego Park, which are predominantly Jewish, although the Forest Hills neighborhood in which they sit, with its old Tudor houses, was originally very WASP. In addition, there are large black neighborhoods here, the slum area of South Jamaica and, overshadowing it, the large middle-class areas of Springfield Gardens and St. Albans. Altogether 44% of the district residents in 1980 were black, which makes them the 7th's largest ethnic group, but Italian–Americans are probably not far behind.

The 7th is a heavily Democratic district, largely because of the Democratic allegiance of its black voters. But the 7th is also, on many issues, conservatively inclined, full of home-owners (not all of them white) who feel oppressed by New York City's high taxes and high cost of living. The whites here were heavily against Mayor John Lindsay and in favor of Senator James Buckley; they switched back to the Democrats in 1974, after Watergate and when the overriding issue in politics, as perceived here, became whether Washington would bail out New York City. By 1980 they had switched back, and while the black neighborhoods continued to support Jimmy Carter, many of the white election districts went for Ronald Reagan.

The 7th district's Congressman, Joseph Addabbo, a Democrat first elected in 1960, had become a very important man by 1979. With the retirement of George Mahon, first elected in 1934, and Bob Sikes, first elected in 1940, and the political disability of Daniel Flood, first elected in 1944, Addabbo became the chairman of the Appropriations subcommittee on Defense. This is the body that handles the Pentagon's appropriations and supplemental appropriations, except military construction, and its chair is a place of considerable potential influence.

Addabbo brings to this important job very different predispositions than his predecessors. Their attitude was one of friendly cooperation with the Pentagon; his is one of skepticism. Addabbo was opposed to the Vietnam war policy and was the floor leader of the successful move in 1973 to stop American bombing of Cambodia. The seniority system tends to elevate men into positions of power long after the events that shaped their attitudes have occurred. Men like Mahon, who controlled defense appropriations during the Vietnam war, had their attitudes shaped in World War II; Addabbo, obviously influenced by Vietnam, came to the chair just when Congress and the nation were moving in the direction of larger defense budgets and a more aggressive military stance.

In 1979 and 1980 five of the ten members of the Appropriations Defense Subcommittee shared at least some of Addabbo's skepticism; it was the toughest panel the Pentagon has had to face in Congress since the days of the buildup following World War II. But two members retired and a third was defeated, and the new members are southern Democrats generally sympathetic to the idea of increasing defense spending. Nevertheless, the fact that a man of Addabbo's views is chairman remains significant. Matters in a body such as this rarely come to an up-or-down vote; rather, the committee tends to work toward a kind of consensus. A skillful and well-prepared chairman can do much to determine the outcome of that consensus. By all accounts, Addabbo is such a chairman. He gives the outward impression of being just another neighborhood politician from a storefront in a slightly seedy neighborhood in Queens. But that impression is misleading, and even with the current composition of the subcommittee he is in a position to frame issues and set the terms of discussion — which is often the real power.

Addabbo has also shown political skill in Queens. He has won the Republican nomination as well as the Democratic and Liberal nominations since 1974; the last time he had a Republican opponent, in 1972, he won 75% of the vote. His district lost population in the 1970s, but he will probably gain territory in southern Queens — in Howard Beach, just west of Kennedy Airport, in Springfield Gardens, Laurelton, and Rosedale, northeast of the airport, and on the Rockaway Peninsula, at the expense of James Scheuer of the 11th district.

Census Data Pop. (1980 final) 424,136, down 9% in 1970s. Median family income, 1970, $11,317, 118% of U.S.

The Voters

  Employment profile 1970 White collar, 59%. Blue collar, 27%. Service, 14%. Farm, -%.
  Ethnic groups Black 1980, 44%. Hispanic 1980, 10%. Asian 1980, 3%. Total foreign stock 1970, 41%. Italy, 7%; USSR, 5%; Poland, Germany, 4% each; Austria, Ireland, 2% each; UK, 1%.

Presidential Vote

1980	Reagan (R)	41,376	(31%)
	Carter (D)	83,385	(63%)
	Anderson (I)	6,466	(5%)
1976	Ford (R)	38,888	(27%)
	Carter (D)	98,095	(73%)

Rep. Joseph P. Addabbo (D) Elected 1960; b. May 17, 1925, Queens; home, Ozone Park; CCNY, 1942–44, St. John's U., LL.B. 1946.

Career Practicing atty., 1946–60.

Offices 2256 RHOB, 202-225-3461. Also 96–11 101st Ave., Ozone Park 11416, 212-845-3131.

Committees *Appropriations* (5th). Subcommittees: Defense (Chairman); Military Construction; Treasury–Postal Service–General Government.

Small Business (3d). Subcommittees: General Oversight; SBA and SBIC Authority, Minority Enterprise and General Small Business Problems.

Group Ratings

	ADA	COPE	PC	LCV	CFA	RPN	NAB	NSI	NTU	ACA	ACU
1980	72	100	70	70	79	—	0	11	10	5	11
1979	79	95	63	63	70	—	—	—	19	8	11
1978	70	95	60	63	64	18	—	20	7	12	5

Key Votes

1) Draft Registn $	AGN	6) Fair Hsg DOJ Enfrc	FOR	11) Cut Socl Incr Dfns $	AGN
2) Ban $ to Nicrgua	AGN	7) Lim PAC Contrbtns	FOR	12) Hosptl Cost Controls	FOR
3) Dlay MX Missile	FOR	8) Cap on Food Stmp $	AGN	13) Gasln Ctrls & Allctns	FOR
4) Nuclr Mortorium	—	9) New US Dep Edcatn	AGN	14) Lim Wndfll Prof Tax	AGN
5) Alaska Lands Bill	FOR	10) Cut OSHA $	AGN	15) Chryslr Loan Grntee	FOR

Election Results

1980 general	Joseph P. Addabbo (D-R-L)	96,137	(95%)	($105,482)
	Francis A. Lees (C-RTL)	4,703	(5%)	($0)
1980 primary	Joseph Addabbo (D-R-L), unopp.			
1978 general	Joseph P. Addabbo (D-R-L)	73,066	(95%)	($41,049)
	Mark Elliot Scott (C)	3,935	(5%)	

EIGHTH DISTRICT

The 8th congressional district of New York encompasses roughly the central part of the borough of Queens. The district's tortuous boundaries were drawn to keep as many conservative and Republican voters as possible within the confines of the adjacent 6th and 9th districts; in effect, the 8th is a district the Republicans conceded to the Democrats. The district radiates in three directions like spokes from a wheel. The hub is Flushing Meadow Park, site of the World's Fairs of 1939–40 and 1964–65, and today the site of Shea Stadium. One of the spokes passes through the middle-class, predominantly Jewish neighborhood of Flushing on its way to Long Island Sound. Another proceeds east through Fresh Meadows and a neighborhood with the real estate promoter's name of Utopia, and on toward the Nassau County line. The third spoke moves west from Flushing Meadow to include the high-rise complex of Lefrak City, a small black ghetto in Corona; and Jackson Heights, a two- and four-family-house neighborhood of lower-middle-income whites and Hispanics. Latin Americans — not just Puerto Ricans but migrants from all parts of Latin America — are the fastest-growing groups in the district, although they have not as yet become an important part of the voting population.

These seemingly disparate areas all have certain things in common. All have large Jewish populations, as if the redistricters took care to gather together all the major Jewish neighborhoods in Queens. And the district lines, as they writhe about, manage to corral most of the borough's big high-rise apartment complexes and many of its public housing projects. Before World War II, most of Queens was given over to neighborhoods of one- and two-family houses, inhabited by Irish, Italian, and German immigrants. It was a conservative Republican stronghold that happened, technically, to be part of a Democratic central city. But after World War II, most of the growth here has been in high rises, a large percentage of whose occupants are Jewish and liberal Democratic voters. So the 8th district may be said to be postwar Queens — and the reason why this once Republican borough is now almost always Democratic.

The district has lapsed from its Democratic faith occasionally. In the early 1970s there were fierce demonstrations here against building low-income high rises in Forest Hills; this hurt John Lindsay, George McGovern, and liberal Democrats generally. In 1980 voters here were scathingly mistrustful of Jimmy Carter. The president suffered the indignity of being criticized and lectured by Jewish community groups in an effort to win back these traditional Democratic votes, and he was largely unsuccessful. The Jewish neighborhoods of Queens, like those in the rest of the New York area, went strongly for Edward Kennedy in the 1980 primary and delivered disappointing majorities — and sometimes not even that — for Carter in the general election.

Back in 1962, Benjamin Rosenthal was elected to Congress in this district. At that time he looked like another Democratic machine hack: a product of local schools, with a Queens law practice, young enough (38) to be interested in holding the seat for a few terms until a judgeship opened up. But Rosenthal has turned out to be a committed and effective congressman. In the middle 1960s he started voting quietly with opponents to the Johnson Administration's war in Vietnam. At the end of the decade he became interested in consumer legislation. He spent much of the 1970s on an ultimately unsuccessful attempt to get a consumer protection agency established, in the process antagonizing some senior members (now retired). He still chairs the Commerce, Consumer, and Monetary Affairs Subcommittee of Government Operations, a primarily investigative body that nonetheless gives him a chance to oversee IRS administration of the windfall profits tax and such items of interest to his constituents as condominium conversions and OPEC investment in the United States. Rosenthal has been more successful in foreign affairs. He was one of the leaders in the move to cut off arms sales to Turkey in retaliation for its invasion of Cyprus. And as second-ranking Democrat on the Foreign Affairs subcommittee on Europe and the Middle East, he is a very important man when it comes to United States support of Israel. Rosenthal is a strong supporter of Israel and often plays a critical leadership role in these matters.

Rosenthal has managed to combine a voting record that is quite distant from the center of the House with an ability to get things done, often without fanfare. He is respected generally, and not only by those who share his views on issues. He does not seem to be ambitious for other office and is reelected every two years by 3-1 margins. His district is, theoretically, vulnerable to dismemberment in redistricting; it is, after all, smack in the middle of Queens and could be divided among its neighbors. But Rosenthal has some political clout and enough strength with his core constituency to survive even a rather severe redistricting.

Census Data   Pop. (1980 final) 462,896, down 1% in 1970s. Median family income, 1970, $12,244, 128% of U.S.

The Voters

Employment profile 1970   White collar, 68%. Blue collar, 23%. Service, 9%. Farm, –%.
Ethnic groups   Black 1980, 8%. Hispanic 1980, 22%. Asian 1980, 10%. Total foreign stock 1970, 59%. Italy, USSR, 8% each; Poland, 6%; Ireland, Germany, 4% each; Austria, 3%; UK, Greece, 2% each; Hungary, Rumania, 1% each.

Presidential Vote	1980	Reagan (R)	59,336	(44%)
		Carter (D)	65,394	(48%)
		Anderson (I)	9,635	(7%)
	1976	Ford (R)	52,024	(33%)
		Carter (D)	104,158	(67%)

Rep. Benjamin S. Rosenthal (D) Elected Feb. 20, 1962; b. June 8, 1923, New York City; home, Elmhurst; Long Island U., CCNY, Brooklyn Law Sch., LL.B. 1949, LL.M. 1952.

Career   Army, WWII; Practicing atty.

Offices   2372 RHOB, 202-225-2601. Also U.S.P.O., 41–65 Main St., Flushing 11351, 212-939-8200.

Committees   *Foreign Affairs* (4th). Subcommittees: Europe and the Middle East; Human Rights and International Organizations.

Government Operations (4th). Subcommittees: Commerce, Consumer and Monetary Affairs (Chairman); Manpower and Housing.

Group Ratings

	ADA	COPE	PC	LCV	CFA	RPN	NAB	NSI	NTU	ACA	ACU
1980	78	100	80	89	79	—	0	0	16	10	11
1979	68	100	48	86	48	—	—	—	20	6	7
1978	90	94	90	77	86	33	0	10	25	8	5

Key Votes

1) Draft Registn $	AGN	6) Fair Hsg DOJ Enfrc	FOR	11) Cut Socl Incr Dfns $	—
2) Ban $ to Nicrgua	AGN	7) Lim PAC Contrbtns	—	12) Hosptl Cost Controls	FOR
3) Dlay MX Missile	FOR	8) Cap on Food Stmp $	AGN	13) Gasln Ctrls & Allctns	FOR
4) Nuclr Mortorium	—	9) New US Dep Edcatn	AGN	14) Lim Wndfll Prof Tax	AGN
5) Alaska Lands Bill	FOR	10) Cut OSHA $	AGN	15) Chryslr Loan Grntee	FOR

Election Results

1980 general	Benjamin S. Rosenthal (D-L)	84,273	(76%)	($35,765)
	Albert Lemishow (R-C-RTL)	27,156	(24%)	($0)
1980 primary	Benj. S. Rosenthal (D-L), unopp.			
1978 general	Benjamin S. Rosenthal (D-L)	74,872	(79%)	($30,220)
	Albert Lemishow (R)	15,165	(16%)	

NINTH DISTRICT

It can be said with some certainty that the durable Archie Bunker lives in the 9th congressional district of New York. The aerial shot taken by TV cameramen of Archie's neighborhood shows the kind of aging, although still neatly maintained, one- and two-family houses that line the streets of Jackson Heights, Long Island City, Ridgewood, or Glendale, Queens. Moreover, Archie's views are a fairly accurate, if stylized, portrayal of attitudes that are often a majority and otherwise a large minority in this district. Geographically, the 9th is the Queens district closest to Manhattan's chic and liberal Upper East Side—but it is far from it in spirit. People here in Queens refer to Manhattan as "the City," as if it were some alien place; to many of them it is.

The boundaries of the 9th district were carefully drawn to include the middle-class heavily Catholic Queens neighborhoods of conservative homeowners—people who live on salaries or wages that make middle-class respectability hard to maintain in New York City. It is ironic—or at least a reversal of the conventional wisdom we inherit from the New Deal era—that the wealthy Upper East Side voted 58% for McGovern in 1972, while across the East River, the factory workers and waiters and doormen and clerks living in Long Island City and Sunnyside and Astoria went 73% for Richard Nixon: the rich voting for economic change, the relatively poor for the status quo.

The ethnic composition is important in shaping attitudes here. There are few blacks or Puerto Ricans in the 9th district, although many of its white homeowners live in neighborhoods near the Brooklyn line, on the other side of which there are large ghetto communities. But there have been recent migrants here: Greeks, Arabs, Colombians. Many of these, particularly those from Latin America, are illegal immigrants, and of necessity they are practitioners of the work ethic. All these groups bring from their native culture a taste for enterprise and a sense that effort will be rewarded; they did not come here to get on the welfare rolls.

This part of Queens was not always so enthusiastically Republican as it was in 1972, nor did it maintain its enthusiasm for long. The historic allegiance of at least a large minority of its residents was to the Democratic Party of Franklin Roosevelt and John Kennedy. But during the time the Democrats appeared more interested in ending the Vietnam war and advocating the interests of blacks and Puerto Ricans than they were in the welfare of such people as Archie Bunker, the 9th shifted solidly to the Republicans. And in the years the district's newfound political heroes, Richard Nixon and Spiro Agnew, were revealed to be the kind of criminals they loved to denounce, the 9th shifted back toward the Democrats. But people here were not happy with the Carter Administration. They favored Edward Kennedy in the Democratic primary and Ronald Reagan in the general election.

For 32 years the congressman from this district was James Delaney, a Democrat who generally matched his constituents' changes of mood. His most significant legislative achievement is the Delaney Amendment, which prohibits the sale of any drug known to produce cancer in animals. It has been attacked by the drug industry but probably — for we do not know all the answers here — has saved quite a few lives. In 1977 Delaney became chairman of the House Rules Committee and, although he had dissented over the years from a number of Democratic positions, worked closely with Speaker O'Neill and made the committee a more effective and rational instrument of majority policy.

Delaney retired in 1978, and the Republicans hoped to pick up the 9th district whose boundaries they had designed for just this eventuality. They had a popular local candidate in Assemblyman Alfred DelliBovi, who despite his youth had served eight years in the legislature. But Democratic nominee Geraldine Ferraro had greater strength. She won her primary with an absolute majority; her experience as a prosecutor gave her good law-and-order credentials. Her campaign was well financed, and she was able to overcome the handicap of endorsing government-paid abortions for the poor. She won a decisive 55% victory in 1978. In 1980, against perennial candidate and sometime Assemblyman and Council member Vito Battista, she won by a larger margin, despite the national trend.

Ferraro's greatest problem for 1980 is redistricting. It would be possible to maintain the 9th district pretty much intact, and the territory at its edges that would have to be added to meet the equal population standard is almost all more Democratic. It is also possible that the district would be carved up among its neighbors, which would mean that Ferraro would have to run against another incumbent in the primary in order to stay in Congress. The advantage for her would be that, if she won, she would have a considerably more Democratic district. In the House Ferraro serves on the Post Office and Civil Service and the Public Works and Transportation Committees, two bodies with practical jurisdiction, and she votes more dependably with her fellow Democrats than her predecessor Delaney sometimes did.

Census Data   Pop. (1980 final) 447,297, down 4% in 1970s. Median family income, 1970, $10,657, 111% of U.S.

The Voters

Employment profile 1970   White collar, 53%. Blue collar, 34%. Service, 13%. Farm, –%.
Ethnic groups   Black 1980, 3%. Hispanic 1980, 14%. Asian 1980, 4%. Total foreign stock 1970, 55%. Italy, 14%; Germany, 8%; Poland, USSR, 3% each; Austria, Greece, UK, 2% each; Czechoslovakia, Hungary, 1% each.

Presidential Vote

1980	Reagan (R)	68,036	(55%)
	Carter (D)	46,748	(38%)
	Anderson (I)	6,338	(5%)
1976	Ford (R)	75,415	(54%)
	Carter (D)	63,412	(46%)

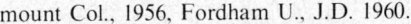

Rep. Geraldine A. Ferraro (D) Elected 1978; b. Aug. 26, 1935, Newburgh; home, Forest Hills; Marymount Col., 1956, Fordham U., J.D. 1960.

Career Practicing atty., 1961–74; Chf., Special Victims' Bureau and Confidential Unit, Ofc. of N.Y. Dist. Atty., 1974–78.

Offices 312 CHOB, 202-225-3965. Also 47-02 47th St., Woodside 11377, 212-826-5714.

Committees *Post Office and Civil Service* (7th). Subcommittees: Human Resources (Chairwoman); Postal Operations and Services.

Public Works and Transportation (18th). Subcommittees: Aviation; Investigations and Oversight; Water Resources.

Select Committee on Aging (17th). Subcommittees: Human Services; Retirement Income and Employment.

Group Ratings

	ADA	COPE	PC	LCV	CFA	RPN	NAB	NSI	NTU	ACA	ACU
1980	72	89	77	72	79	—	8	33	11	17	17
1979	74	88	73	74	78	—	—	—	21	12	16

Key Votes

1) Draft Registn $	FOR	6) Fair Hsg DOJ Enfrc	FOR	11) Cut Socl Incr Dfns $	AGN
2) Ban $ to Nicrgua	AGN	7) Lim PAC Contrbtns	FOR	12) Hosptl Cost Controls	FOR
3) Dlay MX Missile	AGN	8) Cap on Food Stmp $	AGN	13) Gasln Ctrls & Allctns	FOR
4) Nuclr Mortorium	FOR	9) New US Dep Edcatn	AGN	14) Lim Wndfll Prof Tax	AGN
5) Alaska Lands Bill	FOR	10) Cut OSHA $	AGN	15) Chryslr Loan Grntee	FOR

Election Results

1980 general	Geraldine A. Ferraro (D)	63,796	(58%)	($124,743)
	Vito P. Battista (R-C-RTL)	44,473	(41%)	($20,716)
1980 primary	Geraldine A. Ferraro (D), unopp.			
1978 general	Geraldine A. Ferraro (D)	51,350	(54%)	($382,074)
	Alfred A. Dellibovi (R-C)	42,108	(44%)	($110,679)

TENTH DISTRICT

The 10th congressional district of New York covers the east Bronx and the northern fringes of Queens. It is the part of New York the Manhattan-bound traveler sees when coming in a taxi from LaGuardia or from the expressways or parkways from Connecticut. Geographically you are not far from Manhattan, but culturally and politically the distance is usually very great. These areas are not poverty-stricken, and few of the streets are run-down, people here tend to be homeowners, and they work to keep up their property. But the houses seem to be made in the cheapest way possible, with no regard whatever for appearance: row after row of two- and four-family houses, all occupying the maximum space allowed by the zoning code.

The 10th district does not include the slums of the Bronx; its boundaries are roughly the edge of the borough's black and Puerto Rican ghetto. The ethnic flavor of the district, rather, is Italian–American; this may well be the most heavily Italian congressional district in the United States. Its congressman has not only an Italian name, Mario Biaggi, but also a background that is typical of many Italian–Americans in New York City. Biaggi was a police officer for 23 years, and when he retired he was the most decorated officer on the New York police force. He was an attorney—he had finished law school at night, like so many ambitious city employees in New York—but his real interest was politics. In 1968 he was elected to Congress from the predecessor of the 10th district, then entirely in the Bronx.

In his first years in the House, Biaggi seemed to be a kind of urban populist with a law-and-order accent. He voted with Democrats on most issues and went along with the major lobbying groups on the committees on which he served: organized labor on Education and Labor and the maritime industry and unions on Merchant Marine and Fisheries. At home, however, he emphasized the issue of crime and helped to express the hostility his constituents felt toward the Manhattan-based liberalism of Mayor John Lindsay. Biaggi appeared likely to be elected mayor himself in 1973. He was a strong contender for the Democratic nomination, and he had the Conservative nomination as well. But April 1973 newspapers charged that Biaggi had lied when he had said he had not taken the Fifth Amendment before a grand jury. Brazenly Biaggi sued to get some, but not all, of the grand jury records made public; the judge, not to be toyed with, revealed them all. They showed that Biaggi was lying, and his law-and-order candidacy collapsed.

Even after the rout, Biaggi retained a following, particularly in Italian–American neighborhoods like those that are so important in the 10th district. And he has not had serious opposition in elections since then—although the Conservatives, who bent their principles to endorse him in 1973 and then were stuck with him as their candidate in the general election, have not given him their endorsement since. Biaggi has considerable seniority now and is next in line for the chair of Merchant Marine, on which he is an enthusiastic supporter of subsidies to the maritime industry and to merchant seamen. He has made some headlines supporting Irish groups sympathetic to the IRA—groups that have been sternly chastised by such Irish–American leaders as Hugh Carey, Daniel Patrick Moynihan, Edward Kennedy, and Tip O'Neill. As a member of the Education and Labor Committee, he sternly denounced cuts proposed by the Reagan Administration.

Biaggi is somewhat vulnerable in the redistricting process. His district covers two boroughs, so politicians from neither one feel much responsibility for it. His trump card is that most of his territory, particularly in the Bronx, would probably go Republican if he were not the Democratic candidate; so Democrats may want to keep the 10th in something close to its current form to protect their other incumbents, and Republicans may want to do the same in the hope that they can carry the district when Biaggi, who turns 65 in 1982, retires.

Census Data   Pop. (1980 final) 445,159, down 5% in 1970s. Median family income, 1970, $9,988, 104% of U.S.

The Voters

Employment profile 1970   White collar, 52%. Blue collar, 34%. Service, 14%. Farm, –%.

Ethnic groups   Black 1980, 20%. Hispanic 1980, 26%. Asian 1980, 1%. Total foreign stock 1970, 47%. Italy, 17%; Ireland, 6%; Germany, 3%; USSR, Poland, Greece, UK, 2% each; Austria, 1%.

Presidential Vote

1980	Reagan (R)	50,178	(44%)
	Carter (D)	58,412	(51%)
	Anderson (I)	4,545	(4%)
1976	Ford (R)	56,741	(43%)
	Carter (D)	75,681	(57%)

Rep. Mario Biaggi (D) Elected 1968; b. Oct. 16, 1917, New York City; home, Bronx; N.Y. Law Sch., LL.B. 1963.

Career Letter carrier, U.S.P.O., 1936–42; N.Y. City Police Dept., 1942–65; Community Relations Specialist, N.Y. State Div. of Housing, 1961–63; Asst. to the N.Y. Secy. of State, 1961–65; Practicing atty., 1966–; Pres., Natl. Police Officers Assn., 1967.

Offices 2428 RHOB, 202-225-2464. Also 2004 Williamsbridge Rd., Bronx 10461, 212-931-0100.

Committees *Education and Labor* (7th). Subcommittees: Elementary, Secondary and Vocational Education; Labor-Management Relations; Select Education.

Merchant Marine and Fisheries (2d). Subcommittees: Coast Guard and Navigation; Merchant Marine (Chairman).

Select Committee on Aging (3d). Subcommittee: Human Services (Chairman).

Group Ratings

	ADA	COPE	PC	LCV	CFA	RPN	NAB	NSI	NTU	ACA	ACU
1980	50	82	53	34	64	—	11	67	14	15	14
1979	63	88	60	62	67	—	—	—	17	13	18
1978	55	75	55	66	59	44	9	70	10	40	45

Key Votes

1) Draft Registn $	FOR	6) Fair Hsg DOJ Enfrc	FOR	11) Cut Socl Incr Dfns $	AGN
2) Ban $ to Nicrgua	FOR	7) Lim PAC Contrbtns	FOR	12) Hosptl Cost Controls	FOR
3) Dlay MX Missile	AGN	8) Cap on Food Stmp $	AGN	13) Gasln Ctrls & Allctns	FOR
4) Nuclr Mortorium	FOR	9) New US Dep Edcatn	AGN	14) Lim Wndfll Prof Tax	AGN
5) Alaska Lands Bill	FOR	10) Cut OSHA $	AGN	15) Chryslr Loan Grntee	FOR

Election Results

1980 general	Mario Biaggi (D-R-L)...........	95,322	(94%)	($44,707)
1980 primary	Mario Biaggi (D-R-L), unopposed			
1978 general	Mario Biaggi (D-R-L)...........	77,979	(95%)	($71,493)
	Carmen Ricciardi (C)	4,082	(5%)	

ELEVENTH DISTRICT

The 11th congressional district of New York is the southeastern corner of Brooklyn, the extreme southern and southeastern edges of Queens, and Rockaway Peninsula. Separated from each other by marshy Jamaica Bay, and circling Kennedy Airport like a doughnut, these are geographically disparate areas and the neighborhoods contained within them are diverse. East New York in Brooklyn is an aging Italian community, not far from the black ghetto of Brownsville, which is in such miserable condition that it is being rapidly abandoned. To the south, Canarsie and Flatlands are middle-class Italian and Jewish communities. These two areas were developed on marshland sometime after the rest of Brooklyn; here in 1970 the borough's first suburban-style shopping center was opened. More recently Canarsie has been embroiled in controversy over a school busing plan. The Rockaway Peninsula, separating Jamaica Bay from the ocean, is largely Jewish, with a black ghetto at one end. North of Kennedy Airport, entirely cut off from the rest of the district, is the middle-class black neighborhood of Springfield Gardens. In the last ten years, the 11th has seen a large increase in the number of its black residents, both in Brooklyn and Queens.

Historically this seat has been within the gift of the Brooklyn Democratic machine. From 1936 to 1966 it was represented by Eugene Keogh, who retired not because of age but because he wanted to make more money; he left his name on Keogh Plans, which allow self-employed individuals to create their own retirement plans. Keogh's successor was Frank Brasco, a young machine stalwart who seemed likely to match Keogh's tenure. But in 1974 Brasco was convicted of taking bribes and was sentenced to jail.

This time the much overrated Brooklyn organization was unable to hold the seat. The winner was James Scheuer, a former congressman from the faraway Bronx (1965–73), defeated in his primary in 1972 and now a Rockaway resident. A wealthy real estate developer, Scheuer came to office with a reputation as a liberal, but like so many of his constituents he supported Henry Jackson in the 1976 presidential primary. Scheuer was one of the leaders of the ultimately unsuccessful fight to prevent the supersonic Concorde jetliner from landing at Kennedy Airport; the problem was that when the plane was finally allowed to land, the sound did not seem so much louder than that of other planes. The fight was popular here, however: most people in the 11th district seldom fly anywhere, much less to London or Paris in a Concorde.

Scheuer's voting record on most issues is solidly in line with the Democratic majority in the House. But his sometimes abrasive personality irritates many other members, and he has suffered for it. In 1979 he became a subcommittee chairman: the Consumer Protection and Finance Subcommittee of the Commerce Committee. But in 1981 he lost the post. Commerce was overburdened with work and its new chairman, John Dingell of Michigan, wanted to equalize the work of the subcommittees, and new House rules limited the total number of subcommittees. Therefore Dingell abolished Scheuer's subcommittee, claiming that it had little to do; when Scheuer responded angrily, Dingell claimed Scheuer had not another vote on the committee. As a kind of consolation prize, he got the chair of a Science and Technology subcommittee that oversees research and development for some parts of the Department of Energy, Environmental Protection Agency, the oceans agency (NOAA), and the Agriculture Department. That lack of support from colleagues may hurt Scheuer in the redistricting process. He has lost his district once before and the 11th, split almost evenly between two boroughs, could be divided among its neighbors. That would leave Scheuer the unpleasant task of retiring or running against another incumbent, as he did when he lost to Jonathan Bingham ten years ago.

Census Data   Pop. (1980 final) 451,889, down 4% in 1970s. Median family income, 1970, $10,834, 113% of U.S.

The Voters

Employment profile 1970   White collar, 58%. Blue collar, 31%. Service, 11%. Farm, –%.
Ethnic groups   Black 1980, 32%. Hispanic 1980, 15%. Asian 1980, 1%. Total foreign stock 1970, 41%. Italy, 9%; USSR, 8%; Poland, 6%; Germany, Austria, Ireland, 2% each; UK, 1%.

Presidential Vote

1980	Reagan (R)	46,990	(41%)
	Carter (D)	60,006	(53%)
	Anderson (I)	5,576	(5%)
1976	Ford (R)	39,937	(30%)
	Carter (D)	93,240	(70%)

Rep. James H. Scheuer (D) Elected 1974; b. Feb. 6, 1920, New York City; home, Neponsit; Harvard Business Sch., 1943; Swarthmore Col., A.B. 1945, Columbia U., LL.B. 1948.

Career Army Air Corps, WWII; Economist, U.S. Foreign Economic Admin., 1945–46; Mbr., Legal Staff, U.S. Ofc. of Price Stabilization, 1951–52; Pres., N.Y. City Citizens Housing and Planning Cncl.; U.S. House of Reps., 1965–73; Pres. Natl. Housing Conf., 1972–74.

Offices 2402 RHOB, 202-225-5471. Also 1943 Rockaway Pkwy., Brooklyn 11236, 212-251-2222.

Committees *Energy and Commerce* (2d). Subcommittees: Commerce, Transportation and Tourism; Health and the Environment; Telecommunications, Consumer Protection and Finance.

Science and Technology (4th). Subcommittees: Energy Development and Applications; Natural Resources, Agriculture Research and Environment (Chairman).

Select Committee on Narcotics Abuse and Control (7th).

Group Ratings

	ADA	COPE	PC	LCV	CFA	RPN	NAB	NSI	NTU	ACA	ACU
1980	89	94	73	65	93	—	0	25	12	13	5
1979	84	95	75	92	81	—	—	—	14	4	6
1978	70	85	70	67	73	45	0	20	9	12	14

Key Votes

1) Draft Registn $	FOR	6) Fair Hsg DOJ Enfrc	FOR	11) Cut Socl Incr Dfns $	AGN
2) Ban $ to Nicrgua	AGN	7) Lim PAC Contrbtns	FOR	12) Hosptl Cost Controls	FOR
3) Dlay MX Missile	FOR	8) Cap on Food Stmp $	AGN	13) Gasln Ctrls & Allctns	—
4) Nuclr Mortorium	FOR	9) New US Dep Edcatn	AGN	14) Lim Wndfll Prof Tax	AGN
5) Alaska Lands Bill	—	10) Cut OSHA $	AGN	15) Chryslr Loan Grntee	FOR

Election Results

1980 general	James H. Scheuer (D-L)	72,798	(74%)	($61,111)
	Andrew E. Carlan (R-C-RTL)	25,424	(26%)	($0)
1980 primary	James H. Scheuer (D-L), unopposed			
1978 general	James H. Scheuer (D-L)	58,997	(78%)	($24,861)
	Kenneth Huhn (R-C)	16,206	(22%)	

TWELFTH DISTRICT

Celebrity status is fleeting, in politics as in other businesses, and an example is the career of the congresswoman from the 12th district of New York, Shirley Chisholm. A few years ago she was well known as the obstreperous freshman, rebelling against the powers that be — the image she projected when she entitled her autobiography *Unbought and Unbossed.* Her refusal to knuckle under to male political leaders in her home area of Bedford–Stuyvesant had helped her assemble the group of volunteers who elected her to the New York Assembly in 1964 and to Congress in 1968. In 1972 she became a national figure as the first black woman to run for president. She ran in most of the primaries — and even joined the stop-McGovern forces — clear through to the national convention. But it was only a symbolic effort. She failed to win 10% of the vote in any state, and not even her supporters gave much thought to the kind of president she would make. She did, however, get treated on a par with other candidates on television debates and on the convention podium.

During the campaign Chisholm often complained that people were not taking her seriously enough and that she was as qualified as the others. But around Capitol Hill many people sympathetic to her complained that she had done little legislative work, preferring the glamor of the lecture circuit to the hard work of the markup session in the committee room. In the years since 1972 Chisholm has become less of a national celebrity and more of a working legislator. She pushed through a law including domestic workers in the coverage of the federal minimum wage law. She won a seat on the House Rules Committee, and there she usually votes with the Democratic leadership.

Chisholm has talked from time to time about retiring; it sounds more like an effort to get people to pay more attention than a serious projection of what she is likely to do. When she was first elected, in 1968, her district included all of the Bedford–Stuyvesant section of Brooklyn; its lines had been drawn specifically to elect Brooklyn's first black member of Congress. For 1974, an ill-advised lawsuit forced the readjustment of the Brooklyn district lines, supposedly to produce two black-and-Puerto-Rican majority districts. In that respect the effort was entirely unsuccessful, for minority participation is so low here—lower in New York City than anywhere else in the country—that blacks are easily outvoted by others.

The drafters of the new district lines hoped that Chisholm would run in the 46% black (in 1970) 14th district, but she wisely declined; no more than one-quarter of the actual voters there are black. Instead she picked the new 12th, which includes the eastern half of Bedford–Stuyvesant, the huge Brooklyn ghetto; Bushwick, an old Italian neighborhood that is rapidly becoming majority black; and Williamsburgh and Greenpoint, old ethnic Brooklyn neighborhoods whose aged residents are hostile to whatever they consider the forces for change. The real politics here is in the Democratic primary. Chisholm was challenged in 1976 by Assemblyman Samuel Wright and was hard pressed to win. Wright was later indicted, but Chisholm will have to work her constituency hard in the 1980s as she did in the 1960s and 1970s in order to continue to win.

The 12th district lost 148,000 people in the 1970s and must add nearly 200,000 to get up to the district average. But Chisholm's interests should be protected by the Voting Rights Act that applies to Brooklyn because of low voter turnout and prohibits the elimination of minority districts. That means that Chisholm can expect to pick up part of eastern Bedford–Stuyvesant from the 14th district and Brownsville from the 16th and should have a safe seat for 1982.

Census Data   Pop. (1980 final) 320,886, down 31% in 1970s. Median family income, 1970, $6,432, 67% of U.S.

The Voters

Employment profile 1970   White collar, 37%. Blue collar, 45%. Service, 18%. Farm, –%.
Ethnic groups   Black 1980, 54%. Hispanic 1980, 31%. Asian 1980, 1%. Total foreign stock 1970, 16%. Italy, 6%; Poland, 2%.

Presidential Vote

1980	Reagan (R)	8,053	(16%)
	Carter (D)	42,296	(82%)
	Anderson (I)	873	(2%)
1976	Ford (R)	10,513	(18%)
	Carter (D)	49,550	(82%)

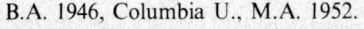

Rep. Shirley Chisholm (D) Elected 1968; b. Nov. 30, 1924, Brooklyn; home, Brooklyn; Brooklyn Col., B.A. 1946, Columbia U., M.A. 1952.

Career Nursery school teacher and dir., 1946–53; Dir., Hamilton Madison Child Care Ctr., 1954–59; Educ. Consultant, N.Y. City Div. of Day Care, 1959–64; N.Y. State Assembly, 1964–68.

Offices 2182 RHOB, 202-225-6230. Also 1360 Fulton St., Suite 400, Brooklyn 11216, 212-330-7588.

Committee *Rules* (5th). Subcommittee: The Legislative Process.

Group Ratings

	ADA	COPE	PC	LCV	CFA	RPN	NAB	NSI	NTU	ACA	ACU
1980	78	95	80	81	86	—	9	0	15	15	6
1979	89	100	85	87	81	—	—	—	22	4	8
1978	100	90	80	73	77	30	0	0	22	7	8

Key Votes

1) Draft Registn $	AGN	6) Fair Hsg DOJ Enfrc	FOR	11) Cut Socl Incr Dfns $	AGN
2) Ban $ to Nicrgua	AGN	7) Lim PAC Contrbtns	—	12) Hosptl Cost Controls	—
3) Dlay MX Missile	FOR	8) Cap on Food Stmp $	AGN	13) Gasln Ctrls & Allctns	FOR
4) Nuclr Mortorium	FOR	9) New US Dep Edcatn	AGN	14) Lim Wndfll Prof Tax	—
5) Alaska Lands Bill	FOR	10) Cut OSHA $	AGN	15) Chryslr Loan Grntee	—

Election Results

1980 general	Shirley Chisholm (D-L)	35,446	(87%)	($31,576)
	Charles Gibbs (R)	3,372	(8%)	($0)
1980 primary	Shirley Chisholm (D)	9,514	(62%)	
	Louis Fernandez (D)............	2,976	(19%)	
	David P. Miller (D)	2,856	(19%)	($0)
1978 general	Shirley Chisholm (D-L)	25,697	(88%)	($14,498)
	Charles Gibbs (R)	3,580	(12%)	

THIRTEENTH DISTRICT

The 13th congressional district of New York, in south central Brooklyn, might be called the Ocean Parkway district: it takes in terrain from both sides of that thoroughfare as it makes its way from Prospect Park to Coney Island. There is a large Italian–American community in Bensonhurst; the 13th according to most recent census figures, is one of the most heavily Italian–American districts in the nation. But most of the neighborhoods here, from Midwood in the north, through the streets lined with low-rise apartment buildings along the Parkway, to Sheepshead Bay, Brighton Beach, and Coney Island in the south, are heavily Jewish. With Flatbush, most of which is in the 16th district, the 13th is the heart of Jewish Brooklyn. Although no reliable data exist, the 13th is probably the nation's most heavily Jewish district, and most likely the 13th and the 16th are the only Jewish-majority districts in the nation. It is, of course, overwhelmingly Democratic by tradition and in most, but not all, elections. During the 1970s the black percentage increased from 2% to 12%. But the overall ethnic tone of the district is still Jewish. And the terrific animus voters felt toward Jimmy Carter is shown by the fact that in 1980 Ronald Reagan carried this usually very Democratic district.

As well as being the heart of Jewish Brooklyn, the 13th district has always been one of the bastions of support for the Democratic machine here. With its patronage jobs in the Brooklyn courts and Borough Hall, the machine used to be able to man all the election districts here with faithful — and hungry — precinct workers who would tell their neighbors who it would be good to vote for; and generally they did. For these are not the wealthy, trendy, assimilated Jews of Manhattan's Upper East Side. These are people who own small stores or work for the city or teach school, and who have been struggling to send their children through college and to accumulate enough for a decent retirement for themselves. There was seldom the time here, or the energy, for a reform politics; elections, like everything else, have been a business — and a tough one.

So from the time the district was created in its present form in 1944 until quite recently the district was represented by machine stalwarts: first Leo Rayfiel (1945–47), who became a federal judge; then Abraham Multer (1947–68), who finally got his state judgeship despite talk that he had been engaged in unsavory banking practices in the Bahamas; and then Bertram Podell (1968–75), who ended up before the bench rather than on it. In 1973 Podell was indicted for taking $41,000 to get the Civil Aeronautics Board to award a Bahama route to a Florida airline; after he lost the primary in 1974 he pleaded guilty.

The current congressman, Stephen Solarz, represents a change from this tradition. He had the reputation of a reformer and beat Podell in the 1974 primary after serving six years in the New York Assembly. Solarz is a serious and ambitious man, a congressman who studies hard on the issues and hopes to have a major impact on them. Much of his effort has been devoted to foreign policy. In 1979 he became chairman of the House's Africa Subcommittee of Foreign Affairs; he was a leading critic of the Muzorewa regime in Zimbabwe–Rhodesia and a supporter of the process that brought Robert Mugabe to power there.

In 1981, Solarz switched to take the chair of the Asian and Pacific Affairs Subcommittee, vacated by the defeat of Nassau County Democrat Lester Wolff. Here the problems are more complex, the choices less clear-cut, and the stakes considerably bigger for the United States. The change removes Solarz from a position where he might have to react to sudden unpleasant crises to one where long-range strategy and subtle negotiation are more important. Solarz has other demanding committee assignments as well. He serves on the House Budget Committee, where he is disposed generally to oppose cuts in aid to the poor and middle income, and chairs its task force on Transportation, Research and Development, and Capital Resources.

The 1970s had a very different demographic effect on different parts of Brooklyn. While Shirley Chisholm's 12th district lost 148,000 residents, or nearly one-third of its 1970 population, Solarz's 13th district lost only 28,000 residents net. That largely reflects the lower number of children in this area, which has had a large elderly population for years now; the number of housing units actually rose. Redistricting here has all the complexity of a huge jigsaw puzzle, but the likelihood is that something closely resembling the current 13th district — another Ocean Parkway district — will emerge from the process. Solarz should have no trouble winning reelection.

Census Data   Pop. (1980 final) 442,616, down 6% in 1970s. Median family income, 1970, $10,294, 107% of U.S.

The Voters

Employment profile 1970 White collar, 64%. Blue collar, 28%. Service, 8%. Farm, –%.
Ethnic groups Black 1980, 12%. Hispanic 1980, 9%. Asian 1980, 3%. Total foreign stock 1970, 61%. Italy, 16%; USSR, 14%; Poland, 9%; Austria, 4%; Germany, Hungary, Rumania, 2% each; Ireland, UK, Czechoslovakia, 1% each.

Presidential Vote

1980	Reagan (R)	56,174	(47%)
	Carter (D)	55,336	(46%)
	Anderson (I)	6,630	(6%)
1976	Ford (R)	44,176	(28%)
	Carter (D)	112,044	(72%)

Rep. Stephen J. Solarz (D) Elected 1974; b. Sept. 12, 1940, New York City; home, Brooklyn; Brandeis U., A.B. 1962, Columbia U., M.A. 1967.

Career N.Y. State Assembly, 1968–74.

Offices 1536 LHOB, 202-225-2361. Also 1628 Kings Hwy., Brooklyn 11229, 212-965-5100.

Committees *Budget* (7th).

Foreign Affairs (8th). Subcommittees: Africa; Asian and Pacific Affairs (Chairman).

Group Ratings

	ADA	COPE	PC	LCV	CFA	RPN	NAB	NSI	NTU	ACA	ACU
1980	78	89	90	65	86	—	0	0	12	20	6
1979	95	90	78	87	85	—	—	—	15	0	3
1978	80	85	78	79	68	42	0	20	10	13	19

Key Votes

1) Draft Registn $	—	6) Fair Hsg DOJ Enfrc FOR	11) Cut Socl Incr Dfns $ AGN
2) Ban $ to Nicrgua	AGN	7) Lim PAC Contrbtns FOR	12) Hosptl Cost Controls FOR
3) Dlay MX Missile	—	8) Cap on Food Stmp $ AGN	13) Gasln Ctrls & Allctns FOR
4) Nuclr Mortorium	—	9) New US Dep Edcatn AGN	14) Lim Wndfll Prof Tax AGN
5) Alaska Lands Bill	FOR	10) Cut OSHA $ AGN	15) Chryslr Loan Grntee FOR

Election Results

1980 general	Stephen J. Solarz (D-L)	81,954	(79%)	($118,916)
	Harry DeMell (R-C)	19,536	(19%)	($0)
1980 primary	Stephen J. Solarz (D L), unopposed			
1978 general	Stephen J. Solarz (D-L)	68,837	(81%)	($21,565)
	Max Carasso (R-C)	16,002	(19%)	

FOURTEENTH DISTRICT

The 14th congressional district of New York, in Brooklyn, is about as polyglot an area as you can find in the United States. The district extends along the Brooklyn waterfront from the Italian neighborhood of Red Hook to the Queens border, past the renovated brownstones of Brooklyn Heights and Cobble Hill, with their affluent (and politically liberal) residents. To the east is downtown Brooklyn, with a skyline that would be impressive anywhere but in New York; it is paled here by the vista of lower Manhattan from Brooklyn Heights. Inland the 14th extends far past the transitional Fort Greene area into Bedford–Stuyvesant. North are parts of Greenpoint and Williamsburgh, with large Orthodox and Hasidic Jewish and Puerto Rican communities in uneasy proximity.

If you were to look at the census statistics about the 14th, you would be seriously mistaken about its political makeup — as were the people who brought the lawsuit to form its present boundaries. In 1970 some 46% of the district's residents were black, 18% were Puerto Ricans; but neither of these groups has much clout here, for the simple reason that they scarcely vote at all. In the 14th, the voting blocs that really matter are the Italians in Red Hook and South Brooklyn, some of the old Hasidic Jews, and a relatively few middle-class blacks. These are the people who vote in Democratic primaries and who therefore control the congressional representation of the district.

For thirty years the 14th and its predecessors were represented by John Rooney, a crusty Democrat who chaired the Appropriations Subcommittee on State, Commerce, and the Judiciary; for years he terrorized the State Department and coddled the FBI. Rooney had tough primary challenges in 1968, 1970, and 1972, but always withstood them — helped by some questionable tactics. Ill and tired, Rooney retired in 1974.

His successor is Frederick Richmond, who ran against Rooney in 1968 and later supported him. Richmond's secret weapon was money — his own — and he was willing to spend plenty of it. He had spent $200,000 on his 1968 campaign, and later a foundation he controlled poured large sums of money into areas that happened to be within the boundaries of the 14th district. By the time he ran in 1974, he had machine and some reform support and was an easy winner. Richmond's electoral clout was tested even more in 1978. He was arrested in the summer of that year and charged with soliciting a young man for sex acts. The charges were dropped after he pleaded not guilty and participated in the first offender program of the D.C. courts. In the district his largesse paid off, and he beat a black primary opponent by a solid margin.

Richmond is a member of the Agriculture Committee in the House — one of the few members from urban areas who has stayed on that body. There is a certain amount of good sense in that: Agriculture controls the food stamp program and a variety of policies that affect food prices and thus are of interest to even the most urban of citizens. Richmond himself heads a subcommittee on consumer issues and nutrition and has gotten much publicity on those subjects. Richmond describes himself as an architect of a rural–urban coalition that supports the food stamp program; he reacted angrily to Budget Director David Stockman's threatened cuts of food stamps.

Richmond's major problem for 1982 is redistricting. The 14th district lost 103,000 people in the 1970s and is 152,000 below the new state district population average. Moreover, the neighboring 12th district, whose population is even lower, cannot be carved up because it is represented by a black and is subject to the Voting Rights Act of 1965. Richmond's district could be preserved if he were to pick up the Manhattan portion of the current 17th district or if Staten Island were combined with part of Leo Zeferetti's district — but that might result in Zeferetti's defeat by Staten Island Republican Guy Molinari. Richmond will have a difficult time saving this seat, but no one should underestimate his talent for political infighting.

Census Data   Pop. (1980 final) 364,356, down 22% in 1970s. Median family income, 1970, $6,874, 71% of U.S.

The Voters

Employment profile 1970   White collar, 47%. Blue collar, 37%. Service, 16%. Farm, –%.
Ethnic groups   Black 1980, 50%. Hispanic 1980, 23%. Asian 1980, 1%. Total foreign stock 1970, 28%. Italy, 5%; Poland, 2%; USSR, Hungary, 1% each.

Presidential Vote

1980	Reagan (R)	14,678	(20%)
	Carter (D)	54,693	(74%)
	Anderson (I)	3,196	(4%)
1976	Ford (R)	17,735	(22%)
	Carter (D)	63,370	(78%)

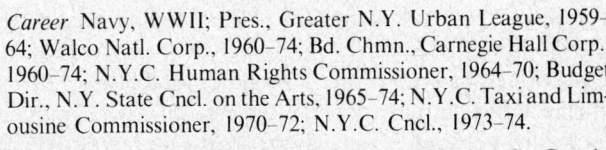

Rep. Frederick W. Richmond (D) Elected 1974; b. Nov. 15, 1923, Mattapan, Mass.; home, Brooklyn; Harvard U., 1942–43, Boston U., B.A. 1945.

Career Navy, WWII; Pres., Greater N.Y. Urban League, 1959–64; Walco Natl. Corp., 1960–74; Bd. Chmn., Carnegie Hall Corp., 1960–74; N.Y.C. Human Rights Commissioner, 1964–70; Budget Dir., N.Y. State Cncl. on the Arts, 1965–74; N.Y.C. Taxi and Limousine Commissioner, 1970–72; N.Y.C. Cncl., 1973–74.

Offices 1707 LHOB, 202-225-5936. Also 1368 Fulton St., Brooklyn 11216, 212-636-4707.

Committees *Agriculture* (8th). Subcommittees: Conservation, Credit and Rural Development; Department Operations, Research and Foreign Agriculture; Domestic Marketing, Consumer Relations and Nutrition (Chairman).

Small Business (7th). Subcommittees: General Oversight; SBA and SBIC Authority, Minority Enterprise and General Small Business Problems.

Joint Economic Committee (6th). Subcommittees: International Trade, Finance, and Security Economics; Trade, Productivity, and Economic Growth.

Group Ratings

	ADA	COPE	PC	LCV	CFA	RPN	NAB	NSI	NTU	ACA	ACU
1980	94	88	80	81	93	—	0	0	17	5	6
1979	95	100	78	91	59	—	—	—	20	4	8
1978	95	95	90	91	77	40	0	0	13	5	4

Key Votes

1) Draft Registn $	AGN	6) Fair Hsg DOJ Enfrc	FOR	11) Cut Socl Incr Dfns $	AGN
2) Ban $ to Nicrgua	AGN	7) Lim PAC Contrbtns	FOR	12) Hosptl Cost Controls	FOR
3) Dlay MX Missile	FOR	8) Cap on Food Stmp $	AGN	13) Gasln Ctrls & Allctns	FOR
4) Nuclr Mortorium	FOR	9) New US Dep Edcatn	AGN	14) Lim Wndfll Prof Tax	AGN
5) Alaska Lands Bill	FOR	10) Cut OSHA $	AGN	15) Chryslr Loan Grntee	—

Election Results

1980 general	Frederick W. Richmond (D-L) ...	45,029	(76%)	($392,751)
	Christopher Lovell (R-C)	8,257	(14%)	($1,622)
	Moses S. Harris (New Alliance) ...	4,151	(7%)	($0)
1980 primary	Frederick W. Richmond (D)	17,474	(74%)	
	Moses S. Harris (D)	6,023	(26%)	
1978 general	Frederick W. Richmond (D-L) ...	31,339	(77%)	($419,663)
	Arthur Bramwell (R)	7,516	(18%)	

FIFTEENTH DISTRICT

To many who have never seen it, Brooklyn means nonstop slums, the tenement apartment of Ralph and Alice Kramden, and the fear of lurking crime. This is not an accurate, or at least not an entirely accurate, picture. Brooklyn has all the diversity one might expect of a city of 2.2 million people. If Brooklyn has some of the nation's most fearsome slums—and it does in Brownsville and parts of Bedford-Stuyvesant—New York's largest borough also has neighborhoods of comfortable, expensive homes. Although its downtown streets are grimy, the parks of Brooklyn are green and its yacht harbors are filled with windblown sails and spinnakers. Nothing is dainty about Brooklyn, but in its pleasant middle-class neighborhoods, the fear of crime is more academic than residents seem to want to admit. In short, a few trees do grow here.

A disproportionate share of Brooklyn's middle-class neighborhoods lies within the boundaries of New York's 15th congressional district. The 15th begins amidst the newly renovated brownstones of Park Slope, a neighborhood just off Prospect Park—one laid out by the architects of Central Park and often considered their masterpiece. To the south is the Sunset Park neighborhood, which has the largest concentration of Norwegian-Americans between Oslo and Minneapolis. In the same area is Borough Park, a middle-class Irish and Italian area with increasing numbers of Spanish-speaking residents. Below that, where New York Harbor spills into the Atlantic and the Verrazano Narrows Bridge arches over to Staten Island, is Bay Ridge.

Bay Ridge is a couple of steps up the ladder for middle-class Brooklynites of Irish and Italian ancestry. It has some impressive housing, but much of it looks like Tony Manero's neighborhood in *Saturday Night Fever.* Bay Ridge is thus not the highest-income neighborhood in Brooklyn, but it is politically the most conservative. People here take their cues from the *Daily News,* not the *Times* nor the *Wall Street Journal.* In most elections, this is the most reliably Republican part of New York City. It is also an area whose mores and cultural attitudes have traditionally been conservative and hostile to Manhattan's. Indeed such attitudes were of cardinal importance throughout the 15th district in the late 1960s and early 1970s and have moved the entire district closer to the Republican column in many elections.

Until 1960 what is now the 15th was a Republican stronghold in congressional elections. Then the Democrats nominated a 41-year-old lawyer named Hugh Carey, who pulled a major upset and was elected to Congress. Despite Republican redistrictings and conservative trends, Carey continued to win here; he was one of the few New York politicians who could win Irish working-class votes and at the same time maintain a voting record acceptable to ideological liberals. He switched from hawk to dove, for example, way back in 1966, reportedly from listening to the arguments of several of his twelve children.

Carey always had the ambition—and aptitude and talent, if he could get well known—for higher office. In 1969 he actually ran for city council president, a mostly honorific post that for some reason gives its holder great publicity. Between bouts of city politics, he became something of a power in the House. In 1971 he led the Brooklyn delegation in supporting Hale Boggs for majority leader; as a reward for being on the winning side, he got a seat on Ways and Means. There he was a major pusher behind revenue sharing and also urged, unsuccessfully, tax breaks for parents with children in private shcools.

Then in 1974 Carey decided to run for governor—and won. That left his House seat up for grabs and in another year—not one when a Republican president was being driven from office for criminal conduct—the Republicans might have made a race of it. But in 1974 the most difficult contest was in the Democratic primary, and the winner there was the machine choice, Leo Zeferetti. He had not come up the usual Brooklyn clubhouse ladder; instead, like the Bronx's Mario Biaggi, he was a well-known cop—in his case president of the Correction Officers Benevolent Association—who moved into electoral politics. Zeferetti won that first general election with 58%. He has served on the Education and Labor Committee, where he was a firm vote for organized labor; and on Merchant Marine and Fisheries, where he voted to maintain the elaborate system of subsidies to business and labor that keep the maritime industry comfortable. In 1979, he won a seat on the House Rules Committee, where he can be expected to vote generally with the House Democratic leadership. In 1981 he got the House to set up a Select Committee on Narcotics Abuse and Control—a problem always of great concern in New York City.

New York City loses four congressional districts, and Zeferetti is one of several congressmen who is in danger of being squeezed out. One possibility is that part of his district might be combined with Staten Island; that might very well give the seat to Staten Island Republican freshman Guy Molinari, particularly if the part of the 15th included is the part closest to Staten Island, Bay Ridge. Zeferetti has had trouble holding onto the current 15th—he won by only 50%–47% in 1980—and Albany Democrats might just consider him expendable.

Census Data   Pop. (1980 final) 416,620, down 13% in 1970s. Median family income, 1970, $9,629, 100% of U.S.

The Voters

Employment profile 1970   White collar, 54%. Blue collar, 34%. Service, 12%. Farm, –%.
Ethnic groups   Black 1980, 6%. Hispanic 1980, 19%. Asian 1980, 3%. Total foreign stock 1970, 50%. Italy, 21%; Ireland, 4%; Poland, 3%; USSR, UK, 2% each; Germany, Canada, Greece, 1% each.

Presidential Vote

1980	Reagan (R)	55,958	(51%)
	Carter (D)	46,323	(42%)
	Anderson (I)	5,583	(5%)
1976	Ford (R)	62,787	(50%)
	Carter (D)	62,332	(50%)

Rep. Leo C. Zeferetti (D) Elected 1974; b. July 15, 1927, Brooklyn; home, Brooklyn; NYU, CCNY.

Career   Navy, WWII; Officer, N.Y.C. Dept. of Correction, 1957–74; Pres., Correction Officers Benevolent Assn., 1969–74; Mbr., N.Y. State Crime Control Planning Bd., 1973.

Offices   2436 RHOB, 202-225-4105. Also 526 86th St., Brooklyn 11209, 212-680-1000.

Committees   *Rules* (6th).

Select Committee on Narcotics Abuse and Control (Chairman).

Group Ratings

	ADA	COPE	PC	LCV	CFA	RPN	NAB	NSI	NTU	ACA	ACU
1980	44	88	57	43	71	—	8	56	13	14	31
1979	37	88	35	35	33	—	—	—	22	15	20
1978	35	80	35	44	36	20	0	89	7	36	46

Key Votes

1) Draft Registn $	FOR	6) Fair Hsg DOJ Enfrc	FOR
2) Ban $ to Nicrgua	FOR	7) Lim PAC Contrbtns	FOR
3) Dlay MX Missile	AGN	8) Cap on Food Stmp $	AGN
4) Nuclr Mortorium	AGN	9) New US Dep Edcatn	AGN
5) Alaska Lands Bill	AGN	10) Cut OSHA $	AGN

11) Cut Socl Incr Dfns $	AGN
12) Hosptl Cost Controls	FOR
13) Gasln Ctrls & Allctns	FOR
14) Lim Wndfll Prof Tax	AGN
15) Chryslr Loan Grntee	—

Election Results

1980 general	Leo C. Zeferetti (D)	49,684	(50%)	($185,458)
	Paul M. Atanasio (R-C-RTL)	46,467	(47%)	($161,803)
1980 primary	Leo C. Zeferetti (D)	16,961	(71%)	
	Peter A. McNeill (D)	6,811	(29%)	($0)
1978 general	Leo C. Zeferetti (D-C)	49,272	(68%)	($67,960)
	Robert Whelan (R)	20,508	(28%)	($15,028)

SIXTEENTH DISTRICT

Flatbush is the heart of Brooklyn, right in the borough's geographical and psychological center. The name Flatbush has become practically synonymous in the public mind with Brooklyn itself. Probably most of the people in Queens or Long Island have some roots in Brooklyn or Flatbush, but a glance at the map shows how these places differ. Freeways crisscross the suburban terrain and most of Queens as well; but Brooklyn has only one, running along its shore. Proposals for another, cutting across the borough, have been killed. Most of Flatbush and Brooklyn were laid out and occupied before the automobile became a necessity; and you can still live in these one- and two-family houses, walk to shopping streets, take the subway to work, and get on quite as comfortably as most New Yorkers with cars.

During the 1910s and 1920s the then new neighborhoods of Flatbush and East Flatbush were attracting thousands of newly middle-income Jews who had grown up on the Lower East Side of Manhattan. They were mostly young people, who raised large families here; many of their children stayed in Flatbush and raised their families there too. Now, as the young people who grew up here increasingly move to Long Island, Westchester, Manhattan, or simply, as many have done, outside the New York metropolitan area altogether, the Jewish population is weighted toward the elderly end of the age scale. Many blacks have been moving into Flatbush from Crown Heights and Bedford–Stuyvesant to the north, and among the older residents there has been much fear of crime. Blacks are now 50% of the population here, but because of age and low voter participation, they are still distinctly a minority of the electorate.

It is not hard to describe the succession in congressional representation over the last six decades here. In the 1920 Harding landslide the area that is now the 16th congressional district—including most of Flatbush and East Flatbush—elected a Republican congressman. Two years later a 36-year-old Jewish lawyer won the Democratic nomination and unseated the incumbent by a small margin. For the next 24 elections the same man, slowly growing older, was elected again and again: Emanuel Celler, chairman of the House Judiciary Committee, and coauthor of the Celler–Kefauver antitrust law. Celler was always a machine

Democrat, and he considered himself invulnerable; he never bothered to provide the kind of constituency services people in other districts had grown accustomed to. So he was more surprised than anyone when he was defeated in the 1972 Democratic primary by Elizabeth Holtzman, a young lawyer and former aide to Mayor John Lindsay.

The Holtzman victory had national significance. If she had lost, it would have been 88-year-old Manny Celler rather than 65-year-old Peter Rodino chairing the Judiciary Committee hearings on the impeachment of Richard Nixon. It also signaled the decline of Democratic machine politics in Flatbush. Numerous machine candidates have been defeated since in Democratic primaries, notably Assembly Speaker Stanley Steingut in 1978.

Holtzman was a serious and liberal legislator; she ran for the Senate in 1980, won an upset victory in the primary, but to almost everyone's surprise lost the general election to Republican Alfonse D'Amato. Her successor in the 16th district, Charles Schumer, is a politician from much the same mold. He won his primary easily, with 54% in a four-candidate race. He is young, liberal, and serious — and must not feel at home among the earnest young conservatives and refugees from midwestern country clubs who predominate among 1981's freshman class. He has a seat on the Banking Committee, and his major worry for 1982 is redistricting. The 16th has not lost much population (and most of it has been in the small part that is in the Brownsville ghetto), and the district will likely survive in somewhat similar form, perhaps with additions from the current 11th. It is possible that there would be a primary between Schumer and 11th district incumbent James Scheuer.

Census Data Pop. (1980 final) 438,615, down 6% in 1970s. Median family income, 1970, $10,504, 110% of U.S.

The Voters

Employment profile 1970 White collar, 64%. Blue collar, 25%. Service, 11%. Farm, -%.
Ethnic groups Black 1980, 50%. Hispanic 1980, 8%. Asian 1980, 2%. Total foreign stock 1970, 49%. USSR, 11%; Poland, 7%; Italy, 6%; Austria, Ireland, 3% each; Germany, UK, 2% each; Rumania, 1%.

Presidential Vote

1980	Reagan (R)	39,344	(49%)
	Carter (D)	55,813	(55%)
	Anderson (I)	5,091	(5%)
1976	Ford (R)	35,378	(29%)
	Carter (D)	88,016	(71%)

Rep. Charles E. Schumer (D) Elected 1980; b. Nov. 23, 1950, Brooklyn; home, Brooklyn; Harvard Col., B.A. 1971, Harvard Law Sch., J.D. 1974.

Career Practicing atty.; N.Y. State Assembly, 1974-80.

Offices 126 CHOB, 202-225-6616. Also 2501 Ave. U, Brooklyn 11229, 212-743-3800.

Committees Banking, Finance and Urban Affairs (22d). Subcommittees: Economic Stabilization; Financial Institutions Supervision, Regulation and Insurance; Housing and Community Development.

Post Office and Civil Service (11th).

Group Ratings and Key Votes: Newly Elected

Election Results

1980 general	Charles E. Schumer (D-L)	67,343	(77%)	($199,805)
	Theodore Silverman (R-C)	17,050	(20%)	($23,268)
1980 primary	Charles E. Schumer (D)	23,260	(59%)	
	Susan Alter (D)	7,385	(19%)	($147,269)
	Theodore Silverman (D)	6,041	(15%)	
	One other (D)	2,842	(7%)	
1978 general	Elizabeth Holtzman (D-L)	59,703	(82%)	($44,428)
	Larry Penner (R)..............	9,405	(13%)	
	John H. Fox (C)	3,782	(5%)	

SEVENTEENTH DISTRICT

Staten Island is the smallest (pop. 349,000) and least densely populated of the five boroughs of New York City (6,000 people per square mile as against 27,000 for the rest of the city). It is also the most parochial, and most atypical, part of New York. Parts of Staten Island retain a rural character, even after the new development spurred by the opening of the Verrazano Narrows Bridge to Brooklyn in 1965. Before that, Staten Island was even more cut off: the only land route from the rest of New York City was through New Jersey, and the only water route was the Staten Island Ferry from the tip of Lower Manhattan.

Most Staten Islanders are quite happy with their comparative isolation. They are in many ways more suburban than real suburbanites. A large proportion are middle-income Italian and Irish Catholics, brought up often in Brooklyn and happy to leave the City (as they call it) behind. Politically, Staten Islanders are intensely conservative, with Conservative Party candidates sometimes outpolling Democrats. Enough people here are ancestral Democrats to elect Democrats to local office, and when the question in an election seems to be aid to New York City, most Staten Islanders will vote Democratic like their compatriots in other boroughs.

Because its population has not merited a full congressional district, Staten Island over the years has been linked politically with various parts of Brooklyn and Manhattan. During the 1950s and 1960s the island was joined to several different parts of Brooklyn. Today it is joined to the lower part of Manhattan. The conservative homeowners of Staten Island find themselves in the same district with elderly Jewish people living in housing projects and the trendy, artsy folk who are extending Greenwich Village southward into the neighborhood known as SoHo. The utter incompatibility of these two portions of the 17th can be shown by the 1980 presidential returns: the Manhattan portion, with one-third of the district's votes, went 61% for Carter, while Staten Island was 59% for Reagan.

For 18 years the congressman from this district was a Staten Island Democrat, John Murphy, who hung on through several redistrictings and won a position of considerable importance. From 1977 to 1980 he was chairman of the Merchant Marine and Fisheries Committee, and he strongly supported maritime subsidies and protective legislation for the maritime unions. Murphy was also interested in Central American affairs. He was a classmate of Nicaragua President Anastasio Somoza at West Point and strongly supported his government; he also opposed the Panama Canal Treaties. In the late 1970s and early 1980s Murphy's career took a bad turn. He was unable to get cargo preference—a measure to require cargoes to be shipped in U.S. flag carriers—through Congress. He saw the Canal Treaties approved and Somoza ousted and assassinated. And Murphy himself was indicted and, just after the 1980 election, convicted in the Abscam scandal.

Murphy's overhanging indictment was the main reason for the election of Republican Guy Molinari in this district. A state legislator from Staten Island, Molinari took predictably conservative stands on cultural and economic issues, although he also took a tough stand on disposal of toxic wastes—a problem in Staten Island and the adjacent industrial areas of New Jersey. Molinari carried the Staten Island part of the district by a 57%–33% margin over Murphy—a sharp reversal of past results. In Manhattan, Molinari finished third with 24%, behind Murphy (39%) and Liberal Party candidate Mary Codd (36%), who had opposed Murphy in the primary. Overall, Molinari was a plurality winner.

The new congressman serves in the House as a junior member of the minority party and as a member of the Public Works Committee. Nevertheless, he stirred a fuss in March 1981 when President Reagan, during a trip to New York, noted that he was paying more attention to Molinari and had persuaded him not to retire from Congress and take a judgeship. Actually, Molinari has less reason for political insecurity than most members of the New York City delegation. His base is the one part of the city with a substantial population gain in the 1970s and has 68% of the population needed for a congressional district. Wherever the remaining 32% comes from, it is certain to be no more unfriendly to Molinari than the Manhattan portion of the current 17th. Quite possibly he could get Bay Ridge in Brooklyn—a Republican middle-class area with a large Italian–American population. That might give him a race against Democratic incumbent Leo Zeferetti, but the odds in such a district would definitely favor the Republican.

Census Data Pop. (1980 final) 529,299, up 13% in 1970s. Median family income, 1970, $10,632, 110% of U.S.

The Voters

Employment profile 1970 White collar, 57%. Blue collar, 28%. Service, 15%. Farm, –%.
Ethnic groups Black 1980, 7%. Hispanic 1980, 11%. Asian 1980, 9%. Total foreign stock 1970, 40%. Italy, 12%; Poland, Ireland, USSR, Germany, UK, 2% each; Austria, 1%.

Presidential Vote

1980	Reagan (R)	77,171	(49%)
	Carter (D)	66,823	(42%)
	Anderson (I)	11,212	(7%)
1976	Ford (R)	68,723	(45%)
	Carter (D)	83,301	(55%)

Rep. Guy V. Molinari (R) Elected 1980; b. Nov. 23, 1928, New York City; home, Staten Island; Wagner Col., B.A. 1949, NY Law Sch., LL.B. 1951.

Career USMC, 1951–53; Practicing atty., 1953–74; N.Y. State Assembly, 1974–80.

Offices 501 CHOB, 202-225-3571. Also 203 Ft. Wadsworth Bldg., Staten Island 10305, 212-981-9800, and 26 Fed. Plaza., 16th Fl., New York 10007, 212-264-9335.

Committees *Public Works and Transportation* (16th). Subcommittees: Investigations and Oversight; Surface Transportation; Water Resources.

Small Business (17th).

Group Ratings and Key Votes: Newly Elected

Election Results

1980 general	Guy V. Molinari (R-C)	69,573	(48%)	($148,993)
	John M. Murphy (D-RTL)	50,954	(35%)	($303,108)
	Mary T. Codd (L)..............	25,118	(17%)	($50,643)
1980 primary	Guy V. Molinari (R-C), unopposed			
1978 general	John M. Murphy (D)	54,228	(54%)	($190,048)
	John M. Peters (R-C)	33,071	(33%)	($45,525)
	Thomas H. Stokes (L)	12,662	(13%)	

EIGHTEENTH DISTRICT

The 18th congressional district of New York has always been known as the Silk Stocking District. The 18th includes most of the skyscrapers of midtown Manhattan and much of Greenwich Village, whose now inaccurate bohemian reputation dates back to the 1910s. The district also includes the middle-income housing developments of Stuyvesant Town and Peter Cooper Village and quaint old squares such as Gramercy Park. If one could measure gross national product by congressional district, the 18th would undoubtedly be number one in the country; despite recent publicity about business leaving, midtown Manhattan is still the center of commerce and media in the United States and, for that matter, the world. The 18th also includes those parts of Manhattan that make it a world class city, whose only rivals are London and Paris: this is one of the places where the really rich live, shop, and entertain. Indeed, increasing numbers of the very rich are moving to Manhattan, fleeing from political instability elsewhere.

Thousands of writers have struggled to describe this part of New York socially, culturally, even physically. It is easier to describe it politically. For as in all of New York, not everyone here votes, and those who do tend to share a set of attitudes that, although they have changed, can be described without great difficulty. The political, although not geographical, center of the 18th district is the Upper East Side of Manhattan, from 59th to 96th Streets, an area that casts more than half the district's votes. This is an area that we associate with the rich, and most of Manhattan's really rich people live here. But it is also an area with a large number of young, single trendy people with professional jobs — the kind of articulate, stylish people who make Manhattan the center of the nation's publishing, entertainment, broadcasting, and communications industries. There is considerable turnover in the district's population: people get married and move to the suburbs, they go to another city, they are replaced by younger people with similar background but perhaps quite different attitudes.

Thus it is possible to discern two basic shifts in political attitudes in the Silk Stocking District over the past 15 years. This was once a Republican district, perhaps the most Republican in New York City. From the 1930s, when rich people here considered Franklin Roosevelt a traitor to his class, up through the early 1960s, when trendy people here considered the Democratic Party as dominated by a bunch of crooked Irish and Italian politicos, the 18th elected a succession of Republican congressmen. Its best-known representative was John Lindsay, elected as a liberal Republican in 1958 and reelected by increasingly wide margins in the next three elections.

Lindsay was exactly the kind of politician Upper East Siders of the time liked. From a WASPy family, a graduate of prep school and Yale, he was obviously the right kind of person. As a Republican, he was not involved in the griminess of Democratic politics; as a procedural reformer and supporter of civil rights, he could be called a liberal. He voted with the

Kennedy Administration on many issues, but in city politics he opposed the pitiable remnants of the Democratic machines. When Lindsay ran for mayor in 1965 he swept the East Side and Manhattan by large enough margins to win, even though Abraham Beame had a plurality in the rest of the city.

Over the next ten years the 18th district swung sharply to the left. One reason was the Vietnam war. People here were opposed, particularly the new young people who moved in off the radicalized campuses; and opposition to the war was expressed almost entirely by the Democratic rather than the Republican Party. There was some fear here of crime, but a greater revulsion against its use by people in the outer boroughs—and by the Republican Party of Richard Nixon and Spiro Agnew—to create an apparent code word for capitalizing on racial prejudice against blacks. As Nixon and Agnew kept campaigning against blacks, intellectuals, and students, the Republican allegiance in the Upper East Side quickly vanished. Nor was Mayor Lindsay keeping people in the Republican Party. He lost the Republican nomination for mayor in 1969, was reelected as a Liberal, and switched to become a Democrat in 1971. The demise of the *New York Herald Tribune* in the late 1960s finished off the voice that once best articulated the Republicanism of the Upper East Side; the increasingly Democratic editorial columns of the *New York Times* replaced it in influence. And by 1968 the 18th district had elected a Democrat, Edward Koch, as its congressman. A product of the reform Democratic movement in Greenwich Village, Koch was reelected easily in 1970, 1972, and 1974 in a district that had last elected a Democratic congressman, and then only by a narrow margin, in 1936.

There was more than a touch of snobbery in the liberalism of the Upper East Side. There was always greater concern here for the problems of lettuce workers in California or the Black Panthers—the honorees at the famous "radical chic" party given by Leonard Bernstein—than there was understanding of the problems faced by the cab drivers, doormen, waiters, sanitation workers, policemen, office clerks, janitors, and others whose work makes life in the Upper East Side possible. This kind of snobbery is what did in the Lindsay Administration. His electoral strategy of combining the top and the bottom of the New York (or Manhattan) electorate worked tactically, but as a formula for providing government in whose good faith people have confidence it was a disaster.

In the early 1970s, voters on the Upper East Side lost their enthusiasm for Lindsay, but they still backed other liberal Democrats. They were strongly for George McGovern in the 1972 primary and for Morris Udall in 1976, just as they had favored Adlai Stevenson over anyone else in the 1950s and Eugene McCarthy over Robert Kennedy in 1968. But now political attitudes here seem to be shifting again—at least enough to permit the election and reelection of a Republican congressman. William Green, an heir to the Grand Union supermarket fortune, had been an assemblyman from the richest part of the Upper East Side until he ran for another office in 1968: a Democrat was elected in his place, and he was thus the last Republican legislator elected in Manhattan. But when Edward Koch was elected mayor in 1977, Green decided to put on a real campaign for the 18th district seat in the special election in early 1978.

Green was blessed in the special and in the 1978 general election as well by his opposition. Apparently acting on the assumption that the seat had become safe Democratic, local Democrats engaged in two fratricidal battles for the nomination. In the special election, the Democrats nominated their candidate by party convention, with dozens of delegates; the contest eventually ended up in court. The winner by court decree was Bella Abzug, fresh from narrow defeats in the 1976 Senate and 1977 mayoral primaries and six years of service in the 20th district seat. Abzug, who could claim a record of hard work and accomplishment in the House, tarnished her own reputation by seeming to shop for offices to run for, and Green's election was as much a rejection of her as anything else.

But in the ensuing months Green's own record became his biggest political asset. In the fall of 1978 he faced Carter Burden, the young millionaire who had lost the earlier nomination to Abzug in court; despite Burden's million-dollar-plus campaign budget, Green won. By this time it had become apparent that his voting record was probably the most liberal of any House Republican, and he proved adept at keeping his constituents informed of his stands. At the same time, he was able to endorse such measures as the Kemp–Roth tax cut, which had support only from Republicans. In 1980, Green faced Democrat Mark Green, head of Ralph Nader's Congress Watch and author of *Who Runs Congress?* Bill Green spent liberally on the race, as he had in 1978; Mark Green spent quite liberally himself. There was a time when Mark Green's kind of liberalism aroused a great enthusiasm in the 18th, but in 1980 the ideas that seemed to be crackling with energy came mostly from the right. Bill Green won with a solid 57% of the vote — his best showing to date and one that indicates that he may very well have made this a safe seat.

Redistricting does not pose too great a danger to the Republican Green. The Republican state Senate will probably see that the boundaries of the 18th are not tampered with greatly, and the district's population held even in the 1970s, which means that it must be expanded only a little bit.

Census Data   Pop. (1980 final) 455,860, down 2% in 1970s. Median family income, 1970, $14,853, 155% of U.S.

The Voters

Employment profile 1970   White collar, 79%. Blue collar, 10%. Service, 11%. Farm, –%.
Ethnic groups   Black 1980, 5%. Hispanic 1980, 11%. Asian 1980, 4%. Total foreign stock 1970, 44%. USSR, 7%; Germany, Poland, Italy, 4% each; Ireland, UK, Austria, 3% each; Hungary, 2%; Canada, France, Czechoslovakia, 1% each.

Presidential Vote

1980	Reagan (R)	62,395	(37%)
	Carter (D)	81,679	(49%)
	Anderson (I)	18,814	(11%)
1976	Ford (R)	63,441	(37%)
	Carter (D)	108,478	(63%)

Rep. S. William (Bill) **Green** (R) Elected Feb. 14, 1978; b. Oct. 16, 1929, New York City; home, New York City; Harvard U., B.A. 1950, J.D. 1953.

Career Army, 1953–55; Law Secy., U.S. Court of Appeals for D.C. Circuit, 1955–56; Practicing atty., 1956–70; N.Y. State Assembly, 1965–70; N.Y. Regional Administrator, HUD, 1970–77.

Offices 1417 LHOB, 202-225-2436. Also 137 E. 57th St., New York 10022, 212-826-4466.

Committee *Appropriations* (18th). Subcommittees: District of Columbia; HUD–Independent Agencies.

Group Ratings

	ADA	COPE	PC	LCV	CFA	RPN	NAB	NSI	NTU	ACA	ACU
1980	94	58	73	83	86	—	17	22	20	29	5
1979	68	55	55	72	54	—	—	—	27	44	29
1978	58	61	56	86	50	90	20	0	13	12	24

Key Votes

1) Draft Registn $	AGN	6) Fair Hsg DOJ Enfrc	FOR	11) Cut Socl Incr Dfns $	AGN
2) Ban $ to Nicrgua	AGN	7) Lim PAC Contrbtns	FOR	12) Hosptl Cost Controls	FOR
3) Dlay MX Missile	FOR	8) Cap on Food Stmp $	AGN	13) Gasln Ctrls & Allctns	AGN
4) Nuclr Mortorium	AGN	9) New US Dep Edcatn	AGN	14) Lim Wndfll Prof Tax	AGN
5) Alaska Lands Bill	FOR	10) Cut OSHA $	AGN	15) Chryslr Loan Grntee	AGN

Election Results

1980 general	S. Wm. Green (R-Ind. Neighbors) .	91,341	(57%)	($330,936)
	Mark J. Green (D-L)	68,786	(43%)	($293,020)
1980 primary	S. William Green (R), unopposed			
1978 general	S. William (Bill) Green (R)	60,867	(53%)	($580,463)
	Carter Burden (D-L)	53,434	(47%)	($1,136,112)

NINETEENTH DISTRICT

In the years following World War I, Harlem, whose tenements had been built just a decade or so earlier for white working-class people, became the center of black American culture. The 1920s were comparatively good years for Harlem, and not just because many Manhattan sophisticates discovered its night spots and jazz music. But the Depression of the 1930s hit Harlem hard, and in many ways it has never recovered. A few middle-class pockets are still left here, in the apartment complexes built along the Harlem River or at the edge of Morningside Heights. But most of Harlem is very poor, and stricken with the problems of heroin, violent crime, and the kind of attitudes that produced the looting during the summer 1977 blackout. For many years now Harlem has been the kind of place people leave if they can; Harlem's population dropped from about 500,000 in 1960 (the exact number depends on where you put the boundaries) to 390,000 in 1970 and only 290,000 in 1980. For all our concentration on the problems of people in Harlem it is apparent that many people there figured out how to solve them—they got out and moved to more comfortable, spread-out, and socially less disorganized neighborhoods. In Harlem the elan of the 1920s has never returned. Black leadership in civil rights battles has dwelled on the handicaps blacks have suffered and the difficulties they have encountered in trying to make progress. One result has been to awaken whites to the injustices they have imposed, but another has been to give a kind of inferiority complex to people who live in such places as Harlem.

Harlem has had representation in Congress that cannot be called inferior by any standard —although at times it has been controversial. For a quarter of a century Harlem was represented by one of the best-known congressmen in the nation, Adam Clayton Powell, Jr. His career peaked in the early 1960s, when he was chairman of the House Education and Labor Committee, which had jurisdiction over most of the social and antipoverty programs of the Kennedy and Johnson administrations. Then in 1966 he refused to pay a libel judgment to a plaintiff he had called a "bag woman." Powell's troubles with the New York courts became regular features of national television newscasts. He got into even more trouble when it was learned that he had diverted staff salaries into his own ample bank account. The House ousted him in 1967, refusing even to let him take his seat—an action the Supreme Court two years later ruled unconstitutional. By that time Harlem voters had elected him in a special election and in the 1968 general election. But he had to stay out of New York except on Sundays, to avoid process servers, and increasingly he spent his time at his luxurious home in Bimini.

When Powell was first elected in 1944, his district was just part of Harlem; with redistricting, the district was expanded to include all of Harlem and a part of Manhattan's white liberal Upper West Side. By 1970 Powell's popularity in Harlem had dropped to the point where he could only barely carry the area over Assemblyman Charles Rangel; the West Side produced enough votes to give Rangel the victory.

In the years since, Rangel has shown at least as much political sensitivity as Powell did in his best years. He speaks in street-wise accents rather than Powell's oratorical style; but where Powell got in trouble with the national television audience, Rangel impressed them favorably as a member of the House Judiciary Committee in the Nixon impeachment hearings. His political acumen is shown by the fact that he managed to get Hugh Carey's old seat on Ways and Means. He has been active legislatively on the committee and the floor on welfare issues and on matters affecting New York City's finances.

Electorally Rangel had no problems in the 1970s, but he could conceivably face problems in redistricting. The predilections of New York legislators and the commands of the Voting Rights Act work against the elimination of the 19th district. But the district's population is down to 367,000 and must be raised to 514,000 by 1982. One way to do that would be to go across the Harlem River and add part of the 21st district in the south Bronx, a district that lost literally half its population in the 1970s. But this would result in the elimination of the 21st, at which the Voting Rights Act might also look askance, and might put Rangel in a primary against 21st district incumbent Robert Garcia—a potentially unpleasant rivalry of black vs. Puerto Rican. The other possibility is to take substantial parts of New York's Upper West Side from the 20th district and add them to the 19th. But this—or a similar procedure with the Upper East Side and the 18th district—would risk creating a district with a large affluent white majority that in the Democratic primary might attract a white liberal challenger. It is not clear yet how the problem will be resolved, but the odds favor Rangel's political survival.

Census Data   Pop. (1980 final) 371,614, down 20% in 1970s. Median family income, 1970, $6,712, 70% of U.S.

The Voters

  Employment profile 1970   White collar, 49%. Blue collar, 27%. Service, 24%. Farm, –%.
  Ethnic groups   Black 1980, 54%. Hispanic 1980, 23%. Asian 1980, 1%. Total foreign stock 1970, 18%. Italy, 2%; USSR, Germany, 1% each.

Presidential Vote

1980	Reagan (R)	12,230	(12%)
	Carter (D)	84,912	(81%)
	Anderson (I)	5,685	(5%)
1976	Ford (R)	14,642	(13%)
	Carter (D)	99,111	(87%)

Rep. Charles B. Rangel (D) Elected 1970; b. June 11, 1930, New York City; home, New York City; NYU, B.S. 1957, St. John's U., LL.B. 1960.

Career Army, 1948–52; Asst. U.S. Atty., So. Dist. of N.Y., 1961; Legal Counsel, N.Y.C. Housing and Redevelopment Bd., Neighborhood Conservation Bureau; Gen. Counsel, Natl. Advisory Comm. on Selective Svc., 1966; N.Y. State Assembly, 1966–70.

Offices 2432 RHOB, 202-225-4365. Also 163 W. 125th St., New York 10027, 212-663-3900.

Committees *Ways and Means* (4th). Subcommittees: Health; Oversight (Chairman).

Select Committee on Narcotics Abuse and Control (3d).

Group Ratings

	ADA	COPE	PC	LCV	CFA	RPN	NAB	NSI	NTU	ACA	ACU
1980	78	95	77	74	79	—	0	0	15	14	15
1979	84	100	75	84	67	—	—	—	20	0	3
1978	80	90	88	86	82	38	0	0	29	8	4

Key Votes

1) Draft Registn $	AGN	6) Fair Hsg DOJ Enfrc	FOR	11) Cut Socl Incr Dfns $	AGN
2) Ban $ to Nicrgua	AGN	7) Lim PAC Contrbtns	FOR	12) Hosptl Cost Controls	FOR
3) Dlay MX Missile	FOR	8) Cap on Food Stmp $	AGN	13) Gasln Ctrls & Allctns	FOR
4) Nuclr Mortorium	FOR	9) New US Dep Edcatn	AGN	14) Lim Wndfll Prof Tax	AGN
5) Alaska Lands Bill	FOR	10) Cut OSHA $		AGN	15) Chryslr Loan Grntee	FOR

Election Results

1980 general	Charles B. Rangel (D-R-L).......	84,062	(96%)	($90,344)
1980 primary	Charles B. Rangel (D-R-L), unopp.			
1978 general	Charles B. Rangel (D-R-L).......	59,731	(100%)	($43,246)

TWENTIETH DISTRICT

The West Side of Manhattan, the funkiest part of New York City, is a polyglot area so diverse that it defies accurate description. It's not a long way from Riverside Park and the Hudson River docks to the invisible line that separates the West Side from midtown or Harlem; but nearly every block in this short stretch seems to have its own peculiar character and so, it sometimes seems, does almost every building on the block. New York's 20th congressional district includes most of the West Side. It begins with a geographic salient into hip, expensive Greenwich Village, then moves up through renovated and raffish Chelsea, past apartment complexes and the obscenity palaces of Times Square, north to the Upper West Side. Here the 20th includes the two blocks from Amsterdam Avenue to the Hudson, north all the way along the Henry Hudson Parkway to the northern tip of Manhattan. Well-known writers and well-paid professionals in the West End Avenue apartments live in close and sometimes uneasy proximity to Puerto Ricans and welfare mothers in the side streets; students occupy cheap apartments around Columbia University, and elderly ethnics live in even cheaper and definitely more dangerous surroundings in Washington Heights. The 20th goes on to include the expensive apartment units and large single-family houses of the Riverdale section of the Bronx. There have been some major shifts in the population here in the 1970s. Below 96th Street, the West Side has become gentrified, increasingly populated by upper-income professionals. North of Columbia, it has become increasingly Hispanic, and the district had the city's biggest increase in Spanish population in the decade.

Because most of the 20th district's votes are cast on the Upper West Side, its politics is worth some examination. For this is the heartland of much of Manhattan's Democratic reform politics. Back in the late 1950s and early 1960s, upper-income Stevenson enthusiasts broke the hold of Tammany Hall up here; the aged ethnics whose votes propped up the machine were either dying or moving elsewhere in search of cheaper rents, and the machine people had no rapport with the growing constituency of affluent liberals. The process of neighborhood change has become known since as gentrification, and in many cities now higher-income young people are replacing lower-income old people (and minority poor) in choice locations near white collar and professional employment and entertainment centers. Much attention and many words were devoted to the Manhattan reform movement because so many writers live in Manhattan; and they, like everyone else, tend to assume that their own experience has instructive value for all. Actually, the clash between gentrification and an old-line political machine is an event not likely to occur in other places, because there are so very few political machines left. In any case, the epic victories the reform groups celebrate were, in retrospect, won rather easily against a machine that had little life left in it.

Today virtually everyone active in Upper West Side politics is a survivor of reform politics. The district has been represented by a succession of reformers. First there was William F. Ryan, the first Manhattan reformer elected to Congress, back in 1960. He was the first congressman to condemn American involvement in Vietnam, and he led the biennial fight against the House Un-American Activities Committee. His views made him an object of derision in the early 1960s; they are the conventional wisdom of American politics today. The 20th district, or part of it, also produced Bella Abzug, who was first elected in 1970. She lost an epic primary battle to Ryan in 1972 (they were redistricted together), but Ryan died before the general, and Abzug was nominated in his place and won reelection.

Since then congressional races have been devoid of the kind of acrimony that used to be synonymous with West Side politics; it is almost as if the reform movement, having achieved most of its objectives and the limits of its possible success, has entered a kind of placid and mellow middle age. Abzug was reelected without incident in 1974 and went on to try for the Senate in 1976, the mayoralty in 1977, and the 18th district House seat in 1978. The 20th district was won by Theodore Weiss. At 34 he had been elected as a reformer to the New York City Council, and he served there 15 years, trying for Congress twice, in 1966 and 1968. His position was strong enough on the West Side that he had no opposition whatever in the primary in 1976, and of course he had no trouble at all winning the general election. Weiss has the sort of liberal record one would predict for a member with his background, including 100% rating from the ADA. He serves on the Education and Labor and Government Operations Committees.

When Ryan first won election to the House, the Upper West Side had three congressional districts; today it has one, and that one is at least possibly threatened with extinction by redistricting. Most likely it will survive; its population held about steady in the 1970s and it will be changed only if its territory is used extensively to increase the size of minority-dominated districts like the 20th and 21st.

Census Data   Pop. (1980 final) 456,195, down 3% in 1970s. Median family income, 1970, $9,743, 102% of U.S.

The Voters

Employment profile 1970 White collar, 64%. Blue collar, 22%. Service, 14%. Farm, –%.
Ethnic groups Black 1980, 17%. Hispanic 1980, 36%. Asian 1980, 3%. Total foreign stock 1970, 52%. USSR, 6%; Germany, 5%; Ireland, 4%; Poland, 3%; Austria, Italy, UK, Greece, 2% each; Hungary, 1%.

Presidential Vote

1980	Reagan (R)	32,400	(25%)
	Carter (D)	80,488	(63%)
	Anderson (I)	10,921	(9%)
1976	Ford (R)	32,250	(23%)
	Carter (D)	105,995	(77%)

Rep. Theodore S. (Ted) **Weiss** (D) Elected 1976; b. Sept. 17, 1927, Gava, Hungary; home, New York City; Syracuse U., B.A. 1951, LL.B. 1952.

Career Army, 1946–47; Practicing atty., 1953–76; Asst. Dist. Atty., N.Y. Co., 1955–59; N.Y.C. Cncl., 1961–77; Candidate for Dem. nomination for U.S. House of Reps., 1966, 1968.

Offices 132 CHOB, 202-225-5635. Also 720 Columbus Ave., New York 10025, 212-850-1500.

Committees *Education and Labor* (12th). Subcommittees: Employment Opportunities; Labor–Management Relations; Post-secondary Education.

Government Operations (15th). Subcommittees: Government Activities and Transportation; Government Information and Individual Rights.

Group Ratings

	ADA	COPE	PC	LCV	CFA	RPN	NAB	NSI	NTU	ACA	ACU
1980	100	89	87	87	93	—	0	0	24	22	11
1979	100	100	88	95	96	—	—	—	27	12	8
1978	100	90	95	90	96	36	0	0	45	8	8

Key Votes

1) Draft Registn $	AGN	6) Fair Hsg DOJ Enfrc	FOR	11) Cut Socl Incr Dfns $	AGN
2) Ban $ to Nicrgua	AGN	7) Lim PAC Contrbtns	FOR	12) Hosptl Cost Controls	FOR
3) Dlay MX Missile	FOR	8) Cap on Food Stmp $	AGN	13) Gasln Ctrls & Allctns	FOR
4) Nuclr Mortorium	FOR	9) New US Dep Edcatn	AGN	14) Lim Wndfll Prof Tax	AGN
5) Alaska Lands Bill	FOR	10) Cut OSHA $	AGN	15) Chryslr Loan Grntee	FOR

Election Results

1980 general	Theodore S. (Ted) Weiss (D-L) ...	86,454	(82%)	($32,092)
	James E. Greene (R)	15,350	(15%)	($0)
1980 primary	Theodore S. Weiss (D-L), unopp			
1978 general	Theodore S. (Ted) Weiss (D-L) ...	64,365	(85%)	($37,859)
	Harry Torczyner (R)	11,661	(15%)	($21,463)

TWENTY-FIRST DISTRICT

The 21st congressional district of New York is the South Bronx, geographically about a mile from Manhattan's posh Upper East Side, but in daily life a world apart. The South Bronx has become known as the nation's quintessential slum. Presidential candidates trudge through here every four years, their mouths agape as they look at destroyed buildings and mouth the inevitable comparisons with Berlin after the war. Candidates for president, governor, senator, and mayor all promise to do something for the South Bronx; but nothing much gets done. Meanwhile, the people of the South Bronx vote with their feet. During the 1970s, the South Bronx lost half its population—the biggest population loss of any congressional district in the country. Social scientists and politicians admonish the rest of the nation that there are South Bronxes all over, waiting to happen. Yet the history of the South Bronx suggests that this is a peculiar New York situation, and that it may not represent as much human misery as at first appears.

The South Bronx was settled in a rush. Most of its housing was built in the years between 1906 and 1917, when the newly built subways opened up the Bronx to settlement by the hundreds of thousands of immigrants who were jammed into Manhattan. By the late 1960s, most of these original Italian, Irish, and Jewish settlers were elderly; their children had long since been dispersed, and they were dying or moving out. Moving in—again in a rush—were blacks and Puerto Ricans who could not find housing in the more stable communities of Harlem or Upper Manhattan. Nearly half the people here in 1970 were under 18, many of them in large fatherless families. With no community institutions and little parental supervision, these teenagers committed hundreds of crimes every day, with relatively little risk of being caught. Arson became an increasingly common crime, committed by kids for kicks or on behalf of landlords who decided that they could never get a return on their buildings in any other way. Historically, the South Bronx was a place for New Yorkers in low-wage jobs—the low-wage economy that helped so many immigrants move upward in the years from 1906 to the 1960s. But the low-wage jobs have largely disappeared from New York City in the 1970s. Union demands, high minimum wages, and high costs of doing business generally in New York have led low-wage employers to take their businesses to the places where their most recent workers have come from, the southeastern states and Puerto Rico. The migrants who had moved to the South Bronx were left to welfare, which tends to split families. In no other part of America have so many low-wage jobs been lost so fast; and nowhere else is there a community as large that was suddenly depopulated as the South Bronx has been.

For this was not an area that showed these signs of rapid decline as late as 1970. In the 1960s the 21st district's population had declined from 480,000 to 467,000—a minimal change, although there was much neighborhood change behind the total figures. But in the 1970s the 21st district's population fell from 467,000 to 234,000. The question arises: what happened to these people? Some of them moved farther out in the Bronx or to other parts of the New York metropolitan area. But the disorganized neighborhoods of the South Bronx did not move out en masse, for the kind of social disorganization apparent there has not spread to the family-oriented neighborhoods on Bruckner Boulevard or up near Fordham University. Some of these people, we may assume, have moved upward in the social scale. Others, it seems certain, have returned to where they came from. New York's welfare payments did not keep up with inflation in the 1970s, and it must have occurred to even the most sluggish welfare recipient after a while that she might be better off back in North Carolina or Puerto Rico, where there are more jobs and the conditions of living—in more stable and settled communities—are better. Puerto Ricans, in particular, seem to have moved back to Puerto Rico. It is relatively easy, after all, to get back and forth, on midnight 747s; and Puerto Ricans in the Bronx have always retained their interest in and identification with Puerto Rican culture. Thus the San Juan newspapers have much higher circulation here than do New York's Spanish language papers. Puerto Ricans in the South Bronx have always had extremely low turnout in mainland elections; the main reason is that they retain their interest in the spirited and hotly contested politics of Puerto Rico. Almost certainly a large percentage of the 233,000 people who left the 21st district in the 1970s are back in Puerto Rico — and are happier and better off there than if they had stayed.

So the depopulation of the South Bronx may make a certain amount of sense: there is no one — or not very many people — who wants to live here anymore. Working-class Americans who make decent livings do not want to live in such close quarters where they have no community ties. The government would probably do well not to try to build housing here but to facilitate the development of sites for small industry. It is actually well located: right on main trucking lines, with access to rail spurs, and not far from the airports and port facilities.

The current congressman from the 21st is Robert Garcia, a Democrat first elected in a 1978 special election. He won the seat held for several years by Herman Badillo and was his political ally; Garcia actually lost the Democratic nomination in the special but won election as a Republican while making it clear that he would vote as a Democrat in the House. Badillo is a man with a steely ambition who ran for mayor in 1969, 1973, and 1977, and would probably run again in 1981 (he broke with Mayor Koch after serving as a deputy mayor under him) if he felt he had any chance to win. But the Puerto Rican vote base in New York seems to be contracting, not expanding; and Badillo has poor prospects. Garcia seems more interested in congressional issues. Ironically, in light of the 21st's population loss, he chairs the Census and Population Subcommittee. He is the cosponsor with Jack Kemp of a plan touted by many Republicans and some Democrats to give tax breaks to businesses that invest in jobs in certain inner-city areas; if such a plan is adopted, obviously the key will be which areas are designated.

Garcia's major political problem is redistricting. The 21st district, with its 50% population loss, is an obvious candidate for elimination, particularly considering that New York state must lose five districts altogether. The district's population would have to more than double, which would require either combining it with the Harlem-based 19th district or spreading it out farther into the Bronx, into white middle-class (and politically very conservative) neighborhoods. Neither alternative is likely to provide the kind of political base Garcia seeks. The Voting Rights Act of 1965, which applies to the Bronx because of its low turnout, seems to require that minority representation be maintained; but it does not say how that can be done when the minority citizens have either moved out into neighborhoods where they are culturally assimilated with the middle class or have left the state altogether. The answer may be to carve up Manhattan's West Side 20th district and divide it between the population-shy 19th and 21st.

Census Data   Pop. (1980 final) 233,787, down 50% in 1970s. Median family income, 1970, $5,613, 58% of U.S.

The Voters

Employment profile 1970   White collar, 37%. Blue collar, 42%. Service, 21%. Farm, -%.
Ethnic groups   Black 1980, 45%. Hispanic 1980, 54%. Total foreign stock 1970, 14%. Italy, USSR, 1% each.

Presidential Vote

1980	Reagan (R)	3,632	(8%)
	Carter (D)	38,723	(89%)
	Anderson (I)	639	(2%)
1976	Ford (R)	4,677	(9%)
	Carter (D)	45,749	(91%)

Rep. Robert Garcia (D) Elected Feb. 14, 1978; b. Jan. 9, 1933, New York City; home, Bronx; CCNY.

Career Army, Korea; Computer engineer, 1957–65; N.Y. State Assembly, 1965–67; N.Y. Senate, 1967–78.

Offices 223 CHOB, 202-225-4361. Also 840 Grand Concourse, Bronx 10451, 212-860-6200.

Committees *Banking, Finance and Urban Affairs* (20th). Subcommittees: Economic Stabilization; Financial Institutions Supervision, Regulation and Insurance; Housing and Community Development.

Post Office and Civil Service (5th). Subcommittees: Census and Population (Chairman); Investigations; Postal Personnel and Modernization.

Group Ratings

	ADA	COPE	PC	LCV	CFA	RPN	NAB	NSI	NTU	ACA	ACU
1980	72	94	77	67	79	—	0	0	16	14	8
1979	84	100	78	90	70	—	—	—	19	4	6
1978	79	83	75	87	50	40	0	0	26	5	16

Key Votes

1) Draft Registn $	AGN	6) Fair Hsg DOJ Enfrc	—	11) Cut Socl Incr Dfns $	AGN
2) Ban $ to Nicrgua	AGN	7) Lim PAC Contrbtns	—	12) Hosptl Cost Controls	FOR
3) Dlay MX Missile	—	8) Cap on Food Stmp $	AGN	13) Gasln Ctrls & Allctns	FOR
4) Nuclr Mortorium	FOR	9) New US Dep Edcatn	AGN	14) Lim Wndfll Prof Tax	AGN
5) Alaska Lands Bill	FOR	10) Cut OSHA $	AGN	15) Chryslr Loan Grntee	FOR

Election Results

1980 general	Robert Garcia (D-R-L)	32,173	(98%)	($115,310)
1980 primary	Robert Garcia (D-R-L), unopposed			
1978 general	Robert Garcia (D-R-L)	23,950	(100%)	($45,068)

TWENTY-SECOND DISTRICT

The 22d congressional district of New York runs from the Grand Concourse to Co-op City —the heart of the Bronx. Unlike Brooklyn, which has its own history as a city, the Bronx is wholly an offspring of Manhattan. It was largely vacant at the turn of the century, but within ten years the subways, which made it an easy commute from Manhattan, had been built. The Bronx quickly filled up. From 1900 to 1930 its population increased from 200,000 to 1,265,000 — higher than the 1,162,000 of today. Initial settlement followed the subway and el lines, as Jews, Italians, and Irish left the crowded tenements of Manhattan for the comparatively spacious and comfortable apartments of the Bronx. There are several large parks and two major universities (NYU and Fordham) here, but few other amenities. The Bronx has never had much white collar employment, nor for that matter all that many factory jobs either; it remains today basically a residential area.

The Grand Concourse was intended to be the showcase of the Bronx. Laid out as a broad boulevard, it was lined in the 1920s with Art Deco apartment houses that were notably more elegant than those on nearby side streets; it was the place you moved when you got that raise or your stock tip paid off. Lately the advancing slums of the South Bronx have shattered the tranquillity—and wrecked the real estate values—of the Concourse. Consequently, the elderly Jews who have been the most numerous residents of the Concourse's buildings are moving out. One place they have headed, assuming they can get in, is Co-op City—a staggeringly vast complex of towering apartment buildings, financed mainly by an offshoot of the Amalgamated Clothing Workers Union. Co-op City is unspeakably ugly, situated on a flat swamp and overlooking a couple of expressways. Like so many buildings in New York —in the posh Upper East Side, as well as out here—it is totally, almost defiantly, lacking in aesthetic merit; it is also miles past the nearest subway stop. But Co-op City has produced clean, safe, relatively inexpensive housing—although not inexpensive enough to suit its tenants, who have conducted a huge rent strike to protest the passing along of increases in the cost of maintaining Co-op City. Like so many other New Yorkers, they assume that simple justice requires that other people pay for things they want and are unwilling to pay for.

Politics and population movements like the one from the Grand Concourse to Co-op City help to explain the convoluted boundaries of the 22d district. The lines threw together in 1972 two reform Democratic congressmen, Jonathan Bingham and James Scheuer, and forced them into a primary fight. Bingham won with Scheuer taking the 11th district seat in Brooklyn and Queens two years later. Bingham has a rather odd background for a Bronx congressman. His father was a wealthy Republican senator from Connecticut; Bingham himself worked for Governor Averell Harriman in the 1950s and UN Ambassador Adlai Stevenson in the early 1960s. As a resident of the posh Riverdale section, in 1964 he challenged Congressman Charles Buckley, boss of the Bronx Democratic machine and chairman of the House Public Works Committee. Bingham won that election, but oldtimers in the House were able to keep him off his favored committee (Foreign Affairs) for several terms. But now Bingham is chairman of the International Economic Policy and Trade Subcommittee. He is regarded not only as thoughtful but as one who on occasion knows how to get a bill passed and can do so without ruffling feathers—and without taking care sometimes to see that he gets the credit he deserves.

But perhaps Bingham's most important moment in Congress came in December 1974 when he moved in the Democratic Steering Committee that all committee chairmen be voted on separately. As a result, two were unseated, and every chairman since has known that he could be ousted if he does not conduct business the way a majority of Democrats want him to. It was a move away from a system of seniority-cum-unaccountability that was indefensible intellectually and not used in any other legislative body in the world. It has done as much as anything else to change the way things are done in the House.

The 22d district did not have a huge population loss in the 1970s—Co-op City mostly made up for the losses on the Grand Concourse. There has been great neighborhood change, however: the district has gone from 18% to 31% black and from 14% to 34% Spanish in the decade. The Grand Concourse area has been largely drained of middle-class whites. That may cause problems for Bingham, and there is always the danger that this district will be eliminated by redistricting. Bingham has shown the capacity before to take on a like-minded colleague and win a hotly contested primary, and he may have to do that again in 1982 if he is thrown in with Robert Garcia of the 21st district or Peter Peyser of the 23d.

Census Data   Pop. (1980 final) 425,822, down 9% in 1970s. Median family income, 1970, $8,850, 92% of U.S.

The Voters

Employment profile 1970   White collar, 58%. Blue collar, 28%. Service, 14%. Farm, –%.
Ethnic groups   Black 1980, 31%. Hispanic 1980, 32%. Total foreign stock 1980, 46%. USSR, 9%; Ireland, Poland, 6% each; Italy, 5%; Austria, 3%; Germany, UK, 2% each; Hungary, Rumania, 1% each.

Presidential Vote

1980	Reagan (R)	28,497	(29%)
	Carter (D)	65,030	(65%)
	Anderson (I)	4,726	(5%)
1976	Ford (R)	29,723	(23%)
	Carter (D)	96,891	(77%)

Rep. Jonathan B. Bingham (D) Elected 1964; b. Apr. 24, 1914, New Haven, Conn.; home, Bronx; Yale U., B.A. 1936, LL.B. 1939.

Career Correspondent, N.Y. *Herald Tribune,* 1935–38; Practicing atty., 1940–61; Army, WWII; Special Asst. to a U.S. Asst. Secy. of State, 1945–46; Asst. Dir., Ofc. of Internatl. Security Affairs, 1951; Secy. to Gov. Averell Harriman, 1955–58; Mbr., U.S. Delegation to U.N., 1961–63; U.S. Rep., U.N. Econ. and Social Cncl., and Chf. Advisor to Amb. Adlai E. Stevenson II, 1963–64.

Offices 2262 RHOB, 202-225-4411. Also Rm. 326 Wagner Bldg., 2488 Grand Concourse, Bronx 10458, 212-933-2310.

Committees *Foreign Affairs* (6th). Subcommittees: International Economic Policy and Trade (Chairman); International Security and Scientific Affairs.

Interior and Insular Affairs (5th). Subcommittees: Energy and the Environment; Public Lands and National Parks.

Group Ratings

	ADA	COPE	PC	LCV	CFA	RPN	NAB	NSI	NTU	ACA	ACU
1980	94	89	83	85	93	—	0	0	17	22	12
1979	100	89	88	95	93	—	—	—	19	4	8
1978	80	83	78	80	68	50	0	20	24	4	6

Key Votes

1) Draft Registn $	AGN	6) Fair Hsg DOJ Enfrc	FOR	11) Cut Socl Incr Dfns $	AGN
2) Ban $ to Nicrgua	AGN	7) Lim PAC Contrbtns	FOR	12) Hosptl Cost Controls	FOR
3) Dlay MX Missile	FOR	8) Cap on Food Stmp $	AGN	13) Gasln Ctrls & Allctns	FOR
4) Nuclr Mortorium	FOR	9) New US Dep Edcatn	AGN	14) Lim Wndfll Prof Tax	AGN
5) Alaska Lands Bill	FOR	10) Cut OSHA $	AGN	15) Chryslr Loan Grntee	FOR

Election Results

1980 general	Jonathan B. Bingham (D-L)......	66,301	(84%)	($6,722)
	Robert Black (R)..............	9,943	(13%)	($0)
198$ primary	Jonathan Bingham (D-L), unopp.			
1978 general	Jonathan B. Bingham (D-L)......	58,727	(84%)	($6,040)
	Anthony J. Geidel, Jr. (R-C)	11,110	(16%)	

TWENTY-THIRD DISTRICT

The line that separates the Bronx from Westchester County marks the end of Democratic New York City and, traditionally, the beginning of the Republican suburbs and upstate. Even in these days of ticket-splitting there is still a major contrast here, and there is no better place to look at it than in the 23d congressional district of New York, one-third of which is in the northern Bronx and two-thirds in Westchester.

The Bronx portion of the district, a large middle-class residential area, is totally cut off from the rest of the 23d by Van Cortlandt Park. Most of the people here are of Italian descent; as in all of New York City, they are more than normally likely to hold government jobs. The Democratic allegiance of this part of the Bronx springs from an immigrant heritage — the days when the Tammany block captain brought around enough coal for the rest of the winter in return for a couple of votes. The Republicans made some gains here in the 1960s, as fear of crime and dislike of the Manhattan-based administration of John Lindsay increased. But in the middle 1970s there was a return to a kind of machine Democratic allegiance: people here vote for the Democrats because their party tends to favor aid to New York City — aid that will keep their salaries and fringe benefits intact without increasing their taxes.

The tradition in the Westchester portion of the 23d is quite different. This includes most of Yonkers, the towns of Greenburgh and Mount Pleasant, and the suburbs along the Hudson River where Washington Irving once lived. With a few exceptions, Republicans have been in control here for as long as anyone can remember; when Democrat Alfred Del Bello was elected county executive in 1973, it was the first time in the nearly fifty years the office had existed that it had not been won by a Republican. People here may have ethnic and sociological backgrounds similar to those of people in the middle-class parts of the Bronx; but they think of themselves as suburbanites, protecting their property from the taxing demands of the masses in the city. Their chosen instrument in that has always been the Republican Party, and continues to be, in state politics. In federal elections, however, the suburbanites are quite happy to see money from people in other states go to New York City, and so they have voted somewhat more Democratic than usual in 1976 and 1978.

The 23d district was established within its present boundaries for the 1972 election. It has since had a series of contests that read like an intricate call for a square dance. Democrat Richard Ottinger, elected to this seat when it was entirely in Westchester in 1964, 1966, and 1968, and defeated in the 1970 Senate race, ran again in 1972 and lost to Republican Peter Peyser. Peyser won again in 1974, while Ottinger was winning the next-door 24th district. Peyser ran for the Senate in 1976, losing the Republican primary to James Buckley, and the 23d district was won by Republican Bruce Caputo. A brainy and ambitious young man, Caputo was the most aggressive member of the House Ethics Committee and constantly complained that Democrats weren't trying to get to the bottom of the Koreagate scandal; he was predictably unpopular with his colleagues and decided to run for lieutenant governor in 1978. When Perry Duryea lost the race, so did Caputo. In the 23d, Peyser was running again, this time as a Democrat, and by a narrow margin he defeated Mayor Angelo Martinelli of Yonkers.

Peyser, as his political history suggests, is something of a maverick, with a brash personality and an unpredictable voting record. Despite his Republican heritage, or perhaps because of his switch in parties, he is one of the more fervent defenders on the Education and Labor Committee of some of the Democratic social programs. In 1981 he also picked up seats on

Government Operations and Post Office and Civil Service, the latter a body that, because of its subject matter, has had a hard time attracting members.

Peyser won in 1970 and 1980 with the aid of large margins (70% in 1980) in the Bronx; he carried the Westchester portion most recently by only 52%–48%. That means that redistricting is vital for him. And that may be a little tricky, given the geographical position of Westchester County. Long Island and New York City between them have 18.71 congressional districts, which means that there will be a large segment of the Bronx left over when redistricting is done — perhaps too large for Peyser's comfort. It could form the nucleus of a Bronx–Westchester district which would choose a Bronx Democrat in the primary. The alternative is to have a number of Bronx–Westchester districts. If Peyser can avoid a primary with another incumbent he will have an improved chance to win the general election; but if the district gets too Democratic, this Democrat may be in trouble.

Census Data   Pop. (1980 final) 446,713, down 5% in 1970s. Median family income, 1970, $12,693, 132% of U.S.

The Voters

Employment profile 1970   White collar, 62%. Blue collar, 26%. Service, 12%. Farm, –%.
Ethnic groups   Black 1980, 21%. Hispanic 1980, 9%. Asian 1980, 2%. Total foreign stock 1970, 42%. Italy, 13%; Ireland, 4%; USSR, Germany, Poland, 3% each; UK, Austria, 2% each; Canada, 1%.

Presidential Vote

1980	Reagan (R)	86,064	(51%)
	Carter (D)	69,720	(41%)
	Anderson (I)	11,381	(7%)
1976	Ford (R)	82,078	(48%)
	Carter (D)	90,623	(52%)

Rep. Peter A. Peyser (D) Elected 1978; b. Sept. 7, 1921, Cedarhurst; home, Irvington; Colgate U., B.A. 1943.

Career   Army, WWII; Life insurance agent; Mgr., Peter A. Peyser Agency, Mutual of N.Y., 1961–70; Mayor of Irvington, 1963–70; U.S. House of Reps., 1971–77; Candidate for Rep. nomination for U.S. Senate, 1976.

Offices   301 CHOB, 202-225-5536. Also 30 S. Broadway, Yonkers 10701, 914-968-8200.

Committees   *Education and Labor* (15th). Subcommittees: Labor–Management Relations; Postsecondary Education.

Government Operations (20th). Subcommittees: Commerce, Consumer, and Monetary Affairs; Government Activities and Transportation.

Post Office and Civil Service (14th). Subcommittees: Census and Population; Compensation and Employee Benefits; Investigations.

Group Ratings

	ADA	COPE	PC	LCV	CFA	RPN	NAB	NSI	NTU	ACA	ACU
1980	94	89	70	69	86	—	0	22	11	14	5
1979	79	95	68	74	74	—	—	—	17	12	8

Key Votes

1) Draft Registn $	AGN	6) Fair Hsg DOJ Enfrc	FOR	11) Cut Socl Incr Dfns $	AGN
2) Ban $ to Nicrgua	AGN	7) Lim PAC Contrbtns	FOR	12) Hosptl Cost Controls	FOR
3) Dlay MX Missile	FOR	8) Cap on Food Stmp $	AGN	13) Gasln Ctrls & Allctns	FOR
4) Nuclr Mortorium	FOR	9) New US Dep Edcatn	AGN	14) Lim Wndfll Prof Tax	AGN
5) Alaska Lands Bill	FOR	10) Cut OSHA $	AGN	15) Chryslr Loan Grntee	FOR

Election Results

1980 general	Peter A. Peyser (D).............	85,749	(56%)	($70,740)
	Andrew A. Albanese (R-C)	66,771	(44%)	($44,031)
1980 primary	Peter A. Peyser (D), unopposed			
1978 general	Peter A. Peyser (D).............	66,354	(52%)	($105,552)
	Angelo A. Martinelli (R-C)	59,455	(46%)	($141,229)

TWENTY-FOURTH DISTRICT

The conventional wisdom has it that New York's Westchester County is *the* suburb for the wealthy: not only the super-rich such as the Rockefellers of Pocantico Hills, but also the ordinary rich, the people who own those large, comfortable houses in Scarsdale and White Plains, with their gently sloping lawns shaded by towering trees; or the glassy contemporary houses in the woodsier hills of Pound Ridge, Armonk, and Briarcliff Manor. All of these places are in New York's 24th congressional district, and the only seat entirely within Westchester County. But the conventional image of Westchester and the 24th is not entirely accurate. Plenty of rich people live here—in 1970 the constituency ranked 18th in median income of the nation's 435 congressional districts. But taken as whole, the 24th is not uniformly wealthy. More typical of Westchester than WASPy Bedford Village or Jewish Scarsdale are the predominantly Italian–American, middle-income neighborhoods of Mount Vernon or Port Chester.

Westchester County and the 24th district are one of the ancestral homes of liberal establishment Republicanism. Upper-income voters have set the tone, if they have not provided most of the votes, of Westchester Republican politics; and here you would have found many of the major backers of Thomas E. Dewey, Dwight D. Eisenhower, and Nelson Rockefeller. In the Nixon years upper-income voters began moving to the left—Scarsdale, for example, went for Humphrey in 1968 and nearly for McGovern in 1972—but they were more than counterbalanced numerically by the middle-income voters moving toward the Nixon version of the politics of law and order. After Watergate and the emergence of the issue of aid to New York City, these ordinary residents of the 24th were moving somewhat toward the Democrats, even though some of the richer residents here found the political style of Jimmy Carter unpalatable.

The passage of the 24th district from a preserve of liberal Republicanism to a battleground between liberal Democrats and conservative Republicans is illustrated by the congressional races of the 1970s. From 1962 the district was represented by Ogden Reid: as heir to the old *New York Herald Tribune* fortune, as Eisenhower's Ambassador to Israel, and as a Nelson Rockefeller appointee, he was the personification of liberal Republican politics. In Congress Reid's voting record was really more liberal than Republican; his main Republican activity was supporting Rockefeller every time he ran for president.

At general election time Reid's brand of Republicanism made him unbeatable, but as time went on it caused him increasing problems in the primary. In 1970 an unknown conservative challenger got 46% against him—evidence, if any was needed, that conservatively inclined Republican primary voters were tired of electing someone who stood against them on most major issues. Reid was souring on Republicans, too, and in 1972 he became a Democrat and survived a Republican challenge financed mainly by his old patron, Nelson Rockefeller. In 1974 Reid ran for governor, as he had wanted to for years; he bowed out early, but too late to run for Congress again.

The congressman from the 24th is a man with a similar background, including a few terms in Congress and a yen for statewide office: Richard Ottinger, former (1965–71) Congressman from the other Westchester district (23d), and Democratic nominee for the U.S. Senate in 1970. Ottinger too comes from a wealthy family with a Republican background (his uncle nearly beat Franklin Roosevelt for governor in 1928), but Ottinger has always run as a Democrat. He was one of the earliest environmentalists in Congress and is an important one today; he has also been a leading opponent of the decontrol of oil and natural gas. Ottinger serves on the Energy and Commerce Committee, perhaps the key House committee on questions of economic regulation in recent years. It handles oil and gas price controls, clean air legislation, health issues, and such regulated industries as broadcasting, telecommunications, airlines, railroads, and trucking. Ottinger is chairman of the Energy Conservation and Power Subcommittee, which has jurisdiction over conservation, solar energy, and nuclear power. These are all areas where Ottinger and a majority or a large minority of his subcommittee is likely to have disputes with the Reagan Administration. The administration's initial budget cut federal conservation and solar energy programs, which Ottinger strongly favors; the Reaganites are strong proponents of nuclear power, of which Ottinger is suspicious. Ottinger is thus in an excellent position to present an alternative on these energy policies to the administration's plan, although he will have close calls getting majorities in the subcommittee, the full committee, and on the floor of the House.

The switch toward the Democrats in Westchester County has not been strong enough to guarantee Ottinger a safe seat, and he has been held below 55% when Republicans have strongly contested this seat. In 1980, the local Republican organization could not come up with a candidate and Ottinger's opponent, a chiropractor and county legislator, had little backing. This produced, against the national trend, the largest Ottinger margin in recent years—59%–40%. For 1982 redistricting will obviously be important. The inclusion of some Democratic areas in the Bronx in this district would help Ottinger somewhat, but whether the Republican Senate would concur with the Democratic Assembly in extending him the favor is unclear. Ottinger has represented virtually all of Westchester at one time or another and has a good chance to win regardless of how the lines are drawn.

Census Data   Pop. (1980 final) 441,639, down 6% in 1970s. Median family income, 1970, $13,577, 141% of U.S.

The Voters

 Employment profile 1970   White collar, 63%. Blue collar, 24%. Service, 13%. Farm, –%.
 Ethnic groups   Black 1980, 16%. Hispanic 1980, 6%. Asian 1980, 2%. Total foreign stock 1970, 39%. Italy, 13%; USSR, Germany, Ireland, UK, 3% each; Poland, 2%; Austria, Canada, 1% each.

Presidential Vote

1980	Reagan (R)	93,842	(52%)
	Carter (D)	68,665	(38%)
	Anderson (I)	15,004	(8%)
1976	Ford (R)	101,587	(53%)
	Carter (D)	90,227	(47%)

Rep. Richard L. Ottinger (D) Elected 1974; b. Jan. 27, 1929, New York City; home, Pleasantville; Cornell U., B.A. 1950, Harvard U., LL.B. 1953, Internatl. Law Study, Georgetown U., 1960–61.

Career Practicing atty., 1955–60, 1972–74; Internatl. corp. contract mgr., 1960–61; Cofounder, 2d Staff Mbr. and Dir, Program for the West Coast of South America, Peace Corps, 1961–64; U.S. House of Reps., 1965–71; Dem. nominee for U.S. Senate, 1970; Organizer, Grassroots Action, Inc., nonprofit consumer and environmental assistance org., 1971–72.

Offices 2241 RHOB, 202-225-6506. Also 10 Fiske Pl., Mt. Vernon 10550, 914-699-2866.

Committees *Energy and Commerce* (3d). Subcommittee: Energy Conservation and Power (Chairman).

Science and Technology (5th). Subcommittees: Energy Development and Applications; Energy Research and Production.

Group Ratings

	ADA	COPE	PC	LCV	CFA	RPN	NAB	NSI	NTU	ACA	ACU
1980	94	95	77	84	93	—	0	0	18	13	11
1979	100	90	85	100	93	—	—	—	20	0	0
1978	80	89	90	92	91	36	0	0	27	4	8

Key Votes

1) Draft Registn $	AGN	6) Fair Hsg DOJ Enfrc	FOR	11) Cut Socl Incr Dfns $	AGN
2) Ban $ to Nicrgua	AGN	7) Lim PAC Contrbtns	FOR	12) Hosptl Cost Controls	FOR
3) Dlay MX Missile	FOR	8) Cap on Food Stmp $	AGN	13) Gasln Ctrls & Allctns	FOR
4) Nuclr Mortorium	FOR	9) New US Dep Edcatn	FOR	14) Lim Wndfll Prof Tax	AGN
5) Alaska Lands Bill	FOR	10) Cut OSHA $	AGN	15) Chryslr Loan Grntee	FOR

Election Results

1980 general	Richard L. Ottinger (D)	100,182	(59%)	($69,281)
	Joseph W. Christiana (R-C-RTL) .	66,689	(40%)	($32,179)
1980 primary	Richard L. Ottinger (D), unopposed			
1978 general	Richard L. Ottinger (D)	75,397	(56%)	($85,769)
	Michael R. Edelman (R)	57,451	(43%)	($64,314)

TWENTY-FIFTH DISTRICT

The 25th congressional district of New York occupies the heart of the Hudson River valley, extending from the Bear Mountain Bridge, some 30 miles north of Manhattan, to a point most of the way to Albany. Like most rivers in this country, the Hudson is badly polluted, but its scenery retains much of the grandeur it had in the early 19th century when it inspired the painters whose school bears its name. In colonial days, and even after independence, this valley was a place that nurtured one of the few feudal systems in the United States. The Dutch who originally colonized the Hudson gave huge land grants to the patroon families whose names are still well known: Schuyler, van Rensselaer, van Cortlandt, Roosevelt.

Since the middle 19th century, the Hudson Valley has been Republican politically, and in the last few years that preference has been strengthened by the arrival of conservative-minded, middle-class people from the New York area, who left the city and its close-in suburbs in disgust and anger. Franklin Roosevelt won an upset victory in a state Senate race in the Democratic year of 1910, but during the 1930s and 1940s he was never able to carry his home area. Even more irritating to FDR, the Hudson Valley persisted in reelecting Congressman Hamilton Fish, an isolationist who hated Roosevelt bitterly and whose hatred was returned in kind. The Fish family was perhaps more socially prominent than the Roosevelts; Hamilton Fishes had been representing the Hudson Valley in Congress since 1842, and an earlier Hamilton Fish had been Secretary of State under Grant. Franklin Roosevelt had the pleasure of seeing the Hamilton Fish of his day finally defeated, in the 1944 election.

The Fish dynasty is again in political control of the Hudson Valley congressional district. The present Hamilton Fish won a tough Republican primary in 1968 — one opponent was Dutchess County assistant DA, G. Gordon Liddy, Jr. — and beat a vigorous and well-financed Democrat in the general election. Unlike his father, Congressman Fish has shown no inclination to roll back the New Deal, although he did share with his father a skepticism about American military involvement in Indochina. Fish has a voting record that works out to about 50% according to most rating groups, and he has proved to be extremely popular in elections. His greatest exposure came in 1974, when he served on the House Judiciary Committee and voted to impeach Richard Nixon — a position his father, nearly 90, publicly opposed.

Fish is poised now near positions of legislative power. He is nearing the ranking minority member positions on the Judiciary and Science Committees, bodies that do not make much news but must deal with problems that could have vast long-term impact on society. Fish is the ranking Republican on the subcommittee that handles one such issue, immigration. Like other members concerned with this issue, he seems torn between trying to control and limit immigration on the one hand and avoiding some of the means necessary to do that (e.g., national identity cards) on the other.

The 25th district may be changed somewhat by redistricting; whatever happens to its boundaries, however, Fish will almost certainly not be hurt.

Census Data   Pop. (1980 final) 524,528, up 12% in 1970s. Median family income, 1970, $11,885, 124% of U.S.

The Voters

Employment profile 1970   White collar, 56%. Blue collar, 30%. Service, 13%. Farm, 1%.
Ethnic groups   Black 1980, 5%. Hispanic 1980, 2%. Asian 1980, 1%. Total foreign stock 1970, 25%. Italy, 6%; Germany, 4%; UK, Ireland, 2% each; Canada, Poland, USSR, 1% each.

Presidential Vote

1980	Reagan (R)	123,585	(58%)
	Carter (D)	65,194	(31%)
	Anderson (I)	19,108	(9%)
1976	Ford (R)	118,585	(58%)
	Carter (D)	86,387	(42%)

Rep. Hamilton Fish, Jr. (R) Elected 1968; b. June 3, 1926, Washington, D.C.; home, Millbrook; Harvard U., A.B. 1949, NYU, LL.B. 1957.

Career Navy, WWII; Practicing atty.; Vice Consul, U.S. Foreign Svc., Ireland, 1951–53; Counsel, N.Y. State Assembly Judiciary Comm., 1961; Dutchess Co. Civil Defense Dir., 1967–68.

Offices 2227 RHOB, 202-225-5441. Also 82 Washington St., Poughkeepsie 12601, 914-452-4220.

Committees *Judiciary* (3d). Subcommittees: Crime; Immigration, Refugees, and International Law.

Science and Technology (3d). Subcommittee: Energy Development and Applications.

Group Ratings

	ADA	COPE	PC	LCV	CFA	RPN	NAB	NSI	NTU	ACA	ACU
1980	61	41	47	70	50	—	45	67	34	52	47
1979	37	53	35	72	26	—	—	—	27	48	49
1978	30	35	35	67	23	75	64	89	18	58	67

Key Votes

1) Draft Registn $	AGN	6) Fair Hsg DOJ Enfrc	FOR	11) Cut Socl Incr Dfns $	AGN
2) Ban $ to Nicrgua	FOR	7) Lim PAC Contrbtns	FOR	12) Hosptl Cost Controls	AGN
3) Dlay MX Missile	AGN	8) Cap on Food Stmp $	AGN	13) Gasln Ctrls & Allctns	AGN
4) Nuclr Mortorium	FOR	9) New US Dep Edcatn	FOR	14) Lim Wndfll Prof Tax	FOR
5) Alaska Lands Bill	FOR	10) Cut OSHA $		AGN	15) Chryslr Loan Grntee	FOR

Election Results

1980 general	Hamilton Fish, Jr. (R-C)	158,936	(81%)	($91,455)
	Gunars M. Ozols (D)	37,369	(19%)	($0)
1980 primary	Hamilton Fish, Jr. (R), unopposed			
1978 general	Hamilton Fish, Jr. (R)	114,641	(78%)	($82,983)
	Gunars M. Ozols (D)	31,213	(21%)	

TWENTY-SIXTH DISTRICT

The 26th congressional district of New York is just at the margin between the New York City suburbs and the vast expanse of Upstate New York. Fast-growing Rockland County, at the southern end of the district, is definitely within the city's orbit. Although it usually goes Republican, Rockland has a Democratic registration edge and a large Jewish population; many of the county's residents work in the city and commute across the George Washington or Tappan Zee Bridges. North of Rockland and separated from it by a mountain ridge is Orange County, once a largely rural area, with one small stagnant city on the Hudson, Newburgh. In recent years Orange County has been experiencing explosive growth, much of it from an exodus of New York City policemen, firemen, and civil servants; they talk of wanting to protect their children from contact with the horrors of the city even as they congratulate themselves quietly for dealing with them.

By long-standing tradition, Orange County has been Republican; and until 1974, the new migrants here were strongly Republican also. But as throughout the New York metropolitan area, the Watergate affair and the crisis over aid to New York City seem to have brought ancestral Democrats back to their party and led them to forget their conservative leanings of the early 1970s. The one-time Republican stronghold of Orange County nearly went for Hugh Carey in 1974 and 1978 and for Jimmy Carter in 1976. In 1980 the pendulum swung again, and Orange County delivered a hefty 57%–33% margin for Ronald Reagan.

The 26th district has been represented since 1972 by Benjamin Gilman, a Republican who seems to span the differences between the two portions of the district. Gilman is Jewish like so many Rockland residents, but he is actually from Orange County himself and served that area in the New York Assembly. He is a Republican, but his voting record has often been rated somewhat higher by Democratic- than Republican-oriented rating groups. He does not receive the Conservative Party endorsement, but in two of the last three elections the Conservatives have not run a candidate against him. Gilman serves on the Foreign Affairs Committee, where he is, among other things, a strong supporter of Israel and ranking minority member of the subcommittee on Latin America. He has been reelected easily and redistricting is unlikely to pose a problem for him. The 26th currently has the second highest population of any New York district and, unless Rockland is joined to one of the Westchester districts (which has never happened in New York history), Gilman's district will just be shorn of a few of its fringe areas on the north.

Census Data　Pop. (1980 final) 541,783, up 16% in 1970s. Median family income, 1970, $11,632, 121% of U.S.

The Voters

Employment profile 1970　White collar, 53%. Blue collar, 32%. Service, 14%. Farm, 1%.
Ethnic groups　Black 1980, 6%. Hispanic 1980, 5%. Asian 1980, 1%. Total foreign stock 1970, 28%. Italy, 6%; Germany, USSR, Ireland, 3% each; Poland, UK, 2% each; Austria, Canada, 1% each.

Presidential Vote

1980	Reagan (R)	115,086	(56%)
	Carter (D)	67,593	(33%)
	Anderson (I)	16,898	(8%)
1976	Ford (R)	106,176	(53%)
	Carter (D)	92,098	(46%)

Rep. Benjamin A. Gilman (R) Elected 1972; b. Dec. 6, 1922, Poughkeepsie; home, Middletown; U. of Penn., B.S. 1946, N.Y. Law Sch., LL.B. 1950.

Career　Army Air Corps, WWII; Asst. Atty. Gen. of N.Y. State, 1953; Practicing atty., 1955–72; Atty., N.Y. State Temp. Comm. on the Courts, 1956–57; N.Y. State Assembly, 1967–72.

Offices　2160 RHOB, 202-225-3776. Also P.O. Bldg., 217 Liberty St., Newburgh 12550, 914-565-6400.

Committees　*Foreign Affairs* (5th). Subcommittees: Inter-American Affairs; International Economic Policy and Trade.

Post Office and Civil Service (3d). Subcommittees: Human Resources; Postal Personnel and Modernization.

Select Committee on Narcotics Abuse and Control (3d).

Group Ratings

	ADA	COPE	PC	LCV	CFA	RPN	NAB	NSI	NTU	ACA	ACU
1980	61	83	57	49	71	—	42	78	24	46	63
1979	53	70	68	74	67	—	—	—	26	46	38
1978	55	75	55	67	68	45	18	90	12	38	43

Key Votes

1) Draft Registn $	AGN	6) Fair Hsg DOJ Enfrc	FOR	11) Cut Socl Incr Dfns $	AGN
2) Ban $ to Nicrgua	FOR	7) Lim PAC Contrbtns	FOR	12) Hosptl Cost Controls	FOR
3) Dlay MX Missile	AGN	8) Cap on Food Stmp $	AGN	13) Gasln Ctrls & Allctns	FOR
4) Nuclr Mortorium	FOR	9) New US Dep Edcatn	AGN	14) Lim Wndfll Prof Tax	AGN
5) Alaska Lands Bill	FOR	10) Cut OSHA $	AGN	15) Chryslr Loan Grntee	FOR

Election Results

1980 general	Benjamin A. Gilman (R)	137,159	(74%)	($120,100)
	Eugene R. Victor (D-L)	37,475	(20%)	($0)
	Edmond W. Farrell (RTL)	8,766	(5%)	($0)
1980 primary	Benjamin A. Gilman (R), unopposed			
1978 general	Benjamin A. Gilman (R)	87,059	(62%)	($92,014)
	Charles E. Holbrook (D-L)	41,870	(30%)	($12,588)
	William R. Schaffer, Jr. (C)	10,708	(8%)	

TWENTY-SEVENTH DISTRICT

New York's 27th congressional district extends along the state's southern border from the Catskills to the Southern Tier. The Catskills are famous for such huge Borscht Belt hotels as Grossinger's and the Concord, for Dutch-descended Rip van Winkle, and for the fashionable little town of Woodstock and the rock festival named after it (which actually took place 50 miles away). The low-lying Catskills occupy most of the eastern half of the 27th district; to the west the mountains subside into the Appalachian plateau. There begins the row of counties along New York's boundary with Pennsylvania known as the Southern Tier. Here is Binghamton, an old manufacturing town with new IBM plants nearby, and Ithaca, the home of Cornell University.

With the exception of Sullivan County in the Borscht Belt — one of three counties in the United States where Jews are the largest religious group — most of the 27th is ancestral Republican territory. It did not move as sharply to the right as parts of the New York metropolitan area during the Nixon years, so for a while it was not much more Republican than the state as a whole. Then in 1974 it did not shift back to the Democrats as did the ethnic middle-class parts of the New York area. But it did come out of the Watergate years willing enough to vote Democratic to elect — for the first time since 1912 — a Democratic congressman.

The new congressman is Matthew McHugh, who had been district attorney in Tompkins County, which includes Ithaca. His tenure covered some of the student riot times at Cornell, where black students once marched around with rifles; and he did a good enough job to win a large local following. McHugh started off on the Agriculture and Interior Committees and won Edward Koch's place on Appropriations when Koch was elected mayor of New York City. McHugh won reelection with a stunning 67% in 1976, but the district is still Republican enough that a young, self-financed challenger was able to hold him to 56% in 1978 and 55% in 1980.

McHugh's problems for 1982 will include redistricting. It is hard to predict just how the jigsaw puzzle of Upstate New York will be carved up, but it is clear that Upstate will lose one district and that the boundaries of almost all the rest will be changed substantially. One possibility is that the 27th will be shifted eastward, toward the Hudson. This would give McHugh some unfamiliar territory that usually goes Republican and might take away from him his home base of Ithaca, which he carried 2–1 in 1980 and is his strongest area in the district. Another possibility is that he will be forced to run against Republican incumbent Gary Lee. In these circumstances it is likely that Republicans will try hard for this district again, even though they fell short the last two times.

In Washington, McHugh, unlike many other junior members, concentrates on problems with broad national implications rather than issues that can give him quick points in his district. He is one of the highest-ranking Democrats on the Appropriations subcommittee that handles foreign aid programs and also serves on the Agricultural Appropriations subcommittee, where he is an important supporter of the food stamp program.

Census Data   Pop. (1980 final) 490,810, up 5% in 1970s. Median family income, 1970, $9,904, 103% of U.S.

The Voters

Employment profile 1970   White collar, 51%. Blue collar, 32%. Service, 14%. Farm, 3%.
Ethnic groups   Black 1980, 3%. Hispanic 1980, 2%. Asian 1980, 1%. Total foreign stock 1970, 19%. Italy, 3%; Germany, UK, Poland, Czechoslovakia, 2% each; USSR, Austria, Canada, 1% each.

Presidential Vote

1980	Reagan (R)	95,553	(48%)
	Carter (D)	75,875	(38%)
	Anderson (I)	21,960	(11%)
1976	Ford (R)	108,821	(55%)
	Carter (D)	88,806	(45%)

Rep. Matthew F. McHugh (D) Elected 1974; b. Dec. 6, 1938, Philadelphia, Pa.; home, Ithaca; Mt. St. Mary's Col., Emmitsburg, Md., B.S. 1960, Villanova U., J.D. 1963.

Career   Practicing atty., 1964–74; Ithaca City Prosecutor, 1968; Tompkins Co. Dist. Atty., 1969–72.

Offices   306 CHOB, 202-225-6335. Also 201 Fed. Bldg., Binghamton 13902, 607-723-4425.

Committee   *Appropriations* (21st). Subcommittees: Agriculture, Rural Development and Related Agencies; Foreign Operations.

Group Ratings

	ADA	COPE	PC	LCV	CFA	RPN	NAB	NSI	NTU	ACA	ACU
1980	83	72	73	82	71	—	0	10	16	21	5
1979	89	90	75	79	78	—	—	—	22	4	11
1978	75	80	75	83	77	45	8	20	24	15	8

Key Votes

1) Draft Registn $	AGN	6) Fair Hsg DOJ Enfrc	FOR	11) Cut Socl Incr Dfns $	AGN
2) Ban $ to Nicrgua	AGN	7) Lim PAC Contrbtns	FOR	12) Hosptl Cost Controls	FOR
3) Dlay MX Missile	FOR	8) Cap on Food Stmp $	AGN	13) Gasln Ctrls & Allctns	—
4) Nuclr Mortorium	FOR	9) New US Dep Edcatn	AGN	14) Lim Wndfll Prof Tax	AGN
5) Alaska Lands Bill	FOR	10) Cut OSHA $	AGN	15) Chryslr Loan Grntee	FOR

Election Results

1980 general	Matthew F. McHugh (D)	103,863	(55%)	($288,061)
	Neil Tyler Wallace (R-C)	83,096	(44%)	($199,966)
1980 primary	Matthew F. McHugh (D), unopp.			
1978 general	Matthew F. McHugh (D)	83,413	(56%)	($199,786)
	Neil Tyler Wallace (R-C)	66,177	(44%)	($139,043)

TWENTY-EIGHTH DISTRICT

The 28th congressional district of New York is the Albany–Schenectady area, where the Mohawk River flows into the Hudson. The district contains virtually all of Albany and Schenectady Counties, plus the aging carpet mill town of Amsterdam in Montgomery County. Of these places, the most interesting and politically significant is Albany, where an old-fashioned Democratic political machine still holds sway over local politics. For fifty years this machine had the same boss, Daniel O'Connell, who operated only from his house much of that time (John Kennedy went there to visit him in 1960); he died finally in 1977 at age 90. Since 1942 the city's mayor has been local aristocrat and machine stalwart Erastus Corning 2d. It remains the practice in Albany for city employees to get clearance from their Democratic ward bosses, who themselves are often blessed with no-show jobs, and there is plenty of favoritism for well-connected contractors. So the antique machine keeps control of the dwindling number of dollars generated by the sagging shopping areas and crumbling brownstone townhouses of Albany; people able to leave the city have been moving out to its more spacious—and better governed—suburbs.

For years Albany has produced the largest Democratic majorities between New York City and Buffalo. There have been exceptions. Governor Nelson Rockefeller poured more than $1 billion of bond money into building the giant Albany Mall, which kept the construction industry here busy for years, and Albany obliged by giving him a solid reelection margin in his last race in 1970. For a while Albany also had a Republican congressman, a liberal named Daniel Button who won on the retirement of a machine loyalist in 1966 and was reelected in 1968. But then redistricting put him in the same district with Democrat Samuel Stratton, who is unbeatable in these parts, and Button's tenure came to an end.

Stratton came out of Schenectady, an industrial town dominated economically by General Electric and more sympathetic than Albany to the Republican politics of GE's corporate leadership. Stratton was elected mayor of Schenectady in 1956 and was a local television news commentator as well; in the 1958 Democratic sweep he was elected to Congress. Twice the Republicans tried to redistrict him out of his seat, and twice failed; his heavy personal campaigning won him 2–1 margins over serious opponents. At one point his district extended most of the way across Upstate New York almost to Rochester; by 1970, the legislature gave him Democratic Albany and in effect conceded him victory.

Stratton has served on the Armed Services Committee since he entered Congress, and he had long been known as something of a maverick. But that was not because he differed from the committee's hawkish view of the world, but rather because of his pesky sniping at congressional sacred cows such as his fight a year ago against extending the west front of the Capitol and in favor of financial disclosure.

Stratton's major interest today is in defense matters. In his first job in public life, Stratton served before Pearl Harbor as an aide to Massachusetts Congressman Thomas Eliot, a supporter of FDR's military preparedness program. Those were the days when aid to Britain was highly controversial, when even Britain seemed likely to be conquered by Hitler, and when the draft passed the House a month before Pearl Harbor by just one vote. Roosevelt himself resorted to some underhanded tactics to aid Britain and to get the United States more involved in the fight against Hitler than most Americans wanted. Those times made a great impression on many young men in Congress then—such men as Lyndon Johnson and Henry Jackson. They seem to have made a deep impression on Samuel Stratton as well.

Stratton, like Johnson and Jackson, seems to see himself as continuing FDR's tradition and opposing today's Neville Chamberlains. He strongly backed the Vietnam war and felt this country should have made a stronger commitment there. He favored the B-1 bomber. He opposed the nomination of Paul Warnke as SALT negotiator and has been worried that the administration is giving up too much in the arms limitation talks. He favored nuclear aircraft carriers. He opposed cuts in military aid to South Korea. He has proposed unsuccessful amendments to increase the defense budget offered by the administration.

Stratton has an excellent chance of becoming Armed Services Committee chairman soon. The two ranking Democrats, Chairman Mel Price and Charles Bennett, turn 77 and 72 respectively in 1982. Stratton's ascendancy would give Armed Services an aggressive, activist leader, one who generally favors the Army when there are differences over priorities among services.

Stratton has weathered the worst that redistricting can do and is not likely to be hurt for 1982. He generally wins reelection in the Albany–Schenectady area by better than 3–1 margins.

Census Data   Pop. (1980 final) 449,019, down 4% in 1970s. Median family income, 1970, $10,764, 112% of U.S.

The Voters

Employment profile 1970   White collar, 58%. Blue collar, 29%. Service, 12%. Farm, 1%.
Ethnic groups   Black 1980, 5%. Hispanic 1980, 1%. Asian 1980, 1%. Total foreign stock 1970, 27%. Italy, 7%; Poland, 4%; Germany, 3%; Canada, UK, Ireland, 2% each; USSR, 1%.

Presidential Vote

1980	Reagan (R)	87,685	(40%)
	Carter (D)	107,364	(49%)
	Anderson (I)	22,429	(10%)
1976	Ford (R)	113,853	(51%)
	Carter (D)	107,602	(49%)

Rep. Samuel S. Stratton (D) Elected 1958; b. Sept. 27, 1916, Yonkers; home, Amsterdam; U. of Rochester, B.A. 1937, Haverford Col., M.A. 1938, Harvard U., M.A. 1940.

Career Secy. to U.S. Rep. Thomas H. Eliot of Mass., 1940–42; Navy, WWII and Korea; Dpty. Secy. Gen., Far Eastern Comm., U.S. Dept. of State, 1946–48; Radio and TV news commentator; College lecturer; Schenectady City Cncl., 1950–56, Mayor, 1956–59.

Offices 2205 RHOB, 202-225-5076. Also U.S.P.O., Jay St., Schenectady 12305, 518-374-4547.

Committee *Armed Services* (3d). Subcommittees: Investigations; Procurement and Military Nuclear Systems (Chairman).

Group Ratings

	ADA	COPE	PC	LCV	CFA	RPN	NAB	NSI	NTU	ACA	ACU
1980	17	58	27	27	38	—	64	90	27	43	28
1979	26	65	30	45	22	—	—	—	29	38	46
1978	15	50	38	51	30	36	42	100	15	44	54

Key Votes

1) Draft Registn $	FOR	6) Fair Hsg DOJ Enfrc	AGN	11) Cut Socl Incr Dfns $	FOR
2) Ban $ to Nicrgua	FOR	7) Lim PAC Contrbtns	AGN	12) Hosptl Cost Controls	FOR
3) Dlay MX Missile	—	8) Cap on Food Stmp $	AGN	13) Gasln Ctrls & Allctns	AGN
4) Nuclr Mortorium	AGN	9) New US Dep Edcatn	AGN	14) Lim Wndfll Prof Tax	AGN
5) Alaska Lands Bill	AGN	10) Cut OSHA $	AGN	15) Chryslr Loan Grntee	FOR

Election Results

1980 general	Samuel S. Stratton (D)	164,088	(78%)	($30,635)
	Frank Wicks (R)	37,504	(18%)	($0)
1980 primary	Samuel S. Stratton (D), unopposed			
1978 general	Samuel S. Stratton (D)	139,575	(76%)	($28,057)
	Paul H. Tocker (R-C)	36,017	(20%)	

TWENTY-NINTH DISTRICT

The 29th congressional district of New York, once a basically rural area, is now on its way to becoming suburban. Although the district extends from the Dutchess County border in the south to a point near Lake Champlain in the north, more than half of its residents live within 20 miles of Albany, the state capital (although Albany itself is in the 28th district). Almost directly across the Hudson from Albany is Troy, in the early 19th century a harbinger of the future as one of the first American cities with an economy based entirely on manufacturing. Troy had major horseshoe and shirt factories; it has been in economic decline for some time, but now young people are renovating some of its old brick mills and stone mansions and townhouses. To the north is Saratoga County, site of the Revolutionary War battle and home of the famous race track, but demographically more significant as the recipient of population spillover from the Albany–Schenectady–Troy metropolitan area. The 29th also includes Columbia County to the south, the home of Martin Van Buren in the 19th century and conservative-minded Dutchmen today, and of the headwaters of the Hudson and the area around Lake George and Fort Ticonderoga.

Politically, the 29th district was designed by a Republican legislature to be a Republican district. All its rural counties are Republican, and Troy's Democratic tendencies are mild enough to be outnumbered usually by the Republican votes in rural Rensselaer County. The new residents of Saratoga County may be ancestrally Democratic, but they are also affluent and wary of high taxes—and usually Republican. What is surprising about this district is that it has had close elections several times in the 1970s, and that a Democrat, Edward Pattison, was elected twice, in 1974 and 1976. In the first case he was helped by Watergate, in the second by a split between the Republican and a Conservative candidate.

The current congressman, Gerald Solomon, had both the Republican and Conservative nominations when he first ran in 1978. He attacked Pattison's liberal voting record strongly, and he may have profited from Pattison's admission that he once smoked marijuana (many congressmen have probably done so, but Pattison is the only one who has publicly admitted it). In November Solomon won with a pretty solid 54% of the vote; Pattison carried little of the district outside Rensselaer County. Solomon was reelected by a 2-1 margin in 1980. It seems unlikely that redistricting will do anything to harm him significantly.

Solomon has one of the more conservative voting records in the New York delegation and fits in well with the Republican minority. He serves on the Public Works and Veterans' Committees.

Census Data   Pop. (1980 final) 523,107, up 12% in 1970s. Median family income, 1970, $9,621, 100% of U.S.

The Voters

Employment profile 1970   White collar, 47%. Blue collar, 38%. Service, 12%. Farm, 3%.
Ethnic groups   Black 1980, 2%. Hispanic 1980, 1%. Total foreign stock 1970, 18%. Italy, Canada, 3% each; Germany, Ireland, 2% each; Poland, 1%.

Presidential Vote

1980	Reagan (R)	139,037	(55%)
	Carter (D)	85,606	(34%)
	Anderson (I)	19,770	(8%)
1976	Ford (R)	136,099	(61%)
	Carter (D)	86,951	(39%)

Rep. Gerald B. H. Solomon (R) Elected 1978; b. Aug. 14, 1930, Birmingham, Ala.; home, Glens Falls; Siena Col., St. Lawrence U.

Career   USMC, Korea; Queensbury Town Supervisor; Chmn., Warren Co. Social Svcs. Comm.; N.Y. State Assembly, 1972–78.

Offices   323 CHOB, 202-225-5614. Also 33 2d St., Troy 12180, 518-274-3121.

Committees   *Public Works and Transportation* (10th). Subcommittees: Investigations and Oversight; Public Buildings and Grounds.

Veterans' Affairs (6th). Subcommittees: Hospitals and Health Care; Oversight and Investigations.

Group Ratings

	ADA	COPE	PC	LCV	CFA	RPN	NAB	NSI	NTU	ACA	ACU
1980	11	29	30	37	14	—	92	100	60	78	82
1979	0	20	18	17	11	—	—	—	60	92	94

Key Votes

1) Draft Registn $	FOR	6) Fair Hsg DOJ Enfrc AGN	11) Cut Socl Incr Dfns $ FOR
2) Ban $ to Nicrgua	FOR	7) Lim PAC Contrbtns AGN	12) Hosptl Cost Controls —
3) Dlay MX Missile	AGN	8) Cap on Food Stmp $ FOR	13) Gasln Ctrls & Alletns FOR
4) Nuclr Mortorium	AGN	9) New US Dep Edcatn AGN	14) Lim Wndfll Prof Tax —
5) Alaska Lands Bill	AGN	10) Cut OSHA $ FOR	15) Chryslr Loan Grntee AGN

Election Results

1980 general	Gerald B. H. Solomon (R-C-RTL)	141,631	(67%)	($112,581)
	Rodger L. Hurley (D-L)	70,697	(33%)	($40,176)
1980 primary	Gerald B. H. Solomon (R), unopp.			
1978 general	Gerald B. H. Solomon (R-C)	99,518	(54%)	($167,723)
	Edward W. Pattison (D-L)	84,705	(46%)	($155,525)

THIRTIETH DISTRICT

The 30th congressional district of New York covers the northernmost reaches of New York state. It includes the counties across the St. Lawrence River from Canada and the ones at the eastern end of Lake Ontario. The large French Canadian population in Clinton and Franklin Counties, just 100 miles south of Montreal, forms the only Democratic voting bloc in the district; as one moves south and west there are fewer French and more Yankees. Here in the farm country of the St. Lawrence and in the Adirondacks, where it gets bitterly cold in the winter and not very warm in the summer, the voting preference is decidedly Republican — enough so to make the entire district Republican in most elections. Geographically, much of the 30th is taken up with the Adirondack Forest Preserve, a giant state park that the New York Constitution stipulates must remain "forever wild." This includes Lake Placid, the site of the 1980 Winter Olympics. North of the Forest Preserve is Massena, on the St. Lawrence River, which has been blessed with the administrative headquarters of the St. Lawrence Seaway. This project was supposed to give the north country an economic boost. But there are continual problems: the Seaway freezes over three months a year; its locks are too small for the large containerized ships that have become the rule in many kinds of trade; and the time it takes to negotiate the locks is longer than most shippers can afford to wait these days. So despite the Seaway the economy of this part of New York has been at best steady since the years early in the 19th century when it was settled by farmers moving west from northern New England or north from the Mohawk River, to seek their own farms even in this agriculturally marginal land.

The politics of this area has also been steady over the years — steadily Republican. Its prime political celebrity was William Wheeler, vice president under Rutherford Hayes, who left office more than 100 years ago. The 30th district does not bulk large in the affairs of New York state and has itself elected a series of Republican congressmen who have reliably conservative voting records and do not achieve much public notice. One such, Robert McEwen, retired in 1980; he was succeeded by David Martin, who appears likely to follow a similar course. The Democrats have made a number of efforts to win here, running serious campaigns against McEwen in 1974 and 1976 and against Martin in 1980. Mary Ann Krupsak, a former lieutenant governor, was the Democratic nominee, but she could manage no better than 33% of the vote. Krupsak has shown unerringly bad political judgment in recent years: in 1978 she took on Governor Hugh Carey in the primary, charging that he had not paid enough attention to her as lieutenant governor; in 1980, she moved from her old base in the Mohawk Valley to run in this district that places a high value on local ties.

Redistricting may alter the district's boundaries somewhat, but the 1970s was a decade of relatively robust growth up north — primarily because people moved year-round into what used to be vacation communities — and little surgery is needed. Martin, who serves on the Interior Committee, is likely to remain in office for a long time.

Census Data   Pop. (1980 final) 492,047, up 5% in 1970s. Median family income, 1970, $8,584, 90% of U.S.

The Voters

Employment profile 1970   White collar, 41%. Blue collar, 37%. Service, 16%. Farm, 6%.
Ethnic groups   Black 1980, 1%. Hispanic 1980, 1%. Am. Ind. 1980, 1%. Total foreign stock 1970, 15%. Canada, 7%; Italy, 2%; UK, 1%.

Presidential Vote

1980	Reagan (R)	71,290	(48%)
	Carter (D)	60,596	(41%)
	Anderson (I)	11,598	(8%)
1976	Ford (R)	104,481	(58%)
	Carter (D)	75,006	(42%)

Rep. David O'B. Martin (R) Elected 1980; b. Apr. 26, 1944, Ogdensburg; home, Canton; U. of Notre Dame, B.B.A. 1966, Albany Law Sch., J.D. 1973.

Career   USMC, 1966–70; St. Lawrence Co. Legislature, 1973–76; N.Y. State Assembly, 1976–80.

Offices   502 CHOB, 202-225-4611. Also 307 Fed. Bldg., Watertown 13601, 315-782-3150; Riverfront Ofc. Bldg., Oswego 13126, 315-342-4688; 104 Fed. Bldg., Plattsburgh 12901, 518-563-1406; and Ogdensburg Mall, Ogdensburg 13669, 315-393-0570.

Committee   *Interior and Insular Affairs* (10th). Subcommittees: Energy and the Environment; Mines and Mining.

Group Ratings and Key Votes: Newly Elected

Election Results

1980 general	David O'B. Martin (R-C)	111,008	(64%)	($244,377)
	Mary Anne Krupsak (D-L)	54,896	(32%)	($54,837)
	John R. Zagame (RTL)	7,985	(5%)	($118,624)
1980 primary	David O'B. Martin (R)	31,661	(70%)	
	John R. Zagame (R)	13,358	(30%)	
1978 general	Robert C. McEwen (R-C)	85,478	(61%)	($56,731)
	Norma A. Bartle (D-L)	55,785	(39%)	($50,692)

THIRTY-FIRST DISTRICT

The 31st congressional district of New York includes most of the Mohawk River Valley, much of the Adirondack Forest Preserve, and a couple of agricultural counties. These other areas add much to its scenic beauty, but most of the people here are concentrated within 30 miles of the Mohawk. During the Revolutionary War, this part of New York was the frontier, where American colonists fought the British and their Iroquois allies, both united in their desire to prevent American penetration of the continent. And this is where they failed as chronicled in, among other places, the movie *Drums Along the Mohawk*.

In the early years of the 19th century, the Mohawk Valley became the major route west for migrating New England Yankees, some of whom stayed to settle the valley. When the Erie Canal, which runs parallel to the river, was opened in 1825, the nation had its first major, and for a long time its most important, path from the coast to the interior. The canal was the cheapest way to get bulky agricultural products out of the Old Northwest (Ohio, Indiana, etc.) and finished goods back into the hinterlands. At first the canal, and then the New York Central Railroad, which followed this same water-level route, accounted for much of the phenomenal growth of New York City and its port. Boston and Philadelphia, with no similar access inland, were left behind.

As migration slowed and trade increased, the Mohawk Valley became one of the early industrial centers of the nation. The little Oneida County hamlets of Utica and Rome grew to become sizable industrial centers. First settled by New England Yankees, these towns attracted a new wave of immigration from the Atlantic coast in the early 20th century. Today they are the most heavily Italian- and Polish-American communities between Albany and Buffalo.

In most parts of the nation, a change in ethnic composition of this magnitude would have moved the area from Republican to Democratic party preference. But not in Upstate New York where suspicion of Democratic New York City has worked to the advantage of the Republican Party since it was founded. Republicans here pay close attention to the sometimes pro-union and pro-abortion, pro-aid to parochial schools sentiments of their blue collar Catholic constituents; theirs is a party that has broadened its base from the all but vanishing white Anglo–Saxon Protestants. Their adaptation has been successful. Only Democrats with the strongest emotional appeal to Catholic voters—for example, Robert Kennedy in 1964 or Hugh Carey in 1974—have carried Mohawk Valley counties.

In 1972, seven-term incumbent Congressman Alexander Pirnie retired. The winner of the Republican primary was Donald Mitchell, a Herkimer County Assemblyman who also had the Conservative Party nomination. Mitchell has won subsequent elections without difficulty and has shown sufficient popularity that he had no Democratic opponent at all in 1978. In the House he votes solidly with his fellow Republicans. Like his predecessor, he serves on the House Armed Services Committee, where he is in a good position to protect the interests of Rome's Griffis Air Force Base. Mitchell is one of the Congress's strongest advocates of measures to strengthen America's civil defense program.

Census Data Pop. (1980 final) 458,792, down 2% in 1970s. Median family income, 1970, $9,388, 92% of U.S.

The Voters

Employment profile 1970 White collar, 44%. Blue collar, 39%. Service, 13%. Farm, 4%.
Ethnic groups Black 1980, 2%. Hispanic 1980, 1%. Total foreign stock 1970, 22%. Italy, 6%; Poland, 3%; Germany, UK, Canada, 2% each.

Presidential Vote

1980	Reagan (R)	97,430	(50%)
	Carter (D)	76,945	(40%)
	Anderson (I)	13,370	(7%)
1976	Ford (R)	107,363	(56%)
	Carter (D)	84,661	(44%)

Rep. Donald J. Mitchell (R) Elected 1972; b. May 8, 1923, Ilion; home, Herkimer; Hobart Col., 1946–47, Columbia U., B.S. 1949, M.A. 1950.

Career Navy, WWII; Optometrist, 1950–72; Herkimer Town Cncl., 1954–57, Mayor, 1957–61; Herkimer Town Zoning Bd. of Appeals, 1963; N.Y. State Assembly, 1965–72, Major. Whip, 1969–72.

Offices 2305 RHOB, 202-225-3665. Also 319 N. Main St., Herkimer 13350, 315-866-1051.

Committee *Armed Services* (5th). Subcommittees: Investigations; Military Personnel and Compensation.

Group Ratings

	ADA	COPE	PC	LCV	CFA	RPN	NAB	NSI	NTU	ACA	ACU
1980	28	44	37	58	21	—	67	100	39	65	61
1979	21	40	38	53	19	—	—	—	40	68	62
1978	25	45	23	49	27	58	67	100	13	70	75

Key Votes

1) Draft Registn $	FOR	6) Fair Hsg DOJ Enfrc	AGN	11) Cut Socl Incr Dfns $	—
2) Ban $ to Nicrgua	FOR	7) Lim PAC Contrbtns	FOR	12) Hosptl Cost Controls	AGN
3) Dlay MX Missile	AGN	8) Cap on Food Stmp $	AGN	13) Gasln Ctrls & Allctns	FOR
4) Nuclr Mortorium	FOR	9) New US Dep Edcatn	AGN	14) Lim Wndfll Prof Tax	FOR
5) Alaska Lands Bill	FOR	10) Cut OSHA $		FOR	15) Chryslr Loan Grntee	FOR

Election Results

1980 general	Donald J. Mitchell (R-RTL)	135,976	(77%)	($78,925)
	Irving A. Schwartz (D-L)	39,589	(23%)	($6,495)
1980 primary	Donald J. Mitchell (R), unopposed			
1978 general	Donald J. Mitchell (R-C), unopp. .			($44,635)

THIRTY-SECOND DISTRICT

From the 1920s until 1974, Upstate and suburban Republicans controlled the New York legislature, except after the Democratic landslides of 1936 and 1964. Republican control was founded on the principle of giving New York City far less representation than its population entitled it to, until the Supreme Court prohibited that practice in 1964; and these same Republicans extended their influence into national affairs by drawing with exceeding care the boundaries of New York's congressional districts so as to maximize the number of Republicans elected. The Upstate cities of Buffalo and Rochester were traditionally divided between two or three districts, each with plenty of suburban and rural territory to overpower any possible Democratic majority. During the 1960s the legislators abandoned this ploy in Buffalo, where one city district became overwhelmingly Democratic, although they retained it in Rochester; in 1970 they applied it to Syracuse.

Until then it had scarcely been necessary. Syracuse and surrounding Onondaga County had been a single district for as long as anyone could remember, and they had the perfect population to continue in that arrangement after the 1970 census. Syracuse is in many ways Upstate New York's most militantly conservative and usually most Republican city (although it voted against Nelson Rockefeller one time because it considered him too big a spender). General Electric, as in much of Upstate New York, is the largest employer here, and it has propagated its conservative Republicanism as much as possible. But the real basis for Syracuse's conservatism — and it has been shared for years by the city's large blue collar Italian–American community, which elsewhere might be Democratic — is fear of and hostility toward New York City. There is a feeling that the city, if it ever got the chance, would tax honest, hardworking Upstaters to bankruptcy to support the welfare cheaters and civil service loafers who, in this view, dominate New York City politics.

So Republicans carried Syracuse during the New Deal. Democrats won here only in 1964, when Lyndon Johnson and Robert Kennedy carried Onondaga County, and in 1966, when there was a local uprising against Nelson Rockefeller. In 1964, the Syracuse area also elected a Democratic congressman, James Hanley, and in this unlikely territory he won reelection and held the seat for 16 years. Hanley skillfully used the advantages of incumbency and survived tough redistricting efforts in 1970 and 1972. The Republican legislature then took half of Syracuse and Onondaga County away from his district (now numbered the 32d) and added the rural and small-town counties of Madison, Cortland, and Chenango.

This accounts for the jagged boundaries of the 32d and 33d districts running through the middle of central New York's largest city. And eventually it caused Hanley serious political trouble. This is a hard district to cover personally, especially after deregulation of the airlines cut the number of flights to Upstate New York. In 1979 Hanley became chairman of the House Committee on Post Office and Civil Service. Committee chairmanships used to be political plums, but this one has turned out to be a kind of rotten apple. Who, after all, wants to be held responsible for the performance of the Post Office? Hanley had been hard pressed by Republicans in the 1976 and 1978 elections; as a chairman he evidently decided to relax, and he declined to run for reelection in 1980.

The race was decided then in the Republican primary. George Wortley, a suburban Syracuse newspaper publisher, did not have the Republican organization endorsement, but he did have lots of local support and was able to beat the 1978 nominee in the district, Peter DelGiorno. The general election was not really seriously contested, even though DelGiorno ran as a candidate of the Right To Life Party.

Wortley's future in the House may depend on redistricting. Upstate New York must lose one of its 15 House seats, and one demographically easy way to redraw the lines is to make Onondaga County and perhaps one rural county back into a single seat, which almost surely will go Republican in today's political climate, and to take the remaining counties in the 32d and 33d districts and distribute them among the districts to the north, south, east, and west. That might put Wortley in a primary with the 33d's Gary Lee, or might give Wortley the Syracuse seat without serious competition (Lee is from the Ithaca area). Neither Wortley nor Lee, who was first elected in 1978, has great legislative importance to New York state in Washington nor great clout in Albany, unless Syracuse's Republican state senators should take it upon themselves to preserve a situation in which Onondaga County has two congressmen.

Census Data   Pop. (1980 final) 485,133, up 4% in 1970s. Median family income, 1970, $10,416, 109% of U.S.

The Voters

Employment profile 1970   White collar, 53%. Blue collar, 32%. Service, 12%. Farm, 3%.
Ethnic groups   Black 1980, 3%. Hispanic 1980, 1%. Asian 1980, 1%. Total foreign stock 1970, 18%. Italy, 4%; Canada, Germany, UK, 2% each; Poland, 1%.

Presidential Vote

1980	Reagan (R)	99,311	(51%)
	Carter (D)	71,354	(37%)
	Anderson (I)	19,834	(10%)
1976	Ford (R)	117,652	(61%)
	Carter (D)	75,658	(39%)

Rep. George C. Wortley (R) Elected 1980; b. Dec. 8, 1926, Syracuse; home, Fayetteville; Syracuse U., B.S. 1948.

Career Navy, WWII; Newspaper publisher, 1949–; Rep. nominee for U.S. House of Reps., 1976; Nat. Commission on Historical Publications and Records, 1977–80; Fayetteville Sr. Citizens Housing Commission, 1977–80.

Offices 508 CHOB, 202-225-3701. Also 1269 Fed. Bldg., Syracuse 13260, 315-423-5657, and Manley Carriage House, 2 Hayes St., Norwich 13815, 607-334-2211.

Committees *Banking, Finance and Urban Affairs* (15th). Subcommittees: Consumer Affairs and Coinage; Economic Stabilization; General Oversight and Renegotiation; Housing and Community Development.

Select Committee on Aging (18th).

Group Ratings and Key Votes: Newly Elected

Election Results

1980 general	George C. Wortley (R-C)	108,128	(60%)	($170,106)
	Jeffrey S. Brooks (D-L)	56,535	(32%)	($15,315)
	Peter J. DelGiorno (RTL)	11,978	(7%)	($65,382)
1980 primary	George C. Wortley (R)	11,521	(40%)	
	Peter J. DelGiorno (R)	8,649	(30%)	
	Pat R. Bombard (R)	4,459	(16%)	($119,500)
	Herbert D. Brewer (R)	4,084	(14%)	($12,653)
1978 general	James M. Hanley (D)	76,251	(52%)	($113,595)
	Peter J. DelGiorno (R-C)	67,071	(46%)	($71,961)

THIRTY-THIRD DISTRICT

The Finger Lakes of upstate New York are long, narrow bodies of water, surrounded by gentle hills. They lie within a triangle, the apexes of which are Syracuse, Rochester, and Elmira. The land above the lakes is dotted with small towns to which some early 19th-century Yankee, proud of his classical education, gave names: Ovid, Scipio, Romulus, Camillus, Pompey, and many others. The Finger Lakes region is pleasant vacation country and is known also for its vineyards; this is where the New York state wine industry thrives. Just north of the Lakes is the line of the Erie Canal, now replaced by one with a name less euphonious: the New York State Barge Canal. Also here are the small industrial cities of Auburn, Geneva, and Canandaigua. The Finger Lakes country is Republican by tradition, the cities heavily Catholic and sometimes Democratic.

The Finger Lakes region accounts for about half of New York's 33d congressional district. The remainder is the west side of Syracuse and surrounding Onondaga County. In its short existence as a district, the 33d has elected three Republican congressmen. John Terry, elected in 1970, decided to retire in 1972 because he didn't want to move his family to Washington. Former Syracuse Mayor William Walsh, elected in 1972, won reelection twice by very large margins. In 1978, at 66, he decided to retire.

The current congressman, Gary Lee, was once director of Cornell University's office of scholarships and served in Tompkins County local government and the New York Assembly. He beat Syracuse-based candidates for the seat in the primary and general elections in 1978 and was reelected without difficulty in 1980. Lee's problem is redistricting. If the legislature decides to place all of Syracuse in a single district, he will either have to run there against Syracuse-based incumbent George Wortley or will have to run in another seat against an incumbent who will have a local advantage. Much depends on the way the lines are drawn, and Lee will be doing his best to affect them. Lee's voting record is basically in line with those of most House Republicans, and he serves on the important Energy and Commerce Committee.

Census Data   Pop. (1980 final) 470,552, up 1% in 1970s. Median family income, 1970, $9,851, 103% of U.S.

The Voters

Employment profile 1970   White collar, 46%. Blue collar, 37%. Service, 14%. Farm, 3%.
Ethnic groups   Black 1980, 4%. Hispanic 1980, 1%. Total foreign stock 1970, 18%. Italy, 5%; Canada, UK, Germany, Poland, 2% each; Ireland, 1%.

Presidential Vote

1980	Reagan (R)	117,783	(52%)
	Carter (D)	84,240	(37%)
	Anderson (I)	19,941	(9%)
1976	Ford (R)	115,166	(56%)
	Carter (D)	75,263	(39%)

Rep. Gary A. Lee (R) Elected 1978; b. Aug. 18, 1933, Buffalo; home, Ithaca; Colgate U., B.A. 1960.

Career Navy, 1952–56; Corning City Alderman, 1961–63; Dryden Town Cncl., 1965–67, Supervisor, 1968–69; Tomkins Co. Supervisor, 1968–69, Bd. of Reps., 1970–74, Chmn., 1974; N.Y. State Assembly, 1974–78.

Offices 322 CHOB, 202-225-3333. Also 1245 Fed. Bldg., Syracuse 13202, 315-423-5333.

Committees *Energy and Commerce* (10th). Subcommittees: Commerce, Transportation, and Tourism; Fossil and Synthetic Fuels.

House Administration (6th). Subcommittees: Accounts; Office Systems; Personnel and Police.

Group Ratings

	ADA	COPE	PC	LCV	CFA	RPN	NAB	NSI	NTU	ACA	ACU
1980	11	19	27	49	7	—	100	100	60	90	94
1979	0	30	13	20	4	—	—	—	55	84	86

800   NEW YORK

Key Votes

1) Draft Registn $	FOR	6) Fair Hsg DOJ Enfrc	AGN	11) Cut Socl Incr Dfns $	FOR
2) Ban $ to Nicrgua	FOR	7) Lim PAC Contrbtns	AGN	12) Hosptl Cost Controls	—
3) Dlay MX Missile	—	8) Cap on Food Stmp $	FOR	13) Gasln Ctrls & Allctns	AGN
4) Nuclr Mortorium	AGN	9) New US Dep Edcatn	AGN	14) Lim Wndfll Prof Tax	—
5) Alaska Lands Bill	AGN	10) Cut OSHA $		FOR	15) Chryslr Loan Grntee	FOR

Election Results

1980 general	Gary A. Lee (R-C)	132,831	(77%)	($128,927)
	Dolores M. Reed (D-L)	39,542	(23%)	($5,326)
1980 primary	Gary A. Lee (R), unopposed			
1978 general	Gary A. Lee (R)	82,501	(56%)	($162,725)
	Roy A. Bernardi (D)............	58,286	(40%)	($69,614)

THIRTY-FOURTH DISTRICT

The 34th congressional district of New York lies along the southern shore of Lake Ontario and includes the east side of the city of Rochester, eastern Monroe County, and Wayne County farther to the east. Rochester's economy, to an extent greater than those of other Upstate New York cities, depends on white collar and highly skilled labor jobs. Major employers here are Eastman Kodak, Xerox, and Bausch & Lomb, all founded in Rochester; Kodak still has its headquarters here. These high technology companies have given the Rochester area a healthier economy over the years than is found in Upstate cities that depend more on heavy industry; its metropolitan area gained more industrial investment in 1980 than Sun Belt cities such as Phoenix and San Antonio.

The city of Rochester by itself is almost large enough to constitute a congressional district, and if it were one it would almost certainly elect a Democrat. Knowing this, Republican legislators for years have split Rochester into two districts, adding plenty of heavily Republican suburban and rural territory to each. Consequently, both the 34th and 35th congressional districts are considered safely Republican. In the 34th, profoundly conservative Wayne County is a particular Republican stronghold and, incidentally, the birthplace of the Mormon Church. Even so, the 39th went Democratic in the 1980 presidential election; it was one of the few districts in the nation to give Jimmy Carter a higher percentage in 1980 than in 1976.

Since 1963, the 34th's congressman has been Frank Horton, on most issues Upstate New York's most liberal Republican. That political coloration has become traditional in the district; some years ago (1947–59) its congressman was Kenneth Keating, later U.S. senator, judge on New York's highest court, and ambassador to India and Israel. Like Keating, Horton is more in tune with New Deal liberals on economic issues than in step with the dovish Democrats who today control their party's caucus in the House; he is not all that far from the politics of, say, Henry Jackson. However you describe his politics, he has proved very popular in the 34th district. In 1974, despite Watergate and an opponent of substance, he won by a 2–1 margin; despite a drunk driving arrest and a week in jail he did as well in 1976. In 1978 he had no Democratic opponent at all, and in 1980 he was reelected by a 3½–1 margin.

Horton is now ranking Republican on the Government Operations Committee. This is an odd legislative body, in the sense that it does not produce very much ongoing legislation but has tremendous discretion to investigate — and therefore to affect — the conduct of government. That makes it potentially a great weapon of the party out of power, and the chairman today is Jack Brooks of Texas, a partisan Democrat if there ever was one. That leaves

Horton with the job of modulating the committee's approach, although he is not a Republican who has ever been thought of as being close to Ronald Reagan.

Redistricting could conceivably change the composition of the districts in this part of the state greatly, but the likelihood is that the 34th will not be altered much. Horton's position appears to be pretty strong and it seems likely that he will survive redistricting.

Census Data Pop. (1980 final) 454,965, down 3% in 1970s. Median family income, 1970, $12,082, 126% of U.S.

The Voters

Employment profile 1970 White collar, 54%. Blue collar, 34%. Service, 11%. Farm, 1%.
Ethnic groups Black 1980, 8%. Hispanic 1980, 3%. Asian 1980, 1%. Total foreign stock 1970, 27%. Italy, 7%; Germany, Canada, 3% each; UK, USSR, Poland, 2% each.

Presidential Vote

1980	Reagan (R)	82,867	(42%)
	Carter (D)	89,911	(46%)
	Anderson (I)	19,877	(10%)
1976	Ford (R)	112,816	(56%)
	Carter (D)	86,580	(43%)

Rep. Frank Horton (R) Elected 1962; b. Dec. 12, 1919, Cuero, Tex.; home, Rochester; La. St. U., B.A. 1941, Cornell U., LL.B. 1947.

Career Army, WWII; Practicing atty., 1947–62; Rochester City Cncl., 1955–61.

Offices 2229 RHOB, 202-225-4916. Also 314 Fed. Bldg., Rochester 14614, 716-263-6270.

Committee *Government Operations* (Ranking Member). Subcommittee: Legislation and National Security.

Group Ratings

	ADA	COPE	PC	LCV	CFA	RPN	NAB	NSI	NTU	ACA	ACU
1980	78	74	30	39	64	—	33	75	28	43	39
1979	47	55	28	39	30	—	—	—	28	48	38
1978	55	50	33	37	32	55	46	80	12	33	46

Key Votes

1) Draft Registn $	AGN	6) Fair Hsg DOJ Enfrc	FOR	11) Cut Socl Incr Dfns $	AGN
2) Ban $ to Nicrgua	FOR	7) Lim PAC Contrbtns	FOR	12) Hosptl Cost Controls	FOR
3) Dlay MX Missile	FOR	8) Cap on Food Stmp $	AGN	13) Gasln Ctrls & Allctns	AGN
4) Nuclr Mortorium	AGN	9) New US Dep Edcatn	FOR	14) Lim Wndfll Prof Tax	AGN
5) Alaska Lands Bill	FOR	10) Cut OSHA $	AGN	15) Chryslr Loan Grntee	FOR

Election Results

1980 general	Frank Horton (R)	133,278	(73%)	($14,669)
	James Toole (D)	37,883	(21%)	($0)
1980 primary	Frank Horton (R), unopposed			
1978 general	Frank Horton (R-D)	122,785	(87%)	($8,262)
	Leo J. Kesselring (C)	18,127	(13%)	

THIRTY-FIFTH DISTRICT

The 35th congressional district of New York includes the western half of the city of Rochester, the western Monroe County suburbs, and the adjacent Upstate counties of Genesee, Wyoming, Livingston, and part of Ontario. This is fertile, rolling countryside, punctuated by such small cities as Batavia, locale of novelist John Gardner's *Sunlight Dialogues,* and Attica, scene of the 1971 prison riot and tragedy. Some 400 miles from New York City, this part of New York state has an almost midwestern feeling to it; celebrity city politicians such as Nelson Rockefeller or Robert Kennedy seemed as out of place campaigning here as they might have in southern Iowa.

There are Democratic margins usually in the city of Rochester and sometimes they are enough to carry Monroe County; in 1980, that was the case and indeed this was one of the few places in the nation that gave Jimmy Carter a higher percentage after he had served as president than it had before. But overall in the 35th district any Democratic margin in Rochester is overwhelmed if not by the suburbs then by the Republican margins in the rural counties.

This is the kind of district that, for the past century, has sent so many men to Washington to tend our national affairs; conservative Republicans, most of them, small-town lawyers with an aptitude for politics, with perhaps a small family fortune behind them, and a few years in the legislature. Typically they have been elected young, returned to office more or less automatically, and have wound up in important committee positions. They have written tariff laws, led the opposition to new federal programs, put together military budgets, and in many cases — remembering what gave birth to the Republican Party — supporting civil rights laws. They have been cautious, serious men, seldom very stylish or fashionable, but often brighter than sophisticated liberals gave them credit for. Through men like these, the people who run the small towns of Upstate New York, central Ohio, outstate Michigan, and downstate Illinois have had a major voice in the way our government has been run.

There are probably fewer such men in the House than there used to be, partly because there are fewer House seats in small-town and rural areas and partly because many that do exist are now represented by Democrats. But the tradition does survive in the person of Barber Conable, Republican congressman from the 35th district of New York. In his first few years he caught the eye of the Republican leadership and won a seat on the Ways and Means Committee. In 1977, when he was only 54, he became ranking Republican on that panel. Conable is respected as a thoughtful, knowledgeable legislator. His voting record is in line with Republican tradition: he likes to balance budgets, to hold down federal spending, to question whether new programs are really necessary. Within that tradition he operates as an intelligent legislative craftsman and compromiser. Conable is also one of the House's most sensitive observers of its own workings, a man with a contemplative bent and an ability to understand and sympathize with the motivations of others even when they are quite different from his own.

Conable does have some strong views, however. On trade issues he is almost invariably a force for free trade and a skeptic when it comes to arguments for protection. He is one of the leading forces on Ways and Means against trade barriers. He is also an advocate of lowering taxes on business and is the chief congressional sponsor of the 10–5–3 (buildings, equipment, vehicles) reform that would increase the depreciation deductions for business, on the theory that they are otherwise understated in a time of inflation. Conable's strong beliefs in free enterprise and the efficacy of the market mechanism do not, however, make him a supporter of all the supply-side economics of Jack Kemp, David Stockman, and Ronald Reagan. He is on record in support of the Kemp–Roth tax cut, as is virtually every congressional Republican. But his native caution is apparent when he discusses the subject; this is an untried strategy, untried in recent memory at least, and Conable appears to be, as many voters are, concerned that any substantial stimulation of consumer demand will result in an increase in inflation. The supply siders, certainly, regard him as a brake on the train they are trying to set in motion; he might reply that he wants to be a little surer of the destination first.

Conable was first elected in 1964 and has not had serious electoral problems since; his closest call came in 1974, when Midge Costanza, later an aide to Jimmy Carter, held him to 59% of the vote. Redistricting poses a possible threat, but the likelihood is that if the 35th district has to give up some of Rochester it will gain some counties in the Finger Lakes area, thus making it more Republican. Another alternative would be to have the 35th, and other districts, carve up the 39th district in Upstate New York's Southern Tier. Conable's importance in Washington virtually assures that the legislature will see that he has a safe district to run in.

Census Data   Pop. (1980 final) 477,377, up 2% in 1970s. Median family income, 1970, $11,528, 120% of U.S.

The Voters

   Employment profile 1970   White collar, 46%. Blue collar, 40%. Service, 12%. Farm, 2%.
   Ethnic groups   Black 1980, 8%. Hispanic 1980, 1%. Total foreign stock 1970, 20%. Italy, 6%; Canada, Germany, 3% each; UK, 2%; Poland, 1%.

Presidential Vote

1980	Reagan (R)	92,312	(46%)
	Carter (D)	88,564	(44%)
	Anderson (I)	15,181	(8%)
1976	Ford (R)	111,399	(56%)
	Carter (D)	85,502	(43%)

Rep. Barber B. Conable, Jr. (R) Elected 1964; b. Nov. 2, 1922, Warsaw; home, Alexander; Cornell U., B.A. 1942, LL.B. 1948.

Career   USMC, WWII and Korea; Practicing atty., 1949–64; N.Y. State Senate, 1963–64.

Offices   237 CHOB, 202-225-3615. Also 311 Fed. Ofc. Bldg., 100 State St., Rochester 14614, 716-263-3156.

Committees   *Standards of Official Conduct* (2d).

Ways and Means (Ranking Member).

Joint Committee on Taxation (Ranking Member).

Group Ratings

	ADA	COPE	PC	LCV	CFA	RPN	NAB	NSI	NTU	ACA	ACU
1980	28	47	27	47	21	—	75	38	58	79	58
1979	26	30	18	20	15	—	—	—	57	60	66
1978	30	25	20	24	18	100	100	80	40	56	70

Key Votes

1) Draft Registn $	AGN	6) Fair Hsg DOJ Enfrc	AGN	11) Cut Socl Incr Dfns $	AGN
2) Ban $ to Nicrgua	AGN	7) Lim PAC Contrbtns	FOR	12) Hosptl Cost Controls	AGN
3) Dlay MX Missile	AGN	8) Cap on Food Stmp $	FOR	13) Gasln Ctrls & Allctns	AGN
4) Nuclr Mortorium	AGN	9) New US Dep Edcatn	AGN	14) Lim Wndfll Prof Tax	FOR
5) Alaska Lands Bill	AGN	10) Cut OSHA $	FOR	15) Chryslr Loan Grntee	AGN

Election Results

1980 general	Barber B. Conable, Jr. (R)	127,623	(72%)	($34,444)
	John M. Owens (D-C)	44,754	(25%)	($0)
1980 primary	Barber B. Conable, Jr. (R), unopp.			
1978 general	Barber B. Conable, Jr. (R)	96,119	(69%)	($59,204)
	Francis C. Repicci (D)	36,428	(26%)	($30,837)

THIRTY-SIXTH DISTRICT

The 36th congressional district of New York includes Niagara County, site of the falls; part of suburban Erie County, just outside Buffalo; and the southern shore of Lake Ontario from the Niagara River to within a few miles of Rochester. From the falls, power lines strung on gigantic pylons hum out to the urban Northeast, Midwest, and eastern Canada. The city of Niagara Falls, despite its tourist business, is mostly industrial, with most of its industries doing not especially well of late. Pollution is high—this is the site of the Love's Canal trage-dy—and the city and its suburbs have been losing population in the 1960s and 1970s. Niaga-ra Falls has large Italian and Polish communities that lean Democratic; the rest of the county subscribes to Upstate New York Republicanism. The Erie County portion of the 36th in-cludes the middle-class and politically marginal suburbs of Tonawanda and Grand Island, as well as a few blocks of the city of Buffalo itself.

On paper the 36th is politically marginal, yet until 1974 it was invariably captured by Re-publicans. One was William Miller, who became famous when he quit Congress in 1964 and was named Barry Goldwater's running mate; he was chosen for his zesty partisan attacks. More recently he was seen on TV in an American Express commercial. Another Republican congressman here was Henry Smith, a frosty former judge who served on the House Judici-ary Committee; he threatened to vote for impeachment because of the bombing of Cambo-dia, but decided not to, and thus missed being a footnote in history. Smith retired voluntarily in that same year, 1974.

Given the Democratic nature of the year and the political leanings of the district, it was almost inevitable that it went Democratic in 1974, and it did in a big way. John LaFalce, a young veteran of both houses of the New York legislature, won the district with a robust 60%. His major interest has been Buffalo area politics; he has used his seats on the Banking and Small Business Committees to seek aid and help projects in the Niagara Frontier. He has won reelection by wide margins even when, as in 1976, he was opposed by a high-spend-ing Republican.

LaFalce's problem for 1982 is redistricting. Erie County no longer has enough population for two whole districts—much less the 2½ it now has. Henry Nowak of the 37th district is well established in Buffalo; Jack Kemp of the 38th district has demonstrated phenomenally high popularity and undoubtedly LaFalce would prefer not to run against him, however favorable the district. Unless Kemp's district is extended east (unlikely, because it would hurt Barber Conable) or south into the Southern Tier, LaFalce will lose his home base in suburban Erie County, and the 36th will have to be extended far into the central city of Rochester. This might suit Rochester area Republicans fine: it would remove Democrats from their districts. But it would force LaFalce to get to know and serve an entirely new metropolitan area.

Census Data Pop. (1980 final) 446,189, down 5% in 1970s. Median family income, 1970, $10,702, 116% of U.S.

The Voters

Employment profile 1970 White collar, 47%. Blue collar, 40%. Service, 12%. Farm, 1%.
Ethnic groups Black 1980, 4%. Hispanic 1980, 1%. Am. Ind. 1980, 1%. Total foreign stock 1970, 27%. Canada, 7%; Italy, 5%; Poland, 4%; UK, Germany, 3% each.

Presidential Vote

1980	Reagan (R)	82,409	(45%)
	Carter (D)	82,183	(45%)
	Anderson (I)	14,001	(8%)
1976	Ford (R)	102,268	(54%)
	Carter (D)	88,063	(46%)

Rep. John J. LaFalce (D) Elected 1974; b. Oct. 6, 1939, Buffalo; home, Tonawanda; Canisius Col., B.S. 1961, Villanova U., J.D. 1964.

Career Law Clerk, Ofc. of Gen. Counsel, U.S. Dept. of the Navy, 1963; Practicing atty.; Army, 1965–67; N.Y. State Senate, 1971–72; N.Y. State Assembly, 1973–74.

Offices 2447 RHOB, 202-225-3231. Also Fed. Bldg., Buffalo 14202, 716-846-4056.

Committees *Banking, Finance and Urban Affairs* (12th). Subcommittees: Financial Institutions Supervision, Regulation and Insurance; Housing and Community Development; International Development Institutions and Finance; International Trade, Investment and Monetary Policy.

Small Business (5th). Subcommittee: General Oversight (Chairman).

Group Ratings

	ADA	COPE	PC	LCV	CFA	RPN	NAB	NSI	NTU	ACA	ACU
1980	56	82	67	74	79	—	20	22	17	25	21
1979	68	80	73	79	74	—	—	—	21	4	8
1978	40	60	78	77	77	67	36	50	15	37	13

Key Votes

1) Draft Registn $	FOR	6) Fair Hsg DOJ Enfrc	FOR	11) Cut Socl Incr Dfns $	AGN
2) Ban $ to Nicrgua	AGN	7) Lim PAC Contrbtns	FOR	12) Hosptl Cost Controls	FOR
3) Dlay MX Missile	AGN	8) Cap on Food Stmp $	AGN	13) Gasln Ctrls & Allctns	FOR
4) Nuclr Mortorium	AGN	9) New US Dep Edcatn	AGN	14) Lim Wndfll Prof Tax	AGN
5) Alaska Lands Bill	FOR	10) Cut OSHA $	AGN	15) Chryslr Loan Grntee	FOR

Election Results

1980 general	John J. LaFalce (D-L)	122,929	(72%)	($66,000)
	H. William Feder (R-C-RTL)	48,428	(28%)	($33,088)
1980 primary	John J. LaFalce (D), unopposed			
1978 general	John J. LaFalce (D-L)	99,497	(74%)	($44,407)
	Francina J. Cartonia (R)	31,527	(24%)	($9,476)

THIRTY-SEVENTH DISTRICT

Buffalo is the second largest city in New York and one of the important industrial centers on the Great Lakes. Huge steel mills line the shores of Lake Erie, as the principal east–west rail lines feed into downtown Buffalo and the industrial areas that circle it. This is the eastern-most American port on the Great Lakes, and here giant freighters unload iron ore from the Mesabi Range and grain from the western prairies. Buffalo is one of the nation's leading steel producers and rivals Minneapolis as a miller of grain.

At the turn of the century, these basic industries were the fastest-growing, most dynamic sector of the economy. There were flush times in Buffalo then. The city sat on the nation's leading transportation lines, and tens of thousands of Italian and Polish immigrants moved here, eager to work in its factories. Today the city's steel mills, grain elevators, and docks, along with its downtown and radial avenues, still look like something out of the 1920s, only a little run-down and shabby. Buffalo no longer enjoys the advantages it once had. Its basic industries now have sluggish growth or none at all. The major transportation routes have shifted to the south, and the great new mode of transportation, the airplane, scarcely touches down in Buffalo at all. In the early part of the century people were willing to put up with the fact that Buffalo receives an unusually heavy snowfall, because of its position at the extreme eastern end of Lake Erie. Now more and more people are trying to get away, to the Sun Belt; and the snow in Buffalo has become a national joke. All of this does not mean that Buffalo is moribund as a city. But its economy is not generating enough jobs for its current residents' children—much less any new migrants. The downtown is in trouble, and even the local branch of the State University of New York has moved to the suburbs.

Nearly all of Buffalo, together with the industrial city of Lackawanna to the south (home of a giant Bethlehem steel mill) and a few precincts in the suburban town of Cheektowaga, make up New York's 37th congressional district. This is a very heavily Democratic district—indeed the most solidly Democratic of any in Upstate New York. Republican voters have died or moved to the suburbs, and Buffalo's relatively depressed economic state has led to desires for the kind of aid programs Democrats tend to favor more than Republicans. The 37th is also the home of a Democratic organization, led by former state Democratic Chairman Joseph Crangle. Unlike its counterparts in New York City, this machine is as interested in winning general elections as it is in controlling judicial nominations.

In 1974 the Erie County machine elected two new congressmen, both still in their 30s. One was Assemblyman John LaFalce, who captured the formerly Republican 36th district; the other was Erie County Controller Henry Nowak, elected here in the 37th. Nowak succeeded Thaddeus Dulski, a 16-year veteran who finally became chairman of the House Post Office and Civil Service Committee but never left much of a legacy. Nowak's election was a cinch; he was easily nominated, with the imprimatur of the machine, and easily elected in this district that even George McGovern easily carried. Nowak was assigned to the Public Works Committee, traditionally a place for practical-minded politicians who want to help their districts. He is considered easy to get along with and politically astute.

For 1982 Nowak will want a district centered on Buffalo, although with the central city's declining population it will have to reach out into the suburbs as well. One thing Nowak does not want is to be placed in the same district with Jack Kemp, the extremely popular Republican. Perhaps the Democrat would prevail, and perhaps Kemp would run for other office, but who wants to take a chance?

Census Data Pop. (1980 final) 360,405, down 23% in 1970s. Median family income, 1970, $8,845, 92% of U.S.

The Voters

Employment profile 1970 White collar, 43%. Blue collar, 43%. Service, 14%. Farm, –%.
Ethnic groups Black 1980, 27%. Hispanic 1980, 3%. Am. Ind. 1980, 1%. Total foreign stock 1970, 28%. Poland, 8%; Italy, 6%; Germany, Canada, 3% each; UK, Ireland, 1% each.

Presidential Vote

1980	Reagan (R)	35,230	(26%)
	Carter (D)	90,367	(67%)
	Anderson (I)	7,036	(5%)
1976	Ford (R)	55,021	(37%)
	Carter (D)	95,413	(63%)

Rep. Henry J. Nowak (D) Elected 1974; b. Feb. 21, 1935, Buffalo; home, Buffalo; Canisius Col., B.B.A. 1957, Buffalo Law Sch., J.D. 1961.

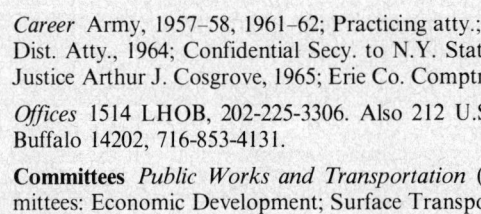

Career Army, 1957–58, 1961–62; Practicing atty.; Erie Co. Asst. Dist. Atty., 1964; Confidential Secy. to N.Y. State Supreme Ct. Justice Arthur J. Cosgrove, 1965; Erie Co. Comptroller, 1966–75.

Offices 1514 LHOB, 202-225-3306. Also 212 U.S. Courthouse, Buffalo 14202, 716-853-4131.

Committees *Public Works and Transportation* (8th). Subcommittees: Economic Development; Surface Transportation; Water Resources.

Small Business (8th). Subcommittee: Tax, Access to Equity Capital and Business Opportunities.

Group Ratings

	ADA	COPE	PC	LCV	CFA	RPN	NAB	NSI	NTU	ACA	ACU
1980	78	89	53	70	64	—	0	10	12	13	12
1979	79	95	73	70	78	—	—	—	18	12	13
1978	70	95	60	61	59	33	0	30	10	15	17

Key Votes

1) Draft Registn $	AGN	6) Fair Hsg DOJ Enfrc	FOR	11) Cut Socl Incr Dfns $	AGN
2) Ban $ to Nicrgua	AGN	7) Lim PAC Contrbtns	FOR	12) Hosptl Cost Controls	FOR
3) Dlay MX Missile	FOR	8) Cap on Food Stmp $	AGN	13) Gasln Ctrls & Allctns	FOR
4) Nuclr Mortorium	AGN	9) New US Dep Edcatn	AGN	14) Lim Wndfll Prof Tax	AGN
5) Alaska Lands Bill	FOR	10) Cut OSHA $	AGN	15) Chryslr Loan Grntee	FOR

Election Results

1980 general	Henry J. Nowak (D-L)	94,890	(83%)	($40,515)
	Roger Heymanowski (R-C)	16,560	(14%)	($0)
1980 primary	Henry J. Nowak (D-L), unopposed			
1978 general	Henry J. Nowak (D-L)	70,911	(79%)	($37,521)
	Charles Poth III (R)	17,585	(20%)	

THIRTY-EIGHTH DISTRICT

The 38th congressional district of New York includes most of suburban Erie County, from the Buffalo city limits to the small state Indian reservations at the northern and southern edges of the county. Altogether the district takes in the most prosperous parts of the so-called Niagara Frontier, the heavily industrial Buffalo–Niagara Falls metropolitan area along the Canadian border. Buffalo and its suburbs are the Democratic bastion of Upstate New York; in fact, the region often produces higher Democratic percentages than Metropolitan New York City, although of course not nearly so many votes. Buffalo is a place much more like Cleveland or Detroit than like New York, and its residents—in large part Polish, Italian, and black—are not as susceptible to either the city's fashionable liberalism nor the Archie Bunker reaction to it as are people in the Big Apple.

A totally suburban district, the 38th is the least Democratic part of Erie County, with most of Buffalo's rather scant supply of wealthy suburban enclaves. Much of the district is working-class Democratic, particularly the suburbs closest to the Buffalo city limits, such as the town of Cheektowaga, which casts about one-quarter of the district's votes. Here are the miles and miles of small tract houses to which people who grew up in immigrant neighborhoods escaped. Overall it is one of the more marginal districts in Upstate New York.

But not in congressional elections. For this is the district that elects Jack Kemp, the Republican who has become one of his party's most forceful intellectual leaders and his district's favorite politician. Kemp was an unlikely candidate for such a role. When he first ran he had only recently been quarterback for the Buffalo Bills; like Ronald Reagan, he was never a top-rank star but worked steadily and competently and became head of his fellow workers' union. Kemp worked briefly in the 1960s for incoming Governor Reagan in California, then returned to the Buffalo area; and when the suburban Democratic congressman ran for the Senate, Kemp ran for Congress. In his first years in the House, Kemp seemed a conventional Republican. He supported the Nixon Administration and, like most young members of both parties, used the advantages of incumbency to help himself win reelection. He was spectacularly successful. But as late as 1974, when Democrats had the political initiative and still seemed to be the party of ideas, most observers would have considered Kemp one of the members of Congress least likely to prove an intellectual leader.

But Jack Kemp, a physical education major in college, started to study economics—and leavened his study with reflections on the America he knew, as the son of a small businessman in southern California and as the representative of suburban Buffalo. Kemp grew up in an area that had one of the highest growth rates in modern American history, and he now represented an area with very little economic growth. He grew up in an environment where government was not a looming presence and where tax rates seemed low; he now lived in a state that, during the 1970s, became more highly taxed than anywhere else in the country. While Democratic economists were concerned about the distribution of wealth, Kemp was concerned about the creation of wealth. He came to believe that the nation was overtaxing the productive (i.e., rich) people in the economy—killing the geese that laid the golden eggs. In conjunction with economist Arthur Laffer, *Wall Street Journal* editorialists Jude Wanniski and Paul Craig Roberts, and others who became identified as supply-side economists, he publicized the so-called Laffer curve, the idea that at some point taxes get so high that an increase in tax rates brings in less revenue. So as Jimmy Carter was summoning the old Democratic economists and applying their prescriptions with disastrous results, Kemp developed what became known as the Kemp–Roth tax cut — the proposal to cut taxes 10% a year for each of three years. He argues that such a tax cut would bring in more, not less, revenue, because it would encorage economic production. Accordingly, there would be no need to cut federal spending — a key point for a Buffalo area congressman, since this is one of the relatively few parts of the country where no great demand exists for cutting federal spending.

Kemp's ideas have gained great currency among the public and have become almost a gospel for the incoming Reagan Administration, although as Reagan took office the focus went off the tax cut and onto David Stockman's budget cuts. Ironically, Kemp–Roth, which seems to promise voters a windfall, is not very popular; too many people suspect that it would just stimulate inflation. But the Reagan Administration is being faithful to what appears to be Kemp's central concern: increasing the vitality and growth of the private economy.

There have been all kinds of scenarios for Kemp to run for statewide or national office. At the Republican National Convention, there was a move among many Reaganites to get him nominated for vice president; there was perhaps a concern that Kemp's ideas, which Reagan has largely embraced, should be carried on even if Reagan is no longer president (and George Bush referred to Kemp–Roth once as "voodoo economics"). When Kemp stepped before the delegates at Detroit to deliver his own speech on economics, there was electricity crackling between the podium and the floor. Delegates cheered lustily when he went into his standard litany — "When you tax something, you get less of it. When you subsidize something, you get more of it. In America today, we are taxing work, saving, investment, enterprise and excellence, as never before. And we are subsidizing non-work, consumption, debt, leisure, and mediocrity. Is it any surprise that we are getting less of the one and more of the other?"

It was a moment of well-deserved triumph: a man who had developed and advanced ideas stood before a party that had embraced them and that was prepared to win an election to put them into effect. It was time for seasoned observers to stop sneering at Jack Kemp; he had proved himself more than just a former football player — just as the man who was the most important popularizer of new ideas for the Democrats for a generation, Hubert Humphrey, had proved himself more than a pharmacist. Kemp sees himself as a man who has brought forward ideas that can turn the country's economy around and can strengthen it beyond people's expectations, and he just may turn out to be right.

At the Detroit convention Kemp also proved himself to be competent dealing with non-economic issues as well. He chaired the platform subcommittee on defense and produced a solid, intellectually respectable plank that expressed most Americans' desire for a stronger, more aggressive defense but did not get candidate Reagan in trouble. Kemp has had some experience on that issue; he served on the Defense Subcommittee of Appropriations in the House. But of course he is much more than just the ninth-ranking Republican on Appropriations, more even than the chairman of the House Republican Conference, a position to which he was elected after the 1980 election. He carries an authority that comes both from a close personal relationship with President Reagan and from his own record as an initiator and articulator of ideas. Undoubtedly other congressmen resent Kemp. He has risen so quickly and has gone so much further than they dreamed; he has influenced the thought of a generation while they are still struggling to influence a majority on their subcommittees.

Like most congressmen, he started off concerned about the problems of his district, but he saw them in a larger perspective than most do and attacked them with much more originality.

Naturally there has been much speculation that Kemp will run for higher office. He seems to have flinched at the prospect, and not without reason. He could hardly have forced himself onto the Republican national ticket in 1980 — a ticket of a former actor and a former football player would not do — and he was not prepared to run for president himself as some of his supply-side friends wanted before it became clear how much Ronald Reagan shared their ideas and would stay committed to them. He was mentioned as a possible candidate for the Senate in 1980, but that would have meant a primary fight against Jacob Javits at a time when Kemp was lining up unanimous Republican support for his tax cut proposal, and it would have been a risky race in the general election. New York is still in many respects a Democratic state, and voters in the New York City area have been suspicious of candidates who can be portrayed as favoring dismantling of federal programs. It is suggested also that Kemp should run for governor in 1982. But why? He has shown little interest in New York state government, which in any case is a kind of holding operation these days. Kemp does not need statewide office to hold a national platform; he already has one. He does not need the quotidian hassles of an office like governor; he has spent his time constructively grappling with major problems. The idea that you can run for president only if you have served as senator or governor should by now be passe.

The only good reason for Kemp to run for statewide office is if his 38th district is eliminated by redistricting. But that is unlikely. The legislature will have to be devious indeed to avoid creating one district that is made up primarily of Buffalo suburbs. And Kemp has demonstrated his capacity to carry the Buffalo suburbs. The same ideas that have captured the national Republican Party have also enabled him to capture in 1980 the votes of 82% of his constituents in this district where most voters are, by heritage, Democrats. No other incumbent is going to want to run against that record. So the prospect is for Jack Kemp to continue in the House — and to continue as one of the more productive thinkers and effective doers in American politics.

Census Data   Pop. (1980 final) 498,233, up 7% in 1970s. Median family income, 1970, $11,583, 121% of U.S.

The Voters

Employment profile 1970   White collar, 52%. Blue collar, 36%. Service, 11%. Farm, 1%.

Ethnic groups   Black 1980, 1%. Hispanic 1980, 1%. Asian 1980, 1%. Total foreign stock 1970, 23%. Poland, 5%; Germany, 4%; Italy, Canada, 3% each; UK, 2%.

Presidential Vote

1980	Reagan (R)	101,559	(48%)
	Carter (D)	92,435	(43%)
	Anderson (I)	16,489	(8%)
1976	Ford (R)	122,219	(55%)
	Carter (D)	98,494	(45%)

Rep. Jack F. Kemp (R) Elected 1970; b. July 13, 1935, Los Angeles, Cal.; home, Hamburg; Occidental Col., B.A. 1957, Long Beach St. U., Cal. Western U.

Career Pro football quarterback, San Diego Chargers and Buffalo Bills, 1957–70, Cofounder and Pres., AFL Players Assn., 1965–70, AFL Most Valuable Player, 1965; Army, 1958; TV and radio commentator; Special Asst. to Gov. Ronald Reagan of Cal., 1967, and to the Chmn., Rep. Natl Comm., 1969.

Offices 2235 LHOB, 202-225-5265. Also 1101 Fed. Bldg., 111 W. Huron St., Buffalo 14202, 716-846-4123.

Committees *Appropriations* (9th). Subcommittee: Foreign Operations.

Budget (5th).

Group Ratings

	ADA	COPE	PC	LCV	CFA	RPN	NAB	NSI	NTU	ACA	ACU
1980	6	12	30	51	21	—	91	100	53	86	82
1979	11	16	20	31	4	—	—	—	59	92	97
1978	15	15	20	13	18	80	100	100	31	96	100

Key Votes

1) Draft Registn $	FOR	6) Fair Hsg DOJ Enfrc	AGN	11) Cut Socl Incr Dfns $	FOR
2) Ban $ to Nicrgua	FOR	7) Lim PAC Contrbtns	AGN	12) Hosptl Cost Controls	AGN
3) Dlay MX Missile	AGN	8) Cap on Food Stmp $	FOR	13) Gasln Ctrls & Allctns	AGN
4) Nuclr Mortorium	AGN	9) New US Dep Edcatn	AGN	14) Lim Wndfll Prof Tax	FOR
5) Alaska Lands Bill	AGN	10) Cut OSHA $	FOR	15) Chryslr Loan Grntee	—

Election Results

1980 general	Jack F. Kemp (R-C-RTL)	167,434	(82%)	($158,061)
	Gale A. Denn (D-L)	37,875	(18%)	
1980 primary	Jack F. Kemp (R-C-RTL), unopp.			
1978 general	Jack F. Kemp (R-C)	113,928	(95%)	($64,251)
	James A. Peck (L).............	6,204	(5%)	($6,418)

THIRTY-NINTH DISTRICT

The 39th congressional district of New York is the western half of the Southern Tier—that is, the counties on the northern side of the boundary between New York and Pennsylvania. Extending from the small city of Elmira to Lake Erie, the district contains the Corning Glass Works in Steuben County, two small Indian reservations, and a point on the western boundary exactly 496 miles from New York City via the Thomas E. Dewey Thruway. The small cities scattered among the district's valleys—Jamestown, Olean, Hornell, Corning—and on the shores of Lake Erie—Dunkirk, Fredonia—tend to be Democratic or politically marginal, reflecting the preference of the Irish and Italian Catholics who came to this part of Upstate New York after it had first been settled by New England Yankees. Outside the towns the Yankee Republicans still predominate and, as in most of Upstate New York, control the district politically.

Historically this has always been a Republican district. It was represented by Daniel Reed, the last Republican chairman of the House Ways and Means Committee; by Charles Goodell, who was appointed to the Senate in 1968 after the death of Robert Kennedy and whose transformation from Upstate moderate to Vietnam dove led to his defeat by Conservative James Buckley in 1970; and James Hastings, who resigned in 1976 and was later convicted on salary kickback charges. Republicans expected to win the seat in the 1976 special election; their candidate, Jack Calkins, longtime head of the Republican Congressional Campaign Committee and a native of the area, seemed like a strong candidate.

But in the middle 1970s, voters were especially anxious to have elected officials who understood their problems closely and from first-hand experience. While Calkins had plenty of experience in Washington, he had not lived in the Southern Tier for years and was plainly out of touch with what was going on there. The Democrat, Stanley Lundine, was not. As mayor of Jamestown, he had made a popular record. He had a strong local base there in Chautauqua County, in the western end of the district, and he was able to make his local experience relevant to people in the eastern counties.

Lundine won that election with a surprising 61% — fully 19 percentage points ahead of where Jimmy Carter finished in the 39th later in the year. With an excellent staff and by keeping in touch with his constituents, he has maintained high standing at home. He won again in the 1976 general election and in 1978, the latter time against a hard-campaigning Catholic priest. Against a Jamestown civic activist, he won 55% of the vote in 1980. The pattern clearly is for a declining percentage; Lundine's work on behalf of the economy of the area is not sufficient to overcome the national trends in the other direction. Redistricting is a big question mark for 1982. The legislature could leave the 39th in pretty much the same shape it is in now. Or it could divide it up among adjacent districts, which would almost certainly result in Lundine's retirement. In any case, he will probably face a tough Republican challenge in 1982, and his success may be determined as much by the fate of the Reagan economic programs as by anything he does himself.

Census Data   Pop. (1980 final) 471,666, up 1% in 1970s. Median family income, 1970, $8,936, 93% of U.S.

The Voters

Employment profile 1970   White collar, 43%. Blue collar, 39%. Service, 14%. Farm, 4%.

Ethnic groups   Black 1980, 2%. Hispanic 1980, 1%. Am. Ind. 1980, 1%. Total foreign stock 1970, 14%. Italy, 3%; Sweden, Germany, Poland, 2% each; UK, Canada, 1% each.

Presidential Vote

1980	Reagan (R)	97,773	(54%)
	Carter (D)	67,886	(37%)
	Anderson (I)	12,049	(7%)
1976	Ford (R)	106,803	(58%)
	Carter (D)	77,776	(42%)

Rep. Stanley N. Lundine (D) Elected March 2, 1976; b. Feb. 4, 1939, Jamestown; home, Jamestown; Duke U. B.A. 1961, NYU, LL.B. 1964.

Career Chautauqua Co. Pub. Defender, 1965–67; Jamestown City Assoc. Corp. Counsel, 1967–69, Mayor, 1969–76.

Offices 231 CHOB, 202-225-3161. Also Fed. Bldg., Jamestown 14702, 716-484-0252.

Committees *Banking, Finance and Urban Affairs* (15th). Subcommittees: Economic Stabilization; Housing and Community Development; International Trade, Investment and Monetary Policy.

Science and Technology (18th). Subcommittees: Energy Research and Production; Science, Research and Technology.

Select Committee on Aging (14th).

Group Ratings

	ADA	COPE	PC	LCV	CFA	RPN	NAB	NSI	NTU	ACA	ACU
1980	83	79	57	65	71	—	18	0	23	13	11
1979	79	79	55	62	44	—	—	—	22	17	11
1978	70	85	63	68	50	67	10	40	24	26	13

Key Votes

1) Draft Registn $	AGN	6) Fair Hsg DOJ Enfrc	FOR	11) Cut Socl Incr Dfns $	AGN
2) Ban $ to Nicrgua	—	7) Lim PAC Contrbtns	FOR	12) Hosptl Cost Controls	FOR
3) Dlay MX Missile	FOR	8) Cap on Food Stmp $	AGN	13) Gasln Ctrls & Allctns	FOR
4) Nuclr Mortorium	AGN	9) New US Dep Edcatn	AGN	14) Lim Wndfll Prof Tax	AGN
5) Alaska Lands Bill	FOR	10) Cut OSHA $	AGN	15) Chryslr Loan Grntee	FOR

Election Results

1980 general	Stanley N. Lundine (D)	93,839	(55%)	($125,269)
	James Abdella (R-C)............	75,039	(44%)	($83,315)
1980 primary	Stanley N. Lundine (D), unopposed			
1978 general	Stanley N. Lundine (D)	79,385	(58%)	($92,454)
	Crispin M. Maguire (R-C)	56,431	(42%)	($65,508)

NORTH CAROLINA

North Carolina, now the tenth largest state, nonetheless does not bulk large in the national consciousness. It is a place with a feel and a vibrancy of its own, which is not well known to most outsiders. North Carolina has no major city to establish the state's identification, no well-known history or monuments, no major vacation spots—no Atlanta, Mount Vernon, or Disney World. Indeed, North Carolina does not have a metropolitan area with a population even approaching one million. But North Carolina is, although few Americans are aware of it, one of the most industrialized states in the nation. This does not mean that it is economically advanced; most of its industry is in textiles with their low wages or furniture making or tobacco. In these three products North Carolina is number one in the nation; in most others it is not important. The state has a proud political tradition, but one that has never produced a major national leader. The closest it has come is Sam Ervin and, perhaps, Jesse Helms.

The political development of North Carolina has been guided by its terrain, but the state really has no clear geographic delineation from its neighbors to the north or south; it is just a slice of land running from coastal barrier islands and the coastal plain up through the rolling Piedmont to the mountains, the highest east of the Rockies. North Carolina was a late-developing colony; it has no major port like Charleston, South Carolina, no inland water route like the rivers that branch off from Chesapeake Bay and reach into Virginia and Maryland. North Carolina's settlers were not as rich as those elsewhere, but they were fiercely independent; they declared independence even before the Declaration in Philadelphia, and they were among the last of the 13 original states to join the Union — because they thought the Constitution might be too constricting. North Carolina was contrary about the Civil War, too. It refused to secede from the Union until Virginia did so, and cut it off from the north; then it contributed more soldiers to the Confederacy than any other state.

This continues to be a state of the common people, not having the kind of aristocrats who dominate business and politics in Virginia nor the brash Ted Turnerish tycoons of Georgia's Atlanta. But it has more people than either of those states, and in the late 1970s it was gaining more new jobs than either as well. North Carolina has had little in-migration from other states or from abroad — except for the slaves brought in before 1808, and North Carolina has always had a lower black percentage than other Deep South states. For many years North Carolina sent migrants elsewhere, from the yeoman farmers (and three presidents, Jackson, Polk, and Andrew Johnson), who were born here and moved to Tennessee, to entire high school classes of young blacks on the bus for New York or Philadelphia in the 1950s and 1960s. Today North Carolina remains overwhelmingly Baptist and Methodist (it was one of the last states to allow liquor by the drink, and most counties still do not), but it is no longer an exporter of people; there are jobs and boom enough to hold people here.

North Carolina is proud of its tradition of support for education, but it is still one of the most heavily blue collar of states. It is proud of its progressive tradition of government, but that tradition has rested on an unspoken policy of not disturbing the state's major economic interests, even if that means not attracting better-paying jobs and technically more advanced industry. North Carolina is proud of its tradition of racial moderation, and proud as well these days that it was the place where the lunch counter sit-in movement started. But it is also the state of the Wilmington Ten case and where Ku Klux Klan members shot and killed self-styled Communists in 1979 in Greensboro. It should be added that the facts of the Wilmington Ten case do not make it clear that an injustice was done and the KKK killers were part of a tiny group without significant support.

And North Carolina in the late 1970s began living up to its traditions much more than it had in the recent past. The growth in the number of jobs was substantial, and they included high-paying jobs that some low-paying local employers were not happy to see come in. Organized labor, traditionally weak in this least unionized of states, achieved a settlement with J. P. Stevens, one of the largest textile makers, and won an organizing fight in Roanoke Rapids, a town that could have been the scene of the movie *Norma Rae*. North Carolina voters elected blacks to statewide office, and blacks generally no longer suffered from overt segregation or the crude racism of the past. Many of these developments were the work of

Democratic Governor Jim Hunt, first elected in 1976 and reelected in 1980 by a large margin despite a Republican trend. He has come to dominate the politics of the state as no other governor has for the past 20 years.

Hunt could not have done as much ten years before, when his support of civil rights and his reputation as a liberal would probably have prevented him from winning high office. But by 1976 they did not prove to be insuperable obstacles. The state then had a Republican governor whose election had come as a surprise, to no one more than himself, and voters were ready for more aggressive leadership. Hunt promised to provide it — and did. He made North Carolina's job recruitment program as aggressive as South Carolina's — which is very aggressive indeed — and in 1980 the state led the nation in foreign business investment. Hunt pushed for competency tests in the schools for both teachers and pupils — tests that ensure that students here, unlike many inner-city schools in the North, can read and write when they graduate. He confounded those who would pigeonhole him ideologically by strongly backing capital punishment and refusing to exonerate the Wilmington Ten; he strongly backed the state university system in disputes with Joseph Califano's HEW. Hunt also succeeded in winning voter approval of an amendment allowing governors to seek a second term, overturning an old North Carolina tradition that was strongly supported by Sam Ervin. He won reelection overwhelmingly in both the Democratic primary and the general election in 1980, despite the Republican tide. A man of great forcefulness and self-confidence, Hunt is likely to continue to dominate North Carolina state politics during his second term, although a raft of ambitious politicians are looking toward the governorship in 1984. Hunt may also become a national figure. It seems almost inevitable that he will run for the Senate against Jesse Helms in 1984, when both of their terms expire.

Jesse Helms is the product of one of the periodic changes of rhythm North Carolina politics has seen in the past decade, although he has come to represent much more than that. He ran for the Senate in 1972, as a recent former Democrat, well known as a Raleigh TV commentator and as a broadcaster with his own hookup on the radio Tobacco Network. He accused Richard Nixon of "appeasing Red China" when he went to Peking; but he was the beneficiary of a pro-Nixon Republican tide in 1972 that also elected a Republican governor and gave Republicans their strongest position ever in the legislature. Then, in 1974, the tide moved the other way. Watergate — and the part that North Carolina's Sam Ervin played in it — was probably a major reason for the Democratic trend. In any case, Democrat Robert Morgan easily won Ervin's Senate seat when Ervin retired, Democrats captured two Republican House seats and virtually eliminated Republicans from the legislature. The Democratic trend continued in 1976, when Jimmy Carter carried the state with a 55%–44% majority and Jim Hunt was elected governor by nearly a 2–1 margin, and in 1978, when Democrats won at almost every level by similar margins. The exception to the pattern in that last year was Jesse Helms's victory. He was fortunate that Luther Hodges, Jr., son of a former governor and a leading North Carolina banker, was beaten in the Democratic runoff by John Ingram, the state insurance commissioner who had a reputation as a populist but virtually no campaign funds and little campaigning skill. Helms, in contrast, spent more than $7 million — although, to be fair, it must be added that most of that money was spent on raising more money (and accumulating lists of donors) by direct mail. The net funds helped Helms to an unimpressive win over Ingram. But they also helped to make him a national power, because he suddenly had the capacity to raise large sums almost overnight, by appealing to his previous contributors.

In his first term in the Senate, Helms was considered an ineffective extremist; in his second term, he has come to be seen as a powerful and dedicated exponent of ideas. Both views are accurate. Helms is a man who believes it is desperately important that America be stronger abroad and fiscally more sound at home, and that the government should promote what he considers to be correct and proper personal morality and religious values. He sees himself as the purest of political conservatives. He stationed himself at the 1976 Republican Platform Committee hearings and as a one-man lobby forced the adoption of platform planks that repudiated the record of the presidential nominee, Gerald Ford. As a member of the Senate majority in the early days of the Reagan Administration, he placed a hold on — and thus delayed — the approval of several of the president's appointments to State Department positions. During his first term Helms had little impact on legislation except perhaps, through his seat on the Agriculture Committee, on tobacco matters. But at the beginning of his second term he won a seat on Foreign Relations, and two years later, as Republicans won a Senate majority, he became chairman of the Agriculture Committee. He will campaign vigorously for tobacco. Northern liberals take particular delight in assailing tobacco programs, in part because they would love to see Helms squirm. Helms argues that there is actually no tobacco subsidy, since the government only makes loans to tobacco producer groups, but actually the loans do not quite pay their way, and the availability of low-interest loans in a time of tight, scarce money is just as much a subsidy as is an outright grant. What Helms does not mention is the system of tobacco allotments that limits the number of people who can grow the crop and receive federal price supports. Among the holders of tobacco allotments: Mrs. Jesse Helms. Helms and other North Carolinians are quite right, however, in saying that the cost of the program is very low — minuscule next to almost any government program that is as often talked about — and that it helps a business that keeps a lot of people on the land.

Helms has been the most hawkish member of an increasingly hawkish Foreign Relations Committee; he was a particular champion of the Muzorewa government of Zimbabwe-Rhodesia. Now he chairs the subcommittee on Latin America and worries about the Red advance in Central American and the Caribbean. On Agriculture, Helms disagreed with committee Democrats and Republican Robert Dole on the food stamp program; Helms wants it cut way back.

Helms is not a man who expects political success; when Ronald Reagan was running, he was fond of saying that maybe God had given America one more chance — with the implication that it probably was not to be. His is the perfect political attitude for direct mail fund-raising: the forebodings of doom, the pessimistic outlook, the grim determination to keep fighting for what is right no matter what the odds. How he will work out as an active participant in government is less clear. Helms does have considerable intelligence and sensitivity to the political process, but does he have the temperament to be part of a majority?

Helms's clout in the Senate was increased substantially in the 1980 elections, and not only because more Republicans were elected. He also was successful in obtaining the election of a like-minded colleague in North Carolina, against considerable odds. The only real political asset John East, the new Republican senator, had when the campaign began was Jesse Helms's support. East was a college professor from the rural eastern (and most Democratic) part of the state; he was originally from the North; he was totally unknown. The Democratic incumbent, Robert Morgan, seemed to be in line with the thinking of the state and had made no mistakes. He had a hard-line record on defense, a moderate record on economic issues, and a reputation as a consumer advocate. He also had a solid campaign treasury.

But East, as it turned out, could more than match him dollar for dollar. He had the benefit of Helms's fund-raising lists, and with that help he was able to spend $600,000 on television advertising in the last six weeks of the campaign. The barrage against Morgan concentrated on a few issues: his support of the Panama Canal Treaties, his support of aid to Nicaragua, his opposition to the B-1 bomber, and his support of aid to New York City. Morgan was unable to match this barrage and ended up running about even with Jimmy Carter, who barely lost the state; East had 50% to Morgan's 49%. This was one of those very close elections, mostly won by Republicans, that gave the Republican Party control of the Senate for the first time in 28 years. East is a member of the Energy and Judiciary Committees and casts a predictably conservative vote on all issues. Incidentally, he is confined to a wheelchair, which seems to have had no effect either on his campaign or his service in the Senate.

North Carolina has 11 congressional districts, with no additions for 1982. The population has risen at about uniform rates throughout the state, so substantial changes will not be required in redistricting—although the Democratic legislature could make them if it wants to. The big question in redistricting is whether the Democrats will concentrate on protecting threatened members of their own party, e.g., Stephen Neal of the 5th district, or try to beat Republicans, such as Eugene Johnston, the upset winner in the 6th in 1980.

Census Data Pop. (1980 final) 5,874,429, up 16% in 1970s: 2.59% of U.S. total, 10th largest. Central city, 20%; suburban, 26%. Median 4-person family income, 1978, $18,058, 88% of U.S., 43d highest.

1979 Share of Federal Tax Burden $9,061,000,000; 2.01% of U.S. total, 16th largest.

1979 Share of Federal Outlays $9,035,017,000; 1.95% of U.S. total, 18th largest.

DOD	$2,227,810,000	15th	(2.10%)	HEW	$3,856,331,000	13th	(2.16%)
DOE	$5,440,000	39th	(0.05%)	ERDA	$2,611,000	38th	(0.09%)
HUD	$128,638,000	14th	(1.95%)	NASA	$3,118,000	30th	(0.07%)
VA	$551,750,000	11th	(2.66%)	DOT	$260,449,000	21st	(1.58%)
EPA	$211,708,000	6th	(3.99%)	DOC	$49,684,000	14th	(1.57%)
DOI	$43,046,000	30th	(0.78%)	USDA	$582,297,000	13th	(2.42%)

Economic Base Textile mill products, especially knitting mills and yarn and thread mills; agriculture, notably tobacco, broilers, hogs, and eggs; apparel and other textile products, especially men's and boys' furnishings; finance, insurance, and real estate; household furniture, and other furniture and fixtures; food and kindred products, especially meat products; electrical equipment and supplies, especially communication equipment.

Political Lineup Governor, James B. Hunt, Jr. (D). Senators, Jesse A. Helms (R) and John P. East (R). Representatives, 11 (7 D and 4 R); 11 in 1982. State Senate, 50 (40 D and 10 R); State House of Representatives, 120 (96 D and 24 R).

The Voters

Registration 2,774,844 Total. 1,974,889 D (71%); 677,077 R (24%); 1,973 others (0%); 120,905 unaffiliated (4%).

Employment profile 1970 White collar, 38%. Blue collar, 46%. Service, 11%. Farm, 5%.

Ethnic groups Black 1980, 22%. Hispanic 1980, 1%. Am. Ind. 1980, 1%. Total foreign stock 1970, 2%.

Presidential Vote

1980	Reagan (R)	915,018	(49%)
	Carter (D)	873,635	(47%)
	Anderson (I)	52,800	(3%)
1976	Ford (R)	741,690	(44%)
	Carter (D)	927,365	(55%)

1980 Democratic Presidential Primary			*1980 Republican Presidential Primary*		
Carter	516,778	(70%)	Reagan	113,854	(68%)
Kennedy	130,684	(18%)	Bush	36,631	(22%)
Brown	21,420	(3%)	Five others	13,368	(8%)
No preference	68,380	(9%)	No preference	4,538	(3%)

SENATORS

Sen. Jesse A. Helms (R) Elected 1972, seat up 1984; b. Oct., 18, 1921, Monroe; home, Raleigh; Wingate Col., Wake Forest Col.

Career Navy, WWII; City Ed., *Raleigh Times*; Admin. Asst. to U.S. Sens. Willis Smith, 1951–53, and Alton Lennon, 1953; Exec. Dir. N.C. Bankers Assn., 1953–60; Raleigh City Cncl., 1957–61; Exec. V.P., WRAL-TV and Tobacco Radio Network, 1960–72.

Offices 4213 DSOB, 202-224-6342. Also Fed. Bldg., Raleigh 27611, 919-755-4630, and Box. 2944, Hickory 28601, 704-322-5170.

Committees *Agriculture, Nutrition, and Forestry* (Chairman). Subcommittee: Agricultural Production, Marketing, and Stabilization of Prices.

Foreign Relations (3d). Subcommittees: African Affairs; East Asian and Pacific Affairs; Near Eastern and South Asian Affairs; Western Hemisphere Affairs (Chairman).

Rules and Administration (5th).

Select Committee on Ethics (2d).

Group Ratings

	ADA	COPE	PC	LCV	CFA	RPN	NAB	NSI	NTU	ACA	ACU
1980	11	5	17	23	0	—	100	100	80	100	100
1979	5	5	26	—	14	—	—	—	80	100	100
1978	5	11	13	18	5	75	100	100	48	96	100

Key Votes

1) Draft Registn $	FOR	6) Fair Housng Cloture	AGN	11) Cut Socl Incr Defns	FOR
2) Ban $ to Nicrgua	AGN	7) Ban $ Rape Abortns	FOR	12) Income Tax Indexing	FOR
3) Dlay MX Missile	AGN	8) Cap on Food Stmp $	FOR	13) Lim Spdg 21% GNP	FOR
4) Nuclr Mortorium	AGN	9) New US Dep Edcatn	AGN	14) Incr Wndfll Prof Tax	AGN
5) Alaska Lands Bill	AGN	10) Cut OSHA Inspctns	FOR	15) Chryslr Loan Grntee	AGN

Election Results

1978 general	Jesse A. Helms (R)	619,151	(55%)	($7,460,966)
	John R. Ingram (D)	516,663	(45%)	($264,088)
1978 primary	Jesse A. Helms (R), unopposed			
1972 general	Jesse A. Helms (R)	795,248	(54%)	($654,246)
	Nick Galifianakis (D)	677,293	(46%)	($470,093)

Sen. John P. East (R) Elected 1980, seat up 1986; b. May 5, 1931, Springfield, Ill.; home, Greenville; Earlham Col., B.A. 1953; U. of Ill., J.D. 1959, U. of Fla., M.A., Ph.D. 1964.

Career USMC, 1953–55; Practicing atty., 1960; Prof., E. Carolina U., 1964–80; Rep. Nat. Committeeman, 1976, 1980, Platform Comm. 1976; Mem. Ed. Bd., *Modern Age* and *Political Science Review.*

Offices 5107 DSOB, 202-224-3154. Also P.O. Drawer 25009, Raleigh 27611, 919-775-4401 and P.O. Box 8087, Greenville 27834, 919-757-1188.

Committees *Energy and Natural Resources* (10th). Subcommittees: Energy Conservation and Supply; Energy Regulation; Energy Research and Development.

Judiciary (7th). Subcommittees: Courts; Security and Terrorism; Separation of Power (Chairman).

Labor and Human Resources (9th). Subcommittees: Labor; Education; Handicapped.

Group Ratings and Key Votes: Newly Elected

Election Results

1980 general	John P. East (R)	898,064	(50%)	($1,175,875)
	Robert Morgan (D)	887,653	(49%)	($948,209)
1980 primary	John P. East (R), unopposed			
1974 general	Robert Morgan (D)	633,775	(62%)	($781,201)
	William E. Stevens (R)	377,618	(37%)	($385,527)

GOVERNOR

Gov. James B. Hunt, Jr. (D) Elected 1976, term expires Jan. 1985; b. May 16, 1937, Greensboro; N.C. St. U., B.S. 1959, M.S. 1962, J.D. 1964.

Career Natl. College Dir., Dem. Natl. Comm., 1962–63, Econ. Advisor to State of Nepal, 1964–66; Practicing atty., 1966–72; Asst. N.C. Dem. Party Chmn., 1969; Lt. Gov. of N.C., 1973–77.

Offices The Capitol, Raleigh 27602, 919-733-5811.

Election Results

1980 gen.	James B. Hunt, Jr. (D)	1,143,145	(62%)
	Beverly Lake (R)	691,449	(37%)
1980 prim.	James B. Hunt, Jr. (D)	524,844	(70%)
	Robert W. Scott (D)	217,289	(29%)
	One other (D)	11,551	(2%)
1976 gen.	James B. Hunt, Jr. (D)	1,081,293	(65%)
	David T. Flaherty (R)	564,102	(34%)

FIRST DISTRICT

If you want to know why tobacco farming is still subsidized and encouraged by a federal government that also seeks to discourage smoking, the best place to come is the eastern coastal plain of North Carolina. This is flat land, not particularly distinguished for its fertili-

ty, yet it is among the most heavily settled rural land in the United States. The reason is to-bacco. It is a most peculiar crop, one that requires much labor and close tending, since dif-ferent tobacco leaves on the same stalk mature at different times. It is also a crop that acre for acre, can be lucrative. But the crop, since the abolition of slavery, has been grown on small farms, not large plantations; fifteen acres of tobacco can produce enough income to support a family. Tobacco production, moreover, is concentrated in a few areas: virtually all of this country's tobacco is grown in North Carolina, South Carolina, and Kentucky. As a result, in these states and in some of their congressional districts there are literally tens of thousands of families whose livelihoods come directly from tobacco. Not surprisingly, their representatives in Congress are not going to allow federal tobacco programs to be cut in any way if they can help it.

For many years tobacco was the only real mainstay of the economy in eastern North Carolina. Job opportunities were so scarce that eastern North Carolina produced thousands of migrants north and has produced very high percentages of volunteers for military service, from the Civil War to the post-Vietnam era. More recently, there have been more jobs: new textile and apparel mills, factories built by European and Japanese companies. But there are virtually no unions here, and wages are still low. Accordingly, tobacco retains its symbolic and most of its economic importance.

North Carolina's 1st congressional district lies entirely within the state's eastern coastal zone. It includes the Outer Banks, the string of coastal islands beyond Pamlico and Albe-marle Sounds, where the Wright brothers flew the first airplane. Also here is Cape Hatteras, where the warm Gulf Stream meets colder currents, creating seas that have sunk countless ships. There is really no good port here (or anywhere else in North Carolina), and most of the people live inland, in small cities such as New Bern, Elizabeth City, and Greenville—at 34,000 the district's largest city. Even more live in the countryside, on small farms or in iso-lated house trailers. Some 25% of the 1st's voters are black, the second largest percentage in North Carolina's 11 districts.

The white voters of the 1st retain from their slaveholding days a Democratic preference. They steadfastly supported Democratic presidential candidates until 1968, when they went for George Wallace, and 1972 when they went for Richard Nixon. After Watergate, the area reverted to its historic Democratic voting habits: Senator Robert Morgan received 79% of the vote here in 1974 and Governor James Hunt got 77% in 1976. Even Senator Jesse Helms who has a following here today, going back to his days as a commentator on the radio Tobacco Network, did not quite carry the district in 1978. The wind seemed to shift sharply in 1980. Jimmy Carter's percentage declined from 60% to 52% in the district, and Robert Morgan, who hoped to win a big margin here in his bid for reelection, instead took only 57% of the vote and lost to East Carolina University professor John East statewide.

The congressman from the 1st is Walter Jones, a Democrat first chosen in a 1966 special election and reelected ever since. Jones is now the chairman of the Merchant Marine and Fisheries Committee, a position his predecessor held. Jones tends to support the elaborate system of subsidies that help the maritime industry and members of the maritime unions escape the rigors of competition. There is a certain irony here: the 1st district has no really important ports, although the Intercoastal Waterway proceeds through Albemarle and Pamlico Sounds, behind the barrier islands of the Carolina Banks and Cape Hatteras.

Jones had not really been expected to become chairman; he did so only after the defeats of John Murphy of New York, an Abscam defendant, and Thomas Ashley of Toledo, Ohio. To get the post, Jones had to give up the chairmanship of the Tobacco Subcommittee of Agriculture, a post arguably of more immediate importance to his district. Of comfort is the fact that the chair went to fellow North Carolinian Charles Rose of the 7th district, who is unlikely to have different views on tobacco issues. Jones is nearing 70 but has not attracted significant opposition and seems likely to continue in the House if he wants to. Redistricting will not much affect the leanings of this conservative Democratic district.

Census Data   Pop. (1980 final) 516,756, up 12% in 1970s. Median family income, 1970, $6,368, 66% of U.S.

The Voters

Employment profile 1970   White collar, 36%. Blue collar, 40%. Service, 13%. Farm, 11%.
Ethnic groups   Black 1980, 34%. Hispanic 1980, 1%. Total foreign stock 1970, 1%.

Presidential Vote

1980	Reagan (R)	72,369	(46%)
	Carter (D)	81,472	(52%)
	Anderson (I)	3,293	(2%)
1976	Ford (R)	52,752	(40%)
	Carter (D)	79,503	(60%)

Rep. Walter B. Jones (D) Elected Feb. 5, 1966; b. Aug. 19, 1913, Fayetteville; home, Farmville; N.C. St. U., B.S. 1934.

Career Office supply business, 1934–49; Mayor of Farmville, 1949–53; N.C. Gen. Assembly, 1955–59; N.C. Senate, 1965.

Offices 241 CHOB, 202-225-3101. Also 108. E. Wilson St., Farmville 27828, 919 753 3082.

Committees *Agriculture* (3d). Subcommittee: Tobacco and Peanuts.

Merchant Marine and Fisheries (Chairman).

Group Ratings

	ADA	COPE	PC	LCV	CFA	RPN	NAB	NSI	NTU	ACA	ACU
1980	22	50	37	35	36	—	73	75	30	38	62
1979	11	37	18	9	15	—	—	—	37	43	45
1978	25	25	28	30	9	64	70	100	18	78	67

Key Votes

1) Draft Registn $	FOR	6) Fair Hsg DOJ Enfrc	AGN	11) Cut Socl Incr Dfns $	AGN
2) Ban $ to Nicrgua	FOR	7) Lim PAC Contrbtns	—	12) Hosptl Cost Controls	—
3) Dlay MX Missile	AGN	8) Cap on Food Stmp $	AGN	13) Gasln Ctrls & Allctns	FOR
4) Nuclr Mortorium	AGN	9) New US Dep Edcatn	FOR	14) Lim Wndfll Prof Tax	—
5) Alaska Lands Bill	AGN	10) Cut OSHA $	FOR	15) Chryslr Loan Grntee	FOR

Election Results

1980 general	Walter B. Jones (D)	108,738	(100%)	($29,126)
1980 primary	Walter B. Jones (D)	66,382	(79%)	
	One other (D)	17,170	(21%)	
1978 general	Walter B. Jones (D)	67,716	(80%)	($24,067)
	James Newcomb (R)	16,814	(20%)	

SECOND DISTRICT

North of Raleigh and south of the Virginia line, the 2d congressional district is situated on an inland portion of the coastal plain where it rises to become the Piedmont. This is a predominantly rural and small-town district; its largest city, Rocky Mount, has only 41,000 people. Like much of North Carolina, the 2d's economy depends almost entirely on textiles and the tobacco crop. What makes the 2d distinctive politically is the size of its black population—almost 40% of its residents (although only 29% of registered voters) are black, the highest percentage in the state, and comparable with what one finds in the Deep South. Black outmigration from this area was great in the decades between World War II and the 1970s; it has substantially stopped in the last ten years, as opportunites have been scarcer in northern cities and more plentiful in North Carolina. The prospect, therefore, is for the black percentage of eligible voters to grow slowly in the next decade—the reversal of almost a century-long trend.

The other distinctive feature of the 2d district is the presence here of Orange County. Most of the nation's Orange Counties, in California, Florida, and even New York, are solidly conservative; this one, which contains the University of North Carolina and its beautiful little city of Chapel Hill, is the state's banner liberal county. It was one of two in the state that went for George McGovern in 1972 (the other was Northampton, a black-majority area with a liberally inclined white boss, also in the 2d).

For nearly three decades the congressman from the 2d has been a man more akin in spirit to the Old South than to its young blacks or Chapel Hill residents, Democrat L. H. Fountain. He is the kind of politician who wears white linen suits in the summertime and speaks with gentle southern courtliness the year round. During his years in Congress, Fountain has compiled a solidly conservative record on economic and social issues. But as chairman of the Intergovernmental Relations and Human Resources Subcommittee of Government Operations, he has been a crusader in one area: drug regulation. For more than a dozen years, Fountain has been holding hearings and arguing that the Food and Drug Administration has been too liberal in allowing possibly dangerous drugs on the market. He has worked to penetrate the layer of secrecy the FDA bureaucracy—convinced that mere laymen cannot understand its workings—puts over its affairs. Fountain's subcommittee has much wider jurisdiction, but apparently he has decided to concentrate on this one area and do a solid job rather than conduct scatter-shot investigations of numerous agencies. He does have other legislative accomplishments, however, notably the writing of a law requiring the setting up of an office of inspector general in each of the Cabinet departments.

For years Fountain had no trouble winning reelection, but he had some significant challenges in the 1970s. They have all come in the Democratic primary; this is not an area where Republicans have provided any significant competition. In 1972 Fountain was opposed by Howard Lee, the black mayor of Chapel Hill; Lee got a creditable 41% in the primary and later was appointed to a top-level job by Governor James Hunt. It would have been fitting if Lee had won this district; it elected a black, Republican George White, in 1898, whose defeat in 1900 began a 28-year period during which no black person served in Congress. In 1976 Fountain had competition from state Senator Russell Kirby. Kirby fell short of winning, but with two minor candidates he held Fountain to 51%—just above what he needed to avoid a runoff. Fountain did not attract serious primary opposition in 1978 or any primary opposition at all in 1980. For 1982, redistricting might result in the removal of Orange County from the district, which would help Fountain. The question is whether, at 69, he chooses to run again and, if so, whether he attracts tough opposition.

Census Data   Pop. (1980 final) 508,097, up 11% in 1970s. Median family income, 1970, $6,550, 68% of U.S.

The Voters

Employment profile 1970   White collar, 36%. Blue collar, 41%. Service, 13%. Farm, 10%.
Ethnic groups   Black 1980, 39%. Hispanic 1980, 1%. Total foreign stock 1970, 1%.

Presidential Vote

1980	Reagan (R)	60,686	(41%)
	Carter (D)	80,482	(57%)
	Anderson (I)	4,872	(3%)
1976	Ford (R)	51,543	(39%)
	Carter (D)	81,050	(61%)

Rep. L. H. Fountain (D) Elected 1952; b. Apr. 23, 1913, Leggett; home, Tarboro; U. of N.C., A.B. 1934, J.D. 1936.

Career   Reading Clerk, N.C. Senate, 1936–41; Practicing atty., 1936–42, 1946–52; Army, WWII; N.C. Senate, 1947–52.

Offices   2188 RHOB, 202-225-4531. Also P.O. Bldg., Tarboro 27886, 919-823-4200.

Committees   *Foreign Affairs* (2d). Subcommittees: Europe and the Middle East; International Security and Scientific Affairs.

Government Operations (2d). Subcommittee: Intergovernmental Relations and Human Resources (Chairman).

Group Ratings

	ADA	COPE	PC	LCV	CFA	RPN	NAB	NSI	NTU	ACA	ACU
1980	17	22	30	43	14	—	83	90	48	61	63
1979	5	30	15	17	8	—	—	—	47	64	71
1978	15	10	25	22	5	58	92	100	29	88	71

Key Votes

1) Draft Registn $	FOR	6) Fair Hsg DOJ Enfrc	AGN	11) Cut Socl Incr Dfns $	FOR
2) Ban $ to Nicrgua	FOR	7) Lim PAC Contrbtns	AGN	12) Hosptl Cost Controls	AGN
3) Dlay MX Missile	AGN	8) Cap on Food Stmp $	AGN	13) Gasln Ctrls & Allctns	FOR
4) Nuclr Mortorium	AGN	9) New US Dep Edcatn	AGN	14) Lim Wndfll Prof Tax	FOR
5) Alaska Lands Bill	AGN	10) Cut OSHA $	FOR	15) Chryslr Loan Grntee	AGN

Election Results

1980 general	L. H. Fountain (D)	99,297	(73%)	($18,370)
	Barry L. Gardner (R)	35,946	(27%)	($6,919)
1980 primary	L. H. Fountain (D), unopposed			
1978 general	L. H. Fountain (D)	61,851	(78%)	($21,984)
	Barry L. Gardner (R)	15,988	(20%)	($7,335)

THIRD DISTRICT

The 3d district of North Carolina is one of small farms, small towns, and Atlantic shore sea-scapes. Lying in the middle of the state's coastal plain, the 3d runs from a point a few miles south of Raleigh and Durham to the Atlantic Ocean near Wilmington. The district's largest city is Goldsboro, with 31,000 people, but an even larger population concentration can be found in Camp Lejeune, the Marine Corps's giant base at the estuary of the New River. One of the Marines' most important installations, Camp Lejeune looms large in the economy of the region, although voters may be disturbed by occasional racial conflict at the base. Also in the 3d is an Air Force base near Goldsboro, with Fort Bragg just over the line in the 7th district.

This is a traditional Democratic area. But with its heavy dependence on the military and its relatively low (27%) black percentage, it was rather conservatively inclined in the late 1960s and early 1970s. In 1972 the district gave George Wallace his highest percentage of any district in the state's Democratic primary, and in the general election that year it delivered a majority for Senate candidate Jesse Helms. After Watergate, it switched back heavily to the Democratic column—except when Helms ran for reelection in 1978. In 1980, it moved back toward the Republicans. Although Ronald Reagan and Senator John East did not carry the district, they cut the Democratic margins enough to score upset victories statewide.

The 3d district seat in the House of Representatives has been handed down in a kind of succession for more than 40 years. From 1934 to 1960 the seat was held by Graham Barden, a stuffy and bigoted conservative. As chairman of the House Education and Labor Com-mittee, Barden refused to recognize the number two Democrat, Adam Clayton Powell, because he was black. Barden retired in 1960 and was succeeded by David Henderson, who had served on his staff. After 14 years Henderson became chairman of the Post Office and Civil Service Committee; in 1976 he decided to retire. His successor was a member of his staff, Charles Whitley.

It would be inaccurate to portray this succession by staffers as automatic. On the contrary, it became more difficult in the 1970s for congressional staffers to win House seats. Voters were less impressed with their experience in local affairs. Whitley wisely made a point of maintaining his actual, not just formal, residence in the 3d district and concentrated on handling district problems.

Whitley's committee assignments were choice ones for a congressman with this kind of district—far better, in fact, than Henderson's or Barden's. He won a seat on the Agriculture Committee and, more important, on its Tobacco Subcommittee; like all North Carolina representatives, he is a strong defender of tobacco. In his first term, he held a seat on Armed Services, useful in a district with so many military bases, but gave it up to spend more time on agricultural matters. He can be expected to be an ardent and assiduous defender of government programs that help tobacco; this is a labor-intensive crop, and thousands of his constituents depend on it for their livings. On issues generally, Whitley is one of the more conservative southern Democrats and thus may be a key man in the 1981–82 sessions. Redistricting will probably not change the complexion of the district much, and Whitley has not had a serious challenge since he was first elected.

Census Data   Pop. (1980 final) 520,027, up 14% in 1970s. Median family income, 1970, $6,193, 65% of U.S.

The Voters

Employment profile 1970   White collar, 34%. Blue collar, 43%. Service, 12%. Farm, 11%.
Ethnic groups   Black 1980, 27%. Hispanic 1980, 2%. Am. Ind. 1980, 1%. Total foreign stock 1970, 2%.

Presidential Vote

1980	Reagan (R)	63,559	(47%)
	Carter (D)	67,875	(51%)
	Anderson (I)	1,993	(2%)
1976	Ford (R)	48,186	(41%)
	Carter (D)	68,612	(59%)

Rep. Charles O. Whitley (D) Elected 1976; b. Jan. 3, 1927, Siler City; home, Mount Olive; Wake Forest U., B.A. 1949, LL.B. 1950, Geo. Wash. U., M.A. 1974.

Career Army, 1944–46; Practicing atty., 1950–60; Mt. Olive Atty., 1961–67; Admin. Asst. to U.S. Rep. David Henderson, 1961–76.

Offices 404 CHOB, 202-225-3415. Also Fed. Bldg., Goldsboro 27530, 919-736-1844.

Committee *Agriculture* (17th). Subcommittees: Cotton, Rice, and Sugar; Livestock, Dairy, and Poultry; Tobacco and Peanuts.

Group Ratings

	ADA	COPE	PC	LCV	CFA	RPN	NAB	NSI	NTU	ACA	ACU
1980	28	53	33	30	50	—	83	67	32	39	56
1979	21	40	23	28	8	—	—	—	33	42	49
1978	25	16	25	34	9	50	91	90	22	95	63

Key Votes

1) Draft Registn $	FOR	6) Fair Hsg DOJ Enfrc	AGN	11) Cut Socl Incr Dfns $	AGN
2) Ban $ to Nicrgua	FOR	7) Lim PAC Contrbtns	AGN	12) Hosptl Cost Controls	AGN
3) Dlay MX Missile	AGN	8) Cap on Food Stmp $	AGN	13) Gasln Ctrls & Allctns	FOR
4) Nuclr Mortorium	AGN	9) New US Dep Edcatn	FOR	14) Lim Wndfll Prof Tax	FOR
5) Alaska Lands Bill	FOR	10) Cut OSHA $	FOR	15) Chryslr Loan Grntee	FOR

Election Results

1980 general	Charles O. Whitley (D)	84,862	(68%)	($33,267)
	Larry J. Parker (R)	39,393	(32%)	($10,268)
1980 primary	Charles O. Whitley (D)	53,337	(80%)	
	Two others (D)	13,705	(20%)	
1978 general	Charles O. Whitley (D)	54,452	(71%)	($44,971)
	William J. Blanchard (R)	22,150	(29%)	($13,583)

FOURTH DISTRICT

The 4th congressional district of North Carolina consists of four counties in the middle of the state, where the coastal plain rises to meet the Piedmont. Raleigh is the state capital and the district's largest city; it is also a tobacco center and the home of North Carolina State University. Durham, another tobacco center and the home of Duke University, has one of North Carolina's largest and most sophisticated urban black communities. Between these two cities and Chapel Hill, which is just outside the district, is the Research Triangle, a collection of think tanks and research businesses attracted to these pleasant surroundings. The other two counties in the district are far smaller: Randolph, in the west, is heavily Republican; Chatham, closer to Raleigh and Durham, is traditionally Democratic.

This has been an area of considerable economic growth in the 1970s, to the point that it had the largest population of any North Carolina district in 1980. The Research Triangle, the universities, and Raleigh generally have attracted new white collar migrants; Durham, with an economy based on cigarette factories, has grown more slowly. This kind of growth in the white collar sector has had two effects. On the one hand it makes the area more liberal in Democratic primaries and nonpartisan elections. This was the district most negative to George Wallace in the 1972 and 1976 Democratic primaries. Raleigh has elected a black mayor and voted for policies to control its booming growth.

The other political effect has been an increase in Republican strength in general elections. Raleigh and surrounding Wake County went for Gerald Ford for president in 1976, for example, although all the surrounding area and Durham as well were strong for Jimmy Carter. By all odds this should mean that congressional elections here should be contests between liberal Democrats and conservative Republicans, each trying to appeal in his own way to the large and growing white collar vote. That was the case in the late 1960s and early 1970s when the 4th district was represented by Democrat Nick Galifianakis. But since Galifianakis ran for the Senate unsuccessfully in 1972, it has been another story

The reason was the victory in the 1972 Democratic primary of Ike Andrews. A state legislator, Andrews was from neither Raleigh nor Durham; his roots are in the town of Siler City in rural Chatham County. His reputation is conservative, like his cultural style, although his voting record is more mixed. He sometimes votes with other Democrats on economic issues and others as well. Andrews sits on the Education and Labor Committee and is chairman of the Human Resources Subcommittee. This would have been the glamor subcommittee a few years ago; it has jurisdiction of the Community Services Administration (the old OEO), the Older Americans Act, juvenile justice and delinquency, and senior volunteer programs in ACTION. Now, however, almost all these programs are being cut mercilessly by the Reagan budget-cutters, and Andrews is not a man who by and large can be expected to fight hard to keep them going. His subcommittee is small; neither of the two Republicans is likely to be very favorable to the programs; and one of the other Democrats is Baltasar Corrada of Puerto Rico, who is likely to be most concerned about the impact of programs and budget cuts on his commonwealth.

Through the bustling 1970s, Andrews did not attract serious opposition; one reason may have been that the period of 1974-78 was heavily Democratic in North Carolina. In 1980 he had more trouble. The Republican candidate was not strong, but the tide of Republican ideas in the district was. Ronald Reagan carried the 4th over Jimmy Carter; Andrews lost Randolph County by nearly 2-1 and did not carry Raleigh and Wake County by an impressive margin.

Given that performance, it is possible that the Republicans will target Andrews's district in 1982, as they did a decade ago. Redistricting may make a difference, and the legislature could change the boundaries to help Andrews. One way would be to return Orange County and Chapel Hill to the district and to slough off Randolph County, perhaps putting it in the 6th district which is now represented by a Republican.

Census Data   Pop. (1980 final) 578,894, up 24% in 1970s. Median family income, 1970, $8,999, 94% of U.S.

The Voters

Employment profile 1970   White collar, 50%. Blue collar, 35%. Service, 12%. Farm, 3%.
Ethnic groups   Black 1980, 23%. Hispanic 1980, 1%. Asian 1980, 1%. Total foreign stock 1970, 3%.

Presidential Vote

1980	Reagan (R)	94,339	(48%)
	Carter (D)	91,223	(46%)
	Anderson (I)	9,551	(5%)
1976	Ford (R)	81,852	(49%)
	Carter (D)	85,541	(51%)

Rep. Ike F. Andrews (D) Elected 1972; b. Sept. 2, 1925, Bonlee; home, Siler City; Mars Hill Col., U. of N.C., B.S. 1950, LL.B. 1952.

Career Army, WWII; Practicing atty., 1952–72; N.C. Senate, 1959–61; N.C. Gen. Assembly, 1961–63, 1967–72, Major. Ldr., Spkr. Pro Tem.

Offices 2201 RHOB, 202-225-1784. Also P O Box 12075, Research Triangle Pk. 27709, 919-541-2981.

Committees *Education and Labor* (8th). Subcommittees: Elementary, Secondary, and Vocational Education; Human Resources (Chairman); Postsecondary Education.

Select Committee on Aging (4th). Subcommittee: Health and Long-Term Care.

Group Ratings

	ADA	COPE	PC	LCV	CFA	RPN	NAB	NSI	NTU	ACA	ACU
1980	28	38	30	31	36	—	64	50	31	41	47
1979	37	58	33	38	16	—	—	—	29	33	41
1978	25	37	38	40	14	64	82	80	20	59	41

Key Votes

1) Draft Registn $	FOR	6) Fair Hsg DOJ Enfrc	AGN	11) Cut Socl Incr Dfns $	AGN
2) Ban $ to Nicrgua	AGN	7) Lim PAC Contrbtns	AGN	12) Hosptl Cost Controls	AGN
3) Dlay MX Missile	AGN	8) Cap on Food Stmp $	AGN	13) Gasln Ctrls & Allctns	—
4) Nuclr Mortorium	AGN	9) New US Dep Edcatn	FOR	14) Lim Wndfll Prof Tax	FOR
5) Alaska Lands Bill	FOR	10) Cut OSHA $	AGN	15) Chryslr Loan Grntee	FOR

Election Results

1980 general	Ike F. Andrews (D).............	97,167	(53%)	($72,446)
	Thurman Hogan (R)............	84,631	(46%)	($59,634)
1980 primary	Ike F. Andrews (D).............	58,370	(77%)	
	Two others (D)	17,817	(23%)	
1978 general	Ike F. Andrews (D), unopposed...			($27,970)

FIFTH DISTRICT

Perhaps the most scenic part of North Carolina is where the mountains begin to rise from the hilly Piedmont. The land is well watered and green, the weather pleasant most of the year, avoiding the extremes of the snowbound winters of the mountains or the humid, muggy summers of the swampy flatlands to the east. Before the Revolution a group of Moravians, a religious sect from Pennsylvania and, before that, Germany, made a settlement here and called it Salem. Later it joined with the Southern Presbyterian settlement of Winston, and together they became one of North Carolina's largest cities, Winston-Salem. The city has given its names to two brands of cigarettes manufactured here by the R. J. Reynolds Company; it is also the headquarters of the Wachovia Bank (the name comes from the Moravians), North Carolina's largest and one of the largest in the South.

Winston-Salem shares to some extent the political habits of the hills to the north and west. Here in hollows surrounded by ridges, there lives a Republicanism that grew up in opposition to the domination of wealthy tobacco farmers on the coastal plain. While recent Republicans in the state, notably Senator Jesse Helms, have styled themselves conservatives, mountain Republicans have been more insurgent in mood. When coastal Republicans talk about law and order, mountain Republicans are likely to think, not entirely with approval, of revenuers driving up into the hills and smashing moonshine stills.

The 5th congressional district of North Carolina extends from Winston-Salem and the furniture manufacturing town of Lexington on the east to the mountains on both sides of the Blue Ridge in the west. The mountain Republican tradition lives on here, particularly in Wilkes County, which only on the most unusual occasions votes Democratic. Winston-Salem shows some signs of mountain Republican influence as well. It has never shown much enthusiasm for Helms, but in the Republican sweep of 1980 it produced majorities not only for Ronald Reagan but for Helms's protege, Senator John East.

The congressman from the 5th, Stephen Neal, is one of those Democrats who was first elected in 1974 and who has held onto the seat ever since. But his hold on the district is anything but secure. He won in an upset in the first place, beating an overconfident Wilmer

(Vinegar Bend) Mizell, a Republican and former major league baseball pitcher. In the 1976 and 1978 elections Neal was reelected with 54% of the vote. He has had some popular accomplishments, funding a program to provide federally subsidized loans to purchasers of solar energy equipment and blocking the building of a dam on the scenic New River. But in 1980 he carried the baggage of being an enthusiastic supporter of President Carter, and he was only barely able to squeak past state Senator Anne Bagnal of Winston-Salem. The Democratic legislature may try to make Neal's district more favorable to him in 1982, although that will take some wholesale redrawing (one possibility is to exclude Davidson County, a furniture manufacturing area that was heavily Republican in 1980). It is almost certain that Republicans will seriously contest this seat in 1982.

Census Data   Pop. (1980 final) 539,949, up 17% in 1970s. Median family income, 1970, $8,191, 85% of U.S.

The Voters

Employment profile 1970   White collar, 38%. Blue collar, 50%. Service, 9%. Farm, 3%.
Ethnic groups   Black 1980, 15%. Hispanic 1980, 1%. Total foreign stock 1970, 1%.

Presidential Vote

1980	Reagan (R)	104,622	(54%)
	Carter (D)	83,043	(43%)
	Anderson (I)	4,510	(2%)
1976	Ford (R)	89,368	(49%)
	Carter (D)	92,010	(51%)

Rep. Stephen L. Neal (D) Elected 1974; b. Nov. 7, 1934, Winston-Salem; home, Winston-Salem; U. of Cal. at Santa Barbara, U. of Hawaii, A.B. 1959.

Career   Mortgage banking business, 1959–66; Newspaper business, 1966–74; Pres., Community Press, Inc., Suburban Newspapers, Inc., King Publishing Co., and Yadkin Printing Co., Inc.

Offices   2463 RHOB, 202-225-2071. Also 421 Fed. Bldg., Winston-Salem 27101, 916-761-3125.

Committees   *Banking, Finance and Urban Affairs* (8th). Subcommittees: Domestic Monetary Policy; International Development Institutions and Finance; International Trade, Investment and Monetary Policy (Chairman).

Government Operations (18th). Subcommittees: Commerce, Consumer, and Monetary Affairs; Intergovernmental Relations and Human Resources.

Group Ratings

	ADA	COPE	PC	LCV	CFA	RPN	NAB	NSI	NTU	ACA	ACU
1980	44	32	43	73	36	—	42	44	29	50	35
1979	32	40	45	49	28	—	—	—	39	58	46
1978	25	25	38	52	23	64	82	88	28	67	43

Key Votes

1) Draft Registn $	FOR	6) Fair Hsg DOJ Enfrc	AGN	11) Cut Socl Incr Dfns $	FOR
2) Ban $ to Nicrgua	AGN	7) Lim PAC Contrbtns	FOR	12) Hosptl Cost Controls	—
3) Dlay MX Missile	AGN	8) Cap on Food Stmp $	AGN	13) Gasln Ctrls & Allctns	FOR
4) Nuclr Mortorium	AGN	9) New US Dep Edcatn	FOR	14) Lim Wndfll Prof Tax	—
5) Alaska Lands Bill	FOR	10) Cut OSHA $	FOR	15) Chryslr Loan Grntee	AGN

Election Results

1980 general	Stephen L. Neal (D)	99,117	(51%)	($179,450)
	Anne Bagnal (R)	94,894	(49%)	($120,022)
1980 primary	Stephen L. Neal (D), unopposed			
1978 general	Stephen L. Neal (D)	68,778	(54%)	($166,643)
	Hamilton C. Horton, Jr. (R)	58,161	(46%)	($118,484)

SIXTH DISTRICT

The 6th congressional district of North Carolina takes in Greensboro, the state's second largest city, High Point, and Burlington—all in the heart of the Piedmont region. One of the textile giants, Burlington Industries, has its southern headquarters here, and most of the other big textile firms have mills in the area. High Point is one of the major furniture manufacturing centers in the nation, and there are tobacco factories in the area as well. This area has also moved beyond the traditional North Carolina industries of textiles, tobacco, and furniture; Western Electric, for example, has a big plant here now. An influx of northern managerial and technical talent has been the standard explanation for increasing Republican strength here in the 1950s and 1960s; but actually most of the new residents are from the South, and their Republican leanings represent a change in local political preference.

The 6th was the scene of one of the most startling upsets in congressional elections in 1980, the defeat of Democratic Congressman Richardson Preyer by Republican Eugene Johnston. Preyer had not been seriously pressed in this district for some time, and he had qualities and credentials that impressed many who did not share all his beliefs. A former federal judge, he had resigned to run for governor in 1964 and was defeated because he was considered too liberal on racial issues. An heir to the Richardson–Merrell drug fortune, he was an eminent figure in Greensboro civic affairs and was elected to Congress without primary opposition when the incumbent retired. In the House Preyer was an exemplarily thoughtful congressman. He tackled such tough problems as busing in schools, seeking legislative rather than judicial solutions; he pressed on the ethics committee for a full investigation of the Koreagate scandal. On the Health Subcommittee of the Commerce Committee he pushed for strong clean air legislation.

But in 1979 Preyer suffered a major setback, when he lost the chairmanship of the Health Subcommittee to Henry Waxman of California by a 15–12 vote of Democratic Commerce Committee members. Waxman charged correctly that Preyer did not favor national health insurance and suggested that his pharmaceutical holdings would place him in conflict-of-interest situations where he would not be able to act. Preyer took his defeat with good humor, but one cannot help believing that it must have hurt him at home: a district that believed with reason that it had a congressman of national stature suddenly saw him unable to gain a position of importance that he had sought. Ironically, Preyer was not entitled to the chair under the seniority principle, although he was more senior than Waxman; the most senior subcommittee member, David Satterfield of Virginia, was too conservative to receive serious consideration, and he chose to retire in 1980. So both Preyer and Satterfield can be seen as casualties of the reform that allows Democrats to elect their subcommittee chairmen rather than have them selected by seniority.

Eugene Johnston was the first tough Republican opponent Preyer had faced in 12 years. A self-made millionaire, he outspent Preyer and emphasized hard-line issues: the incumbent's votes against the B-1 bomber and for food stamps for strikers. He had only the slightest of margins in Guilford County, which includes Greensboro and High Point; he had a bigger margin in smaller Alamance County, where the textile workers tend to be George Wallace Democrats. Johnston now has seats on the Education and Labor and Budget Committees, where he can be expected to take a hard conservative line on just about every issue that arises. The Democratic legislature may choose to safeguard other Democrats by taking Republican Randolph County out of the 4th district and putting it into the 6th—which would be all but conceding the district to Johnston.

Census Data Pop. (1980 final) 499,716, up 9% in 1970s. Median family income, 1970, $9,300, 97% of U.S.

The Voters

Employment profile 1970 White collar, 43%. Blue collar, 45%. Service, 10%. Farm, 2%.
Ethnic groups Black 1980, 23%. Hispanic 1980, 1%. Total foreign stock 1970, 2%.

Presidential Vote

1980	Reagan (R)	82,573	(52%)
	Carter (D)	71,266	(45%)
	Anderson (I)	5,242	(3%)
1976	Ford (R)	67,483	(46%)
	Carter (D)	77,610	(53%)

Rep. Eugene Johnston (R) Elected 1980; b. Mar. 3, 1936, Winston-Salem; home, Greensboro; Wake Forest U., LL.B. 1961, B.B.A. 1963.

Career Army, 1954–57; CPA, A. M. Pullen, 1963–64; Owner, Bd. Chmn., Johnston Properties, 1965–, Fisher–Harrison Corp., 1968–.

Offices 128 CHOB, 202-225-3065. Also 324 W. Market St., Rm. 249, Greensboro 27402, 919-378-5151; 175 N. Point Ave., Rm. 105, High Point 27262, 919-869-5811; and 430 S. Spring St., Burlington 27215, 919-227-0009.

Committees *Budget* (11th).

Education and Labor (11th). Subcommittees: Health and Safety; Labor–Management Relations; Labor Standards.

Group Ratings and Key Votes: Newly Elected

Election Results

1980 general	Eugene Johnston (R)	80,275	(51%)	($302,263)
	Richardson Preyer (D)	76,957	(49%)	($214,850)
1980 primary	Eugene Johnston (R), unopposed			
1978 general	Richardson Preyer (D)	58,193	(68%)	($18,274)
	George Bemus (R)..............	26,882	(32%)	($10,386)

SEVENTH DISTRICT

The 7th congressional district of North Carolina is the southern portion of the state's coastal region, the part of North Carolina most like the Deep South. Wilmington is an old Carolina coastal city that never became a major port—a would-be Charleston or Savannah. It was the site of the 1968 church burnings that led to the arrest and conviction of the Wilmington

Ten — a matter of controversy in North Carolina and indeed around the world. Fayetteville, the district's other population center, lies across the rather sparsely settled coastal plain to the west. The city's population exceeds only slightly that of adjacent Fort Bragg, the huge Army base to which Fayetteville owes much of its prosperity. Bragg is the home of the Army's 82d Airborne paratroopers and nearby, along the garish highway with its X-rated drive-in movies and topless night clubs, is one of the nation's largest concentrations of Vietnamese restaurants.

The 7th has a fairly large percentage of blacks (28%), but its most notable minority consists of American Indians (8%). In fact, more Indians live here that in any other congressional district east of the Mississippi. Most of them are the Lumbees of Robeson County, and their place in the traditional caste system of the South was always unclear. Robeson is about one-third white, one-third black, and one-third Indian, and in the days of segregation the county maintained three school systems. Indians have had their own civil rights demonstrations, but they have also objected to having their children bused to go to school with blacks.

This is an area that has a strong traditional affinity to the Democratic Party, and with the exception of 1968 and 1972 it has supported Democratic presidential candidates, usually by wide margins. Robeson County in particular is heavily Democratic; Wilmington, like many other newly prosperous cities in the South, leans toward the Republicans.

Congressional elections have had few fluctuations, at least since the election of Charles Rose in 1972. Two years before, Rose, a former associate in Terry Sanford's law firm, ran against the conservative incumbent in the Democratic primary and nearly beat him; in 1972 the incumbent retired, and Rose won the seat. He got places on the Agriculture and House Administration Committees, neither normally considered prizes, but he has made something of both of them. He has become an expert on the use of computers to help the legislative process in the House and has chaired House Administration's subcommittee on computers. He also became concerned about protecting the privacy of individuals from the knowledge government can get from its computers and has forced some agencies to change their practices in this area.

In 1981, Rose won the chairmanship of an Agriculture subcommittee that could have been designed for this district: the Tobacco and Peanuts Subcommittee. North Carolina's interest in tobacco is no secret: this is the state that produces the most cigarettes and that grows the most tobacco. What is less well known is that tobacco is a crop that requires hardly any subsidy (there is a program that provides low-interest loans, and hence is an interest subsidy) and which is very labor-intensive. What is crucial is the allotment. A family can live — not well, but live — off 15 acres of tobacco which, however must be cultivated carefully and picked a little at a time throughout the harvest season. North Carolina's tobacco-growing counties, mostly in the east and some in the 7th district, are among the most thickly populated rural areas in the nation, and whatever people here may think of smoking they are not going to be happy with a congressman who does not back tobacco. This is true of peanuts as well. Allotments are critical here, too; there is a whole system, rooted almost in antiquity, that makes some farmers rich and keeps others out of the business entirely. Poor growing conditions resulted in a small crop in 1980 and high prices in 1981 — and in pressures for opening up peanut growing to anyone who wants to try it, a form of deregulation as it were. Rose, as a representative of many existing peanut farmers, seems hardly likely to back this.

Rose's ambitions do not end with his committee assignments, however. He is one of those natural politicians with an affinity for legislative deal-making and seemingly improbable alliances. He was a notable backer of Phillip Burton in his fight for the majority leadership, for example. Rose himself is a possible candidate for a leadership position in the future. He has a safe district and obvious legislative talents; he is acceptable to both northern Democrats and those from the south. Just past 40, he seems to have a long legislative career ahead of him.

Census Data   Pop. (1980 final) 559,395, up 20% in 1970s. Median family income, 1970, $6,875, 72% of U.S.

The Voters

Employment profile 1970   White collar, 40%. Blue collar, 40%. Service, 13%. Farm, 7%.
Ethnic groups   Black 1980, 28%. Hispanic 1980, 2%. Am. Ind. 1980, 8%. Asian 1980, 1%. Total foreign stock 1970, 4%.

Presidential Vote

1980	Reagan (R)	58,352	(43%)
	Carter (D)	73,710	(54%)
	Anderson (I)	3,175	(2%)
1976	Ford (R)	40,560	(33%)
	Carter (D)	81,207	(66%)

Rep. Charles G. (Charlie) **Rose** (D) Elected 1972; b. Aug. 10, 1939, Fayetteville; home, Fayetteville; Davidson Col., A.B. 1961, U. of N.C., LL.B. 1964.

Career   Practicing atty., 1964–72; Chf. Dist. Ct. Prosecutor, 12th Judicial Dist., 1967–70.

Offices   2435 RHOB, 202-225-2731. Also Rm. 208, P.O. Bldg., Wilmington 28401, 919-343-4959.

Committees   *Agriculture* (7th). Subcommittees: Livestock, Dairy and Poultry; Tobacco and Peanuts (Chairman).

House Administration (7th). Subcommittees: Accounts; Services; Policy Group on Information and Computers (Chairman).

Permanent Select Committee on Intelligence (3d). Subcommittee: Oversight and Evaluation (Chairman).

Group Ratings

	ADA	COPE	PC	LCV	CFA	RPN	NAB	NSI	NTU	ACA	ACU
1980	44	50	37	52	43	—	27	43	19	38	47
1979	58	44	45	47	31	—	—	—	31	33	33
1978	50	32	50	43	27	40	20	43	17	43	22

Key Votes

1) Draft Registn $	FOR	6) Fair Hsg DOJ Enfrc	FOR	11) Cut Socl Incr Dfns $	AGN
2) Ban $ to Nicrgua	FOR	7) Lim PAC Contrbtns	FOR	12) Hosptl Cost Controls	FOR
3) Dlay MX Missile	—	8) Cap on Food Stmp $	—	13) Gasln Ctrls & Allctns	FOR
4) Nuclr Mortorium	AGN	9) New US Dep Edcatn	FOR	14) Lim Wndfll Prof Tax	AGN
5) Alaska Lands Bill	FOR	10) Cut OSHA $	FOR	15) Chryslr Loan Grntee	AGN

Election Results

1980 general	Charles G. (Charlie) Rose (D)	88,564	(69%)	($65,576)
	Vivian S. Wright (R)............	40,270	(31%)	($16,992)
1980 primary	Charles G. (Charlie) Rose (D)	56,749	(80%)	
	One other (D)	14,029	(20%)	
1978 general	Charles G. (Charlie) Rose (D)	53,696	(70%)	($57,723)
	Raymond C. Schrump (R).......	23,146	(30%)	($47,933)

EIGHTH DISTRICT

The 8th congressional district of North Carolina consists of two areas: a part of the middle of the Piedmont textile country and the Sand Hills region of the state's coastal plain. The textile counties lie on both sides of Interstate 85 between Charlotte and Greensboro. Along the way the roadway passes through the 8th district towns of Salisbury, Concord, and Kannapolis (a company town, wholly owned by giant Cannon Mills). Here the textile magnates reign supreme. There is no nonsense about unions or workers' rights—the bosses call the shots. That is true in the mills, it is true in the streets of Kannapolis, and it almost seems to be true at the polls. For whatever reasons this area is consistently one of the most Republican parts of North Carolina. The textile counties cast two-thirds of the votes in the 8th district; the rest are from the more sparsely populated Sand Hills counties to the east. Here there has always been a traditional Democratic allegiance—expressed for some years as a preference for the politics of George Wallace.

The 8th has been represented since 1974 by Democrat Bill Hefner. He used to be a country music disc jockey and radio station owner in Kannapolis, and his campaigns have featured a little Democratic oratory and a great deal of country music. He beat a Republican incumbent in 1974—a former basketball coach who was, improbably, named governor of American Samoa by President Ford—and Hefner has not been seriously challenged since. His margins, however, have not been overwhelming, because of the Republican strength in the textile counties.

Hefner is one of those southern Democrats whose vote was not especially important when he was first elected. But now that there are fewer northern Democrats in the House and the Republicans control the Senate and the presidency, people such as Hefner are crucial indeed. In general, he has a record that is rated as highly by conservative as liberal organizations, and he has voted with northern Democrats on some but by no means all important issues. Until 1981 Hefner's committee assignments were pedestrian and uninteresting. But in that year he won seats on both the Appropriations and the Budget Committees. On Budget in particular he is likely to be a swing vote on budget cuts and the question is whether he will go along with Chairman James Jones of Oklahoma or with the Conservative Democratic Forum fellow member Phil Gramm of Texas.

Redistricting could affect Hefner significantly, since the district is irregularly shaped and contains areas with very different political leanings. The Democratic legislature will be inclined to help him, but it is not clear how much they can do—particularly if they are also trying to help Stephen Neal, who is more closely pressed in the 5th district to the north.

Census Data   Pop. (1980 final) 533,306, up 17% in 1970s. Median family income, 1970, $7,872, 82% of U.S.

The Voters

 Employment profile 1970   White collar, 30%. Blue collar, 56%. Service, 10%. Farm, 4%.
 Ethnic groups   Black 1980, 19%. Hispanic 1980, 1%. Am. Ind. 1980, 1%.

Presidential Vote

1980	Reagan (R)	88,044	(52%)
	Carter (D)	75,483	(45%)
	Anderson (I)	3,515	(2%)
1976	Ford (R)	69,653	(45%)
	Carter (D)	85,084	(55%)

Rep. W. G. (Bill) **Hefner** (D) Elected 1974; b.Apr. 11, 1930, Elora, Tenn.; home, Concord.

Career Pres., WRKB Radio, Kannapolis; Mbr., Harvesters Quartet, with weekly TV show on WXII, Winston-Salem; Promoter, "Carolina Sings," gospel music entertainment.

Offices 2161 RHOB, 202-225-3715. Also 2202 S. Cannon Blvd., Kannapolis 28081, 704-933-1615.

Committees *Appropriations* (28th). Subcommittees: Defense; Military Construction.

Budget (13th).

Group Ratings

	ADA	COPE	PC	LCV	CFA	RPN	NAB	NSI	NTU	ACA	ACU
1980	22	47	28	39	36	—	75	44	32	36	63
1979	42	47	40	31	24	—	—	—	33	36	36
1978	25	20	30	51	18	67	83	70	20	63	58

Key Votes

1) Draft Registn $	—	6) Fair Hsg DOJ Enfrc	AGN	11) Cut Socl Incr Dfns $	AGN
2) Ban $ to Nicrgua	AGN	7) Lim PAC Contrbtns	FOR	12) Hosptl Cost Controls	FOR
3) Dlay MX Missile	AGN	8) Cap on Food Stmp $	AGN	13) Gasln Ctrls & Allctns	—
4) Nuclr Mortorium	AGN	9) New US Dep Edcatn	FOR	14) Lim Wndfll Prof Tax	AGN
5) Alaska Lands Bill	FOR	10) Cut OSHA $	FOR	15) Chryslr Loan Grntee	AGN

Election Results

1980 general	W. G. (Bill) Hefner (D)	95,013	(59%)	($79,281)
	L. E. Harris (R)................	67,317	(41%)	($18,530)
1980 primary	W. G. (Bill) Hefner (D)	45,794	(74%)	
	Two others (D)	16,241	(26%)	
1978 general	W. G. (Bill) Hefner (D)	63,168	(59%)	($74,546)
	Roger Austin (R)	43,942	(41%)	($22,949)

NINTH DISTRICT

Charlotte is North Carolina's largest city, a comfortable and prosperous metropolis that has never reached really dominant stature in the state. Charlotte has no particular geographical reason for being: it is on no major river, it stands astride no historically important artery of transportation (although Interstate 85, the spinal column of the American textile industry, now runs through). It is not even in the center of the state but is off to the side, almost in South Carolina. It was not a great city in colonial times nor even in the period following the

Civil War. Charlotte has been described as a town from which traveling salesmen empty out every Monday morning and return every Friday afternoon, and it seems to be a city that has simply outhustled the competition. In blue collar North Carolina it is a city with a substantial white collar job base; it provides the banking, insurance, and white collar services for many of the textile, furniture, and tobacco factories scattered around North Carolina and much of South Carolina as well. Charlotte likes to think of itself as a modern town—a little Atlanta—and a racially progressive place. There was an angry reaction in the early 1970s when a federal judge, in a landmark case upheld by the Supreme Court, ordered massive busing of schoolchildren in Charlotte to achieve integration. But after a time tempers cooled, the plan worked better than expected, and parents who were still unhappy about it got their children into private schools.

Charlotte and its suburban fringe provide most of the votes in North Carolina's 9th congressional district. The district also includes Iredell county, a textile area directly north of Charlotte, and rural Lincoln County, included in the district largely because the longtime congressman from the 9th, Charles Jonas, had his residence there. This represented an unusual degree of comity by a Democratic legislature, since Jonas was a Republican, first elected in 1952. But Democratic efforts to defeat him proved unavailing, and by the 1960s no one really tried; he retired in 1972.

The current congressman is another Republican, James Martin, formerly a chemistry professor at Davidson College. He was first elected easily enough but was pressed closely in 1974 and 1976; his high percentage of 1978 decreased sharply in 1980, although it was still a very respectable 59%. Martin may be hurt slightly by a Democratic trend in the Charlotte area, apparent in returns for most offices; Jimmy Carter, despite his national and state decline, did almost as well here in 1980 (47%) as in 1976 (50%)—and this in a county that has gone Republican for almost 30 years with considerable regularity. This does not necessarily mean that Martin is in trouble, but it is possible that he will attract serious competition. Redistricting will probably remove Lincoln County from the district and may remove Iredell and substitute another county or two, depending on what happens to adjacent districts.

Martin is man with highly important committee assignments. He has a seat on the Budget Committee and on Ways and Means, and on the Oversight Subcommittee. On most national issues, Martin is a pretty reliable Republican vote. On trade issues, he can be expected to be particularly attentive in protecting the textile and apparel industries which, while not the main businesses in Charlotte itself, are the leading industries in the hinterland that Charlotte serves. On Ways and Means he also plays a lead role on health issues and led a move to get Congress to place a moratorium on the ban on saccharin.

Census Data Pop. (1980 final) 529,180, up 15% in 1970s. Median family income, 1970, $9,594, 100% of U.S.

The Voters

Employment profile 1970   White collar, 51%. Blue collar, 37%. Service, 11%. Farm, 1%.
Ethnic groups   Black 1980, 24%. Hispanic 1980, 1%. Asian 1980, 1%. Total foreign stock 1970, 3%.

Presidential Vote

1980	Reagan (R)	92,319	(49%)
	Carter (D)	86,858	(46%)
	Anderson (I)	7,483	(4%)
1976	Ford (R)	79,970	(48%)
	Carter (D)	85,955	(52%)

Rep. James G. Martin (R) Elected 1972; b. Dec. 11, 1935, Savannah, Ga.; home, Davidson; Davidson Col., B.S. 1957, Princeton U., Ph.D. 1960.

Career Asst. Prof. of Chemistry, Davidson Col., 1960–64, Assoc. Prof, 1964–72; Mecklenburg Co. Bd. of Commissioners, 1966–72, Chmn., 1967–68, 1970–71; Founder and First Chmn., Centralina Regional Cncl. of Govts., 1966–69; V.P., Natl. Assoc. of Regional Cncls., 1970–72.

Offices 341 CHOB, 202-225-1976. Also Rm. 248, Jonas Fed. Bldg., Charlotte 28232, 704-372-1976.

Committees *Budget* (6th).

Ways and Means (7th). Subcommittee: Oversight.

Group Ratings

	ADA	COPE	PC	LCV	CFA	RPN	NAB	NSI	NTU	ACA	ACU
1980	11	11	23	48	21	—	100	89	61	88	74
1979	5	5	8	17	4	—	—	—	59	88	95
1978	15	10	23	27	9	58	100	100	45	88	95

Key Votes

1) Draft Registn $	FOR	6) Fair Hsg DOJ Enfrc	AGN	11) Cut Socl Incr Dfns $	FOR
2) Ban $ to Nicrgua	AGN	7) Lim PAC Contrbtns	AGN	12) Hosptl Cost Controls	AGN
3) Dlay MX Missile	AGN	8) Cap on Food Stmp $	FOR	13) Gasln Ctrls & Allctns	AGN
4) Nuclr Mortorium	AGN	9) New US Dep Edcatn	AGN	14) Lim Wndfll Prof Tax	FOR
5) Alaska Lands Bill	AGN	10) Cut OSHA $	FOR	15) Chryslr Loan Grntee	AGN

Election Results

1980 general	James G. Martin (R)............	101,156	(59%)	($279,040)
	Randall R. Kincaid (D).........	71,504	(41%)	($58,955)
1980 primary	James G. Martin (R), unopposed			
1978 general	James G. Martin (R)............	66,157	(68%)	($252,126)
	Charles Maxwell (D)............	29,761	(31%)	($37,657)

TENTH DISTRICT

The 10th congressional district of North Carolina is a collection of seven counties in the western Piedmont and the eastern Appalachian mountains. The southern part of the district, on the South Carolina border, is dominated by the city of Gastonia and surrounding Gaston County—which may be the single American county with the largest number of textile workers. Gaston County is traditionally Democratic and has delivered large Wallace margins in the past. North of Gastonia, the hills rise to mountains around such towns as Morganton, the home of former Senator Sam Ervin. This is furniture manufacturing country, and the farther one gets into the mountains, the more Republican the territory. The political preferences here reflect Civil War allegiances, ones that have continued to be important in election after election.

The 10th took its current shape in the 1968 redistricting and has had only minor boundary changes since. In 1968 two incumbents were thrown together, with relatively senior Democrat Basil Whitener losing to Republican James Broyhill by a solid margin. Broyhill has had a close race only once since, in 1974, when the Watergate issue and perhaps the local prominence of Sam Ervin helped produce a big Democratic sweep in North Carolina.

Although only in his early 50s, Broyhill has now been in Congress for nearly 20 years. He is not often quoted in the press, but he plays an important part in the legislative process. His family owns a prominent furniture company, and he serves as the ranking Republican member on the House Energy and Commerce Committee; he will chair the committee if Republicans win control of the House in 1982. On that body he is almost invariably a voice for less government regulation. He is an opponent of airbags and he worked with John Dingell of Michigan for more relaxed auto emission standards and longer delays on the clean air act. He has opposed measures to increase government regulation of health care costs. He added a sunset provision to the bill creating the Department of Energy, requiring it to go out of existence at the end of 1982 unless Congress reauthorizes it. He has generally been a hardworking advocate of positions espoused by the Chamber of Commerce, the auto industry, the electric utilities, and the nuclear power industry. Broyhill is one of those Republicans whose support of lower federal spending and less government activity has been getting increased political and intellectual support in the past few years.

Given Broyhill's electoral strength in the district, it is not likely that the Democratic legislature will alter its shape much in redistricting, except perhaps to take some Republican territory from other districts and add it to the 10th.

Census Data   Pop. (1980 final) 548,138, up 16% in 1970s. Median family income, 1979, $8,449, 88% of U.S.

The Voters

  Employment profile 1970   White collar, 30%. Blue collar, 59%. Service, 9%. Farm, 2%.
  Ethnic groups   Black 1980, 11%. Hispanic 1980, 1%.

Presidential Vote

1980	Reagan (R)	97,286	(55%)
	Carter (D)	75,087	(42%)
	Anderson (I)	3,802	(2%)
1976	Ford (R)	76,532	(46%)
	Carter (D)	90,939	(54%)

Rep. James T. Broyhill (R) Elected 1962; b. Aug. 19, 1927, Lenoir; home, Lenoir; U. of N.C., B.S. 1950.

Career Personnel Executive, Broyhill Furniture Factories of Lenoir, 1945–62.

Offices 2340 RHOB, 202-225-2576. Also Mulberry St., Lenoir 28645, 704-758-4247.

Committee *Energy and Commerce* (Ranking Member). Subcommittee: Oversight and Investigations.

Group Ratings

	ADA	COPE	PC	LCV	CFA	RPN	NAB	NSI	NTU	ACA	ACU
1980	11	11	27	36	14	—	92	89	61	87	89
1979	5	20	15	17	7	—	—	—	55	84	81
1978	20	5	23	37	18	75	100	100	44	88	91

Key Votes

1) Draft Registn $	FOR	6) Fair Hsg DOJ Enfrc	AGN	11) Cut Socl Incr Dfns $	FOR
2) Ban $ to Nicrgua	FOR	7) Lim PAC Contrbtns	AGN	12) Hosptl Cost Controls	AGN
3) Dlay MX Missile	AGN	8) Cap on Food Stmp $	AGN	13) Gasln Ctrls & Allctns	AGN
4) Nuclr Mortorium	AGN	9) New US Dep Edcatn	AGN	14) Lim Wndfll Prof Tax	FOR
5) Alaska Lands Bill	—	10) Cut OSHA $		FOR	15) Chryslr Loan Grntee	AGN

Election Results

1980 general	James T. Broyhill (R)	120,777	(70%)	($248,354)
	James O. Icenhour (D)	52,485	(30%)	($18,753)
1980 primary	James T. Broyhill (R), unopposed			
1978 general	James T. Broyhill (R), unopposed .			($32,586)

ELEVENTH DISTRICT

The 11th congressional district of North Carolina occupies the western end of the state. Its main features include Asheville, the place to which Thomas Wolfe could not go home again, and the Great Smoky Mountains National Park. The park is the nation's most heavily visited: its roads have become so crowded that the Park Service was forced to install traffic lights — the first ever within a national park. During the summer it is 20° cooler in the mountains than in the lowland towns not far away; the climate and the forested, green, fog-wisped mountains attract some seven million people to the Smokies each year. Over the years the same elements — the mountains, the cool climate — have made western North Carolina a separate unit from the rest of the state. During the Civil War, it was the part of the state most reluctant to secede. With few slaves (only 5% of the people here today are black), many of the small farmers in the hollows remained loyal to the Union, and those who took up the Confederate cause did so largely because of the efforts of Governor Zebulon Vance, an Asheville native and a reluctant secessionist himself.

So there are some ancestral party loyalties here to contend with, Democratic as well as Republican, although this is not monolithically Republican territory like eastern Tennessee on the other side of the mountains. And there is some hostility here to the segregationist Republicanism of eastern North Carolina; Senator Jesse Helms barely carried the district in 1972 and 1978. Even in the Republican sweep of 1980, John East beat Senator Robert Morgan by only a narrow margin.

So strong are the party loyalties here that the 11th district is one of the few places in the country of which it can be said that coattails are still a critical factor in politics. This has definitely been true in House races here. In 1976, when the incumbent retired, Democrat Lamar Gudger won a 51%-49% victory, running behind Jimmy Carter and Jim Hunt. Two years later, Gudger was in more trouble than almost any freshman congressman; at 59, he was not a hard campaigner and could point to no major accomplishments. But at the last minute, Jimmy Carter, still popular from the Camp David agreement earlier in the fall, visit-ed Asheville and stumped for Gudger. The result was a 54% Gudger victory.

Republicans had seriously contested both races, and they were determined to contest the district in 1980. With Carter in clear trouble, they hoped that Reagan would carry the dis-trict and would carry in their candidate, William Hendon, a local businessman who drove a mule-drawn wagon train through every county in the district. Hendon attacked Carter heavily, and the returns in the congressional race closely paralleled the presidential results. Hendon has been described as coming more from the mountain, insurgent tradition of North Carolina Republicanism than from Jesse Helms's ideological conservative wing of the party. He serves on the Interior Committee, which governs the affairs of, among other things, the national parks.

Census Data   Pop. (1980 final) 540,971, up 16% in 1970s. Median family income, 1970, $6,857, 72% of U.S.

The Voters

Employment profile 1970   White collar, 35%. Blue collar, 51%. Service, 11%. Farm, 3%.
Ethnic groups   Black 1980, 5%. Hispanic 1980, 1%. Am. Ind. 1980, 1%. Total foreign stock 1970, 2%.

Presidential Vote

1980	Reagan (R)	100,868	(51%)
	Carter (D)	89,129	(45%)
	Anderson (I)	5,364	(3%)
1976	Ford (R)	84,061	(46%)
	Carter (D)	99,854	(54%)

Rep. William M. Hendon (R) Elected 1980; b. Nov. 9, 1944, Asheville; home, Asheville; U. of Tenn., B.A. 1966, M.B.A. 1968.

Career Instructor, U. of Tenn., 1968–70; Exec., family-owned fu-neral business, 1970–73; Instructor, Western Carolina U., 1971–72; Gen. Mgr., H. Putsch & Co., food equip. supplier, 1974–80; 11th Dist. Chmn., N.C. Rep. Party, 1979.

Offices 212 CHOB, 202-225-6401. Also Asheville Mall, Asheville 28805, 704-298-9437, and Tri-City Mall, Forest City 28043, 704-248-2836.

Committees *Interior and Insular Affairs* (13th). Subcommittees: Oversight and Investigations; Public Lands and National Parks.

Select Committee on Aging (22d). Subcommittees: Housing and Consumer Interests; Retirement Income and Employment.

Group Ratings and Key Votes: Newly Elected

Election Results

1980 general	William M. Hendon (R)	104,485	(54%)	($249,389)
	Lamar Gudger (D)	90,789	(46%)	($125,696)
1980 primary	William M. Hendon (R), unopposed			
1978 general	Lamar Gudger (D)	75,460	(53%)	($156,790)
	R. Curtis Ratcliff (R)	65,832	(47%)	($62,579)

NORTH DAKOTA

North Dakota occupies the northern section of our Great Plains—the world's largest expanse of arable land. Most of North Dakota is wheat country: the state produces about one-twelfth of the nation's crop, and only Kansas grows more. As the North Dakota plains become more arid toward the west, ranching and livestock grazing tend to replace wheat. But both forms of agriculture are demanding and discouraging. North Dakota is a hard, treeless land; its winters are cold with plains open to Arctic blasts from Canada, and its summers are often too short and too dry. Back in 1920 the state had 632,000 people. By 1970 its population had dropped to 617,000, and although it rose to 652,000 in 1980, that may be due only partly to North Dakota's prosperity; the other reason may be the gloomy economic picture in most of the big states where North Dakotans used to move. The demographic history of this state consists of a sudden rush of settlement in the 1890s and the years before World War I, followed by a long period in which the state's young people regularly felt forced to move elsewhere. Even in the 1970s there was still net outmigration from the state.

About 25% of all North Dakotans still live on farms and ranches, the highest percentage of any state. Because the economy of the state depends on the farmers who have little control over the weather or the fluctuations of the commodity markets, North Dakota over the years has seen raging dissatisfaction with the farm programs of the federal government. By tradition the most common topics of the state's political discourse are the minutiae of wheat and feed grain legislation. Agricultural discontent was the driving force behind the most interesting episode in the state's politics, its spell of radicalism in the years around World War I.

Most of North Dakota's settlement occurred between 1890 and 1910. A large portion of the settlers were of immigrant stock: Norwegians to the east, Canadians along the northern border, Volga Germans to the west, and native Germans throughout the state. (Volga Germans were people who had migrated to Russia in the early 1800s, but who retained their German language and character. They are recorded in U.S. census figures as Russian stock.) The new North Dakotans lived on lonely, often marginal farms, cut off in many cases from the wider currents of American culture by the barrier of language. Their economic fate seemed to be at the mercy of the grain millers of Minneapolis, the railroads, the banks, and the commodity traders.

These circumstances led A. C. Townley and William Lemke to organize the North Dakota Non-Partisan League (NPL) in 1915. Its program was frankly socialist—government ownership of the railroads and grain elevators—and, like many North Dakota ethnics, the League opposed going to war with Germany. The positions taken by the NPL won it many adherents in North Dakota and the League spread to neighboring states. But North Dakota was its bastion; the NPL often determined the outcome of the usually decisive Republican primary and sometimes swung its support to the otherwise heavily outnumbered Democrats. It succeeded in some of its goals in North Dakota, such as establishing a state-owned bank. A particular favorite of the NPL was "Wild Bill" Langer, who served intermittently as governor during the 1930s. He was elected to the Senate in 1940 but was allowed to take his seat only after a lengthy investigation of campaign irregularities. His subsequent career was fully as controversial; Langer was the Senate's most unpredictable maverick until his death in 1959. One of his pet projects was to get a North Dakotan on the Supreme Court, and he filibustered every nomination from 1954 until his death in an unsuccessful attempt to achieve that goal.

Another NPL favorite was Congressman Usher Burdick, who served from 1935 to 1945 and then again from 1949 to 1959. Burdick, like Langer, was a nominal Republican but usually voted with New Deal liberals on economic issues. Burdick's son Quentin, a Democrat, was a member of the House when Langer died. The younger Burdick won a special election to fill the Senate seat after waging a campaign against the iniquities of Agriculture Secretary Ezra Taft Benson. The Non-Partisan League of course supported Burdick. By the 1960s its name had become misleading, since it tended to support Democrats in every election.

North Dakota is historically Republican, but it is competitive in many elections. Currently its Senate delegation is split between the parties and its single congressman is a Democrat. Republicans hold most statewide offices and the governorship, but the Democrats held the governorship for 20 years, from 1960 to 1980. In presidential politics North Dakota, like some other farm states, has a tendency to go away from the party in power. In 1976 it was closely contested: Gerald Ford carried the state by only a 52%–46% margin. In the next four years wheat prices did pretty well and the state's economy was in pretty good shape. But wheat-producing counties across the United States reacted angrily to President Carter's embargo on wheat sales to the Russians, and in North Dakota most counties are wheat counties. As a result Ronald Reagan carried this state by a 64%–26% margin. In only two states (Arkansas and Nevada) was there a bigger Republican gain between the two elections, and in only three states (Utah, Idaho, and Nebraska) was Reagan's percentage lead larger.

Republicans have carried North Dakota in every presidential election in the last 30 years except 1964. Yet for more than 20 years the state has had a Democratic senator who is in strong political shape. Quentin Burdick has indeed had strong opposition only once since his first election, in 1970, when Congressman Thomas Kleppe ran one of the Nixon law-and-order campaigns against him. Kleppe spent the then unheard-of sum of $300,000 on his campaign (it is now a modest figure for a state this size), but Burdick won with more than 60% of the vote. In 1976 when other Democratic senators from western states (McGee of Wyoming, Moss of Utah) were defeated, the 68-year-old Burdick was returned almost without a contest. His Republican opponent was an unknown who carried only three counties.

Burdick is not, despite his long incumbency, a real power in the Senate. He has switched committees a number of times, leaving Judiciary and having the Post Office and Civil Service Committee abolished just as he would have become chairman. (The seat was no plum, however; McGee had held it and the chairmanship was used against him in his bid for reelection.) Burdick now has a seat on Appropriations, but he is the tenth-ranking member of the minority party; he is the third-ranking Democrat on the Environment and Public Works Committee. Burdick used to be a reliable Democratic vote on issues; now he has been known to stray, notably on the Panama Canal Treaties, which he opposed. Rumpled, past 70, Burdick does not seem possessed of the political ambition that animates so many other senators, and many people expect him to retire when his term is up in 1982. If he does not he will probably, for the first time in years, attract strong Republican opposition.

The state's other senator, Republican Mark Andrews, was just elected in 1980; it was the first time either North Dakota Senate seat had changed hands in 20 years. The seat had been held by Milton Young, a quiet conservative who specialized in the problems of wheat; he was reelected in 1974 at age 77 in large part because of an ad that showed him splitting a block of wood with a karate chop. Andrews had been the obvious heir apparent for a long time; he was first elected to the House in 1963 and as the state's only congressman in the 1970s was reelected with large margins. His only real detractor was Young, who reacted to him with the resentment and asperity many kings of England expressed toward their princes of Wales. Andrews is a farmer himself and has been something of a specialist in wheat, serving on the Agricultural Appropriations Subcommittee in the Senate. Andrews also serves on the Budget Committee. Tall, with a deep voice and an imposing appearance, Andrews tends to vote with most Republicans on most issues. But he is always ready to desert party orthodoxy when it comes to agricultural issues if he thinks that is in the interests of North Dakota farmers. Andrews did not have a strong opponent in the 1980 race and carried every county in the state; elected at age 54, he has every prospect of having a long Senate career.

North Dakota's at-large congressional seat was one of the four house seats in the country that switched from the Republicans to the Democrats in 1980. That result, like the result of the Senate race, was due more to the popularity of the winner than any other factor. Byron Dorgan, the new congressman-at-large, had been state tax commissioner in North Dakota. That does not sound like an important office, but in this state it is, or can be. Dorgan held that office for 11 years, and his greatest achievement was to force out-of-state corporations to pay higher taxes in North Dakota. That is often a technical, legalistic battle, on which prairie farmers are accustomed to losing to big city lawyers, but Dorgan won victories that brought back echoes of the old Non-Partisan League movement. Dorgan has been reelected to his state office by overwhelming margins and in 1974 gave Andrews himself as close a race as he had had since 1964 (56%–44%). Against a New Right Republican state legislator, Dorgan won an easy 57%–43% victory in 1980, running more than 30% ahead of his party's candidate for president. Dorgan serves on the Agriculture and Small Business Committees, and he represents most vividly North Dakota's prairie populism, its distrust of big institutions (especially banks and grain companies) and its concern for the individual farmer. An opponent of the Vietnam war when that was an issue, Dorgan is skeptical of some defense spending. Should Burdick retire in 1982, Dorgan is the obvious Democratic candidate, and his 1980 showing suggests that he could beat just about any Republican, even in a Republican year. He was only 38 when he was elected to the House; quite possibly he has a very long career ahead of him on Capitol Hill.

Why were the Democrats able to hold the governorship of this Republican state for 20 years? Mostly because of the personal popularity of Governor William Guy, elected in 1960, 1962, 1964, and 1968, and the close election victories of Governor Arthur Link, elected in 1972 and 1976. Link, an upset winner in the western congressional district in 1970, was faced with the unpleasant prospect of running against Mark Andrews when the state was reduced to one House seat by the 1970 census; instead he ran for governor and won two terms. His luck ran out in 1980. The Republican, Allen Olson, was much younger and charged that the state had not been moving ahead. The North Dakota governorship is of importance to people outside the state only because the state has substantial coal and other mineral deposits, and state policy helps to determine if they can be mined. Olson charged that Link favored too high a severance tax and said that he favored more development; he seems to be in line with the Reagan Administration's policy of exploiting American minerals and energy resources more extensively.

Census Data   Pop. (1980 final) 652,695, up 6% in 1970s: 0.29% of U.S. total, 46th largest. Central city, 23%; suburban, 13%. Median 4-person family income, 1978, $18,789, 92% of U.S., 35th highest.

1979 Share of Federal Tax Burden $1,217,000,000; 0.27% of U.S. total, 47th largest.

1979 Share of Federal Outlays $1,580,031,000; 0.34% of U.S. total, 47th largest.

DOD	$280,116,000	44th	(0.26%)	HEW	$472,657,000	46th	(0.26%)
DOE	$10,857,000	36th	(0.09%)	ERDA	$9,977,000	28th	(0.36%)
HUD	$16,677,000	45th	(0.25%)	NASA	—	51st	(0.00%)
VA	$57,130,000	47th	(0.28%)	DOT	$62,951,000	46th	(0.38%)
EPA	$12,938,000	51st	(0.24%)	DOC	$6,568,000	47th	(0.21%)
DOI	$63,217,000	23d	(1.14%)	USDA	$420,914,000	24th	(1.75%)

Economic Base   Agriculture, notably wheat, cattle, barley, and dairy products; finance, insurance, and real estate; food and kindred products, especially dairy products; printing and publishing, especially newspapers; tourism; machinery, especially farm machinery.

Political Lineup   Governor, Allen Olson (R). Senators, Quentin N. Burdick (D) and Mark Andrews (R). Representatives, 1 D at large; 1 in 1982. State Senate, 50 (40 R and 10 D); State House of Representatives, 100 (73 R and 27 D).

The Voters

Registration   No statewide registration.
Employment profile 1970   White collar, 42%. Blue collar, 21%. Service, 16%. Farm, 21%.
Ethnic groups   Hispanic 1980, 1%. Am. Ind. 1980, 3%. Total foreign stock 1970, 24%. Norway, 6%; USSR, 5%.

Presidential Vote

1980	Reagan (R)	193,695	(64%)
	Carter (D)	79,189	(26%)
	Anderson (I)	23,640	(8%)
1976	Ford (R)	153,470	(52%)
	Carter (D)	136,078	(46%)

SENATORS

Sen. Quentin N. Burdick (D) Elected June 28, 1960, seat up 1982; b. June 19, 1908, Munich; home, Fargo; U. of Minn., B.A. 1931, LL.B. 1932.

Career   Practicing atty., 1932–58; Dem. nominee for Gov., 1946; U.S. House of Reps., 1959–60.

Offices   451 RSOB, 202-224-2551. Also Fed. Bldg., Fargo 58102, 701-237-4000, and Fed. Bldg., Bismarck 58501, 701-255-2553.

Committees   *Appropriations* (10th). Subcommittees: Agriculture and Related Agencies; Energy and Water Development; Interior; Labor, Health and Human Services, Education.

Environment and Public Works (3d). Subcommittee: Transportation; Toxic Substances and Environmental Oversight; Regional and Community Development.

Special Committee on Aging (6th).

Group Ratings

	ADA	COPE	PC	LCV	CFA	RPN	NAB	NSI	NTU	ACA	ACU
1980	78	84	53	33	53	—	25	50	30	19	17
1979	63	88	55	—	43	—	—	—	27	30	22
1978	55	74	65	45	55	30	18	60	17	23	30

Key Votes

1) Draft Registn $	FOR	6) Fair Housng Cloture	FOR	11) Cut Socl Incr Defns	AGN
2) Ban $ to Nicrgua	—	7) Ban $ Rape Abortns	AGN	12) Income Tax Indexing	AGN
3) Dlay MX Missile	—	8) Cap on Food Stmp $	AGN	13) Lim Spdg 21% GNP	AGN
4) Nuclr Mortorium	AGN	9) New US Dep Edcatn	FOR	14) Incr Wndfll Prof Tax	FOR
5) Alaska Lands Bill	FOR	10) Cut OSHA Inspctns	AGN	15) Chryslr Loan Grntee	AGN

Election Results

1976 general	Quentin N. Burdick (D)	175,772	(62%)	($117,514)
	Robert Stroup (R)..............	103,466	(37%)	($136,748)
1976 primary	Quentin N. Burdick (D), unopposed			
1970 general	Quentin N. Burdick (D)	134,519	(61%)	
	Thomas S. Kleppe (R)	82,996	(38%)	

Sen. Mark Andrews (R) Elected 1980, seat up 1986; b. May 19, 1926, Cass Co.; home, Mapleton; U.S. Military Acad., 1944–46, N.D. St. U., B.S. 1949, Hon. Doctorate 1978.

Career Farmer; Rep. nominee for Gov., 1962; U.S. House of Reps., 1963–80.

Offices 417 RSOB, 202-224-2043. Also P.O. Box 1915, Bismarck 58502, 701-258-4648; P.O. Box 3004, Fargo 58102, 701-232-8030; Heritage Place, Minot 58701, 701-852-2510; and 106 Fed. Bldg., Grand Forks 58201, 701-775-9601.

Committees *Agriculture, Nutrition, and Forestry* (9th). Subcommittees: Agricultural Credit and Rural Electrification; Agricultural Production, Marketing, and Stabilization of Prices; Agricultural Research and General Legislation; Rural Development, Oversight, and Investigations (Chairman).

Appropriations (9th). Subcommittees: Agriculture and Related Agencies; Defense; Interior; Labor, Health and Human Services, Education; Transportation (Chairman).

Budget (7th).

Select Committee on Indian Affairs (3d).

Group Ratings (as Member of U.S. House of Representatives)

	ADA	COPE	PC	LCV	CFA	RPN	NAB	NSI	NTU	ACA	ACU
1980	17	18	37	27	14	—	73	100	39	67	53
1979	0	20	18	14	7	—	—	—	44	88	81
1978	5	5	5	24	14	50	83	100	19	73	92

Key Votes (as Member of U.S. House of Representatives)

1) Draft Registn $	FOR	6) Fair Hsg DOJ Enfrc	AGN	11) Cut Socl Incr Dfns $	FOR
2) Ban $ to Nicrgua	FOR	7) Lim PAC Contrbtns	AGN	12) Hosptl Cost Controls	AGN
3) Dlay MX Missile	AGN	8) Cap on Food Stmp $	FOR	13) Gasln Ctrls & Allctns	AGN
4) Nuclr Mortorium	AGN	9) New US Dep Edcatn	FOR	14) Lim Wndfll Prof Tax	FOR
5) Alaska Lands Bill	AGN	10) Cut OSHA $	FOR	15) Chryslr Loan Grntee	—

Election Results

1980 general	Mark Andrews (R)	210,347	(70%)	($402,129)
	Kent Johanneson (D)	86,658	(29%)	($139,203)
1980 primary	Mark Andrews (R)	78,833	(100%)	
1974 general	Milton R. Young (R)	114,852	(48%)	($300,121)
	William L. (Bill) Guy (D)	114,675	(48%)	($115,561)

GOVERNOR

Gov. Allen I. Olson (R) Elected 1980, term expires Jan. 1985; b. Nov. 5, 1938, Rolla; home, Bismarck; U. of N.D., B.A. 1960, J.D. 1963.

Career Army, 1963–67; Asst. Dir., N.D. Legis. Cncl., 1967–69; Practicing atty., 1969–72; Atty. Gen. of N.D., 1972–80.

Offices Executive Office, State Capitol, Bismarck 58505, 701-224-2200.

Election Results

1980 gen.	Allen I. Olson (R)	162,230	(54%)
	Arthur A. Link (D)	140,391	(46%)
1980 prim.	Allen I. Olson (R)	60,016	(76%)
	Orville W. Hagen (R)	19,306	(24%)
1976 gen.	Arthur A. Link (D)	153,309	(52%)
	Richard Elkin (R)	138,321	(46%)

Rep. Byron L. Dorgan (D) Elected 1980; b. May 14, 1942, Dickinson; home, Bismarck; U. of N.D., B.S. 1964, U. of Denver, M.A. 1966.

Career Martin-Marietta Exec. Devel. Program, 1966–67; N.D. Dpty. Tax Commissioner, 1967–69, Tax Commissioner, 1969–80; Dem. nominee for U.S. House of Reps., 1974.

Offices 427 CHOB, 202-225-2611. Also P.O. Box 2579, Bismarck 58502, 701-255-4011, ext. 618, and P.O. Box 1664, Fargo 58102, 701-237-5771, ext. 5135.

Committees *Agriculture* (24th). Subcommittees: Conservation, Credit and Rural Development; Forests, Family Farms and Energy; Wheat, Soybeans and Feed Grains.

Small Business (20th). Subcommittee: Tax, Access to Equity Capital and Business Opportunities.

Veterans' Affairs (17th). Subcommittees: Hospitals and Health Care.

Group Ratings and Key Votes: Newly Elected

Election Results

1980 general	Byron L. Dorgan (D)	166,437	(57%)	($195,068)
	Jim Smykowski (R)	124,707	(43%)	($267,525)
1980 primary	Byron L. Dorgan (D)	40,080	(100%)	
1978 general	Mark Andrews (R)	147,746	(67%)	
	Bruce Hagen (D)	68,016	(31%)	

OHIO

If you wanted to send a foreigner to a single state that had within it most of the varying ways of life in America, you could not do better than Ohio. This is a state full of carefully tended farms, God-fearing small towns, and sprawling industrial cities. It has some of the most distressed areas of the United States and some of the most booming. That variety stems in part from its history. Ohio was the first state from the old Northwest Territory admitted to the Union, in 1803, and within 25 years it was the fourth largest state in population. Its patterns of settlement were varied. The first white people here moved up through Kentucky or down the Ohio River to the southwestern corner of the state around Cincinnati. The old-stock Americans were followed by Germans, who were fleeing the consequences of the failed European revolutions of 1848. By the time of the Civil War, Cincinnati was heavily German and pro-Union and was the fourth largest city in the country. Meanwhile, the northeastern corner of Ohio remained placid farmland, settled by Yankee migrants from New England and Upstate New York. Not until the growth of the steel and oil industries in the late 19th century did the huge industrial complexes of Cleveland, Akron, and Youngstown come into being. But they grew rapidly, and by 1910 Cleveland was larger than Cincinnati and was itself, momentarily, the nation's fourth largest city. Cleveland dreamed then, as Houston dreams today, of becoming a world class city; instead, it lost the auto industry to Detroit and became merely a regional center, thriving through the 1950s, in trouble today as its industries decline.

In politics Ohio has a reputation as a profoundly Republican state, and although that is an exaggeration perhaps resulting from the Republican presidents it has produced (Hayes, Garfield, McKinley, Taft, Harding), it is a reputation not entirely undeserved. One factor that helped the Republicans over the years is the decentralization of the state's urban population. Ohio has six metropolitan areas with populations over 500,000; consequently no one city can provide the kind of solid Democratic base that Chicago has in Illinois or Detroit in Michigan. Moreover, some Ohio cities—notably Cincinnati and Columbus—are basically Republican. And Ohio has a tradition of brilliant Republican politicians, such as Senator Mark Hanna, McKinley's mentor and campaign manager; the senior Senator Robert Taft, the idol of his party's conservative wing during the New Deal years and after; and Ray Bliss, a nonideological technician who led the Ohio Republican Party in the 1950s and 1960s and as national chairman helped to turn the party around after the Goldwater debacle of 1964.

It would be accurate today, however, to regard Ohio as a marginal state politically—indeed, with its large number of electoral votes (25 in 1980, 23 in 1984) one of the prime marginal states in the country. Small-town Ohio remains heavily Republican, particularly in the northern and central part of the state; and this is a state where small-town population—in places such as Wapakoneta, home of astronaut Neil Armstrong—remains demographically important. However, in the southern part of the state, in sparsely populated rural counties, remain vestiges of a Democratic tradition that goes back to the Civil War when southern Ohio was copperhead country. These counties, below U.S. 40, the Old National Road, provided critical votes for Jimmy Carter in 1976, when he carried the state by 11,000 votes; and they delivered above-average percentages for him four years later as well. Otherwise Democratic strength in Ohio is concentrated in the industrial cities — in Cleveland, although the number of voters in metropolitan Cleveland has dropped by 56,000 over the past 20 years. Democratic cities also include Akron, Youngstown, Toledo, and Dayton — all at the beginning of the 1980s in serious trouble because of the declines of the auto, rubber, and steel industries. Ohio's oldest city, Cincinnati, has been Republican since the middle 19th century. Columbus, whose economy resembles the Sun Belt more than that of northeastern Ohio — the employment base is white collar, the local economy is booming, and the population has been rising rapidly in the 1960s and 1970s — also has a politics resembling those areas, generally heavily Republican and skeptical of government spending. Altogether, these varying political preferences add up to a pretty even balance — or at least one that comes out almost exactly the same as the nation as a whole.

Indeed, in the last two presidential elections, Ohio has come as close as any state to duplicating the national results. Carter carried the state narrowly in 1976 and lost it by a much wider margin in 1980. The Carter vote dropped particularly in the rural areas in the northern part of the state, where he had run quite well for a Democrat the first time; Carter held his own (and Reagan did not do as well as Ford) in Cincinnati, Columbus, and Dayton. The incumbent president in 1980 was essentially reduced to carrying the parts of the state that had suffered large job losses and serious economic decline during the four years of his presidency: most of northeastern Ohio, Toledo, and Dayton. But the Democratic percentages in these areas ran scarcely above 50%. Despite population loss, turnout in these areas increased, as it did in neighboring Michigan; it was as if people, desperate because of the collapse of the economic underpinnings of their communities, were reaching out and trying to help. But their votes — despite the Democratic margins — showed a lack of faith in the party that for decades has been regarded as more concerned about jobs and prosperity. Ronald Reagan argued during the campaign that he stood for economic growth and regeneration, and many urban Ohio voters — despite Carter's greater support for federal aid programs — apparently believed him.

As Ohio voters gave Reagan a 52%–41% margin, they were reelecting as their senior U.S. senator Democrat John Glenn by a resounding 69%–28% margin. Glenn lost only one of Ohio's 88 counties and ran far ahead of his Republican opponent in rural as well as urban areas. He lost only a few of the highest-income suburbs, (e.g., Indian Hill near Cincinnati) and then not by great margins. It was an awesome victory for a man who had not always won so easily. Glenn had won national fame in the early 1960s as the first astronaut to orbit the earth. He ran for the Senate in 1964 but was forced out of the race by an injury; in 1970 he ran again and was defeated by Howard Metzenbaum, who lost the general election narrowly to Robert Taft, Jr. Then in 1974 Glenn and Metzenbaum ran again. Glenn was helped by a Watergate-type issue: Metzenbaum had paid no income tax in 1969 and was arguing with the IRS about it, while Glenn seemed the picture of integrity. There was also a contrast in their issue positions and personal style. Metzenbaum is a successful lawyer and businessman who takes liberal stands on economic issues and has his strongest backing in the Democratic strongholds of northeastern Ohio. Glenn is a small-town boy who radiates all the virtues of his background; after his service in the military he moved to Columbus where he was a successful businessman. Democratic primaries, with their concentrations of blacks, ethnics, and union members, have always been his weakest political forum; he does much better in general elections, where he wins large numbers of ordinarily Republican votes. Nevertheless he was able to beat Metzenbaum in the 1974 primary by a 54%–46% margin, a victory that proved tantamount to election.

Following the 1980 election, Glenn made moves to suggest he was contemplating a presidential candidacy. It was not the first time he has shown national ambitions. He was one of the finalists for Jimmy Carter's vice presidential selection in 1976; he was effectively ruled out of that slot when he received a less tumultuous response from the convention audience for his keynote speech than Barbara Jordan received for hers. Again, the activist core Democratic constituency did not much care for his all-American style. And that is one of the problems Glenn may face if he does run for president in 1984. He can only hope that events have convinced enough organization Democrats that they cannot elect someone who epitomizes values accepted by only a minority of the population and that they would be well advised to nominate a candidate who, like Glenn, epitomizes the values of the majority.

Whether he makes a national race or not, Glenn has proved to be an important senator. His large margins give him the leeway to devote his attention to matters of broad national and global policy, and by and large he has done so. He is considered a hard worker and one who does not speak to an issue until he has done his homework. On the Foreign Relation Committee, he was part of a critical bloc in the Carter years, eager for example to approve the SALT Treaty but reluctant to do so because of his doubts that the treaty's provisions could be reliably verified. He is concerned as well about nuclear proliferation. As a former military officer, Glenn is much less inclined than are many Democrats who got their starts as opponents of the Vietnam war to be skeptical of the military, and he has favored increases in the defense budget for some time. But he is a man whose temperament is earnest and careful rather than flashy and aggressive, and he is not one who advocates using American military power indiscriminately.

Glenn's views on domestic issues are definitely more moderate than those of most Senate Democrats. He was never an enthusiast for many of the Great Society programs, and he counseled moderation in federal spending long before most of his copartisans favored it. Unions and liberal lobbies do not count Glenn as a sure vote, although he often does favor their positions.

A much surer vote for these positions—indeed one of the most liberal members of the Senate—is Howard Metzenbaum, who has been active in Democratic politics a long time: he was campaign manager for Stephen Young, who was elected to the Senate in 1958 at age 68 and reelected six years later, beating Robert Taft, Jr.; he barely lost to Taft in 1970 himself after beating Glenn in the primary; he was appointed to fill a vacancy in 1974 and then lost to Glenn in the primary; he finally was elected in his own right in 1976, beating Cleveland Congressman James Stanton in the primary and his old antagonist, Senator Taft, in the general. Metzenbaum sees himself as the champion of the little people, those who have been less successful than he—the factory workers and ghetto blacks and urban ethnics and hard-pressed small-town residents. He has made his biggest splash on the Senate Energy Committee, where he has been the most intransigent opponent of oil and gas price deregulation. He even staged a filibuster on this subject with South Dakota Senator James Abourezk. Metzenbaum is unquestionably hardworking and determined, and if he projects any image to his constituents it is one of a fighter. He misses few chances to promote himself and his views and, if he is not always overly popular with his colleagues, he does have considerable popularity with his constitituents.

Metzenbaum seems to be out of step in Ronald Reagan's Washington and in a Republican Senate. He is clearly in the minority position on most issues and is unlikely to prevail. Most of his fellow liberals are too dispirited to resort to a filibuster. Intellectually his views seem out of fashion. But it should not be forgotten that much of Ohio is economically distressed these days. All the certainties that seem represented by the giant factories of Cleveland, Akron, Youngstown, Dayton, and Toledo, now seem to be crumbling. The economic system that once promised them a comfortable life now seems to be collapsing. Some people are simply leaving, migrating out of Ohio's factory cities to places where there is more work. But for those who remain a desperate search for answers goes on. This part of Ohio went for Edward Kennedy over Jimmy Carter in the 1980 primary and mildly favored Carter's lukewarm Democratic politics in the general. The question for 1982 is whether these same voters will show stronger support for the more aggressive and well-defined policies of Howard Metzenbaum. Any number of Republicans are seeking the seat: Governor James Rhodes, barred from a consecutive third term, would like to run at age 73; Congressman John Ashbrook, as strong a conservative as Metzenbaum is a liberal, might like to run statewide, especially if his district is carved up by redistricting. Early 1981 polls showed Rhodes trailing Metzenbaum, which may be significant, since both are well known statewide; Ashbrook would have to make major efforts to become known. This almost certainly will be an expensive and hard-fought Senate race, and perhaps one of the key races to watch in 1982.

Ohio has elected the same governor in four of its last five elections; assuming he serves out his term, James Rhodes will have been governor of this state for 16 of the last 20 years. He is an old-fashioned Republican, one of the last major Republican officeholders who comes from a working-class background and who speaks in the gruff accents of the workingman himself. (Rhodes is already a wealthy man; he was one of the original investors in Wendy's Hamburgers.) Rhodes is thought of as a conservative Republican, but that is more a result of his style than of his policies. In Ohio he has always stressed the need for jobs and has argued that the state should keep taxes and spending low to attract business. The results have been mixed: Ohio enjoyed more industrial growth in the 1950s, before Rhodes became governor, than it has since, although some parts of the state have still grown impressively. In fact, taxes were raised significantly since he was first elected governor in 1962, although much of that was accomplished during the four years (1971–74) that Democrat John Gilligan was governor. In terms of national politics, Rhodes was always skeptical of Richard Nixon and was rather more inclined to such candidates as Nelson Rockefeller; he is not a man, however, to stick forever with a lost cause.

Rhodes has had some good luck. He won an 11,000-vote victory in 1974 largely because Gilligan had antagonized many Democratic voters; the Democrats held big margins in the legislature and in fact still control the state House. Lieutenant Governor Richard Celeste gave Rhodes a close race in 1978 and, with Attorney General William Brown, is one of the leading Democrats in the race to succeed him. The Republican candidate might be George Voinovich, elected mayor of Cleveland in 1979 after serving a year as Rhodes's lieutenant governor. The 1982 election is sure to be hotly contested, for it presents to voters the question of what is to come after nearly 20 years of Rhodes—and when part of the state seems to be in terrible economic trouble.

Ohio is one of the few large states with a Republican plurality in its U.S. House delegation. The state loses two of its 23 House seats through reapportionment, and control of the redistricting process is split between the parties. The Republicans control the governorship and the Senate, the Democrats the lower house. (A state commission controlled by the Democrats is responsible for redistricting the state legislature.) The situation cries out for a brokered solution; the question is whether one side had greater bargaining skill — or the kind of intransigence that might force the issue to the courts. Prime candidates for elimination by redistricting are the 23rd district held by Ronald Mottl, a suburban Cleveland Democrat, and the 17th district held by John Ashbrook, a rural conservative. But there will probably be some furious infighting before those decisions are made.

Census Data   Pop. (1980 final) 10,797,419, up 1% in 1970s: 4.77% of U.S. total, 6th largest. Central city, 28%; suburban, 51%. Median 4-person family income, 1978, $20,959, 103% of U.S., 18th highest.

1979 Share of Federal Tax Burden $22,541,000,000; 5.00% of U.S. total, 6th largest.

1979 Share of Federal Outlays $16,575,578,000; 3.58% of U.S. total, 7th largest.

DOD	$2,724,786,000	12th	(2.57%)	HEW	$7,923,823,000	7th	(4.43%)
DOE	$644,512,000	7th	(5.48%)	ERDA	$50,201,000	12th	(1.85%)
HUD	$338,930,000	5th	(5.14%)	NASA	$189,204,000	7th	(4.05%)
VA	$819,627,000	6th	(3.95%)	DOT	$501,451,000	9th	(3.04%)
EPA	$310,582,000	4th	(5.85%)	DOC	$23,673,000,000	24th	(0.75%)
DOI	$49,090,000	26th	(0.88%)	USDA	$538,638,000	16th	(2.24%)

Economic Base   Machinery, especially metalworking machinery; transportation equipment, especially motor vehicles and equipment; finance, insurance, and real estate; primary metal industries, especially blast furnaces and basic steel products; fabricated metal products, especially metal stampings and structural metal products; electrical equipment and supplies, especially household appliances and electrical industrial apparatus; agriculture, especially dairy products, cattle, soybeans, and corn.

Political Lineup   Governor, James A. Rhodes (R). Senators, John H. Glenn, Jr. (D) and Howard M. Metzenbaum (D). Representatives, 23 (13 R and 10 D), 21 in 1982. State Senate, 33 (18 R and 15 D); State House of Representatives, 99 (56 D and 43 R).

The Voters
Registration   5,887,488 Total. 1,533,704 D (26%); 1,055,033 R (18%); 2,153,506 unaffiliated (37%).
Employment profile 1970   White collar, 45%. Blue collar, 41%. Service, 12%. Farm, 2%.
Ethnic groups   Black 1980, 10%. Hispanic 1980, 1%. Total foreign stock 1970, 12%. Germany, Italy, 2% each; Poland, UK, 1% each.

Presidential Vote

1980	Reagan (R)	2,206,545	(52%)
	Carter (D)	1,752,414	(41%)
	Anderson (I)	254,472	(6%)
1976	Ford (R)	2,000,505	(50%)
	Carter (D)	2,011,621	(50%)

1980 Democratic Presidential Primary			*1980 Republican Presidential Primary*		
Carter	605,744	(51%)	Reagan	692,288	(81%)
Kennedy	523,874	(44%)	Bush	164,485	(19%)
Two others	56,792	(5%)			

SENATORS

Sen. John H. Glenn, Jr. (D) Elected 1974, seat up 1986; b. July 18, 1921, Cambridge; home, Columbus; Muskingum Col., B.S. 1939.

Career USMC, 1942–65; NASA Astronaut, 1959–65, First American to orbit the Earth, 1962; Candidate for Dem. nomination for U.S. Senate, 1964, 1970; V.P., Royal Crown Cola Co., 1966–68, Pres., Royal Crown Internatl., 1967–69.

Offices 2235 DSOB, 202-224-3353. Also Suite 600, 200 N. High St., Columbus 43215, 614-469-6697, and Rm. 104 Fed. Court House, Cleveland 44114, 216-522-7095.

Committees *Foreign Relations* (3d). Subcommittees: African Affairs; East Asian and Pacific Affairs; Near Eastern and South Asian Affairs.

Governmental Affairs (5th). Subcommittees: Permanent Subcommittee on Investigations; Energy, Nuclear Proliferation, and Government Processes.

Special Committee on Aging (2d).

Group Ratings

	ADA	COPE	PC	LCV	CFA	RPN	NAB	NSI	NTU	ACA	ACU
1980	67	72	57	53	53	—	33	20	34	17	15
1979	53	84	52	—	52	—	—	—	24	4	9
1978	65	74	58	76	45	60	33	40	14	25	13

Key Votes

1) Draft Registn $	FOR	6) Fair Housng Cloture	FOR	11) Cut Socl Incr Defns	FOR
2) Ban $ to Nicrgua	—	7) Ban $ Rape Abortns	AGN	12) Income Tax Indexing	AGN
3) Dlay MX Missile	AGN	8) Cap on Food Stmp $	AGN	13) Lim Spdg 21% GNP	AGN
4) Nuclr Mortorium	AGN	9) New US Dep Edcatn	FOR	14) Incr Wndfll Prof Tax	AGN
5) Alaska Lands Bill	FOR	10) Cut OSHA Inspctns	AGN	15) Chryslr Loan Grntee	FOR

Election Results

1980 general	John H. Glenn, Jr. (D)	2,770,786	(69%)	($1,157,965)
	James E. Betts (R)	1,137,695	(28%)	($423,060)
1980 primary	John H. Glenn, Jr. (D)	934,230	(86%)	
	Frances R. Waterman (D)	88,506	(8%)	($1,157)
	Francis Hunstiger (D)	64,270	(6%)	($2,180)
1974 general	John H. Glenn, Jr. (D)	1,930,670	(65%)	($1,149,130)
	Ralph J. Perk (R)	918,133	(31%)	($292,838)

Sen. Howard M. Metzenbaum (D) Elected 1976, seat up 1982; b. June 4, 1917, Cleveland; home, Shaker Heights; Ohio St. U., B.A. 1939, LL.B. 1941.

Career Practicing atty.; Cofounder, Airport Parking Co. of America, ComCorp Communications Corp.; Chmn. of the Bd., ITT Consumer Services Corp.; Ohio House of Reps, 1943–46; Ohio Senate, 1947–50; Campaign Mgr., Sen. Stephen M. Young, 1958 and 1964; Dem. nominee for U.S. Senate, 1970; U.S. Senate, 1974.

Offices 347 RSOB, 202-224-2315. Also Rm. 442, 121 E. State St. Columbus 43215, 614-469-6774.

Committees *Budget* (7th).

Energy and Natural Resources (5th). Subcommittees: Energy Conservation and Supply; Energy Regulation; Public Lands and Reserved Water.

Judiciary (4th). Subcommittees: Agency Administration; Criminal Law; Juvenile Justice.

Labor and Human Resources (7th). Subcommittees: Employment and Productivity; Aging, Family and Human Services.

Group Ratings

	ADA	COPE	PC	LCV	CFA	RPN	NAB	NSI	NTU	ACA	ACU
1980	83	94	87	71	93	—	27	10	34	12	10
1979	84	95	72	—	81	—	—	—	89	13	6
1978	100	84	88	78	90	60	25	10	18	13	13

Key Votes

1) Draft Registn $	AGN	6) Fair Housng Cloture	FOR	11) Cut Socl Incr Defns	AGN
2) Ban $ to Nicrgua	FOR	7) Ban $ Rape Abortns	AGN	12) Income Tax Indexing	AGN
3) Dlay MX Missile	—	8) Cap on Food Stmp $	—	13) Lim Spdg 21% GNP	AGN
4) Nuclr Mortorium	FOR	9) New US Dep Edcatn	FOR	14) Incr Wndfll Prof Tax	FOR
5) Alaska Lands Bill	FOR	10) Cut OSHA Inspctns	AGN	15) Chryslr Loan Grntee	FOR

Election Results

1976 general	Howard M. Metzenbaum (D)	1,941,113	(50%)	($1,092,053)
	Robert A. Taft, Jr. (R)	1,823,774	(47%)	($1,304,207)
1976 primary	Howard M. Metzenbaum (D)	576,124	(54%)	
	James V. Stanton (D)	400,552	(37%)	
	Two others (D)	98,501	(9%)	
1970 general	Robert A. Taft, Jr. (R)	1,565,682	(50%)	
	Howard M. Metzenbaum (D)	1,495,262	(47%)	

GOVERNOR

Gov. James A. Rhodes (R) Elected 1974, term expires Jan. 1983; b. Sept. 13, 1909, Coalton; Ohio St. U.

Career Mayor of Columbus, 1943–53; Ohio St. Auditor, 1953–63; Gov. of Ohio, 1963–70; Writer and novelist; Chmn., Natl. Cncl. for Vocational Educ.

Offices Columbus 43215, 614-466-3555.

Election Results

1978 gen.	James A. Rhodes (R)	1,402,167	(49%)
	Richard Celeste (D)	1,354,631	(48%)
1978 prim.	James A. Rhodes (R)	393,632	(68%)
	Charles Kurfess (R)	187,544	(32%)
1974 gen.	James A. Rhodes (R)	1,493,679	(49%)
	John J. Gilligan (D)	1,482,191	(48%)

FIRST DISTRICT

The 1st district of Ohio is the eastern half of the city of Cincinnati and suburban Hamilton County. This is, by and large, the more prosperous half of the old river city, which was the cultural and commercial capital of the Midwest even before the Tafts arrived. In some neighborhoods within Cincinnati and in the hills beyond the city limits are the fashionable estates of the city's elite. Probably the most prestigious is the suburb of Indian Hill, home of former Senator Robert Taft, Jr. To the north, one finds a mix of shopping centers and high-income suburban terrain. Within the city itself are the formerly Jewish sections of Avondale and Walnut Hills, now predominantly black. Many neighborhoods, such as Norwood, a suburban enclave surrounded by Cincinnati, are inhabited mainly by migrants from the hills of Kentucky and Tennessee. The 1st has most of the city's Jewish population; from its early days as a German river town, Cincinnati has had an important German Jewish community. Politically, it is more conservative and Republican than Jewish communities in other major cities.

Cincinnati has a well-deserved reputation for being a Republican city. Of the nation's 25 largest metropolitan areas, only Dallas–Fort Worth and San Diego turn in Republican margins with greater regularity. That has been the case since before the Civil War, when Cincinnati was a German, pro-Union, and Republican island in a sea of southern Democratic sentiment. Later Cincinnati never attracted large numbers of the ethnic groups that have traditionally voted for Democrats. There are fewer blacks here than in Cleveland, Detroit, or Buffalo, and very few people of Eastern or Southern European origin. Many of the city's Appalachians come from solid Republican mountain counties and bring their politics to the big city here.

Out of Cincinnati have come several prominent Republicans, including U.S. Supreme Court Chief Justice Salmon P. Chase, President and Chief Justice William Howard Taft, Speaker of the House Nicholas Longworth (whose widow, Alice Roosevelt Longworth, lived on until 1980 in Washington), and of course the late Senator Robert Taft. In more recent years the 1st has produced a series of congressmen of both parties who, for some reason or another, have achieved national prominence. That started in 1964, when John Gilligan, then a Cincinnati Council member and later governor of Ohio, was elected in an upset; two

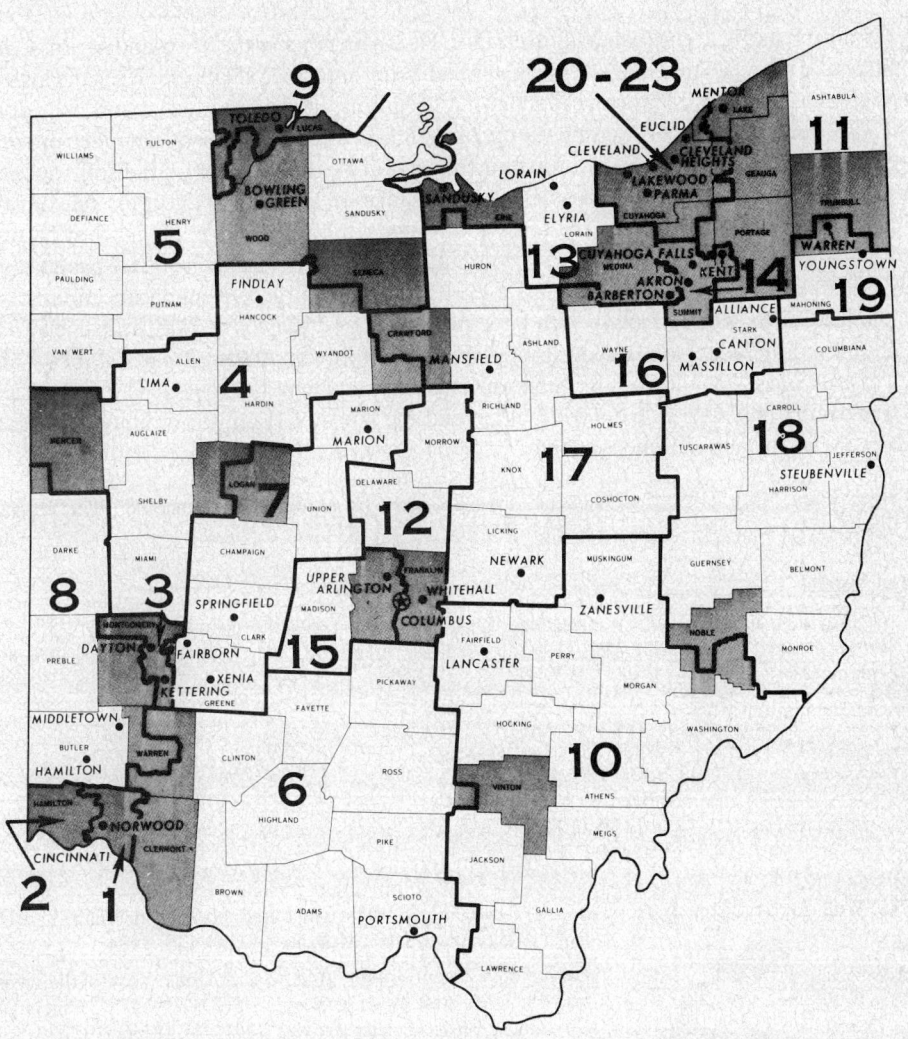

years later he was beaten by Robert Taft, Jr., later U.S. Senator. When Taft moved up to the Senate he was succeeded by William Keating, who in 1974 became president of the *Cincinnati Enquirer,* resigning and thus avoiding service on the Judiciary Committee during the impeachment hearings.

Keating's resignation provided some guidance, however, for Judiciary Committee members, for it required a special election—one of that series in 1974 that showed the vast unpopularity of Richard Nixon. The contenders were two members of the Cincinnati Council, Democrat Thomas Luken and Republican Willis Gradison. Although there was some disagreement on other issues—Luken was against legalized abortion; Gradison wasn't—the main issue was Nixon, and Luken won. This was the only special election that year whose result was overturned in November. With Nixon gone, Gradison captured the seat; two years later, Luken won in the next-door 2d district.

Gradison has held the seat easily ever since. He is a member of the Ways and Means Committee and is considered one of its brighter and better-informed members. He is the kind of congressman who asks basic questions about programs: If we have food stamps, why don't we have energy stamps or housing stamps? If inflation is continuing, why not index our progressive tax rates so that taxes on real incomes don't rise every year? Gradison's answers usually lead him in the direction of less federal regulation and activity; he is for indexing the income tax and for scrapping the food stamp program, for example. He has just become ranking Republican on the Health Subcommittee, which handles Medicare. He has emerged as one of the intellectual and legislative leaders of the resurgent Republican minority.

Gradison has won reelection with large majorities, and there is no way he is likely to be endangered by redistricting. Indeed, the Ohio legislature may trade off parts of the 1st and 2d district so as to make both Republican Gradison and Democrat Luken better off. Gradison's district may also be extended out beyond the limits of Hamilton County in order to meet the equal population standard.

Census Data   Pop. (1980 final) 424,166, down 8% in 1970s. Median family income, 1970, $10,535, 110% of U.S.

The Voters

Employment profile 1970   White collar, 53%. Blue collar, 33%. Service, 14%. Farm, –%.
Ethnic groups   Black 1980, 24%. Hispanic 1980, 1%. Asian 1980, 1%. Total foreign stock 1970, 9%. Germany, 2%.

Presidential Vote

1980	Reagan (R)	92,741	(55%)
	Carter (D)	65,224	(39%)
	Anderson (I)	8,441	(5%)
1976	Ford (R)	98,225	(58%)
	Carter (D)	69,422	(40%)

Rep. Willis D. Gradison, Jr. (R) Elected 1974; b. Dec. 28, 1928, Cincinnati; home, Cincinnati; Yale U., B.A. 1948, Harvard U., M.B.A. 1951, D.C.S. 1954.

Career   Investment broker; Asst. to U.S. Under Secy. of the Treasury, 1953–55; Asst. to U.S. Secy. of HEW, 1955–57; Cincinnati City Cncl., 1961–74, Vice Mayor, 1967–71, Mayor 1971.

Offices   1117 LHOB, 202-225-3164. Also 8008 Fed. Ofc. Bldg., 550 Main St., Cincinnati 45202, 513-684-2456.

Committees *Ways and Means* (10th). Subcommittees: Health; Public Assistance and Unemployment Compensation; Social Security.

Group Ratings

	ADA	COPE	PC	LCV	CFA	RPN	NAB	NSI	NTU	ACA	ACU
1980	22	17	33	52	36	—	67	89	48	67	32
1979	16	20	23	59	11	—	—	—	48	76	76
1978	20	15	28	68	27	91	100	89	37	70	83

Key Votes

1) Draft Registn $	FOR	6) Fair Hsg DOJ Enfrc	FOR	11) Cut Socl Incr Dfns $	FOR
2) Ban $ to Nicrgua	FOR	7) Lim PAC Contrbtns	AGN	12) Hosptl Cost Controls	AGN
3) Dlay MX Missile	AGN	8) Cap on Food Stmp $	FOR	13) Gasln Ctrls & Allctns	AGN
4) Nuclr Mortorium	AGN	9) New US Dep Edcatn	AGN	14) Lim Wndfll Prof Tax	FOR
5) Alaska Lands Bill	FOR	10) Cut OSHA $	AGN	15) Chryslr Loan Grntee	—

Election Results

1980 general	Willis D. Gradison, Jr. (R)	124,080	(75%)	($98,441)
	Donald J. Zwick (D)............	38,529	(23%)	($0)
1980 primary	Willis D. Gradison, Jr. (R)	30,547	(100%)	
1978 general	Willis D. Gradison, Jr. (R)	73,593	(64%)	($84,745)
	Timothy M. Burke (D)	38,669	(34%)	($12,710)

SECOND DISTRICT

The 2d congressional district of Ohio is the western half of Cincinnati and Hamilton County. On the whole, this is the less fashionable half of Cincinnati, although the 2d does have plenty of comfortable neighborhoods, mostly in the suburbs. For the most part, the district consists of middle- and lower-middle-class neighborhoods spread out over Cincinnati's hills. The 2d also includes some of the older and poorer sections of the city, such as the Appalachian Over the Rhine area (a name that recalls Cincinnati's German heritage). At the eastern end of the district winds Mill Creek, and next to it lies Cincinnati's industrial corridor. Here are the great Procter and Gamble soap factories and many of the city's machine tool makers; Cincinnati is a leader in both industries. Here also is the General Electric plant that produces many of the nation's aircraft engines.

Like the 1st district, this is one that has always been strongly Republican. In recent years, Cincinnati itself has become more Democratic, because many of its more affluent citizens have moved to the suburbs; but the suburbs are very heavily Republican. This district has elected Republican congressmen for many years, but now it is represented by a Democrat. One reason is that his Republican predecessor, Donald Clancy, became tired of providing all the services that constituents have come to expect. Instead of returning frequently to the district, he took to spending more time in Florida. First elected in 1960, he had a tough challenge in 1970 and did poorly against a weak opponent in 1974. He was defeated finally in 1976, when Thomas Luken, a veteran of the Cincinnati Council who had won a special election in the 1st district in the spring of 1974 and then lost the district in the 1974 general election, decided to run in the 2d instead.

Luken was a candidate of considerable strength; he had lost in the 1st district to Willis Gradison, a bright and energetic campaigner. Luken beat Clancy despite the latter's long incumbency, and despite the fact that the district was giving 62% of its votes to Gerald Ford. In 1978 he had stronger competition from state Senator Stanley Aronoff but managed to win again by a small margin. In 1980 against former television newscaster Tom Atkins, Luken got his biggest—and first comfortable—margin.

Luken's greatest strength is in Cincinnati's middle-class Catholic neighborhoods. He is a strong foe of abortions and a strong supporter of tuition tax credits. On other issues he has a record that has become considerably more conservative than those of most northern Democrats.

Luken could be helped by redistricting, particularly if the legislature gives some of his more Republican areas to Gradison's 1st district and gives the 2d some of Gradison's Democratic precincts. This is entirely possible since control of redistricting is split between the two parties and the result will probably be a compromise.

Census Data   Pop. (1980 final) 450,691, down 3% in 1970s. Median family income, 1970, $10,439, 109% of U.S.

The Voters

Employment profile 1970   White collar, 53%. Blue collar, 34%. Service, 13%. Farm, –%.
Ethnic groups   Black 1980, 15%. Hispanic 1980, 1%. Total foreign stock 1970, 9%. Germany, 3%.

Presidential Vote

1980	Reagan (R)	102,455	(60%)
	Carter (D)	58,471	(34%)
	Anderson (I)	8,141	(5%)
1976	Ford (R)	107,931	(62%)
	Carter (D)	63,640	(36%)

Rep. Thomas A. Luken (D) Elected 1976; b. July 9, 1925, Cincinnati; home, Cincinnati; Bowling Green U., 1933–34, Xavier U., B.A. 1947, Salmon P. Chase Law Sch., LL.B. 1950.

Career   USMC, WWII; Practicing atty.; Deer Park City Solicitor, 1955–61; U.S. Dist. Atty. for So. Dist. of Ohio, 1961–64; Cincinnati City Cncl., 1964–67, 1969–74, Mayor, 1971–72; U.S. House of Reps., 1974.

Offices   240 CHOB, 202-225-2216. Also Rm. 3409, Fed. Bldg., Cincinnati 45202, 513-684-2723.

Committees   *Energy and Commerce* (11th). Subcommittees: Health and Environment; Oversight and Investigations; Telecommunications, Consumer Protection, and Finance.

Small Business (9th). Subcommittees: Antitrust and Restraint of Trade Activities Affecting Small Business (Chairman); General Oversight.

Select Committee on Aging (16th). Subcommittee: Health and Long-Term Care.

Group Ratings

	ADA	COPE	PC	LCV	CFA	RPN	NAB	NSI	NTU	ACA	ACU
1980	39	68	47	48	57	—	27	56	29	43	33
1979	37	89	55	42	56	—	—	—	32	32	36
1978	25	65	40	51	46	40	50	80	25	60	50

Key Votes

1) Draft Registn $	FOR	6) Fair Hsg DOJ Enfrc	AGN	11) Cut Socl Incr Dfns $	AGN
2) Ban $ to Nicrgua	AGN	7) Lim PAC Contrbtns	AGN	12) Hosptl Cost Controls	AGN
3) Dlay MX Missile	AGN	8) Cap on Food Stmp $	FOR	13) Gasln Ctrls & Allctns	FOR
4) Nuclr Mortorium	AGN	9) New US Dep Edcatn	AGN	14) Lim Wndfll Prof Tax	FOR
5) Alaska Lands Bill	FOR	10) Cut OSHA $	AGN	15) Chryslr Loan Grntee	FOR

Election Results

1980 general	Thomas A. Luken (D)	103,423	(59%)	($290,853)
	Tom (Thearon) Atkins (R)	72,693	(41%)	($120,476)
1980 primary	Thomas A. Luken (D)	26,934	(100%)	
1978 general	Thomas A. Luken (D)	64,522	(52%)	($230,690)
	Stanley J. Aronoff (R)	58,716	(48%)	($275,400)

THIRD DISTRICT

In many ways Dayton, Ohio, is a typical American city. Sitting just below the Old National Road that spans the middle of the Midwest, it is middle sized (metropolitan population 830,000) and middle class. It has given birth to such American phenomena as the Wright brothers and the Phil Donahue show. Dayton was the city picked by analysts Ben Wattenberg and Richard Scammon to illustrate the typical American voters—a housewife whose husband works in a factory and whose brother-in-law is a policeman.

Through most of its history, Dayton has been a prosperous city, with bustling factories and products ranging from National Cash Registers to Dayton Tires. But in the 1970s the slowdown in the growth of the American economy has hit Dayton particularly hard. Like the industrial cities of northern Ohio, Dayton has been losing jobs. Part of the problem is the closedown of big factories, such as the Dayton Tire plant where 1,200 workers suddenly lost their jobs. But another less visible problem is that businesses and jobs are not being created to take the place of those that have failed. Dayton is a city much more diversified economically than Akron or Youngstown, but its decline has been as precipitous—and is even more ominous in its implications for the nation. The ingenuity and energy that produced the Wright brothers' plane and invented the cash register just doesn't seem to be apparent in Dayton anymore.

During the 1970s Dayton has been moving toward the Democrats politically, which is what one might expect: historically the Democrats have been most concerned about easing unemployment and reviving the economy. But support for the Democrats appears to be halfhearted and faltering. Jimmy Carter, for example, carried Dayton and Montgomery County by only small margins in 1976 and 1980.

Dayton's congressional district represents the same trend. The 3d congressional district includes Dayton, the upper-income suburbs of Kettering and Oakwood, and most of the blue collar Montgomery County suburbs directly north and south of the city. It elected a Democrat in 1964 and for a dozen years after 1966 was represented by one of the House's most liberal Republicans, Charles Whalen. He retired in 1978, and the expected successor was Democratic state Senator Tony Hall. But Hall had somewhat more difficulty winning than had been expected. His Republican opponent tried to seize the jobs issue and succeeded in holding Hall to 54%. Hall hoped to do better in 1980. His opponent was not as strong, but nationally the Republican Party was talking about jobs and economic growth while Jimmy Carter's Democrats were arguing that things could not really get much better. In that context Hall was reelected with 57% of the vote.

Things will probably not become any easier for Hall in 1982. After the 1980 election Hall switched from the Foreign Affairs Committee—on which he had sponsored a number of human rights amendments—to the Rules Committee. That means he may play a vital legislative role: the Democrats on Rules control the procedure in the House to a great extent even though the Democratic leadership does not usually have a majority on substantive issues; but, as every parliamentary expert knows, he who controls procedure tends to determine the outcome. Nonetheless, service on that committee is not likely to result in favorable publicity back in the district for Hall. Moreover, the boundaries of the 3d must be expanded substantially, by nearly 100,000 people, to meet the equal population standard; and the legislature, if it wanted to, could make the district considerably more Republican. So it is possible that this district will be hotly contested in 1982.

Census Data   Pop. (1980 final) 425,124, down 8% in 1970s. Median family income, 1970, $11,481, 120% of U.S.

The Voters

Employment profile 1970   White collar, 51%. Blue collar, 37%. Service, 12%. Farm, –%.
Ethnic groups   Black 1980, 18%. Hispanic 1980, 1%. Asian 1980, 1%. Total foreign stock 1970, 7%. Germany, 2%.

Presidential Vote

1980	Reagan (R)	72,684	(45%)
	Carter (D)	77,380	(48%)
	Anderson (I)	10,151	(6%)
1976	Ford (R)	74,128	(48%)
	Carter (D)	78,920	(50%)

Rep. Tony P. Hall (D) Elected 1978; b. Jan. 16, 1942, Dayton; home, Dayton; Denison U., B.A. 1964.

Career   Peace Corps, Thailand, 1964–66; Real estate broker, 1966– ; Ohio House of Reps., 1969–73; Ohio Senate, 1973–79.

Offices   1728 LHOB, 202-225-6465. Also 501 Fed. Bldg., 200 W. 2d St., Dayton 45402, 513-225-2843.

Committee   *Rules* (11th). Subcommittee: Rules of the House.

Group Ratings

	ADA	COPE	PC	LCV	CFA	RPN	NAB	NSI	NTU	ACA	ACU
1980	89	79	73	88	64	—	8	10	19	21	11
1979	84	90	83	88	85	—	—	—	16	4	5

Key Votes

1) Draft Registn $	AGN	6) Fair Hsg DOJ Enfrc	FOR	11) Cut Socl Incr Dfns $	AGN
2) Ban $ to Nicrgua	AGN	7) Lim PAC Contrbtns	FOR	12) Hosptl Cost Controls	FOR
3) Dlay MX Missile	FOR	8) Cap on Food Stmp $	AGN	13) Gasln Ctrls & Allctns	FOR
4) Nuclr Mortorium	FOR	9) New US Dep Edcatn	FOR	14) Lim Wndfll Prof Tax	AGN
5) Alaska Lands Bill	FOR	10) Cut OSHA $	AGN	15) Chryslr Loan Grntee	FOR

Election Results

1980 general	Tony P. Hall (D)..............	95,558	(57%)	($154,725)
	Albert H. Sealy (R)............	66,698	(40%)	($98,305)
1980 primary	Tony P. Hall (D)..............	36,940	(100%)	
1978 general	Tony P. Hall (D)..............	62,849	(54%)	($216,117)
	Dudley P. Kircher (R)	51,833	(44%)	($346,193)

FOURTH DISTRICT

The 4th congressional district of Ohio is a group of counties, mostly rural but usually with small cities, in the western part of the state. This is a deeply conservative part of the nation, a sort of Grant Woodish enclave set in industrial Middle America. It is somehow fitting that the town of Wapakoneta here in the 4th produced the first man to walk on the moon — the straitlaced and taciturn Neil Armstrong. The conservatism of the 4th runs so deep that it is often the most Republican district in Ohio. The district's urban centers, to the extent they can be called that, are as heavily Republican as the countryside, in some cases more so. Findlay is an old Republican town, made newly prosperous as the headquarters of Marathon Oil. Allen County, which contains the district's largest city, Lima, was the largest county east of Chicago and north of Richmond, Virginia, to support the candidacy of Barry Goldwater in 1964. Then there are smaller Republican towns such as Bucyrus, Piqua, and Upper Sandusky (which is nowhere near Sandusky).

For 25 years Republican William McCulloch represented the 4th district. When he retired in 1972, McCulloch was the dean of the Ohio delegation and the ranking Republican on the House Judiciary Committee, which has jurisdiction over civil rights legislation. McCulloch was a cautious, conservative man who shared the passion of some of the founders of the Republican Party for the principle of racial equality. He supported strongly the civil rights bills of the 1950s and 1960s, and his example helped to swing many more dubious Republicans behind the civil rights cause. He is entitled to a great deal of credit for the enactment of the Civil Rights Acts of 1964, 1965, and 1968.

McCulloch retired in 1972. His successor, Tennyson Guyer, a solid conservative, was known for his booming voice, his old-fashioned oratory, and his habit of wearing white shoes and loud-colored clothes; he was both a minister and a former public relations man for a tire company. Guyer died suddenly in the spring of 1981, and in this usually most Republican of districts there was a seriously contested special election to succeed him. Most of the action was on the Republican side. Michael Oxley, a state representative who had backed George Bush in the 1980 primary, narrowly beat Robert Huffman, a local prosecutor who was a strong Reagan backer. The Democrats had a strong candidate, state Representative Dale Locker, who was known as a conservative himself. The area's partisan preference of more than a century prevailed, but only narrowly, and Oxley was elected.

Census Data Pop. (1980 final) 489,043, up 6% in 1970s. Median family income, 1970, $9,710, 101% of U.S.

The Voters

Employment profile 1970 White collar, 38%. Blue collar, 46%. Service, 12%. Farm, 4%.
Ethnic groups Black 1980, 3%. Hispanic 1980, 1%. Total foreign stock 1970, 4%. Germany, 1%.

Presidential Vote

1980	Reagan (R)	127,002	(64%)
	Carter (D)	59,722	(30%)
	Anderson (I)	9,408	(5%)
1976	Ford (R)	104,313	(59%)
	Carter (D)	70,588	(39%)

Rep. Michael Oxley (R) Elected June 25, 1981.

Group Ratings and Key Votes: Newly Elected

Election Results

6/25/81 spc. elc.	Michael Oxley (R).............	41,904	(50%)	
	Dale Locker (D)	41,525	(50%)	
6/2/81 spc. prm.	Michael Oxley (R).............	20,955	(51%)	
	Robert J. Huffman (R)..........	18,512	(45%)	
	Four others (R)	1,637	(4%)	
1980 general	Tennyson Guyer (R)	133,795	(72%)	($41,661)
	Gerry Tebben (D)	51,150	(28%)	($4,832)
1980 primary	Tennyson Guyer (R)	50,183	(100%)	
1978 general	Tennyson Guyer (R)	85,575	(68%)	($23,696)
	John W. Griffin (D)	39,360	(32%)	

FIFTH DISTRICT

Some 150 years ago, New England Yankee farmers settled the flat lands in the northwestern corner of Ohio, together with recently immigrated German Protestants. The land here is more fertile and easier to work than the knobby hills of southern Ohio; its flatness and fertility must have amazed the early settlers. It is the beginning of the great corn and hog belt that stretches into Illinois and Iowa, and it is also one of the heartlands of the Republican Party since it was founded in the 1850s.

Unlike so much of rural America, northwestern Ohio was not in economic decline in the decades after World War II. The fertility of its soil, the industry of its farmers, and, most important, its strategic location prevented the kind of outmigration seen elsewhere. This area is encircled by the giant industrial cities of the Midwest and lies on both sides of the nation's major east–west railroads and interstate highways. Taking advantage of the proximity of these major markets, small factories have sprung up in most of the towns and much of the countryside of northwestern Ohio. They have provided jobs for young people here, who otherwise would probably have migrated to a large city. Even in the 1970s, when the economies of the industrial cities were in trouble, the economic base of northwestern Ohio continued to be relatively strong.

The 5th congressional district covers most of northwestern Ohio. Not included here is the city of Toledo and most of its suburbs, which make up the 9th district. The 5th, as one might expect, is a solidly Republican district that since 1958 has elected and reelected Congressman Delbert Latta. (His name, incidentally, is Welsh, not Italian.) Latta is one of those congressmen who labored for years without much public notice. As a member of the Rules Committee, he was often part, or even the architect, of the coalition of conservative Republicans and southern Democrats who would kill liberal legislation by refusing to schedule it for debate. Always a fierce and aggressive partisan, Latta could be trusted to follow the wishes of the Republican leadership; and within the leadership he was usually an advocate of hard-line opposition to the Democrats.

In the 1970s, Latta has become much more prominent, but his basic orientation has not changed. His well-deserved reputation got him a seat on the Judiciary Committee in 1974; he filled a vacancy just for the hearings on the impeachment of Richard Nixon. Apparently the hope was that Latta would provide a no-holds-barred defense of Richard Nixon, and he did. Again and again he mentioned how much the hearings were costing and he attacked committee counsel Albert Jenner, a Republican favoring impeachment, for having been a member of a committee that recommended the decriminalization of prostitution. Latta's tactics were not particularly effective. These side issues did not bring the angry popular reaction they once might have; the more effective defenses of Nixon, made by Charles Wiggins and others, stuck closer to the facts of the case.

When the congressional budget process was established in 1975, Latta again got a key role. He was named the ranking Republican on the House Budget Committee. The Senate committee has been characterized by cooperation between Chairman Edmund Muskie and ranking Republican Henry Bellmon; the opposite has been the case in the House. Latta has fought the Democrats every step of the way, arguing constantly in committee and then on the floor for lower spending targets in nondefense areas. On occasion he has defeated the budget limits set by the Democrats, although for the most part they have had the votes to prevail. Most commentators compare Latta's stance unfavorably with Bellmon's. But there is something to be said for an adversary process and for requiring the majority to justify their actions against strenuous opposition.

In the Reagan years his role will have to change: it will be his job to help round up enough Democratic votes so that Reagan's budget cuts will prevail in the so-called reconciliation process, which imposes the budget decisions on other committees. This he did in the spring of 1981 as one of the lead sponsors of the successful Gramm–Latta budget resolution. Latta will also play a major role in many fights as a leading Republican on the Rules Committee. On this body the Republicans are heavily outnumbered by Democrats loyal to the leadership; Latta's job will be to prevent them from having complete sway in the procedural decisions they reach and to fight them on the floor when necessary.

These are both positions requiring a sensitive combination of aggressiveness and pugnacity on the one hand and persuasiveness and reasonableness on the other. Latta is a man who has plenty of the former but may have to discipline himself carefully to show the latter. He does seem to be strongly motivated; he is a man who believes that the Democrats are invariably up to mischief and who will take whatever steps he thinks are necessary to stop them. He has been reelected easily every two years, and while it is possible that his district's boundaries will be changed, the legislature will certainly see that this important a Republican congressman has a safe seat.

Census Data   Pop. (1980 final) 513,127, up 11% in 1970s. Median family income, 1970, $9,945, 104% of U.S.

The Voters

    Employment profile 1970   White collar, 37%. Blue collar, 46%. Service, 12%. Farm, 5%.
    Ethnic groups   Black 1980, 1%. Hispanic 1980, 3%. Total foreign stock 1970, 7%. Germany, 2%.

Presidential Vote

1980	Reagan (R)	....	144,298	(59%)
	Carter (D)	....	79,455	(32%)
	Anderson (I)	....	18,840	(8%)
1976	Ford (R)	....	104,202	(54%)
	Carter (D)	....	83,765	(44%)

Rep. Delbert L. Latta (R) Elected 1958; b. Mar. 5, 1920, Weston; home, Bowling Green; Ohio Northern U., A.B. 1943, LL.B. 1946.

Career Practicing atty.; Ohio Senate, 1952–58.

Offices 2309 RHOB, 202-225-6405. Also 100 Fed. Bldg., 280 S. Main St., Bowling Green 43402, 419-353-8871.

Committees *Budget* (Ranking Member).

Rules (2d).

Group Ratings

	ADA	COPE	PC	LCV	CFA	RPN	NAB	NSI	NTU	ACA	ACU
1980	17	11	33	31	7	—	100	89	70	88	100
1979	5	15	5	7	0	—	—	—	64	92	85
1978	5	5	18	30	18	55	100	100	57	89	96

Key Votes

1) Draft Registn $	AGN	6) Fair Hsg DOJ Enfrc	AGN	11) Cut Socl Incr Dfns $	FOR
2) Ban $ to Nicrgua	FOR	7) Lim PAC Contrbtns	AGN	12) Hosptl Cost Controls	AGN
3) Dlay MX Missile	AGN	8) Cap on Food Stmp $	FOR	13) Gasln Ctrls & Allctns	AGN
4) Nuclr Mortorium	AGN	9) New US Dep Edcatn	AGN	14) Lim Wndfll Prof Tax	FOR
5) Alaska Lands Bill	AGN	10) Cut OSHA $		FOR	15) Chryslr Loan Grntee	FOR

Election Results

1980 general	Delbert L. Latta (R)	137,003	(70%)	($57,923)
	James R. Sherck (D)	57,704	(30%)	($17,990)
1980 primary	Delbert L. Latta (R)	49,992	(100%)	
1978 general	Delbert L. Latta (R)	85,547	(63%)	($45,705)
	James R. Sherck (D)	51,071	(37%)	($40,249)

SIXTH DISTRICT

The 6th district of Ohio is a rural district in the southern part of the state. Although the 6th touches the metropolitan areas of Cincinnati to the west and Columbus to the north, little in the 6th partakes of anything metropolitan. From the outer edges of urban Cincinnati and Columbus to the gritty industrial city of Portsmouth on the Ohio River, the district has a southern-accented, small-town feeling. The rolling hill country of the valley of the Scioto River, which runs through Columbus, Chillicothe, and Portsmouth, was once Democratic terrain, reflecting the southern origin of the valley's first settlers. In the 1950s and 1960s, this part of Ohio, like much of the South, became more conservative and much more Republican; only tiny Pike County still delivers Democratic majorities reliably in statewide races. In the western part of the district, some Cincinnati exurban growth spilling into Clermont County has contributed to the Republican trend in the 6th.

Until the late 1950s this district, in line with tradition, sent a Democrat to the House. After his death in 1959, the Ohio Republican organization of Ray Bliss carefully selected the party nominee, William Harsha, the former local prosecutor in Portsmouth, still in his 30s. Harsha won a special election in 1960 and went on to become ranking Republican on the House Public Works Committee, the body that traditionally handles pork barrel projects (federal buildings, dams). It is also responsible for highways and transportation.

There was a much more spirited Republican than Democratic primary to succeed Harsha, an index of the current political balance in the district. The easy winner, with 45% in an eight-candidate primary, was Bob McEwen, a former aide to Harsha who, at age 30, had served six years in the Ohio Senate. McEwen endorsed the national Republican program and had support from fundamentalist Christians. Nevertheless he lost Portsmouth and the river counties and Chillicothe to a candidate Harsha had beaten easily. McEwen's saving margin was his big edge in Clermont County.

Like his predecessor, McEwen serves on the Public Works Committee and is apparently interested in tending to the practical needs of the district. The 6th, after decades of sluggish population growth, is now Ohio's most populous congressional district, and its boundaries must be cut back and perhaps otherwise altered for 1982. McEwen, as a veteran of the Ohio legislature, can be expected to seek as favorable a district as he can get. His major problem may be that Cincinnati area Republican Willis Gradison would like to have some of those Clermont County precincts himself and needs the extra population to bring his district up to the state average.

Census Data   Pop. (1980 final) 543,692, up 17% in 1970s. Median family income, 1970, $8,595, 90% of U.S.

The Voters

   Employment profile 1970   White collar, 37%. Blue collar, 46%. Service, 12%. Farm, 5%.
   Ethnic groups   Black 1980, 2%. Total foreign stock 1970, 2%.

Presidential Vote

1980	Reagan (R)	75,109	(55%)
	Carter (D)	54,904	(40%)
	Anderson (I)	4,431	(3%)
1976	Ford (R)	91,352	(50%)
	Carter (D)	86,984	(48%)

Rep. Bob McEwen (R) Elected 1980; b. Jan. 12, 1950, Hillsboro; home, Hillsboro; U. of Miami, Fla., B.B.A. 1972.

Career   Real estate developer; Ohio House of Reps., 1974–80.

Offices   507 CHOB, 202-225-5705. Also P.O. Bldg., Portsmouth 45662, 614-353-5171; Fed. Bldg., Hillsboro 45133, 513-393-4223; and 190 Main St., Batavia 45103, 513-732-1786.

Committees   *Public Works and Transportation* (18th). Subcommittees: Economic Development; Investigations and Oversight; Surface Transportation.

Veterans' Affairs (9th). Subcommittees: Hospitals and Health Care; Housing and Memorial Affairs.

Group Ratings and Key Votes: Newly Elected

Election Results

1980 general	Bob McEwen (R)	101,288	(55%)	($182,388)
	Ted Strickland (D)	84,235	(45%)	($80,608)
1980 primary	Bob McEwen (R)	21,360	(45%)	
	James T. Christy (R)............	8,221	(17%)	($26,631)
	Don Gingerich (R)	6,545	(14%)	($26,699)
	Five others (R)	11,295	(24%)	
1978 general	William H. Harsha (R)	85,592	(65%)	($107,252)
	Ted Strickland (D)	46,318	(35%)	($32,950)

SEVENTH DISTRICT

Bellefontaine, Ohio, is the site of the first concrete street in the United States. It is still there in the downtown with the old courthouse looming up on one side and a row of stores on the other. Bellefontaine is part of Ohio's 7th congressional district, most of which has enjoyed a similarly stable existence since the turn of the century. It is true that the suburbs of Dayton have begun to encroach on the southwestern corner of the district, where Wright–Patterson Air Force Base is located. But the industrial city of Springfield, the district's largest urban concentration, has neither grown nor changed much in the last fifty years. Neither has the city of Marion, where young Socialist-to-be Norman Thomas delivered newspapers edited by President-to-be Warren Harding.

From 1938 to 1965, the 7th was represented by Republican Clarence Brown, a small-town newspaper editor. He was a man who seemed out of an earlier Republican era, from the days of Harding or even McKinley. For some years he was ranking Republican on the House Rules Committee, and as a strong believer in the free enterprise system he would join Chairman Smith of Virginia and other conservatives in killing or delaying liberal legislation. Brown also followed the venerable Republican tradition of strongly backing civil rights measures. After his death in 1965, he was succeeded by his son, Clarence (Bud) Brown, also a small-town newspaper editor and publisher. The younger Brown also stands solidly in the Republican tradition and has generally followed the majority Republican position on most issues.

In his years in the House Brown has risen to become second-ranking Republican on the Commerce Committee and ranking Republican on its major energy and fuels subcommittee. That latter position plus his own strong beliefs have made Brown a major Republican leader on the energy issue. Pitted against acerbic committee Chairman John Dingell, Brown has argued strongly for deregulation of natural gas and against controls and taxes on the oil industry. He believes that free markets will allocate energy supplies more rationally and economically than will federal bureaucrats, and he has likened the tasks the Carter energy bills set for government to the labor of Sisyphus. Brown's positions are not popular with voters, who would just as soon pay lower prices for gas and not worry about the consequences; but they have succeeded in carrying the day in the intellectual debate on policy in the late 1970s. Brown is in practice the leading House Republican on these issues, and he has seen his free-market position and skepticism about government programs move from being an old-fashioned credo to being, as it is now, the conventional wisdom of official Washington. His own efforts and energy have made some of the difference.

Brown has been mentioned on numerous occasions as a candidate for statewide office, although he has never run. His problem is that he is not well known statewide — a disadvantage to some extent countered by the fact that Ohio has elected numerous Browns to statewide office. One possibility is the 1982 Senate race. The incumbent, Howard Metzenbaum, has been as strong an opponent of energy deregulation as Brown has been a proponent; and Brown like many Republicans probably regards Metzenbaum as a demagogue. A more likely possibility, as this is written, is that Brown would run for governor. In early 1981 he set up a political action committee as a first step toward that end. With his Republican and business ties, Brown has the potential of raising a large campaign treasury, and he seems to have the ability and character to wear well in the spotlight of state politics. If he does run, the legislature will probably decide that his 7th district is the Republican district to be eliminated and divided among neighboring districts.

Census Data   Pop. (1980 final) 487,827, up 3% in 1970s. Median family income, 1970, $10,132, 106% of U.S.

The Voters

   Employment profile 1970   White collar, 44%. Blue collar, 42%. Service, 11%. Farm, 3%.
   Ethnic groups   Black 1980, 6%. Hispanic 1980, 1%. Asian 1980, 1%. Total foreign stock 1970, 5%. Germany, 1%.

Presidential Vote

1980	Reagan (R)	93,553	(54%)
	Carter (D)	67,916	(39%)
	Anderson (I)	10,048	(6%)
1976	Ford (R)	86,785	(52%)
	Carter (D)	75,152	(45%)

Rep. Clarence J. (Bud) **Brown** (R) Elected Nov. 2, 1965; b. June 18, 1927, Columbus; home, Urbana; Duke U., B.A. 1947, Harvard U., M.B.A. 1949.

Career Navy, WWII and Korea; Ed., Blanchester *Star Republican*, 1948–53; Ed. and Coowner, Franklin *Chronicle*, 1953–57; Ed., Urbana *Daily Citizen*, 1957–62, Publisher, 1959–70; Founder and Mgr., WCOM-FM Radio; Pres., Brown Publishing Co., 1955–.

Offices 2217 RHOB, 202-225-4324. Also 220 P.O. Bldg., 150 N. Limestone St., Springfield 45501, 513-325-0474.

Committees *Energy and Commerce* (2d). Subcommittees: Fossil and Synthetic Fuels; Health and the Environment.

Government Operations (3d). Subcommittee: Intergovernmental Relations and Human Resources.

Joint Economic Committee (7th). Subcommittees: Investment, Jobs, and Prices; Trade, Productivity, and Economic Growth (Vice-chairman).

Group Ratings

	ADA	COPE	PC	LCV	CFA	RPN	NAB	NSI	NTU	ACA	ACU
1980	11	20	23	12	14	—	92	100	50	67	63
1979	5	18	8	19	4	—	—	—	54	84	94
1978	15	5	15	19	23	67	92	100	27	80	90

Key Votes

1) Draft Registn $	FOR	6) Fair Hsg DOJ Enfrc	AGN	11) Cut Socl Incr Dfns $	FOR
2) Ban $ to Nicrgua	FOR	7) Lim PAC Contrbtns	AGN	12) Hosptl Cost Controls	—
3) Dlay MX Missile	AGN	8) Cap on Food Stmp $	FOR	13) Gasln Ctrls & Allctns	AGN
4) Nuclr Mortorium	AGN	9) New US Dep Edcatn	AGN	14) Lim Wndfll Prof Tax	—
5) Alaska Lands Bill	—	10) Cut OSHA $	FOR	15) Chryslr Loan Grntee	—

868   OHIO

Election Results

1980 general	Clarence J. (Bud) Brown (R)	124,137	(76%)	($205,446)
	Donald Hollister (D)............	38,952	(24%)	($6,028)
1980 primary	Clarence J. (Bud) Brown (R)	39,292	(100%)	
1978 general	Clarence J. Brown (R), unopposed			($33,877)

EIGHTH DISTRICT

Along the Indiana border, just north of Cincinnati and just west of Dayton, is the 8th congressional district of Ohio. Although the suburban sprawl of both Cincinnati and Dayton spills into the 8th, the district is dominated by two manufacturing cities in Butler County, Hamilton and Middletown. In the 8th the hilly Ohio River country slides into the flatter land of the northern part of the state. Over the years, the district has taken most of its settlers from around the Ohio River and farther south, a fact that shows up in the election returns. In most elections these days, the 8th is heavily Republican and conservative. But a southern Democratic heritage also exists here, one that surfaced in the hefty 18% of the vote cast for George Wallace in the 1968 general election. That was the highest percentage the Alabamian got in any Ohio district that year and, outside of Oklahoma, the best he did in any district that did not allow slavery at the time of the Civil War.

The current Congressman, Republican Thomas Kindness, was elected in an unusual three-cornered race in 1974. The seat had been Republican since its creation ten years before, but one incumbent had left to run for statewide office and another never managed to win a convincing majority. Although 1974 was a Democratic year, Kindness was elected with 42% to 38% for the Democrat and 20% for a Wallace-oriented Independent. The results paralleled almost exactly the standings in the 1968 presidential race in the district.

Kindness has proved more popular than his immediate predecessor and more interested in the House than the one before him. He has taken an active role in Republican affairs, and in 1979 he ran for the chairmanship of the House Republican Conference against John Anderson, although he lost by a decisive margin. Kindness's political skill shows up in his elections in the 8th district; he has been reelected three times with more than 70% of the vote. Redistricting may shift the district northward but is unlikely to make the district less Republican.

Kindness's political skill shows up in his elections in the 8th district; he has been reelected three times with more than 70% of the vote. Redistricting may shift the district northward but is unlikely to make the district less Republican.

Census Data Pop. (1980 final) 515,465, up 11% in 1970s. Median family income, 1970, $10,455, 109% of U.S.

The Voters

Employment profile 1970 White collar, 41%. Blue collar, 45%. Service, 11%. Farm, 3%.
Ethnic groups Black 1980, 6%. Hispanic 1980, 1%. Total foreign stock 1970, 4%. Germany, 1%.

Presidential Vote

1980	Reagan (R)	111,538	(57%)
	Carter (D)	72,266	(37%)
	Anderson (I)	9,392	(5%)
1976	Ford (R)	92,736	(54%)
	Carter (D)	77,534	(45%)

Rep. Thomas N. Kindness (R) Elected 1974; b. Aug. 26, 1929, Knoxville, Tenn.; home, Hamilton; U. of Md., A.B. 1951, Geo. Wash. U., LL.B. 1953.

Career Practicing atty., 1954–57; Asst. Counsel, Legal Dept., Champion Internatl. Corp., 1957–73; Hamilton City Cncl., 1964–69, Mayor 1964–67; Ohio House of Reps., 1971–74.

Offices 2434 RHOB, 202-225-6205. Also 801 High St., Hamilton 45013, 513-895-5656.

Committees *Government Operations* (5th). Subcommittee: Government Information and Individual Rights.

Judiciary (8th). Subcommittees: Administrative Law and Governmental Relations; Criminal Justice.

Group Ratings

	ADA	COPE	PC	LCV	CFA	RPN	NAB	NSI	NTU	ACA	ACU
1980	6	11	23	41	7	—	91	100	64	96	79
1979	11	5	18	20	7	—	—	—	63	96	100
1978	5	5	15	17	14	50	92	90	28	93	96

Key Votes

1) Draft Registn $	FOR	6) Fair Hsg DOJ Enfrc	AGN	11) Cut Socl Incr Dfns $	FOR
2) Ban $ to Nicrgua	FOR	7) Lim PAC Contrbtns	AGN	12) Hosptl Cost Controls	AGN
3) Dlay MX Missile	AGN	8) Cap on Food Stmp $	FOR	13) Gasln Ctrls & Allctns	AGN
4) Nuclr Mortorium	AGN	9) New US Dep Edcatn	AGN	14) Lim Wndfll Prof Tax	FOR
5) Alaska Lands Bill	AGN	10) Cut OSHA $	FOR	15) Chryslr Loan Grntee	AGN

Election Results

1980 general	Thomas N. Kindness (R)	139,590	(76%)	($58,322)
	John W. Griffin (D)	44,162	(24%)	($0)
1980 primary	Thomas N. Kindness (R)	36,650	(100%)	
1978 general	Thomas N. Kindness (R)	81,156	(71%)	($64,077)
	Lou Schroeder (D)	32,493	(29%)	($15,430)

NINTH DISTRICT

The city of Toledo rises incongruously from the flat plains of northwest Ohio and is different from the surrounding countryside in just about every respect. Situated in the middle of rich agricultural country, Toledo is heavily industrial; set among Anglo–Saxon farmers and small-town residents, Toledo is heavily ethnic, with many Polish–Americans; surrounded by one of the nation's staunchest Republican areas, Toledo is solidly Democratic. Toledo is an important factory town: it produces automobile glass, AMC Jeeps, and other bulky products. It is a major Great Lakes port and sits on some of the major east–west railroad lines. Like Detroit, just 60 miles to the north, Toledo experienced its greatest growth between 1910 and 1930, during the initial expansion of the automobile industry. Toledo's industry is a little too diversified to label this a one-industry town, but it was hurt badly by the collapse of the auto industry in the late 1970s and early 1980s. Unemployment was high, people — especially young people — were moving away, and there was an air of uncertainty about Toledo's future.

That uncertainty extended to Toledo's politics. Toledo and Lucas County have been pretty solidly Democratic areas for many years now; the factory workers of the city have outvoted the management types in the few suburbs. Lucas was one of only two Ohio counties that went for George McGovern in 1972. But that Democratic faith seems to have been shaken by the economic slowdown that, after all, did occur at a time when Democrats controlled the presidency and the Congress. Ohio's 9th congressional district, which includes all but a few rural townships of Lucas County, had been electing a Democratic congressman since the early 1950s. But in 1980, he was upset by a Republican, and not by just a narrow margin.

The upset was all the more surprising because the Democrat had a solid legislative record. Thomas Ludlow Ashley was one of the workhorses of the House. A member of the Banking Committee, he was its leading expert on housing programs and was also a leading supporter of banks in their fights with savings institutions. During the 95th Congress, Ashley was tapped by Speaker O'Neill to head the special committee on energy that, although it is largely forgotten now, got President Carter's energy bill through Congress in record time while giving its opponents a fair chance to change its major provisions. Ashley had had problems in past elections, particularly in 1974, when he was nearly beaten a year after a drunk driving arrest. But by 1978 he seemed to have recovered nicely.

Nevertheless Republican Ed Weber won a solid 56%–40% victory. How did he do it? First of all, Weber was an eminently respectable candidate. Despite his lack of experience in public office, he was a solidly successful Toledo lawyer, the kind of man who lends prestige to the civic boards he sits on. He could count on a sympathetic hearing from local media. Second, he worked hard. Weber began campaigning early in 1979. Ashley, not an accomplished speaker or an easy mixer, did not work the district hard. Weber promised to return every weekend — something he may rue, since the district is not easily reachable by plane from Washington. Third, Weber was well financed. He managed to convince national Republicans that he had a chance to win and raised money by direct mail. Altogether he spent $380,000 in this district, money that was especially cost-effective since Toledo has its own television stations. Finally, Weber used the national Republican issues to good advantage in the special economic environment of Toledo. Specific proposals, such as the Kemp–Roth tax cut, were probably less important than the overall message that the Democratic programs weren't working. With 12% unemployment, with young people forced to leave the area to find jobs, with the economic base that people had taken for granted suddenly crumbling, voters were ready to try something new. Ronald Reagan, not Jimmy Carter, carried Lucas County in 1980. And Weber carried the 9th and nearly managed to carry the central city of Toledo itself.

The political skill and hard work Weber showed in his victory should serve him well in the House and in succeeding elections. He is a member of the Banking and Small Business Committees, although it seems unlikely that he will maintain the flow of publicly assisted housing to Toledo that Ashley was able to procure. Weber may try to get more favorable district lines out of the legislature, but there are limits to what he can do there: the Democratic Assembly will want to maintain a Toledo–based district, and Delbert Latta of the 5th district, which entirely surrounds the 9th, is not going to want heavily Democratic territory in his district. Weber will undoubtedly use the advantages of incumbency but his fate may hinge more on the state of the national — and the local — economy. Lyle Williams of the 19th district showed that a Republican incumbent can be reelected in a heavily Democratic seat while it remains in economic distress. But one has the feeling that the party that produces a major improvement in the economy and that appears to restore stability and predictability to the local economies of such places as Toledo will win and hold their political allegiance for a generation. This is, after all, what the Democrats did in the 1930s; Toledo was Republican before that. Now Ronald Reagan and Ed Weber hope that they can make a similar change, in the opposite direction.

Census Data Pop. (1980 final) 442,900, down 4% in 1970s. Median family income, 1970, $10,786, 113% of U.S.

The Voters

Employment profile 1970 White collar, 48%. Blue collar, 39%. Service, 13%. Farm, -%.
Ethnic groups Black 1980, 14%. Hispanic 1980, 3%. Asian 1980, 1%. Total foreign stock 1970, 15%. Poland, Germany, 3% each; Canada, UK, 1% each.

Presidential Vote

1980	Reagan (R)	75,323	(44%)
	Carter (D)	77,661	(46%)
	Anderson (I)	14,808	(9%)
1976	Ford (R)	71,254	(41%)
	Carter (D)	98,925	(57%)

Rep. Ed Weber (R) Elected 1980; b. July 26, 1931, Toledo; home, Toledo; Denison U., B.A. 1953, Harvard U., J.D. 1956.

Career Army, 1956–58; Practicing atty., 1956–80; Asst. Prof., U. of Toledo Law Sch., 1966–79.

Offices 512 CHOB, 202-225-4146. Also 414 N. Erie St., Suite 100, Toledo 43624, 419-259-7579.

Committees Banking, Finance and Urban Affairs (12th). Subcommittees: Domestic Monetary Policy; Financial Institutions Supervision, Regulation and Insurance; General Oversight and Renegotiation.

Small Business (15th). Subcommittees: Export Opportunities and Special Small Business Problems; General Oversight.

Group Ratings and Key Votes: Newly Elected

Election Results

1980 general	Ed Weber (R)	96,927	(56%)	($380,673)
	Thomas Ludlow Ashley (D)	68,728	(40%)	($254,264)
1980 primary	Ed Weber (R)	16,322	(76%)	
	One other (R)	5,153	(24%)	
1978 general	Thomas Ludlow Ashley (D)	71,709	(63%)	($100,223)
	John C. Hoyt (R)	34,326	(30%)	($37,320)

TENTH DISTRICT

The 10th district of Ohio is the state's southeastern corner, a hilly, sparsely populated area. Although the district covers 14% of Ohio's land area, it contains only 5% of the state's residents. Marietta, on the Ohio River here, was the site of the first (1788) permanent American settlement in the Northwest Territory, ceded to the new nation by the British following the Revolutionary War. The town's Republican leanings are evidence of the Yankee origin of its first settlers. Most of the 10th district, however, resembles West Virginia, across the Ohio River. The voters tend to think of themselves as Democrats and vote for Republicans or conservative southern Democrats. This is a district that gave only 39% of its votes to Hubert Humphrey in 1968 but which went 49% for southerner Jimmy Carter in 1976 — one reason Carter carried Ohio's crucial electoral votes. But Carter's percentage here declined to 39% in 1980 — one of the reasons the incumbent president failed to come even close to carrying Ohio a second time.

The 10th's Democratic–conservative tradition produced some frequent changes in the district's representation in the 1950s and 1960s. The 10th ousted a Republican in 1958, a Democrat in 1962, a Republican in 1964, and a Democrat in 1966. Since then it has been represented by Republican Clarence Miller. He has worked to solidify his position in the district and has succeeded in winning reelection by margins around 70% in the 1970s.

Miller is an engineer and seems to approach political problems with a desire for precise, orderly solutions. He established a record of never missing a House roll call since he was elected — an example of stern precision and discipline. As a member of the Appropriations Committee he has introduced numerous amendments to make across-the-board cuts in departmental appropriations — usually 2%, but sometimes 5% or even 8%. On occasion Miller's cuts have passed the House: on unpopular programs, such as foreign aid, or when the vote occurred just after California adopted Proposition 13 in June 1978. The argument made against Miller's motions is that it is irresponsible to order cuts without determining just how and where they should be made. Miller's best argument is that bureaucracies are going to resist cuts until it is absolutely clear that they must be made, and that the only way to do much is by a meat-axe approach.

To some extent, Miller's approach has been vindicated by the Reagan Administration's budget cut proposals. To be sure, the Administration is often more specific about what is to be cut. But on occasions it just leaves the specific content of the cuts up to the states or other decision makers.

Census Data   Pop. (1980 final) 528,320, up 14% in 1970s. Median family income, 1970, $7,894, 82% of U.S.

The Voters

Employment profile 1970   White collar, 39%. Blue collar, 45%. Service, 13%. Farm, 3%.
Ethnic groups   Black 1980, 2%. Total foreign stock 1970, 3%.

Presidential Vote

1980	Reagan (R)	111,879	(55%)
	Carter (D)	79,778	(39%)
	Anderson (I)	8,459	(4%)
1976	Ford (R)	96,410	(50%)
	Carter (D)	92,461	(48%)

Rep. Clarence E. Miller (R) Elected 1966; b. Nov. 1, 1917, Lancaster; home, Lancaster; Internatl. Correspondence Sch.

Career Electrician; Lancaster City Cncl., 1957–63, Mayor, 1964–66.

Offices 2208 RHOB, 202-225-5131. Also 212 S. Broad St., Lancaster 43130, 614-654-5149.

Committee *Appropriations* (6th). Subcommittees: Commerce, Justice, State, and Judiciary; Treasury–Postal Service–General Government.

Group Ratings

	ADA	COPE	PC	LCV	CFA	RPN	NAB	NSI	NTU	ACA	ACU
1980	11	16	30	26	14	—	100	90	70	75	84
1979	0	20	13	7	4	—	—	—	72	92	92
1978	20	15	25	34	27	50	92	90	63	92	91

Key Votes

1) Draft Registn $	AGN	6) Fair Hsg DOJ Enfrc	AGN	11) Cut Socl Incr Dfns $	FOR
2) Ban $ to Nicrgua	FOR	7) Lim PAC Contrbtns	AGN	12) Hosptl Cost Controls	AGN
3) Dlay MX Missile	FOR	8) Cap on Food Stmp $	FOR	13) Gasln Ctrls & Allctns	AGN
4) Nuclr Mortorium	AGN	9) New US Dep Edcatn	AGN	14) Lim Wndfll Prof Tax	FOR
5) Alaska Lands Bill	AGN	10) Cut OSHA $	FOR	15) Chryslr Loan Grntee	AGN

Election Results

1980 general	Clarence E. Miller (R)	143,403	(74%)	($32,336)
	Jack E. Stecher (D).............	49,433	(26%)	($7,647)
1980 primary	Clarence E. Miller (R)	59,937	(100%)	
1978 general	Clarence E. Miller (R)	99,329	(74%)	($22,957)
	James A. Plummer (D)..........	35,039	(26%)	

ELEVENTH DISTRICT

The 11th congressional district of Ohio is the northeastern corner of the state, a district whose lines were drawn by a Republican legislature to include the more heavily Republican parts of heavily industrial and Democratic northeastern Ohio. The district carefully avoids such Democratic areas as the industrial city of Warren, near Youngstown; the close-in suburbs of Lake County near Cleveland (although farther-out Lake County, which is more Republican, is included); and Kent, site of Kent State University. Much of the area is still rural, and some of it is wealthy suburban, as in Geauga County; the only decidedly Democratic portion is Ashtabula, which could hardly be excluded since it lies in the northeastern corner of the state.

The current boundaries of the district were drawn to aid 11th district Congressman William Stanton and the Democrats who then held the seats all around him. But on the evidence, Stanton didn't really need the help. Campaigning as a conventional Republican, he was able to capture this district in 1964, a heavily Democratic year, even though it included all of Lake County, Warren, and Kent, and even though it had elected a Democratic congressman as recently as 1960. In succeeding elections Stanton won easily; in the 1970s, after redistricting, his margins have generally been better than 2–1.

One of Stanton's political assets is a voting record that makes concessions to local opinion. Rather than becoming more conservative since he entered Congress, in his first ten years or so at least he seemed to become more liberal. His ratings from organized labor — an important force in the politics of northeastern Ohio — were unusually high for an Ohio Republican. Stanton nonetheless has an excellent voting record from the point of view of business interests. As ranking Republican on the Banking, Housing, and Urban Affairs Committee, he has generally been sympathetic to the arguments of banking interests and has been skeptical about some federal spending programs, notably aid to New York City. He generally sticks with banks in their fights with savings institutions. And recently, as House Republicans have been growing more cohesive, his record has become more conservative.

In Ohio control of redistricting is split between the parties; the obvious compromise is to protect the maximum number of incumbents. For Stanton that will not be difficult. His current district has a population 12,000 over the state average and a corner geographical position. Only minor adjustments of its boundaries should be necessary.

Census Data   Pop. (1980 final) 525,680, up 14% in 1970s. Median family income, 1970, $11,142, 116% of U.S.

The Voters

   Employment profile 1970   White collar, 41%. Blue collar, 47%. Service, 10%. Farm, 2%.
   Ethnic groups   Black 1980, 2%. Hispanic 1980, 1%. Total foreign stock 1970, 15%. Italy, UK, 2% each; Germany, Hungary, Czechoslovakia, 1% each.

Presidential Vote

1980	Reagan (R)	103,188	(52%)
	Carter (D)	79,137	(40%)
	Anderson (I)	13,683	(7%)
1976	Ford (R)	83,674	(48%)
	Carter (D)	92,298	(52%)

Rep. J. William Stanton (R) Elected 1964; b. Feb. 20, 1924, Painesville; home, Painesville; Georgetown U., B.S. 1949.

Career Army, WWII; Lake Co. Commissioner, 1956–64.

Offices 2466 RHOB, 202-225-5306. Also 170 N. St. Clair St., Painesville 44077, 216-352-6167.

Committees *Banking, Finance and Urban Affairs* (Ranking Member). Subcommittees: Housing and Community Development; International Development Institutions and Finance; International Trade, Investment and Monetary Policy.

Small Business (3d). Subcommittee: General Oversight.

Group Ratings

	ADA	COPE	PC	LCV	CFA	RPN	NAB	NSI	NTU	ACA	ACU
1980	44	21	37	27	29	—	55	60	37	63	37
1979	16	35	23	38	11	—	—	—	39	68	79
1978	15	15	15	30	27	67	92	89	17	52	71

Key Votes

1) Draft Registn $	AGN	6) Fair Hsg DOJ Enfrc	AGN	11) Cut Socl Incr Dfns $	AGN
2) Ban $ to Nicrgua	AGN	7) Lim PAC Contrbtns	AGN	12) Hosptl Cost Controls	AGN
3) Dlay MX Missile	AGN	8) Cap on Food Stmp $	AGN	13) Gasln Ctrls & Allctns	AGN
4) Nuclr Mortorium	FOR	9) New US Dep Edcatn	AGN	14) Lim Wndfll Prof Tax	FOR
5) Alaska Lands Bill	FOR	10) Cut OSHA $	AGN	15) Chryslr Loan Grntee	—

Election Results

1980 general	J. William Stanton (R)	128,507	(69%)	($40,501)
	Patrick J. Donlin (D)	51,224	(28%)	($19,871)
1980 primary	J. William Stanton (R)	34,897	(100%)	
1978 general	J. William Stanton (R)	89,327	(68%)	($24,816)
	Patrick J. Donlin (D)	37,131	(28%)	($11,671)

TWELFTH DISTRICT

In 1960, while campaigning in Columbus, Ohio, John F. Kennedy was greeted by a tumultuous crowd; he was moved to remark that Columbus was the city where he got the loudest cheers and the fewest votes. He was not far off the mark, at least about the votes. Columbus, like Cincinnati, is an urban Republican stronghold. Of all major urban counties in Ohio, Barry Goldwater made his best showing (46%) in Franklin County, which contains Columbus; it is not quite so heavily Republican now, after the enfranchisement of students at Ohio State University, but it certainly has not become Democratic. Columbus's Republicanism can be explained by many of the factors that produce a similar political inclination in the rather similar city of Indianapolis. Like Indianapolis, Columbus does have a significant (18%) black population, but it has few residents of Eastern or Southern European stock. These people who have provided the Democratic base in the big industrial cities of the Midwest are largely absent here. The economy of Columbus is much more white collar than that of most Great Lakes area cities. Major employers here include the state government, Ohio State University, and several big banks and insurance companies. This is a city with a vibrant and growing private economy, in vivid contrast with Cleveland, Youngstown, and Dayton, which are losing jobs and looking for government aid. Columbus is in the midst of an almost Sun Belt–like boom, and it does not want the government taking any more of its money.

Columbus is divided into two congressional districts, the 12th and the 15th, by a line that runs right through the middle of the city. It was carefully drawn by Republican redistricters to keep the city's students and blacks in the district (15th) where they can do the least harm. The 12th district takes in the east side of Columbus and its suburbs, along with two heavily Republican rural and small-town counties.

Despite the district lines and despite Columbus's Republican heritage, the 12th district seat is held by a Democrat — by a Democrat, moreover, who beat an incumbent Republican in the heavily Republican year of 1980. How did this come to happen?

High among the reasons are the deficiencies of the Republican incumbent, Samuel Devine. First elected in 1958, he was certainly familiar in the Columbus area, but he was not necessarily well respected. His reputation as a strong conservative should have been helpful and for eight years he was ranking minority member of the Commerce Committee, which should have given him plenty of business support. But while younger Commerce Republicans such as Bud Brown of Ohio and David Stockman of Michigan took the lead on issues, Devine seemed to do very little. He was nearly beaten by Columbus Council member Fran-

876   OHIO

ces Ryan in 1974 and 1976 and won only 57% of the vote in 1978. Nonetheless, the thinking in Columbus in 1980 was that Devine would survive, if only because it was a heavily Republican year.

Bob Shamansky thought otherwise. A successful Democratic lawyer, he had run against Devine himself in 1966. Although Shamansky had never held public office he was a familiar figure as the liberal side of a point–counterpoint feature on Columbus television. Quick and humorous, Shamansky was politically adept enough to attack Devine for doing nothing and to identify himself with the jobs issue long pushed by Columbus's own leading Republican, Governor James Rhodes. The result surprised Devine; the only other Republican incumbents defeated in the Reagan landslide were a man who acknowledged having had homosexual relations and a man who had won a special election in a Democratic district in unusual circumstances.

Shamansky, who has traveled all over the globe, won a seat on the Foreign Affairs Committee. Whether he will be able to repeat his victory in 1982 depends to some extent on redistricting. At least one Republican state senator who would like to run for the seat wants to remove some of its Democratic precincts and give them to Chalmers Wylie's 15th district. But Wylie is against that and, most likely, so will be the Democratic majority in the Assembly. The political acumen Shamansky showed in winning will probably be enough to hold onto the district if the boundaries drawn are similar to what they are now. So, ironically, Republican Columbus and Cincinnati have at least one Democratic congressman each, while Democratic Toledo and Youngstown are represented by Republicans.

Census Data   Pop. (1980 final) 515,347, up 11% in 1970s. Median family income, 1970, $10,710, 113% of U.S.

The Voters

Employment profile 1970   White collar, 54%. Blue collar, 34%. Service, 11%. Farm, 1%.
Ethnic groups   Black 1980, 15%. Hispanic 1980, 1%. Asian 1980, 1%. Total foreign stock 1970, 7%. Germany, Italy, 1% each.

Presidential Vote

1980	Reagan (R)	130,096	(55%)
	Carter (D)	90,046	(38%)
	Anderson (I)	11,727	(5%)
1976	Ford (R)	105,978	(56%)
	Carter (D)	84,360	(43%)

Rep. Robert N. (Bob) Shamansky (D) Elected 1980; b. Apr. 18, 1927, Columbus; home, Bexley; Ohio St. U., B.A. 1947, Harvard U., J.D. 1950.

Career Army, 1950–52; Practicing atty., 1951–1980; News Commentator, TV Station WBNS, Columbus, 1977–80.

Offices 1022 LHOB, 202-225-5355. Also 200 N. High St., Suite 400, Columbus 43215, 614-469-7318.

Committees *Foreign Affairs* (16th). Subcommittees: Europe and the Middle East; International Economic Policy and Trade.

Science and Technology (20th). Subcommittees: Investigations and Oversight; Science, Research and Technology; Transportation, Aviation and Materials.

Select Committee on Aging (28th). Subcommittee: Housing and Consumer Interests.

Group Ratings and Key Votes: Newly Elected

Election Results

1980 general	Robert N. (Bob) Shamansky (D) ..	108,690	(53%)	($179,321)
	Samuel L. Devine (R)	98,110	(47%)	($132,072)
1980 primary	Robert N. (Bob) Shamansky (D) ..	26,139	(100%)	
1978 general	Samuel L. Devine (R)	81,573	(57%)	($132,634)
	James L. Baumann (D)	61,698	(43%)	($162,162)

THIRTEENTH DISTRICT

The 13th congressional district of Ohio occupies the north central part of the state. It sits between Ohio's industrial, Democratic northeast and its rural, Republican northwest and central areas. The nucleus of the district, with about half its population, is Lorain County, an industrial area just west of metropolitan Cleveland. The dominant places here are the industrial cities of Lorain and Elyria, the latter the only slightly disguised subject of Sherwood Anderson's *Winesburg, Ohio*. Lorain County also contains Oberlin, home of Oberlin College, founded by abolitionists and the first college in the nation to admit both blacks and women, way back in 1833. To the west of Lorain County is the small industrial town of Sandusky in Erie County; to the east are the Akron working-class suburbs of Barberton and Norton. The district has only one traditionally Republican rural county, Medina, and that is fast being transformed by migrants from the Cleveland and Akron areas. While these people are less Democratic than many of the neighbors they left behind, they are more Democratic than their new neighbors, and Medina has been going 50%–50% in recent close statewide elections.

Overall, the 13th district is slightly more Democratic than the state as a whole. For example, when Jimmy Carter barely carried Ohio in 1976, the 13th district was 54% for him. In 1980 the Carter percentage dropped sharply to a point close to his statewide average of 41%.

In congressional elections the district has had a history of representation similar to the 3d district's. For many years, from 1958 to 1974, it elected a Republican, Charles Mosher, whose record became increasingly liberal. Mosher was an opponent of the Vietnam war and on a variety of other issues began voting more often with Democrats than Republicans. He decided at age 70 to retire in 1976. His successor is a Democrat, but one with a similar background and similar views. Donald Pease was editor of the Oberlin newspaper, as Mosher had once been, and he was a member of the state legislature. He was elected in 1976 with more than 60% of the votes in both primary and general elections.

Like Mosher, Pease is especially interested in foreign policy. He serves on the Foreign Affairs Committee and has been one of the leading supporters of applying the concept of human rights to foreign policy decisions. Pease is also the originator of the proposal to boycott Uganda while it was under the rule of Idi Amin and has worked to promote a boycott of the sale of Ugandan coffee by American food companies. In 1981, perhaps reflecting the increasing concern about economic issues in the hard-hit areas of northern Ohio near Lake Erie, Pease won a seat on the Ways and Means Committee. There he is expected to line up with the Democratic stalwarts, who by any reckoning have less than a majority after the 1980 elections, but which will try to persuade the committee and the House not to go along with Republican tax programs that the Democrats claim are inflationary and would give too much of their benefits to people in high-income brackets. On trade issues he will probably be torn between his internationalist leanings and the problems of the local steel and auto industries.

Census Data Pop. (1980 final) 512,747, up 10% in 1970s. Median family income, 1970, $10,795, 113% of U.S.

The Voters

Employment profile 1970 White collar, 40%. Blue collar, 46%. Service, 12%. Farm, 2%.
Ethnic groups Black 1980, 6%. Hispanic 1980, 3%. Total foreign stock 1970, 15%. Germany, Hungary, 2% each; Poland, UK, Italy, Czechoslovakia, Yugoslavia, 1% each.

Presidential Vote

1980	Reagan (R)	98,962	(51%)
	Carter (D)	76,045	(39%)
	Anderson (I)	13,483	(7%)
1976	Ford (R)	79,351	(46%)
	Carter (D)	94,309	(54%)

Rep. Donald J. (Don) **Pease** (D) Elected 1976; b. Sept. 26, 1931, Toledo; home, Oberlin; Ohio U., B.S. 1953, M.A. 1955, Fulbright Scholar, U. of Durham, England, 1954–55.

Career Army, 1955–57; Coed.-pub., Oberlin *News Tribune,* 1957–68, Ed., 1968–77; Oberlin City Cncl., 1961–64; Ohio Senate, 1965–67, 1975–77; Ohio House of Reps., 1969–75.

Offices 1127 LHOB, 202-225-3401. Also 1936 Cooper Park Rd., Lorain 44053, 216-282-5003.

Committee *Ways and Means* (20th). Subcommittees: Public Assistance and Unemployment Compensation; Trade.

Group Ratings

	ADA	COPE	PC	LCV	CFA	RPN	NAB	NSI	NTU	ACA	ACU
1980	83	81	83	88	79	—	18	11	23	17	5
1979	84	85	75	85	81	—	—	—	24	12	5
1978	65	80	73	83	64	50	25	20	16	15	4

Key Votes

1) Draft Registn $	AGN	6) Fair Hsg DOJ Enfrc	FOR	11) Cut Socl Incr Dfns $	AGN
2) Ban $ to Nicrgua	AGN	7) Lim PAC Contrbtns	FOR	12) Hosptl Cost Controls	FOR
3) Dlay MX Missile	FOR	8) Cap on Food Stmp $	AGN	13) Gasln Ctrls & Allctns	FOR
4) Nuclr Mortorium	AGN	9) New US Dep Edcatn	FOR	14) Lim Wndfll Prof Tax	AGN
5) Alaska Lands Bill	FOR	10) Cut OSHA $	AGN	15) Chryslr Loan Grntee	FOR

Election Results

1980 general	Donald J. (Don) Pease (D)	113,439	(64%)	($61,031)
	David Earl Armstrong (R)	64,296	(36%)	($7,511)
1980 primary	Donald J. (Don) Pease (D)	41,632	(69%)	
	Three others (D)	19,083	(31%)	
1978 general	Donald J. (Don) Pease (D)	80,875	(65%)	($44,919)
	Mark W. Whitfield (R)..........	43,269	(35%)	($81,502)

FOURTEENTH DISTRICT

Akron is the rubber capital of America, the place where most of our millions of automobile and truck tires are produced — and a city totally dependent on that one industry. It was an industry that developed relatively late. At the turn of the century Cleveland was one of the nation's biggest cities and Canton, the home of President McKinley, was a bigger urban center than Akron, which lies between them. Akron's growth came in the 1910–30 period and most of its migrants came not from Europe, but from the hills of West Virginia, giving the city a southern-accented atmosphere it retains to this day. The newly booming city liked to cultivate a reputation as an all-American place by doing such things as sponsoring the Soapbox Derby (although it turns out that for years leading entrants cheated). But in reality Akron was one of America's most class-bound cities. It was a giant factory town where management lived as a privileged minority, quite out of contact — except possibly on the job — with the working-class majority.

So it should not be surprising that Akron had a politics of something like class warfare for many years, from the 1930s when the United Rubber Workers organized the tire plants up through the 1960s. In statewide and presidential elections, working-class Akron and surrounding Summit County usually went Democratic. But in local races, and in the race for the 14th congressional district, which for years included all or most of Summit County, Republicans often used their management skills to win. This was the hometown of Ray Bliss, longtime Ohio and sometime national Republican chairman; he made sure that the Republicans had more money in elections and more technical skill. He was also adroit in choosing candidates. One of his first projects in Akron was to rescue the 14th district from the Democrats who had controlled it, with one exception, since New Deal days. His candidate was not a stuffy management type but a garrulous plumber named William Ayres; he won in 1950 and served in Congress for 20 years. Ayres threw just enough votes to labor and the Democrats to keep himself invulnerable here; but as ranking Republican on the Education and Labor Committee, his bottom-line commitment was to management. He was finally defeated in 1970 more for his personal than his political shortcomings.

The breakdown of class warfare politics was signaled by the election of a working-class Republican; it was completed by the election in his place a management-class Democrat. John Seiberling bears the name of one of the smaller rubber companies; his grandfather was one of the founders of Goodyear as well. When he ran for Congress in 1970, he was a lawyer for Goodyear; he avoided crossing the United Rubber Workers picket lines during a strike by taking a leave of absence. Seiberling was also known as an ecology buff — a credential normally of greater interest to upper-income voters — and had worked for some years to keep power lines and highways out of the Cuyahoga River valley. He was respected enough to win the support of the *Akron Beacon Journal,* the flagship paper of the chain founded by John S. Knight, which had backed Ayers for 20 years, his opposition to the Vietnam war and to the Kent State shootings gave him student support.

Seiberling won that election with a solid 56%, and he has been winning since with much larger percentages. He has played some important legislative roles in the years since. He was part of the Judiciary Committee majority that voted to impeach Richard Nixon. As a member of the Interior Committee, he served as a chief sponsor of several bills covering matters of great complexity and importance: the strip mining of coal, the Boundary Waters Canoe Area in Minnesota (a controversial local issue there), and the Alaskan Lands bill. The strip mining bill was successful; the Alaska Lands bill was one of the few successful measures supported by most liberals in the 96th Congress. Seiberling proceeded in each instance in a careful, lawyerlike manner, listening to the arguments of all parties; but he also proceeded with a strong commitment to preserving the environment that is reflected in the final terms of the legislation. He has now taken over the chair of the Public Lands and National Parks Subcommittee from Phillip Burton. That position will put him in the front lines of confrontation with his very development-minded counterparts in the Senate and the Reagan Administration.

In the late 1970s and early 1980s the automobile industry, and therefore the tire industry, practically came to a halt. Workers in Akron were laid off by the thousands, plants were closed down, and the whole underpinning of the economic system that had provided good livings for people in these parts was called into question. Akron continued to turn in Democratic majorities but not especially large ones; it is as if at least a fairly large number of voters here were doubting the efficacy of the Democratic programs they had always supported. That Democratic dropoff even affected the congressional race, pulling Seiberling's percentage down from above 70% to the 65% level. That it still a comfortable margin, and even accounting for the more Republican territory that is likely to be included in the district by redistricting, the chances are that no significant Republican opponent will arise. But this is a district that Seiberling and the Democrats no longer can take entirely for granted — at least if the Reagan economic programs work out well. Democratic incumbents — ones who did not work their districts as hard, to be sure — were defeated in Toledo and Youngstown in recent elections, and the kind of economic upheaval the Akron area is undergoing has the potential of changing established political patterns.

Census Data Pop. (1980 final) 424,452, down 9% in 1970s. Median family income, 1970, $10,876, 114% of U.S.

The Voters

Employment profile 1970 White collar, 49%. Blue collar, 38%. Service, 13%. Farm, -%.
Ethnic groups Black 1980, 13%. Hispanic 1980, 1%. Total foreign stock 1970, 14%. Italy, 2%; Germany, UK, Yugoslavia, Hungary, 1% each.

Presidential Vote

1980	Reagan (R)	68,533	(41%)
	Carter (D)	85,860	(51%)
	Anderson (I)	12,091	(7%)
1976	Ford (R)	61,167	(37%)
	Carter (D)	103,094	(63%)

Rep. John F. Seiberling (D) Elected 1970; b. Sept. 8, 1918, Akron; home, Akron; Harvard U., B.A. 1941, Columbia U., LL.B. 1949.

Career Army, WWII; Practicing atty., 1949–53; Atty., Goodyear Tire and Rubber Co., 1954–70.

Offices 1225 LHOB, 202-225-5231. Also Fed. Bldg., 2 S. Main St., Akron 44308, 216-375-5710.

Committees *Interior and Insular Affairs* (6th). Subcommittees: Energy and the Environment; Insular Affairs; Public Lands and National Parks (Chairman).

Judiciary (6th). Subcommittees: Criminal Justice; Monopolies and Commercial Law.

Group Ratings

	ADA	COPE	PC	LCV	CFA	RPN	NAB	NSI	NTU	ACA	ACU
1980	100	79	77	91	86	—	8	0	21	13	11
1979	95	95	90	97	100	—	—	—	25	0	3
1978	95	84	83	93	86	25	0	0	29	4	8

Key Votes

1) Draft Registn $	AGN	6) Fair Hsg DOJ Enfrc	FOR
2) Ban $ to Nicrgua	AGN	7) Lim PAC Contrbtns	FOR
3) Dlay MX Missile	FOR	8) Cap on Food Stmp $	AGN
4) Nuclr Mortorium	FOR	9) New US Dep Edcatn	FOR
5) Alaska Lands Bill	FOR	10) Cut OSHA $	AGN

11) Cut Socl Incr Dfns $	AGN
12) Hosptl Cost Controls	FOR
13) Gasln Ctrls & Allctns	FOR
14) Lim Wndfll Prof Tax	AGN
15) Chryslr Loan Grntee	FOR

Election Results

1980 general	John F. Seiberling (D)	103,336	(65%)	($29,143)
	Louis A. Mangels (R)	55,962	(35%)	($46,848)
1980 primary	John F. Seiberling (D)	52,805	(100%)	
1978 general	John F. Seiberling (D)	82,356	(72%)	($20,438)
	Walter J. Vogel (R)	31,311	(28%)	($12,352)

FIFTEENTH DISTRICT

The 15th congressional district of Ohio includes the west side of Columbus, its Franklin County suburbs, and Pickaway County to the south. Next to Cincinnati, Columbus is Ohio's most Republican metropolitan area; it is also the state's fastest-growing and most economically buoyant urban area. The 15th district is, marginally, the more Republican of Columbus's two congressional districts, in large part because of Upper Arlington. This suburb, just across the Olentangy River from the Ohio State University campus, is the largest in the Columbus area and one of the most Republican (74% for Ronald Reagan in 1980).

The 15th district was created by redistricting in the middle 1960s, and its first and only congressman has been Chalmers Wylie, a former state legislator and Columbus city attorney (an elective post). Wylie has compiled a generally conservative legislative record in Washington. He is best known among his colleagues for his work on the school prayer issue; Wylie has perennially introduced and pushed an amendment to overturn the Supreme Court decision that prevents state-sponsored prayers in public schools. He serves as second-ranking Republican on the Banking Committee and, unlike his Ohio colleague and ranking Republican William Stanton, tends to favor savings institutions over banks in the constant quarrels between the two.

Wylie has been less controversial in Columbus than his colleague Samuel Devine, and in the early 1970s the Republican legislature gave him a somewhat more Democratic part of the city of Columbus, including most of its black and student populations. But substantial opposition has never materialized, and he has won reelection easily every two years. The only political problem looming for Wylie is redistricting. But Democrats will want to take Democratic precincts away from Wylie and place them in the 12th to help freshman Democrat Bob Shamansky. That will only help Wylie, who can be expected to back such a move. His 15th may be extended into additional rural counties, and since most rural counties in this part of Ohio are among the nation's premier Republican territory, that will help him too.

Census Data Pop. (1980 final) 467,086, up 1% in 1970s. Median family income, 1970, $10,074, 105% of U.S.

The Voters

Employment profile 1970   White collar, 57%. Blue collar, 29%. Service, 13%. Farm, 1%.
Ethnic groups   Black 1980, 12%. Hispanic 1980, 1%. Asian 1980, 1%. Total foreign stock 1970, 7%. Germany, 1%.

Presidential Vote

1980	Reagan (R)	98,309	(55%)
	Carter (D)	66,596	(37%)
	Anderson (I)	11,589	(6%)
1976	Ford (R)	99,481	(57%)
	Carter (D)	69,123	(40%)

Rep. Chalmers P. Wylie (R) Elected 1966; b. Nov. 23, 1920, Norwich; home, Columbus; Otterbein Col., Ohio St. U., B.A., Harvard U., J.D.

Career Army, WWII; Asst. Atty. Gen. of Ohio, 1948, 1951–54; Asst. Columbus City Atty., 1949–50, City Atty., 1953–56; Administrator, Ohio Bureau of Workmen's Comp., 1957; First Asst. to the Gov. of Ohio, 1957–58; Practicing atty., 1959–66; Ohio House of Reps., 1961–67.

Offices 2335 RHOB, 202-225-2015. Also Fed. Bldg., Suite 500, 200 N. High St., Columbus 43215, 614-469-5614.

Committees *Banking, Finance and Urban Affairs* (2d). Subcommittees: Consumer Affairs and Coinage; Financial Institutions Supervision, Regulation and Insurance; Housing and Community Development.

Veterans' Affairs (3d). Subcommittees: Compensation, Pension, and Insurance; Education, Training and Employment.

Joint Economic Committee (10th). Subcommittees: Investment, Jobs, and Prices; Monetary and Fiscal Policy.

Group Ratings

	ADA	COPE	PC	LCV	CFA	RPN	NAB	NSI	NTU	ACA	ACU
1980	28	26	30	22	21	—	91	80	49	65	53
1979	21	32	25	24	15	—	—	—	57	83	77
1978	25	30	40	64	41	67	75	90	28	65	50

Key Votes

1) Draft Registn $	AGN	6) Fair Hsg DOJ Enfrc	AGN	11) Cut Socl Incr Dfns $	AGN
2) Ban $ to Nicrgua	FOR	7) Lim PAC Contrbtns	AGN	12) Hosptl Cost Controls	FOR
3) Dlay MX Missile	AGN	8) Cap on Food Stmp $	FOR	13) Gasln Ctrls & Allctns	AGN
4) Nuclr Mortorium	AGN	9) New US Dep Edcatn	AGN	14) Lim Wndfll Prof Tax	AGN
5) Alaska Lands Bill	FOR	10) Cut OSHA $		FOR	15) Chryslr Loan Grntee	FOR

Election Results

1980 general	Chalmers P. Wylie (R)	129,025	(73%)	($93,073)
	Terry Freeman (D)	48,708	(27%)	($0)
1980 primary	Chalmers P. Wylie (R)	45,790	(100%)	
1978 general	Chalmers P. Wylie (R)	91,023	(71%)	($87,741)
	Henry W. Eckhardt (D)	37,000	(29%)	

SIXTEENTH DISTRICT

Canton, Ohio, is known, to the extent it is known at all today, as the home of the Pro Football Hall of Fame. But to American historians, Canton is most memorable as the home of President William McKinley. It was here that McKinley sat on his famous front porch in 1896 and received delegations of voters carefully selected by Republican organizations throughout the country. And it was also here that he received the news that he had been elected president over William Jennings Bryan. Some historians still cling to the notion that factory workers provided McKinley with the votes he needed to win only because their bosses threatened to fire them if they didn't. No more evidence of such coercion exists for this election than for any other in our history. The fact, however unlikely or unwelcome it may seem, is that McKinley was the heavy choice of northern industrial workers, and they believed that the Republican Party would produce the full dinner pail he promised.

The case can be made further that McKinley delivered admirably on that promise. In any event, a period of protracted prosperity and expansion followed his election. Much has happened since, and political allegiances all over the country have changed. But in Canton, which has not had explosive growth in the 20th century, there is still a significant working-class Republican vote. This muscular city and the nearby towns of Massillon and Alliance, where some of our current National Football League teams got their start, still retain a basic preference for the Republican Party. So does the 16th congressional district of Ohio, which includes Canton, Massillon, and Alliance in Stark County, plus Wayne County, a rural and small-town area to the west.

McKinley was elected to the House six times in the predecessor of today's district. In those more volatile times, he lost the seat twice to Democrats — which didn't prevent him, in those days before the seniority system, from becoming chairman of the House Ways and Means Committee. He is not the only House leader the Canton area has produced. More recently, 16th district Congressman Frank Bow, first elected in 1950, became ranking Republican on the House Appropriations Committee; he decided to retire in 1972 and died just weeks before his last term expired.

The current congressman is Ralph Regula, a former state Senator who is, appropriately, a graduate of the William McKinley School of Law; in the 95th Congress Regula helped retain the name Mount McKinley for the mountain in Alaska against proposals to change it to an Alaskan native alternative. Regula is considered a political moderate and has a fairly high rating from organized labor as well as a very high rating from the Chamber of Commerce. He serves on the Appropriations and Budget Committees, where he is expected to follow the policies of the Reagan Administration pretty faithfully.

Canton has not suffered from the kinds of plant closings and layoffs that have troubled so many other Ohio cities, and the 16th district gained rather than lost population during the 1970s. As a result, the district is unlikely to be altered very substantially by redistricting.

Census Data Pop. (1980 final) 481,871, up 4% in 1970s. Median family income, 1970, $10,197, 106% of U.S.

The Voters

Employment profile 1970 White collar, 41%. Blue collar, 45%. Service, 12%. Farm, 2%.
Ethnic groups Black 1980, 5%. Hispanic 1980, 1%. Total foreign stock 1970, 11%. Poland, 2%; Germany, UK, 1% each.

Presidential Vote

1980	Reagan (R)	107,794	(56%)
	Carter (D)	71,727	(37%)
	Anderson (I)	10,413	(5%)
1976	Ford (R)	90,463	(51%)
	Carter (D)	83,776	(47%)

Rep. Ralph S. Regula (R) Elected 1972; b. Dec. 3, 1924, Beach City; home, Navarre; Mt. Union Col., B.A. 1948, Wm. McKinley Sch. of Law, LL.B. 1952.

Career Navy, WWII; Practicing atty., 1952–73; Ohio Bd. of Educ., 1960–64; Ohio House of Reps., 1965–66; Ohio Senate, 1967–72.

Offices 401 CHOB, 202-225-3876. Also 4150 Belden Village St., Canton 44718, 216-456-2869.

Committees *Appropriations* (10th). Subcommittees: Interior; Military Construction.

Budget (2d).

Select Committee on Aging (5th). Subcommittee: Health and Long-Term Care.

Group Ratings

	ADA	COPE	PC	LCV	CFA	RPN	NAB	NSI	NTU	ACA	ACU
1980	28	21	40	26	29	—	83	80	45	63	63
1979	21	25	25	34	15	—	—	—	52	73	82
1978	20	25	25	47	23	58	83	100	22	63	71

Key Votes

1) Draft Registn $	FOR	6) Fair Hsg DOJ Enfrc	AGN	11) Cut Socl Incr Dfns $	AGN
2) Ban $ to Nicrgua	FOR	7) Lim PAC Contrbtns	FOR	12) Hosptl Cost Controls	AGN
3) Dlay MX Missile	AGN	8) Cap on Food Stmp $	FOR	13) Gasln Ctrls & Allctns	AGN
4) Nuclr Mortorium	AGN	9) New US Dep Edcatn	AGN	14) Lim Wndfll Prof Tax	FOR
5) Alaska Lands Bill	FOR	10) Cut OSHA $	AGN	15) Chryslr Loan Grntee	AGN

Election Results

1980 general	Ralph S. Regula (R)	149,960	(79%)	($23,914)
	Larry V. Slagle (D)	39,219	(21%)	($6,128)
1980 primary	Ralph S. Regula (R)	47,869	(100%)	
1978 general	Ralph S. Regula (R)	105,182	(78%)	($55,300)
	Owen S. Hand, Jr. (D)	29,640	(22%)	($5,309)

SEVENTEENTH DISTRICT

Most congressmen find their way onto committees with whose majorities they are in basic sympathy. They get involved in legislative matters on sides where they have many allies and comrades; they look for fights they can win. Not so John Ashbrook, Republican congressman from the 17th district of Ohio. Ashbrook's political and congressional career is almost a catalogue of lost causes. He is by any measure one of the most conservative members of the House. Yet he serves on its most liberal committees. He managed to take little part in the tax cut offensive of the Republican Party in 1978. Yet he has been fighting hard for lower government spending in less favorable times. Ashbrook's record for 20 years was a continual triumph of idealism over practicality, of principle over effectiveness.

No better example exists than his now nearly forgotten 1972 campaign for president. He fielded no campaign organization; he failed to raise significant amounts of money, despite the large number of committed and affluent conservatives across the country; he failed to win as much as 10% of the vote in any presidential primary and did not get a single delegate vote at the Republican National Convention. Yet Ashbrook's intentions were deadly serious. He believed that the Nixon Administration had done the wrong thing in opening relations with mainland China and in imposing wage and price controls. He decided he had to raise those issues against Nixon and did so in his campaign. But his very lack of success helped to prove the lack of popularity his policies had. He showed conclusively that there was no significant bloc of voters deeply concerned about Nationalist China. He showed conclusively that no significant bloc of voters was opposed to the controls. He proved the opposite of what he intended.

Ashbrook survived these defeats, although his candidacy helped lower his percentage in his heavily Republican district in central Ohio in the fall of 1972, and it was not until 1978 that he was able to get more than 57% of the vote there. In the House he saw the committee on Internal Security (formerly Un-American Activities) abolished out from under him. Since the 1978 election he has served as ranking Republican on the House Education and Labor Committee. His predecessor, Albert Quie of Minnesota, tended to cooperate with committee Democrats and attempted to get them to compromise and whittle back their programs a little — with some limited successes. Ashbrook prefers confrontation. The 1980 election, for the first time in his 20-year congressional career, returned a House with a majority sympathetic to the idea that Education and Labor's programs should be cut back. But the committee majority is still solidly of the opposite opinion. It is Ashbrook's job to oppose the committee majority in a way that will give him a majority on the floor. That has not been his style, but he is a man of intelligence and dedication and perhaps he will see his duty in this way and attempt to do it.

Ashbrook may be distracted, however, by his ambitions to run for the Senate. Although he has served in Congress for 20 years, he is still in his early 50s — much younger than the other leading Republican contender, Governor James Rhodes. He is also much more reliably conservative. Rhodes is a practical man, oriented toward achieving results, ready to trim, careless of ideology. Ashbrook is just the opposite. He would make a fine contrast with Howard Metzenbaum, the Democratic senator who is one of the most vocal proponents of energy price controls and other Democratic economic programs.

If Ashbrook does run for the Senate, his district may or may not survive redistricting. It could be carved up among its neighbors, since Ohio must lose one essentially rural district, or it could maintained pretty much intact for state Senator Tom Van Meter, an Ashbrook ally. It seems unlikely that such a district would go Democratic, although Ashbrook was pressed in the 1970s on occasion.

Census Data   Pop. (1980 final) 498,916, up 8% in 1970s. Median family income, 1970, $9,460, 99% of U.S.

The Voters

Employment profile 1970   White collar, 38%. Blue collar, 46%. Service, 12%. Farm, 4%.
Ethnic groups   Black 1980, 3%. Hispanic 1980, 1%. Total foreign stock 1970, 6%. Germany, 1%.

Presidential Vote

1980	Reagan (R)	111,025	(59%)
	Carter (D)	64,651	(34%)
	Anderson (I)	9,693	(5%)
1976	Ford (R)	92,348	(53%)
	Carter (D)	78,041	(44%)

Rep. John M. Ashbrook (R) Elected 1960; b. Sept. 21, 1928, Johnstown; home, Johnstown; Harvard U., A.B. 1952, Ohio St. U., J.D. 1955.

Career Navy, 1946–48; Pub., *Johnstown Independent,* 1953–60; Practicing atty., 1955–60; Ohio House of Reps., 1956–60.

Offices 1436 LHOB, 202-225-6431. Also 53 S. Main St., Johnstown 43031, 614-967-5941.

Committees *Education and Labor* (Ranking Member). Subcommittee: Labor–Management Relations.

Judiciary (6th). Subcommittee: Crime.

Select Committee on Intelligence (2d). Subcommittees: Legislation; Oversight and Evaluation.

Group Ratings

	ADA	COPE	PC	LCV	CFA	RPN	NAB	NSI	NTU	ACA	ACU
1980	6	10	10	17	14	—	100	100	72	91	100
1979	5	15	10	13	4	—	—	—	73	100	97
1978	5	11	23	10	27	55	100	100	55	100	95

Key Votes

1) Draft Registn $	FOR	6) Fair Hsg DOJ Enfrc	AGN	11) Cut Socl Incr Dfns $	FOR
2) Ban $ to Nicrgua	FOR	7) Lim PAC Contrbtns	AGN	12) Hosptl Cost Controls	AGN
3) Dlay MX Missile	AGN	8) Cap on Food Stmp $	FOR	13) Gasln Ctrls & Allctns	AGN
4) Nuclr Mortorium	AGN	9) New US Dep Edcatn	AGN	14) Lim Wndfll Prof Tax	FOR
5) Alaska Lands Bill	AGN	10) Cut OSHA $	FOR	15) Chryslr Loan Grntee	AGN

Election Results

1980 general	John M. Ashbrook (R)..........	128,870	(73%)	($167,081)
	Donald E. Yunker (D)	47,900	(27%)	($1,877)
1980 primary	John M. Ashbrook (R)..........	45,061	(100%)	
1978 general	John M. Ashbrook (R)..........	87,010	(67%)	($158,543)
	Kenneth R. Grier (D)	42,117	(33%)	

EIGHTEENTH DISTRICT

The 18th congressional district of Ohio, just across the Ohio River from West Virginia, is a land of marginal farms and hills pockmarked by strip mines. The area is part of the great coal and steel belt that stretches from the coal mines of West Virginia to Lake Erie, the destination of the freighters filled with iron ore from Minnesota's Mesabi Range. We tend to think of the belt as a series of large cities, but in fact it is one of the most thickly settled non-metropolitan parts of the United States. Small factories and little mills keep the small towns of western Pennsylvania and eastern Ohio running. These are old towns, mostly, with brick-front stores on their main streets and hills that rise behind the frame houses. There is nothing chic or kicky here: these are gritty places where working people toil long hours for what pay is available.

Some of the people here are from the Scotch–Irish stock of the first migration across the Appalachians. But more are descended from later groups of immigrants: Italians, Poles, Czechs, Germans. The 18th district, sociologically and politically, despite its rural geographical setting, is a kind of ethnic working-class urban neighborhood. Politically, the district is heavily Democratic in most elections, although it voted for Ronald Reagan narrowly in 1980 and Richard Nixon by a wide margin in 1972. Culturally, this is a place where people believe in traditional values, where church, family, home, and hometown are more important than any species of urban-bred liberation. Economically, it is an area that has not thrived in decades but whose lack of really large factories has made it less vulnerable to the kind of economic dislocation experienced recently in such cities as Youngstown, Akron, and Toledo.

This is the district that for 28 years was represented by Wayne Hays, the man who built an empire in the House on his position of chairman of House Administration and the Democratic campaign committee but who was forced to resign by the Elizabeth Ray scandal. The local Democratic Party, forced to name a candidate to replace Hays on the ballot in 1976, chose the man who had long been considered his likely successor, state Senator Douglas Applegate. He has won elections easily since then, doing especially well in 1980. Applegate is a member of the kind of practical committees — Public Works and Veterans' Affairs — that can do something concrete for this district. He tends to have a good voting record by the lights of organized labor but is not at all a liberal on most cultural issues. The 1970s saw population loss in most of Ohio's metropolitan areas but not — in a reversal from previous decades — in rural areas such as the 18th district. Most likely, then, redistricting will not greatly alter the district nor change it from an essentially safe Democratic district that is likely to reelect Applegate for some time.

Census Data   Pop. (1980 final) 484,505, up 5% in 1970s. Median family income, 1970, $8,701, 91% of U.S.

The Voters

Employment profile 1970   White collar, 34%. Blue collar, 51%. Service, 12%. Farm, 3%.
Ethnic groups   Black 1980, 2%. Total foreign stock 1970, 12%. Italy, 3%; UK, 2%; Poland, Czechoslovakia, Germany, 1% each.

Presidential Vote

1980	Reagan (R)	88,934	(49%)
	Carter (D)	82,803	(45%)
	Anderson (I)	9,113	(5%)
1976	Ford (R)	86,513	(44%)
	Carter (D)	106,448	(54%)

Rep. Douglas Applegate (D) Elected 1976; b. Mar. 27, 1928, Steubenville; home, Steubenville.

Career Real estate salesman, 1950–56, broker, 1956–76; Ohio House of Reps., 1961–69; Ohio Senate, 1969–77.

Offices 435 CHOB, 202-225-6265. Also 150 W. Main St., St. Clairsville 43950, 614-695-4600.

Committees *Public Works and Transportation* (17th). Subcommittees: Aviation; Economic Development; Surface Transportation.

Veterans' Affairs (8th). Subcommittees: Compensation, Pension, and Insurance; Hospitals and Health Care.

Group Ratings

	ADA	COPE	PC	LCV	CFA	RPN	NAB	NSI	NTU	ACA	ACU
1980	22	63	30	35	36	—	64	100	47	54	58
1979	11	70	38	39	41	—	—	—	47	60	65
1978	20	55	40	47	41	36	42	80	16	46	48

Key Votes

1) Draft Registn $	AGN	6) Fair Hsg DOJ Enfrc	AGN	11) Cut Socl Incr Dfns $	FOR
2) Ban $ to Nicrgua	FOR	7) Lim PAC Contrbtns	FOR	12) Hosptl Cost Controls	AGN
3) Dlay MX Missile	AGN	8) Cap on Food Stmp $	AGN	13) Gasln Ctrls & Allctns	FOR
4) Nuclr Mortorium	AGN	9) New US Dep Edcatn	AGN	14) Lim Wndfll Prof Tax	FOR
5) Alaska Lands Bill	AGN	10) Cut OSHA $	AGN	15) Chryslr Loan Grntee	FOR

Election Results

1980 general	Douglas Applegate (D)	134,835	(76%)	($44,493)
	Gary L. Hammersley (R)	42,354	(24%)	($24,013)
1980 primary	Douglas Applegate (D)	61,060	(100%)	
1978 general	Douglas Applegate (D)	71,894	(60%)	($75,802)
	Bill Ress (R)	48,931	(40%)	($69,217)

NINETEENTH DISTRICT

The 19th congressional district of Ohio is one of the most heavily industrial districts in the nation. Both Youngstown and Warren, the district's two major cities, are important steel manufacturing centers. Situated about halfway between Cleveland and Pittsburgh, these two cities are also halfway between the docks that unload iron ore from the Great Lakes ranges and the coalfields of western Pennsylvania and West Virginia. This was an area of rapid growth at the turn of the century, when the American steel industry was growing rapidly and using the latest technological developments. Now times have changed. Steel has been anything but a growth industry over the last 20 years. Producers in Japan and West Germany have used newer technology and in some cases can ship steel cheaper to the American Midwest than can Youngstown manufacturers. The steel industry has concentrated on getting presidential permission for price increases (which price it out of foreign markets) and governmental protection for imports (which encourage further inefficiency) rather than improving their product or trying to produce it more cheaply.

The result has been economic disaster for the Youngstown–Warren area. There has been no population growth, and considerable outmigration has occurred since 1960. The late 1970s have been especially rough. Several large steel plants have closed down altogether, putting as many as 5,000 employees out of work at a single time. Local officials have tried to attract new business here, and the area has gotten some new plants, such as General Motors's Lordstown assembly plant, which is not far away—and which served as the model for the Fernwood factory in the Mary Hartman TV series. Local tax revenues have fallen, voters have refused new taxes, and Youngstown schools have had to close for weeks at a time.

For people here it must seem like the collapse of a way of life. They have worked hard for many years and have seen their standard of living rise. Now all seems threatened or about to vanish. In these circumstances, they have begun to question their political loyalties, which have been heavily Democratic since the 1930s. The Democrats strongly supported the unions, which raised wages and improved working conditions. The Democrats stimulated the economy, which kept the steel mills humming. But in the late 1970s Democrats no longer seemed to be the party of jobs and prosperity. The blue collar voters here do not always buy the management line that it was Democratic environmental controls that have ruined the steel industry, but they did see the Democrats in power as the mills were closing. The result here in 1980 was that the Democratic percentage declined drastically. Jimmy Carter still carried the Youngstown area but failed to win an absolute majority of the vote. Carter's percentage was actually about the same as George McGovern's in 1972. And the Democrats, who had lost the 19th district congressional seat (all of Youngstown and Mahoning County and most of Trumbull County, which surrounds Warren) in a fluke election in 1978, were unable to win it back in 1980.

The 1978 election was a fluke because the Democratic incumbent, Charles Carney, was so weak. Like some other Democratic congressmen swept into office in a New Deal year, he seemed content to claim his paycheck and show up on the floor every day. He did nothing to help attract new industry to his district as it was losing thousands of jobs. He provided few of the services that most congressmen use to keep constituents familiar with their names. But he did take the trouble to acquire more than 60,000 surplus books from the Library of Congress, many of which he kept or gave to relatives. The Republican candidate, Lyle Williams, a barber and Trumbull County commissioner, was able to use these things to his advantage and won a narrow victory.

More surprisingly, Williams was able to win in 1980, against a formidable opponent and by an impressive 58%–42% margin. He voted with organized labor on some issues and generally downplayed his party affiliation; he joined the United Steelworkers in a suit to stop U.S. Steel from closing two steel mills in the district. The Democratic nominee, state Senator Harry Meshel, cited the state spending he had directed to the Youngstown area. But voters may have calculated that they would be better off with the hardworking Williams in Washington and the productive Meshel in Columbus. In any case, their verdict was unequivocal; Williams ran far ahead of Reagan. For 1982, the likely redistricting change is to add territory in Trumbull County to the north. This area is more Republican than the current district and is Williams's home county as well. It is hard still to regard this district as a safe Republican seat. But voters here, with the local economy collapsing, seem at least willing to vote Republican, and Lyle Williams must now be regarded as something more than a fluke.

Census Data   Pop. (1980 final) 449,145, down 3% in 1970s. Median family income, 1970, $10,311, 108% of U.S.

The Voters

Employment profile 1970   White collar, 41%. Blue collar, 46%. Service, 12%. Farm, 1%.
Ethnic groups   Black 1980, 12%. Hispanic 1980, 1%. Total foreign stock 1970, 23%. Italy, 6%;
Czechoslovakia, 3%; UK, Poland, 2% each; Yugoslavia, Austria, Germany, Hungary, 1% each.

Presidential Vote

1980	Reagan (R)	76,152	(41%)
	Carter (D)	94,213	(51%)
	Anderson (I)	13,709	(7%)
1976	Ford (R)	69,063	(38%)
	Carter (D)	112,185	(60%)

Rep. Lyle Williams (R) Elected 1978; b. Aug. 23, 1942, Philippi, W.Va.; home, North Bloomfield.

Career Army, 1960–61; Barber; Trumbull Co. Commissioner, 1972–78.

Offices 1004 LHOB, 202-225-5261. Also Suite 204, 4076 Youngstown Rd., S.E., Warren 44484, 216-369-4378.

Committees *Government Operations* (8th). Subcommittee: Commerce, Consumer, and Monetary Affairs.

Small Business (6th). Subcommittee: Antitrust and Restraint of Trade Activities Affecting Small Business.

Group Ratings

	ADA	COPE	PC	LCV	CFA	RPN	NAB	NSI	NTU	ACA	ACU
1980	33	68	33	41	43	—	64	63	28	54	42
1979	16	45	18	29	11	—	—	—	43	59	43

Key Votes

1) Draft Registn $	FOR	6) Fair Hsg DOJ Enfrc	AGN	11) Cut Socl Incr Dfns $	AGN
2) Ban $ to Nicrgua	FOR	7) Lim PAC Contrbtns	FOR	12) Hosptl Cost Controls	AGN
3) Dlay MX Missile	AGN	8) Cap on Food Stmp $	FOR	13) Gasln Ctrls & Allctns	FOR
4) Nuclr Mortorium	AGN	9) New US Dep Edcatn	FOR	14) Lim Wndfll Prof Tax	FOR
5) Alaska Lands Bill	FOR	10) Cut OSHA $	AGN	15) Chryslr Loan Grntee	FOR

Election Results

1980 general	Lyle Williams (R)	107,032	(58%)	($207,760)
	Harry Meshel (D)	77,272	(42%)	($192,887)
1980 primary	Lyle Williams (R)	22,346	(100%)	
1978 general	Lyle Williams (R)	71,890	(51%)	($101,551)
	Charles J. Carney (D)	69,977	(49%)	($168,257)

TWENTIETH DISTRICT

Down the center of Cleveland flows the Cuyahoga River, a waterway so polluted with industrial wastes that it once caught fire. On both sides of the Cuyahoga are Cleveland's giant steel mills and other factories — many of the same operations that made Cleveland the nation's fourth largest city in 1910. In the years that followed, Cleveland lost the auto industry to Detroit and otherwise failed to match the growth rate of other big metropolitan areas; today the Cleveland area is only the 19th largest in the nation. The central city of Cleveland, as is well known, has more than its share of urban problems. Some of them are the result of simple mismanagement: Cleveland has many taxable resources and its budget could have been trimmed in many places to avoid the 1978 and 1979 fiscal crises. And some of them are rooted in cultural differences, symbolized by the Cuyahoga, which divides the races in Cleveland.

East of the Cuyahoga, most of Cleveland is black. Here and there are remnants of ethnic neighborhoods, called cosmo wards in Cleveland, that absorbed the Poles, Czechs, Hungarians, and Italians who came over to work in the grimy steel mills along the Cuyahoga. But the vast majority of Clevelanders living east of the river are black, and some of the neighborhoods are so forbidding that Carl Stokes, the city's first and, so far, only black mayor (1967–71) lived in a Cleveland house that sat on the line separating the city from the posh suburb of Shaker Heights. By glaring contrast, Cleveland west of the Cuyahoga is just about 100% white. Here, in this largely working-class area, are the city's remaining cosmo wards. This is the political homeland of former Mayor Dennis Kucinich, although he gets some black support also. The population west of the river is weighted toward the elderly end of the age scale, as younger people have moved to such suburbs as Parma or Brook Park.

Almost all of the west side of Cleveland, plus a couple of cosmo wards in the east, and a few suburbs to the south (Brook Park, Brooklyn, part of Parma, and Garfield Heights among them), make up the 20th congressional district of Ohio. This is a Democratic district by tradition but not always in practice. In 1967 and 1969, Carl Stokes's Democratic party label gave him only about 20% of the vote here against white Republicans. George Wallace got a surprising 17% here in 1968, and in 1972 Richard Nixon carried the district. Lately the 20th has been more Democratic, but with sharply declining turnout. The older residents, who once believed strongly in the New Deal and in their later days worried about blacks and crime, do not turn out as much any longer; and in many cases the younger people who have replaced them are not voting at all. On the west side, voters see little from the Republicans to attract them but no strong reasons to support Democrats either. Neither the cerebral humor of former Governor John Gilligan nor the southern drawl of Jimmy Carter was particularly attractive to voters on the west side.

In congressional elections, this has been a Democratic district for many, many years. Its last two representatives have come from the Cleveland city council. James Stanton, first elected in 1968, was an opponent of Carl Stokes; he served until he ran unsuccessfully for the Senate in 1976. His successor, the 24% winner in a 12-candidate Democratic primary, was Mary Rose Oakar. She has a solidly liberal record on economic issues but is more conservative on cultural issues. She is competent and popular and was reelected without Republican opposition in 1978 and 1980.

The key question for 1982 is what happens to the district lines. Cuyahoga County must lose one of its four districts. Oakar's 20th district will likely expand into the western suburbs, which could conceivably result in a primary fight with Parma's Ronald Mottl. But unless a great deal of the current 20th in Cleveland is given to the black-majority 21st district, Oakar will have a definite advantage in the new district and is likely to win.

Census Data   Pop. (1980 final) 374,942, down 19% in 1970s. Median family income, 1970, $10,550, 110% of U.S.

892   OHIO

The Voters

Employment profile 1970   White collar, 41%. Blue collar, 47%. Service, 12%. Farm, –%.
Ethnic groups   Black 1980, 6%. Hispanic 1980, 4%. Asian 1980, 1%. Total foreign stock 1970, 32%.
Poland, 6%; Czechoslovakia, Italy, 4% each; Germany, 3%; Hungary, Austria, Yugoslavia, 2% each;
USSR, UK, Ireland, 1% each.

Presidential Vote

1980	Reagan (R)	52,322	(41%)
	Carter (D)	66,223	(53%)
	Anderson (I)	7,623	(6%)
1976	Ford (R)	50,457	(36%)
	Carter (D)	83,949	(60%)

Rep. Mary Rose Oakar (D) Elected 1976; b. Mar. 5, 1940, Cleveland; home, Cleveland; Ursuline Col.,
B.A. 1962, John Carroll U., M.A. 1966.

Career Clerk, Higbee Co., 1956–58; Operator, Ohio Bell Telephone Co., 1957–62; Instructor, Lourdes Acad., 1963–70; Asst. Prof., Cuyahoga Comm. Col., 1968–75; Cleveland City Cncl., 1973–77.

Offices 107 CHOB, 202-225-5871. Also 116 Fed. Court Bldg., 215 Superior Ave., Cleveland 44114, 216-522-4927.

Committees *Banking, Finance and Urban Affairs* (16th). Subcommittees: Economic Stabilization; Financial Institutions Supervision, Regulation and Insurance; General Oversight and Renegotiation; Housing and Community Development; International Development Institutions and Finance.

Post Office and Civil Service (10th). Subcommittees: Census and Population; Compensation and Employee Benefits (Chairwoman); Postal Operations and Services.

Select Committee on Aging (15th). Subcommittees: Health and Long-Term Care; Retirement Income and Employment.

Group Ratings

	ADA	COPE	PC	LCV	CFA	RPN	NAB	NSI	NTU	ACA	ACU
1980	67	89	63	65	86	—	18	38	12	13	13
1979	68	85	75	78	85	—	—	—	20	23	13
1978	60	95	80	72	77	40	0	20	16	20	24

Key Votes

1) Draft Registn $	—	6) Fair Hsg DOJ Enfrc	FOR
2) Ban $ to Nicrgua	AGN	7) Lim PAC Contrbtns	FOR
3) Dlay MX Missile	AGN	8) Cap on Food Stmp $	AGN
4) Nuclr Mortorium	—	9) New US Dep Edcatn	FOR
5) Alaska Lands Bill	FOR	10) Cut OSHA $	AGN

11) Cut Socl Incr Dfns $ AGN
12) Hosptl Cost Controls FOR
13) Gasln Ctrls & Allctns FOR
14) Lim Wndfll Prof Tax AGN
15) Chryslr Loan Grntee FOR

Election Results

1980 general	Mary Rose Oakar (D)	96,217	(100%)	($44,603)
1980 primary	Mary Rose Oakar (D)	44,357	(100%)	
1978 general	Mary Rose Oakar (D), unopposed			($77,081)

TWENTY-FIRST DISTRICT

The 21st congressional district of Ohio is the east side of Cleveland, plus a couple of adjacent suburbs. This area was once a checkerboard of Polish, Czech, Hungarian, and Italian neighborhoods, but today it is heavily black. The central part of the 21st includes some of the poorest black ghettos in the nation, while the black neighborhoods to the north and south are more middle class. There are still a few ethnic ("cosmo" in Cleveland) enclaves left in the 21st, populated mainly by old people who cannot afford to move out of the city. The suburban cities in the district are either already majority black (East Cleveland) or in the process of becoming so (Warrensville Heights). Ironically, some of Cleveland's wealthiest suburbs, such as Shaker Heights and Cleveland Heights, are no more than a mile or two from some of the city's most dilapidated slums.

The representation of this district in Congress has reflected the ethnic changes here. For a decade and a half, until the 1968 election, the district was represented by Charles Vanik, a Democrat with an Eastern European ethnic background. In 1968 Vanik left to run in the suburban 22d district where he ousted the Republican incumbent, and the new congressman in the 21st was Louis Stokes. He is the brother of then Cleveland Mayor (and later New York newscaster) Carl Stokes. Like his brother, Congressman Stokes grew up in poverty and was able to attend college and law school only after serving in the Army during World War II.

Stokes's election was a clear reflection of his brother's popularity on the east side. After the congressional victory of 1968, the two brothers put together their own political machine, the 21st District Caucus. It has suffered some defeats, particularly in elections for mayor, but was the only really effective black political organization in Cleveland during the years in which the city's politics revolved entirely around race and racially oriented issues. Now that has changed. The turbulent politics of former Mayor Dennis Kucinich did not split the city on racial lines, and the Republican who beat Kucinich in 1979, George Voinovich, won with both black and white votes. Cleveland voters no longer believe all their city's problems will be solved by electing a mayor of their own race. As a result, a united black organization no longer exists.

When Louis Stokes first went to Congress, in 1969, he was classified as a militant black congressman; in the years since he has become known as a skilled and intelligent legislator. He was the first black member of the Appropriations Committee and now ranks 10th in seniority among its Democrats. He serves on the subcommittees that handle housing, education, labor, and welfare programs—the whole panoply of public services in which such districts as the 21st are so interested. He is, as might be expected, a supporter of spending on such programs and an opponent of Reagan budget cuts.

In his first years in the House Stokes won the reputation of being smart but also of being lazy. More recently, he has shown that he can work hard and has been entrusted with some difficult assignments that he has carried out well. In 1977 he took over the select committee on presidential assassinations after its first chairman, Henry Gonzalez, quit. Under Stokes's leadership the committee conducted a dignified investigation, came up with a report that was accepted as responsible both by defenders of the Warren Commission and assassination conspiracy buffs, and performed such useful public services as allowing James Earl Ray to discredit himself. In 1981, in the wake of the Abscam scandal, Stokes was called on to chair the Committee on Standards of Official Conduct—the official name of the House ethics committee. This is an extremely sensitive assignment, one that typically in the past has been entrusted to a senior southern Democrat of impeccable conservative credentials. Stokes's selection shows that he is widely respected for fairness, probity, and his ability to handle sensitive matters in a dignified and unreproachable way.

For 1982 Stokes's main problem is that his 21st district must be expanded considerably in size. In the 1970s its population declined from 462,000 to 350,000; now it must go up to 512,000. The key question is whether to expand westward into the cosmo wards of Cleveland or eastward into the suburbs. In either case there will be resistance: the 20th district's Mary Rose Oakar will not want to lose too many cosmo wards, and the 22d district's Dennis Eckard will not want to lose the close-in predominantly Jewish suburbs that are his strongest area. Stokes can absorb some white ethnic areas without much political trouble; racial antagonism is less in the Cleveland area than it was a decade ago, and the district will still have a solid black majority.

Census Data   Pop. (1980 final) 351,997, down 24% in 1970s. Median family income, 1970, $8,573, 89% of U.S.

The Voters

Employment profile 1970   White collar, 37%. Blue collar, 44%. Service, 19%. Farm, –%.
Ethnic groups   Black 1980, 79%. Hispanic 1980, 1%. Total foreign stock 1970, 14%. Yugoslavia, Italy, Hungary, 2% each; Czechoslovakia, Poland, Germany, 1% each:

Presidential Vote

1980	Reagan (R)	12,299	(11%)
	Carter (D)	97,071	(86%)
	Anderson (I)	2,982	(3%)
1976	Ford (R)	17,904	(14%)
	Carter (D)	107,813	(84%)

Rep. Louis Stokes (D) Elected 1968; b. Feb. 23, 1925, Cleveland; home, Cleveland; Western Reserve U., 1946–48, Cleveland-Marshall Law Sch., J.D. 1953.

Career   Practicing atty., 1954–68.

Offices   2465 RHOB, 202-225-7032. Also Rm. 2947 New Fed. Ofc. Bldg., 1240 E. 9th St., Cleveland 44199, 216-522-4900.

Committees   *Appropriations* (10th). Subcommittees: District of Columbia; HUD–Independent Agencies; Labor–Health and Human Services–Education.

Standards of Official Conduct (Chairman).

Group Ratings

	ADA	COPE	PC	LCV	CFA	RPN	NAB	NSI	NTU	ACA	ACU
1980	78	93	77	70	93	—	0	0	14	10	10
1979	95	95	83	91	89	—	—	—	18	0	3
1978	85	100	95	72	77	36	0	10	30	10	5

Key Votes

1) Draft Registn $	AGN	6) Fair Hsg DOJ Enfrc	FOR	11) Cut Socl Incr Dfns $	AGN
2) Ban $ to Nicrgua	AGN	7) Lim PAC Contrbtns	FOR	12) Hosptl Cost Controls	FOR
3) Dlay MX Missile	FOR	8) Cap on Food Stmp $	AGN	13) Gasln Ctrls & Allctns	FOR
4) Nuclr Mortorium	—	9) New US Dep Edcatn	FOR	14) Lim Wndfll Prof Tax	AGN
5) Alaska Lands Bill	FOR	10) Cut OSHA $	AGN	15) Chryslr Loan Grntee	—

Election Results

1980 general	Louis Stokes (D)	83,188	(88%)	($57,984)
	Robert L. Woodall (R)	11,103	(12%)	($0)
1980 primary	Louis Stokes (D)	38,820	(100%)	
1978 general	Louis Stokes (D)	58,934	(86%)	($47,176)
	Bill Mack (R)	9,533	(14%)	

TWENTY-SECOND DISTRICT

The 22d district of Ohio is the eastern half of the ring of suburbs around Cleveland, plus a very small part (14,000 residents) of the city itself. The various suburbs have been settled by people of varying ethnic stock, who have moved here following the radial avenues out of the central city of Cleveland. There are suburbs that are heavily Italian (Mayfield Heights), Serbian (Solon), Hungarian (Euclid), Jewish (University Heights, Beachwood), and high-income WASP (Gates Mills, Pepper Pike). The most well-known of the 22d's communities is one of its most ethnically varied, Shaker Heights. There is little trace of the Shaker group after whom it was named; this close-in suburb instead contains the estatelike homes of some of the city's wealthiest WASPs and Jews, and of some blacks and ethnics as well.

Following Cleveland's suburban migrations, the 22d extends beyond the Cuyahoga County line into adjacent Lake, Geauga, and Summit Counties. The suburbs in Lake (Wickliffe, Willowick, Willoughby) are basically Democratic; those in Geauga, including the high-income community of Chagrin Falls, are solidly Republican. Overall, this is a district most of whose residents have a Democratic tradition, but it is not necessarily that solidly Democratic. Turnout in the older, ethnic areas has been down, and it has been increasing in the Republican areas. As a result, Gerald Ford was able to win this district in 1976, although by less than 1,000 votes.

This district was represented for 30 years by Republican Frances Bolton, a member of one of Cleveland's richest families, and then for 12 years by Democrat Charles Vanik, who moved out from the east side Cleveland district in 1968 when that area became a majority black. Vanik covered most of the district's ethnic bases: of Eastern European stock himself, he was a strong supporter of Israel and had a solid labor voting record for many years. In the House he was chairman of the Trade Subcommittee of Ways and Means, where his basic free-trade inclination tended to conflict with the increasing clamor from Cleveland's industries for protection. Vanik prided himself on spending no money in his campaigns and decided in the high-powered campaign atmosphere of 1980 to retire at age 67.

There was a spirited race to succeed him. Republicans hoped to pick up this seat and clearly had their best chance in years; their candidate, Joseph Nahra, was the winner of a close primary fight. The Democrats had three significant candidates, of whom the winner was state legislator Dennis Eckart. There were some vivid contrasts. Eckart was only 30, Nahra 53. Eckart was an ambitious and successful state legislator, Nahra a former probate judge. Nahra endorsed the national Republican program and got substantial national Republican financing. Eckart emphasized his own issues and raised his own money. Eckart also stressed, in a district with a significant Jewish minority, his strong support for Israel; Nahra is of Lebanese descent.

The result was fairly close, but Eckart won a 55%–41% victory in a Republican year. In the House he won seats on the Foreign Affairs and Education and Labor Committees, and many Democrats considered him one of their most promising freshmen. But to achieve that promise, he must survive redistricting in 1982. The problem is that Cleveland's Cuyahoga County, which has had four congressional districts since 1952, is now entitled to only three under the equal population standard. It is a political certainty that there will continue to be a black-majority 21st district. It is almost certain as well that there will be a 20th district centered in the cosmo wards of the west side of Cleveland. That means that one of the two suburban districts, the 23d or 22d, will likely disappear. There is an alternative: to extend the 23d into adjacent counties or to extend the 22d farther into adjacent counties. But that will raise serious opposition from at least three other northeastern Ohio congressmen, whose political safety it will threaten.

Eckart's problem is that he currently represents only about 290,000 people in the Cuyahoga County suburbs, while the 23d district's Ronald Mottl represents more than 450,000. If approximately equal numbers are borrowed from each district to fatten up the 20th and 21st, Eckart will be forced to run in a district two-thirds of which will have been represented for eight years by his primary opponent. Eckart's strategy must either be to extend the suburban districts into outer counties or to persuade Louis Stokes to shift his district westward into some of Cleveland's white wards. This will not be easy. These wards have strong anti-Stokes feelings dating from the time the congressman's brother, Carl Stokes, was mayor (1969–73). But if that is done, the 20th district will have to take much of Mottl's territory, leaving Eckart much more advantageously positioned for a primary. This will be difficult to do; Eckart's major advantage is that he has many more friends in the Ohio legislature than Mottl does, and blacks may want to see Mottl lose because he keeps pushing antibusing legislation.

Census Data   Pop. (1980 final) 440,617, down 5% in 1970s. Median family income, 1970, $13,427, 140% of U.S.

The Voters

Employment profile 1970   White collar, 63%. Blue collar, 29%. Service, 8%. Farm, –%.
Ethnic groups   Black 1980, 9%. Hispanic 1980, 1%. Asian 1980, 1%. Total foreign stock 1970, 32%. Italy, 5%; USSR, Poland, Germany, Yugoslavia, 3% each; Hungary, UK, Czechoslovakia, Austria, 2% each; Canada, 1%.

Presidential Vote

1980	Reagan (R)	92,016	(48%)
	Carter (D)	84,318	(44%)
	Anderson (I)	15,896	(8%)
1976	Ford (R)	100,076	(50%)
	Carter (D)	99,195	(50%)

Rep. Dennis E. Eckart (D) Elected 1980; b. Apr. 6, 1950, Euclid; home, Euclid; Xavier U., B.A. 1971, John Marshall Law Sch., J.D. 1974.

Career Ohio House of Reps., 1975–80, Chmn., Cuyahoga Co. Delegation, 1979–80.

Offices 1222 LHOB, 202-225-6331. Also 26111 Brush Ave., Euclid 44132, 216-522-2056, and 24700 Chagrin Blvd., Beachwood 44122, 216-522-2158.

Committees *Education and Labor* (20th). Subcommittee: Postsecondary Education.

Foreign Affairs (19th). Subcommittees: Africa; International Economic Policy and Trade.

Small Business (19th). Subcommittees: Antitrust and Restraint of Trade Activities Affecting Small Business; Energy, Environment and Safety Issues Affecting Small Business.

Group Ratings and Key Votes: Newly Elected

Election Results

1980 general	Dennis E. Eckart (D)	108,137	(55%)	($354,048)
	Joseph J. Nahra (R)	80,836	(41%)	($479,874)
1980 primary	Dennis E. Eckart (D)	27,854	(41%)	
	J. Timothy McCormack (D)	16,067	(23%)	($54,315)
	Anthony O. Calabrese, Jr. (D)	12,313	(18%)	($49,212)
	Sheldon D. Schechter (D)	7,325	(11%)	($48,103)
	Three others (D)	4,873	(7%)	
1978 general	Charles A. Vanik (D)	87,551	(66%)	
	Richard W. Sander (R).	30,935	(23%)	($26,715)
	James F. Sexton (I).	7,126	(5%)	
	Robert E. Lehman (I)	6,960	(5%)	

TWENTY-THIRD DISTRICT

The 23d congressional district of Ohio includes most of the suburbs south and west of Cleveland. These can be divided into two parts. The suburbs to the west are such upper-middle-income Protestant towns as Lakewood, Rocky River, and Bay Village—all front on Lake Erie and all cast heavy Republican margins. As one moves farther from the lake, Republican percentages tend to fall; the suburbs to the south are basically Democratic. These were settled more recently, in the 1950s and 1960s, generally by people of Slavic and Hungarian descent who grew up in the smoggier, less spacious streets of the west side of Cleveland.

The largest and best known of these suburbs is Parma, with a population of 92,000, most of which is in the 23d district. It is a town of subdivisions spread out among major avenues; and many bowling alleys are closely monitored by national political reporters for signs of change in public opinion. Parma is heavily Polish, Ukrainian, and Slavic; it is ancestrally Democratic, but when it switches to the Republicans, they usually win. This is what happened in 1980, when Ronald Reagan carried Parma by a 49%–46% margin.

In the 1960s voters in areas such as the 23d disliked the Democrats' heavy emphasis on civil rights and concentration on the disadvantaged, which mostly meant blacks. They still felt that New Deal economic programs basically worked to their benefit; they did not want to stop government action altogether, but to see that its benefits went to ordinary people like themselves. Now these people have less of a sense that government can solve problems. The decade-long failure to stop inflation — a failure as unique in American history as the failure to prevent military defeat in Vietnam — has dried up confidence in the efficacy of government action among people who, for thirty years, saw government action as the way to solve social and economic problems. The result is a sour skepticism toward all politicians and toward most government programs.

From the 1950s until the early 1970s the 23d district was represented in Congress by a Republican, William Minshall. This was, after all, a basically Republican district before all the migration from the cosmo (ethnic) wards of Cleveland to the suburbs. Its transformation to a Democratic district was delayed by the political antics of Dennis Kucinich, later mayor of Cleveland. In 1972, at the age of 25, he came close to Minshall but was unable to defeat him. Two years later Kucinich, whose home ward in Cleveland is in the 23d district, ran as an Independent and nearly managed to defeat the Democrat, state Senator Ronald Mottl of Parma. It was nearly an evenly divided electorate: 37% for Mottl, 32% for the Republican, a creditable 31% for Kucinich.

Mottl's record in the House has reflected many of his constituents' preoccupations. He spends little if any time promoting new federal programs. He has been one of the members most often requesting roll calls, usually on some favorite proposal; it is as if he were reflecting the feeling many of his constituents have that they have been left behind, and that they want recognition. He has devised a number of antibusing amendments, some of which have been adopted, although most of the Cleveland suburbs are not threatened with a busing order. He has sponsored a bill to provide national minimum education standards — reflecting a concern that many parents have that the quality of education today is not high. He serves as chairman of the Veterans' Affairs Hospitals Subcommittee and tends to oppose cuts in the VA hospital budget — a position that will endear him to both traditional veterans' organizations and those who want a more innovative approach. Mottl has been less productive — relatively few of his proposals are adopted — than he has been articulate, expressing the dissatisfactions of an important and often key group in the American electorate whose attitudes have helped to set the tone for our times.

Mottl's problem for 1982 is redistricting. Cuyahoga County is today entitled to only three congressmen, after decades of having four districts, and the chances are that the two suburban congressmen, Mottl and the 22d district's Dennis Eckart, may be thrown together to face each other in what would surely be a bitter Democratic primary. The prospects are examined in detail under the 22d district.

Census Data   Pop. (1980 final) 462,759, no change in 1970s. Median family income, 1970, $13,101, 137% of U.S.

The Voters

Employment profile 1970   White collar, 61%. Blue collar, 30%. Service, 9%. Farm, -%.
Ethnic groups   Black 1980, 1%. Hispanic 1980, 1%. Asian 1980, 1%. Total foreign stock 1970, 28%. Czechoslovakia, 4%; Germany, Poland, Italy, 3% each; UK, Hungary, Austria, 2% each; Yugoslavia, Canada, Ireland, 1% each.

Presidential Vote

1980	Reagan (R)	108,387	(57%)
	Carter (D)	67,942	(35%)
	Anderson (I)	14,714	(8%)
1976	Ford (R)	110,590	(55%)
	Carter (D)	84,525	(42%)

Rep. Ronald M. Mottl (D) Elected 1974; b. Feb. 6, 1934, Cleveland; home, Parma; U. of Notre Dame, B.S. 1956, LL.B. 1957.

Career Army, 1957–58; Practicing atty., 1958–74; Cleveland Asst. Law Dir., 1958–60; Parma City Cncl., 1960–67, Pres., 1962–67; Ohio House of Reps., 1967–69; Ohio Senate; 1969–74.

Offices 2459 RHOB, 202-225-5731. Also Rm. 2951 New Fed. Ofc. Bldg., 1240 E. 9th St., Cleveland 44199, 216-522-4382.

Committees *Energy and Commerce* (15th). Subcommittees: Oversight and Investigations; Telecommunications, Consumer Protection, and Finance.

Veterans' Affairs (5th). Subcommittees: Hospitals and Health Care (Chairman); Housing and Memorial Affairs.

Group Ratings

	ADA	COPE	PC	LCV	CFA	RPN	NAB	NSI	NTU	ACA	ACU
1980	33	72	67	60	43	—	60	89	53	46	72
1979	37	68	68	59	91	—	—	—	54	60	49
1978	30	60	70	73	46	36	42	90	61	50	38

Key Votes

1) Draft Registn $	AGN	6) Fair Hsg DOJ Enfrc	AGN	11) Cut Socl Incr Dfns $	FOR
2) Ban $ to Nicrgua	FOR	7) Lim PAC Contrbtns	FOR	12) Hosptl Cost Controls	FOR
3) Dlay MX Missile	AGN	8) Cap on Food Stmp $	AGN	13) Gasln Ctrls & Allctns	FOR
4) Nuclr Mortorium	FOR	9) New US Dep Edcatn	FOR	14) Lim Wndfll Prof Tax	AGN
5) Alaska Lands Bill	FOR	10) Cut OSHA $	AGN	15) Chryslr Loan Grntee	—

Election Results

1980 general	Ronald M. Mottl (D)	144,365	(100%)	($62,957)
1980 primary	Ronald M. Mottl (D)	43,149	(100%)	
1978 general	Ronald M. Mottl (D)	99,975	(75%)	($40,630)
	Homer S. Taft (R)	33,372	(25%)	($11,197)

OKLAHOMA

Oklahoma has one of the odder and more distinctive state histories, memorialized in the Rodgers and Hammerstein musical, an Edna Ferber novel, and half a dozen Hollywood movies. It was at first a land set apart by the federal government for Indians; the Cherokees and the other Civilized Tribes (as they were called) were herded from their ancestral lands in the South and Midwest and sent here over the Trail of Tears. In 1889 the federal government decided to open what is now Oklahoma to white settlement. On the morning of the great land rush, thousands of would-be homesteaders drove their wagons across the territorial line, in a moment reenacted many times since on film.

The "Sooners," as they were called (for those who crossed the line sooner than they were supposed to), quickly came to outnumber the Indians. Nonetheless, Oklahoma today has the second largest Indian population of any state, but there are no reservations left, and the Indians are about as well assimilated into the rest of the population as they are anywhere in the country. During its first years, Oklahoma held out great promise to its settlers, most of whom were from the South. But for many of the white settlers the promise of Oklahoma turned as sour as it had for the Indians. The Depression and drought of the 1930s drove thousands of Okies, as they were called, from the Dust Bowl of Oklahoma to the greener fields of California. Today the population of Oklahoma stands at almost exactly three million. At statehood in 1907 it was 1.5 million, almost exactly half that; in 1930 it was 2.4 million, and in 1970 2.5 million. That means there was, on balance, rather little population gain for 40 years, and lots of outmigration. During the 1970s Oklahoma's rural counties showed economic buoyancy and population growth for the first time in decades. Still, as in the preceding four decades, most of the state's growth was in and around the state's two largest cities, Oklahoma City and Tulsa.

Linked to the growth of Oklahoma City and Tulsa has been the rise in political strength of the Republican Party. Originally Oklahoma was a Democratic state, as most of its original settlers came from the South. But Oklahoma has always had a Republican minority, especially in the northwestern and north central parts of the state, which were settled largely by people from Republican Kansas. The fast-growing, oil-rich cities of Oklahoma City and Tulsa are now new-rich, conservative strongholds, much like Dallas–Fort Worth in Texas or Phoenix in Arizona. In 1964 Oklahoma City and Tulsa both went for Barry Goldwater, and together they cast 36% of the state's votes; Oklahoma still went Democratic. In 1976, both went for Gerald Ford, and this time they cast 43% of the state's votes—enough to put Oklahoma in the Republican column. In 1980, the Oklahoma City and Tulsa areas, by now spread to formerly rural adjacent counties, cast 50% of the state's votes, and they led Oklahoma to a 60%–35% majority for Reagan—his biggest in the South. Metro Oklahoma City went 65%–29% for Reagan, Metro Tulsa 64%–31%; even the rural areas gave him a substantial absolute majority.

A number of things worked against Carter in Oklahoma. First of all, this is an oil state—the fifth biggest producer, after Texas, Alaska, Louisiana, and California. Oil is very much a part of Oklahoma's lore—there are oil wells on the state Capitol grounds—and in 1976 Oklahomans believed that Carter shared their views on oil and natural gas: that controls should be removed, production should be encouraged. But in the next four years they were disappointed. Carter did finally embrace limited decontrol of oil and natural gas. But he did so only after arguing for and obtaining extensions of controls. The second grievance was that Oklahoma, or at least its northern portion, is a wheat state. Carter's embargo on wheat sales to Russia after the invasion of Afghanistan cost him dearly throughout the wheat belt, which cast percentages against him as large as those in the Rocky Mountain states.

Oklahoma has not gone entirely Republican, however. The rural conservative tradition provides backing for Senator David Boren, elected with an overwhelming margin in 1978, and Governor George Nigh, elected much more narrowly that year. Five of the state's six congressmen are Democrats, not all of them out of sympathy or communication with their party's leadership in the House. Oklahoma is a state that has never really had much of an aristocracy and one with a vibrant tradition of prairie radicalism—there was a big Socialist vote here in the years just after statehood. There is a lack of political steadiness in Oklahoma, which has been represented by liberals and conservatives in quick succession.

The instability of Oklahoma politics is also shown in the young of its current delegation.

As of the 1980 election, the oldest member was Congressman Mickey Edwards of Oklahoma City at 43; there were two 30-year-old congressmen; the senior senator was 39 and the newly elected junior senator 31. The most senior member, Congressman James Jones, was first elected in 1972.

David Boren has reached the position of senior senator before reaching 40 — and after serving four years as governor. He owes his political career largely to an astute reading of the temper of the times in 1974. Not only was that the year of Watergate but of Oklahoma's own scandal in the conduct of Governor David Hall, who was convicted of bribery and extortion after leaving office. Boren's campaign prop was a broom, to symbolize his promise to clean up the mess without committing himself to anything specific. That was enough to give him a victory over Hall and a relative of Will Rogers in the Democratic primary and runoff and an easy victory in the general election.

In office Boren ran a clean and fiscally austere administration. He was an early supporter of Jimmy Carter, but he soon learned to keep his distance from the Carter White House. After four reasonably popular years as governor, it seemed natural for Boren to seek the Senate seat being vacated for reasons of health by Republican Dewey Bartlett, and he would have won easily but for charges made by a minor candidate that he was a homosexual; he eventually swore on a Bible that they were not true. That helped hold him below 50% in the first primary, but in the runoff he beat former congressman and two-time Senate nominee Ed Edmondson. Boren won the general election easily.

In the 1978 campaign Boren was one of the few Democrats to support the Kemp–Roth tax cut plan. He is a believer in measures usually called conservative: cutting federal spending, lowering taxes, decreasing federal regulation, and removing energy price controls. He won seats on the Finance and Agriculture Committees and showed considerable political savvy. He is not a doctrinaire conservative, however, and has considerably less than perfect ratings from conservative organizations. He has joined with senators of considerably different views on some measures; thus with Carl Levin of Michigan he has pushed a bill to provide for legislative veto of regulations issued by administrative agencies. Boren is a member of the Finance subcommittee on trade, and as a general proposition seems to be export-oriented: Oklahoma is a wheat- and, for that matter, oil-exporting state. He also serves on a subcommittee on estate and gift taxation, most of whose members seem inclined to lighten or even eliminate these duties.

Oklahoma now has the youngest member of the Senate, Republican Don Nickles. At the beginning of the 1980 campaign season, he did not seem likely to win; he was a minor Republican contender for the seat being vacated by the retirement of Republican Henry Bellmon. In the Republican primary this freshman state senator was pitted against two older businessmen. But in the first primary he ran first with 35% of the vote, and he won the runoff by a startling margin of nearly 2–1. His weapon was the Moral Majority. Nickles, who is a Catholic rather than a fundamentalist Protestant, is a firm believer in the precepts of the Moral Majority and was able to rally evangelical support all over the state. In the general election the Democratic nominee, former Oklahoma City District Attorney Andy Coats, was favored. He was more mature, better known, well financed, and conservative enough, it seemed, for Oklahoma even at its most conservative. But Nickles's Moral Majority support and the strength of the Republican national issues gave him a victory by the rather surprising margin of 53%–44%. The patterns of support in that election were typical of closely contested Oklahoma elections. Coats got his largest margins in Little Dixie, the southeastern corner of the state, and also carried the rural counties along the Arkansas border and the southern counties on the Red River border with Texas. But Nickles carried Oklahoma City and Tulsa, and he had very wide margins in the wheat-growing country of north central and northwestern Oklahoma.

Nickles will be one of the most militantly conservative members of the Senate. He sees America drifting toward socialism and wants to turn the country around. He wants to preserve the family and uphold traditional moral values. He believes fervently in the free-market system and wants to eliminate any government role in providing energy; he believes the windfall profits tax is unconstitutional and that the synfuels program should be abandoned. Nickles has seats on the Energy and Labor Committees, which have jurisdiction over many of these matters. He is chairman of the Labor subcommittee with jurisdiction over the labor laws, but, without the vote of Vermont moderate Robert Stafford, he may not have a majority. His vote will not be hard to predict; the question is whether the Republican leadership can hold him in line.

The current governor of Oklahoma is George Nigh. A Democrat and a four-term governor, he traveled the state in 1978 in a "white hat brigade"— an apparent attempt to imitate Boren's brooms. Nigh beat Attorney General Larry Derryberry in the Democratic primary and 32-year-old former University of Oklahoma football star Ron Shotts in the general election. Oklahoma has allowed its governors to seek second consecutive terms since the 1960s, but none has won. Nigh will presumably try in 1982. Tthe recent political history of the state suggests that upsets of all kinds are possible. It would be unwise to venture a prediction on the outcome of the race.

Oklahoma has six congressional districts, and the populations of all increased in the 1970s, at not too different rates. This means that the Democratic legislature need not change the boundaries much unless it wants to. There are, however, two or three Democratic congressmen who are not as securely ensconced as they might like. Possibly the legislature will shuffle counties around in an attempt to help them.

Census Data   Pop. (1980 final) 3,025,266, up 18% in 1970s: 1.34% of U.S. total, 26th largest. Central city, 29%; suburban, 28%. Median 4-person income, 1978, $19,069, 93% of U.S., 33d highest.

1979 Share of Federal Tax Burden $5,139,000,000; 1.14% of U.S. total, 27th largest.

1979 Share of Federal Outlays $5,892,275,000; 1.27% of U.S. total, 27th largest.

DOD	$1,475,475,000	24th	(1.39%)	HEW	$2,230,067,000	27th (1.25%)
DOE	$123,939,000	22d	(1.05%)	ERDA	$23,615,000	21st (0.87%)
HUD	$81,719,000	26th	(1.24%)	NASA	$1,414,000	35th (0.03%)
VA	$344,275,000	23d	(1.66%)	DOT	$279,763,000	19th (1.70%)
EPA	$42,715,000	33d	(0.80%)	DOC	$15,236,000	35th (0.48%)
DOI	$89,232,000	18th	(1.61%)	USDA	$310,665,000	33d (1.29%)

Economic Base   Agriculture, notably cattle, wheat, dairy products, and peanuts; finance, insurance, and real estate; oil and gas extraction, especially oil and gas field services and crude petroleum and natural gas; machinery, especially construction and related machinery; fabricated metal products, especially structural metal products; food and kindred products; electrical equipment and supplies, especially communication equipment.

Political Lineup   Governor, George P. Nigh (D). Senators, David Lyle Boren (D) and Don Nickles (R). Representatives, 6 (5 D and 1 R); 6 in 1982. State Senate, 48 (37 D and 11 R); State House of Representatives, 101 (73 D and 28 R).

The Voters

Registration 1,469,320 Total. 1,055,221 D (72%); 382,511 R (26%); 30,713 I (2%); 875 Libertarian (0%).

Employment profile 1970 White collar, 48%. Blue collar, 33%. Service, 14%. Farm, 5%.

Ethnic groups Black 1980, 7%. Hispanic 1980, 2%. Am. Ind. 1980, 6%. Asian 1980, 1%. Total foreign stock 1970, 4%.

Presidential Vote

1980	Reagan (R)	695,570	(60%)
	Carter (D)	402,026	(35%)
	Anderson (I)	38,284	(3%)
1976	Ford (R)	545,708	(50%)
	Carter (D)	532,442	(49%)

SENATORS

Sen. David Lyle Boren (D) Elected 1978, seat up 1984; b. Apr. 24, 1941, Washington, D.C.; home, Seminole; Yale U., B.A., Rhodes Scholar, Oxford U., U. of Okla., LL.B. 1968.

Career Okla. House of Reps., 1966–74; Practicing atty.; Gov. of Okla, 1975–78.

Offices 440 RSOB, 202-224-4721. Also Suite 350, 621 N. Robinson, Oklahoma City 73102, 405-231-4381.

Committees *Agriculture, Nutrition, and Forestry* (6th). Subcommittees: Agricultural Credit and Rural Electrification; Agricultural Research and General Legislation; Foreign Agricultural Policy.

Finance (7th). Subcommittees: International Trade; Social Security and Income Maintenance Programs; Estate and Gift Taxation.

Group Ratings

	ADA	COPE	PC	LCV	CFA	RPN	NAB	NSI	NTU	ACA	ACU
1980	28	37	13	6	20	—	82	80	48	52	67
1979	16	26	26	—	19	—	—	—	44	70	64

Key Votes

1) Draft Registn $	FOR	6) Fair Housng Cloture	AGN	11) Cut Socl Incr Defns	FOR
2) Ban $ to Nicrgua	AGN	7) Ban $ Rape Abortns	FOR	12) Income Tax Indexing	AGN
3) Dlay MX Missile	AGN	8) Cap on Food Stmp $	AGN	13) Lim Spdg 21% GNP	AGN
4) Nuclr Mortorium	—	9) New US Dep Edcatn	FOR	14) Incr Wndfll Prof Tax	AGN
5) Alaska Lands Bill	AGN	10) Cut OSHA Inspctns	FOR	15) Chryslr Loan Grntee	AGN

Election Results

1978 general	David Lyle Boren (D)	493,953	(65%)	($751,286)
	Robert B. Kamm (R)	247,857	(33%)	($443,712)
1978 runoff	David Lyle Boren (D)	251,587	(60%)	
	Ed Edmondson (D)	184,175	(40%)	($129,369)
1978 primary	David Lyle Boren (D)	252,560	(46%)	
	Ed Edmondson (D)	155,626	(28%)	
	Gene Stipe (D)	114,423	(21%)	($370,869)
	Four others (D)	28,409	(5%)	
1972 general	Dewey F. Bartlett (R)	516,934	(51%)	($625,095)
	Ed Edmondson (D)	478,212	(48%)	($512,058)

Sen. Don Nickles (R) Elected 1980, seat up 1986; b. Dec. 6, 1948, Ponca City; home, Ponca City; Okla. St. U., B.A. 1971.

Career Nat. Guard, 1970–76; V.P. and Gen. Mgr., Nickles Machine Corp., 1976–80; Okla. Senate, 1978–80.

Offices 6327 DSOB, 202-224-5754. Also 820 Old P.O. Bldg., Oklahoma City 73102, 405-231-4941; 333 W. 4th, Rm. 3003, Tulsa 74103, 918-581-7651; and 1916 Lake Rd., Ponca City 73601, 405-767-1270.

Committees *Energy and Natural Resources* (9th). Subcommittees: Energy Regulation; Energy Research and Development; Water and Power.

Labor and Human Resources (5th). Subcommittees: Labor (Chairman); Employment and Productivity; Handicapped.

Select Committee on Small Business (7th). Subcommittees: Government Procurement (Chairman); Productivity and Competition.

Group Ratings and Key Votes: Newly Elected

Election Results

1980 general	Don Nickles (R)	587,252	(53%)	($828,346)
	Andy Coats (D)...............	478,283	(44%)	($996,447)
1980 runoff	Don Nickles (R)	81,697	(66%)	
	John Zink (R)	42,818	(34%)	($689,808)
1980 primary	Don Nickles (R)	47,879	(35%)	
	John Zink (R)	45,914	(33%)	
	Ed Noble (R).................	39,839	(29%)	($758,329)
	Two others (R)	4,223	(3%)	
1974 general	Henry Bellmon (R)	390,997	(49%)	($622,480)
	Ed Edmondson (D)............	387,162	(49%)	($195,429)

GOVERNOR

Gov. George P. Nigh (D) Elected 1978, term expires Jan. 1983; b. June 9, 1927, McAlester; Eastern A & M Jr. Col., E. Central St. Teachers Col., B.A. 1950.

Career High school teacher and grocer; Okla. House of Reps., 1951–59; Lt. Gov. of Okla, 1959–63, 1967–79; Gov. of Okla., 1963, 1969.

Offices 212 State Capitol Bldg., Oklahoma City 73105, 405-521-2342.

Election Results

1978 gen.	George P. Nigh (D)	402,240	(52%)
	Ron Shotts (R)	367,055	(47%)
1978 runoff	George P. Nigh (D)	269,681	(58%)
	Larry Derryberry (D)	197,457	(42%)
1978 prim.	George P. Nigh (D)	276,910	(50%)
	Larry Derryberry (D)	208,055	(38%)
	Bob Funston (D)	69,475	(13%)
1974 gen.	David Lyle Boren (D)	514,389	(64%)
	Jim Inhofe (R)	290,459	(36%)

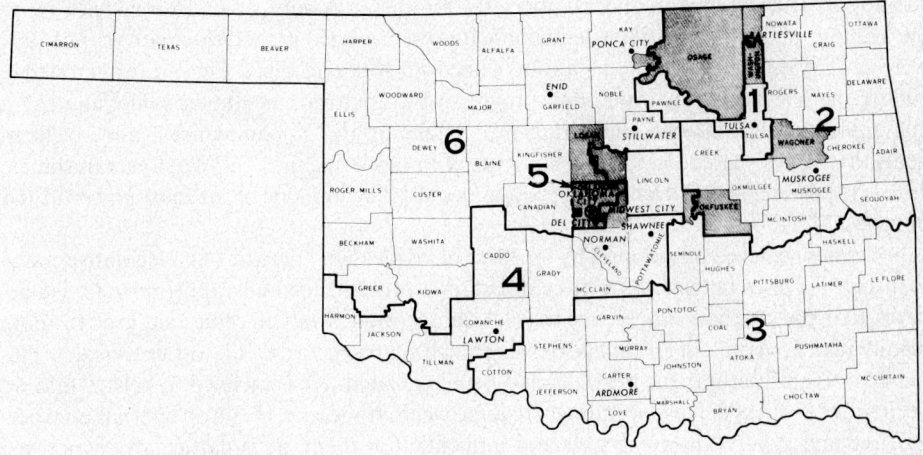

FIRST DISTRICT

Tulsa is a major city that oil built. It has been a major regional center of the oil industry almost since Oklahoma gained statehood in 1907. Even today, years after oil was first discovered in these parts, Tulsa is still growing rapidly. Although its winters are sometimes frigid, Tulsa is very much a part of the Sun Belt in its economic base and in its basic attitudes. For like other oil cities, this is a very conservative place. People here don't resent the big companies and the new rich; they identify with them. They see government as only interfering with efforts to produce goods that people want and are ready to pay for. Tulsa residents also regard some aspects of government policy as antithetical to basic moral values. It is not just an oil town but the home of Oral Roberts University and a center of fundamentalist religion. Tulsa lacks the newfound sophistication of Dallas or Houston; it is closer in spirit to smaller Texas boom towns such as Odessa or Tyler. That is true politically as well. In national politics Tulsa is distinctly Republican. In 1972, for example, it cast a higher percentage of its votes for Richard Nixon (79%) than any other big metropolitan area outside the Deep South. It never cottoned much to Jimmy Carter and gave Ronald Reagan a better than 2–1 margin in 1980.

Tulsa makes up the bulk of Oklahoma's 1st congressional district. The rest consists of parts of neighboring counties, and much of that is suburban. The 1st also includes a part of the city of Bartlesville, a prosperous town that is the headquarters of Phillips Petroleum. The boundaries of the district here and elsewhere in Oklahoma are carefully drawn to maximize the number of Democratic votes, but the 1st remains a solidly Republican district. Jimmy Carter could win only 29% of the vote here in 1980.

The 1st district's congressman, however, is not a Republican but a Democrat, and he might very well turn out to be the single most important member of the 97th Congress. He is James Jones who, although he is barely past 40, has a wealth of political experience, as a congressional aide in his early 20s and as a staff assistant to President Johnson before he was 30. Jones has shown in the House that he is not just a prodigy. He began his congressional career after the 1972 election, when the Democratic majority was relatively united in its opposition to Richard Nixon and his policies—a rather awkward situation for Jones, given the leanings of his district. The Democratic freshmen elected in the Watergate year of 1974 were, at first appearance anyway, far out of line with Jones on issues. They were interested in ending the Vietnam war, promoting progressive tax reform, instituting something like a guaranteed annual income, and stringently regulating the oil companies—none of them goals that Jones shared. Yet within six years of the swearing in of the Watergate freshmen, Jones had persuaded his Democratic colleagues to make him one of the most powerful and influential members of the House.

Jones has achieved his position by the force of his ideas and the skill of his legislative craftsmanship. He does not share the basic orientation of traditional liberal Democrats. He believes that the mechanisms of free-market competition produce economic growth more readily than government spending. He very much shares the belief, almost universal in Tulsa, that oil and natural gas prices should be deregulated. He is inclined to believe that we need more, not less defense spending. He approaches trade issues from an international perspective and is very knowledgeable and influential on them; he is particularly concerned about U.S.–Japan trade relations and generally opposes trade restriction. Jones does not believe he belongs with the Republicans, and indeed his voting record shows him as being far from a perfect conservative. He first got a chance to exhibit his views on the House Ways and Means Committee, where he showed a knack for creative compromise on tax legislation. He became a friendly ally with a group of younger Democrats, including not only southerners but also some northerners elected from historically Republican districts largely on the basis of cultural issues and not convinced of the soundness of traditional Democratic economic positions. The unexpected inflation of 1979 and 1980 made new converts and allies for Jones, and he thereby became a force to be reckoned with.

Thus in 1979, when the Democratic Steering Committee did not give Jones a seat he wanted on the Budget Committee, he put up a fight in the Democratic Caucus—and won. After the shock of the 1980 election Jones ran for chairman of the Budget Committee and, after eliminating several other rivals, narrowly defeated David Obey of Wisconsin. It was a battle between two of the smartest young Democrats, and the Caucus chose the one who tends to favor lower government spending and higher tax incentives. The composition of the Budget Committee in 1981–82 makes Jones a key man in the House. The Democratic margin overall has been reduced, and liberal Democrats are far short of a majority. Republican members are very cohesive, but they are short of a majority too. That leaves the key votes with Jones and several Democrats with similar but not always identical approaches. If anyone can fashion a majority for Democratic budget policies, it is Jones.

Jones's inclination during the opening days of the Reagan Administration was to go along with some, but not all, of the new president's economic program. He appeared genuinely skeptical about the Kemp–Roth tax cut and was not convinced that spending cuts as deep as Reagan's proposals were necessary. He fashioned an artful Democratic alternative to the Reagan budget proposals in the spring of 1981. But, although he got all but one Budget Committee Democrat to go along, he was beaten by a 253–176 vote.

That does not mean, however, that Jones is likely to lose every budget battle. The likelihood is that on budget issues in the early 1980s the Democratic House and the Republican Senate will have significant differences. To iron them out, there will have to be conference committees, where negotiating ability is of critical importance. Jones maintains a friendly working relationship with Pete Domenici of New Mexico, the Republican chairman of the

Senate Budget Committee, but traditionally House members have had greater knowledge of detail and superior negotiating skill.

Jones's national eminence undoubtedly helps him politically in Tulsa. Yet at least through the 1980 election he has never won by really large majorities. The problem is that the district is simply too Republican; probably no other Democrat could hold it. Jones does take pains to keep in touch with voters in Tulsa, and he is not really out of line with the community on any major issues. But he has a significant Republican challenge almost every election and he may face one again in 1982. The New Right was already running television ads against him in 1981. Redistricting is unlikely to change the outlines of the district much. Even if Jones wanted to improve the 1st's Democratic percentage, most of the areas immediately surrounding the district have become increasingly Republican as the Tulsa metropolitan area has moved outward.

Census Data   Pop. (1980 final) 502,274, up 18% in 1970s. Median family income, 1970, $7,720, 81% of U.S.

The Voters

Employment profile 1970   White collar, 55%. Blue collar, 31%. Service, 13%. Farm, 1%.
Ethnic groups   Black 1980, 9%. Hispanic 1980, 2%. Am. Ind. 1980, 4%. Asian 1980, 1%. Total foreign stock 1970, 4%.

Presidential Vote

1980	Reagan (R)	131,916	(66%)
	Carter (D)	58,023	(29%)
	Anderson (I)	8,153	(4%)
1976	Ford (R)	114,485	(62%)
	Carter (D)	71,288	(38%)

Rep. James R. Jones (D) Elected 1972; b. May 5, 1939, Muskogee; home, Tulsa; U. of Okla., A.B. 1961, Georgetown U., LL.B. 1964.

Career   Legis. Asst. to U.S. Rep. Ed Edmondson, 1961–64; Army, 1964–65; White House Staff Asst. to Pres. Lyndon B. Johnson, 1965–69; Practicing atty.

Offices   203 CHOB, 202-225-2211. Also 4536 Fed. Bldg., Tulsa 74103, 918-581-7111.

Committees   *Budget* (Chairman).

Ways and Means (7th). Subcommittee: Trade.

Group Ratings

	ADA	COPE	PC	LCV	CFA	RPN	NAB	NSI	NTU	ACA	ACU
1980	39	47	37	26	29	—	67	50	39	43	22
1979	32	37	35	24	15	—	—	—	53	36	45
1978	25	25	33	16	23	58	92	100	40	92	78

908 OKLAHOMA

Key Votes

1) Draft Registn $	FOR	6) Fair Hsg DOJ Enfrc	FOR	11) Cut Socl Incr Dfns $	AGN
2) Ban $ to Nicrgua	FOR	7) Lim PAC Contrbtns	AGN	12) Hosptl Cost Controls	AGN
3) Dlay MX Missile	AGN	8) Cap on Food Stmp $	AGN	13) Gasln Ctrls & Allctns	AGN
4) Nuclr Mortorium	AGN	9) New US Dep Edcatn	FOR	14) Lim Wndfll Prof Tax	FOR
5) Alaska Lands Bill	AGN	10) Cut OSHA $	FOR	15) Chryslr Loan Grntee	AGN

Election Results

1980 general	James R. Jones (D).............	115,381	(58%)	($239,753)
	Richard C. Freeman (R).........	82,293	(42%)	($153,560)
1980 primary	James R. Jones (D), unopposed			
1978 general	James R. Jones (D).............	73,886	(60%)	($210,179)
	Paula Unruh (R)	49,404	(40%)	($236,437)

SECOND DISTRICT

The 2d congressional district of Oklahoma takes in all the northeastern quadrant of the state, except for the Tulsa area that makes up the 1st district. The 2d is the place where most of Oklahoma's Indians live. Their ancestors were forcibly relocated here from their ancestral lands in the South and Midwest, as early as the 1830s, over the Trail of Tears. This part of Oklahoma remained Indian Territory until it was opened up to white settlement in 1889. Today 12% of the population of the 2d district is Indian, and a larger percentage claim some Indian blood. Even the county names recall the Civilized Tribes: Cherokee, Delaware, Ottawa, Osage, Creek. In 1889, white settlers from the Democratic Deep South and the Republican Ozarks began moving in. As a result, the 2d today is something of a political borderland between Republican and Democratic territory. The Indians, meanwhile, unlike those in the northern plains or Rocky Mountain states, do not vote in any way markedly different from the rest of the population.

The 2d district's largest city is Muskogee, a rather rundown Oklahoma rural center. Anyone who has heard Merle Haggard's "Okie from Muskogee" has a fair idea of the cultural and political attitudes here. There was never much of an establishment in Oklahoma to rebel against (although there was a big Socialist vote in the early years, reflecting hatred of eastern money interests), and people here have been very positive about traditional American values even as they have been questioned elsewhere. The residents of the district are not a particularly solemn folk, however. This part of Oklahoma produced Will Rogers, who is remembered here with favor—and Woody Guthrie, who generally is not.

The 2d has had four congressmen in the last ten years, an unusually high turnover. Twenty-year veteran Ed Edmondson left to run for the Senate in 1972 (he ran also in 1974 and 1978, all without success); Clem Rogers McSpadden, elected in 1972, ran for governor in 1974; Ted Risenhoover, after two close elections and accusations that he had a heart-shaped waterbed, was beaten in the 1978 runoff. The current congressman, Mike Synar, won that runoff at age 27 and was elected in 1978 and 1980. Synar's House career to date is not typical of young Democrats from rural southern districts. Instead of choosing a nuts-and-bolts committee, he served on Judiciary in his first term. There he was a sponsor of a major amendment on the proposed fair housing bill, to provide for enforcement through a system of administrative law judges in the Justice Department. This was considered likely to produce speedier and tougher enforcement and was supported by most strong civil rights advocates.

It passed the House by a 205–204 vote. Fair housing died in 1980 in the Senate, but it may come up again in 1981 or 1982.

Synar also had a voting record as closely attuned to nonsouthern Democrats as any in Oklahoma. The problems that can cause may be tempered by the fact that he got a seat on the Energy and Commerce Committee in 1981. There he sits on two energy subcommittees and is likely to be sympathetic to energy producers.

Although this is historically a Democratic district, Synar has had two tough general elections. Republican Gary Richardson was his opponent both times; he accused Synar of being too liberal and stressed his own affinity with the Moral Majority. In 1980 Synar countered with the value of his constituency service work and the fact that his ranching family is well established in Muskogee County. Synar won both times but by less than overwhelming margins. He carried most of the counties in the district but lost those that encircle Tulsa, where conservative urbanites from that Sun Belt boom town are moving into spanking new subdivisions where once there were only farms and Democratic voters. The 2d district is now the most populous in Oklahoma, and Synar would undoubtedly prefer to shed some of these newly Republican counties. The problem is that Democratic Congressman James Jones of the 1st district probably does not want them either.

Census Data Pop. (1980 final) 542,378, up 27% in 1970s. Median family income, 1970, $9,527, 99% of U.S.

The Voters

Employment profile 1970 White collar, 41%. Blue collar, 39%. Service, 15%. Farm, 5%.
Ethnic groups Black 1980, 5%. Hispanic 1980, 1%. Am. Ind. 1980, 12%. Total foreign stock 1970, 2%.

Presidential Vote

1980	Reagan (R)	114,382	(55%)
	Carter (D)	86,877	(42%)
	Anderson (I)	4,993	(2%)
1976	Ford (R)	85,974	(46%)
	Carter (D)	101,326	(54%)

Rep. Michael Lynn (Mike) **Synar** (D) Elected 1978; b. Oct. 17, 1950, Vinita; home, Muskogee; U. of Okla., B.A. 1972, J.D. 1977, Northwestern U., M.B.A. 1973.

Career Rancher and real estate broker.

Offices 1713 LHOB, 202-225-2701. Also Rm. 2B22 Fed. Bldg., 125 S. Main, Muskogee 74401, 918-681-2533.

Committees *Energy and Commerce* (21st). Subcommittees: Energy Conservation and Power; Fossil and Synthetic Fuels; Oversight and Investigations.

Government Operations (16th). Subcommittee: Environment, Energy, and Natural Resources.

Judiciary (11th). Subcommittee: Administrative Law and Governmental Relations.

Select Committee on Aging (22d). Subcommittee: Retirement Income and Employment.

Group Ratings

	ADA	COPE	PC	LCV	CFA	RPN	NAB	NSI	NTU	ACA	ACU
1980	61	44	67	63	71	—	42	40	23	26	21
1979	58	55	60	66	35	—	—	—	38	35	36

Key Votes

1) Draft Registn $	FOR	6) Fair Hsg DOJ Enfrc	FOR	11) Cut Socl Incr Dfns $	AGN
2) Ban $ to Nicrgua	FOR	7) Lim PAC Contrbtns	FOR	12) Hosptl Cost Controls	AGN
3) Dlay MX Missile	FOR	8) Cap on Food Stmp $	AGN	13) Gasln Ctrls & Allctns	AGN
4) Nuclr Mortorium	FOR	9) New US Dep Edcatn	FOR	14) Lim Wndfll Prof Tax	FOR
5) Alaska Lands Bill	FOR	10) Cut OSHA $	AGN	15) Chryslr Loan Grntee	—

Election Results

1980 general	Michael Lynn (Mike) Synar (D) ..	101,516	(54%)	($270,036)
	Gary Richardson (R)	86,544	(46%)	($205,452)
1980 primary	Michael Lynn Synar (D), unopposed			
1978 general	Michael Lynn (Mike) Synar (D) ..	72,583	(55%)	($190,050)
	Gary Richardson (R)	59,853	(45%)	($130,530)

THIRD DISTRICT

The southern part of Oklahoma is known as Little Dixie. It was first settled, in the period between 1889 and 1907, by white southerners—some of the county names here were taken directly from Mississippi. Ever since statehood Little Dixie has been the most Democratic part of Oklahoma. "Republicans occasionally travel through the district," says a *Congressional Quarterly* writer, "but they seldom settle there." The 3d congressional district of Oklahoma includes most of the Little Dixie counties, and juts up into the center of the state north of Oklahoma City, to include enough people to meet the equal population standard.

This is the district that for 30 years elected Carl Albert to the House of Representatives. Albert was part of the class of World War II veterans first elected in 1946. Others include John Kennedy and Richard Nixon; none is left in the House today. In his early years, as a loyal Democrat from a southern-oriented district, Albert attracted the attention of Speaker Sam Rayburn. He was made majority whip in 1955, and after that his succession to the speakership was, literally, automatic. For eight years, from 1971 to 1977, Albert served as speaker of the House.

Albert's performance as speaker was a disappointment to those who remembered him as a hard-fighting vote counter in the late 1950s and early 1960s. A decade and a half of waiting had only made him cautious, and he deferred to every committee chairman and every hoary tradition. He established no legislative priorities, had little to say about scheduling, essentially provided little leadership of any kind. Those were years in which it was difficult to lead. But it was clear that the time had passed when Albert would have been an effective speaker. His retirement in 1976 spared Democrats the question of whether they wanted to replace him.

Little Dixie had always seemed proud of Albert and reelected him without difficulty. But he proved unable to hand the 3d district seat on to his administrative assistant, Charles Ward. Instead state Senator Wes Watkins won the Democratic primary and captured the district. In his first years in the House Watkins had one of the most conservative voting records of any young Democrat. He has moved somewhat closer to the Democratic Caucus majority recently, even as the Caucus majority has moved somewhat closer to him. In 1980 he faced a difficult decision, whether to risk the uncertainties of a race for the Senate or to stay with the certainties of a career in the House (he has been unopposed since his first election except for token primary opposition in 1980). He chose the House career, and probably wisely, since a Republican won the Senate seat. In 1981 he got a seat on the House Appropriations Committee and serves on the Agriculture and Energy and Water Development (formerly Public

Works) Subcommittees—both bodies of obvious practical interest to Little Dixie. He is a leading participant in the 46-member Conservative Democratic Forum, which seems likely to have a pivotal role in the House in 1981 and 1982. It looks as though Watkins, in his early 40s, has settled in for as long a House career as his predecessor.

Census Data Pop. (1980 final) 508,801, up 19% in 1970s. Median family income, 1970, $6,567, 69% of U.S.

The Voters

Employment profile 1970 White collar, 39%. Blue collar, 40%. Service, 15%. Farm, 6%.
Ethnic groups Black 1980, 5%. Hispanic 1980, 1%. Am. Ind. 1980, 7%. Total foreign stock 1970, 2%.

Presidential Vote

1980	Reagan (R)	92,410	(49%)
	Carter (D)	92,068	(49%)
	Anderson (I)	3,213	(2%)
1976	Ford (R)	66,439	(36%)
	Carter (D)	117,459	(63%)

Rep. Wes Watkins (D) Elected 1976; b. Dec. 15, 1938, DeQueen, Ark.; home, Ada; Okla. St. U., B.S. 1960, M.S. 1961, U. of Md., 1961-63.

Career USDA, 1961-63; Asst. Dir. of Admissions, Okla. St. U., 1963-66; Exec. Dir., Kiamichi Econ. Development Dist. of Okla., 1966-68; Realtor and homebuilder, 1968-; Okla. Senate, 1975-76.

Offices 137 CHOB, 202-225-4565. Also P.O. Box 1607, Ada 74820, 405-436-1980.

Committee *Appropriations* (31st). Subcommittees: Agriculture, Rural Development and Related Agencies; Energy and Water Development.

Group Ratings

	ADA	COPE	PC	LCV	CFA	RPN	NAB	NSI	NTU	ACA	ACU
1980	33	31	37	12	43	—	55	90	36	46	53
1979	0	10	13	24	4	—	—	—	49	68	86
1978	20	37	23	8	14	58	92	89	27	84	81

Key Votes

1) Draft Registn $	FOR	6) Fair Hsg DOJ Enfrc	FOR	11) Cut Socl Incr Dfns $	AGN
2) Ban $ to Nicrgua	FOR	7) Lim PAC Contrbtns	AGN	12) Hosptl Cost Controls	AGN
3) Dlay MX Missile	AGN	8) Cap on Food Stmp $	AGN	13) Gasln Ctrls & Allctns	AGN
4) Nuclr Mortorium	AGN	9) New US Dep Edcatn	FOR	14) Lim Wndfll Prof Tax	FOR
5) Alaska Lands Bill	AGN	10) Cut OSHA $	FOR	15) Chryslr Loan Grntee	AGN

Election Results

1980 general	Wes Watkins (D), unopposed.....			($181,666)
1980 primary	Wes Watkins (D)..............	108,478	(91%)	
	One other (D)	11,373	(9%)	
1978 general	Wes Watkins (D), unopposed.....			($23,999)

FOURTH DISTRICT

The 4th congressional district of Oklahoma is part urban and part rural—a combination of different regions of the state and different political orientations. The rural part is in the southern part of Oklahoma. It includes several counties along the Red River border with Texas, an area that, on both sides of the river, has produced heavy Democratic majorities and some of the nation's most prominent Democratic politicians (including House Speakers Sam Rayburn and Carl Albert). The 4th also includes Lawton, a small city whose major industry is the care and maintenance of the Army's Fort Sill, and several wheat-producing counties near the center of the state. The 4th district also includes some 71,000 people in Oklahoma City and surrounding Oklahoma County. This is a middle-income suburban area, not the most exclusive part of Oklahoma City but filled with people who are at the same time more successful than they expected and financially more hard-pressed than they think they should be. To the south is Norman, the home of the University of Oklahoma. Unlike many midwestern university towns, Norman does not produce a leftish vote; if anything, it is more Republican than the rural counties that surround it on three sides.

All of this makes for a district that is politically marginal. It was about evenly divided in the 1976 presidential election and favored Ronald Reagan, but not by an overwhelming margin, in 1980. Republican strategists targeted the district as long ago as 1966, but they have never quite been able to capture it. For 32 years it was represented by Tom Steed, a former newspaperman and high-ranking Democrat on the Appropriations Committee, who decided to retire at age 76 in 1980.

The new congressman, Dave McCurdy, is a young Democrat who won against the odds. A lawyer from Norman, the closest thing he had to political experience was service in the state attorney general's office. But in the first Democratic primary he was able to run a respectable second to the favored candidate, a former majority leader in the state House. Strong personal campaigning was his secret; he quit his law practice for a year and devoted full time to the campaign. McCurdy won the runoff by carrying the southwestern rural counties solidly and picking up a good margin in Norman; he lost Oklahoma City and Pottawatomie County in the eastern end of the district. The Republican candidate, Howard Rutledge, a former prisoner of war in Vietnam, sounded predictably conservative themes. But McCurdy emphasized his law enforcement experience and talked about cutting taxes and spending. Rutledge carried Oklahoma City, Pottawatomie County, and Norman. McCurdy ran ahead of both President Carter and Democratic Senate candidate Andy Coats, winning solid margins in the rural areas and carrying Lawton. McCurdy won both the runoff and the general election with 51% of the vote—narrow victories, but significant ones in a Republican year. He is a man who bet everything on an outcome that most people said was unlikely, and won against long odds but by only the narrowest of margins.

In the House McCurdy sits on the Armed Services and Science Committees. The former is of considerable practical importance to the district. His long-term ambitions are unclear: elected at age 30, he could have a long House career or could end up seeking one of Oklahoma's Senate seats. The equal population standard will not require much change in the boundaries of the district, but it is possible that McCurdy would swap some areas where he has been weakest—such as Oklahoma City and Pottawatomie County—with more Democratic rural counties in the heavily Democratic 3d district.

Census Data Pop. (1980 final) 517,352, up 21% in 1970s. Median family income, 1970, $5,846, 61% of U.S.

The Voters

Employment profile 1970   White collar, 49%. Blue collar, 32%. Service, 14%. Farm, 5%.
Ethnic groups   Black 1980, 7%. Hispanic 1980, 3%. Am. Ind. 1980, 4%. Asian 1980, 1%. Total foreign stock 1970, 5%.

Presidential Vote

1980	Reagan (R)	92,255	(53%)
	Carter (D)	61,329	(35%)
	Anderson (I)	2,252	(4%)
1976	Ford (R)	73,168	(45%)
	Carter (D)	85,429	(53%)

Rep. Dave McCurdy (D) Elected 1980; b. Mar. 30, 1950, Canadian, Tex.; home, Norman; U. of Okla., B.A. 1972, J.D. 1975.

Career Okla. Asst. Atty. Gen., 1975–77; Practicing atty., 1977–80.

Offices 313 CHOB, 202-225-6165. Also 207 W. Main St., Norman 73069, 405-329-6500, and 103 Fed. Bldg., Lawton 73501, 405-357-2131.

Committees *Armed Services* (22d). Subcommittees: Procurement and Military Nuclear Systems; Readiness.

Science and Technology (22d). Subcommittees: Energy Development and Applications; Science, Research and Technology.

Group Ratings and Key Votes: Newly Elected

Election Results

1980 general	Dave McCurdy (D).............	74,245	(51%)	($229,248)
	Howard Rutledge (R)	71,339	(49%)	($159,115)
1980 runoff	Dave McCurdy (D).............	33,520	(51%)	
	James B. Townsend (D)	31,940	(49%)	($166,643)
1980 primary	James B. Townsend (D)	31,104	(40%)	
	Dave McCurdy (D).............	26,173	(34%)	
	Cuffie Waid (D)	10,722	(14%)	($35,649)
	Clifford O. Marshall (D)	7,035	(9%)	($9,968)
	One other (D)	1,781	(2%)	
1978 general	Tom Steed (D)	62,993	(60%)	($55,854)
	Scotty Robb (R)	41,421	(40%)	($150,420)

FIFTH DISTRICT

Oklahoma City is the capital of Oklahoma and its largest city, with a metropolitan population of more than half a million. During the 1960s the city fathers decided that they would not let the old city limits become a straitjacket, cutting off Oklahoma City from the prosperity and growth of the suburbs. So they annexed so much territory that Oklahoma City now spills over into five counties and three congressional districts. Even without these annexed areas—most of them are still vacant—Oklahoma City is a sprawling and unplanned metropolis. Towering above the dusty plains are a few skyscrapers and, right beside them, huge parking lots. As in the case of Tulsa, the wealth of Oklahoma City comes mainly from oil; on the grounds of the state Capitol there are still a few oil wells pumping away. Like most cities in the Southwest, especially oil cities, Oklahoma City is basically conservative and Republican.

The 5th congressional district, which includes most of Oklahoma City, has had only three different congressmen over the last forty years. The first was Mike Monroney who, as representative from the 5th from 1939 to 1951 and as U.S. senator for three terms, helped get an Air Force base and the FAA Aeronautical Center located here. The second, first elected in 1950, was Democrat John Jarman, a distinguished-looking Ivy League graduate who had a lackluster record and, after being hard-pressed in the 1974 primary and general election, decided to retire and turned Republican for his last two years in Congress.

The current man is the Republican who nearly won in 1974 — a result that would have been very much against the national trend — Mickey Edwards. In the House Edwards quickly became known as one of the most steadfast ideological conservatives — a New Rightist before the emergence of the New Right. He seems to be a man who loves a good fight. He took seats on two of the committees most uncongenial to his own thinking, Education and Labor and Interior, and remained on them for two terms. In 1981 he took a seat on Appropriations. At the beginning of his House career he was part of a small fringe group. But as House Republicans took the initiative in the House, framed the issues and controlled the dialogue, and became an extremely cohesive legislative group, Edwards's views seemed closer to the mainstream.

Edwards has proved very popular in his district and won reelection by overwhelming margins in 1978 and 1980 after taking the seat in a close race in 1976. Edwards considered a race for the Senate in 1980 but declined to run; the upset Republican winner, Don Nickles, is both younger and probably more conservative than Edwards (who, at 45 in 1982, is the oldest member of the youthful Oklahoma delegation). Edwards is thus likely to continue in the House, and the key question is whether he can make the transition from gadfly to leader, from critic to doer.

Census Data   Pop. (1980 final) 459,500, up 79% in 1970s. Median family income, 1970, $7,569, 79% of U.S.

The Voters

   Employment profile 1970   White collar, 56%. Blue collar, 30%. Service, 13%. Farm, 1%.
   Ethnic groups   Black 1980, 13%. Hispanic 1980, 3%. Am. Ind. 1980, 3%. Asian 1980, 1%. Total foreign stock 1970, 4%.

Presidential Vote

1980	Reagan (R)	109,429	(66%)
	Carter (D)	47,118	(28%)
	Anderson (I)	7,367	(4%)
1976	Ford (R)	94,535	(57%)
	Carter (D)	68,288	(41%)

Rep. Mickey Edwards (R) Elected 1976; b. July 12, 1937, Oklahoma City; home, Oklahoma City; U. of. Okla., B.S. 1958, Okla. City U., J.D. 1969.

Career Practicing atty., reporter, and editor; Ed., *Private Practice* magazine; Pub. rel. exec., 1973–76.

Offices 208 CHOB, 202-225-2132. Also 215 3d St., N.W., Oklahoma City 73102, 405-231-4541.

Committee *Appropriations* (16th). Subcommittees: Foreign Operations; Military Construction.

Group Ratings

	ADA	COPE	PC	LCV	CFA	RPN	NAB	NSI	NTU	ACA	ACU
1980	17	6	33	31	14	—	100	100	64	83	100
1979	11	10	23	25	11	—	—	—	69	96	97
1978	10	5	18	13	18	58	100	100	52	92	95

Key Votes

1) Draft Registn $	AGN	6) Fair Hsg DOJ Enfrc	AGN	11) Cut Socl Incr Dfns $	FOR
2) Ban $ to Nicrgua	FOR	7) Lim PAC Contrbtns	AGN	12) Hosptl Cost Controls	AGN
3) Dlay MX Missile	AGN	8) Cap on Food Stmp $	FOR	13) Gasln Ctrls & Allctns	AGN
4) Nuclr Mortorium	FOR	9) New US Dep Edcatn	AGN	14) Lim Wndfll Prof Tax	FOR
5) Alaska Lands Bill	AGN	10) Cut OSHA $	FOR	15) Chryslr Loan Grntee	AGN

Election Results

1980 general	Mickey Edwards (R)	90,053	(68%)	($300,211)
	David Hood (D)	36,815	(28%)	($50,413)
1980 primary	Mickey Edwards (R), unopposed			
1978 general	Mickey Edwards (R)	71,451	(80%)	($247,380)
	Jesse Dennis Knipp (D)	17,978	(20%)	($5,637)

SIXTH DISTRICT

The 6th congressional district of Oklahoma occupies the northwestern and north central parts of the state. It includes the thin Panhandle that goes west to touch the borders of Colorado and New Mexico. Aside from a small portion of Oklahoma City and its suburbs, the 6th is almost entirely small town and rural. Around the turn of the century, the plains west of Tulsa and Oklahoma City attracted thousands of migrants—probably a majority of them from nearby Kansas. Like so many settlers of the Great Plains, these people mistakenly assumed that the land was more fertile and the rainfall more reliable than was actually the case. The Dust Bowl of the 1930s hit already arid northwestern Oklahoma hard, and in many ways it has yet to recover. In 1907, when Oklahoma was admitted to the Union, there were 381,000 people living in the counties now in the 6th and outside the Oklahoma City metropolitan area. By 1970 that number was down to 357,000 and in 1980, after a decade of rural prosperity and lowered outmigration, the count was 395,000.

Due probably to the Kansas origin of its first settlers, the 6th has always been the most Republican part of nonurban Oklahoma. In the late 1960s and early 1970s, when the conservative trend in the state was shifting ancestral Democrats to the party of Richard Nixon and Spiro Agnew, the 6th became for a moment one of the most Republican districts in the nation. In 1972 Nixon won a larger percentage of the vote here (79%) than in any other congressional district outside the Deep South.

But that trend was short-lived, as Watergate had impact out here in Middle America as much as anywhere else. Not only did the traditionally Democratic counties in the southern part of the state switch back to Democrats in statewide races, so too, to a considerable extent, did the traditionally Republican counties of the north central region around Enid and Ponca City. The 6th was still Republican, but narrowly, in the 1976 presidential race; but since 1974 it has been represented in the House by a Democrat.

He is Glenn English, once an aide to liberal Democrats in the California Assembly, but a native of this area who had served as director of the Oklahoma Democratic Party. English won the seat in 1974 against an elderly incumbent, and he has held it by being sensitive to the shifts in public sentiment since that time. The 6th is now again a heavily Republican area; it gave Ronald Reagan an especially large margin, thanks in part to opposition to Jimmy Carter's wheat embargo. English's record over the years seems to have gotten more conservative to the point that he is now one of the most conservative of House Democrats. He continues to serve on the Agriculture Committee, of obvious local importance here, and on Government Operations, on which he chairs a subcommittee on Government Information and Individual Rights, which covers the sensitive area of government recordkeeping and individual privacy. English is continually reelected by large margins, although his percentage did fall noticeably in the Republican year of 1980, and he carried every part of the district except for a portion of Oklahoma City. As it happens, removal of that part would put the 6th pretty close to the population average for Oklahoma districts, so that is what the Democratic legislature will probably do.

Census Data   Pop. (1980 final) 494,961, up 16% in 1970s. Median family income, 1970, $9,305, 96% of U.S.

The Voters

   Employment profile 1970   White collar, 45%. Blue collar, 29%. Service, 15%. Farm, 11%.
   Ethnic groups   Black 1980, 2%. Hispanic 1980, 2%. Am. Ind. 1980, 3%. Total foreign stock 1970, 5%.

Presidential Vote

1980	Reagan (R)	139,828	(68%)
	Carter (D)	54,898	(27%)
	Anderson (I)	6,618	(3%)
1976	Ford (R)	106,437	(54%)
	Carter (D)	86,542	(44%)

Rep. Glenn English (D) Elected 1974; b. Nov. 30, 1940, Cordell; home, Cordell; Southwestern St. Col., B.A. 1964.

Career Chf. Asst. Major. Caucus, Cal. State Assembly; Exec. Dir., Okla. Dem. Party, 1969–73; Petroleum leasing business.

Offices 104 CHOB, 202-225-5565. Also 410 Maple St., Yukon 73099, 405-354-8638.

Committees *Agriculture* (12th). Subcommittees: Conservation, Credit, and Rural Development; Cotton, Rice, and Sugar; Tobacco and Peanuts; Wheat, Soybeans, and Feed Grains.

Government Operations (9th). Subcommittee: Government Information and Individual Rights (Chairman).

Select Committee on Narcotics Abuse and Control (5th).

Group Ratings

	ADA	COPE	PC	LCV	CFA	RPN	NAB	NSI	NTU	ACA	ACU
1980	6	26	37	22	21	—	83	100	47	63	83
1979	11	10	18	24	11	—	—	—	57	73	79
1978	15	16	25	31	9	67	100	90	35	88	74

Key Votes

1) Draft Registn $	FOR	6) Fair Hsg DOJ Enfrc	AGN	11) Cut Socl Incr Dfns $	FOR
2) Ban $ to Nicrgua	FOR	7) Lim PAC Contrbtns	FOR	12) Hosptl Cost Controls	AGN
3) Dlay MX Missile	AGN	8) Cap on Food Stmp $	FOR	13) Gasln Ctrls & Allctns	AGN
4) Nuclr Mortorium	AGN	9) New US Dep Edcatn	FOR	14) Lim Wndfll Prof Tax	FOR
5) Alaska Lands Bill	AGN	10) Cut OSHA $	FOR	15) Chryslr Loan Grntee	AGN

Election Results

1980 general	Glenn English (D)	111,694	(65%)	($81,837)
	Carol McCurley (R)	60,980	(35%)	($0)
1980 primary	Glenn English (D), unopposed			
1978 general	Glenn English (D)	103,512	(74%)	($109,668)
	Harold Hunter (R)	36,031	(26%)	($65,053)

OREGON

Oregon today seems like a distant progressive commonwealth, separated by thousands of miles of mountains and desert from the rest of the United States. The problems and fears that afflict the rest of the country often seem far away, and the state is open to new ideas and new approaches. Going to Oregon is almost like traveling to English-speaking Canada: the society is clearly similar, but everything is arranged in a slightly different way and the assumptions that guide public policy are often noticeably different. Oregon was one of the first states to show that you could decriminalize marijuana without any serious repercussions, and that you can outlaw throwaway bottles and cans without destroying the glass and brewing industries. In a nation that has always equated population growth with prosperity and success, Oregon is a state whose former governor, Tom McCall, urged people to come to visit, "but for heaven's sake don't come to live here."

Despite McCall's plea, Oregon's clean air and uncrowded spaces have been attracting people from the smog of California and the problems of the East. Oregon's population rose 18% during the 1960s and 25% in the 1970s — both rates well above the national average. That was an increase from 1.7 million to 2.6 million people. For all its natural attractions, Oregon still has its population concentrated in a small part of its land area: more than 70% live in the Portland metropolitan area or in the agricultural Willamette Valley directly to the south.

But enough of the current cliches about Oregon are true to merit asking just how this state came to be what it is. Much of the answer lies in the economic history of the West Coast in the years following World War II, when California and, to a lesser extent, Washington were ballooning in population. One reason was the rapid expansion of defense industries, first in World War II and then in the 1950s and 1960s. These brought hundreds of thousands of people to California and Washington, and most of them wanted to stay; when the defense plants shut down, they built the private economy that has made the West Coast an economic empire in its own right rather than a colony. Very little of this kind of growth occurred in Oregon. There is almost no defense industry here, and the Pentagon spends less per capita in

Oregon than almost any other state—one reason, perhaps, that Oregon has been happy to elect such congressional doves as Wayne Morse and Mark Hatfield.

The economy of Oregon is still built on a very old-fashioned commodity—wood. The lumber business provides the state with an economy steady over the long term but subject to violent fluctuations in the short term. When interest rates go up, home construction can almost cease, and suddenly the price of lumber drops and the mills go silent. A substantial market also exists for lumber for shipment to Japan and other East Asian countries, although the Japanese would prefer to import logs and the Oregonians would prefer to ship lumber to keep their mills busy. The lumber-based economy of Oregon did not attract many in-migrants in the 20 years after World War II; rather, it was the physical environment of Oregon that began attracting migrants when the economies of California, Washington, and the rest of the nation produced enough surplus wealth that people could afford the somewhat lower wages available in Oregon. Oregon's growth is the product of, not the cause of, West Coast affluence. That has definitely shaped attitudes here. Oregonians have less regard than people in most states for the need to produce and greater regard for what nature has provided.

If the economy of Oregon has a certain long-term stability, despite some short-term fluctuations, so too does its politics. Unlike most states, there have been no long-standing political differences between different regions. It is true that the coastal areas and the lower Columbia River valleys are marginally more Democratic than the rest of the state, and that Salem, the state capital, is usually more Republican than Eugene, the site of the University of Oregon. Also, the low-lying, less affluent sections of Portland east of the Willamette River are usually Democratic, while the more affluent city neighborhoods and suburbs in the hills to the west tend to be Republican. But there is not all that much difference between these areas—nothing like the difference in outlook between San Francisco and Orange County.

The results of the most recent election for governor, in 1978, seemed to indicate a sharp shift in Oregon's politics, but such was not really the case. Oregon remains concerned to an extraordinary degree with its environment and its own special progressive character—a tradition established during the governorship of Tom McCall (1967–74), whose pungent candor and blunt forcefulness made him the state's most popular political figure. He could have won a third term easily in 1974 had he been eligible to run. His successor was state Treasurer Robert Straub, a Democrat who supported similar policies although without the panache; he beat Victor Atiyeh, a state senator with a conservative reputation who had won the Republican primary in an upset and did not have McCall's strong appeal.

Yet four years later Atiyeh beat both of his predecessors—McCall in the Republican primary, Straub in the general election. In each case Atiyeh was careful to campaign as a supporter, not an opponent, of environmental measures; and he benefited as well from the post-Proposition 13 climate. McCall was handicapped by the composition of the Republican primary electorate, which increasingly has favored candidates of the right; it only barely preferred Gerald Ford over Ronald Reagan in 1976 and in 1980 gave Reagan a comfortable 54%–35% victory over George Bush. In the general election, there was great dispute over taxes, with Atiyeh favoring one ballot measure and Straub getting another, ultimately successful one on the ballot himself. The difference between the two candidates increasingly seemed to be one more of style than substance. Straub was criticized for not providing leadership in McCall's style, while Atiyeh was able to project a forceful image without being under the actual pressures of office. The result was a decisive, but not overwhelming, victory for Atiyeh.

In national politics, Atiyeh may still be identified as a conservative; in Oregon he prefers to accept rather than challenge the environmental orthodoxy. In 1982 he may face an opponent with a contrasting past: former Secretary of Transportation Neil Goldschmidt. As mayor of Portland for six years, Goldschmidt pushed for mass transit and cancelled a major freeway; he became a major hero of and leader for the environmental forces in Oregon politics. He is bright and exceedingly articulate—even the best stenographers cannot get down what he says because he talks so fast—and he is a man whose views are original and challenging. After service in the Carter Administration, he returned to Oregon, and almost everyone there is sure he will run for something. He has talked himself about running for the Multnomah County Commission and he seems unlikely to run for mayor again. The obvious target is the governorship—no U.S. senate seats are up in Oregon in 1982—and if he does run it should be a fascinating battle between two men who have enthusiastic constituencies and widespread respect.

Oregon's two Senate seats are held by Republicans, men who a few years ago would never have been named as among the most powerful of the Senate's members, but who today, by virtue of the positions they hold and their intelligence and ability, are necessarily among the leading senators. They are Mark Hatfield, chairman of the Senate Appropriations Committee, and Bob Packwood, chairman of the Senate Commerce Committee. Both are comparatively young and were first elected to the Senate at young ages: Hatfield in 1966 at age 42, after serving eight years as governor; Packwood in 1968 at age 32, when he upset 24-year incumbent Wayne Morse. Their ratings from various interest groups make them look like similar moderate Republicans. But in fact their views on a wide variety of issues are quite different, as are their basic priorities; and after serving together in the Senate for more than 12 years they are anything but the closest of friends.

Hatfield is one of the senators most devoted to his religion, and that obviously influences his attitudes on major issues. On foreign policy, he has always been among the most dovish of Republicans, concerned about the possibility of nuclear war and the reality of nuclear proliferation. Hatfield cosponsored the McGovern–Hatfield amendment to end the Vietnam war, a measure that almost passed and that launched McGovern's presidential candidacy. It was obviously less useful for any national ambitions Hatfield may have had. In the 1980s, Hatfield is one of the few Republicans who is skeptical about the need for vastly increased defense spending. There is a certain irony here: the Republicans campaigned in 1980 as the party pledged to a more aggressive defense posture, yet the new Secretary of Defense, Caspar Weinberger, is a veteran budget-cutter who seems unlikely to endorse new defense spending without skeptical scrutiny, and the new Senate Appropriations chairman, Hatfield, is a man profoundly concerned about the uses to which new weapons systems might be put. Hatfield has pledged not to obstruct Republican defense spending plans, but he will undoubtedly play some role on those issues.

On domestic issues, Hatfield's basic values do not lead him into the company of liberals so often as they do on defense and foreign policy. For he is a man whose faith is essentially traditional. He is not the kind of Christian who believes that a society with inequalities of income is necessarily immoral, nor one who decries any interference with the natural environment given us. Hatfield is far from being an unqualified believer in free-market economics, but he does work closely with the lumber industry, for example, to promote use of Oregon's forest resources.

Hatfield has served on a Senate Appropriations Committee that, under Chairman Warren Magnuson of Washington, was almost invariably more generous and open-handed than its House counterpart, and he tended to go along with that basic approach, with reservations. Now the terms of discussion may be very different. Appropriations members, including Hatfield, are wary that their committee may be avoided in the budget-cutting process, and that the Budget Committee, through its reconciliation process, may make all the basic decisions. But if Hatfield can be mollified on that issue, he is likely to be a supporter, by and large, of the Reagan Administration's spending plans. He will not be a driving force in pushing them through, for he is not by style an arm-twister, but he is serious enough to command widespread respect.

On the surface, Hatfield's election results make him appear extremely popular in Oregon; actually, he has been close-pressed on occasion. There were serious threats of Republican primary opposition back in 1972, when Hatfield was working to change Richard Nixon's Vietnam war policy, and Hatfield was held to a rather low majority by Wayne Morse, his former colleague, who had endorsed him because of his Vietnam position in 1966. In 1978 Hatfield was luckier and encountered no significant opposition. Assuming he is still Appropriations chairman in 1984, he may once again escape formidable opposition. The chair still gives a senator a lot of ability to help his home state, as Magnuson showed when Mount St. Helen's erupted, and Hatfield will be only 62 then. The thing working most against Hatfield —and working against every member of the Oregon delegation—is that the state is very difficult to reach from Washington, D.C.; there are no nonstop or convenient flights, which means that it is hard to keep in touch with folks back home. Two incumbent congressmen were beaten in 1980, largely because their constituents felt they saw too little of them, and this could someday be a problem for Hatfield, who has gotten quite used to his comfortable life in Washington.

Bob Packwood comes more from the Oregon environmentalist tradition, which was just beginning to be important when he was first elected to the Senate in 1968. In the early 1970s he was the Senate's leading advocate of zero population growth, and he has been a strong opponent of restrictions on abortion. This stand has made him a political hero to the women's rights movement which, through direct mail solicitations, helped to raise hundreds of thousands of dollars for his 1980 campaign. His abortion stand is unpopular among Catholics (of whom there are few in Oregon) but he is very popular with them for cosponsoring with Moynihan of New York a proposal for tax credits for tuition to private schools. Packwood has been something of an innovative thinker among Republicans for some time. He is not one of the key people in the supply-side economics group, however, and at points in his career has had a record on economic issues that has made him acceptable to organized labor. More recently, he has gone along with Kemp–Roth and most of the Reagan economic policies.

Packwood's rise to the chair of the Commerce Committee was somewhat of a surprise. Four years ago Packwood was the fifth-ranking Republican on the committee, when it had a Democratic majority and when it was pretty well run by Warren Magnuson (its chairman before he moved on to the Appropriations chair). Commerce handles a wide range of legislation of great interest to important economic groups: regulated industries such as broadcasting, railroads, and airlines, plus such subsidized industries as the merchant marine, and the space program as well. When Packwood became ranking Republican on the committee in 1979, he began to pay more attention to it and worked closely on major issues with its new chairman, Howard Cannon of Nevada. Now Packwood is at the center of Commerce's issues, without a well-established track record or a set of positions to which he is committed. Deregulation is the order of the day, and Packwood can be expected to go along, probably more readily than Cannon or Magnuson; but he may also lend a sympathetic ear to the plights of industries whose interests have been protected by existing regulation.

Packwood is generally considered a popular senator, yet he won reelection in 1974 and 1980 by margins that have to be considered unimpressive. In both elections, particularly the latter, he had the advantage of substantially outspending his opponents. Moreover, the 1980 opponent, Ted Kulongoski, was an old-fashioned liberal of the kind not very popular in Oregon or elsewhere. Yet Packwood won by only a 52%–44% margin. He failed to win absolute majorities in the Portland metropolitan area or in the area around Eugene. His strongest area was the conservative area of eastern Oregon, which to some extent shares the political leanings of the Rocky Mountain region of which it is a part. True, Packwood ran ahead of Reagan, who got only 48% of the vote in Oregon; but then, after 12 years in the Senate and with his reputation as a moderate, Packwood ought to be running further ahead of Reagan than he did. The distance factor may be playing a part here; and it is possible that Packwood's new prominence in the Senate will help him electorally in Oregon. But in the meantime he has not demonstrated that he holds a safe seat.

Oregon currently elects four congressmen; in 1982 it will elect five. The state experienced considerable turnover in its House delegation. Bob Duncan of Portland, who once represented southwest Oregon and came close to being elected senator in 1966, was defeated in a Democratic primary. Al Ullman, once Oregon's most powerful politician as chairman of the House Ways and Means Committee, was defeated for reelection after 26 years. Only Les AuCoin of the 1st district, a Democrat in a historically Republican seat, was able to win decisively. He has the potential to be a strong statewide candidate someday. Control of redistricting is split between Democrats (who hold the legislature) and Republicans (the governorship). Nevertheless the odds favor the creation of a new Republican seat. The prospect is for the 3d district (Portland) to stay pretty much the same and the 1st, 2d, and 4th districts all ceding territory to create a new 5th district centered on Salem and the Willamette Valley, an area that goes Republican in most elections. Whom it actually elects may depend on the craft with which particular legislators draw the lines.

Census Data   Pop. (1980 final) 2,632,663, up 26% in 1970s: 1.16% of U.S. total, 30th largest. Central city, 23%; suburban, 37%. Median 4-person family income, 1978, $21,534, 105% of U.S., 11th highest.

1979 Share of Federal Tax Burden $5,094,000,000; 1.13% of U.S. total, 28th largest.

1979 Share of Federal Outlays $4,828,408,000; 1.04% of U.S. total, 31st largest.

DOD	$430,443,000	41st	(0.41%)	HEW	$2,039,253,000	28th	(1.14%)
DOE	$154,894,000	20th	(1.32%)	ERDA	$4,168,000	34th	(0.15%)
HUD	$51,979,000	33d	(0.79%)	NASA	$2,620,000	32d	(0.06%)
VA	$255,232,000	31st	(1.23%)	DOT	$160,842,000	31st	(1.00%)
EPA	$90,101,000	19th	(1.70%)	DOC	$30,398,000	20th	(0.96%)
DOI	$236,313,000	7th	(4.26%)	USDA	$673,217,000	9th	(2.80%)

922   OREGON

Economic Base Lumber and wood products, especially millwork, plywood, and related products and sawmills and planing mills; agriculture, notably cattle, dairy products, wheat, and greenhouses; finance, insurance, and real estate; food and kindred products, especially canned, cured, and frozen foods; machinery, especially construction and related machinery; paper and allied products, especially paper mills other than building paper; transportation equipment.

Political Lineup Governor, Victor Atiyeh (R). Senators, Mark O. Hatfield (R) and Robert (Bob) Packwood (R). Representatives, 4 (3 D and 1 R); 5 in 1982. State Senate, 30 (21 D and 9 R); State House of Representatives, 60 (33 D and 27 R).

The Voters

Registration 1,569,222 Total. 784,129 D (50%); 564,771 R (36%); 220,322 I (14%).

Employment profile 1970 White collar, 48%. Blue collar, 34%. Service, 14%. Farm, 4%.
Ethnic groups Black 1980, 1%. Hispanic 1980, 3%. Am. Ind. 1980, 1%. Asian 1980, 1%. Total foreign stock 1970, 14%. Canada, 3%; Germany, 2%. UK, 1%.

Presidential Vote

1980	Reagan (R)	571,044	(48%)
	Carter (D)	456,890	(39%)
	Anderson (I)	112,389	(10%)
1976	Ford (R)	492,120	(48%)
	Carter (D)	490,407	(48%)

1980 Democratic Presidential Primary			*1980 Republican Presidential Primary*		
Carter	208,693	(58%)	Reagan	170,449	(54%)
Kennedy	114,651	(32%)	Bush	109,210	(35%)
Brown	34,409	(10%)	Anderson	32,118	(10%)
			One other	2,324	(1%)

SENATORS

Sen. Mark O. Hatfield (R) Elected 1966, seat up 1984; b. July 12, 1922, Dallas; home, Newport; Willamette U., B.A. 1943, Stanford U., A.M. 1948.

Career Navy, WWII; Assoc. Prof. of Poli. Sci., Willamette U., 1949–56, Dean of Students, 1950–56; Oreg. House of Reps., 1950–54; Oreg. Senate, 1954–56; Secy. of State of Oreg., 1956–58; Gov. of Oreg., 1958–66.

Offices 463 RSOB, 202-224-3753. Also 475 Cottage St., N.E., Salem 97301, 503-399-5731, and 105 Pioneer Courthouse, Portland 97204, 503-221-3386.

Committees *Appropriations* (Chairman). Subcommittees: Energy and Water Development (Chairman); Foreign Operations; Labor, Health and Human Services, Education; Legislative Branch.

Energy and Natural Resources (2d). Subcommittees: Energy Conservation and Supply; Public Lands and Reserved Water; Water and Power.

Rules and Administration (2d).

Joint Committee on the Library (2d).

Joint Committee on Printing (3d).

Group Ratings

	ADA	COPE	PC	LCV	CFA	RPN	NAB	NSI	NTU	ACA	ACU
1980	50	47	57	43	33	—	36	50	36	65	40
1979	58	59	43	—	29	—	—	—	40	40	21
1978	50	86	48	61	35	63	27	0	45	22	20

Key Votes

1) Draft Registn $	AGN	6) Fair Housng Cloture	—	11) Cut Socl Incr Defns	AGN
2) Ban $ to Nicrgua	AGN	7) Ban $ Rape Abortns	FOR	12) Income Tax Indexing	—
3) Dlay MX Missile	FOR	8) Cap on Food Stmp $	AGN	13) Lim Spdg 21% GNP	FOR
4) Nuclr Mortorium	FOR	9) New US Dep Edcatn	FOR	14) Incr Wndfll Prof Tax	FOR
5) Alaska Lands Bill	FOR	10) Cut OSHA Inspctns	FOR	15) Chryslr Loan Grntee	AGN

Election Results

1978 general	Mark O. Hatfield (R)	550,165	(62%)	($223,874)
	Vernon Cook (D)	341,616	(38%)	($38,976)
1978 primary	Mark O. Hatfield (R)	159,617	(66%)	
	Bert W. Hawkins (R)	43,350	(18%)	($64,574)
	Two others (R)	39,922	(16%)	
1972 general	Mark O. Hatfield (R)	494,671	(54%)	($299,626)
	Wayne L. Morse (D)	425,036	(46%)	($251,904)

Sen. Robert W. (Bob) **Packwood** (R) Elected 1968, seat up 1986; b. Sept. 11, 1932, Portland; home, Portland; Willamette U., B.S. 1954, NYU, LL.B. 1957.

Career Practicing atty., 1958–68; Oreg. House of Reps., 1962–68.

Offices 145 RSOB, 202-224-5244. Also 1002 N.E. Holladay St., P.O. Box 3621, Portland 97208, 503-233-4471.

Committees *Commerce, Science, and Transportation* (Chairman). Subcommittee: Business, Trade and Tourism.

Finance (2d). Subcommittees: Health; Savings, Pensions, and Investment Policy; Taxation and Debt Management (Chairman).

Select Committee on Small Business (2d). Subcommittees: Capital Formation and Retention (Chairman); Innovation and Technology.

Joint Committee on Taxation (2d).

Group Ratings

	ADA	COPE	PC	LCV	CFA	RPN	NAB	NSI	NTU	ACA	ACU
1980	56	41	73	75	60	—	46	80	31	43	38
1979	32	47	52	—	43	—	—	—	33	38	57
1978	45	69	25	41	20	88	33	30	12	41	23

Key Votes

1) Draft Registn $	AGN	6) Fair Housng Cloture	AGN	11) Cut Socl Incr Defns	FOR
2) Ban $ to Nicrgua	—	7) Ban $ Rape Abortns	AGN	12) Income Tax Indexing	FOR
3) Dlay MX Missile	AGN	8) Cap on Food Stmp $	AGN	13) Lim Spdg 21% GNP	FOR
4) Nuclr Mortorium	AGN	9) New US Dep Edcatn	FOR	14) Incr Wndfll Prof Tax	FOR
5) Alaska Lands Bill	FOR	10) Cut OSHA Inspctns	FOR	15) Chryslr Loan Grntee	AGN

Election Results

1980 general	Robert W. (Bob) Packwood (R) ..	594,290	(52%)	($1,666,390)
	Ted Kulongoski (D)	501,963	(44%)	($190,047)
1980 primary	Robert W. (Bob) Packwood (R) ..	191,127	(62%)	
	Brenda Jose (R)...............	45,973	(15%)	
	Three others (R)	68,809	(22%)	
1974 general	Robert W. (Bob) Packwood (R) ..	420,984	(55%)	($333,004)
	Betty Roberts (D)	338,591	(44%)	($80,193)

GOVERNOR

Gov. Victor G. Atiyeh (R) Elected 1978, term expires Jan. 1983; b. Feb. 20, 1923, Portland; U. of Oreg.

Career Pres., Atiyeh Bros., rug business; Oreg. House of Reps., 1959–65; Oreg. Senate, 1965–69.

Offices 207 State Capitol, Salem 97310, 503-378-3100.

Election Results

1978 gen.	Victor G. Atiyeh (R)	498,452	(55%)
	Robert W. Straub (D)	409,411	(45%)
1978 prim.	Victor G. Atiyeh (R)	115,593	(47%)
	Tom McCall (R)..........	83,568	(34%)
	Three others (R)	48,850	(20%)
1974 gen.	Robert W. Straub (D)	444,812	(58%)
	Victor G. Atiyeh (R)	324,751	(42%)

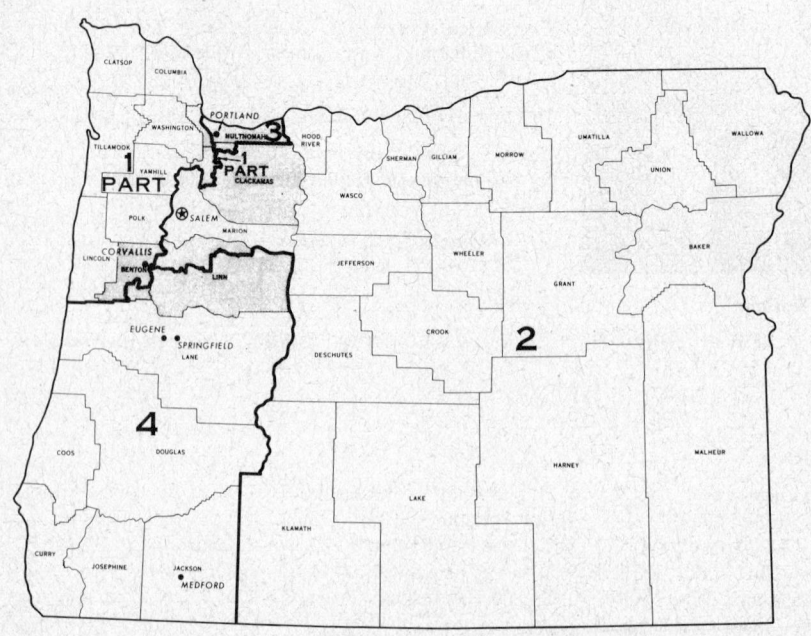

FIRST DISTRICT

The 1st congressional district of Oregon occupies the northwestern corner of the state. It includes the area around the mouth of the Columbia River and the coastal counties of Clatsop, Tillamook, and Lincoln. The countryside here still has frontier ambience to it: rain falls constantly on the weathered frame houses, and men in plaid flannel jackets work in lumber mills or on docks. The towns have an unfinished look to them — a part of Oregon that would still like some economic development. The 1st also includes part of the Willamette Valley south of Portland. This is mostly farmland, and it is more staid, settled-looking territory and has been since this area was settled by New England Yankees more than a century ago.

That is the historical 1st district. More recently, most of the population could be found in the Metropolitan Portland area. The district includes the part of the city of Portland west of the Willamette River. Geographically it is the smaller part of the city; there is only a little flat land before the hills start to rise. But the district includes both the downtown business section and the affluent neighborhoods in the hills overlooking it. About one-third of the district's population is in Washington County, the suburban area directly west of Portland. This is an affluent area where the hills move into the Coast Range; its population increased rapidly during the 1970s. There is developing here a small version of the computer and microchip economy that is so important in California's Silicon Valley, and this is the same kind of place: woodsy, at the foot of mountains, but outfitted with all the comforts and services of modern civilization.

The district was created in almost its present form in 1892, and for 82 years thereafter it always elected Republican congressmen. The progressive era, the Depression of the 1930s, the Goldwater debacle — through all these events the 1st district stayed with the Republicans. Time after time the Yankee-descended Republicans of the Willamette Valley outvoted the lumbermen of the coastal area.

That changed in 1974. The district had been moving toward the Democrats in most noncongressional elections. The environmental and Vietnam war issues worked for Democrats in the highly educated parts of Portland and Washington County. The enfranchisement of the 14,000 students at Oregon State University in Corvallis in the early 1970s initially benefited the Democrats. Watergate hurt the Republicans in this state that has never seen major political scandal. And in 1974 the Republican who represented the district for ten years decided to retire.

The new Democratic Congressman, Les AuCoin, seems tailor-made for the district. At 28 he had been elected to the legislature from Washington County and after one term had become House majority leader. So he had home base appeal in the affluent suburbs that might otherwise go Republican. He had good credentials on environmental issues. He was against the Vietnam war. And he backed traditional Democratic positions on economic issues without alienating traditional Republicans.

AuCoin has seemed to grow more popular since he was first elected. His service on the Banking, Housing, and Urban Affairs Committee was significant for the district, for the state of the housing market is the key variable for Oregon's important lumber industry. On the Merchant Marine and Fisheries Committee he supported subsidies to Oregon's maritime industry and unions, and he has been promoting increased trade between the Pacific Northwest and mainland China. He has emphasized environmental issues that continue to be very important in this part of Oregon. In 1981 AuCoin switched to the Appropriations

Committee and obtained seats on the Interior and Transportation Subcommittees. He is one of the new breed of Democrats who do not necessarily believe in the party's old economic policies and his support of some budget cuts and of deregulation of energy prices led the Democratic leadership to bar him from the Budget Committee.

He has proved to be very popular in his district. At a time when other Oregon congressmen were defeated and Democrats have been in trouble, he has been reelected by increasing margins, and it appears that Republicans have given up targeting him. He has an obvious potential for statewide office, although no Senate seat is up here until 1984. Redistricting will be important for AuCoin, who would like to lose more Republican than Democratic territory.

Census Data   Pop. (1980 final) 699,073, up 34% in 1970s. Median family income, 1970, $10,430, 109% of U.S.

The Voters

Employment profile 1970   White collar, 54%. Blue collar, 30%. Service, 13%. Farm, 3%.
Ethnic groups   Black 1980, 1%. Hispanic 1980, 2%. Am. Ind. 1980, 1%. Asian 1980, 2%. Total foreign stock 1970, 16%. Canada, 3%; Germany, UK, 2% each.

Presidential Vote

1980	Reagan (R)	157,902	(48%)
	Carter (D)	123,866	(38%)
	Anderson (I)	38,527	(12%)
1976	Ford (R)	150,482	(54%)
	Carter (D)	120,319	(45%)

Rep. Les AuCoin (D) Elected 1974; b. Oct. 21, 1942, Portland; home, Forest Grove; Pacific U., B.A. 1969.

Career Army, 1961–64; Newsman, *Portland Oregonian,* 1965–66; Dir. of Pub. Info. and Publications, Pacific U., 1966–73; Oreg. House of Reps., 1971–75, Major. Ldr., 1973–75; Administrator, Skidmore, Owings, and Merrill, engineering firm, 1973–74.

Offices 2446 RHOB, 202-225-0855. Also 1716 Fed. Bldg., 1220 S.W. 3d Ave., Portland 97204, 503-221-2901.

Committee *Appropriations* (29th). Subcommittees: Transportation; Interior.

Group Ratings

	ADA	COPE	PC	LCV	CFA	RPN	NAB	NSI	NTU	ACA	ACU
1980	83	39	50	72	57	—	40	0	27	25	28
1979	68	58	53	70	37	—	—	—	36	29	32
1978	40	60	58	77	41	50	17	38	48	40	20

Key Votes

1) Draft Registn $	AGN	6) Fair Hsg DOJ Enfrc	FOR	11) Cut Socl Incr Dfns $	AGN
2) Ban $ to Nicrgua	AGN	7) Lim PAC Contrbtns	AGN	12) Hosptl Cost Controls	AGN
3) Dlay MX Missile	FOR	8) Cap on Food Stmp $	AGN	13) Gasln Ctrls & Alletns	AGN
4) Nuclr Mortorium	FOR	9) New US Dep Edcatn	FOR	14) Lim Wndfll Prof Tax	FOR
5) Alaska Lands Bill	FOR	10) Cut OSHA $	AGN	15) Chryslr Loan Grntee	AGN

Election Results

1980 general	Les AuCoin (D)	203,532	(66%)	($307,477)
	Lynn Engdahl (R)	105,083	(34%)	($61,045)
1980 primary	Les AuCoin (D)	80,470	(100%)	
1978 general	Les AuCoin (D)	158,706	(63%)	($236,313)
	Nick Bunick (R)	93,640	(37%)	($297,719)

SECOND DISTRICT

The 2d congressional district of Oregon contains 73% of the state's land area and 27% of its population. Most of the land lies east of the Cascade Mountains. To the south, the terrain is desertlike; the only significant settlement here is Klamath Falls. This part of the district contains about one-tenth of its population. To the east, along the Idaho border, are the irrigated farmlands of the Snake River as it flows northwest to the Columbia. This area contains about one-fifth of the 2d's people. The remainder of the intermountain area contains another fifth. This is forested land, with occasional lumber mill towns; settlements are sparse and separated by many miles. The 2d also includes a portion of the Willamette Valley west of the Cascades, originally included to get the district up to the state population average but now helping to make it the most populous district in the state. Here is half the district's present population, in and around the capital city of Salem and in the smaller towns and farms of the Willamette Valley.

The two major portions of the district seem to have been trending in the opposite directions. East Oregon is historically marginal, a place where traditional Rocky Mountain populism on economic issues such as public power development has been overcome since the early 1960s by the mountain country's dislike of an intrusive federal government and environmental activists who want to choke off development. The Willamette Valley, on the other hand, was originally settled by New England Yankees and was a stronghold of Republicanism in the Democratic West for many years. But on such issues as the environment the valley has been getting more liberal, while retaining its conservatism on many economic issues.

These trends would seem to cancel each other out. But in fact both were bad news for Al Ullman, who until the 1980 election was congressman from the 2d. Ullman was first elected in 1956, when eastern Oregon comprised the entire district, and public power was a hot issue here and in neighboring Idaho. He compiled a record in Washington — liberal on most economic issues, conservative on cultural issues — that seemed to please his constituents. But in the Willamette Valley, both his party affiliation and his stands on cultural issues caused him problems. For many years he was not seriously challenged for reelection, and in time — when Wilbur Mills was forced to resign — he became chairman of the House Ways and Means Committee. In the old days, such prominence would make a member stronger. But it seems to have weakened Ullman. It made him seem to all parts of his district a liberal free spender. When he made the innovative proposal that the nation consider a value added tax, Oregonians rose up in wrath; this is one of only four states that has no sales tax, and voters have turned it down overwhelmingly in referendum.

It seemed to many voters here that Ullman had gotten out of touch with his district. This was the main theme of his first serious challenger in years and the new congressman, Denny Smith. Smith pointed out that Ullman owned an apartment in Washington and a vacation condominium in Ocean City, Maryland — but no property in Oregon. Smith had other assets: he is the son of a former Republican governor, he owns a chain of small newspapers,

928   OREGON

he is a former airline pilot and flies his plane around the district. And he was able to raise huge sums of money. Ullman, as chairman of the committee that writes the nation's taxes, was naturally well financed; he spent $670,000. Smith equaled that, with $663,000. He raised his money from conservative contacts and had some help from his cousin, then Congressman and now Senator Steven Symms of Idaho.

Indeed, the Idaho connection in a sense proved vital for Smith. He carried majorities in only two parts of the district: around Klamath Falls in the south and in the counties along the Snake River and near the Idaho border. These areas receive Boise television, and it stands to reason that the very conservative political climate of Idaho had some effect on these Oregonians who are very distant from urban Portland or trendy Eugene. Ullman had a significant margin only in the county around Bend, in the intermountain region. The Willamette Valley area, which Ullman as the more moderate candidate must have hoped to carry, actually went to Smith by 454 votes. Smith's overall margin was a little under 4,000 — but enough to defeat the chairman of the House Ways and Means Committee.

Smith is expected to be one of the more right-leaning of the new Republican members of the House. He serves on the Interior and Veterans' Affairs Committees. Redistricting will have to remove more than 200,000 of the 2d district's residents and perhaps move around more. One plan would be to take Medford and Jackson County from the 4th district and drop Salem and the Willamette Valley area, leaving them to be the nucleus of a new district. That will make the 2d a little tougher for Smith, which is fine with the Democratic legislature but may not please the governor. In any case, it seems hardly likely that there will be another race as expensive and hard-fought as the one in the 2d in 1982.

Census Data Pop. (1980 final) 706,899, up 35% in 1970s. Median family income, 1970, $8,821, 92% of U.S.

The Voters

Employment profile 1970   White collar, 43%. Blue collar, 34%. Service, 14%. Farm, 9%.
Ethnic groups   Hispanic 1980, 4%. Am. Ind. 1980, 2%. Asian 1980, 1%. Total foreign stock 1970, 12%. Canada, Germany, 2% each; UK, 1%.

Presidential Vote

1980	Reagan (R)	162,094	(54%)
	Carter (D)	106,767	(35%)
	Anderson (I)	25,713	(9%)
1976	Ford (R)	124,597	(50%)
	Carter (D)	118,068	(47%)

Rep. Denny Smith (R) Elected 1980; b. Jan. 19, 1938, Ontario; home, Salem; Willamette U., B.A. 1961.

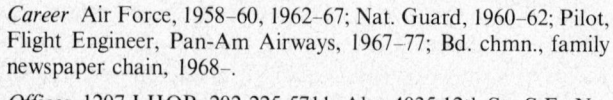

Career Air Force, 1958–60, 1962–67; Nat. Guard, 1960–62; Pilot, Flight Engineer, Pan-Am Airways, 1967–77; Bd. chmn., family newspaper chain, 1968–.

Offices 1207 LHOB, 202-225-5711. Also 4035 12th St., S.E., No. 20, P.O. Box 13089, Salem 97309, 503-399-5756.

Committees *Interior and Insular Affairs* (16th). Subcommittees: Energy and the Environment; Insular Affairs.

Veterans' Affairs (13th). Subcommittees: Compensation, Pension, and Insurance; Education, Training and Employment.

Group Ratings and Key Votes: Newly Elected

Election Results

1980 general	Denny Smith (R)...............	141,854	(49%)	($663,430)
	Al Ullman (D).................	138,089	(47%)	($670,390)
1980 primary	Denny Smith (R)...............	56,718	(77%)	
	Leonard George Roth (R)	16,884	(23%)	
1978 general	Al Ullman (D).................	152,099	(69%)	($55,401)
	Terry L. Hicks (R)	67,547	(31%)	

THIRD DISTRICT

Portland is Oregon's big city. About 40% of the people in the state live within its metropolitan area, and more than half live within 60 miles of its downtown. The 3d congressional district of Oregon takes in most of Portland—the four-fifths of the city east of the Willamette River. The district also includes most of the Portland suburbs along the Willamette and Columbia Rivers. The 3d's eastern borders stretch to a point near the snow-covered peak of Mount Hood, which at 11,000 feet looks down on Portland's green streets and its famous roses.

Portland was founded by New England Yankees (it was nearly called Boston) and had its beginnings as a muscular blue collar town—the place where Oregon unloaded its supplies from the east, on the docks or in the railroad yards, and where it shipped out Oregon's products—lumber, fruit. Portland has gained the reputation of being an almost avant garde city, a place where ecology-minded young marrieds jog together in the mornings, eat health food for dinner, and pray at night that no one else moves to their city. There is some truth to this picture, but it tends to apply to suburbanites and Portland residents west of the Willamette, in the affluent hill areas. On the flat lands east of the river to Mount Hood live Portland's middle-class, blue collar majority. They too have a positive feeling about Oregon's unique environment, but not to the exclusion of more conventional sentiments. The people here tend to be traditional Democrats, and the 3d district went for George McGovern in 1972 and Jimmy Carter in 1976.

The 3d district has been represented by Democrats since 1954 and is seldom the scene of spirited political contests. But 1980 was an exception. Congressman Bob Duncan, a six-year incumbent, seemed superficially popular. A former congressman from the 4th district, he chaired the Transportation Subcommittee of Appropriations, an important body for Portland, the city where former Mayor Neil Goldschmidt expanded mass transit and refused to build a freeway. And Duncan was much less controversial than in the 1960s, when he was an all-out supporter of Lyndon Johnson's Vietnam war policies. Nonetheless Duncan turned out to be vulnerable. It is difficult to get back and forth between Capitol Hill and Portland, and Duncan had come to seem a distant figure to Oregonians. With no Republican or primary opposition in 1976 or 1978, he had not needed to communicate his record to the voters. He turned out to be ripe for an upset and was beaten in the Democratic primary by the extraordinary margin of 60%–40%.

The winner and new congressman is Ron Wyden, who has had a rather unusual career. He achieved wide notice in Portland as director of the Gray Panthers, a militant organization to aid the elderly. He was, among other things, the spark behind the successful referendum to reduce the price of dentures. In the campaign against Duncan he was able to rally a large force of elderly volunteers, and his precinct organization together with his activist reputation and his outspoken campaigning were responsible for victory.

Wyden enters a Congress that is going very much in the opposite direction. He is a strong believer in federal programs to help people—programs that the Reagan Administration and much of the Congress seem bent on dismantling or cutting. As a member of the Health Subcommittee of Energy and Commerce he will be pushing in the other direction. But over the long run, young men who enter Congress at a time when their views are not in favor often have a great advantage in the future. The pendulum almost always swings the other way, and when it does Wyden and other liberals first elected in 1980 will have a significant advantage in seniority and experience over those who are elected later. Wyden's district is not likely to be changed much by redistricting, and his performance in 1980 suggests that he will be a formidable candidate in the future. His energy suggests that he can overcome the problem that so many Oregon congressmen have had: the difficulty of maintaining a visible presence back home.

Census Data   Pop. (1980 final) 540,882, up 4% in 1970s. Median family income, 1970, $10,001, 104% of U.S.

The Voters

Employment profile 1970   White collar, 51%. Blue collar, 34%. Service, 14%. Farm, 1%.
Ethnic groups   Black 1980, 5%. Hispanic 1980, 2%. Am. Ind. 1980, 1%. Asian 1980, 3%. Total foreign stock 1970, 18%. Canada, 3%; Germany, UK, 2% each.

Presidential Vote

1980	Reagan (R)	96,529	(40%)
	Carter (D)	113,273	(47%)
	Anderson (I)	23,902	(10%)
1976	Ford (R)	100,236	(45%)
	Carter (D)	122,743	(53%)

Rep. Ron Wyden (D) Elected 1980; b. May 3, 1949, Wichita, Kans.; home, Portland; U. of Cal., Santa Barbara, 1967–69, Stanford U., A.B. 1971, U. of Oreg., J.D. 1974.

Career Cmpn. Aide to Sen. Wayne Morse, 1972, 1974; Practicing atty., 1974–1980; Codirector, Cofounder, Oreg. Gray Panthers, 1974–80; Dir., Oreg. Legal Svcs. for the Elderly, 1977–79.

Offices 1440 LHOB, 202-225-4811. Also 714 BPA Bldg., 1002 N.E. Holladay, P.O. Box 3621, Portland 97208, 503-231-2300.

Committees *Energy and Commerce* (23d). Subcommittees: Energy, Conservation and Power; Health and the Environment; Oversight and Investigations.

Small Business (18th). Subcommittee: Export Opportunities and Special Small Business Problems.

Select Committee on Aging (29th). Subcommittees: Health and Long-Term Care; Retirement Income and Employment.

Group Ratings and Key Votes: Newly Elected

Election Results

1980 general	Ron Wyden (D)	156,371	(72%)	($183,840)
	Darrell R. Conger (R)...........	60,940	(28%)	($9,724)
1980 primary	Ron Wyden (D)	55,818	(60%)	
	Robert B. Duncan (D)	37,132	(40%)	($172,229)
1978 general	Robert B. Duncan (D)	151,895	(85%)	($38,318)
	Martin Simon (N-P)	27,120	(15%)	

FOURTH DISTRICT

The 4th congressional district of Oregon occupies the southwestern corner of the state. Although the district contains about half of Oregon's rocky and picturesque Pacific coastline, most of its people can be found inland, in the southern end of the Willamette River valley between the Coast Range and the Cascade Mountains. As in most of the West, relatively few people actually live on farms here, although the area produces much of Oregon's famed fruit crop. Instead, most of the people live in small, well-ordered cities including Medford, Grant's Pass, Roseburg, Coos Bay, and Springfield. The largest city here, with 104,000 people, is Eugene, the home of the University of Oregon.

As is the case throughout Oregon, the 4th district has few sharp extremes of political allegiance. Eugene is more Democratic than the rest, particularly since students got the vote in 1972; the southern counties are somewhat more Republican. Overall, the political balance is close enough that party control of the district has changed six times in the last 25 years. In 1956 the district elected Charles Porter, a Democrat who was a strong peace advocate; he was retired by Republican Edwin Durno in 1960, who in turn lost to Democrat Robert Duncan in 1962. Duncan, later congressman from the 3d district, ran for the Senate in 1966 and was succeeded in the House by John Dellenback, who was in turn beaten by Democrat James Weaver in 1974. Dellenback's defeat was a particular surprise and points up a special difficulty incumbents have in holding this seat in an era when constituents expect their congressman to return home almost every weekend: there are no direct flights from Washington, and the quickest route involves eight hours of flying and connection time.

In his first term, Weaver won a seat on the Agriculture Committee, one of special importance to the district, because the Agriculture Department includes the Forestry Service, and this is one of the major lumber-producing districts in the nation. In 1977 Weaver became chairman of the Forests Subcommittee—a position that makes him kind of a czar to the lumber industry.

Many congressmen, given an opportunity to endear themselves to a strong local economic interest, would have seized it gladly. Weaver, on the other hand, has not hesitated to antagonize the big lumber companies. He pushed through a timber bill that provides for sustained yields—less than many lumbermen wanted, because of restrictions on cutting to meet environmental concerns. He has worked to protect large wilderness areas. In a matter less controversial, he has moved to cut timber exports to Japan, so that American rather than Japanese mills can convert the logs into lumber.

These positions have guaranteed vehement opposition to Weaver from major lumber companies. In 1976 and 1978 a local lumberman ran against him and spent liberally, but his strong conservative views may have hurt him; Weaver won decisively each time. In 1980 another Republican, Michael Fitzgerald, spent liberally and waged a harsh negative campaign against Weaver, citing not only the incumbent's support of environment positions but his opposition to discrimination against homosexuals. Weaver lost three of his six major counties but nonetheless won a 55%–45% victory.

That Weaver's margins have diminished and that he continues to generate controversy almost guarantee that he will have strong opposition in 1982. Redistricting will not help. Although the legislature is Democratic, it will have to lop off part of Weaver's district, and he carried all the counties at the edges of the 4th. He would be particularly sorry if he were to lose Eugene, which is currently the heart of the district.

Census Data   Pop. (1980 final) 685,809, up 31% in 1970s. Median family income, 1970, $8,854, 92% of U.S.

The Voters

Employment profile 1970   White collar, 43%. Blue collar, 40%. Service, 13%. Farm, 4%.
Ethnic groups   Hispanic 1980, 2%. Am. Ind. 1980, 1%. Asian 1980, 1%. Total foreign stock 1970, 11%. Canada, Germany, 2% each; UK, 1%.

Presidential Vote

1980	Reagan (R)	154,512	(51%)
	Carter (D)	112,973	(37%)
	Anderson (I)	24,246	(8%)
1976	Ford (R)	116,717	(45%)
	Carter (D)	129,306	(50%)

Rep. James (Jim) Weaver (D) Elected 1974; b. Aug. 8, 1927, Brookings, S.D.; home, Eugene; U. of Oreg., B.S. 1952.

Career   Navy, WWII; Publisher's Rep., Prentice-Hall Co., 1954–58; Staff Dir., Oreg. Legislative Interim Comm. on Agriculture, 1959–60; Builder and apartment complex developer, 1960–75.

Offices   1226 LHOB, 202-225-6416. Also Fed. Bldg., 211 E. 7th Ave., Eugene 97401, 503-687-6732.

Committees   *Agriculture* (9th). Subcommittees: Forests, Family Farms, and Energy (Chairman); Wheat, Soybeans, and Feed Grains.

Interior and Insular Affairs (9th). Subcommittees: Energy and the Environment; Public Lands and National Parks; Water and Power Resources.

Group Ratings

	ADA	COPE	PC	LCV	CFA	RPN	NAB	NSI	NTU	ACA	ACU
1980	83	72	77	93	64	—	40	0	45	35	19
1979	84	77	90	94	93	—	—	—	55	24	17
1978	75	89	80	99	55	45	30	11	50	32	19

Key Votes

1) Draft Registn $	AGN	6) Fair Hsg DOJ Enfrc	FOR	11) Cut Socl Incr Dfns $	AGN
2) Ban $ to Nicrgua	—	7) Lim PAC Contrbtns	FOR	12) Hosptl Cost Controls	FOR
3) Dlay MX Missile	—	8) Cap on Food Stmp $	AGN	13) Gasln Ctrls & Allctns	FOR
4) Nuclr Mortorium	—	9) New US Dep Edcatn	—	14) Lim Wndfll Prof Tax	AGN
5) Alaska Lands Bill	FOR	10) Cut OSHA $	AGN	15) Chryslr Loan Grntee	AGN

Election Results

1980 general	James (Jim) Weaver (D)	158,745	(55%)	($239,432)
	Michael Fitzgerald (R)	130,861	(45%)	($379,056)
1980 primary	James (Jim) Weaver (D)	71,388	(75%)	
	One other (D)	23,758	(25%)	
1978 general	James (Jim) Weaver (D)	124,745	(56%)	($178,950)
	Jerry S. Lausmann (R)	96,953	(44%)	($206,613)

PENNSYLVANIA

Pennsylvania is called the Keystone State, and it is an apt name: the commonwealth connects New York and New England with the rest of the nation. Two hundred years ago, the geography of Pennsylvania promised to make it the commercial and transportation hub of the country, and it was the most populous state of the new nation. But the rugged mountains of central Pennsylvania stalled the early development of transportation arteries west. It was New York City, rather than Philadelphia, that mushroomed most rapidly in the middle 19th century, thanks to the building of the Erie Canal and the first water-level railroad line: it became the New York Central. In 1776 Philadelphia was the nation's capital and largest city. By 1830 it was eclipsed by Washington in government and by New York in commerce, and rivaled by Boston in culture. Philadelphia is still the nation's fourth largest metropolitan area and Pittsburgh is 13th, but neither city looms as large in the national consciousness as seemed likely when the Declaration of Independence was signed.

During the 19th century, Pennsylvania nonetheless had remarkable growth — but for reasons not anticipated by the founders. It became the energy capital of the United States, much as Texas is today, and the major industrial center as well. The key to all this was coal — Pennsylvania probably has enough coal to supply all the nation's needs even today. Northeastern Pennsylvania was the nation's primary source of anthracite, the hard coal used for home heating; and western Pennsylvania was the major source for bituminous coal, the soft coal used in producing steel and other industrial products. As a result, the area around Pittsburgh had become the center of the steel industry by 1890. Immigrants poured into the state to work the mines and the factories, and the very name Pittsburgh became synonymous with industrial prosperity. During this period Pennsylvania was the nation's second largest state and was growing rapidly.

The boom ended conclusively with the Depression of the 1930s, and in much of Pennsylvania good times have never really returned. The coal industry collapsed after World War II, as both home heating and industry switched to oil (a less well-advised decision in retrospect than it seemed at the time). Today, while coal is becoming more important, mining technology is far less labor-intensive, and the population of coal-mining communities continues to diminish. Meanwhile, Pennsylvania steel is no longer a growth industry. Steelmakers here chose to ignore technological advances after World War II, and the state's ancient steel mills are far less efficient than those built in postwar Germany or Japan or even the new mills that have been constructed in other parts of the country.

The leaders of the industry seem to have been afflicted with the notion that they had a monopoly over steel production in the American market, that they could raise wages and prices as much as they wanted, and their customers would be forced to pay. But in time it became cheaper to ship steel to the Midwest from Japan than from Pittsburgh. By the early 1970s the steel companies and the United Steelworkers (who had achieved, with autoworkers, the highest blue collar wages in the nation) were crying for trade barriers against steel imports. A century ago, the steel producers made Pennsylvania the classic high tariff state, when they sought protection for its "infant" industries; now by backing trade restrictions, they seem to be admitting that their industries have grown senile. Steel, which likes to think of itself as a rough, robust industry, has actually demanded protection as if it were some kind of fragile flower. During the 1970s there were some import restrictions, formal (the trigger price system) and informal ("voluntary" import limits by the Japanese). These have not succeeded yet in reviving the domestic steel industry, although they have tended to make every product made with steel more expensive for American consumers.

These economic developments have left Pennsylvania in rather sorry shape. People growing up here are as likely to leave the state as stay, while out-of-staters show little inclination to move in. Compared to the growth areas of the Sun Belt, the cities and small towns of Pennsylvania give the traveler a sense of having gone back 30 or 40 years in time. One can see here, little changed, the suburb where John Updike lived as a boy and the gritty coal town where John O'Hara grew up. Sometimes the trip is pleasant, as in the spanking clean 1920s downtown of Lancaster, surrounded by early 19th-century row house neighborhoods; sometimes it is grim, as in the coal towns where houses stand unoccupied and the woods and brush creep up to the edge of neighborhoods built 60 years ago. In 1930, after its last decade of prosperity, Pennsylvania recorded 9.5 million people. Today the number stands at 11.8 million—by far the smallest long-term growth of the nation's biggest states. By the 1980 census Pennsylvania had slipped behind not only New York and California but also, symbolically important, the nation's new energy capital, Texas. This sluggish growth has had political consequences. As recently as 1950, Pennsylvania had 32 seats in the House of Representatives; in 1982 it will have only 23.

Traditionally Pennsylvania was heavily Republican, the most Republican of all big states. It was for Lincoln and Union, for the steel industry and the high tariff, and in 1932 it was the only big state that stuck with Herbert Hoover when he was beaten by Franklin Roosevelt. For years Philadelphia was governed by not a Democratic but a Republican machine, which held onto the mayor's office until reformer (and later Senator) Joseph Clark won it in 1951. In the industrial cities of northeastern and western Pennsylvania, it was Republicans, not Democrats, who organized and won the votes of the workingmen, both immigrant and native. This was not class politics—although there were some primary fights between progressives and conservatives—as much as it was consensus politics, all elements of Pennsylvania standing under the same party banner and backing the same, seemingly successful programs.

All that changed with the Depression and the New Deal. Since then Pennsylvania has been a classically marginal state. The central part of the state—the Welsh railroad workers in Altoona and the Pennsylvania Dutch farmers around Lancaster—remains the strongest Republican voting bloc in the East. And if Metropolitan Philadelphia has become Democratic in most elections, Republicans are still definitely competitive there; Ronald Reagan carried Metro Philadelphia over Jimmy Carter in 1980. Pennsylvania's great blue collar enclaves—Greater Pittsburgh and the whole western end of the state and the northeastern region around Scranton, Wilkes-Barre, Allentown, Bethlehem, and Reading—are now Democratic bulwarks. These are the places where organized labor, especially the United Steelworkers, exerts most of its political influence.

Pennsylvania has always been a machine state, and to some extent it remains one. Fifteen years ago the state government still had 50,000 patronage employees, appointed for the most part by county political leaders. Their number was whittled down under recent governors, from William Scranton (1963–67) to Milton Shapp (1971–79), who had little use for such largesse. But Pennsylvania politics still has a crass, practical tone. It has also had its share of corruption, particularly under Shapp, who, despite his lack of debt to party leaders, seemed to repose trust in people who did not deserve it. Shapp's administration had some achievements — a notable consumer program, a Volkswagen plant built in western Pennsylvania — but by 1978 voters were ready for something new.

They got that in Richard Thornburgh, a governor who is a strong partisan and who is also impeccably honest. A former federal prosecutor and U.S. deputy attorney general, Thornburgh had the backing of Senator John Heinz; he beat former Philadelphia prosecutor (and now Senator) Arlen Specter in the primary and former Pittsburgh Mayor Pete Flaherty in the general. Flaherty retains a strong following in the Pittsburgh media market from his bureaucracy-cutting days as mayor, although he left that office in 1977. But Flaherty has never raised a sizable campaign budget and has lost two races for the Senate and one for governor. In office Thornburgh proved to have a steady hand and cool judgment during the Three Mile Island nuclear plant crisis in 1979. He was successful enough in his state programs to get, through elections and through conversions, Republican margins in both houses of the legislature, making Pennsylvania the one major state where Republicans control the redistricting process. He is probably in a good position to be reelected in 1982.

Thornburgh's election completed a Republican sweep of the state's top offices, as Republicans have held both of the state's Senate seats. The leading Republican today in Pennsylvania politics is probably John Heinz, who was first elected to the Senate only in 1976. He won in a close-fought election. The contenders were two young (both 38) congressmen. Heinz from the Pittsburgh area where his family founded the H. J. Heinz food company, William J. Green from Philadelphia where his father was a congressman and Democratic party leader before him. The patterns of support ran along geographical rather than party lines, with Heinz carrying western Pennsylvania heavily and Green building huge margins in Philadelphia and other industrial centers in eastern Pennsylvania. The difference was money as much as anything else: Heinz spent some $2.6 million of his own money, and while Green's campaign was amply financed by most standards, he could come nowhere close to matching that figure.

Heinz was considered a liberal Republican when he was first elected, but he has fit in well with the new Republican majority and indeed had some part in creating it. He has concentrated on economic issues, which makes sense for a senator from this economically depressed state. He serves on the Senate Finance Committee and devotes much attention to its International Trade Subcommittee. Heinz does not want to be called a protectionist, but on issue after issue he is perhaps the Senate's most skeptical examiner of trade agreements and its most assiduous backer of forms of trade protection. He pushes for strict enforcement of antidumping laws; he watches particularly closely over the interests of the steel industry; and he is concerned about inexpensive imports of footwear and mushrooms.

Heinz has had major national political success as chairman of the Senate Republican Campaign Committee for the 1980 elections. He does not deserve all the credit, of course, for the fact that Republicans gained 12 seats and won control of the Senate for the first time in 28 years. But he deserves some. Altogether, nine Senate races were decided in 1980 by less than 2% of the vote, and the Republicans won seven of them. That was probably more than luck, or at least a case of luck favoring those who were best prepared. Heinz helped to channel aid to many Senate candidates who at first were given no chance, and he moved adroitly in the last weeks to aid those candidates who seemed about to pull upsets. Most did. Still, Heinz's Republican colleagues were not entirely grateful. After the 1980 elections he sought the post of chairman of the Senate Republican Conference and was defeated by James Mc-

Clure by a margin of 33 to 20. There is something about Heinz that stirs resentment or mis-trust among other politicians: he seems too unruffled, too successful at too young an age, perhaps too self-assured. With so big a big state as Pennsylvania behind him and plenty of money, he has the potential to be a national candidate but not the opening while the Reagan–Bush team is in office.

Heinz has emerged as a kind of powerhouse in Pennsylvania politics. He played a major role in financing Richard Thornburgh's campaign in 1978 and saw to it that Arlen Specter was well financed in 1980 — even though he and Specter had been rather bitter primary op-ponents four years before. Most big-state senators are vulnerable: they do something in their term that irritates almost every group of voters and are not well known personally to their constituents. Yet Heinz seems in good shape going into 1982. He has worked the state hard and his personal wealth tends to deter opposition: who wants to run against a candidate who can spend $2.6 million of his own money? Most likely he will not have a formidable oppo-nent in 1982 and will be reelected about as easily as any senator from this marginal state since the days in the 1920s when the Republican nomination was tantamount to election.

Pennsylvania's other Senate seat was held until 1980 by Richard Schweiker — a generally conservative Republican as a suburban Philadelphia congressman, a liberal senator with a 100% AFL–CIO rating during his first eight years in the Senate, and then a rather conserva-tive Republican after Ronald Reagan picked him as his candidate for vice president in 1976. Schweiker was embarrassed by that ploy, which did not bring him any significant number of votes from the Pennsylvania delegation; even his old friend and political ally, Drew Lewis, did not go with him. All is forgiven now, apparently; both Schweiker and Lewis are members of the Reagan cabinet. Schweiker evidently tired of Senate life or he took a gamble — and it seemed like a long shot at the time he announced his retirement — that Reagan or another Republican would be elected president.

The race for the open seat was one of those free-for-alls that Pennsylvanians have become accustomed to, with big fields in both parties' primaries, just as in the 1978 gubernatorial and 1976 senatorial elections. Again regional bases were of critical importance. In the Dem-ocratic primary, Pete Flaherty won an easy victory, as he had in 1974 and 1978, based on his popularity in the Pittsburgh area and all of western Pennsylvania that gets Pittsburgh tele-vision. In the Republican primary, former state chairman Bub Haabestad had two regional bases — the Pittsburgh area and most of the Philadelphia suburbs. Other candidates had bases at the periphery of the state, most of them areas covered by out-of-state television. Specter carried the rest: his hometown of Philadelphia, central Pennsylvania, the northeast, the far northwestern corner around Erie. Specter has been around the political track many times. He first achieved notice when, fresh from a stint as one of the Warren Commission's leading staffers, he switched to the Republican Party and was elected district attorney in Philadelphia in 1965. It was a stunning upset, but since then Specter has suffered more de-feats than victories. He was beaten for mayor of Philadelphia in 1967 by a beleaguered in-cumbent, James Tate. He was beaten for district attorney in 1973 by Emmet Fitzpatrick, who was later beaten himself. He lost the 1976 nomination for senator to John Heinz by some 26,000 votes, and he lost the 1978 nomination for governor to Richard Thornburgh by a considerably wider margin. By 1980 he had a threadbare look about him, yet the Demo-cratic candidate Flaherty had lost as many statewide races himself. The difference in 1980 is that Specter was better financed and the Republican national philosophy was much more attractive than anything the Democrats could offer.

Specter began his political career with the reputation as a liberal Republican, one who entered the party mainly because of the corruption and cliquishness of Philadelphia Democrats. In today's political climate he is more likely to be a regular Republican, simply because the party retains in early 1981 at least the kind of cohesion and agreement on basic programs that it developed as a minority during the Carter years. Specter, as a former prosecutor, serves on the Judiciary Committee, and it will be interesting to see on civil liberties and civil rights issues the extent to which he sticks with Chairman Strom Thurmond. He also has seats on Appropriations and Veterans' Affairs. By luck of the draw, Specter is one of the least senior of the new Republicans and so has no important subcommittee to chair. It would be idle speculation at this point to evaluate Specter's chances for reelection in 1986.

The defection of a state representative from the Democrats to the Republicans following the 1980 elections left the Republicans in charge of redistricting the 23 House seats Pennsylvania will have in 1982. One seat will almost surely vanish from Philadelphia, which currently has four; the other will likely come from Pittsburgh. The Democrats will probably lose both seats, and their hold on others may be endangered. Still, the Republicans do not have large enough legislative margins to do anything too fancy or that might unduly discommode some of their own incumbents.

The Pennsylvania House delegation has not usually been an especially distinguished one. Not to put too fine a point upon it, it has often been considered, despite the presence of some talented men, as a collection of political hacks. To some extent that image simply reflects the nuts-and-bolts character of Pennsylvania politics. Constituents do not want philosopher kings, but representatives who can bring home the bacon. Nonetheless, there is a striking contrast with even a delegation like that of Illinois, whose politics is no less practical. Abscam has resulted in the criminal convictions of two former Pennsylvania congressmen; both men, Michael Myers and Raymond Lederer, may be considered Frank Rizzo's contribution to Congress, since the former Philadelphia law-and-order mayor more or less personally selected both of them to run in 1976. Pennsylvania presently does not have any especially powerful House committee or subcommittee chairmen. Indeed, there has been considerable turnover in the delegation in the 1970s. Fully 12 of the 25 seats have, during the past decade, been represented by congressmen of both parties—which is remarkable especially when you consider that most of them were intended to be safe for one party or the other. So today the traditionally Republican suburbs of Delaware County are represented by at least one Democrat, while Republicans represent northeastern Philadelphia and the coal country around Scranton and Wilkes-Barre. The Democrats currently hold a 13–12 edge in the delegation, but they are likely to lose as many as five seats in 1982 (although they have a chance to pick up two or three).

Census Data Pop. (1980 final) 11,866,728, up 1% in 1970s: 5.24% of U.S. total, 4th largest. Central city, 25%; suburban, 55%. Median 4-person family income, 1978, $19,753, 97% of U.S., 28th highest.

1979 Share of Federal Tax Burden $24,074,000,000; 5.34% of U.S. total, 5th largest.

1979 Share of Federal Outlays $22,351,452,000; 4.83% of U.S. total, 4th largest.

DOD	$4,002,457,000	7th	(3.77%)	HEW	$10,872,381,000	3d	(6.08%)
DOE	$294,360,000	15th	(2.50%)	ERDA	$141,629,000	7th	(5.22%)
HUD	$416,716,000	3d	(6.32%)	NASA	$98,151,000	10th	(2.10%)
VA	$973,798,000	5th	(4.69%)	DOT	$868,947,000	5th	(5.27%)
EPA	$279,064,000	5th	(5.26%)	DOC	$190,021,000	5th	(6.00%)
DOI	$95,819,000	16th	(1.73%)	USDA	$583,136,000	12th	(2.43%)

Economic Base   Primary metal industries, especially blast furnaces and steel mills; finance, insurance, and real estate; apparel and other textile products, especially women's and misses' outerwear; machinery; electrical equipment and supplies, especially electronic components and accessories; fabricated metal products, especially structural metal products; food and kindred products, especially bakery products.

Political Lineup   Governor, Richard L. Thornburgh (R). Senators, H. John Heinz III (R) and Arlen Specter (R). Representatives, 25 (13 D and 12 R); 23 in 1982. State Senate, 50 (25 R, 23 D, and 2 vacancies); State House of Representatives, 203 (103 R and 100 D).

The Voters

Registration   5,754,287 Total. 3,072,700 D (53%); 2,374,303 R (41%); 307,284 other (5%).
Employment profile 1970   White collar, 45%. Blue collar, 42%. Service, 12%. Farm, 1%.
Ethnic groups   Black 1980, 9%. Hispanic 1980, 1%. Asian 1980, 1%. Total foreign stock 1970, 18%. Italy, 4%; Poland, Germany, UK, 2% each; USSR, Austria, Czechoslovakia, Ireland, 1% each.

Presidential Vote

1980	Reagan (R)	2,261,872	(50%)
	Carter (D)	1,937,540	(42%)
	Anderson (I)	292,921	(6%)
1976	Ford (R)	2,205,604	(48%)
	Carter (D)	2,328,677	(50%)

SENATORS

Sen. H. John Heinz III (R) Elected 1976, seat up 1982; b. Oct. 23, 1938, Pittsburgh; home, Pittsburgh; Yale U., B.A., Harvard U., M.B.A. 1963.

Career Marketing, H.J. Heinz Co., Pittsburgh, 1965-70; Sales Rep., International Harvester, Australia; Special Asst. to U.S. Sen. Hugh Scott, 1964; U.S. House of Reps., 1971-77.

Offices 443 RSOB, 202-224-6324. Also 9456 Wm. J. Green, Jr., Fed. Bldg., 4th and Arch Sts., Philadelphia 19106, 215-925-8750, and 2031 Fed. Bldg., Pittsburgh 15222, 412-562-0533.

Committees *Banking, Housing, and Urban Affairs* (3d). Subcommittees: Housing and Urban Affairs; International Finance and Monetary Policy (Chairman); Economic Policy; Rural Housing and Development.

Energy and Natural Resources (11th). Subcommittees: Energy Conservation and Supply; Energy Regulation; Energy and Mineral Resources.

Finance (6th). Subcommittees: International Trade; Economic Growth, Employment, and Revenue Sharing (Chairman); Health.

Special Committee on Aging (Chairman).

Group Ratings

	ADA	COPE	PC	LCV	CFA	RPN	NAB	NSI	NTU	ACA	ACU
1980	50	67	47	67	33	—	45	80	32	44	55
1979	42	59	46	—	29	—	—	—	26	44	56
1978	60	78	50	66	40	80	8	40	13	18	23

Key Votes

1) Draft Registn $	AGN	6) Fair Housng Cloture	FOR	11) Cut Socl Incr Defns	FOR
2) Ban $ to Nicrgua	AGN	7) Ban $ Rape Abortns	FOR	12) Income Tax Indexing	FOR
3) Dlay MX Missile	AGN	8) Cap on Food Stmp $	AGN	13) Lim Spdg 21% GNP	—
4) Nuclr Mortorium	FOR	9) New US Dep Edcatn	FOR	14) Incr Wndfll Prof Tax	FOR
5) Alaska Lands Bill	FOR	10) Cut OSHA Inspctns	FOR	15) Chryslr Loan Grntee	AGN

Election Results

1976 general	H. John Heinz III (R)	2,381,891	(52%)	($3,004,814)
	William Green (D)	2,126,977	(47%)	($1,269,409)
1976 primary	H. John Heinz III (R)	358,715	(42%)	
	Arlen Specter (R)	332,513	(39%)	
	George Packard (R)	160,379	(19%)	
1970 general	Hugh Scott (R)	1,874,106	(51%)	
	William G. Sesler (D)	1,653,774	(45%)	

Sen. Arlen Specter (R) Elected 1980, seat up 1986; b. Feb. 12, 1930, Wichita, Kans.; home, Philadelphia; U. of Penn., B.A. 1951, Yale U., J.D. 1956.

Career Air Force, 1951–53; Practicing atty.; Warren Commission, 1964; Phila. Dist. Atty., 1966–74, City Cncl., 1979.
Office 342 RSOB, 202-224-4254.

Committees *Appropriations* (15th). Subcommittees: Agriculture and Related Agencies; District of Columbia; Foreign Operations; HUD–Independent Agencies; Labor, Health and Human Services, Education.

Judiciary (10th). Subcommittees: Agency Administration; Criminal Law; Juvenile Justice (Chairman).

Veterans' Affairs (7th).

Group Ratings and Key Votes: Newly Elected

Election Results

1980 general	Arlen Specter (R)	2,230,404	(50%)	($1,588,588)
	Pete Flaherty (D)	2,122,391	(48%)	($633,861)
1980 primary	Arlen Specter (R)	419,372	(36%)	
	Bud Haabestad (R)	382,281	(33%)	($220,364)
	Six others (R)	350,406	(31%)	
1974 general	Richard S. Schweiker (R)........	1,843,317	(53%)	($799,499)
	Pete Flaherty (D)	1,596,121	(46%)	($256,483)

GOVERNOR

Gov. Richard L. Thornburgh (R) Elected 1978, term expires 1983; b. July 16, 1932, Pittsburgh; Yale U., B.S. 1954, U. of Pitt., LL.B. 1957.

Career Atty. and advisor, ALCOA, 1957–59; Practicing atty., 1959–69; U.S. Atty. for W. Pa., 1969–75; Asst. U.S. Atty. Gen., U.S. Department of Justice, 1975–77.

Offices Main Capitol, Harrisburg 17120, 717-787-2121.

Election Results

1978 gen.	Richard L. Thornburgh (R).	1,966,042	(53%)
	Pete Flaherty (D)	1,737,888	(46%)
1978 prim.	Richard L. Thornburgh (R).	323,349	(32%)
	Arlen Specter (R)	206,802	(21%)
	Bob Butera (R)	190,653	(19%)
	David W. Marston (R)	161,813	(16%)
	Three others (R)	113,373	(11%)
1974 gen.	Milton Shapp (D).........	1,878,252	(54%)
	Andrew L. Lewis (R)	1,578,917	(45%)

FIRST DISTRICT

The 1st district of Pennsylvania is the southern end of the city of Philadelphia. The Schuylkill River divides the district into two just about equal parts. On the west bank is the University of Pennsylvania and, beyond the campus, the West Philadelphia black ghetto. On the east side of the river is the heavily Italian–American neighborhood of South Philadelphia, the probable home of "Rocky," the fantasy heavyweight fighter. This has always been the stronghold of former Mayor Frank Rizzo, the first politician of Italian descent in Philadelphia to achieve prominence and still a kind of folk hero in these parts for his spirited opposition to blacks and intellectual liberals.

Back during the Kennedy years of the early 1960s, both South and West Philadelphia voted heavily Democratic. But in the late 1960s and early 1970s, as black areas were voting Democratic with near unanimity, South Philadelphia shifted to the right. Rizzo began his police career here and achieved considerable prominence; he rose enough in society to attend events in black tie, but he was still proud enough of his background as a tough cop to wear a billy club in his cummerbund. Rizzo was elected mayor in 1971 and reelected over weak opposition in 1975. Long before his second term ended, Rizzo was besmirched with scandal; and although he kept South Philadelphia's loyalty to the end, he could not get the city's voters to change the charter to allow him to run for a third term.

This is the kind of district that is more concerned with city politics than with national affairs, and its congressmen have reflected that inclination. For 28 years, until his death in 1976, the district was represented by William Barrett, a man who showed little interest in the business of the Banking Committee on which he ranked just behind the chairman but did find time to come home to Philadelphia every night and hold court for constituents who had problems he could solve. The next congressman, Michael (Ozzie) Myers, a former cargo checker on the Philadelphia waterfront, was Frank Rizzo's hand-picked choice for the district. Myers evidently had an unusual idea of the role of a congressman in society. In 1979 he got into a fistfight with a Washington area restaurant waiter who he believed was not showing proper deference to a member of Congress; in 1980 he accepted apparently as his due a

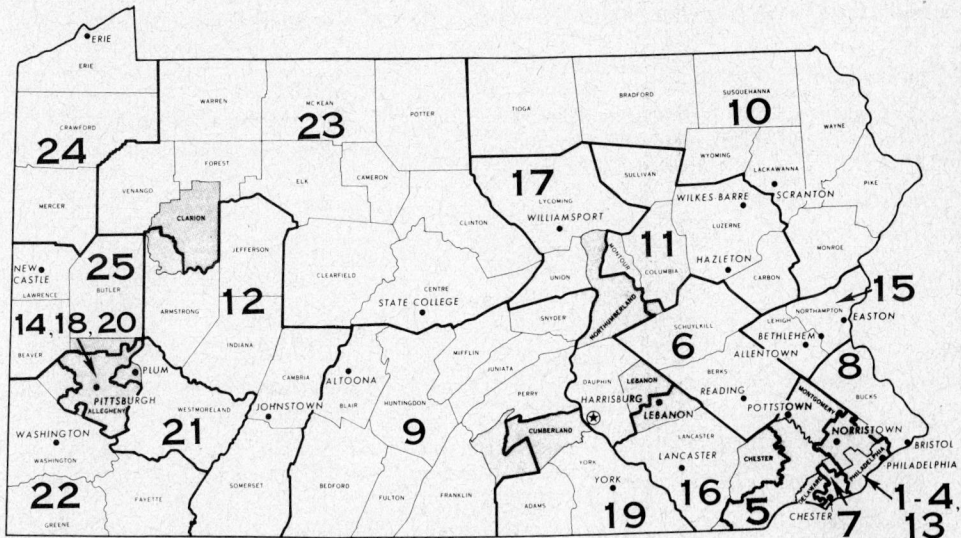

$50,000 bribe from an Arab sheik who turned out to be a government agent. "Money talks in this business," Myers was recorded as saying, "and b---s--- walks." Myers was convicted by a jury on bribery charges but tried to keep his seat in the House; he was expelled almost unanimously, the first member to be so ousted since three Confederate Army volunteers were expelled in 1861. Other members were not only displeased that he was willing to take a bribe, but they were disgusted by his gross language and contempt for any standard of public service.

Myers pleaded for his seat with his colleagues; he fought to be returned to it by his constituents. He had more support among the latter, but not enough to win. The 1st district is not the kind of place to go Republican; the black votes, if nothing else, keep it in the Democratic column, and it delivered solid majorities even for George McGovern in 1972 and Jimmy Carter in 1980. Myers was renominated in the April primary with 30% of the vote against 14 other candidates, and he refused Mayor William Green's demand that he withdraw. So Green supporters backed independent candidate Thomas Foglietta, a longtime Republican member of the Philadelphia Council who appeared likely if elected to vote in the House as a Democrat. On November 4 Myers could win only 34% of the vote; Foglietta had 38% and a hapless Republican, 24%.

Foglietta now serves as a member of the Armed Services and Merchant Marine Committees. Both have importance to Philadelphia. The city has been striving to keep the Defense Department operating the Frankford Arsenal, which is in the 3d district, and the Philadelphia Navy Yard, which is in the 1st; Foglietta will be pushing for both. He sits on the Military Installations and Seapower subcommittees. On Merchant Marine he can be counted on to support maritime subsidies.

For Foglietta 1982 might prove to offer as exacting a race as 1980, although in a different way. The problem is redistricting. The Republican legislature will probably reduce Philadelphia from four districts to three, which means Foglietta may have to run against whoever is Raymond Lederer's successor in the 3d district in the Democratic primary. Since neither candidate will have had much experience, it should be a rip-roaring fight with no clear outcome.

Census Data   Pop. (1980 final) 404,943, down 15% in 1970s. Median family income, 1970, $8,690, 91% of U.S.

The Voters

Employment profile 1970   White collar, 43%. Blue collar, 40%. Service, 17%. Farm, –%.
Ethnic groups   Black 1980, 45%. Hispanic 1980, 1%. Asian 1980, 1%. Total foreign stock 1970, 23%. Italy, 13%; USSR, Ireland, 2% each; UK, 1%.

Presidential Vote

1980	Reagan (R)	53,279	(33%)
	Carter (D)	105,609	(66%)
	Anderson (I)	8,019	(1%)
1976	Ford (R)	50,923	(29%)
	Carter (D)	122,695	(70%)

Rep. Thomas M. Foglietta (D) Elected 1980; b.Dec. 3, 1928, Philadelphia; home, Philadelphia; St. Joseph's Col., B.A. 1949, Temple U., J.D. 1952.

Career   Practicing atty., 1952–80; Phila. City Cncl., 1955–75; Rep. nominee for Mayor of Phila., 1975; Regional Dir., U.S. Dept. of Labor, 1976.

Offices   1217 LHOB, 202-225-4731. Also Wm. J. Green Fed. Bldg., 600 Arch St., Philadelphia 19106, 215-925-6840.

Committees   *Armed Services* (23d). Subcommittees: Military Installations and Facilities; Seapower and Strategic and Critical Materials.

Merchant Marine and Fisheries (17th). Subcommittees: Coast Guard and Navigation; Merchant Marine; Panama Canal and Outer Continental Shelf.

Group Ratings and Key Votes: Newly Elected

Election Results

1980 general	Thomas M. Foglietta (I)	58,737	(38%)	($142,835)
	Michael O. Myers (D)	52,956	(34%)	($45,926)
	Robert R. Burke (R)...........	37,893	(24%)	($37,484)
1980 primary	Thomas M. Foglietta (I), unopposed			
1978 general	Michael O. Myers (D)	104,412	(72%)	($50,069)
	Samuel N. Fanelli (R)...........	37,913	(26%)	

SECOND DISTRICT

The 2d district of Pennsylvania is an oddly shaped chunk of Philadelphia. Although the 2d was designed as the city's black district, it does not center on one of the city's two large black neighborhoods. Instead, the district takes in part of West Philadelphia and then moves across Fairmount Park and the Schuylkill River to encompass part of the North Philadelphia community. The 2d proceeds north to include some of the more middle-class integrated areas of Germantown, which at the time of the Revolution was a town separate from Philadelphia altogether. The district then goes all the way out to the WASP upper-income precincts of Chestnut Hill, where some of Philadelphia's most prominent families have lived for generations. Chestnut Hill usually goes Republican, but its votes are swamped in the 2d by the huge Democratic majorities coming out of the black neighborhoods to the south and east. Altogether, the 2d consistently reports the largest Democratic percentages in Pennsylvania.

For 20 years the 2d district was represented by Robert Nix, a politician who made few waves of any kind. Although in his last term he inherited the chair of the Post Office and Civil Service Committee, he was one of the least active congressmen. It was no surprise when he was defeated in the 1978 Democratic primary; indeed, he had nearly lost in every primary since 1970.

The man who beat Nix is William Gray, a young Baptist minister who had nearly won in 1976. Almost as soon as he got sworn in, Gray was being hailed as one of the most politically astute freshman members. He won a seat on the Budget Committee and also took a seat on Foreign Affairs, generally considered less desirable; but he accumulated some chits from others whom he helped to win a committee seat he might have had himself. After the 1980 election he collected. He obtained a seat on the Appropriations Committee and serves on its subcommittees on Transportation and Foreign Operations.

Gray's voting record is solidly liberal, but he seems, like many of the other younger black members, to be somewhat more pragmatic and less militant in approach than some of the black congressmen elected in the late 1960s and early 1970s. His prospects for continued service seem greater than those of any of Philadelphia's other congressmen. It is unlikely that the Republican legislature will eliminate the 2d in redistricting. Rather, Republicans will be happy to put as many heavily Democratic black precincts in this district as possible, to keep them out of neighboring seats.

Census Data   Pop. (1980 final) 392,550, down 16% in 1970s. Median family income, 1970, $8,670, 90% of U.S.

The Voters

Employment profile 1970   White collar, 49%. Blue collar, 33%. Service, 18%. Farm, –%.
Ethnic groups   Black 1980, 75%. Hispanic 1980, 1%. Total foreign stock 1970, 15%. USSR, 4%; Italy, 2%; Ireland, UK, Germany, 1% each.

Presidential Vote

1980	Reagan (R)	21,639	(13%)
	Carter (D)	130,678	(82%)
	Anderson (I)	6,547	(4%)
1976	Ford (R)	31,264	(19%)
	Carter (D)	128,921	(79%)

Rep. William H. Gray III (D) Elected 1978; b. Aug. 20, 1942, Baton Rouge, La.; home, Philadelphia; Franklin and Marshall Col., B.A. 1963, Drew Theological Seminary, M.A. 1966, 1972, Princeton U. M.A., 1970.

Career   Minister and church history professor.

Offices   429 CHOB, 202-225-4001. Also 6753 Germantown Ave., Philadelphia 19119, 215 438-6070.

Committees *Appropriations* (32d). Subcommittees: Foreign Operations; Transportation.

District of Columbia (6th). Subcommittee: Government Operations and Metropolitan Affairs (Chairman).

Group Ratings

	ADA	COPE	PC	LCV	CFA	RPN	NAB	NSI	NTU	ACA	ACU
1980	72	95	73	81	86	—	0	0	17	19	14
1979	100	100	80	88	81	—	—	—	18	0	5

Key Votes

1) Draft Registn $	—	6) Fair Hsg DOJ Enfrc	FOR	11) Cut Socl Incr Dfns $	AGN
2) Ban $ to Nicrgua	AGN	7) Lim PAC Contrbtns	FOR	12) Hosptl Cost Controls	FOR
3) Dlay MX Missile	FOR	8) Cap on Food Stmp $	AGN	13) Gasln Ctrls & Allctns	FOR
4) Nuclr Mortorium	FOR	9) New US Dep Edcatn	AGN	14) Lim Wndfll Prof Tax	AGN
5) Alaska Lands Bill	FOR	10) Cut OSHA $	AGN	15) Chryslr Loan Grntee	FOR

Election Results

1980 general	William H. Gray III (D)	127,106	(96%)	($182,192)
	Two others (I, Consumer)	5,865	(4%)	
1980 primary	William H. Gray III (D)	52,360	(100%)	
1978 general	William H. Gray III (D)	132,594	(82%)	($225,887)
	Roland Atkins (R)	25,785	(16%)	($24,877)

THIRD DISTRICT

Despite the opinion of W. C. Fields, Center City Philadelphia is one of the more pleasant of American downtowns. The height of buildings here was kept for years to a reasonable 38 stories by an old ordinance that allowed nothing higher than the spire on Philadelphia's ornate City Hall. A large urban renewal project has gone up on the site of old Penn Central tracks, long known as the Chinese wall. Not far from the office buildings are the elegant Victorian neighborhoods around Rittenhouse Square and the restored 18th-century townhouses of Society Hill. But as one moves north a few blocks out of Center City, there are 19th-century suburbs that have long since become slums. Some of these areas along with much of Center City and Society Hill are part of Pennsylvania's 3d congressional district.

At its western fringes, the 3d also takes in part of the black neighborhood of North Philadelphia. But most of the district is made up of white neighborhoods where levels of income and education are little higher than in black ghettos. An example is Kensington, north of Center City, which seems to have been transported intact from the 1930s. Here, in the red brick Philadelphia row houses, live the Irish and Italians left behind after the postwar exodus to the suburbs. Most of these people own their own houses — Philadelphia is a city of homeowners, not renters. But the value of this real estate is pathetically low, since there is little demand for it. According to the Census Bureau, the median value of a homeowner's house here in 1970 was $7,800 — lower than in any other Philadelphia district. Kensington and neighborhoods like it are traditionally Democratic; they also tended to favor Frank Rizzo during his years of prominence in Philadelphia politics.

This area has remained Democratic through all vicissitudes. When Congressman William Green ran for the U.S. Senate in 1976, the new congressman was chosen by then Mayor Frank Rizzo. He was Raymond Lederer, a former football coach and probation officer, and a popular member of the state legislature. Lederer won Green's seat on the Ways and Means Committee and distinguished himself as an opponent of sugar quotas. He seemed to be an amiable, decent backbencher. But then he became famous as one of the Abscam defendants. He was indicted before the Democratic primary (held in April) of 1980 and was tried and convicted after the general election. He won 42% of the vote against six opponents in the primary. In the general, an independent candidate filed against him but withdrew; the candidate of the Consumer Party, a Pennsylvania group that adopted Barry Commoner for its presidential candidate, got 10% of the vote. So for the most part it was a battle of Republican versus Democrat, and the Democrat won handily.

Lederer did not fare so well in the House. After his conviction, the Democrats declined to give him any committee assignments; his Ways and Means seat went to Don Bailey of western Pennsylvania. He resisted a move to oust him from the House on the grounds his appeal has not been heard; but in May 1981 he finally resigned. The prospect at this writing is that there will be a special election some time in 1981 to fill it. The winner of that election may not have long to serve, however. The Republican legislature is likely to eliminate one of Philadelphia's four House seats, and the easiest one to eliminate demographically and politically is the 3d. A Democrat is almost certain to win any special election here, perhaps city chairman David Glancy, an ally of Mayor Green. But if the new congressman wants a second term, he could find himself no sooner elected than launched into a primary fight with Thomas Foglietta of the 1st district or a general election contest with Republican Charles Dougherty of the 4th.

Census Data Pop. (1980 final) 392,084, down 17% in 1970s. Median family income, 1970, $8,368, 87% of U.S.

The Voters

Employment profile 1970 White collar, 40%. Blue collar, 45%. Service, 15%. Farm, –%.
Ethnic groups Black 1980, 32%. Hispanic 1980, 12%. Asian 1980, 1%. Total foreign stock 1970, 22%. Poland, 4%; Italy, USSR, 3% each; Germany, UK, Ireland, 2% each.

Presidential Vote

1980	Reagan (R)	46,147	(32%)
	Carter (D)	86,220	(60%)
	Anderson (I)	8,349	(6%)
1976	Ford (R)	47,471	(31%)
	Carter (D)	101,997	(67%)

Rep. Raymond F. Lederer (D) Resigned in May 1981. Special election for new congressman had not been held by press time.

Election Results

1980 general	Raymond F. Lederer (D)	67,942	(55%)	($158,026)
	William J. Phillips (R)	40,866	(33%)	($33,580)
	Max Weiner (Consumer)	11,849	(10%)	($9,743)
1980 primary	Raymond F. Lederer (D)	20,093	(42%)	
	Dennis Waterman (D)	10,195	(21%)	($125,732)
	Donald P. Sullivan (R)	7,257	(15%)	
	Four others (R)	10,249	(21%)	
1978 general	Raymond F. Lederer (D)	86,015	(72%)	($106,284)
	Raymond S. Kauffman (R)	33,750	(28%)	($6,850)

FOURTH DISTRICT

The 4th congressional district of Pennsylvania is northeastern Philadelphia, the most middle-class and prosperous part of the city. In fact, it is still growing. Geographically, most of the 4th is farther from Center City than the Main Line suburbs. Out here, some 10 to 20 miles from Independence Hall, middle-income suburban tract housing was still going up during the 1960s. In fact, more than half the housing units in northeastern Philadelphia were built after 1950; in the rest of the city, more than 80% went up before that. Most of the 4th's residents once lived in more crowded areas closer to Center City, and the district has a fair ethnic mixture, one representing the outward movement of various groups. Of these, the Jews have been most important politically, with more than half the city's Jewish residents living in this district. There are also plenty of Irish and other Catholics and a few blacks; but the 4th does not include many old-line Italian or other ethnic communities.

The 4th is the only one of Philadelphia's districts to be represented by a Republican, indeed the only district in the city that has elected a Republican congressman since 1956. Republicans made serious efforts to win the district in 1966 and 1972, but they succeeded in 1978 only because of the legal problems of Congressman Joshua Eilberg. A product of machine Democratic politics, Eilberg was first elected in 1966 and served on the Judiciary Committee, where he cast one of the votes to impeach Richard Nixon. He also chaired the Immigration Subcommittee, an area of increasing controversy with rising illegal immigration. Eilberg made the headlines in November 1977 when he called President Carter and complained of the investigating tactics of Philadelphia's holdover U.S. Attorney, David Marston; the call got Carter as well as Eilberg into considerable political trouble.

Republicans smelled opportunity and in 1978 ran a strong candidate: Charles Dougherty, who represented a substantial part of the district in the Pennsylvania Senate. In September Eilberg was charged by the House Ethics Committee with accepting more than $100,000 from his law firm and two affiliated firms that were helping a Philadelphia hospital get a federal grant. Just before the election he was indicted; the result was a 56% victory for Dougherty. After the election Eilberg pleaded guilty and was given five years on probation.

Curiously, Dougherty's biggest problem for 1980 turned out to be not his Democratic opponent but his fellow Republicans. The most prominent Republican in these parts is Billy Meehan, longtime city Republican chairman, who has a map of Ireland for a face and as canny an understanding of politics as anyone in Philadelphia. Meehan and Dougherty feuded; and despite all the advantages of incumbency, Dougherty could get no more than 51% in the primary against Meehan's candidate. In the general, things were much easier. The Democrat, a veteran of the building trades and of the Frank Rizzo political wars (on which he fought on both sides), antagonized many liberal and Jewish voters without getting much support among conservatives and Catholics. The result was nearly a 2–1 Dougherty victory —perhaps the best any Republican has ever done within the bounds of this district.

Can Dougherty repeat in 1982? The first question is whether he can repair his differences with Meehan's Republicans. If he does not, he will probably not get a favorable district out of the legislature. The 4th must add some population, and the addition of some heavily Democratic wards could completely upset the current balance of the district. Even if Dougherty gets a favorable district, he still must run ahead of virtually all Republicans in order to be competitive. It will help if he draws, as he did in 1980, a Democratic opponent with serious weaknesses. He has assets in his committee assignments—Armed Services and Merchant Marine, the same pair as Thomas Foglietta of the 1st district. Both assignments make a difference to Philadelphia, one of the nation's leading ports and home of what it hopes will continue to be the busy Frankford Arsenal. (Dougherty, a former Marine, has also distinguished himself as one of the committee's foremost defenders of the Marine Corps.) Dougherty has already pretty well tailored his voting record to this district which, unlike most, still seems to believe in generous federal spending programs. Accordingly, he is one Republican who could conceivably be hurt by identification with the Reagan Administration's economic programs.

Census Data Pop. (1980 final) 449,684, down 5% in 1970s. Median family income, 1970, $11,069, 115% of U.S.

The Voters

Employment profile 1970 White collar, 57%. Blue collar, 33%. Service, 10%. Farm, –%.
Ethnic groups Black 1980, 8%. Hispanic 1980, 1%. Asian 1980, 1%. Total foreign stock 1970, 32%. USSR, 8%; Italy, Germany, 4% each; Poland, Ireland, UK, 3% each; Austria, 1%.

Presidential Vote

1980	Reagan (R)	107,919	(50%)
	Carter (D)	86,344	(40%)
	Anderson (I)	17,354	(8%)
1976	Ford (R)	96,820	(42%)
	Carter (D)	129,639	(56%)

Rep. Charles F. Dougherty (R) Elected 1978; b. June 26, 1937, Philadelphia; home, Philadelphia; St. Joseph's Col., B.S. 1959, U. of Penn., Temple U.

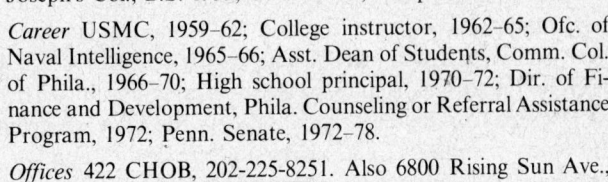

Career USMC, 1959–62; College instructor, 1962–65; Ofc. of Naval Intelligence, 1965–66; Asst. Dean of Students, Comm. Col. of Phila., 1966–70; High school principal, 1970–72; Dir. of Finance and Development, Phila. Counseling or Referral Assistance Program, 1972; Penn. Senate, 1972–78.

Offices 422 CHOB, 202-225-8251. Also 6800 Rising Sun Ave., Philadelphia 19111, 215-742-4479.

Committees *Armed Services* (12th). Subcommittees: Military Installations and Facilities; Seapower and Strategic and Critical Materials.

Merchant Marine and Fisheries (11th). Subcommittees: Coast Guard and Navigation; Fisheries and Wildlife Conservation and the Environment; Merchant Marine.

Group Ratings

	ADA	COPE	PC	LCV	CFA	RPN	NAB	NSI	NTU	ACA	ACU
1980	39	62	33	60	36	—	27	67	17	43	31
1979	5	55	30	45	27	—	—	—	20	42	46

Key Votes

1) Draft Registn $	—	6) Fair Hsg DOJ Enfrc	AGN	11) Cut Socl Incr Dfns $	AGN
2) Ban $ to Nicrgua	AGN	7) Lim PAC Contrbtns	—	12) Hosptl Cost Controls	AGN
3) Dlay MX Missile	AGN	8) Cap on Food Stmp $	AGN	13) Gasln Ctrls & Allctns	FOR
4) Nuclr Mortorium	AGN	9) New US Dep Edcatn	FOR	14) Lim Wndfll Prof Tax	FOR
5) Alaska Lands Bill	AGN	10) Cut OSHA $	AGN	15) Chrysl Loan Grntee	FOR

Election Results

1980 general	Charles F. Dougherty (R)........	127,475	(63%)	($256,961)
	Thomas J. Magrann (D).........	73,895	(37%)	($248,946)
1980 primary	Charles F. Dougherty (R)........	21,923	(51%)	
	Dennis M. O'Brien (R)	21,440	(49%)	($16,590)
1978 general	Charles F. Dougherty (R)........	110,445	(56%)	($130,837)
	Joshua Eilberg (D)	87,555	(44%)	($159,904)

FIFTH DISTRICT

The 5th congressional district of Pennsylvania can be called an exurban Philadelphia district. It takes in the outer edges of suburban Delaware and Montgomery Counties, along with most of Chester County farther out. Although technically all within the Philadelphia metropolitan area, the 5th is really a kind of borderland where the influence of Philadelphia wanes and that of the Pennsylvania Dutch country begins. It is the kind of country John O'Hara described: grimy, small industrial towns surrounded by large suburban estates, and the perfectly tended farms of the Chadds Ford area, where the Wyeth family lives and paints. Not far away is the sleepy town of Oxford, home of Lincoln University, one of the nation's oldest black colleges—and a symbol of the area's Lincoln Republican heritage. Around Kennett Square, in the southern part of the district, is the center of America's mushroom industry. The 5th also contains many of the famed Main Line suburbs of Philadelpha, so named because they lay on the main line of what was once the prosperous Pennsylvania Railroad. The 5th is a Republican district, very Republican. The only time it has been known to go Democratic was in the 1964 presidential election, and then by a very narrow margin.

The current Congressman, Republican Richard Schulze, easily won his party's primary in 1974 after serving three terms in the Pennsylvania legislature. Schulze's predecessors had been conservatives in their 60s; he was first elected at age 45. His record in the House has been in line with conventional Republican philosophy. He is a member of the House Ways and Means Committee, where he works for strict enforcement of antidumping legislation. He tends to support trade barriers of one kind or another, particularly against imports of Japanese steel and Taiwanese mushrooms.

Census Data Pop. (1980 final) 525,619, up 11% in 1970s. Median family income, 1970, $12,148, 127% of U.S.

The Voters

Employment profile 1970 White collar, 54%. Blue collar, 35%. Service, 9%. Farm, 2%.
Ethnic groups Black 1980, 5%. Hispanic 1980, 1%. Asian 1980, 1%. Total foreign stock 1970, 15%. Italy, 3%; UK, Germany, 2% each; Ireland, 1%.

Presidential Vote

1980	Reagan (R)	129,775	(61%)
	Carter (D)	61,107	(29%)
	Anderson (I)	17,512	(8%)
1976	Ford (R)	121,190	(61%)
	Carter (D)	77,048	(39%)

Rep. Richard T. Schulze (R) Elected 1974; b. Aug. 7, 1929, Philadelphia; home, Malvern; U. of Houston, 1949–50, Villanova U., 1952.

Career Army, 1951–53; Proprietor, Home Appliance Ctr., Paoli; Chester Co. Register of Wills and Clerk of Orphans Ct., 1967–69; Penn. House of Reps., 1969–74.

Offices 2444 RHOB, 202-225-5761. Also 2 W. Lancaster Ave., Paoli 19301, 215-648-0555.

Committee *Ways and Means* (9th). Subcommittees: Select Revenue Measures; Trade.

Group Ratings

	ADA	COPE	PC	LCV	CFA	RPN	NAB	NSI	NTU	ACA	ACU
1980	0	17	20	17	21	—	92	100	53	86	89
1979	5	15	15	13	7	—	—	—	58	92	92
1978	10	16	20	27	23	64	83	100	39	88	87

Key Votes

1) Draft Registn $	—	6) Fair Hsg DOJ Enfrc	AGN	11) Cut Socl Incr Dfns $	FOR
2) Ban $ to Nicrgua	FOR	7) Lim PAC Contrbtns	AGN	12) Hosptl Cost Controls	AGN
3) Dlay MX Missile	AGN	8) Cap on Food Stmp $	FOR	13) Gasln Ctrls & Allctns	AGN
4) Nuclr Mortorium	FOR	9) New US Dep Edcatn	AGN	14) Lim Wndfll Prof Tax	FOR
5) Alaska Lands Bill	AGN	10) Cut OSHA $	FOR	15) Chryslr Loan Grntee	AGN

Election Results

1980 general	Richard T. Schulze (R)	148,898	(75%)	($133,815)
	Grady G. Brickhouse (D)	47,092	(24%)	($4,761)
1980 primary	Richard T. Schulze (R)	60,247	(100%)	
1978 general	Richard T. Schulze (R)	110,565	(75%)	($124,390)
	Murray P. Zealor (D)	36,704	(25%)	($5,354)

SIXTH DISTRICT

The 6th congressional district of Pennsylvania includes Berks and Schuylkill Counties and a small portion of Northumberland County. This is a region of both industry and agriculture, on the margin between the industrial Northeast and the Pennsylvania Dutch country. Schuylkill County is anthracite country: on rugged hills, a collection of small towns first set up to scrape the hard coal from underground, now scrambling for whatever industry they can attract. Reading, in Berks County, is a factory town, famous in the 19th century for its black broad-brimmed hats and in the early 20th century for its ironware manufactures. The Reading Railroad once made this one of the major rail centers in the country. It is now a center for light, not heavy, industry, and its old brick factories are used for factory outlet stores that attract buyers from all over the East.

The Dutch country obtrudes into Berks County, but politically the 6th district is more industrial than Dutch. The factory workers of Reading and the anthracite miners, or former miners, of Schuylkill County towns such as Tamaqua and Mahanoy City and Pottsville vote Democratic in most elections. Their votes are usually about evenly matched by Republican margins cast in the southern, more agricultural part of the district. The hard-pressed conditions of local industry have, if anything, strengthened the 6th's Democratic leanings. Even so, the district is more Democratic in local than national elections; it barely went for Jimmy Carter in 1976 and in 1980 was heavily for Reagan.

The current Congressman, Gus Yatron, was first elected in 1968. Owner of a local ice cream business in Reading, he was a 12-year veteran of the state legislature. In the House he serves on the Foreign Affairs Committee; he was part of the group of Greek-American congressmen who led the fight to cut off arms sales to Turkey because of its invasion of Cyprus. In 1977 he became chairman of the panel's Inter-American Affairs Subcommittee. But in 1981 he was voted out of that position by the committee's Democrats by a 10-9 vote. Evidently there was feeling that Yatron was an inactive chairman and did not represent the views of Democrats who, like the new chairman, Michael Barnes of Maryland, are wary of the Reagan Administration's support of right-wing dictators. The sudden loss of the chair

950 PENNSYLVANIA

was undoubtedly a crushing experience for Yatron, but it was a good illustration of the accountability of committee chairmen now that they are not chosen strictly by the seniority system.

Yatron otherwise has not had a particularly controversial career. He votes with Democrats on most economic issues and generally has high labor ratings; he is more conservative on cultural issues. Despite the marginal nature of the district in statewide elections, he is regularly reelected by wide margins. It does not seem likely that the Republican redistricters will try to hurt him; he would be difficult to dislodge, yet if he does not run this is a district a Republican could win. What is not certain is whether Yatron's loss of a chairmanship will hurt him — whether it will be interpreted as a loss of clout or, to the extent it is noticed, as a minor ruckus about an issue most Pennsylvanians do not care much about anyway.

Census Data Pop. (1980 final) 488,524, up 3% in 1970s. Median family income, 1970, $9,009, 94% of U.S.

The Voters

Employment profile 1970 White collar, 35%. Blue collar, 53%. Service, 10%. Farm, 2%.
Ethnic groups Black 1980, 2%. Hispanic 1980, 2%. Total foreign stock 1970, 14%. Poland, 3%; Italy, Germany, 2% each; Austria, Lithuania, 1% each.

Presidential Vote

1980	Reagan (R)	100,019	(56%)
	Carter (D)	65,269	(36%)
	Anderson (I)	12,240	(7%)
1976	Ford (R)	89,194	(49%)
	Carter (D)	90,203	(49%)

Rep. Gus Yatron (D) Elected 1968; b. Oct. 16, 1927, Reading; home, Reading; Kutztown St. Teachers Col., 1950.

Career Pro heavyweight boxer; Proprietor, Yatron's Ice Cream, 1950–69; Mbr., Reading Sch. Bd., 1955–60; Penn. House of Reps., 1956–60; Penn. Senate, 1960–68.

Offices 2267 RHOB, 202-225-5546. Also U.S.P.O. Bldg, 5th and Washington Sts., Reading 19603, 215-375-4573.

Committees *Foreign Affairs* (7th). Subcommittees: Inter-American Affairs; International Operations.

Post Office and Civil Service (9th). Subcommittees: Census and Population; Civil Service.

Group Ratings

	ADA	COPE	PC	LCV	CFA	RPN	NAB	NSI	NTU	ACA	ACU
1980	39	71	37	54	29	—	58	80	34	50	42
1979	26	65	45	47	59	—	—	—	35	42	32
1978	40	60	28	57	41	42	33	78	12	44	54

Key Votes

1) Draft Registn $	AGN	6) Fair Hsg DOJ Enfrc	AGN	11) Cut Socl Incr Dfns $	FOR
2) Ban $ to Nicrgua	FOR	7) Lim PAC Contrbtns	FOR	12) Hosptl Cost Controls	AGN
3) Dlay MX Missile	FOR	8) Cap on Food Stmp $	AGN	13) Gasln Ctrls & Allctns	FOR
4) Nuclr Mortorium	—	9) New US Dep Edcatn	FOR	14) Lim Wndfll Prof Tax	FOR
5) Alaska Lands Bill	AGN	10) Cut OSHA $	AGN	15) Chryslr Loan Grntee	FOR

Election Results

1980 general	Gus Yatron (D)	117,965	(67%)	($66,845)
	George Hulshart (R)	57,844	(33%)	($13,321)
1980 primary	Gus Yatron (D)	51,972	(100%)	
1978 general	Gus Yatron (D)	106,431	(74%)	($55,589)
	Stephen Mazur (R)	37,746	(26%)	

SEVENTH DISTRICT

The 7th congressional district of Pennsylvania contains the larger part of Delaware County, a unit that until the 1980 census has contained more people than the entire state of Delaware just to the south. This is, indeed since the turn of the century has been, a suburban area southwest of Philadelphia, but for the most part not an exclusive one. The towns here are strung out, not on the main line of the old Pennsylvania Railroad, but along less fashionable tracks and radial roads. There are leafy, WASPy suburbs here, such as Swarthmore, around the distinguished college of that name. But the more typical suburb is a place such as Upper Darby, where the grandchildren of immigrants who lived in South or West Philadelphia have moved out from the crowded row-house neighborhoods to the relatively spacious and middle-class streets of Delaware County.

The dominant political institution here for years was the Delaware County War Board, a Republican machine that rivals in age the old Republican machine that for so many years ruled Philadelphia. The War Board's initial strength was among the county's Anglo–Saxon Protestants, but it adapted well to new tides of suburban immigration and won strong support from the Irish– and Italian– and Polish–Americans who moved here over the past four or five decades. But the War Board's power seems to have diminished in the 1970s. It decided to purge the incumbent in the 1974 congressional primary and was only barely able to do so; it was then unable to elect its candidate in the general election.

The winner of that election was 31-year-old Methodist minister Robert Edgar, and despite the district's Republican background he is still the congressman today. He has taken a number of initiatives to build up his local popularity. As a member of the Public Works Committee, he blocked the Rivers and Harbors bill of 1978 and has led the fight against the Tennessee–Tombigbee Waterway. He has pushed for mass transit legislation—this district is still served by commuter rail and public transit lines—and helped organize a "snow-belt" caucus of representatives from northeastern and midwest states. The Northeast-Midwest Caucus has conducted some of the most useful research on federal spending patterns, to document its charges that these older and assertedly needier regions of the country are being shortchanged. Edgar also broke with political protocol when he called for formal investigations of Pennsylvania Democrats Daniel Flood and Joshua Eilberg—a popular move in upper-income precincts. He has been an innovator on the Veterans' Affairs Committee, on which he now heads the Education, Training, and Employment Subcommittee. He tends to support such measures as counseling centers and readjustment programs for Vietnam veterans and elimination of the contribution servicemen must make to get veterans' education benefits. He has been one of the leaders of the innovative approach on this often unnoticed committee.

Yet Edgar has always been poised at the edge of political defeat. He sees himself not as an upper-income voters' congressman but as a man who represents the working class from which he himself sprang; and he has almost impeccable liberal voting records on economic as well as cultural issues. He has been vulnerable for supporting high domestic spending and opposing higher defense spending. Still, in 1980 he was able to reverse the trend of declining percentages. He had won reelection in 1978 by only 1,368 votes, and he was targeted by Republicans. He had an attractive young opponent. But he managed to rally his supporters. Environmentalists conducted a major canvass of voters for him. He stressed his opposition to special interest groups, his fight to cut back the water projects, and his efforts to get jobs for the district. The final result was a 53% Edgar victory.

This is not a large margin, but it went against the national trend. The prospects, however, are that Edgar will be tested again in 1982. The Republican legislature will be redrawing the district lines, and the 7th district lost a lot of population in the 1970s — not so much because of abandonment of neighborhoods as because people's children grew up and moved away. (This is in fact the phenomenon that accounts for most of the population loss that has brought reductions in federal aid to the Northeast and Midwest.) The legislature will probably add to the 7th Haverford and Radnor Townships, Main Line suburbs that are more Republican than the current district and less familiar with Edgar. This almost guarantees Edgar another difficult race, although these are sociologically the kind of suburban areas where he has eaten into Republican strength in the past. It is conceivable that he might, as has sometimes been suggested, run for the Senate, although the odds on a race for John Heinz's seat would seem — simply from the point of view of obtaining campaign funds — forbidding.

Census Data   Pop. (1980 final) 421,368, down 10% in 1970s. Median family income, 1970, $11,383, 119% of U.S.

The Voters

Employment profile 1970   White collar, 57%. Blue collar, 33%. Service, 10%. Farm, –%.
Ethnic groups   Black 1980, 11%. Hispanic 1980, 1%. Asian 1980, 1%. Total foreign stock 1970, 21%. Italy, 6%; Ireland, UK, 3% each; Germany, Poland, USSR, 1% each.

Presidential Vote

1980	Reagan (R)	106,145	(55%)
	Carter (D)	69,706	(36%)
	Anderson (I)	15,100	(8%)
1976	Ford (R)	109,441	(53%)
	Carter (D)	93,411	(45%)

Rep. Robert W. (Bob) Edgar (D) Elected 1974; b. May 29, 1943, Philadelphia; home, Broomall; Lycoming Col., B.A. 1965, Drew U., M.Div. 1968.

Career Minister; Utd. Protestant Chaplain, Drexel U., 1968–71; Codir., People's Emergency Ctr., 1971–75.

Offices 2442 RHOB, 202-225-2011. Also 204 Long Lane, Upper Darby 19082, 215-352-0790.

Committees *Public Works and Transportation* (9th). Subcommittees: Economic Development; Surface Transportation; Water Resources.

Veterans' Affairs (6th). Subcommittees: Education, Training and Employment (Chairman); Hospitals and Health Care.

Group Ratings

	ADA	COPE	PC	LCV	CFA	RPN	NAB	NSI	NTU	ACA	ACU
1980	94	78	73	73	79	—	0	0	22	10	12
1979	89	90	78	87	63	—	—	—	19	4	10
1978	80	89	90	90	91	42	0	11	22	11	9

Key Votes

1) Draft Registn $	—	6) Fair Hsg DOJ Enfrc	FOR	11) Cut Socl Incr Dfns $	AGN
2) Ban $ to Nicrgua	AGN	7) Lim PAC Contrbtns	FOR	12) Hosptl Cost Controls	FOR
3) Dlay MX Missile	FOR	8) Cap on Food Stmp $	AGN	13) Gasln Ctrls & Allctns	FOR
4) Nuclr Mortorium	FOR	9) New US Dep Edcatn	FOR	14) Lim Wndfll Prof Tax	AGN
5) Alaska Lands Bill	FOR	10) Cut OSHA $	AGN	15) Chryslr Loan Grntee	FOR

Election Results

1980 general	Robert W. (Bob) Edgar (D)	99,381	(53%)	($295,529)
	Dennis J. Rochford (R)	87,643	(47%)	($253,406)
1980 primary	Robert W. (Bob) Edgar (D)	21,241	(100%)	
1978 general	Robert W. (Bob) Edgar (D)	79,771	(50%)	($142,238)
	Eugene D. Kane (R)	78,403	(49%)	($216,347)

EIGHTH DISTRICT

The 8th congressional district of Pennsylvania is one of four suburban Philadelphia districts. It includes a small part of Montgomery County, just about directly north of Philadelphia's Center City and all of Bucks County, which has seven-eighths of the district's population. Bucks County is one of those place names that has entered our literary imagination. The northwestern or upper part of the county is rolling farmland, easily reached by train from New York as well as Philadelphia. It has long been the residence of well-known writers and artists, who live in stone Quaker farmhouses near such villages as New Hope and Lumberville. Their neighbors are sometimes Pennsylvania Dutch farmers or, more often, comfortably-off people with jobs somewhere closer-in in the Philadelphia metropolitan area.

But this is not the whole story of Bucks County; indeed, upper Bucks has only about half the county's population. Lower Bucks County is an entirely different place — predominantly industrial and blue collar. Here is U.S. Steel's giant Fairless works; here also is one of the original Levittowns. In the other suburban Philadelphia counties, most of the blue collar immigration took place long ago, when Philadelphia itself was solidly Republican and the suburban county machines adept at enrolling new residents in their party. But in Bucks, the blue collar migration came late, in the 1950s and 1960s, and there is a strong Democratic voting base here in Levittown and Bristol. The Republican tendencies of upper Bucks and Montgomery Counties still dominate: this was a Reagan, not a Carter, district. But there is a sizable Democratic base here too, and sometimes this is the most Democratic (or least Republican) of the suburban Philadelphia districts.

The 8th has switched parties twice in the last three congressional elections, both times rather unexpectedly. In 1976, when moderate Republican Congressman Edward Biester retired, the district was faced with the choice of a much more conservative Republican or a young Democrat who had worked as a press aide to Milton Shapp. By a narrow margin they picked the latter, Peter Kostmayer. During the next four years Kostmayer did just about everything right as far as this district was concerned. He was a visible opponent of the get-along-by-going-along way of doing things in Congress. He pressed for an early investigation of Koreagate and called for investigations of his Pennsylvania Democratic colleagues, Daniel Flood and Joshua Eilberg. He used the advantages of incumbency well, had a sufficiently Democratic voting record to please Lower Bucks, and was enough of a maverick on procedural and some economic issues to please Upper Bucks. He was reelected comfortably in 1978 and looked to be in no great trouble in 1980.

Yet in 1980 the winner was James Coyne, a Republican a year younger than Kostmayer. It would be wrong to say that Coyne was a coattails victor; people here know how to split their tickets if they want to. But he did benefit from the climate of ideas that the national Republican Party had managed, with help from the Carter Administration, to create. This is basically a Republican district on economic issues, and economic issues were in the forefront in 1980. Coyne was helped also by a large, and largely self-financed, campaign budget ($430,000 in all, double Kostmayer's), which enabled him to run television ads attacking Kostmayer's record. They worked. The incumbent had been able to create a positive image when he had more or less a monopoly over information about what he was doing; when the challenger was able to shout louder, he prevailed. Kostmayer, who had been mentioned on occasion as a Senate candidate, is reportedly eager to try again in 1982, and he has proven he has the capacity and the verve to win an upset victory himself. Indeed, in early 1981, Kostmayer won headlines when he continued to try to help 8th district voters solve problems with the government, and Coyne angrily demanded that he cease and desist. The district will probably not change much in redistricting.

Census Data   Pop. (1980 final) 542,042, up 14% in 1970s. Median family income, 1970, $11,807, 123% of U.S.

The Voters

Employment profile 1970   White collar, 52%. Blue collar, 38%. Service, 9%. Farm, 1%.
Ethnic groups   Black 1980, 2%. Hispanic 1980, 1%. Asian 1980, 1%. Total foreign stock 1970, 18%. Germany, Italy, 3% each; UK, 2%; Poland, Ireland, USSR, 1% each.

Presidential Vote

1980	Reagan (R)	113,286	(56%)
	Carter (D)	64,923	(32%)
	Anderson (I)	20,046	(10%)
1976	Ford (R)	101,845	(53%)
	Carter (D)	89,991	(47%)

Rep. James K. Coyne (R) Elected 1980; b. Nov. 17, 1946, Farmville, Va.; home, Washington Crossing; Yale U., B.S. 1968; Harvard U. Bus. Sch., M.A. 1970.

Career   Pres., Coyne Chem. Corp., 1971–81; Lecturer, U. of Penn. Wharton Sch., 1974–78; Founder & Pres., Rechem Co., 1976–80; Founder & Chmn., Energy Management Services Inc., 1977–78; Upper Makefield Twp. Supervisor, 1980–81.

Offices   1513 LHOB, 202-225-4276. Also 126 Cross Keys Ofc. Bldg., 4259 Swamp Rd., Doylestown 18901, 215-345-4040, and 1 Oxford Valley Bldg., Suite 700, Langhorne 19047, 215-752-5900.

Committees   *Banking, Finance and Urban Affairs* (18th). Subcommittees: Domestic Monetary Policy; Economic Stabilization; Housing and Community Development; International Development Institutions and Finance.

House Administration (7th). Subcommittees: Personnel and Police; Services; Policy Group on Information and Computers.

Joint Committee on the Library (5th).

Group Ratings and Key Votes: Newly Elected

Election Results

1980 general	James K. Coyne (R)	103,585	(51%)	($423,002)
	Peter H. Kostmayer (D)	99,593	(49%)	($222,925)
1980 primary	James K. Coyne (R)	45,417	(100%)	
1978 general	Peter H. Kostmayer (D)	89,276	(61%)	($131,010)
	G. Roger Bowers (R)	56,776	(39%)	($52,584)

NINTH DISTRICT

The Appalachian Mountain chains run like a series of backbones through central Pennsylvania. Throughout the state's history, the mountains have constituted a formidable barrier, not so much because of their height, which is unspectacular, but because of their persistence: one rugged chain right after another for 50 to 100 miles. During the 18th century, the mountains provided eastern Pennsylvania with a kind of rampart against Indian attacks, but in the 19th century they proved less useful. The mountains prevented Pennsylvania from ever digging a satisfactory statewide canal system—the boom mode of transportation in the early 19th century. They also delayed, until other states had them, the building of an east–west railroad. Only the aggressive policy of the Pennsylvania Railroad, a relative latecomer to the business, saved the state from branch-line status.

The 9th is the only one of Pennsylvania's congressional districts to lie wholly within these mountains. This part of the Alleghenies (the term is often used interchangeably with Appalachians in Pennsylvania) was first settled by poor Scottish and Ulster Irish farmers just after the Revolutionary War. They were a people of fierce independence and pride, as the Whiskey Rebellion demonstrated. They worked their hardscrabble farms and built their little towns. Sometimes coal was found nearby, and their communities changed. But for the most part the 9th is not really coal country, and the area was spared the boom–bust cycles of northeastern Pennsylvania and West Virginia. This was an important area for the Pennsylvania Railroad, however. Near Altoona was the railroad's famous Horseshoe Curve, and in Altoona itself the railroad built the nation's largest car yards. As the railroad has become less important and its financial condition changed from prosperity to bankruptcy, Altoona's population declined from 82,000 at the end of the 1920s to 57,000 in 1980.

This part of Pennsylvania has been solidly Republican since the election of 1860, and it has not come close to electing a Democrat to Congress in years. The current incumbent, E. G. (Bud) Shuster, is an entrepreneur who made a fortune building up a business and selling it to IBM. He decided to settle in the southern Pennsylvania mountains, became interested in local affairs, decided to run for Congress, and beat the favorite, a local state senator, in the 1972 Republican primary. Shuster has won easily since. He has a solidly conservative voting record, rivaled in that regard in the Pennsylvania delegation only by the 19th district's William Goodling. Shuster has also had some impact on a number of issues. He is the House's leading opponent of the air bag, for example.

Shuster's zeal and conservatism have helped him to a leading role in the House Republican leadership, and he served as chairman of the Republican Policy Committee until 1981. Winning reelection is no problem for Shuster, and the 9th district is not likely to be altered in a politically significant way in redistricting.

Winning reelection is no problem for Shuster, and the 9th district is not likely to be altered in a politically significant way in redistricting.

Census Data Pop. (1980 final) 510,690, up 9% in 1970s. Median family income, 1970, $8,124, 85% of U.S.

The Voters

Employment profile 1970 White collar, 34%. Blue collar, 50%. Service, 12%. Farm, 4%.
Ethnic groups Black 1980, 1%. Total foreign stock 1970, 4%. Italy, 1%.

Presidential Vote

1980	Reagan (R)	103,879	(62%)
	Carter (D)	54,609	(32%)
	Anderson (I)	7,365	(4%)
1976	Ford (R)	96,867	(58%)
	Carter (D)	66,499	(40%)

Rep. E. G. (Bud) **Shuster** (R) Elected 1972; b. Jan. 23, 1932, Glassport; home, W. Providence Twnshp.; U. of Pitt., B.S. 1954, Duquesne U., M.B.A. 1960, American U., Ph.D. 1967.

Career V.P., Radio Corp. of Amer.; Operator, Shuster Farms.

Offices 2455 RHOB, 202-225-2431. Also Suite M, Penn Alto Hotel, Altoona 16603, 814-946-1653.

Committees *Budget* (3d).

Public Works and Transportation (4th). Subcommittees: Aviation; Economic Development; Surface Transportation.

Group Ratings

	ADA	COPE	PC	LCV	CFA	RPN	NAB	NSI	NTU	ACA	ACU
1980	6	11	23	17	14	—	92	100	63	91	100
1979	0	16	13	12	4	—	—	—	66	100	97
1978	5	16	10	20	18	50	100	90	52	96	92

Key Votes

1) Draft Registn $	—	6) Fair Hsg DOJ Enfrc	AGN	11) Cut Socl Incr Dfns $	FOR
2) Ban $ to Nicrgua	FOR	7) Lim PAC Contrbtns	—	12) Hosptl Cost Controls	—
3) Dlay MX Missile	AGN	8) Cap on Food Stmp $	FOR	13) Gasln Ctrls & Allctns	AGN
4) Nuclr Mortorium	AGN	9) New US Dep Edcatn	AGN	14) Lim Wndfll Prof Tax	FOR
5) Alaska Lands Bill	AGN	10) Cut OSHA $	FOR	15) Chryslr Loan Grntee	AGN

Election Results

1980 general	E. G. (Bud) Shuster (R)	157,241	(100%)	($156,048)
1980 primary	E. G. (Bud) Shuster (R)	57,979	(100%)	
1978 general	E. G. (Bud) Shuster (R)	101,151	(75%)	($146,318)
	Blaine L. Havice, Jr. (D)	33,882	(25%)	($16,809)

TENTH DISTRICT

Scranton is the anthracite town par excellence. Back around the turn of the century, anthracite or hard coal was much in demand: it was the fuel used to heat most homes, in furnaces or pot-bellied stoves. Because the only major deposits of anthracite in the United States lie in the Scranton–Wilkes-Barre region of northeastern Pennsylvania, these two cities suddenly came on flush times. Immigrants from Italy, Poland, Austria–Hungary, and Ireland poured in to join the Scots and Welsh already working the mines. Scranton became the third largest city in Pennsylvania, and the region around Scranton and Wilkes–Barre held more than 750,000 people by the end of the 1920s.

Then came the Depression of the 1930s and World War II. Scranton and the anthracite area never really recovered. As the economy began to boom again, Americans were switching from coal to oil or gas furnaces. Demand for anthracite diminished greatly, and the number of miners employed was low. In the 1960s and 1970s there has been some development: textile and apparel mills, mostly bringing low-wage jobs; in the 1980s, a few energy- and cost-conscious householders started to burn anthracite again. But the city of Scranton, isolated in the mountains, can no longer support the numbers it once could. Its population has declined from 143,000 in 1930 to 87,000 in 1980. Just a look at the edges of Scranton shows what happened. On one block stand some large houses, maintained with care, but obviously built in the 1920s — the city's last prosperous decade. On the next block, one finds no new suburban tract housing or shopping centers, only trees and hills. In few parts of the country is such a sudden halt in urban development so apparent.

Scranton and the industrial towns around it make up about half of Pennsylvania's 10th congressional district. The 10th consists of a rather anomalous mix: the heavily ethnic city and surrounding Lackawanna County, combined with several Scots–Irish–Welsh counties in the Pocono Mountains (a favorite resort of many middle-class New Yorkers), along with some of the counties in the state's northern tier. The partisan balance in this area has remained the same over the years. The number of votes in Democratic Scranton has declined, but the rural counties are becoming slightly less Republican. As a result, the district has given Republicans a margin in every presidential election since World War II except 1964.

The district's best-known Congressman, William Scranton, served only two years. He is from the aristocratic family whose name the city bears, and he has been active in efforts to revitalize it economically. He ran for Congress in 1960 to dislodge a Democrat elected in the 1958 landslide, and went on to be elected governor in 1962. Scranton has had an active career in national affairs since, running for president in 1964 and serving on important commissions and in critical posts under various presidents. He continues to maintain his residence in Scranton and is an important presence in the area; his son and namesake was elected lieutenant governor in 1978.

Scranton's successor in the House is Joseph McDade, a Republican in the Scranton mold. The difference is that McDade does not have statewide aspirations; he has represented the 10th district for almost two decades with no apparent intentions to run for anything else. McDade is generally described as a liberal Republican, and usually he has had voting records rated higher by organized labor than by business interests. On the Appropriations Committee he ranks behind only Silvio Conte, who holds the ranking Republican status; just 50, he should be an important member of that committee for years. He serves as ranking

958   PENNSYLVANIA

Republican on the Interior Subcommittee and is a new member of the Defense Subcommittee, on which he reportedly is trying to keep alive an Army ammunition plant in the district.

McDade has proved to be very popular in the 10th district; in the closest race he has had recently, against Democrat Edward Mitchell in 1976, he received 63% of the vote. Redistricting will probably not alter the shape of the district much; while Scranton has continued to lose population, the rural counties for the first time in decades had significant population growth in the 1970s.

Census Data Pop. (1980 final) 519,026, up 10% in 1970s. Median family income, 1970, $8,318, 87% of U.S.

The Voters

Employment profile 1970 White collar, 38%. Blue collar, 47%. Service, 11%. Farm, 4%.
Ethnic groups Black 1980, 1%. Total foreign stock 1970, 20%. Italy, Poland, 4% each; UK, Austria, Germany, 2% each; Ireland, 1%.

Presidential Vote

1980	Reagan (R)	107,138	(54%)
	Carter (D)	76,453	(39%)
	Anderson (I)	10,026	(5%)
1976	Ford (R)	100,938	(50%)
	Carter (D)	97,659	(48%)

Rep. Joseph M. McDade (R) Elected 1962; b. Sept. 29, 1931, Scranton; home, Scranton; U. of Notre Dame, B.A. 1953, U. of Penn., LL.B. 1956.

Career Clerk to Chf. Fed. Judge John W. Murphy, 1956–57; Practicing atty., 1957–62; Scranton City Solicitor, 1962.

Offices 2370 RHOB, 202-225-3731. Also 1223 Northeastern Natl. Bank Bldg., Scranton 18503, 717-346-3834.

Committees *Appropriations* (2d). Subcommittees: Defense; Interior.

Small Business (Ranking Member). Subcommittee: SBA and SBIC Authority, Minority Enterprise and General Small Business Problems.

Group Ratings

	ADA	COPE	PC	LCV	CFA	RPN	NAB	NSI	NTU	ACA	ACU
1980	44	72	40	32	71	—	67	89	34	35	32
1979	26	68	33	54	79	—	—	—	35	48	47
1978	30	45	40	57	32	40	46	70	14	54	50

Key Votes

1) Draft Registn $	AGN	6) Fair Hsg DOJ Enfrc	FOR
2) Ban $ to Nicrgua	FOR	7) Lim PAC Contrbtns	AGN
3) Dlay MX Missile	AGN	8) Cap on Food Stmp $	AGN
4) Nuclr Mortorium	AGN	9) New US Dep Edcatn	AGN
5) Alaska Lands Bill	FOR	10) Cut OSHA $	AGN

11) Cut Socl Incr Dfns $	AGN
12) Hosptl Cost Controls	AGN
13) Gasln Ctrls & Allctns	FOR
14) Lim Wndfll Prof Tax	FOR
15) Chryslr Loan Grntee	FOR

Election Results

1980 general	Joseph M. McDade (R)	145,703	(77%)	($58,582)
	Gene Basalyga (D)	43,152	(23%)	($0)
1980 primary	Joseph M. McDade (R)	49,343	(100%)	
1978 general	Joseph M. McDade (R)	116,003	(76%)	($66,769)
	Gene Basalyga (D)	35,721	(24%)	

ELEVENTH DISTRICT

The 11th congressional district of Pennsylvania is centered on Wilkes-Barre and Luzerne County in northeastern Pennsylvania. This is part of America's great anthracite coal district, which was of great importance to the nation in the days when most houses were heated by coal. There was a kind of boom here, and immigrants were attracted to Wilkes-Barre and the string of communities in the narrow flood plain on both sides of the Susquehanna River. There were almost half a million people in Luzerne County in 1930, most of them in this valley, but some scattered in mining and manufacturing towns in the hills. But the demand for anthracite dropped with the Depression and the conversion to oil and gas heating. Prosperity has never entirely returned to the Wilkes–Barre area. Population has declined, as young people leave to make their livings elsewhere; the new industries that have come in, notably textiles and apparel, pay low wages. This is the kind of congressional district that wants a congressman who will bring federal money and aid to the district and who will do all he can to promote its economy. And that is why the 11th district elected and, in the face of his legal troubles in 1978, reelected Congressman Daniel Flood.

Flood was long a favorite of aficionados of the House. His waxed mustache, his flowing cape, and his staccato oratory that owes something to his years as a Shakespearean actor — all these contributed to Flood's distinctive style. He was also powerful. He was first elected to the House in 1944 and rose in seniority until he became the fourth-ranking Democrat on the House Appropriations Committee. For years he chaired the Labor–HEW Subcommittee, which appropriated money for most social programs; not surprisingly, the Wilkes-Barre area usually got more than its share. He was also the number two man on the Defense Subcommittee and had plenty of friends in the Pentagon. Flood was always working to aid his district. But the high point of his congressional career came in 1972, when Hurricane Agnes and the floods it started devastated the Susquehanna valley. Flood stepped in and took command. Using his Pentagon connections, at one point he even had a fireboat flown in from Boston harbor in a C5–A transport. For such activities Flood was reelected easily every two years.

But he was never known nationally until 1978, when he suddenly found himself in deep trouble. His former administrative assistant, Stephen Elko, accused him of soliciting payments from people for whom he interceded with people in the executive branch; in effect, Flood was accused of selling his clout. To some, the charges seemed dubious. Flood still lived in an old house in Wilkes-Barre and did not spend money lavishly. If he had put a lot of money away, he might have used it to retire; in 1978 he was 75 and had been in poor health. The tendency in Wilkes-Barre was to rally around the congressman. As the best-known public figure in the area, he was a kind of local hero; and he had strong support from local business leaders and the newspaper, which did not print many of the allegations against him. Even when Flood was indicted in October, on ten counts of bribery in Washington and on three counts of perjury in Los Angeles, he was still hailed as a hero in the 11th district. He was renominated in the April primary and reelected over an active Republican in November.

But Flood had already lost his clout in Washington. Younger and some older Democratic members, unwilling to be attacked in their campaigns for condoning corruption in the House, forced Flood to leave his subcommittee chairmanship. He seemed a pathetic, uncomprehending figure at his trial; after his conviction, he resigned from the House.

That set up an unusual situation: a special election in April 1980, 13 days before the primary. The timing was the decision of Governor Richard Thornburgh, who evidently calculated that the Republican would have a better chance in the special if it were not held the same day as the presidential primary; in addition, the Republicans had one significant candidate, James Nelligan, whereas no less than five Democrats were running. In order not to lose their chance at the April 22 primary, all five Democrats ran in the April 9 special, although only one of them, state legislator Ray Musto, had the Democratic Party endorsement. Only half the voters in the special voted for the two candidates endorsed by the major parties, and Musto led Nelligan by a rather small 27% to 23% margin. Musto was apparently not used to such close calls; as a legislator from a Democratic town near Wilkes-Barre, he had never had to worry about general elections. But Nelligan had the edge in all the smaller counties and did not give up after the special. He apparently outcampaigned Musto, who may have relied too much on the Democratic label in a year when the Democratic presidential candidate failed to carry the district. Musto had an additional problem: he had been present at a meeting with purported representatives of an Arab sheik (actually U.S. government agents) and Philadelphia Congressman Ozzie Myers; but no money was offered or accepted at that meeting, and Musto was cleared of all wrongdoing by the Justice Department.

Nelligan can hardly be said to have a safe seat, not in an area with such a strong Democratic heritage. He will probably be helped a little by redistricting, since some additional territory must be added to the district, and almost everything in any direction is heavily Republican. His fate to some extent may depend on the success of the Reagan economic programs and on whether voters here become convinced that the economic and political future belongs to the Republican Party. This is a district that remembers what Dan Flood was able to do and still wants a congressman well connected with the majority in the Congress and the executive branch. Nelligan's chances will be much better if voters here believe the Republicans are in to stay.

Census Data   Pop. (1980 final) 481,355, up 2% in 1970s. Median family income, 1970, $8,161, 85% of U.S.

The Voters

Employment profile 1970   White collar, 35%. Blue collar, 53%. Service, 11%. Farm, 1%.
Ethnic groups   Black 1980, 1%. Total foreign stock 1970, 25%. Poland, 6%; Italy, 4%; Austria, 3%; Czechoslovakia, UK, 2% each; Lithuania, Germany, 1% each.

Presidential Vote

1980	Reagan (R)	95,365	(51%)
	Carter (D)	80,780	(43%)
	Anderson (I)	7,605	(4%)
1976	Ford (R)	85,292	(45%)
	Carter (D)	101,571	(54%)

Rep. James L. Nelligan (R) Elected 1980; b. Feb. 14, 1929, Wilkes-Barre; home, Forty Fort; King's Col., B.S. 1951.

Career Army, 1946–48; U.S. Gen. Acctg. Ofc., 1951–67; Professional Staff Mbr. Foreign Operations and Govt. Operations Subcom. of Govt. Operations Com., U.S. House of Reps., 1967–70; U.S. Ofc. of Econ. Opp., 1970–73; Dir., Ofc. of Property Mgmt., Gen. Svcs. Admin., 1973–75; Operations Dir., Oversight and Investigations Subcom. of Interstate and Foreign Commerce Com., U.S. House of Reps., 1975–79; Rep. nominee for U.S. House of Reps., spec. elect., Apr. 1980.

Offices 1711 LHOB, 202-225-6511. Also 19 N. River St., Wilkes-Barre 18702, 717-824-5796; 7th and Iron Sts., Bloomsburg 17815, 717-784-0241.

Committee *Armed Services* (18th). Subcommittees: Investigations; Readiness.

Group Ratings and Key Votes: Newly Elected

Election Results

1980 general	James L. Nelligan (R)	93,261	(52%)	($120,366)
	Raphael Musto (D)	86,703	(48%)	($298,699)
1980 primary	James L. Nelligan (R)	26,974	(54%)	
	Robert P. Hudock (R)	13,299	(27%)	($35,867)
	Three others (R)	9,495	(19%)	
4/9/80 spc. elct.	Raphael Musto (D)	32,073	(27%)	
	James L. Nelligan (R)	27,496	(23%)	
	Frank Harrison (I)	20,475	(17%)	($85,688)
	Paul E. Kanjorski (I)	18,241	(16%)	($109,877)
	Three others	19,166	(16%)	
1978 general	Daniel J. Flood (D)	61,433	(58%)	($25,794)
	Robert P. Hudock (R)	45,335	(42%)	($19,149)

TWELFTH DISTRICT

The hills of western Pennsylvania, eastern Ohio, and northern West Virginia that encircle the Pittsburgh metropolitan area constitute one of the largest industrial sections of the country without a major city. The easternmost part of these industrial mountains forms Pennsylvania's 12th congressional district: five counties and part of another, the largest city of which is Johnstown, with 35,000 people. More typical of the district are such small towns as Kittanning and Punxsutawney. This area was first settled by Scots–Irish farmers when it was still the frontier in the 1790s, and in the 19th century it became part of the bituminous coal belt. Today coal is still important to the district's economy, but despite the recently improving fortunes of the fuel, the industry employs far fewer people than it did 30 years ago.

In statewide elections, the 12th is as marginal as any district in Pennsylvania; it usually comes in about the same as the state as a whole. In congressional elections it has stayed with its incumbents regardless of party. From 1950 to 1972 it elected Republican John Saylor, one of the leading conservationists in the House. After Saylor's death, the district chose Democrat John Murtha in a special election and has reelected him ever since. This was the first of that series of 1974 special elections that demonstrated the unpopularity of Richard

Nixon during the Watergate crisis; Murtha did not want to use the Watergate issue, but nonetheless it seems to have hurt his Republican opponent.

Murtha is best known to the general public as the one congressman who was named, by unidentified sources, as involved in the Abscam scandal, but who was never indicted. Why government officials leaked Murtha's name is unclear, since even they admitted that there was never anything more than a "flimsy" case against him; their problem was that Murtha never took or agreed to take any money. He had in fact struck his colleagues as an honorable man and, until the scandal broke, had served on the House ethics committee.

Murtha should be remembered as the first Vietnam veteran to be elected to Congress. He served there in the Marines and serves now on the Defense Appropriations Subcommittee, where he remains very much a champion of the Marine Corps. He has also been an eloquent advocate of doing more for Vietnam veterans. The Abscam publicity evidently did not tarnish Murtha's reputation too much in his district, although his Republican opponent argued that it diminished Murtha's effectiveness. His percentage was down but was still a comfortable 59%. Murtha seems to have weathered this unpleasant episode and to be embarked on the continuation of a long House career. Redistricting may actually be kind to him, although the Republicans are in charge; he may receive part of Westmoreland County, which technically is more Democratic than the counties currently in his district.

Census Data   Pop. (1980 final) 491,462, up 5% in 1970s. Median family income, 1970, $8,030, 84% of U.S.

The Voters

Employment profile 1970   White collar, 35%. Blue collar, 50%. Service, 12%. Farm, 3%.
Ethnic groups   Black 1980, 1%. Total foreign stock 1970, 15%. Italy, 3%; Czechoslovakia, Poland, Austria, 2% each; UK, Germany, 1% each.

Presidential Vote

1980	Reagan (R)	90,454	(50%)
	Carter (D)	81,947	(45%)
	Anderson (I)	6,857	(4%)
1976	Ford (R)	88,382	(49%)
	Carter (D)	91,237	(50%)

Rep. John P. Murtha, Jr. (D) Elected Feb. 5, 1974; b. June 17, 1932, New Martinsville, W.Va.; home, Johnstown; U. of Pitt., B.A., Ind. U. of Penn.

Career USMC, Vietnam; Owner, Johnstown Minute Car Wash; Penn. House of Reps., 1969–74.

Offices 2423 RHOB, 202-225-2065. Also 226 Fed. Bldg., Johnstown 15901, 814-535-2642.

Committee *Appropriations* (14th). Subcommittees: Defense; Interior; Legislative.

Group Ratings

	ADA	COPE	PC	LCV	CFA	RPN	NAB	NSI	NTU	ACA	ACU
1980	44	78	40	36	64	—	25	50	22	21	39
1979	37	79	35	28	28	—	—	—	20	8	26
1978	25	65	35	47	27	25	58	90	13	30	50

Key Votes

1) Draft Registn $	FOR	6) Fair Hsg DOJ Enfrc	FOR	11) Cut Socl Incr Dfns $	AGN
2) Ban $ to Nicrgua	FOR	7) Lim PAC Contrbtns	FOR	12) Hosptl Cost Controls	AGN
3) Dlay MX Missile	AGN	8) Cap on Food Stmp $	AGN	13) Gasln Ctrls & Allctns	FOR
4) Nuclr Mortorium	AGN	9) New US Dep Edcatn	FOR	14) Lim Wndfll Prof Tax	FOR
5) Alaska Lands Bill	AGN	10) Cut OSHA $		15) Chryslr Loan Grntee	FOR

Election Results

1980 general	John P. Murtha, Jr. (D)	106,750	(59%)	($133,265)
	Charles A. Getty (R)	72,999	(41%)	($17,675)
1980 primary	John P. Murtha, Jr. (D)	61,180	(100%)	
1978 general	John P. Murtha, Jr. (D)	104,216	(69%)	($33,377)
	Luther V. Elkin (R)	47,442	(31%)	($15,175)

THIRTEENTH DISTRICT

The 13th congressional district of Pennsylvania, part of Montgomery County, is a fair cross-section of the upper-income Philadelphia suburbs. Along with the 5th district, the 13th contains the posh Main Line suburbs, such places as Haverford, Bryn Mawr, and Ardmore — some of them with famous colleges and all with the patina of wealth and social standing and the dignity of age. The 13th also contains the 21st ward of Philadelphia, a well-to-do, Republican part of the city adjacent to the posh Chestnut Hill neighborhood. On the other side of Philadelphia are predominantly Jewish suburbs, such as Cheltenham Township, which were built up mostly in the 1950s. As one moves away from the city limits, the land becomes hillier and more sparsely settled, with the exception of such old industrial towns as Norristown and Conshohocken, right on the banks of the Schuylkill River. Not far away is the growing area around King of Prussia and Valley Forge. Overall, the 13th is increasingly the residence of Pennsylvania's elite. It is also the home of some of the state's leading politicians, e.g.retary Richard Schweiker and Transportation Secretary Drew Lewis.

The 13th is today, as it always has been, a solidly Republican district. Up through the 1950s it was fiercely conservative, and so were its congressmen; since then, they have been more moderate Republicans. Richard Schweiker was elected here from 1960 until he ran for the Senate in 1968; his successor, chosen then and still serving, is Lawrence Coughlin. He is not well known nationally, although he might have become so had he not switched off the House Judiciary Committee in 1973, just a year before the hearings on Richard Nixon's impeachment. Coughlin is an active member of the Appropriations Committee and is seventh ranking among the committee's Republicans. He is the ranking minority member on two Appropriations subcommittees — District of Columbia, which is not considered terribly important, and the Transportation Subcommittee, which is. Coughlin's voting record should be considered moderate; he is rated somewhat better by conservative than liberal groups. He has made no moves toward running for statewide office.

Census Data   Pop. (1980 final) 457,616, down 3% in 1970s. Median family income, 1970, $13,251, 138% of U.S.

The Voters

Employment profile 1970   White collar, 64%. Blue collar, 27%. Service, 9%. Farm, –%.
Ethnic groups   Black 1980, 6%. Hispanic 1980, 1%. Asian 1980, 1%. Total foreign stock 1970, 25%. Italy, 6%; USSR, UK, Germany, 3% each; Poland, Ireland, 2% each.

Presidential Vote

1980	Reagan (R)	117,873	(56%)
	Carter (D)	67,702	(32%)
	Anderson (I)	20,575	(10%)
1976	Ford (R)	120,746	(57%)
	Carter (D)	89,823	(43%)

Rep. Lawrence Coughlin (R) Elected 1968; b. Apr. 11, 1929, Wilkes Barre; home, Villanova; Yale U., B.A. 1950, Harvard U., M.B.A. 1954, Temple U., LL.B. 1958.

Career   USMC, Korea; Practicing atty., 1958–69; Penn. House of Reps., 1965–66; Penn. Senate, 1967–68.

Offices   2467 RHOB, 202-225-6111. Also 700 One Montgomery Plaza, Norristown 19401, 215-277-4040.

Committees   *Appropriations* (7th). Subcommittees: District of Columbia; HUD–Independent Agencies; Transportation.

Select Committee on Narcotics Abuse and Control (5th).

Group Ratings

	ADA	COPE	PC	LCV	CFA	RPN	NAB	NSI	NTU	ACA	ACU
1980	44	21	37	67	43	—	45	78	38	64	38
1979	21	37	33	63	22	—	—	—	40	58	59
1978	25	21	38	65	23	82	92	61	23	56	70

Key Votes

1) Draft Registn $	—	6) Fair Hsg DOJ Enfrc	FOR
2) Ban $ to Nicrgua	AGN	7) Lim PAC Contrbtns	AGN
3) Dlay MX Missile	FOR	8) Cap on Food Stmp $	—
4) Nuclr Mortorium	FOR	9) New US Dep Edcatn	FOR
5) Alaska Lands Bill	FOR	10) Cut OSHA $	AGN

11) Cut Socl Incr Dfns $	FOR
12) Hosptl Cost Controls	AGN
13) Gasln Ctrls & Allctns	FOR
14) Lim Wndfll Prof Tax	FOR
15) Chryslr Loan Grntee	FOR

Election Results

1980 general	Lawrence Coughlin (R)..........	138,212	(71%)	($103,457)
	Pete Slawek (D)	57,745	(29%)	($26,533)
1980 primary	Lawrence Coughlin (R)..........	60,081	(85%)	
	Edward H. Johnson (R)	10,243	(15%)	($0)
1978 general	Lawrence Coughlin (R)..........	112,711	(71%)	($105,534)
	Alan Bendix Rubenstein (D)	47,151	(29%)	($32,279)

FOURTEENTH DISTRICT

Pittsburgh, Pennsylvania's second largest city, was the first urban center in the American interior. Pittsburgh grew because of its propitious site; here the Allegheny and Monongahela Rivers join to form the Ohio. The place where that happens—the Golden Triangle—remains the city's focal point: it is now surrounded by high-rise buildings, products of a downtown renaissance. When most of the nation's commerce moved over water, Pittsburgh's location was ideal; and when traffic switched to the railroads, the city adapted nicely. By the turn of the century, Pittsburgh, with large deposits of coal nearby, was the center of the steel industry, then the nation's largest and also one of the fastest-growing segments of the economy.

Today Pittsburgh remains the headquarters of many of the nation's largest corporations: U.S. Steel and several other steel companies, Westinghouse, Heinz, and the giant concerns associated with the Mellon family: Alcoa, Gulf Oil, and Koppers. But in spite of the city's recent progress—its program of downtown renewal and its relatively successful campaign against air pollution—Pittsburgh has been unable to keep pace with other major metropolitan areas. Its major industry, steel, has not shown much dynamism lately. It does not have the advantage of being a great center of air transportation, like Chicago or Atlanta. Its climate is cold. For these and other reasons, Pittsburgh's economy has not grown very rapidly. As a result, the population not only of the central city but of the entire metropolitan area has been declining since 1960—the only major metropolitan area of which this is true.

The 14th congressional district of Pennsylvania includes most of the city of Pittsburgh, including almost all of the central part of the city between the Allegheny and the Monongahela, plus a few suburbs. The district takes in most of the city's landmarks: the Golden Triangle, the University of Pittsburgh and its skyscraper campus, and Carnegie-Mellon University. Although few of the city's steel mills lie within the 14th, many of the steelworkers do live here, mostly in ethnic neighborhoods nestled among the Pittsburgh hills. The district also includes the Shadyside neighborhood, newly renovated with new shops near some of Pittsburgh's old mansions, and the predominantly Jewish Squirrel Hill neighborhood. Farther out is the main black neighborhood of Pittsburgh. Only 26% of the residents of this district, however, are black, a smaller figure than in most industrial cities because employment opportunities in Pittsburgh peaked before the big wave of black migration from the South. Since the New Deal, the 14th has been solidly Democratic; in 1972, for example, it was one of only four districts in Pennsylvania (the other three were in Philadelphia) that gave George McGovern a majority.

For 22 years the district's congressman was Democrat William Moorhead, who had practically all the credentials Pittsburgh could want. He was a solid Democrat, he was selected in 1958 by then Mayor David Lawrence, the strongest political boss Pittsburgh ever had. Moorhead also had good connections with the Mellon family and was for years a major shareholder in the Mellon National Bank. He was a member of the Banking Committee and presided over the subcommittee that passed on legislation allowing wage and price controls; he was well connected socially and his wife wrote a book on entertaining in the nation's capital. But for all these advantages, Moorhead lacked a certain fire. When, in 1978, he first encountered tough competition from Republican businessman Stan Thomas, he got only 57% of the vote. After that he chose to retire. His son ran for the seat but lost the Democratic primary by a 2–1 margin.

The new congressman has fewer credentials but a more solid base. He is William Coyne, a

Democrat, a former member of the Pittsburgh Council, a faithful follower of Mayor Richard Caligiuri. He did much better against Thomas than Moorhead did and seems to have a safe seat. Coyne serves on the Banking and House Administration committees—the same assignments as Pennsylvania's other freshman Coyne, the Republican from the 8th district, who is no relation. The Pittsburgh Coyne seems likely to have a solid labor voting record and to make no waves.

Census Data   Pop. (1980 final) 388,195, down 17% in 1970s. Median family income, 1970, $8,952, 93% of U.S.

The Voters

   Employment profile 1970   White collar, 53%. Blue collar, 29%. Service, 18%. Farm, -%.
   Ethnic groups   Black 1980, 26%. Hispanic 1980, 1%. Asian 1980, 1%. Total foreign stock 1970, 25%. Italy, 5%; Poland, Germany, 3% each; USSR, UK, Ireland, 2% each; Austria, 1%.

Presidential Vote

1980	Reagan (R)	54,736	(34%)
	Carter (D)	92,226	(57%)
	Anderson (I)	10,389	(6%)
1976	Ford (R)	68,088	(40%)
	Carter (D)	98,609	(58%)

Rep. William J. Coyne (D) Elected 1980; b. Aug. 24, 1936, Pittsburgh; home, Pittsburgh; Robert Morris Col., B.S. 1965.

Career Corporate accountant; Pa. House of Reps., 1970–72; Pittsburgh City Cncl., 1974–80.

Offices 511 CHOB, 202-225-2301. Also 2005 Fed. Bldg., 1000 Liberty Ave., Pittsburgh 15222, 412-644-2870.

Committees *Banking, Finance and Urban Affairs* (25th). Subcommittees: Economic Stabilization; Housing and Community Development; International Trade, Investment and Monetary Policy.

House Administration (11th). Subcommittees: Accounts; Policy Group on Information and Computers.

Joint Committee on the Library (3d).

Group Ratings and Key Votes: Newly Elected

Election Results

1980 general	William J. Coyne (D)	102,545	(70%)	($185,071)
	Stan Thomas (R)...............	126,150	(30%)	($126,150)
1980 primary	William J. Coyne (D)	44,142	(65%)	
	William S. Moorhead (D)	24,209	(35%)	($88,568)
1978 general	William S. Moorhead (D)	68,004	(57%)	($114,623)
	Stan Thomas (R)...............	49,992	(42%)	($119,799)

FIFTEENTH DISTRICT

The 15th congressional district of Pennsylvania is the industrial Lehigh Valley in the eastern part of the state. It is one of only two congressional districts in the country that consist of two and only two whole counties (the other is the 4th of South Carolina). Here in Northampton and Lehigh Counties are the adjoining, but quite different, cities of Allentown and Bethlehem and, to the east, the smaller city of Easton. Allentown is a diversified industrial town, one of the nation's leading cement centers (because of local limestone deposits) and the home of Mack Trucks; drawing its labor force from the Pennsylvania Dutch country around it and to the south, it has grown steadily in the 20th century. Bethlehem has a more complex history. It was founded by the Moravian sect in 1741 (the same people who started the Salem of Winston-Salem, North Carolina) and retains many 18th-century buildings. Across the Lehigh River there was an iron works in the 19th century, which grew eventually to be the central plant for Bethlehem Steel.

Allentown with its steady growth tends to be Republican or about evenly divided between the parties: Bethlehem, with its steelworker population, tends to be Democratic. Overall, the 15th should probably be considered a Democratic district, and it has gone Democratic in close presidential elections in recent years, although it gave Ronald Reagan a solid margin — close to his national average — in the rather lopsided election of 1980.

For years the 15th was reliably Democratic in House elections, but now its congressman is Republican Don Ritter. He won the seat in one of the biggest upsets of 1978, and it was a good example of how prominence and committee positions in Congress can actually work against an incumbent. Fred Rooney, then the Democratic congressman, was chairman of a subcommittee with jurisdiction over railroads; Ritter pointed to the Conrail deficit, freight car shortages, and high shipping costs, and said that Rooney's policies were all wrong. That helped Ritter to a 53% victory, and it was typical of his approach: he is a believer in free-market economics, a Reaganite on economic issues even before Reagan was elected. Other Republicans from blue collar districts like this have tried to court the AFL–CIO; Ritter makes arguments against their policies.

So far, at least, Ritter's arguments seem to be persuasive. This is a district Democrats wanted very much to regain. Their candidate, state Senator Jeanette Reibman, was well known and popular. But Ritter proved to be even more so. Like most freshman congressmen, he used the advantages of incumbency adroitly, but he also made the case for his voting record. Reibman had support from groups of teachers and steelworkers, but evidently she did not have the arguments on issues. Ritter won by a solid 59%–40% margin, which suggests that he has indeed converted the 15th to his point of view. Redistricting will probably help him a little: the district needs to be expanded, and the Republican legislature will probably tack on a few Republican townships from a neighboring county.

Census Data   Pop. (1980 final) 499,000, up 6% in 1970s. Median family income, 1970, $10,171, 106% of U.S.

The Voters

  Employment profile 1970   White collar, 41%. Blue collar, 47%. Service, 11%. Farm, 1%.
  Ethnic groups   Black 1980, 2%. Hispanic 1980, 3%. Asian 1980, 1%. Total foreign stock 1970, 19%. Italy, Austria, 3% each; Hungary, Germany, Czechoslovakia, 2% each; Poland, UK, 1% each.

Presidential Vote

1980	Reagan (R)	86,569	(50%)
	Carter (D)	66,747	(39%)
	Anderson (I)	15,800	(9%)
1976	Ford (R)	79,821	(46%)
	Carter (D)	89,134	(52%)

Rep. Donald L. (Don) **Ritter** (R) Elected 1978; b. Oct. 21, 1940, Bronx, N.Y.; home, Coopersburg; Lehigh U., B.S. 1961, M.I.T. M.S. 1963, Sc.D. 1966.

Career Scientific Exchange Fellow, Moscow, USSR, 1967–78; Asst. Prof., Cal. Poly. U., 1968–76; Mgr., Research Program Development, Lehigh U., 1976–78.

Offices 124 CHOB, 202-225-6411. Also 212 P.O. Bldg., Allentown 18101, 215-439-8861.

Committee *Energy and Commerce* (14th). Subcommittees: Energy Conservation and Power; Health and the Environment; Oversight and Investigations.

Group Ratings

	ADA	COPE	PC	LCV	CFA	RPN	NAB	NSI	NTU	ACA	ACU
1980	22	26	30	46	36	—	100	90	56	74	63
1979	11	30	15	24	4	—	—	—	60	83	84

Key Votes

1) Draft Registn $	—	6) Fair Hsg DOJ Enfrc	AGN	11) Cut Socl Incr Dfns $	FOR
2) Ban $ to Nicrgua	FOR	7) Lim PAC Contrbtns	AGN	12) Hosptl Cost Controls	AGN
3) Dlay MX Missile	AGN	8) Cap on Food Stmp $	FOR	13) Gasln Ctrls & Allctns	AGN
4) Nuclr Mortorium	AGN	9) New US Dep Edcatn	AGN	14) Lim Wndfll Prof Tax	FOR
5) Alaska Lands Bill	FOR	10) Cut OSHA $		FOR	15) Chryslr Loan Grntee	AGN

Election Results

1980 general	Donald L. (Don) Ritter (R)	99,874	(59%)	($318,453)
	Jeanette Reibman (D)	66,626	(40%)	($206,516)
1980 primary	Donald L. (Don) Ritter (R)	36,944	(100%)	
1978 general	Donald L. (Don) Ritter (R)	65,986	(53%)	($63,205)
	Fred B. Rooney (D)	58,077	(47%)	($131,005)

SIXTEENTH DISTRICT

Millions of people know about Pennsylvania Dutch country: farms scrupulously tended and set out among rolling hills, barns decorated with hex signs, and Amish families clad in black, clattering along in horse-drawn carriages. Fewer Americans know that the Pennsylvania Dutch are actually German in origin ("Dutch" is a corruption of "Deutsch"). They are descended from members of Amish, Mennonite, and other pietistic sects who left the principalities of 18th-century Germany for the religious freedom of the Quaker-dominated colony of Pennsylvania. The Quakers were happy to welcome the Germans, but they were not eager to have them in Philadelphia. So they were sent to Germantown, a few miles away, until they could move out to what was then the frontier, where they might help protect the pacifist Quakers against the Indians. Thus the Dutch came to the rolling green hills of Lancaster and York Counties. The land was naturally fertile, and careful cultivation by the Dutch vastly increased its productivity. Today farms in Lancaster County continue to produce some of the highest per-acre yields on earth.

The Pennsylvania Dutch are perhaps the most conservative people in America. They are not like so many residents of the Sun Belt, who seek the reassurance of cultural continuity even as they pursue the economic change inevitably wrought by free-market capitalism. The people here see little need for change of any kind; they believe that they live in a real and present paradise, and aside from the less-than-pleasant tourists much evidence exists to support their belief. Of course most of the Pennsylvania Dutch are not plain people. But the heritage is important: most people here are of German descent and possess a strong work ethic. Small industries have settled here because of the skills and hard work of the labor force, and agriculture continues to be important economically. The brick townhouses of Lancaster, like the frame farmhouses of the Amish, are sparklingly well kept and seem little changed from what they must have looked like 50 years ago.

The Pennsylvania Dutch country has produced one president, James Buchanan, and housed another in his retirement, Dwight Eisenhower. In Buchanan's time the politics of this area was Jeffersonian Democratic. But in the 1850s the Dutch became Republican, a preference they have retained to this day. The laissez-faire of the Jeffersonians seemed less attractive than the antislavery activism of the Republicans; later the Republicans came to exemplify laissez-faire themselves. Today the heart of the Dutch country, Lancaster County, regularly returns Republican majorities on the order of 3–1 — usually the largest of any area of similar size in the East.

The most Dutch of all the Pennsylvania congressional districts is the 16th, which includes all of Lancaster County and parts of Chester and Lebanon Counties. Of all the congressional districts in the East, it has cast the highest Republican percentages in the last three presidential elections. The district's congressman is Robert Walker, a young Republican first elected in 1976, who had been a staff aide to his predecessor, Edwin Eshleman. Walker is one of the more articulate and aggressive proponents of the philosophy that government is too big and ought to be cut back.

Walker has achieved his greatest notice, however, on an issue on which he and almost everyone believes the government should be involved: airplane safety. He is ranking Republican on the Government Operations subcommittee that investigated government regulation of the DC–10, and was as harshly critical of the government's action or inaction as the chairman, liberal Democrat John Burton, whose San Francisco–Marin County represents the polar opposite of the 16th's life-style.

Census Data   Pop. (1980 final) 536,047, up 15% in 1970s. Median family income, 1970, $9,905, 103% of U.S.

The Voters

   Employment profile 1970   White collar, 38%. Blue collar, 46%. Service, 12%. Farm, 4%.
   Ethnic groups   Black 1980, 3%. Hispanic 1980, 2%. Asian 1980, 1%. Total foreign stock 1970, 7%. Germany, Italy, 1% each.

Presidential Vote

1980	Reagan (R)	114,815	(66%)
	Carter (D)	46,372	(27%)
	Anderson (I)	11,419	(7%)
1976	Ford (R)	101,642	(63%)
	Carter (D)	56,814	(35%)

Rep. Robert S. Walker (R) Elected 1976; b. Dec. 23, 1942, Bradford; home, East Petersburg; Wm. and Mary Col., 1960–61, Millersville St. Col., B.S. 1964, U. of Del., M.A. 1968.

Career Teacher, 1964–67; Admin. Asst. to U.S. Rep. Edwin D. Eshleman, 1967–77.

Offices 1028 LHOB, 202-225-2411. Also Lancaster Co. Courthouse, Lancaster 17601, 717-393-0666.

Committees *Government Operations* (6th). Subcommittee: Government Activities and Transportation.

Science and Technology (6th). Subcommittees: Energy Development and Applications; Investigations and Oversight.

Group Ratings

	ADA	COPE	PC	LCV	CFA	RPN	NAB	NSI	NTU	ACA	ACU
1980	17	10	37	43	29	—	100	100	59	92	89
1979	16	25	20	31	7	—	—	—	61	100	97
1978	15	20	23	30	23	73	73	100	56	96	88

Key Votes

1) Draft Registn $	AGN	6) Fair Hsg DOJ Enfrc	AGN	11) Cut Socl Incr Dfns $	FOR
2) Ban $ to Nicrgua	FOR	7) Lim PAC Contrbtns	AGN	12) Hosptl Cost Controls	AGN
3) Dlay MX Missile	AGN	8) Cap on Food Stmp $	FOR	13) Gasln Ctrls & Allctns	AGN
4) Nuclr Mortorium	FOR	9) New US Dep Edcatn	AGN	14) Lim Wndfll Prof Tax	FOR
5) Alaska Lands Bill	AGN	10) Cut OSHA $	FOR	15) Chryslr Loan Grntee	AGN

Election Results

1980 general	Robert S. Walker (R)	129,765	(77%)	($23,719)
	James A. Woodcock (D)	38,891	(23%)	($0)
1980 primary	Robert S. Walker (R)	56,978	(100%)	
1978 general	Robert S. Walker (R)	91,910	(77%)	($40,289)
	Charles W. Boohar (D)	27,386	(23%)	

SEVENTEENTH DISTRICT

The 17th congressional district of Pennsylvania lies at just about the center of the state, taking in a collection of counties along the Susquehanna River. The southern end of the district, around Harrisburg, contains nearly two-thirds of its population. The main industry here, of course, is state government. The 17th also takes in the site of the now famous Three Mile Island nuclear power plant. Farther up the Susquehanna is Northumberland County, the waist, as it were, of the district. Here seams of anthracite once drew ethnics to such towns as Sunbury and Shamokin. Right across the river are the Lewisburg and Allenwood federal prisons, where so many veterans of the Nixon White House, as well as dignitaries such as

Jimmy Hoffa and Carmine DeSapio, did time. To the north is Williamsport, a small manufacturing town on the upper Susquehanna. Its all-American character makes it an appropriate host for the annual Little League World Series and home of the national small-town newspaper, *Grit*.

From the Civil War to the Depression of the 1930s, Pennsylvania was a solidly Republican state. The big capitalists who owned its plants and the workers who toiled in them, the big city machine bosses and the small farmers — virtually everyone voted Republican. The 17th district retains much of that heritage. Harrisburg, a gritty, population-losing state capital, remains heavily Republican in most elections (can that result from the fact that the governorship in this patronage-oriented state was held by Republicans for years?). In Northumberland County, the miners became Democrats in the 1930s, but Williamsport remained true to its ancestral party. Overall, the district remains heavily Republican; Ronald Reagan, for example, carried it easily in 1980.

Nevertheless the 17th has elected a Democrat to the House in the last four elections. He is Allen Ertel, and he ran in 1976 when incumbent Herman Schneebeli, ranking minority member of the House Ways and Means Committee, retired. Ertel's greatest assets that time were the national issues working for Democrats in that Watergate year and his own local popularity in the Williamsport area, where he was district attorney. They were enough to get him elected with 51% of the vote. Since then he has used his seat on the House Public Works Committee to fight for more flood control for this district, which has little in common except the oft-flooding Susquehanna. He has returned constantly to the district and overall has had enough strength to repel significant challenges. His 1978 Republican opponent had the distinction of holding degrees from both Columbia University Law School and McDonald's Hamburger University; nonetheless Ertel was reelected with 60% of the vote. Despite the national Republican trend, Ertel did better in 1980.

Redistricting is really Ertel's major problem, and although the Republican legislature can hardly give him territory that is much more nominally Republican than what he has now, he could have problems if, for example, he were given Perry and Snyder Counties, which are now in the 9th district. These are heavily Republican, and voters there have not been receiving mail about Ertel for the past half dozen years (although they have been seeing him on Harrisburg television). This seat could be as closely contested in 1982 as it was in 1976, when Ertel almost lost.

Census Data Pop. (1980 final) 501,530, up 5% in 1970s. Median family income, 1970, $8,933, 93% of U.S.

The Voters

Employment profile 1970 White collar, 44%. Blue collar, 42%. Service, 12%. Farm, 2%.
Ethnic groups Black 1980, 7%. Hispanic 1980, 1%. Total foreign stock 1970, 8%. Italy, 1%.

Presidential Vote

1980	Reagan (R)	99,371	(59%)
	Carter (D)	56,250	(33%)
	Anderson (I)	10,704	(6%)
1976	Ford (R)	98,920	(56%)
	Carter (D)	73,061	(42%)

Rep. Allen E. Ertel (D) Elected 1976; b. Nov. 7, 1936, Williamsport; home, Montoursville; Dartmouth Col., B.A. 1958, Thayer Sch. of Engr., Dickinson U., 1962–63, Yale U., LL.B. 1965.

Career Navy, 1959–62; Practicing atty.; Lycoming Co. Dist. Atty., 1968–77.

Offices 1211 LHOB, 202-225-4315. Also Rm. 230, 240 W. Third St., Williamsport 17701, 717-326-2814.

Committees *Public Works and Transportation* (13th). Subcommittees: Aviation; Surface Transportation; Water Resources.

Science and Technology (19th). Subcommittees: Energy Development and Applications; Science, Research and Technology.

Group Ratings

	ADA	COPE	PC	LCV	CFA	RPN	NAB	NSI	NTU	ACA	ACU
1980	67	68	53	57	50	—	33	40	22	26	11
1979	53	68	55	60	40	—	—	—	28	31	18
1978	30	56	35	37	32	33	50	60	20	50	27

Key Votes

1) Draft Registn $	AGN	6) Fair Hsg DOJ Enfrc	AGN	11) Cut Socl Incr Dfns $	AGN
2) Ban $ to Nicrgua	AGN	7) Lim PAC Contrbtns	FOR	12) Hosptl Cost Controls	AGN
3) Dlay MX Missile	FOR	8) Cap on Food Stmp $	AGN	13) Gasln Ctrls & Allctns	FOR
4) Nuclr Mortorium	FOR	9) New US Dep Edcatn	FOR	14) Lim Wndfll Prof Tax	FOR
5) Alaska Lands Bill	FOR	10) Cut OSHA $	AGN	15) Chryslr Loan Grntee	FOR

Election Results

1980 general	Allen E. Ertel (D)	97,995	(61%)	($97,999)
	Daniel S. Seiverling (R)	63,790	(39%)	($98,130)
1980 primary	Allen E. Ertel (D)	32,156	(100%)	
1978 general	Allen E. Ertel (D)	79,234	(60%)	($149,236)
	Thomas Rippon (R)	53,613	(40%)	($138,223)

EIGHTEENTH DISTRICT

The 18th congressional district of Pennsylvania is the suburban Pittsburgh district. It covers territory on several sides of downtown Pittsburgh but does not extend farther out into the surrounding counties that, while the census defines them as suburban, are essentially industrial in character. The district does include some closer-in towns along the Allegheny and Ohio Rivers, which include some of the Pittsburgh area's smaller steel mills, and are industrial, blue collar, and Democratic. They are also too numerous to list: at last count Pittsburgh's Allegheny County contained 129 cities, boroughs, and townships, almost half of them in the 18th district. In the hills that rise above both rivers and all the smokestacks are the more comfortable, affluent, and Republican neighborhoods where management personnel live. These include such places as Fox Chapel in the north and Mount Lebanon in the south, as well as many less eminent Republican-leaning places. All in all, the 18th is a little more Republican than Democratic in most elections; certainly it is the least Democratic district in western Pennsylvania.

For many years there were two suburban Pittsburgh districts, represented by two pro-labor Republicans since the early 1940s—James Fulton and Robert Corbett. Both men died in 1971 and their districts were in effect combined and in that form were won by H. John Heinz III of the Heinz "57 Varieties" family. In his four years in Congress, Heinz became exceedingly popular in the Pittsburgh area—so popular that he was able to win election in 1976 to the U.S. Senate in large part because of his strong local base.

But one thing Heinz was not able to accomplish was to turn the 18th district over to a like-minded liberal Republican. Instead the district was captured by Douglas Walgren, who had lost badly in races for the seat in 1970 and 1972. Walgren had the good fortune to face in the 1976 general election an ultraconservative Republican named Robert Casey. The Casey name is familiar—another Robert Casey had been a popular state auditor, and still another one embarrassed Democrats by winning their lieutenant governor nomination in 1978—but in this instance voters learned that this was not the Casey they wanted. Walgren won that race easily; even more easily he beat the same Robert Casey in 1978, that time in the Democratic primary. Walgren's toughest general election was in 1978; in 1980 he won by better than a 2-1 margin. He is a member of Energy and Commerce, which in 1979-80 was the busiest committee in the House; he ranks close to the top of John Dingell's Oversight Subcommittee and Henry Waxman's Health Subcommittee. On the Science Committee, he chairs a subcommittee with jurisdiction over the National Science Foundation, whose billion-plus budget finances so much of the nation's basic science research, and the Offices of Science and Technology Policy and Technology Assessment. Walgren votes pretty solidly with northern Democrats and has a high labor voting record.

For 1982, the problem for Walgren and others in the Pittsburgh area is that the Republican legislature will probably choose to reduce the number of Pittsburgh area House seats by one. From the Republicans' viewpoint, the best strategy is to retain something very much like the 18th district, which after all is a collection of the most Republican-leaning parts of the Pittsburgh area, not so much because they are likely to beat Walgren as because they have a reasonably good chance to win this district if he does not run. Another possibility is that Walgren will be forced into a primary with another Democratic incumbent.

Census Data Pop. (1980 final) 440,840, down 7% in 1970s. Median family income, 1970, $10,770, 112% of U.S.

The Voters

 Employment profile 1970 White collar, 57%. Blue collar, 32%. Service, 11%. Farm, -%.
 Ethnic groups Black 1980, 3%. Asian 1980, 1%. Total foreign stock 1970, 24%. Italy, 5%; Germany, Poland, 3% each; Austria, Czechoslovakia, 2% each; Yugoslavia, Ireland, 1% each.

Presidential Vote

1980	Reagan (R)	98,677	(50%)
	Carter (D)	81,406	(41%)
	Anderson (I)	13,168	(7%)
1976	Ford (R)	108,001	(53%)
	Carter (D)	90,062	(45%)

Rep. Douglas (Doug) **Walgren** (D) Elected 1976; b. Dec. 28, 1940, Rochester, N.Y.; home, Pittsburgh; Dartmouth Col., B.A. 1963, Stanford U., LL.B. 1966.

Career Practicing atty.; Asst. Allegheny Co. Solicitor, 1971–72; Dem. nominee for U.S. House of Reps., 1972.

Offices 117 CHOB, 202-225-2135. Also 2117 Fed. Bldg., 1000 Liberty Ave., Pittsburgh 15222, 412-391-4016.

Committees *Energy and Commerce* (12th). Subcommittees: Energy Conservation and Power; Health and the Environment; Oversight and Investigations.

Science and Technology (9th). Subcommittees: Natural Resources, Agriculture Research and Environment; Science, Research and Technology (Chairman).

Group Ratings

	ADA	COPE	PC	LCV	CFA	RPN	NAB	NSI	NTU	ACA	ACU
1980	78	79	70	78	64	—	18	10	17	8	16
1979	74	85	83	89	85	—	—	—	24	16	16
1978	55	80	65	77	55	58	0	10	15	26	22

Key Votes

1) Draft Registn $	FOR	6) Fair Hsg DOJ Enfrc	FOR	11) Cut Socl Incr Dfns $	AGN
2) Ban $ to Nicrgua	AGN	7) Lim PAC Contrbtns	FOR	12) Hosptl Cost Controls	FOR
3) Dlay MX Missile	FOR	8) Cap on Food Stmp $	AGN	13) Gasln Ctrls & Allctns	FOR
4) Nuclr Mortorium	FOR	9) New US Dep Edcatn	AGN	14) Lim Wndfll Prof Tax	AGN
5) Alaska Lands Bill	FOR	10) Cut OSHA $	AGN	15) Chryslr Loan Grntee	FOR

Election Results

1980 general	Douglas (Doug) Walgren (D)	126,641	(68%)	($98,136)
	Steven R. Snyder (R)	58,821	(32%)	($77,232)
1980 primary	Douglas (Doug) Walgren (D)	68,369	(100%)	
1978 general	Douglas (Doug) Walgren (D)	88,299	(57%)	($171,756)
	Ted Jacob (R)	65,088	(42%)	($187,926)

NINETEENTH DISTRICT

The 19th congressional district of Pennsylvania — Adams and York Counties and most of Cumberland — sits at the western edge of deeply conservative Pennsylvania Dutch country. This is a land of rolling green farmland extending up to the base of the Appalachian ridges that begin to rise at the district's western boundary. The most famous part of this district is also the most sparsely populated, at least by permanent residents: Gettysburg, the tourist-thronged site of the Civil War's northernmost slaughter. Outside the town itself is the retirement home of President Eisenhower, who was of Pennsylvania Dutch stock himself; his father migrated in the late 19th century with a group of Mennonite brethren out into Kansas and Texas.

The largest city in the district is York, with 44,000 people, which, from September 1777 to June 1778, was the capital of the young nation. When the Continental Congress met at York, it passed the Articles of Confederation, received word from Benjamin Franklin in Paris that the French would help with money and ships, and issued the first proclamation calling for a national day of thanksgiving. Today York is less Republican than other cities in the Pennsylvania Dutch area, perhaps because of the lingering influence of the old York *Gazette,* which until a recent change in ownership was one of the most liberal newspapers in the United States.

The other large population center in the 19th district is the fastest growing. This is Cumberland County around Camp Hill, Mechanicsburg, and Carlisle — just across the Susquehanna River from Harrisburg. During the last two decades, Cumberland has absorbed most of the white exodus from the small capital city. The county, already very Republican, is growing more so.

As a result of York's Democratic tendencies, this is a district that was very competitive for years. Democrats won here in 1954, 1958, and 1964; Republicans won narrow victories in 1952, 1956, 1960, and 1966. The last close contest was in 1974. Incumbent George Goodling was retiring at 78. The Republican nominee was his son William, a teacher and school administrator, and he just squeaked by with 52%. Legislatively the younger Goodling's career must have been mostly frustrating. He has served on the Education and Labor Committee, a body dominated by Democratic liberals of whose programs he has often been an acerbic critic. Goodling is now the ranking Republican on the major education subcommittee, ruled still by the iron hand of Chairman Carl Perkins, a solid supporter of Great Society programs; should the Republicans win control of the House and make Goodling chairman, there would be a major change in policies. Yet Goodling does support some federal programs, such as education aid for the handicapped, which he feels the states would not provide on their own. Goodling also serves on Foreign Affairs and is ranking Republican on the subcommittee on Africa.

Goodling has proved to be very popular in his district, and while its demographics have become more Republican, his performance reflects more than that. This is one part of Pennsylvania that has been gaining population, so that the 19th is now the second most populous district in the state. It will have to be pared down a little in redistricting, but that is not likely to change its political balance.

Census Data   Pop. (1980 final) 536,129, up 15% in 1970s. Median family income, 1970, $10,107, 105% of U.S.

The Voters

Employment profile 1970   White collar, 44%. Blue collar, 43%. Service, 10%. Farm, 3%.
Ethnic groups   Black 1980, 2%. Hispanic 1980, 1%. Total foreign stock 1970, 5%.

Presidential Vote

1980	Reagan (R)	111,265	(60%)
	Carter (D)	58,003	(31%)
	Anderson (I)	11,851	(6%)
1976	Ford (R)	105,544	(59%)
	Carter (D)	70,417	(39%)

Rep. William F. (Bill) Goodling (R) Elected 1974; b. Dec. 5, 1927, Logansville; home, Jacobus; U. of Md., B.S. 1953, West Md. Col., M.Ed. 1957, Penn St. U., 1958–62.

Career Army, 1946–48; Public school teacher and administrator.

Offices 109 CHOB, 202-225-5836. Also Fed. Bldg., 200 S. George St., York 17403, 717-843-8887.

Committees *Education and Labor* (4th). Subcommittee: Elementary, Secondary and Vocational Education.

Foreign Affairs (8th). Subcommittees: Africa; Inter-American Affairs.

Group Ratings

	ADA	COPE	PC	LCV	CFA	RPN	NAB	NSI	NTU	ACA	ACU
1980	28	28	33	45	29	—	91	63	49	73	64
1979	26	27	35	42	26	—	—	—	54	78	69
1978	20	21	25	27	23	60	82	75	34	87	86

Key Votes

1) Draft Registn $	—	6) Fair Hsg DOJ Enfrc	AGN	11) Cut Socl Incr Dfns $	AGN
2) Ban $ to Nicrgua	AGN	7) Lim PAC Contrbtns	AGN	12) Hosptl Cost Controls	—
3) Dlay MX Missile	FOR	8) Cap on Food Stmp $	FOR	13) Gasln Ctrls & Allctns	FOR
4) Nuclr Mortorium	FOR	9) New US Dep Edcatn	—	14) Lim Wndfll Prof Tax	—
5) Alaska Lands Bill	FOR	10) Cut OSHA $	—	15) Chryslr Loan Grntee	FOR

Election Results

1980 general	William F. (Bill) Goodling (R)	136,873	(76%)	($40,643)
	Richard P. Noll (D)	41,584	(23%)	($11,274)
1980 primary	William F. (Bill) Goodling (R)	60,760	(100%)	
1978 general	William F. (Bill) Goodling (R)	105,424	(79%)	($37,067)
	Raj Kumar (D)	28,577	(21%)	

TWENTIETH DISTRICT

The 20th congressional district of Pennsylvania could be called the Monongahela district. Most of its residents live in a string of industrial communities along the heavily polluted Monongahela and a tributary, the Youghiogheny. "Monongahela," Walt Whitman once wrote, "it rolls off the tongue like venison." But there are not many deer here; this is a heavily industrialized area. The main product is steel. The 20th district probably makes as much steel as any congressional district in the nation. Here are the operations of Jones & Laughlin and no less than four mills of U.S. Steel. They are found along the banks of the Mononga-hela, which provide just about the only level land available in the Pittsburgh metropolitan area. Most of these mills are ancient and technologically backward; the best known of them is the Homestead Works, site of a great and bloody strike in 1892 when it was owned by Andrew Carnegie.

Not many blacks live in the district, only 7% of the total population, and these live scattered in various Pittsburgh neighborhoods and the smaller towns of McKeesport, Clairton, and Duquesne. Most residents of the 20th are members of the white working class—the children and grandchildren of people who came here from Slovakia, southern Italy, Poland, Wales, and the mountains of West Virginia and Pennsylvania to work in the steel mills. Many of them lived through the 1920s, when the prosperity of the great steel corporations failed to trickle down to its sweat-covered workers, through the deprivations of the 1930s and the exhilaration of the United Steel Workers' organizing drives in the mills, and finally through the slow decline of the industry in the years after World War II. Today these steelworkers live in the same small frame houses found up and down the hills of Braddock, Swissvale, Homestead, and the Hazelwood and St. Clair neighborhoods of Pittsburgh. The populations of all these areas have declined; the children who grew up here have in many cases moved out to find better jobs, sometimes to the outer suburbs, but in many cases away from the Pittsburgh area altogether. As a result, this is an old district, one where an unusual percentage of voters still remember the timbre of Franklin D. Roosevelt's voice.

The image of the melting pot comes to us from the steelmaking process. In one respect, at least, the communities of the 20th district, although separated from one another by hills, have melted into a unit: they all share the preference for the Democratic Party. There are a few white collar suburbs in the 20th, and there has been some dissatisfaction with national Democrats on occasion, as in 1968 when George Wallace got 13% of the vote here. But in most elections, and certainly in local elections, this is a strong Democratic district.

Since the New Deal, the 20th has sent only Democrats to the House of Representatives. The current congressman is Joseph Gaydos, a former state senator and attorney for United Mine Workers District 5. Gaydos had Democratic organization and union backing when he first won the seat in 1968. In Washington his record is what one might expect: solidly liberal on economic issues, more conservative on noneconomic matters. His record with organized labor has often been 100%. Gaydos chairs Education and Labor's subcommittee on Health and Safety, which has jurisdiction over the controversial OSHA. Gaydos can be expected to reflect organized labor's solid support of OSHA; the subcommittee's Republican minority tends toward ideological opposition to government regulation in such matters. This is an area where the difference between management and labor remains the stark basis of politics, and no sophisticated monographs from the American Enterprise Institute or the Heritage Foundation are going to change Gaydos's approach. Indeed, many of OSHA's nitpicking practices were changed not through congressional pressure (although many congressmen were unhappy with the agency), but through administrative action by the OSHA director in the Carter Administration, Eula Bingham.

Gaydos has been reelected effectively without opposition and can count on a similar fate in the 1980s, provided that redistricting is favorable. That may be a problem. The Pittsburgh area must lose one congressman, and one way the Republican legislature can choose to handle the matter is to split the 20th district among its neighbors. For the Republicans, partition of Gaydos's constituency would mean eliminating at least one labor-oriented Democratic congressman. Gaydos, in that eventuality, might find himself running in a primary against William Coyne of the 14th district, Doug Walgren of the 18th, or Don Bailey of the 21st.

Census Data   Pop. (1980 final) 423,739, down 10% in 1970s. Median family income, 1970, $9,937, 104% of U.S.

The Voters

Employment profile 1970   White collar, 50%. Blue collar, 38%. Service, 12%. Farm, -%.
Ethnic groups   Black 1980, 7%. Hispanic 1980, 1%. Total foreign stock 1970, 26%. Italy, Czecho-slovakia, 4% each; Poland, UK, 3% each; Germany, Austria, Hungary, Yugoslavia, 2% each; Ireland, 1%.

Presidential Vote

1980	Reagan (R)	77,245	(43%)
	Carter (D)	90,546	(50%)
	Anderson (I)	9,878	(5%)
1976	Ford (R)	83,713	(44%)
	Carter (D)	102,730	(54%)

Rep. Joseph M. Gaydos (D) Elected 1968; b. July 3, 1926, Braddock; home, McKeesport; Duquesne U., U. of Notre Dame, LL.B. 1951.

Career Navy, WWII; Dpty. Atty. Gen. of Penn.; Asst. Allegheny Co. Solicitor; Gen. Counsel, Utd. Mine Workers of Amer., Dist. 5; Penn. Senate, 1967–68.

Offices 2366 RHOB, 202-225-4631. Also Rm. 207, 224 5th Ave. Bldg., McKeesport 15132, 412-673-7756.

Committees *Education and Labor* (5th). Subcommittees: Health and Safety (Chairman); Postsecondary Education.

House Administration (3d). Subcommittees: Accounts; Contracts and Printing (Chairman).

Joint Committee on Printing (2d).

Group Ratings

	ADA	COPE	PC	LCV	CFA	RPN	NAB	NSI	NTU	ACA	ACU
1980	33	94	40	26	57	—	58	60	34	48	39
1979	47	72	43	45	48	—	—	—	31	27	32
1978	35	75	40	47	46	27	0	33	16	26	30

Key Votes

1) Draft Registn $	FOR	6) Fair Hsg DOJ Enfrc	FOR	11) Cut Socl Incr Dfns $	AGN
2) Ban $ to Nicrgua	FOR	7) Lim PAC Contrbtns	FOR	12) Hosptl Cost Controls	FOR
3) Dlay MX Missile	AGN	8) Cap on Food Stmp $	AGN	13) Gasln Ctrls & Allctns	FOR
4) Nuclr Mortorium	AGN	9) New US Dep Edcatn	AGN	14) Lim Wndfll Prof Tax	AGN
5) Alaska Lands Bill	FOR	10) Cut OSHA $	AGN	15) Chryslr Loan Grntee	FOR

Election Results

1980 general	Joseph M. Gaydos (D)	122,100	(73%)	($98,430)
	Kathleen M. Meyer (R)	46,313	(27%)	($1,624)
1980 primary	Joseph M. Gaydos (D)	80,180	(100%)	
1978 general	Joseph M. Gaydos (D)	97,745	(72%)	($67,339)
	Kathleen M. Meyer (R)	37,745	(28%)	

TWENTY-FIRST DISTRICT

The 21st congressional district of Pennsylvania is Westmoreland County, just to the east of Pittsburgh, plus a small portion of suburban Allegheny County. It is a mixed area: there are a few wealthy enclaves here, for example, Ligonier, but most of Westmoreland is industrial —small factory towns that lie between the hills or along the Allegheny and Monongahela

Rivers at the county's western edge. The district contains an especially large number of Italian–Americans, with other ethnic groups present in smaller numbers. The 21st is part of western Pennsylvania's "black country," so named for the region's bituminous coal deposits. Steel is the major industry here, as it is all over western Pennsylvania; the coal, of course, is a major reason why the steel industry grew here in the first place. Politically, western Pennsylvania in general and the 21st district in particular are heavily Democratic.

Although no one knows for sure, the 21st is probably one of not very many — perhaps 30 — congressional districts in which a majority of the employed persons are members of labor unions. Union membership is taken for granted in these parts; and politicians are expected to vote the union line. That does not mean, however, that particular local labor bosses are all-powerful politically. On the contrary, union members have little sense of being besieged here, where they are in the majority, and generally do not vote together as a bloc. The congressman from the 21st for 20 years before his retirement in 1978, John Dent, illustrated the way politicians here vote the labor line; he was probably the surest AFL–CIO and United Steel Workers vote on the House Education and Labor Committee. But the race to succeed him shows how politics here is not controlled by a single labor machine.

For when Dent retired, there were no fewer than 11 candidates competing in the Democratic primary. One candidate was the Westmoreland County Democratic chairman; he had Dent's support but lost anyway. Another loser was the state House majority leader. The winner was 33-year-old attorney Don Bailey, who spent his own money, assembled his own volunteer force, and won with 23% of the vote. But did Bailey get a free ride in the general elections? Besides having to soothe disgruntled organization Democrats — a time-consuming ordeal that does not necessarily produce many voters — he had to face a well-financed and determined Republican opponent. Robert Miller had received 41% of the vote against Dent in 1976 and probably helped to assure the old Democrat's retirement; Miller talked in 1978 about tax cuts and brought in prominent national Republicans. It is not clear that these were winning tactics. Bailey seemed more on the track when he promised aid to the steel industry, support of nuclear power construction (Westinghouse is a big employer around here), and opposition to unnecessary environmental restrictions. Still, Bailey won with only 53% in this basically Democratic district.

Against a much weaker opponent in 1980 Bailey was reelected by a 2–1 margin. But for 1982 he may face problems in redistricting. It is conceivable that the 21st could be shifted west and, in effect, combined with the 20th, which would put Bailey in a primary fight with 14-year incumbent Joseph Gaydos.

Bailey is not one of those young Democrats whose formative political experience was opposing the Vietnam war. In fact he served in the Army in Vietnam, after attending the University of Michigan and playing in the Rose Bowl on its football team. He served for some time on the Armed Services Committee, where he was a supporter of the Army's interests particularly; he shifted in February 1981 to Ways and Means, to fill the vacancy left by Abscam-convicted Raymond Lederer of Philadelphia. He serves on the Social Security and Public Assistance subcommittees, on which he is likely to go along with organized labor's liberal positions. On trade issues, he almost certainly will be a force for protection of the domestic steel industry.

Census Data   Pop. (1980 final) 485,534, up 3% in 1970s. Median family income, 1970, $9,645, 101% of U.S.

The Voters

Employment profile 1970 White collar, 45%. Blue collar, 43%. Service, 11%. Farm, 1%.
Ethnic groups   Black 1980, 3%. Total foreign stock 1970, 21%. Italy, 6%; Poland, Czechoslovakia, Austria, UK, 2% each; Germany, Yugoslavia, 1% each.

Presidential Vote

1980	Reagan (R)	81,193	(46%)
	Carter (D)	85,062	(48%)
	Anderson (I)	8,341	(5%)
1976	Ford (R)	78,965	(45%)
	Carter (D)	92,450	(53%)

Rep. Don Bailey (D) Elected 1978; b. July 21, 1945, Pittsburgh; home, Greensburg; U. of Mich., B.A. 1967, Duquesne U., J.D. 1976.

Career Army, Vietnam; Practicing atty., 1976–.

Offices 116 CHOB, 202-225-5631. Also 206 N. Main St., Greensburg 15601, 412-837-6420.

Committees *Standards of Official Conduct* (6th).

Ways and Means (23d). Subcommittees: Public Assistance and Unemployment Compensation; Social Security.

Group Ratings

	ADA	COPE	PC	LCV	CFA	RPN	NAB	NSI	NTU	ACA	ACU
1980	50	78	40	48	64	—	25	70	12	21	21
1979	37	85	48	48	63	—	—	—	19	23	36

Key Votes

1) Draft Registn $	FOR	6) Fair Hsg DOJ Enfrc	FOR	11) Cut Socl Incr Dfns $	AGN
2) Ban $ to Nicrgua	FOR	7) Lim PAC Contrbtns	FOR	12) Hosptl Cost Controls	FOR
3) Dlay MX Missile	AGN	8) Cap on Food Stmp $	AGN	13) Gasln Ctrls & Allctns	FOR
4) Nuclr Mortorium	AGN	9) New US Dep Edcatn	AGN	14) Lim Wndfll Prof Tax	AGN
5) Alaska Lands Bill	AGN	10) Cut OSHA $		AGN	15) Chryslr Loan Grntee	FOR

Election Results

1980 general	Don Bailey (D)	112,427	(68%)	($120,891)
	Dirk Matson (R)	51,821	(32%)	($0)
1980 primary	Don Bailey (D)	48,337	(60%)	
	Bernard Scherer (D)	27,007	(33%)	
1978 general	Don Bailey (D)	73,712	(53%)	($125,146)
	Robert H. Miller (R)	65,622	(47%)	($113,186)

TWENTY-SECOND DISTRICT

The 22nd congressional district of Pennsylvania is the northern tip of Appalachia—the southwestern corner of the state between West Virginia and the Pittsburgh suburbs. The region is one of rugged hills and polluted rivers, lined with steel mills and blast furnaces. The operations here are smaller than those in the 20th district, which contains the really big mills;

this is an area of small industrial towns, huddled around a small factory by a river. Residents of Irish, Polish, and Czech descent are found in great numbers, as well as people from West Virginia and the mountain south. This is rough country: it was in a small town here that Joseph Yablonski, the insurgent candidate for president of the United Mine Workers, was found shot to death with his wife and daughter in 1969.

The 22nd remains one of Pennsylvania's safest Democratic districts. It gave a solid majority of its votes in 1980 to Jimmy Carter—one of the few eastern districts outside a central city where this happened. The Democratic leanings of its various ethnic groups are linked with the Democratic tradition of the very large number of union members, and in 1980, with the steel industry in trouble, people here evidently did not want to take a chance with Ronald Reagan's free-market inclinations, which might mean elimination of trade protection for steel.

From 1944 to 1976, the 22d district elected Thomas Morgan, a small-town physician, to Congress. He was chairman of the House Foreign Affairs Committee, criticized by some for not opposing the Vietnam war; he had been brought up in a tradition of bipartisan cooperation on foreign policy and did not deviate from it until it was clear that a majority in the House wanted him to.

The current congressman, Austin Murphy, emerged from the spirited competition that ensued when Morgan retired in 1976. In a 12-candidate Democratic primary Murphy, a state senator then, won with 29%; he won the general election with 56%, not a very high mark in this district. He has won subsequent elections without difficulty. Redistricting should be no problem; this district gained population in the 1970s and, situated as it is in the corner of the state, it is unlikely to have its boundaries changed in any major way.

Murphy chairs the Select Education Subcommittee of Education and Labor, a body that does not handle the big-money education bills but has jurisdiction over a number of sensitive programs where the federal government has become involved, including special education, alcohol and drug abuse, the handicapped, domestic violence, and adoption. Some of these are areas where small, inexpensive programs can improve many people's lives. Others— adoption is a good example—are areas where thoughtless action by the federal government can disrupt personal relationships and institutional arrangements that have served people's needs for many years.

On the full Education and Labor Committee, Murphy is considered a solid supporter of organized labor. He serves also on the Interior Committee, which handles strip mine legislation, of great interest to this heavily coal-producing and -consuming district.

Census Data Pop. (1980 final) 492,584, up 5% in 1970s. Median family income, 1970, $8,396, 88% of U.S.

The Voters

Employment profile 1970 White collar, 40%. Blue collar, 47%. Service, 12%. Farm, 1%.
Ethnic groups Black 1980, 3%. Hispanic 1980, 1%. Total foreign stock 1970, 20%. Italy, 5%; Czechoslovakia, 3%; Poland, Austria, UK, 2% each; Germany, Yugoslavia, 1% each.

Presidential Vote

1980	Reagan (R)	73,735	(42%)
	Carter (D)	92,829	(53%)
	Anderson (I)	7,156	(4%)
1976	Ford (R)	75,161	(42%)
	Carter (D)	103,041	(57%)

Rep. Austin J. Murphy (D) Elected 1976; b. June 17, 1927, North Charleroi; home, Charleroi; Duquesne U., B.A. 1949, U. of Pitt., J.D. 1952.

Career USMC, 1944–46; Practicing atty.; Washington Co. Asst. Dist. Atty., 1956–57; Penn. House of Reps., 1959–71; Penn. Senate, 1971–77.

Offices 204 CHOB, 202-225-4665. Also 308 Fallowfield Ave., Charleroi 15022, 412-489-4217.

Committees *Education and Labor* (11th). Subcommittees: Health and Safety; Labor Standards; Select Education (Chairman).

Interior and Insular Affairs (15th). Subcommittees: Energy and the Environmemt; Mines and Mining.

Veterans' Affairs (16th). Subcommittee: Compensation, Pension, and Insurance.

Group Ratings

	ADA	COPE	PC	LCV	CFA	RPN	NAB	NSI	NTU	ACA	ACU
1980	44	68	47	70	57	—	58	70	27	42	35
1979	42	70	45	55	41	—	—	—	42	38	36
1978	40	72	50	71	59	27	8	60	19	40	26

Key Votes

1) Draft Registn $	FOR	6) Fair Hsg DOJ Enfrc	FOR
2) Ban $ to Nicrgua	FOR	7) Lim PAC Contrbtns	AGN
3) Dlay MX Missile	AGN	8) Cap on Food Stmp $	AGN
4) Nuclr Mortorium	AGN	9) New US Dep Edcatn	FOR
5) Alaska Lands Bill	AGN	10) Cut OSHA $	AGN

11) Cut Socl Incr Dfns $	AGN
12) Hosptl Cost Controls	AGN
13) Gasln Ctrls & Allctns	FOR
14) Lim Wndfll Prof Tax	FOR
15) Chryslr Loan Grntee	FOR

Election Results

1980 general	Austin J. Murphy (D)	118,084	(70%)	($123,663)
	Marilyn Coyle Ecoff (R)	50,020	(29%)	($788)
1980 primary	Austin J. Murphy (D)	55,932	(100%)	
1978 general	Austin J. Murphy (D)	99,559	(72%)	($144,228)
	Marilyn Coyle Ecoff (R)	39,518	(28%)	

TWENTY-THIRD DISTRICT

The 23rd congressional district of Pennsylvania is the rural north central part of the state. The region is not only the most sparsely populated in Pennsylvania, but in the entire East. The district's terrain is mountainous, and its valleys have only a few small towns here and there. The only significant concentrations of people are found in the Nittany Valley in the southern part of the district and around Oil City in the extreme west. The Nittany Valley is the home of Pennsylvania State University, commonly called Penn State, long known for its powerful football teams. Oil City is near the site of the nation's first oil well, sunk in 1859. Today Pennsylvania crude—a relatively scarce but higher quality oil than that found in the Southwest—continues to occupy an important place in the region's economy.

The isolation of this part of Pennsylvania was ended by the opening in the early 1970s of the Keystone Shortway, a superhighway that has replaced the Pennsylvania Turnpike as the main road between New York and Chicago. Some people hoped that the shortway would bring light industrial development to the area; all it seems to have attracted, at least up to now, are gas stations with 60-foot signs and Holiday Inns. So the 23d remains a rural and small-town district, dominated by old-stock farmers.

The area currently covered by the 23d district has a long tradition of electing Republican congressmen, a tradition that goes back to the Civil War. But in the 1970s, it behaved like most other congressional districts in the nation—it was willing to go for one party or the other, depending on the circumstances. Republican Congressman Albert Johnson, despite diminishing margins, declined to retire and was beaten in 1976 by Democratic state Senator Joseph Ammerman. Ammerman's victory looked solid, and he seemed to have the political acumen to hold the district. But in August 1978 Ammerman sustained a broken hip in an automobile accident and was hospitalized for six weeks. He had a strong Republican opponent, William Clinger, who had held a middle-level appointment in the Ford Administration and then returned home to Warren, in the northern part of the district. Clinger attacked Ammerman for his support of a consumer protection agency and his high ADA record; the incumbent was unable to show the kind of vigor and willingness to meet constituents that is so important in so many congressional elections. The result was a 54% Clinger victory.

Clinger appears to be a vigorous, active incumbent, in tune with the philosophy of the Reagan Administration. He was not seriously challenged in 1980 and his district seems unlikely to suffer major dismemberment for 1982.

Census Data Pop. (1980 final) 500,405, up 7% in 1970s. Median family income, 1970, $8,272, 86% of U.S.

The Voters

Employment profile 1970   White collar, 41%. Blue collar, 44%. Service, 13%. Farm, 2%.
Ethnic groups   Total foreign stock 1970, 10%. Italy, 2%; UK, Germany, 1% each.

Presidential Vote

1980	Reagan (R)	93,731	(54%)
	Carter (D)	65,211	(38%)
	Anderson (I)	10,986	(6%)
1976	Ford (R)	91,276	(53%)
	Carter (D)	77,474	(45%)

Rep. William F. (Bill) Clinger, Jr. (R) Elected 1978; b. Apr. 4, 1929, Warren; home, Warren; Johns Hopkins U., B.A. 1951, U. of Va., LL.B. 1965.

Career Adv. Dept., New Process Co., 1955–62; Practicing atty., 1965–75, 1977–78; Chf. Counsel, U.S. Dept. of Commerce Econ. Development Admin., 1975–77.

Offices 1221 LHOB, 202-225-5121. Also 111 S. Allen, State College 16801, 814-238-1776.

Committees *Government Operations* (10th). Subcommittees: Commerce, Consumer and Monetary Affairs; Legislation and National Security.

Public Works and Transportation (9th). Subcommittees: Economic Development; Surface Transportation; Water Resources.

Group Ratings

	ADA	COPE	PC	LCV	CFA	RPN	NAB	NSI	NTU	ACA	ACU
1980	22	26	37	30	43	—	73	80	40	71	53
1979	11	65	20	33	7	—	—	—	42	68	76

Key Votes

1) Draft Registn $	FOR	6) Fair Hsg DOJ Enfrc	FOR	11) Cut Socl Incr Dfns $	FOR
2) Ban $ to Nicrgua	FOR	7) Lim PAC Contrbtns	AGN	12) Hosptl Cost Controls	AGN
3) Dlay MX Missile	AGN	8) Cap on Food Stmp $	AGN	13) Gasln Ctrls & Allctns	AGN
4) Nuclr Mortorium	AGN	9) New US Dep Edcatn	AGN	14) Lim Wndfll Prof Tax	FOR
5) Alaska Lands Bill	AGN	10) Cut OSHA $	FOR	15) Chryslr Loan Grntee	AGN

Election Results

1980 general	William F. (Bill) Clinger, Jr. (R) ..	122,855	(74%)	($86,103)
	Peter Atigan (D)	41,033	(25%)	($0)
1980 primary	William F. (Bill) Clinger, Jr. (R) ..	52,602	(100%)	
1978 general	William F. (Bill) Clinger, Jr. (R) ..	73,194	(54%)	($250,697)
	Joseph S. Ammerman (D)	61,657	(46%)	($174,587)

TWENTY-FOURTH DISTRICT

Situated in the northwestern corner of the state, the 24th congressional district of Pennsylvania is part of the industrial Great Lakes region. It is a long way overland to the East Coast, and the district has none of Metropolitan Philadelphia's seaboard ambience. The city of Erie, with 118,000 people, is the largest in the 24th district. Like most industrial cities on this polluted lake, Erie is a Democratic stronghold. As one goes inland, the territory becomes more Republican. An exception to this pattern is the steel town of Sharon, just a few miles from Youngstown, Ohio; like most towns dependent on steel mills, Sharon votes Democratic. Overall, the political balance in the 24th makes it one of the state's most marginal districts. In the presidential elections of 1976 and 1980, its percentages for the various candidates virtually mirrored the state's results — despite its far from central geographical position.

This was a marginal district for many years, until it was won by Joseph Vigorito in 1964. Through the use of the advantages of incumbency, he won reelection by increasingly safe margins, until in 1973 he was named as one of the "ten dumbest congressmen" by *New Times* magazine. That label — and the nickname of "Jumping Joe" that the article used to describe him — seems to have ended his congressional career. His percentage declined in the Democratic year of 1974 and he was beaten in 1976 by Republican Marc Marks. In 1978 he ran against Marks again and got only 36% of the vote.

Marks has been a smoother candidate and a more articulate congressman. He is adroit enough to receive ratings above 60% from both organized labor and organized business interests. But success of a different sort has caused him political problems as well. In 1979, he considered running for the Senate, and there was even talk of other office. John Connally, then running for president, suggested to Marks that he was the kind of man who might make a good vice president; this was pretty heady stuff for a man who three years before was a successful lawyer in Sharon, Pennsylvania. In the process of all this speculation about higher office, Marks seems to have gotten into a feud with local Republicans, who found his voting record too liberal and Marks himself difficult to deal with; but his liberal ratings declined and he avoided primary opposition.

Marks's real battle in 1980 turned out to be in the general election. David DiCarlo, a young state legislator from Erie, ran a strong campaign against him, and in a less Republican year almost certainly would have won. As it was, Marks won by just 120 votes. That kind of result almost assures him of opposition, if not from DiCarlo then from someone else, in 1982. The district will have to be increased in size slightly, which will help Marks, since the area to the east is Republican. But overall it must be rated a marginal district indeed.

In the meantime Marks is now the ranking Republican on the Oversight and Investigations Subcommittee of Energy and Commerce. This is a potentially important subcommittee of the standing committee that had the most business in the 96th Congress. Marks, who appears to have a strong temperament, will be sitting opposite the chairman, John Dingell, known as one of the House's more competent legislators and also as the possessor of one of the House's shortest fuses.

Census Data Pop. (1980 final) 496,948, up 5% in 1970s. Median family income, 1970, $9,215, 96% of U.S.

The Voters

Employment profile 1970 White collar, 42%. Blue collar, 45%. Service, 11%. Farm, 2%.
Ethnic groups Black 1980, 4%. Hispanic 1980, 1%. Total foreign stock 1970, 16%. Italy, Poland, 3% each; Germany, 2%; Czechoslovakia, 1%.

Presidential Vote

1980	Reagan (R)	87,842	(49%)
	Carter (D)	77,440	(43%)
	Anderson (I)	11,691	(7%)
1976	Ford (R)	87,411	(47%)
	Carter (D)	95,138	(51%)

Rep. Marc Lincoln Marks (R) Elected 1976; b. Feb. 12, 1927, Farrell; home, Sharon; U. of Ala., B.A. 1949, U. of Va., LL.B. 1954.

Career Army Air Corps, WWII; Practicing atty., 1955–76; Mercer Co. Solicitor, 1960–66.

Offices 1424 LHOB, 202-225-5406. Also 108 U.S. Courthouse, Erie 16501, 814-455-1313.

Committees Energy and Commerce (8th). Subcommittees: Oversight and Investigations; Telecommunications, Consumer Protection and Finance.

Select Committee on Aging (4th). Subcommittee: Health and Long-Term Care.

Group Ratings

	ADA	COPE	PC	LCV	CFA	RPN	NAB	NSI	NTU	ACA	ACU
1980	44	37	43	65	29	—	42	70	29	59	39
1979	32	75	35	51	31	—	—		20	31	23
1978	50	55	40	68	50	42	67	80	15	38	42

Key Votes

1) Draft Registn $	FOR	6) Fair Hsg DOJ Enfrc	FOR	11) Cut Socl Incr Dfns $	FOR
2) Ban $ to Nicrgua	FOR	7) Lim PAC Contrbtns	AGN	12) Hosptl Cost Controls	AGN
3) Dlay MX Missile	AGN	8) Cap on Food Stmp $	AGN	13) Gasln Ctrls & Allctns	FOR
4) Nuclr Mortorium	AGN	9) New US Dep Edcatn	FOR	14) Lim Wndfll Prof Tax	FOR
5) Alaska Lands Bill	AGN	10) Cut OSHA $	AGN	15) Chryslr Loan Grntee	FOR

Election Results

1980 general	Marc Lincoln Marks (R)	86,687	(50%)	($172,052)
	David C. Dicarlo (D)	86,567	(50%)	($143,032)
1980 primary	Marc Lincoln Marks (R)	41,501	(100%)	
1978 general	Marc Lincoln Marks (R)	87,041	(64%)	($171,653)
	Joseph P. Vigorito (D)	48,894	(36%)	($35,220)

TWENTY-FIFTH DISTRICT

The 25th congressional district is part of industrial western Pennsylvania. The district adjoins Ohio and the northern tip of the West Virginia panhandle. Almost half the people of the 25th live in Beaver County, where the steel mills sit in little grimy towns along the banks of the Ohio and Beaver Rivers; the best known of these towns is Beaver Falls, the boyhood home of Joe Namath. Like all of western Pennsylvania within a 100-mile radius of Pittsburgh, Beaver County is rich in ethnic diversity, with especially large numbers of Italian–Americans. The county is ordinarily a Democratic bulwark, although it has occasionally gone Republican.

The other two counties in the district are politically more marginal. Lawrence, dominated by the industrial city of New Castle, was Pennsylvania's bellwether county, until the 1974 and 1976 elections when regional loyalties played as much part as partisan labels. Butler County, a few miles north of the industrial concentrations along the rivers, is less thickly settled and tends toward Republicanism. The 25th also includes the northern tier of townships in Pittsburgh's Allegheny County, which usually go Republican.

Altogether, this is about as good an example of a Democratic district as you can find. Yet it had four close elections in the 1970s, and two of them were won by a Republican. Moreover, the Republican was not a sleek management type, but a steel factory foreman and engineer, Gary Myers. He beat 20-year incumbent Frank Clark in 1974, a very Democratic year, by spotlighting Clark's junketeering and his support of a bill to require oil to be shipped in American flag vessels and the maritime industry contributions Clark received, evidently in return. But personal factors were also at work. Clark was obviously not greatly respected: when, after his defeat, he ran for doorkeeper of the House, only 34 of his 244 former Democratic colleagues voted for him. Myers was a management-oriented congressman, although he voted with labor fairly often; he was popular enough in 1976 to beat Beaver County Commissioner Eugene Atkinson by a solid margin. But in 1978 he decided to retire, and to return to being a foreman in the steel mill—a decision no one in Washington could understand.

There was a real contest—or contests—to succeed him. Atkinson was the winner in an 11-candidate Democratic primary, but with only 25% of the vote. The Republican, Butler County Solicitor Tim Shaffer, put on a creditable campaign; and there was an Independent candidate as well, who ended up with 8% of the vote. Atkinson was the winner with less than an absolute majority. He was reelected without difficulty in 1980, and his major problem for 1982 is probably redistricting. There will be some major redrawing of Pittsburgh area congressional districts, but the 25th gained rather than lost population in the 1970s and so may emerge largely unchanged.

Atkinson sits on that most practical of committees, Public Works, and that least concrete of committees, Government Operations. He is not as yet a subcommittee chairman. Atkinson has one of the more conservative voting records among northern Democrats. It was perhaps not an accident that Ronald Reagan, still recovering from his gunshot wound but lobbying for his budget cuts, called Atkinson on the telephone and spoke to him during a radio call-in show. Atkinson is a Democrat who may be inclined to support Reagan on the merits of that issue, and also has a political reason for doing so. Republicans control the redistricting process in Pennsylvania, and Atkinson's major problem for 1980 is probably redistricting. He is not likely to be beaten by a Republican; he won easily in 1980. But he could be thrown into the same district with another Democrat, which would mean a bloody and expensive primary, and one in which Atkinson might very well be defeated. Presumably he—and other Democrats—will find it easier to escape such a fate if they support the president's program.

Census Data   Pop. (1980 final) 488,814, up 3% in 1970s. Median family income, 1970, $9,208, 96% of U.S.

The Voters

Employment profile 1970   White collar, 39%. Blue collar, 48%. Service, 12%. Farm, 1%.
Ethnic groups   Black 1980, 3%. Total foreign stock 1970, 19%. Italy, 5%; Poland, Yugoslavia, 2% each; UK; Germany, Czechoslovakia, Austria, 1% each.

Presidential Vote

1980	Reagan (R)	83,765	(45%)
	Carter (D)	87,982	(48%)
	Anderson (I)	10,690	(6%)
1976	Ford (R)	84,138	(46%)
	Carter (D)	97,466	(53%)

Rep. Eugene V. Atkinson (D) Elected 1978; b. Apr. 5, 1927, Aliquippa; home, Aliquippa; U. of Pitt.

Career Navy, WWII; Owner Atkinson Insurance Agcy.; Dir. of Customs, Port of Pitt., 1962–69; Beaver Co. Comm., 1972–78.

Offices 412 CHOB, 202-225-2565. Also 408 Beaver Valley Mall, Monaca 15061, 412-775-5940.

Committees *Government Operations* (17th). Subcommittees: Commerce, Consumer, and Monetary Affairs; Environment, Energy, and Natural Resources; Manpower and Housing.

Public Works and Transportation (19th). Subcommittees: Aviation; Surface Transportation.

Select Committee on Aging (23d). Subcommittee: Health and Long-Term Care.

Group Ratings

	ADA	COPE	PC	LCV	CFA	RPN	NAB	NSI	NTU	ACA	ACU
1980	28	47	43	50	36	—	67	50	40	42	53
1979	37	75	40	52	33	—	—	—	43	46	46

Key Votes

1) Draft Registn $	AGN	6) Fair Hsg DOJ Enfrc	AGN	11) Cut Socl Incr Dfns $	AGN
2) Ban $ to Nicrgua	FOR	7) Lim PAC Contrbtns	AGN	12) Hosptl Cost Controls	AGN
3) Dlay MX Missile	AGN	8) Cap on Food Stmp $	AGN	13) Gasln Ctrls & Allctns	AGN
4) Nuclr Mortorium	AGN	9) New US Dep Edcatn	FOR	14) Lim Wndfll Prof Tax	FOR
5) Alaska Lands Bill	FOR	10) Cut OSHA $	AGN	15) Chryslr Loan Grntee	FOR

Election Results

1980 general	Eugene V. Atkinson (D)	119,817	(67%)	($51,196)
	Robert Morris (R).............	58,768	(33%)	($89,379)
1980 primary	Eugene V. Atkinson (D)	50,767	(75%)	
	William Kovulenku (D)	8,706	(13%)	($0)
	Gloriann Burick (D)	8,041	(12%)	($0)
1978 general	Eugene V. Atkinson (D)	68,293	(47%)	($106,521)
	Tim Shaffer (R)...............	62,160	(42%)	($91,294)
	John W. Cook (I)	10,588	(7%)	($8,699)

RHODE ISLAND

The state of Rhode Island and Providence Plantations — the full official name — owes its existence to a religious schism in the Massachusetts Bay Colony. Roger Williams, as most schoolchildren know, founded Providence in 1636 as a haven for dissident Calvinists fleeing the regime to the north. Williams had a profound — and for that day unusual — belief in religious and political freedom; he was the New World's first civil libertarian. Williams's colony soon attracted a motley gathering of Baptists, Antinomians, and even some Papists (Roman Catholics), along with a few American Indians. Williams, unlike many of his contemporaries and Americans to follow, was kindly disposed to the native Americans and became a scholar of their languages and customs.

Rhode Island's later history has been almost as idiosyncratic. The descendants of Williams's colonists began to prosper and, as people do, grew more conservative. The "triangle trade" out of Newport — rum, sugar, and slaves — was especially lucrative. After the Revolutionary War Rhode Island was the last of the 13 colonies to ratify the Constitution. It had declined to send delegates to the Convention for fear that any proposed union could impose tariffs inimical to ocean-dependent trade. Only after the new nation threatened to sever commercial relations with Rhode Island did it agree to become the 13th state. As late as 1840, when most other states had given the franchise to free white males, Rhode Island still allowed only large property owners to vote. This situation led to open revolt, the Dorr Rebellion, during which Rhode Island had two separate state governments, each claiming sovereignty.

In the state's economic history the key event occurred in 1793, when Samuel Slater, a British emigre, built the nation's first water-powered cotton mill in Pawtucket and launched America's industrial revolution. During the 19th century the textile industry in Rhode Island boomed, and the tiny state attracted immigrants eager to work the looms and toil on the cutting floor. They came from French Canada, Ireland, and especially from Italy. So by the turn of the century this erstwhile colony of dissident Protestants had become the most heavily Catholic state in the nation. Today 64% of the citizens of Rhode Island are adherents of that faith.

The Protestants and Catholics did not get along very well in politics. Long after they had become a minority numerically, the Protestants, through the Republican Party, were able to maintain control of Rhode Island. The big switch came in 1928, when thousands of immigrants, especially women, who had never before voted, streamed to the polls and carried the state for Al Smith. From that time on Rhode Island has been one of our most Democratic states. It has gone Republican for president only three times in the last 50 years, twice for Eisenhower and once for Nixon; it has elected only one Republican to the U.S. Senate since 1930; and it elected no Republicans to the House of Representatives between 1938 and 1980. In 1980, when most of the nation was going for Ronald Reagan, Rhode Island gave him only 37% of its votes—his worst showing outside the District of Columbia.

The Republicans have done better in gubernatorial elections. They won in 1958, 1962, 1964, and 1966, and have been competitive in four of the last seven elections—Rhode Island is one of the last states with a two-year term for governors. But for most races the decisive battle, when there is one, occurs in the Democratic Party. And the outcome of that contest has, until very recently, almost always been determined by the endorsement of the state Democratic machine. But there are signs that the Democratic machine is losing its omnipotence; in fact, both senators came to office initially over the opposition of the Democratic machine, as did one of the two congressmen. Perhaps not incidentally, both of these senators from ethnic Rhode Island are blue-blood aristocrats.

The first is Claiborne deB. Pell, first elected in 1960, from Bellevue Avenue in Newport, where one finds the Vanderbilt and Auchincloss "cottages." Pell's father was congressman from New York for a term, a friend of Franklin Roosevelt, and minister to Portugal and Hungary during the period around the outbreak of World War II. Pell himself served as a foreign service officer for several years. But such service hardly explains how he was able to beat former Governor (1951–59) Dennis Roberts and former Governor (1941–45), Senator (1947–49), and U.S. Attorney General (1949–52) J. Howard McGrath in the 1960 Democratic primary. (All of them were running for the seat first won by Theodore F. Green in 1936 when he was 69. An entire generation of Rhode Island politicians made plans on the assumption that Green's seat would soon become available. Green, once chairman of the Foreign Relations Committee, finally decided to retire when he reached 93.) Part of the reason for Pell's victory was the odor of scandal that attached itself to both of his rivals. But the win was also attributable to his quiet, aloof, but still vigorous style of campaigning.

That style was one reason Pell was challenged in 1972 by Rhode Island's strongest Republican, John Chafee. Returning from a stint as secretary of the Navy in the Nixon Administration, Chafee was still popular from three terms as governor, and he believed he could attack some of Pell's preoccupations as esoteric (e.g., oceanography and the law of the sea, aid to the arts). But Chafee failed to account for the steel backbone beneath Pell's sometimes halting aristocratic demeanor. Pell had gained attention as an early dove on the Foreign Relations Committee, but he gained support from teachers for steering the higher education bill through the Senate.

Pell won that contest decisively; Chafee went on to win the state's other Senate seat in 1976. Pell is now the ranking minority member on the Senate Foreign Relations Committee, a position he probably never expected to hold. He has always had an interest in foreign policy, and he was one of the committee's doves during the Vietnam period. His role now is harder to define. He probably thinks that the Reagan Administration is pursuing the wrong policies in many areas. But his basic civility, his lack of aggressiveness, and the small number of committee members who share his views have made him an almost silent partner of committee Chairman Charles Percy. On the Human Resources Committee, he will presumably put up a fight for government funding for the arts and for Pell grants (aid to higher education) — with what results it is not clear. Pell comes up for reelection in 1984, and he may then have serious competition, even in this Democratic state; he seems to have a tough race every 12 years.

Rhode Island's junior senator, John Chafee, was elected in 1976 after Senator John Pastore retired and the Democrats split; nevertheless he has considerable popularity in his own right. He survived the embarrassing fact that the Nixon Administration closed down Rhode Island's big naval bases around Newport in 1973 just after he ran for the Senate and after voters were assured that such a thing would happen if McGovern were elected. But this did not hurt Chafee, although as Navy secretary he presumably knew the closings were coming and said nothing about them in his 1972 campaign. Generally, however, he enjoys a reputation for candor and forthrightness; and one must remember that a senator from such a state as Rhode Island — where the Providence newspapers and television stations cover local affairs closely and reach everyone — is subject to very close scrutiny, and Chafee has emerged from that scrutiny as a very popular politician.

In the Senate he is one of the most liberal of Republicans, one who even in the earliest months of the Reagan Administration could be found dissenting from its policies. In March 1981, for example, he led a move to restore funds for various domestic programs that Reagan wanted cut; it got some support from northern Democrats and a few Republicans but fell far short of success, 59–40. Chafee serves on the Finance Committee, where he chairs the subcommittee that handles pensions; he is also a member of the Trade Subcommittee and generally a free trader, although he worries about imports that compete with Rhode Island's main industry, jewelry. He serves as well on the Banking Committee and chairs a subcommittee on Consumer Finance. Chafee is up for reelection in 1982, and at this writing there seems to be no strong Democrat inclined to challenge him.

For the years the Democratic machine solidly controlled Rhode Island politics, the state's congressional delegation kept the kind of ethnic balance one expects from a well-disciplined organization in a very ethnic state. One senator was Italian–American, another a blue-blood WASP; one congressman was of French Canadian descent, the other had an unmistakably Irish name. All were politically safe. Now all that has changed. Both senators today are WASPs, and one of the House members is a Republican, and a woman besides.

The more senior of the House members is Fernand St. Germain of the 1st district. Appropriately, this is the more French Canadian of the two seats; French is still spoken on the streets of Woonsocket and Central Falls, two textile mill towns in the district. The 1st also takes in the wealthier precincts of Providence, including Brown University, all of Pawtucket, and the east side of Narragansett Bay, including Newport. That old city, hit hard in the 1970s by Navy cutbacks, has a large section of restored 18th-century townhouses as well as the robber barons' cottages of the 19th century.

St Germain, first elected in 1960 at the age of 32, has always had machine support and has seldom had significant opposition. After 20 years in the House, he became chairman of the House Banking, Finance, and Urban Affairs Committee, when Henry Reuss decided to take the chair of the Joint Economic Committee instead. This is a little-known committee, with a subject matter that is often highly technical yet also extremely important to society. St. Germain concentrated for some years on the housing programs the committee superintended; this had the happy effect of concentrating much of the nation's supply of federally assisted senior citizen housing in eastern Rhode Island. But housing programs have become less important in recent years, as it has become apparent that the private housing market is increasing the supply more rapidly than population rises. At the same time banking and related issues — the money supply, the policies of the Federal Reserve Board — have become more important as inflation persists. So has banking regulation. The Banking Committee has to referee arguments between the banks and savings institutions; St. Germain, unlike most senior members of the committee, tends to be more sympathetic to the savings institutions. In his approach to these issues he is, if not ostentatiously industrious, then certainly well prepared and knowledgeable.

St. Germain has not experienced any political trouble back in the 1st district, and now that he is a full committee chairman it seems unlikely that he will attract strong opposition.

Rhode Island is the closest thing we have to a city–state. It includes nearly all of Metropolitan Providence, with its population of almost one million, and very little else — just a little strip of rural territory along Long Island Sound. The local media — the *Providence Journal,* the Providence television stations — naturally cover state politics and state government closely, and people get a close picture of the ups and downs of the leading personalities. This sometimes produces great fluctuations in election results over a short period of time — the change in the standing of Congressman Edward Beard is an example. First elected in 1974, he upset an incumbent in the primary by stressing his blue collar roots and the fact that, as a house painter, he had never made as much as $10,000 a year. For a while he was phenomenally popular, but by 1978 he was in trouble. Republican challenger Claudine Schneider charged that he was abrasive and ineffective and that he had become addicted to foreign junkets — the kind of high life he had once spurned. Beard had two years to prepare for a rematch but only lost ground; he won only 57% in the 1980 primary (a poor showing for an incumbent) and he was defeated in the general election. Afterward he bought a tavern in Central Falls in the 1st district and appeared on television tending bar.

Schneider has an odd background for a politician in Rhode Island, or indeed in any state. She got her start as an environmentalist, opposing the construction of a nuclear plant near Narragansett Bay. As a kind of rebel, she perhaps felt more comfortable among Rhode Island's Republicans than among its dominant Democrats; Republicans, who win few elections here, were happy to have her, whatever her views. Her victory in 1980 was impressive, and she will have two years to consolidate her hold on the district and establish her own affirmative popularity, since presumably she will not be running against Beard in 1982. Redistricting need not change the boundaries of the districts much, unless the Democratic legislature wants somehow to make Schneider's race harder.

Rhode Island's governor is Joseph Garrahy, a man who served eight years as lieutenant governor before he was elected governor in 1976. Some may have thought he was not up to the top job, but in fact he has performed very much to voters' satisfaction. No governor in Rhode Island had won a third two-year term since 1966, and in 1980 Garrahy had tough opposition from Providence Mayor Vincent (Buddy) Cianci, a Republican with an aggressive style and considerable popularity. But Cianci also had some problems, and Garrahy was reelected with the astonishing total of 74% of the vote. While it is possible that he will seek John Chafee's Senate seat in 1982, this is a man who has made his career in state government and in Providence, and who seems likely to want to remain where he is.

Census Data   Pop. (1980 final) 947,154, no change in 1970s: 0.42% of U.S. total, 40th largest. Central city, 33%; suburban, 59%. Median 4-person family income, 1978, $21,093, 103% of U.S., 16th highest.

1979 Share of Federal Tax Burden $1,893,000,000; 0.42% of U.S. total, 39th largest.

1979 Share of Federal Outlays $1,926,645,000; 0.41% of U.S. total, 42d largest.

DOD	$431,308,000	40th	(0.41%)	HEW	$903,864,000	38th	(0.51%)
DOE	$2,150,000	46th	(0.02%)	ERDA	$772,000	45th	(0.02%)
HUD	$48,145,000	36th	(0.73%)	NASA	$639,000	40th	(0.01%)
VA	$108,008,000	40th	(0.52%)	DOT	$37,551,000	51st	(0.23%)
EPA	$42,593,000	34th	(0.80%)	DOC	$10,228,000	39th	(0.32%)
DOI	$9,081,000	48th	(0.16%)	USDA	$42,313,000	49th	(0.18%)

Economic Base Miscellaneous manufacturing industries, especially jewelry, silverware, and plated ware; textile mill products, especially narrow fabric mills; finance, insurance, and real estate; primary metal industries, especially nonferrous rolling and drawing; fabricated metal products; electrical equipment and supplies; machinery, especially metalworking machinery.

Political Lineup Governor, J. Joseph Garrahy (D). Senators, Claiborne Pell (D) and John H. Chafee (R). Representatives, 2 (1 D and 1 R); 2 in 1982. State Senate, 50 (43 D and 7 R); State House of Representatives, 90 (72 D and 18 R).

The Voters

Registration 547,472 Total.
Employment profile 1970 White collar, 45%. Blue collar, 42%. Service, 12%. Farm, 1%.
Ethnic groups Black 1980, 3%. Hispanic 1980, 2%. Asian 1980, 1%. Total foreign stock 1970, 33%. Italy, 8%; Canada, 7%; UK, 4%; Portugal, 3%.

Presidential Vote

1980	Reagan (R)	154,793	(37%)
	Carter (D)	198,342	(48%)
	Anderson (I)	59,814	(14%)
1976	Ford (R)	181,249	(44%)
	Carter (D)	227,636	(55%)

1980 Democratic Presidential Primary			*1980 Republican Presidential Primary*		
Kennedy	26,179	(68%)	Reagan	3,839	(72%)
Carter	9,907	(26%)	Bush	993	(19%)
Two others	1,470	(4%)	Uncommitted	348	(6%)
Uncommitted	771	(2%)	Two others	155	(3%)

SENATORS

Sen. Claiborne Pell (D) Elected 1960, seat up 1984; b. Nov. 22, 1918, New York, N.Y.; home, Newport; Princeton U., A.B. 1940, Columbia U., A.M. 1946.

Career Coast Guard, WWII; U.S. Foreign Svc. and State Dept., Czechoslovakia and Italy, 1945–52; Exec. Asst. to R.I. Dem St. Chmn., 1952, 1954; Consultant, Dem. Natl. Comm., 1953–60; Dir., Internatl. Rescue Comm.; Mbr., U.S. Delegation to U.N., 1970.

Offices 325 RSOB, 202-224-4642. Also 418 Fed. Bldg., Providence 02903, 401-528-4547.

Committees *Foreign Relations* (Ranking Member).

Labor and Human Resources (4th). Subcommittees: Education; Employment and Productivity.

Rules and Administration (3d).

Joint Committee on the Library (4th).

Group Ratings

	ADA	COPE	PC	LCV	CFA	RPN	NAB	NSI	NTU	ACA	ACU
1980	78	94	50	65	60	—	0	0	28	10	6
1979	68	100	63	—	71	—	—	—	28	8	10
1978	75	89	83	90	70	60	9	10	14	4	8

Key Votes

1) Draft Registn $	—	6) Fair Housng Cloture	FOR	11) Cut Socl Incr Defns	AGN
2) Ban $ to Nicrgua	FOR	7) Ban $ Rape Abortns	AGN	12) Income Tax Indexing	AGN
3) Dlay MX Missile	FOR	8) Cap on Food Stmp $	AGN	13) Lim Spdg 21% GNP	AGN
4) Nuclr Mortorium	FOR	9) New US Dep Edcatn	FOR	14) Incr Wndfll Prof Tax	FOR
5) Alaska Lands Bill	FOR	10) Cut OSHA Inspctns	—	15) Chryslr Loan Grntee	AGN

Election Results

1978 general	Claiborne Pell (D)	229,557	(75%)	($373,077)
	James G. Reynolds (R)	76,061	(25%)	($85,614)
1978 primary	Claiborne Pell (D)	69,729	(87%)	
	Two others (D)	10,406	(13%)	
1972 general	Claiborne Pell (D)	221,942	(54%)	($528,347)
	John H. Chafee (R)	188,990	(46%)	($457,409)

Sen. John H. Chafee (R) Elected 1976, seat up 1982; b. Oct. 22, 1922, Providence; home, East Greenwich; Yale U., B.A. 1947, Harvard U., LL.B. 1950.

Career USMC, 1942–46, 1950–52; R.I. House of Reps., 1957–63; Gov. of R.I., 1963–69; Secy. of the Navy, 1969–72; Rep. nominee for U.S. Senate, 1972.

Offices 5229 DSOB, 202-224-2921. Also 302 Pastore Bldg., Providence 02903, 401-528-5294.

Committees *Banking, Housing, and Urban Affairs* (7th). Subcommittees: International Finance and Monetary Policy; Economic Policy; Consumer Affairs (Chairman).

Environment and Public Works (4th). Subcommittees: Environmental Pollution (Chairman); Transportation.

Finance (5th). Subcommittees: Taxation and Debt Management; International Trade; Savings, Pensions, and Investment Policy (Chairman).

Select Committee on Intelligence (3d). Subcommittees: Legislation and the Rights of Americans; Collection and Foreign Operations (Chairman).

Group Ratings

	ADA	COPE	PC	LCV	CFA	RPN	NAB	NSI	NTU	ACA	ACU
1980	72	63	70	87	40	—	40	20	38	29	25
1979	47	59	63	—	48	—	—	—	31	22	1/
1978	55	63	53	62	35	100	30	11	20	26	17

Key Votes

1) Draft Registn $	FOR	6) Fair Housng Cloture	FOR	11) Cut Socl Incr Defns	AGN
2) Ban $ to Nicrgua	FOR	7) Ban $ Rape Abortns	AGN	12) Income Tax Indexing	AGN
3) Dlay MX Missile	AGN	8) Cap on Food Stmp $	AGN	13) Lim Spdg 21% GNP	FOR
4) Nuclr Mortorium	FOR	9) New US Dep Edcatn	FOR	14) Incr Wndfll Prof Tax	FOR
5) Alaska Lands Bill	FOR	10) Cut OSHA Inspctns	AGN	15) Chryslr Loan Grntee	AGN

Election Results

1976 general	John H. Chafee (R)	230,329	(58%)	($415,651)
	Richard Lorber (D).............	167,665	(42%)	($782,931)
1976 primary	John H. Chafee (R), unopposed			
1970 general	John O. Pastore (D)	230,469	(68%)	
	John McLaughlin (R)	107,351	(31%)	

GOVERNOR

Gov. J. Joseph Garrahy (D) Elected 1976, term expires Jan. 1983; b. Nov. 26, 1930, Providence; U. of R.I., U. of Buffalo.

Career Air Force, Korea; Sales Rep., Narragansett Brewing Co., 1956–62; R.I. State Senate, 1963–69, Dpty. Major. Ldr., 1967–68; Dem. St. Chmn., 1967–68; R.I. Lt. Gov., 1968–76.

Offices State House, Providence 02903, 401-277-2397.

Election Results

1980 gen.	J. Joseph Garrahy (D)	299,174	(74%)
	Vincent (Buddy) Cianci (R) .	106,729	(26%)
1980 prim.	J. Jos. Garrahy (D), unopp.		
1978 gen.	J. Joseph Garrahy (D)	197,386	(63%)
	Lincoln C. Almond (R)	96,596	(31%)
	Joseph A. Doorley, Jr. (I) ..	20,381	(6%)

FIRST DISTRICT

Census Data Pop. (1980 final) 462,912, down 3% in 1970s. Median family income, 1970, $9,713, 101% of U.S.

The Voters

Employment profile 1970 White collar, 46%. Blue collar, 42%. Service, 12%. Farm, –%.
Ethnic groups Black 1980, 3%. Hispanic 1980, 2%. Asian 1980, 1%. Total foreign stock 1970, 35%. Canada, 9%; Portugal, Italy, 5% each; UK, 4%.

Presidential Vote

1980	Reagan (R)	72,958	(37%)
	Carter (D)	96,087	(48%)
	Anderson (I)	28,689	(14%)
1976	Ford (R)	85,061	(43%)
	Carter (D)	113,522	(57%)

Rep. Fernand J. St. Germain (D) Elected 1960; b. Jan. 9, 1928, Blackstone, Mass.; home, Woonsocket; Providence Col., Ph.B. 1948, Boston U., LL.B. 1955.

Career Army, 1949–52; R.I. House of Reps., 1952–60; Practicing atty., 1956–.

Offices 2108 RHOB, 202-225-4911. Also 200 John E. Fogarty Bldg., Providence 02903, 401-528-4323.

Committee *Banking, Finance and Urban Affairs* (Chairman). Subcommittees: Consumer Affairs and Coinage; Economic Stabilization; Financial Institutions Supervision, Regulation and Insurance (Chairman); Housing and Community Development; International Trade, Investment and Monetary Policy.

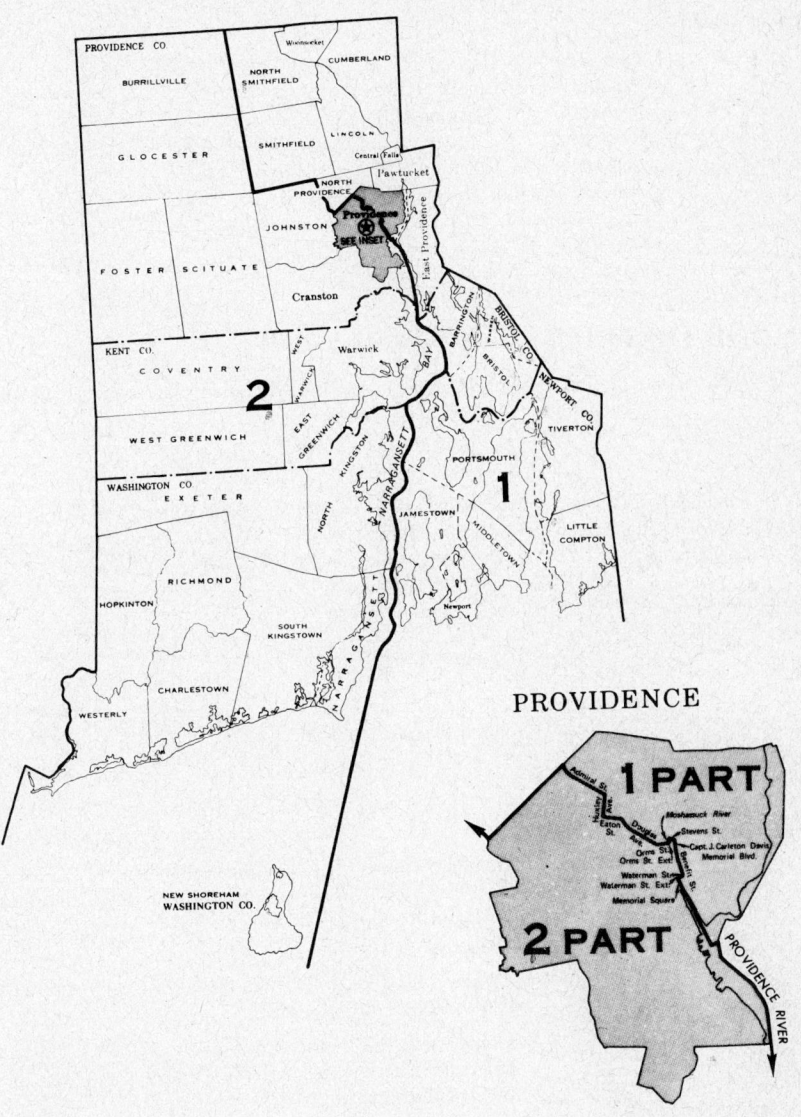

Group Ratings

	ADA	COPE	PC	LCV	CFA	RPN	NAB	NSI	NTU	ACA	ACU
1980	78	84	57	67	79	—	0	33	17	13	7
1979	79	88	75	74	74	—	—	—	21	12	18
1978	65	85	75	69	68	10	0	30	8	15	14

Key Votes

1) Draft Registn $	AGN	6) Fair Hsg DOJ Enfrc	FOR	11) Cut Socl Incr Dfns $	AGN
2) Ban $ to Nicrgua	AGN	7) Lim PAC Contrbtns	FOR	12) Hosptl Cost Controls	FOR
3) Dlay MX Missile	FOR	8) Cap on Food Stmp $	AGN	13) Gasln Ctrls & Allctns	FOR
4) Nuclr Mortorium	FOR	9) New US Dep Edcatn	FOR	14) Lim Wndfll Prof Tax	AGN
5) Alaska Lands Bill	FOR	10) Cut OSHA $	AGN	15) Chryslr Loan Grntee	FOR

Election Results

1980 general	Fernand J. St. Germain (D)	120,756	(68%)	($44,418)
	William Montgomery (R)	57,844	(32%)	($0)
1980 primary	Fernand J. St. Germain (D)	23,105	(79%)	
	Rocha (D)	6,121	(21%)	
1978 general	Fernand J. St. Germain (D)	86,768	(61%)	($125,013)
	John J. Slocum, Jr. (R)	54,912	(39%)	($98,082)

SECOND DISTRICT

Census Data   Pop. (1980 final) 484,242, up 2% in 1970s. Median family income, 1970, $9,755, 102% of U.S.

The Voters

Employment profile 1970   White collar, 45%. Blue collar, 42%. Service, 13%. Farm, –%.
Ethnic groups   Black 1980, 3%. Hispanic 1980, 2%. Asian 1980, 1%. Total foreign stock 1970, 31%. Italy, 10%; Canada, 5%; UK, 3%; Portugal, 1%.

Presidential Vote

1980	Reagan (R)	81,519	(38%)
	Carter (D)	101,008	(47%)
	Anderson (I)	30,677	(14%)
1976	Ford (R)	95,702	(46%)
	Carter (D)	112,877	(54%)

Rep. Claudine Schneider (R) Elected 1980; b. Mar. 25, 1947, Clairton, Pa.; home, Narragansett; Rosemont Col., U. of Barcelona, Spain, Windham Col., B.A. 1969.

Career   Founder, R.I. Committee on Energy, 1973; Exec. Dir., Conservation Law Foundation, 1973; Rep. nominee for U.S. House of Reps., 1978; Producer, Public Affairs Program on Providence TV, 1979–80.

Offices   1431 LHOB, 202-225-2735. Also 307 Pastore Bldg., Providence 02903, 401-528-4861.

Committees   *Merchant Marine and Fisheries* (14th). Subcommittees: Fisheries and Wildlife Conservation and the Environment; Oceanography.

Science and Technology (15th). Subcommittees: Energy Development and Applications; Natural Resources, Agriculture Research and Environment.

Group Ratings and Key Votes: Newly Elected

Election Results

1980 general	Claudine Schneider (R)	115,057	(55%)	($289,937)
	Edward P. Beard (D)	92,970	(45%)	($167,559)
1980 primary	Claudine Schneider (R), unopposed			
1978 general	Edward P. Beard (D)	87,397	(53%)	($84,688)
	Claudine Schneider (R)	78,725	(47%)	($53,879)

SOUTH CAROLINA

South Carolina has one of the most distinctive histories of any state, and to understand it one has to go back to the very beginning. While the other Atlantic seaboard colonies were modeled on life in England or some religious ideal, the model that the first South Carolinians used was Barbados, a sugar-producing island in the West Indies where life for most people was less than idyllic. During the colonial period, South Carolina was the only colony where blacks outnumbered whites massively, for the settlers here were almost all large landholders who could grow their main crops—sugar, rice, indigo—only with the labor of vast numbers of slaves. South Carolina produced a planter elite whose most memorable legacies were such men as the Pinckneys and John C. Calhoun, and whose gravest fears were that their slaves would revolt, as they did in the Denmark Vesey uprising of 1822. And South Carolinians were responsible for the direct cause of the Civil War. The young aristocrats who dominated political life here were hotheaded opponents of any action that in any way restricted slavery. In early 1861 these rebels opened fire on Fort Sumter in Charleston harbor, and so began the Civil War.

It is not hard to understand why, after the war, the state's white minority was enraged to see blacks take political power. For a time during the 1870s blacks controlled the South Carolina legislature and the state's congressional delegation. Such "outrages" of Reconstruction were soon ended, and the blacks—and most poor whites—lost the vote and all political rights. Meanwhile, as the 19th century went on, the once booming port of Charleston settled into economic stagnation, as did the rest of the state. For most of the 20th century South Carolina has been among the lowest-ranking states in per capita income, education levels, and health services. It has also had one of the lowest levels of electoral participation; as late as 1948 only 142,000 South Carolinians voted in the presidential election, in a state with more than two million people.

South Carolina no longer has the same economic base or racial mix that it did in the 19th century. Charleston lives today not on its earnings as a port but largely on the wealth poured in by numerous military bases, and the economic strength of the state has moved inland. Textiles are now the major industry here, with the biggest concentration of mills in the Piedmont region, along Interstate 85 that passes through Greenville and Spartanburg. As in other southern states, there was substantial black migration from the lowlands to the big cities of the North, and substantial increase in the white population, particularly around Columbia and in the Piedmont. South Carolina no longer has a black majority; 30% of its residents are black, a larger percentage than in any other state but Mississippi. But today that number may be on the rise. Black outmigration has slowed to a trickle, because there are now many more job opportunities in South Carolina, and since blacks have more children than whites the long-term prospect is for a higher black percentage.

From the days when the Democrats were the party of the South that stood against civil rights, white South Carolinians were Democrats; up through 1944, this was the single most Democratic state, casting more than 88% of its votes for Franklin Roosevelt. That changed, abruptly, when Hubert Humphrey persuaded the 1948 Democratic National Convention to adopt a strong civil rights plank. Strom Thurmond, then South Carolina's governor, ran as the "Dixiecrat" candidate and, although he won only 1% of the national vote, he carried 39 electoral votes. Since then South Carolina has been a marginal state in presidential elections. Democrats nearly lost it in 1952 and 1960, and Barry Goldwater carried it easily in 1964. And although the Voting Rights Act of 1965 enfranchised hundreds of thousands of South Carolina blacks, Richard Nixon was able to carry the state in a close three-way race in 1968. In 1976 South Carolina gave 56% of its vote to fellow southerner Jimmy Carter, but the electorate was fluid enough that both parties sent their candidates into the state during the last ten days of the campaign. In 1980 South Carolina was again one of the closest states; Reagan carried it by a 49% to 48% margin.

The Voting Rights Act effected as great a change in politics here as in any state of the Union. Today there are three basic voting groups in South Carolina, of roughly equal size. First there are what one might call the country club whites — well-to-do white people in the suburbs or suburban-style neighborhoods of South Carolina's medium and large cities. Their preferences can be gauged best in the returns for Lexington County, a predominantly suburban area outside Columbia; Lexington was 86% for Nixon in 1972 and 68% for Reagan in 1980. Among the affluent in South Carolina, there is no radical chic or sense of noblesse. They believe in the free enterprise system that has helped bring them in many cases to an economic status they never thought they would achieve, and they believe just as strongly in a strong and aggressive defense posture. The country club whites have been going Republican since the 1950s, and their heroes have been Goldwater and Reagan, Strom Thurmond and former Governor and now Energy Secretary James Edwards.

At the other end of the South Carolina electorate are the blacks, who were not a significant political factor until 1965. They now cast more than one-third of the votes in some parts of the state, and all politicians — including Thurmond — seek their support. With few exceptions, however, the blacks prefer Democrats, by overwhelming margins. That leaves as the key element in the electorate what we might call the textile mill whites. These are blue collar workers and farmers; they are found in the mill towns and rural counties and the working-class neighborhoods of large cities. In 1960 enough of them were still Democrats to carry the state for Kennedy; when the Democrats put through the Civil Rights Act, they went for Goldwater in 1964. In 1968 they went solidly for George Wallace, who almost carried the state, and in 1972 they were solidly for Nixon. Then in 1976 a majority of them returned to the Democrats and helped elect Carter. This has been the pattern in most statewide elections, with textile mill whites giving crucial votes to Senator Ernest Hollings in 1966, Governor Robert McNair that same year, and Governor John West in 1970. Just enough of them went Republican in 1980 to deliver the state to Ronald Reagan.

The one constant factor in South Carolina politics for more than thirty years now has been Strom Thurmond. He has a reputation for firmness and steadfastness, yet he has adjusted adroitly enough to remain popular with the vastly expanded and changed South Carolina electorate. Thurmond was elected governor in 1946 as a segregationist, and one of the strongest in the South; he was the Dixiecrat candidate in 1948, and in 1954 he was elected to the Senate in a stunning victory as a write-in candidate. In 1964 Thurmond switched from the Democratic Party to the Republicans out of enthusiasm for Barry Goldwater, and in 1968 he lobbied effectively among southern Republican convention delegations for Richard Nixon, preventing any Reagan breakthrough and getting Nixon his majority on the first ballot.

In the 1970s, Thurmond moved even more adroitly. Noting the increased number of black voters, he hired black staffers early in the decade and took care to make his constituency services available to black South Carolinians. Those moves have never really paid off in large numbers of black votes for him, but they have tended to prevent a large black turnout against him. When the Nixon Administration seemed weak on stopping textile imports, Thurmond attacked the White House strongly and got action. Although born in 1902, he has remained energetic; widowed, he married a young beauty queen and fathered the first of his three children when he was nearly 70.

Thurmond was not an early Reagan supporter; in fact, he stumped South Carolina for John Connally in what turned out to be Connally's last effort at presidential campaigning. But Thurmond has benefited as much from the Republican landslide of 1980 as any senator. For one thing, he is now Senate president pro tempore, an honorific position that nonetheless puts him fourth in line of succession to the presidency. More important, he is chairman of the Judiciary Committee. Only two years before, in 1979, Edward Kennedy had taken over the chair from the retiring James Eastland — a symbolic shift from conservative to liberal control that seemed like the beginning of a new era. But it did not last long. Thurmond laid the groundwork for his chairmanship even then, invoking his right of seniority and displacing Maryland's Charles Mathias as ranking Republican on the committee; thus when the Republicans won Thurmond got the chair without fuss. He moved quickly to cut the committee's staff; that plus the change in party control got rid of the liberal staffers Kennedy had hired by the dozen. He set up an Internal Security Subcommittee and appointed Alabama's Jeremiah Denton to chair it. Thurmond had on occasion worked on a bipartisan basis, as when he had cooperated with Kennedy on revision of the criminal code. But when he got the chair and the votes, he moved aggressively to advance his views on issues such as capital punishment. Thurmond is one of the last lawyers in Congress who studied law by himself at night, and he is not a master of legal nuance. But he is still, although nearly 80, sharp politically and he understands the implications of an adversary's amendment as well as anyone.

Thurmond's other major committee assignment is Armed Services. He is a retired general in the Army, an unabashed enthusiast for things military, a supporter of armed intervention just about anywhere it is conceivable. On Armed Services he is very much an Army man. He backs just about all the positions taken by the New Right. But he is cautious about advancing such issues as abortion to the forefront of public debate when the major goal of the Republican Party is to cut government spending. Thurmond believes very strongly in his principles, but he is a practical, wily politician, not a fanatic.

Thurmond won his most recent election in 1978, at age 76, and against a strong challenger, Democrat Charles Ravenel, who would have been elected governor in 1974 had he not been forced off the ballot by a legal challenge to his residency; Ravenel had an enthusiastic following among younger voters and blacks. But Thurmond's rock-hard strength among the majority of white voters, his unending energy, his substantial campaign budget all paid off, and he won a solid victory. Few people suppose he will run again when his seat comes up in 1984 (although who can tell?), and there is some thinking he would like to see his wife, Nancy Thurmond, succeed him. Although she devotes most of her time to raising their children, she appears to be astute politically and presumably shares his views on issues. Whether she can win as many votes, particularly against a strong Democrat, remains unclear.

South Carolina's junior senator is Ernest Hollings, like Thurmond a former governor but with a rather different sort of career. Hollings won the governorship as a moderate in 1958, and eight years later he beat former Governor Donald Russell in the 1966 primary for the seat vacated by the death of Senator Olin Johnston. That year was the crest of Republican partisan strength in the state, although no one knew it at the time, and Hollings won with only 51%. He has improved his showing substantially since: to 62% in 1968, 70% in 1974 and 1980.

Hollings has been for some years one of the key insiders of the Senate, a man who seldom made headlines but often made things happen. Then, in May 1980, he became chairman of the Senate Budget Committee when Edmund Muskie resigned to become secretary of state. His position was somewhat anomalous, because his views on budgetary matters are not those of a majority of Democratic senators — or at least of a majority of them at that time. Hollings is, for one thing, a strong believer in big defense budgets. Some think he is more hawkish than Thurmond, and he has worked, in the Senate generally and on the Defense Appropriations Subcommittee, to increase defense spending. But Hollings also believes in at least some domestic Democratic programs. He made quite a stir in the late 1960s by spotlighting the malnutrition that was then common in some of South Carolina's coastal counties, and he led the fight for antihunger legislation. He has also led the successful fight to end the oil depletion allowance for large oil producers.

Hollings is, in other words, something of the kind of progressive southern Democrat that flourished in the Roosevelt and Truman years — with the difference that he is a supporter of civil rights. Hollings does favor cutting federal spending substantially on many domestic programs and has proposed such cuts as ranking minority member of the Budget Committee. But he believes that there is a place for government regulation and for government action in behalf of the ordinary person against the forces of the marketplace. He serves as ranking Democrat on one of the most important regulatory subcommittees, Communications, which oversees regulation of the broadcast industry, the telephone company, and telecommunications.

Hollings has sought leadership positions on occasion; for a time in 1976 he was a candidate for majority leader. His current position as Budget's leading Democrat makes him de facto one of the party's leaders; but the position is temporary, and as it happens he holds it at a time when Democrats find it exceedingly difficult to agree on an approach to the Reagan initiatives. Finally, Hollings, more perhaps than any other member, looks like a senator, and he has the demeanor and the deep, commanding voice to match. He may become a more familiar figure to the general public in the years ahead.

Over most of the past decade, South Carolina has had governors outside the usual mold. James Edwards, the Republican orthodontist who won the office when Charles Ravenel was ruled off the ballot in 1974, turned in a more creditable performance than most observers had expected. He won appointment as Ronald Reagan's secretary of Energy in 1981. Again, he began his service with low expectations; at this writing, it remains to be seen whether he will exceed them again. The current governor, Richard Riley, made a name as a reform-minded Democratic state senator from the Republican city of Greenville; in his 14 years in the legislature he had sponsored such measures as aid to the elderly and changes in the composition of the commission that regulates utilities. Riley upset better-known candidates in the 1978 primary and runoff, and swept the general election. In office he has continued South Carolina's exceedingly successful attempts to attract new business (especially from abroad) and has grappled with the difficult problem of nuclear waste disposal (South Carolina, along with Washington and Nevada, disposes of virtually all the nation's nuclear wastes). He is respected by his fellow governors and was one of Jimmy Carter's leading supporters at the 1980 Democratic National Convention. The state's voters in 1980 approved a constitutional amendment allowing their governors to seek a second consecutive term, and Riley will almost certainly be favored to win reelection in 1982.

The Republican Party, however, had its biggest success in a long time in South Carolina in 1980. It has elected popular individuals such as Thurmond and has been positioned to take advantage of Democratic debacles, as in 1974. But it reached its peak in congressional elections as long ago as 1966 — until 1980, that is. Republicans now hold four out of South Carolina's six congressional districts. They have held the 2d district since its incumbent was drummed out of the Democratic Party for supporting Barry Goldwater in 1964, and picked up two others when Democratic incumbents retired: the 4th in 1978 and the 1st in 1980. The other was captured because incumbent Democrat John Jenrette was involved in the Abscam case, but even then the Republican won by only a narrow margin in what is ordinarily the most Democratic district in the state. Still the Republicans begin the 1980s with a majority of the state's congressional delegation for the first time since Reconstruction, and their incumbents are not likely to be hurt by redistricting.

Census Data   Pop. (1980 final) 3,119,208, up 20% in 1980s: 1.38% of U.S. total, 24th largest. Central city, 11%; suburban, 38%. Median 4-person family income, 1978, $18,468, 90% of U.S., 39th highest.

1979 Share of Federal Tax Burden $4,418,000,000; 0.98% of U.S. total, 30th largest.

1979 Share of Federal Outlays $5,378,448,000; 1.16% of U.S. total, 29th largest.

DOD	$1,532,966,000	21st (1.44%)	HEW	$1,946,010,000	29th (1.09%)
DOE	$359,262,000	12th (3.05%)	ERDA	$34,409,000	16th (1.26%)
HUD	$65,573,000	27th (0.99%)	NASA	$551,000	41st (0.01%)
VA	$303,877,000	28th (1.46%)	DOT	$116,431,000	37th (0.71%)
EPA	$63,060,000	26th (1.19%)	DOC	$17,152,000	28th (0.54%)
DOI	$32,572,000	36th (0.59%)	USDA	$306,223,000	35th (1.27%)

Economic Base   Textile mill products, especially cotton weaving mills; apparel and other textile products, especially women's and misses' outerwear; agriculture, notably tobacco, soybeans, cattle, and cotton lint; finance, insurance, and real estate; chemicals and allied products, especially plastics materials and synthetics; machinery, especially special industry machinery; food and kindred products.

Political Lineup   Governor, Richard W. Riley (D). Senators, Strom Thurmond (R) and Ernest F. Hollings (D). Representatives, 6 (4 R and 2 D); 6 in 1982. State Senate, 46 (41 D and 5 R); State House of Representatives, 124 (107 D and 17 R).

The Voters

Registration   1,235,521 Total.
Employment profile 1970   White collar, 37%. Blue collar, 47%. Service, 12%. Farm, 4%.
Ethnic groups   Black 1980, 30%. Hispanic 1980, 1%. Total foreign stock 1970, 2%.

Presidential Vote

1980	Reagan (R)	441,841	(49%)
	Carter (D)	430,385	(48%)
	Anderson (I)	14,071	(2%)
1976	Ford (R)	346,149	(43%)
	Carter (D)	450,807	(56%)

1980 Republican Presidential Primary

Reagan	79,549	(55%)
Connally	43,113	(30%)
Bush	21,569	(15%)
Five others	1,270	(1%)

SENATORS

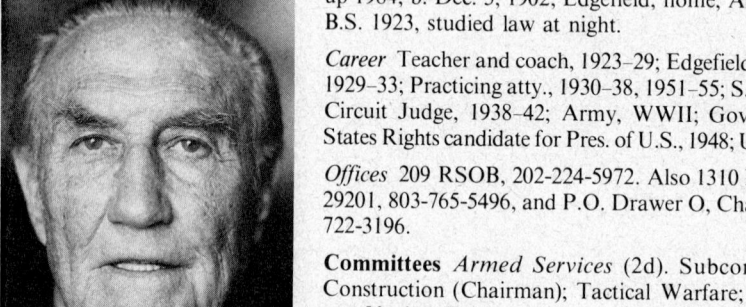

Sen. Strom Thurmond (R) Elected 1956 as Dem., changed party affiliation to Rep. Sept. 16, 1964, seat up 1984; b. Dec. 5, 1902, Edgefield; home, Aiken; Clemson Col., B.S. 1923, studied law at night.

Career Teacher and coach, 1923–29; Edgefield Co. Supt. of Educ., 1929–33; Practicing atty., 1930–38, 1951–55; S.C. Senate, 1933–38; Circuit Judge, 1938–42; Army, WWII; Gov. of S.C., 1947–51; States Rights candidate for Pres. of U.S., 1948; U.S. Senate, 1954–56.

Offices 209 RSOB, 202-224-5972. Also 1310 Lady St., Columbia 29201, 803-765-5496, and P.O. Drawer O, Charleston 29402, 803-722-3196.

Committees *Armed Services* (2d). Subcommittees: Military Construction (Chairman); Tactical Warfare; Strategic and The-atre Nuclear Forces.

Judiciary (Chairman). Subcommittees: Constitution; Courts; Immigration and Refugee Policy.

Veterans' Affairs (2d).

Group Ratings

	ADA	COPE	PC	LCV	CFA	RPN	NAB	NSI	NTU	ACA	ACU
1980	17	11	17	27	0	—	100	100	63	88	86
1979	5	0	18	—	5	—	—	—	61	83	90
1978	10	21	23	11	20	56	80	100	28	87	91

Key Votes

1) Draft Registn $	FOR	6) Fair Housng Cloture	AGN	11) Cut Socl Incr Defns	FOR
2) Ban $ to Nicrgua	AGN	7) Ban $ Rape Abortns	FOR	12) Income Tax Indexing	FOR
3) Dlay MX Missile	AGN	8) Cap on Food Stmp $	FOR	13) Lim Spdg 21% GNP	FOR
4) Nuclr Mortorium	AGN	9) New US Dep Edcatn	FOR	14) Incr Wndfll Prof Tax	AGN
5) Alaska Lands Bill	FOR	10) Cut OSHA Inspctns	FOR	15) Chryslr Loan Grntee	AGN

Election Results

1978 general	Strom Thurmond (R)	351,733	(56%)	($2,013,431)
	Charles D. Ravenel (D)	281,119	(44%)	($1,134,168)
1978 primary	Strom Thurmond (R), unopposed			
1972 general	Strom Thurmond (R)	415,806	(63%)	($666,372)
	Eugene N. Zeigler (D)...........	241,056	(37%)	($167,750)

Sen. Ernest F. Hollings (D) Elected 1966, seat up 1986; b. Jan. 1, 1922, Charleston; home, Charleston; The Citadel, B.A. 1942; U. of So. Car., LL.B. 1947.

Career Practicing atty., 1947–58, 1963–66; S.C. House of Reps., 1949–55, Spkr. Pro Tem, 1951–55; Lt. Gov. of S.C., 1955–59; Gov of S.C., 1959–63.

Offices 115 RSOB, 202-224-6121. Also 306 Fed. Bldg., Columbia 29201, 803-765-5731, and 103 Fed. Bldg., Spartanburg 29301, 803-585-3702.

Committees *Appropriations* (5th). Subcommittees: Defense; Energy and Water Development; Labor, Health and Human Services, Education; Legislative Branch; State, Justice, Commerce, and the Judiciary.

Budget (Ranking Member).

Commerce, Science and Transportation (3d). Subcommittees: Communications; Science, Technology and Space; Surface Transportation.

Group Ratings

	ADA	COPE	PC	LCV	CFA	RPN	NAB	NSI	NTU	ACA	ACU
1980	39	22	33	44	27	—	50	70	44	43	40
1979	32	41	20	—	38	—	—	—	32	35	40
1978	30	39	58	57	60	44	58	56	18	52	50

Key Votes

1) Draft Registn $	FOR	6) Fair Housng Cloture	FOR	11) Cut Socl Incr Defns	FOR
2) Ban $ to Nicrgua	AGN	7) Ban $ Rape Abortns	AGN	12) Income Tax Indexing	AGN
3) Dlay MX Missile	—	8) Cap on Food Stmp $	AGN	13) Lim Spdg 21% GNP	AGN
4) Nuclr Mortorium	AGN	9) New US Dep Edcatn	FOR	14) Incr Wndfll Prof Tax	FOR
5) Alaska Lands Bill	FOR	10) Cut OSHA Inspctns	FOR	15) Chryslr Loan Grntee	—

Election Results

1980 general	Ernest F. Hollings (D)	612,554	(70%)	($736,623)
	Marshall Mays (R)	257,946	(30%)	($62,472)
1980 primary	Ernest F. Hollings (D)	266,796	(81%)	
	Two others (D)	61,072	(19%)	
1974 general	Ernest F. Hollings (D)	356,126	(70%)	($225,678)
	Gwenyfred Bush (R)	146,645	(29%)	($6,754)

GOVERNOR

Gov. Richard W. Riley (D) Elected 1978, term expires Jan. 1983; b. Jan. 2, 1932, Greenville; Furman U., B.A., U. of So. Car., LL.B. 1960.

Career Legal Counsel to U.S. Sen. Olin D. Johnston, 1960–61; Practicing atty., 1961–; S.C. House of Reps., 1963–67; S.C. Senate, 1967–77.

Offices State House, 1st Floor West Wing, Box 11450, Columbia 29211, 803-758-3208.

Election Results

1978 gen.	Richard W. Riley (D)	385,016	(61%)
	Edward L. Young (R)	236,946	(38%)
1978 runoff	Richard W. Riley (D)	180,882	(53%)
	Brantley Harvey (D)	158,655	(47%)
1978 prim.	Brantley Harvey (D)	142,785	(37%)
	Richard W. Riley (D)	125,185	(33%)
	Bryan Dorn (D)	112,793	(30%)
1974 gen.	James B. Edwards (R)	266,109	(51%)
	Bryan Dorn (D)	248,938	(48%)

FIRST DISTRICT

In the spring the pastel row houses of Charleston are wreathed with flowers of the blossoming trees. There are few, if any, more beautiful urban scenes in America. Charleston, founded in 1670 and blessed with one of the finest harbors on the Atlantic, was one of the South's leading cities up to the Civil War. Across its docks went cargoes of rice, indigo, cotton — all crops cultivated by black slaves and designed to enrich the white planters and merchants who dominated the state's economic and political life. In the years following the Civil War, Charleston became an economic backwater. Today the old part of the city, beautifully preserved and still the home of the city's elite, houses fewer people than it did in 1860.

Charleston has always been the center of life for South Carolina's proud aristocracy. These people are not heard from much today, but once they were a leading force in American political life. The Democrats held their national convention in Charleston in 1860, and the hotheaded dandies in the galleries hooted down the northerners and so disrupted the proceedings that the northerners adjourned and reconvened in Baltimore while the southerners nominated a separate ticket. That split in the Democratic Party made possible Lincoln's minority victory, which in turn stimulated Charlestonians to fire on Fort Sumter — and brought Civil War.

Charleston has always had a large black community as well, one whose history and culture has been memorialized in *Porgy and Bess*. Today politics in the Charleston area is largely a matter of blacks on one side supporting the Democrats and whites on the other supporting Republicans. This was not always so. In the 1950s and 1960s there was a white working-class vote in North Charleston, around the Naval Yard, that was particularly strong for Democratic Congressman Mendel Rivers. Rivers was a high-ranking member and eventually chairman of the House Armed Services Committee, and as chairman he worked to make sure that Charleston had plenty of military bases. When he died in 1971, one-third of the payrolls in Charleston and surrounding areas came directly or indirectly from the military.

The 1970s have been as healthy a decade economically as Charleston and lowland South

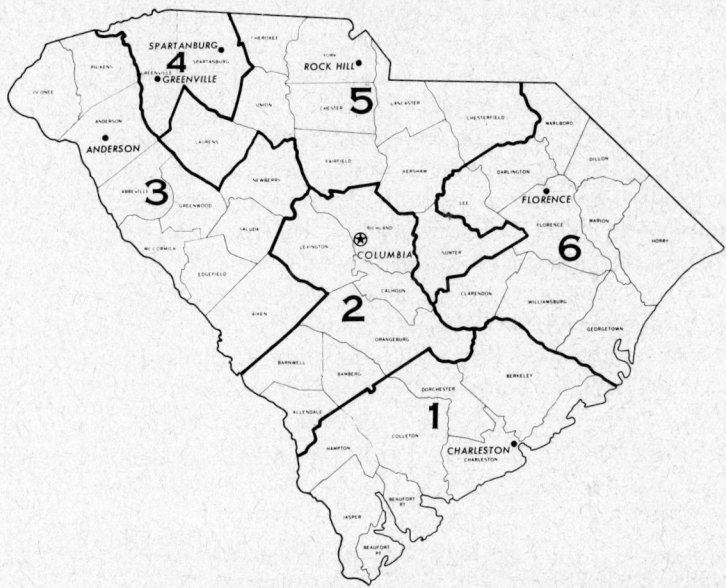

Carolina have seen since Fort Sumter was fired upon. Charleston still has plenty of military bases, but it is not as dependent on the military payrolls as it used to be. South Carolina has had tremendous economic expansion, and while most of the new plants have been inland, in the Piedmont area, some of the growth has been in the lowlands as well. Some developments are controversial, such as Arab-owned Kiawah Island; some developments just quietly provide more jobs. Growth has also provided an increasing economic base for the high-income class of whites who are the modern-day political equivalent of the old Charleston aristocracy. The high-income residential neighborhoods of Charleston itself, whether in the old downtown of the new West of Ashley area, or its suburbs, the pleasant condominiums of Hilton Head and other developments — all these areas are heavily Republican in most elections. They provide a strong political base for such Republicans as Senator Strom Thurmond, former Governor James Edwards, and for Republican presidential candidates.

High-income whites also provide a political base for the new congressman from the 1st district of South Carolina, Tom Hartnett. The 1st district includes Charleston and the surrounding areas and the lowlands to the south, which include the Marine Corps's training base at Parris Island and Hilton Head. They also include some of the poorest black communities in the United States, places where people suffered until a few years ago from malnutrition and where a distinct dialect called Gullah is still spoken.

The 1st district had a seriously contested House race in 1980 when the incumbent, Democrat Mendel Davis, a godson of Mendel Rivers, decided to retire at age 38. The better-known candidate by far was Charles Ravenel. He would have been elected governor in 1974, except that his name was removed from the ballot in the last weeks of the campaign as the result of a lawsuit challenging his residency; in 1978, he had tried to unseat Strom Thurmond and won 44% of the vote. Ravenel brought several assets to the race. He was well known, and his youthfulness and enthusiasm still stirred many voters. He had strong support from virtually all of the district's blacks. But he also had some liabilities. He was running his third race for three different offices, and to some he looked like a perennial candidate. His stands on many issues antagonized many voters like himself—affluent young suburban family people, most of whom here are strongly Republican. He was identified with opposition to the Vietnam war—not a popular position in an area that still depends heavily on military payrolls and expects its congressman to serve on the Armed Services Committee.

The liabilities proved decisive. Ravenel won his primary, but with only 56% of the vote against one serious opponent and two nuisance candidates. In the general, he had a strong opponent in Hartnett, a state senator from an affluent Charleston suburb. Like many other South Carolina Republicans, Hartnett used to be a Democrat; he had served in the legislature for 16 years. During the campaign, it was suggested that Hartnett might have a hard time getting a seat on the Armed Services Committee, on which Republican Floyd Spence of the 2d district already serves. But Hartnett did get a seat on this panel. Redistricting seems likely to make only minor changes in the district's boundaries.

Census Data   Pop. (1980 final) 560,004, up 27% in 1970s. Median family income, 1970, $7,355, 77% of U.S.

The Voters

Employment profile 1970   White collar, 44%. Blue collar, 39%. Service, 15%. Farm, 2%.
Ethnic groups   Black 1980, 33%. Hispanic 1980, 2%. Asian 1980, 1%. Total foreign stock 1970, 4%.

Presidential Vote

1980	Reagan (R)	85,693	(53%)
	Carter (D)	70,952	(44%)
	Anderson (I)	3,027	(2%)
1976	Ford (R)	59,939	(46%)
	Carter (D)	70,124	(53%)

Rep. Thomas F. Hartnett (R) Elected 1980; b. Aug. 7, 1941, Charleston; home, Mount Pleasant; Col. of Charleston, 1960–62, U. of S.C., 1978.

Career   Air Force, 1963, Reserve 1963–69; Pres., Hartnett Realty Co.; S.C. House of Reps., 1965–72; S.C. Senate, 1973–80.

Offices   509 CHOB, 202-225-3176. Also 263 Hampton St., Walterboro 29488, 803-549-5395; 640 Fed. Bldg., 334 Meeting St., Charleston 29403, 803-724-4175; and P.O. Box 1538, Beaufort 29902, 803-524-2166.

Committee   *Armed Services* (19th). Subcommittees: Military Personnel and Compensation; Seapower and Strategic and Critical Materials.

Group Ratings and Key Votes: Newly Elected

Election Results

1980 general	Thomas F. Hartnett (R)	81,988	(52%)	($226,394)
	Charles D. Ravenel (D)	76,743	(48%)	($179,933)
1980 primary	Thomas F. Hartnett (R)	10,510	(75%)	
	Moore (R)	3,428	(25%)	
1978 general	Mendel J. Davis (D)	65,832	(61%)	($124,943)
	C. C. Wanamaker (R)..........	42,811	(39%)	($49,079)

SECOND DISTRICT

Between the coastal swamps and the industrialized Piedmont of South Carolina, square in the middle of the state, is the capital, Columbia. This is South Carolina's largest city, the only one with a population near 100,000, and its fastest growing. Like so many other cities in the South during the 1960s and 1970s, Columbia has been trending Republican. Some observers attributed this phenomenon to an influx of northerners; but this is surely wrong, for there are fewer people from out of state here than in just about any other place in the nation.

The Republican trend was something indigenous, the result of upwardly mobile people from smaller towns and rural areas of the state, moving here to white collar jobs in the growing private sector — insurance agents, computer salesmen, production managers, etc. Uprooted from their traditionally Democratic rural environment and thrust up several notches in social class, these migrants have found the state's Republicans younger, more modern, and generally more congenial than old-style southern Democrats. Raised in the tradition of Franklin D. Roosevelt, they have learned about the glories of the free market and the virtues of the free enterprise system. So most of the white portions of Columbia and its suburbs, particularly those in Lexington County, had by the early 1970s become the bulwark of South Carolina Republicanism.

Columbia, with its suburbs in Richland and Lexington Counties, casts more than 70% of the votes in the state's 2d congressional district. The remainder come from an older part of South Carolina: the black-majority counties closer to the coast. The largest town here is Orangeburg, with only 13,000 people, where white highway patrolmen massacred several black students at South Carolina State College in 1968. These lower counties usually go Democratic but in many elections have been heavily outvoted by the Columbia area.

This seat has been in Republican hands since 1965, when Congressman Albert Watson was stripped of his seniority for backing Barry Goldwater and decided to join the Republican Party. Watson gave up the seat when he ran for governor and lost in 1970, and he was succeeded by Floyd Spence, by then a Republican, but who had lost the 1962 Democratic primary to Watson. A genial man of the good old boy type, Spence won a seat on the Armed Services Committee — a good spot to tend to the needs of Columbia's Fort Jackson — and was also assigned to the Ethics Committee, on which he has served as ranking Republican. Spence is the kind of man whom congressmen have liked to name to ethics posts: personally honest, but not ready to believe anything bad about his colleagues unless he is forced to. He is respected more for his pleasant personality than for intellectual originality.

Spence was unopposed for renomination and reelection, but since the Watergate scandal broke he has not had such an easy time. The disgrace of Richard Nixon moved many rural and blue collar whites in South Carolina back to their ancestral Democratic Party and put such politicians as Spence on the defensive. In the four elections since, he has had significant Democratic opposition and has not won with more than 58%. Some of his opponents have had interesting credentials. Matthew Perry, a black Columbia lawyer who ran in 1974, has since been named to the federal bench on the recommendation of, among others, Strom Thurmond. Jack Bass, the Democratic nominee in 1978, is a top newspaper reporter and writer and the author of the definitive work on the Orangeburg massacre. Tom Turnipseed, the 1980 Democrat, is a former George Wallace backer who has tried to forge a coalition of blacks and populist whites; he ran for governor in 1978 but withdrew before the primary. But none of them could really crack the newly affluent Republican vote in the Columbia area; Turnipseed, for example, could get no better than 28% in Lexington County. One must conclude from Spence's victories over such candidates that he has reasonable safety in this district.

Census Data   Pop. (1980 final) 551,344, up 24% in 1970s. Median family income, 1970, $7,900, 82% of U.S.

The Voters

  Employment profile 1970   White collar, 47%. Blue collar, 36%. Service, 14%. Farm, 3%.
  Ethnic groups   Black 1980, 36%. Hispanic 1980, 1%. Asian 1980, 1%. Total foreign stock 1970, 3%.

Presidential Vote

1980	Reagan (R)	84,354	(52%)
	Carter (D)	73,940	(45%)
	Anderson (I)	2,934	(2%)
1976	Ford (R)	69,827	(47%)
	Carter (D)	76,948	(52%)

Rep. Floyd Spence (R) Elected 1970; b. Apr. 9, 1928, Columbia; home, Lexington; U. of So. Car., B.A. 1952, LL.B. 1956.

Career Navy, Korea; Practicing atty.; S.C. House of Reps., 1956–62; S.C. Senate, 1966–70, Minor. Ldr.

Offices 2427 RHOB, 202-225-2452. Also Rm. 104, 2001 Assembly St., Columbia 29201, 803-765-5871.

Committees *Armed Services* (3d). Subcommittees: Readiness; Seapower and Strategic and Critical Materials.

Standards of Official Conduct (Ranking Member).

Group Ratings

	ADA	COPE	PC	LCV	CFA	RPN	NAB	NSI	NTU	ACA	ACU
1980	11	16	20	30	14	—	83	100	54	83	79
1979	5	5	10	24	4	—	—	—	54	96	87
1978	15	20	15	28	14	50	100	100	21	87	88

Key Votes

1) Draft Registn $	FOR	6) Fair Hsg DOJ Enfrc	AGN	11) Cut Socl Incr Dfns $	FOR
2) Ban $ to Nicrgua	FOR	7) Lim PAC Contrbtns	AGN	12) Hosptl Cost Controls	AGN
3) Dlay MX Missile	AGN	8) Cap on Food Stmp $	FOR	13) Gasln Ctrls & Allctns	AGN
4) Nuclr Mortorium	AGN	9) New US Dep Edcatn	FOR	14) Lim Wndfll Prof Tax	FOR
5) Alaska Lands Bill	FOR	10) Cut OSHA $	FOR	15) Chryslr Loan Grntee	AGN

Election Results

1980 general	Floyd Spence (R)	92,306	(56%)	($275,010)
	Tom Turnipseed (D)	73,353	(44%)	($72,779)
1980 primary	Floyd Spence (R), unopposed			
1978 general	Floyd Spence (R)	71,208	(57%)	($182,995)
	Jack Bass (D)	53,021	(43%)	($136,959)

THIRD DISTRICT

As you move inland from the South Carolina coast, you see fewer and fewer black people. It is a matter of history and economics. The land along the coast is ideal for growing such crops as rice and cotton, which are labor-intensive; so early planters kept thousands of slaves. Inland the terrain is hilly, the rainfall less plentiful, and the soil less fertile; the tradition here is of single-family farms, few of which could afford to support slaves. So while many rural counties along the coast have black majorities today, the population of the Piedmont country of the 3d congressional district is 77% white.

The 3d is an upcountry district, lying mostly along the Savannah River, the boundary with Georgia. The southern part of the district is Strom Thurmond country: he grew up in Edgefield and maintains his residence in Aiken, a prosperous nuclear energy city halfway between Columbia and Augusta, Georgia. Like Thurmond, Aiken became Republican in the 1960s, while the counties farther upriver remained traditionally southern Democratic by backing George Wallace in 1968. Anderson, a heavily white textile mill town and the most populous city in the district with 27,000 people, was the largest South Carolina city carried by Wallace that year. But by 1976 the textile mill whites had gone back to the Democrats; Jimmy Carter took Anderson County with 67% and carried it again in 1980.

The current congressman, Butler Derrick, won the seat in 1974 when the Democrats were suddenly strong again in this area; he is now one of only two Democrats left in the South Carolina House delegation. Derrick has attracted some attention in Washington for taking positions not normally associated with southern congressmen. He was the leadoff speaker in the drive to oust Florida's Bob Sikes from the chair of the Military Construction Subcommittee in 1977. He supported Jimmy Carter's plan to cut funds for water projects, and when Carter announced cancellation of a dam in the 3d district Derrick, instead of squawking, said he agreed. And he has argued for detailed congressional oversight of federal programs with periodic assessment of whether they are doing what they were created to do.

Derrick is a member of the Rules Committee, part of an 11–5 Democratic majority on that body that sets the terms under which almost all bills can be considered and amended by the full House. Derrick is one of the few Democratic members of Rules who is not considered automatically loyal to the Democratic leadership. Although he generally does support leadership positions, he must be persuaded to do so on the merits, and his support cannot be taken for granted. Derrick has been mentioned as a possible candidate for statewide office and may turn out to be a contender for Strom Thurmond's Senate seat in 1984.

Census Data   Pop. (1980 final) 519,823, up 20% in 1970s. Median family income, 1970, $8,002, 84% of U.S.

The Voters

   Employment profile 1970   White collar, 32%. Blue collar, 56%. Service, 10%. Farm, 2%.
   Ethnic groups   Black 1980, 22%. Hispanic 1980, 1%. Total foreign stock 1970, 1%.

Presidential Vote

1980	Reagan (R)	70,256	(48%)
	Carter (D)	73,333	(50%)
	Anderson (I)	2,176	(2%)
1976	Ford (R)	54,640	(41%)
	Carter (D)	78,296	(59%)

Rep. Butler Derrick (D) Elected 1974; b. Sept. 30, 1936, Johnston; home, Edgefield; U. of So. Car., B.A. 1958, U. of Ga., LL.B. 1965.

Career Practicing atty., 1965–74; S.C. House of Reps., 1969–75.

Offices 133 CHOB, 202-225-5301. Also 315 S. McDuffie St., Anderson 29621, 803-224-7401.

Committees *Rules* (7th). Subcommittee: The Legislative Process.

Select Committee on Aging (24th). Subcommittee: Health and Long-Term Care.

Group Ratings

	ADA	COPE	PC	LCV	CFA	RPN	NAB	NSI	NTU	ACA	ACU
1980	56	68	40	55	50	—	50	38	27	50	25
1979	37	44	38	43	30	—	—	—	28	24	23
1978	45	86	58	77	46	36	46	80	20	44	38

Key Votes

1) Draft Registn $	FOR	6) Fair Hsg DOJ Enfrc	FOR	11) Cut Socl Incr Dfns $	AGN
2) Ban $ to Nicrgua	—	7) Lim PAC Contrbtns	FOR	12) Hosptl Cost Controls	AGN
3) Dlay MX Missile	AGN	8) Cap on Food Stmp $	AGN	13) Gasln Ctrls & Allctns	FOR
4) Nuclr Mortorium	AGN	9) New US Dep Edcatn	FOR	14) Lim Wndfll Prof Tax	FOR
5) Alaska Lands Bill	FOR	10) Cut OSHA $	AGN	15) Chryslr Loan Grntee	FOR

Election Results

1980 general	Butler Derrick (D)	87,680	(60%)	($88,255)
	Marshall Parker (R)	57,840	(39%)	($66,047)
1980 primary	Butler Derrick (D), unopposed			
1978 general	Butler Derrick (D)	81,638	(82%)	($84,641)
	Anthony Panuccio (R)	17,973	(18%)	

FOURTH DISTRICT

The major textile producing area in the United States is a strip of land along Interstate 85 in North and South Carolina. Two of the biggest textile centers here are Greenville and Spartanburg, South Carolina — the two cities that, with the counties that surround them, make up South Carolina's 4th congressional district. It will probably come as a surprise to many readers that this is one of the most industrialized and most blue collar parts of the nation; the fact surprises even tourists who drive through the South Carolina Piedmont on their way south. For the mills are not concentrated in a few big factories, like giant steel plants, in the inner part of grimy cities. They are all over, in small towns and suburbs, at interchanges on the Interstate as well as in Greenville and Spartanburg themselves. Few blacks live here — only 19% districtwide, the lowest percentage in South Carolina. And there are even fewer union members: South Carolina has just about the least unionized work force of any state in the nation, and a major reason is the intransigent opposition of the mill owners to unionization. These conditions — low wages, no unions, large work force — have helped South Carolina attract new industry, and many German and French companies now have major installations not far from Interstate 85. It is one of the boom parts of the country.

Politically Greenville and Spartanburg have different traditions. Greenville is the state's premier Republican city; there are lots of textile management types and also a local establishment of considerable distinction, including federal Judge and onetime Supreme Court nominee Clement Haynsworth and former Governor and Senator Donald Russell, himself now a federal judge. Spartanburg is a rougher, more blue collar town, traditionally Democratic. Its most famous citizens were the late Senator (1931–41), Supreme Court Justice (1941–42), Secretary of State (1945–47), and Governor (1951–55) James Byrnes and the late Governor (1935–39, 1943–45) and Senator (1945–65) Olin Johnston, who was something of an oldtime southern populist.

But the dominant fact of political life here for many years was low turnout. In 1972, it cast fewer votes than any other district in the nation except a couple in the New York slums, and 80% of its ballots were for Richard Nixon. The Deering–Milliken executives, the bankers and insurance agents, the country club members were all voting; many white textile workers, with low wages and perhaps no roots in the community other than a lease on a trailer park space, were not. Local population growth and the sudden identification of the Democratic Party, when it nominated Jimmy Carter, with the white South, increased turnout vastly. Between 1972 and 1976, the Republican vote was down 16,000, but the Democratic presidential vote rose by 44,000; Carter carried the district, albeit with only 52%.

That trend seems to have been reversed by four years of the Carter Administration and the booming economic growth of the Interstate 85 corridor. Between 1976 and 1980, Carter's total went down 3,000, while the Republican presidential vote rose by 17,000. This showing records not only population growth but also a kind of buoyant faith in the free enterprise system that seems to be rewarding the Greenville–Spartanburg area for its hard work with all kinds of new plants (many from German firms) and development. Unions have tried to attract the workers here, and at the national level the Textile Workers Union succeeded in winning a contract from J. P. Stevens; but in the textile mills along Interstate 85 people seem happy or at least content with the way things are going. There is a dynamism — and a political conservatism — that recalls the America of the 1920s.

The Republican trend here in the presidential election of 1980 was presaged by the congressional election of 1978. That year the Democratic incumbent, James Mann, a member of the Greenville establishment, retired. Two quite different candidates vied for the right to succeed him. One was Max Heller, the Democratic mayor of Greenville. He had come to the city 40 years before as a refugee from Austria when it was occupied by the Nazis. Starting off as a stock boy, he built his own shirt manufacturing firm; elected mayor, he put together a successful downtown redevelopment program. But Heller was unable to turn his hometown popularity into votes in the congressional race; one reason may have been his Jewish religion in a part of the country where many voters want Christian officeholders.

The winner of the election was the Republican, Carroll Campbell. A generation younger than Heller, he had run for lieutenant governor in 1974 and had been elected to the state Senate in 1976. In both his politics and his personal characteristics he is typical of the young, newly affluent urban voters of such states as South Carolina. He believes in the free enterprise system, he believes taxes are too high, and he believes that government is too big. His party label helped him win a majority in Greenville and he was able to prevent Heller from winning a majority in Spartanburg. Heller and Campbell symbolize two very different approaches to politics, and Greenville–Spartanburg seems clearly to have preferred what has been referred to as the blow-dry conservatism represented by Campbell. He was reelected without Democratic opposition in 1980.

In the House Campbell became a member of the Appropriations Committee in 1981. He is well positioned for a long career in the House, although it is also possible that he might run for statewide office, for governor in 1982, or U.S. senator in 1984.

Census Data   Pop. (1980 final) 489,466, up 18% in 1970s. Median family income, 1970, $8,416, 88% of U.S.

The Voters

Employment profile 1970   White collar, 39%. Blue collar, 49%. Service, 11%. Farm, 1%.
Ethnic groups   Black 1980, 19%. Hispanic 1980, 1%. Total foreign stock 1970, 2%.

Presidential Vote

1980	Reagan (R)	76,147	(54%)
	Carter (D)	60,549	(43%)
	Anderson (I)	2,624	(2%)
1976	Ford (R)	59,555	(48%)
	Carter (D)	63,848	(51%)

Rep. Carroll A. Campbell, Jr. (R) Elected 1978; b. July 24, 1940, Greenville; home, Greenville; U. of So. Car.

Career   Real estate and farming; S.C. House of Reps., 1970–74; Exec. Asst. to Gov. James B. Edwards, 1975–76; S.C. Senate, 1976–78.

Offices   408 CHOB, 202-225-6030. Also P.O. Box 10011, Greenville 29603, 803-232-1411.

Committee   *Appropriations* (21st). Subcommittees: Commerce, Justice, State, and Judiciary; Legislature; Treasury–Postal Service–General Government.

Group Ratings

	ADA	COPE	PC	LCV	CFA	RPN	NAB	NSI	NTU	ACA	ACU
1980	6	11	17	37	21	—	92	100	56	83	81
1979	5	5	13	20	4	—	—	—	57	92	92

Key Votes

1) Draft Registn $	FOR	6) Fair Hsg DOJ Enfrc	AGN	11) Cut Socl Incr Dfns $	FOR
2) Ban $ to Nicrgua	FOR	7) Lim PAC Contrbtns	AGN	12) Hosptl Cost Controls	AGN
3) Dlay MX Missile	AGN	8) Cap on Food Stmp $	FOR	13) Gasln Ctrls & Allctns	AGN
4) Nuclr Mortorium	AGN	9) New US Dep Edcatn	FOR	14) Lim Wndfll Prof Tax	FOR
5) Alaska Lands Bill	FOR	10) Cut OSHA $	FOR	15) Chryslr Loan Grntee	AGN

Election Results

1980 general	Carroll A. Campbell, Jr. (R)	90,941	(93%)	($153,606)
	Thomas Waldenfels (Libertarian) . .	6,984	(7%)	($0)
1980 primary	Carroll A. Campbell, Jr. (R), unopp.			
1978 general	Carroll A. Campbell, Jr. (R)	51,377	(52%)	($182,461)
	Max M. Heller (D)	45,484	(46%)	($240,150)

FIFTH DISTRICT

Stock car racing, one of the nation's most popular sports, thrives most today in such places as the 5th congressional district of South Carolina. After World War II, textile companies fled from the Northeast to shiny new factories on the outskirts of small towns such as Rock Hill and Gaffney in South Carolina. Here plenty of people were eager to work long hours for low wages under poor conditions, and few of them had any funny ideas about joining a union. In the 5th district's textile towns and their outskirts, whites heavily outnumber blacks; although in some smaller, less developed counties, blacks still have a near-majority. But the political spirit prevailing in the 5th is best symbolized by the fan at the stock car races — the yahooing white southerner whom W. J. Cash called "a hell of a fellow."

The 5th is a traditionally Democratic district, but it was one of two South Carolina districts to go for George Wallace in 1968 and went heavily for Richard Nixon in 1972. But the Democratic allegiance returned after the Watergate scandal was exposed and after the Democrats nominated Jimmy Carter. On Labor Day in 1976 Carter appeared at the Southern 500 stock car race, held just next door to the 5th district, on the same day as Republican vice presidential candidate Bob Dole. Dole got only a tepid welcome, while Carter got big cheers. It was a preview of how the two tickets would run in stock car country; the Georgian took 61% of the votes in the 5th district. Even in 1980 he won a solid victory here.

Carter's margin was a political asset for Democratic Congressman Ken Holland. First elected in 1974, he was facing formidable opposition in the person of Bobby Richardson, the longtime scrambling second baseman for the New York Yankees. Richardson was raised in South Carolina and was known locally for his participation in sports programs for youth and for his strong religious beliefs; he represented the evangelical strain in southern culture. Holland, who had been divorced in his first term, represented the hell of a fellow strain. With some help from Carter, Holland was able to win with 52%; this is one of the few districts in the country where coattails may have made the difference in 1976.

Since that election, Holland has gained another political asset: a seat on the House Ways and Means Committee. This is not just a matter of academic interest. Ways and Means has jurisdiction over foreign trade restrictions, and the textile industry, although doing very well, is eager to prevent or reduce imports of textiles from low-wage countries, particularly those in East Asia. Holland is very much textile's man on Ways and Means. He is the senior Democrat on the committee from a textile district and has had a seat on the Trade Subcommittee. He has won a number of victories for the industry and continually applies pressure for restrictions. After his tough election in 1976, Holland did not have Republican opposition at all in 1978 or 1980 — a fact that tells us something about the lack of depth of the South Carolina Republican Party. His importance to the textile industry should help him make this seat safe if he faces any future significant challenges.

Census Data　Pop. (1980 final) 500,296, up 13% in 1970s. Median family income, 1970, $7,623, 80% of U.S.

The Voters

Employment profile 1970　White collar, 30%. Blue collar, 56%. Service, 12%. Farm, 2%.
Ethnic groups　Black 1980, 31%. Hispanic 1980, 1%. Total foreign stock 1970, 1%.

Presidential Vote

1980	Reagan (R)	59,033	(44%)
	Carter (D)	71,387	(54%)
	Anderson (I)	1,761	(1%)
1976	Ford (R)	50,328	(39%)
	Carter (D)	77,715	(60%)

Rep. Kenneth L. (Ken) Holland (D) Elected 1974; b. Nov. 24, 1934, Hickory, N.C.; home, Camden; U. of So. Car., A.B. 1960, LL.B. 1963.

Career　Employee, S.C. St. Hwy. Comm., 1953–55; Instrumentman, Daniel Construction Co., 1956; Practicing atty., 1963–74; Legal Counsel, S.C. Dem. Party.

Offices　2431 RHOB, 202-225-5501. Also P.O. Box 272, CSS, Rock Hill 29730, 803-327-1114.

Committees　*Standards of Official Conduct* (5th).

Ways and Means (10th). Subcommittees: Health; Select Revenue Measures.

Group Ratings

	ADA	COPE	PC	LCV	CFA	RPN	NAB	NSI	NTU	ACA	ACU
1980	22	60	27	42	21	—	45	57	25	41	44
1979	42	53	20	37	11	—	—	—	28	19	26
1978	35	61	33	44	18	57	67	67	18	46	45

Key Votes

1) Draft Registn $	FOR	6) Fair Hsg DOJ Enfrc	AGN	11) Cut Socl Incr Dfns $	AGN
2) Ban $ to Nicrgua	FOR	7) Lim PAC Contrbtns	AGN	12) Hosptl Cost Controls	AGN
3) Dlay MX Missile	AGN	8) Cap on Food Stmp $	AGN	13) Gasln Ctrls & Allctns	AGN
4) Nuclr Mortorium	AGN	9) New US Dep Edcatn	FOR	14) Lim Wndfll Prof Tax	FOR
5) Alaska Lands Bill	FOR	10) Cut OSHA $	FOR	15) Chryslr Loan Grntee	FOR

Election Results

1980 general	Kenneth L. (Ken) Holland (D)....	99,773	(88%)	($89,208)
	Thomas Campbell (Libertarian) ...	14,252	(12%)	($60)
1980 primary	Kenneth L. Holland (D), unopposed			
1978 general	Kenneth L. (Ken) Holland (D)....	63,358	(83%)	($91,690)
	Harold Hough (I)	13,251	(17%)	

SIXTH DISTRICT

The 6th congressional district of South Carolina is the northeastern corner of the state, where the Pee Dee and Santee Rivers flow through lowland country down to the beaches of the South Carolina Strand. This is a region of tobacco farms, textile mills, and ocean beaches. Most of the 6th's residents and voters live in and around such textile mill towns as Florence and Darlington, the latter the site of the Southern 500 stock car race. The fact that this is lowland, not upcountry, makes a big political difference: as in most of coastal South Carolina, there is a large black population, a reminder of the fact that before the Civil War this was an area of large plantations and slave majorities. For many years blacks left the district in large numbers every year, looking for jobs and better opportunities in the North. But the civil rights revolution of the 1960s and the reviving local economy of the 1970s have virtually stopped the black outmigration. The trend of black population is up—blacks here tend to have more children than whites—and this part of South Carolina is where blacks have been the largest percentage of the electorate and where their preferences have most clearly played a role in election results.

The 6th is best known nationally as the home of Congressman John Jenrette, one of the men convicted in the Abscam scandal and the only one of this group whose wife's picture soon thereafter appeared in *Playboy*. He argued that he was an alcoholic and was bribed only after federal agents disguised as Arab sheiks got him drunk; his wife after the trial said she still believed in him but preferred to talk about making love on the steps of the Capitol and to promote her own singing career on talk shows. Jenrette's antics are widely known; less well known is the fact that black voters played a major role in electing him in the first place and in his whole political career.

Jenrette was a small-town lawyer who was elected to the legislature; for some reason, unlike most South Carolina politicians, he always supported equal rights for blacks. That helped him defeat Congressman John McMillan in the 1972 Democratic primary, a defeat that had national significance: McMillan had been chairman of the House District of Columbia Committee for years and as such was the segregationist ruler of a black-majority city. Jenrette lost the general election that year in the Nixon landslide, but he came back and won the seat in 1974 and survived another tough campaign in 1976. In 1980 he came close to being reelected, because of his continued support from black voters. Some might criticize black voters for supporting a convicted felon, but they remembered that he had stood up for them when it was not considered politically profitable to do so, and they stuck with him when things were tough.

The new congressman, John Napier, is a Republican who once served on Senator Strom Thurmond's staff. He was not a strong campaigner and may have trouble in 1982. The district is unlikely to be changed much in redistricting, and the large black population here provides a solid base for a Democratic candidate. The 6th gave Jimmy Carter his largest majority in South Carolina in 1976 and 1980 and could very well be the scene of a closely contested House race in 1982.

Census Data Pop. (1980 final) 498,275, up 21% in 1970s. Median family income, 1970, $6,203, 65% of U.S.

The Voters

Employment profile 1970 White collar, 33%. Blue collar, 43%. Service, 13%. Farm, 11%.
Ethnic groups Black 1980, 41%. Hispanic 1980, 1%. Total foreign stock 1970, 1%.

Presidential Vote

1980	Reagan (R)	66,358	(45%)
	Carter (D)	80,224	(54%)
	Anderson (I)	1,549	(1%)
1976	Ford (R)	51,860	(38%)
	Carter (D)	83,876	(62%)

Rep. John L. Napier (R) Elected 1980; b. May 16, 1947, Marlboro; home, Bennettsville; Davidson Col., B.A. 1969, U. of S.C., J.D. 1972.

Career Army, 1977; Legis. Asst. to Sen. Strom Thurmond, 1972–78; Minority Counsel, U.S. Senate Veterans' Affairs Committee, 1973–76; Practicing atty., 1978–80.

Offices 1511 LHOB, 202-225-3315. Also 201 W. Evans St., P.O. Box 1931, Florence 29503, 803-667-9551, and Horry County Courthouse, Conway 29526, 803-248-6247.

Committee *Agriculture* (13th). Subcommittees: Conservation, Credit, and Rural Development; Cotton, Rice and Sugar; Tobacco and Peanuts.

Group Ratings and Key Votes: Newly Elected

Election Results

1980 general	John L. Napier (R)	75,964	(52%)	($277,856)
	John W. Jenrette, Jr. (D)	70,747	(48%)	($173,059)
1980 primary	John L. Napier (R)	3,735	(60%)	
	Edward Young (R)	2,491	(40%)	
1978 general	John W. Jenrette, Jr. (D), unopp. . .			($100,829)

SOUTH DAKOTA

South Dakota was once the heartland of the Sioux Indians, who roamed the plains hunting buffalo. Then the white man came and exterminated the buffalo and, in such places as Wounded Knee, many Indians as well. Those who survived were herded onto reservations. Today South Dakota still has one of the highest Indian populations in the nation; one out of 14 South Dakotans is a native American. Accordingly, one of the constants in the life of South Dakota has been enmity between Indians and the whites. Sometimes the enmity flares up, as in the 1973 occupation of Wounded Knee by Indian militants, and it is particularly important politically in the western part of the state, where most of the Indians live.

For the Indians, South Dakota was good hunting ground because the buffalo could graze and flourish on the semiarid grassland. But for the white man the region was long considered worthless. The first white settlers decided to come to the state only when gold was found in the Black Hills. Men like Wild Bill Hickok, America's first dime novel hero, made legends in such mining towns as Deadwood, Lead, and Spearfish; and then, as the rich veins petered out, they moved on. They left behind the plains which, as farming methods improved and land became more crowded to the east, were slowly being peopled by homesteaders. Some of them were Scandinavians moving from Wisconsin or Minnesota; but most were White Anglo–Saxon Protestants from Nebraska, Iowa, and points east. South Dakota thereby experienced most of its population growth during two decades of agricultural prosperity, 1880–90 and 1900–10. The decade between, the 1890s, was a period of drought and depression and farm rebellion. By 1910 the population of the state had reached 85% of the current

figure — which is to say that there has been much outmigration and little in-migration during the last 70-odd years.

By 1910 the political character of South Dakota had been pretty well set. During the 1890s
the state flirted briefly with the Populists and William Jennings Bryan; but by the 1920s,
South Dakota had become almost as monolithically Republican as Nebraska. Voters in
South Dakota never had much use for the socialist ideas of the Non-Partisan League, which
caught on in the more Scandinavian soil of North Dakota, and there was never anything
here comparable to the Farmer–Labor Party of Minnesota. As in most other Great Plains
states, voters in South Dakota have sometimes been dissatisfied with the farm programs of
national administrations. Farming is not only of indirect economic importance here; even
today nearly one-quarter of the state's residents actually live on farms. But until the 1970s,
such dissatisfaction had little effect on election outcomes. Between 1936 and 1970 South
Dakota had a Democratic governor for only two years and elected only one Democrat to
Congress, George McGovern.

The period from 1970 to 1980 has, in contrast, been a period of sharp fluctuation in political behavior in South Dakota. First there was a period of Democratic dominance of a sort
never seen here before. Democrats captured the governorship and both House seats in 1970,
they won a second Senate seat (although losing a House seat) in 1972, and they won majorities in both houses of the state legislature. This was part of a general Democratic surge in the
Upper Midwest during the Nixon years, and it undoubtedly owed something to George
McGovern's personal popularity; since the 1950s, he had really personified the Democratic
Party in the state. It owed something also to McGovern's national prominence. Although
he failed to carry South Dakota against Richard Nixon, he came very close; turnout was
high, and Democrats did very well in other races. The switch in focus away from economic
issues (on which South Dakota had long voted Republican) to cultural issues such as the
Vietnam war and Watergate (on which South Dakota was rather liberal) certainly helped
the Democrats.

But just when it looked as if South Dakota was on the verge of becoming a Democratic
constituency, it moved sharply to the right. The shift was foreshadowed by the election of
Congressman James Abdnor in the 2d district (the central and western part of the state), in
1972, and heralded by the election of Congressman Larry Pressler in the 1st district over a
Democratic incumbent in the generally Democratic year of 1974. Both Abdnor and Pressler
are now U.S. senators, elected in 1980 and 1978, respectively. On the state level, Republicans
won a massive victory in 1978, capped by the election of William Janklow, then the gun-
toting attorney general and now governor, who made a great political asset out of his vehement opposition to Indian claims. In 1980 the Republican surge was capped with the election
of Abdnor and the defeat of George McGovern. The margin of Abdnor's victory left no
doubt that the state was in a new era. McGovern, who had been winning elections in South
Dakota or coming in a very close second (as in 1972 and in the 1960 Senate race) won only
39% of the vote, and could carry only three counties (two with Indian majorities and the
other the site of the state university). Republicans won solid 2-1 margins in the legislature.
The Democrats' only consolation was the reelection by a wide margin of 1st district Congressman Thomas Daschle.

As with the Democratic trend a decade earlier, the Republican trend was part of a more
generalized reaction in the Upper Midwest, visible in the election results of North Dakota,
Iowa, Minnesota, and Wisconsin as well as South Dakota. The eclipse of the Vietnam and
Watergate issues brought the economy back to center stage, and there was widespread dis-

content with the performance of the Democratic administration on the economy. The Upper Midwest, moreover, is a region that seems to be temperamentally contrary to parties in power; even with general agricultural prosperity in the Carter years, strong opposition developed to the administration's embargo on grain sales to the Soviet Union after its invasion of Afghanistan. A reaction against the Indians certainly played a role in the Republicans' victory in the state elections in 1978 and may have played a part in McGovern's defeat in 1980 as well. The abortion issue may have entered into the result also. McGovern's troubles became apparent in the 1980 Democratic primary, when an unknown right-to-life candidate won 38% of the vote against him; Democrats traditionally depend on the Catholic vote in the Great Plains states, and when it turns against them on an issue such as abortion there is no way for Democrats to recover.

Despite the seemingly monolithic nature of the Republican trend here, there is still considerable variety in the South Dakota congressional delegation. Senator Pressler, its senior member before he reached age 40, is counted among the more liberal Republicans; Abdnor is a solid conservative. Daschle, a young Vietnam veteran, is hardworking and serious; Clint Roberts, the new 2d district congressman, is best known for having posed for one of the Marlboro Man ads. Pressler's career has been the most dazzling, at least to judge from the vote totals. He upset a Democratic congressman in 1974, he won reelection in 1976 with 80% of the vote, and he was elected to the Senate against respectable opposition in 1978 with 67%. Of all senators, Pressler would seem to have one of the safest seats.

One reason is his extensive cultivation of constituents. He is constantly back in the state and sends out as many press releases as any member of Congress. The definitive work on Pressler's service in the House was written by Albert Hunt of the *Wall Street Journal,* who cited him as a prime example of the congressional show horse (as opposed to workhorse). Pressler's contributions to legislative work in the House were almost nonexistent; in the Senate, with a longer time between elections, he has introduced a flurry of bills, can claim that some measures he has sponsored were passed, but he has not yet steered to passage major and difficult legislation. His committee assignments — Foreign Relations, to which he won assignment in 1981, and Commerce — suggest a desire to work on broad national issues. A man of obvious intelligence and capacity, he is undeniably pleasant; if he has been attacked for changing his views opportunistically to stay in line with the increasing conservative Republican majority, he is not the only one of whom that can be said, and in fact some such conversions represent genuine changes in philosophy. His honesty is not in doubt: he was one senator who turned down cold an Abscam bribe. But Pressler must still live down the episode of his ludicrous and mercifully brief presidential candidacy if he wants to be taken seriously by his colleagues, and he must show the inclination to work as hard on substantive issues as he does on his press releases if he wants to make good use of the position his political hard work and good luck have brought him.

Senator Abdnor is quite another sort: a man certainly too modest to run for president and almost too modest to run for senator. He is a friendly, pleasant man who has strong conservative views on almost every issue. He is not an orator and regularly mangles the English language. He evidently never saw the irony in the fact that as a bachelor he campaigned as a backer of family values against George McGovern, who has five children. His big victory, he would probably be the first to admit, was more a rejection of McGovern than an overwhelming endorsement of Abdnor. Abdnor's performance in the Senate seems altogether predictable. He is unlikely to shine, but he will work doggedly and vote with the Reagan Administration and the Republican leadership. He serves on the Environment and Public Works

Committee and on Appropriations; he chairs the former's subcommittee on Water Resources—the old pork barrel operation.

Congressman Daschle had the distinction of winning his seat in 1978 by the narrowest margin of anyone in the House: only 139 votes after a recount. A former aide to Senator James Abourezk, Daschle waged a door-to door campaign in a state where people still expect to talk personally with congressional candidates. In a Republican year that proved enough—barely enough—for him to defeat former Vietnam prisoner of war Leo Thorsness. In his first term Daschle worked hard to see that he would not be so closely pressed in the future. He won a seat on the House Agriculture Committee and became one of the first backers of gasohol production—which is highly popular in this corn-producing state. He also serves on Veterans' Affairs and there he is one of the leading backers of what is sometimes termed the innovative approach to veterans' issues—concerned with providing more aid to Vietnam veterans and investigating and compensating veterans for damage done by Agent Orange. Hard work and constant communication with voters helped Daschle win reelection in the much more Republican year of 1980 with 66% of the vote—a result startlingly in contrast with the national and local partisan trends.

Clint Roberts has not served long enough in the House to make a clear record at this writing. He won his Republican primary—the decisive race as it turned out—by nearly a 2-1 margin. In the general election he carried all but four counties in the district and won with a solid 58%. Roberts's face is familiar to most Americans from his work as a Marlboro man, but he has also had success in South Dakota as head of the state Cowboy Hall of Fame, as a rancher, and as a state senator and gubernatorial appointee. He specializes in agricultural issues and serves on the House Agriculture Committee.

South Dakota's redistricting task is the easiest possible—except for the two congressmen. The state's number of House seats is reduced from two to one, and Daschle and Roberts will either have to run against each other, retire, or (as North Dakota's Arthur Link did ten years ago in similar circumstances) run for governor. The 1980 returns would suggest that Daschle is the stronger candidate, but Roberts has the advantage of party identification and of having had to run in all the state's media markets (because the 2d district edges into the Sioux Falls and Aberdeen markets). The two congressmen both serve on the Agriculture Committee, and so a close comparison of their records will be possible in a state that has always shown itself capable of sophisticated analysis of agricultural issues.

It probably matters very little to Americans outside South Dakota who the governor of the state is, but it can be very important here—particularly when there is the possibility of armed confrontations between Indians and whites. The current incumbent, Republican William Janklow, made his reputation out of such confrontations, and it is one which is apparently popular in South Dakota. He has been accused of shooting from the hip, figuratively; literally, he has appeared as attorney general of the state at the scene of a crime armed and ready to help. He argued strongly against the demands of the American Indian Movement, and became known as the premier anti-Indian politician in the state. Janklow had the advantage of discord among the Democrats: Governor Kneip resigned to become ambassador to Singapore, and the succeeding Lieutenant Governor, Harvey Wollman, had already been beaten by state Senator Roger McKellips in the primary. McKellips also got into an argument with his party's platform on the Oahe Irrigation Project, a once popular program endorsed by many Democrats but now apparently opposed by most South Dakota voters. In any case, Janklow won the election with a solid 57%. Outsiders will know, by the absence or presence of jarring headlines, whether he has toned down his act.

1020   SOUTH DAKOTA

Census Data   Pop. (1980 final) 690,178, up 4% in 1970s: 0.30% of U.S. total, 45th largest. Central city, 19%; suburban, 11%. Median 4-person family income, 1978, $16,897, 83% of U.S., 47th highest.

1979 Share of Federal Tax Burden $1,172,000,000; 0.26% of U.S. total, 48th largest.

1979 Share of Federal Outlays $1,549,311,000; 0.33% of U.S. total, 48th largest.

DOD	$171,320,000	49th	(0.16%)	HEW	$529,382,000	44th	(0.30%)
DOE	$4,255,000	40th	(0.04%)	ERDA	$401,000	47th	(0.01%)
HUD	$21,445,000	43d	(0.33%)	NASA	$227,000	44th	(0.00%)
VA	$102,686,000	41st	(0.50%)	DOT	$68,186,000	44th	(0.41%)
EPA	$23,028,000	46th	(0.43%)	DOC	$6,190,000	48th	(0.20%)
DOI	$95,328,000	17th	(1.72%)	USDA	$342,153,000	31st	(1.42%)

Economic Base   Agriculture, notably cattle, hogs, wheat, and dairy products; finance, insurance, and real estate; food and kindred products, especially meat packing plants; printing and publishing, especially newspapers; metal mining, especially lode gold; tourism.

Political Lineup   Governor, William J. Janklow (R). Senators, Larry Pressler (R) and James Abdnor (R). Representatives, 2 (1 R and 1 D); 1 in 1982. State Senate, 35 (25 R and 10 D); State House of Representatives, 70 (49 R and 21 D).

The Voters

   Registration   447,508 Total. 202,052 D (45%); 206,411 R (46%); 39,045 other (9%).
   Employment profile 1970   White collar, 41%. Blue collar, 22%. Service, 15%. Farm, 22%.
   Ethnic groups   Hispanic 1980, 1%. Am. Ind. 1980, 7%. Total foreign stock 1970, 16%. Germany, 4%.

Presidential Vote

1980	Reagan (R)	198,343	(61%)
	Carter (D)	103,855	(32%)
	Anderson (I)	21,431	(7%)
1976	Ford (R)	151,505	(50%)
	Carter (D)	147,068	(49%)

1980 Democratic Presidential Primary			*1980 Republican Presidential Primary*		
Kennedy	33,418	(49%)	Reagan	72,861	(88%)
Carter	31,251	(45%)	Two others	4,678	(6%)
Uncommitted	4,094	(6%)	No preference	5,366	(6%)

SENATORS

Sen. Larry Pressler (R) Elected 1978, seat up 1984; b. Mar. 29, 1942, Humboldt; home, Humboldt; U. Of S.D., B.A. 1964, Rhodes Scholar, Oxford U., 1966, Harvard U., M.A., J.D. 1971.

Career   Army, Vietnam; U.S. House of Reps., 1975-78.

Offices   411 RSOB, 202-224-5842. Also 102 S. 2d St., Aberdeen 57401, 605-225-0150, ext. 471; 105 Rushmore Mall, Rapid City 57701, 605-341-1185; 334 S. Phillips Ave., Sioux Falls 57102, 605-336-2980, ext. 433; Raymond 57258, 605-532-3549; Buffalo 57720, 605-375-3355; and R.R. 1, Oldham 57051, 605-482-8538.

Committees   *Commerce, Science, and Transportation* (6th). Subcommittees: Business, Trade and Tourism (Chairman); Communications; Surface Transportation.

Foreign Relations (9th). Subcommittees: Arms Control, Oceans and International Operations and Environment (Chairman); European Affairs; Near Eastern and South Asian Affairs.

Special Committee on Aging (6th).

Group Ratings

	ADA	COPE	PC	LCV	CFA	RPN	NAB	NSI	NTU	ACA	ACU
1980	17	14	17	65	13	—	50	100	40	65	62
1979	32	47	40	—	33	—	—	—	40	58	69
1978	25	44	33	40	32	45	75	80	18	37	62

Key Votes

1) Draft Registn $	FOR	6) Fair Housng Cloture	AGN	11) Cut Socl Incr Defns	—
2) Ban $ to Nicrgua	—	7) Ban $ Rape Abortns	—	12) Income Tax Indexing	FOR
3) Dlay MX Missile	—	8) Cap on Food Stmp $	—	13) Lim Spdg 21% GNP	FOR
4) Nuclr Mortorium	AGN	9) New US Dep Edcatn	FOR	14) Incr Wndfll Prof Tax	AGN
5) Alaska Lands Bill	—	10) Cut OSHA Inspctns	FOR	15) Chryslr Loan Grntee	AGN

Election Results

1978 general	Larry Pressler (R)	170,832	(67%)	($449,541)
	Don Barnett (D)	84,767	(33%)	($152,006)
1978 primary	Larry Pressler (R)	66,893	(74%)	
	Ronald F. Williamson (R)	23,646	(26%)	($24,188)
1972 general	James Abourezk (D)	174,773	(57%)	($427,063)
	Robert Hirsch (R)	131,613	(43%)	($300,800)

Sen. James Abdnor (R) Elected 1980, seat up 1986; b. Feb. 13, 1923, Kennebec; home, Kennebec; U. of Neb., B.A. 1945.

Career Army, WWII; Farmer–rancher; School teacher and coach; S.D Senate, 1956–68, Pres. Pro Tem, 1967–68; Lt. Gov. of S.D., 1969–70; U.S. House of Reps., 1972–80.

Offices 4327 DSOB, 202-224-2321. Also P.O. Box 492, Aberdeen 57401, 605-225-0250; P.O. Box 873, Sioux Falls 57101, 605-336-2890, ext. 474; 507 Kansas City, Rapid City 57701, 605-343-5000; 375 Dakota So., Huron 57350, 605-352-5117; 113 3d Ave. So., Mitchell 57301, 605-996-3601; and Fed. Bldg., Pierre 57501, 605-224-2891.

Committees *Appropriations* (10th). Subcommittees: Agriculture and Related Agencies; Energy and Water Development; Labor, Health and Human Services, Education; Transportation; Treasury, Postal Service, and General Government (Chairman).

Environment and Public Works (6th). Subcommittees: Transportation; Water Resources (Chairman).

Joint Economic Committee (3d).

Group Ratings (as Member of U.S. House of Representatives)

	ADA	COPE	PC	LCV	CFA	RPN	NAB	NSI	NTU	ACA	ACU
1980	11	6	20	29	14	—	91	100	53	72	79
1979	5	16	10	14	0	—	—	—	54	96	95
1978	20	22	18	16	18	73	100	100	24	91	88

Key Votes (as Member of U.S. House of Representatives)

1) Draft Registn $	FOR	6) Fair Hsg DOJ Enfrc	AGN	11) Cut Socl Incr Dfns $	FOR
2) Ban $ to Nicrgua	FOR	7) Lim PAC Contrbtns	AGN	12) Hosptl Cost Controls	AGN
3) Dlay MX Missile	FOR	8) Cap on Food Stmp $	FOR	13) Gasln Ctrls & Allctns	AGN
4) Nuclr Mortorium	AGN	9) New US Dep Edcatn	AGN	14) Lim Wndfll Prof Tax	FOR
5) Alaska Lands Bill	AGN	10) Cut OSHA $	FOR	15) Chryslr Loan Grntee	AGN

Election Results

1980 general	James Abdnor (R)	190,594	(58%)	($1,675,430)
	George McGovern (D)	129,018	(39%)	($3,237,669)
1980 primary	James Abdnor (R)	68,196	(73%)	
	Dale Bell (R)	25,314	(27%)	($758,264)
1974 general	George McGovern (D)	147,929	(53%)	($1,172,831)
	Leo K. Thorsness (R)	130,955	(47%)	($528,817)

GOVERNOR

Gov. William J. Janklow (R) Elected 1978, term expires Jan. 1983; b. Sept. 13, 1939, Chicago, Ill.; U. of S.D., B.S. 1964, J.D. 1966.

Career Staff Atty., Dir. Atty., and Chief Officer, S.D. Legal Svcs. System, Rosebud Indian Reservation, 1966–73; Chief Prosecutor, Ofc. of the Atty. Gen. of S.D., 1973–74; Atty. Gen. of S.D., 1975–78.

Offices State Capitol Bldg., Pierre 57501, 605-773-3212.

Election Results

1978 gen.	William J. Janklow (R)	147,116	(57%)
	Roger D. McKellips (D)	112,679	(43%)
1978 prim.	William J. Janklow (R)	46,423	(51%)
	LeRoy G. Hoffman (R)	30,026	(33%)
	Clint Roberts (R)	14,774	(16%)
1974 gen.	Richard F. Kneip (D)	149,151	(54%)
	John E. Olson (R)	129,077	(46%)

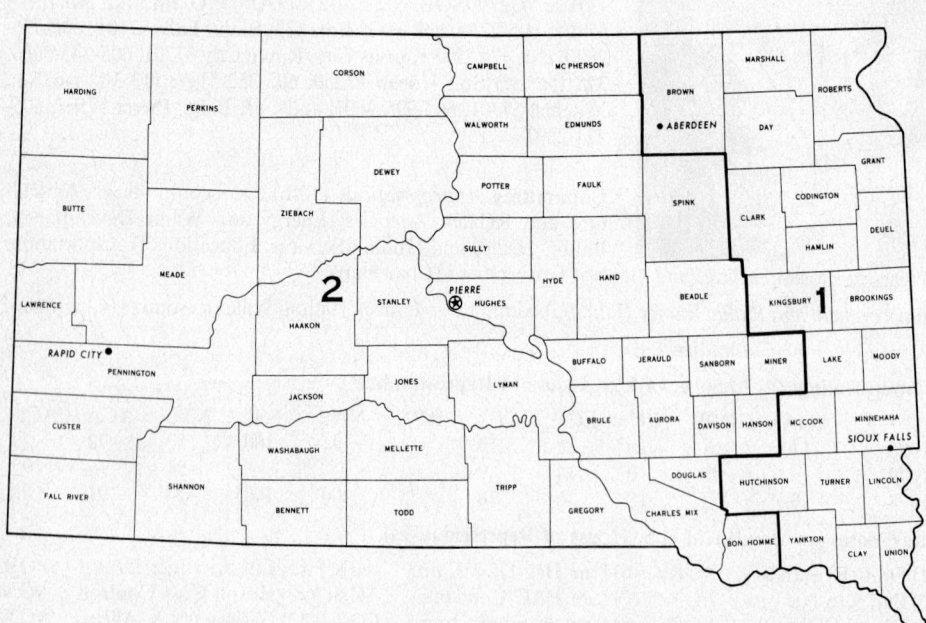

FIRST DISTRICT

Census Data   Pop. (1980 final) 346,630, up 4% in 1970s. Median family income, 1970, $7,095, 80% of U.S.

The Voters

Employment profile 1970   White collar, 42%. Blue collar, 23%. Service, 16%. Farm, 19%.
Ethnic groups   Am. Ind. 1980, 2%. Total foreign stock 1970, 18%. Germany, 4%.

Presidential Vote

1980	Reagan (R)	95,170	(56%)
	Carter (D)	59,684	(35%)
	Anderson (I)	13,181	(8%)
1976	Ford (R)	76,758	(49%)
	Carter (D)	78,680	(50%)

Rep. Thomas A. Daschle (D) Elected 1978; b. Dec. 9, 1947, Aberdeen; home, Aberdeen; S.D. St. U., B.A. 1969.

Career   Air Force, 1969–72; Legis. Asst. to U.S. Sen. James Abourezk, 1973–76, District Aide, 1976–78.

Offices   439 CHOB, 202-225-2801. Also Box 1274, Sioux Falls 57101, 605-334-9596.

Committees   *Agriculture* (19th). Subcommittees: Conservation, Credit, and Rural Development; Forests, Family Farms, and Energy; Wheat, Soybeans, and Feed Grains.

Veterans' Affairs (13th). Subcommittees: Education, Training and Employment; Hospitals and Health Care.

Group Ratings

	ADA	COPE	PC	LCV	CFA	RPN	NAB	NSI	NTU	ACA	ACU
1980	72	74	53	74	64	—	42	10	26	35	24
1979	79	90	70	78	78	—	—	—	37	19	18

Key Votes

1) Draft Registn $	AGN	6) Fair Hsg DOJ Enfrc	FOR	11) Cut Socl Incr Dfns $	AGN
2) Ban $ to Nicrgua	AGN	7) Lim PAC Contrbtns	FOR	12) Hosptl Cost Controls	AGN
3) Dlay MX Missile	FOR	8) Cap on Food Stmp $	AGN	13) Gasln Ctrls & Allctns	FOR
4) Nuclr Mortorium	FOR	9) New US Dep Edcatn	FOR	14) Lim Wndfll Prof Tax	FOR
5) Alaska Lands Bill	FOR	10) Cut OSHA $	AGN	15) Chryslr Loan Grntee	—

Election Results

1980 general	Thomas A. Daschle (D)	109,910	(66%)	($204,380)
	Bart Kull (R)	57,155	(34%)	($83,909)
1980 primary	Thomas A. Daschle (D), unopposed			
1978 general	Thomas A. Daschle (D)	64,683	(50%)	($223,221)
	Leo K. Thorsness (R)	64,544	(50%)	($270,366)

SECOND DISTRICT

Census Data   Pop. (1980 final) 343,548, up 3% in 1970s. Median family income, 1970, $7,283, 76% of U.S.

The Voters

Employment profile 1970   White collar, 40%. Blue collar, 21%. Service, 15%. Farm, 24%.
Ethnic groups   Hispanic 1980, 1%. Am. Ind. 1980, 11%. Total foreign stock 1970, 15%. Germany, 4%.

Presidential Vote

1980	Reagan (R)	103,173	(65%)
	Carter (D)	44,171	(28%)
	Anderson (I)	8,250	(5%)
1976	Ford (R)	74,747	(52%)
	Carter (D)	68,384	(47%)

Rep. Clint Roberts (R) Elected 1980; b. Jan. 30, 1935, Pierre; home, Presho; Black Hills St. Col., 1951–52.

Career   Farmer–rancher; S.D. Senate, 1972–78; S.D. Sec. of Agriculture, 1979–80.

Offices   1009 LHOB, 202-225-5165. Also 621 6th St., Rapid City 57701, 605-342-0042, and 438 S. Pierre, No. 2, Pierre 57501, 605-224-6239.

Committee *Agriculture*   (16th). Subcommittees: Conservation, Credit, and Rural Development; Tobacco and Peanuts; Wheat, Soybeans, and Feed Grains.

Group Ratings and Key Votes: Newly Elected

Election Results

1980 general	Clint Roberts (R)	88,991	(58%)	($217,765)
	Kenneth Stofferahn (D)	63,447	(42%)	($116,776)
1980 primary	Clint Roberts (R)	32,984	(65%)	
	Don Ham (R)	17,970	(35%)	($48,630)
1978 general	James Abdnor (R).............	70,780	(56%)	($160,804)
	Bob Samuelson (D)............	55,516	(44%)	($329,425)

TENNESSEE

To a remarkable extent, Tennessee is a state whose politics has not changed for decades. The political leanings of each of its geographic regions are so well known that many ordinary Tennesseeans are familiar with them. And they are so firmly ingrained that there is virtually no difference in the contours of support between the 1980 presidential election, in which Ronald Reagan edged Jimmy Carter in Tennessee by 4,000 votes, and the 1952 and 1956 elections, in which Dwight Eisenhower edged Adlai Stevenson by 2,000 and 5,000 votes, respectively. Any study of such a durable politics must begin with geography and history.

The state is divisible into three distinct sections, each with its own political heritage and inclination. East Tennessee is part of the Appalachian chain, an area populated almost completely by white mountaineers. Against secession, it was the political base of Andrew Johnson, Lincoln's vice presidential choice and successor. Over the years east Tennessee has remained one of the most dependable Republican areas in the entire nation. Even in 1976, with a southerner on the Democratic ticket, east Tennessee went for Gerald Ford.

The Republicanism of the mountains has usually been matched by the Democratic leanings of middle Tennessee, a region of hilly farmland which, in rough terms, lies between the lower Tennessee River and the mountains. Middle Tennessee was the home of Andrew Jackson, the first president to call himself a Democrat, and since Jackson's time the area has remained Democratic in practically every election. West Tennessee, the flat cotton lands along the Mississippi River, was the part of the state with the largest slave-tended plantations. Like middle Tennessee it is Democratic by tradition; but like the Deep South it has been ready to abandon the Democrats for Republicans (Goldwater, Nixon) or third party candidates (Wallace) who are more palatable to its white residents' traditional views on racial issues.

Urban-rural differences have not been nearly as important in Tennessee as elsewhere. The state's four large cities vote more like the rural territory around them than like each other. Recently Memphis, with its large black vote, has been less conservative than the rest of west Tennessee, while Chattanooga, on the Georgia border, is traditionally less Republican than east Tennessee. Meanwhile, the political behavior of Knoxville and Nashville is virtually indistinguishable from the rural counties around them.

So long as middle and west Tennessee remained strongly Democratic, the Republicans were unable to win a statewide election, no matter how many votes the party of Lincoln piled up in east Tennessee. Between Reconstruction and the 1960s allegiances created by the Civil War were forsaken only twice: once in the 1920 Harding landslide, when a Republican governor was elected, and again in 1928 when Protestant Tennessee rejected Catholic Al Smith for Herbert Hoover. The civil rights revolution touched Tennessee, but it did not affect it as it did other southern states. Its two senators in the 1950s, Estes Kefauver and Albert Gore, refused to sign the Southern Manifesto and were reelected anyway. Tennessee, like the rest of the nation, moved Republican at times. It gave Eisenhower small margins both times, and went for Nixon over Kennedy probably more because of religion than politics. In 1964 Tennessee went comfortably for Johnson over Goldwater.

But in the years since, Tennessee has become increasingly Republican. Not exclusively — Tennessee went for Carter in 1976. The legislature is still Democratic (although Republicans had an even split in one house for a while), and so is party registration. But in the last decade it is clear that, at least on the top levels of statewide politics, the Republicans have usually had greater vitality and stronger candidates. At least one major reason for the Republican success has been the example set by Tennessee's senior Senator, Howard Baker

Baker entered statewide politics at a time when the best exemplars of Tennessee politics were liberal Democrats, men such as Senators Estes Kefauver and Albert Gore and Governor Frank Clement. Their style was often old-fashioned — Gore and Clement were tub-thumping orators, trained in the art of arousing a courthouse crowd in a Democratic county to fever pitch — but their politics was surprisingly modern. In the 1950s they backed civil rights, took liberal stands on economic issues, and, in Kefauver's case, nearly won the Democratic presidential nomination over the objections of most of the party's big city bosses. But in the 1960s their politics was becoming outmoded. Kefauver died in 1963, and Gore had a surprisingly close race in 1964. Clement won his last term as governor in 1962. Young, affluent Tennesseeans found their political style alien and their support of Great Society policies repugnant. The state was ready for another kind of politics.

And that was the kind of politics provided by Howard Baker. He came from a traditional east Tennessee Republican background; his father and his stepmother had served in the House before him. But instead of running for a safe Knoxville area House seat in 1964, Baker chose to make a risky statewide race for the Senate that year — and lost. He did not run the typical Goldwater-coattail race of southern Republicans that year, however; he did not oppose the Civil Rights Act of 1964, even though his Democratic opponent, Ross Bass, had voted for it in the House. Nor was Baker a typical old-time orator. Rather, he had a kind of conversational style well adapted to the increasingly important medium of television. He relied for campaign help not on old courthouse regulars, but on well-dressed young men who applied the latest campaigning techniques.

Baker's loss in 1964 did not prevent him from running in 1966, and this time, facing Frank Clement, he won. It was the last time Baker had electoral problems in Tennessee. Well established as a statewide figure, he beat Ray Blanton with 62% of the vote in 1972, with Baker getting a substantial percentage of the black vote that year. In 1978, his main problem at home was his support of the Panama Canal Treaty, which Democrat Jane Eskind dwelled on. Still, Baker carried every congressional district but the black-majority 8th, winning even in middle Tennessee; his overall percentage was a slightly reduced 58%.

The day after the 1980 election, one of the biggest smiles in Washington was on the face of Howard Baker. The Republicans had, against all expectations, won control of the Senate, and Baker, with characteristic speed and grace, had secured the position of majority leader almost before anyone knew it was available. He asked for and got Paul Laxalt, the president-elect's confidant and Baker's adversary on the Panama Canal Treaties issue, to agree to nominate him for the position. Even while Baker was still saying minority rather than majority, he was working to secure the confidence of the incoming New Right Republican senators and succeeding almost entirely.

But for all the surprise of the 1980 results, Baker had been working for a long time to hold a leadership position. As long ago as 1969, after the death of his father-in-law, Everett Dirksen, he sought the Republican leadership; then and in 1971 he was the candidate of more conservative Republicans opposed to the supposed eastern liberal Hugh Scott. When Scott retired, the favorite to succeed him was Whip Robert Griffin, a hardworking partisan and talented strategist. But Baker put together a coalition of older moderates and new conservatives and upset Griffin. Between those elections, he had become known to the nation as the ranking Republican on the Senate Watergate Committee. Without breaking all ties with the Nixon White House, Baker was able to project himself as a fair-minded and intelligent investigator, whose intention, he said, was to determine what the president knew and when he knew it. As Senate minority leader during the Carter years, Baker again and again successfully maintained relations with people on both sides of an issue, most notably on the Panama Canal. Many Republican conservatives mistrusted him after that vote — his efforts were largely responsible for the treaties' passage — and the hatred of Republican activists would have made it impossible for him to be nominated for president even if his 1980 campaign had gotten a lot farther than it did. But his fellow Republicans in the Senate trusted him, enough to enable Baker to weld them together into a more cohesive partisan force than the Senate has seen for many years.

Baker's success at securing the trust and cooperation of people who disagree with him on issues of fundamental importance is no accident. It is the result of hard work, but more than that, of a confidence that Baker has built in all observers that he takes positions and makes decisions fairly and candidly, in line with a rational set of principles, although not unmindful of the political implications. Baker is in fact a pretty solid Republican on most issues. If he backed the Canal Treaties, he was prepared to oppose the SALT II treaty and has backed high defense spending; he always supported the Vietnam war policy, and he has never been warmly disposed to detente with the Russians. On domestic issues, he always supported civil rights (unlike most southern Republicans) and he was willing, as ranking minority member on the Public Works Committee, to work out constructive compromises with Edmund Muskie on antipollution laws. But he has always believed in balanced budgets, scaling back most federal spending programs, strongly supporting nuclear power.

Many people thought Howard Baker would have been the Republican's strongest presidential candidate in 1980—in the general election. His campaign for the Republican presidential nomination, however, was entirely unsuccessful. He had expert assistance and he had the easy-spoken articulateness that makes him perhaps the most natural television candidate in American politics. But he could not overcome the hostility of many conservatives and, more important, he could not generate an enthusiastic constituency of his own. George Bush out-organized him in Iowa; Ronald Reagan left him in the pack in New Hampshire. Many politicians would have been shattered by such a defeat as this; and Baker himself was genuinely angry for a few days that Bush had tried to exclude him from the Nashua newspaper debate. But he recovered, and even before the general election — and certainly after — he seemed to have a serenity about his role and his worth that few politicians achieve. Bush was mentioned, naturally, as a vice presidential candidate, at which point right wingers threatened vigorous protests; the Reagan people did not discourage such talk. Baker let it be known that he was not interested in the position, thank you, and that he felt he had constructive work elsewhere.

Baker proved that in his first few months as Senate majority leader. It is easy to keep a minority cohesive; it is harder to keep a majority together, and there are plenty of potential philosophic divides among the current Republican majority in the Senate. But Baker presided over a speedy and entirely successful treatment of President Reagan's budget cuts in early 1981, and the esprit of the Senate Republicans continued high. The fissures did not open, and Baker himself emerged as a natural leader. He may still run for president someday, but the odds are against him succeeding; one still has the feeling that this is a man who is comfortable and delighted with what he is doing. He is unquestionably the chief Republican on the Hill; he has a pleasant and trusting relationship with the president and his top aides; he is contributing mightily to the achievement of the policy goals he has long sought and to the intellegent conduct of the business of governance. In the meantime he does not forget Tennessee: it is probably no accident that one major federal project not cut by the Reagan budget is east Tennessee's Clinch River breeder reactor.

Tennessee's junior senator, James Sasser, is far less well known nationally; indeed, he achieved his greatest national notice so far when he defeated incumbent Republican Bill Brock in 1976. Brock's defeat was a blessing in disguise for Republicans; his performance as

Republican national chairman helped the party organize effective fundraising and present to the public a reasonably coherent and intellectually defensible program which helped to topple Jimmy Carter in 1980. For his pains, Brock, who was once mentioned as a possible presidential candidate, was appointed the president's chief trade negotiator. Sasser inevitably is one of the Republicans' major targets in 1982. When he won his seat in 1976, he was one of four congressional Democrats who ran behind Jimmy Carter in their constituencies; one should remember, however, that for all his problems Carter was quite competitive in Tennessee in 1980. Sasser in some ways is an offshoot of the Tennessee Democratic tradition of Estes Kefauver and Albert Gore; he votes more often with northern Democrats than with old-style southern Democrats like John Stennis of Mississippi. Yet he probably owes more to a rural agricultural tradition: his father was an agriculture official who moved all over rural Tennessee, one of those men who symbolize one set of government programs that have helped make American agriculture exceedingly productive (Governor James Hunt of North Carolina has a similar background). For such men, government is more likely to seem a friend than the enemy, and Sasser has a voting record in accordance with that thinking. He serves on the major money committees in the Senate, Budget and Appropriations; he is involved in decisions of considerable practical importance to the state on such matters as the Tennessee Valley Authority and the Clinch River nuclear breeder reactor. He has worked as well for laws to get the government to collect debts owed it and to reform the federal grants system.

Sasser's most formidable opponent in 1982 would probably be Governor Lamar Alexander, who seems however more likely to seek a second term. The leading potential challenger then becomes Congressman Robin Beard, a member of the Armed Services Committee who is an enthusiast for things military and a believer in an assertive — some would say aggressive — foreign policy. Beard comes from east Tennessee, and represents a district that stretches from middle Tennessee near Nashville to the all-white suburbs of Memphis, so he spans the regions of the state; philosophically, however, his hard-edged conservatism is less in line with the state's traditions than the pragmatic, quiet conservatism of a Republican such as Baker or the activist, expansive progressivism of a Democrat like Sasser.

For nearly 20 years (1952-70) the governorship of Tennessee was batted back and forth between two Democrats, Frank Clement and Buford Ellington. In 1970 it was captured by a Memphis dentist, Winfield Dunn; this was the great year of Republican triumph in Tennessee. Watergate changed that in 1974. The Democratic nominee, former Congressman Ray Blanton, was a demonstrated political weakling; he had only got 38% against Howard Baker two years before. But he won the Democratic nomination in a 12-candidate field with 23%, and he was able to beat the Republican, a 34-year-old former baker and Nixon White House aide, by a significant, standard partisan margin.

Blanton's performance in office seems to have soured Tennessee on Democrats. He was criticized for expensive travels in the state executive jet and for taking from jail and putting on his staff the son of a former aide who had shot and killed his former wife and her lover. Alexander this time ran a strong campaign against Blanton as if he were a candidate — which he wisely declined to be — and virtually apologized to the people of the state for not having campaigned harder in 1974 to keep him out of office. Alexander's walk across the state made him seem more in line with Tennessee mores; his opponent was a Knoxville banker, Jake Butcher, who had had dealings with Bert Lance and whose campaign was largely self-financed. Butcher could not shake off his party's connection with Blanton, and

Alexander won by a decisive margin. After the election Blanton began pardoning literally dozens of state prisoners. The U.S. attorney's office was investigating charges that Blanton had been selling pardons, and Democrats were able to persuade Alexander to take the oath of office several days before the planned inauguration day. Nashville country musicians put out a record called "Pardon Me, Ray," and the outgoing governor became national news; his conduct in office was about as disgraceful as Tennessee had ever seen. The contrast with the brainy, articulate, honest Alexander could not have been greater. Alexander by 1981 was the favorite to become the first governor in Tennessee's history to win a second consecutive four-year term.

Tennessee has been batted back and forth by the census in its representation in the House. After the 1970 census the state lost one of its nine seats; two Democrats were thrown together in the same seat, which Republican Robin Beard promptly won. Now, after the 1980 census, Tennessee gains a seat. It will take a little bit of doing, but the Democratic legislature seems likely to create another, probably odd-shaped district in middle Tennessee which will almost certainly go Democratic.

Census Data   Pop. (1980 final) 4,590,750, up 17% in 1970s: 2.03% of U.S. total, 17th largest. Central city, 35%; suburban, 28%. Median 4-person family income, 1978, $17,916, 88% of U.S., 45th highest.

1979 Share of Federal Tax Burden $7,168,000,000; 1.59% of U.S. total, 21st largest.

1979 Share of Federal Outlays $10,417,874,000; 2.25% of U.S. total, 15th largest.

DOD	$1,010,174,000	31st	(0.95%)	HEW	$3,306,032,000	17th	(1.85%)
DOE	$1,357,144,000	1st	(11.54%)	ERDA	$423,087,000	1st	(15.60%)
HUD	$125,349,000	16th	(1.90%)	NASA	$3,898,000	28th	(0.08%)
VA	$482,687,000	14th	(2.33%)	DOT	$272,193,000	20th	(1.65%)
EPA	$83,086,000	22d	(1.56%)	DOC	$25,386,000	22d	(0.80%)
DOI	$25,452,000	42d	(0.46%)	USDA	$568,678,000	15th	(2.37%)

Economic Base   Apparel and other textile products, especially men's and boys' furnishings; agriculture, notably cattle, dairy products, soybeans, and tobacco; finance, insurance, and real estate; chemicals and allied products, especially plastics materials and synthetics; electrical equipment and supplies, especially household appliances; food and kindred products; textile mill products, especially knitting mills.

Political Lineup   Governor, Lamar Alexander (R). Senators, Howard H. Baker, Jr. (R) and James R. (Jim) Sasser (D). Representatives, 8 (5 D and 3 R); 9 in 1982. State Senate, 33 (20 D, 12 R, and 1 I); State House of Representatives, 99 (58 D, 39 R, and 2 I).

The Voters

Registration   2,359,002 Total. No party registration.
Employment profile 1970   White collar, 41%. Blue collar, 42%. Service, 13%. Farm, 4%.
Ethnic groups   Black 1980, 16%. Hispanic 1980, 1%. Total foreign stock 1970, 2%.
Presidential Vote

1980	Reagan (R)	787,761	(49%)
	Carter (D)	783,051	(48%)
	Anderson (I)	35,991	(2%)
1976	Ford (R)	633,969	(43%)
	Carter (D)	825,879	(56%)

1980 Democratic Presidential Primary			*1980 Republican Presidential Primary*		
Kennedy	315,019	(56%)	Reagan	225,959	(81%)
Carter	212,387	(38%)	Bush	47,447	(17%)
One other	13,913	(2%)	One other	4,571	(2%)
Uncommitted	19,499	(3%)			

SENATORS

Sen. Howard H. Baker, Jr. (R) Elected 1966, seat up 1984; b. Nov. 15, 1925, Huntsville; home, Huntsville; Tulane U., U. of the South, U. of Tenn., LL.B. 1949.

Career Navy, WWII; Practicing atty., 1949–66.

Offices 4123 DSOB, 202-224-4944. Also 716 U.S. Courthouse, 801 Broadway, Nashville 37203, 615-749-5129, and 313 P.O. Bldg., Knoxville 37902, 615-546-5486.

Committees *Majority Leader.*

Environment and Public Works (2d). Subcommittees: Transportation; Nuclear Regulation.

Foreign Relations (2d). Subcommittees: Arms Control, Oceans and International Operations and Environment; East Asian and Pacific Affairs; Near Eastern and South Asian Affairs.

Rules and Administration (3d).

Joint Committee on the Library (3d).

Group Ratings

	ADA	COPE	PC	LCV	CFA	RPN	NAB	NSI	NTU	ACA	ACU
1980	17	16	13	25	7	—	67	75	38	81	63
1979	21	29	9	—	5	—	—	—	32	63	60
1978	25	37	30	32	20	100	67	63	15	75	72

Key Votes

1) Draft Registn $	FOR	6) Fair Housng Cloture	AGN	11) Cut Socl Incr Defns	FOR
2) Ban $ to Nicrgua	AGN	7) Ban $ Rape Abortns	—	12) Income Tax Indexing	—
3) Dlay MX Missile	AGN	8) Cap on Food Stmp $	FOR	13) Lim Spdg 21% GNP	FOR
4) Nuclr Mortorium	—	9) New US Dep Edcatn	FOR	14) Incr Wndfll Prof Tax	—
5) Alaska Lands Bill	AGN	10) Cut OSHA Inspctns	FOR	15) Chryslr Loan Grntee	—

Election Results

1978 general	Howard H. Baker, Jr. (R)........	642,644	(56%)	($1,922,573)
	Jane Eskind (D)...............	466,228	(42%)	($1,903,532)
1978 primary	Howard H. Baker, Jr. (R)........	205,680	(83%)	
	Five others (R).................	40,819	(17%)	
1972 general	Howard H. Baker, Jr. (R)........	716,539	(62%)	($830,769)
	Ray Blanton (D)	440,599	(38%)	($224,653)

Sen. James R. (Jim) **Sasser** (D) Elected 1976, seat up 1982; b. Sept. 30, 1936, Memphis; home, Nashville; Vanderbilt U., B.A. 1958, J.D. 1961.

Career Practicing atty.; Chmn., Tenn. State Dem. Comm., 1973–76.

Offices 260 RSOB, 202-224-3344. Also U.S. Courthouse, 801 Broadway, Nashville 37203, 615-251-7353.

Committees *Appropriations* (12th). Subcommittees: Agriculture and Related Agencies; Energy and Water Development; HUD–Independent Agencies; Military Construction.

Budget (5th).

Governmental Affairs (6th). Subcommittees: Permanent Subcommittee on Investigations; Intergovernmental Relations.

Select Committee on Small Business (4th). Subcommittees: Capital Formation and Retention; Government Procurement.

Group Ratings

	ADA	COPE	PC	LCV	CFA	RPN	NAB	NSI	NTU	ACA	ACU
1980	67	68	37	23	47	—	30	20	20	23	5
1979	37	53	32	—	52	—	—	—	22	29	14
1978	55	74	53	47	30	60	27	50	16	57	30

Key Votes

1) Draft Registn $	FOR	6) Fair Housng Cloture	FOR	11) Cut Socl Incr Defns	AGN
2) Ban $ to Nicrgua	—	7) Ban $ Rape Abortns	AGN	12) Income Tax Indexing	—
3) Dlay MX Missile	AGN	8) Cap on Food Stmp $	AGN	13) Lim Spdg 21% GNP	AGN
4) Nuclr Mortorium	AGN	9) New US Dep Edcatn	—	14) Incr Wndfll Prof Tax	FOR
5) Alaska Lands Bill	FOR	10) Cut OSHA Inspctns	FOR	15) Chryslr Loan Grntee	FOR

Election Results

1976 general	James R. (Jim) Sasser (D)	751,180	(52%)	($839,379)
	Bill Brock (R)	673,231	(47%)	($1,301,033)
1976 primary	James R. (Jim) Sasser (D)	244,930	(44%)	
	John J. Hooker, Jr. (D)	171,716	(31%)	
	Five others (D)	137,201	(25%)	
1970 general	Bill Brock (R)	562,645	(51%)	
	Albert Gore (D)................	519,858	(47%)	

GOVERNOR

Gov. Lamar Alexander (R) Elected 1978, term expires Jan. 1983; b. July 3, 1940, Maryville; Vanderbilt U., B.A. 1962, NYU, J.D. 1965.

Career Newspaper reporter, *Knoxville News-Sentinel,* Nashville *Banner, Maryville Alcoa Daily Times.* Practicing atty., 1965, 1971– ; Law Clerk, U.S. Circuit Court of Appeals, 5th Dist., New Orleans, 1965–66; Legis. Asst. to U.S. Sen. Howard H. Baker, Jr., 1967–69; Exec. Asst. to Bryce Harlow, Counselor in charge of congressional relations, 1969; Rep. nominee for Gov. of Tenn., 1974.

Offices State Capitol Bldg., Nashville 37219, 615-741-2001.

Election Results

1978 gen.	Lamar Alexander (R)......	661,959	(56%)
	Jake Butcher (D)	523,495	(44%)
1978 prim.	Lamar Alexander (R)......	230,922	(86%)
	Three others (R)	37,696	(14%)
1974 gen.	Ray Blanton (D)..........	575,205	(55%)
	Lamar Alexander (R)......	457,095	(44%)

FIRST DISTRICT

The 1st district of Tennessee is the far northeastern corner of the state. Most of it is an extension of the Shenandoah Valley of Virginia and the Blue Ridge Mountains of the Appalachian. In fact, the district is closer to Richmond, Virginia, than to Memphis, Tennessee. Although the 1st is part of the Appalachian region, it has not suffered anything like the poverty that recently afflicted the hollows of West Virginia or hills of eastern Kentucky. Because coal has never been very important here, northeastern Tennessee has not gone through the various booms or busts of coal country. Instead, the small towns of the region—Johnson City, Kingsport, Bristol—have been quietly attracting new industries. The region has low

taxes and lots of low wage labor, and its valleys provide reasonably level east-west transportation routes.

The changing economy of the district has not, however, produced much shift in its political inclinations. For more than a century, the 1st has remained solidly Republican, as Republican as any district in Kansas or Nebraska. People up here in the mountains never had many slaves, and they had little use for secession in 1861. They stayed loyal to the Union and continued to send congressmen to Washington. Abraham Lincoln picked a local boy, Andrew Johnson, to be his second vice president in 1864. To this day voters in the 1st continue to support the party of the Union. Even in 1976, after Watergate and with a southerner as the Democratic candidate, the 1st went for Gerald Ford.

For 40 years the congressional politics of this area was dominated by B. Carroll Reece, a Republican who represented the district for most of the period between 1921 and 1961. Reece's successor, first elected in 1962, is Republican Jimmy Quillen. He is one of the quieter senior members of the House. He has a seat on the Rules Committee and is the ranking Republican on that body. Since Democrats still have an 11-5 advantage on that body, and since the Democrats on it are almost all loyal to the party's leadership, Quillen has little ability to overturn their decisions on the procedural matters that Rules handles; in any case, he is less aggressive and vocal than the second ranking Republican on the committee, Delbert Latta of Ohio. Quillen is one of the quiet, pleasant, conservative men who for years provided the backbone for the outnumbered Republicans in the House — a very different breed from the aggressive, brash, ideological young Republicans who now dominate their party's ranks and look forward to the day when the Republicans can win control of the House.

Census Data Pop. (1980 final) 585,624, up 19% in 1970s. Median family income, 1970, $6,820, 71% of U.S.

The Voters

Employment profile 1970 White collar, 36%. Blue collar, 49%. Service, 10%. Farm, 5%.
Ethnic groups Black 1980, 2%. Hispanic 1980, 1%.

Presidential Vote

1980	Reagan (R)	120,203	(61%)
	Carter (D)	70,930	(36%)
	Anderson (I)	5,057	(3%)
1976	Ford (R)	96,233	(53%)
	Carter (D)	83,151	(46%)

Rep. James H.(Jimmy) **Quillen**(R) Elected 1962; b. Jan. 11, 1916, near Gate City, Va.; home, Kingsport.

Career Founder and Pub., *Kingsport Mirror,* 1936–39, *Johnson City Times,* 1939–44; Navy, WWII; Pres. and Bd. Chmn., real estate and insurance businesses, 1946– ; Dir., 1st Tenn. Bank, Kingsport; Tenn. House of Reps., 1955–62, Minor. Ldr., 1959–60.

Offices 102 CHOB, 202-225-6356. Also Rm. 157, 1st Flr., Fed. Bldg., Kingsport 37662, 615-247-8161.

Committee *Rules* (Ranking Member).

Group Ratings

	ADA	COPE	PC	LCV	CFA	RPN	NAB	NSI	NTU	ACA	ACU
1980	17	16	30	46	14	—	80	100	46	57	72
1979	16	26	10	21	4	—	—	—	49	76	73
1978	15	25	15	35	18	58	100	89	25	85	73

Key Votes

1) Draft Registn $	FOR	6) Fair Hsg DOJ Enfrc	AGN	11) Cut Socl Incr Dfns $	—
2) Ban $ to Nicrgua	FOR	7) Lim PAC Contrbtns	AGN	12) Hosptl Cost Controls	AGN
3) Dlay MX Missile	AGN	8) Cap on Food Stmp $	FOR	13) Gasln Ctrls & Allctns	AGN
4) Nuclr Mortorium	AGN	9) New US Dep Edcatn	FOR	14) Lim Wndfll Prof Tax	FOR
5) Alaska Lands Bill	FOR	10) Cut OSHA $	FOR	15) Chryslr Loan Grntee	FOR

Election Results

1980 general	James H. (Jimmy) Quillen (R)	130,296	(86%)	($146,822)
	John Curtis (I)	20,816	(14%)	
1980 primary	James H. (Jimmy) Quillen (R)	43,649	(77%)	
	One other (R)	12,679	(23%)	
1978 general	James H. (Jimmy) Quillen (R)	92,143	(65%)	($218,151)
	Gordon Ball (D)	50,694	(35%)	($46,199)

SECOND DISTRICT

John Gunther called Knoxville, the largest city in east Tennessee, "the ugliest city I ever saw in America." It is indeed an undistinguished looking place, sitting in a hot valley flanked by nondescript hills that do not seem to anticipate the cool green Smokies 40 miles away. Knoxville has a solid blue collar economy and is the home as well of the University of Tennessee. It is also the headquarters of the Tennessee Valley Authority, the federal project that has brought low cost power, recreational lakes, and plenty of jobs to Knoxville. All of these facts would lead one to believe that Knoxville is a Democratic town. Yet for all its factories, despite the university, and despite having one of the most successful examples of government enterprise in the country in TVA, Knoxville is still one of the most heavily Republican cities in the United States.

Knoxville is the center of Tennessee's 2d congressional district, a safe Republican seat if there ever was one. The district has not elected a Democratic congressman since 1853. The 2d is also the home base of Senator Howard Baker, who has a house in the hills and keeps an office in Knoxville. Baker's father represented the district from 1951 until his death in 1963; he was succeeded for the remainder of his term by his widow. Baker Jr., could have had the seat for the asking, but he decided to run for the Senate instead — with results that have already made more than a little history.

So the Republican nomination in 1964 went to Knoxville Mayor John Duncan. He won by a comfortable margin in that Democratic year and has represented the district ever since. Duncan does not make much noise around the Capitol, blending quietly into the conservative folds of the Republican Conference. But he does hold a position of potential power, as second-ranking Republican on the Ways and Means Committee and ranking minority of its Select Revenue Measures Subcommittee. Duncan has a faithful Republican record, and can be counted on to favor lower taxes and greater incentives for business. His own legislative output seems limited to technical matters, perfecting sloppy pieces of legislation and preventing unintended application of new laws.

Census Data   Pop. (1980 final) 586,997, up 19% in 1970s. Median family income, 1970, $7,285, 76% of U.S.

The Voters

   Employment profile 1970   White collar, 43%. Blue collar, 42%. Service, 13%. Farm, 2%.
   Ethnic groups   Black 1980, 6%. Hispanic 1980, 1%. Total foreign stock 1970, 1%.

Presidential Vote

1980	Reagan (R)	119,853	(58%)
	Carter (D)	79,572	(38%)
	Anderson (I)	6,303	(3%)
1976	Ford (R)	98,032	(50%)
	Carter (D)	94,759	(49%)

Rep. John J. Duncan (R) Elected 1964; b. Mar. 24, 1919, Scott Co.; home, Knoxville.

Career Army, WWII; Asst. Atty. Gen. of Tenn., 1947–56; Knoxville Law Dir., 1956–59; Pres., Knoxville Pro Baseball Club, 1956–59; Mayor of Knoxville, 1959–64.

Offices 2458 RHOB, 202-225-5435. Also 318 P.O. Bldg., Knoxville 37902, 615-546-5686.

Committees *Ways and Means* (2d). Subcommittees: Health; Oversight; Select Revenue Measures.

Joint Committee on Taxation (5th).

Group Ratings

	ADA	COPE	PC	LCV	CFA	RPN	NAB	NSI	NTU	ACA	ACU
1980	17	16	27	35	7	—	92	100	41	67	65
1979	11	20	15	21	11	—	—	—	47	72	68
1978	20	20	20	27	23	55	83	80	25	85	79

Key Votes

1) Draft Registn $	FOR	6) Fair Hsg DOJ Enfrc	AGN	11) Cut Socl Incr Dfns $	FOR
2) Ban $ to Nicrgua	FOR	7) Lim PAC Contrbtns	AGN	12) Hosptl Cost Controls	AGN
3) Dlay MX Missile	AGN	8) Cap on Food Stmp $	FOR	13) Gasln Ctrls & Allctns	FOR
4) Nuclr Mortorium	AGN	9) New US Dep Edcatn	FOR	14) Lim Wndfll Prof Tax	FOR
5) Alaska Lands Bill	FOR	10) Cut OSHA $	FOR	15) Chryslr Loan Grntee	FOR

Election Results

1980 general	John J. Duncan (R)	147,947	(76%)	($109,305)
	David H. Dunnaway (D)	46,578	(24%)	($38,018)
1980 primary	John J. Duncan (R)	54,759	(100%)	
1978 general	John J. Duncan (R)	125,082	(82%)	($139,956)
	Margaret Francis (D)	27,745	(18%)	

THIRD DISTRICT

The 3rd congressional district of Tennessee is dominated by the city of Chattanooga. East of the city is rugged hill country, solidly Republican since the Civil War, except for Polk County, where the boundaries of Tennessee, North Carolina, and Georgia meet. This is a place with a political history as violent as any in the United States; three people were killed during the 1948 election. The 3rd also includes Dayton, the site of the Scopes trial of 1925, where William Jennings Bryan and Clarence Darrow debated whether the state of Tennessee could prohibit the teachings of Darwin's theory of evolution. Chattanooga itself was the focus of several Civil War battles (Lookout Mountain, Chickamauga), but it was then only a village; it is one of those southern cities which, like Birmingham and Atlanta, grew into an industrial city during the New South years after the Civil War. Chattanooga therefore does not have a politics rooted as deeply in Civil War sentiments as do most parts of Tennessee. It has been traditionally Democratic, in contrast to the hill counties to the east, but during the 1960s and 1970s it was inclined to the Republicanism of Howard Baker and William Brock.

Indeed, Chattanooga and the 3d district have been the political home base for key figures in postwar Tennessee politics, Estes Kefauver and Bill Brock. Kefauver was first elected to Congress here in 1938, moving on to the Senate — and national fame — in 1948. Brock first won election to the House in 1962, campaigning against the Kennedys, creeping socialism, and civil rights laws. He won election to the Senate in 1970, in a victory which seemed to herald a sleek, articulate Republican future for Tennessee. But not for Brock; he was defeated for reelection in 1976. His successor in the House was a Republican, LaMar Baker, but one with limited political savvy. He barely won in 1970 and 1972 and was defeated in 1974.

The winner that year had not expected to go to Congress. Marilyn Lloyd was the wife of Chattanooga TV personality Mort Lloyd when he won the Democratic congressional nomination in 1974; when he was killed in a plane crash in August, she was given the nomination by local Democrats. The Democratic tide was strong, Baker was weak, and she was elected with 52%.

Marilyn Lloyd Bouquard — the name she uses politically after remarriage — provides a good example of how a member of the House with a pleasing personality, hard work, and shrewd use of the advantages of incumbency can make a marginal district safe. She rapidly achieved the kind of popularity matched by none of her predecessors since Kefauver. She had the advantage of being a Democrat at a time when that label did not require decisions that would be unpopular in this kind of constituency, and she could please most whites and almost all blacks at the same time. As she gained seniority, Bouquard gained positions important to her district on the Public Works and Science Committees. Currently she chairs a subcommittee on Energy Research and Production, which concerns itself primarily with nuclear fission and fusion; this is the home district of the Clinch River breeder reactor. Bouquard has been reelected by comfortable margins, even in the Republican year of 1980. Redistricting will probably remove some of the outer parts of the district, such as the nuclear town of Oak Ridge, and will leave the 3d district centered on Chattanooga.

Census Data　Pop. (1980 final) 575,429, up 18% in 1970s. Median family income, 1970, $7,940, 83% of U.S.

The Voters

Employment profile 1970　White collar, 42%. Blue collar, 45%. Service, 12%. Farm, 1%.
Ethnic groups　Black 1980, 11%. Hispanic 1980, 1%. Total foreign stock 1970, 2%.

Presidential Vote

1980	Reagan (R)	113,363	(56%)
	Carter (D)	82,568	(41%)
	Anderson (I)	4,426	(2%)
1976	Ford (R)	88,578	(48%)
	Carter (D)	96,126	(52%)

Rep. Marilyn Lloyd Bouquard (D) Elected 1974; b. Jan. 3, 1929, Ft. Smith, Ark.; home, Chattanooga; Shorter Col., 1967–70.

Career　Coowner and Mgr., WTTI Radio, Dalton, Ga.; Family agriculture flight service business.

Offices　2334 RHOB, 202-225-3271. Also 230 P.O. Bldg., Chattanooga 37401, 615-483-8611.

Committees　*Public Works and Transportation* (10th). Subcommittees: Economic Development; Public Buildings and Grounds.

Science and Technology (7th). Subcommittees: Energy Development and Applications; Energy Research and Production (Chairwoman); Space Science and Applications.

Select Committee on Aging (11th). Subcommittee: Health and Long-Term Care.

Group Ratings

	ADA	COPE	PC	LCV	CFA	RPN	NAB	NSI	NTU	ACA	ACU
1980	22	53	30	22	29	—	55	90	40	54	58
1979	21	37	20	28	12	—	—	—	35	40	55
1978	15	53	20	33	9	30	73	90	23	68	58

Key Votes

1) Draft Registn $	FOR	6) Fair Hsg DOJ Enfrc	FOR	11) Cut Socl Incr Dfns $	FOR
2) Ban $ to Nicrgua	FOR	7) Lim PAC Contrbtns	AGN	12) Hosptl Cost Controls	AGN
3) Dlay MX Missile	AGN	8) Cap on Food Stmp $	AGN	13) Gasln Ctrls & Allctns	FOR
4) Nuclr Mortorium	AGN	9) New US Dep Edcatn	FOR	14) Lim Wndfll Prof Tax	FOR
5) Alaska Lands Bill	FOR	10) Cut OSHA $	FOR	15) Chryslr Loan Grntee	FOR

Election Results

1980 general	Marilyn Lloyd Bouquard (D).....	117,355	(61%)	($159,440)
	Glen Byers (R).................	74,761	(39%)	($43,236)
1980 primary	Marilyn Lloyd Bouquard (D).....	39,522	(100%)	
1978 general	Marilyn Lloyd (D)	108,282	(89%)	($75,923)
	Dan East (I)...................	13,535	(11%)	

FOURTH DISTRICT

The Tennessee River twice crosses the state that bears its name. The first time the river heads south from its headwaters to Chattanooga; the second time, after turning around in Alabama and Mississippi, the river moves lazily north to its confluence with the Ohio River in Kentucky. Along most of its route the Tennessee is made amenable to the needs of man by the operation of TVA dams. Between the two lengths of the river lies middle Tennessee, with most of its geographical expanse making up the state's 4th congressional district. To the east the district is mountain country, but most of the 4th is part of the hilly farmlands of the Cumberland Plateau, which is known in some quarters as "the dimple of the universe."

For 150 years the Cumberland Plateau has been a region of small- and medium-sized farms and small county seat towns. The 4th district's largest city is Murfreesboro, with a population of 32,000. The first local hero in these parts was Andrew Jackson, victor at the Battle of New Orleans and seventh president of the United States. With the exception of a couple of mountain counties, the 4th has remained loyal to Jackson's party ever since. Indeed, it has produced a number of the party's national leaders, including Congressman (1907-21, 1923-31), Senator (1933-33), and Secretary of State (1933-44) Cordell Hull and Congressman (1939-53) and Senator (1953-71) Albert Gore.

The race issue in the 4th has seldom been the burning issue it has been in other parts of the Deep South. This has always been a region of white small farmers, and only 5% of the district's residents are black. The farmers almost always vote Democratic. Even in 1972 George McGovern got 35% of the vote here—a low figure, but one showing as much support as he had anywhere in the South. Jimmy Carter carried the 4th with 68% of the vote in 1976 and 57% in 1980—both among his best percentages in congressional districts in the nation outside black majority districts in central cities.

The current congressman continues the local tradition of electing national Democrats. He is Albert Gore, Jr., son of the former congressman and senator, Vietnam veteran, a Harvard graduate who returned back to Tennessee to live. He won election to the House in 1976, when the man who succeeded his father, Joe Evins, retired. Currently Gore is a member of the Science Committee and chairman of its Investigations and Oversight Subcommittee, a position that allows him considerable leeway to investigate legislation. Gore is mentioned as a candidate for statewide office, but at this writing he seems unlikely to run either for the governorship in 1982 or for Howard Baker's Senate seat in 1984.

For decades the rural counties of middle Tennessee sent thousands of its sons and daughters north or to cities in search of jobs and opportunities. In the 1970s this outmigration seems to have stopped. In fact, the movement seems to have been in the other direction. The counties around Nashville, for example, gained population as people moved outward from the central city to places with more rural atmospheres and values. Small towns that have stayed the same size for decades have suddenly grown, e.g., Cookeville or Crossville or Lynchburg (the last famous as the home of Jack Daniel's Whiskey, Lem Motlow, Prop.). As a result, Tennessee gained one congressional district out of the 1980 census, and because of the elongated shape of the state the new district will almost certainly be situated in middle Tennessee. In early 1981 the likelihood was that the Democratic legislature would create a district running from the northern end of the 2d district at the northeast down to the boundary of the 4th and the 6th districts in the southeast. This would be a Democratic seat: it went for Carter in 1980 and generally goes Democratic by fairly large margins. There is no shortage of likely Democratic contenders, led by state House Majority Leader Thomas Burnett. The creation of this new district would still leave untouched most of the territory now in the 4th district, which presumably would form the base of a new and even more safely Democratic district for Gore.

Census Data   Pop. (1980 final) 636,253, up 29% in 1970s. Median family income, 1970, $6,451, 67% of U.S.

The Voters

Employment profile 1970   White collar, 34%. Blue collar, 47%. Service, 11%. Farm, 8%.
Ethnic groups   Black 1980, 5%. Hispanic 1980, 1%.

Presidential Vote

1980	Reagan (R)	85,714	(41%)
	Carter (D)	118,789	(56%)
	Anderson (I)	3,734	(2%)
1976	Ford (R)	58,441	(31%)
	Carter (D)	124,267	(67%)

Rep. Albert Gore, Jr. (D) Elected 1976; b. Mar. 31, 1948, Washington, D.C.; home, Carthage; Harvard U., B.A. 1969, Vanderbilt U.

Career   Army, Vietnam; Homebuilding and subdivision business operator, 1971–76.

Offices   1311 LHOB, 202-225-4231. Also U.S. Courthouse, Carthage 37030, 615-735-0173.

Committees   *Energy and Commerce* (13th). Subcommittees: Energy Conservation and Power; Fossil and Synthetic Fuels; Oversight and Investigations.

Science and Technology (12th). Subcommittee: Investigations and Oversight (Chairman).

Permanent Select Committee on Intelligence (8th). Subcommittee: Oversight and Evaluation.

Group Ratings

	ADA	COPE	PC	LCV	CFA	RPN	NAB	NSI	NTU	ACA	ACU
1980	50	79	53	35	71	—	8	40	16	29	11
1979	74	80	70	79	89	—	—	—	15	12	13
1978	65	70	68	58	77	50	33	50	9	15	13

Key Votes

1) Draft Registn $	FOR	6) Fair Hsg DOJ Enfrc	FOR	11) Cut Socl Incr Dfns $	AGN
2) Ban $ to Nicrgua	AGN	7) Lim PAC Contrbtns	FOR	12) Hosptl Cost Controls	FOR
3) Dlay MX Missile	AGN	8) Cap on Food Stmp $	AGN	13) Gasln Ctrls & Allctns	FOR
4) Nuclr Mortorium	FOR	9) New US Dep Edcatn	FOR	14) Lim Wndfll Prof Tax	AGN
5) Alaska Lands Bill	FOR	10) Cut OSHA $	AGN	15) Chryslr Loan Grntee	FOR

Election Results

1980 general	Albert Gore, Jr. (D)	137,612	(79%)	($74,422)
	James Beau Seigneur (R)	35,954	(21%)	($13,870)
1980 primary	Albert Gore, Jr. (D)	65,886	(92%)	
	One other (D)	5,533	(8%)	
1978 general	Albert Gore, Jr. (D), unopposed ..			($47,097)

FIFTH DISTRICT

Nashville is Tennessee's capital and second largest city; after its consolidation with surrounding Davidson County in the 1960s, it reached the impressive population of 450,000. Because of its location near the center of the state, Nashville is in many ways—especially politically—more important to Tennessee than is its larger rival, Memphis. The two newspapers in Nashville reflect neatly the state's two-party politics: the *Banner* is as resolutely Republican as the *Tennessean* is determinedly Democratic. The city is also a major center for industries like printing and insurance. Nashville is best known, however, for country music. It has been the home of the Grand Ole Opry since the 1920s, and today it is the undisputed country and western music capital of the world. It has several major recording studios, and many of the big stars live here or in fabled mansions outside of town. The country music scene is not all that different from that shown in Los Angeles-based Robert Altman's film *Nashville*.

Nashville can claim other cultural ornaments besides country music. The city contains several colleges, including Vanderbilt and Fisk Universities. Also here, not far from the old state Capitol, is the famous replica of the Parthenon. But Nashville's favorite shrine—and the one most significant politically—is the Hermitage, the home of Andrew Jackson. Old Hickory moved to Nashville from the Carolinas when Tennessee was still very much the frontier. He made a small fortune, won election to the House while George Washington was still president, and was elected to the Senate, where he served briefly just after he turned 30; for a few years after that, he served on the state Supreme Court. It was only after this youthful political career, and after some financial setbacks, that Jackson made his national reputation as a merciless Indian fighter, the scourge of the British at the Battle of New Orleans, and the common man's candidate for president. But he had already set Nashville's political preferences. Jackson was a Democrat, and Nashville has remained, with only the most occasional exceptions, Democratic ever since.

The 5th congressional district includes all of Nashville and two small rural counties that are fast becoming suburban. The 5th is usually a reliably Democratic district in statewide elections (although it went once for George Wallace, once for Richard Nixon, and twice for Howard Baker), and it always elects Democrats to Congress. The real contests here are among Democrats. Thus in 1962 liberal Democrat Richard Fulton ousted the reactionary incumbent. Fulton was popular locally and had a seat on the Ways and Means Committee, but in 1975, at age 48, he ran for mayor of Nashville and won easily. Fulton's successor, elected in November 1975, was 63-year-old Tax Assessor Clifford Allen, who had won great popularity by fighting high utility rates. Allen had a national Democratic voting record and was unbeatable locally. But he died in the summer of 1976, after the filing deadline and before the primary election.

The winner of the seat was the only major Democrat who had filed to run against Allen, state Senator Bill Boner. With a somewhat controversial reputation locally, he seemed off to a shaky start and won the general election with only 51% of the vote over a Republican and a former aide to Senator Albert Gore running as an Independent. But in his first term, Boner consolidated his hold on the district. He was strong enough that he had no primary opposition in 1980, and won his general election by nearly a 2–1 margin — the sort that Democrats normally expect out of Nashille. Redistricting may rearrange the boundaries slightly and attach different small counties to Nashville, but that should make no difference in election results. Boner serves on the Public Works and Veterans' Affairs Committee and, in the Tennessee Democratic tradition, has a voting record closer to those of northern Democrats than to those of conservative southerners.

Census Data   Pop. (1980 final) 536,448, up 9% in 1970s. Median family income, 1970, $9,231, 96% of U.S.

The Voters

Employment profile 1970   White collar, 53%. Blue collar, 33%. Service, 13%. Farm, 1%.
Ethnic groups   Black 1980, 21%. Hispanic 1980, 1%. Total foreign stock 1970, 3%.

Presidential Vote

1980	Reagan (R)	76,628	(39%)
	Carter (D)	114,893	(58%)
	Anderson (I)	5,051	(3%)
1976	Ford (R)	64,543	(36%)
	Carter (D)	110,779	(63%)

Rep. William Hill (Bill) **Boner** (D) Elected 1978; b. Feb. 14, 1945, Nashville; home, Nashville; Middle Tenn. St. U., B.S. 1967, Peabody Col., M.A. 1969, YMCA Night Law Sch., Nashville, J.D. 1978.

Career College basketball coach, 1969–71; Tenn. House of Reps., 1970–72, 1974–76; Sr. Staff Asst., Nashville Mayor's Ofc., 1971–72; Asst. V.P. and Dir. of Pub. Rel., 1st Amer. Natl. Bank, Nashville; Law Clerk, 1976–77; Tenn. Senate, 1976–78.

Offices 118 CHOB, 202-225-4311. Also 552 U.S. Courthouse, 801 Broadway, Nashville 37203, 615-251-5296.

Committees *Public Works and Transportation* (21st). Subcommittees: Aviation; Investigations and Oversight; Surface Transportation.

Veterans' Affairs (10th). Subcommittees: Education, Training and Employment; Hospitals and Health Care.

Group Ratings

	ADA	COPE	PC	LCV	CFA	RPN	NAB	NSI	NTU	ACA	ACU
1980	39	79	43	37	43	—	30	50	29	38	47
1979	63	85	55	59	63	—	—	—	22	28	26

Key Votes

1) Draft Registn $	FOR	6) Fair Hsg DOJ Enfrc	AGN	11) Cut Socl Incr Dfns $	AGN
2) Ban $ to Nicrgua	FOR	7) Lim PAC Contrbtns	FOR	12) Hosptl Cost Controls	FOR
3) Dlay MX Missile	—	8) Cap on Food Stmp $	AGN	13) Gasln Ctrls & Allctns	FOR
4) Nuclr Mortorium	AGN	9) New US Dep Edcatn	FOR	14) Lim Wndfll Prof Tax	AGN
5) Alaska Lands Bill	FOR	10) Cut OSHA $	AGN	15) Chryslr Loan Grntee	FOR

Election Results

1980 general	William Hill (Bill) Boner (D)	118,506	(65%)	($237,908)
	Mike Adams (R)	62,746	(35%)	($208,944)
1980 primary	William Hill (Bill) Boner (D)	50,094	(100%)	
1978 general	William Hill (Bill) Boner (D)	68,608	(51%)	($192,960)
	Bill Goodwin (R).	47,288	(35%)	($40,494)
	Henry Haile (I)	17,674	(13%)	($5,838)

SIXTH DISTRICT

The 6th congressional district of Tennessee is a rather odd amalgam, stretching from the Nashville city limits in the heart of middle Tennessee to the city of Memphis on the Mississippi River in the southwestern corner of the state. Its shape is the result of the settlement of a redistricting problem that arose when Tennessee lost one of its nine congressional districts after the 1970 census. The Democratic legislature chose in effect to consolidate two districts: the middle Tennessee district represented by William Anderson and the west Tennessee district represented by Ray Blanton. Both were Democrats, but Blanton was running for Howard Baker's Senate seat that year (he lost, but was later elected governor), and Anderson seemed to be strong enough to win.

But the Democrats failed to anticipate the weakness of their party that year or the strength of Republican Robin Beard. Anderson, the captain of the first nuclear submarine to sail under the North Pole, had a liberal voting record and opposed the war in Vietnam; his constituents in 1972 had different opinions. Particularly critical were the residents of the portion of Shelby County added to the district, a 99% white portion of Memphis and its suburbs. Beard, in contrast, was young, articulate, and aggressively conservative. His identity with the district was tenuous— he was an east Tennessee native and lived in a Nashville suburb just over the Williamson County line. But he strongly opposed busing and strongly backed the Vietnam war. He got 80% in Shelby County; his 20,000-vote edge there wiped out the 3,000-vote edge Anderson had in the rest of the district.

Beard has proved to be one of the most combative members of the House. He is a proud veteran of the Marine Corps and, as a member of the House Armed Services Committee, one of the Marine Corps's strongest boosters. He is also an ardent backer of the draft. Beard reacted very strongly against critics of the Vietnam war and other American policies abroad; he was the congressman who brought charges against Michael Harrington of Massachusetts for allegedly leaking secret testimony about American efforts to subvert the elected government in Chile. He believes that American defenses have become dangerously weak, and is aggressively determined to do something about it.

Beard has been successful politically. He has won reelection by wide margins; in 1980 he had the compliment of not having any Democratic opponent at all. This, in a district some of whose rural counties are so determinedly Democratic that they went for George McGovern in 1972. Beard is considered likely to become a candidate for Senator James Sasser's seat in 1982, and the congressman's strong views should provide an interesting contrast with Sasser's traditional Tennessee progressivism. The 6th district has experienced considerable population growth in the 1970s, gaining about 75,000 people in suburban Memphis and more than 100,000 in the rural counties. This means that redistricting must bring some changes. The Democratic legislature would like to make the district more Democratic by getting rid of the Memphis suburbs (they went for Reagan over Carter by 49,000 to 19,000 in

1980), but there is a risk: if too many of these precincts are placed in the districts of Harold Ford (a Memphis black) or Ed Jones (a rural Democrat), they might be endangered. Most likely the district that will emerge will have the same political balance — with a slight edge to Republicans in an incumbent-less race, thanks to the strong Republican vote in suburban Memphis.

Census Data   Pop. (1980 final) 659,203, up 53% in 1970s. Median family income, 1970, $7,151, 75% of U.S.

The Voters

Employment profile 1970   White collar, 39%. Blue collar, 45%. Service, 11%. Farm, 5%.
Ethnic groups   Black 1980, 14%. Hispanic 1980, 1%. Total foreign stock 1970, 2%.

Presidential Vote

1980	Reagan (R)	123,782	(53%)
	Carter (D)	101,836	(44%)
	Anderson (I)	4,730	(2%)
1976	Ford (R)	94,314	(47%)
	Carter (D)	104,815	(52%)

Rep. Robin L. Beard, Jr. (R) Elected 1972; b. Aug. 21, 1939, Knoxville; home, Franklin; Vanderbilt U., B.A. 1961.

Career USMC, 1962–66; Assoc. Dir. of Alumni Development, Vanderbilt U., 1966–68; Tenn. State Personnel Commissioner, 1970–72.

Offices 229 CHOB, 202-225-2811. Also 22 Public Sq., Columbia 38401, 615-388-2133.

Committees *Armed Services* (4th). Subcommittees: Investigations; Research and Development.

Select Committee on Narcotics Abuse and Control (2d).

Group Ratings

	ADA	COPE	PC	LCV	CFA	RPN	NAB	NSI	NTU	ACA	ACU
1980	11	19	17	27	7	—	100	100	56	91	71
1979	5	20	15	20	4	—	—	—	55	74	80
1978	5	0	13	19	9	64	100	100	29	96	91

Key Votes

1) Draft Registn $	FOR	6) Fair Hsg DOJ Enfrc	—	11) Cut Socl Incr Dfns $	FOR
2) Ban $ to Nicrgua	—	7) Lim PAC Contrbtns	AGN	12) Hosptl Cost Controls	AGN
3) Dlay MX Missile	AGN	8) Cap on Food Stmp $	FOR	13) Gasln Ctrls & Allctns	FOR
4) Nuclr Mortorium	AGN	9) New US Dep Edcatn	AGN	14) Lim Wndfll Prof Tax	FOR
5) Alaska Lands Bill	FOR	10) Cut OSHA $	FOR	15) Chryslr Loan Grntee	AGN

Election Results

1980 general	Robin L. Beard, Jr. (R)	127,945	(100%)	($146,038)
1980 primary	Robin L. Beard, Jr. (R)	26,020	(100%)	
1978 general	Robin L. Beard, Jr. (R)	114,630	(75%)	($156,405)
	Ron Arline (D)	38,954	(25%)	($10,175)

SEVENTH DISTRICT

The 7th congressional district of Tennessee is the northwestern part of the state. The district extends from the TVA lakes of the Tennessee and Cumberland Rivers at the Kentucky state line to the city of Memphis. Physically and politically the 7th resembles the Mississippi Delta or east Arkansas: flat cotton lands and soybean fields, occasional small towns, and a fairly large (19%), mostly rural black population. Outside of Memphis and Shelby County, the district's largest city is Jackson, with a population of 39,000.

Most of the counties here are traditionally Democratic, but only those around the Tennessee River gave statewide Democratic candidates majorities in the years from 1968 to 1972. Indeed, this has been the pivotal part of the state in recent close elections. When it went for Bill Brock in the 1970 Senate election, he won; when it switched and backed Democrat Jim Sasser in 1976, Brock lost. The Shelby County portion of the district, with one-quarter of the 7th's population, is 98% white, relatively high income, and heavily conservative — almost as devoted to the Republican Party as the 6th district's share of Shelby County; it experienced substantial growth in the 1970s, rising from 114,000 to 179,000.

This is a district that has had only one substantial general election contest in the past 20 years. That happened in 1969, in a special election after the incumbent died. Republicans, hoping for new victories for their southern strategy, made a major effort here; so did George Wallace, who came in to campaign for the American Party candidate. But the winner, with 51%, was Democrat Ed Jones. A former state Agriculture Commissioner, he did without national endorsements and ran as a folksy local Democrat.

In Congress Jones received a seat on the Agriculture Committee and Cotton Subcommittee. Agriculture is a body of whose works even most Americans knowledgeable about public affairs are ignorant; and yet its subject matter is very important. In a time when almost everyone is skeptical about government's ability to solve problems, it is worth remembering that government has been heavily involved in agriculture for more than 100 years, and that agricultural products are today America's number one export. Jones is now chairman of the Conservation and Credit Subcommittee, and also sits on subcommittees with jurisdiction over such important crops as livestock, dairy, cotton, rice, and sugar.

Jones has had only one significant challenge in his years in the House, the 1976 Democratic primary. He had no primary opponent in 1980 and won the general election by better than 3–1. He shows no signs of retiring and is in fact younger than the incumbent president. Redistricting need not and probably will not much disturb his district's boundaries except to shear off some of his Memphis suburbs, which will probably only help Jones; what would hurt him, in a general election, is if he should gain part of the Memphis suburbs now in the 6th district, which are heavily Republican.

Census Data   Pop. (1980 final) 584,542, up 20% in 1970s. Median family income, 1970, $7,030, 73% of U.S.

The Voters

Employment profile 1970   White collar, 37%. Blue collar, 44%. Service, 12%. Farm, 7%.
Ethnic groups   Black 1980, 19%. Hispanic 1980, 1%. Total foreign stock 1970, 2%.
Presidential Vote

1980	Reagan (R)	102,092	(50%)
	Carter (D)	96,419	(47%)
	Anderson (I)	3,282	(2%)
1976	Ford (R)	73,714	(42%)
	Carter (D)	100,751	(57%)

Rep. Ed Jones (D) Elected Mar. 25, 1969; b. Apr. 20, 1912, Yorkville; home, Yorkville; U. of Tenn., B.S. 1934.

Career Inspector, Tenn. Dept. of Agric., 1934–41; Supervisor, Tenn. Dairy Products Assn., 1941–43; Agric. Rep., Ill. Central R.R., 1943–48, 1952–69; Tenn. Commissioner of Agric., 1949–52.

Offices 108 CHOB, 202-225-4714. Also P.O. Box 27190, 3179 N. Watkins St., Memphis 38127, 901-358-4094.

Committees *Agriculture* (4th). Subcommittees: Cotton, Rice, and Sugar; Livestock, Dairy, and Poultry.

House Administration (4th). Subcommittees: Contracts and Printing; Services.

Joint Committee on Printing (3d).

Group Ratings

	ADA	COPE	PC	LCV	CFA	RPN	NAB	NSI	NTU	ACA	ACU
1980	22	63	33	17	29	—	50	50	32	45	44
1979	32	55	25	31	15	—	—	—	32	23	28
1978	20	42	18	25	9	45	46	60	17	56	57

Key Votes

1) Draft Registn $	FOR	6) Fair Hsg DOJ Enfrc	AGN	11) Cut Socl Incr Dfns $	FOR
2) Ban $ to Nicrgua	AGN	7) Lim PAC Contrbtns	FOR	12) Hosptl Cost Controls	AGN
3) Dlay MX Missile	AGN	8) Cap on Food Stmp $	AGN	13) Gasln Ctrls & Allctns	FOR
4) Nuclr Mortorium	AGN	9) New US Dep Edcatn	FOR	14) Lim Wndfll Prof Tax	FOR
5) Alaska Lands Bill	FOR	10) Cut OSHA $	AGN	15) Chryslr Loan Grntee	FOR

Election Results

1980 general	Ed Jones (D)	133,606	(77%)	($76,919)
	Daniel H. Campbell (R)	39,227	(23%)	($0)
1980 primary	Ed Jones (D)	47,494	(100%)	
1978 general	Ed Jones (D)	96,863	(73%)	($124,445)
	Ross Cook (R)	36,003	(27%)	($49,769)

EIGHTH DISTRICT

Memphis, Tennessee's largest city with more than 600,000 people, is set in the far southwestern corner of the state. The city is the major financial and commercial center for much of the lower Mississippi Valley. As such, Memphis looks as much south to Mississippi and west to Arkansas as it does east and north to the rest of Tennessee. In recent years Memphis has grown rapidly, doubling its population since World War II. Most of the newcomers are from the Deep South, especially Mississippi. Blacks have found more economic opportunity here, and more political power; for a decade now Memphis has elected black state legislators and even a black judge—Benjamin Hooks, now executive director of the national NAACP.

Memphis is the home of many quintessentially American institutions. Beale Street here gave birth to jazz in the 1920s, and in the 1930s the first supermarket—a Piggly Wiggly—opened in Memphis. In the 1950s Memphis gave us Elvis Presley and the Holiday Inn (the first of which is no longer operated under that aegis, but sports a memorial plaque). Memphis, or at least the white majority here, likes to think of itself as a plain middle American city, but the fact is that the prevailing community opinion, like the accent, remains basically southern.

The city as a whole is dominated by its middle-class whites. Many of these are people from the small-town South, who are now making more money than they ever imagined. They live comfortable lives in the vast suburban tracts that have sprung up inside and outside the expanding city limits in the last 20 years. Their political traditions are Democratic, but they now use their ballots to protect their newfound prosperity—and the whiteness of their neighborhoods—by voting Republican. They are attracted particularly to youngish, lightly accented candidates such as Howard Baker, Bill Brock, and Lamar Alexander, whose sometimes cerebral conservatism and thoughtful articulation symbolize what they hope they have become rather than what they were.

There is one other fact that any political analyst should know about Memphis: this is one of the most segregated cities in the country. There is little of that phenomenon, once so common in Atlanta and still the case in New Orleans, of blacks and whites living in close proximity. The blacks are concentrated entirely in the central portion of the city, while the whites have long since moved to the newer subdivisions. Thirty-odd years ago there were no differences between the voting habits of Memphis blacks and Memphis whites: they both went down the line for candidates endorsed by Boss Ed Crump's machine, which is to say Democrats. But long ago the white neighborhoods started moving toward the Republicans, while the blacks became more Democratic than ever. The result is voting patterns more racially polarized than in any other major American city. In 1980 Jimmy Carter carried Memphis's Shelby County, because of virtually unanimous black support; but more than 60% of the whites voted against him. In the suburban and city areas that are in the 6th congressional district, fully 69% went for Ronald Reagan.

Most of Memphis and virtually none of its suburbs make up Tennessee's 8th congressional district. For some years Tennessee legislators drew the lines to prevent a black-majority district, but in 1972, to maximize Democratic chances, they made a district 47% of whose residents and 41% of whose residents over 18 were black. The percentages have risen since, both because of racial change in some neighborhoods and because of a 1976 redistricting. The latter removed from the 8th seven precincts that had gone 90%, with a margin of nearly 6,000 votes, for the Republican candidate in 1974.

Back in 1972 the 8th still had a white Republican congressman, but it was only a matter of time before he would lose to a black Democrat. The time came earlier than expected, probably because of Watergate, in 1974, when state Representative Harold Ford won by 744 votes.

Ford is part of a local political family. His older brother is a state legislator, and Ford himself seems to have plenty of political savvy. He makes few concessions to Memphis area whites, either his personal style or his voting record. He votes with northern Democrats; he has a seat on Ways and Means and its Health Subcommittee, where he usually is part of the minority that supports progressive taxation and government involvement in health care financing. Ford's percentages in 8th district elections have risen precipitously, as the district's black population has grown and its whites have moved away. That does leave him with a problem for 1982, however. His district lost population in the 1970s, in vivid contrast to other Tennessee districts, and his constituency will have to be expanded out into white precincts of Memphis and its suburban areas. The legislature can add some black areas, but the fact is that almost every white precinct added to the district is likely to go Republican, even if the Republicans nominate only a nuisance candidate. The realities of residential segregation and population movements mean that a new 8th district will probably have a fast-increasing black percentage in the 1980s, so for Ford the real test will be 1982: if he can survive without a strong challenge then, he may be reasonably sure of holding a safe seat for another decade.

Census Data   Pop. (1980 final) 426,254, down 17% in 1970s. Median family income, 1970, $7,874, 82% of U.S.

The Voters

Employment profile 1970   White collar, 47%. Blue collar, 36%. Service, 17%. Farm, –%.
Ethnic groups   Black 1980, 63%. Hispanic 1980, 1%. Total foreign stock 1970, 3%.

Presidential Vote

1980	Reagan (R)	51,121	(29%)
	Carter (D)	118,094	(66%)
	Anderson (I)	3,408	(2%)
1976	Ford (R)	60,114	(35%)
	Carter (D)	111,229	(64%)

Rep. Harold E. Ford (D) Elected 1974; b. May 20, 1945, Memphis; home, Memphis; Tenn. St. U., B.S. 1967, John Gupten Col., L.F.D., L.E.D. 1969.

Career   Mortician, 1969–75; Tenn. House of Reps., 1971–74.

Offices   2445 RHOB, 202-225-3265. Also 369 Fed. Bldg., Memphis 38103, 901-521-4131.

Committees   *Ways and Means* (9th). Subcommittees: Health; Oversight.

Select Committee on Aging (9th). Subcommittee: Health and Long-Term Care.

Group Ratings

	ADA	COPE	PC	LCV	CFA	RPN	NAB	NSI	NTU	ACA	ACU
1980	83	89	63	58	64	—	0	11	17	19	7
1979	79	95	73	88	63	—	—	—	18	0	5
1978	70	90	70	61	46	36	0	10	8	12	9

Key Votes

1) Draft Registn $	AGN	6) Fair Hsg DOJ Enfrc	FOR	11) Cut Socl Incr Dfns $	AGN
2) Ban $ to Nicrgua	AGN	7) Lim PAC Contrbtns	FOR	12) Hosptl Cost Controls	—
3) Dlay MX Missile	FOR	8) Cap on Food Stmp $	AGN	13) Gasln Ctrls & Allctns	FOR
4) Nuclr Mortorium	AGN	9) New US Dep Edcatn	FOR	14) Lim Wndfll Prof Tax	—
5) Alaska Lands Bill	FOR	10) Cut OSHA $	AGN	15) Chryslr Loan Grntee	—

Election Results

1980 general	Harold E. Ford (D)	110,139	(100%)	($187,385)
1980 primary	Harold E. Ford (D)	40,825	(73%)	
	Minerva Johnican (D)...........	11,337	(20%)	($0)
	Two others (D)	3,978	(7%)	
1978 general	Harold E. Ford (D)	80,776	(70%)	($179,244)
	Duncan Ragsdale (R)	33,679	(29%)	($12,372)

TEXAS

Texas is the only state in the Union that was an independent republic for a significant length of time, and today it probably possesses the most distinctive image of any state. Although its border areas are not much different from those of its neighbors — east Texas resembles southern Arkansas, west Texas resembles the Little Texas area of New Mexico — the state as a whole evokes for outsiders and residents a set of images and ideas generally consistent with and not divorced from reality. Texas's distinctive history is well known, and everyone remembers the Alamo — even if it is John Wayne defending it. From the movie *Giant* we have the dusty plains of west Texas cattle ranches and the sudden wealth of oil. By the 1940s Texas jokes — featuring boisterous millionaires and braggarts — were a staple of American humor.

But Texas has always been a more complex and diverse place than cartoon images suggest. We think of the typical Texan as a drawling white Anglo, but at least 21% of the state's residents are of Mexican origin (no one is sure how many, because of heavy illegal immigration) and another 12% are black. And certainly not every Texan has become an oil millionaire. On the contrary, vast differences in income and wealth are especially obvious in fast-growing cities such as Houston — in the same way and for the same reasons that disparities in income have always been most obvious in places with rapid economic development. Those who own or start the successful businesses become rich fast; the growth they help to generate attracts poor people from the rural hinterland to better opportunities in the city.

Texas has been growing more rapidly economically in the 1970s than ever before. The multiplication in oil prices in the 1970s has meant huge prosperity for Texas. This is not so much because of the state's own oil and gas production. It is still the leading oil producer among the states, but of course the U.S. is now an importer, not an exporter, of oil, and until 1978 it was prevented from selling its natural gas beyond its borders at the free market price. Texas prospers because it has become the corporate and operational center of the world oil and gas business. Many of the giants — Exxon, Shell, Gulf — have moved headquarters operations here in the 1970s. Even more important, Texas has literally thousands of specialized companies that can produce oil drill bits or put out oil well fires or construct pipelines. In the 1930s and 1940s, Texas benefited from the good geological luck of having big oil deposits; it now benefits from its skill at getting its own and others' oil and gas out of the ground. In the late 19th century Pennsylvania, with its hard and soft coal deposits, was the nation's energy capital and on that base built the nation's largest mass production industry, steel. In the late 20th century Texas has become the nation's energy capital, and its potential for future growth seems great indeed.

That potential seems especially great because attitudes — at least among the affluent minority that dominates the business community and the media here — are strongly positive about growth. These Texans have the kind of confidence in the future and in their own goodness and fairness and efficiency that most affluent Americans had in the 1950s but lost in the next decade. There is no apology or guilt about wealth here, no notion that it is evil unless it is given away to foundations. The feeling is that it is the God-given reward for building productive businesses and creating a thriving economy where none existed before. So there is very little radical chic or sense of noblesse oblige in Texas. The wealthy west side of Houston and north side of Dallas are strongly Republican; the two congressional districts there were among the most heavily Republican districts in the nation in 1972, 1976, and 1980. The affluent parts of the state are where the growth has been fastest and the elan is most vibrant. They believe that they represent the Texas of the future.

But despite their appreciation for Texas history, politically at least, the rich do not really represent the Texas of the past. Before the oil strikes of the turn of the century, this was a state made up almost entirely of dirt farmers, most of them white Anglos, with some blacks and Mexicans. It was also one of the nation's poorest, least educated, and most strongly Democratic states. As the oil industry grew and some Texans made really big money, there was no immediate move to the Republicans; rather the new rich Texans became Democrats. Their prototype was Jesse Jones, the Houston banker who was Franklin Roosevelt's secretary of Commerce, but never much of a New Dealer. Sam Rayburn and Lyndon Johnson, when they ran the Congress in the 1950s, were in close touch with these men, but did not always share their views; more in line were so-called Tory Democrats, such as Governor and Senator Price Daniel and Governor John Connally. These politicians were not necessarily enemies of big government — particularly when it could subsidize Texas's cotton farmers, irrigate its Lower Rio Grande Valley, or provide a large depletion allowance for its oil. But they believed firmly that the best interests of the state were to serve the best interests of its richest and most successful citizens — to keep taxes and public services low, to provide incentives and low wage labor to business. Texas is the only one of our really major states with a right to work law, and among the big states, its labor unions are the weakest; Texas also has, amid its boom, the lowest wage levels (and lowest costs of living) of the major states. Services recently have been increased while taxes have been cut: the prosperity here has been so great as to generate embarrassingly large revenues.

The Tory Democrats were for years the dominant force in Texas politics. They held onto the governorship for 40 solid years, from 1938 to 1978, and seldom lost effective control of the legislature. They carried the state for the Democratic presidential nominee in close elections like 1960, 1968, and 1976, despite major differences on policy. Their large and usually senior delegations in the House provided crucial aid to Democratic administrations on occasion and protected Texas's interests throughout. Their influential senators, notably Lyndon Johnson, combined liberalism on some issues with a canny appreciation for the Texas power structure and its needs.

The instrument of control was the open Democratic primary. Anyone could vote in the primary, although for years Texas discouraged registration by the poor, first by poll tax and then by onerous requirements. With no contested Republican primaries, conservative voters could participate in Democratic contests; and the mood of a majority of Texas voters in most contests was conservative. Meanwhile, insurgents could never raise the money necessary for sophisticated media campaigns; insiders always could. In general elections, the Tory Democrats won with the help of the liberal vote, mostly from minorities and in working-class sections of the big cities, and with the large rural vote — still more than one-third of the total. Most of the people in the small towns and rural counties of east and central Texas retain Baptist religious and Democratic political affiliation; the loyalty to the party was so strong that even George Wallace failed to crack it in 1968. Tradition-oriented rural Texas provided the key votes for Texas Democrats from Lyndon Johnson through Connally to Senator Lloyd Bentsen and Governor Dolph Briscoe in the 1970s.

Now the pattern of Tory Democratic domination seems to have changed — at least temporarily, quite possibly permanently. The victors have not been the liberal Democrats who had hoped to build a populist coalition of blue collar workers, blacks, and Chicanos, but the Republicans. In 1978 they won two smashing victories, electing William Clements governor and reelecting John Tower senator. In both cases they prevailed over strong Democratic opposition and, in Clements's case, their win was a tremendous upset. To be sure, in both cases the victories were by narrow margins — less than 17,000 votes out of more than two million cast. They were, however, the product of vast differences in turnout. In affluent urban Republican areas, turnout was high, and that is where Clements and Tower were elected; in rural east Texas and in the poorer neighborhoods of Houston, Dallas, Fort Worth, and San Antonio, turnout was low. Both traditional and liberal Democrats seemed to have little elan, little sense that they had the answers for society's problems; the Republicans did.

This trend was confirmed — and strengthened — by the 1980 presidential election. Ronald Reagan carried Texas by a smashing 55%–41% margin. Jimmy Carter, although an incumbent president and a white southerner, could get no larger a percentage than Hubert Humphrey's 12 years before. Once again the affluent areas led the way; the west Houston district cast 74% of its votes for Reagan — his second best percentage in the nation — and turnout was three times higher than in the inner city district next door. Reagan carried most of rural Texas as well, making inroads in counties that Clements and Tower had lost in 1978. Waco, Texarkana, the plains west of Dallas–Fort Worth, the hill country around Austin — all Democratic areas went for Reagan in 1980.

It is too early to say that the Republicans have captured Texas forever. Governor Clements will probably have a tough challenge in 1982, and Democratic Senator Bentsen is favored to retain his seat. Nevertheless, the Reagan triumph here, on top of the Republican victories of 1978, suggests that the philosophy of the Texas Republicans has been accepted here by a solid majority of Texans. It is a philosophy different from — and more consistent than — the thinking of the old Tory Democrats. Texas Republicans believe strongly in an aggressive foreign policy — Reagan's opposition to a Panama Canal Treaty was a big asset — and in untrammeled free enterprise. They believe that private investment has made Texas prosperous and vibrant, while welfare state measures have impoverished the Northeast. They do not believe as many rural Democratic voters do in some traditional values; residents of west Houston and north Dallas are proud of their cultural achievements, their knowledge of foreign wines and gourmet food and tasteful decoration, and they have little use for the evangelical religion and prohibitionism of rural Baptists. At the same time, they do not have the tolerance for the weird cultural styles one sees in affluent Californians. So they do not worry much about civil liberties or civil rights, nor do they pay lip service to causes that are fashionable among affluent northeasterners. When Bill Clements was asked to express some concern about problems of Mexican–Americans, he replied gruffly that he was not running for governor of Mexico. Texas Republicans are not defensive about what they believe.

John Connally shares, indeed exemplifies, much of the confidence these people have; and he played a major role in the Clements campaign. But as Nixon's Treasury secretary he put through wage and price controls and backed the opening to China. George Bush, originally from the Northeast, has a somewhat different attitude. He stressed that his own beliefs on foreign and domestic policies were not significantly different from Ronald Reagan's. But his record as a two-term congressman from Houston showed him supporting the antipoverty program and the federal open housing law. In any case, neither man has been much of a success in Republican politics here. Connally was elected governor as a Democrat, not a Republican; Bush failed twice to be elected senator here, once against a moderate Democrat and once against a liberal.

More successful as a Texas Republican is Governor William Clements. He seemed like a long-shot candidate in 1978, with his gruff manner and lack of experience in elective politics. His Democratic opponent, John Hill, was generally popular although he had a reputation of being somewhat liberal. But Clements had formidable assets. He was smart enough to have served creditably as deputy secretary of Defense — one of the top jobs in Washington. He was full of confidence. And he had plenty of money. Clements founded an extremely successful offshore drilling platform company, and when he decided to run for governor he decided to spend what it would take to win. That turned out to be about $7 million, and Clements was not a bit bashful or apologetic about spending it.

Clements has not accomplished all he wanted as governor but has succeeded in impressing his personality on the state. He has striven to make the Republican Party a major force in state politics, and during the 1980 campaign he worked hard for the Republican ticket — all the while oozing contempt for Jimmy Carter. Democrats charge that Clements has not cut state spending the way he promised, but still seem hard pressed to beat him, assuming he runs for reelection, in 1982. Moreover, the Democrats will probably have a tough primary, while the Republicans are confident and united.

When John Tower was first elected to the Senate in 1961, no one suspected that he would ever be a major force in national policy. He had a reputation as a kind of gadfly candidate, running against Lyndon Johnson when LBJ ran for both vice president and senator in 1960. Tower got a respectable 41% in that race, and in the 1961 special election outpolled an ultra-reactionary Democrat who had been appointed to the seat. Tower again beat a Tory Democrat in 1966, with the help of some liberal voters who figured he might not last as long — they seem to have been proved wrong. Against moderate Democrat Barefoot Sanders he won 55% in 1972, running better than a Republican ever had before in rural counties. His toughest race was in 1978, against Congressman Bob Krueger. A former English professor at Duke who quoted Shakespeare copiously on the campaign trail, Krueger had a tailored-to-Texas voting record. His major achievement was coming as close as anyone ever had to getting the House to vote for deregulating natural gas. His well-financed primary campaign beat an underfinanced liberal, and with his west Texas roots and acceptability to liberal Democrats he was a strong contender. Toward the end the campaign was marred by smear tactics. Tower refused to shake Krueger's hand in October when their paths crossed; and for once the senator's sour personality seems to have worked to his benefit. The result was extremely close, almost an exact duplicate of the gubernatorial race; turnout again was the key factor.

Tower is now chairman of the Senate Armed Services Committee, a post in which he has the potential to exert major influence over the course of policy. Armed Servics was run for years by Mississippi's John Stennis, a courtly southerner who liked to support presidents and kept a bipartisan staff. Tower is a different sort. Although a strong Reagan supporter, he has an acerbic turn of mind and is not the kind to trust anyone entirely. He believes in a strong defense and wants higher defense spending; he is knowledgeable and concerned as well about how the money is spent. One of the first things he did on Armed Serices was to set up partisan staffs — no more bipartisanship for this very partisan Republican. Next he reorganized subcommittee jurisdictions along operational lines. Senate Armed Services has had a distinguished membership in recent years and has the potential to make sure that additional defense outlays are spent well; Tower seems inclined to pursue that goal. Tower has, it should be noted, other important committee positions as well, notably on the Banking Committee. He does not use charm to ingratiate himself with other senators, but he does have influence by virtue of his hard work and brainpower. Back in Texas, his standing is probably as high as it has ever been, thanks to his prominence in Washington; this is a strong defense state and his position on Armed Services will not hurt if he runs for reelection in 1984.

Competence and hard work have also characterized the career of Texas's leading Democratic officeholder, Senator Lloyd Bentsen. His roots are very much in the Tory Democrat tradition. He is from a big landowning family in the Lower Rio Grande Valley and was first elected to the House in 1948 at the age of 27. He left Congress after eight years to make money in business, and returned to electoral politics in 1970. That year he upset Senator Ralph Yarborough, Texas's leading liberal, by running commercials featuring the riots outside the Chicago Democratic National Convention of 1968. For the general election, against George Bush, Bentsen cultivated the support of Barbara Jordan, Congressman Henry Gonzalez, and the state AFL–CIO; he combined rural traditional Democrats and urban minorities in sufficient numbers to win.

As senator Bentsen has toed a careful line between mainstream Democrats and conservatives. He has devoted much attention to complex legislation, such as the pension reform act and the oil depletion allowance (retained for small producers). He combines an ability to deal with complex government regulation with a commitment to free-market capitalism. In 1979 and 1980, Bentsen served as chairman of the Joint Economic Committee and produced its first unanimous report, one advocating lower taxes on capital gains and greater incentives for investment. He serves now on the Finance Committee, where he is ranking minority member of the International Trade Subcommittee. Generally, he supports free trade; Texas, after all, is a major exporter of items from cotton to oil drilling equipment to military airplanes. But he also cosponsored with the committee's Chairman, John Danforth, a measure restricting auto imports that was designed, at the least, to require the Japanese to restrict imports voluntarily.

Bentsen has shown great ability to win elections in Texas, although not on the national level. In 1970 he beat George Bush, then touted as one of the Republicans' leading candidates; in 1976 Bentsen beat Dallas area Congressman Alan Steelman. Neither Republican came from the right wing of the Texas Republican Party, and against each of them Bentsen had large majorities in the small rural counties that have historically formed the bedrock of Democratic strength. Bentsen was less successful in his presidential race. He raised a lot of money in 1975 but failed to win many votes in 1976; Democratic primary voters were receptive to a middle-of-the-road southerner, but they wanted one with less Washington experience than Bentsen and one who seemed closer to the people.

Bentsen is expected to seek a third Senate term in 1982. He could face formidable competition. Governor Clements could conceivably run, although that is unlikely; another possible, although not likely, candidate is former Dallas Cowboys' quarterback Roger Staubach. More likely candidates are Dallas Congressman James Collins and Houston state Senator Walter Mengden, so conservative that liberals call him "Mad Dog" Mengden. Bentsen has the advantage of a philosophy in line with Texas's current mood, and he is not likely to have significant primary opposition, but even against a lesser-known candidate than Clements or Staubach he could face a formidable reelection battle.

Texas has traditionally had a powerful House delegation. Two Texas Democrats have served as speakers of the House—John Nance Garner (1931–33) and Sam Rayburn (1940–

1052   TEXAS

47, 1949–53, 1955–61)—and today a Texan, Jim Wright, is House majority leader. But Texas no longer has many committee chairmen; in 1978 six of its 24 congressmen retired and the state lost 190 years of seniority. The replacements by and large have formed the nucleus of the 40-odd-member Conservative Democratic Forum—known colloquially as the Boll Weevils—a group of rural-based, conservative-minded young members with little seniority and little allegiance to the Democratic leadership, even to Wright.

The Republicans have never entirely succeeded in their hopes of electing many congressmen; currently they hold just five seats. They can expect more in 1982. The state gains three House seats, and two of them—one on the west side of Houston, another between Dallas and Fort Worth—will almost certainly go Republican, and Republicans will have a good chance at another Dallas area seat. But they have never really made a breakthrough outside the big metropolitan areas on a scale comparable to Reagan's performance in 1980. Whether all the talent and money available to Texas's Republican Party will be able to produce major congressional gains is perhaps the critical question about Texas politics in the 1980s.

Census Data   Pop. (1980 final) 14,228,383, up 27% in 1970s: 6.28% of U.S. total, 3d largest. Central city, 46%; suburban, 33%. Median 4-person family income, 1978, $20,455, 100% of U.S., 24th highest.

1979 Share of Federal Tax Burden $26,733,000,000; 5.93% of U.S. total, 4th largest.

1979 Share of Federal Outlays $26,231,553,000; 5.67% of U.S. total, 3d largest.

DOD	$8,646,109,000	2d	(8.15%)	HEW	$8,497,085,000	6th	(4.75%)
DOE	$134,450,000	21st	(1.14%)	ERDA	$41,903,000	13th	(1.54%)
HUD	$332,310,000	6th	(5.04%)	NASA	$433,190,000	3d	(9.26%)
VA	$1,410,977,000	3d	(6.80%)	DOT	$737,427,000	6th	(4.47%)
EPA	$149,551,000	12th	(2.82%)	DOC	$115,966,000	7th	(3.66%)
DOI	$85,250,000	19th	(1.54%)	USDA	$1,683,659,000	3d	(7.01%)

Economic Base   Finance, insurance, and real estate; agriculture, notably cattle, sorghum grain, cotton lint, and dairy products; transportation equipment, especially aircraft; food and kindred products, especially meat products; oil and gas extraction, especially oil and gas field services; boys' furnishings; machinery, especially construction and related machinery.

Political Lineup   Governor, William (Bill) Clements (R). Senators, John G. Tower (R) and Lloyd Bentsen (D). Representatives, 24 (19 D and 5 R); 27 in 1982. State Senate, 31 (24 D and 7 R); State House of Delegates, 150 (114 D and 36 R).

The Voters

Registration   6,639,662 Total.
Employment profile 1970   White collar, 49%. Blue collar, 34%. Service, 13%. Farm, 4%.
Ethnic groups   Black 1980, 12%. Hispanic 1980, 21%. Asian 1980, 1%. Total foreign stock 1970, 11%.

Presidential Vote

1980	Reagan (R)	2,510,705	(55%)
	Carter (D)	1,881,417	(41%)
	Anderson (I)	111,613	(2%)
1976	Ford (R)	1,953,300	(48%)
	Carter (D)	2,082,319	(51%)

1980 Democratic Presidential Primary			*1980 Republican Presidential Primary*		
Carter	769,390	(56%)	Reagan	268,798	(51%)
Kennedy	314,129	(23%)	Bush	249,819	(57%)
One other	35,529	(2%)	Uncommitted	8,162	(2%)
Uncommitted	256,723	(19%)			

SENATORS

Sen. John Tower (R) Elected May 27, 1961, seat up 1984; b. Sept. 29, 1925, Houston; home, Wichita Falls; Southwestern U., B.A. 1948, U. of London, 1952, SMU, M.A. 1953.

Career Navy, WWII; Prof. of Govt., Midwestern U., 1951–61.

Offices 142 RSOB, 202-224-2934. Also 961 Fed. Ofc. Bldg., 300 E. 8th St., Austin 78701, 512-397-5933, and Fed. Bldg., 1114 Commerce St., Dallas 75202, 214-749-7525.

Committees *Armed Services* (Chairman).

Banking, Housing, and Urban Affairs (2d). Subcommittees: Housing and Urban Affairs; Financial Institutions (Chairman); Securities.

Budget (6th).

Group Ratings

	ADA	COPE	PC	LCV	CFA	RPN	NAB	NSI	NTU	ACA	ACU
1980	6	12	13	11	0	—	92	80	58	91	76
1979	11	0	18	—	10	—	—	—	54	88	83
1978	70	6	13	0	15	75	60	100	28	86	91

Key Votes

1) Draft Registn $	FOR	6) Fair Housng Cloture	AGN
2) Ban $ to Nicrgua	AGN	7) Ban $ Rape Abortns	—
3) Dlay MX Missile	AGN	8) Cap on Food Stmp $	FOR
4) Nuclr Mortorium	AGN	9) New US Dep Edcatn	AGN
5) Alaska Lands Bill	AGN	10) Cut OSHA Inspctns	—

11) Cut Socl Incr Defns	FOR
12) Income Tax Indexing	FOR
13) Lim Spdg 21% GNP	FOR
14) Incr Wndfll Prof Tax	AGN
15) Chryslr Loan Grntee	FOR

Election Results

1978 general	John G. Tower (R)	1,151,376	(50%)	($4,324,601)
	Robert Krueger (D).............	1,139,149	(49%)	($2,428,666)
1978 primary	John G. Tower (R)	142,202	(100%)	
1972 general	John G. Tower (R)	1,822,877	(53%)	($2,301,870)
	Barefoot Sanders (D)	1,511,985	(44%)	($629,008)

Sen. Lloyd Bentsen (D) Elected 1970, seat up 1982; b. Feb. 11, 1921, Mission; home, Houston; U. of Tex., LL.B. 1942.

Career Army Air Corps, WWII; Judge, Hidalgo Co., 1946; U.S. House of Reps., 1949–55; Pres., Lincoln Consolidated, financial holding co.

Offices 240 RSOB, 202-224-5922. Also Fed. Bldg., Rm. 912, Austin 78701, 512-397-5834, and Fed. Bldg., Houston 77002, 713-226-5496.

Committees *Environment and Public Works* (2d). Subcommittees: Water Resources; Transportation.

Finance (3d). Subcommittees: Taxation and Debt Management; International Trade; Energy and Agricultural Taxation.

Joint Economic Committee (7th).

Select Committee on Intelligence (7th). Subcommittees: Budget; Analysis and Production.

Group Ratings

	ADA	COPE	PC	LCV	CFA	RPN	NAB	NSI	NTU	ACA	ACU
1980	39	39	27	31	13	—	58	44	39	43	38
1979	26	32	29	—	14	—	—	—	29	38	24
1978	35	26	25	41	30	56	67	50	18	57	38

Key Votes

1) Draft Registn $	FOR	6) Fair Housng Cloture	AGN
2) Ban $ to Nicrgua	FOR	7) Ban $ Rape Abortns	AGN
3) Dlay MX Missile	AGN	8) Cap on Food Stmp $	FOR
4) Nuclr Mortorium	AGN	9) New US Dep Edcatn	FOR
5) Alaska Lands Bill	FOR	10) Cut OSHA Inspctns	—

11) Cut Socl Incr Defns	FOR
12) Income Tax Indexing	AGN
13) Lim Spdg 21% GNP	AGN
14) Incr Wndfll Prof Tax	AGN
15) Chryslr Loan Grntee	FOR

Election Results

1976 general	Lloyd Bentsen (D)..............	2,199,956	(57%)	($1,237,910)
	Alan Steelman (R)	1,636,370	(42%)	($665,058)
1976 primary	Lloyd Bentsen (D)..............	970,983	(64%)	
	Phil Gramm (D)	427,597	(28%)	
	Two others (D)	129,585	(8%)	
1970 general	Lloyd Bentsen (D)..............	1,226,568	(54%)	
	George Bush (R)	1,071,234	(46%)	

GOVERNOR

Gov. William (Bill) Clements (R) Elected 1978, term expires Jan. 1983; b. Apr. 13, 1917, Dallas; SMU.

Career Oil driller, 1937–47; Founder, Chmn. of Bd., Chf. Exec. Officer, SEDCO, Inc., 1947–.

Offices Austin 78711, 512-475-2731.

Election Results

1978 gen.	William (Bill) Clements (R) .	1,183,839	(50%)
	John Hill (D)	1,166,979	(49%)
1978 prim.	William (Bill) Clements (R) .	115,345	(73%)
	Ray Hutchison (R)	38,268	(24%)
	One other (R)	4,790	(3%)
1974 gen.	Dolph Briscoe (D)	1,016,334	(63%)
	Jim Granberry (R)	514,725	(32%)
	R. Muniz (La Raza Unida) .	93,295	(6%)

FIRST DISTRICT

The 1st district of Texas is the northeastern corner of the state. This is not part of the gleaming new urban Texas; the cities here are places such as Marshall, Paris, and the Texas half of Texarkana, with 31,000 people, the largest city in the district. The character of this part of Texas has remained agricultural. It is the part of the state geographically closest to the Deep South, and one of the parts of the state spiritually closest also: it nearly gave a plurality of its votes to George Wallace in 1968. This is a part of the South where the populist tradition retains at least a little life. Like Jim Hogg, the populist governor of Texas in the 1890s,the farmers and townspeople of the 1st are suspicious of bankers, insurance companies, oil men, and Republicans.

Those feelings were exemplified in the congressional career of Wright Patman, who was the 1st's congressman for nearly 50 years. Elected in 1928, he soon made history by moving

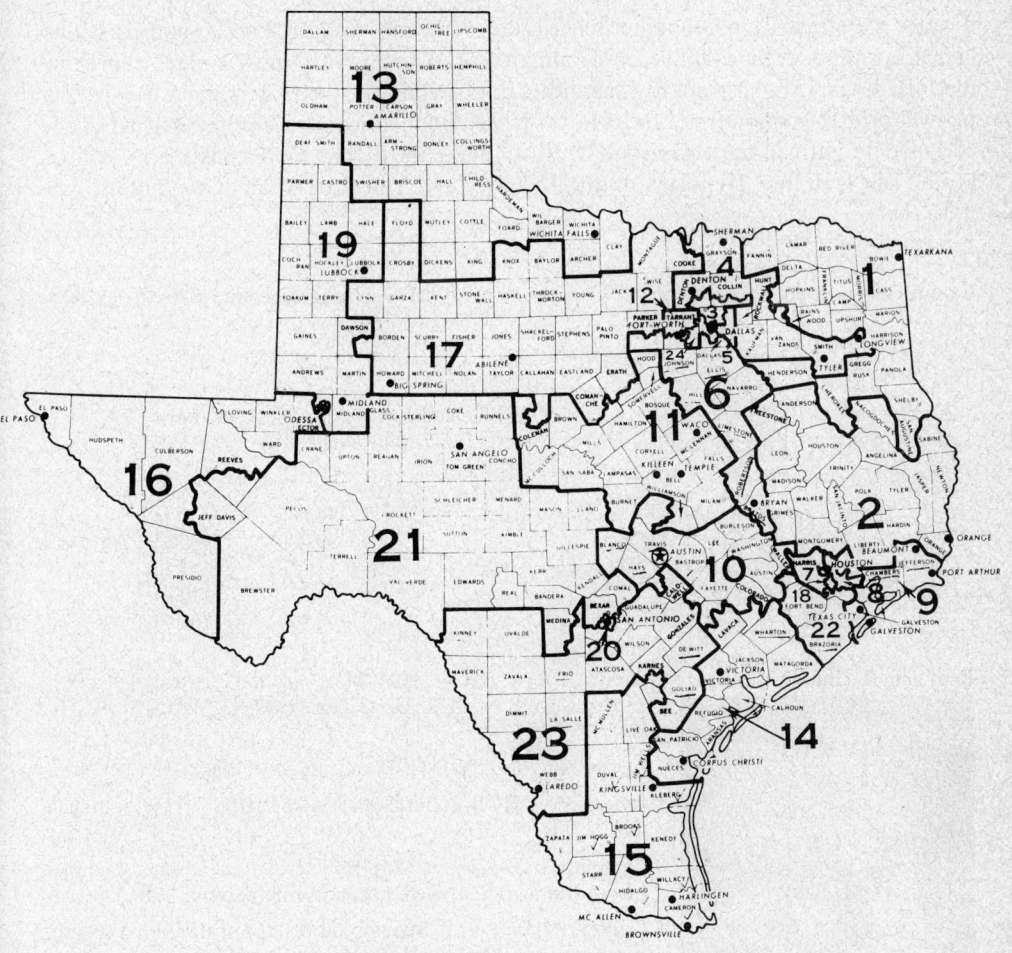

for the impeachment of Treasury Secretary Andrew Mellon; toward the end of his career, in 1972, he tried to launch an investigation of Watergate just before the election. Both efforts failed, although their ultimate goals were achieved. Patman was chairman of the House Banking Committee for many years, and irritated big bankers greatly; but he did not change their business practices as much as he would have liked to.

Patman was ousted from his chairmanship after the 1974 election by the Democratic Caucus; younger members didn't mind his politics, but they felt he was too old to run the committee effectively and would not be an effective spokesman for them on national television. He died in June 1976, and his successor had in effect been chosen in the runoff that had just been held. The winner was Sam Hall, a Democrat who had run against Patman in 1972 and had a local following around his hometown of Marshall. Hall's voting record shows little trace of Patman's kind of populism; he is one of the most conservative of southern Democrats, far more so, for example, than Patman's son William, who is now congressman from the 14th district. Hall has not had significant opposition since the 1976 primary. Redistricting will probably smooth out the district's jagged boundaries (which were designed to accommodate Patman ten years ago). This will make the district more conservative, which should suit Hall fine. He serves on the Judiciary and Veterans' Affairs Committees.

Census Data   Pop. (1980 final) 565,829, up 21% in 1970s. Median family income, 1970, $6,543, 68% of U.S.

The Voters

  Employment profile 1970   White collar, 37%. Blue collar, 44%. Service, 13%. Farm, 6%.
  Ethnic groups   Black 1980, 19%. Hispanic 1980, 2%. Total foreign stock 1970, 1%.

Presidential Vote

1980	Reagan (R)	96,685	(49%)
	Carter (D)	99,203	(50%)
	Anderson (I)	1,580	(1%)
1976	Ford (R)	69,297	(40%)
	Carter (D)	104,400	(60%)

Rep. Sam B. Hall, Jr. (D) Elected June 19, 1976; b. Jan. 11, 1924, Marshall; home, Marshall; E. Tex. Baptist Col., B.A. 1942, U. of Tex., 1942–43, Baylor U., LL.B. 1948.

Career Air Force, WWII; Practicing atty., 1948–76.

Offices 318 CHOB, 202-225-3035. Also P.O. Box 1349, Marshall 75670, 214-938-8386.

Committees *Judiciary* (10th). Subcommittees: Crime; Criminal Justice; Immigration, Refugees, and International Law.

Veterans' Affairs (7th). Subcommittees: Compensation, Pension, and Insurance (Chairman); Oversight and Investigations.

Group Ratings

	ADA	COPE	PC	LCV	CFA	RPN	NAB	NSI	NTU	ACA	ACU
1980	0	22	20	17	7	—	100	89	55	73	89
1979	11	25	18	7	11	—	—	—	51	72	72
1978	20	15	20	10	27	55	91	80	37	92	83

Key Votes

1) Draft Registn $	FOR	6) Fair Hsg DOJ Enfrc	AGN	11) Cut Socl Incr Dfns $	—
2) Ban $ to Nicrgua	FOR	7) Lim PAC Contrbtns	AGN	12) Hosptl Cost Controls	AGN
3) Dlay MX Missile	AGN	8) Cap on Food Stmp $	AGN	13) Gasln Ctrls & Allctns	FOR
4) Nuclr Mortorium	AGN	9) New US Dep Edcatn	AGN	14) Lim Wndfll Prof Tax	FOR
5) Alaska Lands Bill	AGN	10) Cut OSHA $	FOR	15) Chryslr Loan Grntee	AGN

Election Results

1980 general	Sam B. Hall, Jr. (D)	137,665	(100%)	($83,698)
1980 primary	Sam B. Hall, Jr. (D)	89,498	(100%)	
1978 general	Sam B. Hall, Jr. (D)	73,708	(78%)	($44,229)
	Fred Hudson (R)	20,700	(22%)	($76,520)

SECOND DISTRICT

The 2d congressional district of Texas is an almost entirely rural and small town part of east Texas; the largest cities here are Orange and Lufkin, neither with more than 28,000 people. More than any other Texas district, the 2d is an extension of the Deep South. Farmers from that region first settled this none too fertile land; their lot was a hard one, and residents of this part of east Texas retain a streak of populism. During the 1930s, it was here in the 2d district that the first really big Texas oil strikes were made. But for the most part the money seems to have gone elsewhere, to Houston and Dallas and to small east Texas oil cities like Tyler and Longview. Farming and lumber—the kind of scrubby pine that grows rapidly in the humid South—remain the important industries here.

The 2d district elects one of the politically canniest members of the traditionally shrewd Texas delegation Congressman Charles Wilson. Wilson has been known since his days in the state Senate as some kind of liberal; his voting record on economic issues is often in accord with northern Democrats. On oil matters he is, of course, a loyal Texan. He has gotten away with this voting record in even the most conservative years with a personal hell-of-a-fellow style that has always been effective in east Texas campaigns. He first won the seat in 1972, when the incumbent, John Dowdy, had been indicted and convicted on bribery charges; Wilson easily beat Dowdy's wife, who was running as a stand-in.

Wilson is an aggressive and ambitious congressman. He elbowed the more senior Richard White of the 16th district aside to win a seat on the Appropriations Committee. He has looked after interests in his district carefully and has been active on national energy legislation.

For a time Wilson chaired the District of Columbia Appropriations Subcommittee but gave up that chair in return for a seat on the Defense Subcommittee. There he seems less interested in broad matters of policy than he does in protecting Texas interests. Wilson is unlikely to be affected adversely by redistricting. Republican strength in the district is increasing in Montgomery County, immediately north of Houston, but Wilson otherwise seems in tune with district sentiment.

Census Data Pop. (1980 final) 676,069, up 45% in 1970s. Median family income, 1970, $7,259, 76% of U.S

The Voters

Employment profile 1970 White collar, 38%. Blue collar, 44%. Service, 14%. Farm, 4%.
Ethnic groups Black 1980, 15%. Hispanic 1980, 3%. Total foreign stock 1970, 2%.

Presidential Vote

1980	Reagan (R)	111,165	(50%)
	Carter (D)	107,327	(48%)
	Anderson (I)	3,209	(1%)
1976	Ford (R)	76,438	(42%)
	Carter (D)	105,487	(58%)

Rep. Charles Wilson (D) Elected 1972; b. June 1, 1933, Trinity; home, Lufkin; Sam Houston St. U., U.S. Naval Acad., B.S. 1956.

Career Navy, 1956–60; Mgr., retail lumber store; Tex. House of Reps., 1961–66; Tex. Senate, 1967–72.

Offices 1214 LHOB, 202-225-2401. Also Fed. Bldg., Lufkin 75901, 713-634-8247.

Committees *Appropriations* (17th). Subcommittees: Defense; District of Columbia; Foreign Operations.

Standards of Official Conduct (4th).

Group Ratings

	ADA	COPE	PC	LCV	CFA	RPN	NAB	NSI	NTU	ACA	ACU
1980	17	59	30	28	29	—	50	89	30	43	56
1979	21	45	13	24	11	—	—	—	30	44	56
1978	35	68	30	30	9	75	36	75	7	50	37

Key Votes

1) Draft Registn $	FOR	6) Fair Hsg DOJ Enfrc	FOR	11) Cut Socl Incr Dfns $	FOR
2) Ban $ to Nicrgua	FOR	7) Lim PAC Contrbtns	AGN	12) Hosptl Cost Controls	AGN
3) Dlay MX Missile	AGN	8) Cap on Food Stmp $	AGN	13) Gasln Ctrls & Allctns	AGN
4) Nuclr Mortorium	AGN	9) New US Dep Edcatn	FOR	14) Lim Wndfll Prof Tax	FOR
5) Alaska Lands Bill	AGN	10) Cut OSHA $	AGN	15) Chryslr Loan Grntee	FOR

Election Results

1980 general	Charles Wilson (D)	142,496	(69%)	($239,766)
	F. H. Pannill, Sr. (R)	60,742	(30%)	($5,698)
1980 primary	Charles Wilson (D)	88,557	(78%)	
	Allen Summers (D)	25,338	(22%)	($0)
1978 general	Charles Wilson (D)	66,986	(70%)	($218,901)
	James Dillon (R)	28,584	(30%)	($7,091)

THIRD DISTRICT

The rich Texan in all the old rich Texan jokes probably lives on the north side of Dallas. This is where the late right-wing oilman H. L. Hunt lived in his larger than life copy of Mount Vernon, and where other millionaires live in mansions or in pleasant colonial houses on tree-shaded streets. The north side is also the fastest growing part of the Dallas–Fort Worth metroplex. Affluence has pushed the boundaries of development northward, past the Dallas city limits through suburbs like Irving, Farmers Branch, and Richardson, and on into the southern edges of Collin and Denton Counties. Along with most of north Dallas, these suburban areas form the 3d congressional district of Texas.

Dallas is the older and probably the more conservative of Texas's two largest cities. Its initial wealth was based not on oil, which was not discovered in Texas until the turn of the century, but on cotton; indeed, Texas remains one of the major cotton-producing states. By 1900 Dallas was already the banking, financial, and insurance center for the cotton business in Texas; nearby Fort Worth was the urban center of the state's other major industry, cattle. Dallas has continued to be the financial center of Texas and much of the Southwest, although it has strong competition from Houston; it has also continued to be an entrepreneurial center of some note. Of course many of the hugely successful new businesses here are oil-related, such as William Clements's Sedco company; but there are also diverse Dallas–based businesses from giants like Texas Instruments to the well-known retailer Nieman Marcus.

The north side of Dallas and the west side of Houston — basically the areas within the 3d and 7th congressional districts — are not only the most prosperous parts of the state, they also seem increasingly to be the most intellectually influential. The old traditions of Texas populism — the farmers' distrust of banks and insurance companies — seem increasingly to be a thing of the past. Unlike wealthy people in the Northeast, rich people in north Dallas do not feel that they have done something bad because they have grown rich. People here still believe in free markets and that success goes to those who earn it. And unlike much of the rest of affluent America, these are people who believe that things are getting better, that a strong and vibrant future for America is more than a distinct possibility, and that technology and economic growth can produce a better life for all. They do not see the world through Malthusian or Marxist eyes, and they seem to be convincing at least the majority of Texans who do not share all their affluence that their view is the correct one.

Dallas is a free enterprise city, which has little use for big government; and obviously a career in government is not a major aspiration here. This becomes clear when one contrasts the number of bright, articulate people who must live within the 3d district with the congressional representation the seat has had. .In the 1950s it was represented by a Republican best known for shoving Lyndon Johnson and Lady Bird Johnson in a Dallas hotel in the 1960 campaign. Later it was represented by an old-style — rotund, garrulous, bibulous — Democrat named Joe Pool. Since the 1968 election the congressman has been James Collins, a Republican and successful businessman. He votes a predictably conservative line, and has taken some leadership role in recent years. Collins is ranking Republican on the Communications Subcommittee, which regulates the broadcast and telephone industries. He has won reelection every two years and has been mentioned as a possible candidate for the Senate in 1982.

Census Data Pop. (1980 final) 696,081, up 49% in 1970s. Median family income, 1970, $13,395, 140% of U.S.

The Voters

Employment profile 1970 White collar, 74%. Blue collar, 19%. Service, 7%. Farm, -%.
Ethnic groups Black 1980, 3%. Hispanic 1980, 5%. Asian 1980, 1% Total foreign stock 1970, 8%. Germany, 1%.

Presidential Vote

1980	Reagan (R)	210,633	(73%)
	Carter (D)	65,755	(23%)
	Anderson (I)	10,379	(4%)
1976	Ford (R)	172,909	(72%)
	Carter (D)	65,021	(27%)

Rep. James M. (Jim) **Collins** (R) Elected Aug. 24, 1968; b. Apr. 29, 1916, Hallsville; home, Dallas; SMU, B.S.C. 1937, Northwestern U., M.B.A. 1943, American Col., C.L.U. 1940, Harvard U., M.B.A. 1943.

Career Army, WWII; Pres., Consolidated Industries, Inc., and Internatl. Industries, Inc.; Pres., Fidelity Union Life Ins. Co., 1954–65.

Offices 2419 RHOB, 202-225-4201. Also 12900 Preston Rd., Dallas 75230, 214-767-4848.

Committee *Energy and Commerce* (3d). Subcommittees: Energy Conservation and Power; Fossil and Synthetic Fuels; Telecommunications, Consumer Protection and Finance.

Group Ratings

	ADA	COPE	PC	LCV	CFA	RPN	NAB	NSI	NTU	ACA	ACU
1980	11	10	20	35	7	—	100	100	87	96	95
1979	0	5	13	10	7	—	—	—	84	100	97
1978	10	5	23	27	23	83	100	90	75	96	88

Key Votes

1) Draft Registn $	AGN	6) Fair Hsg DOJ Enfrc	AGN	11) Cut Socl Incr Dfns $	FOR
2) Ban $ to Nicrgua	FOR	7) Lim PAC Contrbtns	AGN	12) Hosptl Cost Controls	AGN
3) Dlay MX Missile	AGN	8) Cap on Food Stmp $	FOR	13) Gasln Ctrls & Allctns	AGN
4) Nuclr Mortorium	AGN	9) New US Dep Edcatn	AGN	14) Lim Wndfll Prof Tax	FOR
5) Alaska Lands Bill	AGN	10) Cut OSHA $	FOR	15) Chryslr Loan Grntee	AGN

Election Results

1980 general	James M. (Jim) Collins (R)	218,228	(79%)	($303,229)
	Earle Stephen Porter (D)	49,667	(18%)	($0)
1980 primary	James M. (Jim) Collins (R)	59,446	(100%)	
1978 general	James M. Collins (R), unopposed .			($80,442)

FOURTH DISTRICT

The 4th congressional district of Texas is part of the Red River Valley. This land was settled, on the Texas side, more than a century ago, and soon became thickly populated; it has some of the best farmland in the state. The district remains largely agricultural today, except to the extent that the Dallas–Fort Worth metroplex is growing and reaching out to take over farming acreage. This is the part of Texas where the Deep South turns into the Southwest. The 1st district, just to the east, is 19% black; the 4th is 13% black; the 13th district, to the west, is 5% black. For the most part the 4th is still peopled by small farmers and the residents of small towns.

From the days of its first settlement, with only the most minor of exceptions, the Red River Valley has been staunchly Democratic. It has also produced some of the nation's leading Democratic politicians. From the Oklahoma side of the river came Carl Albert, speaker of the House from 1971 to 1977, and from the Texas side came Sam Rayburn, speaker except during periods of Republican control from 1940 to 1961 and congressman from the 4th district from 1913 to 1961. Rayburn's career spans most of our modern political history. When the young Texan was first elected, Henry Adams still lived on Lafayette Park across from the White House. Rayburn saw Washington grow from the provincial outpost disdained by the Boston Brahmins into the most powerful city in the world.

Rayburn entered the House just after it had freed itself from the iron rule of Speaker Joseph Cannon. In 1961, Rayburn went home to die just a few months after he had led and won a struggle to increase the membership of the Rules Committee — an attempt to restore power to the speaker and to take it away from a reactionary committee chairman. During Rayburn's first term in the House, President Wilson, working with Speaker Champ Clark and Majority Leader Oscar Underwood, enacted the entire Democratic legislative program with automatic votes from the Democratic Caucus. A half century later, the Rules Committee fight exposed all the cracks and fissures that had developed within the caucus since Wilson's time.

"To get along, you have to go along," Mister Sam often said and, in so saying, he admitted that the Democratic Party, split by civil rights and other issues, could no longer operate as a cohesive unit. Members of the party would simply have to take account of the differences among them, and not exacerbate them. Rayburn was speaker for longer than anyone else in American history. Critics said that he did not use his power often or forcefully enough; Rayburn would have replied that a heavy hand would only have led to irrevocable splits within the Democratic Party.

Sam Rayburn also witnessed nearly all the modern political history of Texas. Back in 1912, Texas was still a state of populist farmers and big oil money was not yet a factor in its politics. Fifty years later, oil dominated the state in every conceivable way. Rayburn, as much as anyone, built the politics of oil into the congressional establishment. He made certain that the Ways and Means Committee had a solid majority for the oil depletion allowance, for instance. Rayburn was also largely responsible for the cohesion of the Texas delegation, whether the issue was oil, cotton, or military installations. Texas often elected more Democratic congressmen than any other state, and many of them had great seniority; the result was that Texas usually got what it wanted from the federal government.

Oil changed Sam Rayburn's Texas, and so did shifts in population. In 1912, towns like Rayburn's Bonham (1980 pop. 7,338) were typical of the state — small, dusty agricultural market centers. By 1961, Houston and Dallas–Fort Worth were increasingly important, and in that year they helped elect the first Republican senator here since Reconstruction. Today, Bonham is no longer part of the 4th district; it was moved to the 1st to satisfy the equal population requirement. As it stands now, two-thirds of the 4th is classified as metropolitan, most of it part of the Dallas–Fort Worth metropolitan area. Since Rayburn's death, the 4th has also come to include the archconservative, heavily Republican oil towns of Tyler and Longview.

Rayburn's successor in the House, Ray Roberts, an expert on dams and chairman of the Veterans' Affairs Committee, retired in 1980 at age 67. The new congressman, Ralph Hall, was born when Rayburn had already served in the House for a decade. Hall had a successful career in the Texas legislature and then, after losing the lieutenant governor nomination in 1972, in business. But Hall's election was not automatic. He had serious opposition not only in the Democratic primary but in the general election. Republican John Wright had a solid base in Tyler and Longview, and carried them both; he also ran about even in the parts of the district where affluent people from Dallas are moving into formerly rural counties. Hall won with only 52% of the vote, and he will undoubtedly be paying close attention to redistricting; he would probably like to see Tyler and Longview, or at least one of them, transferred to the 1st district.

Hall is expected to have a conservative voting record in the House and is one of several junior Texas Democrats who are members of the Conservative Democratic Forum. He is also a member of the Energy and Commerce and Science and Technology Committees.

Census Data   Pop. (1980 final) 596,579, up 28% in 1970s. Median family income, 1970, $8,032, 84% of U.S.

The Voters

Employment profile 1970   White collar, 44%. Blue collar, 38%. Service, 14%. Farm, 4%.
Ethnic groups   Black 1980, 13%. Hispanic 1980, 3%. Total foreign stock 1970, 3%.

Presidential Vote

1980	Reagan (R)	117,540	(58%)
	Carter (D)	80,643	(40%)
	Anderson (I)	3,415	(2%)
1976	Ford (R)	84,734	(49%)
	Carter (D)	87,394	(51%)

Rep. Ralph M. Hall (D) Elected 1980; b. May 23, 1923, Rockwall Co.; home, Rockwall; U. of Tex., TCU, SMU, J.D. 1951.

Career   Navy, WWII; Rockwall Co. Judge, 1950–62; Tex. Senate, 1962–72; Pres. and CEO, Texas Aluminum Corp; Gen. Counsel, Texas Extrusion Co., Inc.

Offices   1223 LHOB, 202-225-6673. Also 206 Fed. Bldg., Denton 76201, 817-383-2616; A105 Fed. Bldg., McKinney 75069, 214-542-2617; 104 San Jacinto St., Rockwall 75087, 214-722-9118; 201 Fed. Bldg., Sherman 75090, 214-892-1112; and 211 Fed. Bldg., Tyler 75702, 214-597-3729.

Committees   *Energy and Commerce* (24th). Subcommittees: Energy Conservation and Power; Fossil and Synthetic Fuels.

Science and Technology (21st). Subcommittees: Science, Research and Technology; Space Science and Applications; Transportation, Aviation and Materials.

Group Ratings and Key Votes: Newly Elected

Election Results

1980 general	Ralph M. Hall (D)	102,787	(52%)	($347,903)
	John Wright (R)	93,915	(48%)	($159,152)
1980 primary	Ralph M. Hall (D)	36,874	(57%)	
	Jerdy Gary (D)	27,341	(43%)	($272,524)
1978 general	Ray Roberts (D)	58,336	(61%)	($125,814)
	Frank S. Glenn (R)	36,582	(39%)	($80,606)

FIFTH DISTRICT

The 5th congressional district of Texas includes much of the southern and eastern parts of Dallas and its adjacent suburbs. It includes a significant part of Dallas's black population and its relatively small community of Mexican–Americans; but overall the atmosphere is working-class white. This is not the glittering north Dallas with its millionaires and swimming pools. It is neighborhoods of frame houses where people who grew up in the country now live in air-conditioned comfort. The 5th district contains just about any political strain you can find in Texas. There are ideological liberals, nouveaux riches free market enthusiasts, smug Dallas boosters, black militants, upwardly mobile management types, and union shop stewards. And during the past 20 years just about every strain has been personified by one of the district's congressmen.

The 5th, when it included all of Dallas County, elected Republican Bruce Alger as long ago as 1954; a noisy and sometimes raucous reactionary, he was defeated in 1964 in a wave of remorse over the assassination of President Kennedy. The new congressman was Earle Cabell, a conservative Democrat and mayor of Dallas; he had been installed in the latter post by the city's business leaders who for years successfully guided its politics. Cabell was defeated in 1972 by Alan Steelman, a young Republican with experience in private sector business and the Nixon Administration. He personified many young management types: a free enterpriser on economic policy, but an opponent on environmental grounds of a proposal to build a canal from Dallas to the Gulf of Mexico. That latter position was not popular with big money interests in Texas, however; and when Steelman ran for the Senate in 1976 against Lloyd Bentsen, his campaign fizzled when he could not raise enough money.

The current congressman, Jim Mattox, is a Democrat, who worked summers during college as a dock worker; he has been known in Dallas as a sort of liberal Democrat. His voting record took a turn to the right, however, after the 1978 election, when Republicans swept Texas and Mattox himself was almost beaten. Still, he votes more often with Democrats than Republicans and has not aligned himself with the mostly rural-based southern conservative Democrats.

Mattox has had considerable success in the House. He won a seat on the House Budget Committee as a freshman, and was one of the leaders of his freshman caucus. He has had more difficulty back home in Dallas, where he faced strenuous competition in 1978 and 1980 from Republican Tom Pauken. In two campaigns both candidates spent freely; Mattox won twice with 51% of the vote. These are not secure margins (although some expected Mattox to be swept out with the Reagan tide in 1980), and for the future much will depend on redistricting. Pauken himself seemed in early 1981 likely to get a Reagan Administration appointment, but plenty of other ambitious young Republicans will be watching the line-drawing and wondering whether the new 5th district will have more affluent precincts and fewer working-class ones. Mattox will have trouble getting more favorable territory, since that would mean taking it away from 24th district Democrat Martin Frost.

But this district has not grown much in population, and will have to add territory somewhere. Mattox is an aggressive politician, and with the Republicans charging hard, this is likely to be one of the most seriously contested races in Texas in 1982.

Census Data Pop. (1980 final) 510,041, up 9% in 1970s. Median family income, 1970, $9,480, 99% of U.S.

The Voters

Employment profile 1970 White collar, 48%. Blue collar, 38%. Service, 14%. Farm, -%.
Ethnic groups Black 1980, 18%. Hispanic 1980, 11%. Asian 1980, 1%. Total foreign stock 1970, 5%.

Presidential Vote

1980	Reagan (R)	75,323	(52%)
	Carter (D)	64,706	(44%)
	Anderson (I)	3,477	(2%)
1976	Ford (R)	61,251	(47%)
	Carter (D)	68,944	(53%)

Rep. Jim Mattox (D) Elected 1976; b. Aug. 29, 1943, Dallas; home, Dallas; Baylor U., B.B.A. 1965, SMU, J.D. 1968.

Career Summer dock worker, 1964–66; Intern for U.S. Rep. Earle Cable, 1967; Asst. Dallas Co. Dist. Atty., 1968–70; Practicing atty., 1970–76; Tex. House of Reps., 1973–77.

Offices 1111 LHOB, 202-225-2231. Also Fed. Bldg., Dallas 75201, 214-749-1771.

Committees *Banking, Finance and Urban Affairs* (17th). Subcommittees: Financial Institutions Supervision, Regulation and Insurance; General Oversight and Renegotiation; International Trade, Investment and Monetary Policy.

Budget (6th).

Group Ratings

	ADA	COPE	PC	LCV	CFA	RPN	NAB	NSI	NTU	ACA	ACU
1980	50	44	47	51	43	—	80	40	41	42	50
1979	42	50	48	60	41	—	—	—	37	42	31
1978	40	79	68	77	46	67	36	60	36	50	8

Key Votes

1) Draft Registn $	FOR	6) Fair Hsg DOJ Enfrc	FOR	11) Cut Socl Incr Dfns $	AGN
2) Ban $ to Nicrgua	AGN	7) Lim PAC Contrbtns	FOR	12) Hosptl Cost Controls	AGN
3) Dlay MX Missile	FOR	8) Cap on Food Stmp $	AGN	13) Gasln Ctrls & Allctns	AGN
4) Nuclr Mortorium	AGN	9) New US Dep Edcatn	FOR	14) Lim Wndfll Prof Tax	FOR
5) Alaska Lands Bill	FOR	10) Cut OSHA $	AGN	15) Chryslr Loan Grntee	FOR

Election Results

1980 general	Jim Mattox (D)...............	70,892	(51%)	($529,743)
	Tom Pauken (R)..............	67,848	(49%)	($265,248)
1980 primary	Jim Mattox (D), unopposed			
1978 general	Jim Mattox (D)...............	35,524	(50%)	($269,015)
	Tom Pauken (R)..............	34,672	(49%)	($252,047)

SIXTH DISTRICT

On the map, the 6th district of Texas looks like a basically rural and small-town district. As it stretches south of Dallas and Fort Worth to a point near Houston, the district moves through Waxahachie and Hillsboro to Bryan and College Station, home of Texas A&M. Some blacks live in the rural counties here (they are 15% of the population in the district), as do a few Mexican–Americans (7%). But overall, poor white farmers and their children who have moved to town dominate this part of the 6th. Raised as staunch Democrats, they still vote Democratic from congressman on down. In recent statewide and national elections, however, they have given at least some of their votes to Republicans.

The map of the 6th district is misleading, however. For the majority of the 6th district's population lives in metropolitan areas, and almost precisely half live in either Dallas or Tarrant (Fort Worth) Counties. The shape of the 6th represents the historic response of the Texas legislature to the equal population rule: rather than eliminate an underpopulated rural district, tack on enough metropolitan territory to preserve the seat for the incumbent.

The incumbent in this case was Olin (Tiger) Teague, a Democrat first elected in a 1946 special election. He was a much decorated and severely wounded combat veteran of World War II; from 1963 to 1973 he was chairman of the House Veterans Affairs Committee. In 1973 Teague, a strong backer of the space program, moved to the chair of the Science and Aeronautics Committee. After 32 years in Congress, and after a bout of bad health, Teague retired in 1978.

This was one of several Texas districts that were seriously contested following the retirement of incumbents that year. Here the Democratic primary victory went to Phil Gramm, an economics professor at A&M. Gramm had run two years before in the Senate primary against Lloyd Bentsen, without great success; but since then he has done very well indeed. In 1978 he won a close Democratic runoff and easily beat the Republican nominee; in 1980 he had no serious competition.

In a short time Gramm has become one of the intellectual leaders of what was, at least in the early months of the Reagan Administration, the critical bloc of votes in the House, the younger conservative Democrats who do not have much seniority and who disagree on most issues with most of their Democratic colleagues. Gramm himself is a strong free-market man, an articulate opponent of government spending and government regulation. He had to fight to get a seat on the Budget Committee, and when he succeeded one can see why. Gramm was the only Democrat to oppose the budget plan crafted by Chairman James Jones, and instead in April 1981 cosponsored with Republican Delbert Latta the plan endorsed by President Reagan. Gramm had worked in the House with David Stockman, and admitted he was closer to Stockman than to Tip O'Neill; in fact, he said, if O'Neill is a typical national Democrat then there are not many Democrats in the 6th district. That was rhetorical exaggeration, but Gramm's views do seem closer to his district's voters than O'Neill's or Jones's; and in the House Gramm's positions seemed capable of attracting support from 30 or 40 crucial conservative Democrats who, in the 97th Congress, hold the balance of power.

Gramm's only political problem for 1980 is redistricting. His district could be restructured in any number of ways. Some of the Dallas and Tarrant County portions are likely to be taken away for a new, Republican-oriented district; Gramm will have to be compensated with territory from rural counties. There is enough population indeed to give him a district entirely made up of small rural–oriented counties — a district with the kind of Democratic tradition and conservative ideas that would seem to suit him exactly. It is possible that someday Gramm will seek a Senate seat again, although there has been no talk of his opposing Bentsen again in 1982.

Census Data   Pop. (1980 final) 638,044, up 37% in 1970s. Median family income, 1970, $9,417, 98% of U.S.

The Voters

   Employment profile 1970   White collar, 53%. Blue collar, 32%. Service, 11%. Farm, 4%.
   Ethnic groups   Black 1980, 15%. Hispanic 1980, 7%. Asian 1980, 1%. Total foreign stock 1970, 5%.

Presidential Vote

1980	Reagan (R)	113,504	(54%)
	Carter (D)	90,893	(43%)
	Anderson (I)	4,623	(2%)
1976	Ford (R)	91,676	(49%)
	Carter (D)	95,567	(51%)

Rep. Phil Gramm (D) Elected 1978; b. July 8, 1942, Ft. Benning, Ga.; home, College Station; U. of Ga., B.B.A. 1964, Ph.D. 1967.

Career Prof., Tex. A&M U., 1967–78.

Offices 1721 LHOB, 202-225-2002. Also Suite 102, 5001 S. Hulen, Ft. Worth 76132, 817-294-2040.

Committees *Budget* (18th).

Energy and Commerce (16th). Subcommittees: Energy Conservation and Power; Fossil and Synthetic Fuels; Health and the Environment.

Veterans' Affairs (15th). Subcommittees: Education, Training and Employment; Hospitals and Health Care.

Group Ratings

	ADA	COPE	PC	LCV	CFA	RPN	NAB	NSI	NTU	ACA	ACU
1980	0	10	23	2	7	—	100	100	63	71	89
1979	0	20	18	14	11	—	—	—	56	77	82

Key Votes

1) Draft Registn $	FOR	6) Fair Hsg DOJ Enfrc	AGN	11) Cut Socl Incr Dfns $	FOR
2) Ban $ to Nicrgua	FOR	7) Lim PAC Contrbtns	AGN	12) Hosptl Cost Controls	AGN
3) Dlay MX Missile	AGN	8) Cap on Food Stmp $	FOR	13) Gasln Ctrls & Allctns	AGN
4) Nuclr Mortorium	AGN	9) New US Dep Edcatn	FOR	14) Lim Wndfll Prof Tax	FOR
5) Alaska Lands Bill	AGN	10) Cut OSHA $		FOR	15) Chryslr Loan Grntee	AGN

Election Results

1980 general	Phil Gramm (D)	144,816	(71%)	($21,215)
	Dave (Buster) Haskins (R)	59,503	(29%)	($0)
1980 primary	Phil Gramm (D)	51,693	(100%)	
1978 general	Phil Gramm (D)	66,025	(65%)	($480,778)
	Wesley H. Mowery (R)..........	35,393	(35%)	($116,386)

SEVENTH DISTRICT

In the past few years Houston has become widely known as the nation's leading boom city. It is indubitably the center of the American oil industry, and not just because some of the big giants have moved their headquarters there. More important, Houston is the home of hundreds of businesses that serve and aid the production, transportation, and refining of oil and natural gas—as well as the lawyers who try to interpret the government regulations covering it. The signs of Houston's prosperity are instantly and readily apparent to any visitor. There are new skyscrapers, both downtown and on the well-to-do west side, new hotels, new apartment buildings, and countless new residential subdivisions. Houston is proud that it is attracting some of the world's luxury trade—at the Galleria shopping mall you can find Tiffany's, Gucci, etc.—but even more impressive is the wide range of upper- and upper-middle-income stores and services that are thriving here. The big question for the future is whether Houston is fated to be a one-industry town, another Detroit of Pittsburgh, or whether it will build on this decade of growth the way Los Angeles did on the 1950s or Chicago on the 1880s and become a true world city.

Most of the visible boom in Houston has occurred on the west side of the city. The downtown sits separately, amid a kind of marginal area, and to the east are the great refineries and the Houston Ship Channel. The west and southwest sides are where virtually all of the upper-income people in Houston live. The commercial streets here do not look special: Houston has no zoning laws, and next to a pleasant garden apartment can be a little U-Totem shopping center or a drive-in restaurant. But the neighborhoods behind the main streets preserve their character through protective covenants, and use the lush greenery that thrives in humid Houston to compensate for the uninteresting flatness of the land. The visitor may marvel at the high prices commanded by the mansions of River Oaks or the Memorial Drive area. But there are literally hundreds of newly built subdivisions on the west side of Houston—the city has been expanding its city limits to take part in the growth—where the prices are, by the standards of other large metropolitan areas, quite reasonable.

The 7th congressional district covers most of the west side of Houston, with just a little of the area lying in the neighboring 22d district. This is an area that doubled its population in the 1960s, and nearly doubled it again in the 1970s. In other words, there were about 150,000 people on the west side of Houston and in adjacent suburban areas in 1960 and there are almost 900,000 today. If this is one of the nation's fastest-growing districts, it is also one of the highest status; in 1970 a higher percentage of the workers here held white collar jobs than in all but two of the nation's 434 other congressional districts. It is also a very high-income district, although it does not rank extraordinarily high by national standards; but then the cost of living is much lower in Texas than in the Northeast or California.

The 7th district has one other superlative: it has become one of the most Republican congressional districts in the United States. Fully 74% of its votes went to Gerald Ford in 1976—more than in any other district, and in 1980 74% voted for Ronald Reagan, a percentage exceeded only in the 1st district of Utah. The 7th is distinguished as well as the home of leading national Republicans. George Bush lived here in a home off Memorial Drive and served as the 7th district's congressman for two terms in the late 1960s. Bush's efforts at statewide politics were not successful then; he was beaten in Senate races in 1964 and 1970. Perhaps his eastern style—his father was a Connecticut senator and a partner in Brown Brothers Harriman; he went to prep school and Yale—turned off rural Texans and even those hardy successes who vote in Republican primaries (Bush lost the 1976 Texas presidential primary to Ronald Reagan, although not by much).

The other famous Republican from the district, John Connally, does not quite personify west Houston's voters, either. He spent most of his electoral career as a Democrat and was always ready to use the power of the government—as when he persuaded Richard Nixon to impose wage and price controls—when a free-market purist would have demurred.

Bush's successor in Congress, Bill Archer, was born and grew up in Texas; he was a successful businessman who was elected to the legislature as a Democrat and then became a Republican. Archer became a member of the Ways and Means Committee after the 1972 election, and there he has been an articulate and effective spokesman for positions backed by the oil industry. On issues generally he seems to represent well the free-market ideology that is shared by a large majority of residents of the 7th district. He has been reelected regularly with some of the largest margins in the nation.

The 7th district has enough population now for 1.65 districts, so it will be split up; in effect, the current 7th and the current 22d district will become three separate districts after redistricting. Since the current 7th is almost uniformly heavily Republican, that means that the new 7th and the new district will be as safely Republican as the current constituency.

Census Data   Pop. (1980 final) 867,726, up 86% in 1970s. Median family income, 1970, $13,561, 142% of U.S.

The Voters

Employment profile 1970   White collar, 77%. Blue collar, 16%. Service, 6%. Farm, 1%.
Ethnic groups   Black 1980, 6%. Hispanic 1980, 8%. Asian 1980, 3%. Total foreign stock 1970, 10%. Germany, UK, 1% each.

Presidential Vote

1980	Reagan (R)	220,530	(74%)
	Carter (D)	64,386	(22%)
	Anderson (I)	11,344	(4%)
1976	Ford (R)	186,190	(73%)
	Carter (D)	66,790	(26%)

Rep. Bill Archer (R) Elected 1970; b. Mar. 22, 1928, Houston; home, Houston; Rice U., 1946–47, U. of Tex., B.B.A., L.L.B. 1951.

Career   Air Force, Korea; Pres., Uncle Johnny Mills, Inc., 1953–61; Hunters Creek Village Cncl. and Mayor Pro Tem, 1955–62; Tex. House of Reps., 1966–70; Dir., Heights State Bank, Houston, 1967–70; Practicing atty., 1968–71.

Offices   1135 LHOB, 202-225-2571. Also 5108 Fed. Bldg., 515 Rusk St., Houston 77002, 713-226-4941.

Committee   *Ways and Means* (3d). Subcommittees: Social Security; Trade.

Group Ratings

	ADA	COPE	PC	LCV	CFA	RPN	NAB	NSI	NTU	ACA	ACU
1980	6	11	17	32	14	—	100	100	73	96	94
1979	0	5	13	3	7	—	—	—	70	100	97
1978	10	0	13	17	4	83	100	100	60	100	95

Key Votes

1) Draft Registn $	FOR	6) Fair Hsg DOJ Enfrc	AGN	11) Cut Socl Incr Dfns $	FOR
2) Ban $ to Nicrgua	FOR	7) Lim PAC Contrbtns	AGN	12) Hosptl Cost Controls	AGN
3) Dlay MX Missile	AGN	8) Cap on Food Stmp $	FOR	13) Gasln Ctrls & Allctns	AGN
4) Nuclr Mortorium	AGN	9) New US Dep Edcatn	AGN	14) Lim Wndfll Prof Tax	FOR
5) Alaska Lands Bill	AGN	10) Cut OSHA $	FOR	15) Chryslr Loan Grntee	AGN

Election Results

1980 general	Bill Archer (R)................	242,810	(82%)	($124,687)
	Robert L. Hutchings (D)	48,594	(16%)	($3,877)
1980 primary	Bill Archer (R), unopposed			
1978 general	Bill Archer (R)................	128,214	(85%)	($120,720)
	Robert L. Hutchings (D)	22,415	(15%)	

EIGHTH DISTRICT

The 8th congressional district of Texas is a part of the Houston metropolitan area. Its recent political history gives a good picture of the changes that have come with explosive growth — changes that affect people's way of life and changes that affect their political attitudes. This was a district that was created ten years ago to be dominated by one kind of constituency and which has, due to population growth and changing attitudes, become dominated by another. Politically, that has meant the change from heavily Democratic to marginally Republican; in terms of representation, it has meant the change from liberal Democrat Bob Eckhardt to Republican Jack Fields.

To understand these changes, go back ten years, to the time when the current boundaries of the 8th district were established. The district was intended to include most of the white working class of Houston; most blacks and Mexican–Americans were placed in the 18th district, and most upper-income whites on Houston's west side in the 7th district. The 8th district starts at the Houston Ship Channel, a marvel of engineering that made this inland city a major American port, and a body of water so full of sludge and effluent from the chemical plants and refineries that it is sometimes called a fire hazard. The landscape along the channel is almost surreal: the intricate pipes of refineries and petrochemical plants, the long vistas across parking lots and vacant fields with the skyscrapers of booming downtown Houston in the distance, the slum and working-class houses whose frame walls are so flimsy that they cannot be effectively air conditioned in Houston's muggy summers. The air here is often hazy with smog or so drenched with humidity that it seems almost fluid; it is a long way across town to the kicky boutiques and fancy chocolate stores of the Galleria.

This is the heart of the 8th district. It spreads eastward from central Houston, along the Ship Channel to the towns of Baytown and Pasadena. The latter is the home of Gilley's, the bar made famous in *Urban Cowboy,* which in addition to its artistic merit tells more about life in Houston today than any ten sociological texts. A young man from rural Texas comes to Houston, looking for work, and finds it — high-paying, hard work at long hours, and sometimes dangerous, but far more than he could hope for back home. He also finds Gilley's, where people like himself come to drink beer, dress like cowboys, and ride the mechanical bull. They are acting out their version of the western myth, in an urban setting. There is a political implication here, or rather an implication that there is no politics. There was a time when populist Texas farmers saw in politics the answer to their problems; there was a time much more recently when blue collar workers in Texas saw in labor unions and liberal politics some answers. But the young people in *Urban Cowboy* don't see any answers in politics at all. Society has given them high-wage work, and it has given them the affluence to enjoy a version of the traditional western ways they seek. Their problems are personal; the world around them, even as it changes, they take as unchangeable.

A dozen years ago a certain kind of Texas populism was the dominant politics of the 8th district. You could see it in the 1968 returns here — 46% for the liberal Democrat Humphrey, 28% for fellow southerner Wallace, and only 26% for Richard Nixon, the candidate overwhelmingly favored by the rich and white collar voters across town. In Texas elections this district was solidly for candidates who promised to improve working conditions for the poor and increase taxes on the rich. One such man was Bob Eckhardt, a veteran of the state legislature, who was first elected to Congress in 1966. He is a scholarly lawyer, a man who likes to wear bow ties with his natty suits, a skilled legislator but not a backslapper. In Congress he was the only member of the Texas delegation who consistently voted against the oil companies. On the Commerce Committee he was a sponsor of such agencies as the Consumer Product Safety Commission and in the late 1970s he was, appropriately for someone representing the 8th district, interested in toxic waste management. What Eckhardt was not was a new-style congressman who constantly returns to the district, keeps an innocuous record on the issues, and strives to win reelection by using the advantages of incumbency. He was not afraid to stand for something—and when the district changed, he ended up losing because of it.

The district changed because the affluent, white collar part of Houston was expanding so rapidly that it exceeded the bounds of the 7th district and poured over into part of the 8th. The 8th district includes a large part of suburban Harris County directly north of Houston. In 1970 most of this area was empty, and the people who did live there tended to be poor working folks in ramshackle, jerry-built houses. Then affluent Houston started moving north. A new airport was built here, and dozens of new subdivisions cropped up—most of them with high price tags. The people who moved in identified not with the working class but with the newly successful rich people of Houston; they saw the oil companies not as their exploiters but as fellow pioneers in a battle to provide the country with products it needs; if they came from rural areas, the traditions they wanted to preserve were religious and the tastes they were developing were more urbane than those served at Gilley's. These people were heavy Republican voters, and their votes moved the 8th district far to the right.

That effect was especially pronounced because these upwardly mobile residents of the north Houston suburbs were far more likely to vote than the working-class residents of the part of the district running east from central Houston. One reason Jimmy Carter fell 11 percentage points here between 1976 and 1980 is that turnout in the north part of the district increased and turnout in the east part fell. That is also one of the main reasons why Eckhardt, at age 67, was defeated by 28-year-old Republican Jack Fields.

Fields is in many ways typical of the Republicans who beat Democratic congressmen in the 1980 election. He is young, ambitious, attractive in a way that is unthreatening to those with traditional values. He has genuine roots in the district, and his TV ads featured pictures of his large extended family. His platform was not original, but it did not need to be; the national Republican platform of lower taxes and less government went over well here with the growing number of north suburban voters. Eckhardt's liberal record and opposition to oil companies enraged many conservative Texans; he had had significant Republican opposition in 1976 and 1978 and had been held to 54% and 52% in the 1978 and 1980 Democratic primaries. His work on the toxic waste act and the fact that in the 97th Congress he would have been likely to become one of the highest-ranking members of the Commerce Committee made him a major target for the political action committees of oil companies and other businesses. As a result—and because of good Republican fund-raising efforts—Fields was able to outspend Eckhardt on the order of 2-to-1, even though Eckhardt himself was spending well over $400,000.

The 8th district actually went for Carter in 1980, but by a far reduced margin and with lower turnout than in 1976; and it also elected Fields over Eckhardt by a 52%–48% margin. Affluent Houston, full of enthusiasm for its own achievements and for its ideas for public policy, had triumphed over working-class Houston, unconcerned about public issues and preoccupied with private life. Fields cannot be expected to be as original or distinctive a legislator as Eckhardt; he does not have the Democrat's special talents and he campaigned more as a loyal member of a cohesive challenger party than as an original force himself. Redistricting will not likely hurt him, since affluent Houston has grown so rapidly; he might very well have a safer seat than the current 8th is for him (the district will probably, for example, lose its black minority to the 18th). For the moment, at least, Fields seems clearly to personify the dominant political trend in Houston, and indeed in Texas and much of the nation as well.

Census Data Pop. (1980 final) 612,471, up 31% in 1970s. Median family income, 1970, $9,555, 100% of U.S.

The Voters

   Employment profile 1970 White collar, 40%. Blue collar, 47%. Service, 13%. Farm, –%.
   Ethnic groups Black 1980, 22%. Hispanic 1980, 18%. Asian 1980, 1%. Total foreign stock 1970, 6%.

Presidential Vote

1980	Reagan (R)	62,813	(45%)
	Carter (D)	72,601	(52%)
	Anderson (I)	2,722	(2%)
1976	Ford (R)	52,248	(36%)
	Carter (D)	89,254	(63%)

Rep. Jack Fields (R) Elected 1980; b. Feb. 3, 1952, Humble; home, Humble; Baylor U., B.A. 1974, J.D. 1977.

Career Practicing atty., 1977; Exec. V.P., Rosewood Memorial Park, family business, 1977–79; Tex. Governor's Small Business Advisory Assistance Cncl., 1979–80.

Offices 510 CHOB, 202-225-4901. Also 12605 E. Freeway, Suite 320, First State Bank Bldg., Houston 77015, 713-451-6334.

Committees *Merchant Marine and Fisheries* (13th). Subcommittees: Coast Guard and Navigation; Merchant Marine.

Public Works and Transportation (15th). Subcommittees: Surface Transportation; Water Resources.

Group Ratings and Key Votes: Newly Elected

Election Results

1980 general	Jack Fields (R)	72,856	(52%)	($794,870)
	Bob Eckhardt (D)	67,921	(48%)	($457,630)
1980 primary	Jack Fields (R), unopposed			
1978 general	Bob Eckhardt (D)	39,429	(62%)	($285,214)
	Nick Gearhart (R)	24,673	(38%)	($139,102)

NINTH DISTRICT

The 9th congressional district of Texas is the eastern segment of the state's Gulf Coast — an area of big refineries, petrochemical plants, and other factories. It is, in other words, an area dominated by heavy, oil-related industry, and it has one of the highest concentrations of blue collar workers in Texas. The district is dominated by two urban centers of roughly equal size. On Galveston Bay, which leads into the Houston Ship Channel, are the cities of Galveston and Texas City. Galveston, one of the oldest cities in Texas, is situated on a sand

1072 TEXAS

bar where the bay empties into the Gulf of Mexico. It was the state's first port, but now handles far less tonnage than Houston or Texas City. The other major population center in the 9th is around the oil and petrochemical cities of Beaumont and Port Arthur. These are in the southeastern corner of the state, where there is a little Louisiana Cajun influence.

Most of the residents of this district are migrants, recent or otherwise, from the rural South. Some 23% are black, and another 6% are Cajun. To a surprising extent people here have retained populist Democratic voting habits. This is probably the most unionized part of generally nonunion Texas, and the labor movement here inspires much more loyalty among its members than it does in large industrial states with large union membership. The 9th has stayed Democratic in statewide races, even in 1978, and Jimmy Carter won the district in 1980 as well as 1976.

The district congressman is Democrat Jack Brooks. He has served in the House since the 1952 election, and for the most part has a voting record in line with the Democratic leadership. He is not always a liberal on noneconomic issues, but he has always been a supporter of civil rights measures; he voted for the 1964 Civil Rights Act when his district included some east Texas counties with attitudes very similar to the Deep South. On policy matters and in personality also, Jack Brooks is probably more similar to Lyndon Johnson than any other current member of Congress.

Brooks is extremely partisan, profane, knowledgeable, witty, effective—all qualities he shares with Johnson. They all came out in the House Judiciary Committee hearings on the impeachment of Richard Nixon. Brooks was then the third-ranking Democrat on the committee and is now second behind Chairman Peter Rodino. But his most important post today is the chair of the Government Operations Committee, which has a charter that allows it to investigate most government agencies, although it passes on relatively little legislation, most of it dealing with matters like government reorganization. Government Operations can become a key committee in the hands of an aggressive chairman of the party opposite the president after an administration has been in office for a few years, and that may happen in Brooks's case.

For years Brooks had no difficulty winning reelection. But in 1980 he suddenly had significant primary opposition from one Bubba Pate. Brooks came within 277 votes of being forced into a runoff, which means he will probably have serious opposition again, either in the primary or the general. Brooks is not yet 60, however, and seems hardly likely to retire. He is certainly not the sort to back away from a fight. So the prospect is for a tough race in a similar-shaped district in 1982.

Census Data Pop. (1980 final) 642,276, up 20% in 1970s. Median family income, 1970, $9,344, 97% of U.S.

The Voters

Employment profile 1970   White collar, 45%. Blue collar, 40%. Service, 14%. Farm, 1%.
Ethnic groups   Black 1980, 23%. Hispanic 1980, 7%. Asian 1980, 1%. Total foreign stock 1970, 7%.

Presidential Vote

1980	Reagan (R)	85,646	(48%)
	Carter (D)	88,418	(49%)
	Anderson (I)	4,328	(2%)
1976	Ford (R)	67,280	(41%)
	Carter (D)	97,800	(59%)

Rep. Jack Brooks (D) Elected 1952; b. Dec. 18, 1922, Crowley, La.; home, Beaumont; Lamar Jr. Col., 1939–41, U. of Tex., B.J. 1943, J.D. 1949.

Career USMC, WWII; Tex. House of Reps., 1946–50; Practicing atty., 1949–52.

Offices 2449 RHOB, 202-225-6565. Also 230 Fed. Bldg., Beaumont 77701, 713-838-0271.

Committee *Government Operations* (Chairman). Subcommittee: Legislation and National Security (Chairman).

Judiciary (2d). Subcommittee: Monopolies and Commercial Law

Group Ratings

	ADA	COPE	PC	LCV	CFA	RPN	NAB	NSI	NTU	ACA	ACU
1980	28	50	37	13	15	—	45	43	21	21	18
1979	42	47	20	38	19	—	—	—	29	25	24
1978	30	45	38	34	36	45	58	80	14	40	25

Key Votes

1) Draft Registn $	—	6) Fair Hsg DOJ Enfrc	AGN	11) Cut Socl Incr Dfns $	—
2) Ban $ to Nicrgua	AGN	7) Lim PAC Contrbtns	FOR	12) Hosptl Cost Controls	AGN
3) Dlay MX Missile	AGN	8) Cap on Food Stmp $	AGN	13) Gasln Ctrls & Allctns	AGN
4) Nuclr Mortorium	AGN	9) New US Dep Edcatn	FOR	14) Lim Wndfll Prof Tax	FOR
5) Alaska Lands Bill	FOR	10) Cut OSHA $	AGN	15) Chryslr Loan Grntee	—

Election Results

1980 general	Jack Brooks (D)	103,225	(100%)	($113,569)
1980 primary	Jack Brooks (D)	26,343	(50%)	
	W. L. (Bubba) Pate (D)	22,188	(43%)	($81,295)
	One other (D)	3,600	(7%)	
1978 general	Jack Brooks (D)	50,792	(63%)	($80,171)
	Randy Evans (R)...............	29,473	(37%)	

TENTH DISTRICT

The 10th district of Texas is the LBJ congressional district. Here in central Texas the towns are farther apart and their trees less common than in east Texas; the land is less fertile, and there is much less rain. Lyndon Johnson was born and raised and began his political career amid the rolling hills of central Texas, which yield a living only to those who work hard. The 10th district left its mark on Johnson. The comparative poverty of its people — especially back in the 1930s, when Johnson was a young man — helped to shape his populistic impulses. And the comparatively good relations here between the Anglo white majority and the black (now 12%) and Mexican–American (now 16%) minorities helped shape the Johnson who would push Congress into passing the Civil Rights Acts of 1964 and 1965.

Johnson in turn has certainly left his imprint on the 10th district. Although its boundaries have changed, the district still includes Johnson City and the LBJ Ranch in Blanco County; Southwest Texas State Teachers College in San Marcos, where Johnson got his degree; and

Austin, the state capital, home of the University of Texas, and site of the Lyndon B. Johnson Library. Also in Austin is television station KLBJ — the initial cornerstone of the Johnson family fortune.

Austin has grown substantially since Johnson represented the 10th district. It is now a city of nearly 345,000 people — large enough to dominate a congressional district, but a small town next to Houston or the Dallas–Fort Worth area. Austin is not an oil town or an industrial town or even an agricultural marketing town; economically, its mainstays are state government and higher education. Austin is the home of the state's almost always successful business and oil-oriented lobbyists, but it is also the home of two diverse publications, the very successful *Texas Monthly* and the very liberal *Texas Observer,* which together provide an interesting and continuous view of life in the state.

Unlike Texas's bigger cities, Austin is usually Democratic and liberal in elections. The growing affluent population of the city is Republican, as in most Texas cities, but not by as large a margin. But on the other side is the electorate provided by the University of Texas's 39,000 students. In the early 1970s they were solidly liberal; now they seem more into toga parties and afraid that they might not get a job with Exxon. Nevertheless, the students are more likely than their parents to consider voting against a Republican — if they vote at all.

Since Lyndon Johnson won this seat in a 1937 special election there have been only three congressmen in this district, all of them Democrats who usually voted with their party's majority in the House and who also were adept at getting things done. When Johnson ran for the Senate in 1948, he was succeeded by Homer Thornberry, who was appointed to the federal bench in 1963. Thornberry's succesor in the House is a member in good standing both of the state's Tory Democratic establishment and of the House Democratic Caucus. Congressman Jake Pickle seems sympathetic to the economic interests of Texans, whether rich or poor, and like LBJ does not see why there should be any conflict between the two. He is an able and influential member of the Ways and Means Committee, where he chairs the Social Security Subcommittee and so is charged with the responsibility of dealing with one of our government's most difficult and sensitive problems, the financial soundness of Social Security. Pickle approaches that issue without dogmatic stands on the key issues and with a disposition to compromise if necessary; but tough decisions still need to be made. At home Pickle occasionally has had to look over his shoulder at Austin liberals, but they seem to pose no threat to his tenure.

Census Data Pop. (1980 final) 645,490, up 38% in 1970s. Median family income, 1970, $7,825, 82% of U.S.

The Voters

Employment profile 1970 White collar, 53%. Blue collar, 26%. Service, 16%. Farm, 5%.
Ethnic groups Black 1980, 12%. Hispanic 1980, 16%. Asian 1980, 1%. Total foreign stock 1970, 10%. Germany, 2%; Czechoslovakia, 1%.

Presidential Vote

1980	Reagan (R)	112,687	(48%)
	Carter (D)	107,406	(46%)
	Anderson (I)	11,428	(5%)
1976	Ford (R)	97,640	(46%)
	Carter (D)	115,946	(53%)

Rep. J. J. (Jake) **Pickle** (D) Elected Dec. 17, 1963; b. Oct. 11, 1913, Big Spring; home, Austin; U. of Tex., B.A. 1938.

Career Area Dir., Natl. Youth Admin., 1938–41; Navy, WWII; Coorganizer, KVET Radio, Austin; Adv. and pub. rel. business; Dir., Tex. State Dem. Exec. Comm., 1957–60; Mbr., Tex. Employment Commission, 1961–63.

Offices 242 CHOB, 202-225-4865. Also 763 Fed. Bldg., Austin 78701, 512-397-5921.

Committees *Ways and Means* (3d). Subcommittees: Oversight; Social Security (Chairman).

Joint Committee on Taxation (2d).

Group Ratings

	ADA	COPE	PC	LCV	CFA	RPN	NAB	NSI	NTU	ACA	ACU
1980	22	42	30	30	43	—	63	67	35	33	42
1979	32	37	30	35	15	—	—	—	32	23	46
1978	45	50	35	44	32	55	67	70	20	65	50

Key Votes

1) Draft Registn $	—	6) Fair Hsg DOJ Enfrc	AGN	11) Cut Socl Incr Dfns $	FOR
2) Ban $ to Nicrgua	AGN	7) Lim PAC Contrbtns	AGN	12) Hosptl Cost Controls	AGN
3) Dlay MX Missile	AGN	8) Cap on Food Stmp $	AGN	13) Gasln Ctrls & Allctns	AGN
4) Nuclr Mortorium	AGN	9) New US Dep Edcatn	FOR	14) Lim Wndfll Prof Tax	FOR
5) Alaska Lands Bill	FOR	10) Cut OSHA $		FOR	15) Chryslr Loan Grntee	FOR

Election Results

1980 general	J. J. (Jake) Pickle (D)	135,618	(59%)	($308,661)
	John Biggar (R)	88,940	(39%)	($77,586)
1980 primary	J. J. (Jake) Pickle (D)	65,409	(75%)	
	Greg Stallings (D)	21,271	(25%)	($0)
1978 general	J. J. (Jake) Pickle (D)	94,529	(76%)	($46,726)
	Emmett L. Hudspeth (R)	29,328	(24%)	($19,263)

ELEVENTH DISTRICT

The 11th congressional district is deep in the heart of Texas. Made up of all or part of 19 counties, the district sits slightly off the geographical center of the state, but at just about its center of population. The 11th includes two good-sized cities, Waco and Temple, and a huge Army base, Fort Hood. The rest of the district is classic Texas agricultural country, given over to cotton, livestock, and occasional small towns. People here are descended from settlers who came from the Deep South in the 19th century; they brought Democratic Party identification with them, and maintained it for many years. The 11th district gave even a Yankee liberal, Hubert Humphrey, an absolute majority of its votes in the three-way race of 1968, and it was solidly for Jimmy Carter in 1976. As late as 1978 it voted against Republicans John Tower and William Clements. But in 1980 the 11th switched: it gave Ronald Reagan an absolute majority of its votes and Jimmy Carter only 44%. This may be only a temporary shift, like the one that carried the district for Richard Nixon in 1972; but it appears that this time there will be a concerted effort by the Republican Party to consolidate these gains and make them permanent.

The Republicans missed such a chance in the congressional election of 1978. The incumbent congressman of 42 years, Bob Poage, was retiring. He had chaired the Agriculture Committee until the House Democratic Caucus stripped him of that position after the 1974 election. Poage's voting record on nonagricultural issues had always been conservative. The seat was seriously contested in both the Democratic primary and the general election, but as it turned out the district elected someone pretty much like Poage, businessman Marvin Leath. He beat a liberal in the Democratic primary and a well-financed Republican in the general election. Leath seems well entrenched in the district; he had no opposition at all in 1980.

But the question remains whether Leath can represent the district with the effectiveness and clout Poage once had. Leath does indeed seem likely, as one of 40-odd members of the Conservative Democratic Forum, to cast some key votes in the current Congress. But he is not likely to win choice committee assignments from the House Democratic Caucus, most of whose members disagree with him on most issues. Nor is he going to get much power if Republicans win a majority in the House. Leath is a member now of the Armed Services and Veterans' Affairs Committees, useful posts for a member with a military-oriented district like the 11th. Redistricting is not likely to change the basic outlook of the district; the real question is how a conservative Democrat can build an influential as well as a long career in the House.

Census Data   Pop. (1980 final) 604,540, up 30% in 1970s. Median family income, 1970, $6,755, 71% of U.S.

The Voters

Employment profile 1970   White collar, 44%. Blue collar, 33%. Service, 15%. Farm, 8%.
Ethnic groups   Black 1980, 13%. Hispanic 1980, 10%. Asian 1980, 1%. Total foreign stock 1970, 8%. Germany, 2%.

Presidential Vote

1980	Reagan (R)	101,035	(53%)
	Carter (D)	84,009	(44%)
	Anderson (I)	4,126	(2%)
1976	Ford (R)	71,096	(43%)
	Carter (D)	94,548	(57%)

Rep. J. Marvin Leath (D) Elected 1978; b. May 6, 1931, Rusk Co.; home, Marlin; U. of Tex., B.A. 1954.

Career Army, 1954–56; High school teacher and coach, 1956–58; Banker, 1962–72, 1975–78; Spec. Asst. to U.S. Rep. Bob Poage, 1972–75.

Offices 336 CHOB, 202-225-6105. Also 205 Fed. Bldg., Waco 76701, 817-752-9609.

Committees *Armed Services* (21st). Subcommittees: Procurement and Military Nuclear Systems; Readiness.

Veterans' Affairs (9th). Subcommittees: Education, Training and Employment; Housing and Memorial Affairs (Chairman); Oversight and Investigations.

Group Ratings

	ADA	COPE	PC	LCV	CFA	RPN	NAB	NSI	NTU	ACA	ACU
1980	0	19	20	1	0	—	89	100	62	71	86
1979	5	20	3	7	0	—	—	—	57	84	83

Key Votes

1) Draft Registn $	FOR	6) Fair Hsg DOJ Enfrc	AGN	11) Cut Socl Incr Dfns $	FOR
2) Ban $ to Nicrgua	FOR	7) Lim PAC Contrbtns	AGN	12) Hosptl Cost Controls	AGN
3) Dlay MX Missile	AGN	8) Cap on Food Stmp $	FOR	13) Gasln Ctrls & Allctns	AGN
4) Nuclr Mortorium	AGN	9) New US Dep Edcatn	AGN	14) Lim Wndfll Prof Tax	FOR
5) Alaska Lands Bill	AGN	10) Cut OSHA $		FOR	15) Chryslr Loan Grntee	AGN

Election Results

1980 general	J. Marvin Leath (D)	128,520	(100%)	($171,978)
1980 primary	J. Marvin Leath (D)	68,472	(100%)	
1978 general	J. Marvin Leath (D)	53,354	(52%)	($588,492)
	Jack Burgess (R)	49,965	(48%)	($320,084)

TWELFTH DISTRICT

Between Fort Worth and Dallas, through the new Dallas–Fort Worth Regional Airport and near the Freeway Stadium and Six Flags Over Texas park in the suburb of Arlington, runs an invisible line marking the geological divide known as the Balcones Escarpment. It divides dry west Texas from humid east Texas; it separates the treeless grazing lands that run west from Fort Worth from the green croplands that run east from Dallas. Fort Worth and Dallas are only 30 miles apart, but they are very different cities, from their geology to their recent development and their politics. As the old saying has it, Dallas is the end of the East and Fort Worth is the beginning of the West.

Fort Worth got its start as a cattle town. It was once the western end of the railroad here, and cowboys drove their stock into Fort Worth to have them shipped east. Then Fort Worth built its own railroad, the Texas Pacific, and its own stockyards, the largest in Texas. While Dallas was concentrating on cotton and banking, Fort Worth was concentrating on railroads and meat-packing. Fort Worth developed more as a blue collar town, although of course it had its management class and town fathers; Dallas of course also had its factories, but became more white collar. The differences even extend to recent defense contracts. Dallas tends to produce high technology items; Fort Worth has the General Dynamics assembly plant that produces air frames for many of the nation's military aircraft. Dallas residents sometimes look down on Fort Worth and call it Cowtown. But Fort Worth has its own strong civic culture and a set of art museums far superior to any others in Texas. Among them is the Amon Carter Museum of Western Art, the premier collection of its kind; looking west from one of Fort Worth's hills, toward the treeless skyline in the distance, you can almost see some of those scenes come to life again on the high plains.

As the differences between Fort Worth and Dallas suggest, Fort Worth tends to be more Democratic and Dallas more Republican. But the differences have tended to become more muted in recent years, as Fort Worth's Tarrant County sprouts affluent suburbs, and as some of the most affluent Dallasites move to the counties to the north and east. Thus in 1980 both went for Reagan, Dallas County by a 59%–37% margin and Tarrant County by a slightly smaller 57%–40% margin. The 12th congressional district, which includes most of Fort Worth and the Tarrant County suburbs to the north, is somewhat more Democratic than the county as a whole, although it went for Reagan over Carter in 1980. Although it includes Fort Worth's affluent west side neighborhoods, it has generally supported Democrats who in Texas are considered liberal, and that has certainly been true in congressional races.

This is the district that elects Congressman Jim Wright, the House majority leader. He was first elected in 1954, and in the 1950s he was considered the most liberal member of the Texas delegation. He has remained a strong supporter of national Democratic policies on most economic issues, and has generally had a good labor voting record. But on other issues, he has often parted company with other Democrats. A strong supporter of American policy in Vietnam, he has also been skeptical about many environmental causes. These stances have undoubtedly been in line with majority opinion in his district, and have helped make him more accepted in the Texas delegation. Since his election as majority leader, however, his ratings from national liberal groups have increased, as he has gotten more in line with his new constituency in the House Democratic Caucus.

Wright has proven himself again and again as a skilled legislative tactician. He is an adroit and sometimes eloquent speaker, he does his homework, he is pleasant and ingratiating — and he usually wins on issues he concentrates on. He had less luck early in his congressional career when he ran for the Senate. In 1961 he ran for the seat vacated by Lyndon Johnson and just missed making the runoff; if he had he might very well have won and by now would surely have become an important senator. In 1966 he wanted to run again. But he was unable to raise money from the state's big economic interests. He went on television and asked for $10 contributions, and got a lot of them — but not enough for a Senate race in Texas.

After the 1976 elections, Wright expected to become chairman of the House Public Works Committee; he was in line for the post under the seniority system and would not have been seriously opposed. He decided also to run for the majority leadership, and at first his chances looked dim. He had the support of the Texas delegation and of some, but by no means all, southerners, but not much beyond that. But on the second ballot he edged Richard Bolling of Missouri for second place by two votes; on the third he beat Phillip Burton of California, 148–147. Suddenly he was a national figure, summoned regularly to the White House, speaking regularly on national television.

Can he become speaker? He has as good a chance as any other House Democrat of succeeding Tip O'Neill, but he has some problems as well. Balancing the views of a Texas constituency, even a relatively liberal one, with those of most northern House Democrats is difficult — perhaps increasingly difficult if the Reagan Administration is adept and the Republican trend continues in Texas. At the same time, Wright may have difficulty attracting the votes of conservative southern Democrats, as he did in the budget cut fight of early 1981 — and the ability to attract such votes is the main argument for many northerners to support him. There was some dissatisfaction too with Wright's willingness to cosponsor fiscal measures with Republican whip Trent Lott and his strong support of the synfuels program. Wright has as good a chance as any House member to become the next speaker, but he does not have a lock on the job.

From the 1950s until 1980 Wright never had to worry much about elections in the 12th district. Suddenly, after the Republicans' big success here in 1978, a surge of enthusiasm swept their ranks and Jim Bradshaw, then mayor pro tem of Fort Worth, decided to take Wright on. Bradshaw could raise lots of money, but so did Wright; the majority leader ultimately spent more than $1 million on his reelection campaign. The result makes one wonder why the Republicans decided to commit resources here anyway. Wright won with a solid

60% of the vote and proved that he still has a strong base in the district. Redistricting should proceed to his liking; there will probably be only minor adjustments to the district's boundaries. It would be surprising if the Republicans, after failing to win under the most favorable of circumstances, should try again here soon.

Census Data Pop. (1980 final) 507,160, up 9% in 1970s. Median family income, 1970, $9,441, 98% of U.S.

The Voters

Employment profile 1970 White collar, 47%. Blue collar, 39%. Service, 13%. Farm, 1%.
Ethnic groups Black 1980, 16%. Hispanic 1980, 10%. Asian 1980, 1%. Total foreign stock 1970, 6%.

Presidential Vote

1980	Reagan (R)	82,561	(52%)
	Carter (D)	72,992	(46%)
	Anderson (I)	3,401	(2%)
1976	Ford (R)	58,562	(44%)
	Carter (D)	74,381	(55%)

Rep. Jim Wright (D) Elected 1954; b. Dec. 22, 1922, Fort Worth; home, Fort Worth; Weatherford Col., U. of Tex.

Career Army Air Corps, WWII; Partner, trade extension and adv. firm; Tex. House of Reps.; Mayor of Weatherford; Pres., Tex. League of Municipalities, 1953.

Offices 1236 LHOB, 202-225-5071. Also 1 Fed. Bldg., 819 Taylor St., Fort Worth 76102, 817-334-3212.

Committees *Majority Leader.*

Budget (2d).

Group Ratings

	ADA	COPE	PC	LCV	CFA	RPN	NAB	NSI	NTU	ACA	ACU
1980	39	71	37	31	50	—	17	38	14	29	24
1979	37	58	25	24	19	—	—	—	17	8	6
1978	35	83	55	28	36	40	0	50	6	29	10

Key Votes

1) Draft Registn $	FOR	6) Fair Hsg DOJ Enfrc	FOR	11) Cut Socl Incr Dfns $	AGN
2) Ban $ to Nicrgua	AGN	7) Lim PAC Contrbtns	FOR	12) Hosptl Cost Controls	—
3) Dlay MX Missile	AGN	8) Cap on Food Stmp $	AGN	13) Gasln Ctrls & Allctns	FOR
4) Nuclr Mortorium	AGN	9) New US Dep Edcatn	FOR	14) Lim Wndfll Prof Tax	—
5) Alaska Lands Bill	AGN	10) Cut OSHA $	AGN	15) Chryslr Loan Grntee	FOR

Election Results

1980 general	Jim Wright (D)	99,104	(60%)	($1,256,142)
	Jim Bradshaw (R)	65,005	(40%)	($645,289)
1980 primary	Jim Wright (D), unopposed			
1978 general	Jim Wright (D)	46,456	(68%)	($283,125)
	Claude K. Brown (R)	21,364	(32%)	($12,571)

THIRTEENTH DISTRICT

The 13th congressional district of Texas is an entity that is totally the creation of politics, an amalgam of two old congressional districts that, because of the equal population rule, had to be combined, but that had always been separate and rather different regions. The old 13th district, which forms the eastern part of the current seat, is part of the agricultural land of the Red River Valley; like all of that valley, it is traditionally and heavily Democratic. It is dusty land, with empty skylines; it only grudgingly yields a living. Virtually all the people here are white Anglos; few blacks got this far west and few Mexican–Americans this far north. Population has been declining here not only in the rural counties, but also in the district's second largest city, Wichita Falls, whose population has fallen below 100,000.

The other half of the 13th district is the old 18th, situated on the high plains of the Texas Panhandle, drier and less fertile land than the Red River Valley. West of the 100th meridian, the land is full of dry gullies that swell to floods when it rains. But it seldom does; instead, the wind blows as hard and unremittingly as anywhere in the United States. Over the years, most of the Panhandle farmers and ranchers seem to have moved into Amarillo, the district's largest city with 149,000 people, and smaller towns such as Pampa and Borger. First settled by people from neighboring northwest Oklahoma and western Kansas, the Panhandle has always been one of the most Republican parts of Texas. In recent years the heavily conservative leanings of Amarillo, the helium capital of the world, have strengthened the area's traditional Republicanism.

The two parts of the district result in a pretty even balance; the 13th was nearly evenly split in the 1976 presidential election. At the beginning of the 1970s it combined the seats of two incumbents, Democrat Graham Purcell and Republican Bob Price. They lost in successive elections, Purcell in 1972 and Price in 1974.

The current congressman is Democrat Jack Hightower. He was helped in 1974 by low turnout in the traditionally Republican Panhandle part of the district; evidently voters there were dispirited after the Watergate scandal and the resignation of Richard Nixon. After serving on the Agriculture and Small Business Committees for two terms, he has moved to the Appropriations Committee. His voting record is rated higher by conservative than liberal groups. He was reelected without any great difficulty in 1976 and 1978. In 1980 Hightower ran into unexpected trouble from Republican Ron Slover, an Amarillo salesman and broker. It was not so much Reagan coattails as it was a reassertion of the Republican trend in the Panhandle. Hightower carried Amarillo, but he lost the smaller towns of the Panhandle, places solidly Republican in most elections and less accessible to a busy congressman.

The result may whet Republicans' appetites for 1982. The Democrats control redistricting, and they can shift some counties around; but the Republican heart of the Panhandle will be hard to remove without creating a new, safe Republican district. Hightower is one of those conservative Democrats who may support the Reagan Administration on key votes; the question may be whether the Republicans will ease up on him if he does, or whether they will gamble and wage an aggressive campaign here.

Census Data   Pop. (1980 final) 505,613, up 8% in 1970s. Median family income, 1970, $8,182, 85% of U.S.

The Voters

Employment profile 1970   White collar, 46%. Blue collar, 32%. Service, 14%. Farm, 8%.
Ethnic groups   Black 1980, 5%. Hispanic 1980, 8%. Asian 1980, 1%. Total foreign stock 1970, 4%.

Presidential Vote

1980	Reagan (R)	113,453	(62%)
	Carter (D)	64,474	(35%)
	Anderson (I)	3,021	(2%)
1976	Ford (R)	87,302	(50%)
	Carter (D)	85,220	(49%)

Rep. Jack Hightower (D) Elected 1974; b. Sept. 6, 1926, Memphis; home, Vernon; Baylor U., B.A. 1949, LL.B. 1951.

Career Navy, WWII; Practicing atty., 1951–74; Tex. House of Reps., 1953–54; Dist. Atty., 1955–61; Tex. Senate, 1965–74.

Offices 2348 RHOB, 202-225-3706. Also 109 Fed. Bldg., Amarillo 79101, 806-376-2381.

Committee *Appropriations* (24th). Subcommittees: Agriculture, Rural Development and Related Agencies; Commerce, Justice, State and Judiciary.

Group Ratings

	ADA	COPE	PC	LCV	CFA	RPN	NAB	NSI	NTU	ACA	ACU
1980	17	33	27	15	21	—	92	60	36	43	47
1979	16	25	13	17	4	—	—	—	39	60	68
1978	30	35	30	34	32	64	67	90	16	67	50

Key Votes

1) Draft Registn $	FOR	6) Fair Hsg DOJ Enfrc	AGN	11) Cut Socl Incr Dfns $	AGN
2) Ban $ to Nicrgua	AGN	7) Lim PAC Contrbtns	AGN	12) Hosptl Cost Controls	AGN
3) Dlay MX Missile	—	8) Cap on Food Stmp $	AGN	13) Gasln Ctrls & Allctns	AGN
4) Nuclr Mortorium	AGN	9) New US Dep Edcatn	AGN	14) Lim Wndfll Prof Tax	FOR
5) Alaska Lands Bill	AGN	10) Cut OSHA $		FOR	15) Chryslr Loan Grntee	FOR

Election Results

1980 general	Jack Hightower (D)	98,779	(55%)	($145,292)
	Ron Slover (R)	80,819	(45%)	($67,863)
1980 primary	Jack Hightower (D)	61,362	(100%)	
1978 general	Jack Hightower (D)	75,271	(75%)	($44,551)
	Clifford A. Jones (R)	25,275	(25%)	($30,086)

FOURTEENTH DISTRICT

The 14th congressional district of Texas moves along the state's steamy Gulf Coast from the Brazosport area just south of Houston all the way to Padre Island, the National Seashore below Corpus Christi. Behind the sand bars that protect the harbors from the Gulf are some of the largest oil refineries and chemical plants in Texas, in places like Brazosport, Port Lavaca, Victoria, and Corpus Christi. The latter, with more than 200,000 people, is by far the district's largest city, and has a large Mexican–American population.

The 14th is sweaty, heavy industry country. It is one of the few parts of Texas where the state's labor unions have much influence. Few blacks live this far south and west in Texas, but there is a large Mexican–American minority here (39% of the district's population). On economic issues, this is one of the state's more liberal districts, although it is hardly similar in attitude to places in New York or Massachusetts.

The 14th district has elected three congressmen in the last three elections, of three very different kinds of politics. John Young, last elected in 1976, was an oldtimer (first elected in 1954), a member of the Rules Committee who generally got along with the Democratic leadership; he ultimately left after a woman who once served on his staff charged him with improprieties. Joe Wyatt, a former legislator elected in 1978, was a solid conservative; he withdrew abruptly from the 1980 race because of personal problems. That meant a good old-fashioned political fight in both the Democratic primary and—new for this area—in the general election.

The winner was state Senator William Patman, son of longtime 1st district Congressman Wright Patman and a formidable figure in Texas politics in his own right. He was one of the leaders of the "killer bees," a group of liberally inclined state senators who absented themselves from the Senate and prevented a quorum from being formed for a bill that would hold Texas's presidential and state primaries on separate days. (Conservatives wanted Reagan primary voters to be able to vote for Democrats in the state primary; the killer bees wanted them to have to choose between one party and the other.) Patman is a man of great probity, accustomed to fighting losing battles with little attention or acclaim. The Texas liberal tradition from which he comes is not one rich in experience winning elections. Yet he was able to win in a year when Democrats and liberals all over the country were losing. In both the runoff against conservative Democrat Bob Barnes and the general election against Republican Charles Concklin, Patman was able to win large majorities in the mostly Anglo northern part of the district, his home territory, and to combine them with at least an even break in the Corpus Christi area, thanks to Mexican–American votes. Patman's victory was one of the few gains for national Democrats in the 1980 elections. Like his father, he sits on the Banking Committee; and if the current Congress does not seem attuned to his thinking he may reflect that the first Congress Wright Patman sat in, after he was first elected in 1928, was not much attuned to the elder Patman's thinking either.

Redistricting poses some problems for William Patman. If the district shifts too far south, he may get opposition from Mexican–Americans; if it goes too far north, it may provide a good base for conservatives. He has some old friends among the killer bees in Austin but will need to fight hard to get a favorable district.

Census Data   Pop. (1980 final) 544,736, up 17% in 1970s. Median family income, 1970, $7,683, 80% of U.S.

The Voters

Employment profile 1970   White collar, 44%. Blue collar, 36%. Service, 15%. Farm, 5%.
Ethnic groups   Black 1980, 6%. Hispanic 1980, 39%. Total foreign stock 1970, 13%. Germany, 1%.

Presidential Vote

1980	Reagan (R)	87,979	(51%)
	Carter (D)	80,040	(46%)
	Anderson (I)	3,406	(2%)
1976	Ford (R)	68,780	(41%)
	Carter (D)	95,485	(58%)

Rep. William N. Patman (D) Elected 1980; b. Mar. 26, 1927, Texarkana; home, Ganado; U. of Tex., B.B.A. 1953, J.D. 1953.

Career USMC, WWII; Air Force Reserve, 1953–56; Dipl. Courier, U.S. Foreign Svc., 1949–50; Practicing atty., 1955–80; Tex. Senate, 1961–81.

Offices 1408 LHOB, 202-225-2831. Also 307 U.S. Court House, 521 Star St., Corpus Christi 78401, 512-888-3381, and 218 U.S. P.O. & Court House, Victoria 77901, 512-578-9954.

Committees *Banking, Finance and Urban Affairs* (24th). Subcommittees: Consumer Affairs and Coinage; Domestic Monetary Policy; Financial Institutions Supervision, Regulation and Insurance.

Merchant Marine and Fisheries (18th). Subcommittees: Fisheries and Wildlife Conservation and the Environment; Merchant Marine.

Group Ratings and Key Votes: Newly Elected

Election Results

1980 general	William N. Patman (D)	93,884	(57%)	($665,984)
	C. L. Concklin (R)	71,495	(43%)	($182,572)
1980 runoff	William N. Patman (D)	25,480	(52%)	
	Robert N. Barnes (D)	23,923	(48%)	($414,075)
1980 primary	William N. Patman (D)	32,258	(35%)	
	Robert N. Barnes (D)	28,660	(31%)	
	Joe Salem (D)	21,974	(24%)	($18,468)
	Jason Luby (D)	8,600	(9%)	($0)
1978 general	Joe Wyatt, Jr. (D)	63,953	(72%)	($310,890)
	Jay Yates (R)	24,325	(28%)	($10,766)

FIFTEENTH DISTRICT

South Texas lives closer to the feudal ages than any other region of the United States. Here are the fabled Texas ranches: the King Ranch covers more acreage than the state of Rhode Island and produces an annual income of $25 million — mostly from oil, not cattle. Just down the road (which is to say, in the next county) is a spread, not too much smaller, belonging to former Ambassador to Britain Anne Armstrong and her husband, who is now a top aide to Governor Clements. Farther south is the Lower Rio Grande Valley. Here, thanks to irrigation water and the semitropical climate, are fields of cotton, fruits, and vegetables tended by Mexican farmhands. The United Farm Workers have tried to do some organizing here but with little success. Inevitably, many of the workers are Mexican nationals, and many of those are illegal immigrants; they are interested in receiving what are, by their standards, generous wages and not interested in making trouble.

This is the land of Texas's 15th congressional district. It includes not only the Lower Rio Grande, but also some of the interior counties between Corpus Christi and Laredo, although it contains neither of these two cities. Although 77% of the residents of the district are of Mexican stock, virtually all the important decisions here are made by Anglo ranchers, bankers, lawyers, and farmers. Evidence of Anglo power is apparent in the election returns. Richard Kleberg, owner of the King Ranch, represented this part of Texas in the House from 1931 to 1945: a young poor boy named Lyndon Johnson from the hills around Austin got his first government job in Kleberg's office.

Another Lower Rio Grande Valley congressman was Lloyd Bentsen. His father had made a fortune in land in the Valley (and was accused of selling parcels without water or sewers to northern retirees); young Lloyd was elected county judge at 25 and congressman at 27, in 1946. Bentsen retired from the House in 1954 to make a fortune of his own in Houston; his successor was Joe M. Kilgore, a pillar of the Connally Tory Democratic establishment. Kilgore wanted to run against Ralph Yarborough in the 1964 Senate primary; LBJ persuaded him not to, and six years later Yarborough was beaten by Bentsen.

In the smaller counties of the district, the votes are easy to manipulate. Almost all of them are cast by Mexican–American fieldhands whose jobs depend on a single landowner. The evidence is plain from the election returns: Jim Hogg County, for example, went 82% for Humphrey in 1968 and 47% for Nixon in 1972. Most interesting is the voting history of Duval County, long the fiefdom of the Parr family. Its most famous performance came in the 1948 Senate runoff. After some delay, Duval reported 4,622 votes for Lyndon Johnson and 40 for his opponent. Inasmuch as the county had gone the other way a few weeks before, people were suspicious of the result; but it was certified, and "Landslide Lyndon" carried the state by 87 votes. George Parr, the last "Duke of Duval," was sentenced to jail on an income tax charge and killed himself in 1974. But the same kind of power is now being exerted by a Mexican–American family that used to be allied with the Parrs.

When Kilgore retired from the House in 1964, someone apparently decided that it was time the 15th had a Mexican–American congressman. Accordingly Eligio de la Garza was elected. He had shown his reliability through 12 years in the legislature; he is by no means a favorite of the militant Chicanos and generally votes like other Texas rural Democrats. The seniority system has been kind to de la Garza. He is chairman of the House Agriculture Committee, a position he won after Thomas Foley became majority whip in 1981; there was some opposition to de la Garza, but no rival candidacy arose. He is not really a controversial chairman and seems likely to allow subcommittee chairmen great latitude. De la Garza has been reelected every two years without difficulty. Because the district rose in population during the 1970s (and even though many of the new residents are aliens), the 15th will have to be cut back in size for 1982.

Census Data   Pop. (1980 final) 659,265, up 41% in 1970s. Median family income, 1970, $5,059, 53% of U.S.

The Voters

   Employment profile 1970   White collar, 40%. Blue collar, 34%. Service, 13%. Farm, 13%.
   Ethnic groups   Hispanic 1980, 77%. Total foreign stock 1970, 36%.

Presidential Vote

1980	Reagan (R)	67,517	(42%)
	Carter (D)	89,487	(56%)
	Anderson (I)	2,464	(2%)
1976	Ford (R)	49,873	(34%)
	Carter (D)	94,926	(65%)

Rep. E. (Kika) de la Garza (D) Elected 1964; b. Sept. 22, 1927, Mercedes; home, Mission; Edinburg Jr. Col., St. Mary's U., San Antonio, LL.B. 1952.

Career Navy, WWII; Army, Korea; Practicing atty., 1952–64; Tex. House of Reps., 1952–64.

Offices 1434 LHOB, 202-225-2531. Also 1418 Beach St., La Posada Village, McAllen 78501, 512-682-5545.

Committee *Agriculture* (Chairman).

Group Ratings

	ADA	COPE	PC	LCV	CFA	RPN	NAB	NSI	NTU	ACA	ACU
1980	22	40	37	8	43	—	64	57	30	52	35
1979	5	32	23	29	11	—	—	—	47	64	75
1978	10	39	15	23	27	50	60	90	19	83	68

Key Votes

1) Draft Registn $	FOR	6) Fair Hsg DOJ Enfrc	FOR	11) Cut Socl Incr Dfns $	AGN
2) Ban $ to Nicrgua	AGN	7) Lim PAC Contrbtns	AGN	12) Hosptl Cost Controls	—
3) Dlay MX Missile	AGN	8) Cap on Food Stmp $	AGN	13) Gasln Ctrls & Allctns	—
4) Nuclr Mortorium	AGN	9) New US Dep Edcatn	AGN	14) Lim Wndfll Prof Tax	—
5) Alaska Lands Bill	AGN	10) Cut OSHA $		15) Chryslr Loan Grntee	AGN

Election Results

1980 general	E. (Kika) de la Garza (D)	105,325	(70%)	($66,324)
	Robert L. McDonald (R)	45,090	(30%)	($17,639)
1980 primary	E. (Kika) de la Garza (D)	71,521	(100%)	
1978 general	E. (Kika) de la Garza (D)	54,560	(66%)	($85,164)
	Robert L. McDonald (R)	27,853	(34%)	($30,535)

SIXTEENTH DISTRICT

"West of the Pecos" is a phrase associated with the frontier justice of Judge Roy Bean, but it is also a pretty fair description of the location of the 16th congressional district of Texas. When Bean held his court in his barroom in the town of Langtry, there was precious little of anything except uninhabited desert west of the Pecos. Today there is not much more—except for the city of El Paso. With 425,000 residents, El Paso dominates the 16th district. Aside from the little town of Pecos and the 50,000 residents of the oil drilling and mechanics' town of Odessa, El Paso is the only significant population center of the 16th. Typical of the landscape beyond is the harsh desert of Loving County, which in 1980 had a population of 191 people—the lowest population of any county in the nation.

El Paso is a Sun Belt city that mushroomed after World War II. Its economy was fueled by the nearby presence of giant military installations like Fort Bliss and the White Sands

Proving Ground. But its chief economic asset is low wage labor. Just across the Rio Grande from El Paso is the city of Juarez, which has a population considerably larger than El Paso's and is separated from any other concentration of population in Mexico by as great a distance as El Paso is in the United States. This is the part of the Mexican border that gave us the word "wetback," the 1940s' synonym for illegal immigrant; and the fact is that you don't even have to get very wet to cross the Rio Grande, which is just a trickle most of the year. A majority of El Paso's residents are Mexican in origin, and no one knows for sure how many are U.S. citizens. As befits the border between two free countries, hundreds or even thousands of people cross the line every day, and many live on one side and work on the other.

Even subminimum wages in the United States look good to people brought up in rural Mexico, and so thousands of Mexicans have moved to Juarez, looking for jobs in El Paso. The Texas city has become a center for the apparel business and for other low-wage, low-skill industries; if wages are low enough, it pays to to ship raw materials into El Paso and finished goods out. A few years ago there was a long and bitter strike at the Farah pants plant, and Catholic bishops backed the strikers. But basic conditions haven't changed and aren't likely to in the future.

Although El Paso has a Mexican majority, most of its voters are Anglos — in part because many of the Mexicans are not American citizens at all. Accordingly, the 16th is not all that liberal a district; it went Republican for president not only in 1980 but in 1976 as well. In congressional races, except for the two-year tenure of a Republican congressman after the Billie Sol Estes scandal, the 16th has gone Democratic. The current congressman, Richard White, was first elected in 1964. He has a variety of concessions in his voting record to the Mexican–Americans; he supported civil rights, and some years ago he had high ratings from organized labor. But his basic instincts seem to be more in the traditional Texas Tory Democratic mold. He is a member in good standing of the Conservative Democratic Forum.

White has not been a particularly forceful congressman. Several years ago he lost an Appropriations seat to the more junior and more aggressive Charles Wilson of east Texas. Now a relatively senior member of Armed Services, he chairs the Subcommittee on Investigations. White had liberal primary opposition in 1976 and managed to win 57%–35%. That year he won the general election with only 58%. But in most elections he does not have such opposition; in 1978 and 1980 he won easily.

Census Data   Pop. (1980 final) 599,857, up 29% in 1970s. Median family income, 1970, $7,936, 83% of U.S.

The Voters

Employment profile 1970   White collar, 49%. Blue collar, 36%. Service, 13%. Farm, 2%.
Ethnic groups   Black 1980, 4%. Hispanic 1980, 57%. Asian 1980, 1%. Total foreign stock 1970, 34%. Germany, 2%.

Presidential Vote

1980	Reagan (R)	74,138	(56%)
	Carter (D)	51,743	(39%)
	Anderson (I)	5,565	(4%)
1976	Ford (R)	60,264	(50%)
	Carter (D)	59,349	(49%)

Rep. Richard C. White (D) Elected 1964; b. Apr. 29, 1923, El Paso; home, El Paso; U. of Tex., B.A. 1946, LL.B. 1949.

Career USMC, WWII; Practicing atty., 1949–64; Tex. House of Reps., 1955–58.

Offices 2186 RHOB, 202-225-4831. Also 146 U.S. Courthouse, El Paso 79901, 915-543-7650.

Committees *Armed Services* (4th). Subcommittees: Investigations (Chairman); Military Personnel and Compensation; Research and Development.

Science and Technology (14th). Subcommittees: Energy Development and Applications; Natural Resources, Agriculture Research and Environment.

Group Ratings

	ADA	COPE	PC	LCV	CFA	RPN	NAB	NSI	NTU	ACA	ACU
1980	11	26	23	22	14	—	60	100	33	55	83
1979	0	20	13	21	7	—	—	—	37	73	72
1978	25	20	28	30	23	58	70	100	13	80	70

Key Votes

1) Draft Registn $	FOR	6) Fair Hsg DOJ Enfrc	AGN	11) Cut Socl Incr Dfns $	FOR
2) Ban $ to Nicrgua	FOR	7) Lim PAC Contrbtns	AGN	12) Hosptl Cost Controls	AGN
3) Dlay MX Missile	AGN	8) Cap on Food Stmp $	AGN	13) Gasln Ctrls & Allctns	AGN
4) Nuclr Mortorium	AGN	9) New US Dep Edcatn	FOR	14) Lim Wndfll Prof Tax	FOR
5) Alaska Lands Bill	AGN	10) Cut OSHA $	FOR	15) Chryslr Loan Grntee	—

Election Results

1980 general	Richard C. White (D)	104,734	(85%)	($49,964)
	Catherine McDivitt (Libertarian) . .	19,010	(15%)	($0)
1980 primary	Richard C. White (D)	42,709	(100%)	
1978 general	Richard C. White (D)	53,090	(70%)	($107,976)
	Michael Giere (R)	22,743	(30%)	($34,881)

SEVENTEENTH DISTRICT

The 17th congressional district is the geographical heart of Texas. Here are thousands and thousands of acres of arid farming and grazing land stretching west from Fort Worth to the horizon. The 17th is primarily cattle grazing country, although there is some oil here and some raising of cotton and grain. Its largest city is Abilene, with 98,000 people. As is often the case on the plains, the town is more conservative than the countryside; all the bankers, lawyers, and professionals are concentrated in town, and they form the bulk of the conservative vote. Like most of central Texas, this area was settled originally by southerners who brought their Democratic politics with them, and it remained pretty solidly Democratic up through 1978. Then, in 1980, it shifted sharply to the Republicans. Jimmy Carter's share of the vote dropped from 57% to 44% in four years; the Republican share rose from 42% to 54%. These results may prove simply a temporary revulsion toward Carter, but they could also be part of a longer-term trend. The 1982 elections should tell. This was an area carried by Democrats in the 1978 Senate and governor races, and it will be interesting to see if Senator Lloyd Bentsen and the Democratic gubernatorial nominee can still carry the west Texas plains.

Unfortunately for the Republicans, this seat became open in 1978, while it was still going Democratic in statewide contests, but not in 1980. The longtime congressman, Omar Burleson, retired after 32 years of placid and conservative service; he consistently won ratings of zero from liberal groups, gave up the only committee chairmanship he won (to get a seat on Ways and Means). He had no opposition in primary or general elections from 1964 to 1976.

The new congressman, Charles Stenholm, is a much younger man than Burleson but has similar views on most issues; the difference is the way they get along in the House. Burleson always went along quietly, sometimes cooperating with the Democratic leadership, never taking a visible role or causing trouble. The seniority system protected him and others like him in high positions against assaults from the liberal majority of House Democrats. Stenholm is not so protected. He complained during his first term that southern conservatives were not getting good committee assignments from the Democratic Caucus, and he was right; the best posts were reserved for those who agreed with the majority on issues. Stenholm evidently felt he must apply some public pressure, and he was one of those younger southerners who formed the Conservative Democratic Forum, of which he is coordinator.

In the first months of the Reagan Administration, Stenholm and his conservative colleagues seemed in a powerful position. CDF had 46 members, more than enough to hold the balance of power between Republicans and Democrats; and through Phil Gramm, a member of the Budget Committee, CDF had a definite impact on the budget cut program the Reagan Administration finally endorsed. But opposing Democratic positions is not the way to power in the Democratic Caucus (although the caucus may be forced to concede positions to conservatives from time to time), and CDF members will probably get short shrift if the Republicans should gain a majority in the House. But under the circumstances Stenholm probably has no choice but to take a more public, riskier approach than Burleson ever did, if he is to serve faithfully his own conservative views on issues and those of his constitutents.

Census Data   Pop. (1980 final) 504,029, up 8% in 1970s. Median family income, 1970, $7,144, 75% of U.S.

The Voters

Employment profile 1970   White collar, 40%. Blue collar, 34%. Service, 15%. Farm, 11%.
Ethnic groups   Black 1980, 4%. Hispanic 1980, 11%. Total foreign stock 1970, 4%.

Presidential Vote

1980	Reagan (R)	95,818	(54%)
	Carter (D)	77,774	(44%)
	Anderson (I)	1,992	(1%)
1976	Ford (R)	71,103	(42%)
	Carter (D)	95,482	(57%)

Rep. Charles W. Stenholm (D) Elected 1978; b. Oct. 26, 1938, Stamford; home, Stamford; Tarleton St. Jr. Col., 1959, Tex. Tech. U., B.S. 1961.

Career Vo. ag. teacher, 1962–64; Farm mgr., 1961–.

Offices 1232 LHOB, 202-225-6605. Also 903 E. Hamilton, Stamford 79553, 915-773-3623.

Committees *Agriculture* (21st). Subcommittees: Cotton, Rice and Sugar; Livestock, Dairy and Poultry; Tobacco and Peanuts; Wheat, Soybeans and Feed Grains.

Small Business (13th). Subcommittee: Export Opportunities and Special Small Business Problems.

Group Ratings

	ADA	COPE	PC	LCV	CFA	RPN	NAB	NSI	NTU	ACA	ACU
1980	0	11	20	4	7	—	100	100	68	74	89
1979	0	20	8	10	0	—	—	—	54	83	81

Key Votes

1) Draft Registn $	FOR	6) Fair Hsg DOJ Enfrc	AGN	11) Cut Socl Incr Dfns $	FOR
2) Ban $ to Nicrgua	FOR	7) Lim PAC Contrbtns	AGN	12) Hosptl Cost Controls	AGN
3) Dlay MX Missile	AGN	8) Cap on Food Stmp $	FOR	13) Gasln Ctrls & Allctns	AGN
4) Nuclr Mortorium	AGN	9) New US Dep Edcatn	AGN	14) Lim Wndfll Prof Tax	FOR
5) Alaska Lands Bill	AGN	10) Cut OSHA $	FOR	15) Chryslr Loan Grntee	FOR

Election Results

1980 general	Charles W. Stenholm (D)	130,465	(100%)	($98,134)
1980 primary	Charles W. Stenholm (D)	75,951	(100%)	
1978 general	Charles W. Stenholm (D)	69,030	(68%)	($331,516)
	Billy Lee Fisher (R)	32,302	(32%)	($149,705)

EIGHTEENTH DISTRICT

The 18th congressional district of Texas covers the central part of the city of Houston. It includes within its boundaries most of the city's blacks and many of its Mexican–Americans. In 1980, 43% of its residents were black and 31% of Spanish origin: during the 1970s, the number of Mexican–Americans rose significantly, but the number of blacks actually dropped, as blacks became more prosperous and moved out to other parts of Houston. This is a very different part of Houston from the gleaming west side. Like many rapidly growing cities in developing countries, Houston seems to have unusually great disparities of income and wealth. While entrepreneurs are getting rich in the oil business and living in $500,000 houses near the Galleria, many black and Mexican–American residents live east and south of downtown in unpainted frame houses complete with cracks wide enough to let in Houston's humid, smoggy air. The Houston slums look like something out of the sharecropper 1930s, and they remind us that although this is one of our fastest-growing cities, its growth is based in large part on cheap labor. Houston has a strong developing economy, and eventually perhaps everyone will benefit, perhaps is benefiting already; but in the meantime, it is a fact that some people are getting rich a lot faster than others.

Houston's black neighborhoods cast higher Democratic percentages—on the order of 98%—than any other part of the United States. The voting habits here in the 18th district are thus a considerable contrast from the 7th district, immediately to the west, which is one of the most Republican districts in the country. The real question in Houston politics is, who will outvote whom? In 1976, there were enough votes cast in the 18th—nearly half as many as in the 7th—to help carry Texas for Jimmy Carter. But in 1978 enthusiasm and elan belonged entirely to the Republicans. More than four times as many people voted in the 7th district as in the 18th. If the ratio of turnout had been the same as in 1976, the statewide results would have been different; Senator John Tower would have been defeated, and William Clements would not have been elected Texas's first Republican governor in more than 100 years. The year 1980 was more like 1978 than 1976. Three times as many people voted in the 7th district as in the 18th, and the Carter margin of 44,000 in the 18th was wiped out by the Reagan margin of 176,000 in the 7th.

The black part of Houston is the place that gave political birth to Barbara Jordan. She was a familiar figure in the middle 1970s, from her stirring speech at the House Judiciary Committee impeachment hearings and even more from her tumultuously greeted keynote speech at the 1976 Democratic National Convention. Jordan was the first black state senator in Texas; and a powerful state senator at that, one who could get the ear of the ruling powers and who could get herself chosen acting governor. She also demonstrated clout by constructing a congressional district, the 18th, tailored to her ambitions. Although it did not have a black voting majority in 1972, she was elected easily—and never had any electoral problems after, until she decided to retire in 1978. Jordan's career can almost be taken as a metaphor for the fate of liberalism in the 1970s. She performed ably, inspired some, and had some positive accomplishments. But she left behind no major legislation and no unrealized dreams.

Jordan's successor in the House, Mickey Leland, seems likely to be more comfortable in the Congressional Black Caucus. He does not have Jordan's taste for getting along with powerful conservatives nor her disdain for militant speechmaking. He is a pharmacist, and in the Texas legislature and in the House he has advocated replacing name brand with generic brand drugs. He was chosen in a fierce primary and runoff in 1978, and had no significant opposition in 1980. The 18th district has lost population, but the legislature will presumably add heavily Democratic precincts to it. Leland has the most liberal voting record in the Texas delegation; only one other member, Henry Gonzalez of San Antonio, is even close.

Census Data   Pop. (1980 final) 427,491, down 8% in 1970s. Median family income, 1970, $7,288, 76% of U.S.

The Voters

Employment profile 1970   White collar, 40%. Blue collar, 40%. Service, 20%. Farm, –%.
Ethnic groups   Black 1980, 43%. Hispanic 1980, 31%. Asian 1980, 1%. Total foreign stock 1970, 12%.

Presidential Vote

1980	Reagan (R)	23,051	(25%)
	Carter (D)	67,361	(72%)
	Anderson (I)	2,613	(3%)
1976	Ford (R)	26,606	(24%)
	Carter (D)	82,608	(75%)

Rep. Mickey Leland (D) Elected 1978; b. Nov. 27, 1944, Lubbock; home, Houston; Tex. So. U., B.S. 1970.

Career Instructor, Tex. So. U., 1970–71; Dir. of Spec. Development Projects, Hermann Hosp., 1971–78; Tex. House of Reps., 1972–79.

Offices 419 CHOB, 202-225-3816. Also Suite 101, 4101 San Jacinto Ctr., Houston 77004, 713-527-9692.

Committees *District of Columbia* (5th). Subcommittee: Judiciary and Education.

Energy and Commerce (18th). Subcommittees: Energy Conservation and Power; Fossil and Synthetic Fuels.

Post Office and Civil Service (6th). Subcommittees: Census and Population; Postal Personnel and Modernization (Chairman).

Group Ratings

	ADA	COPE	PC	LCV	CFA	RPN	NAB	NSI	NTU	ACA	ACU
1980	83	100	73	81	71	—	0	0	17	5	12
1979	84	84	83	79	93	—	—	—	18	0	3

Key Votes

1) Draft Registn $	AGN	6) Fair Hsg DOJ Enfrc	FOR	11) Cut Socl Incr Dfns $	AGN
2) Ban $ to Nicrgua	AGN	7) Lim PAC Contrbtns	FOR	12) Hosptl Cost Controls	FOR
3) Dlay MX Missile	FOR	8) Cap on Food Stmp $	AGN	13) Gasln Ctrls & Allctns	FOR
4) Nuclr Mortorium	AGN	9) New US Dep Edcatn	FOR	14) Lim Wndfll Prof Tax	AGN
5) Alaska Lands Bill	FOR	10) Cut OSHA $	AGN	15) Chryslr Loan Grntee	FOR

Election Results

1980 general	Mickey Leland (D)	71,985	(80%)	($132,490)
	C. L. Kennedy (R)	16,128	(18%)	($0)
1980 primary	Mickey Leland (D), unopposed			
1978 general	Mickey Leland (D)	36,783	(97%)	($258,366)
	Deborah Vernier (Soc. Wrkrs.) ...	1,235	(3%)	

NINETEENTH DISTRICT

The 19th congressional district of Texas takes in part of the flat, dusty plains and the distant, treeless skyline of west Texas. This is the high plains, land of little rainfall and giant gullies, of parching hot summers, snowbound winters, and tremendous winds. There is relatively little farming here; the land is used primarily for grazing—and for oil. For this is also the center of the Permian Basin, one of the greatest areas for oil exploration and development in the decades after World War II. Even as the agricultural communities here were declining in population, their young people going off to cities to find jobs, two significant urban centers were developing as the Permian Basin was being explored. One was Lubbock, which has always been the main commercial center for farming and grazing in the area, and the home of Texas Tech as well; it is a sort of regional capital of west Texas. The other is Midland, a much smaller town created almost entirely by the Permian Basin boom. This is a rich man's town, a part of north Dallas or west Houston transplanted to the desert, with expensive stores and restaurants and all the accoutrements of cultured living that affluent Texans are growing used to.

Politically, this is a part of Texas that is ancestrally Democratic, but that increasingly has been going Republican in recent elections. Lubbock, like many fast-growing cities in the Southwest, is considerably more Republican than the rural area around it, particularly in national elections. Midland is as heavily Republican as the rich neighborhoods in the big cities it resembles. The result is a district solidly Republican in national and now in statewide contests — it gave 70% of its votes to Ronald Reagan — but has remained Democratic in congressional elections.

The main reason has been the strength of the Democratic candidates. This is the district that for 34 years was represented by George Mahon. First elected in 1934, he chaired the House Appropriations Committee. His austere personality and sense of fairness made him invulnerable.

Naturally Mahon did not work his district the way junior congressmen do and in 1976, when he was 76 years old, he must have been somewhat surprised when Republican Jim Reese, a Lubbock stockbroker with no previous electoral experience, held him to 55% of the vote. Mahon's decision to retire followed, and most Republican strategists eagerly awaited picking up the district. But their plans fell victim to intraparty competition. Reese ran again, but he was challenged in the primary by George W. Bush, the 32-year-old son of the vice president. The elder Bush had participated in the Permian boom and had lived in Midland for some years, and the younger Bush had a solid electoral base there. Not many people vote in Texas Republican primaries, and in the 19th district enough people voted in Midland to give Bush a large enough majority to win the nomination even though he failed to carry another county in the district.

Bush had plenty of money in the general election, but he also had a shrewd and competent opponent, state Senator Kent Hance. Hance's base was Lubbock; he had grown up in the area and graduated from Texas Tech. The contrast with Bush — a graduate of an eastern prep school who attended Harvard and Yale — was obvious. Hance's policies seemed in line with district opinion, and he ended up winning with almost the same percentage Mahon had had two years before.

In the House, Hance now occupies a pivotal position. He is a member of the Ways and Means Committee, and one of the few committee members who is also part of the 46-member Conservative Democratic Forum. This makes Hance a crucial negotiating partner for Reagan Republicans. His vote does not necessarily give Republicans a majority on Ways and Means, but with his support they can probably win enough conservative Democratic votes on the floor to prevail. Thus this rather junior congressman for at least a moment is likely to occupy center stage in national politics.

Theoretically, Hance has little to fear from Republicans. His record is almost as conservative as most Republicans', and he has shown that he can withstand a serious Republican challenge in a year when Republicans at the top of the ticket were carrying his district. Yet he will also undoubtedly be more comfortable if the legislature, in the course of redistricting, removes Midland from his district. That is entirely possible. It makes sense from a demographic point of view; the only problem is that the district it would be added to — perhaps a new district in the desert plains of west Texas — would almost certainly be Republican, which is not what the Democratic legislature would like to see.

Census Data   Pop. (1980 final) 543,553, up 16% in 1970s. Median family income, 1970, $8,315, 87% of U.S.

The Voters

Employment profile 1970   White collar, 47%. Blue collar, 29%. Service, 13%. Farm, 11%.
Ethnic groups   Black 1980, 6%. Hispanic 1980, 23%. Total foreign stock 1970, 7%.

Presidential Vote

1980	Reagan (R)	122,673	(70%)
	Carter (D)	48,082	(27%)
	Anderson (I)	3,461	(2%)
1976	Ford (R)	93,985	(57%)
	Carter (D)	68,836	(42%)

Rep. Kent Hance (D) Elected 1978; b. Nov. 14, 1942, Dimmitt; home, Lubbock; Tex. Tech. U., B.B.A. 1965, U. of Tex., LL.B. 1968.

Career Practicing atty., 1968– ; Tex. Senate, 1974–78.

Offices 1039 LHOB, 202-225-4005. Also 611 Fed. Ofc. Bldg., 1205 Texas Ave., Lubbock 79401, 806-763-1611.

Committee *Ways and Means* (21st). Subcommittees: Public Assistance and Unemployment Compensation; Trade.

Group Ratings

	ADA	COPE	PC	LCV	CFA	RPN	NAB	NSI	NTU	ACA	ACU
1980	11	26	20	12	21	—	73	100	42	43	78
1979	0	20	8	6	4	—	—	—	55	83	80

Key Votes

1) Draft Registn $	FOR	6) Fair Hsg DOJ Enfrc	FOR	11) Cut Socl Incr Dfns $	FOR
2) Ban $ to Nicrgua	FOR	7) Lim PAC Contrbtns	AGN	12) Hosptl Cost Controls	AGN
3) Dlay MX Missile	AGN	8) Cap on Food Stmp $	FOR	13) Gasln Ctrls & Allctns	AGN
4) Nuclr Mortorium	AGN	9) New US Dep Edcatn	AGN	14) Lim Wndfll Prof Tax	FOR
5) Alaska Lands Bill	AGN	10) Cut OSHA $	FOR	15) Chryslr Loan Grntee	AGN

Election Results

1980 general	Kent Hance (D)................	126,632	(94%)	($106,573)
	J. D. Webster (Libertarian)	8,792	(6%)	($0)
1980 primary	Kent Hance (D)................	45,205	(100%)	
1978 general	Kent Hance (D)................	54,729	(53%)	($314,110)
	George W. Bush (R)	48,070	(47%)	($434,909)

TWENTIETH DISTRICT

San Antonio was the most important town in Texas when the state was part of Mexico. It was here, of course, that Santa Ana and his troops wiped out Davy Crockett, Jim Bowie, and 184 others at the Alamo in 1836. (Crockett was a Tennessee congressman in 1827–31 and 1833–35; if he had not lost his bid for reelection in 1835, he would never have left Tennessee for Texas.) Today San Antonio is Texas's third largest city, with 785,000 people and a metropolitan population over one million. Because it has never been a center of the Texas boom industries of oil, electronics, or cattle, San Antonio has not been growing as fast as Houston or Dallas–Fort Worth. But this is not a withering city, either. It also has its own special atmosphere, particularly along the banks of the San Antonio River as it wanders through the center of town. The Alamo is nearby, thronged with tourists — a monument to patriotism, although it represents a defeat nearly unparalleled in our history.

Only 130 miles from the Mexican border, San Antonio has a Mexican–American majority within its city limits; it is, in fact, the most Hispanic major city in the country. That is the single demographic fact one needs to understand most of the electoral politics here. The other thing that is politically important about San Antonio is that this is a city heavily dependent on government, primarily military, payrolls. San Antonio has Fort Sam Houston, with 10,000 men; the Brooks Aero Medical Center, the major medical facility of the Air Force; and no less than three Air Force bases either within the city limits or just outside them. San Antonio politics for years was a struggle between liberals, who depend on Mexican–Americans for most of their votes, and conservatives, whose constituency is the well-to-do Anglo middle class that is sympathetic with and often dependent on the military establishment here. Recently it has gotten more complicated. In the spring of 1981 San Antonio elected Henry Cisneros as its first Mexican–American mayor. But Cisneros is no militant; he wants to create a good climate for growth for business and investment, and sees that as the best way to create a vibrant economy that will raise up everyone as a rising tide lifts all ships.

The 20th congressional district includes the central part of San Antonio, leaving the mostly Anglo northern residential sections as part of the 21st and some low-income Mexican areas in the south as part of the 23d. Some two-thirds of the residents of the 20th are of Spanish origin, and this, together with the inner city 18th district in Houston, are Texas's two most liberal congressional districts. Gonzalez was first elected back in 1961, when Mexican–American candidates were far less common than they are now; in those days he was the patron saint of Texas liberalism. That has long since ceased to be the case. Gonzalez does in fact have high ratings from liberal organizations. But he is not a man who bends his principles easily. He backed Lyndon Johnson's conduct of the Vietnam war, and he had little but scorn for the younger generation of Chicano militants who preached various kinds of political separatism in the early 1970s.

Gonzalez's stubbornness — or adherence to principle — got him into an uncomfortable position when as chairman of the House committee investigating assassinations, he got into a fight with his counsel; after an embarrassing episode, he resigned the chairmanship. He serves now as a high-ranking member of the Banking, Finance, and Urban Affairs Committee, next in line for the chair after Chairman Fernand St. Germain. He chairs a subcommittee on Housing and Community Development, an interesting task but one that will be less so if the Reagan Administration's budget-cutting proposals are passed.

Gonzalez has had no trouble winning reelection. The 20th district lost population in the 1970s, and new territory will have to be added, but there are plenty of Mexican–American neighborhoods adjacent to but not included in the current district, primarily in the 23d. Even if Texas legislators were inclined to try to redistrict Gonzalez out of his seat, they would probably be prevented from doing so by the Voting Rights Act.

Census Data   Pop. (1980 final) 423,610, down 9% in 1970s. Median family income, 1970, $6,566, 69% of U.S.

The Voters

Employment profile 1970   White collar, 42%. Blue collar, 40%. Service, 18%. Farm, –%.
Ethnic groups   Black 1980, 10%. Hispanic 1980, 68%. Total foreign stock 1970, 25%. Germany, 1%.

Presidential Vote

1980	Reagan (R)	22,903	(22%)
	Carter (D)	79,282	(76%)
	Anderson (I)	2,002	(2%)
1976	Ford (R)	26,711	(26%)
	Carter (D)	77,691	(73%)

Rep. Henry B. Gonzalez (D) Elected Nov. 4, 1961; b. May 3, 1916, San Antonio; home, San Antonio; San Antonio Col., U. of Tex., St. Mary's U., San Antonio, LL.B.

Career Army, WWII; Bexar Co. Chf. Probation Ofcr., 1946; Work with bilingual publications; Teacher, San Antonio Night Sch.; San Antonio City Cncl., 1953–56, Mayor Pro Tem, 1955–56; Tex. Senate, 1956–61.

Offices 2252 RHOB, 202-225-3236. Also B-124 Fed. Bldg., 727 E. Durango, San Antonio 78205, 512-229-6199.

Committees *Banking, Finance and Urban Affairs* (3d). Subcommittees: Consumer Affairs and Coinage; General Oversight and Renegotiation; Housing and Community Development (Chairman).

Small Business (4th). Subcommittees: Antitrust and Restraint of Trade Activities Affecting Small Business; SBA and SBIC Authority, Minority Enterprise and General Small Business Problems.

Group Ratings

	ADA	COPE	PC	LCV	CFA	RPN	NAB	NSI	NTU	ACA	ACU
1980	72	79	73	35	79	—	8	33	11	17	5
1979	74	84	70	70	67	—	—	—	11	8	11
1978	70	95	63	37	64	42	9	88	7	26	38

Key Votes

1) Draft Registn $	AGN	6) Fair Hsg DOJ Enfrc	FOR	11) Cut Socl Incr Dfns $	AGN
2) Ban $ to Nicrgua	AGN	7) Lim PAC Contrbtns	AGN	12) Hosptl Cost Controls	FOR
3) Dlay MX Missile	AGN	8) Cap on Food Stmp $	AGN	13) Gasln Ctrls & Allctns	FOR
4) Nuclr Mortorium	FOR	9) New US Dep Edcatn	FOR	14) Lim Wndfll Prof Tax	AGN
5) Alaska Lands Bill	FOR	10) Cut OSHA $	AGN	15) Chryslr Loan Grntee	FOR

Election Results

1980 general	Henry B. Gonzalez (D)	84,113	(82%)	($51,385)
	Merle Nash (R)	17,725	(17%)	($17,190)
1980 primary	Henry B. Gonzalez (D), unopposed			
1978 general	Henry B. Gonzalez (D), unopposed			($28,703)

TWENTY-FIRST DISTRICT

Most of the physical expanse of the 21st congressional district of Texas is unpopulated — a vast near-desert given over to the raising of cattle and cotton, the pumping of oil, and the extraction of natural gas. In the middle of this vast expanse is the small city of San Angelo, a place less picturesque than its name, which shares the conservative Democratic political tradition and inclination of much of rural Texas. In the eastern part of the district is a noteworthy area, the Texas German district around (but not including) San Antonio. Such towns as New Braunfels and Fredericksburg (where Lyndon Johnson used to go to church) were founded by '48ers—liberal Germans who left Europe after the failure of the revolutions of 1848 and settled on the frontier of southern Texas. Because the Germans considered slaveholding barbarous, they soon became attracted to the then radical Republican Party, and their opposition to secession solidified their allegiance to the party of Lincoln. To this day, the counties in which the descendants of the '48ers are still a majority—Comal, Kendall, Gillespie, Kerr—cast huge Republican margins in almost every election.

But the most significant part of the 21st district is the small geographical segment in Bexar County that casts nearly 60% of the district's votes. This is the north side of San Antonio and its suburbs. A majority of San Antonio's residents are Mexican–American, and although most of them live in the inner-city 20th district, quite a few have moved to the north and east sides within the 21st; altogether, 24% of the residents of the 21st district portion of Bexar County are of Spanish origin. This is in line with patterns of neighborhood settlement in other cities: although there are recognizable Hispanic concentrations, there are also Hispanics living scattered all over the metropolitan area.

One must conclude that Mexican–Americans who move to the north side of San Antonio are much more likely to vote Republican than those who live in the central part of the city; for this part of San Antonio is almost as heavily Republican as affluent areas of other major Texas cities. The north side is not as affluent as the booming west side of Houston and north side of Dallas; there is not the profusion of fancy shops, restaurants, and other signs of sudden wealth and sophistication. The boom is not so pronounced here. But the basic philosophy is the same.

Yet until 1978 this district had never elected a Republican congressman. From 1942 until 1972 it elected O. C. Fisher, as conservative a Democrat as ever sat in the House, a quiet man who stayed in until he qualified for the maximum pension. His successor, elected in 1974 and 1976, was Robert Krueger, a young Shakespearean scholar and hosiery mill heir from New Braunfels, by way of Duke and Oxford Universities. Krueger spent what then were considered huge sums of money (more than $350,000 in 1974), beat a strong Republican candidate and made a name for himself in the House by nearly persuading that body to deregulate natural gas. It was a bravura performance, and Krueger seemed to have a fine legislative future, but he decided he wanted it to be in the Senate. In 1978 he came heartbreakingly close to beating Senator John Tower; perhaps he will run again.

The Republicans finally captured this seat in 1978. Their candidate, Tom Loeffler, came from the German country and had a background in the Ford White House. He showed a sturdy loyalty to conservative principles, expressing reservations about bilingual education in a district with a significant Spanish minority and questioning federal aid to schools in areas impacted by federal installations in an area loaded with military bases. Nevertheless Loeffler was able to win a large enough margin in Bexar County to overcome his Democratic opponent's edge in many of the rural counties. In his first term Loeffler served on the Energy and Commerce Committee—the busiest in the House those years—and proved politically adept. He won reelection against weak opposition by a wide margin. In 1981 he was one of the key forgers of the alliance between the Reagan Administration and the conservative Democrats led by Texan Phil Gramm. For 1982, Loeffler may have a choice of districts. One way the Texas legislature could resolve the embarrassment of riches it has in the form of three new congressional districts is essentially to split the 21st into two parts, centering one district on San Angelo (and possibly including heavily Republican Midland and Odessa) and basing the other in suburban Bexar County. Loeffler would be able to win either such district; indeed, both would likely go Republican whoever is the candidate.

Census Data   Pop. (1980 final) 678,379, up 45% in 1970s. Median family income, 1970, $8,789, 92% of U.S.

The Voters

Employment profile 1970   White collar, 57%. Blue collar, 26%. Service, 11%. Farm, 6%.
Ethnic groups   Black 1980, 3%. Hispanic 1980, 26%. Asian 1980, 1%. Total foreign stock 1970, 14%. Germany, 2%.

Presidential Vote

1980	Reagan (R)	156,904	(64%)
	Carter (D)	80,296	(33%)
	Anderson (I)	5,978	(3%)
1976	Ford (R)	127,268	(59%)
	Carter (D)	85,953	(40%)

Rep. Thomas G. (Tom) **Loeffler** (R) Elected 1978; b. Aug. 1, 1946, Fredericksburgh; home, Hunt; U. of Tex., B.B.A. 1968, J.D. 1971.

Career Practicing atty. and rancher; Chf. Legis. Counsel to U.S. Sen. John Tower, 1972–74; Spec. Asst. for Legis. Affairs, Fed. Energy Admin., 1974–75; Spec. Asst. for Legis. Affairs to Pres. Gerald Ford, 1975.

Offices 1212 LHOB, 202-225-4236. Also B-209 Fed. Bldg., 727 E. Durango, San Antonio 78205, 512-229-5880.

Committee *Appropriations* (19th). Subcommittees: Interior; Military Construction.

Group Ratings

	ADA	COPE	PC	LCV	CFA	RPN	NAB	NSI	NTU	ACA	ACU
1980	0	10	13	26	7	—	100	100	65	92	95
1979	0	10	10	10	0	—	—	—	63	100	97

Key Votes

1) Draft Registn $	FOR	6) Fair Hsg DOJ Enfrc	AGN	11) Cut Socl Incr Dfns $	FOR
2) Ban $ to Nicrgua	FOR	7) Lim PAC Contrbtns	AGN	12) Hosptl Cost Controls	AGN
3) Dlay MX Missile	AGN	8) Cap on Food Stmp $	FOR	13) Gasln Ctrls & Allctns	AGN
4) Nuclr Mortorium	AGN	9) New US Dep Edcatn	AGN	14) Lim Wndfll Prof Tax	FOR
5) Alaska Lands Bill	AGN	10) Cut OSHA $	FOR	15) Chryslr Loan Grntee	AGN

Election Results

1980 general	Thomas G. (Tom) Loeffler (R) ...	196,424	(76%)	($344,199)
	Joe Sullivan (D)	58,425	(23%)	($45,382)
1980 primary	Thomas G. (Tom) Loeffler (R) ...	36,576	(100%)	
1978 general	Thomas G. (Tom) Loeffler (R) ...	84,336	(57%)	($402,299)
	Nelson W. Wolff (D)	63,501	(43%)	($438,013)

TWENTY-SECOND DISTRICT

The 22d district of Texas moves from the south side of Houston across the coastal plain to the Brazosport area on the Gulf of Mexico. This territory was almost vacant 20 years ago. Like so many other Sun Belt boom areas, its development was dependent on the technology of the air conditioner. Life here goes on inside: in air conditioned houses, air conditioned shopping malls, and in the air conditioned Houston Astrodome. Outside, at least during the summer, is the shimmering heat and almost eerie silence.

The 22d takes in the prosperous, middle-income, and rapidly growing suburban tracts of the south side of Houston. It includes the cultural complex around Rice University and the vast and impressive Houston Medical Center. In the eastern parts of the district are the suburbs of Pasadena and Baytown, places where people who grew up in rural surroundings have moved to find good jobs and during the evenings, in bars like Gilley's, live the lives of urban cowboys. There are some blacks here, 17% of the population in 1980, but the overall complexion is basically white and the accent east Texas. Down the Gulf Freeway the 22d stretches toward Galveston, and includes the NASA Manned Spacecraft Center. Beyond to the southwest are Fort Bend and Brazoria Counties, which are experiencing now the phenomenal growth that has shaped the south and west sides of Houston.

Over the past six years congressional elections in this district have centered around Congressman Ron Paul, one of the most original (to his admirers) and most oddball (to detractors) members of the House. Paul is a physician from Lake Jackson, in the part of the district farthest from Houston. He is also the Congress's leading gold bug, an advocate of the gold standard, and perhaps the member of the House most inclined to a libertarian philosophy. He has obviously been controversial in his district. He won his first contest, a special election in 1976, by some 8,000 votes but was beaten by the same Democrat in the 1976 general election by 236 votes. In 1978, with lower turnout and great enthusiasm for the Republican state ticket, he won by 1,200 votes; in 1980, an even better Republican year, he won by the landslide margin of 5,703 votes. In his first three contests he faced Democrat Bob Gammage, a liberal by Texas standards; in 1980 his opponent, Mike Andrews, appealed to the business community and conservative instincts.

Paul is not the kind of congressman who quietly seeks influence or waits to get seniority. He evidently sees himself as a man engaged in a battle of ideas, and he is obviously willing to take risks with his career. Nevertheless, it is possible that redistricting will help him win re-election in 1982. His district's black minority may become part of the 18th district, which needs additional black population. The west side of Houston has grown so much that it is entitled now to almost a whole new congressional district; in effect the 7th and 22d districts, taken together, will be three districts in 1982. That means that southwest Houston will probably be detached from Brazoria and Fort Bend Counties; this should be fine with Paul, who lost the former but carried the latter two in 1982. In any case, it will be interesting to see if the Congress's foremost gold bug is able to keep his seat.

Census Data Pop. (1980 final) 711,212, up 52% in 1970s. Median family income, 1970, $11,022, 115% of U.S.

The Voters

Employment profile 1970 White collar, 54%. Blue collar, 34%. Service, 11%. Farm, 1%.
Ethnic groups Black 1980, 17%. Hispanic 1980, 14%. Asian 1980, 1%. Total foreign stock 1970, 9%.

Presidential Vote

1980	Reagan (R)	118,063	(57%)
	Carter (D)	81,843	(40%)
	Anderson (I)	6,308	(3%)
1976	Ford (R)	95,998	(50%)
	Carter (D)	95,479	(49%)

Rep. Ron Paul (R) Elected Apr. 6, 1976; b. Aug. 20, 1935, Pittsburgh, Pa.; home, Lake Jackson; Gettysburg Col., B.A. 1957; Duke U., M.D. 1961.

Career Flight Surgeon, U.S. Air Force, 1963–65; Practicing physician.

Offices 1234 LHOB, 202-225-5951. Also Suite 406, 1110 NASA Rd. One, Houston 77058, 713-333-2566.

Committee *Banking, Finance and Urban Affairs* (8th). Subcommittees: Domestic Monetary Policy; Economic Stabilization; General Oversight and Renegotiation.

Group Ratings

	ADA	COPE	PC	LCV	CFA	RPN	NAB	NSI	NTU	ACA	ACU
1980	22	5	27	47	7	—	100	60	94	92	94
1979	21	10	30	31	19	—	—	—	91	92	97

Key Votes

1) Draft Registn $	AGN	6) Fair Hsg DOJ Enfrc	AGN	11) Cut Socl Incr Dfns $	FOR
2) Ban $ to Nicrgua	FOR	7) Lim PAC Contrbtns	AGN	12) Hosptl Cost Controls	AGN
3) Dlay MX Missile	FOR	8) Cap on Food Stmp $	FOR	13) Gasln Ctrls & Allctns	AGN
4) Nuclr Mortorium	AGN	9) New US Dep Edcatn	AGN	14) Lim Wndfll Prof Tax	FOR
5) Alaska Lands Bill	AGN	10) Cut OSHA $		FOR	15) Chryslr Loan Grntee	AGN

Election Results

1980 general	Ron Paul (R)...................	106,797	(51%)	($359,558)
	Mike Andrews (D)	101,094	(48%)	($750,836)
1980 primary	Ron Paul (R)...................	23,059	(100%)	
1978 general	Ron Paul (R)...................	54,643	(51%)	($322,156)
	Bob Gammage (D)	53,443	(49%)	($476,852)

TWENTY-THIRD DISTRICT

From San Antonio south, Texas is majority Mexican–American. Much of the territory can be called feudal: desertlike rural counties where big landowners effectively run the lives of their Mexican field hands. This is one part of the United States where there is a stark disparity between the power conferred by money and the power at least theoretically conferred by numbers and votes. In general, money wins. There have been so-called "brown power" movements in some of the small towns and counties here, and one in Zavala County has taken over the local government. But the problem remains of how to finance services and provide jobs when the wherewithal lies in the hands of the people who have been defined as the enemy. The future for most Mexican–Americans, at least to judge from their own behavior,

1100   TEXAS

seems to be in the larger urban centers where there are jobs, not in the parched reaches of south Texas where there is little economic activity of any kind.

The 23d congressional district of Texas covers much of the Mexican–American rural counties of south Texas. It also includes about 210,000 people in Bexar County — the south side of San Antonio and its suburbs, also a predominantly Mexican–American area. The rest of the district is a group of counties east and southeast of San Antonio. The area contains some Texas Germans and a fairly large Mexican–American minority; but the political preferences tend to fall more along the lines of John Connally, who comes from Wilson County in the 23d.

The 23d district has existed in basically its present form since the middle 1960s and has had only one congressman. He is Abraham Kazen, who is of Lebanese rather than Mexican descent, but who has always had Mexican–American support in elections. Kazen spent 20 years in the Texas legislature before being elected to Congress, and he seems to have developed a Lyndon Johnsonlike knack for pleasing both the powerful and the minorities in his district. He has not had major legislative acomplishments, although he does chair an often busy subcommittee, on Water and Power Resources (an ironic assignment, given the desert nature of his district). Kazen has not had significant electoral opposition in years.

Census Data   Pop. (1980 final) 601,823, up 29% in 1970s. Median family income, 1970, $6,512, 68% of U.S.

The Voters

Employment profile 1970   White collar, 43%. Blue collar, 35%. Service, 13%. Farm, 9%.
Ethnic groups   Black 1980, 5%. Hispanic 1980, 53%. Total foreign stock 1970, 23%. Germany, 2%.

Presidential Vote

1980	Reagan (R)	74,449	(49%)
	Carter (D)	75,143	(49%)
	Anderson (I)	2,734	(2%)
1976	Ford (R)	57,139	(40%)
	Carter (D)	83,251	(59%)

Rep. Abraham Kazen, Jr. (D) Elected 1966; b. Jan. 17, 1919, Laredo; home, Laredo; U. of Tex., 1937–40, Cumberland U. Law Sch., 1941.

Career Air Force, WWII; Practicing atty., 1945–66; Tex. House of Reps., 1947–53; Tex. Senate, 1953–66, Pres. Pro Tem, 1959.

Offices 2408 RHOB, 202-225-4511. Also 201 Fed. Bldg., Laredo 78040, 512-723-4336.

Committees *Armed Services* (13th). Subcommittees: Investigations; Military Installations and Facilities.

Interior and Insular Affairs (4th). Subcommittees: Mines and Mining; Public Lands and National Parks; Water and Power Resources (Chairman).

Group Ratings

	ADA	COPE	PC	LCV	CFA	RPN	NAB	NSI	NTU	ACA	ACU
1980	22	44	27	31	50	—	50	75	27	30	29
1979	21	25	18	24	7	—	—	—	30	42	59
1978	10	33	18	16	18	42	46	100	15	64	58

Key Votes

1) Draft Registn $	—	6) Fair Hsg DOJ Enfrc	AGN	11) Cut Socl Incr Dfns $	—
2) Ban $ to Nicrgua	AGN	7) Lim PAC Contrbtns	AGN	12) Hosptl Cost Controls	AGN
3) Dlay MX Missile	AGN	8) Cap on Food Stmp $	AGN	13) Gasln Ctrls & Allctns	AGN
4) Nuclr Mortorium	AGN	9) New US Dep Edcatn	FOR	14) Lim Wndfll Prof Tax	FOR
5) Alaska Lands Bill	AGN	10) Cut OSHA $	FOR	15) Chryslr Loan Grntee	FOR

Election Results

1980 general	Abraham Kazen, Jr. (D).........	104,595	(70%)	($317,815)
	Bobby Locke (R)...............	45,139	(30%)	($8,516)
1980 primary	Abraham Kazen, Jr. (D).........	59,210	(76%)	
	Paul Rich (D)	18,275	(24%)	($2,231)
1978 general	Abraham Kazen, Jr. (D).........	62,649	(90%)	($55,734)
	Augustin Mata (La Raza Unida) ..	7,185	(10%)	($5,337)

TWENTY-FOURTH DISTRICT

The 24th congressional district of Texas is known as the mid-cities district. It sits between Fort Worth and Dallas and contains parts of both. Geographically the district appears to consist of two tentacles emanating from the Dallas–Fort Worth Regional Airport — a Texas-sized establishment where everything (telephones and an ingenious but confusing mass transit system) costs a quarter and where the dollar-changing machines return 95 cents. One tentacle reaches into Dallas, which contains about half the district's population. This is not the wealthy, Republican north side of Dallas, however; that is in the 3d district to the north. Rather, this is part of the city south of the Trinity River, an old neighborhood with funky Victorian houses and an interesting history called Oak Cliff. This is becoming increasingly a black neighborhood, and more than half of the 24th district's portion of Dallas is black. Thus in this district, if not in statewide elections, Dallas is a liberal force; it has supported the liberal candidate in primaries and has voted heavily Democratic in the general election. The Dallas tentacle also contains the suburb of Grand Prairie, a prosperous place many of whose residents grew up in rural Texas, and Irving, which stands a little higher on the socioeconomic scale.

The Fort Worth tentacle moves south and west from the airport. It includes the western edge of Fort Worth and the suburbs of Euless and Arlington. The latter shows what has happened to this area in recent years. This was a town of 7,000 in 1950 and has 160,000 people today. Situated on the Dallas–Fort Worth Turnpike, it attracts thousands each year to the Six Flags Over Texas park and is the smallest city with a major league baseball team, the Texas Rangers who play in Turnpike Stadium. This Tarrant County part of the district, with its many middle-income and upwardly mobile residents, is several shades to the right of the Dallas County portion of the 24th; it tends to favor conservative candidates in the Democratic primary and Republicans in the general election.

Martin Frost, the congressman from the 24th, won the district on his second try. In 1974 he lost to Congressman Dale Milford, a former television weathercaster, in the Democratic primary; in 1978 he beat Milford by a 55%–45% margin. In the general election, he beat retired Air Force officer Leo Berman by a similar margin. Frost's secret was hard campaigning. He was liberal enough to get large margins in Oak Cliff in the primary and conservative enough to hold down the Republican margin in Arlington in the general.

In the House, Frost seems to follow a similar strategy. He is a follower of Majority Leader

Jim Wright and the House Democratic leadership, and a reliable enough one to have been rewarded with a seat on the House Rules Committee in his first term. On this body he can be counted on to carry out the leadership's tactics. On issues Frost has a record that is rated higher by liberal groups than conservatives, but he is not uniformly on one side or the other.

Redistricting created this seat, and redistricting will be vital in determining whether Frost will stay in Congress. Initial reports in early 1981 were that the Texas legislature would excise most of the Tarrant County portion of the district and give the 24th some of the Dallas County areas that are now in the 6th district — working-class areas that either lean Democratic or are not too heavily Republican. There is some talk, however, that Republicans, conservative Democrats, and blacks will get together and draw a heavily black district in Dallas that presumably will elect a black congressman; the new 24th, in that event, would be much more Republican than the present district. Frost probably wants quite a few blacks in the district, to help him in the general election, but not too many, because that would hurt him in the primary. In any case, it seems likely that Arlington, the southern part of Tarrant County, and parts of Dallas County and the newly affluent areas just to the north will be combined in a new mid-cities district, this one leaning strongly Republican.

Census Data   Pop. (1980 final) 547,498, up 17% in 1970s. Median family income, 1970, $9,583, 100% of U.S.

The Voters

Employment profile 1970   White collar, 48%. Blue collar, 38%. Service, 14%. Farm, –%.
Ethnic groups   Black 1980, 26%. Hispanic 1980, 12%. Am. Ind. 1980, 1%. Asian 1980, 1%. Total foreign stock 1970, 5%.

Presidential Vote

1980	Reagan (R)	78,005	(50%)
	Carter (D)	72,013	(46%)
	Anderson (I)	3,714	(2%)
1976	Ford (R)	60,373	(44%)
	Carter (D)	75,161	(55%)

Rep. Martin Frost (D) Elected 1978; b. Jan. 1, 1942, Glendale, Cal.; home, Dallas; U. of Mo., B.A., B.J. 1964, Georgetown U., LL.B. 1970.

Career   Practicing atty., 1970–.

Offices   1238 LHOB, 202-225-3605. Also Suite 1319, Oakcliff Bank Tower, Dallas 75208, 214-941-6032.

Committee   *Rules* (9th). Subcommittee: Rules of the House.

Group Ratings

	ADA	COPE	PC	LCV	CFA	RPN	NAB	NSI	NTU	ACA	ACU
1980	50	58	47	17	50	—	9	60	18	23	31
1979	37	65	43	49	30	—	—	—	20	31	26

Key Votes

1) Draft Registn $	FOR	6) Fair Hsg DOJ Enfrc	FOR	11) Cut Socl Incr Dfns $	AGN
2) Ban $ to Nicrgua	FOR	7) Lim PAC Contrbtns	AGN	12) Hosptl Cost Controls	AGN
3) Dlay MX Missile	AGN	8) Cap on Food Stmp $	AGN	13) Gasln Ctrls & Allctns	AGN
4) Nuclr Mortorium	AGN	9) New US Dep Edcatn	FOR	14) Lim Wndfll Prof Tax	FOR
5) Alaska Lands Bill	FOR	10) Cut OSHA $	AGN	15) Chryslr Loan Grntee	FOR

Election Results

1980 general	Martin Frost (D)	93,690	(61%)	($406,096)
	Clay Smothers (R)	59,172	(39%)	($126,092)
1980 primary	Martin Frost (D)	18,104	(100%)	
1978 general	Martin Frost (D)	39,201	(54%)	($347,177)
	Leo Berman (R)	33,314	(46%)	($228,740)

UTAH

In 1827 Joseph Smith, a young Palmyra, New York, farmer, experienced a vision in which the Angel Moroni appeared to him. Moroni was a prophet of the lost tribe of Israel (the American Indians) that had presumably found its way to the New World some 600 years before the birth of Christ. Moroni told Smith where to unearth several golden tablets inscribed with hieroglyphic writings. With the aid of magical spectacles, Smith translated the tablets and published them as the Book of Mormon in 1830. He then declared himself a prophet and founded a religious group he called the Church of Jesus Christ of Latter Day Saints.

The group was just one wave in a wash of religious revivalism, prophecy, and utopianism that swept across upstate New York — Palmyra is just east of Rochester — during the 1820s and 1830s; the region was so alive with religious enthusiasm that it was known as the "burned-over district." Very quickly the prophet's new sect attracted hundreds of converts. Persecuted for their beliefs, these Mormons, as they were called, moved west to Ohio, Missouri, and then Illinois. In 1844 the Mormon colony at Nauvoo, Illinois, had some 15,000 members, all living under the strict theocratic rule of Joseph Smith. In secular Illinois politics Nauvoo — then the largest city in the state — held the balance of power between contending Democrats and Whigs. It was here that Smith received a revelation sanctioning the practice of polygamy, which led to his death at the hands of a mob in 1844.

After the murder, the new president of the church, Brigham Young, decided to move the faithful, "the saints," farther west into territory that was still part of Mexico and far beyond the pale of white settlement. Young led a well-organized migration across the Great Plains and into the Rocky Mountains. In 1847 the prophet and his followers stopped along the western slope of the Wasatch Range, and as Brigham Young viewed the valley of the Great Salt Lake spread out below, he uttered the now-famous words "This is the place."

The place was Utah. And it is the only state that continues to live by the teachings of the church responsible for its founding. Throughout the 19th century "Zion" attracted thousands of converts from the Midwest, the north of England, and Scandinavia. The object of religious fear, prejudice, and perhaps some envy, Utah was not granted statehood until 1896, after the church renounced polygamy. Presently more than 70% of all Utah citizens are members of the Church of Jesus Christ of Latter Day Saints (LDS).

The distinctive features of the LDS Church dominate Utah politics. Leaders of the church have always exerted great political influence. For one thing, Utah has sent very few Gentiles (non-Mormons) to Congress during 80 years of statehood. Today the church owns one of the two leading Salt Lake City newspapers and a statewide television station. It has holdings in an insurance company, various banks, and real estate, and runs the largest department store in Salt Lake City. The Mormon hierarchy confidently takes stands on secular matters, economic and political. For example, it strongly supports Utah's right-to-work law and strongly opposes abortion on demand. And it came out against the MX missile system that the Carter Administration proposed placing in Utah and Nevada.

One church doctrine in particular has embarrassed many Mormons—the faith denied blacks, supposedly cursed in the Bible, the "priesthood," i.e., full church membership. All Mormons are lay persons, as the church does not employ a professional clergy; but laymen may be called to service and seldom refuse. (That is what happened to former Congressman Wayne Owens, a Democrat who lost the 1974 Senate race. He was sent by the church to eastern Canada in 1975 and effectively removed from Utah politics.) The church doctrine toward blacks was finally changed in 1978, when LDS president Spencer Kimball received a revelation. The president is the most senior member of the church's ruling body, and for some years the post was held by men over 90. The man next in line for the post is Ezra Taft Benson, Eisenhower's secretary of Agriculture in the 1950s, a member of the board of the John Birch Society and a very conservative Republican.

LDS doctrine carries the virtues of 19th-century upstate New York to their logical ends. Even today Mormons are forbidden to consume alcohol, tobacco, coffee, or tea; apparently as a result incidence of cancer is lower than average among them. Mormons are strong upholders of traditional sexual morality, as millions have learned from the most famous Mormon entertainers, the Osmond family. Many young Mormons give two years of their lives to "missions" at home and in some of the unlikeliest places overseas, in which they attempt to win new converts to the faith. And members are required to pledge a 10% tithe of their income to the church.

That income is often substantial, for Mormons have a well-deserved reputation for hard work and tend to do well in business and the professions. And it seems that their very traditional cultural attitudes with their general affluence (there is little poverty in Utah) have made Mormons generally and Utah voters in particular increasingly conservative and Republican in the 1960s and 1970s. Utahans in the 1930s had voted for Franklin Roosevelt and elected New Deal senators and congressmen. But with the coming of the Kennedy Administration, as national Democrats became increasingly identified with the causes of racial minorities and with detractors of traditional morality, Utah moved hard to the right. As late as 1960 John Kennedy got a respectable, if losing, 45% here. Barry Goldwater won 45% himself four years later—one of his best showings in the nation. In 1972 Richard Nixon carried the state with a record 72%. This was the trend of the future; Utah's young people, at least those who stay close to the church, are probably more conservative than their parents. At Brigham Young University, a Mormon institution known for its conservatism, Nixon took 79%, Schmitz 15%, and McGovern 6% in 1972. In 1976 Utah gave Gerald Ford 62% of its vote— his largest percentage in any state in the nation. It was the first time, but not the last, that Utah was the most Republican of states: in 1980 Ronald Reagan won fully 73% of

Utah's votes, compared to 21% for Jimmy Carter. The result was almost as one-sided as the Democrats' typical lead in the District of Columbia.

The mood in Utah is sharply hostile to the federal government and fiercely supportive of the free enterprise system and of traditional moral values. Utahans believe they have found the way to run a society successfully — and there is much here to support that contention. In the 1930s Utah was economically depressed, out of the main lines of trade, and there was reason for Utah voters to seek assistance from a friendly federal government. But today Utah is economically buoyant. Its population rose 38% in the 1970s, and its economy grew even faster. Most Utahans do not believe in building big fortunes: successful Mormons usually give liberally to the church and divide their fortunes among the rest of their large families. But the standard of living among ordinary people and the affluent here has clearly risen. While most of the country is plagued by doubt, Utah has found certainty; while most of the country is depressed by falling productivity and looser moral standards, Utah has shown what hard work and clean living can accomplish. Eastern liberals who like to sneer at people with traditional values and conservative attitudes have to explain why Utah works and New York doesn't.

So in a period of a few years, Utah has become the most Republican of states. Yet it is still willing to elect an occasional Democrat; in fact the state has had Democratic governors since 1964. Not surprisingly, they have been men of considerable ability and conservative attitudes. The current incumbent, Scott Matheson, was a Salt Lake City lawyer whose clients included the Union Pacific Railroad and Anaconda, and who in his first term jousted repeatedly with the federal government. He claimed credit for saving the Central Utah Project during the Carter Administration and fought plans for storing nerve gas bombs and locating the MX missile system in Utah (the outcome of that latter fight is, at this writing, unclear). Matheson cut spending and taxes; he was out of line with local opinion primarily because of his support of the Equal Rights Amendment. Against a not especially strong Republican opponent, he was reelected in 1980.

Utah's congressional delegation is now made up entirely of Republicans, and it likely will be in 1982, when it will be enlarged; the state's population growth has gained it an additional House seat. Its two current congressmen are relatively junior — one was just elected in 1980, replacing the last Democrat elected here — and wield relatively little power. But the state's two senators are both chairmen of important committees and, more important, men with a force of character and conviction who have considerable influence on the conduct of government. They are Jake Garn, the former mayor of Salt Lake City, elected to his second Senate term in 1980, and now chairman of the Senate Committee on Banking, Housing, and Urban Affairs; and Orrin Hatch, first elected in 1976 in one of the big upsets of the year, and now chairman in his first term of the Senate Committee on Labor and Human Resources. They are men of similar views on issues — part of the New Right contingent of the Republican Party — but they have sharply different temperaments and, like many senators of the same party and similar views, they are not necessarily the closest of friends.

Garn is bright, aggressive, and strongly committed, a man with a sense of humor but also with a noted temper. As a former mayor, he is familiar with many of the housing programs the Banking Committee superintends. He has always tended to oppose heavy federal funding and federal control. On banking issues, he is one who may lean a little more to savings institutions than to banks in their disputes. But Garn does not have clear-cut control over his committee on either count: the presence of such northern liberal Republicans as Heinz and

Chafee and the fact that all the committee's Democrats (save possibly William Proxmire) are northern liberals means he does not have automatic majorities on housing issues. On banking matters the full-service banks tend to have more advocates than the savings and loans. He also chairs the HUD–Independent Agencies Appropriations Subcommittee, which makes him a virtual czar of HUD.

Garn indeed seems to reserve much of his interest and drive for foreign and defense issues. He is by most measures a hawk: a man who believes fervently in a strong defense, who strongly opposed both the Panama Canal and SALT II Treaties, who particularly favors increasing the Air Force budget but generally favors across-the-board increases in defense spending. He may very well prove to be the decisive influence on the Defense Subcommittee of Appropriations—although he is not chairman—because of his strength of commitment and depth of knowledge. He may also prove to be decisive on the difficult question of the siting of the MX missile. The Carter Administration proposed building a huge railroad-track-type base for the MX that would occupy much of the Utah and Nevada desert. Garn and Nevada's Paul Laxalt, both strong defense advocates, have chaired subcommittees with a critical voice in the MX program and must face constituencies that increasingly seem hostile to the system, at least in the form proposed by the Carter Administration.

Orrin Hatch has had one of the most rapid rises in American politics. As late as the filing day for the 1976 Senate election, he was neither a public officeholder nor a candidate; he decided at the last minute to run and, as a Reagan delegate-seeker, campaigned as the most Reaganlike candidate. That was enough to win first the primary and then, against three-term Democrat Frank Moss, the general election. During his first years in the Senate Hatch seemed almost feverish in his advocacy of New Right causes, and many of his colleagues seemed to regard him as a fanatic. He led fights that other senators shunned—for example, the battle to repeal the Davis–Bacon Act, which props up wages on federal construction projects. He failed in 1979 to get elected chairman of the Republican Senatorial Campaign Committee, losing to the much more moderate John Heinz by one vote. Toward the end of the 1980 campaign, Democratic campaigners were mentioning as the most unthinkable of the horrible things that would happen if Republicans gained a majority in the Senate the likelihood that Hatch would become chairman of the Labor Committee.

He has, and the Republic still stands. Hatch has in fact gone out of his way to assure Washington that he was a reasonable man who would proceed with due regard for the feelings and prerogatives of other senators. He established a satisfactory working relationship with the committee's ranking minority member, Edward Kennedy. He agreed to defer consideration of some of the most controversial items on the New Right agenda, including revision of the labor laws. He agreed to defer some of the more controversial cultural issues, such as abortion, pending resolution of the major economic and budgetary issues raised by the Reagan Administration. He advised business lobbyists not to seek a youth minimum wage, arguing that the move would be bad public relations and might trigger demands to raise the minimum wage for others. He even went to bat for the Job Corps, interceding with Budget Director David Stockman and saving the program from crippling cuts; he cited the program's success in helping young people acquire job skills and become productive citizens, although some cynics suggested his stand was motivated by the fact that one of the nation's largest Job Corps centers is in Clearfield, Utah.

But for all these apparent concessions to liberals, the fact remains that Hatch as chairman of Labor represents a clear break with the past, and he can be expected to fight hard to change national policies he has long believed mistaken. His committee has jurisdiction over many of the antipoverty and welfare policies, and Hatch will strive to make them more efficient, less costly, and less generous to most recipients. His committee has jurisdiction over labor laws and Hatch, who likes to recall that he was once a labor union member himself, will strive to reduce unions' bargaining power, to repeal such statutes as Davis–Bacon and to institute other changes in various labor laws that organized labor has strenuously opposed. He lived much of his adult life in Pittsburgh before moving to Salt Lake City, and he was undoubtedly impressed by the difference between the stagnant and troubled economy of the former and the buoyancy of the latter. Hatch's views on noneconomic issues are rooted in strong religious beliefs; he is a bishop in the Mormon Church.

There has been talk that Hatch faces trouble in his 1982 reelection campaign, and that his concessions to liberals and labor in early 1981 were motivated by a desire to disarm their opposition. There are Democrats in Utah with the potential to give him a tough race — Governor Scott Matheson, should he choose to run, or former Governor Calvin Rampton — but it is not clear that Hatch will get formidable opposition. Even if he does, Utah has become an overwhelmingly Republican state and there is no indication that Hatch is seriously out of line with opinion in the state on any major issue. His major problem would be if Utah voters were to conclude that he is ineffective in advancing what are his and their views.

Utah has two congressional districts, and although they both stretch far from the Wasatch Front — the land between the mountains and the Great Salt Lake where 88% of the state's people live — that is where the battles are really fought. The 1st district covers geographically the eastern half of the state, but its two main population concentrations are separated by Salt Lake City, which is in the 2d district. To the north are the well-to-do suburbs of Davis County and the working-class town of Ogden, near which the Golden Spike was pounded, linking the nation by transcontinental railroad in 1869. To the south is Utah County, whose main town is Provo, the home of Brigham Young University and of the Osmonds. Utah County is perhaps the most solidly conservative part of the United States. Ronald Reagan got 83% of the vote here in 1980 — the highest he received in any county with a population as substantial (207,000).

Politically the 1st is the more conservative and Republican of the two districts, yet through the 1970s it was represented by a Democrat, Gunn McKay. He was helped by his conservative voting record and because he was related to a former LDS president and had served as an aide to former Governor Rampton. But in 1980 he was no longer able to overcome his liabilities. The Republican candidate, James Hansen, was widely respected for his legislative skill as speaker of the Utah House, and he was able to convince enough voters that McKay was Democratic enough to be rejected in a district that was giving Jimmy Carter only 19% of its votes. Hansen is a member of the Interior Committee — always important in a western state — and, an unusual thing for a freshman, was assigned to the ethics committee.

The 2d district includes several of the state's western counties, but for all practical purposes it is the Salt Lake City district; 85% of the vote is cast in Salt Lake County. It is also something of a jinx seat: in four elections in the 1970–76 period it elected four different congressmen, one of the few districts in the nation with such high turnover. This was the district whose congressman, Democrat Allan Howe, had the misfortune to have been arrested and charged with soliciting an undercover policewoman for an act of prostitution on a notorious

Salt Lake City street, West Second South; predictably, Howe lost the next election. The winner was Dan Marriott, a Republican who is now a three-term incumbent. Marriott is a member of the Interior and Small Business Committees and a solid conservative.

Utah will have three congressional districts for 1982, and in early 1981 there was no agreement on how the districts should be drawn. One district almost certainly will be wholly within Salt Lake County. Technically, such a seat would be a little less Republican than the state as a whole, but in practice it would likely reelect Marriott without difficulty. Population figures suggest that the part of the state north of Salt Lake City would make up another district, which would include not only Ogden but the Salt Lake City suburbs between the capital and Ogden. This would be Hansen's home district, where he would probably win reelection without difficulty. That would leave the southern part of the state — two-thirds of it in area, one-third in population — as a third district. Almost half its population would be in Utah County, and in terms of national elections it would be one of the most Republican districts in the nation.

Census Data Pop. (1980 final) 1,461,037, up 38% in 1970s: 0.65% of U.S. total, 36th largest. Central city, 24%; suburban, 55%. Median 4-person family income, 1978, $20,202, 99% of U.S., 26th highest.

1979 Share of Federal Tax Burden $2,164,000,000; 0.48% of U.S. total, 36th largest.

1979 Share of Federal Outlays $2,849,390,000; 0.61% of U.S. total, 38th largest.

DOD	$838,486,000	32d	(0.79%)	HEW	$757,082,000	40th	(0.42%)
DOE	$46,659,000	26th	(0.40%)	ERDA	$6,942,000	32d	(0.25%)
HUD	$22,534,000	40th	(0.34%)	NASA	$71,243,000	11th	(1.52%)
VA	$113,170,000	39th	(0.55%)	DOT	$110,522,000	38th	(0.67%)
EPA	$26,266,000	41st	(0.49%)	DOC	$10,049,000	40th	(0.32%)
DOI	$167,831,000	8th	(3.02%)	USDA	$198,178,000	40th	(0.82%)

Economic Base Finance, insurance, and real estate; agriculture, notably cattle, dairy products, turkeys, and sheep; primary metal industries; metal mining; food and kindred products; transportation equipment, especially aircraft and parts; apparel and other textile products, especially women's and misses' outerwear.

Political Lineup Governor, Scott M. Matheson (D). Senators, Jacob (Jake) Garn (R) and Orrin G. Hatch (R). Representatives, 2 R; 3 in 1982. State Senate, 29 (22 R and 7 D); State House of Representatives, 75 (58 R and 17 D).

The Voters

Registration 781,711 Total.
Employment profile 1970 White collar, 50%. Blue collar, 33%. Service, 13%. Farm, 4%.
Ethnic groups Black 1980, 1%. Hispanic 1980, 4%. Am. Ind. 1980, 1%. Asian 1980, 1%. Total foreign stock 1970, 12%. UK, 2%.

Presidential Vote

1980	Reagan (R)	439,687	(73%)
	Carter (D)	124,266	(21%)
	Anderson (I)	30,284	(5%)
1976	Ford (R)	337,908	(62%)
	Carter (D)	182,110	(34%)

SENATORS

Sen. Jacob (Jake) **Garn** (R) Elected 1974, seat up 1986; b. Oct, 12, 1932, Richfield; home, Salt Lake City; U. of Utah, B.S. 1955.

Career Navy, 1956–60; Asst. Mgr., Salt Lake City Ofc. Home Life Insurance Co. of N.Y., 1961–66; Salt Lake City Commission, 1967–71; Mayor of Salt Lake City, 1971–74.

Offices 5207 DSOB, 202-224-5444. Also 4225 Fed. Bldg., 125 S. State St., Salt Lake City 84138, 801-524-5933, and Fed. Bldg., Ogden 84401, 801-399-6208.

Committees *Appropriations* (6th). Subcommittees: Defense; Energy and Water Development; HUD–Independent Agencies (Chairman); Interior; Military Construction.

Banking, Housing, and Urban Affairs (Chairman). Subcommittees: Housing and Urban Affairs; Financial Institutions; International Finance and Monetary Policy.

Select Committee on Intelligence (2d). Subcommittees: Budget; Analysis and Production; Legislation and the Rights of Americans; Collection and Foreign Operations.

Group Ratings

	ADA	COPE	PC	LCV	CFA	RPN	NAB	NSI	NTU	ACA	ACU
1980	17	10	13	13	7	—	92	100	68	96	95
1979	11	5	29	—	14	—	—	—	70	100	91
1978	5	5	18	11	20	60	75	100	51	95	100

Key Votes

1) Draft Registn $	AGN	6) Fair Housng Cloture	AGN	11) Cut Socl Incr Defns	FOR
2) Ban $ to Nicrgua	—	7) Ban $ Rape Abortns	FOR	12) Income Tax Indexing	FOR
3) Dlay MX Missile	AGN	8) Cap on Food Stmp $	FOR	13) Lim Spdg 21% GNP	FOR
4) Nuclr Mortorium	AGN	9) New US Dep Edcatn	FOR	14) Incr Wndfll Prof Tax	AGN
5) Alaska Lands Bill	AGN	10) Cut OSHA Inspctns	FOR	15) Chryslr Loan Grntee	AGN

Election Results

1980 general	Jacob (Jake) Garn (R)	434,675	(74%)	($1,048,137)
	Dan Berman (D)	151,454	(26%)	($237,882)
1980 primary	Jacob (Jake) Garn (R), unopposed			
1974 general	Jacob (Jake) Garn (R)	210,299	(50%)	($363,162)
	Wayne Owens (D)	185,377	(44%)	($445,400)
	Bruce Bangerter (Amer.)	24,966	(6%)	($1,488)

Sen. Orrin G. Hatch (R) Elected 1976, seat up 1982; b. Mar. 22, 1934, Pittsburgh, Pa.; home, Salt Lake City; Brigham Young U., B.S. 1959, U. of Pittsburgh, J.D. 1962.

Career Practicing atty., 1962–77.

Offices 125 RSOB, 202-224-5251. Also Fed. Bldg., 125 S. State St., Salt Lake City 84138, 801-524-4380.

Committees *Budget* (5th).

Judiciary (4th). Subcommittees: Constitution (Chairman); Security and Terrorism; Separation of Power.

Labor and Human Resources (Chairman). Subcommittees: Labor; Employment and Productivity; Alcoholism and Drug Abuse.

Select Committee on Small Business (3d). Subcommittees: Capital Formation and Retention; Government Regulation and Paperwork (Chairman).

Group Ratings

	ADA	COPE	PC	LCV	CFA	RPN	NAB	NSI	NTU	ACA	ACU
1980	17	10	13	17	7	—	82	100	60	96	90
1979	11	5	26	—	14	—	—	—	73	96	97
1978	5	11	15	7	15	50	92	100	51	96	96

Key Votes

1) Draft Registn $	AGN	6) Fair Housng Cloture	AGN	11) Cut Socl Incr Defns	FOR
2) Ban $ to Nicrgua	—	7) Ban $ Rape Abortns	FOR	12) Income Tax Indexing	FOR
3) Dlay MX Missile	—	8) Cap on Food Stmp $	FOR	13) Lim Spdg 21% GNP	FOR
4) Nuclr Mortorium	AGN	9) New US Dep Edcatn	FOR	14) Incr Wndfll Prof Tax	AGN
5) Alaska Lands Bill	AGN	10) Cut OSHA Inspctns	FOR	15) Chryslr Loan Grntee	AGN

Election Results

1976 general	Orrin G. Hatch (R)	290,221	(54%)	($370,517)
	Frank E. Moss (D)	241,948	(45%)	($343,598)
1976 primary	Orrin G. Hatch (R)	104,490	(65%)	
	Jack Carlson (R)	57,249	(35%)	
1970 general	Frank E. Moss (D)	210,207	(56%)	
	Laurence J. Burton (R)	159,004	(42%)	

GOVERNOR

Gov. Scott M. Matheson (D) Elected 1976, term expires Jan. 1985; b. Jan. 8, 1929, Chicago, Ill.; U. of Utah, B.S. 1950, Stanford U., J.D. 1952.

Career Practicing atty., 1953–54, 1956–68; Parowan City Atty. and Dpty. Iron Co. Atty., 1953–54; Law Clerk for U.S. Dist. Judge, Salt Lake City, 1954–56; Dpty. Salt Lake Co. Atty. 1956–57; Atty., Union Pacific R.R., 1958–69, Gen. Solicitor, 1972–76; Counsel, Anaconda Co., 1969–70, Asst. Gen. Counsel, 1970–72.

Offices 210 State Capitol, Salt Lake City 84114, 801-533-5231.

Election Results

1980 gen.	Scott M. Matheson (D)	330,974	(55%)
	Bob Wright (R)	266,578	(44%)
1980 prim.	Scott Matheson (D), unopp.		
1976 gen.	Scott M. Matheson (D)	280,606	(52%)
	Vernon B. Romney (R)	248,027	(46%)

FIRST DISTRICT

Census Data Pop. (1980 final) 742,709, up 40% in 1970s. Median family income, 1970, $9,080, 95% of U.S.

The Voters

Employment profile 1970 White collar, 50%. Blue collar, 33%. Service, 13%. Farm, 4%.
Ethnic groups Black 1980, 1%. Hispanic 1980, 4%. Total foreign stock 1970, 10%. UK, 2%.

Presidential Vote

1980	Reagan (R)	236,439	(77%)
	Carter (D)	56,592	(19%)
	Anderson (I)	9,628	(3%)
1976	Ford (R)	170,399	(64%)
	Carter (D)	82,741	(31%)

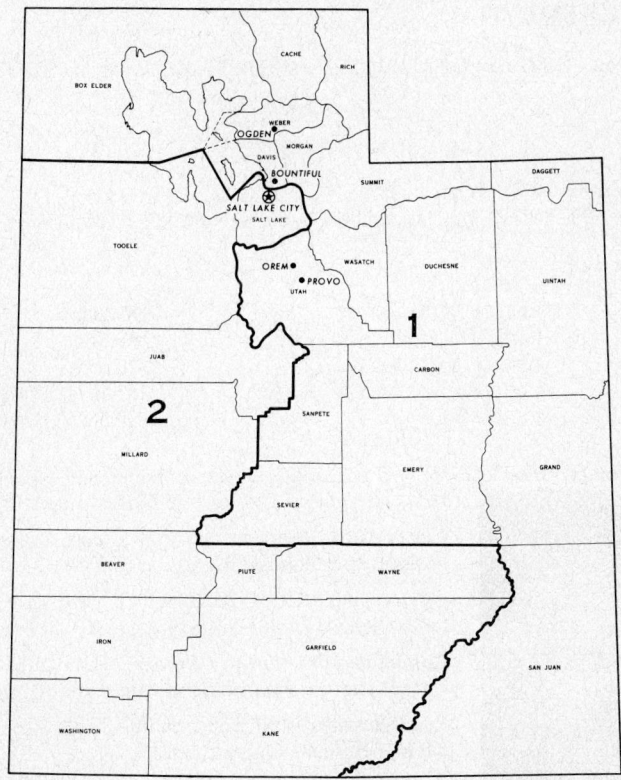

Rep. James V. Hansen (R) Elected 1980; b. Aug. 14, 1932, Salt Lake City; home, Farmington; U. of Utah, B.A. 1960.

Career Navy, 1951–53; Farmington City Cncl., 1962–72; Utah House of Reps., 1972–80, Spkr., 1978–80.

Offices 1407 LHOB, 202-225-0453. Also 1017 Fed. Bldg., 324 25th St., Ogden 84401, 801-626-2151, and West Park Bldg., 750 N. 200 West, Suite 204, Provo 84601, 801-375-0370.

Committees *Interior and Insular Affairs* (17th). Subcommittees: Public Lands and National Parks; Water and Power Resources.

Standards of Official Conduct (6th).

Group Ratings and Key Votes: Newly Elected

Election Results

1980 general	James V. Hansen (R)	157,111	(52%)	($232,206)
	K. Gunn McKay (D)	144,459	(48%)	($275,313)
1980 primary	James V. Hansen (R), unopposed			
1978 general	K. Gunn McKay (D)	93,892	(51%)	($149,143)
	Jed J. Richardson (R).	85,028	(46%)	($147,556)

SECOND DISTRICT

Census Data   Pop. (1980 final) 718,328, up 36% in 1970s. Median family income, 1970, $9,537, 99% of U.S.

The Voters

Employment profile 1970   White collar, 53%. Blue collar, 32%. Service, 13%. Farm, 2%.
Ethnic groups   Black 1980, 1%. Hispanic 1980, 5%. Total foreign stock 1970, 14%. UK, 3%.

Presidential Vote

1980	Reagan (R)	203,248	(68%)
	Carter (D)	67,674	(22%)
	Anderson (I)	20,656	(7%)
1976	Ford (R)	167,509	(61%)
	Carter (D)	99,369	(36%)

Rep. Dan Marriott (R) Elected 1976; b. Nov. 2, 1939, Bingham; home, Salt Lake City; U. of Utah, B.S. 1967, Amer. Col. of Life Underwriters, C.L.U.

Career Pres., Marriott Associates, corp. benefit planners and business consultants, 1976–77.

Offices 1133 LHOB, 202-225-3011. Also 2311 Fed. Bldg., Salt Lake City 84138, 801-524-4394.

Committees *Interior and Insular Affairs* (5th). Subcommittees: Energy and the Environment; Mines and Mining.

Small Business (5th). Subcommittee: Tax, Access to Equity Capital and Business Opportunities.

Group Ratings

	ADA	COPE	PC	LCV	CFA	RPN	NAB	NSI	NTU	ACA	ACU
1980	17	7	20	40	14	—	100	100	44	74	81
1979	5	18	10	12	4	—	—	—	58	96	94
1978	5	15	10	1	14	64	100	100	35	100	90

Key Votes

1) Draft Registn $	AGN	6) Fair Hsg DOJ Enfrc	AGN	11) Cut Socl Incr Dfns $	FOR
2) Ban $ to Nicrgua	FOR	7) Lim PAC Contrbtns	AGN	12) Hosptl Cost Controls	—
3) Dlay MX Missile	FOR	8) Cap on Food Stmp $	FOR	13) Gasln Ctrls & Allctns	AGN
4) Nuclr Mortorium	AGN	9) New US Dep Edcatn	AGN	14) Lim Wndfll Prof Tax	FOR
5) Alaska Lands Bill	AGN	10) Cut OSHA $	FOR	15) Chryslr Loan Grntee	FOR

Election Results

1980 general	Dan Marriott (R)	194,885	(67%)	($352,435)
	Arthur L. Monson (D)	87,967	(30%)	($27,669)
1980 primary	Dan Marriott (R), unopposed			
1978 general	Dan Marriott (R)	121,492	(62%)	($353,520)
	Edwin B. Firmage (D)	68,899	(35%)	($230,760)

VERMONT

In many ways Vermont still seems part of the 19th century. The classic New England town squares still stand here; the cows still graze on the hillsides; the taciturn Yankee farmers still tap sugar maple trees in early spring; and the autumn foliage is perhaps the most magnificent in the world. Vermont remains, by census definition, our most rural state, with two-thirds of the population living outside urban areas. But even so the 1960s and 1970s have brought change here. There are now large IBM and General Electric complexes around Burlington, the state's largest city, whose metropolitan population has passed 100,000. The ski resort and summer home industries have boomed so much that the price of rural land has skyrocketed and led many farmers to sell. And so, the very things that attract people to Vermont threaten to vanish. From 1850 to 1960 Vermont's population hovered between 300,000 and 400,000; only in 1963 were there finally more people than cows in the state. But in 1970 there were 444,000 people living in Vermont, and in 1980, 511,000.

There have also been massive political changes here—massive enough that this state, long the most Republican in the nation, today has a Democratic senator and for most of the 1960s and 1970s had Democratic governors. Before 1960 the only areas of Democratic strength were the small Irish and French Canadian communities in Burlington and other towns near the Canadian border; it was almost as if all the Catholic minority were Democrats and all the Protestant majority Republicans. As long as that was the case, there was no suspense about election outcomes. This is one part of New England that still has a Yankee majority, and Democrats have won—Governor Philip Hoff in 1962, 1964, and 1966; Governor Thomas Salmon in 1972 and 1974; Senator Patrick Leahy in 1974 and 1980—only when they have cracked the Yankee vote. The Democrats on occasion have been split between their culturally traditional Catholic base and the culturally liberal newcomers who are enthusiastic about Vermont's natural environment. In terms of registration and also in terms of most election results this is still basically a Republican state, and the most successful politicians here are Republicans, particularly those Republicans who identify themselves with Vermont's life-style and environment. Vermont voters show some resistance to Republicans who, like Ronald Reagan, emphasize conservative positions on cultural issues. Reagan carried the state but with only 44% of the vote; in only six states was his percentage lower. Vermont was also one of Jimmy Carter's weakest states and, after Massachusetts, John Anderson's strongest. Anderson did well here in both primary and general elections—he is, after all, the kind of Republican Vermonters seem to like best.

One of the most successful Vermont politicians is Senator Robert Stafford, who has held statewide office since 1954. He was elected governor in 1958, congressman in 1960 and was appointed senator when incumbent Winston Prouty died in 1971. Stafford is a taciturn Yankee, neither aggressive nor overbearing; yet he holds one of the more important positions in the Senate now as chairman of the Environment and Public Works Committee. This committee writes most of our antipollution bills, and its attentions will be directed in 1981 to rewriting the Clean Air Act, which comes up for renewal. This complex legislation deals with the very different atmospheric—and economic—conditions in various parts of the country. Stafford has been considered over the years sympathetic to environmental concerns, and environmental groups see him as their major champion. But he is also mindful of the need for economic growth and development and will work to see that the act does not stifle either. Stafford is also a member of the Labor and Human Resources Committee, where his vote is likely to be critical to the outcome of issues: all the other Republicans but one are pretty firmly identified with the party's conservative wing while all the Democrats are solidly prolabor.

Stafford has never seriously antagonized any segment of the Vermont electorate, and on paper he seems ideally suited to the state. Yet he had a more serious challenge than he probably expected in 1976 from then Governor Salmon; there were some differences on issues but the most vivid contrast was between the quiet Stafford and the hard-driving Salmon. The general assumption for 1982 is that Stafford will be reelected; some Democratic-oriented lobbying groups, including labor and environmentalists, might even be tempted to support him on the theory that they need some members who will consider their claims among the Republican ranks. It is possible that Stafford, who turns 69 in 1982, will choose to retire, in which case the clear favorites to succeed him would be two popular Republicans, Governor Richard Snelling and Congressman-at-Large James Jeffords.

Vermont's junior senator is a Democrat — the only Democrat Vermont has ever sent to the Senate. Patrick Leahy first won the seat in 1974, when the quintessential Vermont Yankee, George Aiken, retired after 34 years in the Senate. Leahy had made a name for himself in Vermont as the Burlington area prosecutor who tried all major felony cases personally and attacked the big oil companies during the gasoline crisis of 1974. He had a solid base in Democratic (and Catholic) Burlington together with the kind of quiet, thoughtful temperament Yankee Vermonters like in their public officials. In that heavily Democratic year he was able to outpoll Republican Congressman-at-Large Richard Mallary by a narrow margin.

Leahy kept his seat in the very Republican year of 1980 by almost the same margin. Why was a Democrat able to win again in this Republican state? The main reason is that Leahy had established, not just in 1980 but over the preceding seven years, that he shared basic values with most Vermonters. His basic instincts are parsimonious, as residents of Washington, D.C., learned when he chaired the District of Columbia Appropriations Subcommittee. He was attacked in 1980 for opposing weapons systems but was able to reply convincingly that they were not good buys. On the Agriculture Committee he was one of the leading advocates of the interests of dairy farmers — a numerous and economically important group in Vermont. In 1980, Leahy had substantial opposition from Republican Stewart Ledbetter, who was able to wage an expensive and sophisticated campaign. But the result came out almost a carbon copy of the 1974 results — and left Leahy no longer part of a confident Democratic majority but a part of a beleaguered and confused Democratic minority. His own values and goals seem strongly enough rooted, however, that his position on issues can be fairly readily predicted. What cannot be predicted, with any certainty, are the political prospects of a Democrat in Vermont.

Vermont's congressman-at-large is James Jeffords, a Republican with one of the more liberal records in his party. First elected in 1974, he has won reelection with overwhelming majorities. His home state popularity has not been matched by legislative productivity, although it must be said that it is difficult for a Republican to get his name on successful legislation in a Democratic House. His defenders argue that he has done valuable work on reforming CETA and encouraging solar energy (the latter a favorite project of many congressmen) but admit that some of his most creative proposals have not been enacted. Should Stafford choose to retire, Jeffords could almost certainly be elected to the Senate, unless Governor Snelling, who is also highly popular, runs. It should be noted that Vermont's most popular Democrat, after Leahy, is Lieutenant Governor Madeleine Kunin; this is one of the few states that still elects its lieutenant governors separately, as well as one of the few that elects governors every two years. It is not out of the realm of possibility that Kunin could be elected governor or senator someday.

Census Data   Pop. (1980 final) 511,456, up 15% in 1970s: 0.23% of U.S. total, 48th largest. Median 4-person family income, 1978, $18,458, 90% of U.S., 40th highest.

1979 Share of Federal Tax Burden $766,000,000; 0.17% of U.S. total, 50th largest.

1979 Share of Federal Outlays $918,215,000; 0.19% of U.S. total, 51st largest.

DOD	$138,777,000	51st	(0.13%)	HEW	$440,231,000	47th	(0.25%)
DOE	$487,000	51st	(0.00%)	ERDA	$10,000	51st	(0.00%)
HUD	$11,251,000	49th	(0.17%)	NASA	$151,000	45th	(0.00%)
VA	$54,327,000	49th	(0.26%)	DOT	$46,611,000	50th	(0.28%)
EPA	$26,345,000	42d	(0.50%)	DOC	$3,646,000	50th	(0.12%)
DOI	$7,184,000	51st	(0.13%)	USDA	$43,115,000	48th	(0.18%)

Economic Base   Agriculture, notably dairy products, cattle, eggs, and forest products; finance, insurance, and real estate; electrical equipment and supplies, especially electronic components and accessories; machinery, especially metalworking machinery; printing and publishing, especially book printing; lumber and wood products; cut stone and stone products, and other stone, clay, and glass products.

Political Lineup   Governor, Richard A. Snelling (R). Senators, Robert T. Stafford (R) and Patrick J. Leahy (D). Representatives, 1 R at large; 1 in 1982. State Senate, 30 (16 R and 14 D); State House of Representatives, 150 (83 R, 65 D, and 2 I).

The Voters

   Registration   311,919 Total.
   Employment profile 1970   White collar, 46%. Blue collar, 35%. Service, 14%. Farm, 5%.
   Ethnic groups   Hispanic 1980, 1%. Total foreign stock 1970, 18%. Canada, 10%.

Presidential Vote

1980	Reagan (R)	94,628	(44%)
	Carter (D)	81,952	(38%)
	Anderson (I)	31,761	(15%)
1976	Ford (R)	100,387	(55%)
	Carter (D)	78,789	(43%)

1980 Democratic Presidential Primary			*1980 Republican Presidential Primary*		
Carter	29,015	(73%)	Reagan	19,720	(30%)
Kennedy	10,135	(26%)	Anderson	19,030	(29%)
Scattering	553	(1%)	Bush	14,226	(22%)
			Baker	8,055	(12%)
			3 others & scattering	4,580	(7%)

SENATORS

Sen. Robert T. Stafford (R) Appointed Sept. 16, 1971, elected Jan. 7, 1972, seat up 1982; b. Aug. 8, 1913, Rutland; home, Rutland; Middlebury Col., B.S. 1935, U. of Mich., Boston U. LL.B. 1938.

Career Rutland City Prosecuting Atty., 1938–42; Navy, WWII and Korea; Rutland Co. States Atty., 1947–51; Dpty. Atty. Gen. of Vt., 1953–55; Atty. Gen. of Vt., 1955–57; Lt. Gov. of Vt., 1957–59; Gov. of Vt., 1959–61; U.S. House of Reps., 1961–71.

Offices 5219 DSOB, 202-224-5141. Also 501 Fed . Bldg., Burlington 05401, 802-951-6707, and 27 S. Main St., Rutland 05701, 802-775-5446.

Committees *Environment and Public Works* (Chairman). Subcommittee: Transportation.

Labor and Human Resources (2d). Subcommittees: Labor; Education (Chairman); Handicapped.

Veterans' Affairs (3d).

Group Ratings

	ADA	COPE	PC	LCV	CFA	RPN	NAB	NSI	NTU	ACA	ACU
1980	61	58	60	71	33	—	36	44	35	38	25
1979	47	75	55	—	57	—	—	—	23	9	18
1978	55	58	55	74	35	88	17	34	13	29	25

Key Votes

1) Draft Registn $	FOR	6) Fair Housng Cloture	FOR	11) Cut Socl Incr Defns	AGN
2) Ban $ to Nicrgua	FOR	7) Ban $ Rape Abortns	AGN	12) Income Tax Indexing	FOR
3) Dlay MX Missile	AGN	8) Cap on Food Stmp $	AGN	13) Lim Spdg 21% GNP	FOR
4) Nuclr Mortorium	AGN	9) New US Dep Edcatn	—	14) Incr Wndfll Prof Tax	FOR
5) Alaska Lands Bill	FOR	10) Cut OSHA Inspctns	AGN	15) Chryslr Loan Grntee	FOR

Election Results

1976 general	Robert T. Stafford (R)	94,481	(50%)	($157,927)
	Thomas P. Salmon (D)	85,682	(45%)	($169,296)
	Nancy Kaufman (LU)	8,801	(5%)	
1976 primary	Robert T. Stafford (R), unopposed			
1972 special	Robert T. Stafford (R)	45,888	(64%)	
	Randolph T. Major (D)	23,842	(33%)	
1972 spec. prim.	Robert T. Stafford (R), unopposed			
1970 general	Winston L. Prouty (R)	91,198	(59%)	
	Phillip H. Hoff (D)	62,271	(40%)	

Sen. Patrick J. Leahy (D) Elected 1974, seat up 1986; b. Mar. 31, 1940, Montpelier; home, Burlington;

St. Michael's Col., Winooski, B.A. 1961, Georgetown U., J.D. 1964.

Career Practicing atty., 1964–74; Chittenden Co. States Atty., 1966–74.

Offices 427 RSOB, 202-224-4242. Also Box 2, Burlington 05401, 802-863-2525.

Committees *Agriculture, Nutrition, and Forestry* (2d). Subcommittees: Agricultural Production, Marketing, and Stabilization of Prices; Rural Development, Oversight, and Investigations; Nutrition.

Appropriations (11th). Subcommittees: District of Columbia; Foreign Operations; HUD–Independent Agencies; Interior.

Judiciary (6th). Subcommittees: Constitution; Regulatory Reform; Security and Terrorism.

Select Committee on Intelligence (6th). Subcommittees: Budget; Legislation and the Rights of Americans (Vice-chairman).

Group Ratings

	ADA	COPE	PC	LCV	CFA	RPN	NAB	NSI	NTU	ACA	ACU
1980	83	83	87	90	53	—	30	0	30	16	0
1979	89	79	72	—	76	—	—	—	30	19	9
1978	65	79	80	94	55	60	8	22	15	21	8

Key Votes

1) Draft Registn $	AGN	6) Fair Housng Cloture	FOR	11) Cut Socl Incr Defns	—
2) Ban $ to Nicrgua	—	7) Ban $ Rape Abortns	AGN	12) Income Tax Indexing	FOR
3) Dlay MX Missile	FOR	8) Cap on Food Stmp $	AGN	13) Lim Spdg 21% GNP	AGN
4) Nuclr Mortorium	FOR	9) New US Dep Edcatn	FOR	14) Incr Wndfll Prof Tax	FOR
5) Alaska Lands Bill	FOR	10) Cut OSHA Inspctns	AGN	15) Chryslr Loan Grntee	FOR

Election Results

1980 general	Patrick J. Leahy (D)	104,176	(50%)	($434,644)
	Stewart M. Ledbetter (R)	101,421	(49%)	($532,904)
1980 primary	Patrick J. Leahy (D)	27,548	(100%)	
1974 general	Patrick J. Leahy (D)	70,629	(49%)	($152,817)
	Richard W. Mallary (R)	66,223	(46%)	($90,617)

GOVERNOR

Gov. Richard A. Snelling (R) Elected 1976, term expires Jan. 1983; b. Feb. 18, 1927, Allentown, Pa.; U. of Havana, Cuba, Lehigh U., Harvard U., A.B. 1948.

Career Army, WWII; Founder and Chmn., Shelburne Industries, Inc.; Vt. House of Reps., 1959–60, 1973–76, Major. Ldr., 1975–76.

Offices Governor's Office, Montpelier 05602, 802-828-3333,

Election Results

1980 gen.	Richard A. Snelling (R)	123,229	(59%)
	M. Jerome Diamond (D)...	77,363	(37%)
1980 prim.	Richard A. Snelling (R)	38,228	(87%)
	Two others (R)	5,705	(13%)
1978 gen.	Richard A. Snelling (R)	78,181	(63%)
	Edwin C. Granai (D)	42,482	(34%)

Rep. James M. Jeffords (R) Elected 1974; b. May 11, 1934, Rutland; home, Montpelier; Yale U., B.S. 1956, Harvard U., LL.B. 1962.

Career Navy, 1956–59; Law Clerk to U.S. Dist. Ct. Judge Ernest W. Gibson, 1962; Practicing atty., 1963–75; Chmn., Rutland Co. Bd. of Property Tax Appeals, 1964–66; Vt. Senate, 1967–68; Atty. Gen. of Vt., 1969–73.

Offices 1524 LHOB, 202-225-4115. Also P.O. Box 676, Fed. Bldg., Montpelier 05602, 802-223-5274.

Committees *Agriculture* (3d). Subcommittees: Conservation, Credit, and Rural Development; Livestock, Dairy, and Poultry.

Education and Labor (3d). Subcommittees: Elementary, Secondary, and Vocational Education; Employment Opportunities; Select Education.

Select Committee on Aging (12th). Subcommittees: Health and Long-Term Care; Retirement Income and Employment.

Group Ratings

	ADA	COPE	PC	LCV	CFA	RPN	NAB	NSI	NTU	ACA	ACU
1980	67	18	60	91	57	—	27	56	32	30	17
1979	63	65	55	89	41	—	—	—	41	35	39
1978	40	30	58	84	64	82	36	67	17	25	50

Key Votes

1) Draft Registn $	AGN	6) Fair Hsg DOJ Enfrc	AGN	11) Cut Socl Incr Dfns $	AGN
2) Ban $ to Nicrgua	AGN	7) Lim PAC Contrbtns	FOR	12) Hosptl Cost Controls	AGN
3) Dlay MX Missile	FOR	8) Cap on Food Stmp $	AGN	13) Gasln Ctrls & Allctns	AGN
4) Nuclr Mortorium	FOR	9) New US Dep Edcatn	FOR	14) Lim Wndfll Prof Tax	FOR
5) Alaska Lands Bill	FOR	10) Cut OSHA $	AGN	15) Chryslr Loan Grntee	AGN

Election Results

1980 general	James M. Jeffords (R)	154,274	(79%)	($58,781)
	Robin Lloyd (D)	24,758	(13%)	($0)
	Peter Isaac Diamondstone (LU)...	15,218	(8%)	($0)
1980 primary	James M. Jeffords (R)	41,785	(100%)	
1978 general	James M. Jeffords (R)	90,688	(75%)	($66,589)
	S. Marie Dietz (D)	23,228	(19%)	($8,768)
	Peter Isaac Diamondstone (LU)...	6,505	(5%)	

VIRGINIA

Twenty years ago any analysis of Virginia politics began and ended with the Byrd machine, the unique group of conservative Democrats who utterly dominated the politics of this large and variegated state. Today, after more than a decade of political turmoil and uncertainty, the Byrd machine in its old form is gone. It has been replaced, however, by an organization that serves its basic objectives, the Virginia Republican Party. The party carries the state for Republicans in presidential elections (it has gone Democratic only once since 1952), and it holds onto the governorship (Republicans won in 1969, 1973, 1977). The Republicans have the Senate seat not held by Harry Byrd, Jr., a man who runs as an Independent, votes to organize the Senate as a Democrat, and votes like a Republican. Finally, the Virginia congressional delegation — 9-1 Republican — is probably the most conservative in the nation. On the local level, Byrd-type Democrats continue to dominate the politics of most of Virginia's small county courthouses but face turbulence and competition in some of the state's urban and suburban areas.

The replacement of the Byrd machine by this somewhat untidy but congenial arrangement has been a major political accomplishment. For 15 years ago the Byrd machine and the ideas it represented seemed in very serious trouble indeed. The Massive Resistance that the machine had sponsored against school integration in the 1950s had failed; the strategy had first disgraced Virginia by closing public schools and then had to be ignominiously abandoned. The bulwark of the machine — small towns of Southside Virginia or the Shenandoah Valley — were increasingly unable to deliver votes as the electorate increased vastly in size. Areas that had never been friendly to the Byrd machine were growing in importance: the Washington suburbs were 5% of the state in 1940 and 21% in 1970; the Tidewater area was 13% of the state in 1940 and 22% in 1970. Massive Resistance was the Byrd machine's one appeal to a mass vote — otherwise they had worked to keep the electorate small — and combined with the impact of the Voting Rights Act, it seemed to produce a body of voters too big for the oldtime Byrd leaders to control. Senator Harry Byrd, Sr., himself, after forty years of dominance of state public life, resigned in 1965.

Into this vacuum sprang a number of talented Republican politicians, of which the most notable was the party's state chairman, Richard Obenshain. Republicans began as a regional party in Virginia, with a base in the western mountains where they were competitive with anti-Byrd Democrats and in the valley area around Roanoke. These traditional Republicans came from a background that was antislavery, and they had opposed the Byrd machine both in policy and politics. This traditional base was the origin of Linwood Holton, the party's gubernatorial candidate in 1965, when he was beaten by the last Byrd Democrat Governor, Mills Godwin, and in 1969, when he won following a divisive Democratic primary and runoff. The Obenshain Republicans, with the Nixon Administration, wanted to use the famous southern strategy in Virginia, identifying their party with resistance to integration. But Holton made a point of accompanying his young daughter to the majority-black elementary school to which a court order assigned her. That essentially finished Holton in the new style of Virginia Republican politics; he was not considered for a gubernatorial nomination again and ran third among three major candidates in the race for the 1978 Senate nomination.

The transformation of Virginia politics was signaled by the gubernatorial election of 1973. The Republicans nominated Mills Godwin, until then a stalwart of the Byrd machine although as a governor one who abandoned some of its segregationist policies. The Democrats had no candidate at all — a sorry state that resulted from the vogue for independent candidacies here in the early 1970s. Running against Godwin was Henry Howell, a self-styled populist from Norfolk who had managed to get himself elected lieutenant governor in a three-way race. Howell had a vision of a new kind of Virginia politics. As a folksy personal injury lawyer, he was accustomed to make stirring pleas to juries; he combined country cornpone and generous social policy into what he hoped would become a new populism. The end of the Byrd machine, Howell thought, would turn the state's politics over to the little people, white and black, and to him as their representative. With his Norfolk base, he had run a respectable third-place race for governor in the 1969 primary. Against a Godwin who was visibly ailing and less than eager to run, and in the Watergate year, he looked like a formidable candidate in 1973.

Howell nevertheless managed to lose. Godwin and state Chairman Obenshain raised the school busing issue and capitalized on a statement Howell made that seemed to endorse court-ordered busing plans. Instead of reemphasizing his populist refrain, Howell went on the defensive and concentrated on busing in the last few weeks. It was enough to defeat him by one of the narrowest margins in Virginia history—and to destroy any chances of success for the kind of politics he represented. Four years later Howell ran again and had enough support to win an upset victory over Attorney General Andrew Miller in the primary; Miller came from an old anti-Byrd family and had a progressive record of his own but did not match Howell's fiery advocacy. In the 1977 general election, however, Howell ran out of steam. The Republican candidate, Lieutenant Governor John Dalton, came from the mountain branch of the party; his father, like Miller's father, had run against Senator Byrd himself. But Dalton was a loyal follower of Godwin and the new Virginia Republicans. He ran a campaign almost totally devoid of content except to point out that there was a candidate running against Henry Howell. The strategy worked. Dalton carried not only the mountains and the Byrd strongholds but the Washington suburbs as well, and he held down Howell's edge in the Tidewater to a pittance.

The governor to be elected in 1981 seems sure to be one of the two young men who won Virginia's other statewide offices in 1977. One of them, Lieutenant Governor Charles Robb, has a national reputation because he married Lynda Bird Johnson; he also has Virginia roots and had worked diligently in the vineyards of state politics. With a reputation as a moderate, he was one of the few Democrats who have been able to carry the state. The other, Attorney General Marshall Coleman, was an upset winner. A mountain Republican, he beat a Byrd Democrat associated with segregationist policies; he did particularly well in the Washington suburbs where the old-fashioned Byrd machine has never been popular. For 1981 Coleman seems to be aligning himself solidly with the Republican establishment. Some of Virginia's activist liberals complain that Robb is not one of them, and in fact he is pursuing a more independent course. The Virginia establishment has no doubts about whom it favors, however; like the Right in France, it feels that it must win every election without exception or all will be lost, and it sees Robb as an adversary and someone it cannot control.

One of the new Virginia Republicans' greatest triumphs was the election in 1972 of Senator William Scott. A Washington area congressman, he had seemed likely to lose to scholarly Democratic incumbent William Spong; but Scott got a last-minute injection of money and ran a series of controversial ads attacking Spong as a liberal. They said little about Scott, and you will hear little about him from Virginia Republicans today. For shortly into his term he was named the dumbest member of Congress by *New Times* magazine—in response to which he called a press conference. His efforts at refutation were generally considered unsuccessful. An inveterate junketeer, Scott was able to sum up his insights succinctly; he understood the Panama Canal, he said, because he had seen ships going both ways. Scott's shrewdest political move was his decision not to run for reelection in 1978.

The Democratic nomination that year went to Andrew Miller; after his narrow defeat in the gubernatorial primary the year before and Howell's defeat afterward, he had no opposition. The Republicans, however—and this is a sign of the vitality of their party—had a spirited race. It was conducted not in a primary but in a state party convention with some

9,000 delegates—a bigger convention, as far as anyone can remember, than any American political party has ever conducted before. Running were former Governor Holton, who finished third, and former Navy Secretary and Bicentennial Commission Chairman John Warner, who finished second. The winner was Richard Obenshain, the architect of Virginia's Republican Party. He had been more successful in his party work than in his own candidacies—he lost the 3d district Congress seat in 1964 and the attorney generalship in 1969, both narrowly—but he looked like at least an even bet in 1978. Then one August night he was killed in a plane crash outside Richmond.

The Obenshain forces were not particularly happy with replacing him with the convention's number two candidate, Warner, but they had little choice. Warner was widely regarded as a lukewarm conservative, although he had served the Nixon Administration faithfully enough; he had few roots in state politics, and his campaign had been helped by the money of his first wife (a Mellon) and the celebrity of his second (Elizabeth Taylor). Many Virginia ladies cringed at the thought of a candidate whose wife had had seven husbands. But Warner seemed as strong a candidate as the party had (Godwin refused to run) and he had quietly offered to help Obenshain after he had lost the nomination himself (when he seemed to have nothing to gain from such an offer).

Warner ended up winning that election by the smallest of margins—another of those victories produced by superior campaigning in 1978 that set the stage for the Republican capture of the Senate in 1980. Warner was expected to be a lightweight as senator, but in fact he has turned in a stronger performance than anticipated. On the Armed Services Committee, his service as secretary of the Navy seems to have given him some genuine expertise as well as a strong propensity to emphasize Navy programs, but he is known as well as one of the strongest supporters of the MX missile system and the proposed basing system in the Nevada and Utah desert and chairs the subcommittee that handles it. As might be expected, he believes there should be higher defense spending, especially for the Navy. Warner is the fourth-ranking Republican on the committee, with as much seniority in two years as his colleague Harry Byrd, Jr., accumulated in 15; he is younger than Chairman John Tower and much younger than the next two Republicans, Strom Thurmond and Barry Goldwater. Warner serves also on the Energy and Natural Resources Committee, where he supports deregulation of energy prices and increased exploration for mineral resources.

Virginia's senior senator is Harry Byrd, Jr., who was destined for the Senate from the beginning of his career, and who was appointed to the seat when his father resigned. With a distinguished appearance and white hair, he looks like a senator; with his slow-paced, careful tones, he talks like one. He initially had somewhat more trouble in Virginia elections than he must have anticipated but found a winning formula. Byrd had tough competition for the Democratic nomination in 1966; and in 1970, when it appeared that the Democratic primary electorate might reject him, he decided to run as an Independent instead. He had the covert support of many Republican activists, although Governor Holton insisted the party run a candidate, and from the Nixon Administration as well; he won an absolute majority of the vote and easily outclassed his liberal Democratic opponent. The Republicans, pleased to see him reelected, ran no candidate against him in 1976; against the Democrat, former Chief of Naval Operations Elmo Zumwalt, he increased his percentage somewhat from 1970.

There was much talk before the 1980 election that Byrd could have the pivotal vote in the organization of the Senate and speculation that he might vote with the Republicans in re-

1122   VIRGINIA

turn for choice committee positions. But the Republicans unexpectedly achieved a majority without Byrd's help, and with every prospect of increasing their margin in 1982 they do not seem interested in it now. Byrd is in any case not the kind of man to engage in hardheaded bargaining. Like his father, he is parsimonious and concerned about saving the government money. Unlike his father, who chaired the Finance Committee for years, he does not have much impact on major national policies. He seems more interested in matters such as his successful bill to restore posthumously Robert E. Lee's citizenship, and he seems to make no effort to persuade other senators to vote with him. Evidently he sees his duty as showing up and casting votes, but not trying to influence the outcome of any issue in any other way.

Byrd's seat is up in 1982, and the general assumption is that he will be reelected as an Independent. Governor Dalton in early 1981 announced that he would not run, and Congressman Paul Trible — obviously very ambitious for the office — said he would not run against Byrd. Republicans might like to win an extra Republican vote in the Senate, but they must be wary about running a candidate against Byrd lest they split the conservative vote and let a more or less liberal Democrat in. Democrats must be wary lest they run a candidate too liberal to win in any circumstances. So this is not an entirely predictable race: Byrd will turn 68 in 1982, he obviously has limited clout in the Senate, and there is the possibility of spirited and substantial opposition.

Virginia's Republicans have made steady gains in the state's U.S. House delegation since they first won seats in 1952, to the point that today they hold nine of the state's ten seats. They won some by surprising inattentive incumbents and others by replacing a retiring conservative Democrat with a conservative Republican; they recaptured in 1980 the two northern Virginia districts that Democrats had held for six years. Democrats theoretically have control of the redistricting process, but the Democrats in the Virginia legislature are divided among many factions, and they cannot do much to defeat many of the incumbents anyway. The state has had fairly uniform population growth, so that substantial changes in the boundaries are not necessary, and each district may very well end up having the same basic political balance as before.

Census Data Pop. (1980 final) 5,346,279, up 15% in 1970s: 2.36% of U.S. total, 14th largest. Central city, 26%; suburban, 40%. Median 4-person family income, 1978, $20,729, 101% of U.S., 21st highest.

1979 Share of Federal Tax Burden $10,324,000,000; 2.29% of U.S. total, 12th largest.

1979 Share of Federal Outlays $15,079,175,000; 3.26% of U.S. total, 9th largest.

DOD	$6,650,798,000	3d	(6.27%)	HEW	$3,257,830,000	18th	(1.82%)
DOE	$1,126,621,000	2d	(9.58%)	ERDA	$32,188,000	17th	(1.19%)
HUD	$127,245,000	15th	(1.93%)	NASA	$224,659,000	5th	(4.80%)
VA	$528,234,000	13th	(2.55%)	DOT	$424,783,000	13th	(2.57%)
EPA	$125,223,000	14th	(2.36%)	DOC	$108,876,000	8th	(3.44%)
DOI	$148,133,000	10th	(2.67%)	USDA	$362,424,000	29th	(1.51%)

Economic Base Finance, insurance, and real estate; agriculture, notably dairy products, tobacco, cattle, and broilers; textile mill products, especially cotton weaving mills; apparel and other textile products, especially men's and boys' furnishings, and women's and misses' outerwear; chemicals and synthetics; food and kindred products; electrical equipment and supplies.

Political Lineup Governor, John N. Dalton (R). Senators, Harry F. Byrd, Jr. (I) and John W. Warner (R). Representatives, 10 (9 R and 1 D); 10 in 1982. State Senate, 40 (31 D and 9 R); State House of Delegates, 100 (74 D, 25 R, and 1 I).

The Voters

Registration 2,309,181 Total. No party registration.
Employment profile 1970 White collar, 49%. Blue collar, 36%. Service, 12%. Farm, 3%.
Ethnic groups Black 1980, 19%. Hispanic 1980, 1%. Asian 1980, 1%. Total foreign stock 1970, 5%.

Presidential Vote

1980	Reagan (R)	989,609	(53%)
	Carter (D)	752,174	(40%)
	Anderson (I)	95,418	(5%)
1976	Ford (R)	836,554	(49%)
	Carter (D)	813,896	(48%)

SENATORS

Sen. Harry F. Byrd, Jr. (I) Appointed Nov. 12, 1965, elected 1966 as Dem., reelected as Ind., seat up 1982; b. Dec. 20, 1914, Winchester; home, Winchester; Va. Mil. Inst., 1931–33, U. of Va., 1933–35.

Career Newspaper editor; Orchardist; Navy, WWII; Va. Senate, 1948–65.

Offices 245 RSOB, 202-224-4024. Also Winchester 22601, 703-662-7745.

Committees *Armed Services* (4th). Subcommittees: Tactical Warfare; Sea Power and Force Projection; Manpower and Personnel.

Finance (2d). Subcommittees: Taxation and Debt Management; International Trade; Estate and Gift Taxation.

Joint Committee on Taxation (5th).

Group Ratings

	ADA	COPE	PC	LCV	CFA	RPN	NAB	NSI	NTU	ACA	ACU
1980	22	21	33	16	0	—	100	80	80	69	86
1979	0	10	29	—	14	—	—	—	75	74	74
1978	10	11	25	35	20	40	100	90	50	100	92

Key Votes

1) Draft Registn $	FOR	6) Fair Housng Cloture	AGN	11) Cut Socl Incr Defns	FOR
2) Ban $ to Nicrgua	AGN	7) Ban $ Rape Abortns	AGN	12) Income Tax Indexing	AGN
3) Dlay MX Missile	AGN	8) Cap on Food Stmp $	FOR	13) Lim Spdg 21% GNP	FOR
4) Nuclr Mortorium	AGN	9) New US Dep Edcatn	AGN	14) Incr Wndfll Prof Tax	AGN
5) Alaska Lands Bill	AGN	10) Cut OSHA Inspctns	FOR	15) Chryslr Loan Grntee	AGN

1124   VIRGINIA

Election Results

1976 general	Harry F. Byrd, Jr. (I)	890,778	(57%)	($802,928)
	Elmo R. (Bud) Zumwalt (D)	596,009	(38%)	($443,107)
	Martin H. Perper (I)	70,559	(5%)	
1976 primary	Harry F. Byrd, Jr., qualified for ballot as Independent			
1970 general	Harry F. Byrd, Jr. (I)	506,327	(53%)	
	George C. Rawlings, Jr. (D)......	294,582	(31%)	
	Ray Garland (R)	144,765	(15%)	

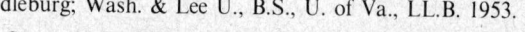

Sen. John W. Warner (R) Elected 1978, seat up 1984; b. Feb. 18, 1927, Washington, D.C.; home, Middleburg; Wash. & Lee U., B.S., U. of Va., LL.B. 1953.

Career Navy, WWII; Law Clerk, U.S. Ct. of Appeals Chf. Judge E. Barrett Prettyman, 1953-54; Practicing atty., 1954-56, 1960-69; Asst. U.S. Atty, 1956-60; Cattle farm owner and operator, 1961-; U.S. Secy. of Navy, 1972-74; Dir., Am. Rev. Bicenten. Commn., 1974-77.

Offices 405 RSOB, 202-224-2023. Also Rm. 8000 Fed. Bldg., Richmond 23240, 804-782-2579.

Committees *Armed Services* (4th). Subcommittees: Military Construction; Tactical Warfare; Strategic and Theatre Nuclear Forces (Chairman).

Energy and Natural Resources (6th). Subcommittees: Energy Research and Development; Energy and Mineral Resources (Chairman); Public Lands and Reserved Water.

Rules and Administration (6th).

Joint Committee on Printing (2d).

Group Ratings

	ADA	COPE	PC	LCV	CFA	RPN	NAB	NSI	NTU	ACA	ACU
1980	22	21	27	27	13	—	100	80	51	77	86
1979	5	10	15	—	10	—	—	—	56	83	91

Key Votes

1) Draft Registn $	FOR	6) Fair Housng Cloture	AGN	11) Cut Socl Incr Defns	FOR
2) Ban $ to Nicrgua	AGN	7) Ban $ Rape Abortns	FOR	12) Income Tax Indexing	FOR
3) Dlay MX Missile	AGN	8) Cap on Food Stmp $	FOR	13) Lim Spdg 21% GNP	FOR
4) Nuclr Mortorium	AGN	9) New US Dep Edcatn	AGN	14) Incr Wndfll Prof Tax	AGN
5) Alaska Lands Bill	FOR	10) Cut OSHA Inspctns	FOR	15) Chryslr Loan Grntee	AGN

Election Results

1978 general	John W. Warner (R)............	613,232	(50%)	($2,897,237)
	Andrew P. Miller (D)	608,511	(50%)	($832,773)
1978 primary	John W. Warner (R), nominated by Republican Party Richard Obenshain (R), nominated by convention			
1972 general	William Lloyd Scott (R)	718,337	(51%)	($619,908)
	William B. Spong, Jr. (D)	643,963	(46%)	($380,921)

GOVERNOR

Gov. John N. Dalton (R) Elected 1977, term expires Jan. 1982; b. July 11, 1931, Emporia; Col. of Wm. and Mary, B.A. 1953, U. of Va., J.D. 1957.

Career Army, 1953–54; Practicing atty., 1957–; Va. House of Delegates, 1965–73; Va. Senate, 1973–74; Lt. Gov. of Va., 1974–78.

Offices State Capitol, Richmond 23219, 804-786-2211.

Election Results

1977 gen.	John N. Dalton (R)	699,302	(56%)
	Henry Howell (D)	541,319	(43%)
1977 prim.	John N. Dalton (R), nominated by convention		
1973 gen.	Mills E. Godwin, Jr. (R) . . .	525,075	(51%)
	Henry Howell (I)	510,103	(49%)

FIRST DISTRICT

The 1st congressional district is part of Tidewater Virginia, the lowlands by the wide tidal marshes of the Atlantic Ocean and Chesapeake Bay. The district includes the southern tip of the Delmarva Peninsula, site of the annual roundup of wild Chincoteague ponies and the rural Northern Neck counties that have changed little since George Washington's time — when they produced such worthies as Washington himself and the various Lees. But the district's population is concentrated not in these essentially rural areas but in the Hampton Roads area, where two-thirds of the 1st district's residents live, most of them in Newport News and Hampton, which have more than 120,000 residents each.

This has been a fast-growing, industrialized area that owes much of its prosperity to the federal government. Hampton Roads — the strait that separates Newport News and Hampton on the north from Norfolk and Portsmouth on the south — is one of the best natural harbors on the Atlantic seaboard and is the headquarters of the Navy's Atlantic Fleet. Most of the naval bases are on the south side of the Roads, but here in the 1st is Tenneco's Newport News Shipbuilding and Dry Dock Company, which for years has been one of the nation's largest shipbuilders, and one heavily dependent on Navy business. Altogether the Defense Department has regularly spent more than $500 million a year in this district — obviously the basis of its current economy.

The current congressman, Republican Paul Trible, was a surprise winner in this seat when he first ran in 1976, at age 29. The Democratic incumbent had retired, and most attention was centered on the Democratic primary; Trible outhustled and outcampaigned the Democrat and won. He built on his own rural base and also did well in Newport News and Hampton. That same formula has paid off for Trible ever since. He has served on the Armed Services Committee and fought hard and effectively — surprisingly so for a member of the minority party — for the interests of the district. He is, naturally enough, a booster of the Navy and of Newport News Shipbuilding; he is ranking Republican on the Military Installations and Facilities Subcommittee. On domestic issues, he is a solid backer of Republican programs and serves now on the Budget Committee. His enthusiasm and hard work have

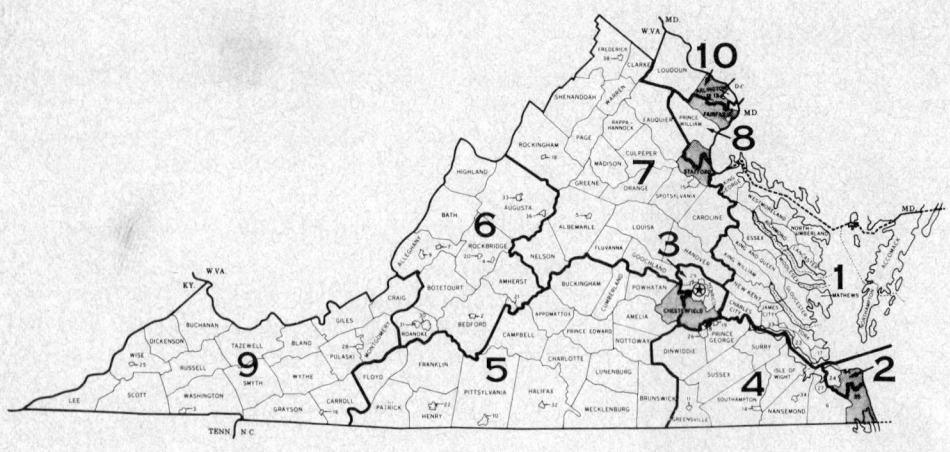

paid off on election day; he won easily in 1978 against a war hero, although Trible himself had no experience in the military, and in 1980 had no Democratic opponent.

Trible should have no difficulty holding this seat in the 1980s. He may, however, run for the Senate in 1982, particularly if Harry Byrd, Jr., decides to retire at age 68. Trible is indeed the most plausible Senate candidate of any of Virginia's Republican House members and so may very well move onto the Senate sometime in the decade.

Census Data   Pop. (1980 final) 517,181, up 11% in 1970s. Median family income, 1970, $8,490, 89% of U.S.

The Voters

   Employment profile 1970   White collar, 45%. Blue collar, 38%. Service, 14%. Farm, 3%.
   Ethnic groups   Black 1980, 31%. Hispanic 1980, 1%. Asian 1980, 1%. Total foreign stock 1970, 5%.

Presidential Vote

1980	Reagan (R)	88,022	(50%)
	Carter (D)	77,510	(44%)
	Anderson (I)	7,324	(4%)
1976	Ford (R)	75,601	(47%)
	Carter (D)	80,485	(50%)

Rep. Paul S. Trible, Jr. (R) Elected 1976; b. Dec. 29, 1946, Baltimore, Md.; home, Tappahannock; Hampden-Sydney Col., B.A. 1968, Wash. & Lee U., J.D. 1971.

Career   Law Clerk, U.S. Dist. Judge Albert Bryan, Jr., 1971–72; Asst. U.S. Atty. for East. Dist. of Va., 1972–74; Essex Co. Commonwealth's Atty., 1974–76.

Offices   326 CHOB, 202-225-4261. Also Tower Box 59, Exec. Tower, 2101 Executive Dr., Hampton 23666, 804-838-3287.

Committees   *Armed Services* (10th). Subcommittees: Military Installations and Facilities; Seapower and Strategic and Critical Materials.

Budget (7th).

Group Ratings

	ADA	COPE	PC	LCV	CFA	RPN	NAB	NSI	NTU	ACA	ACU
1980	6	16	17	13	7	—	100	100	55	79	78
1979	5	10	13	13	7	—	—	—	52	92	92
1978	20	21	28	30	18	50	92	100	25	88	79

Key Votes

1) Draft Registn $	FOR	6) Fair Hsg DOJ Enfrc	AGN	11) Cut Socl Incr Dfns $	FOR
2) Ban $ to Nicrgua	FOR	7) Lim PAC Contrbtns	AGN	12) Hosptl Cost Controls	AGN
3) Dlay MX Missile	AGN	8) Cap on Food Stmp $	FOR	13) Gasln Ctrls & Allctns	AGN
4) Nuclr Mortorium	AGN	9) New US Dep Edcatn	FOR	14) Lim Wndfll Prof Tax	FOR
5) Alaska Lands Bill	FOR	10) Cut OSHA $		FOR	15) Chryslr Loan Grntee	AGN

Election Results

1980 general	Paul S. Trible, Jr. (R)	130,130	(90%)	($38,697)
	Sharon D. Grant (I)	13,688	(10%)	($0)
1980 primary	Paul S. Trible, Jr. (R),			
	nominated by convention			
1978 general	Paul S. Trible, Jr. (R)	89,158	(72%)	($257,257)
	Lew Puller (D)	34,578	(28%)	($134,051)

SECOND DISTRICT

Norfolk, Virginia, is the headquarters of the Navy's Atlantic Fleet. Within its city limits are one of the world's largest naval bases and more than half a dozen other naval installations, not to mention the dozen or so military facilities in nearby Portsmouth, Virginia Beach, or Hampton and Newport News across Hampton Roads. The naval buildup during and after World War II made Norfolk what it is today. Before the war it was a city of 144,000 with perhaps another 100,000 in adjacent areas; today Norfolk is the center of an urban area of nearly a million people. Suburban homes have been built in the low-lying land near the wide inlets off the bay, and shopping centers have sprouted up at freeway interchanges. During the 1960s and 1970s the area of fastest growth has been in the east, in the relatively high-income suburb of Virginia Beach.

Politically Norfolk is a working-class town. For the most part Navy personnel do not vote here, and their absence from the electorate shows up in low turnout figures. The Norfolk voter is more likely to be a blue collar worker, who moved here from a small town in Southside Virginia or eastern North Carolina looking for a job. This is a definitely segregated city, and the large black minority is reliably Democratic in most elections. The whites are a swing vote: they have gone for George Wallace and Richard Nixon, but they have also given big margins to Jimmy Carter and Henry Howell.

Virginia Beach is quite different politically. If Norfolk, with its rough bars and burly downtown, appeals to the enlisted man, Virginia Beach caters to officers — and their families. The atmosphere here is comfortably suburban, although many of the new subdivisions and shopping centers have been reclaimed only recently from the swamp. The old beach resort — always a family-style place — is overshadowed by the suburban territory just inland. As the Navy has become staffed increasingly with experts and officers and less with manual laborers and enlisted men, so too the Norfolk area has become less centralized in Norfolk and more suburbanized in Virginia Beach. In the 1980 election, Virginia Beach cast more votes than Norfolk, and its solid margin for Reagan easily overcame Norfolk's margin for Carter.

Norfolk and most of Virginia Beach make up Virginia's 2d congressional district. Historically, this is a Democratic seat; it went for Hubert Humphrey in 1968. But now, as Virginia Beach has eclipsed Norfolk, the district has become essentially a Republican constituency. That transformation was anticipated by the election of Congressman William Whitehurst here in 1968, when a conservative Democratic incumbent retired. Whitehurst was a professor at a local college and commentator on a local television station when he was first elected. His major political assets have been his seat on the House Armed Services Committee and a willingness to return frequently to the district. He is now second in seniority among Republicans on that body and ranking minority member of its Readiness Subcommittee. As one might expect, he favors increased defense expenditures and is generally considered partial to the Navy. Of course he looks after the interests of Norfolk and its naval bases. Whitehurst has been reelected easily or without opposition and seems likely to continue to do so. He has shown no inclination to run for statewide office. If Republicans should achieve their dream of controlling the House in the 1980s, he has a good chance of becoming chairman of the House Armed Services Committee.

Census Data   Pop. (1980 final) 494,049, up 6% in 1970s. Median family income, 1970, $8,733, 91% of U.S.

The Voters

Employment profile 1970   White collar, 55%. Blue collar, 30%. Service, 15%. Farm, -%.
Ethnic groups   Black 1980, 24%. Hispanic 1980, 2%. Asian 1980, 3%. Total foreign stock 1970, 8%. UK, 1%.

Presidential Vote

1980	Reagan (R)	71,129	(51%)
	Carter (D)	57,164	(41%)
	Anderson (I)	7,728	(6%)
1976	Ford (R)	60,261	(47%)
	Carter (D)	62,494	(49%)

Rep. G. William Whitehurst (R) Elected 1968; b. Mar. 12, 1925, Norfolk; home, Virginia Beach; Wash. & Lee U., B.A. 1950, U. of Va., M.A. 1951, W.Va. U., Ph.D. 1962.

Career   Navy, WWII; Prof. of History, Old Dominion Col., 1950–68, Dean of Students, 1963–68; News analyst, WTAR-TV, Norfolk, 1962–68.

Offices   2469 RHOB, 202-225-4215. Also Rm. 815 Fed. Bldg., Norfolk 23510, 804-441-3340.

Committees   *Armed Services* (2d). Subcommittees: Military Installations and Facilities; Readiness.

Permanent Select Committee on Intelligence (4th). Subcommittee: Program and Budget Authorization.

Group Ratings

	ADA	COPE	PC	LCV	CFA	RPN	NAB	NSI	NTU	ACA	ACU
1980	0	12	17	13	7	—	100	89	54	87	68
1979	16	11	13	21	4	—	—	—	52	88	83
1978	15	25	23	33	14	55	100	100	21	89	79

Key Votes

1) Draft Registn $	FOR	6) Fair Hsg DOJ Enfrc	AGN	11) Cut Socl Incr Dfns $	FOR
2) Ban $ to Nicrgua	FOR	7) Lim PAC Contrbtns	AGN	12) Hosptl Cost Controls	AGN
3) Dlay MX Missile	AGN	8) Cap on Food Stmp $	FOR	13) Gasln Ctrls & Allctns	—
4) Nuclr Mortorium	AGN	9) New US Dep Edcatn	AGN	14) Lim Wndfll Prof Tax	FOR
5) Alaska Lands Bill	FOR	10) Cut OSHA $	FOR	15) Chryslr Loan Grntee	FOR

Election Results

1980 general	G. William Whitehurst (R)	97,319	(90%)	($43,672)
	Kenneth P. Morrison (I)	11,003	(10%)	
1980 primary	G. William Whitehurst (R), nominated by convention			
1978 general	G. William Whitehurst (R), unopp.			($37,796)

THIRD DISTRICT

Richmond, the capital of the Confederacy, remains the capital of Virginia and a major tobacco producing center. In many ways Richmond is Virginia's most important city, although it is eclipsed in size by the Washington suburbs and the Tidewater area around Norfolk. But Richmond is not only the state capital; it is also Virginia's ideological center and the headquarters of its major economic interests. The state government continues in the hands of men sympathetic to friends who run the Virginia Electric and Power Company and the big Richmond banks. The Richmond newspapers provide a sometimes stylishly articulated defense of the status quo and of free enterprise; during the 1950s, they provided the most intellectually phrased defense of racial segregation. In the words of columnist Mark Shields, Richmond is a famous center of social rest.

Virginia's 3d congressional district consists of Richmond and almost all of its two principal suburban counties, Henrico and Chesterfield. This was the area covered by the Richmond school busing case in the early 1970s, a decision that was ultimately reversed to the great relief of Richmond area whites. There is now a black majority in the city—which has controlled the city council because members are elected by district—and sometimes the city goes for liberal candidates; Jimmy Carter carried it with 55% in both 1976 and 1980. But the Richmond suburbs, nearly all white, are among the most conservative areas in the United States. Carter was beaten 2½-1 here in 1980, and some Democrats have lost the suburban counties by margins as high as 7-1.

The Richmond area's traditional political preference is conservative Democratic; its present voting behavior is Republican. Long after it went Republican in statewide elections, it was still electing a Democrat to Congress; that ended when incumbent David Satterfield retired in 1980. Satterfield's retirement was probably due more to events in the House than in Richmond. His very conservative views are far out of line with those of most House Democrats; and no one even seemed to think it worthy of comment when in 1979 he was passed over for the chairmanship of the Health Subcommittee, one of the most important House panels.

The succession to Satterfield's seat was more or less automatic. Thomas Bliley had been a nominal Democrat while mayor of Richmond between 1970 and 1977; now he ran for the House as a Republican. He captured the party's nomination without a primary and easily won the general election, although the Democrat barely carried Richmond. Bliley, a mem-

1130   VIRGINIA

ber of the Energy and Commerce and District of Columbia Committees, can be expected to remain in the House for some time.

Census Data   Pop. (1980 final) 500,491, up 8% in 1970s. Median family income, 1970, $9,945, 104% of U.S.

The Voters

Employment profile 1970   White collar, 55%. Blue collar, 32%. Service, 13%. Farm, –%.
Ethnic groups   Black 1980, 30%. Hispanic 1980, 1%. Asian 1980, 1%. Total foreign stock 1970, 5%.

Presidential Vote

1980	Reagan (R)	109,864	(55%)
	Carter (D)	78,826	(40%)
	Anderson (I)	7,704	(4%)
1976	Ford (R)	101,624	(56%)
	Carter (D)	77,387	(42%)

Rep. Thomas J. Bliley, Jr. (R) Elected 1980; b. Jan. 28, 1932, Chesterfield Co.; home, Richmond; Georgetown U., B.A. 1952.

Career Navy, 1952–55; Owner, funeral home, 1955–80; Richmond City Cncl., 1968, Vice Mayor, 1968–70, Mayor, 1970–77.

Offices 214 CHOB, 202-225-2815. Also 510 E. Main St., Richmond 23219, 804-771-2809.

Committees *District of Columbia* (3d). Subcommittees: Fiscal Affairs and Health; Judiciary and Education.

Energy and Commerce (18th). Subcommittees: Health and the Environment; Telecommunications, Consumer Protection, and Finance.

Group Ratings and Key Votes: Newly Elected

Election Results

1980 general	Thomas J. Bliley, Jr. (R)	96,524	(52%)	($259,131)
	John A. Mapp (D)	60,962	(33%)	($0)
	Howard H. Carwile (I)	19,549	(10%)	($0)
	James B. Turney (I)	9,852	(5%)	($10,432)
1980 primary	Thomas J. Bliley, Jr. (R), nominated by convention			
1978 general	David E. Satterfield III (D)	104,550	(88%)	($5,626)
	Alan R. Ogden (I)	14,453	(12%)	

FOURTH DISTRICT

The 4th congressional district is part of Southside Virginia — the southern part of the state that is also the northern edge of the Deep South. This is not, however, one of those sections of the Deep South where the rich white community leaders always dominate. The southern coastal region, where the flat lands that once produced tobacco now produce peanuts, also contains some of Virginia's grittiest cities. Both rural Southside counties and the cities have large black populations. The 4th includes the blue collar city of Portsmouth, right next to Norfolk, and the blue collar suburb of Chesapeake; the old city of Petersburg, a major urban center when it was the focus of several Civil War battles and not much bigger now; and

Hopewell, the site in the middle 1970s of the dumping of the chemical kepone into the James River, which forced bans on fishing in Chesapeake Bay.

The 4th is in fact one of the most Democratic Virginia districts, the only one to favor Jimmy Carter in the 1980 general election. Yet throughout the 1970s the district has been Republican in congressional elections. Congressman Robert Daniel, a former CIA agent and local farmer and businessman, was first elected in 1972, with a minority vote in a six-candidate race. In the next two elections he had serious Democratic challenges but managed to hold on; in 1978 and 1980 he won with ease. Daniel is one of the large group of Virginians who serve on the Armed Services Committee, where he supports higher defense spending and tends particularly to favor the Navy. Redistricting will require some additions to the 4th district, and almost any possible change is likely to benefit Daniel.

Census Data Pop. (1980 final) 511,154, up 10% in 1970s. Median family income, 1970, $8,294, 87% of U.S.

The Voters

Employment profile 1970 White collar, 39%. Blue collar, 43%. Service, 15%. Farm, 3%.
Ethnic groups Black 1980, 38%. Hispanic 1980, 1%. Asian 1980, 1%. Total foreign stock 1970, 3%.

Presidential Vote

1980	Reagan (R)	76,999	(46%)
	Carter (D)	84,300	(50%)
	Anderson (I)	4,647	(3%)
1976	Ford (R)	62,961	(40%)
	Carter (D)	89,112	(57%)

Rep. Robert W. Daniel, Jr. (R) Elected 1972; b. Mar. 17, 1936, Richmond; home, Spring Grove; U. of Va., B.A. 1958, Columbia U., M.B.A. 1961.

Career Practicing financial analyst, 1961–62; Instructor of Economics, U. of Richmond Business Sch., 1963; CIA, 1964–68; Owner and operator, Brandon agricultural enterprise.

Offices 2236 RHOB, 202-225-6365. Also 209 P.O. Bldg., Petersburg 23803, 804-732-2544.

Committee *Armed Services* (7th). Subcommittees: Investigations; Research and Development.

Group Ratings

	ADA	COPE	PC	LCV	CFA	RPN	NAB	NSI	NTU	ACA	ACU
1980	6	10	23	22	7		100	100	63	100	94
1979	0	10	10	3	4	—	—	—	63	100	97
1978	10	11	13	17	18	58	100	100	36	93	91

Key Votes

1) Draft Registn $	FOR	6) Fair Hsg DOJ Enfrc	AGN	11) Cut Socl Incr Dfns $	FOR
2) Ban $ to Nicrgua	FOR	7) Lim PAC Contrbtns	AGN	12) Hosptl Cost Controls	AGN
3) Dlay MX Missile	AGN	8) Cap on Food Stmp $	FOR	13) Gasln Ctrls & Allctns	AGN
4) Nuclr Mortorium	AGN	9) New US Dep Edcatn	AGN	14) Lim Wndfll Prof Tax	FOR
5) Alaska Lands Bill	AGN	10) Cut OSHA $	FOR	15) Chryslr Loan Grntee	AGN

Election Results

1980 general	Robert W. Daniel, Jr. (R)	92,557	(61%)	($186,334)
	Cecil Y. Jenkins (D)	59,930	(39%)	($84,109)
1980 primary	Robert W. Daniel, Jr. (R), nominated by convention			
1978 general	Robert W. Daniel, Jr. (R), unopp.			($31,644)

FIFTH DISTRICT

The 5th congressional district of Virginia covers most of Southside Virginia, from the Richmond city limits out to the Blue Ridge near Roanoke. The eastern counties are flat and humid and the most heavily black part of the district. Slowly, as the land gets hillier, the terrain rises into the Piedmont and moves past the textile and furniture manufacturing centers of Danville and Martinsville. As one goes west, there is more livestock and less tobacco, more whites with mountain accents and fewer blacks. Altogether the 5th is 26% black — significantly less than the figure for the 4th district, which takes in Southside and Tidewater counties just to the east.

Southside Virginia was always a stronghold for Byrd Democrats, with its politics firmly in the hands of prosperous bankers and planters who still remember the Civil War. More recently Southside has fallen into the racially polarized patterns that characterize the Deep South. This is one of two Virginia districts that went for George Wallace in 1968 and the one that gave him his largest percentage here. Since then, at least some of the Wallace vote has been trending Republican. In the close presidential race of 1976 and the close Senate race of 1978, the Republican candidates won small margins in the 5th district — and were able to carry the state.

For more than twelve years the 5th district has been represented by the last survivor in the Virginia delegation of the Byrd Democratic tradition. Dan Daniel, a former executive at Danville's Dan River Mills, was first elected in 1968 over spirited Republican and Independent competition; since then he has won easily or has been unopposed. Daniel is a member of the District of Columbia Committee, where his voting record may be confused with that of fellow committee member Robert Daniel, the Republican congressman from the 4th district. Dan Daniel is also an active member of Armed Services, a believer in higher defense expenditures, and chairman of the new Readiness Subcommittee, a body of great significance given the current state of the armed forces and the desire of many in the Reagan Administration to establish a credible American force in the Persian Gulf.

Census Data Pop. (1980 final) 545,615, up 18% in 1970s. Median family income, 1970, $7,471, 78% of U.S.

The Voters

Employment profile 1970 White collar, 32%. Blue collar, 52%. Service, 10%. Farm, 6%.
Ethnic groups Black 1980, 26%. Hispanic 1980, 1%. Total foreign stock 1970, 1%.

Presidential Vote

1980	Reagan (R)	106,318	(57%)
	Carter (D)	74,486	(40%)
	Anderson (I)	4,254	(2%)
1976	Ford (R)	82,011	(51%)
	Carter (D)	75,894	(46%)

Rep. W. C. (Dan) **Daniel** (D) Elected 1968; b. May 12, 1914, Chatham; home, Danville.

Career Asst. to Bd. Chmn., Dan River Mills, Inc., and various other business positions, 1939–68; Va. House of Delegates, 1959–68.

Offices 2368 RHOB, 202-225-4711. Also 315 P.O. Bldg., Danville 24541, 804-792-1280.

Committee *Armed Services* (8th). Subcommittees: Investigations; Readiness (Chairman).

Group Ratings

	ADA	COPE	PC	LCV	CFA	RPN	NAB	NSI	NTU	ACA	ACU
1980	6	10	23	17	7	—	92	100	61	92	89
1979	5	10	5	3	0	—	—	—	56	100	95
1978	0	5	13	13	9	50	100	100	36	96	96

Key Votes

1) Draft Registn $	FOR	6) Fair Hsg DOJ Enfrc	AGN	11) Cut Socl Incr Dfns $	FOR
2) Ban $ to Nicrgua	FOR	7) Lim PAC Contrbtns	AGN	12) Hosptl Cost Controls	AGN
3) Dlay MX Missile	AGN	8) Cap on Food Stmp $	FOR	13) Gasln Ctrls & Allctns	AGN
4) Nuclr Mortorium	AGN	9) New US Dep Edcatn	FOR	14) Lim Wndfll Prof Tax	FOR
5) Alaska Lands Bill	AGN	10) Cut OSHA $		FOR	15) Chryslr Loan Grntee	AGN

Election Results

1980 general	W. C. (Dan) Daniel (D)	112,143 (100%)	($7,747)
1980 primary	W. C. (Dan) Daniel (D), nominated by convention		
1978 general	W. C. (Dan) Daniel (D), unopp. . .		($4,991)

SIXTH DISTRICT

Traditionally the most Republican parts of Virginia are in the great valley west of the Blue Ridge around Roanoke. Because this fertile land was never given over to slave-tended plantations, the hardy farmers here were not especially sympathetic to the Confederacy. In the hundred years that followed the Civil War, the Roanoke area was usually the most Republican — or least Democratic — part of the state. Unlike places farther north in the valley, this part of Virginia was always suspicious of the Byrd machine and, to some extent, of its alliance with the state's largest and most powerful economic interests. There has always been a tinge of populism, of insurgency to the Republicanism of these hills; it is not the political faith of a comfortable majority, as it was in the rich farmlands of the Midwest, but of people who believe they have been excluded from power.

The 6th congressional district is centered on Roanoke and this vestigially Republican part of Virginia. Its traditional Republicanism can be seen by its presidential performance in 1968, when it was the only Virginia district to give Richard Nixon an absolute majority. In more recent elections, as the state's Republicans have made alliances with former Byrd

Democrats, the 6th is no longer the most Republican part of the state, although some traces of insurgency persist.

That is true too of the congressional career of 6th district Congressman Caldwell Butler. First elected in 1972 to replace a Republican who had been elected in the first Eisenhower year and who had made the district safely Republican, Butler came from the mountain tradition; he was the law partner of Governor Linwood Holton, who earned the enduring wrath of many Virginia Republicans by escorting his daughter to a school integrated by court order. On most issues Butler is a conventional Republican. He favors free enterprise and market mechanisms over government decision making, he is cautious about new federal spending programs, he tends to favor tough measures against crime. But he is also a careful lawyer. As a member of the Judiciary Committee during the impeachment hearings, he studied the evidence thoroughly, reportedly aided by his wife, who read *All the President's Men* to him in the evening. Butler came to the conclusion that Nixon should be impeached, and he was one of those who worked to draw up articles of impeachment that Republicans and southern Democrats could agree on. He was the leader in the fight to block Reagan Administration cuts in legal assistance to the poor. In the public hearings his rapid-fire delivery, his peppery voice, his occasional sense of humor, and his lawyer's instinct for the main issue helped to cinch the case against the president.

As a matter of strict politics, Butler was probably the least likely impeachment vote on the committee. He was a Republican in a Republican district in the South, where Nixon's popularity sagged least. Faced as he had been in 1972 with an Independent as well as a Democratic opponent, Butler saw his share of the vote drop from 55% to 46%. Since then, he has not been presented with such grave issues and on most matters has voted with most Republicans. He was reelected comfortably in 1976 and without opposition in 1978 and 1980.

Census Data   Pop. (1980 final) 501,748, up 8% in 1970s. Median family income, 1970, $8,594, 90% of U.S.

The Voters

Employment profile 1970   White collar, 43%. Blue collar, 42%. Service, 13%. Farm, 2%.
Ethnic groups   Black 1980, 12%. Hispanic 1980, 1%. Total foreign stock 1970, 2%.

Presidential Vote

1980	Reagan (R)	96,026	(53%)
	Carter (D)	74,842	(42%)
	Anderson (I)	6,566	(4%)
1976	Ford (R)	85,448	(49%)
	Carter (D)	82,077	(48%)

Rep. M. Caldwell Butler (R) Elected 1972; b. June 22, 1925, Roanoke; home, Roanoke; U. of Richmond, A.B. 1948, U. of Va., LL.B. 1950.

Career Practicing atty., 1950–72; Va. House of Delegates, 1962–71, Minor. Ldr., 1966–71.

Offices 2330 RHOB, 202-225-5431. Also 313 U.S.P.O. and Courthouse Bldg., 900 Church St., Lynchburg 24505, 804-845-1378.

Committees *Government Operations* (7th). Subcommittees: Legislation and National Security; Manpower and Housing.

Judiciary (4th). Subcommittees: Courts, Civil Liberties, and the Administration of Justice; Monopolies and Commercial Law.

Group Ratings

	ADA	COPE	PC	LCV	CFA	RPN	NAB	NSI	NTU	ACA	ACU
1980	17	16	20	17	14	—	83	78	60	91	72
1979	16	25	13	14	4	—	—	—	55	83	68
1978	10	0	18	8	14	91	100	90	36	96	96

Key Votes

1) Draft Registn $	FOR	6) Fair Hsg DOJ Enfrc	FOR	11) Cut Socl Incr Dfns $	FOR
2) Ban $ to Nicrgua	AGN	7) Lim PAC Contrbtns	AGN	12) Hosptl Cost Controls	AGN
3) Dlay MX Missile	AGN	8) Cap on Food Stmp $	FOR	13) Gasln Ctrls & Allctns	AGN
4) Nuclr Mortorium	AGN	9) New US Dep Edcatn	AGN	14) Lim Wndfll Prof Tax	FOR
5) Alaska Lands Bill	AGN	10) Cut OSHA $	FOR	15) Chryslr Loan Grntee	AGN

Election Results

1980 general	M. Caldwell Butler (R)	123,125	(99%)	($114,929)
1980 primary	M. Caldwell Butler (R), nominated by convention			
1978 general	M. Caldwell Butler (R), unopposed			($16,307)

SEVENTH DISTRICT

East and west of the Blue Ridge Mountains in northern Virginia is some of the most beautiful countryside in the United States. Away from the tidal flatlands, the climate is cool and salubrious; the flowering bushes and trees in the spring provide an even greater riot of color than the turning leaves in the fall; the mountains to the west protect against icy blasts. The Piedmont, on the eastern side of the Blue Ridge, was once the property of large landowners, such as Lord Fairfax, George Washington's patron; much of the land here now is the property of some of the nation's wealthiest families, who spend their winters riding in the hunt. West of the Blue Ridge is the Shenandoah Valley, once the granary of the Confederacy and still marvelously fertile land, although now more often given over to orchards than to grain. The region's major towns — Winchester and Harrisonburg in the Valley, Charlottesville and Fredericksburg in the Piedmont, none with a population as high as 40,000 — still retain an old-fashioned air at least in the narrow streets of their downtowns, although a McDonald's culture has developed on the bypass roads on their outskirts.

This is the land of the 7th congressional district of Virginia — the northern part of the state beyond the Washington metropolitan area. It was the home of three presidents (Jefferson, Madison, and Monroe) and the scene of more carnage and killing in the Civil War than any other area of comparable size in the nation. The district is also the home turf of the 20th-century Byrd dynasty. The late Senator Harry Byrd, Sr., developed one of the world's largest and most productive apple orchards in the Shenandoah Valley and also acquired newspapers in Winchester and Harrisonburg; his son, the current senator, retains these interests. The 7th continues today to be solid Byrd country in most elections — which means that it has long since shifted from its traditional Democratic preference to conservative Republicanism in most presidential and statewide races. This was a solid district for Gerald Ford in 1976, John Dalton in 1977, John Warner (a resident of the hunt country) in 1978, and Ronald Reagan in 1980.

Nowhere has the trend from Byrd Democrat to Ford Republican been better illustrated than in the 7th district's congressional representation. From 1963 to 1971 the congressman here was John Marsh, a nominal Democrat who became a top White House aide to President Ford. Marsh declined to seek renomination in 1970 — the year Byrd first ran as an Independent — because it appeared that liberals had got control of the Democratic primary. The Byrd imprimatur — unofficial, but not open to doubt — went to the Republican nominee, state Senator Kenneth Robinson. Back in 1962 he had nearly defeated Marsh; later he had been elected to the state Senate vacancy caused by the elevation of Harry Byrd, Jr., to the U.S. Senate. The Byrd machine, driven out of the Democratic Party, thus reappeared in Republican guise.

A solid conservative, Robinson serves on the Appropriations Committee and on its Agriculture and Defense Subcommittees. His one tough general election occurred in 1974, when a Democrat held him to 53%. Some observers expected him to have trouble in 1978, but his opponent carried only Fredericksburg, and Robinson won by nearly a 2-1 margin. He was unopposed in 1980. Redistricting will change the shape of the 7th district somewhat but not its political leanings.

Census Data   Pop. (1980 final) 599,915, up 29% in 1970s. Median family income, 1970, $7,952, 83% of U.S.

The Voters

   Employment profile 1970   White collar, 40%. Blue collar, 42%. Service, 13%. Farm, 5%.
   Ethnic groups   Black 1980, 13%. Hispanic 1980, 1%. Total foreign stock 1970, 3%.

Presidential Vote

1980	Reagan (R)	117,538	(57%)
	Carter (D)	74,608	(36%)
	Anderson (I)	9,577	(5%)
1976	Ford (R)	96,884	(54%)
	Carter (D)	79,319	(44%)

Rep. J. Kenneth Robinson (R) Elected 1970; b. May 14, 1916, Winchester; home, Winchester; Va. Polytech. Inst , B.S. 1937.

Career Family fruit growing and packing business, 1937–42; Army, WWII; Dir., Winchester Cold Storage, R & T Packing Corp., Inc., Winchester Apple Growers Assn., and Green Chemical Co.; Va. Senate, 1965–70.

Offices 2233 RHOB, 202-225-6561. Also 112 N. Cameron St., P.O. Box 136, Winchester 22601, 703-667-0990.

Committees *Appropriations* (5th). Subcommittees: Agriculture, Rural Development and Related Agencies; Defense.

Permanent Select Committee on Intelligence (Ranking Member). Subcommittee: Program and Budget Authorization.

Group Ratings

	ADA	COPE	PC	LCV	CFA	RPN	NAB	NSI	NTU	ACA	ACU
1980	6	10	17	13	7	—	100	100	59	92	95
1979	0	10	5	7	0	—	—	—	59	100	97
1978	10	10	18	10	18	67	100	100	36	93	91

Key Votes

1) Draft Registn $	FOR	6) Fair Hsg DOJ Enfrc	AGN	11) Cut Socl Incr Dfns $	FOR
2) Ban $ to Nicrgua	FOR	7) Lim PAC Contrbtns	AGN	12) Hosptl Cost Controls	AGN
3) Dlay MX Missile	AGN	8) Cap on Food Stmp $	FOR	13) Gasln Ctrls & Allctns	AGN
4) Nuclr Mortorium	AGN	9) New US Dep Edcatn	AGN	14) Lim Wndfll Prof Tax	FOR
5) Alaska Lands Bill	AGN	10) Cut OSHA $	FOR	15) Chryslr Loan Grntee	AGN

Election Results

1980 general	J. Kenneth Robinson (R)	139,957	(100%)	($33,173)
1980 primary	J. Kenneth Robinson (R), nominated by convention			
1978 general	J. Kenneth Robinson (R)	84,517	(64%)	($87,087)
	Lewis Fickett (D)	46,950	(36%)	($58,493)

EIGHTH DISTRICT

The 8th congressional district covers the southern portion of the Virginia suburbs of Washington, D.C. Just across the Potomac from Washington is Alexandria, whose old town section recalls the tobacco port George Washington once frequented. Today, it is more significant politically that Alexandria has its own little black ghetto and that about two-thirds of its residents live in multifamily units, usually high-rise apartments. These two groups make Alexandria the most Democratic part of northern Virginia. Beyond Alexandria, in Fairfax County, are the suburbs of Springfield, Annandale, and Mount Vernon. These are affluent places, with large colonial or, occasionally, contemporary houses built for large families; voters here are wary both of new developments and higher taxes, and they have the cautious and sometimes reactionary feelings you find in parents of teenage children. South of Fairfax is Prince William County. Here zoning requirements are less stringent and there are fewer minimum acreage requirements. You could not call this a poor area, but it is where the blue collar and lower-paid federal employees are moving; the cheapest new housing in Metropolitan Washington is in places like this, 30 miles from the White House.

The 8th district was one of the fastest-growing congressional districts in the nation in the 1960s; and despite the efforts of some Fairfax County officials it is still one of the faster-growing areas on the eastern seaboard. The primary reason for this growth is of course the federal government. Federal paychecks have more than doubled since 1960, and here in the 8th about 30% of all wage earners have such checks to cash every two weeks.

In the 1960s, the 8th district spread far into the Virginia countryside. But its fast-growing suburban areas made a political revolution when in 1966 they ousted Congressman Howard Smith in the Democratic primary. Smith was chairman of the House Rules Committee, a reactionary who could often control the pace and substance of House debate by commanding a committee majority—or simply by refusing to convene the committee at all. Smith's political demise was followed by a period of political instability, which continues to this day. The Democrat who beat him in 1966 was beaten in turn by the Republican in the general election—William Scott, later elevated to the Senate and named as the dumbest member of Congress. Scott was succeeded in 1972 in the district by Republican Stanford Parris, who in turn lost to Democrat Herb Harris in 1974, who was beaten himself by Parris in 1980.

Harris and Parris presented a nice contrast in attitudes and issues. Harris had voted mostly with northern Democrats, although he emphasized such issues as federal employees' pay and civil service reform (he was for high pay and against any reforms that would make employees accountable for their work). He also favored home rule for the District but of course opposed any commuter tax. Parris, a kind of old-fashioned Gerald Ford Republican, has exhibited the distrust of old-line suburbanites for the District, but he campaigned mostly on less parochial matters: he argued to this district full of people dependent on government that there should be less government spending and fewer government programs. In 1980, at least, that proved to be a winning platform. Support for Jimmy Carter fell here to 33%, the lowest in any Virginia district. Harris carried Alexandria and its renters by a wide margin, but Parris took the homeowning parts of the district by enough to win, overall, by 1,094 votes.

There is no telling what will happen in — or to — this district in 1982. The one part of the state where redistricting might make a real difference is in northern Virginia. Some liberal Democrats want to create an inner and an outer suburban district; they hope to carry the former and are willing to concede the latter. The greater likelihood, however, is that the 8th will be altered slightly, and that there will be another close race here.

Census Data Pop. (1980 final) 587,054, up 27% in 1970s. Median family income, 1970, $13,146, 137% of U.S.

The Voters

Employment profile 1970 White collar, 68%. Blue collar, 21%. Service, 10%. Farm, 1%.
Ethnic groups Black 1980, 10%. Hispanic 1980, 3%. Asian 1980, 3%. Total foreign stock 1970, 11%. Germany, UK, 1% each.

Presidential Vote

1980	Reagan (R)	113,676	(56%)
	Carter (D)	67,754	(33%)
	Anderson (I)	18,994	(9%)
1976	Ford (R)	83,943	(51%)
	Carter (D)	78,914	(47%)

Rep. Stanford E. Parris (R) Elected 1980; b. Sept. 9, 1929, Champaign, Ill.; home, Woodbridge; U. of Ill., B.S. 1950, Geo. Wash. U., J.D. 1958.

Career Air Force; Commercial pilot; Practicing atty.; Fairfax Co. Bd. of Supervisors, 1964–67; Va. House of Delegates, 1969–72; U.S. House of Reps., 1972–74; Secy., Commonwealth of Va., 1978; Dir., Va. Fed. Liaison Ofc., 1978–80.

Offices 428 CHOB, 202-225-4376. Also 6701 Lois Dale Rd., Suite 116, Springfield 22150, 703-922-7640.

Committees *Banking, Finance and Urban Affairs* (12th). Subcommittees: Economic Stabilization; Housing and Community Development; International Trade, Investment and Monetary Policy.

District of Columbia (2d). Subcommittees: Fiscal Affairs and Health; Government Operations and Metropolitan Affairs.

Group Ratings and Key Votes: Newly Elected

Election Results

1980 general	Stanford E. Parris (R)	95,624	(49%)	($410,291)
	Herbert E. Harris II (D)	94,530	(48%)	($238,680)
1980 primary	Stanford E. Parris (R)	9,930	(60%)	
	Robert L. Thoburn (R).........	6,564	(40%)	($33,055)
1978 general	Herbert E. Harris II (D)	56,137	(51%)	($164,352)
	John F. Herrity (R)............	52,396	(47%)	($223,973)

NINTH DISTRICT

The southwestern corner of Virginia is perhaps the only part of the nation sometimes known in ordinary discourse by the number of its congressional district: the Fighting Ninth. Part of the Appalachian mountain country, the 9th probably has more in common with neighboring eastern Kentucky or Tennessee than with the rest of Virginia. It is not, however, one of the poorest regions of Appalachia. Except for a few counties, the area has never been as dependent on coal as southern West Virginia; and it has benefited recently from economic development in the valley that reaches from the Shenandoah to Knoxville, Tennessee, along Interstate 81. The mountain area of southwestern Virginia is a place with its own cultural traditions, where the federal government can still mean the hated revenuers, and where the kind of music most favored is still what is heard from fiddlers and guitar, banjo, and mandolin pickers at the annual Galax Old Time Fiddlers' Convention.

The Fighting Ninth never did cotton much to the Byrd organization. In fact, its Republican tradition goes back to the days of the Civil War, when the virtually all-white mountains had little use for slavery and the Confederacy. The local breed of Democrats dates mostly from New Deal days, and a devotion to Franklin D. Roosevelt was quite exclusive with a devotion to Harry Byrd, Sr. The political alignments here are really closer to those of West Virginia than those of most of Virginia. This was the only part of the state that Harry Byrd did not carry in his 1970 Senate race, and he nearly lost it again in 1976. The Fighting Ninth has a taste for raucous, noisy politics; it has favored the loud conservatism of William Scott, the yahooing populism of Henry Howell, and in 1976 the southern accents of Jimmy Carter.

The current congressman from the Fighting Ninth is Republican William Wampler. First elected in 1952, when he was only 26, Wampler was defeated in 1954 and 1956 by liberal Democrat Pat Jennings. For a while Wampler returned to his furniture and carpet business, but by 1966 he apparently sensed the public's disenchantment with Lyndon Johnson's Great Society and Vietnam war. Wampler ran once again and this time defeated Jennings, who later became clerk of the House.

Wampler is one of only three Republican congressmen who can remember serving in a House in which his party had the majority. He is also the ranking minority member on the House Agriculture Committee and, incidentally, the brother-in-law of Senator Howard Baker of Tennessee. Wampler had tough opposition from the same candidate in 1974 and 1976 and has won more easily since then.

Census Data   Pop. (1980 final) 554,494, up 19% in 1970s. Median family income, 1970, $6,608, 69% of U.S.

The Voters

Employment profile 1970   White collar, 32%. Blue collar, 52%. Service, 11%. Farm, 5%.
Ethnic groups   Black 1980, 2%. Hispanic 1980, 1%. Total foreign stock 1970, 1%.

Presidential Vote

1980	Reagan (R)	89,709	(49%)
	Carter (D)	86,013	(47%)
	Anderson (I)	4,625	(3%)
1976	Ford (R)	79,376	(45%)
	Carter (D)	90,065	(51%)

Rep. William C. Wampler (R) Elected 1966; b. Apr. 21, 1926, Pennington Gap; home, Bristol; Va. Polytech. Inst., B.S. 1948, U. of Va. Law Sch., 1949–50.

Career Navy, WWII; Newspaperman, *Bristol Herald Courier* and *Virginia-Tennesseean*; U.S. House of Reps., 1953–55; Rep. nominee for U.S. House of Reps., 1954, 1956; Special Asst. to the Gen. Mgr., Atomic Energy Comm., 1955; Furniture and carpet business, 1955–66; Bristol Utilities Bd. and Redevelopment and Housing Auth., 1965–66.

Offices 2407 RHOB, 202-225-3861. Also Reynolds Arcade Bldg., Bristol 24201, 703-466-9451.

Committees *Agriculture* (Ranking Member). Subcommittees: Department Operations, Research, and Foreign Agriculture; Tobacco and Peanuts.

Select Committee on Aging (2d). Subcommittee: Retirement Income and Employment.

Group Ratings

	ADA	COPE	PC	LCV	CFA	RPN	NAB	NSI	NTU	ACA	ACU
1980	28	21	17	17	7	—	83	78	43	71	72
1979	0	16	5	13	0	—	—	—	46	77	79
1978	10	20	18	23	23	58	92	100	20	85	92

Key Votes

1) Draft Registn $	FOR	6) Fair Hsg DOJ Enfrc	AGN	11) Cut Socl Incr Dfns $	AGN
2) Ban $ to Nicrgua	FOR	7) Lim PAC Contrbtns	AGN	12) Hosptl Cost Controls	AGN
3) Dlay MX Missile	AGN	8) Cap on Food Stmp $	FOR	13) Gasln Ctrls & Allctns	AGN
4) Nuclr Mortorium	AGN	9) New US Dep Edcatn	FOR	14) Lim Wndfll Prof Tax	FOR
5) Alaska Lands Bill	AGN	10) Cut OSHA $	FOR	15) Chryslr Loan Grntee	FOR

Election Results

1980 general	William C. Wampler (R)	119,196	(69%)	($89,461)
	Roosevelt Ferguson (D)	52,636	(31%)	($17,198)
1980 primary	William C. Wampler (R), nominated by convention			
1978 general	William C. Wampler (R)	76,877	(62%)	($112,016)
	Champ Clark (D)	47,367	(38%)	($56,121)

TENTH DISTRICT

The 10th congressional district — a portion of the commonwealth's suburbs of Washington, D.C. — is one of those places where recent trends in political thinking and social attitudes can be told through the perspective of its congressional representation. This is a district that did not exist before the 1952 election; its creation is owed to the steady expansion of the Washington metropolitan area into the Virginia countryside during World War II and the years immediately afterward. The district's initial representation reflected the attitudes of these initial suburban settlers. Congressman Joel Broyhill was a Republican first elected in the Eisenhower landslide of 1952. He adhered to the conservative wing of his party on national issues but made his greatest impression on local matters: resolutely opposing home rule for the District of Columbia, opposing any D.C. commuter tax, maintaining control by white segregationists of the affairs of the nation's black-majority capital city. In this he clearly reflected majority opinion in suburban Virginia, whose residents, busy raising families and tending lawns, feared the district's blacks and wanted them kept far away—and away from power.

Broyhill also should be remembered as one of the first congressmen to grasp the notion that the best way to get reelected was not to wait around for your party label to become popular, but to go to bat for your constituents when they have problems with the government—federal, state, or local. In his 22 years in Congress Broyhill resolved more than 100,000 constituent complaints, many of them of course from aggrieved government employees. This opponent of federal spending generally was not going to allow any of his constituents to be fired from the government payroll if he could prevent it.

Broyhill's high profile on local issues ultimately defeated him. By the early 1970s, Virginia suburbanites no longer wanted to think of themselves as hostile to the District. Washington had an elected city government that seemed not to be doing them any harm and Broyhill's hostility seemed out of date. Increasingly, the Virginia suburbs began voting on national issues and, regardless of how well their congressman was handling constituency services, were willing to vote against him. So Broyhill lost in 1974 to Joseph Fisher, a member of the Arlington local government and a professional economist. A veteran of the economic planning movement spawned in the New Deal years, Fisher won a seat on the Ways and Means Committee and exerted great influence on a number of tax bills. The disappointing economic performance of the nation during the Carter years seems to have eroded his standing; his claims of expertise were devalued, and in 1980 he was defeated by Republican Frank Wolf.

Broyhill and Fisher both had their political bases in Arlington, the closest-in suburb of the 10th district; Wolf's base was farther out, in the Fairfax and Vienna and McLean sections of Fairfax County. The Broyhill backers of the 1950s were young people with many children; Fisher's base was among these people when they were older and their children had moved away and in the new apartment dwellers. Wolf, a persistent man who ran three times before he finally won, is deeply religious; he has his strongest support in the newer subdivisions, among young and religious families looking for a nation more open to economic innovation and more respectful of traditional values.

Whether this will remain a majority constituency in this district is an open question. Wolf has a seat on the Post Office and Civil Service Committee—important in this district with its very high percentage of government employees—and he undoubtedly has put together an efficient constituency service operation. But redistricting is an imponderable: liberal Democrats would like to see a 10th district that includes both Alexandria and Arlington and only the innermost suburbs of Fairfax County, a district within whose boundaries the congressional vote went Democratic in 1980. And there is always the possibility of yet another shift on national issues. How kindly, one wonders, would the people of suburban Virginia look on really serious efforts to legislate and enforce the moral precepts of evangelical Christians? In any case, no congressman in the 30 years this district has existed has ever received as much as 60% of the vote, and it is likely that the 1982 election will be seriously contested.

Census Data   Pop. (1980 final) 534,494, up 15% in 1970s. Median family income, 1970, $14,457, 151% of U.S.

The Voters

   Employment profile 1970   White collar, 75%. Blue collar, 15%. Service, 9%. Farm, 1%.
   Ethnic groups   Black 1980, 4%. Hispanic 1980, 4%. Asian 1980, 4%. Total foreign stock 1970, 15%. UK, Germany, 2% each.

Presidential Vote

1980	Reagan (R)	120,328	(54%)
	Carter (D)	76,676	(34%)
	Anderson (I)	23,999	(11%)
1976	Ford (R)	100,521	(51%)
	Carter (D)	92,341	(48%)

Rep. Frank R. Wolf (R) Elected 1980; b. Jan. 30, 1939, Philadelphia, Pa.; home, Vienna; Penn. St. U., B.A. 1961; Georgetown U., J.D. 1965.

Career Army, 1962–63; Army Reserve, 1963–; Practicing atty., 1965–; Legis. Asst to U.S. Rep. Edward Biester, 1968–71; Asst. to Sec. of Interior Rogers Morton, 1971–74; Dpty. Asst. Secy., Congress./Legis. Affairs Dept. of Interior, 1974–75.

Offices 414 CHOB, 202-225-5136. Also 1651 Old Meadow Rd., Suite 115, McLean 22102, 703-734-1500; 19 E. Market St., Rm. 4B, Leesburg 22075, 703-777-4422.

Committees *Post Office and Civil Service* (10th). Subcommittees: Civil Service; Human Resources; Postal Operations and Services.

Public Works and Transportation (19th). Subcommittees: Aviation; Water Resources.

Group Ratings and Key Votes: Newly Elected

Election Results

1980 general	Frank R. Wolf (R)	110,840	(51%)	($460,504)
	Joseph L. Fisher (D)............	105,883	(49%)	($270,920)
1980 primary	Frank R. Wolf (R)	13,782	(75%)	
	Two others (R)	4,566	(25%)	
1978 general	Joseph L. Fisher (D)............	70,892	(53%)	($147,340)
	Frank R. Wolf (R)	61,981	(47%)	($232,286)

WASHINGTON

In the far northwestern corner of the continental United States is the state of Washington, which the massive Cascade Range separates into two topographical and economic regions. To the east is the so-called Inland Empire. Here the Columbia River winds through plateau country, its waters backed up into giant reservoirs by dams and distributed through irrigation canals to many of the area's farms. There are some urban areas here—Spokane, the smaller city of Yakima, the complex around the nuclear Hanford Works—but the Inland Empire is primarily agricultural. Wheat is the biggest crop here, and apples and hops are also important—Washington is a big exporter of apples and beer. Like most of rural America, this area had outmigration in the 1950s and 1960s but has had some population growth in the 1970s.

The more populous region of Washington is the land west of the mountains, around Puget Sound. Here there is a strip of continuous urban development for more than 50 miles, from Everett south through Seattle and beyond Tacoma; in this area nearly two-thirds of the people of Washington live. The physical environment here is unique in the United States. The Olympic Mountains west of Puget Sound are the rainiest part of the nation, and the Sound itself is bathed in what sometimes seems a constant drizzle. The result is hills that were covered with green firs when the first white men arrived, and to a considerable extent they still are, for this is prime lumber country. The hills of Seattle and its suburbs, covered now with often colorful houses, dive down toward the Sound or the inland lakes not far away; ferries ply from Seattle and other harbors across the Sound. The valleys are dense with factories, warehouses, railroad yards; for railroads made the Puget Sound what it is. This is the closest continental U.S. port to Alaska and the Orient, a major point for exports (wheat from the Northwest and Great Plains) and imports (Japanese goods, Alaskan oil) as well as a major fishing center (salmon). The railroads did not reach the Sound until the 1880s, and it was not clear which port — Seattle, Tacoma, Everett — would emerge dominant until Seattle grew, in a flash, with the 1898 Alaska gold strike. It quickly became and has remained the major city of the Northwest.

In that booming, young, lusty Seattle there developed a turbulent politics. This was the major center of the Industrial Workers of the World (the IWW or Wobblies) in the years before World War I; Seattle's business and civic leaders decided to exterminate the movement and in brutal fashion did so. Adding to the distinctiveness of the area were its large numbers of Scandinavian immigrants. They rode the Great Northern or Northern Pacific west from Minneapolis after the long trip from Bergen or Goteborg. The Scandinavians brought with them attitudes favorable to cooperative enterprises (Washington has more businesses owned by workers than any other part of the country). They had no suspicions of public power development, and Washington, blessed with the hydroelectric resources of the Columbia, became the leader in public power in the United States in the 1930s. Also, despite the experience of the IWW, Washington proved hospitable to the trade union movement from the 1930s on; today it has one of the largest percentages of workers in unions of any state (less than West Virginia, roughly equal with Michigan and Pennsylvania).

All of these factors led Washington voters to support the New Deal, and the state — especially the Puget Sound counties — piled up large margins for Franklin Roosevelt and his fellow Democrats. With only one exception in 50 years, Washington elected only Democrats to the Senate. But since World War II this became a two-party state in just about every other respect. Republicans have held the governorship more often than not, probably because their almost always rather liberal candidates have been personally more attractive than the intensely political Democratic nominees they have beaten. In the 1950s the Republicans controlled the state's House delegation; since 1964 it has been heavily Democratic. The legislature is usually closely divided. Republicans won control of both houses after the 1980 elections only because one maverick Democratic state senator switched parties.

Seattle, once a Democratic stronghold, as it has grown more prosperous and white collar has also grown more Republican in many elections. It is the smaller cities in the Puget Sound area — Tacoma, Everett, Bremerton — that ordinarily deliver the largest Democratic percentages. The result is that in the last three close presidential elections, Washington's electoral votes have been determined by very small margins — and have gone to the losing candidate each time. This is a state far from the rest of America — the nearest big city to Seattle is Vancouver, British Columbia — and Washington's political rhythms are not necessarily those of the rest of the country.

With World War II there came to be another major force in Washington's economy: the aircraft industry. The giant here is Boeing, and its prosperity helped Washington achieve substantial growth in the 1950s and 1960s. But building airplanes is anything but a steady business; there are few potential customers and demand can vanish suddenly, even for so accomplished a manufacturer as Boeing. That is what happened here in 1970. The year before, Boeing employed 101,000 people in Washington — 8% of the state's total work force. By the end of 1970 Boeing's payroll had shrunk to 38,000. Unemployment lines were jammed, 55,000 people left the state, and the Seattle area real estate market went into depression. Now Boeing tries not to hire as many people here as it did in the 1960s boom and attempts to keep its business steadier. By the late 1970s the Seattle area and Washington generally have seen some of the kind of growth that has been the common experience of most of the West throughout the decade.

Just as one of the biggest national political stories in 1980 was the election of a Republican Senate, so one of the biggest political stories in Washington was the election of a Republican Senator, Slade Gorton, to replace Democrat Warren Magnuson. Magnuson, along with his colleague Henry Jackson, provided Washington for many years with the most powerful and politically adept pair of senators in the nation — and a pair that cooperated and worked amicably together. They knew their way around Capitol Hill: Magnuson was first elected to the House in 1936 and to the Senate in 1944; Jackson was first elected to the House in 1940 and to the Senate in 1952. By the 1980 election they had 64 years of Senate seniority and 84 years of experience in Congress. Both were important committee chairmen. Magnuson chaired the Commerce Committee for years — an important body since it covers almost all direct federal regulation of business — and in time became chairman of Appropriations and Senate president pro tempore. Through a subcommittee he controlled the budget of what was then HEW and was responsible for much of the funding of the National Institutes of Health. He was a prolific legislator, responsible for such measures as truth-in-packaging, the 200-mile fishing limit, safety standards for children's clothes. He was one of the last New Dealers: a gifted wheeler-dealer who also cared deeply about ordinary people and sought to help them.

Magnuson's defeat in the 1980 election may turn out to be one of the important symbols of the end of an era, one that began almost 50 years before when he was just beginning his career in Congress. It was not so much that voters rejected Magnuson's views on issues, although they were plainly more concerned about high levels of government spending in general and less concerned about the kind of programs he had sponsored in particular, nor was the problem that voters no longer felt warmly toward Magnuson. The big problem was simply age: Magnuson was 75, he could walk only slowly, and his hearing was not good. Gorton subtly pointed up the contrast by jogging ostentatiously. But Gorton's campaign was by no means entirely negative, as his slogan, "the next great senator," suggested. Magnuson in fact led right up to the last week before the election, but then the bottom fell out all at once: Magnuson lost in all but one of the state's congressional districts, and Gorton was elected with a decisive, although not overwhelming, 54% of the vote.

A cerebral man with the reputation of a moderate, Gorton may represent the Washington electorate's self-image today better than the burly Magnuson with his working-class roots. Gorton is in fact something of an aristocrat, from the Gorton's of Gloucester fish products family; he is liberal on environmental matters, on consumer issues, and on some procedural issues but has throughout his career been unsympathetic to unions despite a large membership in the state. If he is not entirely at home in Ronald Reagan's Washington, he is not entirely out of place either: as a member of the Budget Committee, he backed, at least initially, the Reagan Administration's budget cuts. He serves also on Commerce, Magnuson's old committee, and on Environment and Public Works.

The capture of the Senate by the Republicans has made Henry Jackson, for a long time one of our most prolific and skillful legislators, at least for a time something of a backbencher. He has lost the choice chairmanships he once held — the old Interior Committee (now Energy and Natural Resources), the Permanent Investigations Subcommittee of Government Operations, the Armed Services subcommittee on arms control. In the 1970s Jackson made his mark in all these areas. He authored the Environmental Protection Act and, as much as any senator, mediated intelligently between the goals of protecting the environment and encouraging economic growth. That balance, combined with his iron control of the Interior Committee, will be missed now that western Republicans, eager to encourage development and convinced that talk of the environment is subterfuge, dominate the committee. Jackson was often an antagonist of the oil companies and an advocate of energy price controls — a cause that has largely been lost.

Jackson was always a backer of a strong defense. He extracted concessions from the Nixon Administration before he agreed to support the first SALT Treaty; he vocally opposed the second. He authored the Jackson–Vanik Amendment, cutting off the Soviet Union from most favored nation trade status if it did not allow emigration of Jews, against the wishes of the Nixon Administration; eventually emigration was allowed. That measure gave him the reputation of being one of the Senate's staunchest opponents of the Soviets and backers of Israel. Jackson was attacked by some Democrats as a conservative; but he could reply, with justice, that he was merely following the basic policies of the Roosevelt, Truman, Kennedy, and Johnson Administrations. He is, now, literally one of the last New Dealers, one of five members of Congress who also served when Franklin Roosevelt was president.

A superb legislator, Jackson turned out to be less than a brilliant presidential candidate. In 1972 he started off too late and had the handicap of being a strong supporter of the Vietnam war at a time when most Democratic activists were dedicated, above all else, to oppose it. In 1976 he was the candidate with the most experience in Washington in a year when voters, fresh from Richard Nixon, were sick of experienced candidates and wanted someone fresh and presumably close to the ordinary person.

Jackson is a senator who has spent most of his life in the majority party and must now somehow adapt to being part of the minority. He will suffer less than some colleagues from losing the staff resources of majority senators; he knows the details of difficult issues thoroughly and does not have to be prompted to make compelling arguments. On some issues, at least, Jackson is very much in line with the new majority — defense is the most notable example. On the Armed Services Committee he is an especially strong advocate of nuclear submarine programs and an increased number of ships. He used to be known as the senator from Boeing but, as no less an adversary than Eugene McCarthy has conceded, Jackson would support exactly the same defense budget even if not a penny of defense money was spent in Washington state. Jackson is in superb health and physical condition, and although he turns 70 in 1982 no one doubts that he can win reelection to a sixth term rather easily. The question is whether he will attract significant Republican opposition. For the longer term, the possibility has been raised of Jackson receiving a major appointment, such as secretary of Defense, in the Reagan Administration; he did not get one in 1981, but if an offer were made in the future, and if it appeared the Democrats were not about to regain a majority in the Senate, Jackson might very well take it.

After four tempestuous years of Governor Dixy Lee Ray, Washington now has a much more conventional governor, Republican John Spellman. Ray raised hackles for her strong defense of nuclear power and her feuds with legislators and reporters; an intelligent and articulate woman, she always seemed to be on the defensive in a controversy and so was not really able to lead the state in the direction — more economic development — that she wanted. She was beaten in the 1980 Democratic primary by state Senator James McDermott, a liberal Seattle psychiatrist; he was beaten pretty soundly in the general election by Spellman, as it became apparent that voters wanted neither a liberal nor an urbanite nor a psychiatrist in the governor's mansion. Spellman made his mark as a competent but colorless head of the King County (Seattle) government.

The new governor now has the advantage of a Republican majority in the legislature. Democrats lost control of the state House in 1978 (it was actually split 49–49 for two years, with Democratic and Republican cospeakers); they lost the state Senate in February 1981 when state Senator Peter von Reichbauer switched to the Republican Party. That gives the Republicans at least theoretical control over congressional redistricting. Washington gains one district from the 1980 census, and von Reichbauer and the Republicans, aided by the Rose Institute of Claremont, California, drew a plan that undermined several Democrats and created a new, Republican-leaning district in von Reichbauer's home area. It went a little too far, however. The state's two Republican congressmen got a lot of new and not very friendly territory. And it was not clear that Washington's civic leaders really wanted to endanger such Democratic congressmen as Majority Whip Thomas Foley and Norman Dicks, who saved the Import-Export Bank loan program (the major recipient of which is Boeing) from extinction in the Reagan budget. So in the late spring of 1981 the Republican congressional redistricting plan was actually vetoed by the Republican governor. Presumably whatever plan is finally adopted will accommodate most of the incumbents and will not go to such great lengths to accommodate von Reichbauer.

Census Data   Pop. (1980 final) 4,130,163, up 21% in 1970s: 1.82% of U.S. total, 20th largest. Central city, 25%; suburban, 47%. Median 4-person family income, 1978, $21,494, 105% of U.S., 12th highest.

1979 Share of Federal Tax Burden $8,701,000,000; 1.93% of U.S. total, 17th largest.

1979 Share of Federal Outlays $9,920,443,000; 2.14% of U.S. total, 16th largest.

DOD	$3,160,245,000	11th	(2.98%)	HEW	$2,929,433,000	21st	(1.64%)
DOE	$783,493,000	6th	(6.66%)	ERDA	$354,805,000	3d	(13.09%)
HUD	$89,597,000	25th	(1.36%)	NASA	$41,322,000	17th	(0.88%)
VA	$393,265,000	18th	(1.90%)	DOT	$461,573,000	11th	(2.80%)
EPA	$139,803,000	13th	(2.63%)	DOC	$92,317,000	10th	(2.92%)
DOI	$134,549,000	12th	(2.42%)	USDA	$412,693,000	25th	(1.72%)

Economic Base   Finance, insurance, and real estate; transportation equipment, especially aircraft and parts; agriculture, notably wheat, dairy products, cattle, and apples; lumber and wood products, especially sawmills and planing mills; food and kindred products, especially canned, cured, and frozen foods; paper and allied products; primary metal industries, especially primary nonferrous metals.

Political Lineup   Governor, John D. Spellman (R). Senators, Henry M. Jackson (D) and Slade Gorton (R). Representatives, 7 (5 D and 2 R); 8 in 1982. State Senate, 49 (25 R and 24 D); State House of Representatives, 98 (56 R and 42 D).

The Voters

Registration   2,236,603 Total. No party registration.
Employment profile 1970   White collar, 51%. Blue collar, 33%. Service, 13%. Farm, 3%.
Ethnic groups   Black 1980, 3%. Hispanic 1980, 3%. Am. Ind. 1980, 1%. Asian 1980, 2%. Total foreign stock 1970, 19%. Canada, 4%; Germany, Norway, 2% each; Sweden, 1%.

Presidential Vote

1980	Reagan (R)	865,244	(50%)
	Carter (D)	650,193	(37%)
	Anderson (I)	185,073	(11%)
1976	Ford (R)	777,732	(50%)
	Carter (D)	717,323	(46%)

SENATORS

Sen. Henry M. Jackson (D) Elected 1952, seat up 1982; b. May 31, 1912, Everett; home, Everett; U. of Wash., LL.B. 1935.

Career Practicing atty., 1936–38; Snohomish Co. Prosecuting Atty., 1938–40; U.S. House of Reps., 1941–53.

Offices 137 RSOB, 202-224-3441. Also 802 U.S. Courthouse, Seattle 98104, 206-442-7476.

Committees *Armed Services* (2d). Subcommittees: Military Construction; Strategic and Theatre Nuclear Forces; Preparedness.

Energy and Natural Resources (Ranking Member).

Governmental Affairs (2d). Subcommittees: Permanent Subcommittee on Investigations; Energy, Nuclear Proliferation, and Government Processes; Federal Expenditures, Research, and Rules.

Select Committee on Intelligence (5th). Subcommittees: Budget; Analysis and Production (Vicechairman); Collection and Foreign Operations.

Group Ratings

	ADA	COPE	PC	LCV	CFA	RPN	NAB	NSI	NTU	ACA	ACU
1980	72	84	67	33	87	—	0	30	21	19	14
1979	68	95	49	—	67	—	—	—	12	11	9
1978	55	84	55	71	45	40	8	50	7	8	13

Key Votes

1) Draft Registn $	FOR	6) Fair Housng Cloture	FOR	11) Cut Socl Incr Defns	FOR
2) Ban $ to Nicrgua	FOR	7) Ban $ Rape Abortns	AGN	12) Income Tax Indexing	AGN
3) Dlay MX Missile	AGN	8) Cap on Food Stmp $	AGN	13) Lim Spdg 21% GNP	AGN
4) Nuclr Mortorium	AGN	9) New US Dep Edcatn	FOR	14) Incr Wndfll Prof Tax	FOR
5) Alaska Lands Bill	FOR	10) Cut OSHA Inspctns	AGN	15) Chryslr Loan Grntee	FOR

Election Results

1976 general	Henry M. Jackson (D)	1,071,219	(72%)	($198,375)
	George M. Brown (R)...........	361,546	(24%)	($10,841)
1976 primary	Henry M. Jackson (D)	549,974	(87%)	
	Two others (D)	79,029	(13%)	
1970 general	Henry M. Jackson (D)	879,385	(82%)	
	Charles W. Elicker (R)	170,790	(16%)	

Sen. Slade Gorton (R) Elected 1980, seat up 1986; b. Jan. 8, 1928, Chicago, Ill.; home, Olympia; Dartmouth Col., B.A. 1950, Columbia U., LL.B. 1953.

Career Army, WWII; Air Force, 1953–56; Air Force Res., 1956–; Practicing atty., 1956–68; Wash. House of Reps., 1958–68; Wash. Atty. Gen., 1968–76.

Offices 3327 DSOB, 202-224-2621. Also 2988 Fed. Ofc. Bldg., 915 2d Ave., Seattle 98174, 206-442-5545, and S770 U.S. Courthouse, W. 920 Riverside Dr., Spokane 99201, 509-456-6816.

Committees *Budget* (12th).

Commerce, Science, and Transportation (7th). Subcommittees: Merchant Marine and Tourism (Chairman); Science, Technology, and Space; Surface Transportation.

Environment and Public Works (8th). Subcommittees: Environmental Pollution; Water Resources.

Select Committee on Indian Affairs (4th).

Select Committee on Small Business (6th). Subcommittees: Government Regulation and Paperwork; Productivity and Competition.

Group Ratings and Key Votes: Newly Elected

Election Results

1980 general	Slade Gorton (R)	936,317	(54%)	($907,317)
	Warren G. Magnuson (D)	792,052	(46%)	($1,614,999)
1980 primary	Slade Gorton (R)	313,560	(57%)	
	Lloyd Cooney (R)	229,178	(42%)	($277,035)
	One other (R)	7,112	(1%)	
1974 general	Warren G. Magnuson (D)	611,811	(61%)	($463,116)
	Jack Metcalf (R)	363,626	(36%)	($63,153)

GOVERNOR

Gov. John D. Spellman (R) Elected 1980, term expires Jan. 1985; b. Dec. 29, 1926, Bellevue; home, King Co.; Seattle U., B.S.S., 1949, Georgetown U., J.D. 1953.

Career Navy, WWII; Practicing atty., 1954–67; King Co. Commissioner, 1967–69, Co. Exec., 1969–77; 1st V.P. and Bd. of Dirs., Nat. Assn. of Counties, 1969–80.

Offices Legislative Bldg., Olympia 98504, 206-753-6780.

Election Results

1980 gen.	John D. Spellman (R)	981,083	(57%)
	Jim McDermott (D)	749,813	(43%)
1980 prim.	John D. Spellman (R)	162,426	(41%)
	Duane Berentson (R)	154,724	(39%)
	Bruce K. Chapman (R)	70,875	(18%)
1976 gen.	Dixy Lee Ray (D)	821,787	(53%)
	John D. Spellman (R)	687,017	(44%)

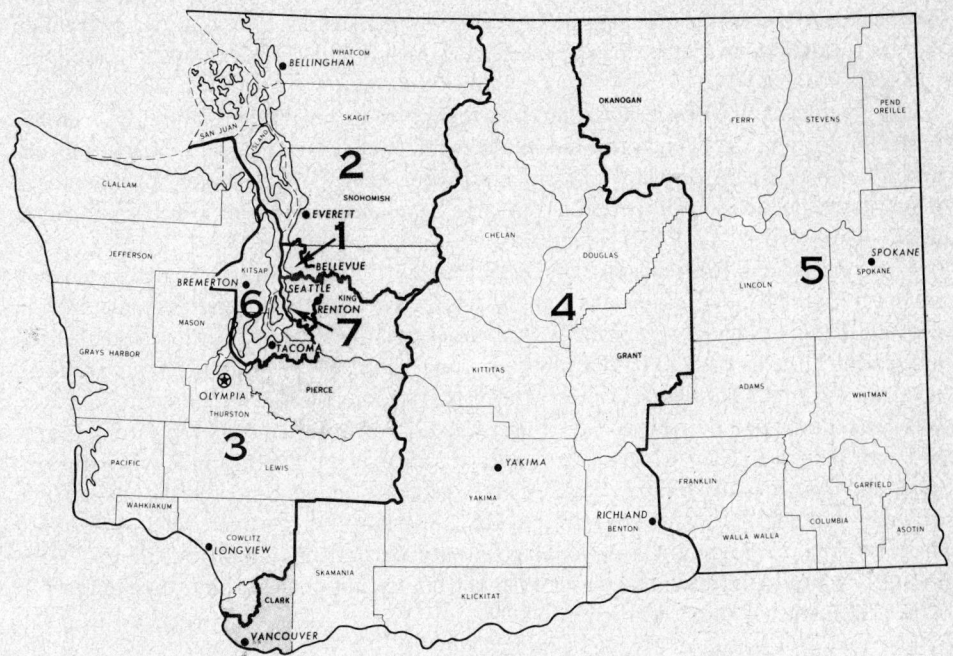

FIRST DISTRICT

Like most large American cities, Seattle has its own personality. If its high-rise downtown buildings are not that dissimilar to those of many cities elsewhere — although they are impressive for a metropolitan area with less than two million people — then a few blocks below them is the city's funky waterfront, with stands where you can get salmon and dungenesse crab. Nearby is the Pioneer Square area, where stores and warehouses from the turn of the century have been restored and renovated. Some people have compared Seattle to San Francisco, and there is some similarity in the topography; Seattle too has steep hills, with picturesque views overlooking a bay and other bodies of water.

There are other similarities. Seattle's upper class, like San Francisco's, continues to be anchored downtown and has kept residential quarters not so far away; it favors conservative clothes and outdoor recreation. Seattle's working class, like San Francisco's, has maintained many comfortable neighborhoods of frame houses on steep hillsides. The ethnic groups here are less distinctive, however — partly because so many are of Scandinavian background and to most outward appearances have assimilated with the Yankee Protestants.

Like every city, Seattle is divided into distinct neighborhoods, mostly by voluntary residential choices. Generally blue collar workers live on the south side of the city, near the factories, warehouses, and railroad yards in the valley near Puget Sound. The wealthier, more white collar, better-educated people tend to live on the north side of the city, in such neighborhoods as Broadmoor and Magnolia Bluff that sit on the hills between Puget Sound and Lake Washington. There are less wealthy neighborhoods here too, for example, the Scandinavian Ballard section, but overall the north side is the more affluent area. The north side of

Seattle is also the heart of Washington's 1st congressional district — the only part of the state (except for the 7th district in one special election) to send a Republican to Congress in the 1970s.

The 1st takes in the north side, extends farther north to a middle-class suburb in Snohomish County, and then bends east to Lake Washington to take in most of the affluent suburb of Bellevue. There are plenty of Democratic votes in the 1st — it has gone Democratic in many statewide races — but there is also a large Republican base here, which is not true in many other parts of the Puget Sound area.

The congressman from this district is Joel Pritchard, a Republican who has gotten high ratings from the Ripon Society, a group that has several important Republican members in the state. Pritchard had served in the Washington legislature for 12 years when he challenged incumbent Thomas Pelly in the Republican primary in 1970; Pelly, although high ranking on an important committee, returned to the district seldom because he refused to fly, and he was weaker than had been expected. He retired in 1972. Pritchard did not win automatically, however; he had to beat strong challenges from a member of the Boeing family in the primary and from an aide to Henry Jackson in the general election. Since then he has had little difficulty winning. As a Ripon–type Republican, Pritchard has been increasingly in line with his party's majority in recent years, as it has shifted its focus from cultural to economic issues. He is on record to the effect that no member of Congress should serve more than 12 years — which means he probably will retire in 1984.

Census Data   Pop. (1980 final) 470,180, down 2% in 1970s. Median family income, 1970, $12,084, 126% of U.S.

The Voters

Employment profile 1970   White collar, 65%. Blue collar, 23%. Service, 12%. Farm, –%.
Ethnic groups   Black 1980, 2%. Hispanic 1980, 2%. Am. Ind. 1980, 1%. Asian 1980, 4%. Total foreign stock 1970, 25%. Canada, 6%; Norway, UK, 3% each; Germany, Sweden, 2% each.

Presidential Vote

1980	Reagan (R)	107,925	(43%)
	Carter (D)	97,899	(39%)
	Anderson (I)	35,829	(14%)
1976	Ford (R)	126,588	(52%)
	Carter (D)	104,738	(43%)

Rep. Joel Pritchard (R) Elected 1972; b. May 5, 1925, Seattle; home, Seattle; Marietta Col., 1946–48.

Career Army, WWII; Griffin Envelope Co., 1948–72, Pres., 1970–72; Wash. House of Reps., 1958–66; Wash. Senate, 1966–70.

Offices 2263 RHOB, 202-225-6311. Also 2888 Fed. Bldg., 915 2d Ave., Seattle 98174, 206-442-4220.

Committees *Foreign Affairs* (9th). Subcommittees: Asian and Pacific Affairs; Human Rights and International Organizations; International Operations.

Merchant Marine and Fisheries (4th). Subcommittees: Fisheries and Wildlife Conservation and the Environment; Oceanography.

Group Ratings

	ADA	COPE	PC	LCV	CFA	RPN	NAB	NSI	NTU	ACA	ACU
1980	72	33	43	62	29	—	46	25	30	42	16
1979	32	30	33	44	30	—	—	—	33	46	44
1978	40	32	50	53	36	100	60	38	18	39	46

Key Votes

1) Draft Registn $	AGN	6) Fair Hsg DOJ Enfrc	FOR	11) Cut Socl Incr Dfns $	AGN
2) Ban $ to Nicrgua	AGN	7) Lim PAC Contrbtns	FOR	12) Hosptl Cost Controls	AGN
3) Dlay MX Missile	FOR	8) Cap on Food Stmp $	AGN	13) Gasln Ctrls & Allctns	AGN
4) Nuclr Mortorium	AGN	9) New US Dep Edcatn	FOR	14) Lim Wndfll Prof Tax	FOR
5) Alaska Lands Bill	AGN	10) Cut OSHA $	AGN	15) Chryslr Loan Grntee	AGN

Election Results

1980 general	Joel Pritchard (R)	180,475	(78%)	($40,045)
	Robin Drake (D)...............	41,830	(18%)	($21,573)
1980 primary	Joel Pritchard (R)	97,329	(100%)	
1978 general	Joel Pritchard (R)	99,942	(64%)	($125,399)
	Janice Niemi (D)	52,706	(34%)	($60,121)

SECOND DISTRICT

The 2d congressional district of Washington constitutes the far northwestern corner of the continental United States. This is a region of green mountains, of heavily wooded inlets, and of gentle rain and fog. The 2d takes in sparsely populated islands in the Puget Sound and the Strait of Juan de Fuca, along with the counties just east of the Sound from Seattle to the Canadian border. Most of the population of the district is concentrated in a narrow strip of land between the Sound and the Cascade Mountains, in or near such cities as Bellingham, Everett, and several suburbs of Seattle. Traditionally this has been blue collar country; for years affluent people in Seattle stayed in the city or moved east, across Lake Washington, rather than north into the 2d. But the affluence of the 1970s and the growth of Washington in that decade have changed the character of the 2d somewhat. Everett and Bellingham remain rather grimy paper mill towns (with the big Boeing plants that produce the 747s near Everett). But in the once vacant territory south and east of Everett are an increasing number of above-average-income suburbs, to accommodate the growing affluent population of Metropolitan Seattle. And in the valleys or coastal inlets in agricultural Skagit County or in the islands in the Sound are small communities of dropouts from the late 1960s, living quiet lives now, their once unconventional apparel and hair styles now common, their desire to live natural lives now integrated, as advertisements show, into the broader popular culture.

The 2d historically has tended to favor Democrats. It was represented for 12 years (1941–53) by Henry Jackson. But the most important issue here in the middle 1970s was not a standard partisan matter, but a question virtually unheard of in the rest of the United States: Indian fishing rights. Several years ago a federal judge in Seattle recognized the right of some Indian tribes to half the salmon catch in some of the state's major waterways. Commercial fishermen were faced with the prospect of bankruptcy; sports fishermen and others were worried that the supply of fish would be depleted. Democratic Congressman Lloyd Meeds was nearly beaten on this issue in 1976 by Republican John Nance Garner, a grandnephew of Franklin Roosevelt's first vice president; rather than run and face angry constituents, Meeds retired in 1978.

1152　　WASHINGTON

Garner tried again, but the winner was a Democrat, former Meeds aide and local newscaster Al Swift. In his first two years in office, Swift appears to have succeeded in overshadowing the fishing rights issue. He devoted much of his attention to legislation reorganizing the supply of electric power in the Pacific Northwest — a technical matter with massive practical effects. He impressed local voters with his mastery of detail and attention to local matters, even in a district so distant from Washington, D.C.; he was reelected easily against a conservative Republican. He serves on the busy Energy and Commerce Committee and has earned a reputation as a skillful and hardworking legislator.

Census Data　Pop. (1980 final) 658,523, up 37% in 1970s. Median family income, 1970, $10,563, 110% of U.S.

The Voters

Employment profile 1970　White collar, 48%. Blue collar, 37%. Service, 12%. Farm, 3%.
Ethnic groups　Black 1980, 1%. Hispanic 1980, 2%. Am. Ind. 1980, 2%. Asian 1980, 2%. Total foreign stock 1970, 20%. Canada, 5%; Norway, UK, Germany, Sweden, 2% each.

Presidential Vote

1980	Reagan (R)	138,265	(50%)
	Carter (D)	101,857	(37%)
	Anderson (I)	29,902	(11%)
1976	Ford (R)	116,274	(51%)
	Carter (D)	107,031	(47%)

Rep. Al Swift (D) Elected 1978; b. Sept. 12, 1935, Tacoma; home, Bellingham; Whitman Col., 1953–55, Cent. Wash. U., B.A. 1957.

Career　Broadcaster and Dir. of Pub. Affairs, KVOS-TV, Bellingham, 1957–62, 1969–77; Admin. Asst. to U.S. Rep. Lloyd Meeds, 1965–69, 1977.

Offices　1511 LHOB, 202-225-2605. Also Fed. Bldg., 3002 Colby, Everett 98201, 206-252-3188.

Committees　Energy and Commerce (17th). Subcommittees: Energy Conservation and Power; Fossil and Synthetic Fuels; Telecommunications, Consumer Protection, and Finance.

House Administration (10th). Subcommittees: Accounts; Office Systems.

Joint Committee on the Library (2d).

Group Ratings

	ADA	COPE	PC	LCV	CFA	RPN	NAB	NSI	NTU	ACA	ACU
1980	94	58	73	70	71	—	0	22	14	17	0
1979	79	85	70	67	74	—	—	—	17	12	15

Key Votes

1) Draft Registn $　AGN	6) Fair Hsg DOJ Enfrc　FOR	11) Cut Socl Incr Dfns $　AGN
2) Ban $ to Nicrgua　AGN	7) Lim PAC Contrbtns　FOR	12) Hosptl Cost Controls　AGN
3) Dlay MX Missile　FOR	8) Cap on Food Stmp $　AGN	13) Gasln Ctrls & Allctns　FOR
4) Nuclr Mortorium　FOR	9) New US Dep Edcatn　FOR	14) Lim Wndfll Prof Tax　FOR
5) Alaska Lands Bill　AGN	10) Cut OSHA $　AGN	15) Chryslr Loan Grntee　AGN

Election Results

1980 general	Al Swift (D)...................	162,002	(64%)	($143,100)
	Neal Snider (R)	82,639	(33%)	($15,003)
1980 primary	Al Swift (D)...................	84,552	(92%)	
	One other (D)	7,736	(8%)	
1978 general	Al Swift (D)...................	70,620	(51%)	($150,435)
	John Nance Garner (R)	66,793	(49%)	($324,456)

THIRD DISTRICT

Lumber is one of Washington's most important industries. And nowhere in the state is lumber a more important part of the economy than in the damp, mountainous region along the Pacific coast and the lower Columbia River. This is Washington's 3d congressional district, which encircles the Seattle and Tacoma metropolitan areas and just fails to include the industrial town of Vancouver, right across the Columbia from Portland, Oregon. This not an urban district; the largest cities are Longview, with 31,000 people, and the state capital of Olympia, with 27,000; another large concentration of population, in the Army's Fort Lewis, which sits at the district's edge near Tacoma, is not part of the 3d's electoral politics.

The political atmosphere in the 3d has not changed too much since the turn of the century, when the lumberjacks first attacked the firs and the sawmill towns grew up on the bays off the Pacific and Puget Sound. It is an atmosphere that retains a kind of rough-hewn populism, reminiscent of the days when the Industrial Workers of the World were trying to organize the lumber camps. People usually vote Democratic here, and have since the New Deal, for basic economic reasons: they think the Democrats are on the side of the little guy. Politics here has sometimes been radical, but it has never been chic.

The importance of lumber here apparently helped the current Congressman, Democrat Don Bonker, to win the seat in 1974. Bonker's Republican opponent backed unlimited exports of timber to Japan. Bonker opposed them, arguing that the timber should be milled into lumber first in the United States or should otherwise be left standing in American forests. Bonker won that election with a solid 62%. He is a member of the Merchant Marine and Fisheries Committee—of obvious local import—and of the Foreign Affairs Committee. On the latter, he became chairman of the International Organizations Subcommittee in 1979. An indication of his basic orientation can be gained from the fact that he led the move to rename the subcommittee Human Rights and International Organizations after the Reagan Administration announced its foreign policy plans. Bonker can be counted on to continue to stress the importance of human rights considerations in foreign policy and to joust with Reagan Administration appointees who try ostentatiously to downplay it.

Redistricting may change the boundaries of the district, but the Republicans in charge of the process will have to work hard to hurt Bonker. The move suggested by the population figures would actually strengthen him: to move the district southward to include industrial Vancouver, just across the river from Portland. Such a change might also remove Republican-leaning parts of the district near Olympia (which trended Republican in 1980) and Tacoma; they in turn might help fatten a new Republican-leaning Puget Sound district.

Census Data Pop. (1980 final) 695,204, up 33% in 1970s. Median family income, 1970, $9,736, 102% of U.S.

1154   WASHINGTON

The Voters

Employment profile 1970   White collar, 42%. Blue collar, 42%. Service, 13%. Farm, 3%.
Ethnic groups   Black 1980, 2%. Hispanic 1980, 2%. Am. Ind. 1980, 2%. Asian 1980, 2%. Total foreign stock 1970, 15%. Canada, 3%; Germany, 2%; UK, Norway, Sweden, 1% each.

Presidential Vote

1980	Reagan (R)	133,405	(50%)
	Carter (D)	101,699	(38%)
	Anderson (I)	26,864	(10%)
1976	Ford (R)	105,441	(46%)
	Carter (D)	113,587	(50%)

Rep. Don Bonker (D) Elected 1974; b. Mar. 7, 1937, Denver, Colo.; home, Olympia; Clark Col., Vancouver, Wash., A.A. 1962, Lewis & Clark Col., B.A. 1964, American U., 1964–66.

Career Coast Guard, 1955–59; Research Asst. to U.S. Sen. Maurine B. Neuberger of Oreg., 1964–66; Clark Co. Auditor, 1966–74; Candidate for Secy. of State of Wash., 1972.

Offices 434 CHOB, 202-225-3536. Also 209 Fed. Bldg., Olympia 98501, 206-753-9528.

Committees Foreign Affairs (9th). Subcommittees: Human Rights and International Organizations (Chairman); International Economic Policy and Trade.

Merchant Marine and Fisheries (8th). Subcommittees: Coast Guard and Navigation; Fisheries and Wildlife Conservation and the Environment.

Select Committee on Aging (6th). Subcommittee: Health and Long-Term Care.

Group Ratings

	ADA	COPE	PC	LCV	CFA	RPN	NAB	NSI	NTU	ACA	ACU
1980	83	67	60	77	71	—	18	0	16	30	11
1979	84	90	68	78	67	—	—	—	20	4	6
1978	65	89	50	79	46	50	17	13	7	21	20

Key Votes

1) Draft Registn $	AGN	6) Fair Hsg DOJ Enfrc	FOR	11) Cut Socl Incr Dfns $	AGN
2) Ban $ to Nicrgua	AGN	7) Lim PAC Contrbtns	FOR	12) Hosptl Cost Controls	FOR
3) Dlay MX Missile	FOR	8) Cap on Food Stmp $	AGN	13) Gasln Ctrls & Allctns	—
4) Nuclr Mortorium	FOR	9) New US Dep Edcatn	FOR	14) Lim Wndfll Prof Tax	AGN
5) Alaska Lands Bill	FOR	10) Cut OSHA $	AGN	15) Chryslr Loan Grntee	FOR

Election Results

1980 general	Don Bonker (D)	155,906	(63%)	($96,112)
	Rod Culp (R)	92,872	(37%)	($32,871)
1980 primary	Don Bonker (D)	88,001	(91%)	
	One other (D)	8,832	(9%)	
1978 general	Don Bonker (D)	82,607	(59%)	($43,324)
	Rick Bennett (R)	58,270	(41%)	($51,753)

FOURTH DISTRICT

For most of its length in Washington, the Columbia River flows either within or along the borders of the 4th congressional district. To the west the district expands to the city of Vancouver, an industrial town across the Columbia from Portland, Oregon. Upriver the 4th cuts through the Cascade Mountains at Bonneville Dam, past McNary Dam, to the town of Richland. This is the site of one of the major nuclear power areas in the United States; the Hanford Works here house government nuclear projects and one of the nation's three significant nuclear waste disposal sites. Jobs and the area's recent growth depend on the health of the nuclear industry, and few parts of the country are so strongly in favor of nuclear power—and bitter about the successes of nuclear opponents. Farther upriver one comes to the Yakima River, along which exists one of Washington's most fertile agricultural valleys, the producer of so many of the famous Washington apples. Still farther upriver, past Wenatchee, is the Grand Coulee Dam: one of the greatest federal construction projects during the New Deal that produced cheap hydroelectric power and plentiful irrigation water for much of this Inland Empire of interior Washington.

This is an area much indebted to the federal government: for Grand Coulee, the heavily subsidized nuclear industry, government support of agriculture. Yet the 4th district is extremely sour and negative in its attitude toward government generally. Government support of agriculture is taken for granted or details of it are the subject of complaint while Grand Coulee is part of the landscape. The nuclear industry arouses strong feelings, but during the Carter Administration at least the dominant sentiment here was that the federal government was not doing enough to encourage the nuclear industry or to discourage opponents of nuclear power.

The 1980 election saw the district not only go heavily for Ronald Reagan but also reject a ten-year Democratic congressman by a wide margin. This was all the more startling since the congressman, Mike McCormack, was one of Capitol Hill's most vigorous and enthusiastic boosters of nuclear power. McCormack was also well positioned, as chairman of a subcommittee on energy research, to advance the nuclear cause. Perhaps the problem was that, while nuclear was winning most of the battles—prevailing in referenda, receiving continued federal funding—it was losing the war—private investors, for a variety of reasons, no longer see utilities with nuclear expansion plans as an attractive place to put their money. McCormack had other problems; he was abrasive, and he backed a project to increase salmon spawning in the Yakima Valley at the expense of irrigation water. In general, he was hurt by the Democratic unpopularity on major economic and foreign policy issues.

Yet it is unlikely that even his Republican opponent, state Senator Sid Morrison, expected so big a Republican victory. Morrison won with a solid 57%. He carried the Yakima Valley by more than 2–1 and carried the area around Richland and the Hanford Works, McCormack's home base. The Democrat carried the Vancouver area. But that could easily be removed from the district in the redistricting process, which is controlled by Republicans. In that case Morrison, who is a member of the Agriculture Committee and seems likely to be a solid member of the Reagan Republican Party, would look like an excellent bet for reelection.

Census Data Pop. (1980 final) 629,637, up 32% in 1970s. Median family income, 1970, $9,206, 96% of U.S.

The Voters

Employment profile 1970   White collar, 44%. Blue collar, 34%. Service, 12%. Farm, 10%.
Ethnic groups   Black 1980, 1%. Hispanic 1980, 6%. Am. Ind. 1980, 2%. Asian 1980, 1%. Total foreign stock 1970, 14%. Canada, 3%; Germany, 2%; UK, 1%.

Presidential Vote

1980	Reagan (R)	131,717	(55%)
	Carter (D)	85,906	(36%)
	Anderson (I)	19,219	(9%)
1976	Ford (R)	111,182	(52%)
	Carter (D)	93,783	(44%)

Rep. Sid Morrison (R) Elected 1980; b. May 13, 1933, Yakima; home, Zillah; Wash. St. U., B.S. 1954.

Career Army, 1954–56; Orchardist, Morrison Fruit Co., Inc., 1956– ; Wash. House of Reps., 1966–74; Wash. Senate, 1974–80.

Offices 1330 LHOB, 202-225-5816. Also 212 E. E St., Yakima 98901, 509-575-5891; 176 Fed. Bldg., Richland 99352, 509-376-9702; and 314 Arts Bldg., Vancouver 98660, 206-696-7838.

Committee *Agriculture* (15th). Subcommittees: Conservation, Credit, and Rural Development; Cotton, Rice, and Sugar; Forests, Family Farms, and Energy.

Group Ratings and Key Votes: Newly Elected

Election Results

1980 general	Sid Morrison (R)	134,691	(57%)	($402,884)
	Mike McCormack (D)	100,114	(43%)	($250,728)
1980 primary	Sid Morrison (R)	39,673	(59%)	
	Claude Oliver (R)	27,547	(41%)	($129,386)
1978 general	Mike McCormack (D)	85,602	(61%)	($132,190)
	Susan Roylance (R)	54,389	(39%)	($65,371)

FIFTH DISTRICT

The 5th congressional district is the western part of Washington state. It is the heart of the Inland Empire and centers on Spokane, with 171,000 people the state's second largest city. Lying between the Cascades and the Rockies, the land here was originally arid plateau, but with the help of irrigation it has become one of the major wheat-growing areas of the United States. Much of the water is provided by the Grand Coulee Dam, the engineering marvel of the New Deal; the reclamation project also furnishes cheap public power. Washington, blessed with the nation's greatest hydroelectric resources, has always been a big backer of public power development.

In the intermountain West, Spokane is the largest city north of Salt Lake City. Spokane County, which contains the city and its suburbs, has about 60% of the 5th district's people and voters. Spokane is more Republican than the Puget Sound area in national races; in the 1980 race Carter was competitive with Reagan in the Puget Sound area, but Reagan carried

Spokane solidly. Strengthening the Republican tendencies of the 5th are small counties and towns such as Walla Walla near the Idaho and Oregon borders.

This district has elected only two congressmen in the last 40 years: Republican Walt Horan, who served from 1943 to 1965, and Democrat Thomas Foley, who defeated him in 1964 and has won reelection ever since. Foley is now one of the leading Democrats in the Congress as the House majority whip, the number three position in the leadership; and for six years before that he was chairman of the House Agriculture Committee. Yet he has had serious challenges in each of the last three elections and cannot count on automatic reelection in 1982.

Foley has climbed to his position in the House not so much by ambition nor certainly by ruthlessness, but by having the good fortune to be in the right place at the right time — and by developing great competence as a legislator. He did not even have ten years' seniority in 1974 when he won the Agriculture chair. The newly elected freshman Democrats that year deposed the incumbent, Bob Poage of Texas, for his conservative voting record, and Foley, thanks to a number of timely retirements, was next in seniority. Actually, as chairman he often deferred to Poage and got on with him well; Agriculture is a committee on which few issues, even food stamps, are decided on liberal–conservative lines. Foley's elevation to the whip position came after the defeat of its incumbent, John Brademas of Indiana, and by appointment — this is one of the last positions that is not elective — of Speaker Tip O'Neill and Majority Leader Jim Wright. Foley is widely respected by Democrats as a parliamentarian who is knowledgeable, careful in his rulings, and scrupulously fair; he is in line with the majority on issues and is considered a zealot by no one. He works hard and, despite his national leadership posts, makes great efforts to keep in touch with his district. He is probably one of the best natural legislators in the House, a man who is respectful of the opinions of others even as he is forceful in the advocacy of his own.

Why then does he have trouble winning reelection? One reason is that the 5th simply is a Republican district in national politics. In the late 1950s and early 1960s, the area now covered by the 5th district was voting pretty close to the national average; now it is about 6% more Republican and less Democratic than the national average. Another problem for Foley has been the presence of persistent and well-financed opponents, tire dealer Duane Alton in 1976 and 1978 and surgeon John Sonneland in 1980 (he lost to Alton in the 1978 primary). Foley's margin was small in 1978, when an Indian running as an Independent undoubtedly cost him some votes; it was similar, although his percentage was higher, in 1980.

Foley's high profile on national issues evidently has hurt him in a district where the Democratic position on most national issues is not popular; national prominence is evidently not a political asset anymore. Redistricting could shear off part of the district least favorable to Foley, the area around the nuclear city of Pasco, but he seems likely to have a serious challenge again in 1982. Foley is conceivably in line for the speakership and might indeed be most Democrats' choice should a battle develop between more polarizing figures; but in the meantime he must reflect on the fact that the last two men to hold the whip position were defeated for reelection.

Census Data   Pop. (1980 final) 579,374, up 19% in 1970s. Median family income, 1970, $9,164, 96% of U.S.

The Voters

Employment profile 1970   White collar, 49%. Blue collar, 28%. Service, 16%. Farm, 7%.
Ethnic groups   Black 1980, 1%. Hispanic 1980, 3%. Am. Ind. 1980, 2%. Asian 1980, 1%. Total foreign stock 1970, 16%. Canada, 4%; Germany, 2%; UK, Norway, Sweden, 1% each.

Presidential Vote

1980	Reagan (R)	132,936	(56%)
	Carter (D)	80,554	(34%)
	Anderson (I)	18,973	(8%)
1976	Ford (R)	114,988	(54%)
	Carter (D)	91,796	(43%)

Rep. Thomas S. Foley (D) Elected 1964; b. Mar. 6, 1929, Spokane; home, Spokane; U. of Wash., B.A. 1951, LL.B. 1957.

Career Practicing atty.; Spokane Co. Dpty. Prosecuting Atty., 1958–60; Instructor, Gonzaga U. Law Sch., 1958–60; Asst. Atty. Gen. of Wash., 1960–61; Asst. Chf. Clerk and Special Counsel, U.S. Senate Comm. on Interior and Insular Affairs, 1961–63.

Offices 1201 LHOB, 202-225-2006. Also 574 U.S. Courthouse, Spokane 99201, 509-456-4680.

Committees *Majority Whip.*

Agriculture (2d). Subcommittees: Cotton, Rice, and Sugar; Domestic Operations, Research, and Foreign Agriculture; Domestic Marketing, Consumer Relations, and Nutrition; Forests, Family Farms, and Energy; Wheat, Soybeans, and Feed Grains (Chairman).

Group Ratings

	ADA	COPE	PC	LCV	CFA	RPN	NAB	NSI	NTU	ACA	ACU
1980	61	72	53	49	64	—	17	11	15	17	5
1979	58	60	43	43	35	—	—	—	16	8	15
1978	30	65	48	47	41	42	42	40	12	22	36

Key Votes

1) Draft Registn $	AGN	6) Fair Hsg DOJ Enfrc	FOR	11) Cut Socl Incr Dfns $	AGN
2) Ban $ to Nicrgua	AGN	7) Lim PAC Contrbtns	AGN	12) Hosptl Cost Controls	AGN
3) Dlay MX Missile	AGN	8) Cap on Food Stmp $	AGN	13) Gasln Ctrls & Allctns	FOR
4) Nuclr Mortorium	AGN	9) New US Dep Edcatn	FOR	14) Lim Wndfll Prof Tax	FOR
5) Alaska Lands Bill	AGN	10) Cut OSHA $	AGN	15) Chryslr Loan Grntee	FOR

Election Results

1980 general	Thomas S. Foley (D)	120,530	(52%)	($361,234)
	John Sonneland (R)	111,705	(48%)	($213,853)
1980 primary	Thomas S. Foley (D)	55,967	(100%)	
1978 general	Thomas S. Foley (D)	77,201	(48%)	($347,573)
	Duane Alton (R)	68,761	(43%)	($174,978)
	Mel Tonasket (I)	14,887	(9%)	($18,141)

SIXTH DISTRICT

Tacoma, the second largest city on Puget Sound, has always lived in the shadow of its larger neighbor, Seattle. Back in 1900, just before the state's most explosive decade of growth, Tacoma was still a credible rival—it had 37,000 people to Seattle's 80,000. But in the years that followed, Seattle's growth continued, while Tacoma got itself embroiled in an unsuccessful attempt to rewrite history and change the name of Mount Rainier (which is in Pierce County like the city) to Mount Tacoma. Seattle was diversifying, adding white collar employment to its basic industries of shipping, fishing, lumber, and railroading. Tacoma remained primarily a lumber town, headquarters of the giant Weyerhaeuser firm, with only about one-quarter the population of its larger neighbor. Tacoma sits today on the hills rising from Commencement Bay, not as grim an environment as many mill towns, but not the city it once hoped it would become.

Tacoma is the heart of Washington's 6th congressional district, which includes the city and virtually all of its suburbs. The 6th also crosses the Puget Sound Narrows (where the Tacoma Straits Bridge collapsed in 1940) to include Kitsap County and its major city, Bremerton, a naval repair port, which lies across the Sound from Seattle. The 6th is a Democratic area in most elections—blue collar territory that is often the most Democratic part of the state.

But in 1980 the whole area—both the Tacoma area and Kitsap County—swung heavily to the Republicans. It gave strong margins to Ronald Reagan (he lost central-city Tacoma only narrowly), it failed to support 36-year Democratic Senator Warren Magnuson, and it gave a solid margin to Republican gubernatorial candidate John Spellman over Seattle psychiatrist James McDermott. No one is sure whether these results were just a one-time phenomenon or the beginning of a basic realignment. It does seem that this blue collar area was reacting against candidates it deemed too soft on defense (Carter) or too liberal on cultural issues (McDermott). Save Magnuson, who had an age problem, no one at the top of the Democratic ticket seemed to symbolize the values and beliefs that had kept these blue collar voters faithful Democrats for so many years.

The district still has a Democratic congressman, however. Norman Dicks was considered one of the state's most politically knowledgeable Democrats even while he was a member of Magnuson's staff; he won election to the district without difficulty in 1976 when the incumbent received the judgeship he had been hankering after for 12 years. Dicks has the record one would expect of a Democrat from a blue collar district. He has a liberal and prolabor record on economic issues; he is more conservative on many cultural issues; he supports, as most Washingtonians do, many environmental causes. He has, moreover, committee and subcommittee assignments that suggest that he has the high regard of his colleagues. He is a member of the Appropriations Committee and of its two subcommittees that are of greatest importance to his district: Defense and Interior. On Defense, Dicks generally supports increased defense spending and naturally looks after the Navy's interests in Bremerton and the Army's Fort Lewis outside Tacoma, which is just beyond the district's boundaries. On Interior, he has some clout and leverage on a wide variety of environmental issues. He is generally considered a constructive and knowledgeable legislator. And he is very sensitive to Washington state issues: in 1981, for example, he organized the drive to save the Export-Import Bank loan program, of which Boeing is the chief recipient.

Yet Dicks had a rather tough contest in the 1980 election—difficulty that can be explained only by shifts in his constituents' attitudes toward national issues. His percentage declined somewhat in 1978, although it was still over 60%. In 1980 the same opponent, with more financing this time thanks to national Republican efforts, narrowed his margin significantly. Dicks lost the suburban Lakewood area outside Tacoma and nearly lost southern Kitsap County. The prospect for 1982 is not entirely clear. Redistricting could change the boundaries of the district considerably. State Senator Peter von Reichbauer of Vashon Island switched from the Democratic to Republican Party in 1981 and gave the Republicans control of the redistricting process; the price may be the creation of Washington's new House seat with boundaries that will be most favorable to von Reichbauer's election to Congress. This would

1160 WASHINGTON

suggest that he would get Kitsap County and the Lakewood area, to be combined perhaps with some of the more Republican suburbs of Seatle and some of the Olympic peninsula. This would strengthen Democrats in surrounding districts, including Dicks. But all this is highly hypothetical; and if Republicans want to contend seriously for control of the House, the 6th is a district they will probably target. Dicks, in turn, will be fighting hard; his is a promising legislative career, whether he stays in the House or whether, as some suggest, he runs someday for the Senate.

Census Data Pop. (1980 final) 608,396, up 27% in 1970s. Median family income, 1970, $10,481, 109% of U.S.

The Voters

Employment profile 1970 White collar, 50%. Blue collar, 36%. Service, 13%. Farm, 1%.
Ethnic groups Black 1980, 4%. Hispanic 1980, 2%. Am. Ind. 1980, 1%. Asian 1980, 3%. Total foreign stock 1970, 19%. Canada, Germany, 3% each; Norway, UK, 2% each; Sweden, 1%.

Presidential Vote

1980	Reagan (R)	123,867	(50%)
	Carter (D)	88,831	(36%)
	Anderson (I)	28,621	(12%)
1976	Ford (R)	103,846	(48%)
	Carter (D)	106,107	(49%)

Rep. Norman D. Dicks (D) Elected 1976; b. Dec. 16, 1940, Bremerton; home, Port Orchard; U. of Wash., B.A. 1963, J.D. 1968.

Career Staff Mbr., Ofc. of U.S. Sen. Warren G. Magnuson, Legis. Asst., 1968–73, Admin. Asst., 1973–76.

Offices 1122 LHOB, 202-225-5916. Also Security Bldg., Tacoma 98402, 206-593-6536.

Committee *Appropriations* (20th). Subcommittees: Defense; Interior; Legislative.

Group Ratings

	ADA	COPE	PC	LCV	CFA	RPN	NAB	NSI	NTU	ACA	ACU
1980	67	76	53	44	57	—	17	33	18	26	5
1979	63	75	60	42	70	—	—	—	20	4	6
1978	45	90	58	55	59	50	27	33	6	19	13

Key Votes

1) Draft Registn $	FOR	6) Fair Hsg DOJ Enfrc	FOR	11) Cut Socl Incr Dfns $	AGN
2) Ban $ to Nicrgua	AGN	7) Lim PAC Contrbtns	FOR	12) Hosptl Cost Controls	FOR
3) Dlay MX Missile	AGN	8) Cap on Food Stmp $	AGN	13) Gasln Ctrls & Allctns	FOR
4) Nuclr Mortorium	AGN	9) New US Dep Edcatn	FOR	14) Lim Wndfll Prof Tax	AGN
5) Alaska Lands Bill	AGN	10) Cut OSHA $	AGN	15) Chryslr Loan Grntee	FOR

Election Results

1980 general	Norman D. Dicks (D)...........	122,903	(54%)	($234,650)
	James E. Beaver (R)	106,236	(46%)	($165,330)
1980 primary	Norman D. Dicks (D)...........	71,407	(91%)	
	One other (D)	7,059	(9%)	
1978 general	Norman D. Dicks (D)...........	71,057	(61%)	($166,731)
	James E. Beaver (R)	43,640	(37%)	($19,308)

SEVENTH DISTRICT

The 7th congressional district of Washington is the south side of Seattle and most of its southern suburbs, from Lake Washington and downtown Seattle about halfway down to Tacoma. This is the more blue collar side of Seattle. The city's industrial area is concentrated in a flat plain that slides into Puget Sound; here the railroads and freeways come in from the south and east and serve the factories and warehouses that are everywhere. At the southern end of this valley are the major Boeing plants, built some years after the initial industrial boom but for some years—from the 1940s through 1969, when Boeing employment plummeted, and again in the late 1970s—the biggest industry in town.

Seattle's blue collar workers live in hilly neighborhoods on either side of the industrial flatlands. And if their houses are architecturally undistinguished, their streets look out often on pleasant views of Lake Washington or Puget Sound. Farther south of the city, one comes on newer and newer suburbs—Renton, Burien, Kent—that have filled up with the sons and daughters of those who settled the working-class neighborhoods of Seattle itself. There is a small black community in the 7th, which includes nearly half the state's black population, but it still amounts to only 9% of the district's population; there are also small Mexican-American and Asian communities.

The 7th district also includes some higher-income, more Republican areas. The district lines cross Lake Washington to the east to include the woodsy suburb of Mercer Island and part of the more settled area of Bellevue, the most Republican part of the Seattle area. Also, south of the city, along the hills between Puget Sound and the valley that contains the Boeing plants, one comes eventually to pleasant suburbs overlooking the water: Burien, Normandy Park, Des Moines, Zenith. These are all more Republican than Democratic.

Politics in the Seattle area—much as in Metropolitan Minneapolis, another area settled heavily by Scandinavians—remains correlated highly to economic status. The predominantly blue collar nature of the 7th district has made it Democratic in most elections. Yet there is also a substantial Republican base here. The district went for Jimmy Carter in 1976, but only by a narrow margin, and Ronald Reagan carried it in 1980. It elected a Democratic congressman by large margins for 12 years, Brock Adams. But when he became Carter's first secretary of Transportation, the 7th in the 1977 special election chose a Republican, and a right-wing one at that, Jack Cunningham.

That choice was reversed in the 1978 election, and the district is now held by a Democrat who is an unabashed liberal and supporter of prolabor legislation. Mike Lowry was able to beat Cunningham in 1978, although the incumbent spent half a million dollars, and to prevail against a conservative opponent in 1980, in essentially the same way: he won overwhelming margins in the minority areas, carried all the working-class districts, and more than compensated for the margins by which he lost the upper-income areas. It was an old-fashioned

1162   WASHINGTON

victory of a liberal Democrat in a historically Democratic area. Lowry serves on the Banking and Merchant Marine Committees. His prospects for reelection in 1982 are good and may be improved by redistricting if the area around Bellevue is removed from the district; he could be hurt, however, if the Republican legislature puts too many Republican areas in his district.

Census Data Pop. (1980 final) 488,611, up 2% in 1970s. Median family income, 1970, $11,706, 122% of U.S.

The Voters

Employment profile 1970 White collar, 54%. Blue collar, 33%. Service, 13%. Farm, –%.
Ethnic groups Black 1980, 9%. Hispanic 1980, 3%. Am. Ind. 1980, 1%. Asian 1980, 7%. Total foreign stock 1970, 22%. Canada, 4%; UK, Germany, Norway, 2% each; Sweden, 1%.

Presidential Vote

1980	Reagan (R)	97,129	(44%)
	Carter (D)	93,447	(42%)
	Anderson (I)	25,665	(12%)
1976	Ford (R)	99,388	(48%)
	Carter (D)	100,271	(48%)

Rep. Michael E. (Mike) **Lowry** (D) Elected 1978; b. Mar. 8, 1939, St. John; home, Mercer Island; Wash. St. U., B.A. 1962.

Career Chf. Fiscal Analyst and Staff Dir., Wash. Senate Ways & Means Comm., 1969–73; Govt. Affairs Dir., Puget Sound Group Health Coop., 1974–75; King Co. Cncl., 1975–78, Chmn., 1977.

Offices 1206 LHOB, 202-225-3106. Also 3400 Rainier Ave. S., Seattle 98118, 206-442-7170.

Committees *Banking, Finance and Urban Affairs* (21st). Subcommittees: Housing and Community Development; International Development Institutions and Finance; International Trade Investment and Monetary Policy.

Merchant Marine and Fisheries (13th). Subcommittees: Coast Guard and Navigation; Fisheries and Wildlife Conservation and the Environment.

Group Ratings

	ADA	COPE	PC	LCV	CFA	RPN	NAB	NSI	NTU	ACA	ACU
1980	100	68	67	87	79	—	8	20	16	17	11
1979	84	85	68	79	81	—	—	—	14	15	15

Key Votes

1) Draft Registn $	AGN	6) Fair Hsg DOJ Enfrc	FOR	11) Cut Socl Incr Dfns $	AGN
2) Ban $ to Nicrgua	AGN	7) Lim PAC Contrbtns	FOR	12) Hosptl Cost Controls	FOR
3) Dlay MX Missile	FOR	8) Cap on Food Stmp $	AGN	13) Gasln Ctrls & Allctns	AGN
4) Nuclr Mortorium	AGN	9) New US Dep Edcatn	FOR	14) Lim Wndfll Prof Tax	AGN
5) Alaska Lands Bill	FOR	10) Cut OSHA $	AGN	15) Chryslr Loan Grntee	FOR

Election Results

1980 general	Michael E. (Mike) Lowry (D)	112,848	(57%)	($236,351)
	Ron Dunlap (R)	84,218	(43%)	($221,223)
1980 primary	Michael E. (Mike) Lowry (D)	66,209	(94%)	
	One other (D)	4,092	(6%)	
1978 general	Michael E. (Mike) Lowry (D)	67,450	(53%)	($214,609)
	John E. Cunningham (R)	59,052	(47%)	($523,905)

WEST VIRGINIA

West Virginia lies in the middle of the Appalachian chain that separates the East Coast from the vast Mississippi Valley of Middle America. This is a state with scarcely a square mile of level ground, and it has been said that if all the mountains were ironed out, the resulting surface area would cover the entire nation. Maybe so, but in any case, the mountains and the narrow, twisting roads that wind through them give West Virginia an isolation and a sense of distance from the rest of the country. This is not a state that thinks of itself as part of the East or Midwest or even the South; the term Appalachian (with a hard "ch" sometimes) is heard occasionally, but people here really think of themselves as West Virginians.

It is an identity hard won. Until 1863 the mountain counties were part, a misfit part, of the commonwealth of Virginia. There were few slaves here; in the late 1820s legislators from the mountain counties teamed up with Jeffersonian aristocrats and almost abolished slavery in Virginia. But the spectre of slave rebellions and the increasing profitability of breeding slaves for sale in the cotton belts of the Deep South strengthened the peculiar institution east of the Blue Ridge, and the mountain counties went their own way. They opposed secession; they stayed part of the Union and continued to send congressmen to Washington. In 1863, after a dispute over the name (it was nearly called Kanawha), West Virginia was admitted to the Union as a separate state.

The new state contained about one-quarter of the residents of old Viriginia. But in the years that followed the Civil War, West Virginia grew much more rapidly than its parent. The reason was simple: coal. Under virtually all the mountains here and often near the surface are rich veins of bituminous coal, the essential fuel for industry and home heating in the late 19th and early 20th centuries. West Virginia was then a kind of frontier. Men from all over the Appalachian region and even some immigrants from southern and eastern Europe came to work the booming mines.

The working conditions in the mines were never very good and were sometimes deadly. Lovers of country music know something of life in the coal company towns and the credit practices of company stores, where workers and their families had to buy everything. Immigrant communities in the big cities of the time had some geographical proximity and exposure to other kinds of American life. The coal mining communities of West Virginia, often literally up a creek or in a hollow, were effectively cut off from the rest of the world. Conditions were bad enough that a union movement developed, and during the 1930s John L. Lewis's United Mine Workers organized most of West Virginia's mines — so successfully that West Virginia is now the most heavily unionized state in the nation. But just as unionization was complete, the coal industry entered a decades-long decline. The railroads switched from coal-powered steam engines to oil-powered diesels. Homes switched from messy coal to clean oil or gas. After World War II Lewis worked with the companies to encourage mechanization of the industry and to reduce the work force. The program was a vast success — but something of a disaster for West Virginia. In 1950 the state's population exceeded two million; by 1970, as thousands left to look for work elsewhere, it was down to 1.7 million. Almost a whole generation of young people had found themselves forced to leave the state.

Recently the coal industry has come on better times. As other fuels — oil and gas — become more expensive, coal becomes more attractive. And there is plenty of it: West Virginia alone has enough coal to supply the nation for hundreds of years. But the new prosperity has a price. Now that labor is relatively expensive, companies look for capital-intensive ways to mine the coal. One solution is strip mining: much of the coal is near the surface and can be scooped up with giant steam shovels. But strip mining often leaves ugly, sometimes irreparable scars on the landscape. The big companies have claimed they use sound reclamation methods, which are sometimes clearly less than successful. Many of the smaller operators do not bother. Nor are federal or state regulations automatically an answer. The Buffalo Creek disaster of 1972—when a company-constructed dam burst and flood waters destroyed a small town—shows how negligent or corrupt regulators can be. Companies are also careless about wastes, and hundreds of the narrow valleys and hollows of West Virginia suffer from serious air and water pollution. This is a state that operates very near the margin and the incentive for profit is often desperate.

The proliferation of small operators in the coal business has helped to create a few local millionaires, but it has also helped change the conditions of West Virginia life; the big companies were easier to regulate and easier to unionize. The United Mine Workers represents a smaller percentage of the mine work force than it used to, and it appears in danger of breaking up as well. Lewis's successor, Tony Boyle, who ran a cozy and corrupt operation, has been convicted of murdering a rival who ran against him in the 1968 union election. In 1972 Boyle was beaten by Arnold Miller who was in turn forced out when he utterly failed to keep the union under control. In 1981 union members rejected a contract settlement and went out on strike—likely a self-defeating course, since one thing that deters industry from switching to coal is unreliability of supply.

Politics in West Virginia is a rough—and often corrupt—business. Many state jobs are filled by patronage, and bribery is not uncommon. One recent former governor, W. W. Barron (1961–64) has gone to jail, and another, Arch Moore, was tried and acquitted on charges of taking $25,000 from a savings and loan executive seeking a bank charter. Vote fraud has been so much a matter of course that returns from Mingo County, to take the most flagrant example, have traditionally been interpreted as indicating who paid off the county leaders rather than which candidate the voters actually preferred. As in underdeveloped nations, so in this impoverished state, idealism and altruism are scarce in politics. In a state where most of the executive positions are held by outsiders in companies headquartered elsewhere, the best local avenues to riches are through public and union office.

Yet the state's governorship is currently held by a man against whom charges of greed have no credibility: John D. Rockefeller IV, universally called Jay. He first moved to West Virginia in 1964 to work in an antipoverty program, at the time an expert in East Asian affairs. He decided to stay and enter politics, as a Democrat rather than a Republican like his uncles, the governors of New York and Arkansas. He was elected to the legislature in 1966 and to statewide office in 1968. His one setback occurred in 1972, when he ran against Arch Moore, the first West Virginia governor eligible for a second consecutive term. Moore was running in good times and was able to point to rising employment, rising population, and new roads; he called Rockefeller a carpetbagger (one ad showed people on a New York street being asked whether they would elect an outsider from West Virginia as governor). Moore won that race with 55% and Rockefeller spent several years as president of a small West Virginia college.

In 1976 Rockefeller ran again. In a strong primary field, Rockefeller won 50% of the vote. Against former Governor Cecil Underwood in the general he won overwhelmingly. There were some difficult moments during his first term, but by and large Rockefeller was successful. He built 10,000 miles of roads, removed the sales tax on food, he recruited industry for the state, and he sold other states on using West Virginia coal. He excelled at providing emergency services when severe flooding hit the state, although he could do relatively little to ameliorate the effects of UMW and wildcat strikes. In 1980 Rockefeller faced his toughest opponent, Arch Moore, and this time beat him. The margin was decisive but not overwhelming, and Rockefeller spent more than $9 million in his campaign. His television advertisements were aired in Pittsburgh (whose stations cover much of northern West Virginia) and Washington (whose stations cover several fast-growing counties in the eastern part of the state). There is always speculation that Rockefeller will run for president, but that presumably must wait for at least a couple more years. The likelier betting is that he will run for the Senate seat that Jennings Randolph is likely to vacate in 1984. If he does, he may face Moore again—if Moore doesn't run for governor once again.

If Rockefeller is West Virginia's most famous governor for some time, its best known congressional representative ever is certainly Senator Robert Byrd. If you look back to the beginning of his political career, his rise seems most improbable. He had once been a Ku Klux Klan member (he quit in 1945), he voted against civil rights laws in the House and the Senate, he was not exactly well connected with the Washington establishment. Byrd made his career and created his leadership role through one little secret: hard work. He cultivated his constituents in West Virginia assiduously; he still keeps file cards with thousands of names and telephone numbers and calls constituents every night, to ask their opinions on issues and to find out what is happening back home. In 1969 and 1970, when Edward Kennedy was Senate majority whip, Byrd was secretary of the Senate Democratic Conference. After Kennedy was distracted from his duties by Chappaquiddick, Byrd paid meticulous attention to the petty details that can make the lives of senators easier: keeping them informed of the pace of floor debate and the schedule of upcoming votes, helping them to get amendments before the Senate, arranging pairs, and even getting taxicabs. He showed his colleagues elaborate courtesy, writing them thank-you notes on the slightest pretext. It all paid off in 1971, when Byrd suddenly challenged Kennedy for the whip post. All of Byrd's hard work got him critical votes from senators whose voting records were much closer to Kennedy's, and he was even careful to round up Richard Russell's deathbed proxy.

Before his election as whip, Byrd had one of the most conservative voting records of Senate Democrats; afterward, he took more liberal positions on issues generally. His attention to detail gave him a critical role in uncovering the Watergate scandal: it was Byrd who got L. Patrick Gray to admit that John Dean "probably lied" about the affair, an admission that sparked Dean's determination to tell the truth. By 1976 it was clear that Byrd would be elected majority leader when Mike Mansfield retired. Hubert Humphrey ran a last-minute campaign against him but was not able to win away from Byrd many liberal votes that had long been committed to him. Byrd has not had any challenge for the Democratic leadership since.

Byrd's four years as majority leader during the Carter presidency were undoubtedly frustrating ones. He did succeed in streamlining Senate proceedings to some extent—although the Senate by its nature is inherently inefficient. But increasingly the Senate became the burying ground for Democratic legislation. Byrd himself supported on most occasions the administration and liberal positions, partly probably out of a conviction that a leader should not get out of line from his followers, partly out of simple conviction. But with 59 Democrats—one short of the number needed to break a filibuster—and a united Republican Party, he was often stymied. Moreover, the failure of the Carter Administration to bring forward and then really fight for a program hobbled a leader such as Byrd who had always seen his role as one who expedited other Democrats' bills rather than as one who initiated a whole program himself.

Now Byrd is minority leader. He has fewer votes and seems to regard himself as under a greater obligation to enunciate policy. In the early days of the Reagan Administration he was one of the senators most critical of some of its appointments (he was one of the handful opposing the confirmation of Secretary of State Haig) and of its policies of cutting back on domestic programs. Byrd evidently was attempting to rally his 46 Democrats around a particular point of view and, perhaps, attract some defecting Republicans. For the long run that is a strategy that may work. In the short run, however, it did not. Democrats showed little capacity to unite around anything, while Republicans still acted as if they were a beleaguered minority and held together. Byrd had the pleasure of insisting that all but three Republicans vote to raise the ceiling on the national debt. But on most issues the Republicans had 53 votes and Byrd could do very little.

Byrd's careful cultivation of West Virginia voters has not stopped, despite his high position in Washington. Although he is an accomplished country fiddle player, Byrd is not part of any old boy network in the state, but he is West Virginia's champion vote-getter nonetheless. In 1970 he whipped a liberal primary challenger with 88%; in the general election that year he became the first candidate in history to carry all 55 of West Virginia's counties. In 1976 he was prepared to do that all over again, but no one filed to run against him. No one doubts that he will be reelected easily in 1982.

West Virginia's other senator, Jennings Randolph, is one of the most experienced war horses on Capitol Hill. He first came to Congress in 1932, as a 30-year-old freshman New Deal congressman. Defeated in the Republican year of 1946, he became a Hill lobbyist, but he kept a hand in West Virginia politics. In 1958 he won election to the Senate, and he had little trouble winning full terms in 1960, 1966, and 1972.

For many years Randolph was chairman of the Environment and Public Works Committee. Under its old name, Public Works, this was the key pork barrel committee, and its chairman had a great deal of clout from doling out dams and post offices and other federal building projects to his colleagues. This was a role Randolph found congenial. Naturally a generous and amiable man, he was pleased to help his friends. He remains an old-fashioned New Dealer, convinced that public works projects create jobs and help the little people of the nation. More recently the committee has taken on matters suggested by the first half of its new name; it is the body that passes on most air and water pollution legislation. On such matters the legislative workload for years was hefted by Edmund Muskie. Now the lead role will be taken by Chairman Robert Stafford of Vermont; but this is not a committee that operates in a very partisan fashion, and Randolph will be in on the negotiations to renew the Clean Air Act in 1981 and will be careful to protect the interests of West Virginia coal.

Most of Randolph's legislative work has been with this committee, but he does have other interests. Since the 1930s he has been Congress's leading backer of projects to help the handicapped; it was he, for example, who wrote the law requiring candy stands in federal buildings to be run by blind persons.

Many people expected Randolph to retire in 1978, when he turned 76 years old — and when the irrepressible Arch Moore was the Republican candidate. But he decided to run just one more time. Moore naturally contrasted their ages and argued that he as governor, not Randolph as senator, built the roads West Virginia needed and got its economy moving again. Randolph for the first time used professional television advertisements and public opinion polling, and emphasized his own strengths. He argued that he had done more for

West Virginia, that he was still vigorous and powerful, and some of his commercials — although not featuring the polite Randolph himself — went so far as to attack Moore. Robert Byrd made a very strong endorsement of Randolph and campaigned extensively for him — a rare example of colleagues of the same party from the same state working closely for each other. It was one of the closest Senate elections in the country, but Randolph won by some 4,000 votes. Assuming his continued good health, he can expect to celebrate his 80th birthday and the 50th anniversary of his first election to Congress in 1982.

Before 1980, West Virginia had not been represented by a Republican in Congress since Arch Moore left the House to run for governor in 1968. Suddenly, in 1980, two Republicans were elected here, one to replace the retiring Harley Staggers, the other to replace the winner of a 1980 special election in the Charleston district. Neither owed their elections to Ronald Reagan's coattails: West Virginia was one of six states carried by Jimmy Carter, and Carter in fact carried all four of its congressional districts. The Democrats could try to hurt the Republicans in redistricting, but they do not have too much room to maneuver. All four districts are close to the average statewide population, and any attempt to make one more Democratic will make another more Republican. The prospect is for seriously contested House races — an oddity here — in one, two, or perhaps even three districts in 1982.

Census Data   Pop. (1980 final) 1,949,644, up 12% in 1970s: 0.86% of U.S. total, 34th largest. Central city, 12%; suburban, 23%. Median 4-person family income, 1978, $18,493, 91% of U.S., 38th highest.

1979 Share of Federal Tax Burden $3,201,000,000; 0.71% of U.S. total, 34th largest.

1979 Share of Federal Outlays $3,544,810,000; 0.76% of U.S. total, 36th largest.

DOD	$211,730,000	46th	(0.20%)	HEW	$1,693,727,000	34th	(0.95%)
DOE	$24,825,000	31st	(0.21%)	ERDA	$24,000,000	20th	(0.88%)
HUD	$49,121,000	34th	(0.75%)	NASA	$17,000	49th	(0.00%)
VA	$236,952,000	33d	(1.14%)	DOT	$164,105,000	30th	(0.99%)
EPA	$109,902,000	17th	(2.07%)	DOC	$8,112,000	41st	(0.26%)
DOI	$38,358,000	32d	(0.69%)	USDA	$158,809,000	42d	(0.66%)

Economic Base   Bituminous coal mining; chemicals and allied products, especially industrial chemicals; primary metal industries, especially blast furnaces and basic steel products; stone, clay, and glass products, especially glassware, pressed or blown; finance, insurance, and real estate; agriculture, especially cattle, dairy products, apples, and eggs.

Political Lineup   Governor, John D. (Jay) Rockefeller IV (D). Senators, Jennings Randolph (D) and Robert C. Byrd (D). Representatives, 4 (2 D and 2 R); 4 in 1982. State Senate, 34 (27 D and 7 R); State House of Delegates, 99 (77 D and 22 R).

The Voters

Registration   1,034,546 Total. 691,382 D (67%); 319,286 R (31%); 23,878 other (2%).
Employment profile 1970   White collar, 40%. Blue collar, 45%. Service, 13%. Farm, 2%.
Ethnic groups   Black 1980, 3%. Hispanic 1980, 1%. Total foreign stock 1970, 4%.

Presidential Vote

1980	Reagan (R)	334,206	(45%)
	Carter (D)	367,462	(50%)
	Anderson (I)	31,691	(4%)
1976	Ford (R)	314,726	(42%)
	Carter (D)	435,864	(58%)

1980 Democratic Presidential Primary			*1980 Republican Presidential Primary*		
Carter	197,687	(62%)	Reagan	115,407	(84%)
Kennedy	120,247	(38%)	Bush	19,509	(14%)
			One other	3,100	(2%)

SENATORS

Sen. Jennings Randolph (D) Elected 1958, seat up 1984; b. Mar. 8, 1902, Salem; home, Elkins; Salem Col., B.A. 1924.

Career Ed. Staff, *Clarksburg Daily Telegram,* 1924–25; Assoc. Ed., W.Va. *Review,* 1925–26; Prof. and Athletic Dir., Davis & Elkins Col., 1926–32; Instructor and Business Col. Dean, Southeastern U.; U.S. House of Reps., 1933–47; Asst. to the Pres. and Dir. of Pub. Rel., Capital Airlines, 1947–48.

Offices 3203 DSOB, 202-224-6472. Also 328–329 Fed. Bldg., 300 3d St., Elkins 26241, 304-636-5100.

Committees *Environment and Public Works* (Ranking Member). Subcommittee: Transportation.

Labor and Human Resources (2d). Subcommittees: Labor; Education; Handicapped.

Veterans' Affairs (2d).

Group Ratings

	ADA	COPE	PC	LCV	CFA	RPN	NAB	NSI	NTU	ACA	ACU
1980	72	89	57	49	60	—	36	67	28	12	19
1979	32	88	52	—	38	—	—	—	22	29	33
1978	30	68	43	51	50	11	45	70	14	38	43

Key Votes

1) Draft Registn $	FOR	6) Fair Housng Cloture	FOR	11) Cut Socl Incr Defns	AGN
2) Ban $ to Nicrgua	AGN	7) Ban $ Rape Abortns	FOR	12) Income Tax Indexing	AGN
3) Dlay MX Missile	AGN	8) Cap on Food Stmp $	AGN	13) Lim Spdg 21% GNP	AGN
4) Nuclr Mortorium	FOR	9) New US Dep Edcatn	FOR	14) Incr Wndfll Prof Tax	FOR
5) Alaska Lands Bill	FOR	10) Cut OSHA Inspctns	AGN	15) Chryslr Loan Grntee	FOR

Election Results

1978 general	Jennings Randolph (D)..........	249,034	(50%)	($684,605)
	Arch A. Moore, Jr. (R)	244,317	(50%)	($458,823)
1978 primary	Jennings Randolph (D), unopposed			
1972 general	Jennings Randolph (D)..........	486,310	(66%)	($133,670)
	Louise Leonard (R).............	245,531	(34%)	($45,513)

Sen. Robert C. Byrd (D) Elected 1958, seat up 1982; b. Jan. 15, 1918, North Wilkesboro, N.C.; home, Sophia; Beckley Col., Concord Col., Morris Harvey Col., Marshall Col.

Career W.Va. House of Reps., 1946–50; W.Va. Senate, 1950–52; U.S. House of Reps., 1953–59; U.S. Senate Major. Whip, 1971–77, Major. Ldr. 1978–80.

Office 133 RSOB, 202-224-3954.

Committees *Minority Leader.*

Appropriations (3d). Subcommittees: Agriculture and Related Agencies; Energy and Water Development; Interior; Labor, Health and Human Services, Education; Transportation.

Judiciary (3d). Subcommittee: Regulatory Reform.

Rules and Administration (4th).

Group Ratings

	ADA	COPE	PC	LCV	CFA	RPN	NAB	NSI	NTU	ACA	ACU
1980	56	57	47	23	53	—	8	30	34	15	14
1979	53	58	38	—	38	—	—	—	17	26	16
1978	45	78	63	56	40	40	50	50	15	29	21

Key Votes

1) Draft Registn $	FOR	6) Fair Housng Cloture	FOR
2) Ban $ to Nicrgua	FOR	7) Ban $ Rape Abortns	AGN
3) Dlay MX Missile	AGN	8) Cap on Food Stmp $	AGN
4) Nuclr Mortorium	AGN	9) New US Dep Edcatn	FOR
5) Alaska Lands Bill	FOR	10) Cut OSHA Inspctns	AGN

11) Cut Socl Incr Defns	FOR
12) Income Tax Indexing	AGN
13) Lim Spdg 21% GNP	AGN
14) Incr Wndfll Prof Tax	FOR
15) Chryslr Loan Grntee	FOR

Election Results

1976 general	Robert C. Byrd (D).............	338,444	(100%)	($94,335)
1976 primary	Robert C. Byrd (D), unopposed			
1970 general	Robert C. Byrd (D).............	345,965	(78%)	
	Elmer H. Dodson (R)...........	99,663	(22%)	

GOVERNOR

Gov. John D. (Jay) **Rockefeller IV** (D) Elected 1976, term expires Jan. 1985; b. June 18, 1937, New York City; International Christian U., Tokyo, 1957–60, Harvard U., B.A. 1961.

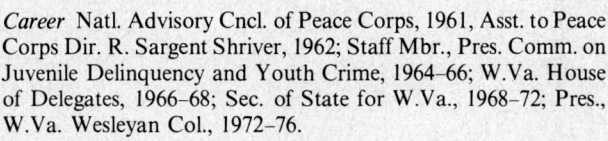

Career Natl. Advisory Cncl. of Peace Corps, 1961, Asst. to Peace Corps Dir. R. Sargent Shriver, 1962; Staff Mbr., Pres. Comm. on Juvenile Delinquency and Youth Crime, 1964–66; W.Va. House of Delegates, 1966–68; Sec. of State for W.Va., 1968–72; Pres., W.Va. Wesleyan Col., 1972–76.

Offices Charleston 25305, 304-348-2000.

Election Results

1980 gen.	John Rockefeller IV (D) ...	401,863	(54%)
	Arch A. Moore, Jr. (R)	337,240	(45%)
1980 prim.	John D. Rockefeller IV (D).	240,550	(78%)
	H. John Rogers (D)	70,452	(22%)
1976 gen.	John D. Rockefeller IV (D).	495,600	(66%)
	Cecil H. Underwood (R) ...	253,398	(34%)

FIRST DISTRICT

West Virginia's northern panhandle is the least isolated part of the state. The terrain here is hilly, not mountainous, and the panhandle is in steel country that sits along the Ohio River just west of Pittsburgh and south of Youngstown, Ohio. Along the river are giant blast furnaces in Wheeling, the hometown of Walter Reuther, and Weirton. With the Pittsburgh area, the panhandle is one of the leading glassmaking areas of the country as well. Not surprisingly, industrial pollution here has been a big problem. The Ohio River valley around Wheeling has some of the most polluted air in the United States, and the Ohio itself is not clean. Another problem is the periodically sagging and seldom surging economy. Steel was once American's leading industry; its performance now is lackluster.

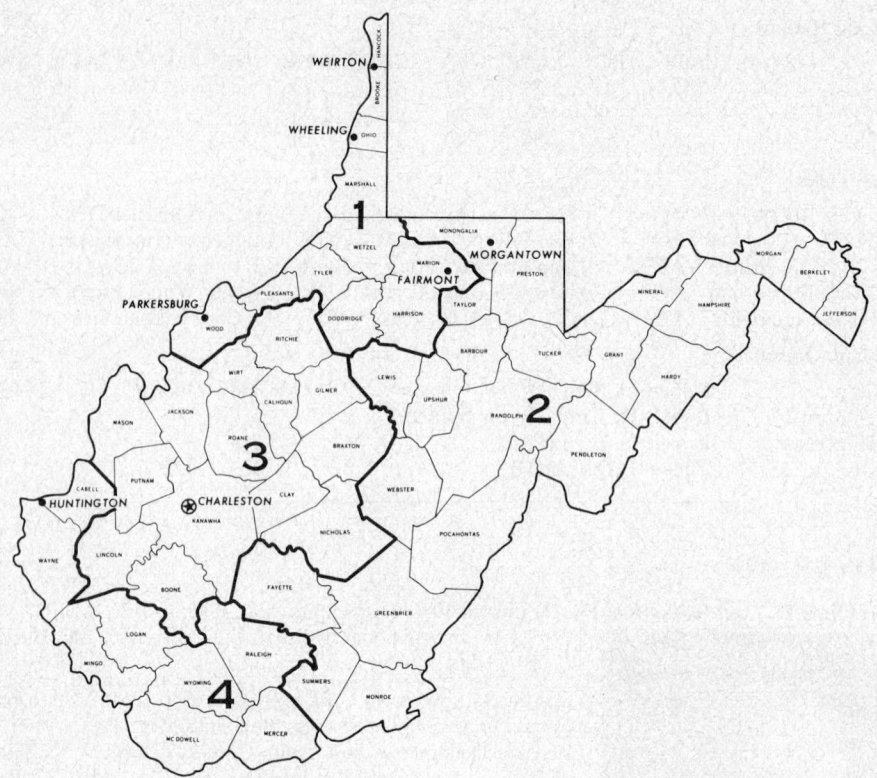

The industrial towns of Clarksburg and Fairmont in the Monongahela River valley south of Pittsburgh, the northern panhandle, and the Ohio River counties as far south as Parkersburg make up West Virginia's 1st congressional district. Aside from a few rural counties and Parkersburg, which tend to go Republican, the 1st district is Democratic territory in most elections. But that has not always been the case in congressional elections, thanks to the vote-getting prowess of Arch Moore, who was elected to Congress here from 1956 to 1966 and was elected governor in 1968 and 1972.

Moore's successor in Congress is also his predecessor: Democrat Robert Mollohan. A veteran of West Virginia political wars, Mollohan was elected here in 1952 and 1954 and then ran unsuccessfully for governor in 1956, when Moore won in the House. Mollohan tried to beat Moore, but even in the Democratic year of 1958 he could not do so; he went into the insurance business and ran for the House when Moore ran for governor in 1968. A member of the Armed Services and House Administration Committees, he has a voting record that wins approval both in the Pentagon and in the halls of organized labor.

Mollohan has not always shown great prowess as a vote-getter, however. His margins in 1974 and 1976 were not particularly impressive. Although he did somewhat better in 1978 and 1980, he turns 73 in 1982, and he must be considered a possible candidate for retirement soon.

Census Data   Pop. (1980 final) 460,542, up 5% in 1970s. Median family income, 1970, $8,457, 88% of U.S.

The Voters

Employment profile 1970 White collar, 39%. Blue collar, 47%. Service, 13%. Farm, 1%.
Ethnic groups Black 1980, 2%. Hispanic 1980, 1%. Total foreign stock 1970, 9%.

Presidential Vote

1980	Reagan (R)	85,216	(46%)
	Carter (D)	88,697	(48%)
	Anderson (I)	8,370	(5%)
1976	Ford (R)	84,374	(44%)
	Carter (D)	105,377	(56%)

Rep. Robert H. Mollohan (D) Elected 1968; b. Sept. 18, 1909, Grantsville; home, Fairmont; Glenville Col., Shepherd Col.

Career Chf., W.Va. Misc. Tax Div., and Cashier, IRS, 1933–36; Dist. Mgr. and State Personnel Dir., Works Projects Admin., 1937–40; State Dir., U.S. Census, 1940; Supt., W.Va. Industrial Sch. for Boys, 1945–49; U.S. Marshal, No. Dist. of W.Va., 1949–51; Clerk, U.S. Senate Comm. on the Dist. of Columbia; U.S. House of Reps., 1953–57.

Offices 339 CHOB, 202-225-4172. Also Rm. 603 Deveny Bldg., Fairmont 26554, 304-363-3356.

Committees *Armed Services* (7th). Subcommittees: Investigations; Research and Development; Seapower and Strategic and Critical Materials.

House Administration (5th). Subcommittees: Office Systems (Chairman); Services.

Group Ratings

	ADA	COPE	PC	LCV	CFA	RPN	NAB	NSI	NTU	ACA	ACU
1980	56	68	43	17	57	—	17	56	16	20	16
1979	37	90	48	42	48	—	—	—	25	19	20
1978	30	55	45	54	27	25	50	80	12	48	42

Key Votes

1) Draft Registn $	FOR	6) Fair Hsg DOJ Enfrc	AGN	11) Cut Socl Incr Dfns $	AGN
2) Ban $ to Nicrgua	AGN	7) Lim PAC Contrbtns	FOR	12) Hosptl Cost Controls	AGN
3) Dlay MX Missile	AGN	8) Cap on Food Stmp $	AGN	13) Gasln Ctrls & Allctns	FOR
4) Nuclr Mortorium	AGN	9) New US Dep Edcatn	FOR	14) Lim Wndfll Prof Tax	FOR
5) Alaska Lands Bill	FOR	10) Cut OSHA $	AGN	15) Chryslr Loan Grntee	FOR

Election Results

1980 general	Robert H. Mollohan (D)	107,471	(64%)	($57,941)
	Joe Bartlett (R)	61,438	(36%)	($60,925)
1980 primary	Robert H. Mollohan (D)	64,998	(100%)	
1978 general	Robert H. Mollohan (D)	76,372	(63%)	($37,680)
	Gene A. Haynes (R)	44,062	(37%)	($14,129)

SECOND DISTRICT

The 2d congressional district of West Virginia occupies the eastern part of the state and contains the most mountainous and most sparsely populated counties of West Virginia. The district extends from Harpers Ferry, not far from Washington, D.C., where John Brown's raiders seized the arsenal and tried to free the slaves in 1859, south and west to Fayette County, near the state capital of Charleston, and not far from the Kentucky line. In the northwestern part of the district, not far from Pittsburgh, is the 2d's only significant city, Morgantown, with a population of only 27,000 — part of the industrial Monongahela River valley and home of West Virginia University.

The 1970s were the best decade this part of West Virginia has seen for some time — perhaps ever. The population as recorded by the census grew 20% in ten years; and, while some of this change evidently reflected better census-taking in remote hollows and hills, it seems also to indicate an end to the outmigration that has been the pattern of life in West Virginia for so many years. People left because there were few good jobs here and many opportunities in northern cities; now the northern cities are in trouble, and West Virginia, despite some turbulence, is doing better than ever. The coal industry has been booming, other businesses have moved in, four-lane highways have been built, and some of the pollution from coal mining and paper milling has been cleaned up or prevented.

These developments may have created a change in basic political attitudes and have certainly helped to produce a change in congressional representation. The political map of the 2d district is an odd-looking patchwork of Democratic industrial and mining areas and Republican mountain strongholds. In most statewide elections the district has been marginal; it gave Jimmy Carter a very small plurality in 1980. In congressional elections for many years it was reliably Democratic. This was essentially the district that sent Jennings Randolph to the House during the New Deal, and from 1948 until 1980 it elected Democrat Harley Staggers, who for more than a decade chaired the House Commerce (now Energy and Commerce) Committee. Staggers was never, however, one of the real powers in Washington, and after his percentage dropped sharply in 1978, he decided to retire in 1980. He tried to pass the district along to his son, but he was narrowly beaten in the Democratic primary by state Senator Pat Hamilton.

The winner in 1980 was Cleveland Benedict, a Republican and longtime associate of former Governor Arch Moore. Benedict is the man who gave Staggers the close race in 1978, and in 1980 he carried all but three counties in the district against Hamilton. Benedict campaigned as a dairy farmer and rural resident; actually he is an heir to the Procter & Gamble fortune and about as rural as Jay Rockefeller. The solidness of his victory suggests that he has much of Moore's political acumen. He won Staggers's old seat on the Energy and Commerce Committee. The outlook for 1982 is unclear. Democrats would like to regain this seat, and they have control of the redistricting process. But Benedict's large 1980 margin — well ahead of Ronald Reagan in the district — and his access to generous campaign funds may mean that he is unbeatable. In that event, Democrats would be better off taking some of the more Democratic counties from the 2d district and swapping them for more Republican counties in the 3d, where Republican incumbent Mick Staton looks more vulnerable. In that event the 2d might end up with a much more attenuated shape than it has now; even more so if it swaps Democratic Morgantown for the 1st district's Republican Parkersburg.

Census Data   Pop. (1980 final) 522,835, up 20% in 1970s. Median family income, 1970, $6,437, 67% of U.S.

The Voters

   Employment profile 1970   White collar, 37%. Blue collar, 45%. Service, 14%. Farm, 4%.
   Ethnic groups   Black 1980, 3%. Hispanic 1980, 1%. Total foreign stock 1970, 3%.

Presidential Vote

1980	Reagan (R)	93,228	(47%)
	Carter (D)	94,094	(48%)
	Anderson (I)	9,313	(5%)
1976	Ford (R)	84,374	(43%)
	Carter (D)	105,377	(57%)

Rep. Cleveland K. (Cleve) **Benedict** (R) Elected 1980; b. Mar. 21, 1935, Harrisburg, Pa.; home, Lewisburg; Princeton U., B.A. 1957.

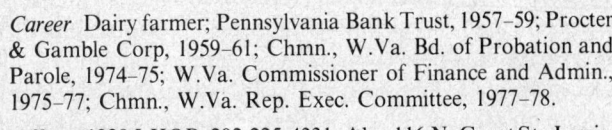

Career Dairy farmer; Pennsylvania Bank Trust, 1957–59; Procter & Gamble Corp, 1959–61; Chmn., W.Va. Bd. of Probation and Parole, 1974–75; W.Va. Commissioner of Finance and Admin., 1975–77; Chmn., W.Va. Rep. Exec. Committee, 1977–78.

Offices 1229 LHOB, 202-225-4331. Also 116 N. Court St., Lewisburg 24901, 304-645-6028; 307 Fed. Bldg. 225 W. King St., Martinsburg 25401, 304-263-6679; and 201 Prairie Ave., Rm. 209, Morgantown 26505, 304-292-3005.

Committee *Energy and Commerce* (16th). Subcommittees: Energy Conservation and Power; Fossil and Synthetic Fuels; Health and the Environment.

Group Ratings and Key Votes: Newly Elected

Election Results

1980 general	Cleveland K. (Cleve) Benedict (R) .	102,805	(56%)	($231,377)
	Pat R. Hamilton (D)............	80,940	(44%)	($447,450)
1980 primary	Cleveland K. (Cleve) Benedict (R) .	24,593	(62%)	
	Edgar Heiskell (R)..............	14,778	(38%)	($39,641)
1978 general	Harley O. Staggers (D)	69,683	(55%)	($37,481)
	Cleveland K. (Cleve) Benedict (R) .	56,272	(45%)	($168,782)

THIRD DISTRICT

Charleston is West Virginia's capital, the center of its largest metropolitan area, and the state's largest city. Along the banks of the Kanawha River (pronounced kan-AW locally) stands the Capitol building, one of the largest and most beautiful in the country. But a little more typical of Charleston are the large Union Carbide plants a little farther downriver. Like most West Virginia cities, Charleston is situated in a narrow river valley, hemmed in by mountains; so situated, the city is a victim to a smog that can rival that of Los Angeles. It is primarily an industrial city, with large chemical plants. Although there are a few skyscrapers here, the country atmosphere still prevails; this is where irate fundamentalist parents literally started riots over the allegedly liberal and pornographic contents of school textbooks in the middle 1970s.

Charleston and surrounding Kanawha County are the population center and political pivot of West Virginia's 3d congressional district. Upriver in the mountains is coal mining country, the kind of destitute hollows where Jay Rockefeller lived when he first came to the state as an antipoverty worker. The territory below Charleston, down to the Ohio River, is less mountainous and also less densely populated. The coal counties are usually heavily Democratic; the Ohio River counties seem to retain a Republicanism that goes back to the days when West Virginia first became a state during the Civil War. Charleston itself, perhaps surprisingly for an industrial city, often leans a little more to the Republicans than the Democrats. In 1980, for example, when West Virginia was one of the few states to give a plurality to Jimmy Carter, Kanawha County was almost dead even.

This was a solidly Democratic district for many years—since 1926—and one of those districts whose capture by the Republicans has put control of the House within their reach. For more than 20 years the congressman here was John Slack, a former real estate man and local assessor, whose conservative politics and position as an Appropriations subcommittee chairman made him seem politically unbeatable. Slack died suddenly in March 1980, just before the filing deadline for the seat; numerous local politicians scrambled to succeed him, first in a special election held on June 3 and then in the general election in November. One was John Hutchinson, the mayor of Charleston. He captured the seat in the special election and seemed likely to hold it for the Democrats in November. But Hutchinson got some nasty publicity: he took a vacation almost as soon as he was sworn in, while Congress was in session, and, after he fired one attractive aide, his wife was revealed to have written a memo insisting he hire only homely women.

The result was an upset victory for Republican Mick Staton. A political self-starter whose underfinanced campaign against Slack in 1978 had gotten him a respectable 41% of the vote, Staton had attracted support from the national Republican Party and from the Moral Majority group. With a professional effort, he was able to raise the national Republican issues and to profit from Hutchinson's problems. Staton's victory was not a matter of coattails: he ran ahead of Ronald Reagan, while Hutchinson ran behind Jimmy Carter in the district.

The question for 1982 is whether Staton can hold onto this district—or whatever district the Democratic legislature draws for him. He carried Kanawha County in 1980, but not by a wide enough margin to overcome Hutchinson's edge in the coal counties; the real Republican margin came from the counties toward the Ohio River. These could conceivably be removed by the legislature and placed within the 2d district (thereby conceding it to Republican Cleve Benedict), and coal counties right on the border of the current 3d district could be added to it. In these circumstances, Staton would have to run far ahead of his 1980 showing to hold onto the seat.

Census Data   Pop. (1980 final) 478,741, up 10% in 1970s. Median family income, 1970, $7,574, 79% of U.S.

The Voters

Employment profile 1970   White collar, 44%. Blue collar, 43%. Service, 12%. Farm, 1%.
Ethnic groups   Black 1980, 3%. Hispanic 1980, 1%. Total foreign stock 1970, 2%.

Presidential Vote

1980	Reagan (R)	88,693	(47%)
	Carter (D)	91,695	(48%)
	Anderson (I)	8,728	(5%)
1976	Ford (R)	81,613	(42%)
	Carter (D)	111,688	(58%)

Rep. David Michael (Mick) **Staton** (R) Elected 1980; b. Feb. 11, 1940, Parkersburg; home, South Charleston; Concord Col., 1961–63.

Career Army Nat. Guard, 1958–65; V.P., Data Processing and Mktg., Kanawha Valley Bank, 1970–80.

Offices 425 CHOB, 202-225-2711. Also 1206 Virginia St. E., Charleston 25301, 304-345-6425.

Committees *Interior and Insular Affairs* (15th). Subcommittees: Energy and the Environment; Mines and Mining.

Small Business (11th). Subcommittees: Export Opportunities and Special Small Business Problems; SBA and SBIC Authority, Minority Enterprise and General Small Business Problems.

Group Ratings and Key Votes: Newly Elected

Election Results

1980 general	David Michael (Mick) Staton (R) .	94,583	(53%)	($155,579)
	John G. Hutchinson (D)	84,980	(47%)	($246,961)
1980 primary	David Michael (Mick) Staton (R) .	28,259	(74%)	
	Richie Robb (R)	7,457	(20%)	($0)
	One other (R)	2,435	(6%)	
1980 special	John G. Hutchinson (D)	51,169	(54%)	
	David Michael (Mick) Staton (R) .	43,950	(46%)	
1980 spec. prim.	John G. Hutchinson (D), nominated by convention			
1978 general	John M. Slack (D)	74,837	(59%)	($34,433)
	David Michael (Mick) Staton (R) .	51,584	(41%)	($14,878)

FOURTH DISTRICT

The 4th district of West Virginia is the southern part of the state. This is coal country. The eight counties of the 4th probably have produced more bituminous coal over the years than any other single congressional district in the United States. Not quite all the district is mining country, however; it also contains the state's largest city, Huntington, with 63,000 people, a manufacturing and railroad junction town on the Ohio River. But from the banks of the Ohio the mountains rise steeply, and the heart of the 4th is in the small coal towns sitting between the mountainsides. This was a boom area around the turn of the century, with lots of in-migration, mostly from the South. But after World War II employment in the mines declined drastically, and the decline continued through the 1950s and 1960s. The population of the counties now in the 4th declined from 579,000 in 1950 to 437,000 in 1970. Recently the economy of this area has bounced back somewhat, as coal prices rose and mining—or at least strip mining—actively increased and the population is now up to 487,000. But the number of coal mining jobs is still far from its old peak, and many of the jobs are now non-union. The United Mine Workers has split into several factions, and this has been the site of major wildcat strikes, of varying effectiveness.

The politics of this sometimes poverty-stricken area has little of the altruism that some liberal reformers expect to find among the poor. In such places as southern West Virginia there are few ways for a bright young man to make money except by owning a coal mine or winning public or union office. Public office is often more lucrative than published salaries suggest; corruption is common, and there are counties where one is still supposed to be able to buy votes. Under such circumstances maximum feasible participation of the poor amounts to the survival of the fittest — not necessarily of the one who does the most for the ordinary person. In the struggle to get ahead, the ordinary politician has little concern for matters such as unsafe mine conditions, black lung disease, or air and water pollution. People are inclined to get what they can and not to worry about others.

The district's last two congressmen, in very different ways, have provided contrasts with this kind of political background. Ken Hechler was first elected here in 1958, shortly after he came to West Virginia as a professor at Huntington's Marshall University; he had a background as a speech writer for Adlai Stevenson. A resourceful campaigner, Hechler opposed the UMW leadership of Tony Boyle when it was physically dangerous to do so, and he advocated a complete ban on strip mining. Without organized backing, and against all the local politicos, he beat another incumbent with whom he had been redistricted in 1972. Hechler's congressional career ended abruptly in 1976. He announced early that he would run for governor and for Congress as well — an entirely legal procedure here. Later he opted out of the House race, even as it was becoming clear that he had no chance against front-runner Jay Rockefeller in the gubernatorial primary. Defeated then, he ran as a write-in for the House and won a phenomenal 37% — not enough to win. In 1978 he ran in the Democratic House primary and, when he was solidly beaten, announced that he would not try again.

If Hechler's advantage was idealism and real empathy with people, his successor's real strength has been hard work and hard cash. Nick Joe Rahall comes from a family that owns broadcasting stations in West Virginia and Florida. In 1976, at 27, he ran in the Democratic primary. With Hechler out of the race, and after spending more than $100,000 of his own money, he won with 37% in a five-candidate field. That fall Rahall had to spend again to repel Hechler's effort, although this time he had the aid of labor, Democratic politicos, and Rockefeller. During his first two years in the House, Rahall provided the kind of constituency services and attention to district matters that enabled him to overcome Hechler in the Democratic primary. That is testimony again to his strength. Now, just over 30, he seems to have vanquished all the tough opposition, and a long congressional career may have opened up ahead of him. Rahall is a member of the Public Works and Interior Committees, bread-and-butter assignments for a congressman from a coal mining district such as the 4th. He is also a member of the House ethics committee, which says something positive about his colleagues' respect for him.

Census Data Pop. (1980 final) 487,526, up 11% in 1970s. Median family income, 1970, $7,039, 73% of U.S.

The Voters

Employment profile 1970 White collar, 42%. Blue collar, 46%. Service, 12%. Farm, –%.
Ethnic groups Black 1980, 6%. Hispanic 1980, 1%. Total foreign stock 1970, 2%.

Presidential Vote

1980	Reagan (R)	67,069	(40%)
	Carter (D)	92,976	(56%)
	Anderson (I)	5,300	(3%)
1976	Ford (R)	62,505	(37%)
	Carter (D)	105,407	(63%)

Rep. Nick Joe Rahall II (D) Elected 1976; b. May 20, 1949, Beckley; home, Beckley; Duke U., B.A. 1971, Geo. Wash. U., 1973.

Career Sales Rep. and Mbr. of the Bd., Rahall Communications Corp.; Pres., Mountaineer Tour and Travel Agency.

Offices 440 CHOB, 202-225-3452. Also Bair Bldg., Main and N. Fayette Sts., Beckley 25801, 304-252-5000.

Committees *Interior and Insular Affairs* (16th). Subcommittees: Energy and the Environment; Mines and Mining.

Public Works and Transportation (16th). Subcommittees: Aviation; Surface Transportation; Water Resources.

Standards of Official Conduct (2d).

Group Ratings

	ADA	COPE	PC	LCV	CFA	RPN	NAB	NSI	NTU	ACA	ACU
1980	67	94	57	41	64	—	8	33	21	13	24
1979	74	79	60	48	63	—	—	—	21	17	15
1978	60	79	58	66	36	18	25	60	15	29	25

Key Votes

1) Draft Registn $	FOR	6) Fair Hsg DOJ Enfrc	FOR	11) Cut Socl Incr Dfns $	AGN
2) Ban $ to Nicrgua	AGN	7) Lim PAC Contrbtns	FOR	12) Hosptl Cost Controls	FOR
3) Dlay MX Missile	FOR	8) Cap on Food Stmp $	AGN	13) Gasln Ctrls & Allctns	FOR
4) Nuclr Mortorium	FOR	9) New US Dep Edcatn	FOR	14) Lim Wndfll Prof Tax	AGN
5) Alaska Lands Bill	AGN	10) Cut OSHA $		AGN	15) Chryslr Loan Grntee	FOR

Election Results

1980 general	Nick Joe Rahall II (D)	117,595	(77%)	($155,285)
	Winton G. Covey, Jr. (R)	36,020	(23%)	($0)
1980 primary	Nick Joe Rahall II (D)	61,228	(100%)	
1978 general	Nick Joe Rahall II (D), unopposed			($242,298)

WISCONSIN

Wisconsin is a state of political anomalies. It spawned both Bob LaFollette and the Progressive movement and Joe McCarthy and his campaign against communism in high places. Richard Nixon carried Wisconsin, the state where the Republican Party was founded, three times; yet the state in the 1970s became one of the most Democratic at all levels. It provided 11 crucial electoral votes for Jimmy Carter in 1976 and came close to favoring him in 1980. Wisconsin is heavily industrial, although it is also the nation's leading producer of dairy products; a heavily urban state, yet filled with lakes and forests.

Wisconsin owes much of its unique politics to the German and Scandinavian immigrants who formed such a large percentage of its original settlers. Here, as in Minnesota and North

Dakota, the immigrants left a distinctive political stamp. In all three states there developed —against the background of an overwhelming preference for the Republican Party—a politics of near radical economic reform and an isolationist foreign policy. The term "progressive" was coined in Wisconsin, and it was personified by Robert "Fighting Bob" LaFollette. Elected governor in 1900, he completely revamped the state government before going into the Senate in 1906. There LaFollette supported other insurgent reformers and voted against American entry into World War I. In 1924 he ran for president under the banner of the Progressive Party and won 18% of the nation's votes—the best third party showing in the last 60 years. LaFollette's sons maintained the traditions of Wisconsin progressivism. Robert LaFollette, Jr., served in the Senate from 1925 to 1947, and Philip LaFollette was governor of Wisconsin from 1935 to 1939. During the 1930s the LaFollettes ran on the Progressive Party line in Wisconsin and dreamed of forming a national third party. But the onset of World War II destroyed the plans of the isolationist reformers. In 1946 Senator LaFollette, busy with congressional reorganization in Washington, was upset in the Republican primary by one Joseph McCarthy.

How did the state produce politicians as different as LaFollette and McCarthy at roughly the same time? Part of the answer lies in the leanings of Wisconsin's ethnic groups, particularly the largest—the German–Americans. As Samuel Lubell pointed out, much of the impetus behind postwar anticommunism came from those who believed that we should not have fought a war allied with the Communists against Germany. In any case, McCarthy proved to be less typical of Wisconsin in the long run than the LaFollettes. "Tail gunner Joe" won his first primary in an upset; his two victories in the general elections of 1946 and 1952 occurred in heavily Republican years, and only the first did he win by a large margin. If McCarthy had not died a broken man in 1957, after his censure by the Senate in 1954, he would probably have been defeated in the 1958 election.

During the McCarthy years Republicans dominated Wisconsin elections more or less by default. The party's progressive side was dormant, and the Democrats had usually been not much of a factor in the state's politics. But in the early 1950s a group of liberal Democrats — none of whom had held major office—assumed control over the husk of the party and laid plans to become a majority force. A simple recitation of their names gives evidence of their success: Senator William Proxmire, Governor and Senator Gaylord Nelson, Governor Patrick Lucey, and Congressman Robert Kastenmeier. The group's first victory occurred in the 1957 special election to fill McCarthy's Senate vacancy. The Republican nominee was former Governor Walter Kohler; the Democrat was Proxmire, fresh from three defeats in three consecutive gubernatorial campaigns. But by the summer of 1957 the booming economy of the middle Eisenhower years had begun to turn sour: factories were laying off workers and farm income was declining because of government surpluses. Proxmire's years of campaigning finally paid off, and he beat Kohler by a 56%–41% margin. From that time until 1980, when Nelson was upset, Democrats won every U.S. Senate election in the state, and Proxmire is heavily favored to win a fifth full term in 1982.

How has Proxmire come to be so popular among his constituents (although not always among his colleagues)? One reason is his reputation as a pinch-penny. He is consistently the senator rated highest by the National Taxpayers Union, because he votes against just about any money bill that there is a shred of a reason to oppose. He has never been a liberal spender: he is a business school graduate and a man who prizes discipline and hard work. His personal habits are legend. He is the only senator who runs four miles from his home to the Capitol every morning and the only one to stand rather than sit at his desk. He is in superb health and looks years younger than his age. Proxmire combines parsimoniousness with an utter disdain for the camaraderies most politicians enjoy. He is the last man in the Senate who will go along to get along; he constantly finds himself as the lone man on votes.

These characteristics have sometimes isolated him from power, but they have also produced some of his greatest victories. An example was his fight to kill the supersonic transport (SST) in the late 1960s and early 1970s. He took on the big boys — the Johnson and Nixon Administrations, the nation's most reliable aircraft contractor (Boeing), the two powerful senators from the state of Washington, Warren Magnuson and Henry Jackson — and won. Proxmire does not limit his targets to the aerospace industry. He has also gone after big defense contractors, the Pentagon, social scientists, and HHS. For several years he has issued a monthly "golden fleece" award to some person or group he feels has wasted federal money in the most outrageous fashion.

For his attacks on the SST and the defense budget, Proxmire was labeled a liberal. Businessmen sometimes consider Proxmire antibusiness when he attacks big companies for charging the government too much or for bribing foreign officials. Actually he believes strongly in the free enterprise system. He just hates to see money wasted.

Proxmire undoubtedly sacrifices some of his potential effectiveness by his way of doing business. His colleagues often consider him a grandstander, but his thorough preparation and hard work make him a force to be reckoned with.

Proxmire has held a number of important committee positions. In the Carter years he was chairman of the Senate Banking, Housing and Urban Affairs Committee. Bankers initially feared that he would be their nemesis, but that did not occur. Often he found himself out on a limb: he was the only vote, for example, against confirming Patricia Harris as secretary of HUD on the grounds — uncharacteristic for Proxmire — that she was not part of the small group of recognized experts on housing programs. The Banking Committee also handled legislation on loan guarantees. Despite Proxmire's qualms, it reported out measures to bail out New York City and the Chrysler Corporation although, because of Proxmire's work, the terms were tougher than they might otherwise have been. Going into the Reagan years, Proxmire became ranking minority member on the Appropriations Committee — a seemingly ideal place from which to cut the budget. But most of the action now is in the Budget Committee, and at the beginning of the Reagan Administration Proxmire seemed very much in the shadow of Budget Director David Stockman. Proxmire's spotlighting of frivolous research projects and his crusade against first class air travel paled into insignificance beside Stockman's massive budget cuts. Ironically, Proxmire voted against the first budget-cutting measure to come to the floor; it affected dairy price supports, and no Wisconsin senator votes against dairy farmers. Proxmire will have plenty of opportunities to hack at the Labor, HHS, Education, and Defense budgets over the next few years; the question is how much effect his work will have.

Proxmire appears to remain one of the most popular and invincible of senators at home. With his incredible energy, he has continued to work the state hard; the saying is that you can't get into a Green Bay Packers' football game without shaking Proxmire's hand. His reputation as a budget cutter is helpful in the frugal Upper Midwest and his skepticism about defense budgets has not hurt in a state that has virtually no defense industry or military bases. In the last two elections Proxmire has beaten well-known opponents with more than 70% of the vote and has carried every county. It seems unlikely that a serious Republican challenger can be found to face him in 1982.

Yet it was not long ago that Senator Gaylord Nelson seemed almost as invincible. Nelson was never as widely popular as Proxmire, nor did he have an issue that went across party lines as much as Proxmire's budget cutting. But Nelson had worn well with the state's voters for years, since he was elected governor in 1958. He was one of the first politicians in the country to concern himself with environmental issues and remained identified as an environmentalist throughout his career. He was one of the brightest and best-liked senators, but he lacked the ambition so many of his colleagues had and he never showed the kind of intensive hard work characteristic of Proxmire. In 1980 Nelson was opposed by former Congressman Robert Kasten, a young suburban Milwaukee conservative who had lost the 1978 gubernatorial primary; only in the later weeks did Nelson run an all-out campaign. By then it was apparently too late. The problem was not simply Reagan coattails (Carter had 43% of the vote in the state, and Nelson had run far ahead of other Democrats before) as it was Nelson's identification with what voters had come to regard as outdated ideas. To Nelson this was outrageous: he was ahead of his time on the environment and the Vietnam war. But his skepticism about some defense programs and his support of generous government spending programs hurt in 1980. Narrowly defeated, Nelson went on to become head of the Wilderness Society.

Kasten, a few years ago an obscure backbencher in the House, is now part of the majority party in the Senate, a member of the Budget and Appropriations Committees. He is chairman of the subcommittee with jurisdiction over foreign aid and sits on subcommittees that handle defense and agriculture spending. He is a member of the Commerce Committee as well and of Veterans' Affairs. Kasten's record in the House suggests that he will be a solid Reagan conservative, but he is not a charter member of the New Right. Nor is he politically suicidal. Along with Proxmire, he opposed cuts in the levels of dairy price supports.

In the middle 1970s Democrats controlled just about every Wisconsin office they could control. They had the governorship, other statewide offices, and big margins in both houses of the legislature. Now that has changed. Republicans made only minor gains in legislative seats, but they have captured the governorship. They did so with an unorthodox candidate whose chances were heavily discounted before the Republican primary, Lee Dreyfus. As chancellor of the Wisconsin State University campus at Stevens Point, he had made a reputation as an opponent of campus rebels and of stuffed shirts at the same time. Dreyfus's zest for campaigning and his hard-hitting speaking style — he is a professor of speech — attracted favorable attention and enabled him to upset the primary favorite, Robert Kasten. The Democratic candidate was Martin Schreiber, who had inherited the governorship when Patrick Lucey became ambassador to Mexico in 1977. The Democrat had taken some of the state's surplus revenue and given it back to voters as property tax relief and retained some of the rest against a rainy day. Schreiber had planned to run against Kasten as a candidate of the wealthy and the well-placed; instead he had to run against a small-town professor who simply asked that the state refrain from collecting any more withholding tax in order to cut the surplus. Dreyfus's spirited attacks, his trademark red vest, and the momentum from the primary gave him control of the dialogue of the campaign. He made big inroads among upper-income liberals in both the Milwaukee area and in Madison's Dane County, which he actually carried over Schreiber. The Democrat was able to carry only a few industrial enclaves and the north woods counties that receive Minnesota television—where Dreyfus had accordingly made little impression. The result was a solid Dreyfus victory.

How well Dreyfus's appeal will wear over the long run is unclear. The Democrats still control the legislature by large margins, and Dreyfus almost inevitably is involved in some feuds with them. For the moment anyway it is like a basketball game in which the Republicans have got a dominant star but the Democrats have the stronger bench. Almost certainly there will be a spirited contest for the governorship in 1982.

Congressional redistricting presents relatively few problems for Wisconsin. The state loses no seats, and the only ones to lose substantial population are the two based in Milwaukee. If territory is added to them in the suburbs, the rest of the districts can be handled with minor adjustments that are unlikely to affect their incumbents' political security much.

Census Data   Pop. (1980 final) 4,705,335, up 7% in 1970s: 2.08% of U.S. total, 16th largest. Central city, 29%; suburban, 33%. Median 4-person family income, 1978, $21,034, 103% of U.S., 17th highest.

1979 Share of Federal Tax Burden $9,332,000,000; 2.07% of U.S. total, 15th largest.

1979 Share of Federal Outlays $6,834,608,000; 1.47% of U.S. total, 24th largest.

DOD	$571,832,000	36th	(0.54%)	HEW	$4,024,250,000	12th	(2.25%)
DOE	$8,593,000	37th	(0.07%)	ERDA	$3,286,000	36th	(0.12%)
HUD	$101,284,000	23d	(1.54%)	NASA	$4,727,000	27th	(0.10%)
VA	$387,662,000	19th	(1.87%)	DOT	$212,011,000	26th	(1.28%)
EPA	$80,616,000	23d	(1.52%)	DOC	$17,084,000	29th	(0.54%)
DOI	$31,278,000	38th	(0.56%)	USDA	$432,958,000	22d	(1.80%)

Economic Base   Agriculture, notably dairy products, cattle, hogs, and corn; machinery, especially engines and turbines; finance, insurance, and real estate; food and kindred products, especially dairy products and beverages; electrical equipment and supplies, especially electrical industrial apparatus; fabricated metal products; paper and allied products, especially paper mills, other than building paper.

Political Lineup   Governor, Lee Sherman Dreyfus (R). Senators, William Proxmire (D) and Robert W. Kasten, Jr. (R). Representatives, 9 (5 D and 4 R); 9 in 1982. State Senate, 33 (19 D and 14 R); State Assembly, 99 (58 D, 40 R, and 1 vacancy).

The Voters

Registration   3,372,000 Total.
Employment profile 1970   White collar, 43%. Blue collar, 37%. Service, 14%. Farm, 6%.
Ethnic groups   Black 1980, 4%. Hispanic 1980, 1%. Am. Ind. 1980, 1%. Total foreign stock 1970, 17%. Germany, 5%; Poland, 2%; Norway, 1%.

Presidential Vote

1980	Reagan (R)	1,088,845	(48%)
	Carter (D)	981,584	(43%)
	Anderson (I)	160,657	(7%)
1976	Ford (R)	1,004,987	(48%)
	Carter (D)	1,040,232	(49%)

1980 Democratic Presidential Primary			1980 Republican Presidential Primary		
Carter	353,662	(56%)	Reagan	364,898	(40%)
Kennedy	189,520	(30%)	Bush	276,164	(30%)
Brown	74,496	(12%)	Anderson	248,623	(27%)
2 others & scattering	9,247	(1%)	5 others & scattering	15,573	(2%)
None	2,694	(0%)	None	2,595	(0%)

SENATORS

Sen. William Proxmire (D) Elected Aug. 1957, seat up 1982; b. Nov. 11, 1915, Lake Forest, Ill.; home, Madison; Yale U., B.A. 1938, Harvard U., M.B.A. 1940, M.P.A. 1948.

Career Wis. House of Reps., 1951; Dem. nominee for Gov., 1952, 1954, 1956; Pres., Artcraft Press, 1953–57.

Offices 5241 DSOB, 202-224-5653. Also Rm. 301, 30 W. Mifflin St., Madison 53703, 608-252-5338, and Fed. Court Bldg., 517 E. Wisconsin Ave., Milwaukee 53202, 414-272-0388.

Committees *Appropriations* (Ranking Member). Subcommittees: Defense; HUD–Independent Agencies; Labor, Health and Human Services, Education; Treasury, Postal Service, and General Government.

Banking, Housing, and Urban Affairs (2d). Subcommittees: Housing and Urban Affairs; Financial Institutions; International Finance and Monetary Policy.

Joint Economic Committee (8th).

Group Ratings

	ADA	COPE	PC	LCV	CFA	RPN	NAB	NSI	NTU	ACA	ACU
1980	56	52	80	93	73	—	83	60	87	54	71
1979	42	53	89	—	76	—	—	—	83	59	52
1978	60	63	70	91	70	60	83	10	73	46	29

Key Votes

1) Draft Registn $	AGN	6) Fair Housng Cloture	FOR	11) Cut Socl Incr Defns	FOR
2) Ban $ to Nicrgua	AGN	7) Ban $ Rape Abortns	FOR	12) Income Tax Indexing	FOR
3) Dlay MX Missile	FOR	8) Cap on Food Stmp $	FOR	13) Lim Spdg 21% GNP	FOR
4) Nuclr Mortorium	FOR	9) New US Dep Edcatn	AGN	14) Incr Wndfll Prof Tax	FOR
5) Alaska Lands Bill	FOR	10) Cut OSHA Inspctns	AGN	15) Chryslr Loan Grntee	AGN

Election Results

1976 general	William Proxmire (D)	1,396,970	(72%)	($697)
	Stanley York (R)	521,902	(27%)	($62,210)
1976 primary	William Proxmire (D), unopposed			
1970 general	William Proxmire (D)	948,445	(71%)	
	John E. Erickson (R)	381,297	(28%)	

Sen. Robert W. Kasten, Jr. (R) Elected 1980, seat up 1986; b. June 19, 1942, Milwaukee; home, Milwaukee; U. of Ariz., B.A. 1964, Columbia U., M.A. 1966.

Career Air Force, 1967; Wis. Air Nat. Guard; Wis. Senate, 1972; U.S. House of Reps., 1974–78.

Offices 328 RSOB, 202-224-5323. Also 120 Bishops Way, Brookfield 53005, 414-784-5315.

Committees *Appropriations* (11th). Subcommittees: Agriculture and Related Agencies; Defense; Energy and Water Development; Foreign Operations (Chairman); Transportation.

Budget (10th).

Commerce, Science, and Transportation (9th). Subcommittees: Consumer (Chairman); Merchant Marine and Tourism; Science, Technology, and Space.

Veterans' Affairs (4th).

Group Ratings (as Member of U.S. House of Representatives)

	ADA	COPE	PC	LCV	CFA	RPN	NAB	NSI	NTU	ACA	ACU
1978	15	23	23	36	23	63	78	89	33	90	83

Key Votes: Newly Elected

Election Results

1980 general	Robert W. Kasten, Jr. (R)	1,106,311	(50%)	($686,758)
	Gaylord A. Nelson (D)	1,065,487	(48%)	($897,774)
1980 primary	Robert W. Kasten, Jr. (R)	134,586	(37%)	
	Terry J. Kohler (R)	106,270	(29%)	($524,929)
	Douglass Cofrin (R)	84,355	(23%)	($1,497,508)
	One other (R)	40,823	(11%)	
1974 general	Gaylord A. Nelson (D)	740,700	(62%)	($247,555)
	Thomas E. Petri (R)	429,327	(36%)	($80,590)

GOVERNOR

Gov. Lee Sherman Dreyfus (R) Elected 1978, term expires Jan. 1983; b. June 20, 1926, Milwaukee; U. of Wis., B.A. 1949, M.A. 1952, Ph.D. 1957.

Career Navy, WWII; Instr., Asst. Prof., Assoc. Prof., Wayne St. U., and Gen. Mgr., WDET Radio, U. Station, 1952–62; Chmn., Wis. Educ. TV Comm., 1962–65; Prof., U. of Wis., and Gen. Mgr., WHA-TV, U. Station, 1962–67; Pres. Wis. St. U. at Stevens Point, 1967–72, Chancellor, 1972–78.

Offices State Capitol, Madison 53702, 608-266-1212.

Election Results

1978 gen.	Lee Sherman Dreyfus (R) ..	816,056	(54%)
	Martin J. Schreiber (D)	673,813	(45%)
1978 prim.	Lee Sherman Dreyfus (R) ..	197,279	(58%)
	Robert W. Kasten (R)	143,361	(42%)
1974 gen.	Patrick J. Lucey (D).......	628,639	(53%)
	William D. Dyke (R)	497,195	(42%)

FIRST DISTRICT

The 1st congressional district of Wisconsin is the southeastern corner of the state. The district contains a fairly good microcosm of Wisconsin as a whole. In the eastern part of the 1st, along Lake Michigan, are the industrial cities of Racine and Kenosha, the homes of such companies as Johnson's Wax and American Motors. These tend to be Democratic areas, particularly Kenosha. Farther inland is Walworth County, an area of small farms around the posh resort town of Lake Geneva. This is one of the most heavily Republican parts of the state. To the west are the cities of Janesville and Beloit. Like Racine and Kenosha they are industrial. But the workers here are less ethnic and more likely to be Anglo–Saxon Protestants. Unions are not so heavily entrenched, and the dairy farming country around includes a significant percentage of the area's total population. This area, like so much of small-city Wisconsin, is basically Republican.

All of this produces a congressional district with a pretty even partisan balance. In the past two presidential elections, it has differed less than 2% from the statewide percentage. During the 1960s this was one of the most marginal congressional districts in the country,

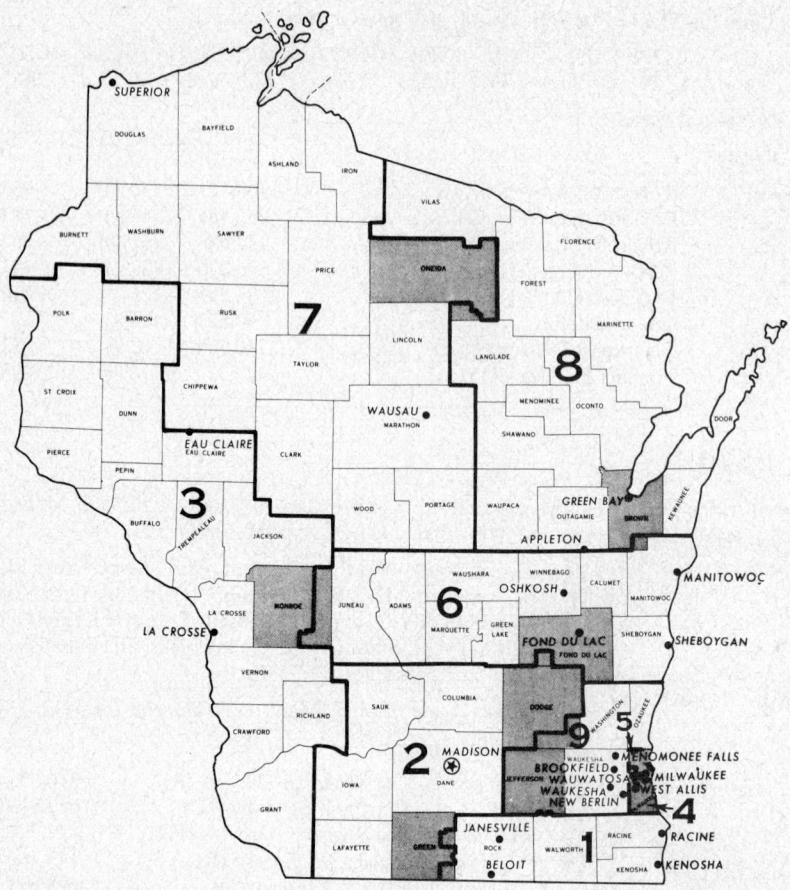

election after election. This was not true in the 1970s, but the pattern could reemerge in the 1980s.

The congressman here, Les Aspin, had an unusual career path: he made his way up not as a small officeholder in Wisconsin but as a staffer in Washington. His resume is distinctive: he worked for Senator William Proxmire, for Walter Heller when he was chairman of the Council of Economic Advisers, and (while he was in the Army) for Robert McNamara in the Pentagon. After two years as an economics professor in Wisconsin, he ran for Congress in 1970 against a weak Republican incumbent and won, with a stunningly large percentage.

The House Aspin entered at age 32 was considerably different from the House of today. The top committee positions were still held in many cases by men born in the 19th century; virtually the entire membership solidly supported the Vietnam war; the House as a whole was much more sympathetic to and controllable by the Nixon Administration. That was particularly true of the Armed Services Committee, on which Aspin got a seat. He was one of its few certified doves and one of the few sympathetic to the management techniques and method of analysis McNamara had introduced to the Pentagon. In these surroundings Aspin could not hope to prevail by legislative maneuver. So he resorted to what might be called legislation by press release. For some years he was one of the most prolific sources of news stories on Capitol Hill, since his press releases broke interesting stories and stood up under scrutiny.

By the middle 1970s the House had changed and so did Aspin. The House as a whole voted to cut off military aid to Cambodia and refused to flinch when the Thieu government was forced out of South Vietnam. Not just a few but many members, often a majority, were skeptical about many military spending programs. Armed Services, even in these years, stayed pretty solidly hawkish, but it was not always able to get its way on the floor. Then, in the later Carter years, there was a reaction against these trends. Aspin felt it most forcefully when he saw his percentage, against the same opponent, decline from 66% to 54% between 1976 and 1978. One reason was dissatisfaction with Democratic economic programs. Another was a shift in the national mood — and the local mood even in Wisconsin — from dovishness and revulsion at foreign involvements to aggressiveness and a desire to demonstrate American strength.

The Republicans targeted Aspin's seat for 1980. The incumbent responded by concentrating on district matters to an extent greater than he had in some time. Aspin evidently quit attending Armed Services meetings; one old-timer on the committee was surprised to hear that Aspin was still on it. His campaign efforts paid off, however. In 1980, against the national Republican trend, Aspin increased his percentage in the district, with a particularly large gain in the marginal Janesville and Beloit area. Aspin will probably have a significant challenge again in 1982. But assuming he wins, he will be an interesting man to watch, to see what one of the smartest and most innovative Democrats of the 1970s does to handle and help define the problems of the 1980s.

Census Data   Pop. (1980 final) 515,298, up 5% in 1970s. Median family income, 1970, $10,478, 109% of U.S.

The Voters

   Employment profile 1970   White collar, 41%. Blue collar, 42%. Service, 14%. Farm, 3%.
   Ethnic groups   Black 1980, 4%. Hispanic 1980, 3%. Total foreign stock 1970, 18%. Germany, 4%; Italy, 2%; Poland, 1%.

Presidential Vote

1980	Reagan (R)	115,995	(50%)
	Carter (D)	97,626	(42%)
	Anderson (I)	16,233	(7%)
1976	Ford (R)	107,457	(49%)
	Carter (D)	106,274	(48%)

Rep. Les Aspin (D) Elected 1970; b. July 21, 1938, Milwaukee; home, Racine; Yale U., B.A. 1960, Oxford U., M.A. 1962, MIT, Ph.D. 1965.

Career   Staff Asst. to U.S. Sen. William Proxmire, 1960; Staff Asst. to Walter Heller, Pres. Cncl. of Econ. Advisers, 1963; Army, 1966–68; Asst. Prof. of Economics, Marquette U., 1969–70.

Offices   443 CHOB, 202-225-3031. Also Rm. 200, 603 Main St., Racine 52403, 414-632-4446.

Committees   *Armed Services* (10th). Subcommittees: Investigations; Military Personnel and Compensation.

Budget (12th).

Group Ratings

	ADA	COPE	PC	LCV	CFA	RPN	NAB	NSI	NTU	ACA	ACU
1980	67	61	60	85	64	—	8	10	21	25	11
1979	74	80	60	80	50	—	—	—	25	13	16
1978	60	85	83	90	68	50	8	33	10	12	8

Key Votes

1) Draft Registn $	FOR	6) Fair Hsg DOJ Enfrc	FOR	11) Cut Socl Incr Dfns $	AGN
2) Ban $ to Nicrgua	AGN	7) Lim PAC Contrbtns	FOR	12) Hosptl Cost Controls	FOR
3) Dlay MX Missile	FOR	8) Cap on Food Stmp $	AGN	13) Gasln Ctrls & Allctns	AGN
4) Nuclr Mortorium	—	9) New US Dep Edcatn	FOR	14) Lim Wndfll Prof Tax	AGN
5) Alaska Lands Bill	FOR	10) Cut OSHA $	AGN	15) Chryslr Loan Grntee	FOR

Election Results

1980 general	Les Aspin (D)	126,222	(56%)	($152,364)
	Kathryn H. Canary (R)	96,047	(43%)	($75,766)
1980 primary	Les Aspin (D)	27,619	(100%)	
1978 general	Les Aspin (D)	77,146	(54%)	($73,570)
	William W. Petrie (R)	64,437	(46%)	($102,205)

SECOND DISTRICT

Madison is Wisconsin's second largest city, with nearly 200,000 people, and the state capital. Madison is also one of the nation's most important university communities — home of the University of Wisconsin and its 30,000 students. The university was a factor in Wisconsin politics long before the 18-year-old vote of the early 1970s. Back in 1900, Robert LaFollette, a Madison native, was elected governor. Once in office, he called on professors from the university to set up the Wisconsin Tax Commission and to draft a workmen's compensation law — both the first in the nation. Wisconsin's progressive movement, including the *Progressive* magazine, which is published in Madison, has always relied heavily on the university community. As a result, Madison, not the much bigger city of Milwaukee, has always been the major center of Wisconsin liberalism.

In the early 1950s, when LaFollette progressives had completely lost control of the Republican Party here, Madison became the center of a new liberal movement in the minority and moribund Democratic Party. Today the city remains the home base of Senators William Proxmire and of former Governor Patrick Lucey, who was John Anderson's running mate in the 1980 general election. Anderson in fact carried Madison heavily (it was the only part of the state he carried) in the 1980 Republican presidential primary. That happened because students vote in large numbers here, and Wisconsin's primary has traditionally allowed people to participate without registering in a party — a procedure that national Democrats have ruled cannot be used to select delegates to their 1984 national convention. Madison's city elections have been struggles among former students and various radical groups, although the appeal went out of radicalism here in 1970 when a group of radicals blew up a laboratory and killed a student who was working late in it.

Madison is the center of Wisconsin's 2d congressional district, with Madison and surrounding Dane County casting 63% of the district's votes. Since the 1958 election the 2d has been represented by Robert Kastenmeier, one of the youngest members of the group of Madison liberals of the 1950s. With a rural background, Kastenmeier was nonetheless one of the most liberal members of Congress in the early 1960s; he was not able to win reelection by a wide margin until after the redistricting of 1964.

Until 1974 Kastenmeier was little known outside his district, climbing slowly to a high seniority position on the House Judiciary Committee. Suddenly the impeachment hearings focused national attention on the committee and its members. Kastenmeier, as fourth-ranking Democrat, was considered the most senior member absolutely sure for impeachment. Kastenmeier's rather languid speaking style may have bothered some of those most strongly partial to his position; he does not look like a fiery liberal. He made one important contribution to the proceedings by insisting that each article of impeachment be voted on separately, after evidence pertaining to it was discussed. Some of the Republicans and conservative Democrats favoring impeachment wanted to wait and hold all the roll calls at the end, as if then people would somehow not notice. Kastenmeier's firm stance ensured an orderly procedure and enabled the public to make an easy connection between members' interpretations of the facts and their decisions. Judiciary has not been such an exciting place since, of course. Kastenmeier has concentrated on such matters as shepherding through the copyright reform of 1976—the first major revision since 1909.

Kastenmeier experienced little trouble or even visible opposition in elections between 1964 and 1976. But in 1978 Republican James Wright, a Baraboo yo-yo manufacturer, waged a strenuous campaign. Kastenmeier had been accustomed to winning by nearly 2–1 margins; Wright reduced his share of the vote to 58%. Encouraged by this comparative success, Wright tried again in 1980 and national Republicans targeted this seat. Kastenmeier stepped up his own efforts, returning to the district more frequently and hiring national campaign consultants. The Republicans had some success—but not enough to win. As in 1978, Wright carried every county outside Dane, and held Kastenmeier to just 42% of the vote in them. But Kastenmeier carried Dane County by a 61%–38% margin.

This district is now one of the most polarized in the nation, with one distinctive geographic part—Dane County—going strongly in one direction and the other—the rural counties—almost equally strongly in the other. The 2d recorded almost precisely the same results in the 1980 presidential, senatorial, and congressional races. Redistricting can obviously play a critical role for 1982. Democrats control the legislature and there is no chance that Kastenmeier will lose any part of his Dane County base. But he may have to swap some rural counties with the 3d district, in order to accommodate population changes, which would cause him additional problems in 1982. There is no sign, however, that his Dane County base is weakening; and so long as it remains strong Republicans will have little chance of carrying this district.

Census Data Pop. (1980 final) 537,933, up 10% in 1970s. Median family income, 1970, $10,397, 108% of U.S.

The Voters

Employment profile 1970 White collar, 49%. Blue collar, 28%. Service, 14%. Farm, 9%.
Ethnic groups Black 1980, 1%. Hispanic 1980, 1%. Asian 1980, 1%. Total foreign stock 1970, 13%. Germany, 4%; Norway, 2%.

Presidential Vote

1980	Reagan (R)	....	110,374	(41%)
	Carter (D)	....	123,451	(47%)
	Anderson (I)	....	25,815	(10%)
1976	Ford (R)	....	113,143	(46%)
	Carter (D)	....	125,639	(51%)

Rep. Robert W. Kastenmeier (D) Elected 1958; b. Jan. 24, 1924, Beaver Dam; home, Sun Prairie; U. of Wis., LL.B. 1952.

Career Practicing atty., 1952–58.

Offices 2232 RHOB, 202-225-2906. Also 119 Monona Ave., Madison 53703, 608-252-5206.

Committees *Interior and Insular Affairs* (3d). Subcommittee: Public Lands and National Parks.

Judiciary (3d). Subcommittees: Civil and Constitutional Rights; Courts, Civil Liberties, and the Administration of Justice (Chairman); Crime.

Group Ratings

	ADA	COPE	PC	LCV	CFA	RPN	NAB	NSI	NTU	ACA	ACU
1980	100	79	80	91	79	—	8	0	24	13	11
1979	95	95	85	97	89	—	—	—	29	4	11
1978	95	95	95	87	96	50	8	0	27	4	4

Key Votes

1) Draft Registn $	AGN	6) Fair Hsg DOJ Enfrc	FOR	11) Cut Socl Incr Dfns $	AGN
2) Ban $ to Nicrgua	AGN	7) Lim PAC Contrbtns	FOR	12) Hosptl Cost Controls	FOR
3) Dlay MX Missile	FOR	8) Cap on Food Stmp $	AGN	13) Gasln Ctrls & Allctns	FOR
4) Nuclr Mortorium	FOR	9) New US Dep Edcatn	AGN	14) Lim Wndfll Prof Tax	AGN
5) Alaska Lands Bill	FOR	10) Cut OSHA $	AGN	15) Chryslr Loan Grntee	FOR

Election Results

1980 general	Robert W. Kastenmeier (D)	142,037	(54%)	($225,706)
	James A. Wright (R)............	119,514	(45%)	($282,348)
1980 primary	Robert W. Kastenmeier (D)	14,232	(100%)	
1978 general	Robert W. Kastenmeier (D)	99,631	(58%)	($43,643)
	James A. Wright (R)............	71,412	(41%)	($86,041)

THIRD DISTRICT

The 3d district of Wisconsin occupies the western and southwestern parts of the state. This is rolling farmland, stretching some 200 miles along the Mississippi and St. Croix Rivers. The countryside here probably looks little different from when it first attracted white settlers in the 1840s and 1850s — in the south is gentle, hilly dairy land; in the north, more forests. The district has only two significant urban centers, LaCrosse and Eau Claire, both with names that recall the French chevaliers who came paddling down the Mississippi and St. Croix in the 17th century. The 3d of Wisconsin is one of the nation's premier dairy districts; there are more dairy cows in this district than in any other in the nation. Its congressman inevitably finds himself concerned with the arcane details of milk marketing regulations and import restrictions on Dutch and Swiss cheese.

Most Americans would guess that this district is heavily Republican; in fact, it is a place with very close competition between the parties. The southern part of the 3d is ancestrally Republican, the counties north and west of Eau Claire, which are part of the Minneapolis–

St. Paul media market, are pretty solidly Democratic. In the 1960s, when the Democratic Party seemed preoccupied with expensive programs to help big cities, the 3d district trended toward the Republicans. In the 1970s, when the Nixon Administration seemed interested in helping the Sun Belt and violated basic standards of honesty in the Watergate crisis, the 3d district trended toward the Democrats. All the while, the dairy lobby in Washington was quietly winning major battles, and this part of western Wisconsin began to enjoy an era of prosperity it has not experienced in living memory. In contrast to past decades, the 1970s saw a sharp rise in population here and an end to net outmigration.

The congressional representation in this district has oscillated between Republicans and Democrats and is now Republican. This is a bit of a surprise. Democratic Congressman Al Baldus, first elected in 1974, seemed to have developed a lock on the district. He beat a tough opponent by a wide margin in 1976, and by 1980 he had become chairman of the subcommittee handling the dairy program — a more important position for the district could not be imagined. Moreover, while Jimmy Carter was in trouble nationally, he was holding on pretty well in this area. Rural Wisconsin had given him votes critical to his important victories in the 1976 Wisconsin primary and for Wisconsin's 11 electoral votes in the 1976 general election; and as it turned out Carter ran ahead of his national average in the 3d district in the 1980 general election as well.

Nevertheless 29-year-old Republican Steven Gunderson beat Baldus in the House election. His secret seemed to be sheer hard work, plus a good personal appeal. Gunderson won his primary much more solidly than expected. He campaigned in the general election with a 40-foot semitrailer truck decorated with his picture and accompanied by a "swing choir." He used standard Republican themes on foreign and domestic issues, and to a considerable extent he rallied standard Republican majorities in the southern part of the district. But he added to that big gains in his home area and a majority in Eau Claire, which Jimmy Carter was carrying at the same time. Overall, Gunderson ran ahead of Ronald Reagan.

Gunderson is evidently ambitious. He was elected to the legislature at age 23 and told one reporter that he was running for the House only because he was not old enough to run for the Senate. There are those who see him as a kind of Scandinavian Sammy Glick. Yet his popularity is undoubted in a part of the country where voters like to meet candidates personally and where they are alert to candidates who put on airs. Gunderson has a seat on the Agriculture Committee, which may help him in the 1982 election; he may lose some of the more Republican counties in the southern part of the district in redistricting, which will hurt him. It is generally expected that he will run for statewide office someday, although it seems doubtful that he would be audacious enough to challenge Senator William Proxmire in 1982.

Census Data Pop. (1980 final) 557,065, up 13% in 1970s. Median family income, 1970, $8,485, 89% of U.S.

The Voters

Employment profile 1970 White collar, 37%. Blue collar, 33%. Service, 15%. Farm, 15%
Ethnic groups Total foreign stock 1970, 13%. Norway, Germany, 4% each; Sweden, 1%.

Presidential Vote

1980	Reagan (R)	130,635	(48%)
	Carter (D)	116,758	(43%)
	Anderson (I)	19,528	(7%)
1976	Ford (R)	119,607	(48%)
	Carter (D)	121,904	(49%)

Rep. Steven Gunderson (R) Elected 1980; b. May 10, 1951, Eau Claire; home, Pleasantville; U. of Wis., B.A. 1973, Brown Sch. of Broadcasting, 1974.

Career Wis. Assembly, 1974–79.

Offices 416 CHOB, 202-225-5506. Also 438 N. Water St., Black River Falls 54615, 715-284-7431.

Committee *Agriculture* (17th). Subcommittees: Conservation, Credit, and Rural Development; Cotton, Rice, and Sugar; Livestock, Dairy, and Poultry.

Group Ratings and Key Votes: Newly Elected

Election Results

1980 general	Steven Gunderson (R)............	132,001	(51%)	($177,782)
	Alvin Baldus (D)	126,859	(49%)	($136,320)
1980 primary	Steven Gunderson (R)...........	35,710	(69%)	
	Gary K. Madson (R)	11,515	(22%)	($42,473)
	One other (R)	4,487	(9%)	
1978 general	Alvin Baldus (D)	96,326	(63%)	($75,983)
	Michael S. Ellis (R)............	57,060	(37%)	($5,414)

FOURTH DISTRICT

The 4th district of Wisconsin is the south side of Milwaukee and the Milwaukee County suburbs to the south and west. The Milwaukee River splits the city into two different sections. Traditionally the north side has been German; today, it includes all of Milwaukee's medium-sized black community. Like all of Wisconsin, the south side has large numbers of German–Americans, but since the days of industrial growth at the turn of the century, south side Milwaukee has been known as the Polish part of town. Today the south remains all white and has a large Polish community, while the suburbs to the south are filled mainly with the newly prosperous blue and white collar descendants of the original Polish and German immigrants. The western suburbs, Wauwatosa and West Allis, are more German and white collar.

Milwaukee's south side has attracted national attention in many presidential election years. Because Wisconsin has had one of the nation's earliest presidential primaries, Milwaukee has often been the first large city to participate in the process. So observers come to the south side to see how the Polish and other ethnics are voting this year. In 1964 they found many supporting George Wallace — but the percentage was about the same as in the rest of the state and was due more to a state tax revolt than to racial issues. In 1972 the 4th actually went for George McGovern — a result clearly out of line with the ethnic stereotype reached for by the press.

The south side had a Democratic tradition before the rest of Wisconsin developed one. Its current congressman, Clement Zablocki, was first elected more than 30 years ago, in 1948. Most of Zablocki's attitudes seem closer to those of machine Democrats from Chicago or Philadelphia than to those of the ideological liberals in the rest of the Wisconsin delegation. He was the only Wisconsin Democrat to support the Vietnam war policies of the Johnson and Nixon Administrations, and he was considerably more conservative on cultural issues than his state colleagues.

Zablocki is now chairman of the House Foreign Affairs Committee. He owes this position mainly to seniority; there is little likelihood that he would have been elected to it de novo, although the caucus declined to take it away from him. The bulk of House Democrats, after all, were elected in the 1970s and campaigned as opponents of the Vietnam war. Zablocki came to office at a time when many of his constituents were convinced, unrealistically but understandably, that the United States could liberate Poland and other Eastern European countries from Soviet domination. Zablocki has been flexible enough to do a workmanlike job of shepherding the war powers act through the House in the 1970s. But he has made enemies by being at best a lukewarm supporter of aid to Israel.

In the old days when committee chairmen got their positions automatically and were effectively accountable to no one, such views might have had important consequences. But in this case they have not. When committee Chairman Thomas Morgan retired in 1976, it was made clear to Zablocki that he would have to expedite policies favored by a majority of the committee's Democrats. He has. Rather than exert great power as chairman, he has presided over a college of powerful subcommittee chairmen, including several young liberals elected after the 1980 election (Michael Barnes on Latin American Affairs, Howard Wolpe on Africa) in at least one case over Zablocki's opposition. Zablocki has expedited aid to Israel and has not tried to block objections to the Reagan Administration's policy in El Salvador.

Zablocki can be reelected indefinitely. Redistricting will require adding some suburban territory to this district (or adding some of Milwaukee from the 5th, and adding suburbs to the even more Democratic 5th), but it is still likely to be a heavily Democratic seat. If Zablocki does retire in 1982 or 1984, as many expect, there should be a spirited Democratic primary to determine the succession.

Census Data Pop. (1980 final) 455,899, down 7% in 1970s. Median family income, 1970, $11,285, 118% of U.S.

The Voters

Employment profile 1970 White collar, 47%. Blue collar, 40%. Service, 13%. Farm, -%.
Ethnic groups Hispanic 1980, 4%. Asian 1980, 1%. Total foreign stock 1970, 24%. Germany, Poland, 6% each; Austria, 1%.

Presidential Vote

1980	Reagan (R)	99,267	(44%)
	Carter (D)	108,816	(48%)
	Anderson (I)	15,912	(7%)
1976	Ford (R)	97,686	(44%)
	Carter (D)	119,386	(53%)

Rep. Clement J. Zablocki (D) Elected 1948; b. Nov. 18, 1912, Milwaukee; home, Milwaukee; Marquette U., Ph.B. 1936.

Career Organist and choir dir., 1932–48; High school teacher, 1938–40; Wis. Senate, 1942–48.

Offices 2183 RHOB, 202-225-4572. Also 1401 W. Lincoln Ave., Milwaukee 53215, 414-383-4000.

Committees *Foreign Affairs* (Chairman). Subcommittee: International Security and Scientific Affairs (Chairman).

Permanent Select Committee on Intelligence (2d). Subcommittee: Program and Budget Authorization.

Group Ratings

	ADA	COPE	PC	LCV	CFA	RPN	NAB	NSI	NTU	ACA	ACU
1980	61	83	53	43	71	—	0	22	10	13	11
1979	53	79	38	40	29	—	—	—	17	12	17
1978	40	65	48	47	50	42	8	60	5	33	25

Key Votes

1) Draft Registn $	FOR	6) Fair Hsg DOJ Enfrc	FOR	11) Cut Socl Incr Dfns $	AGN
2) Ban $ to Nicrgua	AGN	7) Lim PAC Contrbtns	FOR	12) Hosptl Cost Controls	FOR
3) Dlay MX Missile	AGN	8) Cap on Food Stmp $	AGN	13) Gasln Ctrls & Allctns	FOR
4) Nuclr Mortorium	AGN	9) New US Dep Edcatn	AGN	14) Lim Wndfll Prof Tax	AGN
5) Alaska Lands Bill	FOR	10) Cut OSHA $	AGN	15) Chryslr Loan Grntee	FOR

Election Results

1980 general	Clement J. Zablocki (D)	146,437	(70%)	($14,592)
	Elroy C. Honadel (R)	61,027	(30%)	($10,201)
1980 primary	Clement J. Zablocki (D)	29,411	(89%)	
	One other (D)	3,489	(11%)	
1978 general	Clement J. Zablocki (D)	101,575	(66%)	($10,398)
	Elroy C. Honadel (R)	52,125	(34%)	($14,665)

FIFTH DISTRICT

The 5th congressional district of Wisconsin is made up of the north side of Milwaukee, from the center of town to the city limits. The north side is the traditionally German half of Milwaukee; the gemutlichkeit atmosphere of old Milwaukee is now part of our common heritage, thanks to beer advertisements. For years Milwaukee has been famous for its beer, and it is still the home of Schlitz, Miller's, Pabst, Blatz, and others. Not as well known is that for years Milwaukee had its own unique politics, with roots deep in the German tradition. During the years Robert LaFollette and his progressive Republicans were governing the rest of Wisconsin, Milwaukee was electing a series of Socialist mayors and congressmen. The most notable of them was Victor Berger, who served in the House from 1911 to 1913 and again from 1923 to 1929.

After the 1918 and 1920 elections Berger was denied his seat because of his opposition to American entry into World War I. For those who think the prosecution of antiwar dissenters is a phenomenon only of the 1960s, it should be recalled that Berger was sentenced in

1919 to 20 years in prison for having written antiwar articles. The prosecution was brought by the Wilson Administration and, after the conviction was reversed by the Supreme Court, all charges were dropped by the "return to normalcy" Harding Administration. It is a measure of the strength of German Milwaukee's opposition to World War I that Berger was reelected to Congress while his case was on appeal and after he had been denied his seat.

Today many descendants of the first German immigrants have left the north side for the suburbs to the north and west, and some of them have been replaced by blacks from the rural South. In 1980, some 33% of the 5th's population was black, which may not seem an especially high figure for a big city district; but it includes 80% of the black population of the entire state.

Since the 1954 election the 5th district has been represented in the House by Henry Reuss, member of an aristocratic Milwaukee German family. Reuss is now one of the most senior and intellectually distinguished liberals in the House, completing a career in which he has seen most of his ideas prevail despite the current problems of liberalism. Over the years Reuss has had leadership positions in several areas of policy. For years he was congressional Democrats' leading expert on international finance. Later, heading a Government Operations subcommittee, he unearthed the 1899 Refuse Act, which baldly prohibits the dumping of pollutants in interstate waterways, and got the executive branch to revive it as a weapon against industrial polluters. As a member of and, from 1974 to 1980, chairman of the House Banking Committee he was one of the leading figures in loan guarantees to such diverse entities as New York City and the Chrysler Corporation. Reuss is a Keynesian, a veteran of the Office of Price Administration in World War II, a firm believer that government should exert some control over private economic institutions. He has championed wage and price controls and helped see that they were available to the Nixon Administration in 1971; he has argued for credit controls, which means government determination of whom banks should loan money to; he would like to see much more national economic planning of the type the young economists of the TNEC were so interested in when he began his public career.

Reuss, never a favorite on Wall Street, never had a majority on the Banking Committee for his more ambitious plans; it is a body that tends to attract members more concerned about the practical commercial needs of banks and savings institutions, home builders and property developers. Accordingly, Reuss has used his seniority to try to stimulate liberal thinking on issues he cares about. For a while his vehicle was a subcommittee called the City. In 1981 he relinquished the chair of the Banking Committee for that of the Joint Economic Committee, a body that passes no legislation and is generally considered powerless. However, it had some attraction for Reuss. In the previous Congress the JEC had been controlled by a bipartisan coalition urging tax cuts and less government regulation of business. Reuss hired an entirely new staff and positioned himself as the one liberal in the Congress with a real platform and the ability to articulate liberal ideas.

Reuss also announced early that he would retire in 1982. His district is now, thanks to its black voters, the most Democratic in Wisconsin. It also has the smallest population. But even the addition of several Republican suburbs is not going to make it marginal. Reportedly Reuss's choice for the seat is state legislator Bill Broydick, who as an aide to Congressman Les Aspin worked on many of his ubiquitous press releases. But undoubtedly there will be a spirited primary for this seat.

Census Data Pop. (1980 final) 439,126, down 11% in 1970s. Median family income, 1970, $10,067, 105% of U.S.

The Voters

Employment profile 1970   White collar, 47%. Blue collar, 38%. Service, 15%. Farm, –%.
Ethnic groups   Black 1980, 33%. Hispanic 1980, 3%. Am. Ind. 1980, 1%. Asian 1980, 1%. Total foreign stock 1970, 21%. Germany, 7%; Poland, 2%; Italy, Austria, 1% each.

Presidential Vote

1980	Reagan (R)	61,322	(31%)
	Carter (D)	117,147	(60%)
	Anderson (I)	13,972	(7%)
1976	Ford (R)	68,240	(36%)
	Carter (D)	116,332	(61%)

Rep. Henry S. Reuss (D) Elected 1954; b. Feb. 22, 1912, Milwaukee; home, Milwaukee; Cornell U., A.B. 1933, Harvard U., LL.B. 1936

Career Practicing atty.; Asst. Corp. Counsel, Milwaukee Co., 1939–40; Asst. Gen. Counsel, OPA, 1941–42; Army, WWII; Chf., Price Control Branch Ofc. of Military Govt. for Germany, 1945; Dpty. Gen. Counsel, Marshall Plan, 1949; Milwaukee Co. Grand Jury Spec. Prosecutor, 1950.

Offices 2413 RHOB, 202-225-3571. Also 400 Fed. Bldg., Milwaukee 53202, 414-291-1331.

Committees *Banking, Finance and Urban Affairs* (2d). Subcommittees: Domestic Monetary Policy; International Development Institutions and Finance.

Joint Economic Committee (Chairman). Subcommittees: Investment, Jobs, and Prices (Chairman); Monetary and Fiscal Policy.

Group Ratings

	ADA	COPE	PC	LCV	CFA	RPN	NAB	NSI	NTU	ACA	ACU
1980	89	83	57	82	82	—	9	11	17	22	6
1979	95	95	83	83	89	—	—	—	18	0	3
1978	80	90	83	87	82	45	17	0	26	8	4

Key Votes

1) Draft Registn $	AGN	6) Fair Hsg DOJ Enfrc	—	11) Cut Socl Incr Dfns $	AGN
2) Ban $ to Nicrgua	AGN	7) Lim PAC Contrbtns	FOR	12) Hosptl Cost Controls	FOR
3) Dlay MX Missile	FOR	8) Cap on Food Stmp $	AGN	13) Gasln Ctrls & Allctns	FOR
4) Nuclr Mortorium	FOR	9) New US Dep Edcatn	FOR	14) Lim Wndfll Prof Tax	AGN
5) Alaska Lands Bill	FOR	10) Cut OSHA $	AGN	15) Chryslr Loan Grntee	FOR

Election Results

1980 general	Henry S. Reuss (D).............	129,574	(77%)	($36,250)
	David Bathke (R)	37,267	(22%)	($1,107)
1980 primary	Henry S. Reuss (D).............	20,977	(88%)	
	One other (D)	2,842	(12%)	
1978 general	Henry S. Reuss (D).............	85,067	(73%)	($68,092)
	James R. Medina (R)	30,185	(26%)	($4,952)

SIXTH DISTRICT

The 6th district of Wisconsin is an almost perfectly rectangular slice of the central part of the state, which extends from Lake Michigan west to a point near the Mississippi River. On the lake are the small industrial cities of Manitowoc and Sheboygan, both of which lean Democratic. During the 1950s Sheboygan was the scene of a bitter, eight-year-long UAW strike against the Kohler Company. To the west are the quiet, more Republican cities of Oshkosh and Fond du Lac, both on Lake Winnebago, the state's largest inland lake. All around is dairy country, with small paper mill towns here and there. The 6th district also includes the small town of Ripon, where the Republican Party is said to have been founded in 1854. (Jackson, Michigan, also claims this distinction.) The 6th has consistently been one of Wisconsin's most Republican districts, but it has been known to elect Democrats on occasion.

This district was represented by William Steiger, a Republican who made a substantial impact on the legislative process although he died suddenly at age 40. He was one of the leading forces behind the creation of the volunteer army, a leader in reforming the presidential delegate selection rules of the Republican Party, and the driving force behind the lowering of the capital gains tax in 1978. That last move may be seen in history as a turning point: before, most legislative efforts were devoted to making taxes more progressive; afterward, most of the effort has gone to reducing taxes of those who seem likely to use their money for investment. Steiger was very popular in his district and could have been reelected indefinitely.

Steiger died shortly after the 1978 election; a special election was held early in 1979 to fill the seat. In most of the country, the Democrats would have been pretty dispirited; in Wisconsin, they still had enough vitality to put up, in the person of state Senator Gary Goyke, a strong fight for the seat. But Republican state Senator Thomas Petri prevailed by 1,223 votes out of more than 140,000 cast. Petri increased his margin substantially by the 1980 general election, when he faced Goyke again and this time carried every county. Petri serves on the Education and Labor Committee, where he is considered a thoughtful moderate. He goes along with Republicans on major initiatives, such as the Kemp–Roth tax cut, but toes his own line on other issues. He seems to be following Steiger's philosophy: a wariness toward government action combined with an open mind or even liberal attitude on some cultural issues. Redistricting is not likely to affect his chances of reelection very much.

Census Data Pop. (1980 final) 520,319, up 6% in 1970s. Median family income, 1970, $9,727, 102% of U.S.

The Voters

Employment profile 1970 White collar, 38%. Blue collar, 41%. Service, 13%. Farm, 8%.
Ethnic groups Hispanic 1980, 1%. Total foreign stock 1970, 14%. Germany, 6%.

Presidential Vote

1980	Reagan (R)	131,522	(53%)
	Carter (D)	98,007	(39%)
	Anderson (I)	15,707	(6%)
1976	Ford (R)	118,126	(51%)
	Carter (D)	108,920	(47%)

Rep. Thomas E. Petri (R) Elected Apr. 9, 1979; b. May 28, 1940, Marinette; home, Fond du Lac; Harvard Col., A.B. 1962, Harvard Law Sch., J.D. 1965.

Career Instructor, Kennedy Sch.; Peace Corps, 1966–67; Practicing atty., 1972–.

Offices 1024 LHOB, 202-225-2476. Also 20 Forest Ave., Fond du Lac 54935, 414-922-1180.

Committees *Education and Labor* (8th). Subcommittees: Elementary, Secondary, and Vocational Education; Employment Opportunities; Human Resources.

Select Committee on Aging (15th). Subcommittee: Human Services.

Group Ratings

	ADA	COPE	PC	LCV	CFA	RPN	NAB	NSI	NTU	ACA	ACU
1980	39	44	47	44	36	—	83	56	55	57	53
1979	39	37	44	77	30	—	—	—	58	71	64

Key Votes

1) Draft Registn $	FOR	6) Fair Hsg DOJ Enfrc	AGN	11) Cut Socl Incr Dfns $	AGN
2) Ban $ to Nicrgua	AGN	7) Lim PAC Contrbtns	FOR	12) Hosptl Cost Controls	AGN
3) Dlay MX Missile	AGN	8) Cap on Food Stmp $	FOR	13) Gasln Ctrls & Allctns	AGN
4) Nuclr Mortorium	FOR	9) New US Dep Edcatn	FOR	14) Lim Wndfll Prof Tax	FOR
5) Alaska Lands Bill	FOR	10) Cut OSHA $	AGN	15) Chryslr Loan Grntee	AGN

Election Results

1980 general	Thomas E. Petri (R)	143,980	(59%)	($524,122)
	Gary R. Goyke (D)	98,628	(41%)	($234,563)
1980 primary	Thomas E. Petri (R)	43,628	(100%)	
1979 special	Thomas E. Petri (R)	71,715	(50%)	
	Gary R. Goyke (D)	70,492	(50%)	
1979 spec. prim.	Thomas E. Petri (R)	22,293	(35%)	
	Tommy Thompson (R)	11,850	(19%)	
	Jack D. Steinhilber (R)	11,810	(19%)	
	Kenneth B. Benson (R)	10,965	(17%)	
	Three others (R)	6,316	(10%)	
1978 general	William A. Steiger (R)	114,742	(70%)	($67,664)
	Robert J. Steffes (D)	48,785	(30%)	

SEVENTH DISTRICT

Northern Wisconsin is a land of forests and lakes and mines. Two natural resources are of key importance here, the dairy cow and the tree; without them, there would be few people here at all. This is the land of Wisconsin's 7th congressional district, which stretches from a point near Green Bay in the south up to the city limits of Duluth, Minnesota. Superior, the Wisconsin town directly next to Duluth, is like its neighbor an iron ore port, with scarcely any other reason to exist there on the icy fastness of Lake Superior. In contrast, most of the jobs in towns like Wausau, Stevens Point, and Wisconsin Rapids, in the southern part of the district, depend on the lumber and paper mills. All these places were off the beaten track of east–west migration; they attracted their own unusual ethnic groups, like the Finns of Superior and the Poles of Stevens Point. The politics of northern Wisconsin and the 7th district has always had a rough-hewn quality about it, a certain populist flavor; although this is an ancestrally Republican area, it is also part of the state that always favored the progressivism of the LaFollettes.

The current congressman from the 7th, however, is a Democrat, and probably one of the most important young members of the House. He is David Obey, who in his early 40s has spent more than a decade in the House. He was elected in something of an upset in a 1969 special election, in the seat vacated by Defense Secretary Melvin Laird. Obey showed signs of political talent early. He won election to the Wisconsin legislature when he was 24. He used issues shrewdly in his special election campaign. Once in office, he behaved like a textbook model for the young congressmen of the 1970s: working hard on constituent problems, keeping in touch with the voters and returning to the district regularly, voting solidly with the majority of his party but avoiding ridiculous positions. In 1972 redistricting placed him in the same district with an aging Republican incumbent first elected 30 years before; Obey won that election with 63% of the vote.

Obey is now one of the leading legislators in the House, one of the dozen or two members of the national Republican trend in 1980. His chances of being hurt by redistricting are small, because his district has gained population in the 1970s—another example of the recent economic vitality of the northlands—and he is the Democrat who will work with all members of the congressional delegation to come up with a mutually agreeable plan.

Obey is now one of the leading legislators in the House, one of the dozen or so members whose positions and leads on major issues must be considered and can be crucial. To some extent he owes his prominence to committee position. He got a seat on the Appropriations Committee early and now is the eighth-ranking Democrat of 33, and he is 13 years younger than the youngest more senior Democrat. He does not yet chair an Appropriations sub-committee, but he is number two on Foreign Operations and number three on Labor–HHS–Education, and on quite a few occasions effectively takes the lead on their bills.

The way the House used to work, these committee positions would have made Obey powerful, but his prominence would still be far in the future. But in the House of the 1970s power moved more fluidly to those who understood how to exercise it. Obey was one of those younger members called on repeatedly to undertake difficult special projects, and he performed ably on all of them. In 1977 and 1978 he was chairman of a special committee on ethics and came up with a new ethics code that was backed by reformers and passed by the House—a substantial achievement, and one virtually without precedent. In 1979 he was elected head of the liberal Democratic Study Group, to uphold its principles after its members were hurt somewhat by the 1978 elections. In 1977 he won a seat on the Budget Committee, and in 1980 he came within a few votes of becoming chairman. After a spirited campaign, he was tied twice with James Jones of Oklahoma and finally lost to Jones on the third ballot by a 121–116 margin.

That election represented a significant decision by House Democrats, although the result was clouded by the fact that running in the race were a number of Democrats with views similar to Obey's. Obey represents the traditional liberal Democrats, who have supported without major reservations the programs of the Great Society and the principle that government should take an active role to protect individuals against the unregulated workings of the free market. Obey is anything but a bleeding heart in temperament, and there is nothing sloppy about his generosity. He takes pride in being thoroughly prepared and will not be backed into taking a position before he has become convinced of the merits. But he is also capable of acting rapidly as he did in 1980 and 1981 to come up with alternatives to administration budgets.

In the initial stages of the Reagan Administration Obey seemed unlikely to be playing a decisive role. Liberal Democrats were clearly outnumbered on the Budget Committee, on which Obey remains a ranking member, and the task of preparing alternatives to the Reagan budget fell primarily on Jones, who is less favorable toward government programs than Obey. Obey recognized that Democrats of his stripe had little chance to achieve a majority on the floor of the House in early 1981. But as time goes on, if the Republicans become less united, if some Democrats are disaffected with Reagan policies or unhappy with cuts on specific programs, Obey will probably be a leader in bringing forward budget alternatives that represent the position of his kind of Democrats. By dint of hard work, thorough preparation, and mastery of details, he has become the effective leader of a large and important bloc in the House.

Census Data　Pop. (1980 final) 553,658, up 13% in 1970s. Median family income, 1970, $8,424, 88% of U.S.

The Voters

Employment profile 1970　White collar, 38%. Blue collar, 38%. Service, 14%. Farm, 10%.
Ethnic groups　Am. Ind. 1980, 1%. Total foreign stock 1970, 19%. Germany, 6%; Poland, Sweden, Norway, 2% each; Canada, 1%.

Presidential Vote

1980	Reagan (R)	123,451	(46%)
	Carter (D)	124,011	(46%)
	Anderson (I)	16,805	(6%)
1976	Ford (R)	105,666	(43%)
	Carter (D)	134,210	(55%)

Rep. David R. Obey (D) Elected Apr. 1, 1969; b. Oct. 3, 1938, Okmulgee, Okla.; home, Wausau; U. of Wis., Marathon, U. of Wis., Madison, M.A. 1960.

Career　Wis. House of Reps., 1962–68.

Offices　2230 RHOB, 202-225-3365. Also Fed. Bldg., Wausau 54401, 715-842-5606.

Committees　*Appropriations* (8th). Subcommittees: Foreign Operations; Labor–Health and Human Services–Education; Treasury–Postal Service–General Government.

Budget (3d).

Group Ratings

	ADA	COPE	PC	LCV	CFA	RPN	NAB	NSI	NTU	ACA	ACU
1980	94	75	77	78	79	—	8	0	23	15	5
1979	89	95	80	79	81	—	—	—	27	9	11
1978	60	80	83	87	73	50	18	20	33	22	13

Key Votes

1) Draft Registn $	AGN	6) Fair Hsg DOJ Enfrc	FOR	11) Cut Socl Incr Dfns $	AGN
2) Ban $ to Nicrgua	AGN	7) Lim PAC Contrbtns	FOR	12) Hosptl Cost Controls	FOR
3) Dlay MX Missile	FOR	8) Cap on Food Stmp $	AGN	13) Gasln Ctrls & Allctns	FOR
4) Nuclr Mortorium	FOR	9) New US Dep Edcatn	AGN	14) Lim Wndfll Prof Tax	AGN
5) Alaska Lands Bill	FOR	10) Cut OSHA $	AGN	15) Chryslr Loan Grntee	FOR

Election Results

1980 general	David R. Obey (D)	164,340	(65%)	($134,287)
	Vinton A. Vesta (R)	89,745	(35%)	($38,835)
1980 primary	David R. Obey (D)	33,060	(100%)	
1978 general	David R. Obey (D)	110,874	(62%)	($53,463)
	Vinton A. Vesta (R)	65,750	(37%)	($13,403)

EIGHTH DISTRICT

The 8th of Wisconsin might be called the Packers' district. Centered on the midwestern metropolis of Green Bay, with less than 100,000 people, it is the home of the Green Bay Packers and the smallest city with any kind of bigtime athletic franchise in the United States. That the team is here is a reminder of the early days of pro football, when the National Football League included teams from a number of towns such as Green Bay and Canton, Ohio. During the late 1960s "the Pack" under Vince Lombardi was the first team to dominate the NFL during the Super Bowl era. The Packers in the swirling snows of Lambeau Field are the aspect of the 8th district best known to the outside world, although this 13-county district in northeastern Wisconsin has other features of note. It includes the city of Appleton, somewhat smaller than Green Bay, which was Joe McCarthy's hometown. As in all of Wisconsin there is good dairy country here, and in the north, near the Upper Peninsula of Michigan, are forests and prime vacation country. The 8th also contains the most recently formed county in the United States, Menominee, which was created when the Menominee Indian Reservation was abolished under the termination policy of the Eisenhower Administration.

Although the 8th is generally considered a solid Republican district, that is not quite right. Green Bay, which usually goes Republican, is a German Catholic town that went for John Kennedy in 1960 and came fairly close to going for Jimmy Carter in 1976. There are some heavily Republican counties here (Shawano, Waupaca), but also some that usually go Democratic (Forest, Florence). The balance, and more than half the votes, are cast in Brown and Outgamie Counties, which contain Green Bay and Appleton.

For nearly three decades the 8th had a very stable congressional representation, but during the 1970s it was the scene of one close race after another. The steady years were when John Byrnes, a Republican, represented the district. First elected in 1944, he was for years ranking Republican on the House Ways and Means Committee and worked closely with Chairman Wilbur Mills in fashioning legislation. In 1970 Byrnes was held to 55% of the vote by Jesuit priest Robert Cornell; in 1972 Byrnes retired.

Since then Cornell ran four more races in which the district went Democratic twice and Republican twice. Republican Harold Forehlich was elected in 1972 and got a seat on the House Judiciary Committee. That turned out to be a hot spot for him. He seemed visibly reluctant to support impeachment of Richard Nixon but in fact voted for the first two articles; his apparent ambivalence probably hurt him more than any position he took. Cornell won in 1974 with 54%. That was his high mark. He managed to hold on in 1976 with 52%, but he apparently did not use the advantages of incumbency as effectively as many of his colleagues in the Democratic freshman class of 1974 and was defeated solidly in 1978.

The current congressman, Toby Roth, seems to have as solid a lock on the district as Byrnes did in the 1950s and 1960s. He won by better than a 2–1 margin in 1980, and redistricting is not likely to change the district boundaries significantly in 1982. Roth is a solidly conservative Republican. In 1981 he switched from the Science and Small Business Committees to Foreign Affairs. As yet he is not high ranking on any subcommittee.

Census Data   Pop. (1980 final) 547,408, up 11% in 1970s. Median family income, 1970, $9,190, 96% of U.S.

The Voters

Employment profile 1970   White collar, 39%. Blue collar, 40%. Service, 13%. Farm, 8%.
Ethnic groups   Am. Ind. 1980, 2%. Total foreign stock 1970, 14%. Germany, 5%; Poland, Canada, 1% each.

Presidential Vote

1980	Reagan (R)	146,595	(56%)
	Carter (D)	96,188	(37%)
	Anderson (I)	15,293	(6%)
1976	Ford (R)	122,174	(52%)
	Carter (D)	105,904	(465)

Rep. Toby Roth (R) Elected 1978; b. Oct. 10, 1938; home, Appleton; Marquette U., B.A. 1961.

Career Realtor; Wis. House of Reps., 1972–78.

Offices 215 CHOB, 202-225-5665. Also Rm. 202, 325 E. Walnut, Green Bay 54305, 414-465-3931.

Committee *Foreign Affairs* (14th). Subcommittees: Europe and the Middle East; International Operations.

Group Ratings

	ADA	COPE	PC	LCV	CFA	RPN	NAB	NSI	NTU	ACA	ACU
1980	22	10	27	48	14	—	91	90	62	75	84
1979	16	21	23	28	7	—	—	—	62	96	95

Key Votes

1) Draft Registn $	AGN	6) Fair Hsg DOJ Enfrc	AGN	11) Cut Socl Incr Dfns $	FOR
2) Ban $ to Nicrgua	FOR	7) Lim PAC Contrbtns	AGN	12) Hosptl Cost Controls	AGN
3) Dlay MX Missile	AGN	8) Cap on Food Stmp $	FOR	13) Gasln Ctrls & Allctns	AGN
4) Nuclr Mortorium	AGN	9) New US Dep Edcatn	AGN	14) Lim Wndfll Prof Tax	FOR
5) Alaska Lands Bill	FOR	10) Cut OSHA $	FOR	15) Chryslr Loan Grntee	AGN

Election Results

1980 general	Toby Roth (R)	169,664	(68%)	($144,146)
	Michael R. Monfils (D)	81,043	(32%)	($20,233)
1980 primary	Toby Roth (R)	41,229	(100%)	
1978 general	Toby Roth (R)	101,856	(58%)	($202,021)
	Robert J. Cornell (D)	73,925	(42%)	($72,202)

NINTH DISTRICT

The 9th is Wisconsin's only predominantly suburban congressional district. It was first created in 1963 when population changes and the Supreme Court's one-person-one-vote decision required the elimination of a rural district and full recognition of the growth of Milwaukee's suburbs. Today—the district lines were redrawn after the 1970 census—the 9th forms a kind of arc north and west of Milwaukee. The district includes the wealthy, long-established suburbs of Shorewood and Whitefish Bay, just north of downtown Milwaukee on Lake Michigan, and a ring of suburbs around Milwaukee in Ozaukee, Washington, and Waukesha Counties: Mequon, Germantown, Menomonee Falls, Brookfield, and New Berlin. The territory combines country clubs, tree-shaded streets, shopping centers, and starkly new suburban housing. Although the 9th also includes some of the dairy country between Milwaukee and Madison, about half of its residents live in suburban Waukesha County.

The district was originally designed to remove Republican voters from Robert Kastenmeier's 2d and Henry Reuss's 5th districts. The job was done so well that the 9th is the state's most heavily Republican district. It has always elected Republican congressmen, and except for 1964 has delivered solid Republican margins in presidential elections.

The current congressman, James Sensenbrenner, was first elected in 1978 when the incumbent, Robert Kasten, ran for governor. Kasten lost that race in the primary but in an upset was elected U.S. senator in 1980. Sensenbrenner's only tough race was the 1978 primary, in which he barely beat moderate Susan Engeleiter; since then he has won easily. Sensenbrenner is a solid conservative vote in the House. He serves on the Judiciary Committee and on its subcommittee on Civil and Constitutional Rights; on the latter he is part of the Republican minority that backs right-to-life positions on the abortion issue. He is ranking Republican on the Criminal Justice Subcommittee.

Redistricting will probably change the shape of the 9th district as much as any Wisconsin seat. The two Milwaukee-based districts have lost population and will have to expand out into the suburbs; the 9th will lose some of its close-in territory (including probably Sensenbrenner's hometown) and will move somewhat farther out into the dairying countryside of southern Wisconsin. All the areas involved, however, are pretty heavily Republican, so the election outcomes here should not be much affected.

Census Data Pop. (1980 final) 578,629, up 18% in 1970s. Median family income, 1970, $12,479, 130% of U.S.

The Voters

Employment profile 1970 White collar, 51%. Blue collar, 35%. Service, 11%. Farm, 3%.
Ethnic groups Black 1980, 1%. Hispanic 1980, 1%. Total foreign stock 1970, 16%. Germany, 6%.

Presidential Vote

1980	Reagan (R)	167,684	(58%)
	Carter (D)	97,580	(34%)
	Anderson (I)	21,392	(7%)
1976	Ford (R)	152,888	(59%)
	Carter (D)	101,663	(39%)

Rep. F. James Sensenbrenner, Jr. (R) Elected 1978; b. June 14, 1943, Chicago, Ill.; home, Shorewood; Stanford U., A.B. 1965, U. of Wis., J.D. 1968.

Career Staff of U.S. Rep. Arthur Younger of Cal., 1965; Asst. to Wis. Senate Minor. Ldr., 1967; Practicing atty., 1968– ; Wis. Assembly, 1968–76.

Offices 315 CHOB, 202-225-5101. Also 333 Bishops Way, Brookfield 53005, 414-784-1111.

Committees *Judiciary* (11th). Subcommittees: Civil and Constitutional Rights; Criminal Justice.

Science and Technology (10th). Subcommittees: Energy Development and Applications; Natural Resources, Agriculture Research and Environment.

Group Ratings

	ADA	COPE	PC	LCV	CFA	RPN	NAB	NSI	NTU	ACA	ACU
1980	22	5	27	48	14	—	100	90	67	79	89
1979	16	15	38	54	15	—	—	—	66	100	97

Key Votes

1) Draft Registn $	AGN	6) Fair Hsg DOJ Enfrc	AGN	11) Cut Socl Incr Dfns $	FOR
2) Ban $ to Nicrgua	FOR	7) Lim PAC Contrbtns	AGN	12) Hosptl Cost Controls	AGN
3) Dlay MX Missile	AGN	8) Cap on Food Stmp $	FOR	13) Gasln Ctrls & Allctns	AGN
4) Nuclr Mortorium	—	9) New US Dep Edcatn	AGN	14) Lim Wndfll Prof Tax	FOR
5) Alaska Lands Bill	FOR	10) Cut OSHA $	FOR	15) Chryslr Loan Grntee	AGN

Election Results

1980 general	F. James Sensenbrenner, Jr. (R) ..	206,227	(78%)	($143,524)
	Gary C. Benedict (D)	56,838	(22%)	($2,678)
1980 primary	F. James Sensenbrenner, Jr. (R) ..	52,385	(100%)	
1978 general	F. James Sensenbrenner, Jr. (R) ..	118,386	(61%)	($197,749)
	Matthew J. Flynn (D)	75,207	(39%)	($41,028)

WYOMING

Wyoming is the closest thing we have to the old Wild West—one of the few states where ranchers, organized in the Wyoming Stock Growers' Association, and a railroad, the Union Pacific, have managed to remain political powers. The ranchers were the first white settlers here and consolidated their power in the Johnson County land war of the 1890s; the railroad's clout comes from the land it received for building the transcontinental line through the southern part of the state in the 1860s. Politically, the ranchers, small businessmen, and farmers who work the irrigated land in the north have usually voted Republican. The people who came to build the UP, their lives more remote from their employers, were usually Democrats, and the counties along the state's southern edge are Democratic — or as close as anything in Wyoming comes to being Democratic. This is the basic partisan split in the state. There are no big urban concentrations and only seven "cities" with populations over 10,000. More common are Ten Sleep (405) or Medicine Bow (952). Between the Wyoming settlements, for stretches of 50 to 100 miles, is the high desolate, serene plateau; to the west and north are the Rockies.

Yet Wyoming today finds itself in the midst of a boom — an oil and mining boom — the likes of which it has never seen before. This is almost totally the product of the 1960s. There has been strip mining of coal in the northeastern part of the state, minerals in Johnson County and around Rock Springs (uranium, coal, sodium), oil exploration centering around Casper, and, most important, the oil discoveries in the Overthrust Belt that is centered in southwestern Wyoming. The 1980 census tells the story: there are now nearly 500,000 people in Wyoming, and the state's population increased more in the 10 years between 1970 and 1980 than it did in the 50 years between 1920 and 1970.

Such explosive growth obviously has an effect on a state's life — and quality of life. Lots of people in Wyoming, or people who have come to Wyoming, have gotten quite rich. They see their wealth as a just reward for developing oil and minerals the nation needs. Others are disturbed at the ticky-tacky growth at the edge of Wyoming's towns or near its mineral sites. Many who have flocked here live in grimy trailers, linked precariously to civilization's utilities and unprotected against the winds and snows that come out of the enormous sky. Wyoming simply does not have the infrastructure to protect itself against the pollution that even a small influx of people brings. There is another kind of pollution as well: the mining camp atmosphere that builds around suddenly sprung-up camps near drilling rigs or mines. Wyoming is one of the few states that has always had more men than women — a sure sign that it has never gotten far from a frontier atmosphere (and also the reason it was the first state to give women the vote). In the 1970s around such towns as Rock Springs there grew a subculture of prostitution, gambling, and violent crime, which would have been familiar to anyone acquainted with the heyday of Virginia City, Nevada, or Cripple Creek, Colorado.

Those two developments — rapid growth and local crime — have changed Wyoming's state politics beyond recognition. This state, increasingly Republican in national politics, has had a Democratic governor since 1974. Ed Herschler won his first election largely because he opposed a slurry pipeline — a device to mix coal with water and pipe it out of the state to market for use in highway and street surfacing. Coal operators wanted the slurry pipeline, but it had numerous opponents, including environmentalists (not a major force in this state), the railroads (who want to ship the coal themselves), along with farmers and ranchers in the northern part of the state who feared depletion of Wyoming's meager water supply and a disastrous rise in the price of the West's most precious commodity

In 1978 Herschler seemed in great political trouble because of the situation in Rock Springs. One of the state's leading crime investigators was fired and then went on *60 Minutes* to charge that Herschler was involved. A grand jury indicted the state attorney general, the governor's appointee, and there were charges that the state Democratic chairman was involved in corruption. Then the Rock Springs police chief shot and killed an undercover investigator. But Herschler managed to win by firing the attorney general and ousting the party chairman and by shifting the focus of the campaign to his proposal to increase Wyoming's severance tax on minerals by 5% — and use the proceeds to reduce property taxes. This his Republican opponent opposed; it then turned out the Republican had profitable business dealings with one of the mining companies. Thus Herschler won a second term in Republican Wyoming. What will happen in 1982, indeed whether Herschler will run or not, is unclear; Wyoming may again provide some of the most turbulent state politics in the country.

In national politics, Wyoming is more serene — and solidly Republican. This was not always so: it was Democratic during the New Deal and had a majority–Democratic congressional delegation as recently as 1976. But Wyoming has delivered some of the nation's biggest majorities for Gerald Ford (59%) and Ronald Reagan (63%) and has two Republican senators and a Republican congressman who hold some of the safest seats in the nation. The state's political attitudes are based on a pervasive mistrust of the federal government. Out here on the frontier, people — especially those who have done well — think of themselves as self-sufficient pioneers. The irony is that sparsely populated Wyoming, even in the midst of an energy boom, would be even more vacant and economically dependent without the feds. The federal government, which still owns 48% of the land in Wyoming, maintains national parks and national forests in a way Wyoming could not itself afford, and leases land at bargain rates to cattle and sheep ranchers; the Bureau of Reclamation provides cheap water; the federal government has subsidized highways, feeder airlines, and agriculture.

Yet those who look askance on the federal government can argue, correctly, that the gap between the tax dollars Wyoming sends to Washington and what it gets back in federal spending has steadily narrowed, while at the same time federal intrusions into the lives of ordinary Wyomingites have increased. This is a state whose legislature once risked loss of federal highway funds to protest the 55-mile-per-hour speed limit. One of the reasons Senator Malcolm Wallop was elected in 1976 was an ad protesting an Occupational Safety and Health Administration regulation requiring a certain number of portable toilets for farm workers (the ad showed a cowboy riding a horse with a portajohn attached awkwardly to the saddle). Wyoming ranchers chafe at federal regulations against poisoning coyotes (which kill sheep) and at any hint of federal gun controls. Given these attitudes, the only surprise about Wyoming's congressional delegation is that it is not more stridently part of the New Right than it is.

The senior member of the delegation now is Malcolm Wallop, who is serving his first term in the Senate. His election in 1976 was something of an upset; he beat Gale McGee, an 18-year veteran, who did not bother to spend his whole campaign budget and apparently assumed that his seniority and committee positions would pull him through. Unfortunately, one of his committee positions was chairmanship of the Post Office and Civil Service Committee, which allowed Wallop to ask voters whether they were satisfied with postal service. (The committee has since been abolished; no senator wanted to chair it.) Wallop campaigned as a north Wyoming rancher; he emphasized less that his parents were born in England and that he went to Yale. He is in fact basically in line with the Republican majority in the Senate and is a solid backer of free-market measures on the Finance and Energy Committee. Wallop chairs a number of subcommittees: one on Energy Taxation, handling such matters as depletion allowances; and one on Public Lands, which is of course very important in western states. There he can have much to say about the practices that have led some westerners to advocate the extreme solutions of the Sagebrush Rebellion. He serves on the Trade Subcommittee and is basically a free trader, interested in promoting agricultural exports. As a member of the Intelligence Committee, he supports a stronger and more expensive defense. On some issues, however, he parts company with the New Right. He is one of the few Rocky Mountain Republicans who is not opposed to all abortions, and he favors reclamation of strip-mined land, as many ranchers do (you can't graze sheep or cattle on a denuded slope). He has shown himself to be a thoughtful senator on a number of issues, and there seems to be no reason to believe he will have trouble winning reelection in 1982.

Wyoming's junior senator, Alan Simpson, won his seat in 1978 with wonderfully little competition when Republican Clifford Hansen retired. It helped that the new senator's father, Milward Simpson, had served as senator and governor, but Alan Simpson had strong qualifications himself. Simpson had served in the state legislature for 14 years and had won a leadership position; more important, in a state where most voters still expect to meet a politician before they vote for him, he is personable, friendly, and intelligent. He also has a sense of humor as good as any senator's and a willingness to examine problems afresh that has made him, despite his lack of seniority, a man other senators listen to when they are looking for good judgment and good sense.

Simpson is a member of the Environment and Public Works Committee, which has jurisdiction over, among other things, the Clean Air Act. That law is up for renewal in 1981 and one provision that will be challenged is that allowing no degradation of air quality in areas where it is very high already — a provision that effectively prevents many kinds of development in states like Wyoming. Simpson also chairs the Nuclear Regulation Subcommittee and is a cautious but convinced advocate of nuclear power. He serves on the Judiciary Committee and is chairman of the subcommittee on Immigration and Refugee Policy; he brings a thoughtful approach to this difficult issue and a recognition that it is not possible to achieve all objectives (controlling the inflow without a national identification card system). And, after only two years in the Senate, Simpson became a full committee chairman, of the Veterans' Affairs Committee. This is not the Senate's largest committee (it was nearly abolished in the early 1970s) nor its best publicized, but it does handle a large chunk of the federal budget and has a lot to say about the quality of life of many Americans. Under its previous chairman, Alan Cranston, the Senate committee pioneered in setting up counseling centers for Vietnam era veterans, promoted judicial review of VA decisions, and worked to increase other benefits. Simpson takes an approach somewhat closer to that of traditional veterans' organizations, which were skeptical about these changes; he would abide by Reagan budget ceilings on overall veterans' spending but would shift cuts away from medical services. He seems likely on most veterans' issues to come out somewhere between the Cranston approach and the traditional approach of the majority of the House committee.

Wyoming's one and only congressman is Richard Cheney, who brings to office an unusual credential: he was White House chief of staff under Gerald Ford. Cheney achieved that position in his middle 30s as a protege of Donald Rumsfeld; and in the ordinary course of things, he could have been expected to live a comfortable life in Washington, earning a good living as a lobbyist. Instead he returned to Wyoming and ran for the U.S. House of Representatives. His race was not easy: he had a serious Republican opponent and suffered a mild heart attack during the campaign. Nevertheless he won convincingly.

Cheney could hardly have moved from a more powerful position to a less powerful one. Yet after one term he had become chairman of the House Republican Policy Committee and had become one of the most thoughtful members of the Republican leadership. He worked closely with Reagan Administration aides, and he seems likely to be one of the most influential House members in years to come. He was reelected easily in 1980 and obviously has a safe seat (yet Wyoming voters will expect to see him with some frequency); his possibilities for the Senate, however, seem limited so long as Wyoming's seats are held by two popular Republicans, both first elected in their 40s, who show no inclination to retire.

Census Data   Pop. (1980 final) 470,816, up 42% in 1970s: 0.21% of U.S. total, 49th largest. Median 4-person family income, 1978, $22,452, 110% of U.S., 4th highest.

1979 Share of Federal Tax Burden $992,000,000; 0.22% of U.S. total, 49th largest.

1979 Share of Federal Outlays $953,524,000; 0.20% of U.S. total, 50th largest.

DOD	$144,255,000	50th	(0.14%)	HEW	$224,153,000	50th	(0.13%)
DOE	$54,787,000	25th	(0.47%)	ERDA	$29,879,000	18th	(1.10%)
HUD	$7,250,000	51st	(0.45%)	NASA	$327,000	43d	(0.01%)
VA	$49,719,000	50th	(0.24%)	DOT	$56,110,000	49th	(0.34%)
EPA	$14,906,000	50th	(0.28%)	DOC	$2,315,000	51st	(0.07%)
DOI	$140,293,000	11th	(2.53%)	USDA	$64,378,000	46th	(0.27%)

Economic Base   Agriculture, notably cattle, sheep, sugar beets, and dairy products; oil and gas extraction, especially oil and gas field services; finance, insurance, and real estate; metal mining, especially uranium–radium–vanadium ores; petroleum refining and other petroleum and coal products; food and kindred products.

Political Lineup   Governor, Ed Herschler (D). Senators, Malcolm Wallop (R) and Alan K. Simpson (R). Representatives, 1 R at large; 1 in 1982. State Senate, 30 (19 R and 11 D); State House of Representatives, 62 (39 R and 23 D).

The Voters

Registration   219,423 Total. 81,204 D (37%); 108,485 R (49%); 29,734 unclassified (14%).
Employment profile 1970   White collar, 47%. Blue collar, 30%. Service, 14%. Farm, 9%.
Ethnic groups   Black 1980, 1%. Hispanic 1980, 5%. Am. Ind. 1980, 2%. Total foreign stock 1970, 11%.

Presidential Vote

1980	Reagan (R)	110,700	(63%)
	Carter (D)	49,427	(28%)
	Anderson (I)	12,072	(7%)
1976	Ford (R)	92,717	(59%)
	Carter (D)	62,239	(40%)

SENATORS

Sen. Malcolm Wallop (R) Elected 1976, seat up 1982; b. Feb. 27, 1933, New York, N.Y.; home, Big Horn; Yale U., B.A. 1954.

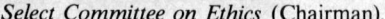

Career   Rancher; Army, 1955–57; Wyo. House of Reps., 1969–73; Wyo. Senate, 1973–77; Candidate for Rep. nomination for Gov., 1974.

Offices   204 RSOB, 202-224-6441. Also 2201 Fed. Bldg., Casper 82601, 307-266-3240, and 2009 Fed. Ctr., Cheyenne 82001, 307-634-0626.

Committees   *Energy and Natural Resources* (5th). Subcommittees: Energy and Mineral Resources; Water and Power; Public Lands and Reserved Water.

Finance (7th). Subcommittees: Taxation and Debt Management; International Trade; Energy and Agricultural Taxation (Chairman).

Select Committee on Ethics (Chairman).

Select Committee on Intelligence (5th). Subcommittees: Budget (Chairman); Analysis and Production.

Group Ratings

	ADA	COPE	PC	LCV	CFA	RPN	NAB	NSI	NTU	ACA	ACU
1980	22	5	27	28	0	—	75	100	63	92	86
1979	11	10	20	—	10	—	—	—	61	88	84
1978	10	11	15	21	15	63	92	100	29	78	92

Key Votes

1) Draft Registn $	FOR	6) Fair Housng Cloture	AGN	11) Cut Socl Incr Defns	FOR
2) Ban $ to Nicrgua	AGN	7) Ban $ Rape Abortns	AGN	12) Income Tax Indexing	FOR
3) Dlay MX Missile	—	8) Cap on Food Stmp $	FOR	13) Lim Spdg 21% GNP	FOR
4) Nuclr Mortorium	—	9) New US Dep Edcatn	AGN	14) Incr Wndfll Prof Tax	AGN
5) Alaska Lands Bill	AGN	10) Cut OSHA Inspctns	FOR	15) Chryslr Loan Grntee	AGN

Election Results

1976 general	Malcolm Wallop (R)............	84,810	(55%)	($301,595)
	Gale McGee (D)	70,558	(45%)	($181,028)
1976 primary	Malcolm Wallop (R)............	41,445	(77%)	
	Two others (R)	12,696	(23%)	
1970 general	Gale McGee (D)	67,207	(56%)	
	John S. Wold (R)	53,279	(44%)	

Sen. Alan K. Simpson (R) Elected 1978, seat up 1984; b. Sept. 2, 1931, Denver, Colo.; home, Cody; U. of Wyo., B.S. 1954, J.D. 1958.

Career Practicing atty., 1958; Cody City Atty., 1959–69; Wyo. House of Reps., 1964–78, Major. Whip, 1973–75, Major. Ldr., 1975–77, Spkr. Pro Tem, 1977.

Offices 4107 DSOB, 202-224-3424. Also 1731 Sheridan Ave., Cody 82414, 307-587-5323.

Committees *Environment and Public Works* (5th). Subcommittees: Environmental Pollution; Nuclear Regulation.

Judiciary (6th). Subcommittees: Courts; Immigration and Refugee Policy (Chairman); Regulatory Reform.

Veterans' Affairs (Chairman).

Group Ratings

	ADA	COPE	PC	LCV	CFA	RPN	NAB	NSI	NTU	ACA	ACU
1980	17	5	33	45	0	—	100	100	64	91	95
1979	11	0	18	—	10	—	—	—	61	81	76

Key Votes

1) Draft Registn $	FOR	6) Fair Housng Cloture	AGN	11) Cut Socl Incr Defns	FOR
2) Ban $ to Nicrgua	AGN	7) Ban $ Rape Abortns	AGN	12) Income Tax Indexing	FOR
3) Dlay MX Missile	AGN	8) Cap on Food Stmp $	FOR	13) Lim Spdg 21% GNP	FOR
4) Nuclr Mortorium	AGN	9) New US Dep Edcatn	FOR	14) Incr Wndfll Prof Tax	AGN
5) Alaska Lands Bill	AGN	10) Cut OSHA Inspctns	—	15) Chryslr Loan Grntee	AGN

Election Results

1978 general	Alan K. Simpson (R)	82,908	(62%)	($439,805)
	Raymond B. Whitaker (D).......	50,456	(38%)	($142,749)
1978 primary	Alan K. Simpson (R)	37,332	(55%)	
	Hugh Binford (R)	20,768	(30%)	($245,064)
	Two others (R)	10,203	(15%)	
1972 general	Clifford P. Hansen (R)	101,314	(71%)	($169,878)
	Mike M. Vinich (D)	40,753	(29%)	($10,411)

GOVERNOR

Gov. Ed Herschler (D) Elected 1974, term expires Jan. 1983; b. Oct. 27, 1918, Lincoln Co.; U. of Colo., B.A., U. of Wyo., LL.B. 1949.

Career USMC, WWII; Practicing atty., 1949–74; Kemmerer Town Atty., 1949–74; Lincoln Co. Prosecuting Atty.; Wyo. House of Reps., 1960–69.

Offices Capitol Bldg., Cheyenne 82002, 307-777-7434.

Election Results

1978 gen.	Ed Herschler (D)	69,972	(51%)
	John C. Ostlund (R)	67,595	(49%)
1978 prim.	Ed Herschler (D)	28,406	(65%)
	Margaret McKinstry (D) ...	15,111	(35%)
1974 gen.	Ed Herschler (D)	71,741	(56%)
	Dick Jones (R)	56,645	(44%)

Rep. Richard Bruce (Dick) **Cheney** (R) Elected 1978; b. Jan. 30, 1941, Lincoln, Neb.; home, Casper; U. of Wyo., B.A. 1965, M.A. 1966, U. of Wis., 1968.

Career Spec. Asst. to the Dir. of OEO; Dpty. to White House Pres. Counselor Donald Rumsfeld; Asst. Dir. for Operations, Cost of Living Cncl.; V.P., Bradley, Woods & Co., investment advisors, 1973–74, 1976–78; Asst. to Pres. Gerald Ford, 1974–76.

Offices 225 CHOB, 202-225-2311. Also Rm. 4005 Fed. Bldg., Casper 82601, 307-265-5550.

Committee *Interior and Insular Affairs* (7th). Subcommittees: Energy and the Environment; Public Lands and National Parks.

Group Ratings

	ADA	COPE	PC	LCV	CFA	RPN	NAB	NSI	NTU	ACA	ACU
1980	6	10	30	12	21	—	91	100	64	95	74
1979	11	10	18	28	19	—	—	—	60	100	89

Key Votes

1) Draft Registn $	FOR	6) Fair Hsg DOJ Enfrc	AGN	11) Cut Socl Incr Dfns $	FOR
2) Ban $ to Nicrgua	FOR	7) Lim PAC Contrbtns	AGN	12) Hosptl Cost Controls	AGN
3) Dlay MX Missile	AGN	8) Cap on Food Stmp $	FOR	13) Gasln Ctrls & Allctns	AGN
4) Nuclr Mortorium	AGN	9) New US Dep Edcatn	AGN	14) Lim Wndfll Prof Tax	FOR
5) Alaska Lands Bill	AGN	10) Cut OSHA $	FOR	15) Chryslr Loan Grntee	AGN

Election Results

1980 general	Richard Bruce (Dick) Cheney (R) .	116,361	(69%)	($97,959)
	Jim Rogers (D)	53,338	(31%)	($0)
1980 primary	Richard Bruce (Dick) Cheney (R) .	60,615	(100%)	
1978 general	Richard Bruce (Dick) Cheney (R) .	75,855	(59%)	($209,064)
	Bill Bagley (D)	53,522	(41%)	($175,297)

PUERTO RICO, VIRGIN ISLANDS, GUAM, AMERICAN SAMOA

Four American insular territories are represented in Congress by elected delegates who — like the District of Columbia representative — have floor privileges and votes on committees but may not vote on the floor. They are Puerto Rico, the Virgin Islands, Guam, and American Samoa, and they are a diverse lot.

The largest by far is Puerto Rico, a Caribbean island with more than three million people. (It has about the same population as Connecticut, South Carolina, or Oklahoma.) Puerto Rico was one of Spain's last colonial possessions; the United States gained it in the Spanish–American War of 1898. Until the 1940s it was desperately poor: heavily populated, devoted almost entirely to sugar cultivation. Then in the 1940s, 1950s, and early 1960s Puerto Rico was transformed by Governor Luis Munoz Marin and his Popular Democratic Party. Munoz initiated Operation Bootstrap, a program to lure businesses to Puerto Rico with promises of low-wage labor and government assistance; it took advantage of the fact that Puerto Rico is within the United States for trade purposes but is not subject to federal taxes. Munoz also developed what is known in English as the Commonwealth form of government (in Spanish it is estado liberado associado, free associated state). Under Commonwealth, Puerto Rico is part of the United States for purposes of international trade, foreign policy, and war, but it has its own separate laws, taxes, and representative government. Puerto Rico has also developed its own political parties: Munoz's Popular Democrats, the New Progressives (originally associated with the mainland Republicans), and two independence parties. Munoz himself could have been reelected president for life. Instead, in 1964 he retired, like George Washington; his funeral in 1979 was an occasion for an islandwide outpouring of emotion.

Puerto Rico has developed a vibrant politics in the years since Munoz's retirement. The central question, to which Puerto Ricans always return, is status. Some mainlanders suppose that Puerto Ricans yearn for independence, but in fact in the several referenda on status that have taken place over the years, independence has been the choice of fewer than 10% of the voters. (Nor is there any large number of independence-minded abstentions. Puerto Rico's voter turnout is much higher than on the mainland.) The big argument is between Commonwealth and statehood. In crafting Commonwealth, Munoz artfully preserved a way for Puerto Rico to retain its Hispanic culture and the advantages of its association with the United States. But many Puerto Ricans, particularly the younger and more highly educated people and residents of the growing San Juan metropolitan area, are proud of their American citizenship and want to be part of a state. Statehood has always had fewer backers than Commonwealth, however. In the 1976 election, the New Progressive candidate, Carlos Romero Barcelo carefully downplayed the status issue; he won election over Popular Democratic incumbent Rafael Hernandez Colon largely on economic issues. In 1980, Romero was expected to beat Hernandez easily. But actually the election was very close. One reason was that Romero had promised, if reelected, to stage a referendum on status, and there was no question that he was going to push statehood hard. But he was nearly defeated (there was a lengthy recount) and his party lost control of the Puerto Rican legislature; Romero in turn promised not to push statehood during the next four years. That promise is a good indication of where Puerto Ricans stand on this issue today.

The other major issue in Puerto Rico is the state of the economy. The island's rapid growth during the Operation Bootstrap period gave it the highest income level in Latin America — even higher than oil-producing Venezuela. But the 1970s were difficult years. Much of the island's prosperity was based on oil refining (because of quirks in the U.S. laws) and required cheap energy; the rise in energy prices hurt Puerto Rico badly. Romero Barcelo during his first term, on the advice of the same supply-side economists who advise the Reagan Administration, systematically lowered tax rates and claimed that the economy was as a result growing rapidly. His opponents claimed that all people were seeing was more inflation. The truth is that no one knows for sure. Economic measurements are not so well developed here; there may be traces left of a subsistence economy and, because of high taxes, perhaps a cash economy as well. More than half of Puerto Ricans receive food stamps, because eligibility is based on mainland income standards; the cupones, as the stamps are called, presumably reduce work incentives and are part of the reason for the very high unemployment rate. Things cannot be too bad, though; during the 1970s the net migration of Puerto Ricans was away from the mainland (particularly New York) and toward Puerto Rico.

Puerto Rico's delegate (his official title is resident commissioner) to the House of Representatives is Baltasar Corrada, elected in 1976 and 1980 (the term is for four years) as the candidate of Romero's New Progressive Party. Romero was a political ally of Jimmy Carter, and Corrada votes as a Democrat on congressional committees. Like two others of the four insular delegates, he is a member of the Interior and Insular Affairs Committee, which handles most of the specialized legislation concerning Puerto Rico. He is also on Education and Labor.

The United States' other insular area in the Caribbean is the Virgin Islands, a very different sort of place. It is much smaller than Puerto Rico, with a population under 100,000. Puerto Rico is multiracial and not self-conscious about it; most of the Virgin Islanders are black, and there is a pretty clear divide between the races, much resented by the blacks. Puerto Rico has attracted all kinds of light industry; the Virgin Islands lives off tourism and refineries (although the major refinery on St. Croix is in trouble). The Virgin Islands has had an elected governor only since 1976; before that he was appointed by the president. The delegate from the Virgin Islands is Ron de Lugo, who votes with the Democrats; in 1980 he defeated Melvin Evans, who voted with the Republicans. De Lugo serves on the Interior and Insular Affairs Committee and two others — Post Office and Civil Service and Public Works and Transportation.

It takes some 19 hours to fly from Washington, D.C., to Guam, the place where, as every viewer of political conventions knows, America's day begins. Guam lies just west of the International Date Line, and it is indeed the early hours of Tuesday there when the rest of us are just trying to get through Monday afternoon. Guam is geographically in the center of the Marianas, but juridically it is separate; Guam is an integral part of the United States, while the Marianas and the islands around them were for years United Nations trust territories administered by the United States. With a population just over 100,000, Guam is a more advanced society than most of the Marianas, but economically it is not yet self-supporting. More than two-thirds of the workers are employed by the federal government (there are big defense bases here) or by the Guamanian government. The people are of mixed ethnic stock

(Spanish and Pacific Islander), their religion is almost always Catholic, and they speak English, Spanish, and a local language called Chamorro.

The governor, Paul Calvo, is a successful businessman and a Republican; he would like to see Guam develop a stronger and more self-sufficient economy. In 1978 he defeated Democrat Richard Bordallo. The delegate to the House, however, is a Democrat: Antonio Borja Won Pat, first elected in 1972 and the senior insular delegate in Congress. He is a close ally of Phillip Burton, the San Francisco Democrat who for years chaired the Insular Affairs Subcommittee. "The sun never sets on the Burton empire," the saying went, and Burton labored hard to help the insular areas. He persuaded Congress to allow food stamps and other aid programs to be distributed with the same income cutoffs in the insular possessions as on the mainland, with the result that in Guam, as in Puerto Rico, a very large percentage of the population has come to depend on food stamps. Some argue that these programs are too generous, that they make the islanders too dependent and reduce their incentive to work at either traditional or modern tasks. Burton, Won Pat, and other defenders of the programs would argue that they are simple justice, just a matter of seeing that hungry people get food.

In 1981, Burton, at the request of organized labor, took the chairmanship of a labor subcommittee and gave up Insular Affairs. Now Won Pat is chairman — a fact that must have elevated his already high standing on Guam. He was reelected without difficulty in 1980.

In 1981, for the first time, American Samoa has representation in Congress. This Southern Pacific island, unlike Guam, has been little influenced by western settlers; it is almost as Polynesian as it was when the United States took possession in 1900. The new delegate is Fofo I. F. Sunia. He votes as a Democrat on the Merchant Marine and Fisheries and Public Works and Transportation Committees. In his first term he is something of an unknown quantity in Washington.

SENATE COMMITTEES

STANDING COMMITTEES

AGRICULTURE, NUTRITION, AND FORESTRY

Majority (9 R): Helms (N.C), Chmn.; Dole (Kan.), Hayakawa (Cal.), Lugar (Ind.), Cochran (Miss.), Boschwitz (Minn.), Jepsen (Iowa), Hawkins (Fla.), Andrews (N.D.).

Minority (8 D): Huddleston (Ky.), Leahy (Vt.), Zorinsky (Neb.), Melcher (Mont.), Pryor (Ark.), Boren (Okla.), Dixon (Ill.), Heflin (Ala.).

Subcommittees

[Helms and Huddleston are ex officio members of all subcommittees of which they are not regular members.]

SOIL AND WATER CONSERVATION

Majority (3 R): Jepsen, Chmn.; Cochran, Hayakawa.
Minority (2 D): Heflin, Huddleston.

AGRICULTURAL CREDIT AND RURAL ELECTRIFICATION

Majority (3 R): Hawkins, Chwmn.; Jepsen, Andrews.
Minority (3 D): Zorinsky, Heflin, Boren.

AGRICULTURAL PRODUCTION, MARKETING, AND STABILIZATION OF PRICES

Majority (5 R): Cochran, Chmn.; Helms, Andrews, Boschwitz, Hawkins.
Minority (5 D): Huddleston, Zorinsky, Melcher, Dixon, Leahy.

AGRICULTURAL RESEARCH AND GENERAL LEGISLATION

Majority (5 R): Lugar, Chmn.; Dole, Hayakawa, Boschwitz, Andrews.
Minority (4 D): Boren, Huddleston, Pryor, Heflin.

RURAL DEVELOPMENT, OVERSIGHT, AND INVESTIGATIONS

Majority (3 R): Andrews, Chmn.; Lugar, Boschwitz.
Minority (2 D): Pryor, Leahy.

FOREIGN AGRICULTURAL POLICY

Majority (6 R): Boschwitz, Chmn.; Lugar, Cochran, Dole, Jepsen, Hawkins.
Minority (4 D): Dixon, Pryor, Boren, Zorinsky.

NUTRITION

Majority (4 R): Dole, Chmn.; Hayakawa, Lugar, Hawkins.
Minority (3 D): Leahy, Melcher, Dixon.

FORESTRY, WATER RESOURCES, AND ENVIRONMENT

Majority (2 R): Hayakawa, Chmn.; Jepsen.
Minority (1 D): Melcher

APPROPRIATIONS

Majority (15 R): Hatfield (Oreg.), Chmn.; Stevens (Alaska), Weicker (Conn.), McClure (Ida.), Laxalt (Nev.), Garn (Utah), Schmitt (N.M.), Cochran (Miss.), Andrews (N.D.), Abdnor (S.D.), Kasten (Wis.), D'Amato (N.Y.), Mattingly (Ga.), Rudman (N.H.), Specter (Pa.).

Minority (14 D): Proxmire (Wis.), Stennis (Miss.), Byrd (W.Va.), Inouye (Hawaii), Hollings (S.C.), Eagleton (Mo.), Chiles (Fla.), Johnston (La.), Huddleston (Ky.), Burdick (N.D.), Leahy (Vt.), Sasser (Tenn.), DeConcini (Ariz.), Bumpers (Ark.).

Subcommittees

[Hatfield and Proxmire are nonvoting ex officio members of all subcommittees of which they are not regular members.]

AGRICULTURE AND RELATED AGENCIES

Majority (7 R): Cochran, Chmn.; McClure, Andrews, Abdnor, Kasten, Mattingly, Spencer.
Minority (6 D): Eagleton, Stennis, Byrd, Chiles, Burdick, Sasser.

DEFENSE

Majority (9 R): Stevens, Chmn.; Weicker, Garn, McClure, Schmitt, Andrews, Kasten, D'Amato, Rudman.
Minority (8 D): Stennis, Proxmire, Inouye, Hollings, Eagleton, Chiles, Johnston, Huddleston.

DISTRICT OF COLUMBIA

Majority (3 R): D'Amato, Chmn.; Weicker, Specter.
Minority (2 D): Leahy, Bumpers.

ENERGY AND WATER DEVELOPMENT

Majority (8 R): Hatfield, Chmn.; McClure, Garn, Schmitt, Cochran, Abdnor, Kasten, Mattingly.
Minority (7 D): Johnston, Stennis, Byrd, Hollings, Huddleston, Burdick, Sasser.

FOREIGN OPERATIONS

Majority (5 R): Kasten, Chmn.; Hatfield, D'Amato, Rudman, Specter.
Minority (4 D): Inouye, Johnston, Leahy, DeConcini.

HUD–INDEPENDENT AGENCIES

Majority (6 R): Garn, Chmn.; Weicker, Laxalt, Schmitt, D'Amato, Specter.
Minority (5 D): Huddleston, Stennis, Proxmire, Leahy, Sasser.

INTERIOR

Majority (8 R): McClure, Chmn.; Stevens, Laxalt, Garn, Schmitt, Cochran, Andrews, Rudman.
Minority (7 D): Byrd, Johnston, Huddleston, Leahy, DeConcini, Burdick, Bumpers.

LABOR, HEALTH AND HUMAN SERVICES, EDUCATION

Majority (8 R): Schmitt, Chmn.; Hatfield, Weicker, Stevens, Andrews, Abdnor, Rudman, Specter.
Minority (7 D): Proxmire, Byrd, Hollings, Eagleton, Chiles, Burdick, Inouye.

LEGISLATIVE BRANCH

Majority (3 R): Mattingly, Chmn.; Stevens, Hatfield.
Minority (2 D): Bumpers, Hollings.

MILITARY CONSTRUCTION

Majority (3 R): Laxalt, Chmn.; Garn, Mattingly.
Minority (2 D): Sasser, Inouye.

STATE, JUSTICE, COMMERCE, AND THE JUDICIARY

Majority (5 R): Weicker, Chmn.; Stevens, Laxalt, Cochran, Rudman.
Minority (4 D): Hollings, Inouye, DeConcini Bumpers.

TRANSPORTATION

Majority (5 R): Andrews, Chmn.; Cochran, Abdnor, Kasten, D'Amato.
Minority (4 D): Chiles, Stennis, Byrd, Eagleton.

TREASURY, POSTAL SERVICE, AND GENERAL GOVERNMENT

Majority (3 R): Abdnor, Chmn.; Laxalt, Mattingly.
Minority (2 D): DeConcini, Proxmire.

ARMED SERVICES

Majority (9 R): Tower (Tex.), Chmn.; Thurmond (S.C.), Goldwater (Ariz.), Warner (Va.), Humphrey (N.H.), Cohen (Maine), Jepsen (Iowa), Quayle (Ind.), Denton (Ala.).
Minority (8 D): Stennis (Miss.), Jackson (Wash.), Cannon (Nev.), Byrd (Va.), Nunn (Ga.), Hart (Colo,), Exon (Neb.), Levin (Mich.).

Subcommittees
MILITARY CONSTRUCTION

Majority (4 R): Thurmond, Chmn.; Warner, Humphrey, Denton.
Minority (4 D): Hart, Jackson, Cannon, Exon.

TACTICAL WARFARE

Majority (4 R): Goldwater, Chmn.; Thurmond, Warner, Jepsen.
Minority (3 D): Cannon, Byrd, Levin.

STRATEGIC AND THEATER NUCLEAR FORCES

Majority (5 R): Warner, Chmn.; Thurmond, Goldwater, Cohen, Quayle.
Minority (5 D): Jackson, Cannon, Nunn, Hart, Exon.

PREPAREDNESS

Majority (3 R): Humphrey, Chmn.; Goldwater, Jepsen.
Minority (2 D): Levin, Jackson.

SEA POWER AND FORCE PROJECTION

Majority (4 R): Cohen, Chmn.; Humphrey, Quayle, Denton.
Minority (3 D): Byrd, Nunn, Hart.

MANPOWER AND PERSONNEL

Majority (4 R): Jepsen, Chmn.; Cohen, Quayle, Denton.
Minority (3 D): Exon, Byrd, Nunn.

BANKING, HOUSING, AND URBAN AFFAIRS

Majority (8 R): Garn (Utah), Chmn.; Tower (Tex.), Heinz (Pa.), Armstrong (Colo.), Lugar (Ind.), D'Amato (N.Y.), Chafee (R.I.), Schmitt (N.M.)
Minority (7 D): Williams (N.J.), Proxmire (Wis.), Cranston (Cal.), Riegle (Mich.), Sarbanes (Md.), Dodd (Conn.), Dixon (Ill.).

HOUSING AND URBAN AFFAIRS

Majority (6 R): Lugar, Chmn.; Garn, Tower, Heinz, Armstrong, D'Amato.
Minority (5 D): Williams, Proxmire, Cranston, Sarbanes, Riegle.

FINANCIAL INSTITUTIONS

Majority (5 R): Tower, Chmn.; Garn, Lugar, D'Amato, Schmitt.
Minority (4 D): Cranston, Williams, Proxmire, Dixon.

INTERNATIONAL FINANCE AND MONETARY POLICY

Majority (4 R): Heinz, Chmn.; Garn, Armstrong, Chafee.
Minority (3 D): Proxmire, Williams, Dodd.

ECONOMIC POLICY

Majority (4 R): Armstrong, Chmn.; Heinz, Lugar, Chafee.
Minority (3 D): Riegle, Cranston, Sarbanes.

SECURITIES

Majority (3 R): D'Amato, Chmn.; Tower, Schmitt.
Minority (2 D): Sarbanes, Riegle.

RURAL HOUSING AND DEVELOPMENT

Majority (3 R): Schmitt, Chmn.; Heinz, Lugar.
Minority (2 D): Dixon, Dodd.

CONSUMER AFFAIRS

Majority (3 R): Chafee, Chmn.; D'Amato, Schmitt.
Minority (2 D): Dodd, Dixon.

BUDGET

Majority (12 R): Domenici (N.M.), Chmn.; Armstrong (Colo.), Kassebaum (Kans.), Boschwitz (Minn.), Hatch (Utah), Tower (Tex.), Andrews (N.D.), Symms (Ida.), Grassley (Iowa), Kasten (Wis.), Quayle (Ind.), Gorton (Wash.).
Minority (10 D): Hollings (S.C.), Chiles (Fla.), Biden (Del.), Johnston (La.), Sasser (Tenn.), Hart (Colo.), Metzenbaum (Ohio), Riegle (Mich.), Moynihan (N.Y.), Exon (Neb.).

No Subcommittees

COMMERCE, SCIENCE, AND TRANSPORTATION

Majority (9 R): Packwood (Oreg.), Chmn.; Goldwater (Ariz.), Schmitt (N.M.), Danforth (Mo.), Kassebaum (Kans.), Pressler (S.D.), Gorton (Wash.), Stevens (Alaska), Kasten (Wis.).
Minority (8 D): Cannon (Nev.), Long (La.), Hollings (S.C.), Inouye (Hawaii), Ford (Ky.), Riegle (Mich.), Exon (Neb.), Heflin (Ala.).

Subcommittees
[Packwood and Cannon are ex officio members of all subcommittees of which they are not regular members.]

AVIATION

Majority (4 R): Kassebaum, Chmn.; Goldwater, Danforth, Stevens.
Minority (3 D): Cannon, Inouye, Exon.

BUSINESS, TRADE, AND TOURISM

Majority (2 R): Pressler, Chmn.; Packwood.
Minority (1 D): Exon.

COMMUNICATIONS

Majority (4 R): Goldwater, Chmn.; Schmitt, Pressler, Stevens.
Minority (3 D): Hollings, Inouye, Ford.

CONSUMER

Majority (2 R): Kasten, Chmn.; Danforth.
Minority (1 D): Ford.

MERCHANT MARINE AND TOURISM

Majority (3 R): Gorton, Chmn.; Stevens, Kasten.
Minority (2 D): Inouye, Long.

Majority (5 R): Schmitt, Chmn.; Goldwater, Kassebaum, Gorton, Kasten.
Minority (4 D): Riegle, Ford, Hollings, Heflin.

SURFACE TRANSPORTATION

Majority (5 R): Danforth, Chmn.; Pressler, Schmitt, Kassebaum, Gorton.
Minority (4 D): Long, Hollings, Riegle, Heflin.

ENERGY AND NATURAL RESOURCES

Majority (11 R): McClure (Ida.), Chmn.; Hatfield (Oreg.), Weicker (Conn.), Domenici (N.M.), Wallop (Wyo.), Warner (Va.), Humphrey (N.H.), Murkowski (Alaska), Nickles (Okla.), East (N.C.), Heinz (Pa.).
Minority (9 D): Jackson (Wash.), Johnston (La.), Bumpers (Ark.), Ford (Ky.), Metzenbaum (Ohio), Matsunaga (Hawaii), Melcher (Mont.), Tsongas (Mass.), Bradley (N.J.).

Subcommittees
[McClure and Jackson are ex officio members of all subcommittees.]

ENERGY CONSERVATION AND SUPPLY

Majority (5 R): Weicker, Chmn.; Hatfield, Humphrey, East, Heinz.
Minority (4 D): Metzenbaum, Matsunaga, Tsongas, Bradley.

ENERGY REGULATION

Majority (5 R): Humphrey, Chmn.; Nickles, Domenici, East, Heinz.
Minority (4 D): Johnston, Ford, Metzenbaum, Melcher.

ENERGY RESEARCH AND DEVELOPMENT

Majority (5 R): Domenici, Chmn.; East, Nickles, Weicker, Warner.
Minority (4 D): Ford, Johnston, Bumpers, Tsongas.

ENERGY AND MINERAL RESOURCES

Majority (5 R): Warner, Chmn.; Heinz, Humphrey, Wallop, Murkowski.
Minority (4 D): Matsunaga, Johnston, Bumpers, Bradley.

WATER AND POWER

Majority (5 R): Murkowski, Chmn.; Hatfield, Weicker, Wallop, Nickles.
Minority (4 D): Melcher, Ford, Tsongas, Bradley.

PUBLIC LANDS AND RESERVED WATER

Majority (5 R): Wallop, Chmn.; Hatfield, Warner, Murkowski, Domenici.
Minority (4 D): Bumpers, Metzenbaum, Matsunaga, Melcher.

ENVIRONMENT AND PUBLIC WORKS

Majority (9 R): Stafford (Vt.), Chmn.; Baker (Tenn.), Domenici (N.M.), Chafee (R.I.), Simpson (Wyo.), Abdnor (S.D.), Symms (Ida.), Gorton (Wash.), Murkowski (Alaska).
Minority (7 D): Randolph (W.Va.), Bentsen (Tex.), Burdick (N.D), Hart (Colo.), Moynihan (N.Y.), Mitchell (Maine), Baucus (Mont.).

Subcommittees
ENVIRONMENTAL POLLUTION

Majority (4 R): Chafee, Chmn.; Simpson, Symms, Gorton.
Minority (3 D): Mitchell, Hart, Moynihan.

WATER RESOURCES

Majority (4 R): Abdnor, Chmn.; Domenici, Gorton, Murkowski.
Minority (3 D): Moynihan, Bentsen, Baucus.

TRANSPORTATION

Majority (5 R): Symms, Chmn.; Stafford, Baker, Chafee, Abdnor.
Minority (4 D): Bentsen, Randolph, Burdick, Moynihan.

NUCLEAR REGULATION

Majority (4 R): Simpson, Chmn.; Baker, Domenici, Symms.
Minority (3 D): Hart, Mitchell, Baucus.

FINANCE

Majority (11 R): Dole (Kans.), Chmn.; Packwood (Oreg.), Roth (Del.), Danforth (Mo.), Chafee (R.I.), Heinz (Pa.), Wallop (Wyo.), Durenberger (Minn.), Armstrong (Colo.), Symms (Ida.), Grassley (Iowa).
Minority (9 D): Long (La.), Byrd (Va.), Bentsen (Tex.), Matsunaga (Hawaii), Moynihan (N.Y.), Baucus (Mont.), Boren (Okla.), Bradley (N.J.), Mitchell (Maine).

Subcommittees
TAXATION AND DEBT MANAGEMENT

Majority (5 R): Packwood, Chmn.; Danforth, Chafee, Wallop, Armstrong.
Minority (4 D): Byrd, Bentsen, Matsunaga, Long.

INTERNATIONAL TRADE

Majority (8 R): Danforth, Chmn.; Roth, Chafee, Heinz, Wallop, Armstrong, Grassley, Symms.
Minority (7 D): Bentsen, Matsunaga, Moynihan, Boren, Bradley, Byrd, Baucus.

SAVINGS, PENSIONS, AND INVESTMENT POLICY

Majority (3 R): Chafee, Chmn.; Packwood, Roth.
Minority (2 D): Matsunaga, Mitchell.

ECONOMIC GROWTH, EMPLOYMENT, AND REVENUE SHARING

Majority (2 R): Heinz, Chmn.; Roth.
Minority (2 D): Mitchell, Moynihan.

ENERGY AND AGRICULTURAL TAXATION

Majority (3 R): Wallop, Chmn.; Symms, Durenberger.
Minority (3 D): Bradley, Mitchell, Bentsen.

HEALTH

Majority (4 R): Durenberger, Chmn.; Dole, Packwood, Heinz.
Minority (3 D): Baucus, Bradley, Long.

SOCIAL SECURITY AND INCOME MAINTENANCE PROGRAMS

Majority (4 R): Armstrong, Chmn.; Durenberger, Danforth, Dole.
Minority (3 D): Moynihan, Boren, Long.

ESTATE AND GIFT TAXATION

Majority (2 R): Symms, Chmn.; Grassley.
Minority (2 D): Boren, Byrd.

OVERSIGHT OF THE INTERNAL REVENUE SERVICE

Majority (2 R): Grassley, Chmn.; Dole.
Minority (1 D): Baucus.

FOREIGN RELATIONS

Majority (9 R): Percy (Ill.), Chmn.; Baker (Tenn.), Helms (N.C.), Hayakawa (Cal.), Lugar (Ind.), Mathias (Md.), Kassebaum (Kans.), Boschwitz (Minn.), Pressler (S.D.).
Minority (8 D): Pell (R.I.), Biden (Del.), Glenn (Ohio), Sarbanes (Md.), Zorinsky (Neb.), Tsongas (Mass.), Cranston (Cal.), Dodd (Conn.).

Subcommittees

[Percy is an ex officio member of all subcommittees of which he is not a regular member; Pell is an ex officio member of all subcommittees.]

INTERNATIONAL ECONOMIC POLICY

Majority (4 R): Mathias, Chmn.; Percy, Lugar, Kassebaum.
Minority (3 D): Dodd, Biden, Sarbanes.

ARMS CONTROL, OCEANS AND INTERNATIONAL OPERATIONS, AND ENVIRONMENT

Majority (3 R): Pressler, Chmn.; Percy, Baker.
Minority (2 D): Cranston, Zorinsky.

AFRICAN AFFAIRS

Majority (4 R): Kassebaum, Chwmn.; Helms, Hayakawa, Mathias.
Minority (3 D): Tsongas, Glenn, Dodd.

EUROPEAN AFFAIRS

Majority (4 R): Lugar, Chmn.; Mathias, Boschwitz, Pressler.
Minority (3 D): Biden, Sarbanes, Zorinsky.

EAST ASIAN AND PACIFIC AFFAIRS

Majority (4 R): Hayakawa, Chmn.; Baker, Helms, Boschwitz.
Minority (3 D): Glenn, Tsongas, Cranston.

NEAR EASTERN AND SOUTH ASIAN AFFAIRS

Majority (4 R): Boschwitz, Chmn.; Baker, Helms, Pressler.
Minority (3 D): Sarbanes, Glenn, Cranston.

WESTERN HEMISPHERE AFFAIRS

Majority (4 R): Helms, Chmn.; Hayakawa, Lugar, Kassebaum.
Minority (3 D): Zorinsky, Tsongas, Dodd.

GOVERNMENTAL AFFAIRS

Majority (9 R): Roth (Del.), Chmn.; Percy (Ill.), Stevens (Alaska), Mathias (Md.), Danforth (Mo,),
Cohen (Maine), Durenberger (Minn.), Mattingly (Ga.), Rudman (N.H.).
Minority (8 D): Eagleton (Mo.), Jackson (Wash.), Chiles (Fla.), Nunn (Ga.), Glenn (Ohio), Sasser
(Tenn.), Pryor (Ark.), Levin (Mich.)

Subcommittees

PERMANENT SUBCOMMITTEE ON INVESTIGATIONS

Majority (6 R): Roth, Chmn.; Rudman, Vice Chmn.; Percy, Mathias, Danforth, Cohen.
Minority (5 D): Nunn, Jackson, Chiles, Glenn, Sasser.

GOVERNMENTAL EFFICIENCY AND THE DISTRICT OF COLUMBIA

Majority (2 R): Mathias, Chmn.; Rudman.
Minority (1 D): Eagleton.

ENERGY, NUCLEAR PROLIFERATION, AND GOVERNMENT PROCESSES

Majority (4 R): Percy, Chmn.; Durenberger, Cohen, Mattingly.
Minority (3 D): Glenn, Jackson, Levin.

FEDERAL EXPENDITURES, RESEARCH, AND RULES

Majority (3 R): Danforth, Chmn.; Percy, Durenberger.
Minority (2 D): Chiles, Jackson.

INTERGOVERNMENTAL RELATIONS

Majority (3 R): Durenberger, Chmn.; Danforth, Mattingly.
Minority (2 D): Sasser, Nunn.

CIVIL SERVICE, POST OFFICE, AND GENERAL SERVICES

Majority (2 R): Stevens, Chmn.; Mathias.
Minority (1 D): Pryor.

OVERSIGHT OF GOVERNMENT MANAGEMENT

Majority (3 R): Cohen, Chmn.; Stevens, Rudman.
Minority (2 D): Levin, Pryor.

CONGRESSIONAL OPERATIONS AND OVERSIGHT

Majority (2 R): Mattingly, Chmn.; Stevens.
Minority (1 D): Pryor.

JUDICIARY

Majority (10 R): Thurmond (S.C.), Chmn.; Mathias (Md.), Laxalt (Nev.), Hatch (Utah), Dole (Kans.), Simpson (Wyo.), East (N.C.), Grassley (Iowa), Denton (Ala.), Specter (Pa.).
Minority (8 D): Biden (Del.), Kennedy (Mass.), Byrd (W.Va.), Metzenbaum (Ohio), DeConcini (Ariz.), Leahy (Vt.), Baucus (Mont.), Heflin (Ala.).

Subcommittees
AGENCY ADMINISTRATION

Majority (3 R): Grassley, Chmn.; Laxalt, Specter.
Minority (2 D): Metzenbaum, Baucus.

CONSTITUTION

Majority (3 R): Hatch, Chmn.; Thurmond, Grassley.
Minority (2 D): DeConcini, Leahy.

COURTS

Majority (4 R): Dole, Chmn.; Thurmond, Simpson, East.
Minority (2 D): Heflin, Baucus.

CRIMINAL LAW

Majority (4 R): Mathias, Chmn.; Laxalt, Specter, Dole.
Minority (2 D): Biden, Metzenbaum.

IMMIGRATION AND REFUGEE POLICY

Majority (3 R): Simpson, Chmn.; Thurmond, Grassley.
Minority (2 D): Kennedy, DeConcini.

JUVENILE JUSTICE

Majority (3 R): Specter, Chmn.; Denton, Mathias.
Minority (2 D): Metzenbaum, Kennedy.

REGULATORY REFORM

Majority (4 R): Laxalt, Chmn.; Dole, Mathias, Simpson.
Minority (2 D): Leahy, Byrd.

SECURITY AND TERRORISM

Majority (3 R): Denton, Chmn.; Hatch, East.
Minority (2 D): Biden, Leahy.

SEPARATION OF POWER

Majority (3 R): East, Chmn.; Hatch, Denton.
Minority (2 D): Baucus, Heflin.

LABOR AND HUMAN RESOURCES

Majority (9 R): Hatch (Utah), Chmn.; Stafford (Vt.), Quayle (Ind.), Hawkins (Fla.), Nickles (Okla.), Weicker (Conn.), Humphrey (N.H.), Denton (Ala.), East (N.C.).
Minority (7 D): Kennedy (Mass.), Randolph (W.Va.), Williams (N.J.), Pell (R.I.), Eagleton (Mo.), Riegle (Mich.), Metzenbaum (Ohio).

Subcommittees

[Hatch and Kennedy are ex officio members of all subcommittees of which they are not regular members.]

LABOR

Majority (6 R): Nickles, Chmn.; Hatch, East, Stafford, Quayle, Hawkins.
Minority (4 D): Williams, Kennedy, Randolph, Riegle.

EDUCATION

Majority (5 R): Stafford, Chmn.; East, Quayle, Weicker, Denton.
Minority (2 D): Pell, Kennedy, Randolph, Eagleton.

EMPLOYMENT AND PRODUCTIVITY

Majority (4 R): Quayle, Chmn.; Hawkins, Nickles, Hatch.
Minority (3 D): Metzenbaum, Kennedy, Pell.

HANDICAPPED

Majority (4 R): Weicker, Chmn.; Stafford, East, Nickles.
Minority (3 D): Randolph, Williams, Eagleton.

ALCOHOLISM AND DRUG ABUSE

Majority (3 R): Humphrey, Chmn.; Denton, Hatch.
Minority (2 D): Riegle, Williams.

AGING, FAMILY, AND HUMAN SERVICES

Majority (3 R): Denton, Chmn.; Weicker, Humphrey.
Minority (2 D): Eagleton, Metzenbaum.

INVESTIGATION AND GENERAL OVERSIGHT

Majority (2 R): Hawkins, Chwmn.; Humphrey.
Minority (1 D): Kennedy.

RULES AND ADMINISTRATION

Majority (7 R): Mathias (Md.), Chmn.; Hatfield (Oreg.), Baker (Tenn.), McClure (Ida.), Helms (N.C.), Warner (Va.), Dole (Kans.).
Minority (5 D): Ford (Ky.), Cannon (Nev.), Pell (R.I.), Byrd (W.Va.), Williams (N.J.).

No Subcommittees

VETERANS' AFFAIRS

Majority (7 R): Simpson (Wyo.), Chmn.; Thurmond (S.C.), Stafford (Vt.), Kasten (Wis.), Denton (Ala.), Murkowski (Alaska), Specter (Pa.).
Minority (5 D): Cranston (Cal.), Randolph (W.Va.), Matsunaga (Hawaii), DeConcini (Ariz.), Mitchell (Maine).

No Subcommittees

SELECT COMMITTEES

SELECT COMMITTEE ON ETHICS
[Created by S.Res.4, 95th Cong.]

Majority (3 R): Wallop (Wyo.), Chmn.; Helms (N.C.), Mattingly (Ga.).
Minority (3 D): Heflin (Ala.), Pryor (Ark.), Eagleton (Mo.)

No Subcommittees

SELECT COMMITTEE ON INDIAN AFFAIRS
[Created by S.Res.4, 95th Cong.]

Majority (4 R): Cohen (Maine), Chmn.; Goldwater (Ariz.), Andrews (N.D.), Gorton (Wash.).
Minority (3 D): Melcher (Mont.), Inouye (Hawaii), DeConcini (N.M.).

No Subcommittees

SELECT COMMITTEE ON INTELLIGENCE
[Created pursuant to S.Res.400, 94th Cong.]
[Senate Majority Leader Baker (Tenn.) and Senate Minority Leader Byrd (W.Va.) are ex officio members of the committee.]

Majority (8 R): Goldwater (Ariz.), Chmn.; Garn (Utah), Chafee (R.I.), Lugar (Ind.), Wallop (Wyo.), Durenberger (Minn.), Roth (Del.), Schmitt (N.M.).
Minority (7 D): Moynihan (N.Y.), Vice Chmn.; Huddleston (Ky.), Biden (Del.), Inouye (Hawaii), Jackson (Wash.), Leahy (Vt.), Bentsen (Tex.).

Subcommittees
[Goldwater and Moynihan are ex officio members of all subcommittees.]

BUDGET
Majority (4 R): Wallop, Chmn.; Garn, Durenberger, Roth.
Minority (4 D): Inouye, Vice Chmn.; Jackson, Leahy, Bentsen.

ANALYSIS AND PRODUCTION
Majority (4 R): Lugar, Chmn.; Garn, Wallop, Durenberger.
Minority (2 D): Jackson, Vice Chmn.; Bentsen.

LEGISLATION AND THE RIGHTS OF AMERICANS
Majority (3 R): Schmitt, Chmn.; Garn, Chafee.
Minority (2 D): Leahy, Vice Chmn.; Huddleston.

COLLECTION AND FOREIGN OPERATIONS
Majority (5 R): Chafee, Chmn.; Garn, Lugar, Durenberger.
Minority (4 D): Huddleston, Vice Chmn.; Biden, Inouye, Jackson.

SELECT COMMITTEE ON SMALL BUSINESS
[Created pursuant to S.Res.58, 81st Cong.]

Majority (9 R): Weicker (Conn.), Chmn.; Packwood (Oreg.), Hatch (Utah), Hayakawa (Cal.), Boschwitz (Minn.), Gorton (Wash.), Nickles (Okla.), Rudman (N.H.), D'Amato (N.Y.).
Minority (8 D): Nunn (Ga.), Huddleston (Ky.), Bumpers (Ark.), Sasser (Tenn.), Baucus (Mont.), Levin (Mich.), Tsongas (Mass.), Dixon (Ill.).

Subcommittees
[Weicker and Nunn are ex officio members of all subcommittees of which they are not regular members.]

SENATE COMMITTEES 1225

CAPITAL FORMATION AND RETENTION

Majority (3 R): Packwood, Chmn.; Hatch, Boschwitz.
Minority (2 D): Nunn, Sasser.

GOVERNMENT REGULATION AND PAPERWORK

Majority (3 R): Hatch, Chmn.; D'Amato, Gorton.
Minority (2 D): Bumpers, Huddleston.

URBAN AND RURAL ECONOMIC DEVELOPMENT

Majority (2 R): D'Amato, Chmn.; Weicker.
Minority (1 D): Dixon.

GOVERNMENT PROCUREMENT

Majority (2 R): Nickles, Chmn.; Weicker.
Minority (1 D): Sasser.

PRODUCTIVITY AND COMPETITION

Majority (2 R): Gorton, Chmn.; Nickles.
Minority (1 D): Baucus.

INNOVATION AND TECHNOLOGY

Majority (2 R): Rudman, Chmn.; Packwood.
Minority (1 D): Levin.

EXPORT PROMOTION AND MARKET DEVELOPMENT

Majority (2 R): Boschwitz, Chmn.; Hayakawa.
Minority (1 D): Huddleston.

ADVOCACY AND THE FUTURE OF SMALL BUSINESS

Majority (2 R): Hayakawa, Chmn.; Rudman.
Minority (1 D): Tsongas.

SPECIAL COMMITTEE

SPECIAL COMMITTEE ON AGING

[Created pursuant to S.Res.33, 87th Cong. and amended by S.Res.4, 95th Cong.]

Majority (8 R): Heinz (Pa.), Chmn.; Domenici (N.M.), Percy (Ill.), Kassebaum (Kans.), Cohen (Maine), Pressler (S.D.), Grassley (Iowa), Durenberger (Minn.).
Minority (7 D): Chiles (Fla.), Glenn (Ohio), Melcher (Mont), Pryor (Ark.), Bradley (N.J.), Burdick (N.D.), Dodd (Conn.).

No Subcommittees

JOINT COMMITTEES OF THE CONGRESS

JOINT ECONOMIC COMMITTEE

[Created pursuant to sec. 5(a) of Public Law. 204, 79th Cong.]

Senate (10): Jepsen (Iowa), Vice Chmn.; Roth (Del.), Abdnor (S.D.), Symms (Ida.), Hawkins (Fla.), Mattingly (Ga.), Bentsen (Tex.), Proxmire (Wis.), Kennedy (Mass.), Sarbanes (Md.).
House (9): Reuss (Wis.), Chmn.; Bolling (Mo.), Hamilton (Ind.), Long (La.), Mitchell (Md.), Brown (Ohio), Heckler (Mass.), Rousselot (Cal.), Wylie (Ohio).

HOUSE COMMITTEES

STANDING COMMITTEES

AGRICULTURE

Majority (24 D): De la Garza (Tex.), Chmn.; Foley (Wash.), Jones (N.C.), Jones (Tenn.), Brown (Cal.), Bowen (Miss.), Rose (N.C.), Richmond (N.Y.), Weaver (Oreg.), Harkin (Iowa), Bedell (Iowa), English (Okla.), Fithian (Ind.), Panetta (Cal.), Huckaby (La.), Glickman (Kans.), Whitley (N.C.), Coelho (Cal.), Daschle (S.D.), Anthony (Ark.), Stenholm (Tex.), Volkmer (Mo.), Hatcher (Ga.), Dorgan (N.D.).

Minority (19 R): Wampler (Va.), Findley (Ill.), Jeffords (Vt.), Hagedorn (Minn.), Coleman (Mo.), Marlenee (Mont.), Hopkins (Ky.), Thomas (Cal.), Hansen (Ida.), Stangeland (Minn.), Roberts (Kans.), Emerson (Mo.), Napier (S.C.), Skeen (N.M.), Morrison (Wash.), Roberts (S.D.), Gunderson (Wis.), Evans (Iowa), Chappie (Cal.).

Subcommittees

[De la Garza is ex officio member of all subcommittees; Wampler is ex officio member of all subcommittees of which he is not a regular member.]

CONSERVATION, CREDIT, AND RURAL DEVELOPMENT

Majority (12 D): Jones (Tenn.), Chmn.; Bedell, Glickman, Daschle, Dorgan, Bowen, Harkin, English, Fithian, Panetta, Anthony, Richmond.

Minority (9 R): Jeffords, Coleman, Roberts (Kans.), Napier, Skeen, Morrison, Roberts (S.D.), Gunderson, Evans.

COTTON, RICE, AND SUGAR

Majority (10 D): Bowen, Chmn.; Huckaby, Coelho, Anthony, Stenholm, Hatcher, Jones (Tenn.), Whitley, Foley, English.

Minority (7 R): Thomas, Stangeland, Emerson, Napier, Morrison, Gunderson, Chappie.

DEPARTMENT OPERATIONS, RESEARCH, AND FOREIGN AGRICULTURE

Majority (6 D): Brown, Chmn.; Richmond, Foley, Bowen, Fithian, Volkmer.

Minority (5 R): Wampler, Thomas, Roberts (Kans.), Emerson, Evans.

DOMESTIC MARKETING, CONSUMER RELATIONS, AND NUTRITION

Majority (6 D): Richmond, Chmn.; Panetta, Glickman, Coelho, Harkin, Foley.

Minority (4 R): Coleman, Findley, Hansen, Chappie.

FORESTS, FAMILY FARMS, AND ENERGY

Majority (9 D): Weaver, Chmn.; Foley, Brown, Bedell, Huckaby, Panetta, Daschle, Anthony, Dorgan.

Minority (6 R): Marlenee, Hansen, Stangeland, Skeen, Morrison, Chappie.

LIVESTOCK, DAIRY, AND POULTRY

Majority (8 D): Harkin, Chmn.; Volkmer, Jones (Tenn.), Rose, Whitley, Coelho, Stenholm, Hatcher.

Minority (6 R): Hagedorn, Jeffords, Hopkins, Hansen, Skeen, Gunderson.

TOBACCO AND PEANUTS

Majority (6 D): Rose, Chmn.; Jones (N.C.), Whitley, Hatcher, English, Stenholm.

Minority (4 R): Hopkins, Wampler, Napier, Roberts (S.D.).

WHEAT, SOYBEANS, AND FEED GRAINS

Majority (11 D): Foley, Chmn.; English, Fithian, Weaver, Glickman, Daschle, Stenholm, Volkmer, Dorgan, Bedell, Huckaby.

Minority (8 R): Findley, Hagedorn, Marlenee, Stangeland, Roberts (Kans.), Emerson, Roberts (S.D.), Evans.

APPROPRIATIONS

Majority (33 D): Whitten (Miss.), Chmn.; Boland (Mass.), Natcher (Ky.), Smith (Iowa), Addabbo (N.Y.), Long (Md.), Yates (Ill.), Obey (Wis.), Roybal (Cal.), Stokes (Ohio), Bevill (Ala.), Chappell (Fla.), Alexander (Ark.), Murtha (Pa.), Traxler (Mich.), Early (Mass.), Wilson (Tex.), Boggs (La.), Benjamin (Ind.), Dicks (Wash.), McHugh (N.Y.), Ginn (Ga.), Lehman (Fla.), Hightower (Tex.), Sabo (Minn.), Dixon (Ill.), Fazio (Cal.), Hefner (N.C.), AuCoin (Oreg.), Akaka (Hawaii), Watkins (Okla.), Gray (Pa.), Dwyer (N.J.).

Minority (22 R): Conte (Mass.), McDade (Pa.), Edwards (Ala.), Myers (Ind.), Robinson (Va.), Miller (Ohio), Coughlin (Pa.), Young (Fla.), Kemp (N.Y.), Regula (Ohio), Burgener (Cal.), O'Brien (Ill.), Smith (Neb.), Rudd (Ariz.), Pursell (Mich.), Edwards (Okla.), Livingston (La.), Green (N.Y.), Loeffler (Tex.), Lewis (Cal.), Campbell (S.C.), Porter (Ill.).

Subcommittees

[Whitten and Conte are ex officio members of all subcommittees on which they do not hold a regular assignment.]

AGRICULTURE, RURAL DEVELOPMENT AND RELATED AGENCIES

Majority (8 D): Whitten, Chmn.; Traxler, Alexander, McHugh, Natcher, Hightower, Akaka, Watkins.

Minority (4 R): Smith, Robinson, Myers, Lewis.

COMMERCE, JUSTICE, STATE, AND JUDICIARY

Majority (5 D): Smith, Chmn.; Alexander, Early, Hightower, Dwyer.

Minority (3 R): O'Brien, Miller, Campbell.

DEFENSE

Majority (7 D): Addabbo, Chmn.; Chappell, Murtha, Dicks, Wilson, Hefner, Ginn.

Minority (4 R): Edwards (Ala.), Robinson, McDade, Young.

DISTRICT OF COLUMBIA

Majority (5 D): Dixon, Chmn.; Natcher, Stokes, Wilson, Lehman.

Minority (3 R): Coughlin, Green, Porter.

ENERGY AND WATER DEVELOPMENT

Majority (7 D): Bevill, Chmn.; Boland, Boggs, Chappell, Fazio, Watkins, Benjamin.

Minority (4 R): Myers, Burgener, Smith, Rudd.

FOREIGN OPERATIONS

Majority (8 D): Long, Chmn.; Obey, Yates, McHugh, Lehman, Wilson, Dixon, Gray.

Minority (5 R): Kemp, Edwards (Okla.), Livingston, Lewis, Porter.

HUD–INDEPENDENT AGENCIES

Majority (5 D): Boland, Chmn.; Traxler, Stokes, Boggs, Sabo.

Minority (3 R): Green, Coughlin, Young.

INTERIOR

Majority (5 D): Yates, Chmn.; Long, Murtha, Dicks, AuCoin.

Minority (3 R): McDade, Regula, Loeffler.

LABOR–HEALTH AND HUMAN SERVICES–EDUCATION

Majority (7 D): Natcher, Chmn.; Smith, Obey, Roybal, Stokes, Early, Dwyer.
Minority (5 R): Conte, O'Brien, Pursell, Livingston, Porter.

LEGISLATIVE

Majority (5 D): Fazio, Chmn.; Murtha, Traxler, Benjamin, Dicks.
Minority (4 R): Burgener, Conte, Lewis, Campbell.

MILITARY CONSTRUCTION

Majority (7 D): Ginn, Chmn.; Bevill, Hefner, Addabbo, Long, Chappell, Alexander.
Minority (4 R): Regula, Burgener, Edwards (Okla.), Loeffler.

TRANSPORTATION

Majority (5 D): Benjamin, Chmn.; Lehman, Sabo, AuCoin, Gray.
Minority (4 R): Coughlin, Conte, Edwards (Ala.), Pursell.

TREASURY–POSTAL SERVICE–GENERAL GOVERNMENT

Majority (5 D): Roybal, Chmn.; Addabbo, Akaka, Yates, Obey.
Minority (3 R): Miller, Rudd, Campbell.

ARMED SERVICES

Majority (26 D): Price (Ill.), Chmn.; Bennett (Fla.), Stratton (N.Y.), White (Tex.), Nichols (Ala.), Brinkley (Ga.), Mollohan (W.Va.), W. Daniel (Va.), Montgomery (Miss.), Aspin (Wis.), Dellums (Cal.), Schroeder (Colo.), Kazen (Tex.), Won Pat (Guam), McDonald (Ga.), Stump (Ariz.), Byron (Md.), Mavroules (Mass.), Hutto (Fla.), Skelton (Mo.), Leath (Tex.), McCurdy (Okla.), Foglietta (Pa.), Dyson (Md.), Hertel (Mich.), one vacancy.
Minority (19 R): Dickinson (Ala.), Whitehurst (Va.), Spence (S.C.), Beard (Tenn.), Mitchell (N.Y.), Holt (Md.), R. Daniel (Va.), Hillis (Ind.), Emery (Maine), Trible (Va.), Badham (Cal.), Dougherty (Pa.), Courter (N.J.), Hopkins (Ky.), Davis (Mich.), Kramer (Colo.), Hunter (Cal.), Nelligan (Pa.), Hartnett (S.C.).

Subcommittees
INVESTIGATIONS

Majority (8 D): White, Chmn.; Mollohan, Aspin, Kazen, Mavroules, Stratton, Brinkley, W. Daniel.
Minority (6 R): Beard, R. Daniel, Mitchell, Hopkins, Davis, Nelligan.

MILITARY INSTALLATIONS AND FACILITIES

Majority (8 D): Brinkley, Chmn.; Montgomery, Kazen, Won Pat, Hutto, Foglietta, Dyson, Bennett.
Minority (6 R): Trible, Whitehurst, Mitchell, Dickinson, Dougherty, Kramer.

MILITARY PERSONNEL AND COMPENSATION

Majority (8 D): Nichols, Chmn.; Montgomery, Aspin, Won Pat, Byron, Skelton, Bennett, White.
Minority (6 R): Mitchell, Holt, Hillis, Hopkins, Hunter, Hartnett.

PROCUREMENT AND MILITARY NUCLEAR SYSTEMS

Majority (7 D): Stratton, Chmn.; Byron, Mavroules, Leath, McCurdy, Hertel, Price.
Minority (6 R): Holt, Hillis, Badham, Courter, Kramer, Hunter.

READINESS

Majority (6 D): W. Daniel, Chmn.; Schroeder, Stump, Skelton, Leath, McCurdy.
Minority (5 R): Whitehurst, Dickinson, Spence, Hillis, Nelligan.

RESEARCH AND DEVELOPMENT

Majority (9 D): Price, Chmn.; Mollohan, Dellums, Schroeder, McDonald, Stump, Hutto, White, Nichols.
Minority (7 R): Dickinson, Courter, Beard, R. Daniel, Emery, Badham, Davis.

SEAPOWER AND STRATEGIC AND CRITICAL MATERIALS

Majority (7 D): Bennett, Chmn.; Mollohan, McDonald, Hutto, Foglietta, Dyson, Hertel.
Minority (5 R): Spence, Emery, Trible, Dougherty, Hartnett.

BANKING, FINANCE, AND URBAN AFFAIRS

Majority (26 D): St. Germain (R.I.), Chmn.; Reuss (Wis.), Gonzalez (Tex.), Minish (N.J.), Annunzio (Ill.), Mitchell (Md.), Fauntroy (D.C.), Neal (N.C.), Patterson (Cal.), Blanchard (Mich.), Hubbard (Ky.), LaFalce (N.Y.), Evans (Ind.), D'Amours (N.H.), Lundine (N.Y.), Oakar (Ohio), Mattox (Tex.), Vento (Minn.), Barnard (Ga.), Garcia (N.Y.), Lowry (Wash.), Schumer (N.Y.), Frank (Mass.), Patman (Tex.), W. Coyne (Pa.), one vacancy.
Minority (19 R): Stanton (Ohio), Wylie (Ohio), McKinney (Conn.), Hansen (Ida.), Hyde (Ill.), Leach (Iowa), Evans (Del.), Paul (Tex.), Bethune (Ark.), Shumway (Cal.), Parris (Va.), Weber (Ohio), McCollum (Fla,), Carman (N.Y.), Wortley (N.Y.), Roukema (N.J.), Lowery (Cal.), J. Coyne (Pa.), Bereuter (Neb.).

Subcommittees
CONSUMER AFFAIRS AND COINAGE

Majority (5 D): Annunzio, Chmn.; St. Germain, Gonzalez, Minish, Patman.
Minority (4 R): Evans, Wylie, Wortley, Carman.

DOMESTIC MONETARY POLICY

Majority (8 D): Fauntroy, Chmn.; Mitchell, Neal, Barnard, Reuss, Blanchard, Hubbard, Patman.
Minority (6 R): Hansen, Paul, McCollum, Lowery, Weber, J. Coyne.

ECONOMIC STABILIZATION

Majority (13 D): Blanchard, Chmn.; Lundine, Vento, Evans, D'Amours, Oakar, Garcia, St. Germain, Minish, Annunzio, Fauntroy, Schumer, W. Coyne.
Minority (9 R): McKinney, Shumway, Paul, Bethune, Parris, Wortley, Roukema, J. Coyne, one vacancy.

FINANCIAL INSTITUTIONS SUPERVISION, REGULATION AND INSURANCE

Majority (14 D): St. Germain, Chmn.; Annunzio, Hubbard, D'Amours, Mattox, Minish, Barnard, LaFalce, Evans, Oakar, Vento, Garcia, Schumer, Patman.
Minority (10 R): Wylie, Hyde, Hansen, Leach, Bethune, McKinney, Shumway, Weber, McCollum, Lowery.

GENERAL OVERSIGHT AND RENEGOTIATION

Majority (9 D): Minish, Chmn.; Gonzalez, Annunzio, Mitchell, Barnard, Fauntroy, Oakar, Mattox, Frank.
Minority (7 R): Paul, McCollum, Weber, Roukema, Carman, Wortley, one vacancy.

1230   HOUSE COMMITTEES

HOUSING AND COMMUNITY DEVELOPMENT

Majority (19 D): Gonzalez, Chmn.; St. Germain, Fauntroy, Patterson, LaFalce, Blanchard, Evans, Lundine, Oakar, Vento, Garcia, Lowry, Mitchell, Hubbard, D'Amours, Schumer, Frank, W. Coyne, one vacancy.
Minority (14 R): Stanton, Wylie, McKinney, Evans, Leach, Bethune, Parris, Roukema, J. Coyne, Wortley, Carman, McCollum, Lowery, one vacancy.

INTERNATIONAL DEVELOPMENT INSTITUTIONS AND FINANCE

Majority (6 D): Patterson, Chmn.; LaFalce, Oakar, Neal, Reuss, Lowry.
Minority (4 R): Hyde, Evans, Stanton, J. Coyne.

INTERNATIONAL TRADE, INVESTMENT AND MONETARY POLICY

Majority (10 D): Neal, Chmn.; Lundine, Barnard, Patterson, LaFalce, Mattox, Lowry, Frank, W. Coyne, St. Germain.
Minority (7 R): Leach, Hyde, Hansen, Shumway, Stanton, Parris, Carman.

BUDGET

Majority (18 D): Jones (Okla.), Chmn.; Wright (Tex.), Obey (Wis.), Simon (Ill.), Mineta (Cal.), Mattox (Tex.), Solarz (N.Y.), Wirth (Colo.), Panetta (Cal.), Gephardt (Mo.), Nelson (Fla.), Aspin (Wis), Hefner (N.C.), Downey (N.Y.), Benjamin (Ind.), Donnelly (Mass.), Anthony (Ark.), Gramm (Tex.).
Minority (12 R): Latta (Ohio), Regula (Ohio), Shuster (Pa.), Frenzel (Minn.), Kemp (N.Y.), Martin (N.C.), Trible (Va.), Bethune (Ark.), Martin (Ill.), Smith (Ala.), Johnston (N.C.),   Fiedler (Cal.).

No Subcommittees

DISTRICT OF COLUMBIA

Majority (8 D): Dellums (Cal.), Chmn.; Fauntroy (D.C.), Mazzoli (Ky.), Stark (Cal.), Leland (Tex.), Gray (Pa.), Barnes (Md.), Dymally (Cal.).
Minority (4 R): McKinney (Conn.), Parris (Va.), Bliley (Va.), Holt (Md.).

Subcommittees
[Dellums is an ex officio member (with vote) of each subcommittee counted for purposes of compliance with the ratio requirement.]

FISCAL AFFAIRS AND HEALTH

Majority (3 D): Dellums, Chmn.; , Fauntroy, one vacancy.
Minority (3 R): McKinney, Bliley, Parris.

GOVERNMENT OPERATIONS AND METROPOLITAN AFFAIRS

Majority (3 D): Gray, Chmn.; Stark, Barnes.
Minority (3 R): Parris, McKinney, Holt.

JUDICIARY

Majority (3 D): Dymally, Chmn.; Mazzoli, Leland.
Minority (2 R): Bliley, Holt.

EDUCATION AND LABOR

Majority (20 D): Perkins (Ky.), Chmn.; Hawkins (Cal.), Ford (Mich.), P. Burton (Cal.), Gaydos (Pa.), Clay (Mo.), Biaggi (N.Y.), Andrews (N.C.), Simon (Ill.), Miller (Cal.), Murphy (Pa.), Weiss (N.Y.), Corrada (P.R.), Kildee (Mich.), Peyser (N.Y.), Williams (Mont.), Ratchford (Conn.), Kogovsek (Colo.), Washington (Ill.), Eckart (Ohio).

Minority (14 R): Ashbrook (Ohio), Erlenborn (Ill.), Jeffords (Vt.), Goodling (Pa.), Coleman (Mo.), Kramer (Colo.), Erdahl (Minn.), Petri (Wis.), Fenwick (N.J.), Roukema (N.J.), Johnston (N.C.), DeNardis (Conn.), Craig (Ida.), Bailey (Mo.).

Subcommittees
[Perkins and Ashbrook (or his designee) are ex officio voting members of all subcommittees of which they are not regular members. Designees are indicated by an asterisk (*).]

ELEMENTARY, SECONDARY AND VOCATIONAL EDUCATION

Majority (11 D): Perkins, Chmn.; Ford, Andrews, Miller, Corrada, Kildee, Williams, Hawkins, Biaggi, Ratchford, Washington.
Minority (8 R): Goodling, Jeffords, Coleman, Erdahl, Petri,* Roukema, DeNardis, Craig.

EMPLOYMENT OPPORTUNITIES

Majority (6 D): Hawkins, Chmn.; Clay, Weiss, Corrada, Simon, Washington.
Minority (4 R): Jeffords, Petri, Fenwick, DeNardis.*

HEALTH AND SAFETY

Majority (4 D): Gaydos, Chmn.; Murphy, Kogovsek, Washington.
Minority (3 R): Kramer, Johnston, Craig.

HUMAN RESOURCES

Majority (3 D): Andrews, Chmn.; Corrada, Williams.
Minority (2 R): Petri, Coleman.*

LABOR-MANAGEMENT RELATIONS

Majority (7 D): P. Burton, Chmn.; Clay, Ford, Biaggi, Kildee, Weiss, Peyser.
Minority (5 R): Ashbrook, Erlenborn, Kramer, Fenwick, Johnston.

LABOR STANDARDS

Majority (6 D): Miller, Chmn.; P. Burton, Williams, Ratchford, Murphy, Kildee.
Minority (5 R): Erlenborn, Fenwick, Roukema,* Johnston, Bailey.

POSTSECONDARY EDUCATION

Majority (7 D): Simon, Chmn.; Ford, Peyser, Gaydos, Weiss, Andrews, Eckart.
Minority (5 R): Coleman, Erdahl,* DeNardis, Bailey.

SELECT EDUCATION

Majority (4 D): Murphy, Chmn.; Miller, Biaggi, Simon.
Minority (3 R): Erdahl, Jeffords, Bailey.*

ENERGY AND COMMERCE

Majority (24 D): Dingell (Mich.), Chmn.; Scheuer (N.Y.), Ottinger (N.Y.), Waxman (Cai.), Wirth (Colo.), Sharp (Ind.), Florio (N.J.), Moffett (Conn.), Santini (Nev.), Markey (Mass.), Luken (Ohio), Walgren (Pa.), Gore (Tenn.), Mikulski (Md.), Mottl (Ohio), Gramm (Tex.), Swift (Wash.), Leland (Tex.), Shelby (Ala.), Collins (Ill.), Synar (Okla.), Tauzin (La.), Wyden (Oreg.), Hall (Tex.).
Minority (18 R): Broyhill (N.C.), Brown (Ohio), Collins (Tex.), Lent (N.Y.), Madigan (Ill.), Moorhead (Cal.), Rinaldo (N.J.), Marks (Pa.), Corcoran (Ill.), Lee (N.Y.), Dannemeyer (Cal.), Whittaker (Kans.), Tauke (Iowa), Ritter (Pa.), Rogers (Ky.), Benedict (W.Va.), Coats (Ind.), Bliley (Va.).

COMMERCE, TRANSPORTATION, AND TOURISM

Majority (5 D): Florio, Chmn.; Santini, Mikulski, Scheuer, Moffett.
Minority (3 R): Lent, Madigan, Lee.

ENERGY CONSERVATION AND POWER

Majority (13 D): Ottinger, Chmn.; Moffett, Markey, Gore, Gramm, Swift, Leland, Shelby, Synar, Wyden, Hall, Walgren, Collins.
Minority (9 R): Moorhead, Rinaldo, Collins, Corcoran, Whittaker, Tauke, Ritter, Rogers, Benedict.

FOSSIL AND SYNTHETIC FUELS

Majority (13 D): Sharp, Chmn.; Moffett, Markey, Gore, Gramm, Swift, Leland, Shelby, Collins, Synar, Tauzin, Hall, Wirth.
Minority (9 R): Brown, Collins, Corcoran, Lee, Dannemeyer, Tauke, Rogers, Benedict, Coats.

HEALTH AND THE ENVIRONMENT

Majority (11 D): Waxman, Chmn.; Scheuer, Luken, Walgren, Mikulski, Wyden, Florio, Moffett, Shelby, Gramm, Leland.
Minority (7 R): Madigan, Brown, Dannemeyer, Whittaker, Ritter, Benedict, Bliley.

OVERSIGHT AND INVESTIGATIONS

Majority (10 D): Dingell, Chmn.; Santini, Walgren, Gore, Mottl, Luken, Shelby, Synar, Tauzin, Wyden.
Minority (7 R): Marks, Lent, Whittaker, Ritter, Rogers, Coats, Broyhill.

TELECOMMUNICATIONS, CONSUMER PROTECTION, AND FINANCE

Majority (9 D): Wirth, Chmn.; Mottl, Scheuer, Markey, Luken, Swift, Waxman, Collins, Tauzin.
Minority (6 R): Collins, Rinaldo, Moorhead, Marks, Tauke, Bliley.

FOREIGN AFFAIRS

Majority (21 D): Zablocki (Wis.), Chmn.; Fountain (N.C.), Fascell (Fla.), Rosenthal (N.Y.), Hamilton (Ind.), Bingham (N.Y.), Yatron (Pa.), Solarz (N.Y.), Bonker (Wash.), Studds (Mass.), Ireland (Fla.), Mica (Fla.), Barnes (Md.), Wolpe (Mich.), Crockett (Mich.), Shamansky (Ohio), Gejdenson (Conn.), Dymally (Cal.), Eckart (Ohio), Lantos (Cal.), Bowen (Miss.).
Minority (16 R): Broomfield (Mich.), Derwinski (Ill.), Findley (Ill.), Winn (Kans.), Gilman (N.Y.), Lagomarsino (Cal.), Goodling (Pa.), Pritchard (Wash.), Fenwick (N.J.), Dornan (Cal.), Leach (Iowa), Erdahl (Minn.), Roth (Wis.), Snowe (Maine), LeBoutillier (N.Y.), one vacancy.

AFRICA

Majority (5 D): Wolpe, Chmn.; Crockett, Solarz, Studds, Eckart.
Minority (4 R): Goodling, Erdahl, Snowe, Dornan.

ASIAN AND PACIFIC AFFAIRS

Majority (5 D): Solarz, Chmn.; Dymally, Ireland, Lantos, Bowen.
Minority (4 R): Pritchard, Dornan, Leach, one vacancy.

EUROPE AND THE MIDDLE EAST

Majority (5 D): Hamilton, Chmn.; Fountain, Rosenthal, Shamansky, Lantos.
Minority (4 R): Findley, Fenwick, Roth, Snowe.

HUMAN RIGHTS AND INTERNATIONAL ORGANIZATIONS

Majority (5 D): Bonker, Chmn.; Rosenthal, Barnes, Gejdenson, Dymally.
Minority (4 R): Leach, Dornan, LeBoutillier, Pritchard.

INTER-AMERICAN AFFAIRS

Majority (5 D): Barnes, Chmn.; Yatron, Studds, Mica, Gejdenson.
Minority (4 R): Gilman, Lagomarsino, Goodling, one vacancy.

INTERNATIONAL ECONOMIC POLICY AND TRADE

Majority (5 D): Bingham, Chmn.; Eckart, Bonker, Wolpe, Shamansky.
Minority (4 R): Lagomarsino, Erdahl, Gilman, Fenwick.

INTERNATIONAL OPERATIONS

Majority (5 D): Fascell, Chmn.; Ireland, Yatron, Mica, Crockett.
Minority (4 R): Derwinski, Winn, Pritchard, Roth.

INTERNAL SECURITY AND SCIENTIFIC AFFAIRS

Majority (5 D): Zablocki, Chmn.; Fountain, Fascell, Hamilton, Bingham.
Minority (4 R): Broomfield, Winn, LeBoutillier, Derwinski.

GOVERNMENT OPERATIONS

Majority (23 D): Brooks (Tex.), Chmn.; Fountain (N.C.), Fascell (Fla.), Rosenthal (N.Y.), Fuqua (Fla.), Conyers (Mich.), Collins (Ill.), J. Burton (Cal.), English (Okla.), Levitas (Ga.), Evans (Ind.), Moffett (Conn.), Waxman (Cal.), Fithian (Ind.), Weiss (N.Y.), Synar (Okla.), Atkinson (Pa.), Neal (N.C.), Barnard (Ga.), Peyser (N.Y.), Frank (Mass.), Washington (Ill.), Lantos (Cal.).
Minority (17 R): Horton (N.Y.), Erlenborn (Ill.), Brown (Ohio), McCloskey (Cal.), Kindness (Ohio), Walker (Pa.), Butler (Va.), Williams (Ohio), Deckard (Ind.), Clinger (Pa.), McGrath (N.Y.), Daub (Neb.), Hiler (Ind.), Dreier (Cal.), Bailey (Mo.), DeNardis (Conn.), Gregg (N.H.).

Subcommittees

[Brooks and Horton are ex officio members of all subcommittees on which they do not hold a regular assignment.]

COMMERCE, CONSUMER, AND MONETARY AFFAIRS

Majority (6 D): Rosenthal, Chmn.; Conyers, Atkinson, Neal, Barnard, Peyser.
Minority (4 R): Williams, Daub, Clinger, Hiler.

ENVIRONMENT, ENERGY, AND NATURAL RESOURCES

Majority (6 D): Moffett, Chmn.; Fithian, Synar, Lantos, Atkinson, Frank.
Minority (4 R): Deckard, Hiler, Dreier, Gregg.

GOVERNMENT ACTIVITIES AND TRANSPORTATION

Majority (6 D): J. Burton, Chmn.; Evans, Weiss, Peyser, Lantos, one vacancy.
Minority (4 R): Walker, Bailey, McGrath, Daub.

GOVERNMENT INFORMATION AND INDIVIDUAL RIGHTS

Majority (5 D): English, Chmn.; Weiss, Waxman, J. Burton, one vacancy.
Minority (3 R): Kindness, Erlenborn, Bailey.

INTERGOVERNMENTAL RELATIONS AND HUMAN RESOURCES

Majority (5 D): Fountain, Chmn.; Frank, Levitas, Fithian, Neal.
Minority (3 R): Brown, McGrath, DeNardis.

LEGISLATION AND NATIONAL SECURITY

Majority (6 D): Brooks, Chmn.; Fascell, Fuqua, Levitas, Evans, Waxman.
Minority (4 R): Horton, Erlenborn, Butler, Clinger.

MANPOWER AND HOUSING

Majority (5 D): Collins, Chwmn.; Washington, Conyers, Atkinson, Rosenthal.
Minority (3 R): McCloskey, Butler, Dreier.

HOUSE ADMINISTRATION

Majority (11 D): Hawkins (Cal.), Chmn.; Annunzio (Ill.), Gaydos (Pa.), Jones (Tenn.), Mollohan (W.Va.), Minish (N.J.), Rose (N.C.), J. Burton (Cal.), Ratchford (Conn.), Swift (Wash.), W. Coyne (Pa.).
Minority (8 R): Frenzel (Minn.), Dickinson (Ala.), Badham (Cal.), Gingrich (Ga.), Thomas (Cal.), Lee (N.Y.), J. Coyne (Pa.), Martin (Ill.).

Subcommittees

ACCOUNTS

Majority (7 D): Annunzio, Chmn.; Rose, J. Burton, Ratchford, Swift, W. Coyne, Gaydos.
Minority (5 R): Badham, Thomas, Lee, Martin, Frenzel.

CONTRACTS AND PRINTING

Majority (3 D): Gaydos, Chmn.; Jones, Minish.
Minority (2 R): Gingrich, Martin.

OFFICE SYSTEMS

Majority (3 D): Mollohan, Chmn.; J. Burton, Swift.
Minority (2 R): Thomas, Lee.

PERSONNEL AND POLICE

Majority (3 D): Minish, Chmn.; Annunzio, Ratchford.
Minority (2 R): Lee, J. Coyne.

SERVICES

Majority (3 D): Jones, Chmn.; Mollohan, Rose.
Minority (2 R): Dickinson, J. Coyne.

POLICY GROUP ON INFORMATION AND COMPUTERS

Majority (3 D): Rose, Chmn.; J. Burton, W. Coyne.
Minority (2 R): J. Coyne, Thomas.

INTERIOR AND INSULAR AFFAIRS

Majority (26 D): Udall (Ariz.), Chmn.; P. Burton (Cal.), Kastenmeier (Wis.), Kazen (Tex.), Bingham (N.Y.), Seiberling (Ohio), Won Pat (Guam), Santini (Nev.), Weaver (Oreg.), Miller (Cal.), Florio (N.J), Sharp (Ind.), Markey (Mass.), Corrada (P.R.), Murphy (Pa.), Rahall (W.Va.), Vento (Minn.), Huckaby (La.), Patterson (Cal.), Kogovsek (Colo.), Williams (Mont.), Kildee (Mich.), Coelho (Cal.), Byron (Md.), de Lugo (V.I.), Gejdenson (Conn.).

Minority (17 R): Lujan (N.M.), Clausen (Cal.), Young (Alaska), Lagomarsino (Cal.), Marriott (Utah), Marlenee (Mont.), Cheney (Wyo.), Pashayan (Cal.), Bereuter (Neb), Martin (N.Y.), Craig (Ida.), Hendon (N.C.), Brown (Colo.), Staton (W.Va.), Smith (Oreg.), Hansen (Utah), one vacancy.

Subcommittees

[Udall and Lujan are nonvoting ex officio members of all subcommittees on which they do not hold a regular assignment.]

ENERGY AND THE ENVIRONMENT

Majority (13 D): Udall, Chmn.; Bingham, Seiberling, Weaver, Sharp, Markey, Corrada, Murphy, Rahall, Vento, Huckaby, Williams, Gejdenson.
Minority (8 R): Lujan, Marriott, Cheney, Bereuter, Martin, Staton, Smith, one vacancy.

INSULAR AFFAIRS

Majority (7 D): Won Pat, Chmn.; P. Burton, Seiberling, Corrada, Kildee, de Lugo, Udall.
Minority (4 R): Lagomarsino, Clausen, Bereuter, Smith.

MINES AND MINING

Majority (7 D): Santini, Chmn.; Kazen, Murphy, Rahall, Huckaby, Kogovsek, Byron.
Minority (5 R): Marriott, Young, Martin, Craig, Staton.

OVERSIGHT AND INVESTIGATIONS

Majority (6 D): Markey, Chmn.; , Coelho, Patterson, Florio, Byron, Gejdenson.
Minority (4 R): Merlenee, Hendon, Brown, one vacancy.

PUBLIC LANDS AND NATIONAL PARKS

Majority (16 D): Seiberling, Chmn.; P. Burton, Kastenmeier, Kazen, Bingham, Won Pat, Santini, Weaver, Florio, Vento, Kogovsek, Williams, Kildee, Byron, de Lugo, Gejdenson.
Minority (10 R): Young, Clausen, Lagomarsino, Marlenee, Cheney, Pashayan, Craig, Hendon, Brown, Hansen.

WATER AND POWER RESOURCES

Majority (7 D): Kazen, Chmn.; Udall, Weaver, Miller, Patterson, Kogovsek, Coelho.
Minority (5 R): Clausen, Lujan, Pashayan, Bereuter, Hansen.

JUDICIARY

Majority (16 D): Rodino (N.J.), Chmn.; Brooks (Tex.), Kastenmeier (Wis.), Edwards (Cal.), Conyers (Mich.), Seiberling (Ohio), Danielson (Cal.), Mazzoli (Ky.), Hughes (N.J.), Hall (Tex.), Synar (Okla.), Schroeder (Colo.), Evans (Ga.), Glickman (Kans.), Washington (Ill.), Frank (Mass.).
Minority (12 R): McClory (Ill.), Railsback (Ill.), Fish (N.Y.), Butler (Va.), Moorhead (Cal.), Ashbrook (Ohio), Hyde (Ill.), Kindness (Ohio), Sawyer (Mich.), Lungren (Cal.), Sensenbrenner (Wis.), McCollum (Fla.).

Subcommittees

ADMINISTRATIVE LAW AND GOVERNMENTAL RELATIONS

Majority (4 D): Danielson, Chmn.; Synar, Evans, Glickman.
Minority (3 R): Moorhead, Kindness, McClory.

CIVIL AND CONSTITUTIONAL RIGHTS

Majority (4 D): Edwards, Chmn.; Kastenmeier, Schroeder, Washington.
Minority (3 R): Hyde, Sensenbrenner, Lungren.

COURTS, CIVIL LIBERTIES, AND THE ADMINISTRATION OF JUSTICE
Majority (4 D): Kastenmeier, Chmn.; Brooks, Danielson, Frank.
Minority (3 R): Railsback, Sawyer, Butler.

CRIME
Majority (4 D): Hughes, Chmn.; Kastenmeier, Conyers, Hall.
Minority (3 R): Sawyer, Ashbrook, Fish.

CRIMINAL JUSTICE
Majority (4 D): Conyers, Chmn.; Edwards, Seiberling, Hall.
Minority (3 R): Sensenbrenner, Kindness, McCollum.

IMMIGRATION, REFUGEES, AND INTERNATIONAL LAW
Majority (4 D): Mazzoli, Chmn.; Hall, Schroeder, Frank.
Minority (3 R): Fish, Lungren, McCollum.

MONOPOLIES AND COMMERCIAL LAW
Majority (7 D): Rodino, Chmn.; Brooks, Edwards, Seiberling, Mazzoli, Hughes, Evans.
Minority (5 R): McClory, Butler, Railsback, Moorhead, Hyde.

MERCHANT MARINE AND FISHERIES

Majority (21 D): Jones (N.C.), Chmn.; Biaggi (N.Y.), Anderson (Cal.), Breaux (La.), Studds (Mass.), Bowen (Miss.), Hubbard (Ky.), Bonker (Wash.), D'Amours (N.H.), Oberstar (Minn.), Hughes (N.J.), Mikulski (N.J.), Lowry (Wash.), Hutto (Fla.), Donnelly (Mass.), Tauzin (La.), Foglietta (Pa.), Patman (Tex.), Sunia (Am. Samoa), Hertel (Mich.), Dyson (Md.).

Minority (15 R): Snyder (Ky.), McCloskey (Cal.), Forsythe (N.J.), Pritchard (Wash.), Young (Alaska), Lent (N.Y.), Emery (Maine), Evans (Del.), Davis (Mich.), Carney (N.Y.), Dougherty (Pa.), Shumway (Cal.), Fields (Tex.), Schneider (R.I.), Shaw (Fla.).

Subcommittees
[Jones and Snyder are ex officio members, with vote, of all subcommittees.]

COAST GUARD AND NAVIGATION
Majority (11 D): Studds, Chmn.; Hughes, Tauzin, Biaggi, Bonker, Oberstar, Mikulski, Lowry, Hutto, Foglietta, Dyson.
Minority (8 R): Young, Lent, Evans, Davis, Dougherty, Shumway, Fields, Shaw.

FISHERIES AND WILDLIFE CONSERVATION AND THE ENVIRONMENT
Majority (16 D): Breaux, Chmn.; Bowen, Bonker, Oberstar, Lowry, Hutto, Donnelly, Patman, Sunia, Dyson, Anderson, Studds, D'Amours, Hughes, Tauzin, Hertel.
Minority (11 R): Forsythe, McCloskey, Pritchard, Young, Emery, Evans, Davis, Carney, Dougherty, Shumway, Schneider.

MERCHANT MARINE
Majority (10 D): Biaggi, Chmn.; Anderson, Mikulski, Foglietta, Hertel, Hubbard, Donnelly, Patman, Sunia, Breaux.
Minority (7 R): McCloskey, Young, Davis, Dougherty, Shumway, Fields, Shaw.

OCEANOGRAPHY
Majority (6 D): D'Amours, Chmn.; Dyson, Studds, Hughes, Mikulski, Hertel.
Minority (4 R): Pritchard, Emery, Carney, Schneider.

PANAMA CANAL AND OUTER CONTINENTAL SHELF

Majority (4 D): Hubbard, Chmn.; Breaux, Bowen, Foglietta.
Minority (2 R): Lent, Forsythe.

POST OFFICE AND CIVIL SERVICE

Majority (16 D): Ford (Mich.), Chmn.; Udall (Ariz.), Clay (Mo.), Schroeder (Colo.), Garcia (N.Y.), Leland (Tex.), Ferraro (N.Y.), Albosta (Mich.), Yatron (Pa.), Oakar (Ohio), Schumer (N.Y.), Danielson (Cal.), Dellums (Cal.), Peyser (N.Y.), de Lugo (V.I.), Savage (Ill.).
Minority (11 R): Derwinski (Ill.), Taylor (Mo.), Gilman (N.Y.), Corcoran (Ill.), Courter (N.J.), Pashayan (Cal.), Dannemeyer (Cal.), D. Crane (Ill.), Grisham (Cal.), Wolf (Va.), one vacancy.

Subcommittees
[Ford and Derwinski are ex officio voting members of all legislative subcommittees on which they do not hold a regular assignment.]

CENSUS AND POPULATION

Majority (5 D): Garcia, Chmn.; Yatron, Leland, Oakar, Peyser.
Minority (3 R): Courter, D. Crane, Grisham.

CIVIL SERVICE

Majority (6 D): Schroeder, Chwmn.; Udall, Clay, Yatron, Danielson, one vacancy.
Minority (4 R): Pashayan, Taylor, Courter, Wolf.

COMPENSATION AND EMPLOYEE BENEFITS

Majority (5 D): Oakar, Chwmn.; Albosta, Danielson, Peyser, one vacancy.
Minority (3 R): Dannemeyer, D. Crane, one vacancy.

HUMAN RESOURCES

Majority (5 D): Ferraro, Chwmn.; Dellums, Danielson, two vacancies.
Minority (3 R): Corcoran, Gilman, Wolf.

INVESTIGATIONS

Majority (5 D): Ford, Chmn.; Clay, Udall, Garcia, Peyser.
Minority (3 R): Derwinski, Pashayan, Grisham.

POSTAL OPERATIONS AND SERVICES

Majority (6 D): Clay, Chmn.; Albosta, Ferraro, Oakar, de Lugo, Dellums.
Minority (4 R): Taylor, Corcoran, Wolf, one vacancy.

POSTAL PERSONNEL AND MODERNIZATION

Majority (5 D): Leland, Chmn.; Garcia, Clay, Dellums, one vacancy.
Minority (3 R): Gilman, Dannemeyer, Grisham.

PUBLIC WORKS AND TRANSPORTATION

Majority (27 D): Howard (N.J.), Chmn.; Anderson (Cal.), Roe (N.J.), Breaux (La.), Mineta (Cal.), Levitas (Ga.), Oberstar (Minn.), Nowak (N.Y.), Edgar (Pa.), Bouquard (Tenn.), Fary (Ill.), Young (Mo,), Ertel (Pa.), Evans (Ga.), Flippo (Ala.), Rahall (W.Va.), Applegate (Ohio), Ferraro (N.Y.), Atkinson (Pa.), Albosta (Mich.), Boner (Tenn.), de Lugo (V.I.), Savage (Ill.), Sunia (Am. Samoa), Roemer (La.), Donnelly (Mass.), Kogovsek (Colo.).

Minority (19 R): Clausen (Cal.), Snyder (Ky.), Hammerschmidt (Ark.), Shuster (Pa.), Goldwater (Cal.), Hagedorn (Minn.), Stangeland (Minn.), Gingrich (Ga.), Clinger (Pa.), Solomon (N.Y.), Hollenbeck (N.J.), Deckard (Ind.), Grisham (Cal.), Jeffries (Kans.), Fields (Tex.), Molinari (N.Y.), Shaw (Fla.), McEwen (Ohio), Wolf (Va.).

Subcommittees

[Howard and Clausen are ex officio members of all subcommittees.]

AVIATION

Majority (16 D): Mineta, Chmn.; Levitas, Ferraro, Atkinson, Boner, de Lugo, Roemer, Anderson, Oberstar, Fary, Young, Ertel, Rahall, Applegate, Sunia, Nowak.
Minority (10 R): Snyder, Hammerschmidt, Shuster, Goldwater, Hagedorn, Gingrich, Hollenbeck, Deckard, Grisham, Wolf.

ECONOMIC DEVELOPMENT

Majority (11 D): Oberstar, Chmn.; Bouquard, Roe, Flippo, Applegate, Albosta, Savage, Sunia, Donnelly, Nowak, Edgar.
Minority (7 R): Hagedorn, Hammerschmidt, Shuster, Clinger, Hollenbeck, Deckard, McEwen.

INVESTIGATIONS AND OVERSIGHT

Majority (10 D): Levitas, Chmn.; Mineta, Roe, Ferraro, Albosta, Boner, Savage, Roemer, Fary, Flippo.
Minority (7 R): Goldwater, Stangeland, Gingrich, Solomon, Hollenbeck, Molinari, McEwen.

PUBLIC BUILDINGS AND GROUNDS

Majority (5 D): Fary, Chmn.; Mineta, Levitas, Donnelly, Bouquard.
Minority (3 R): Stangeland, Solomon, Jeffries.

SURFACE TRANSPORTATION

Majority (17 D): Anderson, Chmn.; Edgar, Ertel, Rahall, Applegate, Atkinson, Boner, Nowak, Young, Evans, Albosta, de Lugo, Savage, Sunia, Donnelly, Kogovsek, Breaux.
Minority (11 R): Shuster, Snyder, Hagedorn, Stangeland, Gingrich, Clinger, Deckard, Fields, Molinari, Shaw, McEwen.

WATER RESOURCES

Majority (14 D): Roe, Chmn.; Breaux, Flippo, Ferraro, Roemer, Anderson, Oberstar, Nowak, Edgar, Fary, Young, Ertel, Evans, Rahall.
Minority (10 R): Hammerschmidt, Snyder, Clinger, Solomon, Grisham, Jeffries, Fields, Molinari, Shaw, Wolf.

RULES

Majority (11 D): Bolling (Mo.), Chmn.; Pepper (Fla.), Long (La.), Moakley (Mass.), Chisholm (N.Y.), Zeferetti (N.Y.), Derrick (S.C.), Beilenson (Cal.), Frost (Tex.), Bonior (Mich.), Hall (Ohio).
Minority (5 R): Quillen (Tenn.), Latta (Ohio), Lott (Miss.), Taylor (Mo.), Rhodes (Ariz.).

Subcommittees
RULES OF THE HOUSE

Majority (6 D): Moakley, Chmn.; Beilenson, Frost, Pepper, Bonior, Hall.
Minority (3 R): Taylor, Rhodes, Lott.

THE LEGISLATIVE PROCESS

Majority (4 D): Long, Chmn.; Chisholm, Zeferetti, Derrick.
Minority (2 R): Lott, Taylor.

SCIENCE AND TECHNOLOGY

Majority (23 D): Fuqua (Fla.), Chmn.; Roe (N.J.), Brown (Cal.), Scheuer (N.Y.), Ottinger (N.Y.), Harkin (Iowa), Bouquard (Tenn.), Blanchard (Mich.), Walgren (Pa.), Flippo (Ala.), Glickman (Kans.), Gore (Tenn.), Young (Mo.), White (Tex.), Volkmer (Mo.), Wolpe (Mich.), Nelson (Fla.), Lundine (N.Y.), Ertel (Pa.), Shamansky (Ohio), Hall (Tex.), McCurdy (Okla.), Dymally (Cal.).
Minority (17 R): Winn (Kans.), Goldwater (Cal.), Fish (N.Y.), Lujan (N.M.), Hollenbeck (N.J.), Walker (Pa.), Forsythe (N.J.), Carney (N.Y.), Heckler (Mass.), Sensenbrenner (Wis.), Weber (Minn.), Gregg (N.H.), McGrath (N.Y.), Skeen (N.M.), Schneider (R.I.), Dunn (Mich.), Lowery (Cal.).

Subcommittees
[Fuqua and Winn are ex officio members, with vote, of all subcommittees.]

ENERGY DEVELOPMENT AND APPLICATIONS

Majority (14 D): Fuqua, Chmn.; Harkin, Blanchard, White, Volkmer, Wolpe, Nelson, Ertel, McCurdy, Roe, Scheuer, Ottinger, Bouquard, Young.
Minority (9 R): Fish, Sensenbrenner, Weber, Gregg, Skeen, Schneider, McGrath, Dunn, Walker.

ENERGY RESEARCH AND PRODUCTION

Majority (8 D): Bouquard, Chwmn.; Roe, Ottinger, Young, Lundine, Flippo, Volkmer, Wolpe.
Minority (5 R): Lujan, Forsythe, Lowery, Goldwater, Hollenbeck.

INVESTIGATIONS AND OVERSIGHT

Majority (3 D): Gore, Chmn.; Shamansky, Volkmer.
Minority (2 R): Walker, Lujan.

NATURAL RESOURCES, AGRICULTURAL RESEARCH AND ENVIRONMENT

Majority (5 D): Scheuer, Chmn.; Brown, Blanchard, Walgren, White.
Minority (3 R): Carney, Sensenbrenner, Schneider.

SCIENCE, RESEARCH AND TECHNOLOGY

Majority (8 D): Walgren, Chmn.; Brown, Shamansky, Dymally, Lundine, Ertel, Hall, McCurdy.
Minority (5 R): Heckler, Weber, Gregg, Skeen, Forsythe.

SPACE SCIENCE AND APPLICATIONS

Majority (5 D): Flippo, Chmn.; Nelson, Brown, Bouquard, Hall.
Minority (3 R): Hollenbeck, McGrath, Lowery.

TRANSPORTATION, AVIATION AND MATERIALS

Majority (6 D): Glickman, Chmn.; Hall, Harkin, Shamansky, Dymally, Flippo.
Minority (4 R): Goldwater, Dunn, Hollenbeck, Carney.

SMALL BUSINESS

Majority (23 D): Mitchell (Md.), Chmn.; Smith (Iowa), Addabbo (N.Y.), Gonzalez (Tex.), LaFalce (N.Y.), Bedell (Iowa), Richmond (N.Y.), Nowak (N.Y.), Luken (Ohio), Ireland (Fla.), Skelton (Mo.), Evans (Ga.), Stenholm (Tex.), Mazzoli (Ky.), Mavroules (Mass.), Crockett (Mich.), Hatcher (Ga.), Wyden (Oreg.), Eckart (Ohio), Dorgan (N.D.), Savage (Ill.), Roemer (La.), Fary (Ill.).
Minority (17 R): McDade (Pa.), Conte (Mass.), Stanton (Ohio), Broomfield (Mich.), Marriott (Utah), Williams (Ohio), Snowe (Maine), Bereuter (Neb.), D. Crane (Ill.), Hiler (Ind.), Staton (W.Va.), Weber (Minn.), Daub (Neb.), Smith (N.J.), Weber (Ohio), Dreier (Cal.), Molinari (N.Y.).

Subcommittees

ANTITRUST AND RESTRAINT OF TRADE ACTIVITIES AFFECTING SMALL BUSINESS

Majority (4 D): Luken, Chmn.; Eckart, Gonzalez, Bedell.
Minority (3 R): Williams, Daub, one vacancy.

ENERGY, ENVIRONMENT AND SAFETY ISSUES AFFECTING SMALL BUSINESS

Majority (4 D): Bedell, Chmn.; Mavroules, Hatcher, Eckart.
Minority (3 R): Conte, Bereuter, Hiler.

EXPORT OPPORTUNITIES AND SPECIAL SMALL BUSINESS PROBLEMS

Majority (6 D): Ireland, Chmn.; Skelton, Stenholm, Wyden, Crockett, Smith.
Minority (4 R): Broomfield, Staton, Weber (Ohio), Dreier.

GENERAL OVERSIGHT

Majority (7 D): LaFalce, Chmn.; Mazzoli, Addabbo, Richmond, Luken, Roemer, Crockett.
Minority (5 R): Stanton, Bereuter, Smith, Weber (Ohio), Dreier.

SBA AND SBIC AUTHORITY, MINORITY ENTERPRISE AND GENERAL SMALL BUSINESS PROBLEMS

Majority (7 D): Mitchell, Chmn.; Smith, Addabbo, Gonzalez, Richmond, Hatcher, Savage.
Minority (5 R): McDade, Hiler, Staton, Daub, Smith.

TAX, ACCESS TO EQUITY CAPITAL AND BUSINESS OPPORTUNITIES

Majority (6 D): Nowak, Chmn.; Evans, Dorgan, Savage, Roemer, Fary.
Minority (4 R): Marriott, Snowe, D. Crane, Weber (Minn.).

STANDARDS OF OFFICIAL CONDUCT

Majority (6 D): Stokes (Ohio), Chmn.; Rahall (W.Va.), Alexander (Ark.), Wilson (Tex.), Holland (S.C.), Bailey (Pa.)
Minority (6 R): Spence (S.C.), Conable (N.Y.), Myers (Ind.), Forsythe (N.J.), Brown (Colo.), Hansen (Utah).

No Subcommittees

VETERANS' AFFAIRS

Majority (17 D): Montgomery (Miss.), Chmn.; Edwards (Cal.), Danielson (Cal.), Brinkley (Ga.), Mottl (Ohio), Edgar (Pa.), Hall (Tex.), Applegate (Ohio), Leath (Tex.), Boner (Tenn.), Shelby (Ala.), Mica (Fla.), Daschle (S.D.), Stump (Ariz.), Gramm (Tex.), Murphy (Pa.), Dorgan (N.D.).
Minority (14 R): Hammerschmidt (Ark.), Heckler (Mass.), Wylie (Ohio), Hillis (Ind.), Sawyer (Mich.), Solomon (N.Y.), Jeffries (Kans.), McEwen (Ohio), Dunn (Mich.), Smith (N.J.), Smith (Ala.), Smith (Oreg.), Siljander (Mich.), one vacancy.

Subcommittees
[Montgomery and Hammerschmidt are ex officio members of all subcommittees of which they are not regular members.]

COMPENSATION, PENSION, AND INSURANCE

Majority (6 D): Hall, chmn.; Montgomery, Danielson, Brinkley, Applegate, Murphy.
Minority (5 R): Wylie, Hammerschmidt, Smith (Ala.), Smith (Oreg.), one vacancy.

EDUCATION, TRAINING AND EMPLOYMENT

Majority (6 D): Edgar, Chmn.; Edwards, Leath, Boner, Daschle, Gramm.
Minority (5 R): Heckler, Wylie, Sawyer, Jeffries, Smith (Oreg.).

HOSPITALS AND HEALTH CARE

Majority (10 D): Mottl, Chmn.; Edwards, Applegate, Boner, Shelby, Mica, Daschle, Gramm, Edgar, Dorgan.
Minority (8 R): Hammerschmidt, Heckler, Hillis, Solomon, McEwen, Dunn, Smith (N.J.), Smith (Ala.).

HOUSING AND MEMORIAL AFFAIRS

Majority (5 D): Leath, Chmn.; Brinkley, Mottl, Shelby, Mica.
Minority (4 R): McEwen, Smith (N.J.), Dunn, one vacancy.

OVERSIGHT AND INVESTIGATIONS

Majority (6 D): Montgomery, Chmn.; Danielson, Stump, Hall, Mica, Leath.
Minority (5 R): Hillis, Hammerschmidt, Sawyer, Solomon, Jeffries.

WAYS AND MEANS

Majority (23 D): Rostenkowski (Ill.), Chmn.; Gibbons (Fla.), Pickle (Tex.), Rangel (N.Y.), Cotter (Conn.), Stark (Cal.), Jones (Okla.), Jacobs (Ind.), Ford (Tenn.), Holland (S.C.), Brodhead (Mich), Jenkins (Ga.), Gephardt (Mo.), Downey (N.Y.), Heftel (Hawaii), Fowler (Ga.), Guarini (Ga.), Shannon (Mass.), Russo (Ill.), Pease (Ohio), Hance (Tex.), Matsui (Cal.), Bailey (Pa.).
Minority (12 R): Conable (N.Y.), Duncan (Tenn.), Archer (Tex.), Vander Jagt (Mich.), P. Crane (Ill.), Frenzel (Minn.), Martin (N.C.), Bafalis (Fla.), Schulze (Pa.), Gradison (Ohio), Rousselot (Cal.), Moore (La.).

Subcommittees
HEALTH

Majority (5 D): Jacobs, Chmn.; Rangel, Ford, Heftel, Holland.
Minority (3 R): Gradison, Duncan, P. Crane.

OVERSIGHT

Majority (7 D): Rangel, Chmn.; Gibbons, Pickle, Ford, Heftel, Brodhead, Fowler.
Minority (4 R): P. Crane, Moore, Duncan, Martin.

PUBLIC ASSISTANCE AND UNEMPLOYMENT COMPENSATION

Majority (7 D): Stark, Chmn.; Brodhead, Russo, Pease, Hance, Matsui, Bailey.
Minority (4 R): Bafalis, Rousselot, Gradison, Moore.

SELECT REVENUE MEASURES

Majority (7 D): Cotter, Chmn.; Holland, Stark, Fowler, Russo, Matsui, Jenkins.
Minority (4 R): Duncan, Schulze, Vander Hagt, Moore.

SOCIAL SECURITY

Majority (7 D): Pickle, Chmn.; Jacobs, Cotter, Gephardt, Guarini, Shannon, Bailey.
Minority (4 R): Archer, Gradison, Rousselot, P. Crane.

TRADE

Majority (9 D): Gibbons, Chmn.; Rostenkowski, Jones, Jenkins, Downey, Guarini, Shannon, Pease, Hance.
Minority (5 R): Vander Jagt, Archer, Frenzel, Bafalis, Schulze.

SELECT COMMITTEES

SELECT COMMITTEE ON AGING

Majority (31 D): Pepper (Fla.), Chmn.; Roybal (Cal.), Biaggi (N.Y.), Andrews (N.C), J. Burton (Cal.), Bonker (Wash.), Downey (N.Y.), Florio (N.J.), Ford (Tenn.), Hughes (N.J.), Bouquard (Tenn.), Santini (Nev.), Evans (Ind.), Lundine (N.Y.), Oakar (Ohio), Luken (Ohio), Ferraro (N.Y.), Byron (Md.), Ratchford (Conn.), Mica (Fla.), Waxman (Cal.), Synar (Okla.), Atkinson (Pa.), Derrick (S.C.), Vento (Minn.), Frank (Mass.), Lantos (Cal.), Shamansky (Ohio), Wyden (Oreg.), Albosta (Mich.), Crockett (Mich.).

Minority (23 R): Rinaldo (N.J.), Wampler (Va.), Hammerschmidt (Ark.), Marks (Pa.), Regula (Ohio), Dornan (Cal.), Hollenbeck (N.J.), Shumway (Cal.), Snowe (Maine), Lungren (Cal.), Fenwick (N.J.), Jeffords (Vt.), Bereuter (Neb.), Tauke (Iowa), Petri (Wis.), Gregg (N.H.), Coats (Ind.), Wortley (N.Y.), Daub (Neb.), Craig (Ida.), Roberts (Kans.), Hendon (N.C.), Carman (N.Y.).

Subcommittees
[Pepper and Rinaldo are ex officio members of all subcommittees.]

HEALTH AND LONG-TERM CARE

Majority (14 D): Pepper, Chmn.; Andrews, Bonker, Ford, Bouquard, Luken, Ratchford, Mica, Atkinson, Derrick, Wyden, Florio, Evans, Oakar.
Minority (9 R): Marks, Regula, Lungren, Fenwick, Jeffords, Wortley, Daub, Craig, Roberts.

HOUSING AND CONSUMER INTERESTS

Majority (8 D): Roybal, Chmn.; Santini, Byron, Lantos, Shamansky, Crockett, Lundine, Synar.
Minority (6 R): Hammerschmidt, Dornan, Bereuter, Wortley, Hendon, Carman.

HUMAN SERVICES

Majority (9 D): Biaggi, Chmn.; Florio, Hughes, Lundine, Vento, Albosta, Ferraro, Ratchford, Crockett.
Minority (8 R): Rinaldo, Hammerschmidt, Shumway, Snowe, Lungren, Tauke, Petri, Craig.

RETIREMENT INCOME AND EMPLOYMENT

Majority (11 D): J. Burton, Chmn.; Downey, Evans, Oakar, Ferraro, Waxman, Synar, Frank, Vento, Lantos, Wyden.
Minority (8 R): Wampler, Hollenbeck, Shumway, Jeffords, Gregg, Coats, Hendon, Carman.

PERMANENT SELECT COMMITTEE ON INTELLIGENCE

Majority (9 D): Boland (Mass.), Chmn.; Zablocki (Wis.), Rose (N.C.), Mazzoli (Ky.), Mineta (Cal.), Fowler (Ga.), Hamilton (Ind.), Gore (Tenn.), Stump (Ariz.).
Minority (5 R): Robinson (Va.), Ashbrook (Ohio), McClory (Ill.). Whitehurst (Va.), Young (Fla.)

Subcommittees
[Boland is a member of all subcommittees.]

LEGISLATION

Majority (3 D): Mazzoli, Chmn.; Fowler, Hamilton.
Minority (2 R): McClory, Ashbrook.

OVERSIGHT AND EVALUATION

Majority (3 D): Rose, Chmn.; Fowler, Gore.
Minority (2 R): Ashbrook, Young.

PROGRAM AND BUDGET AUTHORIZATION

Majority (4 D): Boland, Chmn.; Zablocki, Mineta, Stump.
Minority (3 R): Robinson, Whitehurst, Young.

SELECT COMMITTEE ON NARCOTICS ABUSE AND CONTROL

Majority (11 D): Zeferetti (N.Y.), Chmn.; Rodino (N.J.), Rangel (N.Y.), Stark (Cal.), English (Okla.), Evans (Ga.), Scheuer (N.Y.), Collins (Ill.), Akaka (Hawaii), Guarini (N.J.), Matsui (Cal.).
Minority (8 R): Railsback (Ill.), Beard (Tenn.), Gilman (N.Y.), Coughlin (Pa.), Dornan (Cal.), De-Nardis (Conn.), Shaw (Fla.), one vacancy.

No Subcommittees

INDEX OF TOPICS

INDEX OF PERSONS

THE AUTHORS

MICHAEL BARONE, coauthor and publisher of *The Almanac of American Politics,* is also senior vice president of Peter D. Hart Research Associates, Inc., a public opinion research firm. He has served as a consultant to CBS News. He is a graduate of Harvard College and Yale Law School and is a native of the Detroit area. He lives in Washington, D.C., with his wife Joan, who is producer of *Face the Nation* for CBS News, and their daughter Sarah.

GRANT UJIFUSA, a 1965 graduate of Harvard College, is a Sansei native of Worland, Wyoming. He now lives in New York City with his wife Amy and their sons Steven and Andrew. A book editor at Random House, he has recently handled such titles as *Energy Future, All You Need to Know about the IRS,* and *Everything We Had: An Oral History of the Vietnam War.*